International Dictionary of Films and Filmmakers-5

TITLE INDEX

International Dictionary of Films and Filmmakers

International Dictionary of Films and Filmmakers - 5

TITLE INDEX

SECOND EDITION

EDITOR
SAMANTHA COOK

St J

St James Press

Detroit   London   Washington DC

Front cover – **Trans-Lux Theatre, New York,** c.**1930,**
courtesy of the Ronald Grant Archive, London

Gale Research International Ltd.
PO Box 699
Cheriton House, North Way, Andover
Hants SP10 5YE
or
Gale Research Inc.
835 Penobscot Bldg.
Detroit. MI 48226-4094

ST JAMES PRESS is an imprint of Gale Research
International Ltd.
An Affiliated Company of Gale Research Inc.

A CIP catalogue record for this book is available from the
British Library.

ISBN 1-55862-041-9

First edition published 1987; second edition 1994;

Typeset by Tradespools Ltd., Frome, Somerset.
Printed in the United States of America.

The paper used in this publication meets the minimum
requirements of American National Standard for
Information Sciences—Permanence Paper for printed
Library Materials, ANSI Z39.48-1984. ⊗™

Published simultaneously in the United Kingdom and the
United States of America

I⟨T⟩P™

The trademark **ITP** is used under license.

10 9 8 7 6 5 4 3 2 1

INTRODUCTION

The following list of titles cites all films included in the first four volumes of this series, including cross-references for alternative or English-language titles. The name(s) and numbers(s) in parenthesis following the title and date refer the reader to the appropriate entry or entries, where full information is given:

1 — Films (all entries in this volume have titles appearing in **bold** in the index)
2 — Directors
3 — Actors and Actresses
4 — Writers and Production Artists

International Dictionary of Films and Filmmakers - 5
TITLE INDEX

$, 1971 (Brooks 2, Beatty 3, Hawn 3, Jones 4)

1 April 2000, 1952 (Wagner 4)

1 Berlin-Harlem, 1974 (Fassbinder 2)

1×1 der Ehe, 1949 (Herlth 4)

1–100, 1978 (Greenaway 2)

1.42.08, 1915 (Lucas 2)

2 Août 1914, 1914 (Linder 3)

2-Buldi-2, 1929 (Maretskaya 3)

2 Drops of Water. See Do boond pani, 1972

2 Gun Rusty, 1944 (Pal 4)

''2×4'', 1989 (Emshwiller 2)

2nd Hand Love, 1923 (Wellman 2)

3-Ring Wing-Ding, 1968 (Blanc 4)

3:10 to Yuma, 1957 (Daves 2, Ford 3, Cohn 4, Duning 4)

4×4, 1965 (Von Sydow 2)

5% de risque, 1979 (Cassel 3, Ganz 3)

6 in Paris. See Paris vu par . . ., 1965

6×2: sur et sous la communication, 1977 (Godard 2)

6.18.67, 1915 (Lucas 2)

6:30 Collection, 1934 (Watt 2)

7 Morts sur ordonnance, 1975 (Depardieu 3)

7–9–13, 1934 (Holger-Madsen 2)

8a. Bienal de São Paulo, 1965 (Diegues 2)

8 Ball Bunny, 1950 (Blanc 4, Jones 4, Maltese 4, Stalling 4)

8 Million Ways to Die, 1986 (Ashby 2, Stone 2, Bridges 3, Curtis 3)

8½, 1963 (Fellini 2, Wertmüller 2, Aimée 3, Cardinale 3, Mastroianni 3, Di Venanzo 4, Flaiano 4, Gherardi 4, Levine 4, Pinelli 4, Rota 4)

8×8, 1926 (Richter 2)

9 dnei odnogo goda, 1962 (Batalov 3)

9½ Weeks, 1986 (Rourke 3)

9/30/55, 1977 (Rosenman 4)

009 Mission to Hong Kong. See Geheimnis der drei Dschunken, 1965

10, 1979 (Edwards 2, Andrews 3, Moore 3, Mancini 4)

10 Korkusuz adam, 1964 (Güney 2)

10 Modern Commandments, 1927 (Arzner 2)

10 Rillington Place, 1970 (Attenborough 3, Hurt 3)

10 to Midnight, 1982 (Bronson 3)

10th Victim. See Decima vittima, 1965

10:30 P.M. Summer, 1966 (Dassin 2, Duras 2, Finch 3, Mercouri 3, Schneider 3)

11:30 P.M., 1915 (Walsh 2)

12 dicembre, 1972 (Pasolini 2, Volonté 3)

12 O'Clock, 1958 (Dutt 2)

13 at Dinner, 1985 (Dunaway 3, Ustinov 3)

13 Rue Madeleine, 1946 (Hathaway 2, Cagney 3, Jaffe 3, Malden 3, Basevi 4, De Rochement 4, Newman 4, Zanuck 4)

14 Carrot Rabbit, 1952 (Blanc 4, Foster 4, Freleng 4, Stalling 4)

14 dage i jernalderen, 1977 (Roos 2)

15/18, 1973 (Akerman 2)

15 from Rome. See Mostri, 1963

15 Jahre schweren Kerker. See Frauen aus der Wiener Vorstadt, 1925

15 Maiden Lane, 1936 (Dwan 2, Seitz 4)

15 Song Traits. See Songs, 1964–69

17 minutter Grønland, 1967 (Roos 2)

17ᶜ ciel, 1966 (Dalio 3, Trintignant 3)

19th Hole Club, 1936 (Terry 4)

$20 a Week, 1924 (Arliss 3, Colman 3)

£20 a Ton, 1955 (Anderson 2)

20 Juli, 1955 (Schell 3)

20 let sovetskogo kino. See Kino za XX liet, 1940

20 Million Miles to Earth, 1957 (Harryhausen 4)

20 Mule Team, 1940 (Baxter 3, Beery 3)

21 Carat Snatch. See Popsy Pop, 1970

21 Days. See First and the Last, 1937

21 Days Together. See First and the Last, 1937

$21.00 a Day Once a Month, 1941 (Lantz 4)

21 Miles, 1942 (Watt 2)

22 Misfortunes. See Dvadzatdva neshchastia, 1930

23½ Hours Leave, 1919 (King 2, Zukor 4)

23½ Hours Leave, 1937 (Bond 3, Carré 4)

23rd Psalm Branch: Parts I and II. See Songs, 1969

24 Hours in an Underground Market. See Chikagai 24-jikan, 1947

24 Hours of a Woman's Life, 1952 (Saville 2, Oberon 3, Challis 4, Francis 4)

24 Stunden aus dem Leben einer Frau, 1931 (Porten 3)

25 Fireman's Street. See Tüzoltó utca 25, 1973

25e Heure, 1967 (Quinn 3, Reggiani 3, Rosay 3, Delerue 4, Mankowitz 4, Ponti 4)

25th Hour. See 25e Heure, 1967

26 es también 19, 1981 (Alvarez 2)

27 Down, 1973 (Chandragupta 4)

27, Rue de la Paix, 1936 (Berry 3)

32 Rue Montmartre. See Derrière la façade, 1939

33-go-sha oto nashi, 1955 (Tsukasa 3)

33.333, 1924 (Molander 2)

35 Boulevard General Koenig, 1971 (Markopoulos 2)

36 Chowringhee Lane, 1977 (Chandragupta 4)

36 Fillette, 1988 (Léaud 3)

36 Hours, 1965 (Garner 3, Saint 3, Head 4, Tiomkin 4)

36 Hours to Kill, 1936 (Burnett 4, Miller 4)

40 Carats, 1973 (Kelly 3, Ullmann 3, Lang 4, Legrand 4)

40-Horse Hawkins, 1924 (Miller 4)

42nd Street, 1933 (Bacon 2, Berkeley 2, Daniels 3, Keeler 3, Powell 3, Rogers 3, Walthall 3, Orry-Kelly 4, Polito 4, Wallis 4, Warner 4, Zanuck 4)

45 dias, 1978 (Díaz 2)

45 Minutes from Hollywood, 1926 (Laurel and Hardy 2, Roach 4)

47 Loyal Ronin. See Chushingura, 1954

47 morto che parla, 1950 (Age and Scarpelli 4)

48 heures d'amour, 1968 (De Beauregard 4)

48-Hour Prison Break. See Shutsugoku yonjuhachi jikan, 1969

48 Hours. See Went the Day Well?, 1942

48 HRS., 1982 (Hill 2, Murphy 3, Nolte 3)

48-Year-Old Rebel. See Yonjuhachi-sai no teiko, 1956

49th Man, 1953 (Katzman 4)

49th Parallel, 1941 (Lean 2, Howard 3, Olivier 3, Walbrook 3, Mathieson 4, Young 4)

50–50, 1945 (Fleming 2)

50 Ans de Don Juan, 1922 (Vanel 3)

52 Pick-Up, 1986 (Scheider 3, Golan and Globus 4)

52nd Street, 1937 (Newman 4, Raksin 4, Reynolds 4, Wanger 4)

53 Stations of the Wind of Love. See Koikaze gojusan-tsugi, 1952

55 Days at Peking, 1962 (Hamer 2, Heston 2, Itami 2, Ray 2, Lukas 3, Gardner 3, Niven 3, Fisher 4, Tiomkin 4)

58–59, 1959 (Almendros 4)

60 Minutos con el primer mundial de boxeo amateur, 1974 (Alvarez 2)

65, 66, och jag, 1936 (Fischer 4)

66, 1966 (Breer 4)

69, 1968 (Breer 4)

70, 1970 (Breer 4)

70-Talets Människor, 1975 (Watkins 2)

72 gradusa nizhe nulia, 1976 (Yankovsky 3)

77, 1977 (Breer 4)

84 Charing Cross Road, 1986 (Brooks 2, Bancroft 3, Hopkins 3)

99, 1918 (Lugosi 3)

99 and 44/100% Dead!, 1974 (Frankenheimer 2, Harris 3, O'Brien 3, Mancini 4)

99 mujeres, 1969 (McCambridge 3, Lom 3, Schell 3)

99 River Street, 1953 (Planer 4)

100 Adventures, 1929 (Ptushko 4)

100 Men and a Girl, 1937 (Menjou 3, Kräly 4, Pasternak 4)

100 Rifles, 1969 (Reynolds 3, Welch 3, Goldsmith 4)

100 to 1 Shot, 1906 (Blackton 2)

102 Boulevard Haussman, 1990 (Bates 3)

111-es, 1919 (Korda 2, Korda 4)

113, 1935 (Clothier 4)

122 rue de Provence, 1978 (Morricone 4)

125, rue Montmartre, 1959 (Audiard 4)

300 Din Ke Baad, 1938 (Biswas 4)

317e Section, 1964 (Coutard 4, De Beauregard 4)

365 Days, 1922 (Roach 4)

365 Nights in Hollywood, 1934 (Faye 3)

365 Nights in Osaka. *See* Sanbyaku-rokujugo-ya, 1948

365 Nights in Tokyo. *See* Sanbyaku-rokujugo-ya, 1948

400 Blows. *See* **Quatre Cents Coups, 1959**

400 Million, 1939 (March 3, Nichols 4, Van Dongen 4)

491, 1964 (Fischer 4)

500 Hats of Bartholomew Cubbins, 1943 (Pal 4)

633 Squadron, 1964 (Koch 4)

711 Ocean Drive, 1950 (O'Brien 3, Planer 4)

800 Leguas por el Amazona, 1960 (Armendáriz 3)

813, 1976 (Mizoguchi 2)

813: The Adventures of Arsene Lupin. *See* 813, 1976

999 Nacht, 1919 (Albers 3)

1000 Carat Diamond. *See* Supercolpo da 7 miliard, 1966

$1000 a Minute, 1935 (Lewis 2, Pangborn 3)

1001 Arabian Nights, 1959 (Bosustow 4)

1001 Drawings, 1960 (Vukotić 4)

1001 Nacht, 1918 (Albers 3)

1001 Nights with Toho. *See* Toho senichi-ya, 1947

1492: The Conquest of Paradise, 1992 (Vangelis 4)

1776, 1909 (Griffith 2, Pickford 3, Blitzer 4)

1776, 1972 (Jenkins 4, Warner 4)

1814, 1910 (Gaumont 4)

1848, 1948 (Risi 2)

1877: The Grand Army of Starvation, 1985 (Jones 3)

1900, 1976 (Bertolucci 2, Bertini 3, DeNiro 3, Depardieu 3, Hayden 3, Lancaster 3, Sanda 3, Sutherland 3, Valli 3, Morricone 4, Storaro 4)

1914, die letzten Tage vor dem Weltbrand, 1931 (Homolka 3)

1919, A Russian Funeral, 1971 (Le Grice 2)

1941, 1979 (Fuller 2, Landis 2, Spielberg 2, Zemeckis 2, Belushi 3, Lee 3, Mifune 3, Oates 3, Rourke 3, Fraker 4, Williams 4)

1944, 1984 (Tyszkiewicz 3)

1969, 1988 (Dern 3)

1984, 1956 (O'Brien 3, Pleasence 3, Redgrave 3, Arnold 4)

1984, 1984 (Burton 3, Cusack 3, Hurt 3)

2000 B.C., 1931 (Terry 4)

2,000 Women, 1944 (Rank 4)

2000 Years After, 1969 (Terry-Thomas 3)

2001: A Space Odyssey, 1968 (Kubrick 2, Alcott 4, Trumbull 4, Unsworth 4)

2010, 1984 (Scheider 3, Edlund 4)

$5,000 Reward—Dead or Alive, 1911 (Dwan 2)

5000 Fingers of Dr. T, 1953 (Kramer 2, Planer 4, Salter 4)

10,000 Kids and a Cop, 1948 (Stewart 3)

20,000 Leagues under the Sea, 1954 (Douglas 3, Lorre 3, Lukas 3, Mason 3, Disney 4, Ellenshaw 4, Iwerks 4, Planer 4)

70,000 Witnesses, 1932 (Fort 4, Krasner 4)

$500,000 Reward, 1911 (Sennett 2)

600,000 Francs par mois, 1926 (Vanel 3)

660214, the Story of an IBM Card, 1961 (De Palma 2)

A, 1964 (Delerue 4, Lenica 4)
A & B in Ontario, 1966 (Frampton 2)
A & B in Ontario, 1984 (Wieland 4)
A.B.C., 1958 (Lassally 4)
A.B.C.A., 1943 (Alwyn 4)
A bout de souffle, 1960 (Broca 2, Chabrol 2, Godard 2, Melville 2, Belmondo 3, Seberg 3, Coutard 4, De Beauregard 4)
A Double Tour, 1959 (Broca 2, Chabrol 2, Belmondo 3, Decaë 4, Evein 4, Gegauff 4, Hakim 4, Rabier 4, Saulnier 4)
A la conquête du Pôle, 1912 (Méliès 2)
A la Mode, 1958 (Vanderbeek 2)
A nous deux, 1979 (Lelouch 2)
A Nous la liberté, 1931 (Clair 2, Auric 4, Meerson 4, Périnal 4, Trauner 4)
A Pied, à cheval et en voiture, 1957 (Belmondo 3, Cassel 3)
A propos de Nice, 1930 (Vigo 2)
A Proposito Lucky Luciano, 1973 (O'Brien 3, Steiger 3, Volonté 3, Cristaldi 4, Guerra 4)
. . . à Valparaiso, 1963 (Ivens 2, Delerue 4)
Aa furusato, 1938 (Mizoguchi 2, Yoda 4)
Aa, kaigun, 1969 (Mori 3)
Aamour, 1978 (Brdečka 4)
Aadha din aadhi raat, 1977 (Azmi 3)
Aadmi, 1968 (Kumar 3)
Aage Badho, 1947 (Anand 3)
Aaghat, 1985 (Nihalani 4)
Aah, 1953 (Kapoor 2)
Aaj ka M.L.A. Ram Avtaar, 1984 (Azmi 3)
Aakash, 1953 (Biswas 4)
Aan, 1952 (Kumar 3)
Aanasi yiğit doğurmus, 1966 (Güney 2)
Aandhiya, 1952 (Anand 3)
Aaraam, 1951 (Biswas 4)
Aaram, 1951 (Anand 3)
Aarohan, 1982 (Chandragupta 4)
Aaron Slick from Punkin Crick, 1952 (Bumstead 4, Head 4, Lang 4)
Aashik, 1962 (Kapoor 2)
Aashiyana, 1952 (Kapoor 2)
Aasman Mahal, 1965 (Abbas 4)
Aasraa, 1941 (Biswas 4)
Aath Din, 1946 (Burman 4)
Ab Dilli Dur Nahin, 1957 (Kapoor 2)
Ab Mitternacht, 1938 (Hoffmann 4)
Ab Morgen sind wir reich und ehrlich, 1977 (Baker 3, Kennedy 3)
Abajo el telón, 1954 (Cantinflas 3)
Abalone Industry, 1913 (Sennett 2)
Abandon Ship, 1956 (Zetterling 2, Power 3)
Abandonadas, 1944 (Fernández 2, Armendáriz 3, Del Rio 3, Figueroa 4)

Abandonado, 1949 (Armendáriz 3)
Abandoned, 1949 (Boyle 4, Daniels 4)
Abare andon, 1956 (Kagawa 3)
Abare Goemon, 1966 (Mifune 3)
Abare-jishi, 1953 (Yamada 3)
Abarenbo kaido, 1957 (Yamada 3, Yoda 4)
Abarenbou taishou, 1960 (Yoda 4)
Abastecimento, nova política, 1968 (Pereira Dos Santos 2)
Abbandano, 1940 (Stallich 4)
Abbasso la miseria, 1945 (Magnani 3)
Abbasso la ricchezza!, 1946 (De Sica 2, Magnani 3)
Abbé Constantin, 1925 (Duvivier 2)
Abbé Constantin, 1933 (Rosay 3, Burel 4, Spaak 4)
Abbott and Costello Go to Mars, 1953 (Abbott and Costello 3, Boyle 4)
Abbott and Costello in Hollywood, 1945 (Walters 2, Abbott and Costello 3, Ball 3, Irene 4)
Abbott and Costello in the Foreign Legion, 1950 (Abbott and Costello 3)
Abbott and Costello Meet Captain Kidd, 1952 (Aldrich 2, Abbott and Costello 3, Laughton 3, Cortez 4)
Abbott and Costello Meet Dr. Jekyll and Mr. Hyde, 1954 (Abbott and Costello 3, Karloff 3, Salter 4, Westmore Family 4)
Abbott and Costello Meet Frankenstein, 1948 (Abbott and Costello 3, Lugosi 3, Price 3, Pierce 4)
Abbott and Costello Meet the Ghosts. See Abbott and Costello Meet Frankenstein, 1948
Abbott and Costello Meet the Invisible Man, 1951 (Abbott and Costello 3, Salter 4)
Abbott and Costello Meet the Keystone Cops, 1955 (Abbott and Costello 3)
Abbott and Costello Meet the Killer, Boris Karloff, 1949 (Abbott and Costello 3, Karloff 3)
Abbott and Costello Meet the Mummy, 1955 (Abbott and Costello 3, Salter 4)
Abdication, 1974 (Cusack 3, Finch 3, Ullmann 3, Rota 4, Unsworth 4)
Abduction, 1975 (Malone 3)
Abduction of Saint Anne, 1973 (Duning 4)
Abduction of St. Anne, 1975 (Wagner 3)
Abductors, 1957 (McLaglen 3, La Shelle 4)
Abdul the Damned, 1935 (Kortner 3, Eisler 4)
Abdullah, 1981 (Kapoor 2)
Abdullah the Great, 1954 (Kendall 3, Auric 4, Garmes 4)

Abdullah's Harem. See Abdullah the Great, 1954
Abe Gets Even With Father, 1911 (Sennett 2)
Abe Lincoln in Illinois, 1940 (Gordon 3, Massey 3, Howe 4, Plunkett 4, Polglase 4, Sherwood 4)
Abeille et les hommes, 1960 (Braunberger 4)
Abeilles, 1956 (Braunberger 4)
Abel Gance—The Charm of Dynamite, 1968 (Anderson 2, Menges 4)
Abend . . . Nacht . . . Morgen, 1920 (Murnau 2, Veidt 3)
Abenteuer: Die Affenbrücke See Doktor Dolittle und seine Tiere, 1928
Abenteuer: Die Reise nach Afrika. See Doktor Dolittle und seine Tiere, 1928
Abenteuer der Sybille Brant, 1925 (Porten 3)
Abenteuer der Thea Roland, 1933 (Dagover 3)
Abenteuer des Dr. Kircheisen, 1920 (Wiene 2)
Abenteuer des Königs Pausole, 1933 (Jannings 3, Rathaus 4)
Abenteuer des Prinzen Achmed. See Geschichte des Prinzen Achmed, 1922
Abenteuer des Till Ulenspiegel, 1956 (Matras 4)
Abenteuer einer schönen Frau. See Abenteuer der Thea Roland, 1933
Abenteuer eines Heimgekehrten. See Rinaldo Rinaldini, 1927
Abenteuer eines jungen Herrn in Polen, 1934 (Fröhlich 3, Tschechowa 3)
Abenteuer eines Zehnmarkscheinen, 1927 (Homolka 3, Balàzs 4, Freund 4)
Abenteuer geht weiter, 1939 (Gallone 2)
Abenteuer in Wien. See Gefährliches Abenteuer, 1953
Abenteurer, 1921 (Courant 4)
Abgrund der Seelen, 1920 (Gad 2)
Abhagin, 1938 (Roy 2)
Abhijan, 1962 (Chatterjee 3, Chandragupta 4)
Abhilasha, 1938 (Biswas 4)
Abhimaan, 1973 (Bachchan 3, Burman 4)
Abhiman, 1957 (Biswas 4)
Abidjan, port de pêche, 1962 (Rouch 2)
Abie's Irish Rose, 1929 (Fleming 2, Banton 4, Furthman 4, Mankiewicz 4, Rosson 4, Schulberg 4)
Abilene Town, 1946 (Scott 3)
Abito nero da sposa, 1943 (Flaiano 4)
Able Man. See Karl för sin hatt, 1940
Ableminded Lady, 1922 (Walthall 3)
Abominable Dr. Phibes, 1971 (Cotten 3, Price 3, Terry-Thomas 3)

3

Abominable Homme des douanes, 1963
(Brasseur 3, Dalio 3, Delerue 4)

Abominable Snow Rabbit, 1961 (Blanc 4,
Jones 4)

Abominable Snowman. *See* Jujin Kuki-
Otoko, 1955

Abominable Snowman, 1957 (Cushing 3,
Carreras 4, Trumbo 4)

Abominable Snowman of the Himalayas.
See Abominable Snowman, 1957

About Face, 1942 (Dumont 3, Roach 4)

About Face, 1951 (Glennon 4, Prinz 4)

About Fakes. *See* F for Fake, 1975

About Mrs. Leslie, 1954 (Ryan 3, Head 4,
Laszlo 4, Wallis 4, Young 4)

About 'The White Bus', 1967 (Anderson 2)

Above All Law. *See* Indische Grabmal, 1921

Above and Beyond, 1952 (Taylor 3, Frank 4,
Friedhofer 4, Rose 4)

Above Suspicion, 1943 (Saville 2,
Crawford 3, MacMurray 3, Rathbone 3,
Veidt 3, Irene 4, Kaper 4, Mayer 4)

Above the Abyss. *See* Nad propastí, 1921

Above Us the Waves, 1955 (Mills 3, Rank 4)

Abracadabra, 1958 (Vukotić 4)

Abraham Bosse, 1972 (Leenhardt 2)

Abraham Lincoln, 1924 (Marion 4)

Abraham Lincoln, 1930 (Griffith 2,
Bosworth 3, Huston 3, Walthall 3,
Menzies 4, Schenck 4, Struss 4)

Abraham's Gold, 1990 (Schygulla 3)

Abrégeons les formalités!, 1917 (Feyder 2)

Abril de Giron, 1966 (Alvarez 2)

Abril de Vietnam en el año del gato, 1975
(Alvarez 2)

Abroad with Two Yanks, 1944 (Dwan 2,
Bendix 3)

Abschied, 1930 (Siodmak 2, Schüfftan 4)

Abseits vom Blück, 1916 (Freund 4)

Abseits vom Glück, 1914 (Porten 3,
Messter 4)

Absence, 1975 (Brakhage 2)

Absence of Malice, 1981 (Pollack 2, Field 3,
Newman 3, Roizman 4)

Absent-Minded Bootblack, 1903
(Hepworth 2)

Absent-Minded Professor, 1960
(Stevenson 2, MacMurray 3, Disney 4,
Ellenshaw 4)

Absent-Minded Waiter, 1979 (Martin 3,
Hamlisch 4, Henry 4)

Absinthe, 1914 (Brenon 2)

Absolute Quiet, 1936 (Waxman 4)

Absolution, 1978 (Burton 3)

Absturz, 1922 (Nielsen 3)

Abul Hasan, 1931 (Mehboob 2)

Abus de confiance, 1937 (Darrieux 3
Vanel 3, Burel 4)

Abused Confidence. *See* Abus de confiance,
1937

Abyss, 1914 (Selig 4)

Abyss. *See* Oeuvre au noir, 1988

Academician Ivan Pavlov. *See* Akademik
Ivan Pavlov, 1949

Academy Awards Film, 1951 (Clarke 4)

Academy Decides, 1937 (Baxter 2)

Acadie, L'Acadie!, 1970 (Perrault 2)

Acapulco, 1951 (Fernández 2)

Accadde al commissariato, 1954 (Sordi 3)

Accadde al penitenziario, 1955 (Fabrizi 3,
Sordi 3, Delli Colli 4)

**Accattone, 1961 (Bertolucci 2, Pasolini 2,
Delli Colli 4)**

Accent on Love, 1941 (Clarke 4, Day 4,
Trumbo 4)

Accent on Youth, 1935 (Marshall 3,
Sidney 3, Shamroy 4)

Acciaio, 1931 (Ruttman 2)

Accident. *See* Uberfall, 1928

Accident, 1961 (Kosma 4)

**Accident, 1967 (Losey 2, Baker 3,
Bogarde 3, Seyrig 3, Dillon 4, Fisher 4,
Pinter 4)**

Accident d'auto, 1907 (Feuillade 2)

Accident Insurance, 1910 (White 3)

Accidental Accidents, 1924 (McCarey 2,
Roach 4)

Accidental Tourist, 1988 (Kasdan 2, Hurt 3,
Turner 3, Williams 4)

Accidents Will Happen, 1938 (Reagan 3)

Accord final, 1939 (Sirk 2, Berry 3, Blier 3)

Accordéon et ses vedettes, 1946 (Decaë 4)

Accordeon Song, 1974 (Brdečka 4)

According to Hoyle, 1922 (Van Dyke 2)

Accordion Joe, 1938 (Fleischer 4)

Accounting, 1915 (Bushman 3)

Accounts of Affection. *See* Aijo no kessan,
1956

Accroche-coeur, 1938 (Guitry 2)

Accursed. *See* Traitors, 1957

Accusation of Broncho Billy, 1913
(Anderson 3)

Accused, 1936 (Del Rio 3, Withers 3,
Akins 4)

Accused, 1948 (Dieterle 2, Jaffe 3, Young 3,
Dreier 4, Head 4, Krasner 4, Wallis 4,
Young 4)

Accused, 1988 (Foster 3)

Accused of Murder, 1956 (Van Cleef 3,
Burnett 4)

Accusée, levez-vous, 1930 (Tourneur 2,
Vanel 3, Douy 4, Spaak 4)

Accusing Finger, 1936 (Carey 3, Head 4)

Ace Eli and Rodger of the Skies, 1973
(Spielberg 2, Robertson 3, Goldsmith 4,
Smith 4)

Ace High, 1918 (Mix 3)

Ace High. *See* Quattro dell'ave Maria, 1968

Ace in the Hole, 1951 (Wilder 2, Douglas 3,
Edouart 4, Friedhofer 4, Lang 4)

Ace in the Saddle, 1919 (Carey 3)

Ace of Aces, 1933 (Bellamy 3, Cooper 4,
Plunkett 4, Polglase 4, Saunders 4,
Steiner 4)

Ace of Aces. *See* As des as, 1982

Ace of Cads, 1926 (Menjou 3, Hunt 4)

Ace of Hearts, 1921 (Chaney 3)

Ace of Hearts, 1974 (Rooney 3)

Ace of Spades, 1931 (Fleischer 4)

Ace of Spades, 1935 (Pearson 2)

Ace of the Saddle, 1919 (Ford 2)

Ace Up Your Sleeve. *See* Crime and Passion,
1976

Aces High, 1976 (Gielgud 3, Howard 3,
McDowell 3, Milland 3, Fisher 4)

Aces Wild, 1937 (Carey 3)

Achanak, 1973 (Abbas 4)

Ache in Every Stake, 1941 (Three Stooges 3)

Aching Youth, 1928 (Roach 4)

Achoo Mr. Keroochev, 1959 (Vanderbeek 2)

Acht Mädels im Boot, 1932 (Junge 4)

Acht Tage Gluck. *See* Liebesexpress, 1931

Acht und Siebzig, 1980 (Tyszkiewicz 3)

Achte Gebot, 1915 (Leni 2)

Achte Wochentag. *See* Osmy dzień tygodnia,
1957

Achtung! Bandit!, 1951 (Lollobrigida 3, Di
Venanzo 4)

Achtung Harry! Augen auf!, 1926 (Galeen 4)

Achtung! Lieb-Lebensgefahr!, 1929
(Metzner 4)

Achtzehnjährigen, 1927 (Planer 4)

Acid Test, 1914 (Costello 3)

Aciéries de la marine et d'Homécourt, 1925
(Grémillon 2)

Ack, du är some en ros, 1967 (Fischer 4)

Acoso, 1964 (Solas 2)

Acostates første Offer. *See* Krigens Fjende,
1915

Acqua, 1960 (Almendros 4)

Acquaintances of the Street. *See* Známosti z
ulice, 1929

Acque di primavera, 1942 (Cervi 3)

Acquittal, 1923 (Brown 2, Furthman 4)

Acquitted, 1916 (Love 3)

Acres of Alfalfa, 1914 (Sennett 2)

Acrobate, 1940 (Fernandel 3)

Acrobatic Toys. *See* Freres Boutdebois, 1908

Acrobatty Bunny, 1946 (Blanc 4,
McKimson 4, Stalling 4)

Across 110th Street, 1972 (Quinn 3)

Across the Alley, 1913 (Sennett 2)

Across the Araks. *See* Po tu storonu Araksa,
1946

Across the Atlantic, 1914 (Brenon 2)

Across the Atlantic, 1928 (Blanke 4)

Across the Border. *See* Special Inspector,
1939

Across the Bridge, 1957 (Steiger 3,
Greene 4, Rank 4)

Across the Continent, 1922 (Reid 3)

Across the Great Divide, 1913 (Anderson 3)

Across the Hall, 1914 (Sennett 2)

Across the Heart, 1986 (Branco 4)

Across the Lake, 1988 (Hopkins 3)

Across the Line, 1931 (Carey 3)

Across the Mexican Line, 1911 (Guy 2)

Across the Pacific, 1926 (Loy 3, Haskin 4,
Zanuck 4)

Across the Pacific, 1942 (Huston 2, Astor 3,
Bogart 3, Greenstreet 3, Deutsch 4,
Edeson 4, Haskin 4, Wald 4)

Across the Pacific, 1957 (Bernard 4)

Across the Plains. *See* War on the Plains,
1912

Across the Rio Grande, 1913 (Anderson 3)

Across the Rio Grande, 1980 (Johnson 3)

Across the River and Into the Trees, 1987
(Frankenheimer 2)

Across the Wide Missouri, 1951
(Wellman 2, Gable 3, Keel 3, Menjou 3,
Basevi 4, Jennings 4, Plunkett 4,
Raksin 4)

Across to Singapore, 1928 (Crawford 3,
Novarro 3, Wong 3, Gibbons 4, Mayer 4,
Seitz 4)

Act of Aggression. *See* Agression, 1975

Act of Betrayal, 1988 (Gould 3)

Act of Deceit. *See* French Kiss, 1981

Act of God, 1981 (Greenaway 2)

Act of Love, 1954 (Litvak 2, Bardot 3,
Douglas 3, Reggiani 3, Hornbeck 4,
Trauner 4)

Act of Love, 1980 (Rourke 3)

Act of Murder, 1948 (March 3, O'Brien 3,
Boyle 4, Mohr 4)

Act of the Heart. *See* Acte du coeur, 1970

Act of Vengeance ... A True Story, 1989
(Bronson 3, Burstyn 3)

Act of Violence, 1948 (Zinnemann 2, Astor 3, Leigh 3, Ryan 3, Kaper 4, Rose 4, Surtees 4)

Act One, 1963 (Robards 3, Segal 3, Wallach 3, Schary 4)

Actas de Marusia, 1985 (Volonté 3)

Actas de Merusia, 1976 (Theodorakis 4)

Acte d'amour. *See* Act of Love, 1954

Acte du coeur, 1970 (Bujold 3, Sutherland 3)

Action, 1921 (Ford 2)

Action for Slander, 1937 (Saville 2, Withers 3, Dalrymple 4, Korda A. 4, Korda V. 4, Stradling 4)

Action in Arabia, 1944 (Dalio 3, Sanders 3, Hunt 4)

Action in the North Atlantic, 1943 (Bacon 2, Bogart 3, Gordon 3, Massey 3, Burnett 4, Deutsch 4, Gaudio 4, McCord 4, Wald 4, Warner 4)

Action Man. *See* Soleil des voyous, 1967

Action of the Tiger, 1957 (Connery 3, Johnson 3, Lom 3)

Action under Arsenal. *See* Akcja pod Arsenalem, 1977

Actor, 1978 (Kidd 4)

Actor, 1989 (Piccoli 3, Quinn 3)

Actor Finney's Finish, 1914 (Beery 3)

Actors and Sin, 1952 (Robinson 3, Garmes 4, Hecht 4)

Actor's Revenge. *See* Yokino-jo henge, 1963

Actress. *See* Szinèszno, 1920

Actress, 1928 (Shearer 3, Daniels 4, Day 4, Gibbons 4, Lewin 4, Mayer 4)

Actress. *See* Aktrisa, 1943

Actress. *See* Joyu, 1947

Actress, 1953 (Cukor 2, Gordon 3, Perkins 3, Simmons 3, Tracy 3, Wright 3, Gibbons 4, Kaper 4, Plunkett 4, Rosson 4)

Actress and the Angel. *See* Butter and Egg Man, 1928

Actress and the Cowboys, 1911 (Dwan 2)

Actress and the Singer, 1911 (Lawrence 3)

Acts of Love, 1978 (Kazan 2)

Actualités burlesques, 1948 (Braunberger 4)

Actualités: ça c'est des nouvelles!, 1949 (Braunberger 4)

Acusation, 1965 (Solas 2)

A.D., 1985 (Houseman 4)

Ad ogni costo, 1967 (Kinski 3, Leigh 3, Robinson 3, Morricone 4)

Ada, 1961 (Hayward 3, Martin 3, Kaper 4, Rose 4, Ruttenberg 4)

Ada dans la jungle, 1988 (Blier 3)

Adalat, 1977 (Bachchan 3)

Adam and Eva, 1922 (Davies 3, Gaudio 4)

Adam and Evelyn. *See* Adam and Evelyne, 1949

Adam and Evelyne, 1949 (Granger 3, Simmons 3, Green 4, Rank 4)

Adam and Evil, 1927 (Day 4, Gibbons 4)

Adam at 6.00 a.m., 1970 (Douglas 3)

Adam Had Four Sons, 1941 (Bergman 3, Hayward 3, Wray 3, Cohn 4)

Adam und Eva, 1923 (Krauss 3)

Adamo e Eva, 1950 (De Laurentiis 4)

Adam's Apple, 1928 (Launder and Gilliat 2)

Adam's Rib, 1923 (De Mille 2, Buckland 4, Gillespie 4, Macpherson 4)

Adam's Rib, 1949 (Cukor 2, Gordon 3, Hepburn 3, Holliday 3, Sinatra 3, Tracy 3, Folsey 4, Gibbons 4, Kanin 4, Mayer 4, Plunkett 4, Rozsa 4)

Adam's Woman, 1970 (Mills 3)

Adamson i Sverige, 1966 (Fischer 4)

Adam 2. *See* Adam II, 1969

Adam II, 1969 (Lenica 4)

Adauchi goyomi, 1940 (Hasegawa 3)

Adauchi hizakurige, 1936 (Yoda 4)

Adauchi kokyogaku, 1940 (Shimura 3)

Adauchi kyodai kagami, 1933 (Hasegawa 3)

Adauchi senshu, 1931 (Yamada 3)

Addams Family, 1990 (Roizman 4)

Adding Machine, 1968 (Lassally 4)

Addio, amore!, 1944 (Amidei 4)

Addio fratello credele, 1971 (Morricone 4, Storaro 4)

Addio Kira, 1942 (Valli 3)

Addio mia bella signora, 1953 (Cervi 3)

Addio Mimì, 1947 (Pangborn 3)

Address Unknown, 1944 (Wood 2, Lukas 3, Maté 4, Menzies 4)

Adéla Hasn't Had Her Supper Yet. *See* Adéla ještě nevečerela, 1977

Adéla ještě nevečerela, 1977 (Kučera 4, Švankmajer 4)

Adelaide, 1968 (Thulin 3)

Adelita, 1937 (Armendáriz 3, Figueroa 4)

Adéma i aviateur, 1933 (Fernandel 3, Schüfftan 4)

Adémaï au moyen age, 1935 (Spaak 4)

Ademat au Moyen-Age, 1935 (Simon 3)

Adhemar, 1951 (Guitry 2, Fernandel 3)

Adhémar Lampiot, 1932 (Christian-Jaque 2)

Adieu Blaireau, 1985 (Girardot 3)

Adieu Bonaparte, 1984 (Piccoli 3)

Adieu Chérie, 1945 (Darrieux 3)

Adieu l'ami, 1968 (Bronson 3, Delon 3)

Adieu Léonard, 1943 (Brasseur 3, Signoret 3, Douy 4, Kosma 4, Prévert 4)

Adieu les beaux jours, 1933 (Gabin 3, Gründgens 3)

Adieu Philippine, 1960 (De Beauregard 4)

Adieu poulet, 1976 (Sarde 4)

Adios. *See* Lash, 1930

Adios Amigo, 1975 (Pryor 3)

Adios companeros. *See* Conde Dracula, 1970

Adiós Nicanor, 1937 (Fernández 2)

Adios Sabata. *See* Indio Black, 1970

Adjudant des Zaren, 1929 (Mozhukin 3)

Adjunkt Vrba, 1929 (Heller 4)

Adjustment and Work, 1986 (Wiseman 2)

Adjutant seiner Hoheit, 1933 (Heller 4)

Admirable Crichton. *See* Male and Female, 1919

Admirable Crichton, 1957 (More 3, Dalrymple 4)

Admiral Nakhimov. *See* Amiral Nakhimov, 1946

Admiral Ushakov, 1953 (Bondarchuk 3)

Admiral Was a Lady, 1950 (O'Brien 3, Cortez 4, Polglase 4)

Admiral Yamamoto. *See* Yamamoto Isoruku, 1968

Admission Free, 1932 (Fleischer 4)

Adolescent. *See* Adolescente, 1982

Adolescent Girl. *See* Adolescente, 1979

Adolescente, 1979 (Moreau 3, Sarde 4)

Adolescente, 1982 (Signoret 3)

Adolescents. *See* Fleur de l'age, ou les adolescents, 1964

Adolf & Marlene, 1976 (Ballhaus 4)

Adolphe, ou l'âge tendre, 1968 (Noiret 3, Evein 4, Stawiński 4)

Adoption, 1978 (Chaplin 3)

Adoptivkind, 1914 (Porten 3)

Adorabili e bugiarde, 1957 (Delli Colli 4)

Adorable, 1933 (Dieterle 2, Wilder 2, Gaynor 3, Seitz 4)

Adorable Creatures. *See* Adorable Créatures, 1952

Adorable Créatures, 1952 (Darrieux 3, Feuillère 3, Gélin 3, Matras 4, Spaak 4)

Adorable Idiot. *See* Ravissante Idiote, 1964

Adorable Julia, 1962 (Boyer 3)

Adorable Savage, 1920 (Johnson 3)

Adoration, 1928 (Biro 4, Seitz 4)

Adressatin verstorben, 1911 (Porten 3, Messter 4)

Adriana Lecouvreur, 1955 (Vitti 3)

Adrien, 1943 (Fernandel 3, Aurenche 4)

Adrienne Lecouvreur, 1938 (L'Herbier 2, Fresnay 3)

Adua e le compagne, 1960 (Mastroianni 3, Signoret 3, Pinelli 4)

A-Ducking They Did Go, 1939 (Three Stooges 3)

Adultera, 1945 (Pinelli 4)

Adultery, 1983 (Brocka 2)

Adultress. *See* Thérèse Raquin, 1953

Advance to the Rear, 1964 (Blondell 3, Douglas 3, Ford 3, Krasner 4)

Advent of Jane, 1912 (Lawrence 3)

Adventure, 1925 (Fleming 2, Beery 3, Johnson 3)

Adventure. *See* Aventyret, 1936

Adventure, 1945 (Fleming 2, Blondell 3, Gable 3, Garson 3, Irene 4, Mayer 4, Ruttenberg 4, Stothart 4, Veiller 4)

Adventure à Paris, 1936 (Arletty 3, Berry 3)

Adventure for Two. *See* Demi-Paradise, 1943

Adventure for Two. *See* Nous deux, 1979

Adventure in Algiers, 1952 (Raft 3)

Adventure in Baltimore, 1949 (Temple 3, Young 3, D'Agostino 4)

Adventure in Diamonds, 1940 (Head 4, Lang 4)

Adventure in Hearts, 1919 (Cruze 2)

Adventure in Manhattan, 1936 (Arthur 3, McCrea 3, Buchman 4)

Adventure in Sahara, 1938 (Fuller 2, Planer 4)

Adventure in the Autumn Woods, 1912 (Griffith 2, Barrymore 3, Bitzer 4, Carey 3)

Adventure of Mark Twain, 1944 (Crisp 3)

Adventure of Sherlock Holmes' Smarter Brother, 1975 (Finney 3, Wilder 3, Fisher 4)

Adventure of the Shooting Party. *See* Pickwick Papers, 1913

Adventure of Westgate Siminary. *See* Pickwick Papers, 1913

Adventure Starts Here. *See* Här börjar äventyret, 1965

Adventurer, 1917 (Chaplin 2, Guy 2, (Purviance 3)

Adventurer, 1927 (Van Dyke 2)

Adventurer. *See* Äventyrare, 1942

Adventurers, 1950 (Hawkins 3, Morris 4)

Adventurers, 1970 (Borgnine 3, Brazzi 3, De Havilland 3, Rey 3, Levine 4, Renoir 4)

Adventures d'Arsène Lupin, 1956 (Cloquet 4)

Adventure's End, 1937 (Wayne 3)

Adventures in History. *See* Guerre est finie, 1966

Adventures in the Far North, 1923 (Fleischer 4)

Adventures in Washington, 1941 (Marshall 3)

Adventures of *, 1957 (Hubley 4)

Adventures of a Brown Man in Search of
  Civilisation, 1972 (Ivory 2, Lassally 4)

Adventures of a Private Eye, 1977 (Dors 3)

Adventures of a Ten-Mark Note. *See*
  Abenteuer Eines Zehnmarkscheines, 1928

Adventures of a Young Man. *See*
  Hemingway's Adventures of A Young
  Man, 1962

Adventures of an Old Flirt, 1909 (Porter 2)

Adventures of Arsène Lupin. *See*
  Adventures d'Arsène Lupin, 1956

Adventures of Baron Munchausen, 1988
  (Gilliam 2, Reed 3, Williams 3,
  Rotunno 4)

Adventures of Barry MacKenzie, 1972
  (Beresford 2)

Adventures of Billy, 1911 (Griffith 2,
  Crisp 3, Bitzer 4)

Adventures of Buckaroo Banzai: Across the
  Eighth Dimension, 1984 (Curtis 3)

Adventures of Bullwhip Griffin, 1966
  (Malden 3, McDowall 3, Disney 4,
  Ellenshaw 4)

Adventures of Captain Africa, 1954
  (Katzman 4)

Adventures of Captain Fabian, 1951
  (Flynn 3, Moorehead 3, Presle 3, Price 3,
  Douy 4, Lourié 4)

Adventures of Casanova, 1948
  (Friedhofer 4)

Adventures of Colonel Heezaliar—He's a
  Daredevil, 1915 (Bray 4)

Adventures of Dr. Dolittle. *See* Doktor
  Dolittle und seine Tiere, 1928

Adventures of Dolly, 1908 (Griffith 2)

Adventures of Don Juan, 1949 (Florey 2,
  Flynn 3, Steiner 4, Wald 4)

Adventures of Don Quixote, 1973
  (Harrison 3, Legrand 4)

Adventures of Francois Villon. *See*
  Oubliette, 1914

Adventures of Frank and Jesse James, 1948
  (Canutt 4)

Adventures of Gerard, 1970 (Skolimowski 2,
  Cardinale 3, Hawkins 3)

Adventures of Girard, 1971 (Wallach 3)

Adventures of Goopi and Bagha. *See* Goopy
  Gyne Bagha Byne, 1969

Adventures of Hajji Baba, 1954 (Tiomkin 4,
  Wanger 4)

Adventures of Huckleberry Finn, 1939
  (Mankiewicz 2, Rooney 3, Mayer 4,
  Waxman 4)

Adventures of Huckleberry Finn, 1960
  (Curtiz 2, Keaton 2, Carradine 3, Hall 4,
  McCord 4)

Adventures of Huckleberry Finn, 1986
  (Gish 3, Lassally 4)

Adventures of Ichabod and Mr. Toad. *See*
  Ichabod and Mr. Toad, 1949

Adventures of Kathlyn, 1914 (Selig 4)

Adventures of King Pausole. *See* Aventures
  du roi Pausole, 1933

Adventures of Marco Polo, 1938 (Cooper 3,
  Rathbone 3, Turner 3, Basevi 4, Day 4,
  Friedhofer 4, Glennon 4, Goldwyn 4,
  Maté 4, Newman 4, Sherwood 4)

Adventures of Mark Twain, 1944 (Siegel 2,
  Carradine 3, March 3, Lasky 4, Polito 4,
  Steiner 4)

Adventures of Mark Twain, 1986 (Murch 4,
  Vinton 4)

Adventures of Martin Eden, 1942 (Ford 3,
  Trevor 3, Planer 4, Schulberg 4)

Adventuress of Milo and Otis, 1989
  (Moore 3)

Adventures of Mr. Wonderful, 1959
  (Ustinov 3)

Adventures of Nick Carter, 1972
  (Crawford 3, Winters 3, Bumstead 4)

Adventures of PC 49, 1949 (Carreras 4)

Adventures of Pinocchio. *See* Pinocchiova
  dobrodružstvi, 1971

Adventures of Popeye, 1935 (Fleischer 4)

Adventures of Prince Achmed. *See*
  Geschichte des Prinzen Achmed, 1922

Adventures of Quentin Durward. *See*
  Quentin Durward, 1955

Adventures of Rex and Rinty, 1935
  (Lewis 2, Eason 4)

Adventures of Robin Hood, 1938
  (Curtiz 2, De Havilland 3, Flynn 3,
  Rains 3, Rathbone 3, Blanke 4,
  Eason 4, Friedhofer 4, Gaudio 4,
  Korngold 4, Miller 4, Polito 4, Raine 4,
  Wallis 4)

Adventures of Robinson Crusoe, 1922
  (Johnson 3)

Adventures of Sadie. *See* Our Girl Friday,
  1953

Adventures of Sherlock Holmes, 1939
  (Lupino 3, Rathbone 3, Day 4, Raksin 4,
  Shamroy 4)

Adventures of Shorty, 1914 (Ince 4)

Adventures of Sir Galahad, 1950
  (Katzman 4)

Adventures of Takla Makan. *See* Kiganjo no
  boken, 1966

Adventures of Tartu, 1943 (Donat 3)

Adventures of the Queen, 1975 (Bellamy 3)

Adventures of Till Eulenspiegel. *See*
  Abenteuer des Till Ulenspiegel, 1956

Adventures of Togo and Dinky, 1925
  (Bray 4)

Adventures of Tom Sawyer, 1938
  (Brennan 3, Howe 4, Menzies 4,
  Plunkett 4, Selznick 4, Steiner 4,
  Wheeler 4)

Adventures of Two Swedish Emigrants in
  America. *See* Två Svenska emigranters
  aventyr i Amerika, 1912

Adventuress, 1920 (Valentino 3)

Adventuress. *See* I See a Dark Stranger,
  1946

Adventurous Automobile Trip. *See* Raid
  Paris-Monte Carlo en deux heures, 1905

Adventurous Sex, 1925 (Bow 3)

Adversary. *See* Pratidwandi, 1970

Advice to the Lovelorn, 1933 (Newman 4,
  Zanuck 4)

Advise and Consent, 1962 (Preminger 2,
  Ayres 3, Fonda 3, Laughton 3,
  Meredith 3, Pidgeon 3, Tierney 3, Bass 4,
  Wheeler 4)

Adviser of the World's Adviser. *See* Tenka
  no goikenban o Ikensuru otoko, 1947

Aelita, 1924 (Protazanov 2)

Aerial Gunner, 1944 (Gable 3, Mitchum 3)

Aeriel Joyride, 1916 (Laurel and Hardy 3)

Aero-Engine, 1933 (Grierson 2)

Aerogard, 1935 (Gerasimov 2, Tisse 4)

Aeropuerto, 1953 (Rey 3)

Aesop's Fable, 1950 (Terry 4)

Aesop's Fable: Golden Egg Goosie, 1951
  (Terry 4)

Aesop's Fable: The Mosquito, 1945
  (Terry 4)

Afanasi Nikitin, 1957 (Biswas 4)

Affair, 1973 (Wagner 3, Wood 3)

Affair in Havana, 1957 (Armendáriz 3)

Affair in Monte Carlo. *See* Twenty-four
  Hours of a Woman's Life, 1952

Affair in Trinidad, 1952 (Ford 3,
  Hayworth 3, Cohn 4, Duning 4,
  Walker 4)

Affair Lafont. *See* Conflit, 1938

Affair of Hearts, 1910 (Griffith 2, Sennett 2)

Affair of Susan, 1935 (Waxman 4)

Affair of the Follies, 1927 (Gaudio 4,
  Wilson 4)

Affair of the Heart. *See* Dole plotovi, 1962

Affair of the Skin, 1963 (Grant 3, Fields 4,
  Maddow 4)

Affair to Remember, 1957 (Daves 2,
  McCarey 2, Grant 3, Kerr 3,
  Friedhofer 4, Krasner 4, LeMaire 4,
  Smith 4, Wald 4, Wheeler 4)

Affair with a Stranger, 1953 (Darwell 3,
  Mature 3, Simmons 3)

Affaire classée, 1932 (Spaak 4)

Affaire Clémenceau, 1918 (Bertini 3)

Affaire Coquelet, 1934 (Matras 4)

Affaire de la Rue de Courcine, 1923
  (Chevalier 3)

Affaire des femmes, 1988 (Chabrol 2,
  Huppert 3, Rabier 4)

Affaire des poisons, 1955 (Darrieux 3,
  D'Eaubonne 4)

Affaire des poissons, 1965 (Braunberger 4)

Affaire Dominici, 1972 (Depardieu 3,
  Gabin 3)

Affaire Dreyfus, 1899 (Méliès 2, Pathé 4)

Affaire du collier de la reine, 1946
  (L'Herbier 2, Annenkov 4, Douy 4,
  Ibert 4, Spaak 4)

Affaire du courrier de Lyon, 1937
  (Aurenche 4)

Affaire d'une nuit, 1960 (Bardot 3,
  Aurenche 4)

Affaire est dans le sac, 1932 (Jaubert 4,
  Prévert 4, Trauner 4)

Affaire Lafarge, 1937 (Von Stroheim 2,
  Dalio 3, Aurenche 4, Auric 4, Fradetal 4,
  Lourié 4)

Affaire Manet, 1950 (Astruc 2)

Affaire Maurizius, 1954 (Duvivier 2,
  Gélin 3, Vanel 3, Walbrook 3,
  Douy 4)

Affaire Nina B, 1962 (Siodmak 2,
  D'Eaubonne 4, Delerue 4)

Affaires publiques, 1934 (Bresson 2,
  Dalio 3)

Affaires sont les affaires, 1943 (Vanel 3)

Affairs de coeur, 1909 (Cohl 4)

Affairs of a Gentleman, 1934 (Lukas 3)

Affairs of Anatol, 1921 (Daniels 3, Reid 3,
  Swanson 3, Macpherson 4, Struss 4,
  Zukor 4)

Affairs of Annabel, 1938 (Ball 3, Metty 4,
  Polglase 4)

Affairs of Cappy Ricks, 1937 (Brennan 3)

Affairs of Cellini, 1934 (La Cava 2, Ball 3,
  Calhern 3, March 3, Wray 3, Day 4,
  Meredyth 4, Newman 4, Rosher 4,
  Zanuck 4)

Affairs of Dobie Gillis, 1953 (Fosse 2,
  Reynolds 3)

Affairs of Geraldine, 1946 (Alton 4)

Affairs of Hearts. *See* Affairs de coeur, 1909

Affairs of Jimmy Valentine, 1942 (Alton 4)

Affairs of Martha, 1942 (Kaper 4, Lennart 4, Schary 4)

Affairs of Sally. *See* Fuller Brush Girl, 1950

Affairs of Susan, 1945 (Fontaine 3, Dreier 4, Head 4, Wallis 4)

Affectionately Yours, 1941 (Bacon 2, Bellamy 3, Hayworth 3, McDaniel 3, McQueen 3, Oberon 3, Gaudio 4, Grot 4, Orry-Kelly 4, Wallis 4)

Affiche, 1924 (Epstein 2)

Affichés animés, 1908 (Pathé 4)

Affinities, 1922 (Moore 3)

Affreux, 1959 (Fresnay 3)

Afghanistan porquoi, 1983 (Papas 3)

Afgrunden, 1910 (Nielsen 3)

Aflame in the Sky, 1927 (Walker 4)

Afraid to Love, 1927 (Schulberg 4)

Afraid to Talk, 1932 (Calhern 3, Freund 4)

Africa, 1930 (Lantz 4)

Africa, 1967 (North 4)

Africa Before Dark, 1928 (Disney 4)

Africa Express, 1975 (Palance 3)

Africa Screams, 1949 (Abbott and Costello 3, Three Stooges 3)

Africa sotto i mari, 1952 (Loren 3)

Africa Squawks, 1939 (Terry 4)

Africa Squeaks, 1932 (Iwerks 4)

Africa Squeaks, 1940 (Blanc 4, Clampett 4, Stalling 4)

Africa—Texas Style!, 1967 (Mills 3, Arnold 4)

Africa under the Seas. *See* Africa sotto i mari, 1952

Africain, 1983 (Deneuve 3, Noiret 3)

African. *See* Africain, 1983

African Fury. *See* Cry, the Beloved Country, 1951

African in London, 1941 (Pearson 2)

African Jungle, 1924 (Lantz 4)

African Lion, 1955 (Iwerks 4)

African Queen, 1951 (Huston 2, Bogart 3, Hepburn 3, Cardiff 4, Spiegel 4)

African Queen, 1977 (Oates 3)

African Treasure, 1962 (Mirisch 4)

Africana. *See* Ruckkehr, 1990

Afskedens timme, 1973 (Andersson 3)

Aftenlandet, 1977 (Watkins 2)

After a Lifetime, 1971 (Loach 2, Menges 4)

After All, 1912 (Lawrence 3)

After Dark, My Sweet, 1990 (Dern 3, Jarre 4)

After Darkness, 1985 (Hurt 3)

After Five, 1914 (Darwell 3, Hayakawa 3)

After Hours, 1985 (Scorsese 2, Ballhaus 4)

After Laughter, 1981 (Vanderbeek 2)

After Leonardo, 1973 (Le Grice 2)

After Leslie Wheeler, 1973 (Le Grice 2)

After Lumiere, L'Arroseur Arrosé, 1974 (Le Grice 2)

After Manet, After Giorgione, Le Dejeuner sur l'herbe, 1975 (Le Grice 2)

After Many Years, 1908 (Griffith 2, Lawrence 3, Bitzer 4)

After Midnight, 1927 (Shearer 3, Day 4, Gibbons 4)

After Midnight. *See* Captain Carey, U.S.A., 1950

After My Last Move. *See* Nach Meinem letzten Umzug, 1970

After Office Hours, 1932 (Launder and Gilliat 2)

After Office Hours, 1935 (Gable 3, Adrian 4, Mankiewicz 4, Rosher 4)

After School, 1911 (Dwan 2)

After the Ball. *See* Aprés le bal, 1897

After the Ball, 1926 (Fleischer 4)

After the Ball, 1932 (Balcon 4, Junge 4)

After the Ball, 1957 (Harvey 3, Mathieson 4)

After the Dance, 1935 (August 4)

After the Fall, 1974 (Dunaway 3)

After the Fox. *See* Caccia alla volpe, 1966

After the Rehearsal, 1984 (Josephson 3, Thulin 3)

After the Storm, 1915 (Eason 4)

After the Storm, 1928 (Bosworth 3, Walker 4)

After the Thin Man, 1936 (Van Dyke 2, Loy 3, Powell 3, Stewart 3, Brown 4, Freed 4, Goodrich 4, Mayer 4, Stothart 4, Stromberg 4)

After the Verdict, 1929 (Tschechowa 3, Galeen 4, Reville 4)

After the War, 1989 (Raphael 4)

After Tomorrow, 1932 (Borzage 2, Howe 4, Levien 4)

After Tonight, 1933 (Cooper 4, Murfin 4, Polglase 4, Rosher 4, Steiner 4)

After Winter: Sterling Brown, 1985 (Gerima 2)

After Your Own Heart, 1921 (Mix 3)

Aftermath, 1914 (Eason 4)

Aftermath. *See* Mädchen ohne Heimat, 1926

Aftermath, 1980 (Brakhage 2)

Aftermath: A Test of Love, 1991 (Rosenman 4)

Afternoon, 1965 (Warhol 2)

Agaguk, 1990 (Mifune 3)

Against All. *See* Proti všem, 1957

Against All Flags, 1952 (Flynn 3, O'Hara 3, Quinn 3, Metty 4, Salter 4)

Against All Odds, 1984 (Bridges 3, Widmark 3)

Against the Law, 1934 (Bond 3)

Against the Wind, 1948 (Crichton 2, Signoret 3, Balcon 4, Clarke 4, Rank 4)

Agatha, 1978 (Hoffman 3, Redgrave 3, Russell 4, Storaro 4)

Agatha Christie's Dead Man's Folly, 1986 (Addison 4)

Agatha Christie's Ordeal By Innocence, 1984 (Donaggio 4, Golan and Globus 4)

Agaton and Fina. *See* Agaton och Fina, 1912

Agaton och Fina, 1912 (Jaenzon 4)

Age des artères, 1959 (Delerue 4)

Age d'or, 1930 (Buñuel 2, Modot 3, Braunberger 4)

Age for Love, 1931 (Newman 4, Seitz 4, Sherwood 4)

Age ingrat, 1964 (Fernandel 3, Gabin 3, Delerue 4)

Age of Consent, 1932 (La Cava 2, Berman 4, Hunt 4, Selznick 4, Steiner 4)

Age of Consent, 1969 (Powell and Pressburger 2, Mason 3)

Age of Curiosity, 1963 (Farrow 3)

Age of Daydreaming. *See* Álmodozások kora, 1964

Age of Desire, 1923 (Borzage 2, Coffee 4)

Age of Indiscretion, 1935 (Lukas 3, Coffee 4, Haller 4)

Age of Infidelity. *See* **Muerte de un ciclista, 1955**

Age of Innocence, 1934 (Dunne 3, Berman 4, Plunkett 4, Steiner 4)

Age of Love, 1931 (Horton 3)

Age tendre, 1974 (Guillemot 4)

Age vermeil, 1984 (Darrieux 3)

Age Versus Youth, 1911 (Lawrence 3)

Agee, 1980 (Huston 2)

Agence Cacahuete, 1978 (Raimu 3)

Agence matrimoniale, 1951 (Blier 3, Noiret 3, Douy 4, Kosma 4)

Agency, 1981 (Mitchum 3)

Agent 8 3/4. *See* Hot Enough for June, 1963

Agent de poche, 1909 (Cohl 4)

Agent et le violoniste. *See* Violoniste, 1908

Agent Nr. 1, 1971 (Ścibor-Rylski 4)

Agent Orange: Policy of Poison, 1987 (Christie 3)

Agents tels qu'on nous les présente, 1908 (Feuillade 2)

Agent Trouble, 1987 (Deneuve 3)

Agget är löst, 1974 (Von Sydow 3)

Aggie Appleby, Maker of Men, 1933 (Hunt 4, Plunkett 4, Steiner 4)

Aggressionen, 1968 (Schroeter 2)

Aggressor, 1911 (Ince 4)

Aggrippès à la terre, 1968 (Ivens 2)

Agguato a Tangeri, 1958 (Cervi 3)

Agitator, 1912 (Emerson 4)

Agitpoezd VTsIK, 1921 (Vertov 2)

Agit-Train of the Central Committee. *See* Agitpoezd VTsIK, 1921

Agkadyanchi Mouj, 1914 (Phalke 2)

Agnes of God, 1985 (Jewison 2, Bancroft 3, Fonda 3, Adam 4, Delerue 4, Nykvist 4)

Agnese va a morire, 1977 (Age and Scarpelli 4, Morricone 4)

Agnese Visconti, 1910 (Pastrone 2)

Agonie de Byzance, 1913 (Feuillade 2, Gaumont 4)

Agonie de Jerusalem, 1926 (Duvivier 2)

Agonie des aigles, 1920 (Duvivier 2)

Agonie des aigles, 1933 (Pagnol 2, Wakhévitch 4)

Agonies of Agnes, 1918 (Dressler 3)

Agonizing Adventure. *See* Angoissante Aventure, 1919

Agony and the Ecstasy, 1965 (Reed 2, Harrison 3, Heston 3, Dunne 4, Goldsmith 4, North 4, Shamroy 4, Smith 4)

Agosta, 1986 (Branco 4, De Almeida 4)

Agostino, 1962 (Thulin 3)

Agostino di Ippona, 1972 (Rossellini 2)

Agression, 1975 (Deneuve 3, Trintignant 3, Braunberger 4)

Agua, 1959 (Gómez 2)

Aguila o sol, 1937 (Cantinflas 3)

Aguirre, der Zorn Göttes, 1973 (Herzog 2, Kinski 3)

Aguirre, the Wrath of God. *See* **Aguirre, der Zorn Göttes, 1973**

Agulha no palheiro, 1952 (Pereira Dos Santos 2)

Ah, Cradle, 1980 (Xie 2)

Ah, My Home Town. *See* Aa furusato, 1938

Ah! Nango shosa, 1938 (Tsuburaya 4)

Ah Sweet Mouse-Story of Life, 1965 (Jones 4)

Ah, Wilderness, 1935 (Brown 2, Barrymore 3, Beery 3, Rooney 3, Goodrich 4, Mayer 4, Stothart 4, Stromberg 4)

A-Haunting We Will Go, 1942 (Laurel and Hardy 3, Day 4)

A-Haunting We Will Go, 1966 (McKimson 4)

Ahava Ilemeth, 1982 (Golan and Globus 4)

Ahen senso, 1943 (Shindo 3, Takamine 3)
Ahí está el detalle, 1940 (Cantinflas 3)
Ahí viene Martín Corona, 1952 (Infante 3, Figueroa 4)
Ahijado de la muerte, 1946 (Alcoriza 4)
Ahora mis pistolas hablan, 1980 (Fernández 2)
Ahora soy rico, 1952 (Infante 3)
A-Hunting We Will Go, 1932 (Fleischer 4)
A-Hunting We Won't Go, 1943 (Fleischer 4)
Ai margini della metropoli, 1952 (Di Venanzo 4)
Ai Midori no nakama, 1954 (Mori 3)
Ai ni yomigaeru hi, 1976 (Mizoguchi 2)
Ai no borei, 1978 (Takemitsu 4, Toda 4)
Ai no corrida, 1976 (Toda 4)
Ai no kane, 1959 (Kagawa 3)
Ai no onimotsu, 1955 (Yamada 3, Yamamura 3)
Ai no rekishi, 1955 (Tsukasa 3)
Ai no sanga, 1950 (Yamamura 3, Miyagawa 4)
Ai no sekai, 1943 (Takamine 3)
Ai to honoho to, 1961 (Mori 3, Shimura 3)
Ai to nikushimi no kaneta e, 1951 (Mifune 3)
Ai vostri ordini, signora!, 1938 (De Sica 2)
Ai wa dokomaremo, 1932 (Yamada 3)
Ai wa furu hoshi no kanata ni, 1956 (Mori 3)
Ai yo hoshi to tomoni, 1947 (Takamine 3, Hayasaka 4)
Ai yo jinrui to tomo ni are, 1931 (Takamine 3, Tanaka 3)
Aid to the Nation, 1947 (De Mille 2)
Aida, 1953 (Loren 3)
Aide-toi, 1918 (Feuillade 2)
Aienkyo, 1937 (Mizoguchi 2, Yoda 4)
Aigle à deux têtes, 1947 (Cocteau 2, Feuillère 3, Marais 3, Auric 4, Matras 4, Wakhévitch 4)
Aiglon, 1931 (Burel 4, Planer 4)
Aigrette Hunter, 1910 (Olcott 2)
Aiguille rouge, 1950 (Wakhévitch 4)
Aija no musume, 1938 (Yoda 4)
Aijo dudou, 1959 (Yoda 4)
Aijo no keifu, 1961 (Yamamura 3)
Aijo no kessan, 1956 (Mifune 3)
Aijo no miyako, 1958 (Tsukasa 3)
Aijo shindansho, 1948 (Takamine 3)
Aijo-fudo, 1959 (Kagawa 3, Yamada 3)
Aile ou la cuisse, 1976 (Dalio 3, Renoir 4)
Ailes de la Colombe, 1981 (Huppert 3, Sanda 3)
Ailes du désir. *See* Himmel über Berlin, 1987
Aimez-vous Brahms?. *See* Goodbye Again, 1961
Aimez-vous les femmes?, 1964 (Feuillère 3, Evein 4, Vierny 4)
Ainé des Ferchaux, 1963 (Melville 2, Belmondo 3, Vanel 3, Decaë 4, Delerue 4)
Ain't It the Truth, 1915 (Beery 3)
Ain't Love Funny?, 1926 (Plunkett 4)
Ain't Misbehavin', 1955 (Cahn 4)
Ain't She Sweet, 1933 (Fleischer 4)
Ain't She Tweet, 1952 (Blanc 4, Foster 4, Freleng 4, Stalling 4)
Ain't That Ducky, 1945 (Blanc 4, Freleng 4, Maltese 4, Stalling 4)
Ain't We Got Fun, 1937 (Avery 4, Stalling 4)
Air, 1972 (Driessen 4)
Air America, 1990 (Gibson 3)
Air Cadet, 1951 (Hudson 3)

Air Circus, 1928 (Hawks 2, Carré 4, Miller 4)
Air City. *See* Aerogard, 1935
Air de Paris, 1954 (Carné 2, Arletty 3, Gabin 3)
Air Express, 1937 (Lantz 4)
Air Force, 1943 (Hawks 2, Carey 3, Garfield 3, Kennedy 3, Haskin 4, Howe 4, Nichols 4, Wald 4, Wallis 4, Warner 4, Waxman 4)
Air Fright, 1933 (Roach 4)
Air Hawks, 1935 (Bellamy 3)
Air Hostess, 1933 (Darwell 3, Walker 4)
Air Legion, 1929 (Glennon 4, Plunkett 4)
Air Mail, 1932 (Bellamy 3, Freund 4, Laemmle 4)
Air Outpost, 1937 (Alwyn 4)
Air pur, 1939 (Clair 2, Douy 4, Lourié 4)
Air Raid Wardens, 1943 (Laurel and Hardy 3)
Air Tonic, 1933 (Grable 3)
Air Waves, 1939 (Vorkapich 4)
Airborne, 1973 (Jarre 4)
Aire de un crimen, 1988 (Rey 3)
Aires de renovación en el meridiano 37, 1986 (Alvarez 2)
Airman's Letter to His Mother, 1941 (Powell and Pressburger 2, Gielgud 3)
Airplane, 1980 (Bernstein 4)
Airplane II: The Sequel, 1982 (Bernstein 4, Biroc 4)
Airport, 1969 (Dunn 4, Laszlo 4)
Airport, 1970 (Hathaway 2, Lancaster 3, Martin 3, Seberg 3, Ames 4, Head 4, Hunter 4, Newman 4, Westmore Family 4)
Airport 1975, 1974 (Andrews 3, Black 3, Heston 3, Loy 3, Swanson 3, Head 4)
Airport '77, 1977 (Cotten 3, De Havilland 3, Grant 3, Lemmon 3, Stewart 3, Head 4, Whitlock 4)
Airport '80—The Concorde. *See* Concorde—Airport '79, 1979
Airs, 1975 (Brakhage 2)
Aisai monogatari, 1951 (Shindo 2)
Aisai-ki, 1959 (Tsukasa 3)
Aisureba koso, 1955 (Yoshimura 2, Kagawa 3, Yamada 3, Yamamura 3)
Aiyoku no ki, 1930 (Tanaka 3)
Aiyoku no sabaki, 1953 (Kagawa 3)
Aizen katsura, 1954 (Kyo 3)
Aizen katsura: Kanketsu-hen, 1939 (Tanaka 3)
Aizen tsubaki, 1940 (Tanaka 3)
Aizen-bashi, 1951 (Tanaka 3, Yoda 4)
Aizo toge, 1934 (Mizoguchi 2, Yamada 3)
Aizome-gasa, 1956 (Hasegawa 3)
Ajos vandados, 1978 (Chaplin 3)
A.K., 1985 (Marker 2)
Akademik Ivan Pavlov, 1949 (Cherkassov 3, Enei 4)
Akadou Suzunosuke, 1958 (Miyagawa 4)
Akage, 1969 (Iwashita 3, Mifune 3)
Akahige, 1965 (Kagawa 3, Mifune 3, Ryu 3, Shimura 3, Tanaka 3, Muraki 4)
Akai jinbaori, 1958 (Kagawa 3)
Akai shuriken, 1965 (Miyagawa 4)
Akai yuhi ni terasarete, 1925 (Mizoguchi 2)
Akanegumo, 1967 (Shinoda 2, Iwashita 3, Takemitsu 4, Toda 4)
Akanishi Kakita, 1936 (Shimura 3)
Akasen chitai, 1956 (Mizoguchi 2, Kyo 3, Shindo 3, Miyagawa 4)
Akasen no hi wa kiezu, 1958 (Kyo 3)

Akash Kusum, 1965 (Mitra 4)
Akatsuki ni inoru, 1940 (Tanaka 3)
Akatsuki no dasso, 1950 (Hayasaka 4)
Akatsuki, no Gassho, 1955 (Kagawa 3)
Akatsuki no gassho, 1963 (Yamamura 3)
Akatsuki no hatakaze, 1938 (Yoda 4)
Akatsuki no shi, 1924 (Mizoguchi 2)
Akatsuki no yushi, 1973 (Hasegawa 3)
Akatsuki wa tokedo, 1937 (Tanaka 3)
Akcja pod Arsenalem, 1977 (Stawiński 4)
Aken senso, 1943 (Tsuburaya 4)
Akibiyori, 1960 (Hara 3, Iwashita 3, Ryu 3, Tsukasa 3)
Akitsu onsen, 1962 (Yamamura 3)
Akogare, 1966 (Takemitsu 4)
Ako-jo, 1952 (Yamada 3)
Akrobat na hrazdě, 1953 (Stallich 4)
Akrobat schö-ö-ön, 1943 (Staudte 2)
Akrosh, 1981 (Patil 3, Nihalani 4)
Akt, 1961 (Skolimowski 2)
Aku no tanoshisa, 1954 (Mori 3)
Aku Ryoto. *See* Akuma-to, 1980
Akujo no kisetsu, 1958 (Yamada 3)
Akuma no kanpai, 1947 (Miyagawa 4)
Akuma-to, 1980 (Shinoda 2, Miyagawa 4)
Akumyo, 1961 (Miyagawa 4, Yoda 4)
Akumyo hatoba, 1963 (Yoda 4)
Akumyo ichiba, 1963 (Yoda 4)
Akumyo ichidai, 1967 (Yoda 4)
Akumyo juhachi-ban, 1968 (Yoda 4)
Akumyo muteki, 1965 (Miyagawa 4, Yoda 4)
Akumyo nawabari arashi, 1974 (Miyagawa 4, Yoda 4)
Akumyo niwaka, 1965 (Miyagawa 4, Yoda 4)
Akumyo zakura, 1966 (Miyagawa 4, Yoda 4)
Akuto, 1965 (Shindo 2)
Al caer de la tarde, 1948 (Armendáriz 3)
Al Capone, 1959 (Steiger 3, Ballard 4, Raksin 4)
Al Capone im deutschen Wald, 1969 (Fassbinder 2)
Al diavolo la celebrità, 1949 (Monicelli 2)
Al di là del bene a del male, 1980 (Donaggio 4)
Al di là della legge, 1968 (Van Cleef 3)
Al Jennings of Oklahoma, 1951 (Duryea 3)
Al Mas à la Al Kubra. *See* Great Question, 1983
Al otro lado de la ciudad, 1962 (Valli 3)
Al sole, 1935 (Gallone 2)
Al Treleor Muscle Exercises, 1905 (Bitzer 4)
Alaap, 1977 (Bachchan 3)
Alabama—2000 Light Years, 1969 (Wenders 2, Müller 4)
Aladdin, 1953 (Reiniger 4)
Aladdin, 1958 (Porter 4)
Aladdin, 1989 (Jones 3)
Aladdin and His Lamp, 1952 (Wagner 4)
Aladdin and His Wonderful Lamp, 1939 (Fleischer 4)
Aladdin and the Wonderful Lamp, 1934 (Iwerks 4)
Aladdin's Lamp, 1931 (Terry 4)
Aladdin's Lamp, 1935 (Terry 4)
Aladdin's Lamp, 1943 (Terry 4)
Aladdin's Lamp, 1947 (Terry 4)

Aladin, 1900 (Pathé 4)

Aladin, 1906 (Pathé 4)

Alamo, 1960 (Harvey 3, Wayne 3, Widmark 3, Clothier 4, Tiomkin 4)

Alamo Bay, 1985 (Malle 2)

Alan and Apple, 1967 (Warhol 2)

Alan and Dickin, 1967 (Warhol 2)

Alarcosbal, 1918 (Lugosi 3)

Alarm, 1914 (Sennett 2, Arbuckle 3, Normand 3)

Alarm, 1941 (Rasp 3)

Alarm, 1969 (Fassbinder 2)

Alarm auf Gleis B. *See* Gleisdreieck, 1936

Alarm aus Station III, 1939 (Fröhlich 3)

Alarm Clock Andy, 1919 (Ince 4)

Alarm in Peking, 1937 (Fröhlich 3)

Alarme!, 1943 (Ivens 2)

Alarmstufe V, 1941 (Hoffmann 4)

Alas and Alack, 1915 (Chaney 3)

Alas, Poor Yorick, 1913 (Bosworth 3)

Alaska, 1930 (Lantz 4)

Alaska, 1944 (Carradine 3)

Alaska Love, 1932 (Sennett 2)

Alaska Seas, 1954 (Ryan 3, Head 4)

Alaska Sweepstakes, 1936 (Lantz 4)

Alaskafüchse, 1964 (Mueller-Stahl 3)

Alaskan, 1924 (Brenon 2, Wong 3, Howe 4)

Älaskarinnan, 1962 (Andersson 3)

Alauddin Khan, 1963 (Ghatak 2)

Alba, 1917 (Bertini 3)

Albany Bunch, 1931 (Sennett 2)

Albergo Luna, Camera 34, 1947 (Rota 4)

Albero degli zoccoli, 1978 (Olmi 2)

Alberobello, ''Au pays des trulli'', 1957 (Braunberger 4)

Albert Ier, Roi des Belges, 1950 (Spaak 4)

Albert Pinto ko gussa kyon aata hai, 1981 (Azmi 3, Patil 3)

Albert, R. N., 1953 (Arnold 4)

Albert Schweitzer, 1957 (March 3, Meredith 3)

Albertfalvai történet, 1955 (Mészáros 2)

Alberto Express, 1990 (Moreau 3)

Albigeois, 1964 (Braunberger 4)

Albuquerque, 1948 (Scott 3)

Albur de amor, 1947 (Armendáriz 3)

Alby's Delight. *See* Over the Brooklyn Bridge, 1984

Alcalde de Zalamea, 1953 (Rey 3)

Alcatraz Island, 1938 (Sheridan 3)

Alchimie, 1966 (Delerue 4)

Alcofrisbas, the Master Magician. *See* Enchanteur Alcofrisbas, 1903

Alcohol Abuse: The Early Warning Signs, 1977 (Fonda 3)

Alcool tue, 1947 (Resnais 2)

Alcoolisme engendre la tuberculose, 1905 (Pathé 4)

Aldebran, 1935 (Blasetti 2, Cervi 3)

Aldrig i livet, 1957 (Thulin 3)

Ale doktore, 1978 (Brejchová 3)

Aleksandr Nevskii. *See* **Alexander Nevsky, 1938**

Alenka, 1962 (Shukshin 3)

Alerte au sud, 1953 (Von Stroheim 2, Kosma 4)

Alerte en Méditerranée, 1938 (Fresnay 3)

Alex and the Gypsy, 1976 (Bujold 3, Lemmon 3, Mancini 4)

Alex in Wonderland, 1970 (Fellini 2, Mazursky 2, Burstyn 3, Moreau 3, Sutherland 3, Kovacs 4)

Alex the Great, 1928 (Miller 4)

Alexander Calder, 1963 (Richter 2)

Alexander den Store, 1917 (Stiller 2, Madsen and Schenstrøm 3, Jaenzon 4)

Alexander Hamilton, 1931 (Arliss 3)

Alexander Nevsky, 1938 (Eisenstein 2, Cherkassov 3, Prokofiev 4, Tisse 4)

Alexander Parkhomenko, 1942 (Dovzhenko 2)

Alexander Popov, 1949 (Cherkassov 3)

Alexander the Great. *See* Alexander den Store, 1917

Alexander the Great, 1956 (Rossen 2, Baker 3, Bloom 3, Burton 3, Cushing 3, Darrieux 3, March 3, Andrejeu 4, Krasker 4)

Alexander the Great, 1991 (Anhalt 4)

Alexander's Ragtime Band, 1931 (Fleischer 4)

Alexander's Ragtime Band, 1938 (King 2, Ameche 3, Carradine 3, Faye 3, Power 3, Berlin 4, Brown 4, Leven 4, Newman 4, Trotti 4, Zanuck 4)

Alexandra, 1914 (Porten 3, Messter 4)

Alexandre i Chanakya, 1967 (Tyszkiewicz 3)

Alexandre le bienheureux, 1968 (Noiret 3)

Alfabeto notturno, 1951 (Birri 2)

Alf, Bill, and Fred, 1964 (Godfrey 4)

Alfie, 1966 (Caine 3, Elliott 3, Winters 3, Heller 4)

Alfredo, Alfredo, 1972 (Germi 2, Hoffman 3, Pinelli 4)

Alf's Button, 1920 (Hepworth 2)

Alf's Button, 1930 (Crazy Gang 3, Oberon 3)

Alf's Button Afloat, 1938 (Launder and Gilliat 2, Crazy Gang 3, Slim 3, Rank 4, Vetchinsky 4)

Alf's Carpet. *See* Rocket Bus, 1929

Algie on the Force, 1913 (Sennett 2)

Algiers, 1933 (Lamarr 3)

Algiers, 1938 (Cromwell 2, Boyer 3, Howe 4, Irene 4, Reynolds 4, Wanger 4)

Algol, 1920 (Jannings 3)

Algy, the Watchman, 1911 (Sennett 2)

Ali Baba, 1936 (Iwerks 4)

Ali Baba. *See* Ali Baba et les 40 voleurs, 1954

Ali Baba Bound, 1940 (Blanc 4, Clampett 4, Stalling 4)

Ali Baba Bunny, 1957 (Blanc 4, Jones 4, Maltese 4, Stalling 4)

Ali Baba et les 40 voleurs, 1954 (Fernandel 3, Wakhévitch 4, Zavattini 4)

Ali Baba Goes to Town, 1937 (Cantor 3, Carradine 3, Cobb 3, Del Rio 3, Canutt 4)

Ali Baba Nights, 1953 (Wong 3)

Alibaba, 1940 (Mehoob 2, Biswas 4)

Alibaba and Forty Thieves, 1962 (Mehboob 2)

Alía en el bajia, 1941 (Armendáriz 3)

Alias a Gentleman, 1948 (Beery 3)

Alias Aladdin, 1920 (Roach 4)

Alias Bulldog Drummond. *See* Bulldog Jack, 1935

Alias French Gertie, 1930 (Daniels 3, Hunt 4)

Alias Jesse James, 1959 (McLeod 2, Bond 3, Cooper 3, Crosby 3, Hope 3, Rogers 3, Head 4)

Alias Jimmy Valentine, 1915 (Tourneur 2, Carré 4)

Alias Jimmy Valentine, 1920 (Polito 4)

Alias Jimmy Valentine, 1929 (Barrymore 3, Gibbons 4, Mayer 4)

Alias John Preston, 1956 (Lee 3)

Alias Ladyfingers. *See* Ladyfingers, 1921

Alias Mary Dow, 1935 (Carradine 3, Milland 3)

Alias Mary Flynn, 1925 (Berman 4)

Alias Mary Smith, 1932 (Walthall 3)

Alias Mike Moran, 1919 (Cruze 2, Reid 3)

Alias Mr. Twilight, 1947 (Sturges 2)

Alias Nick Beal, 1949 (Milland 3, Dreier 4, Waxman 4)

Alias Texas Pete Owens. *See* Sell 'em Cowboy, 1924

Alias the Deacon. *See* Half a Sinner, 1934

Alias the Deacon, 1940 (Cortez 4, Salter 4)

Alias the Doctor, 1932 (Bacon 2, Curtiz 2, Barthelmess 3, Karloff 3, Grot 4)

Alibi, 1929 (Menzies 4, Schenck 4, Sullivan 4)

Alibi, 1937 (Von Stroheim 2, Dalio 3, Jouvet 3, Achard 4, Auric 4, Fradetal 4, Lourié 4)

Alibi, 1942 (Lockwood 3, Mason 3, Heller 4)

Alibi, 1969 (Gassman 3, Morricone 4)

Alibi Ike, 1935 (Brown 3, De Havilland 3)

Alibi Inn, 1935 (Box 4)

Alice Series, 1923–27 (Disney 4)

Alice. *See* Alicja, 1979

Alice, 1981 (York 3)

Alice, 1988 (Švankmajer 4)

Alice, 1991 (Farrow 3, Hurt 3)

Alice Adams, 1923 (Barnes 4)

Alice Adams, 1935 (Stevens 2, Hepburn 3, MacMurray 3, McDaniel 3, Berman 4, Murfin 4, Plunkett 4, Polglase 4, Steiner 4)

Alice au pays des merveilles, 1948 (Renoir 4)

Alice Be Good, 1926 (Sennett 2)

Alice Doesn't Live Here Anymore, 1975 (Scorsese 2, Burstyn 3, Foster 3)

Alice in den Städten, 1974 (Wenders 2, Vogler 3, Müller 4)

Alice in Switzerland, 1939 (Cavalcanti 2)

Alice in the Cities. *See* Alice in den Städten, 1974

Alice in Wonderland, 1903 (Hepworth 2)

Alice in Wonderland, 1933 (Mankiewicz 2, McLeod 2, Cooper 3, Fields 3, Grant 3, Horton 3, Marsh 3, Edouart 4, Glennon 4, Menzies 4, Tiomkin 4, Westmore Family 4, Zukor 4)

Alice in Wonderland. *See* Alice au pays des merveilles, 1948

Alice in Wonderland, 1951 (Disney 4, Lewin 4)

Alice, or the Last Escapade. *See* Alice, ou la dernière fugue, 1977

Alice, ou la dernière fugue, 1977 (Chabrol 2, Rabier 4)

Alice's Adventures in Wonderland, 1972 (Moore 3, Richardson 3, Sellers 3, Barry 4, Shankar 4, Unsworth 4)

Alice's Restaurant, 1969 (Penn 2, Allen 4)

Alicja, 1979 (Cassel 3)

Alien, 1915 (Ince 4)

Alien, 1979 (Hill 2, Scott 2, Hurt 3, Stanton 3, Weaver 3 Goldsmith 4)

Alien Encounter, 1976 (Lee 3)

Alien from LA, 1988 (Golan and Globus 4)

Alien Nation, 1988 (Caan 3, Stamp 3)

Alien III, 1991 (Weaver 3)

Alien Souls, 1916 (Hayakawa 3)

Alien Thunder, 1975 (Sutherland 3)

Aliens, 1986 (Hill 2, Weaver 3)

Alien's Invasion, 1905 (Hepworth 2)

Aliki, 1962 (Maté 4)

Aliki in the Navy. See Aliki sto naftiko, 1960

Aliki sto naftike, 1960 (Lassally 4)

Alimony, 1918 (Valentino 3)

Alimony Madness, 1933 (Eason 4)

Alina, 1950 (Lollobrigida 3, Delli Colli 4)

Alive and Kicking, 1958 (Harris 3)

Alive by Night. See Evil Spawn, 1987

Alkali Bests Broncho Billy. See Alkali Ike Bests Broncho Billy, 1912

Alkali Ike Bests Broncho Billy, 1912 (Anderson 3)

Alkali Ike's Boarding House, 1912 (Anderson 3)

Alkali Ike's Misfortunes, 1913 (Anderson 3)

Alkony, 1971 (Szabó 2)

All Abir-r-rd, 1950 (Blanc 4, Freleng 4, Stalling 4)

All Aboard, 1917 (Daniels 3, Lloyd 3, Roach 4)

All About Dogs, 1942 (Terry 4)

All About Eve, 1950 (Mankiewicz 2, Baxter 3, Davis 3, Monroe 3, Ritter 3, Sanders 3, Head 4, Krasner 4, LeMaire 4, Newman 4, Wheeler 4, Zanuck 4)

All About People, 1967 (Fonda 3, Heston 3, Lancaster 3)

All American Chump, 1936 (Clarke 4)

All American Co-ed, 1941 (Langdon 3, Prinz 4, Roach 4)

All American Kickback, 1931 (Sennett 2)

All American Toothache, 1935 (Roach 4)

All Ashore, 1952 (Edwards 2, Rooney 3, Duning 4)

All at Sea, 1914 (Sennett 2)

All at Sea, 1919 (Roach 4)

All at Sea, 1929 (Gibbons 4)

All at Sea, 1935 (Harrison 3, Withers 3)

All at Sea. See Barnacle Bill, 1957

All by Myself, 1943 (Beavers 3)

All Creatures Great and Small, 1974 (Hopkins 3)

All Dogs Go to Heaven, 1989 (Reynolds 3)

All Dressed Up, 1920 (Roach 4)

All Fall Down, 1962 (Frankenheimer 2, Beatty 3, Lansbury 3, Malden 3, Saint 3, Ames 4, Houseman 4, Jeakins 4, North 4)

All for a Girl, 1916 (Laurel and Hardy 3)

All for a Woman. See Danton, 1920

All for Her, 1912 (Brenon 2)

All for Love, 1912 (Lawrence 3)

All for Mary, 1955 (Rank 4)

All for Old Ireland, 1915 (Olcott 2)

All for Peggy, 1915 (Chaney 3)

All Fowled Up, 1955 (Blanc 4, McKimson 4, Stalling 4)

All God's Children, 1980 (Widmark 3)

All Good Countrymen. See Všichni dobří rodáci, 1968

All Gummed Up, 1947 (Three Stooges 3)

All Hands, 1940 (Mills 3, Balcon 4)

All Hands on Deck, 1961 (Smith 4)

All I Desire, 1953 (Sirk 2, O'Sullivan 3, Stanwyck 3, Hunter 4, Westmore Family 4)

All In, 1936 (Balcon 4, Vetchinsky 4)

All in a Day, 1920 (Roach 4)

All in a Night's Work, 1961 (MacLaine 3,

Martin 3, Robertson 3, Head 4, Previn 4, La Shelle 4, Wallis 4)

All Is Confusion. See Riding on Air, 1937

All Is Well. See Tenka taihai, 1955

All Lit Up, 1920 (Roach 4)

All Lit Up, 1959 (Halas and Batchelor 4)

All Man, 1916 (Marion 4)

All Men Are Enemies, 1934 (Hoffenstein 4, Seitz 4)

All Mine to Give, 1956 (Jaffe 3, Steiner 4)

All Mixed Up. See Sac de noeuds, 1985

All My Darling Daughters, 1972 (Massey 3, Young 3)

All My Life, 1966 (Baillie 2)

All My Sons, 1948 (Lancaster 3, Robinson 3, Metty 4)

All Night, 1918 (Valentino 3)

All Night Long, 1924 (Capra 2, Sennett 2)

All Night Long, 1961 (Dearden 2, Attenborough 3, Rank 4)

All Night Long, 1981 (Girardot 3, Hackman 3, Langdon 3, Streisand 3)

All of Me, 1934 (Hopkins 3, March 3, Raft 3, Banton 4, Buchman 4)

All of Me, 1984 (Martin 3)

All on Account of a Laundry Mark, 1910 (Porter 2)

All on Account of the Milk, 1910 (Sennett 2, Pickford 3, Sweet 3)

All One Night. See Love Begins at Twenty, 1936

All Out for ''V'', 1942 (Terry 4)

All Over the Top, 1949 (Cusack 3)

All Over the Town, 1949 (Baker 3, Rank 4)

All Over Town, 1937 (Ladd 3, Pangborn 3)

All Quiet on the Western Front, 1930 (Cukor 2, Milestone 2, Zinnemann 2, Ayres 3, Edeson 4, Freund 4, Gaudio 4, Laemmle 4)

All Quiet on the Western Front, 1979 (Neal 3, Pleasence 3)

All Russian Elder Kalinin. See Vserusski starets Kalinin, 1920

All Screwed Up. See Tutto a posto e niente in ordine, 1974

All Souls Day, 1961 (Konwicki 4)

All Square. See Gang War, 1928

All Star Bond Rally, 1945 (Crosby 3, Darnell 3, Grable 3, Hope 3, Sinatra 3)

All-Star Musical Revue, 1945 (Pan 4, Prinz 4)

All Star Production of Patriotic Episodes for the Second Liberty Loan, 1917 (Hart 3)

All Teed Up, 1930 (Roach 4)

All That Heaven Allows, 1955 (Sirk 2, Hudson 3, Moorehead 3, Wyman 3, Hunter 4, Metty 4)

All That I Have, 1951 (Biroc 4)

All That Jazz, 1979 (Fosse 2, Lange 3, Scheider 3, Rotunno 4)

All That Money Can Buy, 1941 (Darwell 3, Huston 3, Simon 3, August 4, Herrmann 4, Polglase 4)

All the Brothers Were Valiant, 1923 (Chaney 3)

All the Brothers Were Valiant, 1953 (Granger 3, Taylor 3, Berman 4, Folsey 4, Plunkett 4, Rozsa 4)

All the Drawings of the Town, 1959 (Vukotić 4)

All the Fine Young Cannibals, 1960 (Beavers 3, Wagner 3, Wood 3, Berman 4, Daniels 4, Rose 4)

All the King's Horses, 1935 (Horton 3, Wyman 3, Banton 4, Prinz 4)

All the King's Men, 1949 (Rossen 2, Crawford 3, McCambridge 3, Cohn 4, Guffey 4)

. . . All the Marbles, 1981 (Falk 3, Biroc 4)

All the President's Men, 1976 (Pakula 2, Hoffman 3, Redford 3, Robards 3, Goldman 4, Jenkins 4, Willis 4)

All the Right Moves, 1983 (Cruise 3)

All the Right Noises, 1969 (Fisher 4)

All These Women. See För att inte tala om alla dessa kvinnor, 1964

All the Way Boys. See Piu forte ragazzi!, 1972

All the Way Home, 1963 (Preston 3, Simmons 3, Kaufman 4, Smith 4, Sylbert 4)

All the World's a Stage, 1910 (Lawrence 3)

All the World's a Stooge, 1941 (Three Stooges 3)

All the World to Nothing, 1918 (Furthman 4)

All the Young Men, 1960 (Ladd 3, Poitier 3, Duning 4)

All This and Heaven Too, 1940 (Orry-Kelly 4, Litvak 2, Boyer 3, Davis 3, Friedhofer 4, Haller 4, Haskin 4, Robinson 4, Steiner 4, Wallis 4)

All This and Money Too. See Love Is a Ball, 1963

All This and Rabbit Stew, 1941 (Avery 4, Blanc 4, Stalling 4)

All This and Rabbit Stew, 1950 (Terry 4)

All Through the Night, 1942 (Bogart 3, Darwell 3, Lorre 3, Veidt 3, Deutsch 4, Mercer 4, Wald 4)

All Tied Up, 1987 (Gould 3)

All Wet, 1924 (McCarey 2, Roach 4)

All Wet, 1927 (Disney 4)

All Women, 1918 (Marsh 3)

All Women Have Secrets, 1939 (Lake 3, Head 4)

All Wool, 1925 (Roach 4)

Allá en el rancho grande, 1936 (De Fuentes 2, Fernández 2, Heston 3, Lancaster 3, Figueroa 4)

Alla en el Rancho Grande, 1948 (De Fuentes 2)

Alla en el tropico, 1940 (De Fuentes 2, Figueroa 4)

Alla ricerca di Tadzio, 1970 (Visconti 2)

All-American, 1932 (Brennan 3)

All-American, 1953 (Curtis 3)

All-American Boy, 1973 (Voight 3)

Allan Quatermain and the Lost City of Gold, 1987 (Golan and Globus 4, Jones 3)

Alle man på post, 1940 (Björnstrand 3)

Allegheny Uprising, 1939 (Sanders 3, Trevor 3, Wayne 3, Musuraca 4, Plunkett 4, Polglase 4)

Allegory, 1989 (Ruiz 2)

Allegretto, 1936 (Fischinger 2, Ford 2)

Allegro squadrone, 1954 (De Sica 2, Gélin 3, Sordi 3, Audiard 4, Cecchi D'Amico 4)

Aller simple, 1971 (Giannini 3)

Allergic to Love, 1944 (Pangborn 3, Salter 4)

Alles für Geld, 1923 (Jannings 3, Kräly 4)

Alles für Papa, 1953 (Tschechowa 3)

Alles Schwindel, 1940 (Fröhlich 3)

Alley in Paradise. See Ulička v Ráji, 1936

Alley of the World. See Ukiyo kouji, 1939

Allez France, 1966 (Dors 3)

Allez Oop, 1934 (Keaton 2)

Alliance, 1970 (Karina 3, Carière 4)

Alligator, 1980 (Sayles 2)
Alligator Named Daisy, 1955 (Dors 3,
    Rutherford 3, Rank 4)
Alligator People, 1959 (Struss 4)
'Allo Berlin, ici Paris, 1931 (Rathaus 4)
Allo! Hallo! Alo!, 1962 (Popescu-Gopo 4)
Allonsanfan, 1974 (Taviani 2, Mastroianni 3,
    Morricone 4)
Allotment Wives, 1945 (Francis 3)
Allotria, 1936 (Walbrook 3)
All's Fair, 1988 (Segal 3)
All's Fair at the Fair, 1938 (Fleischer 4)
All's Well, 1941 (Fleischer 4)
All's Well That Ends Well, 1940 (Terry 4)
Allskande par, 1964 (Björnstrand 3)
Alltägliche Geschichte, 1944 (Fröhlich 3)
Allumettes animées, 1908 (Cohl 4)
Allumettes fantaisies, 1912 (Cohl 4)
Allumettes magiques. See Allumettes
    fantaisies, 1912
Allumorphoses, 1960 (Delerue 4)
Allvarsamma leken, 1945 (Dahlbeck 3)
Allvarsamma leken, 1977 (Josephson 3)
Alma de bronce, 1944 (Armendáriz 3)
Alma de Gaucho, 1930 (Shamroy 4)
Almas encontradas, 1933 (Figueroa 4)
Álmodozások kora, 1964 (Szabó 2)
Almonds and Raisins, 1983 (Welles 2,
    Mankowitz 4)
Almost a Gentleman, 1939 (Hunt 4)
Almost a Hero, 1910 (Porter 2)
Almost a Husband, 1919 (Rogers 3)
Almost a Lady, 1926 (Rosson 4)
Almost an Actress, 1913 (Chaney 3)
Almost an Angel, 1990 (Heston 3,
    Bumstead 4)
Almost Angels, 1962 (Disney 4)
Almost Human, 1926 (Adrian 4,
    Buckland 4)
Almost Human. See Shock Waves, 1975
Almost Married, 1932 (Bellamy 3,
    Friedhofer 4, Menzies 4)
Almost Perfect Affair, 1979 (Vitti 3,
    Decaë 4, Delerue 4)
Alô, alô, Brasil!, 1935 (Miranda 3)
Alô, alô carnaval!, 1936 (Miranda 3)
Aloha Bobby and Rose, 1975 (Fraker 4)
Aloha Hooey, 1942 (Avery 4, Blanc 4,
    Stalling 4)
Aloha, le chant des îles, 1936 (Arletty 3,
    Spaak 4)
Aloha Oe, 1915 (Ince 4)
Aloha Oe, 1933 (Fleischer 4)
Alois vyhrál los, 1919 (Heller 4)
Alois Won a Prize. See Alois vyhrál los,
    1919
Aloise, 1975 (Huppert 3, Seyrig 3)
Alom a házröl. See Budapest, amiért
    szeretem, 1971
Aloma of the South Seas, 1926 (Tourneur 2,
    Johnson 3, Powell 3, Zukor 4)
Aloma of the South Seas, 1941 (Johnson 3,
    Lamour 3, Dreier 4, Edouart 4, Head 4,
    Siodmak 4, Struss 4, Young 4)
Alone. See Odna, 1931
Alone. See Samac, 1958
Alone in a City. See Sam pósród miasta,
    1965
Alone in the Dark, 1982 (Palance 3,
    Pleasence 3)
Alone in the Jungle, 1913 (Selig 4)
Alone in the Pacific. See Taiheiyo
    hitoribotchi, 1963
Alone in the World, 1916 (Weber 2)

Alone on the Pacific. See Taiheiyo
    hitoribotchi, 1963
Alone Together. See Crisscross, 1990
Alone with the Monsters, 1958 (Lassally 4)
Along Came Auntie, 1926 (Laurel and
    Hardy 3, Roach 4)
Along Came Daffy, 1947 (Blanc 4,
    Freleng 4)
Along Came Jones, 1945 (Cooper 3,
    Duryea 3, Young 3, Fields 4,
    Friedhofer 4, Johnson 4, Krasner 4,
    Plunkett 4)
Along Came Sally. See Aunt Sally, 1933
Along Came Youth, 1930 (McLeod 2,
    Head 4)
Along Flirtation Walk, 1935 (Freleng 4)
Along the Border, 1916 (Mix 3)
Along the Great Divide, 1950 (Walsh 2,
    Brennan 3, Douglas 3, Veiller 4)
Along the Navajo Trail, 1945 (Rogers 3)
Along the River Nile, 1912 (Olcott 2)
Alouette, je te plumerai, 1988 (Presle 3)
Alpagueur, 1976 (Belmondo 3, Evein 4)
Alpentragödie, 1927 (Kortner 3,
    Andrejew 4)
Alpha Beta, 1972 (Finney 3)
Alpha Beta, 1976 (Roberts 3)
Alpha Caper, 1973 (Fonda 3)
Alphabet, 1968 (Lynch 2)
Alphabet Murders, 1965 (Tashlin 2,
    Rutherford 3)
Alphaville, 1965 (Godard 2,
    Constantine 3, Karina 3, Léaud 3,
    Coutard 4, Guillemot 4)
Alpine Yodeler, 1936 (Terry 4)
Alraune, 1918 (Curtiz 2)
Alraune, 1927 (Wegener 3, Galeen 4,
    Planer 4)
Alraune, 1930 (Kaper 4)
Alraune, 1952 (Von Stroheim 2, Herlth 4,)
Als tween druppels water, 1963 (Coutard 4)
Alsace, 1915 (Burel 4)
Alsino and the Condor. See Asino y el
    condor, 1981
Alskande par, 1964 (Zetterling 2,
    Andersson 3, Dahlbeck 3, Nykvist 4)
Alskarinnen, 1962 (Von Sydow 3)
Älskling, jag ger mig, 1943 (Molander 2)
Alskling på vågen, 1956 (Nykvist 4)
Also es war so..., 1976 (Karina 3,
    Ballhaus 4)
Alt paa ét Kort, 1912 (Psilander 3)
Alta infedeltà, 1964 (Monicelli 2, Blier 3,
    Bloom 3, Cassel 3, Vitti 3, Age
    and Scarpelli 4, Di Venanzo 4,
    Gherardi 4)
Altar of Death, 1912 (Ince 4, Sullivan 4)
Altar of Love, 1915 (Costello 3)
Altar of the Aztecs, 1913 (Bosworth 3)
Altar Stairs, 1922 (Karloff 3, Laemmle 4)
Altars of Desire, 1927 (Daniels 4, Gibbons 4,
    Gillespie 4)
Altars of the East, 1955 (Ayres 3)
Altars of the World, 1976 (Ayres 3)
Alte Balhaus, 1925 (Tschechowa 3)
Alte Gesetz, 1923 (Krauss 3, Porten 3,
    Junge 4)
Alte Herzen, neue Zeiten, 1926 (Pick 2)
Alte Lied, 1930 (Dagover 3)
Alte und der junge König, 1935 (Jannings 3,
    Von Harbou 4)
Altered Message, 1911 (Guy 2)
Altered States, 1980 (Russell 2, Hurt 3,
    Chayefsky 4, Smith 4)

Altes Herz wird wieder jung, 1943
    (Jannings 3, Wagner 4)
Altgermanische Bauernkultur, 1934
    (Ruttman 2)
Alt-Heidelberg, 1923 (Krauss 3, Metzner 4)
Although There Are Millions of Women. See
    Onna wa ikuman aritotemo, 1966
Altitude 3.200, 1938 (Barrault 3, Blier 3,
    Jaubert 4)
Altitude 8625, 1964 (Braunberger 4)
Altra, 1947 (Amidei 4)
Altri, gli altri e noi, 1967 (De Sica 2)
Altri tempi, 1952 (Fabrizi 3, Lollobrigida 3,
    Cecchi D'Amico 4)
Alum and Eve, 1932 (Roach 4)
Aluminité, 1910 (Gance 2)
Alvarez Kelly, 1966 (Dmytryk 2, Holden 3,
    Widmark 3, Green 4, Mercer 4)
Always, 1989 (Spielberg 2, Dreyfuss 3,
    Hepburn 3, Williams 4)
Always a Bride, 1953 (Rank 4)
Always a Way, 1911 (Lawrence 3)
Always Audacious, 1920 (Cruze 2, Reid 3)
Always Faithful, 1929 (Sweet 3)
Always Goodbye, 1931 (Edeson 4,
    Friedhofer 4, Menzies 4)
Always Goodbye, 1938 (Marshall 3,
    Pangborn 3, Stanwyck 4)
Always in My Heart, 1942 (Francis 3,
    Huston 3)
Always Kickin', 1939 (Fleischer 4)
Always Leave Them Laughing, 1949
    (Cahn 4, Haller 4, Mercer 4, Wald 4)
Always on Sunday, 1965 (Russell 2)
Always Tell Your Wife, 1923 (Hitchcock 2)
Always Together, 1947 (Bogart 3, Flynn 3,
    Diamond 4)
Alye parusa, 1961 (Ptushko 4)
Alyonka, 1961 (Barnet 2)
Alzire oder der Neue Kontinent, 1978
    (Vogler 3)
Am Abend auf der Heide, 1941 (Von
    Harbou 4)
Am Meer, 1924 (Nielsen 3)
Ama a tu prójimo, 1958 (Cantinflas 3)
Ama no yugao, 1948 (Hayasaka 4)
Amada, 1983 (Solas 2)
Amadeus, 1984 (Forman 2, Ondřiček 4,
    Smith 4)
Amagi kara kita otoko, 1950 (Yamada 3)
Amai himitsu, 1971 (Yoshimura 2)
Amai shiru, 1964 (Kyo 3)
Amami, Alfredo!, 1940 (Gallone 2)
Amanat, 1955 (Roy 2)
Aman Ke Farishte, 1990 (Anand 3)
Amant de Bornéo, 1942 (Arletty 3)
Amant de cinq jours, 1961 (Cassel 3,
    Presle 3, Seberg 3, Delerue 4, Evein 4)
Amant de Lady Chatterley, 1955
    (Darrieux 3, Kosma 4, Périnal 4,
    Trauner 4)
Amant de Madame Vidal, 1936
    (D'Eaubonne 4)
Amante della città Sepolta. See Atlantide,
    1960
Amante di Paride. See Eterna femmina, 1954
Amante italiana. See Sultans, 1966
Amante segreta, 1941 (Gallone 2, Valli 3)
Amantes, 1983 (Fernández 2)
Amanti, 1968 (Dunaway 3, Mastroianni 3,
    Guerra 4, Ponti 4), Van Runkle 4,
    Zavattini 4)
Amanti del deserto, 1956 (Cervi 3)
Amanti del mostro, 1974 (Kinski 3)

Amanti di Gramigna, 1969 (Volonté 3)
Amanti di Ravello, 1950 (Baarová 3)
Amanti d'oltretombo, 1965 (Morricone 4)
Amanti senza amore, 1947 (Gherardi 4,
  Rota 4)
Amantia Pestilens, 1963 (Bujold 3)
Amants, 1958 (Cuny 3, Modot 3, Moreau 3,
  Decaë 4, Evein 4, Saulnier 4)
Amants de Bras-Mort, 1950 (Auric 4)
Amants de demain, 1957 (Brasseur 3,
  Manès 3)
Amants de la Villa Borghese, 1954
  (Philipe 3)
Amants de minuit, 1931 (Allégret 2,
  Braunberger 4)
Amants de Teruel, 1961 (Renoir 4,
  Theodorakis 4)
Amants de Tolède, 1953 (Armendáriz 3,
  Valli 3, Barsacq 4)
Amants de Vérone, 1948 (Aimée 3,
  Brasseur 3, Dalio 3, Reggiani 3,
  Alekan 4, Kosma 4, Prévert 4)
Amants de villa Borghese. See Villa
  Borghese, 1953
Amants du Pont Saint-Jean, 1947 (Simon 3,
  Aurenche 4)
Amants du Tage, 1955 (Armendáriz 3,
  Dalio 3, Gélin 3, Howard 3,
  D'Eaubonne 4, Legrand 4)
Amants et voleurs, 1935 (Arletty 3,
  Simon 3)
Amants terribles, 1984 (Branco 4)
Amapola del Camino, 1937 (Armendáriz 3)
Amar, 1954 (Mehboob 2, Kumar 3)
Amar, Akbar, Anthony, 1977 (Azmi 3,
  Bachchan 3)
Amar Deep, 1958 (Anand 3)
Amar Lenin, 1970 (Ghatak 2)
Amarcord, 1974 (Fellini 2, Cristaldi 4,
  Donati 4, Guerra 4, Rota 4, Rotunno 4)
Amardeep, 1979 (Azmi 3)
Amarilly of Clothes-Line Alley, 1918
  (Neilan 2, Pickford 3, Marion 4)
Amarrando el Cordon, 1968 (Alvarez 2)
Amateur Broadcast, 1935 (Lantz 4)
Amateur Daddy, 1932 (Friedhofer 4,
  Howe 4)
Amateur Film. See Pärlorna, 1922
Amateur Gentleman, 1926 (Olcott 2,
  Barthelmess 3)
Amateur Gentleman, 1936 (Lockwood 3)
Amateur Night, 1927 (Love 3)
Amateur Night, 1935 (Terry 4)
Amator, 1978 (Zanussi 2)
Amature Nite, 1929 (Lantz 4)
Amazing Captain Nemo, 1978 (Ferrer 3,
  Meredith 3)
Amazing Colossal Man, 1957 (Biroc 4)
Amazing Dobermans, 1977 (Astaire 3)
Amazing Dr. Clitterhouse, 1938 (Huston 2,
  Litvak 2, Bogart 3, Bond 3, Crisp 3,
  Hayward 3, Robinson 3, Trevor 3,
  Gaudio 4, Steiner 4, Warner 4)
Amazing Dr. G, 1965 (Rey 3)
Amazing Grace, 1974 (McQueen 3)
Amazing Grace and Chuck, 1987 (Curtis 3,
  Peck 3, Bernstein 4)
Amazing Mrs. Holliday, 1943 (Durbin 3,
  Fitzgerald 3, O'Brien 3, Levien 4,
  Salter 4)
Amazing Mr. Beecham. See Chiltern
  Hundreds, 1949
Amazing Mr. Blunden, 1972 (Dors 3,
  Bernstein 4, Fisher 4)

Amazing Mr. Forrest. See Gang's All Here,
  1939
Amazing Mr. Williams, 1939 (Blondell 3,
  Douglas 3)
Amazing Mr Forrest. See Gang's All Here,
  1939
Amazing Monsieur Fabre. See Monsieur
  Fabre, 1951
Amazing Quest of Ernest Bliss, 1936
  (Grant 3, Balderston 4, Heller 4)
Amazing Stories. See Secret Cinema, 1985
Amazing Transparent Man, 1960 (Ulmer 2,
  Pierce 4)
Amazing Vagabond, 1929 (Miller 4,
  Plunkett 4)
Amazing What Color Can Do, 1954
  (Kaufman 4)
Amazon Women on the Moon, 1987
  (Dante 2, Landis 2, Bellamy 3,
  Pfeiffer 3)
Amazonas Amazonas, 1965 (Rocha 2)
Amazons, 1917 (Menjou 3, Marion 4)
Amazons of Rome. See Vergine di Roma,
  1961
Amazonus de pueblo embravecido, 1980
  (Alvarez 2)
Amazzone mascherata, 1914 (Bertini 3)
Ambar, 1952 (Kapoor 2)
Ambassador, 1984 (Burstyn 3, Mitchum 3,
  Golan and Globus 4)
Ambassador at Large, 1964 (Homolka 3)
Ambassador Bill, 1931 (Milland 3, Rogers 3)
Ambassadors, 1977 (Remick 3)
Ambassador's Daughter, 1956 (De
  Havilland 3, Loy 3, Menjou 3, Barsacq 4,
  Krasna 4)
Ambassador's Despatch. See Valise
  diplomatique, 1909
Ambassador's Disappearance, 1913
  (Costello 3)
Ambassador's Envoy, 1914 (Hayakawa 3,
  Ince 4)
Ambiciosos. See Fièvre monte à El Pao,
  1959
Ambitieuse, 1959 (Allégret 2, O'Brien 3,
  Wakhévitch 4)
Ambition, 1990 (Rosenman 4)
Ambition of the Baron, 1915 (Bushman 3,
  Swanson 3)
Ambitious. See Bakumatsu, 1970
Ambitious Butler, 1912 (Sennett 2,
  Normand 3)
Ambitious Ethel, 1916 (Laurel and Hardy 3)
Ambrose Series, 1914–16 (Sennett 2)
Ambulance, 1990 (Cohen 2)
Ambulance Corps Drill, 1899 (Bitzer 4)
Ambush, 1939 (Crawford 3)
Ambush, 1949 (Wood 2, Taylor 3,
  Plunkett 4)
Ambush. See Machibuse, 1970
Ambush at Cimarron Pass, 1957
  (Eastwood 3)
Ambush Bay, 1966 (Rooney 3)
Ambushers, 1967 (Martin 3, Guffey 4)
Ame d'argile, 1955 (Delerue 4)
Ame d'artiste, 1925 (Dulac 2, Manès 3,
  Vanel 3)
Ame de bronze, 1918 (Baur 3)
Ame de clown, 1933 (Fresnay 3,
  D'Eaubonne 4)
Ame de Pierre, 1912 (Modot 3)
Amelia and the Angel, 1957 (Russell 2)
Amère victoire, 1957 (Ray 2, Burton 3,
  Lee 3, D'Eaubonne 4)

America, 1924 (Barrymore 3, Bitzer 4)
America, 1982 (Rosenblum 4)
America, America, 1963 (Kazan 2, Allen 4,
  Wexler 4)
America and Lewis Hine, 1984 (Robards 3)
America at the Movies, 1977 (Delon 3,
  Heston 3)
America Can Give It, 1942 (Huston 3)
America Is Hard to See, 1969 (De
  Antonio 2)
America: Isn't Life Wonderful, 1924
  (Griffith 2)
America Is Waiting, 1982 (Conner 2)
America Revisited, 1971 (Ophuls 2)
America 3000, 1986 (Golan and Globus 4)
Américain, 1970 (Signoret 3, Trintignant 3)
Américain se détend, 1957 (Braunberger 4)
American, 1927 (Love 3)
American Aristocracy, 1916 (Fleming 2,
  Fairbanks 3, Loos 4)
American Aristocracy, 1945 (Fleming 2)
American Autobahn, 1983 (Jarmusch 2)
American Beauty, 1927 (Folsey 4, Wilson 4)
American Boy, 1979 (Scorsese 2)
American Christmas Carol, 1979 (Baker 4)
American Chronicles: Farewell to the Flesh,
  1990 (Dreyfuss 3)
American Citizen, 1914 (Barrymore 3)
American Creed, 1946 (Jones 3)
American Dream, 1966 (Leigh 3)
American Dreamer, 1971 (Kovacs 4)
American Dreamer, 1984 (Giannini 3,
  Rotunno 4)
American Empire, 1942 (Harlan 4)
American Film, 1967 (Heston 3)
American Flyers, 1985 (Badham 2,
  Costner 3)
American Friend. See **Amerikanische
  Freund, 1977**
American Gigolo, 1980 (Schrader 2, Gere 3)
American Girls, 1978 (Andrews 3)
American Gothic, 1987 (De Carlo 3,
  Steiger 3)
**American Graffiti, 1973 (Coppola 2,
  Lucas 2, Dreyfuss 3, Ford 3, Fields 4,
  Murch 4, Wexler 4)**
American Guerilla in the Philippines, 1950
  (Lang 2, Power 3, Presle 3, LeMaire 4,
  Trotti 4, Wheeler 4)
American Heiress, 1917 (Hepworth 2)
American Hot Wax, 1977 (Fraker 4)
**American in Paris, 1951 (Minnelli 2,
  Caron 3, Kelly 3, Alton 4, Ames 4,
  Edens 4, Freed 4, Gibbons 4, Green 4,
  Orry-Kelly 4, Plunkett 4, Sharaff 4,
  Smith 4)**
American Madness, 1932 (Capra 2,
  Huston 3, Cohn 4, Riskin 4, Walker 4)
American March, 1941 (Fischinger 2,
  Ford 2)
American Matchmaker. See Americaner
  Schadchen, 1939
American Ninja II, 1987 (Golan and
  Globus 4)
American People, 1945 (Huston 3)
American Pop, 1981 (Bakshi 4)
American Portrait, 1949 (Ladd 3)
American Prisoner, 1929 (Carroll 3)
American Raspberry. See Prime Time, 1977
American Road, 1954 (North 4)
American Romance, 1944 (Vidor 2, Irene 4,
  Rosson 4)
American Soldier in Love and War, 1903
  (Bitzer 4)

American Success. *See* American Success Company, 1979

American Success Company, 1979 (Bridges 3, Jarre 4)

American Tail 2: Fievel Goes West, 1991 (Spielberg 2, Stewart 3)

American 30's Song. *See* Songs, 1964–69

American Tragedy, 1931 (Von Sternberg 2, Sidney 3, Banton 4, Dreier 4, Garmes 4, Hoffenstein 4)

American Venus, 1926 (Brooks 3, Hunt 4)

American Way, 1961 (Emshwiller 2)

American Way, 1986 (Hooper 3)

American Werewolf in London, 1981 (Landis 2, Baker 4, Bernstein 4)

American West of John Ford, 1971 (Stewart 3)

American Widow, 1917 (Barrymore 3)

Americaner Schadchen, 1939 (Ulmer 2)

Americanization of Emily, 1964 (Andrews 3, Coburn 3, Douglas 3, Garner 3, Challis 4, Chayefsky 4, Mercer 4)

Americano, 1916 (Fleming 2, Fairbanks 3, Emerson 4, Loos 4)

Americano, 1945 (Fleming 2)

Americano, 1954 (Ford 3)

Americano a Roma, 1954 (Scola 2, Sordi 3, Ponti 4)

Americano in vacanza, 1945 (Ponti 4, Rota 4)

America's Cup Race, 1946 (Porter 2)

America's Sweetheart: The Mary Pickford Story, 1978 (Fonda 3)

Amerikanische Freund, 1977 (Fuller 2, Wenders 2, Ganz 3, Hopper 3, Müller 4)

Amerikanische Soldat, 1970 (Von Trotta 2)

Amérique insolite, 1958 (Braunberger 4, Legrand 4)

Amérique Lunaire, 1962 (Braunberger 4)

Amérique vue par un français. *See* Amérique insolite, 1960

Ames de fous, 1917 (Dulac 2)

Ames d'orient, 1919 (Gaumont 4)

Ametralladora, 1943 (Infante 3)

Ami de Vincent, 1983 (Karina 3, Noiret 3)

Ami Fritz, 1933 (D'Eaubonne 4)

Ami retrouvé, 1989 (Robards 3, Pinter 4, Sarde 4, Trauner 4)

Ami viendra ce soir, 1945 (Gélin 3, Simon 3, Honegger 4,)

Amica, 1969 (Lattuada 2)

Amiche, 1955 (Cecchi d'Amico 4, Di Venanzo 4, Fusco 4)

Amici miei, 1975 (Germi 2, Monicelli 2, Blier 3, Noiret 3, Pinelli 4)

Amici miei, atto due, 1982 (Monicelli 2, Noiret 3, Pinelli 4)

Amici miei atto III, 1985 (Blier 3)

Amici per la pelle, 1955 (Rota 4)

Amico del giaguaro, 1958 (Delli Colli 4)

Amiga, 1988 (Ullmann 3)

Amigos, 1972 (Delli Colli 4)

Amiral Nakhimov, 1946 (Golovnya 4)

Amir Garib, 1974 (Anand 3)

Amitie noire, 1946 (Cocteau 2)

Amitiés particulières, 1964 (Aurenche 4, Bost 4, Matras 4)

Amityville Horror, 1979 (Steiger 3, Schifrin 4)

Amityville II: The Possession, 1982 (Schifrin 4)

Amleto e il suo clown, 1920 (Gallone 2)

Amo non amo, 1979 (Schell 3, Stamp 3)

Amo te sola, 1935 (De Sica 2)

Am Rande der Gross-stadt, 1922 (Kortner 3)

Am Rande der Welt, 1927 (Dieterle 2, Wagner 4)

Am roten Kliff, 1921 (Kortner 3)

Am seidenen Faden, 1950 (Staudte 2)

Am Tor des Lebens, 1918 (Wiene 2)

Am Tor des Todes. *See* Am Tor des Lebens, 1918

Am Webstuhl der Zeit, 1921 (Holger-Madsen 2)

Amoire volante, 1948 (Modot 3)

Amok, 1934 (Courant 4, Meerson 4, Rathaus 4, Trauner 4)

Amok, 1944 (Félix 3)

Among the Living, 1941 (Carey 3, Farmer 3, Hayward 3, Fort 4, Head 4)

Among the Missing, 1934 (August 4)

Among the Mourners, 1914 (Sennett 2, Arbuckle 2)

Among Those Present, 1919 (Sennett 2)

Among Those Present, 1921 (Lloyd 3, Roach 4)

Among Vultures. *See* Unter Geiern, 1964

Amoozin' But Confoozin', 1944 (Fleischer 2)

Amor, amor, amor, 1965 (Figueroa 4)

Amor brujo, 1985 (Saura 2)

Amor de Don Juan, 1956 (Rey 3)

Amor de perdicao, 1981 (Branco 4)

Amor en el aire, 1967 (Rey 3)

Amor libre, 1978 (Hermosillo 2)

Amor non ho … pero … pero, 1951 (Lollobrigida 3)

Amor tiene cara de mujer, 1973 (Figueroa 4)

Amor und das standhafte Liebespaar, 1920 (Reiniger 4)

Amor y deditos del pie, 1990 (Cassel 3)

Amor y sexo, 1963 (Félix 3)

Amore, 1923 (Gallone 2)

Amore, 1935 (Cervi 3, Feuillère 3)

Amore, 1947 (Magnani 3, Pinelli 4)

Amore, 1965 (Brazzi 3)

Amore a Roma, 1960 (De Sica 2, Flaiano 4)

Amore audaz. *See* Enigmatique Monsieur Parkes, 1930

Amore canta, 1941 (De Laurentiis 4)

Amore difficile, 1962 (Gassman 3)

Amore e chiacchiere, 1957 (Blasetti 2, De Sica 2, Cervi 3, Zavattini 4)

Amore e ginnastica, 1973 (Cecchi D'Amico 4)

Amore e guai, 1958 (Mastroianni 3)

Amore e rabbia, 1969 (Pasolini 2, Fusco 4, Guillemot 4)

Amore Imperiale, 1941 (Volkov 2)

Amore in citta, 1953 (Fellini 2, Ferreri 2, Di Venanzo 4, Pinelli 4, Zavattini 4)

Amore in quattro dimensioni, 1963 (Delli Colli 4)

Amore mio, aiutami, 1969 (Sordi 3, Vitti 3)

Amore pericolosi, 1964 (Delli Colli 4)

Amore, piombo, e furore, 1978 (Peckinpah 2, Oates 3, Donaggio 4)

Amore primitivo, 1964 (Mansfield 3)

Amore vince amore, 1921 (Bertini 3)

Amores de une viuda, 1948 (Alcoriza 4)

Amori di Ercole, 1960 (Mansfield 3)

Amori di Manon Lescaut, 1954 (Pinelli 4)

Amori di mezzo secolo, 1953 (Delli Colli 4)

Amori di mezzo secolo, 1954 (Rossellini 2, Sordi 3)

Amorosa, 1986 (Zetterling 2, Josephson 3)

Amorosa menzogna, 1949 (Antonioni 2, Fusco 4)

Amorous Adventures of Moll Flanders, 1965 (De Sica 2, Lansbury 3, Novak 3, Sanders 3, Addison 4, Vetchinsky 4)

Amorous General. *See* Waltz of the Toreadors, 1962

Amorous Mr. Prawn. *See* Amorous Prawn, 1962

Amorous Prawn, 1962 (Greenwood 3, Barry 4)

Amos, 1985 (Douglas 3)

Amour, 1973 (Warhol 2, Vangelis 4)

Amour à la chaîne, 1964 (Delerue 4)

Amour à la mer, 1964 (Delon 3)

Amour à l'américaine, 1931 (Allégret 2, Fejös 2, Braunberger 4)

Amour à mort, 1984 (Resnais 2, Vierny 4)

Amour à tous les étages, 1902 (Pathé 4)

Amour a vingt ans, 1962 (Truffaut 2, Wajda 2, Cybulski 3, Léaud 3, Coutard 4, Delerue 4, Stawiński 4, Takemitsu, 4)

Amour autour de la maison, 1946 (Brasseur 3, Kosma 4)

Amour avec des si, 1963 (Braunberger 4)

Amour blessé, 1975 (Lefebvre 2)

Amour c'est gai, l'amour c'est triste, 1968 (Dalio 3)

Amour chante, 1930 (Florey 2)

Amour d'automne, 1912 (Feuillade 2)

Amour de Jeanne Ney. *See* Liebe der Jeanne Ney, 1927

Amour de pluie, 1974 (Schneider 3, Carrière 4, Lai 4)

Amour de poche, 1957 (Melville 2, Marais 3, Cloquet 4)

Amour de Swann. *See* Swann in Love, 1984

Amour d'une femme, 1954 (Grémillon 2, Presle 3)

Amour d'un métier, 1950 (Colpi 4)

Amour en Allemagne, 1983 (Mueller-Stahl 3)

Amour en cage, 1934 (Heller 4)

Amour en fuite, 1979 (Truffaut 2, Léaud 3, Almendros 4, Delerue 4)

Amour en question, 1978 (Cayatte 2, Andersson 3, Girardot 3)

Amour est en jeu, 1957 (Girardot 3)

Amour et discipline, 1931 (D'Eaubonne 4)

Amour et la veine, 1932 (D'Eaubonne 4)

Amour existe, 1961 (Pialat 2, Braunberger 4, Delerue 4)

Amour fou, 1968 (Rivette 2, De Beauregard 4)

Amour interdit, 1984 (Rey 3)

Amour l'après-midi, 1972 (Almendros 4)

Amour, madame …, 1951 (Arletty 3)

Amour par terre, 1984 (Rivette 2, Chaplin 3)

Amour tenace, 1912 (Linder 3)

Amoureux du France, 1963 (Legrand 4)

Amoureux sont seuls au monde, 1948 (Jouvet 3, Jeanson 4)

Amours célèbres, 1961 (Bardot 3, Belmondo 3, Brasseur 3, Delon 3, Feuillère 3, Girardot 3, Noiret 3, Signoret 3, Achard 4, Audiard 4, Jarre 4, Prévert 4, Wakhévitch 4)

Amours de Casanova, 1933 (Mozhukin 3)

Amours finissent à l'aube, 1953 (Alekan 4)

Ampélopède, 1974 (Huppert 3)

Amphitryon, 1935 (Herlth 4, Röhrig 4, Wagner 4)

Amsterdam Affair, 1968 (Fisher 4)

Amsterdam Kill, 1977 (Mitchum 3)

Amuletten, 1911 (Magnusson 4)

Amy, 1981 (O'Brien 3)

Amy and the Angel, 1986 (Jones 3, Rosenblum 4)

Amy Goes to Buy Some Bread, 1979 (Vukotić 4)

An der schönen blauen Donau, 1926 (Albers 3, Andrejew 4)

An heiligen Wassern, 1960 (Heller 4)

An jedem Finger zehn, 1954 (Albers 3)

An quarante, 1940 (Berry 3)

An uns glaubt Gott nicht mehr, 1981 (Mueller-Stahl 3)

Ana, 1957 (Kyo 3, Yamamura 3)

Ana, 1981 (Branco 4)

Ana, 1982 (De Almeida 4)

Ana and the Wolves. See Ana y los lobos, 1973

Ana y los lobos, 1973 (Saura 2, Chaplin 3)

Anadi, 1959 (Kapoor 2)

Analfabeto, 1960 (Cantinflas 3)

Anam, 1956 (Sharif 3)

Anand, 1971 (Bachchan 3)

Anand nur Anand, 1984 (Anand 3, Patil 3)

Anarchie chez Guignol, 1906 (Méliès 2)

Anarchist, 1913 (Brenon 2)

Anarchistes ou la Bande à Bonnot, 1967 (Girardot 3)

Anastasia, 1956 (Litvak 2, Bergman 3, Brynner 3, Andrejew 4, Newman 4)

Anastasia nio fratello, 1973 (Amidei 4)

Anastasia: The Mystery of Anna, 1986 (De Havilland 3, Harrison 3, Sharif 3)

Anata to watashi no ai-kotoba: Sayonara, konnichiwa, 1959 (Kyo 3)

Anatahan, 1953 (Von Sternberg 2, Tsuburaya 4)

Anatolian, 1982 (Kazan 2)

Anatolian Smile. See America, America, 1964

Anatomie d'un livreur, 1969 (Vierny 4)

Anatomie stunde, 1977 (Zanussi 2)

Anatomist, 1961 (Sim 3)

Anatomy Lesson. See Anatomie stunde, 1977

Anatomy of a Murder, 1959 (Preminger 2, Arden 3, Remick 3, Scott 3, Stewart 3, Bass 4, Leven 4)

Anatomy of an Illness, 1983 (Wallach 3)

Anatomy of Cindy Fink, 1965 (Leacock 2)

Anatomy of Love. See Tempi nostri, 1953

Anatomy of Love, 1972 (Nowicki 3)

Anatra all'orancia, 1975 (Vitti 3)

Anche se volessi lavorare che faccio?, 1972 (Morricone 4)

Anchors Aweigh, 1945 (Donen 2, Grayson 3, Kelly 3, Sinatra 3, Cahn 4, Hanna and Barbera 4, Irene 4, Lennart 4, Mayer 4, Pasternak 4)

Anciens de Saint-Loup, 1950 (Blier 3, Reggiani 3)

Ancient Law. See Alte Gesetz, 1923

Ancient Mariner, 1925 (Bow 3, August 4)

Ancient Temples of Egypt, 1912 (Olcott 2)

And a Little Child Shall Lead Them, 1909 (Griffith 2)

And a Still Small Voice, 1918 (Walthall 3)

And Baby Makes Six, 1979 (Oates 3)

And Baby Makes Three, 1949 (Young 3, Duning 4, Guffey 4)

And . . . God Created Woman. See Et . . . **Dieu créa la femme, 1956**

And God Said to Cain. See E Dio disse a Caino . . ., 1969

And Happiness Will Be Possible. See Shchastiya bylo tak vozmotzno, 1916

And His Wife Came Back, 1913 (Bunny 3)

And Hope to Die. See Course du lièvre à travers les champs, 1971

And Justice for All, 1979 (Jewison 2, Levinson 2, Pacino 3)

And Life Goes On. See Život jde dál, 1935

. . . and Nobody Was Ashamed. See . . . und keiner schämte sich, 1960

And No One Could Save Her, 1973 (Remick 3)

And Nothing But the Truth, 1984 (Jackson 3)

And Now for Something Completely Different, 1971 (Gilliam 2, Cleese 3, Godfrey 4)

And Now My Love. See Toure une vie, 1974

And Now the Screaming Starts, 1973 (Cushing 3, Lom 3)

And Now Tomorrow, 1944 (Bondi 3, Hayward 3, Ladd 3, Young 3, Chandler 4, Dreier 4, Head 4, Young 4)

And So They Were Married, 1935 (Astor 3, Douglas 3, Schulberg 4)

And So They Were Married. See Johnny Doesn't Live Here Anymore, 1944

And Sudden Death, 1936 (Scott 3)

. . . and Suddenly It's Murder. See Crimen, 1960

And the Angels Sing, 1943 (Hutton 3, Lamour 3, MacMurray 3, Dreier 4, Frank 4, Head 4, Struss 4, Young 4)

And the Dance Goes On, 1990 (Bujold 3)

And the Earth Shall Give Back Life, 1953 (Kaufman 4)

And the Green Grass Grew All Around, 1931 (Fleischer 4)

And Then There Were None, 1945 (Clair 2, Fitzgerald 3, Huston 3, Nichols 4)

And Then There Were None, 1974 (Attenborough 3, Audran 3, Lom 3, Reed 3)

And the Pursuit of Happiness, 1986 (Malle 2)

And There Came a Man. See E venne un uomo, 1965

And the Ship Sails On. See E la nave va, 1983

And the Wild, Wild Women. See Nella città l'inferno, 1958

And to Think I Saw It on Mulberry Street, 1944 (Pal 4)

And Yet They Go. See Shikamo karera wa yuku, 1931

And You Act Like One, Too, 1989 (Seidelman 2)

Andaz, 1949 (Kapoor 2, Kumar 3, Nargis 3)

Andechser Gefühl, 1975 (Von Trotta 2)

Andělský kabát, 1948 (Brdečka 4)

Andere, 1913 (Warm 4)

Andere, 1924 (Hoffmann 4)

Andere, 1930 (Wiene 2, Kortner 3)

Andere Ich, 1918 (Kortner 3)

Andere Seite, 1931 (Veidt 3)

Anders als die Andern, 1919 (Veidt 3)

Andersen hos fotografen, 1975 (Roos 2)

Andersens hemmelighed, 1971 (Roos 2)

Anderson Tapes, 1971 (Lumet 2, Connery 3, Jones 4)

Anderssonskans Kalle, 1950 (Andersson 3)

Andhaa Kaanoon, 1983 (Bachchan 3)

Ando volando bajo, 1957 (Armendáriz 3)

André Masson et les quatre éléments, 1958 (Grémillon 2, Delerue 4)

Andreas Hofer, 1909 (Porten 3, Messter 4)

Andreas Schlüter, 1942 (Tschechowa 3, Herlth 4)

Andrei Kozhukhov, 1917 (Protazanov 2, Mozhukin 3)

Andreina, 1917 (Bertini 3)

Andrei Rublev, 1964 (Mikhalkov-Konchalovsky 2, Tarkovsky 2)

Andremo in città, 1966 (Chaplin 3, Delli Colli 4, Stawiński 4, Zavattini 4)

Andrew Jackson, 1913 (Dwan 2)

Andrew Logan Kisses the Glitterati, 1972 (Jarman 2)

Andriesh, 1954 (Paradzhanov 2)

Androclès, 1912 (Feuillade 2)

Androcles and the Lion, 1952 (Lanchester 3, Mature 3, Newton 3, Simmons 3, Dunn 4, Horner 4, Stradling 4, D'Agostino 4)

Android, 1983 (Kinski 3)

Andromeda Strain, 1970 (Wise 2, Leven 4, Trumbull 4)

Andy Clyde Gets Spring Chicken, 1939 (Bruckman 4)

Andy Hardy Comes Home, 1958 (Rooney 3)

Andy Hardy Gets Spring Fever, 1939 (Van Dyke 2, Rooney 3)

Andy Hardy Meets Debutante, 1940 (Garland 3, Rooney 3)

Andy Hardy Steps Out. See Andy Hardy's Double Life, 1942

Andy Hardy's Blonde Trouble, 1944 (Marshall 3, Irene 4)

Andy Hardy's Double Life, 1942 (Rooney 3, Williams 3, Folsey 4)

Andy Hardy's Double Trouble, 1944 (Rooney 3)

Andy Hardy's Private Secretary, 1941 (Grayson 3, Rooney 3, Murfin 4, Stothard 4)

Andy of the Royal Mounted, 1915 (Anderson 3)

Andy Plays Hookey, 1946 (Bruckman 4)

Andy Warhol Films Jack Smith Filming Normal Love, 1963 (Warhol 2)

Andy Warhol's Bad, 1977 (Corman 2, Warhol 2, Baker 3)

Andy Warhol's Dracula. See Dracula cerca sangue di vergine e . . . mori di sete!!!, 1974

Andy Warhol's Frankenstein. See Carne per Frankenstein, 1974

Ane de Bruidan, 1932 (Douy 4)

Ane jaloux. See Max et son âne, 1911

Ane no shussei, 1940 (Takamine 3)

Ane to imoto, 1965 (Iwashita 3, Yamamura 3)

Anfisa, 1912 (Protazanov 2)

Angarey, 1954 (Burman 4)

Ange de la nuit, 1943 (Barrault 3, Signoret 3)

Ange gardien, 1933 (Meerson 4)

Ange que j'ai vendu, 1938 (Barsacq 4)

Angeklagt nach N.218, 1965 (Schüfftan 4)

Angeklagt nach Paragraph 218, 1966 (Lomnicki 3)

Angel, 1937 (Lubitsch 2, Dietrich 3, Douglas 3, Horton 3, Marshall 3, Banton 4, Dreier 4, Lang 4, Raphaelson 4)

Angel, 1982 (Menges 4)

Angel and Sinner. *See* Boule de suif, 1945

Angel and the Badman, 1947 (Carey 3, Wayne 3, Canutt 4)

Angel, Angel, Down We Go, 1969 (Jones 3)

Angel Baby, 1961 (Blondell 3, McCambridge 3, Reynolds 3, Wexler 4)

Angel Child, 1908 (Porter 2)

Angel Dust, 1980 (Woodward 3)

Angel Esquire, 1919 (Pearson 2)

Ángel exterminador, 1962 (Alcoriza 4, Figueroa 4)

Angel Face, 1952 (Preminger 2, Marshall 3, Mitchum 3, Simmons 3, D'Agostino 4, Nugent 4, Stradling 4, Tiomkin 4)

Angel from Texas, 1940 (Reagan 3, Wyman 3)

Angel Heart, 1987 (Parker 2, De Niro 3, Rourke 3)

Angel in Exile, 1948 (Dwan 2)

Angel Levine, 1970 (Kadár 2, Wallach 3, Jenkins 4)

Angel of Broadway, 1926 (Adrian 4)

Angel of Broadway, 1927 (Weber 2, Coffee 4, Miller 4)

Angel of Contention, 1914 (Gish 3)

Angel of Darkness. *See* Donne proibite, 1953

Angel of Death, 1913 (Brenon 2)

Angel of Death. *See* Egy Barany, 1970

Angel of Paradise Ranch, 1911 (Dwan 2)

Angel of the Canyons, 1913 (Dwan 2)

Angel of the Studio, 1912 (Lawrence 3)

Angel on Earth. *See* Engel auf Erden, 1959

Angel on My Shoulder, 1946 (Baxter 3, Muni 3, Rains 3, Tiomkin 4)

Angel Out of the Slums, 1910 (White 3)

Angel over Brooklyn. *See* Angel paso sobre Brooklyn, 1957

Angel paso sobre Brooklyn, 1957 (Ustinov 3)

Angel Puss, 1944 (Blanc 4, Jones 4, Stalling 4)

Angel Street. *See* Gaslight, 1940

Angel with the Trumpet, 1951 (Schell 3, Werner 3, Korda 4, Krasker 4)

Angel Wore Red, 1960 (Bogarde 3, Cotten 3, Fabrizi 3, Gardner 3, Johnson 4, Kaper 4, Rotunno 4)

Angela, 1954 (Brazzi 3)

Angela. *See* Tarots, 1972

Angela, 1973 (Delerue 4)

Angela, 1976 (Loren 3)

Angela, 1977 (Huston 2)

Angela, 1984 (Mancini 4)

Angela Markado, 1980 (Brocka 2)

Angelas Krig, 1984 (Josephson 3)

Angela's War. *See* Angelas Krig, 1984

Angèle, 1934 (Pagnol 2, Fernandel 3, Honegger 4)

Angeles de Puebla, 1966 (Figueroa 4)

Angelica, 1939 (Ibert 4)

Angelic Attitude, 1916 (Mix 3)

Angelic Conversation, 1985 (Jarman 2)

Angeli dalle mani bendate, 1975 (Brazzi 3)

Angelika, 1940 (Tschechowa 3)

Angelika, 1954 (Schell 3)

Angelina. *See* Onorevole Angelina, 1947

Angelitos negros, 1948 (Infante 3)

Angelo bianco, 1955 (Delli Colli 4)

Angelo e il Diavolo, 1946 (Camerini 2, Cervi 3, Zavattini 4)

Angelo, My Love, 1983 (Duvall 3)

Angels and the Pirates. *See* Angels in the Outfield, 1951

Angels Brigade, 1979 (Palance 3)

Angel's Coat. *See* Andělský kabát, 1948

Angels Die Hard, 1970 (Corman 2)

Angels' Door, 1971 (Brakhage 2)

Angels Hard as They Come, 1971 (Corman 2, Demme 2)

Angels in the Outfield, 1951 (Brown 2, Crosby 3, Leigh 3)

Angels of Darkness. *See* Donne proibite, 1953

Angels of Mercy, 1942 (Crosby 3)

Angels One Five, 1952 (Hawkins 3, Challis 4, Francis 4)

Angels over Broadway, 1940 (Hayworth 3, Cohn 4, Garmes 4, Hecht 4)

Angels Wash Their Faces, 1939 (Reagan 3, Sheridan 3, Buckner 4, Deutsch 4)

Angels with Dirty Faces, 1938 (Curtiz 2, Bogart 3, Cagney 3, Sheridan 3, Friedhofer 4, Orry-Kelly 4, Polito 4, Steiner 4)

Angélus, 1897 (Guy 2, Gaumont 4)

Angelus, 1922 (Astor 3)

Anger in His Eyes. *See* Con la rabbia agli occhi, 1976

Angkor. *See* Grande Cité, 1954

Anglais tel que Max le parle, 1914 (Linder 3)

Anglers, 1914 (Sennett 2)

Anglia, 1970 (Schroeter 2)

Angoissante Aventure, 1919 (Protazanov 2, Mozhukin 3)

Angoisse, 1913 (Feuillade 2, Gaumont 4)

Angoisse au foyer, 1915 (Feuillade 2)

Angokugai no kaoyaku, 1959 (Mifune 3)

Angola, 1984 (Branco 4)

Angora Love, 1929 (Laurel and Hardy 3, Roach 4)

Angriff der Gegenwart auf die Ubrige Zeit, 1985 (Kluge 2, Mueller-Stahl 3)

Angry Age. *See* Diga sul Pacifico, 1958

Angry Barbara. *See* Bařbora rádí, 1935

Angry Harvest. *See* Bittere Ernte, 1986

Angry Hills, 1959 (Aldrich 2, Baker 3, Mitchum 3, Adam 4)

Angry Man. *See* Homme en colère, 1979

Angry Red Planet, 1960 (Cortez 4)

Angry Sea. *See* Chino hate ni ikiru mono, 1960

Angry Silence, 1960 (Attenborough 3, Reed 3, Arnold 4, Green 4)

Angst, 1928 (Fröhlich 3)

Angst, 1954 (Bergman 3, Amidei 4)

Angst des Tormanns beim Elfmeter, 1971 (Wenders 2, Vogler 3, Müller 4)

Angst essen Seele auf, 1973 (Fassbinder 2)

Angulimaal, 1960 (Biswas 4)

Anhonee, 1952 (Kapoor 2, Nargis 3, Abbas 4)

Ani imoto, 1953 (Kyo 3, Mori 3)

Ani no hanayome, 1941 (Yamada 3)

Ani Ohev Otach Rosa, 1971 (Golan and Globus 4)

Ani to sono imoto, 1956 (Tsukasa 3)

Anichti epistoli, 1968 (Lassally 4)

Anicka, Come Back!. *See* Aničko, vrať se!, 1926

Aničko, vrať se!, 1926 (Ondra 3, Heller 4)

Aniki-Bóbó, 1942 (Oliveira 2)

Anillo de compromiso, 1951 (Alcoriza 4)

Anima allegra, 1918 (Bertini 3)

Anima del demi-monde, 1913 (Bertini 3)

Anima nera, 1962 (Rossellini 2, Gassman 3)

Anima persa, 1976 (Deneuve 3, Gassman 3, Delli Colli 4, Lai 4)

Anima redenta, 1917 (Bertini 3)

Anima selvaggia, 1920 (Bertini 3)

Animal, 1913 (Dwan 2, Reid 3)

Animal, 1977 (Belmondo 3, Welch 3, Audiard 4)

Animal Crackers, 1930 (Dumont 3, Marx Brothers 3, Folsey 4, Green 4, Ryskind 4)

Animal Farm, 1954 (De Rochemont 4, Halas and Batchelor 4)

Animal Kingdom, 1932 (Cukor 2, Howard 3, Loy 3, Folsey 4, Glazer 4, Irene 4, Mandell 4, Selznick 4, Steiner 4)

Animal Vegetable Mineral, 1955 (Halas and Batchelor 4)

Animal Within, 1911 (Dwan 2)

Animal World, 1955 (Harryhausen 4)

Animals, 1980 (Halas and Batchelor 4)

Animals and the Brigands. *See* Zvířátka a Petrovští, 1946

Animals Film, 1981 (Christie 3)

Animals of Eden and After, 1970 (Brakhage 2)

Animas Trujano, 1961 (Mifune 3)

Animas Trujano, el hombre importante, 1961 (Figueroa 4)

Animated Coins, 1914 (Phalke 2)

Animated Luncheon, 1900 (Porter 2)

Animated Matches. *See* Allumettes animées, 1908

Animated Poster, 1903 (Porter 2)

Animated Self-Portraits, 1989 (Švankmajer 4)

Animaux, 1963 (Jarre 4)

Anita Garibaldi. *See* Camicie rosse, 1951

Anita in Paradise. *See* Anita v Ráji, 1934

Anita v Ráji, 1934 (Heller 4)

Anjangarh, 1948 (Roy 2)

Anjo-ke no butokai, 1947 (Shindo 2, Yoshimura 2, Hara 3, Mori 3)

Anjou, 1977 (Leenhardt 2)

Anjuta, the Dancer. *See* Balettprimadonnan, 1916

Anju to Zushio-maru, 1961 (Yamada 3, Yamamura 3)

Ankoku-gai, 1956 (Mifune 3)

Ankoku-gai no taiketsu, 1960 (Mifune 3, Tsukasa 3)

Ankur, 1974 (Azmi 3, Nihalani 4)

An-Magritt, 1968 (Ullmann 3)

Ann Carver's Profession, 1933 (Wray 3, Riskin 4)

Ann Vickers, 1933 (Dunne 3, Huston 3, Berman 4, Cooper 4, Murfin 4, Plunkett 4, Polglase 4, Steiner 4)

Anna, 1952 (Lattuada 2, Risi 2, Gassman 3, Loren 3, Mangano 3, De Laurentiis 4, Ponti 4, Rota 4)

Anna, 1965 (Karina 3)

Anna, 1970 (Donner 2, Andersson 3)

Anna and the King of Siam, 1946 (Cromwell 2, Cobb 3, Darnell 3, Dunne 3, Harrison 3, Day 4, Herrmann 4, Jennings 4, Miller 4, Wheeler 4)

Anna Ascends, 1922 (Fleming 2)

Anna Boleyn, 1920 (Lubitsch 2, Jannings 3, Porten 3, Messter 4, Zukor 4)

Anna Christie, 1923 (Sweet 3, Ince 4)

Anna Christie, 1930 (Brown 2, Feyder 2, Florey 2, Dressler 3, Garbo 3, Adrian 4, Daniels 4, Day 4, Gibbons 4, Marion 4, Mayer 4, Shearer 4, Thalberg 4)

Anna di Brooklyn, 1958 (De Sica 2, Lollobrigida 3, Rotunno 4)

Anna Karenina. *See* Love, 1927 (Gibbons 4)

Anna Karenina, 1935 (Brown 2, Von Stroheim 2, Garbo 3, March 3, O'Sullivan 3, Rathbone 3, Adrian 4, Behrman 4, Daniels 4, Gibbons 4, Levien 4, Mayer 4, Selznick 4, Stothart 4)

Anna Karenina, 1947 (Duvivier 2, Cervi 3, Leigh 3, Richardson 3, Alekan 4, Andrejew 4, Beaton 4, Korda 4)

Anna la bonne, 1959 (Jutra 2)

Anna la bonne, 1963 (Cocteau 2)

Anna Lucasta, 1949 (Crawford 3, Goddard 3, Homolka 3, Cahn 4, Polito 4)

Anna Lucasta, 1958 (Ballard 4, Bernstein 4)

Anna of Brooklyn. See Anna di Brooklyn, 1958

Anna the Adventurer, 1920 (Colman 3)

Anna the Adventuress, 1920 (Hepworth 2)

Annabel Takes a Tour, 1939 (Ball 3, Metty 4)

Annabelle Lee, 1972 (O'Brien 3)

Annabelle's Affairs, 1931 (Beavers 3, MacDonald 3, McLaglen 3, Clarke 4)

Annabel's Romance, 1916 (White 3)

Annapolis, 1928 (Bosworth 3, Miller 4)

Annapolis Farewell, 1935 (Beavers 3)

Annapolis Salute, 1937 (Carey 3, Metty 4)

Annapolis Story, 1955 (Siegel 2, Mirisch 4)

Anne Against the World, 1929 (Karloff 3)

Anne and Muriel. See Deux Anglaises et le continent, 1971

Anne Boleyn, 1920 (Kräly 4)

Anne of Green Gables, 1919 (Goodrich 4, Marion 4)

Anne of Green Gables, 1934 (MacGowan 4, Plunkett 4, Steiner 4)

Anne of the Golden Heart, 1914 (Daniels 3)

Anne of the Indies, 1951 (Tourner 2, Jourdan 3, Marshall 3, Dunne 4, LeMaire 4, Waxman 4, Wheeler 4)

Anne of the Thousand Days, 1969 (Bujold 3, Burton 3, Papas 3, Quayle 3, Taylor 3, Delerue 4, Wallis 4)

Anneau fatal, 1912 (Feuillade 2)

Anneaux d'or, 1956 (Cardinale 3)

Année dernière à Marienbad, 1961 (Seyrig 3, Colpi 4, Evein 4, Robbe-Grillet 4, Saulnier 4, Vierny 4)

Année prochaine si tout va bien, 1981 (Adjani 3)

Année sainte, 1975 (Darrieux 3, Gabin 3)

Année se meurt, 1951 (Fradetal 4)

Années lumières, 1981 (Tanner 2, Howard 3)

Annelie, 1941 (Krauss 3, Von Harbou 4)

Anne-Marie, 1936 (D'Eaubonne 4, Honegger 4, Ibert 4)

Anni difficili, 1948 (Amidei 4)

Anni facili, 1953 (Amidei 4, De Laurentiis 4, Gherardi 4, Ponti 4, Rota 4)

Anni rugenti, 1962 (Amidei 4)

Anni ruggenti, 1962 (Cervi 3)

Annibale, 1960 (Mature 3)

Annie, 1982 (Huston 2, Finney 3, Booth 4, Stark 4)

Annie Bell. See Mørke Punkt, 1911

Annie Get Your Gun, 1950 (Calhern 3, Hutton 3, Keel 3, Alton 4, Berlin 4, Deutsch 4, Edens 4, Freed 4, Gibbons 4, Mayer 4, Plunkett 4, Rose 4, Rosher 4)

Annie Hall, 1977 (Allen 2, Keaton 3, Weaver 3, Rosenblum 4, Willis 4)

Annie Laurie, 1916 (Hepworth 2)

Annie Laurie, 1927 (Bosworth 3, Gish 3, Gibbons 4)

Annie Moved Away, 1934 (Lantz 4)

Annie Oakley, 1935 (Stevens 2, Douglas 3, Stanwyck 3, Hunt 4, Plunkett 4, Polglase 4)

Anniversary, 1963 (Pidgeon 3)

Anniversary, 1968 (Davis 3, Carreras 4, Sangster 4)

Anniversary of the Revolution. See Godovshchina revoliutsiya, 1919

Anniversary Trouble, 1935 (Roach 4)

Anno Domini 1573. See Seljačka buna 1573, 1975

Anno uno, 1975 (Rossellini 2)

Annushka, 1959 (Barnet 2)

Año de libertad, 1960 (Alvarez 2)

Ano hashi no tamoto de, Part III: Ano hito was ima, 1963 (Yamamura 3)

Ano hata o ute, 1944 (Hayasaka 4, Tsuburaya 4)

Ano kumo no hate ni hoshi wa matataku, 1962 (Yamamura 3)

Ano nami no hate made, 1961 (Iwashita 3)

Año Siete, 1966 (Alvarez 2)

Ano uno, 1972 (Gómez 2)

Anohito wa ima, 1963 (Iwashita 3)

Anokha bandham, 1982 (Azmi 3)

Anokha Pyar, 1948 (Kumar 3, Biswas 4)

Anokhi Ada, 1948 (Mehboob 2)

Anonimo, 1932 (De Fuentes 2)

Anonyme, 1957 (Alexeieff and Parker 4)

Anonymes du ciel, 1951 (Kosma 4)

Anote konote, 1952 (Mori 3)

Another Air. See Carmen fra i rossi, 1939

Another Chance, 1914 (Reid 3)

Another Dawn, 1937 (Dieterle 2, Flynn 3, Francis 3, Brown 4, Friedhofer 4, Gaudio 4, Korngold 4, Orry-Kelly 4)

Another Face, 1935 (McDaniel 3, Plunkett 4)

Another Fine Mess, 1930 (Laurel and Hardy 3)

Another 48 HRS., 1990 (Hill 2, Murphy 3, Nolte 3)

Another Language, 1933 (Montgomery 3, Adrian 4, Mankiewicz 4, Stewart 4, Wanger 4)

Another Man, Another Chance. See Autre Homme, une autre chance, 1977

Another Man, Another Woman. See Autre Homme, une autre chance, 1977

Another Man's Poison, 1951 (Davis 3, Krasker 4)

Another Man's Shoes, 1922 (Laemmle 4)

Another Man's Wife, 1913 (Dwan 2)

Another Man's Wife, 1924 (Beery 3)

Another Part of the Forest, 1948 (Duryea 3, March 3, O'Brien 3, Boyle 4, Mohr 4)

Another Shore, 1948 (Crichton 2, Auric 4, Balcon 4, Slocombe 4)

Another Sky, 1955 (Lassally 4)

Another Thin Man, 1939 (Van Dyke 2, Loy 3, Powell 3, Daniels 4, Gibbons 4, Goodrich 4, Stromberg 4)

Another Time, Another Place, 1958 (Connery 3, Turner 3)

Another to Conquer, 1941 (Ulmer 2)

Another Wild Idea, 1934 (Roach 4)

Another Woman, 1988 (Allen 2, Farrow 3, Hackman 3, Rowlands 3, Houseman 4, Nykvist 4)

Another You, 1990 (Pryor 3, Wilder 3)

Ansatsu, 1964 (Shinoda 2, Iwashita 3, Okada 3, Takemitsu 4)

Ansichten eines Clowns, 1975 (Schygulla 3, Lassally 4)

Ansiedad, 1952 (Infante 3, Figueroa 4)

Ansikte mot ansikte, 1976 (Björnstrand 3, Josephson 3, Ullmann 3, De Laurentiis 4, Nykvist 4)

Ansiktet, 1958 (Andersson 3, Björnstrand 3, Jospehson 3, Thulin 3, Von Sydow 3, Fischer 4)

Answer, 1980 (Lee 2)

Answer to Violence. See Zamach, 1958

Ant and the Aardvark, 1968 (Freleng 4)

Ant Pasted, 1953 (Blanc 4, Freleng 4, Stalling 4)

Antagonists, 1982 (O'Toole 3)

Anton Špelec, ostrostřelec, 1932 (Heller 4)

Anton Spelec, Sharpshooter. See Anton Špelec, ostrostřelec, 1932

Anton the Terrible, 1916 (Rosher 4)

Antonieta, 1982 (Saura 2, Adjani 3)

Antonín Dvořák, 1990 (Jireš 2)

Antonio di Padova, 1949 (Fabrizi 3)

Antonio Gaudi, 1961 (Russell 2)

Antonio Gaudi, 1985 (Takemitsu 4)

Antonito, 1961 (Finch 3)

Antony and Cleopatra, 1972 (Heston 3, Rey 3)

Antarctica. See Nankyoku monogatari, 1983

Anthony Adverse, 1936 (LeRoy 2, De Havilland 3, March 3, Rains 3, Blanke 4, Gaudio 4, Grot 4, Korngold 4, Wallis 4, Warner 4)

Anthony and Cleopatra, 1908 (Costello 3)

Anthony of Padua. See Antonio di Padova, 1949

Anti-Cats, 1950 (Terry 4)

Antichrist. See anticristo, 1974

Anticipation of the Night, 1958 (Brakhage 2)

Anticristo, 1974 (Kennedy 3, Valli 3, Morricone 4)

Antigone, 1960 (Papas 3)

Antimiracolo, 1965 (Cristaldi 4)

Antinea. See Atlantide, 1960

Antípodas de la victoria, 1986 (Alvarez 2)

Antiquités de l'Asie occidentale, 1943 (Honegger 4)

Antoine et Antoinette, 1947 (Becker 2, Modot 3)

Antoinette Sabrier, 1926 (Dulac 2)

Ants in His Pants, 1939 (Finch 3, Rafferty 3)

Ants in the Pantry, 1936 (Three Stooges 3)

Ants in the Plants, 1940 (Fleischer 4)

Ants in Your Pantry, 1945 (Terry 4)

Anugraham, 1978 (Patil 3)

Anuraag, 1972 (Burman 4)

Anuradha, 1960 (Shankar 4)

Anuschka, 1942 (Käutner 2)

Anvil Chorus, 1922 (Roach 4)

Anwalt des Herzens, 1927 (Dagover 3)

Anxious Years. See Dark Journey, 1937

Any Bonds Today, 1942 (Clampett 4)

Any Friend of Nicholas Nickleby Is a Friend of Mine, 1982 (Rosenblum 4)

Any Little Girl That's a Nice Little Girl, 1931 (Fleischer 4)

Any Man's Death, 1990 (Borgnine 3)

Any Man's Wife. See Michael O'Halloran, 1937

Any Night, 1922 (Anderson 3)

Any Number Can Play, 1949 (Brooks 2, LeRoy 2, Astor 3, Gable 3, Freed 4, Mayer 4, Rosson 4)

Any Number Can Win. See Mélodie en soussol, 1962

Any Old Port, 1920 (Roach 4)

Any Old Port, 1932 (Laurel and Hardy 3)

Any Rags, 1932 (Fleischer 4)

Any Second Now, 1969 (Granger 3)

Any Wednesday, 1966 (Fonda 3, Robards 3, Duning 4, Epstein 4, Jeakins 4)

Any Which Way You Can, 1980 (Eastwood 3, Gordon 3)

Any Wife, 1922 (Brenon 2)

Any Woman, 1925 (King 2, Furthman 4, Haller 4)

Any Woman's Choice, 1914 (Bushman 3)

Anya és leánya, 1981 (Nowicki 3)

Anybody Here Seen Kelly, 1928 (Wyler 2)

Anybody's Blonde, 1931 (Walthall 3)

Anybody's Goat, 1932 (Arbuckle 3)

Anybody's Woman, 1930 (Arzner 2, Lukas 3, Akins 4, Lang 4, Zukor 4)

Anyone Can Kill Me. See Tous peuvent me tuer, 1957

Anyone Lived in a Pretty How town, 1964–66 (Lucas 2)

Anything Can Happen, 1952 (Ferrer 3, Head 4, Young 4)

Anything Goes, 1936 (Milestone 2, Carradine 3, Crosby 3, Dumont 3, Lupino 3, Wyman 3, Carmichael 4, Dreier 4, Glazer 4, Struss 4, Young 4)

Anything Goes, 1956 (Crosby 3, O'Connor 3, Cahn 4, Head 4)

Anything Once, 1917 (Chaney 3)

Anything Once, 1927 (Normand 3)

Anzio. See Sbarco di Anzio, 1968

Anzukko, 1958 (Naruse 2, Kagawa 3, Yamamura 3)

Aoba-jo no oni, 1962 (Hasegawa 3)

Aogashima no kodomotachi: Onnakyoshi no kiroku, 1955 (Kagawa 3)

Aoi me, 1956 (Tsukasa 3, Muraki 4)

Aoi sanmyaku, 1949 (Hara 3)

Aoi sanmyaku: enpen, 1957 (Tsukasa 3)

Aoi yaju, 1960 (Tsukasa 3)

Aos, 1964 (Kuri 4)

Aozora roshi, 1936 (Yamada 3)

Apa, 1966 (Szabó 2)

Apache, 1928 (Johnson 3)

Apache, 1954 (Aldrich 2, Bronson 3, Lancaster 3, Laszlo 4, Raksin 4)

Apache Country, 1952 (Autry 3, Bushman 3)

Apache Drums, 1951 (Lewton 4, Salter 4)

Apache Rifles, 1964 (Murphy 3)

Apache Rose, 1947 (Rogers 3)

Apaches de Paris, 1905 (Pathé 4)

Apache's Gratitude, 1913 (Mix 3)

Apaches pas veinards, 1903 (Guy 2)

Apache Trail, 1942 (Reed 3, Schary 4)

Apache War Smoke, 1952 (Alton 4)

Apache Woman, 1955 (Corman 2, Crosby 4)

Apachentanz, 1906 (Porten 3, Messter 4)

Aparadhi Kaun, 1957 (Roy 2)

Aparajito, 1956 (Chandragupta 4, Datta 4, Mitra 4, Shankar 4)

Apariencias enganan, 1977 (Hermosillo 2)

Apartment, 1960 (Wilder 2, Lemmon 3, MacLaine 3, MacMurray 3, Deutsch 4, Diamond 4, La Shelle 4, Mandell 4, Mirisch 4, Trauner 4)

Apartment for Peggy, 1948 (Holden 3, LeMaire 4, Raksin 4)

Ape, 1940 (Karloff 3, Siodmak 4)

Ape Man, 1943 (Lugosi 3, Brown 4, Katzman 4)

Ape Woman. See Donna scimmia, 1964

Apes of Wrath, 1959 (Blanc 4, Freleng 4)

Apfel ist ab, 1948 (Käutner 2)

A-Plumbing We Will Go, 1940 (Three Stooges 3)

Apna Haath Jaganath, 1960 (Burman 4)

Apna Paraya, 1942 (Biswas 4)

Apne paraye, 1980 (Azmi 3)

Apocalypse des animaux, 1973 (Vangelis 4)

Apocalypse Now, 1979 (Coppola 2, Brando 3, Duvall 3, Ford 3, Hopper 3, Sheen 3, Murch 4, Storaro 4, Tavoularis 4)

Apokalypse, 1918 (Reiniger 4)

Apostasy. See Hakai, 1948

Apostle of Vengeance, 1916 (Gilbert 3, Hart 3, August 3)

Appaloosa, 1966 (Fernández 2, Brando 3)

Apparatus, 1989 (Cohen 2)

Apparatus Sum, 1972 (Frampton 2)

Appare binanshi, 1928 (Tanaka 3)

Appare Isshin Tasuke, 1945 (Kurosawa 2)

Apparences, 1964 (Delerue 4)

Apparition. See Revenant, 1903

Apparitions fugitives, 1904 (Méliès 2)

Apparizione, 1943 (Fellini 2, Valli 3)

Appassionata, 1944 (Björnstrand 3)

Appassionata. See Taková láska, 1959

Appassionata, 1989 (Morricone 4)

Appât. See Köder, 1975

Appearances, 1921 (Hitchcock 2, Crisp 3)

Appel du sang, 1920 (Novello 3)

Appelez-moi Mathilde, 1968 (Blier 3)

Appelkriget, 1971 (Von Sydow 3)

Applause, 1929 (Mamoulian 2, Folsey 4, Fort 4, Ruttenberg 4, Wanger 4)

Apple, 1961 (Dunning 4)

Apple, 1963 (Dinov 4)

Apple, 1980 (Golan and Globus 4)

Apple Game, 1977 (Menzel 2)

Apple War. See Appelkriget, 1971

Apples and Oranges, 1962 (Bass 4)

Apples to You!, 1934 (Roach 4)

Appointment, 1969 (Lumet 2, Aimée 3, Sharif 3, Barry 4, Gherardi 4)

Appointment for Love, 1941 (Boyer 3, Sullavan 3)

Appointment in Berlin, 1943 (Sanders 3, Planer 4)

Appointment in Honduras, 1953 (Tourner 2, Ford 3, Sheridan 3, Biroc 4)

Appointment in London, 1952 (Bogarde 3)

Appointment with a Shadow. See Midnight Story, 1957

Appointment with Crime, 1946 (Lom 3)

Appointment with Danger, 1951 (Ladd 3, Dreier 4, Seitz 4, Young 4)

Appointment with Death, 1988 (Bacall 3, Gielgud 3, Ustinov 3, Donaggio 4, Golan and Globus 4)

Appointment with Venus, 1951 (More 3, Niven 3, Box 4, Rank 4)

Apprenez à soulever une charge, 1949 (Decaë 4)

Apprenti, 1907 (Gaumont 4)

Apprenticeship of Duddy Kravitz, 1974 (Dreyfuss 3, Elliott 3)

Apprentice to Murder, 1988 (Sutherland 3)

Apprentis, 1964 (Tanner 2)

Apprentissages de Boireau, 1907 (Pathé 4)

Apprentis sorciers, 1977 (Hopper 3)

Apprezzato professionista di sicuro avvenire, 1972 (De Santis 2)

Approach to Science, 1947 (Alwyn 4)

Appuntamento col disonore, 1970 (Kinski 3, Sanders 3)

Appuntamento per le spie, 1965 (Andrews 3)

Appunti per un film indiano, 1969 (Pasolini 2)

Appunti su un fatto di cronaca, 1951 (Ferreri 2, Visconti 2)

Après après-demain, 1990 (Presle 3)

Après l'amour, 1947 (Tourneur 2)

Après le bal, 1897 (Méliès 2)

Après le vent des sables, 1974 (Lassally 4)

Après l'orage, 1942 (Berry 3)

April, April, 1935 (Sirk 2)

April Folly, 1920 (Davies 3)

April Fool, 1924 (Roach 4)

April Fools, 1969 (Boyer 3, Deneuve 3, Loy 3, Hamlisch 4, Sylbert 4)

April in Paris, 1952 (Day 3, Prinz 4)

April in Portugal, 1954 (Howard 3)

April Love, 1957 (LeMaire 4, Newman 4)

April Showers, 1923 (Moore 3, Schulberg 4)

April Showers, 1926 (Jolson 3)

April Showers, 1948 (Prinz 4)

April to Paris, 1952 (Cahn 4)

Apur Sansar, 1959 (Chatterjee 3, Chandragupta 4, Datta 4, Mitra 4, Shankar 4)

Aqua Duck, 1963 (Blanc 4, McKimson 4)

Aquarians, 1970 (Ferrer 3, Schifrin 4)

Aquarien, 1974 (Brakhage 2)

Aquarium, 1895 (Lumière 2)

Aquella casa en las afueras, 1980 (Maura 3, Valli 3)

Aquí está Heraclio Bernal, 1957 (Figueroa 4)

Aquila Nera, 1946 (Brazzi 3, Cervi 3, Lollobrigida 3)

Aquila Nera, 1987 (Monicelli 2)

Är aldrig för sent, 1956 (Björnstrand 3)

Ara nonkida ne, 1926 (Tanaka 3)

Arab, 1915 (Buckland 4)

Arab, 1924 (Novarro 3, Mayer 4, Seitz 4)

Arab, 1988 (De Mille 2)

Arabella, 1916 (Negri 3)

Arabella, 1924 (Marsh 3, Metzner 4)

Arabella, 1967 (Giannini 3, Marsh 3, Rutherford 3, Terry-Thomas 3, Morricone 4)

Arabella, der Roman eines Pferdes, 1924 (Rasp 3)

Arabeski na temu Pirosmani, 1986 (Paradzhanov 2)

Arabesque, 1966 (Donen 2, Loren 3, Peck 3, Challis 4, Mancini 4)

Arabia, 1922 (Fox 4)

Arabian Adventure, 1979 (Cushing 3, Lee 3, Rooney 3)

Arabian Bazaar. See World Window, 1977

Arabian Jewish Dance, 1903 (Porter 2)

Arabian Knight, 1920 (Hayakawa 3)

Arabian Love, 1922 (Gilbert 3, August 4, Fox 4, Furthman 4)

Arabian Nights, 1942 (Three Stooges 3, Krasner 4, Wanger 4)

Arabian Tights, 1933 (Roach 4)

Arabian Tragedy, 1912 (Olcott 2)

Arabics, 1982 (Brakhage 2)

Arabie interdite, 1937 (Clement 2)

Arab's Bride, 1912 (Cruze 2)

Aradhana, 1969 (Burman 4)

Araignées rouges, 1955 (Rabier 4)

Araignée verte, 1941 (Volkov 2)

Arakawa no Sakichi, 1936 (Hasegawa 3)

Araki Mataemon, 1931 (Yamada 3)

Araki Mataemon, 1955 (Yamada 3)

Arakure, 1957 (Mori 3)

Arakure daimyo, 1960 (Kagawa 3)

Aranyak, 1963 (Ghatak 2)

Aranyer Din Ratri, 1970 (Chatterjee 3, Chandragupta 4, Datta 4)
Arashi, 1956 (Tanaka 3)
Arashi nisakuhana, 1940 (Yamada 3)
Arashi no maki, 1956 (Yamamura 3)
Arashi no naka no haha, 1952 (Kagawa 3)
Arashi no naka no otoko, 1957 (Kagawa 3, Mifune 3)
Arbeitstag, 1965 (Zavattini 4)
Arbejdet kalder, 1941 (Henning-Jensen 2)
Arboles de Buenos-Aires, 1957 (Torre Nilsson 2)
Arbor Day, 1935 (Krasner 4, Roach 4)
Arbre de Noel, 1969 (Holden 3, Auric 4, Alekan 4)
Arbres aux champignons, 1951 (Markopoulos 2)
Arcadian Maid, 1910 (Griffith 2, Sennett 2, Pickford 3, Bitzer 4)
Arcadians, 1927 (Saville 2)
Arcagelo, 1969 (Gassman 3)
Arch of Triumph, 1948 (Aldrich 2, Milestone 2, Bergman 3, Boyer 3, Calhern 3, Laughton 3, Alekan 4, Head 4, Menzies 4, Metty 4)
Arch of Triumph, 1985 (Hopkins 3, Pleasence 3)
Archanděl Gabriel a paní Husa, 1964 (Trnka 4)
Archangel Gabriel and Mistress Goose. See Archanděl Gabriel a paní Husa, 1964
Arche, 1919 (Freund 4)
Arche de Noë, 1946 (Brasseur 3, Kosma 4, Prévert 4)
Arche de Noé, 1967 (Grimault 4)
Archimède, le clochard, 1959 (Blier 3, Gabin 3, Audiard 4)
Archipel des amours, 1983 (Presle 3)
Architects of England, 1941 (Alwyn 4)
Architecture, art de l'espace, 1961 (Barrault 3)
Architecture de lumière, 1953 (Colpi 4)
Architecture et chauffage d'aujourd'hui, 1960 (Delerue 4)
Architecture of Entertainment, 1960 (Russell 2)
Architecture of Frank Lloyd Wright, 1983 (Baxter 3)
Arcidiavolo, 1966 (Gassman 3, Rooney 3)
Arctic Rivals, 1954 (Terry 4)
Ard el Salam, 1955 (Sharif 3)
Ardha Satya, 1983 (Patil 3, Nihalani 4)
Arditi civili, 1940 (Amidei 4)
Are Blond Men Bashful?, 1924 (Roach 4)
Are Brunettes Safe?, 1927 (Roach 4)
Are Crooks Dishonest?, 1918 (Daniels 3, Lloyd 3, Roach 4)
Are ga minato no tomoshibi da, 1961 (Yamamura 3)
Are Husbands Human?, 1925 (Roach 4)
Are Husbands Necessary?, 1942 (Milland 3, Head 4, Lang 4)
Are Parents People?, 1925 (Menjou 3, Glennon 4)
Are Parents Pickles?, 1925 (Roach 4)
Are These Our Children?. See Age of Consent, 1932
Are Waitresses Safe, 1917 (Sennett 2)
Are Women to Blame?, 1928 (Negri 3)
Are You a Failure?, 1923 (Lang 4, Schulberg 4)
Are You a Mason, 1915 (Barrymore 3)
Are You Legally Married?, 1919 (Polito 4)
Are You Listening?, 1932 (Rosson 4)

Are You with It?, 1948 (O'Connor 3)
Arena, 1953 (Van Cleef 3)
Arena, 1973 (Corman 2)
Arène de la vengeance, 1941 (Volkov 2)
Arènes joyeuses, 1935 (Stradling 4)
Aren't We All, 1932 (Oberon 3)
Argent, 1928 (Artaud 3, Berry 3, Meerson 4)
Argent, 1929 (L'Herbier 2)
Argent, 1936 (Matras 4)
Argent, 1983 (Bresson 2)
Argent de poche, 1976 (Truffaut 2)
Argent des autres, 1978 (Deneuve 3, Trintignant 3)
Argentine Love, 1924 (Dwan 2, Daniels 3, Hunt 4)
Argentine Nights, 1940 (Cahn 4)
Argila, 1968 (Schroeter 2)
Argine, 1937 (Cervi 3)
Aria, 1987 (Altman 2, Godard 2, Jarman 2, Roeg 2, Russell 2, Hurt 3, Henry 4)
Ariane, 1931 (Bergner 3, Mayer 4)
Arie prérie, 1949 (Brdečka 4, Trnka 4)
Arise, My Love, 1940 (Leisen 2, Wilder 2, Colbert 3, Milland 3, Brackett 4, Dreier 4, Glazer 4, Head 4, Irene 4)
Aristo, 1934 (D'Eaubonne 4)
Aristo-Cat, 1943 (Blanc 4, Jones 4, Stalling 4)
Aristocats, 1970 (Chevalier 3)
Aristocrates, 1955 (Fresnay 3)
Aristocrat's Stairs. See Kizoku no kaidan, 1959
Aristotle. See Pomsta, 1968
Arivano i nostri, 1951 (Age and Scarpelli 4)
Arizona, 1919 (Fairbanks 3)
Arizona. See Men Are Like That, 1930
Arizona, 1940 (Arthur 3, Holden 3, Cohn 4, Walker 4, Young 4)
Arizona Bound, 1927 (Cooper 3)
Arizona Bushwackers, 1968 (De Carlo 3, Cagney 3, Keel 3)
Arizona Cyclone, 1928 (Laemmle 4)
Arizona Cyclone, 1941 (Lewis 2, Salter 4)
Arizona Escapade, 1912 (Anderson 3)
Arizona Express, 1924 (Fox 4)
Arizona Kid, 1930 (Lombard 3, Fox 4)
Arizona Kid, 1939 (Rogers 3)
Arizona Mahoney, 1937 (Crabbe 3, Head 4)
Arizona Mission. See Gun the Man Down, 1956
Arizona Raiders, 1936 (Crabbe 3)
Arizona Raiders, 1965 (Crabbe 3, Murphy 3)
Arizona Ranger, 1948 (Hunt 4)
Arizona Romeo, 1925 (Fox 4)
Arizona Slim, 1975 (De Carlo 3)
Arizona to Broadway, 1933 (Bennett 3)
Arizona Trail, 1943 (Salter 4)
Arizona Wildcat, 1927 (Mix 3, Fox 4)
Arizona Wooing, 1915 (Mix 3)
Arizonian, 1935 (Vidor 2, Calhern 3, Nichols 4, Plunkett 4)
Arjun Pandit, 1976 (Burman 4)
Arjun Sardar, 1958 (Ghatak 2)
Arkansas Judge, 1941 (Rogers 3, Lardner 4)
Arkansas Traveler, 1938 (Dreier 4, Head 4)
Arlésienne, 1922 (Duvivier 2, Burel 4)
Arlésienne, 1930 (Vanel 3)
Arlésienne, 1942 (Jourdan 3, Raimu 3, Archard 4)
Arlette et ses papas, 1933 (Berry 3)
Arm Drenthe, 1929 (Ivens 2)
Arm of Vengeance, 1914 (Anderson 3)
Arma, 1978 (Cardinale 3)

Arma dei vigliacchi, 1913 (Bertini 3)
Armageddon, 1977 (Delon 3)
Arman, 1953 (Anand 3, Burman 4)
Armand and Michaela Denis, 1955 (Balcon 4)
Armata assura, 1932 (Cervi 3)
Armata Brancaleone, 1966 (Monicelli 2, Gassman 3, Volonté 3, Age and Scarpelli 4, Gherardi 4)
Arme à gauche, 1965 (Sautet 2)
Arme Eva. See Frau Eva, 1915
Arme Jenny, 1912 (Gad 2, Nielsen 3)
Arme Kleine Sif, 1927 (Wegener 3)
Arme Marie, 1915 (Lubitsch 2, Wiene 2)
Arme Sünderin, 1923 (Kortner 3)
Arme Violetta, 1920 (Negri 3, Kräly 4, Wagner 4)
Armed and Dangerous, 1987 (Carpenter 2)
Armed Intervention, 1913 (Eason 4)
Armed Police Force. See Busou keikantai, 1948
Armed Response, 1986 (Van Cleef 3)
Armée d'Agenor, 1909 (Cohl 4)
Armée des ombres, 1969 (Melville 2, Cassel 3, Reggiani 3, Signoret 3)
Armée populaire arme le peuple, 1969 (Ivens 2)
Armes kleines Mädchen, 1924 (Kortner 3)
Armistice, 1929 (Balcon 4)
Armoire, 1969 (Braunberger 4)
Armoire volante, 1948 (Fernandel 3)
Armored Attack. See North Star, 1943
Armored Car, 1937 (Cortez 4)
Armored Command, 1961 (Keel 3, Reynolds 3, Haller 4, Haskin 4)
Armor of God. See Lunghing fudai, 1987
Armor of God II. See Lunghing fudai tsuktsap, 1990
Armour chante, 1930 (Braunberger 4)
Arms and the Gringo, 1914 (Reid 3)
Arms and the Man, 1932 (Launder and Gilliat 2)
Arms and the Man. See Helden, 1959
Arms and the Woman, 1916 (Grot 4, Miller 4)
Arms and the Woman. See Mr. Winkle Goes to War, 1944
Armstrong's Wife, 1915 (Cruze 2)
Army. See Rikugun, 1944
Army, 1991 (Reed 3)
Army Girl, 1938 (Eason 4, Young 4)
Army Surgeon, 1912 (Sullivan 4)
Army Surgeon, 1942 (Metty 4)
Arnelo Affair, 1947 (Arden 3, Irene 4)
Arnold, 1974 (Lanchester 3, McDowall 3, Duning 4)
Aroma of the South Seas, 1931 (Balcon 4)
Around Is Around, 1949 (McLaren 4)
Around Sennichimae. See Sennichimae fukin, 1945
Around the Corner, 1930 (Glennon 4, Walker 4)
Around the World, 1931 (Terry 4)
Around the World, 1943 (Dwan 2, Metty 4)
Around the World, 1967 (Kapoor 2)
Around the World in Eighteen Days, 1923 (Eason 4)
Around the World in Eighty Days. See Reise um die Erde in 80 Tagen, 1919
Around the World in Eighty Days, 1956 (Keaton 2, Boyer 3, Brown 3, Cantinflas 3, Carradine 3, Coburn 3, Colman 3, Dietrich 3, Fernandel 3, Gielgud 3, Howard 3, Lorre 3, MacLaine 3,

McLaglen 3, Mills 3, Newton 3, Niven 3, Raft 3, Sinatra 3, Adam 4, Bass 4, Coward 4, Menzies 4, Young 4)

Around the World in 80 Days, 1989 (Remick 3, Ustinov 3, Wagner 3)

Around the World in Eighty Minutes with Douglas Fairbanks, 1931 (Fairbanks 3, Newman 4, Sherwood 4)

Around the World with Orson Welles, 1956 (Constantine 3)

Arouse and Beware. *See* Man from Dakota, 1940

Arousers. *See* Sweet Kill, 1972

Arrah-na-Pogue, 1911 (Olcott 2)

Arrangement, 1969 (Kazan 2, Douglas 3, Dunaway 3, Kerr 3, Surtees 4, Van Runkle 4, Westmore Family 4)

Arrest Bulldog Drummond, 1939 (Dreier 4, Head 4)

Arrêtez les tambours, 1961 (Blier 3, Delerue 4)

Arriba el campesino, 1960 (Zavattini 4)

Arriba las mujeres, 1943 (Infante 3)

'Arriet's Baby, 1913 (Talmadge 3)

Arriva Dorellik, 1967 (Terry-Thomas 3)

Arrival from the Dark. *See* Příchozí z temnot, 1921

Arrivano i dollari!, 1957 (Sordi 3)

Arrivano i miei, 1983 (Cristaldi 4)

Arrivano i Titani, 1962 (Armendáriz 3, Cristaldi 4)

Arrivederci, Baby, 1966 (Curtis 3)

Arrivederci Papà, 1948 (Rota 4)

Arrivée d'un bateau à vapeur, 1895 (Lumière 2)

Arrivée d'un train à La Ciotat, 1895 (Lumière 2)

Arrivée d'un train de Vincennes, 1896 (Pathé 4)

Arrivée d'un train en gare de La Ciotat, 1936 (Lumière 2)

Arrivée du Président de la République au pesage, 1949 (Gaumont 4)

Arriving Tuesday, 1986 (Grant 3)

Arrivista, 1913 (Bertini 3)

Arrivistes. *See* Trübe Wasser, 1958

Arrivistes, 1959 (Barsacq 4)

Arroseur arrosé, 1895 (Lumière 2)

Arroseur arrosé, 1897 (Guy 2)

Arroseur arrosé, 1907 (Gaumont 4)

Arrow in the Dust, 1954 (Hayden 3, Van Cleef 3)

Arrowhead, 1953 (Heston 3, Palance 3, Head 4)

Arrowsmith, 1931 (Ford 2, Bondi 3, Colman 3, Loy 3, Day 4, Goldwyn 4, Howard 4, Newman 4)

Arruza, 1971 (Boetticher 2, Quinn 3, Ballard 4)

Ars, 1959 (Demy 2)

Ars Gratia Artis, 1970 (Vukotić 4)

Arsenal Stadium Mystery, 1939 (Dickinson 2, Rank 4)

Arsene Lupin, 1932 (Barrymore 3, Barrymore 3, Adrian 4, Coffee 4, Wilson 4)

Arsène Lupin contre Arsène Lupin, 1962 (Cassel 3)

Arsène Lupin, détective, 1936 (Berry 3, Fradetal 4)

Arsène Lupin et la toison d'or, 1959 (Valli 3)

Arsene Lupin Returns, 1938 (Douglas 3, Folsey 4, Gibbons 4, Waxman 4)

Arsenic and Old Lace, 1944 (Capra 2,

Grant 3, Horton 3, Lorre 3, Massey 3, Burks 4, Epstein 4, Friedhofer 4, Haskin 4, Mandell 4, Orry-Kelly 4, Polito 4, Steiner 4)

Art de la turlutte, 1969 (Braunberger 4)

Art d'etre Papa, 1956 (Fernandel 3)

Art Director, 1948 (Wheeler 4)

Art for Art's Sake, 1980 (Halas and Batchelor 4)

Art Haut-Rhénan, 1951 (Braunberger 4)

Art Lovers, 1980 (Halas and Batchelor 4)

Art of Crime, 1975 (Clayburgh 3, Ferrer 3)

Art of Deceit, 1981 (Vadim 2)

Art of Hollywood, 1944 (Day 4)

Art of Love. *See* Prinzessin Olala, 1928

Art of Love, 1965 (Jewison 2, Dickinson 3, Garner 4, Hunter 4, Metty 4)

Art of the English Craftsman, 1933 (Flaherty 2)

Art of Vision, 1965 (Brakhage 2)

Art pour l'art, 1965 (Godfrey 4)

Art Scene USA, 1966 (Emshwiller 2)

Art Versus Music, 1911 (Lawrence 3)

Artamonov Affair. *See* Delo Artamonovykh, 1941

Arte del tobaco, 1974 (Guitérrez Alea 2)

Arte di arrangiarsi, 1955 (Sordi 3)

Arte e realtà, 1950 (Delli Colli 4)

Arte in Sicilia, 1948 (Fusco 4)

Arteres de France, 1939 (Epstein 2)

Artful Kate, 1911 (Pickford 3, Gaudio 4, Ince 4)

Arth, 1983 (Azmi 3, Patil 3)

Arthur, 1969 (Terry-Thomas 3)

Arthur, 1981 (Gielgud 3, Minnelli 3, Moore 3)

Arthur Arthur, 1969 (Pleasence 3, Winters 3)

Arthur Honegger, 1955 (Demy 2)

Arthur Miller on Home Ground, 1979 (Cobb 3, Dunaway 3, Lancaster 3, Robinson 3, Scott 3)

Arthur Penn, 1970 (Bancroft 3, Hoffman 3)

Arthur Penn Films "Little Big Man", 1970 (Hoffman 3)

Arthur 2: On the Rocks, 1988 (Gielgud 3, Minnelli 3, Moore 3)

Arthur's Hallowed Ground, 1983 (Puttnam 4, Young 4)

Arthur's Island. *See* Isola di Arturo, 1962

Article Fifty-Five, 1952 (Ferrer 3)

Article 99, 1990 (Wallach 3)

Article 330, 1934 (Pagnol 2)

Artifices, 1963 (Braunberger 4)

Artificial Light, 1969 (Frampton 2)

Artisan, 1989 (Brandauer 3)

Artist, 1918 (Laurel and Hardy 3)

Artist and Models, 1955 (Edouart 4, Head 4)

Artist and the Brute, 1913 (Bosworth 3)

Artistic Atmosphere, 1916 (Laurel and Hardy 3)

Artists and Models, 1915 (Laurel and Hardy 3)

Artists and Models, 1937 (Walsh 2, Lupino 3, Banton 4, Dreier 4, Head 4, Prinz 4, Young 4)

Artists and Models, 1955 (Lewis 2, Tashlin 2, MacLaine 3, Malone 3, Martin 3, Fulton 4, Wallis 4)

Artists and Models Abroad, 1938 (Leisen 2, Bennett 3, Dreier 4, Head 4, Prinz 4)

Artist's Dream, 1900 (Porter 2)

Artist's Dream, 1910 (Bray 4)

Artist's Great Madonna, 1913 (Ingram 2)

Arturo's Island. *See* Isola di Arturo, 1962

Aru eiga kantoku no shogai: Mizoguchi Kenji no kiroku, 1975 (Shindo 2, Tanaka 3)

Aru fujinkai no kokuhaku, 1950 (Yoda 4)

Aru kengo no shogai, 1959 (Mifune 3, Tsukasa 3)

Aru koroshiya, 1967 (Miyagawa 4)

Aru koroshiya no kagi, 1967 (Miyagawa 4)

Aru Onna, 1942 (Tanaka 3)

Aru Onna, 1954 (Kyo 3, Mori 3)

Aru Osaka no onna, 1962 (Yoda 4)

Aru rakujitsu, 1959 (Mori 3)

Aru sonan, 1961 (Kagawa 3)

Aru to sono no baai, 1956 (Tsukasa 3)

Aruba, Bonaire, Curazao. *See* A.B.C., 1958

Aruhi watashi wa, 1959 (Muraki 4)

Arupusu no wakadaisho, 1966 (Tanaka 3)

Aruyo no tonosama, 1946 (Hasegawa 3, Shindo 3, Takamine 3, Yamada 3)

Aryan, 1916 (Hart 3, Love 3, August 4, Sullivan 4)

Arzoo, 1950 (Kumar 3, Biswas 4)

Arzt aus Halberstadt, 1969 (Kluge 2)

As a Father Spareth His Son, 1913 (Bosworth 3)

As armas e o Povo, 1975 (De Almeida 4)

As a Wife. *See* Tsuma to shite haha to shite, 1961

As a Woman. *See* Tsuma to shite haha to shite, 1961

As Dark As the Night, 1959 (Lassally 4)

As des as, 1982 (Belmondo 3)

As Fate Ordained. *See* Enoch Arden, 1915

As Good As Married, 1937 (Pidgeon 3, Krasna 4, Raksin 4)

As Husbands Go, 1934 (Behrman 4, Friedhofer 4, Lasky 4, Levien 4, Mohr 4)

As in a Looking Glass, 1911 (Griffith 2, Bitzer 4)

As It Is in Life, 1910 (Griffith 2, Pickford 3, Bitzer 4)

As Long as They're Happy, 1955 (Buchanan 3, Dors 3, Rank 4)

As Long as We Live. *See* Inochi aru kagiri, 1947

As Man Made Her, 1917 (Marion 4)

As negro, 1944 (Figueroa 4)

As Old as the Hills, 1950 (Halas and Batchelor 4)

As Summer Dies, 1989 (Davis 3, Legrand 4)

As Summers Die. *See* As Summer Dies, 1989

As the Bells Rang Out, 1910 (Griffith 2, Bitzer 4)

As the Devil Commands, 1932 (August 4)

As the Earth Turns, 1934 (Haskin 4, Orry-Kelly 4)

As the Sea Rages. *See* Hellas, 1959

As the Sea Rages, 1960 (Robertson 3)

As Told by Princess Bess, 1912 (Bosworth 3)

As You Desire Me, 1932 (Von Stroheim 2, Douglas 3, Garbo 3, Adrian 4, Daniels 4, Mayer 4)

As You Like It, 1912 (Costello 3)

As You Like It, 1936 (Lean 2, Bergner 3, Olivier 3, Cardiff 4, Meerson 4, Rosson 4, Schenck 4, Walton 4)

As Young As We Are, 1958 (Bumstead 4)

As Young As You Are, 1958 (Head 4)

As Young As You Feel, 1951 (Monroe 3, Ritter 3, Chayefsky 4, LeMaire 4)

Asa no hamon, 1952 (Kagawa 3, Takamine 3)

Asahi wa kagayaku, 1929 (Mizoguchi 2)
Asakusa kurenai-dan, 1952 (Kyo 3)
Asakusa monogatari, 1953 (Mori 3)
Asakusa no hada, 1950 (Kyo 3)
Asakusa no yoru, 1954 (Kyo 3)
Asakusa yonin shimai, 1952 (Yamamura 3)
Asama no mozu, 1953 (Hasegawa 3)
Asamblea general, 1960 (Almendros 4)
Asani Sanket, 1973 (Datta 4)
Ascending Scale. See Aarohan, 1982
Ascenseur pour l'échafaud, 1958 (Moreau 3,
   Decaë 4)
Ascension du Mont-Blanc, 1900
   (Gaumont 4)
Aschenbrödel, 1914 (Gad 2, Nielsen 3)
Aschenputtel, 1922 (Reiniger 4)
Asemblea General, 1960 (Gutiérrez Alea 2)
Asesino se embarca, 1966 (Figueroa 4)
Asfar, 1950 (Anand 3, Burman 4)
Ash Can Fleet, 1939 (Zinnemann 2)
Ash Wednesday, 1973 (Fonda 3, Taylor 3,
   Head 4, Jarre 4)
Ashani Sanket, 1973 (Chatterjee 3)
Ashanti, 1979 (Caine 3, Harrison 3, Sharif 3,
   Ustinov 3)
Ashanti, 1982 (Azmi 3)
Ashes, 1922 (Anderson 3)
Ashes, 1930 (Balcon 4)
Ashes. See Popióły, 1965
Ashes and Diamonds. See **Popiół i diament,
1958**
Ashes and Embers, 1982 (Gerima 2)
Ashes of Desire, 1919 (Borzage 2)
Ashes of Hope, 1914 (Bushman 3)
Ashes of the Past, 1914 (Sweet 3)
Ashes of Three, 1913 (Dwan 2)
Ashes of Vengeance, 1923 (Beery 3,
   Talmadge 3, Gaudio 4, Schenck 4)
Ashi ni sawatta onna, 1952 (Yamamura 3)
Ashi ni sawatta onna, 1960 (Kyo 3)
Ashi o arrata otoko, 1949 (Hasegawa 3)
Ashibi, 1928 (Tsuburaya 4)
Ashik kerib, 1988 (Paradzhanov 2)
Ashita kuru hito, 1955 (Yamamura 3)
Ashizuri misaki, 1954 (Yoshimura 2)
Ashura hangan, 1951 (Hasegawa 3)
Asi era Pancho Villa, 1957 (Armendáriz 3)
Asi es mi tierra, 1937 (Cantinflas 3)
Asi se quiere en Jalisco, 1942 (De Fuentes 2)
Asino y el condor, 1981 (Herrera 4)
Ask a Policeman, 1939 (Launder and
   Gilliat 2, Hay 3)
Ask Any Girl, 1959 (Walters 2, MacLaine 3,
   Niven 3, Pasternak 4, Rose 4)
Ask Father, 1918 (Daniels 3, Lloyd 3,
   Roach 4)
Ask Grandma, 1925 (Roach 4)
Asleep at the Switch, 1923 (Sennett 2)
Asleep in the Feet, 1933 (Roach 4)
Asli Nagli, 1962 (Anand 3)
Aspern, 1982 (Valli 3, De Almeida 4,
   Branco 4)
Asphalt, 1929 (Fröhlich 3, Herlth 4,
   Pommer 4, Röhrig 4)
**Asphalt Jungle, 1950 (Huston 2,
   Calhern 3, Hayden 3, Jaffe 3,
   Monroe 3, Gibbons 4, Maddow 4,
   Mayer 4, Rosson 4, Rozsa 4,
   Shearer 4)**
Ass and the Stick, 1974 (Halas and
   Batchelor 4)
Assam Garden, 1985 (Kerr 3)
Assassin. See Venetian Bird, 1952
Assassin. See Ansatsu, 1964

Assassin a peur la nuit, 1942 (Delannoy 2,
   Berry 3, Auric 4)
Assassin connait la musique, 1963 (Schell 3)
Assassin est dans l'annuaire, 1961
   (Fernandel 3)
Assassin habite au 21, 1942 (Clouzot 2,
   Fresnay 3, Gélin 3, Andrejew 4)
Assassin musicien, 1975 (Karina 3)
Assassin n'est pas coupable, 1946 (Berry 3)
Assassin of the Tsar, 1991 (McDowell 3)
Assassinat de la rue du Temple, 1904
   (Gaumont 4)
Assassinat de Mac Kinley, 1901 (Pathé 4)
Assassinat de Trotsky, 1972 (Losey 2,
   Burton 3, Delon 3, Schneider 3)
Assassinat du Courrier de Lyon, 1904
   (Guy 2, Gaumont 4)
Assassinat du Duc de Guise, 1902 (Pathé 4)
Assassinat du Père Noël, 1941 (Baur 3,
   Blier 3, Spaak 4)
Assassination. See Ansatsu, 1964
Assassination. See Assassination at Sarajevo,
   1975
Assassination, 1987 (Bronson 3, Golan and
   Globus 4)
Assassination at Sarajevo, 1975 (Schell 3)
Assassination Bureau, 1969 (Dearden 2,
   Noiret 3, Reed 3, Mankowitz 4,
   Unsworth 4)
Assassination of Trotsky. See Assassinat de
   Trotsky, 1972
Assassinio made in Italy. See Segreto del
   vestito rosso, 1963
Assassino, 1961 (Mastroianni 3, Presle 3,
   Cristaldi 4, Guerra 4)
Assassins de l'ordre, 1971 (Carné 2)
Assassins et voleurs, 1957 (Guitry 2)
Assault, 1936 (Vanel 3)
Assault and Peppered, 1965 (Blanc 4,
   McKimson 4)
Assault Force. See Ffolkes, 1980
Assault on a Queen, 1966 (Sinatra 3,
   Daniels 4, Head 4)
Assault on Paradise. See Maniac, 1978
Assault on Precinct 13, 1977 (Carpenter 2)
Assault on the Wayne, 1970 (Cotten 3)
Assayer of Lone Gap, 1915 (Eason 4)
Assedio dell'Alcazar, 1940 (Stallich 4)
Assedio di Siracusa, 1960 (Brazzi 3, Cervi 3)
Assenza ingiustificata, 1939 (Valli 3)
Assiettes tournantes, 1895 (Lumière 2)
Assigned to Danger, 1948 (Boetticher 2)
Assignment, 1978 (Rey 3)
Assignment Children, 1954 (Kaye 3)
Assignment in Britanny, 1943 (Irene 4,
   Rosher 4, Veiller 4)
Assignment K, 1968 (Redgrave 3)
Assignment Munich, 1972 (Scheider 3)
Assignment Paris, 1952 (Andrews 3,
   Sanders 3, Dunning 4, Guffey 4)
Assignment Skybolt, 1966 (Lassally 4)
Assignment to Kill, 1967 (Gielgud 3, Lom 3)
Assignment to Kill, 1969 (Homolka 3)
Assignments. See Assignment to Kill, 1967
Assisi Underground, 1984 (Giannini 3,
   Mason 3, Papas 3, Schell 3, Rotunno 4)
Assistant Wives, 1927 (Laurel and Hardy 3,
   Roach 4)
Assisted Elopement, 1911 (Dwan 2)
Associate. See Associé, 1979
Association de malfaiteurs, 1986 (Lai 4)
Associé, 1979 (Carrière 4)
Assoluto naturale, 1969 (Harvey 3, Schell 3,
   Morricone 4)

Assommoir, 1910 (Baur 3, Pathé 4)
Assunta spina, 1915 (Bertini 3)
Assunta spina, 1947 (Magnani 3)
Astonished Heart, 1949 (Fisher 2,
   Coward 4)
Astonished Heart, 1950 (Johnson 3, Box 4,
   Rank 4)
Astragale, 1968 (Braunberger 4)
Astral Man, 1957 (Vanderbeek 2)
Astray from the Steerage. See Away from
   the Steerage, 1921
Astroduck, 1966 (Blanc 4, McKimson 4)
Astrologie ou Le Miroir de la vie, 1952
   (Grémillon 2)
Astromutts, 1963 (Vukotić 4)
Astronautes, 1960 (Marker 2)
Astronomer's Dream. See Lune à un mètre,
   1898
Astro-Zombies, 1968 (Carradine 3)
Asu aru kagiri, 1962 (Kagawa 3)
Asu e no seiso, 1959 (Takemitsu 4)
Asu no odoriko, 1939 (Yoshimura 2)
Asu no taiyo, 1959 (Oshima 2)
Asu o tsukuru hitobito, 1946 (Mori 3)
Asu wa docchi da, 1953 (Kagawa 3,
   Takamine 3)
Asunaro monogatari, 1955 (Hayasaka 4)
Aswa medher ghora, 1981 (Patil 3)
Asylum, 1972 (Cushing 3, Lom 3)
Asymvivastos, 1979 (Theodorakis 4)
At a Quarter to Two, 1911 (Pickford 3,
   Gaudio 4)
At Bay, 1915 (Miller 4)
At Breakneck Speed, 1900 (Bitzer 4)
At Coney Island, 1912 (Sennett 2)
At Cripple Creek, 1912 (Reid 3)
At Dawn, 1914 (Reid 3)
At Dawn We Die. See Tomorrow We Live,
   1942
At First Sight, 1917 (Rosher 4)
At First Sight, 1923 (Roach 4)
At First Sight. See Coup de foudre, 1983
At Gunpoint, 1955 (Brennan 3,
   MacMurray 3, Malone 3)
At hirsizi banus, 1967 (Güney 2)
At It Again, 1912 (Sennett 2, Normand 3)
At Land, 1944 (Deren 2)
At Long Last Love, 1975 (Bogdanovich 2,
   Reynolds 3, Kovacs 4)
At Midnight, 1913 (Meredyth 4)
At Midnight in the Tomb. See V polnotch na
   kladbische, 1914
At Play in the Fields of the Lord, 1990
   (Carrière 4)
At Scrogginses' Corner, 1912 (Bunny 3)
At Sea Ashore, 1935 (Roach 4)
At Sword's Point, 1952 (O'Hara 3, Wilde 3)
At the Altar, 1909 (Griffith 2, Bitzer 4)
At the Bottom of the Swimming Pool. See In
   fondo ala piscina, 1971
At the Break of Dawn, 1911 (Anderson 3)
At the Circus, 1939 (LeRoy 2, Arden 3,
   Dumont 3, Marx Brothers 3, Waxman 4)
At the Circus, 1944 (Terry 4)
At the Duke's Command, 1911 (Pickford 3,
   Gaudio 4)
At the Earth's Core, 1976 (Cushing 3)
At the Eleventh Hour. See Hvem var
   Forbryderen?, 1912
At the End of a Perfect Day, 1915
   (Swanson 3)
At the End of the Trail, 1912 (Bushman 3)
At the French Ball, 1908 (Bitzer 4)
At the Front, 1943 (Zanuck 4)

At the Grey House. *See* Zur Chronik von Grieshuus, 1925

At the Lariat's End, 1913 (Anderson 3)

At the Monkey House, 1906 (Bitzer 4)

At the Old Maid's Ball, 1913 (Beery 3)

At the Old Stage Door, 1919 (Daniels 3, Lloyd 3, Roach 4)

At the Phone, 1912 (Guy 2)

At the Photographer's. *See* Kod fotografa, 1959

At the Prison Gates. *See* Ved Faengslets Port, 1911

At the Ringside, 1921 (Roach 4)

At Twelve O'Clock, 1913 (Sennett 2)

At War with the Army, 1950 (Lewis 2, Martin 3, Jenkins 4)

At Whose Door?, 1952 (Lassally 4)

At Yale. *See* Hold 'em Yale, 1928

At Your Service, 1935 (Lantz 4)

At Your Service Madame, 1936 (Freleng 4)

At žije nebožtik, 1935 (Stallich 4)

At ziji duchove, 1976 (Brodský 3)

Atake-ke no hitobito, 1952 (Tanaka 3, Yamamura 3)

Atala, 1912 (Bosworth 3)

Atalante, 1934 (Vigo 2, Simon 3, Douy 4, Grimault 4, Jaubert 4, Kaufman 4)

¡Atame!, 1989 (Morricone 4)

Atanka, 1987 (Chatterjee 3)

Atarashiki tsuchi, 1937 (Hara 3, Hayakawa 3, Tsuburaya 4)

Atelier de Fernard Léger, 1954 (Borowczyk 2)

Ateliers de La Ciotat, 1895 (Lumière 2)

Aten, 1989 (Delerue 4, Lai 4)

Atencion prenatal, 1972 (Gómez 2)

Atentat u Sarajevu. *See* Assassination at Sarajevo, 1975

Athena, 1954 (Calhern 3, Reynolds 3, Pasternak 4, Plunkett 4, Rose 4)

Athens, 1982 (Angelopoulos 2)

Athlete, 1932 (Lantz 4)

Athlète incomplet, 1932 (Autant-Lara 2)

Athleten, 1925 (Nielsen 3, Junge 4)

Athletes, 1928 (Rooney 3)

Athletic Ambitions, 1915 (Mix 3)

Athletic Girl and Burglar, 1905 (Bitzer 4)

Atilla. *See* Attila, Flagello di dio, 1954

Atilla 74, 1975 (Cacoyannis 2)

Atithee, 1978 (Azmi 3)

Atividades politicas em Sao Paolo, 1950 (Pereira Dos Santos 2)

Atlanta Child Murders, 1985 (Jones 3, Robards 3, Sheen 3)

Atlantic, 1929 (Dupont 2, Carroll 3, Rosher 4)

Atlantic Adventure, 1935 (Langdon 3)

Atlantic City, 1944 (Dandridge 3, Alton 4)

Atlantic City, 1981 (Malle 2, Lancaster 3, Piccoli 3, Sarandon 3, Legrand 4)

Atlantic Episode. *See* Catch as Catch Can, 1937

Atlantic Ferry, 1941 (Love 3, Redgrave 3)

Atlantide, 1932 (Metzner 4, Schüfftan 4)

Atlantide, 1960 (Ulmer 2, Trintignant 3, Volonté 3)

Atlantik, 1929 (Dupont 2, Kortner 3)

Atlantis, 1913 (Blom 2, Curtiz 2)

Atlantis, 1930 (Dupont 2)

Atlantis, the Lost Continent, 1960 (Gillespie 4, Pal 4)

Atlas, 1960 (Corman 2)

Ato ni tsuzuku o shinzu, 1945 (Hasegawa 3)

Atoll K, 1950 (Laurel and Hardy 3)

Atom, 1918 (Borzage 2)

Atom Man vs. Superman, 1950 (Katzman 4)

Atomic Cafe, 1982 (Rozsa 4)

Atomic City, 1952 (Lang 4)

Atomic Kid, 1954 (Edwards 2, Rooney 3)

Atonement, 1914 (Anderson 3)

Atonement of Gösta Berling. *See* **Gösta Berlings Saga, 1924**

Atout coeur à Tokyo pour OSS 177, 1966 (Douy 4)

Atragon. *See* Kaitei gunkan, 1964

Atre, 1920 (Gance 2)

Atre, 1922 (Vanel 3)

Atroce menace, 1934 (Christian-Jaque 2)

Atsui yoru, 1968 (Yoshimura 2)

Att älska, 1964 (Andersson 3, Cybulski 3, Nykvist 4)

Atta Boy, 1926 (Laurel and Hardy 3)

Atta Boy's Last Race, 1916 (Browning 2)

Attack!, 1956 (Aldrich 2, Marvin 3, Palance 3, Bass 4, Biroc 4)

Attack and Retreat. *See* Italiani brava gente, 1964

Attack Force Z, 1980 (Gibson 3)

Attack in the Pacific, 1945 (Raksin 4)

Attack of the Crab Monsters, 1957 (Corman 2, Crosby 4)

Attack of the Puppet People, 1958 (Laszlo 4)

Attack of the Robots, 1967 (Rey 3)

Attack Squadron. *See* Taiheiyo no tsubasa, 1963

Attaque du feu, 1895 (Lumière 2)

Attaque d'un diligence, 1904 (Guy 2)

Attaque nocturne, 1931 (Fernandel 3)

Attendant l'auto, 1970 (Braunberger 4)

Attendat, 1973 (Scheider 3)

Attendenti, 1961 (De Sica 2, Cervi 3)

Attentat, 1972 (Noiret 3, Piccoli 3, Seberg 3, Trintignant 3, Volonté 3, Morricone 4)

Attenti al buffone!, 1975 (Wallach 3, Morricone 4)

Attention Bandits, 1987 (Lelouch 2, Lai 4)

Attention, les enfants regardent, 1977 (Delon 3, Renoir 4)

Attention les yeux, 1975 (Braunberger 4)

Attention, Tortoise!. *See* Vnimanie, cherpakha!, 1969

Atti degli apostoli, 1968 (Rossellini 2)

Attic, 1980 (Milland 3)

Attila. *See* Attila flagello di dio, 1955

Attila flagello di dio, 1955 (Loren 3, Papas 3, Quinn 3, Levine 4, Ponti 4, Rotunno 4, Struss 4)

Attila the Hun. *See* Attila flagello di dio, 1955

Atto di accusa, 1951 (Mastroianni 3)

Atto di dolore, 1990 (Cardinale 3)

Attrait du bouge, 1912 (Feuillade 2)

Au bagne, 1905 (Pathé 4)

Au Bal de Flore, 1900 (Guy 2)

Au bal de flore, 1901 (Gaumont 4)

Au bon coin, 1958 (Braunberger 4)

Au bonheur des chiens. *See* C'era un castello con 40 cani, 1990

Au bonheur des Dames, 1929 (Christian-Jaque 2, Duvivier 2)

Au bonheur des Dames, 1943 (Simon 3, Andrejew 4)

Au bout de monde, 1933 (Gabin 3)

Au bout du fil. *See* Cat's Cradle, 1974

Au bout du monde, 1933 (Vanel 3)

Au cabaret, 1897 (Guy 2)

Au carrefour de la vie, 1949 (Storck 2)

Aucassin et Nicolette, 1976 (Reiniger 4)

Au champ de vapeur, 1969 (Braunberger 4)

Au Clair de la lune ou Pierrot malheureux, 1904 (Méliès 2)

Au coeur de la Casbah, 1951 (Decaë 4)

Au coeur de la ville, 1969 (Jutra 2)

Au cœur de l'Ile de France, 1954 (Grémillon 2)

Au deuil du Harem, 1922 (Modot 3)

Au fil de l'eau, 1932 (Matras 4)

Au Fou!, 1966 (Kuri 4)

Au grand balcon, 1949 (Fresnay 3, Kosma 4)

Au gré des flots, 1913 (Feuillade 2)

Au Guadalquiviz, 1965 (Braunberger 4)

Au hasard, Balthazar, 1966 (Cloquet 4)

Au joli coin, 1932 (Vanel 3)

Au nom de la loi, 1932 (Tourneur 2, Vanel 3, Douy 4)

Au pays de George Sand, 1926 (Epstein 2, Périnal 4)

Au pays de Guillaume le Conquérant, 1954 (Delerue 4)

Au pays de Porgy and Bess, 1957 (Braunberger 4)

Au pays des grandes causses, 1951 (Fradetal 4)

Au pays des lions, 1912 (Feuillade 2)

Au pays des mages noirs, 1947 (Rouch 2)

Au pays du Roi Lépreux, 1927 (Feyder 2)

Au pays du scalp, 1931 (Cavalcanti 2, Jaubert 4)

Au pays noir, 1905 (Pathé 4)

Au peril de la mer, 1968 (Braunberger 4, Coutard 4)

Au petit bonheur, 1945 (L'Herbier 2, Darrieux 3)

Au Poulailler!, 1905 (Guy 2)

Au réfectoire, 1897 (Guy 2)

Au rendez-vous de la mort joyeuse, 1972 (Depardieu 3, Cloquet 4)

Au royaume des cieux, 1949 (Duvivier 2, Reggiani 3, Jeanson 4)

Au rythme du siècle, 1953 (Delerue 4)

Au secours!, 1923 (Gance 2, Linder 3)

Au service du Tsar. *See* Adjudant des Zaren, 1929

Au sommet de la gloire, 1941 (Volkov 2)

Aube d'un monde, 1956 (Cocteau 2)

Aube du troisième jour, 1963 (Kosma 4)

Auberge du bon repos, 1903 (Méliès 2)

Auberge du Petit-Dragon, 1934 (Modot 3, Burel 4)

Auberge ensorcelée, 1897 (Méliès 2)

Auberge rouge, 1910 (Gance 2)

Auberge rouge, 1923 (Epstein 2, Manès 3)

Auberge rouge, 1951 (Fernandel 3, Rosay 3, Aurenche 4, Bost 4, Douy 4)

Aubervilliers, 1946 (Kosma 4, Prévert 4)

Auction Sale of Run-Down Ranch, 1915 (Mix 3)

Auctioneer, 1927 (Fox 4)

Audace colpo dei soliti ignoti, 1959 (Cardinale 3, Gassman 3, Age and Scarpelli 4, Cristaldi 4)

Audaces du cœur, 1913 (Feuillade 2)

Audacious Mr. Squire, 1923 (Buchanan 3)

Au-delà de la Mort, 1922 (Modot 3)

Au-delà des grilles, 1949 (Clement 2, Gabin 3, Aurenche 4, Bost 4, Cecchi D'Amico 4, Zavattini 4)

Au-delà du bien et du mal, 1977 (Sanda 3)

Au-delà du visible, 1943 (Decaë 4)

Auditions, 1980 (Loach 2, Menges 4)

Audrey Rose, 1977 (Wise 2, Hopkins 3, Horner 4, Jeakins 4)

Auf Befehl der Pompadour, 1924 (Albers 3)
Auf der Alm da gibt's ka Sünd, 1915
   (Porten 3, Messter 4)
Auf der Radrennbahn, 1903 (Messter 4)
Auf der Reeperbahn nachts um halb eins,
   1954 (Albers 3)
Auf gefährlichen Spuren, 1924 (Galeen 4)
Auf Wiedersehen, Franziska, 1941
   (Käutner 2)
Auferstehung, 1958 (Herlth 4)
Aufruhr im Paradise, 1950 (Tschechowa 3)
Aufruhr in Indien. See Mistero del tempio
   indiano, 1963
Aufs Eis geführt, 1914 (Lubitsch 2)
Aufstand, 1980 (Ballhaus 4)
Aufzeichnungen zu Kleidern und Städten,
   1989 (Wenders 2, Müller 4)
Auge des Buddha, 1919 (Kortner 3)
Auge des Toten, 1922 (Banky 3)
Augen aus einem anderen Land, 1975
   (Kluge 2)
Augen der Liebe. See Zwischen Nacht und
   Morgen, 1944
Augen der Mumie Mâ, 1918 (Lubitsch 2,
   Jannings 3, Negri 3, Kräly 4)
Augen der Welt, 1920 (Veidt 3)
Augen des Ole Brandis, 1914 (Wegener 3)
Augh! Augh!, 1980 (Donaggio 4)
Auguri e figli maschi, 1951 (Age and
   Scarpelli 4)
August der Starke, 1936 (Dagover 3,
   Wegener 3)
Augustina de Aragón, 1950 (Rey 3)
Augustirapsodi, 1939 (Sucksdorff 2)
August Rhapsody. See Augustirapsodi, 1939
Auld Lang Syne, 1917 (Buchanan 3)
Auld Lang Syne, 1929 (Dickinson 2,
   Pearson 2)
Aunt Bill, 1916 (Laurel and Hardy 3)
Aunt Clara, 1954 (Rutherford 3, Korda 4)
Aunt Green, Aunt Brown, and Aunt Lilac.
   See Tant Grun, Tant Brun, och Tant
   Gredelin, 1945
Aunt Jane's Legacy, 1911 (Lawrence 3)
Aunt Julia and the Scriptwriter, 1990 (Falk 3,
   Henry 4)
Aunt Sally, 1933 (Balcon 4, Rank 4,
   Vetchinsky 4)
Auntie and the Cowboys, 1911 (Dwan 2)
Auntie Lee's Meat Pies, 1990 (Black 3)
Auntie Mame, 1958 (Dumont 3, Russell 3,
   Comden and Green 4, Kaper 4, Orry-
   Kelly 4, Stradling 4, Warner 4)
Aunty's Romance, 1912 (Costello 3)
Aurat, 1940 (Biswas 4)
Aurelia Steiner series, 1978 (Duras 2)
Aurelia Steiner—Vancouver, 1979
   (Branco 4)
Aurora, 1966 (Braunberger 4)
Aurora, 1984 (Loren 3, Noiret 3)
Aus dem Leben der Marionetten, 1980
   (Nykvist 4)
Aus dem Schwarzbuch eines
   Polizeikommissars, 1921 (Kortner 3)
Aus dem Tagebuch einer Frauenärztin. See
   Erste Recht des Kindes, 1932
Aus dem Tagebuch eines Verführers. See
   Liebesnächte, 1929
Aus den Erinnerungen eines Frauenarztes,
   1921 (Pick 2)
Aus der Familie der Panzerechsen, 1974
   (Wenders 2)
Aus eines Mannes Mädchenjahren, 1919
   (Albers 3)

Aus erster Ehe, 1940 (Wagner 4)
Aus erster Ehe, 1950 (Staudte 2)
Aus Mangel an Beweisen, 1916 (Jannings 3)
Ausgestossenen, 1927 (Kortner 3, Planer 4)
Aussagen nach einer Verhaftung, 1978
   (Schygulla 3)
Aussi loin que l'amour, 1971 (Chabrol 2,
   Audran 3, Dalio 3)
Aussi Longue Absence, 1961 (Valli 3,
   Colpi 4, Delerue 4)
Auster und die Perle, 1961 (Herlth 4)
Austeria, 1982 (Kawalerowicz 2,
   Konwicki 4)
Austerlitz, 1960 (De Sica 2, Gance 2,
   Welles 2, Brazzi 3, Cardinale 3, Caron 3,
   Gélin 3, Marais 3, Palance 3, Simon 3,
   Trintignant 3, Alekan 4)
Austerprinzessin, 1919 (Kräly 4)
Australia, 1989 (Morricone 4)
Austreibung, 1923 (Dieterle 2, Murnau 2,
   Freund 4, Von Harbou 4)
Austreibung—Die Macht der zweiter Frau,
   1923 (Pommer 4)
Author! Author!, 1982 (Pacino 3, Weld 3,
   Reynolds 4, Winkler 4)
Auto Antics, 1939 (Roach 4)
Auto Boat on the Hudson, 1904 (Bitzer 4)
Auto chiese, 1959 (Olmi 2)
Autobahn, 1979 (Halas and Batchelor 4)
Autobiography of a Princess, 1975 (Ivory 2,
   Jhabvala 3, Lassally 4)
Autocrat of Flapjack Junction, 1913
   (Bunny 3)
Autogram, 1984 (Ballhaus 4)
Autogrimpeurs, 1962 (Delerue 4)
Automania 2000, 1963 (Halas and
   Batchelor 4)
Automate, 1908 (Cohl 4)
Automation, 1959 (Alexeieff and Parker 4)
Automation Blues, 1980 (Halas and
   Batchelor 4)
Automobile Ride, 1921 (Fleischer 4)
Automobile Thieves, 1905 (Blackton 2)
Auto-portrait, 1963 (Braunberger 4)
Autopsia de un fantasma, 1968 (Carradine 3,
   Rathbone 3)
Autopsie d'un monstre. See Chacun son
   enfer, 1976
Autopsy on a Ghost. See Autopsia de un
   fantasma, 1968
Autostop rosso sangue, 1977 (Morricone 4)
Autour de l'arbre, 1982 (Moreau 3)
Autour de minuit. See 'Round Midnight,
   1986
Autour d'une bague, 1915 (Feyder 2)
Autour d'une enquête, 1931 (Modot 3)
Autre, 1917 (Feuillade 2)
Autre, 1970 (Braunberger 4)
Autre aile, 1924 (Vanel 3)
Autre Femme, 1964 (Girardot 3, Valli 3,
   Delerue 4)
Autre Homme, une autre chance, 1977
   (Bujold 3, Caan 3, Lai 4)
Autre Victoire, 1915 (Musidora 3)
Autresville d'art, 1969 (Rabier 4)
Autumn Afternoon. See **Samma no aji, 1962**
Autumn Crocus, 1934 (Hawkins 3,
   Novello 3, Dean 4)
Autumn Leaves, 1956 (Aldrich 2,
   Crawford 3, Robertson 3, Lang 4,
   Salter 4)
Autumn Sonata. See Herbstsonate, 1978
Autumnal Equinox, 1974 (Frampton 2)
Auvergne, 1925 (Grémillon 2, Périnal 4)

Aux confins d'une ville, 1952 (Fradetal 4)
Aux deux colombes, 1949 (Guitry 2)
Aux frontières de l'homme, 1952
   (Cloquet 4)
Aux lions les chrétiens, 1911 (Feuillade 2,
   Carré 4, Gaumont 4)
Aux portes de Paris, 1934 (Spaak 4)
Aux Quatre Coins, 1950 (Rivette 2)
Aux yeux du souvenir, 1948 (Marais 3,
   Morgan 3, Auric 4, Jeanson 4)
Av de många, 1915 (Sjöström 2)
Availing Prayer, 1914 (Crisp 3)
Avalanche, 1919 (Miller 4)
Avalanche, 1928 (Mankiewicz 4)
Avalanche, 1946 (Anhalt 4)
Avalanche, 1950 (Cloquet 4)
Avalanche. See Nadare, 1952
Avalanche, 1978 (Corman 2, Farrow 3,
   Hudson 3)
Avalanche Express, 1979 (Polonsky 2,
   Marvin 3, Schell 3, Shaw 3)
Avalon, 1990 (Levinson 2, Mueller-Stahl 3)
Avant la musique, 1962 (Cervi 3,
   Fernandel 3)
Avant le déluge, 1954 (Cayatte 2, Blier 3,
   Spaak 4)
Avant-Garde Home Movie, 1961
   (Brakhage 2)
Avanti!, 1972 (Wilder 2, Lemmon 3,
   Diamond 4)
Avanti, c'e posto, 1942 (Fellini 2, Fabrizi 3)
Avanti la musica. See Avant la musique,
   1962
Avant-Scène, 1973 (Spaak 4)
Avant-veille du grand soir, 1969
   (Braunberger 4)
Avanzi di galera, 1954 (Constantine 3,
   Fusco 4)
Avaro, 1990 (Lee 3, Sordi 3)
Avatar, 1915 (Gallone 2)
Avatar botanique de Mlle. Flora, 1964
   (Braunberger 4, Coutard 4)
Avatar, the Return of the Wolf, 1977
   (Müller 4)
Ave Caesar!, 1919 (Korda 2, Korda 4)
Ave Maria, 1936 (Ophüls 2, Planer 4)
Ave Maria, 1984 (Karina 3)
Avec amour et avec rage. See Costanza della
   ragione, 1964
Avec André Gide, 1952 (Philipe 3,
   Braunberger 4)
Avec Claude Monet, 1966 (Gélin 3)
Avec les gens de voyage, 1953 (Decaë 4)
Avec le sourire, 1936 (Tourneur 2,
   Chevalier 3)
Avec les peaux des autres, 1965
   (D'Eaubonne 4)
Avec les pilotes de porte-avions, 1953
   (Delerue 4)
Avenger. See Hämnaren, 1915
Avenger. See Mstitel, 1959
Avengers. See Day Will Dawn, 1942
Avenging Angels. See Messenger of Death,
   1988
Avenging Arrow, 1921 (Van Dyke 2)
Avenging Bill, 1915 (Laurel and Hardy 3)
Avenging Conscience, 1914 (Griffith 2,
   Crisp 3, Marsh 3, Sweet 3, Walthall 3,
   Bitzer 4, Brown 4)
Avenging Force, 1986 (Golan and Globus 4)
Avenging Rider, 1928 (Musuraca 4)
Avenging Rider, 1942 (Hunt 4)
Avenging Trail, 1917 (Gaudio 4)
Avenging Waters, 1936 (Bond 3)

Avenir d'Emilie, 1984 (Vierny 4)
Avenir devoile par les lignes des pieds, 1917 (Cohl 4)
Aventura de Gil Blas, 1956 (Rey 3)
Aventura de Musidora en España, 1922 (Musidora 3)
Aventuras de Juan Lucas, 1949 (Rey 3)
Aventure à Paris, 1936 (Lourié 4)
Aventure à Pigalle, 1949 (Dalio 3)
Aventure c'est l'aventure, 1972 (Lai 4)
Aventure de Billy le Kid, 1973 (Léaud 3)
Aventure de Cabassou, 1946 (Fernandel 3)
Aventure de Moutonnet. See Moutonnet, 1936
Aventure des millions, 1916 (Feuillade 2)
Aventure est au coin de la rue, 1943 (Renoir 4)
''Aventure'' et ses Terre-Nuevas, 1953 (Delerue 4)
Aventures de Clementine, 1916 (Cohl 4)
Aventures de Holly and Wood, 1978 (Vierny 4)
Aventures de Rabbi Jacob, 1973 (Dalio 3, Decaë 4)
Aventures de Robert Macaire, 1925 (Epstein 2, Meerson 4)
Aventures de Salavin, 1963 (Saulnier 4)
Aventures de Till l'Espiègle, 1956 (Philipe 3, Auric 4, Barsacq 4)
Aventures des Pieds-Nickelés, 1948 (Braunberger 4)
Aventures du roi Pausole, 1933 (Delannoy 2, Baranovskaya 3, Feuillère 3, Amidei 4, Jeanson 4, Maté 4, Rathaus 4)
Aventures d'un bout de papier, 1911 (Cohl 4)
Aventures d'un voyageur trop pressé, 1903 (Guy 2)
Aventures en Laponie, 1960 (Braunberger 4)
Aventurier, 1934 (L'Herbier 2)
Aventurière, 1912 (Feuillade 2)
Aventurière, dame de compagnie, 1911 (Feuillade 2)
Aventuriers, 1966 (Delon 3, Reggiani 3)
Äventyrare, 1942 (Björnstrand 3)
Aventyret, 1936 (Fischer 4, Jaenzon 4)
Avenue de l'Opéra, 1900 (Guy 2)
Average Husband, 1930 (Sennett 2)

Average Man. See Borghese piccolo piccolo, 1977
Aveu, 1970 (Montand 3, Signoret 3, Coutard 4, Evein 4)
Aveugle, 1897 (Guy 2)
Aveugle, 1907 (Gaumont 4)
Aveugle de Jerusalem, 1909 (Feuillade 2)
Aveux les plus doux, 1971 (Noiret 3, Coutard 4, Delerue 4)
Aviatikeren og Journalistens Hustru. See Lektion, 1911
Aviation Vacation, 1941 (Avery 4, Blanc 4, Stalling 4)
Aviator, 1929 (Horton 3)
Aviator and the Journalist's Wife. See Lektion, 1911
Avignon, bastion de la provence, 1951 (Philipe 3)
Avion de minuit, 1938 (Berry 3)
Avisen, 1954 (Roos 2)
Avoir 16 ans, 1978 (Lefebvre 2)
Avtaar, 1983 (Azmi 3)
Avventura, 1959 (Antonioni 2, Vitti 3, Fusco 4, Guerra 4)
Avventura di Annabella, 1943 (Magnani 3)
Avventura di Salvator Rosa, 1940 (Blasetti 2, Castellani 2, Cervi 3)
Avventure di Pinocchio, 1947 (Gassman 3)
Avventure di Pinocchio, 1971 (Comencini 2, Lollobrigida 3, Gherardi 4)
Avventure e gli amori di Miguel Cervantes. See Cervantes, 1968
Avventure nell 'arcipelago, 1958 (Fusco 4)
Avventuriera del piano di sopra, 1941 (De Sica 2)
Avventuriero. See Rover, 1967
Avventurosa fuga. See Ultimi angeli, 1977
Avvoltoio nero, 1913 (Bertini 3)
Awa no odoriko, 1941 (Hasegawa 3, Takamine 3)
Awaara. See **Awara, 1951**
Awakened Conscience. See Probuzené svědomí, 1919
Awakening, 1909 (Griffith 2, Pickford 3, Bitzer 4)
Awakening, 1928 (Fleming 2, Banky 3, Barnes 4, Berlin 4, Goldwyn 4, Marion 4, Menzies 4, Wilson 4)
Awakening. See Suor Letizia, 1956

Awakening. See Probuzeni, 1959
Awakening, 1980 (Heston 3, York 3, Savini 4)
Awakening of Bess, 1909 (Lawrence 3)
Awakening of Helena Ritchie, 1916 (Barrymore 3)
Awakening of Jones, 1912 (Bunny 3)
Awakenings, 1990 (De Niro 3, Von Sydow 3, Williams 3, Ondříček 4)
Awara, 1951 (Kapoor 2, Nargis 3, Abbas 4)
Award Presentation to Andy Warhol, 1964 (Mekas 2)
Away All Boats, 1956 (Daniels 4)
Away from the Steerage, 1921 (Sennett 2)
Away Out West, 1910 (Anderson 3)
Awaz, 1956 (Mehboob 2)
Awful Moment, 1908 (Griffith 2, Lawrence 3)
Awful Orphan, 1949 (Blanc 4, Jones 4, Stalling 4)
Awful Skate, 1907 (Anderson 3)
Awful Spook, 1921 (Bray 4)
Awful Truth, 1929 (Neilan 2)
Awful Truth, 1937 (McCarey 2, Bellamy 3, Dunne 3, Grant 3, Cohn 4, Walker 4)
Awwal Number, 1990 (Anand 3)
Axe and the Lamp, 1963 (Halas and Batchelor 4)
Axe Me Another. See Adventures of Popeye, 1935
Ay! Carmela, 1990 (Saura 2, Maura 3)
Ay, qué tiempos, señor don Simón, 1941 (Figueroa 4)
Aya ni kanashiki, 1956 (Yamada 3)
Ayako. See Aru Osaka no onna, 1962
Ayamna el Hilwa, 1954 (Sharif 3)
Aysa, 1965 (Sanjinés 2)
Az aranyember, 1918 (Korda 2, Korda 4)
Az azredes, 1917 (Lugosi 3)
Az egymillió fontos bankó, 1916 (Korda 2, Korda 4)
Az elet kiralya, 1918 (Lugosi 3)
Az idö ablakai, 1970 (Tyszkiewicz 3)
Až přijde kocour, 1963 (Brodský 3, Brdečka 4, Kučera 4)
Azad, 1955 (Kumar 3)
Azais, 1930 (D'Eaubonne 4)
Aztecas, 1976 (Figueroa 4)

B

B. Must Die. *See* Hay que matar a B., 1973
B.F.'s Daughter, 1948 (Coburn 3, Stanwyck 3, Irene 4, Kaper 4, Ruitenberg 4)
Baag ki Jyoti, 1953 (Biswas 4)
Baaji, 1951 (Burman 4)
Baal, 1969 (Fassbinder 2, Schlöndorff 2, Von Trotta 2, Schygulla 3)
Baap Beti, 1954 (Roy 2)
Baat Ek Raat Ki, 1962 (Anand 3, Burman 4)
Baaz, 1953 (Dutt 2)
Baazi, 1951 (Anand 3)
Baba-Ali, 1952 (Colpi 4)
Baba Yaga—Devil Witch, 1973 (Baker 3)
Babatu, 1976 (Rouch 2)
Babbitt, 1934 (McDaniel 3, Orry-Kelly 4)
Babe, 1975 (Ames 4, Goldsmith 4)
Babe, 1990 (Wexler 4)
Babe Comes Home, 1927 (Struss 4)
Babe Ruth Story, 1948 (Bendix 3, Trevor 3)
Babel Opera, ou la répétition de Don Juan, 1985 (Delvaux 2)
Babel Yemen, 1977 (Howard 3)
Babes in Arms, 1939 (Berkeley 2 , Garland 3, Brown 4, Edens 4, Freed 4)
Babes in Bagdad, 1952 (Ulmer 2, Goddard 3, Lee 3)
Babes in the Goods, 1934 (Roach 4)
Babes in the Wood. *See* Perníková chaloupka, 1927
Babes in Toyland, 1934 (Laurel and Hardy 3, Roach 4)
Babes in Toyland, 1961 (Disney 4)
Babes on Broadway, 1941 (Berkeley 2, Garland 3, O'Brien 3, Reed 3, Rooney 3, Edens 4, Freed 4, Mayer 4)
Babe's School Days, 1915 (Laurel and Hardy 3)
Babette Goes to War. *See* Babette s'en va-t-en guerre, 1959
Babette s'en va-t-en guerre, 1959 (Bardot 3, Audiard 4)
Babette's Feast. *See* Babette's Gastebud, 1987
Babette's Gastebud, 1987 (Andersson 3, Audran 3)
Babies, 1928 (Rooney 3)
Babies for Sale, 1940 (Ford 3)
Babies Having Babies, 1991 (Sheen 3)
Babla, 1953 (Burman 4)
Bab's Burglar, 1917 (Barthelmess 3)
Bab's Diary, 1917 (Barthelmess 3)
Babul, 1950 (Kumar 3)
Baby, 1915 (Laurel and Hardy 3)
Baby, 1932 (Ondra 3, Walbrook 3, Heller 4)
Baby. *See* Bebek, 1973
Baby, 1985 (Alcott 4)

Baby and the Battleship, 1956 (Attenborough 3, Mills 3)
Baby and the Stork, 1911 (Griffith 2, Bitzer 4)
Baby Be Good, 1935 (Fleischer 4)
Baby Be Good. *See* Brother Rat and a Baby, 1940
Baby Blue Marine, 1976 (Gere 3, Kovacs 4)
Baby Boogie, 1955 (Bosustow 4)
Baby Boom, 1987 (Keaton 3, Fraker 4, Shepard 4)
Baby Bottleneck, 1946 (Blanc 4, Clampett 4, Stalling 4)
Baby Buggy Bunny, 1954 (Blanc 4, Jones 4, Maltese 4)
Baby Butch, 1953 (Hanna and Barbera 4)
Baby Clothes, 1926 (Roach 4)
Baby Cyclone, 1928 (Gibbons 4)
Baby Day, 1913 (Sennett 2, Normand 3)
Baby Doll, 1916 (Laurel and Hardy 3)
Baby Doll, 1956 (Kazan 2, Baker 3, Malden 3, Wallach 3, Kaufman 4, Sylbert 4)
Baby Face, 1933 (Brennan 3, Stanwyck 3, Wayne 3, Grot 4, Orry-Kelly 4, Zanuck 4)
Baby Face Harrington. *See* Baby Face, 1933
Baby Face Harrington, 1935 (Walsh 2, Johnson 4)
Baby Face Nelson, 1957 (Siegel 2, Rooney 3, Mohr 4)
Baby, It's You, 1983 (Sayles 2, Ballhaus 4)
Baby l'indiavolate. *See* My Little Baby, 1916
Baby Love, 1968 (Dors 3)
Baby Love. *See* Roman Zair, 1983
Baby Mine, 1917 (Edeson 4)
Baby Mine, 1928 (Gibbons 4)
Baby on the Barge, 1915 (Hepworth 2)
Baby Puss, 1943 (Hanna and Barbera 4)
Baby Review, 1903 (Porter 2)
Baby Seal, 1941 (Terry 4)
Baby—Secret of the Lost Legend, 1984 (Goldsmith 4)
Baby Sitters' Jitters, 1951 (Three Stooges 3)
Baby Story, 1978 (Bozzetto 4)
Baby, Take a Bow, 1934 (Temple 3, Trevor 3)
Baby the Rain Must Fall, 1964 (Mulligan 2, Pakula 2, McQueen 3, Remick 3, Bernstein 4, Laszlo 4)
Baby Wants a Bottle-ship, 1942 (Fleischer 4)
Babylon, 1980 (Menges 4)
Babylon Series, 1989 (Brakhage 2)
Babylon Series 2, 1990 (Brakhage 2)
Baby's Birthday, 1929 (Sennett 2)
Baby's Pets, 1926 (Sennett 2)

Baby's Ride, 1914 (Reid 3)
Baby's Shoe, 1909 (Griffith 2, Lawrence 3, Bitzer 4)
Baby-Sitter, 1975 (Clement 2, Lai 4, Ponti 4)
Babysitter, 1980 (Houseman 4)
Bacall to Arms, 1946 (Blanc 4, Clampett 4, Stalling 4)
Baccara, 1936 (Berry 3, Lourié 4)
Bacchantin, 1924 (Tschechowa 3)
Bacciamo le mani, 1973 (Kennedy 3)
Bach Millionnaire, 1933 (Jeanson 4)
Bach to Bach, 1967 (May 4, Rosenblum 4)
Bach y sus intérpretes, 1975 (Leduc 2)
Bachelor. *See* Mio caro Dr. Gräsler, 1990
Bachelor and the Bobby-Soxer, 1947 (Grant 3, Loy 3, Temple 3, Musuraca 4, Schary 4)
Bachelor Apartment, 1931 (Dunne 3)
Bachelor Bait, 1934 (Stevens 2, Plunkett 4, Polglase 4, Steiner 4)
Bachelor Brides, 1926 (Fort 4, Sullivan 4)
Bachelor Butt-in, 1926 (Sennett 2)
Bachelor Buttons, 1912 (Bunny 3)
Bachelor Daddy, 1941 (Horton 3, Pangborn 3, Krasner 4, Salter 4)
Bachelor Father, 1931 (Davies 3, Milland 3, Adrian 4)
Bachelor Father. *See* Ungkarlspappan, 1934
Bachelor Flat, 1962 (Tashlin 2, Terry-Thomas 3, Weld 3, Smith 4, Williams 4)
Bachelor Girl Apartment. *See* Any Wednesday, 1966
Bachelor in Paradise, 1961 (Hope 3, Moorehead 3, Turner 3, Mancini 4, Rose 4, Ruttenberg 4)
Bachelor Knight. *See* Bachelor and the Bobby-Soxer, 1947
Bachelor Mother, 1939 (Coburn 3, Niven 3, Rogers 3, Irene 4, Kanin 4, Krasna 4, Polglase 4)
Bachelor of Arts, 1934 (Marsh 3, Walthall 3, Trotti 4)
Bachelor of Hearts, 1958 (Rank 4, Raphael 4, Unsworth 4)
Bachelor Party, 1957 (Chayefsky 4, La Shelle 4, North 4)
Bachelor Party, 1984 (Hanks 3)
Bachelor's Affairs, 1932 (Menjou 3)
Bachelor's Baby, 1915 (Anderson 3)
Bachelor's Baby, 1927 (Fort 4)
Bachelor's Brides. *See* Bachelor Brides, 1926
Bachelor's Burglar, 1915 (Anderson 3)
Bachelor's Daughter, 1946 (Menjou 3, Trevor 3)
Bachelor's Folly. *See* Calendar, 1931
Bacher, 1967 (Müller 4)

Bacio di Cirano, 1913 (Gallone 2)
Bacio di Cirano, 1920 (Gallone 2)
Back Alley Oproar, 1948 (Blanc 4, Freleng 4, Stalling 4)
Back and Forth. *See* Standard Time, 1967
Back at the Front, 1952 (Boyle 4)
Back Door to Heaven, 1939 (Howard 2, Head 4, Mohr 4)
Back Door to Hell, 1964 (Nicholson 3)
Back from Eternity, 1956 (Bondi 3)
Back from Eternity, 1956 (Ryan 3, Steiger 3, D'Agostino 4, Waxman 4)
Back from the Dead, 1957 (Haller 4)
Back From the Front, 1943 (Three Stooges 3)
Back in Circulation, 1937 (Blondell 3, Miller 4, Wallis 4)
Back in the Saddle, 1941 (Autry 3)
Back of the Man, 1917 (Ince 4)
Back Page, 1931 (Arbuckle 3)
Back Pay, 1922 (Borzage 2, Marion 4)
Back Pay, 1930 (Beavers 3, Seitz 4)
Back Roads, 1981 (Ritt 2, Field 3, Alonzo 4, Mancini 4)
Back Room Boy, 1942 (Withers 3, Rank 4)
Back Stage, 1917 (Laurel and Hardy 3)
Back Stage, 1919 (Keaton 2, Arbuckle 3)
Back Stage, 1923 (Roach 4)
Back Street, 1932 (Stahl 2, Darwell 3, Dunne 3, Freund 4, Laemmle 4)
Back Street, 1941 (Stevenson 2, Boyer 3, Sullavan 3, Daniels 4)
Back Street, 1961 (Hayward 3, Cortez 4, Hunter 4, Lourié 4)
Back Streets of Paris. *See* Macadam, 1946
Back to Back, 1989 (Johnson 3)
Back to Bataan, 1945 (Dmytryk 2, Bondi 3, Quinn 3, Wayne 3, D'Agostino 4, Musuraca 4,)
Back to God's Country, 1920 (Walker 4)
Back to God's Country, 1927 (Laemmle 4)
Back to God's Country, 1953 (Hudson 3)
Back to Life, 1913 (Dwan 2, Chaney 3)
Back to the Farm, 1914 (Laurel and Hardy 3)
Back to the Future, 1985 (Spielberg 2, Zemeckis 2, Fox 3)
Back to the Future II, 1989 (Zemeckis 2, Fox 3)
Back to the Future III, 1990 (Zemeckis 2, Fox 3)
Back to the Kitchen, 1919 (Sennett 2)
Back to the Primitive, 1911 (Mix 3)
Back to the Soil, 1911 (Pickford 3, Gaudio 4)
Back to the Soil, 1941 (Terry 4)
Back to the Wall. *See* Dos au mur, 1958
Back to the Woods, 1919 (Daniels 3, Lloyd 3, Normand 3, Roach 4)
Back to the Woods, 1937 (Three Stooges 3)
Back Yard, 1920 (Laurel and Hardy 3)
Back Yard Theater, 1914 (Sennett 2)
Backdraft, 1991 (De Niro 3, Sutherland 3)
Backfire, 1950 (O'Brien 3, Grot 4, Veiller 4)
Backfire. *See* Echappement libre, 1964
Background to Danger, 1943 (Walsh 2, Greenstreet 3, Lorre 3, Raft 3, Burnett 4, Gaudio 4, Wald 4)
Backlash, 1956 (Sturges 2, Reed 3, Van Cleef 3, Widmark 3, Chase 4)
Backs to Nature, 1933 (Roach 4)
Backstage. *See* Limelight, 1936
Backstairs. *See* Hintertreppe, 1921
Backtrack, 1969 (Lupino 3, Chase 4)
Backtrack, 1989 (Foster 3, Hopper 3, Price 3)

Backwoods Bunny, 1959 (Blanc 4, McKimson 4)
Backwoodsman's Suspicions, 1911 (Anderson 3)
Backyard. *See* Två trappor över gården, 1950
Bacon Grabbers, 1929 (Harlow 3, Laurel and Hardy 3, Roach 4)
Bacquet de Mesmer, 1905 (Méliès 2)
Bad and the Beautiful, 1952 (Minnelli 2, Bushman 3, Calhern 3, Douglas 3, Grahame 3, Pidgeon 3, Powell 3, Turner 3, Gibbons 4, Houseman 4, Raksin 4, Rose 4, Schnee 4, Surtees 4)
Bad Bascomb, 1946 (Beery 3, O'Brien 3, Irene 4)
Bad Blonde. *See* Flanagan Boy, 1953
Bad Blood. *See* First Offence, 1936
Bad Blood. *See* Blood Feud, 1983
Bad Blood. *See* Mauvais Sang, 1986
Bad Boy, 1917 (Moore 3)
Bad Boy, 1925 (McCarey 2, Roach 4)
Bad Boy, 1935 (Bondi 3, Carradine 3, Glennon 4)
Bad Boy, 1949 (Murphy 3, Struss 4)
Bad Boys. *See* Furyo shonen, 1961
"Bad Buck" of Santa Ynez, 1915 (Hart 3)
Bad Charleston Charlie, 1973 (Carradine 3)
Bad Company, 1931 (Garnett 2, Carey 3, Miller 4)
Bad Company. *See* Mauvaises Fréquentations, 1967
Bad Company, 1972 (Benton 2, Bridges 3, Rosenblum 4, Willis 4)
Bad Day at Black Rock, 1954 (Sturges 2, Borgnine 3, Brennan 3, Marvin 3, Ryan 3, Tracy 3, Gibbons 4, Previn 4, Schary 4)
Bad Day at Cat Rock, 1965 (Jones 4)
Bad Eggs. *See* Rötägg, 1946
Bad for Each Other, 1953 (Heston 3, Planer 4, Wald 4)
Bad Game, 1913 (Sennett 2)
Bad Girl, 1931 (Borzage 2)
Bad Investment, 1911 (Dwan 2)
Bad Jim, 1989 (Golan and Globus 4)
Bad Lands, 1925 (Carey 3, Polito 4, Stromberg 4)
Bad Little Angel, 1939 (Seitz 4)
Bad Lord Byron, 1948 (Zetterling 2, Greenwood 3, Rank 4)
Bad Luck. *See* Zezowate szczęście, 1960
Bad Luck Blackie, 1949 (Avery 4)
Bad Man. *See* "Bad Buck" of Santa Ynez, 1915
Bad Man, 1930 (Huston 3, Estabrook 4, Seitz 4)
Bad Man, 1941 (Barrymore 3, Beery 3, Reagan 3, Waxman 4)
Bad Man and Others, 1915 (Walsh 2)
Bad Man and the Ranger, 1911 (Dwan 2)
Bad Man Bobbs, 1915 (Mix 3)
Bad Man From Cheyenne, 1980 (Johnson 3)
Bad Man of Brimstone, 1938 (Beery 3)
Bad Man of Deadwood, 1941 (Rogers 3, Canutt 4)
Bad Man of Wyoming. *See* Wyoming, 1940
Bad Man's Christmas Gift, 1910 (Anderson 3)
Bad Man's Downfall, 1911 (Anderson 3)
Bad Man's First Prayer, 1911 (Anderson 3)
Bad Man's Last Deed, 1910 (Anderson 3)
Bad Man's River, 1972 (Mason 3)
Bad Medicine, 1985 (Arkin 3, Schifrin 4)

Bad Men of Missouri, 1941 (Kennedy 3, Wyman 3)
Bad Men of Tombstone, 1948 (Crawford 3, Harlan 4)
Bad Men's Money, 1929 (Canutt 4)
Bad Names. *See* Akumyo, 1961
Bad Names' Best Trick. *See* Akumyo juhachi-ban, 1968
Bad Names' Breaking of Territories. *See* Akumyo nawabari arashi, 1974
Bad Names' Cherry Blossoms. *See* Akumyo zakura, 1966
Bad News Bears, 1976 (Matthau 3, Alonzo 4)
Bad News Bears Go to Japan, 1978 (Curtis 3)
Bad Ol' Putty Tat, 1949 (Blanc 4, Freleng 4, Stalling 4)
Bad One, 1930 (Del Rio 3, Karloff 3, Berlin 4, Menzies 4, Schenck 4, Struss 4, Wilson 4)
Bad Seed, 1956 (LeRoy 2, North 4, Rosson 4)
Bad Sister, 1931 (Bogart 3, Davis 3, Freund 4, Laemmle 4)
Bad Sister. *See* White Unicorn, 1947
Bad Sleep Well. *See* Warui yatsu hodo yoku nemuru, 1960
Bad Son. *See* Mauvais Fils, 1980
Bad Timber, 1931 (Bosworth 3)
Bad Timing, 1980 (Roeg 2, Elliott 3)
Badarna, 1968 (Thulin 3)
Badban, 1954 (Anand 3)
Badge 373, 1973 (Duvall 3)
Badge of Honor, 1934 (Crabbe 3)
Badge of Marshall Brennan, 1957 (Van Cleef 3)
Badger. *See* Tanuki, 1956
Badger General. *See* Tanuki no taishou, 1965
Badger's Holiday. *See* Tanuki no kyujitsu, 1966
Badger's Tea Pot. *See* Bunbuku chagama, 1939
Badi Bahu, 1951 (Biswas 4)
Badi Didi, 1939 (Roy 2)
Badlanders, 1958 (Daves 2, Borgnine 3, Ladd 3, Seitz 4)
Badlanders, 1991 (Golan and Globus 4)
Badlands, 1973 (Malick 2, Oates 3, Sheen 3, Spacek 4)
Badlands of Dakota, 1941 (Crawford 3, Farmer 3, Cortez 4, Salter 4)
Badman, 1923 (Polito 4)
Badman's Country, 1958 (Crabbe 3)
Badman's Territory, 1946 (Johnson 3, Scott 3, D'Agostino 4)
Baeus, 1987 (Bozzetto 4)
Baffled!, 1973 (Roberts 3)
Bag and Baggage, 1923 (Mohr 4)
Bagarres, 1948 (Kosma 4)
Bagdad, 1949 (O'Hara 3, Price 3, Metty 4)
Bagdad Cafe, 1987 (Palance 3)
Baggage Smasher, 1914 (Sennett 2, Arbuckle 3)
Bagnosträfling, 1949 (Fröhlich 3)
Bagpipes, 1989 (Halas and Batchelor 4)
Bague, 1947 (Resnais 2)
Bague qui tue, 1915 (Feuillade 2)
Bagula bhagat, 1979 (Azmi 3)
Bahama Passage, 1941 (Carroll 3, Dandridge 3, Hayden 3, Dreier 4, Head 4)
Bahar, 1951 (Burman 4)
Bahen, 1941 (Biswas 4)

Bahurani, 1963 (Dutt 2)

Baia di Napoli. *See* It Started in Naples, 1960

Baie des anges, 1963 (Moreau 3, Evein 4, Legrand 4, Rabier 4)

Baignade dans le torrent, 1897 (Guy 2)

Baignade en mer, 1895 (Lumière 2)

Baignades dans le torrent, 1901 (Gaumont 4)

Baignoire, 1917 (Cohl 4)

Bailiff. *See* **Sansho Dayu, 1954**

Bailiffs, 1932 (Crazy Gang 3)

Baîllonnée, 1922 (Fresnay 3)

Bain d'X, 1956 (Alexeieff and Parker 4)

Bains en mer, 1895 (Lumière 2)

Bairaag, 1976 (Kumar 3)

Baiser. *See* Ronde, 1974

Baisers, 1963 (Coutard 4, De Beauregard 4)

Baisers volés, 1968 (Truffaut 2, Léaud 3, Seyrig 3, Guillemot 4)

Bait, 1921 (Tourneur 2)

Baited Trap, 1927 (Walker 4)

Baited Trap. *See* Trap, 1959

Baja Oklahoma, 1988 (Ballhaus 4)

Bajaja, 1950 (Trnka 4)

Bajazzo. *See* Sehnsucht, 1920

Báječni muži s klikou, 1979 (Menzel 2)

Bajka w Ursusie, 1952 (Munk 2)

Bajo el cielo de Mexico, 1937 (De Fuentes 2, Figueroa 4)

Baka ga sensha de yattekuru, 1964 (Iwashita 3)

Baked at the Altar, 1935 (Sennett 2)

Baker's Wife. *See* **Femme de boulanger, 1938**

Bakom Jalusin, 1984 (Josephson 3)

Baku wa Toukichiroh, 1955 (Miyagawa 4)

Bakui ichidai, 1951 (Shimura 3)

Bakumatsu, 1970 (Mifune 3)

Bakuon to daichi, 1957 (Yamamura 3)

Bakuro ichidai, 1951 (Mifune 3, Hayasaka 4)

Bakushu, 1951 (Hara 3, Ryu 3)

Bakuto ichidai, 1951 (Kyo 3)

Bal, 1931 (Darrieux 3, Siodmak 4)

Bal, 1982 (Scola 2, Age and Scarpelli 4)

Bal d'enfants, 1895 (Lumière 2)

Bal des espions, 1960 (Piccoli 3)

Bal du Comte d'Orgel, 1970 (Presle 3, Matras 4)

Bal paré, 1940 (Röhrig 4)

Bala, 1976 (Ray 2, Datta 4)

Bala peridida, 1959 (Alcoriza 4)

Balaclava, 1930 (Balcon 4)

Balada da Praia dos Cães, 1986 (De Almeida 4)

Balalaika, 1939 (De Toth 2, Eddy 3, Adrian 4, Bennett 4, Freund 4, Gibbons 4, Ruttenberg 4, Shearer 4, Stothart 4)

Balança mas nao caid, 1953 (Pereira Dos Santos 2)

Balance, 1982 (Baye 3)

Balance, 1984 (Baye 3)

Balao, 1913 (Gaumont 4)

Balatli arif, 1967 (Güney 2)

Balatum, 1938 (Alexeieff and Parker 4)

Balayeur, 1961 (Delerue 4)

Balboa, 1982 (Curtis 3)

Balcony, 1963 (Falk 3, Grant 3, Winters 3, Fields 4, Folsey 4, Maddow 4)

Balena bianca, 1964 (Di Venanzo 4)

Balettprimadonnan, 1916 (Stiller 2, Jaenzon 4, Magnusson 4)

Baleydier, 1931 (Simon 3, Braunberger 4)

Bali, 1984 (Szabó 2)

Balidann, 1963 (Ghatak 2)

Balked at the Altar, 1908 (Griffith 2)

Ball, 1931 (Meerson 4)

Ball. *See* Bal, 1982

Ball at the Anjo House. *See* Anjoke no butokai, 1947

Ball der Nationen, 1954 (Fröhlich 3)

Ball of Fire, 1941 (Hawks 2, Wilder 2, Andrews 3, Cooper 3, Duryea 3, Homolka 3, Stanwyck 3, Brackett 4, Goldwyn 4, Head 4, Mandell 4, Newman 4, Toland 4)

Ball of the Anjo Family. *See* Anjo-ke no butokai, 1947

Ball Player and the Bandit, 1912 (Ince 4)

Ballad. *See* Sorvanetch, 1914

Ballad for the Kid, 1974 (Seberg 3)

Ballad in Blue, 1964 (Henreid 3)

Ballad of Andy Crocker, 1969 (Moorehead 3)

Ballad of a Soldier. *See* **Balada o Soldate, 1959**

Ballad of Cable Hogue, 1970 (Peckinpah 2, Robards 3, Ballard 4, Goldsmith 4)

Ballad of Josie, 1967 (Day 3, Krasner 4, Needham 4, Whitlock 4)

Ballad of Narayama. *See* Narayamabushi-ko, 1958

Ballad of Orin. *See* Hanare-goze Orin, 1977

Ballad of Smokey the Bear, 1966 (Cagney 3)

Ballad of the Sad Café, 1991 (Redgrave 3, Steiger 3, Lassally 4)

Ballad to Paducah Jail, 1934 (Roach 4)

Ballade de Mamlouk, 1982 (Papas 3)

Ballade parisienne, 1954 (Braunberger 4)

Ballade pour un chien, 1969 (Vanel 3)

Ballade pour un voyou, 1963 (Noiret 3)

Ballade sur les fils, 1957 (Braunberger 4)

Ballade vom Kleinen Soldaten, 1985 (Herzog 2)

Ballata di un milliardo, 1964 (Bertolucci 2)

Balle au coeur, 1965 (Theodorakis 4)

Ballerina e buon Dio, 1958 (De Sica 2)

Ballet adagio, 1972 (McLaren 4)

Ballet Black, 1986 (Johnson 3)

Ballet Dancer. *See* Balletdanserinden, 1911

Ballet do Brasil, 1962 (Pereira Dos Santos 2)

Ballet Girl. *See* Ballettens born, 1954

Ballet Japonais, 1900 (Guy 2)

Ballet Libella, 1897 (Guy 2)

Ballet Master's Dream. *See* Rêve du maître de ballet, 1903

Ballet-Oop, 1954 (Bosustow 4)

Balletdanserinden, 1911 (Nielsen 3, Psilander 3)

Ballettens born, 1954 (Fischer 4)

Ballo al castello, 1939 (Valli 3)

Balloon, 1959 (Leacock 2)

Balloonatic, 1923 (Keaton 2)

Balloonland, 1935 (Iwerks 4)

Balloons, 1923 (Fleischer 4)

Ballot Box Bunny, 1951 (Blanc 4, Freleng 4, Stalling 4)

Ballroom Tragedy, 1905 (Bitzer 4)

Ballyhoo Buster, 1928 (Brennan 3)

Balthasar. *See* Au hasard, Balthazar, 1966

Balthazar, 1938 (Berry 3)

Baltic Deputy. *See* Deputat Baltiki, 1936

Baltimore Bullet, 1979 (Coburn 3, Sharif 3)

Balún Canán, 1976 (Figueroa 4)

Bambai Ka Babu, 1960 (Anand 3)

Bambi, 1942 (Disney 4, Hubley 4)

Bambina. *See* faró da padre, 1974

Bambini chiedono perchè, 1972 (Morricone 4)

Bambini ci guardano, 1943 (De Sica 2, Mastroianni 3, Zavattini 4)

Bambini in cittá, 1946 (Comencini 2)

Bambole, 1964 (Lollobrigida 3, Vitti 3, Gherardi 4, Pinelli 4)

Bamboo Blonde, 1946 (Mann 2)

Bamboo Cross, 1955 (Ford 2)

Bamboo Doll of Echizen. *See* Echizen take ningyo, 1963

Bamboo Prison, 1954 (Guffey 4)

Bamboo Saucer, 1968 (Duryea 3, Mohr 4)

Banana da terra, 1939 (Miranda 3)

Banana Peel. *See* Peau de banane, 1963

Bananas, 1971 (Allen 2, Stallone 3, Hamlisch 4, Rosenblum 4)

Banarasi Babu, 1973 (Anand 3)

Banba no Chutaro, 1955 (Yamada 3)

Bancho sarayashiki, 1937 (Hasegawa 3, Tanaka 3)

Banco de prince, 1950 (Burel 4)

Band Master, 1917 (Laurel and Hardy 3)

Band Master, 1931 (Lantz 4)

Band of Angels, 1957 (Walsh 2, De Carlo 3, Gable 3, Poitier 3, Ballard 4, Steiner 4)

Band of Assassins. *See* Shinsen-gumi, 1969

Band of Outsiders. *See* Bande à part, 1964

Band Plays On, 1934 (Young 3)

Band Waggon, 1940 (Rank 4)

Band Wagon, 1953 (Minnelli 2, Astaire 3, Buchanan 3, Charisse 3, Gardner 3, Ames 4, Comden and Green 4, Deutsch 4, Edens 4, Freed 4, Gibbons 4, Kidd 4)

Banda degli onesti, 1956 (Age and Scarpelli 4, De Laurentiis 4)

Banda de Jaider. *See* Verflucht dies Amerika, 1973

Banda J & S, 1972 (Morricone 4)

Bande à Bébel, 1967 (Belmondo 3)

Bande à part, 1964 (Godard 2, Karina 3, Coutard 4, Guillemot 4, Legrand 4)

Bande des quatre, 1989 (Rivette 2)

Bande von Hoheneck, 1950 (Staudte 2)

Bandeau sur les yeux, 1917 (Feuillade 2)

Bandeirantes, 1940 (Mauro 2)

Bandera, 1935 (Duvivier 2, Gabin 3, Modot 3, Spaak 4)

Banderas del amanecer, 1983 (Sanjinés 2)

Bandhe Haath, 1972 (Bachchan 3)

Bandida, 1962 (Fernández 2, Armendáriz 3, Félix 3, Figueroa 4)

Bandido, 1956 (Mitchum 3, Laszlo 4, Smith 4, Steiner 4)

Bandini, 1963 (Roy 2, Burman 4)

Bandit, 1913 (Sennett 2, Arbuckle 3)

Bandit. *See* Cucaracha, 1958

Bandit and the Preacher. *See* On the Night Stage, 1914

Bandit General. *See* Torch, 1949

Bandit General. *See* Del odio nace el amor, 1950

Bandit King, 1907 (Anderson 3)

Bandit Makes Good, 1907 (Anderson 3)

Bandit of Point Loma, 1911 (Dwan 2)

Bandit of Sherwood Forest, 1946 (Wilde 3, Friedhofer 4, Gaudio 4)

Bandit of Zhobe, 1959 (Mature 3)

Bandit Trail, 1941 (Polglase 4)

Banditi a Milano, 1968 (Volonté 3, De Laurentiis 4)

Banditi a Roma. *See* Roma come Chicago, 1968

Bandito, 1946 (Lattuada 2, Magnani 3, De Laurentiis 4)

Bandit's Child, 1912 (Anderson 3)
Bandits of Corsica, 1954 (Van Cleef 3)
Bandits on the Wind. *See* Yato kaze no naka
  o hashiru, 1961
Bandit's Son, 1927 (Plunkett 4)
Bandit's Wager, 1916 (Ford 2)
Bandit's Waterloo, 1908 (Griffith 2,
  Lawrence 3)
Bandit's Wife, 1910 (Anderson 3)
Bandolero!, 1968 (Martin 3, Stewart 3,
  Welch 3, Cahn 4, Clothier 4,
  Goldsmith 4, Needham 4, Smith 4)
Bang, 1967 (Godfrey 4)
Bang!, 1986 (Breer 4)
Bang! Bang! You're Dead. *See* Our Man in
  Marrakesh, 1966
Bang the Drum Slowly, 1973 (De Niro 3)
Bangville Police, 1913 (Sennett 2)
Banished. *See* Hanare-goze Orin, 1977
Banished Orin. *See* Hanare-goze Orin, 1977
Banjo, 1947 (Beavers 3)
Banjo on My Knee, 1936 (Cromwell 2,
  Brennan 3, McCrea 3, Stanwyck 3,
  Johnson 4)
Banjun no santo-kocho, 1959 (Yamada 3)
Bank, 1915 (Bacon 2, Chaplin 2,
  Purviance 3)
Bánk bán, 1914 (Curtiz 2)
Bank Breaker. *See* Kaleidoscope, 1966
Bank Detective. *See* **Bank Dick, 1940**
Bank Dick, 1940 (Fields 3, Pangborn 3,
  Three Stooges 3, Krasner 4)
Bank Holiday, 1937 (Launder and Gilliat 2,
  Vetchinsky 4)
Bank Holiday, 1938 (Lockwood 3, Rank 4)
Bank of Departure. *See* Ruri no kishi, 1956
Bank Robbery. *See* Skok, 1969
Bank Shot, 1974 (Scott 3)
Banka, 1957 (Mori 3)
Banker's Daughter, 1910 (Walsh 2)
Banker's Daughter, 1927 (Disney 4)
Banker's Daughter, 1933 (Terry 4)
Banker's Daughters, 1910 (Griffith 2,
  Bitzer 4)
Bankkrasch Unter den Linden, 1925
  (Albers 3)
Bankokku no yuro, 1966 (Shimura 3)
Bankomatt, 1989 (Ganz 3)
Bankraub in der Rue Latour, 1961
  (Kinski 3)
Bankrupt Honeymoon, 1926 (Laurel and
  Hardy 3)
Banner, 1974 (Frampton 2)
Banner in the Sky. *See* Third Man on the
  Mountain, 1959
Bannerline, 1951 (Barrymore 3, Schnee 4)
Banner of Youth. *See* Sztandar młodych,
  1958
Banning, 1967 (Hackman 3, Wagner 3,
  Bumstead 4, Jones 4)
Banović Strahinja, 1981 (Mimica 4)
Banque, 1955 (Rabier 4)
Banque Nemo, 1934 (Meerson 4)
Banquet des fraudeurs, 1952 (Storck 2,
  Rosay 3, Schüfftan 4, Spaak 4)
Banquière, 1980 (Schneider 3, Trintignant 3)
Banshun, 1949 (Hara 3, Ryu 3)
Bansi Birju, 1972 (Bachchan 3)
Bantam Cowboy, 1928 (Plunkett 4)
Banty Raids, 1963 (Blanc 4, McKimson 4)
Banwara, 1950 (Kapoor 2)
Banware Nayan, 1950 (Kapoor 2)
Banyon, 1971 (Ferrer 3)
Banzai, 1913 (Ince 4)

Bar de la fourche, 1972 (Huppert 3, De
  Beauregard 4)
Bar du Sud, 1938 (Vanel 3)
Bar Fly, 1924 (Roach 4)
Bar L Ranch, 1930 (Canutt 4)
Bar 20, 1943 (Mitchum 3, Harlan 4,
  Wilson 4)
Bar 20 Justice, 1938 (Head 4)
Bara en danserska, 1927 (Albers 3,
  Dagover 3)
Bara en mor, 1949 (Sjöberg 2, Dahlbeck 3,
  Von Sydow 3)
Bara ikutabika, 1955 (Kyo 3)
Bara wa ikutabika, 1955 (Hasegawa 3)
Barabba, 1961 (Borgnine 3, Gassman 3,
  Kennedy 3, Mangano 3, Palance 3,
  Quinn 3, De Laurentiis 4)
Barabbas, 1953 (Sjöberg 2, Dahlbeck 3,
  Nykvist 4)
Barabbas. *See* Barabba, 1961
Barajas, aeropuerto internacional, 1950
  (Bardem 2)
Bärande hav, 1951 (Dahlbeck 3)
Barbablu, Barbablu, 1987 (Gielgud 3,
  York 3)
Barbara, 1961 (Andersson 3)
Barbara Frietchie, 1915 (Guy 2)
Barbara Frietchie, 1924 (Ince 4)
Barbara's Blindness, 1965 (Wieland 2)
Barbarella, 1968 (Vadim 2, Fonda 3, De
  Laurentiis 4, Jarre 4, Renoir 4)
Barbarian, 1921 (Crisp 3)
Barbarian, 1933 (Wood 2, Loy 3,
  Novarro 3, Adrian 4, Brown 4, Freed 4,
  Loos 4, Mayer 4, Rosson 4,
  Stothart 4)
Barbarian and the Geisha, 1958 (Huston 2,
  Jaffe 3, Wayne 3, Clarke 4, Friedhofer 4,
  LeMaire 4, Smith 4, Wheeler 4)
Barbarian, Ingomar, 1908 (Griffith 2,
  Lawrence 3, Bitzer 4)
Barbarian Queen, 1985 (Corman 2)
Barbarians. *See* Revak, lo schiavo di
  Cartagine, 1960
Barbarians, 1987 (Donaggio 4, Golan and
  Globus 4)
Barbaro del Ritmo, 1963 (Alvarez 2)
Barbarosa, 1981 (Schepisi 2)
Barbary Coast, 1935 (Hawks 2, Brennan 3,
  Carey 3, Hopkins 3, McCrea 3, Niven 3,
  Robinson 3, Day 4, Goldwyn 4, Hecht 4,
  Newman 4)
Barbary Coast Bunny, 1956 (Blanc 4,
  Jones 4, Maltese 4, Stalling 4)
Barbary Coast Gent, 1944 (Beavers 3,
  Beery 3, Carradine 3)
Barbary Pirate, 1949 (Katzman 4)
Barbary Sheep, 1917 (Tourneur 2, Carré 4,
  Zukor 4)
Barbe-Bleue. *See* Charlatan, 1901
Barbe-Bleue, 1935 (Jaubert 4)
Barbe-Bleue, 1951 (Brasseur 3, Jeanson 4,
  Matras 4, Wakhévitch 4)
Barbe-Bleue, 1972 (Burton 3, Welch 3,
  Legrand 4, Morricone 4)
Barbed Water, 1969 (Welles 2)
Barbed Wire, 1927 (Stiller 2, Negri 3,
  Banton 4, Furthman 4, Glennon 4,
  Pommer 4, Schulberg 4)
Barbed Wire, 1952 (Autry 3)
Barbeque Brawl, 1956 (Hanna and
  Barbera 4)
Barber, 1918 (Laurel and Hardy 3)
Barber Shop, 1933 (Sennett 2, Fields 3)

Barberina, die Tänzerin von Sanssouci. *See*
  Tänzerin von Sanssouci, 1933
Barberousse, 1916 (Gance 2, Burel 4,
  Gaumont 4)
Barber's Daughter, 1929 (Sennett 2)
Barboni, 1946 (Risi 2)
Barbora Hlavsová, 1942 (Frič 2)
Barbora rádí, 1935 (Heller 4)
Barbouzes, 1964 (Blier 3, Audiard 4)
Barca de oro, 1947 (Infante 3)
Barcarole. *See* Brand in der Oper, 1930
Barcarole, 1935 (Baarová 3, Feuillère 3,
  Fröhlich 3, Manès 3, Herlth 4, Röhrig 4)
Barcarolle d'amour, 1929 (Boyer 3)
Bardame, 1922 (Wagner 4)
Bardelys the Magnificent, 1926 (Florey 2,
  Vidor 2, Gilbert 3, Daniels 4, Day 4,
  Gibbons 4, Mayer 4)
Bare Essence, 1982 (Ames 4)
Bare Fists, 1919 (Ford 2, Carey 3)
Bare Knees, 1927 (Robinson 4)
Barefaced Flatfoot, 1950 (Bosustow 4,
  Burness 4, Hubley 4)
Barefoot Battalion, 1953 (Theodorakis 4)
Barefoot Boy, 1924 (Cohn 4)
Barefoot Boy, 1938 (Brown 4)
Barefoot Contessa, 1954 (Mankiewicz 2,
  Bogart 3, Brazzi 3, Gardner 3, Love 3,
  O'Brien 3, Cardiff 4, Hornbeck 4)
Barefoot in the Park, 1967 (Boyer 3,
  Fonda 3, Redford 3, Edouart 4, Head 4,
  La Shelle 4, Mercer 4, Wallis 4,
  Westmore Family 4)
Barefoot Mailman, 1951 (Duning 4)
Barfly, 1987 (Dunaway 3, Rourke 3, Golan
  and Globus 4, Müller 4)
Bargain, 1914 (Hart 3, Sullivan 4)
Bargain, 1931 (Rooney 3, Polito 4)
Bargain Daze, 1953 (Terry 4)
Bargain Hunt, 1928 (Sennett 2)
Bargain Hunters, 1914 (Beery 3)
Bargain of the Century, 1933 (Roach 4)
Bariera, 1966 (Skolimowski 2, Lomnicki 3),
  Nowicki 3)
Bariri, 1958 (Olmi 2)
Barish, 1957 (Anand 3)
Barker, 1928 (Garmes 4, Glazer 4, Grot 4,
  Mankiewicz 4)
Barking-Donkey Sonichi. *See* Shiriboe
  Sonichi, 1969
Barkleys of Broadway, 1949 (Walters 2,
  Astaire 3, Rogers 3, Alton 4, Comden
  and Green 4, Freed 4, Irene 4, Mayer 4,
  Pan 4, Stradling 4)
Barn Dance, 1929 (Disney 4, Iwerks 4)
Barnabé, 1938 (Fernandel 3)
Barnaby series, 1962 (Halas and
  Batchelor 4)
Barnaby and Me, 1977 (Frank and
  Panama 4)
Barnacle Bill, 1938 (Fleischer 4)
Barnacle Bill, 1941 (Beery 3, Gibbons 4,
  Kaper 4)
Barnacle Bill, 1957 (Guinness 3,
  Pleasence 3, Addison 4, Clarke 4,
  Slocombe 4)
Barnen från Frostmofjället, 1945 (Nykvist 4)
Barnet, 1912 (Stiller 2, Sjöström 2,
  Jaenzon 4, Magnusson 4)
Barnet, 1940 (Christensen 2)
Barney Oldfield's Race for a Life, 1913
  (Sennett 2, Normand 3)
Barnförbjudet, 1979 (Andersson 3)
Barnstormers, 1905 (Bitzer 4)

Barnum, 1986 (Schygulla 3)

Barnum and Ringling Inc., 1927 (Laurel and Hardy 3, Roach 4)

Barnum Was Right, 1929 (Beavers 3)

Barnyard series, 1936–55 (Terry 4)

Barnyard Battle, 1929 (Disney 4, Iwerks 4)

Barnyard Brat, 1939 (Fleischer 4)

Barnyard Concert, 1930 (Disney 4)

Barnyard Five, 1936 (Lantz 4)

Barnyard Flirtation. See Barnyard Flirtations, 1914

Barnyard Flirtations, 1914 (Sennett 2, Arbuckle 3)

Barocco, 1925 (Vanel 3)

Barocco, 1976 (Adjani 3, Depardieu 3, Sarde 4)

Baromètre de la fidélité, 1909 (Linder 3)

Baron, 1911 (Sennett 2)

Baron Blood. See Orrori del castello di Norimberga, 1972

Baron de Crac. See Monsieur de Crac, 1910

Baron de l'écluse, 1959 (Delannoy 2, Gabin 3, Presle 3, Audiard 4)

Baron fantôme, 1942 (Cocteau 2, Cuny 3)

Baron Munchausen. See Baron Prášil, 1961

Baron of Arizona, 1950 (Fuller 2, Bondi 3, Price 3, Howe 4)

Baron Prášil, 1961 (Brejchová 3, Brdečka 4, Zeman 4)

Baroness and the Butler, 1938 (Powell 3, La Shelle 4, Miller 4, Trotti 4)

Baroni, 1974 (Fabrizi 3)

Baroon, 1976 (Burman 4)

Baroud, 1931 (Henreid 3, Burel 4, Wakhévitch 4)

Barque en mer, 1895 (Lumière 2)

Barque sortant du port, 1895 (Lumière 2)

Barquero, 1970 (Oates 3, Van Cleef 3)

Barrabas, 1919 (Feuillade 2)

Barrage contre le Pacifique, 1958 (Mangano 3, Perkins 3, Vallie 3, De Laurentiis 4, Rota 4)

Barrage de l'Aigle, 1946 (Leenhardt 2)

Barrage du Châtelot, 1953 (Colpi 4, Fradelal 4)

Barrandov Nocturne, or How Films Dance and Sing. See Barrandovské nocturno, aneb Jak film tančil a zpíval, 1984

Barravento, 1962 (Pereira Dos Santos 2)

Barrel Full of Dollars. See Conde Dracula, 1970

Barren Gain, 1915 (Eason 4)

Barrendero, 1981 (Cantinflas 3)

Barretts of Wimpole Street, 1934 (Laughton 3, March 3, O'Sullivan 3, Shearer 3, Adrian 4, Booth 4, Daniels 4, Gibbons 4, Mayer 4, Stewart 4, Stothart 4, Thalberg 4, Vajda 4)

Barretts of Wimpole Street, 1956 (Gielgud 3, Jones 4, Junge 4, Kaper 4, Young 4)

Barricade, 1939 (Faye 3, Freund 4, Newman 4, Veiller 4)

Barricade, 1950 (Massey 3)

Barricade du point du jour, 1978 (Noiret 3)

Barrier, 1926 (Barrymore 3, Walthall 3, Mayer 4)

Barrier, 1937 (Barnes 4, Head 4)

Barrier. See Bariera, 1966

Barrier of Faith, 1915 (Talmadge 3)

Barriera delle legge, 1953 (Brazzi 3)

Barrière, 1915 (Feuillade 2, Musidora 3)

Barrières, 1949 (Christian-Jaque 2)

Barriers Burned Away. See Chicago Fire, 1925

Barrings, 1955 (Dagover 3, Tschechowa 3)

Barry, 1948 (Fresnay 3)

Barry Lyndon, 1975 (Kubrick 2, Adam 4, Alcott 4, Rosenman 4)

Barry MacKenzie Holds His Own, 1974 (Beresford 2, Pleasence 3)

Barsaat, 1949 (Kapoor 2, Nargis 3)

Barsaat Ki Ek Raat, 1981 (Bachchan 3)

Bartered Bride. See Prodaná nevěsta, 1933

Bartholomew versus the Wheel, 1964 (Blanc 4, McKimson 4)

Bartok, 1964 (Russell 2)

Baruch. See Alte Gesetz, 1923

Baruffe Chiozzotte. See Paese senza pace, 1943

Baruten Bukvar, 1977 (Dinov 4)

Barwy ochronne, 1976 (Zanussi 2)

Basant, 1943 (Biswas 4)

Baseball Bugs, 1946 (Blanc 4, Freleng 4, Maltese 4, Stalling 4)

Baseball Madness, 1917 (Swanson 3)

Bas-fonds, 1936 (Becker 2, Visconti 2, Gabin 3, Jouvet 3, Lourié 4, Spaak 4)

Bashful, 1917 (Roach 4)

Bashful Buccaneer, 1925 (Brown 4)

Bashful Buzzard, 1945 (Blanc 4, Clampett 4, Stalling 4)

Bashful Jim, 1925 (Sennett 2)

Bashful Suitor, 1921 (Astor 3)

Basic Instinct, 1992 (Goldsmith 4, Winkler 4)

Basic Training, 1971 (Wiseman 2)

Basil the Great Mouse Detective. See Great Mouse Detective, 1986

Basileus Quartet, 1984 (Cuny 3)

Basilischi, 1963 (Wertmüller 2, Di Venanzo 4, Morricone 4)

Basilisk, 1914 (Hepworth 2)

Basketball Fix, 1951 (Cortez 4, Leven 4)

Bassae, 1964 (Astruc 2)

Basta che non si sappia in giro, 1976 (Comencini 2, Age and Scarpelli 4)

Bastardi, 1968 (Hayworth 3, Kinski 3)

Bat, 1926 (Edeson 4, Menzies 4)

Bat, 1959 (Moorehead 3, Price 3, Biroc 4)

Bat 21, 1988 (Hackman 3)

Bat Whispers, 1929 (Schenck 4)

Bata no zeni: Ogon oni ranbu no maki, 1931 (Hasegawa 3)

Bataan, 1943 (Garnett 2, Taylor 3, Walker 3, Gibbons 4, Gillespie 4, Kaper 4, Mayer 4, Schary 4, Wheeler 4)

Bataille, 1923 (Hayakawa 3)

Bataille, 1933 (L'Herbier 2, Boyer 3)

Bataille d'Austerlitz, 1909 (Cohl 4)

Bataille de boules de neige, 1897 (Guy 2)

Bataille de boules de neige, 1901 (Gaumont 4)

Bataille de San Sébastian, 1967 (Bronson 3, Jaffe 3, Quinn 3, Morricone 4)

Bataille des trois rois, 1989 (Bondarchuk 3, Cardinale 3, Rey 3)

Bataille d'oreillers, 1897 (Guy 2)

Bataille d'oreillers, 1907 (Gaumont 4)

Bataille du rail, 1945 (Clement 2, Alekan 4)

Bataille silencieuse, 1937 (Fresnay 3, Simon 3)

Bataille sur le grand fleuve, 1951 (Rouch 2)

Bataillon du ciel, 1946 (Dalio 3)

Batalia pentru Roma. See Kampf um Rom, 1968

Batalla de Chile: La lucha de un pueblo sin armas, 1974 (Guzmán 2)

Batavernas trohetsed, 1957 (Fischer 4)

Batavians' Oath of Fidelity. See Batavernas trohetsed, 1957

Bateau à soupe, 1946 (Vanel 3)

Bateau d'Emile, 1961 (Brasseur 3, Girardot 3, Simon 3, Audiard 4)

Bateau de verre, 1928 (Rosay 3)

Bateau ivre, 1949 (Barrault 3)

Bateau sur l'herbe, 1971 (Cassel 3, Evein 4)

Bateliers de la Volga, 1936 (Vanel 3)

Bateliers de la Volga, 1959 (Vanel 3)

Bathers, 1900 (Hepworth 2)

Bathhouse Beauty. See Bathing Beauty, 1914

Bathhouse Blunder, 1916 (Sennett 2)

Bathhouse Scandal, 1918 (Beery 3)

Bathing Beauty, 1914 (Arbuckle 3)

Bathing Beauty, 1914 (Sennett 2)

Bathing Beauty, 1944 (Dumont 3, Rathbone 3, Williams 3, Alton 4, Green 4, Irene 4, Mayer 4, Sharaff 4, Stradling 4)

Bathroom, 1970 (Kuri 4)

Bathtub Perils, 1916 (Sennett 2)

Bâtir à notre âge, 1956 (Leenhardt 2)

Batisseurs, 1938 (Epstein 2, Honegger 4)

Batman, 1966 (Meredith 3, Smith 4)

Batman, 1989 (Nicholson 3, Palance 3)

Batman and Robin, 1949 (Katzman 4)

Batman Dracula, 1964 (Warhol 2)

Bato no zeni: Kesho-bosatsu no maki, 1931 (Hasegawa 3)

Bâton, 1946 (Braunberger 4)

Baton Bunny, 1959 (Blanc 4, Jones 4, Maltese 4)

Baton Rouge, 1988 (Maura 3)

Bats in the Belfry, 1960 (Lantz 4)

Battaglia del Sinai, 1969 (Fusco 4)

Battaglia di Algeri, 1966 (Pontecorvo 2, Morricone 4, Solinas 4)

Battaglia di Maratona, 1959 (Tourneur 2)

Battaglia di Mareth. See Grande attaco, 1977

Battaglia d'Inghilterra, 1969 (Johnson 3)

Battant, 1982 (Delon 3)

Battement de coeur, 1939 (Darrieux 3, Barsacq 4)

Battered! See Intimate Strangers, 1977

Battered, 1978 (Blondell 3)

Batticuore, 1938 (Castellani 2)

Battle, 1911 (Barrymore 3)

Battle, 1911 (Griffith 2, Crisp 3, Sweet 3, Bitzer 4)

Battle, 1923 (Fleischer 4)

Battle, 1927 (Rooney 3)

Battle, 1934 (Boyer 3, Oberon 3)

Battle at Apache Pass, 1952 (Hunter 4)

Battle at Bloody Beach, 1961 (Murphy 3)

Battle at Elderberry Gulch, 1914 (Walthall 3)

Battle at Elderbush Gulch, 1914 (Griffith 2, Gish 3, Bitzer 4)

Battle Beneath the Earth, 1967 (Love 3)

Battle Beyond the Stars, 1980 (Sayles 2, Jaffe 3)

Battle Beyond the Sun, 1962 (Corman 2, Coppola 2)

Battle Circus, 1953 (Brooks 2, Allyson 3, Bogart 3, Alton 4, Basevi 4, Berman 4)

Battle Cry, 1955 (Walsh 2, Malone 3, Massey 3, Steiner 4)

Battle Cry of Peace, 1915 (Talmadge 3)

Battle Dust. See Senjin, 1935

Battle Flag. *See* Standarte, 1977

Battle for Anzio. *See* Sbarco di Anzio, 1968

Battle for Britain, 1957 (Hawkins 3)

Battle for Midway. *See* Midway, 1976

Battle for the Planet of the Apes, 1973 (Huston 2, Landis 2, Ayres 3, McDowall 3, Dehn 4, Rosenman 4)

Battle for Tsaritsin. *See* Boi pod Tsaritsinom, 1920

Battle Hymn, 1957 (Sirk 2, Duryea 3, Hudson 3, Hunter 4, Metty 4)

Battle Hymn of the Republic, 1911 (Costello 3)

Battle in Outer Space. *See* Uchu daisensu, 1959

Battle of Algiers. *See* **Battaglia di Algeri, 1966**

Battle of Ambrose and Walrus, 1915 (Sennett 2)

Battle of Anzio. *See* Sbarco di Anzio, 1968

Battle of Apache Pass, 1952 (Salter 4)

Battle of Austerlitz. *See* Bataille d'Austerlitz, 1909

Battle of Austerlitz. *See* Austerlitz, 1960

Battle of Blood Island, 1959 (Corman 2)

Battle of Britain. *See* **Why We Fight series, 1943–45**

Battle of Britain, 1969 (Caine 3, Howard 3, More 3, Olivier 3, Richardson 3, Shaw 3, York 3, Arnold 4, Walton 4, Young 4)

Battle of Broadway, 1938 (Darwell 3, McDaniel 3, McLaglen 3)

Battle of Chile: The Struggle of an Unarmed People. *See* **Batalla de Chile: La lucha de un pueblo sin armas, 1974**

Battle of China. *See* **Why We Fight series, 1943–45**

Battle of Elderbush Gulch, 1914 (Barrymore 3, Marsh 3)

Battle of Gettysburg, 1913 (Ince 4, Sullivan 4)

Battle of Gettysburg, 1956 (Deutsch 4, Folsey 4, Schary 4)

Battle of Hawaii. *See* Hawaii marei oki haisen, 1942

Battle of Kawanakajima. *See* Kawanakajima gassen, 1941

Battle of Love, 1914 (Bushman 3)

Battle of Marathon. *See* Battaglia di Maratona, 1959

Battle of Midway, 1942 (Ford 2, Crisp 3, Darwell 3, Newman 4,

Battle of Midway. *See* Midway, 1976

Battle of Neretva. *See* Bitka na Neretvi, 1969

Battle of Neretva, 1970 (Welles 2)

Battle of New Orleans, 1960 (Godfrey 4)

Battle of Paris, 1929 (Porter 4, Ruttenberg 4)

Battle of Rogue River, 1954 (Katzman 4)

Battle of Russia. *See* **Why We Fight series, 1943–45**

Battle of San Pietro, 1944 (Tiomkin 4)

Battle of Stalingrad. *See* Stalingradskaya bitva, 1949

Battle of the Astros. *See* Kaiju daisenso, 1966

Battle of the Bulge, 1965 (Andrews 3, Bronson 3, Fonda 3, Ryan 3, Shaw 3, Lourié 4)

Battle of the Century, 1927 (Stevens 2, Laurel and Hardy 3, Bruckman 4, Roach 4)

Battle of the Coral Sea, 1959 (Robertson 3)

Battle of the Japan Sea. *See* Nippon-kai dai-kaisen, 1969

Battle of the Rails. *See* **Bataille du rail, 1945**

Battle of the Red Men, 1912 (Ince 4)

Battle of the River Plate, 1956 (Finch 3, Lee 3, Quayle 3, Challis 4, Heckroth 4, Rank 4)

Battle of the Sexes, 1914 (Griffith 2, Crisp 3, Gish 3, Bitzer 4)

Battle of the Sexes, 1928 (Griffith 2, Bitzer 4, Schenck 4, Struss 4)

Battle of the Sexes, 1959 (Crichton 2, Pleasence 3, Sellers 3, Francis 4)

Battle of the V 1, 1958 (Lee 3, Adam 4)

Battle of the Villa Fiorita, 1965 (Daves 2, Brazzi 3, O'Hara 3, Dillon 4, Morris 4)

Battle of the Worlds. *See* Planet degli uomini spenti, 1960

Battle of Three Kings. *See* Bataille des trois rois, 1989

Battle of Who Run, 1913 (Sennett 2, Normand 3)

Battle of Wills, 1913 (Dwan 2)

Battle on the Neretva. *See* Bitka na Neretvi, 1969

Battle Royal, 1916 (Laurel and Hardy 3)

Battle Royal, 1918 (Sennett 2)

Battle Royal, 1936 (Lantz 4, Terry 4)

Battle Squadron. *See* Battaglia d'Inghilterra, 1969

Battle Stations, 1944 (Cagney 3, Rogers 3, Tracy 3, Kanin 4)

Battle Stations, 1956 (Bendix 3, Guffey 4)

Battle Taxi, 1954 (Hayden 3)

Battle under the Walls of Kerchenetz, 1971 (Ivanov-Vano 4, Norstein 4)

Battle without Weapons. *See* Buki naki tatakai, 1960

Battle Zone, 1952 (Wanger 4)

Battleground, 1911 (Dwan 2)

Battleground, 1949 (Wellman 2, Johnson 3, Gibbons 4, Schary 4)

Battles of Chief Pontiac, 1952 (Bernstein 4)

Battleship Gallactica, 1978 (Astaire 3)

Battleship Potemkin. *See* **Bronenosets Potemkin, 1925**

Battleship Potemkin Survivor, 1968 (Lassally 4)

Battleships, 1911 (Dwan 2)

Battleshock. *See* Woman's Devotion, 1956

Battlestar Galactica, 1978 (Milland 3)

Battletruck, 1981 (Menges 4)

Battling Buckaroos, 1933 (Canutt 4)

Battling Butler, 1926 (Keaton 2, Schenck 4)

Battling Fool, 1924 (Van Dyke 2)

Battling Jane, 1918 (Zukor 4)

Battling Oriole, 1970 (Stevens 2)

Battling Orioles, 1924 (Roach 4)

Battling with Buffalo Bill, 1931 (Canutt 4)

Baty Baseball, 1944 (Avery 4)

Bauer von Babylon, 1983 (Moreau 3)

Baule-les-pins, 1990 (Baye 3, Sarde 4,)

Bavu, 1923 (Beery 3)

Bawdy Adventures of Tom Jones, 1975 (Howard 3, Terry-Thomas 3)

Baxter, 1972 (Cassel 3, Neal 3, Unsworth 4)

Baxter, Vera Baxter, 1977 (Duras 2, Depardieu 3, Seyrig 3, Vierny 4)

Bay Boy, 1985 (Ullmann 3)

Bay of Angels. *See* Baie des anges, 1963

Bay of Rocks, 1976 (Xie 2)

Bay of St. Michel, 1963 (Zetterling 2)

Bay of the Angels. *See* Baie des anges, 1963

Bayaya. *See* Bajaja, 1950

Baza ludzi umarllych, 1959 (Lomnicki 3)

Bazaar, 1982 (Patil 3)

Bazoku geisha, 1954 (Kyo 3)

BBC: Droitwich, 1934 (Grierson 2, Watt 2)

BBC: The Voice of Britain, 1935 (Grierson 2)

Be Big, 1930 (Laurel and Hardy 3)

Be Careful. *See* Hansom Cabman, 1924

Be Careful!, 1944 (Gable 3)

Be Happy These Two Lovers. *See* Kono futari ni sachi are, 1957

Be Honest, 1923 (Roach 4)

Be Human, 1936 (Fleischer 4)

Be Kind to Animals, 1935 (Fleischer 4)

Be Mine Tonight, 1932 (Litvak 2)

Be My Wife, 1919 (Daniels 3, Lloyd 3, Roach 4)

Be My Wife, 1921 (Linder 3)

Be Reasonable, 1922 (Sennett 2)

Be Safe or Be Sorry, 1955 (Peries 2)

Be Up to Date, 1938 (Fleischer 4)

Be Your Age, 1926 (McCarey 2, Laurel and Hardy 3, Roach 4)

Be Yourself, 1930 (Menzies 4, Schenck 4, Struss 4)

Beach Ball, 1965 (Corman 2)

Beach Blanket Bingo, 1965 (Keaton 2, Crosby 4)

Beach Club, 1928 (Sennett 2, Lombard 3)

Beach Combers, 1936 (Lantz 4)

Beach House. *See* Cassoto, 1980

Beach Nut, 1919 (Beery 3)

Beach Nuts, 1918 (Lloyd 3, Roach 4)

Beach Pajamas, 1931 (Arbuckle 3)

Beach Party, 1963 (Malone 3, Price 3)

Beach Red, 1967 (Wilde 3)

Beachcomber, 1915 (Bosworth 3)

Beachcomber. *See* Vessel of Wrath, 1938

Beachcomber, 1939 (Head 4)

Beachcomber, 1954 (Newton 3, Pleasence 3, Rank 4)

Beachcomber, 1955 (Box 4)

Beaches, 1988 (Midler 3, Delerue 4)

Beachhead, 1954 (Curtis 3)

Beaded Buckskin Bag, 1913 (Bosworth 3)

Beaks to the Grindstone, 1985 (Godfrey 4)

Beanstalk Bunny, 1955 (Blanc 4, Jones 4, Maltese 4, Stalling 4)

Beanstalk Jack, 1933 (Terry 4)

Beanstalk Jack, 1946 (Terry 4)

Bear, 1984 (Stanton 3)

Bear. *See* Ours, 1988

Bear Affair, 1915 (Sennett 2)

Bear Escape, 1912 (Sennett 2)

Bear Facts. *See* Porky's Baseball Broadcast, 1940

Bear Feat, 1949 (Blanc 4, Jones 4, Stalling 4)

Bear for Punishment, 1951 (Blanc 4, Jones 4, Stalling 4)

Bear Hug, 1963 (Hanna and Barbera 4)

Bear Island, 1979 (Redgrave 3, Lee 3, Sutherland 3, Widmark 3)

Bear Knuckles, 1963 (Hanna and Barbera 4)

Bear of a Story, 1916 (Mix 3)

Bear That Wasn't, 1967 (Jones 4)

Bear Up, 1963 (Hanna and Barbera 4)

Bear Ye One Another's Burden, 1910 (Lawrence 3)

Bearded Bandit, 1910 (Anderson 3)

Bearded Youth, 1911 (Sennett 2)

Bearer of the Golden Star. *See* Knight of the Gold Star, 1950

Bearly Able, 1962 (Hanna and Barbera 4)

Bearn, 1983 (Rey 3)

Bears and Bad Men, 1918 (Laurel and Hardy 3)

Bear's Tale, 1940 (Avery 4, Blanc 4, Stalling 4)

Bear's Wedding. *See* Medvezhya svadba, 1926

Beast. *See* Bête, 1974

Beast Alley. *See* Kemonomichi, 1965

Beast at Bay, 1912 (Griffith 2, Pickford 3, Bitzer 4)

Beast from a Haunted Cave, 1959 (Corman 2)

Beast from 20,000 Fathoms, 1953 (Van Cleef 3, Boyle 4, Harryhausen 4, Lourié 4)

Beast Must Die, 1974 (Cushing 3)

Beast of Hollow Mountain, 1956 (O'Brien 4)

Beast of Prey. *See* Dravci, 1948

Beast of the City, 1932 (Harlow 3, Huston 3, Rooney 3, Burnett 4)

Beast with Five Fingers, 1947 (Florey 2, Lorre 3, Friedhofer 4, Siodmak 4, Steiner 4)

Beast with 1,000,000 Eyes, 1955 (Corman 2)

Beastmaster, 1982 (Alcott 4)

Beasts of Berlin. *See* Hitler, Beast of Berlin, 1939

Beasts of the Jungle, 1913 (Guy 2)

Beat Girl, 1960 (Lee 3, Reed 3, Barry 4, Lassally 4)

Beat It, 1918 (Daniels 3, Lloyd 3, Roach 4)

Beat Me Daddy, Eight to the Bar!, 1940 (Krasner 4)

Beat the Devil, 1954 (Clayton 2, Huston 2, Bogart 3, Jones 3, Lollobrigida 3, Lorre 3, Francis 4, Morris 4)

Beat 13. *See* Třináctý revír, 1945

Beata Loro, 1975 (Cristaldi 4)

Beating Hearts and Carpets, 1915 (Sennett 2)

Beating He Needed, 1912 (Sennett 2)

Beating the Game, 1921 (Gibbons 4)

Beatnik et le minet, 1967 (Leenhardt 2)

Beatrice, 1919 (Bertini 3)

Beatrice Cenci, 1926 (Amidei 4)

Beatrice Cenci, 1941 (Stallich 4)

Beatrice Cenci, 1956 (Cervi 3, Presle 3)

Beatrice devant le désir, 1944 (Berry 3, Signoret 3, Wakhévitch 4)

Beau and Arrows, 1932 (Lantz 4)

Beau Beste, 1933 (Lantz 4)

Beau Broadway, 1928 (Gibbons 4)

Beau Brummel, 1913 (Ingram 2)

Beau Brummel, 1924 (Astor 3, Barrymore 3)

Beau Brummell, 1954 (Granger 3, Love 3, Taylor 3, Ustinov 3, Francis 4, Junge 4, Morris 4)

Beau Chumps, *See* Beau Hunks, 1931

Beau fixe, 1953 (Legrand 4)

Beau Geste, 1926 (Brenon 2, Colman 3, McLaglen 3, Powell 3, Hunt 4, Zukor 4)

Beau Geste, 1939 (Wellman 2, Milland 3, Crawford 3, Hayward 3, Milland 3, O'Connor 3, Preston 3, Dreier 4, Head 4, Newman 4)

Beau Geste, 1966 (Bumstead 4, Needham 4, Salter 4, Whitlock 4)

Beau Hunks, 1931 (Laurel and Hardy 3, Roach 4)

Beau Ideal, 1931 (Brenon 2, Young 3, Hunt 4, Steiner 4)

Beau James, 1957 (Durante 3, Hope 3, Cahn 4, Head 4)

Beau Jour de noces, 1932 (Fernandel 3)

Beau père, 1981 (Blier 2, Baye 3, Sarde 4, Vierny 4)

Beau Plaisir, 1969 (Perrault 2)

Beau Revel, 1921 (Ince 4)

Beau Sabreur, 1928 (Cooper 3, Powell 3, Banton 4, Zukor 4)

Beau Serge, 1958 (Broca 2, Chabrol 2, Decaë 4, Rabier 4)

Beau temps, mais orageux en fin de journée, 1986 (Presle 3)

Beau Voyage, 1947 (Matras 4)

Beaubourg, 1977 (Almendros 4)

Beauté de l'effort, 1953 (Decaë 4)

Beauté du diable, 1949 (Clair 2, Modot 3, Philipe 3, Simon 3, Barsacq 4, Di Venanzo 4)

Beauties of the Night. *See* Belles de nuit, 1952

Beautiful Banff and Lake Louise, 1935 (Hoch 4)

Beautiful Blonde from Bashful Bend, 1949 (Sturges 2, Grable 3, Trumbo 4)

Beautiful Budapest, 1938 (Hoch 4)

Beautiful But Dangerous. *See* She Couldn't Say No, 1954

Beautiful But Dangerous. *See* Donna più bella del mondo, 1955

Beautiful But Deadly. *See* Don Is Dead, 1973

Beautiful But Poor. *See* La Belle ma povere, 1957

Beautiful Cheat, 1945 (Banton 4)

Beautiful City, 1925 (Goulding 2, Barthelmess 3, Powell 3)

Beautiful Fraud. *See* American Beauty, 1927

Beautiful Gambler, 1921 (Barnes 4)

Beautiful Katya. *See* Krasavice Kaťa, 1919

Beautiful Liar, 1921 (Schulberg 4)

Beautiful Margaret. *See* Tout Petit Faust, 1910

Beautiful Nuisance. *See* On peut le dire sans se fâcher!, 1978

Beautiful Rebel. *See* Janice Meredith, 1924

Beautiful Sinner, 1924 (Van Dyke 2)

Beautiful Stranger, 1954 (Baker 3, Ferrer 3, Lom 3, Rogers 3, Arnold 4)

Beautiful Swindlers. *See* Plus Belles Escroqueries du monde, 1964

Beautiful Voice, 1911 (Sennett 2)

Beauty. *See* Beauty for Sale, 1933

Beauty. *See* Reijin, 1946

Beauty and the Barge, 1937 (Hawkins 3, Rutherford 3)

Beauty and the Beast, 1934 (Freleng 4)

Beauty and the Beast. *See* **Belle et la bête, 1946**

Beauty and the Beast, 1962 (Friedhofer 4, Pierce 4)

Beauty and the Beast, 1976 (Scott 3)

Beauty and the Beast, 1983 (Kinski 3)

Beauty and the Beast, 1987 (Golan and Globus 4)

Beauty and the Bunglers, 1915 (Sennett 2)

Beauty and the Bus, 1933 (Roach 4)

Beauty and the Devil. *See* Beauté du Diable, 1949

Beauty and the Dragon. *See* Bijo to kairyu, 1955

Beauty and the Robot. *See* Sex Kittens Go to College, 1960

Beauty and the Rogue, 1918 (King 2, Seitz 4)

Beauty Capital. *See* Bibou no miyako, 1957

Beauty for Sale, 1934 (Adrian 4, Howe 4)

Beauty for the Asking, 1939 (Ball 3)

Beauty on the Beach, 1950 (Terry 4)

Beauty Prize. *See* Prix de beauté, 1930

Beauty Shop. *See* Schönheit-spflästerchen, 1937

Beauty Shop, 1950 (Terry 4)

Beauty Shoppe, 1936 (Lantz 4)

Beauty Treatment, 1980 (Halas and Batchelor 4)

Beauty's Daughter, 1935 (Dwan 2, Bellamy 3, Darwell 3, Trevor 3, Levien 4, Maté 4, Seitz 4)

Beauty's Worth, 1922 (Davies 3)

Beaux Arts mysterieux, 1910 (Cohl 4)

Beaux Jours, 1935 (Barrault 3, Simon 3, D'Eaubonne 4, Meerson 4, Spaak 4)

Beaux-Arts de Jocko, 1909 (Cohl 4)

Beaver Trouble, 1951 (Terry 4)

Bébé series, 1910 (Feuillade 2)

Bébé de l'escadron, 1935 (Brasseur 3, Simon 3, Douy 4, Lourié 4)

Bébé embarrassant, 1905 (Guy 2)

Bebek, 1973 (Andersson 3)

Bebo's Girl. *See* Ragazza di Bube, 1963

Because He Loved Her, 1916 (Sennett 2)

Because He's My Friend, 1978 (Black 3)

Because I Loved You. *See* Dich hab' ich geliebt, 1929

Because of Him, 1946 (Durbin 3, Laughton 3, Mohr 4, Plunkett 4, Rozsa 4)

Because of You, 1952 (Young 3, Metty 4)

Because They're Young, 1960 (Weld 3, Williams 4)

Because You're Mine, 1952 (Green 4, Pasternak 4, Rose 4, Ruttenberg 4,)

Because You're Mine, 1953 (Cahn 4)

Becket, 1964 (Burton 3, Cervi 3, Gielgud 3, O'Toole 3, Anhalt 4, Mathieson 4, Unsworth 4, Wallis 4)

Beckoning Flame, 1916 (Sullivan 4)

Becky, 1927 (Gibbons 4)

Becky Sharp, 1935 (Mamoulian 2, Hopkins 3, Cooper 4, MacGowan 4, Steiner 4)

Becoming Colette, 1991 (Huppert 3)

Becsapott újságíró, 1914 (Korda 2, Korda 4)

Bed. *See* Secrets d'alcove, 1954

Bed and Board. *See* Domicile conjugal, 1970

Bed of Roses, 1922 (Roach 4)

Bed of Roses, 1933 (Darwell 3, McCrea 3, Pangborn 3, Cooper 4, Polglase 4, Rosher 4, Steiner 4)

Bed Sitting Room, 1969 (Lester 2, Moore 3, Richardson 3, Watkin 4)

Bed's Breakfast, 1930 (Launder and Gilliat 2)

Bedazzled, 1967 (Donen 2, Moore 3, Welch 3)

Bedelia, 1930 (Fleischer 4)

Bedelia, 1946 (Lockwood 3, Young 4)

Bedevilled, 1955 (Leisen 2, Baxter 3, Alwyn 4, Junge 4, Rose 4)

Bedevilled Rabbit, 1957 (Blanc 4, McKimson 4)

Bedford Incident, 1965 (Poitier 3, Sutherland 3, Widmark 3)

Bedingung—Kein Anhang, 1914 (Lubitsch 2)

Bedknobs and Broomsticks, 1971 (Stevenson 2, Jaffe 3, Lansbury 3, McDowall 3, Ellenshaw 4)

Bedlam, 1946 (Karloff 3, D'Agostino 4, Lewton 4, Musuraca 4)

Bedlam in Paradise, 1955 (Three Stooges 3)

Bedroom Blunder, 1917 (Sennett 2)

Bedroom Window, 1987 (Huppert 3, Towne 4)

Bedside, 1934 (Florey 2, Beavers 3, Orry-Kelly 4)

Bedtime, 1923 (Fleischer 4)

Bedtime for Bonzo, 1951 (Reagan 3, Fleischer 4)

Bedtime for Sniffles, 1940 (Blanc 4, Jones 4, Stalling 4)

Bedtime Story, 1933 (Chevalier 3, Horton 3, Glazer 4, Johnson 4, Lang 4, Young 4)

Bedtime Story, 1941 (Arden 3, March 3, Benchley 4, Irene 4, Schulberg 4, Walker 4, Young 4)

Bedtime Story, 1964 (Brando 3, Dern 3, Niven 3, Salter 4)

Bedtime with Rosie, 1974 (Dors 3)

Bedtime Worries, 1933 (Roach 4)

Bee and the Dove, 1950 (Popescu-Gopo 4)

Bee-devilled Bruin, 1949 (Blanc 4, Jones 4, Stalling 4)

Beef and the Banana. See Biffen och Bananen, 1951

Beef-for and After, 1962 (Hanna and Barbera 4)

Beekeeper. See O Melissokomos, 1986

Beekeeper Dies—The Other Tale. See Melissokomos Patheni—O Alles Mythos, 1986

Beelzebub's Daughters. See Filles du Diable, 1903

Beep Beep, 1952 (Jones 4, Maltese 4, Stalling 4)

Beep Prepared, 1961 (Blanc 4, Jones 4)

Beer and Pretzels, 1933 (Three Stooges 3)

Beer Barrel Polecats, 1946 (Three Stooges 3)

Bees, 1978 (Corman 2, Carradine 3)

Bee's Buzz, 1929 (Sennett 2)

Bees in His Bonnet, 1918 (Daniels 3, Lloyd 3, Roach 4)

Bees in Paradise, 1944 (Rank 4)

Beethoven, 1927 (Kortner 3)

Beethoven, le voleur de femmes. See Grand Amour de Beethoven, 1937

Beethoven's Nephew. See Neveu de Beethoven, 1985

Beetlejuice, 1988 (Sidney 3)

Before Breakfast, 1919 (Daniels 3, Lloyd 3, Roach 4)

Before Dawn, 1933 (Darwell 3, Fort 4, Steiner 4)

Before Him All Rome Trembled. See Devanti a lui tremava tutta Roma, 1946

Before I Hang, 1940 (Karloff 3, Brown 4)

Before Matriculation. See Pred maturitou, 1932

Before Midnight, 1925 (Furthman 4)

Before Midnight, 1934 (Bellamy 3)

Before She Met Me, 1991 (Shepard 4)

Before the Dawn. See Yoake mae, 1953

Before the Monsoon, 1979 (Menges 4)

Before the Nickelodeon, 1982 (Sweet 3)

Before the Public, 1922 (Roach 4)

Before the Raid, 1943 (Weiss 2, Dalrymple 4)

Before the Revolution. See Prima della revoluzione, 1964

Before the White Man Came, 1912 (Reid 3)

Before Winter Comes, 1969 (Hurt 3, Karina 3, Niven 3, Quayle 3, Topol 3)

Befriete Hände, 1939 (Hoffmann 4)

Beg, 1971 (Batalov 3)

Beg, Borrow, or Steal, 1937 (Daniels 4)

Begegnung in Rom. See Parigina a Roma, 1954

Begegnung mit Fritz Lang, 1963 (Godard 2)

Beggar. See Tainstvennie nekto, 1914

Beggar Life. See Svět, kde se žebrá, 1938

Beggar Maid, 1921 (Astor 3)

Beggar of Cawnpore, 1916 (Sullivan 4)

Beggar on Horseback, 1925 (Cruze 2, Horton 3, Brown 4)

Beggar Prince, 1920 (Hayakawa 3)

Beggar's Deceit, 1900 (Hepworth 2)

Beggars in Ermine, 1934 (Walthall 3)

Beggars of Life, 1928 (Wellman 2, Beery 3, Brooks 3, Glazer 4)

Beggar's Opera. See **Dreigroschenoper, 1931**

Beggar's Opera, 1953 (Olivier 3, Green 4, Wakhévitch 4)

Beggar's Uproar, 1980 (Halas and Batchelor 4)

Beggar's Uproar, 1989 (Halas and Batchelor 4)

Beginning of the End, 1947 (Edwards 2, Walker 3, Gillespie 4, Irene 4)

Begone Dull Care, 1949 (McLaren 4)

Begreite Hände, 1939 (Tschechowa 3)

Begstvo Puankare, 1932 (Ptushko 4)

Beguiled, 1971 (Siegel 2, Eastwood 3, Page 3, Schifrin 4, Westmore Family 4)

Behave Yourself, 1951 (Winters 3, Howe 4, Krasna 4, Orry-Kelly 4, Wald 4)

Behemoth, the Sea Monster. See Giant Behemoth, 1959

Behind Closed Doors, 1931 (Wilson 4)

Behind Closed Doors. See S vyloučenim veřejnosti, 1933

Behind Closed Doors, 1988 (Jarman 2)

Behind Closed Shutters. See Persiane chiuse, 1951

Behind Jury Doors, 1932 (Eason 4)

Behind Locked Doors, 1948 (Boetticher 2)

Behind Office Doors, 1931 (Astor 3, Hunt 4)

Behind That Curtain, 1929 (Karloff 3, Fox 4, Levien 4)

Behind the Closed Shutters. See Persiane chiuse, 1951

Behind the Counter, 1927 (Horton 3)

Behind the Door, 1919 (Beery 3, Bosworth 3, Ince 4)

Behind the Door. See Man with Nine Lives, 1940

Behind the Door. See Oltre la porta, 1982

Behind the Front, 1926 (Beery 3)

Behind the Green Lights, 1935 (Lewis 2)

Behind the Headlines, 1937 (Metty 4)

Behind the High Wall, 1956 (Sidney 3)

Behind the Iron Mask, 1977 (De Havilland 3)

Behind the Iron Mask. See Fifth Musketeer, 1979

Behind the Lines, 1980 (Johnson 3)

Behind the Make-Up, 1930 (Arzner 2, Francis 3, Lukas 3, Powell 3, Wray 3, Estabrook 4, Lang 4, Miller 4)

Behind the Mask, 1917 (Guy 2)

Behind the Mask, 1932 (Karloff 3, Swerling 4)

Behind the Mask, 1958 (Redgrave 3, Redgrave 3, Krasker 4)

Behind the Meat Ball, 1945 (Blanc 4, Stalling 4)

Behind the News, 1940 (Schary 4)

Behind the Rising Sun, 1943 (Dmytryk 2, Ryan 3, Metty 4)

Behind the Scenes, 1908 (Griffith 2, Lawrence 3)

Behind the Scenes, 1914 (Pickford 3)

Behind the Screen. See Kulissi ekrana, 1916

Behind the Screen, 1916 (Bacon 2, Chaplin 2, Purviance 3)

Behind the Shutters. See Corrupcion de Chris Miller, 1973

Behind the Shutters. See Bakom Jalusin, 1984

Behind the Silence. See Detras del silencio, 1972

Behind the Spanish Lines, 1938 (Dickinson 2)

Behind the Stockade, 1911 (Ince 4)

Behind the Veil, 1914 (Weber 2)

Behind the Wall. See Za sciana, 1971

Behold a Pale Horse, 1964 (Zinnemann 2, Peck 3, Quinn 3, Sharif 3, Jarre 4, Trauner 4)

Behold My Wife, 1935 (Leisen 2, Sheridan 3, Sidney 3, Schulberg 4, Shamroy 4, Zukor 4)

Behold This Woman, 1924 (Blackton 2)

Behold Thy Son. See Kiiroi karasu, 1957

Behold We Live. See If I Were Free, 1933

Beichte einer Toten, 1920 (Krauss 3)

Beiden Gatten der Frau Ruth, 1919 (Galeen 4)

Beiden Rivalen, 1914 (Warm 4)

Beil von Wandsbek, 1949 (Staudte 2)

Being, 1983 (Ferrer 3, Malone 3)

Being There, 1979 (Ashby 2, Douglas 3, MacLaine 3, Sellers 3)

Beispiellose Verteidigung der Festung Deutschkreuz, 1966 (Herzog 2)

Bekenntnis der Ina Kahr, 1954 (Pabst 2)

Bekenntnisse des Hochstaplers Felix Krull, 1957 (Dagover 3, Herlth 4)

Bel Age, 1958 (Cloquet 4, Delerue 4, Vierny 4)

Bel ami, 1939 (Tschechowa 3)

Bel Ami, 1954 (Eisler 4, Barsacq 4)

Bel Indifférent, 1957 (Demy 2, Cocteau 4, Evein 4, Fradetal 4, Jarre 4)

Bela Lugosi Meets a Brooklyn Gorilla, 1952 (Lugosi 3)

Belges et la mer, 1954 (Storck 2)

Belgian, 1918 (Olcott 2)

Belgian Grand Prix, 1955 (Haanstra 2)

Belgique nouvelle, 1937 (Storck 2)

Believe in Me, 1971 (Winkler 4)

Believe It or Else, 1939 (Avery 4)

Believe Me Xanthippe. See Believe Me Xantippe, 1918

Believe Me Xantippe, 1918 (Cruze 2, Crisp 3, Reid 3)

Believed Violent. See Presumé dangereux, 1990

Believers, 1987 (Schlesinger 2, Sheen 3, Müller 4)

Belinski, 1953 (Kozintsev 2, Moskvin 4, Shostakovich 4)

Belizaire the Cajun, 1986 (Duvall 3)

Bell, Book, and Candle, 1958 (Lanchester 3, Lemmon 3, Novak 3, Stewart 3, Duning 4, Howe 4, Taradash 4)

Bell Boy, 1918 (Keaton 2, Arbuckle 3)

Bell for Adano, 1945 (King 2, Bendix 3, Dalio 3, Tierney 3, La Shelle 4, Newman 4, Raine 4, Trotti 4)

Bell Hoppy, 1954 (Blanc 4, McKimson 4, Stalling 4)

Bell of Austi, 1914 (Ince 4)

Bell ouvrage, 1943 (Alekan 4)
Bella di Lodi, 1962 (Delli Colli 4)
Bella di Roma, 1955 (Comencini 2, Sordi 3, Rota 4)
Bella Donna, 1915 (Porter 2)
Bella Donna, 1923 (Menjou 3, Negri 3, Miller 4, Zukor 4)
Bella Donna, 1934 (Veidt 3)
Bella Donna, 1982 (Josephson 3)
Bella mugnaia, 1955 (De Sica 2, Loren 3, De Laurentiis 4, Ponti 4)
Belladonna, 1981 (Theodorakis 4)
Bellamy Trial, 1929 (Gibbons 4, Miller 4)
Bell' Antonio, 1960 (Pasolini 2, Brasseur 3, Cardinale 3, Mastroianni 3)
Bella's Elopement, 1914 (Costello 3)
Bell-Bottom George, 1943 (Formby 3)
Bellboy, 1960 (Lewis 2, Bumstead 4, Head 4)
Belle, 1973 (Delvaux 2, Cloquet 4)
Belle Américaine, 1961 (Cloquet 4)
Belle au bois dormant, 1935 (Alexeieff and Parker 4)
Belle Aventure. See Schöne Abenteuer, 1932
Belle Aventure, 1942 (Presle 3, Jourdan 3, Achard 4, Auric 4, Burel 4)
Belle Captive, 1983 (Alekan 4, Robbe-Grillet 4)
Belle Comme la mort, 1941 (Volkov 2)
Belle Dame sans merci, 1920 (Dulac 2)
Belle de Cadix, 1953 (Barsacq 4)
Belle de jour, 1966 (Buñuel 2, Deneuve 3, Piccoli 3, Carrière 4, Hakim 4, Vierney 4)
Belle de Paris. See Under My Skin, 1949
Belle della notte. See Belles de nuit, 1952
Belle dell'aria, 1958 (Cervi 3)
Belle Emmerdeuse. See On peut le dire sans se fâther!, 1978
Belle Equipe, 1936 (Duvivier 2, Gabin 3, Vanel 3, Spaak 4)
Belle et la bête, 1946 (Cocteau 2, Marais 3, Alekan 4, Auric 4)
Belle et le bête, 1899 (Pathé 4)
Belle et l'empereur, 1959 (Matras 4)
Belle Etoile, 1938 (Simon 3, Wakhévitch 4)
Belle étoile, 1966 (Prévert 4)
Belle famiglie, 1964 (Girardot 3)
Belle Fille comme moi, 1972 (Truffaut 2, Delerue 4)
Belle frégate, 1942 (Spaak 4)
Belle Garce, 1930 (Manès 3)
Belle Garce, 1947 (Spaak 4)
Belle humeur series, 1921–22 (Feuillade 2)
Belle Journée, 1954 (Cloquet 4)
Belle Journée, 1972 (Colpi 4)
Belle le Grand, 1951 (Dwan 2, Young 4)
Belle ma povere, 1957 (Delli Colli 4)
Belle Marinière, 1932 (Delannoy 2, Gabin 3, Archard 4, Maté 4)
Belle Marinière, 1963 (Cloquet 4)
Belle Meunière, 1948 (Pagnol 2)
Belle mugnaia, 1955 (Mastroianni 3)
Belle Nivernaise, 1923 (Epstein 2)
Belle Noiseuse, 1990 (Rivette 2, Piccoli 3)
Belle of New York, 1919 (Davies 3, Freed 4, Mercer 4)
Belle of New York, 1952 (Walters 2, Astaire 3, Alton 4, Deutsch 4, Freed 4, Mercer 4, Rose 4, Smith 4)
Belle of Siskiyou, 1913 (Anderson 3)
Belle of the Nineties, 1934 (Dmytryk 2, McCarey 2, West 3, Banton 4, Dreier 4, Struss 4, Zukor 4)

Belle of the Yukon, 1944 (Scott 3, Fields 4)
Belle of Yorktown, 1913 (Ince 4)
Belle Otéro, 1954 (Félix 3)
Belle que voilà, 1949 (Morgan 3, Douy 4, Kosma 4)
Belle Russe, 1919 (Bara 3)
Belle Starr, 1941 (Andrews 3, Beavers 3, Scott 3, Tierney 3, Banton 4, Day 4, MacGowan 4, Newman 4, Trotti 4)
Belle Starr, 1980 (Alonzo 4)
Belle Starr's Daughter, 1948 (Burnett 4)
Belle's Beau, 1910 (White 3)
Belles dents, 1966 (Gélin 3)
Belles de nuit, 1952 (Clair 2, Lollobrigida 3, Philipe 3, Barsacq 4)
Belles of St. Clement's, 1936 (Havelock-Allan 4)
Belles of St. Trinian's, 1954 (Launder and Gilliat 2, Sim 3, Arnold 4, Korda 4)
Belles on Their Toes, 1952 (Loy 3, Carmichael 4, Jeakins 4, LeMaire 4)
Bellezza del mondo, 1926 (De Sica 2)
Bellissima, 1951 (Rosi 2, Visconti 2, Zeffirelli 2, Magnani 3, Cecchi D'Amico 4, Zavattini 4)
Bellissimo novembre, 1968 (Lollobrigida 3, Morricone 4)
Bellman. See Sortiléges, 1944
Bello mia bellezza mia, 1982 (Giannini 3, Rotunno 4)
Bello, onesto, emigrato Australia sposerebbe compaesana illibata, 1971 (Cardinale 3)
Bells, 1926 (Barrymore 3, Johnson 3, Karloff 3)
Bells, 1982 (Houseman 4)
Bells Are Ringing, 1960 (Minnelli 2, Holliday 3, Martin 3, Ames 4, Comden and Green 4, Freed 4, Krasner 4, Plunkett 4, Previn 4)
Bells Go Down, 1943 (Dearden 2, Mason 3, Balcon 4)
Bells of Capistrano, 1942 (Autry 3)
Bells of Colorado, 1950 (Rogers 3)
Bells of Rosarita, 1945 (Rogers 3)
Bells of St. Mary's, 1945 (McCarey 2, Bergman 3, Crosby 3, Barnes 4, D'Agostino 4, Head 4, Nichols 4)
Bells of San Angelo, 1947 (Rogers 3)
Belly of an Architect, 1987 (Greenaway 2, Vierny 4)
Beloe solntse pustiny, 1969 (Yankovsky 3)
Beloved, 1934 (Rooney 3)
Beloved. See Del odio nació el amor, 1949
Beloved, 1971 (Hawkins 3)
Beloved. See Restless, 1978
Beloved Adventuress, 1917 (Marion 4)
Beloved Bachelor, 1931 (Lukas 3, Rosher 4)
Beloved Bozo, 1925 (Sennett 2)
Beloved Brat, 1938 (Negulesco 2, Costello 3, Crisp 3, Barnes 4)
Beloved Brute, 1924 (Blackton 2, McLaglen 3)
Beloved Enemy, 1936 (Crisp 3, Niven 3, Oberon 3, Balderston 4, Day 4, Goldwyn 4, Newman 4, Toland 4)
Beloved Infidel, 1959 (King 2, Kerr 3, Peck 3, Reynolds 4, Shamroy 4, Wald 4, Waxman 4)
Beloved Jim, 1917 (Carey 3)
Beloved Rogue, 1927 (Barrymore 3, Veidt 3, August 4, Menzies 4)
Beloved Traitor, 1918 (Marsh 3)
Beloved Vagabond, 1923 (Matthews 3)
Beloved Vagabond, 1936 (Chevalier 3,

Lockwood 3, Andrejew 4, Milhaud 4, Planer 4)
Below the Chinese Restaurant. See Sotto il ristorante Cinese, 1987
Below the Sea, 1933 (Bellamy 3, Wray 3, Swerling 4, Walker 4)
Below the Surface, 1920 (Bosworth 3)
Below Zero, 1930 (Laurel and Hardy 3, Roach 4)
Belstone Fox, 1973 (Roberts 3)
Belva, 1970 (Kinski 3)
Bemisal, 1982 (Bachchan 3)
Ben, 1972 (Metty 4)
Ben Bolt, 1913 (Guy 2)
Ben Hur, 1907 (Olcott 2)
Benaam, 1974 (Bachchan 3)
Benazir, 1964 (Roy 2, Burman 4)
Bend of the River, 1952 (Mann 2, Hudson 3, Kennedy 3, Stewart 3, Chase 4, Salter 4)
Beneath a Stony Sky, See Pod kamennym nebom, 1974
Beneath the Czar, 1914 (Guy 2)
Beneath the Planet of the Apes, 1968 (Krasner 4)
Beneath the Planet of the Apes, 1970 (Heston 3, McDowall 3, Dehn 4, Rosenman 4, Smith 4)
Beneath the 12-Mile Reef, 1953 (Wagner 3, Cronjager 4, Herrmann 4, Jeakins 4, LeMaire 4, Reynolds 4)
Benefit of the Doubt, 1965 (Jackson 3)
Bengal Brigade, 1954 (Hudson 3, Miller 4, Salter 4)
Bengal Famine, 1943 (Roy 2)
Bengal Lancers, 1984 (Lassally 4)
Bengali Night. See Nuit Bengali, 1988
Bengazi, 1955 (McLaglen 3, Biroc 4)
Ben-Hur, 1926 (Niblo 2, Bushman 3, Johnson 3, Loy 3, Novarro 3, Eason 4, Gibbons 4, Gillespie 4, Goldwyn 4, Mathis 4, Mayer 4, Meredyth 4, Struss 4, Thalberg 4, Wilson 4)
Ben-Hur, 1959 (Wyler 2, Hawkins 3, Heston 3, Jaffe 3, Adam 4, Canutt 4, Gillespie 4, Rozsa 4, Surtees 4)
Beni komori, 1951 (Kinugasa 2, Hasegawa 3)
Benikmori, 1931 (Tsuburaya 4)
Benito Cereno, 1969 (Guerra 2)
Benjamin, 1968 (Deneuve 3, Morgan 3, Piccoli 3, Cloquet 4)
Benjy, 1951 (Zinnemann 2, Fonda 3)
Benny from Panama, 1934 (Roach 4)
Benny Goodman Story, 1955 (Reed 3, Daniels 4, Mancini 4)
Benson Murder Case, 1930 (Lukas 3, Powell 4)
Benten Boy. See Benten kozou, 1958
Benten kozou, 1958 (Miyagawa 4)
Benten-kozo, 1928 (Hasegawa 3)
Benvenuta, 1983 (Delvaux 2, Gassman 3)
Benvenuto Cellini, 1910 (Feuillade 2)
Benvenuto Cellini, or a Curious Evasion. See Benvenutto Cellini ou une curieuse évasion, 1904
Benvenuto reverendo!, 1950 (Fabrizi 3)
Benvenutto Cellini ou une curieuse évasion, 1904 (Méliès 2)
Beqasoor, 1950 (Biswas 4)
Bequest to the Nation, 1973 (Finch 3, Jackson 3, Quayle 3, Dillon 4, Fisher 4, Legrand 4, Rattigan 4, Wallis 4)
Berammee geisha makaridoru, 1961 (Yamamura 3)

Between the Lines, 1977 (Silver 2)
Between Three and Five Minutes, 1972 (Nemec 2)
Between Two Women, 1937 (Von Stroheim 2, O'Sullivan 3, Adrian 4, Seitz 4)
Between Two Women, 1944 (Barrymore 3, Johnson 3, Irene 4, Rosson 4, Wilson 4)
Between Two Worlds. See Müde Tod, 1921
Between Two Worlds, 1944 (Garfield 3, Greenstreet 3, Henreid 3, Friedhofer 4, Korngold 4)
Between Us Girls, 1942 (Francis 3)
Between Us Thieves. See Oss tjuvar emellan eller En burk ananas, 1945
Between Worlds. See Müde Tod, 1921
Betwixt Love and Fire, 1913 (Sennett 2)
Beute der Erinnyen, 1921 (Krauss 3)
Beverley of Graustark, 1926 (Day 4)
Beverly Hills Brats, 1989 (Goldberg 3, Sheen 3)
Beverly Hills Cop, 1984 (Murphy 3)
Beverly Hills Cop II, 1987 (Murphy 3)
Beverly Hills Madam, 1986 (Dunaway 3, Jourdan 3, Schifrin 4)
Beverly of Graustark, 1926 (Davies 3, Gibbons 4)
Bewaqoof, 1960 (Burman 4)
Beware My Lovely, 1952 (Lupino 3, Ryan 3, D'Agostino 4, Horner 4)
Beware of a Holy Whore. See Warnung vor einer heiligen Nutte, 1970
Beware of Barnacle Bill, 1935 (Fleischer 4)
Beware of Blondes, 1928 (Walker 4)
Beware of Children. See No Kidding, 1960
Beware of Married Men, 1928 (Loy 3)
Beware of Pity, 1946 (Beaton 4, Rank 4, Vetchinsky 4)
Beware of the Dog, 1923 (La Cava 2)
Beware of Widows, 1927 (Laemmle 4)
Beware Spooks!, 1939 (Brown 3)
Beware the Boarders, 1918 (Sennett 2)
Bewitched, 1945 (Kaper 4)
Bewitched Bunny, 1954 (Blanc 4, Jones 4, Maltese 4, Stalling 4)
Bewitched Inn. See Auberge ensorcelée, 1897
Bewitched Matches, 1912 (Cohl 4)
Bewitched Trunk. See Coffre enchanté, 1904
Beyaz atli adam, 1965 (Güney 2)
Beyoğlu canavari, 1968 (Güney 2)
Beyond a Reasonable Doubt, 1956 (Lang 2, Andrews 3, Fontaine 3)
Beyond All Limits. See Flor de mayo, 1957
Beyond Evil. See Al di là del bene a del male, 1980
Beyond Glory, 1948 (Ladd 3, Murphy 3, Reed 3, Dreier 4, Head 4, Seitz 4)
Beyond Good and Evil. See Oltre il bene e il male, 1977
Beyond London, 1928 (Berman 4)
Beyond Love and Hate. See Ai to nikushimi no kaneta e, 1951
Beyond Mombasa, 1956 (Lee 3, Reed 3, Wilde 3)
Beyond Price, 1921 (Fox 4, Ruttenberg 4)
Beyond the Aegean, 1989 (Kazan 2)
Beyond the Bermuda Triangle, 1975 (MacMurray 3)
Beyond the Blue Horizon, 1942 (Lamour 3, Dreier 4, Head 4, Westmore Family 4, Young 4)
Beyond the Border, 1925 (Carey 3, Polito 4, Stromberg 4)

Beyond the City, 1914 (Eason 4)
Beyond the Door. See Oltre la porta, 1982
Beyond the Forest, 1949 (Vidor 2, Cotten 3, Davis 3, Blanke 4, Burks 4, Coffee 4, Head 4, Steiner 4)
Beyond the Last Frontier, 1943 (Mitchum 3)
Beyond the Law. See Al di là della legge, 1968
Beyond the Limit. See Honorary Consul, 1983
Beyond the Mountains. See Más allá de las montañas, 1967
Beyond the Mountains: The Desperate Ones. See Más allá de las montañas, 1967
Beyond the Ocean, 1990 (Clayburgh 3)
Beyond the Poseidon Adventure, 1979 (Caine 3, Field 3, Malden 3, Ames 4)
Beyond the Purple Hills, 1950 (Autry 3)
Beyond the Rainbow, 1922 (Bow 3)
Beyond the Reef, 1981 (Lai 4)
Beyond the River. See Bottom of the Bottle, 1956
Beyond the Rockies, 1932 (McCord 4)
Beyond the Rocks, 1922 (Wood 2, Swanson 3, Valentino 3)
Beyond the Time Barrier, 1960 (Ulmer 2, Pierce 4)
Beyond the Tropopause, 1968 (Menges 4)
Beyond the Valley of the Dolls, 1970 (Smith 4)
Beyond the Wall. See Müde Tod, 1921
Beyond Therapy, 1987 (Altman 2, Jackson 3)
Beyond This Place, 1959 (Johnson 3, Adam 4, Cardiff 4)
Beyond Tomorrow, 1940 (Carey 3, Garmes 4)
Beyond Victory, 1931 (Mandell 4)
Bez znieczulenia, 1977 (Wajda 2)
Bezdětná, 1935 (Heller 4)
Bharat Mata, 1957 (Nargis 3, Mehboob 2)
Bharosa, 1963 (Dutt 2)
Bhavna, 1984 (Azmi 3)
Bhavni bhavai, 1981 (Patil 3)
Bhookh, 1947 (Biswas 4)
Bhowani Junction, 1956 (Cukor 2, Gardner 3, Granger 3, Berman 4, Levien 4, Rozsa 4, Young 4)
Bhumika, 1977 (Patil 3, Nihalani 4)
Biala Wizytowka, 1986 (Nowicki 3)
Bianchi cavalli d'Agosto, 1975 (Seberg 3)
Bianco, il giallo, il nero, 1975 (Wallach 3)
Bianco, rosso, e . . . , 1972 (Rey 3, Loren 3, Guerra 4, Ponti 4)
Bianco, rosso, e verdone, 1981 (Morricone 4)
Bibbia, 1965 (Gardner 3, Harris 3, O'Toole 3, Scott 3, De Laurentiis 4, Dunn 4, Rotunno 4)
Bible. See Bibbia, 1965
Bible, 1975 (Jarman)
Bible, 1976 (Carné 2)
Bible for Girls, 1934 (Zhao dan 3)
Bible . . . in the Beginning. See Bibbia, 1965
Bible Stories, 1980 (Halas and Batchelor 4)
Bibliothèques, 1963 (Borowczyk 2)
Bibo no miyako, 1957 (Tsukasa 3, Muraki 4)
Bibo no umi, 1950 (Kyo 3)
Bice skoro propast sveta, 1968 (Girardot 3)
Biches, 1968 (Chabrol 2, Audran 3, Trintignant 3, Gégauff 4, Rabier 4)
Bicycle Flirt, 1928 (Sennett 2, Lombard 3)

Bicycle Thief. See Ladri di biciclette, 1948
Bid of Roses, 1933 (La Cava 2)
Bidaya wa Nihaya, 1960 (Sharif 3)
Bidon d'or, 1931 (Christian-Jaque 2)
Bidone, 1955 (Fellini 2, Crawford 3, Masina 3, Flaiano 4, Pinelli 4, Rota 4)
Bidrohi, 1935 (Burman 4)
Bien amada, 1951 (Fernández 2, Figueroa 4)
Bien pho, 1991 (Pleasence 3)
Bien-aimée, 1967 (Morgan 3)
Bienamados, 1965 (Figueroa 4)
Bienfaiteur, 1941 (Raimu 3)
Bienfaits du cinématographe, 1904 (Guy 2)
Bientôt j'espère, 1969 (Marker 2)
Bienvenido, Mr. Marshall, 1952 (Rey 3)
Bienvenuto Cellini, 1910 (Gaumont 4)
Bière, 1924 (Grémillon 2, Périnal 4)
Bièvre, fille perdue, 1939 (Clement 2)
Biff Bang Buddy, 1924 (Arthur 3)
Biffen and the Banana. See Biffen och Bananen, 1951
Biffen och Bananen, 1951 (Andersson 3, Fischer 4)
Big, 1988 (Hanks 3, Bass 4, Hamlisch 4)
Big Adventure, 1921 (Eason 4, Miller 4)
Big Bad Mama, 1974 (Corman 2, Dickinson 3)
Big Bad Mama II, 1986 (Corman 2, Dickinson 3)
Big Bankroll. See King of the Roaring Twenties, 1961
Big Barrier. See Schloss Hubertus: Der Fischer von Heiligensee, 1955
Big Beat, 1957 (Mancini 4)
Big Bird Cage, 1972 (Corman 2)
Big Blockade, 1942 (Cavalcanti 2, Crichton 2, Hay 3, Mills 3, Redgrave 3, Balcon 4)
Big Boodle, 1957 (Armendáriz 3, Flynn 3, Garmes 4)
Big Boss. See Ankokugai no kaoyaku, 1959
Big Boss. See Fists of Fury, 1971
Big Bounce, 1968 (Grant 3)
Big Boy, 1930 (Jolson 3, Mohr 4)
Big Brain, 1933 (Wray 3, Edeson 4)
Big Brawl, 1980 (Chan 3, Ferrer 3, Schifrin 4)
Big Broadcast of 1932, 1932 (Crosby 3, Rooney 3, Folsey 4, Head 4)
Big Broadcast of 1936, 1935 (Crosby 3, Robinson 3, Glazer 4, Head 4, Prinz 4)
Big Broadcast of 1937, 1936 (Leisen 2, Milland 3, Banton 4, Dreier 4, Head 4, Young 4)
Big Broadcast of 1938, 1938 (Leisen 2, Fields 3, Hope 3, Lamour 3, Dreier 4, Head 4)
Big Brother, 1923 (Dwan 2)
Big Brown Eyes, 1936 (Walsh 2, Bennett 3, Grant 3, Pidgeon 3, Reynolds 4, Wanger 4)
Big Build-Up, 1942 (Terry 4)
Big Bus, 1976 (Ferrer 3, Gordon 3)
Big Business, 1924 (Roach 4)
Big Business, 1929 (Stevens 2, Laurel and Hardy 3, Roach 4)
Big Business, 1932 (Rooney 3)
Big Business, 1988 (Midler 3)
Big Business Girl, 1931 (Blondell 3, Young 3, Polito 4)
Big Cage, 1933 (Rooney 3)
Big Calibre, 1937 (Katzman 4)
Big Carnival. See Ace in the Hole, 1951

Big Chance, 1933 (Rooney 3)

Big Chief. *See* Grand Chef, 1958

Big Chief Ko-Ko, 1925 (Fleischer 4)

Big Chief Ugh-Amugh-Ugh, 1938 (Fleischer 4)

Big Chill, 1983 (Kasdan 2, Close 3, Costner 3, Hurt 3)

Big Circus, 1959 (Lorre 3, Mature 3, Price 3, Bennett 4, Hoch 4)

Big City, 1928 (Browning 2, Chaney 3, Day 4, Gibbons 4, Young 4)

Big City, 1937 (Borzage 2, Rainer 3, Tracy 3, Gibbons 4, Krasna 4, Schary 4)

Big City, 1948 (Donen 2, O'Brien 3, Preston 3, Ames 4, Pasternak 4, Surtees 4)

Big City. *See* Mahanagar, 1963

Big City Blues, 1932 (LeRoy 2, Blondell 3, Bogart 3, Grot 4)

Big Clock, 1948 (Lanchester 3, Laughton 3, Milland 3, O'Sullivan 3, Dreier 4, Head 4, Seitz 4, Young 4)

Big Combo, 1955 (Lewis 2, Van Cleef 3, Wilde 3, Alton 4, Raksin 4)

Big Country, 1958 (Ashby 2, Wyler 2, Baker 3, Heston 3, Peck 3, Simmons 3, Bass 4, Planer 4)

Big Crash. *See* Stora Skrällen, 1943

Big Cube, 1969 (Turner 3, Figueroa 4)

Big Dan, 1923 (Wellman 2, August 4, Fox 4)

Big Day, 1937 (Ruttenberg 4)

Big Day, 1960 (Pleasence 3)

Big Day in Bogo, 1958 (Dickinson 2)

Big Deal at Dodge City. *See* Big Hand for the Little Lady, 1966

Big Deal on Madonna Street. *See* Soliti ignoti, 1958

Big Deal on Madonna Street . . . Twenty Years Later. *See* Soliti ignoti vent' anni dopo, 1985

Big Deal on Madonna Street—Update. *See* Soliti ignoti vent'anni dopo, 1985

Big Decision. *See* Basketball Fix, 1951

Big Diamond, 1929 (Mix 3)

Big Diamond Robbery, 1929 (Plunkett 4)

Big Doll House, 1971 (Corman 2)

Big Ears, 1931 (Roach 4)

Big Fella, 1937 (Robeson 3, Rutherford 3)

Big Fibber, 1933 (Sennett 2)

Big Fisherman, 1959 (Borzage 2, Bondi 3, Keel 3, Lom 3, Eastbrook 4, Garmes 4)

Big Fix, 1947 (Miller 4)

Big Fix, 1978 (Dreyfuss 3, Head 4)

Big Flame, 1969 (Loach 2)

Big Flash, 1932 (Langdon 3)

Big Frame. *See* Lost Hours, 1952

Big Gamble, 1931 (Niblo 2, Mohr 4)

Big Gamble, 1960 (D'Eaubonne 4, Jarre 4, Zanuck 4)

Big Game, 1921 (Roach 4)

Big Game, 1936 (Berman 4, Polglase 4)

Big Game, 1972 (Milland 3)

Big Game Haunt, 1968 (Blanc 4)

Big Game Hunt, 1928 (Rooney 3)

Big Game Hunt, 1937 (Terry 4)

Big Gundown. *See* Resa dei conti, 1967

Big Guns, 1973 (Delon 3)

Big Guy, 1939 (Cooper 3, McLaglen 3, Salter 4)

Big Hand for the Little Lady, 1966 (Fonda 3, Meredith 3, Robards 3, Woodward 3, Garmes 4, Mercer 4, Raksin 4)

Big Hangover, 1950 (Johnson 3, Taylor 3, Deutsch 4, Folsey 4, Krasna 4, Rose 4)

Big Heart. *See* Miracle on 34th Street, 1947

Big Hearted Herbert, 1934 (Orry-Kelly 4)

Big Heat, 1953 (Lang 2, Ford 3, Grahame 3, Marvin 3, Cohn 4, Wald 4)

Big Heel-watha, 1944 (Avery 4)

Big House, 1930 (Beery 3, Montgomery 3, Gibbons 4, Marion 4, Mayer 4, Shearer 4, Thalberg 4)

Big House Bunny, 1950 (Blanc 4, Stalling 4)

Big House, U.S.A., 1955 (Bronson 3, Crawford 3)

Big Hug. *See* Stora famnen, 1939

Big Idea, 1918 (Daniels 3, Lloyd 3, Mohr 4, Roach 4)

Big Idea, 1923 (Roach 4)

Big Idea, 1934 (Three Stooges 3)

Big Jack, 1949 (Beery 3, Stothart 4, Surtees 4)

Big Jake, 1971 (O'Hara 3, Wayne 3, Bernstein 4, Clothier 4)

Big Jim Garrity, 1916 (Miller 4)

Big Jim McLain, 1952 (Wayne 3)

Big Kick, 1925 (Roach 4)

Big Kick, 1930 (Langdon 3, Roach 4)

Big Killing, 1928 (Beery 3, Mankiewicz 4, Schulberg 4)

Big Knife, 1955 (Aldrich 2, Lupino 3, Palance 3, Sloane 3, Steiger 3, Winters 3, Bass 4, Laszlo 4)

Big Land, 1957 (Ladd 3, O'Brien 3, Seitz 4)

Big Leaguer, 1953 (Aldrich 2, Robinson 3)

Big Life, 1950 (Newman 4)

Big Lift, 1950 (Clift 3, Clarke 4, Reynolds 4)

Big Little Person, 1919 (Valentino 3)

Big Li, Young Li, and Old Li, 1962 (Xie 2)

Big Man, 1990 (Morricone 4)

Big Moment, 1929 (Rooney 3)

Big Moments from Little Pictures, 1924 (Rogers 3, Roach 4)

Big Money, 1937 (Cavalcanti 2, Watt 2)

Big Money, 1958 (Rank 4)

Big Mouse-Take, 1963 (Hanna and Barbera 4)

Big Mouth, 1967 (Lewis 2, Wheeler 4)

Big News, 1929 (La Cava 2, Lombard 3, Miller 4)

Big Night, 1951 (Losey 2, Lardner 4, Mohr 4)

Big Noise, 1928 (Dwan 2, Hecht 4)

Big Noise, 1936 (Sim 3)

Big Noise, 1944 (Laurel and Hardy 3)

Big Operator, 1959 (Rooney 3, Ames 4)

Big Pal, 1925 (Furthman 4)

Big Palooka, 1929 (Sennett 2)

Big Parade, 1925 (Vidor 2, Bosworth 3, Gilbert 3, Basevi 4, Gibbons 4, Mayer 4, Thalberg 4)

Big Parade, 1952 (Godfrey 4)

Big Party, 1930 (Fox 4)

Big Picture, 1989 (Cleese 3, Gould 3, McDowall 3)

Big Pond, 1930 (Sturges 2, Chevalier 3, Colbert 3, Folsey 4, Fort 4, Green 4, Zukor 4)

Big Punch, 1920 (Ford 2, Fox 4, Furthman 4)

Big Race. *See* Texan, 1930

Big Race, 1937 (Lantz 4)

Big Race, 1980 (Halas and Batchelor 4)

Big Rally, 1950 (Vukotić 4)

Big Red, 1962 (Pidgeon 3, Disney 4)

Big Red One, 1980 (Fuller 2, Audran 3, Marvin 3)

Big Red Riding Hood, 1925 (McCarey 2, Roach 4)

Big Rip-Off, 1975 (Curtis 3)

Big Ripoff. *See* Controrapina, 1978

Big Risk. *See* Classe tous risques, 1960

Big Rose, 1974 (Winters 3)

Big Sam. *See* Great Scout and Cathouse Thursday, 1976

Big Shakedown, 1934 (Davis 3)

Big Shave, 1967 (Scorsese 2)

Big Shot, 1931 (O'Sullivan 3, Miller 4)

Big Shot, 1937 (Musuraca 4, Polglase 4)

Big Shot, 1942 (Bogart 3, Deutsch 4)

Big Shots, 1987 (Ondříček 4)

Big Show, 1923 (Roach 4)

Big Show, 1936 (Autry 3, Rogers 3, Canutt 4)

Big Show, 1961 (Robertson 3, Williams 3, Heller 4)

Big Sky, 1952 (Hawks 2, Douglas 3, D'Agostino 4, Harlan 4, Jeakins 4, Nichols 4, Tiomkin 4)

Big Sleep, 1946 (Hawks 2, Bacall 3, Bogart 3, Malone 3, Brackett 4, Chandler 4, Faulkner 4, Furthman 4, Steiner 4)

Big Sleep, 1978 (Mills 3, Mitchum 3, Reed 3, Stewart 3, Chandler 4)

Big Snatch. *See* Mélodie en sous-sol, 1962

Big Snooze, 1946 (Blanc 4, Stalling 4)

Big Sombrero, 1949 (Autry 3)

Big Squawk, 1929 (Roach 4)

Big Stampede, 1932 (Wayne 3, McCord 4)

Big Steal, 1949 (Siegel 2, Bendix 3, Mitchum 3, Novarro 3)

Big Store, 1941 (Dumont 3, Marx Brothers 3)

Big Street, 1942 (Ball 3, Beavers 3, Fonda 3, Moorehead 3, Metty 4)

Big Timber, 1917 (Reid 3)

Big Time, 1929 (Ford 2, Fox 4)

Big Time Operators. *See* Smallest Show on Earth, 1957

Big Time Vaudeville Reels, 1936 (McDaniel 3)

Big Timer, 1932 (Riskin 4)

Big Top, 1938 (Terry 4)

Big Top Bunny, 1951 (McKimson 4, Stalling 4)

Big Top Pee Wee, 1988 (Edlund 4)

Big Town, 1924 (Roach 4)

Big Town, 1987 (Cern 3, Dillon 3, Grant 3)

Big Town Czar, 1939 (Arden 3)

Big Town Girl, 1937 (Trevor 3)

Big Town Round-up, 1921 (Mix 3)

Big Trail, 1930 (Walsh 2, Bond 3, Wayne 3, Edeson 4, Friedhofer 4)

Big Trees, 1952 (Douglas 3, Glennon 4)

Big Tremaine, 1916 (Glaudio 4)

Big Trouble, 1986 (Cassavetes 2, Arkin 3, Falk 3)

Big Trouble in Little China, 1986 (Carpenter 2, Edlund 4)

Big Wave, 1962 (Hayakawa 3)

Big Wheel, 1949 (McDaniel 3, Rooney 3, Laszlo 4)

Big Yellow Schooner to Byzantium, 1978 (Fonda 3)

Bigamist, 1953 (Darwell 3, Fontaine 3, Lupino 3, O'Brien 3)

Bigamist. *See* Bigamo, 1955

Bigamo, 1955 (De Sica 2, Rosi 2, Mastroianni 3, Age and Scarpelli 4, Amidei 4)

Bigfoot, 1973 (Carradine 3)

Bigger and Better Blondes, 1927 (Arthur 3, Roach 4)

Bigger than Life, 1956 (Ray 2, Mason 3, Mathau 3, LeMaire 4, Raksin 4, Smith 4, Wheeler 4)

Biggest Bank Robbery. *See* Nightingale Sang in Berkeley Square, 1980

Biggest Bundle of Them All, 1968 (De Sica 2, Wagner 3, Welch 3)

Biggest Fight on Earth. *See* Sandai kaiju chikyu saidai no kessen, 1965

Biggest Show on Earth, 1918 (Barnes 4)

Biggles, 1985 (Cushing 3)

Bijo no tokudane, 1952 (Kyo 3)

Bijo to ekitai ningen, 1958 (Tsuburaya 4)

Bijo to kairyu, 1955 (Shindo 2, Yosimura 2)

Bijo to tozoku, 1952 (Kyo 3, Mori 3)

Bijo to yaju, 1952 (Shimura 3)

Bijobu Sakyo, 1931 (Hasegawa 3)

Bijoutiers du clair de lune, 1958 (Vadim 2, Bardot 3, Rey 3, Valli 3, Auric 4)

Bike Boy, 1967 (Warhol 2)

Bike Bug, 1921 (Roach 4)

Bikini Beach, 1964 (Karloff 3, Crosby 4)

Bikini Paradise, 1964 (Lourié 4)

Bílá nemoc, 1937 (Heller 4)

Bilá spona, 1960 (Frič 2)

Bilans kwartalny, 1975 (Zanussi 2)

Bild der Zeit, 1921 (Lang 2)

Bildnis, 1925 (Banky 3)

Bildnis einer Unbekannten, 1954 (Käutner 2)

Bilet powrotny, 1978 (Stawinski 4)

Bilitis, 1977 (Colpi 4, Lai 4)

Biljett till paradiset, 1962 (Dahlbeck 3)

Bill, 1981 (Rooney 3)

Bill Apperson's Boy, 1919 (Polito 4)

Bill Bumper's Bargain, 1911 (Bushman 3)

Bill Haywood, Producer, 1915 (Mix 3)

Bill of Divorcement, 1932 (Cukor 2, Barrymore 3, Hepburn 3, Estabrook 4, Selznick 4, Steiner 4, Westmore Family 4)

Bill of Divorcement, 1940 (Marshall 3, Menjou 3, O'Hara 3, Musuraca 4, Trumbo 4)

Bill of Hare, 1962 (Blanc 4, McKimson 4)

Bill: On His Own, 1983 (Rooney 3, Wright 3)

Bill Sharkley's Last Game, 1990 (Carey 3)

Billard cassé, 1917 (Feyder 2)

Billboard Frolics, 1936 (Freleng 4)

Billboard Girl, 1932 (Sennett 2, Crosby 3, Hornbeck 4)

Bille de clown, 1950 (Burel 4)

Bille en tete, 1989 (Darrieux 3)

Billet de banque, 1906 (Feuillade 2)

Billet de faveur, 1906 (Pathé 4)

Billet de mille, 1932 (Rosay 3, Matras 4)

Billion Dollar, 1933 (Brown 4)

Billion Dollar Brain, 1967 (De Toth 2, Russell 2, Caine 3, Homolka 3, Malden 3, Russell 4)

Billion Dollar Threat, 1979 (Bellamy 3)

Billion for Boris, 1984 (Grant 3)

Billionaire. *See* Okuman-choja, 1954

Billionaire, 1989 (Halas and Batchelor 4)

Billions, 1920 (Nazimova 3)

Billy and the Butler, 1912 (Bushman 3)

Billy Bathgate, 1990 (Hoffman 3, Almendros 4)

Billy Blazes, Esq., 1919 (Daniels 3, Lloyd 3, Roach 4)

Billy Boy, 1954 (Avery 4)

Billy Budd, 1962 (Douglas 3, Ryan 3, Stamp 3, Ustinov 3, Bodeen 4, Krasker 4)

Billy Dodges Bills, 1913 (Sennett 2)

Billy Galvin, 1986 (Malden 3)

Billy Goat Whiskers, 1937 (Terry 4)

Billy Jack Goes to Washington, 1977 (Bernstein 4)

Billy Jim, 1922 (Borzage 2)

Billy Liar, 1963 (Schlesinger 2, Christie 3)

Billy Mouse's Akwakade, 1940 (Terry 4)

Billy Rose's Diamond Horseshoe, 1945 (Dumont 3, Grable 3, Newman 4, Pan 4, Raksin 4)

Billy Rose's Jumbo, 1962 (Zanuck 4)

Billy the Kid series, 1941–42 (Crabbe 3)

Billy the Kid, 1930 (Vidor 2, Beery 3, Hart 3, Gibbons 4, MacArthur 4, Mayer 4)

Billy the Kid, 1941 (Taylor 3, Mayer 4)

Billy the Kid Returns, 1938 (Rogers 3)

Billy the Kid vs. Dracula, 1966 (Carradine 3)

Billy Two Hats, 1973 (Jewison 2, Peck 3)

Billy's Rival, 1914 (Loos 4)

Billy's Strategem, 1911 (Griffith 2, Bitzer 4)

Bilocation, 1973 (Lassally 4)

Biloxi Blues, 1988 (Nichols 2, Delerue 4, Stark 4)

Bílý Ráj, 1924 (Ondra 3, Heller 4)

Bimbo's Express, 1931 (Fleischer 4)

Bimbo's Initiation, 1931 (Fleischer 4)

Bimi. *See* King of the Wild, 1930

Bin defa ölürüm, 1969 (Güney 2)

Binettoscope, 1910 (Cohl 4)

Bing Crosby in Cinerama's Russian Adventure. *See* Cinerama's Russian Adventure, 1965

Bing Crosby's Washington State, 1968 (Crosby 3)

Bing Presents Oreste, 1955 (Dmytryk 2, Crosby 3)

Bingo, Bridesmaids and Braces, 1988 (Armstrong 2)

Bingo Crosbyana, 1936 (Freleng 4)

Bingo Long Traveling All-Stars and Motor Kings, 1976 (Badham 2, Jones 3, Pryor 3)

Bink Runs Away. *See* Bink's Vacation, 1913

Bink's Vacation, 1913 (Loos 4)

Bio Woman, 1980 (Godfrey 4)

Biografía de un carnaval, 1983 (Alvarez 2)

Biography of a Bachelor Girl, 1935 (Horton 3, Mongomery 3, Howe 4, Loos 4, Stothart 4, Thalberg 4)

Bionda sottochiave, 1939 (Zavattini 4)

Bip Goes to Town, 1941 (Ivens 2)

Biraghin, 1946 (Gallone 2)

Biraj Bahu, 1954 (Roy 2)

Birch Interval, 1976 (Rosenman 4)

Birch-wood. *See* Brzezina, 1970

Bird, 1978 (Brakhage 2)

Bird, 1987 (Eastwood 3)

Bird Came C.O.D., 1942 (Blanc 4, Jones 4, Stalling 4)

Bird in a Bonnet, 1958 (Blanc 4, Freleng 4)

Bird in a Guilty Cage, 1952 (Blanc 4, Freleng 4, Stalling 4)

Bird in the Head, 1946 (Three Stooges 3)

Bird of Paradise, 1932 (Berkeley 2, Vidor 2, Del Rio 3, McCrea 3, Dunn 4, Selznick 4, Steiner 4)

Bird of Paradise, 1951 (Daves 2, Jourdan 3, Sloane 3, Hoch 4, LeMaire 4, Wheeler 4)

Bird of Prey. *See* Epervier, 1933

Bird on a Wire, 1990 (Badham 2, Gibson 3, Hawn 3)

Bird Symphony, 1955 (Terry 4)

Bird Tower, 1941 (Terry 4)

Bird with the Crystal Plumage. *See* Uccello dalle piume di cristallo, 1969

Birdcall. *See* Lockfågeln, 1971

Birdland, 1935 (Terry 4)

Birdman of Alcatraz, 1962 (Frankenheimer 2, Lancaster 3, Malden 3, O'Brien 3, Ritter 3, Bernstein 4, Guffey 4)

Birds, 1963 (Hitchcock 2, Boyle 4, Burks 4, Head 4, Herrmann 4, Iwerks 4, Whitlock 4)

Bird's a Bird, 1915 (Sennett 2)

Birds and the Bees. *See* Three Daring Daughters, 1948

Birds and the Bees, 1956 (Sturges 2, Niven 3, Head 4)

Birds Anonymous, 1957 (Blanc 4, Foster 4, Freleng 4)

Birds at Sunrise, 1972 (Wieland 2)

Birds Bees and Storks, 1989 (Halas and Batchelor 4)

Bird's Eye View of Budh Gaya, 1914 (Phalke 2)

Birds in Peru. *See* Oiseaux vont mourir aux Pérou, 1968

Birds of a Father, 1961 (Blanc 4, McKimson 4)

Birds of a Feather, 1917 (Daniels, Lloyd 3, Roach 4)

Birds of a Feather, 1935 (Baxter 2)

Birds of Passage. *See* Tažní ptáci, 1961

Birds of Prey, 1930 (Hawkins 3, Dean 4)

Birds, the Bees, and the Italians. *See* Signore e signori, 1966

Birdy, 1985 (Parker 2)

Birdy and the Beast, 1944 (Blanc 4, Clampett 4, Foster 4, Stalling 4)

Birgitt Haas Must Be Killed. *See* Il Faut tuer Birgitt Haas, 1981

Birha Ki Raat, 1950 (Anand 3)

Birichino di Papà, 1943 (Rota 4, Zavattini 4)

Birth of a Flivver, 1916 (O'Brien 4)

Birth of a Nation, 1915 (Griffith 2, Ford 2, Von Stroheim 2, Walsh 2, Crisp 3, Gish 3, Love 3, Marsh 3, Reid 3, Walthall 3, Bitzer 4, Brown 4)

Birth of a Notion, 1947 (Blanc 4, McKimson 4)

Birth of a Robot, 1936 (Jennings 2, Lye 4)

Birth of a Star, 1944 (Kaye 3)

Birth of Magellan: Fourteen Cadenzas, 1980 (Frampton 2)

Birth of Mankind, 1946 (Lee 3)

Birth of the Blues, 1941 (Crosby 3, Dreier 4, Head 4, Mercer 4)

Birth of the Year, 1938 (Alwyn 4)

Birthday, 1922 (Fleischer 4)

Birthday Cake, 1989 (Halas and Batchelor 4)

Birthday Gift. *See* Fødselsdagsgaven, 1912

Birthday of the Young Inhabitants of Warsaw. *See* Urodziny młodego warszawiaka, 1980

Birthday Party, 1937 (Lantz 4)

Birthday Party, 1968 (Friedkin 2, Shaw 3, Pinter 4)

Birthday Party, 1987 (Pinter 4)

Birthday Treat, 1980 (Halas and Batchelor 4)

Birthright, 1924 (Micheaux 2)

Birthright, 1939 (Micheaux 2)

Biruma no tategoto, 1956 (Ichikawa 2)

Bis ans Ende der Welt, 1992 (Hurt 3, Mitchum 3, Moreau 3, Vogler 3, Von Sydow 3)
Bis wir uns Wiederschen, 1953 (Schell 3)
Bisarca, 1950 (Baarová 3)
Bisbetica domata, 1942 (Amidei 4)
Biscuit Eater, 1940 (Dreier 4, Head 4)
Biscuit Eater, 1972 (Ayres 3)
Bishop Misbehaves, 1935 (O'Sullivan 3)
Bishop Murder Case, 1930 (Davies 2, Rathbone 3, Coffee 4, Gibbons 4)
Bishop of the Ozarks, 1923 (Polito 4)
Bishop's Candlesticks, 1929 (Huston 3)
Bishop's Wife, 1947 (Grant 3, Lanchester 3, Niven 3, Young 3, Friedhofer 4, Goldwyn 4, Jenkins 4, Sharaff 4, Sherwood 4, Toland 4)
Bismarck, 1940 (Dagover 3)
Bisschen Liebe, 1974 (Müller 4)
Bisschen Liebe für dich, 1932 (Metzner 4)
Bist du es lachendes Gluck. See Mascottchen, 1929
Bit of Blarney, 1944 (Fleischer 4)
Bitch, 1965 (Warhol 2)
Bitch. See Garce, 1989
Bite and Run. See Mordi e fuggi, 1972
Bite the Bullet, 1975 (Brooks 2, Coburn 3, Hackman 3, Johnson 3, Boyle 4, North 4)
Bite the Dust, 1969 (Van Cleef 3)
Bite to Eat. See Sousto, 1960
Biter Bit, 1943 (Korda 4)
Bitka na Neretvi, 1969 (Bondarchuk 3, Brynner 3, Herrmann 4)
Bits of Life, 1921 (Neilan 2, Chaney 3, Wong 3)
Bitter Apples, 1927 (Loy 3, Mohr 4)
Bitter Grass. See Gorge trave, 1965
Bitter Moon, 1992 (Delli Colli 4)
Bitter Reunion. See Beau Serge, 1958
Bitter Rice. See Riso amaro, 1948
Bitter Spirit. See Eien no hito, 1961
Bitter Springs, 1950 (Rafferty 3, Balcon 4)
Bitter Sweet, 1933 (Wilcox 2, Neagle 3, Young 4)
Bitter Sweet, 1940 (Saville 2, Van Dyke 2, Eddy 3, MacDonald 3, Sanders 4, Adrian 4, Stothart 4)
Bitter Sweets, 1928 (Shamroy 4)
Bitter Tea of General Yen, 1933 (Capra 2, Stanwyck 3, Cohn 4, Walker 4, Wanger 4)
Bitter Tears of Petra von Kant. See Bitteren Tranen der Petra von Kant, 1972
Bitter Victory. See Amère victoire, 1957
Bittere Ernte, 1986 (Mueller-Stahl 3)
Bitteren Tränen der Petra von Kant, 1972 (Schygulla 3, Ballhaus 4)
Bittersweet Love, 1976 (Turner 3)
Bivio, 1950 (Vanel 3)
Biwi O Biwi, 1981 (Kapoor 2)
Bix Snooze, 1946 (Clampett 4)
Bizalom, 1979 (Szabó 2)
Bizarre Bizarre. See Drôle de drame, 1937
B.J. Lang Presents, 1971 (Rooney 3)
Black Abbot. See Schwarze Abt, 1963
Black Ace, 1928 (Johnson 3)
Black and White. See Fantasmagorie, 1908
Black and White Like Day and Night. See Schwarz und Weiss wie Tage und Nächte, 1978
Black Angel, 1946 (Crawford 3, Duryea 3, Lorre 3)
Black Angel. See Paroxismus, 1969
Black Bag, 1922 (Miller 4)

Black Bart, 1948 (De Carlo 3, Duryea 3, Friedhofer 4)
Black Bart, Highwayman. See Black Bart, 1948
Black Beauty, 1946 (Hunt 4, Tiomkin 4)
Black Beauty, 1971 (Mankowitz 4, Menges 4)
Black Belt History of Three Countries. See Kuroobi sangoku-shi, 1956
Black Bird, 1975 (Audran 3, Segal 3, Booth 4, Horner 4)
Black Book. See Reign of Terror, 1949
Black Buccaneer. See Gordon, il Pirato Nero, 1961
Black Camel, 1931 (Lugosi 3, Young 3, Carré 4)
Black Castle, 1952 (Karloff 3, Salter 4)
Black Cat, 1934 (Ulmer 2, Carradine 3, Karloff 3, Lugosi 3, Pierce 4)
Black Cat, 1941 (Crawford 3, Ladd 3, Lugosi 3, Rathbone 3, Cortez 4, Salter 4)
Black Cat. See Gatto nero, 1981
Black Cat. See Due occhi diabolici, 1990
Black Cat in the Bush. See Yabu no naka no kuroneko, 1968
Black Cauldron, 1985 (Hurt 3, Bernstein 4)
Black Chancellor. See Sorte Kansler, 1912
Black Coin, 1936 (Canutt 4)
Black Crows. See Svarte fugler, 1983
Black Cyclone, 1925 (Stevens 2, Roach 4)
Black Diamond. See Cerný démant, 1955
Black Diamond Express, 1927 (Zunuck 4)
Black Diamonds, 1940 (Salter 4)
Black Doll, 1938 (Cortez 4)
Black Dragons, 1942 (Lugosi 3, Katzman 4)
Black Dream. See Sorte Drøm, 1911
Black Eagle. See Aquila Nera, 1987
Black Eyes, 1939 (Brenon 2)
Black Eyes and Blues, 1941 (Bruckman 4)
Black Feather, 1928 (Costello 3)
Black Flame. See Cerný plamen, 1930
Black Flowers for the Bride. See Something for Everyone, 1970
Black Fox, 1962 (Dietrich 3)
Black Friday, 1940 (Karloff 3, Lugosi 3, Salter 4, Siodmak 4)
Black Fury, 1935 (Curtiz 2, Bond 3, Marsh 3, Muni 3, Haskin 4)
Black Fury. See Mitsuyu-sen, 1954
Black Ghost. See Last Frontier, 1932
Black Ghost Bandit, 1915 (Eason 4)
Black Girl from .... See Noire de ..., 1966
Black Glove. See Face the Music, 1954
Black Gold, 1947 (Quinn 3, Eason 4)
Black Hand, 1906 (Bitzer 4)
Black Hand, 1950 (Kelly 3, Plunkett 4)
Black Hand Blues, 1925 (Roach 4)
Black Hole, 1979 (Borgnine 3, Perkins 3, Schell 3, Barry 4, Ellenshaw 4)
Black Horse Canyon, 1954 (McCrea 3, Salter 4)
Black Hussar. See Schwarze Husar, 1932
Black Imp. See Diable noir, 1905
Black Is White, 1920 (White 3)
Black Jack, 1927 (Fox 4)
Black Jack, 1950 (Duvivier 2, Dalio 3, Marshall 3, Kosma 4, Spaak 4)
Black Jack, 1979 (Loach 2, Cushing 3, Menges 4)
Black Journal. See Signora della ororo, 1977
Black Killer, 1971 (Kinski 3)
Black Knight, 1954 (Garnett 2, Cushing 3, Ladd 3, Addison 4, Box 4, Vetchinsky 4)

Black Leather Jacket, 1990 (Hopper 3)
Black Legion, 1935 (Sheridan 3)
Black Legion, 1937 (Bogart 3, Barnes 4)
Black Lightning, 1924 (Bow 3)
Black Limelight, 1939 (Massey 3)
Black Magic, 1929 (Walthall 3, Fox 4)
Black Magic, 1949 (Welles 2, Mangano 3, Annankov 4, Bennett 4, D'Eaubonne 4)
Black Marble, 1980 (Stanton 3, Jarre 4, Roizman 4)
Black Mask, 1935 (Launder and Gilliat 2)
Black Masks. See Svarta maskerna, 1912
Black Midnight, 1949 (Boetticher 2, McDowall 3)
Black Moon, 1934 (Wray 3, August 4)
Black Moon, 1975 (Malle 2, Nykvist 4)
Black Moon Rising, 1986 (Carpenter 2, Schifrin 4)
Black Narcissus, 1947 (Powell and Pressburger 2, Kerr 3, Simmons 3, Cardiff 4, Challis 4, Ellenshaw 4, Heckroth 4, Junge 4, Rank 4)
Black Noon, 1971 (Grahame 3, Milland 3, Duning 4)
Black Oak Conspiracy, 1977 (Corman 2)
Black on White, 1954 (Alwyn 4)
Black Orchid, 1916 (Selig 4)
Black Orchid. See Trifling Woman, 1922
Black Orchid, 1959 (Ritt 2, Loren 3, Quinn 3, Burks 4, Head 4, Ponti 4)
Black Oxen, 1924 (Bow 3, Kräly 4)
Black Oxfords, 1924 (Sennett 2)
Black Palm Trees. See Svarta palmkronor, 1968
Black Panthers, 1968 (Varda 2)
Black Parachute, 1944 (Carradine 3)
Black Paradise, 1926 (Fox 4)
Black Patch, 1957 (Goldsmith 4)
Black Pirate, 1926 (Crisp 3, Fairbanks 3)
Black Rain, 1989 (Scott 2, Douglas 3)
Black Rainbow, 1989 (Robards 3)
Black Room, 1935 (Karloff 3)
Black Rose, 1950 (Hathaway 2, Welles 2, Harvey 3, Hawkins 3, Lom 3, Power 3, Cardiff 4, Jennings 4, Mathieson 4)
Black Roses, 1921 (Hayakawa 3)
Black Roses. See Svarta rosor, 1932
Black Roses. See Svarta rosor, 1945
Black Sabbath, 1964 (Karloff 3)
Black Sail. See Chornyi parus, 1929
Black Scorpion, 1957 (O'Brien 4)
Black Sea Fighters, 1942 (March 3)
Black Secret, 1919 (White 3)
Black Sheep, 1909 (Anderson 3)
Black Sheep, 1912 (Griffith 2, Bitzer 4)
Black Sheep, 1934 (Terry 4)
Black Sheep, 1935 (Dwan 2, Trevor 3, Miller 4)
Black Sheep, 1956 (Carradine 3)
Black Sheep of Whitehall, 1941 (Dearden 2, Hay 3, Mills 3, Balcon 4)
Black Shield of Falworth, 1954 (Curtis 3, Leigh 3, Marshall 3, Maté 4, Salter 4)
Black Sleep, 1956 (Lugosi 3, Rathbone 3)
Black Spider, 1920 (Colman 3)
Black Spider, 1931 (Terry 4)
Black Spurs, 1964 (Darnell 3)
Black Stallion, 1979 (Coppola 2, Rooney 3)
Black Stallion Returns, 1982 (Coppola 2, Rooney 3, Delerue 4)
Black Sunday, 1977 (Frankenheimer 2, Dern 3, Shaw 3, Alonzo 4, Williams 4)

Black Swan, 1942 (King 2, O'Hara 3, Power 3, Quinn 3, Sanders 3, Basevi 4, Day 4, Hecht 4, Miller 4, Newman 4, Shamroy 4)

Black Tent, 1956 (Pleasence 3, Alwyn 4, Rank 4)

Black Tights, 1960 (Charisse 3, Chevalier 3, Alekan 4, Wakhévitch 4)

Black Tuesday, 1954 (Robinson 3, Cortez 4)

Black Tulip. See Tulipe noire, 1963

Black Veil for Lisa. See Morte non ha sesso, 1969

Black Viper, 1908 (Bitzer 4)

Black Vision, 1965 (Brakhage 2)

Black Watch, 1929 (Ford 2, Loy 3, McLaglen 3, Scott 3, August 4, Fox 4)

Black Waters, 1929 (Neilan 2, Johnson 3)

Black Whip, 1956 (Dickinson 3, Biroc 4)

Black Widow, 1951 (Carreras 4)

Black Widow, 1954 (Raft 3, Rogers 3, Tierney 3, Clarke 4, LeMaire 4)

Black Widow, 1987 (Rafelson 2, Hopper 3, Hall 4)

Black Windmill, 1974 (Siegel 2, Caine 3, Pleasence 3, Seyrig 3)

Black Wings. See Czarne skrzydła, 1962

Black Zoo, 1963 (Crosby 4)

Blackbeard, 1911 (Bosworth 3)

Blackbeard the Pirate, 1952 (Walsh 2, Bendix 3, Darnell 3, Newton 3, Young 4)

Blackbeard's Ghost, 1968 (Stevenson 2, Lanchester 3, Ustinov 3, Ellenshaw 4)

Blackbird, 1926 (Browning 2, Chaney 3, Gibbons 4, Gillespie 4, Mayer 4, Young 4)

Blackbird Descending, 1977 (Le Grice 2)

Blackbirds, 1916 (Rosher 4)

Blackboard Jungle, 1955 (Brooks 2, Mazursky 2, Calhern 3, Ford 3, Poitier 3, Berman 4, Gibbons 4, Harlan 4)

Blackboard Revue, 1940 (Iwerks 4)

Blackened Hills, 1911 (Dwan 2)

Blackguard, 1925 (Balcon 4)

Blackjack Ketchum Desperado, 1956 (Katzman 4)

Blacklist, 1916 (Sweet 3, Rosher 4)

Blacklist. See Liste noire, 1985

Blackmail, 1929 (Hitchcock 2, Ondra 3, Bennett 4)

Blackmail, 1939 (Robinson 3)

Blackmailed, 1950 (Zetterling 2, Bogarde 3)

Blackout. See Contraband, 1940

Blackout. See Murder By Proxy, 1955

Blackout, 1978 (Allyson 3, Milland 3)

Blackout, 1985 (Widmark 3)

Blacks and Whites in Days and Nights, 1960 (Vanderbeek 2)

Blacksmith, 1922 (Keaton 2)

Blackwell's Island, 1939 (Garfield 3)

Blade Runner, 1982 (Scott 2, Ford 3, Trumbull 4, Vangelis 4)

Blague dans le coin, 1963 (Fernandel 3, Spaak 4)

Blaho lásky, 1966 (Brdečka 4, Trnka 4)

Blaise Pascal, 1975 (Rossellini 2)

Blåjackor, 1945 (Fischer 4)

Blake of Scotland Yard, 1937 (Katzman 4)

Blame It on Father, 1953 (Lee 3)

Blame it on Love, 1940 (Ladd 3)

Blame It on Rio, 1984 (Donen 2, Caine 3)

Blame it on the Bellboy, 1991 (Moore 3)

Blame the Woman, 1932 (Niblo 2, Menjou 3)

Blänande hav, 1956 (Nykvist 4)

Blanc comme neige, 1947 (Cloquet 4)

Blanc de chine, 1988 (Piccoli 3, Coutard 4)

Blanc et le noir, 1930 (Fernandel 3)

Blanc et le noir, 1931 (Florey 2, Guitry 2, Rainu 3, Braunberger 4)

Blanche, 1970 (Borowczyk 2, Simon 3)

Blanche comme neige, 1908 (Cohl 4)

Blanche Fury, 1947 (Granger 3, Green 4, Havelock-Allan 4, Rank 4, Unsworth 4)

Blanchisserie Américaine, 1915 (Cohl 4)

Blandt byens børn, 1922 (Madsen and Schenstrøm 3)

Blankt Vapen, 1990 (Andersson 3)

Blarney, 1926 (Gibbons 4, Lewin 4, Mayer 4)

Blarney Stone, 1913 (Bunny 3)

Blason, 1915 (Feuillade 2)

Blaubart, 1951 (Albers 3, Kortner 3)

Blaubart, 1984 (Von Trotta 2, Zanussi 2)

Blaue Engel, 1930 (Von Sternberg 2, Albers 3, Dietrich 3, Jannings 3, Hunte 4, Pommer 4, Waxman 4)

Blaue Hand, 1967 (Kinski 3)

Blaue Laterne, 1918 (Porten 3, Messter 4)

Blaue Maus, 1913 (Warm 4)

Blaue von Himmel, 1932 (Wilder 2)

Blaze, 1989 (Newman 3, Wexler 4)

Blaze Away, 1922 (Roach 4)

Blaze o' Glory, 1929 (Walthall 3)

Blaze of Noon, 1947 (Baxter 3, Bendix 3, Hayden 3, Holden 3, Deutsch 4, Dreier 4, Head 4)

Blazes, 1961 (Breer 4)

Blazing Days, 1927 (Wyler 2, Laemmle 4)

Blazing Forest, 1952 (Moorehead 3)

Blazing Frontier, 1943 (Crabbe 3)

Blazing Guns, 1934 (Canutt 4)

Blazing Saddles, 1974 (Brooks 2, Wilder 3, Biroc 4)

Blazing Saddles, 1990 (Pryor 3)

Blazing Stewardesses, 1976 (De Carlo 3)

Blazing Sun, 1950 (Autry 3)

Blázni, vodníci, a podvodníci, 1980 (Švankmajer 4)

Bláznova kronika, 1964 (Zeman 4)

Blechtrommel, 1978 (Schlöndorff 2, Winkler 3)

Blechtrommel, 1979 (Olbrychski 3, Carrière 4, Jarre 4)

Blé en herbe, 1953 (Feuillère 3, Aurenche 4, Bost 4, Douy 4)

Blé en liasses, 1969 (Dalio 3)

Bled, 1929 (Becker 2, Renoir 2)

Bleierne Zeit, 1981 (Von Trotta 2, Vogler 3)

Bleka Greven, 1937 (Madsen and Schenstrøm 3)

Błękitny krzyż, 1955 (Munk 2)

Bless the Beasts and Children, 1971 (Kramer 2, Wheeler 4)

Bless the Children, 1953 (Zhao 3)

Blessed Event, 1932 (Powell 3, Polito 4)

Blessure, 1921 (Bertini 3)

Bleu gang . . . , 1972 (Storaro 4)

Bleu perdu, 1972 (Driessen 4)

Bleus de la marine, 1934 (Fernandel 3)

Bleus de l'amour, 1932 (Wakhévitch 4)

Blick zurück, 1944 (Stallich 4)

Blighty, 1927 (Balcon 4)

Blind, 1986 (Wiseman 2)

Blind Adventure, 1933 (Schoedsack 2, Bellamy 3, Plunkett 4, Steiner 4)

Blind Alibi, 1938 (Musuraca 4)

Blind Alley, 1939 (Vidor 2, Bellamy 3, Ballard 4)

Blind Bargain, 1922 (Chaney 3)

Blind Chance. See Przypadek, 1982

Blind Date, 1934 (Darwell 3, Rooney 3)

Blind Date, 1954 (Terry 4)

Blind Date, 1959 (Baker 3, Presle 3, Challis 4)

Blind Date, 1987 (Edwards 2, Mancini 4)

Blind Deception, 1911 (Lawrence 3)

Blind Desire. See Part de l'ombre, 1945

Blind Director. See Angriff der Gegenwart aud die Ubrige Zeit, 1985

Blind Fate, 1914 (Hepworth 2)

Blind Goddess, 1926 (Fleming 2, Banton 4)

Blind Goddess, 1948 (Bloom 3, Box 4, Rank 4)

Blind Hearts, 1921 (Bosworth 3)

Blind Husbands, 1918 (Von Stroheim 2, Carey 3, Daniels 4, Day 4)

Blind Justice, 1934 (Mills 3)

Blind Love, 1912 (Sweet 3)

Blind Love, 1979 (Legrand 4)

Blind Man's Bluff, 1936 (Mason 3)

Blind Man's Bluff, 1971 (Karloff 3)

Blind Man's Tact, 1910 (Lawrence 3)

Blind Passion. See V boynoi slepote strastei, 1916

Blind Princess and the Poet, 1911 (Griffith 2, Sweet 3, Bitzer 4)

Blind Spot. See Flüsternde Tod, 1975

Blind Terror, 1971 (Farrow 3, Bernstein 4, Fisher 4)

Blind White Duration, 1967 (Le Grice 2)

Blinde, 1911 (Porten 3, Messter 4)

Blinde Passagerer. See Blinde Passagiere, 1936

Blinde Passagiere, 1936 (Madsen and Schenstrøm 3)

Blinded by the Light, 1980 (Alonzo 4)

Blindfold, 1928 (Fox 4)

Blindfold, 1966 (Cardinale 3, Hudson 3, Bumstead 4, Dunne 4, Schifrin 4, Whitlock 4)

Blindfold. See Ojos vendados, 1978

Blindkuh, 1914 (Lubitsch 2)

Blindness of Devotion, 1915 (Ingram 2)

Blindness of Fortune, 1918 (Hepworth 2)

Blinkeyes, 1926 (Pearson 2)

Blinkity Blank, 1952 (McLaren 4)

Blinky, 1923 (Miller 4)

Bliss, 1917 (Daniels 3, Lloyd 3)

Bliss, 1967 (Markopoulos 2)

Bliss of Love. See Blaho lásky, 1966

Bliss of Mrs. Blossom, 1968 (Attenborough 3, MacLaine 3, Godfrey 4, Unsworth 4)

Blithe Spirit, 1945 (Lean 2, Harrison 3, Rutherford 3, Coward 4)

Blithe Spirit, 1966 (Bogarde 3)

Blitz on the Fritz, 1943 (Langdon 3, Bruckman 4)

Blitz Wolf, 1942 (Avery 4)

Blitzzug de Liebe, 1925 (Hoffmann 4)

Blixt och dunder, 1938 (Fischer 4)

Blizzard, 1921 (Laurel and Hardy 3)

Blob, 1958 (McQueen 3)

Block Busters, 1944 (Langdon 3, Katzman 4)

Block Signal, 1926 (Arthur 3)

Blockade, 1938 (Dieterle 2, Carroll 3, Fonda 3, Basevi 4, Irene 4, Maté 4, Wanger 4)

Blockade. See Bloko, 1964

Block-Heads, 1938 (Langdon 3, Laurel and Hardy 3, Roach 4)

Blockhouse, 1973 (Sellers 3)

Block-Notes di un regista, 1969
(Mastroianni 3)

Blodets röst, 1913 (Sjöström 2, Jaenzon 4)

Bloko, 1964 (Theodorakis 4)

Blomstertid, 1940 (Sjöberg 2)

Blond Cheat, 1938 (Fontaine 3, Hunt 4)

Blonde and Groom, 1943 (Langdon 3)

Blonde Bombshell. See Bombshell, 1933

Blonde Crazy, 1931 (Blondell 3, Cagney 3,
Calhern 3, Milland 3, Haller 4)

Blonde de Pekin, 1968 (Robinson 3)

Blonde Dream. See Blonder Traum, 1932

Blonde Dynamite. See She's Dangerous,
1936

Blonde Fever, 1944 (Astor 3, Gardner 3,
Grahame 3, Irene 4)

Blonde Fist, 1991 (Baker 3)

Blonde for a Night, 1928 (Pangborn 3)

Blonde for Danger. See Sois belle et tais-toi,
1958

Blonde from Brooklyn, 1945 (Guffey 4)

Blonde from Peking. See Blonde de Pekin,
1968

Blonde in Black Leather, 1977 (Cardinale 3)

Blonde Inspiration, 1941 (Berkeley 2,
Kaper 4)

Blonde Menace. See Scattergood Meets
Broadway, 1941

Blonde or Brunette, 1927 (Menjou 3,
Schulberg 4)

Blonde Saint, 1926 (Gaudio 4)

Blonde Sinner. See Yield to the Night, 1956

Blonde Trouble, 1937 (Head 4)

Blonde Venus, 1932 (Von Sternberg 2,
Dietrich 3, Grant 3, Marshall 3,
McDaniel 3, Banton 4, Furthman 4,
Glennon 4, Zukor 4)

Blonder Traum, 1932 (Wilder 2, Pommer 4,
Reisch 4)

Blondes for Danger, 1938 (Wilcox 2)

Blonde's Revenge, 1926 (Sennett 2)

Blondie Goes to College, 1942 (Bruckman 4,
Cahn 4)

Blondie Johnson, 1933 (Blondell 3,
Gaudio 4, Orry-Kelly 4)

Blondie Knows Best, 1946 (Three
Stooges 3)

Blondie of the Follies, 1932 (Goulding 2,
Davies 3, Durante 3, Montgomery 3,
Barnes 4, Freed 4, Loos 4, Marion 4)

Blondie on a Budget, 1940 (Hayworth 3)

Blondie Plays Cupid, 1940 (Ford 3)

Blondie's Blessed Event, 1942 (Cahn 4)

Blondy, 1975 (Andersson 3)

Blood. See Occhio nel labarinto, 1970

Blood Alley, 1955 (Wellman 2, Bacall 3,
Wayne 3, Clothier 4)

Blood and Lace, 1970 (Grahame 3)

Blood and Roses. See Et mourir de plaisir,
1960

Blood and Sand, 1922 (Arzner 2, Niblo 2,
Valentino 3, Mathis 4, Westmore
Family 4)

Blood and Sand, 1941 (Mamoulian 2,
Carradine 3, Darnell 3, Hayworth 3,
Nazimova 3, Power 3, Quinn 3,
Banton 4, Day 4, Newman 4, Swerling 4,
Zanuck 4)

Blood and Soul. See Chi to rei, 1976

Blood and Steel, 1959 (Crosby 4)

Blood and Water, 1913 (Guy 2)

Blood Barrier, 1920 (Blackton 2)

Blood Bath, 1965 (Corman 2)

Blood Beast Terror, 1968 (Cushing 3)

Blood Brother. See Rodnoi brat, 1929

Blood Brothers. See Guappi, 1973

Blood Brothers, 1978 (Mulligan 2, Gere 3,
Bernstein 4, Surtees 4)

Blood Demon. See Schlangengrube und das
Pendel, 1967

Blood Feast. See Fin de fiesta, 1959

Blood Feud, 1983 (Wertmüller 2,
Borgnine 3, Ferrer 3)

Blood Fiend. See Theatre of Death, 1967

Blood for Dracula, 1974 (Polanski 2)

Blood from the Mummy's Tomb, 1971
(Carreras 4)

Blood in the Streets, 1976 (Reed 3,
Morricone 4)

Blood Kin, 1969 (Lumet 2, Coburn 3,
Howe 4, Jones 4)

Blood Money, 1933 (Ball 3, D'Agostino 4,
Newman 4, Zanuck 4)

Blood Money. See Moneda sangrienta, 1974

Blood Need Not Be Spilled. See Ni nado
kruvi, 1917

Blood of a Poet. See **La Sang d'un poète,
1930**

Blood of Dracula's Castle, 1967
(Carradine 3, Kovacs 4)

Blood of Frankenstein. See Dracula vs.
Frankenstein, 1969

Blood of Fu Manchu, 1968 (Lee 3)

Blood of Ghastly Horror, 1972 (Carradine 3)

Blood of Hussain, 1977 (Lassally 4)

Blood of Others. See Sang des autres, 1983

Blood of the Children, 1915 (Meredyth 4)

Blood of the Condor. See **Yawar Mallku,
1969**

Blood of the Iron Maiden, 1970
(Carradine 3)

Blood of the Man Devil. See House of the
Black Death, 1965

Blood of the Vampire, 1958 (Sangster 4)

Blood on My Hands. See Kiss the Blood off
My Hands, 1948

Blood on the Moon, 1948 (Wise 2,
Brennan 3, Mitchum 3, Preston 3,
D'Agostino 4, Musuraca 4)

Blood on the Sun, 1945 (Cagney 3, Sidney 3,
Rozsa 4)

Blood Orange, 1953 (Fisher 2, Carreras 4)

Blood Red, 1990 (Giannini 3, Hopper 3)

Blood Relatives. See Liens du sang, 1978

Blood Ruby, 1914 (Costello 3)

Blood Seekers. See Dracula vs.
Frankenstein, 1969

Blood Ship, 1927 (Bosworth 3, Cohn 4)

Blood Sisters. See Sister, 1972

Blood Suckers. See Dr. Terror's Gallery of
Horrors, 1967

Blood Tide, 1982 (Ferrer 3, Jones 3)

Blood Wedding. See Bodas de sangre, 1981

Blood Will Tell, 1912 (Ince 4)

Blood Will Tell, 1914 (Bushman 3)

Blood Will Tell, 1927 (Fox 4)

Bloodbath in the House of Death, 1983
(Price 3)

Bloodhounds of Broadway, 1952
(Bronson 3, Cronjager 4, LeMaire 4)

Bloodhounds of the North, 1913 (Dwan 2,
Chaney 3)

Bloodlaw, 1990 (Curtis 3)

Bloodline, 1979 (Hepburn 3, Papas 3,
Schneider 3, Sharif 3, Morricone 4,
Young 4)

Bloodsport, 1973 (Johnson 3)

Bloodsport, 1988 (Golan and Globus 4)

Bloodstain, 1912 (Guy 2)

Bloodsuckers. See Incense for the Damned,
1970

Bloody Birthday, 1986 (Ferrer 3)

Bloody Brood, 1959 (Falk 3, Schüfftan 4)

Bloody Chamber, 1983 (Stamp 3)

Bloody Hands of the Law. See Mano spietat
della legge, 1973

Bloody Judge. See Processo de las brujas,
1970

Bloody Kids, 1979 (Menges 4)

Bloody Mama, 1970 (De Niro 3, Dern 3,
Winters 3, Alonzo 4)

Bloomfield, 1970 (Harris 3, Schneider 3,
Heller 4, Mankowitz 4)

Blossom Time. See Blomstertid, 1940

Blossoms in the Dust, 1941 (LeRoy 2,
Garson 3, Pidgeon 3, Adrian 4, Freund 4,
Gibbons 4, Loos 4, Mayer 4, Stothart 4)

Blossoms on Broadway, 1937 (Head 4,
Schulberg 4, Shamroy 4)

Blot, 1921 (Weber 2, Calhern 3)

Blot on the Scutcheon, 1911 (Griffith 2,
Bitzer 4)

Blot on the Shield, 1915 (Eason 4)

Blotted Brand, 1911 (Dwan 2)

Blotto, 1930 (Laurel and Hardy 3, Roach 4)

Bloudĕni, 1965 (Menzel 2, Brejchová 3)

Blow By Blow, 1928 (McCarey 2, Roach 4)

Blow 'em Up, 1922 (Roach 4)

Blowing Hot and Cold, 1984 (Giannini 3)

Blowing Wild, 1953 (Bond 3, Cooper 3,
Quinn 3, Stanwyck 3, Tiomkin 4)

Blow Me Down, 1939 (Fleischer 4)

Blow Out, 1981 (De Palma 2, Travolta 3,
Donaggio 4, Zsigmond 4)

Blow! The Spring Breeze. See Fukeyo
harukaze, 1953

Blow to the Heart. See Colpa al cuore, 1982

Blow Job, 1963 (Warhol 2)

Blow-out, 1936 (Avery 4)

Blow-Out. See Grande Bouffe, 1973

**Blow-Up, 1966 (Antonioni 2, Redgrave 3,
Guerra 4, Ponti 4)**

Blue, 1968 (Malden 3, Stamp 3, Cortez 4,
Winkler 4)

Blue and the Gold. See Annopolis Story,
1955

Blue and the Gray, 1982 (Hayden 3, Peck 3)

Blue Angel. See **Blaue Engel, 1930**

Blue Angel, 1959 (Dmytryk 2, Friedhofer 4,
Shamroy 4)

Blue Beard. See Charlatan, 1901

Blue Beast. See Aoi yaju, 1960

Blue Bird, 1918 (Tourneur 2, Carré 4)

Blue Bird, 1940 (Temple 3, Day 4, Miller 4,
Newman 4, Zanuck)

Blue Blazes, 1936 (Keaton 2)

Blue Blazes Rawden, 1918 (Hart 3,
August 4)

Blue Blood, 1973 (Reed 3)

Blue Blood and Red, 1916 (Walsh 2)

Blue Bud. See Aoi me, 1956

Blue Canadian Rockies, 1952 (Autry 3)

Blue Cat Blues, 1956 (Hanna and
Barbera 4)

Blue City, 1986 (Hill 2)

Blue Collar, 1978 (Schrader 2, Pryor 3)

Blue Dahlia, 1946 (Ladd 3, Lake 3,
Chandler 4, Dreier 4, Head 4,
Houseman 4, Young 4)

Blue Danube, 1928 (Adrian 4, Grot 4,
Miller 4)

Blue Danube, 1931 (Wilcox 2, Young 4)

Blue Denim, 1959 (Brackett 4, Dunne 4, Herrmann 4, Reynolds 4, Wheeler 4)
Blue Eagle, 1926 (Ford 2, Gaynor 3, Fox 4)
Blue Electrico, 1988 (Cardinale 3)
Blue Envelope Mystery, 1916 (Menjou 3)
Blue Field Duration, 1972 (Le Grice 2)
Blue Gardenia, 1953 (Lang 2, Baxter 3, Musuraca 4)
Blue Grass Romance, 1913 (Ince 4)
Blue Hawaii, 1961 (Lansbury 3, Presley 3, Edouart 4, Fulton 4, Head 4, Lang 4, Wallis 4)
Blue Jeans. See Blue Denim, 1959
Blue Knight, 1975 (Holden 3, Mancini 4)
Blue Lagoon, 1949 (Launder and Gilliat 2, Cusack 3, Simmons 3, Rank 4, Unsworth 4)
Blue Lagoon, 1979 (Almendros 4)
Blue Lamp, 1950 (Dearden 2, Mackendrick 2, Bogarde 3, Balcon 4, Clarke 4)
Blue Light, 1931 (Balàzs 4)
Blue Man, 1986 (Black 3)
Blue Max, 1966 (Mason 3, Goldsmith 4, Slocombe 4)
Blue Monday, 1938 (Hanna and Barbera 4)
Blue Monday, 1988 (Breer 4)
Blue Montana Skies, 1939 (Autry 3, Eason 4)
Blue Moon Murder Case, 1932 (Florey 2)
Blue Moses, 1962 (Brakhage 2)
Blue Mountains. See Aoi sanmyaku, 1949
Blue Movie, 1968 (Warhol 2)
Blue Murder at St. Trinian's, 1957 (Launder and Gilliat 2, Sim 3, Terry-Thomas 3, Arnold 4)
Blue of the Night, 1933 (Sennett 2, Crosby 3)
Blue or the Gray, 1913 (Gish 3)
Blue Peter, 1958 (Lassally 4)
Blue Planet, 1990 (Burtt 4)
Blue Plate Symphony, 1954 (Terry 4)
Blue Rose, 1913 (Talmadge 3)
Blue Skies, 1929 (Fox 4)
Blue Skies, 1946 (Astaire 3, Crosby 3, Berlin 4, Head 4, Lang 4, Pan 4)
Blue Sky, 1991 (Richardson 2, Lange 3)
Blue Smoke, 1935 (Bennett 4)
Blue Steel, 1934 (Wayne 3, Canutt 4)
Blue Steel, 1990 (Curtis 3)
Blue Streak McCoy, 1920 (Carey 3, Eason 4)
Blue Thunder, 1983 (McDowell 3, Oates 3, Scheider 3, Alonzo 4)
Blue Vanguard, 1957 (Dickinson 2)
Blue Veil, 1951 (Blondell 3, Cusack 3, Laughton 3, Moorehead 3, Sloane 3, Wood 3, Wyman 3, Hakim 4, Krasna 4, Planer 4, Wald 4, Waxman 4, Westmore Family 4)
Blue Velvet, 1986 (Lynch 2, Hopper 3, De Laurentiis 4)
Blue Wall, 1989 (Emshwiller 2)
Blue Water, 1924 (Shearer 3)
Blue, White, and Perfect, 1941 (Marsh 3, Chase 4)
Bluebeard, 1944 (Ulmer 2, Carradine 3)
Bluebeard. See Barbe-Bleue, 1951
Bluebeard. See Landru, 1963
Bluebeard. See Barbe-Bleue, 1972
Bluebeard. See Blaubart, 1984
Bluebeard's Brother, 1932 (Terry 4)
Bluebeard's Castle. See Herzog Blaubart's Burg, 1964

Bluebeard's Eighth Wife, 1923 (Wood 2, Swanson 3)
Bluebeard's Eighth Wife, 1938 (Guitry 2, Lubitsch 2, Wilder 2, Colbert 3, Cooper 3, Horton 3, Niven 3, Pangborn 3, Banton 4, Brackett 4, Dreier 4, Prinz 4)
Bluebeard's Seven Wives, 1926 (Sweet 3, Haller 4)
Bluebeard's Six Wives. See Sei mogli di Barbablu', 1950
Bluebeard's Ten Honeymoons, 1960 (Sanders 3)
Bluebird, 1917 (Zukor 4)
Bluebird, 1976 (Cukor 2, Fonda 3, Gardner 3, Taylor 3, Head 4, Young 4)
Bluebottles, 1928 (Lanchester 3, Laughton 3)
Bluegrass, 1987 (Rooney 3)
Bluejackets. See Blåjackor, 1945
Blueprint for Murder, 1953 (Cotten 3, Marsh 3, LeMaire 4)
Blues, 1931 (Terry 4)
Blues Brothers, 1980 (Landis 2, Spielberg 2, Belushi 3, Whitlock 3)
Blues for Lovers. See Ballad in Blue, 1964
Blues in the Night, 1941 (Kazan 2, Litvak 2, Rossen 2, Siegel 2, Blanke 4, Haller 4, Mercer 4)
Bluets dans la tête, 1969 (Almendros 4)
Bluff, 1916 (Feyder 2, Gaumont 4)
Bluff, 1924 (Wood 2)
Bluff, 1976 (Quinn 3)
Bluff Stop, 1978 (Donner 2)
Bluffer, 1930 (Sennett 2)
Bluffers, 1915 (Eason 4)
Blume in Love, 1973 (Mazursky 2, Segal 3, Winters 3)
Blumenfrau von Lindenau, 1931 (Lamarr 3)
Blumenfrau von Potsdamer Platz, 1925 (Dieterle 2)
Blunder Below, 1942 (Fleischer 4)
Blunder Boys, 1955 (Three Stooges 3)
Blunt, 1986 (Hopkins 3)
Blusen König, 1917 (Lubitsch 2, Kräly 4)
Blushing Bride, 1921 (Fox 4, Furthman 4)
Blut der Ahnen, 1920 (Wiene 2, Dagover 3, Warm 4)
Blut und Boden, 1933 (Ruttman 2)
Blutsbrüderschaft, 1950 (Staudte 2)
Blutschande die 173 St. G.B., 1929 (Tschechowa 3)
Bly jednou jeden Král, 1955 (Brdečka 4)
Boadicea, 1927 (Asquith 2)
Boardwalk, 1979 (Gordon 3, Leigh 3)
Boat, 1921 (Keaton 2)
Boatniks, 1970 (Ameche 3)
Boats under Oars, 1901 (Bitzer 4)
Bob and Carol and Ted and Alice, 1969 (Mazursky 2, Gould 3, Wood 3, Jones 4, Lang 4)
Bob and the Pirates, 1959 (Haller 4)
Bob Hampton of Placer, 1921 (Neilan 2, Carré 4)
Bob Hope Reports to the Nation, 1947 (Kaye 3)
Bob Kick, l'enfant terrible, 1903 (Méliès 2)
Bob Kick the Mischievous Kid. See Bob Kick, l'enfant terrible, 1903
Bob le flambeur, 1956 (Melville 2, Decaë 4)
Bob Mathias Story, 1954 (Bond 3)
Bob, Son of Battle. See Thunder in the Valley, 1947

Bobbed Hair, 1925 (Costello 3, Haskin 4)
Bobbie of the Ballet, 1916 (Chaney 3)
Bobby, 1974 (Kapoor 2, Abbas 4)
Bobby Deerfield, 1977 (Pollack 2, Pacino 3, Decaë 4, Sargent 4)
Bobby the Coward, 1911 (Bitzer 4)
Bobby's Kodak, 1908 (Bitzer 4)
Bobo, 1967 (Brazzi 3, Sellers 3, Cahn 4, Lai 4)
Bobo Jacco, 1979 (Girardot 3)
Bobosse, 1958 (Presle 3)
Bobs, 1928 (Grémillon 2)
Bocal aux poissons-rouges, 1895 (Lumière 2)
Boccaccio, 1920 (Curtiz 2)
Boccaccio, 1972 (Blier 3)
Boccaccio '70, 1962 (De Sica 2, Monicelli 2, Visconti 2, Loren 3, Schneider 3, Cecchi D'Amico 4, Flaiano 4, Gherardi 4, Pinelli 4, Ponti 4, Rota 4, Rotunno 4, Zavattini 4)
Bocchan dohyo-iri, 1943 (Tanaka 3)
Bocchan kisha, 1955 (Yamamura 3)
Bodakunden, 1956 (Molander 2)
Bodas de Fuego, 1949 (Armendáriz 3)
Bodas de sangre, 1976 (Papas 3)
Bodas de sangre, 1981 (Saura 2)
Bødes der for. See Haevnet, 1911
Body. See Ratai, 1962
Body. See Take This—My Body, 1974
Body and Soul, 1925 (Micheaux 2, Robeson 3)
Body and Soul, 1927 (Barrymore 3, Gibbons 4, Gillespie 4)
Body and Soul, 1931 (Bogart 3, Loy 3, Furthman 4, Grot 4)
Body and Soul, 1947 (Aldrich 2, Polonsky 2, Rossen 2, Garfield 3, Friedhofer 4, Howe 4)
Body and Soul, 1981 (Golan and Globus 4)
Body Disappears, 1942 (Horton 3, Wyman 3)
Body Double, 1984 (De Palma 2, Donaggio 4)
Body Heat, 1981 (Kasdan 2, Hurt 3, Rourke 3, Turner 3, Barry 4)
Body of My Enemy. See Corps de mon ennemi, 1976
Body Rock, 1984 (Müller 4)
Body Slam, 1987 (Needham 4)
Body Snatcher, 1945 (Wise 2, Karloff 3, Lugosi 3, D'Agostino 4, Lewton 4)
Body Stealers, 1969 (Sanders 3)
Bodyguard, 1944 (Hanna and Barbera 4)
Bodyguard. See Yojimbo, 1961
Boefje, 1939 (Sirk 2)
Boeing Boeing, 1965 (Lewis 2, Curtis 3, Ritter 3, Anhalt 4, Ballard 4, Head 4, Wallis 4)
Boeuf sur la langue, 1933 (Christian-Jaque 2)
Bof!, 1969 (Vierny 4)
Bofuu no bara, 1931 (Takamine 3)
Bogie, 1980 (Taradash 4)
Bohdan Khmelnytsky, 1941 (Dovzhenko 2)
Boheme, 1923 (Dreier 4, Kräly 4)
Bohème, 1926 (Florey 2, Vidor 2, Gilbert 3, Gish 3, Horton 3, Carré 4, Gibbons 4, Gillespie 4, Mayer 4)
Bohème, 1982 (Zeffirelli 2)
Boheme, 1989 (Comencini 2)
Boheme—Künstlerliebe, 1923 (Dieterle 2)
Bohemian Dancer, 1929 (Young 4)
Bohemian Girl, 1922 (Novello 3)

Bohemian Girl, 1936 (Laurel and Hardy 3, Roach 4)
Bohus bataljon, 1949 (Nykvist 4)
Boi pod Tsaritsinom, 1920 (Vertov 2)
Boia di Lilla, 1952 (Brazzi 3)
Boilesk, 1933 (Fleischer 4)
Boireau déménage, 1906 (Pathé 4)
Bois des amants, 1960 (Autant-Lara 2, Rosay 3, Douy 4)
Bois et cuivres, 1958 (Decaë 4)
Bois sacré, 1939 (Dalio 3)
Boîte à malice, 1903 (Méliès 2)
Boîte aux rêves, 1943 (Allégret 2, Philipe 3, Signoret 3, Wakhévitch 4)
Boite diabolique. See Jobard fiance par interim, 1911
Bojo, 1950 (Yamada 3)
Bojo no hito, 1961 (Hara 3)
Boks, 1961 (Skolimowski 2)
Bokser, 1966 (Olbrychski 3)
Boku wa san-nin mae, 1958 (Kagawa 3)
Bokura no otouto, 1933 (Yoda 4)
Bokyaku no hanabira: Kanketsu-hen, 1957 (Tsukasa 3)
Bold and the Brave, 1956 (Rooney 3)
Bold Caballero, 1937 (Canutt 4)
Bold Cavalier. See Bold Caballero, 1937
Bold Emmett, 1915 (Olcott 2)
Bold King Cole, 1936 (Messmer 4)
Bolero, 1934 (Lombard 3, Milland 3, Raft 3, Sheridan 3, Banton 4, Prinz 4, Wilson 4, Zukor 4)
Bolero, 1942 (Arletty 3, Signoret 3)
Bolero. See Uns et les autres, 1981
Bolero, 1984 (Bernstein 4, Golan and Globus 4)
Bolero de Raquel, 1956 (Cantinflas 3, Figueroa 4)
Bolivar 63–29, 1963 (Gélin 3)
Bolivia, 1946 (Ferrer 3)
Bolly, 1968 (Halas and Batchelor 4)
Bolshaya semya, 1955 (Batalov 3)
Bolwieser, 1977 (Fassbinder 2, Ballhaus 4)
Boman på utstallningen, 1923 (Magnusson 4)
Bomarzo, 1949 (Antonioni 2)
Bom Povo Português, 1980 (De Almeida 4)
Bom the Flyer. See Flyg-Bom, 1952
Bomb for a Dictator. See Fanatiques, 1957
Bomb Mania. See Bombománie, 1959
Bomb Was Stolen. See S-a furat o bomba, 1961
Bomba and the African Treasure. See African Treasure, 1962
Bomba and the Elephant Stampede. See Elephant Stampede, 1951
Bomba and the Hidden City. See Hidden City, 1950
Bomba and the Jungle Girl, 1962 (Mirisch 4)
Bomba and the Lion Hunters. See Lion Hunters, 1962
Bomba Kemal, 1967 (Güney 2)
Bomba on Panther Island, 1950 (Mirisch 4)
Bomba the Jungle Boy, 1949 (Mirisch 4)
Bombay Clipper, 1941 (Cortez 4, Salter 4)
Bombai Ka Babu, 1960 (Burman 4)
Bombardier, 1943 (Ryan 3, Scott 3, Dunn 4, Musuraca 4)
Bombardment of Monte Carlo. See Bomben auf Monte Carlo, 1931
Bombay Talkie, 1970 (Ivory 2, Jhabvala 4, Mitra 4)
Bombay to Goa, 1972 (Bachchan 3)
Bombe, 1909 (Linder 3)

Bombe après l'obtention de son bachot. See Bombe, 1909
Bombe par hasard, 1969 (Grimault 4)
Bomben auf Monte Carlo, 1931 (Albers 3, Pommer 4)
Bomben auf Monte Carlo, 1931 (Lorre 3)
Bomben auf Monte Carlo, 1960 (Constantine 3)
Bombero atómico, 1950 (Cantinflas 3, Figueroa 4)
Bomber-pilot, 1970 (Schroeter 2)
Bombers B-52, 1957 (Malden 3, Wood 3, Clothier 4, Rosenman 4)
Bomber's Moon, 1943 (Florey 2, Ballard 4, Basevi 4)
Bombomania. See Bombománie, 1959
Bombománie, 1959 (Brdečka 4, Trnka 4)
Bombs, 1916 (Sennett 2)
Bombs and Bangs, 1914 (Sennett 2)
Bombs and Banknotes, 1916 (Beery 3)
Bombs over Burma, 1942 (Lewis 2, Wong 3)
Bombs over Japan. See Wild Blue Yonder, 1951
Bombs over London. See Midnight Menace, 1936
Bombshell, 1933 (Beavers 3, Harlow 3, Adrian 4, Booth 4, Furthman 4, Mayer 4, Rosson 4, Stromberg 4)
Bombsight Stolen. See Cottage to Let, 1941
Bon baisers de Hong Kong, 1975 (Rooney 3)
Bon Dieu sans confession, 1953 (Autant-Lara 2, Darrieux 3, Douy 4)
Bon et les méchants, 1976 (Reggiani 3, Lai 4)
Bon Plaisir, 1983 (Deneuve 3, Trintignant 3)
Bon propriétaire, 1913 (Feuillade 2)
Bon Roi Dagobert, 1963 (Cervi 3, Fernandel 3)
Bon Voyage, 1944 (Hitchcock 2)
Bon Voyage. See Schastlivogo plavaniya, 1949
Bon Voyage, 1962 (MacMurray 3, Wyman 3, Disney 4)
Bona, 1980 (Brocka 2)
Bonanza Bunny, 1959 (Blanc 4, McKimson 4)
Bonaparte et la révolution, 1971 (Gance 2)
Bonaventure. See Thunder on the Hill, 1951
Bonbon, 1947 (Hasegawa 3)
Bonchi, 1960 (Ichikawa 2, Kyo 3, Yamada 3, Miyagawa 4)
Bond, 1918 (Chaplin 2, Purviance 3)
Bond Between, 1917 (Crisp 3)
Bond Between Us, 1953 (Metty 4)
Bond Boy, 1922 (King 2, Barthelmess 3)
Bond Street, 1948 (Clayton 2, De Grunwald 4, Heller 4, Rattigan 4)
Bondage, 1917 (Chaney 3)
Bondage, 1933 (Darwell 3, Friedhofer 4)
Bondage of Barbara, 1919 (Marsh 3)
Bondman, 1929 (Wilcox 2, Steiner 4)
Bonds of Honor, 1919 (Hayakawa 3)
Bonds That Chafe. See Erotikon, 1920
Bone Dry, 1922 (Roach 4)
Bone for a Bone, 1951 (Blanc 4, Freleng 4, Stalling 4)
Bone, Sweet Bone, 1948 (Blanc 4)
Bonfire of the Vanities, 1990 (Hanks 3, Sylbert 4, Zsigmond 4)
Bonheur, 1934 (L'Herbier 2, Boyer 3, Marais 3, Simon 3, Douy 4, Stradling 4)
Bonheur, 1965 (Varda 2, Rabier 4)
Bonheur des autres, 1918 (Dulac 2)
Bonheur d'être aimée, 1962 (Storck 2)

Bonheur est pour demain, 1962 (Delerue 4)
Boniface somnambule, 1950 (Fernandel 3)
Bonita of El Cajon, 1911 (Dwan 2)
Bonjour cinéma, 1948 (Epstein 2)
Bonjour Mr. Lewis, 1982 (Scorsese 2, Martin 3)
Bonjour, Monsieur La Bruyère, 1958 (Braunberger 4)
Bonjour New York!, 1928 (Florey 2, Chevalier 3)
Bonjour sourire, 1956 (Sautet 2, Burel 4)
Bonjour Tristesse, 1957 (Preminger 2, Kerr 3, Niven 3, Seberg 3, Auric 4, Bass 4, Périnal 4)
Bonne à tout faire. See Difficulté d'être infidèle, 1963
Bonne Absinthe, 1897 (Guy 2)
Bonne Absinthe, 1899 (Gaumont 4)
Bonne année, 1913 (Feuillade 2)
Bonne Année, 1973 (Lai 4)
Bonne Aventure, 1932 (Fradetal 4)
Bonne chance, 1935 (Guitry 2)
Bonne Chance, Charlie, 1962 (Constantine 3)
Bonne Etoile, 1942 (Fernandel 3)
Bonne Farce avec ma tête, 1904 (Méliès 2)
Bonne Occase, 1965 (Trinignant 3)
Bonne pour monsieur, un domestique pour madame, 1909 (Linder 3)
Bonne Soupe, 1964 (Blier 3, Gélin 3, Girardot 3, Saulnier 4)
Bonne Tisane, 1957 (Blier 3)
Bonnes à tuer, 1954 (Darrieux 3, D'Eaubonne 4)
Bonnes Causes, 1963 (Brasseur 3, Jeanson 4)
Bonnes Femmes, 1960 (Chabrol 2, Audran 3, Decaë 4, Gégauff 4, Hakim 4)
Bonnie and Clyde, 1967 (Benton 2, Penn 2, Beatty 3, Dunaway 3, Hackman 3, Wilder 3, Allen 4, Guffey 4, Tavoularis 4, Towne 4, Van Runkle 4, Warner 4)
Bonnie, Bonnie Lassie, 1919 (Browning 2)
Bonnie Brier Bush. See Beside the Bonnie Brier Bush, 1921
Bonnie of the Hills, 1913 (Anderson 3)
Bonnie Prince Charlie, 1923 (Novello 3)
Bonnie Prince Charlie, 1948 (Hawkins 3, Niven 3, Korda, A. 4, Korda, V. 4, Krasker 4)
Bonnie Scotland, 1935 (Laurel and Hardy 3, Roach 4)
Bonny May, 1920 (Love 3)
Bons baisers à lundi, 1974 (Blier 3, Audiard 4)
Bons baisers de Dinard, 1949 (Decaë 4)
Bons Vivants, 1965 (Blier 3, Audiard 4)
Bonsoir mesdames, bonsoir messieurs, 1943 (Renoir 4)
Bonsoir Paris, bonjour l'amour, 1956 (Gélin 3, D'Eaubonne 4)
Bonsoirs, 1910 (Cohl 4)
Bonsoirs russes, 1910 (Cohl 4)
Bonzo Goes to College, 1952 (O'Sullivan 3)
Boo, Boo, Theme Song, 1933 (Fleischer 4)
Boob, 1926 (Wellman 2, Crawford 3, Daniels 4, Gibbons 4)
Boobs and Bricks, 1913 (Dwan 2)
Boobs in Arms, 1940 (Three Stooges 3)
Boobs in the Woods, 1925 (Capra 2, Sennett 2, Langdon 3)
Boobs in the Woods, 1950 (Blanc 4, McKimson 4, Stalling 4)
Booby Dupes, 1945 (Three Stooges 3)

Booby Hatched, 1944 (Blanc 4, Foster 4, Stalling 4)
Booby Traps, 1943 (Clampett 4)
Boogey Man, 1980 (Carradine 3)
Boogie Doodle, 1939 (McLaren 4)
Boogie Man Will Get You, 1942 (Karloff 3, Lorre 3)
Boogie Woogie Bugle Boy of Company B, 1941 (Lantz 4)
Boogie Woogie Dream, 1942 (Horne 3)
Book, 1926 (Carré 4)
Book Agents, 1910 (White 3)
Book Agent's Romance, 1916 (Anderson 3)
Book Bargain, 1935 (Cavalcanti 2)
Book Bargain, 1976 (McLaren 4)
Book in the Country, 1929 (Ptushko 4)
Book Revue, 1946 (Blanc 4, Clampett 4, Stalling 4)
Book Shop, 1937 (Terry 4)
Bookworm, 1939 (Freleng 4)
Bookworms, 1920 (Howard 3)
Booloo, 1938 (Head 4)
Boom, 1963 (De Sica 2, Sordi 3, De Laurentiis 4, Zavattini 4)
Boom!, 1968 (Losey 2, Burton 3, Taylor 3, Barry 4, Coward 4, Slocombe 4)
Boom. See Kondura, 1977
Boom Town, 1940 (Colbert 3, Gable 3, Lamarr 3, Tracy 3, Adrian 4, Canutt 4, Gibbons 4, Gillespie 4, Mayer 4, Rosson 4, Waxman 4)
Boomerang, 1913 (Ince 4)
Boomerang, 1919 (Walthall 3)
Boomerang, 1925 (Schulberg 4)
Boomerang, 1947 (Kazan 2, Andrews 3, Cobb 3, LeMaire 4)
Boomerang, 1947 (Kennedy 3, Malden 3, Basevi 4, Day 4, De Rochemont 4, Newman 4, Zanuck 4)
Boomerang Bill, 1922 (Barrymore 3)
Boon. See Anugraham, 1978
Boop-Oop-a-Doop, 1932 (Fleischer 4)
Booster, 1928 (Roach 4)
Bootlegger, 1911 (Bosworth 3)
Bootlegger, 1922 (Laurel and Hardy 3)
Bootleggers, 1922 (Shearer 3)
Boot Polish, 1954 (Kapoor 2)
Boots, 1919 (Barthelmess 3)
Boots and Saddles, 1937 (Autry 3)
Boots! Boots!, 1934 (Formby 3)
Boots Malone, 1952 (Dieterle 2, Holden 3, Bernstein 4, Guffey 4)
Booty and the Beast, 1953 (Three Stooges 3)
Boquetière des Innocents, 1922 (Modot 3)
Boquitas pintadas, 1974 (Torre Nilsson 2)
Boran—Zeit zum zielen, 1987 (Léaud 3)
Border, 1982 (Richardson 2, Nicholson 3, Oates 3, Zsigmond 4)
Border Badmen, 1945 (Crabbe 3)
Border Cafe, 1937 (Carey 3, Musuraca 4)
Border Cavalier, 1927 (Wyler 2, Laemmle 4)
Border Devils, 1932 (Carey 3)
Border Feud. See Gränsfolken, 1913
Border Film, 1990 (Branco 4)
Border Flight, 1936 (Farmer 3, Dreier 4, Head 4)
Border G-Man, 1938 (August 4)
Border Incident, 1949 (Mann 2, Alton 4, Koch 4, Previn 4)
Border Justice, 1925 (Eason 4)
Border Legion, 1919 (Bosworth 3)
Border Legion, 1924 (Hathaway 2, Howard 2)
Border Legion, 1930 (Wray 3)

Border Legion, 1940 (Rogers 3)
Border Patrol, 1928 (Carey 3, Polito 4)
Border Patrol, 1943 (Mitchum 3, Harlan 4, Wilson 4)
Border Ranger, 1911 (Anderson 3)
Border River, 1954 (Armendáriz 3, DeCarlo 3, McCrea 3)
Border Treasure, 1950 (Hunt 4)
Border Vigilantes, 1941 (Harlan 4, Head 4)
Border Weave, 1942 (Alwyn 4, Cardiff 4)
Border Wireless, 1918 (Hart 3, August 4, Sullivan 4)
Border Wolves, 1938 (Lewis 2)
Borderland, 1937 (Head 4)
Borderline, 1925 (Robeson 3)
Borderline, 1950 (MacMurray 3, Trevor 3, Cahn 4, Salter 4)
Borderline, 1980 (Bronson 3)
Borderlines. See Caretakers, 1963
Bordertown, 1935 (Armendáriz 3, Davis 3, Muni 3, Orry-Kelly 4, Gaudio 4, Westmore Family 4)
Bored of Education, 1935 (Roach 4)
Borghese piccolo piccolo, 1977 (Monicelli 2, Sordi 3, Winters 3, Amidei 4)
Borgne, 1981 (Ruiz 2)
Borgo a Mozzano, 1958 (Rotunno 4)
Borinage. See Misère au Borinage, 1934
Boring Afternoon. See Fádní odpoledne, 1965
Boris Godunov, 1986 (Bondarchuk 3)
Born Again, 1978 (Andrews 3)
Born for Glory. See Brown on Resolution, 1935
Born for Trouble. See Murder in the Big House, 1942
Born Free, 1966 (Barry 4, Foreman 4)
Born in Sin. See Kawano hotoride, 1962
Born Losers, 1967 (Russell 3)
Born Lucky, 1932 (Powell and Pressburger 2)
Born on the Fourth of July, 1989 (Stone 2, Cruise 3, Mancini 4, Williams 4)
Born Reckless, 1930 (Ford 2, Bond 3, Brown 3, Fox 4, Nichols 4)
Born Reckless, 1937 (Carey 3)
Born Reckless, 1959 (Biroc 4)
Born Rich, 1924 (Folsey 4)
Born to Battle, 1926 (Arthur 3)
Born to Be Bad, 1934 (Grant 3, Young 3, Day 4, Newman 4, Zanuck 4)
Born to Be Bad, 1950 (Ray 2, Fontaine 3, Ryan 3, Musuraca 4, Schnee 4)
Born to Be Wild, 1938 (Bond 3)
Born to Buck, 1968 (Fonda 3)
Born to Dance, 1936 (Powell 3, Stewart 3, Adrian 4, Edens 4, Mayer 4, Newman 4, Porter 4)
Born to Kill, 1947 (Wise 2, Trevor 3)
Born to Kill. See Cockfighter, 1974
Born to Love, 1931 (McCrea 3)
Born to Peck, 1952 (Lantz 4)
Born to Sing, 1941 (Berkeley 2, Dumont 3)
Born to Sing. See Almost Angels, 1962
Born to the West, 1938 (Wayne 3, Head 4)
Born to Win, 1971 (Passer 2, Black 3, De Niro 3, Segal 3, Rosenblum 4)
Born Yesterday, 1950 (Cukor 2, Crawford 3, Holden 3, Holliday 3, Cohn 4, Horner 4, Kanin 4, Walker 4)
Børnevennerne, 1914 (Psilander 3)
Boro no kesshitai, 1942 (Hara 3)
Borom Sarret, 1963 (Sembene 2)
Borrasca humana, 1939 (Armendáriz 3)

Borrowed Clothes, 1918 (Weber 2)
Borrowed Finery, 1914 (Ingram 2)
Borrowed Identity, 1913 (Anderson 3)
Borrowers, 1973 (Allen 4, Trumbull 4)
Borsalino, 1970 (Belmondo 3, Delon 3, Carrière 4)
Borsalino & Co., 1974 (Delon 3)
Börsenkönigin, 1917 (Nielsen 3)
Bortsføraelse, 1912 (Psilander 3)
Boryoku, 1952 (Yoshimura 2)
Borza, 1935 (Van Dongen 4)
Bosambo. See Sanders of the River, 1935
Bosko in Dutch, 1933 (Freleng 4)
Bosphore, 1963 (Delerue 4)
Bosque animado, 1987 (Rey 3)
Boss, 1915 (Carré 4)
Boss, 1956 (Haskin 4, Mohr 4, Trumbo 4)
Boss of Boomtown, 1944 (Salter 4)
Boss of Camp Four, 1922 (Van dyke 2, Fox 4)
Boss of Hangtown Mesa, 1942 (Lewis 2, Salter 4)
Boss of the Katy Mine, 1912 (Anderson 3)
Boss Said No See Blondie Goes to College, 1942
Boss Tweed, 1933 (Coburn 3)
Bossu, 1934 (Lourié 4)
Bossu, 1944 (Delannoy 2, Modot 3, Annenkov 4, Auric 4, Matras 4)
Bossu de Rome See Il Gobbo, 1960
Boston Blackie, 1923 (Fox 4)
Boston Quackie, 1957 (Blanc 4, Mckimson 4)
Boston Strangler, 1968 (Curtis 3, Fonda 3, Anhalt 4, Day 4, Smith 4)
Boston Tea Party, 1908 (Porter 2)
Bostonians, 1984 (Ivory 2, Redgrave 3, Jhabvala 4, Lassally 4)
Botab dourou, 1968 (Yoda 4)
Botany Bay, 1953 (Ladd 3, Mason 3, Seitz 4, Waxman 4)
Both Ends of the Candle. See Helen Morgan Story, 1957
Both Sides of the Law. See Street Corner, 1953
Botschafterin, 1960 (Warm 4)
Botta di vita, 1989 (Blier 3, Sordi 3)
Botta e risposta, 1949 (Fernandel. 3)
Botta e risposta, 1951 (De laurentiis 4)
Bottle, 1915 (Hepworth 2)
Bottle Babies, 1924 (Roach 4)
Bottle Imp, 1917 (Neilan 2, Hayakawa 3)
Bottleneck. See Ingorgo, 1979
Bottom Line. See On aura tout vu!, 1976
Bottom of the Bottle, 1956 (Cotten 3, Johnson 3, Garmes 4, LeMaire 4, Wheeler 4)
Bottoms Up, 1934 (Ball 3, Tracy 3, Miller 4)
Boucher, 1969 (Chabrol 2, Audran 3, Rabier 4)
Boucher, la star, et l'orpheline. See Evlalie quitte les champs, 1973
Bouclette, 1917 (L'Herbier 2)
Boudoir Brothers, 1932 (Sennett 2)
Boudoir Diplomat, 1930 (Freund 4, Glazer 4, Laemmle 4)
Boudu sauvé des eaux, 1932 (Becker 2, Simon 3, Renoir 4)
Boudu Saved from Drowning. See **Boudu sauvé des eaux, 1932**
Bouevard du Rhum, 1971 (Douy 4)
Bought, 1931 (Milland 3)
Bought and Paid For, 1916 (Edeson 4, Marion 4)

Boulanger de Valorgue, 1952 (Fernandel 3)
Boulangerie de Monceau, 1963 (Rohmer 2)
Boulder Wham, 1965 (Blanc 4)
Boule de suif, 1945 (Presle 3, Barsacq 4,
    Jeanson 4, Matras 4)
Boulevard, 1960 (Duvivier 2)
Boulevard des assassins, 1982 (Audran 3,
    Trintignant 3)
Boulevard du rhum, 1971 (Bardot 3)
Boulevard Nights, 1979 (Schifrin 4)
Boulevardier from the Bronx, 1936
    (Freleng 4, Stalling 4)
Boulevards d'Afrique—bac ou mariage,
    1988 (Rouch 2)
Boulot aviateur, 1937 (Simon 3)
Bouncer, 1925 (Roach 4)
Bouncing Babies, 1929 (Roach 4)
Bound and Gagged, 1919 (Grot 4)
Bound for Glory, 1976 (Ashby 2,
    Rosenman 4, Wexler 4, Whitlock 4)
Bound In Morocco, 1918 (Dwan 2)
Bound in Morocco, 1918 (Fairbanks 3)
Bound on the Wheel, 1915 (Chaney 3,
    Furthman 4)
Boundary House, 1918 (Hepworth 2)
Bounty, 1982 (Vangelis. 4)
Bounty, 1984 (Day Lewis 3, Gibson 3,
    Hopkins 3, Olivier 3, De Laurentiis 4)
Bounty Hunter, 1954 (De Toth 2,
    Borgnine 3, Scott 3)
Bounty Killer, 1919 (Anderson 3)
Bounty Killer, 1965 (Duryea 3)
Bounty Killers, 1965 (Crabbe 3)
Bouquet, 1915 (Beery 3)
Bouquetière des Catalans, 1915
    (Musidora. 3)
Bouquets de fleurs, 1913 (Gaumont 4)
Bourbon Street Blues, 1978 (Fassbinder 2)
Bourbon Street Blues, 1979 (Sirk 2)
Bourdelle, 1950 (Honegger 4)
Bourdelle, sculpteur monumental, 1962
    (Coutard 4)
Bourgeois Gentilhomme, 1958 (Alekan 4)
Bourgogne, 1936 (Epstein 2)
Bourne Identity, 1988 (Quayle 3)
Bourreau turc, 1904 (Méliès 2)
Bourse. See Valise diplomatique, 1909
Bourse et la vie, 1965 (Fernandel 3)
Bourse ou la vie. See Piednadze albo zycie,
    1961
Bout de Zan et le poilu, 1915 (Musidora 3)
Bout de Zan et l'espion, 1915 (Musidora 3)
Bout-de-chou, 1935 (Brasseur 3)
''Bout-de-Zan'' series, from 1912
    (Feuillade 2)
Boutique de l'Orfèvre. See Jeweller's Shop,
    1990
Bow Bells, 1954 (Lassally 4)
Bowery, 1914 (Walsh 2)
Bowery, 1933 (Walsh 2, Ball 3, Beery 3,
    Cooper 3, Raft 3, Wray 3, Day 4,
    Estabrook 4, Newman 4, Zanuck 4)
Bowery at Midnight, 1942 (Lugosi 3,
    Katzman 4)
Bowery Bimboes, 1930 (Lantz 4)
Bowery Bishop, 1924 (Walthall 3)
Bowery Blitzkrieg, 1941 (Katzman 4)
Bowery Boy, 1940 (Fuller 2)
Bowery Boys, 1914 (Sennett 2, Arbuckle 3)
Bowery Bugs, 1949 (Blanc 4, Stalling 4)
Bowery Champs, 1944 (Katzman 4)
Bowery to Broadway, 1944 (O'Connor 3)
Bowled Over, 1923 (Roach 4)
Bowling Bimboes, 1930 (Lantz 4)

Bowling Match, 1913 (Sennett 2,
    Normand 3)
Bowling-Alley Cat, 1942 (Hanna and
    Barbera 4)
Bow Wow, 1922 (Sennett 2)
Bow Wows, 1922 (Roach 4)
Boxcar Bertha, 1972 (Corman 2, Scorsese 2,
    Carradine 3)
Boxe de la France, 1943 (Honegger 4)
Boxer. See Bokser, 1966
Boxer. See Uomo dalle pelle dura, 1971
Boxing. See Boks, 1961
Boxing Gloves, 1929 (Roach 4)
Boxing Kangaroo, 1920 (Fleischer 4)
Boy. See Shonen, 1969
Boy, a Girl and a Bike, 1949 (Rank 4)
Boy and a Bike, 1951 (Buchanan 3)
Boy and His Dog, 1948 (Prinz 4)
Boy and His Dog, 1976 (Robards 3)
Boy and the Fog. See Nino y la niebla, 1953
Boy and the Law, 1914 (Stahl 2)
Boy and the Sea, 1953 (Brakhage 2)
Boy Crazy, 1922 (Stromberg 4)
Boy Detective, 1908 (Bitzer 4)
Boy, Did I Get a Wrong Number!, 1966
    (Hope 3, Lewin 4)
Boy Friend, 1926 (Gibbons 4)
Boy Friend, 1928 (McCarey 2, Roach 4)
Boy Friend, 1971 (Russell 2, Jackson 3,
    Russell 4, Watkin 4)
Boy From Barnado's. See Lord Jeff, 1938
Boy from Oklahoma, 1954 (Curtiz 2,
    Burks 4, Steiner 4)
Boy in Blue. See Knabe in Blau, 1919
Boy in the Barrel, 1903 (Bitzer 4)
Boy in the Plastic Bubble, 1976 (Bellamy 3,
    Travolta 3)
Boy in the Tree. See Pojken i trädet, 1961
Boy Meets Girl, 1938 (Bacon 2, Bellamy 3,
    Cagney 3, Reagan 3, Edeson 4, Polito 4,
    Wallis 4)
Boy of Mine, 1923 (Walthall 3)
Boy of the Revolution, 1911 (Cruze 2)
Boy of the Sea. See Kaikoku danji, 1926
Boy of the Street, 1937 (Cooper 3)
Boy on a Dolphin, 1957 (Negulesco 2,
    Ladd 3, Loren 3, Webb 3, Friedhofer 4,
    Krasner 4, Smith 4)
Boy Rider, 1927 (Plunkett 4)
Boy Slaves, 1939 (Berman 4, Hunt 4)
Boy Ten Feet Tall. See Sammy Going South,
    1963
Boy Ten Feet Tall, 1965 (Robinson 3)
Boy Trouble, 1939 (O'Connor 3, Head 4)
Boy Who Could Fly, 1986 (Edlund 4)
Boy Who Stole a Million, 1960 (Crichton 2,
    Slocombe 4)
Boy Who Turned Yellow, 1972 (Powell and
    Pressburger 2, Challis 4)
Boy with Green Hair, 1948 (Losey 2,
    Ryan 3, Barnes 4, D'Agostino 4,
    Schary 4)
Boyars' Plot. See Ivan Grozny II: Boyarskii
    Zagovor, 1958
Boycotted Baby, 1917 (Laurel and Hardy 3)
Boyhood Daze, 1957 (Blanc 4, Jones 4)
Boykott, 1930 (Dagover 3)
Boys from Brazil, 1978 (Schaffner 2,
    Elliott 3, Ganz 3, Mason 3, Olivier 3,
    Peck 3, Decaë 4, Goldsmith 4)
Boys from Brooklyn. See Bela Lugosi Meets
    a Brooklyn Gorilla, 1952
Boys in Brown, 1949 (Attenborough 3,
    Bogarde 3, Rank 4)

Boys in the Band, 1970 (Friedkin 2)
Boys' Night Out, 1962 (Bendix 3, Garner 3,
    Homolka 3, Novak 3, Cahn 4)
Boys of the City, 1940 (Lewis 2)
Boys' Ranch, 1946 (Irene 4)
Boys School. See Disparus de Saint-Agil,
    1938
Boys to Board, 1923 (Roach 4)
Boys Town, 1938 (Rooney 3, Tracy 3,
    Mayer 4, Schary 4)
Boys Will Be Boys, 1921 (Rogers 3)
Boys Will Be Boys, 1932 (Stevens 2)
Boys Will Be Boys, 1935 (Hay 3, Balcon 4,
    Rank 4, Vetchinsky 4)
Boys Will Be Joys, 1925 (Roach 4)
Bra flicka reder sig själv, 1914 (Sjöström 2)
Braccia aperte, 1922 (Gallone 2)
Braccio violento della mala. See Dinero
    Maldito, 1978
Braconniers, 1903 (Guy 2)
Bracos de Sologne, 1933 (Aurenche 4)
Braddock: Missing in Action III, 1988
    (Golan and Globus 4)
Brahim, 1956 (Cloquet 4)
Brahma Diamond, 1909 (Griffith 2,
    Lawrence 3, Bitzer 4)
Brahmane et le papillon, 1901 (Méliès 2)
Brahmin and the Butterfly. See Brahmane et
    le papillon, 1901
Brain. See Vengeance, 1962
Brain. See Cerveau, 1969
Brain Eaters, 1958 (Corman 2)
Brains Repaired. See Retapeur de Cervelles,
    1911
Brainsnatcher. See Man Who Lived Again,
    1936
Brainstorm, 1965 (Andrews 3, Duning 4)
Brainstorm, 1983 (Robertson 3, Wood 3,
    Trumbull 4)
Brainwashed. See Schachnovelle, 1960
Brainwashed. See Droit d'aimer, 1972
Brainwaves, 1982 (Curtis 3)
Brakhage Lectures, 1990 (Brakhage 2)
Bramble Bush, 1960 (Burton 3, Dickinson 3,
    Ballard 4, Rosenman 4)
Bramy raju, 1967 (Wajda 2)
Brancaleone alla crusada. See Brancaleone
    alle Crociate, 1970
Brancaleone alle Crociate, 1970
    (Monicelli 2, Gassman 3, Age and
    Scarpelli 4)
Branches, 1970 (Emshwiller 2)
Branches of the Tree. See Shakha Proshakha,
    1990
Brand, 1911 (Dwan 2)
Brand im Ozean, 1950 (Staudte 2)
Brand in der Oper, 1930 (Fröhlich 3,
    Gründgens 3, Reisch 4, Wagner 4)
Brand New Hero, 1914 (Sennett 2,
    Arbuckle 3)
Brand of Cowardice, 1916 (Barrymore 3)
Brand of Fear, 1911 (Dwan 2)
Brand of Hate, 1934 (Katzman 4)
Brand of Lopez, 1920 (Hayakawa 3)
Branded, 1950 (Ladd 3, Dreier 4, Head 4,
    Lang 4, Maté 4)
Branded a Bandit, 1924 (Canutt 4)
Branded Sombrero, 1928 (Fox 4)
Branded Woman, 1920 (Talmadge 3,
    Emerson 4, Hunt 4, Loos 4)
Brandherd. See Verlogene Moral, 1921
Branding a Bad Man, 1911 (Dwan 2)
Branding Broadway, 1918 (Hart 3, August 4,
    Sullivan 4)

Brandos Costumes, 1974 (De Almeida 4)

Brandstifter, 1969 (Von Trotta 2)

Brandy for the Parson, 1951 (Grierson 2, More 3, Addison 4)

Branle-bas de combat, 1936 (Ibert 4)

Brannigan, 1975 (Attenborough 3, Wayne 3, Fisher 4)

Brannigar, 1935 (Bergman 3, Jaenzon 4)

Branningar, eller Stulen lycka, 1912 (Jaenzon 4, Magnusson 4)

Braque, 1950 (Cloquet 4)

Bras de la nuit, 1961 (Darrieux 3)

Brasher Doubloon, 1947 (Kortner 3, Basevi 4, Chandler 4)

Brasier ardent, 1923 (Mozhukin 3)

Brass Bottle, 1923 (Tourneur 2)

Brass Bottle, 1964 (Bumstead 4)

Brass Bowl, 1924 (Fox 4)

Brass Buttons, 1919 (King 2, Furthman 4)

Brass Check, 1918 (Bushman 3)

Brass Commandments, 1923 (Fox 4)

Brass Knuckles, 1927 (Bacon 2, Blanke 4)

Brass Monkey, 1917 (Selig 4)

Brass Monkey. See Lucky Mascot, 1948

Brass Target, 1978 (Loren 3, Von Sydow 3)

Brat, 1919 (Guy 2, Nazimova 3, Mathis 4)

Brat, 1931 (Ford 2, August 4, Behrman 4, Levien 4)

Bratichka, 1927 (Kozintsev 2, Enei 4, Moskvin 4)

Brats, 1930 (Laurel and Hardy 3, Roach 4)

Bratya, 1912 (Mozhukin 3)

Bratya razbotchniki, 1912 (Mozhukin 3)

Bräutigam, die Komödiantin und der Zuhälter, 1968 (Straub and Huillet 2, Schygulla 3)

Bravade legendaire, 1978 (Vierny 4)

Bravados, 1958 (King 2, Peck 3, Van Cleef 3, Friedhofer 4, LeMaire 4, Newman 4, Shamroy 4, Wheeler 4)

Brave and Bold, 1911 (Sennett 2)

Brave and the Beautiful. See Magnificent Matador, 1955

Brave Bulls, 1951 (Rossen 2, Quinn 3, Crosby 4, Howe 4, Trumbo 4)

Brave Deserve the Fair, 1915 (Mix 3)

Brave Don't Cry, 1952 (Grierson 2)

Brave Hare, 1955 (Ivanov-Vano 4)

Brave Hunter, 1912 (Sennett 2, Normand 3)

Brave Little Bat, 1941 (Blanc 4, Jones 4, Stalling 4)

Brave One, 1956 (Cardiff 4, Trumbo 4, Young 4)

Brave Ones, 1916 (Laurel and Hardy 3)

Brave Rifles, 1966 (Kennedy 3)

Brave Sünder, 1931 (Kortner 3)

Brave Tin Soldier, 1934 (Iwerks 4)

Brave Warrior, 1952 (Katzman 4)

Braver Than the Bravest, 1916 (Roach 4)

Braves Gens, 1912 (Gaumont 4)

Braves Petits Soldats de plomb, 1915 (Cohl 4)

Bravest Girl in the South, 1910 (Olcott 2)

Bravest Way, 1918 (Hayakawa 3)

Bravissimo, 1955 (Sordi 3, Age and Scarpelli 4)

Bravo Alpha, 1957 (Jarre 4)

Bravo di Venezia, 1941 (Brazzi 3)

Bravo for Billy, 1979 (Halas and Batchelor 4)

Bravo, Mr. Strauss, 1945 (Pal 4)

Brawn of the North, 1922 (Murfin 4)

Brazen Beauty, 1918 (Browning 2)

Brazen Bell, 1962 (Cobb 3)

Brazil, 1944 (Horton 3, Rogers 3)

Brazil, 1985 (Gilliam 2, De Niro 3, Hoskins 3)

Brazil: A Report on Torture, 1971 (Wexler 4)

Breach of Promise, 1932 (Miller 4, Veiller 4)

Bread, 1924 (Bosworth 3, Coffee 4, Lewin 4, Mayer 4)

Bread and Chocolate. See Pane e cioccolata, 1973

Bread of the Border, 1924 (Arzner 2)

Breadline. See Heros for Sale, 1933

Break, Break, Break, 1914 (Eason 4)

Break in the Circle, 1955 (Carreras 4)

Break of Hearts, 1935 (Boyer 3, Hepburn 3, Berman 4, Biroc 4, Polglase 4, Steiner 4, Veiller 4)

Break the News, 1937 (Clair 2, Buchanan 3, Chevalier 3, Meerson 4)

Break to Freedom. See Albert, R. N., 1953

Breakaway, 1956 (Rank 4)

Breakaway, 1966 (Conner 2)

Breakdance 2: Electric Boogaloo, 1984 (Golan and Globus 4)

Breakdown. See Si j'étais un espion, 1967

Breaker Morant, 1980 (Beresford 2)

Breakers Ahead, 1935 (Green 4)

Breakers, or Stolen Happiness. See Branningar, eller Stulen lycka, 1912

Breakfast, 1972 (Snow 2)

Breakfast at Sunrise, 1918 (Dressler 3)

Breakfast at Sunrise, 1927 (Schenck 4)

Breakfast at Tiffany's, 1961 (Edwards 2, Hepburn 3, Neal 3, Rooney 3, Axelrod 4, Edouart 4, Fulton 4, Head 4, Mancini 4, Mercer 4, Planer 4, Westmore Family 4)

Breakfast Club, 1985 (Hughes 2, Allen 4)

Breakfast for Two, 1937 (Marshall 3, Stanwyck 3, Hunt 4)

Breakfast in Hollywood, 1945 (Bondi 3, Metty 4)

Breakheart Pass, 1975 (Bronson 3, Johnson 3, Ballard 4, Canutt 4, Goldsmith 4)

Breaking Away, 1979 (Yates 2)

Breaking Home Ties, 1988 (Robards 3, Saint 3, Trevor 3)

Breaking In, 1989 (Forsyth 2, Sayles 2, Reynolds 3)

Breaking into Society, 1923 (Stromberg 4)

Breaking Point, 1924 (Brenon 2, Howe 4)

Breaking Point, 1950 (Curtiz 2, Garfield 3, Neal 3, McCord 4, Wald 4)

Breaking the Ice, 1925 (Sennett 2)

Breaking the Ice, 1938 (Costello 3, Young 4)

Breaking the Sound Barrier. See Sound Barrier, 1952

Breaking Up, 1978 (Remick 3)

Breakout. See Danger Within, 1959

Breakout, 1975 (Huston 2, Bronson 3, Duvall 3, Ballard 4, Goldsmith 4, Winkler 4)

Breakthrough, 1979 (Mitchum 3, Steiger 3)

Breakthrough Steiner, 1979 (Burton 3)

Break-Up, 1968 (Ferreri 2)

Breakup. See Rupture, 1970

Breath of Scandal, 1924 (Schulberg 4)

Breath of Scandal, 1960 (Chevalier 3, Lansbury 3, Loren 3, Head 4, Lardner 4, Ponti 4)

Breathdeath, 1964 (Vanderbeek 2)

Breathing, 1963 (Breer 4)

Breathless. See A bout de souffle, 1960

Breathless, 1983 (Black 3, Gere 3, Lourié 4, Sylbert 4)

Bred in the Bone, 1915 (Crisp 3)

Breed Apart, 1984 (Pleasence 3, Turner 3)

Breed of Men, 1919 (Hart 3, August 4)

Breed of the Mountains, 1914 (Reid 3)

Breed o' the North, 1914 (Ince 4)

Breezing Home, 1937 (Dunne 4)

Breezy, 1973 (Eastwood 3, Holden 3, Legrand 4)

Breite Weg, 1917 (Gad 2)

Brelan d'As, 1952 (Simon 3)

Bremen Freedom. See Bremer Freiheit, 1972

Bremen Town Musicians, 1935 (Iwerks 4)

Bremer Freiheit, 1972 (Schygulla 3)

Brenda Starr, 1976 (Schifrin 4)

Brenda Starr, 1988 (Francis 4)

Brennende Acker, 1922 (Murnau 2, Krauss 3, Pommer 4, Von Harbou 4, Wagner 4)

Brennende Acker, 1922 (Freund 4)

Brennende Betten, 1988 (Coutard 4)

Brennende Grenze, 1926 (Homolka 3, Tschechowa 3, Junge 4)

Brennende Herz, 1929 (Fröhlich 3, Courant 4)

Brennendes Geheimnis, 1933 (Siodmak 2)

Bretagne, 1936 (Epstein 2)

Breve stagione, 1969 (Castellani 2, De Laurentiis 4, Morricone 4)

Breve vacanza, 1973 (Zavattini 4)

Brevet de pilote No. 1: Bleriot, 1960 (Delerue 4)

Brevi amori a Palma di Majorca, 1959 (Cervi 3, Sordi 3)

Brewster McCloud, 1970 (Altman 2, Ames 4)

Brewster's Millions, 1914 (De Mille 2, Darwell 3, Buckland 4)

Brewster's Millions, 1921 (Arbuckle 3, Brown 4)

Brewster's Millions, 1935 (Wilcox 2, Buchanan 3)

Brewster's Millions, 1945 (Dwan 2, Friedhofer 4)

Brewster's Millions, 1985 (Hill 2, Pryor 3)

Brian's Song, 1971 (Caan 3, Biroc 4, Legrand 4)

Bribe, 1949 (Gardner 3, Laughton 3, Price 3, Taylor 3, Berman 4, Brown 4, Irene 4, Rozsa 4, Ruttenberg 4)

Bric-a-Brac, 1935 (Brennan 3)

Bric a Brac et Cie, 1931 (Fernandel 3)

Bridal Bail, 1934 (Stevens 2)

Bridal Path, 1959 (Launder and Gilliat 2)

Bridal Suite, 1939 (Young 3, Hoffenstein 4)

Bride, 1914 (Lawrence 3)

Bride, 1985 (Page 3, Jarre 4, Russell 4)

Bride and Gloom, 1918 (Daniels 3, Lloyd 3, Roach 4)

Bride and Groom, 1955 (Godfrey 4)

Bride by Mistake, 1944 (Langdon 3, Krasna 4, Musuraca 4)

Bride Came C.O.D., 1941 (Cagney 3, Epstein 4, Friedhofer 4, Haller 4, Haskin 4, Orry-Kelly 4, Steiner 4, Wallis 4, Warner 4)

Bride Came Through the Ceiling. See Bruden kom genom taket, 1947

Bride Comes Home, 1935 (Colbert 3, MacMurray 3, Young 3, Banton 4)

Bride for Sale, 1949 (Colbert 3, Young 3)

Bride Goes Wild, 1948 (Allyson 3, Johnson 3, Rose 4)

Bride Is Much Too Beautiful. *See* Mariée est trop belle, 1956

Bride Is Too Beautiful. *See* Mariée est trop belle, 1956

Bride of Frankenstein, 1935 (Whale 2, Brennan 3, Carradine 3, Karloff 3, Lanchester 3, Balderston 4, Fulton 4, Laemmle 4, Pierce 4, Waxman 4)

Bride of the Gorilla, 1951 (Siodmak 4)

Bride of the Monster, 1955 (Lugosi 3)

Bride of the Regiment, 1930 (Loy 3, Pidgeon 4)

Bride of the Storm, 1926 (Blackton 2, Costello 3, Musuraca 4)

Bride of Vengeance, 1949 (Leisen 2, Goddard 3, Dreier 4, Friedhofer 4)

Bride 68. *See* Land Ohne Frauen, 1929

Bride sur le cou, 1961 (Vadim 2, Bardot 3)

Bride Talks in Her Sleep. *See* Hanayome no negoto, 1933

Bride to Be. *See* Petita Jimenez, 1976

Bride Walks Out, 1936 (Bond 3, McDaniel 3, Stanwyck 3, Young 3, Epstein 4, Hunt 4)

Bride Wasn't Willing. *See* Frontier Gal, 1945

Bride Wore Black. *See* Mariée était en noir, 1967

Bride Wore Boots, 1946 (Stanwyck 3, Wood 3, Benchley 4, Dreier 4, Head 4)

Bride Wore Crutches, 1941 (Clarke 4, Day 4)

Bride Wore Red, 1937 (Arzner 2, Mankiewicz 2, Crawford 3, Young 3, Adrian 4, Folsey 4, Waxman 4)

Bridegroom, the Comedienne, and the Pimp. *See* Bräutigam, die Komödiantin, und der Zuhalter, 1968

Bridegroom's Taiheiki. *See* Hanamuko Taiheiki, 1945

Brideless Grooms, 1947 (Three Stooges 3, Bruckman 4)

Bride's Mistake, 1931 (Sennett 2)

Brides of Dracula, 1960 (Fisher 2, Cushing 3, Carreras 4, Sangster 4)

Brides of Fu Manchu, 1966 (Lee 3)

Bride's Play, 1922 (Davies 3)

Bride's Relation, 1929 (Sennett 2)

Bride's Silence, 1918 (King 2)

Brideshead Revisited, 1981 (Olivier 3)

Bride-to-Be, 1922 (Roach 4)

Bridge. *See* Brug, 1928

Bridge, 1931 (Vidor 2)

Bridge, 1942 (Van Dyke 2, Maddow 4)

Bridge. *See* Brücke, 1949

Bridge Ahoy!, 1936 (Fleischer 4)

Bridge at Remagen, 1969 (Segal 3, Bernstein 4, Cortez 4, Needham 4)

Bridge Came C.O.D., 1941 (Davis 3)

Bridge in the Jungle, 1971 (Huston 3)

Bridge of Love. *See* Aizen-bashi, 1951

Bridge of San Luis Rey, 1929 (Walthall 3, Adrian 4, Booth 4, Day 4, Gibbons 4, Stromberg 4)

Bridge of San Luis Rey, 1944 (Calhern 3, Nazimova 3, Estabrook 4, Tiomkin 4)

Bridge of Time, 1950 (Korda 4)

Bridge on the River Kwai, 1957 (Lean 2, Guinness 3, Hawkins 3, Hayakawa 3, Holden 3, Arnold 4, Cohn 4, Fisher 4, Foreman 4, Spiegel 4, Wilson 4)

Bridge that Gap, 1965 (De Palma 2)

Bridge Too Far, 1977 (Attenborough 3, Bogarde 3, Caan 3, Caine 3, Connery 3, Elliott 3, Gould 3, Hackman 3, Hopkins 3, Olivier 3, Redford 3, Schell 3, Ullmann 3, Addison 4, Goldman 4, Levine 4, Unsworth 4)

Bridge to Silence, 1989 (Remick 3)

Bridge to the Sun, 1961 (Baker 3, Auric 4)

Bridge Wives, 1932 (Arbuckle 3)

Bridger, 1976 (Field 3)

Bridges at Toko-Ri, 1954 (Holden 3, Kelly 3, March 3, Rooney 3, Bumstead 4, Clarke 4, Fulton 4, Head 4)

Bridges-Go-Round, 1959 (Clarke 2)

Brief Ecstasy, 1937 (Lukas 3)

Brief einer Toten, 1917 (Kortner 3)

Brief Encounter, 1945 (Lean 2, Howard 3, Johnson 3, Coward 4, Havelock-Allan 4, Krasker 4, Mathieson 4, Rank 4)

Brief Encounter, 1974 (Burton 3, Loren 3, Ponti 4)

Brief Moment, 1933 (Lombard 3, Banton 4, Behrman 4)

Brief Season. *See* Breve stagione, 1969

Brief Vacation. *See* Breve vacanza, 1973

Briefe, die ihn nicht erreichten, 1925 (Andrejew 4)

Brig, 1964 (Mekas 2)

Brigade mondaine, 1979 (Gégauff 4)

Brigade mondaine, vaudou aux Caraïbes, 1980 (Dalio 3)

Brigade sauvage, 1939 (Vanel 3)

Brigadier Gerard. *See* Fighting Eagle, 1927

Brigadoon, 1954 (Minnelli 2, Charisse 3, Johnson 3, Kelly 3, Ames 4, Freed 4, Green 4, Ruttenberg 4, Sharaff 4)

Brigady, 1947 (Zeman 4)

Brigand, 1952 (Quinn 3)

Brigand of Kandahar, 1965 (Reed 3, Carreras 4)

Brigante, 1961 (Castellani 2, Rota 4)

Brigante di Tacca del Lupo, 1952 (Fellini 2, Germi 2)

Brigante Musolino, 1950 (Mangano 3)

Brigante Mussolini, 1950 (De Laurentiis 4, Ponti 4)

Briganti italiani, 1961 (Blier 3, Borgnine 3, Gassman 3, Presle 3)

Brigaten Rache, 1920 (Nielsen 3)

Brigham Young. *See* Brigham Young—Frontiersman, 1940

Brigham Young—Frontiersman, 1940 (Astor 3, Carradine 3, Darnell 3, Darwell 3, Power 3, Price 3, La Shelle 4, MacGowan 4, Miller 4, Newman 4, Trotti 4, Zanuck 4)

Bright and Early, 1918 (Laurel and Hardy 3)

Bright Angel, 1990 (Shepard 4)

Bright Day of My Life. *See* Waga shogai no kagayakeru hi, 1948

Bright Eyes, 1922 (Sennett 2)

Bright Eyes, 1934 (Darwell 3, Temple 3, Miller 4)

Bright Leaf, 1950 (Curtiz 2, Bacall 3, Cooper 3, Crisp 3, Neal 3, Blanke 4, Freund 4, Young 4)

Bright Lights, 1916 (Sennett 2, Arbuckle 3, Normand 3)

Bright Lights, 1925 (Day 4, Gibbons 4)

Bright Lights, 1928 (Disney 4)

Bright Lights, 1930 (Curtiz 2, Carradine 3, Garmes 4, Grot 4)

Bright Lights, 1935 (Berkeley 2, Brown 3, Brown 4, Grot 4, Orry-Kelly 4)

Bright Lights, Big City, 1988 (Pollack 2, Fox 3, Robards 3, Willis 4)

Bright Prospects. *See* Ljusnande framtid, 1940

Bright Road, 1953 (Dandridge 3)

Bright Shawl, 1923 (Goulding 2, Astor 3, Barthelmess 3, Powell 3, Robinson 3, Folsey 4)

Bright Victory, 1951 (Hudson 3, Kennedy 3, Buckner 4, Daniels 4)

Brighton Beach Memoirs, 1986 (Stark 4)

Brighton Rock, 1947 (Attenborough 3, Greene 4)

Brighton Story, 1956 (Lassally 4)

Brighton Strangler, 1945 (D'Agostino 4, Hunt 4)

Brighty of the Grand Canyon, 1967 (Cotten 3)

Brigitte et Brigitte, 1965 (Chabrol 2, Fuller 2)

Brigitte Horney, 1977 (Zanussi 2)

Brillanten, 1937 (Röhrig 4)

Brillantenschiff, 1920 (Dagover 3)

Brilliant Murder. *See* Kenran taru satsujin, 1951

Brimstone, 1949 (Brennan 3)

Brimstone and Treacle, 1982 (Elliott 3)

Bring Back 'em Sober, 1932 (Sennett 2)

Bring Himself Back Alive, 1940 (Fleischer 4)

Bring Home the Turkey, 1927 (Roach 4)

Bring Me the Head of Alfredo Garcia, 1974 (Fernández 2, Peckinpah 2, Oates 3)

Bring on the Dancing Girls, 1965 (Scorsese 2)

Bring on the Girls, 1945 (De Carlo 3, Lake 3, Head 4, Struss 4)

Bring Your Smile Along, 1955 (Edwards 2)

Bringing Home the Bacon, 1941 (Terry 4)

Bringing Up Baby, 1938 (Hawks 2, Fitzgerald 3, Grant 3, Hepburn 3, Dunn 4, Metty 4, Nichols 4, Polglase 4)

Bringing Up Father, 1928 (Dressler 3, Booth 4, Daniels 4, Gibbons 4, Marion 4)

Bringing Up Mother, 1954 (Bosustow 4)

Bringin' Home the Bacon, 1924 (Arthur 3)

Brink of Life. *See* Nära livet, 1958

Brink's Job, 1978 (Friedkin 2, Falk 3, Oates 3, Rowlands 3, De Laurentiis 4, Tavoularis 4)

Briseur de chaînes, 1941 (Fresnay 3, Matras 4)

Brita i grosshandlarhuset, 1946 (Dahlbeck 3)

Britain at Bay, 1940 (Watt 2)

Brita in the Wholesaler's House. *See* Brita i grosshandlarhuset, 1946

Britannia Hospital, 1981 (Anderson 2, McDowell 3)

Britannia Mews. *See* Forbidden Street, 1949

Britannia of Billingsgate, 1933 (Mills 3, Balcon 4, Junge 4)

British Agent, 1934 (Curtiz 2, Francis 3, Howard 3, Blanke 4, Grot 4, Haller 4, Orry-Kelly 4)

British—Are They Artistic?, 1947 (Donat 3)

British Family in Peace and War, 1940 (Pearson 2)

British Intelligence, 1940 (Karloff 3, Salter 4)

British Youth, 1941 (Pearson 2)

Briton and Boer, 1910 (Mix 3)

Broad Daylight, 1922 (Laemmle 4)

Broadcast News, 1987 (Hurt 3, Nicholson 3, Ballhaus 4, Bass 4)

Broad-Minded, 1930 (LeRoy 2, Brown 3, Lugosi 3)

Broadside: Taking on the Bomb, 1984 (Christie 3)

Broadway, 1929 (Fejös 2, Laemmle 4, Mohr 4)

Broadway, 1942 (Crawford 3, Raft 3, Barnes 4)

Broadway after Dark, 1924 (LeRoy 2, Menjou 3, Shearer 3)

Broadway Babies, 1929 (Polito 4)

Broadway Bad, 1933 (Blondell 3, Crisp 3, Rogers 3, Barnes 4, Friedhofer 4)

Broadway Bill, 1918 (Gaudio 4)

Broadway Bill, 1934 (Capra 2, Ball 3, Bond 3, Loy 3, Buchman 4, Cohn 4, Riskin 4, Walker 4)

Broadway Billy, 1926 (Brown 4)

Broadway Blues, 1929 (Sennett 2)

Broadway by Light, 1957 (Resnais 2)

Broadway Danny Rose, 1984 (Allen 2, Farrow 3, Willis 4)

Broadway Folly, 1930 (Lantz 4)

Broadway Gold, 1923 (Gibbons 4)

Broadway Gondolier, 1935 (Bacon 2, Blondell 3, Menjou 3, Powell 3, Barnes 4, Epstein 4, Grot 4, Kräly 4, Orry-Kelly 4, Wald 4)

Broadway Hoofers, 1930 (Walker 4)

Broadway Hostess, 1935 (Orry-Kelly 4)

Broadway Jones, 1920 (Zukor 4)

Broadway Kid. See Ginsberg the Great, 1927

Broadway Limited, 1941 (McLaglen 3, Roach 4)

Broadway Love, 1918 (Chaney 3)

Broadway Melody, 1929 (Goulding 2, Love 3, Brown 4, Freed 4, Gibbons 4, Mayer 4, Shearer 4)

Broadway Melody. See No Man of Her Own, 1932

Broadway Melody of 1936, 1935 (Powell 3, Taylor 3, Adrian 4, Brown 4, Edens 4, Freed 4, Mayer 4, Newman 4, Rosher 4)

Broadway Melody of 1938, 1937 (Garland 3, Powell 3, Taylor 3, Adrian 4, Benchley 4, Brown 4, Daniels 4, Edens 4, Freed 4, Gibbons 4, Mayer 4, Vorkapich 4)

Broadway Melody of 1940, 1940 (Astaire 3, Powell 3, Adrian 4, Mayer 4, Newman 4, Porter 4, Ruttenberg 4, Schary 4)

Broadway Musketeers, 1938 (Sheridan 3, Deutsch 4)

Broadway Nights, 1927 (Sidney 3, Stanwyck 3, Haller 4)

Broadway or Bust, 1924 (Miller 4)

Broadway Peacock, 1922 (Fox 4)

Broadway Rhythm, 1944 (Walters 2, Horne 3, Alton 4, Green 4, Irene 4, Mayer 4, Sharaff 4)

Broadway Rose, 1922 (Goulding 2)

Broadway Scandal, 1918 (Chaney 3)

Broadway Serenade, 1939 (Berkeley 2, Ayres 3, MacDonald 3, Pangborn 3, Adrian 4, Kräly 4, Lederer 4, Stothart 4)

Broadway Singer. See Torch Singer, 1933

Broadway Thru a Keyhole, 1933 (Ball 3, Newman 4, Zanuck 4)

Broadway to Hollywood, 1933 (Cooper 3, Durante 3, Eddy 3, Rooney 3, Daniels 4, Tiomkin 4)

Broadway's Like That, 1930 (Blondell 3, Bogart 3)

Broceliande, 1969 (Jarre 4)

Brock's Last Case, 1973 (Widmark 3)

Bröderna, 1913 (Stiller 2, Jaenzon 4)

Broke in China, 1927 (Sennett 2)

Broken Arrow, 1950 (Daves 2, Stewart 3, Friedhofer 4, Newman 4, Wheeler 4)

Broken Barriers, 1924 (Menjou 3, Shearer 3)

Broken Blossoms, 1919, (Griffith 2, Barthelmess 3, Crisp 3, Gish 3, Bitzer 4, Brown 4)

Broken Blossoms, 1936 (Courant 4, Rathaus 4)

Broken Butterfly, 1919 (Tourneur 2, Carré 4)

Broken Chains, 1922 (Garnett 2, Moore 3, Haskin 4, Wilson 4)

Broken Cloud, 1915 (Eason 4)

Broken Coin, 1915 (Ford 2)

Broken Cross, 1911 (Griffith 2, Bitzer 4)

Broken Doll, 1910 (Griffith 2, Bitzer 4)

Broken Doll, 1921 (Dwan 4)

Broken Dreams, 1933 (Scott 3)

Broken English, 1979 (Jarman 2)

Broken Gate, 1927 (Arthur 3)

Broken Hearts of Broadway, 1921 (Moore 3)

Broken Hearts of Hollywood, 1926 (Bacon 2, Miller 4)

Broken in the Wars, 1918 (Hepworth 2)

Broken Journey, 1948 (Rank 4)

Broken Jug. See Zerbrochene Krug, 1937

Broken Lance, 1954 (Dmytryk 2, Tracy 3, Wagner 3, Widmark 3, LeMaire 4)

Broken Land, 1961 (Nicholson 3, Crosby 4)

Broken Leghorn, 1959 (Blanc 4, McKimson 4)

Broken Locket, 1909 (Griffith 2, Pickford 3, Bitzer 4)

Broken Lullaby. See Man I Killed, 1932

Broken Melody, 1934 (Oberon 3)

Broken Oath, 1910 (Lawrence 3)

Broken Parole, 1913 (Anderson 3)

Broken Pledge, 1915 (Beery 3, Swanson 3)

Broken Rainbow, 1985 (Sheen 3)

Broken Sabre, 1966 (Carradine 3)

Broken Sky. See Brusten Himmel, 1982

Broken Spell, 1910 (Costello 3, Talmadge 3, White 3)

Broken Spur, 1912 (Bosworth 3)

Broken Ties, 1911 (Dwan 2)

Broken Violin. See Lulli ou le violon brisé, 1908

Broken Ways, 1913 (Griffith 2, Carey 3, Sweet 3, Bitzer 4)

Broken Wing, 1923 (Schulberg 4)

Broken Wing, 1932 (Douglas 3)

Broken Wings, 1913 (Walthall 3)

Bröllopet på Ulfåsa, 1909 (Magnusson 4)

Bröllopet på Ulfåsa, 1911 (Jaenzon 4)

Brölloppsnatt. See Noc Poslubna, 1959

Bröllopsdagen, 1960 (Andersson 3, Von Sydow 3)

Bröllöpsresan, 1935 (Molander 2, Jaenzon 4)

Brolly. See Paraplíčko, 1957

Bromo and Juliet, 1926 (McCarey 2, Roach 4)

Broncho Billy series, 1910–16 (Anderson 3)

Broncho Buster, 1927 (Laemmle 4)

Broncho Buster's Bride, 1911 (Dwan 2)

Broncho Busting for Flying A Pictures, 1911 (Dwan 2)

Broncho Twister, 1927 (Mix 3, Fox 4)

Bronco Billy, 1980 (Eastwood 3, Lourié 4)

Bronco Bullfrog, 1970 (Shepard 4)

Bronco Buster, 1935 (Lantz 4)

Bronco Buster, 1952 (Boetticher 2, Boyle 4)

Bronenosets Potemkin, 1925 (Eisenstein 2, Tisse 4)

Brontë Sisters. See Soeurs Brontë, 1979

Bronx Tale, 1991 (De Niro 3)

Bronze Bell, 1921 (Johnson 3, Barnes 4)

Bronze Venus. See Duke Is Tops, 1938

Brood, 1979 (Cronenberg 2, Reed 3)

Brooding Eyes, 1926 (Barrymore 3)

Brookfield Recreation Center, 1964 (Baillie 2)

Brooklyn Orchid, 1942 (Bendix 3, Roach 4)

Broomstick Bunny, 1955 (Blanc 4, Maltese 4)

Brother Brat, 1944 (Blanc 4, Stalling 4)

Brother Brigands. See Bratya razbotchniki, 1912

Brother, Can You Spare a Dime, 1975 (Cagney 3)

Brother from Another Planet, 1984 (Sayles 2)

Brother John, 1949 (Fleischer 4)

Brother John, 1971 (Poitier 3, Jones 4)

Brother of the Bear, 1921 (Astor 3)

Brother Orchid, 1940 (Bacon 2, Bellamy 3, Bogart 3, Crisp 3, Robinson 3, Burks 4, Gaudio 4, Haskin 4, Wallis 4)

Brother Rat, 1938 (Beavers 3, Reagan 3, Wyman 3, Haller 4, Wald 4, Wallis 4)

Brother Rat and a Baby, 1940 (Ladd 3, Reagan 3, Wyman 3, Rosher 4, Wald 4, Wallis 4)

Brother Sun, Sister Moon. See Fratelli sole sorella luna, 1972

Brother, the Sister, and the Cowpuncher, 1910 (Anderson 3)

Broth of a Boy, 1959 (Fitzgerald 3)

Brotherhood, 1968 (Ritt 2, Douglas 3, Papar 3, Kaufman 4, Schifrin 4)

Brotherhood of Man, 1946 (Bosustow 4, Hubley 4, Lardner 4)

Brotherhood of the Bell, 1970 (Ford 3, Goldsmith 4)

Brotherhood of the Rose, 1989 (Mitchum 3)

Brotherly Love, 1928 (Arthur 3, Gibbons 4)

Brotherly Love, 1936 (Fleischer 4)

Brotherly Love. See Country Dance, 1969

Brothers, 1912 (Griffith 2, Carey 3, Reid 3, Bitzer 4)

Brothers. See Bratya, 1912

Brothers, 1913 (Dwan 2)

Brothers. See Bröderna, 1913

Brothers, 1947 (Box 4, Rank 4)

Brothers and Sisters of the Toda Family. See Toda-ke no kyodai, 1941

Brothers in Law, 1957 (Boulting 2, Schlesinger 2, Attenborough 3, Terry-Thomas 3)

Brothers in the Saddle, 1949 (Hunt 4)

Brothers Karamazov. See Brüder Karamasoff, 1920

Brothers Karamazov. See Morder Dimitri Karamazov, 1930

Brothers Karamazov, 1954 (Epstein 4)

Brothers Karamazov, 1958 (Brooks 2, Bloom 3, Brynner 3, Cobb 3, Schell 3, Alton 4, Berman 4, Epstein 4, Kaper 4, Plunkett 4)

Brother's Keeper, 1939 (McDowall 3)

Brother's Loyalty, 1913 (Bushman 3)

Brothers Rico, 1957 (Boyle 4, Duning 4, Guffey 4)

Brother's Sacrifice, 1917 (Selig 4)

Brothers under the Chin, 1924 (Laurel and Hardy 3, Roach 4)

Brothers Wood. *See* Freres Boutdebois, 1908

Brother's Wrong, 1909 (Olcott 2)

Brott i Paradiset, 1959 (Andersson 3, Björnstrand 3)

Brouillard sur la ville. *See* Gaz mortels, 1916

Brown Bread Sandwiches, 1989 (Giannini 3)

Brown Derby, 1929 (Rooney 3)

Brown of Harvard, 1926 (Wayne 3, Gibbons 4, Gillespie 4, Mayer 4, Stewart 4)

Brown on Resolution, 1935 (Mills 3, Balcon 4, Junge 4)

Brown Wallet, 1936 (Powell and Pressburger 2, Dalrymple 4)

Browning, 1913 (Feuillade 2)

Browning Version, 1951 (Asquith 2, Redgrave 3, Dillon 4, Rank 4, Rattigan 4)

Brown's Seance, 1912 (Sennett 2, Normand 3)

Brubaker, 1980 (Rafelson 2, Redford 3, Schifrin 4)

Bruce Gentry, 1949 (Katzman 4)

Bruce Lee's Game of Death. *See* Game of Death, 1979

Brücke, 1949 (Wagner 4)

Bruden kom genom taket, 1947 (Björnstrand 3)

Brüder Karamasoff, 1920 (Jannings 3, Kortner 3, Krauss 3)

Brüder Schellenberg, 1926 (Dagover 3, Veidt 3)

Bruegel, 1967 (Gélin 3)

Brug, 1928 (Ivens 2, Van Dongen 4)

Bruna indiavolata, 1951 (Age and Scarpelli 4)

Brune piquante, 1932 (Fernandel 3)

Brunes ou blondes, 1950 (Audiard 4)

Brunkul, 1941 (Henning-Jensen 2)

Brunnen des Wahnsinns, 1921 (Planer 4)

Bruno Bozzetto: Animazione primo amore, 1990 (Bozzetto 4)

Brushfire, 1962 (Sloane 3)

Brussels ''Loops'', 1958 (Clarke 2)

Brusten Himmel, 1982 (Thulin 3)

Brutal Justice. *See* Roma a mano armato, 1976

Brutality, 1912 (Griffith 2, Barrymore 3, Bitzer 4)

Brute, 1914 (Olcott 2)

Brute. *See* Bruto, 1953

Brute, 1987 (Guillemot 4)

Brute Force, 1912 (Marsh 3)

Brute Force. *See* McVeagh of the South Seas, 1914

Brute Force, 1947 (Brooks 2, Dassin 2, De Carlo 3, Lancaster 3, Daniels 4, Rozsa 4)

Brute Island. *See* McVeagh of the South Seas, 1914

Brute Man, 1946 (Salter 4)

Brute Master, 1920 (Bosworth 3)

Bruto, 1952 (Buñuel 2, Armendáriz 3, Alcoriza 4)

Brutti, sporchi, cattivi, 1976 (Ponti 4)

Bruyère, 1964 (Rohmer 2)

Bryllupsaften Paa Hotel, 1913 (Psilander 3)

Brzezina, 1970 (Wajda 2, Olbrychski 3)

B2 Tape/Film, 1983 (Jarman 2)

Bubble Trouble, 1953 (Three Stooges 3)

Bubbles, 1922 (Fleischer 4)

Bubbles of Song, 1951 (Fleischer 4)

Bubbling Over, 1921 (Roach 4)

Buccaneer, 1938 (De Mille 2, Bondi 3, Brennan 3, March 3, Quinn 3, Dreier 4, Head 4, Macpherson 4, Prinz 4, Sullivan 4)

Buccaneer, 1958 (De Mille 2, Bloom 3, Boyer 3, Brynner 3, Heston 3, Bernstein 4, Head 4, Westmore Family 4)

Buccaneer, 1991 (Quinn 3)

Buccaneer Bunny, 1948 (Blanc 4, Freleng 4, Maltese 4, Stalling 4)

Buccaneers, 1911 (Bosworth 3)

Buccaneers, 1924 (Roach 4)

Buccaneer's Girl, 1950 (De Carlo 3, Lanchester 3, Boyle 4, Metty 4)

Buch des Lasters, 1917 (Hoffmann 4)

Buchanan Rides Alone, 1958 (Boetticher 2, Scott 3, Ballard 4, Boyle 4, Brown 4)

Buchhalterin, 1918 (Dupont 2)

Buchse der Pandora, 1928 (Pabst 2, Brooks 3, Kortner 3, Andrejew 4, Vajda 4)

Buck and the Preacher, 1972 (Poitier 3)

Buck Benny Rides Again, 1940 (Bond 3, Dreier 4, Head 4, Lang 4, Young 4)

Buck Privates, 1928 (Laemmle 4)

Buck Privates, 1941 (Abbott and Costello 3, Three Stooges 3, Krasner 4)

Buck Privates Come Home, 1947 (Abbott and Costello 3)

Buck Richard's Bride, 1913 (Bosworth 3)

Buck Rogers, 1939 (Crabbe 3)

Buck Rogers in the 25th Century, 1979 (Palance 3)

Buckaroo Bugs, 1944 (Blanc 4, Clampett 4, Stalling 4)

Buckaroo Kid, 1926 (Laemmle 4)

Bucket of Blood, 1959 (Corman 2)

Bucking Broadway, 1917 (Ford 2, Carey 3)

Bucking Society, 1916 (Sennett 2)

Bucking the Barrier, 1923 (Fox 4)

Bucking the Line, 1921 (Fox 4)

Bucking the Truth, 1926 (Laemmle 4)

Bucklige und die Tanzerin, 1920 (Murnau 2, Krauss 3, Freund 4, Mayer 4)

Buckskin Frontier, 1943 (Cobb 3, Harlan 4, Young 4)

Budapest, amiért szeretem, 1971 (Szabó 2)

Budapest Tales. *See* Budapesti mesék, 1976

Budapesti mesék, 1976 (Szabó 2)

Budd Doble Comes Back, 1913 (Mix 3)

Buddenbrooks, 1959 (Dagover 3, Herlth 4)

Buddenbrooks, 1984 (Gielgud 3)

Buddha. *See* Shaka, 1961

Buddy and Towser, 1934 (Freleng 4)

Buddy Buddy, 1981 (Wilder 2, Kinski 3, Lemmon 3, Matthau 3, Diamond 4, Schifrin 4)

Buddy System, 1983 (Dreyfuss 3, Sarandon 3)

Buddy the Gob, 1934 (Freleng 4)

Buddy's Trolley Troubles, 1934 (Freleng 4)

Budo kagami, 1934 (Yamada 3)

Budo sen-ichi-ya, 1938 (Yamada 3)

Buenos dias, Buenos Aires, 1960 (Birri 2)

Bufera, 1913 (Bertini 3)

Bufere, 1952 (Gabin 3, Reggiani 3)

Buffalo Bill, 1944 (Wellman 2, Darnell 3, McCrea 3, O'Hara 3, Quinn 3, Basevi 4, Shamroy 4)

Buffalo Bill and the Indians, or Sitting Bull's History Lesson, 1976 (Altman 2, Rudolph 2, Chaplin 3, Lancaster 3, Newman 3, De Laurentiis 4)

Buffalo Bill on the U.P. Trail, 1926 (Pierce 4)

Buffalo Hunting, 1914 (Mix 3)

Bufferin, 1966 (Warhol 2)

Buffet froid, 1979 (Blier 2, Blier 3, Depardieu 3)

Bug, 1975 (Smith 4)

Bug Carnival, 1937 (Terry 4)

Bug Parade, 1941 (Avery 4, Blanc 4, Stalling 4)

Bug Vaudeville, 1921 (McCay 4)

Bugambilia, 1944 (Fernández 2, Armendáriz 3, Del Rio 3, Figueroa 4)

Bugged By a Bee, 1969 (Blanc 4, McKimson 4)

Bughouse Bell Hops, 1914 (Lloyd 3, Roach 4)

Bugiarda, 1989 (Olbrychski 3)

Bugle Call, 1916 (Sullivan 4)

Bugle Call, 1927 (Gibbons 4, Sullivan 4)

Bugle Sounds, 1941 (Beery 3, Reed 3)

Bugles in the Afternoon, 1951 (Milland 3, Tiomkin 4)

Bugs and Thugs, 1954 (Blanc 4, Freleng 4)

Bugs Beetle and His Orchestra, 1938 (Terry 4)

Bugs Bonnets, 1956 (Blanc 4, Jones 4, Maltese 4)

Bugs Bunny and the Three Bears, 1944 (Blanc 4, Jones 4, Stalling 4)

Bugs Bunny Gets the Boid, 1942 (Blanc 4, Clampett 4, Stalling 4)

Bugs Bunny Nips the Nips, 1944 (Blanc 4, Freleng 4, Stalling 4)

Bugs Bunny Rides Again, 1948 (Blanc 4, Freleng 4, Maltese 4, Stalling 4)

Bugs Bunny's 3rd Movie: 1001 Rabbit Tales, 1982 (Freleng 4, Jones 4)

Bugs Bunny—Superstar, 1975 (Welles 2, Clampett 4)

Bugsy, 1991 (Morricone 4)

Bugsy and Mugsy, 1957 (Blanc 4, Freleng 4, Stalling 4)

Bugsy Malone, 1976 (Parker 2, Foster 3, Puttnam 4)

Build Me a World, 1979 (Jackson 3)

Build My Gallows High. *See* **Out of the Past, 1947**

Build Thy House, 1920 (Rains 3)

Builders, 1954 (Altman 2)

Building the Great Los Angeles Aqueduct, 1913 (Dwan 2)

Building the Pyramids, 1973 (Jarman 2)

Buio in sala, 1950 (Risi 2)

Buisson ardent, 1955 (Alexeieff and Parker 4)

Buki naki tatakai, 1960 (Yoda 4)

Bulbule Baghdad, 1933 (Mehboob 2)

Bull and Sand, 1924 (Sennett 2)

Bull Dog, 1937 (Biswas 4)

Bull Durham, 1988 (Costner 3, Sarandon 3)

Bull Fighter, 1927 (Sennett 2)

Bull Rushes, 1931 (Balcon 4)

Bulldog Breed, 1960 (Caine 3, Reed 3, Wisdom 3, Rank 4)

Bulldog Courage, 1925 (Love 3)

Bulldog Drummond, 1929 (Ball 3, Bennett 3, Colman 3, Barnes 4, Goldwyn 4, Howard 4, Menzies 4, Toland 4)

Bulldog Drummond Comes Back, 1937 (Barrymore 3, Dreier 4, Head 4)

Bulldog Drummond Escapes, 1937 (Milland 3, Head 4)

Bulldog Drummond in Africa, 1938 (Quinn 3, Dreier 4, Head 4)

Bulldog Drummond's Bride, 1939 (Dreier 4, Head 4)

Bulldog Drummond's Peril, 1938 (Dmytryk 2, Barrymore 3, Dreier 4, Head 4)

Bulldog Drummond's Revenge, 1937 (Barrymore 3, Head 4)

Bulldog Drummond's Secret Police, 1939 (Head 4)

Bulldog Drummond's Third Round, 1925 (Buchanan 3)

Bulldog Drummond Strikes Back, 1934 (Ball 3, Colman 3, Young 3, Day 4, Johnson 4, Newman 4, Zanuck 4)

Bulldog Drummond Strikes Back, 1947 (Anhalt 4)

Bulldog Jack, 1935 (Richardson 3, Wray 3, Balcon 4, Junge 4, Rank 4)

Bulldog Sees It Through, 1940 (Buchanan 3, Newton 3, Withers 3)

Bulldozing the Bull, 1938 (Fleischer 4)

Bulldozing the Bull, 1951 (Terry 4)

Bulle und das Mädchen, 1985 (Olbrychski 3)

Bullero, 1932 (Terry 4)

Bullet, 1976 (Anand 3)

Bullet for a Badman, 1964 (Murphy 3, Biroc 4, Bumstead 4)

Bullet for Berlin, 1918 (Hart 3)

Bullet for Joey, 1955 (Raft 3, Robinson 3)

Bullet for Sandoval. See Desperados, 1970

Bullet for Stefano. See Passatore, 1947

Bullet for the General. See Quien sabe?, 1967

Bullet Is Waiting, 1954 (Simmons 3, Planer 4, Robinson 4, Tiomkin 4)

Bullet Proof, 1920 (Carey 3)

Bullets and Brown Eyes, 1916 (Gilbert 3)

Bullet Scars, 1942 (Bosworth 3, McCord 4)

Bullet Wound. See Dankon, 1969

Bulletin d'Information ASIFA, 1962 (Alexeieff and Parker 4)

Bullets for O'Hara, 1941 (Howard 2, Bosworth 3, McCord 4)

Bullets or Ballots, 1921 (Astor 3)

Bullets or Ballots, 1936 (Beavers 3, Blondell 3, Bogart 3, Robinson 3, Miller 4, Mohr 4)

Bullfight, 1935 (Terry 4)

Bullfight. See Course de taureaux, 1951

Bullfight, 1955 (Clarke 2)

Bullfight at Málaga, 1958 (Leacock 2)

Bullfighter and the Lady, 1951 (Boetticher 2, Young 4)

Bullfighters, 1945 (Laurel and Hardy 3)

Bullitt, 1968 (Yates 2, Duvall 3, McQueen 3, Fraker 4, Schifrin 4, Van Runkle 4)

Bulloney, 1933 (Iwerks 4)

Bulls and Bears, 1930 (Sennett 2)

Bull's Eye, 1918 (Johnson 3)

Bullseye!, 1990 (Caine 3, Cleese 3, Golan and Globus 4)

Bully, 1932 (Iwerks 4)

Bully Beef, 1930 (Terry 4)

Bully for Bugs, 1953 (Blanc 4, Jones 4, Maltese 4, Stalling 4)

Bully Frog, 1936 (Terry 4)

Bully Romance, 1939 (Terry 4)

Bum Bandit, 1931 (Fleischer 4)

Bum Voyage, 1934 (Roach 4)

Bummelstudenten, 1916 (Freund 4)

Bump, 1920 (Howard 3)

Bumping into Broadway, 1919 (Daniels 3, Lloyd 3, Roach 4)

Bunbuku chagama, 1939 (Yoda 4)

Bunch of Flowers, 1914 (Loos 4)

Bunch That Failed, 1910 (White 3)

Bunco Game at Lizardhead, 1911 (Anderson 3)

Buncoed Stage Johnnie, 1908 (Méliès 2)

Bundle of Joy, 1956 (Reynolds 3, Krasna 4)

Bundled Bungalow, 1950 (Burness 4)

Bungalow Boobs, 1924 (McCarey 2, Roach 4)

Bungalow Troubles, 1920 (Sennett 2)

Bungle Uncle, 1961 (Hanna and Barbera 4)

Bungled Bungalow, 1949 (Bosustow 4)

Bungles series, 1916 (Laurel and Hardy 3)

Bungs and Bunglers, 1919 (Laurel and Hardy 3)

Bunker, 1981 (Hopkins 3)

Bunker Bean, 1936 (Ball 3)

Bunker Hill Bunny, 1950 (Blanc 4, Freleng 4, Stalling 4)

Bunker Palace Hotel, 1989 (Léaud 3, Trintignant 3)

Bunkie, 1912 (Bosworth 3)

Bunnies Abundant, 1962 (Hanna and Barbera 4)

Bunny series, 1912–14 (Bunny 3)

Bunny and Claude, 1968 (Blanc 4, McKimson 4)

Bunny Hugged, 1951 (Blanc 4, Jones 4, Maltese 4, Stalling 4)

Bunny Lake Is Missing, 1965 (Preminger 2, Olivier 3, Bass 4, Coward 4, Fisher 4)

Bunny O'Hare, 1971 (Borgnine 3, Davis 3)

Bunny-mooning, 1937 (Fleischer 4)

Buon appetito, 1956 (Delli Colli 4)

Buona Sera, Mrs. Campbell, 1968 (Grant 3, Lollobrigida 3, Winters 3, Frank 4)

Buone notizie, 1979 (Morricone 4)

Buongiorno, elefante!, 1952 (Cecchi D'Amico 4, Zavattini 4)

Buongiorno natura, 1955 (Olmi 2)

Buono, il brutto, il cattivo, 1966 (Leone 2, Eastwood 3, Van Cleef 3, Wallach 3, Age and Scarpelli 4, Delli Colli 4, Morricone 4)

Buraikan. See Scandalous Adventures of Buraikan, 1970

Burari burabura monogatari, 1962 (Takamine 3)

'Burbs, 1989 (Dante 2, Dern 3, Hanks 3, Goldsmith 4)

Burcak tarlasi, 1966 (Güney 2)

Burden of Dreams, 1982 (Herzog 2, Cardinale 3, Kinski 3, Robards 3)

Burden of Fate. See Gnet roka, 1917

Burden of Life. See Jinsei ni onimotsu, 1935

Burden of Proof, 1917 (Davies 3)

Bureau des mariages, 1962 (Delerue 4)

Bureau of Missing Persons, 1933 (Davis 3, Blanke 4)

Burglar, 1928 (Sennett 2, Hornbeck 4)

Burglar, 1957 (Duryea 3, Mansfield 3)

Burglar, 1987 (Goldberg 3, Fraker 4)

Burglar By Proxy, 1919 (Polito 4)

Burglar Catcher, 1980 (Halas and Batchelor 4)

Burglar Godfather, 1915 (Anderson 3)

Burglarized Burglar, 1911 (Bushman 3)

Burglar on the Roof, 1898 (Blackton 2)

Burglars. See Casse, 1971

Burglars Bold, 1921 (Roach 4)

Burglar's Dilemma, 1912 (Griffith 2, Barrymore 3, Gish 3, Walthall 3, Bitzer 4)

Burglar's Mistake, 1909 (Bitzer 4)

Burgtheater, 1936 (Krauss 3, Tschechowa 3)

Burial Path, 1978 (Brakhage 2)

Buried Hand, 1915 (Walsh 2)

Buried Loot, 1935 (Taylor 3)

Buried Treasure, 1921 (Davies 3, Rosson 4)

Buried Treasure, 1926 (Roach 4)

Burlesque, 1925 (Balcon 4)

Burlesque, 1928 (Brown 3)

Burlesque, 1932 (Terry 4)

Burlesque, 1944 (Brown 3)

Burlesque on Carmen, 1915 (Purviance 3)

Burlesque Suicide, 1902 (Porter 2)

Burma Convoy, 1941 (Salter 4)

Burma Victory, 1945 (Boulting 2)

Burmese Harp. See **Biruma no tategoto, 1956**

Burn!. See Queimada!, 1969

Burn 'em Up O'Connor, 1939 (Carey 3)

Burn, Witch, Burn. See Night of the Eagle, 1961

Burn Witch Burn. See Mark of the Devil, 1970

Burned Hand, 1915 (Browning 2)

Burn-'em-Up Barnes, 1934 (Canutt 4)

Burning, 1967 (Frears 2)

Burning, 1980 (Savini 4)

Burning Autumn. See Moeru aki, 1978

Burning Beds. See Brennende Betten, 1988

Burning Bridges, 1928 (Carey 3, Polito 4)

Burning Chrome, 1991 (Gibson 3)

Burning Court. See Chambre ardente, 1962

Burning Daylight, 1914 (Bosworth 3)

Burning Daylight, 1927 (Polito 4)

Burning Heart. See Brennende Herz, 1929

Burning Hills, 1956 (Wood 3, McCord 4)

Burning Sands, 1922 (Clarke 4, Glennon 4, Howe 4, Young 4)

Burning Secret. See Brennendes Geheimnis, 1933

Burning Secret, 1988 (Brandauer 3, Dunaway 3)

Burning Soil. See Brennende Acker, 1922

Burning Stable, 1900 (Hepworth 2)

Burning the Candle, 1917 (Walthall 3)

Burning the Wind, 1929 (Karloff 3)

Burning Words, 1923 (Johnson 3, Laemmle 4)

Burning Youth. See Yama no sanka: Moyuru wakamono-tachi, 1962

Burnt Cork, 1912 (Bunny 3)

Burnt Fingers, 1927 (Stradling 4)

Burnt Offering. See Passport to Hell, 1932

Burnt Offerings, 1976 (Black 3, Davis 3, Meredith 3, Reed 3, Lourié 4, Smith 4)

Burnt Out Case, 1992 (Greene 4)

Burro, 1989 (Guerra 4)

Burroughs, 1982 (Jarmusch 2)

Burschenlied aus Heidelberg, 1930 (Herlth 4, Hoffmann 4, Röhrig 4)

Burton, 1966 (Burton 3)

Bury Me Dead, 1947 (Alton 4)

Bus, 1965 (Fields 4, Wexler 4)

Bus Riley's Back in Town, 1965 (Metty 4)

Bus Stop, 1956 (Monroe 3, Axelrod 4, Krasner 4, LeMaire 4, Newman 4, Reynolds 4, Wheeler 4)

Bus Terminal. See Florence 13.30, 1957

Bus II, 1983 (Wexler 4)

Busby Berkeley Book, 1970 (Berkeley 2)

Bush Christmas, 1947 (Rafferty 3)

Bush Christmas, 1947 (Rank 4)

Bush Mama, 1975 (Gerima 2)

Busher, 1919 (Gilbert 3, Moore 3, Ince 4)

Bushido. *See* Bushido zankoku monogatari, 1963

Bushido Blade, 1978 (Jones 3, Mifune 3)

Bushido zankoku monogatari, 1963 (Mori 3, Yoda 4)

Bushwackers, 1952 (Biroc 4)

Bushy Hare, 1950 (Blanc 4, Foster 4, McKimson 4, Stalling 4)

Business and Pleasure, 1932 (Karloff 3, McCrea 3, Rogers 3)

Business as Usual, 1987 (Jackson 3, Golan and Globus 4)

Business Is a Pleasure, 1934 (Grable 3)

Business Must Not Interfere, 1917 (Cohl 4)

Business of Love, 1925 (Horton 3)

Busker, 1976 (Menges 4)

Busman's Holiday, 1940 (Young 4)

Busman's Honeymoon, 1940 (Montgomery 3, Newton 3, Withers 3, Junge 4)

Busou keikantai, 1948 (Yoda 4)

Büssende Magdalena, 1915 (Wiene 2)

Busted Blossoms, 1934 (Terry 4)

Busted Hearts, 1916 (Laurel and Hardy 3)

Buster, 1923 (Fox 4)

Buster, 1988 (Quayle 3, Jarre 4)

Buster Keaton Rides Again, 1965 (Keaton 2)

Buster Keaton Story, 1957 (De Mille 2, Lorre 3, O'Connor 3, Head 4, Westmore Family 4, Young 4)

Buster se marie, 1930 (Autant-Lara 2, Rosay 3)

Buster's Bedroom, 1991 (Chaplin 3, Sutherland 3, Nykvist 4)

Bustin' Loose, 1981 (Pryor 3)

Busting, 1973 (Gould 3, Winkler 4)

Busting the Beanery, 1916 (Roach 4)

Busy Bakers, 1940 (Blanc 4, Stalling 4)

Busy Barber, 1932 (Lantz 4)

Busy Bee, 1936 (Terry 4)

Busy Bees, 1922 (Roach 4)

Busy Bodies, 1933 (Laurel and Hardy 3, Roach 4)

Busy Body, 1967 (Baxter 3, Pryor 3, Ryan 3, Green 4)

Busy Buddies, 1944 (Three Stooges 3)

Busy Buddies, 1956 (Hanna and Barbera 4)

Busy Day, 1914 (Sennett 2)

Busy Day, 1932 (Rooney 3)

Busybody, 1923 (La Cava 2)

But I Don't Want to Get Married!, 1967 (Duning 4)

But Not for Me, 1959 (Baker 3, Cobb 3, Gable 3, Burks 4, Hayes 4, Head 4)

But the Flesh Is Weak, 1932 (Horton 3, Montgomery 3, Adrian 4)

But the Greatest of These Is Charity, 1912 (Cruze 2)

Butai sugata, 1940 (Tanaka 3)

Butch and Sundance: The Early Days, 1979 (Lester 2, Goldman 4, Kovacs 4)

Butch Cassidy and the Sundance Kid, 1969 (Hill 2, Newman 3, Redford 3, Goldman 4, Hall 4, Head 4, Smith 4)

Butch Minds the Baby, 1942 (Crawford 3, Three Stooges 3)

Butcher. *See* **Boucher, 1969**

Butcher Boy, 1917 (Keaton 2, Arbuckle 3, Schenck 4)

Butcher Boy, 1932 (Lantz 4)

Butcher of Seville, 1944 (Terry 4)

Butley, 1973 (Bates 3, Dillon 4, Fisher 4, Pinter 4)

Butter and Egg Man, 1928 (Folsey 4)

Butter Fingers, 1925 (Sennett 2)

Buttercup Chain, 1970 (Slocombe 4)

Butterfield 8, 1960 (Harvey 3, Taylor 3, Berman 4, Hayes 4, Kaper 4, Rose 4, Ruttenberg 4, Schnee 4)

Butterflies Are Free, 1972 (Hawn 3, Lang 4)

Butterflies in the Rain, 1926 (Laemmle 4)

Butterfly, 1924 (Brown 2, Laemmle 4)

Butterfly, 1981 (Welles 2, Morricone 4)

Butterfly Ball, 1974 (Halas and Batchelor 4)

Butterfly Ball, 1976 (Price 3)

Butterfly Net, 1912 (Bushman 3)

Butterfly on the Wheel, 1915 (Tourneur 2, Carré 4)

Button My Back, 1929 (Sennett 2, Hornbeck 4)

Buttons, 1915 (Pearson 2)

Buttons, 1927 (Gibbons 4, Gillespie 4)

Buwana Toshi no uta, 1965 (Takemitsu 4)

Buy and Cell, 1988 (McDowell 3)

Buy Me That Town, 1941 (Dreier 4, Head 4)

Büyük cellatlar, 1967 (Güney 2)

Buzzin' Around, 1933 (Arbuckle 3)

Buzzy Boop, 1938 (Fleischer 4)

Buzzy Boop at the Concert, 1938 (Fleischer 4)

Bwana Devil, 1952 (Biroc 4, Clampett 4)

Bwana Magoo, 1958 (Bosustow 4, Burness 4)

Bwana Toshi. *See* Buwana Toshi no uta, 1965

By Candlelight, 1934 (Whale 2, Lukas 3, Kräly 4, Laemmle 4)

By Design, 1980 (Jutra 2, Rosenblum 4)

By Divine Right, 1957 (Von Sternberg 2)

By Golly, 1920 (Sennett 2)

By Heck, 1922 (Sennett 2)

By Hook or by Crook. *See* I Dood It, 1943

By Indian Post, 1919 (Ford 2, Carey 3)

By Love Possessed, 1961 (Sturges 2, Robards 3, Sloane 3, Turner 3, Bernstein 4, Cahn 4, Metty 4, Mirisch 4)

By Right of Purchase, 1918 (Talmadge 3)

By Rocket to the Moon. *See* Frau im Mond, 1929

By St. Matthias. *See* U sv. Matěje, 1928

By Stork Delivery, 1916 (Sennett 2)

By Super Strategy. *See* Restitution, 1918

By the Beautiful Sea, 1931 (Fleischer 4)

By the Governor's Order, 1914 (Costello 3)

By the Lake. *See* U ozera, 1969

By the Light of the Moon, 1911 (Porter 2)

By the Light of the Silvery Moon, 1926 (Fleischer 4)

By the Light of the Silvery Moon, 1931 (Fleischer 4)

By the Light of the Silvery Moon, 1953 (Day 3, Steiner 4)

By the Sad Sea Waves, 1917 (Daniels 3, Lloyd 3, Roach 4)

By the Sea, 1915 (Chaplin 2, Purviance 3)

By the Sea, 1931 (Terry 4)

By the Shortest of Heads, 1915 (Formby 3)

By the Sun's Rays, 1914 (Chaney 3)

By Whose Hand?, 1932 (Walker 4)

By Word of Mouse, 1954 (Blanc 4, Freleng 4)

By Your Leave, 1934 (Grable 3, Berman 4, Musuraca 4, Plunkett 4, Steiner 4)

Byakko-tai, 1927 (Tanaka 3)

Byakuran no uta, 1939 (Hasegawa 3)

Byakuya no kyoen, 1932 (Yamada 3)

Bye Bye Birdie, 1963 (Leigh 3, Biroc 4, Green 4)

Bye Bye Bluebeard, 1949 (Blanc 4, Stalling 4)

Bye Bye Brasil, 1980 (Diegues 2)

Bye Bye Braverman, 1968 (Lumet 2, Segal 3, Kaufman 4, Rosenblum 4)

Bye Bye Monkey. *See* Ciao maschio, 1978

Bye-Bye Red Riding Hood. *See* Piroska és a farkas, 1988

Byosai monogatari: Aya ni kanashiki, 1956 (Tanaka 3, Yamada 3)

Byl jednou jeden král, 1954 (Trnka 4)

Był sobie raz . . ., 1957 (Lenica 4)

Byt, 1968 (Švankmajer 4)

C.A.S.H. *See* Whiffs, 1975
C.I.D., 1956 (Dutt 2, Anand 3)
C.O.D., 1932 (Powell and Pressburger 2)
Ça aussi c'est Paris, 1930 (Fresnay 3)
Ça colle, 1933 (Christian-Jaque 2, Fernandel 3)
Ca n'arrive qu'a moi, 1985 (Blier 3)
Ca n'arrive qu'aux autres, 1971 (Deneuve 3, Mastroianni 3)
Ça va barder!, 1955 (Constantine 3)
Ca va etre ta fête, 1961 (Constantine 3)
Caballero a la medida, 1953 (Cantinflas 3)
Caballero del dragon, 1986 (Kinski 3, Rey 3)
Cabane aux souvenirs, 1946 (Vanel 3)
Cabaret, 1916 (Sennett 2)
Cabaret, 1953 (Rey 3)
Cabaret, 1972 (Fosse 2, Minnelli 3, Allen 4, Unsworth 4)
Cabaret du grand large, 1946 (Hayakawa 3)
Cabaret Singer, 1910 (White 3)
Cabareteras, 1980 (Fernández 2)
Cabeza de la hidra, 1981 (Leduc 2)
Cabin in the Cotton, 1932 (Curtiz 2, Barthelmess 3, Davis 3, Walthall 3, Orry-Kelly 4)
Cabin in the Sky, 1943 (Minnelli 2, Horne 3, McQueen 3, Edens 4, Freed 4, Gibbons 4, Irene 4, Lewin 4, Mayer 4)
Cabina, 1973 (Bozzetto 4)
Cabinet of Dr. Caligari. *See* **Kabinett des Dr. Caligari, 1920**
Cabinet of Dr. Ramirez, 1990 (Watkin 4)
Cabinets de physique au XVIIIème siècle, 1964 (Rohmer 2)
Cabiria, 1914 (Pastrone 2)
Cabiria. *See* Notti di Cabiria, 1956
Cable Car Murder. *See* Cable Car Mystery, 1971
Cable Car Mystery, 1971 (Ferrer 3, Wagner 3, Goldsmith 4)
Cable Laying, 1940 (Balcon 4)
Cabo Blanco, 1979 (Bronson 3, Rey 3, Robards 3, Sanda 3, Goldsmith 4)
Cabos Blancos, 1954 (Van Dyke 2)
Cabrioles ou la journée d'une danseuse, 1963 (Cassel 3)
Caccia alla volpe, 1938 (Blasetti 2)
Caccia alla volpe, 1966 (Mature 3, Sellers 3, Zavattini 4)
Caccia all'uomo. *See* Miserabili, 1947
Caccia in brughiera, 1949 (Risi 2)
Caccia tragica, 1947 (Zavattini 4)
Cache. *See* Battant, 1982
Cactus, 1986 (Huppert 3)
Cactus Cure, 1925 (Canutt 4)
Cactus Flower, 1969 (Bergman 3, Hawn 3, Matthau 3, Diamond 4, Jones 4, Lang 4)

Cactus Jack. *See* Villain, 1979
Cactus Jack Heartbreaker, 1914 (Mix 3)
Cactus Jim's Shopgirl, 1915 (Mix 3)
Cactus Kid, 1930 (Disney 4)
Cactus Makes Perfect, 1942 (Three Stooges 3)
Cactus Nell, 1917 (Sennett 2, Beery 3)
Cadaveri eccellenti, 1976 (Cuny 3, Rey 3, Vanel 3, Von Sydow 3, Guerra 4)
Caddies, 1980 (Halas and Batchelor 4)
Caddy, 1953 (Lewis 2, Martin 3, Reed 3, Head 4)
Caddy's Dream, 1911 (Pickford 3)
Cadeau, 1982 (Cardinale 3, Legrand 4)
Cadena de Amor, 1970 (Brocka 2)
Cadence, 1990 (Sheen 3, Delerue 4)
Cadet Girl, 1941 (Ladd 3, Clarke 4)
Cadet Rousselle, 1946 (Dunning 4)
Cadets de l'océan, 1941 (Gélin 3)
Cadetti di guascogna, 1950 (Age and Scarpelli 4)
Cadillac Man, 1990 (Williams 3)
Cadres fleuris, 1910 (Cohl 4)
Caduta degli angeli ribelli, 1981 (Valli 3)
Caduta degli dei, 1969 (Visconti 2, Bogarde 3, Thulin 3, Jarre 4)
Caduta di Troia, 1910 (Pastrone 2)
Caesar and Cleopatra, 1946 (Granger 3, Kendall 3, Leigh 3, Rains 3, Simmons 3, Auric 4, Cardiff 4, Heckroth 4, Krasker 4, Mathieson 4, Young 4)
Caf'Conc 1954, 1954 (Chevalier 3)
Café Colón, 1958 (Félix 3, Figueroa 4)
Café Colón de la Cerna, 1958 (Armendáriz 3)
Café de Paris, 1938 (Berry 3, Brasseur 3, Matras 4)
Café du Cadran, 1946 (Blier 3)
Café Electric, 1927 (Dietrich 3)
Café Express, 1980 (Cristaldi 4)
Café in Cairo, 1924 (Polito 4, Stromberg 4)
Cafe in the Main Street. *See* Kavárna na hlavni třídě, 1954
Cafe Metropole, 1937 (Menjou 3, Power 3, Young 3, Johnson 4)
Cafe Society, 1939 (Carroll 3, MacMurray 3, Dreier 4, Head 4)
Café tabac, 1965 (Piccoli 3)
Café Waiter's Dream. *See* Songe d'un garçon de café, 1910
Cage, 1975 (Thulin 3, Sarde 4, Saulnier 4)
Cage aux Folles, 1978 (Morricone 4)
Cage aux Folles II, 1980 (Morricone 4)
Cage aux Folles III, 1985 (Audran 3, Morricone 4)
Cage of Doom. *See* Terror from the Year 5000, 1958

Cage of Gold, 1950 (Dearden 2, Lom 3, Simmons 3, Auric 4, Balcon 4, Slocombe 4)
Caged, 1950 (Cromwell 2, Darwell 3, Moorehead 3, Steiner 4, Wald 4)
Caged Fury, 1948 (Crabbe 3)
Caged Heat, 1974 (Corman 2, Demme 2)
Cagey Canary, 1941 (Avery 4, Blanc 4, Clampett 4, Stalling 4)
Cagliostro, 1928 (Meerson 4)
Cagliostro. *See* Black Magic, 1947
Cagna, 1972 (Deneuve 3, Mastroianni 3, Piccoli 3, Carrière 4, Flaiano 4, Sarde 4)
Cahill. *See* Cahill, United States Marshall, 1973
Cahill, United States Marshall, 1973 (Bernstein 4, Biroc 4)
Caicara, 1950 (Cavalcanti 2)
Caïd, 1960 (Fernandel 3)
Cáida, 1959 (Torre Nilsson 2)
Caïds, 1972 (Reggiani 3, Douy 4)
Caimano del Piave, 1950 (Cervi 3)
Cain and Mabel, 1936 (Bacon 2, Davies 3, Gable 3, Wyman 3, Barnes 4, Orry-Kelly 4, Westmore Family 4)
Caine, 1967 (Fuller 2)
Caine Mutiny, 1954 (Dmytryk 2, Kramer 2, Bogart 3, Ferrer 3, Johnson 3, MacMurray 3, Marvin 3, Cohn 4, Planer 4, Steiner 4, Wald 4)
Cain's Cutthroats, 1970 (Carradine 3)
Cain's Way. *See* Cain's Cutthroats, 1970
Cairo, 1942 (Mankiewicz 2, Van Dyke 2, MacDonald 3, Young 3, Stothart 4, Wheeler 4)
Cairo, 1963 (Sanders 3)
Cairo Road, 1950 (Harvey 3, Morris 4)
Caissière du Grand Cafe, 1946 (Fernandel 3)
Caissounbouw Rotterdam, 1929 (Ivens 2)
Cake Eater, 1924 (Rogers 3, Roach 4)
Cake-Walk de la pendule, 1904 (Guy 2, Gaumont 4)
Cake-walk infernal, 1903 (Méliès 2)
Cal, 1984 (Puttnam 4)
Calaboose, 1942 (Roach 4)
Calabuch, 1956 (García Berlanga 2, Flaiano 4)
Calais-Douvre, 1931 (Litvak 2, Planer 4)
Calamitous Elopement, 1908 (Griffith 2, Lawrence 3, Bitzer 4)
Calamity Anne series, 1911–13 (Dwan 2)
Calamity Jane, 1953 (Day 3, Keel 3)
Calamity Jane and Sam Bass, 1949 (De Carlo 3)
Calamity Jane's Love Affair, 1914 (Eason 4)
Calamity the Cow, 1967 (Dalrymple 4)
Cala naprzód, 1966 (Cybulski 3)

Calandria, 1933 (De Fuentes 2)
Calaveras del terror, Guadalajara, 1943 (Armendáriz 3)
Calcutta, 1947 (Bendix 3, Ladd 3, Dreier 4, Head 4, Miller 4, Seitz 4, Young 4)
Calcutta, 1969 (Malle 2)
Calcutta, My El Dorado, 1990 (Sen 2)
Calcutta 71, 1972 (Sen 2)
Calendar, 1931 (Marshall 3, Balcon 4)
Calendar, 1948 (Dors 3, Rank 4)
Calendar Girl, 1947 (Dwan 2, McLaglen 3, Pangborn 3)
Calendar of the Year, 1936 (Cavalcanti 2, Grierson 2)
Calibre 44, 1959 (Armendáriz 3)
Calico Vampire, 1916 (Loos 4)
Caliente Love, 1933 (Sennett 2)
Califfa, 1971 (Schneider 3, Morricone 4)
California, 1927 (Van Dyke 2)
California, 1947 (Fitzgerald 3, Milland 3, Quinn 3, Stanwyck 3, Dreier 4, Head 4, Miller 4, Young 4)
California Conquest, 1952 (Wilde 3, Wright 3, Katzman 4)
California Dolls. See All the Marbles, 1981
California in '49. See Days of '49, 1924
California Kid, 1974 (Nolte 3, Sheen 3)
California Mail, 1929 (Brown 4)
California or Bust, 1923 (Roach 4)
California Romance, 1922 (Gilbert 3, August 4, Fox 4, Furthman 4)
California Split, 1974 (Altman 2, Rudolph 2, Gould 3, Segal 3)
California Straight Ahead, 1925 (Mandell 4)
California Straight Ahead, 1937 (Wayne 3)
California Suite, 1978 (Caine 3, Coburn 3, Fonda 3, Matthau 3, Pryor 3, Smith 3, Booth 4, May 4, Stark 4)
Caligula, 1980 (Gielgud 3, McDowell 3, O'Toole 3, Donati 4)
Caliph Storch, 1954 (Reiniger 4)
Call, 1909 (Griffith 2, Walthall 3, Bitzer 4)
Call a Cop, 1921 (Sennett 2)
Call a Cop!, 1931 (Stevens 2, Roach 4)
Call a Messenger, 1939 (Crabbe 3, Salter 4)
Call a Taxi, 1920 (Roach 4)
Call for Mr. Caveman, 1919 (Roach 4)
Call from Home, 1910 (White 3)
Call from Space, 1989 (Cardiff 4, Murch 4)
Call Girl. See Models, Inc., 1952
Call Harry Crown. See 99 and 44/100% Dead!, 1974
Call Her Mom, 1971 (Charisse 3, Johnson 3)
Call Her Savage, 1932 (Bow 3, Garmes 4)
Call Him Mr. Shatter, 1975 (Cushing 3)
Call It a Day, 1937 (De Havilland 3, Blanke 4, Haller 4, Orry-Kelly 4, Robinson 4, Wallis 4)
Call It Luck, 1934 (Nichols 4, Trotti 4)
Call me Anna, 1990 (Malden 3)
Call Me Bwana, 1963 (Hope 3)
Call Me Genius. See Rebel, 1961
Call Me Madam, 1953 (O'Connor 3, Sanders 3, Alton 4, Berlin 4, Newman 4, Shamroy 4, Sharaff 4, Wheeler 4)
Call Me Mister, 1951 (Bacon 2, Berkeley 2, Grable 3, LeMaire 4, Lewin 4, Newman 4, Wheeler 4)
Call Northside 777, 1948 (Hathaway 2, Cobb 3, Ritter 3, Stewart 3, LeMaire 4, Newman 4, Wheeler 4, Zanuck 4)
Call of Flesh. See Jotai, 1964
Call of Her People, 1917 (Barrymore 3)
Call of the Blood. See Appel du sang, 1920

Call of the Canyon, 1923 (Fleming 2, LeRoy 2, Howe 4)
Call of the Canyon, 1942 (Autry 3)
Call of the Circus, 1910 (Lawrence 3)
Call of the Circus, 1930 (Bushman 3)
Call of the Cuckoo, 1927 (Laurel and Hardy 3, Bruckman 4, Roach 4)
Call of the East, 1917 (Cruze 2, Hayakawa 3)
Call of the Flesh, 1930 (Dressler 3, Novarro 3, Gibbons 4, Shearer 4, Stothart 4)
Call of the Heart, 1927 (Laemmle 4)
Call of the Mate, 1924 (Furthman 4)
Call of the North, 1914 (De Mille 2, Buckland 4)
Call of the Open Range, 1911 (Dwan 2)
Call of the Plains, 1913 (Anderson 3)
Call of the Road, 1920 (McLaglen 3)
Call of the Song, 1911 (Pickford 3, Gaudio 4)
Call of the Wild, 1908 (Griffith 2, Lawrence 3)
Call of the Wild, 1923 (Roach 4)
Call of the Wild, 1935 (Wellman 2, Gable 3, Young 3, Day 4, Newman 4, Rosher 4, Zanuck 4)
Call of the Wild, 1972 (Heston 3)
Call of the Yukon, 1938 (Eason 4)
Call of Youth, 1920 (Hitchcock 2)
Call Out the Marines, 1942 (McLaglen 3, Pangborn 3, Hunt 4, Musuraca 4)
Call the Witness, 1921 (Roach 4)
Call to Arms, 1902 (Hepworth 2)
Call to Arms, 1910 (Griffith 2, Sennett 2, Pickford 3, Bitzer 4)
Call to Arms, 1913 (Dwan 2)
Call to Glory, 1966 (Van Cleef 3)
Callahans and the Murphys, 1918 (Dressler 3)
Callahans and the Murphys, 1927 (Gibbons 4, Marion 4)
Callas Text mit Doppel-beleuchtung, 1968 (Schroeter 2)
Callas Walking Lucia, 1968 (Schroeter 2)
Callaway Went Thataway, 1952 (Gable 3, Keel 3, MacMurray 3, Taylor 3, Williams 3, Frank 4, Rose 4)
Calle Mayor, 1956 (De Beauregard 4, Kosma 4)
Called Back, 1912 (Cruze 2)
Callejón sin salida, 1964 (Fernández 2)
Caller, 1987 (McDowell 3)
Calligraphie japonaise, 1961 (Braunberger 4)
Calling All Curs, 1939 (Three Stooges 3)
Calling All Husbands, 1940 (McCord 4)
Calling All Tars, 1936 (Hope 3)
Calling Bulldog Drummond, 1951 (Saville 2, Pidgeon 3, Junge 4)
Calling Dr. Death, 1943 (Miller 4)
Calling Dr. Gillespie, 1942 (Barrymore 3, Gardner 3, Reed 3)
Calling Dr. Kildare, 1939 (Ayres 3, Barrymore 3, Turner 3)
Calling Dr. Magoo, 1956 (Bosustow 4, Burness 4)
Calling Dr. Porky, 1940 (Blanc 4, Freleng 4, Stalling 4)
Calling Hubby's Bluff, 1929 (Sennett 2)
Calling Mr. Death, 1943 (Salter 4)
Calling of Dan Matthews, 1935 (Brown 4)
Calling of Jim Barton, 1914 (Anderson 3)
Calling the Shots, 1988 (Zetterling 2, Moreau 3)
Calling the Tune, 1936 (Dickinson 2)
Calling Wild Bill Hickok, 1943 (Canutt 4)

Callisto, 1943 (Honegger 4)
Calm Yourself, 1935 (Young 3)
Calmos, 1975 (Blier 3, Delerue 4)
Calvaire, 1914 (Feuillade 2, Musidora 3)
Calveras, 1969 (Grimault 4)
Calvert's Folly. See Calvert's Valley, 1922
Calvert's Valley, 1922 (Gilbert 3, Fox 4, Furthman 4)
Calypso Heat Wave, 1957 (Katzman 4)
Calypso Joe, 1957 (Dickinson 3)
Camacchio, 1942 (Fusco 4)
Cambiale, 1959 (Gassman 3)
Cambio della guardia, 1962 (Cervi 3)
Cambio de sexo, 1976 (Almendros 4)
Cambrick Mask, 1919 (Costello 3)
Cambriolage sur les toits, 1898 (Pathé 4)
Cambrioleur et agent, 1904 (Guy 2)
Cambrioleurs, 1897 (Guy 2)
Cambrioleurs de Paris, 1904 (Guy 2)
Came the Brawn, 1938 (Roach 4)
Came the Dawn, 1928 (McCarey 2, Roach 4)
Camée, 1913 (Tourneur 2)
Camelia, 1953 (Félix 3, Figueroa 4)
Camelot, 1967 (Harris 3, Redgrave 3, Newman 4, Warner 4)
Camels Are Coming, 1934 (Balcon 4, Rank 4)
Cameo Kirby, 1914 (De Mille 2)
Cameo Kirby, 1923 (Ford 2, Arthur 3, Gilbert 3, Johnson 3, Fox 4)
Cameo Kirby, 1930 (Loy 3, Fox 4)
Camera Bluff. See Amator, 1978
Camera d'Afrique, 1983 (Sembene 2)
Camera d'albergo, 1980 (Monicelli 2, Gassman 3, Vitti 3)
Camera Makes Woopee, 1976 (McLaren 4)
Cameraman, 1928 (Keaton 2, Bruckman 4, Mayer 4)
Cameramen at War, 1944 (Lye 4)
Cameriera bella presenza offresi, 1951 (De Sica 2, Fellini 2, Cervi 3, Fabrizi 3, Sordi 3, Pinelli 4)
Cameriere, 1959 (Delli Colli 4)
Camicie rosse, 1952 (Rosi 2, Cuny 3, Magnani 3, Reggiani 3, Gherardi 4)
Camila, 1984 (Bemberg 2)
Camilla, 1955 (Cristaldi 4, Flaiano 4)
Camille, 1915 (Gordon 3, Carré 4, Marion 4)
Camille, 1917 (Bara 3)
Camille, 1919 (Negri 3)
Camille, 1921 (Nazimova 3, Valentino 3, Mathis 4)
Camille, 1927 (Niblo 2, Costello 3, Talmadge 3, Menzies 4, Schenck 4)
Camille. See Dame aux camélias, 1934
Camille, 1937 (Cukor 2, Barrymore 3, Garbo 3, Taylor 3, Adrian 4, Akins 4, Booth 4, Daniels 4, Freund 4, Gibbons 4, Marion 4, Mayer 4, Stothart 4, Thalberg 4)
Camille, 1984 (Gielgud 3)
Camille Claudel, 1988 (Adjani 3, Cuny 3, Depardieu 3)
Camille ou La Comédie catastrophique, 1971 (Miller 2)
Camille without Camelias. See Signora senza camelie, 1953
Camino de infierno, 1950 (Armendáriz 3)
Camion, 1977 (Duras 2, Depardieu 3)
Camion blanc, 1942 (Cayatte 2, Berry 3)
Camisards, 1970 (Allio 2)
Cammelli, 1988 (Morricone 4)
Cammina, cammina, 1983 (Olmi 2)

Cammino degli eroi, 1936 (Fusco 4)

Cammino della speranza, 1950 (Fellini 2, Pinelli 4)

Cammorista, 1986 (Morricone 4)

Camorra, 1972 (Seberg 3, Vanel 3)

Camorra, 1986 (Wertmüller 2)

Camouflage, 1943 (Terry 4)

Camouflage. See Barwy ochronne, 1976

Camouflage Kiss, 1918 (Furthman 4)

Camp, 1965 (Warhol 2)

Camp de Thiaroye, 1987 (Sembene 2)

Camp Followers. See Soldatesse, 1965

Camp on Blood Island, 1958 (Carreras 4)

Campagne de France 1814–(?), 1916 (Cohl 4)

Campagne electorale, 1909 (Linder 3)

Campanadas a medianoche. See **Chimes at Midnight, 1966**

Campana de mi pueblo, 1944 (Armendáriz 3)

Campanas tambien pueden doblar mañana, 1983 (Alvarez 2)

Campane a martello, 1949 (Lollobrigida 3, Gherardi 4, Ponti 4, Rota 4)

Campbell Soups, 1912 (Cohl 4)

Campbell's Kingdom, 1957 (Baker 3, Bogarde 3, Box 4, Rank 4)

Campement 13, 1938 (Alekan 4)

Campi sperimentali, 1957 (Olmi 2)

Camping, 1957 (Zeffirelli 2, Ponti 4)

Campo dei fiori, 1943 (Fellini 2, Fabrizi 3, Magnani 3)

Campo di maggio. See Hundert Tage, 1935

Campus a Go-Go. See Eriki no wakadaisho, 1966

Campus Carmen, 1928 (Sennett 2, Lombard 3)

Campus Cinderella, 1938 (Hayward 3)

Campus Confessions, 1938 (Grable 3, Dreier 4, Head 4)

Campus Crushes, 1930 (Sennett 2)

Campus Flirt, 1926 (Daniels 3)

Campus Sweetheart, 1922 (Rogers 3)

Campus Sweetheart, 1931 (Newman 4)

Campus Vamp, 1928 (Sennett 2)

Can, 1972 (Müller 4)

Can Heironymus Merkin Ever Forget Mercy Humppe and Find True Happiness?, 1969 (Heller 4)

Can Horses Sing?, 1971 (Lassally 4)

Can She Bake A Cherry Pie?, 1983 (Black 3)

Can This Be Dixie?, 1936 (McDaniel 3, Glennon 4, Trotti 4)

Can You Take It?, 1934 (Fleischer 4)

Canada Is My Piano, 1967 (Dunning 4)

Canadian Capers, 1931 (Terry 4)

Canadian Moonshiners, 1910 (Olcott 2)

Canadian Officers in the Making, 1917 (Pearson 2)

Canadian Pacific, 1949 (Scott 3, Tiomkin 4)

Canadian Pacific Railroad Shots, 1899 (Bitzer 4)

Canadians, 1961 (Ryan 3, Mathieson 4)

Canal. See **Kanal, 1957**

Canal Zone, 1942 (Planer 4)

Canal Zone, 1977 (Wiseman 2)

Canale, 1964 (Bertolucci 2)

Cananea, 1976 (Figueroa 4)

Canard aux cérises, 1951 (Kosma 4)

Canary Bananas, 1935 (Leacock 2)

Canary Murder Case, 1929 (Arthur 3, Brooks 3, Powell 3, Banton 4, Mankiewicz 4)

Canary Row, 1950 (Blanc 4, Freleng 4, Stalling 4)

Canasta de cuentos mexicanos, 1956 (Armendáriz 3, Félix 3, Figueroa 4)

Canasta uruguaya, 1951 (Alcoriza 4)

Canby Hill Outlaws, 1916 (Mix 3)

Can-Can, 1960 (Chevalier 3, Dalio 3, Jourdan 3, MacLaine 3, Sinatra 3, Daniels 4, Lederer 4, Pan 4, Sharaff 4, Smith 4, Wheeler 4)

Canção de Lisboa, 1933 (Oliveira 2)

Cancel My Reservation, 1972 (Bellamy 3, Crosby 3, Hope 3, Saint 3, Wayne 3, Metty 4)

Cancer, 1968 (Rocha 2)

Canción de cuna, 1952 (De Fuentes 2)

Canción del alma, 1938 (Figueroa 4)

Canción del milagro, 1940 (Figueroa 4)

Candid Camera, 1932 (Sennett 2)

Candid Candidate, 1937 (Fleischer 4)

Candidate, 1972 (Crawford 3, Douglas 3, Redford 3, Wood 3)

Candidate for a Killing. See Candidato per un assassino, 1969

Candidato per un assassino, 1969 (Rey 3)

Candide, 1960 (Brasseur 3, Simon 3)

Candide ou l'optimisme au XXe siecle, 1960 (Cassel 3)

Candle and the Moth. See Evangeliemandens Liv, 1914

Candle in the Wind. See Fuzen no tomoshibi, 1957

Candlelight in Algeria, 1943 (Fisher 2, Mason 3, Heller 4)

Candlemaker, 1956 (Halas and Batchelor 4)

Candles at Nine, 1944 (Matthews 3)

Candleshoe, 1978 (Foster 3, Niven 3)

Candy, 1968 (Huston 2, Brando 3, Burton 3, Coburn 3, Matthau 3, Henry 4, Rotunno 4, Tavoularis 4, Trumbull 4)

Candy House, 1934 (Lantz 4)

Candy Kid, 1917 (Laurel and Hardy 3)

Candy Lamb, 1935 (Lantz 4)

Candy Man, 1969 (Sanders 3)

Candy Stripe Nurses, 1974 (Corman 2)

Candy Trail, 1916 (Laurel and Hardy 3)

Cani del Sinai. See Fortini/Cani, 1976

Canicule, 1983 (Marvin 3, Audiard 4, Lai 4)

Canker of Jealousy, 1915 (Hepworth 2)

Canned Feud, 1951 (Blanc 4, Foster 4, Freleng 4, Stalling 4)

Canned Fishing, 1938 (Roach 4)

Cannery Row, 1982 (Huston 2, Nolte 3, Nykvist 4)

Cannery Woe, 1961 (Blanc 4, McKimson 4)

Cannibal Attack, 1954 (Weissmuller 3, Katzman 4)

Cannibal King, 1915 (Laurel and Hardy 3)

Cannibali, 1970 (Morricone 4)

Cannon Ball, 1915 (Sennett 2)

Cannon Ball Express, 1924 (Sennett 2)

Cannon for Cordoba, 1970 (Bernstein 4)

Cannonball, 1931 (Sennett 2)

Cannonball, 1976 (Scorsese 2)

Cannonball Carquake. See Death Race 2000, 1975

Cannonball Run, 1981 (Chan 3, Martin 3, Reynolds 3, Needham 4)

Cannonball Run II, 1984 (Chan 3, MacLaine 3, Martin 3, Reynolds 3, Sinatra 3, Needham 4)

Canon, 1964 (McLaren 4)

Canon City, 1948 (Alton 4)

Canpazari, 1968 (Güney 2)

Can't Help Singing, 1944 (Durbin 3, Plunkett 4, Salter 4)

Canta delle marane, 1960 (Pasolini 2)

Cantaclaro, 1944 (Figueroa 4)

Cantata de Chile, 1975 (Solas 2, Villagra 3, Herrera 4)

Cantate pour deux généraux, 1990 (Rouch 2)

Canterbury Tale, 1944 (Powell and Pressburger 2, Junge 4, Rank 4)

Canterbury Tales. See Racconti di Canterbury, 1972

Canterville Ghost, 1944 (Dassin 2, Laughton 3, O'Brien 3, Young 3)

Canterville Ghost, 1986 (Gielgud 3)

Cantiere d'inverno, 1955 (Olmi 2)

Cantiflas boxeador, 1940 (Cantinflas 3)

Cantiflas ruletero, 1940 (Cantinflas 3)

Canto a mi tierra, 1938 (Armendáriz 3)

Canto della vita, 1945 (Gallone 2, Valli 3)

Canto ma sottovoce, 1945 (Zavattini 4)

Cantoria d'Angeli, 1949 (Di Venanzo 4)

Canyon Dweller, 1911 (Dwan 2)

Canyon Hawks, 1930 (Canutt 4)

Canyon of Adventure, 1928 (Brown 4, McCord 4)

Canyon of Light, 1926 (Mix 3, Fox 4)

Canyon of the Fools, 1923 (Carey 3)

Canyon Pass. See Raton Pass, 1951

Canyon Passage, 1946 (Tourneur 2, Andrews 3, Bond 3, Hayward 3, Banton 4, Carmichael 4, Cronjager 4, Wanger 4)

Canzone di Werner, 1914 (Bertini 3)

Canzoni a due voci, 1953 (Fusco 4)

Canzoni, canzoni, canzoni, 1953 (Sordi 3, Flaiano 4)

Cap de l'Espérance, 1951 (Feuillère 3, Kosma 4)

Cap du sud, 1935 (Storck 2)

Cap perdu, 1930 (Dupont 2, Baur 3)

Capable Lady Cook, 1916 (Beery 3)

Cape Ashizuri. See Ashizuri misaki, 1954

Cape Fear, 1962 (Mitchum 3, Peck 3, Boyle 4, Herrmann 4)

Cape Fear, 1991 (Scorsese 2, Spielberg 2, De Niro 3, Lange 3, Nolte 3, Peck 3, Bass 4, Bernstein 4, Bumstead 4, Francis 4)

Cape Forlorn, 1930 (Junge 4)

Cape Town Affair, 1953 (Fuller 2)

Cape Town Affair, 1967 (Trevor 3)

Capello a tre punte, 1935 (Valli 3)

Caper of the Golden Bulls, 1967 (Head 4, Levine 4)

Capestro degli Asburgo, 1915 (Bertini 3)

Capitaine Corsaire. See Mollenard, 1938

Capitaine Fracasse, 1928 (Cavalcanti 2, Boyer 3)

Capitaine Fracasse, 1942 (Gance 2, Honegger 4)

Capitaine Fracasse, 1961 (Marais 3, Noiret 3)

Capitaine jaune, 1930 (Vanel 3)

Capitaine Mollenard. See Mollenard, 1938

Capitaine Singrid, 1968 (Tavernier 2)

Capital Punishment, 1925 (Bow 3, Schulberg 4)

Capital Story, 1945 (Kaufman 4)

Capital versus Labor, 1909 (Porter 2)

Capitan, 1960 (Marais 3)

Capitan Fantasma, 1953 (Age and Scarpelli 4)

Capitan Fracassa, 1940 (Zavattini 4)

Capitan Malacara, 1944 (Armendáriz 3)

Capitana Allegria. *See* Pour Don Carlos, 1921

Capitani di Venezia, 1951 (Di Venanzo 4)

Capitol Affair, 1971 (McCambridge 3)

Capitu, 1968 (Diegues 2)

Capkovy povĭdky, 1947 (Trnka 4)

Cap'n Abe's Niece, 1917 (Costello 3)

Capone, 1975 (Corman 2, Stallone 3)

Caporal épinglé, 1962 (Cassel 3, Kosma 4, Spaak 4)

Cappello da prete, 1945 (Baarová 3, Amidei 4)

Cappotto, 1952 (Ferreri 2, Zavattini 4)

Cappotto di Astrakan, 1980 (Cristaldi 4)

Cappriccio all'italiana, 1967 (Pasolini 2)

Cappucetto rosso, Cenerentola … et voi ci credete, 1972 (Brazzi 3)

Cappy Ricks, 1921 (Young 4)

Caprelles et pantopodes, 1930 (Jaubert 4)

Capriccio, 1938 (Röhrig 4)

Capriccio all'italiana, 1968 (Launder and Gilliat 4, Monicelli 2, Mangano 3, Delli Colli 4, Zavattini 4)

Capriccio Espagnol. *See* Spanish Fiesta, 1941

Caprice, 1913 (Pickford 3)

Caprice, 1967 (Tashlin 2, Day 3, Harris 3, Shamroy 4, Smith 4)

Caprice de Noël, 1963 (McLaren 4)

Caprice de princesse, 1933 (Clouzot 2, Planer 4)

Caprices, 1941 (Cayatte 2, Blier 3, Darrieux 3, Andrejew 4)

Caprices de Maria, 1969 (Noiret 3, Delerue 4)

Caprices of Kitty, 1915 (Bosworth 3, Marion 4)

Capricious Summer. *See* Rozmarné lĕto, 1968

Capricorn One, 1977 (Black 3, Gould 3, Goldsmith 4)

Capriolen, 1937 (Gründgens 3, Planer 4)

Captain America, 1990 (Golan and Globus 4)

Captain Apache, 1971 (Baker 3, Van Cleef 3)

Captain Barnacle's Baby, 1911 (Bunny 3)

Captain Barnacle's Courtship, 1911 (Bunny 3)

Captain Barnacle's Messmate, 1912 (Bunny 3, Talmadge 3)

Captain Blackjack, 1950 (Moorehead 3, Sanders 3)

Captain Blood, 1935 (Curtiz 2, De Havilland 3, Flynn 3, Rathbone 3, Brown 4, Friedhofer 4, Grot 4, Haller 4, Korngold 4, Mohr 4, Robinson 4, Wallis 4, Warner 4, Westmore Family 4)

Captain Blood, Fugitive. *See* Captain Pirate, 1952

Captain Boycott, 1947 (Launder and Gilliat 2 Donat 3, Granger 3, Sim 3, Alwyn 4, Morris 4, Rank 4)

Captain Cap, 1963 (Braunberger 4)

Captain Careless, 1928 (Miller 4, Plunkett 4)

Captain Carey, U.S.A., 1950 (Leisen 2, Ladd 3, Dreier 4, Friedhofer 4, Seitz 4)

Captain Caution, 1940 (Ladd 3, Mature 3, Plunkett 4, Roach 4)

Captain China, 1949 (Alton 4)

Captain Clegg, 1962 (Cushing 3, Reed 3, Carreras 4)

Captain Courageous, 1937 (Hawks 2)

Captain Courageous, 1952 (Burness 4)

Captain Courtesy, 1915 (Bosworth 3, Marion 4)

Captain Cowboy, 1929 (Canutt 4)

Captain Eddie, 1945 (Bacon 2, MacMurray 3)

Captain Eo, 1986 (Huston 3, Storaro 4)

Captain Fly-by-Night, 1922 (Howard 2)

Captain Fracassa, 1940 (Stallich 4)

Captain from Castile, 1947 (King 2, Cobb 3, Power 3, Basevi 4, Clarke 4, Day 4, LeMaire 4, Newman 4, Trotti 4)

Captain Fury, 1939 (Carradine 3, Lukas 3, McLaglen 3, Canutt 4, Roach 4)

Captain Grant's Children. *See* Deti kapitana Granta, 1936

Captain Hareblower, 1954 (Blanc 4, Freleng 4, Stalling 4)

Captain Hates the Sea, 1934 (Milestone 2, Gilbert 3, McLaglen 3, Three Stooges 3, August 4)

Captain Horatio Hornblower, 1951 (Walsh 2, Baker 3, Lee 3, Peck 3, Green 4)

Captain Hurricane, 1935 (Plunkett 4)

Captain Is a Lady, 1940 (Bondi 3, Coburn 3, Kaper 4)

Captain Jack's Dilemma, 1912 (Bunny 3)

Captain Jack's Diplomacy, 1912 (Bunny 3)

Captain James Cook, 1988 (Rey 3)

Captain January, 1924 (Bosworth 3)

Captain January, 1936 (Carradine 3, Darwell 3, Temple 3, Seitz 4, Zanuck 4)

Captain Kate, 1911 (Mix 3)

Captain Kidd, 1926 (Bray 4)

Captain Kidd, 1945 (Carradine 3, Laughton 3, Scott 3, Raine 4)

Captain Kidd, Jr., 1919 (Pickford 3, Marion 4, Rosher 4)

Captain Kidd's Kids, 1919 (Daniels 3, Lloyd 3, Roach 4)

Captain Kleinschmidt's Adventures in the Far North. *See* Adventures in the Far North, 1923

Captain Lash, 1929 (McLaglen 3, Fox 4)

Captain Lightfoot, 1955 (Sirk 2, Hudson 3, Burnett 4, Hunter 4, Salter 4)

Captain Macklin, 1915 (Gish 3)

Captain McLean, 1914 (Von Stroheim 2)

Captain Nemo and the Underwater City, 1970 (Ryan 3)

Captain Newman, M.D., 1963 (Curtis 3, Dickinson 3, Duvall 3, Peck 3, Metty 4, Westmore Family 4, Whitlock 4)

Captain of the Guard, 1930 (Laemmle 4, Mohr 4)

Captain Pirate, 1952 (Brown 4, Duning 4)

Captain Salvation, 1927 (Daniels 4, Gibbons 4)

Captain Sinbad, 1963 (Armendáriz 3, Haskin 4, Schüfftan 4)

Captain Thunder, 1931 (Wray 3)

Captain Tugboat Annie, 1945 (Darwell 3)

Captain Video, 1951 (Katzman 4)

Captain Yankee. *See* Jungle Raiders, 1985

Captain's Captain, 1918 (Costello 3)

Captains Courageous, 1937 (Fleming 2, Barrymore 3, Carradine 3, Douglas 3, Rooney 3, Tracy 3, Gibbons 4, Gillespie 4, Mayer 4, Rosson 4, Waxman 4)

Captains Courageous, 1977 (Malden 3)

Captain's Kid, 1936 (Haller 4)

Captains of the Clouds, 1942 (Curtiz 2, Cagney 3, Haskin 4, Hoch 4, Mercer 4, Polito 4, Raine 4, Steiner 4, Wallis 4)

Captains Outrageous, 1952 (Bosustow 4)

Captain's Paradise, 1953 (De Carlo 3, Guinness 3, Johnson 3, Arnold 4, Korda 4)

Captain's Table, 1959 (Challis 4, Rank 4)

Captivating Mary Carstairs, 1915 (Talmadge 3)

Captive, 1915 (De Mille 2, Sweet 3, Buckland 4, Macpherson 4)

Captive, 1986 (Reed 3)

Captive City, 1952 (Garmes 4)

Captive City. *See* Citta prigioniera, 1962

Captive Girl, 1950 (Crabbe 3, Weissmuller 3, Katzman 4)

Captive God, 1916 (Hart 3, August 4)

Captive Heart, 1946 (Dearden 2, Redgrave 3, Balcon 4, Rank 4, Slocombe 4)

Captive Island. *See* Shokei no shima, 1966

Captive Rage, 1988 (Reed 3)

Captive Wild Woman, 1943 (Dmytryk 2, Carradine 3, Pierce 4, Salter 4)

Capture, 1950 (Sturges 2, Ayres 3, Wright 3, Cronjager 4)

Capture of Aquinaldo, 1913 (Darwell 3)

Capture of the Biddle Brothers, 1902 (Porter 2)

Capture of Yegg Bank Burglars, 1904 (Porter 2)

Captured!, 1933 (Howard 3, Lukas 3, Orry-Kelly 4)

Captured by Bedouins, 1912 (Olcott 2)

Car, 1977 (Rosenman 4, Whitlock 4)

Car 99, 1935 (MacMurray 3, Sheridan 3, Head 4, Sullivan 4)

Car of Chance, 1917 (Young 4)

Car of Dreams, 1935 (Mills 3, Balcon 4, Junge 4, Rank 4)

Car of Tomorrow, 1951 (Avery 4)

Car Wash, 1975 (Pryor 3)

Cara del terror, 1962 (Rey 3)

Carabina 30–30, 1958 (Figueroa 4)

Carabiniere, 1963 (Rossellini 2)

Carabiniere a cavallo, 1961 (Di Venanzo 4, Gherardi 4)

Carabiniers, 1963 (Godard 2, Coutard 4, De Beauregard 4, Guillemot 4, Ponti 4)

Carambolages, 1962 (Delon 3, Audiard 4)

Caravaggio, 1940 (Stallich 4)

Caravaggio, 1986 (Jarman 2)

Caravan. *See* Caravane, 1934

Caravan, 1946 (Granger 3, Rank 4)

Caravan, 1980 (Johnson 3)

Caravane, 1934 (Boyer 3, Brasseur 3, Young 3, Raphaelson 4)

Caravane au Jardin d'Acclimatation, 1949 (Gaumont 4)

Caravane de la lumière, 1947 (Fradetal 4)

Caravans, 1978 (Cotten 3, Lee 3, Quinn 3, Slocombe 4)

Carbine Williams, 1952 (Stewart 3, Plunkett 4)

Carbon Arc Projection, 1947 (Hoch 4)

Carbon Copy, 1981 (Segal 3)

Carbunara, 1955 (Taviani 2)

Carcasse et le Tord-Cou, 1947 (Simon 3)

Cárcel de Cananca, 1960 (Armendáriz 3)

Card, 1952 (Guinness 3, Alwyn 4, Morris 4)

Card Game. *See* Poker, 1920

Cardboard Baby, 1909 (Olcott 2)

Cardboard Cavalier, 1949 (Lockwood 3, Dillon 4, Rank 4)

Cardboard City. *See* Ciudad de carton, 1932

Cardboard City, 1934 (Barrymore 3)

Cardboard Lover, 1928 (Gibbons 4, Wilson 4)

Cardenal, 1951 (Bennett 4)

Cardeuse de Matelas, 1906 (Méliès 2)

Cardigan's Last Case. *See* State's Attorney, 1932

Cardinal, 1963 (Huston 2, Preminger 2, Meredith 3, Schneider 3, Bass 4, Shamroy 4, Smith 4, Wheeler 4)

Cardinal Richelieu, 1935 (Arliss 3, Carradine 3, O'Sullivan 3, Day 4, Johnson 4, Newman 4, Zanuck 4)

Cardinal Richelieu's Ward, 1914 (Cruze 2)

Cardinale Lambertini, 1955 (Cervi 3)

Cardinal's Conspiracy, 1909 (Griffith 2, Lawrence 3, Pickford 3, Bitzer 4, Ince 4)

Cardinal's Visit, 1970 (Baillie 2)

Cards on the Table. *See* Cartas boca arriba, 1965

Care Bears Movie, 1985 (Rooney 3, Stanton 3)

Career, 1939 (Trumbo 4)

Career. *See* Kariera, 1955

Career, 1959 (MacLaine 3, Martin 3, Cahn 4, Head 4, La Shelle 4, Wallis 4, Waxman 4)

Career: Medical Technologists, 1954 (Bernstein 4)

Career of Pavel Camrda. *See* Kariéra Pavla Camrdy, 1931

Career Woman, 1936 (Trevor 3, Trotti 4)

Careers, 1929 (Seitz 4)

Carefree, 1938 (Astaire 3, Bellamy 3, Pangborn 3, Rogers 3, Berlin 4, Berman 4, Nichols 4, Pan 4, Polglase 4)

Careful, Soft Shoulders, 1942 (Clarke 4, Day 4)

Careless Age, 1929 (Young 3)

Careless Lady, 1932 (Bennett 3, Friedhofer 4, Seitz 4)

Careless Love. *See* Bonne Soupe, 1964

Careless Youth. *See* Leichtsinnige Jugend, 1931

Caretaker, 1963 (Roeg 2, Bates 3, Pleasence 3, Shaw 3, Pinter 4)

Caretakers, 1963 (Crawford 3, Marshall 3, Ballard 4, Bernstein 4)

Caretaker's Daughter, 1925 (McCarey 2, Roach 4)

Caretaker's Daughter, 1934 (Roach 4)

Carey Treatment, 1972 (Coburn 3, Ravetch 4)

Cargaison blanche, 1937 (Siodmak 2, Berry 3, Dalio 3, Jeanson 4)

Cargaison blanche, 1957 (Broca 2)

Cargamento prohibibo, 1965 (Figueroa 4)

Cargo from Jamaica, 1933 (Grierson 2, Wright 2)

Cargo of Innocents. *See* Stand By for Action, 1942

Cargo to Capetown, 1950 (Crawford 3, Duning 4)

Caribbean, 1952 (Head 4)

Cariboo Trail, 1950 (Scott 3)

Carillons, 1936 (Storck 2)

Carillons sans joie, 1962 (Auric 4, Cloquet 4)

Cariñoso, 1958 (Alcoriza 4)

Carl Dreyer, Le Celluloid et la marbre, 1965 (Rohmer 2)

Carl Nielsen 1865–1931, 1978 (Roos 2)

Carl Th. Dreyer, 1966 (Roos 2)

Carlo Pisacane, 1955 (Taviani 2)

Carlos, 1971 (Müller 4)

Carlos und Elisabeth—Eine Herrschertragödie, 1924 (Dieterle 2, Veidt 3)

Carlton-Browne of the F.O., 1958 (Terry-Thomas 3, Sellers 3, Addison 4)

Carmen, 1900 (Guy 2)

Carmen, 1915 (De Mille 2, Walsh 2, Bara 3, Reid 3, Buckland 4, Macpherson 4, Zukor 4)

Carmen, 1918 (Lubitsch 2, Negri 3, Kräly 4)

Carmen, 1926 (Feyder 2, Modot 3, Meerson 4)

Carmen, 1933 (Reiniger 4)

Carmen, 1943 (Christian-Jaque 2, Marais 3, Jeanson 4, Spaak 4)

Carmen, 1960 (Gassman 3)

Carmen, 1967 (Wakhévitch 4)

Carmen, 1983 (Saura 2)

Carmen, 1984 (Guerra 4)

Carmen, Baby, 1967 (Kinski 3)

Carmen Comes Home. *See* Karumen Kokyo ni kaeru, 1951

Carmen di Trastavere, 1962 (Gallone 2)

Carmen fra i rossi, 1939 (Stallich 4)

Carmen Jones, 1954 (Preminger 2, Dandridge 3, Bass 4)

Carmen von St. Pauli, 1928 (Rasp 3, Junge 4)

Carmenita the Faithful, 1911 (Anderson 3)

Carmen's Pure Love. *See* Karumen Junjo su, 1951

Carmen's Veranda, 1944 (Terry 4)

Carnal Knowledge, 1971 (Nichols 2, Nicholson 3, Levine 4, Rotunno 4, Sylbert 4)

Carnaval, 1953 (Pagnol 2, Fernandel 3)

Carnaval à la Nouvelle Orléans, 1957 (Braunberger 4)

Carnaval à Nice, 1913 (Gaumont 4)

Carnaval des vérités, 1919 (Autant-Lara 2, L'Herbier 2)

Carnavals, 1950 (Storck 2)

Carne de horca, 1954 (Brazzi 3)

Carne de presidio, 1951 (Armendáriz 3, Alcoriza 4)

Carne inquieta, 1952 (Baarová 3)

Carne per Frankenstein, 1974 (Warhol 2, Guerra 4, Ponti 4)

Carnegie Hall, 1947 (Ulmer 2, Schüfftan 4)

Carnet de bal, 1937 (Duvivier 2, Baur 3, Fernandel 3, Jouvet 3, Raimu 3, Rosay 3, Jaubert 4, Jeanson 4)

Carnet de viaje, 1961 (Ivens 2)

Carnets du Major Thompson, 1957 (Sturges 2, Buchanan 3, Matras 4)

Carnevale di Venezia, 1927 (Amidei 4)

Carnival, 1911 (Olcott 2)

Carnival, 1921 (McLaglen 3, Novello 3)

Carnival, 1932 (Wilcox 2)

Carnival, 1935 (Ball 3, Durante 3, Riskin 4)

Carnival, 1946 (Dillon 4, Green 4, Rank 4)

Carnival. *See* Karneval, 1961

Carnival Boat, 1932 (Bosworth 3, Rogers 3, McCord 4)

Carnival Capers, 1932 (Lantz 4)

Carnival Girl, 1926 (Garmes 4)

Carnival in Costa Rica, 1947 (Cobb 3, Hoffenstein 4, Reynolds 4)

Carnival in Flanders. *See* **Kermesse héroïque, 1935**

Carnival in the Clothes Cupboard, 1940 (Halas and Batchelor 4)

Carnival Man, 1929 (Huston 3)

Carnival of Killers. *See* Spie contro il mondo, 1966

Carnival of Sinners. *See* Main du diable, 1942

Carnival of Thieves. *See* Caper of the Golden Bulls, 1966

Carnival on Costa Rica, 1947 (Basevi 4)

Carnival Rock, 1957 (Corman 2, Crosby 4)

Carnival Story, 1954 (Baxter 3, Haller 4, Trumbo 4)

Carnival Week, 1927 (Terry 4)

Carny, 1980 (Foster 3, North 4)

Caro Michele, 1976 (Monicelli 2, Seyrig 3, Cecchi D'Amico 4, Delli Colli 4, Guerra 4, Rota 4)

Caro Papà, 1979 (Gassman 3, Delli Colli 4)

Carobni zvuci, 1957 (Vukotić 4)

Carodějuv učen, 1977 (Zeman 4)

Carol, 1970 (Emshwiller 2)

Carol for Another Christmas, 1964 (Hayden 3, Saint 3)

Carola, 1975 (Caron 3, Lourié 4)

Carola Lamberti—Eine vom Zirkus, 1954 (Porten 3)

Carolina, 1934 (King 2, Barrymore 3, Gaynor 3, Temple 3, Young 3, Mohr 4)

Carolina Blues, 1944 (Miller 3, Cahn 4, Duning 4, Planer 4)

Carolina Moon, 1940 (Autry 3)

Carolina Rediviva, 1920 (Magnusson 4)

Caroline, 1990 (Neal 3)

Caroline au pays natal, 1951 (Decaë 4)

Caroline chérie, 1950 (Auric 4)

Caroline chérie, 1967 (De Sica 2, Blier 3, Saulnier 4, Vierny 4)

Caroline du Sud, 1952 (Decaë 4)

Carolyn of the Corners, 1918 (Love 3)

Caronna nera. *See* Corona negra, 1952

Carosella napolitano, 1953 (Rosi 2, Loren 3)

Carosello di varietà, 1955 (Fabrizi 3)

Carousel, 1956 (King 2, Clarke 4, Glazer 4, Newman 4, Reynolds 4, Smith 4, Wheeler 4)

Carpenter, 1922 (Laurel and Hardy 3)

Carpetbaggers, 1964 (Dmytryk 2, Ayres 3, Baker 3, Ladd 3, Bernstein 4, Edouart 4, Hayes 4, Head 4, Levine 4, Westmore Family 4)

Carpocapse des pommes, 1955 (Rabier 4)

Carradines in Concert, 1980 (Carradine 3)

Carrara, 1950 (Di Venanzo 4)

Carré de valets, 1947 (Jeanson 4)

Carrefour, 1938 (Berry 3, Vanel 3, Burel 4, D'Eaubonne 4)

Carrefour de passion. *See* Uomini sono nemici, 1948

Carrefour des enfants perdus, 1943 (Reggiani 3)

Carrefour des passion, 1948 (Kosma 4)

Carrefour du crime, 1947 (Burel 4)

Carrie, 1951 (Wyler 2, Hopkins 3, Jones 3, Oliver 3, Head 4, Raksin 4)

Carrie, 1976 (De Palma 2, Spacek 3, Travolta 3, Donaggio 4)

Carried Away By the Current. *See* Proudy, 1922

Carro armata dell'otto settembre, 1960 (Pasolini 2, Guerra 4)

Carrosse d'or, 1953 (Magnani 3, Renoir 4)

Carrots and Peas, 1969 (Frampton 2)

Carry Harry, 1942 (Langdon 3)

Carry on Constable, 1960 (Dillon 4)

Carry on Cruising, 1962 (Dillon 4)

Carry On George, 1939 (Formby 3)

Carry On Milkmaids, 1974 (Halas and Batchelor 4)

Carry on Nurse, 1959 (Vetchinsky 4)

Carry on Sergeant, 1958 (Vetchinsky 4)

Carry on Spying, 1964 (Vetchinsky 4)

Carry on Teacher, 1959 (Vetchinsky 4)

Carry on Up the Khyber, 1968 (Vetchinsky 4)

Carrying the Mail, 1934 (Canutt 4)

Cars That Ate Paris, 1974 (Weir 2)

Cars That Ate People. *See* Cars That Ate Paris, 1974

Carson City, 1952 (De Toth 2, Massey 3, Scott 3)

Carson City Kid, 1940 (Rogers 3)

Carson City Raiders, 1948 (Canutt 4)

Carta, 1930 (Fort 4)

Cartagine in fiamme, 1959 (Gallone 2, Brasseur 3, Cervi 3, Gélin 3)

Cartas boca arriba, 1965 (Rey 3)

Cartas marcadas, 1947 (Infante 3)

Carte américaine, 1917 (Cohl 4)

Carte a Sara, 1956 (Bardem 2)

Carter Case, 1941 (Pangborn 3)

Carters, 1939 (Barnes 4)

Carter's Army, 1970 (Pryor 3)

Cartes sur table, 1965 (Constantine 3, Carrière 4, D'Eaubonne 4)

Cartes vivants, 1905 (Méliès 2)

Carthage in Flames. *See* Cartagine in fiamme, 1959

Cartoon Factory, 1925 (Fleischer 4)

Cartoonland, 1921 (Fleischer 4)

Cartouche, 1934 (Fradetal 4)

Cartouche, 1962 (Broca 2, Belmondo 3, Cardinale 3, Dalio 3, Delerue 4, Matras 4, Spaak 4)

Car-Tune Portrait, 1937 (Fleischer 4)

Carve Her Name with Pride, 1958 (Aimée 3, Caine 3, Alwyn 4, Box 4, Rank 4)

Carved in Ivory, 1974 (Lassally 4)

Cas de conscience, 1939 (Berry 3)

Cas de malheur, 1958 (Bardot 3, Cassel 3, Feuillère 3, Gabin 3, Aurenche 4, Bost 4, Douy 4, Saulnier 4)

Cas du Docteur Laurent, 1956 (Gabin 3, Alekan 4, Kosma 4)

Casa chica, 1950 (Del Rio 3)

Casa colorado, 1947 (Armendáriz 3, Figueroa 4)

Casa de cristal, 1967 (Alcoriza 4)

Casa dei Pulcini, 1924 (Camerini 2)

Casa del ángel, 1957 (Torre Nilsson 2)

Casa del ogro, 1938 (De Fuentes 2, Figueroa 4)

Casa del peccato, 1938 (Valli 3)

Casa del pelicano, 1977 (Figueroa 4)

Casa del rencor, 1941 (Figueroa 4)

Casa del tappeto giallo, 1983 (Josephson 3)

Casa de mujeres, 1966 (Del Rio 3)

Casa Ricordi, 1954 (Mastroianni 3, Presle 3, Age and Scarpelli 4)

Casa sin fronteras, 1972 (Chaplin 3)

Casablanca, 1942 (Curtiz 2, Siegel 2, Bergman 3, Bogart 3, Dalio 3, Greenstreet 3, Henreid 3, Lorre 3, Rains 3, Veidt 3, Edeson 4, Epstein 4, Friedhofer 4, Koch 4, Orry-Kelly 4, Steiner 4, Wallis 4, Warner 4, Westmore Family 4)

Casablanca, 1961 (Solas 2)

Casablanca, Casablanca, 1984 (Olbrychski 3)

Casanova, 1927 (Delannoy 2, Volkov 2, Mozhukin 3, Simon 3, Burel 4)

Casanova, 1976 (Sutherland 3, De Laurentiis 4, Donati 4, Rota 4)

Casanova, 1987 (Dunaway 3, Schygulla 3)

Casanova & Co., 1977 (Curtis 3)

Casanova Brown, 1944 (Wood 2, Cooper 3, Wright 3, Fields 4, Johnson 4, Seitz 4)

Casanova Cat, 1950 (Hanna and Barbera 4)

Casanova de Federico Fellini, 1976 (Rotunno 4)

Casanova farebbe cosi, 1942 (Sordi 3)

Casanova's Big Night, 1954 (McLeod 2, Carradine 3, Fontaine 3, Hope 3, Price 3, Rathbone 3)

Casanova '70, 1965 (Ferreri 2, Monicelli 2, Mastroianni 3, Age and Scarpelli 4, Cecchi D'Amico 4, Guerra 4, Levine 4, Ponti 4)

Casanove wider willen, 1931 (Rosay 3)

Casbah, 1948 (De Carlo 3, Lorre 3)

Cascade de Feu, 1904 (Méliès 2)

Case Against Calvin Cooke. *See* Act of Murder, 1948

Case Against Ferro, 1976 (Signoret 3)

Case Against Mrs. Ames, 1936 (Bondi 3, Carroll 3, Wanger 4)

Case Dismissed, 1924 (Arthur 3)

Case for PC 49, 1951 (Carreras 4)

Case of Becky, 1915 (Sweet 3)

Case of Becky, 1921 (Folsey 4)

Case of Colonel Redl. *See* Fall des Generalstabsoberst Redl, 1931

Case of Gabriel Perry, 1935 (Lockwood 3)

Case of Irresponsibility. *See* Caso di incoscienza, 1984

Case of Jonathan Drew. *See* Lodger, 1926

Case of Lena Smith, 1929 (Von Sternberg 2, Banton 4, Dreier 4, Furthman 4, Rosson 4)

Case of Marcel Duchamp, 1983 (Lassally 4)

Case of Sergeant Grischa, 1930 (Brenon 2, Hunt 4, Plunkett 4)

Case of the Black Parrot, 1941 (McCord 4)

Case of the Curious Bride, 1935 (Curtiz 2, Flynn 3, Brown 4, Grot 4, Laszlo 4, Orry-Kelly 4)

Case of the Howling Dog, 1934 (Astor 3, Orry-Kelly 4)

Case of the Lost Sheep, 1935 (Lantz 4)

Case of the Lucky Legs, 1935 (Gaudio 4)

Case of the Missing Blonde. *See* Lady in the Morgue, 1938

Case of the Missing Hare, 1942 (Blanc 4, Jones 4, Stalling 4)

Case of the Mukkinese Battlehorn, 1955 (Sellers 3)

Case of the Stuttering Pig, 1937 (Blanc 4, Stalling 4)

Case of the Velvet Claw, 1936 (Blanke 4)

Casey and His Neighbor's Goat, 1903 (Porter 2)

Casey at the Bat, 1912 (Talmadge 3)

Casey at the Bat, 1927 (Beery 3, Furthman 4)

Casey's Frightful Dream, 1904 (Porter 2)

Casey's Shadow, 1978 (Ritt 2, Matthau 3, Alonzo 4, Stark 4)

Casey's Vendetta, 1914 (Browning 2)

Cash, 1933 (Donat 3, Korda 4)

Cash and Carry, 1937 (Three Stooges 3, Bruckman 4)

Cash Customers, 1921 (Roach 4)

Cash McCall, 1960 (Garner 3, Wood 3, Blanke 4, Coffee 4, Folsey 4, Steiner 4)

Cash on Delivery. *See* To Dorothy, a Son, 1954

Cash on Demand, 1961 (Cushing 3, Carreras 4)

Cash on the Barrel Head, 1962 (Bendix 3)

Cash Parrish's Pal, 1915 (Hart 3, August 4)

Casimir, 1950 (Fernandel 3)

Casino de Paree. *See* Go into Your Dance, 1935

Casino de Paris, 1957 (De Sica 2)

Casino Murder Case, 1935 (Lukas 3, Russell 3, Clarke 4, Tiomkin 4)

Casino Royale, 1967 (Allen 2, Huston 2, Roeg 2, Welles 2, Belmondo 3, Boyer 3, Holden 3, Kerr 3, Niven 3, O'Toole 3, Raft 3, Sellers 3, Fisher 4, Mankowitz 4, Williams 4)

Caso di incoscienza, 1984 (Josephson 3, Vogler 3)

Caso Haller, 1933 (Blasetti 2)

Caso Mattei, 1972 (Volonté 3, Cristaldi 4, Guerra 4)

Caso Moro, 1986 (Volonté 3, Donaggio 4)

Caso Raoul, 1975 (Valli 3)

Casotto, 1977 (Deneuve 3)

Casque d'or, 1952 (Becker 2, Modot 3, Reggiani 3, Signoret 3, D'Eaubonne 4, Hakim 4)

Cass Timberlane, 1947 (Astor 3, Pidgeon 3, Tracy 3, Turner 3, Irene 4, Levien 4, Mayer 4, Stewart 4)

Cassandra Crossing, 1977 (Gardner 3, Harris 3, Lancaster 3, Loren 3, Sheen 3, Thulin 3, Valli 3, Goldsmith 4, Ponti 4)

Casse, 1971 (Belmondo 3, Sharif 3, Morricone 4, Renoir 4, Saulnier 4)

Casse-pieds, 1948 (Blier 3, Burel 4)

Cassette de l'emigrée, 1912 (Feuillade 2)

Cassidy of Bar 20, 1938 (Head 4)

Cassis, 1966 (Mekas 2)

Cassis Colank, 1958 (Breer 4)

Cassoto, 1980 (Foster 3)

Cast a Dark Shadow, 1955 (Bogarde 3, Lockwood 3)

Cast a Giant Shadow, 1966 (Brynner 3, Dickinson 3, Douglas 3, Douglas 3, Sinatra 3, Topol 3, Wayne 3, Bernstein 4)

Cast a Long Shadow, 1959 (Murphy 3, Mirisch 4)

Cast Iron. *See* Virtuous Sin, 1929

Cast Iron. *See* Virtuous Sin, 1930

Cast Iron, 1964 (Ioseliani 2)

Cast of the Die, 1914 (Anderson 3)

Casta Diva, 1935 (Planer 4)

Casta Diva, 1955 (Gallone 2, Age and Scarpelli 4)

Casta e pura, 1981 (Rey 3)

Castagnino, diario romano, 1966 (Birri 2)

Castaway, 1986 (Roeg 2, Reed 3)

Castaway Cowboys, 1974 (Garner 3)

Castel Sant' Angelo, 1946 (Blasetti 2)

Castelli in aria, 1938 (Castellani 2)

Castelli in aria, 1938 (De Sica 2)

Castello dei morti vivi, 1964 (Lee 3, Sutherland 3)

Castello di paura, 1972 (Brazzi 3)

Castiglione, 1954 (Brazzi 3, De Carlo 3)

Castilian, 1962 (Crawford 3)

Castillian. *See* Valle de las espadas, 1963

Casting, 1972 (Pasternak 4)

Castle. *See* Schloss, 1968

Castle, 1991 (Jackson 3, Sharif 3)
Castle in the Air, 1952 (Rutherford 3)
Castle in the Desert, 1942 (Miller 4)
Castle Keep, 1969 (Pollack 2, Dern 3, Falk 3, Lancaster 3, Douy 4, Decaë 4, Legrand 4, Taradash 4)
Castle of Fu Manchu, 1970 (Lee 3)
Castle of Otranto. See Otrantský zámek, 1977
Castle of Terror. See Vergine de Norimberga, 1964
Castle of the Living Dead. See Castello dei morti viva, 1964 (Reeves 2)
Castle of the Spider's Web. See Kumonosu-jo, 1957
Castle on the Hudson, 1940 (Litvak 2, Garfield 3, Meredith 3, Sheridan 3, Deutsch 4, Edeson 4, Haskin 4, Miller 4)
Castle 1, 1966 (Le Grice 2)
Castle 2, 1968 (Le Grice 2)
Castle Without A Name, 1920 (Lukas 3)
Castro Street, 1966 (Baillie 2)
Casualties of War, 1989 (De Palma 2, Fox 3, Morricone 4)
Cat, 1921 (Laemmle 4)
Cat. See Chatte, 1958
Cat Above and the Mouse Below, 1964 (Jones 4, Maltese 4)
Cat and Duplicat, 1967 (Jones 4)
Cat and Mouse, 1958 (Rotha 2)
Cat and Mouse. See Mousey, 1974
Cat and Mouse. See Chat et la souris, 1975
Cat and the Canary, 1927 (Leni 2, Laemmle 4)
Cat and the Canary, 1939 (Goddard 3, Hope 3, Dreier 4, Head 4, Lang 4)
Cat and the Fiddle, 1934 (Howard 2, MacDonald 3, Novarro 3, Adrian 4, Clarke 4, Rosson 4, Stothart 4)
Cat and the Mermouse, 1949 (Hanna and Barbera 4)
Cat Ballou, 1965 (Fonda 3, Marvin 3)
Cat Came Back, 1936 (Freleng 4)
Cat Came Back, 1944 (Terry 4)
Cat Concerto, 1946 (Hanna and Barbera 4)
Cat Creature, 1973 (Carradine 3)
Cat Creeps, 1930 (Laemmle 4, Mohr 4)
Cat, Dog, & Co., 1929 (Roach 4)
Cat Feud, 1959 (Blanc 4, Jones 4)
Cat Fishin', 1946 (Hanna and Barbera 4)
Cat from Outer Space, 1978 (McDowall 3, Ames 4, Schifrin 4)
Cat Happy, 1950 (Terry 4)
Cat Meets Mouse, 1942 (Terry 4)
Cat Napping, 1950 (Hanna and Barbera 4)
Cat Nipped, 1932 (Lantz 4)
Cat 'o Nine Tails. See Gatto a nove code, 1969
Cat on a Hot Tin Roof, 1958 (Brooks 2, Newman 3, Taylor 3, Daniels 4, Rose 4)
Cat on a Hot Tin Roof, 1976 (Olivier 3, Wagner 3, Wood 3)
Cat on a Hot Tin Roof, 1984 (Lange 3)
Cat People, 1942 (Tourneur 2, Simon 3, Bodeen 4, D'Agostino 4, Dunn 4, Lewton 4, Musuraca 4)
Cat People, 1982 (Schrader 2, Kinski 3, McDowell 3, Whitlock 4)
Cat, Shozo, and the Two Women. See Neko to Shozo to futaru no onna, 1956
Cat That Hated People, 1948 (Avery 4)
Cat Trouble, 1947 (Terry 4)
Cat Women of the Moon, 1953 (Bernstein 4)
Catacombs, 1965 (Andrews 3)

Catacombs, 1988 (Donaggio 4)
Catacombs. See Setta, 1991
Catacumba. See Setta, 1991
Catalan, 1984 (Jarman 2)
Catalina, Here I Come, 1927 (Sennett 2)
Catamount Killing, 1974 (Zanussi 2)
Catapult and the Kite. See Prak a drank, 1960
Cat-astrophe, 1916 (Terry 4)
Catastrophe de la Martinique, 1902 (Pathé 4)
Catch As Catch Can, 1927 (Shamroy 4)
Catch-as-Catch-Can, 1931 (Roach 4)
Catch as Catch Can, 1937 (Mason 3, Rutherford 3)
Catch as Catch Can. See Scatenato, 1967
Catch As Cats Can, 1947 (Blanc 4, Stalling 4)
Catch Him!. See Chytte ho!, 1924
Catch Me a Spy, 1971 (Blier 3, Douglas 3, Howard 3, Braunberger 4, Challis 4, Dillon 4)
Catch Meow, 1961 (Hanna and Barbera 4)
Catch My Smoke, 1922 (Mix 3, Fox 4)
Catch My Soul, 1973 (Hall 4)
Catch the Heat, 1987 (Steiger 3)
Catch-22, 1970 (Nicholas 2, Welles 2, Arkin 3, Dalio 3, Perkins 3, Sheen 3, Voight 3, Henry 4, Sylbert 4, Watkin 4, Whitlock 4)
Catcher, 1971 (Baxter 3)
Catchfire. See Backtrack, 1989
Catching a Coon, 1921 (Roach 4)
Cate naria, 1969 (Ruiz 2)
Catene invisibili, 1942 (Valli 3)
Catered Affair, 1956 (Brooks 2, Borgnine 3, Davis 3, Fitzgerald 3, Reynolds 3, Alton 4, Previn 4, Westmore Family 4)
Catfood, 1968 (Wieland 2)
Cathedral. See Chiesa, 1989
Cathédrale, 1947 (Braunberger 4)
Catherine, 1964 (Loach 2)
Catherine and I. See Io e Caterina, 1980
Catherine the Great. See Katherina die Grosse, 1920
Catherine the Great, 1934 (Bergner 3, Biro 4, Korda 4, Korda 4, Krasker 4, Mathieson 4, Périnal 4)
Catholic Boys. See Heaven Help Us, 1985
Catholics, 1973 (Cusack 3, Howard 3, Sheen 3, Fisher 4)
Cathy Come Home, 1966 (Loach 2)
Catlow, 1971 (Brynner 3, Love 3)
Catnip Capers, 1940 (Terry 4)
Catnip Gang, 1949 (Terry 4)
Cats, 1956 (Breer 4)
Cats. See Kattorna, 1965
Cats. See Bastardi, 1968
Cats. See Sons of Satan, 1971
Cats and Bruises, 1965 (Blanc 4, Freleng 4)
Cats and Dogs, 1932 (Lantz 4)
Cats A-Weigh, 1953 (Blanc 4, McKimson 4, Stalling 4)
Cat's Bah, 1954 (Blanc 4, Jones 4, Stalling 4)
Cat's Cradle, 1959 (Brakhage 2)
Cat's Cradle, 1974 (Driessen 4)
Cat's Eye, 1985 (Cardiff 4, De Laurentiis 4)
Cats in the Bag, 1936 (Terry 4)
Cat's Me-Ouch, 1965 (Jones 4)
Cat's Meow, 1924 (Capra 2, Sennett 2)
Cat's Meow, 1956 (Avery 4)
Cat's Meow, 1980 (Langdon 3)
Cat's Nine Lives, 1927 (Lantz 4)
Cat's Pajamas, 1926 (Wellman 2, Banton 4, Vajda 4)

Cat's Paw, 1914 (Cruze 2)
Cat's Paw, 1934 (Lloyd 3, Newman 4)
Cat's Paw, 1959 (Blanc 4)
Cat's Revenge, 1954 (Terry 4)
Cat's Tale, 1941 (Blanc 4, Freleng 4, Stalling 4)
Cat's Tale, 1951 (Terry 4)
Cat's Whiskers, 1923 (Terry 4)
Cat's Whiskers, 1926 (Lantz 4)
Cat-Tails for Two, 1953 (Blanc 4, McKimson 4, Stalling 4)
Cattivo soggetto, 1933 (De Sica 2)
Cattle Annie and Little Britches, 1979 (Lancaster 3, Steiger 3)
Cattle Drive, 1951 (McCrea 3)
Cattle Empire, 1958 (McCrea 3)
Cattle, Gold and Oil, 1911 (Dwan 2)
Cattle King, 1963 (Taylor 3)
Cattle King's Daughter, 1912 (Anderson 3)
Cattle Queen of Montana, 1954 (Dwan 2, Reagan 3, Stanwyck 3, Alton 4, Estabrook 4, Polglase 4)
Cattle Rustler's End, 1911 (Dwan 2)
Cattle Rustler's Father, 1911 (Anderson 3)
Cattle Stampede, 1943 (Crabbe 3)
Cattle Station. See Phantom Stockman, 1953
Cattle Thief, 1936 (Bond 3)
Cattle Thief's Brand, 1911 (Dwan 2)
Cattle Thieves, 1909 (Olcott 2)
Cattle Town, 1952 (McCord 4)
Cattleman's Daughter, 1911 (Anderson 3)
Catty Cornered, 1953 (Blanc 4, Freleng 4, Stalling 4)
Cauchemar de Max, 1909 (Linder 3)
Cauche-mar du Fantoche, 1908 (Cohl 4)
Caudillo, 1967 (Fernández 2)
Caught, 1931 (Lang 4)
Caught, 1949 (Ophüls 2, Mason 3, Ryan 3, Garmes 4)
Caught Bluffing, 1922 (Laemmle 4)
Caught by Television. See Trapped by Television, 1936
Caught by Wireless, 1908 (Bitzer 4)
Caught Courting, 1913 (Costello 3)
Caught in a Cabaret, 1914 (Sennett 2, Normand 3)
Caught in a Flue, 1914 (Sennett 2, Arbuckle 3)
Caught in a Jam, 1916 (Roach 4)
Caught in a Taxi, 1929 (Sennett 2, Hornbeck 4)
Caught in the Act, 1910 (White 3)
Caught in the Act, 1915 (Sennett 2)
Caught in the Act, 1981 (Brocka 2)
Caught in the Draft, 1941 (Hope 3, Lamour 3, Dreier 4, Head 4, Struss 4, Young 4)
Caught in the Fog, 1928 (Haskin 4)
Caught in the Kitchen, 1928 (Sennett 2, Hornbeck 4)
Caught in the Night. See Zastihla me noc, 1985
Caught in the Park, 1915 (Sennett 2)
Caught in the Rain, 1914 (Sennett 2)
Caught in Tights, 1914 (Sennett 2)
Caught Short, 1930 (Dressler 3, Gibbons 4)
Caught with the Goods, 1911 (Sennett 2)
Cauldron of Blood. See Blind Man's Bluff, 1971
Cause commune, 1940 (Cavalcanti 2)
Cause for Alarm, 1951 (Garnett 2, Young 3, Previn 4, Ruttenberg 4)
Cause for Concern, 1974 (Howard 3)

C'est pour les orphelins, 1917 (Musidora 3)
Cesta do pravěku, 1955 (Zeman 4)
Cesta duga godinu dana, 1958 (Guerra 4)
Cesta ka barikádám, 1945 (Stallich 4)
Cesty k výšinam, 1921 (Heller 4)
Cet homme est dangereux, 1953
    (Constantine 3, D'Eaubonne 4)
Cet obscur objet de désir, 1977 (Carrière 4)
C'était moi. See Ernest le rebelle, 1938
C'était un jour comme les autres, 1970
    (Cloquet 4)
C'était un musicien, 1933 (Bresson 2)
C'était un Québécois en Bretagne, madame!,
    1977 (Perrault 2)
Cette nuit-là, 1958 (Burel 4)
Cette Sacrée gamine, 1955 (Bardot 3)
Cette vieille canaille, 1933 (Litvak 2, Baur 3,
    Andrejew 4, Courant 4)
Ceux de chez nous, 1915 (Guitry 2)
Ceux du deuxième bureau. See Homme à
    abattre, 1937
Ceux du rail, 1942 (Clement 2, Alekan 4)
Cézanne, 1989 (Straub and Huillet 2)
Chaar Dil Chaar Rahen, 1959 (Abbas 4)
Chacal de Nahueltoro, 1968 (Villagra 3)
Chacals, 1917 (Musidora 3)
Cha-Cha-Boom!, 1956 (Katzman 4)
Chacun sa chance, 1931 (Gabin 3)
Chacun son enfer, 1977 (Cayatte 2,
    Girardot 3)
Chad Hanna, 1940 (King 2, Carradine 3,
    Darnell 3, Darwell 3, Fonda 3, Lamour 3,
    Banton 4, Day 4, Johnson 4, Zanuck 4)
Chadwick Family, 1974 (MacMurray 3)
Chagall, 1953 (Braunberger 4, Kosma 4)
Chagall, 1963 (Price 3)
Chagrin et la pitié, 1971 (Chevalier 3)
Chaim—to Life!, 1974 (Wallach 3)
Chain. See Zanjeer, 1973
Chain Gang, 1950 (Katzman 4)
Chain Letters, 1935 (Terry 4)
Chain Lightning, 1927 (Fox 4)
Chain Lightning, 1950 (Bogart 3, Massey 3,
    Haller 4, Veiller 4)
Chain Reaction, 1971 (Dinov 4)
Chain Reaction, 1980 (Miller 2)
Chained, 1934 (Brown 2, Crawford 3,
    Gable 3, Rooney 3, Folsey 4, Mayer 4,
    Stothart 4, Stromberg 4)
Chaines, 1910 (Cohl 4)
Chaines d'or. See Anneaux d'or, 1956
Chains, 1912 (Bushman 3)
Chains of Evidence, 1920 (Brenon 2)
Chains of Gold, 1989 (Travolta 3)
Chair, 1961 (Kuri 4)
Chair, 1962 (Leacock 2)
Chair, 1967 (Dunning 4)
Chair de l'orchidée, 1974 (Feuillère 3,
    Signoret 3, Valli 3, Carrière 4)
Chair de poule, 1963 (Duvivier 2, Burel 4,
    Delerue 4, Hakim 4)
Chair et le diable, 1953 (Brazzi 3, Auric 4,
    Wakhévitch 4)
Chairman. See Most Dangerous Man in the
    World, 1969 (Maddow 4)
Chairy Tale, 1957 (McLaren 4, Shankar 4)
Chaise à porteurs enchantée, 1905 (Méliès 2)
Chakkari fujin to ukkari fujin, 1952
    (Kagawa 3)
Chakra, 1980 (Patil 3)
Chaleur du foyer, 1955 (Auric 4)
Chaleur du sein, 1938 (Arletty 3, Simon 3)
Chaliapin, 1972 (Donskoi 2)
Chalis Baba Ek Chor, 1954 (Burman 4)

Chaliya, 1960 (Kapoor 2)
Chalk Garden, 1964 (Evans 3, Kerr 3,
    Mills 3, Arnold 4, Dillon 4, Hayes 4,
    Hunter 4)
Chalk Line, 1972 (Emshwiller 2)
Chalk Marks, 1924 (Walker 4)
Challenge, 1922 (Fleischer 4)
Challenge, 1938 (Korda, A. 4, Korda, V. 4,
    Krasker 4, Périnal 4)
Challenge, See Sfida, 1958
Challenge, 1960 (Mansfield 3, Quayle 3)
Challenge, 1970 (Crawford 3, Lukas 3,
    Smith 4)
Challenge, 1982 (Frankenheimer 2, Sayles 2,
    Mifune 3, Goldsmith 4)
Challenge for Robin Hood, 1967
    (Carreras 4)
Challenge of Greatness, 1976 (Welles 2)
Challenge—Science Against Cancer, 1950
    (Massey 3)
Challenge to be Free, 1975 (Garnett 2)
Challenge to Lassie, 1949 (Crisp 3, Previn 4)
Challenge to Live. See Ai to honoo to, 1961
Challenger. See Lady and Gent, 1932
Challengers, 1970 (Baxter 3, Mineo 3)
Chalti Ka Naam Gaddi, 1958 (Burman 4)
Chamade, 1968 (Deneuve 3, Piccoli 3)
Chamber of Horrors, 1966 (Curtis 3)
Chamberlain. See Kammarjunkaren, 1914
Chambre, 1964 (Cloquet 4)
Chambre, 1972 (Akerman 2)
Chambre à part, 1989 (Sarde 4)
Chambre ardente, 1962 (Duvivier 2, Auric 4,
    Spaak 4)
Chambre de bonne, 1970 (Braunberger 4)
Chambre en ville, 1982 (Darrieux 3,
    Piccoli 3, Sanda 3, Evein 4)
Chambre 34, 1945 (Braunberger 4)
Chambre verte, 1978 (Truffaut 2, Baye 3,
    Almendros 4)
Champ, 1931 (Vidor 2, Beery 3, Cooper 3,
    Marion 4, Mayer 4, Terry 4)
Champ, 1979 (Zeffirelli 2, Blondell 3,
    Dunaway 3, Voight 3)
Champ du possible, 1962 (Delerue 4)
Champagne, 1928 (Hitchcock 2, Launder
    and Gilliat 2)
Champagne Charlie, 1944 (Cavalcanti 2,
    Kendall 3, Balcon 4, Clarke 4)
Champagne for Caesar, 1950 (Colman 3,
    Price 3, Tiomkin 4)
Champagne Murders. See Scandale, 1967
Champagne Safari, 1951 (Hayworth 3)
Champagne Waltz, 1937 (Wilder 2,
    MacMurray 3, Banton 4, Prinz 4,
    Young 4)
Champeen, 1922 (Roach 4)
Champignon, 1969 (Valli 3)
Champion, 1913 (Sennett 2, Normand 3)
Champion, 1915 (Bacon 2, Anderson 3,
    Purviance 3)
Champion, 1949 (Kramer 2, Douglas 3,
    Kennedy 3, Foreman 4, Planer 4,
    Tiomkin 4)
Champion du jeu à la mode, 1910 (Cohl 4)
Champion of Justice, 1944 (Terry 4)
Champions, 1983 (Hurt 3, Johnson 3)
Champions: A Love Story, 1979 (Alonzo 4)
Champions juniors, 1950 (Fradetal 4,
    Kosma 4)
Champlain, 1962 (Arcand 2)
Champs-Elysées, 1928 (Kaufman 4)
Chamsin, 1972 (Schell 3)
Chanayaka Chandragupta, 1980 (Kumar 3)

Chance, 1931 (Rosay 3)
Chance at Heaven, 1933 (McCrea 3,
    Rogers 3, Cooper 4, Musuraca 4,
    Plunkett 4, Polglase 4, Steiner 4)
Chance Deception, 1912 (Griffith 2, Sweet 3,
    Bitzer 4)
Chance et l'amour, 1964 (Chabrol 2,
    Tavernier 2, Blier 3, Chevalier 3,
    Piccoli 3, De Beauregard 4)
"Chance explosive", 1964 (Tavernier 2)
Chance Meeting. See Young Lovers, 1954
Chance Meeting. See Blind Date, 1959
Chance of a Lifetime, 1950 (More 3)
Chance of a Night Time, 1931 (Wilcox 2)
Chance Shot, 1912 (Lawrence 3)
Chance to Live, 1990 (Hepburn 3)
Chances, 1931 (Dwan 2, Haller 4, Young 4)
Chances Are, 1989 (Fraker 4, Jarre 4)
Chandi Sona, 1977 (Kapoor 2)
Chandler, 1971 (Caron 3, Grahame 3,
    Oates 3)
Chandu on the Magic Island. See Return of
    Chandu, 1934
Chandu the Magician, 1932 (Lugosi 3,
    Walthall 3, Howe 4, Menzies 4)
Chanel solitaire, 1981 (Black 3, Caron 3)
Chang, 1927 (Schoedsack 2, Cooper 4,
    Zukor 4)
Change, 1974 (Schell 3)
Change in Baggage, 1914 (Bunny 3)
Change of Habit, 1969 (Presley 3, Metty 4)
Change of Heart, 1909 (Griffith 2, Bitzer 4)
Change of Heart, 1934 (Darwell 3, Gaynor 3,
    Rogers 3, Temple 3, Friedhofer 4,
    Hoffenstein 4, Levien 4, Mohr 4)
Change of Heart, 1938 (Darwell 3)
Change of Heart. See Two and Two Make
    Six, 1962
Change of Seasons, 1980 (Hopkins 3,
    MacLaine 3)
Change of Spirit, 1912 (Griffith 2, Sweet 3,
    Walthall 3)
Change the Needle, 1925 (Roach 4)
Changeling, 1979 (Douglas 3, Scott 3)
Changing Husbands, 1924 (Glennon 4)
Channel Crossing, 1933 (Junge 4, Rank 4)
Channel Incident, 1940 (Asquith 2,
    Newton 3)
Channing of the Northwest, 1922 (Shearer 3)
Chanson d'armor, 1934 (Epstein 2)
Chanson de gestes, 1966 (Braunberger 4)
Chanson de Roland, 1978 (Cuny 3, Kinski 3,
    Sanda 3)
Chanson de rue, 1945 (Decaë 4)
Chanson des peupliers, 1931 (Epstein 2)
Chanson du pavé, 1951 (Colpi 4)
Chanson du souvenir, 1936 (Sirk 2)
Chanson d'une nuit, 1932 (Clouzot 2,
    Litvak 2, Brasseur 3, Wagner 4)
Chansons de Paris, 1934 (Barsacq 4)
Chant de l'amour, 1935 (D'Eaubonne 4)
Chant des ondes, 1943 (Leenhardt 4)
Chant du départ. See Desert Song, 1943
Chant du marin, 1932 (Gallone 2, Planer 4)
Chant du monde, 1965 (Deneuve 3, Vanel 3)
Chant du Styrène, 1958 (Resnais 2,
    Braunberger 4, Delerue 4)
Chantelouve, 1921 (Boyer 3)
Chanteur de minuit, 1937 (Matras 4,
    Renoir 4, Wakhévitch 4)
Chanteur de Seville. See Call of the Flesh,
    1930
Chanteur inconnu, 1931 (Simon 3,
    Courant 4, Wakhévitch 4)

Chanteur inconnu, 1947 (Cayatte 2, Barsacq 4)

Chanteur inconnu, 1968 (Clouzot 2)

Chanteurs des cours, 1899 (Gaumont 4)

Chantier en ruines, 1945 (Leenhardt 2)

Chantons sous l'occupation, 1976 (Colpi 4)

Chantons sous l'Occupation, 1990 (Rouch 2)

Chants populaires, 1943–46 (Dunning 4)

Chants retrouvés, 1948 (Colpi 4)

Chaos. *See* **Kaos, 1984**

Chapayev, 1934 (Vasiliev 2)

Chapayev Is with Us, 1939 (Gerasimov 2)

Chapeau-Claqué, 1909 (Linder 3)

Chapeau de Max, 1913 (Linder 3)

Chapeau de paille d'Italie, 1927 (Clair 2, Tschechowa 3, Meerson 4)

Chapeau de paille d'Italie, 1940 (Fernandel 3)

Chapeaux des belles dames, 1909 (Cohl 4)

Chaperon, 1916 (Van Dyke 2)

Chaplin, 1991 (Attenborough 3, Nykvist 4)

Chaplin Revue, 1957 (Chaplin 2)

Chapman Report, 1962 (Cukor 2, Bloom 3, Fonda 3, Winters 3, Orry-Kelly 4, Rosenman 4)

Chappaqua, 1966 (Barrault 3, Shankar 4, Schüfftan 4)

Chapter in Her Life, 1923 (Weber 2)

Chapter Two, 1979 (Caan 3, Booth 4, Hamlisch 4, Stark 4)

Char Ankhen, 1944 (Biswas 4)

Char Dil Char Rahen, 1959 (Kapoor 2, Biswas 4)

Charade, 1953 (Mason 3, Biroc 4)

Charade, 1963 (Donen 2, Coburn 3, Grant 3, Hepburn 3, Matthau 3, D'Eaubonne 4, Lang 4, Mancini 4, Mercer 4)

Charandas Chor, 1975 (Nihalani 4)

Charandas the Thief. *See* Charandas Chor, 1975

Charcuterie mécanique, 1895 (Lumière 2)

Charcutier de Machonville, 1946 (Decaë 4, Fradetal 4)

Charette fantôme, 1939 (Ibert 4)

Charge at Feather River, 1953 (Steiner 4)

Charge Is Murder. *See* Twilight of Honor, 1963

Charge of the Gauchos, 1928 (Bushman 3, Musuraca 4)

Charge of the Lancers, 1954 (Goddard 3, Katzman 4)

Charge of the Light Brigade, 1936 (Curtiz 2, Crisp 3, De Havilland 3, Flynn 3, Niven 3, Canutt 4, Eason 4, Friedhofer 4, Polito 4, Steiner 4, Wallis 4)

Charge of the Light Brigade, 1968 (Richardson 2, Redgrave 3, Gielgud 3, Howard 3, Addison 4, Watkin 4, Williams 4)

Charing Cross Road, 1935 (Mills 3)

Chariot de Thespis, 1941 (Alekan 4)

Chariots of Fire, 1981 (Anderson 2, Gielgud 3, Puttnam 4, Vangelis 4, Watkin 4)

Charité, 1927 (Vanel 3)

Charité du prestidigitateur, 1905 (Guy 2)

Charity, 1932 (Rooney 3)

Charlatan, 1901 (Méliès 2)

Charlemagne, 1933 (Raimu 3, Douy 4)

Charles and Diana: A Royal Love Story, 1982 (Lee 3, Addison 4)

Charles, Dead or Alive. *See* Charles, mort ou vif, 1969

Charleston. *See* Sur un air de Charleston, 1927

Charleston, 1977 (Lom 3)

Charleston, 1979 (Bernstein 4)

Charleston Chain Gang, 1902 (Porter 2)

Charley series, 1989 (Halas and Batchelor 4)

Charley and the Angel, 1973 (MacMurray 3)

Charley My Boy, 1926 (McCarey 2, Roach 4)

Charley Varrick, 1973 (Siegel 2, Schifrin 4)

Charley's American Aunt. *See* Charley's Aunt, 1941

Charley's Aunt, 1915 (Laurel and Hardy 3)

Charley's Aunt, 1941 (Baxter 3, Francis 3, Banton 4, Day 4, Newman 4, Vetchinsky 4)

Charley's Tante, 1934 (Rasp 3)

Charlie. *See* Chaplin, 1991

Charlie and the Sausage. *See* Mabel's Busy Day, 1914

Charlie at the Races. *See* Gentlemen of Nerve, 1914

Charlie Bubbles, 1967 (Frears 2, Finney 3, Minnelli 3)

Charlie Chan and the Curse of the Dragon Queen, 1981 (Dickinson 3, Grant 3, Hayden 3, McDowall 3, Pfeiffer 3, Roberts 3, Ustinov 3)

Charlie Chan at the Olympics, 1937 (Miller 4)

Charlie Chan at the Opera, 1936 (Karloff 3, Meredyth 4)

Charlie Chan at the Wax Museum, 1940 (Day 4, Miller 4)

Charlie Chan at Treasure Island, 1939 (Day 4, Miller 4)

Charlie Chan in Egypt, 1935 (Hayworth 3)

Charlie Chan in Honolulu, 1938 (Clarke 4, Day 4)

Charlie Chan in London, 1934 (Milland 3)

Charlie Chan in Panama, 1940 (Day 4, Miller 4)

Charlie Chan in Reno, 1939 (Miller 4)

Charlie Chan in Rio, 1941 (Day 4)

Charlie Chan in the City of Darkness, 1939 (Miller 4)

Charlie Chan's Chance, 1931 (August 4)

Charlie Chan's Courage, 1934 (Miller 4, Mohr 4)

Charlie Chan's Murder Cruise, 1940 (Miller 4)

Charlie Chan's Secret, 1936 (Maté 4)

Charlie Cobb: Nice Night for a Hanging, 1977 (Bellamy 3)

Charlie et ses deux nénettes, 1973 (Sarde 4)

Charlie Fadden, 1913 (Zukor 4)

Charlie McCarthy, Detective, 1939 (Calhern 3)

Charlie Varrick, 1973 (Matthau 3)

Charlotte. *See* Jeune Fille assassinée, 1974

Charlotte et son Jules, 1958 (Cocteau 2, Godard 2, Belmondo 3, Braunberger 4)

Charlotte et Véronique ou Tous les garçons s'appellent Patrick, 1957 (Godard 2)

Charlotte Löwenskjöld, 1930 (Molander 2, Jaenzon 4)

Charlotte's Web, 1972 (Moorehead 3, Reynolds 3, Hanna and Barbera 4)

Charly, 1968 (Bloom 3, Robertson 3, Shankar 4)

Charm of Life, 1953 (Harrison 3)

Charm School, 1920 (Cruze 2, Reid 3)

Charm School. *See* Collegiate, 1936

Charmant FrouFrou, 1901 (Guy 2)

Charmants garcons, 1957 (Broca 2, Gélin 3, Legrand 4, Spaak 4)

Charme discrèt de la bourgeoisie, 1972 (Audran 3, Cassel 3, Piccoli 3, Rey 3, Seyrig 3, Carrière 4)

Charmer, 1915 (Johnson 3)

Charmer, 1925 (Olcott 2, Negri 3, Howe 4)

Charmer. *See* Moonlight Sonata, 1937

Charmes de l'existence, 1949 (Grémillon 2)

Charmes de l'existence. *See* Charm of Life, 1953

Charmeuse de serpents, 1949 (Gaumont 4)

Charmides. *See* Du sang de la volupté et de la mort, 1947

Charming Sinners, 1929 (Arzner 2, Powell 3, Banton 4)

Charrette fantôme, 1939 (Duvivier 2, Epstein 2, Fresnay 3, Jouvet 3)

Charro!, 1969 (Presley 3)

Charro negro, 1940 (Fernández 2, Armendáriz 3)

Chartres, 1923 (Périnal 4)

Chartreuse de Parme, 1948 (Philipe 3, Annenkov 4, D'Eaubonne 4)

Charulata, 1964 (Chatterjee 3, Chandragupta 4, Datta 4, Mitra 4)

Chase, 1913 (Dwan 2)

Chase, 1946 (Lorre 3, Morgan 3, Planer 4)

Chase, 1966 (Penn 2, Brando 3, Dickinson 3, Duvall 3, Fonda 3, Hopkins 3, Redford 3, Barry 4, Day 4, La Shelle 4, Spiegel 4)

Chase. *See* Caza, 1966

Chase a Crooked Shadow, 1957 (Baxter 3, Lom 3, Warner 4)

Chase After Adam. *See* Pogoń za Adamem, 1970

Chased by Bloodhounds, 1912 (Bunny 3)

Chaser, 1928 (Langdon 3)

Chaser, 1938 (Turner 3)

Chaser on the Rocks, 1965 (Blanc 4)

Chasers. *See* Dragueurs, 1959

Chases of Pimple Street, 1935 (Roach 4)

Chasing Danger, 1939 (Miller 4)

Chasing Rainbows, 1930 (Dressler 3, Love 3, Gibbons 4, Meredyth 4)

Chasing the Chaser, 1925 (Roach 4)

Chasing the Limited, 1915 (Furthman 4)

Chasing the Moon, 1922 (Mix 3, Fox 4)

Chasing Through Europe, 1929 (Fox 4)

Chasing Yesterday, 1935 (Plunkett 4)

Chasse à l'hippopotame, 1946 (Rouch 2)

Chasse à l'homme, 1964 (Belmondo 3, Blier 3, Deneuve 3, Presle 3, Audiard 4)

Chasse au cambrioleur, 1903 (Guy 2)

Chasse au lion à l'arc, 1965 (Braunberger 4)

Chassé-croisé, 1931 (Fradetal 4)

Chasseur, 1970 (Braunberger 4)

Chasseur de chez Maxim's, 1927 (Meerson 4)

Chasseurs de lions, 1913 (Feuillade 2)

Chaste Suzanne, 1937 (Raimu 3, D'Eaubonne 4)

Chastity, 1923 (Schulberg 4)

Chastity, 1969 (Cher 3)

Chastity Belt. *See* Cintura di castita, 1967

Chat, 1971 (Gabin 3, Signoret 3, Sarde 4, Saulnier 4)

Chat et la souris, 1975 (Morgan 3, Reggiani 3, Lai 4)

Chatarra, 1990 (Maura 3)

Chateau de la peur, 1912 (Feuillade 2)

Chateau de rêve, 1933 (Clouzot 2, Darrieux 3)

Chateau de verre, 1950 (Clement 2, Marais 3, Morgan 3, Barsacq 4, Bost 4)

Château des amants maudits. *See* Beatrice Cenci, 1956

Château du passé, 1958 (Decaë 4, Rabier 4)

Château en Suede, 1963 (Vadim 2, Trintignant 3, Vitti 3)

Châteaux de France, 1948 (Resnais 2)

Châteaux en Espagne, 1953 (Darrieux 3)

Chateaux stop . . . sur la Loire, 1962 (Delerue 4)

Châtelaine du Liban, 1926 (Modot 3)

Chatelaine du Liban, 1933 (Epstein 2, Matras 4)

Chato's Land, 1971 (Bronson 3, Palance 3)

Chatpatee, 1983 (Patil 3)

Chattahoochee, 1989 (Hopper 3)

Chatte, 1958 (Blier 3, Kosma 4)

Chatte métamorphosée en femme, 1909 (Feuillade 2)

Chatte sort ses griffes, 1959 (Kosma 4)

Chatte sur un doigt brûlant, 1974 (Dalio 3)

Chatterbox, 1936 (Ball 3, Plunkett 4)

Chatterbox, 1943 (Brown 3)

Chaudhwin ka Chand, 1960 (Dutt 2)

Chaudron infernal, 1903 (Méliès 2)

Chaudronnier, 1948 (Fradetal 4)

Chauncy Explains, 1905 (Bitzer 4)

Chausette surprise, 1978 (Dalio 3, Karina 3, Carrière 4)

Chaussette, 1906 (Guy 2)

Chaussures matrimoniales, 1909 (Cohl 4)

Chauve-souris, 1931 (Heller 4)

Che!, 1969 (Palance 3, Sharif 3, Schifrin 4, Smith 4, Wilson 4)

Che?, 1972 (Mastroianni 3, Ponti 4)

Che, Buenos Aires, 1962 (Birri 2)

Che c'entriamo noi con la rivoluzione?, 1972 (Gassman 3, Morricone 4)

Che distinta famiglia, 1943 (Cervi 3)

Che gioia vivere, 1961 (Cervi 3, Delon 3, Bost 4, Decaë 4)

Che ora e?, 1990 (Scola 2, Mastroianni 3)

Che si dice a Roma, 1979 (Scola 2)

Che Tempi!, 1948 (Sordi 3)

Cheap, 1974 (Corman 2)

Cheap Detective, 1978 (Falk 3, Alonzo 4, Booth 4, Houseman 4, Stark 4)

Cheap Kiss, 1924 (Sullivan 4)

Cheaper By the Dozen, 1950 (Loy 3, Webb 3, LeMaire 4, Shamroy 4, Trotti 4, Wheeler 4)

Cheaper to Marry, 1925 (Gibbons 4, Mayer 4)

Cheat, 1915 (De Mille 2, Hayakawa 3, Buckland 4, Zukor 4)

Cheat, 1923 (Negri 3, Miller 4)

Cheat, 1931 (Folsey 4)

Cheat. *See* Manèges, 1950

Cheated Hearts, 1921 (Karloff 3, Laemmle 4, Miller 4)

Cheated Love, 1921 (Glennon 4, Levien 4)

Cheater, 1920 (Valentino 3)

Cheater Reformed, 1921 (Fox 4, Furthman 4)

Cheaters, 1934 (Beavers 3)

Cheaters. *See* Tricheurs, 1958

Cheating Cheaters, 1919 (Dwan 2, Edeson 4)

Cheating Cheaters, 1927 (Laemmle 4)

Cheating Cheaters, 1934 (Wray 3)

Check and Double Check, 1930 (Crosby 3, Steiner 4)

Check to Song, 1989 (Halas and Batchelor 4)

Check Your Baggage, 1918 (Roach 4)

Checkered Flag or Crash, 1978 (Sarandon 3)

Checkmate, 1911 (Dwan 2)

Checkmate, 1935 (Pearson 2, Havelock-Allan 4)

Checkpoint, 1956 (Baker 3, Box 4, Dillon 4, Rank 4)

Cheech and Chong's Next Movie, 1980 (Whitlock 4)

Cheer Boys Cheer, 1939 (Balcon 4)

Cheer Up and Smile, 1930 (Wayne 3, Fox 4)

Cheerful Alley. *See* Yokina uramachi, 1939

Cheerful Fraud, 1927 (Laemmle 4)

Cheerful Givers, 1917 (Love 3)

Cheering a Husband, 1914 (Beery 3)

Cheers for Miss Bishop, 1941 (Garnett 2, Mohr 4)

Cheers of the Crowd, 1935 (Krasner 4)

Cheese Chasers, 1951 (Blanc 4, Jones 4, Stalling 4)

Cheese It, the Cat, 1957 (Blanc 4, McKimson 4, Stalling 4)

Chef at Circle G, 1915 (Mix 3)

Chef de famille, 1981 (Feuillère 3)

Chef-Lieu du Canton, 1910 (Gaumont 4)

Chefs de demain, 1944 (Clement 2, Alekan 4)

Chefs d'oeuvres de Bébé, 1910 (Cohl 4)

Chelovek, drama nachidnya, 1912 (Mozhukin 3)

Chelovek iz restorana, 1929 (Protazanov 2, Golovnya 4)

Chelovek s drugoi storoni, 1972 (Andersson 3)

Chelovek s kinoapparatom, 1929 (Vertov 2)

Chelovek s ruzhyom, 1938 (Cherkassov 3, Shostakovich 4)

Chelsea Girls, 1966 (Warhol 2)

Chemin de Damas, 1952 (Simon 3, Schüfftan 4)

Chemin de la croix est coupable, 1941 (Volkov 2)

Chemin de la terre, 1962 (Delerue 4)

Chemin de l'honneur, 1939 (Brasseur 3)

Chemin de Rio. *See* Cargaison blanche, 1937

Chemin des écoliers, 1959 (Delon 3, Aurenche 4, Barsacq 4, Bost 4, Matras 4)

Chemin du bonheur, 1933 (Kaufman 4)

Chemin du paradis, 1930 (Planer 4)

Chemin perdu, 1979 (Vanel 3, Seyrig 3, Vierny 4)

Chemins de Katmandou, 1969 (Cayatte 2)

Chemist, 1936 (Keaton 2)

Cher Inconnu, 1981 (Seyrig 3, Signoret 3, Cloquet 4, Evein 4, Sarde 4)

Cher Victor, 1975 (Valli 3)

Cher vieux Paris!, 1950 (Decaë 4)

Cherchez la femme, 1921 (Curtiz 2)

Chère Louise, 1972 (Broca 2, Moreau 3, Delerue 4)

Chères vieilles choses, 1957 (Colpi 4, Delerue 4)

Cherí, 1984 (Morgan 3)

Chéri Bibi, 1954 (Auric 4)

Cheri de sa concierge, 1934 (Fernandel 3)

Chéri-Bibi, 1938 (Dalio 3, Fresnay 3)

Chernyi barak, 1933 (Maretskaya 3)

Cherokee Kid, 1927 (Musuraca 4)

Cherokee Strip, 1940 (Harlan 4, Head 4)

Cherry Blossoms, 1970 (Brocka 2)

Cherry Picker, 1970 (Terry-Thomas 3)

Cherry 2000, 1988 (Johnson 3)

Cheryomushki, 1963 (Shostakovich 4)

Chess Fever. *See* Shakmatnaya goryachka, 1925

Chess Game, 1983 (Stamp 3)

Chess Player. *See* Joueur d'échecs, 1938

Chess Players. *See* Shatranj Ke Khilari, 1977

Chess Players, 1978 (Attenborough 3)

Chess-nuts, 1932 (Fleischer 4)

Chesty: A Tribute to a Legend, 1970 (Ford 2, Wayne 3)

Chetniks!, 1943 (Day 4, Friedhofer 4)

Chetniks—The Fighting Guerillas. *See* Chetniks!, 1943

Chetyre vizity Samuelya Vulfa, 1934 (Maretskaya 3)

Cheval, 1950 (Decaë 4)

Cheval d'orgueil, 1980 (De Beauregard 4, Rabier 4)

Chevalier de Gaby, 1920 (Modot 3)

Chevalier de Ménilmontant, 1953 (Chevalier 3)

Chevalier des neiges, 1912 (Méliès 2)

Chevaliers de la table ronde, 1990 (Braunberger 4)

Chevaux d'acier. *See* Moissons d'aujourd'hui, 1949

Chevaux de Vaugirard, 1961 (Delerue 4)

Chevaux du Vercors, 1942 (Alekan 4)

Chevelure, 1961 (Piccoli 3)

Chèvre, 1961 (Fradetal 4)

Chèvre, 1981 (Depardieu 3)

Chèvre d'or, 1942 (Bost 4)

Chewin' Bruin, 1940 (Blanc 4, Clampett 4, Stalling 4)

Cheyenne, 1929 (Brown 4)

Cheyenne, 1947 (Walsh 2, Kennedy 3, Wyman 3, Buckner 4, Friedhofer 4, Steiner 4)

Cheyenne Autumn, 1964 (Ford 2, Baker 3, Carradine 3, Del Rio 3, Johnson 3, Kennedy 3, Malden 3, Marsh 3, Mineo 3, Robinson 3, Stewart 3, Widmark 3, Clothier 4, Day 4, North 4)

Cheyenne Cyclone, 1932 (Canutt 4)

Cheyenne Kid, 1933 (Musuraca 4, Steiner 4)

Cheyenne Roundup, 1943 (Salter 4)

Cheyenne Social Club, 1970 (Fonda 3, Kelly 3, Stewart 3, Clothier 4)

Cheyenne's Pal, 1917 (Ford 2)

Chez le magnétiseur, 1897 (Guy 2)

Chez le Maréchal-Ferrant, 1897 (Guy 2)

Chez le photographe, 1900 (Guy 2)

Chhipa Rustom, 1973 (Anand 3)

Chhoti Chhoti Baten, 1965 (Biswas 4)

Chhou Dance of Puralia, 1970 (Ghatak 2)

Chhupa Rustam, 1973 (Burman 4)

Chi dice donna dice . . . donna, 1975 (Audran 3)

Chi è senza peccato, 1952 (Rosay 3)

Chi l'ha vista morire?, 1972 (Morricone 4)

Chi l'ha visto?, 1942 (Fellini 2, Sordi 3)

Chi legge?, 1960 (Zavattini 4)

Chi ni somuku mono, 1929 (Hasegawa 3)

Chi to rei, 1976 (Mizoguchi 2)

Chi to suna, 1965 (Mifune 3)

Chiamavano Cosetta, 1917 (Gallone 2)

Chiamavano King . . . , 1971 (Kinski 3)

Chiameremo Andrea, 1972 (De Sica 2, Zavattini 4)

Chiave, 1983 (Morricone 4)

Chica del lunes, 1966 (Torre Nilsson 2, Kennedy 3, Page 3)

Chicago, 1927 (Adrian 4, Coffee 4)

Chicago after Midnight, 1928 (Plunkett 4)

Chicago Calling, 1951 (Duryea 3)

Chicago, Chicago, 1969 (Hecht 4)
Chicago Deadline, 1949 (Kennedy 3, Ladd 3, Reed 3, Seitz 4, Young 4)
Chicago Fire, 1925 (Van Dyke 2)
Chicago Kid, 1945 (Brown 4)
Chicago Masquerade. See Little Egypt, 1951
Chicago Story, 1981 (Schifrin 4)
Chicago Streets, 1975 (Menges 4)
Chicago-Digest, 1950 (Gélin 3, Piccoli 3)
Chicas de club, 1972 (Rey 3)
Chichi, 1930 (Takamine 3)
Chichi ariki, 1942 (Ryu 3)
Chichi kaeru haha no kokoro, 1935 (Yamada 3)
Chichiko-daka, 1956 (Yoda 4)
Chicken, 1928 (Sennett 2)
Chicken à la King, 1919 (Garmes 4)
Chicken à la King, 1928 (Fox 4)
Chicken à la King, 1937 (Fleischer 4)
Chicken Chaser, 1914 (Sennett 2, Arbuckle 3)
Chicken Every Sunday, 1949 (Wood 3, Epstein 4, LeMaire 4, Newman 4, Wheeler 4)
Chicken Feed, 1927 (Roach 4)
Chicken Fracas-see, 1962 (Hanna and Barbera 4)
Chicken Jitters, 1939 (Blanc 4, Clampett 4, Stalling 4)
Chicken Reel, 1934 (Lantz 4)
Chicken Thief, 1921 (Bray 4)
Chicken-Hearted Jim, 1916 (Ford 2)
Chicken-Hearted Wolf, 1962 (Hanna and Barbera 4)
Chickens, 1916 (Laurel and Hardy 3)
Chickens Come Home, 1931 (Laurel and Hardy 3)
Chicken-Wagon Family, 1939 (Cronjager 4)
Chickie, 1925 (Bosworth 3)
Chicos, 1959 (Ferreri 2)
Chidambaram, 1985 (Patil 3)
Chiedo asilo, 1979 (Sarde 4)
Chief, 1933 (Rooney 3)
Chief Cook, 1917 (Laurel and Hardy 3)
Chief Crazy Horse, 1955 (Mature 3, Boyle 4)
Chief from Göinge. See Göingehövdingen, 1953
Chiefs, 1969 (Leacock 2)
Chiefs, 1983 (Heston 3)
Chief's Blanket, 1912 (Barrymore 3, Sweet 3)
Chief's Daughter, 1911 (Griffith 2, Bosworth 3, Bitzer 4)
Chief's Predicament, 1913 (Sennett 2, Normand 3)
Chieko Story. See Chieko-sho, 1957
Chieko-sho, 1957 (Hara 3, Yamamura 3)
Chieko-sho, 1967 (Iwashita 3, Okada 3)
Chiemi no haihiiru, 1956 (Muraki 4)
Chiemi no hatsukoi chaccha musume, 1956 (Tsukasa 3)
Chiemi's High Heeled Shoes. See Chiemi no haihiiru, 1956
Chien, 1984 (Presle 3)
Chien andalou, 1929 (Buñuel 2, Braunberger 4)
Chien dans un jeu de quilles, 1962 (Gégauff 4)
Chien de Monsieur Michel, 1977 (Beineix 2)
Chien de pique, 1960 (Allégret 2, Constantine 3, Legrand 4)
Chien fou, 1966 (Guillemot 4)
Chien jouant á la balle, 1905 (Guy 2)
Chien Mélomane, 1973 (Grimault 4)

Chien qui rapporte, 1909 (Linder 3)
Chien qui rapporte, 1931 (Arletty 3)
Chienne, 1931 (Allégret 2, Renoir 2, Simon 3, Braunberger 4)
Chiens, 1978 (Depardieu 3)
Chiens contrebandiers, 1906 (Pathé 4)
Chiens perdus sans collier, 1955 (Delannoy 2, Guerra 2, Gabin 3, Aurenche 4, Bost 4)
Chiens savants, 1902 (Guy 2)
Chiesa, 1989 (Argento 4)
Chiffonier, 1897 (Guy 2)
Chiffonniers d'Emmaüs, 1954 (Kosma 4)
Chigo no kenpo, 1927 (Tsuburaya 4)
Chigo no kenpo, 1973 (Hasegawa 3)
Chiheisen, 1984 (Shindo 2)
Chiisai tobosha, 1966 (Kyo 3)
Chiisaki tabigeinin, 1925 (Tanaka 3)
Chiisana tobosha, 1967 (Miyagawa 4)
Chijin no ai, 1949 (Kyo 3, Mori 3)
Chijo, 1957 (Yoshimura 2, Kagawa 3, Tanaka 3)
Chijo no seiza: Chijo-hen, Seizahen, 1934 (Tanaka 3)
Chika-gai no dankon, 1949 (Kyo 3)
Chikagai no nijuyo-jikan, 1947 (Yamamura 3)
Chikagai 24-jikan, 1947 (Hayasaka 4)
Chikamatsu monogatari, 1954 (Mizoguchi 2, Hasegawa 3, Kagawa 3, Shindo 3, Hayasaka 4, Miyagawa 4, Yoda 4)
Chikashitsu, 1927 (Tanaka 3)
Chikita, 1961 (Ganz 3)
Chikuzan hitori-tabi, 1977 (Shindo 2)
Chikyu boeigun, 1957 (Tsuburaya 4)
Child. See Barnet, 1912
Child, 1954 (Mason 3)
Child and the Killer, 1959 (Roeg 2)
Child Crusoes. See His Sister's Children, 1911
Child Influence, 1910 (White 3)
Child in the House, 1956 (Baker 3, Adam 4, Heller 4)
Child Is Born, 1940 (Bacon 2, Rossen 2, Arden 3, Rosher 4, Wallis 4)
Child Is Waiting, 1962 (Cassavetes 2, Kramer 2, Garland 3, Lancaster 3, Rowlands 3, La Shelle 4)
Child of Manhattan, 1933 (Sturges 2, Darwell 3, Grable 3)
Child of Resistance, 1972 (Gerima 2)
Child of the Ghetto, 1910 (Griffith 2, Bitzer 4)
Child of the Paris Streets, 1916 (Marsh 3)
Child of the Prairie, 1913 (Mix 3)
Child of the Prairie, 1915 (Mix 3)
Child of the Purple Sage, 1912 (Anderson 3)
Child of the Streets, 1967 (Benegal 2)
Child of the West, 1912 (Anderson 3)
Child of the Wilderness, 1912 (Bosworth 3)
Child Psykolojiky, 1941 (Fleischer 4)
Child Sock-ology, 1961 (Hanna and Barbera 4)
Child, The Dog, and the Villain, 1915 (Mix 3)
Child Thou Gavest Me, 1920 (Stahl 2, Mayer 4)
Child under a Leaf, 1974 (Lai 4)
Child Went Forth, 1941 (Losey 2, Eisler 4)
Childhood's Vow, 1900 (Bitzer 4)
Childless. See Bezdětná, 1935
Children, 1974 (Davies 2)
Children. See Enfants, 1985

Children, 1990 (Black 3, Chaplin 3, Novak 3)
Children and Cars, 1971 (Halas and Batchelor 4)
Children at School, 1937 (Grierson 2, Wright 2)
Children Feeding Ducklings, 1899 (Bitzer 4)
Children Galore, 1954 (Fisher 2)
Children Hand in Hand. See Te o tsunaqu kora, 1948
Children Hand in Hand. See Te o tsunagu ko-ra, 1964
Children in the Crossfire, 1984 (Lassally 4)
Children in the Holocaust, 1983 (Ullmann 3)
Children in the House, 1916 (Talmadge 3)
Children in the Surf, 1904 (Bitzer 4)
Children Making Cartoons, 1973 (Halas and Batchelor 4)
Children Must Learn, 1940 (Van Dyke 2)
Children of a Lesser God, 1986 (Hurt 3)
Children of Chance, 1930 (Launder and Gilliat 2)
Children of Change. See Campane a martello, 1949
Children of Chaos. See Carrefour des enfants perdus, 1943
Children of China, 1939 (Zhao 3)
Children of Divorce, 1927 (Von Sternberg 2, Bow 3, Cooper 3, Banton 4)
Children of Frostmofjället, 1945 (Nykvist 4)
Children of Mata Hari. See Peau de Torpédo, 1969
Children of Paradise. See **Enfants du paradis, 1945**
Children of Pleasure, 1930 (Gibbons 4)
Children of Rage, 1975 (Cusack 3)
Children of Sanchez, 1978 (Davis 3, Del Rio 3, Quinn 3, Figueroa 4, Zavattini 4)
Children of the Atomic Bomb. See Genbakuno-Ko, 1952
Children of Theatre Street, 1977 (Kelly 3)
Children of the Century, 1933 (Zhao 3)
Children of the City. See Ditya bolchogo goroda, 1914
Children of the Damned, 1963 (Love 3)
Children of the Dust, 1923 (Borzage 2)
Children of the Earth. See Dharti Ke Lal, 1947
Children of the Forest, 1913 (Anderson 3)
Children of the Night, 1921 (Fox 4)
Children of the Night. See Nattbarn, 1956
Children of the Street. See Gatans barn, 1914
Children of the Sun, 1960 (Hubley 4)
Children of the Whirlwind, 1925 (Barrymore 3)
Children Pay, 1916 (Gish 3)
Children Upstairs, 1955 (Anderson 2, Lassally 4)
Children Were Watching, 1961 (Leacock 2)
Children's Corner, 1939 (L'Herbier 2)
Children's Corner, 1956 (Lassally 4)
Children's Friend, 1909 (Griffith 2, Bitzer 4)
Children's Hour, 1962 (Wyler 2, Garner 3, Hepburn 3, Hopkins 3, MacLaine 3, Hayes 4, Jeakins 4, North 4, Planer 4)
Child's Faith, 1910 (Griffith 2, Bitzer 4)
Child's Impulse, 1910 (Griffith 2, Pickford 3, Bitzer 4)
Child's Play, 1972 (Lumet 2, Mason 3, Preston 3)
Child's Remorse, 1912 (Griffith 2, Bitzer 4)
Child's Strategem, 1910 (Griffith 2, Bitzer 4)
Chile con Carmen, 1930 (Lantz 4)
Chile, Land of Charm, 1937 (Hoch 4)

Chili con Corny, 1965 (Blanc 4, McKimson 4)

Chili Weather, 1963 (Blanc 4, Freleng 4)

Chilly Scenes of Winter. *See* Head Over Heels, 1979

Chilly Willy in the Legend of Rockabye Point, 1955 (Avery 4)

Chiltern Country, 1938 (Cavalcanti 2)

Chiltern Hundreds, 1949 (Rank 4)

Chimatsuri, 1929 (Tsuburaya 4)

Chimes at Midnight, 1966 (Welles 2, Gielgud 3, Moreau 3, Rey 3, Richardson 3, Rutherford 3)

Chimmie Fadden, 1915 (De Mille 2, Buckland 4)

Chimmie Fadden Out West, 1915 (De Mille 2, Buckland 4, Macpherson 4)

Chimney's Secret, 1915 (Chaney 3)

Chimp, 1932 (Laurel and Hardy 3, Roach 4)

Chimp and Zee, 1968 (Blanc 4)

China, 1931 (Lantz 4, Terry 4)

China, 1943 (Bendix 3, Ladd 3, Young 3, Dreier 4, Head 4, Young 4)

China Bound, 1929 (Gibbons 4)

China Clipper, 1936 (Bogart 3, Walthall 3, Edeson 4, Orry-Kelly 4)

China Corsair, 1951 (Borgnine 3)

China Doll, 1958 (Borzage 2, Bond 3, Mature 3, Clothier 4)

China Fights, 1942 (Eisler 4)

China Gate, 1957 (Fuller 2, Dalio 3, Dickinson 3, Van Cleef 3, Biroc 4, Steiner 4, Young 4)

China Girl, 1942 (Hathaway 2, McLaglen 3, Tierney 3, Basevi 4, Day 4, Friedhofer 4, Garmes 4, Hecht 4, Newman 4, Zanuck 4)

China hilaria, 1939 (Armendáriz 3)

China Is Near. *See* Cine è vicina, 1967

China Jones, 1959 (Blanc 4, McKimson 4)

China 9, Liberty 37. *See* Amore, piombo, e furore, 1978

China Passage, 1937 (Musuraca 4)

China poblana, 1943 (Félix 3)

China Rose, 1983 (Scott 3)

China Seas, 1935 (Garnett 2, Beery 3, Gable 3, Harlow 3, McDaniel 3, Russell 3, Adrian 4, Benchley 4, Brown 4, Freed 4, Furthman 4, Gibbons 4, Lewin 4, Mayer 4, Stothart 4, Thalberg 4)

China Sky, 1945 (Quinn 3, Scott 3, Musuraca 4)

China Story. *See* Satan Never Sleeps, 1961

China Strikes Back, 1937 (Maddow 4)

China Syndrome, 1979 (Douglas 3, Fonda 3, Lemmon 3, Edlund 4, Jenkins 4)

China Tea, 1966 (Le Grice 2)

China Venture, 1953 (Siegel 2, O'Brien 3)

Chinaman, 1920 (Fleischer 4)

Chinaman's Chance, 1933 (Iwerks 4)

China's 400 Million. *See* 400 Million, 1939

China's Little Devils, 1945 (Carey 3, Tiomkin 4)

Chinasisches Roulette, 1976 (Ballhaus 4)

Chinatown, 1974 (Huston 2, Polanski 2, Dunaway 3, Nicholson 3, Alonzo 4, Goldsmith 4, Sylbert 4, Towne 4)

Chinatown at Midnight, 1949 (Katzman 4)

Chinatown Charlie, 1928 (Wong 3)

Chinatown My Chinatown, 1926 (Fleischer 4)

Chinatown Mystery, 1915 (Hayakawa 3)

Chinatown Nights, 1929 (Wellman 2, Beery 3, Selznick 4)

Chinatown Squad, 1935 (Schary 4)

Chinchoge, 1933 (Tanaka 3)

Chinese Adventures in China. *See* Tribulations d'un chinois en Chine, 1965

Chinese Bungalow, 1931 (Neagle 3)

Chinese Bungalow, 1941 (Lukas 3)

Chinese Connection, 1972 (Lee 3)

Chinese Den. *See* Chinese Bungalow, 1941

Chinese Honeymoon, 1917 (Bray 4)

Chinese Parrot, 1927 (Leni 2, Bosworth 3, Wong 3, Laemmle 4)

Chinese Room, 1966 (Figueroa 4)

Chinese Roulette. *See* Chinesisches Roulette, 1976

Chinesisches Roulette, 1976 (Karina 3)

Ching Lin Foo Outdone, 1900 (Porter 2)

Chinjara monogatari, 1962 (Iwashita 3)

Chink, 1921 (Roach 4)

Chinmoko, 1971 (Shinoda 2, Iwashita 3, Miyagawa 4, Takemitsu 4)

Chino. *See* Valdez il mezzosangue, 1973

Chino hate ni ikiru mono, 1960 (Tsukasa 3)

Chinois à Paris, 1974 (Blier 3)

Chinoise, 1967 (Léaud 3, Coutard 4, Guillemot 4)

Chinoise ou Plutôt à la chinoise, 1967 (Godard 2)

Chintao yosai bakugeki merrei, 1963 (Tsuburaya 4)

Chip of the Flying U, 1914 (Mix 3)

Chip Off the Old Block, 1913 (Sennett 2)

Chip Off the Old Block, 1944 (O'Connor 3)

Chips Are Down. *See* Jeux sont faits, 1947

Chiqué, 1930 (Vanel 3)

Chiriakhana, 1967 (Datta 4)

Chirimen kuyo, 1934 (Yamada 3)

Chirurgie fin de siècle, 1900 (Guy 2)

Chirurgien distrait, 1909 (Cohl 4)

Chiseler, 1931 (Sennett 2)

Chisto angliskoe ubiistvo, 1973 (Batalov 3)

Chisum, 1970 (Johnson 3, Wayne 3, Clothier 4)

Chithod Vijay, 1947 (Kapoor 2)

Chittor Vijay, 1947 (Burman 4)

Chitty Chitty Bang Bang, 1968 (Adam 4, Challis 4)

Chiuzoi pidzak, 1927 (Enei 4)

Chivato, 1961 (Haller 4)

Chiyoda Castle on Fire. *See* Chiyoda-jo enjo, 1959

Chiyoda no ninjo, 1930 (Hasegawa 3)

Chiyoda-jo enjo, 1959 (Yoda 4)

Chlen pravitelstva, 1939 (Maretskaya 3)

Chloe, 1934 (Neilan 2)

Chloe in the Afternoon. *See* Amour l'après-midi, 1972

Chobotnice Z II. Patra, 1987 (Brodský 3)

Choc, 1982 (Audran 3, Delon 3, Deneuve 3)

Choc en retour, 1937 (Simon 3)

Choca, 1973 (Fernández 2)

Chocolate Soldier, 1941 (Saville 2, Eddy 3, Freund 4, Gibbons 4, Kaper 4, Mayer 4, Stothart 4)

Chohichiro matsudaira, 1930 (Tsuburaya 4)

Choice Chance Woman Dance, 1971 (Emshwiller 2)

Choice of a Goal, 1975 (Bondarchuk 3)

Choice of Arms. *See* Choix des armes, 1981

Choice of Weapons. *See* Trial by Combat, 1976

Choices, 1986 (Scott 3)

Choices of the Heart, 1983 (Sheen 3, Houseman 4)

Choirboys, 1977 (Aldrich 2, Biroc 4)

Choito neesan omoide yanagi, 1952 (Yamamura 3)

Choix d'assassins, 1966 (De Beauregard 4)

Choix des armes, 1981 (Deneuve 3, Depardieu 3, Montand 3, Sarde 4)

Chokon yasha, 1928 (Hasegawa 3)

Chokoreito to heitai, 1938 (Takamine 3)

Cholly Polly, 1929 (Fleischer 4)

Chômeur de Clochemerle, 1957 (Fernandel 3)

Choo Choo Swing, 1948 (Fleischer 4)

Choo-Choo, 1932 (Roach 4)

Choose Me, 1984 (Rudolph 2, Bujold 3)

Choose Your Partner. *See* Two Girls on Broadway, 1940

Choose Your Partners. *See* Two Girls on Broadway, 1940

Choose Your Weppins, 1935 (Fleischer 4)

Choosing a Husband, 1909 (Griffith 2, Bitzer 4)

Chop Suey, 1930 (Terry 4)

Chop Suey and Co., 1919 (Daniels 3, Lloyd 3, Roach 4)

Chopin, 1958 (Cloquet 4)

Choral von Leuthen, 1933 (Tschechowa 3, Planer 4)

Choral von Leuthen, 1950 (Staudte 2)

Chori Chori, 1956 (Kapoor 2)

Chornyi parus, 1929 (Enei 4)

Chorus, 1974 (Sen 2)

Chorus Girl, 1910 (White 3)

Chorus Kid, 1927 (Robinson 4)

Chorus Lady, 1915 (Reid 3)

Chorus Lady, 1924 (LeRoy 2)

Chorus Line, 1985 (Attenborough 3, Douglas 3, Hamlisch 4)

Chorus of Disapproval, 1989 (Hopkins 3, Irons 3)

Chosen, 1978 (Douglas 3, Quayle 3)

Chosen, 1982 (Schell 3, Steiger 3, Bernstein 4)

Chosen Survivors, 1974 (Cooper 3)

''Chosen'' yoi: Ali to honoo to, 1961 (Tsukasa 3)

Choses de la vie, 1970 (Sautet 2, Piccoli 3, Schneider 3, Sarde 4)

Chotard et Cie, 1933 (Becker 2, Renoir 2, Douy 4)

Chouans, 1946 (Marais 3, Kosma 4, Renoir 4, Spaak 4)

Chouans, 1988 (Broca 2, Cassel 3, Noiret 3, Delerue 4)

Chouchou Yuji no meoto zenzai, 1965 (Yoda 4)

Chouette aveugle, 1987 (Ruiz 2)

Chouki the Bar Owner. *See* Izakaya Chouji, 1983

Chow Hound, 1951 (Blanc 4, Jones 4, Stalling 4)

Chr. IV—Tegselver icke mig, 1988 (Roos 2)

Chris Columbo, 1938 (Terry 4)

Chris Columbus, Jr., 1934 (Lantz 4)

Christ en croix, 1910 (Feuillade 2)

Christ Stopped at Eboli. *See* Cristo si è fermato a Eboli, 1979

Christa, 1970 (Gélin 3)

Christa Hartungen, 1916 (Freund 4)

Christening Party. *See* Křtiny, 1981

Christian, 1923 (Tourneur 2)

Christian Licorice Store, 1971 (Renoir 2)

Christian Wahnschaffe, 1921 (Gad 2, Krauss 3, Veidt 3)

Christina, 1929 (Howard 2, Gaynor 3, Fox 4)

Christine, 1958 (Delon 3, Presle 3, Schneider 3, Auric 4, D'Eaubonne 4, Matras 4, Spaak 4)

Christine, 1983 (Carpenter 2, Stanton 3)

Christine of the Big Tops, 1926 (Levien 4)

Christmas at the Brothel. See Natale in Casa di Appuntamento, 1976

Christmas Burglars, 1908 (Griffith 2, Lawrence 3, Bitzer 4)

Christmas Carol, 1938 (Mankiewicz 2, Waxman 4)

Christmas Carol. See Scrooge, 1951

Christmas Carol, 1965 (Depardieu 2)

Christmas Carol, 1971 (Jones 4, Williams 4)

Christmas Carol, 1984 (Scott 3, York 3)

Christmas Coal Mine Miracle, 1977 (Carradine 3)

Christmas Comes But Once a Year, 1936 (Fleischer 4)

Christmas Crackers. See Caprice de Noël, 1963

Christmas Day in the Workhouse, 1914 (Pearson 2)

Christmas Dream. See Rêve de Noël, 1900

Christmas Dream. See Vánocni, 1946

Christmas Eve. See Notch pered Rozdcstvom, 1913

Christmas Eve, 1947 (Raft 3, Scott 3)

Christmas Eve. See Przedświąteczny wieczór, 1966

Christmas Eve, 1986 (Howard 3, Young 3)

Christmas Feast, 1974 (Halas and Batchelor 4)

Christmas Gift, 1980 (Vinton 4)

Christmas Holiday, 1944 (Siodmak 2, Durbin 3, Kelly 3, Berlin 4, Mankiewicz 4, Salter 4)

Christmas in Connecticut, 1945 (Greenstreet 3, Stanwyck 3, Head 4, Warner 4)

Christmas in July, 1940 (Sturges 2, Pangborn 3, Powell 3, Dreier 4, Head 4)

Christmas Lilies of the Field, 1979 (Schell 3)

Christmas Memories, 1915 (Daves 2)

Christmas Miracle in Caufield, U.S.A. See Christmas Coal Mine Miracle, 1977

Christmas Party. See Jackie Cooper's Christmas, 1932

Christmas Revenge, 1915 (Anderson 3)

Christmas Story, 1966 (Burton 3)

Christmas That Almost Wasn't, 1966 (Brazzi 3)

Christmas to Remember, 1978 (Robards 3, Saint 3, Woodward 3)

Christmas Tree. See Arbre de Noel, 1969

Christmas Under Fire, 1941 (Watt 2, Dalrymple 4)

Christmas Visitor, 1958 (Halas and Batchelor 4)

Christmas without Snow, 1980 (Houseman 4)

Christoph Colomb, 1904 (Pathé 4)

Christopher Bean, 1933 (Wood 2, Barrymore 3)

Christopher Bean, 1933 (Bondi 3, Dressler 3, Daniels 4)

Christopher Columbus, 1949 (Cusack 3, March 3, Box 4, Mathieson 4, Rank 4)

Christopher Crumpet, 1953 (Bosustow 4)

Christopher Crumpet's Playmate, 1955 (Bosustow 4)

Christopher Strong, 1933 (Arzner 2, Hepburn 3, Akins 4, Berman 4, Glennon 4, Plunkett 4, Polglase 4, Selznick 4, Steiner 4, Vorkapich 4)

Christo's Valley Curtain, 1972 (Maysles 2)

Christus, 1919 (Krauss 3)

Chronicle of a Death Foretold. See Cronica di una morte annunciata, 1987

Chronicle of a Love Affair. See Kronika wypadkow milosnych, 1986

Chronicle of Anna Magdalena Bach. See **Chronik der Anna Magdalena Bach, 1968**

Chronicle of Flaming Years. See Povest plamennykh, 1961

Chronicle of May Rain. See Samidare zoshi, 1924

Chronicles of the Grey House. See Zur Chronik von Grieshuus, 1925

Chronik der Anna Magdalena Bach, 1968 (Straub and Huillet 2)

Chronique d'un été, 1960 (Coutard 4)

Chronique provinciale, 1958 (Jarre 4, Rappeneau 4)

Chrysalis, 1973 (Emshwiller 2)

Chrysanthemums. See Krisantemi, 1914

Chto delat', 1928 (Ptushko 4)

Chu Chu and the Philly Flash, 1981 (Arkin 3, Jarre 4)

Chu-Chin-Chow, 1923 (Wilcox 2)

Chu-Chin-Chow, 1934 (Launder and Gilliat 2, Kortner 3, Wong 3, Balcon 4, Metzner 4, Rank 4)

Chudá holka, 1929 (Stallich 4)

Chuji uridasu, 1935 (Shimura 3)

Chuka, 1967 (Borgnine 3, Mills 3, Head 4)

Chump at Oxford, 1940 (Cushing 3, Langdon 3, Laurel and Hardy 3, Roach 4)

Chump Champ, 1950 (Avery 4)

Chumps, 1912 (Bunny 3, Reid 3)

Chumps, 1930 (Sennett 2)

Chunmiao, 1975 (Xie 2)

Chupke Chupke, 1975 (Bachchan 3, Burman 4)

Church. See Chiesa, 1989

Churchill and the Generals, 1979 (Cotten 3)

Churetsu nikudan sanyushi, 1936 (Shimura 3)

Churning. See Manthan, 1976

Chushingura, 1932 (Hasegawa 3, Tanaka 3)

Chushingura, 1934 (Yamada 3)

Chushingura, 1939 (Hasegawa 3, Takamine 3)

Chushingura, 1954 (Yamada 3, Yoda 4)

Chushingura, 1958 (Hasegawa 3, Kyo 3, Shimura 3, Shindo 3, Yamamura 3)

Chushingura, 1962 (Hara 3, Mifune 3, Shimura 3)

Chushingura: Hana no maki, Yuki no maki, 1962 (Tsukasa 3)

Chushingura, Part II, 1939 (Yamada 3)

Chute dans le bonheur. See Chacun sa chance, 1931

Chute de la maison Usher, 1928 (Buñuel 2, Epstein 2)

Chute d'un corps, 1973 (Buñuel 2, Rey 3, Carrière 4)

Chutes de pierres, danger du mort, 1958 (Breer 4)

Chuzhie pisma, 1975 (Yankovsky 3)

Chuzhoy pidzhak, 1927 (Moskvin 4)

Chwila pokoju, 1965 (Konwicki 4)

Chyortovo koleso, 1926 (Kozintsev 2, Enei 4, Moskvin 4)

Chytte ho, 1924 (Ondra 3, Heller 4)

Ci risiamo, vero Provvidenza, 1973 (Morricone 4)

Ci troviamo in galleria, 1953 (Loren 3, Sordi 3)

Ciao Gulliver, 1970 (Ferreri 2)

Ciao maschio, 1978 (Depardieu 3, Mastroianni 3, Sarde 4)

Ciascuno il sou, 1967 (Papas 3)

Ciascuno il suo, 1967 (Volonté 3)

Cible humaine, 1904 (Guy 2)

Ciboulette, 1933 (Allégret 2, Autant-Lara 2, Courant 4, Meerson 4, Prévert 4, Trauner 4)

Cicala, 1980 (Lattuada 2)

Ciclon, 1963 (Alvarez 2)

Ciclon, 1977 (Baker 3, Kennedy 3)

Cid, 1961 (Mann 2, Heston 3, Lom 3, Loren 3, Canutt 4, Fields 4, Krasker 4, Rozsa 4)

Cidade mulher, 1934 (Mauro 2)

Cieca di Sorrento, 1934 (Magnani 3)

Ciel est à vous, 1944 (Grémillon 2, Vanel 3, Douy 4, Spaak 4)

Ciel est pardessus le toit, 1956 (Cloquet 4)

Ciel, la terre. See Threatening Sky, 1965

Cielito lindo, 1936 (Figueroa 4)

Cielo è rosso, 1950 (Cervi 3, Zavattini 4)

Cielo negro, 1951 (Rey 3)

Cielo sulla palude, 1949 (Aldo 4, Cecchi D'Amico 4)

Cień, 1956 (Ścibor-Rylski 4)

Cifte tabancali kabadayi, 1969 (Güney 2)

Cifte yürekli, 1970 (Güney 2)

Cigale et la fourmi, 1909 (Feuillade 2)

Cigale et la fourmi, 1953 (Kosma 4)

Cigalon, 1935 (Pagnol 2)

Cigarette, 1919 (Dulac 2)

Cigarette Tests, 1934 (Fischinger 2, Ford 2)

Cigarette, That's All, 1915 (Weber 2)

Cigarettes Bastos, 1938 (Alexeieff and Parker 4)

Ciklámen, 1916 (Korda 2, Korda 4)

Cimarron, 1930 (Dunne 3, Clothier 4, Cronjager 4, Dunn 4, Eason 4, Estabrook 4, Plunkett 4, Steiner 4, Westmore Family 4)

Cimarron, 1960 (Mann 2, Baxter 3, Ford 3, McCambridge 3, Schell 3, Gillespie 4, Plunkett 4, Surtees 4, Waxman 4)

Cimarron Kid, 1952 (Boetticher 2, Murphy 3)

Cimego. See San Massenza, 1955

Cimetière dans la falaise, 1951 (Rouch 2)

Cin Cin. See Tchin-tchin, 1991

Cina è vicina, 1967 (Delli Colli 4, Morricone 4)

Cinch for the Gander, 1925 (Wray 3)

Cincinnati Kid, 1965 (Ashby 2, Jewison 2, Blondell 3, Malden 3, McQueen 3, Robinson 3, Weld 3, Lardner 4, Schifrin 4)

Cinco de la tarde, 1960 (Bardem 2, Rey 3)

Cinco Vêzes Favela, 1962 (Diegues 2)

Cinderella, 1911 (Selig 4)

Cinderella, 1914 (Pickford 3)

Cinderella, 1922 (Disney 4)

Cinderella, 1925 (Lantz 4)

Cinderella, 1933 (Terry 4)

Cinderella, 1937 (Kaufman 4)

Cinderella, 1950 (Disney 4, Iwerks 4)

Cinderella, 1963 (Reiniger 4)

Cinderella Italian Style. *See* C'era una volta, 1967

Cinderella Jones, 1946 (Berkeley 2, Horton 3, Cahn 4, Polito 4)

Cinderella Liberty, 1973 (Caan 3, Wallach 3, Williams 4, Zsigmond 4)

Cinderella Man, 1917 (Marsh 3)

Cinderella Meets Fella, 1938 (Avery 4)

Cinderella of the Hills, 1921 (Fox 4)

Cinderfella, 1960 (Lewis 2, Tashlin 2, Bumstead 4, Head 4)

Cinders of Love, 1916 (Sennett 2)

Cindy Eller: A Modern Fairy Tale, 1985 (Grant 3)

Cine è vicina, 1967 (Cristaldi 4)

Cinegiornale della pace, 1963 (Zavattini 4)

Cinéma, 1941 (Alekan 4)

Cinéma 57, 1962 (Alexeieff and Parker 4)

Cinema According to Bertolucci, 1977 (Sutherland 3, Valli 3)

Cinéma au service de l'histoire, 1927 (Dulac 2)

Cinéma cinéma, 1969 (Braunberger 4)

Cinema d'altri tempi, 1953 (Age and Scarpelli 4, Gherardi 4)

Cinéma de papa, 1970 (Broca 2)

Cinéma du diable, 1948 (Epstein 2)

Cinéma du diable, 1967 (L'Herbier 2)

Cinema Girl's Romance, 1915 (Pearson 2)

Cinema in the Country, 1930 (Ptushko 4)

Cinema Murder, 1919 (Davies 3, Marion 4, Rosson 4)

Cinema Paradiso, 1990 (Noiret 3, Cristaldi 4, Morricone 4)

Cinéma Pratique, 1941 (Alekan 4)

Cinéma Pratique, 1962 (Alexeieff and Parker 4)

Cinema secondo Bertolucci. *See* Bertolucci secondo il cinema, 1975

Cinématographe, 1990 (Vitti 3)

Cinématographe vu de l'Etna, 1948 (Epstein 2)

Cinema-Truth. *See* **Kino-Pravda, 1922**

Cinerama Holiday, 1955 (De Rochemont 4)

Cinerama's Russian Adventure, 1965 (Crosby 3)

Cinétracts, 1968 (Godard 2)

Cinq cents balles, 1961 (Braunberger 4)

Cinq gars pour Singapour, 1967 (Amidei 4)

Cinq gentilshommes maudits, 1931 (Duvivier 2, Baur 3, Walbrook 3, Ibert 4, Meerson 4)

Cinq jours en juin, 1989 (Girardot 3, Legrand 4)

Cinq sous de Lavarède, 1938 (Fernandel 3)

Cinque giornate, 1973 (Argento 4)

Cinque ore in contanti, 1961 (Charisse 3, Sanders 3, Challis 4)

Cinque per l'inferno, 1968 (Kinski 3)

Cinque pistole di violenca. *See* Mio nome è Shanghai Joe, 1973

Cinque poveri in automobile, 1952 (Fabrizi 3, Zavattini 4)

Cintura, 1989 (Morricone 4)

Cintura di castità, 1949 (Flaiano 4)

Cintura di castita, 1968 (Curtis 3, Vitti 3, Donati 4)

Ciociara, 1960 (Belmondo 3, Loren 3, Levine 4, Ponti 4, Zavattini 4)

Ciphers. *See* Číslice, 1966

Cipola Colt, 1975 (Hayden 3)

Circe the Enchantress, 1924 (Gibbons 4)

Circle, 1925 (Borzage 2, Crawford 3, Basevi 4, Gibbons 4)

Circle, 1957 (Mills 3, Heller 4)

Circle, 1976 (Hayworth 3, Houseman 4)

Circle C Ranch Wedding Present, 1910 (Anderson 3)

Circle of Children, 1977 (Roberts 3)

Circle of Danger, 1951 (Tourneur 2, Milland 3, Harrison 4, Morris 4)

Circle of Death, 1935 (Canutt 4)

Circle of Deceit. *See* Fälschung, 1981

Circle of Iron. *See* Silent Flute, 1977

Circle of Love. *See* **Ronde, 1950**

Circle of Love. *See* Ronde, 1964

Circle of Two, 1980 (Dassin 2, Burton 3)

Circle of Violence: A Family Drama, 1986 (Weld 3)

Circo, 1942 (Cantinflas 3, Figueroa 4)

Circo, 1954 (García Berlanga 2)

Circo equestre Za-Bum, 1944 (Fabrizi 3, Sordi 3, Valli 3)

Circoncision, 1949 (Rouch 2)

Circonstances atténuantes, 1939 (Arletty 3, Simon 3)

Circostanza, 1974 (Olmi 2)

Circular Fence, 1911 (Dwan 2)

Circular Panorama of the Electric Tower, 1901 (Porter 2)

Circular Path, 1915 (Walthall 3)

Circulez!, 1931 (Brasseur 3)

Circumstance. *See* Circostanza, 1974

Circumstantial Evidence, 1990 (Micheaux 2)

Circus, 1920 (Fleischer 4)

Circus, 1927 (Chaplin 2)

Circus, 1932 (Iwerks 4)

Circus Ace, 1927 (Mix 3, Fox 4)

Circus and the Boy, 1914 (Ingram 2)

Circus Clown, 1934 (Brown 3, Orry-Kelly 4)

Circus Comes to Town. *See* Under the Big Top, 1938

Circus Cowboy, 1924 (Wellman 2, Fox 4)

Circus Days, 1935 (Terry 4)

Circus Drawings, 1964 (Williams 4)

Circus Fever, 1925 (Roach 4)

Circus Friends, 1956 (Heller 4)

Circus Hoodoo, 1934 (Langdon 3)

Circus Kid, 1928 (Brown 3, Plunkett 4)

Circus King. *See* Zirkuskönig, 1924

Circus Man, 1914 (De Mille 2)

Circus of Fear, 1967 (Kinski 3, Lee 3)

Circus of Horrors, 1960 (Pleasence 3, Mathieson 4, Slocombe 4)

Circus of Love. *See* Carnival Story, 1954

Circus of Sin. *See* Salto mortale, 1931

Circus Queen Murder, 1933 (Menjou 3, August 4)

Circus Rookies, 1928 (Day 4, Gibbons 4)

Circus Shadow. *See* Shadow, 1937

Circus Star, 1989 (Halas and Batchelor 4)

Circus Today, 1926 (Sennett 2)

Circus Today, 1940 (Avery 4, Blanc 4, Stalling 4)

Circus World, 1964 (Cardinale 3, Hayworth 3, Wayne 3, Fisher 4, Hecht 4, Renoir 4, Tiomkin 4)

Cirkin kiral, 1966 (Güney 2)

Cirkin kiral affetmez, 1967 (Güney 2)

Cirkin ve cesur, 1971 (Güney 2)

Cirkus Hurvínek, 1955 (Trnka 4)

Cirkus v cirkuse, 1975 (Kučera 4)

Cirque de la mort, 1918 (Florey 2)

Císařuv pekař a pekařuv cisař, 1951 (Brdečka 4, Stallich 4, Trnka 4)

Císařuv slavík, 1948 (Brdečka 4, Trnka 4)

Císařv pekař a Pekařuv pekař, 1951 (Frič 2)

Cisco Kid and the Lady, 1940 (Bond 3)

Cisco Pike, 1971 (Black 3, Hackman 3, Stanton 3)

Ciske—A Child Wants Love. *See* Ciske—Ein Kind braucht Liebe, 1955

Ciske—Ein Kind braucht Liebe, 1955 (Staudte 2)

Číslice, 1966 (Švankmajer 4)

Cita de amor, 1956 (Fernández 2, Figueroa 4)

Citadel, 1938 (Saville 2, Vidor 2, Donat 3, Harrison 3, Richardson 3, Russell 3, Dalrymple 4, Junge 4, Mayer 4, Meerson 4, Stradling 4)

Citadel of Crime. *See* Man Betrayed, 1941

Citadelle du silence, 1937 (Andrejew 4, Honegger 4, Milhaud 4)

Cité d'argent, 1955 (Delerue 4)

Cité de l'indiciblepeur. *See* Grande frousse, 1964

Cités du ciel, 1959 (Fradetal 4)

Citizen Kane, 1941 (Welles 2, Wise 2, Cotten 3, Ladd 3, Moorehead 3, Sloane 3, Dunn 4, Herrmann 4, Mankiewicz 4, Polglase 4, Toland 4)

Citizen of Tomorrow, 1942 (Alwyn 4)

Citlivá místa, 1988 (Brejchová 3)

Città dei traffici, 1949 (Risi 2)

Citta delle donne, 1980 (Mastroianni 3, Rotunno 4)

Città di notte, 1958 (Rota 4)

Città di Stendhal, 1949 (Fusco 4)

Città dolente, 1948 (Fellini 2, Delli Colli 4)

Citta prigioniera, 1962 (Niven 3)

Città si difende, 1951 (Fellini 2, Lollobrigida 3, Pinelli 4)

Città violenta, 1970 (Bronson 3, Morricone 4)

City, 1914 (Ince 4)

City, 1926 (Fox 4)

City, 1939 (Cavalcanti 2, Lorentz 2, Van Dyke 2, Copland 4)

City, 1971 (Quinn 3)

City Across the River, 1949 (Curtis 3, Ritter 3)

City Beautiful, 1914 (Reid 3)

City Beneath the Sea, 1953 (Boetticher 2, Quinn 3, Ryan 3)

City Beneath the Sea, 1970 (Cotten 3, Wagner 3)

City Butterfly. *See* Grosstadt Schmetterling, 1929

City for Conquest, 1940 (Kazan 2, Litvak 2, Siegel 2, Cagney 3, Crisp 3, Kennedy 3, Quinn 3, Sheridan 3, Friedhofer 4, Haskin 4, Howe 4, Polito 4, Steiner 4, Wallis 4)

City Girl, 1930 (Brown 3, Carré 4, Fox 4)

City Gone Wild, 1927 (Cruze 2, Brooks 3, Furthman 4, Glennon 4, Mankiewicz 4)

City Government. *See* City Speaks, 1947

City Hall to Harlem in Fifteen Seconds via the Subway Route, 1904 (Porter 2)

City Heat, 1984 (Eastwood 3, Reynolds 3)

City in Fear, 1980 (Rourke 3, Rosenman 4)

City in the Night, 1956 (O'Brien 3)

City in the Sea, 1965 (Price 3)

City is Dark. *See* Crime Wave, 1954

City Jungle. *See* Young Philadelphians, 1959

City Lights, 1931 (Chaplin 2, Harlow 3, Newman 4)

City Limits, 1985 (Jones 3)

City Map. *See* Várostérkép, 1977

City of Bad Men, 1953 (Clarke 4, Jeakins 4, LeMaire 4)

City of Chance, 1939 (Day 4)

City of Darkness, 1915 (August 4, Ince 4)

City of Darkness, 1939 (Day 4)

City of Desire. *See* Joen no chimata, 1976

City of Dim Faces, 1918 (Hayakawa 3, Marion 4)

City of Fear, 1958 (Ballard 4, Goldsmith 4)

City of Joy, 1992 (Morricone 4)

City of Masks, 1920 (Brown 4)

City of Pirates. *See* Ville de pirates, 1984

City of Play, 1929 (Balcon 4)

City of Secrets. *See* Stadt ist voller Geheimnisse, 1955

City of Shadows, 1955 (McLaglen 3)

City of the Dead, 1960 (Lee 3)

City of Torment. *See* Und über und der Himmel, 1947

City of Women. *See* Citta delle donne, 1980

City on Fire, 1979 (Gardner 3, Winters 3)

City Park, 1934 (Walthall 3, Brown 4)

City Slicker, 1918 (Daniels 3, Lloyd 3, Roach 4)

City Slicker, 1952 (Terry 4)

City Slickers, 1991 (Palance 3)

City Sparrow, 1920 (Wood 2)

City Speaks, 1947 (Rotha 2, Alwyn 4)

City Story, 1954 (Ford 3)

City Streaming, 1990 (Brakhage 2)

City Streets, 1931 (Mamoulian 2, Cooper 3, Goddard 3, Lukas 3, Sidney 3, Garmes 4, Zukor 4)

City That Never Sleeps, 1924 (Cruze 2, Brown 4)

City Under the Sea. *See* War Gods of the Deep, 1965

City Vamp, 1915 (Marion 4)

City without Men, 1943 (Darnell 3, Raksin 4, Schulberg 4)

Citydreams. *See* Dear Mr. Wonderful, 1982

Ciudad de carton, 1932 (Gaynor 3, Young 3)

Civilian, 1912 (Ince 4)

Civilization, 1916 (Ince 4, Sullivan 4)

Civilization's Child, 1916 (August 4, Sullivan 4)

Claim Jumper, 1913 (Ince 4)

Claim Jumpers, 1911 (Dwan 2)

Clair de femme, 1979 (Montand 3, Schneider 3)

Clair de lune, 1932 (Fradetal 4)

Clair de lune espagnol, 1909 (Cohl 4)

Clair de lune sous Richelieu, 1911 (Gance 2)

Clair de terre, 1970 (Feuillère 3, Girardot 3, Presle 3)

Claire's Knee. *See* Genou de Claire, 1970

Clairvoyant, 1935 (Rains 3, Wray 3, Balcon 4, Bennett 4, Junge 4, Rank 4)

Clambake, 1967 (Presley 3)

Clan de los immorales, 1973 (Ferrer 3)

Clan des Siciliens, 1969 (Delon 3, Gabin 3, Decaë 4, Morricone 4, Saulnier 4)

Clan of the Cave Bear, 1985 (Sayles 2)

Clancy, 1974 (Brakhage 2)

Clancy at the Bat, 1929 (Sennett 2)

Clancy Street Boys, 1943 (Katzman 4)

Clancy's Kosher Wedding, 1927 (Plunkett 4)

Clandestino destino, 1987 (Hermosillo 2)

Clap Your Hands, 1948 (Fleischer 4)

Claque, 1932 (Fernandel 3)

Clara and Her Mysterious Toys, 1912 (Cohl 4)

Clara Cleans Her Teeth, 1925 (Disney 4)

Clara de Montargis, 1950 (Renoir 4)

Clara et les chics types, 1980 (Adjani 3)

Clara et les méchants, 1957 (Wakhévitch 4)

Clara's Heart, 1988 (Mulligan 2, Goldberg 3, Francis 4)

Clarence, 1922 (Menjou 3, Reid 3)

Clarence, 1937 (Head 4)

Claretta, 1984 (Cardinale 3)

Claretta and Ben. *See* Permettete che ami vostre figlia?, 1974

Clarissa, 1941 (Fröhlich 3)

Claro, 1975 (Rocha 2)

Clash, 1984 (Vierny 4)

Clash by Night, 1952 (Lang 2, Monroe 3, Ryan 3, Stanwyck 3, D'Agostino 4, Krasna 4, Musuraca 4, Wald 4)

Clash of the Titans, 1981 (Bloom 3, Meredith 3, Olivier 3, Smith 3, Harryhausen 4)

Clash of the Wolves, 1925 (Walker 4)

Class. *See* You Never Can Tell, 1920

Class, 1983 (Robertson 3, Bernstein 4)

Class Action, 1991 (Hackman 3, Hall 4)

Class Enemy. *See* Klassenfeind, 1984

Class of Miss MacMichael, 1979 (Jackson 3, Reed 3)

Class of 1984, 1983 (Fox 3, McDowall 3, Schifrin 4)

Class of 1999, 1990 (McDowell 3)

Class Relations. *See* Klassenverhältnisse, 1985

Classe, 1897 (Guy 2)

Classe de lettres, 1953 (Cloquet 4)

Classe de mathematiques, 1953 (Cloquet 4)

Classe d'histoire, 1953 (Cloquet 4)

Classe operaia va in paradiso, 1971 (Volonté 3, Morricone 4)

Classe tous risques, 1960 (Sautet 2, Belmondo 3, Dalio 3, Cloquet 4, Delerue 4)

Classification des plantes, 1982 (Ruiz 2)

Classified, 1925 (Mathis 4, Rosson 4)

Classmates, 1908 (Bitzer 4)

Classmates, 1913 (Barrymore 3, Sweet 3, Walthall 3, Gaudio 4)

Classmates, 1924 (Barthelmess 3, Seitz 4)

Claudelle Inglish, 1961 (Kennedy 3)

Claudia von Geiserhof, 1917 (Veidt 3)

Claudia, 1943 (Goulding 2, Young 3, Basevi 4, Newman 4, Ryskind 4, Shamroy 4)

Claudia and David, 1946 (Astor 3, Young 3, Basevi 4, La Shelle 4)

Claudine. *See* Claudine à l'école, 1938

Claudine, 1974 (Jones 3)

Claudine à l'école, 1938 (Brasseur 3)

Claudi vom Geisterhof, 1915 (Messter 4)

Clavigo, 1970 (Ophuls 2)

Claw, 1927 (Olcott 2, Laemmle 4)

Claws for Alarm, 1954 (Blanc 4, Jones 4, Stalling 4)

Claws in the Lease, 1963 (Blanc 4, McKimson 4)

Clay Pigeon, 1949 (Foreman 4)

Clay Pigeon, 1971 (Meredith 3)

Claymation series, 1978–91 (Vinton 4)

Clé sur la porte, 1978 (Girardot 3)

Clean Heart, 1924 (Blackton 2)

Clean Pastures, 1937 (Freleng 4, Stalling 4)

Clean Shaven Man, 1936 (Fleischer 4)

Clean Slate. *See* Coup de torchon, 1981

Clean Sweep, 1957 (Carreras 4)

Cleaning Time, 1915 (Laurel and Hardy 3)

Cleaning Up, 1926 (Arbuckle 3)

Clean-Up, 1917 (Young 4)

Clean-Up Man, 1928 (Laemmle 4)

Clear All Wires, 1933 (Daves 2, Marshall 3)

Clear the Decks for Action. *See* Klart till drabbning, 1937

Clearing, 1991 (Segal 3)

Clearing the Trail, 1928 (Eason 4)

Clef sur la porte, 1978 (Sarde 4)

Clemenceau Case, 1915 (Brenon 2, Bara 3)

Clémentine Chérie, 1963 (Noiret 3)

Cléo de cinq à sept, 1962 (Godard 2, Varda 2, Constantine 3, Karina 3, De Beauregard 4, Evein 4, Legrand 4, Ponti 4, Rabier 4)

Cleo from 5 to 7. *See* **Cléo de cinq à sept, 1962**

Cleopatra, 1917 (Bara 3)

Cleopatra, 1934 (De Mille 2, Carradine 3, Colbert 3, Banton 4, Dreier 4, Prinz 4, Young 4, Zukor 4)

Cleopatra, 1963 (Mankiewicz 2, Burton 3, Harrison 3, McDowall 3, Taylor 3, Buchman 4, North 4, Pan 4, Renoir 4, Shamroy 4, Sharaff 4, Smith 4, Wanger 4, Zanuck 4)

Cleopatra Jones, 1973 (Winters 3)

Cléopâtre, 1899 (Méliès 2)

Cleopatsy, 1918 (Roach 4)

Clérambard, 1969 (Noiret 3)

Clever Dummy, 1917 (Sennett 2, Beery 3)

Clever Girl Takes Care of Herself. *See* Bra flicka reder sig själv, 1914

Clever Mrs. Carfax, 1917 (Crisp 3)

Client sérieux, 1932 (Autant-Lara 2)

Cliente seductor, 1931 (Chevalier 3)

Climats, 1962 (Piccoli 3, Fusco 4, Vierny 4)

Climax, 1930 (Laemmle 4)

Climax, 1944 (Costello 3, Karloff 3, Mohr 4, Siodmak 4)

Climax. *See* Immorale, 1967

Climb an Angry Mountain, 1972 (Duning 4)

Climber, 1917 (King 2)

Climbers, 1927 (Loy 3)

Climbers. *See* Ambitieuse, 1959

Climbing High, 1939 (Reed 2, Matthews 3, Redgrave 3, Sim 3, Junge 4, Rank 4)

Clinging Vine, 1926 (Miller 4, Sullivan 4)

Clinic. *See* Sanitarium, 1910

Clippety Clobbered, 1966 (Blanc 4)

Clive of India, 1935 (Carradine 3, Colman 3, Young 3, Day 4, Guffey 4, Newman 4, Zanuck 4)

Cloak. *See* Shinel, 1926

Cloak and Dagger, 1946 (Lang 2, Cooper 3, Friedhofer 4, Lardner 4, Polito 4, Steiner 4)

Cloches de Paques, 1912 (Feuillade 2)

Clock, 1945 (Garland 3, Walker 3, Folsey 4, Freed 4, Gillespie 4, Irene 4, Mayer 4)

Clockmaker. *See* Horloger de Saint-Paul, 1974

Clockmaker's Dream. *See* Rêve d'horloger, 1904

Clockwise, 1986 (Cleese 3)

Clockwork Orange, 1971 (Kubrick 2, McDowell 3, Alcott 4, Barry 4)

Clod, 1912 (Ince 4)

Clodoche, 1938 (Berry 3)

Cloister's Touch, 1909 (Griffith 2, Walthall 3, Bitzer 4)

Clone Master, 1978 (Bellamy 3, Biroc 4)

Cloportes. *See* Métamorphose des cloportes, 1964

Cloportes, 1966 (Rosay 3)

Close Call, 1911 (Sennett 2)

Close Call, 1916 (Mix 3)

Close Call for Boston Blackie, 1946 (Guffey 4)

Close Encounters of the Third Kind, 1977 (Schrader 2, Spielberg 2, Truffaut 2, Dreyfuss 3, Alonzo 4, Fraker 4, Kovacs 4, Slocombe 4, Trumbull 4, Williams 4, Zsigmond 4)

Close Harmony, 1929 (Cromwell 2, Harlow 3, Hunt 4)

Close Quarters, 1943 (Dalrymple 4)

Close Relations, 1933 (Arbuckle 3)

Close Shave, 1929 (Sennett 2, Hornbeck 4)

Close Shave, 1937 (Terry 4)

Close to My Heart, 1951 (Milland 3, Tierney 3, Burks 4, Steiner 4)

Close to Nature, 1968 (Benegal 2)

Closed Circuit. See System ohne Schatten, 1983

Closed Door, 1912 (Lawrence 3)

Closed Mondays, 1974 (Vinton 4)

Closed Road, 1916 (Tourneur 2, Carré 4)

Closely Watched Trains. See **Ostře sledované vlaky, 1966**

Closet, 1965 (Warhol 2)

Close-Up: The Movie Star Book, 1966 (Burton 3)

Clothes and the Woman, 1937 (Sim 3)

Clothes Make the Man, 1915 (Laurel and Hardy 3)

Clothes Make the Pirate, 1925 (Tourneur 2)

Clothes Make the Woman, 1928 (Pidgeon 3)

Cloud in the Sky, 1940 (Ulmer 2)

Cloudburst, 1951 (Baker 3, Preston 3, Carreras 4)

Clouded Name, 1923 (Shearer 3)

Clouded Yellow, 1950 (Howard 3, More 3, Simmons 3, Box 4, Unsworth 4)

Clouds, 1917 (Van Dyke 2)

Clouds at Sunset. See Akanegumo, 1967

Clouds at Twilight. See Yuyake-gume, 1956

Clouds Like White Sheep, 1962 (Frampton 2)

Clouds of Glory, Parts I and II, 1978 (Russell 2, Russell 4)

Clouds over Europe. See Q Planes, 1939

Clouds Will Roll Away. See Není stále zamračeno, 1950

Clověk pod vodou, 1961 (Brdečka 4)

Clown, 1916 (Rosher 4)

Clown. See Klovnen, 1917

Clown, 1931 (Lantz 4)

Clown. See Ansichten eines Clowns, 1975

Clown and Policeman, 1900 (Hepworth 2)

Clown and the Alchemist, 1900 (Porter 2)

Clown and the Primadonna, 1913 (Costello 3)

Clown Bux, 1935 (Modot 3, D'Eaubonne 4, Douy 4)

Clown en sac, 1904 (Guy 2)

Clown Must Laugh. See Pagliacci, 1936

Clown Princes, 1939 (Roach 4)

Clowning, 1931 (Terry 4)

Clowns, 1902 (Guy 2)

Clowns. See Clowns, 1970

Clowns, 1970 (Donati 4, Rota 4)

Clowns. See Ansichten eines Clowns, 1975

Clowns de dieu, 1986 (Theodorakis 4)

Clown's Little Brother, 1920 (Fleischer 4)

Clown's Pup, 1942 (Fleischer 4)

Clown's Triumph, 1912 (Brenon 2)

Club, 1981 (Beresford 2)

Club de femmes, 1936 (Delannoy 2, Darrieux 3)

Club de femmes, 1956 (Trintignant 3)

Club de rencontres, 1987 (Legrand 4)

Club des aristocrates, 1937 (Berry 3)

Club des soupirants, 1941 (Cayatte 2, Fernandel 3, Burel 4, Wakhévitch 4)

Club Extinction. See Dr. M, 1990

Club Fed, 1990 (Black 3)

Club Havana, 1945 (Ulmer 2)

Club Life, 1987 (Curtis 3)

Club Life in Stone Age, 1940 (Terry 4)

Club of the Big Deed. See S.V.D., 1927

Club Paradise, 1986 (O'Toole 3, Williams 3)

Club Sandwich, 1931 (Terry 4)

Clubman and the Tramp, 1908 (Griffith 2, Lawrence 3, Bitzer 4)

Clubs Are Trump, 1917 (Lloyd 3, Roach 4)

Clue, 1915 (Hayakawa 3, Sweet 3)

Clue, 1985 (Landis 2, Whitlock 4)

Clue of the New Pin, 1929 (Gielgud 3)

Clumsy Robber. See Chytte ho!, 1924

Clunked on the Corner, 1929 (Sennett 2, Hornbeck 4)

Cluny Brown, 1946 (Lubitsch 2, Boyer 3, Jones 3, Hoffenstein 4, La Shelle 4, Wheeler 4)

Clutching Hand, 1936 (Canutt 4)

C-Man, 1949 (Carradine 3)

Coal Black and de Sebben Dwarfs, 1943 (Foster 4, Blanc 4, Clampett 4, Stalling 4)

Coal Miner's Daughter, 1980 (Spacek 3)

Coalface, 1935 (Cavalcanti 2, Grierson 2)

Coals of Fire, 1911 (Bosworth 3)

Coals of Fire, 1918 (Niblo 2)

Coartada en disco rojo, 1970 (Rey 3)

Coast Guard, 1939 (Bellamy 3, Scott 3, Ballard 4)

Coast of Folly, 1925 (Dwan 2, Swanson 3)

Coast Patrol, 1925 (Wray 3)

Coastal Command, 1942 (Dalrymple 4)

Coat's Tale, 1914 (Sennett 2)

Cobbler, 1923 (Roach 4)

Cobbler Stay at Your Bench. See Skomakare bliv vid din läst, 1915

Cobra, 1925 (Valentino 3, Adrian 4, Menzies 4, Westmore Family 4, Zukor 4)

Cobra, 1967 (Andrews 3)

Cobra, 1986 (Stallone 3, Golan and Globus 4)

Cobra Mission, 1986 (Pleasence 3)

Cobra Verde, 1987 (Herzog 2, Kinski 3)

Cobra Woman, 1944 (Brooks 2, Siodmak 2)

Cobweb, 1916 (Hepworth 2)

Cobweb, 1955 (Minnelli 2, Bacall 3, Boyer 3, Gish 3, Grahame 3, Widmark 3, Wray 3, Folsey 4, Houseman 4, Paxton 4, Rosenman 4)

Cobweb Castle. See Kumonosu-jo, 1957

Cobweb Hotel, 1936 (Fleischer 4)

Coca Cola Cartoons, 1960 (Lantz 4)

Coca Cola Kid, 1985 (Makavejev 2)

Cocagne, 1960 (Fernandel 3)

Cocaine Cowboys, 1979 (Palance 3)

Cocaine Wars, 1986 (Corman 2)

Cocardiers, 1967 (Carrière 4)

Cocher de fiacre endormi, 1897 (Guy 2)

Cocher de fiacre endormi, 1907 (Gaumont 4)

Cock o' the North, 1935 (Crazy gang 3)

Cock o' the Walk, 1930 (Loy 3)

Cock of the Air, 1932 (Lederer 4, Newman 4, Sherwood 4)

Cockaboody, 1973 (Hubley 4)

Cock-a-Doodle Deaux Deaux, 1966 (McKimson 4)

Cock-a-Doodle Dog, 1951 (Avery 4)

Cockeyed Cavaliers, 1934 (Pangborn 3, Plunkett 4)

Cockeyed Cowboys of Calico County, 1970 (Rooney 3)

Cock-Eyed World, 1929 (Walsh 2, Brown 3, McLaglen 3, Carre 4, Edeson 4, Fox 4)

Cockfighter, 1974 (Oates 3, Stanton 3, Almendros 4)

Cockleshell Heroes, 1955 (Ferrer 3, Howard 3, Lee 3, Addison 4, Box 4)

Cuckoo Cavaliers, 1940 (Three Stooges 3)

Cockpit. See Lost People, 1949

Cockroach. See Sváb, 1946

Cocktail, 1937 (Henning-Jensen 2)

Cocktail, 1988 (Cruise 3)

Cocktail Hour, 1933 (Daniels 3, Scott 3, August 4)

Cocktails, 1927 (Madsen and Schenstrøm 3)

Cocktails, 1928 (Launder and Gilliat 2)

Cocktails for Three, 1978 (Cardinale 3)

Cocktails in the Kitchen. See For Better, For Worse, 1954

Cocky Bantam, 1943 (Fleischer 4)

Cocky Cockroach, 1932 (Terry 4)

Cocoanut Grove, 1938 (Arden 3)

Cocoanuts, 1929 (Florey 2, Dumont 3, Marx Brothers 3, Berlin 4, Folsey 4, LeMaire 4, Ruttenberg 4, Ryskind 4, Wanger 4, Zukor 4)

Cocoanuts, 1991 (Francis 3)

Coconut Grove, 1938 (MacMurray 3, Head 4)

Cocoon, 1985 (Ameche 3, Baker 4)

Cocoon II: The Return, 1988 (Ameche 3)

Cocorico Monsieur Poulet, 1977 (Rouch 2)

Cocotiers, 1963 (Rouch 2)

Cocotte d'azur, 1959 (Kosma 4)

Cocu magnifique, 1946 (Barrault 3)

Coda. See Songs, 1964–69

Code. See Szyfry, 1966

Code Name: Emerald, 1985 (Von Sydow 3, Francis 4)

Code Name Heraclitus, 1967 (Baker 3)

Code of Honor, 1911 (Bosworth 3)

Code of Honor, 1916 (Borzage 2)

Code of Scotland Yard. See Shop at Sly Corner, 1946

Code of Silence, 1960 (Cushing 3, Sanders 3)

Code of the Scarlet, 1928 (Brown 4, McCord 4)

Code of the Sea, 1924 (Fleming 2)

Code of the Secret Service, 1939 (Reagan 3, McCord 4)

Code of the Streets, 1938 (Carey 3)

Code of the West, 1925 (Howard 2)

Codename Wildgeese, 1984 (Borgnine 3, Kinski 3, Van Cleef 3)

Codfish Balls, 1930 (Terry 4)

Codine, 1963 (Colpi 4)

Cody of the Pony Express, 1950 (Katzman 4)

Coeur à l'envers, 1980 (Girardot 3)

Coeur battant, 1962 (Trintignant 3, Legrand 4, Matras 4)

Coeur de coq, 1946 (Fernandel 3)

Coeur de Gueux, 1936 (Epstein 2)

Coeur de la France, 1962 (Leenhardt 2)

Coeur de Lilas, 1932 (Litvak 2, Fernandel 3, Gabin 3, Courant 4)

Coeur de mal, 1941 (Volkov 2)

Coeur de Paris, 1931 (Fradetal 4)

Coeur de Tzigane, 1909 (Modot 3)
Coeur des pierres, 1967 (Colpi 4)
Coeur et l'argent, (Feuillade 2)
Coeur fidèle, 1923 (Epstein 2, Manès 3)
Coeur fragile, 1916 (Musidora 3)
Coeur gros comme ça, 1961 (Morgan 3, Braunberger 4)
Coeur joie, 1967 (Bardot 3)
Coeur joyeux, 1931 (Gabin 3)
Coeurs farouches, 1924 (Duvivier 2)
Coffee and Cigarettes, 1986 (Jarmusch 2)
Coffee and Cigarettes II, 1989 (Müller 4)
Coffee House. See Kaffeehaus, 1970
Coffre enchanté, 1904 (Méliès 2)
Coffre-fort, 1908 (Cohl 4)
Coffret de laque, 1932 (Darrieux 3)
Coffret de Tolède, 1914 (Feuillade 2)
Cohen and Tate, 1988 (Scheider 3)
Cohen at Coney Island, 1912 (Sennett 2, Normand 3)
Cohen Collects a Debt. See Cohen at Coney Island, 1912
Cohen's Advertising Scheme, 1904 (Porter 2)
Cohens and Kellys in Africa, 1930 (Mohr 4)
Cohens and Kellys in Hollywood, 1932 (Ayres 3, Karloff 3)
Cohens and Kellys in Paris, 1928 (Laemmle 4)
Cohens and Kellys in Scotland, 1930 (Laemmle 4)
Cohens and the Kellys, 1927 (Florey 2)
Cohens and the Kellys in Trouble, 1933 (Stevens 2, O'Sullivan 3)
Cohen Saves the Flag, 1913 (Sennett 2, Normand 3)
Cohen's Outing, 1913 (Sennett 2)
Coiffeur pour dames, 1952 (Fernandel 3)
Coïncidences, 1946 (Reggiani 3)
Col cuore in gola, 1967 (Trintignant 3)
Col ferro e col fuoco, 1961 (Fusco 4)
Col. Heezaliar series, 1924 (Lantz 4)
Colbys, 1985 (Heston 3)
Cold Comfort, 1957 (Sellers 3)
Cold Deck, 1917 (Hart 3, August 4)
Cold Feet, 1930 (Lantz 4)
Cold Front, 1989 (Sheen 3)
Cold Heaven, 1990 (Roeg 2)
Cold Hunters, 1915 (Johnson 3)
Cold Night's Death, 1973 (Wallach 3)
Cold Romance, 1949 (Terry 4)
Cold Room, 1984 (Segal 3)
Cold Sweat, 1969 (Ullmann 3)
Cold Sweat. See De la part des copains, 1970
Cold Sweat. See Uomo dalle due ombre, 1971
Cold Turkey, 1925 (Sennett 2)
Cold Turkey, 1929 (Lantz 4)
Cold Turkey, 1940 (Langdon 3)
Cold Turkey, 1971 (Horton 3)
Cold Wind in August, 1961 (Crosby 4)
Cold-blooded Beast. See Bestia uccide a sangue freddo, 1971
Colditz Story, 1955 (Mills 3, Vetchinsky 4)
Cólera del viente, 1970 (Rey 3)
Colère des dieux, 1947 (Annenkov 4, Burel 4)
Colette, 1950 (Cocteau 2)
Collants noirs. See Black Tights, 1960
Collars and Cuffs, 1923 (Laurel and Hardy 3, Roach 4)
Colle universelle, 1907 (Méliès 2)
Collection particulière, 1973 (Borowczyk 2)

Collectionneuse, 1967 (Rohmer 2, Almendros 4, De Beauregard 4)
Collections privées, 1979 (Borowczyk 2, Braunberger 4)
Collector, 1965 (Wyler 2, Stamp 3, Jarre 4, Krasker 4, Surtees 4)
Colleen, 1927 (Fox 4)
Colleen, 1936 (Blondell 3, Keeler 3, Powell 3, Haskin 4, Orry-Kelly 4, Polito 4)
Colleen Bawn, 1911 (Olcott 2)
College, 1927 (Keaton 2, Schenck 4)
College, 1931 (Lantz 4)
College Boob, 1926 (Arthur 3)
College Chums, 1910 (White 3)
College Coach, 1933 (Wellman 2, Powell 3, Wayne 3, Freed 4, Mercer 4, Orry-Kelly 4)
College Confidential, 1960 (Marshall 3)
College Days, 1926 (Montgomery 3)
College Days, 1929 (Zukor 4)
College Hero, 1927 (Walker 4)
College Holiday, 1936 (Head 4, Prinz 4, Young 4)
College Humor, 1933 (Crosby 3)
College Is a Nice Place. See Daigaku yoi toko, 1936
College Kiddo, 1927 (Sennett 2)
College Love, 1929 (Laemmle 4)
College Rhythm, 1934 (Dmytryk 2, Pangborn 3, Sheridan 3, Wyman 3, Prinz 4)
College Scandal, 1935 (Brackett 4)
College Spirit, 1932 (Terry 4)
College Swing, 1938 (Walsh 2, Grable 3, Hope 3, Horton 3, Carmichael 4, Dreier 4, Head 4, Prinz 4)
College Vamp, 1931 (Sennett 2)
College Widow, 1927 (Costello 3, Blanke 4)
Collegians, 1926 (Gable 3)
Collegiate, 1936 (Grable 3, Head 4, Prinz 4)
Collégiennes, 1956 (Deneuve 3)
Collier de la reine, 1909 (Feuillade 2)
Collier de perles, 1915 (Feuillade 2, Musidora 3)
Collier vivant, 1909 (Modot 3)
Collision Course. See Bamboo Saucer, 1968
Collisions, 1976 (Emshwiller 2)
Colloids, 1969 (Godfrey 4)
Colomba, 1918 (Veidt 3)
Colomba, 1933 (Modot 3)
Colombine, 1920 (Jannings 3)
Colombo Plan, 1967 (Halas and Batchelor 4)
Colonel Blimp. See **Life and Death of Colonel Blimp, 1943**
Colonel Bogey, 1948 (Fisher 2)
Colonel Bontemps, 1915 (Musidora 3)
Colonel Chabert, 1943 (Raimu 3)
Colonel Effingham's Raid, 1945 (Bennett 3, Coburn 3, Cronjager 4, Trotti 4)
Colonel Heezaliar series, 1914–24 (Bray 4)
Colonel March Investigates, 1953 (Karloff 3)
Colonel March of Scotland Yard. See Colonel March Investigates, 1953
Colonel Redl. See Redl Ezredes, 1985
Colonello Chabert, 1920 (Gallone 2)
Colonel's Cup. See Sports Day, 1945
Colonel's Ward, 1912 (Ince 4)
Colonia penal, 1971 (Villagra 3)
Colonialskandal, 1927 (Warm 4)
Colonie Sicedison, 1958 (Olmi 2)
Colonna di ferro, 1940 (Mastroianni 3)
Color Box, 1935 (Lye 4)

Color Cry, 1953 (Lye 4)
Color Fields, 1977 (Vanderbeek 2)
Color of Evening, 1990 (Burstyn 3, McDowall 3)
Color of Money, 1986 (Scorsese 2, Cruise 3, Newman 3, Ballhaus 4, Bernstein 4)
Color Purple, 1985 (Spielberg 2, Goldberg 3, Jones 4)
Color Rhythm, 1942 (Fischinger 2, Ford 2)
Colorado, 1915 (Bosworth 3)
Colorado, 1921 (Eason 4, Laemmle 4, Miller 4)
Colorado, 1940 (Rogers 3)
Colorado Jim. See Colorado Pluck, 1920
Colorado Legend and the Ballad of the Colorado Ute, 1961 (Brakhage 2)
Colorado Pluck, 1920 (Furthman 4)
Colorado Sundown, 1952 (Beavers 3)
Colorado Sunset, 1939 (Autry 3, Crabbe 3)
Colorado Territory, 1939 (Autry 3, Crabbe 3)
Colorado Territory, 1949 (Walsh 2, Malone 3, McCrea 3, Veiller 4)
Colored Girl's Love, 1914 (Sennett 2)
Colored Villainy, 1915 (Sennett 2)
Colorful Bombay, 1937 (Hoch 4)
Colorful Islands—Madagascar and Seychelles, 1936 (Hoch 4)
Colors, 1988 (Duvall 3, Hopper 3, Wexler 4)
Colosseum and Juicy Lucy, 1970 (Baker 3)
Colossus of New York, 1958 (Edouart 4, Lourié 4)
Colossus: The Forbin Project, 1970 (Head 4)
Colour Box. See Color Box, 1935
Colour Cocktail, 1976 (McLaren 4)
Colour Flight, 1938 (Lye 4)
Colour in Clay, 1942 (Cardiff 4)
Coloured Villiany, 1915 (Arbuckle 3)
Colpa al cuore, 1982 (Trintignant 3)
Colpa altrui, 1914 (Bertini 3)
Colpa e la pena, Abbasso lo zio, 1958 (Bellocchio 2)
Colpe rovente, 1969 (Flaiano 4)
Colpevoli, 1957 (De Sica 2)
Colpo di pistola, 1941 (Castellani 2)
Colpo di sole, 1968 (Amidei 4)
Colpo di vento, 1936 (Berry 3)
Colt Comrades, 1943 (Mitchum 3, Harlan 4, Wilson 4)
Colt 45, 1950 (Scott 3)
Coltello di ghiaccio, 1972 (Baker 3)
Colter Craven Story, 1960 (Ford 2)
Columbo series, 1989–90 (Falk 3)
Column South, 1953 (Murphy 3)
Coma, 1978 (Bujold 3, Douglas 3, Widmark 3, Goldsmith 4)
Comanche, 1956 (Andrews 3)
Comanche Station, 1960 (Boetticher 2, Scott 3, Brown 4)
Comanche Territory, 1950 (O'Hara 3)
Comancheros, 1961 (Curtiz 2, Marvin 3, Bernstein 4, Clothier 4, Smith 4)
Comancho blanco, 1969 (Cotten 3)
Comandamenti per un gangster, 1968 (Morricone 4)
Comata, the Sioux, 1909 (Griffith 2, Bitzer 4)
Combat America, 1944 (Gable 3)
Combat dans l'île, 1961 (Schneider 3, Trintignant 3, Evein 4, Rappeneau 4)
Combat naval en Grèce, 1897 (Méliès 2)
Combats sans haine, 1948 (Spaak 4)
Combourg, visage de pierre, 1948 (Fresnay 3)

Come Across, 1929 (Laemmle 4)

Come Along With Me, 1982 (Woodward 3)

Come and Get It, 1929 (Miller 4, Plunkett 4)

Come and Get It, 1936 (Hawks 2, Wyler 2, Brennan 3, Farmer 3, McCrea 3, Day 4, Furthman 4, Goldwyn 4, Maté 4, Murfin 4, Newman 4, Toland 4)

Come Back, 1983 (Vadim 2)

Come Back Charleston Blue, 1972 (Jones 4)

Come Back, Little Sheba, 1952 (Lancaster 3, Bumstead 4, Head 4, Howe 4, Wallis 4, Waxman 4)

Come Back, Little Sheba, 1977 (Olivier 3, Woodward 3)

Come Back to Erin, 1914 (Olcott 2)

Come Back to Me. See Doll Face, 1946

Come Back to the Five and Dime, Jimmy Dean, Jimmy Dean, 1982 (Altman 2, Black 3, Cher 3)

Come Blow Your Horn, 1963 (Cobb 3, Martin 3, Sinatra 3, Cahn 4, Daniels 4, Head 4)

Come Clean, 1931 (Laurel and Hardy 3, Mayer 4, Roach 4)

Come Dance with Me. See Voulez-vous danser avec moi, 1959

Come Fill the Cup, 1951 (Cagney 3, Massey 3, Blanke 4, Burks 4, Steiner 4)

Come Fly with Me, 1963 (Malden 3, Cahn 4, De Grunwald 4, Morris 4)

Come Live with Me, 1941 (Brown 2, Lamarr 3, Stewart 3, Folsey 4, Stothart 4)

Come Next Spring, 1956 (Brennan 3, Sheridan 3, Steiner 4)

Come on Cowboys, 1937 (Canutt 4)

Come on Danger, 1932 (Musuraca 4)

Come On, George!, 1939 (Dearden 2)

Come On In, 1918 (Emerson 4, Loos 4, Zukor 4)

Come on Leathernecks, 1938 (Cruze 2, Ladd 3)

Come on Marines!, 1934 (Hathaway 2, Lupino 3, Sheridan 3, Prinz 4)

Come on Over, 1922 (Moore 3, Gibbons 4)

Come On, Rangers, 1938 (Rogers 3)

Come Out Fighting, 1945 (Katzman 4)

Come Out of the Kitchen, 1919 (Goodrich 4)

Come Out of the Pantry, 1935 (Buchanan 3, Wray 3)

Come persi la guerra, 1948 (Pinelli 4, Rota 4)

Come Play with Me. See Grazia, zia, 1968

Come See the Paradise, 1990 (Parker 2)

Come September, 1961 (Mulligan 2, Hudson 3, Lollobrigida 3, Bumstead 4, Daniels 4, Salter 4)

Come Take a Trip in My Airship, 1929 (Fleischer 4)

Come Take a Trip in My Airship, 1930 (Fleischer 4)

Come to My House, 1927 (August 4, Fox 4)

Come to the Stable, 1949 (Lanchester 3, Young 3, La Shelle 4, LeMaire 4, Newman 4, Reynolds 4)

Come una rosa al naso, 1976 (Gassman 3)

Come un bambino, 1990 (Risi 2, Gassman 3, Sanda 3)

Come Up Smiling. See Sing Me a Love Song, 1936

Come Up Smiling. See Ants in His Pants, 1939

Comeback, 1970 (Hopkins 3)

Comedians. See Komedianty, 1961

Comédians, 1964 (Brasseur 3)

Comedians. See Comedians in Africa, 1967

Comedians in Africa, 1967 (Burton 3, Gish 3, Guinness 3, Jones 3, Taylor 3, Ustinov 3, Decaë 4, Greene 4)

Comédie!, 1987 (Sarde 4)

Comédie d'amour, 1989 (Trauner 4)

Comedie du bonheur, 1940 (Cocteau 2, L'Herbier 2, Jourdan 3, Novarro 3, Presle 3, Simon 3, Ibert 4)

Comédie Française, 1934 (Fradetal 4)

Comédien, 1948 (Guitry 2)

Comedienne. See Komediantka, 1920

Comédiens ambulants, 1950 (Fernandel 3, Jouvet 3)

Comedy!. See Comédie!, 1987

Comedy Man, 1963 (More 3)

Comedy of Death. See Komedia smerti, 1915

Comedy of Terrors, 1963 (Tourneur 2, Brown 3, Karloff 3, Lorre 3, Price 3, Rathbone 3, Crosby 4)

Comedy Tale of Fanny Hill, 1963 (Cortez 4)

Comedy-Graph. See Binettoscope, 1910

Comenzo a retumbar el Momtombo, 1981 (Alvarez 2)

Come-On, 1956 (Baxter 3, Hayden 3, Haller 4, Head 4)

Comes a Horseman, 1978 (Pakula 2, Caan 3, Fonda 3, Robards 3, Jenkins 4, Willis 4, Winkler 4)

Comet over Broadway, 1938 (Berkeley 2, Crisp 3, Francis 3, Hayward 3, Buckner 4, Howe 4, Orry-Kelly 4)

Cometogether, 1971 (Delli Colli 4)

Comets, 1930 (Lanchester 3)

Comfort and Joy, 1984 (Forsyth 2, Menges 4)

Comfort of Strangers, 1990 (Schrader 2, Pinter 4)

Comic, 1969 (Rooney 3, Wilde 3)

Comic Book Land, 1950 (Terry 4)

Comic Grimacer, 1901 (Hepworth 2)

Comic History of Aviation. See Jak se člověk naučil létat, 1958

Comical Sculpture. See Jodai no chokoku, 1950

Cómicos, 1952 (Rey 3)

Comin' Round the Mountain, 1936 (Autry 3)

Comin' round the Mountain, 1940 (Dreier 4, Head 4)

Comin' Round the Mountain, 1951 (Abbott and Costello 3)

Comin' Thro' the Rye, 1916 (Hepworth 2)

Comin' Thro' the Rye, 1922 (Hepworth 2)

Comin' Through the Rye, 1926 (Fleischer 4)

Coming Home, 1978 (Ashby 2, Dern 3, Fonda 3, Voight 3, Salt 4, Wexler 4)

Coming of Amos, 1925 (Fort 4, Miller 4)

Coming of Angelo, 1913 (Griffith 2, Sweet 3, Bitzer 4)

Coming of Columbus, 1912 (Selig 4)

Coming of the Dial, 1933 (Grierson 2)

Coming of the Law, 1919 (Mix 3)

Coming Out of the Ice, 1982 (Jarre 4)

Coming Out Party, 1934 (Friedhofer 4, Lasky 4, Seitz 4)

Coming Out Party, 1965 (Loach 2)

Coming Through, 1925 (Beery 3)

Coming to America, 1988 (Landis 2, Bellamy 3, Jones 3, Murphy 3, Baker 4)

Coming-Out Party. See Very Important Person, 1961

Comizi d'amore, 1964 (Pasolini 2, Delli Colli 4)

Commancheros, 1961 (Wayne 3)

Command, 1953 (Fuller 2, Tiomkin 4)

Command Decision, 1948 (Wood 2, Gable 3, Johnson 3, Pidgeon 3, Gibbons 4, Gillespie 4, Mayer 4, Rosson 4, Rozsa 4)

Command Performance, 1937 (Pearson 2)

Commandamenti per un gangster, 1968 (Argento 4)

Commander, 1988 (Pleasence 3, Van Cleef 3)

Commander of the Navy. See Flottans överman, 1958

Commanding Officer, 1915 (Dwan 2, Crisp 3)

Commando. See Marcia o crepa, 1963

Commando, 1985 (Schwarzenegger 3)

Commando Attack. See Leopardi di Churchill, 1970

Commando Leopard. See Kommando Leopard, 1985

Commandoes Strike at Dawn, 1943 (Plunkett 4)

Commandos, 1968 (Van Cleef 3, Argento 4)

Commandos Strike at Dawn, 1942 (Gish 3, Muni 3)

Commare secca, 1962 (Pasolini 2)

. . . Comme Icare, 1979 (Morricone 4)

Comme je te veux, 1969 (Braunberger 4)

Comme on fait son lit on se couche, 1903 (Guy 2)

Comme s'il en pleuvait, 1963 (Constantine 3)

Comme un boomerang, 1976 (Delon 3, Vanel 3, Fisher 4)

Comme un poisson dans l'eau, 1962 (Noiret 3, Legrand 4)

Comme un pot de fraises, 1974 (Braunberger 4, Coutard 4)

Comme une carpe, 1932 (Fernandel 3, Prévert 4)

Comme une lettre à la poste, 1938 (Storck 2)

Commencement Day, 1924 (Roach 4)

Comment ça va, 1976 (Godard 2)

Comment épouser un premier ministre, 1964 (Evein 4)

Comment Max fait le tour du monde, 1913 (Linder 3)

Comment monsieur prend son bain, 1903 (Guy 2)

Comment on disperse les foules, 1903 (Guy 2)

Comment on dort á Paris!, 1905 (Guy 2)

Comment qu'elle est!, 1960 (Constantine 3)

Comment reussir dans la vie quand on est con et pleurnichard, 1974 (Audran 3, Braunberger 4)

Comment Yukong déplaça les montagnes, 1976 (Ivens 2)

Commissaire est bon enfant, le gendarme est sans pitie, 1935 (Becker 2)

Commissario, 1962 (Comencini 2, Sordi 3, Age and Scarpelli 4)

Commissario Pepe, 1968 (Scola 2)

Common Cause, 1918 (Blackton 2)

Common Clay, 1919 (Miller 4)

Common Clay, 1930 (Fleming 2, Ayres 3, Fox 4, Furthman 4)

Common Enemy, 1962 (Daniels 3)

Common Ground, 1916 (Rosher 4)

Common Heritage, 1940 (Howard 3)

Common Law, 1923 (Bosworth 3)

Common Law, 1931 (McCrea 3, Mohr 4)

Common Property, 1919 (Moore 3)

Common Scents, 1962 (Hanna and Barbera 4)

Common Sin, 1920 (Haller 4)

Common Threads, 1989 (Hoffman 3)

Common Touch, 1941 (Baxter 2)

Commonwealth, 1967 (Halas and Batchelor 4)

Commotion on the Ocean, 1956 (Three Stooges 3)

Communale, 1965 (Auric 4)

Commune de Paris, 1951 (Kosma 4)

Communicants. See Nattsvardsgästerna, 1963

Communion solennelle, 1976 (Baye 3, Dalio 3)

Communo senso del pudore, 1976 (Cardinale 3, Noiret 3, Sordi 3)

Como, por qué y para qué asesina a un general?, 1971 (Alvarez 2)

Compact, 1910 (White 3)

Compadre Mendoza, 1933 (De Fuentes 2)

Compagni, 1963 (Monicelli 2, Blier 3, Girardot 3, Mastroianni 3, Age and Scarpelli 4, Cristaldi 4, Rotunno 4)

Compagnia dei Matti, 1928 (Amidei 4)

Compagno Don Camillo, 1964 (Comencini 2, Cervi 3)

Compagnons de la marguerite, 1966 (Burel 4)

Compagnons de voyage encombrants, 1903 (Guy 2)

Compañeros. See Vamos a matar, compañeros!, 1970

Companion, 1977 (Friedhofer 4)

Companions in Nightmare, 1968 (Baxter 3, Douglas 3, Herrmann 4)

Company Business, 1991 (Hackman 3, Fisher 4)

Company of Cowards. See Advance to the Rear, 1963

Company of Killers, 1970 (Johnson 3, Milland 3)

Company of Wolves, 1984 (Jordan 2, Lansbury 3, Stamp 3)

Company She Keeps, 1951 (Cromwell 2, Bridges 3, Houseman 4, Musuraca 4)

Comparison of Heights. See Takekurabe, 1955

Compartiment de dames seules, 1934 (Stradling 4)

Compartiment pour dames seules, 1934 (Christian-Jaque 2)

Compartiment tueurs, 1965 (Gélin 3, Montand 3, Piccoli 3, Reggiani 3, Signoret 3, Trintignant 3)

Compassionate Marriage, 1927 (Robinson 4)

Compères, 1983 (Depardieu 3)

Competition, 1915 (Eason 4)

Competition, 1980 (Dreyfuss 3, Remick 3, Schifrin 4)

Compleat Beatles, 1982 (McDowell 3)

Complementos, 1977 (Almodóvar 2)

Complessi, 1965 (Sordi 3, Age and Scarpelli 4)

Completely Different Way of Life, 1971 (Menges 4)

Complicato intrigo di Donne, Vicoli e delitti, 1985 (Wertmüller 2)

Compliments of Mister Flow. See Mister Flow, 1936

Compliments of Mr. Flow. See Mister Flow 1936

Complot petrolero, 1981 (Leduc 2)

Compositeur toqué, 1905 (Méliès 2)

Compressed Hare, 1961 (Blanc 4, Jones 4)

Compromis, 1978 (Blier 3)

Compromised, 1931 (Haller 4, Young 4)

Compromising Positions, 1985 (Sarandon 3)

Comptes à rebours, 1970 (Moreau 3, Reggiani 3, Signoret 3, Vanel 3, Delerue 4)

Comptesse Doddy, 1919 (Negri 3)

Compulsion, 1959 (Welles 2, LeMaire 4, Reynolds 4, Wheeler 4)

Compulsory Husband, 1930 (Launder and Gilliat 2)

Computer Generation, 1973 (Vanderbeek 2)

Computer Glossary, 1967 (Bernstein 4)

Computer Graphics No. 1, 1972 (Emshwiller 2)

Computers. See Komputery, 1967

Comrade X, 1940 (Vidor 2, Arden 3, Gable 3, Homolka 3, Lamarr 3, Adrian 4, Gillespie 4, Hecht 4, Kaper 4, Lederer 4, Mayer 4, Reisch 4, Ruttenberg 4)

Comrades, 1911 (Sennett 2)

Comrades, 1986 (Redgrave 3)

Comrades of 1918. See Westfront 1918, 1930

Comradeship. See **Kameradschaft, 1931**

Comte de Monte-Cristo, 1914 (Modot 3)

Comte de Monte-Cristo, 1942 (Spaak 4)

Comte de Monte-Cristo, 1953 (Marais 3)

Comte de Monte Cristo, 1961 (Jourdan 3, Douy 4)

Comte Kostia, 1925 (Veidt 3)

Comtesse Doddy, 1919 (Kräly 4)

Comtesse Maria, 1928 (Meerson 4)

Comunicados del comité nacional de huelga, 1968 (Leduc 2)

Con Artists, 1981 (Quinn 3)

Con la División del Norte. See Los de abajo, 1940

Con la rabbia agli occhi, 1976 (Brynner 3)

Con los dorados de Pancho Villa, 1939 (Fernández 2, Armendáriz 3)

Con su amable permiso, 1940 (Figueroa 4)

Conan the Barbarian, 1982 (Stone 2, Jones 3, Schwarzenegger 3, Von Sydow 3, De Laurentiis 4)

Conan the Destroyer, 1984 (Schwarzenegger 3, Cardiff 4, De Laurentiis 4)

Concealing a Burglar, 1908 (Griffith 2, Lawrence 3, Bitzer 4)

Concealment. See Secret Bride, 1934

Conceit, 1921 (Costello 3)

Concentratin' Kid, 1930 (Laemmle 4)

Concert. See Koncert, 1961

Concert, 1962 (Borowczyk 2)

Concerto. See I've Always Loved You, 1946

Concerto Brandenbourgeois, 1967 (Braunberger 4, Coutard 4)

Concerto for Sub-Machine Gun. See Koncert za mašinsku pušku, 1958

Concerto in X Minor, 1968 (Kuri 4)

Concerto per pistola solista, 1970 (Valli 3)

Concierge, 1900 (Guy 2)

Concierge revient de suite, 1978 (Guillemot 4)

Concorde affaire, 1979 (Cotten 3)

Concorde—Airport '79, 1979 (Andersson 3, Delon 3, McCambridge 3, Wagner 3, Bumstead 4, Schifrin 4)

Concours de bébés, 1904 (Guy 2)

Concours de boules, 1895 (Lumière 2)

Concrete Cowboys, 1979 (Sangster 4)

Concrete Jungle. See Criminal, 1960

Condamné à mort s'est échappé, 1956 (Straub and Huillet 2, Burel 4)

Condamnés, 1947 (Fresnay 3)

Conde Dracula, 1970 (Kinski 3, Lee 3, Lom 3)

Condemned, 1923 (Furthman 4)

Condemned, 1929 (Colman 3, Barnes 4, Goldwyn 4, Howard 4, Menzies 4, Toland 4)

Condemned Man Escapes. See **Condamné à mort s'est échappé, 1956**

Condemned of Altona. See Sequestrati di Altona, 1962

Condemned to Life. See Life for Ruth, 1962

Condemned Women, 1938 (Musuraca 4, Polglase 4)

Condition of Man, 1980 (Halas and Batchelor 4)

Condominium, 1979 (Bellamy 3)

Condor, 1970 (Cohen 2, De Toth 2, Van Cleef 3, Jarre 4)

Condorman, 1981 (Reed 3, Mancini 4)

Conduct Report on Professor Ishinaka. See Ishinaka-sensei gyojoki datsugoko, 1950

Conduct Unbecoming, 1975 (Attenborough 3, Howard 3, York 3)

Conductor. See Dyrygent, 1979 (Gielgud 3)

Conduisez-moi madame, 1932 (Meerson 4)

Coney Island, 1943 (Grable 3, Day 4, Newman 4, Pan 4, Rose 4, Zanuck 4)

Coney Island, 1950 (Rosenblum 4)

Coney Island Police Patrol Chicken Thief, 1904 (Bitzer 4)

Confederate Honey, 1940 (Blanc 4, Freleng 4, Stalling 4)

Confession, 1920 (Walthall 3)

Confession, 1929 (Barrymore 3)

Confession, 1937 (Crisp 3, Francis 3, Rathbone 3, Blanke 4, Epstein 4, Grot 4, Wallis 4, Orry-Kelly 4)

Confession, 1964 (Gould 3, Rogers 3)

Confession. See Aveu, 1970

Confession, 1986 (Brakhage 2)

Confession de minuit, 1963 (Saulnier 4)

Confessional, 1989 (Quayle 3)

Confessions from the David Galaxy Affair, 1979 (Dors 3)

Confessions of a Co-ed, 1931 (Crosby 3, Sidney 3, Garmes 4)

Confessions of a Driving Instructor, 1975 (Dors 3)

Confessions of a Frustrated Housewife. See Moglie di mio padre, 1976

Confessions of a Nazi Spy, 1939 (Litvak 2, Lukas 3, Robinson 3, Sanders 3, Polito 4, Steiner 4, Warner 4)

Confessions of a Nutzy Spy, 1943 (Blanc 4)

Confessions of a Queen, 1925 (Sjöström 2, Basevi 4, Gibbons 4, Mayer 4)

Confessions of an Opium Eater, 1962 (Price 3, Biroc 4, Lourié 4)

Confessions of Felix Krull. See Bekenntnisse des Hochstaplers Felix Krull, 1957

Confessions of Gynecologist. See Aru fujinkai no kokuhaku, 1950

Confessions of Winifred Wagner. See Winifred Wagner und die Geschichte des Hauses Wahnfried von 1914–1975, 1975

Confetti, 1927 (Buchanan 3)

Confidence, 1909 (Griffith 2, Lawrence 3, Bitzer 4)

Confidence, 1922 (Laemmle 4)

Confidence, 1933 (Lantz 4)

Confidence. See Bizalom, 1979

Confidence Girl, 1952 (Clothier 4)

Confidences d'un piano, 1957 (Decaë 4)

Conversations with Willard Van Dyke, 1981 (Ivens 2, Copland 4)

Conversion d'Irma, 1913 (Feuillade 2)

Conversion of Ferdys Pistora. See Obrácení Ferdyše Pištory, 1931

Conversion of Frosty Blake, 1915 (Hart 3, August 4, Sullivan 4)

Conversion of Smiling Tom, 1915 (Mix 3)

Convert. See Conversion of Frosty Blake, 1915

Convert of San Clemente, 1911 (Bosworth 3)

Converts, 1910 (Griffith 2, Walthall 2, Bitzer 4)

Convict 993, 1918 (Miller 4)

Convict 99, 1938 (Launder and Gilliat 2, Hay 4, McDowall 3, Withers 3, Rank 4, Vetchinsky 4)

Convict Thirteen, 1920 (Keaton 2)

Convicted, 1938 (Hayworth 3)

Convicted, 1950 (Crawford 3, Ford 3, Malone 3, Duning 4, Guffey 4)

Convicted Woman, 1940 (Ford 3)

Convicts, 1962 (Steiger 3)

Convicts, 1988 (Duvall 3)

Convict's Daughter, 1910 (White 3)

Convicts Four, 1962 (Crawford 3, Price 3, Biroc 4, Rosenman 4)

Convict's Sacrifice, 1909 (Griffith 2, Walthall 3, Bitzer 4)

Convict's Threat, 1915 (Anderson 3)

Convoy, 1927 (Haller 4)

Convoy, 1940 (Granger 3, Balcon 4)

Convoy, 1978 (Peckinpah 2, Borgnine 3, Coburn 3)

Conway the Kerry Dancer, 1912 (Olcott 2)

Coocoo Murder Case, 1931 (Iwerks 4)

Coo-Coo Nut Grove, 1936 (Freleng 4, Stalling 4)

Coo-Coo the Magician, 1933 (Iwerks 4)

Coogan's Bluff, 1968 (Siegel 2, Cobb 3, Eastwood 3, Schifrin 4)

Cook, 1918 (Keaton 2, Arbuckle 3)

Cook and Peary: The Race to the North Pole, 1983 (Steiger 3)

Cook of Canyon Camp, 1917 (Crisp 3)

Cook, the Thief, His Wife and Her Lover, 1989 (Greenaway 2, Vierny 4)

Cooked Trails, 1916 (Mix 3)

Cookery Nook, 1951 (Terry-Thomas 3)

Cookie, 1989 (Seidelman 2, Falk 3)

Cool Cat, 1967 (Blanc 4)

Cool Hand Luke, 1967 (Hopper 3, Newman 3, Stanton 3, Hall 4, Schifrin 4)

Cool of the Day, 1962 (Finch 3)

Cool Ones, 1967 (McDowall 3, Cahn 4, Crosby 4)

Cool World, 1964 (Clarke 2, Wiseman 2)

Coonskin, 1975 (Bakshi 4, Fraker 4)

Coolie, 1983 (Bachchan 3)

Cooperativas agrícolas, 1959 (Gómez 2)

Cooperativas agropecurias, 1960 (Almendros 4)

Cop, 1928 (Garnett 2, Crisp 3, Miller 4)

Cop. See Ripoux, 1984

Cop au Vin. See Poulet au vinaigre, 1985

Cop Fools the Sergeant, 1904 (Porter 2)

Cop Killer. See Order of Death, 1983

Cop or Hood. See Flic ou voyou, 1979

Cop 2. See Ripoux contre Ripoux, 1990

Copacabana, 1947 (Marx brothers 3, Miranda 3, Glennon 4)

Copacabana Palace, 1962 (Amidei 4)

Copain suavé sa peau, 1967 (Blier 3)

Copains, 1964 (Noiret 3)

Copains du dimanche, 1958 (Belmondo 3, Piccoli 3)

Copenhagen, 1956 (Carreras 4)

Copenhagen Ballet, 1960 (Robinson 4)

Copie conforme, 1946 (Jouvet 3, Jeanson 4)

Coplan ouverte le feu à Mexico, 1967 (Tavernier 2)

Coplan sauve sa peau, 1967 (Kinski 3)

Cop-Out. See Stranger in the House, 1967

Copper Canyon, 1950 (Lamarr 3, Milland 3, Dreier 4, Head 4, Lang 4)

Copper Coin King. See Doka o, 1926

Copperhead, 1920 (Barrymore 3)

Coppie, 1970 (Monicelli 2, Sordi 3, Vitti 3, Zavattini 4)

Cops, 1922 (Keaton 2, Schenck 4)

Cops. See When Comedy was King, 1960

Cops and Robbers. See Guardie e ladri, 1951

Cops and Robbers, 1973 (Legrand 4)

Cops and Robin, 1978 (Borgnine 3)

Cops Is a Business, 1910 (White 3)

Cops Is Always Right, 1938 (Fleischer 4)

Copy Cat, 1941 (Fleischer 4)

Coq du regiment, 1933 (Fernandel 3)

Coquecigrole, 1932 (Darrieux 3, D'Eaubonne 4)

Coquette, 1929 (Beavers 3, Pickford 3, Berlin 4, Menzies 4, Struss 4)

Coquette's Suitors, 1910 (Lawrence 3)

Coquille et le clergyman, 1927 (Artaud 3)

Cor, 1931 (Epstein 2)

Coraggio, 1955 (Cervi 3, De Laurentiis 4)

Coraje del pueblo, 1971 (Sanjinés 2)

Coralie et Cie, 1933 (Cavalcanti 2, Rosay 3, Burel 4, D'Eaubonne 4)

Corazón bandolero, 1934 (Fernández 2)

Corazón de la noche, 1983 (Hermosillo 2, Figueroa 4)

Corazón salvaje, 1968 (Figueroa 4)

Corazón sobre la tierra, 1985 (Villagra 3)

Corbeau, 1943 (Clouzot 2, Fresnay 3, Andrejew 4, Fleischer 4, Warm 4)

Corbeille enchantée, 1903 (Méliès 2)

Corbusier, l'architecte du bonheur, 1956 (Delerue 4)

Cord of Life, 1909 (Griffith 2, Bitzer 4)

Corde raide, 1960 (Girardot 3, Jarre 4)

Cordon-bleu, 1931 (Feuillère 3)

Corinthian Jack, 1921 (McLaglen 3)

Coriolan, 1950 (Cocteau 2)

Cork and Vicinity, 1912 (Bunny 3)

Corky, 1972 (Johnson 3, McDowall 3, Willis 4)

Corleone, 1978 (Cardinale 3, Morricone 4)

Corleone, 1985 (Cardinale 3)

Corn Is Green, 1945 (Davis 3, Friedhofer 4, Orry-Kelly 4, Polito 4, Robinson 4, Steiner 4)

Corn Is Green, 1979 (Cukor 2, Hepburn 3, Barry 4, Dillon 4, Slocombe 4)

Corn on the Cop, 1965 (Blanc 4)

Corn Plastered, 1951 (Blanc 4, McKimson 4, Stalling 4)

Corne d'or, 1963 (Delerue 4)

Corner in Colleens, 1916 (Sullivan 4)

Corner in Cotton, 1916 (Loos 4)

Corner in Hats, 1914 (Browning 2, Loos 4)

Corner in Water, 1916 (Mix 3)

Corner in Wheat, 1909 (Griffith 2, Sweet 3, Walthall 3, Bitzer 4, Macpherson 4)

Corner of Great Tokyo. See Dai-Tokyo no ikkaku, 1930

Corner Pocket, 1921 (Roach 4)

Cornered, 1932 (Eason 4)

Cornered, 1945 (Dmytryk 2, Powell 3, D'Agostino 4, Paxton 4)

Cornet, 1955 (Rasp 3, Reisch 4)

Corniaud, 1964 (Decaë 4, Delerue 4)

Corny Casanovas, 1952 (Three Stooges 3)

Corny Concerto, 1943 (Blanc 4, Clampett 4, Stalling 4)

Corona di ferro, 1940 (Castellani 2, Cervi 3)

Corona negra, 1950 (Brazzi 3, Félix 3, Gassman 4)

Coronación, 1975 (Figueroa 4)

Coronado, 1935 (Mcleod 2, Prinz 4)

Coronation of Edward VII. See Sacré d'Édouard VII, 1902

Coronation of King Edward VII, 1901 (Hepworth 2)

Coronation Parade, 1953 (Hathaway 2, Clarke 4)

Coroner Creek, 1948 (Scott 3, Brown 4)

Corot, 1965 (Leenhardt 2)

Corpi presentano tracce di violenza carnale, 1973 (Ponti 4)

Corpo. See Take This—My Body, 1974

Corpo d'amore, 1971 (Storaro 4)

Corporal Kate, 1926 (Sullivan 4)

Corporation and the Ranch Girl, 1911 (Anderson 3)

Corps célestes, 1973 (Sarde 4)

Corps de Diane, 1969 (Moreau 3)

Corps de mon ennemi, 1976 (Belmondo 3, Blier 3, Audiard 4, Lai 4)

Corps et biens, 1986 (Darrieux 3, Léaud 3, Sanda 3)

Corpse Came C.O.D., 1947 (Blondell 3, Duning 4)

Corpse Vanished. See Revenge of the Zombies, 1944

Corpse Vanishes, 1942 (Lugosi 3, Katzman 4)

Corregidor, 1943 (Ulmer 2)

Correva l'anno di grazio 1870 . . . , 1972 (Morricone 4)

Corri uomo corri, 1968 (Morricone 4)

Corrida d'hier et d'aujourd'hui, 1965 (Braunberger 4)

Corridor of Mirrors, 1948 (Lee 3, Auric 4, Rank 4)

Corridors of Blood, 1963 (Karloff 3, Lee 3)

Corriere del re, 1947 (Brazzi 3)

Corrupcion de Chris Miller, 1973 (Bardem 2, Seberg 3)

Corruption. See Going Straight, 1916

Corruption, 1968 (Cushing 3)

Corruption in the Halls of Justice. See Corruzione al palazzo di giustizia, 1975

Corruption of Chris Miller. See Corrupcion de Chris Miller, 1973

Corruzione, 1963 (Fusco 4)

Corruzione al palazzo di giustizia, 1975 (Donaggio 4)

Corsair, 1931 (Newman 4)

Corsaire, 1939 (Dalio 3, Jourdan 3)

Corsaire, 1983 (Thulin 3)

Corsario negro, 1944 (Armendáriz 3, Figueroa 4)

Corsaro, 1924 (Gallone 2)

Corsican Brothers. See Frères corses, 1939

Corsican Brothers, 1941 (Estabrook 4, Plunkett 4, Stradling 4, Tiomkin 4)

Corsican Brothers, 1985 (Chaplin 3, Pleasence 3)

Corso rouge, 1913 (Tourneur 2)

Corta notte della bambole di vetro, 1971 (Morricone 4)

Cortili, 1947 (Risi 2)

Corvette K-225, 1943 (Fitzgerald 3, Mitchum 3, Scott 3, Gaudio 4)

Corvette Port Arthur. See Alarme!, 1943

Coryphee, 1914 (Lawrence 3)

Cosa avete fatto a Solange, 1972 (Morricone 4)

Cosa buffa, 1973 (Morricone 4)

Cosa Nostra, An Arch Enemy of the F.B.I., 1967 (Duvall 3, Pidgeon 3)

Cosacchi, 1959 (Fusco 4)

Cose da pazzi, 1953 (Pabst 2, Fabrizi 3)

Cose dell'altro mondo, 1939 (Amidei 4)

Cose di Cosa Nostra, 1970 (De Sica 2, Fabrizi 3)

Cosi come sei, 1978 (Lattuada 2, Kinski 3, Mastroianni 3, Morricone 4)

Cosi dolce cosi perversa, 1969 (Baker 3, Trintignant 3)

Cosi fan tutte, 1970 (Stallich 4)

Cosmic Man, 1959 (Carradine 3)

Cosmic Ray, 1958 (Conner 2)

Cossacks, 1928 (Gilbert 3, Gibbons 4, Marion 4)

Cossacks Across the Danube. See Zaporosch Sa Dunayem, 1938

Cossacks in Exile. See Zaporosch Sa Dunayem, 1938

Costa azzurra, 1959 (Sordi 3)

Costanza della ragione, 1964 (Deneuve 3)

Coster Bill of Paris. See Crainquebille, 1933

Costly Exchange, 1915 (Browning 2)

Costumi e bellezze d'Italia, 1948 (Risi 2)

Côte d'Adam, 1963 (Grimault 4)

Côte d'Azur, 1948 (Leenhardt 2)

Coton, 1935 (Storck 2)

Cottage to Let, 1941 (Mills 3, Sim 3, De Grunwald 4, Rank 4, Vetchinsky 4)

Cotton Club, 1984 (Coppola 2, Gere 3, Hoskins 3, Barry 4, Sylbert 4)

Couch, 1961 (Edwards 2)

Couch, 1964 (Warhol 2)

Couch Trip, 1988 (Matthau 3)

Coucher d'une Parisienne, 1900 (Guy 2)

Coucher d'Yvette, 1897 (Guy 2)

Coucher d'Yvette et Pierreuse, 1897 (Pathé 4)

Cough and Sneeze. See Kǎslání a kýchani, 1950

Could I But Live. See Ware hitotsubu no mugi naredo, 1965

Couldn't Possibly Happen. See Phantom Empire, 1935

Couleur chair, 1978 (Hopper 3, Ullmann 3)

Couleur de feu, 1957 (Storck 2)

Couleur de temps. See Démons de midi, 1978

Couleur du vent, 1988 (Sarde 4)

Couleurs de Venise, 1945 (Aldo 4)

Coulomb's Law, 1959 (Leacock 2)

Council Bluffs to Omaha—Train Scenic, 1900 (Bitzer 4)

Counsel for the Defense, 1912 (Costello 3, Talmadge 3)

Counsel on De Fence, 1934 (Langdon 3)

Counsellor-at-Law, 1933 (Wyler 2, Barrymore 3, Daniels 3, Douglas 3, Mandell 4)

Counsel's Opinion, 1933 (Dwan 2, Korda 4)

Count, 1916 (Chaplin 2, Purviance 3)

Count and the Cowboys, 1911 (Anderson 3)

Count Down Clown, 1960 (Hanna and Barbera 4)

Count Downe. See Son of Dracula, 1974

Count Dracula. See Conde Dracula, 1970

Count Dracula and his Vampire Bride. See Satanic Rites of Dracula, 1973

Count Dracula and his Vampire Brides. See Satanic Rites of Dracula, 1973

Count of Monk's Bridge. See Munkbrogreven, 1934

Count of Monte Cristo, 1908 (Selig 4)

Count of Monte Cristo, 1913 (Porter 2, Bosworth 3, Zukor 4)

Count of Monte Cristo, 1934 (Calhern 3, Donat 3, Dunne 4, Newman 4)

Count of Monte Cristo. See Comte de Monte Cristo, 1961

Count of Monte Cristo, 1975 (Curtis 3, Howard 3, Jourdan 3, Pleasence 3)

Count of Ten, 1928 (Laemmle 4, Miller 4)

Count Takes the Count, 1935 (Roach 4)

Count the Hours, 1953 (Siegel 2, Wright 3, Alton 4)

Count the Votes, 1919 (Daniels 3, Lloyd 3)

Count Three and Pray, 1955 (Woodward 3, Duning 4, Guffey 4)

Count Vim's Last Exercise, 1967 (Weir 2)

Count Your Blessings, 1959 (Negulesco 2, Brazzi 3, Chevalier 3, Kerr 3, Folsey 4, Krasner 4, Rose 4, Waxman 4)

Count Your Change, 1919 (Daniels 3, Lloyd 3, Roach 4)

Countdown, 1967 (Altman 2, Caan 3, Duvall 3, Rosenman 4)

Countdown. See Comptes à rebours, 1970

Counter Jumper, 1922 (Laurel and Hardy 3)

Counter-Attack, 1945 (Muni 3, Howe 4)

Counter-Espionage, 1942 (Dmytryk 2)

Counterfeit, 1919 (Miller 4)

Counterfeit, 1936 (Schulberg 4)

Counterfeit Cat, 1949 (Avery 4)

Counterfeit Constable. See Allez France, 1966

Counterfeit Killer, 1968 (McCambridge 3, Jones 4)

Counterfeit Lady, 1937 (Bellamy 3)

Counterfeit Traitor, 1962 (Dahlbeck 3, Holden 3, Kinski 3, Newman 4)

Counterfeiter, 1913 (Ince 4)

Counterfeiter Traitor, 1962 (Head 4)

Counterfeiters, 1914 (Lawrence 3)

Counterfeiters of Paris. See Cave se rebiffe, 1961

Counterforce. See Escuadron, 1988

Counterplan. See Vstrechnyi, 1932

Counterplot, 1959 (Struss 4)

Counterpoint, 1968 (Heston 3, Schell 3, Kaper 4, Metty 4, Whitlock 4)

Countess, 1914 (Bushman 3)

Countess Betty's Mine, 1914 (Reid 3)

Countess Charming, 1917 (Crisp 3)

Countess Donelli. See Gräfin Donelli, 1924

Countess Dracula, 1971 (Carreras 4)

Countess from Hong Kong, 1967 (Chaplin 2, Brando 3, Chaplin 3, Loren 3, Rutherford 3, Ponti 4)

Countess from Podskali. See Hrabĕnka z Podskalí, 1926

Countess of Monte Cristo, 1934 (Lukas 3, Wray 3, Freund 4, Laemmle 4)

Countess of Monte Cristo, 1948 (Henie 3, Cronjager 4, Reisch 4)

Countess Sweedie, 1914 (Beery 3)

Countless Families, 1953 (Lee 3)

Country, 1984 (Greenwood 3, Lange 3, Shepard 4)

Country Beyond, 1926 (Fox 4)

Country Beyond, 1936 (Trotti 4)

Country Boy, 1915 (De Mille 2)

Country Boy, 1934 (Freleng 4)

Country Boy, 1966 (Fields 4)

Country Bumpkin. See All American Chump, 1936

Country Chairman, 1914 (Dwan 2)

Country Comes to Town, 1931 (Grierson 2, Wright 2)

Country Courtship, 1905 (Bitzer 4)

Country Cupid, 1911 (Griffith 2, Bitzer 4)

Country Dance, 1969 (Cusack 3, O'Toole 3, York 3, Addison 4)

Country Doctor, 1909 (Griffith 2, Lawrence 3, Pickford 3, Bitzer 4)

Country Doctor, 1927 (Adrian 4, Grot 4)

Country Doctor, 1936 (King 2, Darwell 3, Johnson 4, Levien 4, Seitz 4, Zanuck 4)

Country Doctor. See Fundoshi isha, 1960

Country Fair, 1934 (Lantz 4)

Country Flapper, 1922 (Goodrich 4)

Country Girl, 1954 (Crosby 3, Holden 3, Kelly 3, Alton 4, Head 4, Young 4)

Country Hero, 1917 (Keaton 2, Arbuckle 3)

Country Lovers, 1911 (Sennett 2, Sweet 3)

Country Mouse, 1914 (Bosworth 3)

Country Mouse, 1935 (Freleng 4)

Country Mouse and the City Mouse, 1921 (Terry 4)

Country Music Holiday, 1958 (Rosenblum 4)

Country Music U.S.A. See Las Vegas Hillbillies, 1966

Country of Bells. See Paese dei campanelli, 1953

Country School, 1931 (Lantz 4)

Country Schoolmaster, 1906 (Bitzer 4)

Country Store, 1937 (Lantz 4)

Country That God Forgot, 1916 (Neilan 2)

Country Town, 1944 (Alwyn 4)

Countrywomen, 1942 (Alwyn 4)

Counts of Pocci—Some Chapters Towards the History of a Family. See Grafen Pocci—Einige Kapitel zur Geschichte einer Familie, 1967

County Chairman, 1935 (Rooney 3, Mohr 4)

County Fair, 1920 (Tourneur 2)

County Fair, 1932 (Bosworth 3)

County Fair, 1950 (Mirisch 4)

County Hospital, 1932 (Laurel and Hardy 3, Roach 4)

Coup de bambou, 1962 (Presle 3, Matras 4)

Coup de berger, 1956 (Chabrol 2, Godard 2, Rivette 2, Straub and Huillet 2, Braunberger 4)

Coup de foudre, 1976 (Deneuve 3, Noiret 3)

Coup de foudre, 1983 (Huppert 3)

Coup de grâce, 1965 (Darrieux 3, Piccoli 3)

Coup de Jarnac, 1909 (Cohl 4)

Coup de roulis, 1931 (D'Eaubonne 4)

Coup de téléphone, 1931 (Lourié 4, Meerson 4, Spaak 4)

Coup de torchon, 1981 (Tavernier 2, Audran 3, Huppert 3, Noiret 3, Aurenche 4, Sarde 4, Trauner 4)

Coup du fakir, 1915 (Feuillade 2, Musidora 3)

Coup du parapluie, 1980 (Decaë 4)

Coup pur pour rien, 1970 (Braunberger 4)

Coupable, 1936 (Barsacq 4, Ibert 4)

Coupe de Ville, 1990 (Arkin 3)

Coupe franche, 1989 (Reggiani 3)
Couple, 1951 (Zhao 3)
Couple, 1960 (Schüfftan 4)
Couple idéal, 1945 (Cayatte 2, Signoret 3, Renoir 4)
Couple Takes a Wife, 1972 (Loy 3)
Couple témoin, 1977 (Constantine 3)
Couples and Robbers, 1981 (Menges 4)
Couple's Drum. *See* Meoto daiko, 1941
Coups de feu à l'aube, 1932 (Artaud 3, Modot 3)
Cour des miracles, 1902 (Guy 2)
Courage, 1921 (Menjou 3)
Courage, 1986 (Loren 3)
Courage for Every Day, 1989 (Menzel 2)
Courage for Everyday. *See* Každý den odvahu, 1964
Courage, fuyons, 1980 (Deneuve 3)
Courage Mountain, 1989 (Caron 3)
Courage of Black Beauty, 1957 (Leven 4)
Courage of Lassie, 1946 (Taylor 3, Irene 4, Kaper 4)
Courage of Marge O'Doone, 1919 (Karloff 3)
Courage of the West, 1937 (Lewis 2)
Courageous Coward, 1919 (Hayakawa 3)
Courageous Dr. Christian, 1940 (Alton 4, Lardner 4)
Courageous Mr. Penn. *See* Penn of Pennsylvania, 1942
Coureurs de brousse, 1956 (Decaë 4)
Courier of Lyons. *See* Affaire du courrier de Lyon, 1937
Courier to the Tsar. *See* Strogoff, 1968
Couronnes, 1909 (Cohl 4)
Courrier Sud, 1936 (Bresson 2, Vanel 3, Barsacq 4, Ibert 4)
Cours après moi que je t'attrape, 1976 (Girardot 3)
Cours de route. *See* Utközben, 1979
Cours d'une vie, 1966 (Delerue 4)
Cours privé, 1986 (Sarde 4)
Course a l'abîme, 1915 (Feuillade 2)
Course à l'échalotte, 1975 (Decaë 4)
Course au petrole, 1938 (Leenhardt 2)
Course au potiron, 1906 (Feuillade 2)
Course aux millions, 1912 (Feuillade 2)
Course aux potirons, 1907 (Carré 4)
Course des belles-mères, 1907 (Feuillade 2, Gaumont 4)
Course de taureaux, 1951 (Braunberger 4, Decaë 4)
Course de taureaux à Nîmes, 1906 (Guy 2)
Course du lièvre à travers les champs, 1971 (Ryan 3, Trintignant 3, Lai 4)
Course en sac, 1895 (Lumière 2)
Courses d'obstacles, 1957 (Delerue 4)
Court House Crooks, 1915 (Sennett 2)
Court Intrigue. *See* Hofintrige, 1912
Court Jester, 1956 (Carradine 3, Kaye 3, Lansbury 3, Rathbone 3, Cahn 4, Frank 4, Head 4)
Court Martial, 1928 (Walker 4)
Court Martial. *See* Carrington, V.C., 1954
Court Martial of Billy Mitchell, 1955 (Bellamy 3, Cooper 3, Steiger 3, Tiomkin 4)
Courte échelle, 1897 (Guy 2)
Courte tête, 1956 (Audiard 4)
Courtes Jambes, 1938 (Dalio 3)
Courtesans of Bombay, 1982 (Ivory 2, Jhabvala 4)
Courtin' of Calliope Clew, 1916 (Borzage 2)
Courtin' Wildcats, 1929 (Laemmle 4)

Courting of Mary, 1911 (Pickford 3)
Courting Trouble, 1932 (Sennett 2)
Court-Martialled, 1915 (Hepworth 2)
Courtneys of Curzon Street, 1947 (Wilcox 2, Neagle 3)
Courtroom, 1967 (Warhol 2)
Courtship of Andy Hardy, 1942 (Reed 3, Rooney 3)
Courtship of Eddie's Father, 1963 (Minnelli 2, Ford 3, Krasner 4, Pasternak 4, Rose 4)
Courtship of Miles Sandwich, 1923 (Roach 4)
Courtship of Miles Standish, 1910 (Bosworth 3)
Courtship of Miles Standish, 1923 (Johnson 3)
Courtship of O San, 1914 (Ince 4)
Courtship of O'Sann. *See* O Mimi san, 1914
Courtship of the Newt, 1938 (Benchley 4)
Cousin Angelica. *See* Prima Angélica, 1974
Cousin cousine, 1975 (Guillemot 4)
Cousin de Callao, 1962 (Delerue 4)
Cousin Pons, 1923 (Modot 3)
Cousin Wilbur, 1939 (Roach 4)
Cousins, 1959 (Broca 2, Chabrol 2, Audran 3, Decaë 4, Evein 4, Gégauff 4, Rabier 4, Saulnier 4)
Couteau dans la plaie, 1962 (Loren 3, Perkins 3, Alekan 4, Theodorakis 4, Trauner 4)
Couteaux tirés, 1962 (Dalio 3)
Couturier de ces dames, 1956 (Fernandel 3)
Couturière de Linevile, 1931 (Maté 4)
Covenant with Death, 1967 (Hackman 3, Burks 4, Rosenman 4)
Cover Girl, 1944 (Donen 2, Vidor 2, Arden 3, Hayworth 3, Kelly 3, Banton 4, Cohn 4, Cole 4, Guffey 4, Maté 4)
Cover Girl Models, 1975 (Corman 2)
Cover Me, Babe, 1970 (Smith 4)
Cover to Cover, 1936 (Rotha 2)
Cover Up, 1984 (Jourdan 3)
Covered Pushcart, 1949 (Terry 4)
Covered Wagon, 1923 (Arzner 2, Cruze 2, Brown 4, Lasky 4, Zukor 4)
Covered Wagon, 1933 (Rooney 3)
Covert Action. *See* Sono stato un'agente CIA, 1978
Cover-Up, 1949 (Bendix 3, Laszlo 4, Salter 4)
Cover-Up. *See* Crime, 1983
Cow and I. *See* Vache et le prisonnier, 1959
Cow Country, 1953 (O'Brien 3)
Cow on the Moon. *See* Krava na mjescu, 1959
Cow Town, 1950 (Autry 3)
Coward, 1911 (Dwan 2, White 3)
Coward, 1915 (August 4, Ince 4, Sullivan 4)
Coward. *See* Zbabělec, 1962
Coward and the Holy Man. *See* Kapurush-o-Mahapurush, 1965
Coward and the Saint. *See* Kapurush-o-Mahapurush, 1965
Cowboy, 1958 (Daves 2, Ford 3, Lemmon 3, Bass 4, Duning 4, Trumbo 4)
Cowboy, 1985 (Sarde 4)
Cowboy and the Artist, 1911 (Dwan 2)
Cowboy and the Blonde, 1941 (Clarke 4, Day 4)
Cowboy and the Countess, 1926 (Fox 4)
Cowboy and the Girl. *See* Lady Takes a Chance, 1943
Cowboy and the Indians, 1949 (Autry 3)

Cowboy and the Lady, 1922 (Johnson 3)
Cowboy and the Lady, 1938 (McCarey 2, Brennan 3, Cooper 3, Oberon 3, Basevi 4, Behrman 4, Day 4, Goldwyn 4, Levien 4, Newman 4, Toland 4)
Cowboy and the Outlaw, 1911 (Dwan 2)
Cowboy and the Senorita, 1944 (Rogers 3)
Cowboy and the Squaw, 1910 (Anderson 3)
Cowboy Commandos, 1943 (Bond 3)
Cowboy Cop, 1926 (Arthur 3)
Cowboy Coward, 1911 (Anderson 3)
Cowboy from Brooklyn, 1938 (Bacon 2, Powell 3, Reagan 3, Sheridan 3, Deutsch 4, Edeson 4, Mercer 4, Wallis 4)
Cowboy in Manhattan, 1943 (Salter 4)
Cowboy Jimmy, 1957 (Mimica 4, Vukotić 4)
Cowboy Kid, 1928 (Fox 4, Miller 4)
Cowboy Quarterback, 1939 (McCord 4)
Cowboy Samaritan, 1913 (Anderson 3)
Cowboy Serenade, 1942 (Autry 3)
Cowboy Sheik, 1924 (Rogers 3, Roach 4)
Cowboy Socialist, 1911 (Dwan 2)
Cowboys, 1971 (Dern 3, Wayne 3, Ravetch 4, Surtees 4, Williams 4)
Cowboys Cry for It, 1923 (Laurel and Hardy 3)
Cowboy's Deliverance, 1911 (Dwan 2)
Cow-boys français, 1953 (Decaë 4)
Cowboys from Texas, 1939 (Canutt 4)
Cowboy's Mother-in-Law, 1910 (Anderson 3)
Cowboy's Ruse, 1911 (Dwan 2)
Cowboy's Sweetheart, 1910 (Anderson 3)
Cowboy's Vindication, 1910 (Anderson 3)
Cowcatcher's Daughter, 1931 (Sennett 2)
Cowgirls, 1986 (Dunaway 3)
Cowpuncher's Law, 1911 (Anderson 3)
Cowpuncher's Peril, 1916 (Mix 3)
Cowpuncher's Ward, 1910 (Anderson 3)
Cow's Husband, 1931 (Fleischer 4)
Cow's Kimono, 1926 (Roach 4)
Coy Decoy, 1941 (Blanc 4, Clampett 4, Stalling 4)
Crabe-Tambour, 1977 (Coutard 4, De Beauregard 4, Sarde 4)
Crack in the Mirror, 1960 (Welles 2, D'Eaubonne 4, Jarre 4, Zanuck 4)
Crack in the World, 1965 (Andrews 3, Lourié 4)
Crack o' Dawn, 1925 (Garmes 4)
Crack Your Heels, 1919 (Daniels 3, Lloyd 3, Roach 4)
Cracked Ice Man, 1933 (Roach 4)
Cracked Nuts, 1931 (Karloff 3, Musuraca 4, Steiner 4)
Cracked Quack, 1952 (Blanc 4, Freleng 4, Stalling 4)
Cracked Wedding Bells, 1920 (Roach 4)
Cracker Factory, 1979 (Wood 3)
Crackerjack, 1938 (Rank 4)
Crackers, 1984 (Malle 2, Sutherland 3, Kovacs 4)
Crackpot King, 1946 (Terry 4)
Crackpot Quail, 1941 (Avery 4, Blanc 4, Stalling 4)
Cracks, 1968 (Delerue 4)
Cracksman, 1963 (Sanders 3)
Cracksman Santa Claus, 1913 (Reid 3)
Crack-Up, 1937 (Lorre 3)
Crack-Up, 1946 (Marshall 3, Trevor 3, Paxton 4)
Cradle, 1922 (Rosson 4)
Cradle of Courage, 1920 (Hart 3, Hayakawa 3, August 4)

Cradle of Genius, 1959 (Rotha 2, Fitzgerald 3)

Cradle Robbers, 1924 (Roach 4)

Cradle Snatchers, 1927 (Hawks 2, Pangborn 3, Fox 4)

Cradle Song, 1933 (Leisen 2, Head 4, Lang 4)

Craig's Wife, 1936 (Arzner 2, Darwell 3, Russell 3, Ballard 4)

Crainquebille, 1922 (Feyder 2, Rosay 3)

Crainquebille, 1933 (Modot 3)

Cranes Are Flying. See Letyat zhuravli, 1957

Cranks at Work, 1960 (Russell 2)

Crash, 1928 (McCord 4)

Crash, 1932 (Dieterle 2, Haller 4, Orry-Kelly 4)

Crash, 1976 (Carradine 3, Ferrer 3)

Crash Dive, 1943 (Andrews 3, Baxter 3, Power 3, Burnett 4, Day 4, Shamroy 4, Swerling 4)

Crash Donovan, 1936 (Bond 3, Krasner 4)

Crash Goes the Hash, 1944 (Three Stooges 3)

Crash Landing, 1958 (Katzman 4)

Crash of Silence. See Mandy, 1952

Crashing Hollywood, 1931 (Arbuckle 3, Grable 3)

Crashing Hollywood, 1938 (Musuraca 4)

Crashout, 1955 (Bendix 3, Kennedy 3, Metty 4)

Craven, 1915 (Reid 3)

Crawling Eye. See Trollenberg Terror, 1958

Crawlspace, 1971 (Kennedy 3, Wright 3, Goldsmith 4)

Crawlspace, 1986 (Kinski 3, Donaggio 4)

Crayono, 1907 (Bitzer 4)

Craze, 1974 (Dors 3, Evans 3, Howard 3, Palance 3, Francis 4)

Crazed Fruit. See Kurutta kajitsu, 1956

Crazy Composer. See Compositeur toqué, 1905

Crazy Cruise, 1942 (Avery 4, Blanc 4, Clampett 4, Maltese 4, Stalling 4)

Crazy Desire. See Voglia matta, 1962

Crazy Feet, 1929 (Roach 4)

Crazy for Love. See Trou normand, 1952

Crazy Gang Argue About Lending Money, 1941 (Crazy Gang 3)

Crazy House, 1928 (Roach 4)

Crazy House, 1940 (Lantz 4)

Crazy House, 1943 (Pangborn 3, Rathbone 3, Three Stooges 3, Cahn 4)

Crazy House. See House in Nightmare Park, 1973

Crazy Joe, 1974 (Wallach 3)

Crazy Knights, 1944 (Katzman 4)

Crazy Like a Fox, 1926 (McCarey 2, Laurel and Hardy 3, Roach 4)

Crazy Mama, 1975 (Corman 2, Demme 2)

Crazy Mixed-Up Pup, 1954 (Avery 4)

Crazy People, 1990 (Moore 3)

Crazy Prospector, 1913 (Anderson 3)

Crazy Quilt, 1966 (Meredith 3)

Crazy That Way, 1930 (Bennett 3, Fox 4)

Crazy to Act, 1927 (Laurel and Hardy 3, Sennett 2)

Crazy to Marry, 1921 (Cruze 2, Arbuckle 3, Brown 4)

Crazy Town, 1932 (Fleischer 4)

Crazy World, 1968 (Kuri 4)

Crazy World of Laurel and Hardy, 1967 (Roach 4)

Crazylegs, 1953 (Miller 4)

Cream Puff Romance, 1916 (Sennett 2, Arbuckle 3)

Creation, 1979 (Brakhage 2)

Creation, 1982 (Vinton 4)

Création d'ulcères artificiels chez le chien, 1934 (Storck 2)

Creation of the Humanoids, 1962 (Mohr 4, Pierce 4)

Creator, 1985 (Passer 2, O'Toole 3)

Creature. See Titan Find, 1984

Creature from the Black Lagoon, 1954 (Mancini 4, Salter 4, Westmore Family 4)

Creature from the Haunted Sea, 1960 (Corman 2)

Creature Walks Among Us, 1956 (Mancini 4, Salter 4, Westmore Family 4)

Creature with the Atom Brain, 1955 (Siodmak 4)

Creature with the Blue Hand. See Blaue Hand, 1967

Créatures, 1966 (Varda 2, Dahlbeck 3, Deneuve 3, Piccoli 3)

Creatures of the Prehistoric Planet. See Horror of the Blood Monsters, 1970

Creatures of the Red Planet. See Horror of the Blood Monsters, 1970

Creatures the World Forgot, 1971 (Carreras 4)

Credo ou La Tragédie de Lourdes, 1924 (Duvivier 2)

Creed of Violence, 1969 (Van Cleef 3)

Creepers. See Phenomena, 1984

Creeping Flesh, 1972 (Cushing 3, Lee 3, Francis 4)

Creeping Unknown. See Quatermass Experiment, 1955

Creeping Unknown. See Shock, 1972

Creeps, 1956 (Three Stooges 3)

Creepshow, 1982 (Romero 2, Savini 4)

Creepshow 2, 1990 (Romero 2, Lamour 3, Savini 4)

Creepy Time Pal, 1960 (Hanna and Barbera 4)

Crème Simon, 1937 (Alexeieff and Parker 4)

Creo en Dios, 1940 (De Fuentes 2, Figueroa 4)

Creosoot, 1931 (Van Dongen 4)

Creosote. See Creosoot, 1931

Crepúscolo de un Dios, 1968 (Fernández 2)

Crépuscule d'épouvante, 1921 (Duvivier 2, Vanel 3)

Crescendo, 1969 (Carreras 4, Sangster 4)

Crescete e moltiplicatevi, 1973 (Morricone 4)

Crest of the Wave. See Seagulls over Sorrento, 1954

Cresus, 1960 (Fernandel 3, Kosma 4)

Crête sans les Dieux, 1934 (Leenhardt 2, Jaubert 4)

Crève-Coeur, 1954 (Decaë 4, Rabier 4)

Crew, 1990 (Scorsese 2)

Cri de coeur, 1974 (Audran 3, Seyrig 3)

Cri du cormoran le soir au-dessus des jonques, 1970 (Blier 3, Depardieu 3, D'Eaubonne 4)

Cri du hibou, 1987 (Chabrol 2, Rabier 4)

Cria Cuervos, 1976 (Saura 2, Chaplin 3)

Cricca dorata, 1913 (Bertini 3)

Cricket in Times Square, 1971 (Jones 4)

Cricket on the Heart, 1914 (Gaudio 4)

Cricket on the Hearth, 1909 (Griffith 2, Bitzer 4)

Cricket on the Hearth, 1914 (Guy 2)

Cries and Whispers. See **Viskningar och rop, 1972**

Crime, 1983 (Trintignant 3)

Crime and Passion, 1976 (Black 3, Sharif 3)

Crime and Punishment. See Raskolnikoff, 1923

Crime and Punishment. See Crime et châtiment, 1935

Crime and Punishment. See Crime et châtiment, 1956

Crime and Punishment, U.S.A., 1959 (Corman 2, Crosby 4)

Crime at a Girls' School. See Zločin v dívčí škole, 1965

Crime au concert Mayol, 1954 (Manès 3)

Crime by Night, 1944 (Wyman 3)

Crime Club, 1973 (Sheen 3)

Crime Control, 1941 (Benchley 4)

Crime de Grand-père, 1910 (Gance 2)

Crime de Monsieur Lange, 1936 (Becker 2, Berry 3, Grimault 4, Kosma 4, Prévert 4)

Crime de Monsieur Pégotte, 1935 (Berry 3)

Crime Doctor, 1934 (Crisp 3, Murfin 4, Plunkett 4, Steiner 4)

Crime Doctor's Diary, 1949 (Anhalt 4)

Crime Doctor's Manhunt, 1946 (Brackett 4)

Crime Does Not Pay. See Crime ne paie pas, 1962

Crime d'Ovide Plouffe, 1983 (Arcand 2)

Crime du bouif, 1951 (Braunberger 4)

Crime et châtiment, 1935 (Von Sternberg 2, Baur 3, Lorre 3, Ballard 4, Cohn 4, Honegger 4, Lourié 4, Schulberg 4)

Crime et châtiment, 1956 (Blier 3, Gabin 3, Renoir 4, Spaak 4)

Crime in a Night Club. See Zločin v šantánu, 1968

Crime in Paradise. See Brott i Paradiset, 1959

Crime in the Streets, 1956 (Cassavetes 2, Siegel 2, Mineo 3, Waxman 4)

Crime ne paie pas, 1962 (Brasseur 3, Cervi 3, Darrieux 3, Feuillère 3, Girardot 3, Morgan 3, Noiret 3, Aurenche 4, Bost 4, Delerue 4, Jeanson 4, Matras 4, Wakhévitch 4)

Crime Nobody Saw, 1937 (Ayres 3, McDaniel 3, Head 4)

Crime of Cain, 1914 (Ingram 2)

Crime of Dr. Crespi, 1935 (Von Stroheim 2)

Crime of Dr. Hallet, 1938 (Bellamy 3, Krasner 4)

Crime of Helen Stanley, 1934 (Bellamy 3, Bond 3)

Crime of Monsieur Lange. See **Crime de Monsieur Lange, 1936**

Crime of Passion, 1957 (Hayden 3, Stanwyck 3, Wray 3, La Shelle 4)

Crime of the Century, 1933 (Banton 4, Head 4)

Crime on a Summer Morning. See Par un beau matin d'été, 1965

Crime on Their Hands, 1948 (Three Stooges 3)

Crime Over London, 1936 (Withers 3)

Crime School, 1938 (Bogart 3, Friedhofer 4, Steiner 4)

Crime Wave, 1954 (Bronson 3, Hayden 3, Glennon 4)

Crime without Passion, 1934 (Rains 3, Garmes 4, Hecht 4, MacArthur 4, Vorkapich 4, Zukor 4)

Crimebusters, 1961 (Dern 3)

Crimen, 1960 (Blier 3, Mangano 3, Sordi 3, De Laurentiis 4, Di Venanzo 4, Gherardi 4)

Crimen de Oribe, 1950 (Torre Nilsson 2)

Crimen y castigo, 1950 (De Fuentes 2)

Crimes and Misdemeanors, 1990 (Allen 2, Bloom 3, Farrow 3, Huston 3, Nykvist 4)

Crimes de l'amour. See Rideau carmoisi, 1952

Crime's End. See My Son is Guilty, 1939

Crimes of Passion, 1984 (Russell 2, Perkins 3, Turner 3)

Crimes of the Future, 1970 (Cronenberg 2)

Crimes of the Heart, 1986 (Beresford 2, Keaton 3, Lange 3, Spacek 3, Adam 4, De Laurentiis 4, Delerue 4, Shepard 4)

Criminal, 1915 (Costello 3, Talmadge 3, Sullivan 4)

Criminal, 1960 (Baker 3, Krasker 4, Sangster 4)

Criminal at Large. See Frightened Lady, 1932

Criminal Code, 1931 (Hawks 2, Huston 3, Karloff 3, Cohn 4, Howe 4, Miller 4)

Criminal Court, 1946 (Wise 2)

Criminal Hypnotist, 1908 (Griffith 2, Bitzer 4)

Criminal Law, 1988 (Goldsmith 4)

Criminals, 1913 (Dwan 2)

Criminals. See Once Upon a Crime, 1992

Criminals of the Air, 1937 (Hayworth 3)

Criminals Within, 1941 (Lewis 2)

Criminel, 1932 (Baur 3)

Crimson Blade. See Scarlet Blade, 1963

Crimson City, 1928 (Loy 3, Wong 3)

Crimson Cult, 1970 (Karloff 3, Lee 3)

Crimson Curtain. See Rideau cramoisi, 1953

Crimson Dove, 1917 (Marion 4)

Crimson Dynasty. See Koenigsmark, 1936

Crimson Kimono, 1959 (Fuller 2, Boyle 4)

Crimson Notebook. See Piros bugyelláris, 1917

Crimson Pirate, 1952 (Siodmak 2, Lancaster 3, Lee 3, Adam 4, Alwyn 4, Heller 4, Mathieson 4)

Crimson Romance, 1934 (Von Stroheim 2)

Crinoline, 1906 (Guy 2)

Cripta de l'incubo, 1963 (Lee 3)

Crise est finie, 1934 (Siodmak 2, Darrieux 3, Schüfftan 4, Siodmak 4)

Crisis, 1912 (Ince 4)

Crisis, 1950 (Brooks 2, Ferrer 3, Grant 3, Novarro 3, Ames 4, Freed 4, Mayer 4, Rozsa 4)

Crisis, 1954 (Xie 2)

Crisis, 1963 (Leacock 2)

Crisis at Central High, 1981 (Woodward 3)

Crisis en el Caribe, 1962 (Alvarez 2)

Criss Cross, 1949 (Siodmak 2, Curtis 3, De Carlo 3, Duryea 3, Lancaster 3, Leven 4, Planer 4, Rozsa 4)

Crisscross, 1991 (Hawn 3, Menges 4)

Cristo proibito, 1951 (Cervi 3, Cuny 3)

Cristo si è fermato a Eboli, 1979 (Cuny 3, Papas 3, Volonté 3, Cristaldi 4, Guerra 4)

Cristoforo Colombo, 1985 (Brazzi 3, Dunaway 3)

Critic, 1906 (Bitzer 4)

Critic, 1963 (Brooks 2)

Critical Condition, 1987 (Pryor 3)

Critical List, 1978 (Wagner 3)

Critical Mass, 1971 (Frampton 2)

Critic's Choice, 1963 (Ball 3, Hope 3, Duning 4, Head 4, Lang 4)

Crockett-Doodle-Do, 1960 (Blanc 4, McKimson 4)

Croisée des chemins, 1942 (Brasseur 3)

Croisière de L'Atalante, 1926 (Grémillon 2)

Croisière pour l'inconnu, 1947 (Brasseur 3)

Croisières sidérales, 1942 (Bost 4)

Croissance de Paris, 1954 (Braunberger 4)

Croix de bois, 1931 (Artaud 3, Vanel 3, Douy 4)

Croix des vivants, 1960 (Cuny 3, Barsacq 4)

Croix du Sud, 1931 (Christian-Jaque 2)

Cromwell, 1911 (Berry 3)

Cromwell, 1970 (Guinness 3, Harris 3, Unsworth 4)

Cronaca criminale del Far West. See Banda J & S, 1972

Cronaca di un amore, 1950 (Fusco 4)

Cronaca di una morte annunciata, 1987 (Cuny 3, Papas 3, Volonté 3, Guerra 4)

Cronaca familiare, 1962 (Mastroianni 3)

Cronaca nera, 1947 (Cervi 3)

Cronache di poveri amanti, 1954 (Mastroianni 3, Amidei 4, Di Venanzo 4)

Cronica familiare, 1962 (Rotunno 4)

Cronoca nera, 1946 (Amidei 4)

Crook. See Voyou, 1970

Crook Buster, 1925 (Wyler 2)

Crook That Cried Wolf, 1963 (Hanna and Barbera 4)

Crooked Billet, 1930 (Carroll 3, Balcon 4)

Crooked Hearts, 1972 (O'Sullivan 3, Russell 3, Biroc 4)

Crooked Road, 1911 (Griffith 2, Bitzer 4)

Crooked Road, 1965 (Granger 3, Ryan 3)

Crooked to the End, 1915 (Sennett 2)

Crooked Way, 1949 (Florey 2, Alton 4, Polglase 4)

Crooks and Coronets, 1969 (Evans 3, Oates 3)

Crooks Anonymous, 1962 (Christie 3)

Crooks Can't Win, 1928 (Brown 3)

Crooks in Clover. See Penthouse, 1933

Crook's Tour, 1933 (Roach 4)

Crook's Tour, 1940 (Baxter 2)

Crooner, 1932 (Bacon 2, Orry-Kelly 4)

Crop Chasers, 1939 (Iwerks 4)

Croquemitaine et Rosalie, 1916 (Cohl 4)

Cross By the Brook. See Kríž u potoka, 1921

Cross Country Cruise, 1934 (Ayres 3)

Cross Country Detours, 1940 (Avery 4)

Cross Country Doctors, 1940 (Blanc 4, Stalling 4)

Cross Country Romance, 1940 (Ladd 3, Hunt 4)

Cross Creek, 1983 (Ritt 2, McDowell 3, Alonzo 4)

Cross Currents, 1935 (Havelock-Allan 4)

Cross My Heart, 1937 (Havelock-Allan 4)

Cross My Heart, 1947 (Hutton 3, Head 4, Lang 4, Schnee 4)

Cross of Iron, 1977 (Peckinpah 2, Burton 3, Coburn 3, Schell 3, Epstein 4)

Cross of Lorraine, 1943 (Garnett 2, Kelly 3, Lorre 3, Freund 4, Gibbons 4, Kaper 4, Lardner 4)

Cross of the Living. See Croix des vivants, 1960

Cross of Valour. See Krzyż walecznych, 1959

Cross Purposes, 1913 (Reid 3)

Cross Red Nurse, 1918 (Dressler 3)

Cross Shot, 1976 (Cobb 3)

'Cross the Mexican Line, 1914 (Reid 3)

Cross Your Heart, 1912 (Cruze 2)

Crossbeams. See Tvärbalk, 1967

Cross-Country original, 1909 (Linder 3)

Crosscurrent. See Cable Car Mystery, 1971

Crossed Love and Swords, 1915 (Sennett 2)

Crossed Swords. See Maestro di Don Giovanni, 1953

Crossed Swords. See Prince and the Pauper, 1977

Crossed Wires, 1923 (Laemmle 4)

Crossfire, 1933 (Musuraca 4, Plunkett 4)

Crossfire, 1947 (Dmytryk 2, Grahame 3, Mitchum 3, Ryan 3, Young 3, D'Agostino 4, Hunt 4, Paxton 4, Schary 4)

Crossing Delancey, 1988 (Silver 2)

Crossing Fox River, 1976 (Bondi 3)

Crossing the Line. See Big Man, 1990

Crossing to Freedom. See Pied Piper, 1989

Crossings and Meetings, 1974 (Emshwiller 2)

Crossroads. See **Jujiro, 1928**

Crossroads. See Shizi jietou, 1937

Crossroads. See Carrefour, 1939

Crossroads, 1942 (Lamarr 3, Powell 3, Rathbone 3, Trevor 3, Kaper 4, Ruttenberg 4)

Crossroads, 1955 (Lee 3)

Crossroads, 1976 (Conner 2)

Crossroads, 1986 (Hill 2)

Crossroads of Life. See I Livets Braending, 1915

Crossroads of New York, 1922 (Sennett 2, Hornbeck 4)

Crosswinds, 1951 (Head 4)

Crouching Beast, 1935 (Kortner 3)

Croulants se portent bien, 1961 (Auric 4)

Crow, 1919 (Eason 4)

Crow on a Moonlit Night. See Tsukiyo garasu, 1939

Crowd, 1928 (Vidor 2, Gibbons 4, Gillespie 4, Mayer 4, Thalberg 4)

Crowd Roars, 1932 (Hawks 2, Blondell 3, Cagney 3, Miller 4, Zanuck 4)

Crowd Roars, 1938 (Fleming 2, O'Sullivan 3, Taylor 3, Wyman 3, Mayer 4, Seitz 4)

Crowded Day, 1954 (Roberts 3)

Crowded Hour, 1925 (Daniels 3, Hunt 4)

Crowded Paradise, 1956 (Kaufman 4, Sylbert 4)

Crowded Sky, 1960 (Andrews 3, Rosenman 4, Schnee 4, Stradling 4)

Crowded Snores, 1932 (Lantz 4)

Crowhaven Farm, 1970 (Carradine 3)

Crowing Pains, 1947 (Blanc 4, McKimson 4, Stalling 4)

Crown of Lies, 1926 (Negri 3, Glennon 4, Vajda 4)

Crown of the Year, 1943 (Alwyn 4)

Crown of Thorns. See I.N.R.I., 1923

Crown Prince's Double, 1916 (Costello 3, Talmadge 3)

Crown Versus Stevens, 1936 (Powell and Pressburger 2, Withers 3)

Crows and Sparrows. See Wuya yu Maque, 1948

Crow's Feat, 1962 (Blanc 4, Freleng 4)

Crow's Fete, 1963 (Hanna and Barbera 4)

Crucial Test, 1912 (Bosworth 3)

Crucial Test, 1916 (Menjou 3, Marion 4)

Crucible. See Sorcières de Salem, 1957

Crucifer of Blood, 1991 (Heston 3)

Crucified Lovers. *See* **Chikamatsu monogatari, 1954**
Crudeli, 1966 (Cotten 3, Morricone 4)
Cruel, Cruel Love, 1914 (Sennett 2)
Cruel Sea, 1953 (Baker 3, Elliott 3, Hawkins 3)
Cruel Story of the Samurai Code. *See* Bushidou zankku monogatari, 1963
Cruel Tower, 1956 (Haller 4)
Cruise, 1967 (Hubley 4)
Cruise Cat, 1950 (Hanna and Barbera 4)
Cruise into Terror, 1978 (Milland 3)
Cruise Missile. *See* Teheran Incident, 1979
Cruise of the Jasper B., 1926 (Garnett 2)
Cruise of the Zaca, 1952 (Flynn 3)
Cruisin' Down the River, 1953 (Edwards 2)
Cruising, 1980 (Friedkin 2, Pacino 3)
Crumbs for the Poor. *See* Ulička v Ráji, 1936
Crusader, 1922 (Howard 2, Fox 4)
Crusaders, 1931 (Rooney 3)
Crusades, 1935 (De Mille 2, Bosworth 3, Carradine 3, Sheridan 3, Young 3, Banton 4, Brackett 4, Dreier 4, Head 4, Macpherson 4, Nichols 4, Prinz 4, Young 4)
Crush Proof, 1971 (Hopper 3)
Crushin' Thru, 1923 (Carey 3)
Cruz de Ferro, 1968 (De Almeida 4)
Cruz diablo, 1934 (De Fuentes 2, Fernández 2, Hayworth 3)
Cruz na praça, 1958 (Rocha 2)
Cruzada ABC, 1966 (Pereira Dos Santos 2)
.Cry. *See* Křik, 1963
Cry Baby, 1958 (Corman 2)
Cry Baby, 1990 (Waters 2)
Cry Baby Killer, 1958 (Nicholson 3, Crosby 4)
Cry Blood, Apache, 1970 (McCrea 3)
Cry Danger, 1951 (Powell 3, Biroc 4, Day 4)
Cry for Happy, 1961 (Ford 3, O'Connor 3, Duning 4, Guffey 4)
Cry for Help, 1912 (Griffith 2, Barrymore 3, Carey 3, Gish 3, Bitzer 4)
Cry Freedom, 1987 (Attenborough 3)
Cry from the Streets, 1958 (Dalrymple 4)
Cry from the Wilderness, 1909 (Porter 2)
Cry Havoc, 1943 (Blondell 3, Mitchum 3, Sullavan 3, Freund 4, Irene 4)
Cry in the Dark, 1988 (Streep 3, Golan and Globus 4)
Cry in the Night, 1956 (Ladd 3, Wood 3, Seitz 4)
Cry of Battle, 1963 (Fields 4)
Cry of the Banshee, 1970 (Bergner 3, Price 3)
Cry of the Children, 1912 (Cruze 2)
Cry of the City, 1948 (Siodmak 2, Mature 3, Winters 3, LeMaire 4, Newman 4, Wheeler 4)
Cry of the Hunted, 1953 (Lewis 2, Gassman 3)
Cry of the Innocent, 1978 (Cusack 3)
Cry of the Penguins. *See* Mr. Forbush and the Penguins, 1971
Cry of the Weak, 1919 (Miller 4)
Cry of the World, 1933 (De Rochemont 4)
Cry of Triumph. *See* Hempas bar, 1977
Cry Onion. *See* Cipola Colt, 1975
Cry Terror, 1958 (Dickinson 3, Marsh 3, Mason 3, Steiger 3)
Cry, The Beloved Country, 1952 (Poitier 3, Korda 4, Krasker 4)
Cry Wolf, 1947 (Flynn 3, Stanwyck 3, Blanke 4, Burks 4, Head 4, Waxman 4)

Cry Wolf, 1980 (Krasker 4)
Crying and Laughing. *See* Gens qui pleurent et gens qui rient, 1900
Crying Wolf, 1947 (Terry 4)
Cryptogramme rouge, 1915 (Feuillade 2)
Crystal Ball, 1943 (Bendix 3, De Carlo 3, Goddard 3, Milland 3, Dreier 4, Head 4, Young 4)
Crystal Eye, 1988 (Lom 3)
Crystals, 1959 (Leacock 2)
Csak egy mozi, 1985 (Léaud 3)
Csardasfürstin, 1934 (Herlth 4, Hoffmann 4, Röhrig 4)
Csibi, der Fratz. *See* Früchten, 1933
Csikós, 1917 (Korda 4)
Csillagosok, katonák, 1967 (Jancsó 2)
Csoda vege, 1983 (Brodský 3)
Cuando corre el alazán, 1967 (Fernández 2)
Cuando corrió el alazán, 1985 (Fernández 2)
Cuando el amor rie. *See* Ladron de amor, 1930
Cuando habla el corazón, 1943 (Infante 3)
Cuando levanta la niebla, 1952 (Fernández 2, Figueroa 4)
Cuando viajan las estrellas, 1942 (Figueroa 4)
Cuando viva villa es la muerte, 1958 (Armendáriz 3)
Cuandolloran los valientes, 1945 (Infante 3)
Cuatro Juanes, 1964 (Figueroa 4)
Cuatro milpas, 1937 (Fernández 2, Armendáriz 3)
Cuatro puentes, 1974 (Alvarez 2)
Cuatro Robinsones, 1940 (Rey 3)
Cub, 1915 (Tourneur 2)
Cub, 1917 (Carré 4)
Cuba, 1979 (Lester 2, Connery 3, Elliott 3)
Cuba Cabana, 1952 (Warm 4)
Cuba dos de enero, 1965 (Alvarez 2)
Cuba Si!, 1961 (Marker 2, Braunberger 4, Grimault 4)
Cuban Love Song, 1931 (Van Dyke 2, Durante 3, Booth 4, Lewin 4, Meredyth 4, Rosson 4, Sullivan 4)
Cuban Rebel Girls, 1959 (Flynn 3)
Cubisme. *See* Statues d'épouvante, 1953
Cucaracha, 1934 (Cooper 4, MacGowan 4)
Cucaracha, 1958 (Fernández 2, Armendáriz 3, Del Rio 3, Félix 3, Figueroa 4)
Cuccagne, 1962 (Morricone 4)
Cuckoo. *See* Jihi shincho, 1927
Cuckoo. *See* Hototogisu, 1932
Cuckoo Bird, 1939 (Terry 4)
Cuckoo Clock, 1950 (Avery 4)
Cuckoo in a Choo Choo, 1952 (Three Stooges 3)
Cuckoo in the Nest, 1933 (Junge 4)
Cuckoo Love, 1925 (Roach 4)
Cuckoos, 1930 (Musuraca 4, Plunkett 4)
Cuckoo's Egg: Milos Forman, 1985 (Jireš 2)
Cue Ball Cat, 1950 (Hanna and Barbera 4)
Cuenca, 1958 (Saura 2)
Cuentos de Alhambra, 1963 (Gómez 2)
Cuerpo de mujer, 1949 (Alcoriza 4, Figueroa 4)
Cueva de los tiburones. *See* Bermuda: la fossa maledetta, 1978
Cugina, 1974 (Morricone 4)
Cuidado con el amor, 1954 (Infante 3)
Cuidado con el ser, 1954 (Infante 3)
Cuisine au beurre, 1963 (Fernandel 3)
Cuivres à la voix d'or, 1958 (Decaë 4)

Culastrice nobile veneziano, 1976 (Mastroianni 3)
Cul-de-Sac, 1966 (Polanski 2, Pleasence 3, Lenica 4)
Culloden, 1964 (Watkins 2)
Culpables, 1958 (Rey 3)
Culpepper Cattle Company, 1972 (Goldsmith 4, Needham 4, Smith 4)
Cult of the Cobra, 1955 (Metty 4)
Cult of the Damned. *See* Angel, Angel, Down We Go, 1969
Cultured Ape, 1989 (Halas and Batchelor 4)
Culture intensive ou Le Vieux Mari, 1904 (Guy 2)
Cumberland Story, 1947 (Jennings 2)
Cumbite, 1964 (Gutiérrez Alea 2)
Cumbre que nos une, 1979 (Alvarez 2)
Cummington Story, 1945 (Copland 4)
Cumpleanos del Perro, 1974 (Hermosillo 2)
Cumplimos, 1962 (Alvarez 2)
Cunegonde, 1932 (Fernandel 3)
Cuore, 1948 (De Sica 2)
Cuore, 1984 (Comencini 2, Cecchi D'Amico 4)
Cuore di cane, 1975 (Von Sydow 3)
Cuore di mamma, 1969 (Morricone 4)
Cuore rivelatore, 1935 (Monicelli 2)
Cuore rivelatore, 1948 (Risi 2)
Cuore semplice, 1977 (Valli 3, Zavattini 4)
Cuori nella tormenta, 1940 (Sordi 3, Amidei 4)
Cuori senza frontiere, 1950 (Lollobrigida 3, Ponti 4)
Cuori sul mare, 1950 (Loren 3, Mastroianni 3, Vanel 3)
Cup of Bitterness, 1916 (Ingram 2)
Cup of Cold Water, 1911 (Bosworth 3, Bosworth 3)
Cup of Kindness, 1934 (Balcon 4, Junge 4, Rank 4)
Cup of Life, 1915 (Sullivan 4)
Cup of Life, 1921 (Bosworth 3, Wilson 4)
Cup of Life and Death. *See* Kubok zhizhni i smerti, 1912
Cupboard Was Bare. *See* Armoire volante, 1948
Cupid and the Motor Boat, 1910 (Bunny 3)
Cupid and the Pest, 1915 (Browning 2)
Cupid Forecloses, 1919 (Love 3)
Cupid in Chaps, 1911 (Dwan 2)
Cupid Incognito, 1914 (Reid 3)
Cupid in the Dental Parlor, 1913 (Sennett 2)
Cupid in the Rough. *See* Aggie Appleby, Maker of Men, 1933
Cupid Never Ages, 1913 (Dwan 2)
Cupid Takes a Holiday, 1938 (Kaye 3)
Cupid the Cowpuncher, 1920 (Rogers 3)
Cupid Through Padlocks, 1911 (Dwan 2)
Cupid Throws a Brick, 1913 (Dwan 2)
Cupid Versus Money, 1914 (Talmadge 3)
Cupid Versus Women's Rights, 1913 (Costello 3)
Cupid's Boots, 1925 (Sennett 2)
Cupid's Day Off, 1919 (Sennett 2)
Cupid's Fireman, 1923 (Wellman 2, August 4, Fox 4)
Cupid's Hired Man, 1913 (Bunny 3)
Cupid's Joke, 1911 (Sennett 2)
Cupid's Rival, 1917 (Laurel and Hardy 3)
Cupid's Roundup, 1918 (Mix 3)
Cupid's Target, 1915 (Laurel and Hardy 3)
Curare et curarisants de synthèse, 1950 (Cloquet 4)
Cure, 1917 (Chaplin 2, Purviance 3)

Cure, 1924 (Fleischer 4)
Curé de Cucugnan, 1967 (Pagnol 2)
Cure for Love, 1949 (Donat 3, Alwyn 4, Korda 4)
Cure for Pokeritus, 1912 (Bunny 3)
Cure for Suffragettes, 1913 (Loos 4)
Cure for Timidity. See Timidité vaincue, 1909
Cure That Failed, 1913 (Sennett 2, Normand 3)
Cured, 1911 (Sennett 2)
Cured in the Excitement, 1927 (Sennett 2)
Curée, 1966 (Vadim 2, Fonda 3, Piccoli 3, Renoir 4)
Curfew Shall Not Ring Tonight, 1912 (Reid 3)
Curing a Husband, 1914 (Beery 3)
Curing of Myra May, 1914 (Talmadge 3)
Curiosity, 1911 (Sennett 2)
Curious Conduct of Judge Legarde, 1915 (Barrymore 3)
Curious Pets of Our Ancestors, 1917 (O'Brien 4)
Curious Puppy, 1939 (Jones 4)
Curious Way to Love. See Morte, la fatto, l'uovo, 1967
Curley, 1947 (Roach 4)
Curly, 1958 (Romero 2)
Curly Sue, 1991 (Delerue 4)
Curly Top, 1935 (Darwell 3, Temple 3, Friedhofer 4, Seitz 4)
Curlytop, 1924 (Fox 4)
Curse of Frankenstein, 1957 (Fisher 2, Cushing 3, Lee 3, Bernard 4, Carreras 4, Sangster 4)
Curse of Humanity, 1914 (Ince 4)
Curse of Iku, 1918 (Borzage 2)
Curse of King Tut's Tomb, 1980 (Saint 3)
Curse of the Cat People, 1944 (Wise 2, Simon 3, Bodeen 4, D'Agostino 4, Lewton 4, Musuraca 4)
Curse of the Crimson Affair. See Crimson Cult, 1970
Curse of the Crimson Altar. See Crimson Cult, 1970
Curse of the Demon. See Night of the Demon, 1957
Curse of the Living Corpse, 1964 (Scheider 3)
Curse of the Mummy's Tomb, 1964 (Carreras 4, Heller 4)
Curse of the Pink Panther, 1983 (Edwards 2, Lom 3, Niven 3, Wagner 3, Freleng 4, Mancini 4)

Curse of the Redman. See Little Circus Rider, 1911
Curse of the Starving Class, 1990 (Scott 3)
Curse of the Stone Hand, 1964 (Carradine 3)
Curse of the Werewolf, 1961 (Fisher 2, Reed 3, Carreras 4)
Cursed Millions. See Prokliatiye millioni, 1917
Curses! They Remarked, 1914 (Sennett 2)
Curtain Call, 1940 (Metty 4, Polglase 4, Trumbo 4)
Curtain Call at Cactus Creek, 1950 (Arden 3, Brennan 3, O'Connor 3, Price 3, Metty 4)
Curtain Falls, 1934 (Brown 4)
Curtain Pole, 1908 (Griffith 2, Sennett 2, Lawrence 3, Bitzer 4)
Curtain Razor, 1949 (Blanc 4, Freleng 4, Stalling 4)
Curtain Rises. See Entrée des artistes, 1938
Curtain Up, 1952 (Kendall 3, Rutherford 3, Rank 4)
Curtatone e Montanara, 1955 (Taviani 2)
Curtiss's School of Aviation, 1911 (Dwan 2)
Curucu, Beast of the Amazon, 1956 (Siodmak 4)
Custard Cup, 1923 (Brenon 2, Fox 4)
Custer of the West, 1968 (Siodmak 2, Ryan 3, Shaw 3, D'Eaubonne 4, Lourié 4)
Custer's Last Raid, 1912 (Ince 4)
Custer's Last Stand. See On the Little Big Horn, 1910
Custer's Last Stand. See Bob Hampton of Placer, 1921
Customers Wanted, 1939 (Fleischer 4)
Customs Officer Bom. See Tull-Bom, 1951
Cut and Run. See Inferno in Diretta, 1985
Cut Passes, 1982 (Emshwiller 2)
Cut the Cards, 1920 (Roach 4)
Cutter and Bone, 1981 (Bridges 3)
Cutter's Trail, 1969 (Cotten 3)
Cutter's Way. See Cutter and Bone, 1981
Cutting California Redwoods, 1912 (Anderson 3)
Cutting Class, 1989 (McDowall 3)
Cutts. See Woman to Woman, 1923
Cybèle, ou les dimanches de Ville d'Avray, 1961 (Evein 4, Jarre 4)
Cybernetic Granny. See Kybernetická babička, 1962

Cyborg, 1988 (Golan and Globus 4)
Cyclamen. See Ciklámen, 1916
Cycle of Fate, 1916 (Neilan 2)
Cycle Savages, 1970 (Dern 3)
Cyclone, 1920 (Mix 3, Moore 3)
Cyclone, 1946 (Canutt 4)
Cyclone. See Ciclon, 1977
Cyclone Higgins, 1918 (Bushman 3)
Cyclone of the Range, 1927 (Musuraca 4)
Cyclone of the Saddle, 1935 (Canutt 4)
Cyclone on Horseback, 1941 (Polglase 4)
Cykledrengene i Tørvegraven, 1940 (Henning-Jensen 2)
Cymbeline, 1913 (Cruze 2)
Cynara, 1932 (Vidor 2, Colman 3, Francis 3, Day 4, Goldwyn 4, Marion 4, Newman 4)
Cynara, 1943 (Stewart 4)
Cynthia, 1947 (Astor 3, Taylor 3, Irene 4, Kaper 4, Mayer 4)
Cyrano de Bergerac, 1900 (Gaumont 4)
Cyrano de Bergerac, 1950 (Kramer 2, Ferrer 3, Foreman 4, Planer 4, Tiomkin 4)
Cyrano de Bergerac, 1990 (Depardieu 3, Carrière 4, Rappeneau 4)
Cyrano et d'Artagnan, 1963 (Gance 2, Cassel 3, Ferrer 3, Noiret 3, Simon 3)
Cyrano et D'Assoucy, 1911 (Gance 2)
Cyril Stapleton and the Show Band, 1955 (Carreras 4)
Cytherea, 1924 (Carré 4, Goldwyn 4, Marion 4, Miller 4)
Czar Durandai, 1934 (Ivanov-Vano 4)
Czar of Broadway, 1930 (Laemmle 4, Mohr 4)
Czar of the Slot Machines. See King of Gamblers, 1937
Czardasfürsten, 1927 (Courant 4)
Czardas-König, 1958 (Wagner 4)
Czarina. See Royal Scandal, 1945
Czarna Ksiazka, 1915 (Negri 3)
Czarne skrzydla, 1962 (Tyszkiewicz 3, Ścibor-Rylski 4)
Czas przeszly, 1961 (Lomnicki 3)
Czech Connection, 1975 (Nemec 2)
Czech Year. See Spalíček, 1947
Czechoslovakia on Parade, 1938 (Hoch 4)
Człowiek na torze, 1956 (Munk 2, Stawiński 4)
Człowiek z marmuru, 1977 (Wajda 2, Lomnicki 3, Scibor-Rylski 4)
Człowiek z żelaza, 1981 (Wajda 2)

D

D.A.R.Y.L, 1985 (Hamlisch 4)
D.C. Follies, 1988 (Golan and Globus 4)
D.F., 1978 (Figueroa 4)
D.O.A., 1950 (O'Brien 3, Laszlo 4, Maté 4, Tiomkin 4)
Da, 1988 (Sheen 3, Bernstein 4)
Da grande, 1988 (Sarandon 3)
Da hält die Welt den Aten an, 1927 (Krauss 3, Vanel 3, Junge 4)
Da qui all 'eredità, 1956 (Sordi 3)
Da uomo a uomo, 1967 (Van Cleef 3, Morricone 4)
Da veni . . . Don Calogero. See Filo d'erba, 1952
Daag, 1952 (Kumar 3)
Dabbling in Art, 1921 (Sennett 2)
Dábelské libánky, 1970 (Brejchová 3)
Dachshund and the Sausage. See Artist's Dream, 1910
Dactylo, 1931 (Heller 4)
Dactylo se marie, 1934 (Douy 4, Planer 4)
Dad, 1989 (Lemmon 3)
Dad and Dave Come to Town, 1938 (Finch 3)
Dad Rudd, M.P., 1940 (Rafferty 3)
Dadah is Death, 1988 (Christie 3)
Dadascope, 1926 (Richter 2)
Daddies, 1924 (Marsh 3)
Daddy Boy, 1927 (Sennett 2)
Daddy Goes a-Grunting, 1925 (Roach 4)
Daddy Knows Best, 1933 (Sennett 2)
Daddy Long Legs, 1919 (Neilan 2, Pickford 3, Rosher 4)
Daddy Long Legs, 1931 (Gaynor 3, Behrman 4, Friedhofer 4, Levien 4)
Daddy Long Legs, 1955 (Negulesco 2, Astaire 3, Caron 3, Ritter 3, LeMaire 4, Mercer 4, Newman 4, Reynolds 4, Shamroy 4, Wheeler 4)
Daddy Nostalgie, 1990 (Tavernier 2, Bogarde 3)
Daddy's Boys, 1988 (Corman 2)
Daddy's Gone A-Hunting, 1925 (Borzage 2, Gibbons 4, Mayer 4)
Daddy's Gone A-Hunting, 1969 (Cohen 2, Laszlo 4, Williams 4)
Daddy Wanted. See Pappa sökes, 1947
Dad's Choice, 1927 (Horton 3)
Dad's Day, 1929 (McCarey 2, Roach 4)
Dadu Mansoor, 1934 (Roy 2)
Daemon, 1986 (York 3)
Daesh vozkukh, 1924 (Vertov 2)
Daffodil Killer. See Geheimnis der gelben Narzissen, 1961
Daffy Commando, 1943 (Maltese 4)
Daffy Dilly, 1948 (Blanc 4, Jones 4, Stalling 4)
Daffy Doc, 1938 (Blanc 4, Clampett 4, Stalling 4)

Daffy Doodles, 1946 (Blanc 4, Foster 4, McKimson 4, Stalling 4)
Daffy Duck and Egghead, 1938 (Avery 4, Blanc 4, Stalling 4)
Daffy Duck and the Dinosaur, 1939 (Blanc 4, Jones 4)
Daffy Duck Hunt, 1949 (Blanc 4, Foster 4, McKimson 4, Stalling 4)
Daffy Duck in Hollywood, 1938 (Avery 4, Blanc 4, Stalling 4)
Daffy Duck Slept Here, 1948 (Blanc 4, Foster 4, McKimson 4, Stalling 4)
Daffy Rents, 1966 (Blanc 4, McKimson 4)
Daffy Duckaroo, 1942 (Blanc 4, Stalling 4)
Daffy Duck's Movie: Fantastic Island, 1983 (Freleng 4, Jones 4)
Daffy Duck's Quackbusters, 1988 (Blanc 4, Freleng 4, Jones 4)
Daffy the Commando, 1943 (Blanc 4, Freleng 4, Stalling 4)
Daffy's Diner, 1967 (Blanc 4)
Daffy's Diner, 1967 (McKimson 4)
Daffy's Inn Trouble, 1961 (Blanc 4, McKimson 4)
Daffy's Romance, 1938 (Avery 4)
Daffy's Southern Exposure, 1942 (Blanc 4, Stalling 4)
Dagfin, 1926 (Wegener 3, Schüfftan 4)
Dagger. See Dolken, 1915
Dağlarin oğlu, 1965 (Güney 2)
Dagny, 1976 (Olbrychski 3, Ścibor-Rylski 4)
Daguerre ou la naissance de la photographie, 1964 (Leenhardt 2)
Daguerrotypes, 1975 (Varda 2)
Dai go fukuryu-maru, 1959 (Shindo 2)
Dai kusen, 1966 (Tsuburaya 4)
Daiboken, 1965 (Tsuburaya 4)
Daibosatsu toge, 1966 (Mifune 3)
Daibutsu kaigen, 1952 (Hasegawa 3, Kyo 3)
Daichi no komoriuta, 1976 (Okada 3, Tanaka 3)
Daichi wa hohoemu, 1925 (Mizoguchi 2)
Dai-Chushingura, 1930 (Yamada 3)
Dai Chushingura, 1957 (Yamada 3)
Daigaku no kotengu, 1952 (Kagawa 3)
Daigaku no nijuhachi-nin shu, 1959 (Tsukasa 3)
Daigaku no oneichan, 1959 (Tsukasa 3, Muraki 4)
Daigaku no samuri-tachi, 1957 (Tsukasa 3)
Daigaku yoi toko, 1936 (Ryu 3)
Daikaiju Baran, 1958 (Tsuburaya 4)
Daikon to ninjin, 1965 (Iwashita 3, Ryu 3, Tsukasa 3)
Daimler-Benz Limuzyna, 1982 (Lomnicki 3)
Dainah la métisse, 1931 (Grémillon 2, Vanel 3, Périnal 4, Spaak 4)

Dai-ni no jinsei, 1948 (Yamamura 3)
Dai-ni no seppun, 1954 (Takamine 3)
Daisan no Akumyo, 1963 (Miyagawa 4, Yoda 4)
Dai-san no shikaku, 1959 (Mori 3)
Daisies. See Sedmikrásky, 1966
Daisy, 1965 (Dinov 4)
Daisy Bell, 1925 (Fleischer 4)
Daisy Kenyon, 1947 (Preminger 2, Andrews 3, Crawford 3, Fonda 3, LeMaire 4, Raksin 4, Shamroy 4, Wheeler 4)
Daisy Miller, 1974 (Bogdanovich 2, Fields 4, Raphael 4)
Dai-tatsumaki, 1964 (Mifune 3, Tsuburaya 4)
Daitokai: Bakuhatsu-hen, 1929 (Tanaka 3)
Daitokai no kao, 1949 (Yamamura 3)
Dai-tokai no ushimitsu-doki, 1949 (Mori 3)
Dai-Tokyo no ikkaku, 1930 (Takamine 3)
Dai-Tokyo tanjo: Oedo no kane, 1958 (Yamada 3)
Daitozuku, 1964 (Mifune 3, Shimura 3, Tsuburaya 4)
Dakota, 1945 (Bond 3, Brennan 3, Wayne 3, Canutt 4, Foreman 4)
Dakota Dan. See Tools of Providence, 1915
Dakota Incident, 1956 (Bond 3, Darnell 3, Haller 4)
Dakota Lil, 1950 (Leven 4, Tiomkin 4)
Daleko ot voiny, 1969 (Yankovsky 3)
Daleks—Invasion Earth AD 2150, 1966 (Cushing 3)
Dallas, 1950 (Cooper 3, Massey 3, Eason 4, Haller 4, Steiner 4, Veiller 4)
Dalle Ardenne all'inferno, 1968 (Morricone 4)
Dam Busters, 1955 (Redgrave 3, Shaw 3, Sherriff 4)
Dam the Delta, 1958 (Halas and Batchelor 4)
Dama del Alba, 1966 (Del Rio 3)
Dáma s malou nožkou, 1919 (Ondra 3)
Dama s sobachkoi, 1960 (Batalov 3, Moskvin 4)
Damaged Lives, 1933 (Ulmer 2)
Damals, 1942 (Brazzi 3)
Dame à la longue vue, 1963 (Braunberger 4)
Dame aus Berlin, 1925 (Dieterle 2, Krauss 3)
Dame aus der Cottage-Villa. See Villa im Tiergarten, 1926
Dame aux camélias, 1934 (Gance 2, Fresnay 3, Stradling 4)
Dame aux camélias, 1952 (Cervi 3, Presle 3, Barsacq 4)
Dame aux camélias, 1962 (Pagnol 2)
Dame aux camélias, 1980 (Ganz 3)
Dame aux milles et une vies, 1983 (Darrieux 3)

Dame dans l'auto avec des lunettes et un fusil. *See* Lady in the Car with Glasses and a Gun, 1970

Dame de chez Maxim's, 1933 (Korda 2, Jeanson 4)

Dame de Chez Maxim's, 1950 (D'Eaubonne 4)

Dame de Haut-le-Bois, 1946 (Rosay 3)

Dame de l'ouest, 1942 (Simon 3)

Dame de Malacca, 1937 (Blier 3, Feuillère 3, Trauner 4)

Dame de Monsoreau, 1923 (Manès 3)

Dame de Montsoreau, 1913 (Tourneur 2)

Dame de Pique, 1937 (Rathaus 4)

Dame, der Teufel, und die Probiermamsell, 1917 (Wiene 2, Messter 4)

Dame des Dunes, 1986 (Karina 3)

Dame d'onze heures, 1947 (Kosma 4)

Dame en couleurs, 1985 (Jutra 2)

Dame mit den Sonnenblum, 1920 (Curtiz 2)

Dame mit der Maske, 1928 (Galeen 4)

Dame vraiment bien, 1908 (Feuillade 2)

Damen i svart, 1958 (Nykvist 4)

Damen med de lyse Handsker, 1942 (Christensen 2, Henning-Jensen 2)

Dames, 1934 (Berkeley 2, Daves 2, Blondell 3, Keeler 3, Powell 3, Barnes 4, Orry-Kelly 4)

Dames Ahoy!, 1930 (Laemmle 4)

Dames and Dentists, 1920 (Laurel and Hardy 3)

Dames de la côte, 1984 (Feuillère 3)

Dames du Bois de Boulogne, 1945 (Cocteau 2, Melville 2, Douy 4)

Damien—Omen II, 1978 (Ayres 3, Grant 3, Holden 3, Sidney 3, Goldsmith 4)

Damme in Glashaus, 1921 (Negri 3)

Damn Citizen, 1958 (Mancini 4)

Damn the Defiant!. *See* H.M.S. Defiant, 1962

Damnation Alley, 1977 (Sanda 3, Ames 4, Goldsmith 4)

Damnation du Docteur Faust, 1904 (Méliès 2)

Damnation of Faust. *See* Faust aux enfers, 1903

Damned. *See* Maudits, 1947

Damned, 1963 (Losey 2, Reed 3, Bernard 4, Carreras 4)

Damned. *See* **Caduta degli dei, 1969**

Damned Don't Cry, 1950 (Crawford 3, McCord 4, Wald 4)

Damned in Venice. *See* Nero Veneziamo, 1978

Damoi, 1949 (Kagawa 3)

Dämon der Frauen. *See* Rasputin, 1932

Dämon des Himalaya, 1935 (Honegger 4)

Dämon des Meeres, 1931 (Curtiz 2)

Damon the Mower, 1972 (Dunning 4)

Dämonische Liebe, 1950 (Herlth 4)

D'amore si muore, 1972 (Mangano 3, Morricone 4)

D'amour et d'eau fraîche, 1933 (Fernandel 3)

D'amour et d'eau fraîche, 1975 (Girardot 3)

Dams and Waterways, 1911 (Dwan 2)

Damsel in Distress, 1937 (Stevens 2, Astaire 3, Fontaine 3, August 4, Berman 4, Pan 4, Polglase 4)

Damy, 1955 (Gerasimov 2)

Dan, 1965 (Lassally 4)

Dan chez les gentlemen. *See* Residencia para espias, 1967

Dan Cupid, Assayer, 1914 (Anderson 3)

Dan the Dandy, 1911 (Griffith 2, Bitzer 4)

Dan Candy's Law. *See* Alien Thunder, 1975

Dance at Eagle Pass, 1913 (Anderson 3)

Dance at Silver Gulch, 1912 (Anderson 3)

Dance Chromatic, 1959 (Emshwiller 2)

Dance Contest, 1934 (Fleischer 4)

Dance, Fools, Dance, 1931 (Crawford 3, Gable 3, Rosher 4)

Dance, Girl, Dance, 1940 (Arzner 2, Wise 2, Ball 3, Bellamy 3, O'Hara 3, Metty 4, Polglase 4, Pommer 4)

Dance Hall, 1929 (Murfin 4, Plunkett 4)

Dance Hall, 1941 (Day 4)

Dance Hall, 1950 (Crichton 2, Dors 3, Kendall 3, Slocombe 4)

Dance Hall Hostess, 1933 (Eason 4)

Dance Hall Marge, 1931 (Sennett 2)

Dance in the Sun, 1954 (Clarke 2)

Dance Little Lady, 1954 (Zetterling 2)

Dance Madness, 1926 (Florey 2, Basevi 4, Daniels 4, Gibbons 4)

Dance Movie, 1963 (Warhol 2)

Dance Music, 1927 (Haller 4)

Dance of Death, 1969 (Olivier 3, Unsworth 4)

Dance of Life, 1929 (Cromwell 2, Banton 4, Glazer 4, Hunt 4, Selznick 4)

Dance of the Heron, 1966 (Vierny 4)

Dance of the Looney Spoons, 1959 (Vanderbeek 4)

Dance of the Seven Veils, 1970 (Russell 2)

Dance of the Vampires. *See* Fearless Vampire Killers, or Pardon Me, But Your Teeth Are in My Neck, 1967

Dance, Pretty Lady, 1931 (Asquith 2)

Dance—Steigler & Steigler, 1981 (Lee 3)

Dance Team, 1931 (Howe 4)

Dance with Me, Henry, 1956 (Abbott and Costello 3)

Dance with My Doll. *See* Dansa min docka, 1953

Dancing in the Dark, 1949 (Menjou 3, Powell 3, LeMaire 4, Newman 4, Wheeler 4)

Dancer. *See* Maihime, 1989

Dancer of Paris, 1926 (Haller 4)

Dancers, 1925 (Goulding 2, Johnson 3, Fox 4)

Dancers, 1930 (Friedhofer 4)

Dancers, 1987 (Donaggio 4, Golan and Globus 4, Reynolds 4)

Dancers in the Dark, 1932 (Hopkins 3, Raft 3, Mankiewicz 4, Struss 4, Zukor 4)

Dancers of Tomorrow. *See* Asu no odoriko, 1939

Dances with Wolves, 1990 (Costner 3, Barry 4)

Danchi nanatsu-no taizai, 1964 (Tsukasa 3)

Dancin' Fool, 1920 (Daniels 3, Reid 3)

Dancing Bear, 1937 (Terry 4)

Dancing Co-Ed, 1939 (Turner 3, Walker 3)

Dancing Craze, 1910 (White 3)

Dancing Dynamite, 1931 (Brennan 3)

Dancing Fool, 1920 (Wood 2)

Dancing Fool, 1932 (Fleischer 4)

Dancing Foot. *See* Harold Teen, 1933

Dancing Girl, 1915 (Dwan 2)

Dancing Girl of Butte, 1909 (Griffith 2, Sennett 2, Bitzer 4)

Dancing Girls of Izu. *See* Izu no odoriko, 1933

Dancing in a Harem. *See* Danse au sérail, 1897

Dancing Instructor, 1929 (Brown 3)

Dancing Lady, 1933 (Arden 3, Astaire 3,

Crawford 3, Eddy 3, Gable 3, Three Stooges 3, Adrian 4, Benchley 4, Booth 4, Mayer 4, Selznick 4, Vorkapich 4)

Dancing Machine, 1990 (Delon 3)

Dancing Masters, 1943 (Dumont 3, Laurel and Hardy 3, Mitchum 3, Basevi 4)

Dancing Mothers, 1926 (Brenon 2, Goulding 2, Bow 3, Banton 4, Hunt 4)

Dancing on a Dime, 1940 (Head 4, Lang 4, Young 4)

Dancing on the Moon, 1935 (Fleischer 4)

Dancing Pirate, 1936 (Benchley 4, Cooper 4, Newman 4, O'Brien 4, Raksin 4)

Dancing Shoes, 1949 (Terry 4)

Dancing with Crime, 1947 (Attenborough 3, Bogarde 3, Dors 3, Lassally 4)

Dandin, 1988 (Gélin 3)

Dandy Dick, 1935 (Hay 3)

Dandy in Aspic, 1968 (Mann 2, Farrow 3, Harvey 3, Challis 4, Dillon 4, Jones 4)

Dandy Lion, 1940 (Fleischer 4)

Danger, 1923 (Walker 4)

Danger Ahead, 1921 (Laemmle 4)

Danger Ahead, 1923 (Howard 2)

Danger Ahead, 1935 (Katzman 4)

Danger: Diabolik. *See* Diabolik, 1968

Danger Girl, 1916 (Sennett 2, Swanson 3)

Danger—Go Slow, 1918 (Chaney 3)

Danger Grows Wild. *See* Poppy Is Also a Flower, 1966

Danger in the Pacific, 1942 (Salter 4)

Danger Island, 1939 (Lorre 3)

Danger Lights, 1930 (Arthur 3, Dunn 4, Struss 4)

Danger Line. *See* Bataille, 1923

Danger List, 1957 (Carreras 4)

Danger, Love at Work, 1937 (Preminger 2, Carradine 3, Horton 3, Pangborn 3, Miller 4)

Danger on the Air, 1938 (Cobb 3, Cortez 4)

Danger Patrol, 1937 (Carey 3, Musuraca 4)

Danger Rider, 1928 (Eason 4)

Danger Rides the Range. *See* Three Texas Steers, 1939

Danger Route, 1967 (Dors 3)

Danger Signal, 1945 (Florey 2, Deutsch 4, Howe 4)

Danger Stalks Near. *See* Fuzen no tomoshibi, 1957

Danger Within, 1959 (Caine 3)

Danger! Women at Work, 1943 (Ulmer 2)

Dangerous, 1935 (Davis 3, Brown 4, Haller 4, Orry-Kelly 4)

Dangerous Adventure, 1922 (Warner 4)

Dangerous Age, 1922 (Stahl 2, Mayer 4, Meredyth 4)

Dangerous Age. *See* Beloved Brat, 1938

Dangerous Business, 1921 (Emerson 4, Loos 4)

Dangerous Business, 1946 (Three Stooges 3)

Dangerous Cargo. *See* Forbidden Cargo, 1925

Dangerous Comment, 1940 (Mills 3, Balcon 4)

Dangerous Corner, 1934 (Douglas 3, Hunt 4, Plunkett 4, Steiner 4)

Dangerous Coward, 1924 (Brown 4)

Dangerous Crossing, 1953 (La Shelle 4, LeMaire 4, Reynolds 4, Wheeler 4)

Dangerous Curves, 1929 (Bow 3)

Dangerous Curves, 1991 (Francis 3)

Dangerous Curves Behind, 1925 (Sennett 2)

Dangerous Dan McFoo, 1939 (Avery 4)

Dangerous Days. *See* Wild Boys of the Road, 1933

Dangerous Dude, 1926 (Brown 4)

Dangerous Exile, 1957 (Jourdan 3, Auric 4, Rank 4, Unsworth 4)

Dangerous Females, 1929 (Dressler 3)

Dangerous Flirt, 1924 (Browning 2)

Dangerous Game, 1922 (Laemmle 4)

Dangerous Game, 1941 (Cortez 4, Salter 4)

Dangerous Hero. *See* Kiken no eiyu, 1957

Dangerous Holiday, 1937 (Pangborn 3)

Dangerous Hours, 1919 (Niblo 2, Barnes 4, Sullivan 4)

Dangerous Inheritance. *See* Girls' School, 1950

Dangerous Intrigue, 1936 (Bellamy 3)

Dangerous Liaisons, 1988 (Frears 2, Close 3, Pfeiffer 3)

Dangerous Lies, 1921 (Hitchcock 2)

Dangerous Love, 1988 (Gould 3)

Dangerous Maid, 1923 (Schenck 4, Sullivan 4)

Dangerous Mission, 1954 (Bendix 3, Mature 3, Price 3, Bennett 4, Burnett 4)

Dangerous Mists. *See* U-Boat Prisoner, 1944

Dangerous Moment, 1921 (Glennon 4, Laemmle 4)

Dangerous Money, 1924 (Daniels 3, Powell 3, Hunt 4)

Dangerous Moonlight, 1941 (Beaton 4, Krasker 4, Mathieson 4)

Dangerous Moves. *See* Diagonale du fou, 1984

Dangerous Nan McGrew, 1930 (Folsey 4, Fort 4)

Dangerous Number, 1937 (Pangborn 3, Young 3, Wilson 4)

Dangerous Paradise, 1920 (Goulding 2)

Dangerous Paradise, 1930 (Wellman 2)

Dangerous Partners, 1945 (Freund 4, Irene 4)

Dangerous Profession, 1949 (Raft 3)

Dangerous Quest, 1926 (Brown 4)

Dangerous Secrets, 1938 (Lukas 3)

Dangerous to Know, 1938 (Florey 2, Quinn 3, Wong 3, Head 4)

Dangerous When Wet, 1953 (Walters 2, Williams 3, Hanna and Barbera 4, Mercer 4, Rose 4, Rosson 4, Smith 4)

Dangerous Woman, 1929 (Dreier 4)

Dangerous Years, 1948 (Monroe 3)

Dangerous Years of Kiowa Jones, 1966 (Mineo 3)

Dangerously Close, 1986 (Golan and Globus 4)

Dangerously They Live, 1941 (Florey 2, Garfield 3, Massey 3)

Dangerously Yours, 1933 (Friedhofer 4, Seitz 4)

Dangerously Yours, 1937 (Darwell 3)

Dangers de l'acoolisme, 1897 (Guy 2)

Dangers de l'alcoolisme, 1899 (Gaumont 4)

Dangers of a Bride, 1917 (Sennett 2, Swanson 3)

Dangers of the Canadian Mounted, 1948 (Canutt 4)

Daniel, 1983 (Lumet 2)

Daniel and the Devil. *See* All That Money Can Buy, 1941

Daniel Boone, 1936 (Carradine 3)

Daniel Boone, or Pioneer Days in America, 1907 (Porter 2, Lawrence 3)

Daniele Cortis, 1947 (Cervi 3, Gassman 3, Gherardi 4, Rota 4)

Danish Design, 1960 (Roos 2)

Danites, 1912 (Bosworth 3)

Danjuro sandai, 1944 (Mizoguchi 2, Kyo 3, Tanaka 3)

Dankon, 1969 (Okada 3, Muraki 4, Takemitsu 4)

Dann schon lieber Lebertran, 1930 (Ophüls 2, Schüfftan 4)

Danny Kaye Story. *See* Birth of a Star, 1944

Danny the Champion of the World, 1989 (Irons 3)

Danny Travis. *See* Last Word, 1979

Danryu, 1939 (Yoshimura 2)

Dans Arles où sont les Alyscamps, 1966 (Braunberger 4)

Dans Bankett der Schmugger. *See* Banquet des fraudeurs, 1952

Dans la brousse, 1912 (Feuillade 2)

Dans la nuit, 1929 (Vanel 3)

Dans la poussière du soleil, 1971 (Schell 3, Lai 4)

Dans la réserve africaine, 1961 (Braunberger 4)

Dans la Vallée d'Ossau, 1912 (Cohl 4)

Dans la vie, 1911 (Feuillade 2, Gaumont 4)

Dans la vie tout s'arrange. *See* Pardon My French, 1950

Dans la ville blanche, 1983 (Tanner 2, Ganz 3, Branco 4, De Almeida 4)

Dans les coulisses, 1900 (Guy 2)

Dans les rues, 1933 (Andrejew 4, Maté 4)

Dans l'ouragan de la vie, 1916 (Dulac 2)

Dans un miroir, 1985 (De Almeida 4)

Dansai Hyoe issho-tabi, 1933 (Yamada 3)

Dansa min docka, 1953 (Björnstrand 3)

Danse au sérail, 1897 (Méliès 2)

Danse basque, 1901 (Guy 2)

Danse de l'ivresse, 1900 (Guy 2)

Danse de mort, 1947 (Von Stroheim 2, Wakhévitch 4)

Danse des Saisons, 1900 (Guy 2)

Danse du papillon, 1900 (Guy 2)

Danse du pas des foulards par des almées, 1900 (Guy 2)

Danse du ventre, 1900 (Guy 2)

Danse fleur de lotus, 1897 (Guy 2)

Danse Macabre. *See* Tanyets smerti, 1916

Danse mauresque, 1902 (Guy 2)

Danse serpentine, 1900 (Guy 2)

Danse serpentine par Mme Bob Walter, 1897 (Guy 2)

Dansei No. 1, 1955 (Mifune 3)

Dansei tai josei, 1936 (Tanaka 3)

Danses, 1900 (Guy 2)

Danses espagnoles, 1900 (Lumière 2)

Danseuse de Marrakech, 1949 (Manès 3)

Danseuse nue, 1952 (Evein 4)

Danseuse orchidé, 1927 (Burel 4)

Danseuse rouge, 1937 (Alekan 4, Auric 4)

Danseuse voilée, 1916 (Modot 3)

Danshum, 1965 (Iwashita 3)

Dansk politi i Sverige, 1945 (Henning-Jensen 2)

Danssalongen, 1955 (Thulin 3)

Dante n'avait rien vu, 1962 (Braunberger 4)

Dante Quartet, 1987 (Brakhage 2)

Dante's Inferno, 1924 (Goulding 2, August 4, Fox 4)

Dante's Inferno, 1935 (Hayworth 3, Tracy 3, Trevor 3, Walthall 3, Canutt 4, Carré 4, Friedhofer 4, Maté 4)

Dante's Inferno, 1967 (Russell 2, Reed 3)

Danton, 1920 (Gründgens 3, Jannings 3, Kortner 3, Krauss 3, Dreier 4)

Danton, 1932 (Gründgens 3, Kortner 3, Burel 4, Trauner 4)

Danton, 1982 (Wajda 2, Depardieu 3, Carrière 4)

Danube—Fishes—Birds. *See* Budapest, amiért szeretem, 1971

Danza del fuoco, 1942 (Flaiano 4)

Danza delle lancette, 1936 (Lattuada 2, Zavattini 4)

Daphne, 1936 (Rossellini 2)

Daphne. *See* Jinchoge, 1966

Daphne and the Pirate, 1916 (Gish 3, Brown 4)

Daphne, the Virgin of the Golden Laurels, 1951 (Barrymore 3)

Daraku suru onna, 1967 (Yoshimura 2)

Dařbuján a Pandrhola, 1960 (Frič 2)

Darby O'Gill and the Little People, 1959 (Stevenson 2, Connery 3, Disney 4, Hoch 4)

Darby's Rangers, 1958 (Wellman 2, Garner 3, Clothier 4, Steiner 4)

Dard ka rishta, 1983 (Patil 3)

Dare ga watashi o sabakunoka, 1951 (Yamamura 3)

Dare no tame ni aisuruka, 1971 (Muraki 4)

Daredevil, 1920 (Mix 3)

Dare-Devil, 1923 (Sennett 2)

Daredevil Drivers, 1938 (Eason 4, McCord 4)

Dare-Devil Droopy, 1951 (Avery 4)

Daredevil in the Castle. *See* Osaka-jo monogatari, 1961

Daredevil Jack, 1920 (Van Dyke 2, Chaney 3)

Daredevils of the Red Circle, 1939 (Canutt 4)

Daredevil's Reward, 1928 (Mix 3, Fox 4)

Dárek, 1946 (Brdečka 4, Trnka 4)

Dareka-san to dareka-san go zeiin shugo!, 1970 (Iwashita 3)

Dåres försvarstal, 1976 (Andersson 3)

Daring Days, 1925 (Laemmle 4)

Daring Hearts, 1919 (Bushman 3)

Daring Years, 1923 (Bow 3)

Daring Young Man, 1942 (Brown 3, Planer 4)

Daring Youth, 1924 (Daniels 3)

Dark Angel, 1925 (Banky 3, Colman 3, Barnes 4, Goldwyn 4, Marion 4, Menzies 4)

Dark Angel, 1935 (March 3, Marshall 3, Oberon 3, Day 4, Goldwyn 4, Newman 4, Toland 4)

Dark Angel, 1989 (O'Toole 3)

Dark at the Top of the Stairs, 1960 (Arden 3, Lansbury 3, Preston 3, Ravetch 4, Steiner 4, Stradling 4)

Dark Avenger, 1955 (Finch 3, Flynn 3, Lee 3, Green 4, Mirisch 4)

Dark Before Dawn, 1988 (Johnson 3, Henry 4)

Dark City, 1950 (Dieterle 2, Heston 3, Dreier 4, Head 4, Wallis 4, Waxman 4)

Dark Command, 1940 (Walsh 2, Pidgeon 3, Rogers 3, Trevor 3, Wayne 3, Canutt 4, Young 4)

Dark Corner, 1945 (Bendix 3)

Dark Corner, 1946 (Hathaway 2, Ball 3, Webb 3, Basevi 4)

Dark Crystal, 1982 (Burtt 4, Morris 4)

Dark Delusion, 1947 (Barrymore 3, Irene 4, Rosher 4, Wilson 4)

Dark Eyes. *See* Yeux noirs, 1935

Dark Eyes. *See* Oci ciorinia, 1987

Dark Eyes of London. *See* Human Monster, 1939

Dark Half, 1990 (Romero 2)

Dark Hazard, 1934 (Robinson 3, Walthall 3, Orry-Kelly 4, Polito 4)

Dark Horse, 1932 (LeRoy 2, Davis 3, Polito 4, Zanuck 4)

Dark Horse, 1946 (Darwell 3, Salter 4)

Dark Hour, 1937 (Bosworth 3)

Dark House, 1923 (Laurel and Hardy 3)

Dark Intruder, 1965 (Schifrin 4)

Dark Journey, 1937 (Saville 2, Leigh 3, Newton 3, Veidt 3, Biro 4, Hornbeck 4, Korda 4, Périnal 4)

Dark Light, 1951 (Carreras 4)

Dark Lover's Play, 1915 (Sennett 2)

Dark Magic, 1939 (Benchley 4)

Dark Man, 1950 (Rank 4)

Dark Mansions, 1986 (Fontaine 3)

Dark Mirror, 1920 (White 3)

Dark Mirror, 1946 (Siodmak 2, Ayres 3, De Havilland 3, Irene 4, Johnson 4, Krasner 4, Schüfftan 4, Sharaff 4, Tiomkin 4)

Dark Night. *See* Noche oscura, 1989

Dark of the Sun. *See* Mercenaries, 1968

Dark Page. *See* Scandal Sheet, 1952

Dark Passage, 1947 (Daves 2, Bacall 3, Bogart 3, Moorehead 3, Wald 4, Waxman 4)

Dark Past, 1949 (Cobb 3, Holden 3, Duning 4, Maté 4, Walker 4)

Dark Places, 1974 (Lee 3, Lom 3)

Dark Purpose, 1964 (Brazzi 3, Presle 3, Sanders 3)

Dark Road, 1917 (Ince 4)

Dark Romance of a Tobacco Tin, 1911 (Bushman 3)

Dark Secret of Harvest Home, 1978 (Pleasence 3)

Dark Secrets, 1923 (Fleming 2, Goulding 2, Rosson 4)

Dark Silence, 1916 (Carré 4)

Dark Star, 1919 (Dwan 2, Davies 3)

Dark Star, 1974 (Carpenter 2)

Dark Streets, 1929 (Haller 4)

Dark Streets of Cairo, 1941 (Salter 4)

Dark the Mountain Snow. *See* Rokujo yukiyama tsumugi, 1965

Dark Tower, 1943 (Fisher 2, Lom 3, Heller 4)

Dark Tower, 1988 (Francis 4)

Dark Town Strutters, 1975 (Corman 2)

Dark Venture, 1956 (Carradine 3)

Dark Victory, 1939 (Goulding 2, Bogart 3, Davis 3, Reagan 3, Friedhofer 4, Haller 4, Orry-Kelly 4, Robinson 4, Steiner 4, Wallis 4)

Dark Victory, 1976 (Hopkins 3)

Dark Waters, 1944 (De Toth 2, Oberon 3, Harrison 4, Rozsa 4)

Dark Wave, 1956 (Clarke 4)

Dark World, 1935 (Withers 3)

Darkening Trail, 1915 (Hart 3, August 4)

Darker Side of Terror, 1979 (Milland 3)

Darker Than Amber, 1970 (Russell 3)

Darkest Africa, 1936 (Eason 4)

Darkest Hour, 1923 (Roach 4)

Darkest Hour. *See* Hell on Frisco Bay, 1955

Darkest Russia, 1917 (Marion 4)

Darkfeather's Strategy, 1912 (Bosworth 3)

Darkness. *See* Temno, 1950

Darkness. *See* Tamas, 1987

Darkness and Daylight, 1923 (August 4)

Darkness at Noon. *See* Mahiru no ankoku, 1956

Darktown Belle, 1913 (Sennett 2)

Darling, 1965 (Schlesinger 2, Bogarde 3, Christie 3, Harvey 3, Raphael 4)

Darling Darling, 1977 (Anand 3)

Darling Dolly Gray, 1926 (Fleischer 4)

Darling, How Could You?, 1951 (Leisen 2, Fontaine 3, Head 4)

Darling I Surrender. *See* Älskling, jag ger mig, 1943

Darling Lili, 1970 (Edwards 2, Andrews 3, Hudson 3, Dunn 4, Harlan 4, Mancini 4, Mercer 4, Pan 4)

Darling of Paris, 1917 (Bara 3)

Darling of the Gods. *See* Liebling der Götter, 1930

Darling of the Rich, 1922 (Goodrich 4)

Darò un millione, 1935 (De Sica 2, Zavattini 4)

Dårskab, dyd og driverter, 1923 (Madsen and Schenstrøm 3)

Dårskapens hus, 1951 (Andersson 3)

Dartozoku, 1963 (Tsuburaya 4)

Darwin Was Right, 1924 (Fox 4)

Dash for Liberty. *See* Højt Spil, 1913

Dash of Courage, 1916 (Sennett 2, Beery 3, Swanson 3)

Dash through the Clouds, 1911 (Sennett 2, Normand 3)

Dastaan, 1950 (Kapoor 2)

Date, 1971 (Cortez 4)

Date for Dinner, 1947 (Terry 4)

Date to Skate, 1938 (Fleischer 4)

Date with a Dream, 1948 (Terry-Thomas 3, Wisdom 3)

Date with a Lonely Girl. *See* T.R. Baskin, 1971

Date with an Angel, 1987 (Edlund 4)

Date with Destiny. *See* Mad Doctor, 1940

Date with Destiny. *See* Return of October, 1949

Date with Dizzy, 1957 (Hubley 4)

Date with Duke, 1947 (Pal 4)

Date with Judy, 1948 (Donen 2, Beery 3, Miranda 3, Taylor 3, Pasternak 4, Rose 4, Surtees 4)

Date with the Falcon, 1941 (Sanders 3)

Dates and Nuts, 1937 (Allyson 3)

Datsugoku, 1950 (Mifune 3)

Daughter of Asia. *See* Aija no musume, 1938

Daughter of Deceit. *See* Hija del angaño, 1951

Daughter of Destiny. *See* Alraune, 1927

Daughter of Dr. Jekyll, 1957 (Ulmer 2)

Daughter of Eve, 1919 (Colman 3)

Daughter of Israel, 1914 (Talmadge 3)

Daughter of Israel. *See* Dots Izrila, 1917

Daughter of Liberty, 1911 (Dwan 2)

Daughter of Luxury. *See* Five and Ten, 1931

Daughter of MacGregor, 1916 (Olcott 2)

Daughter of Rosie O'Grady, 1950 (Darwell 3, Reynolds 3)

Daughter of Shanghai, 1937 (Crabbe 3, Quinn 3, Wong 3, Head 4)

Daughter of the City, 1915 (Van Dyke 2)

Daughter of the Confederacy, 1913 (Olcott 2)

Daughter of the Congo, 1930 (Micheaux 2)

Daughter of the Dragon, 1931 (Hayakawa 3, Wong 3, Buchman 4)

Daughter of the Gods, 1916 (Brenon 2, Hunt 4)

Daughter of the Law, 1921 (Glennon 4)

Daughter of the Mind, 1969 (Carradine 3, Milland 3, Tierney 3, Smith 4)

Daughter of the Mountains. *See* Högfjällets dotter, 1914

Daughter of the Navajos, 1911 (Guy 2)

Daughter of the Night. *See* Tanz auf dem Vulkan, 1921

Daughter of the Poor, 1917 (Love 3, Loos 4)

Daughter of the Railway. *See* Jernbanens Datter, 1911

Daughter of the Sheriff, 1913 (Anderson 3)

Daughter of the South, 1910 (White 3)

Daughter of Two Worlds, 1920 (Goulding 2, Talmadge 3)

Daughter-in-Law. *See* Snotchak, 1912

Daughters Courageous, 1939 (Curtiz 2, Crisp 3, Garfield 3, Rains 3, Blanke 4, Epstein 4, Howe 4, Steiner 4, Wallis 4)

Daughters of Darkness. *See* Rouge aux lèvres, 1971

Daughters of Destiny. *See* Destinées, 1952

Daughters of Destiny. *See* Destini di donne, 1953

Daughters of Pleasure, 1924 (Bow 3)

Daughters of Senor Lopez, 1911 (Dwan 2)

Daughters of the Night, 1924 (Fox 4)

Daughters of the Rich, 1923 (Schulberg 4, Struss 4)

Daughters of Yoshiwara. *See* Takekurabe, 1955

Daughter's Strange Inheritance, 1915 (Talmadge 3)

Daughters Who Pay, 1925 (Lugosi 3)

Daughters, Wives, and a Mother. *See* Musume tsuma haha, 1960

Daumier, 1958 (Leenhardt 2)

Dauphine Java, 1960 (Alexeieff and Parker 4)

Davdas, 1955 (Burman 4)

Dave's Love Affair, 1911 (Sennett 2)

David, 1977 (Driessen 4)

David and Bathsheba, 1951 (King 2, Bushman 3, Hayward 3, Massey 3, Peck 3, Cole 4, Dunne 4, LeMaire 4, Newman 4, Shamroy 4, Wheeler 4, Zanuck 4)

David and Lisa, 1962 (Perry 4)

David Copperfield, 1935 (Barrymore 3, Fields 3, Lanchester 3, O'Sullivan 3, Rathbone 3, Estabrook 4, Gibbons 4, Mayer 4, Selznick 4, Stothart 4, Vorkapich 4)

David Copperfield, 1970 (Attenborough 3, Cusack 3, Evans 3, Olivier 3, Redgrave 3, Richardson 3, Arnold 4, Vetchinsky 4)

David e Golia, 1959 (Welles 2)

David Garrick, 1914 (Ingram 2)

David Golder, 1930 (Duvivier 2, Baur 3, Meerson 4, Périnal 4, Trauner 4)

David Harum, 1915 (Dwan 2, Rosson 4)

David Harum, 1934 (Cruze 2, Darwell 3, Rogers 3, Mohr 4)

David Lynn's Sculpture, 1961 (Baillie 2)

David Niven, 1973 (Alcott 4)

Davudo, 1965 (Güney 2)

Davy, 1957 (Dearden 2, Slocombe 4)

Davy Crockett, 1910 (Bosworth 3, Selig 4)

Davy Crockett and the River Pirates, 1955 (Disney 4, Glennon 4)

Davy Crockett at the Fall of the Alamo, 1926
(Pierce 4)
Davy Crockett, King of the Wild Frontier,
1954 (Ellenshaw 4)
Davy Jones' Locker, 1934 (Iwerks 4)
Dawn, 1914 (Crisp 3, Selig 4)
Dawn, 1919 (Blackton 2)
Dawn, 1928 (Marshall 3)
Dawn. *See* Svítání, 1933
Dawn. *See* Gryning, 1945
Dawn. *See* Hajnal, 1971
Dawn All Night. *See* Svítalo celou noc,
1980
Dawn and Twilight, 1914 (Bushman 3)
Dawn at Socorro, 1954 (Van Cleef 3)
Dawn Guard, 1941 (Boulting 2)
Dawn Maker, 1916 (Hart 3, Sullivan 4)
Dawn of a Tomorrow, 1924 (Clarke 4)
Dawn of Manchukuo and Mongolia. *See*
Mammo Kenkoku no Reimei, 1932
Dawn of Passion, 1911 (Dwan 2)
Dawn of the Dead, 1978 (Savini 4)
Dawn of Tomorrow, 1915 (Pickford 3)
Dawn of Understanding, 1918 (Gilbert 3,
Love 3)
Dawn Patrol, 1930 (Hawks 2, Barthelmess 3,
Haller 4, Miller 4, Saunders 4, Wallis 4)
Dawn Patrol, 1938 (Goulding 2, Crisp 3,
Fitzgerald 3, Flynn 3, Niven 3,
Rathbone 3, Friedhofer 4, Gaudio 4,
Miller 4, Saunders 4, Steiner 4, Wallis 4)
Dawn Rider, 1935 (Wayne 3, Canutt 4)
Dawn Trail, 1930 (McCord 4)
Dawning, 1988 (Hopkins 3, Howard 3,
Simmons 3)
Day. *See* Antonito, 1961
Day After, 1909 (Sweet 3)
Day After. *See* Up from the Beach, 1965
Day After, 1983 (Robards 3, Raksin 4)
Day and the Hour. *See* Jour et l'heure, 1962
Day at Santa Anita, 1936 (De Havilland 3)
Day at School, 1916 (Laurel and Hardy 3)
Day at the Beach, 1938 (Freleng 4)
Day at the Beach, 1969 (Polanski 2,
Sellers 3)
Day at the Circus, 1901 (Porter 2)
Day at the Races, 1937 (Wood 2,
Dandridge 3, Dumont 3, Marx
Brothers 3, O'Sullivan 3, Edens 4,
Gibbons 4, Kaper 4, Mayer 4,
Ruttenberg 4, Waxman 4)
Day at the Zoo, 1939 (Avery 4)
Day Before. *See* Giorno prima, 1987
Day by Day, 1913 (Beery 3)
Day Christ Died, 1980 (Anhalt 4)
Day Dreams, 1922 (Keaton 2)
Day for Night. *See* Nuit américaine, 1973
Day in Court. *See* Giorno in pretura, 1953
Day in Jerusalem, 1912 (Olcott 2)
Day in June, 1944 (Terry 4)
Day in the Country. *See* **Partie de
campagne, 1946**
Day in the Death of Joe Egg, 1971
(Bates 3)
Day in the Life of Wood Newton, 1990
(Reynolds 3)
Day Nurse, 1932 (Lantz 4)
Day Nursing. *See* Children's Corner, 1956
Day of a Man of Affairs, 1929 (Rogers 3)
Day of Anger. *See* Giorno dell'ira, 1967
Day of Faith, 1923 (Browning 2)
Day of Fury, 1956 (Boyle 4)
Day of Grace, 1957 (Carreras 4)
Day of Happiness. *See* Den stchastia, 1964

Day of Marriage. *See* Totsugu hi, 1956
Day of Reckoning, 1915 (Eason 4)
Day of Rest, 1939 (Benchley 4)
Day of the Animals, 1976 (Schifrin 4)
Day of the Bad Man, 1958 (MacMurray 3,
Van Cleef 3, Salter 4)
Day of the Dead, 1985 (Romero 2, Savini 4)
Day of the Dolphin, 1973 (Nichols 2,
Scott 3, Delerue 4, Fraker 4, Henry 4,
Levine 4, Sylbert 4)
Day of the Evil Gun, 1968 (Ford 3,
Kennedy 3, Stanton 3)
Day of the Fight, 1952 (Kubrick 2)
Day of the Jackal, 1973 (Zinnemann 2,
Cusack 3, Seyrig 3, Delerue 4)
Day of the Locust, 1975 (Schlesinger 2,
Black 3, Meredith 3, Page 3,
Sutherland 3, Barry 4, Hall 4, Salt 4,
Whitlock 4)
Day of the Outlaw, 1959 (De Toth 2, Ryan 3,
Harlan 4)
Day of the Triffids, 1963 (Keel 3)
Day of Triumph, 1954 (Cobb 3)
Day of Wrath. *See* **Vredens dag, 1943**
Day Shall Dawn. *See* Jago hua savera, 1958
Day She Paid, 1919 (Ingram 2)
Day That Shook the World. *See*
Assassination at Sarajevo, 1975
Day the Bookies Wept, 1939 (Grable 3)
Day the Clown Cried, 1972 (Lewis 2)
Day the Earth Caught Fire, 1961 (Caine 3,
Mankowitz 4)
Day the Earth Moved, 1974 (Cooper 3)
Day the Earth Stood Still, 1951 (Wise 2,
Jaffe 3, Neal 3, Herrmann 4, LeMaire 4,
Reynolds 4, Wheeler 4)
Day the Fish Came Out, 1967 (Cacoyannis 2,
Lassally 4, Theodorakis 4)
Day the Hot Line Got Hot, 1969 (Boyer 3,
Taylor 3)
Day the Sun Rose. *See* Gion-matsuri, 1968
Day the World Ended, 1955 (Corman 2)
Day They Gave Babies Away. *See* All Mine
to Give, 1956
Day They Robbed the Bank of England,
1960 (O'Toole 3, Périnal 4)
Day Time Ended, 1980 (Malone 3)
Day to Live, 1931 (Terry 4)
Day to Remember, 1953 (Box 4)
Day to Wed. *See* Totsugu hi, 1956
Day Will Come. *See* Es kommt ein Tag,
1950
Day Will Dawn, 1942 (Kerr 3, Richardson 3,
Rank 4, Rattigan 4)
Day with the Boys, 1969 (Kovacs 4)
Daybreak, 1931 (Feyder 2, Novarro 3)
Daybreak. *See* **Jour se lève, 1939**
Daybreak, 1947 (Box 4, Rank 4)
Daybreak and Whiteye, 1957 (Brakhage 2)
Daybreak in Udi, 1949 (Alwyn 4)
Daydreamer, 1966 (Hayakawa 3, Karloff 3,
Terry-Thomas 3)
Daydreams, 1928 (Lanchester 3,
Laughton 3)
Daylight Burglar, 1913 (Crisp 3)
Days and Nights in the Forest. *See* Aranyar
din Ratri, 1970
Days in the Trees. *See* Des journées entières
dans les arbres, 1976
Days of '49, 1913 (Ince 4, Sullivan 4)
Days of '49, 1924 (Canutt 4)
Days of Fury. *See* Giorno del furore,
1973
Days of Fury, 1978 (Price 3)

Days of Glory, 1944 (Tourneur 2, Peck 3,
Dunn 4, Gaudio 4, Robinson 4)
Days of Hate. *See* Días de odio, 1954
**Days of Heaven, 1978 (Malick 2, Gere 3,
Almendros 4, Morricone 4, Shepard 4,
Wexler 4)**
Days of Hope, 1976 (Loach 2)
Days of Jesse James, 1939 (Rogers 3)
Days of October. *See* Oktiabr' dni, 1958
Days of Old, 1922 (Roach 4)
Days of the Pony Express, 1913
(Anderson 3)
Days of Thunder, 1990 (Cruise 3, Duvall 3,
Mancini 4, Towne 4)
Days of Volochayev. *See* Volochayevskiye
dni, 1937
Days of Wilfred Owen, 1965 (Burton 3)
Days of Wine and Roses, 1962 (Edwards 2,
Lemmon 3, Remick 3, Mancini 4,
Mercer 4)
Day's Pleasure, 1919 (Chaplin 2,
Purviance 3)
Daytime Wife, 1939 (Darnell 3, Power 3,
Day 4, Zanuck 4)
Daytime Wives, 1923 (Coffee 4)
Dayu san yori: Jotai wa kanashiku, 1957
(Tanaka 3)
Daze in the West, 1927 (Wyler 2)
Dcery Eviny, 1928 (Heller 4)
D-Day, the Sixth of June, 1956 (O'Brien 3,
Taylor 3, Brackett 4, Garmes 4,
LeMaire 4)
De abajo, 1940 (Figueroa 4)
De aire y fuego, 1972 (Brazzi 3)
De America soy hijo . . . y a ella me debo,
1972 (Alvarez 2)
De Babord à Tribord, 1926 (Matras 4)
De blå undulater, 1965 (Henning-Jensen 2)
De bouche à oreille, 1957 (Decaë 4)
De brandende straal, 1911 (Ivens 2)
De brug, 1928 (Van Dongen 4)
De cierta manera, 1977 (Gómez 2)
De Dans van de Reiger, 1966 (Vierny 4)
De Drapeau noir flotte sur le marmite, 1971
(Gabin 3)
De Flyngande Djavlarna. *See* Flying Devils,
1985
De guerre lasse, 1987 (Aurenche 4, Sarde 4)
De haut à bas, 1933 (Lorre 3)
De Ijsallon, 1985 (Ganz 3)
De Kalte ham Skarven, 1965 (Ullmann 3)
De keder sig pålandet. *See* Et
sommereventyr, 1919
De la Canebière, 1938 (D'Eaubonne 4)
De la ferraille a l'acier victorieux, 1940
(Auric 4)
De la Légion, 1936 (Christian-Jaque 2,
Fernandel 3)
De l'amour, 1964 (Karina 3, Piccoli 3,
Braunberger 4, Guillemot 4)
De Landsflyktige, 1921 (Stiller 2,
Magnusson 4)
De la part des copains, 1970 (Bronson 3)
De la poudre et des balles. *See* Bonne
Chance, Charlie, 1962
De l'autre côté de l'eau, 1951 (Cortez 4)
De Lengte van een Ster, 1964 (Müller 4)
De man die zijn haar kort liet knippen, 1966
(Tyszkiewicz 3, Cloquet 4)
De Mayerling à Sarajevo, 1940 (Feuillère 3,
Courant 4, D'Eaubonne 4, Heller 4)
De Pisis, 1957 (Fusco 4)
De Renoir à Picasso, 1950 (Brasseur 3)
De Sade, 1969 (Corman 2, Huston 2)

De sista stegen, 1960 (Dahlbeck 3, Nykvist 4)

De unge gamle, 1984 (Roos 2)

Dea del mare, 1950 (Bertini 3)

Deacon Outwitted, 1913 (Sennett 2)

Deacon's Troubles, 1912 (Sennett 2, Normand 3)

Deacon's Whiskers, 1915 (Loos 4)

Dead, 1960 (Brakhage 2)

Dead, 1987 (Huston 2, Huston 3, Jeakins 4, North 4)

Dead Again, 1991 (Schygulla 3, Williams 3)

Dead Bang, 1989 (Frankenheimer 2, Adam 4)

Dead Cert, 1973 (Richardson 2)

Dead Don't Die, 1975 (Milland 3)

Dead Don't Scream, 1975 (Blondell 3)

Dead End, 1937 (Wyler 2, Bogart 3, Bond 3, McCrea 3, Sidney 3, Trevor 3, Basevi 4, Day 4, Goldwyn 4, Mandell 4, Newman 4, Toland 4, Westmore Family 4)

Dead Eyes of London. See Toten Augen von London, 1961

Dead Heat, 1988 (Price 3)

Dead Heat on a Merry-Go-Round, 1966 (Coburn 3, Ford 3)

Dead Image. See Dead Ringer, 1964

Dead Letter, 1915 (Laurel and Hardy 3)

Dead Line. See Gray Horizon, 1919

Dead Live. See Mrtví žijí, 1922

Dead Man's Claim, 1912 (Anderson 3)

Dead Man's Folly, 1986 (Ustinov 3)

Dead Man's Return. See Manželé paní Mileny, 1921

Dead Man's Shoes, 1913 (Reid 3)

Dead Men Are Dangerous, 1939 (Newton 3)

Dead Men Don't Die, 1990 (Gould 3)

Dead Men Don't Wear Plaid, 1982 (Martin 3, Head 4, Rozsa 4)

Dead Men Tell, 1941 (Clarke 4, Raksin 4)

Dead Men Tell No Tales, 1920 (Haller 4)

Dead Men's Shoes, 1939 (McDowall 3)

Dead of Night, 1945 (Hamer 2, Redgrave 3, Withers 3, Auric 4, Balcon 4, Clarke 4, Slocombe 4)

Dead of Night. See Deathdream, 1972

Dead of Summer. See Ondata di calore, 1970

Dead of Winter, 1987 (Penn 2, McDowall 3)

Dead on Arrival, 1979 (Palance 3)

Dead on Course. See Wings of Danger, 1952

Dead Ones, 1948 (Markopoulos 2)

Dead or Alive. See Minuto per pregare, un instante per morire, 1968

Dead Pays, 1912 (Ince 4)

Dead Pigeon on Beethoven Street, 1973 (Fuller 2, Audran 3)

Dead Poets Society, 1989 (Weir 2, Williams 3, Jarre 4)

Dead Pool, 1988 (Eastwood 3, Schifrin 4)

Dead Reckoning, 1947 (Cromwell 2, Bogart 3, Cohn 4)

Dead Ringer, 1964 (Davis 3, Henreid 3, Malden 3, Haller 4, Previn 4)

Dead Ringers, 1988 (Bujold 3, Irons 3)

Dead Yesterday, 1937 (Darwell 3)

Dead Zone, 1983 (Cronenberg 2, Lom 3, Sheen 3, De Laurentiis 4)

Deadend Cats, 1947 (Terry 4)

Deadfall, 1968 (Caine 3, Barry 4)

Deadhead Miles, 1972 (Arkin 3, Lupino 3, Raft 3)

Deadhead Miles, 1982 (Malick 2)

Deadlier Sex, 1920 (Karloff 3, Sweet 3)

Deadlier Than the Male, 1966 (Box 4, Sangster 4, Vetchinsky 4)

Deadliest Season, 1977 (Streep 3)

Deadline, 1930 (Haskin 4)

Deadline. See Deadline U.S.A., 1952

Deadline at Dawn, 1946 (Hayward 3, Lukas 3, Eisler 4, Musuraca 4)

Deadline at Eleven, 1920 (Costello 3)

Deadline U.S.A., 1952 (Brooks 2, Barrymore 3, Bogart 3, Krasner 4, LeMaire 4, Wheeler 4)

Deadlock, 1931 (Bennett 4)

Deadlock, 1964 (Halas and Batchelor 4)

Deadly Affair, 1967 (Lumet 2, Andersson 3, Mason 3, Schell 3, Signoret 3, Dehn 4, Jones 4, Young 4)

Deadly Bees, 1966 (Francis 4)

Deadly Blessing, 1981 (Craven 2, Borgnine 3)

Deadly Business, 1986 (Arkin 3)

Deadly Companions, 1961 (O'Hara 3, Clothier 4)

Deadly Dreams, 1971 (Leigh 3)

Deadly Friend, 1986 (Craven 2)

Deadly Game. See Third Party Risk, 1955

Deadly Game, 1982 (Howard 3)

Deadly Glass of Beer, 1917 (Loos 4)

Deadly Hero, 1976 (Jones 3)

Deadly Honeymoon, 1972 (Bernstein 4)

Deadly Is the Female. See Gun Crazy, 1949

Deadly Lessons, 1983 (Reed 3)

Deadly Mantis, 1957 (Westmore Family 4)

Deadly Pursuit. See Shoot to Kill, 1988

Deadly Ray from Mars. See Flash Gordon's Trip to Mars, 1938

Deadly Roulette, 1966 (Pidgeon 3, Wagner 3, Schifrin 4)

Deadly Roulette, 1968 (Schifrin 4)

Deadly Sting. See Evil Spawn, 1987

Deadly Strangers, 1974 (Hayden 3)

Deadly Sweet. See Col cuore in gola, 1967

Deadly Trackers, 1973 (Harris 3)

Deadly Trap. See Maison sous les arbres, 1971

Deadwood Coach, 1924 (Mix 3, Fox 4)

Deadwood Dick, 1939 (Canutt 4)

Deadwood '76, 1965 (Zsigmond 4)

Deadwood Sleeper, 1905 (Bitzer 4)

Deaf, 1986 (Wiseman 2)

Deaf Burglar, 1913 (Sennett 2)

Deaf, Dumb, and Daffy, 1924 (Roach 4)

Deaf Smith and Johnny Ears. See Amigos, 1972

Deaf Smith and Johnny Ears, 1973 (Quinn 3)

Deaf-Mutes Ball, 1907 (Bitzer 4)

Deal of the Century, 1983 (Weaver 3)

Dealing for Daisy. See Mr. "Silent" Haskins, 1915

Dear America: Letters Home from Vietnam, 1987 (Burstyn 3, De Niro 3)

Dear Brat, 1951 (Wood 3, Ames 4, Head 4, Krasna 4, Seitz 4)

Dear Brigitte, 1965 (Bardot 3, Stewart 3, Ballard 4, Duning 4, Smith 4)

Dear Dead Delilah, 1972 (Moorehead 3)

Dear! Deer!, 1942 (Metty 4)

Dear Departed, 1920 (Roach 4)

Dear Detective. See Tendre poulet, 1978

Dear Dr. Gräsler. See Mio caro Dr. Gräsler, 1990

Dear Father. See Caro Papà, 1979

Dear Heart, 1964 (Ford 3, Lansbury 3, Page 3, Harlan 4, Mancini 4)

Dear Hearts. See Mrs. Soffel, 1985

Dear Inspector. See Tendre Poulet, 1978

Dear Margery Boobs, 1977 (Godfrey 4)

Dear Mr. Prohack, 1949 (Bogarde 3, Elliott 3, Dalrymple 4, Rank 4)

Dear Mr. Wonderful, 1982 (Ballhaus 4)

Dear Murderer, 1947 (Box, B. 4, Box, M. 4, Mathieson 4, Rank 4)

Dear Octopus, 1943 (Johnson 3, Lockwood 3)

Dear Old Girl, 1913 (Bushman 3)

Dear Old Girl, 1915 (Bushman 3)

Dear Old Switzerland, 1944 (Terry 4)

Dear Phone, 1977 (Greenaway 2)

Dear Relatives. See Kära släkten, 1933

Dear Ruth, 1947 (Holden 3, Dreier 4, Head 4, Krasna 4, Laszlo 4, Mercer 4)

Dear Summer Sister. See Natsu no imoto, 1972

Dear Wife, 1949 (Holden 3, Dreier 4, Krasna 4)

Dearie, 1927 (Blanke 4)

De-as fi Harap Alb, 1965 (Popescu-Gopo 4)

Death Among Friends, 1975 (Henreid 3)

Death and Transfiguration, 1983 (Davies 2)

Death at 45 RPM. See Meurtre en 45 tours, 1960

Death at Broadcasting House, 1934 (Hawkins 3)

Death at Dawn. See Akatsuki no shi, 1924

Death at Love House, 1976 (Blondell 3, Carradine 3, Lamour 3, Sidney 3, Wagner 3)

Death Bite, 1982 (Reed 3)

Death By Hanging. See **Koshikei, 1968**

Death Cliff. See Shi no dangai, 1951

Death Corps. See Shock Waves, 1977

Death Day. See Que Viva Mexico!, 1931

Death Day, 1933 (Eisenstein 2)

Death Dice, 1915 (Walsh 2)

Death Disk, 1909 (Griffith 2, Bitzer 4)

Death Drives Through, 1935 (Huston 2)

Death Flight. See SST—Death Flight, 1977

Death Hunt, 1981 (Bronson 3, Dickinson 3, Marvin 3)

Death in Canaan, 1978 (Richardson 2, Addison 4)

Death in the Garden. See Mort en ce jardin, 1956

Death in the Sun. See Flüsternde Tod, 1975

Death in the Vatican. See Morte in Vaticano, 1982

Death in Venice. See **Morte a Venezia, 1971**

Death Kiss, 1933 (Lugosi 3)

Death Leaps from the Dome of the Circus. See Dødspringet Til Hest fra Curkuskuplen, 1912

Death Line, 1972 (Lee 3, Pleasence 3)

Death of a Champion, 1939 (Florey 2, O'Connor 3, Head 4)

Death of a Corrupt Man. See Morte di un operatore, 1978

Death of a Cyclist. See **Muerte de un ciclista, 1955**

Death of a Gunfighter, 1969 (Siegel 2, Horne 3, Widmark 3, Westmore Family 4)

Death of a Provincial. See Smierc prowincjala, 1966

Death of a Salesman, 1951 (Kramer 2, March 3, Cohn 4, North 4, Planer 4)

Death of a Salesman, 1957 (Sellers 3)

Death of a Salesman, 1985 (Schlöndorff 2, Hoffman 3, Ballhaus 4)

Death of a Scoundrel, 1956 (De Carlo 3, Sanders 3, Howe 4, Steiner 4)

Death of a Soldier, 1986 (Coburn 3)

Death of a Teamaster. *See* Sen no rikyu, 1989

Death of an Angel, 1952 (Carreras 4)

Death of an Expert Witness, 1983 (Cusack 3)

Death of Hemingway, 1965 (Markopoulos 2)

Death of Her Innocence. *See* Our Time, 1974

Death of Innocence, 1971 (Kennedy 3, Winters 3)

Death of Mario Ricci. *See* Mort de Mario Ricci, 1984

Death of Mr. Baltisberger. *See* Smrt pana Baltisbergra, 1965

Death of Stalinism in Bohemia, 1990 (Švankmajer 4)

Death of the Fly. *See* Smrt mouchy, 1975

Death on the Diamond, 1934 (Rooney 3, Young 3, Krasner 4)

Death on the Freeway, 1979 (Needham 4)

Death on the Mountain. *See* Aru sonan, 1961

Death on the Nile, 1978 (Davis 3, Farrow 3, Lansbury 3, Niven 3, Smith 3, Ustinov 3, Cardiff 4, Rota 4)

Death on the Road, 1935 (Rotha 2)

Death Race 2000, 1975 (Corman 2, Landis 2, Stallone 3, Baker 4)

Death Rage. *See* Con la rabbia agli occhi, 1976

Death Ray. *See* Luch smerti, 1925

Death Rides a Horse. *See* Da uomo a uoma, 1967

Death Sentence, 1974 (Nolte 3)

Death Squad, 1974 (Douglas 3)

Death Takes a Holiday, 1934 (Leisen 2, March 3, Banton 4, Lang 4, Zukor 4)

Death Takes a Holiday, 1971 (Douglas 3, Loy 3, Lourié 4)

Death Travels Too Much. *See* Humour noir, 1965

Death Valley, 1927 (Walker 4)

Death Wheelers. *See* Living Dead, 1972

Death Wish, 1974 (Bronson 3, De Laurentiis 4)

Death Wish II, 1981 (Bronson 3)

Death Wish III, 1985 (Bronson 3)

Death Wish IV: The Crackdown, 1987 (Bronson 3, Golan 4)

Death Woman. *See* Senora Muerte, 1967

Deathdream, 1972 (Savini 4)

Death's Marathon, 1913 (Griffith 2, Barrymore 3, Sweet 3, Walthall 3, Bitzer 4)

Deathsport, 1978 (Corman 2)

Deathtrap, 1982 (Lumet 2, Caine 3, Allen 4)

Deathwatch, 1966 (Mazursky 2, Fields 4)

Deathwatch. *See* Mort en direct, 1979

Deathwatch, 1982 (Stanton 3)

Débrouille-toi, 1917 (Feuillade 2, Musidora 3)

Débroussaillage chimique, 1955 (Rabier 4)

Debshishu, 1986 (Patil 3)

Debt, 1910 (Lawrence 3)

Debt. *See* His Debt, 1919

Debt of Honor, 1918 (Ruttenberg 4)

Deburau, 1951 (Guitry 2)

Debussy Film, 1965 (Russell 2)

Début du siècle, 1968 (Braunberger 4)

Debut in the Secret Service, 1914 (Cruze 2)

Debut of Thomas Cat, 1917 (Bray 4)

Debutantinden, 1913 (Psilander 3)

Débuts au cinématographe. *See* Débuts de Max au cinéma, 1909

Débuts de Max au cinéma, 1909 (Linder 3)

Débuts d'un aviateur. *See* Max dans les airs, 1914

Débuts d'un patineur, 1908 (Linder 3, Pathé 4)

Débuts d'un yachtman, 1909 (Linder 3)

Decade prodigieuse, 1972 (Chabrol 2, Welles 2, Perkins 3, Piccoli 3, Gégauff 4, Rabier 4)

Decameron. *See* Decamerone, 1971

Decameron, 1971 (Mangano 3, Delli Colli 4, Donati 4, Morricone 4)

Decameron Nights. *See* Dekameron-Nächte, 1924

Decameron Nights, 1953 (Fontaine 3, Green 4, Jourdan 3)

Deccan Queen, 1936 (Mehboob 2)

Deceit, 1921 (Micheaux 2)

Deceived Slumming Party, 1908 (Bitzer 4)

Deceiver, 1914 (Loos 4)

Deceiver, 1920 (Mohr 4)

Deceiver, 1930 (Wayne 3)

Deceivers, 1914 (Browning 2)

Deceivers, 1987 (Adam 4)

Deceiving Costume. *See* Itsuwareru seiso, 1951

December Flower, 1984 (Simmons 3)

December 7th, 1943 (Ford 2, Andrews 3, Huston 3, Newman 4, Toland 4)

Décembre, mois des enfants, 1956 (Franju 2, Storck 2)

Deception, 1909 (Griffith 2, Lawrence 3, Bitzer 4)

Deception. *See* Anna Boleyn, 1920

Deception, 1946 (Davis 3, Henreid 3, Rains 3, Blanke 4, Grot 4, Haller 4, Korngold 4)

Deception, 1956 (Howard 3)

Deception. *See* Richter und sein Henker, 1975

Deception Against Time. *See* Man in the Sky, 1957

Deceptions, 1985 (Lollobrigida 3, McDowall 3)

Déchaînés, 1950 (Colpi 4)

Décharge, 1970 (Cloquet 4, Legrand 4)

Deciding Kiss, 1918 (Browning 2)

Decima vittima, 1965 (Mastroianni 3, Di Venanzo 4, Flaiano 4, Guerra 4, Levine 4, Ponti 4)

Decimals of Love. *See* Kärlekens decimaler, 1960

Decimo clandestino, 1989 (Wertmüller 2)

Decimo clandestino, 1989 (Sanda 3)

Decision Against Time. *See* Man in the Sky, 1956

Decision at Sundown, 1957 (Boetticher 2, Scott 3, Brown 4, Guffey 4)

Decision Before Dawn, 1951 (Litvak 2, Kinski 3, Malden 3, Werner 3, Planer 4, Waxman 4)

Decision of Christopher Blake, 1948 (Freund 4, Steiner 4)

Decisions! Decisions, 1972 (Carradine 3)

Decisive Battle. *See* Kessen, 1944

Decks Ran Red, 1958 (Crawford 3, Dandridge 3, Mason 3)

Declassée, 1925 (Gable 3, Gaudio 4)

Declic et des claques, 1965 (Girardot 3)

Décolleté dans le dos, 1975 (Nemec 2)

Decorator, 1920 (Laurel and Hardy 3)

Decree of Destiny, 1910 (Griffith 2, Pickford 3, Bitzer 4)

Dĕdĕckem proti své vuli, 1939 (Stallich 4)

Dédée, 1934 (Darrieux 3)

Dédée. *See* Dédée d'Anvers, 1948

Dédée d'Anvers, 1948 (Blier 3, Dalio 3, Signoret 3, Wakhévitch 4)

Dédé la tendresse, 1972 (Dalio 3)

Dedicated to the Kinks. *See* Summer in the City, 1970

Dedicato al mare Eglo, 1979 (Morricone 4)

Deduce, You Say, 1956 (Blanc 4, Jones 4)

Deedar, 1951 (Kumar 3)

Deep, 1970 (Welles 2)

Deep, 1977 (Yates 2, Nolte 3, Shaw 3, Wallach 3, Barry 4, Challis 4)

Deep Blue Sea, 1955 (Litvak 2, Leigh 3, More 3, Arnold 4, Korda, A. 4, Korda, V. 4, Rattigan 4)

Deep End, 1970 (Skolimowski 2, Dors 3)

Deep in My Heart, 1954 (Donen 2, Astaire 3, Charisse 3, Ferrer 3, Henreid 3, Keel 3, Kelly 3, Miller 3, Oberon 3, Pidgeon 3, Deutsch 4, Edens 4, Folsey 4, Friedhofer 4, Plunkett 4, Rose 4)

Deep in the Heart of Texas, 1942 (Salter 4)

Deep Purple, 1916 (Carré 4, Edeson 4)

Deep Purple, 1920 (Walsh 2, Menzies 4)

Deep Red. *See* Profondo rosso, 1976

Deep Sea Fishing, 1952 (Flynn 3)

Deep Six, 1958 (Bendix 3, Ladd 3, Maté 4, Seitz 4)

Deep Valley, 1947 (Negulesco 2, Lupino 3, Blanke 4, McCord 4, Steiner 4)

Deep Waters, 1920 (Tourneur 2, Gilbert 3)

Deep Waters, 1948 (King 2, Andrews 3, Marsh 3, La Shelle 4, LeMaire 4)

Deer Hunter, 1978 (Cimino 2, De Niro 3, Streep 3, Smith 4, Williams 4, Zsigmond 4)

Deer Stalking with Camera, 1905 (Bitzer 4)

Deerslayer, 1913 (Reid 3)

Deerslayer. *See* Lederstrumpf, 1918

Deerslayer, 1943 (De Carlo 3)

Deerslayer, 1957 (Struss 4)

Deewanjee, 1976 (Burman 4)

Deewar, 1975 (Bachchan 3)

Defeated People, 1946 (Jennings 2)

Defection of Simas Kurdirka, 1978 (Arkin 3, Pleasence 3)

Defective Detectives, 1944 (Langdon 3)

Defector. *See* Espion, 1966

Defence of the Realm, 1985 (Elliott 3, Puttnam 4)

Defend My Love. *See* Difendo il mio amore, 1956

Defendant, 1989 (Menzel 2)

Defending Your Life, 1991 (Grant 3, Streep 3, Henry 4)

Defense de savoir, 1973 (Trintignant 3)

Defense of Madrid, 1976 (McLaren 4)

Defense of Sebastopol. *See* Oborono Sevastopolya, 1911

Defense of Tsaritsyn. *See* Oborona Tsaritsina, 1942

Defense Rests, 1934 (Arthur 3, Bond 3, August 4, Swerling 4)

Defenseless, 1991 (Shepard 4)

Défenseur, 1930 (D'Eaubonne 4)

Defiance. *See* Trots, 1952

Defiant Ones, 1958 (Kramer 2, Curtis 3, Poitier 3)

Deficit, 1989 (Seidelman 2)

Défilé d'artillerie à la revue du 14 juillet 1896, 1949 (Gaumont 4)

Défilé de vaches laitières, 1901 (Gaumont 4)

Definitive afslag på anmodningen om et kys, 1949 (Roos 2)

Defizit, 1917 (Hoffmann 4)

Défroqué, 1953 (Fresnay 3)

Dégourdis de la onzième, 1937 (Christian-Jaque 2, Fernandel 3, Aurenche 4)

Degree of Hygiene and Safety in a Copper Mine. *See* Podstawy w kopalni miedzi, 1972

Dein Herz ist meine Heimat, 1953 (Von Harbou 4)

Dein Schicksal, 1928 (Fischinger 2, Metzner 4)

Déjà vu, 1984 (Bloom 3, Winters 3, Donaggio 4, Golan and Globus 4)

Déjeuner de bébé. *See* Repas de bébé, 1895

Déjeuner des enfants, 1897 (Guy 2)

Déjeuner des oiseaux au Kursaal de Vienne, 1949 (Gaumont 4)

Déjeuner de soleil, 1937 (Berry 3, Auric 4, D'Eaubonne 4)

Déjeuner du chat, 1895 (Lumière 2)

Déjeuner sur l'herbe, 1959 (Kosma 4)

Dekalog 3, 1988 (Olbrychski 3, Lomnicki 3)

Dekameron-Nächte, 1924 (Wilcox 2, Barrymore 3, Krauss 3, Pommer 4)

Dekkai dekkai yaro, 1969 (Iwashita 3)

Del mismo barro, 1930 (Furthman 4)

Del odio nació el amor. *See* Torch, 1949

Del ranco a la capital, 1941 (Armendáriz 3)

Delancey Street: The Crisis Within, 1975 (Schifrin 4)

Delayed Proposal, 1911 (Sennett 2)

Delessi Affair, 1979 (More 3)

Delfini, 1960 (Cardinale 3, Cristaldi 4, Di Venanzo 4, Fusco 4)

Delhi. *See* World Window, 1977

Delhi Way, 1964 (Ivory 2)

Délibábok országa, 1983 (Mészáros 2, Nowicki 3)

Delicate Balance, 1973 (Richardson 2, Cotten 3, Hepburn 3, Remick 3, Watkin 4)

Delicate Delinquent, 1957 (Lewis 2, Head 4)

Delicious, 1931 (Gaynor 3, Behrman 4, Levien 4)

Delicious Little Devil, 1919 (Valentino 3)

Delightful Rogue, 1929 (Plunkett 4)

Delightfully Dangerous, 1945 (Tashlin 2, Beavers 3, Bellamy 3, Krasner 4)

Delinquents, 1955 (Altman 2)

Délit de fuite, 1958 (Renoir 4)

Delitto, 1984 (Gélin 3)

Delitto al circolo del tennis, 1969 (Storaro 4)

Delitto d'amore, 1974 (Comencini 2)

Delitto di Giovanni Episcopo, 1947 (Fellini 2, Fabrizi 3, Lollobrigida 3, Mangano 3, Sordi 3, Cecchi D'Amico 4, Rota 4)

Delitto Matteotti, 1973 (De Sica 2)

Delitto quasi perfetto, 1966 (Camerini 2, Blier 3)

Deliverance, 1972 (Boorman 2, Reynolds 3, Voight 3, Zsigmond 4)

Deliverance. *See* Sadgati, 1981

Della nube alla resistenza, 1979 (Straub and Huillet)

Delo Artamonovykh, 1941 (Maretskaya 3)

Delo Rumiantseva, 1956 (Batalov 3)

Delphi Bureau, 1972 (Lourié 4)

Delphica, 1962 (Braunberger 4)

Delphine, 1968 (Gégauff 4)

Delta de sel, 1967 (Braunberger 4)

Delta Factor, 1970 (Garnett 2, De Carlo 3)

Delta Force, 1986 (Marvin 3, Schygulla 3, Winters 3, Golan and Globus 4)

Delta Force II: The Columbian Connection. *See* Stranglehold: Delta Force II, 1990

Delta Phase I, 1962 (Haanstra 2)

Deluded Wife, 1916 (Eason 4)

Deluge. *See* Potop, 1915

Deluge. *See* Potop, 1974

Delusion, 1980 (Cotten 3)

Delusions of Grandeur. *See* Folie des grandeurs, 1971

Deluxe Annie, 1918 (Talmadge 3)

Demain Paris, 1964 (Leenhardt 2)

Démanty noci, 1964 (Kučera 4, Ondříček 4)

Demaskierung. *See* Nacht der Verwandlung, 1935

Déménagement à la cloche de bois, 1897 (Guy 2)

Déménagement à la cloche de bois, 1907 (Guy 2)

Dément du Lac Jean Jeune, 1947 (Jutra 2)

Demetrius and the Gladiators, 1954 (Daves 2, Bancroft 3, Borgnine 3, Burton 3, Hayward 3, Mature 3, Dunne 4, Krasner 4, LeMaire 4, Waxman 4, Wheeler 4)

Demi-Bride, 1927 (Shearer 3, Gibbons 4, Gillespie 4)

Demi-Paradise, 1943 (Olivier 3, Rutherford 3, De Grunwald 4, Dillon 4, Rank 4)

Demoiselle du notaire, 1912 (Feuillade 2)

Demoiselle et le violoncelliste, 1965 (Grimault 4)

Demoiselle et son revenant, 1951 (Burel 4)

Demoiselles de Rochefort, 1967 (Darrieux 3, Deneuve 3, Kelly 3, Piccoli 3, Cloquet 4, Evein 4, Legrand 4)

Démolition d'un mur, 1895 (Lumière 2)

Demon, 1925 (Laemmle 4)

Demon, 1976 (Sidney 3)

Demon Cathedral. *See* Chiesa, 1989

Demon Doctor. *See* Juggernaut, 1936

Demon for Trouble, 1934 (Katzman 4)

Demon in My View, 1991 (Perkins 3)

Demon of Fear, 1916 (Borzage 2)

Demon Pond. *See* Yashagaike, 1979

Demon Seed, 1977 (Christie 3)

Demoni, 1985 (Argento 4)

Demoni 2—L'incuba ritorna, 1986 (Argento 4)

Demoniaque. *See* Louves, 1957

Demons. *See* Demoni, 1985

Demons 2—The Nightmare is Back. *See* Demoni 2—L'incuba ritorna, 1986

Démons de l'aube, 1946 (Allégret 2, Signoret 3, Honegger 4 Wakhévitch 4)

Démons de midi, 1978 (Presle 3)

Démons de minuit, 1961 (Boyer 3)

Demons of the Mind, 1972 (Carreras 4)

Demütiger und die Sängerin, 1925 (Dagover 3)

Den of Thieves, 1905 (Hepworth 2)

Den of Thieves, 1914 (Reid 3)

Den pervyi, 1958 (Enei 4)

Dendai inchiki monogatari: Dotanuki, 1963 (Kyo 3)

Denen Kokyogaku, 1938 (Hara 3)

Dengeki Shutsudo, 1944 (Mori 3)

Denial, 1925 (Gibbons 4, Mayer 4)

Denmark Grows Up, 1947 (Henning-Jensen 2)

Dénonciation, 1961 (Braunberger 4, Delerue 4)

Denso ningen, 1960 (Tsuburaya 4)

Dent récalcitrante, 1902 (Guy 2)

Dentellière, 1977 (Goretta 2, Huppert 3)

Dentist, 1919 (Sennett 2)

Dentist, 1932 (Sennett 2, Fields 3)

Dents du diable. *See* Savage Innocents, 1960

Dents longues, 1952 (Bardot 3, Gélin 3, Audiard 4)

Denture Adventure, 1980 (Halas and Batchelor 4)

Denver and Rio Grande, 1952 (Hayden 3, O'Brien 3, Head 4)

Denver Dude, 1927 (Eason 4, Laemmle 4)

Denwa wa yugata ni naru, 1959 (Yoshimura 2)

Départ, 1967 (Skolimowski 2, Léaud 3)

Départ en voiture, 1895 (Lumière 2)

Départ pour l'Allemagne, 1946 (Leenhardt 2)

Départ pour les vacances, 1904 (Guy 2)

Départment 66, 1963 (Braunberger 4)

Department Store. *See* Univermag, 1922

Departure of Train from Station, 1905 (Bitzer 4)

Deported, 1950 (Siodmak 2, Buckner 4, Daniels 4, Orry-Kelly 4)

Depraved. *See* Adelaide, 1968

Depressed Area, 1963 (Van Dyke 2)

Deprisa, deprisa, 1980 (Saura 2)

Deputat Baltiki, 1936 (Cherkassov 3)

Deputy and the Girl, 1912 (Anderson 3)

Deputy Droopy, 1955 (Avery 4)

Deputy's Love. *See* Deputy's Love Affair, 1910

Deputy's Love Affair, 1910 (Anderson 3)

Deranged, 1987 (Savini 4)

Derby, 1919 (Dupont 2)

Derby Day, 1923 (Roach 4)

Derby Day, 1951 (Wilcox 2, Neagle 3, Withers 3)

Derecho de asilo, 1972 (Fernández 2)

Derek and Clive Get the Horn, 1980 (Moore 3)

Derelitta, 1981 (Olbrychski 3)

Derkovitz Gyula 1894–1934, 1958 (Jancsó 2)

Dermis Probe, 1965 (Williams 4)

Dernier amour, 1948 (Moreau 3)

Dernier atout, 1942 (Becker 2, Modot 3, Bost 4, Douy 4)

Dernier Baiser, 1977 (Girardot 3)

Dernier Choc, 1932 (Clouzot 2)

Dernier des six, 1941 (Clouzot 2, Fresnay 3, Andrejew 4)

Dernier été a Tangier, 1987 (Karina 3)

Dernier Metro, 1980 (Truffaut 2, Deneuve 3, Depardieu 3, Almendros 4, Delerue 4)

Dernier Milliardaire, 1934 (Clair 2, Jaubert 4, Maté 4)

Dernier Papillon, 1991 (North 4)

Dernier Pardon, 1913 (Tourneur 2)

Dernier Refuge, 1947 (Modot 3, Burel 4)

Dernier Refuge, 1965 (Braunberger 4, Delerue 4)

Dernier Soir, 1964 (Chaplin 3)

Dernier Sou, 1946 (Andrejew 4)

Dernier Soul, 1946 (Cayatte 2)

Dernier Tango à Paris. *See* **Last Tango in Paris, 1972**

Dernier Tiercé, 1964 (Burel 4)

Dernier Tournant, 1939 (Simon 3, Matras 4, Renoir 4, Spaak 4, Wakhévitch 4)

Dernière chanson, 1986 (Karina 3)

Dernière Femme. *See* Ultima donna, 1975

Dernière jeunesse, 1939 (Brasseur 3, Raimu 3)

Dernière la façade, 1939 (Spiegel 4)

Dernière Valse, 1936 (Burel 4)

Dernières Cartouches, 1899 (Pathé 4)

Dernières Vacances, 1949 (Leenhardt 2, Barsacq 4)

Derniers Jours de Pompéi, 1948 (Presle 3, Aldo 4)

Déroute, 1957 (Colpi 4)

Derrière la façade, 1939 (Von Stroheim 2, Berry 3, Simon 3)

Derrière la fenêtre, 1966 (Delerue 4)

Dersu Uzala, 1975 (Kurosawa 2)

Des jeunes filles dans la nuit, 1943 (Berry 3)

Des journées entières dans les arbres, 1976 (Almendros 4)

Des Pardes, 1979 (Anand 3)

Des pissenlits par la racine, 1964 (Delerue 4)

Des rails sous les palmiers, 1951 (Colpi 4)

Des ruines et des hommes, 1958 (Delerue 4)

Des Teufels Advokat, 1977 (Audran 3, Mills 3, Green 4)

Des Teufels General, 1955 (Käutner 2)

Desafio, 1979 (Alvarez 2)

Desarraigados, 1958 (Armendáriz 3)

Desarroi, 1946 (Berry 3)

Desaster, 1973 (Von Trotta 2)

Désastres de la guerre, 1951 (Grémillon 2)

Descanse en piezas, 1986 (Malone 3)

Descendants of Taro Urashima. See Urashima Taro no koei, 1946

Déscente aux enfers, 1986 (Delerue 4)

Description d'un combat, 1960 (Marker 2, Cloquet 4)

Desdemona, 1908 (Porten 3, Messter 4)

Desdemona, 1911 (Blom 2, Psilander 3)

Deseada, 1951 (Del Rio 3)

Desert, 1975 (Brakhage 2)

Desert Attack. See Ice Cold in Alex, 1958

Desert Bloom, 1986 (Voight 3)

Desert Blossoms, 1921 (Fox 4)

Desert Breed, 1915 (Chaney 3)

Desert Calls Its Own, 1916 (Mix 3)

Desert Claim, 1911 (Anderson 3)

Desert Command. See Three Musketeers, 1933

Désert de Pigalle, 1957 (Girardot 3)

Désert des Tartares, 1976 (Gassman 3, Noiret 3, Rey 3, Trintignant 3, Von Sydow 3, Morricone 4)

Desert Driven, 1923 (Carey 3)

Desert Dust, 1927 (Wyler 2, Laemmle 4)

Desert Flower, 1925 (LeRoy 2, Moore 3, Mathis 4, McCord 4)

Desert Fox, 1951 (Sloane 3, Johnson 4, Wheeler 4)

Desert Fury, 1947 (Rossen 2, Astor 3, Lancaster 3, Cronjager 4, Head 4, Lang 4, Rozsa 4, Wallis 4)

Desert Gold, 1914 (Ince 4)

Desert Gold, 1926 (Powell 3, Schulberg 4)

Desert Gold, 1936 (Crabbe 3, Dreier 4)

Desert Greed, 1926 (Canutt 4)

Desert Hawk, 1924 (Canutt 4)

Desert Hawk, 1944 (Eason 4)

Desert Hawk, 1950 (De Carlo 3, Hudson 3, Metty 4)

Desert Hero, 1919 (Arbuckle 3)

Desert Honeymoon, 1980 (Johnson 3)

Desert Legion, 1953 (Ladd 3, Seitz 4)

Desert Love, 1920 (Mix 3)

Desert Man, 1917 (Hart 3, August 4)

Desert Man, 1934 (Canutt 4)

Desert Mice, 1959 (Dearden 2)

Desert Nights, 1929 (Gilbert 3, Coffee 4, Gibbons 4, Howe 4)

Desert of the Tartars. See Desert des Tartares, 1976

Desert of the Tartars. See Deserto dei Tartari, 1977

Desert Outlaw, 1924 (Fox 4)

Desert Passage, 1952 (Hunt 4)

Desert Patrol. See Sea of Sand, 1958

Desert Rats, 1953 (Wise 2, Burton 3, Mason 3, Newton 3, LeMaire 4, Newman 4)

Desert Rider, 1923 (Pierce 4)

Desert Rose. See Rosa de areia, 1989

Desert Sands, 1955 (Carradine 3)

Desert Shield, 1990 (Golan and Globus 4)

Desert Song, 1929 (Loy 3)

Desert Song, 1943 (Florey 2, Dalio 3, Johnson 3, Buckner 4, Glennon 4, Prinz 4)

Desert Song, 1953 (Grayson 3, Massey 3, Burks 4, Prinz 4, Steiner 4)

Desert Sweetheart, 1912 (Anderson 3)

Desert Trail, 1935 (Wayne 3)

Desert Tribesman, 1914 (Cruze 2)

Desert Valley, 1926 (Fox 4)

Desert Vengeance, 1931 (McCord 4)

Desert Victory, 1943 (Boulting 2, Alwyn 4)

Desert Warrior. See Amanti del deserto, 1956

Desert Wooing, 1918 (Niblo 2, Barnes 4)

Deserted at the Altar, 1922 (Howard 2, Love 3)

Deserter, 1912 (Ince 4)

Deserter, 1916 (August 4, Ince 4)

Deserter. See Dezertir, 1933

Deserter. See Dezerter, 1958

Deserter. See Dezertér, 1965

Deserter, 1971 (Huston 2, De Laurentiis 4)

Deserter. See Disertore, 1983

Déserteur, 1906 (Pathé 4)

Déserteur, 1939 (Honegger 4)

Déserteuse, 1917 (Feuillade 2)

Deserto dei tartari. See Désert des Tartares, 1976

Deserto rosso, 1964 (Antonioni 2, Harris 3, Vitti 3, Fusco 4, Guerra 4)

Desert's Price, 1925 (Van Dyke 2, Fox 4)

Desert's Sting, 1914 (Macpherson 4, Meredyth 4)

Desert's Toll, 1926 (Stevens 2, Wong 3)

Desh Premee, 1982 (Bachchan 3)

Déshabillé du modèle, 1897 (Pathé 4)

Desideria, la vita interiore, 1980 (Donaggio 4)

Desiderio, 1943 (De Santis 2, Rossellini 2)

Desiderio, 1984 (Rotunno 4)

Design for Leaving, 1954 (Blanc 4, McKimson 4, Stalling 4)

Design for Living, 1933 (Lubitsch 2, Cooper 3, Darwell 3, Hopkins 3, Horton 3, March 3, Pangborn 3, Banton 4, Dreier 4, Hecht 4, Zukor 4)

Design for Scandal, 1941 (Pidgeon 3, Russell 3, Daniels 4, Waxman 4)

Designing Woman, 1941 (Cole 4)

Designing Woman, 1957 (Minnelli 2, Bacall 3, Peck 3, Alton 4, Ames 4, Previn 4, Rose 4, Schary 4)

Designs on Jerry, 1956 (Hanna and Barbera 4)

Désir mène les hommes, 1957 (Decaë 4)

Desirable, 1934 (Brennan 3, Darwell 3, Haller 4, Orry-Kelly 4)

Desire, 1923 (Barnes 4)

Desire, 1936 (Borzage 2, Lubitsch 2, Cooper 3, Dietrich 3, Banton 4, Dreier 4, Hoffenstein 4, Lang 4, Young 4)

Désiré, 1937 (Guitry 2, Arletty 3)

Desire. See Yokubo, 1953

Desire, 1954 (Brando 3, Oberon 3, Simmons 3, Krasner 4, LeMaire 4, Newman 4, North 4, Reynolds 4, Taradash 4, Wheeler 4)

Desire. See Touha, 1958

Desire in the Dust, 1960 (Bennett 3, Ballard 4)

Desire Me, 1947 (Cukor 2, LeRoy 2, Garson 3, Mitchum 3, Akins 4, Irene 4, Robinson 4, Ruttenberg 4, Stothart 4)

Desire, the Interior Life. See Desideria, la vita interiore, 1980

Desire under the Elms, 1958 (Loren 3, Perkins 3, Bernstein 4)

Desired Woman, 1927 (Curtiz 2, Blanke 4, Zanuck 4)

Desistfilm, 1954 (Brakhage 2)

Desk Set, 1957 (Blondell 3, Hepburn 3, Tracy 3, LeMaire 4, Shamroy 4)

Désordre, 1961 (Welles 2)

Désordre et la nuit, 1958 (Cassel 3, Darrieux 3, Gabin 3, Audiard 4)

Despair, 1979 (Bogarde 3, Ballhaus 4)

Despegue a la 18.00, 1969 (Alvarez 2)

Desperado, 1910 (Anderson 3)

Desperado, 1954 (Van Cleef 3)

Desperado: Avalanche at Devil's Ridge, 1988 (Steiger 3)

Desperado Outpost. See Dokuritsu gurenta, 1959

Desperadoes, 1943 (Vidor 2, Ford 3, Scott 3, Trevor 3, Brown 4)

Desperados, 1969 (Palance 3)

Desperados, 1970 (Borgnine 3)

Desperate, 1947 (Mann 2)

Desperate Adventure, 1938 (Novarro 3)

Desperate Case, 1981 (Lee 3)

Desperate Chance. See "Bad Buck" of Santa Ynez, 1915

Desperate Characters, 1971 (MacLaine 3)

Desperate Hours, 1955 (Wyler 2, Bogart 3, Kennedy 3, March 3, Garmes 4, Head 4)

Desperate Hours, 1990 (Hopkins 3, Rourke 3, De Laurentiis 4)

Desperate Journey, 1942 (Walsh 2, Flynn 3, Kennedy 3, Massey 3, Reagan 3, Friedhofer 4, Glennon 4, Steiner 4, Wald 4, Wallis 4)

Desperate Lives, 1982 (Biroc 4)

Desperate Living, 1977 (Waters 2)

Desperate Lover, 1912 (Sennett 2, Normand 3)

Desperate Moment, 1953 (Zetterling 2, Bogarde 3, Rank 4)

Desperate Moves, 1986 (Lee 3)

Desperate Ones. See Más allá de las montañas, 1967

Desperate Search, 1952 (Lewis 2, Keel 3)

Desperate Trails, 1921 (Ford 2, Carey 3, Laemmle 4)

Desperately Seeking Susan, 1985 (Seidelman 2)

Dessin de perspective. See Perspective, 1949

Dessous des cartes, 1948 (Cayatte 2, Reggiani 3, Korda 4, Spaak 4)

Destination Fury. See Pleine bagarre, 1961

Destination Gobi, 1952 (Wise 2, Widmark 3, Clarke 4, LeMaire 4, Newman 4)

Destination Magoo, 1954 (Bosustow 4, Burness 4)

Destination Meatball, 1951 (Lantz 4)

Destination Moon, 1950 (Pal 4)

Destination Murder, 1949 (Leven 4)

Destination Tokyo, 1944 (Daves 2, Garfield 3, Grant 3, Glennon 4, Wald 4, Warner 4, Waxman 4)

Destination Unknown, 1933 (Garnett 2, Bellamy 3)

Destination Unknown, 1942 (Salter 4)

Destin fabuleux de Desirée Clary, 1941 (Guitry 2, Barrault 3)

Destinées, 1952 (Colbert 3, Morgan 3, Piccoli 3, Aurenche 4, Bost 4, D'eaubonne 4, Jeanson 4, Matras 4)

Destini di donne, 1953 (Amidei 4, Flaiano 4)

Destino e il timoniere, 1919 (Gallone 2)

Destins de Manoel, 1984 (Branco 4, De Almeida 4)

Destiny. See Müde Tod, 1921

Destiny of a Man. See Sudba cheloveka, 1959

Destiny of a Spy, 1969 (Quayle 3, Roberts 3)

Deštivý den, 1963 (Kučera 4)

Destroy All Monsters. See Kaiju soshingeki, 1968

Destroy, She Said. See Détruire, dit-elle, 1969

Destroyer, 1943 (Ford 3, Robinson 3, Chase 4, Planer 4)

Destroyer, 1988 (Perkins 3)

Destroying Angel, 1923 (Van Dyke 2)

Destruction, 1916 (Bara 3)

Destruction of Sakura-Jima. See Wrath of the Gods, 1914

Destructors. See Marseilles Contract, 1974

Destry, 1955 (Murphy 3)

Destry Rides Again, 1932 (Mix 3)

Destry Rides Again, 1939 (Dietrich 3, Stewart 3, Mohr 4, Pasternak 4)

Det är min modell, 1946 (Molander 2)

Det är min musik, 1942 (Fischer 4)

Det brinner en eld, 1943 (Molander 2, Sjöström 2)

Detained, 1924 (Laurel and Hardy 3)

Detained While Waiting for Justice, Why?. See Detenuto in attesa di giudizio, 1971

Detective, 1928 (Rooney 3)

Detective, 1930 (Lantz 4)

Detective. See Father Brown, 1954

Detective, 1968 (Duvall 3, Sinatra 3, Biroc 4, Goldsmith 4, Smith 4)

Détective, 1985 (Godard 2, Baye 3, Cuny 3, Léaud 3)

Detective Clive, Bart. See Scotland Yard, 1930

Detective Craig's Coup, 1910 (White 3)

"Détective Dervieux", 1912–13 (Feuillade 2)

Detective Story, 1951 (Wyler 2, Bendix 3, Douglas 3, Grant 3, Garmes 4, Head 4)

Detective Swift, 1910 (White 3)

Detectives, 1968 (Remick 3)

Detektiv des Kaisers, 1930 (Tschechowa 3)

Detenuto in attesa di giudizio, 1970 (Amidei 4)

Detenuto in attesa di giudizio, 1971 (Sordi 3)

Determination, 1922 (Costello 3)

Determined Woman, 1910 (Lawrence 3)

Déterminés à vaincre, 1968 (Ivens 2)

Deti kapitana Granta, 1936 (Cherkassov 3)

Deti Vanyousina, 1915 (Mozhukin 3)

Detour, 1945 (Ulmer 2)

Detour, 1978 (Cushing 3)

Detouring America, 1939 (Avery 4)

Detras de esa puerta, 1972 (Brazzi 3)

Detras del silencio, 1972 (Baker 3)

Détruire, dit-elle, 1969 (Gélin 3, Colpi 4)

Deuce of Spades, 1922 (Buckland 4)

Deus Ex. See Pittsburgh Documents, 1971

Deutsche Herzen am Deutschen Rhein, 1925 (Albers 3)

Deutscher Frühling, 1979 (Ballhaus 4)

Deutscher Traum. See Hitler: Ein Film aus Deutschland, 1977

Deutsches Mann Geil! Die Geschichte von Ilona und Kurti, 1991 (Morricone 4)

Deutschland im Herbst, 1978 (Winkler 3, Ballhaus 4)

Deutschmeister, 1955 (Schneider 3)

Deux, 1989 (Depardieu 3)

Deux Anglaises et le continent, 1971 (Truffaut 2, Léaud 3, Almendros 4, Delerue 4)

Deux bobines et un fil, 1954 (Cloquet 4)

Deux Canards, 1933 (Douy 4)

Deux Combinards, 1937 (Berry 3)

Deux coverts, 1935 (Guitry 2, Fradetal 4)

Deux Crocodiles, 1987 (Sarde 4)

Deux Françaises, 1915 (Feuillade 2, Musidora 3)

Deux Gamines, 1920 (Clair 2, Feuillade 2)

Deux Gosses, 1906 (Feuillade 2)

Deux grandes filles dans un pyjama, 1974 (Presle 3)

Deux heures à tuer, 1965 (Brasseur 3, Simon 3)

Deux hommes dans la ville, 1973 (Delon 3, Depardieu 3, Gabin 3, Sarde 4)

Deux hommes dans Manhattan, 1959 (Melville 2)

Deux Mondes, 1930 (Dupont 2)

Deux "Monsieurs" de Madame, 1933 (Burel 4)

Deux Orphelines, 1933 (Tourneur 2, Douy 4, Ibert 4)

Deux ou trois choses que je sais d'elle, 1967 (Godard 2, Coutard 4)

Deux Pigeons, 1962 (Barsacq 4)

Deux Rivaux, 1903 (Guy 2)

Deux Saisons de la vie, 1972 (Morricone 4)

Deux sous de violettes, 1951 (Barsacq 4)

Deux Timides, 1928 (Clair 2, Rosay 3, Meerson 4)

Deux Timides, 1942 (Brasseur 3, Achard 4, Alekan 4)

Deux Verités, 1950 (Simon 3)

Deuxième Ciel, 1969 (Braunberger 4)

Deuxième Procès d'Artur London, 1969 (Montand 3)

Deuxième Souffle, 1966 (Melville 2)

Devanti a lui tremava tutta Roma, 1946 (Magnani 3)

Devata, 1978 (Azmi 3)

Děvčata, nedejte se!, 1937 (Heller 4)

Děvčátko, neříkej ne!, 1932 (Stallich 4)

Devdas, 1935 (Roy 2)

Devdas, 1955 (Roy 2, Kumar 3)

Development History of the Southern Sea: Tribes of the Ocean. See Mampou hattenshi: Umi no gouzoku, 1942

Devi, 1960 (Chatterjee 3, Chandragupta 4, Datta 4, Mitra 4)

Deviatoe yanvaria, 1926 (Moskvin 4)

Devices and Desires, 1991 (York 3)

Devil, 1908 (Griffith 2, Lawrence 3, Bitzer 4)

Devil, 1920 (Goulding 2, Arliss 3)

Devil and Daniel Webster. See All That Money Can Buy, 1941

Devil and Max Devlin, 1981 (Gould 3, Hamlisch 4, Sangster 4)

Devil and Miss Jones, 1941 (Wood 2, Arthur 3, Coburn 3, Krasna 4, Menzies 4, Stradling 4)

Devil and the Deep, 1932 (Cooper 3, Grant 3, Laughton 3, Lang 4, Zukor 4)

Devil and the Ten Commandments. See Diable et les dix commandements, 1962

Devil at Four O'Clock, 1961 (LeRoy 2, Dalio 3, Sinatra 3, Tracy 3, Biroc 4)

Devil at His Elbow, 1916 (Menjou 3, Duning 4)

Devil Bat, 1941 (Lugosi 3)

Devil by the Tail. See Diable par la queue, 1968

Devil Commands, 1941 (Dmytryk 2, Karloff 3)

Devil Dancer, 1927 (Niblo 2, Wong 3, Barnes 4, Goldwyn 4)

Devil Dodger, 1917 (Gilbert 3)

Devil Dogs of the Air, 1935 (Bacon 2, Bond 3, Cagney 3, Edeson 4, Saunders 4)

Devil Doll, 1936 (Browning 2, Von Stroheim 2, Barrymore 3, O'Sullivan 3, Walthall 3, Fort 4, Gibbons 4, Waxman 4)

Devil Girl from Mars, 1954 (Korda 4)

Devil Goddess, 1955 (Weissmuller 3, Katzman 4)

Devil Has Seven Faces. See Diavolo a sette face, 1971

Devil Horse, 1926 (Stevens 2, Canutt 4, Roach 4)

Devil Horse, 1932 (Carey 3, Canutt 4)

Devil in Evening Dress, 1973 (Miller 2)

Devil in Love. See Arcidiavolo, 1966

Devil in Silk. See Teufel in Seide, 1955

Devil in the Brain. See Diavolo nel cervello, 1972

Devil in the Flesh. See Diable au corps, 1947

Devil in the Flesh, 1986 (Bellocchio 2, Sarde 4)

Devil Is an Empress. See Joueur d'échecs, 1938

Devil Is a Sissy, 1936 (Van Dyke 2, Cooper 3, Rooney 3, Brown 4, Freed 4, Rosson 4, Stothart 4)

Devil Is a Woman, 1935 (Von Sternberg 2, Dietrich 3, Horton 3, Ballard 4, Banton 4, Dreier 4, Zukor 4)

Devil Is a Woman. See Soriso del grande tentatore, 1973

Devil Makes Three, 1952 (Kelly 3)

Devil May Care, 1929 (Novarro 3, Adrian 4, Day 4, Gibbons 4, Kräly 4, Lewin 4, Shearer 4, Stothart 4, Tiomkin 4)

Devil May Hare, 1954 (Blanc 4, McKimson 4, Stalling 4)

Devil Never Sleeps. See Satan Never Sleeps, 1962

Devil of a Fellow. See Teufelskerl, 1935

Devil of the Deep, 1938 (Terry 4)

Devil on Horseback, 1936 (Lewis 2, Miller 3)

Devil on Horseback, 1954 (Withers 3)

Devil on Wheels. See Indianapolis Speedway, 1939

Devil Pays Off, 1941 (Alton 4)

Devil, Probably. *See* Diable, probablement, 1977

Devil Riders, 1943 (Crabbe 3)

Devil Rides Out, 1968 (Lee 3, Bernard 4, Carreras 4)

Devil Strikes at Night. *See* Nachtswann der Teufel Kamm, 1957

Devil Takes the Count. *See* Devil Is a Sissy, 1936

Devil Thumbs a Ride, 1947 (Hunt 4)

Devil to Pay, 1930 (Colman 3, Loy 3, Young 3, Barnes 4, Day 4, Goldwyn 4, Newman 4, Toland 4)

Devil with Hitler, 1942 (Roach 4)

Devil with Women, 1930 (Bogart 3, McLaglen 3, Fox 4, Friedhofer 4, Nichols 4)

Devil Within Her. *See* I Don't Want to be Born, 1975

Devilish Honeymoon. *See* Kam čert nemuže, 1970

Devils, 1970 (Jarman 2)

Devils, 1971 (Russell 2, Redgrave 3, Reed 3, Russell 4, Watkin 4)

Devil's Advocate. *See* Des Teufels Advokat, 1977

Devil's Agent, 1962 (Cushing 3, Lee 3)

Devil's Angels, 1967 (Cassavetes 2, Corman 2)

Devil's Bait, 1959 (Alwyn 4)

Devil's Bishop, 1988 (Pontecorvo 2)

Devil's Bride. *See* Devil Rides Out, 1968

Devil's Brigade, 1968 (Andrews 3, Holden 3, Robertson 3, Clothier 4, Needham 4, North 4)

Devil's Brother. *See* Fra Diavolo, 1933

Devil's Canyon, 1953 (D'Agostino 4, Musuraca 4)

Devil's Cargo, 1925 (Fleming 2, Beery 3)

Devil's Chaplain, 1929 (Karloff 3)

Devil's Circus, 1926 (Christensen 2, Shearer 3)

Devil's Claim, 1920 (Hayakawa 3, Moore 3)

Devil's Cross. *See* Cruz diablo, 1934

Devil's Daffodil, 1962 (Kinski 3, Lee 3)

Devil's Daughter, 1915 (Bara 3)

Devil's Daughter. *See* Fille du diable, 1945

Devil's Daughter, 1972 (Cotten 3, Winters 3)

Devil's Disciple, 1959 (Douglas 3, Lancaster 3, Olivier 3, Fisher 4)

Devil's Doorway, 1950 (Mann 2, Calhern 3, Taylor 3, Alton 4, Canutt 4, Mayer 4, Plunkett 4)

Devil's Double, 1916 (Hart 3, August 4)

Devil's Envoy. *See* Visiteurs du soir, 1942

Devil's Eye. *See* Djävulens öga, 1960

Devil's Feud Cake, 1963 (Blanc 4, Freleng 4)

Devil's Garden, 1920 (Barrymore 3, Stradling 4)

Devil's Garden. *See* Coplan sauve sa peau, 1967

Devil's Hairpin, 1957 (Astor 3, Wilde 3, Head 4)

Devil's Hand, 1961 (Pierce 4)

Devil's Holiday, 1930 (Goulding 2, Bosworth 3, Lukas 3)

Devil's Imposter. *See* Pope Joan, 1972

Devil's in Love, 1933 (Dieterle 2, Lugosi 3, Young 3, Mohr 4)

Devil's Instrument. *See* Djävulens instrument, 1967

Devil's Island, 1940 (Karloff 3)

Devil's Island. *See* Gokumon-to, 1977

Devil's Island. *See* Akuma-to, 1980

Devil's Lottery, 1932 (McLaglen 3, Friedhofer 4)

Devil's Men, 1976 (Cushing 3, Pleasence 3)

Devil's Messenger, 1962 (Siodmak 4)

Devil's Mill. *See* Certuv mlýn, 1950

Devil's Needle, 1916 (Talmadge 3)

Devil's Own. *See* Witches, 1966

Devil's Own Envoy. *See* Visiteurs du soir, 1942

Devil's Partner, 1923 (Shearer 3)

Devil's Partner, 1958 (Cronjager 4)

Devil's Party, 1938 (McLaglen 3, Krasner 4)

Devil's Pass, 1957 (Adam 4)

Devil's Passkey, 1919 (Von Stroheim 2, Daniels 4, Day 4)

Devil's Pipeline, 1940 (Salter 4)

Devil's Playground. *See* Lady Who Dared, 1931

Devil's Playground, 1937 (Bond 3, Del Rio 3, Ballard 4, Trumbo 4)

Devil's Playground, 1976 (Schepisi 2)

Devil's Rain, 1975 (Borgnine 3, Lupino 3, Travolta 3)

Devil's Stone, 1917 (De Mille 2, Bosworth 3, Reid 3, Buckland 4, Macpherson 4)

Devil's Tail. *See* Mal d'aimer, 1986

Devil's Temple. *See* Oni no sumu yakata, 1969

Devil's Toast. *See* Akuma no kanpai, 1947

Devil's Toy, 1916 (Edeson 4)

Devil's Triangle, 1974 (Price 3)

Devil's Wheel. *See* Chyortovo koleso, 1926

Devil's Widow. *See* Tam Lin, 1971

Devil-Ship Pirates, 1964 (Lee 3, Carreras 4, Sangster 4)

Devoir de Zouzou, 1955 (Kosma 4)

Devonsville Terror, 1983 (Pleasence 3)

Devoradora, 1946 (De Fuentes 2, Félix 3)

Devotion, 1913 (Ince 4)

Devotion, 1931 (Howard 3, Mandell 4, Mohr 4, Stewart 4)

Devotion, 1946 (De Havilland 3, Greenstreet 3, Henreid 3, Kennedy 3, Lupino 3, Buckner 4, Friedhofer 4, Haller 4, Korngold 4)

Devushka s dalekoi reki, 1928 (Enei 4)

Dezerter, 1958 (Stawiński 4)

Dezertér, 1965 (Brdečka 4)

Dezertir, 1933 (Golovnya 4)

D'Fightin' Ones, 1961 (Blanc 4, Freleng 4)

Dhadram Karam, 1975 (Kapoor 2)

Dharam Ki Devi, 1935 (Biswas 4)

Dharti Ke Lal, 1945 (Abbas 4, Shankar 4)

D'homme à hommes, 1948 (Barrault 3, Blier 3, Kosma 4, Matras 4, Spaak 4)

Dhoon, 1953 (Kapoor 2)

Dhrupad, 1984 (Kaul 2)

Di, 1978 (Rocha 2)

Di padre in figlio, 1982 (Gassman 3)

Di quelle, 1953 (Fabrizi 3)

Día con el diablo, 1945 (Cantinflas 3, Figueroa 4)

Dia de Noviembre, 1972 (Solas 2)

Dia de vida, 1950 (Figueroa 4)

Día Paulino, 1963 (Sanjinés 2)

Diable au coeur, 1927 (Autant-Lara 2, L'Herbier 2)

Diable au corps, 1947 (Autant-Lara 2, Tati 2, Philipe 3, Presle 3, Aurenche 4, Bost 4, Douy 4)

Diable boiteaux, 1949 (Guitry 2)

Diable dans la boîte, 1976 (Presle 3, Carrière 4, Vierny 4)

Diable dans la ville, 1924 (Dulac 2)

Diable et les dix commandements, 1962 (Duvivier 2, Dalio 3, Darrieux 3, Delon 3, Fernandel 3, Modot 3, Presle 3, Simon 3, Audiard 4, Jeanson 4)

Diable noir, 1905 (Méliès 2)

Diable par la queue, 1968 (Montand 3, Schell 3, Delerue 4)

Diable probablement, 1977 (Bresson 2, Sarde 4)

Diable souffle, 1947 (Vanel 3, Alekan 4)

Diablo bajo la Almohada, 1969 (Thulin 3)

Diablo del desierto, 1954 (Armendáriz 3)

Diabolical Dr. Z. *See* Miss Muerte, 1966

Diabolical Honeymoon. *See* Dábelské libánky, 1970

Diabolical Wedding, 1971 (O'Brien 3)

Diabolic Tenant. *See* Locataire diabolique, 1910

Diabolically Yours. *See* Diaboliquement vôtre, 1967

Diabolik, 1968 (Piccoli 3, Terry-Thomas 3, De Laurentiis 4, Gherardi 4, Morricone 4)

Diabolique. *See* **Diaboliques, 1954**

Diaboliquement vôtre, 1967 (Duvivier 2, Delon 3, Barsacq 4, Decaë 4, Gégauff 4)

Diaboliques, 1954 (Clouzot 2, Signoret 3, Vanel 3, Barsacq 4)

Diadalmas elet, 1923 (Lukas 3)

Diadiouskina kvartira, 1913 (Mozhukin 3)

Diagnosis: Murder, 1975 (Lee 3)

Diagnosis for Murder. *See* Diagnosis: Murder, 1975

Diagnostic C.I.V., 1960 (Delerue 4)

Diagnoza X, 1933 (Stallich 4)

Diagonale du fou, 1984 (Caron 3, Olbrychski 3, Piccoli 3, Ullmann 3, Coutard 4, Guillemot 4)

Dial M for Murder, 1954 (Hitchcock 2, Kelly 3, Milland 3, Burks 4, Tiomkin 4)

Dial M for Murder, 1981 (Dickinson 3)

Dial 1119, 1950 (Previn 4)

Dial ''P'' for Pink, 1965 (Freleng 4)

Dialectique, 1966 (Guillemot 4)

Dialog, 1968 (Léaud 3, Skolimowski 2)

Dialogo de exilados. *See* Dialogue d'exilés, 1974

Dialogue. *See* Dialog, 1968

Dialogue des Carmélites, 1960 (Barrault 3, Brasseur 3, Moreau 3, Valli 3)

Dialogue d'exiles, 1974 (Gélin 3)

Diamant, 1969 (Grimault 4)

Diamant du Sénéchal, 1914 (Feuillade 2)

Diamant noir, 1922 (Fresnay 3)

Diamant noir, 1940 (Delannoy 2, Vanel 3)

Diamanti che nessuno voleva rubare, 1968 (Andrews 3)

Diamond City, 1949 (Dors 3, Rank 4)

Diamond Cut Diamond, 1912 (Bunny 3, Reid 3)

Diamond Cut Diamond, *See* Blame the Woman, 1932

Diamond Frontier, 1940 (McLaglen 3, Krasner 4, Salter 4)

Diamond Handcuffs, 1928 (Johnson 3, Wilson 4)

Diamond Head, 1962 (Heston 3, Green 4, Williams 4)

Diamond Horseshoe. *See* Billy Rose's Diamond Horseshoe, 1945

Diamond Jim, 1935 (Sturges 2, Arthur 3, Mandell 4, Waxman 4)

Diamond Mercenaries. *See* Killer Force, 1975

Diamond Queen, 1953 (Cortez 4, Lourié 4)

Diamond Ship. *See* Brillantenschiff, 1920

Diamond Star, 1910 (Griffith 2, Bitzer 4)

Diamonds, 1976 (Shaw 3, Winters 3, Golan and Globus 4)

Diamonds Are Brittle. *See* Millard un billard, 1965

Diamonds Are Forever, 1971 (Connery 3, Barry 4, Whitlock 4)

Diamonds for Breakfast, 1968 (Mastroianni 3)

Diamonds of the Night. *See* Démanty noci, 1964

Diana, l'affascinatrice, 1915 (Bertini 3)

Diane, 1929 (Tschechowa 3, Andrejew 4)

Diane, 1955 (Armendáriz 3, Turner 3, Plunkett 4, Rozsa 4)

Diane of the Follies, 1916 (Gish 3)

Diaries, Notes, and Sketches. *See* Walden, 1968

Diario de invierno, 1988 (Rey 3)

Diario de la guerra del cerdo, 1975 (Torre Nilsson 2)

Diario di un italiano, 1973 (Valli 3)

Diary, 1981 (Vinton 4)

Diary For My Children. *See* Napló gyermekeimnek, 1982

Diary For My Lovers. *See* Napló szerelmeimnek, 1987

Diary for Timothy, 1945 (Jennings 2, Wright 2, Gielgud 3, Redgrave 3, Mathieson 4)

Diary of a Chambermaid, 1946 (Renoir 2, Goddard 3, Meredith 3, Lourié 4)

Diary of a Chambermaid. *See* Journal d'une femme de chambre, 1964

Diary of a Country Priest. *See* **Journal d'un curé de campagne, 1950**

Diary of a Lost Girl. *See* Tagebuch einer Verlorenen, 1929

Diary of a Lost Woman. *See* Tagebuch einer Verlorenen, 1918

Diary of a Lover. *See* Tagebuch einer Verliebten, 1953

Diary of a Mad Housewife, 1970 (Perry 4)

Diary of a Madman. *See* Para gnedych, 1915

Diary of a Madman, 1963 (Price 3, Williams 4)

Diary of a Nobody, 1964 (Russell 2)

Diary of a Shinjuku Thief. *See* Shinjuku dorobo nikki, 1969

Diary of a Young Man, 1964 (Loach 2)

Diary of Anne Frank, 1959 (Ashby 2, Stevens 2, Winters 3, Cardiff 4, Goodrich 4, LeMaire 4, Newman 4, Wheeler 4)

Diary of Anne Frank, 1980 (Schell 3, Goodrich 4)

Diary of an Unknown Soldier, 1959 (Watkins 2)

Diary of Forbidden Dreams. *See* Che?, 1972

Diary of Major Thompson. *See* French They Are a Funny Race, 1956

Diary of the Pig War. *See* Diario de la guerra del cerdo, 1975

Días de odio, 1954 (Torre Nilsson 2)

Días de otoño, 1962 (Figueroa 4)

Dias del agua, 1971 (Herrera 4)

Diavolo, 1963 (Sordi 3, De Laurentiis 4)

Diavolo a sette face, 1971 (Baker 3)

Diavolo bianco, 1947 (Brazzi 3)

Diavolo innamorato. *See* Arcidiavolo, 1966

Diavolo nel cervello, 1972 (Presle 3, Cecchi D'Amico 4, Morricone 4)

Dice of Destiny, 1920 (King 2)

Dicen que soy mujeriego, 1948 (Infante 3)

Diceria dell'untore, 1989 (Redgrave 3, Rey 3)

Dich hab' ich geliebt, 1929 (Reisch 4)

Diciotteni al sole, 1962 (Morricone 4)

Diciottenni, 1956 (Ponti 4)

Dick Barton at Bay, 1950 (Carreras 4)

Dick Barton—Special Agent, 1948 (Carreras 4)

Dick Barton Strikes Back, 1949 (Adam 4, Carreras 4)

Dick Tracy, 1937 (Bushman 3)

Dick Tracy, 1990 (Beatty 3, Hoffman 3, Pacino 3, Storaro 4, Sylbert 4)

Dick Tracy Meets Gruesome, 1947 (Karloff 3, D'Agostino 4)

Dick Tracy Returns, 1938 (Canutt 4)

Dick Tracy's Amazing Adventure. *See* Dick Tracy Meets Gruesome, 1947

Dick Tracy's G-Men, 1939 (Jones 3)

Dick Turpin, 1925 (Lombard 3, Mix 3, Fox 4)

Dick Turpin, 1933 (McLaglen 3)

Dick Turpin, 1981 (Dors 3)

Dick Turpin—Highwayman, 1956 (Carreras 4)

Dick Whittington and His Cat, 1913 (Guy 2)

Dick Whittington's Cat, 1936 (Iwerks 4)

Dictator, 1922 (Cruze 2, Reid 3, Brown 4)

Dictator, 1935 (Saville 2, Carroll 3, Andrejew 4, Planer 4, Rathaus 4)

Dictionnaire de Joachim, 1965 (Borowczyk 2)

Dictionnaire des pin-up girls, 1951 (Braunberger 4)

Did Mother Get Her Wash, 1911 (Sennett 2)

Did You Ever See a Dream Walking?, 1943 (Balcon 4)

Dida Ibsens Geschichte, 1918 (Veidt 3)

Die! Die! My Darling. *See* Fanatic, 1968

Die—oder Keine, 1932 (Courant 4)

Diebe, 1928 (Dieterle 2)

Diebe von Günsterburg. *See* Springende Hirsch, 1915

Diece minuti di vita, 1943 (De Sica 2)

Dieci comandamenti, 1945 (Germi 2, Brazzi 3)

Dieci italiani per un Tedesco, 1962 (Cervi 3)

Diesel, 1942 (Wegener 3)

Diese Machine ist mein antihumanistisches Kunstwerk, 1982 (Jarman 2)

Diese Mann gehört mir, 1950 (Fröhlich 3)

Diese Nacht vergess' ich nie, 1949 (Fröhlich 3)

Dieses Leid bleibt bei dir. *See* Kabarett, 1954

Dieu a besoin des hommes, 1950 (Fresnay 3, Gélin 3, Aurenche 4, Bost 4)

Dieu a choisi Paris, 1969 (Belmondo 3, Milhaud 4)

Dieux du feu, 1961 (Storck 2)

Difanzati della morte, 1956 (Solinas 4)

Difendo il mio amore, 1956 (Gassman 3, Di Venanzo 4)

Different Man, 1914 (Crisp 3)

Different Sons. *See* Futari no musuko, 1962

Difficile morire, 1977 (Jancsó 2)

Difficulté d'être infidèle, 1963 (Braunberger 4, Coutard 4)

Difficult Years. *See* Anni difficili, 1948

Difficult Years, 1950 (Garfield 3)

Dig Up, 1922 (Roach 4)

Diga sul Pacifico. *See* Barrage contre le Pacifique, 1958

Digging for Victory, 1942 (Halas and Batchelor 4)

Digi sul ghiaccio, 1953 (Olmi 2)

Digital Dreams, 1983 (Coburn 3)

Digue, ou Pour sauver la Hollande, 1911 (Gance 2)

Dil Diya Dard Liya, 1966 (Kumar 3)

Dil e Nadaan, 1982 (Patil 3)

Dil Hi To Hai, 1963 (Kapoor 2)

Dil Ki Rani, 1947 (Kapoor 2, Burman 4)

Dilawar, 1931 (Mehboob 2)

Dilemma, 1982 (Halas and Batchelor 4)

Dillinger, 1945 (Tiomkin 4)

Dillinger, 1973 (Dreyfuss 3, Johnson 3, Oates 3, Stanton 3)

Dillinger è morto, 1968 (Girardot 3, Piccoli 3)

Dillinger est mort. *See* Dillinger è morto, 1968

Dillinger Is Dead. *See* Dillinger è morto, 1968

Dilruba, 1950 (Anand 3)

Dim Little Island, 1949 (Jennings 2)

Dimanche à la campagne, 1984 (Tavernier 2)

Dimanche à Pekin, 1956 (Marker 2, Delerue 4)

Dimanche de flics, 1983 (Mueller-Stahl 3, Müller 4)

Dimanche de la vie, 1965 (Darrieux 3)

Dimanche Matin. *See* Niedzielny poranek, 1955

Dimanche nous volerons, 1956 (Belmondo 3)

Dime a Dance, 1937 (Allyson 3, Kaye 3)

Dimensions of a Dialogue. *See* Jan Svankmajer: Alchemist of the Surreal, 1990

Dimensions of Dialogue. *See* Možnosti dialogu, 1982

Dimenticare Palermo, 1990 (Rosi 2, Gassman 3, Noiret 3, Guerra 4, Morricone 4)

Dimenticare Venezia, 1979 (Josephson 3)

Dime to Retire, 1955 (Blanc 4, McKimson 4)

Dimmi che fai tutto per mei, 1976 (Cecchi D'Amico 4)

Dimples, 1936 (Carradine 3, Temple 3, Glennon 4, Johnson 4)

Dimples, 1943 (Robinson 3)

Din stund pa jorden, 1972 (Fischer 4)

Din tillvaros land, 1940 (Sucksdorff 2)

Dina chez les lois, 1967 (Arletty 3)

Dina e Django, 1981 (De Almeida 4)

Dinah, 1933 (Fleischer 4)

Diner, 1982 (Levinson 2, Rourke 3)

Diner des bustes, 1988 (Vangelis 4)

Dinero Maldito, 1978 (Widmark 3)

Ding Dog Daddy, 1942 (Blanc 4, Freleng 4, Stalling 4)

Ding Dong Doggie, 1937 (Fleischer 4)

Dingaka, 1965 (Baker 3)

Dingbat Land, 1949 (Terry 4)

Dinky, 1935 (Astor 3, Cooper 3, Edeson 4)

Dinky Doodle series, 1925–26 (Lantz 4)

Dinky Finds a Home, 1946 (Terry 4)

Dinner at Eight, 1933 (Cukor 2, Barrymore, J. 3, Barrymore, L. 3, Beery 3, Dressler 3, Harlow 3, Adrian 4, Daniels 4, Gibbons 4, Mankiewicz 4, Marion 4, Mayer 4, Selznick 4, Stewart 4)

Dinner at the Ritz, 1937 (Lukas 3, Niven 3)

Dinner Date, 1980 (Halas and Batchelor 4)

Dinner Hour, 1920 (Roach 4)

Dinner Jest, 1926 (Sennett 2)

Dinner Under Difficulties. *See* Salle à manger fantastique, 1898

Dino, 1957 (Mineo 3, Waxman 4)

Dinosaur, 1980 (Vinton 4)

Dinosaur and the Missing Link, 1914 (O'Brien 4)

Dinosaurs, 1989 (Adam 4)

Dinosaurus!, 1960 (Cortez 4)

Dinty, 1920 (Neilan 2, Moore 3, Wong 3, Carré 4)

Dio, sei proprio un padreterno, 1973 (Van Cleef 3)

Dionysos, 1984 (Rouch 2, Braunberger 4)

Dionysus in '69, 1970 (De Palma 2)

Dios eligió sus viajeros, 1963 (Rey 3)

Diosa arrodillada, 1947 (Felix 3)

Diplomacy, 1926 (Neilan 2, Sweet 3, Glazer 4)

Diplomacy, 1931 (Rooney 3)

Diplomaniacs, 1933 (Mankiewicz 2, Calhern 3, Cronjager 4, Steiner 4)

Diplomatic Courier, 1952 (Hathaway 2, Bronson 3, Malden 3, Marvin 3, Neal 3, Ballard 4, Robinson 4, Wheeler 4)

Diplomatic Encounter, 1952 (Power 3)

Diplomatic Flo, 1914 (Lawrence 3)

Dippy Daughter, 1918 (Roach 4)

Dippy Dentist, 1920 (Roach 4)

Dipsy Gypsy, 1941 (Pal 4)

Diptyque, 1967 (Borowczyk 2)

Direct au coeur, 1933 (Pagnol 2)

Directed by Andrei Tarkovsky, 1989 (Josephson 3)

Directed by John Ford, 1971 (Bogdanovich 2, Welles 2, Fonda 3, Stewart 3, Wayne 3, Kovacs 4)

Direction d'acteurs par Jean Renoir, 1966 (Braunberger 4)

Director, 1915 (Barrymore 3)

Directors, 1963 (Germi 2, Godard 2, Hitchcock 2, Huston 2)

Director's Notebook. *See* Block-Notes di un regista, 1969

Dirftin' Thru, 1926 (Carey 3, Polito 4)

Dirigible, 1931 (Capra 2, Bosworth 3, Karloff 3, Wray 3, Cohn 4, Saunders 4, Swerling 4, Walker 4)

Dirnenlied. *See* Ich glaub' nie mehr an eine Frau, 1929

Dirnenmörder von London. *See* Jack the Ripper, 1976

Dirnentragödie, 1927 (Homolka 3, Nielsen 3)

Dirnentragödie. *See* Zwischen Nacht und Morgen, 1931

Dirordine, 1962 (Jourdan 3)

Dirt, 1939 (McDowall 3)

Dirty Agents. *See* Guerre secrète, 1966

Dirty Angels. *See* Vergogna schifosi, 1968

Dirty Dingus Magee, 1970 (Sinatra 3)

Dirty Dozen, 1967 (Aldrich 2, Cassavetes 2, Borgnine 3, Bronson 3, Marvin 3, Ryan 3, Sutherland 3, Johnson 4)

Dirty Dozen: Fatal Mission, 1988 (Borgnine 3)

Dirty Dozen—The Next Mission, 1985 (Borgnine 3, Marvin 3)

Dirty Duck, 1977 (Corman 2)

Dirty Game. *See* Guerre secrète, 1966

Dirty Hands. *See* Mains sales, 1951

Dirty Hands. *See* Innocents aux mains sales, 1975

Dirty Harry, 1971 (Siegel 2, Eastwood 3, Schifrin 4)

Dirty Heroes. *See* Dalle Ardenne all'inferno, 1968

Dirty Knight's Work. *See* Trial by Combat, 1976

Dirty Little Billy, 1972 (Warner 4)

Dirty Money. *See* Flic, 1972

Dirty Rotten Scoundrels, 1988 (Caine 3, Martin 3, Ballhaus 4)

Dirty Story, 1984 (Josephson 3)

Dirty Tricks, 1981 (Gould 3)

Dirty Two. *See* Dito nell piaga, 1969

Dirty Weekend. *See* Mordi e fuggi, 1972

Dirty Work, 1933 (Laurel and Hardy 3, Roach 4)

Dirty Work, 1934 (Johnson 3, Balcon 4, Junge 4, Rank 4)

Dirty Work in a Laundry, 1915 (Sennett 2)

Disamistade; O Re, 1989 (Morricone 4)

Disappearance, 1977 (Hurt 3, Alcott 4)

Disappearance, 1981 (Hurt 3, Sutherland 3)

Disappearance of Aimee, 1976 (Davis 3, Dunaway 3, Head 4)

Disappearance of Flight 412, 1974 (Ford 3)

Disbarred, 1939 (Florey 2, Preston 3, Dreier 4, Head 4)

Discard, 1916 (Van Dyke 2)

Discarded Woman, 1920 (Haller 4)

Disciple, 1915 (Hart 3, August 4)

Disco volante, 1965 (Mangano 3, Sordi 3, Vitti 3)

Discontent, 1916 (Weber 2)

Discord. *See* Hans engelska frau, 1926

Discord. *See* Roztržka, 1956

Discord and Harmony, 1914 (Dwan 2, Chaney 3)

Discours de bienvenue de McLaren. *See* Opening Speech, 1960

Discover America, 1967 (Meredith 3)

Discovering the Movies, 1962 (Alexeieff and Parker 4)

Discovery, 1913 (Bushman 3)

Discovery of Zero, 1961 (Kuri 4)

Discovery on the Shaggy Mountain. *See* Objec na střapaté hurce, 1962

Discreet Charm of the Bourgeoisie. *See* **Charme discrèt de la bourgeoisie, 1972**

Discussion, 1895 (Lumière 2)

Discussion de M. Janssen et de M. Lagrange, 1895 (Lumière 2)

Disenchantment, 1914 (Lawrence 3)

Disertore, 1983 (Papas 3)

Disgraced, 1933 (Banton 4, Struss 4)

Disguises, 1933 (Rooney 3)

Dishonor Bright, 1936 (Sanders 3)

Dishonorable Discharge. *See* Ces dames preferent le Mambo, 1958

Dishonored, 1931 (Hathaway 2, Von Sternberg 2, Dietrich 3, McLaglen 3, Banton 4, Dreier 4, Garmes 4, Zukor 4)

Dishonored Lady, 1947 (De Toth 2, Lamarr 3, Stromberg 4)

Dishonoured Lady, 1947 (Stevenson 2)

Disillusioned, 1912 (Bosworth 3)

Disillusioned Bluebird, 1944 (Fleischer 4)

Dislocations mystérieuses, 1901 (Méliès 2)

Dis-moi, 1980 (Akerman 2)

Dis-moi qui tuer, 1965 (Morgan 3)

Disobedient Robot. *See* Playful Robot, 1956

Disorder. *See* Dirordine, 1962

Disorder in the Court, 1936 (Three Stooges 3)

Disorderlies, 1987 (Bellamy 3)

Disorderly Conduct, 1932 (Bellamy 3, Tracy 3)

Disorderly Orderly, 1964 (Lewis 2, Tashlin 2, Sloane 3, Edouart 4, Fulton 4, Head 4)

Disordine, 1962 (Valli 3)

Disparus de Saint-Agil, 1938 (Von Stroheim 2, Simon 3)

Dispatch Bearer, 1907 (Lawrence 3)

Dispatch from Reuters, 1940 (Robinson 3, Blanke 4, Burks 4, Grot 4, Howe 4, Orry-Kelly 4, Steiner 4, Wallis 4)

Disputation, 1986 (Lee 3)

Disputed Passage, 1939 (Borzage 2, Lamour 3, Dreier 4, Head 4, Veiller 4)

Disque 413, 1936 (Berry 3)

Disque 927, 1928 (Dulac 2)

Disques d'hier et d'aujourd'hui, 1951 (Colpi 4)

Disraeli, 1921 (Arliss 3)

Disraeli, 1929 (Arliss 3, Bennett 3, Garmes 4, Warner 4, Zanuck 4)

Distance. *See* Faasla, 1974

Distant Clouds. *See* Tooi kumo, 1955

Distant Drums, 1951 (Walsh 2, Cooper 3, Steiner 4)

Distant Harmony, 1987 (Ondříček 4)

Distant Relative, 1911 (Dwan 2)

Distant Thames, 1951 (Alwyn 4)

Distant Thunder. *See* Ashani Sanket, 1973

Distant Thunder, 1988 (Jarre 4)

Distant Trumpet, 1952 (Fisher 2)

Distant Trumpet, 1964 (Walsh 2, Clothier 4, Steiner 4)

Distant Voices, Still Lives, 1988 (Davies 2)

Distinto amanecer, 1943 (Armendáriz 3, Figueroa 4)

Distractions, 1960 (Chabrol 2, Belmondo 3)

Distrait, 1970 (Blier 3)

Distress Call, 1938 (Cavalcanti 2)

District Attorney, 1947 (Menjou 3)

Disturbed, 1990 (McDowell 3)

Disubbidienza, 1981 (Morricone 4)

Dit Vindarna Bär, 1948 (Thulin 3)

Dita Saxová, 1967 (Menzel 2, Kučera 4)

Dites cariatides, 1984 (Varda 2)

Dites-le avec des fleurs, 1974 (Rey 3, Seyrig 3, Cloquet 4, Guerra 4)

Dites-lui que je l'aime, 1977 (Depardieu 3)

Dito nell piaga, 1969 (Kinski 3)

Ditto, 1937 (Keaton 2)

Ditya bolchogo goroda, 1914 (Mozhukin 3)

Diva, 1981 (Beineix 2)

Dive Bomber, 1941 (Curtiz 2, Bellamy 3, Flynn 3, MacMurray 3, Buckner 4, Friedhofer 4, Glennon 4, Haskin 4, Hoch 4, Steiner 4, Wallis 4)

Divers at Work on the Wreck of the Maine. *See* Visite sous-marine du Maine, 1898

Diverse Reports: We Should Have Won, 1985 (Loach 2)

Divertissement, 1952 (Rivette 2)

Divertissement, 1962 (Alexeieff and Parker 4)

Divide and Conquer. *See* **Why We Fight series, 1943–45**

Divide and Conquer, 1943 (Capra 2, Litvak 2, Hornbeck 4, Tiomkin 4, Veiller 4)

Divided Heart, 1954 (Crichton 2,
Schlesinger 2, Auric 4, Heller 4)
Divided World. *See* kluven värld, 1948
Dividend, 1916 (Ince 4)
Dividing Line. *See* Lawless, 1950
Divina comedia, 1991 (Branco 4)
Divina creatura, 1976 (Mastroianni 3,
Stamp 3, Morricone 4, Rotunno 4)
Divinas palabras, 1977 (Figueroa 4)
Divine, 1935 (Ophüls 2, Manès 3)
Divine, 1975 (Darrieux 3)
Divine Comedy. *See* Divina comedia,
1991
Divine croisière, 1929 (Duvivier 2)
Divine Damnation, 1967 (Markopoulos 2)
Divine Emma, 1983 (Ondříček 4)
Divine Lady, 1929 (Bennett 3, Dressler 3,
Seitz 4)
Divine Lover, 1933 (Bosworth 3)
Divine Madness, 1980 (Midler 3, Fraker 4)
Divine Mr. J, 1974 (Midler 3)
Divine Nymph. *See* Divina creatura, 1976
Divine Sinner, 1928 (Lombard 3)
Divine Spark. *See* Casta Diva, 1935
Divine Woman, 1928 (Sjöström 2,
Garbo 3, Day 4, Gibbons 4, Gillespie 4,
Mayer 4)
Diviners, 1983 (Altman 2)
Diving for Roman Plunder: The Cousteau
Odyssey, 1980 (Mercouri 3)
Diving Girl, 1911 (Sennett 2, Crisp 3,
Normand 3)
Divino Boemo, 1975 (Jireš 2)
Divisions de la nature, 1978 (Ruiz 2)
Dívka v modrém, 1940 (Baarová 3)
Divorce, 1914 (Ince 4)
Divorce, 1945 (Francis 3)
Divorce. *See* Divorce His, Divorce Hers,
1973
Divorce a la Mode, 1932 (Sennett 2)
Divorce American Style, 1967 (Grant 3,
Johnson 3, Reynolds 3, Robards 3,
Simmons 3, Hall 4)
Divorce Courtship, 1933 (Stevens 2)
Divorce Dodger, 1926 (Sennett 2)
Divorce Game, 1917 (Marion 4)
Divorce heureux, 1975 (Sarde 4)
Divorce His, Divorce Hers, 1973 (Burton 3,
Taylor 3, Head 4)
Divorce in the Family, 1932 (Daves 2,
Beavers 3, Cooper 3)
Divorce Italian Style. *See* Divorzio
all'italiana, 1962
Divorce of Lady X, 1938 (Oberon 3,
Olivier 3, Richardson 3, Biro 4,
Dalrymple 4, Hornbeck 4, Korda 4,
Meerson 4, Rozsa 4, Sherwood 4,
Stradling 4)
Divorce Scandal, 1913 (Eason 4)
Divorced. *See* Frånskild, 1951
Divorced Sweethearts, 1930 (Sennett 2)
Divorcee, 1919 (Guy 2, Barrymore 3)
Divorcee, 1930 (Montgomery 3, Shearer 3,
Adrian 4, Gibbons 4, Mayer 4)
Divorcement, 1979 (Piccoli 3)
Divorzio, 1970 (Gassman 3)
Divorzio all'italiana, 1962 (Mastroianni 3,
Cristaldi 4)
Divot Diggers, 1935 (Roach 4)
Diwana, 1967 (Kapoor 2)
Dix Femmes pour un mari, 1905 (Pathé 4)
Dix Siècles d'elegance, 1910 (Cohl 4)
Dixiana, 1930 (Daniels 3, Robinson 3,
Hunt 4, Plunkett 4, Steiner 4)

Dixie, 1925 (Fleischer 4)
Dixie, 1943 (Crosby 3, Lamour 3)
Dixie Dugan, 1943 (Marsh 3, Day 4)
Dixie Dynamite, 1976 (Oates 3)
Dixie Flyer, 1926 (Walker 4)
Dixie Fryer, 1960 (Blanc 4, McKimson 4)
Dixie Handicap, 1925 (Gibbons 4, Mayer 4,
Young 4)
Dixie Jamboree, 1944 (Beavers 3)
Dixie Lanes, 1988 (Black 3)
Dixie Merchant, 1926 (Borzage 2, Fox 4)
Dixie Mother, 1910 (Costello 3,
Talmadge 3)
Dixieland Droopy, 1954 (Avery 4)
Dixième Symphonie, 1918 (Gance 2,
Burel 4, Gaumont 4)
Dizzy Daddies, 1926 (Roach 4)
Dizzy Detectives, 1943 (Three Stooges 3)
Dizzy Dishes, 1938 (Fleischer 4)
Dizzy Divers, 1935 (Fleischer 4)
Dizzy Doctors, 1937 (Three Stooges 3)
Dizzy Dwarf, 1934 (Lantz 4)
Dizzy Heights and Daring Hearts, 1916
(Sennett 2)
Dizzy Joe's Career, 1914 (Browning 2)
Dizzy Kitty, 1941 (Lantz 4)
Dizzy Newsreel, 1943 (Fleischer 4)
Dizzy Pilots, 1943 (Three Stooges 3,
Bruckman 4)
Dizzy Red Riding Hood, 1931
(Fleischer 4)
Django Reinhardt, 1958 (Cocteau 2)
Django Strikes Again. *See* Grande ritorno
di Django, 1987
Djävulens instrument, 1967 (Fischer 4)
Djävulens öga, 1960 (Andersson 3,
Björnstrand 3, Fischer 4)
Djevojka sz sve, 1959 (Mimica 4)
Djungelsaga, 1957 (Sucksdorff 2,
Shankar 4)
Dlinnoe, dlinnoe delo, 1976
(Yankovsky 3)
Dlugoszewski Concert, 1965
(Emshwiller 2)
Dnes večer všechno skončí, 1955
(Kučera 4)
Do a Good Deed, 1935 (Lantz 4)
Do and Dare, 1922 (Mix 3, Fox 4)
Do Anjanne, 1976 (Bachchan 3)
Do Aur Do Paanch, 1980 (Bachchan 3)
Do Bhai, 1947 (Burman 4)
Do Bigha Zamin, 1953 (Roy 2)
Do Boond Pani, 1972 (Abbas 4)
Do Detectives Think?, 1927 (Laurel and
Hardy 3, Roach 4)
Do Dooni Char, 1968 (Roy 2)
Do Gentlemen Snore?, 1928 (McCarey 2,
Roach 4)
Do Husbands Deceive?, 1918 (Roach 4)
Do I Love You?. *See* Lyubliu tebya, 1934
Do Jasoos, 1975 (Kapoor 2)
Do lesíčka na čekanou, 1966 (Brdečka 4)
Do Me a Favor, 1922 (Roach 4)
Do Not Disturb, 1965 (Day 3, Welch 3,
Boyle 4, Shamroy 4, Smith 4)
Do Not Fold, Spindle, or Mutilate, 1971
(Loy 3, Sidney 3, Cortez 4,
Goldsmith 4)
Do panskeho stavu, 1925 (Ondra 3)
Do pivnice, 1982 (Švankmajer 4)
Do Raha, 1952 (Biswas 4)
Do Sitare, 1951 (Anand 3, Biswas 4)
Do the Right Thing, 1989 (Lee 2)
Do widzenia do jutra, 1960 (Cybulski 3)

Do You Know This Voice?, 1963 (Duryea 3)
Do You Like Women?, 1964 (Polanski 2)
Do You Love Me?, 1946 (Grable 3,
O'Hara 3, Cronjager 4)
Do You Love Your Wife?, 1919 (Laurel and
Hardy 3, Roach 4)
Do You Mean There Are Still Real
Cowboys?, 1987 (Close 3, Redford 3)
Do You Remember?. *See* Ty pomnis li?,
1914
Do You Remember Love, 1985
(Woodward 3)
Do You Take This Stranger?, 1970
(Cotten 3)
Do Your Duty, 1926 (Roach 4, Robinson 4)
Do Your Stuff, 1923 (Roach 4)
Do Yourself Some Good, 1975 (Hurt 3)
Dobrý tramp Bernasek, 1933 (Heller 4)
Dobrý voják Svejk, 1931 (Frič 2, Heller 4,
Stallich 4)
Dobu, 1954 (Shindo 2, Yamamura 3)
Doc, 1971 (Dunaway 3)
Doc Hollywood, 1991 (Fox 3)
Doc Savage, the Man of Bronze, 1975
(Pal 4)
Doce mujeres, 1939 (Alton 4)
Dochu sugoruku bune, 1926 (Kinugasa 2)
Dock Brief, 1962 (Attenborough 3, Sellers 3)
Docks of New York, 1928 (Von Sternberg 2,
Banton 4, Dreier 4, Furthman 4,
Rosson 4, Saunders 4)
Docks of New York, 1945 (Katzman 4)
Docteur Carnaval, 1909 (Cohl 4)
Docteur Françoise Gailland, 1975 (Cassel 3,
Girardot 3, Huppert 3, Renoir 4)
Docteur Jekyll et les femmes, 1981
(Borowczyk 2)
Docteur Laënnac, 1948 (Renoir 4)
Docteur M, 1990 (Chabrol 2)
Docteur Popaul, 1972 (Chabrol 2,
Belmondo 3, Farrow 3, Gégauff 4,
Rabier 4)
Doctor, 1991 (Hurt 3, Adam 4)
Doctor and the Debutante. *See* Dr. Kildare's
Victory, 1941
Doctor and the Devils, 1985 (Brooks 2,
Francis 4)
Doctor and the Girl, 1949 (Coburn 3, Ford 3,
Leigh 3, Ames 4, Berman 4)
Doctor and the Woman, 1918 (Weber 2)
Doctor at Large, 1957 (Bogarde 3, Box 4,
Rank 4)
Doctor at Sea, 1955 (Bardot 3, Bogarde 3,
Box 4, Dillon 4, Rank 4)
Doctor Bridget, 1912 (Bunny 3)
Dr. Broadway, 1942 (Mann 2, Dreier 4)
Doctor Bull, 1933 (Ford 2, Rogers 3)
Dr. Cadman's Secret. *See* Black Sheep,
1956
Dr. Christian Meets the Women, 1940
(Alton 4)
Dr. Cook's Garden, 1971 (Crosby 3)
Dr. Crippen, 1962 (Roeg 2, Pleasence 3)
Doctor Cupid, 1911 (Bunny 3)
Dr. Cyclops, 1940 (Schoedsack 2, Dreier 4),
Edouart 4, Head 4, Hoch 4)
Doctor Death, Seeker of Souls, 1973 (Three
Stooges 3)
Doctor Detroit, 1983 (Schifrin 4)
Doctored Affair, 1913 (Sennett 2,
Normand 3)
Dr. Devil and Mr. Hare, 1964 (Blanc 4,
McKimson 4)
Dr. Dippy's Sanitarium, 1906 (Bitzer 4)

Dr. Dolittle, 1967 (Attenborough 3, Harrison 3, Smith 4, Surtees 4)

Dr. Ehrlich's Magic Bullet. *See* Story of Dr. Ehrlich's Magic Bullet, 1940

Dr. Evans' Silence, 1973 (Bondarchuk 3)

Doctor Faustus, 1966 (Burton 3, Taylor 3)

Dr. Fischer of Geneva, 1984 (Bates 3, Cusack 3, Mason 3, Greene 4)

Dr. Gillespie's Criminal Case, 1943 (Barrymore 3, Johnson 3, O'Brien 3, Reed 3, Irene 4)

Dr. Gillespie's New Assistant, 1942 (Barrymore 3, Johnson 3, Folsey 4)

Dr. Goldfoot and the Bikini Machine, 1965 (Price 3)

Dr. Goldfoot and the Girl Bombs, 1966 (Price 3)

Dr. Grässler. *See* Mio caro Dr. Grässler, 1990

Dr. Heckyl and Mr. Hype, 1980 (Reed 3)

Dr. Holl, 1951 (Herlth 4, Von Harbou 4)

Doctor in Clover, 1966 (Box 4)

Doctor in Distress, 1963 (Bogarde 3, Box 4, Vetchinsky 4)

Doctor in Love, 1960 (Box 4, Rank 4)

Doctor in the House, 1954 (Bogarde 3, Kendall 3, More 3, Box 4, Dillon 4, Rank 4)

Doctor in Trouble, 1970 (Box 4)

Dr. Jack, 1921 (Lloyd 3)

Dr. Jack, 1922 (Roach 4)

Dr. Jekyll and Mr. Hyde, 1908 (Olcott 2, Selig 4)

Dr. Jekyll and Mr. Hyde, 1912 (Cruze 2)

Dr. Jekyll and Mr. Hyde. *See* Januskopf, 1918

Dr. Jekyll and Mr. Hyde, 1920 (Barrymore 3, Zukor 4)

Dr. Jekyll and Mr. Hyde, 1931 (Mamoulian 2, Hopkins 3, March 3, Banton 4, Drier 4, Hoffenstein 4, Mayer 4, Struss 4, Westmore family 4, Zukor 4)

Dr. Jekyll and Mr. Hyde, 1941 (Fleming 2, Saville 2, Bergman 3, Crisp 3, Tracy 3, Turner 3, Adrian 4, Mayer 4, Ruttenberg 4, Waxman 4)

Dr. Jekyll and Mr. Hyde, 1972 (Palance 3)

Dr. Jekyll and Mr. Hyde. *See* Edge of Sanity, 1989

Dr. Jekyll and Mr. Mouse, 1946 (Hanna and Barbera 4)

Dr. Jekyll and Sister Hyde, 1971 (Carreras 4)

Dr. Jerkyl's Hyde, 1953 (Blanc 4, Foster 4, Freleng 4, Stalling 4)

Dr. Justice, 1975 (Christian-Jaque 2)

Dr. Kildare Goes Home, 1940 (Ayres 3, Barrymore 3, Rosson 4)

Dr. Kildare's Crisis, 1940 (Ayres 3, Barrymore 3, Young 3, Seitz 4)

Dr. Kildare's Strange Case, 1940 (Ayres 3, Barrymore 3, Seitz 4)

Dr. Kildare's Victory, 1941 (Van Dyke 2, Ayres 3, Barrymore 3, Daniels 4)

Dr. Kildare's Wedding Day, 1941 (Ayres 3, Barrymore 3, Folsey 4, Kaper 4)

Dr. Kotnis Ki Amar Kahani, 1946 (Abbas 4)

Dr. Le Fleur's Theory, 1907 (Costello 3)

Dr. M, 1990 (Bates 3, Rabier 4)

Dr. Mabuse, der Spieler, 1922 (Dagover 3, Hoffmann 4, Hunte 4, Pommer 4, Von Harbou 4)

Dr. Mabuse, The Gambler. *See* **Dr. Mabuse, der Spieler, 1922**

Dr. Maniac. *See* Man Who Lived Again, 1936

Dr. Max, 1974 (Cobb 3)

Dr. Med. Hiob Preaetorius, 1965 (Rasp 3)

Dr. Monica, 1934 (Dieterle 2, Beavers 3, Francis 3, Blanke 4, Grot 4, Orry-Kelly 4, Polito 4)

Dr. Morelle—the Case of the Missing Heiress, 1949 (Carreras 4)

Dr. Neighbor, 1916 (Bosworth 3)

Dr. Nicola I–III, 1909 (Blom 2)

Dr. No, 1962 (Connery 3, Adam 4, Barry 4)

Doctor of Seven Dials. *See* Corridors of Blood, 1963

Doctor Oswald, 1935 (Lantz 4)

Dr. Phibes Rises Again, 1972 (Cushing 3, Price 3, Terry-Thomas 3)

Dr. Phil Döderlein, 1945 (Wegener 3)

Dr. Pickle and Mr. Pryde, 1925 (Laurel and Hardy 3)

Dr. Renault's Secret, 1942 (Day 4, Miller 4, Raksin 4)

Doctor Rhythm, 1938 (Crosby 3, Pangborn 3, Crosby 4, Head 4, Lang 4, Swerling 4)

Doctors. *See* Hommes en blanc, 1955

Doctors at War, 1943 (Goodrich 4)

Doctor Says. *See* Angeklagt nach N.218, 1965

Dr. Skinum, 1907 (Bitzer 4)

Dr. Smith's Baby, 1914 (Costello 3)

Dr. Socrates, 1935 (Dieterle 2, Muni 3, Gaudio 4, Grot 4)

Dr. Strangelove; or, How I Learned to Stop Worrying and Love the Bomb., 1964 (Kubrick 2, Hayden 3, Jones 3, Sellers 3, Scott 3, Adam 4)

Dr. Syn, 1937 (Launder and Gilliat 2, Arliss 3, Lockwood 3, Vetchinsky 4)

Doctor Takes a Wife, 1940 (Milland 3, Young 3)

Dr. Terror's Gallery of Horrors, 1967 (Carradine 3)

Dr. Terror's House of Horrors, 1964 (Cushing 3, Lee 3, Sutherland 3, Francis 4)

Dr. Vidya, 1962 (Burman 4)

Dr. Who and the Daleks, 1965 (Cushing 3)

Dr. Wislizenus, 1924 (Kortner 3)

Doctor X, 1932 (Curtiz 2, Wray 3, Grot 4)

Dr. Zhivago, 1965 (Christie 3, Richardson 3, Sharif 3, Steiger 3)

Doctor Zhivago, 1965 (Lean 2, Chaplin 3, Guinness 3, Kinski 3, Box 4, Jarre 4, Ponti 4, Young 4)

Doctor's Diary, 1937 (Vidor 2, D'Agostino 4, Head 4, Schulberg 4)

Doctor's Dilemma, 1959 (Asquith 2, Bogarde 3, Caron 3, Sim 3, Beaton 4, De Grunwald 4, Kosma 4, Krasker 4)

Doctors Don't Tell, 1941 (Tourneur 2, Bond 3)

Doctor's Duty, 1913 (Anderson 3)

Doctor's Orders, 1934 (Mills 3)

Doctor's Perfidy, 1910 (Lawrence 3)

Doctor's Secret. *See* Hydrothérapie fantastique, 1910

Doctor's Secret, 1913 (Talmadge 3)

Doctor's Secret, 1929 (Hunt 4)

Doctor's Testimony, 1914 (Lawrence 3)

Doctor's Trouble, 1912 (Ince 4)

Doctors' Wives, 1931 (Borzage 2, Bennett 3, Edeson 4)

Doctors' Wives, 1970 (Bellamy 3, Hackman 3, Roberts 3, Bernstein 4, Lang 4, Taradash 4, Wheeler 4)

Document in Cipher, 1928 (Ptushko 4)

Documental a proposito del transito, 1971 (Gómez 2)

Documenteur: An Emotion Picture, 1981 (Varda 2)

Documento, 1939 (Castellani 2)

Documento Fatale, 1939 (Camerini 2)

Documento mensile. *See* Appunti su un fatto di cronaca, 1951

Documento Z3, 1941 (Fellini 2)

Dodeskaden. *See* Dodesukaden, 1970

Dodes'ka-den, 1970 (Ichikawa 2)

Dodesukaden, 1970 (Muraki 4, Takemitsu 4)

Dodge City, 1939 (Curtiz 2, Bond 3, De Havilland 3, Flynn 3, Sheridan 3, Buckner 4, Canutt 4, Friedhofer 4, Haskin 4, Polito 4, Steiner 4)

Dodge your Debts, 1921 (Roach 4)

Dodging a Million, 1918 (Normand 3)

Dodging His Doom, 1917 (Sennett 2)

Dødsbokseren, 1926 (Madsen and Schenstrøm 3)

Dodshoppet farn circkuskupolen, 1912 (Magnusson 4)

Dodskyssen, 1917 (Sjöström 2, Jaenzon 4)

Dødspringet Til Hest fra Curkuskuplen, 1912 (Psilander 3)

Dødssejleren or Dynamitattentatet paa Fyrtaarnet, 1911 (Holger-Madsen 2)

Does. *See* Biches, 1968

Does It Pay, 1923 (Fox 4, Ruttenberg 4)

Dog, 1977 (Bardem 2)

Dog and the Bone, 1937 (Terry 4)

Dog Catcher's Love, 1917 (Sennett 2)

Dog Collared, 1950 (Blanc 4, McKimson 4, Stalling 4)

Dog Day. *See* Canicule, 1983

Dog Day Afternoon, 1975 (Lumet 2, Pacino 3, Allen 4)

Dog Days, 1925 (Roach 4)

Dog Daze, 1937 (Freleng 4, Stalling 4)

Dog Daze, 1939 (Roach 4)

Dog Doctor, 1931 (Sennett 2)

Dog Done Dog Catcher, 1989 (Halas and Batchelor 4)

Dog Eat Dog. *See* Einer frisst den anderern, 1964

Dog Gone It, 1927 (Lantz 4)

Dog Gone Modern, 1938 (Jones 4)

Dog Gone South, 1950 (Blanc 4, Jones 4, Stalling 4)

Dog in a Mansion, 1940 (Terry 4)

Dog it was that Died, 1988 (Bates 3)

Dog Justice, 1928 (Musuraca 4)

Dog of Flanders, 1935 (Hunt 4, Plunkett 4)

Dog of Flanders, 1959 (Crisp 3, Heller 4)

Dog Heaven, 1929 (Roach 4)

Dog Pound, 1980 (Hanna and Barbera 4)

Dog Pounded, 1954 (Blanc 4, Freleng 4, Stalling 4)

Dog Show, 1934 (Terry 4)

Dog Show, 1950 (Terry 4)

Dog Shy, 1926 (McCarey 2)

Dog Snatcher, 1952 (Bosustow 4, Burness 4)

Dog Soldiers. *See* Who'll Stop the Rain, 1978

Dog Star Man, 1964 (Brakhage 2)

Dog Tales, 1958 (Blanc 4, McKimson 4)

Dog Tired, 1942 (Blanc 4, Jones 4, Stalling 4)

Dog Trouble, 1942 (Hanna and Barbera 4)

Dog Watch, 1914 (Meredyth 4)

Dogadaj, 1969 (Mimica 4)

Doggone Cats, 1947 (Blanc 4)

Doggone Mixup, 1938 (Langdon 3)

Doggone People, 1960 (Blanc 4, McKimson 4)

Doggone Tired, 1949 (Avery 4)

Doggy and the Four. See Punt'a a čtyřlístek, 1954

Dog-Heads. See Psohlavci, 1954

Dog-House, 1952 (Hanna and Barbera 4)

Dogo no kishi, 1932 (Hasegawa 3)

Do-Good Wolf, 1960 (Hanna and Barbera 4)

Dogora—The Space Monster. See Uchu daikaiju Dogora, 1964

Dogpound Shuffle, 1974 (Fisher 4)

Dogs and People. See Psi a lidé, 1971

Dog's Dream, 1941 (Terry 4)

Dogs Is Dogs, 1931 (Roach 4)

Dog's Life, 1918 (Chaplin 2, Purviance 3)

Dogs of War, 1923 (Roach 4)

Dogs of War, 1981 (Jewison 2, Cardiff 4, Smith 4)

Dogsday. See Canicule, 1983

Dohyo-matsuri, 1944 (Kurosawa 2, Miyagawa 4)

Doigts de lumière, 1947 (Fradetal 4)

Doigts qui voient, 1911 (Feuillade 2)

Doin' Time on Planet Earth, 1988 (McDowall 3, Golan and Globus 4)

Doing Her Bit, 1917 (Gilbert 3)

Doing Imposikible Stunts, 1940 (Fleischer 4)

Doing Their Bit, 1918 (Ruttenberg 4)

Doing Their Bit, 1942 (Terry 4)

Doing Time, 1920 (Roach 4)

Do-It-Yourself Cartoon Kit, 1959 (Godfrey 4)

Do-It-Yourself Democracy, 1963 (Zetterling 2)

Dojoyaburi, 1964 (Iwashita 3)

Doka o, 1926 (Mizoguchi 2)

Dokhunda, 1935 (Kuleshov 2)

Dokoku, 1952 (Hayasaka 4)

Doktor Dolittle und seine Tiere, 1928 (Reiniger 4)

Doktor Eva, 1970 (Nowicki 3)

Doktor Glas, 1967 (Zetterling 2)

Doktor Mabuze—Igrok, 1924 (Eisenstein 2)

Doktor Satansohn, 1915 (Lubitsch 2)

Doku azami, 1973 (Hasegawa 3)

Dokuga, 1950 (Yamamura 3)

Dokuritsu bijin-tai, 1963 (Kagawa 3)

Dokuritsu gurenta, 1959 (Mifune 3)

Dolandiricilar sahi, 1961 (Güney 2)

Dolce cinema, 1983 (Fontaine 3, Hayden 3)

Dolce corpo di Deborah, 1968 (Baker 3)

Dolce vita, 1960 (Fellini 2, Aimée 3, Cuny 3, Mastroianni 3, Flaiano 4, Gherardi 4, Pinelli 4, Rota 4)

Dolci inganni, 1960 (Lattuada 2)

Dolci signore, 1967 (Cassel 3)

Doldertal 7, 1971 (Markopoulos 2)

Dole plotovi, 1962 (Makavejev 2)

Dolina Issy, 1982 (Konwicki 4)

Dolken, 1915 (Stiller 2, Jaenzon 4)

Doll. See Puppe, 1919

Doll, 1961 (Vukotić 4)

Doll. See Lalka, 1968

Doll Face, 1946 (Miranda 3, La Shelle 4, Leven 4)

Doll That Took the Town. See Donna del giorno, 1957

Dollar, 1937 (Molander 2, Bergman 3)

Dollar-a-Year Man, 1921 (Cruze 2, Arbuckle 3, Brown 4)

Dollar Dance, 1943 (McLaren 4)

Dollar Did It, 1913 (Sennett 2)

Dollar Down, 1925 (Browning 2, Walthall 3)

Dollar Mark, 1914 (Carré 4, Edeson 4)

Dollaro a testa, 1966 (Rey 3, Reynolds 3, Morricone 4)

Dollaro per 7 vigliacchi, 1967 (Hoffman 3)

Dollarprinzessin und ihre sechs Freier, 1927 (Albers 3, Reisch 4)

Dollars. See $, 1971

Dollars of Dross, 1916 (Borzage 2)

Dollmaker, 1984 (Fonda 3, Page 3, Jenkins 4)

Dolls. See Bambole, 1964

Doll's Eye, 1973 (Pinter 4)

Doll's House, 1916 (Chaney 3)

Doll's House, 1918 (Tourneur 2, Carré 4, Zukor 4)

Doll's House, 1922 (Nazimova 3)

Doll's House, 1973 (Losey 2, Bloom 3, Elliott 3, Evans 3, Fonda 3, Hopkins 3, Howard 3, Richardson 3, Seyrig 3, Barry 4, Fisher 4, Head 4, Legrand 4)

Dolly macht Karriere, 1930 (Litvak 2, Wagner 4)

Dolly Put the Kettle On, 1947 (Halas and Batchelor 4)

Dolly Sisters, 1945 (Grable 3, Newman 4, Orry-Kelly 4, Wheeler 4)

Dolly's Papa, 1907 (Selig 4)

Dolly's Scoop, 1916 (Chaney 3)

Dolorosa, 1934 (Grémillon 2)

Dolwyn. See Last Days of Dolwyn, 1948

Dom, 1958 (Lenica 4)

Dom bez okien, 1962 (Ścibor-Rylski 4)

Dom, kotoryi postroil svift, 1982 (Yankovsky 3)

Dom na Trubnoi, 1928 (Maretskaya 3)

Dom v sugribakh, 1928 (Enei 4)

Dom Wariatow, 1984 (Lomnicki 3)

Domain of the Moment, 1977 (Brakhage 2)

Domani accadra, 1988 (Morricone 4)

Domani è troppo tardi, 1950 (De Sica 2)

Domani e un altro giorno, 1951 (Aldo 4)

Domani non siamo più qui, 1967 (Thulin 3, Fusco 4)

Domani si balla, 1982 (Cristaldi 4)

Domaren, 1960 (Nykvist 4)

Domaren, 1960 (Sjöberg 2)

Domburi-ike, 1963 (Tsukasa 3)

Dömen icke, 1914 (Sjöström 2)

Domenica d'agosto, 1950 (Rosi 2, Amidei 4, Zavattini 4)

Domenica d'agosto, 1950 (Mastroianni 3)

Domenica della buona gente, 1954 (Loren 3, Rota 4)

Domenica d'estate, 1962 (Amidei 4)

Domenica è sempre domenica, 1958 (De Sica 2, Sordi 3)

Domenica specialmente, 1991 (Guerra 4, Morricone 4)

Domestic Relations, 1922 (Glennon 4, Schulberg 4)

Domicile conjugal, 1970 (Truffaut 2, Léaud 3, Almendros 4, Guillemot 4)

Domik v Kolomna, 1913 (Mozhukin 3)

Dominant Sex, 1937 (Brenon 2)

Dominatore dei sette mari, 1960 (Maté 4)

Domingo, 1961 (Diegues 2)

Domingo à Tarde, 1965 (De Almeida 4)

Domingo salvaje, 1966 (Figueroa 4)

Dominick and Eugene, 1988 (Curtis 3, Sargent 4)

Dominika's Name Day. See Když má svátek Dominika, 1967

Dominion, 1974 (Brakhage 2)

Dominique, 1978 (Robertson 3, Simmons 3)

Domino, 1943 (Blier 3, Achard 4, Aurenche 4)

Domino Killings. See Domino Principle, 1976

Domino Principle, 1976 (Kramer 2, Hackman 3, Wallach 3, Widmark 3, Laszlo 4)

Domino vert, 1935 (Darrieux 3, Vanel 3)

Domyaku retto, 1975 (Yamamura 3)

Don, 1978 (Bachchan 3)

Don Bosco, 1935 (Amidei 4)

Don Camillo, 1983 (Ayres 3, Cusack 3)

Don Camillo à Moscou. See Don Camillo en Russie, 1965

Don Camillo e i giovani d'oggi, 1972 (Camerini 2, Cervi 3)

Don Camillo e l'onorevole Peppone, 1955 (Gallone 2, Cervi 3)

Don Camillo en Russie, 1965 (Fernandel 3)

Don Camillo et les contestataires, 1970 (Christian-Jaque 4)

Don Camillo Monseigneur, 1961 (Fernandel 3)

Don Camillo Monsignore ma non troppo, 1961 (Gallone 2, Cervi 3)

Don Cesar de Bazan, 1957 (Enei 4)

Don Cesare di Bazan, 1942 (Cervi 3, Amidei 4, Zavattini 4)

Don Giovanni, 1979 (Losey 2, Fisher 4, Trauner 4)

Don Giovanni della Costa Azzurra, 1962 (Belmondo 3)

Don Giovanni in Sicilia, 1967 (Lattuada 2)

Don Is Dead, 1973 (Quinn 3, Ames 4, Goldsmith 4, Head 4, Wallis 4)

Don Juan, 1922 (Metzner 4)

Don Juan, 1926 (Astor 3, Barrymore 3, Loy 3, Carré 4, Haskin 4, Meredyth 4, Warner 4)

Don Juan, 1955 (Fernandel 3, Rey 3, Wakhévitch 4)

Don Juan. See Don Sajn, 1970

Don Juan et Faust, 1922 (Autant-Lara 2, L'Herbier 2)

Don Juan, Karl-Liebeknecht-Strasse 78. See Acht und Siebzig, 1980

Don Juan 1973 ou si Don Juan était une femme, 1973 (Vadim 2, Bardot 3, Decaë 4)

Don Juan Quilligan, 1945 (Bendix 3, Blondell 3, Raksin 4)

Don Juan 68, 1968 (Jireš 2)

Don Kikhot, 1957 (Kozintsev 2, Cherkassov 3, Enei 4, Moskvin 4)

Don Lucio y el harmano pio, 1960 (Rey 3)

Don Pasquale, 1940 (De Santis 2)

Don Pietro Caruso, 1917 (Bertini 3)

Don Q, Son of Zorro, 1925 (Astor 3, Crisp 3, Fairbanks 3, Grot 4)

Don Quichotte, 1909 (Cohl 4)

Don Quichotte, 1933 (Pabst 2, Andrejew 4, Ibert 4, Reiniger 4, Wakhévitch 4)

Don Quichotte, 1964 (Rohmer 2)

Don Quichotte, le chat botté, 1903 (Pathé 4)

Don Quickshot of the Rio Grande, 1923 (Laemmle 4)

Don Quijote cabalga de nuevo, 1972 (Cantinflas 3)

Don Quintin el amargao, 1935 (Buñuel 2)
Don Quixote. *See* Don Quichotte, 1909
Don Quixote, 1926 (Madsen and
  Schenstrøm 3)
Don Quixote. *See* Don Quichotte, 1933
Don Quixote, 1934 (Iwerks 4)
Don Quixote, 1955 (Welles 2)
Don Quixote. *See* Don Kikhot, 1957
Don Quixote, 1966 (Rey 3)
Don Quixote de la Mancha, 1947 (Rey 3)
Don Sajn, 1970 (Švankmajer 4)
Don Winslow of the Coast Guard, 1943
  (Brooks 2)
Dona Barbara, 1943 (De Fuentes 2, Félix 3)
Doña Diabla, 1949 (Félix 3)
Doña Herlinda y su hijo, 1984
  (Hermosillo 2)
Dona Juana, 1927 (Bergner 3, Balàzs 4,
  Freund 4)
Dona mentiras, 1930 (Fort 4)
Doña Perfecta, 1951 (Del Rio 3)
Donatella, 1956 (Monicelli 2, Fabrizi 3,
  Delli Colli 4)
Donauwalzer, 1930 (Reisch 4)
Doncella de piedra, 1955 (Figueroa 4)
Donde van nuestros hijos, 1958 (Del Rio 3)
Done in Oil, 1934 (Roach 4)
Done in Wax, 1915 (Beery 3)
Dong Kingman, 1955 (Howe 4)
Donkey Skin. *See* Peau d'âne, 1971
Donna!, 1914 (Bertini 3)
Donna alla frontiera. *See* Frauen, die durch
  die Hölle gehen, 1966
Donna che inventà l'amore, 1952 (Brazzi 3)
Donna che venne del mare, 1957 (De Sica 2)
Donna dei Faraoni, 1960 (Fusco 4)
Donna del fiume, 1954 (Pasolini 2, De
  Laurentiis 4, Flaiano 4, Ponti 4)
Donna del giorno, 1957 (Reggiani 3,
  Zavattini 4)
Donna del mondo, 1963 (Ustinov 3)
Donna del Montagna, 1943 (Castellani 2)
Donna della domenica, 1975 (Trintignant 3,
  Age and Scarpelli 4, Mastroianni 3,
  Morricone 4)
Donna della montagne, 1943 (De
  Laurentiis 4)
Donna delle meraviglie, 1985 (Cardinale 3)
Donna di una notte, 1930 (Bertini 3)
Donna è una cosa meravigliosa, 1964
  (Fabrizi 3, Di Venanzo 4, Guerra 4)
Donna, il diavolo, il tempo, 1921 (Bertini 3)
Donna invisible, 1969 (Morricone 4)
Donna libera, 1953 (Cervi 3)
Donna nuda, 1913 (Gallone 2)
Donna nuda, 1918 (Bertini 3)
Donna più bella del mondo, 1955
  (Gassman 3, Lollobrigida 3, Solinas 4)
Donna scimmia, 1964 (Girardot 3, Ponti 4)
Donna senza nome, 1951 (Simon 3)
Donna spezzata, 1988 (Josephson 3)
Donnaren, 1960 (Thulin 3)
Donne del fiume, 1954 (Loren 3)
Donne e briganti, 1950 (Rota 4)
Donne e soldati, 1954 (Ferreri 2, Di
  Venanzo 4)
Donne proibite, 1953 (De Santis 2,
  Darnell 3, Masina 3, Quinn 3,
  Zavattini 4)
Donne senza nome, 1950 (Cervi 3, Rosay 3)
Donne-moi la main, 1958 (Jarre 4)
Donne-moi tes yeux, 1943 (Guitry 2)
Donogoo Tonka, 1936 (Ondra 3)
Donovan Affair, 1929 (Capra 2, Cohn 4)

Donovan's Brain, 1953 (Ayres 3, Biroc 4,
  Leven 4)
Donovan's Kid. *See* Young Donovan's Kid,
  1931
Donovan's Kid, 1979 (Rooney 3)
Donovan's Reef, 1963 (Ford 2, Dalio 3,
  Lamour 3, Marsh 3, Marvin 3, Wayne 3,
  Clothier 4, Edouart 4, Head 4, Nugent 4)
Don's Party, 1975 (Beresford 2)
Don't Axe Me, 1958 (Blanc 4, McKimson 4)
Don't Be Blue. *See* Tout peut arriver, 1969
Don't Be Jealous, 1928 (Brown 3)
Don't Bet on Blondes, 1935 (Florey 2,
  Flynn 3)
Don't Bet on Love, 1933 (Ayres 3, Rogers 3,
  Laemmle 4)
Don't Bet On Women, 1931 (MacDonald 3)
Don't Bite Your Dentist, 1930 (Sennett 2)
Don't Bother to Knock, 1952 (Bancroft 3,
  Monroe 3, Widmark 3, Ballard 4,
  Lemaire 4, Taradash 4)
Don't Bother to Knock, 1961 (Raphael 4,
  Unsworth 4)
Don't Change Your Husband, 1919 (De
  Mille 2, Swanson 3, Buckland 4,
  Macpherson 4)
Don't Cry, It's Only Thunder, 1982 (Jarre 4)
Don't Drink the Water, 1969 (Allen 2,
  Rosenblum 4, Williams 4)
Don't Ever Leave Me, 1949 (Box 4, Rank 4)
Don't Ever Marry, 1921 (Neilan 2, Carré 4)
Don't Fence Me In, 1945 (Rogers 3)
Don't Flirt, 1923 (Roach 4)
Don't Forget, 1924 (Roach 4)
Don't Gamble With Love, 1936
  (Pangborn 3)
Don't Get Gay with Your Manicure, 1903
  (Bitzer 4)
Don't Get Jealous, 1929 (Sennett 2,
  Hornbeck 4)
Don't Get Personal, 1922 (Laemmle 4)
Don't Get Personal, 1936 (Waxman 4)
Don't Give In, Girls!. *See* Děvčata, nedejte
  se!, 1937
Don't Give Up. *See* Tappa inte sugen, 1947
Don't Give Up the Sheep, 1953 (Blanc 4,
  Jones 4, Maltese 4, Stalling 4)
Don't Give Up the Ship, 1959 (Lewis 2,
  Head 4, Wallis 4)
Don't Go Near the Water, 1957 (Walters 2,
  Ford 3, Cahn 4, Kaper 4, Rose 4)
Don't Go to Sleep, 1982 (Gordon 3)
Don't Hook Now, 1938 (Crosby 3, Hope 3)
Don't Just Stand There, 1968 (Wagner 3,
  Krasner 4)
Don't Knock the Rock, 1957 (Katzman 4)
Don't Knock the Twist, 1962 (Katzman 4)
Don't Look Now, 1936 (Avery 4, Stalling 4)
**Don't Look Now, 1973 (Roeg 2, Christie 3,
  Sutherland 3, Donaggio 4)**
Don't Make Grandfather Angry. *See*
  Nezlobte dědečka, 1934
Don't Make Waves, 1967 (MacKendrick 2,
  Cardinale 3, Curtis 3)
Don't Marry, 1928 (August 4, Fox 4)
Don't Marry for Money, 1923 (Brown 2)
Don't Miss, Miss Pizz, 1968 (Müller 4)
Don't Open the Window. *See* Fin de semana
  para los muertos, 1974
Don't Panic Chaps!, 1959 (Carreras 4)
Don't Park There!, 1924 (Garnett 2,
  Rogers 3, Roach 4)
Don't Play Bridge with Your Wife, 1933
  (Sennett 2)

Don't Play with Love. *See* Man spielt nicht
  mit der Liebe, 1926
Don't Pull Your Punches. *See* Kid Comes
  Back, 1937
Don't Raise the Bridge, Lower the River,
  1967 (Lewis 2, Terry-Thomas 3,
  Heller 4)
Don't Rock the Boat, 1920 (Roach 4)
Don't Say, 1973 (Le Grice 2)
Don't Say Die, 1923 (Roach 4)
Don't Say It. *See* Kung Fu Master, 1988
Don't Shoot, 1922 (Laemmle 4, Miller 4)
Don't Shoot, 1926 (Wyler 2)
Don't Shoot the Composer, 1966 (Russell 2)
Don't Shove, 1919 (Daniels 3, Lloyd 3,
  Roach 4)
Don't Take It to Heart, 1944 (Rank 4,
  Vetchinsky 4)
Don't Tease the Mosquito. *See* Non
  stuzzicate la zanzara, 1967
Don't Tell Dad, 1925 (Sennett 2)
Don't Tell Everything, 1921 (De Mille 2,
  Wood 2, Reid 3, Swanson 3)
Don't Tell Everything, 1927 (Roach 4)
Don't Tell the Wife, 1927 (Blanke 4)
Don't Tell the Wife, 1937 (Ball 3,
  McDaniel 3)
Don't Tempt the Devil. *See* Bonnes Causes,
  1963
Don't Throw That Knife, 1951 (Three
  Stooges 3)
Don't Trust Your Husband, 1948 (Carroll 3,
  MacMurray 3, Cronjager 4, Salter 4)
Don't Turn 'em Loose, 1936 (Grable 3)
Don't Turn the Other Cheek. *See* Viva la
  muerte. . . tua!, 1972
Don't Weaken, 1920 (Sennett 2, Roach 4)
Don't Worry, We'll Think of a Title, 1966
  (Three Stooges 3)
Donto okoze, 1959 (Oshima 2)
Donzoko, 1957 (Kagawa 3, Mifune 3,
  Yamada 3, Muraki 4)
Dooley Scheme, 1911 (Sennett 2)
Doolhan, 1983 (Azmi 3)
Doolins of Oklahoma, 1949 (Scott 3,
  Brown 4, Canutt 4, Duning 4)
Doombeach, 1990 (Jackson 3)
Doomed. *See* **Ikiru, 1952**
Doomed Battalion, 1931 (Fulton 4)
Doomed Caravan, 1941 (Harlan 4, Head 4)
Doomed Cargo. *See* Seven Sinners, 1936
Doomed to Die, 1940 (Karloff 3)
Doomsday, 1928 (Cooper 3, Banton 4)
Doomsday, 1938 (Terry 4)
Doomsday Flight, 1966 (Johnson 3,
  O'Brien 3, Schifrin 4)
Doomsday Voyage, 1972 (Cotten 3)
Doomwatch, 1972 (Sanders 3)
Door, 1968 (Blanc 4)
Door, 1972 (Xie 2)
Door in the Wall, 1956 (Bernard 4)
Doorbell Rang, 1977 (Baxter 3)
Doors, 1991 (Stone 2)
Doorway of Destruction, 1915 (Ford 2)
Doorway to Hell, 1930 (Ayres 3, Cagney 3,
  Zanuck 4)
Doosri, 1983 (Azmi 3)
Dopey Dicks, 1950 (Three Stooges 3)
Doppelganger, 1969 (Lom 3)
Doppelgängerin, 1925 (Dagover 3)
Doppelte Lottchen, 1950 (Herlth 4)
Doppia faccia. *See* Double Face, 1969
Doppia taglia per Monnesota Stinky, 1972
  (Kinski 3)

Doppio delitto, 1978 (Mastroianni 3, Ustinov 3)

Dora, 1909 (Olcott 2)

Dora, 1943 (Bertini 3)

Dora Brandes, 1916 (Nielsen 3)

Dora Thorne, 1915 (Barrymore 3)

Dora's Dunkin' Doughnuts, 1933 (Temple 3)

Do-Re-Mi-Fa, 1915 (Sennett 2)

Dorf unter Himmel, 1953 (Herlth 4)

Dorian Gray, 1970 (Lom 3)

Dorian Gray im Spiegel der Boulevardpresse, 1984 (Constantine 3, Seyrig 3)

Dorian Grays Portraet, 1910 (Psilander 3)

Dorian's Divorce, 1916 (Barrymore 3)

Dormeuse, 1962 (Rabier 4)

Dornenweg einer Fürstin, 1928 (Albers 3)

Dornröschen, 1917 (Leni 2)

Dornröschen, 1918 (Wegener 3)

Dornröschen, 1922 (Reiniger 4)

Doroga k zvezdam. See Faisons le point sur les Spoutniks, 1957

Dorogoi moi chelovek, 1958 (Batalov 3)

Dorothea, 1974 (Sarde 4)

Dorothea Angermann, 1959 (Siodmak 2, Herlth 4)

Dorothea Tanning, ou le regard ébloui, 1960 (Delerue 4)

Dorotheas Rache, 1974 (Carrière 4)

Dorothée cherche l'amour, 1945 (Berry 3)

Dorothy Vernon of Haddon Hall, 1924 (Neilan 2, Pickford 3, Grot 4, Rosher 4, Young 4)

Dortoir des grandes, 1953 (Marais 3, Moreau 3)

Dos au mur, 1958 (Moreau 3)

Dos de la Mafia. See Due mafiosi contre Goldginger, 1965

Dos hijos desobedientes, 1960 (Armendáriz 3)

Dos mundos y un amor, 1954 (Armendáriz 3)

Dos rostros y una sola imagen, 1984 (Alvarez 2)

Dos tipos de cuidado, 1952 (Infante 3, Figueroa 4)

Dos y media y veinuno, 1959 (Rey 3)

Dodsworth, 1936 (Wyler 2, Astor 3, Huston 3, Lukas 3, Niven 3, Day 4, Goldwyn 4, Howard 4, Mandell 4, Maté 4)

Doshaburi, 1957 (Yamamura 3, Takemitsu 4)

Doss House, 1933 (Baxter 2)

Dossier noir, 1955 (Cayatte 2, Blier 3, Spaak 4)

Dostana, 1980 (Bachchan 3)

Dosworth, 1936 (Newman 4)

Dot and the Line, 1965 (Jones 4)

Dotanba, 1957 (Shimura 3)

Dotknięcie nocy, 1960 (Ścibor-Rylski 4)

Doto ichi man kairi, 1966 (Mifune 3)

Dots, 1939 (McLaren 4)

Dots Izrila, 1917 (Mozhukin 3)

Dottor Antonio, 1937 (Fusco 4)

Dotty World of James Lloyd, 1964 (Russell 2)

Double Adventure, 1921 (Van Dyke 2)

Double Amour, 1925 (Epstein 2)

Double Chaser, 1942 (Blanc 4, Freleng 4, Stalling 4)

Double Confession, 1950 (Lorre 3, Unsworth 4)

Double Crime sur la Ligne Maginot, 1938 (Blier 3, Fradetal 4)

Double Crossbones, 1951 (O'Connor 3)

Double Crossed. See Cash Parrish's Pal, 1915

Double Cross Roads, 1930 (August 4, Estabrook 4, Fox 4)

Double Daring, 1926 (Arthur 3)

Double Date, 1941 (Salter 4)

Double Dealing, 1923 (Laemmle 4)

Double Deception. See Magiciennes, 1960

Double Destin, 1954 (Simon 3)

Double Door, 1934 (Vidor 2)

Double Dynamite, 1951 (Marx Brothers 3, Russell 3, Sinatra 3, Cahn 4)

Double Exposure, 1935 (Hope 3)

Double Face, 1969 (Kinski 3)

Double Harness, 1933 (Powell 3, Cooper 4, Hunt 4, MacGowan 4, Murfin 4, Plunkett 4, Steiner 4)

Double Indemnity, 1974 (Cobb 3, Winters 3)

Double Indemnity, 1944 (Wilder 2, Darwell 3, MacMurray 3, Robinson 3, Stanwyck 3, Chandler 4, Dreier 4, Head 4, Rozsa 4, Seitz 4)

Double jeu, 1916 (Feuillade 2)

Double Knot, 1913 (Walsh 2)

Double Life, 1947 (Cukor 2, Colman 3, Gordon 3, O'Brien 3, Winters 3, Banton 4, Horner 4, Kanin 4, Krasner 4, Rozsa 4)

Double McGuffin, 1979 (Borgnine 3)

Double Man, 1967 (Schaffner 2, Brynner 3)

Double Murders. See Doppio delitto, 1978

Double Negative, 1979 (Perkins 3)

Double or Mutton, 1955 (Blanc 4, Jones 4, Maltese 4)

Double or Nothing, 1937 (Dmytryk 2, Crosby 3, Glazer 4, Head 4, Lederer 4, Prinz 4, Struss 4, Young 4)

Double Pursuit, 1948 (Rank 4)

Double Reward, 1912 (Ince 4)

Double Sixes, 1931 (Carey 3)

Double Speed, 1920 (Wood 2, Reid 3)

Double Speed, 1965 (LeRoy 2)

Double Suicide. See Shinju Ten-no-amijima, 1969

Double Suicide of Sonezaki. See Sonezaki shinjuh, 1981

Double Trouble, 1915 (Fairbanks 3, Loos 4)

Double Trouble, 1941 (Langdon 3)

Double Trouble, 1967 (Presley 3, Rafferty 3, Winkler 4)

Double Up, 1943 (Metty 4)

Double Wedding, 1913 (Sennett 2)

Double Wedding, 1937 (Mankiewiez 2, Loy 3, Powell 3, Adrian 4, Daniels 4, Swerling 4)

Double Whoopee, 1929 (Harlow 3, Laurel and Hardy 3, Roach 4)

Doubling for Romeo, 1921 (Rogers 3)

Doubling in the Quickies, 1932 (Sennett 2)

Doubting Thomas, 1935 (Rogers 3)

Douce, 1943 (Aurenche 4, Bost 4)

Doucement les basses!, 1971 (Delon 3)

Douceur d'aimer, 1930 (Arletty 3)

Douceur du village, 1963 (Braunberger 4)

Douche aprés le bain, 1895 (Lumière 2)

Douche d'eau bouillanie, 1907 (Méliès 2)

Doug and Dynamite, 1914 (Sennett 2)

Dough for the Do-Do, 1949 (Blanc 4, Stalling 4)

Dough Ray Me-ow, 1948 (Blanc 4, Stalling 4)

Doughboys, 1930 (Keaton 2, Gibbons 4)

Doughboys in Ireland, 1943 (Mitchum 3)

Doughgirls, 1944 (Arden 3, Sheridan 3, Wyman 3, Deutsch 4, Haller 4)

Dough-Nuts, 1917 (Laurel and Hardy 3)

Doughnuts and Society, 1936 (Pangborn 3)

Doulos, 1963 (Melville 2, Belmondo 3, Piccoli 3, Reggiani 3, De Beauregard 4, Ponti 4)

Doulos—the Finger Man. See Doulos, 1963

Dourman, 1912 (Mozhukin 3)

Douze heures de bonheur, 1952 (Evein 4)

Douze heures d'horloge, 1959 (Alekan 4)

Douze mois en France, 1970 (Leenhardt 2)

Douze Travaux d'Hercule, 1910 (Cohl 4)

Dove, 1927 (Talmadge 3, Menzies 4, Schenck 4)

Dove, 1974 (Peck 3, Barry 4, Nykvist 4)

Dove in the Eagle's nest, 1913 (Cruze 2)

Dov'è la libertà?, 1953 (Rossellini 2, De Laurentiis 4, Delli Colli 4, Flaiano 4)

Dove scenda il sole. See Unter Geiern, 1964

Dove vai in vacanza?, 1978 (Sordi 3, Morricone 4)

Dove vai tutta nuda?, 1969 (Gassman 3)

Dover Boys, 1942 (Blanc 4, Jones 4, Stalling 4)

Dover Revisited, 1942 (Watt 2)

Dover Road. See Little Adventuress, 1927

Dover Road. See Where Sinners Meet, 1934

Doverie, 1976 (Yankovsky 3)

Dovolená s andělem, 1952 (Stallich 4)

Down a Long Way, 1954 (Halas and Batchelor 4)

Down among the Sheltering Palms, 1952 (Goulding 2, Johnson 3, Marvin 3, LeMaire 4, Lewin 4, Shamroy 4)

Down among the Sugar Cane, 1932 (Fleischer 4)

Down among the Z Men, 1952 (Sellers 3)

Down and Dirty. See Brutti, sporchi, cattivi, 1976

Down and Out, 1922 (Roach 4)

Down and Out in America, 1985 (Grant 3)

Down and Out in Beverly Hills, 1986 (Mazursky 2, Dreyfuss 3, Midler 3, Nolte 3)

Down Argentine Way, 1940 (Ameche 3, Grable 3, Miranda 3, Banton 4, Brown 4, Day 4, Shamroy 4, Zanuck 4)

Down Beat Bear, 1956 (Hanna and Barbera 4)

Down By Law, 1986 (Jarmusch 2, Müller 4)

Down by the Old Mill Stream, 1933 (Fleischer 4)

Down by the Sounding Sea, 1914 (Reid 3)

Down Dakota Way, 1949 (Rogers 3)

Down Melody Lane, 1943 (Crazy Gang 3)

Down Memory Lane, 1949 (Sennett 2, Pangborn 3)

Down Mexico Way, 1941 (Autry 3)

Down Missouri Way, 1946 (Carradine 3)

Down on the Farm, 1920 (Sennett 2)

Down on the Levee, 1933 (Terry 4)

Down River, 1931 (Laughton 3)

Down the Ancient Stairs. See Per le antiche scale, 1976

Down the Hill to Creditville, 1914 (Crisp 3, Reid 3)

Down the River, 1951 (Fleischer 4)

Down the Stretch, 1926 (Laemmle 4)

Down the Stretch, 1936 (Rooney 3)

Down There in the Jungle, 1987 (Johnson 3)

Down Three Dark Streets, 1954
(Crawford 3)
Down to Earth, 1917 (Fleming 2,
Fairbanks 3, Loos 4)
Down to Earth, 1932 (Rogers 3)
Down to Earth, 1947 (Hayworth 3, Horton 3,
Cohn 4, Cole 4, Duning 4, Maté 4)
Down to the Cellar. *See* Do pivnice, 1982
Down to the Cellar. *See* Jan Svankmajer:
Alchemist of the Surreal, 1990
Down to Their Last Yacht, 1934
(Cronjager 4, Dunn 4, Plunkett 4,
Steiner 4)
Down to the Sea in Ships, 1923 (Bow 3)
Down to the Sea in Ships, 1949
(Hathaway 2, Barrymore 3, Widmark 3,
LeMaire 4, Newman 4, Wheeler 4)
Down to the Sea in Shoes, 1923 (Sennett 2)
Down Twisted, 1987 (Golan and Globus 4)
Down with Cats, 1943 (Terry 4)
Down with the Fences. *See* Dole plotovi,
1962
Downey Girl. *See* Dunungen, 1920
Downfall of Osen. *See* Orizuru osen, 1934
Downhearted Duckling, 1953 (Hanna and
Barbera 4)
Downhill, 1927 (Novello 3, Balcon 4)
Downhill Racer, 1969 (Hackman 3,
Redford 3, Head 4)
Downstairs, 1932 (Gilbert 3, Lukas 3,
Rosson 4)
Downtown. *See* Shitamachi, 1957
Downy Girl. *See* Dunungen, 1941
Dozen Socks, 1927 (Sennett 2)
**Dracula, 1931 (Browning 2, Lugosi 3,
Fort 4, Freund 4, Laemmle 4, Pierce 4)**
**Dracula, 1958 (Fisher 2, Cushing 3, Lee 3,
Bernard 4, Carreras 4, Sangster 4)**
Dracula, 1974 (Palance 3)
Dracula, 1979 (Badham 2, Olivier 3,
Pleasence 3, Mirisch 4, Whitlock 4,
Williams 4)
Dracula A.D, 1972, 1972 (Cushing 3, Lee 3,
Carreras 4)
Dracula cerca sangue di vergine e . . . mori di
sete!!!, 1974 (Warhol 2, Ponti 4)
Dracula Has Risen from the Grave, 1968
(Lee 3, Bernard 4, Carreras 4, Francis 4)
Dracula im Schloss des Schreckens. *See* Nell
stretta morsa del ragno, 1971
Dracula—Prince of Darkness, 1965
(Fisher 2, Lee 3, Bernard 4, Carreras 4)
Dracula vs. Frankenstein, 1969 (Carradine 3)
Dracula's Daughter, 1936 (D'Agostino 4,
Fort 4)
Dracula's Dog. *See* Zoltan . . . Hound of
Dracula, 1977
Dracula's Son, 1975 (Lee 3)
Draft Horse, 1942 (Blanc 4, Jones 4,
Stalling 4)
Draftee Daffy, 1945 (Blanc 4, Clampett 4,
Stalling 4)
Drag, 1929 (Barthelmess 3, Haller 4)
Drag Net, 1928 (Von Sternberg 2)
Drag-a-long Droopy, 1953 (Avery 4)
Dragée haute, 1959 (Piccoli 3)
Dragées au poivre, 1963 (Belmondo 3,
Karina 3, Signoret 3, Vitti 3, Decaë 4)
Dragnet, 1928 (Powell 3, Dreier 4,
Furthman 4, Mankiewicz 4, Rosson 4)
Dragnet, 1987 (Hanks 3, Rozsa 4)
Dragnet Girl. *See* Hijosen no onna, 1933
Dragon de Komodo, 1958 (Delerue 4)
Dragon First, 1978 (Chan 3)

Dragon Lord. *See* Lung siuye, 1982
Dragon Murder Case, 1934 (Blanke 4,
Gaudio 4, Orry-Kelly 4)
Dragon of Pendragon Castle, 1950
(Baxter 2)
Dragon Painter, 1919 (Hayakawa 3)
Dragon Seed, 1944 (Van Dyke 2,
Barrymore 3, Hepburn 3, Huston 3,
Moorehead 3, Berman 4, Murfin 4,
Stothart 4, Wheeler 4)
Dragonard, 1987 (Lom 3, Reed 3)
Dragonen, 1925 (Blom 2)
Dragonerliebchen, 1928 (Reisch 4)
Dragones de Ha-Long, 1976 (Alvarez 2)
Dragons de Villars, 1900 (Guy 2)
Dragon's Gold, 1953 (Cortez 4)
Dragonslayer, 1981 (Richardson 3, North 4)
Dragonwyck, 1946 (Mankiewicz 2,
Huston 3, Price 3, Tierney 3, Miller 4,
Newman 4, Wheeler 4, Zanuck 4)
Dragoon Wells Massacre, 1957 (Clothier 4)
Dragstrip Riot, 1958 (Wray 3)
Dragueurs, 1959 (Aimée 3, Douy 4, Jarre 4)
Drahoušek Klementýna, 1959 (Brdečka 4)
Drama della gelosia, 1970 (Mastroianni 3)
Drama of Jealousy—and Other Things. *See*
Dramma della gelosia, 1970
Drama von Mayerling. *See* Tragodie im
Haus Habsburg, 1924
Drama's Dreadful Deal, 1916 (Lloyd 3)
Dramatic School, 1938 (LeRoy 2,
Goddard 3, Rainer 3, Turner 3, Adrian 4,
Daniels 4, Vajda 4, Waxman 4)
Dramatic School, 1939 (Dumont 3)
Drame à Venise, 1906 (Pathé 4)
Drame au château d'Acre, 1915 (Gaumont 4)
Drame au pays basque, 1913 (Feuillade 2)
Drame chez les fantoches, 1908 (Cohl 4,
Gaumont 4)
Drame de Shanghai, 1938 (Pabst 2, Jouvet 3,
Alekan 4, Andrejew 4, Annenkov 4,
Courant 4, Jeanson 4, Schüfftan 4)
Drame du taureau, 1965 (Braunberger 4)
Drame sur la planche à chaussures, 1915
(Cohl 4)
Drames du Bois de Boulogne, 1947
(Decaë 4)
Dramma della Casbah, 1953 (Papas 3)
Dramma della gelosia—tutti i particolari in
cronaca, 1970 (Giannini 3, Vitti 3, Age
and Scarpelli 4)
Dranem, 1900 (Guy 2)
Drango, 1957 (Crisp 3, Bernstein 4,
Howe 4)
Drapeau noir flotte sur la marmite, 1971
(Audiard 4, D'Eaubonne 4)
Drastic Demise, 1945 (Anger 2)
Dráteníček, 1920 (Ondra 3, Heller 4)
Draufgänger, 1931 (Albers 3)
**Draughtsman's Contract, 1982
(Greenaway 2)**
Dravci, 1948 (Weiss 2)
Draw, 1984 (Coburn 3, Douglas 3)
Drawing Lesson. *See* Statue animée, 1903
Drawing the Line, 1915 (Eason 4)
Dream, 1911 (Pickford 3, Gaudio 4, Ince 4)
Dream a Little Dream, 1989 (Robards 3,
Stanton 3)
Dream Child, 1914 (Eason 4)
Dream Circus, 1939 (Reiniger 4)
Dream Doll, 1979 (Godfrey 4, Halas and
Batchelor 4)
Dream Flights. *See* Polety vo sne i nayavu,
1982

Dream Girl, 1916 (De Mille 2, Buckland 4,
Macpherson 4)
Dream Girl, 1948 (Leisen 2, Hutton 3,
Dreier 4, Head 4, Young 4)
Dream House, 1932 (Sennett 2, Crosby 3,
Hornbeck 4)
Dream Kids, 1944 (Fleischer 4)
Dream Lover, 1986 (Pakula 2, Jenkins 4)
Dream Machine, 1983 (Jarman 2)
Dream, NYC, The Return, The Flower, 1975
(Brakhage 2)
Dream of a Rarebit Fiend, 1906 (Porter 2)
Dream of David Gray. *See* **Vampyr, 1932**
Dream of Happiness. *See* Lyckodrömmen,
1963
Dream of Kings, 1969 (Papas 3, Quinn 3,
Leven 4, North 4)
Dream of Love, 1928 (Niblo 2, Crawford 3,
Adrian 4, Daniels 4, Gibbons 4)
Dream of Passion, 1978 (Dassin 2,
Burstyn 3, Mercouri 3)
Dream of the Racetrack Fiend, 1905
(Bitzer 4)
Dream of Zorro. *See* Sogno di Zorro, 1951
Dream One, 1984 (Boorman 2)
Dream Path of Youth. *See* Seishun no
yumeji, 1976
Dream Street, 1921 (Griffith 2)
Dream Stuff, 1933 (Sennett 2)
Dream Valley. *See* Drömda dalen, 1947
Dream Walking, 1934 (Fleischer 4)
Dream Walking, 1950 (Terry 4)
Dream Wife, 1953 (Grant 3, Kerr 3,
Pidgeon 3, Krasner 4, Rose 4, Schary 4)
Dream Woman, 1914 (Guy 2)
Dreamboat, 1952 (Lanchester 3, Rogers 3,
Webb 3, Krasner 4, LeMaire 4)
Dreamers, 1933 (Crazy Gang 3)
Dreamer's Walk. *See* Drömmares vandring,
1957
Dreaming, 1944 (Baxter 2, Crazy Gang 3,
Kendall 3)
Dreaming, 1980 (Vanderbeek 2)
Dreaming Lips. *See* Traümende Mund, 1932
Dreaming Lips, 1937 (Lean 2, Bergner 3,
Massey 3, Andrejew 4, Garmes 4,
Mayer 4)
Dreaming Lips. *See* Traumende Mund, 1953
Dreams, 1940 (Cushing 3)
Dreams. *See* Kvinnodröm, 1955
Dreams, 1990 (Kurosawa 2, Scorsese 2,
Ryu 3)
Dreams, Journey into Autumn. *See*
Kvinnodröm, 1955
Dreams of a Rarebit Fiend, 1921 (McCay 4)
Dreams of Gold: The Mel Fisher Story, 1986
(Robertson 3)
Dreams of Monte Carlo. *See* Monte Carlo,
1926
Dreams of Youth. *See* Wakodo no yume,
1928
Dreams That Money Can Buy, 1926
(Richter 2)
Dreams That Money Can Buy, 1946
(Milhaud 4)
Dreamscape, 1984 (Von Sydow 3, Jarre 4)
Dreamy Knights, 1916 (Laurel and Hardy 3)
Drei amerikanische LPs, 1969 (Wenders 2)
Drei Kuckucksuhren, 1926 (Wagner 4)
Drei machen ihr Glück. *See* Teure Heimat,
1929
Drei Mannequins, 1926 (Albers 3)
Drei Probiermamsells. *See* Drei Mannequins,
1926

Drei Seelen und ein Gedanke, 1927
(Albers 3)
Drei Tage Liebe, 1931 (Albers 3)
Drei Tänze der Mary Wilford, 1920
(Wiene 2)
Drei um Edith, 1929 (Rasp 3, Junge 4)
Drei Unteroffiziere, 1950 (Staudte 2)
Drei van Hells, 1918 (Kräly 4)
Drei von der Stempelstelle, 1932
(Walbrook 3)
Drei von der Tankstelle. See Chemin du
paradis, 1930
Drei von der Tankstelle, 1930
(Tschechowa 3, Planer 4, Pommer 4)
Dreigroschenoper, 1931 (Artaud 3, Modot 3,
Rasp 3, Andrejew 4, Balàzs 4, Wagner 4)
Dreigroschenoper, 1963 (Staudte 2,
Heckroth 4)
Dreiklang, 1938 (Sirk 2, Dagover 3)
Dreimäderlhaus, 1918 (Veidt 3)
Dreizehn, 1918 (Albers 3)
Dreizehn alte Esel, 1958 (Albers 3)
Dresden Doll, 1922 (Fleischer 4)
Dress. See Klänningen, 1964
Dress Parade, 1927 (Crisp 3, Love 3,
Adrian 4)
Dress Returns to Glory, 1947 (Zhao 3)
Dressage de chevaux sauvages, 1970
(Braunberger 4)
Dressed to Kill, 1928 (Astor 3, Brown 3,
Estabrook 4, Fox 4)
Dressed to Kill, 1941 (Day 4)
Dressed to Kill, 1946 (Rathbone 3, Salter 4)
Dressed to Kill, 1980 (De Palma 2, Caine 3,
Dickinson 3, Donaggio 4)
Dressed to Thrill, 1935 (Maté 4,
Raphaelson 4)
Dresser, 1984 (Yates 2, Finney 3)
Dressmaker from Paris, 1925 (Hawks 2,
Banton 4, Glennon 4)
Dressmaker's Bill, 1910 (White 3)
Dreyfus, 1930 (Homolka 3, Kortner 3,
Rasp 3, Warm 4)
Dreyfus Affair. See Affaire Dreyfus, 1899
Dreyfus Case. See Dreyfus, 1930
Drift Fence, 1936 (Crabbe 3, Miller 4)
Drifter, 1929 (Mix 3)
Drifter, 1944 (Crabbe 3)
Drifter, 1988 (Corman 3)
Drifters, 1929 (Grierson 2)
Drifting, 1923 (Browning 2, Beery 3,
Wong 3, Laemmle 4)
Driftwood, 1911 (Dwan 2)
Driftwood, 1928 (Walker 4)
Driftwood, 1947 (Dwan 2, Brennan 3,
Wood 3, Alton 4)
Drink Hearty, 1920 (Roach 4)
Drink's Lure, 1912 (Griffith 2, Crisp 3,
Bitzer 4)
Drip-Along Daffy, 1951 (Blanc 4, Jones 4,
Maltese 4, Stalling 4)
Dripping Water, 1969 (Snow 2, Wieland 2)
Drishti, 1991 (Nihalani 4)
Dritte, 1958 (Vitti 3)
Dritte, 1972 (Mueller-Stahl 3)
Dritte Generation, 1979 (Constantine 3)
Drive a Crooked Road, 1954 (Edwards 2,
Rooney 3)
Drive for Life, 1909 (Griffith 2, Bitzer 4)
Drive, He Said, 1972 (Rafelson 2, Black 3,
Dern 3, Nicholson 3)
Driven from Home. See Austreibung,
1923
Driven from Home, 1927 (Wong 3)

Driver, 1978 (Hill 2, Adjani 3, Dern 3,
Horner 4)
Driver dagg faller Regn, 1946 (Zetterling 2)
Driver's Seat, 1975 (Taylor 3)
Driving Home the Cows, 1912 (Olcott 2)
Driving Miss Daisy, 1989 (Beresford 2)
Droga do nieba, 1958 (Zanussi 2)
Droga llamada. Helen. See Paranoia, 1969
Droit à aimer, 1972 (Sarde 4)
Droit à la vie, 1917 (Gance 2, Burel 4,
Gaumont 4)
Droit d'aimer, 1972 (Sharif 3, Carrière 4,
Decaë 4)
Droit d'asile, 1970 (Braunberger 4)
Drôle de dimanche, 1958 (Arletty 3,
Belmondo 3, Darrieux 3)
Drôle de drame, 1937 (Barrault 3, Jouvet 3,
Rosay 3, Simon 3, Alekan 4, Jaubert 4,
Prévert 4, Schüfftan 4, Trauner 4)
Drole d'endroit pour une rencontre, 1988
(Deneuve 3, Depardieu 3, Morricone 4)
Drole de paroissien, 1963 (Burel 4,
Kosma 4)
Drôles d'actualités, 1959 (Braunberger 4)
Drömda dalen, 1947 (Sucksdorff 2)
Drömmares vandring, 1957 (Nykvist 4)
Droopy's Double Trouble, 1951 (Avery 4)
Droopy's Good Deed, 1951 (Avery 4)
Drop Dead, Darling. See Arrivederci, Baby,
1966
Drop Kick, 1927 (Barthelmess 3, Wayne 3,
Edeson 4)
Drop Too Much. See O skleničku vic, 1953
Dropout. See Vacanza, 1969
Droppington's Devilish Dream, 1915
(Sennett 2)
Droppington's Family Tree, 1915
(Sennett 2)
Drottningholm Palace Theatre. See
Drottningholms slottsteater, 1965
Drottningholms slottsteater, 1965 (Fischer 4)
Drowning by Numbers, 1988 (Greenaway 2,
Vierny 4)
Drowning Pool, 1975 (Hill 2, Newman 3,
Woodward 3, Willis 4)
Drugstore Cowboy, 1925 (Arthur 3)
Drugstore Cowboy, 1989 (Dillon 3)
Druides, 1906 (Guy 2)
Drum, 1938 (Massey 3, Biro 4, Hornbeck 4,
Korda, A. 4, Korda, V. 4, Krasker 4,
Périnal 4, Unsworth 4)
Drum, 1976 (Frampton 2, Oates 3, Ballard 4,
De Laurentiis 4)
Drum Beat, 1954 (Daves 2, Bronson 3,
Ladd 3, Young 4)
Drummer of the Eighth, 1913 (Ince 4)
Drummer's Notebook, 1910 (White 3)
Drummer's Vacation, 1912 (Sennett 2)
Drums. See Drum, 1938
Drums Across the River, 1954 (Brennan 3,
Murphy 3)
Drums Along the Mohawk, 1939 (Ford 2,
Bond 3, Carradine 3, Colbert 3, Fonda 3,
Day 4, Glennon 4, Levien 4, Newman 4,
Trotti 4, Zanuck 4)
Drums for a Queen, 1961 (Quayle 3)
Drums in the Deep South, 1951 (Menzies 4,
Tiomkin 4)
Drums of Destiny. See Drums of Fate, 1922
Drums of Fate, 1923 (Johnson 3, Howe 4)
Drums of Jeopardy, 1923 (Beery 3)
Drums of Love, 1928 (Griffith 2,
Barrymore, 3, Bitzer 4, Menzies 4,
Struss 4)

Drums of Tahiti, 1954 (Katzman 4)
Drums of the Congo, 1942 (Dandridge 3,
Salter 4)
Drum-Sticked, 1962 (Hanna and Barbera 4)
Drunk, 1965 (De Antonio 2, Warhol 2)
Drunkard's Reformation, 1909 (Griffith 2,
Lawrence 3, Bitzer 4)
Drunken Angel. See Yoidore tenshi, 1948
Drunken Master. See Drunken Monkey in a
Tiger's Eye, 1978
Drunken Monkey in a Tiger's Eye, 1978
(Chan 3)
Drunken Music. See Yoidore bayashi,
1955
Drunkenness and Its Consequences. See
Pianstvo i yevo pozledstvia, 1913
Druzya, 1938 (Cherkassov 3)
Drvoštěp, 1922 (Ondra 3)
Dry Martini, 1928 (D'Arrast 2, Astor 3,
Fox 4)
Dry Rot, 1956 (Clayton 2, Francis 4)
Dry White Season, 1989 (Brando 3,
Sarandon 3, Sutherland 3)
Du är mitt äventyr, 1958 (Andersson 3,
Björnstrand 3, Fischer 4)
Du Barry Was a Lady, 1943 (Ball 3,
Beavers 3, Costello 3, Gardner 3,
Kelly 3, Turner 3, Freed 4, Freund 4)
Du charbon et des hommes, 1952
(Leenhardt 2)
Du côté de la côte, 1958 (Varda 2, Colpi 4,
Delerue 4)
Du Crépuscule à l'aube, 1922 (Vanel 3)
Du cuir en juin, 1968 (Braunberger 4)
Du fil à l'aiguille, 1924 (Grémillon 2)
Du grabuge chez les veuves, 1963
(Darrieux 3, Delerue 4)
Du haut en bas, 1933 (Gabin 3, Simon 3,
Metzner 4, Schüfftan 4)
Du mou dans la gachette, 1966 (Blier 3)
Du mouron pour les petits oiseaux, 1962
(Carné 2, Saulnier 4)
Du plaisir à la joie, 1978 (Leenhardt 2)
Du point de vue d'Anton, 1954 (Colpi 4)
Du Rififi à Paname, 1966 (Gabin 3, Raft 3)
Du Rififi chez les femmes, 1959
(Constantine 3, Rosay 3)
**Du Rififi chez les hommes, 1955 (Dassin 2,
Auric 4, Trauner 4)**
Du sang dans la sciure. See Chicago-Digest,
1950
Du sang de la volupté et de la mort, 1947
(Markopoulos 2)
Du Sel sur la peau, 1984 (Coutard 4)
Du skal elske din Naeste, 1915 (Psilander 3)
Du soleil plein les yeux, 1970 (Lai 4)
Dual Alibi, 1947 (Lom 3)
Dub, 1918 (Cruze 2, Reid 3, Rosher 4)
Duba, 1972 (Rey 3)
DuBarry von Heute, 1926 (Albers 3,
Dietrich 3, Korda 4, Wagner 4)
DuBarry, Woman of Passion, 1930
(Bosworth 3, Talmadge 3, Menzies 4,
Schenck 4)
Dublin Through Different Eyes, 1964
(Lassally 4)
Dubliners. See Dead, 1987
Dubs, 1978 (Emshwiller 2)
Ducháček to zaridi, 1938 (Heller 4)
Duchacek Will See to It. See Ducháček to
zaridi, 1938
Duchess and the Dirtwater Fox, 1976
(Hawn 3, Segal 3, Biroc 4, Cahn 4,
Frank 4)

Duchess of Buffalo, 1926 (Kräly 4, Schenck 4)

Duchess of Idaho, 1950 (Horne 3, Johnson 3, Powell 3, Williams 3, Mayer 4, Pasternak 4, Rose 4)

Duchesse de Langeais, 1941 (Feuillère 3, Annenkov 4, Douy 4, Matras 4)

Duck Amuck, 1953 (Blanc 4, Jones 4, Maltese 4, Stalling 4)

Duck Doctor, 1952 (Hanna and Barbera 4)

Duck Dodgers in the 24½th Century, 1953 (Blanc 4, Jones 4, Maltese 4, Stalling 4)

Duck Fever, 1955 (Terry 4)

Duck Hunt, 1937 (Lantz 4)

Duck Hunter, 1922 (Sennett 2)

Duck in Orange Sauce. See Anatra all'orancia, 1975

Duck! Rabbit! Duck, 1953 (Blanc 4, Jones 4, Maltese 4, Stalling 4)

Duck Soup, 1927 (Laurel and Hardy 3, Roach 4)

Duck Soup, 1933 (McCarey 2, Calhern 3, Dumont 3, Marx Brothers 3, Dreier 4, Head 4, Mankiewicz 4, Zukor 4)

Duck Soup to Nuts, 1944 (Blanc 4, Freleng 4, Stalling 4)

Duck You Sucker. See Giù la testa, 1972

Ducking the Devil, 1957 (Blanc 4, McKimson 4)

Ducks and Drakes, 1921 (Daniels 3)

Ducksters, 1950 (Blanc 4, Jones 4, Stalling 4)

Ducktators, 1942 (Blanc 4, Stalling 4)

Dude and the Burglar, 1903 (Bitzer 4)

Dude Goes West, 1948 (Struss 4, Tiomkin 4)

Dudes Are Pretty People, 1942 (Roach 4)

Dude Wrangler, 1930 (Bushman 3)

Due compari, 1955 (Fabrizi 3)

Due cuori felici, 1932 (De Sica 2)

Due cuori sotto sequestro, 1941 (Fusco 4)

Due Foscari, 1942 (Brazzi 3)

Due lettere anonime, 1944 (Ponti 4)

Due madri, 1938 (De Sica 2)

Due mafiosi contre Goldginger, 1965 (Rey 3)

Due marescialli, 1961 (De Sica 2)

Due milioni per un sorriso, 1939 (Castellani 2)

Due mogli sono troppe, 1951 (Cecchi D'Amico 4, Rota 4)

Due nemici, 1961 (Niven 3, Sordi 3, Age and Scarpelli 4, Cecchi D'Amico 4, De Laurentiis 4, Rota 4, Rotunno 4)

Due notti con Cleopatra, 1954 (Loren 3, Sordi 3, Struss 4)

Due occhi diabolici, 1990 (Romero 2, Argento 4, Donaggio 4, Savini 4)

Due orfanelle, 1942 (Valli 3)

Due orfanelle, 1942 (Stallich 4)

Due orfanelle, 1954 (Rota 4)

Due orfanelli, 1947 (Age and Scarpelli 4)

Due pezzi di pane, 1979 (Gassman 3, Noiret 3)

Due sergenti, 1936 (Cervi 3, Valli 3)

Due soldi di speranza, 1951 (Rota 4)

Due vite di Mattia Pascal, 1985 (Monicelli 2, Blier 3, Mastroianni 3, Cecchi D'Amico 4, Morricone 4)

Due volte Giuda, 1968 (Kinski 3)

Due volti della paura. See Coartada en disco rojo, 1970

Duel, 1912 (Sennett 2, Normand 3)

Duel, 1939 (Clouzot 2, Fresnay 3, Matras 4)

Duel, 1941 (Raimu 3)

Duel, 1971 (Spielberg 2)

Duel a mort, 1950 (Keaton 2)

Duel at Diablo, 1966 (Andersson 3, Garner 3, Poitier 3)

Duel at Ichijoji Temple. See Zoko Miyamoto Musashi, 1955

Duel à travers les âges, 1952 (Audiard 4)

Duel at Silver Creek, 1952 (Siegel 2, Marvin 3, Murphy 3, Salter 4)

Duel at the Rio Grande. See Segno di Zorro, 1963

Duel de Max, 1913 (Linder 3)

Duel de Monsieur Myope, 1908 (Linder 3)

Duel in the Forest. See Schinderhannes, 1958

Duel in the Jungle, 1954 (Andrews 3)

Duel in the Sun, 1946 (Dieterle 2, Vidor 2, Von sternberg 2, Welles 2, Barrymore 3, Carey 3, Cotten 3, Gish 3, Huston 3, Jones 3, Marshall 3, McQueen 3, Peck 3, Basevi 4, Eason 4, Garmes 4, Menzies 4, Plunkett 4, Rosson 4, Selznick 4, Tiomkin 4)

Duel of Champions. See Orazi e Curiazi, 1962

Duel of Love, 1990 (Chaplin 3)

Duel of the Candles, 1911 (Dwan 2)

Duel Personality, 1966 (Jones 4)

Duel tragique, 1904 (Guy 2)

Duellists, 1977 (Scott 2, Finney 3, Puttnam 4)

Duello nel mundo, 1966 (Blier 3)

Duelo de pistoleros, 1965 (Fernández 2)

Duelo en las montañas, 1949 (Fernández 2, Figueroa 4)

Duena y señora, 1948 (Figueroa 4)

Dueños del silencio, 1987 (Andersson 3, Falk 3)

Duet for One, 1981 (Friedkin 2)

Duet for One, 1986 (Mikhalkov-Konchalovsky 2, Andrews 3, Bates 3, Von Sydow 3, Golan and Globus 4)

Duffy, 1968 (Coburn 3, Mason 3, York 3, Heller 4)

Duffy of San Quentin, 1954 (O'Sullivan 3, Alton 4)

Duffy's Tavern, 1945 (Crosby 3, Fitzgerald 3, Goddard 3, Hutton 3, Ladd 3, Lake 3, Lamour 3, Benchley 4, Dreier 4, Frank 4, Head 4)

Duggie Fields, 1974 (Jarman 2)

Duke de Ribbon Counter, 1911 (Lawrence 3)

Duke for a Day, 1934 (Roach 4)

Duke Is Tops, 1938 (Horne 3)

Duke of Chimney Butte, 1921 (Borzage 2)

Duke of West Point, 1939 (Fontaine 3)

Duke Steps Out, 1929 (Cruze 2, Daves 2, Crawford 3, Gibbons 4)

Duke Wore Jeans, 1958 (Heller 4)

Duke's Plan, 1909 (Griffith 2, Bitzer 4)

Dukhiyari, 1937 (Biswas 4)

Dulces horas, 1981 (Saura 2)

Dulcima, 1971 (Mills 3)

Dulcimer Street. See London Belongs to Me, 1948

Dulcinea, 1962 (Fusco 4)

Dulcinea del Toboso, 1966 (Rey 3)

Dulcy, 1923 (Emerson 4, Loos 4, Sullivan 4)

Dulcy. See Not So Dumb, 1930

Dulcy, 1940 (Kaper 4)

Dulha Dulhan, 1964 (Kapoor 2)

Dum Bom, 1953 (Andersson 3)

Dum no předměstí, 1933 (Stallich 4)

Dům v Kaprové ulici, 1967 (Brejchová 3)

Dumb Cluck, 1937 (Lantz 4)

Dumb Daddies, 1928 (McCarey 2, Roach 4)

Dumb Dicks, 1986 (Golan and Globus 4)

Dumb Girl of Portici, 1916 (Weber 2, Karloff 3, Rosher 4)

Dumb Half Breed's Defense, 1910 (Anderson 3)

Dumb Patrol, 1964 (Blanc 4)

Dumb Waiter, 1928 (Sennett 2, Hornbeck 4)

Dumb Waiter, 1989 (Altman 2, Travolta 3, Pinter 4)

Dumb-Bells, 1922 (Roach 4)

Dumbconscious Mind, 1929 (Fleischer 4)

Dumbconscious Mind, 1940 (Hubley 4)

Dumb-Hounded, 1942 (Avery 4)

Dumbo, 1941 (Disney 4)

Dummkopf, 1920 (Mayer 4)

Dummy, 1929 (Cromwell 2, March 3, Hunt 4, Mankiewicz 4)

Dummy Owner, 1938 (Metty 4)

Dune, 1984 (Lynch 2, Ferrer 3, Mangano 3, Von Sydow 3, De Laurentiis 4, Francis 4, Whitlock 4)

Dungeon, 1922 (Micheaux 2)

Dungeon. See Scarf, 1951

Duniya, 1968 (Anand 3)

Dunked in the Deep, 1949 (Three Stooges 3)

Dunkirk, 1957 (Crazy Gang 3)

Dunkirk, 1958 (Attenborough 3, Mills 3, Arnold 4)

Dunoyer de Segonzac, 1965 (Braunberger 4)

Dunungen, 1920 (Jaenzon 4, Magnusson 4)

Dunungen, 1941 (Fischer 4)

Dunwich Horror, 1970 (Corman 2, Jaffe 3)

Duo colonelli, 1962 (Pidgeon 3)

Duomo di Milano, 1946 (Blasetti 2)

Dupe, 1916 (Sweet 3)

Duped Journalist. See Becsapott újságíró, 1914

Duplicity series, 1978–80 (Brakhage 2)

Duplizität der Ereignisse, 1919 (Dreier 4)

Dupont-Barbès, 1951 (Kosma 4)

Dupont Lajoie, 1974 (Huppert 3)

Durand of the Bad Lands, 1917 (Mix 3)

Durand of the Badlands, 1925 (Lombard 3, Fox 4)

Durante l'estate, 1971 (Olmi 2)

Durbargati Padma, 1971 (Ghatak 2)

Durch die Walder, durch die Auen, 1956 (Pabst 2)

Dürfen wir schweigen, 1926 (Kortner 3, Veidt 3)

During Cherry Time, 1911 (Lawrence 3)

During the Round-Up, 1913 (Griffith 2, Gish 3, Walthall 3, Bitzer 4)

During the Summer. See Durante l'estate, 1971

Durs à cuire, 1964 (Chabrol 2, Audran 3)

Dushman, 1957 (Anand 3)

Dusk to Dawn, 1922 (Vidor 2, Barnes 4)

Dust, 1985 (Howard 3)

Dust Be My Destiny, 1939 (Rossen 2, Bond 3, Garfield 3, Haskin 4, Howe 4, Steiner 4)

Dust Fever, 1962 (Watkins 2)

Dust of Desire. See Song of Love, 1923

Dustbin Parade, 1941 (Halas and Batchelor 4)

Dusty and Sweets McGee, 1970 (Fraker 4)

Dusty Ermine, 1937 (Rutherford 3, Courant 4)

Dutch at the Double. See Nederland in 7 Lessen, 1964

Dutch Gold Mine, 1911 (Sennett 2)

Dutch Treat, 1930 (Terry 4)

E arrivato il cavaliere, 1950 (Monicelli 2, Ponti 4)

E arrivato l'accordatore, 1952 (Loren 3, Sordi 3)

E caduta una donna, 1941 (Brazzi 3, Zavattini 4)

. . . e continuavano a fregarsi il millione di dollari, 1971 (Van Cleef 3)

E Dio disse a Caino . . . , 1969 (Kinski 3)

. . . e eontinuavano a fregarsi il milione di dollari, 1970 (Lollobrigida 3)

E la nave va, 1983 (Cristaldi 4, Guerra 4, Rotunno 4)

E la vita continua, 1984 (Risi 2)

E' Lollipop, 1975 (Ferrer 3)

E' più facile che un cammello, 1950 (Gabin 3, Cecchi D'Amico 4, Rota 4, Zavattini 4)

E primavera, 1950 (Cecchi D'Amico 4, Rota 4, Zavattini 4)

E ropeya del camino, 1941 (Armendáriz 3)

E.T.—The Extraterrestrial, 1982 (Spielberg 2, Burtt 4, Williams 4)

E tanta paura, 1976 (Wallach 3)

E tornato Sabata . . . hai chiuso, 1972 (Van Cleef 3)

E una Domenica sera di novembre, 1981 (Wertmüller 2)

E venne l'ora della vendetta, 1970 (Cotten 3)

E venne un uomo, 1965 (Olmi 2, Steiger 3)

Each Dawn I Crow, 1949 (Blanc 4, Freleng 4, Stalling 4)

Each Dawn I Die, 1939 (Cagney 3, Holden 3, Raft 3, Edeson 4, Raine 4, Steiner 4)

Each for All, 1946 (Alwyn 4)

Each to His Kind, 1917 (Hayakawa 3)

Each to His Own Way. See Var sin väg, 1948

Eadie Was a Lady, 1945 (Miller 3, Guffey 4)

Eager Beaver, 1946 (Blanc 4, Jones 4)

Eagle, 1925 (Brown 2, Banky 3, Valentino 3, Adrian 4, Barnes 4, Kräly 4, Menzies 4, Westmore Family 4)

Eagle and the Hawk, 1933 (Leisen 2, Grant 3, Lombard 3, March 3, Banton 4, Miller 4, Saunders 4)

Eagle and the Hawk, 1950 (Howe 4)

Eagle Has Landed, 1976 (Sturges 2, Caine 3, Duvall 3, Pleasence 3, Quayle 3, Sutherland 3, Schifrin 4)

Eagle in a Cage, 1970 (Gielgud 3, Richardson 3)

Eagle of the Night, 1928 (Costello 3)

Eagle of the Pacific. See Taiheiyo no washi, 1953

Eagle of the Sea, 1926 (Karloff 3, Schulberg 4)

Eagle Squadron, 1942 (Cooper 4, Cortez 4, Raine 4, Wanger 4)

Eagle with Two Heads. See Aigle à deux têtes, 1947

Eagle's Mate, 1914 (Pickford 3)

Eagles of the Fleet. See Flat Top, 1952

Eagles over Britain. See Battaglia d'Inghilterra, 1969

Eagle's Wings, 1980 (Audran 3, Johnson 3, Sheen 3)

Eames Lounge Chair, 1956 (Bernstein 4)

Earl Carroll Vanities, 1945 (Arden 3)

Earl Carroll's Sketch Book, 1946 (Horton 3, Cahn 4)

Earl of Chicago, 1940 (Saville 2, Montgomery 3)

Early Bird, 1965 (Wisdom 3)

Early Bird Dood it, 1942 (Avery 4)

Early Cinema of Edwin S. Porter, 1982 (Sweet 3)

Early Days, 1981 (Richardson 3)

Early Days of Communication, 1958 (Halas and Batchelor 4)

Early Days Out West, 1912 (Rosher 4)

Early Frost, 1985 (Rowlands 3, Sidney 3)

Early Spring. See Shoshun, 1956

Early Summer. See Bakushu, 1951

Early to Bed, 1928 (Laurel and Hardy 3, Roach 4)

Early to Bed. See Ich bei Tag und Du bei Nacht, 1932

Early to Bed, 1936 (McLeod 2)

Early to Bet, 1951 (Blanc 4, Foster 4, McKimson 4, Stalling 4)

Early to Wed, 1926 (Borzage 2, Fox 4)

Early Worm Gets the Bird, 1940 (Avery 4, Blanc 4, Stalling 4)

Earrings of Madame de . . . . See **Madame de . . . , 1953**

Ears of Experience, 1938 (Metty 4)

Earth Dies Screaming, 1964 (Fisher 2)

Earth Girls Are Easy, 1989 (Lai 4)

Earth in Labour, 1950 (Halas and Batchelor 4)

Earth Smiles. See Daichi wa hohoemu, 1925

Earth II, 1971 (Schifrin 4)

Earth vs. the Flying Saucers, 1956 (Harryhausen 4, Katzman 4, Siodmak 4)

Earthbottom, 1989 (Romero 2)

Earthbound, 1940 (Day 4, Newman 4)

Earthling, 1981 (Holden 3)

Earthquake, 1974 (Bujold 3, Gardner 3, Heston 3, Matthau 3, Ames 4, Whitlock 4, Williams 4)

Earth's Final Fury. See When Time Ran Out, 1980

Earthworm Tractors, 1936 (Brown 3)

Easiest Profession. See Chômeur de Clochemerle, 1957

Easiest Way, 1931 (Gable 3, Menjou 3, Montgomery 3, Mayer 4)

East End Chant. See Limehouse Blues, 1935

East Is East, 1916 (Evans 3)

East Is West, 1922 (Gaudio 4, Marion 4, Schenck 4)

East Is West, 1930 (Ayres 3, Robinson 3, Laemmle 4)

East Lynne, 1912 (Cruze 2)

East Lynne, 1916 (Bara 3)

East Lynne, 1925 (Coffee 4, Fox 4)

East Lynne, 1931 (Seitz 4)

East Lynne in Bugville, 1910 (White 3)

East Lynne on the Western Front, 1931 (Pearson 2)

East Lynne with Variations, 1919 (Sennett 2)

East Meets West, 1936 (Arliss 3, Balcon 4, Rank 4)

East of Borneo, 1931 (Johnson 3, Fulton 4)

East of Broadway, 1924 (Howard 2)

East of Eden, 1955 (Kazan 2, Dean 3, Massey 3, Basevi 4, McCord 4, Rosenman 4, Warner 4)

East of Elephant Rock, 1976 (Hurt 3)

East of Java, 1935 (Waxman 4)

East of Java. See South Sea Sinner, 1950

East of Shanghai. See Rich and Strange, 1931

East of Sudan, 1964 (Quayle 3)

East of Suez, 1925 (Walsh 2, Negri 3, Dreier 4)

East of Sumatra, 1953 (Boetticher 2, Quinn 3, Boyle 4)

East of the Rising Sun. See Malaya, 1949

East of the River, 1940 (Garfield 3, Deutsch 4)

East of the Water Plug, 1924 (Sennett 2)

East 103rd Street, 1981 (Menges 4)

East Side Kids, 1940 (Katzman 4)

East Side of Heaven, 1939 (Blondell 3, Crosby 3)

East Side, West Side, 1927 (Dwan 2, Fleischer 4, Fox 4)

East Side, West Side, 1949 (LeRoy 2, Charisse 3, Gardner 3, Mason 3, Stanwyck 3, Lennart 4, Rose 4, Rosher 4, Rozsa 4)

Easter Celebration at Jerusalem, 1912 (Olcott 2)

Easter Egg Hunt, 1981 (Altman 2)

Easter Parade, 1948 (Walters 2, Astaire 3, Garland 3, Miller 3, Alton 4, Berlin 4, Edens 4, Freed 4, Goodrich 4, Green 4, Irene 4, Mayer 4, Smith 4, Stradling 4)

Easter Yeggs, 1947 (Blanc 4, McKimson 4, Stalling 4)

Eastern Cowboy, 1911 (Dwan 2)

Eastern Flower, 1913 (Dwan 2)

Eastern Girl, 1911 (Dwan 2)

Eastern Westerner, 1920 (Lloyd 3)

Eastern Westerner, 1920 (Roach 4)

Easy Come, Easy Go, 1928 (Arthur 3, Cronjager 4)

Easy Come, Easy Go, 1947 (Fitzgerald 3, Dreier 4, Head 4, MacGowan 4)

Easy Come, Easy Go, 1967 (Lanchester 3, Presley 3, Head 4, Wallis 4)

Easy Life. See Snadný život, 1957

Easy Life. See Sorpasso, 1962

Easy Living, 1937 (Leisen 2, Sturges 2, Arthur 3, Milland 3, Pangborn 3, Dreier 4, Head 4)

Easy Living, 1949 (Tourneur 2, Ball 3, Mature 3, Schnee 4)

Easy Money, 1910 (White 3)

Easy Money, 1925 (Brown 4)

Easy Money, 1948 (Box 4, Rank 4)

Easy on the Eyes, 1933 (Sennett 2)

Easy Peckin's, 1953 (Blanc 4, McKimson 4, Stalling 4)

Easy Rider, 1969 (Rafelson 2, Black 3, Hopper 3, Nicholson 3, Kovacs, 4)

Easy Road. See Asymvivastos, 1979

Easy Street, 1917 (Chaplin 2, Purviance 3)

Easy Street, 1928 (Micheaux 2)

Easy to Look At, 1945 (Salter 4)

Easy to Love, 1934 (Astor 3, Horton 3, Menjou 3, Grot 4, Haller 4, Orry-Kelly 4)

Easy to Love, 1953 (Berkeley 2, Walters 2, Baker 3, Charisse 3, Johnson 3, Williams 3, Pasternak 4, Rose 4, Smith 4)

Easy to Take, 1936 (Dmytryk 2)

Easy to Wed, 1946 (Ball 3, Johnson 3, Williams 3, Green 4, Irene 4, Stradling 4)

Easy Virtue, 1927 (Hitchcock 2, Balcon 4)

Easy Years. See Anni facili, 1953

Eat Me, Kitty, Eight to the Bar, 1942 (Terry 4)

Eat My Dust, 1976 (Corman 2)

Eat Your Makeup, 1968 (Waters 2)

Eatin' on the Cuff, 1942 (Blanc 4, Clampett 4, Stalling 4)

Eating Raoul, 1982 (Landis 2, Henry 4)

Eating Too Fast, 1966 (Warhol 2)

Eau, 1966 (Alexeieff and Parker 4)

Eau à la bouche, 1959 (Braunberger 4)

Eau d'Evian, 1938 (Alexeieff and Parker 4)

Eau vive, 1938 (Epstein 2, Jaubert 4)

Eau vive, 1941 (Decaë 4)

Eaux d'artifice, 1953 (Anger 2)

Eaux profondes, 1981 (Huppert 3, Trintignant 3)

Eaux troublés, 1949 (Kosma 4)

Eaux vives. See Fleuve: Le Tarn, 1951

Eavesdropper, 1909 (Griffith 2, Bitzer 4)

Eavesdropper, 1914 (Sennett 2)

Eavesdropper. See Ojo de la cerradura, 1964

Ebb Tide, 1922 (Clarke 4, Glennon 4, Young 4)

Ebb Tide, 1932 (Oberon 3)

Ebb Tide, 1937 (Farmer 3, Fitzgerald 3, Homolka 3, Milland 3, Head 4, Young 4)

Ebberød Bank. See Ebberöds Bank, 1926

Ebberöds Bank, 1926 (Madsen and Schenstrøm 3)

Ebirah—Terror of the Deep. See Nankai no daiketto, 1966

Ebony Parade, 1947 (Dandridge 3)

Ebony Tower, 1984 (Olivier 3)

Ebreo errante, 1947 (Fellini 2, Gassman 3)

Ecce Homo, 1915 (Gance 2)

Ecce Homo, 1966 (Fresnay 3)

Ecce Homo, 1968 (Papas 3)

Ecce Homo—I soparavvissuti, 1969 (Morricone 4)

Eccentric Dancer, 1900 (Hepworth 2)

Ecco, 1963 (Sanders 3, Simon 3)

Echappement libre, 1964 (Belmondo 3, Rey 3, Seberg 3, Wakhévitch 4)

Echec au porteur, 1957 (Moreau 3, Reggiani 3)

Echec au roi, o Le Roi s'ennui, 1931 (Rosay 3)

Echec au roy, 1943 (Alekan 4)

Echigo-jishi, 1929 (Tanaka 3)

Echigo-jishi matsuri, 1939 (Hasegawa 3)

Echiquier de Dieu, 1964 (Welles 2)

Echivoier de dieu, 1964 (Saulnier 4)

Echizen take ningyo, 1963 (Yoshimura 2, Miyagawa 4)

Echo, 1915 (Eason 4)

Echo, 1985 (Reggiani 3)

Echo and Narcissus, 1929 (Fleischer 4)

Echo of a Song, 1913 (Dwan 2)

Echo Passes, 1982 (Emshwiller 2)

Echoes, 1980 (McCambridge 3)

Echoes of a Summer, 1976 (Foster 3, Harris 3)

Echos de plateau, 1952 (Gabin 3, Gélin 3)

Eclipse, 1911 (Guy 2)

Eclipse. See **Eclisse, 1962**

Eclipse sur un ancien chemin vers Compostelle, 1977 (Vierny 4)

Eclisse, 1962 (Antonioni 2, Delon 3, Vitti 3, Di Venanzo 4, Fusco 4, Guerra 4, Hakim 4)

Ecole, 1962 (Tanner 2)

Ecole buissonnière, 1948 (Blier 3, Modot 3, Kosma 4)

Ecole communale, 1939 (Carné 2)

Ecole de Paris. See Statues d'épouvante, 1953

Ecole des cocottes, 1935 (Raimu 3, Douy 4)

Ecole des cocottes, 1958 (Blier 3)

Ecole des detectives, 1934 (Delannoy 2)

Ecole des facteurs, 1947 (Tati 2)

Ecole des femmes, 1940 (Ophüls 2)

Ecole des journalistes, 1936 (Christian-Jaque 2)

Ecole du soldat. See Armée d'Agenor, 1909

Ecoles, 1963 (Borowczyk 2)

Ecoute voir . . . , 1978 (Deneuve 3)

Ecran, 1966 (Burton 3)

Ecran d'épingles, 1973 (McLaren 4)

Ecriture, 1963 (Borowczyk 2)

Ecstasy. See Extase, 1932

Ed Murrow: This Reporter, 1990 (Bacall 3)

Eddie Cantor, 1929 (Florey 2)

Eddie Cantor Story, 1953 (Cantor 3, Prinz 4)

Eddie Duchin Story, 1956 (Novak 3, Power 3, Cohn 4, Duning 4, Stradling 4, Wald 4)

Eddie Macon's Run, 1983 (Douglas 3)

Eddie Murphy Raw, 1987 (Murphy 3)

Eden et après, 1971 (Robbe-Grillet 4)

Eden-misère, 1986 (Branco 4)

Edgar Allan Poe, 1909 (Griffith 2, Bitzer 4)

Edgar Allan Poe. See Due occhi diabolici, 1990

Edgar and Goliath, 1937 (Metty 4)

Edgar Poë, 1964 (Rohmer 2)

Edgar Runs Again, 1940 (Terry 4)

Edge of Darkness, 1943 (Milestone 2, Rossen 2, Siegel 2, Flynn 3, Gordon 3, Huston 3, Sheridan 3, Blanke 4, Orry-Kelly 4, Waxman 4)

Edge of Doom, 1950, (Andrews 3, Day 4, Friedhofer 4, Goldwyn 4, Mandell 4, Stradling 4)

Edge of Eternity, 1959 (Siegel 2, Wilde 3, Guffey 4)

Edge of Fury, 1956 (Hall 4)

Edge of Sanity, 1989 (Perkins 3)

Edge of the Abyss, 1915 (Sullivan 4)

Edge of the City, 1957 (Cassavetes 2, Poitier 3, Bass 4, Rosenman 4, Sylbert 4)

Edge of the Wind, 1985 (Mills 3, Sharif 3)

Edge of the World, 1937 (Powell and Pressburger 2)

Edge of Things, 1913 (Anderson 3)

Edged Tools, 1915 (Seitz 4)

Edinburgh, 1952 (Korda 4)

Edipo Re, 1967 (Mangano 3, Valli 3)

Edison Bugg's Invention, 1916 (Laurel and Hardy 3)

Edison, Marconi, & Co., 1928 (Roach 4)

Edison the Man, 1940 (Brown 2, Coburn 3, Tracy 3, Jennings 4, Mayer 4, Rosson 4, Schary 4, Stothart 4)

Edith and Marcel. See Edith et Marcel, 1983

Edith et Marcel, 1982 (Lelouch 2, Lai 4)

Edithes Tagebuch, 1983 (Winkler 3, Ballhaus 4)

Edith's Diary. See Edithes Tagebuch, 1983

Edmund Kean—Prince among Lovers. See Kean, 1924

Edmundo Ross Half Hour, 1957 (Carreras 4)

Edo bishonen-roku, 1931 (Yamada 3)

Edo gonomi Ryogoku-zoshi, 1932 (Hasegawa 3, Takamine 3)

Edo iroha matsuri, 1953 (Yamada 3)

Edo mujo, 1963 (Hasegawa 3)

Edo saigo no hi, 1941 (Shimura 3)

Edo sodachi, 1928 (Hasegawa 3)

Edo wa utsuru, 1934 (Hasegawa 3)

Edokko ichiba, 1931 (Yamada 3)

Edokko Kenchan, 1937 (Takamine 3)

Edokko matsuri, 1958 (Hasegawa 3)

Édouard et Caroline, 1951 (Becker 2, Gélin 3)

Educated Evans, 1936 (Launder and Gilliat 2)

Educated Fish, 1937 (Fleischer 4)

Educating Rita, 1983 (Caine 3)

Education, 1915 (Beery 3)

Education de prince, 1926 (Purviance 3)

Education de prince, 1938 (Jouvet 3, Burel 4)

Education of Aunt Georgina, 1913 (Costello 3)

Education of Elizabeth, 1920 (Folsey 4)

Education professionelle des conducteurs de tramway, 1925 (Grémillon 2)

Education sentimentale, 1962 (Astruc 2, Saulnier 4)

Education sentimentale, 1985 (Léaud 3)

Educazione civica, 1974 (Comencini 2)

Edvard Munch, 1974 (Watkins 2)

Edward, My Son, 1949 (Cukor 2, Kerr 3, Tracy 3, Junge 4, Stewart 4, Young 4)

Edward Scissorhands, 1990 (Arkin 3, Price 3)

Een blandt mange, 1961 (Henning-Jensen 2, Fischer 4)

Een zwoele zomeravond, 1982 (Müller 4)

Effect of Gamma Rays on Man-in-the-Moon Marigolds, 1972 (Newman 3, Woodward 3, Jarre 4, Sargent 4)

Effects, 1978 (Savini 4)

Effeuillant la Marguerite, 1956 (Bardot 3, Gélin 3, Trauner 4)

Effi Briest. *See* Rosen im Herbst, 1955

Effi Briest. *See* Fontane: Effi Briest, 1974

Effroi, 1913 (Feuillade 2)

E-Flat Man, 1935 (Keaton 2)

Egen ingång, 1956 (Andersson 3, Fischer 4)

Egg, 1922 (Laurel and Hardy 3)

Egg, *See* Jaje, 1959

Egg and I, 1947 (Colbert 3, MacMurray 3, Krasner 4)

Egg and Jerry, 1956 (Hanna and Barbera 4)

Egg Collector, 1940 (Blanc 4, Jones 4, Stalling 4)

Egg! Egg! A Hardboiled Story. *See* Agget är löst, 1974

Egg Hunt, 1940 (Iwerks 4)

Egg Scramble, 1950 (Blanc 4, Foster 4, McKimson 4, Stalling 4)

Egg-cited Rooster, 1952 (Blanc 4, McKimson 4, Stalling 4)

Egg-Crate Wallop, 1919 (Moore 3)

Egghead Rides Again, 1937 (Avery 4, Stalling 4)

Egg-Laying Man, 1900 (Hepworth 2)

Eggs, 1970 (Hubley 4, Jones 4)

Eglantine, 1971 (Charbrol 2)

Eglises romanes en Saintange, 1958 (Braunberger 4)

Ego, 1969 (Bozzetto 4)

Ego prevoskhoditelstvo, 1927 (Cherkassov 3)

Ego zovut Sukhe-Bator, 1942 (Cherkassov 3)

Egouts du paradis, 1978 (Audiard 4)

Egret Hunt. *See* Aigrette Hunter, 1910

Egy Barany, 1970 (Olbrychski 3)

Egy fiunak a fele, 1923 (Lukas 3)

Egy örült éjszaka, 1969 (Tyszkiewicz 3)

Egy tukor, 1971 (Szabó 2)

Egypt, 1912 (Olcott 2)

Egypt by Three, 1953 (Constantine 3, Cotten 3)

Egypt the Mysterious, 1912 (Olcott 2)

Egypte éternelle, 1953 (Decaë 4)

Egyptian, 1954 (Curtiz 2, Carradine 3, Mature 3, Simmons 3, Tierney 3, Ustinov 3, Dunne 4, Herrmann 4, LeMaire 4, Newman 4, Robinson 4, Shamroy 4, Wheeler 4, Zanuck 4)

Egyptian Series, 1984 (Brakhage 2)

Egyptian Sports, 1912 (Olcott 2)

Egyptologists, 1965 (Heston 3)

Ehe, 1929 (Dagover 3)

Ehe der Luise Rohrbach, 1917 (Jannings 3, Porten 3, Freund 4, Messter 4)

Ehe der Maria Braun, 1978 (Fassbinder 2, Schygulla 3, Ballhaus 4)

Ehe des Dr. Med. Danwitz, 1956 (Schell 3)

Ehe für eine Nacht, 1953 (Fröhlich 3)

Ehi, amico ... c'e Sabata, hai chiuso?, 1969 (Van Cleef 3)

Ehne el Talamza, 1959 (Sharif 3)

Ehrengard, 1982 (Cassel 3)

Ehrengard, 1986 (Cassel 3)

Ei des Fürsten Ulrich. *See* Spitzen, 1926

Ei gerochsky podvig, 1914 (Mozhukin 3)

Eien no hito, 1961 (Takamine 3)

Eien no kokoro, 1928 (Tanaka 3)

Eifersucht, 1925 (Krauss 3, Schüfftan 4)

Eiger Sanction, 1975 (Eastwood 3, Williams 4)

Eight Bells, 1935 (Bellamy 3, Pangborn 3, Walker 4)

Eight Cylinder Bull, 1926 (Arthur 3)

Eight Girls in a Boat, 1934 (Robinson 4)

Eight Iron Men, 1952 (Dmytryk 2, Kramer 2, Marvin 3, Anhalt 4, Hunt 4)

Eight Men Out, 1988 (Sayles 2)

Eight O'Clock Walk, 1953 (Attenborough 3)

Eight on the Lam, 1967 (Hope 3, Lewin 4)

Eighteen in the Sun. *See* Diciottenni al sole, 1962

Eighteen-Year Old Girl. *See* Osmnáctiletá, 1939

Eighth Day of the Week. *See* Osmy dzień tygodnia, 1957

Eight-Thirteen, 1920 (Beery 3)

Eighty Days, 1944 (Jennings 2)

Eighty Steps to Jonah, 1969 (Mineo 3, Rooney 3, La Shelle 4)

Eighty Thousand Suspects, 1963 (Cusack 3)

Eika Katappa, 1969 (Schroeter 2)

Eiko eno 5000 kiro, 1969 (Mifune 3)

Eiko eno kurohyo, 1969 (Ryu 3)

Eikyu no ai, 1935 (Tanaka 3)

Eiland, 1966 (Müller 4)

Eileen of the Trees. *See* Glorious Youth, 1929

Einbrecher, 1930 (Pommer 4)

Einbruch, 1927 (Planer 4)

Eindringling, 1911 (Porten 3, Messter 4)

Eine Nacht der Liebe. *See* Liebesnächte, 1929

Eine Nacht im Grandhotel, 1931 (Metzner 4)

Eine Nacht im Paradise, 1932 (Ondra 3)

Eine Nacht im Separée, 1950 (Tschechowa 3)

Eine Nacht in London, 1928 (Warm 4)

Eine Rose für Jane, 1970 (Müller 4)

Eine Stunde glück, 1930 (Dieterle 2)

Einer frisst den anderern, 1964 (Mansfield 3)

Einer zuviel an Bord, 1935 (Baarová 3)

Einleitung zu Arnold Schoenberg Begleit Musik zu einer Lichtspielscene, 1969 (Straub and Huillet 2)

Einmal werd'ich Dir geffallende, 1937 (Rasp 3)

Einsichten eines Clowns, 1976 (Schell 3)

Einsteiger, 1985 (Morricone 4)

Einstein Theory of Relativity, 1923 (Fleischer 4)

Eisenbahnkönig, 1921 (Kortner 3)

Eisenstein in Mexico. *See* Que Viva Mexico!, 1931

Eisenstein's Mexican Project, 1958 (Eisenstein 2)

Ek baar kaho, 1980 (Azmi 3)

Ek Dil Sou Afsane, 1963 (Kapoor 2)

Ek din achanak, 1989 (Sen 2)

Ek hi bhool, 1981 (Azmi 3)

Ek Hi Raasta, 1939 (Biswas 4)

Ek Hi Rasta, 1939 (Mehboob 2)

Ek hi rasta, 1977 (Azmi 3)

Ek Ke Baad Ek, 1960 (Anand 3, Burman 4)

Ek Naujawan, 1951 (Burman 4)

Ek Nazar, 1972 (Bachchan 3)

Ekel, 1931 (Schüfftan 4)

Ekimae onsen, 1962 (Tsukasa 3)

Ekti Jiban, 1988 (Chatterjee 3)

El, 1952 (Buñuel 2, Alcoriza 4, Figueroa 4)

El Dorado, 1921 (L'Herbier 2, Gaumont 4)

El Dorado, 1963 (Golan and Globus 4)

El Dorado, 1967 (Hawks 2, Caan 3, Mitchum 3, Wayne 3, Brackett 4, Edouart 4, Rosson 4)

El Dorado, 1985 (Bozzetto 4)

El Dorado, 1987 (Saura 2)

Elakoon Itsemurhaaja, 1984 (Olbrychski 3)

Elan, 1947 (Mehboob 2)

Elanprostekt nr. 4, 1986 (Constantine 3)

Elastic Affair, 1930 (Hitchcock 2)

Elbowing, 1980 (Driessen 4)

Eld ombord, 1923 (Sjöström 2, Jaenzon 4, Magnusson 4)

Elder Brother, 1914 (Bushman 3)

Elder Vasili Gryaznov. *See* Starets Vasili Gryaznov, 1924

Eldora, 1953 (Markopoulos 2)

Eldorado, 1921 (Autant-Lara 2)

Eldorado, 1963 (Topol 3)

Eleanor and Franklin, 1977 (Barry 4)

Eleanor, First Lady of the World, 1982 (Addison 4)

Eleanora Duse, 1947 (Brazzi 3)

Electra. *See* Lektro, 1927

Electra, 1962 (Cacoyannis 2, Papas 3, Lassally 4, Theodorakis 4)

Electra Glide in Blue, 1973 (Hall 4)

Electric Alarm, 1915 (Browning 2)

Electric Horseman, 1979 (Pollack 2, Fonda 3, Redford 3, Roizman 4, Sargent 4, Stark 4)

Electric House, 1922 (Keaton 2)

Electric Man. *See* Man Made Monster, 1940

Electricity Cure, 1900 (Hepworth 2)

Electrification de la ligne Bruxelles-Anvers, 1935 (Storck 2)

Electrification de la ligne Paris-Vierzon, 1925 (Grémillon 2)

Électrocuté, 1911 (Gance 2)

Électrocutée, 1904 (Guy 2)

Electronic Mouse Trap, 1946 (Terry 4)

Electron's Tale, 1970 (Godfrey 4)

Electroshow, 1966 (Guzmán 2)

Elegant John and His Ladies. *See* Last of the Cowboys, 1977

Elegy. *See* Ereji, 1951

Eléna et les hommes, 1956 (Straub and Huillet 2, Bergman 3, Marais 3, Modot 3, Kosma 4, Renoir 4, Saulnier 4)

Eleni, 1985 (Yates 2)

Elephant. *See* Barnförbjudet, 1979

Elephant Boy, 1937 (Crichton 2, Flaherty 2, Hornbeck 4, Korda, A. 4, Korda, V. 4)

Elephant Called Slowly, 1969 (Launder and Gilliat 2)

Elephant Games, 1986 (Meredith 3)

Elephant God. *See* Joi Baba Felunath, 1978

Elephant Gun. *See* Nor the Moon by Night, 1958

Elephant Man, 1980 (Brooks 2, Lynch 2, Bancroft 3, Gielgud 3, Hopkins 3, Hurt 3, Francis 4, Previn 4)

Elephant Mouse, 1951 (Terry 4)

Elephant Never Forgets, 1935 (Fleischer 4)

Elephant Shooting the Chutes at Luna Park, 1904 (Porter 2)

Elephant Stampede, 1951 (Mirisch 4)

Elephant Walk, 1954 (Dieterle 2, Andrews 3, Finch 3, Taylor 3, Fulton 4, Head 4, Waxman 4)

Elephant Walk. *See* Barnförbjudet, 1979

Elephantastic, 1964 (Hanna and Barbera 4)

Elephantrio, 1986 (Driessen 4)

Elet, halál, szerelem, 1929 (Lubitsch 2, Barrymore 3, Bosworth 3, Kräly 4, Schenck 4)

Elevator, 1971 (Breer 4)
Elevator, 1974 (Loy 3, McDowall 3, Wright 3)
Eleven, 1927 (Rooney 3)
Eleven Harrowhouse, 1974 (Gielgud 3, Howard 3, Mason 3)
Eleventh Commandment. See Jedenácté přikazání, 1935
Eleventh Hour, 1923 (Fox 4)
Eleventh Hour Reformation, 1914 (Ince 4)
Eleventh Year. See Odinnadtsatii, 1928
Elèves-maîtres, 1958 (Braunberger 4)
Elf Teufel, 1927 (Fröhlich 3, Reisch 4)
Elfrida and the Pig, 1968 (Young 4)
Elgar, 1962 (Russell 2)
Elgar, 1984 (Russell 2)
Eliette, ou instants de la vie d'une femme, 1971 (Braunberger 4)
Eliminator. See Teheran Incident, 1979
Elinor Norton, 1934 (Trevor 3)
Elisa, 1956 (Reggiani 3)
Elisa, My Love. See Elisa, vida mía, 1977
Elisa, vida mía, 1977 (Saura 2, Chaplin 3, Rey 3)
Elisabeth und der Narr, 1934 (Von Harbou 4)
Elisabeth von Osterreich, 1931 (Dagover 3)
Elisir d'amore, 1939 (Reiniger 4)
Elisir d'amore, 1947 (Lollobrigida 3, Mangano 3)
Elite Ball, 1913 (Sennett 2)
"Elite" Group. See Race des "Seigneurs", 1976
Eliza Fraser, 1976 (Howard 3)
Eliza on the Ice, 1944 (Terry 4)
Eliza Runs Again, 1938 (Terry 4)
Elizabeth of Austria. See Elisabeth von Osterreich, 1931
Elizabeth of Ladymead, 1949 (Wilcox 2, Neagle 3)
Eliza's Horoscope, 1971 (Lourié 4)
Ella Cinders, 1926 (Leroy 2, Langdon 3, Moore 3)
Elle, 1918 (Modot 3)
Elle boit pas, elle fume pas, elle drague pas ... mais elle cause, 1970 (Blier 3, Girardot 3, Audiard 4, D'Eaubonne 4)
Elle cause plus ... elle flingue, 1972 (Blier 3, Girardot 3, Audiard 3)
Elle court, elle court, la banliue, 1973 (Braunberger 4)
Elle disait non, 1932 (Fernandel 3)
Elle et moi, 1952 (Audiard 4)
Ellehammer, 1957 (Roos 2)
Ellery Queen, 1975 (Milland 3, Bernstein 4)
Ellery Queen and the Murder Ring, 1941 (Bellamy 3)
Ellery Queen and the Perfect Crime, 1941 (Bellamy 3)
Ellery Queen, Master Detective, 1940 (Niblo 2, Bellamy 3)
Ellery Queen's Penthouse Mystery, 1941 (Bellamy 3, Wong 3)
Elles étaient douze femmes, 1940 (Presle 3, Rosay 3, Andrejew 4)
Elles se marient. See Cage aux folles III, 1985
Ellie, 1984 (Winters 3)
Ellis Island, 1984 (Dunaway 3, Greenwood 3)
Elly y yo, 1951 (Armendáriz 3)
Elmer Fudd's Comedy Capers, 1987 (Freleng 4)
Elmer Gantry, 1960 (Brooks 2, Kennedy 3,

Lancaster 3, Simmons 3, Alton 4, Jeakins 4, Previn 4)
Elmer the Great, 1933 (Leroy 2, Brown 3, Wyman 3)
Elmer the Great Dane, 1935 (Lantz 4)
Elmer's Candid Camera, 1940 (Blanc 4, Jones 4, Stalling 4)
Elmer's Pet Rabbit, 1941 (Blanc 4, Maltese 4, Stalling 4)
Elogia della pazzia di desiderio erasmo, 1984 (Rey 3)
Elope If You Must, 1922 (Fox 4)
Elopement, 1907 (Bitzer 4)
Elopement, 1915 (Dressler 3)
Elopement, 1951 (Webb 3, La Shelle 4, LeMaire 4)
Elopement at Home, 1913 (Talmadge 3)
Elopements on Double L Ranch, 1911 (Dwan 2)
Eloping with Auntie, 1909 (Griffith 2, Lawrence 3, Bitzer 4)
Else von Erlenhof, 1919 (Kortner 3)
Elskovs Magt, 1912 (Holger-Madsen 2, Psilander 3)
Elskovsleg, 1913 (Psilander 3)
Elstree Calling, 1930 (Hitchcock 2, Wong 3)
Elus de la mer, 1925 (Modot 3)
Elusive Corporal. See Caporal epinglé, 1962
Elusive Isabel, 1914 (Lawrence 3)
Elusive Pimpernel, 1950 (Cusack 3, Hawkins 3, Niven 3, Challis 4, Francis 4, Heckroth 4)
Elvira, Mistress of the Dark, 1988 (Edlund 4)
Elvis, 1978 (Winters 3)
Elvis! Elvis!, 1977 (Donner 2)
Elvis on Tour, 1972 (Presley 3)
Elvis—That's the Way It Is, 1970 (Grant 3, Presley 3, Ballard 4)
Embajador, 1949 (Figueroa 4)
Embarkation at Midnight. See Imbarco a mezzanotte, 1952
Embarquement pour le promenade, 1895 (Lumière 2)
Embarrassing Moments, 1930 (Laemmle 4)
Embarrassing Moments, 1934 (Darwell 3, Mandell 4)
Embassy, 1972 (Crawford 3, Milland 3, Von Sydow 3, Coutard 4)
Embezzler, 1914 (Dwan 2, Chaney 3, Ince 4)
Embryo, 1976 (Hudson 3, McDowall 3)
Embuscade, 1941 (Berry 3)
Emerald Forest, 1985 (Boorman 2)
Emergency Call, 1933 (Mankiewicz 2, Darwell 3, Hunt 4, Mandell 4, Plunkett 4, Polglase 4, Steiner 4)
Emergency Squad, 1940 (Dmytryk 2, Quinn 3, Dreier 4, Head 4)
Emergency Wedding, 1950 (Guffey 4)
Émigrante, 1939 (Allégret 2, Feuillère 3, Alekan 4, Aurenche 4, Schüfftan 4)
Emigrantes, 1949 (Fabrizi 3)
Emigrants. See Utvandrarna, 1971
Emil and the Detectives. See Emil und die Detektive, 1931
Emil and the Detectives, 1935 (Launder and Gilliat 2)
Emil and the Detectives, 1964 (Disney 4)
Emil und die Detektive, 1931 (Wilder 2, Rasp 3)
Emile et les détectives. See Emil und die Detektive, 1931
Emile l'africain, 1947 (Fernandel 3)
Emilie Högqvist, 1939 (Molander 2, Fischer 4, Jaenzon 4)

Eminent Domain, 1990 (Sutherland 3)
Emitai, 1971 (Sembene 2)
Emma, 1932 (Brown 2, Dressler 3, Loy 3, Rooney 3, Adrian 4, Marion 4)
Emma Hamilton. See Lady Hamilton—zwischen Smach und Liebe, 1969
Emmanuelle, 1974 (Cuny 3, Lai 4)
Emmanuelle 5, 1987 (Borowczyk 2)
Emmanuelle on Taboo Island. See Spiaggia del desiderio, 1976
Emmanuelle II: Joys of a Woman. See Emmanuelle II: L'Anti-vierge, 1975
Emmanuelle II: L'Anti-vierge, 1975 (Lai 4)
Emma's War, 1986 (Remick 3)
Emmerdeur, 1973 (Coutard 4)
Empereur de Perou, 1981 (Rooney 3)
Emperor, 1915 (Lucas 2)
Emperor and a General. See Nippon no ichiban nagai hi, 1967
Emperor Jones, 1925 (Robeson 3)
Emperor Jones, 1933 (Haller 4)
Emperor of Peru. See Empereur de Perou, 1981
Emperor of Portugal. See Kejsaren av Portugallien, 1944
Emperor of the North. See Emperor of the North Pole, 1973
Emperor of the North Pole, 1973 (Aldrich 2, Borgnine 3, Marvin 3, Biroc 4, Smith 4)
Emperor Waltz, 1948 (Wilder 2, Crosby 3, Fontaine 3, Barnes 4, Brackett 4, Dreier 4, Edouart 4, Head 4, Young 4)
Emperor's Baker and the Baker's Emperor. See Císaŕuv pekaŕ a pekaŕuv cisaŕ, 1951
Emperor's Candlesticks, 1937 (O'Sullivan 3, Powell 3, Rainer 3, Young 3, Gibbons 4, Rosson 4, Waxman 4)
Emperor's New Clothes, 1953 (Bosustow 4)
Emperor's New Clothes, 1966 (Carradine 3)
Emperor's New Clothes, 1987 (Golan and Globus 4)
Emperor's Nightingale. See Císaŕuv slavík, 1948
Emperor's Nightingale, 1951 (Karloff 3)
Empire, 1964 (Warhol 2)
Empire de la nuit, 1962 (Constantine 3, Legrand 4)
Empire of Passion. See Ai no borei, 1978
Empire of the Sun, 1987 (Spielberg 2, Williams 4)
Empire Strikes Back, 1980 (Kasdan 2, Lucas 2, Ford 3, Guinness 3, Jones 3, Brackett 4, Burtt 4, Edlund 4, Menges 4, Williams 4)
Emploi du temps, 1967 (Braunberger 4)
Employees Entrance, 1932 (Young 3, Orry-Kelly 4)
Empreinte de Dieu, 1940 (Heller 4)
Empreinte des géants, 1980 (Reggiani 3)
Empreinte du Dieu, 1940 (Spaak 4)
Empress, 1917 (Guy 2)
Empty Canvas. See Noia, 1963
Empty Gun, 1917 (Chaney 3)
Empty Hands, 1924 (Fleming 2, Shearer 3, Wilson 4)
Empty Hearts, 1924 (Bow 3, Haller 4)
Empty Holsters, 1937 (Eason 4)
Empty Pockets, 1917 (Brenon 2)
Empty Saddles, 1936 (Brooks 3)
Empty Socks, 1927 (Disney 4)
Empty Star. See Estrella vacia, 1958
En, men ett lejon, 1940 (Molander 2, Jaenzon 4)
En Natt, 1931 (Molander 2)

Enamorada, 1946 (Fernández 2, Armendáriz 3, Félix 3, Figueroa 4)

Enamorado, 1951 (Infante 3, Figueroa 4)

Enchanted April, 1935 (Cronjager 4, Hoffenstein 4, MacGowan 4, Plunkett 4, Steiner 4)

Enchanted Barn, 1919 (Love 3)

Enchanted Basket. *See* Corbeille enchantée, 1903

Enchanted Castle in Dudinci, 1952 (Vukotić 4)

Enchanted Cottage, 1924 (Barthelmess 3, Folsey 4)

Enchanted Cottage, 1945 (Cromwell 2, Marshall 3, Young 3, Bodeen 4, Mankiewicz 4)

Enchanted Drawing, 1900 (Blackton 2, Porter 2)

Enchanted Forest, 1945 (D'Agostino 4)

Enchanted Island, 1927 (Walthall 3)

Enchanted Island, 1958 (Dwan 2, Andrews 3)

Enchanted Sedan Chair. *See* Chaise à porteurs enchantée, 1905

Enchanted Well. *See* Puits fantastique, 1903

Enchanteur Alcofrisbas, 1903 (Méliès 2)

Enchantment, 1916 (Borzage 2)

Enchantment, 1921 (Davies 3)

Enchantment, 1948 (Niven 3, Wright 3, Friedhofer 4, Goldwyn 4, Head 4, Jenkins 4, Mandell 4, Toland 4)

Encontra a Mallorca, 1962 (Dors 3)

Encore, 1951 (Clarke 4, Rank 4)

Encore Paris, 1965 (Jarre 4)

Encounter. *See* Stranger on the Prowl, 1952

Encounter at the Elbe. *See* Vstrecha na Elbe, 1949

Encrucijada para una monja, 1967 (Fusco 4)

Encuentro, 1964 (Gómez 2)

Encyclopédie filmée—Alchimie, Azur, Absence, 1952 (Grémillon 2)

End. *See* Slut, 1966

End, 1978 (Field 3, Loy 3, Reynolds 3, Woodward 3, Needham 4, Williams 4)

End as a Man. *See* Strange One, 1957

End of a Circle, 1913 (Anderson 3)

End of a Day. *See* Fin du jour, 1938

End of a Priest. *See* Faŕáruv konee, 1968

End of Arthur's Marriage, 1965 (Loach 2)

End of Battle Fire. *See* Senka no hate, 1950

End of Dawn, 1964 (Warhol 2)

End of Day. *See* Fin du jour, 1938

End of Desire. *See* Vie, 1958

End of Innocence. *See* Casa del ángel, 1957

End of St. Petersburg. *See* **Konyets Sankt-Peterburga, 1927**

End of Summer. *See* Kohayagawa-ke no aki, 1961

End of the Affair, 1955 (Dmytryk 2, Cushing 3, Johnson 3, Kerr 3, Mills 3, Coffee 4, Greene 4)

End of the Chieftain, 1970 (Mikhalkov-Konchalovsky 2)

End of the Day. *See* Fin du jour, 1938

End of the Feud, 1912 (Dwan 2, Bushman 3)

End of the Feud, 1914 (Dwan 2, Chaney 3)

End of the Game. *See* Richter und sein Henker, 1975

End of the Good Old Days. *See* Koneč starych casu, 1989

End of the Lonely Farm Berhof. *See* Zánik samoty Berhof, 1983

End of the Night. *See* Koniec nocy, 1957

End of the Rainbow. *See* Northwest Outpost, 1947

End of the River, 1947 (Challis 4, Rank 4)

End of the Road, 1954 (Addison 4)

End of the Road, 1969 (Jones 3, Willis 4)

End of the Romance, 1912 (Bosworth 3)

End of the Tour, 1917 (Barrymore 3)

End of the World, 1924 (Edeson 4)

End of the World, 1978 (Lee 3)

End of the World in Our Usual Bed in a Night Full of Rain, 1978 (Wertmüller 2, Giannini 3, Rotunno 4)

Enda natt, 1938 (Molander 2, Bergman 3)

Endangered Species, 1982 (Rudolph 2)

Ende eines Wintermärchens, 1977 (Syberberg 2)

Ende vom Lied, 1914 (Porten 3, Messter 4)

Ende von Liede, 1919 (Nielsen 3)

Ending Up, 1990 (Mills 3)

Endless Game, 1989 (Finney 3, Quayle 3, Segal 3, Morricone 4)

Endless Love, 1981 (Zeffirelli 2, Cruise 3, Watkin 4)

Endless Night, 1972 (Launder and Gilliat 2, Sanders 3, Herrmann 4)

Endormi, 1963 (Braunberger 4)

Endowing Your Future, 1957 (Allen 4)

Eneide, 1970 (Storaro 4)

Enemies, a Love Story, 1989 (Mazursky 2, Huston 3, Jarre 4)

Enemies of Women, 1923 (Barrymore 3, Bow 3)

Enemigo principal, 1974 (Sanjinés 2)

Enemy, 1927 (Niblo 2, Gish 3, McCrea 3, Booth 4, Day 4, Gibbons 4, Mayer 4)

Enemy Agent. *See* British Intelligence, 1940

Enemy Air Attack. *See* Tekki kushu, 1943

Enemy Below, 1957 (Mitchum 3, Powell 3, LeMaire 4, Rosson 4)

Enemy from Space. *See* Quatermass II, 1957

Enemy General, 1960 (Johnson 3, Katzman 4)

Enemy of Soap, 1918 (Roach 4)

Enemy of the People. *See* **Public Enemy, 1931**

Enemy of the People. *See* Minshu no teki, 1946

Enemy of the People, 1977 (Andersson 3, McQueen 3, Lourié 4, Rosenman 4)

Enemy of the People. *See* Ganashatru, 1989

Enemy Sex, 1924 (Cruze 2, Brown 4)

Énergie et vous, 1961 (Storck 2)

Energy First, 1955 (Anderson 2)

Energy Picture, 1959 (Halas and Batchelor 4)

Enesorabilia, 1950 (Brazzi 3)

Enez Eussa, 1961 (Delerue 4)

Enfance de l'art, 1910 (Cohl 4)

Enfance nue, 1967 (Pialat 2)

Enfant aimé, 1971 (Akerman 2)

Enfant au fennec, 1956 (Decaë 4)

Enfant de l'amour, 1929 (L'Herbier 2, Simon 3)

Enfant de la roulotte, 1914 (Feuillade 2)

Enfant de la tourmente. *See* Retour au bonheur, 1939

Enfant de ma soeur, 1932 (Artaud 3)

Enfant de Paris, 1913 (Gaumont 4)

Enfant du carnaval, 1921 (Vanel 3)

Enfant du carnaval, 1934 (Mozhukin 3)

Enfant du miracle, 1932 (Fradetal 4)

Enfant et chien, 1895 (Lumière 2)

Enfant prodigue, 1901 (Pathé 4)

Enfant sauvage, 1969 (Truffaut 2, Almendros 4, Guillemot 4)

Enfants, 1985 (Gélin 3)

Enfants au bord de la mer, 1895 (Lumière 2)

Enfants aux jouets, 1895 (Lumière 2)

Enfants de l'amour, 1953 (Kosma 4)

Enfants dorment la nuit, 1948 (Colpi 4)

Enfants du miracle, 1903 (Guy 2)

Enfants du paradis, 1945 (Arletty 3, Barrault 3, Brasseur 3, Modot 3, Barsacq 4, Kosma 4, Prévert 4, Trauner 4)

Enfants du silence, 1963 (Jutra 2)

Enfants gâtés, 1977 (Tavernier 2, Huppert 3, Piccoli 3, Sarde 4)

Enfants terribles, 1950 (Cocteau 2, Melville 2, Decaë 4)

Enfany du carnaval, 1934 (Volkov 2)

Enfer de Dien Bien Phu. *See* Jump Into Hell, 1955

Enfer de Rodin, 1957 (Alekan 4)

Enfer des anges, 1939 (Christian-Jaque 2, Blier 3, D'Eaubonne 4, Heller 4, Renoir 4)

Enfer du jeu. *See* Macao, l'enfer du jeu, 1939

Enforcer, 1951 (Walsh 2, Bogart 3, Sloane 3, Burks 4)

Enforcer, 1975 (Eastwood 3)

Engagement Italiano. *See* Ragazza in prestito, 1965

Engagement Ring, 1911 (Sennett 2)

Engagement Ring. *See* Konyaku yubiwa, 1950

Engeiji ringu, 1950 (Mifune 3, Tanaka 3)

Engel auf Erden. *See* Mademoiselle Ange, 1959

Engel aus Eisen, 1981 (Lassally 4)

Engel mit der Posaune, 1948 (Schell 3, Werner 3)

Engelein, 1913 (Gad 2, Nielsen 3, Freund 4, Kräly 4)

Engeleins Hochzeit, 1914 (Gad 2, Nielsen 3, Freund 4)

England Made Me, 1972 (Finch 3, Greene 4)

English without Tears, 1944 (Rutherford 3, Rank 4, Rattigan 4)

Englische Heirat, 1934 (Walbrook 3)

Englishman Abroad, 1985 (Bates 3)

Englishman and the Girl, 1910 (Griffith 2, Sennett 2, Pickford 3, Bitzer 4, Ince 4)

Englishman's Home, 1939 (Henreid 3)

Engrenage, 1919 (Feuillade 2, Gaumont 4)

Enhörningen, 1955 (Molander 2)

Enigma, 1983 (Sheen 3)

Enigma, 1987 (Rouch 2)

Enigma of Kaspar Hauser. *See* Jeder für sich und Gott gegen alle, 1974

Enigmatique Monsieur Parkes, 1930 (Colbert 3, Menjou 3)

Enigme, 1919 (Gaumont 4)

Enigme de dix heures, 1916 (Gance 2, Burel 4)

Enjo, 1958 (Miyagawa 4)

Enlèvement de Dejanire Goldbois, 1917 (Cohl 4)

Enlèvement en automobile et mariage précipite, 1903 (Guy 2)

Enlèvement en hydroplane, 1913 (Linder 3)

Enlevez-moi, 1932 (Arletty 3, Douy 4)

Enlisted Man's Honor, 1911 (Guy 2)

Enmeiin no semushiotoko, 1924 (Tsuburaya 4)

Ennemi public, 1937 (Storck 2)

Ennemi public No 1, 1953 (Fernandel 3, Audiard 4, Rota 4)

Ennemis, 1960 (Brasseur 3)

Ennemis intimes, 1987 (Sarde 4)

Enoch Arden, 1911 (Griffith 2, Bitzer 4, MacPherson 4)

Enoch Arden, 1915 (Gish 3, Reid 3)

Enola Gay: The Men, the Mission, the Atomic Bomb, 1980 (Jarre 4)

Enough Rope. *See* Meurtrier, 1963

Enough Simplicity in Every Wise Man. *See* Inspector Clouseau, 1967

Enough to Do, 1925 (Laurel and Hardy 3)

Enquête aboutit, 1954 (Colpi 4)

Enquête de l'inspecteur Morgan. *See* Blind Date, 1959

Enquête sur le 58, 1944 (Gélin 3, Vanel 3)

Enquiry into General Practice, 1959 (Lassally 4)

Enredate y veras, 1948 (Alcoriza 4)

Enredos de una gallega, 1951 (Alcoriza 4)

Enrico Caruso, leggenda di una voce, 1951 (Lollobrigida 3)

Enrico cuisinier, 1955 (Grimault 4)

Enrico IV, 1984 (Cardinale 3, Mastroianni 3, Guerra 4)

Ensign Pulver, 1964 (Matthau 3, Nicholson 3, Duning 4, Jeakins 4, Reynolds 4)

Entanglement. *See* Karami-ai, 1962

Entebbe: Operation Thunderbolt, 1977 (Kinski 3, Golan and Globus 4)

Entends-tu les chiens aboyer?, 1974 (Vangelis 4)

Entente cordiale, 1939 (L'Herbier 2, Fradetal 4)

Enter Arsene Lupin, 1944 (Mohr 4)

Enter Laughing, 1966 (Ferrer 3, Winters 3, Biroc 4, Jones 4, May 4)

Enter Madam, 1935 (Grant 3, Sheridan 3, Banton 4, Brackett 4, Dreier 4, Glazer 4)

Enter the Dragon, 1973 (Lee 3, Schifrin 4)

Enter the Ninja, 1981 (Golan 4)

Entertainer, 1960 (Richardson 2, Yates 2, Bates 3, Finney 3, Olivier 3, Addison 4, Morris 4)

Entertainer, 1976 (Lemmon 3, Reynolds 4)

Entertaining the Troops, 1988 (Lamour 3, Blanc 4)

Entfesselte Wein. *See* Seine Hoheit, der Eintänzer, 1927

Entführung, 1936 (Fröhlich 3)

Enthusiasm: Symphony of the Don Basin. *See* Entuziazm: Simfoniia Donbassa, 1931

Enticement, 1925 (Astor 3, Ince 4)

Entity, 1983 (Bernstein 4)

Entlassung, 1942 (Jannings 3, Krauss 3, Wagner 4)

Entotsu no mieru basho, 1953 (Gosho 2, Takamine 3, Tanaka 3)

Entr'acte, 1924 (Clair 2, Achard 4, Auric 4, Braunberger 4)

Entrainement du toréro, 1968 (Braunberger 4)

Entraîneuse, 1938 (Morgan 3, Spaak 4)

Entrance Examination, 1965 (Konwicki 4)

Entre Calais et Douvres, 1897 (Méliès 2)

Entre Hermanos, 1944 (Armendáriz 3)

Entre la mer et l'eau douce, 1967 (Arcand 2, Bujold 3)

Entre la terre et le ciel, 1959 (Delerue 4, Rappeneau 4)

Entre Nous. *See* Coup de foudre, 1983

Entre onze heures et minuit, 1948 (Jouvet 3, Jeanson 4)

Entre Seine et mer, 1960 (Leenhardt 2)

Entre Tinieblas, 1983 (Maura 3)

Entrée des artistes, 1938 (Cayatte 2, Blier 3, Dalio 3, Jouvet 3, Auric 4, Jeanson 4, Matras 4, Trauner 4)

Entrega immediata, 1963 (Cantinflas 3, Figueroa 4)

Entres angen, ur Dollarprinsessan, 1910 (Magnusson 4)

Entrez dans la danse, 1948 (Leenhardt 2)

Entuziazm: Simfoniia Donbassa, 1931 (Vertov 2)

Envers du paradis, 1953 (Von Stroheim 2, Burel 4)

Eperon d'or, 1930 (Matras 4)

Epervier, 1933 (Boyer 3, Marais 3)

Epic That Never Was, 1963 (Bogarde 3)

Epidemic, 1914 (Beery 3)

Epilepsy, 1976 (Benegal 2)

Epilog, 1950 (Kortner 3)

Episode, 1935 (Reisch 4, Stradling 4)

Episode of Cloudy Canyon, 1913 (Anderson 3)

Epitaph to My Love. *See* Waga Koi no tabiji, 1961

Epitome. *See* Shukuzu, 1953

Epouse infernale, 1963 (Braunberger 4)

Epouvantail, 1943 (Aurenche 4, Grimault 4)

Epoux scandaleux, 1935 (Spaak 4)

Épreuve, 1914 (Feuillade 2)

Equilibre, 1952 (Ibert 4)

Equilibriste, 1902 (Guy 2)

Equine Spy, 1912 (Guy 2)

Equinox Flower. *See* **Higanbana, 1958**

Equipage, 1927 (Tourneur 2, Burel 4)

Equipage, 1935 (Litvak 2, Vanel 3, Honegger 4, Jaubert 4)

Equivoque 1900, 1966 (Braunberger 4)

Equus, 1977 (Lumet 2, Burton 3, Canutt 4, Morris 4)

Er oder ich. *See* Sein grösster Bluff, 1927

Er tilladt at vaere ǻndssvag, 1969 (Roos 2)

Er und seine Schwester, 1931 (Ondra 3, Heller 4)

Era di venerdi 17, 1956 (Zavattini 4)

Era du venerdi 17, 1956 (Sordi 3)

Era lui, sì! sì!, 1951 (Loren 3, Rota 4)

Era notte a Roma, 1960 (Rossellini 2, Bondarchuk 3)

Eradicating Auntie, 1909 (Griffith 2, Bitzer 4)

Eran trecento, 1952 (Brazzi 3)

Eraserhead, 1978 (Lynch 2)

Erbe der Van Diemen, 1921 (Hoffmann 4)

Erbe von Pretoria, 1934 (Gründgens 3)

Erbföster, 1915 (Dieterle 2)

Ercole al centro della terra, 1961 (Lee 3)

Ercole alla conquista di Atlantide, 1961 (Volonté 3)

Erdenschwer, 1989 (Volger 3)

Erdgeist, 1923 (Nielsen 3, Mayer 4)

Eredità Ferramonti, 1976 (Quinn 3, Sanda 3, Morricone 4)

Ereji, 1951 (Mifune 3)

Erendira, 1983 (Guerra 2, Papas 3)

Erfinder, 1980 (Ganz 3)

Eric, 1975 (Neal 3)

Eric the Great. *See* Last Performance, 1928

Eric Winstone Band Show, 1955 (Carreras 4)

Eric Winstone's Coach, 1957 (Unsworth 4)

Eric Winstone's Stagecoach, 1956 (Carreras 4)

Erik the Viking, 1989 (Cleese 3, Rooney 3)

Eriki no wakadaisho, 1966 (Tanaka 3)

Eriko to tomoni, 1951 (Yamamura 3)

Erlebnis einer Nacht, 1929 (Warm 4)

Erlebnisse einer Nacht, 1930 (Baranovskaya 3)

Ernani, 1911 (Bertini 3)

Ernest Hemingway's Adventures of a Young Man, 1962 (Garmes 4)

Ernest le rebelle, 1938 (Fernandel 3, Prévert 4)

Ernst Fuchs, 1976 (Lassally 4)

Ernst Thälman Führer seiner Klasse, 1955 (Piccoli 3)

Eroe dei nostri tempi, 1955 (Lattuada 2, Monicelli 2, Sordi 3, Cristaldi 4, Fusco 4, Rota 4)

Eroe sono io, 1951 (Age and scarpelli 4)

Eroi, 1972 (Terry-Thomas 3)

Eroi della domenica, 1952 (Risi 2, Mastroianni 3, Solinas 4)

Eroica, 1949 (Werner 3)

Eroica, 1958 (Munk 2, Lomnicki 3, Stawiński 4)

Eroica, 1960 (Cacoyannis 2, Lassally 4)

Eroismo d'amore, 1914 (Bertini 3)

Eros, O Basileus, 1967 (Markopoulos 2)

Erosion, 1971 (Greenaway 2)

Erótica, 1978 (Fernández 2)

Erotikon, 1920 (Stiller 2, Magnusson 4)

Érotique. *See* Erotyk, 1960

Erotissimo, 1968 (Girardot 3, Braunberger 4)

Erotyk, 1960 (Skolimowski 2)

Errand Boy, 1961 (Lewis 2, Head 4)

Erreur de poivrot, 1904 (Guy 2)

Erreur judiciaire, 1897 (Guy 2)

Erreur judiciaire, 1947 (Dalio 3)

Erreur tragique, 1913 (Feuillade 2, Gaumont 4)

Ersatz, 1961 (Vukotić 4)

Ersbsünde. *See* Vererbte Triebe: Der Kampf ums neue Geschlecht, 1929

Erste Frühlingstag, 1956 (Fröhlich 3)

Erste Kuss, 1928 (Ondra 3, Heller 4)

Erste Liebe, 1970 (Sanda 3, Schell 3, Nykvist 4)

Erste Polka, 1979 (Josephson 3, Schell 3, Ballhaus 4)

Erste Recht des Kindes, 1932 (Planer 4, Von Harbou 4)

Eruption of Mount Pelée. *See* Eruption volcanique à la Martinique, 1902

Eruption volcanique à la Martinique, 1902 (Méliès 2)

Ervinka, 1974 (Topol 3)

Erzehog Otto und das Wäschermadel, 1930 (Heller 4)

Erzieherin gesucht, 1950 (Von Harbou 4)

Es blasen die Trompetten, 1926 (Albers 3)

Es Dach überem Chopf, 1962 (Ganz 3)

Es flüstert die liebe, 1935 (Fröhlich 3)

Es flüstert die Nacht, 1929 (Dagover 3)

Es geschah am hellichten Tag, 1959 (Simon 3)

Es gibt eine Frau, die Dich niemals vergisst, 1930 (Dagover 3)

Es herrscht Ruhe im Land, 1976 (Müller 4)

Es hilft nicht, wo Gewalt herrscht. *See* Nicht versöhnt oder Es hilft nur Gewalt, wo Gewalt herrscht, 1965

Es kommt alle Tage vor . . . , 1930 (Warm 4)

Es kommt ein Tag, 1950 (Dagover 3, Schell 3, Von Harbou 4)

Es leuchtet meine Liebe, 1922 (Dieterle 2)

Es war eine rauschende Ballnacht, 1939 (Rasp 3)

Es war einmal ein Walzer, 1932 (Wilder 2)

Es werde Licht, 1917 (Pick 2)

Es werde Licht, 1918 (Krauss 3)

Es wird schon wieder besser, 1932 (Kaper 4, Wagner 4)

Es zogen drei Burschen, 1927 (Albers 3)

Esa pareja feliz, 1951 (Rey 3)

Escalada del chantaje, 1965 (Alvarez 2)

Escalation, 1968 (Morricone 4)

Escale, 1959 (Delerue 4)

Escale à Paris, 1951 (Decaë 4)

Escale au soleil, 1947 (Fernandel 3)

Escalier C, 1985 (Guillemot 4)

Escalier de service, 1954 (Darrieux 3)

Escalier sans fin, 1943 (Fresnay 3, Matras 4, Spaak 4)

Escambray, 1961 (Alvarez 2)

Escamotage d'une dame chez Robert-Houdin, 1896 (Méliès 2)

Escándalo, 1934 (Figueroa 4)

Escándalo de estrellas, 1944 (Infante 3)

Escapade, 1935 (Powell 3, Rainer 3, Kaper 4, Mankiewicz 4, Reisch 4)

Escapade, 1955 (Mills 3, Sim 3, Stewart 4)

Escapade, 1957 (Jourdan 3, Wakhévitch 4)

Escapade, 1974 (Trintignant 3)

Escapade de Filoche, 1915 (Feuillade 2, Musidora 3)

Escapade in Japan, 1957 (Eastwood 3, Wright 3, Steiner 4)

Escapades of Eva. See Eva tropí hlouposti, 1939

Escape, 1914 (Griffith 2, Crisp 3, Gish 3, Marsh 3, Sweet 3, Bitzer 4)

Escape, 1925 (Florey 2, Laemmle 4)

Escape, 1930 (Carroll 3, Dean 4)

Escape, 1940 (LeRoy 2, Nazimova 3, Shearer 3, Taylor 3, Veidt 3, Adrian 4, Cronjager 4, Day 4, Mayer 4, Waxman 4)

Escape, 1948 (Mankiewicz 2, Cusack 3, Harrison 3, Alwyn 4, Dunne 4, LeMaire 4, Vetchinsky 4, Young 4)

Escape, 1971 (Grahame 3, Schifrin 4)

Escape Artist, 1982 (Coppola 2, Delerue 4, Tavoularis 4)

Escape at Dawn. See Red Sky at Morning, 1945

Escape at Dawn. See Akatsuki no dasso, 1950

Escape by Night, 1937 (Bond 3)

Escape Episode, 1944 (Anger 2)

Escape Episode, 1946 (Anger 2)

Escape from Alcatraz, 1979 (Siegel 2, Eastwood 3)

Escape from Andersonville, 1909 (Olcott 2)

Escape from Devil's Island, 1935 (Johnson 3)

Escape from East Berlin. See Tunnel 28, 1962

Escape from Fort Bravo, 1953 (Sturges 2, Holden 3, Surtees 4)

Escape from Japan. See Nihon dashutsu, 1964

Escape from New York, 1981 (Carpenter 2, Borgnine 3, Pleasence 3, Stanton 3, Van Cleef 3)

Escape from Prison. See Datsugoku, 1950

Escape from San Quentin, 1957 (Katzman 4)

Escape from Sobibor, 1987 (Arkin 3)

Escape from the Dark, 1975 (Sim 3)

Escape from the Planet of the Apes, 1971 (McDowall 3, Mineo 3, Biroc 4, Dehn 4, Goldsmith 4, Smith 4)

Escape from Yesterday. See Bandera, 1935

Escape from Zahrain, 1962 (Brynner 3, Mason 3, Mineo 3, Fulton 4, Head 4)

Escape in the Desert, 1944 (Florey 2, Burks 4, Deutsch 4)

Escape into Dreams. See Natale al campo 119, 1948

Escape Me Never, 1935 (Lean 2, Bergner 3, Périnal 4, Walton 4)

Escape Me Never, 1947 (Flynn 3, Lupino 3, Blanke 4, Friedhofer 4, Korngold 4, Polito 4, Prinz 4)

Escape of Broncho Billy, 1915 (Anderson 3)

Escape of Jim Dolan, 1913 (Mix 3)

Escape of Nicholas and Alexandra, 1973 (Fontaine 3)

Escape on the Fog, 1945 (Boetticher 2)

Escape to Athena, 1979 (Cardinale 3, Gould 3, Niven 3, Anhalt 4, Schifrin 4)

Escape to Bermuda, 1955 (Ryan 3)

Escape to Burma, 1955 (Dwan 2, Stanwyck 3, Alton 4, Jennings 4, Polglase 4)

Escape to Danger, 1943 (Alwyn 4, Green 4)

Escape to Glory, 1940 (Irene 4, Planer 4)

Escape to Happiness. See Intermezzo: A Love Story, 1939

Escape to Paradise, 1939 (Young 4)

Escape to the Sun. See Habrichka el hashemersh, 1972

Escape to Victory. See Victory, 1981

Escape to Witch Mountain, 1975 (Milland 3, Pleasence 3)

Escapes, 1987 (Price 3)

Escapulario, 1966 (Figueroa 4)

Escarpins de Max, 1913 (Linder 3)

Esclave, 1923 (Boyer 3)

Esclave, 1953 (Gélin 3, Auric 4)

Esclave blanche, 1927 (Vanel 3)

Esclave blanche, 1938 (Dalio 3, Alekan 4, Andrejew 4, Jaubert 4)

Escondida, 1955 (Armendáriz 3, Félix 3, Figueroa 4)

Escondido. See Minuto per pregare, un instante per morire, 1968

Escort West, 1959 (Mature 3, Clothier 4)

Escuadró de la muerte, 1966 (Crawford 3)

Escuadron, 1988 (Jourdan 3)

Escuela de música, 1955 (Infante 3)

Escuela de rateros, 1956 (Infante 3, Alcoriza 4)

Escuela de vagabundos, 1954 (Infante 3)

Escuela en el campo, 1961 (Gómez 2)

Escuela para solteras, 1964 (Figueroa 4)

Escuela rural, 1960 (Almendros 4)

Esercito di cinque uomini, 1969 (Argento 4, Morricone 4)

Esfinge de cristal, 1968 (Taylor 3)

Eshaet Hub, 1960 (Sharif 3)

Eskapade, 1936 (Von Harbou 4)

Eskimo, 1933 (Van Dyke 2, Gillespie 4, Mayer 4)

Eskimo-Baby, 1917 (Nielsen 3)

Eskimo Limon, 1977 (Golan and Globus 4)

Eskimo Limon 6. See Eskimo Ohgen, 1985

Eskimo Ohgen, 1985 (Golan and Globus 4)

Eskimo Village, 1933 (Grierson 2)

Eskiya celladi, 1967 (Güney 2)

Esleuchten die Sterne, 1938 (Tschechowa 3)

Esli khochesh byt schastlivym, 1974 (Shukshin 3)

Esmeralda, 1905 (Guy 2, Gaumont 4)

Esmerelda, 1915 (Pickford 3)

Espagne 1937/España leal en armas!, 1937 (Buñuel 2)

España insolita, 1965 (Rey 3)

Especially on Sunday. See Domenica specialmente, 1991

Espectro de la novia, 1943 (Figueroa 4)

Esperanza; El muro de silencio, 1972 (Alcoriza 4)

Esperienza del cubismo, 1949 (Delli Colli 4)

Espion, 1966 (Clift 3, McDowall 3, Coutard 4)

Espion, lève-toi, 1981 (Piccoli 3, Audiard 4, Morricone 4)

Espionage, 1937 (Lukas 3)

Espionage Agent, 1939 (Bacon 2, McCrea 3, Buckner 4, Deutsch 4, Rosher 4)

Espions. See Spione, 1928

Espions, 1957 (Clouzot 2, Jaffe 3, Ustinov 3, Auric 4, Matras 4)

Espoir, 1939 (Milhaud 4)

Espoir au village, 1950 (Cloquet 4)

Espontánes, 1963 (Rey 3)

Esprit de cinéma, 1948 (Epstein 2)

Esqueleto de la señora Morales, 1959 (Alcoriza 4)

Esrefpasali, 1966 (Güney 2)

Essence. See Susman, 1985

Essene, 1972 (Wiseman 2)

Esso, 1954 (Alexeieff and Parker 4)

Essor, 1920 (Fresnay 3)

Esta tierra nuestra, 1959 (Gutiérrez Alea 2)

Estafa de amor, 1954 (Figueroa 4)

Estambul 65, 1965 (Kinski 3)

Estampida, 1971 (Alvarez 2)

Estate in quattro, 1969 (Andersson 3, Björnstrand 3)

Estate violenta, 1959 (Trintignant 3, Cecchi D'Amico 4)

Est-ce bien raisonnable, 1980 (Audiard 4, Decaë 4)

Este pueblo no hay ladrones, 1964 (Buñuel 2)

Esther, 1910 (Feuillade 2, Gaumont 4)

Esther, 1962 (Eisler 4)

Esther, 1986 (Alekan 4)

Esther and the King, 1960 (Walsh 2)

Esther Waters, 1948 (Bogarde 3, Cusack 3, Dalrymple 4, Rank 4)

Estouffade à la Carabei, 1967 (Seberg 3)

Estrange M. Victor, 1938 (Achard 4)

Estrangeira, 1981 (Rey 3, Branco 4, De Almeida 4)

Estrella vacia, 1958 (Félix 3)

Estudantes, 1935 (Miranda 3)

Et år med Henry, 1967 (Roos 2)

Et cetera, 1966 (Švankmajer 4)

Et crac!, 1969 (Chabrol 2)

Et . . . Dieu créa la femme, 1956 (Vadim 2, Bardot 3, Trintignant 3)

Et Dieu créa la femme, 1987 (Vadim 2)

Et Drama par Havet, 1912 (Psilander 3)

Et forfejlet Spring. See Højt Spil, 1913

Et Laereaar, 1914 (Psilander 3)

Et moi j'te dis qu'elle t'a fait de l'oeil, 1935 (Berry 3)

Et mourir de plaisir, 1960 (Vadim 2, Renoir 4)

Et per tetto un cielo di stelle, 1968 (Morricone 4)

Et quand vient le soir, 1969 (Braunberger 4)

Et Satan conduit le bal, 1962 (Deneuve 3, Coutard 4)
Et si nous buvions un coup, 1908 (Cohl 4)
Et si on faisait l'amour. *See* Scusi, facciamo l'amore, 1968
Et sommereventyr, 1919 (Madsen and Schenstrøm 3)
Et ta soeur?, 1958 (Arletty 3, Cassel 3, Fresnay 3)
Eta del ferro, 1964 (Rossellini 2)
Età dell'amore, 1953 (Fabrizi 3)
Etat de grace, 1986 (Sarde 4)
Etat de siège, 1972 (Montand 3, Solinas 4, Theodorakis 4)
Etat sauvage, 1978 (Piccoli 3)
Etc., 1975 (Breer 4)
Été dernier à Tangier, 1987 (Sarde 4)
Été indien, 1957 (Braunberger 4)
Été meurtrier, 1983 (Adjani 3, Delerue 4)
Été prochain, 1986 (Cardinale 3, Noiret 3, Trintignant 3)
Eterna femmina, 1954 (Lamarr 3)
Eternal. *See* Amar, 1954
Eternal City, 1915 (Porter 2)
Eternal City, 1923 (Barrymore 3, Colman 3, Goldwyn 4, Miller 4)
Eternal Fire. *See* World Window, 1977
Eternal Flame, 1922 (Menjou 3, Talmadge 3, Gaudio 4, Marion 4, Schenck 4)
Eternal Grind, 1916 (Pickford 3)
Eternal Love. *See* Elet, halál, szerelem, 1929
Eternal Melodies. *See* Melodie eterne, 1940
Eternal Mother, 1911 (Griffith 2, Normand 3, Sweet 3, Bitzer 4)
Eternal Mother, 1917 (Barrymore 3)
Eternal Prague, 1941 (Weiss 2)
Eternal Return. *See* Eternel Retour, 1943
Eternal Sappho, 1916 (Bara 3)
Eternal Sea, 1955 (Hayden 3, Bernstein 4)
Eternal Sin, 1917 (Brenon 2, Barthelmess 3, Hunt 4)
Eternal Struggle, 1923 (Beery 3, Mayer 4)
Eternal Three, 1923 (Neilan 2, Bosworth 3, Love 3, Wilson 4)
Eternal Triangle, 1910 (Lawrence 3)
Eternal Triangle, 1922 (Terry 4)
Eternal Woman, 1929 (Walker 4)
Eternally Yours, 1939 (Garnett 2, Arden 3, Crawford 3, Niven 3, Young 3, Banton 4, Irene 4, Wanger 4)
Eternel Conflit, 1947 (Modot 3, Barsacq 4, Matras 4, Spaak 4)
Eternel Retour, 1943 (Cocteau 2, Marars 3, Annenkov 4, Auric 4, Wakhévitch 4)
Eternity, 1990 (Legrand 4)
Eternity of Love. *See* Wakaret ikiru toki mo, 1961
Etes-vous fiancée à un marin grec ou à un pilote de ligne?, 1970 (Braunberger 4, Coutard 4)
Etes-vous jalouse?, 1937 (Kaufman 4)
Ethel's Romeos, 1915 (Laurel and Hardy 3)
Ethel's Teacher, 1914 (Browning 2)
Etienne of the Glad Heart, 1914 (Mix 3)
Étirage des ampoules électriques, 1924 (Grémillon 2)
Etnocidio: notas sobre el Mezquital, 1978 (LeDuc 2)
Etoile au soleil, 1942 (Bost 4)
Etoile de mer, 1926 (Artaud 3)
Etoile de mer, 1959 (Delerue 4)
Etoile de mer, 1967 (Braunberger 4)

Etoile de Valencia, 1933 (Gabin 3, Simon 3)
Etoile disparaît, 1932 (Delannoy 2, Achard 4)
Etoile du nord, 1982 (Noiret 3, Signoret 3, Aurenche 4, Sarde 4)
Etoile du sud, 1969 (Welles 2, Segal 3, Coutard 4)
Etoile filant, 1930 (Brasseur 3)
Etoile sans lumière, 1945 (Montand 3, Reggiani 3, D'Eaubonne 4)
Etoiles de Midi, 1959 (Jarre 4)
Etoiles ne meurent jamais, 1957 (Raimu 3)
Etoiles sans lumière, 1946 (Berry 3)
Etrange Affaire, 1981 (Baye 3, Piccoli 3)
Etrange aventure de Lemmy Caution. *See* **Alphaville, 1965**
Etrange Désir de Monsieur Bard, 1953 (Simon 3, Burel 4)
Etrange destin, 1945 (Burel 4)
Etrange Madame X, 1951 (Grémillon 2, Morgan 3)
Etrange Mr. Steve, 1957 (Moreau 3)
Etrange Monsieur Victor, 1938 (Grémillon 2, Raimu 3, Spaak 4)
Etranger. *See* Straniero, 1967
Etrangère, 1930 (Burel 4, Meerson 4)
Etroit mousquetaire. *See* Three Must-Get-Theres, 1922
Etruscologia, 1961 (Storaro 4)
Etta of the Footlights, 1914 (Costello 3)
Ettaro di cielo, 1958 (Mastroianni 3, Cristaldi 4, Di Venanzo 4, Flaiano 4, Guerra 4, Rota 4)
Ettore Fieramosca, 1938 (Blasetti 2, Cervi 3)
Ettore lo fusto, 1972 (De Sica 2, Giannini 3)
Etude, 1961 (Gaál 2)
Etude cinégraphique sur une arabesque, 1929 (Dulac 2)
Etudes de mouvements, 1928 (Ivens 2)
Etudiante d'aujourd'hui, 1966 (Rohmer 2)
Etudiants, 1960 (Delerue 4)
Etwas wird sichtbar, 1981 (Ganz 3)
Euberfall in Feindesland, 1915 (Messter 4)
Euclidean Illusions, 1978 (Vanderbeek 2)
Eugene, the Jeep, 1940 (Fleischer 4)
Eugenia de Montijo, 1944 (Rey 3)
Eugenia Grandet, 1946 (Valli 3, Gherardi 4)
Eugenie—The Story of Her Journey into Perversion, 1970 (Lee 3)
Eulogy to 5.02, 1965 (Burton 3)
Eureka, 1984 (Roeg 2, Hackman 3, Rourke 3)
Eureka Stockade, 1949 (Watt 2, Finch 3, Rafferty 3, Balcon 4, Rank 4)
Europa, 1990 (Constantine 3)
Europa Abends, 1989 (Constantine 3)
Europa '51, 1952 (Fellini 2, Rossellini 2, Bergman 3, Masina 3, De Laurentiis 4, Ponti 4, Stewart 4)
Europe, 1958 (Delerue 4)
Europe, 1964 (Leenhardt 2)
Europe continentale avant 1900, 1969 (Braunberger 4)
Europe méridionale au temps des rois, 1969 (Braunberger 4)
European Rest Cure, 1904 (Porter 2)
Europeans, 1979 (Ivory 2, Remick 3, Jhabvala 4)
Eusèbe Deputé, 1939 (Berry 3, Simon 3)
Eva, 1913 (Porten 3, Messter 4)
Eva, 1935 (Henreid 3)
Eva, 1948 (Bergman 2, Molander 2, Dahlbeck 3)
Eva, 1953 (Theodorakis 4)

Eva, 1962 (Losey 2, Baker 3, Moreau 3, Di Venanzo 4, Hakim 4, Legrand 4)
Eva and the Grasshopper. *See* Jugendrausch, 1927
Eva tropí hlouposti, 1939 (Frič 2)
Evadée, 1929 (Burel 4)
Evadés, 1954 (Fresnay 3, Kosma 4)
Evangeliemandens Liv, 1914 (Psilander 3)
Evangelimann, 1923 (Bergner 3, Pommer 4)
Evangeline, 1911 (Bosworth 3)
Evangeline, 1919 (Walsh 2)
Evangeline, 1929 (Del Rio 3)
Evangelist. *See* Evangeliemandens Liv, 1914
Evangelium, 1923 (Holger-Madsen 2)
Evariste Galois, 1965 (Astruc 2)
Evas Töchter, 1928 (Heller 4)
Evasion de Vidocq, 1990 (Baur 3)
Evasion du mort, 1915 (Feuillade 2)
Evasions de Bob Walter, 1916 (Cohl 4)
Eve. *See* Eva, 1962
Eve. *See* Face of Eve, 1968
Eve Knew Her Apples, 1945 (Miller 3, Guffey 4)
Eve of St. Mark, 1944 (Edwards 2, Stahl 2, Baxter 3, Price 3, Basevi 4, La Shelle 4)
Eve sans trêve, 1963 (Braunberger 4)
Eveil d'un monde, 1951 (Rabier 4)
Eveillé du Pont de l'Alma, 1985 (Ruiz 2, Branco 4)
Evelyn Prentice, 1934 (Howard 2, Loy 3, Powell 3, Russell 3, Clarke 4, Coffee 4)
Even as I.O.U., 1942 (Three Stooges 3)
Even As You and I, 1917 (Weber 2)
Even Break, 1917 (Menjou 3, August 4)
Even in My Heart, 1933 (Stanwyck 3)
Evènement le plus important depuis que l'homme a marché sur la lune, 1973 (Deneuve 3, Mastroianni 3, Presle 3, Evein 4, Legrand 4)
Evening Alone, 1938 (Benchley 4)
Evening Clothes, 1927 (Brooks 3, Menjou 3, Rosson 4, Schulberg 4)
Evening for Sale, 1932 (Banton 4)
Evening Glory of Heaven. *See* Ama no yugao, 1948
Evening Land. *See* Aftenlandet, 1977
Evening with the Royal Ballet, 1963 (Asquith 2, Challis 4, Havelock-Allan 4, Unsworth 4)
Evenings for Sale, 1932 (Marshall 3)
Evenings with Jindrich Plachta. *See* Večery s Jindřichem Plachtou, 1954
Evensong, 1934 (Saville 2, Guinness 3, Kortner 3, Balcon 4, Junge 4, Rank 4)
Event. *See* Dogadaj, 1969
Event in the Stadium, 1929 (Ptushko 4)
Eventail animé, 1909 (Cohl 4)
Eventful Elopement, 1912 (Bunny 3)
Eventful Evening, 1916 (Mix 3)
Ever in My Heart, 1933 (Bellamy 3, Grot 4)
Ever Since Eve, 1921 (Fox 4)
Ever Since Eve, 1934 (Miller 4)
Ever Since Eve, 1937 (Bacon 2, Davies 3, Montgomery 3, Barnes 4, Orry-Kelly 4)
Ever-Changing Motor Car, 1961 (Dunning 4)
Evergreen, 1934 (Saville 2, Matthews 3, Balcon 4, Junge 4)
Evergreen Tree, 1958 (Zhao 3)
Everlasting Whisper, 1925 (Johnson 3, Mix 3, Fox 4)
Every Bastard a King, 1968 (Topol 3)
Every Day Except Christmas, 1957 (Anderson 2, Reisz 3, Lassally 4)

Every Day's a Holiday, 1938 (West 3, Carmichael 4, Struss 4)

Every Day's a Holiday. *See* Oro di Napoli, 1955

Every Day's a Holiday, 1964 (Roeg 2)

Every Five Minutes, 1950 (Lassally 4)

Every Girl Should Be Married, 1948 (Grant 3, Sharaff 4)

Every Girl Should Have One, 1978 (Faye 3)

Every Inch a King, 1914 (Bushman 3)

Every Inch a Man, 1912 (Reid 3)

Every Inch a Man. *See* Tools of Providence, 1915

Every Little Crook and Nanny, 1972 (Mature 3)

Every Man for Himself, 1924 (Roach 4)

Every Man for Himself. *See* Sauve qui peut, 1979

Every Man for Himself and God Against All. *See* Jeder für sich und Gott gegen alle, 1974

Every Man's Wife, 1925 (Fox 4)

Every Minute Counts. *See* Count the Hours, 1953

Every Mother's Son, 1919 (Walsh 2)

Every Night at Eight, 1935 (Walsh 2, Faye 3, Raft 3, Wanger 4)

Every Other Weekend. *See* Week-End sur deux, 1990

Every Revolution Is a Throw of the Dice. *See* Toute révolution est un coup de dés, 1977

Every Saturday Night, 1936 (August 4)

Every Sunday, 1936 (Durbin 3, Garland 3)

Every Sunday Afternoon. *See* Every Sunday, 1936

Every Time We Say Goodbye, 1986 (Hanks 3, Sarde 4)

Every Which Way But Loose, 1977 (Eastwood 3, Gordon 3)

Every Woman For Herself and All For Art, 1977 (Jarman 2)

Every Woman's Man. *See* Prizefighter and the Lady, 1933

Everybody at His Station. *See* Alle man på post, 1940

Everybody Dance, 1936 (Fisher 2, Balcon 4, Rank 4, Vetchinsky 4)

Everybody Does It, 1949 (Goulding 2, Coburn 3, Darnell 3, Johnson 4, La Shelle 4, LeMaire 4, Newman 4)

Everybody Go Home!. *See* Tutti a casa, 1960

Everybody Sing, 1938 (Garland 3, Edens 4, Kaper 4, Ruttenberg 4)

Everybody Sings, 1937 (Lantz 4)

Everybody Wins, 1990 (Reisz 2, Nolte 3)

Everybody Works But Father, 1905 (Bitzer 4)

Everybody's Acting, 1926 (Neilan 2, Walthall 3, Glazer 4, Hughes 4)

Everybody's All-American, 1988 (Lange 3, Van Runkle 4)

Everybody's Baby, 1939 (McDaniel 3)

Everybody's Changing. *See* Take Me Out to the Ball Game, 1949

Everybody's Cheering. *See* Take Me Out to the Ball Game, 1949

Everybody's Dancing, 1950 (McDowall 3)

Everybody's Doing It, 1916 (Browning 2)

Everybody's Doing It, 1938 (Musuraca 4)

Everybody's Fine. *See* Stanno tutti bene, 1990

Everyday, 1929 (Eisenstein 2)

Everyday. *See* Ich dzień powszedni, 1963

Everyday Courage. *See* Každý den odvahu, 1964

Everyday—Sunday. *See* Neděle ve všedni, 1962

Everyman, 1962 (Baillie 2)

Everything But the Truth, 1956 (O'Hara 3)

Everything Ends Tonight. *See* Dnes večer všechno skončí, 1955

Everything for Sale, 1921 (Howe 4, Rosson 4)

Everything for Sale. *See* Wszystko na sprzedaż, 1968

Everything Happens at Night, 1939 (Henie 3, Milland 3, Brown 4, Cronjager 4, Day 4)

Everything I Have Is Yours, 1953 (Mercer 4)

Everything Is Thunder, 1936 (Homolka 3, Balcon 4, Junge 4, Rank 4)

Everything Remains for the People. *See* Vse ostaetsia lyudyam, 1963

Everything You Always Wanted to Know About Sex But Were Afraid to Ask, 1972 (Allen 2, Carradine 3, Quayle 3, Reynolds 3, Wilder 3)

Everything's Ducky, 1962 (Cooper 3, Rooney 3)

Everything's in Order but Nothing Works. *See* Tutto a posto e niente in ordine, 1974

Everything's on Ice, 1939 (Metty 4)

Everything's Rosie, 1931 (Bruckman 4, Musuraca 4)

Everywoman, 1919 (Daniels 3)

Everywoman's Husband, 1918 (Swanson 3)

Eve's Daughter, 1914 (Ingram 2)

Eve's Daughters. *See* Dcery Eviny, 1928

Eves Futures, 1963 (Delerue 4)

Eve's Leaves, 1926 (Miller 4)

Eve's Love Letters, 1926 (Laurel and Hardy 3, Roach 4)

Eve's Lover, 1925 (Bow 3)

Evidence, 1929 (Loy 3)

Evidence Enclosed. *See* Settled Out of Court, 1925

Evidence in Camera. *See* Headline Shooter, 1933

Evil Eden. *See* Mort en ce jardin, 1956

Evil Eye, 1917 (Sweet 3)

Evil Inheritance, 1911 (Dwan 2)

Evil Men Do, 1914 (Ingram 2, Costello 3)

Evil Mind. *See* Clairvoyant, 1935

Evil of Frankenstein, 1964 (Cushing 3, Carreras 4, Francis 4)

Evil Roy Slade, 1972 (Rooney 3)

Evil Spawn, 1987 (Carradine 3)

Evil That Men Do, 1984 (Bronson 3, Ferrer 3)

Evil under the Sun, 1981 (Mason 3, McDowall 3, Smith 3, Ustinov 3, Challis 4)

Evils of Chinatown. *See* Confessions of an Opium Eater, 1962

Evils of the Night, 1985 (Carradine 3)

Evintrude: Die Geschichte eines Abenteurers, 1914 (Wegener 3)

Eviny Evas Töchter, 1928 (Ondra 3)

Evita, 1991 (Stone 2)

Evita Peron, 1981 (Dunaway 3, Ferrer 3)

Evitez le désordre, 1949 (Decaë 4)

Evlalie quitte les champs, 1973 (Lee 3, Seyrig 3, Simon 3, Cloquet 4)

Evolution, 1925 (Fleischer 4)

Evolution of Fashion, 1917 (Laurel and Hardy 3)

Ewige Fluch, 1921 (Warm 4)

Ewige Klang, 1943 (Tschechowa 3)

Ewige Maske, 1935 (Tschechowa 3)

Ewige Nacht, 1914 (Gad 2, Nielsen 3, Freund 4, Kräly 4)

Ewige Spiel, 1951 (Warm 4)

Exalted Flapper, 1929 (Clarke 4, Fox 4)

Examination Day at School, 1910 (Griffith 2, Pickford 3, Bitzer 4)

Ex-Bad Boy, 1931 (Arthur 3, Loos 4)

Excalibur, 1981 (Boorman 2)

Excess Baggage, 1928 (Cruze 2, Daves 2, Day 4, Gibbons 4, Marion 4)

Ex-Champ, 1939 (McLaglen 3)

Exchange Is No Robbery, 1898 (Hepworth 2)

Excitement, 1924 (Laemmle 4)

Exciters, 1923 (Daniels 3, Levien 4)

Exciting Adventure. *See* Kouzelné dobrodružství, 1982

Exciting Courtship, 1914 (Browning 2)

Exclusive, 1937 (Farmer 3, MacMurray 3, Glazer 4, Head 4)

Exclusive Story, 1935 (Gillespie 4)

Ex-Convict, 1904 (Porter 2)

Excursion a Vueltabajo, 1965 (Gómez 2)

Excursion House, 1954 (Van Dyke 2)

Excuse Me, 1925 (Gibbons 4, Mayer 4)

Excuse Me. . . . *See* Scusi, lei e favorevole o contrario, 1967

Excuse My Dust, 1920 (Wood 2, Reid 3)

Excuse My Dust, 1951 (Darwell 3, Pan 4, Rose 4)

Excuse My Glove, 1925 (Roach 4)

Exécution, 1960 (Cloquet 4)

Execution, 1972 (Robards 3)

Exécution capitale à Berlin, 1897 (Pathé 4)

Execution of Private Slovik, 1974 (Sheen 3)

Execution Squad. *See* Mano spietata della legge, 1976

Executioner. *See* **Verdugo, 1964**

Executioner, 1970 (Homolka 3)

Executioner's Song, 1982 (Wallach 3)

Executive Action, 1973 (Lancaster 3, Ryan 3, Trumbo 4)

Executive Suite, 1954 (Wise 2, Allyson 3, Calhern 3, Holden 3, March 3, Pidgeon 3, Stanwyck 3, Winters 3, Folsey 4, Gibbons 4, Houseman 4, Rose 4)

Exemple Etretat, 1962 (Braunberger 4, Delerue 4)

Exhumation of the Remains of Sergius of Radonezh. *See* Vskrytie moschei Sergeia Radonezhskogo, 1919

Exile, 1917 (Tourneur 2, Carré 4)

Exile, 1931 (Micheaux 2)

Exile, 1947 (Ophüls 2, Planer 4)

Exile of "Bar-K" Ranch, 1915 (Eason 4)

Exiles. *See* De Landsflyktige, 1921

Exiles, 1923 (Gilbert 3)

Existentialist, 1964 (Emshwiller 2)

Exit Smiling, 1926 (Pangborn 3, Gibbons 4)

Ex-Lady, 1933 (Florey 2, Davis 3, Gaudio 4, Orry-Kelly 4, Riskin 4)

Ex-Mrs. Bradford, 1936 (Arthur 3, Powell 3, Hunt 4, Polglase 4, Veiller 4)

Exode, 1910 (Feuillade 2)

Exodus, 1960 (Preminger 2, Cobb 3, Mineo 3, Newman 3, Richardson 3, Saint 3, Bass 4, Day 4, Trumbo 4)

Exo-Man, 1977 (Ferrer 3)

Exorcist, 1973 (Friedkin 2, Burstyn 3, Cobb 3, McCambridge 3, Von Sydow 3, Baker 4, Roizman 4, Smith 4)

Exorcist II: The Heretic, 1977 (Boorman 2, Burton 3, Henreid 3, Jones 3, Von Sydow 3, Fisher 4, Fraker 4, Morricone 4, Smith 4, Whitlock 4)

Exorcist III, 1990 (Scott 3, Sidney 3)

Expedition. *See* Abhijan, 1962

Expensive Husbands, 1970 (Negulesco 2)

Expensive Visit, 1915 (Laurel and Hardy 3)

Expensive Women, 1931 (Costello 3)

Experience, 1921 (Barthelmess 3, Miller 4, Young 4)

Experience Preferred But Not Essential, 1982 (Puttnam 4)

Experiment, 1943 (Frič 2)

Experiment in Terror, 1962 (Ford 3, Remick 3, Mancini 4)

Experiment Perilous, 1944 (Tourneur 2, Lamarr 3, Lukas 3, Dunn 4, Gaudio 4)

Experimental Animation, 1962 (Alexeieff and Parker 4)

Experimental Animation: Peanut Vendor, 1933 (Lye 4)

Expert, 1932 (Beavers 3)

Experts, 1989 (Travolta 3, Hamlisch 4)

Expert's Opinion, 1935 (Havelock-Allan 4)

Expiated Innocence. *See* Sonad oskuld, 1915

Expiation, 1909 (Griffith 2, Bitzer 4)

Expiation, 1915 (Feuillade 2)

Exploit on the Ice. *See* Podvig vo idach, 1928

Exploits de Farfadet, 1916 (Cohl 4)

Exploits de feu-follet. *See* Jobard fiance par interim, 1911

Exploits d'un jeune Don-Juan, 1987 (Carrière 4, Morricone 4)

Exploits of Elaine, 1915 (Barrymore 3, White 3)

Explorers, 1929 (Rooney 3)

Explorers, 1931 (Terry 4)

Explorers, 1986 (Dante 2, Goldsmith 4)

Exploring England with Will Rogers, 1927 (Rogers 3)

Explosion, 1971 (Coutard 4)

Explosion of a Motor Car, 1900 (Hepworth 2)

Explosive Generation, 1961 (Crosby 4)

Explosive Mr. Magoo, 1958 (Bosustow 4, Burness 4)

Ex-Plumber, 1931 (Arbuckle 3)

Exposed, 1938 (Cortez 4)

Exposed, 1983 (Andersson 3, Kinski 3, Decaë 4, Delerue 4)

Exposition de Caricatures. *See* Unforeseen Metamorphosis, 1912

Exposition de 1900, 1900 (Méliès 2)

Exposition Française à Moscou, 1962 (Delerue 4)

Exposition 1900, 1967 (Braunberger 4)

Expostulations, 1958 (Romero 2)

Exposure, 1958 (Dickinson 2)

Express Sedan. *See* Sutobi kago, 1952

Express Train in a Railway Cutting, 1899 (Hepworth 2)

Expresso Bongo, 1959 (Harvey 3, Mankowitz 4)

Exquisite Sinner, 1926 (Florey 2, Von Sternberg 2, Loy 3, Gibbons 4)

Exquisite Thief, 1919 (Browning 2)

Ex-Sweeties, 1931 (Sennett 2, Grable 3)

Extase, 1933 (Lamarr 3, Stallich 4)

Extenuating Circumstances. *See* Circonstances atténuantes, 1939

Exterminating Angel. *See* Ángel exterminador, 1962

Exterminator, 1945 (Terry 4)

Exterminator 1, 1984 (Golan and Globus 4)

Extra, 1962 (Cantinflas 3)

Extra Day, 1956 (Simon 3)

Extra Dollars, 1954 (Holliday 3)

Extra! Extra!, 1922 (Howard 2)

Extra Girl, 1923 (Sennett 2, Normand 3, Hornbeck 4)

Extraconiugale, 1964 (Delli Colli 4)

Extramuros, 1985 (Maura 3)

Extraordinaires Exercices de la famille Coeur-de-Bois, 1912 (Cohl 4)

Extraordinary Case of Mr. West in the Land of the Bolsheviks. *See* **Neobychanye priklucheniya Mistera Vesta v stranye bolshevikov, 1924**

Extraordinary Child, 1954 (Brakhage 2)

Extraordinary Illusions. *See* Dislocations mystérieuses, 1901

Extraordinary Illusions. *See* Illusions funambulesques, 1903

Extraordinary Seaman, 1968 (Frankenheimer 2, Dunaway 3, Niven 3, Rooney 3, Jarre 4)

Extravagante Mission, 1945 (Renoir 4)

Extreme Prejudice, 1987 (Hill 2, Nolte 3, Goldsmith 4)

Extremities, 1913 (Costello 3, Talmadge 3)

Ex-voto, 1919 (Autant-Lara 2)

Eye for an Eye, 1918 (Nazimova 3, Mathis 4)

Eye for an Eye. *See* Oeil pour oeil, 1956

Eye for an Eye, 1966 (Ballard 4)

Eye for an Eye, 1981 (Lee 3)

Eye Myth, 1972 (Brakhage 2)

Eye Myth, 1981 (Brakhage 2)

Eye of Conscience, 1911 (Bosworth 3)

Eye of the Cat, 1969 (Head 4, Metty 4, Schifrin 4)

Eye of the Cat. *See* Attenti al buffone!, 1975

Eye of the Devil, 1966 (Kerr 3, Niven 3, Pleasence 3)

Eye of the Government, 1914 (Olcott 2)

Eye of the Needle. *See* Smania addosso, 1963

Eye of the Needle, 1981 (Sutherland 3, Rozsa 4)

Eye of the Night, 1916 (Gilbert 3, Sullivan 4)

Eye of the Spider. *See* Occhio del ragno, 1971

Eye on Emily, 1964 (Kanin 4)

Eye That Never Sleeps, 1912 (Bushman 3)

Eye Witness. *See* Your Witness, 1950

Eyes. *See* Pittsburgh Documents, 1971

Eyes in the Night, 1942 (Zinnemann 2, Reed 3, Schary 4)

Eyes of a Stranger, 1981 (Savini 4)

Eyes of Charles Sand, 1972 (Bennett 3)

Eyes of God, 1913 (Weber 2)

Eyes of Hell. *See* Mask, 1961

Eyes of Hollywood, 1949 (Ladd 3)

Eyes of Laura Mars, 1978 (Carpenter 2, Dunaway 3)

Eyes of Mystery, 1918 (Browning 2)

Eyes of Texas, 1948 (Rogers 3)

Eyes of the Forest, 1923 (Mix 3, Fox 4)

Eyes of the Mummy. *See* Augen der Mumie Ma, 1918

Eyes of the Totem, 1926 (Van Dyke 2)

Eyes of the Underworld, 1943 (Salter 4)

Eyes of the World, 1930 (King 2)

Eyes of Youth, 1919 (Valentino 3, Edeson 4)

Eyes That Could Not Close, 1913 (Guy 2)

Eyes That See Not, 1912 (Porter 2)

Eyes, The Mouth. *See* Occhi, la bocca, 1983

Eyes Without a Face. *See* **Yeux sans visage, 1959**

Eyewash, 1959 (Breer 4)

Eyewitness, 1956 (Box 4, Rank 4)

Eyewitness, 1980 (Yates 2, Hurt 3, Weaver 3)

Eygalières, commune de France, 1957 (Braunberger 4)

F comme Fairbanks, 1976 (Piccoli 3)
F for Fake, 1975 (Bogdanovich 2, Welles 2, Cotten 3, Harvey 3, Legrand 4)
F. Murray Abraham: Man and Actor, 1987 (Jireš 2)
F. Scott Fitzgerald and the Last of the Belles, 1974 (Sarandon 3)
F. Scott Fitzgerald in Hollywood, 1976 (Weld 3)
F.I.S.T., 1978 (Jewison 2, Stallone 3, Steiger 3, Kovacs 4)
F.P. 1. *See* F.P. 1 antwortet nicht, 1932
F.P. 1 antwortet nicht, 1932 (Albers 3, Boyer 3, Brasseur 3, Lorre 3, Veidt 3, Pommer 4, Reisch 4, Siodmak 4)
F.P. 1 Does Not Answer. *See* F.P. 1 antwortet nicht, 1932
F.P. 1 Does Not Reply. *See* F.P. 1 antwortet nicht, 1933
F.P. 1 Doesn't Answer. *See* F.P. 1 antwortet nicht, 1932
F.P. 1 ne répond plus, *See* F.P. 1 antwortet nicht, 1932
F.T.A. *See* FTA Show, 1972
Faasla, 1974 (Abbas 4)
Fabbrica del Duomo, 1948 (Risi 2)
Fabiola, 1948 (Blasetti 2, Cervi 3, Morgan 3, Simon 3, Cecchi D'Amico 4, Zavattini 4)
Fabiola, 1960 (Rey 3)
Fable of Elvira and Farina and the Meal Ticket, 1915 (Swanson 3)
Fable of Napoleon and the Bumpkin, 1914 (Beery 3)
Fable of the Brash Drummer and the Nectarine, 1914 (Beery 3)
Fable of the Bush League Lover Who Failed to Qualify, 1914 (Beery 3, Bushman 3)
Fable of the Business Boy and the Droppers-in, 1914 (Beery 3)
Fable of the Coming Champion Who Was Delayed, 1914 (Beery 3)
Fable of the Roystering Blades, 1915 (Beery 3)
Fabrication du ciment artificiel, 1924 (Grémillon 2)
Fabrication du fil, 1924 (Grémillon 2)
Fabrication industrielle des comrimés et dragées, 1952 (Colpi 4)
Fabrication industrielle des solutés injectables, 1951 (Colpi 4)
Fabror Johannes ankomst till Stockholm, 1912 (Jaenzon 4)
Fabuleuse Aventure de Marco Polo. *See* Echiquier de Dieu, 1964
Fabuleuse Aventure de Marco Polo, 1965 (Quinn 3, Sharif 3, Rappeneau 4, Smith 4)

Fabulous Adventures of the Legendary Baron Munchausen, 1979 (Legrand 4)
Fabulous Baker Boys, 1989 (Bridges 3, Pfeiffer 3, Ballhaus 4)
Fabulous Joe, 1947 (Daniels 3, Roach 4)
Fabulous World of Jules Verne. *See* Vynález zkásy, 1958
Faccia a faccia, 1967 (Volonté 3, Morricone 4)
Face. *See* Ansiktet, 1958
Face, 1961 (Kuri 4)
Face, 1965 (Warhol 2)
Face. *See* Tvár, 1973
Face at the Window, 1910 (Griffith 2, Walthall 3, Bitzer 4)
Face at the Window, 1912 (Guy 2)
Face at the Window, 1915 (Mix 3)
Face au destin, 1941 (Berry 3)
Face Behind the Mask, 1941 (Florey 2, Lorre 3, Cohn 4, Planer 4)
Face Between, 1922 (Coffee 4)
Face in the Crowd, 1957 (Kazan 2, Neilan 2, Matthau 3, Neal 3, Remick 3, Stradling 4, Sylbert 4)
Face in the Dark, 1918 (Marsh 3)
Face in the Fog, 1922 (Barrymore 3)
Face in the Fog, 1936 (Katzman 4)
Face in the Rain, 1963 (Fields 4, Wexler 4)
Face in the Sky, 1933 (Tracy 3, Friedhofer 4, Garmes 4)
Face of a Fugitive, 1959 (Coburn 3, MacMurray 3, Goldsmith 4)
Face of Another, *See* Tanin no kao, 1966
Face of Britain, 1935 (Rotha 2)
Face of Eve, 1968 (Lee 3, Lom 3)
Face of Fu Manchu, 1965 (Lee 3)
Face of Marble, 1946 (Carradine 3)
Face of Scotland, 1938 (Grierson 2, Wright 2)
Face of Terror. *See* Cara del terror, 1962
Face of the Enemy. *See* Fashizm budet razbit, 1941
Face Off, 1977 (Emshwiller 2)
Face on the Barroom Floor, 1908 (Porter 2)
Face on the Barroom Floor, 1914 (Sennett 2)
Face on the Barroom Floor, 1923 (Ford 2, Walthall 3, Fox 4)
Face on the Ceiling, 1915 (Ince 4)
Face That Launched a Thousand Ships. *See* Eterna femmina, 1954
Face the Camera, 1922 (Roach 4)
Face the Music, 1954 (Carreras 4)
Face to Face, 1952 (Mason 3, Preston 3, Friedhofer 4, Struss 4)
Face to Face. *See* Faccia a faccia, 1967
Face to Face. *See* Twarza w twarz, 1968
Face to Face. *See* Ansikte mot Ansikte, 1976

Face to Face, 1990 (Schifrin 4)
Face Value, 1927 (Florey 2)
Faceless Man. *See* Counterfeit Killer, 1968
Faces, 1968 (Cassavetes 2, Schroeter 2, Rowlands 3)
Faces in the Dark, 1960 (Zetterling 2, Theodorakis 4)
Faces of America, 1965 (Emshwiller 2)
Faces of Love, *See* Repérages, 1977
Facing the Music, 1933 (Launder and Gilliat 2)
Facteur trop ferré, 1907 (Feuillade 2, Gaumont 4)
Faction, 1902 (Guy 2)
Factory Front, 1940 (Cavalcanti 2)
Factory Girl, 1909 (Olcott 2)
Facts in the Case of M. Valdemar. *See* Due occhi diabolici, 1990
Facts of Life, 1960 (Ball 3, Beavers 3, Hope 3, Bass 4, Frank 4, Head 4, Lang 4, Mercer 4)
Fada, 1932 (Burel 4)
Fade In, 1968 (Reynolds 3, Fraker 4)
Fade to Black, 1980 (Rourke 3)
Fadeaway, 1926 (Fleischer 4)
Faded Lilies, 1909 (Griffith 2, Pickford 3, Bitzer 4)
Fader og Søn, 1911 (Psilander 3)
Fadern, 1969 (Sjöberg 2)
Faderulla, ur Göteborgssystemet I . . . , 1910 (Magnusson 4)
Fádní odpoledne, 1965 (Kučera 4)
Fahlstrom, 1980 (Ruiz 2)
Fahrendes Volk, 1921 (Dreier 4)
Fahrendes Volk, 1938 (Albers 3, Rosay 3)
Fahrenheit 451, 1966 (Truffaut 2, Christie 3, Cusack 3, Herrmann 4)
Fahrt ins Abenteuer, 1926 (Courant 4)
Fahrt ins Blaue, 1919 (Kräly 4)
Fahrt ins Glück, 1948 (Von Harbou 4)
Fai in fretta ad ucidermi . . . ho Freddo!, 1965 (Vitti 3)
Faibles femmes, 1959 (Delon 3)
Fail Safe, 1964 (Lumet 2, Fonda 3, Matthau 3, Rosenblum 4)
Failing of Raymond, 1971 (Henreid 3, Wyman 3)
Faille, 1975 (Piccoli 3, Carrière 4, Morricone 4)
Failure, 1911 (Griffith 2, Crisp 3, Bitzer 4)
Failure's Song is Sad. *See* Haizan no uta wa kanashi, 1976
Faim de loup, 1932 (Brasseur 3)
Faim du monde, 1958 (Grimault 4, Prévert 4)
Faim . . . L'occasion . . . L'herbe tendre, 1904 (Guy 2)
Faint Heart, 1922 (La Cava 2)

Faint Perfume, 1925 (Powell 3)
Fainting Lover, 1931 (Sennett 2)
Fair and Muddy, 1928 (Roach 4)
Fair and Worm-er, 1946 (Blanc 4, Jones 4, Stalling 4)
Fair Co-ed, 1927 (Tourneur 2, Wood 2, Davies 3, McCrea 3, Gibbons 4, Gillespie 4, Seitz 4)
Fair Dentist, 1911 (Pickford 3, Gaudio 4)
Fair Exchange, 1909 (Griffith 2, Bitzer 4)
Fair Exchange. See Getting Acquainted, 1914
Fair Lady, 1922 (Stradling 4)
Fair Sussex, 1913 (Pearson 2)
Fair Today, 1941 (Lantz 4)
Fair Week, 1922 (Roach 4)
Fair Wind to Java, 1953 (MacMurray 3, McLaglen 3, Young 4)
Fairfax Avenue, 1984 (Lewis 2)
Fair-Haired Hare, 1951 (Blanc 4, Freleng 4, Stalling 4)
Faisons le point sur les Spoutniks, 1957 (Gélin 3)
Faisons un rêve, 1936 (Guitry 2, Arletty 3, Raimu 3, Simon 3)
Faites soigner vos égratignures, 1949 (Decaë 4)
Faites vos jeux, mesdames. See Feu à volonte, 1965
Faith Healer, 1921 (Menjou 3)
Faith, Hope and Hogan, 1953 (Crosby 3)
Faithful, 1910 (Griffith 2, Bitzer 4)
Faithful Heart, 1932 (Saville 2, Marshall 3, Balcon 4, Biro 4, Vetchinsky 4)
Faithful Hearts. See Faithful Heart, 1932
Faithful in My Fashion, 1946 (Reed 3, Irene 4)
Faithful Indian, 1911 (Anderson 3)
Faithful Narrative of the Capture, Sufferings, and Miraculous Escape of Eliza Fraser. See Eliza Fraser, 1976
Faithful Servant, 1913 (Costello 3)
Faithful Taxicab, 1913 (Sennett 2)
Faithfully in My Fashion, 1946 (Horton 3)
Faithless, 1932 (Montgomery 3, Adrian 4, Wilson 4)
Faits d'hiver, 1951 (Decaë 4)
Faits divers, 1923 (Autant-Lara 2, Artaud 3, Honegger 4)
Faits divers à Paris, 1949 (Fradetal 4)
Fakers. See Hell's Bloody Devils, 1970
Faking with Society. See Caught in a Cabaret, 1914
Fakira, 1976 (Azmi 3)
Fakir du Grand Hotel, 1933 (Burel 4)
Fala Brasilia, 1965 (Pereira Dos Santos 2)
Falak, 1968 (Theodorakis 4)
Falbalas, 1945 (Presle 3, Douy 4)
Falchivi koupon, 1912 (Mozhukin 3)
Falcon, 1981 (Mimica 4)
Falcon and the Co-Eds, 1943 (Malone 3, Hunt 4)
Falcon and the Snowman, 1985 (Schlesinger 2)
Falcon in Hollywood, 1944 (Musuraca 4)
Falcon in San Francisco, 1945 (Lewis 2, Miller 4)
Falcon Strikes Back, 1943 (Dmytryk 2)
Falcon Takes Over, 1942 (Bond 3, Sanders 3, Chandler 4)
Falcon's Adventure, 1946 (D'Agostino 4)
Falcon's Brother, 1942 (Sanders 3, Metty 4)
Falcon's Gold, 1982 (Schifrin 4)
Falena, 1916 (Gallone 2)

Falešná kočička, 1926 (Heller 4)
Fall. See Cáida, 1959
Fall des Generalstabsoberst Redl, 1931 (Dagover 3)
Fall Franza, 1986 (Mueller-Stahl 3)
Fall Guy, 1921 (Laurel and Hardy 3)
Fall Guy, 1930 (Plunkett 4)
Fall Guy, 1947 (Mirisch 4)
Fall In, 1942 (Roach 4)
Fall Lena Christ, 1968 (Müller 4)
Fall Molander, 1944 (Pabst 2, Wegener 3)
Fall of Berlin, See Padeniye Berlina, 1949
Fall of Eve, 1929 (Emerson 4, Loos 4)
Fall of Montezuma, 1912 (Bushman 3)
Fall of the House of Usher. See House of Usher, 1960
Fall of the House of Usher. See Zanik domu Usheru, 1981
Fall of the Rebel Angels. See Caduta degli angeli ribelli, 1981
Fall of the Roman Empire, 1964 (Mann 2, Guinness 3, Loren 3, Mason 3, Quayle 3, Sharif 3, Krasker 4, Tiomkin 4)
Fall of the Romanoffs, 1917 (Brenon 2, Hunt 4)
Fall of the Romanov Dynasty. See Padenye dinastii romanovykh, 1927
Fall Rainer, 1942 (Wagner 4)
Fall Rosentopf, 1918 (Lubitsch 2)
Fall Tokeramo. See Polizeiakte 909, 1933
Falle. See Salon Dora Green, 1933
Fällen, 1975 (Watkins 2)
Fallen Angel, 1945 (Preminger 2, Andrews 3, Carradine 3, Darnell 3, Faye 3, La Shelle 4, Raksin 4, Wheeler 4)
Fallen Arches, 1933 (Roach 4)
Fallen Hero, 1913 (Browning 2, Loos 4)
Fallen Idol, 1919 (Ruttenberg 4)
Fallen Idol, 1948 (Reed 2, Hawkins 3, Morgan 3, Richardson 3, Alwyn 4, Greene 4, Korda, A. 4, Korda, V. 4, Périnal 4)
Fallen Sparrow, 1943 (Garfield 3, O'Hara 3, Musuraca 4, Polglase 4)
Fallen Star, 1916 (Hepworth 2)
Fallende Stern, 1950 (Krauss 3)
Fallible Fable, 1962 (Hanna and Barbera 4)
Falling for You, 1933 (Launder and Gilliat 2, Stevenson 2, Balcon 4, Vetchinsky 4)
Falling Hare, 1943 (Blanc 4, Clampett 4, Stalling 4)
Falling in Love, 1984 (De Niro 3, Streep 3)
Falling in Love Again, 1980 (Gould 3, Pfeiffer 3, York 3, Legrand 4)
Falling Leaves, 1912 (Guy 2)
Falls, 1980 (Greenaway 2)
Falsche Bewegung, 1974 (Wenders 2, Kinski 3, Schygulla 3, Vogler 3, Müller 4)
Falsche Dimitry, 1922 (Albers 3)
Falsche Ehemann, 1931 (Wilder 2, Herlth 4, Hoffmann 4, Röhrig 4)
Falsche Feldmarschall, 1930 (Heller 4)
Falschspieler, 1920 (Albers 3)
Fälschung, 1981 (Ganz 3, Schygulla 3, Carrière 4, Jarre 4)
Falschung, 1981 (Schlöndorff 2, Skolimowski 2)
False Alarm, 1923 (Fleischer 4)
False Alarms, 1936 (Three Stooges 3)
False Bride, 1914 (Lawrence 3)

False Colors, 1914 (Weber 2, Bosworth 3, Marion 4)
False Colors, 1943 (Mitchum 3, Harlan 4)
False Faces, 1919 (Chaney 3, Walthall 3)
False Faces, 1932 (McCord 4)
False Faces, 1943 (Siodmak 4)
False Hare, 1964 (Blanc 4, McKimson 4)
False Identity, 1990 (Bujold 3)
False Idol. See False Madonna, 1932
False Impressions, 1932 (Sennett 2)
False Kisses, 1921 (Laemmle 4)
False Kitten. See Falešná kočička, 1926
False Madonna, 1932 (Francis 3)
False Millionaire. See Pour mon coeur et ses millions, 1931
False Note. See Falchivi koupon, 1912
False Road, 1920 (Niblo 2, Barnes 4, Sullivan 4)
False Step. See Schritt vom Wege, 1939
False Suspicion, 1911 (Bushman 3)
False Witness. See Transient Lady, 1935
False Witness. See Arkansas Judge, 1941
Falsely Accused, 1905 (Hepworth 2)
Falsely Accused, 1907 (Bitzer 4)
Falstaff, 1913 (Rosay 3)
Falstaff. See **Chimes at Midnight, 1966**
Fama, 1921 (Bertini 3)
Famalicão, 1940 (Oliveira 2)
Fame, 1936 (Wilcox 2)
Fame. See Sláva, 1960
Fame, 1980 (Parker 2)
Fame and Fortune, 1918 (Mix 3)
Fame Is the Name of the Game, 1966 (Duvall 3, Wagner 3)
Fame Is the Spur, 1947 (Boulting 2, Rank 4)
Fame Street, 1932 (Walthall 3)
Famiglia, 1987 (Gassman 3, Noiret 3)
Famiglia impossible, 1940 (Zavattini 4)
Famiglia Passaguai, 1951 (Fabrizi 3)
Famiglia Passaguai fa fortuna, 1952 (Fabrizi 3)
Familia Dressel, 1935 (De Fuentes 2)
Familia Pichilin, 1978 (Solanas 2)
Familia provisional, 1955 (García Berlanga 2)
Familiar, 1973 (Solanas 2)
Familie Buchholz, 1944 (Fröhlich 3, Porten 3)
Familie Raffke, 1923 (Albers 3)
Familie Schimecl, 1926 (Tschechowa 3)
Familientag im Hause Prellstein, 1927 (Courant 4)
Familjens hemlighet, 1936 (Molander 2)
Familjens traditioner, 1920 (Magnusson 4)
Famille duraton, 1939 (Berry 3)
Famille Pont-Biquet, 1935 (Christian-Jaque 2)
Family. See Città violenta, 1970
Family. See Kareinaru Ichizoku, 1974
Family, 1976 (Kovacs 4)
Family. See Famiglia, 1987
Family Affair, 1917 (Bray 4)
Family Affair, 1937 (Barrymore 3, Rooney 3, Mayer 4)
Family Affair, See Life with the Lyons, 1954
Family Affair, 1955 (Kaufman 4)
Family Business, 1984 (Akerman 2)
Family Business, 1985 (Costa-Gavras 2)
Family Business, 1989 (Lumet 2, Connery 3, Hoffman 3)
Family Circus, 1951 (Bosustow 4)
Family Diary. See Cronaca familiare, 1962
Family Doctor, 1975 (Menges 4)
Family Entrance, 1924 (Roach 4)

Family Entrance, 1925 (McCarey 2)
Family Feud, 1943 (Darwell 3)
Family Focus, 1975 (Emshwiller 2)
Family Group, 1928 (Roach 4)
Family Home. *See* His Trysting Place, 1914
Family Honeymoon, 1948 (Colbert 3, MacMurray 3, McDaniel 3, Daniels 4, Orry-Kelly 4)
Family Honor, 1920 (Vidor 2)
Family Jewels, 1965 (Lewis 2, Baxter 3, Head 4)
Family Life. *See* Zycie rodzinne, 1970
Family Life, 1971 (Loach 2)
Family Mixup, 1912 (Sennett 2)
Family Next Door, 1939 (Krasner 4)
Family of Women. *See* Jokei kazoku, 1963
Family Plot, 1976 (Hitchcock 2, Black 3, Dern 3, Bumstead 4, Head 4, Williams 4)
Family Portrait, 1950 (Jennings 2, Dalrymple 4)
Family Reunion, 1981 (Davis 3)
Family Rico, 1972 (Mineo 3)
Family Secret, 1924 (Laemmle 4)
Family Secret. *See* Familjens hemlighet, 1936
Family Secret, 1951 (Cobb 3, Duning 4, Guffey 4)
Family Secrets, 1979 (Blondell 3)
Family Swedenhielms. *See* Swedenhielms, 1935
Family Tree, 1948 (Dunning 4)
Family Troubles, 1932 (Stevens 2)
Family Upside Down, 1978 (Astaire 3, Ames 4, Biroc 4, Hunter 4, Mancini 4)
Family Upstairs, 1926 (Fox 4)
Family Way, 1966 (Boulting 2, Mills 3)
Family without a Dinner Table. *See* Shokutaku no nai ie, 1985
Family's Honor, 1913 (Ingram 2)
Family's Situation. *See* Kazoku no jijo, 1962
Famine, 1915 (Hayakawa 3)
Famous All Over Town, 1988 (Demme 2)
Famous Box Trick. *See* Illusions fantasmagoriques, 1898
Famous Escape, 1908 (Bitzer 4)
Famous Ferguson Case, 1932 (Bacon 2, Blondell 3)
Famous Mrs. Fair, 1923 (Niblo 2, Marion 4, Mayer 4)
Famous Soviet Heroes. *See* Slava Sovetskim Geroiniam, 1938
Famous Sword Bijomaru. *See* Meito Bijomaru, 1945
FAMU Newsreel. *See* Zurnál FAMU, 1961
Fan, 1949 (Carroll 3, Sanders 3, La Shelle 4, LeMaire 4, Reisch 4, Wheeler 4)
Fan, 1981 (Bacall 3, Garner 3, Donaggio 4, Hamlisch 4, Smith 4)
Fanatic, 1968 (Sutherland 3, Carreras 4)
Fanatiques, 1957 (Fresnay 3, Burel 4)
Fanatisme, 1934 (Negri 3)
Fanchon, the Cricket, 1915 (Pickford 3)
Fanciulla di Amalfi, 1921 (Bertini 3)
Fanciulla di portici, 1940 (Amidei 4, Delli Colli 4)
Fanciulla, il poeta e la laguna, 1920 (Gallone 2)
Fanciulle di lusso, 1952 (Flaiano 4, Rota 4)
Fancy Answers, 1941 (Gardner 3)
Fancy Baggage, 1929 (Loy 3)
Fancy Pants, 1950 (Ball 3, Hope 3, Dreier 4, Head 4, Lang 4)
Fandango, 1985 (Costner 3)

Fanfan la Tulipe, 1951 (Lollobrigida 3, Philipe 3, Jeanson 4, Matras 4)
Fanfan the Tulip. *See* Fanfan la Tulipe, 1951
Fanfare, 1958 (Haanstra 2)
Fanfare d'amour, 1935 (Fradetal 4)
Fangens Søn, 1914 (Psilander 3)
Fangerfamilie i Thuledistriktet, 1967 (Roos 2)
Fangio, 1971 (Alcott 4)
Fango sulla metropoli, 1965 (Giannini 3)
Fangs of Destiny, 1927 (Laemmle 4)
Fangs of the Wild, 1928 (Berman 4)
Fangschuss, 1976 (Von Trotta 2)
Fanny, 1932 (Pagnol 2, Fresnay 3, Raimu 3, Junge 4, Korda 4)
Fanny, 1961 (Boyer 3, Caron 3, Chevalier 3, Cardiff 4, Epstein 4, Reynolds 4)
Fanny and Alexander *See* **Fanny och Alexander, 1982**
Fanny By Gaslight, 1944 (Granger 3, Mason 3, Rank 4)
Fanny Foley Herself. *See* Top of the Bill, 1931 (Steiner 4, Wilson 4)
Fanny Hill, 1964 (Hopkins 3)
Fanny Hill, 1983 (Reed 3, Winters 3)
Fanny Hill: Memoirs of a Woman of Pleasure. *See* Fanny Hill, 1964
Fanny in the Lion's Den, 1933 (Terry 4)
Fanny och Alexander, 1982 (Andersson 3, Björnstrand 3, Josephson 3, Nykvist 4)
Fanny's Conspiracy, 1913 (Talmadge 3)
Fanny's Wedding Day, 1933 (Terry 4)
Fanrik Stals Sagner, 1909 (Magnusson 4)
Fan's Note, 1972 (Meredith 3)
Fantaisie d'un jour, 1954 (Kosma 4)
Fantaisie sur quatre cordes, 1957 (Braunberger 4)
Fantaisies d'Agenor maltrace, 1911 (Cohl 4)
Fantaisies truquées, 1915 (Cohl 4)
Fantasia, 1940 (Disney 4, Hubley 4)
Fantasia chez les ploucs, 1971 (Delon 3, Braunberger 4)
Fantasia sottomarina, 1939 (Rossellini 2)
Fantasma d'amore, 1981 (Mastroianni 3, Schneider 3)
Fantasma del convento, 1934 (De Fuentes 2)
Fantasmagorie, 1908 (Cohl 4)
Fantasmi a Roma, 1961 (Gassman 3, Mastroianni 3, Amidei 4, Cristaldi 4, Flaiano 4, Rota 4, Rotunno 4)
Fantastic Voyage, 1966 (Kennedy 3, O'Brien 3, Pleasence 3, Welch 3, Laszlo 4, Rosenman 4, Smith 4)
Fantastica, 1980 (Reggiani 3)
Fantasy for Piano, 1972 (Kuri 4)
Fanteuil 47, 1937 (Rosay 3)
Fantoche cherche un logement. *See* Maison du Fantoche, 1916
Fantômas, 1913 (Feuillade 2, Gaumont 4)
Fantômas, 1931 (Allégret 2, Fejos 2, Modot 3, Braunberger 4)
Fantômas, 1947 (Signoret 3)
Fantômas, 1964 (Marais 3)
Fantômas contre Fantômas, 1914 (Feuillade 2, Gaumont 4)
Fantômas contre Scotland Yard, 1967 (Marais 3, Douy 4)
Fantômas se déchaine, 1965 (Marais 3, Douy 4)
Fantôme de bonheur, 1929 (Modot 3)
Fantôme de la liberté, 1974 (Piccoli 3, Vitti 3, Carrière 4)
Fantôme du Moulin Rouge, 1924 (Clair 2)

Fantômes du Chapelier, 1982 (Chabrol 2, Rabier 4)
Fantorro, le dernier justicier, 1972 (Lenica 4)
Fantorro, the Last Just Man. *See* Fantorro, le dernier justicier, 1972
Far Call, 1929 (Dwan 2, Scott 3, Fox 4, Miller 4, Rosson 4)
Far Country, 1955 (Mann 2, Brennan 3, Stewart 3, Chase 4, Daniels 4, Salter 4)
Far Cry, 1926 (Bosworth 3, Sweet 3)
Far Cry, 1959 (Finch 3)
Far East. *See* Volochayevskiye dni, 1937
Far from Dallas, 1972 (Gélin 3)
Far from the Madding Crowd, 1967 (Roeg 2, Schlesinger 2, Bates 3, Christie 3, Finch 3, Stamp 3, Raphael 4)
Far From Vietnam. *See* Loin du Vietnam, 1967
Far Frontier, 1948 (Rogers 3)
Far Horizons, 1955 (Heston 3, MacMurray 3, Reed 3, Canutt 4, Head 4, Maté 4, Salter 4)
Får jag låna din fru?, 1959 (Nykvist 4)
Far North, 1988 (Lange 3, Shepard 4)
Far Out West, 1967 (Sheridan 3)
Far Pavilions, 1984 (Lee 3, Sharif 3)
Far Shore, 1976 (Wieland 2)
Far West Story, *See* Banda J & S, 1972
Faraar, 1975 (Bachchan 3)
Farandole, 1945 (Cayatte 2, Blier 3, Auric 4, Jeanson 4)
Faraon, 1965 (Konwicki 4)
Farar, 1955 (Anand 3, Biswas 4)
Faráŕuv konec, 1968 (Brejchová 3, Brodský 3)
Faraway Love, 1947 (Zhao 3)
Farces de cuisinière, 1902 (Guy 2)
Farces de Jocko, 1897 (Guy 2)
Farceur, 1961 (Aimée 3, Cassel 3, Delerue 4, Saulnier 4)
Fardier, 1949 (Gaumont 4)
Farenheit 451, 1966 (Roeg 2, Werner 3)
Farewell. *See* Proshchanie, 1981
Farewell Again, 1937 (Newton 3, Howe 4, Korda 4, Pommer 4)
Farewell Friend. *See* Adieu l'ami, 1968
Farewell My Lovely. *See* Murder, My Sweet, 1944
Farewell My Lovely, 1975 (Mitchum 3, Stallone 3, Stanton 3, Alonzo 4, Chandler 4, Tavoularis 4, Westmore Family 4)
Farewell Party. *See* Morals for Women, 1931
Farewell To Arms, 1932 (Borzage 2, Cooper 3, Menjou 3, Banton 4, Dreier 4, Head 4, Lang 4, Glazer 4, Zukor 4)
Farewell To Arms, 1957 (De Sica 2, Huston 2, Vidor 2, Homolka 3, Hudson 3, Jones 3, McCambridge 3, Sordi 3, Dreier 4, Hecht 4, Junge 4, Morris 4, Selznick 4, Wheeler 4)
Farewell to Childhood, 1950 (Peries 2)
Farewell to the King, 1989 (Nolte 3, Edlund 4)
Fargo. *See* Wild Seed, 1964
Farib, 1953 (Biswas 4)
Farina del diavolo, 1975 (Brazzi 3)
Farinet, oder das falsche Geld, 1939 (Barrault 3, Honegger 4)
Farinet, ou la fausse monnaie. *See* Farinet, oder das falsche Geld, 1939
Farlig vår, 1947 (Sjöström 2)
Farlige Alder, 1911 (Psilander 3)
Farm Frolics, 1941 (Blanc 4, Clampett 4)

Farm of the Year. *See* Miles from Home, 1988

Farm of Tomorrow, 1954 (Avery 4)

Farmer, 1931 (Lantz 4)

Farmer Alfalfa series, 1932 (Terry 4)

Farmer aux Texas, 1925 (Leni 2)

Farmer: Feast or Famine, 1965 (Van Dyke 2)

Farmer for a Day, 1943 (Bruckman 4)

Farmer in the Dell, 1936 (Ball 3, Musuraca 4)

Farmer Takes a Wife, 1935 (Fleming 2, Fonda 3, Gaynor 3, Canutt 4, Reynolds 4)

Farmer Takes a Wife, 1953 (Grable 3, Ritter 3, Cole 4, LeMaire 4, Wheeler 4)

Farmer's Daughter, 1913 (Bushman 3)

Farmer's Daughter, 1928 (August 4, Fox 4)

Farmer's Daughter, 1940 (Daves 2, Dreier 4, Head 4)

Farmer's Daughter, 1947 (Barrymore 3, Cotten 3, Young 3, Krasner 4, Schary 4)

Farmers of Fermathe, 1960 (Dickinson 2)

Farmer's Wife, 1928 (Hitchcock 2)

Farming Fools, 1936 (Lantz 4)

Faró da padre, 1974 (Papas 3)

Farrebique, 1947 (Fradetal 4)

Far-West, 1973 (Piccoli 3)

Faschingsprinz, 1928 (Reisch 4)

Faschingzauber, 1927 (Reisch 4)

Fascinante Amazônie, 1964 (Colpi 4)

Fascinating Bachelor, 1911 (Lawrence 3)

Fascinating Mrs. Frances, 1909 (Griffith 2, Bitzer 4)

Fascinating Youth, 1926 (Wood 2, Menjou 3)

Fascination, 1922 (Goulding 2)

Fascination, 1931 (Carroll 3, Oberon 3)

Fascination of the Fleur de Lis, 1915 (Chaney 3)

Fascism Will Be Destroyed. *See* Fashizm budet razbit, 1941

Fascist. *See* Federale, 1961

Fashion, 1960 (Kuri 4)

Fashion Follies of 1934. *See* Fashions of 1934, 1934

Fashions for Men. *See* Fine Clothes, 1925

Fashions for Women, 1927 (Arzner 2, Furthman 4, Mankiewicz 4)

Fashions in Love, 1929 (Menjou 3, Cronjager 4)

Fashions of 1934, 1934 (Berkeley 2, Dieterle 2, Darwell 3, Davis 3, Powell 3, Blanke 4, Orry-Kelly 4)

Fashizm budet razbit, 1941 (Shub 2)

Faslah, 1975 (Azmi 3)

Fast and Furious, 1927 (Laemmle 4)

Fast and Furious, 1939 (Berkeley 2)

Fast and Furry-ous, 1949 (Blanc 4, Jones 4, Maltese 4, Stalling 4)

Fast and Loose, 1930 (Sturges 2, Hopkins 3, Lombard 3, Banton 4)

Fast and Loose, 1939 (Montgomery 3, Russell 3, Folsey 4)

Fast and Loose, 1954 (Kendall 3, Rank 4)

Fast and Sexy, 1958 (Rotunno 4)

Fast and the Furious, 1954 (Corman 2, Crosby 4)

Fast Black, 1924 (Roach 4)

Fast Buck Duck, 1963 (Blanc 4, McKimson 4)

Fast Companions, 1932 (O'Sullivan 3, Rooney 3, Edeson 4)

Fast Company, 1918 (Chaney 3, Young 4)

Fast Company, 1924 (Roach 4)

Fast Company, 1929 (Mankiewicz 2, Cronjager 4, Selznick 4)

Fast Company, 1938 (Calhern 3, Douglas 3)

Fast Company, 1953 (Sturges 2, Keel 3)

Fast Company, 1978 (Cronenberg 2)

Fast Drive in the Country: The Heydays of Le Mans, 1976 (Coburn 3)

Fast Forward, 1985 (Poitier 3, Jones 4)

Fast Freight, 1921 (Arbuckle 3)

Fast Lady, 1963 (Christie 3)

Fast Life, 1929 (Young 3)

Fast Mail, 1922 (Menjou 3, Fox 4)

Fast Play. *See* Campus Confession, 1938

Fast Set, 1924 (Menjou 3)

Fast Work, 1930 (Roach 4)

Fast Worker, 1924 (Laemmle 4)

Fast Workers, 1933 (Browning 2, Gilbert 3, Brown 4)

Fasters miljoner, 1934 (Molander 2)

Fastest Guitar Alive, 1967 (Katzman 4)

Fastest Gun Alive, 1956 (Crawford 3, Ford 3, Folsey 4, Plunkett 4, Previn 4)

Fastest with the Mostest, 1960 (Blanc 4, Jones 4)

Fästman i taget, 1952 (Björnstrand 3)

Fästmö uthyres, 1951 (Molander 2, Björnstrand 3, Dahlbeck 3)

Fastnachtsbeichte, 1960 (Dieterle 2)

Fast-Walking, 1982 (Schifrin 4)

Fat and Fickle, 1917 (Laurel and Hardy 3)

Fat City, 1972 (Huston 2, Bridges 3, Booth 4, Hall 4, Hamlisch 4, Jeakins , 4, Stark 4, Sylbert 4)

Fat Man, 1951 (Hudson 3)

Fat Man and Little Boy, 1989 (Newman 3, Morricone 4, Zsigmond 4)

Fat Spy, 1966 (Mansfield 3)

Fat Wives for Thin, 1930 (Sennett 2)

Fata Morgana, 1970 (Herzog 2)

Fatal Attraction, 1987 (Close 3, Douglas 3, Jarre 4)

Fatal Beauty, 1988 (Goldberg 3)

Fatal Chocolate, 1911 (Sennett 2, Normand 3)

Fatal Desire. *See* Cavalleria Rusticana, 1953

Fatal Dress Suit, 1914 (Loos 4)

Fatal Finger Prints, 1915 (Loos 4)

Fatal Flirtation, 1914 (Sennett 2)

Fatal Glass of Beer, 1933 (Sennett 2, Fields 3, Bruckman 4)

Fatal High, 1914 (Sennett 2)

Fatal Hour, 1908 (Griffith 2)

Fatal Hour, 1937 (Pearson 2, Havelock-Allan 4)

Fatal Hour, 1940 (Karloff 3)

Fatal Lady, 1936 (Pidgeon 3, Shamroy 4, Wanger 4, Young 4)

Fatal Lie. *See* Fru Potifar, 1911

Fatal Mallet, 1914 (Sennett 2, Normand 3)

Fatal Mirror, 1911 (Dwam 2)

Fatal Passions, 1921 (Lang 2)

Fatal Ring, 1917 (White 3)

Fatal Sweet Tooth, 1914 (Sennett 2)

Fatal Taxicab, 1913 (Arbuckle 3, Normand 3)

Fatal Vision, 1984 (Malden 3, Saint 3)

Fatal Warning, 1929 (Karloff 3)

Fatal Wedding, 1913 (Barrymore 3)

Fatalità, 1947 (Amidei 4)

Fate, 1912 (Griffith 2, Barrymore 3, Marsh 3, Bitzer 4)

Fate, 1966 (Monicelli 2, Cardinale 3, Sordi 3, Vitti 3, Welch 3, Cecchi D'Amico 4, Gherardi 4, Guerra 4)

Fate Fashions a Letter, 1913 (Bosworth 3)

Fate Is the Hunter, 1964 (Ford 3, Malone 3, Russell 3, Goldsmith 4, Krasner 4, Smith 4)

Fate largo ai moschettieri, 1953 (Cervi 3)

Fate of a Flirt, 1925 (Lewin 4)

Fate's Fathead, 1934 (Roach 4)

Fate's Funny Frolic, 1911 (Bushman 3)

Fate's Interception, 1912 (Griffith 2, Pickford 3, Bitzer 4)

Fate's Turning, 1910 (Griffith 2, Crisp 3, Bitzer 4)

Father. *See* Apa, 1966

Father. *See* Fadern, 1969

Father, 1990 (Von Sydow 3)

Father and Son. *See* Otets i syn, 1917

Father and the Boys, 1915 (Chaney 3)

Father Bom. *See* Pappa Bom, 1949

Father Brown, 1954 (Finch 3, Greenwood 3, Guinness 3, Auric 4, Mathieson 4)

Father Brown, Detective, 1935 (Lukas 3, Head 4, Sullivan 4, Zukor 4)

Father Buys a Ladder, 1907 (Gaumont 4)

Father Christopher's Prayer. *See* Promessi sposi, 1941

Father Gets in the Game, 1908 (Griffith 2, Bitzer 4)

Father Gets in the Game, 1935 (Sennett 2)

Father Goose, 1964 (Caron 3, Grant 3, Howard 3, Bumstead 4, Fraker 4, Lang 4)

Father Is a Bachelor, 1950 (Holden 3, Guffey 4)

Father Is a Prince, 1940 (McCord 4)

Father Master. *See* Padre padrone, 1977

Father of the Bride, 1950 (Minnelli 2, Bennett 3, Taylor 3, Tracy 3, Alton 4, Berman 4, Deutsch 4, Goodrich 4, Mayer 4, Plunkett 4, Rose 4)

Father Sergius. *See* Otets Sergii, 1918

Father Takes a Wife, 1941 (Menjou 3, Swanson 3)

Father Vojtech. *See* Páter Vojtěch, 1929

Father Was a Fullback, 1949 (Stahl 2, MacMurray 3, O'Hara 3, Ritter 3, Wood 3, Robinson 4)

Fatherhood, 1915 (Bosworth 3)

Fatherland, 1986 (Loach 2, Menges 4)

Fathers and Sons. *See* Padre e figli, 1957

Father's Bride, 1914 (Meredyth 4)

Father's Choice, 1913 (Sennett 2, Normand 3)

Father's Devotion, 1910 (White 3)

Father's Dilemma. *See* Prima comunione, 1950

Father's Doing Fine, 1952 (Attenborough 3)

Father's Favorite, 1911 (Dwan 2)

Father's Flirtation, 1914 (Bunny 3)

Father's Husband, 1913 (Talmadge 3)

Father's Lesson, 1913 (Barrymore 3)

Father's Little Dividend, 1951 (Minnelli 2, Bennett 3, Taylor 3, Tracy 3, Alton 4, Berman 4, Goodrich 4, Rose 4)

Father's New Maid, 1915 (Beery 3)

Father's Son, 1930 (Miller 4)

Father's Wild Game, 1950 (Darwell 3, Struss 4)

Father-Son Falcons. *See* Chichiko-daka, 1956

Fathom, 1967 (Welch 3)

Fatso, 1989 (Bancroft 3)

Fattened for the Market, 1901 (Bitzer 4)

Fatti di gente per bene, 1974 (Deneuve 3, Giannini 3, Morricone 4)

Fatto di sangue fra due uomini per causa di una vedova, 1978 (Mastroianni 3)

Fatty series, 1913–16 (Sennett 2, Arbuckle 3, Normand 3)

Fatty's Fatal Fun, 1915 (Laurel and Hardy 3)

Faubourg Montmartre, 1931 (Artaud 3, Vanel 3)

Faubourg St. Martin, 1985 (Branco 4)

Faun, 1918 (Korda 2, Korda 4)

Fausse alerte, 1940 (Presle 3, Lourié 4)

Fausse Maîtresse, 1942 (Cayatte 2, Darrieux 3, Andrejew 4)

Fausses confidences, 1984 (Presle 3)

Faust, 1900 (Guy 2)

Faust, 1907 (Pathé 4)

Faust, 1926 (Murnau 2, Annenkov 4, Herlth 4, Hoffmann 4, Pommer 4, Röhrig 4)

Faust, 1958 (Švankmajer 4)

Faust, 1960 (Gründgens 3)

Faust, 1970 (Syberberg 2)

Faust 3: Candida Albacore, 1988 (Brakhage 2)

Faust 4, 1989 (Brakhage 2)

Faust and Marguerite, 1900 (Porter 2)

Faust aux enfers, 1903 (Méliès 2)

Faust des Riesen, 1917 (Dupont 2, Porten 3, Messter 4)

Faust: Eine Deutsche Volkssage, 1926 (Dieterle 2, Jannings 3)

Faust et Méphistophélès, 1903 (Guy 2)

FaustFilm: An Opera, 1987 (Brakhage 2)

Faustina, 1957 (Félix 3, Rey 3)

Faustine and the Beautiful Summer. See Faustine et le bel été, 1972

Faustine et le bel été, 1971 (Adjani 3, Huppert 3, Cloquet 4)

Faustrecht der Freiheit, 1975 (Ballhaus 4)

Faust's Other: An Idyll, 1988 (Brakhage 2)

Faut ce qu'il faut, 1940 (Wakhévitch 4)

Faut pas prendre les enfants du Bon Dieu pour des canards sauvages, 1968 (Blier 3, Rosay 3, Audiard 4, D'Eaubonne 4)

Faut réparer Sophie, 1933 (Trauner 4)

Faute de l'Abbé Mouret, 1970 (Fradetal 4)

Faute des autres, 1953 (Guillemot 4)

Faute d'orthographe, 1919 (Feyder 2, Gaumont 4)

Fauteuil 47. See Parkettsessel 47, 1926

Fauteuil 47, 1937 (Raimu 3)

Faut-il les marier?, 1932 (Clouzot 2, Heller 4)

Fauves et Bandits, 1909 (Modot 3)

Faux et usage de faux, 1990 (Noiret 3, Sarde 4)

Faux Magistrat, 1914 (Gaumont 4)

Faux monnayeurs. See Farinet, oder das falsche Geld, 1939

Faux-Cul, 1975 (Blier 3, Dalio 3)

Favoris de la Lune, 1984 (Ioseliani 2)

Favorit der Kaiserin, 1936 (Tschechowa 3)

Favorit der Königin, 1922 (Planer 4)

Favorita, 1952 (Loren 3)

Favorita del Re, 1990 (Adjani 3, Raphael 4)

Favorite. See Favorita, 1952

Favorite Fool, 1915 (Sennett 2)

Favorite Son, 1913 (Ince 4)

Fayette, 1961 (Hawkins 3)

Fayette. See Victory at Yorktown, 1965

Fazil, 1927 (Hawks 2, Fox 4, Miller 4)

FBI Code 98, 1964 (Steiner 4)

FBI Story, 1959 (LeRoy 2, Stewart 3, Biroc 4, Steiner 4)

FDR: The Last Year, 1980 (Sidney 3)

Fe, esperanza y caridad, 1979 (Alcoriza 4)

Fear, 1911 (Dwan 2)

Fear. See Angst, 1954

Fear, 1965 (Ghatak 2)

Fear, 1989 (Mancini 4)

Fear and Desire, 1953 (Kubrick 2, Mazursky 2)

Fear Chamber, 1971 (Karloff 3)

Fear City, 1984 (Brazzi 3)

Fear Eats the Soul. See **Angst essen Seele auf, 1973**

Fear in the Night. See Michael Carmichael, 1972

Fear Market, 1919 (Folsey 4)

Fear No Evil, 1969 (Jourdan 3)

Fear No Evil, 1991 (Scorsese 2, Ballhaus 4)

Fear No More, 1961 (Haller 4)

Fear o' God. See Mountain Eagle, 1926

Fear on Trial, 1975 (Scott 3, Houseman 4)

Fear over the City. See Peur sur la ville, 1975

Fear Strikes Out, 1957 (Mulligan 2, Pakula 2, Malden 3, Perkins 3, Bernstein 4, Head 4)

Fearless Fagan, 1952 (Donen 2, Leigh 3, Lederer 4)

Fearless Frank. See Frank's Greatest Adventure, 1967

Fearless Hyena. See Siukun gwaitsiu, 1979

Fearless Rider, 1928 (Laemmle 4)

Fearless Vampire Killers, or Pardon Me, But Your Teeth Are in My Neck, 1967 (Polanski 3, Godfrey 4, Slocombe 4)

Fearmakers, 1958 (Tourneur 2, Andrews 3)

Feast and Famine, 1914 (Eason 4)

Feast at Zhirmunka. See Pir v Girmunka, 1941

Feast of Life, 1916 (Marion 4)

Feather Bluster, 1958 (Blanc 4, McKimson 4, Stalling 4)

Feather Dusted, 1955 (Blanc 4, McKimson 4)

Feather Finger, 1966 (Blanc 4, McKimson 4)

Feather Gets in the Game, 1908 (Lawrence 3)

Feather in Her Hat, 1935 (Rathbone 3, Walker 4)

Feather in Her Heart, 1935 (Niven 3)

Feather in His Hare, 1948 (Blanc 4, Jones 4)

Feather Letter, 1953 (Xie 2)

Feather Your Nest, 1937 (Formby 3, Dean 4)

Featherweight Champ, 1953 (Terry 4)

Febbre di vivere, 1953 (Mastroianni 3, Cecchi D'Amico 4)

Fede, 1916 (Gallone 2)

Federal Bullets, 1937 (Brown 4)

Federal Man-Hunt, 1938 (Fuller 2)

Federal Operator 99, 1945 (Canutt 4)

Federale, 1961 (Morricone 4)

Federico Fellini's Intervista, 1987 (Rota 4)

Fediha fil Zamalek, 1958 (Sharif 3)

Fedora. See Fehér éjszakák, 1916

Fedora, 1978 (Wilder 2, Ferrer 3, Fonda 3, Holden 3, Diamond 4, Fisher 4, Rozsa 4, Trauner 4)

Fée au printemps, 1906 (Guy 2)

Fée aux choux. See Sage-femme de première classe, 1902

Fee Fie Foes, 1961 (Hanna and Barbera 4)

Feed 'em and Weep, 1929 (Roach 4)

Feed 'em and Weep, 1938 (Roach 4)

Feed the Kitty, 1952 (Blanc 4, Jones 4, Stalling 4)

Feedback, 1965 (Vanderbeek 2)

Feeder de l'est. See Chaleur du foyer, 1955

Feedin' the Kiddie, 1957 (Hanna and Barbera 4)

Feeding Time, 1913 (Sennett 2)

Feel My Pulse, 1928 (La Cava 2, Daniels 3, Powell 3, Hunt 4)

Feel the Heat. See Catch the Heat, 1987

Feenhände, 1912 (Messter 4)

Feet First, 1930 (Lloyd 3, Bruckman 4, Zukor 4)

Feet of Clay, 1924 (De Mille 2)

Feet of Mud, 1924 (Capra 2, Sennett 2)

Feet of Mud, 1980 (Langdon 3)

Fehér éjszakák, 1916 (Korda 2, Bertini 3, Korda 4)

Fehér rózsa, 1919 (Korda 2)

Feind im Blut, 1931 (Ruttman 2)

Feinde, 1940 (Wagner 4)

Feine Gesellschaft—Beschränkte Haftung, 1982 (Bergner 3)

Feldgrau. See Mann aus dem jenseits, 1925

Feldherrenhügel, 1926 (Tschechowa 3)

Felices Pascuas, 1954 (Bardem 2)

Félicie Nanteuil, 1942 (Jourdan 3, Presle 3, Achard 4, Ibert 4)

Felicità perduta, 1946 (Delli Colli 4)

Feline Follies, 1919 (Messmer 4)

Feline Frame-Up, 1954 (Blanc 4, Jones 4, Stalling 4)

Félins, 1964 (Delon 3, Fonda 3, Decaë 4, Schifrin 4)

Felix, 1987 (Von Trotta 2)

Félix Leclerc, troubadour, 1959 (Jutra 2)

Felix on the Job, 1916 (Chaney 3)

Felix the Cat series, 1916–30 (Messmer 4)

Felix the Fox, 1947 (Terry 4)

Fella with the Fiddle, 1937 (Freleng 4, Stalling 4)

Fellini Roma. See Roma, 1972

Fellini Satyricon, 1969 (Cuny 3, Rey 3)

Fellini's Casanova. See Casanova, 1976

Fellow Americans, 1942 (Stewart 3, Kanin 4)

Fellow Citizens, 1920 (Roach 4)

Fellow Countrymen. See Zemliaka, 1975

Fellow Romans, 1921 (Roach 4)

Fellow Voyagers, 1913 (Costello 3)

Fellows Who Ate the Elephant. See Zo o kutta renchu, 1947

Fem raske Piger, 1933 (Holger-Madsen 2)

Female, 1924 (Wood 2)

Female, 1933 (Curtiz 2, Dieterle 2, Brennan 3, Blanke 4, Orry-Kelly 4)

Female. See Femme et le pantin, 1958

Female Animal, 1957 (Lamarr 3, Metty 4, Salter 4)

Female Artillery, 1973 (Lupino 3)

Female Cop, 1914 (Laurel and Hardy 3)

Female Highwayman, 1906 (Selig 4)

Female Instinct. See Snoop Sisters, 1972

Female Jungle, 1956 (Carradine 3, Mansfield 3)

Female of the Species, 1912 (Griffith 2, Webber 2, Pickford 3, Bitzer 4)

Female on the Beach, 1955 (Crawford 3, Lang 4)

Female: 70 Times 7. See Setenta veces siete, 1962

Female Trouble, 1974 (Waters 2)

Females Is Fickle, 1940 (Fleischer 4)

Femeile zilelor noastre, 1958 (Mészáros 2)

Feminine Touch, 1941 (Mankiewicz 2, Van Dyke 2, Ameche 3, Francis 3, Adrian 4, Waxman 4)

Feminine Touch, 1956 (Balcon 4, Rank 4)

Femme à sa fenêtre, 1976 (Noiret 3, Schneider 3)

Femme au volant, 1933 (Maté 4)

Femme aux bottes rouges, 1974 (Deneuve 3, Carrière 4)

Femme chipée, 1934 (Berry 3)

Femme coquette, 1955 (Godard 2)

Femme d'à côté, 1981 (Truffaut 2, Depardieu 3, Delerue 4)

Femme dans la nuit, 1941 (Alekan 4, Kosma 4)

Femme de boulanger, 1938 (Pagnol 2, Raimu 3)

Femme de Jean, 1973 (Delerue 4)

Femme de ma vie, 1986 (Trintignant 3)

Femme de mes amours, 1988 (Guerra 4)

Femme de mon pote, 1982 (Huppert 3)

Femme de nulle part, 1922 (Delluc 2)

Femme de papier, 1989 (Léaud 3)

Femme de Rose Hill, 1989 (Tanner 2)

Femme disparait, 1942 (Rosay 3, D'Eaubonne 4)

Femme douce, 1969 (Bresson 2, Sanda 3, Cloquet 4)

Femme du bout du monde, 1937 (Epstein 2, Vanel 3)

Femme du Ganges, 1974 (Duras 2, Depardieu 3)

Femme d'une nuit, 1930 (L'Herbier 2, Artaud 3, Bertini 3, Burel 4)

Femme écarlate, 1968 (Chabrol 2, Vitti 3, Gégauff 4)

Femme en blanc se révolte. See Nouveau Journal d'une femme en blanc, 1966

Femme en bleu, 1972 (Piccoli 3, Simon 3)

Femme en homme, 1932 (Rosay 3, Meerson 4, Périnal 4)

Femme en rouge, 1946 (Gélin 3)

Femme enfant, 1982 (Kinski 3)

Femme est passée. See Nunca pasa nada, 1963

Femme est une femme, 1961 (Godard 2, Belmondo 3, Karina 3, Moreau 3, Coutard 4, De Beauregard 4, Evein 4, Guillemot 4, Legrand 4, Ponti 4)

Femme et la fauve, 1955 (Auric 4)

Femme et le pantin, 1958 (Duvivier 2, Bardot 3, Achard 4, Aurenche 4, Wakhévitch 4)

Femme et le rossignol, 1930 (Christian-Jaque 2)

Femme fardeé, 1990 (Moreau 3, Coutard 4)

Femme fatale, 1917 (Feuillade 2)

Femme fatale, 1945 (Brasseur 3)

Femme fidèle, 1976 (Vadim 2)

Femme idéale, 1933 (D'Eaubonne 4)

Femme inconnue, 1923, (Burel 4)

Femme infidèle, 1969 (Chabrol 2, Audran 3, Rabier 4)

Femme invisible, 1933 (Meerson 4)

Femme mariée, 1964 (Leenhardt 2)

Femme noire, femme nue, 1969 (Colpi 4)

Femme nue, 1932 (Burel 4, Meerson 4)

Femme nue et Satan, 1959 (Simon 3)

Femme ou deux, 1985 (Depardieu 3, Weaver 3)

Femme ou mère, 1941 (Volkov 2)

Femme publique, 1984 (Vierny 4)

Femme que j'ai assassinée, 1949 (Vanel 3)

Femme que j'ai le plus aimée, 1942 (Arletty 3, Blier 3)

Femme qui se partage, 1936 (Brasseur 3)

Femme rêvée, 1927 (Vanel 3)

Femme sans importance, 1936 (Spaak 4)

Femme secrete, 1986 (Noiret 3)

Femme spectacle, 1964 (Braunberger 4)

Femme sur la lune. See Frau im Mond, 1929

Femme-Fleur, 1965 (Lenica 4)

Femmes, 1969 (Bardot 3)

Femmes au soleil, 1973 (Almendros 4)

Femmes d'abord, 1963 (Constantine 3)

Femmes de Paris, 1952 (Simon 3)

Femmes de personne, 1984 (Trintignant 3, Delerue 4)

Femmes et des fleurs, 1963 (Leenhardt 2)

Femmes fatales. See Calmos, 1975

Femmes Fatales, 1979 (Tavernier 2)

Femmes s'en balancent, 1954 (Constantine 3)

Femmes sont marrantes, 1957 (Presle 3)

Femmina. See Grande Sauterelle, 1967

Femmine di lusso, 1960 (Cervi 3)

Femmine tre volte, 1957 (Delli Colli 4, Ponti 4)

Fence at Bar Z Ranch, 1910 (Anderson 3)

Fencing Master, 1907 (Bitzer 4)

Fencing Master, 1915 (Walsh 2)

Fenêtre ouverte, 1952 (Storck 2)

Fer à cheval, 1915 (Feuillade 2, Musidora 3)

Ferdinand, 1986 (Ustinov 3)

Ferdinand Lassale, 1918 (Dupont 2)

Ferdinand le noceur, 1935 (Fernandel 3)

Ferdinando I, re di Napoli, 1959 (De Sica 2, Mastroianni 3)

Ferdydurke, 1991 (Skolimowski 2)

Ferghana Canal, 1939 (Eisenstein 2, Tisse 4)

Feri, 1954 (Anand 3)

Feria de las flores, 1942 (Infante 3)

Feriebørn, 1952 (Roos 2)

Ferien auf Immenhof, 1957 (Wagner 4)

Ferita, 1921 (Bertini 3)

Fermata Etna, 1981 (Ganz 3)

Ferme aux loups, 1942 (Andrejew 4)

Ferme des sept péchés, 1949 (Kosma 4)

Ferme du pendu, 1945 (Vanel 3, Douy 4)

Fermière à Montfaucon, 1967 (Rohmer 2)

Fernandel the Dressmaker. See Couturier de ces dames, 1956

Feroce Saladino, 1937 (Valli 3)

Ferrente. See Bacciamo le mani, 1973

Ferréol, 1916 (Bertini 3)

Ferris Bueller's Day Off, 1986 (Hughes 2)

Ferroviere, 1956 (Ponti 4)

Ferry Pilot, 1941 (Dalrymple 4)

Ferry to Hong Kong, 1959 (Welles 2, Heller 4, Mathieson 4, Rank 4)

Fertilizzanti complessi, 1956 (Olmi 2)

Fertiluzzanti produtti dalla Societa del Gruppo Edison, 1959 (Olmi 2)

Fès, 1950 (Auric 4)

Fesche Erzherzog, 1927 (Courant 4)

Fessée, 1937 (Fradetal 4)

Festa di maggio, 1957 (Fabrizi 3)

Festin de Balthazar, 1910 (Feuillade 2, Carré 4)

Festin des mots, 1965 (Cuny 3)

Festival, 1952 (Lassally 4)

Festival acrobatique, 1951 (Kosma 4)

Festival Game, 1969 (Heston 3, Hopper 3)

Festival of Claymation, 1987 (Vinton 4)

Festival of Nyan-nyan-myan. See Nyan-nyan-myan-hoi, 1940

Fête à Henriette, 1952 (Duvivier 2, Auric 4, D'Eaubonne 4, Jeanson 4)

Fête des mères, 1969 (Braunberger 4)

Fête des morts, 1969 (Braunberger 4)

Fête des pères. See Mords pas, on t'aime, 1975

Fête des pères, 1989 (Presle 3)

Fête espagnole, 1919 (Delluc 2, Dulac 2, Modot 3)

Fête sauvage, 1975 (Vangelis 4)

Fêtes de Belgiques, 1968 (Storck 2)

Fêtes de France, 1939 (Leenhardt 2)

Fêtes du centenaire, 1930 (Storck 2)

Fêtes galantes, 1965 (Clair 2, Cassel 3, Matras 4, Wakhévitch 4)

Fetita mincinoasa, 1953 (Popescu-Gopo 4)

Feu!, 1926 (Brasseur 3, Vanel 3)

Feu!, 1937 (Delannoy 2, Feuillère 3, Ibert 4, Wakhévitch 4)

Feu. See Forêt calcinée, 1971

Feu à volonte, 1965 (Constantine 3)

Feu aux poudres, 1957 (Vanel 3)

Feu d'artifice improvisé, 1905 (Méliès 2)

Feu follet, 1963 (Cloquet 4, Moreau 3, Evein 4)

Feu la mère de madame, 1936 (Arletty 3)

Feu Mathias Pascal, 1925 (Cavalcanti 2, Mozhukin 3, Simon 3, Burel 4, Meerson 4)

Feu Nicolas, 1943 (Douy 4)

Feu quelque part, 1952 (Audiard 4)

Feu sacré, 1920 (Linder 3)

Feu sacré, 1942 (Burel 4)

Feud, 1910 (Olcott 2)

Feud, 1919 (Mix 3)

Feud, 1936 (Terry 4)

Feud and the Turkey, 1908 (Griffith 2, Lawrence, 3, Bitzer 4)

Feud in the Kentucky Hills, 1912 (Griffith 2, Pickford 3, Walthall 3, Bitzer 4)

Feud of the West, 1936 (McCord 4)

Feud There Was, 1938 (Avery 4)

Feud with a Dude, 1968 (Blanc 4)

Feudin', Fussin', and A-Fightin', 1948 (O'Connor 3)

Feuding Hillbillies, 1947 (Terry 4)

Feudists, 1913 (Bunny 3)

Feuer, 1914 (Gad 2, Nielsen 3, Freund 4, Kräly 4)

Feuerlöscher E.A. Winterstein, 1968 (Kluge 2)

Feuerwerk, 1954 (Schneider 3)

Feuerzangenbowle, 1970 (Käutner 2)

Feux de la chandeleur, 1972 (Girardot 3, Legrand 4)

Feux de la mer, 1948 (Epstein 2)

Feux Follets, 1928 (Vanel 3)

Fever, 1985 (Brooks 2)

Fever in the Blood, 1961 (Ameche 3, Dickinson 3, Marshall 3)

Fever Pitch, 1985 (Giannini 3, Fraker 4)

Ffolkes, 1980 (Mason 3, Perkins 3)

Fi Baitina Rajul, 1961 (Sharif 3)

Fiacre nr. 13, 1941 (Stallich 4)

Fiaker Nr. 13, 1926 (Leni 2)

Fiamma che no si spegne, 1949 (Cervi 3)

Fiammata, 1924 (Gallone 2)

Fiammata, 1952 (Blasetti 2)

Fiançailles d'Agénor, 1916 (Feuillade 2, Musidora 3)

Fiançailles de Flambeau, 1916 (Cohl 4)

Fiancé ensorcelé, 1903 (Guy 2)

Fiancée du diable, 1915 (Gaumont 4)

Fiancée du pirate, 1969 (Malle 2)

Fiancée for Hire. See Fästmö uthyres, 1951

Fiancés. See Fidanzati, 1963

Fiancés de 1914, 1914 (Feuillade 2, Musidora 3)

Fiancés de Séville, 1914 (Feuillade 2)

Fiancés du Pont Macdonald, 1961 (Karina 3)

Fiasco in Milan. See Audace colpo dei soliti ignoti, 1959

Fibre e civilta, 1957 (Olmi 2)

Fickle Fancy, 1920 (Sennett 2)

Fickle Fatty's Fall, 1915 (Sennett 2, Arbuckle 3)

Fickle Spaniard, 1911 (Sennett 2)

Fickleness of Sweedie, 1914 (Beery 3)

Fidanzati, 1963 (Olmi 2)

Fidanzati della morte, 1956 (Albers 3)

Fiddle-de-dee, 1947 (McLaren 4)

Fiddler on the Roof, 1971 (Jewison 2, Topol 3, Boyle 4, Morris 4, Williams 4)

Fiddlers Three, 1944 (Hamer 2, Watt 2, Kendall 3, Balcon 4)

Fiddlers Three, 1948 (Three Stooges 3)

Fiddle's Requiem, 1911 (Olcott 2)

Fiddlesticks, 1927 (Capra 2, Sennett 2, Langdon 3)

Fiddlesticks, 1931 (Iwerks 4)

Fiddling Around. See Just Mickey, 1930

Fiddling Buckaroo, 1933 (McCord 4)

Fiddling Fool, 1923 (La Cava 2)

Fiddling Fuel. See Nero, 1944

Fidel en la URSS, 1963 (Alvarez 2)

Fidele Bauer, 1927 (Krauss 3)

Fidele Gefängnis, 1917 (Jannings 3)

Fideles Gefängnis, 1918 (Lubitsch 2)

Fidelio, 1956 (Eisler 4)

Fidélité romaine, 1911 (Feuillade 2)

Fidelity, 1911 (Dwan 2)

Fido's Fate, 1916 (Sennett 2)

Fido's Tin-Type Tangle, 1915 (Sennett 2)

Field, 1990 (Harris 3, Hurt 3, Bernstein 4)

Field and Scream, 1955 (Avery 4)

Field of Dreams, 1989 (Costner 3, Jones 3, Lancaster 3)

Field of Honor, 1973 (Zemeckis 2)

Field of Honor, 1986 (Golan and Globus 4)

Field of Red, 1958 (Watkins 2)

Fields of Honour, 1918 (Marsh 3)

Fiend Who Walked the West, 1958 (LeMaire 4, Wheeler 4)

Fiend with the Electronic Brain. See Psycho A-Go-Go!, 1965

Fiend with the Electronic Brain. See Blood of Ghastly Horror, 1972

Fiendish Ghouls. See Flesh and the Fiends, 1960

Fiendish Plot of Dr. Fu Manchu, 1980 (Sellers 3, Trauner 4)

Fiends. See Diaboliques, 1954

Fiercest Heart, 1961 (Massey 3)

Fiery Introduction, 1915 (Furthman 4)

Fiery Summer. See Ohnivé léto, 1939

Fiesco, 1921 (Kortner 3, Hoffmann 4, Metzner 4)

Fiesko, 1913 (Dieterle 2, Hoffmann 4)

Fiesta, 1941 (Prinz 4, Roach 4)

Fiesta, 1947 (Astor 3, Charisse 3, Williams 3, Copland 4, Green 4, Irene 4, Mayer 4, Plunkett 4, Rosher 4)

Fiesta, 1972 (Hayworth 3)

Fiesta de Santa Barbara, 1936 (Keaton 2, Cooper 3, Garland 3)

Fiesta del diablo, 1930 (Goulding 2)

Fiesta Fiasco, 1967 (Blanc 4)

Fiesta Story, 1977 (Alcott 4)

Fièvre, 1921 (Delluc 2, Modot 3)

Fièvre monte à El Pao, 1959 (Felix 3, Philipe 3, Alcoriza 4, Figueroa 4)

Fièvres, 1941 (Delannoy 2)

Fifi Blows Her Top, 1958 (Three Stooges 3)

Fifi tambour, 1915 (Feuillade 2, Musidora 3)

Fifres et tambours d'Entre-Sambre-et-Meuse, 1968 (Storck 2)

Fifteen Minutes, 1921 (Roach 4)

Fifteen Wives, 1935 (Dumont 3)

Fifth Avenue, 1916 (Miller 4)

Fifth Avenue, 1926 (Wong 3)

Fifth Avenue Girl, 1939 (La Cava 2, Calhern 3, Pangborn 3, Rogers 3, Polglase 4)

Fifth Avenue Models, 1925 (Laemmle 4)

Fifth Chair. See It's in the Bag, 1945

Fifth Column Mouse, 1943 (Blanc 4, Freleng 4, Stalling 4)

Fifth Man, 1914 (Mix 3, Selig 4)

Fifth Monkey, 1990 (Golan and Globus 4)

Fifth Musketeer, 1979 (Ferrer 3, Harrison 3, Wilde 3)

Fifty Fantastics, 1965 (Warhol 2)

Fifty Fathoms Deep, 1931 (Walker 4)

Fifty Mile Auto Contest, 1911 (Dwan 2)

Fifty Million Frenchmen, 1931 (Bacon 2, Lugosi 3)

Fifty Personalities, 1965 (Warhol 2)

Fifty Roads to Town, 1937 (Ameche 3, Darwell 3, August 4)

Fifty Years of Action, 1986 (Schlesinger 2)

Fig Leaves, 1926 (Hawks 2, Adrian 4, August 4, Fox 4, Menzies 4)

Fight to the Finish, 1925 (Eason 4)

Fight to the Finish, 1937 (Bond 3)

Fight to the Finish, 1947 (Terry 4)

Fifty-Fifty, 1916 (Dwan 2, Fleming 2, Talmadge 3)

Fifty-Fifty, 1925 (Florey 2, Barrymore 3)

Fifty-Fifty Girl, 1928 (Daniels 3, Banton 4, Hunt 4)

Fight for Freedom, 1908 (Bitzer 4)

Fight for Life, 1940 (Lorentz 2, Crosby 4)

Fight for Love, 1919 (Ford 2, Carey 3)

Fight for Rome. See Kampf um Rom, 1968

Fight for Rome II. See Kampf um Rom II, 1969

Fight for the Glory. See Eiko eno kurohyo, 1969

Fight for Your Lady, 1937 (Lupino 3, Polglase 4)

Fight for Your Lady, 1970 (Negulesco 2)

Fight Goes On. See Striden går vidare, 1941

Fight Night, 1926 (Sennett 2)

Fight Pest, 1928 (Roach 4)

Fighter, 1952 (Cobb 3, Howe 4)

Fighter Attack, 1953 (Hayden 3)

Fighter Squadron, 1948 (Walsh 2, Hudson 3, O'Brien 3, Miller 4, Steiner 4)

Fightin' Pals, 1940 (Fleischer 4)

Fighting American, 1924 (Astor 3, Laemmle 4)

Fighting Bill Carson, 1945 (Crabbe 3)

Fighting Bill Fargo, 1942 (Salter 4)

Fighting Blade, 1923 (Barthelmess 3, Folsey 4)

Fighting Blood, 1911 (Griffith 2, Barrymore 3)

Fighting Blood series, 1923 (Garmes 4)

Fighting Breed. See Jackaroo of Coolabong, 1920

Fighting Breed, 1921 (Meredyth 4)

Fighting Brothers, 1919 (Ford 2, Carey 3)

Fighting Buckaroo, 1926 (Fox 4)

Fighting Caravans, 1930 (Darwell 3)

Fighting Caravans, 1931 (Cooper 3, Garmes 4, Zukor 4)

Fighting Cheat, 1926 (Arthur 3)

Fighting Code, 1934 (Bond 3)

Fighting Colleen, 1919 (Love 3)

Fighting Courage, 1925 (Walker 4)

Fighting Coward, 1924 (Cruze 2, Astor 3, Brown 4)

Fighting Cressy, 1919 (Sweet 3)

Fighting Dervishes, 1912 (Olcott 2)

Fighting Dude, 1926 (Arbuckle 3)

Fighting Eagle, 1927 (Crisp 3, Lombard 3, Adrian 4, Miller 4, Sullivan 4)

Fighting Engineers, 1943 (Eason 4)

Fighting Fathers, 1927 (Roach 4)

Fighting Film Albums. See Pir v Girmunka, 1941

Fighting Fluid, 1925 (McCarey 2, Roach 4)

Fighting for Gold, 1919 (Mix 3)

Fighting for Justice, 1933 (Brennan 3)

Fighting For Love, 1919 (Johnson 3)

Fighting For Love, 1980 (Johnson 3)

Fighting Gringo, 1917 (Carey 3)

Fighting Guardsman, 1945 (Guffey 4)

Fighting Heart, 1919 (Eason 4)

Fighting Heart, 1925 (Ford 2, McLaglen 3, August 4, Fox 4)

Fighting Kentuckian, 1949 (Laurel and Hardy 3, Marsh 3, Wayne 3, Garmes 4)

Fighting Lady, 1944 (De Rochemont 4, Newman 4)

Fighting Lady, 1945 (Taylor 3)

Fighting Legion, 1930 (Brown 4, Laemmle 4, McCord 4)

Fighting Line, 1919 (Eason 4)

Fighting Love, 1927 (Walthall 3)

Fighting Mad, 1976 (Corman 2, Demme 2)

Fighting Man of the Plains, 1949 (Scott 3)

Fighting Marine, 1935 (Canutt 4, Eason 4)

Fighting Marshall. See Cherokee Strip, 1940

Fighting Odds, 1917 (Dwan 2)

Fighting O'Flynn, 1948 (Edeson 4)

Fighting Parson, 1930 (Langdon 3, Roach 4)

Fighting Peacemaker, 1926 (Laemmle 4)

Fighting Pimpernel. See Elusive Pimpernel, 1950

Fighting Prince of Donegal, 1966 (Disney 4, Ellenshaw 4)

Fighting Rangers, 1934 (Bond 3)

Fighting Rats of Tobruk. See Rats of Tobruk, 1944

Fighting Sap, 1924 (Brown 4)

Fighting Seabees, 1944 (Hayward 3, Wayne 3, Chase 4)

Fighting Shadows, 1935 (Bond 3)

Fighting Shepherdess, 1920 (Gaudio 4)

Fighting 69th, 1940 (Cagney 3, Deutsch 4, Friedhofer 4, Gaudio 4, Haskin 4, Raine 4, Wallis 4)

Fighting 69½th, 1941 (Blanc 4, Freleng 4, Stalling 4)

Fighting Smile, 1925 (Arthur 3, Brown 4)

Fighting Stallion, 1926 (Canutt 4)

Fighting Stock, 1935 (Balcon 4, Rank 4)

Fighting Stranger, 1921 (Selig 4)

Fighting Streak, 1922 (Mix 3, Fox 4)

Fighting Sullivans. See Sullivans, 1944

Fighting Test, 1931 (Canutt 4)

Fighting Texans, 1933 (Canutt 4)

Fighting the Flames, 1925 (Eason 4)

Fighting Thorobreds, 1926 (Brown 4)

Fighting Three, 1927 (Laemmle 4)

Fighting Through, 1934 (Canutt 4)

Fighting Westerner. *See* Rocky Mountain Mystery, 1935

Fighting with Kit Carson, 1933 (Canutt 4)

Fighting Youth, 1925 (Eason 4)

Fighting Youth, 1935 (Sheridan 3)

Fights of Nations, 1907 (Bitzer 4)

Figli chiedono perche, 1972 (Cecchi D'Amico 4)

Figli del marchese Lucera, 1938 (Cervi 3)

Figli di nessuno, 1951 (Rosi 2, Rosay 3)

Figlia del capitano, 1947 (Gassman 3, De Laurentiis 4, Pinelli 4)

Figlia del corsaro verde, 1940 (Stallich 4)

Figlia del tempesta, 1920 (Gallone 2)

Figlia di Frankenstein, 1971 (Cotten 3)

Figlia di Mata Hari, 1955 (Gallone 2)

Figlie del mare, 1919 (Gallone 2)

Figlio del Capitano Blood, 1962 (Brown 4, Robinson 4)

Figlio del corsaro rosso, 1942 (Amidei 4)

Figlio di Lagardere, 1952 (Brazzi 3)

Figlio d'oggi, 1961 (Cervi 3)

Figures de cire, 1912 (Tourneur 2)

Figures de cire et tetes de bois, 1916 (Cohl 4)

Figures Don't Lie, 1927 (Mankiewicz 4, Schulberg 4)

Figures in a Landscape, 1970 (Losey 2, McDowell 3, Shaw 3, Alekan 4)

File of the Golden Goose, 1969 (Brynner 3)

File of Thelma Jordan, 1949 (Siodmak 2, Stanwyck 3, Barnes 4, Dreier 4, Head 4, Wallis 4, Young 4)

Filer, 1988 (Yankovsky 3)

Fill It Up, Premium. *See* Plein de super, 1976

Fille à croquer, 1950 (Reggiani 3)

Fille à la dérive, 1964 (Guillemot 4)

Fille à papa, 1936 (Morgan 3)

Fille au fouet, 1952 (Simon 3)

Fille bien gardée, 1924 (Feuillade 2)

Fille consue de fil blanc, 1977 (Reggiani 3)

Fille dangereuse. *See* Bufere, 1952

Fille dans la montagne, 1964 (Leenhardt 2)

Fille de Hambourg, 1957 (Gélin 3)

Fille de Jephté, 1910 (Feuillade 2, Gaumont 4)

Fille de la mer morte, 1966 (Brasseur 3, Golan and Globus 4)

Fille de l'eau, 1925 (Renoir 2, Braunberger 4)

Fille de Madame Angot, 1935 (Arletty 3)

Fille des chiffonniers, 1990 (Baur 3)

Fille d'Eve, 1916 (Musidora 3)

Fille du cantonnier, 1909 (Gaumont 4)

Fille du diable, 1945 (Fresnay 3)

Fille du margrave, 1912 (Feuillade 2)

Fille du puisatier, 1940 (Pagnol 2, Fernandel 3, Raimu 3)

Fille du régiment, 1933 (Heller 4)

Fille du samourai. *See* Tochter des Samurai, 1937

Fille du sonneur, 1906 (Pathé 4)

Fille du torrent, 1960 (Valli 3)

Fille et des fusils, 1964 (Braunberger 4)

Fille nommée Madeleine. *See* Maddalena, 1953

Fille pour l'été, 1959 (Presle 3, Delerue 4)

Fille Prodigue, 1980 (Piccoli 3)

Fille sage, 1963 (Borowczyk 2)

Filles de la concierge, 1934 (Tourneur 2, Wakhévitch 4)

Filles du cantonnier, 1909 (Feuillade 2)

Filles du Diable, 1903 (Méliès 2)

Filles du Rhone, 1938 (Burel 4, Jaubert 4)

Filling the Gap, 1941 (Halas and Batchelor 4)

Film, 1965 (Keaton 2, Kaufman 4)

Film About a Woman Who . . . , 1974 (Rainer 2)

Film and Reality, 1952 (Cavalcanti 2)

Film Biographies, 1990 (Brakhage 2)

Film comme les autres, 1968 (Godard 2)

Film Comment, 1966 (Burton 3)

Film Concert No. One. *See* Koncert na ekrane, 1939

Film Culture, 1962 (Alexeieff and Parker 4)

Film d'amore e d'anarchia, 1973 (Wertmüller 2, Giannini 3, Rota 4, Rotunno 4)

Film den Niemand sieht, 1964 (Thulin 3)

Film der Menschlichkeit. *See* I.N.R.I., 1923

Film Elation of Spejbl. *See* Spejblovo filmové opojení, 1931

''Film Esthétique'' series, 1910–11 (Feuillade 2)

Film Fan, 1939 (Blanc 4, Clampett 4, Stalling 4)

Film, flirt og forlovelse, 1921 (Madsen and Schenstrøm 3)

Film Form No. 1, 1970 (Vanderbeek 2)

Film Form No. 2, 1970 (Vanderbeek 2)

Film gegen die Volkskrankheit Krebs—jeder Achte . . . , 1941 (Ruttman 2)

Film ist Rhythmus. *See* Rhythmus 21, 1964

Film Johnnie, 1914 (Sennett 2, Arbuckle 3)

Film Magazine No. 1, 1963 (Emshwiller 2)

Film Magazine of the Arts, 1963 (Mekas 2)

Film Making Techniques: Acting, 1973 (Fonda 3)

Film of Love and Anarchy. *See* **Film d'amore e d'anarchia, 1973**

Film ohne Titel, 1947 (Käutner 2, Herlth 4)

Film without Title. *See* Film ohne Titel, 1947

Film with Three Dancers, 1970 (Emshwiller 2)

Filmcritica, 1962 (Alexeieff and Parker 4)

Filmens Helte, 1928 (Madsen and Schenstrøm 3)

Filmmaker, 1968 (Lucas 2)

Filmprimadonna, 1913 (Gad 2, Nielsen 3, Freund 4, Kräly 4)

Films By Stan Brakhage:, 1961 (Brakhage 2)

Films comiques, 1903 (Pathé 4)

Films in Review, 1972 (Cervi 3)

Filmstudie, 1926 (Richter 2)

Film-Truth. *See* **Kino-Pravda, 1922**

Filo d'erba, 1952 (Fizgerald 3)

Filosofská historie, 1937 (Heller 4)

Fils, 1972 (Montand 3, Sarde 4, Saulnier 4)

Fils d'Amerique, 1932 (Gallone 2, Simon 3, Courant 4)

Fils de Caroline chérie, 1954 (Bardot 3)

Fils de la sunamité, 1911 (Feuillade 2)

Fils de l'eau, 1951 (Braunberger 4)

Fils de l'eau, 1955 (Rouch 2)

Fils de Locuste, 1911 (Feuillade 2)

Fils du chiek. *See* Amanti del deserto, 1956

Fils du diable, 1906 (Pathé 4)

Fils du flibustier, 1922 (Feuillade 2)

Fils du garde-chasse, 1906 (Guy 2)

Fils du Rajah, 1931 (Autant-Lara 2)

Fils improvisé, 1932 (Delannoy 2)

Fils puni, 1978 (Vierny 4)

Filumena Marturano, 1951 (Rota 4)

Fim de estação, 1981 (Branco 4)

Fin de Don Juan, 1911 (Gaumont 4)

Fin de fiesta, 1959 (Torre Nilsson 2)

Fin de jour, 1939 (Simon 3)

Fin de Paganini, 1910 (Gance 2)

Fin de semana para los muertos, 1974 (Kennedy 3)

Fin des Pyrénées, 1971 (Braunberger 4)

Fin du jour, 1938 (Jouvet 3, Modot 3, Jaubert 4, Matras 4, Spaak 4)

Fin du monde, 1931 (Gance 2, Honegger 4, Meerson 4)

Fin 'n' Catty, 1943 (Blanc 4, Jones 4, Stalling 4)

Final Accord. *See* Schlussakkord, 1936

Final Appointment, 1954 (Fisher 2)

Final Assignment, 1980 (Bujold 3, Meredith 3)

Final Comedown, 1972 (Corman 2)

Final Conflict, 1981 (Brazzi 3)

Final Countdown, 1980 (Douglas 3, Sheen 3)

Final Hour, 1936 (Bellamy 3)

Final Judgment, 1915 (Barrymore 3)

Final Justice, 1985 (Brazzi 3)

Final Option, 1982 (Widmark 3)

Final Pardon, 1912 (Porter 2)

Final Program, 1973 (Hayden 3)

Final Programme, 1973 (Puttnam 4)

Final Reckoning, 1914 (Ince 4)

Final Settlement, 1910 (Griffith 2, Bitzer 4)

Final Take: The Golden Age of Movies. *See* Kinema no tenchi, 1986

Final Test, 1952 (Asquith 2, Rattigan 4)

Final Verdict, 1914 (Walsh 2)

Finale der Liebe, 1925 (Planer 4)

Finally, Sunday. *See* Vivement dimanche!, 1983

Finalmente sì, 1943 (Delli Colli 4)

Finalmente soli, 1941 (Magnani 3)

Finanzen des Grossherzogs, 1924 (Murnau 2, Freund 4, Planer 4, Pommer 4, Von Harbou 4)

Finanzen des Grossherzogs, 1934 (Gründgens 3)

Finche c'è guerra c'è speranza, 1974 (Sordi 3)

Finchè dura la tempesta, 1964 (Mason 3)

Finders Keepers, 1928 (Miller 4)

Finders Keepers, 1951 (Salter 4)

Finders Keepers, 1984 (Lester 2)

Find, Fix and Strike, 1941 (Cavalcanti 2, Crichton 2)

Find the Girl, 1920 (Roach 4)

Find the King, 1927 (Horton 3)

Find the Lady, 1936 (Sanders 3)

Find the Lady, 1976 (Rooney 3)

Find the Witness, 1937 (Miller 4)

Find Your Man, 1924 (Garmes 4, Zanuck 4)

Finding His Voice, 1929 (Fleischer 4)

Fine and Dandy. *See* West Point Story, 1950

Fine Clothes, 1925 (Stahl 2, Booth 4, Gibbons 4, Glazer 4, Mayer 4)

Fine combine, 1931 (Fernandel 3, Feuillère 3)

Fine di Montecarlo. *See* Monte Carlo, 1928

Fine Feathered Friend, 1942 (Hanna and Barbera 4)

Fine Feathers Make Fine Birds, 1914 (Ingram 2)

Fine Madness, 1966 (Connery 3, Seberg 3, Woodward 3, Addison 4, McCord 4)

Fine Manners, 1926 (Swanson 3)

Fine Mess, 1986 (Mancini 4)

Fine Pair. *See* Ruba al prossimo tuo, 1968

Fine Snow, 1983 (Ichikawa 2)

Fine Tolerance, 1979 (Nihalani 4)

Finer Things, 1913 (Dwan 2)

Finest Hours, 1964 (Welles 2)

Finestra sul Luna Park, 1956 (Comencini 2, Cecchi D'Amico 4)
Fingal's Cave, 1946 (Vorkapich 4)
Finger of Guilt. *See* Intimate Stranger, 1956
Finger Points, 1931 (Barthelmess 3, Gable 3, Wray 3, Burnett 4, Haller 4, Saunders 4)
Finger Prints, 1923 (Roach 4)
Finger Prints, 1927 (Bacon 2, Loy 3, Pangborn 3, Miller 4)
Fingerprints, 1914 (Bushman 3)
Fingers, 1977 (Cahn 4)
Fingers at the Window, 1942 (Ayres 3, Rathbone 3, Kaper 4, Lederer 4, Schary 4, Stradling 4)
Finian's Rainbow, 1968 (Coppola 2, Astaire 3, Jeakins 4, Pan 4)
Finis terrae, 1929 (Epstein 2)
Finisce sempre cosí, 1939 (De Sica 2)
Finish of Bridget McKeen, 1901 (Porter 2)
Finished Actor, 1927 (Sennett 2)
Finishing School, 1934 (Bondi 3, Darwell 3, Rogers 3, Cooper 4, D'Agostino 4, Hunt 4, MacGowan 4, Plunkett 4, Polglase 4, Steiner 4)
Finishing Touch, 1928 (Laurel and Hardy 3, Bruckman 4, Roach 4)
Finishing Touch, 1932 (Stevens 2)
Finlande, 1951 (Colpi 4)
Finn and Hattie, 1931 (Mankiewicz 2, McLeod 2)
Finnegan, Begin Again, 1985 (Silver 2, Preston 3, Sidney 3, Müller 4)
Finnegan's Bomb, 1914 (Sennett 2)
Finsternis und ihr Eigentum, 1922 (Kortner 3)
Fiole enchantée, 1902 (Guy 2)
Fior di male, 1915 (Gallone 2)
Fiore dai petali d'acciaio, 1973 (Baker 3)
Fiore delle mille e una notte, 1974 (Donati 4, Morricone 4)
Fiore sotto gli occhi, 1943 (Magnani 3)
Fiorina la vacca, 1973 (Morricone 4)
Fioritures, 1916 (Burel 4)
Fiorno piu'corto, 1962 (Cervi 3)
Fire Alarm. *See* Flames, 1932
Fire and Ice. *See* Combat dans l'île, 1961
Fire and Ice, 1983 (Bakshi 4)
Fire and Steel, 1927 (Walker 4)
Fire Barrier, 1926 (Wyler 2)
Fire Brigade, 1926 (Gibbons 4)
Fire Bugs, 1930 (Fleischer 4)
Fire Cheese, 1941 (Fleischer 4)
Fire Chief, 1916 (Sennett 2)
Fire Down Below, 1957 (Hayworth 3, Lemmon 3, Lom 3, Mitchum 3, Box 4, Cohn 4)
Fire Eater, 1921 (Eason 4)
Fire Fighters, 1922 (Roach 4)
Fire! Fire, 1932 (Iwerks 4)
Fire Flingers, 1919 (Young 4)
Fire Has Been Arranged, 1935 (Crazy Gang 3, Sim 3)
Fire in the Opera House. *See* Brand in der Oper, 1930
Fire Island, 1974 (Jarman 2)
Fire of Waters, 1965 (Brakhage 2)
Fire over Africa. *See* Malaga, 1954
Fire over England, 1936 (Howard 2, Leigh 3, Mason 3, Massey 3, Newton 3, Olivier 3, Howe 4, Korda 4, Meerson 4, Pommer 4)
Fire Patrol, 1924 (Fort 4, Stromberg 4)
Fire Raisers, 1933 (Balcon 4, Junge 4, Rank 4, Powell and Pressburger 2)
Fire Sale, 1977 (Arkin 3)

Fire the Cook, 1918 (Roach 4)
Fire the Fireman, 1922 (Roach 4)
Fire the Flag!. *See* Ano hata o ute, 1944
Fire the Kaiser, 1918 (Fairbanks 3)
Fire Within. *See* Feu follet, 1963
Fireball, 1950 (Garnett 2, Monroe 3, Rooney 3, Polglase 4, Young 4)
Fireball 500, 1965 (Crosby 4)
Fireball Forward, 1972 (Smith 4)
Firebird, 1934 (Dieterle 2, Darwell 3, Blanke 4, Grot 4, Haller 4, Orry-Kelly 4)
Firebrand, 1962 (Crosby 4)
Firebrand Jordan, 1930 (Canutt 4)
Firebug, 1905 (Bitzer 4)
Firebugs, 1913 (Sennett 2)
Firecreek, 1968 (Fonda 3, Stewart 3, Clothier 4, Newman 4)
Fired, 1918 (Dressler 3)
Fired Man, 1940 (Hunt 4)
Firefall. *See* Cascade de Feu, 1904
Firefly, 1937 (MacDonald 3, Adrian 4, Gibbons 4, Goodrich 4, Mayer 4, Stothart 4, Stromberg 4, Vorkapich 4)
Firefly of France, 1918 (Crisp 3, Reid 3)
Firefox, 1982 (Jarre 4)
Fireman, 1916 (Bacon 2, Chaplin 2, Purviance 3)
Fireman, 1931 (Lantz 4)
Fireman, Save My Child, 1918 (Daniels 3, Lloyd 3, Roach 4)
Fireman, Save My Child, 1927 (Beery 3, Schulberg 4)
Fireman Save My Child, 1932 (Bacon 2, Brown 3, Polito 4)
Fireman Save My Child, 1935 (Terry 4)
Fireman's Bride, 1931 (Terry 4)
Fireman's Picnic, 1937 (Lantz 4)
Firemen's Ball. *See* Hoří, má penenko, 1967
Firemen to the Rescue, 1903 (Hepworth 2)
Firepower, 1979 (Coburn 3, Loren 3, Mature 3, Wallach 3)
Fires of Conscience, 1914 (Reid 3)
Fires of Fate, 1913 (Reid 3)
Fires of Rebellion, 1916 (Chaney 3)
Fires of Youth. *See* Up for Murder, 1931
Fires on the Plain. *See* Nobi, 1959
Fires Were Started, 1943 (Jennings 2, Alwyn 4, Dalrymple 4, Mathieson 4)
Fires Within, 1991 (Jarre 4)
Fireside Brewer, 1920 (Sennett 2)
Fireside Theater. *See* Bamboo Cross, 1955
Firestarter, 1984 (Scott 3, Sheen 3, De Laurentiis 4)
Firewalker, 1986 (Golan and Globus 4)
Fireworks, 1947 (Anger 2)
Firma Heiratet, 1914 (Lubitsch 2, Freund 4)
Firma Heiratet, 1930 (Metzner 4)
First a Girl, 1935 (Saville 2, Matthews 3, Balcon 4)
First and Last, 1988 (Schlesinger 2)
First and the Last, 1937 (Leigh 3, Newton 3, Olivier 3, Dean 4, Greene 4, Hornbeck 4, Korda, A. 4, Korda, V. 4, Stallich 4)
First Auto, 1927 (Zanuck 4)
First Baby, 1904 (Bitzer 4)
First Baby, 1936 (Darwell 3, McDaniel 3, Trotti 4)
First Bad Man, 1955 (Avery 4)
First Blood, 1982 (Stallone 3)
First Born, 1921 (Hayakawa 3, Wong 3)
First Born, 1928 (Carroll 3, Balcon 4, Reville 4)
First Charge of the Machete. *See* **Primera carga al machete, 1969**

First Comes Courage, 1943 (Arzner 2, Oberon 3, Brown 4, Walker 4)
First Day. *See* Den pervyi, 1958
First Day of Freedom. *See* Pierwszy dzień wolności, 1964
First Days, 1939 (Cavalcanti 2, Watt 2)
First Deadly Sin, 1980 (Dunaway 3, Sinatra 3)
First Degree, 1923 (Laemmle 4)
First Echelon. *See* Pervye eshelon, 1956
First Family, 1980 (Henry 4)
First Flying Fish, 1955 (Terry 4)
First Great Train Robbery. *See* Great Train Robbery, 1978
First Hundred Years, 1924 (Capra 2, Sennett 2)
First Hundred Years, 1938 (Montgomery 3, Krasna 4, Ruttenberg 4)
First Hundred Years, 1980 (Langdon 3)
First in War, 1932 (Roach 4)
First Kiss, 1928 (Cooper 3, Wray 3)
First Lady, 1937 (Francis 3, Brown 4, Orry-Kelly 4, Steiner 4, Wallis 4)
First Legion, 1951 (Sirk 2, Boyer 3)
First Line of Defence, 1947 (Halas and Batchelor 4)
First Love, 1921 (Levien 4)
First Love. *See* Pervaya lyubov, 1933
First Love, 1939 (Durbin 3, Pasternak 4, Salter 4)
First Love. *See* Erste Liebe, 1970
First Love, 1977 (Barry 4)
First Love. *See* Primo amore, 1978
First Man to the Moon, 1921 (Fleischer 4)
First Men in the Moon, 1964 (Finch 3, Harryhausen 4)
First Mission, 1985 (Chan 3)
First Mrs. Fraser, 1932 (Dickinson 2)
First Misunderstanding, 1911 (Pickford 3)
First Monday in October, 1981 (Clayburgh 3, Matthau 3)
First Name Carmen. *See* Prénom Carmen, 1983
First Ninety-Nine, 1958 (Halas and Batchelor 4)
First of the Few, 1942 (Howard 3, Niven 3, De Grunwald 4, Dillon 4, Mathieson 4, Périnal 4, Walton 4)
First Offence, 1936 (Mills 3, Balcon 4)
First Olympics: Athens 1896, 1984 (Jourdan 3)
First Piano Quartet, 1954 (La Shelle 4)
First Polka. *See* Erste Polka, 1979
First Prize. *See* Högsta vinsten, 1915
First Rebel. *See* Allegheny Uprising, 1939
First Robin, 1939 (Terry 4)
First Round-Up, 1934 (Roach 4)
First Seven Years, 1930 (Roach 4)
First Snow, 1935 (Terry 4)
First Snow, 1947 (Terry 4)
First Steps, 1981 (Halas and Batchelor 4)
First Texan, 1956 (McCrea 3, Haskin 4, Mirisch 4)
First Time, 1952 (Tashlin 2, Laszlo 4)
First Time, 1968 (Laszlo 4)
First to Fight, 1967 (Hackman 3)
First Traveling Saleslady, 1956 (Eastwood 3, Rogers 3)
First Tuesday in November, 1945 (Houseman 4)
First Violin, 1912 (Bunny 3, Costello 3, Talmadge 3)
First Woman Jury in America, 1912 (Bunny 3)

Flaming Hour, 1922 (Laemmle 4)
Flaming Signal, 1933 (Walthall 3)
Flaming Sky. *See* Moyuru oozora, 1940
Flaming Star, 1960 (Siegel 2, Del Rio 3,
    Presley 3, Clarke 4, Johnson 4)
Flaming Sword, 1915 (Barrymore 3)
Flaming Torch. *See* Bob Mathias Story, 1954
Flaming Years. *See* Povest plamennykh,
    1961
Flaming Youth, 1923 (Moore 3)
Flamingo, 1947 (Dandridge 3)
Flamingo Kid, 1984 (Dillon 3)
Flamingo Road, 1949 (Curtiz 2, Crawford 3,
    Greenstreet 3, McCord 4, Steiner 4,
    Wald 4)
Flamme, 1923 (Lubitsch 2, Negri 3, Kräly 4)
Flamme, 1925 (Vanel 3)
Flamme, 1936 (Vanel 3, D'Eaubonne 4)
Flamme cachée, 1920 (Musidora 3)
Flamme dans mon coeur, 1987 (Tanner 2)
Flamme lügen, 1926 (Porten 3)
Flamme merveilleuse, 1903 (Méliès 2)
Flammen, 1928 (Tschechowa 3)
Flammende Völker, 1921 (Wegener 3)
Flammes sur l'Adriatique, 1968 (Astruc 2)
Flanagan, 1985 (Page 3)
Flanagan Boy, 1953 (Carreras 4)
Flap, 1970 (Reed 2, Quinn 3, Winters 3,
    Hamlisch 4)
Flapper, 1920 (Shearer 3, Marion 4)
Flapper Wives, 1924 (Horton 3, Murfin 4)
Flareup, 1969 (Welch 3)
Flash Back, 1975 (Huppert 3)
Flash Gordon, 1936 (Crabbe 3)
Flash Gordon, 1980 (Topol 3, Von Sydow 3,
    De Laurentiis 4, Donati 4)
Flash Gordon Conquers the Universe, 1940
    (Crabbe 3)
Flash Gordon's Trip to Mars, 1938
    (Crabbe 3)
Flash in the Dark, 1914 (Reid 3)
Flash of Fate, 1918 (Young 4)
Flash of Light, 1910 (Griffith 2, Bitzer 4)
Flashback, 1989 (Hopper 3)
Flashes Festivals, 1965 (Harrison 3)
Flashing Spikes, 1962 (Wayne 3)
Flashing Spurs, 1924 (Eason 4)
Flashlight Girl, 1916 (Chaney 3)
Flat. *See* Byt, 1968
Flat. *See* Jan Svankmajer: Alchemist of the
    Surreal, 1990
Flat Broke, 1920 (Roach 4)
Flat Foot Fledgling, 1952 (Terry 4)
Flat Foot Stooges, 1938 (Three Stooges 3)
Flat Hatting, 1946 (Bosustow 4, Hubley 4)
Flat Top, 1952 (Hayden 3)
Flat Top, 1962 (Mirisch 4)
Flatbed Annie and Sweetiepie: Lady
    Truckers, 1979 (Stanton 3)
Flavor of Green Tea over Rice. *See*
    Ochazuke no aji, 1952
Flaw, 1955 (Fisher 2)
Flea Circus, 1954 (Avery 4)
Flea in Her Ear. *See* Puce à l'oreille, 1967
Flea in Her Ear, 1968 (Harrison 3, Jourdan 3,
    Roberts 3, Cahn 4, Lang 4)
Fledermaus, 1931 (Ondra 3, Heller 4)
Fledermaus, 1937 (Baarová 3)
Fledermaus, 1946 (Herlth 4)
Fledermaus '55. *See* Oh Rosalinda, 1955
Fledged Shadows. *See* Opeřené stíny, 1930
Fleet Air Arm, 1943 (Balcon 4)
Fleet That Came to Stay, 1946 (Boetticher 2)
Fleet's In, 1928 (Bow 3, Banton 4)

Fleet's In, 1942 (Holden 3, Hutton 3,
    Lamour 3, Head 4, Mercer 4, Young 4)
Fleets of Stren'th, 1942 (Fleischer 4)
Fleetwing, 1928 (Fox 4)
Flemish Farm, 1943 (Rank 4, Vetchinsky 4)
Flesh, 1932 (Ford 2, Goulding 2, Beery 3,
    Edeson 4)
Flesh, 1968 (Warhol 2)
Flesh and Blood, 1912 (Guy 2)
Flesh and Blood, 1922 (Chaney 3)
Flesh and Blood, 1951 (Clayton 2,
    Greenwood 3, De Grunwald 4, Heller 4,
    Korda 4)
Flesh and Bullets, 1985 (Wilde 3)
Flesh and Desire. *See* Fuco nelle vene, 1953
Flesh and Fantasy, 1943 (Duvivier 2,
    Boyer 3, Robinson 3, Stanwyck 3,
    Benchley 4, Boyle 4, Cortez 4, Head 4,
    Hoffenstein 4)
Flesh and Fury, 1951 (Curtis 3, Salter 4)
Flesh and the Devil, 1926 (Brown 2,
    Garbo 3, Gilbert 3, Daniels 4, Gibbons 4,
    Glazer 4, Mayer 4, Thalberg 4)
Flesh and the Fiends, 1960 (Cushing 3,
    Pleasence 3)
Flesh and Woman. *See* Grand Jeu, 1954
Flesh Creatures. *See* Horror of the Blood
    Monsters, 1970
Flesh Creatures of the Red Planet. *See*
    Horror of the Blood Monsters, 1970
Flesh Feast, 1973 (Lake 3)
Flesh for Frankenstein. *See* Carne per
    Frankenstein, 1973
Flesh of Morning, 1956 (Brakhage 2)
Flesh Will Surrender. *See* Delitto di
    Giovanni Episcopo, 1947
Fletch, 1985 (Leven 4)
Fleuchtweg nach Marseille, 1977 (Vogler 3)
Fleur au fusil, 1959 (Rosay 3)
Fleur de l'âge, 1947 (Carné 2, Aimée 3,
    Reggiani 3, Trauner 4)
Fleur de l'age, 1964 (Bujold 3, Takemitsu 4)
Fleur de l'age, ou les adolescents, 1964
    (Braunberger 4)
Fleur de peau, 1962 (Kosma 4)
Fleur de Rubis, 1990 (Adjani 3, Belmondo 3,
    Deneuve 3)
Fleur d'eau, 1970 (Braunberger 4)
Fleur des ruines, 1916 (Gance 2, Burel 4,
    Gaumont 4)
Fleur d'oseille, 1967 (Audiard 4,
    D'Eaubonne 4)
Fleuve Dieu, 1956 (Fresnay 3)
Fleuve invisible, 1960 (Delerue 4)
Fleuve: Le Tarn, 1951 (Fradetal 4)
Flic, 1972 (Melville 2, Delon 3, Deneuve 3)
Flic ou voyou, 1978 (Belmondo 3,
    Audiard 4, Decaë 4, Sarde 4)
Flic Story, 1975 (Delon 3, Trintignant 3)
Flickan från fjällbyn, 1948 (Dahlbeck 3)
Flickan från tredje raden, 1949
    (Björnstrand 3)
Flickan i fönstret mittemot, 1942 (Fischer 4)
Flickan i frack, 1956 (Nykvist 4)
Flickan i regnet, 1955 (Andersson 3)
Flicker Fever, 1935 (Sennett 2)
Flickering Youth, 1924 (Capra 2, Sennett 2)
Flickorna, 1968 (Andersson, B. 3,
    Andersson, H. 3, Björnstrand 3,
    Josephson 3)
Fliegende Klassenzimmer, 1954 (Herlth 4)
Fliegende Koffer, 1921 (Reiniger 4)
Fliegenden Briganten, 1921 (Warm 4)
Fliehende Schatten, 1922 (Pick 2)

Flies, 1923 (Fleischer 4)
Flies Ain't Human, 1941 (Fleischer 4)
Flight, 1929 (Capra 2, Cohn 4, Walker 4)
Flight. *See* Beg, 1971
Flight, 1974 (Brakhage 2)
Flight Angels, 1940 (Bellamy 3, Wyman 3,
    Haskin 4, Wald 4)
Flight Command, 1941 (Borzage 2,
    Pidgeon 3, Taylor 3, Gillespie 4,
    Rosson 4, Waxman 4)
Flight Commander, 1927 (Saville 2)
Flight 54321, 1971 (Vukotić 4)
Flight for Freedom, 1943 (MacMurray 3,
    Marshall 3, Russell 3, Garmes 4,
    Murfin 4)
Flight from Ashiya, 1964 (Brynner 3,
    Widmark 3, Guffey 4, Lourié 4, Salt 4)
Flight from Folly, 1944 (Fisher 2,
    Goulding 2, Heller 4)
Flight from Glory, 1937 (Musuraca 4)
Flight from Terror. *See* Satan Never Sleeps,
    1962
Flight in the Night. *See* Flucht in die Nacht,
    1926
Flight into Darkness. *See* Equipage, 1935
Flight into France. *See* Fuga in Francia, 1948
Flight into Nowhere, 1938 (Bond 3)
Flight Lieutenant, 1942 (Dalio 3, Ford 3,
    Cohn 4, Planer 4, Schulberg 4)
Flight Nurse, 1954 (Dwan 2, Young 4)
Flight of Ludlows Aerodrome, 1905
    (Bitzer 4)
Flight of the Eagle. *See* Ingenjör Andrees
    luftfärd, 1981
Flight of the Phoenix, 1965 (Aldrich 2,
    Attenborough 3, Borgnine 3, Duryea 3,
    Finch 3, Stewart 3, Biroc 4, Westmore
    Family 4)
Flight of the Spruce Goose, 1986 (Black 3)
Flight (or Desertion) of Poincaré, 1932
    (Ptushko 4)
Flight to Berlin. *See* Fluchtpunkt Berlin,
    1984
Flight to Fame, 1938 (Ballard 4)
Flight to Fury, 1966 (Nicholson 3)
Flight to Mars, 1951 (Mirisch 4)
Flight to Tangier, 1953 (Dalio 3, Fontaine 3,
    Palance 3)
Flim-Flam Man, 1967 (Scott 3, Goldsmith 4,
    Jeakins 4, Lang 4, Smith 4)
Fling in the Ring, 1955 (Three Stooges 3)
Flip Flops, 1923 (Sennett 2)
Flipper Frolics, 1952 (Terry 4)
Flipping, 1973 (Chabrol 2)
Flips and Flops, 1919 (Laurel and Hardy 3)
Flip's Circus, 1918 (McCay 4)
Flip's Lunch Room, 1933 (Iwerks 4)
Flirt, 1917 (Weber 2, Daniels 3, Lloyd 3,
    Roach 4)
Flirt, 1922 (Laemmle 4)
Flirt, 1983 (Vitti 3)
Flirtation Walk, 1934 (Borzage 2, Daves 2,
    Keeler 3, Pangborn 3, Powell 3, Power 3,
    Barnes 4, Orry-Kelly 4, Polito 4,
    Wallis 4)
Flirting Husband, 1912 (Sennett 2,
    Normand 3)
Flirting in the Park, 1933 (Stevens 2)
Flirting Widow, 1930 (Rathbone 3)
Flirting with Fate, 1916 (Fairbanks 3,
    Gish 3)
Flirting with Fate, 1938 (Brown 3, Young 4)
Flirting with Love, 1924 (Moore 3,
    McCord 4)

Folketingsvalg 1945, 1945 (Henning-
Jensen 2)

Folle à tuer, 1975 (Sarde 4)

Folle Aventure, 1930 (Albers 3, Planer 4)

Føllet, 1943 (Henning-Jensen 2)

''Follia'' de Zavattini, 1982 (Zavattini 4)

Follie d'estate, 1966 (Scola 2)

Follie per l'opera, 1948 (Lollobrigida 3,
Fusco 4)

Follies, 1927 (Cantor 3)

Follow a Star, 1959 (Wisdom 3, Rank 4)

Follow Me, 1972 (Farrow 3, Topol 3,
Barry 4, Challis 4, Wallis 4)

Follow Me, Boys!, 1966 (Gish 3,
MacMurray 3, Disney 4)

Follow That Car, 1964 (Halas and
Batchelor 4)

Follow That Dream, 1962 (Presley 3,
Lederer 4, Salter 4)

Follow the Band, 1943 (Mitchum 3)

Follow the Boys, 1944 (Welles 2, Beavers 3,
Dietrich 3, Fields 3, MacDonald 3,
O'Connor 3, Raft 3, Cahn 4)

Follow the Crowd, 1918 (Daniels 3, Lloyd 3,
Roach 4)

Follow the Fleet, 1936 (Astaire 3, Ball 3,
Grable 3, Rogers 3, Scott 3, Berlin 4,
Berman 4, Pan 4, Polglase 4, Steiner 4)

Follow the Leader, 1930 (Rogers 3, Green 4,
Head 4)

Follow the Leader, 1944 (Katzman 4)

Follow the Sun, 1951 (Baxter 3, Ford 3,
LeMaire 4)

Follow Thru', 1930 (Banton 4)

Follow Your Star, 1938 (Pearson 2)

Following the Fuhrer. See Mitlaufer, 1984

Folly of Anne, 1914 (Gish 3)

Folly of Vanity, 1924 (August 4, Fox 4)

Folly to Be Wise, 1952 (Launder and
Gilliat 2, Sim 3, Korda 4)

Foma Gordeyev, 1959 (Donskoi 2)

Fond de l'air est rouge, 1977 (Marker 2)

Fonderies Martin, 1938 (Alexeieff and
Parker 4)

Foney Fables, 1942 (Blanc 4, Freleng 4,
Stalling 4)

Fontane: Effi Briest, 1974 (Schygulla 3)

Foo Foo's New Hat, 1980 (Halas and
Batchelor 4)

Foo Foo's Sleepless Night, 1980 (Halas and
Batchelor 4)

Food for Scandal, 1920 (Cruze 2)

Food of the Gods, 1976 (Lupino 3)

Fool, 1913 (Pearson 2)

Fool, 1925 (Goulding 2, Fox 4,
Ruttenberg 4)

Fool, 1990 (Cusack 3)

Fool and His Money, 1914 (Weber 2)

Fool Coverage, 1952 (Blanc 4, McKimson 4,
Stalling 4)

Fool for Love, 1985 (Altman 2, Stanton 3,
Shepard 4)

Fool Killer, 1965 (Perkins 3, Jeakins 4,
Rosenblum 4)

Fool There Was, 1915 (Bara 3, Fox 4)

Fool There Was, 1922 (Fox 4)

Foolish Age, 1919 (Sennett 2)

Foolish Age, 1921 (Stromberg 4)

Foolish Duckling, 1952 (Terry 4)

Foolish Husbands, 1929 (Sennett 2,
Hornbeck 4)

Foolish Husbands. See Historie de rire, 1941

Foolish Matrons, 1921 (Brown 2,
Tourneur 2, Bosworth 3)

**Foolish Wives, 1922 (Von Stroheim 2,
Brown 4, Daniels 4, Day 4, Laemmle 4,
Mandell 4, Thalberg 4)**

Fools, 1970 (Robards 3)

Fools First, 1922 (Neilan 2, Struss 4)

Fools for Luck, 1928 (Fields 3)

Fools for Scandal, 1938 (LeRoy 2,
Bellamy 3, Lombard 3, Wyman 3,
Banton 4, Deutsch 4, Grot 4)

Fool's Gold. See Krakguldet, 1968

Fool's Highway, 1924 (Coffee 4,
Laemmle 4)

Fool's Luck, 1926 (Arbuckle 3)

Fools of Fate, 1909 (Griffith 2, Bitzer 4)

Fools of Fortune, 1990 (Christie 3)

Fools' Parade, 1971 (Baxter 3)

Fool's Paradise, 1921 (De Mille 2, Struss 4,
Zukor 4)

Fool's Paradise, 1971 (Stewart 3, Westmore
Family 4)

Fool's Revenge, 1909 (Griffith 2, Bitzer 4)

Fools Rush In, 1949 (Rank 4, Unsworth 4)

Fools, Water Sprites, and Imposters. See
Blázni, vodníci, a podvodníci, 1980

Foot and Mouth, 1955 (Anderson 2,
Lassally 4)

Foot of Romance, 1914 (Beery 3)

Football, 1935 (Terry 4)

Football, 1962 (Decaë 4)

Football Coach. See College Coach, 1933

Football Fever, 1937 (Lantz 4)

Football Freaks, 1971 (Halas and
Batchelor 4)

Football Romeo, 1938 (Roach 4)

Football Toucher Downer, 1937
(Fleischer 4)

Footfalls, 1921 (Fox 4)

Footlight Glamour. See Upstream, 1926

Footlight Parade, 1933 (Bacon 2, Berkeley 2,
Blondell 3, Cagney 3, Garfield 3,
Keeler 3, Powell 3, Barnes 4, Grot 4,
Wallis 4, Warner 4)

Footlight Ranger, 1923 (Fox 4)

Footlight Serenade, 1942 (Grable 3,
Mature 3, Wyman 3, Day 4, Garmes 4,
Pan 4)

Footlight Varieties, 1951 (Hunt 4)

Footlights. See Sunny Side Up, 1926

Footlights and Fools, 1929 (March 3,
Moore 3, Grot 4, Wilson 4)

Footloose, 1979 (Von Sydow 3)

Footloose Heiress, 1937 (Sheridan 3,
Edeson 4)

Footloose Widows, 1926 (Zanuck 4)

Footpath, 1953 (Kumar 3)

Footsteps, 1973 (Parker 2)

Footsteps in the Dark, 1941 (Bacon 2,
Bellamy 3, Flynn 3, Haller 4,
Wallis 4)

Footsteps in the Fog, 1955 (Granger 3,
Simmons 3, Challis 4, Coffee 4)

Footsteps in the Night. See Honeymoon
Adventure, 1931

Footsteps in the Snow, 1966 (Lake 3)

Foozle at a Tea Party, 1914 (Roach 4)

For a Cop's Hide. See Pour la peau d'un flic,
1970

For a Few Dollars More. See Per qualche
dollaro in più, 1966

For a Joyful Life. See Za život radostný,
1951

For a Night of Love, 1988 (Makavejev 2)

For a Wife's Honor, 1908 (Griffith 2)

For a Woman's Honor, 1910 (Olcott 2)

For Alimony Only, 1926 (Adrian 4,
Coffee 4, Miller 4)

For Art's Sake, 1923 (Roach 4)

För att inte tala om alla dessa kvinnor, 1964
(Andersson, B. 3, Andersson, H. 3,
Dahlbeck 3, Josephson 3, Nykvist 4)

For Auld Lang Syne, 1938 (Cagney 3)

For Beauty's Sake, 1941 (Dumont 3,
Clarke 4, Day 4)

For Better, 1919 (Swanson 3)

For Better—But Worser, 1915 (Sennett 2)

For Better, For Worse, 1954
(Bogarde 3, Green 4)

For Better For Worse, 1959 (Halas and
Batchelor 4)

For Better, For Worser, 1919 (De Mille 2,
Buckland 4, Howe 4, Macpherson 4)

For Better or Worse. See That Little Band of
Gold, 1915

For Better or Worse, 1935 (Fleischer 4)

For Big Stakes, 1922 (Mix 3, Fox 4)

For Cash, 1915 (Chaney 3)

For Crimin' Out Loud, 1956 (Three
Stooges 3)

For De Andre. See Du skal elske din Naeste,
1915

For France, 1917 (Von Stroheim 2)

For Freedom, 1940 (Terry-Thomas 3)

For Freedom of Cuba, 1912 (Ince 4)

For Friendship. See För vänskaps skull, 1963

For fuld Fart. See Cocktails, 1927

For Fun—for Play. See Kaleidoskop:
Valeska Gert, 1979

For Georgia O'Keeffe, 1976 (Frampton 2)

For God and Country, 1943 (Huston 3)

For Guests Only, 1923 (Roach 4)

For Heaven's Sake, 1926 (Lloyd 3,
Bruckman 4, Zukor 4)

For Heaven's Sake, 1950 (Bennett 3,
Blondell 3, Webb 3, LeMaire 4,
Newman 4)

För hennes skull, 1930 (Jaenzon 4)

For Her Boy's Sake, 1913 (Cruze 2)

For Her Brother's Sake, 1911 (Pickford 3,
Gaudio 4, Ince 4)

For Her Brother's Sake, 1914 (Ince 4)

For Her Father's Sins, 1914 (Reid 3,
Sweet 3, Loos 4)

For Her Sake. See För hennes skull, 1930

For His Country's Honour. See For sit Lands
Aere, 1915

For His Son, 1911 (Griffith 2, Sweet 3,
Bitzer 4)

For Honor of the Name, 1910 (White 3)

For Husbands Only, 1917 (Weber 2)

For Ladies Only, 1981 (Grant 3)

For Lizzie's Sake, 1913 (Sennett 2,
Normand 3)

For Love . . . For Magic. See Per amore . . .
per magia, 1966

For Love of a Queen. See Dictator, 1935

For Love of Gold, 1908 (Griffith 2)

For Love of Ivy, 1968 (Poitier 3, Jones 4)

For Love of Mabel, 1913 (Sennett 2,
Normand 3)

For Love of You, 1933 (Dickinson 2,
Gallone 2)

For Love or Money. See Crossroads of New
York, 1922

For Love or Money. See Cash, 1933

For Love or Money, 1939 (Cortez 4,
Taradash 4)

For Love or Money, 1963 (Bendix 3,
Douglas 3, Ritter 3)

Forever Yours, 1944 (Tiomkin 4)

Forfaiture, 1937 (Allégret 2, L'Herbier 2, Hayakawa 3, Jouvet 3, Braunberger 4, Schüfftan 4)

Forgerons, 1895 (Lumière 2)

Forgery. See Southside 1–1000, 1950

Forget-Me-Not, 1917 (Marion 4)

Forget Me Not, 1922 (Van Dyke 2, Love 3)

Forget-Me-Not, 1936 (Hornbeck 4, Korda 4, Krasker 4)

Forget Mozart!. See Zabudnite na Mozarta, 1985

Forget Palermo. See Dimenticare Palermo, 1990

Forgiven in Death, 1911 (Anderson 3)

Forgotten Babies, 1933 (Roach 4)

Forgotten Commandments, 1932 (Carradine 3, Struss 4, Zukor 4)

Forgotten Faces, 1928 (Powell 3, Estabrook 4, Hunt 4, Selznick 4)

Forgotten Faces, 1936 (Dupont 2, Marshall 3)

Forgotten Faces, 1961 (Watkins 2)

Forgotten Man, 1941 (Benchley 4)

Forgotten Patriots, See Zapadlí vlastenci, 1932

Forgotten Prayer, 1916 (Borzage 2)

Forgotten Story, 1983 (Johnson 3)

Forgotten Sweeties, 1927 (Roach 4)

Forgotten Victory, 1939 (Zinnemann 2)

Forgotten Village, 1941 (Meredith 3, Eisler 4)

Forgotten Woman, 1939 (Arden 3, Cortez 4)

Forjadores de la paz, 1962 (Alvarez 2)

Forked Trails, 1915 (Mix 3)

Forlorn River, 1937 (Crabbe 3, Head 4)

Form Phases, 1952–54 (Breer 2)

Formal Kimono. See Harekodose, 1940

Formal Kimono. See Harekodose, 1961

Formation, 1952 (Godfrey 4)

Formula, 1980 (Brando 3, Gielgud 3, Scott 3)

Formula for a Murder. See Formula for Murder, 1985

Formula for Murder, 1985 (Brazzi 3)

Formula I, febbre della velocità, 1978 (Hackman 3)

Fornaretto di Venezia, 1964 (Morgan 3)

Fornarina, 1942 (Baarová 3)

Føroyar Faerøerne, 1961 (Roos 2)

Forsaking All Others, 1922 (Moore 3, Laemmle 4)

Forsaking All Others, 1934 (Mankiewicz 2, Van Dyke 2, Crawford 3, Gable 3, Montgomery 3, Russell 3, Adrian 4, Folsey 4, Toland 4)

Förseglade löppar, 1927 (Molander 2, Jaenzon 4)

Forstenbuben, 1985 (Morricone 4)

Försterchristel, 1926 (Dieterle 2, Andrejew 4)

Försterchristl, 1952 (Herlth 4)

Forsyte Saga. See That Forsyte Woman, 1949

Fort Algiers, 1953 (De Carlo 3)

Fort Apache, 1948 (Ford 2, Armendáriz 3, Bond 3, Fonda 3, McLaglen 3, Temple 3, Wayne 3, Basevi 4, Clothier 4, Cooper 4, Nugent 4)

Fort Apache, the Bronx, 1981 (Newman 3, Alcott 4)

Fort Bowie, 1957 (Johnson 3)

Fort Defiance, 1951 (Johnson 3, Cortez 4)

Fort Dobbs, 1958 (Clothier 4, Steiner 4)

Fort Graveyard. See Chi to suna, 1965

Fort Massacre, 1958 (McCrea 3, Mirisch 4)

Fort Osage, 1951 (Mirisch 4)

Fort Saganne, 1983 (Deneuve 3, Depardieu 3, Noiret 3)

Fort Ti, 1953 (Katzman 4)

Fort Vengeance, 1953 (Wanger 4)

Fort Worth, 1951 (Scott 3)

Fort Yuma, 1955 (Koch 4)

Fort-Dolorès, 1938 (Kaufman 4)

Forties Gals, 1967 (Sheridan 3)

Fortieth Door, 1921 (Van Dyke 2)

Fortieth Door, 1924 (Wong 3)

Fortini/Cani, 1976 (Straub and Huillet 2)

Fortuna, 1973 (Stawiński 4)

Fortuna di essere donna, 1955 (Boyer 3, Loren 3, Mastroianni 3, Cecchi D'Amico 4, Flaiano 4)

Fortuna viene dal cielo, 1943 (Magnani 3)

Fortunat, 1960 (Morgan 3)

Fortunate Pilgrim, 1988 (Loren 3)

Fortune, 1913 (Bunny 3)

Fortune, 1975 (Nichols 2, Beatty 3, Nicholson 3, Alonzo 4, Sylbert 4)

Fortune Cookie, 1966 (Wilder 2, Lemmon 3, Matthau 3, Diamond 4, La Shelle 4, Mandell 4, Previn 4)

Fortune Hunter. See Lyckoriddare, 1921

Fortune Hunters, 1913 (Guy 2)

Fortune Hunters, 1946 (Terry 4)

Fortune in Diamonds. See Adventurers, 1951

Fortune Is a Woman, 1957 (Launder and Gilliat 2, Hawkins 3, Lee 3, Alwyn 4)

Fortune Lane, 1947 (Baxter 2)

Fortune Teller, 1923 (Fleischer 4)

Fortunella, 1958 (Fellini 2, Masina 3, Sordi 3, De Laurentiis 4, Flaiano 4, Pinelli 4, Rota 4)

Fortune's Fool. See Alles für Geld, 1923

Fortune's Mask, 1922 (Laurel and Hardy 3)

Fortunes of a Composer, 1912 (Talmadge 3)

Fortunes of War, 1914 (Ince 4)

Forty Carats, 1973 (Kelly 3, Lang 4)

Forty Guns, 1957 (Fuller 2, Stanwyck 3, Biroc 4, LeMaire 4)

Forty Guns to Apache Pass, 1967 (Murphy 3)

Forty Leagues from Paradise, 1970 (Peries 2)

Forty Little Mothers. See Mioche, 1936

Forty Little Mothers, 1940 (Berkeley 2, Cantor 3, Lake 3)

Forty Naughty Girls, 1937 (Metty 4, Polglase 4)

Forty Pounds of Trouble, 1962 (Jewison 2, Curtis 3)

Forty Thieves, 1932 (Terry 4)

Forty Thieves, 1944 (Harlan 4, Wilson 4)

Forty Thousand Horsemen, 1940 (Rafferty 3)

Forty Winks, 1925 (Wong 3)

Forty Years. See Veertig Jaren, 1938

Forty Years of Experiment, 1926 (Richter 2)

Forty-Five Fathers, 1937 (McDaniel 3)

Forward a Century, 1951 (Lassally 4)

Forward into the Future, 1964 (Peries 2)

Forward March Hare, 1953 (Blanc 4, Jones 4, Maltese 4, Stalling 4)

Forward Pass, 1929 (Young 3)

Forza bruta, 1940 (Brazzi 3)

Forza del destino, 1950 (Gallone 2)

Forza G, 1971 (Morricone 4)

Forza Italia!, 1978 (Morricone 4)

Fossils. See Kaseki, 1975

Foster and Laurie, 1975 (Schifrin 4)

Foto proibite de una signora per bene, 1971 (Morricone 4)

Fou de Labo 4, 1967 (Brasseur 3)

Fou de la falaise, 1916 (Gance 2, Burel 4)

Fou du Labo 4, 1967 (Blier 3)

Fougères bleues, 1975 (De Beauregard 4)

Foul Ball Player, 1942 (Fleischer 4)

Foul Play, 1976 (Bardem 2)

Foul Play, 1978 (Hawn 3, Meredith 3, Moore 3, Roberts 3, Needham 4)

Foule hurle, 1932 (Gabin 3)

Found Film No. 1, 1968 (Vanderbeek 2)

Foundation of Ordination. See Seishoku no ishique, 1978

Foundations of Progress, 1972 (Benegal 2)

Foundling, 1915 (Dwan 2, Crisp 3)

Foundling, 1916 (Pickford 3, Marion 4)

Fountain, 1934 (Cromwell 2, Lukas 3, Berman 4, Hoffenstein 4, Murfin 4, Plunkett 4, Polglase 4, Steiner 4)

Fountainhead, 1949 (Vidor 2, Cooper 3, Massey 3, Neal 3, Blanke 4, Burks 4, Steiner 4)

Fountains of Bakhisarai, 1909 (Protazanov 2)

Four Against Fate. See Derby Day, 1952

Four American Composers, 1983 (Greenaway 2)

Four around a Woman. See Kamfende Herzen, 1920

Four Bags Full. See Traversée de Paris, 1956

Four Barriers, 1937 (Cavalcanti 2, Grierson 2, Watt 2)

Four Chimneys. See **Entotsu no mieru basho, 1953**

Four Companions. See Die vier gesellen, 1938

Four Dark Hours. See Green Cockatoo, 1937

Four Daughters, 1938 (Curtiz 2, Garfield 3, Rains 3, Blanke 4, Coffee 4, Epstein 4, Friedhofer 4, Haller 4, Orry-Kelly 4, Steiner 4, Wallis 4)

Four Days in November, 1964 (Bernstein 4)

Four Days Leave, 1949 (Signoret 3, Wilde 3, Lardner 4, Siodmak 4)

Four Days of Naples. See Quattro giornate de Napoli, 1962

Four Days' Wonder, 1936 (Cortez 4)

Four Deuces, 1975 (Palance 3)

Four Devils, 1928 (Murnau 2, Gaynor 3, Fox 4, Mayer 4)

Four Faces of India. See Chaar dil chaar rahen, 1959

Four Faces West, 1948 (McCrea 3, Harlan 4)

Four Feathers, 1929 (Schoedsack 2, Johnson 3, Powell 3, Wray 3, Banton 4, Cooper 4, Estabrook 4, Selznick 4, Zukor 4)

Four Feathers, 1939 (Richardson 3, Biro 4, Hornbeck 4, Korda 4, Krasker 4, Périnal 4, Rozsa 4, Saunders 4, Sherriff 4, Unsworth 4)

Four Flights to Love. See Paradis perdu, 1940

Four for Texas, 1963 (Aldrich 2, Bronson 3, Martin 3, Sinatra 3, Three Stooges 3, Biroc 4, Cahn 4, Guffey 4, Laszlo 4)

Four Friends, 1981 (Penn 2, Cloquet 4)

Four Frightened People, 1934 (De Mille 2, Colbert 3, Marshall 3, Coffee 4, Struss 4, Zukor 4)

Four Girls in Town, 1956 (Hudson 3, North 4)

Four Guns to the Border, 1954 (Brennan 3, Mancini 4, Metty 4, Salter 4)

Four Hearts, Four Roads. *See* Chaar dil chaar rahen, 1959

Four Horsemen of the Apocalypse, 1921 (Ingram 2, Beery 3, Johnson 3, Novarro 3, Valentino 3, Mathis 4, Mohr 4, Seitz 4)

Four Horsemen of the Apocalypse, 1962 (Minnelli 2, Boyer 3, Cobb 3, Ford 3, Henreid 3, Lansbury 3, Lukas 3, Thulin 3, Gillespie 4, Krasner 4, Orry-Kelly 4, Périnal 4, Plunkett 4, Previn 4)

Four Hours to Kill, 1935 (Leisen 2, Barthelmess 3, Milland 3, Head 4, Krasna 4, Zukor 4)

Four Hundred Blows. *See* **Quatre Cent Coups, 1959**

Four in the Morning, 1965 (Barry 4)

Four Jacks and a Jill, 1941 (Metty 4)

Four Jills in a Jeep, 1944 (Niblo 2, Faye 3, Francis 3, Grable 3, Miranda 3, Basevi 4, Friedhofer 4)

Four Just Men, 1939 (Balcon 4)

Four Kinds of Love. *See* Bambole, 1965

Four Little Tailors. *See* Quatre Petits Tailleurs, 1910

Four Love Stories. *See* Yottsu no koi no monogatari, 1947

Four Masked Men, 1934 (Pearson 2)

Four Men and a Girl. *See* Kentucky Moonshine, 1938

Four Men and a Prayer, 1938 (Ford 2, Carradine 3, Fitzgerald 3, Niven 3, Sanders 3, Young 3, Levien 4, MacGowan 4)

Four Minutes Late, 1914 (Mix 3)

Four Mothers, 1940 (Blanke 4)

Four Mothers, 1941 (Rains 3, Rosher 4)

Four Musicians of Bremen, 1922 (Disney 4)

Four Musketeers, 1974 (Lester 2, Cassel 3, Chaplin 3, Dunaway 3, Heston 3, Lee 3, Reed 3, Welch 3, Schifrin 4, Watkin 4)

Four Orphans, 1923 (La Cava 2)

Four Parts, 1934 (Roach 4)

Four Poster, 1952 (Kramer 2, Harrison 3, Bosustow 4, Hubley 4, Mohr 4, Tiomkin 4)

Four Seasons of Tateshina. *See* Tateshina no shiki, 1966

Four Shall Die, 1940 (Dandridge 3)

Four Sided Triangle, 1953 (Fisher 2, Carreras 4)

Four Sons, 1928 (Ford 2, Clarke 4, Fox 4)

Four Sons, 1940 (Ameche 3, Brown 4, Day 4, Shamroy 4, Zanuck 4)

Four Star Boarder, 1935 (Roach 4)

Four Stars. *See* ****, 1967

**** (Four Stars), 1967 (Warhol 2)

Four Steps in the Clouds. *See* Quattro passi fra le nuvole, 1942

Four Troublesome Heads. *See* Homme de tête, 1898

Four Wall Duration, 1973 (Le Grice 2)

Four Walls, 1928 (Crawford 3, Gilbert 3, Gibbons 4, Howe 4)

Four Wheels and No Brake, 1955 (Bosustow 4)

Four Wives, 1939 (Curtiz 2, Rains 3, Blanke 4, Epstein 4, Polito 4, Steiner 4, Wallis 4)

Fourberies de Pingouin, 1916 (Feuillade 2, Musidora 3)

Four-Bit Man, 1919 (Eason 4)

Fourchambault, 1929 (Vanel 3)

Fourflusher, 1927 (Laemmle 4)

Four-Footed Ranger, 1927 (Laemmle 4)

Fourmi, 1964 (Douy 4)

Four's a Crowd, 1938 (Curtiz 2, De Havilland 3, Flynn 3, Pangborn 3, Russell 3, Deutsch 4, Haller 4, Orry-Kelly 4, Robinson 4)

Fourteen Hours, 1951 (Cassavetes 2, Hathaway 2, Darwell 3, Kelly 3, Moorehead 3, LeMaire 4, Newman 4, Paxton 4, Wheeler 4)

Fourteen's Good, Eighteen's Better, 1980 (Armstrong 2)

Fourteenth Man, 1920 (Daniels 3, Brown 4)

Fourth Alarm, 1926 (Roach 4)

Fourth Commandment, 1927 (Laemmle 4)

Fourth Estate, 1940 (Rotha 2, Mayer 4)

Fourth Horseman, 1932 (Mix 3)

Fourth Mrs. Anderson, 1971 (Baker 3)

Fourth Musketeer, 1923 (Howard 2)

Fourth Protocol, 1987 (Caine 3, Axelrod 4, Schifrin 4)

Fourth War, 1990 (Frankenheimer 2, Scheider 3, Stanton 3)

Fourth Wise Man, 1985 (Arkin 3, Bellamy 3, Sheen 3)

Fourvière, 1948 (Colpi 4)

Fowl Ball, 1930 (Lantz 4)

Fowl Play, 1937 (Fleischer 4)

Fowl Play, 1973 (McKimson 4)

Fowl Weather, 1953 (Blanc 4, Foster 4, Freleng 4, Stalling 4)

Fox, 1921 (Carey 3)

Fox, 1967 (Fraker 4, Koch 4, Schifrin 4)

Fox and his Friends. *See* Faustrecht der Freiheit, 1975

Fox and the Duck, 1945 (Terry 4)

Fox and the Grapes, 1921 (Terry 4)

Fox and the Hounds, 1981 (Rooney 3)

Fox and the Jug. *See* Liska a džbán, 1947

Fox and the Rabbit, 1935 (Lantz 4)

Fox Chase, 1928 (Disney 4)

Fox Chase, 1952 (Lye 4)

Fox Hunt, 1906 (Bitzer 4)

Fox Hunt, 1925 (Roach 4)

Fox Hunt, 1936 (Korda 4)

Fox Hunt, 1950 (Terry 4)

Fox in a Fix, 1951 (Blanc 4, McKimson 4, Stalling 4)

Fox Movietone Follies of 1929, 1929 (Cooper 3, Fox 4)

Fox Movietone Follies of 1930, 1930 (Grable 3, Fox 4)

Fox Pop, 1942 (Blanc 4, Jones 4)

Fox Talent Movietone, 1928 (Gaynor 3)

Fox Terror, 1957 (Blanc 4, McKimson 4, Stalling 4)

Foxed By a Fox, 1955 (Terry 4)

Foxes, 1980 (Foster 3, Puttnam 4)

Foxes of Harrow, 1947 (Stahl 2, Harrison 3, McLaglen 3, O'Hara 3, La Shelle 4, LeMaire 4, Newman 4, Wheeler 4)

Foxfire, 1955 (Duryea 3, Russell 3, Daniels 4)

Foxfire Childwatch, 1971 (Brakhage 2)

Foxhole in Cairo, 1960 (Caine 3)

Foxiest Girl in Paris. *See* Nathalie, 1957

Foxtrot, 1975 (O'Toole 3, Von Sydow 3)

Foxtrot Tango Alpha. *See* F.T.A., 1972

Foxy By Proxy, 1952 (Blanc 4, Freleng 4, Stalling 4)

Foxy Duckling, 1947 (Blanc 4)

Foxy Hunter, 1937 (Fleischer 4)

Foxy Pup, 1937 (Iwerks 4)

Foxy-Fox, 1935 (Terry 4)

Fozzle at a Tee Party, 1914 (Lloyd 3)

Fra Diavolo, 1906 (Messter 4)

Fra Diavolo, 1912 (Guy 2)

Fra Diavolo, 1922 (Metzner 4)

Fra Diavolo, 1930 (Metzner 4)

Fra Diavolo, 1933 (Laurel and Hardy 3, Macpherson 4, Roach 4)

Fra Manisco cerca quai, 1964 (Fabrizi 3)

Fra Mørken Til Lys, 1914 (Psilander 3)

Fra Vincenti, 1909 (Feuillade 2)

Fractured Leghorn, 1950 (Blanc 4, Foster 4, McKimson 4, Stalling 4)

Fragilité, ton nom est femme, 1965 (Trintignant 3)

Fragment of an Empire. *See* Oblomok imperii, 1929

Fragment of Fear, 1970 (Dehn 4, Morris 4)

Fragments of Isabella, 1989 (Lassally 4)

Fraidy Cat, 1924 (Roach 4)

Fraidy Cat, 1942 (Hanna and Barbera 4)

Framed, 1939 (Guffey 4, Salter 4)

Framed, 1947 (Ford 3, Guffey 4, Maddow 4)

Framed Cat, 1950 (Hanna and Barbera 4)

Frame-Up, 1917 (Furthman 4)

Frame-Up, 1938 (Terry 4)

Framing Father, 1942 (Metty 4)

Framing Youth, 1937 (Roach 4)

Från yttersta skären, 1931 (Molander 2)

Français vus par . . . , 1988 (Lynch 2)

Française et l'amour, 1960 (Belmondo 3, Girardot 3, Audiard 4, Delerue 4, Kosma 4, Rappeneau 4, Spaak 4)

France d'abord, 1915 (Fresnay 3)

France est un jardin, 1952 (Leenhardt 2)

France, nouvelle patrie, 1948 (Kosma 4)

France. S.A., 1973 (Carrière 4)

Frances, 1982 (Costner 3, Lange 3, Barry 4, Kovacs 4, Shepard 4, Sylbert 4)

Francesca da Rimini, 1911 (Bertini 3)

Francesco, 1989 (Rourke 3, Vangelis 4)

Francesco e mia, 1986 (Vitti 3)

Francesco—guillare di Dio, 1950 (Fellini 2, Fabrizi 3)

Franches lippées, 1933 (Delannoy 2)

Franchise Affair, 1951 (More 3)

Francis, 1949 (Curtis 3, O'Connor 3, Fleischer 4)

Francis Covers the Big Town, 1953 (O'Connor 3)

Francis Goes to the Races, 1951 (O'Connor 3)

Francis Goes to West Point, 1952 (O'Connor 3)

Francis in the Haunted House, 1956 (Rooney 3)

Francis in the Navy, 1955 (Eastwood 3, O'Connor 3)

Francis Joins the Wacs, 1954 (O'Connor 3)

Francis of Assisi, 1961 (Curtiz 2, Armendáriz 4)

Francis the First. *See* François Ier, 1937

Francisca, 1981 (Oliveira 2, Branco 4)

Franciscain de Bourges, 1967 (Autant-Lara 2, Aurenche 4, Bost 4, Douy 4)

Franck Aroma, 1937 (Alexeieff and Parker 4)

François Ier, 1937 (Fernandel 3)

François le rhinocéros, 1953 (Kosma 4)

François Mauriac, 1954 (Leenhardt 2)

François Simon—La présence, 1986 (Tanner 2, Moreau 3)

François Villon, 1945 (Reggiani 3, Auric 4, Douy 4)

Frank Hansens Glück, 1917 (Wiene 2)

Frankenstein, 1931 (Florey 2, Whale 2, Karloff 3, Balderston 4, Edeson 4, Fort 4, Fulton 4, Laemmle 4, Pierce 4)

Frankenstein, 1958 (Karloff 3)

Frankenstein, 1984 (Gielgud 3)

Frankenstein and the Monster from Hell, 1973 (Fisher 2, Cushing 3, Bernard 4)

Frankenstein Conquers the World. *See* Furankenshutain tai Baragon, 1966

Frankenstein Created Woman, 1967 (Fisher 2, Cushing 3, Bernard 4, Carreras 4)

Frankenstein cum Cannabis, 1970 (Müller 4)

Frankenstein Island, 1977 (Carradine 3)

Frankenstein Meets the Wolf Man, 1943 (Lugosi 3, Pierce 4, Salter 4, Siodmak 4)

Frankenstein Must Be Destroyed, 1969 (Fisher 2, Cushing 3, Bernard 4, Carreras 4)

Frankenstein—The True Story, 1973 (Gielgud 3, Mason 3, Moorehead 3, Richardson 3)

Frankenstein Trestle, White Mts., 1899 (Bitzer 4)

Frankenstein Unbound, 1989 (Corman 2)

Frankenstein vs. the Giant Devilfish. *See* Furankenshutain tai Barogon, 1966

Frankenstein's Castle of Freaks. *See* House of Freaks, 1973

Frankenstein's Cat, 1942 (Terry 4)

Frankenstein's Great Aunt Tillie, 1985 (Pleasence 3)

Frankie and Johnnie, 1928 (Laughton 3)

Frankie and Johnnie, 1935 (Ruttenberg 4, Young 4)

Frankie and Johnny, 1966 (Presley 3)

Frankie and Johnny, 1991 (Pacino 3, Pfeiffer 3)

Franks, 1909 (Griffith 2)

Frank's Greatest Adventure, 1967 (Voight 3)

Frånskild, 1951 (Molander 2, Andersson 3)

Frantic. *See* Ascenseur pour l'échafaud, 1958

Frantic, 1988 (Polanski 2, Ford 3, Morricone 4)

Franziskus. *See* Francesco, 1988

Fratelli, 1985 (Vogler 3)

Fratelli d'italia, 1951 (Delli Colli 4)

Fratello sole, sorella luna, 1972 (Zeffirelli 2, Guinness 3, Cecchi D'Amico 4, Donati 4)

Fraternity Row, 1977 (Robertson 3)

Frau, 1936 (Von Harbou 4)

Frau am Scheidewege, 1938 (Von Harbou 4)

Frau auf der Folter, 1928 (Wiene 2, Kortner 3)

Frau Blackburn, geb. 5. Jan, 1872, wird gefilmt, 1967 (Kluge 2)

Frau Cheney's Ende, 1961 (Rosay 3)

Frau, die jeder liebt, bist du!, 1929 (Reisch 4)

Frau, die nicht ''nein'' sagen kann, 1926 (Albers 3, Fröhlich 3)

Frau, die weiss was sie will, 1934 (Walbrook 3)

Frau Eva, 1915 (Wiene 2, Jannings 3, Freund 4, Messter 4)

Frau für drei Tage, 1944 (Von Harbou 4)

Frau fürs ganze Leben, 1960 (Herlth 4)

Frau gegenüber, 1978 (Lassally 4)

Frau Holle, 1985 (Masina 3)

Frau im Delphin, oder 30 Tage auf dem Meeresgrund, 1918 (Lugosi 3)

Frau im Feuer, 1924 (Nielsen 3, Tschechowa 3)

Frau im Mond, 1929 (Gründgens 3, Rasp 3, Courant 4, Pommer 4, Von Harbou 4)

Frau im Mond, 1929 (Fischinger 2, Ford 2, Hunte 4)

Frau im Strom, 1939 (Rasp 3)

Frau im Talar, 1929 (Kortner 3)

Frau mit dem schlechten Ruf, 1925 (Barrymore 3, Fröhlich 3, Hoffmann 4)

Frau mit den Millionen, 1923 (Dreier 4)

Frau mit den Orchiden, 1919 (Krauss 3, Hoffmann 4, Pommer 4)

Frau mit Herz, 1951 (Tschechowa 3)

Frau mit Vergangenheit, 1920 (Hoffmann 4)

Frau, nach der Man sich sehnt, 1929 (Dietrich 3, Kortner 3, Courant 4)

Frau nach Mass, 1940 (Käutner 2)

Frau ohne Bedeutung, 1936 (Gründgens 3, Von Harbou 4)

Frau ohne Namen, 1926 (Warm 4)

Frau ohne Seele, 1921 (Krauss 3)

Frau Sixta, 1938 (Fröhlich 3)

Frau Sorge, 1928 (Dieterle 2, Kortner 3)

Frau über Bord, 1945 (Staudte 2)

Frau von vierzig Jahren, 1925 (Leni 2)

Fraud that Failed, 1913 (Dwan 2)

Frauds and Frenzies, 1918 (Laurel and Hardy 3)

Frauen am Abgrund, 1929 (Planer 4)

Frauen aus der Wiener Vorstadt, 1925 (Reisch 4)

Frauen, die durch die Hölle gehen, 1966 (Baxter 3)

Frauen in New York, 1977 (Ballhaus 4)

Frauen sind keine Engel, 1943 (Stallich 4)

Frauen von Folies Bergères, 1926 (Warm 4)

Frauen von Gnadenstein, 1921 (Von Harbou 4)

Frauenarzt Dr. Prätorius, 1950 (Wagner 4)

Frauenarzt Dr. Schäfer, 1927 (Albers 3)

Frauenehre, 1918 (Kortner 3)

Frauenhaus von Brescia, 1920 (Dreier 4)

Frauenhaus von Rio, 1927 (Planer 4)

Frauennot-Frauenglück, 1930 (Tisse 4)

Frauenopfer, 1922 (Dieterle 2, Leni 2, Porten 3)

Frauenschicksale, 1952 (Eisler 4)

Fräulein aus Argentinien, 1928 (Albers 3)

Fräulein Barbier, 1915 (Wiene 2)

Fraulein Berlin, 1983 (Jarmusch 2)

Fräulein Doktor, 1968 (Lattuada 2, Giannini 3, More 3, De Laurentiis 4, Morricone 4)

Fräulein Else, 1929 (Bergner 3, Balàzs 4, Freund 4)

Fräulein Fähnrich, 1929 (Reisch 4)

Fräulein Hoffmanns Erzahlungen, 1933 (Ondra 3, Heller 4)

Fräulein Josette, meine Frau, 1926 (Warm 4)

Fräulein Julie, 1922 (Dieterle 2, Nielsen 3, Herlth 4, Röhrig 4)

Fräulein Pfiffikus, 1919 (Krauss 3)

Fräulein Piccolo, 1914 (Lubitsch 2)

Fräulein Raffke, 1923 (Krauss 3)

Fräulein Seifenschaum, 1914 (Lubitsch 2)

Fräulein vom Amt, 1925 (Galeen 4, Wagner 4)

Fräulein von Barnhelm, 1940 (Hoffmann 4)

Fräulein von Scuderi, 1955 (Porten 3)

Fraungasse von Algier, 1927 (Hoffmann 4)

Frayle, 1959 (Olmi 2)

Freak Orlando, 1981 (Seyrig 3)

Freaks, 1932 (Browning 2, Beavers 3, Gibbons 4, Mayer 4, Thalberg 4)

Freaks of the Deep, 1932 (Sennett 2)

Freaky Friday, 1976 (Foster 3)

Freccia nel fianco, 1945 (Lattuada 2, Flaiano 4, Ponti 4, Rota 4, Zavattini 4)

Freckled Fish, 1919 (Laurel and Hardy 3)

Freckled Rascal, 1929 (Musuraca 4, Plunkett 4)

Freckles, 1912 (Bunny 3)

Freckles, 1917 (Neilan 2, Bosworth 3)

Freckles, 1928 (Bosworth 3)

Freckles, 1935 (Berman 4, Plunkett 4)

Freckles, 1960 (Crosby 4)

Fred Barry, comédien, 1959 (Jutra 2)

Fredaines de Pierrette, 1901 (Guy 2, Gaumont 4)

Freddie Steps Out, 1946 (Katzman 4)

Free. *See* Azad, 1955

Free and Easy, 1930 (De Mille 2, Niblo 2, Barrymore 3, Montgomery 3, Gibbons 4)

Free and Easy, 1941 (Folsey 4)

Free at Last, 1985 (Hurt 3)

Free, Blond, and 21, 1940 (Barnes 4)

Free Eats, 1932 (Roach 4)

Free Enterprise, 1947 (Terry 4)

Free Fall, 1967 (Vanderbeek 2)

Free for All, 1950 (Buckner 4)

Free Man. *See* Homme libre, 1973

Free Radicals, 1957 (Lye 4)

Free School. *See* Jiyu gakko, 1951

Free Soul, 1931 (Brown 2, Barrymore 3, Gable 3, Howard 3, Shearer 3, Adrian 4, Daniels 4, Mayer 4)

Free Spirit. *See* Belstone Fox, 1973

Free the Army. *See* F.T.A., 1972

Free to Live. *See* Holiday, 1938

Free to Love, 1925 (Bow 3, Schulberg 4)

Free Wheeling, 1932 (Roach 4)

Freebie and the Bean, 1974 (Arkin 3, Caan 3, Kovacs 4, Lourié 4)

Freed 'em and Weep, 1929 (McCarey 2)

Freedom, 1970 (Black 3)

Freedom Fighter. *See* Wall of Tyrrany, 1988

Freedom Must Have Wings, 1941 (Balcon 4)

Freedom of the Press, 1928 (Walthall 3)

Freedom Radio, 1940 (Dillon 4, Rank 4)

Freedom Road, 1978 (Kadár 2)

Freehände, 1912 (Porten 3)

Freejack, 1991 (Hopkins 3)

Freeze Out, 1921 (Ford 2, Carey 3)

Frei bis zum nächsten Mal, 1969 (Fassbinder 2)

Freibuter, 1985 (Thulin 3)

Freie Fahrt, 1928 (Metzner 4)

Freighters of Destiny, 1931 (McCord 4)

Freiheit, 1915 (Lucas 2)

Freiheit in Fesseln, 1929 (Warm 4)

Freiwild, 1928 (Holger-Madsen 2)

Fremde, 1917 (Pick 2, Hoffmann 4)

Fremde, 1917 (Krauss 3)

Fremde, 1930 (Burel 4)

Fremde Frau, 1950 (Staudte 2)

Fremde Furst, 1918 (Wegener 3)

Fremde Vogel, 1911 (Gad 2, Nielsen 3, Freund 4)

Fremdenlegionär. *See* Wenn die Schwalben heimwärts ziehn, 1928

French Cancan, 1955 (Rivette 2, Straub and Huillet 2, Félix 3, Gabin 3, Modot 3, Piccoli 3, Douy 4)

French Communique, 1940 (Hamer 2)

French Connection, 1971 (Friedkin 2, Hackman 3, Rey 3, Scheider 3, Roizman 4)

French Connection II, 1975 (Frankenheimer 2, Hackman 3, Rey 3, Needham 4, Renoir 4, Saulnier 4)

French Conspiracy. See Attentat, 1972

French Cops Learning English, 1908 (Méliès 2)

French Doll, 1923 (Marion 4)

French Downstairs, 1916 (Weber 2)

French Dressing, 1927 (Dwan 2, Haller 4)

French Dressing, 1963 (Russell 2, Delerue 4, Russell 4)

French Duel, 1909 (Griffith 2, Bitzer 4)

French Fried, 1930 (Terry 4)

French Game. See Coeur battant, 1962

French Kiss, 1981 (Douglas 3)

French Leave, 1930 (Carroll 3)

French Leave, 1948 (Cooper 3)

French Leave. See Poudre d'escampette, 1971

French Lieutenant's Woman, 1981 (Reisz 2, Irons 3, Streep 3, Francis 4, Pinter 4)

French Line, 1954 (Bacon 2, Novak 3, Russell 3, D'Agostino 4, Dunn 4)

French Lunch, 1969 (Douglas 3)

French Maid, 1907 (Crisp 3)

French Milliner, 1916 (Loos 4)

French Mistress, 1960 (Boulting 2, Addison 4)

French Promoter. See Great White Hope, 1970

French Provincial. See Souvenirs d'en France, 1975

French Rabbit, 1951 (Blanc 4)

French Rarebit, 1951 (McKimson 4)

French They Are a Funny Race. See Carnets du Major Thompson, 1957

French Touch. See Coiffeur pour dames, 1952

French Way. See Mouton enragé, 1974

French White Cargo. See Cargaison blanche, 1937

French without Tears, 1939 (Asquith 2, Lean 2, Milland 3, Dalrymple 4, De Grunwald 4, Dillon 4, Head 4, Rattigan 4)

Frenchie, 1950 (Lanchester 3, McCrea 3, Winters 3, Salter 4)

Frenchman's Creek, 1944 (Leisen 2, Fontaine 3, Rathbone 3, Barnes 4, Dreier 4, Jennings 4, Young 4)

Frenchy, 1914 (Crisp 3)

Frenesia dell'estate, 1963 (Gassman 3, Age and Scarpelli 4)

Frenzied Finance, 1916 (Laurel and Hardy 3)

Frenzy. See Hets, 1944

Frenzy, 1972 (Hitchcock 2)

Frequence meurtre, 1988 (Deneuve 3)

Frère de lait, 1916 (Feyder 2)

Frères Boutdebois, 1908 (Cohl 4)

Frères corses, 1939 (Brasseur 3)

Frères d'Afrique, 1939 (Brasseur 3)

Frères Karamazov, 1930 (Rathaus 4)

Frères Karamazov. See Mörder Dimitri Karamasoff, 1931

Fresh Airedale, 1945 (Blanc 4, Jones 4, Stalling 4)

Fresh as a Freshman, 1941 (Bruckman 4)

Fresh Eggs, 1923 (Roach 4)

Fresh Fish, 1939 (Avery 4)

Fresh from the City, 1920 (Sennett 2)

Fresh from the Farm, 1914 (Lloyd 3, Roach 4)

Fresh Hare, 1942 (Blanc 4, Freleng 4, Maltese 4, Stalling 4)

Fresh Paint, 1920 (Roach 4)

Fresh Vegetable Mystery, 1939 (Fleischer 4)

Freshman, 1925 (Lloyd 3, Zukor 4)

Freshman, 1990 (Brando 3, Adam 4, Fraker 4)

Freshman Love, 1935 (Orry-Kelly 4)

Freshman Year, 1938 (Ladd 3)

Freud. See Freud: The Secret Passion, 1962

Freud: The Secret Passion, 1962 (Clift 3, York 3, Goldsmith 4, Slocombe 4)

Freudlose Gasse, 1925 (Dietrich 3, Garbo 3, Krauss 3, Nielsen 3)

Freudy Cat, 1964 (Blanc 4, McKimson 4)

Freundin eines grossen Mannes, 1934 (Wegener 3)

Freundin so goldig wie du, 1930 (Ondra 3, Heller 4)

Fric-Frac, 1939 (Autant-Lara 2, Arletty 3, Fernandel 3, Simon 3)

Frida's Songs. See Fridas visor, 1930

Fridas visor, 1930 (Jaenzon 4)

Friday the 13th, 1922 (Roach 4)

Friday the 13th, 1953 (Terry 4)

Friday the Thirteenth, 1933 (Saville 2, Launder and Gilliat 2, Matthews 3, Richardson 3, Balcon 4, Junge 4, Vetchinsky 4)

Friday the Thirteenth, 1980 (Savini 4)

Friday the Thirteenth, Part II, 1981 (Savini 4)

Fridays of Eternity. See Viernes de la eternidad, 1981

Fridericus, 1936 (Dagover 3)

Fridericus Rex, 1921 (Metzner 4)

Fridericus Rex, 1923 (Krauss 3)

Fridericus Rex: Ein Königsschicksal, 1922 (Dreier 4)

Fried Chicken, 1930 (Terry 4)

Frieda, 1947 (Dearden 2, Zetterling 2, Balcon 4, Rank 4)

Friedemann Bach, 1941 (Gründgens 3)

Friedemann Bach, 1950 (Staudte 2)

Friedensreiter, 1917 (Krauss 3)

Friederike, 1932 (Warm 4)

Friedrich Schiller, 1940 (Dagover 3, Wagner 4)

Friedrich Werders Sendung, 1916 (Hoffmann 4)

Friend. See Przy Jaciel, 1960

Friend Fleeing, 1962 (Baillie 2)

Friend Husband, 1918 (Sennett 2)

Friend Husband, 1924 (Roach 4)

Friend in Need Is Friend Indeed, 1906 (Bitzer 4)

Friend Indeed, 1938 (Zinnemann 2)

Friend of the Family, 1909 (Griffith 2, Bitzer 4)

Friend of the Family, 1949 (Mills 3)

Friend of the Family, 1954 (Lassally 4)

Friend of the Family. See Patate, 1964

Friend Will Come Tonight. See Ami viendra ce soir, 1945

Friendly Enemies, 1925 (Clarke 4)

Friendly Enemies, 1942 (Dwan 2, Cronjager 4)

Friendly Husband, 1922 (Fox 4)

Friendly Persuasion, 1956 (Wyler 2, Cooper 3, Perkins 3, Jeakins 4, Tiomkin 4, Wilson 4)

Friends, 1912 (Griffith 2, Barrymore 3, Carey 3, Pickford 3, Walthall 3, Bitzer 4)

Friends. See Druzya, 1938

Friends and Husbands. See Heller Wahn, 1982

Friends and Lovers, 1931 (Von Stroheim 2, Menjou 3, Olivier 3, Hunt 4, Murfin 4, Steiner 4)

Friends for Life. See Amici per la pelle, 1955

Friends of Eddie Coyle, 1973 (Yates 2, Mitchum 3)

Friends of Mr. Sweeney, 1934 (Orry-Kelly 4)

Friesenblut, 1925 (Fröhlich 3)

Frieze, an Underground Film, 1973 (Miller 2)

Fright Night, 1947 (Three Stooges 3, Bruckman 4)

Fright Night, 1985 (McDowall 3, Edlund 4)

Fright Night II, 1988 (McDowall 3)

Frightened Bride. See Tall Headlines, 1952

Frightened City. See Killer That Stalked New York, 1950

Frightened City, 1961 (Connery 3, Lom 3)

Frightened Lady, 1932 (Balcon 4)

Frigid Hare, 1949 (Blanc 4, Jones 4, Stalling 4)

Fringe Dwellers, 1985 (Beresford 2)

Frios ojos miedo, 1970 (Rey 3)

Fripons, voleurs, et cie. See Boulot aviateur, 1937

Friquet, 1912 (Tourneur 2)

Frischer Wind aus Kanada, 1935 (Herlth 4, Röhrig 4)

Frisco Jenny, 1933 (Wellman 2, Calhern 3, Orry-Kelly 4)

Frisco Kid, 1935 (Bacon 2, Cagney 3, Miller 4, Orry-Kelly 4, Polito 4)

Frisco Kid, 1979 (Aldrich 2, Ford 3, Wilder 3)

Frisco Lil, 1942 (Salter 4)

Frisco Sal, 1945 (Siodmak 4)

Frisco Sally Levy, 1927 (Gibbons 4)

Frisky Mrs. Johnson, 1920 (Folsey 4)

Frissons partout, 1964 (Constantine 3)

Fritz Kortner, 1966 (Syberberg 2)

Fritz the Cat, 1972 (Bakshi 4)

Frivolité, 1901 (Guy 2)

Frivolités, 1929 (Burel 4)

Frivolous Wives. See Married Virgin, 1920

Frog, 1937 (Wilcox 2, Hawkins 3)

Frog and the Princess, 1944 (Terry 4)

Frog on the Swing, 1988 (Breer 4)

Frog Pond, 1938 (Iwerks 4)

Frog Prince, 1954 (Reiniger 4)

Frog Prince, 1961 (Reiniger 4)

Frog Prince, 1985 (Puttnam 4)

Frog That Wanted a King, 1921 (Terry 4)

Frogmen, 1951 (Bacon 2, Andrews 3, Wagner 3, Widmark 3, LeMaire 4, Reynolds 4, Wheeler 4)

Frogs, 1972 (Milland 3)

Fröken April, 1958 (Björnstrand 3)

Fröken Julie, 1951 (Von Sydow 3)

From a Far Country, 1981 (Zanussi 2)

From A to Z-Z-Z, 1954 (Blanc 4, Jones 4, Stalling 4)

From a Whisper to a Scream, 1986 (Price 3)

From Bad to Worse, 1937 (Ballard 4)

From Beyond the Grave, 1973 (Cushing 3, Dors 3, Pleasence 3)

From Blitzkrieg to the Bomb, 1985 (Sheen 3)

From Champion To Tramp, 1980 (Johnson 3)

From Doric to Gothic, 1952 (Ibert 4)

From Earth to the Moon, 1958 (Sanders 3)

From Hand to Mouse, 1944 (Blanc 4, Jones 4, Stalling 4)

From Hand to Mouth, 1919 (Lloyd 3, Roach 4)

From Hare to Heir, 1960 (Blanc 4, Freleng 4)

From Headquarters, 1929 (Walthall 3)

From Headquarters, 1933 (Dieterle 2, Brennan 3, Grot 4)

From Hell to Heaven, 1933 (Lombard 3, Banton 4, Buchman 4)

From Hell to Texas, 1958 (Hopper 3, Buckner 4, LeMaire 4, Wheeler 4)

From Here to Eternity, 1953 (Zinnemann 2, Borgnine 3, Clift 3, Kerr 3, Lancaster 3, Reed 3, Sinatra 3, Cohn 4, Duning 4, Guffey 4, Taradash 4, Wald 4)

From Here to There, 1964 (Bass 4)

From Jerusalem to the Dead Sea, 1912 (Olcott 2)

From Noon Till Three, 1976 (Bronson 3, Ballard 4, Bernstein 4)

From Now On, 1920 (Walsh 2, Ruttenberg 4)

From Nurse to Worse, 1940 (Three Stooges 3, Bruckman 4)

From Patches to Plenty, 1915 (Sennett 2)

From Plan into Action, 1951 (Lassally 4)

From Rags to Britches, 1925 (Sennett 2)

From Russia with Love, 1963 (Armendáriz 3, Connery 3, Shaw 3, Barry 4)

From Soup to Nuts, 1928 (Laurel and Hardy 3, Roach 4)

From the Bottom of the Sea, 1911 (Pickford 3, Gaudio 4)

From the Cloud to the Resistance. See Della nube alla resistenza, 1979

From the Czech Mills. See Z českých mlýnu, 1929

From the Drain, 1967 (Cronenberg 2)

From the Earth to the Moon, 1958 (Cotten 3, Haskin 4)

From the Four Corners, 1941 (Launder and Gilliat 2, Howard 3, Havelock-Allan 4)

From the Four Hundred to the Herd, 1911 (Dwan 2)

From the Hip, 1987 (Hurt 3)

From the Life of the Marionettes. See Aus dem Leben der Marionetten, 1980

From the Manger to the Cross, 1912 (Olcott 2)

From the Mixed-Up Files of Mrs. Basil E. Frankweiler, 1973 (Bergman 3)

From the Other Side of the Water. See De l'autre côté de l'eau, 1951

From the Shadows, 1913 (August 4)

From the Terrace, 1960 (Loy 3, Newman 3, Woodward 3, Bernstein 4, Wheeler 4)

From This Day Forward, 1946 (Fontaine 3, Barnes 4, D'Agostino 4, Kanin 4)

From Wash to Washington, 1914 (Cruze 2)

From Whom Cometh My Help, 1949 (Poitier 3)

Fromme Lüge, 1938 (Negri 3)

Front, 1943 (Vasiliev 2)

Front, 1976 (Allen 2, Ritt 2)

Front de mer, 1951 (Auric 4)

Front Line, 1940 (Watt 2)

Front Page, 1931 (Milestone 2, Horton 3, Menjou 3, Day 4, Hecht 4, Hughes 4, Lederer 4)

Front Page, 1974 (Wilder 2, Lemmon 3, Matthau 3, Sarandon 3, Bumstead 4, Diamond 4, Hecht 4)

Front Page Story, 1953 (Hawkins 3)

Front Page Story, 1978 (Horton 3)

Front Page Woman, 1935 (Curtiz 2, Davis 3, Gaudio 4, Orry-Kelly 4)

Frontier. See Aerogard, 1935

Frontier Badmen, 1943 (Salter 4)

Frontier Doctor, 1911 (Anderson 3)

Frontier Gal, 1945 (De Carlo 3, Banton 4)

Frontier Girl's Courage, 1911 (Bosworth 3)

Frontier Hellcat. See Unter Geiern, 1964

Frontier Horizon. See New Frontier, 1939

Frontier Marshal, 1934 (Bond 3)

Frontier Marshal, 1939 (Dwan 2, Bond 3, Carradine 3, Scott 3, Clarke 4, Day 4, Raksin 4)

Frontier Outlaws, 1944 (Crabbe 3)

Frontier Pony Express, 1939 (Johnson 3, Rogers 3)

Frontier Rangers, 1959 (Tourneur 2, Dickinson 3)

Frontier Scout. See Quincannon, Frontier Scout, 1956

Frontier Trail, 1926 (Carey 3, Polito 4)

Frontier Vengeance, 1939 (Canutt 4)

Frontier Wife, 1913 (Ince 4)

Frontiere, 1934 (Cervi 3)

Frontière, 1961 (Braunberger 4)

Frontiers. See Grens, 1984

Frontiers of News, 1964 (Van Dyke 2)

Frontiersman, 1938 (Harlan 4, Head 4)

Frontline Cameras 1935–1965, 1965 (Van Dyke 2)

Frosch mit der Maske, 1959 (Rasp 3)

Frou Frou, 1914 (Cruze 2)

Frou Frou, 1918 (Bertini 3)

Frou Frou. See Toy Wife, 1938

Frou-Frou, 1955 (Cervi 3, Alekan 4)

Frozen Dead, 1967 (Andrews 3)

Frozen Feet, 1939 (Terry 4)

Frozen Ghost, 1945 (Salter 4)

Frozen Hearts, 1923 (Laurel and Hardy 3, Roach 4)

Frozen Justice, 1929 (Dwan 2, Carré 4, Fox 4, Levien 4, Rosson 4)

Frozen Limits, 1939 (Launder and Gilliat 2, Crazy Gang 3, Rank 4)

Frozen Logger. See Zmrzly dřevař, 1962

Frozen North, 1922 (Keaton 2)

Frozen North, 1941 (Terry 4)

FRPS, 1973 (Le Grice 2)

Fru Potifar, 1911 (Psilander 3)

Früchten, 1933 (Pasternak 4)

Fruehlings Erwachen, 1929 (Rasp 3)

Frühjahrsparade, 1934 (Pasternak 4)

Frühling auf Immenhof, 1974 (Tschechowa 3)

Frühlingssinfonie, 1985 (Kinski 3)

Fruillo del passero, 1988 (Noiret 3)

Fruit défendu, 1952 (Fernandel 3, Alekan 4)

Fruit of Evil, 1914 (Reid 3)

Fruit of Paradise. See Ovoce stromů rajských jíme, 1969

Fruitful Vine, 1921 (Rathbone 3)

Fruits amers, 1966 (Kosma 4)

Fruits communs, 1960 (Delerue 4)

Fruits de la passion, 1981 (Kinski 3, Colpi 4)

Fruits de l'été, 1954 (Feuillère 3, Barsacq 4)

Fruits de saison, 1902 (Guy 2)

Fruits et légumes animés, 1915 (Cohl 4)

Fruits et légumes vivants, 1912 (Cohl 4)

Fruits of Passion. See Fruits de la passion, 1981

Fruits of the Faith, 1922 (Rogers 3, Roach 4)

Fruits Sauvages, 1953 (Kosma 4)

Frumento, 1958 (Olmi 2)

Frusta e il corpo, 1963 (Lee 3)

Frustration. See Die Lady, 1964

FTA Show, 1972 (Fonda 3, Sutherland 3, Trumbo 4)

Fubuki ni sakebu ookami, 1931 (Hasegawa 3)

Fubuki to tomo ni keiyukinu, 1959 (Mori 3, Yamada 3)

Fubuki-toge, 1929 (Hasegawa 3)

Fuchs von Glenarvon, 1940 (Tschechowa 3, Wagner 4)

Fuck. See Blue Movie, 1968

Fuck the Army. See F.T.A., 1972

Fucking Fernand, 1987 (Aurenche 4)

Fuco nelle vene. See Chair et le diable, 1953

Fuddy Duddy Buddy, 1951 (Bosustow 4, Hubley 4)

Fudget's Budget, 1954 (Bosustow 4)

Fuefuki-gawa, 1960 (Iwashita 3, Takamine 3)

Fuegos, 1987 (Coutard 4, Guillemot 4)

Fuelin' Around, 1949 (Three Stooges 3)

Fuente magica, 1961 (Williams 3)

Fuentovejuna, 1947 (Rey 3)

Fuera de aquí, 1976 (Sanjinés 2)

Fuerza vivas, 1974 (Alcoriza 4)

Fuga, 1960 (Diegues 2)

Fuga, 1964 (Aimée 3, Amidei 4)

Fuga in città, 1950 (Risi 2)

Fuga in Francia, 1948 (Germi 2, Flaiano 4, Gherardi 4, Ponti 4, Rota 4)

Fuggitiva, 1941 (Magnani 3)

Fugitif, 1946 (Burel 4)

Fugitifs, 1986 (Depardieu 3)

Fugitive, 1910 (Griffith 2, Bitzer 4)

Fugitive, 1913 (Dwan 2)

Fugitive. See Taking of Luke McVane, 1915

Fugitive. See Return of Draw Egan, 1916

Fugitive, 1935 (Shamroy 4)

Fugitive. See On the Night of the Fire, 1939

Fugitive, 1947 (Ford 2, Armendáriz 3, Bond 3, Del Rio 3, Fonda 3, Cooper 4, Figueroa 4, Greene 4, Nichols 4)

Fugitive Apparitions. See Apparitions fugitives, 1904

Fugitive Family, 1980 (Wallach 3)

Fugitive for a Night, 1938 (Trumbo 4)

Fugitive from Chicago. See Flüchtling aus Chicago, 1934

Fugitive from Matrimony, 1919 (King 2)

Fugitive from Montreal. See Inconnue de Montréal, 1950

Fugitive in 6B. See Brigante Musolino, 1950

Fugitive in the Sky, 1937 (McCord 4)

Fugitive Kind, 1960 (Lumet 2, Brando 3, Magnani 3, Woodward 3, Kaufman 4, Sylbert 4)

Fugitive Lady, 1934 (Ball 3)

Fugitive Lady. See Strada, 1949

Fugitive Lovers, 1934 (Montgomery 3, Three Stooges 3, Gillespie 4, Goodrich 4)

Fugitive of the Prairies, 1943 (Crabbe 3)

Fugitive Road, 1934 (Von Stroheim 2, McCord 4)

Fugitives, 1929 (Harlow 3, Fox 4)

Fugue de Jim Baxter. See Son Oncle de Normandie, 1939

Fugue de Lily, 1917 (Feuillade 2)

Fugue de Mahmoud, 1950 (Leenhardt 2)

Fuite de gaz, 1912 (Linder 3)

Fuji, 1974 (Breer 4)

Fuji sancho, 1948 (Hayasaka 4)

Fujicho, 1947 (Tanaka 3)

Fujinka-i no kokuhaku, 1957 (Yamamura 3)

Fujinkai no himitsu, 1959 (Hara 3)

Fukei-zu, 1934 (Tanaka 3)

Fukei-zu, 1942 (Hasegawa 3, Takamine 3, Yamada 3)

Fukei-zu, 1949 (Hasegawa 3)

Fukeizu, 1962 (Yoda 4)

Fukeyo harukaze, 1953 (Mifune 3, Yamamura 3)

Fukkatsu, 1950 (Kyo 3, Yoda 4)

Fukushu no shichikamen, 1955 (Yamamura 3)

Fukushu suruwa ware ni ari, 1979 (Imamura 2)

Full Ahead. See Cala naprzód, 1966

Full Circle, 1976 (Farrow 3)

Full Confession, 1939 (Fitzgerald 3, McLaglen 3, Hunt 4)

Full Fathom Five, 1934 (Gielgud 3)

Full House, 1920 (Cruze 2)

Full House. See O. Henry's Full House, 1952

Full Life. See Mitasareta seikatsu, 1961

Full Metal Jacket, 1987 (Kubrick 2)

Full Moon High, 1981 (Cohen 2)

Full Moon in Blue Water, 1988 (Hackman 3, Meredith 3)

Full o' Pep, 1922 (Roach 4)

Full of Life, 1956 (Holliday 3, Cohn 4, Duning 4)

Full Rich Life. See Cynthia, 1947

Full Treatment, 1961 (Rosay 3, Carreras 4)

Full Value, 1911 (Dwan 2)

Fulla Bluff Man, 1942 (Fleischer 4)

Fuller Brush Girl, 1950 (Bacon 2, Tashlin 2, Ball 3)

Fuller Brush Man, 1947 (Tashlin 2)

Fully Insured, 1923 (Roach 4)

Fultah Fisher's Boarding House, 1922 (Capra 2)

Fumée, histoire et fantaisie, 1962 (Piccoli 3)

Fumée noire, 1920 (Delluc 2)

Fumées, 1951 (Alexeieff and Parker 4)

Fumetsu no nekkyu, 1955 (Tsukasa 3)

Fumetsu so ai, 1928 (Tanaka 3)

Fumo di Londra, 1966 (Sordi 3, Amidei 4)

Fun and Fancy Free, 1947 (Disney 4, Iwerks 4)

Fun from the Press, 1923 (Fleischer 4)

Fun House, 1936 (Lantz 4)

Fun in a Bakery Shop, 1902 (Porter 2)

Fun in Acapulco, 1963 (Lukas 3, Presley 3, Head 4, Wallis 4)

Fun of Your Life, 1975 (Heston 3)

Fun on the Joy Line, 1905 (Bitzer 4)

Fun with Dick and Jane, 1977 (Fonda 3, Segal 3)

Functions and Relations, 1968 (Halas and Batchelor 4)

Fundoshi isha, 1960 (Hara 3, Yamamura 3)

Fundvogel, 1930 (Wegener 3, Warm 4)

Funebrák, 1932 (Heller 4, Stallich 4)

Funérailles à Bongo: Le Vieux Anai, 1979 (Rouch 2)

Funeral Attendant. See Funebrák, 1932

Funeral in Berlin, 1966 (Caine 3, Homolka 3, Adam 4, Heller 4)

Funeral of Queen Victoria, 1901 (Hepworth 2)

Funeral Rites. See Osokoshi, 1985

Fünf Patronenhülsen, 1960 (Mueller-Stahl 3)

Funf verfluchten Gentlemen, 1931 (Duvivier 2)

Fünf von der Jazzband, 1932 (Lorre 3)

Fünf von Titan. See Vors uns liegt das Leben, 1948

Funfuhrtee in zerin, 1926 (Planer 4)

Funhouse, 1981 (Baker 4)

Funivia del Faloria, 1950 (Antonioni 2)

Funkausstellung 1971—Hitparade, 1971 (Schroeter 2)

Funkzauber, 1927 (Krauss 3)

Funny, 1986 (Pryor 3)

Funny About Love, 1990 (Wilder 3)

Funny Boy, 1987 (Sarde 4)

Funny Bunny Business, 1942 (Terry 4)

Funny Face, 1933 (Iwerks 4)

Funny Face. See Bright Lights, 1935

Funny Face, 1957 (Donen 2, Astaire 3, Hepburn 3, Deutsch 4, Edens 4, Head 4)

Funny Farm. See Hashigaon Hagadol, 1988

Funny Girl, 1968 (Wyler 2, Pidgeon 3, Sharif 3, Streisand 3, Lennart 4, Sharaff 4, Stark 4, Stradling 4)

Funny Lady, 1975 (Caan 3, McDowall 3, Sharif 3, Streisand 3, Allen 4, Howe 4, Jenkins 4, Stark 4)

Funny Thing Happened on the Way to the Crusades. See Cintura di castita, 1967

Funny Thing Happened on the Way to the Forum, 1966 (Keaton 2, Lester 2, Roeg 2, Frank 4, Williams 4)

Funny, You Don't Look 200, 1987 (Dreyfuss 3)

Funnymooners, 1926 (Sennett 2)

Funtoosh, 1956 (Anand 3, Burman 4)

Fununjo shi, 1928 (Tsuburaya 4)

Fuoco, 1915 (Pastrone 2)

Fuorilegge, 1949 (Gassman 3)

Fuorilegge del matrimonio, 1963 (Taviani 2, Girardot 3)

Fuorilegge del matrimonio, 1963 (Fusco 4)

Furai monogatari: Abare Hisha, 1960 (Hasegawa 3, Yamada 3)

Furai monogatari: Ninkyo-hen, 1959 (Hasegawa 3, Yamada 3)

Furankenshutain no kaiju—Sanda tai Gailah, 1966 (Tsuburaya 4)

Furankenshutain tai Baragon, 1966 (Shimura 3, Tsuburaya 4)

Furcht, 1917 (Veidt 3)

Furia, 1947 (Brazzi 3, Cervi 3)

Furie des S.S. See Dieci italiani per un Tedesco, 1962

Furies, 1950 (Mann 2, Bondi 3, Huston 3, Stanwyck 3, Bumstead 4, Dreier 4, Head 4, Schnee 4, Wallis 4, Waxman 4)

Furin kaza, 1969 (Mifune 3, Shimura 3)

Furisode kenpo, 1955 (Yamada 3)

Furisode kyojo, 1952 (Hasegawa 3)

Furnace Trouble, 1929 (Benchley 4)

Furniture Movers, 1918 (Roach 4)

Furoncle, 1915 (Feuillade 2)

Furs, 1911 (Sennett 2)

Fürst der Nacht, 1919 (Albers 3)

Fürst oder Clown, 1927 (Homolka 3)

Fürstin Woronzoff, 1920 (Dreier 4)

Further Adventures of the Girl Spy, 1910 (Olcott 2)

Further Up the Creek, 1958 (Carreras 4)

Furto e l'anima del commercio, 1971 (Blier 3)

Furto su misura, 1962 (Valli 3)

Furusato, 1930 (Mizoguchi 2)

Furusato, 1976 (Mizoguchi 2)

Furusato no uta, 1925 (Mizoguchi 2)

Fury, 1922 (Goulding 2, King 2, Barthelmess 3)

Fury, 1936 (Lang 2, Mankiewicz 2, Brennan 3, Sidney 3, Tracy 3, Gibbons 4, Krasna 4, Mayer 4, Ruttenberg 4, Waxman 4)

Fury, 1978 (Cassavetes 2, De Palma 2, Douglas 3, Baker 4, Smith 4, Williams 4)

Fury at Furnace Creek, 1948 (Mature 3, Newman 4, Raksin 4)

Fury at Showdown, 1956 (La Shelle 4)

Fury at Smuggler's Bay, 1961 (Cushing 3)

Fury Is a Woman. See Sibirska Ledi Magbet, 1972

Fury of the Congo, 1951 (Weissmuller 3, Katzman 4)

Fury of the Jungle, 1933 (Schary 4)

Fury Unleashed. See Hot Rod Gang, 1958

Furyo shojo, 1960 (Yamamura 3)

Furyo shonen, 1961 (Takemitsu 4)

Furyu Fukagawa uta, 1960 (Yamada 3, Yamamura 3)

Furyu katsujin-ken, 1934 (Yamada 3)

Furyu onsen: banto nikki, 1962 (Tsukasa 3)

Furyu onsen nikki, 1958 (Tsukasa 3)

Fusée, 1933 (Tourneur 2)

Fusen, 1956 (Mori 3)

Fusetsu ni ju-nen, 1951 (Okada 3)

Fusion, 1967 (Emshwiller 2)

Fuss and Feathers, 1909 (Porter 2)

Fuss and Feathers, 1918 (Niblo 2, Barnes 4)

Fussgänger, 1974 (Bergner 3, Dagover 3, Rosay 3, Schell 3)

Futamabatu, 1933 (Tanaka 3)

Futari de aruita ikutoshitsuki, 1962 (Takamine 3)

Futari no Iida, 1976 (Takamine 3)

Futari no Musashi, 1960 (Hasegawa 3)

Futari no musuko, 1962 (Shimura 3)

Futate no maki, 1938 (Yamada 3)

Futatsu dore, 1933 (Hasegawa 3)

Futore e donna, 1984 (Schygulla 3, Delli Colli 4)

Future Is a Woman. See Futore e donna, 1984

Future of Emily. See Avenir d'Emilie, 1984

Future Women. See Rio '70, 1970

Future's in the Air, 1936 (Rotha 2, Alwyn 4, Greene 4)

Futures vedettes, 1954 (Bardot 3, Marais 3)

Futureworld, 1976 (Brynner 3)

Futz!, 1969 (Zsigmond 4)

Fuun Konpira-san, 1950 (Yamada 3)

Fuun senryo-bune, 1952 (Hasegawa 3)

Fuun tenman-zoshi, 1930 (Yamada 3)

Fuunji: Oda Nobunaga, 1959 (Kagawa 3)

Fuunjo-shi, 1928 (Hasegawa 3)

Fuyaki shinju, 1934 (Kinugasa 2)

Fuyard, 1941 (Volkov 2)

Fuyuki shinju, 1931 (Hasegawa 3, Yamada 3)

Fuzen no tomoshibi, 1957 (Takamine 3)

Fuzis, 1964 (Guerra 2)

Fuzz, 1972 (Brynner 3, Reynolds 3, Welch 3, Jeakins 4)

Fuzzy Pink Nightgown, 1957 (Menjou 3, Russell 3, La Shelle 4)

Fuzzy Settles Down, 1944 (Crabbe 3)

F/X, 1986 (Ondříček 4)

FX2: The Deadly Art of Illusion, 1991 (Schifrin 4)

Fy og Bi i Kantonnement, 1931 (Madsen and Schenstrøm 3)

Fy og Bi i Paradis. See Insel wird entdeckt, 1937

Fy og Bi Prøvefilm, 1930 (Madsen and Schenstrøm 3)

G.E. Television Theatre, 1958 (Brakhage 2)
G.I. Blues, 1960 (Presley 3, Head 4, Wallis 4)
G.I. Joe. *See* Story of G.I. Joe, 1945
G.I. Wanna Go Home, 1946 (Three Stooges 3)
G.m.b.H. Tenor, 1916 (Lubitsch 2)
G.P.U., 1942 (Röhrig 4)
G.S.O., 1958 (Kosma 4)
Ga, Ga—chwala bohaterom, 1985 (Nowicki 3, Olbrychski 3)
Gaa med mig hjem, 1941 (Christensen 2)
Gabbia, 1985 (Morricone 4)
Gabbiano, 1977 (Bellocchio 2)
Gabby Goes Fishing, 1941 (Fleischer 4)
Gable and Lombard, 1976 (Clayburgh 3, Head 4, Legrand 4)
Gabriel over the White House, 1933 (La Cava 2, Huston 3, Adrian 4, Glennon 4, Mayer 4, Wanger 4, Wilson 4)
Gabriela, 1983 (Mastroianni 3)
Gabriele ein, zwei, drei, 1937 (Fröhlich 3)
Gabrielle, 1954 (Björnstrand 3, Fischer 4)
Gab's nur einmal, 1958 (Albers 3)
Gaby, 1956 (Caron 3, Goodrich 4, Lederer 4, Rose 4)
Gaby: A True Story, 1987 (Jarre 4, Ullmann 3)
Gadfly. *See* Poprigunya, 1955
Gaest fra en anden Verden. *See* Tugthusfange No. 97, 1914
Gaestespillet, 1913 (Psilander 3)
Gaétan ou le commis audacieux, Lahire ou le valet de cœur, 1921 (Feuillade 2)
Gage d'amour, 1904 (Guy 2)
Gagnant, 1935 (Allégret 2, Fradetal 4)
Gagnant, 1979 (Audran 3)
Gai Dimanche, 1935 (Tati 2)
Gai Savoir, 1968 (Godard 2, Léaud 3)
Gaiety George, 1945 (Heller 4)
Gaiety Girl, 1924 (Laemmle 4)
Gaiety Girls. *See* Paradise for Two, 1937
Gaijo no suketchi, 1925 (Mizoguchi 2)
Gaily, Gaily, 1969 (Ashby 2, Mercouri 3, Boyle 4, Mancini 4)
Gaines Roussel, 1939 (Alexeieff and Parker 4)
Gaité Parisienne. *See* Gay Parisian, 1941
Gaités de la finance, 1935 (Fernandel 3, Spaak 4)
Gaités de l'escadron, 1913 (Tourneur 2, Douy 4)
Gaités de l'escadron, 1932 (Tourneur 2, Fernandel 3, Gabin 3, Raimu 3)
Gaités de l'exposition, 1938 (Kaufman 4)
Gaiwak, 1983 (Chan 3)
Gaiwatsuktsap, 1987 (Chan 3)

Gajre, 1948 (Biswas 4)
Gakusei geisha: Koi to kenka, 1962 (Iwashita 3)
Gakuso o idete, 1925 (Mizoguchi 2)
Gal Who Took the West, 1949 (Coburn 3, De Carlo 3, Boyle 4, Daniels 4, Salter 4)
Galápagos Islands, 1938 (Leacock 2)
Galathea, 1921 (Banky 3)
Galathea, 1935 (Reiniger 4)
Galaxie, 1966 (Markopoulos 2)
Galaxy of Terror, 1981 (Corman 2)
Galeerensträfling, 1918 (Wegener 3, Wagner 4)
Galerie des monstres, 1924 (Calvalcanti 2)
Galeries Lévy et Cie, 1931 (Christian-Jaque 2)
Galettes de Pont Aven, 1975 (Sarde 4)
Galgamannen, 1945 (Molander 2)
Galia, 1965 (D'Eaubonne 4)
Galileo, 1968 (Cusack 3, Morricone 4, Pinelli 4)
Galileo, 1975 (Losey 2, Gielgud 3, Topol 3)
Gallant Blade, 1948 (Duning 4, Guffey 4)
Gallant Defender, 1935 (Rogers 3)
Gallant Gringo. *See* Adventurer, 1927
Gallant Hours, 1960 (Cagney 3, Montgomery 3)
Gallant Hussar, 1928 (Novello 3)
Gallant Journey, 1946 (Wellman 2, Ford 3, Guffey 4)
Gallant Lady, 1933 (La Cava 2, Day 4, Newman 4, Zanuck 4)
Gallant Little Tailor, 1954 (Reiniger 4)
Gallant Man. *See* That's My Man, 1947
Gallant Sons, 1941 (Cooper 3)
Gallego, 1987 (Gómez 2)
Gallery Murders. *See* Uccello dalle piume di cristallo, 1969
Galley Slave, 1915 (Ingram 2, Bara 3)
Gallina clueca, 1941 (De Fuentes 2, Figueroa 4)
Gallina muy ponedora, 1980 (Fernández 2)
Gallina Vogelbirdie. *See* Spatně namalovaná slepice, 1963
Gallipoli, 1981 (Weir 2, Gibson 3)
Gallo de oro, 1964 (Figueroa 4)
Gallo en corral ajeno, 1952 (Figueroa 4)
Gallopin' Gals, 1940 (Hanna and Barbera 4)
Gallopin' Gaucho, 1929 (Disney 4, Iwerks 4)
Galloping Bungalows, 1924 (Sennett 2)
Galloping Fury, 1927 (Eason 4, Laemmle 4)
Galloping Gallagher, 1924 (Brown 4)
Galloping Ghost, 1931 (Canutt 4, Eason 4)
Galloping Ghosts, 1927 (Laurel and Hardy 3, Roach 4)
Galloping Justice, 1927 (Wyler 2)
Galloping Major, 1951 (More 3)

Galope sobre la historia, 1982 (Alvarez 2)
Galose Statsia, 1985 (Brejchová 3)
Galveston Hurricane Shots, 1900 (Bitzer 4)
Gaman, 1978 (Patil 3)
Gamberge, 1961 (Arietty 3, Cassel 3, Saulnier 4)
Gambit, 1966 (Caine 3, Lom 3, MacLaine 3, Jarre 4, Sargent 4)
Gamble, *See* Partita, 1988
Gambler, 1971 (Anand 3, Burman 4)
Gambler, 1974 (Reisz 2, Caan 3, Winkler 4)
Gambler and the Lady, 1952 (Carreras 4)
Gambler of the West, 1910 (Anderson 3)
Gambler Wore a Gun, 1960 (Crosby 4, Hall 4)
Gamblers, 1929 (Curtiz 2)
Gamblers Sometimes Win. *See* March Hare, 1956
Gamblers' Story of Saruga: Broken Iron Fire. *See* Suruga yuhkyou-den: Yabure takka, 1964
Gambler's Way, 1914 (Anderson 3)
Gambling Hell. *See* Macao, l'enfer du jeu, 1939
Gambling House, 1950 (Bendix 3, Mature 3)
Gambling in the High Seas, 1940 (Wyman 3)
Gambling Lady, 1934 (McCrea 3, Stanwyck 3, Barnes 4, Blanke 4, Grot 4, Orry-Kelly 4)
Gambling Rube, 1914 (Sennett 2)
Gambling Samurai. *See* Kunisada Chuji, 1960
Gambling Ship, 1933 (Grant 3, Head 4, Lang 4)
Gambling Wives, 1924 (Lawrence 3)
Game Called Scruggs. *See* Scruggs, 1965
Game Chicken, 1922 (Daniels 3, Folsey 4)
Game for Six Lovers. *See* Eau à la bouche, 1959
Game for Two, 1910 (Lawrence 3)
Game for Vultures, 1980 (Elliott 3, Harris 3, Milland 3)
Game Is Over. *See* Curée, 1966
Game of Death, 1946 (Wise 2, Johnson 3, Barry 4, Dunn 4, Hunt 4)
Game of Death, 1979 (Lee 3)
Game of Deception, 1911 (Lawrence 3)
Game of Love. *See* Blé en herbe, 1953
Game of Poker, 1913 (Sennett 2)
Game of Pool, 1913 (Sennett 2)
Game of Wits, 1917 (King 2)
Game Old Knight, 1915 (Sennett 2)
Game That Kills, 1937 (Hayworth 3)
Game with Stones. *See* Spiel mit Steinen, 1965
Gamekeeper, 1980 (Loach 2, Menges 4)
Games, 1967 (Caan 3, Signoret 3, Fraker 4)

Games, 1969 (Baker 3, Lai 4)

Games of Desire. *See* Lady, 1964

Games of Love and Loneliness. *See* Allvarsamma Leken, 1977

Gametsui yatsu, 1960 (Mori 3)

Gamila Bohraid, 1958 (Chahine 2)

Gamin de Paris, 1923 (Feuillade 2)

Gamine. *See* Uličnice, 1936

Gamla Historie, 1913 (Psilander 3)

Gamma People, 1956 (Box 4)

Gammelion, 1967 (Markopoulos 2)

Gan, 1953 (Takamine 3)

Ganashatru, 1989 (Chatterjee 3)

Gancia, 1963 (Borowczyk 2)

Gander at Mother Goose, 1940 (Avery 4, Blanc 4, Stalling 4)

Gandhi, 1982 (Attenborough 3, Day Lewis 3, Gielgud 3, Howard 3, Mills 3, Sheen 3, Nihalani 4, Shankar 4)

Gandy Goose and the Chipper Chipmunk, 1947 (Terry 4)

Gandy the Goose, 1938 (Terry 4)

Gandy's Dream Girl, 1944 (Terry 4)

Ganesh Utsava, 1914 (Phalke 2)

Gang, 1976 (Delon 3, Carrière 4)

Gang Buster, 1931 (Mankiewicz 2, Arthur 3)

Gang des otages, 1972 (Coutard 4, Legrand 4)

Gang des tractions-arrière, 1950 (Berry 3)

Gang in die Nacht, 1921 (Murnau 2, Veidt 3, Mayer 4)

Gang Show, 1937 (Wilcox 2)

Gang That Couldn't Shoot Straight, 1971 (De Niro 3, Roizman 4, Salt 4, Winkler 4)

Gang War, 1928 (Glennon 4, Miller 4)

Gang War, 1958 (Bronson 3)

Ganga Jamuna, 1961 (Kumar 3)

Ganga Ki Saugand, 1978 (Bachchan 3)

Ganga Sagar, 1979 (Chandragupta 4)

Ganga Zumba, 1964 (Diegues 2)

Gangavataran, 1937 (Phalke 2)

Gang-Busters, 1955 (Clothier 2)

Gang's All Here, 1939 (Buchanan 3, Horton 3, Withers 3)

Gang's All Here, 1943 (Berkeley 2, Faye 3, Horton 3, Miranda 3, Basevi 4, Cronjager 4, Friedhofer 4, Newman 4, Raksin 4)

Gangs Inc. *See* Paper Bullets, 1941

Gangs of Chicago, 1940 (Ladd 3, Brown 4)

Gangs of New York, 1938 (Cruze 2, Fuller 2)

Gangs of the Waterfront. *See* Gangs of New York , 1938

Gangs of the Waterfront, 1945 (Edwards 2)

Gangster, 1913 (Sennett 2)

Gangster, 1947 (Winters 3)

Gangster, 1964 (Alcoriza 4)

Gangster in London. *See* Rätsel der roten Orchidee, 1961

Gangster maigré lui, 1935 (Rosay 3)

Gangster '70, 1968 (Cotten 3)

Gangster Story. *See* Dio, sei proprio un padreterno, 1973

Gangster Story, 1991 (Matthau 3)

Gangstergirl. *See* Gangstermeisje, 1967

Gangstermeisje, 1967 (Volonté 3)

Gangsters, 1913 (Arbuckle 3)

Gangsters and the Girl, 1914 (Ince 4)

Gangster's Boy, 1938 (Cooper 3, Brown 4)

Gangster's Den, 1945 (Crabbe 3)

Gangsters du Chateau d'If, 1938 (D'Eaubonne 4)

Gangsters of New York, 1914 (Loos 4)

Gangster's Song. *See* Gurentai no uta, 1934

Gangway, 1937 (Matthews 3, Sim 3, Junge 4)

Gangway for Tomorrow, 1943 (Carradine 3, Ryan 3, Musuraca 4)

Ganovenehre, 1966 (Staudte 2)

Ganpeki, 1953 (Yamamura 3)

Gantelet vert. *See* Green Glove, 1951

Gaou utaggasen, 1939 (Miyagawa 4)

Garage, 1919 (Keaton 2, Arbuckle 3)

Garbage. *See* Sal Gordo, 1983

Garbo Talks, 1984 (Lumet 2, Bancroft 3)

Garce, 1984 (Coutard 4)

Garce, 1989 (Huppert 3)

Garçon!, 1983 (Sautet 2, Montand 3, Sarde 4)

Garçon sauvage, 1951 (Jeanson 4)

Garçonne, 1936 (Arletty 3)

Garçonne, 1957 (Achard 4)

Garçonnière, 1960 (De Santis 2)

Garde a vue, 1980 (Miller 2, Schneider 3, Audiard 4, Delerue 4)

Garde-chasse, 1951 (Decaë 4)

Garden. *See* Zahrada, 1968

Garden, 1990 (Jarman 2)

Garden Gopher, 1950 (Avery 4)

Garden Murder Case, 1936 (Walthall 3, Clarke 4)

Garden of Allah, 1916 (Selig 4)

Garden of Allah, 1927 (Ingram 2, Garmes 4, Mayer 4)

Garden of Allah, 1936 (Boyer 3, Carradine 3, Dietrich 3, Rathbone 3, Miller 4, Rosson 4, Selznick 4, Steiner 4, Wheeler 4)

Garden of Delights. *See* Jardín de las delicias, 1970

Garden of Earthly Delights, 1981 (Brakhage 2)

Garden of Eden, 1928 (Milestone 2, Kräly 4, Menzies 4)

Garden of Eden, 1954 (Kaufman 4)

Garden of Eden, 1990 (Raphael 4)

Garden of Evil, 1954 (Hathaway 2, Cooper 3, Hayward 3, Widmark 3, Brackett 4, Herrmann 4, Krasner 4, LeMaire 4, Wheeler 4)

Garden of the Finzi-Contini. *See* **Giardino dei Finzi-Contini, 1970**

Garden of the Moon, 1938 (Berkeley 2, Mercer 4, Wald 4)

Garden of Weeds, 1924 (Cruze 2, Brown 4)

Garden of Women. *See* Onna no sono, 1954

Gardener. *See* Trädgárrdsmaästaren, 1912

Gardener, 1922 (Laurel and Hardy 3)

Gardener, 1980 (Halas and Batchelor 4)

Gardens of England, 1942 (Unsworth 4)

Gardens of Stone, 1987 (Coppola 2, Caan 3, Huston 3, Jones 3, Tavoularis 4)

Gardens of the Moon, 1938 (Gaudio 4)

Gardeoffizier. *See* Leibgardist, 1925

Gardien de la nuit, 1985 (Branco 4)

Gardienne du feu, 1913 (Feuillade 2)

Gardiens de phare, 1929 (Feyder 2, Grémillon 2, Périnal 4)

Gareeb, 1942 (Biswas 4)

Gargousse, 1938 (Jeanson 4)

Gargoyles, 1971 (Wilde 3)

Garibaldino al convento, 1942 (De Sica 2)

Garibaldi—The General, 1986 (Josephson 3, Cristaldi 4)

Garlands at the Foot of the Mountain, 1984 (Xie 2)

Garment Jungle, 1957 (Aldrich 2, Cobb 3, Biroc 4)

Garnison amoureuse, 1933 (Brasseur 3, Fernandel 3)

Garou-Garou, le passe-muraille, 1950 (Greenwood 3, Audiard 4)

Garrison amoureuse, 1933 (Planer 4)

Garrison's Finish, 1914 (Mix 3)

Garrison's Finish, 1923 (Pickford 3, Rosson 4)

Garryowen, 1920 (Pearson 2)

Gars des vues, 1975 (Lefebvre 2)

Garten, 1985 (Bergner 3)

Gas and Air, 1923 (Laurel and Hardy 3, Roach 4)

Gasbags, 1940 (Crazy Gang 3, Rank 4)

Gaslight, 1940 (Newton 3, Walbrook 3, Junge 4)

Gaslight, 1944 (Cukor 2, Bergman 3, Boyer 3, Cotten 3, Lansbury 3, Balderston 4, Gibbons 4, Irene 4, Kaper 4, Reisch 4, Ruttenberg 4)

Gaslight Ridge, 1957 (Raksin 4)

Gasmann, 1941 (Ondra 3)

Gas-Oil, 1955 (Gabin 3, Moreau 3, Audiard 4)

Gasoline Engagement, 1911 (Pickford 3, Gaudio 4)

Gasoline Gus, 1921 (Cruze 2, Arbuckle 3, Brown 4)

Gasoline Love, 1923 (Wray 3)

Gasoline Wedding, 1918 (Lloyd 3, Roach 4)

Gaspard a un rendez-vous, 1963 (Braunberger 4)

Gaspard de Besse, 1935 (Raimu 3)

Gaspard et Robinson, 1990 (Legrand 4)

Gaspard fait du cheval, 1963 (Braunberger 4)

Gaspard se marie, 1964 (Braunberger 4)

Gaspards, 1974 (Depardieu 3, Noiret 3)

Gasparone, 1955 (Eisler 4)

Gassenhauer, 1931 (Pick 2, Staudte 2, Schüfftan 4)

Gassi, 1960 (Delerue 4)

Gass-s-s-s, or It Became Necessary to Destroy the World in Order to Save it, 1970 (Corman 2)

Gäst i eget hus, 1957 (Nykvist 4)

Gastone, 1959 (De Sica 2, Sordi 3)

Gasu ningen daiichigo, 1960 (Tsuburaya 4)

Gatans barn, 1914 (Magnusson 4)

Gatans barn, 1914 (Sjöström 2)

Gate of Hell. *See* **Jigokumon, 1953**

Gate of Youth. *See* Seishun no mon, 1975

Gate of Youth: Independence. *See* Seishun no mon: Jiritsu hen, 1977

Gates of Heaven. *See* Bramy raju, 1967

Gates of Paris. *See* Porte de Lilas, 1957

Gates of the Forest, 1980 (Ullmann 3)

Gates of the Night. *See* Portes de la nuit, 1946

Gates to Paradise. *See* Bramy raju, 1967

Gateway, 1938 (Ameche 3, Carey 3, Carradine 3, Cronjager 4, Reisch 4, Trotti 4)

Gateway of the Moon, 1928 (Del Rio 3, Johnson 3, Pidgeon 3, Fox 4)

Gateway to Glory. *See* Aa, kaigun, 1969

Gateway to the Catskills, 1906 (Bitzer 4)

Gathering, 1977 (Barry 4)

Gathering of Eagles, 1963 (Hudson 3, Bumstead 4, Goldsmith 4, Harlan 4, Irene 4)

Gathering of Old Men, 1987 (Widmark 3)

Gatling Gun, 1973 (Carradine 3)

Gator, 1976 (Reynolds 3, Fraker 4, Needham 4)

Gatti. *See* Bastardi, 1968

Gattin, 1943 (Von Harbou 4)

Gatto, 1977 (Comencini 2, Leone 2, Morricone 4)

Gatto a nove code, 1969 (Malden 3, Argento 4, Morricone 4)

Gatto nero, 1981 (Donaggio 4)

Gattopardo, 1962 (Visconti 2, Cardinale 3, Delon 3, Lancaster 3, Reggiani 3, Cecchi D'Amico 4, Rota 4, Rotunno 4)

Gaucho, 1928 (Fernández 2, Fairbanks 3, Gaudio 4)

Gaucho, 1964 (Gassman 3)

Gaucho Serenade, 1940 (Autry 3)

Gauchos judíos, 1975 (Torre Nilsson 2)

Gauchos of Eldorado, 1941 (Canutt 4)

Gauguin, 1950 (Resnais 2, Braunberger 4)

Gauguin the Savage, 1980 (Lassally 4)

Gauloises bleues, 1968 (Girardot 3, Guillemot 4)

Gaunt Stranger, 1938 (Balcon 4)

Gaunt Stranger, 1938 (Launder and Gilliat 2)

Gaunt Woman. *See* Destiny of a Spy, 1969

Gauntlet, 1975 (Eastwood 3)

Gautama the Buddha, 1967 (Roy 2)

Gaven. *See* Fødselsdagsgaven, 1912

Gavilanes, 1954 (Infante 3)

Gavilán pollero, 1950 (Infante 3, Figueroa 4)

Gavotte, 1902 (Guy 2)

Gavotte, 1967 (Borowczyk 2)

Gay Adventure, 1953 (Meredith 3)

Gay and Devilish, 1922 (Fort 4)

Gay Anties, 1947 (Blanc 4, Freleng 4, Stalling 4)

Gay Back Alley. *See* Yokina uramachi, 1939

Gay Bride, 1934 (Benchley 4)

Gay Bride, 1935 (Lombard 3)

Gay Caballero, 1932 (McLaglen 3)

Gay Caballero, 1940 (Cronjager 4, Day 4)

Gay Corinthian, 1925 (McLaglen 3)

Gay Deceiver, 1926 (Stahl 2, Booth 4, Gaudio 4, Gibbons 4, Glazer 4)

Gay Deception, 1935 (Wyler 2, Lasky 4, Reynolds 4)

Gay Defender, 1927 (La Cava 2, Cronjager 4, Mankiewicz 4)

Gay Desperado, 1936 (Mamoulian 2, Lupino 3, Day 4, Lasky 4, Newman 4)

Gay Diplomat, 1931 (Berman 4, Steiner 4)

Gay Divorce. *See* Gay Divorcee, 1934

Gay Divorcee, 1934 (Astaire 3, Grable 3, Horton 3, Rogers 3, Benchley 4, Berman 4, Biroc 4, Hoffenstein 4, Pan 4, Plunkett 4, Polglase 4, Steiner 4)

Gay Duellist. *See* Meet Me at Dawn, 1947

Gay Falcon, 1941 (Sanders 3, Musuraca 4, Polglase 4)

Gay Imposters. *See* Gold Diggers in Paris, 1938

Gay Knighties, 1941 (Pal 4)

Gay Lady. *See* Battle of Paris, 1929

Gay Lady. *See* Trottie True, 1949

Gay Love, 1934 (Bennett 4)

Gay Mrs. Trexel. *See* Susan and God, 1940

Gay Nineties. *See* Floradora Girl, 1930

Gay Old Bird, 1927 (Miller 4)

Gay Parisian, 1941 (Friedhofer 4, Haller 4)

Gay Purr-ee, 1962 (Garland 3, Jones 4)

Gay Ranchero, 1948 (Rogers 3)

Gay Retreat, 1927 (Fox 4)

Gay Senorita, 1945 (Guffey 4)

Gay Shoe Clerk, 1903 (Porter 2)

Gay Sisters, 1942 (Crisp 3, Stanwyck 3, Blanke 4, Coffee 4, Head 4, Polito 4, Steiner 4)

Gaz, 1939 (Alexeieff and Parker 4)

Gaz de Lacq, 1960 (Guillemot 4)

Gaz mortels, 1916 (Burel 4, Gaumont 4)

Gazebo, 1960 (Hitchcock 2, Ford 3, Reynolds 3, Rose 4)

… gdziekolwiek jestés, Panie Prezydencie, 1978 (Lomnicki 3)

Gebissen wird nur Nachts—Happening der Vampire, 1971 (Francis 4)

Gedächtnis: Ein Film für Curt Bois und Bernhard Minetti, 1982 (Ganz 3)

Gee, If Me Mudder Could See Me, 1905 (Bitzer 4)

Gee Whiz, 1920 (Sennett 2)

Gee Whiz, Genevieve, 1924 (Rogers 3, Roach 4)

Gee Whiz-z-z, 1956 (Blanc 4, Jones 3)

Geese and Ducks' Singing Contest. *See* Gaou utaggasen, 1939

Gefahren der Brautzeit. *See* Liebesnächte, 1929

Gefährliche Alter, 1911 (Porten 3, Messter 4)

Gefährliche Alter, 1927 (Nielsen 3)

Gefährliche Spiel, 1919 (Wiene 2)

Gefährlicher Frühling, 1943 (Tschechowa 3, Röhrig 4)

Gefährliches Abenteuer, 1953 (Fröhlich 3)

Gefährliches Spiel, 1937 (Warm 4)

Gefährten meines Sommers, 1943 (Von Harbou 4)

Gefangene Seele, 1912 (Porten 3, Messter 4)

Gefangene Seele, 1916 (Freund 4)

Geheimaktion schwarze Kapelle, 1961 (Cervi 3)

Geheime Kurier, 1926 (Dagover 3, Mozhukin 3)

Geheimnis auf Schloss Almshoh, 1925 (Walbrook 3)

Geheimnis der alten Mamsell, 1925 (Andrejew 4)

Geheimnis der chinesischen Nelke, 1964 (Kinski 3)

Geheimnis der drei Dschunken, 1965 (Granger 3)

Geheimnis der gelben Mönche, 1966 (Granger 3, Kinski 3)

Geheimnis der gelben Narzissen. *See* Devil's Daffodil, 1962

Geheimnis der schwarzen Witwe, 1963 (Kinski 3)

Geheimnis des blauen Zimmers, 1950 (Staudte 2)

Geheimnis des Carlo Cavelli. *See* Hohe Schule, 1934

Geheimnis des indischen Tempels. *See* Mistero del tempio indiano, 1963

Geheimnis einer Ehe, 1951 (Tschechowa 3)

Geheimnis um Johann Orth, 1932 (Wegener 3)

Geheimnis von Bergsee, 1950 (Dagover 3)

Geheimnis von Bombay, 1920 (Dagover 3, Veidt 3, Herlth 4, Röhrig 4)

Geheimnis von London. *See* Toten Augen von London, 1961

Geheimnisse des Blutes. *See* Verfuhrte, 1914

Geheimnisse des Orients, 1928 (Volkov 2, Courant 4)

Geheimnisse einer Seele, 1926 (Krauss 3, Metzner 4)

Geheimnistrager, 1975 (Theodorakis 4)

Geheimnisvolle Spiegel, 1928 (Rasp 3, Hoffmann 4)

Geheimnisvolle Tiefen, 1949 (Pabst 2)

Gehetzte Frauen, 1927 (Fröhlich 3, Nielsen 3)

Gehetzte Menschen, 1924 (Albers 3, Messter 4, Planer 4)

Gehetzte Menschen, 1932 (Warm 4)

Gehetzter Gaukler. *See* Fahrendes Volk, 1938

Gehri Chaal, 1973 (Bachchan 3)

Geidou ichidai otoko, 1941 (Yoda 4)

Geier-Wally, 1921 (Dieterle 2, Leni 2, Porten 3)

Geierwally, 1940 (Warm 4)

Geiger von Florenz, 1926 (Bergner 3, Veidt 3, Pommer 4)

Geisha, 1914 (Hayakawa 3, Ince 4)

Geisha. *See* Gion bayashi, 1953

Geisha Boy, 1958 (Lewis 2, Tashlin 2, Hayakawa 3, Head 4)

Geisha Konatsu, 1955 (Shimura 3)

Geisha Who Saved Japan, 1909 (Olcott 2)

Gekido no Showa-shi: Gunbatsu, 1970 (Yamamura 3)

Gekiryu, 1952 (Mifune 3)

Gekiryu, 1967 (Iwashita 3)

Gekitsu no sakebi, 1925 (Tanaka 3)

Gekka no kyoba, 1927 (Tsuburaya 4)

Gekka no kyoba, 1973 (Hasegawa 3)

Gekka no wakamusha, 1937 (Hasegawa 3)

Gelbe Flagge, 1937 (Albers 3, Tschechowa 3)

Gelbe Haus des King-Fu, 1930 (Douy 4)

Gelbe Schein, 1918 (Negri 3, Kräly 4)

Geld auf der Strasse, 1930 (Lamarr 3)

Geliebte, 1927 (Wiene 2)

Geliebte Corinna, 1956 (Kinski 3)

Geliebte des Gouverneurs, 1927 (Kortner 3)

Geliebte Feindin, 1954 (Herlth 4)

Geliebte Roswolskys, 1921 (Nielsen 3, Wegener 3, Galeen 4)

Geliebter Lügner, 1949 (Herlth 4)

Gelignite Gang, 1956 (Fisher 2, Fisher 2)

Gelosia, 1943 (Amidei 4)

Gelosia, 1953 (Germi 2)

Gelöste Ketten, 1915 (Wiene 2, Porten 3, Freund 4)

Gem of a Jam, 1943 (Three Stooges 3)

Gemischte Frauenchor, 1916 (Lubitsch 2)

Gemma orientale di Papi, 1946 (Blasetti 2)

Gems, 1930 (Balcon 4)

Gemütlich beim Kaffee, 1898 (Messter 4)

Gen to Fudo-myoh, 1961 (Mifune 3, Ryu 3, Tsuburaya 4)

Genbakuno-ko, 1952 (Shindo 2)

Genboerne, 1939 (Henning-Jensen 2)

Gendai mushuku, 1958 (Yamamura 3)

Gendai no joo, 1924 (Mizoguchi 2)

Gendai no yokubo, 1956 (Tsukasa 3)

Gendai shinshi yaro, 1964 (Tsukasa 3)

Gendaijin, 1952 (Yamada 3, Yamamura 3)

Gendarme desconocido, 1941 (Cantinflas 3, Figueroa 4)

Gendarme est sans culotte, 1914 (Feuillade 2)

Gendarme est sans pitié, 1932 (Autant-Lara 2)

Gendarmes, 1907 (Guy 2)

Gendre de Monsieur Poirier, 1934 (Pagnol 2)

Gene Autry and the Mounties, 1951 (Autry 3)

Gene Krupa Story, 1959 (Mineo 3)

Gene of the Northland, 1915 (Rosher 4)
General, 1926 (Keaton 2, Bruckman 4, Schenck 4)
General Crack, 1929 (Barrymore 3, Bosworth 3, Gaudio 4)
Général de l'armée morte, 1982 (Mastroianni 3, Piccoli 3)
General Della Rovere. *See* Generale Della Rovere, 1959
General Died at Dawn, 1936 (Milestone 2, Carroll 3, Cooper 3, Dreier 4, Westmore Family 4)
General Idi Amin Dada, 1974 (Almendros 4)
General Line. *See* Staroie i novoie, 1929
General Nogi and Kuma-san. *See* Nogi Taisho to Kuma-san, 1926
General Nuisance, 1941 (Keaton 2, Bruckman 4)
General Spanky, 1936 (Beavers 3, Bosworth 3, Roach 4)
General von Döbeln, 1942 (Björnstrand 3)
Generala, 1970 (Félix 3)
Generale della Rovere, 1959 (De Sica 2, Rossellini 2, Amidei 4)
Generale dell'armata morta, 1983 (Aimée 3)
General's Daughter, 1911 (Talmadge 3)
Generation. *See* Pokolenie, 1954
Génération du désert, 1958 (Jarre 4)
Génération spontanée, 1909 (Cohl 4)
Générations comiques. *See* Génération spontanée, 1909
Genesis, 1968 (Carradine 3)
Genesis, 1986 (Sen 2, Azmi 3, Shankar 4)
Genesis I. *See* Genesis, 1968
Genevieve, 1953 (Kendall 3, More 3, Challis 4, Rank 4)
Genghis Khan, 1965 (Mason 3, Sharif 3, Wallach 3, Mathieson 4, Unsworth 4)
Genio due compari e un pollo, 1975 (Leone 2, Kinski 3)
Genius, 1917 (Laurel and Hardy 3)
Genius, 1970 (Markopoulos 2)
Genius at Work, 1946 (Lugosi 3)
Genius in the Family. *See* So Goes My Love, 1946
Genji monogatari, 1951 (Yoshimura 2, Hasegawa 3, Kyo 3, Shindo 3)
Genji monogatari, 1951 (Shindo 2)
Genji monogatari: Ukifune, 1957 (Hasegawa 3)
Genki de ikauyo, 1941 (Tanaka 3)
Genocide, 1981 (Taylor 3)
Genocide, 1985 (Welles 2)
Genopstandelsen. *See* Opstandelse, 1914
Genou de Claire, 1970 (Almendros 4)
Genroku bushido, 1940 (Shimura 3)
Genroku chushingura, 1941 (Yoda 4)
Genroku onna, 1924 (Tanaka 3)
Gens d'Abitibi, 1979 (Perrault 2)
Gens de voyage. *See* Fahrendes Volk, 1938
Gens du mil, 1951 (Rouch 2)
Gens du voyage, 1938 (Feyder 2, Rosay 3, D'Eaubonne 4)
Gens qui pleurent et gens qui rient, 1900 (Méliès 2)
Gens sans importance, 1955 (Gabin 3, Kosma 4)
Gente da Praia da Vieira, 1975 (De Almeida 4)
Gente del Po, 1947 (Antonioni 2)
Gente dell'aria, 1942 (Cervi 3)
Gente di rispetto, 1975 (Morricone 4)
Gente en la playa, 1961 (Almendros 4)
Gente moderna, 1964

Genti così, 1949 (Fusco 4)
Gentile Alouette, 1985 (Chaplin 3)
Gentle Annie, 1944 (Reed 3)
Gentle Arm. *See* Street Corner, 1953
Gentle Art of Seduction. *See* Chasse à l'homme, 1964
Gentle Corsican, 1956 (Lassally 4)
Gentle Creature. *See* Femme douce, 1969
Gentle Cyclone, 1926 (Van dyke 2, Laurel and Hardy 3)
Gentle Gunman, 1952 (Dearden 2, Bogarde 3, Mills 3)
Gentle Julia, 1923 (Love 3)
Gentle Julia, 1936 (McDaniel 3)
Gentle Sergeant. *See* Three Stripes in the Sun, 1955
Gentle Sex, 1943 (Greenwood 3, Howard 3, Dillon 4, Krasker 4, Rank 4)
Gentle Touch. *See* Feminine Touch, 1956
Gentleman after Dark, 1942 (Hopkins 3, Krasner 4, Tiomkin 4)
Gentleman at Heart, 1942 (Clarke 4)
Gentleman Burglar, 1908 (Porter 2)
Gentleman Burglar, 1914 (Sennett 2)
Gentleman Daku, 1937 (Biswas 4)
Gentleman de Cocody, 1965 (Marais 3)
Gentleman d'Epsom, 1962 (Gabin 3, Legrand 4)
Gentleman from America, 1923 (Karloff 3, Miller 4)
Gentleman from Blue Gulch. *See* Conversion of Frosty Blake, 1915
Gentleman from Mississippi, 1914 (Edeson 4)
Gentleman from Nowhere, 1948 (Anhalt 4)
Gentleman in Paradise. *See* Kedlubnový kavalír v ráji, 1928
Gentleman in Room 6, 1951 (Kaufman 4)
Gentleman Jim, 1942 (Walsh 2, Bond 3, Flynn 3, Buckner 4)
Gentleman Jo . . . uccidi, 1967 (Morricone 4)
Gentleman Misbehaves, 1946 (Three Stooges 3)
Gentleman of Fashion, 1913 (Bunny 3)
Gentleman of Leisure, 1915 (De Mille 2)
Gentleman of Paris, 1927 (D'Arrast 2, Menjou 3, Glazer 4, Mankiewicz 4, Rosson 4)
Gentleman of Paris, 1931 (Launder and Gilliat 2)
Gentleman of the Room. *See* Kammarjunkaren, 1913
Gentleman or Thief, 1913 (Loos 4)
Gentleman Tramp, 1975 (Bogdanovich 2, Harrison 3, Matthau 3, Almendros 4)
Gentleman's Agreement, 1935 (Pearson 2, Leigh 3, Havelock-Allan 4)
Gentleman's Agreement, 1947 (Kazan 2, Garfield 3, Jaffe 3, Peck 3, LeMaire 4, Miller 4, Newman 4, Zanuck 4)
Gentleman's Fate, 1931 (Gilbert 3)
Gentlemen Are Born, 1934 (Darwell 3, Orry-Kelly 4)
Gentlemen d'Epsom, 1962 (Audiard 4)
Gentlemen from Blue Gulch. *See* Roughneck, 1915
Gentlemen Marry Brunettes, 1955 (Russell 3, Cole 4, Loos 4)
Gentlemen of Nerve, 1914 (Sennett 2, Normand 3)
Gentlemen of the Press, 1929 (Huston 3, Folsey 4, Zukor 4)
Gentlemen of the Press, 1991 (Francis 3)
Gentlemen Prefer Blondes, 1928

(Emerson 4, Loos 4, Mankiewicz 4, Rosson 4, Zukor 4)
Gentlemen Prefer Blondes, 1953 (Hawks 2, Coburn 3, Dalio 3, Monroe 3, Russell 3, Carmichael 4, Cole 4, Lederer 4, LeMaire 4, Loos 4, Wheeler 4)
Gentlemen, the Queen;, 1953 (Rank 4)
Gentlemen Tramp, 1975 (Chaplin 3)
Gentlemen with Guns, 1946 (Crabbe 3)
Gentlemen's Agreement, 1947 (Wheeler 4)
Gents in a Jam, 1952 (Three Stooges 3)
Gents Without Cents, 1944 (Three Stooges 3)
Genuine: Die Tragödie eines seltsamen Hauses, 1920 (Wiene 2, Mayer 4)
Genuine Risk, 1990 (Stamp 3)
Genzaburo ihen: Hissatsuken oni no maki, 1934 (Hasegawa 3)
Genzaburo ihen: Shokuran renbo no maki, 1934 (Hasegawa 3)
Geo le mysterieux, 1916 (Dulac 2)
Geography Films Series, 1946 (Leacock 2)
Geole, 1921 (Musidora 3)
Geordie, 1955 (Launder and Gilliat 2, Sim 3, Alwyn 4)
George and Margaret, 1940 (Fisher 2)
George Bernard Shaw, 1956 (Lassally 4)
George Dumpson's Place, 1964 (Emshwiller 2)
George in Civvie Street, 1946 (Formby 3)
George Raft Story, 1961 (Mansfield 3)
George Takes the Air. *See* It's in the Air, 1938
George Washington, 1984 (Ferrer 3, Howard 3)
George Washington's Escape, 1911 (Bosworth 3)
George Washington Slept Here, 1942 (Coburn 3, McDaniel 3, Pangborn 3, Sheridan 3, Deutsch 4, Haller 4, Orry-Kelly 4, Wald 4)
George White's 1935 Scandals, 1935 (Faye 3, Powell 3, Friedhofer 4)
George White's Scandals, 1934 (Durante 3, Faye 3, Friedhofer 4, Garmes 4, LeMaire 4)
Georgia's Friends. *See* Four Friends, 1981
Georgie and the Dragon, 1951 (Bosustow 4, Hubley 4)
Georgina's Gründe, 1974 (Von Trotta 2)
Georgy Girl, 1966 (Bates 3, Mason 3)
Gerald Cranston's Lady, 1924 (Goulding 2)
Gerald McBoing Boing series, 1951–56 (Bosustow 4)
Geraldine, 1929 (Wilson 4)
Gerald's Film, 1976 (Jarman 2)
Geranium, 1911 (Costello 3)
Gerarchi si muore, 1962 (Fabrizi 3)
Gerard Has His Hair Removed with Nair, 1967 (Warhol 2)
Gerard Malanga Reads Poetry. *See* Bufferin, 1966
Gerechtigkeit, 1920 (Kortner 3)
Gerechtigkeit, 1925 (Dieterle 2)
German Calling, 1942 (Lye 4)
German Manpower, 1943 (Kanin 4)
German Sisters. *See* Bleieren Zeit, 1982
Germania, anno zero, 1947 (Rossellini 2, Amidei 4)
Germanin, 1943 (Stallich 4)
Germany in Autumn. *See* Deutschland in Herbst, 1978
Germany, Year Zero. *See* Germania, anno zero, 1947

Germinal, 1963 (Allégret 2, Blier 3, Saulnier 4, Spaak 4)

Germination d'un haricot, 1928 (Dulac 2)

Gern hab' ich die Frau'n gekillt. *See* Spie control il mondo, 1966

Geroite na Shipka, 1954 (Vasiliev 2)

Geronimo, 1939 (Dreier 4, Head 4)

Geronimo, 1962 (Friedhofer 4)

Geronimo's Last Raid, 1912 (Emerson 4)

Gertie on Tour, 1918 (McCay 4)

Gertie the Dinosaur, 1914 (McCay 4)

Gertie the Trained Dinosaur. *See* **Gertie the Dinosaur, 1914**

Gertrud, 1964 (Dreyer 2)

Gervaise, 1955 (Clement 2, Schell 3, Aurenche 4, Auric 4, Bost 4)

Geschäft, 1917 (Jannings 3)

Geschäft nit Amerika. *See* Yes Mr. Brown, 1932

Geschichte der stillen Mühle, 1914 (Warm 4)

Geschichte des kleinen Muck, 1953 (Staudte 2)

Geschichte des Prinzen Achmed, 1922 (Reiniger 4)

Geschichte des Prinzen Achmed. *See* Scheintote Chinese, 1928

Geschichte einer Leidenschaft. *See* Weib in Flammen, 1928

Geschichte einer Liebe, 1981 (Ganz 3)

Geschichte eines Lebens. *See* Annelie, 1941

Geschichten aus dem Wienerwald, 1981 (Dagover 3, Schell 3)

Geschichtsunterricht, 1972 (Straub and Huillet 2)

Geschiendene Frau, 1953 (Herlth 4)

Geschlecht derer von Ringwall, 1918 (Wiene 2, Freund 4)

Geschlossene Kette, 1920 (Negri 3, Wagner 4)

Geschwader Fledermaus, 1958 (Eisler 4)

Gesicht im Dunkeln. *See* Double Face, 1969

Gespensterschiff, 1921 (Leni 2)

Gespensterstunde, 1917 (Gad 2)

Gestapo. *See* Night Train to Munich, 1940

Gestärtes Rendez-vous, 1897 (Messter 4)

Gestes de France, 1963 (Braunberger 4)

Gestes du silence, 1960 (Storck 2)

Gestohlene Gesicht, 1930 (Schüfftan 4)

Gestohlene Herz, 1934 (Reiniger 4)

Gestohlene Jahr, 1951 (Werner 3)

Gestos e Fragmentos, 1982 (De Almeida 4)

Gesu di Nazareth. *See* Jesus of Nazareth, 1977

Gesucht: Monika Ertl, 1989 (Rozsa 4)

Gesunkenen, 1925 (Dieterle 2, Albers 3, Nielsen 3, Tschechowa 3)

Get Busy, 1924 (Roach 4)

Get Carter, 1970 (Caine 3)

Get Charlie Tully. *See* Ooh . . . You Are Awful, 1972

Get Cracking, 1943 (Formby 3)

Get Crazy, 1983 (McDowell 3)

Get 'em Young, 1926 (Laurel and Hardy 3, Roach 4)

Get Going, 1943 (Salter 4)

Get Help to Love, 1942 (O'Connor 3)

Get Off My Back. *See* Synanon, 1965

Get Off My Foot, 1935 (Launder and Gilliat 2)

Get Out and Get Under, 1920 (Lloyd 3)

Get Out Your Handkerchiefs. *See* Préparez vos mouchoirs, 1978

Get Rich Quick, 1913 (Sennett 2)

Get Rich Quick Porky, 1937 (Blanc 4, Clampett 4, Stalling 4)

Get That Venus, 1933 (Arthur 3)

Get to Know Your Rabbit, 1972 (De Palma 2, Welles 2, Alonzo 4)

Get Your Man, 1921 (Howard 2)

Get Your Man, 1923 (Roach 4)

Get Your Man, 1927 (Arzner 2, Bow 3, Schulberg 4)

Get Your Man, 1934 (Harrison 3)

Get Yourself a College Girl, 1964 (Katzman 4)

Get-Away, 1941 (Reed 3, Burnett 4)

Getaway, 1972 (Hill 2, Peckinpah 2, Johnson 3, McQueen 3, Ballard 4, Jones 4)

Get-Rich-Quick Wallingford, 1915 (Niblo 2)

Get-Rich-Quick Wallingford, 1921 (Borzage 2)

Getting Acquainted, 1914 (Sennett 2, Normand 3)

Getting an Eyeful, 1938 (Kaye 3)

Getting a Start in Life, 1915 (Mix 3)

Getting a Ticket, 1929 (Cantor 3)

Getting Atmosphere, 1912 (Bosworth 3)

Getting Away from It All, 1972 (Meredith 3)

Getting Even, 1909 (Griffith 2, Pickford 3, Bitzer 4)

Getting Gertie's Garter, 1927 (Garnett 2, Pangborn 3, Rosson 4)

Getting Gertie's Garter, 1945 (Dwan 2, Friedhofer 4)

Getting His Goat, 1920 (Roach 4)

Getting it Right, 1989 (Gielgud 3)

Getting Married, 1978 (Johnson 3)

Getting Mary Married, 1919 (Dwan 2, Davies 3, Emerson 4, Loos 4)

Getting of Wisdom, 1977 (Beresford 2)

Getting Reuben Back, 1910 (White 3)

Getting Straight, 1970 (Ford 3, Gould 3, Kovacs 4)

Gewehr über, 1950 (Staudte 2)

Gewisser Herr Gran, 1933 (Albers 3)

Gewisser Judas, 1958 (Herlth 4)

Gewitter im Mai, 1919 (Veidt 3)

Gewitterflug zu Claudia, 1937 (Tschechowa 3)

Ghaltit Habibi, 1957 (Sharif 3)

Ghar Ki Izzat, 1948 (Kumar 3)

Gharam el Asyad, 1960 (Sharif 3)

Ghare Bahire, 1982 (Chatterjee 3, Datta 4)

Ghev, 1974 (Yankovsky 3)

Ghidrah. *See* Sandai kaiju chikyu saidai no kessen, 1965

Ghosks in the Bunk, 1939 (Fleischer 4)

Ghost, 1911 (Sennett 2)

Ghost, 1990 (Goldberg 3, Edlund 4, Jarre 4, Murch 4, North 4)

Ghost and Mrs. Muir, 1947 (Mankiewicz 2, Harrison 3, Sanders 3, Tierney 3, Wood 3, Day 4, Dunne 4, Herrmann 4, Lang 4, LeMaire 4)

Ghost Breaker, 1914 (Buckland 4, Macpherson 4)

Ghost Breaker, 1914 (De Mille 2)

Ghost Breaker, 1922 (LeRoy 2, Johnson 3, Reid 3)

Ghost Breakers, 1940 (Goddard 3, Hope 3, Johnson 3, Lukas 3, Quinn 3, Dreier 4, Head 4, Lang 4)

Ghost Camera, 1933 (Lupino 3, Mills 3)

Ghost Dad, 1990 (Poitier 3, Bumstead 4, Mancini 4)

Ghost Flower, 1918 (Borzage 2)

Ghost Goes West, 1935 (Clair 2, Donat 3, Lanchester 3, Cardiff 4, Hornbeck 4, Korda, A. 4, Korda, V. 4, Mathieson 4, Rosson 4, Sherwood 4)

Ghost Goes Wild, 1947 (Horton 3, Alton 4)

Ghost in Monte Carlo, 1989 (Reed 3)

Ghost in the Invisible Bikini, 1966 (Bushman 3, Karloff 3, Rathbone 3)

Ghost in the Noonday Sun, 1974 (Sellers 3)

Ghost of Flight 401, 1978 (Raksin 4)

Ghost of Folly, 1926 (Sennett 2)

Ghost of Frankenstein, 1942 (Bellamy 3, Lugosi 3, Krasner 4, Pierce 4, Salter 4)

Ghost of Hidden Valley, 1946 (Crabbe 3)

Ghost of Love. *See* Fantasma d'amore, 1981

Ghost of St. Michael's, 1941 (Hay 3, Balcon 4)

Ghost of Slumber Mountain, 1918 (O'Brien 4)

Ghost of the Twisted Oaks, 1915 (Olcott 2)

Ghost Parade, 1931 (Sennett 2)

Ghost Patrol, 1923 (Love 3)

Ghost Ship, 1943 (D'Agostino 4, Lewton 4, Musuraca 4)

Ghost Steps Out, 1946 (Abbott and Costello 3)

Ghost Story, 1981 (Astaire 3, Douglas 3, Neal 3, Cardiff 4, Houseman 4, Sarde 4, Smith 4, Whitlock 4)

Ghost Talks, 1929 (Brown 3)

Ghost Talks, 1949 (Three Stooges 3)

Ghost Town, 1937 (Carey 3)

Ghost Town, 1944 (Terry 4)

Ghost Town, 1955 (Biroc 4)

Ghost Town Gold, 1936 (Canutt 4)

Ghost Train, 1931 (Launder and Gilliat 2, Balcon 4, Biro 4)

Ghost Train, 1941 (Launder and Gilliat 2, Rank 4, Vetchinsky 4)

Ghost Train. *See* Yuhrei ressha, 1949

Ghost Valley Raiders, 1939 (Canutt 4)

Ghost Wanted, 1940 (Blanc 4, Jones 4, Stalling 4)

Ghostbusters, 1984 (Weaver 3, Bernstein 4, Edlund 4, Kovacs 4)

Ghostbusters II, 1989 (Weaver 3)

Ghosts, 1915 (Von Stroheim 2, Walthall 3)

Ghosts Can't Do It, 1990 (Quinn 3)

Ghosts; In Old Heidelberg, 1915 (Emerson 4)

Ghosts in Rome. *See* Fantasmi a Roma, 1961

Ghosts in the Night. *See* Ghosts on the Loose, 1943

Ghosts—Italian Style. *See* Questi fantasmi, 1967

Ghosts of Rome. *See* Fantasmi a Roma, 1961

Ghosts of Yesterday, 1918 (Talmadge 3)

Ghosts on the Loose, 1943 (Gardner 3, Lugosi 3, Katzman 4)

Ghoul, 1933 (Karloff 3, Richardson 3, Balcon 4, Junge 4)

Ghoul, 1975 (Cushing 3, Hurt 3, Francis 4)

Ghum Bhangaar Gaan, 1964 (Shankar 4)

Ghungroo, 1983 (Patil 3)

Giacomo l'idealista, 1942 (Lattuada 2, Risi 2, Ponti 4)

Giaconda Smile. *See* Woman's Vengeance, 1948

Giallo, 1933 (Camerini 2)

Giallo automatico, 1980 (Bozzetto 4)

Giallo napoletano, 1979 (Mastroianni 3, Piccoli 3)

Gian Burrasca, 1943 (Zavattini 4)

Giant, 1956 (Stevens 2, Baker 3, Dean 3, Hopper 3, Hudson 3, McCambridge 3, Mineo 3, Taylor 3, Hornbeck 4, Leven 4, Tiomkin 4, Warner 4)
Giant Behemoth, 1958 (Lourié 4)
Giant Behemoth, 1959 (O'Brien 4)
Giant Claw, 1957 (Katzman 4)
Giant Killer, 1924 (Lantz 4)
Giants vs. Yanks, 1923 (Roach 4)
Giarabub, 1942 (Sordi 3)
Giardino dei Finzi-Contini, 1970 (Sanda 3, Pinelli 4)
Giardino delle delizie, 1967 (Morricone 4)
Giarrettiera Colt, 1968 (Fusco 4)
Gibier de potence, 1951 (Arletty 3, Aurenche 4)
Gibraltar, 1932 (Wright 2)
Gibraltar, 1938 (Fradetal 4, Wakhévitch 4)
Gibson Goddess, 1909 (Griffith 2, Sennett 2, Pickford 3, Bitzer 4)
Giddap, 1925 (Sennett 2)
Giddy Age, 1932 (Sennett 2)
Giddy, Gay and Ticklish, 1915 (Sennett 2)
Giddy Yap, 1949 (Bosustow 4)
Giddyap, 1950 (Raksin 4)
Giddy-yapping, 1944 (Fleischer 4)
Gideon of Scotland Yard. See Gideon's Day, 1958
Gideon's Day, 1958 (Cusack 3, Hawkins 3, Adam 4, Clarke 4, Young 4)
Gideon's Trumpet, 1980 (Wray 3, Houseman 4)
Gidget, 1959 (Robertson 3, Duning 4, Guffey 4, Williams 4)
Gidget Gets Married, 1972 (Bennett 3, Biroc 4)
Gidget Goes Hawaiian, 1961 (Duning 4)
Gidget Goes to Rome, 1963 (Williams 4)
Gidslet, 1913 (Christensen 2)
Gifle, 1974 (Adjani 3, Girardot 3, Delerue 4)
Gift. See Dárek, 1946
Gift, 1973 (Brakhage 2)
Gift, 1979 (Ford 3)
Gift. See Cadeau, 1982
Gift for Love, 1964 (Heller 4)
Gift Horse, 1952 (Attenborough 3, Howard 3)
Gift of Gab, 1934 (Karloff 3, Lugosi 3, Lukas 3, Freund 4, Wald 4)
Gift of Green, 1946 (Van Dongen 4)
Gift of Love, 1958 (Negulesco 2, Bacall 3, Brackett 4, Krasner 4, LeMaire 4)
Gift of Love: A Christmas Story, 1983 (Lansbury 3, Remick 3)
Gift o'Gab, 1917 (Van Dyke 2)
Gift Supreme, 1920 (Chaney 3)
Gift Wrapped, 1952 (Blanc 4, Foster 4, Freleng 4, Stalling 4)
Giftas, 1956 (Zetterling 2)
Giftasvuxnar döttrar, 1933 (Jaenzon 4)
Giftgas, 1929 (Baranovskaya 3, Kortner 3)
Giftpilen, 1915 (Psilander 3)
Gigantis the Fire Monster. See Gojira no gyakushu, 1955
Gigi, 1948 (Noiret 3)
Gigi, 1958 (Minnelli 2, Caron 3, Chevalier 3, Jourdan 3, Ames 4, Beaton 4, Freed 4, Previn 4, Ruttenberg 4)
Gigolette, 1935 (Bellamy 3, Ruttenberg 4)
Gigolette, 1937 (Morgan 3)
Gigolettes, 1932 (Arbuckle 3)
Gigolo, 1926 (Howard 2, Adrian 4, Fort 4, Sullivan 4)
Gigolo, 1960 (Valli 3)

Gigot, 1962 (Kelly 3, Cahn 4)
Gilbert and Sullivan. See Story of Gilbert and Sullivan, 1953
Gilda, 1946 (Vidor 2, Ford 3, Hayworth 3, Cohn 4, Cole 4, Friedhofer 4, Maté 4, Polglase 4)
Gilded Cage, 1916 (Edeson 4, Marion 4)
Gilded Highway, 1926 (Blackton 2, Loy 3, Musuraca 4)
Gilded Lily, 1921 (Haller 4, Zukor 4)
Gilded Lily, 1935 (Colbert 3, MacMurray 3, Milland 3, Banton 4, Zukor 4)
Gilded Spider, 1916 (Chaney 3)
Gildersleeve's Bad Day, 1943 (Darwell 3)
Gillekop, 1919 (Blom 2, Dreyer 2)
Gilly y Praze, 1920 (Ondra 3)
Gimme, 1923 (Walthall 3, Gibbons 4)
Gimme Shelter, 1970 (Maysles 2, Murch 4, Wexler 4)
Gina. See Mort en ce jardin, 1956
Gina, 1974 (Arcand 2)
Ginecologo della mutua, 1977 (Fabrizi 3)
Gingchat gusi, 1985 (Chan 3)
Gingchat gusi tsuktsap, 1988 (Chan 3)
Ginger, 1935 (Glennon 4)
Ginger Bread Boy, 1934 (Lantz 4)
Ginger e Fred, 1986 (Fellini 2, Masina 3, Mastroianni 3, Delli Colli 4, Donati 4, Guerra 4, Morricone 4, Pinelli 4)
Ginger in the Morning, 1973 (Spacek 3)
Gingerbread Hut. See Perníková chaloupka, 1951
Gingham Girl, 1920 (Sennett 2)
Gingham Girl, 1927 (Plunkett 4)
Gink at the Sink, 1948 (Bruckman 4)
Ginpei the Outlaw. See Muhoumono Ginpei, 1938
Ginrei no hate, 1947 (Mifune 3, Shimura 3)
Ginrin, 1955 (Takemitsu 4)
Ginsberg the Great, 1927 (Blanke 4, Haskin 4)
Gin-Shinju, 1956 (Shindo 2)
Ginza Cosmetics. See Ginza gesho, 1951
Ginza gesho, 1951 (Kagawa 3, Tanaka 3)
Ginza kankan musume, 1949 (Takamine 3)
Ginza no onna, 1955 (Yoshimura 2)
Ginza no yanagi, 1932 (Tanaka 3)
Giocattolo, 1979 (Morricone 4)
Giochi di Colonia, 1958 (Olmi 2)
Giochi particolari, 1970 (Mastroianni 3, Guerra 4, Morricone 4)
Gioco al massacro, 1989 (Baye 3, Gould 3)
Gioco pericoloso, 1942 (Amidei 4)
Gion bayashi, 1953 (Mizoguchi 2, Shindo 3, Miyagawa 4, Yoda 4)
Gion Festival. See Gion matsuri, 1933
Gion Festival Music. See Gion bayashi, 1953
Gion matsuri, 1933 (Mizoguchi 2)
Gion matsuri, 1968 (Iwashita 3, Mifune 3, Shimura 3)
Gion no shimai, 1936 (Mizoguchi 2, Shindo 3, Yamada 3, Yoda 4)
Gion no shimai, 1956 (Yoda 3)
Giordano Bruno, 1973 (Volonté 3, Morricone 4, Storaro 4)
Giornata balorda, 1960 (Pasolini 2)
Giornata nera per l'ariete, 1971 (Morricone 4, Storaro 4)
Giornata speciale, 1977 (Loren 3, Mastroianni 3, Ponti 4)
Giorni contati, 1962 (Guerra 4)
Giorni d'amore, 1954 (Mastroianni 3)
Giorni di fuoco. See Winnetou: II Teil, 1964

Giorni di gloria, 1945 (Visconti 2)
Giorno da leone, 1961 (Cristaldi 4)
Giorno del furore, 1973 (Cardinale 3, Reed 3)
Giorno della civetta, 1968 (Cardinale 3, Cobb 3, Reggiani 3, Delli Colli 4, Fusco 4)
Giorno dell'ira, 1967 (Van Cleef 3)
Giorno in pretura, 1954 (Loren 3, Sordi 3, De Laurentiis 4, Ponti 4)
Giorno nella vita, 1946 (Blasetti 2, Zavattini 4)
Giorno per giorno disperatamente, 1961 (Cristaldi 4)
Giorno più corto, 1963 (Aimée 3, Belmondo 3, Girardot 3, Granger 3, Mastroianni 3, Niven 3, Pidgeon 3)
Giorno prima, 1987 (Josephson 3, Lancaster 3, Thulin 3, Morricone 4)
Giovane leone, 1959 (Sordi 3)
Giovane Toscanini, 1988 (Zeffirelli 2, Taylor 3)
Giovani mariti, 1958 (Rota 4)
Giovanna d'Arco al rogo, 1954 (Bergman 3)
Giovanna e le altre, 1960 (De Laurentiis 4)
Giovanni delle Bande Nere, 1956 (Gassman 3)
Giovanni Mariti, 1958 (Pasolini 2)
Giovanni Senzapensieri, 1986 (Fabrizi 3)
Gioventù alla sbarra, 1951 (Delli Colli 4)
Gioventù perduta, 1947 (Monicelli 2, Ponti 4)
Giovinezza, 1952 (Sordi 3)
Giovinezza del diavolo, 1921 (Bertini 3)
Giovinezza, giovinezza, 1969 (Storaro 4)
Gipsy Angel, 1989 (Baker 3)
Gipsy Joe, 1916 (Sennett 2)
Girasoli, 1970 (Loren 3, Mastroianni 3, Guerra 4, Levine 4, Mancini 4, Ponti 4, Rotunno 4, Zavattini 4)
Girl, 1987 (Lee 3)
Girl, a Guy, and a Gob, 1941 (Ball 3, Lloyd 3, O'Brien 3, Pangborn 3, Metty 4)
Girl and Her Money, 1913 (Lawrence 3)
Girl and Her Trust, 1912 (Griffith 2, Bitzer 4)
Girl and the Bronco Buster, 1911 (Guy 2)
Girl and the Fugitive, 1910 (Anderson 3)
Girl and the Gambler, 1939 (Metty 4)
Girl and the General. See Ragazza e il generale, 1967
Girl and the Gun, 1911 (Dwan 2)
Girl and the Judge, 1913 (Bosworth 3)
Girl and the Legend. See Robinson soll nicht sterben, 1957
Girl and the Mail Bag, 1915 (Mix 3)
Girl and the Outlaw, 1908 (Griffith 2, Lawrence 3)
Girl and the Shoes. See Pigen og skoene, 1959
Girl at Home, 1917 (Neilan 2)
Girl at the Curtain, 1914 (Bushman 3)
Girl at the Ironing Board, 1934 (Freleng 4)
Girl at the Lunch Counter, 1913 (Bunny 3)
Girl Back East, 1911 (Anderson 3)
Girl Back Home, 1911 (Dwan 2)
Girl Can't Help It, 1956 (Tashlin 2, Mansfield 3, O'Brien 3, Kanin 4, LeMaire 4, Shamroy 4, Wheeler 4)
Girl Crazy, 1929 (Sennett 2)
Girl Crazy, 1932 (Hunt 4, Mankiewicz 4)
Girl Crazy, 1938 (Allyson 3)

Girl Crazy, 1943 (Berkeley 2, Walters 2, Garland 3, Rooney 3, Daniels 4, Freed 4, Irene 4, Mayer 4, Sharaff 4)

Girl Downstairs, 1938 (Pangborn 3)

Girl Friend. *See* Kanojo, 1926

Girl Friend, 1935 (Walker 4)

Girl Friends. *See* Podrugi, 1935

Girl Friends. *See* Amiche, 1955

Girl from Avenue A, 1940 (Barnes 4, Day 4)

Girl from Chicago, 1927 (Loy 3, Mohr 4)

Girl from Chicago, 1932 (Micheaux 2)

Girl from China. *See* Shanghai Lady, 1928

Girl from Everywhere, 1927 (Sennett 2, Lombard 3)

Girl from Flanders. *See* Mädchen aus Flandern, 1956

Girl from God's Country, 1921 (Walker 4)

Girl from Havana, 1940 (Brown 4)

Girl from Hong Kong, 1931 (Robinson 4)

Girl from Jones Beach, 1948 (Reagan 3, Diamond 4)

Girl from Lorraine. *See* Provinciale, 1980

Girl from Manhattan, 1948 (Lamour 3, Laughton 3, Laszlo 4)

Girl from Maxim's, 1933 (Crichton 2, Korda 2, Korda, A. 4, Korda, V. 4, Périnal 4)

Girl from Mexico, 1939 (Bond 3, Polglase 4)

Girl from Missouri, 1934 (Barrymore 3, Harlow 3, Adrian 4, Emerson 4, Gillespie 4, Loos 4)

Girl from Nowhere, 1928 (Sennett 2, Lombard 3)

Girl from Petrovka, 1974 (Hawn 3, Hopkins 3, Mancini 4, Zsigmond 4)

Girl from Rio, 1927 (Pidgeon 3)

Girl from Scotland Yard, 1937 (Head 4, Schary 4)

Girl from State Street. *See* State Street Sadie, 1928

Girl from Tenth Avenue, 1935 (Davis 3, Blanke 4, Orry-Kelly 4)

Girl from the Distant River. *See* Devushka s dalekoi reki, 1928

Girl from the Moon. *See* Spadla s mĕsice, 1966

Girl from the Mountain Village. *See* Flickan från fjällbyn, 1948

Girl from the Third Row. *See* Flickan från tredje raden, 1949

Girl from the Triple X, 1910 (Anderson 3)

Girl Game. *See* Copacabana Palace, 1962

Girl Getters. *See* System, 1964

Girl Grief, 1932 (Goddard 3, Roach 4)

Girl Guardian, 1916 (Sennett 2)

Girl Habit, 1931 (Dumont 3, Goddard 3)

Girl Happy, 1965 (Presley 3, Pasternak 4)

Girl He Left Behind, 1921 (Johnson 3)

Girl He Left Behind. *See* Gang's All Here, 1943

Girl He Left Behind, 1956 (Garner 3, Wood 3, McCord 4)

Girl I Loved. *See* Waga koiseshi otome, 1946

Girl I Made. *See* Made on Broadway, 1933

Girl in 313, 1940 (Cronjager 4, Day 4)

Girl in 419, 1933 (Furthman 4, Struss 4)

Girl in a Dressing Gown. *See* Flickan i frack, 1956

Girl in a Million, 1946 (Greenwood 3)

Girl in Black. *See* To koritsi me ta mavra, 1955

Girl in Black, 1957 (Cacoyannis 2)

Girl in Black Stockings, 1956 (Bancroft 3)

Girl in Danger, 1934 (Bellamy 3, Bond 3)

Girl in Distress. *See* Jeannie, 1941

Girl in Every Port, 1928 (Hawks 2, Brooks 3, McLaglen 3, Miller 4)

Girl in Every Port, 1952 (Bendix 3, Marx Brothers 3, Musuraca 4)

Girl in Lover's Lane, 1959 (Cronjager 4)

Girl in Number 29, 1920 (Ford 2)

Girl in Overalls. *See* Swing Shift Maisie, 1943

Girl in Pants, 1910 (White 3)

Girl in Question, 1914 (Eason 4)

Girl in Room 17. *See* Vice Squad, 1953

Girl in Room Seventeen. *See* Vice Squad, 1953

Girl in the Bikini. *See* Manina, la fille sans voiles, 1952

Girl in the Case, 1914 (Costello 3)

Girl in the Checkered Coat, 1916 (Chaney 3)

Girl in the Crowd, 1934 (Powell and Pressburger 2, Withers 3)

Girl in the Glass Cage, 1929 (Young 3, Haller 4)

Girl in the Headlines, 1963 (Addison 4)

Girl in the Kremlin, 1957 (Bodeen 4)

Girl in the Limousine, 1924 (Laurel and Hardy 3)

Girl in the Moon. *See* Frau im Mond, 1929

Girl in the News, 1940 (Reed 2, Launder and Gilliat 2, Lockwood 3)

Girl in the Painting. *See* Portrait from Life, 1948

Girl in the Pullman, 1927 (Pangborn 3)

Girl in the Rain. *See* Flickan i regnet, 1955

Girl in the Red Velvet Swing, 1955 (Milland 3, Brackett 4, Krasner 4, LeMaire 4, Reisch 4, Wheeler 4)

Girl in the Shack, 1914 (Loos 4)

Girl in the Show, 1929 (Love 3, Day 4, Gibbons 4)

Girl in the Taxi. *See* Chaste Suzanne, 1937

Girl in the Tonneau, 1932 (Sennett 2)

Girl in the Web, 1920 (Sweet 3, Young 4)

Girl in the Window Opposite. *See* Flickan i fönstret mittemot, 1942

Girl in the Yellow Pajamas. *See* Ragazza in Pigiamo Giallo, 1978

Girl in White, 1952 (Sturges 2, Allyson 3, Kennedy 3, Raksin 4, Rose 4)

Girl Loves Boy, 1937 (Brown 4)

Girl Missing, 1932 (Florey 2, Beavers 3)

Girl Most Likely, 1957 (Leisen 2, Robertson 3)

Girl Must Live, 1939 (Reed 2, Launder and Gilliat 2, Lockwood 3, Vetchinsky 4)

Girl Named Sooner, 1975 (Remick 3, Goldsmith 4)

Girl Named Tamiko, 1962 (Sturges 2, Harvey 3, Anhalt 4, Bernstein 4, Head 4, Lang 4, Wallis 4)

Girl Next Door, 1923 (Van Dyke 2)

Girl Next Door, 1953 (Kidd 4, LeMaire 4, Lennart 4, Shamroy 4)

Girl Next Room, 1910 (White 3)

Girl o' the Woods, 1913 (Lawrence 3)

Girl of Gold Gulch, 1916 (Mix 3)

Girl of My Dreams. *See* Sweetheart of Sigma Chi, 1933

Girl of the Golden West, 1915 (De Mille 2, Buckland 4, Macpherson 4)

Girl of the Golden West, 1923 (Polito 4)

Girl of the Golden West, 1930 (Polito 4, Young 4)

Girl of the Golden West, 1938 (Eddy 3, MacDonald 3, Pidgeon 3, Adrian 4, Canutt 4, Gibbons 4, Stothart 4, Vorkapich 4)

Girl of the Lighthouse, 1912 (Bosworth 3)

Girl of the Limberlost, 1934 (Walthall 3)

Girl of the Limberlost, 1945 (Guffey 4)

Girl of the Mountains, 1912 (Bosworth 3)

Girl of the Night, 1915 (Chaney 3)

Girl of the Ozarks, 1936 (Dreier 4)

Girl of the Port, 1930 (Glennon 4)

Girl of the Rio, 1932 (Brenon 2, Del Rio 3, Steiner 4)

Girl of the West, 1911 (Anderson 3)

Girl of Vaniousine. *See* Deti Vanyousina, 1915

Girl of Yesterday, 1915 (Dwan 2, Crisp 3, Pickford 3, Marion 4)

Girl on a Motorcycle, 1968 (Delon 3, Cardiff 4, D'Eaubonne 4)

Girl on Approval, 1962 (Roberts 3)

Girl on the Boat, 1961 (Wisdom 3)

Girl on the Canal. *See* Painted Boats, 1945

Girl on the Front Page, 1936 (Krasner 4)

Girl on the Late, Late Show, 1974 (De Carlo 3, Grahame 3, Johnson 3, Pidgeon 3)

Girl on the Stairs, 1924 (Walker 4)

Girl on the Subway, 1958 (Furthman 4)

Girl on Triple X Ranch. *See* Girl from the Triple X, 1910

Girl Overboard, 1936 (Pidgeon 3)

Girl Reporter, 1910 (White 3)

Girl Rush, 1944 (Mitchum 3, Musuraca 4)

Girl Rush, 1955 (Russell 3, Alton 4, Daniels 4, Head 4, Hornbeck 4)

Girl Said No, 1930 (Wood 2, Dressler 3, Gibbons 4, MacArthur 4)

Girl Scout, 1909 (Olcott 2)

Girl Shy, 1924 (Lloyd 3, Roach 4, Zukor 4)

Girl Spy Before Vicksburg, 1910 (Olcott 2)

Girl Stroke Boy, 1971 (Greenwood 3)

Girl Swappers. *See* Two and Two Make Six, 1962

Girl Trouble, 1942 (Ameche 3, Bennett 3, Cronjager 4, Day 4, Newman 4)

Girl Was Young. *See* Young and Innocent, 1937

Girl Who Came Back, 1923 (Schulberg 4)

Girl Who Couldn't Say No. *See* Suo modo di fare, 1968

Girl Who Had Everything, 1953 (Powell 3, Taylor 3, Previn 4)

Girl Who Rode in the Palio. *See* Ragazza del Palio, 1957

Girl Who Stayed at Home, 1919 (Griffith 2, Barthelmess 3, Bitzer 4)

Girl Who Won, 1914 (Lawrence 3)

Girl Who Wouldn't Work, 1925 (Barrymore 3, Walthall 3)

Girl with a Gun. *See* Ragazza con la pistola, 1968

Girl with a Suitcase. *See* Ragazza con la valigia, 1961

Girl with Green Eyes, 1964 (Richardson 2, Finch 3, Addison 4)

Girl with Ideas, 1937 (Pidgeon 3, Krasner 4)

Girl with the Devil in Her. *See* Jsem děvče s čertem v tĕle, 1933

Girl with the Green Eyes, 1916 (Guy 2)

Girl with the Pistol. *See* Ragazza con la pistola, 1968

Girl without a Room, 1933 (Banton 4)

Girl Woman, 1919 (Costello 3)

Girl Worth While, 1913 (Cruze 2)

Girlfriends. *See* Biches, 1968

Girlfriends, 1978 (Wallach 3)

Girlish Impulse, 1911 (Lawrence 3)

Girls, 1957 (Cukor 2, Kelly 3, Kendall 3, Cole 4, Deutsch 4, Orry-Kelly 4, Porter 4, Surtees 4)

Girls. *See* Flickorna, 1968

Girls about Town, 1931 (Cukor 2, Beavers 3, Francis 3, McCrea 3, Banton 4, Haller 4, Vorkapich 4)

Girls and a Daddy, 1908 (Griffith 2, Bitzer 4)

Girls Can Play, 1937 (Hayworth 3, Ballard 4)

Girls Demand Excitement, 1930 (Wayne 3, Clarke 4)

Girls' Dormitory, 1936 (Marshall 3, Power 3, Simon 3)

Girl's Folly, 1917 (Tourneur 2, Carré 4, Marion 4)

Girls from Wilko. *See* Panny z Wilka, 1979

Girls! Girls! Girls!, 1962 (Presley 3, Anhalt 4, Head 4, Wallis 4)

Girls Gone Wild, 1929 (MacMurray 3, Edeson 4)

Girls Growing Up, 1967 (Halas and Batchelor 4)

Girls He Left Behind. *See* Gang's All Here, 1943

Girls in Chains, 1943 (Ulmer 2)

Girls in Prison, 1956 (Darwell 3, Marsh 3)

Girls in the Night, 1952 (Boyle 4)

Girls Marked Danger. *See* Tratta delle bianche, 1952

Girls of Huntington House, 1973 McCambridge 3, Spacek 3)

Girls of Pleasure Island, 1953 (Lanchester 3)

Girls of the Big House, 1945 (Alton 4)

Girls on Probation, 1938 (Hayward 3, Reagan 3)

Girls on the Beach, 1965 (Corman 2)

Girls on the Loose, 1958 (Henreid 3)

Girl's School, 1938 (Bellamy 3, Planer 4)

Girls School, 1949 (Dutt 2, Biswas 4)

Girls' School, 1950 (Beavers 3)

Girl's Stratagem, 1913 (Griffith 2, Barrymore 3, Marsh 3, Bitzer 4)

Girl's Way, 1923 (Lukas 3)

Girls Will Be Boys, 1910 (White 3)

Girls Will Be Boys, 1934 (Siodmak 4)

Girl-Shy Cowboy, 1928 (Miller 4)

Giro City, 1982 (Jackson 3)

Giro del monde degli innamorati di Paynet, 1974 (Morricone 4)

Girovaghi, 1956 (Ustinov 3)

Gisants, 1949 (Fresnay 3)

Giselle, 1952 (Buchanan 3)

Giselle, 1970 (Alekan 4)

Gishi shimatsu-ki, 1962 (Iwashita 3, Yamamura 3)

Gishiki, 1971 (Takemitsu 4, Toda 4)

Git Along Little Dogies, 1937 (Autry 3)

Gitan, 1975 (Delon 3, Girardot 3)

Gitana tenias que ser, 1953 (Infante 3, Alcoriza 4)

Gitane, 1986 (Audran 3)

Gitanella, 1914 (Feuillade 2)

Gitanes, 1932 (Vanel 3)

Gitanilla, 1940 (Rey 3)

Gitans d'Espagne, 1945 (Braunberger 4)

Gitta entdeckt ihr Herz, 1932 (Fröhlich 3, Courant 4)

Giù la testa, 1972 (Coburn 3, Steiger 3, Morricone 4)

Giù le mani . . . carogna, 1970 (Kinski 3)

Giudizio universale, 1961 (De Sica 2, Aimée 3, Borgnine 3, Durante 3, Fernandel 3, Gassman 3, Mercouri 3, Sordi 3, De Laurentiis 4, Zavattini 4)

Giulia e Giulia, 1987 (Turner 3, Jarre 4, Rotunno 4)

Giulietta degli spiriti, 1965 (Masina 3, Di Venanzo 4, Flaiano 4, Gherardi 4, Pinelli 4, Rota 4)

Giulietta e Romeo. *See* Romeo and Juliet, 1954

Giungla, 1942 (Amidei 4)

Giuseppe Verdi, 1938 (Gallone 2, Brasseur 3)

Giuseppe w Warzawie, 1964 (Cybulski 3)

Giustiziere sfida la citta, 1975 (Cotten 3)

Give a Girl a Break, 1953 (Donen 2, Fosse 2, Reynolds 3, Goodrich 4, Previn 4)

Give and Take. *See* Singing in the Corn, 1946

Give and Take, 1956 (Hanna and Barbera 4)

Give Her a Ring, 1934 (Granger 3)

Give Her the Moon. *See* Caprices de Maria, 1969

Give Me a Sailor, 1938 (Grable 3, Hope 3, Dreier 4, Head 4, Prinz 4)

Give Me Liberty, 1937 (Eason 4)

Give Me Your Heart, 1936 (Francis, Orry-Kelly 4, Robinson 4)

Give My Regards, 1948 (LeMaire 4)

Give My Regards to Broad Street, 1984 (Richardson 3)

Give My Regards to Broadway, 1948 (Bacon 2, Hoffenstein 4, Reynolds 4, Wheeler 4)

Give Out Sisters, 1942 (O'Connor 3)

Give Us Air. *See* Daesh vozkukh, 1924

Give Us the Moon, 1944 (Lockwood 3, Simmons 3, Rank 4)

Give Us This Day. *See* Ingeborg Holm, 1913

Give Us This Day, 1949 (Vetchinsky 4)

Give Us This Night, 1936 (Dreier 4, Korngold 4)

Give Us Wings, 1936 (Weiss 2)

Give Us Wings, 1940 (Three Stooges 3, Salter 4)

Giving the Bride Away, 1919 (Roach 4)

Giving Them Fits, 1915 (Daniels 3, Lloyd 3, Roach 4)

Givoi troup, 1912 (Mozhukin 3)

Giwaku, 1982 (Iwashita 3)

Glace a trois faces, 1927 (Epstein 2)

Glaciers, 1942 (Decaë 4)

Glad Eye, 1927 (Saville 2)

Glad Rag Doll, 1929 (Curtiz 2, Beavers 3, Costello 3, Haskin 4)

Glad Rags, 1923 (Bruckman 4)

Glad Rags to Riches, 1932 (Temple 3)

Glade Gøglere. *See* Lumpenkavaliere, 1932

Gladiator, 1938 (Brown 3, D'Agostino 4, Young 4)

Gladiatorerna, 1969 (Watkins 2)

Gladiators. *See* Gladiatorerna, 1969

Glaede Lojtnant, 1912 (Psilander 3)

Glaive et la balance, 1963 (Perkins 3, Jeanson 4, Spaak 4)

Glamour, 1934 (Wyler 2, Beavers 3, Lukas 3, Laemmle 4)

Glamour Boy, 1941 (Cooper 3, Dreier 4, Head 4, Young 4)

Glamour for Sale, 1940 (Planer 4)

Glamour Girl, 1948 (Katzman 4)

Glanz gegen Gluck, 1923 (Veidt 3)

Glanz und Elend der Kurtisanen, 1927 (Wegener 3, Planer 4)

Glas du Père Césaire, 1909 (Gance 2)

Glas Wasser. *See* Spiel der Königin, 1923

Glas Wasser, 1960 (Käutner 2, Gründgens 3)

Glasberget, 1953 (Molander 2, Björnstrand 3)

Gläserne Zelle, 1981 (Müller 4)

Glass Bottom Boat, 1966 (Tashlin 2, Day 3, Shamroy 4)

Glass Cage, 1955 (Carreras 4)

Glass Cell. *See* Gläserne Zelle, 1981

Glass Houses, 1970 (Folsey 4, Raksin 4)

Glass Key, 1935 (Milland 3, Raft 3, Sheridan 3, Head 4)

Glass Key, 1942 (Bendix 3, Ladd 3, Lake 3, Dreier 4, Head 4, Young 4)

Glass Menagerie, 1950 (Douglas 3, Kennedy 3, Wyman 3, Burks 4, Steiner 4, Wald 4)

Glass Menagerie, 1973 (Hepburn 3, Barry 4)

Glass Menagerie, 1987 (Newman 3, Woodward 3, Ballhaus 4, Mancini 4)

Glass Mountain, 1948 (Rota 4)

Glass of Water. *See* Glas Wasser, 1960

Glass of Wine. *See* Glass vin, 1960

Glass Slipper, 1938 (Terry 4)

Glass Slipper, 1954 (Caron 3, Plunkett 4, Rose 4)

Glass Slipper, 1955 (Walters 2, Lanchester 3, Pidgeon 3, Kaper 4)

Glass Sphinx. *See* Esfinge de cristal, 1968

Glass Tomb. *See* Glass Cage, 1955

Glass vin, 1960 (Fischer 4)

Glass Wall, 1953 (Gassman 3, Grahame 3, Biroc 4)

Glass Web, 1953 (Robinson 3)

Glass Works, 1914 (Phalke 2)

Glassmakers of England, 1933 (Flaherty 2)

Glaze of Cathexis, 1990 (Brakhage 2)

Gleam O'Dawn, 1922 (Gilbert 3, Furthman 4)

Glee Quartette, 1930 (Buchanan 3)

Gleisdreieck, 1936 (Fröhlich 3)

Gleisdreieck, 1950 (Staudte 2)

Glen or Glenda?, 1952 (Lugosi 3)

Glenn Miller Story, 1954 (Mann 2, Allyson 3, Stewart 3, Daniels 4, Mancini 4)

Glimpse of Austria, 1938 (Hoch 4)

Glimpse of Los Angeles, 1914 (Sennett 2, Normand 3)

Glimpse of the San Diego Exposition, 1915 (Sennett 2)

Glimpses of Java and Ceylon, 1937 (Hoch 4)

Glimpses of New Brunswick, 1938 (Hoch 4)

Glimpses of Peru, 1937 (Hoch 4)

Glimpses of the Moon, 1923 (Dwan 2, Costello 3, Daniels 3, Rosson 4)

Glimpses of the U.S.A., 1959 (Bernstein 4)

Glimpses of West Bengal, 1978 (Chandragupta 4)

Glinka. *See* Kompozitor Glinka, 1952

Glissements progressifs du plaisir, 1974 (Huppert 3, Robbe-Grillet 4)

Glitter. *See* Drop Kick, 1927

Glitter, 1984 (Neal 3)

Global Affair, 1964 (De Carlo 3, Hope 3, Ames 4, Lederer 4, Ruttenberg 4)

Globalny Pressing, 1987 (Mastroianni 3)

Gloria, 1913 (Bertini 3)

Gloria. *See* Gloria, 1931 (Fröhlich 3, Gabin 3)

Gloria, 1977 (Autant-Lara 2, Frampton 2)

Gloria, 1980 (Cassavetes 2, Rowlands 3, Henry 4)

Gloria Alley, 1952 (Caron 3)

Gloria's Romance, 1916 (Barthelmess 3)

Glorifying the American Girl, 1929 (Cantor 3, Berlin 4, Folsey 4)

Glorifying the Show Girl. *See* Glorifying the American Girl, 1929

Glorious Adventure, 1918 (Marsh 3)

Glorious Adventure, 1922 (Blackton 2, McLaglen 4)

Glorious Betsy, 1928 (Costello 3, Mohr 4)

Glorious Campaign. *See* Spanilá jízda, 1963

Glorious Days. *See* Lilacs in the Spring, 1955

Glorious Fourth, 1927 (Roach 4)

Glorious Lady, 1919 (Goulding 2)

Glorious Life, 1923 (Lukas 3)

Glorious Musketeers, 1973 (Halas and Batchelor 4)

Glorious Sixth of June, 1934 (Jennings 2)

Glorious Youth, 1929 (Ondra 3)

Glory, 1956 (Brennan 3, O'Brien 3)

Glory, 1988 (Francis 4)

Glory Alley, 1952 (Daniels 4, Rose 4)

Glory at Sea. *See* Gift Horse, 1952

Glory Boy. *See* My Old Man's Place, 1971

Glory Boys, 1984 (Perkins 3, Steiger 3)

Glory Brigade, 1953 (Marvin 3, Mature 3)

Glory! Glory!, 1988 (Anderson 2)

Glory Guys, 1965 (Caan 3, Howe 4)

Glory of Love. *See* While Paris Sleeps, 1923

Glory on the Summit. *See* Yama no sanka: Moyuru wakamono-tachi, 1962

Glory Stompers, 1967 (Hopper 3)

Glory to Me, Death to the Enemy!. *See* Slava nam, smert vragam!, 1914

Glove, 1978 (Blondell 3)

Glove Birds, 1942 (Bruckman 4)

Glove Taps, 1937 (Roach 4)

Glow Worm, 1930 (Fleischer 4)

Glowa, 1953 (Borowczyk 2)

Gluck auf der Alm, 1958 (Schell 3)

Glück bei Frauen, 1944 (Stallich 4)

Glückliche Mutter, 1928 (Dietrich 3)

Glücklichen Jahre der Thorwalds, 1962 (Staudte 2, Bergner 3)

Glücklicher Mensch, 1943 (Wagner 4)

Glühende Gasse, 1927 (Albers 3)

Glut, 1983 (Mueller-Stahl 3)

Glutton's Nightmare, 1901 (Hepworth 2)

G-Man Jitters, 1939 (Terry 4)

G-Man's Wife. *See* Public Enemy's Wife, 1936

G-Men, 1935 (Cagney 3, Miller 4, Orry-Kelly 4, Polito 4, Wallis 4, Zanuck 4)

G-Men Never Forget, 1947 (Canutt 4)

Gnet roka, 1917 (Baranovskaya 3)

Gniazdo, 1974 (Ścibor-Rylski 4)

Gnome-Mobile, 1967 (Stevenson 2, Brennan 3, Disney 4, Ellenshaw 4)

Go and Get It, 1920 (Neilan 2, Carré 4)

Go As You Please, 1920 (Roach 4)

Go Away Stowaway, 1967 (Blanc 4)

Go Chase Yourself, 1938 (Ball 3)

Gô chez les oiseaux, 1939 (Grimault 4)

Go Fly a Kit, 1957 (Blanc 4, Jones 4)

Go for Broke, 1951 (Johnson 3, Schary 4)

Go Getter, 1937 (Berkeley 2, Daves 2, Edeson 4, Orry-Kelly 4, Wallis 4)

Go Go Amigo, 1965 (Blanc 4, McKimson 4)

Go Go Mania. *See* Pop Gear, 1965

Go Home, 1966 (Terry-Thomas 3)

Go Into Your Dance, 1935 (Berkeley 2, Florey 2, Jolson 3, Keeler 3, Gaudio 4, Polito 4)

Go, Man, Go, 1954 (Poitier 3, Howe 4, North 4)

Go Naked in the World, 1961 (Borgnine 3, Lollobrigida 3, Deutsch 4, Krasner 4, Rose 4)

Go See Mother . . . Father Is Working. *See* Va voir Maman . . . Papa travaille, 1977

Go Tell the Spartans, 1978 (Lancaster 3)

Go to Blazes, 1942 (Balcon 4)

Go to Blazes, 1962 (Smith 3, Addison 4)

Go to Nowhere, 1966 (Ivanov-Vano 4)

Go West, 1925 (Keaton 2, Arbuckle 3, Mayer 4, Roach 4, Schenck 4)

Go West, 1940 (Marx Brothers 3, Cahn 4, Edens 4, Kaper 4)

Go West, Big Boy, 1931 (Terry 4)

Go West, Young Lady, 1941 (Ford 3, Miller 3, Plunkett 4)

Go West, Young Man, 1936 (Hathaway 2, Scott 3, West 3, Banton 4, Dreier 4, Struss 4)

Goal Rush, 1932 (Iwerks 4)

Goalie's Anxiety at the Penalty Kick. *See* Angst des Tormanns beim Elfmeter, 1971

Goalkeeper's Fear of the Penalty. *See* Angst des Tormanns beim Elfmeter, 1971

Goat, 1918 (Crisp 3, Laurel and Hardy 3, Novarro 3, Marion 4)

Goat, 1921 (Keaton 2)

Goat Getter, 1925 (Garmes 4)

Gobbo, 1960 (Pasolini 2, Blier 3, De Laurentiis 4, Gherardi 4)

Goben no tsubaki, 1965 (Iwashita 3, Okada 3)

Go-Between, 1971 (Losey 2, Bates 3, Christie 3, Redgrave 3, Dillon 4, Fisher 4, Legrand 4, Pinter 4)

GoBots: Battle of the Rock Lords, 1986 (McDowall 3, Hanna and Barbera 4)

Gobu no tamashii, 1938 (Shindo 3)

God Does Not Believe In Us Anymore, 1988 (Mueller-Stahl 3)

God Gave Me Twenty Cents, 1926 (Brenon 2)

God Is My Co-Pilot, 1945 (Florey 2, Massey 3, Buckner 4, Burks 4, Waxman 4)

God is My Partner, 1957 (Brennan 3)

God King, 1973 (Peries 2)

God Needs Men. *See* Dieu a besoin des hommes, 1950

God Rot Tunbridge Wells, 1985 (Howard 3)

God Shiva, 1955 (Haanstra 2)

God Told Me To, 1976 (Corman 2)

God Within, 1912 (Griffith 2, Barrymore 3, Sweet 3, Walthall 3, Bitzer 4)

Goda vänner, trogna grannar, 1938 (Fischer 4)

Godan, 1962 (Shankar 4)

Godchild, 1974 (Palance 3)

Goddag Dyr!, 1947 (Roos 2)

Goddess, 1958 (Cromwell 2, Beavers 3, Chayefsky 4, Thomson 4)

Goddess. *See* Devi, 1960

Goddess of Sagebrush Gulch, 1912 (Griffith 2, Sweet 3, Bitzer 4)

Godelureaux, 1961 (Chabrol 2, Audran 3, Gégauff 4, Rabier 4)

Godfather, 1972 (Coppola 2, Brando 3, Caan 3, Duvall 3, Hayden 3, Keaton 3, Pacino 3, Murch 4, Reynolds 4, Rota 4, Smith 4, Tavoularis 4, Willis 4)

Godfather, Part II, 1974 (Coppola 2, Corman 2, Caan 3, De Niro 3, Duvall 3, Keaton 3, Pacino 3, Stanton 3, Murch 4, Rota 4, Smith 4, Tavoularis 4, Van Runkle 4, Willis 4)

Godfather, Part III, 1991 (Coppola 2, Keaton 3, Pacino 3, Wallach 3, Murch 4, Rota 4, Tavoularis 4, Willis 4)

Godless Girl, 1929 (De Mille 2, Adrian 4, Grot 4, Macpherson 4)

Godmothers, 1973 (Rooney 3)

Godovshchina revoliutsiya, 1919 (Vertov 2)

God's Clay, 1928 (Ondra 3)

God's Country, 1946 (Keaton 2)

God's Country, 1985 (Malle 2)

God's Country and the Law, 1921 (Olcott 2)

God's Country and the Woman, 1936 (Friedhofer 4, Gaudio 4, Raine 4, Steiner 4, Wallis 4)

God's Gift to Women, 1931 (Blondell 3, Brooks 3)

God's Gun, 1978 (Palance 3, Van Cleef 3)

God's Inn by the Sea, 1911 (Bushman 3)

God's Little Acre, 1958 (Mann 2, Ryan 3, Bernstein 4, Haller 4, Maddow 4)

Gods of the Plague. *See* Gotter der Pest, 1969

God's Outlaw, 1919 (Bushman 3)

God's Stepchildren, 1938 (Micheaux 2)

God's Tomorrow. *See* Restitution, 1918

God's Unfortunate, 1911 (Dwan 2)

Godsforvalteren, 1915 (Psilander 3)

Godson. *See* Cose di Cosa Nostra, 1971

Goduria, 1976 (Monicelli 2)

Godzilla. *See* Gojira, 1954

Godzilla vs. The Thing. *See* Gojira tai Mosura, 1964

Godzina szczytu, 1973 (Stawiński 4)

Godzina W, 1979 (Stawiński 4)

Gog, 1954 (Marshall 3)

Gøgleren. *See* Elskovs Magt, 1912

Goha, 1958 (Cardinale 3, Sharif 3)

Goiken Gomuyo, 1925 (Tanaka 3)

Goin' South, 1978 (Belushi 3, Nicholson 3, Almendros 4)

Goin' to Heaven on a Mule, 1934 (Freleng 4)

Goin' to Town, 1935 (West 3, Banton 4, Dreier 4, Struss 4, Zukor 4)

Going and Coming Back. *See* Partir, revenir, 1985

Going Ape!, 1981 (Bernstein 4)

Going Ashore. *See* Strandhugg, 1950

Going Bananas, 1987 (Lom 3, Donaggio 4, Golan and Globus 4)

Going Bye-Bye, 1934 (Laurel and Hardy 3, Roach 4)

Going Crooked, 1926 (Love 3, Clarke 4)

Going Ga-ga, 1928 (McCarey 2)

Going Gay, 1934 (Gallone 2)

Going Gently, 1981 (Wisdom 3)

Going! Going! Gone!, 1918 (Daniels 3, Lloyd 3, Roach 4)

Going! Going! Gosh!, 1952 (Blanc 4, Jones 4, Stalling 4)

Going Highbrow, 1935 (Florey 2, Horton 3, Edeson 4, Orry-Kelly 4)

Going Hollywood, 1933 (Walsh 2, Crosby 3, Davies 3, Adrian 4, Brown 4, Folsey 4, Freed 4, Marion 4, Stewart 4, Stothart 4, Wanger 4)

Going Home, 1972 (Mitchum 3)

Going My Way, 1944 (McCarey 2, Crosby 3, Fitzgerald 3, Dreier 4, Head 4)

Going of the White Swan, 1914 (Mix 3)

Going Places, 1939 (Dandridge 3, Powell 3, Reagan 3, Glazer 4, Mercer 4, Wald 4, Wallis 4)

Going Places. See Valseuses, 1973

Going Some, 1910 (White 3)

Going Spanish, 1934 (Hope 3)

Going Steady, 1958 (Katzman 4)

Going Steady. See Yotz 'im Kavua, 1979

Going Straight, 1916 (Talmadge 3)

Going to Blazes, 1933 (Lantz 4)

Going to Congress, 1924 (Rogers 3, Roach 4)

Going Undercover, 1988 (Simmons 3)

Going Up, 1923 (LeRoy 2)

Going West to Make Good, 1916 (Mix 3)

Going Wild, 1931 (Brown 3, Pidgeon 3, Polito 4)

Goingehov dingen, 1953 (Thulin 3)

Göingehövdingen, 1953 (Dahlbeck 3)

Gojira, 1954 (Shimura 3, Tsuburaya 4)

Gojira no gyakushu, 1955 (Tsuburaya 4)

Gojira no musuko, 1967 (Tsuburaya 4)

Gojira tai Mosura, 1964 (Tsuburaya 4)

Goju man-nin no isan, 1990 (Mifune 3)

Gojuman-nin no isan, 1963 (Muraki 4)

Gokudo No Tumatachi, 1986 (Iwashita 3)

Gokumoncho, 1955 (Kagawa 3)

Gokumon-to, 1977 (Tsukasa 3)

Gokuraku hanayome-juku, 1936 (Miyagawa 4)

Gokurosama, 1929 (Tanaka 3)

Gold, 1913 (Bitzer 4)

Gold, 1933 (Albers 3)

Gold, 1974 (Gielgud 3, Milland 3, York 3, Bernstein 4, Vetchinsky 4)

Gold and Glitter, 1912 (Griffith 2, Barrymore 3, Gish 3, Bitzer 4)

Gold and the Girl, 1925 (Lombard 3)

Gold and the Woman, 1916 (Bara 3)

Gold Digger of Weepah, 1927 (Sennett 2)

Gold Diggers, 1970 (Ford 3)

Gold Diggers, 1984 (Christie 3)

Gold Diggers in Paris, 1938 (Berkeley 2, Barnes 4, Mercer 4, Polito 4, Wald 4, Wallis 4, Warner 4)

Gold Diggers of Broadway, 1929 (Beavers 3)

Gold Diggers of 1933, 1933 (Berkeley 2, Leroy 2, Blondell 3, Keeler 3, Powell 3, Rogers 3, Grot 4, Orry-Kelly 4, Polito 4, Wallis 4, Warner 4)

Gold Diggers of 1935, 1935 (Berkeley 2, Menjou 2, Powell 3, Barnes 4, Cortez 4, Grot 4, Orry-Kelly 4, Warner 4)

Gold Diggers of 1937, 1936 (Bacon 2, Berkeley 2, Blondell 3, Powell 3, Wyman 3, Edeson 4, Orry-Kelly 4, Warner 4)

Gold Diggers of '49, 1936 (Avery 4, Stalling 4)

Gold Dust and the Squaw, 1915 (Mix 3)

Gold Dust Gertie, 1931 (Bacon 2)

Gold from the Gutter. See Alt paa ét Kort, 1912

Gold Ghost, 1934 (Keaton 2)

Gold Heels, 1924 (Van Dyke 2)

Gold Hunters, 1925 (Johnson 3)

Gold in New Frisco, 1939 (Hoffmann 4)

Gold Is Not All, 1910 (Griffith 2, Walthall 3, Bitzer 4)

Gold Is Where You Find It, 1938 (Curtiz 2,

De Havilland 3, Rains 3, Buckner 4, Friedhofer 4, Polito 4, Steiner 4, Wallis 4)

Gold Lust, 1911 (Dwan 2)

Gold Mine in the Sky, 1938 (Autry 3)

Gold Necklace, 1910 (Pickford 3)

Gold of Naples. See oro di Napoli, 1955

Gold of the Amazon Women, 1979 (Pleasence 3)

Gold of the Seven Saints, 1961 (Biroc 4, Brackett 4)

Gold Raiders, 1951 (Three Stooges 3)

Gold Reserve, 1925 (Tisse 4)

Gold Ring. See Zlote kolo, 1971

Gold Rush, 1925 (Chaplin 2)

Gold Seekers, 1910 (Griffith 2, Walthall 3, Bitzer 4)

Gold von Sam Cooper. See Ognuno per se, 1968

Goldbergs, 1950 (Bumstead 4, Seitz 4)

Golddiggers, 1923 (Beavers 3)

Golden Arrow, 1936 (Davis 3, Edeson 4, Grot 4, Orry-Kelly 4)

Golden Arrow. See Three Men and a Girl, 1952

Golden Bed, 1925 (De Mille 2, Walthall 3, Head 4, Macpherson 4)

Golden Blade, 1953 (Hudson 3)

Golden Boat, 1990 (Ruiz 2)

Golden Boy, 1939 (Mamoulian 2, Cobb 3, Holden 3, Menjou 3, Stanwyck 3, Cohn 4, Freund 4, Musuraca 4, Taradash 4, Young 4)

Golden Calf, 1930 (Friedhofer 4)

Golden Chance, 1915 (De Mille 2, Reid 3, Buckland 4, Macpherson 4)

Golden Child, 1986 (Murphy 3)

Golden Claw, 1915 (Ince 4, Sullivan 4)

Golden Coach. See **Carrosse d'or, 1953**

Golden Cocoon, 1925 (Haskin 4)

Golden Days, 1914 (Brown 4)

Golden Earrings, 1947 (Leisen 2, Polonsky 2, Dietrich 3, Milland 3, Dreier 4, Young 4)

Golden Eighties, 1986 (Seyrig 3)

Golden Fern. See Zbabělec, 1962

Golden Fetter, 1917 (Reid 3)

Golden Fish. See O zlaté rybce, 1951

Golden Flame, 1967 (Fonda 3)

Golden Fleecing, 1940 (Ayres 3)

Golden Follies, 1938 (Menjou 3)

Golden Fortress. See Sonar Kella, 1974

Golden Gate, 1981 (Simmons 3)

Golden Gate Murders, 1979 (York 3, Foreman 4)

Golden Girl, 1951 (Bacon 2, Clarke 4, LeMaire 4, Wheeler 4)

Golden Gloves, 1940 (Dmytryk 2, Ryan 3, Dreier 4, Head 4)

Golden Goose, 1914 (Ince 4)

Golden Harvest, 1933 (Krasner 4, Robinson 4)

Golden Hawk, 1952 (Hayden 3, Katzman 4)

Golden Head, 1964 (Sanders 3)

Golden Helmet. See **Casque d'or, 1952**

Golden Hen, 1946 (Terry 4)

Golden Hills. See Zlaty gori, 1931

Golden Honeymoon, 1980 (Wright 3)

Golden Horde, 1951 (Metty 4, Salter 4)

Golden Hour. See Pot o' Gold, 1941

Golden Key, 1939 (Ptushko 4)

Golden Lake. See Goldene See, 1919

Golden Louis, 1909 (Griffith 2)

Golden Marie. See **Casque d'or, 1952**

Golden Mask. See South of Algiers, 1953

Golden Needles, 1974 (Meredith 3, Schifrin 4)

Golden Pathway, 1913 (Costello 3)

Golden Pavement, 1915 (Hepworth 2)

Golden Princess, 1925 (Lang 4)

Golden Rendezvous, 1977 (Carradine 3, Harris 3, Malone 3, Meredith 3, Francis 4)

Golden River. See Rio del oro, 1986

Golden Rule, 1932 (Rooney 3)

Golden Rule Kate, 1917 (Gilbert 3, August 4)

Golden Salamander, 1949 (Aimée 3, Howard 3, Lom 3, Alwyn 4, Francis 4, Morris 4, Rank 4)

Golden Snare, 1921 (Beery 3)

Golden Spider. See Zlatý pavouk, 1956

Golden Squadron. See Zolotoi eshelon, 1959

Golden Stallion, 1949 (Rogers 3)

Golden Strain, 1925 (Bosworth 3)

Golden Supper, 1910 (Griffith 2, Bitzer 4)

Golden Thought, 1916 (Mix 3)

Golden Touch, 1935 (Disney 4)

Golden Trail, 1920 (Mohr 4)

Golden Trail. See Riders of the Whistling Skull, 1937

Golden Vampire, 1974 (Cushing 3, Bernard 4)

Golden Virgin. See Story of Esther Costello, 1957

Golden Vision, 1968 (Loach 2)

Golden Voyage of Sinbad, 1973 (Harryhausen 4, Rozsa 4)

Golden Web, 1926 (Karloff 3)

Golden West, 1932 (McDaniel 3)

Golden West, 1939 (Terry 4)

Golden Yeggs, 1950 (Blanc 4, Freleng 4, Stalling 4)

Goldene Gans, 1944 (Reiniger 4)

Goldene Kalb, 1924 (Porten 3)

Goldene Krone, 1920 (Messter 4)

Goldene Schmetterling, 1926 (Leni 2)

Goldene See, 1919 (Dagover 3)

Goldengirl, 1979 (Caron 3, Coburn 3)

Goldenrod, 1977 (Pleasence 3)

Goldfinger, 1964 (Connery 3, Adam 4, Barry 4, Dehn 4)

Goldfish, 1924 (Carré 4, Schenck 4, Sullivan 4)

Goldie, 1931 (Harlow 3, Tracy 3)

Goldie Gets Along, 1933 (Irene 4)

Goldie Locks and the Three Bears, 1922 (Disney 4)

Goldielocks and the Three Bears, 1934 (Lantz 4)

Goldilocks and the Jivin' Bears, 1944 (Blanc 4, Freleng 4, Stalling 4)

Goldimouse and the Three Cats, 1960 (Blanc 4, Freleng 4)

Goldpuppen. See Pleasure Girls, 1965

Goldsmith's Shop. See Jeweller's Shop, 1990

Goldtown Ghost Raiders, 1953 (Autry 3)

Goldwyn Follies, 1938 (Ladd 3, Day 4, Goldwyn 4, Hecht 4, Newman 4, Toland 4)

Golem, 1914 (Wegener 3, Galeen 4)

Golem. See Golem, wie er in die Welt kam, 1920

Golem, 1935 (Baur 3, Andrejew 4, Stallich 4)

Golem und die Tänzerin, 1917 (Wegener 3)

Golem, wie er in die Welt kam, 1920
(Wegener 3, Freund 4, Galeen 4,
Röhrig 4)
Golf, 1922 (Laurel and Hardy 3)
Golf Bug, 1922 (Roach 4)
Golf Game and the Bonnet, 1913 (Bunny 3)
Golf Link Champion "Chick" Evans Links
with Sweedie, 1914 (Beery 3)
Golf Nut, 1927 (Sennett 2)
Golf Nuts, 1930 (Terry 4)
Golf Specialist, 1930 (Fields 3)
Golfa, 1957 (Figueroa 4)
Golfers, 1929 (Sennett 2)
Golfers, 1937 (Lantz 4)
Golfos, 1960 (Saura 2)
Golf's Golden Years, 1970 (Crosby 3)
Golgotha, 1935 (Duvivier 2, Baur 3,
Feuillère 3, Gabin 3, Ibert 4)
Goliat contra los gigantes, 1961 (Rey 3)
Goliath Against the Giants. See Goliat contra
los gigantes, 1961
Goliath and the Dragon. See Vendetta di
Ercole, 1960
Goliath and the Vampire. See Maciste contre
il vampiro, 1961
Golod . . . golod . . . golod, 1921 (Tisse 4)
Golowin geht durch die Stadt, 1940
(Hoffmann 4)
Golpeando en la selva, 1967 (Alvarez 2)
Gólyakalifa, 1917 (Korda 2, Korda 4)
Goma 2, 1984 (Van Cleef 3)
Gommes, 1968 (Delerue 4)
Gomorron Bill, 1945 (Nykvist 4)
Gondole delle chimera, 1936 (Burel 4)
Gone Are the Days!, 1963 (Kaufman 4,
Rosenblum 4)
Gone Batty, 1954 (Blanc 4, McKimson 4,
Stalling 4)
Gone to Earth, 1950 (Cotten 3, Cusack 3,
Jones 3, Challis 4, Francis 4, Heckroth 4,
Korda 4, Selznick 4)
Gone to the Country, 1921 (Roach 4)
Gone with the West, 1975 (Caan 3)
**Gone with the Wind, 1939 (Cukor 2,
Fleming 2, Hawks 2, Wood 2, Bond 3,
Darwell 3, De Havilland 3, Gable 3,
Howard 3, Leigh 3, McDaniel 3,
McQueen 3, Canutt 4, Deutsch 4,
Eason 4, Friedhofer 4, Garmes 4,
Haller 4, Hecht 4, Howard 4, Mayer 4,
Menzies 4, Plunkett 4, Rosson 4,
Ruttenberg 4, Selznick 4, Steiner 4,
Swerling 4, Westmore Family 4,
Wheeler 4)**
Gonin no kyodai, 1939 (Yoshimura 2)
Gonin no mokugekisha, 1948 (Yoda 4)
Gonin no totsugekitai, 1961 (Yamamura 3)
Gonshchiki, 1972 (Yankovsky 3)
Gönül kusu, 1965 (Güney 2)
Gonza the Spearman. See Yari no Gonza,
1985
Gonzague, 1923 (Chevalier 3)
Gonzague ou L'Accordeur, 1933
(Grémillon 2)
Gonzales' Tamales, 1957 (Blanc 4,
Freleng 4, Stalling 4)
Goo Goo Goliath, 1954 (Blanc 4, Freleng 4,
Stalling 4)
Good Against Evil, 1977 (Sangster 4,
Schifrin 4)
Good and Naughty, 1926 (Negri 3,
Glennon 4)
Good and the Bad. See Bon et les méchants,
1976

Good Bad Girl. See Inez from Hollywood,
1924
Good Bad Man, 1916 (Fairbanks 3, Love 3)
Good Business Deal, 1915 (Eason 4)
Good Catch, 1912 (Bushman 3)
Good Cheer, 1926 (Roach 4)
Good Companions, 1933 (Pearson 2,
Saville 2, Gielgud 3, Hawkins 3,
Matthews 3, Balcon 4, Dalrymple 4,
Friedhofer 4, Junge 4, Mercer 4)
Good Companions, 1957 (Johnson 3,
Roberts 3)
Good Dame, 1934 (Brennan 3, March 3,
Sidney 3, Schulberg 4, Shamroy 4)
Good Day for a Hanging, 1958
(MacMurray 3)
Good Day for Fighting. See Custer of the
West, 1968
Good Deed Daily, 1955 (Terry 4)
Good Die Young, 1954 (Clayton 2, Baker 3,
Grahame 3, Harvey 3, Auric 4)
Good Earth, 1937 (Fleming 2, Muni 3,
Rainer 3, Freund 4, Gibbons 4,
Gillespie 4, Jennings 4, Lewin 4,
Mayer 4, Stothart 4, Thalberg 4,
Vorkapich 4)
Good Egg, 1939 (Jones 4)
Good Fairy, 1935 (Sturges 2, Bondi 3,
Marshall 3, Sullavan 3, Laemmle 4,
Mandell 4)
Good Fairy. See Zemma, 1951
Good Father, 1986 (Hopkins 3)
Good Fellows, 1943 (Dreier 4, Head 4)
Good Fight: The Abraham Lincoln Brigade
in the Spanish Civil War, 1984
(Houseman 4)
Good Friends and Faithful Neighbors. See
Goda vänner, trogna grannar, 1938
Good Girls Go to Paris, 1939 (Blondell 3,
Douglas 3, Coffee 4, Cohn 4)
Good Guys and the Bad Guys, 1969
(Carradine 3, Mitchum 3, Stradling 4)
Good Guys Wear Black, 1977 (Andrews 3)
Good Housekeeping, 1933 (Darwell 3)
Good Humor Man, 1950 (Bacon 2,
Tashlin 2)
Good Indian, 1913 (Mix 3)
Good Intentions, 1930 (Howard 2)
Good Little Devil, 1913 (Porter 2,
Pickford 3, Zukor 4)
Good Love and the Bad, 1911 (Dwan 2)
Good Luck, Miss Wyckoff, 1979
(Pleasence 3)
Good Luck, Mr. Yates, 1943 (Trevor 3)
Good Luck of a Souse. See Il y a un dieu
pour les ivrognes, 1908
Good Mad Man, 1980 (Johnson 3)
Good Medicine, 1929 (Horton 3)
Good Men and True, 1922 (Carey 3)
Good Morning. See Ohayo, 1959
Good Morning Babilonia, 1986 (Taviani 2,
Guerra 4, Morricone 4)
Good Morning Babylon. See Good Morning
Babilonia, 1986
Good Morning, Boys, 1937 (Launder and
Gilliat 2, Hay 3, Vetchinsky 4)
Good Morning Doctor. See You Belong to
Me, 1941
Good Morning, Judge, 1922 (Roach 4)
Good Morning, Judge, 1943 (Beavers 3,
Boyle 4)
Good Morning, Madam, 1925 (Sennett 2)
Good Morning, Miss Dove, 1955 (Jones 3,
Reynolds 4, Shamroy 4)

Good Morning, Nurse!, 1925 (Sennett 2)
Good Morning, Vietnam, 1987 (Williams 3,
North 4)
Good Mother, 1988 (Bellamy 3, Keaton 3,
Robards 3, Wright 3, Bernstein 4,
Watkin 4)
Good Mouse Keeping, 1952 (Terry 4)
Good Neighbor Sam, 1964 (Lemmon 3,
Robinson 3, Schneider 3, Guffey 4)
Good News, 1930 (Daves 2, Crabbe 3,
Love 3, Brown 4, Freed 4, Gibbons 4,
Marion 4, Mayer 4)
Good News, 1947 (Walters 2, Allyson 3,
Comden and Green 4, Edens 4, Freed 4,
Mayer 4, Rose 4)
Good Night Elmer, 1940 (Blanc 4, Jones 4,
Stalling 4)
Good Night, Nurse, 1918 (Keaton 2,
Arbuckle 3)
Good Night, Rusty, 1943 (Pal 4)
Good Noose, 1962 (Blanc 4, McKimson 4)
Good Old Irish Tunes, 1941 (Terry 4)
Good Old School Days. See Those Were the
Days, 1940
Good Old Soak, 1937 (Beery 3)
Good People's Sunday. See Domenica della
buona gente, 1953
Good Provider, 1922 (Borzage 2)
Good Riddance, 1923 (Roach 4)
Good Sam, 1948 (McCarey 2, Beavers 3,
Cooper 3, Sheridan 3, Barnes 4)
Good Scout, 1934 (Iwerks 4)
Good Soldier Schweik. See Dobrý voják
švejk, 1931
Good Soldier Schweik. See Osudy dobrého
vojáka Svejkova, 1955
Good Soldier Svejk. See Dobrý voják Švejk,
1926
Good Sport, 1931 (Beavers 3, Clarke 4)
Good Sport, 1984 (Remick 3)
Good, the Bad and the Ugly. See **Buono, il
bruto, il Cattivo, 1966**
Good Time Charley, 1927 (Curtiz 2)
Good Times, 1967 (Friedkin 2, Cher 3,
Sanders 3)
Good Tramp Bernasek. See Dobrý tramp
Bernasek, 1933
Good Turn, 1911 (Lawrence 3)
Good Will to Men, 1955 (Hanna and
Barbera 4)
Good Women, 1921 (Edeson 4, Sullivan 4)
Good-Bad Wife, 1921 (Goodrich 4)
Good-by Girls!, 1923 (August 4)
Goodbye Again, 1933 (Curtiz 2, Blondell 3,
Barnes 4)
Goodbye Again, 1961 (Bergman 3,
Brynner 3, Montand 3, Perkins 3,
Auric 4, Trauner 4)
Goodbye and Amen, 1977 (Cardinale 3)
Good-Bye Bill, 1918 (Emerson 4,
Loos 4)
Goodbye Charlie, 1964 (Minnelli 2,
Burstyn 3, Curtis 3, Matthau 3,
Reynolds 3, Day 4, Krasner 4, Previn 4,
Rose 4, Smith 4)
Goodbye Columbus, 1969 (Midler 3,
Rosenblum 4)
Goodbye Gemini, 1970 (Redgrave 3,
Unsworth 4)
Goodbye Girl, 1977 (Dreyfuss 3, Booth 4,
Stark 4)
Good-Bye Kiss, 1928 (Sennett 2,
Hornbeck 4)
Goodbye Legs, 1930 (Sennett 2)

Grand Cirque s'en va, 1953 (Decaë 4)

Grand Combat, 1942 (Berry 3)

Grand Concert, 1989 (Halas and
  Batchelor 4)

Grand Délire, 1974 (Huppert 3)

Grand Départ, 1971 (Hayden 3)

Grand Duchess and the Waiter, 1926
  (Menjou 3, Banton 4, Garmes 4)

Grand Duel. See Gran duelo, 1972

Grand Duke's Finances. See Finanzen des
  Grossherzogs, 1924

Grand Duke's Finances. See Finanzen des
  Grossherzogs, 1934

Grand Élan, 1939 (Christian-Jaque 2,
  Heller 4)

Grand Erg oriental, 1960 (Kosma 4)

Grand Escapade, 1946 (Baxter 2)

Grand Escogriffe, 1976 (Montand 3,
  Audiard 4)

Grand Escroc, 1963 (Seberg 3)

Grand Finale, 1936 (Havelock-Allan 4)

Grand Frère, 1982 (Depardieu 3, Colpi 4)

Grand Hotel, 1932 (Goulding 2, Barrymore,
  J. 3, Barrymore, L. 3, Beery 3,
  Crawford 3, Garbo 3, Adrian 4,
  Daniels 4, Gibbons 4, Mayer 4,
  Thalberg 4)

Grand Hotel. See Menschen im Hotel, 1960

Grand Hotel Babylon, 1919 (Dupont 2,
  Albers 3)

Grand Hotel to Big Indian, 1906 (Bitzer 4)

Grand Illusion. See Grande Illusion, 1937

Grand Jeu, 1934 (Feyder 2, Rosay 3,
  Vanel 3, Eisler 4, Meerson 4, Spaak 4,
  Stradling 4)

Grand Jeu, 1954 (Siodmak 2, Arletty 3,
  Barsacq 4, Spaak 4)

Grand Jury, 1936 (August 4, Epstein 4)

Grand Jury Secrets, 1939 (Darwell 3,
  Dreier 4, Head 4)

Grand Larceny, 1922 (Meredyth 4)

Grand Larceny, 1988 (Jourdan 3, Sharif 3)

Grand Machin et le petit chose, 1910
  (Cohl 4)

Grand Maneuver. See Grandes Manoeuvres,
  1955

Grand Matin, 1975 (Guillemot 4)

Grand Méliès, 1952 (Franju 2)

Grand Oeuvre, 1958 (Jarre 4)

Grand Old Girl, 1935 (MacMurray 3,
  Plunket 4)

Grand Parade, 1930 (Goulding 2)

Grand Pardon, 1982 (Trintignant 3)

Grand Passion, 1918 (Chaney 3)

Grand Passion. See Grande Passion, 1929

Grand Patron, 1951 (Fresnay 3, Kosma 4)

Grand Pavois, 1953 (Cloquet 4)

Grand Piano, 1989 (Legrand 4)

Grand Prix, 1966 (Frankenheimer 2,
  Garner 3, Mifune 3, Montand 3, Saint 3,
  Bass 4, Jarre 4, Sylbert 4)

Grand Refrain, 1936 (Lourié 4, Stradling 4)

Grand Refrain, 1936 (Siodmak 2)

Grand Restaurant, 1966 (Blier 3)

Grand Silence, 1955 (Jarre 4)

Grand Silence. See Grande silenzio, 1968

Grand Slam, 1933 (Dieterle 2, Lukas 3,
  Young 3, Grot 4, Orry-Kelly 4)

Grand Slam. See Ad ogni costo, 1967

Grand Slam Opera, 1936 (Keaton 2)

Grand Souffle, 1915 (Musidora 3)

Grand Sud, 1956 (Braunberger 4)

Grand Theft Auto, 1977 (Corman 2,
  Dante 2)

Grand Trunk Railroad Scenes, 1900
  (Bitzer 4)

Grand Uproar, 1930 (Fleischer 4)

Grand Uproar, 1933 (Terry 4)

Granddaughter of Dracula. See Nocturna,
  1979

Grande abbuffata, 1973 (Mastroianni 3,
  Noiret 3, Piccoli 3, Sarde 4)

Grande allure, 1986 (Perrault 2)

Grande attaco, 1977 (Fonda 3)

Grande aurora, 1947 (Brazzi 3, Zavattini 4)

Grande avventura, 1953 (Cervi 3)

Grande Bagarre de Don Camillo, 1955
  (Fernandel 3)

Grande Bouffe. See Grande abbuffata, 1973

Grande Bourgeoise. See Fatti di gente
  perbene, 1974

Grande Bourgeoise, 1975 (Rey 3)

Grande-Bretagne et les Etats-Unis de 1896 à
  1900, 1968 (Braunberger 4)

Grande Carnaval, 1983 (Noiret 3)

Grande Case, 1952 (Rabier 4)

Grande Chartreuse, 1938 (Clement 2)

Grande cidade, 1966 (Rocha 2)

Grande Cité, 1954 (Delerue 4)

Grande Délire, 1975 (Seberg 3)

Grande Époque, 1959 (Clair 2)

Grande feira, 1965 (Rocha 2)

Grande Fille tout simple, 1947 (L'Herbier 2)

Grande Frousse, 1964 (Barrault 3,
  Schüfftan 4)

Grande giuoco, 1954 (Lollobrigida 3)

Grande guerra, 1959 (Monicelli 2, Blier 3,
  Gassman 3, Mangano 3, Sordi 3, Age
  and Scarpelli 4, De Laurentiis 4, Rota 4)

Grande Guerre. See grande guerra, 1959

Grande Illusion, 1937 (Becker 2, Von
  Stroheim 2, Dalio 3, Fresnay 3, Gabin 3,
  Modot 3, Kosma 4, Lourié 4, Matras 4,
  Renoir 4, Spaak 4, Wakhévitch 4)

Grande Illusion, 1973 (Spaak 4)

Grande Mare, 1930 (Chevalier 3, Colbert 3,
  Fort 4)

Grande paese d'Acciaio, 1960 (Olmi 2)

Grande Passion, 1929 (Christian-Jaque 2,
  Delannoy 2, Dagover 3)

Grande Pastorale, 1943 (Clement 2,
  Alekan 4)

Grande ritorno di Django, 1987
  (Pleasence 3)

Grande Sauterelle, 1967 (Audiard 4)

Grande scrofa nera, 1972 (Cuny 3)

Grande silenzio, 1968 (Kinski 3,
  Trintignant 3, Morricone 4)

Grande speranza, 1954 (Rota 4)

Grande strada azzurra, 1957 (Valli 3,
  Gherardi 4, Solinas 4)

Grande Terre, 1955 (Decaë 4)

Grande tormenta, 1920 (Gallone 2)

Grande Trouille. See Tendre Dracula, 1974

Grande Vadrouille, 1966 (Auric 4, Renoir 4)

Grande Vie, 1960 (Masina 3)

Grande Voliere, 1947 (Renoir 4)

Grandes Eaux de Versailles, 1949
  (Gaumont 4)

Grandes Familles, 1958 (Blier 3, Brasseur 3,
  Gabin 3, Audiard 4)

Grandes Manoeuvres, 1955 (Clair 2,
  Bardot 3, Morgan 3, Philipe 3,
  Barsacq 4)

Grandes Personnes, 1960 (Presle 3,
  Seberg 3, Coutard 4, Evein 4)

Grandeur et Decadence d'un petit commerce
  du cinéma, 1986 (Léaud 3)

Grandeur nature, 1974 (Piccoli 3, Carrière 4,
  Jarre 4, Trauner 4)

Grandi condottieri, 1965 (Guerra 4)

Grandi magazzini, 1939 (Castellani 2, De
  Sica 2)

Grandi naïf jugoslavi, 1973 (Storaro 4)

Grandma's Boy, 1922 (Lloyd 3, Roach 4)

Grandma's Girl, 1930 (Sennett 2)

Grandma's Pet, 1932 (Lantz 4)

Grandmother. See Nagymama, 1916

Grandmother, 1970 (Lynch 2)

Grandmother Sabella. See Nonna Sabella,
  1957

Grandmother's War Story, 1911 (Olcott 2)

Grandpa, 1989 (Ustinov 3)

Grandpa Involuntarily. See Dědečkem proti
  své vuli, 1939

Grandpa Planted a Beet. See Zasadil dědek
  řepu, 1945

Grands, 1936 (Vanel 3)

Grands Chemins, 1962 (Aimée 3,
  Gégauff 4)

Grands Feux, 1937 (Alexeieff and Parker 4)

Grands Moments, 1965 (Lelouch 2,
  Braunberger 4)

Grands Seigneurs. See Gentleman d'Epsom,
  1962

Grandview, U.S.A., 1984 (Curtis 3)

Granges brûlées, 1973 (Delon 3, Signoret 3,
  Vierny 4)

Granica, 1977 (Lomnicki 3)

Granite Hotel, 1942 (Fleischer 4)

Granitsa, 1935 (Cherkassov 3)

Granny Takes Over. See Páté kolo u vozu,
  1958

Gränsfolken, 1913 (Stiller 2, Jaenzon 4,
  Magnusson 4)

Grant Wood, 1950 (Fonda 3)

Granton Trawler, 1934 (Cavalcanti 2,
  Grierson 2)

**Grapes of Wrath, 1940 (Ford 2, Bond 3,
  Carradine 3, Darwell 3, Fonda 3,
  Marsh 3, Day 4, Johnson 4, Newman 4,
  Toland 4, Zanuck 4)**

Grasp of Greed, 1916 (Chaney 3)

Grass, 1924 (Zukor 4)

Grass, 1925 (Schoedsack 2)

Grass, 1968 (Le Grice 2)

Grass: A Nation's Battle for Life, 1925
  (Cooper 4)

Grass Country Goes Dry, 1914 (Beery 3)

Grass Is Greener, 1960 (Donen 2, Black 3,
  Grant 3, Kerr 3, Mitchum 3, Simmons 3,
  Challis 4)

Grass: The Epic of a Lost Tribe. See Grass:
  A Nation's Battle for Life, 1925

Grasshopper. See Poprigunya, 1955

Grasshopper, 1969 (Cotten 3)

Grasshopper, 1975 (Vukotić 4)

Grasshopper and the Ant, 1954 (Reiniger 4)

Grassy Shires, 1944 (Alwyn 4)

Grateful Outcast, 1910 (White 3)

Gratitude of Wanda, 1913 (Reid 3)

Gratuités, 1927 (Grémillon 2, Périnal 4)

Grausame Freundin. See Faut-il les marier?,
  1932

Grausame Freundin, 1932 (Ondra 3, Rasp 3,
  Heller 4)

Grausame Job. See Peau d'espion, 1967

Grausige Nächte, 1921 (Pick 2, Krauss 3,
  Mayer 4)

Graustark, 1915 (Bushman 3)

Graustark, 1925 (Talmadge 3, Gaudio 4,
  Marion 4, Menzies 4, Schenck 4)

Great Scott, 1920 (Sennett 2)

Great Scout and Cathouse Thursday, 1976 (Marvin 3, Reed 3, Smith 4)

Great Secret, 1917 (Bushman 3, Mayer 4)

Great Silence, 1915 (Bushman 3)

Great Singer, 1949 (Gibbons 4)

Great Sinner, 1949 (LeRoy 2, Siodmak 2, Barrymore 3, Douglas 3, Gardner 3, Huston 3, Moorehead 3, Peck 3, Folsey 4, Irene 4, Kaper 4, Previn 4)

Great Sioux Massacre, 1965 (Cotten 3)

Great Sioux Uprising, 1953 (Bacon 2)

Great Smokey Roadblock, 1978 (Fonda 3, Sarandon 3)

Great Spy Chase. See Barbouzes, 1964

Great Spy Hunt. See Barbouzes, 1964

Great Spy Mission. See Operation Crossbow, 1965

Great Stone Face, 1970 (Keaton 2)

Great Swordsmen of Japan. See Nippon kengo-den, 1945

Great Toe Mystery, 1914 (Sennett 2)

Great Train Robbery, 1903 (Porter 2, Anderson 3)

Great Train Robbery, 1941 (Canutt 4)

Great Train Robbery, 1978 (Connery 3, Sutherland 3, Goldsmith 4)

Great Universal Mystery, 1914 (Dwan 2)

Great Vacuum Robbery, 1915 (Sennett 2)

Great Van Robbery, 1959 (Roeg 2)

Great Victor Herbert, 1939 (Dreier 4, Head 4, Prinz 4)

Great Waldo Pepper, 1975 (Hill 2, Redford 3, Sarandon 3, Bumstead 4, Goldman 4, Head 4, Mancini 4, Reynolds 4, Surtees 4)

Great Wall. See Shin no shi-kotei, 1962

Great Waltz. See Number Seventeen, 1932

Great Waltz, 1938 (Fleming 2, Rainer 3, Gibbons 4, Hoffenstein 4, Reisch 4, Ruttenberg 4, Tiomkin 4)

Great Waltz, 1972 (Brazzi 3)

Great War. See Grande guerra, 1959

Great Water Peril, 1918 (Roach 4)

Great While It Lasted, 1914 (Lloyd 3, Roach 4)

Great White Hope, 1970 (Ritt 2, Dalio 3, Jones 3, Guffey 4, Reynolds 4, Sharaff 4)

Great Who Dood It, 1952 (Lantz 4)

Great Wind Cometh, 1984 (Minnelli 3)

Great Ziegfeld, 1936 (Loy 3, Powell 3, Rainer 3, Adrian 4, Edens 4, Folsey 4, Freund 4, Gibbons 4, Mayer 4, Stromberg 4)

Greater Devotion, 1914 (Reid 3)

Greater Glory, 1926 (Karloff 3, Lawrence 3, Mathis 4)

Greater Influence, 1910 (White 3)

Greater Love, 1913 (Dwan 2)

Greater Love Hath No Man, 1915 (Guy 2)

Greater than a Crown, 1925 (Costello 3, August 4)

Greater than Love, 1921 (Niblo 2, Stahl 2, Sullivan 4)

Greater Wealth, 1913 (Bosworth 3)

Greatest, 1977 (Borgnine 3, Duvall 3, Johnson 3, Jones 3, Lardner 4)

Greatest Battle on Earth. See Sandai kaiju chikyu saidai no kessen, 1965

Greatest Gift, 1974 (Ford 3)

Greatest Love. See Europa '51, 1952

Greatest Power, 1917 (Barrymore 3)

Greatest Question, 1919 (Griffith 2, Gish 3, Bitzer 4)

Greatest Show on Earth, 1952 (De Mille 2, Crosby 3, Grahame 3, Heston 3, Hope 3, Hutton 3, Lamour 3, O'Brien 3, Stewart 3, Wilde 3, Barnes 4, Head 4, Jeakins 4, Young 4)

Greatest Story Ever Told, 1965 (Ashby 2, Stevens 2, Baker 3, Ferrer 3, Heston 3, Lansbury 3, McDowall 3, Mineo 3, Pleasence 3, Poitier 3, Rains 3, Von Sydow 3, Wayne 3, Winters 3, Day 4, Friedhofer 4, Gillespie 4, Newman 4)

Greatest Thing in Life, 1918 (Griffith 2, Gish 3, Bitzer 4, Zukor 4)

Greatest Thing That Almost Happened, 1977 (Jones 3)

Greco, 1966 (Rey 3, Donati 4, Morricone 4)

Greed, 1924 (Ingram 2, Von Stroheim 2, Daniels 4, Day 4, Gibbons 4, Goldwyn 4, Mathis 4, Mayer 4)

Greed for Gold, 1913 (Anderson 3)

Greed in the Sun. See Cent Mille Dollars au Soleil, 1963

Greed of Gold. See Desert Greed, 1926

Greedy for Tweety, 1957 (Blanc 4, Freleng 4)

Greedy Humpty Dumpty, 1936 (Fleischer 4)

Greek Meets Greek, 1921 (Roach 4)

Greek Sculpture, 1959 (Wright 2)

Greek Tycoon, 1978 (Quinn 3)

Greeks, 1965 (Lassally 4)

Greeks Had a Word for Them, 1932 (Blondell 3, Grable 3, Barnes 4, Day 4, Goldwyn 4, Howard 4, Newman 4)

Green and Pleasant Land, 1955 (Anderson 2, Lassally 4)

Green Berets, 1968 (LeRoy 2, Pryor 3, Wayne 3, Hoch 4, Rozsa 4)

Green Bird. See Grüne Vogel, 1979

Green Book. See Zelená knížka, 1948

Green Card, 1990 (Weir 2, Depardieu 3)

Green Carnation. See Trials of Oscar Wilde, 1960

Green Cat, 1922 (Roach 4)

Green Cockatoo, 1937 (Mills 3, Newton 3, Withers 3, Greene 4, Menzies 4, Rozsa 4)

Green Cockatoo. See Four Dark Hours, 1939

Green Dolphin Street, 1947 (Saville 2, Reed 3, Turner 3, Folsey 4, Gillespie 4, Irene 4, Kaper 4, Mayer 4, Plunkett 4, Raphaelson 4, Shearer 4, Wilson 4)

Green Earth. See Midori no daichi, 1942

Green Fields, 1937 (Ulmer 2)

Green Fire, 1954 (Granger 3, Kelly 3, Gillespie 4, Rose 4, Rozsa 4)

Green for Danger, 1946 (Launder and Gilliat 2, Howard 3, Sim 3, Alwyn 4, Mathieson 4, Morris 4, Rank 4)

Green Ghost. See Unholy Night, 1929

Green Girdle, 1941 (Cardiff 4)

Green Glove, 1951 (Ford 3, Bennett 4, Cloquet 4, Kosma 4, Maté 4, Renoir 4, Trauner 4)

Green Goddess, 1923 (Olcott 2, Arliss 3)

Green Goddess, 1930 (Arliss 3)

Green Grass of Wyoming, 1948 (Coburn 3, McDowall 3, Clarke 4, LeMaire 4)

Green Grow the Rushes, 1951 (Burton 3)

Green Hell, 1940 (Whale 2, Bennett 3, Price 3, Sanders 3, Freund 4, Marion 4)

Green Horizons. See Zelené obzory, 1962

Green Hornet, 1939 (Ladd 3)

Green Ice, 1981 (Sharif 3, Anhalt 4)

Green Light, 1937 (Borzage 2, Flynn 3, Blanke 4, Friedhofer 4, Haskin 4, Orry-Kelly 4, Steiner 4, Wallis 4)

Green Line, 1944 (Terry 4)

Green Man, 1956 (Dearden 2, Launder and Gilliat 2, Sim 3, Terry-Thomas 3)

Green Man, 1990 (Finney 3)

Green Mansions, 1959 (Cobb 3, Hayakawa 3, Hepburn 3, Perkins 3, Ames 4, Jeakins 4, Kaper 4, Ruttenberg 4)

Green Manuela. See Grüne Manuela, 1923

Green Mare. See Jument verte, 1959

Green Mountain Land, 1950 (Flaherty 2)

Green Murder Case, 1929 (Powell 3)

Green Native Country. See Midorino furusato, 1946

Green Necklace. See Gröna halsbandet, 1912

Green Pastures, 1936 (Blanke 4, Friedhofer 4, Korngold 4, Mohr 4, Wallis 4)

Green Promise, 1949 (Brennan 3, Wood 3)

Green Queen. See Reine verte, 1964

Green Room. See Chambre verte, 1978

Green Scarf, 1954 (Redgrave 3, Korda 4)

Green Shadow, 1913 (Ince 4)

Green Spider. See Zelyonyi pauk, 1916

Green Swamp, 1916 (Sullivan 4)

Green Years, 1946 (Saville 2, Coburn 3, Folsey 4, Gibbons 4, Gillespie 4, Irene 4, Levien 4, Stothart 4)

Greene Murder Case, 1929 (Arthur 3)

Green-Eyed Blonde, 1957 (Trumbo 4)

Green-Eyed Devil, 1914 (Gish 3)

Green Eyed Monster, 1911 (Dwan 2)

Green Eyed Woman. See Take a Letter, Darling, 1942

Greengage Summer, 1961 (Saville 2, Darrieux 3, Love 3, More 3, York 3, Koch 4, Young 4)

Greenhorn, 1913 (Ince 4)

Greenwich Village, 1944 (Ameche 3, Bendix 3, Holliday 3, Miranda 3, Basevi 4, Brown 4, Comden and Green 4, Shamroy 4)

Greetings, 1969 (De Palma 2, De Niro 3)

Greetings Bait, 1943 (Blanc 4, Freleng 4, Stalling 4)

Gregor Marold, 1918 (Kortner 3)

Gregory's Girl, 1980 (Forsyth 2)

Grehut na Malitsa, 1986 (Dinov 4)

Greifer, 1930 (Albers 3)

Greifer, 1958 (Albers 3)

Grekh, 1916 (Mozhukin 3)

Greluchon delicat, 1934 (Baur 3)

Gremlins, 1984 (Dante 2, Spielberg 2, Goldsmith 4, Jones 4)

Gremlins 2: The New Batch, 1990 (Dante 2, Lee 3, Baker 4, Goldsmith 4, Jones 4)

Grendel, Grendel, Grendel, 1981 (Ustinov 3)

Grenoble. See Treize jours en France, 1968

Grens, 1984 (Winkler 3, Branco 4)

Grenzfeuer, 1934 (Rasp 3)

Gretel, 1973 (Armstrong 2)

Grève, 1904 (Pathé 4)

Grève, 1911 (Gaumont 4)

Grève des apaches, 1908 (Feuillade 2)

Grey Gardens, 1975 (Maysles 2)

Grey Sentinel, 1913 (Ince 4)

Greystoke: The Legend of Tarzan, Lord of the Apes, 1984 (Close 3, Richardson 3, Alcott 4, Baker 4, Russell 4, Towne 4, Whitlock 4)

Gribiche, 1925 (Rosay 3, Meerson 4)

Gribouille, 1937 (Blier 3, Dalio 3, Morgan 3, Raimu 3, Achard 4, Auric 4, Trauner 4)

Gricheux, 1909 (Cohl 4)

Gridiron Flash, 1934 (Dumont 3, Berman 4, Plunkett 4, Steiner 4)

Grido, 1957 (Valli 3, Di Venanzo 4, Fusco 4)

Grido della città, 1950 (Risi 2)

Grief in Bagdad, 1925 (Roach 4)

Grierson, 1972 (Haanstra 2, Ivens 2)

Griff nach den Sternen, 1955 (Käutner 2)

Griffin and Phoenix: A Love Story, 1976 (Clayburgh 3, Falk 3)

Grifters, 1990 (Frears 2, Scorsese 2, Huston 3, Bernstein 4)

Grihadaha, 1936 (Roy 2)

Grihalaxmi, 1934 (Mehboob 2)

Grillon du foyer, 1923 (Boyer 3)

Grim Comedian, 1921 (Meredyth 4)

Grim Game, 1919 (Buckland 4)

Grim Pastures, or the Fight for Fodder, 1944 (Dunning 4)

Grim Prairie Tales, 1990 (Jones 3)

Grimace, 1966 (Blier 2)

Grin and Bear It, 1933 (Stevens 2)

Grind, 1915 (Chaney 3)

Gringalet, 1946 (Vanel 3)

Gringuita en Mexico, 1951 (Alcoriza 4)

Grip of Fear. See Experiment in Terror, 1962

Grip of Jealousy, 1916 (Chaney 3)

Grip of the Strangler. See Haunted Strangler, 1958

Grip of the Yukon, 1928 (Bushman 3)

Grips, Grunts, and Groans, 1937 (Three Stooges 3, Bruckman 4)

Grisbi. See Touchez pas au Grisbi, 1954

Grisbi. See Touchez pas au Grisbi, 1988

Grisou, 1938 (Blier 3, Brasseur 3)

Grissom Gang, 1971 (Aldrich 2, Biroc 4)

Grit, 1915 (August 4)

Grit, 1924 (Bow 3)

Grizzly Golfer, 1951 (Bosustow 4, Burness 4, Hubley 4)

Grizzly Gulch Chariot Race, 1915 (Mix 3)

Grocery Clerk's Romance, 1912 (Sennett 2, Normand 3)

Gromaire, 1970 (Braunberger 4)

Gröna halsbandet, 1912 (Jaenzon 4, Magnusson 4)

Grønkøbings glade gavtyve, 1925 (Madsen and Schenstrøm 3)

Grønland, 1980 (Roos 2)

Grønlandske dialektoptagelser og trommedanse fra Thuledistriktet, 1967 (Roos 2)

Groom Wore Spurs, 1951 (Rogers 3)

Groove Room, 1974 (Dors 3)

Gros Coup, 1964 (Delerue 4, Gégauff 4)

Gros Lot, 1933 (Fernandel 3)

Gross Fog, 1973 (Le Grice 2)

Gross Paris, 1973 (De Beauregard 4)

Gross und Klein, 1980 (Ballhaus 4)

Grosse Abenteuerin, 1928 (Wiene 2)

Grosse Atlantik, 1962 (Welles 2)

Grosse Attraktion, 1931 (Kaper 4)

Grosse Fall, 1944 (Fröhlich 3)

Grosse Freiheit Nr. 7, 1944 (Käutner 2, Albers 3)

Grosse Gafahr, 1915 (Kortner 3)

Grosse König, 1942 (Fröhlich 3, Wegener 3)

Grosse Licht, 1920 (Jannings 3)

Grosse Liebe, 1931 (Preminger 2)

Grosse Mandarin, 1949 (Wegener 3)

Grosse Pause, 1927 (Porten 3)

Grosse Schweigen, 1922 (Porten 3)

Grosse Sehnsucht, 1930 (Dagover 3, Kortner 3, Ondra 3, Rasp 3, Tschechowa 3, Veidt 3, Pasternak 4)

Grosse Spiel, 1950 (Staudte 2)

Grosse Sprung, 1927 (Riefenstahl 2)

Grosse Sünderin, 1913 (Porten 3, Messter 4)

Grosse Tête, 1962 (Constantine 3, Guillemot 4, Legrand 4)

Grosse Unbekannte, 1927 (Planer 4)

Grosse und die kleine Welt, 1921 (Albers 3, Dreier 4)

Grosse Verhau, 1970 (Kluge 2)

Grosse Zapfeinstreich, 1952 (Herlth 4)

Grossindustrielle, 1923 (Wagner 4)

Grossreinemachen, 1935 (Ondra 3, Heller 4)

Gross-stadtkavaliere. See Kleine aus der Kongektion, 1925

Grosstadtnacht, 1931 (Rathaus 4)

Grosstadt Schmetterling, 1929 (Wong 3)

Grösste Gauner des Jahrhunderts, 1927 (Albers 3)

Grotesk—Burlesk—Pittoresk, 1968 (Schroeter 2)

Grotesque Chicken. See Spatně namalovaná slepice, 1963

Ground Zero, 1987 (Pleasence 3)

Grounds for Divorce, 1925 (Banton 4)

Grounds for Marriage, 1950 (Grayson 3, Johnson 3, Alton 4, Kaper 4, Raksin 4, Rose 4)

Group, 1966 (Lumet 2, Buchman 4, Kaufman 4, Rosenblum 4)

Group One, 1967 (Warhol 2)

Group Picture with Lady. See Gruppenbild mit Dame, 1977

Growing Pains, 1928 (Roach 4)

Growing Pains, 1953 (Terry 4)

Growing Pains, 1984 (Black 3)

Growing Up. See Takekurabe, 1955

Growing Years, 1951 (Fonda 3)

Growth of a Pea Plant, 1986 (Phalke 2)

Grub Stake, 1923 (Walker 4)

Grubstake Mortgage, 1911 (Dwan 2)

Grudge, 1915 (Hart 3)

Gruesome Twosome, 1945 (Blanc 4, Clampett 4, Stalling 4)

Gruft mit dem Räselschloss, 1964 (Kinski 3)

Grumpy, 1930 (Cukor 2, Lukas 3, Zukor 4)

Grüne Manuela, 1923 (Dieterle 2, Junge 4)

Grüne Vogel, 1979 (Szabó 2)

Gruppenbild mit Dame, 1977 (Schneider 3)

Gruppo di famiglia in un interno, 1974 (Visconti 2, Cardinale 3, Lancaster 3, Mangano 3, Sanda 3, Cecchi D'Amico 4)

Grüss and küss Veronika, 1934 (Pasternak 4, Waxman 4)

Gryning, 1945 (Sucksdorff 2)

Guacanayabo, 1961 (Gómez 2)

Guadalcanal Diary, 1943 (Bendix 3, Quinn 3, Basevi 4, Clarke 4, Trotti 4)

Guaglio. See Proibito rubare, 1948

Guantes de Oro, 1959 (Alcoriza 4)

Guapo del 900, 1960 (Torre Nilsson 2)

Guappi, 1973 (Cardinale 3)

Guard That Girl, 1935 (Bond 3)

Guardia del corpo, 1942 (De Sica 2)

Guardia, guardia scelta, brigadiere e maresciallo, 1956 (Cervi 3, Fabrizi 3, Sordi 3)

Guardian, 1984 (Sheen 3)

Guardian, 1990 (Alonzo 4)

Guardians of the Wild, 1928 (Miller 4)

Guardie e ladri, 1951 (Monicelli 2, Fabrizi 3, De Laurentiis 4, Flaiano 4)

Guardsman. See Testör, 1918

Guardsman, 1931 (Adrian 4, Lewin 4, Mayer 4, Vajda 4)

Guayana: Crime of the Century. See Guayana: Cult of the Damned, 1979

Guayana: Cult of the Damned, 1979 (Cotten 3)

Gubben Kommer, 1939 (Sjöström 2)

Gubecziana, 1974 (Vukotić 4)

Gubijinso, 1935 (Mizoguchi 2)

Gubijinso, 1941 (Hayasaka 4)

Gubijinso, 1984 (Ryu 3)

Guddobai, 1949 (Mori 3, Takamine 3)

Güemes—La terra en armas, 1970 (Torre Nilsson 2)

Guendalina, 1956 (Lattuada 2, De Laurentiis 4, Ponti 4)

Guêpes, 1961 (Braunberger 4, Delerue 4)

Guerillas. See American Guerilla in the Philippines, 1950

Guérillera, 1982 (Cassel 3)

Guerilleros. See Briganti italiani, 1961

Guérisseur, 1954 (Marais 3, Bost 4)

Guernica, 1950 (Resnais 2, Braunberger 4)

Guerra alle guerra, 1948 (Zavattini 4)

Guerra continua, 1961 (Palance 3, Reggiani 3)

Guerra de los pasteles, 1943 (Armendáriz 3)

Guerra del cerdo. See Diario de la guerra del cerdo, 1975

Guerra e pace. See War and Peace, 1956

Guerra necessaria, 1980 (Alvarez 2)

Guerra segreta. See Guerre secrète, 1966

Guerre des karts. See Grosse Tête, 1962

Guerre des valses. See Walzerkrieg, 1933

Guerre du feu, 1981 (Sarde 4)

Guerre du silence, 1959 (Lelouch 2)

Guerre du Transvaal, 1900 (Pathé 4)

Guerre est finie, 1966 (Bujold 3, Montand 3, Piccoli 3, Thulin 3, Fusco 4, Saulnier 4, Vierny 4)

Guerre la plus glorieuse, 1989 (Huppert 3, Josephson 3)

Guerre Lasse, 1988 (Baye 3)

Guerre populaire au Laos, 1969 (Ivens 2)

Guerre Russo-Japonais, 1904 (Pathé 4)

Guerre secrète, 1966 (Fonda 3, Girardot 3, Gassman 3, Kinski 3, Ryan 3)

Guerriers et captives, 1989 (Caron 3, Sanda 3)

Guerrilla, 1908 (Griffith 2, Bitzer 4)

Guess Who's Coming to Dinner?, 1967 (Kramer 2, Hepburn 3, Poitier 3, Tracy 3)

Guest, 1951 (Newman 4)

Guest. See Caretaker, 1963

Guest in the House, 1944 (De Toth 2, Baxter 3, Bellamy 3, Wilde 3, Garmes 4, Stromberg 4)

Guest Wife, 1945 (Wood 2, Ameche 3, Colbert 3)

Guests of Honour, 1941 (Cavalcanti 2, Crichton 2)

Guests of the Nation, 1934 (Cusack 3)

Guet-apens, L'écrin du rajah, 1912 (Feuillade 2)

Gueule d'amour, 1937 (Grémillon 2, Gabin 3, Spaak 4)

Gueule de l'emploi, 1973 (Gélin 3, Presle 3)

Gueule ouverte, 1974 (Pialat 2, Baye 3, Almendros 4)

Gueux au paradis, 1945 (Fernandel 3, Raimu 3)

Guglielmo Tell, 1949 (Cervi 3)

Guide, 1965 (Anand 3, Burman 4)

Guide for the Married Man, 1967 (Ball 3, Jaffe 3, Kelly 3, Mansfield 3, Matthau 3, Terry-Thomas 3, Smith 4, Williams 4)

Guided Muscle, 1955 (Blanc 4, Jones 4, Stalling 4)

Guiding Conscience. *See* Lykken, 1916

''Guidizio'' di Michelangelo, 1949 (Fusco 4)

Guidizio universale, 1961 (Mangano 3, Palance 3)

Guignolo, 1979 (Belmondo 3, Audiard 4, Decaë 4)

Guile of Women, 1921 (Rogers 3)

Guilietta e Romeo, 1911 (Bertini 3)

Guillaume Apollinaire, 1955 (Kosma 4)

Guillaume Tell, 1903 (Pathé 4)

Guillotine, 1924 (Albers 3)

Guilt Is Not Mine. *See* Ingiusta condanna, 1952

Guilt of Janet Ames, 1947 (Douglas 3, Russell 3, Coffee 4, Duning 4, Walker 4)

Guilt of Vladimir Olmer. *See* Vina Vladimira Olmera, 1956

Guilty as Charged, 1932 (McLaglen 3)

Guilty as Hell, 1932 (Struss 4)

Guilty Bystander, 1950 (Harlan 4, Tiomkin 4)

Guilty By Suspicion, 1991 (De Niro 3, Ballhaus 4, Winkler 4)

Guilty Conscience, 1985 (Hopkins 3)

Guilty Generation, 1931 (Karloff 3, Young 3, Haskin 4)

Guilty Hands, 1931 (Van Dyke 2, Barrymore 3, Francis 3, Stromberg 4)

Guilty Melody, 1936 (Stallich 4)

Guilty of Treason, 1950 (Friedhofer 4)

Guilty Ones, 1916 (Laurel and Hardy 3)

Guilty or Innocent: The Sam Sheppard Murder Case, 1975 (Schifrin 4)

Guinea Pig, 1948 (Attenborough 3)

Guinguette, 1958 (Delannoy 2, Jeanson 4)

Guirlande merveilleuse, 1903 (Méliès 2)

Guitar Craze, 1959 (Russell 2)

Gulag, 1985 (McDowell 3)

Guldmønten. *See* Alt paa ét Kort, 1912

Guldspindeln, 1914 (Sjöström 2)

Gulf Stream, 1939 (Alexeieff and Parker 4, Milhaud 4)

Gull!. *See* Trut!, 1944

Gullible Canary, 1929 (Fleischer 4)

Gulliver's Travels, 1939 (Young 4)

Gulliver's Travels, 1977 (Harris 3, Love 3, Legrand 4)

Gulls and Buoys, 1972 (Breer 4)

Gumshoe, 1971 (Frears 2, Finney 3, Menges 4)

Gumshoe Magoo, 1958 (Bosustow 4)

Gun. *See* Dio, sei proprio un padreterno, 1973

Gun Battle at Monterey, 1957 (Hayden 3, Van Cleef 3)

Gun Before Butter, 1972 (Lassally 4)

Gun Brothers, 1956 (Crabbe 3)

Gun Crazy, 1949 (Harlan 4, Trumbo 4, Young 4)

Gun Fightin' Gentleman, 1919 (Ford 2, Carey 3)

Gun for a Coward, 1957 (MacMurray 3)

Gun Fury, 1953 (Walsh 2, Marvin 3, Reed 3, Wald 4)

Gun Glory, 1957 (Granger 3, Plunkett 4)

Gun Gospel, 1927 (Brown 4, Polito 4)

Gun in His Hand, 1945 (Losey 2)

Gun Justice, 1927 (Wyler 2)

Gun Justice, 1934 (McCord 4)

Gun Law, 1919 (Ford 2, Carey 3)

Gun Law, 1929 (Musuraca 4, Plunkett 4)

Gun Law, 1938 (Bond 3, August 4)

Gun Moll. *See* Poopsie, 1974

Gun o' Gunga Din, 1910 (White 3)

Gun Packer, 1919 (Carey 3)

Gun Play, 1951 (Hunt 4)

Gun Pusher. *See* Gun Packer, 1919

Gun Riders. *See* Five Bloody Graves, 1970

Gun Runner. *See* Santiago, 1956

Gun Runners, 1958 (Siegel 2, Murphy 3, Sloane 3, Mohr 4)

Gun Smugglers, 1948 (Hunt 4)

Gun That Won the West, 1955 (Katzman 4)

Gun the Man Down, 1956 (Dickinson 3, Clothier 4)

Gun Woman, 1918 (Borzage 2)

Gunbatsu, 1970 (Mifune 3, Shimura 3)

Güney ölüm saciyor, 1969 (Güney 2)

Gunfight, 1971 (Black 3, Douglas 3)

Gunfight at Comanche Creek, 1963 (Biroc 4)

Gunfight at Commanche Creek, 1962 (Murphy 3)

Gunfight at Dodge City, 1959 (McCrea 3, Mirisch 4, Salter 4)

Gunfight at Sandoval, 1959 (Duryea 3)

Gunfight at the O.K. Corral, 1957 (Sturges 2, Douglas 3, Hopper 3, Lancaster 3, Van Cleef 3, Head 4, Lang 4, Tiomkin 4, Wallis 4)

Gunfighter, 1917 (Hart 3, August 4)

Gunfighter, 1950 (De Toth 2, King 2, Malden 3, Marsh 3, Peck 3, Johnson 4, LeMaire 4, Miller 4, Newman 4, Zanuck 4)

Gunfighters, 1947 (Scott 3, Brown 4)

Gunfighters of Abilene, 1960 (Crabbe 3)

Gunfighters of Casa Grande. *See* Pistoleros de Casa Grande, 1965

Gung Ho!, 1943 (Mitchum 3, Scott 3, Krasner 4, Salter 4, Wanger 4)

Gunga Din, 1939 (Hawks 2, Stevens 2, Fontaine 3, Grant 3, Jaffe 3, McLaglen 3, August 4, Berman 4, Clothier 4, Dunn 4, Hecht 4, MacArthur 4, Newman 4, Polglase 4)

Gunkan sudeni kemuri nashi, 1950 (Yamamura 3)

Gunki hatameku shitani, 1972 (Shindo 2)

Gunless Bad Man, 1926 (Wyler 2)

Gunman, 1911 (Dwan 2)

Gunman, 1913 (Walsh 2)

Gunman in the Streets. *See* Traqué, 1950

Gunman's Walk, 1958 (Duning 4, Nugent 4)

Gunn, 1967 (Edwards 2, Mancini 4)

Gunnar Hede's Saga. *See* Gunnar Hedes saga, 1922

Gunnar Hedes saga, 1922 (Stiller 2, Jaenzon 4, Magnusson 4)

Gunpoint!. *See* At Gunpoint!, 1955

Gunpoint, 1966 (Murphy 3, Bumstead 4, Salter 4)

Gunpowder Plot, 1900 (Hepworth 2)

Gunro no machi, 1952 (Yamamura 3)

Guns. *See* **Fuzis, 1964**

Guns and Guitars, 1936 (Autry 3)

Guns A-Poppin', 1956 (Three Stooges 3)

Guns at Batasi, 1964 (Attenborough 3, Farrow 3, Hawkins 3, Addison 4, Fisher 4, Slocombe 4)

Guns for San Sebastian. *See* Bataille de San Sébastian, 1967

Guns for the Dictator. *See* Arme à gauche, 1965

Guns in the Afternoon. *See* **Ride the High Country, 1962**

Guns of Darkness, 1962 (Asquith 2, Caron 3, Niven 3, Fisher 4, Krasker 4)

Guns of Diablo, 1964 (Bronson 3)

Guns of Fort Petticoat, 1957 (Murphy 3, Brown 4)

Guns of Loos, 1928 (Carroll 3)

Guns of Navarone, 1961 (Yates 2, Baker 3, Harris 3, Niven 3, Papas 3, Peck 3, Quayle 3, Quinn 3, Foreman 4, Halas and Batchelor 4, Morris 4, Tiomkin 4)

Guns of the Magnificent Seven, 1968 (Rey 3, Bernstein 4)

Guns of the Pecos, 1937 (McCord 4)

Guns of the Timberland, 1960 (Ladd 3, Seitz 4)

Guns of the Trees, 1961 (Mekas 2)

Guns of Zangara, 1960 (Van Cleef 3)

Guns, Sin, and Bathtub Gin. *See* Lady in Red, 1979

Guns West, 1954 (Corman 2)

Gunsaulus Mystery, 1921 (Micheaux 2)

Gunsight Ridge, 1957 (McCrea 3, Jennings 4, Laszlo 4)

Gunslinger, 1956 (Corman 2)

Gunsmoke, 1953 (Murphy 3, Boyle 4)

Gunsmoke Ranch, 1937 (Canutt 4)

Günstling von Schönbrunn, 1929 (Dagover 3, Junge 4)

Guraida, 1943 (Tsuburaya 4)

Gurentai no uta, 1934 (Yoda 4)

Guru, 1968 (Ivory 2, Jhabvala 4, Mitra 4)

Gus and the Anarchists, 1915 (Laurel and Hardy 3)

Gus Edwards' Song Revue, 1929 (Day 4)

Gusher, 1913 (Sennett 2, Normand 3)

Gussie series, 1914–15 (Sennett 2)

Gustav Adolfs Page, 1960 (Herlth 4)

Gutter. *See* Dobu, 1954

Guv'nor, 1934 (Arliss 3, Balcon 4, Junge 4, Rank 4)

Guy, a Girl, and a Pal, 1945 (Boetticher 2, Edwards 2, Hunter 4)

Guy Could Change, 1946 (Howard 2)

Guy de Maupassant, 1978 (Gélin 3)

Guy Named Joe, 1943 (Edwards 2, Fleming 2, Barrymore 3, Bond 3, Dunne 3, Johnson 3, Tracy 3, Williams 3, Folsey 4, Freund 4, Gibbons 4, Irene 4, Mayer 4, Stothart 4, Trumbo 4)

Guy Upstairs, 1915 (Eason 4)

Guy Who Came Back, 1951 (Bennett 3, Darnell 3, La Shelle 4, LeMaire 4, Wheeler 4)

Guyana: Crime of the Century. *See* Guyana: Cult of the Damned, 1979

Guyana: Cult of the Damned, 1979 (De Carlo 3)

Guyrkoviscarna, 1920 (Magnusson 4)

Guys and Dolls, 1955 (Mankiewicz 2, Brando 3, Simmons 3, Sinatra 3, Goldwyn 4, Kidd 4, Mandell 4, Sharaff 4, Stradling 4)

Guys of the Sea. *See* Umi no yarodomo, 1957

Gweisser Herr Grant, 1933 (Tschechowa 3)

Gwiazdy muszą płonąć, 1954 (Munk 2)

Gyangu chushingura, 1963 (Yamamura 3)

Gyarmat a föld alatt, 1951 (Fábri 2)

Gycklarnas afton, 1953 (Andersson 3, Björnstrand 3, Fischer 4, Nykvist 4)

Gymnasium Jim, 1922 (Sennett 2)

Gymnasts, 1961 (Baillie 2)

Gypped in the Penthouse, 1955 (Three Stooges 3)

Gypsy, 1911 (Lawrence 3)

Gypsy, 1962 (LeRoy 2, Malden 3, Russell 3, Wood 3, Orry-Kelly 4, Stradling 4)

Gypsy and the Gentleman, 1958 (Losey 2, Mercouri 3, Rank 4)

Gypsy Blood. *See* Zügelloses Blut, 1917

Gypsy Blood. *See* Carmen, 1918

Gypsy Cavalier, 1922 (Blackton 2)

Gypsy Colt, 1954 (Bond 3, Van Cleef 3)

Gypsy Fiddler, 1933 (Terry 4)

Gypsy Girl. *See* Sky, West, and

Crooked, 1966

Gypsy Life, 1945 (Terry 4)

Gypsy Moths, 1969 (Frankenheimer 2, Hackman 3, Kerr 3, Lancaster 3, Bernstein 4)

Gypsy Queen, 1913 (Sennett 2, Arbuckle 3, Normand 3)

Gypsy Romance, 1914 (Reid 3)

H

H is for House, 1973 (Greenaway 2)

H + 2, 1971 (Lancaster 3)

H. 2 S., 1968 (Morricone 4)

H.M. Pulham, Esquire, 1941 (Coburn 3, Lamarr 3, Young 3, Gibbons 4, Kaper 4)

H.M.S. Defiant, 1962 (Bogarde 3, Guinness 3, Challis 4, Mathieson 4)

Ha fatto tredici!, 1951 (Fusco 4)

Ha fatto una signora, 1939 (Valli 3)

Ha! Ha! Ha!, 1934 (Fleischer 4)

Haadsaa, 1983 (Patil 3)

Haar Jeet, 1939 (Roy 2)

Haares und der Liebe Wellen, 1929 (Ruttman 2)

Hääyö. See Noc Poslubna, 1959

Habanera, 1937 (Sirk 2)

Habeas Corpus, 1928 (Laurel and Hardy 3, Roach 4)

Habit of Happiness, 1916 (Fairbanks 3, Menjou 3)

Habit Rabbit, 1963 (Hanna and Barbera 4)

Habit vert, 1937 (Berry 3, Blier 3, D'Eaubonne 4)

Habitantes de la casa deshabitada, 1958 (Rey 3)

Habrichka el hashemersh, 1972 (Harvey 3, Hawkins 3, Golan and Globus 4)

Haceldama ou Le Prix du Sang, 1919 (Duvivier 2)

Hachyyuhachinenme no taiyo, 1941 (Tsuburaya 4)

Hacienda de la flor, 1948 (Armendáriz 3)

Hadaka no jukyu-sai, 1970 (Shindo 2)

Hadaka no shima, 1960 (Shindo 2)

Hadaka no taiyo, 1958 (Shindo 2)

Haevnet, 1911 (Psilander 3)

Hag in a Leather Jacket, 1964 (Waters 2)

Hagiographia, 1971 (Markopoulos 2)

Haha, 1929 (Takamine 3)

Haha, 1958 (Kyo 3)

Haha, 1963 (Shindo 2)

Haha nareba onna nareba, 1952 (Yamada 3)

Haha no ai, 1935 (Hasegawa 3, Takamine 3)

Haha no chizu, 1942 (Mori 3, Hayasaka 4)

Haha no hatsukoi, 1954 (Kagawa 3)

Haha no saigetsu, 1965 (Tanaka 3)

Haha no uta, 1938 (Tanaka 3)

Haha san-nin, 1958 (Yamada 3)

Haha shirayuki, 1956 (Yoda 4)

Haha to ko, 1938 (Tanaka 3)

Haha yo kimi no na o kegasu nakare, 1928 (Tanaka 3)

Haha yo ko yo, 1933 (Yoda 4)

Hahakogusa, 1959 (Tanaka 3, Yamamura 3)

Hahako-zo, 1956 (Yamada 3)

Haha-tsubaki, 1950 (Yamamura 3)

Hahn im Korb, 1925 (Dieterle 2)

Hai hun, 1957 (Zhao 3)

Haikyo no naka, 1976 (Mizoguchi 2)

Hail, Hero!, 1969 (Douglas 3, Kennedy 3, Wright 3)

Hail Mafia. See Je vous salue, Mafia, 1965

Hail Mary, 1985 (Godard 2)

Hail the Conquering Hero, 1944 (Sturges 2, Pangborn 3, Dreier 4, Head 4, Seitz 4)

Hail the Woman, 1921 (Ince 4, Sullivan 4)

Haim Soutine, 1959 (Delerue 4)

Haine, 1918 (Gaumont 4)

Haine, 1979 (Kinski 3)

Hair, 1979 (Forman 2, Ray 2, Ondříček 4)

Hair Cut-Ups, 1953 (Terry 4)

Hair Trigger Baxter, 1926 (Haller 4)

Hair Trigger Casey, 1922 (Borzage 2)

Hair Trigger Stuff, 1920 (Eason 4)

Haircut, 1963 (Warhol 2)

Hairless Hector, 1941 (Terry 4)

Hairpins, 1920 (Niblo 2, Barnes 4, Sullivan 4)

Hair-Raising Hare, 1946 (Blanc 4, Jones 4, Stalling 4)

Hairspray, 1988 (Waters 2)

Hairy Ape, 1944 (Bendix 3, Hayward 3)

Hairy Hercules, 1989 (Halas and Batchelor 4)

Haitoku no mesu, 1961 (Yamamura 3)

Haizan no uta wa kanashi, 1976 (Mizoguchi 2)

Hajnal, 1971 (Szabó 2)

Hakai, 1948 (Mori 3)

Hakai, 1962 (Miyagawa 4)

Hakoiri musume, 1935 (Tanaka 3)

Hakone fuun-roku, 1952 (Yamada 3)

Hakuchi, 1951 (Hara 3, Mifune 3, Mori 3, Shimura 3, Hayasaka 4)

Hakuchu no ketto, 1950 (Yamamura 3)

Hakuchu no torima, 1966 (Toda 4)

Hakufujin no yoren, 1956 (Tsuburaya 4)

Hakugy, 1953 (Hara 3)

Hakuji no hito, 1957 (Yamamura 3)

Halbblut, 1919 (Hoffmann 4, Pommer 4)

Halbseide, 1925 (Albers 3)

Halbzart, 1959 (Schneider 3)

Hale and Hearty, 1922 (Roach 4)

Half a Bride, 1928 (La Cava 2, Cooper 3, Lombard 3)

Half a Loaf of Kung-Fu, 1978 (Chan 3)

Half a Man, 1925 (Garnett 2, Laurel and Hardy 3)

Half a Sinner, 1934 (Brennan 3, McCrea 3, Rooney 3)

Half a Sinner, 1940 (Trumbo 4)

Half a Sixpence, 1968 (Unsworth 4)

Half Angel, 1936 (Carradine 3, Glennon 4, MacGowan 4, Meredyth 4, Zanuck 4)

Half Angel, 1951 (Cotten 3, Young 3, Krasner 4, Newman 4, Riskin 4)

Half Breed, 1922 (Clarke 4)

Half Caste. See Halbblut, 1919

Half Holiday, 1931 (Sennett 2)

Half Human, 1957 (Carradine 3)

Half Life, 1988 (Corman 2)

Half Marriage, 1929 (Murfin 4, Plunkett 4)

Half Moon Street, 1986 (Caine 3, Weaver 3)

Half Shot at Sunrise, 1930 (Plunkett 4, Steiner 4)

Half Shot at Sunset, 1930 (Musuraca 4)

Half Shot Shooters, 1936 (Three Stooges 3, Bruckman 4)

Half Way to Shanghai, 1942 (Salter 4)

Half-a-Dollar Bill, 1923 (Van Dyke 2)

Half-Back of Notre Dame, 1924 (Sennett 2)

Halfbreed. See Halvblod, 1913

Half-Breed, 1916 (Dwan 2, Fleming 2, Fairbanks 3, Loos 4)

Half-Breed, 1945 (Fleming 2)

Half-Breed, 1952 (Young 3, Eason 4)

Half-Fare Hare, 1956 (Blanc 4, McKimson 4, Stalling 4)

Half-Naked Truth, 1932 (La Cava 2, Berman 4, Glennon 4, Selznick 4, Steiner 4)

Half-Nelson, 1985 (Martin 3)

Half-Pint Pygmy, 1948 (Avery 4)

Half-Way Girl, 1925 (Bosworth 3, Folsey 4)

Halfway House, 1944 (Cavalcanti 2, Dearden 2, Rosay 3, Balcon 4, Clarke 4)

Half-Way to Heaven, 1929 (Arthur 3, Lukas 3, Lang 4)

Half-Wit's Holiday, 1947 (Three Stooges 3)

Halimeden mektup var, 1964 (Güney 2)

Halkas Gelöbnis, 1918 (Albers 3)

Hall on Devil's Island, 1957 (Haller 4)

Hallelujah, 1929 (Vidor 2, Berlin 4, Gibbons 4, Mayer 4, Shearer 4, Thalberg 4)

Hallelujah, I'm a Bum, 1933 (Milestone 2, Jolson 3, Langdon 3, Behrman 4, Day 4, Hecht 4, Newman 4)

Hallelujah I'm a Tramp. See Hallelujah, I'm a Bum, 1933

Hallelujah the Hills, 1963 (Emshwiller 2)

Hallelujah Trail, 1965 (Sturges 2, Lancaster 3, Pleasence 3, Remick 3, Bernstein 4, Head 4, Surtees 4)

Halles, 1929 (Kaufman 4)

Halliday Brand, 1957 (Lewis 2, Bond 3, Cotten 3)

Hallo, Afrika forude, 1929 (Madsen and Schenstrøm 3)

Hallo Everybody, 1933 (Milhaud 4)

Hallo! Hallo! Hier spricht Berlin!. *See* 'Allo Berlin, ici Paris, 1931

Halloween. *See* Zaduszki, 1961

Halloween, 1978 (Carpenter 2, Curtis 3, Pleasence 3)

Halloween II, 1981 (Carpenter 2, Curtis 3, Pleasence 3)

Halloween III: Season of the Witch, 1983 (Carpenter 2)

Halloween IV: The Return of Michael Myers, 1988 (Pleasence 3)

Halloween V: The Revenge of Michael Myers, 1989 (Pleasence 3)

Hallroom Boys, 1906 (Bitzer 4)

Hallroom Girls, 1910 (White 3)

Halls of Anger, 1970 (Bridges 3, Guffey 4, Mirisch 4)

Halls of Montezuma, 1951 (Milestone 2, Malden 3, Palance 3, Wagner 3, Widmark 3, Hoch 4, LeMaire 4, Reynolds 4, Wheeler 4)

Hallucinations du Baron Münchausen, 1911 (Méliès 2)

Hallucinations sadiques, 1969 (Gélin 3)

Hallucinators. *See* Naked Zoo, 1971

Halvblod, 1913 (Sjöström 2, Magnusson 4)

Ham and Eggs. *See* Ham and Eggs at the Front, 1927

Ham and Eggs, 1933 (Lantz 4)

Ham and Eggs at the Front, 1927 (Loy 3, Clarke 4)

Ham Dard, 1953 (Biswas 4)

Ham in a Role, 1949 (Blanc 4, McKimson 4, Stalling 4)

Hamagure no komoriuta, 1973 (Yoshimura 2)

Hamari Baat, 1943 (Kapoor 2, Biswas 4)

Hamateur Night, 1938 (Avery 4)

Hambone and Hillie, 1984 (Gish 3)

Hamburg, 1961 (Roos 2)

Hame Khelne Do, 1962 (Biswas 4)

Hamilton in the Musical Festival, 1961 (Halas and Batchelor 4)

Hamilton the Musical Elephant, 1961 (Halas and Batchelor 4)

Hamles, 1960 (Skolimowski 2)

Hamlet, 1910 (Blom 2)

Hamlet, 1920 (Nielsen 3, Courant 4)

Hamlet, 1939 (Gielgud 3, Hawkins 3)

Hamlet, 1948 (Cushing 3, Lee 3, Olivier 3, Quayle 3, Simmons 3, Dillon 4, Mathieson 4, Rank 4, Walton 4)

Hamlet, 1960 (Schell 3)

Hamlet, 1963 (Kozintsev 2, Enei 4, Moskvin 4, Shostakovich 4)

Hamlet, 1964 (Burton 3, Gielgud 3)

Hamlet, 1969 (Dmytryk 2, Richardson 2, Hopkins 3, Huston 3, Addison 4, Fisher 4)

Hamlet, 1990 (Zeffirelli 2, Bates 3, Close 3, Gibson 3, Morricone 4, Watkin 4)

Hammerhead, 1968 (Dors 3)

Hammersmith Is Out, 1972 (Burton 3, Raft 3, Taylor 3, Ustinov 3, Head 4)

Hammett, 1982 (Coppola 2, Wenders 2, Sidney 3, Barry 4, Biroc 4, Tavoularis 4)

Hammond Mystery. *See* Undying Monster, 1942

Hämnaren, 1915 (Stiller 2)

Hamnstad, 1948 (Fischer 4)

Hampelmann, 1930 (Courant 4)

Hampi, 1960 (Rouch 2)

Hamrahi, 1945 (Roy 2)

Hams That Couldn't Be Cured, 1942 (Lantz 4)

Hamster. *See* Křeček, 1946

Hamusse Hanussen, 1955 (Warm 4)

Han, Hun og Hamlet, 1922 (Madsen and Schenstrøm 3)

Han, Hun og Hamlet, 1932 (Madsen and Schenstrøm 3)

Hana, 1941 (Yoshimura 2, Tanaka 3)

Hana aru zasso, 1939 (Tanaka 3)

Hana futatabi, 1956 (Yamamura 3)

Hana hiraku, 1948 (Hayasaka 4)

Hana hiraku, 1955 (Yamada 3)

Hana no Banzui-in, 1959 (Yamada 3)

Hana no bojo, 1958 (Tsukasa 3)

Hana no kenka-jo, 1953 (Hasegawa 3)

Hana no Kodo-kan, 1953 (Hasegawa 3)

Hana no nagawakizashi, 1954 (Hasegawa 3)

Hana no Oedo no musekinin, 1964 (Shindo 3)

Hana no saku ie, 1963 (Iwashita 3, Yamamura 3)

Hana no sugao, 1949 (Okada 3, Yamamura 3)

Hana no tsukihi, 1949 (Yamada 3)

Hana no wataridori, 1956 (Hasegawa 3)

Hana no Yoshiwara hyakunin-giri, 1960 (Yoda 4)

Hana no yukyo-den, 1958 (Hasegawa 3)

Hanahagi sensei to Santa, 1952 (Yamada 3)

Hanakago no uta, 1937 (Takamine 3, Tanaka 3)

Hanako-sen, 1943 (Takamine 3)

Hanakurabe tanuki-goten, 1949 (Kyo 3)

Hanamuko Taiheiki, 1945 (Yoda 4)

Hanano sandogasa, 1954 (Hasegawa 3)

Hananoren, 1959 (Tsukasa 3)

Hanaoko Seishu no tsuma, 1967 (Shindo 2, Takamine 3)

Hanare-goze Orin, 1977 (Shinoda 2, Iwashita 3, Miyagawa 4, Takemitsu 4)

Hanasake jijii, 1923 (Kinugasa 2)

Hanataba no yume, 1938 (Takamine 3)

Hanatsumi nikki, 1939 (Shindo 3)

Hanauta ojosan, 1938 (Tanaka 3)

Hanayome kaigi, 1956 (Tsukasa 3)

Hanayome karuta, 1937 (Takamine 3)

Hanayome kurabe, 1935 (Tanaka 3)

Hanayome no negoto, 1933 (Tanaka 3)

Hanayome no negoto, 1935 (Hasegawa 3)

Hanayome san wa sekai-ichi, 1959 (Shindo 2)

Hand. *See* Ruka, 1965

Hand, 1981 (Stone 2, Caine 3)

Hand in the Trap. *See* Mano en la trampa, 1961

Hand Movie, 1968 (Rainer 2)

Hand of Death, 1961 (Crosby 4)

Hand of Destiny, 1910 (White 3)

Hand of Fate, 1912 (Bosworth 3)

Hand of Peril, 1916 (Tourneur 2, Carré 4)

Hand Organ Man, 1909 (Olcott 2)

Hand Painted Abstraction, 1976 (McLaren 4)

Hand That Rocks the Cradle, 1917 (Weber 2)

Handcuffs or Kisses, 1921 (Colman 3)

Handful of Clouds. *See* Doorway to Hell, 1930

Handful of Dust, 1988 (Guinness 3, Huston 3)

Handful of Love. *See* Handfull kaerlek, 1973

Handfull kaerlek, 1973 (Thulin 3)

Handle With Care, 1965 (Lancaster 3)

Händler der vier Jahreszeiten, 1971 (Schygulla 3)

Handling Ships, 1943 (Halas and Batchelor 4)

Handmaid's Tale, 1990 (Schlöndorff 2, Dunaway 3, Duvall 3, Pinter 4)

Hands Across the Border, 1943 (Rogers 3)

Hands Across the Table, 1935 (Leisen 2, Bellamy 3, Lombard 3, MacMurray 3, Krasna 4)

Hands, Knees, and Bumps-a-Daisy, 1969 (Dunning 4)

Hands of Cormac Joyce, 1972 (Cusack 3)

Hands of Orlac. *See* Orlacs Hande, 1924

Hands of Orlac. *See* Mad Love, 1935

Hands of Orlac, 1960 (Lee 3, Pleasence 3)

Hands of the Ripper, 1971 (Carreras 4)

Hands Off, 1921 (Mix 3)

Hands over the City. *See* Mani sulla citta, 1963

Hands Up!, 1917 (Browning 2, Moore 3)

Hands Up!, 1926 (Johnson 3)

Hands Up!. *See* Rece do gory, 1967

Handsome Boy Trying to Rule the World. *See* Tenka o nerau bishounen, 1955

Handy Andy, 1934 (Rogers 3, Taylor 3, Miller 4)

Handy Man, 1918 (Laurel and Hardy 3)

Handy Man, 1923 (Laurel and Hardy 3)

Hang 'em High, 1967 (Dern 3, Eastwood 3, Hopper 3, Johnson 3)

Hanged Man, 1964 (Siegel 2, O'Brien 3)

Hanging Out Yonkers, 1973 (Akerman 2)

Hanging Tree, 1959 (Daves 2, Cooper 3, Malden 3, Schell 3, Scott 3, McCord 4, Orry-Kelly 4, Steiner 4)

Hängivelse, 1965 (Thulin 3)

Hangman, 1959 (Curtiz 2, Taylor 3, Bumstead 4, Head 4, Nichols 4)

Hangman's House, 1928 (Ford 2, Bosworth 3, McLaglen 3, Wayne 3)

Hangman's Knot, 1952 (Marvin 3, Reed 3, Scott 3, Brown 4, Canutt 4)

Hangmen Also Die!, 1943 (Lang 2, Brennan 3, Eisler 4, Howe 4)

Hangover. *See* Female Jungle, 1956

Hangover Square, 1945 (Darnell 3, McDowall 3, Sanders 3, Herrmann 4, La Shelle 4, Wheeler 4)

Hangup, 1974 (Hathaway 2)

Hangyaboly, 1971 (Fábri 2)

Hangyaku-ji, 1961 (Shindo 3)

Hanjo, 1961 (Yamamura 3, Takemitsu 4)

Hanka, 1955 (Vorkapich 4)

Hanky Panky, 1982 (Poitier 3, Widmark 3, Wilder 3)

Hanna K, 1983 (Costa-Gavras 2, Clayburgh 3, Solinas 4)

Hannah and Her Sisters, 1986 (Allen 2, Caine 3, Farrow 3, O'Sullivan 3, Von Sydow 3)

Hannah Dusten, 1910 (Olcott 2)

Hanna's War, 1988 (Burstyn 3, Pleasence 3, Golan and Globus 4)

Hanneles Himmelfahrt, 1922 (Gad 2)

Hanneles Himmelfahrt, 1934 (Von Harbou 4)

Hannerl und ihre Liebhaber, 1936 (Tschechowa 3)

Hannibal. *See* Annibale, 1960 (Ulmer 2)

Hannibal Brooks, 1969 (Reed 3, Lai 4)

Hannie Caulder, 1971 (Borgnine 3, Dors 3, Lee 3, Welch 3)

Hanno rapito un uomo, 1937 (De Sica 2)

Hanno rubato un tram, 1955 (Fabrizi 3)

Hanoi Hilton, 1987 (Golan and Globus 4)

Hanoi, martes 13, 1967 (Alvarez 2)

Hanover Street, 1979 (Ford 3, Barry 4, Watkin 4)

Hanran, 1954 (Kagawa 3, Hayasaka 4)

Hans Brinker, or the Silver Skates, 1959 (Fischer 4)

Hans bröllopsnatt, 1915 (Stiller 2, Magnusson 4)

Hans Christian Andersen, 1952 (Vidor 2, Kaye 3, Day 4, Goldwyn 4, Mandell 4, Stradling 4)

Hans engelska fru, 1926 (Molander 2, Dagover 3, Jaenzon 4)

Hans Hartung, 1971 (Braunberger 4)

Hans, Hein, und Henny, 1914 (Porten 3)

Hans, hon, och pengarna, 1936 (Fischer 4)

Hans hustrus förflutna, 1915 (Stiller 2, Jaenzon 4)

Hans im Glück, 1936 (Herlth 4, Röhrig 4)

Hans in allen Gassen. See Folle Aventure, 1930

Hans le marin, 1948 (Dalio 3, D'Eaubonne 4, Kosma 4)

Hans nåds testamente, 1919 (Sjöström 2, Magnusson 4)

Hans Store Chance, 1915 (Psilander 3)

Hans Trutz in Schlaraffenland, 1917 (Lubitsch 2, Rasp 3, Wegener 3)

Hans Westmar, 1933 (Wegener 3)

Hansel and Gretel, 1909 (Porter 2)

Hansel and Gretel, 1933 (Terry 4)

Hansel and Gretel, 1952 (Terry 4)

Hansel and Gretel, 1955 (Reiniger 4)

Hansel and Gretel, 1987 (Golan and Globus 4)

Hansom Cabman, 1924 (Capra 2, Sennett 2, Langdon 3)

Hansom Driver, 1913 (Sennett 2)

Hantise, 1912 (Feuillade 2, Gaumont 4)

Hanussen, 1955 (Kinski 3, Herlth 4)

Hanussen, 1989 (Szabó 2, Brandauer 3, Josephson 3)

Hanya: Portrait of a Dance Legend, 1984 (Andrews 3)

Hapax Legomena, 1972 (Frampton 2)

Happening, 1966 (Chabrol 2, Dunaway 3, Homolka 3, Quinn 3, Day 4, Spiegel 4)

Happening in Calcutta, 1980 (Chandragupta 4)

Happidrome, 1943 (Buchanan 3)

Happiest Days of Your Life, 1950 (Launder and Gilliat 2, Rutherford 3, Sim 3, Korda 4)

Happiest Millionaire, 1967 (Garson 3, MacMurray 3, Page 3, Ellenshaw 4)

Happily Ever After. See C'era una volta, 1967

Happiness, 1917 (Gilbert 3, Ince 4, Sullivan 4)

Happiness, 1924 (Vidor 2)

Happiness. See Schastye, 1932

Happiness Ahead, 1928 (Goulding 2, Moore 3, Glazer 4)

Happiness Ahead, 1934 (LeRoy 2, Darwell 3, Powell 3, Gaudio 4, Orry-Kelly 4)

Happiness of Us Alone. See Namonaku mazushiku utsukushiku, 1961

Happy, 1933 (Launder and Gilliat 2)

Happy and Joyous Story of Colinot, the Man Who Pulls Up Skirts. See Histoire très

bonne et très joyeuse de Colinot Trousse-Chemise, 1973

Happy and Lucky, 1938 (Terry 4)

Happy Anniversary, 1959 (Niven 3, Garmes 4)

Happy As the Grass Was Green, 1973 (Page 3)

Happy Birthday. See Forever My Heart, 1954

Happy Birthday, 1979 (Bozzetto 4)

Happy Birthday Harry!, 1981 (Terry-Thomas 3)

Happy Birthday to Me, 1981 (Ford 3)

Happy Birthday Wanda June, 1971 (Steiger 3, York 3, Leven 4)

Happy Circus Days, 1942 (Terry 4)

Happy Cobblers, 1952 (Terry 4)

Happy Days, 1930 (Gaynor 3, Grable 3, Rogers 3, Friedhofer 4)

Happy Days, 1936 (Iwerks 4)

Happy Divorce. See Divorce heureux, 1975

Happy Easter. See Joyeuses Pâques, 1984

Happy End, 1958 (Mimica 4)

Happy Ending, 1924 (Buchanan 3)

Happy Ending, 1931 (Launder and Gilliat 2)

Happy Ending, 1969 (Brooks 2, Rowlands 3, Simmons 3, Wright 3, Hall 4, Legrand 4)

Happy Ever After, 1932 (Stevenson 2, Pommer 4)

Happy Ever After, 1954 (De Carlo 3, Fitzgerald 3, Niven 3)

Happy Families, 1939 (Balcon 4)

Happy Family. See Merry Frinks, 1934

Happy Family, 1952 (Box 4)

Happy Go Ducky, 1956 (Hanna and Barbera 4)

Happy Go Loopy, 1960 (Hanna and Barbera 4)

Happy Go Lovely, 1950 (Niven 3)

Happy Go Lucky, 1943 (Hutton 3, Powell 3, Dreier 4, Frank 4, Head 4, Struss 4)

Happy Go Lucky, 1947 (Terry 4)

Happy Haunting Grounds, 1940 (Terry 4)

Happy Holland, 1952 (Terry 4)

Happy Hooldini and Lampoons, 1917 (Bray 4)

Happy Hooligan Earns His Dinner, 1903 (Bitzer 4)

Happy Hooligan Surprised, 1901 (Porter 2)

Happy Hooligan Turns Burglar, 1902 (Porter 2)

Happy in the Morning, 1938 (Cavalcanti 2)

Happy Is the Bride, 1957 (Boulting 2, Terry-Thomas 3)

Happy Lads of the Fleet. See Flottans glada gossar, 1954

Happy Land, 1943 (Ameche 3, Carey 3, Wood 3, Basevi 4, La Shelle 4, MacGowan 4)

Happy Landing, 1938 (Ameche 3, Henie 3, Zanuck 4)

Happy Landing, 1949 (Terry 4)

Happy Lion. See Stastny lev, 1959

Happy Mother's Day, 1963 (Leacock 2)

Happy Mother's Day ... Love George, 1973 (Neal 3, Lassally 4)

Happy New Year. See Bonne Année, 1973

Happy New Year, 1988 (Lelouch 2, Falk 3)

Happy Road, 1956 (Cassel 3, Chevalier 3, Redgrave 3, Trauner 4)

Happy Thieves, 1962 (Harrison 3, Hayworth 3, Valli 3)

Happy Though Married, 1919 (Niblo 2, Barnes 4, Sullivan 4)

Happy Time, 1952 (Kramer 2, Boyer 3, Dalio 3, Jourdan 3, Tiomkin 4)

Happy Valley, 1952 (Terry 4)

Happy Warrior, 1917 (Howard 3)

Happy Warrior, 1925 (Blackton 2)

Happy Years, 1950 (Wagner 3, Plunkett 4, Wilson 4)

Happy You and Merry Me, 1936 (Fleischer 4)

Happyakuman-goku ni idomu otoko, 1961 (Yamamura 3)

Happy-Go-Lucky. See Pechkolavochki, 1973

Happy-Go-Nutty, 1944 (Avery 4)

Här börjar äventyret, 1965 (Andersson 3)

Här har du ditt liv, 1966 (Björnstrand 3)

Här Har du Ditt Liv, 1968 (Von Sydow 3)

Här kommer vi, 1947 (Björnstrand 3)

Haracima dokunma, 1965 (Güney 2)

Hara-Kiri, 1919 (Lang 2, Dagover 3, Hoffmann 4)

Hara-Kiri. See Battle, 1934

Harakiri. See **Seppuku, 1962**

Harald Sæverud—1 en alder af 88 år, 1985 (Roos 2)

Harbor Island, 1912 (Bosworth 3)

Harbor Scenes, 1935 (Maddow 4)

Hard, 1988 (Edlund 4)

Hard Boiled, 1925 (McCarey 2, Mix 3, Roach 4)

Hard Boiled Egg, 1947 (Terry 4)

Hard Boiled Mahoney, 1948 (Johnson 3)

Hard Cash, 1913 (Ingram 2)

Hard Choices, 1984 (Sayles 2)

Hard Cider, 1914 (Sennett 2)

Hard Contract, 1969 (Black 3, Coburn 3, Hayden 3, Meredith 3, Remick 3, North 4)

Hard Day's Night, 1964 (Lester 2)

Hard, Fast, and Beautiful, 1951 (Lupino 3, Trevor 3)

Hard Fists, 1927 (Wyler 2)

Hard Guy, 1930 (Tracy 3)

Hård klang, 1952 (Sjöström 2)

Hard Knocks, 1924 (Roach 4)

Hard Knocks and Love Taps, 1921 (Sennett 2)

Hard Luck, 1921 (Keaton 2)

Hard Promises, 1990 (Grant 3, Spacek 3)

Hard Times, 1975 (Bronson 3, Coburn 3)

Hard Times for Vampires. See Tempi duri per vampiri, 1959

Hard to Be a God, 1989 (Carrière 4, Delerue 4)

Hard to Beat, 1909 (Porter 2)

Hard to Get, 1929 (Seitz 4)

Hard to Get, 1938 (De Havilland 3, Powell 3, Grot 4, Mercer 4, Rosher 4, Wald 4, Wallis 4)

Hard to Handle, 1933 (Leroy 2, Cagney 3, Orry-Kelly 4)

Hard Wash, 1896 (Bitzer 4)

Hard Way, 1942 (Lupino 3, Orry-Kelly 4, Howe 4, Prinz 4, Wald 4)

Hard Way, 1979 (Van Cleef 3, Decaë 4)

Hårda leken, 1955 (Fischer 4)

Harda viljor, 1923 (Magnusson 4)

Hardboiled, 1929 (Plunkett 4)

Hard-Boiled Haggerty, 1927 (Plunkett 4, Polito 4, Wilson 4)

Hardboiled Rose, 1929 (Loy 3)

Hard-Boiled Tenderfoot, 1924 (Roach 4)

Hardcore, 1979 (Schrader 2, Scott 3)

Harder They Fall, 1956 (Bogart 3, Steiger 3, Cohn 4, Friedhofer 4, Guffey 4, Wald 4)

Hardhat and Legs, 1980 (Kanin 4)

Hardly Working, 1980 (Lewis 2)

Hardship of Miles Standish, 1940 (Blanc 4, Freleng 4, Stalling 4)

Hard-Shoemakers. See Skalní ševci, 1931

Hardys Ride High, 1939 (Rooney 3)

Hare and the Hounds, 1940 (Terry 4)

Hare Brush, 1955 (Blanc 4, Freleng 4)

Hare Conditioned, 1945 (Blanc 4, Jones 4, Stalling 4)

Hare Do, 1949 (Blanc 4, Freleng 4, Stalling 4)

Hare Force, 1944 (Blanc 4, Freleng 4, Stalling 4)

Hare Grows in Manhattan, 1947 (Blanc 4, Freleng 4, Stalling 4)

Hare Krishna, 1966 (Mekas 2)

Hare Lift, 1952 (Blanc 4, Freleng 4, Stalling 4)

Hare Mail, 1931 (Lantz 4)

Hare Rama Hare Krishna, 1972 (Anand 3)

Hare Remover, 1946 (Blanc 4, Stalling 4)

Hare Ribbin', 1944 (Blanc 4, Clampett 4, Stalling 4)

Hare Splitter, 1948 (Blanc 4, Freleng 4, Stalling 4)

Hare Tonic, 1945 (Blanc 4, Jones 4, Stalling 4)

Hare Trigger, 1945 (Blanc 4, Freleng 4, Maltese 4, Stalling 4)

Hare Trimmed, 1953 (Blanc 4, Freleng 4, Stalling 4)

Hare We Go, 1951 (Blanc 4, Freleng 4, Stalling 4)

Hare-abian Nights, 1959 (Blanc 4)

Hare-Brained Hypnotist, 1942 (Blanc 4, Freleng 4, Maltese 4, Stalling 4)

Hare-Breadth Hurry, 1963 (Blanc 4, Jones 4)

Haredevil Hare, 1948 (Blanc 4, Jones 4, Stalling 4)

Harekodose, 1940 (Yoda 4)

Harekodose, 1961 (Hasegawa 3, Yoda 4)

Hare-less Wolf, 1958 (Blanc 4, Freleng 4)

Harem, 1967 (Ferreri 2, Baker 3, Morricone 4)

Harem, 1986 (Gardner 3, Kinski 3, Sharif 3, Sarde 4, Trauner 4)

Harem Knight, 1926 (Sennett 2)

Harem Scarem, 1927 (Disney 4)

Harems Devoid of Magic. See Harémy kouzla zbavené, 1922

Harémy kouzla zbavené, 1922 (Heller 4)

Hare-Um Scare-Um, 1939 (Blanc 4, Stalling 4)

Hare-Way to the Stars, 1958 (Blanc 4, Jones 4, Maltese 4)

Hari Hondal Burgadar, 1980 (Nihalani 4)

Harikiri shacho, 1956 (Tsukasa 3)

Harikomi, 1958 (Takamine 3)

Harlekin, 1931 (Reiniger 4)

Harlem, 1942 (Gallone 2, Amidei 4)

Harlem Globetrotters, 1951 (Dandridge 3)

Harlem Hotshots, 1940 (Horne 3)

Harlem in Heaven, 1938 (Robinson 3)

Harlem Nights, 1989 (Murphy 3, Pryor 3)

Harlem on Parade, 1942 (Horne 3)

Harlem Wednesday, 1958 (Hubley 4)

Harlequin, 1980 (Crawford 3)

Harley Davidson and the Marlboro Man, 1991 (Rourke 3)

Harlot, 1964 (Warhol 2)

Harlow, 1965 (Baker 3, Lansbury 3, Rogers 3, Hayes 4, Head 4, Levine 4, Ruttenberg 4, Westmore Family 4)

Harmonikář, 1953 (Stallich 4)

Harmony at Home, 1930 (Miller 4)

Harmony Heaven, 1930 (Launder and Gilliat 2)

Harmony Lane, 1935 (Lewis 2)

Harmony Parade. See Pigskin Parade, 1936

Harold and Maude, 1971 (Ashby 2, Cusack 3, Gordon 3, Alonzo 4)

Harold Lloyd's Funny Side of Life, 1966 (Lloyd 3)

Harold Lloyd's World of Comedy, 1962 (Lloyd 3)

Harold Teen, 1928 (Leroy 2, Haller 4)

Harold Teen, 1933 (Orry-Kelly 4)

Harold's Bad Man, 1915 (Mix 3)

Harp in Hock, 1927 (Love 3, Levien 4)

Harp of Burma. See Biruma no tategoto, 1956

Harp of Tara, 1914 (Ince 4)

Harper, 1966 (Bacall 3, Leigh 3, Newman 3, Wagner 3, Winters 3, Goldman 4, Hall 4, Previn 4)

Harried and Hurried, 1965 (Blanc 4)

Harriet and the Piper, 1920 (Mayer 4)

Harriet Craig, 1950 (Crawford 3, Duning 4, Walker 4)

Harrigan's Kid, 1943 (Chase 4, Schary 4)

Harrison and Barrison. See Harrison es Barrison, 1917

Harrison és Barrison, 1917 (Korda 2, Korda 4)

Harry and Son, 1984 (Newman 3, Woodward 3, Allen 4, Bumstead 4, Mancini 4)

Harry and the Hendersons, 1987 (Ameche 3, Baker 4)

Harry and Tonto, 1974 (Mazursky 2, Burstyn 3)

Harry and Walter Go to New York, 1976 (Caan 3, Caine 3, Gould 3, Horner 4, Kovacs 4)

Harry Black, 1958 (Granger 3)

Harry Black and the Tiger. See Harry Black, 1958

Harry in Your Pocket, 1973 (Coburn 3, Pidgeon 3, Schifrin 4)

Harry Lauder Songs, 1931 (Balcon 4)

Harry Never Holds. See Harry in Your Pocket, 1973

Harry Tracy, 1982 (Dern 3)

Harry's War, 1981 (Page 3)

Hart to Hart, 1979 (McDowall 3, Wagner 3)

Haru ichiban, 1966 (Iwashita 3)

Haru no tawamure, 1949 (Takamine 3, Hayasaka 4)

Haru no uzumaki, 1954 (Kyo 3)

Haru o matsu hitobito, 1959 (Takemitsu 4)

Haru ramman, 1966 (Mori 3, Tsukasa 3)

Harubiyori, 1967 (Iwashita 3)

Haruka nari haha no kuni, 1950 (Kyo 3, Yamada 3)

Haruka narishi haha no kuni, 1950 (Yoda 4)

Harukanaru soro, 1980 (Tsukasa 3)

Harum Scarum, 1965 (Presley 3, Katzman 4)

Harun al Raschid, 1924 (Curtiz 2)

Harusugata gonin-otoko, 1936 (Hasegawa 3)

Harvard, Here I Come, 1942 (De Carlo 3, Brown 4, Planer 4)

Harvest. See Regain, 1937

Harvest Hands, 1923 (Roach 4)

Harvest Help, 1940 (Wright 2)

Harvest of Flame, 1913 (Reid 3)

Harvest of My Lai, 1970 (Ophuls 2)

Harvest of Sin, 1913 (Ince 4)

Harvest Shall Come, 1942 (Alwyn 4)

Harvest Time, 1940 (Terry 4)

Harvester, 1936 (Lewis 2)

Harvey, 1950 (Stewart 3, Daniels 4, Orry-Kelly 4)

Harvey Girls, 1946 (Walters 2, Lansbury 3, Charisse 3, Garland 3, Alton 4, Edens 4, Folsey 4, Freed 4, Irene 4, Mayer 4, Mercer 4, Raphaelson 4, Rose 4)

Harvey Middleman, Fireman, 1965 (Smith 4)

Has Anybody Here Seen Kelly?, 1926 (Fleischer 4)

Has Anybody Here Seen Kelly, 1929 (Love 3)

Has Anybody Seen My Gal?, 1952 (Sirk 2, Coburn 3, Dean 3, Hudson 3)

Hasard et l'amour, 1913 (Linder 3)

Hasard et la violence, 1974 (Montand 3, Evein 4)

Hasegawa Roppa no Iemitsu to Hikosa, 1941 (Hasegawa 3)

Hash House Fraud, 1915 (Sennett 2)

Hash House Mashers, 1915 (Sennett 2)

Hash Shop, 1930 (Lantz 4)

Hasher's Delirium. See Songe d'un garçon de café, 1910

Hashigaon Hagadol, 1988 (Hill 2, Bernstein 4, Bumstead 4, Golan and Globus 4, Ondříček 4)

Hashimura Togo, 1917 (Hayakawa 3, Rosher 4)

Hasshu kyokakujin, 1936 (Shimura 3)

Hasta que perdio Jalisco, 1945 (De Fuentes 2)

Hasty Hare, 1952 (Blanc 4, Jones 4, Maltese 4, Stalling 4)

Hasty Heart, 1950 (Neal, 3, Reagan 3)

Hasty Marriage, 1931 (Roach 4)

Hat, 1964 (Moore 3, Hubley 4)

Hat, a Coat, and a Glove, 1934 (Plunkett 4)

Hat Check Girl, 1932 (Rogers 3)

Hat Check Honey, 1944 (Krasner 4, Salter 4)

Hat, Coat, and Glove, 1934 (Beavers 3, Hunt 4, MacGowan 4, Steiner 4)

Hatamoto kenka-daka, 1961 (Yamamura 3)

Hatamoto taikutsu otoko, 1956 (Shindo 3)

Hatamoto to Banshiin: Otoko no Taiketsu, 1960 (Yamamura 3)

Hataoka junsa, 1940 (Yoda 4)

Hatari!, 1962 (Hawks 2, Wayne 3, Brackett 4, Fulton 4, Harlan 4, Head 4, Mancini 4, Mercer 4)

Hatarnegol, 1971 (Topol 3)

Hatch Up Your Troubles, 1948 (Hanna and Barbera 4)

Hatchet Man, 1932 (Wellman 2, Robinson 3, Young 3, Grot 4)

Hate, 1922 (Mathis 4)

Hater of Men, 1917 (Gilbert 3)

Haters, 1911 (Dwan 2)

Haters. See Grudge, 1915

Hatfields and the McCoys, 1975 (Palance 3)

Hatful of Dreams, 1945 (Pal 4)

Hatful of Rain, 1957 (Zinnemann 2, Saint 3, Herrmann 4, LeMaire 4, Wheeler 4)

Hatred. See Mollenard, 1938

Hats Off, 1927 (Laurel and Hardy 3, Roach 4)

Hats Off, 1936 (Fuller 2, Pangborn 3)

Hatsugaro-ondo, 1936 (Shimura 3)

Hatsukoi jigokuhen, 1968 (Takemitsu 4)

Hatsukoi no haru, 1933 (Takamine 3)
Hatsukoi san-nin masuko, 1955 (Tsukasa 3)
Hatta Marri, 1932 (Sennett 2)
Hatter's Castle, 1941 (Kerr 3, Mason 3, Newton 3)
Hauen Sie ab mit Heldentum. See Kinder, Mütter, und ein General, 1954
Haunted Bedroom, 1919 (Niblo 2, Barnes 4, Sullivan 4)
Haunted Castle. See Schloss Vogelöd, 1921
Haunted Cat, 1951 (Terry 4)
Haunted Gold, 1932 (Wayne 3, Musuraca 4)
Haunted Hat, 1915 (Laurel and Hardy 3)
Haunted Homestead, 1927 (Wyler 2)
Haunted Honeymoon, 1925 (Roach 4)
Haunted Honeymoon. See Busman's Honeymoon, 1940
Haunted Honeymoon, 1986 (Wilder 3)
Haunted Hotel, 1907 (Blackton 2)
Haunted House, 1921 (Keaton 2)
Haunted House, 1928 (Christensen 2, Biro 4, Polito 4)
Haunted House, 1929 (Disney 4, Iwerks 4)
Haunted Mouse, 1941 (Avery 4, Blanc 4, Stalling 4)
Haunted Mouse, 1965 (Jones 4)
Haunted Pajamas, 1917 (Gaudio 4)
Haunted Palace, 1963 (Corman 2, Price 3, Crosby 4)
Haunted Spooks, 1920 (Lloyd 3, Roach 4)
Haunted Strangler, 1958 (Karloff 3)
Haunted Summer, 1988 (Passer 2, Golan and Globus 4, Rotunno 4)
Haunted World. See Ercole al centro della terra, 1961
Haunting, 1963 (Wise 2, Bloom 3)
Haunting of Julia, 1981 (Farrow 3)
Haunting of Rosalind, 1973 (Sarandon 3)
Haunting Shadows, 1919 (King 2)
Haunting We Will Go, 1966 (Blanc 4)
Haunts of the Very Rich, 1972 (Lourié 4)
Haupt des Juarez, 1920 (Warm 4)
Hauptmann Kreutzer, 1977 (Vogler 3)
Hauptmann von Köpenick, 1907 (Freund 4)
Hauptmann von Köpenick, 1956 (Käutner 2)
Haus am Meer, 1971 (Schygulla 3)
Haus der Frauen, 1977 (Zanussi 2)
Haus der Lüge, 1925 (Pick 2, Krauss 3)
Haus der tausend Freuden, 1967 (Price 3)
Haus der Unseligen, 1922 (Tschechowa 3)
Haus des Lebens, 1952 (Fröhlich 3, Rasp 3)
Haus in der Karpfengasse, 1964 (Brejchová 3)
Haus in Montevideo, 1963 (Käutner 2)
Haus ohne Lachen, 1923 (Galeen 4)
Haus zum Mond, 1920 (Kortner 3, Hoffmann 4)
Hauser's Memory, 1970 (Siodmak 4)
Haut des marches, 1983 (Darrieux 3, Presle 3)
Haut les mains!, 1912 (Feuillade 2)
Haut les mains!. See Pleine bagarre, 1961
Haut sur ces montagnes, 1945 (McLaren 4)
Haute Lisse, 1956 (Grémillon 2)
Hautes solitudes, 1974 (Seberg 3)
Haut-le-Vent, 1944 (Vanel 3)
Hautnah, 1986 (Mueller-Stahl 3)
Havana, 1990 (Pollack 2, Arkin 3, Redford 3, Roizman 4)
Havana Widows, 1933 (Blondell 3, Barnes 4)
Havarist, 1984 (Vogler 3)
Have a Heart, 1934 (Howe 4)

Have Rocket, Will Travel, 1958 (Three Stooges 3)
Have You Thought of Talking to the Director?, 1962 (Baillie 2)
Havets Son, 1949 (Thulin 3)
Having a Go, 1983 (Armstrong 2)
Having it All, 1982 (Sidney 3)
Having Wonderful Time, 1938 (Arden 3, Ball 3, Miller 3, Rogers 3, Berman 4, Polglase 4)
Havoc, 1925 (Goulding 2)
Havre sac, 1963 (Braunberger 4)
Havsbandet, 1971 (Andersson 3, Von Sydow 3)
Havsgammar. See Rösen på Tistelön, 1916
Hawaii, 1966 (Hill 2, Andrews 3, Hackman 3, Harris 3, Midler 3, Von Sydow 3, Bernstein 4, Dunn 4, Harlan 4, Jeakins 4, Mirisch 4, Taradash 4, Trumbo 4, Van Runkle 4)
Hawaii Calls, 1938 (Bond 3)
Hawaiian Aye Aye, 1964 (Blanc 4)
Hawaiian Birds, 1936 (Fleischer 4)
Hawaiian Nights. See Down to Their Last Yacht, 1934
Hawaiian Nights, 1939 (Cortez 4)
Hawaiian Pineapple, 1930 (Terry 4)
Hawaiians, 1970 (Chaplin 3, Heston 3, Ballard 4, Mancini 4, Mirisch 4)
Hawai-Marei oki kaisen, 1942 (Shindo 3, Tsuburaya 4)
Hawk. See Ride Him Cowboy, 1932
Hawk, 1935 (Dmytryk 2)
Hawk the Slayer, 1980 (Palance 3)
Hawkins and Watkins, 1932 (Sennett 2)
Hawkins on Murder, 1973 (Stewart 3, Goldsmith 4)
Hawks and the Sparrows. See Uccellacci e uccellini, 1966
Hawk's Nest, 1928 (Christensen 2, Polito 4, Robinson 4)
Hawk's Trail, 1920 (Van Dyke 2)
Hawleys of High Street, 1933 (Launder and Gilliat 2, Bennett 4)
Hawthorne of the U.S.A., 1919 (Cruze 2, Reid 3)
Hay Foot, 1941 (Roach 4)
Hay que matar a B., 1973 (Audran 3, Meredith 3, Neal 3)
Hay Ride, 1937 (Terry 4)
Hay un niño en su futuro, 1952 (Figueroa 4)
Hayabusa daimyo, 1961 (Yamamura 3)
Hayfoot, Strawfoot, 1926 (Sennett 2)
Hayl-Moskau, 1932 (Moskvin 4)
Hayseed, 1919 (Keaton 2, Arbuckle 3)
Hayseed Romance, 1935 (Keaton 2)
Haystacks and Steeples, 1916 (Sennett 2, Swanson 3)
Haywire, 1980 (Remick 3, Robards 3)
Hazard, 1948 (Goddard 3, Dreier 4)
Hazard of Hearts, 1987 (Granger 3)
Hazard's People, 1976 (Houseman 4)
Hazel Kirke, 1916 (White 3)
Hazel's People. See Happy As the Grass Was Green, 1973
Hazukashiiyume, 1927 (Tanaka 3)
He, 1933 (Rosay 3)
He and His Sister. See On a jeho sestra, 1931
He and She. See Kanojo to kare, 1963
He and She. See Assoluto naturale, 1969
He Answered the Ad, 1913 (Bunny 3)
He Called Her In, 1913 (Dwan 2)
He Can't Make It Stick, 1943 (Fleischer 4, Hubley 4)

He Comes Up Smiling, 1918 (Dwan 2, Fairbanks 3, August 4, Marion 4)
He Cooked His Goose, 1952 (Three Stooges 3)
He Couldn't Take It, 1933 (Darwell 3, Schary 4)
He Did and He Didn't, 1916 (Sennett 2, Arbuckle 3, Normand 3)
He Died after the War. See Tokyo senso sengo hiwa, 1970
He Died with His Eyes Open. See On ne meurt que deux foix, 1985
He Doesn't Care to Be Photographed, 1917 (Cohl 4)
He Dood It Again, 1943 (Terry 4)
He Forgot to Remember, 1926 (Roach 4)
He Fought for the U.S.A., 1911 (Bushman 3)
He Found a Star, 1941 (Greenwood 3, Junge 4)
He Hired the Boss, 1943 (Day 4)
He Is My Brother, 1976 (Dmytryk 2)
He Knew Women, 1930 (Cronjager 4)
He Knows You're Alone, 1980 (Hanks 3)
He Laughed Last, 1956 (Edwards 2)
He Laughs Last, 1920 (Laurel and Hardy 3)
He Leads, Others Follow, 1919 (Daniels 3, Lloyd 3, Roach 4)
He Learned about Women, 1932 (Banton 4, Head 4, Lang 4)
He Likes Things Upside-Down, 1917 (Cohl 4)
He Loved an Actress, 1938 (Langdon 3)
He Loved the Ladies, 1914 (Sennett 2)
He Loves to Be Amused, 1917 (Cohl 4)
He Loves to Watch the Flight of Time, 1917 (Cohl 4)
He Married His Wife, 1940 (McCrea 3, Day 4, Zanuck 4)
He Poses for His Portrait, 1917 (Cohl 4)
He Ran All the Way, 1951 (Garfield 3, Winters 3, Horner 4, Howe 4, Trumbo 4, Waxman 4)
He Rides Tall, 1963 (Duryea 3)
He Ruins His Family Reputation, 1917 (Cohl 4)
He, She, and the Money. See Hans, hon, och pengarna, 1936
He Slept Well, 1917 (Cohl 4)
He Snoops to Conquer, 1944 (Formby 3)
He Stands in the Desert Counting the Seconds of His Life, 1986 (Mekas 2)
He Stayed for Breakfast, 1940 (Douglas 3, Young 3, Cohn 4, Vajda 4, Walker 4)
He Trumped Her Ace, 1930 (Sennett 2)
He Walked by Night, 1948 (Mann 2)
He Wants What He Wants When He Wants It, 1917 (Cohl 4)
he was born, he suffered, he died, 1974 (Brakhage 2)
He Was Her Man, 1934 (Bacon 2, Blondell 3, Cagney 3, Barnes 4, Grot 4, Orry-Kelly 4)
He Was Her Man, 1937 (Freleng 4, Stalling 4)
He Was Not Ill, Only Unhappy, 1917 (Cohl 4)
He Who Gets Slapped, 1924 (Sjöström 2, Chaney 3, Gilbert 3, Shearer 3, Gibbons 4, Mayer 4, Thalberg 4, Wilson 4)
He Who Gets Smacked, 1925 (Sennett 2)
He Who Laughs Last, 1910 (Bunny 3)
He Who Laughs Last, 1925 (Mohr 4)

He Who Must Die. *See* Celui qui doit mourir, 1958

He Who Rides a Tiger, 1965 (Crichton 2)

He Winked and Won, 1917 (Laurel and Hardy 3)

He Would a Hunting Go, 1913 (Sennett 2, Arbuckle 3)

He Wouldn't Stay Down, 1915 (Sennett 2)

Head. *See* Femme nue et Satan, 1959

Head, 1968 (Rafelson 2, Hopper 3, Mature 3, Nicholson 3)

Head for Business, 1911 (Lawrence 3)

Head Guy, 1929 (Roach 4)

Head Guy, 1930 (Langdon 3)

Head Man, 1928 (Young 3)

Head of the Family, 1927 (Robinson 4)

Head of the Family. *See* Padre di famiglia, 1967

Head of the House, 1916 (Eason 4)

Head of the House, 1952 (Leacock 2)

Head On, 1980 (Huston 2)

Head over Heels, 1922 (Menjou 3, Normand 3)

Head over Heels, 1937 (Matthews 3, Balcon 4, Junge 4)

Head over Heels, 1979 (Grahame 3)

Head over Heels in Love. *See* Head over Heels, 1937

Headdresses of Different Periods. *See* Histoire de chapeaux, 1910

Headin' East, 1937 (Three Stooges 3)

Headin' for Danger, 1928 (Miller 4, Plunkett 4)

Headin' South, 1918 (Fairbanks 3)

Headless Horseman, 1922 (Rogers 3)

Headless Horseman, 1934 (Iwerks 4)

Headleys at Home, 1938 (Beavers 3)

Headline Bands, 1939 (Hutton 3)

Headline Shooter, 1933 (Bellamy 3, Pangborn 3, Walthall 3, Benchley 4, D'Agostino 4, Musuraca 4, Polglase 4, Steiner 4)

Headline Woman, 1935 (Lewis 2, Bond 3, Pangborn 3)

Headlines of Destruction. *See* Je suis un sentimental, 1955

Headquarters United Nations, 1947 (Rathaus 4)

Heads or Tails. *See* Pile ou face, 1980

Heads Up, 1930 (Green 4)

Heads Up, Charly. *See* Kopf hoch, Charly, 1926

Healer, 1935 (Bellamy 3, Rooney 3)

Health, 1979 (Altman 2, Bacall 3, Garner 3, Jackson 3)

Health Farm, 1936 (Terry 4)

Health for the Nation, 1940 (Richardson 3)

Health in Industry, 1938 (Watt 2)

Healthy and Happy, 1919 (Laurel and Hardy 3)

Healthy Neighborhood, 1913 (Sennett 2)

Healthy, Wealthy, and Dumb, 1938 (Three Stooges 3)

Heap Big Chief, 1919 (Daniels 3, Lloyd 3, Roach 4)

Hear 'em Rave, 1918 (Daniels 3, Lloyd 3, Roach 4)

Hear Me Good, 1957 (Head 4)

Hearse, 1980 (Cotten 3)

Hearst and Davies Affair, 1985 (Mitchum 3)

Heart. *See* Kokoru, 1973

Heart and Soul, 1917 (Bara 3)

Heart and Soul, 1988 (Jones 4)

Heart Beat, 1978 (Kovacs 4)

Heart Beat, 1980 (Nolte 3, Spacek 3)

Heart Beats of Long Ago, 1910 (Griffith 2, Bitzer 4)

Heart Buster, 1924 (Mix 3)

Heart Condition, 1990 (Hoskins 3)

Heart for a Song. *See* Srdce za písničku, 1933

Heart in Pawn, 1919 (Hayakawa 3)

Heart Is a Lonely Hunter, 1968 (Arkin 3, Howe 4)

Heart Line, 1921 (Barnes 4)

Heart of a Child, 1920 (Nazimova 3)

Heart of a Child, 1958 (Pleasence 3, Rank 4)

Heart of a Cowboy, 1909 (Anderson 3)

Heart of a Cracksman, 1913 (Reid 3)

Heart of a Gambler, 1913 (Anderson 3)

Heart of a Man, 1959 (Wilcox 2, Neagle 3, Rank 4)

Heart of a Nation. *See* Untel Pere et Fils, 1943

Heart of a Painted Woman, 1915 (Guy 2)

Heart of Alaska, 1924 (Costello 3)

Heart of Arizona, 1938 (Harlan 4, Head 4)

Heart of a Siren, 1925 (Webb 3, LeMaire 4)

Heart of a Texan, 1922 (Canutt 4)

Heart of a Tigress, 1980 (Johnson 3)

Heart of Flame, 1915 (Eason 4)

Heart of Gold, 1915 (Eason 4)

Heart of Jim Brice, 1913 (Costello 3)

Heart of Maryland, 1915 (Brenon 2)

Heart of Maryland, 1927 (Bacon 2, Costello 3, Loy 3, Mohr 4)

Heart of New York, 1932 (LeRoy 2)

Heart of Nora Flynn, 1916 (De Mille 2, Buckland 4, Macpherson 4)

Heart of Oyama, 1908 (Griffith 2, Lawrence 3)

Heart of Paris. *See* Gribouille, 1937

Heart of Princess Mitsari, 1915 (Cruze 2)

Heart of Salome, 1926 (Pidgeon 3)

Heart of Scotland, 1959 (Grierson 2)

Heart of Show Business, 1957 (De Mille 2, Chevalier 3, Crosby 3, Horne 3, Lancaster 3)

Heart of Spain, 1937 (Maddow 4, North 4)

Heart of Texas Ryan, 1917 (Mix 3)

Heart of the Golden West, 1942 (Rogers 3)

Heart of the Hills, 1914 (Reid 3)

Heart of the Matter, 1953 (Elliott 3, Finch 3, Howard 3, Schell 3, Dalrymple 4, Greene 4, Korda 4)

Heart of the Matter, 1983 (Greene 4)

Heart of the Mountains. *See* Kokoro no sanmyaku, 1966

Heart of the North, 1938 (Deutsch 4)

Heart of the Rio Grande, 1942 (Autry 3)

Heart of the Rockies, 1938 (Canutt 4)

Heart of the Rockies, 1951 (Rogers 3)

Heart of the Sheriff, 1915 (Mix 3)

Heart of the Stag, 1984 (Rosenman 4)

Heart of the Wilds, 1918 (Neilan 2)

Heart of the Yukon, 1926 (Van Dyke 2)

Heart of Variety, 1969 (Heston 3)

Heart of Wetona, 1918 (Talmadge 3)

Heart o' the Hills, 1919 (Gilbert 3, Pickford 3, Rosher 4)

Heart Punch, 1932 (Eason 4)

Heart Song. *See* Only Girl, 1933

Heart Thief, 1927 (Levien 4)

Heart to Heart, 1928 (Astor 3, Polito 4)

Heart to Let, 1921 (Folsey 4)

Heart Trouble, 1928 (Langdon 3)

Heartbeat. *See* Schpountz, 1937

Heartbeat, 1946 (Wood 2, Menjou 3, Rathbone 3, Rogers 3, Ryskind 4)

Heartbeat, 1968 (Hakim 4)

Heartbeeps, 1981 (Van Runkle 4, Whitlock 4, Williams 4)

Heartbreak, 1931 (August 4, Friedhofer 4, Grot 4)

Heartbreak Hotel, 1988 (Weld 3, Delerue 4)

Heartbreak House, 1989 (Harrison 3)

Heartbreak Kid, 1972 (Cahn 4, May 4, Roizman 4, Sylbert 4)

Heartbreak Ridge, 1986 (Eastwood 3)

Heartbreakers, 1984 (Ballhaus 4)

Heartburn, 1986 (Nichols 2, Nicholson 3, Streep 3, Almendros 4)

Hearth Fires. *See* Feux de la chandeleur, 1972

Heartland, 1985 (Hopkins 3)

Hearts, 1990 (Fonda 3)

Hearts Adrift, 1914 (Porter 2, Pickford 3)

Hearts Afire. *See* Hearts in Exile, 1915

Hearts Aflame, 1923 (Mayer 4)

Hearts and Diamonds, 1914 (Bunny 3)

Hearts and Dollars, 1924 (Litvak 2)

Hearts and Flowers, 1914 (Bushman 3)

Hearts and Flowers, 1919 (Sennett 2)

Hearts and Horses, 1913 (Dwan 2, Reid 3)

Hearts and Masks, 1914 (Mix 3)

Hearts and Minds. *See* Uomo da rispettare, 1973

Hearts and Planets, 1915 (Sennett 2)

Hearts and Saddles, 1917 (Mix 3)

Hearts and Sparks, 1916 (Sennett 2, Swanson 3)

Hearts and Spurs, 1925 (Van Dyke 2, Lombard 3)

Hearts Are Thumps, 1937 (Roach 4)

Hearts Are Trumps, 1920 (Ingram 2, Mathis 4, Seitz 4)

Heart's Desire, 1915 (Mix 3)

Hearts Divided, 1936 (Borzage 2, Bondi 3, Davies 3, Horton 3, McDaniel 3, Powell 3, Rains 3, Brown 4, Folsey 4, Korngold 4, Orry-Kelly 4, Robinson 4)

Hearts in Bondage, 1936 (Ayres 3, Walthall 3, Brown 4)

Hearts in Exile, 1915 (Carré 4, Edeson 4)

Hearts in Exile, 1929 (Curtiz 2, Costello 3)

Hearts in Shadow, 1915 (Eason 4)

Hearts in Springtime. *See* Glamour Boy, 1941

Hearts of Age, 1934 (Welles 2)

Hearts of Fire, 1987 (Barry 4)

Hearts of Humanity, 1936 (Baxter 2)

Hearts of Lieutenants. *See* Löjtnantshjärtan, 1941

Hearts of Oak, 1924 (Ford 2, Bosworth 3)

Hearts of the Jungle, 1915 (Mix 3)

Hearts of the West, 1975 (Arkin 3, Bridges 3, Pleasence 3)

Hearts of the World, 1918 (Griffith 2, Von Stroheim 2, Gish 3, Bitzer 4, Coward 4)

Hearts or Diamonds, 1918 (King 2)

Hearts Up, 1921 (Carey 3)

Hearts Upon the Sea. *See* Cuori su mare, 1950

Heat, 1972 (Warhol 2)

Heat, 1987 (Reynolds 3, Goldman 4, Tavoularis 4)

Heat and Dust, 1982 (Ivory 2, Christie 3, Jhabvala 4, Lassally 4)

Heat Haze. *See* Kagero, 1969

Heat Lightning, 1934 (LeRoy 2, Darwell 3, Orry-Kelly 4)

Heat of Anger, 1971 (Cobb 3, Hayward 3)

Heat of the Day, 1989 (Pinter 4)

Heat Wave, 1935 (Rank 4)

Heat Wave. *See* House Across the Lake, 1954

Heathcliff: The Movie, 1986 (Blanc 4)

Heat's On, 1943 (West 3, Cahn 4, Planer 4, Plunkett 4)

Heave Away My Johnny, 1948 (Halas and Batchelor 4)

Heave Ho!. *See* Hej rup!, 1934

Heaven, 1987 (Keaton 3, Mancini 4)

Heaven and Earth, 1956 (Slocombe 4)

Heaven and Hell. *See* Tengoku to jigoku, 1963

Heaven and Hell of Bohemia. *See* Plameny života, 1920

Heaven and Pancakes. *See* Himmel och pannkaka, 1959

Heaven Avenges, 1912 (Griffith 2, Bitzer 4)

Heaven Can Wait, 1943 (Lubitsch 2, Ameche 3, Calhern 3, Coburn 3, Tierney 3, Basevi 4, Cronjager 4, Newman 4, Raphaelson 4)

Heaven Can Wait, 1978 (Beatty 3, Christie 3, Mason 3, Fraker 4, Henry 4, May 4, Van Runkle 4)

Heaven Fell That Night. *See* Bijoutiers du clair de lune, 1958

Heaven Help Us, 1985 (Sutherland 3, Ondříček 4)

Heaven Knows, Mr. Allison, 1957 (Huston 2, Kerr 3, Mitchum 3, Auric 4, Morris 4)

Heaven on Earth, 1927 (Gibbons 4, Gillespie 4)

Heaven on Earth, 1931 (Ayres 3, Carradine 3)

Heaven Only Knows, 1947 (Struss 4)

Heaven Scent, 1956 (Blanc 4, Jones 4)

Heaven with a Barbed Wire Fence, 1939 (Bond 3, Ford 3, Cronjager 4, Trumbo 4)

Heaven with a Gun, 1969 (Ford 3)

Heavenly Body, 1943 (Lamarr 3, Powell 3, Gillespie 4, Irene 4, Kaper 4, Mayer 4, Reisch 4)

Heavenly Days, 1944 (Estabrook 4, Hunt 4)

Heavenly Daze, 1948 (Three Stooges 3)

Heavenly Puss, 1948 (Hanna and Barbera 4)

Heavens Above, 1963 (Boulting 2, Sellers 3)

Heaven's Gate, 1980 (Cimino 2, Bridges 3, Cotten 3, Huppert 3, Hurt 3, Rourke 3, Reynolds 4, Zsigmond 4)

Heavens! My Husband!, 1932 (Sennett 2)

Heavy Petting, 1988 (Mancini 4)

Heavy Seas, 1923 (Roach 4)

Heavy Traffic, 1973 (Bakshi 4)

Hebihime douchuh, 1949 (Hasegawa 3, Kyo 3, Yamada 3, Miyagawa 4, Yoda 4)

Hebihime-sama, 1940 (Hasegawa 3, Yamada 3)

Hebihime-sama, 1951 (Hasegawa 3)

Hebrew Lesson, 1972 (Mankowitz 4)

Heckling Hare, 1941 (Avery 4, Blanc 4, Maltese 4, Stalling 4)

Hectic Days. *See* Goryachie dyenechki, 1935

Hedda, 1975 (Jackson 3, Slocombe 4)

Hedda Gabler, 1919 (Pastrone 2)

Hedda Gabler, 1924 (Nielsen 3)

Hedgehog in the Mist, 1976 (Norstein 4)

Hedy, 1965 (Warhol 2)

Hedy the Shoplifter or The Fourteen Year Old Girl. *See* Hedy, 1965

Heer, 1956 (Biswas 4)

Heera Panna, 1974 (Anand 3)

Heerak Rajar Deshe, 1979 (Datta 4)

Heeren der Meere, 1922 (Korda 2)

Heideschulmeister Uwe Karsten, 1933 (Tschechowa 3)

Heideschulmeister Uwe Karsten, 1954 (Wagner 4)

Heidi, 1937 (Dwan 2, Temple 3, Miller 4)

Heidi, 1968 (Redgrave 3, Schell 3, Simmons 3)

Heidi's Song, 1982 (Cahn 4, Hanna and Barbera 4)

Height of Battle. *See* Senka no hate, 1950

Height of Glory. *See* Na viershina slavy, 1916

Heiji happy-aku-ya-cho, 1949 (Hasegawa 3)

Heilige Berg, 1926 (Riefenstahl 2)

Heilige Flamme, 1931 (Fröhlich 3)

Heilige Lüge, 1927 (Holger-Madsen 2, Homolka 3)

Heilige Simplizie, 1920 (Von Harbou 4)

Heilige und der Narr, 1928 (Manès 3)

Heilige und ihr Narr, 1928 (Andrejew 4)

Heimkehr, 1928 (Fröhlich 3, Pommer 4)

Heimkehr, 1941 (Röhrig 4)

Heimkehr des alten Herrn, 1977 (Schygulla 3)

Heimkehr des Odysseus, 1918 (Wiene 2)

Heimkehr ins Glück, 1950 (Staudte 2)

Heimlich nach St. Pauli, 1964 (Mansfield 3)

Heimliche Ehen, 1956 (Mueller-Stahl 3)

Heimlichkeiten, 1968 (Staudte 2)

Heimweh, 1927 (Dieterle 2)

Heinrich der Vierte, 1926 (Courant 4)

Heinze's Resurrection, 1913 (Sennett 2, Normand 3)

Heir Conditioned, 1955 (Blanc 4, Freleng 4)

Heir to Genghis Khan. *See* **Potomok Chingis-Khan, 1928**

Heiratsnest, 1927 (Reisch 4)

Heiress, 1949 (Wyler 2, Clift 3, De Havilland 3, Hopkins 3, Richardson 3, Copland 4, Head 4, Hornbeck 4, Horner 4)

Heiress at Coffee Dan's, 1917 (Love 3)

Heiresses. *See* Schimbul de miine, 1959

Heiresses. *See* Orökseg, 1980

Heirs. *See* Herederos, 1969

Heisse Ernte, 1956 (Herlth 4)

Heisses Blut, 1911 (Gad 2, Nielsen 3, Freund 4)

Heisses Spiel fur Hart Manner. *See* Rebus, 1968

Heist. *See* $, 1971

Hej rup!, 1934 (Heller 4)

Held aller Mädchenträume, 1929 (Reisch 4)

Held By the Enemy, 1920 (Crisp 3)

Held Up for the Makin's, 1920 (Eason 4)

Helden, 1959 (Warm 4)

Heldorado, 1946 (Rogers 3)

Helen la Belle, 1957 (Reiniger 4)

Helen Morgan Story, 1957 (Newman 3, McCord 4, Prinz 4)

Helen of Four Gates, 1920 (Hepworth 2)

Helen of Troy. *See* Sköna Helena, 1951

Helen of Troy, 1955 (Wise 2, Baker 3, Bardot 3, Adam 4, Steiner 4, Stradling 4)

Helena, 1990 (Winters 3)

Hélène, 1936 (Barrault 3, Burel 4)

Helen's Babies, 1924 (Bow 3, Horton 3, Daniels 4)

Helen's Marriage, 1911 (Sennett 2)

Helicon, 1991 (Coburn 3)

Helicopter, 1944 (Terry 4)

Helicopter Spies, 1968 (Carradine 3)

Heliotrope, 1921 (Rosson 4)

Hell and High Water, 1954 (Fuller 2, LeMaire 4, Newman 4, Wheeler 4)

Hell Below, 1933 (Durante 3, Huston 3, Montgomery 3, Young 3, Rosson 4)

Hell Below Zero, 1954 (Baker 3, Ladd 3, Vetchinsky 4)

Hell Bent, 1918 (Ford 2, Carey 3)

Hell Bent for Glory. *See* Lafayette Escadrille, 1957

Hell Bent for Heaven, 1926 (Blackton 2, Musuraca 4)

Hell Bent for Leather, 1960 (Murphy 3)

Hell Bound for Alaska. *See* Darkening Trail, 1915

Hell Canyon Outlaws, 1957 (Crosby 4)

Hell Diggers, 1921 (Reid 3)

Hell Divers, 1931 (Beery 3, Gillespie 4)

Hell Drivers, 1931 (Gable 3)

Hell Drivers, 1957 (Baker 3, Connery 3, Lom 3, Rank 4, Unsworth 4)

Hell Harbor, 1930 (King 2)

Hell, Heaven and Hoboken. *See* I Was Monty's Double, 1958

Hell Hound of Alaska. *See* Darkening Trail, 1915

Hell Hunters, 1988 (Granger 3)

Hell in Korea. *See* Hill in Korea, 1956

Hell in the City. *See* Nella città l'inferno, 1958

Hell in the Heavens, 1934 (Glennon 4)

Hell in the Pacific, 1968 (Boorman 2, Marvin 3, Mifune 3, Hall 4, Schifrin 4)

Hell Is a City, 1960 (Baker 3, Pleasence 3, Carreras 4)

Hell Is for Heroes, 1962 (Siegel 2, Coburn 3, McQueen 3, Blanke 4, Rosenman 4)

Hell Is Sold Out, 1951 (Attenborough 3, Lom 3)

Hell Morgan's Girl, 1916 (Chaney 3)

Hell on Frisco Bay, 1956 (Ladd 3, Mansfield 3, Robinson 3, Wray 3, Seitz 4, Steiner 4)

Hell or High Water, 1954 (Widmark 3)

Hell River. *See* Partizani, 1974

Hell River Bad Company, 1979 (Theodorakis 4)

Hell Ship Mutiny, 1957 (Carradine 3, Lorre 3)

Hell Spit Flexion, 1981 (Brakhage 2)

Hell to Eternity, 1960 (Hayakawa 3)

Hell Unlimited, 1976 (McLaren 4)

Hell Up in Harlem, 1973 (Cohen 2)

Hell with Heroes, 1968 (Cardinale 3, Jones 4)

Hellas, 1959 (Schell 3)

Hellbenders. *See* Crudeli, 1966

Hell-Bent for Election, 1944 (Hubley 4)

Hellcats of the Navy, 1957 (Reagan 3)

Helldorado, 1935 (Cruze 2, Bellamy 3, Walthall 3, Lasky 4, Seitz 4)

Hellé, 1972 (Vadim 2, Gégauff 4, Renoir 4)

Heller in Pink Tights, 1960 (Cukor 2, Loren 3, Novarro 3, O'Brien 3, Quinn 3, Head 4, Nichols 4, Ponti 4)

Heller Wahn, 1982 (Von Trotta 2, Schygulla 3, Vogler 3, Müller 4)

Hellfighters, 1968 (Wayne 3, Clothier 4, Head 4, Needham 4, Rosenman 4, Whitlock 4)

Hellfire, 1949 (Canutt 4)

Hell-Fire Austin, 1932 (McCord 4)

Hellfire Club, 1961 (Cushing 3, Sangster 4)

Hellgate, 1952 (Bond 3, Hayden 3)

Her First Egg, 1931 (Terry 4)
Her First Elopement, 1921 (Wood 2)
Her First Mate, 1933 (Wyler 2)
Her First Mistake, 1918 (Sennett 2)
Her First Romance, 1940 (Dmytryk 2, Ladd 3)
Her First Romance, 1951 (O'Brien 3)
Her Forgotten Past, 1933 (Walthall 3)
Her Friend the Bandit, 1914 (Sennett 2, Normand 3)
Her Gallant Knights, 1913 (Cruze 2)
Her Generous Way, 1909 (Lawrence 3)
Her Gilded Cage, 1923 (Wood 2, Swanson 3)
Her Good Name, 1917 (Van Dyke 2)
Her Grave Mistake, 1914 (Chaney 3)
Her Great Adventure, 1918 (Love 3)
Her Greatest Love, 1917 (Bara 3)
Her Great Scoop, 1914 (Ingram 2, Costello 3)
Her Guardian, 1913 (Bosworth 3)
Her Harem. See Harem, 1967
Her Heritage, 1919 (Buchanan 3)
Her Hero, 1911 (Bunny 3, Costello 3, Talmadge 3)
Her Highness and the Bellboy, 1945 (Walters 2, Allyson 3, Lamarr 3, Moorehead 3, Walker 3, Mercer 4, Pasternak 4, Stradling 4)
Her Highness' Young Washerwoman. See Pradlenka Jeho Jasnosti, 1930
Her Hour of Triumph, 1912 (Bushman 3)
Her Humble Ministry, 1911 (Lawrence 3)
Her Husband Lies, 1937 (Calhern 3, D'Agostino 4, Head 4, Schulberg 4, Shamroy 4)
Her Husband's Affairs, 1947 (Ball 3, Horton 3, Duning 4, Hakim 4, Hecht 4, Lederer 4)
Her Husband's Friend, 1920 (Niblo 2, Barnes 4)
Her Husband's Honor, 1918 (Polito 4)
Her Husband's Trademark, 1922 (Wood 2, Swanson 3)
Her Indian Hero, 1909 (Olcott 2)
Her Innocent Marriage, 1913 (Dwan 2)
Her Jungle Love, 1938 (Lamour 3, Milland 3, Head 4, Siodmak 4)
Her Kid Sister, 1910 (White 3)
Her Kind of Man, 1946 (Waxman 4)
Her Kingdom of Desire, 1922 (Mayer 4)
Her Kingdom of Dreams, 1920 (Neilan 2, Gaudio 4)
Her Last Affair, 1935 (Powell and Pressburger 2, Withers 3, Dalrymple 4)
Her Last Chance, 1914 (Sennett 2)
Her Legacy, 1913 (Ince 4)
Her Lesson, 1916 (Anderson 3)
Her Life's Story, 1914 (Chaney 3)
Her Little Slipper, 1910 (White 3)
Her Love Story, 1924 (Dwan 2, Swanson 3)
Her Lucky Night, 1945 (Bruckman 4, Mohr 4)
Her Mad Bargain, 1921 (Mayer 4)
Her Majesty, 1931 (Dieterle 2)
Her Majesty, Love, 1931 (Fields 3)
Her Man, 1930 (Garnett 2)
Her Man Gilbey. See English Without Tears, 1944
Her Man o' War, 1926 (Fort 4, Sullivan 4)
Her Marble Heart, 1916 (Sennett 2)
Her Master's Voice, 1936 (Reynolds 4, Schary 4, Wanger 4)
Her Melody. See Hennes melodi, 1940

Her Mother Interferes, 1911 (Sennett 2)
Her Mother's Necklace, 1914 (Crisp 3)
Her Mother's Oath, 1913 (Griffith 2, Walthall 3, Bitzer 4)
Her Nature Dance, 1917 (Sennett 2)
Her Necklace, 1910 (White 3)
Her New Beau, 1913 (Sennett 2)
Her New Hat, 1910 (White 3)
Her Night of Promise, 1924 (Kräly 4)
Her Night of Romance, 1924 (Colman 3, Schenck 4)
Her Old Sweetheart, 1912 (Bunny 3)
Her Only Way, 1918 (Talmadge 3)
Her Own Country, 1911 (Dwan 2)
Her Own Free Will, 1924 (Hunt 4)
Her Painted Hero, 1915 (Sennett 2)
Her Panelled Door. See Woman with No Name, 1950
Her Pet, 1911 (Sennett 2)
Her Photograph, 1910 (White 3)
Her Polished Family, 1912 (Sullivan 4)
Her Primitive Man, 1944 (Horton 3, Benchley 4)
Her Primitive Mate. See No Place to Go, 1927
Her Private Life, 1929 (Korda 2, Pidgeon 3, Grot 4, Korda 4, Seitz 4)
Her Ragged Knight, 1914 (Lawrence 3)
Her Realization, 1915 (Anderson 3)
Her Reputation. See Broadway Bad, 1933
Her Resale Value, 1933 (Eason 4)
Her Return, 1915 (Anderson 3)
Her Sacrifice, 1911 (Griffith 2, Bitzer 4)
Her Screen Idol, 1918 (Sennett 2)
Her Second Husband, 1917 (Polito 4)
Her Secretary, 1910 (White 3)
Her Sister, 1925 (Adrian 4)
Her Sister from Paris, 1925 (Colman 3, Edeson 4, Menzies 4, Schenck 4)
Her Sister's Children, 1911 (Bunny 3)
Her Sister's Secret, 1913 (Cruze 2)
Her Sister's Secret, 1946 (Ulmer 2, Planer 4)
Her Slight Mistake, 1915 (Mix 3)
Her Soldier Sweetheart, 1910 (Olcott 2)
Her Splendid Folly, 1933 (Beavers 3)
Her Strange Desire. See Potiphar's Wife, 1931
Her Summer Hero, 1927 (Plunkett 4)
Her Sweetheart. See Christopher Bean, 1933
Her Terrible Ordeal, 1909 (Griffith 2, Bitzer 4)
Her Torpedoed Love, 1917 (Sennett 2)
Her Twelve Men, 1954 (Garson 3, Ryan 3, Houseman 4, Kaper 4, Rose 4, Ruttenberg 4)
Her Twin Brother, 1910 (White 3)
Her Twin Brother, 1914 (Meredyth 4)
Her Two Sons, 1911 (Lawrence 3)
Her Unwilling Husband, 1920 (Sweet 3)
Her Wedding Bell, 1913 (Sweet 3)
Her Wedding Night, 1930 (Bow 3)
Her Wild Oat, 1927 (Neilan 2, Moore 3, Young 3, Folsey 4, Robinson 4)
Hera Pheri, 1976 (Bachchan 3)
Herakles, 1962 (Herzog 2)
Herb Alpert and the Tijuana Brass Double Feature, 1966 (Hubley 4)
Herbe rouge, 1985 (Léaud 3)
Herbie, 1915 (Lucas 2)
Herbie Rides Again, 1974 (Stevenson 2)
Herbier. See Citadelle du silence, 1937
Herbstonate, 1978 (Bergman 3, Björnstrand 3, Josephson 3, Ullmann 3, Nykvist 4)

Hercule, 1938 (Berry 3, Fernandel 3)
Hercule ou l'incorruptible, 1938 (Brasseur 3)
Hercules, 1983 (Donaggio 4, Golan and Globus 4)
Hercules and the Big Stick. See Douze Travaux d'Hercule, 1910
Hercules and the Captive Women. See Ercole alla conquista di Atlantide, 1961
Hercules at the Center of the Earth. See Ercole al centro della terra, 1961
Hercules Goes Bananas. See Hercules Goes to New York, 1970
Hercules Goes to New York, 1970 (Schwarzenegger 3)
Herdsman, 1982 (Xie 2)
Here and There, 1961 (Kuri 4)
Here Come the Co-eds, 1945 (Abbott and Costello 3)
Here Come the Girls, 1918 (Daniels 3, Lloyd 3, Roach 4)
Here Come the Girls, 1953 (Hope 3, Head 4)
Here Come the Huggetts, 1947 (Box 4, Rank 4)
Here Come the Jets, 1959 (Struss 4)
Here Come the Nelsons, 1952 (Hudson 3)
Here Come the Waves, 1944 (Crosby 3, De Carlo 3, Hutton 3, Head 4, Mercer 4)
Here Comes Carter, 1936 (Orry-Kelly 4)
Here Comes Cookie, 1935 (McLeod 2, Head 4)
Here Comes Mr. Jordan, 1941 (Costello 3, Horton 3, Montgomery 3, Rains 3, Buchman 4, Cohn 4, Head 4, Miller 4, Walker 4)
Here Comes Mr. Zerk, 1943 (Langdon 3)
Here Comes Santa Claus. See J'ai recontré le Père Noel, 1984
Here Comes the Bride, 1919 (Barrymore 3)
Here Comes the Groom, 1934 (Bond 3, Brown 4, Robinson 4)
Here Comes the Groom, 1951 (Capra 2, Crosby 3, Lamour 3, Wyman 3, Barnes 4, Carmichael 4, Head 4, Mercer 4, Riskin 4)
Here Comes the Huggetts, 1948 (Dors 3)
Here Comes the Navy, 1934 (Bacon 2, Cagney 3, Edeson 4, Orry-Kelly 4)
Here Comes the Sun, 1945 (Baxter 2, Crazy Gang 3)
Here Comes the Waves, 1944 (Dreier 4, Lang 4)
Here Comes Troubles, 1948 (Roach 4)
Here I Am, 1962 (Baillie 2)
Here I Am a Stranger, 1939 (Brown 4, Miller 4)
Here I Come. See Harvard, Here I Come, 1941
Here Is a Man. See All That Money Can Buy, 1941
Here Is My Heart, 1934 (Crosby 3, Banton 4, Struss 4, Zukor 4)
Here Is the Land, 1937 (Rotha 2)
Here Is Tomorrow, 1941 (Maddow 4)
Here Is Your Life. See Här har du ditt liv, 1966
Here Kiddie Kiddie, 1960 (Hanna and Barbera 4)
Here Today, Gone Tamale, 1959 (Freleng 4)
Here We Come. See Här kommer vi, 1947
Here We Go, 1951 (McKimson 4)
Here We Go Again, 1942 (Dwan 2)
Here We Go Round the Mulberry Bush, 1967 (Elliott 3)
Herederos, 1969 (Léaud 3)

Heredity, 1912 (Griffith 2, Carey 3, Bitzer 4)

Here's Las Vegas. *See* Spree, 1967

Here's to Good Old Jail, 1938 (Terry 4)

Here's to Romance, 1935 (Friedhofer 4, Lasky 4, Levien 4)

Here's to the Girls. *See* Ojosan kampai, 1949

Here's Your Life. *See* Här Har du Ditt Liv, 1968

Hergün ölmektense, 1964 (Güney 2)

Heritage, 1953 (Hubley 4)

Héritage du croissant, 1950 (Leenhardt 2)

Heritage of Eve, 1913 (August 4)

Heritage of Five Hundred Thousand People. *See* Gojuman-nin no isan, 1963

Heritage of the Desert, 1924 (Hathaway 2, Daniels 3)

Heritage of the Desert, 1932 (Hathaway 2, Scott 3)

Heritage of the Desert, 1939 (Harlan 4, Head 4, Young 4)

Héritier, 1973 (Belmondo 3)

Héritier des Mondésir, 1939 (Becker 2, Berry 3, Fernandel 3, Aurenche 4, Bost 4)

Héritières. *See* Orökseg, 1980

Herman Teirlinck, 1953 (Storck 2)

Hermann und Dorothea von heute. *See* Liebesleute, 1935

Hermanos del hierro, 1963 (Fernández 2, Armendáriz 3, Figueroa 4)

Hermanos Muerte, 1964 (Fernández 2)

Hermit, 1914 (Eason 4)

Hermit's Gold, 1911 (Dwan 2)

Hero, 1917 (Laurel and Hardy 3)

Hero, 1923 (Schulberg 4, Struss 4)

Hero. *See* Nayak, 1966

Hero. *See* Bloomfield, 1970

Hero Ain't Nothin' But a Sandwich, 1977 (Corman 2)

Hero and the Terror, 1988 (Golan and Globus 4)

Hero for a Day, 1953 (Terry 4)

Hero for a Night. *See* Jrdina jedné noci, 1935

Hero for Hire, 1990 (Welch 3)

Hero of Liao Yang, 1904 (Bitzer 4)

Hero of Little Italy, 1913 (Griffith 2, Carey 3, Sweet 3, Bitzer 4)

Hero of the Hour, 1980 (Johnson 3)

Hérodiade, 1910 (Gaumont 4)

Héroe desconocido, 1981 (Figueroa 4)

Heroes, 1916 (Laurel and Hardy 3)

Heroes. *See* Eroi, 1972

Heroes, 1977 (Field 3, Ford 3)

Heroes and Husbands, 1922 (Schulberg 4)

Heroes and Sinners. *See* Héros sont fatigués, 1955

Heroes Are Tired. *See* Héros sont fatigués, 1955

Heroes for Sale, 1933 (Wellman 2, Barthelmess 3, Bond 3, Orry-Kelly 4)

Heroes in Yellow and Blue. *See* Hjältar i gult och blått, 1940

Heroes of Shipka. *See* Geroite na Shipka, 1954

Heroes of Telemark, 1965 (Mann 2, Douglas 3, Harris 3, Redgrave 3, Arnold 4, Fulton 4)

Heroes of the Hills, 1938 (Canutt 4)

Heroes of the Mine, 1913 (Pearson 2)

Heroes of the Street, 1922 (Goulding 2)

Héroes sont fatigués, 1955 (Alekan 4)

Heroic Harold, 1910 (White 3)

Heroine of Mons, 1914 (Howard 3)

Héroines du mal, 1978 (Borowczyk 2, Braunberger 4)

Héroïque Monsieur Boniface, 1949 (Fernandel 3)

Heroïsme de Paddy, 1916 (Gance 2, Burel 4, Gaumont 4)

Heroismus einer Franzosin, 1913 (Porten 3, Messter 4)

Heron and the Crane, 1975 (Norstein 4)

Héros de l'air, 1962 (Delerue 4)

Héros de la Marne, 1938 (Raimu 3, Ibert 4)

Heros for Sale, 1933 (Young 3)

Hero's Island, 1962 (Mason 3, Oates 3, Stanton 3, McCord 4)

Héros sont fatigués, 1955 (Félix 3, Montand 3)

Herr Arnes Pengar, 1919 (Molander 2, Stiller 2, Jaenzon 4, Magnusson 4)

Herr Arnes penningar, 1954 (Andersson 3)

Herr auf Bestellung, 1930 (Reisch 4)

Herr Bürovorsteher, 1931 (Planer 4)

Herr der Bestien, 1921 (Hoffmann 4)

Herr der Galgenleiter. *See* Bankkrasch Unter den Linden, 1925

Herr der Liebe, 1919 (Hoffmann 4, Pommer 4)

Herr Doktor, 1917 (Feuillade 2)

Herr Finanz-direktor, 1930 (Warm 4)

Herr Meets Hare, 1945 (Blanc 4, Freleng 4, Maltese 4, Stalling 4)

Herr Meister und Frau Meisterin, 1928 (Albers 3)

Herr och fru Stockholm, 1921 (Garbo 3)

Herr Puntila und sein Knecht Matti, 1955 (Cavalcanti 2, Eisler 4)

Herr Sanders lebt gefährlich, 1943 (Wagner 4)

Herr Tartuff. *See* Tartuff, 1925

Herr über Leben und Tod, 1919 (Pick 2)

Herr über Leben und Tod, 1955 (Schell 3)

Herr und Hund, 1963 (Herlth 4)

Herren der Meere, 1920 (Korda 4)

Herren mit der weissen Weste, 1970 (Staudte 2)

Herrenpartie, 1964 (Staudte 2)

Herrin der Welt, 1920 (Hunte 4)

Herrin der Welt, 1960 (Cervi 3, Presle 3)

Herrin von Atlantis. *See* Atlantide, 1932

Herring Murder Case, 1931 (Fleischer 4)

Herring Murder Mystery, 1944 (Fleischer 4)

Herringbone Clouds. *See* Iwashigumo, 1958

Herrliches Dasein, 1974 (Staudte 2)

Herrscher, 1937 (Jannings 3, Herlth 4, Von Harbou 4)

Hers to Hold, 1943 (Cotten 3, Durbin 3, Adrian 4)

Herz der Welt, 1952 (Herlth 4, Warm 4)

Herz des Königin, 1940 (Röhrig 4)

Herz geht vor Anker, 1940 (Fröhlich 3)

Herz kehrt Heim, 1956 (Schell 3)

Herz modern möbliert, 1940 (Frölich 3)

Herz vom Hochland, 1920 (Hoffmann 4)

Herz von St. Pauli, 1957 (Albers 3)

Herzbube. *See* King, Queen, Knave, 1972

Herzensphotograph, 1928 (Andrejew 4)

Herzog Blaubart's Burg, 1964 (Powell and Pressburger 2, Heckroth 4)

Herzog Ferrantes Ende, 1922 (Wegener 3, Freund 4)

Herzog von Reichstadt, 1931 (Planer 4)

Herzogin Satanella, 1920 (Curtiz 2)

Herzogin von Langeais. *See* Liebe, 1926

Herztrumpt, 1920 (Dupont 2)

He's a Cockeyed Wonder, 1950 (Rooney 3)

Hesitating Houses, 1926 (Sennett 2)

Hesokuri shacho, 1956 (Tsukasa 3)

Hessian Renegades, 1909 (Griffith 2)

Hest pá sommerferie. *See* Horse on Holiday, 1959

Hesten paa Kongens Nytorv, 1941 (Henning-Jensen 2)

Hester Street, 1974 (Silver 2)

Het bezoek, 1971 (Müller 4)

Heterodyne, 1967 (Frampton 2)

Hets, 1944 (Sjöberg 2, Zetterling 2, Björnstrand 3)

Hetszàzeves szerelem, 1921 (Lukas 3)

Hetty King—Performer, 1970 (Anderson 2)

Heure de rêve, 1930 (Brasseur 3)

Heure exquise. *See* Nuit de Décembre, 1939

Heure exquise, 1982 (Allio 2)

Heures, 1909 (Feuillade 2)

Heureuse Intervention, 1919 (Florey 2)

Heureux anniversaire, 1961 (Carrière 4)

Heureux qui comme Ulysse, 1970 (Fernandel 3, Colpi 4, Delerue 4)

Heut' kommt's drauf an, 1933 (Rainer 3, Kaper 4)

Heut Spielt der Strauss, 1928 (Wiene 2, Planer 4)

Heut tanzt Mariett, 1928 (Andrejew 4)

Heut war ich bei der Frieda, 1928 (Albers 3)

Heute heiratet mein Mann, 1956 (Herlth 4)

Heute Kommt es drauf an, 1933 (Albers 3)

Heute Nacht—Eventuell, 1930 (Planer 4)

Heute nacht passiert's, 1953 (Tschechowa 3)

Hex, 1973 (Carradine 3)

Hex on Fogg's Millions, 1914 (Talmadge 3)

Hexen bis aufs Blutgeqvält. *See* Mark of the Devil, 1970

Hexer, 1932 (Rasp 3, Heller 4)

Hey Diddle Diddle, 1935 (Terry 4)

Hey Good Lookin!, 1982 (Bakshi 4)

Hey! Hey! U.S.A.!, 1938 (Launder and Gilliat 2, Hay 3, McDowall 3, Rank 4, Vetchinsky 4)

Hey, Pop!, 1932 (Arbuckle 3)

Hey Rookie, 1944 (Donen 2, Miller 3)

Hey Rube!, 1928 (Plunkett 4)

Hey There, 1918 (Daniels 3, Lloyd 3, Roach 4)

Hey There, It's Yogi Bear, 1963 (Hanna and Barbera 4)

Hi, Beautiful, 1944 (McDaniel 3)

Hi Diddle Diddle, 1943 (Menjou 3, Negri 3, Adrian 4)

Hi Gang, 1941 (Daniels 3, Green 4, Rank 4)

Hi, Gaucho!, 1935 (Plunkett 4)

Hi, Good Lookin', 1944 (Salter 4)

Hi, Mom!, 1970 (De Palma 2, De Niro 3)

Hi mo tsuki, 1969 (Mori 3)

Hi mo tsuki mo, 1969 (Iwashita 3)

Hi Neighbor!, 1934 (Roach 4)

Hi, Nellie!, 1934 (LeRoy 2, Muni 3, Orry-Kelly 4)

Hi no tori, 1950 (Hasegawa 3, Kyo 3)

Hi Ya, Chum, 1943 (Salter 4)

Hi Ya, Sailor, 1943 (Salter 4)

Hiawatha, 1962 (Mirisch 4)

Hiawatha's Rabbit Hunt, 1941 (Blanc 4, Freleng 4, Maltese 4, Stalling 4)

Hibari no hanagata tantei gassen, 1958 (Yamamura 3)

Hibari no komori-uta, 1951 (Yamamura 3)

Hibari no zoku beranmee geisha, 1960 (Yamamura 3)

Hibernatus, 1969 (Delerue 4)

Hibiscus Town, 1987 (Xie 2)

Hic-Cup Pup, 1952 (Hanna 4)

Hick, a Slick and a Chick, 1948 (Blanc 4, Stalling 4)

Hick Chick, 1946 (Avery 4)

Hickey and Boggs, 1972 (Hill 2)

Hickory Hill, 1968 (Leacock 2)

Hickory Hiram, 1918 (Laurel and Hardy 3)

Hicksville Epicure, 1913 (Loos 4)

Hickville's Finest, 1914 (Loos 4)

Hidden Aces, 1927 (Shamroy 4)

Hidden Agenda, 1990 (Loach 2, Zetterling 2)

Hidden Children, 1917 (Gaudio 4)

Hidden City, 1915 (Ford 2)

Hidden City, 1950 (Mirisch 4)

Hidden Eye, 1945 (Irene 4)

Hidden Fear, 1957 (De Toth 2)

Hidden Fires, 1918 (Marsh 3)

Hidden Fortress. See Kakushitoride no san akunin, 1958

Hidden Gold, 1932 (Mix 3)

Hidden Gold, 1940 (Harlan 4, Head 4)

Hidden Guns, 1956 (Carradine 3, Dickinson 3)

Hidden Homicide, 1959 (Rank 4)

Hidden in the Fog. See Dimma dold, 1952

Hidden Letters, 1914 (Talmadge 3)

Hidden Master, 1940 (Cushing 3)

Hidden Menace. See Star of the Circus, 1938

Hidden Mine, 1911 (Anderson 3)

Hidden Pearls, 1918 (Cruze 2, Hayakawa 3)

Hidden Power. See Sabotage, 1937

Hidden River. See Rio escondido, 1947

Hidden Room. See Obsession, 1949

Hidden Scar, 1916 (Marion 4)

Hidden Spring, 1917 (Gaudio 4)

Hidden Trail, 1912 (Ince 4)

Hidden Valley Outlaws, 1944 (Canutt 4)

Hidden Woman, 1922 (Dwan 2)

Hidden Woman. See Escondida, 1955

Hidden World, 1958 (Rosenman 4)

Hide and Seek, 1913 (Sennett 2)

Hide and Seek, 1932 (Fleischer 4)

Hide and Seek Detectives, 1918 (Sennett 2)

Hide and Shriek, 1938 (Roach 4)

Hide in Plain Sight, 1979 (Caan 3, Rosenman 4)

Hideaway, 1937 (Polglase 4)

Hideaway Girl, 1937 (Head 4, Young 4)

Hideko no oendancho, 1940 (Takamine 3)

Hideko no shasho-san, 1941 (Takamine 3)

Hideko the Bus Conductor. See Hideko no shasho-san, 1941

Hide-Out, 1934 (Van Dyke 2, Montgomery 3, O'Sullivan 3, Rooney 3, Brown 4, Freed 4, Goodrich 4, Stromberg 4)

Hideout. See Small Voice, 1948

Hideout in the Alps. See Dusty Ermine, 1936

Hier et aujourd'hui. See Paris d'hier et d'aujourd'hui, 1956

Hieroglyphic, 1912 (Reid 3)

Higan sen-nin giri, 1927 (Tanaka 3)

Higanbana, 1958 (Ryu 3, Tanaka 3)

Higegi no shogun Yamashita Yasubumi, 1953 (Hayakawa 3)

Higginses Versus Judsons, 1911 (Lawrence 3)

High, 1950 (Young 4)

High and Dizzy, 1920 (Lloyd 3)

High and Dry, 1920 (Roach 4)

High and Dry. See Maggie, 1954

High and Handsome, 1925 (Haller 4)

High and Low, 1913 (Dwan 2)

High and Low. See Du haut en bas, 1933

High and Low. See Tengoku to jigoku, 1963

High and Mighty, 1954 (Newton 3)

High and the Flighty, 1956 (Blanc 4, McKimson 4, Stalling 4)

High and the Mighty, 1954 (Wellman 2, Trevor 3, Wayne 3, Clothier 4, Tiomkin 4)

High Anxiety, 1977 (Brooks 2, Levinson 2, Whitlock 4)

High Ashbury, 1967 (Warhol 2)

High Barbaree, 1947 (Allyson 3, Johnson 3, Irene 4, Stothart 4)

High Bright Sun, 1964 (Bogarde 3, Elliott 3, Box 4)

High Brow Stuff, 1924 (Rogers 3, Roach 4)

High Command, 1937 (Dickinson 2, Heller 4)

High Commissioner. See Nobody Runs Forever, 1968

High Conquest, 1947 (Bondi 3)

High Cost of Loving, 1958 (Ferrer 3, Rowlands 3, Folsey 4, Rose 4)

High Diving Hare, 1949 (Blanc 4, Freleng 4, Stalling 4)

High Encounters of the Ultimate Kind. See Cheech and Chong's Next Movie, 1980

High Finance, 1933 (Lupino 3)

High Flies the Hawk, I and II. See Píseň o sletu I, II, 1949

High Flight, 1956 (Milland 3, Box 4)

High Flyer, 1926 (Brown 4)

High Flyers, 1938 (Dumont 3)

High Frequency, 1988 (Donaggio 4)

High Fury. See White Cradle Inn, 1947

High Gear, 1931 (Stevens 2, Roach 4)

High Gear Jeffrey, 1920 (Furthman 4)

High Hand, 1926 (Mohr 4)

High Hat, 1937 (Pangborn 3)

High Infidelity. See Alta infideltà, 1964

High Journey, 1959 (Welles 3)

High Noon, 1952 (Kramer 2, Zinnemann 2, Cooper 3, Kelly 3, Van Cleef 3, Crosby 4, Foreman 4, Tiomkin 4)

High Note, 1961 (Blanc 4, Jones 4)

High on the Range, 1985 (Canutt 4)

High Pavement, 1948 (Rank 4)

High Plains Drifter, 1972 (Eastwood 3, Bumstead 4)

High Pressure, 1932 (LeRoy 2, Powell 3)

High Rise Donkey, 1979 (Clarke 4)

High Risk, 1981 (Coburn 3, Quinn 3)

High Road. See Lady of Scandal, 1930

High Road to China, 1983 (Barry 4)

High Rollers, 1921 (Roach 4)

High Rollers. See Bluff, 1976

High School, 1968 (Wiseman 2)

High School Hero, 1927 (Miller 4)

High School Hero, 1946 (Katzman 4)

High School Student and Woman Teacher: Merciless Youth. See Koukousei to onna kyoushi: hijou no seishun, 1962

High School U.S.A. See Class of 1984, 1983

High Season, 1987 (Papas 3, Menges 4)

High Sierra, 1941 (Huston 2, Walsh 2, Bogart 3, Kennedy 3, Lupino 3, Wilde 3, Burnett 4, Deutsch 4, Gaudio 4, Haskin 4, Wallis 4)

High Sign, 1917 (Young 4)

High Sign, 1921 (Keaton 2)

High Society, 1924 (Roach 4)

High Society, 1956 (Walters 2, Calhern 3, Crosby 3, Kelly 3, Sinatra 3, Gibbons 4, Green 4, Porter 4, Rose 4)

High Society Blues, 1930 (Gaynor 3)

High Speed, 1932 (Bond 3, Rooney 3)

High Speed, 1953 (Lassally 4)

High Spirits, 1988 (Jordan 2, O'Toole 3)

High Spots on Broadway, 1914 (Sennett 2)

High Stakes, 1931 (Hunt 4)

High Steppers, 1926 (Astor 3, Del Rio 3)

High Tension, 1936 (Dwan 2, McDaniel 3)

High Tension. See Sånt händer inte här, 1950

High Tide, 1922 (Roach 4)

High Tide, 1987 (Armstrong 2)

High Tide at Noon, 1957 (Rank 4)

High Time, 1960 (Edwards 2, Crosby 3, Weld 3, Brackett 4, Cahn 4, Kanin 4, Mancini 4)

High Treason. See Hochverrat, 1929

High Treason, 1951 (Boulting 2, Addison 4, Rank 4, Vetchinsky 4)

High Velocity, 1976 (Goldsmith 4)

High Vermilion. See Silver City, 1951

High Voltage, 1929 (Lombard 3)

High Wall, 1948 (Marshall 3, Taylor 3, Kaper 4, Mayer 4)

High, Wide, and Handsome, 1937 (Mamoulian 2, Dunne 3, Lamour 3, Scott 3, Banton 4, Dreier 4, Prinz 4)

High Wind in Jamaica, 1965 (MacKendrick 2, Coburn 3, Quinn 3, Slocombe 4)

High Window. See Brasher Doubloon, 1947

Highbinders, 1915 (Browning 2)

Highbrow Love, 1913 (Loos 4)

Higher and Higher, 1943 (Morgan 3)

Higher Law, 1911 (Cruze 2)

Higher Principle. See Vyšší princip, 1960

Higher Than a Kite, 1943 (Three Stooges 3)

Highland Fling, 1936 (Crazy Gang 3)

Highlander, 1986 (Connery 3)

Highlander II, 1990 (Connery 3)

Highly Dangerous, 1950 (Lockwood 3, Rank 4, Vetchinsky 4)

Highpoint, 1984 (Harris 3)

High-Powered Rifle, 1960 (Crosby 4)

Highs, 1975 (Brakhage 2)

Highway Dragnet, 1954 (Corman 2, Bennett 3)

Highway Patrol, 1938 (Ballard 4)

Highway Pickup. See Chair de poule, 1963

Highway Runnery, 1965 (Blanc 4)

Highway to Freedom. See Joe Smith, American, 1942

Highway West, 1941 (Kennedy 3, Burks 4, McCord 4)

Highwayman, 1951 (Coburn 3)

Highways by Night, 1942 (Darwell 3)

Higuchi Ichiyo, 1939 (Takamine 3, Yamada 3)

Hiho, 1960 (Yamada 3)

Hija de Juan Simón, 1935 (Buñuel 2)

Hija del angaño, 1951 (Alcoriza 4)

Hijacking of the Achille Lauro, 1989 (Grant 3, Lancaster 3, Malden 3, Saint 3, Sanda 3)

Hijazo de mi vidaza, 1971 (Figueroa 4)

Hijo de papa, 1933 (Alton 4)

Hijo del crack, 1953 (Torre Nilsson 2)

Hijos de Fierro, 1976 (Solanas and Getino 2)

Hijos de Maria Morales, 1952 (De Fuentes 2, Infante 3)

Hijos de Satanas, 1971 (Figueroa 4)

Hijosen no onna, 1933 (Tanaka 3)

Hijo-toshi, 1960 (Tsukasa 3)

Hikage no musume, 1957 (Kagawa 3, Yamada 3)

Hikaritokage, 1946 (Hara 3)

Hikaru umi, 1963 (Mori 3, Tanaka 3)

Hiking Through Holland with Will Rogers, 1927 (Rogers 3)

Hikinige, 1966 (Naruse 2, Takamine 3, Tsukasa 3)

Hikoki wa naze tobuka, 1943 (Tsuburaya 4)

Hilda Crane, 1956 (Simmons 3, Dunne 4, LeMaire 4, Raksin 4)

Hilde Warren und der Tod, 1917 (Courant 4, Hoffmann 4)

Hildegard, 1948 (Zetterling 2)

Hill, 1965 (Lumet 2, Connery 3, Redgrave 3, Morris 4)

Hill Billy, 1924 (Young 4)

Hill in Korea, 1956 (Baker 3, Caine 3, Shaw 3, Dalrymple 4, Francis 4)

Hill Tillies, 1935 (Roach 4)

Hill Twenty-Four Doesn't Answer, 1955 (Dickinson 2)

Hillbilly, 1935 (Lantz 4)

Hillbilly Hare, 1950 (Blanc 4, McKimson 4, Stalling 4)

Hillbillys in a Haunted House, 1967 (Carradine 3, Rathbone 3)

Hillcrest Mystery, 1918 (Miller 4)

Hills Are Calling, 1914 (Hepworth 2)

Hills Have Eyes, 1977 (Craven 2)

Hills Have Eyes, Part II, 1983 (Craven 2)

Hills of Home, 1948 (Crisp 3, Leigh 3, Stothart 4)

Hills of Old Wyomin', 1936 (Fleischer 4)

Hills of Old Wyoming, 1937 (Head 4)

Hills of Peace, 1914 (Anderson 3)

Hills of Utah, 1951 (Autry 3)

Hills Run Red. See Fiume di dollari, 1966

Hilly Billy, 1951 (Fleischer 4)

Himawari-musume, 1953 (Mifune 3)

Himegimi to ronin, 1953 (Kagawa 3)

Himetaru kakugo, 1943 (Hasegawa 3, Yamada 3)

Hime-yasha gyojo-ki, 1959 (Yamada 3)

Himeyuri no to, 1953 (Kagawa 3, Okada 3)

Himiko, 1974 (Shinoda 2, Iwashita 3, Takemitsu 4)

Himitsu, 1952 (Tanaka 3)

Himlaspelet, 1942 (Sjöberg 2)

Himmel Hoch, 1968 (Schroeter 2)

Himmel och pannkaka, 1959 (Björnstrand 3)

Himmel og Helvede, 1988 (Andersson 3)

Himmel ohne Sterne, 1955 (Käutner 2)

Himmel über Berlin, 1987 (Wenders 2, Falk 3, Ganz 3, Alekan 4)

Himmel, wir erben ein Schloss, 1943 (Ondra 3)

Himself as Herself, 1967 (Markopoulos 2)

Hin och smålänningen, 1949 (Nykvist 4)

Hinarai naku sato, 1929 (Tanaka 3)

Hindenburg, 1975 (Wise 2, Bancroft 3, Meredith 3, Scott 3, Jeakins 4, Surtees 4, Whitlock 4)

Hindle Wakes, 1931 (Saville 2, Balcon 4)

Hindoo Charm, 1913 (Costello 3)

Hindoo Dagger, 1908 (Griffith 2, Bitzer 4)

Hindu, 1953 (Karloff 3)

Hindustan Hamara, 1950 (Anand 3)

Hinoki butai, 1946 (Hasegawa 3, Yamada 3)

Hinotori, 1977 (Legrand 4)

Hinter Kostermann, 1952 (Tschechowa 3, Herlth 4)

Hintertreppe, 1921 (Dieterle 2, Mayer 4)

Hintertreppe, 1921 (Kortner 3, Porten 3, Junge 4)

Hip Action, 1933 (Fields 3)

Hip Hip—Hurry!, 1959 (Blanc 4, Jones 4)

Hipolito el de Santa, 1949 (De Fuentes 2)

Hipoteza, 1972 (Zanussi 2)

Hippety Hopper, 1949 (Blanc 4, Foster 4, Stalling 4)

Hippocampe, 1934 (Milhaud 4)

Hippydrome Tiger, 1968 (Blanc 4)

Hips, Hips, Hooray!, 1934 (Grable 3, Steiner 4)

Hira aur Patthar, 1977 (Azmi 3)

Hirameku yaiba, 1926 (Tanaka 3)

Hiram's Bride, 1909 (Olcott 2)

Hirate Miki, 1951 (Yamada 3, Yamamura 3)

Hired and Fired, 1916 (Laurel and Hardy 3)

Hired and Fired, 1922 (Roach 4)

Hired Hand. See Porky's Baseball Broadcast, 1940

Hired Hand, 1971 (Oates 3, Zsigmond 4)

Hired to Kill, 1989 (Ferrer 3, Reed 3)

Hired Wife, 1940 (Russell 3, Benchley 4, Krasner 4)

Hireling, 1973 (Shaw 3, Mankowitz 4)

Hiren hikui-zuka, 1931 (Hasegawa 3)

Hirondelle et la mésange, 1921 (Burel 4)

Hirondelle et la mésange, 1983 (Colpi 4)

Hiroshima, 1953 (Yamada 3)

Hiroshima mon amour, 1959 (Duras 2, Resnais 2, Okada 3, Colpi 4, Delerue 4, Fusco 4, Vierny 4)

Hiroshima: Out of the Ashes, 1990 (Von Sydow 3)

Hirt von Maria Schnee, 1919 (Hoffmann 4)

Hiryuh no ken, 1937 (Miyagawa 4)

His Affair. See This Is My Affair, 1937

His Alibi, 1916 (Sennett 2, Arbuckle 3)

His and Hers, 1961 (Reed 3, Terry-Thomas 3)

His Athletic Wife, 1913 (Beery 3)

His Aunt Emma, 1910 (White 3)

His Auto Ruination, 1916 (Sennett 2)

His Awful Daughter, 1910 (White 3)

His Awful Vengeance, 1914 (Loos 4)

His Best Girl, 1921 (Roach 4)

His Better Self, 1911 (Guy 2, Ince 4)

His Birthday, 1910 (White 3)

His Birth Right, 1918 (Hayakawa 3)

His Bitter Half, 1950 (Blanc 4, Freleng 4, Stalling 4)

His Bitter Pill, 1916 (Sennett 2)

His Bogus Uncle, 1911 (Lawrence 3)

His Bread and Butter, 1916 (Sennett 2)

His Bridal Night, 1919 (Folsey 4)

His Bridal Sweet, 1935 (Langdon 3)

His Brother's Ghost, 1945 (Crabbe 3)

His Brother's Wife, 1936 (Van Dyke 2, Stanwyck 3, Taylor 3, Waxman 4)

His Busted Trust, 1916 (Sennett 2)

His Busy Day, 1918 (Roach 4)

His Butler's Sister, 1943 (Borzage 2, Durbin 3, Pangborn 3, Adrian 4, Hoffenstein 4, Salter 4)

His Captive Woman, 1929 (Garmes 4, Wilson 4)

His Children's Children, 1923 (Wood 2, Daniels 3)

His Chorus Girl Wife, 1911 (Lawrence 3)

His Chum, the Baron, 1913 (Sennett 2)

His Country. See Ship Comes In, 1928

His Country's Bidding, 1914 (Hepworth 2)

His Crooked Career, 1913 (Sennett 2)

His Daredevil Queen. See Mabel at the Wheel, 1914

His Daughter, 1911 (Griffith 2, Bitzer 4)

His Day of Rest, 1908 (Bitzer 4)

His Day Out, 1918 (Laurel and Hardy 3)

His Debt, 1919 (Hayakawa 3)

His Diving Beauty. See Sea Nymphs, 1914

His Dog, 1927 (Adrian 4, Brown 4)

His Double Life, 1933 (Gish 3, Edeson 4)

His Dress Shirt, 1911 (Pickford 3, Gaudio 4)

His Duty, 1909 (Griffith 2, Bitzer 4)

His Duty. See Man from Nowhere, 1915

His English Wife. See Hon den enda, 1926

His Ex Marks the Spot, 1940 (Keaton 2)

His Excellency. See Ego prevoskhoditelstvo, 1927

His Excellency, 1951 (Hamer 2, Slocombe 4)

His Family Tree, 1935 (Vidor 2, Plunkett 4)

His Father's Deputy, 1913 (Mix 3)

His Father's Footsteps, 1915 (Sennett 2)

His Father's Son, 1917 (Barrymore 3)

His Favorite Pastime, 1914 (Sennett 2, Arbuckle 3)

His Fight, 1914 (Mix 3)

His First Command, 1929, (La Cava 2, Miller 4)

His First False Step, 1916 (Sennett 2)

His First Flame, 1927 (Sennett 2, Langdon 3, Hornbeck 4)

His First Job, 1908 (Méliès 2)

His Friend, The Burglar, 1911 (Lawrence 3)

His Friend's Wife, 1911 (Bushman 3)

His Girl Friday, 1940 (Hawks 2, Bellamy 3, Grant 3, Russell 3, Cohn 4, Hecht 4, Lederer 4, Walker 4)

His Glorious Night, 1929 (Barrymore 3, Gilbert 3, Gibbons 4, Mayer 4)

His Glorious Night. See Si l'empereur savait ça!, 1930

His Greatest Bluff. See Seine grösster Bluff, 1927

His Greatest Gamble, 1934 (Buchman 4, Plunkett 4, Steiner 4)

His Guardian Auto, 1915 (Cruze 2)

His Halted Career, 1914 (Sennett 2)

His Hare Raising Tale, 1951 (Blanc 4, Freleng 4, Stalling 4)

His Hereafter, 1916 (Sennett 2)

His Heroic Action. See Ei gerochsky podvig, 1914

His Hidden Purpose, 1918 (Sennett 2)

His Highness' Adjutant. See Pobočnik jeho výsosti, 1933

His Hoodoo, 1913 (Loos 4)

His Hour, 1924 (Vidor 2, Gilbert 3, Gibbons 4, Mayer 4)

His Hour of Manhood, 1914 (Hart 3, August 4, Ince 4)

His House Friday, 1950 (Hanna and Barbera 4)

His House in Order, 1920 (Miller 4)

His Inspiration, 1913 (Barrymore 3)

His Jonah Day, 1920 (Laurel and Hardy 3)

His Kind of Woman, 1951 (Mitchum 3, Price 3, Russell 3)

His Lady. See When a Man Loves, 1927

His Last Adventure. See Battling Buckaroos, 1933

His Last Burglary, 1910 (Griffith 2, Walthall 3, Bitzer 4)

His Last False Step, 1919 (Sennett 2)

His Last Haul, 1928 (Neilan 2)

His Last Laugh, 1916 (Sennett 2)

His Last Legs, 1917 (Bray 4)

His Last Race, 1923 (Eason 4)

His Last Scent, 1916 (Sennett 2)

His Last Twelve Hours. *See* E più facile che un camello, 1950

His Last Twelve Hours. *See* Mondo le condanna, 1952

His Late Excellency. *See* Selige Excellenz, 1926

His Lesson, 1912 (Griffith 2, Bitzer 4)

His Lesson, 1914 (Crisp 3, Gish 3)

His Little Page, 1913 (Talmadge 3)

His Lordship, 1932 (Powell and Pressburger 2)

His Lordship, 1936 (Arliss 3, Balcon 4, Junge 4)

His Lordship's Dilemma, 1915 (Fields 3)

His Lordship's White Feather, 1912 (Guy 2)

His Lost Love, 1909 (Griffith 2, Pickford 3, Bitzer 4)

His Luckless Love, 1915 (Sennett 2)

His Lying Heart, 1916 (Sennett 2)

His Majesty, Bunker Bean, 1925 (Haskin 4)

His Majesty Bunker Bean. *See* Bunker Bean, 1936

His Majesty O'Keefe, 1954 (Lancaster 3, Chase 4, Haskin 4, Heller 4, Tiomkin 4)

His Majesty, the American, 1919 (Fairbanks 3, Karloff 3)

His Marriage Mixup, 1935 (Langdon 3)

His Marriage Wow, 1925 (Capra 2, Sennett 2, Langdon 3)

His Master's Voice, 1936 (Horton 3)

His Mother, 1912 (Olcott 2)

His Mother-in-Law, 1912 (Bunny 3)

His Mother's Scarf, 1911 (Griffith 2, Bitzer 4)

His Mother's Son, 1913 (Griffith 2, Reid 3, Bitzer 4)

His Mother's Trust, 1914 (Crisp 3)

His Move, 1905 (Bitzer 4)

His Musical Career, 1914 (Sennett 2)

His Name Is Sukhe-Bator. *See* Ego zovut Sukhe-Bator, 1942

His Naughty Thought, 1917 (Sennett 2)

His Neighbor's Wife, 1913 (Porter 2)

His Nemesis, 1912 (Ince 4)

His New Job, 1915 (Chaplin 2, Swanson 3)

His New Lid, 1910 (Ince 4)

His New Mama, 1924 (Capra 2, Sennett 2)

His New Mama, 1980 (Langdon 3)

His New Profession, 1914 (Sennett 2)

His New Stenographer, 1928 (Sennett 2, Hornbeck 4)

His New York Wife, 1926 (Musuraca 4)

His Nibs, 1922 (La Cava 2, Moore 3)

His Night Out, 1915 (Purviance 3)

His Night Out, 1935 (Bond 3, Horton 3, Mandell 4, Waxman 4)

His Off Day, 1938 (Terry 4)

His Official Appointment, 1913 (Talmadge 3)

His Old-Fashioned Mother, 1913 (Dwan 2)

His Only Father, 1919 (Daniels 3, Lloyd 3, Roach 4)

His Only Son, 1912 (Reid 3)

His Other Woman. *See* Desk Set, 1957

His Own Fault, 1911 (Sennett 2)

His Own Law, 1920 (Bosworth 3)

His Picture in the Papers, 1916 (Fleming 2, Von Stroheim 2, Fairbanks 3, Emerson 4, Loos 4)

His Picture in the Papers, 1945 (Fleming 2)

His Precious Life, 1917 (Sennett 2)

His Prehistoric Past, 1914 (Sennett 2)

His Pride and Shame, 1916 (Sennett 2)

His Private Life, 1926 (Arbuckle 3)

His Private Life, 1928 (Menjou 3, Vajda 4)

His Private Secretary, 1933 (Wayne 3)

His Reformation, 1909 (Anderson 3)

His Regeneration, 1914 (Chaplin 2, Anderson 3)

His Return, 1915 (Walsh 2)

His Rich Uncle, 1910 (White 3)

His Robe of Honor, 1918 (Ingram 2, Walthall 3)

His Royal Flush. *See* Mr. "Silent" Haskins, 1915

His Royal Shyness, 1932 (Sennett 2)

His Royal Slyness, 1919 (Lloyd 3, Roach 4)

His Second Childhood, 1914 (Sennett 2)

His Secretary, 1925 (Shearer 3, Day 4, Gibbons 4, Wilson 4)

His Sense of Duty, 1912 (Ince 4)

His Sick Friend, 1910 (Lawrence 3)

His Silver Bachelorhood, 1913 (Talmadge 3)

His Sister from Paris, 1925 (Kräly 4)

His Sister-in-Law, 1910 (Griffith 2, Bitzer 4)

His Sister's Children, 1911 (Costello, 3 Talmadge 3)

His Sister's Kids, 1913 (Sennett 2, Arbuckle 3)

His Sister's Sweetheart, 1911 (Guy 2)

His Smothered Love, 1918 (Sennett 2)

His Squaw, 1912 (Ince 4)

His Stolen Fortune, 1914 (Bushman 3)

His Supreme Moment, 1925 (Colman 3, Sweet 3, Wong 3, Goldwyn 4, Marion 4, Miller 4)

His Sweetheart, 1917 (Crisp 3)

His Taking Ways, 1914 (Sennett 2)

His Talented Wife, 1914 (Sennett 2)

His Tiger Lady, 1928 (Banton 4, Mankiewicz 4, Vajda 4)

His Tiger Wife, 1928 (Menjou 3)

His Tired Uncle, 1913 (Bunny 3)

His Trust, 1910 (Griffith 2, Bitzer 4)

His Trust Fulfilled, 1910 (Griffith 2, Bitzer 4)

His Trysting Place, 1914 (Sennett 2, Normand 3)

His Uncle Dudley, 1917 (Sennett 2)

His Unlucky Night, 1928 (Sennett 2, Lombard 3, Hornbeck 4)

His Ups and Downs, 1913 (Sennett 2)

His Ward's Love, 1909 (Griffith 2, Bitzer 4)

His Wedded Wife, 1914 (Ingram 2)

His Wedding Night. *See* Hans bröllopsnatt, 1915

His Wedding Night, 1917 (Keaton 2, Arbuckle 3)

His Wife's Child, 1913 (Lawrence 3)

His Wife's Friend, 1918 (Sennett 2)

His Wife's Husband, 1922 (Stradling 4)

His Wife's Mistake, 1916 (Sennett 2, Arbuckle 3)

His Wife's Mother, 1909 (Griffith 2, Lawrence 3)

His Wife's Past. *See* Hans hustrus förflutna, 1915

His Wife's Stratagem, 1910 (White 3)

His Wife's Visitor, 1909 (Griffith 2, Pickford 3, Bitzer 4)

His Wild Oats, 1916 (Sennett 2)

His Winning Punch, 1915 (Sennett 2)

His Woman, 1931 (Colbert 3, Cooper 3)

His Wooden Wedding, 1925 (McCarey 2, Roach 4)

His Young Wife. *See* Miserie del signor Travet, 1946

His Youthful Fancy, 1920 (Sennett 2)

Hi-sen-ryo, 1960 (Hasegawa 3, Kagawa 3)

Hiss and Make Up, 1943 (Blanc 4, Freleng 4, Stalling 4)

Hissatsu shikake-nin, 1973 (Yamamura 3)

Hissatsu shikake-nin: Shinsetsu shikake-bari, 1974 (Iwashita 3, Yamamura 3)

Hissatsu shikaki-nin: Baiko ari-jigoku, 1973 (Yamamura 3)

Hisshoka, 1945 (Mizoguchi 2, Tanaka 3)

Histadruth, 1945 (Rathaus 4)

Histadruth II, 1946 (Rathaus 4)

Histérico, 1952 (Figueroa 4)

Histoira de una traición, 1970 (Rey 3)

Histoire comique. *See* Félicie Nanteuil, 1942

Histoire d'Adèle H., 1975 (Truffaut 2, Adjani 3, Almendros 4)

Histoire d'amour, 1933 (Ophüls 2)

Histoire d'amour, 1951 (Gélin 3, Jouvet 3, Audiard 4)

Histoire d'eau, 1958 (Godard 2, Truffaut 2, Braunberger 4)

Histoire de chapeaux, 1910 (Cohl 4)

Histoire de pin-up girls, 1950 (Braunberger 4)

Histoire de puce, 1909 (Feuillade 2)

Histoire de vent, 1988 (Ivens 2)

Histoire du soldat inconnu, 1932 (Storck 2)

Histoire d'un crime, 1901 (Pathé 4)

Histoire d'un crime, 1904 (Gaumont 4)

Histoire d'un crime, 1906 (Méliès 2)

Histoire d'un petit garçon devenu grand, 1963 (Braunberger 4)

Histoire d'un Pierrot, 1913 (Bertini 3)

Histoire simple, 1978 (Sautet 2, Schneider 3, Sarde 4)

Histoire très bonne et très joyeuse de Colinot Trousse-Chemise, 1973 (Bardot 3, Cloquet 4)

Histoires d'Amérique: Food, Family and Philosophy/American Stories, 1989 (Akerman 2)

Histoires extraordinaires, 1949 (Berry 3)

Histoires extraordinaires, 1968 (Malle 2, Vadim 2, Bardot 3, Delon 3, Fonda 3, Price 3, Stamp 3, Delli Colli 4, Renoir 4, Rota 4, Rotunno 4)

Histoires insolites, 1974 (Chabrol 2)

Historia de un amor, 1955 (Figueroa 4)

Historia de un gran amor, 1942 (Figueroa 4)

Historia de una mala mujer, 1948 (Del Rio 3)

Historia naturae, 1967 (Švankmajer 4)

Historia współczesna, 1961 (Stawiński 4)

Historias de la revolucion, 1961 (Gutiérrez Alea 2)

Historias prohibidas de Pulgarcito, 1979 (Leduc 2)

Histórias Selvagens, 1978 (De Almeida 4)

Historical Fan. *See* Eventail animé, 1909

Historie blechatého psa, 1958 (Brdečka 4)

Historie de rire, 1941 (Presle 3)

Historien om en moder, 1979 (Karina 3, Gégauff 4)

Historien om et slot, J.F. Willumsen, 1951 (Roos 2)

History. *See* Storia, 1985

History and Romance of Transportation, 1939 (Maddow 4)

History Is Made at Night, 1937 (Borzage 2, Arthur 3, Boyer 3, Basevi 4, Newman 4, Toland 4)

History Lessons. *See* Geschichtsunterricht, 1972

History of Adventure, 1964 (Bass 4)

History of Inventions, 1960 (Halas and Batchelor 4)

Holiday Camp, 1947 (Dors 3, Box 4, Rank 4)

Holiday for Drumsticks, 1949 (Blanc 4, Stalling 4)

Holiday for Henrietta. *See* Fête à Henriette, 1952

Holiday for Lovers, 1959 (Henreid 3, Webb 3, Wyman 3, Cahn 4, Clarke 4)

Holiday for Shoestrings, 1946 (Blanc 4, Freleng 4, Stalling 4)

Holiday for Sinners, 1952 (Houseman 4, Rose 4)

Holiday Highlights, 1940 (Avery 4, Blanc 4, Stalling 4)

Holiday in Mexico, 1946 (Donen 2, McDowall 3, Pidgeon 3, Brown 4, Hanna and Barbera 4, Irene 4, Lennart 4, Pasternak 4, Smith 4, Stradling 4)

Holiday in Spain. *See* Scent of Mystery, 1960

Holiday in Storyland, 1930 (Garland 3)

Holiday in Tokyo. *See* Tokyo no kyujitsu, 1958

Holiday Inn, 1942 (Astaire 3, Beavers 3, Crosby 3, Berlin 4, Dreier 4, Head 4)

Holiday Inn. *See* Riding High, 1943

Holiday's End, 1937 (Havelock-Allan 4)

Holidays in Spain. *See* Scent of Mystery, 1959

Holidays with an Angel. *See* Dovolená s andělem, 1952

Holland Days, 1934 (Terry 4)

Holland Submarine Torpedo Boat, 1904 (Bitzer 4)

Hölle der Jungfrauen, 1927 (Krauss 3)

Hölle der Liebe—Erlebnisse aus einem Tanzpalais, 1926 (Dieterle 2)

Höllenspuk in 6 Akten. *See* Kurfürstendamm, 1920

Höllische Macht, 1922 (Wiene 2)

Hollow Triumph, 1948 (Bennett 3, Henreid 3, Alton 4)

Hollow Triumph, 1987 (Henreid 3)

Holly and the Ivy, 1952 (Elliott 3, Johnson 3, Richardson 3, De Grunwald 4, Korda, A. 4, Korda, V. 4)

Hollywood, 1923 (Cruze 2, De Mille 2, Arbuckle 3, Astor 3, Hart 3, Negri 3, Rogers 3)

Hollywood and Vine, 1945 (Pangborn 3)

Hollywood Blue, 1970 (Rooney 3)

Hollywood Boulevard, 1936 (Florey 2, Bushman 3, Cooper 3, Costello 3, Marsh 3, Dreier 4, Head 4, Struss 4)

Hollywood Boulevard, 1976 (Corman 2, Dante 2)

Hollywood Bowl, 1950 (Hanna and Barbera 4)

Hollywood Canine Canteen, 1946 (Blanc 4, McKimson 4, Stalling 4)

Hollywood Canteen, 1944 (Daves 2, Brown 3, Cantor 3, Crawford 3, Davis 3, Garfield 3, Greenstreet 3, Henreid 3, Lorre 3, Lupino 3, Malone 3, Rogers 3, Stanwyck 3, Wyman 3, Glennon 4, Prinz 4)

Hollywood Cavalcade, 1934 (Cantor 3)

Hollywood Cavalcade, 1939 (Keaton 2, Sennett 2, Ameche 3, Faye 3, Jolson 3, Brown 4, Day 4, Raksin 4, Zanuck 4)

Hollywood Cowboys. *See* Hearts of the West, 1975

Hollywood Daffy, 1946 (Blanc 4, Freleng 4, Maltese 4, Stalling 4)

Hollywood Diet, 1932 (Terry 4)

Hollywood Double, 1932 (Sennett 2)

Hollywood Extra Girl, 1935 (De Mille 2)

Hollywood Fathers, 1954 (Brown 3)

Hollywood Gad-About, 1934 (Astor 3, Cagney 3, Hart 3)

Hollywood Goes A-Fishing, 1956 (Andrews 3)

Hollywood Goes to Church, 1949 (Ford 3)

Hollywood Handicap, 1932 (Wayne 3)

Hollywood Handicap, 1938 (Keaton 2)

Hollywood Happenings, 1931 (Sennett 2)

Hollywood Hero, 1927 (Sennett 2)

Hollywood Hoodlum, 1934 (Eason 4)

Hollywood Horror House. *See* Comeback, 1970

Hollywood Hotel, 1937 (Berkeley 2, Hayward 3, Powell 3, Reagan 3, Barnes 4, Mercer 4, Orry-Kelly 4, Rosher 4, Wald 4, Wallis 4)

Hollywood in Uniform, 1943 (Ford 3, Gable 3)

Hollywood Kid, 1924 (Sennett 2)

Hollywood Knights, 1980 (Pfeiffer 3, Fraker 4)

Hollywood Lights, 1932 (Arbuckle 3, Grable 3)

Hollywood Luck, 1932 (Arbuckle 3, Grable 3)

Hollywood Matador, 1942 (Lantz 4)

Hollywood on Parade, 1932 (Rogers 3)

Hollywood on Parade, 1933 (Cagney 3, Crabbe 3, Three Stooges 3)

Hollywood on Parade, No. 8, 1933 (Brown 3)

Hollywood on Parade, No. 13, 1934 (Del Rio 3, Dressler 3)

Hollywood on Parade Nos. 3–4, 1932 (Mix 3)

Hollywood on Trial, 1976 (Dmytryk 2)

Hollywood or Bust, 1956 (Lewis 2, Tashlin 2, Martin 3, Bumstead 4, Head 4, Wallis 4)

Hollywood Park, 1946 (Grable 3)

Hollywood Party, 1934 (Dwan 2, Goulding 2, Durante 3, Laurel and Hardy 3, Three Stooges 3, Young 3, Brown 4, Freed 4, Howe 4)

Hollywood Players: The Thirties, 1943 (Buchanan 3)

Hollywood Revue of 1929, 1929 (Keaton 2, Barrymore 3, Crawford 3, Davies 3, Dressler 3, Gilbert 3, Love 3, Shearer 3, Brown 4, Day 4, Freed 4, Gibbons 4, Mayer 4)

Hollywood Rodeo, 1949 (Wayne 3)

Hollywood Roundup, 1938 (Three Stooges 3)

Hollywood Shower of Stars, 1955 (Bendix 3)

Hollywood Speaks, 1932 (Krasna 4)

Hollywood Star, 1929 (Sennett 2)

Hollywood Steps Out, 1941 (Avery 4, Blanc 4, Stalling 4)

Hollywood Story, 1951 (McCrea 3)

Hollywood Ten, 1950 (Dmytryk 2, Lardner 4)

Hollywood Theme Song, 1930 (Sennett 2)

Hollywood Today Number Four, 1928 (Mix 3)

Hollywood Victory Caravan, 1945 (Crosby 3, Hope 3, Hutton 3, Ladd 3)

Hollywood Wives, 1985 (Dickinson 3)

Hollywood You Never See, 1935 (De Mille 2)

Hollywood's Wild Angel, 1979 (Scorsese 2)

Hollywood/Sunset. *See* Good Morning Babilonia, 1986

Holocaust 2000, 1977 (Morricone 4)

Holy Apes. *See* Bramy raju, 1967

Holy Matrimony, 1943 (Stahl 2, Fields 3, Pangborn 3, Ballard 4, Basevi 4, Johnson 4)

Holy Smoke, 1963 (Borowczyk 2)

Holy Terror, 1929 (Roach 4)

Holy Terror, 1931 (Bogart 3)

Homage at Siesta Time. *See* Homenaje a la hora de la siesta, 1962

Homage to Jean Tinguely's Homage to New York, 1960 (Breer 4)

Homard Flambé. *See* Bateau d'Emile, 1961

Hombre, 1966 (Ritt 2, March 3, Newman 3, Howe 4, Ravetch 4, Smith 4)

Hombre de Alazan, 1958 (Alcoriza 4)

Hombre de exito, 1986 (Solas 2)

Hombre de papel, 1963 (Figueroa 4)

Hombre neustra de cada dia, 1959 (Armendáriz 3, Alcoriza 4)

Home, 1916 (Ince 4, Sullivan 4)

Home, 1919 (Weber 2)

Home Again, 1958 (Kaufman 4)

Home Alone, 1990 (Williams 4)

Home and Eddie, 1989 (Black 3)

Home and School, 1946 (Alwyn 4)

Home at Seven, 1952 (Hawkins 3, Richardson 3, De Grunwald 4, Korda, A. 4, Korda, V. 4, Sherriff 4)

Home Before Dark, 1958 (LeRoy 2, Simmons 3, Biroc 4, Cahn 4, Waxman 4)

Home Breakers, 1915 (Sennett 2)

Home Breaking Hound, 1915 (Sennett 2)

Home Brew. *See* Fireside Brewer, 1920

Home Cured, 1926 (Arbuckle 3)

Home Early, 1939 (Benchley 4)

Home Folks, 1912 (Griffith 2, Barrymore 3, Pickford 3, Bitzer 4)

Home for Christmas, 1990 (Rooney 3)

Home for the Holidays, 1972 (Brennan 3, Field 3)

Home from Babylon. *See* Hem från Babylon, 1941

Home from the Hill, 1960 (Minnelli 2, Mitchum 3, Sloane 3, Ames 4, Kaper 4, Krasner 4, Plunkett 4, Ravetch 4)

Home from the Sea, 1915 (Walsh 2)

Home from the Sea, 1962 (Peries 2)

Home Girl, 1928 (Hopkins 3)

Home Grown, 1989 (Johnson 3)

Home Guard, 1941 (Terry 4)

Home in Indiana, 1944 (Hathaway 2, Bond 3, Brennan 3, Basevi 4, Cronjager 4, Friedhofer 4)

Home in Oklahoma, 1946 (Rogers 3)

Home in Wyomin', 1942 (Autry 3)

Home Is the Hero, 1959 (Kennedy 3)

Home Movies, 1939 (Benchley 4)

Home Movies, 1980 (De Palma 2, Douglas 3, Donaggio 4)

Home of the Brave, 1949 (Kramer 2, Foreman 4, Tiomkin 4)

Home of the Hopeless, 1950 (Fonda 3)

Home on the Prairie, 1939 (Autry 3)

Home on the Rails, 1982 (Driessen 4)

Home on the Range, 1935 (Scott 3, Sheridan 3)

Home on the Range, 1938 (Ballard 4)

Home Stretch, 1920 (Roach 4)

Home, Sweet Home, 1910 (White 3)

Home, Sweet Home, 1914 (Griffith 2, Crisp 3, Gish 3, Marsh 3, Sweet 3, Walthall 3, Bitzer 4)

Home Sweet Homicide, 1946 (Bacon 2, Scott 3, Basevi 4, Leven 4, Seitz 4)

Home Talent, 1921 (Sennett 2, Hornbeck 4)

Home to Danger, 1951 (Fisher 2, Baker 3)

Home to Stay, 1978 (Fonda 3)

Home Town. See Furusato, 1930

Home Town Story, 1951 (Crisp 3, Monroe 3)

Home Trail, 1927 (Wyler 2)

Home Tweet Home, 1950 (Blanc 4, Freleng 4, Stalling 4)

Homeboy, 1989 (Rourke 3)

Homebreaker, 1919 (Valentino 3, Ince 4)

Homecoming. See Heimkehr, 1928

Homecoming, 1948 (LeRoy 2, Baxter 3, Gable 3, Turner 3, Kaper 4, Mayer 4, Rose 4, Rosson 4)

Homecoming, 1973 (Cusack 3, Pinter 4, Watkin 4)

Homecoming: A Christmas Story, 1971 (Neal 3, Goldsmith 4)

Homeless, 1989 (Grant 3)

Homeless Hare, 1950 (Blanc 4, Jones 4, Maltese 4, Stalling 4)

Homeless Pup, 1937 (Terry 4)

Home-Made Movies, 1922 (Sennett 2)

Homenaje a la hora de la siesta, 1962 (Torre Nilsson 2, Valli 3)

Homer and Eddie, 1989 (Mikhalkov-Konchalovsky 2, Goldberg 3)

Homesdale, 1971 (Weir 2)

Homesick for a Mountain Village, 1934 (Zhao 3)

Homespun Vamp, 1922 (Rosson 4)

Homesteader, 1990 (Micheaux 2)

Homesteader Droopy, 1954 (Avery 4)

Homestretch, 1947 (O'Hara 3, Wilde 3, Basevi 4, LeMaire 4, Raksin 4)

Hometown. See Furusato, 1976

Homeward Bound, 1923 (Haller 4)

Homicidal, 1961 (Friedhofer 4, Guffey 4)

Homicide Bureau, 1938 (Hayworth 3)

Hommage à Debussy, 1963 (L'Herbier 2)

Hommage irrespectueux comme tous les hommages, 1974 (Dalio 3)

Homme, 1946 (Braunberger 4, Kosma 4)

Homme, 1972 (Lai 4)

Homme à abattre, 1937 (Berry 3, Dalio 3)

Homme à abattre, 1967 (Trintignant 3)

Homme à femmes, 1960 (Darrieux 3, Deneuve 3)

Homme à la barbiche, 1932 (Fradetal 4)

Homme à la Buick, 1967 (Darrieux 3, Fernandel 3, Legrand 4)

Homme à la cagoule noire. See Bête aux sept manteaux, 1936

Homme à la mer, 1948 (Decaë 4)

Homme à la pipe, 1962 (Leenhardt 2)

Homme à la tête de caoutchouc, 1902 (Méliès 2)

Homme à la valise, 1984 (Akerman 2)

Homme à l'Hispano, 1926 (Duvivier 2)

Homme à l'Hispano, 1933 (Epstein 2, Wakhévitch 4)

Homme à l'imperméable, 1957 (Duvivier 2, Blier 3, Fernandel 3)

Homme à l'oeillet blanc, 1953 (Cloquet 4)

Homme à l'oreille cassée, 1935 (Burel 4)

Homme aimanté, 1907 (Feuillade 2, Gaumont 4)

Homme amoreux, 1987 (Cardinale 3, Curtis 3, Delerue 4, Tavoularis 4)

Homme au cerveau greffé, 1971 (Trintignant 3)

Homme au chapeau rond, 1946 (Raimu 3, Spaak 4, Wakhévitch 4)

Homme au crâne rasé, 1968 (Tyszkiewicz 3)

Homme au foulard à pois, 1916 (Feyder 2)

Homme aux clefs d'or, 1956 (Fresnay 3, Girardot 3, D'Eaubonne 4)

Homme aux gants blancs, 1908 (Pathé 4)

Homme aux yeux d'argent, 1985 (Trintignant 3, Sarde 4)

Homme de compagnie, 1916 (Feyder 2, Gaumont 4)

Homme de la Jamaique, 1950 (Brasseur 3)

Homme de Londres, 1943 (Berry 3, Modot 3)

Homme de ma vie, 1951 (Moreau 3, Audiard 4, Jeanson 4)

Homme de nulle part, 1936 (Ibert 4)

Homme de proie, 1912 (Feuillade 2)

Homme de Rio, 1964 (Belmondo 3, Delerue 4, Rappeneau 4)

Homme de tête, 1898 (Méliès 2)

Homme de trop, 1967 (Costa-Gavras 2, Hondo 2, Piccoli 3, Vanel 3)

Homme des poisons, 1915 (Feuillade 2)

Homme du jour, 1936 (Duvivier 2, Chevalier 3, Spaak 4)

Homme du large, 1920 (Autant-Lara 2, L'Herbier 2, Boyer 3, Gaumont 4)

Homme du Niger, 1940 (Baur 3, Burel 4)

Homme en colère, 1979 (Dickinson 3, Pleasence 3)

Homme en marche, 1952 (Fradetal 4)

Homme en or, 1934 (Baur 3, Burel 4)

Homme est mort, 1973 (Dickinson 3, Scheider 3, Trintignant 3, Carrière 4, Legrand 4)

Homme et la bête, 1953 (Decaë 4)

Homme et l'enfant, 1956 (Constantine 3)

Homme et une femme, 1966 (Aimée 3, Trintignant 3, Lai 4)

Homme et une femme: vingt ans déja, 1986 (Aimée 3, Morgan 3, Trintignant 3, Lai 4)

Homme libre, 1973 (Lai 4)

Homme mysterieux. See Obsession, 1934

Homme nu, 1978 (Raimu 3)

Homme orchestre, 1900 (Méliès 2)

Homme orchestre, 1969 (Rabier 4)

Homme presse, 1977 (Delon 3)

Homme qui a perdu son ombre, 1991 (Branco 4)

Homme qui aimait les femmes, 1977 (Leenhardt 2, Truffaut 2, Baye 3, Caron 3, Almendros 4)

Homme qui assassina, 1930 (Courant 4)

Homme qui cherche la verité, 1939 (Raimu 3)

Homme qui joue avec le feu, 1942 (Bost 4)

Homme qui me plait, 1969 (Belmondo 3, Girardot 3, Lai 4)

Homme qui ment, 1968 (Trintignant 3, Robbe-Grillet 4)

Homme qui ne sais pas dire non, 1932 (Courant 4)

Homme sans coeur, 1936 (Kaufman 4)

Homme sans nom, 1932 (Fernandel 3)

Homme sans nom, 1937 (D'Eaubonne 4)

Homme sans visage, 1919 (Feuillade 2, Manès 3, Gaumont 4)

Homme sur la voie. See Człowiek na torze, 1956

Homme voilé, 1987 (Piccoli 3)

Hommes d'aujourd'hui, 1952 (Fradetal 4)

Hommes de la baleine, 1958 (Colpi 4)

Hommes de la croix bleue. See Błękitny krzyż, 1955

Hommes de la Wahgi, 1963 (Braunberger 4, Guillemot 4)

Hommes des oasis, 1950 (Cloquet 4)

Hommes du Champagne, 1950 (Leenhardt 2)

Hommes du pétrole, 1961 (Delerue 4)

Hommes du Sepik, 1965 (Braunberger 4)

Hommes en blanc, 1955 (Moreau 3)

Hommes et bêtes, 1946 (Decaë 4)

Hommes et les autres, 1954 (Guerra 2)

Hommes nouveaux, 1936 (L'Herbier 2, Baur 3, Fradetal 4, Lourié 4)

Hommes qui font la pluie, 1951 (Rouch 2)

Hommes sans nom, 1937 (Kaufman 4)

Hommes . . . une doctrine, 1960 (Delerue 4)

Hommes veulent vivre, 1961 (Kosma 4)

Homo eroticus, 1971 (Blier 3, Delli Colli 4)

Homo Sapiens, 1960 (Popescu-Gopo 4)

Homo Technologicus, 1984 (Bozzetto 4)

Homo Technologicus, 1985 (Bozzetto 4)

Homoman, 1964 (Lefebvre 2)

Homunculus, 1916 (Pick 2, Hoffman 4)

Hon den enda, 1926 (Molander 2, Jaenzon 4)

Hon segrade, 1916 (Sjöström 4)

Hondo, 1953 (Bond 3, Page 3, Wayne 3, Burks 4, Friedhofer 4)

Honest Hutch, 1920 (Rogers 3)

Honest Love and True, 1938 (Fleischer 4)

Honest Man, 1918 (Borzage 2)

Honesty Is the Best Policy, 1908 (Porter 2)

Honesty—the Best Policy, 1926 (Hawks 2)

Honey, 1930 (Mankiewicz 4)

Honey Pot, 1967 (Mankiewicz 2, Harrison 3, Hayward 3, Robertson 3, Smith 3, Addison 4, Di Venanzo 4)

Honeychile, 1951 (Young 4)

Honeycomb. See Madriguera, 1969

Honeymood Blues, 1946 (Bruckman 4)

Honeymoon, 1928 (Von Stroheim 2, Gibbons 4)

Honeymoon, 1931 (Wray 3)

Honeymoon, 1947 (Temple 3, Cronjager 4)

Honeymoon. See Luna de miel, 1959

Honeymoon Academy, 1990 (Lee 3)

Honeymoon Adventure, 1931 (Dean 4)

Honeymoon Deferred. See Due mogli sono troppe, 1951

Honeymoon for Three, 1915 (Evans 3)

Honeymoon for Three, 1941 (Bacon 2, Sheridan 3, Wyman 3, Epstein 4, Haller 4)

Honeymoon Hardships, 1925 (Garnett 2, Sennett 2)

Honeymoon Hate, 1927 (Mankiewicz 4)

Honeymoon Hotel, 1964 (Lanchester 3, Berman 4, Cahn 4)

Honeymoon in Bali, 1939 (Carroll 3, MacMurray 3, Head 4, Reynolds 4)

Honeymoon Limited, 1935 (Krasner 4)

Honeymoon Lodge, 1943 (Pangborn 3, Bruckman 4)

Honeymoon Machine, 1961 (McQueen 3, Ames 4, La Shelle 4, Rose 4)

Honeymoon Trio, 1931 (Arbuckle 3)

Honeymoon Trip. See Bröllopsresan, 1935

Honeymoon Trip. See Jalousie 1976, 1976

Honeymoon with a Stranger, 1969 (Leigh 3)

Honeymoon Zeppelin, 1930 (Sennett 2)

Honeymooners, 1914 (Bunny 3, Lawrence 3)

Honeymoons. See Voyage des noces, 1975

Honeymoon's Over, 1939 (Day 4, Miller 4)

Honey-mousers, 1956 (Blanc 4, McKimson 4)

Honey's Money, 1962 (Blanc 4, Freleng 4)

Honeysuckle Rose, 1980 (Pollack 2, Rooney 3, Müller 4)

Hong Kong, 1951 (Reagan 3, Head 4)

Hong Kong un addio, 1962 (Flaiano 4)

Honkers, 1972 (Coburn 3)

Honkon no hoshi, 1962 (Yamamura 3)

Honkon no yoru, 1961 (Tsukasa 3)

Honky, 1971 (Jones 4)

Honky Tonk, 1929 (Bacon 2)

Honky Tonk, 1941 (Gable 3, Trevor 3, Turner 3, Berman 4, Gibbons 4, Rosson 4, Waxman 4)

Honky Tonk, 1974 (Biroc 4, Bumstead 4)

Honky Tonk Freeway, 1981 (Schlesinger 2, Page 3, Bernstein 4)

Honky-Donkey, 1934 (Roach 4)

Honkytonk Man, 1982 (Eastwood 3)

Honneur du Corse, 1906 (Guy 2)

Honneur d'un capitaine, 1982 (De Beauregard 4)

Honneurs de la guerre, 1960 (Cloquet 4)

Honno, 1966 (Shindo 2)

Honolulu, 1939 (Powell 3, Young 3, Waxman 4)

Honolulu Lu, 1942 (Cahn 4, Planer 4)

Honoo no hada, 1951 (Yamamura 3)

Honor among Lovers, 1931 (Arzner 2, Colbert 3, March 3, Rogers 3, Folsey 4)

Honor Bound, 1928 (August 4)

Honor First, 1922 (Gilbert 3, August 4)

Honor of His Family, 1909 (Griffith 2, Walthall 3)

Honor of His House, 1918 (Hayakawa 3, Rosher 4)

Honor of the District Attorney, 1915 (Eason 4)

Honor of the Family, 1909 (Bitzer 4)

Honor of the Family, 1931 (Bacon 2, Daniels 3, Grot 4, Haller 4)

Honor of the Humble, 1914 (Lawrence 3)

Honor of the Mounted, 1914 (Dwan 2, Chaney 3)

Honor of the Nation. See Ei gerochsky podvig, 1914

Honor of the Press, 1932 (Eason 4)

Honor of the Regiment, 1913 (Meredyth 4)

Honor of Thieves, 1908 (Griffith 2, Bitzer 4)

Honor System, 1917 (Walsh 2)

Honor Thy Father, 1912 (Pickford 3)

Honor Thy Father, 1973 (Duning 4)

Honorable Algernon, 1913 (Talmadge 3)

Honorable Billy. See Society For Sale, 1918

Honorable Catherine, 1942 (L'Herbier 2, Feuillère 3, Barsacq 4, Jeanson 4)

Honorable Event. See Pickwick Papers, 1913

Honorable Friend, 1916 (Hayakawa 3)

Honorable Mr. Buggs, 1927 (Laurel and Hardy 3, Roach 4)

Honorable Société, 1978 (Dalio 3, Gélin 3)

Honorable Stanislas, agent secret, 1963 (Delerue 4)

Honorary Consul, 1983 (Caine 3, Gere 3, Hoskins 3, Greene 4)

Honoré de Marseilles, 1956 (Fernandel 3)

Honoring a Hero, 1910 (White 3)

Honor's Altar, 1916 (Sullivan 4)

Honour above All. See Blue Danube, 1928

Honour Redeemed. See Victoria Cross, 1917

Honourable Mr. Wong. See Hatchet Man, 1932

Honours Easy, 1935 (Brenon 2, Lockwood 3)

Honryu, 1926 (Tanaka 3)

Hoodlum, 1919 (Pickford 3, Rosher 4)

Hoodlum Empire, 1952 (Trevor 3)

Hoodlum Priest, 1961 (Wexler 3)

Hoodlum Saint, 1946 (Lansbury 3, Powell 3, Williams 3)

Hoodlum's Honor. See Ganovenehre, 1966

Hoodman Blind, 1923 (Ford 2)

Hoodoo, 1910 (White 3)

Hoodoo Ann, 1916 (Marsh 3)

Hoofs and Goofs, 1956 (Three Stooges 3)

Hook, 1963 (Douglas 3, Ruttenberg 4)

Hook, 1992 (Hoffman 3, Smith 3, Williams 3)

Hook and Hand, 1914 (Guy 2)

Hook and Ladder, 1924 (Miller 4)

Hook and Ladder, 1932 (Roach 4)

Hook and Ladder Number One, 1932 (Terry 4)

Hook, Line, and Sinker, 1922 (Roach 4)

Hook, Line, and Sinker, 1930 (Musuraca 4)

Hook, Line, and Sinker, 1939 (Terry 4)

Hook, Line, and Sinker, 1969 (Lewis 2)

Hook, Line, and Stinker, 1958 (Blanc 4, Jones 4)

Hooked at the Altar, 1926 (Sennett 2)

Hookibi, 1928 (Hasegawa 3)

Hooks and Jabs, 1933 (Langdon 3)

Hoola Boola, 1941 (Pal 4)

Hooligans. See Golfos, 1960

Hooper, 1978 (Field 3, Reynolds 3, Needham 4)

Hoopla, 1933 (Bow 3)

Hooray for Love, 1935 (Robinson 3, Plunkett 4)

Hoose-Gow, 1929 (Laurel and Hardy 3, Roach 4)

Hoosier Romance, 1918 (Moore 3, Selig 4)

Hoosier Schoolboy, 1937 (Rooney 3)

Hoosiers, 1986 (Hackman 3, Hopper 3, Goldsmith 4)

Hoot Mon, 1919 (Laurel and Hardy 3, Roach 4)

Hootchy Kootchy Parlais Vous, 1930 (Messmer 4)

Hootenanny Hoot, 1963 (Katzman 4)

Hop and Go, 1943 (Blanc 4, Stalling 4)

Hop, Look and Listen, 1948 (Blanc 4, Foster 4, McKimson 4)

Hop Pickers. See Starci na chmelu, 1964

Hop, Skip and a Chump, 1942 (Blanc 4, Freleng 4)

Hop the Bell-Hop, 1919 (Laurel and Hardy 3)

Hop, the Devil's Brew, 1916 (Weber 2)

Hop to It, 1925 (Laurel and Hardy 3)

Hopalong Casualty, 1960 (Blanc 4, Jones 4)

Hopalong Rides Again, 1937 (Harlan 4, Head 4)

Hope, 1922 (Astor 3)

Hope and Glory, 1987 (Boorman 2)

Hope Chest, 1918 (Barthelmess 3, Garmes 4)

Hope Diamond Mystery, 1921 (Karloff 3)

Hope for the Hungry, 1953 (Rotha 2)

Hope Is Not Dead Yet. See Nozomi naki ni arazu, 1949

Hope of Blue Sky. See Kibo no aozora, 1960

Hopeful Donkey, 1943 (Terry 4)

Hopes of Blind Alley, 1914 (Dwan 2)

Hopi Legend, 1913 (Reid 3)

Hôpital de Leningrad, 1983 (Vogler 3)

Hoppity Pop, 1946 (McLaren 4)

Hoppla, jetzt kommt Eddie!, 1958 (Constantine 3)

Hoppsan!, 1955 (Andersson 3, Thulin 3)

Hoppy Daze, 1961 (Blanc 4, McKimson 4)

Hoppy Go Lucky, 1952 (Blanc 4, McKimson 4, Stalling 4)

Hoppy Serves a Writ, 1943 (Mitchum 3, Harlan 4)

Hopscotch, 1980 (Jackson 3, Lom 3, Matthau 3)

Hora de los hornos, 1968 (Solanas 2)

Horace Greeley, Jr., 1925 (Capra 2, Langdon 3)

Horace '62, 1962 (Trintignant 3)

Horde, 1928 (Tschechowa 3)

Hordubalové, 1937 (Frič 2)

Hordubals. See Hordubalové, 1937

Horizon, 1966 (Coutard 4)

Horizon. See Chiheisen, 1984

Horizon du Sud, 1924 (Modot 3)

Horizons nouveaux, 1961 (Delerue 4)

Horizons West, 1952 (Boetticher 2, Hudson 3, Ryan 3)

Horizontal Lieutenant, 1962 (Gillespie 4, Pasternak 4)

Horloger de Saint-Paul, 1974 (Tavernier 2, Noiret 3, Aurenche 4, Bost 4, Sarde 4)

Horn Blows at Midnight, 1945 (Walsh 2, Dumont 3, Pangborn 3, Waxman 4)

Horn i norr, 1950 (Sucksdorff 2)

Horňák and Koebner. See Muž bez srdce, 1923

Hornets' Nest, 1970 (Hudson 3, Morricone 4)

Horns and Hoofs. See Pinto Ben, 1915

Horoki, 1954 (Okada 3)

Horoki, 1962 (Naruse 2, Takamine 3, Tanaka 3, Tsukasa 3)

Horoscope for a Child, 1970 (Benegal 2)

Horror Castle. See Vergine de Norimberga, 1964

Horror Chamber of Dr. Faustus. See **Yeux sans visage, 1959**

Horror Express. See Panico en el Transiberiano, 1972

Horror Express, 1974 (Lee 3)

Horror Film 1, 1970 (Le Grice 2)

Horror Film 2, 1972 (Le Grice 2)

Horror Island, 1941 (Salter 4)

Horror Motel. See City of the Dead, 1960

Horror of Dracula. See **Dracula, 1958**

Horror of Frankenstein, 1970 (Bernard 4, Carreras 4, Sangster 4)

Horror of It All, 1964 (Fisher 2)

Horror of the Blood Monsters, 1970 (Carradine 3, Zsigmond 4)

Horror Show, 1979 (Perkins 3)

Horse. See Uma, 1941

Horse, 1965 (Warhol 2)

Horse, 1969 (Saulnier 4)

Horse, 1970 (Gabin 3)

Horse Collars, 1935 (Bruckman 4)

Horse Feathers, 1932 (McLeod 2, Marx Brothers 3, Mankiewicz 4, Zukor 4)

Horse Fly Opera, 1941 (Terry 4)

Horse Hare, 1960 (Blanc 4, Freleng 4)

Horse Hoofs, 1931 (Carey 3)

Horse on Bill, 1913 (Loos 4)

Horse on Holiday, 1959 (Henning-Jensen 2, Greenwood 3)

Horse on the Merry-Go-Round, 1938 (Iwerks 4)

Horse Over Tea Kettle, 1962 (Breer 4)
Horse Patrol. *See* Jízdní hlídka, 1936
Horse Play, 1924 (Lantz 4)
Horse Shoes, 1927 (Arthur 3, Bruckman 4)
Horse Shoo, 1964 (Hanna and Barbera 4)
Horse Soldiers, 1959 (Ford 2, Holden 3,
    Wayne 3, Clothier 4, Mirisch 4)
Horse Thief, 1905 (Bitzer 4)
Horse Thief, 1911 (Dwan 2)
Horse Thief, 1913 (Sennett 2)
Horse Thief's Bigamy, 1911 (Dwan 2)
Horse Trader, 1927 (Wyler 2)
Horse without a Head, 1963 (Lom 3,
    Clarke 4)
Horsefly Fleas, 1947 (Blanc 4, McKimson 4)
Horseherder. *See* Csikós, 1917
Horseman, 1971 (Sharif 3)
Horseman of the Plains, 1928 (Mix 3)
Horseman, The Woman and The Moth, 1968
    (Brakhage 2)
Horsemasters, 1961 (Pleasence 3, Francis 4)
Horsemen, 1970 (Frankenheimer 2,
    Palance 3, Delerue 4, Renoir 4,
    Trumbo 4)
Horsemen of the Wind. *See* Vsadniki vetra,
    1930
Horse-Race and Wife. *See* Kyouba to
    nyoubou, 1932
Horses and Their Ancestors, 1962
    (Hubley 4)
Horses Collars, 1935 (Three Stooges 3)
Horseshoe for Luck. *See* Podkova pro štěstí,
    1946
Horseshoe Nail, 1940 (Dickinson 2)
Horse's Mouth, 1958 (Guinness 3)
Horses of Death, 1972 (Dunning 4)
Horsing Around, 1956 (Three Stooges 3)
Horské volání SOS, 1929 (Stallich 4)
Hors-la-loi, 1985 (Sarde 4)
Horst Wessel. *See* Hans Westmar, 1933
Horton Hatches the Egg, 1942 (Blanc 4,
    Clampett 4, Maltese 4)
Horton Hears a Who, 1971 (Jones 4)
Hose, 1927 (Krauss 3)
Hosen des Ritters von Bredow, 1973
    (Mueller-Stahl 3)
Hospital, 1970 (Wiseman 2)
Hospital, 1971 (Scott 3, Chayefsky 4)
Hospital Massacre, 1982 (Golan and
    Globus 4)
Hospitaliky, 1937 (Fleischer 4)
Hostage, 1917 (Novarro 3, Reid 3)
Hostage, 1967 (Carradine 3, Stanton 3)
Hostage, 1987 (Black 3)
Hostage Tower, 1980 (Johnson 3, Roberts 3)
Hostages, 1943 (Bendix 3, Homolka 3,
    Lukas 3, Rainer 3, Dreier 4, Head 4,
    Young 4)
Hostile Guns, 1967 (De Carlo 3)
Hostile Witness, 1967 (Milland 3)
Höstsonaten. *See* Herbstsonate, 1978
Hot Air Salesman, 1937 (Fleischer 4)
Hot and Cold, 1933 (Lantz 4)
Hot Angel, 1958 (Struss 4)
Hot Blood, 1956 (Ray 2, Russell 3,
    Wilde 3)
Hot Box, 1972 (Corman 2, Demme 2)
Hot Cakes for Two, 1926 (Sennett 2)
Hot Car Girl, 1958 (Corman 2)
Hot Cross Bunny, 1948 (Blanc 4,
    McKimson 4, Stalling 4)
Hot Dog, 1928 (Disney 4)
Hot Dog, 1930 (Fleischer 4)
Hot Dogs. *See* Mabel's Busy Day, 1914

Hot Enough for June, 1963 (Bogarde 3,
    Box 4)
Hot Feet, 1931 (Lantz 4)
Hot Finish. *See* Mabel at the Wheel, 1914
Hot for Hollywood, 1930 (Lantz 4)
Hot for Paris, 1929 (Walsh 2, McLaglen 3,
    Carré 4)
Hot Heels, 1924 (Roach 4)
Hot Heir, 1931 (Balcon 4)
Hot Heiress, 1931 (Pidgeon 3, Polito 4)
Hot Ice, 1955 (Three Stooges 3)
Hot Lead, 1951 (Musuraca 4)
Hot Millions, 1968 (Malden 3, Smith 3,
    Ustinov 3)
Hot Money, 1935 (Edeson 4, Roach 4)
Hot Money Girl. *See* Treasure of San Teresa,
    1959
Hot Money Girls. *See* Treasure of San
    Teresa, 1959
Hot News, 1928 (Daniels 3, Lukas 3)
Hot Night. *See* Atsui yoru, 1968
Hot Off the Press, 1922 (Roach 4)
Hot Off the Press, 1934 (Katzman 4)
Hot Pepper, 1933 (McLaglen 3, Clarke 4,
    Nichols 4)
Hot Property, 1983 (Brocka 2)
Hot Resort, 1984 (Golan and Globus 4)
Hot Rhythm, 1944 (Langdon 3)
Hot Rock, 1972 (Yates 2, Redford 3, Segal 3,
    Goldman 4, Jones 4)
Hot Rod Action, 1969 (Zsigmond 4)
Hot Rod and Reel, 1959 (Blanc 4, Jones 4)
Hot Rod Gang, 1958 (Crosby 4)
Hot Rods, 1953 (Terry 4)
Hot Rods to Hell, 1967 (Andrews 3,
    Katzman 4)
Hot Sands, 1934 (Terry 4)
Hot Saturday, 1932 (Darwell 3, Grant 3,
    Scott 3, Head 4)
Hot Scots, 1948 (Three Stooges 3)
Hot Shots!, 1991 (Scott 3)
Hot Spell, 1936 (Terry 4)
Hot Spell, 1958 (Cukor 2, MacLaine 3,
    Quinn 3, Head 4, North 4, Wallis 4,
    Westmore Family 4)
Hot Spot, 1932 (Roach 4)
Hot Spot, 1941 (Grable 3, Mature 3,
    Cronjager 4)
Hot Spot, 1990 (Hopper 3)
Hot Stuff, 1911 (Sennett 2)
Hot Stuff, 1924 (Roach 4)
Hot Stuff, 1929 (Leroy 2)
Hot Stuff, 1956 (Three Stooges 3)
Hot Summer Game, 1965 (Zsigmond 4)
Hot Summer Night, 1957 (Previn 4)
Hot Time in the Old Town Tonight, 1930
    (Fleischer 4)
Hot Tip, 1935 (Plunkett 4)
Hot Touch, 1980 (Vadim 2)
Hot Turkey, 1930 (Terry 4)
Hot Water, 1924 (Lloyd 3, Roach 4,
    Zukor 4)
Hot Wind. *See* Neppu, 1943
Hotel, 1967 (Douglas 3, Malden 3, Oberon 3,
    Head 4, Lang 4)
Hotel Adlon, 1955 (Wagner 4)
Hotel Berlin, 1945 (Lorre 3, Massey 3,
    Waxman 4)
Hotel Colonial, 1987 (Duvall 3, Donaggio 4,
    Rotunno 4)
Hotel Continental, 1931 (Walthall 3)
Hôtel de la gare, 1914 (Feuillade 2)
Hotel des Amériques, 1982 (Deneuve 3)
Hotel des étudiants, 1932 (Périnal 4)

Hôtel des Invalides, 1951 (Franju 2,
    Fradetal 4, Jarre 4)
Hotel du Lac, 1985 (Elliott 3)
Hôtel du libre-échange, 1934 (Fernandel 3,
    Grimault 4, Meerson 4, Prévert 4,
    Trauner 4)
Hôtel du Nord, 1938 (Carné 2, Arletty 3,
    Blier 3, Jouvet 3, Aurenche 4, Jaubert 4,
    Jeanson 4, Trauner 4)
Hotel du paradis, 1986 (Rey 3)
Hôtel du silence, 1908 (Cohl 4)
Hotel for Women, 1939 (Darnell 3,
    Zanuck 4)
Hotel Geheimnisse, 1928 (Metzner 4)
Hotel Haywire, 1937 (Sturges 2, Pangborn 3,
    Head 4)
Hotel Honeymoon, 1912 (Guy 2)
Hotel Imperial, 1927 (Stiller 2, Negri 3,
    Furthman 4, Glennon 4, Pommer 4)
Hotel Imperial, 1939 (Florey 2, Milland 3,
    Head 4)
Hotel Mixup. *See* Mabel's Strange
    Predicament, 1914
Hotel Modrá hvězda, 1941 (Frič 2)
Hotel Monterey, 1972 (Akerman 2)
Hotel New Hampshire, 1984 (Richardson 2,
    Foster 3, Kinski 3, Watkin 4)
Hotel of the Americas. *See* Hotel des
    Amériques, 1982
Hotel Paradiso, 1966 (Guinness 3,
    Lollobrigida 3, Carrière 4, Decaë 4)
Hotel Potemkin, 1924 (Banky 3)
Hotel Reserve, 1944 (Lom 3, Mason 3)
Hotel Sahara, 1951 (De Carlo 3, Ustinov 3)
Hotel Splendide, 1932 (Powell and
    Pressburger 2)
Hotel Terminus: Klaus Barbie, His Life and
    Times, 1988 (Ophuls 2)
Hothouse, 1981 (Pinter 4)
Hothouse, 1988 (Allen 4)
Hotlips Jasper, 1945 (Pal 4)
Hotori musuko, 1936 (Ryu 3)
Hototogisu, 1932 (Hasegawa 3, Takamine 3)
Hotsy Footsy, 1952 (Bosustow 4, Burness 4)
Hotsy Toty, 1925 (Sennett 2)
Hottentot, 1922 (Garnett 2)
Hottentot, 1929 (Horton 3)
Hotter Than Hot, 1929 (Langdon 3, Roach 4)
Houat, 1963 (Fradetal 4)
Houdini, 1953 (Curtis 3, Leigh 3, Head 4,
    Laszlo 4, Pal 4)
Hound Dog Man, 1959 (Siegel 2, Darwell 3,
    Clarke 4, Wald 4, Wheeler 4)
Hound for Trouble, 1951 (Blanc 4, Jones 4,
    Stalling 4)
Hound Hunters, 1947 (Avery 4)
Hound of the Baskervilles, 1939
    (Carradine 3, Rathbone 3, Day 4)
Hound of the Baskervilles, 1959 (Fisher 2,
    Cushing 3, Lee 3, Bernard 4, Carreras 4)
Hound of the Baskervilles, 1969 (Granger 3)
Hound of the Baskervilles, 1977 (Elliott 3,
    Greenwood 3, Matthews 3, Moore 3,
    Terry-Thomas 3)
Hounded. *See* Johnny Allegro, 1949
Hounding the Hares, 1947 (Terry 4)
Hounds of Zaroff. *See* Most Dangerous
    Game, 1932
Hour after Hour, 1974 (Nowicki 3)
Hour and the Man, 1914 (Bushman 3)
Hour Before the Dawn, 1944 (Lake 3,
    Dreier 4, Head 4, Rozsa 4, Seitz 4)
Hour for Lunch, 1938 (Benchley 4)
Hour Glass, 1972 (Popescu-Gopo 4)

Hour of Parting. *See* Afskedens timme, 1973
Hour of Terror, 1910 (White 3)
Hour of the Furnace. *See* Hora de los hornos, 1968
Hour of the Gun, 1967 (Sturges 2, Garner 3, Robards 3, Ryan 3, Voight 3, Anhalt 4, Ballard 4, Goldsmith 4)
Hour of the Trial. *See* I. Prövningens stund, 1916
Hour of the Wolf. *See* Vargtimmen, 1968
Hour of 13, 1952 (Addison 4, Green 4, Junge 4)
Hours Between. *See* Twenty-Four Hours, 1931
House. *See* Dom, 1958
House Across the Bay, 1940 (Hitchcock 2, Bennett 3, Pidgeon 3, Raft 3, Irene 4, Wanger 4)
House Across the Lake, 1954 (Carreras 4)
House, after Five Years of Living, 1955 (Bernstein 4)
House at the End of the World. *See* Die, Monster, Die!, 1965
House Behind the Cedars, 1925 (Micheaux 2)
House Broken, 1936 (Havelock-Allan 4)
House Builder-Upper, 1938 (Fleischer 4)
House Built Upon Sand, 1917 (Gish 3)
House Busters, 1952 (Terry 4)
House by the River, 1950 (Lang 2, Cronjager 4, Leven 4)
House Calls, 1978 (Jackson 3, Matthau 3, Bumstead 4, Epstein 4, Mancini 4)
House Cleaning Blues, 1937 (Fleischer 4)
House Divided, 1919 (Blackton 2)
House Divided, 1931 (Huston 2, Wyler 2, Huston 3, Fulton 4)
House Hunting Mice, 1947 (Blanc 4, Jones 4)
House I Live In, 1945 (Leroy 2, Sinatra 3)
House in Bayswater, 1960 (Russell 2)
House in Nightmare Park, 1973 (Milland 3)
House in the Snow-Drifts. *See* Dom v sugribakh, 1928
House in the Square, 1951 (Alwyn 4)
House Is Not a Home, 1964 (Crawford 3, Taylor 3, Welch 3, Winters 3, Head 4)
House No. 44. *See* Makan no. 44, 1955
House of a Thousand Candles, 1915 (Selig 4)
House of a Thousand Candles, 1936 (Lewis 2)
House of a Thousand Dolls. *See* Haus der tausend Freuden, 1967
House of Bamboo, 1955 (Fuller 2, Hayakawa 3, Ryan 3, LeMaire 4, Wheeler 4)
House of Blackmail, 1953 (Lassally 4)
House of Bondage, 1913 (Ince 4)
House of Cards, 1916 (Guy 2)
House of Cards, 1969 (Welles 2, Head 4, Lai 4, Ravetch 4)
House of Connelly. *See* Carolina, 1934
House of Crazies. *See* Asylum, 1972
House of Dark Shadows, 1970 (Bennett 3, Smith 4)
House of Darkness, 1913 (Griffith 2, Barrymore 3, Gish 3, Bitzer 4)
House of Darkness, 1948 (Harvey 3)
House of Death. *See* Smerti doma, 1915
House of Discord, 1913 (Barrymore 3, Sweet 3)
House of Doom. *See* Black Cat, 1934

House of Dracula, 1945 (Carradine 3, Pierce 4, Salter 4)
House of Dracula's Daughter, 1973 (Carradine 3, Crawford 3)
House of Errors, 1942 (Langdon 3)
House of Evil, 1972 (Karloff 3)
House of Evil. *See* House on Sorority Row, 1982
House of Exorcism. *See* Lisa e il diavolo, 1972
House of Fate. *See* Muss 'em Up, 1936
House of Fear, 1939 (Krasner 4)
House of Fear, 1945 (Rathbone 3, Lourié 4, Miller 4, Salter 4)
House of Folly. *See* Dårskapens hus, 1951
House of Frankenstein, 1944 (Carradine 3, Karloff 3, Fulton 4, Pierce 4, Salter 4, Siodmak 4)
House of Freaks, 1973 (Brazzi 3)
House of Fright. *See* Two Faces of Doctor Jekyll, 1960
House of Hate, 1918 (White 3)
House of Horror, 1929 (Christensen 2, Haller 4, Polito 4)
House of Horror, 1946 (Salter 4)
House of Long Shadows, 1983 (Carradine 3, Cushing 3)
House of Lovers. *See* Pot bouille, 1957
House of Magic, 1937 (Lantz 4)
House of Marney, 1927 (Hepworth 2)
House of Mystery, 1910 (White 3)
House of Numbers, 1957 (Palance 3, Folsey 4, Previn 4, Schnee 4)
House of Pleasure. *See* Plaisir, 1952
House of Pride, 1912 (Bushman 3)
House of Ricordi. *See* Casa Ricordi, 1954
House of Rothschild, 1934 (Arliss 3, Karloff 3, Young, L. 3, Young, R. 3, Day 4, Johnson 4, Newman 4, Westmore Family 4, Zanuck 4)
House of Secrets, 1956 (Buckner 4, Green 4, Rank 4, Vetchinsky 4)
House of Settlement. *See* Mr. Soft Touch, 1949
House of Seven Gables, 1940 (Price 3)
House of Silence, 1918 (Crisp 3, Reid 3)
House of Silence, 1962 (Bernstein 4)
House of Strangers, 1949 (Mankiewicz 2, Hayward 3, Krasner 4, LeMaire 4, Wheeler 4)
House of the Angel. *See* casa del ángel, 1957
House of the Arrow, 1953 (Homolka 3)
House of the Black Death, 1965 (Carradine 3)
House of the Long Shadows, 1983 (Lee 3, Price 3, Golan and Globus 4)
House of the Seven Corpses, 1974 (Carradine 3)
House of the Seven Gables, 1940 (Sanders 3, Krasner 4)
House of the Seven Hawks, 1959 (Taylor 3)
House of the Sleeping Virgins. *See* Nemurero bijo, 1968
House of the Spaniard, 1936 (Dickinson 2)
House of the Tolling Bell, 1920 (Blackton 2)
House of the Yellow Carpet. *See* Casa del tappetto giallo, 1983
House of Tomorrow, 1949 (Avery 4)
House of Trent, 1933 (Bennett 2)
House of Usher, 1960 (Price 3, Crosby 4)
House of Usher. *See* Jan Svankmajer: Alchemist of the Surreal, 1990
House of Wax, 1953 (De Toth 2, Bronson 3, Price 3, Glennon 4, Warner 4)

House of Women. *See* Kvinnohuset, 1953
House of Women. *See* Haus der Frauen, 1977
House of Wrath, 1924 (Sullivan 4)
House on Carroll Street, 1988 (Yates 2, Ballhaus 4, Delerue 4)
House on Chelouche Street, 1973 (Golan and Globus 4)
House on 56th Street, 1933 (Florey 2, Francis 3, Haller 4, Orry-Kelly 4)
House on Garibaldi Street, 1979 (Topol 3)
House on Green Apple Road, 1970 (Leigh 3, Pidgeon 3)
House on Haunted Hill, 1959 (Price 3)
House on 92nd Street, 1945 (Hathaway 2, De Rochemont 4, Wheeler 4, Zanuck 4)
House on Sorority Row, 1982 (Goldsmith 4)
House on Telegraph Hill, 1951 (Wise 2, Ballard 4, LeMaire 4, Newman 4, Wheeler 4)
House That Dinky Built, 1925 (Lantz 4)
House That Dripped Blood, 1970 (Cushing 3, Elliott 3, Lee 3)
House that Jack Built, 1911 (Dwan 2)
House That Wouldn't Die, 1970 (Stanwyck 3)
House with the Closed Shutters, 1910 (Griffith 2, Walthall 3, Bitzer 4)
House with the Golden Windows, 1916 (Reid 3)
House Without a Christmas Tree, 1972 (Robards 3)
House without Windows. *See* Dom bez okien, 1962
Houseboat, 1916 (Sennett 2)
Houseboat, 1958 (Grant 3, Loren 3, Duning 4, Edouart 4, Fulton 4, Head 4, Westmore Family 4)
Housebreakers, 1914 (Browning 2)
Household Pest, 1910 (Talmadge 3)
Householder, 1963 (Ivory 2, Jhabvala 4, Mitra 4)
Housekeeper of Circle C, 1913 (Anderson 3)
Housekeeper's Daughter, 1939 (Bennett 3, Mature 3, Menjou 3, Irene 4, Roach 4)
Housemaster, 1938 (Brenon 2)
Housewife, 1934 (Brennan 3, Orry-Kelly 4)
Housewife Herman, 1938 (Terry 4)
Housewife Herman, 1938 (Terry 4)
Housing Problem, 1946 (Terry 4)
Houston Story, 1956 (Katzman 4)
Houston Texas, 1956 (Braunberger 4)
Houston Texas, 1976 (Jarman 2)
How a Man Loves. *See* Woman He Loved, 1922
How a Mosquito Operates, 1912 (McCay 4)
How Awful about Allan, 1970 (Perkins 3)
How Cissy Made Good, 1915 (Bunny 3)
How Could William Tell, 1919 (La Cava 2)
How Could You, Caroline?, 1918 (Love 3)
How Could You, Jean?, 1918 (Pickford 3, Marion 4, Rosher 4)
How Did a Nice Girl Like You Get into This Business. *See* Wie kommt ein so reizendes Mädchen zu diesem Gewerbe?, 1970
How Do I Know It's Sunday, 1934 (Freleng 4)
How Do I Love Thee?, 1970 (O'Hara 3, Winters 3, Metty 4)
How Dry I Am, 1920 (Roach 4)
How Ducks Are Fattened, 1899 (Bitzer 4)
How Films Are Made, 1914 (Phalke 2)
How Funny Can Sex Be?. *See* Sesso matto, 1973

How Grandpa Changed Till Nothing Was Left. *See* Jak stařeček měnil až vyměnil, 1953

How Green Was My Valley, 1941 (Ford 2, Crisp 3, Fitzgerald 3, McDowall 3, O'Hara 3, Pidgeon 3, Banton 4, Day 4, Dunne 4, La Shelle 4, Miller 4, Newman 4, Zanuck 4)

How Hazel Got Even, 1915 (Crisp 3)

How He Lied to Her Husband, 1930 (Launder and Gilliat 2)

How He Prepared the Room, 1912 (Bunny 3)

How Heroes Are Made, 1914 (Sennett 2)

How High Is Up?, 1940 (Three Stooges 3)

How Hiram Won Out, 1913 (Sennett 2, Arbuckle 3)

How I Became Krazy, 1921 (Bray 4)

How I Flew from London to Paris in 25 Hrs and 11 Minutes, 1965 (Terry-Thomas 3)

How I Play Golf, 1931 (Cagney 3)

How I Play Golf No. 7: The Spoon, 1933 (Huston 3)

How I Spent My Summer Vacation. *See* Deadly Roulette, 1966

How I Won the War, 1967 (Lester 2, Watkin 4)

How It Feels to be Run Over, 1900 (Hepworth 2)

How It Happened, 1913 (Mix 3)

How Jones Lost His Roll, 1905 (Porter 2)

How Kico Was Born, 1951 (Vukotić 4)

How Man Learned to Fly. *See* Jak se člověk naučil létat, 1958

How Max Went Around the World. *See* Comment Max fait le tour du monde, 1913

How Mike Got the Soap in His Eyes, 1903 (Bitzer 4)

How Motion Pictures Are Made, 1914 (Sennett 2)

How Much Do You Owe?. *See* Jackpot, 1950

How Much Wood Would a Woodchuck Chuck, 1976 (Herzog 2)

How Nerves Are Made, 1914 (Normand 3)

How Not to Dress. *See* Herr och fru Stockholm, 1921

How Not to Lose Your Head While Shotfiring, 1973 (Dunning 4)

How Not to Succeed in Business, 1975 (Halas and Batchelor 4)

How Now Boing Boing, 1954 (Bosustow 4)

How Rastus Gets His Turkey, 1910 (White 3)

How Rulers Live, 1932 (Ptushko 4)

How She Triumphed, 1911 (Griffith 2, Sweet 3, Bitzer 4)

How Sweet It Is!, 1968 (Dalio 3, Garner 3, Reynolds 3, Terry-Thomas 3, Ballard 4, Rose 4)

How the Burglar Tricked the Bobby, 1901 (Hepworth 2)

How the Day Was Saved, 1913 (Loos 4)

How the F-100 Got Its Tail, 1955 (Leacock 2)

How the Grinch Stole Christmas, 1970 (Jones 3)

How the West Was Won, 1963 (Ford 2, Hathaway 2, Baker 3, Brennan 3, Cobb 3, Fonda 3, Malden 3, Massey 3, Moorehead 3, Peck 3, Preston 3, Reynolds 3, Ritter 3, Stewart 3, Tracy 3, Van Cleef 3, Wallach 3, Wayne 3, Widmark 3, Cahn 4, Canutt 4, Daniels 4,

Gillespie 4, Krasner 4, Lang 4, La Shelle 4, Mercer 4, Newman 4, Plunkett 4)

How to . . . series, 1935–41 (Benchley 4)

How to Be a Hostess, 1959 (Halas and Batchelor 4)

How to be a Woman and Survive, 1990 (Maura 3)

How to Be Loved. *See* Jak być kochana, 1962

How to Be Very, Very Popular, 1955 (Grable 3, Cahn 4, Johnson 4, Krasner 4, LeMaire 4)

How to Beat the High Cost of Living, 1980 (Lange 3)

How to Break Ninety. *See* Hip Action, 1933

How to Commit Marriage, 1969 (Hope 3, Wyman 3, Frank 4, Lang 4)

How to Destroy the Reputation of the Greatest Secret Agent. . . . *See* Magnifique, 1974

How to Fill a Wild Bikini. *See* How to Stuff a Wild Bikini, 1965

How to Fire a Lewis Gun, 1918 (Fleischer 4)

How to Fire a Stokes Mortar, 1918 (Fleischer 4)

How to Furnish a Flat. *See* Jak zařídit byt, 1960

How to Handle Women, 1928 (Lugosi 3)

How to Have Love Flame on the Spot, even for the Deceased. *See* Tu Ten Kámen, 1923

How to Keep a Husband, 1914 (Loos 4)

How to Keep Cool, 1953 (Terry 4)

How to Keep Slim. *See* Jak na to, 1963

How to Make a French Dish. *See* Bonne Soupe, 1963

How to Marry a Millionaire, 1953 (Negulesco 2, Bacall 3, Grable 3, Monroe 3, Powell 3, Johnson 4, LeMaire 4, Newman 4, Wheeler 4)

How to Murder a Rich Uncle, 1957 (Caine 3, Coburn 3, Box 4, Paxton 4)

How to Murder Your Wife, 1965 (Lemmon 3, Trevor 3, Terry-Thomas 3, Axelrod 4, Stradling 4, Sylbert 4)

How to Read an Army Map, 1918 (Fleischer 4)

How to Relax, 1954 (Terry 4)

How to Save a Marriage—and Ruin Your Life, 1968 (Martin 3, Wallach 3, Garmes 4, Legrand 4)

How to Score a Movie, 1978 (Howard 3)

How to Steal a Diamond in Four Uneasy Lessons. *See* Hot Rock, 1972

How to Steal a Million, 1966 (Wyler 2, Boyer 3, Dalio 3, Hepburn 3, O'Toole 3, Wallach 3, Lang 4, Trauner 4, Williams 4)

How to Steal an Airplane, 1971 (Mineo 3)

How to Stop a Motor Car, 1902 (Hepworth 2)

How to Stuff a Wild Bikini, 1965 (Keaton 2, Rooney 3, Crosby 4)

How to Succeed in Business without Really Trying, 1967 (Boyle 4, Guffey 4)

How to Succeed with Sex, 1972 (Katzman 4)

How Villains Are Made. *See* Race, 1914

How Weary Went Wooing, 1915 (Mix 3)

How Wet Was My Ocean, 1940 (Terry 4)

How Women Love, 1922 (Stradling 4)

Howard the Duck, 1986 (Lucas 2, Barry 4, Blanc 4)

Howard's End, 1991 (Hopkins 3, Jhabvala 4)

Howards of Virginia, 1940 (Grant 3, Ladd 3, Buchman 4, Glennon 4, Vorkapich 4)

Howling, 1980 (Corman 2, Dante 2, Sayles 2, Carradine 3, Baker 4, Bottin 4, Donaggio 4)

Howling II: Your Sister is a Werewolf, 1985 (Lee 3)

Howling Success, 1954 (Terry 4)

How's About It, 1943 (Three Stooges 3)

How've You Been?, 1933 (Arbuckle 3)

Hoyden, 1911 (Lawrence 3)

Hoyo, 1953 (Mifune 3)

Hr. Tell og Søn, 1929 (Madsen and Schenstrøm 3)

Hra o život, 1956 (Weiss 2)

Hraběnka z Podskali, 1925 (Ondra 3, Heller 4)

Hrabina Cosel, 1968 (Olbrychski 3)

Hranjenik, 1970 (Mimica 4)

Hrátky s čertem, 1956 (Stallich 4)

Hřích, 1929 (Heller 4)

Hřichy v manželstvi, 1924 (Ondra 3)

Hu Man, 1974 (Moreau 3, Stamp 3)

Huang Baomei, 1958 (Xie 2)

Huang Tudi, 1984 (Chen 2)

Hubbi el Wahid, 1960 (Sharif 3)

Hubby Buys a Baby, 1913 (Bunny 3)

Hubby to the Rescue, 1914 (Browning 2)

Hubby's Job, 1913 (Sennett 2, Normand 3)

Hubby's Latest Alibi, 1928 (Sennett 2, Hornbeck 4)

Hubby's Quiet Little Game, 1926 (Sennett 2)

Hubby's Toothache, 1913 (Bunny 3)

Hubby's Week End Trip, 1928 (Sennett 2, Hornbeck 4)

Huckleberry Finn, 1930 (Darwell 3, Zukor 4)

Huckleberry Finn. *See* Adventures of Huckleberry Finn, 1939 (Seitz 4)

Huckleberry Finn, 1974 (Kovacs 4)

Hucksters, 1947 (Gable 3, Gardner 3, Greenstreet 3, Kerr 3, Menjou 3, Irene 4, Mayer 4, Rosson 4)

Hud, 1963 (Ritt 2, Douglas 3, Neal 3, Newman 3, Bernstein 4, Edouart 4, Head 4, Howe 4, Ravetch 4, Westmore Family 4)

Hud, 1986 (Stamp 3)

Huddle, 1932 (Wood 2, Novarro 3, Adrian 4, Gillespie 4, Sullivan 4)

Hudson Hawk, 1991 (Coburn 3)

Hudson's Bay, 1940 (Muni 3, Price 3, Tierney 3, Banton 4, Barnes 4, Day 4, MacGowan 4, Newman 4, Trotti 4)

Hue and Cry, 1947 (Crichton 2, Sim 3, Auric 4, Balcon 4, Clarke 4, Slocombe 4)

Huellas del pasado, 1950 (Alcoriza 4)

Huey. *See* Black Panthers, 1968

Hug Bug, 1926 (Roach 4)

Huggetts Abroad, 1949 (Box 4, Rank 4)

Hughie at the Victory Derby, 1919 (Pearson 2)

Hugo architecte, 1964 (Rohmer 2)

Hugs and Mugs, 1950 (Three Stooges 3)

Huguenot, 1909 (Feuillade 2, Carré 4, Gaumont 4)

Huilor, 1938 (Alexeieff and Parker 4, Auric 4)

Huis clos, 1954 (Arletty 3, Kosma 4)

Huit hommes dans un château, 1942 (Aurenche 4, Honegger 4)

Huit Jours de bonheur. *See* Liebesexpress, 1931

Huitième Jour, 1960 (Fradetal 4, Kosma 4)

Hula, 1927 (Fleming 2, Hathaway 2, Bow 3, Schulberg 4)

Hula from Hollywood, 1954 (Kaye 3)

Hula Hula Land, 1917 (Sennett 2)

Hula Hula Land, 1949 (Terry 4)

Hula La La, 1951 (Three Stooges 3)

Hulchul, 1951 (Kumar 3)

Hulda from Holland, 1916 (Pickford 3)

Hulda's Lovers, 1908 (Bitzer 4)

Hullabaloo over Georgie and Bonnie's Pictures, 1978 (Ivory 2, Jhabvala 4, Lassally 4)

Hullo Everybody. See Getting Acquainted, 1914

Hullo Fame, 1941 (Ustinov 3)

Hulyeseg nem Akadaly, 1985 (Nowicki 3)

Hum, 1990 (Bachchan 3)

Hum Bhi Insaan Hai, 1948 (Anand 3)

Hum Dono, 1961 (Anand 3)

Hum ek Hain, 1946 (Dutt 2)

Hum Naujawan, 1985 (Anand 3)

Hum paanch, 1981 (Azmi 3)

Hum Safar, 1953 (Anand 3)

Hum Tum aur Woh, 1938 (Biswas 4)

Humain trop humain, 1972 (Malle 2)

Human Beast. See **Bête humaine, 1938**

Human Being. See Ningen, 1925

Human Cargo, 1936 (Dwan 2, Hayworth 3, Trevor 3)

Human Collateral, 1920 (Costello 3)

Human Comedy, 1943 (Brown 2, Johnson 3, Mitchum 3, Reed 3, Rooney 3, Estabrook 4, Gibbons 4, Irene 4, Stothart 4, Stradling 4)

Human Condition. See **Ningen no joken, 1959–61**

Human Desire, 1919 (Mayer 4)

Human Desire, 1954 (Lang 2, Crawford 3, Ford 3, Grahame 3, Guffey 4, Wald 4)

Human Driftwood, 1915 (Tourneur 2)

Human Face Is a Monument, 1965 (Vanderbeek 2)

Human Factor, 1975 (Dmytryk 2, Mills 3, Morricone 4)

Human Factor, 1979 (Preminger 2, Attenborough 3, Gielgud 3, Greene 4)

Human Fish, 1932 (Sennett 2, Bruckman 4)

Human Growth, 1947 (Hubley 4)

Human Highway, 1982 (Hopper 3)

Human Hounds, 1916 (Laurel and Hardy 3)

Human Hound's Triumph, 1915 (Sennett 2)

Human Jungle, 1954 (Salter 4)

Human Kindness, 1913 (Dwan 2)

Human Monster, 1939 (Lugosi 3)

Human Revolution. See Ningen kakumei, 1973

Human Revolution: Sequel. See Zoku ningen kakumai, 1976

Human Sabotage. See Murder in the Big House, 1942

Human Side, 1934 (Bond 3, Menjou 3)

Human Sparrows. See Sparrows, 1926

Human Stuff, 1920 (Carey 3, Eason 4)

Human Tornado, 1925 (Canutt 4)

Human Vapor. See Gasu ningen daiichigo, 1960

Human Wreckage, 1923 (Love 3, Ince 4, Sullivan 4)

Human Zoo, 1961 (Kuri 4)

Humanity. See Insaniyat, 1955

Humanoid. See Unanoide, 1979

Humanoids from the Deep, 1980 (Bottin 4)

Humayun, 1945 (Mehboob 2)

Humdrum Brown, 1918 (Ingram 2, Walthall 3)

Hume Ek Hai, 1946 (Anand 3)

Humming Bird, 1924 (Olcott 2, Swanson 3)

Humoresque, 1920 (Borzage 2, Marion 4, Zukor 4)

Humoresque, 1946 (Negulesco 2, Crawford 3, Garfield 3, Adrian 4, Haller 4, Wald 4, Waxman 4)

Humoresques. See Iumoreski, 1924

Humorous Phases of Funny Faces, 1906 (Blackton 2)

Humour noir, 1964 (Autant-Lara 2, Brasseur 3, Valli 3, Aurenche 4, Bost 4, Douy 4)

Hump Back Angel, 1984 (Woodward 3)

Humpty Dumpty, 1935 (Iwerks 4)

Hun Within, 1918 (Von Stroheim 2)

Hunchback, 1914 (Gish 3, Loos 4)

Hunchback and the Dancer. See Bucklige und die Tänzerin, 1920

Hunchback of Notre Dame, 1923 (Chaney 3, Sherwood 4, Thalberg 4)

Hunchback of Notre Dame, 1939 (Dieterle 2, Laughton 3, O'Brien 3, O'Hara 3, August 4, Berman 4, Dunn 4, Levien 4, Newman 4, Plunkett 4, Polglase 4, Pommer 4, Westmore Family 4)

Hunchback of Notre Dame. See Notre Dame de Paris, 1956

Hunchback of Notre Dame, 1981 (Gielgud 3, Hopkins 3)

Hunchback of Rome. See Gobbo, 1960

Hund von Baskerville, 1914 (Freund 4, Warm 4)

Hund von Baskerville, 1929 (Rasp 3)

Hund von Baskerville, 1936 (Rasp 3)

Hundert Tage, 1935 (Gründgens 3, Krauss 3)

Hundra, 1983 (Morricone 4)

Hundred Men and a Girl, 1937 (Durbin 3)

Hundred Pound Window, 1943 (Fisher 2, Attenborough 3, Heller 4)

Hundred Thousand Children, 1955 (Anderson 2, Lassally 4)

Hundstage, 1944 (Stallich 4)

Hungarian Goulash, 1930 (Terry 4)

Hungarian Nights. See Es flüstert die Nacht, 1929

Hungarian Rhapsody. See Ungarische Rhapsodie, 1913

Hungarian Rhapsody. See Ungarische Rhapsodie, 1928

Hungarn in Flammen, 1957 (Kovacs 4, Zsigmond 4)

Hunger. See Tex, 1982

Hunger, 1984 (Deneuve 3, Love 3, Sarandon 3, Smith 4)

Hunger … Hunger … Hunger. See Gold … gold … gold, 1921

Hunger of the Blood, 1921 (Selig 4)

Hungers, 1987 (Emshwiller 2)

Hungry Dog, 1989 (Halas and Batchelor 4)

Hungry Heart, 1917 (Marion 4)

Hungry Hearts, 1916 (Laurel and Hardy 3)

Hungry Hill, 1947 (Lockwood 3, Simmons 3, Rank 4, Vetchinsky 4)

Hungry Hoboes, 1928 (Disney 4)

Hunky and Spunky, 1938 (Fleischer 4)

Huns and Hyphens, 1918 (Laurel and Hardy 3)

Hunt, 1915 (Sennett 2)

Hunt. See Caza, 1966

Hunt for Red October, 1990 (Connery 3, Jones 3)

Hunt the Man Down, 1950 (Musuraca 4)

Hunted, 1947 (Glazer 4)

Hunted, 1951 (Bogarde 3, Rank 4, Vetchinsky 4)

Hunted in Holland, 1961 (Dalrymple 4)

Hunted Men, 1938 (Crabbe 3, Quinn 3, Dreier 4, Head 4)

Hunted Through the Everglades, 1911 (Olcott 2)

Hunted Woman, 1925 (August 4)

Hunter, 1931 (Lantz 4)

Hunter, 1973 (Schifrin 4)

Hunter, 1980 (Belmondo 3, Johnson 3, McQueen 3, Wallach 3, Legrand 4, Stark 4)

Hunter of the Sun. See Taiyo no karyudo, 1970

Hunters, 1958 (Mitchum 3, Powell 3, Wagner 3, Clarke 4, LeMaire 4, Wheeler 4)

Hunters Are for Killing, 1970 (Douglas 3, Reynolds 3)

Hunters Are the Hunted. See Jagdszenden aus Niederbayern, 1969

Hunters Bold, 1924 (Roach 4)

Hunting Big Game in Africa, 1909 (Selig 4)

Hunting Flies. See Polowanie na muchy, 1969

Hunting for Germans in Berlin with Will Rogers, 1927 (Rogers 3)

Hunting of the Hawk, 1917 (Miller 4)

Hunting Party, 1971 (Hackman 3, Reed 3)

Hunting Scenes in Bavaria. See Jagdszenden aus Niederbayern, 1969

Hunting Scenes in Lower Bavaria. See Jagdszenden aus Niederbayern, 1969

Hunting Trouble, 1933 (Stevens 2)

Hunting We Will Go, 1980 (Halas and Batchelor 4)

Huntingtower, 1927 (Dickinson 2, Pearson 2)

Huntress, 1923 (Moore 3)

Hurdy Gurdy, 1929 (McCarey 2, Lantz 4, Roach 4)

Hurdy Gurdy Hare, 1950 (Blanc 4, McKimson 4, Stalling 4)

Hurly-Burly in the Circus. See Cirkus v cirkuse, 1975

Hurrah for Soldiers, 1962 (Baillie 2)

Hurrah! Ich lebe!, 1928 (Fröhlich 3, Courant 4)

Hurrah I'm Alive. See Hurrah! Ich lebe!, 1928

Hurra! Ich bin Papa!, 1939 (Von Harbou 4)

Hurricane, 1930 (Bosworth 3)

Hurricane, 1937 (Ford 2, Astor 3, Carradine 3, Lamour 3, Massey 3, Basevi 4, Day 4, Glennon 4, Goldwyn 4, Newman 4, Nichols 4)

Hurricane, 1979 (Farrow 3, Howard 3, Robards 3, Von Sydow 3, De Laurentiis 4, Donati 4, Nykvist 4, Rota 4)

Hurricane Express, 1932 (Wayne 3, Canutt 4)

Hurricane Horseman, 1925 (Arthur 3)

Hurricane Horseman, 1931 (Canutt 4)

Hurricane Island, 1951 (Katzman 4)

Hurricane Kid, 1925 (Miller 4)

Hurricane Rider, 1931 (Carey 3)

Hurricane Smith, 1952 (De Carlo 3, Head 4)

Hurricane's Girl, 1922 (Beery 3)

Hurricane's Pal, 1922 (Haskin 4)

Hurry Call, 1932 (Hunt 4)

Hurry, Charlie, Hurry, 1941 (Johnson 3, Musuraca 4)

Hurry, Doctor, 1925 (Sennett 2)

Hurry Doctor, 1931 (Fleischer 4)

Hurry, Hurry. *See* Deprisa, deprisa, 1980

Hurry Sundown, 1966 (Preminger 2, Caine 3, Dunaway 3, Fonda 3, Meredith 3, Krasner 4)

Hurry Up, Or I'll Be Thirty, 1973 (Levine 4)

Hurry West, 1921 (Roach 4)

Hurvínek's Circus. *See* Cirkus Hurvínek, 1955

Husarenliebe. *See* Es blasen die Trompetten, 1926

Husband Hunters, 1927 (Arthur 3)

Husbands, 1970 (Cassavetes 2, Falk 3)

Husbands and Lovers, 1924 (Stahl 2, Booth 4, Gaudio 4)

Husbands Beware, 1956 (Three Stooges 3, Bruckman 4)

Husbands or Lovers. *See* Nju, 1924

Husbands or Lovers. *See* Honeymoon in Bali, 1939

Husband's Reunion, 1933 (Sennett 2)

Huse til mennesker, 1972 (Roos 2)

Hush, 1920 (Edeson 4)

Hush … Hush, Sweet Charlotte, 1964 (Aldrich 2, Astor 3, Cotten 3, Davis 3, De Havilland 3, Dern 3, Moorehead 3, Biroc 4)

Hush Money, 1931 (Bennett 3, Loy 3, Raft 3, Nichols 4, Seitz 4)

Hush My Mouse, 1946 (Blanc 4, Jones 4, Stalling 4)

Hushed Hour, 1919 (Sweet 3, Edeson 4)

Hushing the Scandal, 1915 (Sennett 2)

Husmenna, 1986 (Andersson 3)

Hussards, 1955 (Blier 3, Auric 4)

Hussards et grisettes, 1901 (Guy 2)

Hussite Warrior. *See* Jan Žižka, 1955

Hustle, 1975 (Aldrich 2, Borgnine 3, Deneuve 3, Johnson 3, Reynolds 3, Biroc 4)

Hustler, 1921 (Roach 4)

Hustler, 1961 (Rossen 2, Newman 3, Scott 3, Allen 4, Horner 4, Schüfftan 4)

Hustlin' Hawk, 1923 (Rogers 3, Roach 4)

Hustling, 1975 (Clayburgh 3, Remick 3)

Hustling for Health, 1919 (Laurel and Hardy 3, Roach 4)

Hustruens Ret, 1913 (Psilander 3)

Hvem var Forbryderen?, 1912 (Psilander 3)

Hvězda zvaná Pelyněk, 1964 (Frič 2)

Hvide Hingst, 1962 (Watt 2)

Hvorledes Jeg Kom Till Filmen, 1919 (Psilander 3)

Hyakuman-nin no musume-tachi, 1963 (Iwashita 3)

Hyas, 1930 (Jaubert 4)

Hyde and Go Tweet, 1960 (Blanc 4, Freleng 4)

Hyde and Hare, 1955 (Blanc 4, Foster 4, Freleng 4, Stalling 4)

Hydrothérapie fantastique, 1910 (Méliès 2)

Hyena's Laugh, 1927 (Lantz 4)

Hymn of Nations, 1946 (Meredith 3)

Hymn to Her, 1974 (Brakhage 2)

Hyoroku yume monogatari, 1943 (Takamine 3, Tsuburaya 4)

Hypnotic Eyes, 1933 (Terry 4)

Hypnotist, 1922 (Fleischer 4)

Hypnotist. *See* London After Midnight, 1927

Hypnotist, 1980 (Halas and Batchelor 4)

Hypnotist's Revenge, 1907 (Bitzer 4)

Hypnotized, 1932 (Sennett 2, McDaniel 3, Hornbeck 4)

Hypnotized, 1952 (Terry 4)

Hypnotizing the Hypnotist, 1911 (Bunny 3)

Hyp-nut-tist, 1935 (Fleischer 4)

Hypochondriac. *See* Malato imaginario, 1979

Hypochondri-Cat, 1950 (Blanc 4, Jones 4, Maltese 4, Stalling 4)

Hypocrites, 1914 (Weber 2, Bosworth 3, Marion 4)

Hypothèse du tableau volé, 1978 (Vierny 4)

Hypothesis. *See* Hipoteza, 1972

Hypothesis of the Stolen Painting. *See* Hypothèse du tableau volé, 1978

Hysteria, 1964 (Carreras 4, Francis 4, Sangster 4)

Hysterical High Spots in American History, 1941 (Lantz 4)

I.N.R.I., 1923 (Wiene 2, Krauss 3, Nielsen 3, Porten 3, Metzner 4)

I Accuse!, 1957 (Ferrer 3, Lom 3, Walbrook 3, Alwyn 4)

I Aim at the Stars, 1960 (Lom 3)

I Ain't Got Nobody, 1932 (Fleischer 4)

I Am a Camera, 1955 (Clayton 2, Harvey 3, Winters 3, Arnold 4, Dehn 4, Green 4, Korda 4, Mathieson 4)

I Am a Fugitive from a Chain Gang, 1932 (Leroy 2, Muni 3, Orry-Kelly 4, Polito 4, Wallis 4, Warner 4, Zanuck 4)

I Am a Girl with the Devil in My Body. *See* Jsem děvče s čertem v těle, 1933

I Am a Thief, 1934 (Florey 2, Orry-Kelly 4, Astor 3, Blanke 4)

I Am Suzanne, 1934 (Garmes 4, Lasky 4)

I Am the Cheese, 1983 (Wagner 3)

I Am the Law, 1922 (Beery 3)

I Am the Law, 1938 (Robinson 3, Swerling 4)

I Am the Man, 1924 (Barrymore 3)

I Am Tokichiro. *See* Baku wa Toukichiroh, 1955

I and My Lovers. *See* Galia, 1965

I Became a Criminal. *See* They Made Me a Fugitive, 1947

I Beg a Word. *See* Proshu slova, 1976

I Believe in You, 1951 (Dearden 2, Harvey 3, Johnson 3)

I Believed in You, 1934 (Beavers 3)

I Blush. *See* Jag rödnar, 1981

I Bombed Pearl Harbor. *See* Taiheiyo no arashi, 1960

I Call First, 1967 (Scorsese 2)

I Can Get It for You Wholesale, 1951 (Polonsky 2, Hayward 3, Jaffe 3, Sanders 3, Krasner 4, LeMaire 4)

I Can Hardly Wait, 1943 (Three Stooges 3, Bruckman 4)

I Cannot Say That Person's Name. *See* Sono hito no na wa ienai, 1951

I Can't Escape from You, 1936 (Fleischer 4)

I Can't Give You Anything But Love, Baby, 1940 (Crawford 3, Salter 4)

I Changed My Sex. *See* Glen or Glenda?, 1952

I chitaro yaai, 1931 (Takamine 3)

I, Claudius, 1937 (Laughton 3, Newton 3, Korda 4, Krasker 4, Périnal 4)

I Confess, 1953 (Hitchcock 2, Baxter 3, Clift 3, Malden 3, Orry-Kelly 4, Burks 4, Reville 4, Tiomkin 4)

I Could Go On Singing, 1963 (Bogarde 3, Garland 3, Head 4)

I Cover the Underworld, 1955 (Van Cleef 3)

I Cover the War, 1937 (Wayne 3)

I Cover the Waterfront, 1933 (Cruze 2, Colbert 3, D'Agostino 4, Newman 4)

I de gode gamle Dage, 1940 (Madsen and Schenstrøm 3)

I Deal in Danger, 1966 (Cohen 2, Schifrin 4, Smith 4)

I den store pyramide, 1974 (Roos 2)

I Did It, Mama, 1909 (Griffith 2, Bitzer 4)

I Didn't Do It, 1945 (Formby 3)

I Died a Thousand Times, 1955 (Hopper 3, Marvin 3, Palance 3, Winters 3, Burnett 4, McCord 4)

I dimma dold, 1952 (Fischer 4)

I Do, 1921 (Lloyd 3, Roach 4)

I Don't Care Girl, 1953 (Bacon 2, Cole 4, Wheeler 4)

I Don't Remember, 1935 (Langdon 3)

I Don't Want to be Born, 1975 (Pleasence 3)

I Don't Want to Make History, 1936 (Fleischer 4)

I Dood It, 1943 (Horne 3, McQueen 3, Powell 3, Sharaff 4)

I Dream of Jeannie, 1952 (Beavers 3)

I Dream Too Much, 1935 (Cromwell 2, Ball 3, Fonda 3, Berman 4, Pan 4, Polglase 4, Steiner 4)

I . . . Dreaming, 1988 (Brakhage 2)

I Eats My Spinach. *See* Adventures of Popeye, 1935

I Eats My Spinach, 1939 (Fleischer 4)

I Escaped from Devil's Island, 1973 (Corman 2)

I Escaped from the Gestapo, 1943 (Carradine 3)

I Feel Like a Feather in the Breeze, 1936 (Fleischer 4)

I Flunked, But . . . *See* Rakudai wa shita keredo, 1930

I Found Stella Parrish, 1935 (LeRoy 2, Francis 3, Lukas 3, Brown 4, Orry-Kelly 4, Saunders 4)

I Give My Heart, 1936 (Siodmak 4, Launder and Gilliat 2)

I Give My Life. *See* Port Arthur, 1936

I Give My Love, 1934 (Beavers 3, Lukas 3, Freund 4)

I Gopher You, 1954 (Blanc 4, Freleng 4)

I Got Plenty of Mutton, 1944 (Blanc 4, Stalling 4)

I Graduated, But . . . *See* Yokina uta Daigaku wa detakeredo, 1929

I Hate Actors. *See* Je hais les acteurs, 1986

I hatt eller aldrig, 1941 (Molander 2)

I Have a New Master. *See* Ecole buissonière, 1949

I Haven't Got a Hat, 1935 (Freleng 4)

I Heard, 1933 (Fleischer 4)

I Hired a Contract Killer, 1990 (Léaud 3, Reggiani 3)

I, I, I . . . and the Others. *See* Io, io, io . . . e gli altri, 1966

I Killed. *See* Jag dräpte, 1943

I Killed Rasputin. *See* J'ai tué Raspoutine, 1967

I Kiss Your Hand, Madame. *See* Ich küsse Ihre Hand, Madame, 1929

I Knew Her Well. *See* Io la conoscevo bene, 1965

I Know That You Know That I Know. *See* Io so che tu sai che io so, 1982

I Know Where I'm Going, 1945 (Powell and Pressburger 2, Junge 4, Rank 4)

I Like Babies and Infinks, 1937 (Fleischer 4)

I Like It That Way, 1934 (Rooney 3)

I Like Mike, 1963 (Topol 3)

I Like Money. *See* Mr. Topaze, 1961

I Like Mountain Music, 1933 (Fleischer 4)

I Like Your Nerve, 1931 (Karloff 3, Young 3, Haller 4)

I Live Again, 1936 (Love 3)

I Live But, 1984 (Ryu 3)

I Live for Love, 1935 (Berkeley 2, Del Rio 3, Barnes 4, Epstein 4, Orry-Kelly 4, Wald 4)

I Live for You. *See* I Live for Love, 1935

I Live in Fear. *See* Ikimono no kiroku, 1955

I Live in Grosvenor Square. *See* Yank in London, 1945

I Live My Life, 1935 (Mankiewicz 2, Van Dyke 2, Crawford 3, Adrian 4, Folsey 4, Tiomkin 4)

I Lived with You, 1923 (Lupino 3, Novello 3)

I Lived Without You, 1933 (Hawkins 3)

I Livets Braending, 1915 (Psilander 3)

I livets vår, 1912 (Sjöström 2)

I livets var, eller Forsta alskarinnan, 1912 (Jaenzon 4, Magnusson 4)

I Liza kai i alli, 1961 (Lassally 4)

I Look at You, 1941 (Ladd 3)

I Love a Bandleader, 1945 (Planer 4)

I Love a Lassie, 1925 (Fleischer 4)

I Love a Mystery, 1945 (Guffey 4)

I Love a Mystery, 1973 (Lupino 3)

I Love a Soldier, 1944 (Bondi 3, Fitzgerald 3, Goddard 3, Head 4, Lang 4)

I Love Melvin, 1953 (O'Connor 3, Reynolds 3, Taylor 3, Alton 4, Rose 4, Rosson 4, Smith 4)

I Love My Wife, 1970 (Gould 3, Schifrin 4)

I Love N.Y., 1987 (Henry 4)

I Love N.Y., Sidney Lumet, 1987 (Jireš 2)

I Love That Man, 1933 (Brown 4, Krasner 4, Robinson 4)

I Love to Singa, 1936 (Avery 4)

I Love Trouble, 1947 (Duning 4)

I Love You Again, 1940 (Van Dyke 2, Loy 3, Powell 3, Lederer 4, Mayer 4, Waxman 4)

I Love You, Alice B. Toklas!, 1968 (Bernstein 4, Van Runkle 4)

I Love You, I Love You Not. See Amo non Amo, 1978

I Love, You Love. See Io amo, tu ami, 1961

I Love You, Rosa. See Ani Ohev Otach Rosa, 1971

I Love You to Death, 1990 (Kasdan 2, Hurt 3, Roizman 4)

I Love You Wednesday, 1933 (King 2)

I Loved a Soldier, 1936 (Hathaway 2, Dietrich 3)

I Loved a Woman, 1933 (Francis 3, Robinson 3, Blanke 4)

I Loved You Wednesday, 1933 (Menzies 4, Mohr 4)

I Married a Communist. See Woman on Pier 13, 1950

I Married a Doctor, 1936 (Brown 4, Haskin 4, Orry-Kelly 4, Robinson 4)

I Married a Monster from Outer Space, 1958 (Bumstead 4, Fulton 4, Head 4)

I Married a Shadow. See J'ai épousé une ombre, 1983

I Married a Spy. See Secret Lives, 1937

I Married a Witch, 1942 (Clair 2, Hayward 3, Lake 3, March 3, Benchley 4, Dreier 4, Head 4, Waxman 4)

I Married a Woman, 1958 (Dickinson 3, Dors 3, Menjou 3, Wayne 3, Ballard 4, D'Agostino 4)

I Married an Angel, 1942 (Van Dyke 2, Eddy 3, Horton 3, MacDonald 3, Loos 4, Mayer 4, Stothart 4, Stromberg 4)

I Married Too Young. See Married Too Young, 1961

I Married You for Fun. See Ti ho sposato per allegria, 1967

I Met a Murderer, 1939 (Mason 3)

I Met Him in Paris, 1937 (Colbert 3, Douglas 3, Young 3, Banton 4, Dreier 4)

I Met My Love Again, 1938 (Bennett 3, Fonda 3, Mohr 4, Wanger 4)

I, Mobster, 1958 (Crosby 4)

I, Monster, 1970 (Cushing 3, Lee 3)

I Need a Woman. See Adamson i Sverige, 1966

I Never Changes My Altitude, 1937 (Fleischer 4)

I Never Promised You a Rose Garden, 1977 (Corman 2, Andersson 3, Sidney 3)

I Never Sang for My Father, 1969 (Douglas 3, Hackman 3)

I Only Arsked, 1959 (Carreras 4)

I Only Have Eyes for You, 1937 (Avery 4, Stalling 4)

I Only Want You to Love Me. See Ich will doch nur, das Ihr mich liebt, 1976

I Ought to be in Pictures, 1982 (Matthau 3, Hamlisch 4)

I Passed for White, 1960 (Folsey 4, Williams 4)

I Played it For You, 1985 (Wenders 2)

I Promise to Pay, 1937 (Ballard 4)

I Prövningens stund, 1916 (Sjöström 2)

I Remember Mama, 1948 (Stevens 2, Dunne 3, Homolka 3, Bodeen 4, D'Agostino 4, Musuraca 4)

I Rok och Dans, 1954 (Thulin 3)

I Saw the New World Born. See Red Bells: I've Seen the Birth of the New World, 1983

I Saw What You Did, 1965 (Crawford 3, Biroc 4, Westmore Family 4)

I See a Dark Stranger, 1946 (Launder and Gilliat 2, Howard 3, Kerr 3, Alwyn 4, Rank 4)

I See Ice, 1938 (Formby 3, McDowall 3, Dean 4)

I Sell Anything, 1934 (Florey 2, Orry-Kelly 4)

I Sent a Letter to My Love. See Cher Inconnu, 1981

I Shall Return. See American Guerilla in the Philippines, 1950

I Shot Jesse James, 1948 (Fuller 2)

I Should Have Stood in Bedlam, 1984 (Lewis 2)

I Stand Condemned. See Moscow Nights, 1935

I Stole a Million, 1939 (Raft 3, Trevor 3, Krasner 4)

I Surrender Dear, 1931 (Sennett 2, Crosby 3, Hornbeck 4)

I Surrender Dear, 1948 (Katzman 4)

I Survived Certain Death. See Prezil isem svou smrt, 1960

I Take This Woman, 1931 (Von Sternberg 2, Cooper 3, Lombard 3, Vorkapich 4, Zukor 4)

I Take This Woman, 1940 (Van Dyke 2, Calhern 3, Lamarr 3, Tracy 3, Kaper 4, MacArthur 4, Rosson 4)

I Taw a Putty Tat, 1948 (Blanc 4, Freleng 4, Stalling 4)

I Thank a Fool, 1962 (Cusack 3, Finch 3, Hayward 3, De Grunwald 4)

I Thank You, 1941 (Rank 4, Vetchinsky 4)

I, the Jury, 1953 (Saville 2, Alton 4, Waxman 4)

I, The Jury, 1981 (Cohen 2)

I Think They Call Him John, 1964 (Love 3)

I Vor Pittfalks, 1967 (Williams 4)

I Wake Up Screaming. See Hot Spot, 1941

I Walk Alone, 1947 (Douglas 3, Lancaster 3, Dreier 4, Haskin 4, Head 4, Schnee 4, Wallis 4, Young 4)

I Walk the Line, 1970 (Frankenheimer 2, Peck 3, Weld 3, Sargent 4)

I Walked with a Zombie, 1943 (Tourneur 2, D'Agostino 4, Hunt 4, Lewton 4, Siodmak 4)

I Wanna Be a Life Guard, 1936 (Fleischer 4)

I Wanna Be a Sailor, 1937 (Avery 4, Stalling 4)

I Wanna Hold Your Hand, 1978 (Zemeckis 2)

I Wanna Mink, 1989 (Halas and Batchelor 4)

I Wanna Play House with You, 1936 (Freleng 4)

I Want a Divorce, 1940 (Beavers 3, Blondell 3, Powell 3, Dreier 4, Head 4, Young 4)

I Want My Dinner, 1903 (Bitzer 4)

"I Want My Hat!", 1909 (Griffith 2)

I Want to Be a Shellfish. See Watash iwa kai ni naritai, 1959

I Want to Go Home. See Je veux rentrer à la maison, 1989

I Want to go Home, 1989 (Chaplin 3)

I Want to Hold Your Hand, 1978 (Spielberg 2)

I Want to Live!, 1958 (Wise 2, Hayward 3, Hornbeck 4, Wanger 4)

I Want to Live, 1983 (Stanton 3)

I Want You, 1951 (Andrews 3, Day 4, Goldwyn 4, Mandell 4, Stradling 4)

I Wanted Wings, 1941 (Leisen 2, Holden 3, Lake 3, Milland 3, Dreier 4, Edouart 4, Head 4, Young 4)

I Was a Communist for the FBI, 1951 (Steiner 4)

I Was a Fireman. See **Fires Were Started, 1943**

I Was a Mail Order Bride, 1981 (Addison 4)

I Was a Male War Bride, 1949 (Grant 3, Sheridan 3, Lederer 4, Wheeler 4)

I Was an Adventuress, 1940 (Von Stroheim 2, Lorre 3, Cronjager 4, Day 4, Johnson 4, Shamroy 4, Zanuck 4)

I Was a Prisoner on Devil's Island, 1941 (Brown 4)

I Was a Shoplifter, 1950 (Curtis 3, Hudson 3)

I Was a Spy, 1933 (Saville 2, Carroll 3, Marshall 3, Veidt 3, Balcon 4, Junge 4)

I Was a Teenage Thumb, 1963 (Jones 4)

I Was a Teenage Werewolf, 1957 (La Shelle 4)

I Was Born, But . . . . See Umarete wa mita keredo, 1932

I Was Framed, 1942 (Bosworth 3, McCord 4)

I Was Happy Here. See Passage of Love, 1965

I Was Monty's Double, 1958 (Mills 3, Addison 4)

I Will, I Will . . . for Now, 1976 (Gould 3, Keaton 3, Alonzo 4, Cahn 4, Frank 4)

I Will If You Will. See Infermiera, 1975

I Will Not Take Any More Boring Art, 1989 (Snow 2)

I Wished on the Moon, 1935 (Fleischer 4)

I Wonder Who's Kissing Her Now, 1931 (Fleischer 4)

I Wonder Who's Kissing Her Now, 1947 (Bacon 2, Day 4, LeMaire 4, Leven 4, Newman 4, Pan 4)

I Won't Forget That Night. See Sono yo wa wasurenai, 1962

I Wouldn't Be in Your Shoes, 1948 (Mirisch 4)

I Yam Love Sick, 1938 (Fleischer 4)

I Yam What I Yam, 1939 (Fleischer 4)

I, Zorba, 1987 (Wise 2)

Ibañez' Torrent. See Torrent, 1926

Ibaragi Ukon, 1939 (Miyagawa 4)

Ibis rouge, 1975 (Simon 3)

IBM at the Fair, 1965 (Bernstein 4)

IBM Mathematics Peep Show, 1961 (Bernstein 4)

IBM Puppet Show, 1965 (Bernstein 4)

Ibo-kyodai, 1957 (Tanaka 3, Yoda 4)

Ibun Sarutobi sasuke, 1965 (Shinoda 2, Takemitsu 4)

Icarus, 1961 (De Palma 2)

Ice. See Is, 1970

Ice Capades Revue, 1942 (Alton 4)

Ice Carnival, 1941 (Terry 4)

Ice Castles, 1978 (Hamlisch 4)

Ice Cold Cocos, 1926 (Sennett 2)

Ice Cold in Alex, 1958 (Mills 3, Quayle 3)

Ice Flood, 1927 (Walthall 3)

Ice Follies of 1939, 1939 (Ayres 3, Crawford 3, Stewart 3, Adrian 4, Brown 4, Freed 4, Ruttenberg 4, Waxman 4)

Ice Man's Luck, 1929 (Lantz 4)

Ice Palace, 1960 (Burton 3, Ryan 3, Biroc 4, Blanke 4, Steiner 4)

Ice Pirates, 1983 (Carradine 3, Huston 3)

Ice Pond, 1939 (Terry 4)

Ice Station Zebra, 1968 (Sturges 2, Borgnine 3, Hudson 3, Legrand 4)

Icebound, 1924 (Buckland 4)

Ice-Breaker Krassnin. See Podvig vo idach, 1928

Iced Bullet, 1917 (Sullivan 4)

Iceland, 1942 (Henie 3, Day 4, Miller 4)

Iceman, 1984 (Jewison 2, Schepisi 2)

Iceman Cometh, 1973 (Frankenheimer 2, Bridges 3, Marvin 3, Ryan 3, Jeakins 4)

Iceman Ducketh, 1964 (Blanc 4)

Iceman's Ball, 1932 (Brennan 3)

Icepick. See Coltello di ghiaccio, 1972

Ich bei Tag und Du bei Nacht, 1932 (Pommer 4)

Ich bin auch nur eine Frau, 1962 (Schell 3)

Ich bin du, 1934 (Röhrig 4)

Ich bin Sebastian Ott, 1939 (Hoffmann 4)

Ich dzień powszedni, 1963 (Cybulski 3, Ścibor-Rylski 4)

Ich glaub' nie mehr an eine Frau, 1929 (Gründgens 3)

Ich hab' von Dir geträumt, 1944 (Staudte 2)

Ich habe im Mai von der Liebe geträumt, 1927 (Dieterle 2)

Ich hatte einen Kamaraden, 1926 (Albers 3)

Ich hierate meine Frau, 1927 (Fröhlich 3)

Ich heirate meine Frau, 1934 (Dagover 3)

Ich kenn' dich nicht und liebe dich. See Toi que j'adore, 1933

Ich küsse Ihre Hand, Madame, 1929 (Dietrich 3)

Ich lebe für dich, 1929 (Junge 4)

Ich liebe all Frauen, 1935 (Warm 4)

Ich liebe dich, 1925 (Ondra 3, Courant 4)

Ich möchte kein Mann sein!, 1920 (Lubitsch 2)

Ich puti razoshchlis, 1932 (Enei 4)

Ich suche dich, 1955 (Aimée 3)

Ich und die Kaiserin, 1933 (Veidt 3, Herlth 4, Reisch 4, Rohrig 4, Waxman 4)

Ich verweigere die Aussage, 1939 (Tschechowa 3)

Ich war ein hässliches Mädchen, 1955 (Tschechowa 3)

Ich war Jack Mortimer, 1935 (Walbrook 3, Von Harbou 4)

Ich werde dich auf Händen tragen, 1943 (Wagner 4)

Ich wiess, wofür ich lebe, 1955 (Dagover 3)

Ich will dich liebe lehren, 1933 (Courant 4)

Ich will doch nur, das Ihr mich liebt, 1976 (Ballhaus 4)

Ichabod and Mr. Toad, 1949 (Crosby 3, Rathbone 3, Disney 4, Glennon 4, Iwerks 4)

Ichiban utsukushiku, 1944 (Shimura 3)

Ichijoji no ketto, 1955 (Mifune 3)

Ici et ailleurs, 1976 (Godard 2)

Ici et maintenant, 1968 (Alekan 4)

Ickle Meets Pickle, 1942 (Terry 4)

ICOGRADA Congress, 1966 (Halas and Batchelor 4)

Iconoclast, 1909 (Porter 2)

Iconoclast, 1910 (Griffith 2, Bitzer 4)

Iconoclast, 1913 (Ince 4)

I'd Climb the Highest Mountain, 1931 (Fleischer 4)

I'd Climb the Highest Mountain, 1951 (King 2, Hayward 3, Cronjager 4, LeMaire 4, Trotti 4)

I'd Love to Take Orders from You, 1936 (Avery 4)

I'd Rather Be Rich, 1964 (Chevalier 3, Hunter 4, Krasna 4, Metty 4, Whitlock 4)

Ide ku słońcu, 1955 (Wajda 2)

Idaho, 1943 (Rogers 3)

Idaho Red, 1928 (Musuraca 4)

Ida's Christmas, 1912 (Bunny 3, Costello 3)

Idaten kaido, 1944 (Hasegawa 3)

Idaten kisha, 1953 (Kagawa 3)

Idea di un 'isola, 1967 (Rossellini 2)

Ideal Husband, 1947 (Clayton 2, Korda 2, Goddard 3, Beaton 4, Biro 4, Korda, A. 4, Korda, V. 4, Périnal 4)

Ideál Septimy, 1938 (Stallich 4)

Ideal Teacher. See Kantor Idéal, 1932

Ideale Gattin, 1914 (Lubitsch 2)

Idealer Gatte, 1935 (Von Harbou 4)

Idée, 1934 (Honegger 4)

Idée fixe, 1962 (Braunberger 4)

Idée fixe, 1968 (Fresnay 3)

Idée folle, 1932 (Arletty 3)

Identification Marks: None. See Rysopis, 1964

Identificazione di una donna, 1982 (Antonioni 2, Guerra 4)

Identikit, 1973 (Storaro 4)

Identikit. See Driver's Seat, 1975

Identité judicaire, 1951 (Jeanson 4)

Identities, 1973 (Emshwiller 2)

Identity Unknown. See Girl in 419, 1933

Idillio tragico, 1912 (Bertini 3)

Idiot, 1914 (Crisp 3)

Idiot. See Dummkopf, 1920

Idiot, 1946 (Feuillère 3, Philipe 3, Barsacq 4, Matras 4, Spaak 4)

Idiot. See Hakuchi, 1951

Idiot à Paris, 1966 (Blier 3, Audiard 4, Rabier 4)

Idiot qui se croit Max, 1909 (Linder 3)

Idiot's Delight, 1939 (Brown 2, Coburn 3, Gable 3, Meredith 3, Shearer 3, Adrian 4, Daniels 4, Sherwood 4, Stothart 4, Stromberg 4, Vorkapich 4)

Idiots Deluxe, 1945 (Three Stooges 3)

Idle Class, 1921 (Chaplin 2, Purviance 3)

Idle on Parade, 1959 (Bendix 3)

Idle Rich, 1921 (Mathis 4)

Idle Rich, 1929 (Love 3, Day 4, Gibbons 4)

Idle Roomers, 1931 (Arbuckle 3)

Idle Roomers, 1944 (Three Stooges 3)

Idle Tongues, 1924 (Struss 4, Sullivan 4)

Idlers That Work, 1949 (Anderson 2, Copland 4)

Ido Zero daisakusen, 1969 (Cotten 3, Tsuburaya 4)

Idoire, 1932 (Tourneur 2)

Idol. See Dots Izrila, 1917

Idol, 1966 (Jones 3, Levine 4)

Idol Dancer, 1920 (Griffith 2, Barthelmess 3, Bitzer 4)

Idol of Hope, 1941 (Eisenstein 2)

Idol of the Crowds, 1937 (Wayne 3)

Idol of the Hour, 1913 (Cruze 2)

Idol on Parade. See Idle on Parade, 1959

Idole, 1948 (Montand 3)

Idolo infranto, 1913 (Bertini 3)

Idols in the Dust. See Saturday's Hero, 1951

Idols of Clay, 1920 (Miller 4)

Idyll of the Hills, 1915 (Chaney 3)

Idylle, 1897 (Guy 2)

Idylle à la ferme, 1912 (Linder 3)

Idylle à la plage, 1931 (Storck 2)

Idylle interrompue, 1897 (Guy 2)

Idylle sous un tunnel, 1901 (Pathé 4)

Iemitsu to Hikosa to Isshin Sasuke, 1961 (Shindo 3)

Ieri, oggi, domani, 1963 (Loren 3, Mastroianni 3, Ponti 4, Zavattini 4)

If ..., 1968 (Anderson 2, Frears 2, McDowell 3, Menges 4, Ondříček 4)

If a Body Meets a Body, 1945 (Three Stooges 3)

If All the Guys in the World. See Si tous les gars du monde, 1955

If a Man Answers, 1962 (Presle 3, Hunter 4, Metty 4, Salter 4)

If a Thousand Clarinets. See Kdyby tisic karinetu, 1964

If Cats Could Sing, 1950 (Terry 4)

If I Had a Million, 1932 (Cruze 2, Lubitsch 2, Mankiewicz 2, McLeod 2, Cooper 3, Fields 3, Laughton 3, Raft 3, Buchman 4, Miller 4, Zukor 4)

If I Had My Way, 1940 (Crosby 3)

If I Had to Do It All Over Again. See Si c'était à refaire, 1976

If I Marry Again, 1925 (Bosworth 3)

If I'm Lucky, 1946 (Miranda 3, Basevi 4)

If I Was a Daddy. See Kdybych byl tátou, 1939

If I Were a Spy. See Si j'étais un espion, 1967

If I Were Boss, 1938 (Withers 3)

If I Were Free, 1933 (Dunne 3, Cronjager 4, MacGowan 4, Polglase 4, Steiner 4)

If I Were King, 1938 (Sturges 2, Colman 3, Rathbone 3, Dreier 4)

If I Were Single, 1927 (Loy 3)

If I Were Young Again, 1914 (Mix 3)

If It Were Raining. See Comme s'il en pleuvait, 1963

If It's Tuesday, This Must Be Belgium, 1969 (Cassavetes 2, De Sica 2)

If Marriage Fails, 1925 (Sullivan 4)

If My Country Should Call, 1916 (Chaney 3)

If One Thousand Clarinets, 1989 (Menzel 2)

"If Only" Jim, 1921 (Carey 3)

If This Be Sin. See That Dangerous Age, 1950

If Tomorrow Comes, 1971 (Baxter 3)

If We Only Knew, 1913 (Sweet 3, Walthall 3)

If Winter Comes, 1923 (Ruttenberg 4)

If Winter Comes, 1947 (Saville 2, Kerr 3, Lansbury 3, Leigh 3, Pidgeon 3, Berman 4, Folsey 4, Irene 4, Stothart 4)

If You Believe It, It's So, 1922 (Young 4)

If You Could Only Cook, 1935 (Arthur 3, Marshall 3)

If You Feel Like Singing. See Summer Stock, 1950

If You Had a Wife Like This, 1907 (Bitzer 4)

If You Knew Susie, 1948 (Cantor 3)

If You Love Me. Because I Love. See Aisureba koso, 1955

If You Want to Be Happy. See Esli khochesh byt schastlivym, 1974

Iga Kottou gunryu, 1941 (Yoda 4)

Iga Kottou Military Style. See Iga Kottou gunryu, 1941

Igano minatsuki, 1958 (Hasegawa 3)

Igloo for Two, 1955 (Terry 4)

Ignace, 1937 (Fernandel 3)

Igrok, 1972 (Batalov 3)

Ihr grosse Fall. *See* grosse Fall, 1944
Ihr Privatsekretär, 1940 (Fröhlich 3)
Ihr Sport, 1919 (Wiene 2)
Ihre Durchlaucht, die Verkäuferin. *See* Caprice de Princesse, 1933
Ihre Hoheit befiehlt, 1931 (Wilder 2, Pommer 4)
Ihre Majestät die Liebe, 1931 (Andrejew 4)
Iikagen baka, 1964 (Iwashita 3)
I'Ile de sein, 1958 (Delerue 4)
Ikari no umi, 1944 (Tsuburaya 4)
Ike, 1979 (Duvall 3)
Ikimono no kiroku, 1955 (Mifune 3, Shimura 3, Hayasaka 4, Muraki 4)
Ikiru, 1952 (Kurosawa 2, Shimura 3, Hayasaka 4)
Ikiteiru gazo, 1948 (Hayasaka 4)
Ikiteiru ningyo, 1957 (Yamada 3)
Ikitoshi ikeru mono, 1955 (Yamamura 3)
Ikonostast, 1969 (Dinov 4)
Il a été perdu une mariée, 1932 (Burel 4, Meerson 4, Spaak 4)
Il aime le bruit, 1917 (Cohl 4)
Il est charmant, 1931 (Stradling 4)
Il est minuit, Docteur Schweitzer, 1952 (Fresnay 3, Moreau 3, Cloquet 4)
Il était une chaise. *See* Chairy Tale, 1957
Il était une fois, 1933 (Douy 4)
Il était une fois un flic, 1972 (Delon 3)
Il faut tuer Birgitt Haas, 1981 (Noiret 3, Sarde 4)
Il faut vivre dangereusement, 1975 (Girardot 3)
Il gèle en enfer, 1990 (Coutard 4)
Il joue avec Dodo, 1917 (Cohl 4)
Il n'y a pas de fumée sans feu, 1972 (Girardot 3)
Il pleut sur Santiago, 1975 (Andersson 3, Girardot 3, Trintignant 3)
Il ya des jours … et des lunes, 1990 (Girardot 3, Lai 4)
Il y a des pieds au plafond, 1912 (Gance 2)
Il y a longtemps que je t'aime, 1979 (Guillemot 4)
Il y a un dieu pour les ivrognes, 1908 (Méliès 2)
Ile au trésor, 1985 (Branco 4, De Almeida 4)
Ile de Pâques, 1935 (Storck 2, Jaubert 4)
Ile d'Ouessant. *See* Enez Eussa, 1961
Ile Maurice, 1960 (Braunberger 4)
Ile mystérieuse, 1973 (Colpi 4)
Iles, 1983 (Müller 4)
Iles enchantées, 1965 (Rabier 4)
Ilha dos Amores, 1982 (De Almeida 4)
Ilhas Encantadas, 1965 (De Almeida 4)
Iliac Passion, 1967 (Markopoulos 2)
I'll Be Glad When You're Dead, You Rascal, 1932 (Fleischer 4)
I'll Be Home for Christmas, 1988 (Saint 3)
I'll Be Seeing You, 1944 (Cukor 2, Dieterle 2, Cotten 3, Rogers 3, Temple 3, Gaudio 4, Head 4, Schary 4)
I'll Be Suing You, 1934 (Roach 4)
I'll Be Your Sweetheart, 1945 (Lockwood 3, Rank 4)
I'll Be Yours, 1947 (Sturges 2, Bendix 3, Durbin 3, Menjou 3, Pangborn 3, Banton 4, Mohr 4)
I'll Cry Tomorrow, 1955 (Hayward 3, Gibbons 4, Mercer 4, North 4, Rose 4)
I'll Defend You My Love. *See* Difendo il mio amore, 1956
I'll Dig Your Grave. *See* Sono Sartana, il vostro bechino, 1969

I'll Get By, 1950 (Mature 3, Ritter 3, Clarke 4, LeMaire 4)
I'll Get Him Yet, 1919 (Barthelmess 3, Garmes 4)
I'll Get You, 1951 (Raft 3)
I'll Get You for This. *See* Lucky Nick Cain, 1951
I'll Give a Million, 1938 (Carradine 3, Lorre 3, MacGowan 4, Zanuck 4, Zavattini 4)
I'll Give My Life, 1960 (Dickinson 3)
I'll Love You Always, 1935 (August 4, Buchman 4)
I'll Never Crow Again, 1941 (Fleischer 4)
I'll Never Forget You, 1951 (Welles 2, Love 3, Power 3, Reed 3, Balderston 4, Heller 4, Lai 4, Périnal 4)
I'll Never Heil Again, 1941 (Three Stooges 3, Bruckman 4)
I'll Say So, 1918 (Walsh 2)
I'll See You in My Dreams, 1952 (Curtiz 2, Day 3, McCord 4, Prinz 4)
I'll Take Romance, 1937 (Douglas 3, Pangborn 3, Cohn 4, Murfin 4)
I'll Take Sweden, 1965 (Hope 3, Weld 3)
I'll Take Vanilla, 1922 (Roach 4)
I'll Take Vanilla, 1934 (Roach 4)
I'll Tell the World, 1934 (Mandell 4)
I'll Tell the World, 1945 (Salter 4)
I'll Wait for You, 1941 (Kaper 4)
Ill Met By Moonlight, 1957 (Bogarde 3, Cusack 3, Lee 3, Challis 4, Rank 4, Theodorakis 4, Vetchinsky 4)
Illegal, 1955 (Mansfield 3, Burnett 4, Steiner 4)
Illegal Divorce. *See* Second Hand Wife, 1932
Illegal Entry, 1949 (Daniels 4)
Illegal Traffic, 1938 (Crabbe 3, Preston 3, Dreier 4, Head 4)
Illegally Yours, 1987 (Bogdanovich 2)
Illicit, 1931 (Blondell 3, Stanwyck 3, Zanuck 4)
Illuminacja, 1973 (Zanussi 2)
Illumination, 1912 (Reid 3)
Illumination. *See* Illuminacja, 1973
Illuminations, 1963 (Braunberger 4)
Illusion, 1929 (Lukas 3, Schulberg 4)
Illusion, 1947 (Braunberger 4)
Illusion, 1991 (Francis 3)
Illusion in Moll, 1952 (Pommer 4)
Illusion of Blood. *See* Yotsuya kaidan, 1965
Illusión viaja en tranvía, 1953 (Buñuel 2, Alcoriza 4)
Illusioniste renversant, 1903 (Guy 2, Gaumont 4)
Illusions. *See* Time Out of Mind, 1947
Illusions fantaisistes, 1910 (Méliès 2)
Illusions fantasmagoriques, 1898 (Méliès 2)
Illusions funambulesques, 1903 (Méliès 2)
Illustrated Man, 1969 (Bloom 3, Steiger 3, Goldsmith 4, Sylbert 4)
Illustrious Corpses. *See* Cadaveri eccellenti, 1976
Illustrious Prince, 1919 (Hayakawa 3)
Ils, 1970 (Vanel 3)
Ils étaient neuf célibataires, 1939 (Guitry 2)
Ils étaient tous des volontaires, 1954 (Milhaud 4)
Ils sont foux, ces sorciers!, 1978 (Decaë 4)
Ils sont grands ces petits, 1979 (Deneuve 3, Carrière 4)
Ils vont tous bien. *See* Stanno tutti bene, 1990

Ilya Mourometz. *See* Sword and the Dragon, 1960
Ilya Muromets, 1956 (Ptushko 4)
Im 1812, 1928 (Tschechowa 3)
I'm a Big Shot Now, 1936 (Freleng 4)
I'm a Civilian Here Myself, 1945 (Benchley 4)
I'm a Monkey's Uncle, 1948 (Three Stooges 3)
I'm a Stranger Here Myself, 1972 (Wood 3)
I'm Afraid to Come Home in the Dark, 1930 (Fleischer 4)
I'm All Right, Jack, 1959 (Boulting 2, Attenborough 3, Rutherford 3, Sellers 3, Terry-Thomas 3)
I'm Almost Not Crazy: John Cassavetes—the Man and His Work, 1984 (Golan and Globus 4)
Im Angesicht des Toten, 1916 (Jannings 3)
Im Banne der Kralle, 1921 (Pabst 2)
Im Banne der Vergangenheit, 1915 (Kortner 3)
I'm Cold, 1955 (Avery 4)
I'm Dancing As Fast As I Can, 1982 (Clayburgh 3, Page 3)
Im Dienste der Menschheit, 1938 (Ruttman 2)
Im Exil der ertrunkenen Tiger, 1988 (Alekan 4)
I'm Forever Blowing Bubbles, 1930 (Fleischer 4)
I'm from Missouri, 1939 (Head 4)
I'm from the City, 1938 (Polglase 4)
Im Geheimdienst, 1931 (Homolka 3, Herlth 4, Reisch 4, Röhrig 4)
Im grossen Augenblick, 1910 (Nielsen 3)
I'm in the Army Now, 1936 (Fleischer 4)
I'm Just Wild about Jerry, 1965 (Jones 4)
Im Lauf der Zeit, 1976 (Wenders 2, Vogler, 3, Müller 4)
Im letzten Augenblick, 1920 (Banky 3)
Im Luxuszug, 1927 (Andrejew 4)
I'm No Angel, 1933 (Beavers 3, Grant 3, McDaniel 3, West 3, Dreier 4, Head 4, Zukor 4)
I'm Nobody's Sweetheart Now, 1940 (Salter 4)
I'm Not Feeling Myself Tonight, 1975 (Godfrey 4)
I'm on My Way, 1919 (Daniels 3, Lloyd 3, Roach 4)
Im Schützengraben, 1914 (Jannings 3)
Im Sonneschein, 1936 (Planer 4)
I'm Still Alive, 1940 (Niblo 2, Hunt 4, Polglase 4)
Im weissen Rössl, 1952 (Herlth 4)
Image. *See* Bildnis, 1925 (Feyder 2, Burel 4)
Image By Images, 1954–56 (Breer 4)
Image, Flesh and Voice, 1969 (Emshwiller 2)
Images, 1972 (Altman 2, Emshwiller 2, York 3, Williams 4, Zsigmond 4)
Images de Sologne, 1959 (Delerue 4)
Images des mondes perdus, 1959 (Delerue 4)
Images d'hier et d'aujourd'hui, 1960 (Decaë 4)
Images d'Ostende, 1986 (Storck 2)
Images gothiques, 1949 (Renoir 4)
Images pour Baudelaire, 1958 (Delerue 4)
Imaginary Baron. *See* Juxbaron, 1927
Imagination, 1943 (Fleischer 4)
Imagination, 1969 (Kuri 4)
Imagination in Motion, 1958 (Mohr 4)
Imagine, 1973 (Astaire 3)

Imagine My Embarrassment, 1928 (Roach 4)

Imagining October, 1984 (Jarman 2)

Imago, 1970 (Schifrin 4)

Imbarco a mezzanotte, 1952 (Muni 3)

Imi Hageneralit, 1979 (Golan and Globus 4)

Imitation General, 1958 (Ford 3, Folsey 4)

Imitation of Christ, 1967 (Warhol 2)

Imitation of Life, 1934 (Stahl 2, Sturges 2, Beavers 3, Colbert 3, McDaniel 3, Pangborn 3, Laemmle 4)

Imitation of Life, 1959 (Sirk 2, Turner 3, Hunter 4, Metty 4)

Immaculate Road, 1960 (Maté 4)

Immagini Populari Siciliane Profane, 1952 (Birri 2)

Immagini Populari Siciliane Sacre, 1952 (Birri 2)

Immature Punter, 1898 (Hepworth 2)

Immediate Disaster. See Stranger from Venus, 1954

Immediate Family, 1989 (Close 3)

Immigrant, 1917 (Chaplin 2, Purviance 3)

Immigrant Experience: The Long Long Journey, 1972 (Silver 2)

Immobile Love. See Aijou dudou, 1959

Immoral Charge. See Serious Charge, 1959

Immoral Moment. See Dénonciation, 1961

Immorale, 1967 (Pinelli 4)

Immoralità, 1978 (Morricone 4)

Immortal, 1969 (Bellamy 3)

Immortal Bachelor. See Qui comincia l'avventura, 1975

Immortal Garrison, 1956 (Tisse 4)

Immortal Land, 1958 (Wright 2, Gielgud 3, Redgrave 3, Bernard 4)

Immortal Love. See Eien no hito, 1961

Immortal Sergeant, 1943 (Stahl 2, Fonda 3, O'Hara 3, Day 4, Miller 4, Newman 4, Trotti 4)

Immortal Story, 1968 (Welles 2, Moreau 3)

Immortal Story of Dr. Kotnis. See Dr. Kotnis Ki Amar Kahani, 1946

Immortal Stupa, 1961 (Roy 2)

Immortal Swan, 1935 (Green 4)

Immortal Vagabond. See Unsterbliche Lump, 1930

Immortel Amour. See Miracle in the Rain, 1956

Immortelle, 1963 (Delerue 4, Robbe-Grillet 4)

Imp, 1919 (Goulding 2)

Impaciencia del corazon, 1958 (Figueroa 4)

Impact, 1949 (Coburn 3, Marsh 3, Wong 3, Laszlo 4)

Impalement, 1910 (Bitzer 4)

Impasse, 1969 (Reynolds 3)

Impasse des deux anges, 1948 (Tourneur 2, Signoret 3, D'Eaubonne 4, Renoir 4)

Impasse d'un matin, 1964 (Delerue 4)

Impassive Footman, 1932 (Dean 4)

Impatient Maiden, 1932 (Whale 2, Ayres 3, Edeson 4)

Impatient Patient, 1942 (Blanc 4, Clampett 4, Stalling 4)

Impatient Years, 1944 (Arthur 3, Coburn 3, Darwell 3, Walker 4)

Imperative. See Uerreichbare, 1982

Imperativo categorio: control il crimine con rabbia, 1973 (Kinski 3)

Imperatore di Capri, 1949 (Comencini 2, Ponti 4)

Imperceptible Transformations. See Transmutations imperceptibles, 1904

Imperfect Lady, 1947 (Milland 3, Quinn 3, Wright 3, Dreier 4, Seitz 4, Young 4)

Imperfect Wife, 1947 (Head 4)

Imperial Grace. See Ko-on, 1927

Impersonation of Tom, 1915 (Mix 3)

Impetuous Youth. See Geiger von Florenz, 1926

Impiegata di papa, 1934 (Blasetti 2)

Implement, 1910 (Griffith 2)

Importance of Being Earnest, 1952 (Asquith 2, Evans 3, Greenwood 3, Redgrave 3, Rutherford 3, Dillon 4, Rank 4)

Importancia universal del hueco, 1981 (Alvarez 2)

Important Business, 1944 (Benchley 4)

Important c'est d'aimer, 1974 (Kinski 3, Schneider 3, Delerue 4)

Important Man. See Animas Trujano, 1961

Important News, 1935 (Stewart 3)

Important Witness, 1933 (Pangborn 3)

Imposibrante, 1968 (Guzmán 2)

Impossible. See Anhonee, 1951

Impossible aveu, 1935 (Vanel 3)

Impossible Convicts, 1905 (Bitzer 4)

Impossible M. Pipelet, 1955 (Simon 3)

Impossible Mrs. Bellew, 1922 (Wood 2, Swanson 3)

Impossible Object. See Impossible Objet, 1973

Impossible Object: Story of a Love Story. See Impossible Objet, 1973

Impossible Objet, 1973 (Frankenheimer 2, Bates 3, Sanda 3, Legrand 4, Renoir 4, Trauner 4)

Impossible Years, 1968 (Niven 3, Ames 4, Daniels 4)

Imposter, 1914 (August 4)

Imposter, 1918 (Polito 4)

Imposter, 1931 (Fort 4)

Imposter, 1944 (Duvivier 2, Gabin 3, Lourié 4, Tiomkin 4)

Imposter, 1956 (Fernández 2, Armendáriz 3)

Impostor, 1936 (Fernández 2)

Impotence. See Xala, 1974

Impractical Joker, 1937 (Fleischer 4)

Imprécateur, 1977 (Piccoli 3)

Impression of John Steinbeck—Writer, 1969 (Fonda 3)

Impressionable Years, 1952 (Fonda 3)

Impressioniste fin de siècle, 1899 (Méliès 2)

Impressions de L'Ile des Morts, 1986 (Leacock 2)

Impressions de New York, 1955 (Braunberger 4)

Imprevisto, 1961 (Lattuada 2, Aimée 3)

Imprint of Giants. See Empreinte des géants, 1980

Improper Channels, 1981 (Arkin 3)

Improper Conduct. See Mauvaise conduite, 1984

Impulse, 1954 (Kennedy 3)

Impures, 1954 (Presle 3, Alekan 4)

Imus, 1973 (Kuri 4)

In a Fantastic Vision. See V blouznění, 1928

In a Hempen Bag, 1909 (Griffith 2, Bitzer 4)

In a Lonely Place, 1950 (Ray 2, Bogart 3, Grahame 3, Cohn 4, Guffey 4)

In a Monastery Garden, 1929 (Balcon 4)

In Again—Out Again, 1917 (Von Stroheim 2, Fairbanks 3, Edeson 4, Emerson 4, Loos 4)

In and Out, 1914 (Beery 3)

In Anfang war das Wort, 1928 (Metzner 4)

In Another's Nest, 1913 (Dwan 2)

In Bermuda, 1914 (Rosher 4)

In Between, 1955 (Brakhage 2)

In Between, 1978 (Mekas 2)

In Black and White, 1969 (Loach 2)

In Blossom Time, 1911 (Olcott 2)

In Caliente, 1935 (Bacon 2, Berkeley 2, Del Rio 3, Horton 3, Barnes 4, Epstein 4, Orry-Kelly 4, Polito 4, Wald 4)

In Celebration, 1974 (Anderson 2, Bates 3)

In Cold Blood, 1967 (Brooks 2, Boyle 4, Hall 4, Jones 4)

In Conference, 1931 (Sennett 2)

In Country, 1989 (Jewison 2)

In Cupid's Realm, or A Game of Hearts, 1908 (Lawrence 3)

In Dalarna and Jerusalem. See Ingmarsarvet, 1925

In Defiance of the Law, 1914 (Mix 3)

In dem grossen Augenblick, 1911 (Gad 2)

In Dickens Land, 1913 (Pearson 2)

In einer Fremden Stadt, 1963 (Herlth 4)

In Enemy Country, 1968 (Anhalt 4, Head 4, Whitlock 4)

In faccia al destino, 1913 (Bertini 3)

In Fast Company, 1924 (Fort 4)

In fondo ala piscina, 1971 (Baker 3)

In for Treatment. See Opname, 1979

In From the Cold, 1988 (Bacall 3)

In Gay Madrid, 1930 (Novarro 3, Adrian 4, Day 4, Gibbons 4, Meredyth 4, Stothart 4)

In Geheimdienst, 1931 (Hoffmann 4)

In geheimer Mission, 1938 (Fröhlich 3, Wegener 3)

In God We Trust, 1913 (Bosworth 3)

In God We Trust, 1980 (Pryor 3)

In Harm's Way, 1965 (Preminger 2, Andrews 3, Douglas 3, Fonda 3, Meredith 3, Neal 3, Wayne 3, Bass 4, Edouart 4, Goldsmith 4, Wheeler 4)

In His Steps, 1936 (Brown 4)

In Hollywood with Potash and Perlmutter, 1924 (Carré 4, Goldwyn 4, Marion 4, Miller 4)

In jenen Tagen, 1947 (Käutner 2)

In Life's Cycle, 1910 (Griffith 2, Walthall 3, Bitzer 4)

In Like Flint, 1967 (Cobb 3, Coburn 3, Daniels 4, Goldsmith 4, Smith 4)

In Line of Duty, 1931 (Glennon 4)

In Little Italy, 1909 (Griffith 2, Walthall 3, Bitzer 4)

In Little Italy, 1912 (Bosworth 3)

In Love, 1928 (Rooney 3)

In Love and War, 1913 (Reid 3)

In Love and War, 1958 (Wagner 3, Anhalt 4, Canutt 4, Dunne 4, Friedhofer 4, LeMaire 4, Reynolds 4, Wald 4)

In Memoriam, 1977 (Chaplin 3)

In Memory of Sergo Ordzhonikidze. See Pamyati Sergo Ordzhonikidze, 1937

In My Merry Oldsmobile, 1931 (Fleischer 4)

In Name Only, 1939 (Cromwell 2, Coburn 3, Francis 3, Grant 3, Lombard 3, Banton 4, Berman 4, Hunt 4, Polglase 4)

In Name Only, 1969 (Lancaster 3)

In Neighboring Kingdoms, 1911 (Talmadge 3)

In nome del popolo italiano, 1971 (Age and Scarpelli 4)

In nome della legge, 1949 (Fellini 2, Monicelli 2, Vanel 3, Pinelli 4, Rota 4)

In Old Amarillo, 1951 (Rogers 3)

In Old Arizona, 1929 (Walsh 2, Brown 3, Edeson 4)
In Old Caliente, 1939 (Rogers 3)
In Old California, 1910 (Griffith 2, Walthall 3, Bitzer 4)
In Old California, 1929 (Walthall 3)
In Old California, 1942 (Wayne 3)
In Old California When the Gringos Came, 1911 (Mix 3)
In Old Cheyenne, 1941 (Rogers 3)
In Old Chicago, 1938 (King 2, Ameche 3, Faye 3, Power 3, Canutt 4, Levien 4, MacGowan 4, Trotti 4, Zanuck 4)
In Old Colorado, 1941 (Harlan 4, Head 4)
In Old Florida, 1911 (Olcott 2)
In Old Kentucky, 1909 (Griffith 2, Pickford 3, Walthall 3, Bitzer 4)
In Old Kentucky, 1920 (Neilan 2, Carré 4, Gaudio 4, Mayer 4)
In Old Kentucky, 1927 (Stahl 2, Booth 4, Gibbons 4)
In Old Kentucky, 1935 (Robinson 3, Rogers 3)
In Old Madrid, 1911 (Pickford 3, Gaudio 4, Ince 4)
In Old Mexico, 1938 (Harlan 4, Head 4)
In Old Missouri, 1940 (Ladd 3)
In Old Monterey, 1939 (Autry 3)
In Old Oklahoma, 1943 (Wayne 3, Canutt 4, Plunkett 4)
In Old Santa Fe, 1934 (Autry 3)
In Old Santa Fe, 1958 (Lewis 2)
In Olden Days. See Altri tempi, 1952
In Our Hands, 1959 (Dickinson 2)
In Our Time, 1944 (Henreid 3, Lupino 3, Nazimova 3, Koch 4, Wald 4, Waxman 4)
In Paris Parks, 1954 (Clarke 2)
In Person, 1935 (Rogers 3, Berman 4, Cronjager 4, Pan 4, Polglase 4)
In Praise of Love, 1976 (Rattigan 4)
In Praise of Older Women, 1977 (Black 3)
In Prehistoric Days, 1913 (Griffith 2, Bitzer 4)
In School, 1928 (Rooney 3)
In Search of a Sinner, 1920 (Emerson 4, Loos 4)
In Search of America, 1971 (Bridges 3, Mineo 3)
In Search of Dracula, 1971 (Lee 3)
In Search of Gregory, 1969 (Christie 3, Hurt 3, Guerra 4, Heller 4)
In Search of Opportunity, 1967 (Menges 4)
In Search of the Castaways, 1962 (Stevenson 2, Chevalier 3, Sanders 3, Alwyn 4, Disney 4, Ellenshaw 4)
In Society, 1944 (Abbott and Costello 3, Lourié 4)
In Soft in a Studio, 1916 (Roach 4)
In Spite of Danger, 1935 (Cohn 4)
In Swift Waters, 1912 (Lawrence 3)
In the Aisles of the Wild, 1912 (Griffith 2, Carey 3, Gish 3, Walthall 3, Bitzer 4)
In the Arctic Night, 1911 (Bunny 3)
In the Beginning, 1975 (Lassally 4)
In the Bishop's Carriage, 1913 (Porter 2, Pickford 3)
In the Blood, 1923 (McLaglen 3)
In the Border States, 1910 (Griffith 2, Bitzer 4)
In the Candlelight, 1914 (Eason 4)
In the Cellar, 1989 (Halas and Batchelor 4)
In the Clutches of a Vapor Bath, 1911 (Bunny 3)

In the Clutches of the Gang, 1914 (Sennett 2, Arbuckle 3, Normand 3)
In the Cool of the Day, 1963 (Fonda 3, Lansbury 3, Houseman 4, Orry-Kelly 4)
In the Cool of the Night, 1962 (Adam 4)
In the Course of Time. See **Im Lauf der Zeit, 1976**
In the Custody of Strangers, 1982 (Sheen 3)
In the Days of '49, 1911 (Griffith 2, Bitzer 4)
In the Days of Daring, 1916 (Mix 3)
In the Days of Gold, 1911 (Bosworth 3, Mix 3)
In the Days of the Thundering Herd, 1914 (Mix 3)
In the Days of Witchcraft, 1913 (Bosworth 3)
In the Diplomatic Service, 1916 (Bushman 3)
In the Doghouse, 1961 (Rank 4)
In the Dough, 1933 (Arbuckle 3)
In the Employ of the Secret Service. See Im Geheimdienst, 1931
In the Face of Demolition, 1954 (Lee 3)
In the French Style, 1963 (Baker 3, Seberg 3, Kosma 4)
In the Glare of the Lights, 1914 (Bushman 3)
In the Good Old Summertime, 1926 (Fleischer 4)
In the Good Old Summertime, 1949 (Keaton 2, Garland 3, Johnson 3, Minnelli 3, Alton 4, Goodrich 4, Irene 4, Pasternak 4, Stradling 4)
In the Grazing Country, 1901 (Bitzer 4)
In the Grease!, 1925 (Roach 4)
In the Hands of a Pitiless Destiny. See V roukatch bespotchadnogo roka, 1914
In the Haunts of Rip Van Winkle, 1906 (Bitzer 4)
In the Heart of a Fool, 1921 (Dwan 2)
In the Heart of the Catskills, 1906 (Bitzer 4)
In the Heat of the Night, 1967 (Ashby 2, Jewison 2, Grant 3, Oates 3, Poitier 3, Steiger 3, Jones 4, Mirisch 4, Wexler 4)
In the Jungle, 1989 (Halas and Batchelor 4)
In the King of Prussia, 1983 (De Antonio 2)
In the Maiden's Room. See Diadiouskina kvartira, 1913)
In the Meantime, Darling, 1944 (Preminger 2, Basevi 4)
In the Midst of the Jungle. See In the Midst of the Wilds, 1913
In the Midst of the Wilds, 1913 (Bosworth 3)
In the Money, 1934 (Beavers 3)
In the Moonlight, 1914 (Eason 4)
In the Mountains of Ala-Tau. See V gorakh Ala-Tau, 1944
In the Mountains of Yugoslavia, 1946 (Tisse 4)
In the Name of Life. See Vo imya zhizni, 1946
In the Name of Love, 1925 (Beery 3)
In the Name of the Father. See Nel nome del padre, 1971
In the Name of the Italian People. See In nome del popolo italiano, 1971
In the Name of the Law. See In nome della legge, 1949
In the Name of the People, 1985 (Sheen 3)
In the Navy, 1941 (Abbott and Costello 3, Powell 3, Three Stooges 3)
In the N.Y. Subway, 1903 (Bitzer 4)
In the Next Room, 1930 (Seitz 4)
In the Nick, 1959 (Adam 4)
In the Open, 1914 (Eason 4)

In the Palace of the King, 1923 (Bosworth 3, Johnson 3, Sweet 3, Mathis 4)
In the Park, 1915 (Bacon 2, Purviance 3)
In the Power of the Ku-Klux-Klan, 1913 (Olcott 2)
In the Purple Hills, 1915 (Eason 4)
In the Ranks, 1913 (Ince 4)
In the Realm of the Senses. See Ai no corrida, 1976
In the Ruins. See Haikyo no naka, 1976
In the Sage Brush Country, 1914 (Hart 3)
In the Season of Buds, 1910 (Griffith 2, Pickford 3, Bitzer 4)
In the Shade of the Old Apple Sauce, 1931 (Fleischer 4)
In the Shadow of the Pines, 1911 (Bosworth 3)
In the Shadow of the Sun, 1980 (Jarman 2)
In the Spirit, 1990 (Falk 3, May 4)
In the Spring of Life, or His First Love. See I livets var, eller Forsta alskarinnan, 1912
In the Storm. See U oluji, 1952
In the Sultan's Garden, 1911 (Pickford 3, Gaudio 4, Ince 4)
In the Sultan's Power, 1909 (Bosworth 3, Selig 4)
In the Sweet Pie and Pie, 1941 (Three Stooges 3, Bruckman 4)
In the Tents of the Assa, 1912 (Bosworth 3)
In the Twilight, 1915 (Eason 4)
In the Villain's Power, 1917 (O'Brien 4)
In the Wake of the Bounty, 1933 (Flynn 3)
In the Watches of the Night, 1909 (Griffith 2, Pickford 3, Bitzer 4)
In the White City. See Dans la ville blanche, 1983
In the Window Recess, 1909 (Griffith 2, Bitzer 4)
In the Year of the Pig, 1968 (De Antonio 2)
In the Year 2000, 1912 (Guy 2)
In This Corner, 1978 (Brocka 2)
In This House of Brede, 1975 (Dillon 4)
In This Our Life, 1942 (Huston 2, Astor 3, Bogart 3, Bond 3, Coburn 3, Davis 3, De Havilland 3, Huston 3, McDaniel 3, Burks 4, Friedhofer 4, Haller 4, Haskin 4, Koch 4, Orry-Kelly 4, Steiner 4, Wallis 4)
In Time of Pestilence, 1989 (Halas and Batchelor 4)
In Time with Industry. See Trade Tattoo, 1937
In Times Like These, 1956 (Wray 3)
In Trust, 1915 (Eason 4)
In Two Minds, 1967 (Loach 2)
In una notta di chiaro di luna, 1989 (Wertmüller 2, O'Toole 3, Sanda 3)
In una notte piena di Pioggia, 1977 (Giannini 3)
In Venice, 1933 (Terry 4)
In viaggio con papa, 1982 (Sordi 3)
In Walked Charley, 1932 (Roach 4)
In Which We Serve, 1942 (**Lean 2, Attenborough 3, Howard 3, Johnson 3, Mills 3, Coward 4, Green 4, Rank 4**)
In Wrong, 1919 (Gaudio 4)
Ina no Kantaro, 1943 (Hasegawa 3, Yamada 3)
Ina Song. See Ina-bushi, 1940
Ina-bushi, 1940 (Hayasaka 4)
Ina-bushi jinji. See Ina no Kantaro, 1943
Inadmissible Evidence, 1968 (Anderson 2)
Inadmissible Evidence, 1991 (Moore 3)

Inauguration de l'Exposition universelle, 1900 (Lumière 2)

Inauguration of the Pleasure Dome, 1954 (Anger 2)

Inay, 1977 (Brocka 2)

Inazuma, 1952 (Kagawa 3, Takamine 3)

Inazuma-zoshi, 1951 (Tanaka 3)

Inbad the Sailor, 1923 (Sennett 2)

Incantesimo tragico, 1951 (Brazzi 3, Félix 3, Vanel 3)

Incantevole nemica, 1953 (Sordi 3, Age and Scarpelli 4)

Ince cumali, 1967 (Güney 2)

Incendiaire, 1905 (Pathé 4)

Incendiary Blonde, 1945 (Fitzgerald 3, Hutton 3, Dreier 4, Head 4)

Incense for the Damned, 1970 (Cushing 3)

Incensurati. See It Started in Naples, 1960

Incertaine Vocation de Médéric de Plougastel, 1966 (Braunberger 4)

Inchiesa, 1971 (Bertolucci 2)

Inchiesta, 1987 (Cecchi D'Amico 4)

Inchon, 1981 (Mifune 3, Olivier 3, Sharif 3, Goldsmith 4)

Incident, 1967 (Ritter 3, Sheen 3)

Incident at Blood Pass. See Machibuse, 1970

Incident at Phantom Hill, 1966 (Duryea 3, Nugent 4, Salter 4)

Incident in Shanghai, 1938 (Havelock-Allan 4)

Incident on a Dark Street, 1973 (Bernstein 4)

Incidents in the Great European War, 1914 (Pearson 2)

Incognito, 1933 (Brasseur 3)

Incognito, 1958 (Constantine 3)

Income Tax Sappy, 1954 (Three Stooges 3)

Incompetent Hero, 1914 (Sennett 2, Arbuckle 3)

Incompreso, 1967 (Quayle 3)

Inconnue de Monte-Carlo, 1938 (Berry 3)

Inconnue de Montréal, 1950 (Kosma 4)

Inconnue des six jours, 1926 (Simon 3)

Inconnus dans la maison, 1941 (Clouzot 2, Fresnay 3, Raimu 3)

Incontro, 1971 (Morricone 4)

Incorrigible, 1975 (Broca 2, Belmondo 3, Bujold 3, Audiard 4, Delerue 4)

Incorrigible Dukane, 1915 (Barrymore 3, Folsey 4)

Incorruptible. See Hercule, 1937

Incredible Floridas, 1972 (Weir 2)

Incredible Invasion, 1971 (Karloff 3)

Incredible Journey, 1963 (Disney 4)

Incredible Journey of Dr. Meg Laurel, 1979 (Wyman 3, Green 4)

Incredible Melting Man, 1977 (Baker 4)

Incredible Mr. Limpet, 1964 (McKimson 4)

Incredible Petrified World, 1960 (Carradine 3)

Incredible Sarah, 1976 (Jackson 3, Bernstein 4, Challis 4)

Incredible Shrinking Man, 1957 (Salter 4)

Incredible Shrinking Woman, 1981 (Baker 4)

Incredible Two-Headed Transplant, 1970 (Dern 3)

Incredibly Strange Creatures Who Stopped Living and Became Crazy Mixed-Up Zombies!!?, 1964 (Zsigmond 4)

Incubus, 1965 (Hall 4)

Indagine su un cittadino al di sopra di ogni sospetto, 1970 (Volonté 3, Morricone 4)

Indagine su un delitto perfetto, 1976 (Valli 3)

Inde fantôme, 1969 (Malle 2)

Indée d'apache, 1907 (Linder 3)

Independence, 1976 (Huston 2, Wallach 3)

Index Hans Richter, 1969 (Markopoulos 2)

India, 1958 (Rossellini 2)

India, 1972 (De Almeida 2)

India favolosa, 1954 (Renoir 4)

India on Parade, 1937 (Hoch 4)

India Rubber Head. See Homme à la tête de caoutchouc, 1902

India Song, 1975 (Duras 2, Seyrig 3)

India vista da Rossellini, 1958 (Rossellini 2)

Indian Agent, 1948 (Hunt 4)

Indian and the Child, 1912 (Anderson 3)

Indian Brothers, 1911 (Griffith 2, Bitzer 4)

Indian Chief and the Seidlitz Powder, 1901 (Hepworth 2)

Indian Durbar. See World Window, 1977

Indian Fighter, 1955 (De Toth 2, Douglas 3, Matthau 3, Hecht 4, Waxman 4)

Indian Friendship, 1912 (Anderson 3)

Indian Girl's Love, 1910 (Anderson 3)

Indian Jealousy, 1911 (Dwan 2)

Indian Legend, 1912 (Ince 4)

Indian Maiden's Lesson, 1911 (Anderson 3)

Indian Massacre, 1912 (Inec 4)

Indian Mother, 1910 (Olcott 2)

Indian Paint, 1964 (Crosby 4)

Indian Pudding, 1930 (Terry 4)

Indian Raiders, 1912 (Reid 3)

Indian Romeo and Juliet, 1912 (Reid 3)

Indian Runner, 1991 (Bronson 3, Hopper 3)

Indian Runner's Romance, 1909 (Griffith 2, Pickford 3, Bitzer 4)

Indian Summer, 1912 (Griffith 2, Pickford 3, Bitzer 4)

Indian Summer, 1978 (Delon 3, Giannini 3)

Indian Summer, 1987 (Lassally 4)

Indian Sunbeam, 1912 (Anderson 3)

Indian Temples. See World Window, 1977

Indian Territory, 1950 (Autry 3)

Indian Tomb. See Indische Grabmal, 1921

Indian Trailer, 1909 (Anderson 3)

Indian Vestal, 1911 (Bosworth 3)

Indian Village. See Indisk by, 1951

Indian Wife's Devotion, 1910 (Mix 3)

Indian Youth—An Exploration, 1968 (Benegal 2)

Indiana Jones and the Last Crusade, 1989 (Lucas 2, Spielberg 2, Connery 3, Elliott 3, Ford 3, Burtt 4, Slocombe 4, Williams 4)

Indiana Jones and the Temple of Doom, 1984 (Lucas 2, Spielberg 2, Ford 3, Slocombe 4, Williams 4)

Indianapolis Speedway, 1939 (Bacon 2, Sheridan 3, Deutsch 4, Orry-Kelly 4)

Indian's Gratitude, 1913 (Ince 4)

Indian's Lament, 1980 (Johnson 3)

Indian's Loyalty, 1913 (Griffith 2, Gish 3, Bitzer 4)

Indian's Narrow Escape, 1915 (Anderson 3)

Indian's Sacrifice, 1911 (Anderson 3)

Indict and Convict, 1974 (Loy 3, Wallach 3, Goldsmith 4)

Indiens sont encore loin, 1977 (Huppert 3)

Indifferente, 1989 (Morricone 4)

Indifferenti, 1963 (Cardinale 3, Goddard 3, Steiger 3, Winters 3, Cecchi D'Amico 4, Cristaldi 4, Di Venanzo 4, Fusco 4)

Indio, 1939 (Armendáriz 3)

Indio, 1971 (Fernández 2)

Indio, 1989 (Donaggio 4)

Indio Black, 1970 (Brynner 3)

Indische Grabmal, 1921 (Veidt 3, Hunte 4, Pommer 4, Von Harbou 4)

Indische Tuch, 1963 (Kinski 3)

Indiscreet, 1931 (McCarey 2, Swanson 3, Day 4, Newman 4, Toland 4)

Indiscreet, 1958 (Donen 2, Bergman 3, Grant 3, Cahn 4, Krasna 4, Young 4)

Indiscreet, 1988 (Wagner 3)

Indiscretion. See Christmas in Connecticut, 1945

Indiscretion. See Stazione termini, 1953

Indiscretion of an American Wife. See Stazione termini, 1953

Indisk by, 1951 (Sucksdorff 2)

Indiskrete Frau, 1927 (Reisch 4)

Indomitable Teddy Roosevelt, 1985 (Scott 3)

Indonesia Calling, 1946 (Ivens 2, Finch 3)

Induito, 1960 (Armendáriz 3)

Industrial Britain, 1931–32 (Grierson 2)

Industrial Britain, 1933 (Flaherty 2)

Industrial Research, 1976 (Benegal 2)

Industrial Symphony. See Philips-Radio, 1931

Industrie de la tapisserie et du meuble sculpté, 1935 (Storck 2)

Industrie du verre, 1913 (Burel 4)

Inesorabili, 1951 (Vanel 3)

Inez from Hollywood, 1924 (Arzner 2, Astor 3, Edeson 4)

Infancy, 1951 (Lee 3)

Infant at Snakeville, 1911 (Anderson 3)

Infanzia, vocazione, e prime esperienze di Giacomo Casanova, Veneziano, 1969 (Comencini 2, Cecchi D'Amico 4, Gherardi 4)

Infascelli. See Zuppa di pesce, 1992

Infatuation, 1926 (Rosson 4)

Infedeli, 1953 (Lollobrigida 3)

Inferior Sex, 1919 (Gaudio 4, Mayer 4)

Infermiera, 1975 (Ponti 4)

Infernal Cake Walk. See Cake-walk infernal, 1903

Infernal Cauldron. See Chaudron infernal, 1903

Infernal Triangle, 1935 (Roach 4)

Infernal Trio. See Trio infernal, 1973

Inferno, 1953 (Ryan 3, Jeakins 4, LeMaire 4)

Inferno, 1979 (Valli 3, Argento 4)

Inferno in Diretta, 1985 (Black 3)

Infidel, 1922 (Karloff 3, Schulberg 4)

Infideli, 1953 (Monicelli 2, Papas 3)

Infidelity. See Altri tempi, 1952

Infidelity. See Amant de cinq jours, 1960

Infinity, 1977 (Popescu-Gopo 4)

Infirmière, 1914 (Gance 3)

Inflation, 1926 (Richter 2)

Influence of Broncho Billy, 1913 (Anderson 3)

Influence of Sympathy, 1913 (Lawrence 3)

Information, 1966 (Frampton 2)

Information Kid. See Fast Companions, 1932

Information Machine, 1957 (Bernstein 4)

Information Please, 1940 (Gordon 3)

Information Please, 1942 (Carradine 3)

Information Please Number Eight, 1941 (Karloff 3)

Information Please Number Twelve, 1941 (Karloff 3)

Information Received, 1961 (Roeg 2)

Informer, 1912 (Griffith 2, Barrymore 3, Carey 3, Pickford 3, Walthall 3, Bitzer 4)

Informer, 1929 (Milland 3, Cardiff 4, Herlth 4, Röhrig 4)

Informer, 1935 (Ford 2, Bond 3, McLaglen 3, August 4, Guffey 4, Nichols 4, Plunkett 4, Polglase 4, Steiner 4)

Inge bliver voksen, 1954 (Roos 2)

Ingeborg Holm, 1913 (Sjöström 2, Magnusson 4)

Inge Larsen, 1924 (Albers 3, Porten 3)

Inge und die Millionen, 1933 (Wegener 3, Hoffmann 4)

Ingen dans på rosor. See I Never Promised You a Rose Garden, 1977

Ingénieurs de la mer, 1952 (Delerue 4)

Ingénieux Attendat, 1909 (Linder 3)

Ingenium Nobis Ipsa Puella Fecit, 1975 (Frampton 2)

Ingenjör Andrees luftfärd, 1981 (Von Sydow 3)

Ingens Mans Kvinna, 1953 (Von Sydow 3)

Ingénu, 1971 (Delerue 4)

Ingiusta condanna, 1952 (Brazzi 3)

Ingmar Bergman, 1971 (Andersson 3, Gould 3)

Ingmar Inheritance. See Ingmarsarvet, 1925

Ingmarsarvet, 1925 (Molander 2, Veidt 3, Jaenzon 4, Magnusson 4)

Ingmarsönerna, 1919 (Jaenzon 4)

Ingmarsönerna, Parts I and II, 1919 (Sjöström 2, Magnusson 4)

Ingomar of the Hills, 1915 (Anderson 3)

Ingorgo, 1979 (Comencini 2, Cardinale 3, Depardieu 3, Girardot 3, Mastroianni 3, Rey 3, Sordi 3)

Ingrate, 1908 (Griffith 2, Lawrence 3, Bitzer 4)

Ingrid, 1984 (Gielgud 3, Lansbury 3, Quinn 3)

Inherit the Wind, 1960 (Kramer 2, Kelly 3, March 3, Tracy 3, Laszlo 4)

Inherit the Wind, 1988 (Douglas 3, Robards 3)

Inheritance. See Uncle Silas, 1947

Inheritance. See Karamiai, 1962

Inheritance, 1963 (Burton 3, Ryan 3)

Inheritance. See Eredità Ferramonti, 1976

Inheritor. See Héritier, 1973

Inhumaine, 1923 (Autant-Lara 2, Cavalcanti 2, L'Herbier 2, Milhaud 4)

Initiation, 1929 (Rooney 3)

Initiation, 1978 (Clarke 2)

Initiation à la danse des Possédés, 1949 (Rouch 2)

Initiation of Sarah, 1978 (Winters 3)

Iniwa Hachiro, 1933 (Yamada 3)

Injun Trouble, 1937 (Blanc 4, Clampett 4, Stalling 4)

Injun Trouble, 1951 (Terry 4)

Injun Trouble, 1969 (Blanc 4, McKimson 4)

Inki and the Lion, 1941 (Blanc 4, Jones 4, Stalling 4)

Inki and the Minah Bird, 1943 (Blanc 4, Jones 4, Stalling 4)

Inki at the Circus, 1947 (Blanc 4, Jones 4)

Inklings, 1927 (Fleischer 4)

Inkognito, 1936 (Fröhlich 3)

In-Laws, 1979 (Arkin 3, Falk 3)

Inmaan Dharam, 1977 (Bachchan 3)

Inmates: A Love Story, 1981 (Curtis 3)

Inn of Evil. See Inochi bonifuro, 1970

Inn of the Sixth Happiness, 1958 (Bergman 3, Donat 3, Arnold 4, Box 4, Lennart 4, Young 4)

Inn Where No Man Rests. See Auberge du bon repos, 1903

Innamorati, 1955 (Cervi 3)

Inner and Outer Space, 1960 (Breer 4)

Inner Circle, 1912 (Griffith 2, Pickford 3, Bitzer 4)

Inner Eye, 1972 (Ray 2, Datta 4)

Inner Shrine, 1917 (Bosworth 3)

Inner Voice, 1920 (Haller 4)

Innerspace, 1987 (Dante 2, Goldsmith 4, Jones 4)

Innocence Is Bliss. See Miss Grant Takes Richmond, 1949

Innocent, 1918 (Menzies 4)

Innocent, 1921 (Rathbone 3)

Innocent. See Innocente, 1976

Innocent Affair. See Don't Trust Your Husband, 1948

Innocent Bystanders, 1972 (Andrews 3, Baker 3, Chaplin 3, Pleasence 3)

Innocent Grafter, 1911 (Dwan 2)

Innocent Heroes. See Hanna's War, 1988

Innocent Husbands, 1925 (McCarey 2, Roach 4)

Innocent Lie, 1916 (Olcott 2)

Innocent Magdalene, 1916 (Dwan 2, Fleming 2, Gish 3)

Innocent Magdalene, 1945 (Fleming 2)

Innocent Maid. See Hakoiri musume, 1935

Innocent Man, 1989 (Yates 2, Fraker 4)

Innocent Sinner, 1917 (Walsh 2)

Innocent Sinners, 1958 (Rank 4)

Innocent Sorcerers. See Niewinni czarodzieje, 1960

Innocente, 1976 (Visconti 2, Giannini 3, Cecchi D'Amico 4)

Innocente Casimiro, 1945 (Sordi 3)

Innocenti pagano, 1953 (Baarová 3)

Innocents. See Neviňátka, 1929

Innocents, 1961 (Clayton 2, Kerr 3, Redgrave 3, Auric 4, Dehn 4, Francis 4)

Innocents, 1987 (Sarde 4)

Innocents aux mains sales, 1975 (Chabrol 2, Schneider 3, Steiger 3, Rabier 4)

Innocents in Paris, 1953 (Bloom 3, Harvey 3, Lee 3, Rutherford 3, Sim 3, De Grunwald 4, Kosma 4, Wakhévitch 4)

Innocents of Paris, 1929 (Chevalier 3, Lang 4, Vajda 4, Zukor 4)

Innocent's Progress, 1918 (Borzage 2)

Inocente, 1955 (Infante 3, Alcoriza 4)

Inocentes, 1962 (Bardem 2)

Inochi aru kagiri, 1946 (Yamamura 3, Hayasaka 4)

Inochi bonifuro, 1970 (Takemitsu 4)

Inochi hateru hi made, 1966 (Iwashita 3)

Inochi no minato, 1944 (Hasegawa 3)

Inochi o kakeru otoko, 1958 (Hasegawa 3)

Inondation, 1923 (Cavalcanti 2, Delluc 2)

Inquest. See Voruntersuchung, 1931

Inquest, 1940 (Boulting 2)

Inquilab, 1935 (Kapoor 2, Bachchan 3)

Insaan Jag Utha, 1959 (Burman 4)

Insaf, 1937 (Biswas 3)

Insaniyat, 1955 (Anand 3, Kumar 3)

Insaziabili, 1969 (Malone 3)

Insel, 1934 (Rosay 3)

Insel, 1974 (Wenders 2)

Insel der Träume, 1926 (Courant 4)

Insel der verbotenen Küsse, 1926 (Warm 4)

Insel der Verschollenen, 1921 (Gad 2)

Insel wird entdeckt, 1937 (Madsen and Schenstrøm 3)

Inserts, 1975 (Dreyfuss 3, Hoskins 3, Russell 4)

Insh' Allah, 1965 (Bates 3)

Insiang, 1976 (Brocka 2)

Inside a Girls' Dormitory. See Dortoir des grandes, 1953

Inside Daisy Clover, 1965 (Mulligan 2, Pakula 2, Gordon 3, McDowall 3, Redford 3, Wood 3, Head 4, Lang 4, Previn 4, Tavoularis 4)

Inside Edges, 1975 (Emshwiller 2)

Inside Information, 1939 (Carey 3)

Inside Job, 1946 (Browning 2)

Inside Job. See Alpha Caper, 1973

Inside Man, 1984 (Hopper 3)

Inside Moves, 1980 (Levinson 2, Barry 4, Kovacs 4)

Inside Out, 1986 (Gould 3)

Inside Rooms—The Bathroom, 1985 (Greenaway 2)

Inside Story, 1938 (Darwell 3, Miller 4)

Inside Story, 1948 (Dwan 2)

Inside Straight, 1951 (McCambridge 3)

Inside the Gelatin Factory, 1972 (Emshwiller 2)

Inside the Line, 1930 (Musuraca 4)

Inside the Third Reich, 1981 (Gielgud 3)

Insignificance, 1985 (Roeg 2, Curtis 3)

Insolent, 1972 (Douy 4)

Insolent Matador, 1989 (Halas and Batchelor 4)

Insomnia Is Good for You, 1957 (Sellers 3)

Insomniac at the Bridge. See Eveillé du Pont de l'Alma, 1985

Insomnie, 1963 (Carrière 4)

Insoumis, 1964 (Delon 3, Delerue 4, Evein 4, Renoir 4)

Inspecteur aime la bagarre, 1956 (Kosma 4)

Inspecteur La Bavure, 1980 (Depardieu 3, Decaë 4)

Inspecteur Lavardin, 1985 (Chabrol 2)

Inspector. See Revisor, 1933

Inspector, 1961 (Pleasence 3, Arnold 4, Dunne 4)

Inspector Calls, 1954 (Sim 3)

Inspector Clouseau, 1968 (Edwards 2, Arkin 3)

Inspector General, 1949 (Kaye 3, Lanchester 3, Green 4, Wald 4)

Inspector Goes Home. See Inspektor se vraća kući, 1959

Inspector Hornleigh, 1939 (Sim 3)

Inspector Hornleigh Goes to It, 1941 (Cusack 3, Launder and Gilliat 2, Sim 3)

Inspector Hornleigh on Holiday, 1939 (Launder and Gilliat 2, Sim 3)

Inspector Lavardin, 1986 (Rabier 4)

Inspector Maigret. See Maigret tend un piège, 1957

Inspektor se vraća kući, 1959 (Mimica 4)

Inspirace, 1949 (Zeman 4)

Inspiration, 1931 (Brown 2, Garbo 3, Montgomery 3, Adrian 4, Daniels 4, Mayer 4)

Inspiration. See Inspirace, 1949

Instant Sex, 1979 (Godfrey 4)

Instinct. See Honno, 1966

Instinct est maître, 1917 (Feyder 2, Gaumont 4)

Institute for Revenge, 1979 (Schifrin 4)

Instructional Steamer 'Red Star'. See Instruktorii Parokhod 'Krasnaia Zvezda', 1920

Instructive Story. *See* Shido monogatari, 1941

Instruktorii Parokhod 'Krasnaia Zvezda', 1920 (Vertov 2)

Instruments of the Orchestra, 1946 (Mathieson 4)

Insult, 1932 (Gielgud 3)

Insultin' the Sultan, 1934 (Iwerks 4)

Insulting the Sultan, 1920 (Roach 4)

Insurance, 1930 (Cantor 3)

Insured for Life, 1980 (Halas and Batchelor 4)

Insurrección de la burguesia, 1974 (Guzmán 2)

Insurrection of the Bourgeoisie. *See* Insurrección de la burguesia, 1974

Intelligence d'une machine, 1948 (Epstein 2)

Intelligence Men, 1965 (Dillon 4)

Intent to Kill, 1958 (Lom 3, Cardiff 4, Sangster 4)

Interdit de séjour, 1953 (Piccoli 3)

Interference, 1929 (Powell 3, Banton 4, Hunt 4)

Interference of Broncho Billy, 1914 (Anderson 3)

Interim, 1952 (Brakhage 2)

Interim Balance. *See* Věrni zustaneme, 1945

Interior of a Railway Carriage, 1901 (Hepworth 2)

Interiors, 1978 (Allen 2, Keaton 3, Page 3, Rosenblum 4, Willis 4)

Interlude, 1957 (Sirk 2, Allyson 3, Brazzi 3, Rosay 3, Daniels 4, Hunter 4)

Interlude, 1968 (Cleese 3, Sutherland 3, Werner 3, Delerue 4, Fisher 4)

Intermezzo, 1936 (Molander 2, Bergman 3)

Intermezzo, 1939 (Bergman 3, Howard 3, Irene 4, Menzies 4, Selznick 4, Steiner 4, Toland 4, Westmore Family 4, Wheeler 4)

Intermezzo, 1974 (Popescu-Gopo 4)

Intermezzo einer Ehe in sieben Tagen. *See* Soll man heiraten, 1925

Internal Affairs, 1990 (Gere 3, Alonzo 4)

International Hotel. *See* V.I.P.s, 1963

International House, 1933 (Fields 3, Lugosi 3, Pangborn 3, Banton 4, Haller 4)

International Lady, 1941 (Rathbone 3, Estabrook 4, Mohr 4)

International Settlement, 1938 (Carradine 3, Del Rio 3, Sanders 3)

International Sneak, 1917 (Sennett 2)

International Squadron, 1941 (Reagan 3)

International Velvet, 1978 (Hopkins 3, Lai 4)

Internecine Project, 1974 (Coburn 3, Grant 3, Unsworth 4)

Interno di un convento, 1977 (Borowczyk 2)

Interns, 1962 (Robertson 3, Metty 4)

Interns Can't Take Money, 1937 (McCrea 3, Stanwyck 3, Dreier 4, Head 4)

Interpol, 1957 (Howard 3, Mature 3, Paxton 4)

Interrupted Elopement, 1911 (Sennett 2)

Interrupted Game, 1911 (Sennett 2)

Interrupted Journey, 1949 (Havelock-Allan 4, Korda 4)

Interrupted Melody, 1955 (Ford 3, Deutsch 4, Levien 4, Rose 4, Ruttenberg 4)

Interrupted Message, 1900 (Bitzer 4)

Interrupted Picnic, 1898 (Hepworth 2)

Interrupted Solitude, 1974 (Emshwiller 2)

Interval, 1967 (Oberon 3)

Interval, 1973 (Figueroa 4, Levine 4)

Intervals, 1969 (Greenaway 2)

Intervention in the Far East. *See* Volochayevskiye dni, 1937

Interview, 1971 (Sen 2)

Interview. *See* Intervista, 1987

Interview with President Allende, 1971 (Wexler 4)

Interviews with My Lai Veterans, 1970 (Wexler 4)

Intervista, 1987 (Mastroianni 3, Morricone 4)

Intimades en un cuarto de baño, 1989 (Hermosillo 2)

Intimate. *See* Stranger in Love, 1932

Intimate Dream. *See* Hazukashiiyume, 1927

Intimate Interview, 1930 (Cagney 3)

Intimate Lighting. *See* Intimni osvetleni, 1965

Intimate Moments. *See* Madame Claude 2, 1981

Intimate Stranger, 1956 (Losey 2, Koch 4)

Intimate Strangers, 1977 (Douglas 3)

Intimni osvetleni, 1965 (Ondříček 4)

Into Her Kingdom, 1926 (Wilson 4)

Into the Blue, 1951 (Wilcox 2)

Into the Dark. *See* Entre Tinieblas, 1983

Into the Desert, 1912 (Cruze 2)

Into the Light. *See* Wise Guy, 1926

Into the Night, 1985 (Cronenberg 2, Landis 2, Mazursky 2, Siegel 2, Papas 3, Pfeiffer 3, Baker 4)

Into Thin Air, 1985 (Burstyn 3)

Into Thin Air, 1990 (Cohen 2, Jones 3)

Into Your Dance, 1935 (Freleng 4)

Intoccabili, 1968 (Falk 3, Rowlands 3, Morricone 4)

Intolerance, 1916 (Browning 2, Griffith 2, Van Dyke 2, Von Stroheim 2, Crisp 3, Fairbanks 3, Gish 3, Johnson 3, Love 3, Marsh 3, Bitzer 4, Brown 4, Loos 4)

Intolerance. *See* Mother and the Law, 1919

Intrepid Davy, 1911 (Bunny 3)

Intrepid Mr. Twigg, 1968 (Francis 4)

Intriguantes, 1953 (Moreau 3)

Intrigue, 1948 (Raft 3)

Intrigue. *See* Dark Purpose, 1964

Intriguen der Madame de la Pommeraye, 1921 (Herlth 4, Hoffmann 4, Röhrig 4)

Introducing Audrey Hepburn, 1953 (Hepburn 3)

Introducing the Dial, 1935 (Grierson 2)

Introduction to Arnold Schoenberg's Accompaniment for a Cinematographic Scene. *See* Einleitung zu Arnold Schoenberg Begleit Musik zu einer Lichtspielscene, 1969

Introduction to Feedback, 1960 (Bernstein 4)

Introduction to the Enemy, 1974 (Fonda 3, Wexler 4)

Intruder, 1913 (Costello 3)

Intruder, 1914 (Reid 3)

Intruder, 1953 (Hawkins 3, Adam 4, Mathieson 4)

Intruder in the Dust, 1949 (Brown 2, Deutsch 4, Faulkner 4, Maddow 4, Mayer 4, Surtees 4)

Intruders, 1947 (Terry 4)

Intruders, 1970 (Ford 3, O'Brien 3)

Intrusa, 1955 (Delli Colli 4)

Intruse, 1913 (Feuillade 2)

Intrusion at Lompoc, 1911 (Dwan 2)

Inubue, 1978 (Yamamura 3)

Interval, 1973 (Figueroa 4, Levine 4)

Invader, 1935 (Schüfftan 4, Spiegel 4)

Invader, 1991 (Golan and Globus 4)

Invader from Mars, 1953 (Menzies 4)

Invaders, 1912 (Ince 4, Sullivan 4)

Invaders. *See* 49th Parallel, 1941

Invaders from Mars, 1953 (Leven 4, Seitz 4)

Invaders from Mars, 1986 (Black 3, Golan and Globus 4)

Invasion, 1970 (Allégret 2, Piccoli 3)

Invasion of the Animal People, 1962 (Carradine 3)

Invasion of the Astro-Monsters. *See* Kaiju daisenso, 1966

Invasion of the Astros. *See* Kaiju daisenso, 1966

Invasion of the Body Snatchers, 1956 (Peckinpah 2, Siegel 2, Wanger 4)

Invasion of the Body Snatchers, 1978 (Siegel 2, Duvall 3, Sutherland 3)

Invasion of the Body Stealers. *See* Body Stealers, 1969

Invasion U.S.A., 1985 (Golan and Globus 4, Savini 4)

Invasore, 1943 (Rossellini 2)

Inventiamo l'amore, 1938 (Cervi 3)

Invention for Destruction. *See* Vynález zkásy, 1958

Inventor. *See* Erfinder, 1980

Inventor's Secret, 1911 (Sennett 2)

Invenzione di Morel, 1974 (Karina 3)

Investigation, 1990 (Schrader 2)

Investigation of a Citizen above Suspicion. *See* Indagine su un cittadino al di sopra di ogni sospetto, 1970

Investigation of Murder. *See* Laughing Policeman, 1973

Inviati speciali, 1943 (Flaiano 4)

Invincibili sette, 1964 (Guerra 4)

Invincible Bad Names. *See* Akumyo muteki, 1965

Invisible Agent, 1942 (Lorre 3, Salter 4, Siodmak 4)

Invisible Avenger, 1958 (Howe 4)

Invisible Enemy, 1931 (Buchanan 3)

Invisible Enemy. *See* Neviditelní nepřátelé, 1950

Invisible Fear, 1921 (Mayer 4)

Invisible Fluid, 1908 (Bitzer 4)

Invisible Ghost, 1941 (Lewis 2, Lugosi 3, Katzman 4)

Invisible Ink, 1921 (Fleischer 4)

Invisible Invaders, 1959 (Carradine 3)

Invisible Kid, 1988 (Black 3)

Invisible Man, 1933 (Whale 2, Carradine 3, Rains 3, Edeson 4, Fulton 4, Laemmle 4, Pierce 4, Sherriff 4)

Invisible Man. *See* Tomei ningen, 1954

Invisible Man, 1975 (Cooper 3)

Invisible Man Returns, 1940 (Price 3, Fulton 4, Krasner 4, Salter 4, Siodmak 4)

Invisible Man's Revenge, 1944 (Carradine 3, Fulton 4, Krasner 4, Salter 4)

Invisible Menace, 1938 (Karloff 3)

Invisible Mouse, 1947 (Hanna and Barbera 4)

Invisible Opponent. *See* Unsichtbare Gegner, 1933

Invisible Power, 1921 (Gibbons 4)

Invisible Ray, 1936 (Bondi 3, Karloff 3, Lugosi 3, D'Agostino 4, Fulton 4, Waxman 4)

Invisible Stripes, 1940 (Bacon 2, Bogart 3, Holden 3, Raft 3, Haller 4, Haskin 4, Wallis 4)

Invisible Wall. *See* Osynliga muren, 1944

Invisible Woman, 1941 (Barrymore 3, Homolka 3, Three Stooges 3, Fulton 4, Siodmak 4)

Invisibles, 1906 (Pathé 4)

Invitata, 1969 (Piccoli 3)

Invitation, 1952 (Calhern 3, Johnson 3, Kaper 4, Rose 4)

Invitation à la chasse, 1974 (Von Trotta 2, Gégauff 4)

Invitation au voyage, 1927 (Dulac 2)

Invitation to a Gunfighter, 1964 (Kramer 2, Brynner 3, Segal 3, Raksin 4)

Invitation to a Wedding, 1982 (Gielgud 3)

Invitation to Happiness, 1939 (Dunne 3, MacMurray 3, Dreier 4, Head 4)

Invitation to Monte Carlo, 1959 (Sinatra 3)

Invitation to the Dance, 1956 (Charisse 3, Kelly 3, Freed 4, Hanna and Barbera 4, Ibert 4, Junge 4, Previn 4, Ruttenberg 4, Young 4)

Invitation to the Inside. *See* Zaproszenie do wnętrza, 1978

Invitation to the Wedding, 1983 (Gielgud 3, Richardson 3, Young 4)

Invité de la lle, 1945 (Wakhévitch 4)

Invité du Mardi, 1949 (Blier 3)

Invite Monsieur à dîner, 1932 (Autant-Lara 2)

Invité surprise, 1989 (Sarde 4)

Invitée, 1969 (Guerra 4)

Invocation of My Demon Brother, 1969 (Anger 2)

Io amo, tu ami, 1961 (De Laurentiis 4)

Io e Caterina, 1980 (Sordi 3)

Io e il duce, 1985 (Girardot 3, Hopkins 3, Sarandon 3)

Io, io, io … e gli altri, 1966 (De Sica 2, Lollobrigida 3, Mangano 3, Mastroianni 3, Age and Scarpelli 4, Cecchi D'Amico 4, Flaiano 4)

Io la conoscevo bene, 1965 (Scola 2, Salter 4)

Io non vedo, tu non parli, lui non sente, 1971 (Camerini 2, De Sica 2)

Io piaccio, 1955 (Fabrizi 3)

Io so che tu sai che io so, 1982 (Sordi 3, Vitti 3)

Io sono il Capataz!, 1950 (Loren 3, Delli Colli 4)

Io uccido, tu uccidi, 1965 (Trintignant 3)

Iolanda la figlia del corsaro nero, 1951 (Gherardi 4)

Iola's Promise, 1912 (Griffith 2, Pickford 3, Bitzer 4)

Ipcress File, 1965 (Caine 3, Adam 4, Barry 4, Heller 4)

Iphigenia, 1977 (Cacoyannis 2, Papas 3, Theodorakis 4)

Ippocampo, 1943 (De Sica 2, Baarová 3, Zavattini 4)

Ippodromi all'Alba, 1950 (Blasetti 2)

Ippon-gatana dohyo-iri, 1934 (Hasegawa 3)

Ippon-gatana dohyo-iri, 1960 (Hasegawa 3)

Ire a Santiago, 1964 (Gómez 2)

Ireland or Bust, 1932 (Terry 4)

Ireland the Oppressed, 1912 (Olcott 2)

Ireland, the Tear and the Smile, 1960 (Van Dyke 2)

Ireland's Martyr, 1915 (Olcott 2)

Irene, 1926 (LeRoy 2, Moore 3, Mathis 4, McCord 4)

Irene, 1940 (Wilcox 2, Milland 3, Neagle 3, Metty 4)

Irene, Irene, 1976 (Cuny 3)

Irene's Infatuation, 1912 (Bunny 3)

Irezumi, 1966 (Miyagawa 4)

Irezumi chohan, 1936 (Shimura 3)

Irezumi hangan, 1933 (Hasegawa 3)

Irezumi hangan: Hyaku-san kiki no maki, 1933 (Hasegawa 3)

Irezumi hangan: Kanketsu-hen, 1933 (Hasegawa 3)

Irgendwo in Berlin, 1946 (Rasp 3)

Irgendwo in Europa. *See* Valahol Europaban, 1947

Iris, 1915 (Hepworth 2)

Iris and the Lieutenant. *See* Iris och Lojtnantshjarta, 1946

Iris and the Lieutenant. *See* Iris och Lojtnantshjarta, 1946

Iris och Lojtnantshjarta, 1946 (Zetterling 2, Sjöberg 2)

Irish Eyes Are Smiling, 1944 (Quinn 3, Newman 4, Pan 4)

Irish for Luck, 1936 (Lockwood 3)

Irish Girl's Love, 1912 (Olcott 2)

Irish Hearts, 1927 (Haskin 4, Meredyth 4, Miller 4, Zanuck 4)

Irish Honeymoon, 1911 (Olcott 2)

Irish in America, 1915 (Olcott 2)

Irish in Us, 1935 (Bacon 2, Cagney 3, De Havilland 3, Barnes 4, Orry-Kelly 4)

Irish Stew, 1930 (Terry 4)

Irish Sweepstakes, 1934 (Terry 4)

Irma La Douce, 1963 (Wilder 2, Caan 3, Lemmon 3, MacLaine 3, Diamond 4, La Shelle 4, Mandell 4, Orry-Kelly 4, Previn 4, Trauner 4, Westmore Family 4)

Irma la voyante, 1945 (Fernandel 3)

Iron and Steel, 1914 (Costello 3)

Iron Angel. *See* Engel aus Eisen, 1981

Iron Claw, 1916 (White 3)

Iron Crown. *See* corona di ferro, 1940

Iron Curtain, 1948 (Wellman 2, Andrews 3, Tierney 3, Clarke 4, LeMaire 4, Newman 4, Wheeler 4)

Iron Duke, 1934 (Saville 2, Arliss 3, Balcon 4, Courant 4, Junge 4, Rank 4)

Iron Glove, 1954 (Katzman 4)

Iron Hand, 1916 (Bosworth 3)

Iron Heart, 1917 (Grot 4, Miller 4)

Iron Heel, 1912 (Bushman 3)

Iron Horse, 1924 (Ford 2)

Iron Maiden, 1963 (Dillon 4)

Iron Major, 1943 (Ryan 3)

Iron Man, 1931 (Browning 2, Ayres 3, Harlow 3)

Iron Man, 1951 (Hudson 3, Boyle 4, Chase 4)

Iron Mask, 1929 (Dwan 2, Fairbanks 3, Carré 4, Menzies 4)

Iron Master, 1913 (August 4)

Iron Mistress, 1952 (Ladd 3, Blanke 4, Seitz 4, Steiner 4)

Iron Nag, 1925 (Sennett 2)

Iron Petticoat, 1956 (Hepburn 3, Hope 3, Box 4, Dillon 4, Hecht 4)

Iron Rider, 1920 (Furthman 4)

Iron Ring. *See* Kanawa, 1972

Iron Road, 1925 (Barrymore 3)

Iron Road. *See* Buckskin Frontier, 1943

Iron Sheriff, 1957 (Hayden 3)

Iron Strain, 1915 (August 4, Ince 4, Sullivan 4)

Iron Trail, 1921 (Haller 4)

Iron-Carrier. *See* Järnbäraren, 1911

Ironside, 1967 (Jones 4)

Ironweed, 1987 (Babenco 2, Baker 3, Nicholson 3, Streep 3)

Irony of Fate, 1910 (Lawrence 3)

Iro-zange, 1956 (Mori 3, Tanaka 3)

Irrashaimase, 1955 (Kagawa 3)

Irreconcilible Differences, 1984 (Fraker 4)

Irrende Seelen, 1920 (Nielsen 2, Herlth 4, Röhrig 4)

Irrepressible Brightness of Spring, 1948 (Zhao 3)

Irresistible Lover, 1927 (Laemmle 4)

Irresistible Man. *See* Unwiderstehliche, 1937

Irrfahrt ins Glück, 1914 (Hoffmann 4)

Irrungen, 1918 (Porten 3)

Irrwege der Liebe, 1918 (Albers 3)

Irving Berlin's America, 1986 (Faye 3, O'Connor 3)

Is, 1970 (Fischer 4)

Is Everybody Happy?, 1928 (Roach 4)

Is Marriage the Bunk?, 1925 (McCarey 2, Laurel and Hardy 3, Roach 4)

Is Matrimony a Failure?, 1922 (Cruze 2, Menjou 3, Brown 4)

Is My Face Red, 1932 (Krasner 4, Robinson 4, Steiner 4)

Is My Palm Read, 1933 (Fleischer 4)

Is Paris Burning?. *See* Paris brûle-t-il?, 1966

Is There a Doctor in the Mouse, 1964 (Jones 4)

Is There Justice?, 1931 (Walthall 3)

Is There Sex after Death, 1971 (Henry 4)

Is This a Record, 1973 (Godfrey 4)

Is This Trip Really Necessary. *See* Blood of the Iron Maiden, 1970

Is Your Honeymoon Really Necessary?, 1953 (Dors 3)

Isabel, 1968 (Bujold 3)

Isabelle, 1951 (Kosma 4)

Isabelle devant le désir, 1974 (Decaë 4)

Isabelle Eberhardt, 1990 (Wenders 2, O'Toole 3)

Isabel's Choice, 1981 (Green 4)

Isadora, 1968 (Love 3, Redgrave 3, Robards 3, Hakim 4, Jarre 4)

Isadora Duncan, The Biggest Dancer in the World, 1966 (Russell 2)

Ise ondo, 1929 (Hasegawa 3)

Isen brydes, 1947 (Roos 2)

Ishi, the Last of His Tribe, 1978 (Jarre 4, Trumbo 4)

Ishi-gassen, 1955 (Yamada 3)

Ishii Tsuneemon, 1934 (Hasegawa 3)

Ishimatsu of Mori. *See* Mori no Ishimatsu, 1949

Ishimatsu of the Forest. *See* Mori no Ishimatsu, 1949

Ishin no uta, 1938 (Yoda 4)

Ishinaka-sensei gyojoki datsugoko, 1950 (Mifune 3)

Ishk Ishk Ishk, 1975 (Anand 3)

Ishq, Ishq, Ishq, 1974 (Azmi 3)

Ishq par Zor Nahin, 1970 (Burman 4)

Ishtar, 1987 (Adjani 3, Beatty 3, Hoffman 3, May 4, Reynolds 4, Storaro 4)

Isidore a la deveine, 1919 (Florey 2)

Isidore sur le lac, 1919 (Florey 2)

I-ski Love-ski You-ski, 1936 (Fleischer 4)

Isla de la pasion, 1941 (Armendáriz 3)

Isla de mujeres, 1952 (Alcoriza 4)

Isla del tesero, 1969 (Gómez 2)

Island, 1960 (Shindo 2)

Island. *See* Ön, 1966

Island. *See* Eiland, 1966

Island, 1976 (Hurt 3)

Island, 1980 (Caine 3, Decaë 4, Morricone 4)
Island, 1989 (Papas 3)
Island at the Top of the World, 1973
  (Stevenson 2, Ellenshaw 4, Jarre 4)
Island in the Sky, 1938 (Cronjager 4)
Island in the Sky, 1953 (Wellman 2,
  Wayne 3, Basevi 4, Clothier 4,
  Friedhofer 4)
Island in the Sun, 1957 (Rossen 2,
  Dandridge 3, Fontaine 3, Mason 3,
  Arnold 4, Young 4, Zanuck 4)
Island of Desire. *See* Saturday Island, 1952
Island of Despair. *See* 99 mujeres, 1969
Island of Dr. Moreau, 1977 (Lancaster 3,
  Fisher 4)
Island of Doomed Men, 1940 (Lorre 3)
Island of Horrors. *See* Gokumon-to, 1977
Island of Lost Men, 1939 (Crawford 3,
  Quinn 3, Wong 3, Head 4, Raine 4,
  Struss 4)
Island of Lost Souls, 1933 (Laughton 3,
  Lugosi 3, Scott 3, Struss 4, Westmore
  Family 4, Young 4)
Island of Lost Women, 1959 (Seitz 4)
Island of Lost Women. *See* 99 mujeres, 1969
Island of Love, 1963 (Matthau 3, Preston 3,
  Duning 4, Stradling 4)
Island of Mutations. *See* Isola degli uomini
  pesci, 1979
Island of Terror, 1966 (Fisher 2, Cushing 3)
Island of the Alive: It's Alive III, 1987
  (Cohen 2)
Island of the Blue Dolphins, 1964
  (Whitlock 4)
Island of the Burning Damned. *See* Night of
  the Big Heat, 1967
Island of Treasure, 1965 (Welles 2)
Island Rescue. *See* Appointment with Venus,
  1951
Island Unknown, 1971 (Quayle 3)
Islanders, 1939 (Milhaud 4)
Islands, 1984 (Maysles 2)
Islands in the Stream, 1977 (Schaffner 2,
  Bloom 3, Scott 3, Goldsmith 4)
Isla para dos, 1958 (Figueroa 4)
Islas Marías, 1950 (Fernández 2, Infante 3,
  Figueroa 4)
Isle of Conquest, 1919 (Talmadge 3,
  Emerson 4, Loos 4)
Isle of Escape, 1930 (Johnson 3, Loy 3)
Isle of Forgotten Sins, 1943 (Ulmer 2,
  Carradine 3)
Isle of Forgotten Women, 1927 (Walker 4)
Isle of Fury, 1936 (Bogart 3, Orry-Kelly 4)
Isle of Lost Ships, 1923 (Tourneur 2)
Isle of Lost Ships, 1929 (Polito 4)
Isle of Lost Women. *See* 99 mujeres, 1969
Isle of Pingo Pongo, 1938 (Avery 4)
Isle of Retribution, 1926 (McLaglen 3)
Isle of the Dead, 1945 (Karloff 3,
  D'Agostino 4, Lewton 4)
Isle of the Snake People, 1970 (Karloff 3)
Ismael Bey, 1941 (Volkov 2)
Isn't It Romantic?, 1948 (McLeod 2, Lake 3,
  Dreier 4, Head 4)
Isn't it Shocking, 1973 (Gordon 3,
  O'Brien 3)
Isn't Life Terrible?, 1925 (McCarey 2,
  Laurel and Hardy 3, Roach 4)
Isn't Love Cuckoo, 1925 (Sennett 2)
Isola. *See* Una estate in quattro, 1969
Isola, 1986 (Audran 3)
Isola bianca, 1950 (Risi 2)
Isola degli uomini pesci, 1979 (Cotten 3)

Isola del tesoro, 1986 (Borgnine 3, Quinn 3)
Isola di Arturo, 1962 (Ponti 4, Rota 4,
  Zavattini 4)
Isola di Montecristo, 1948 (Delli Colli 4)
Isola misteriosa e il capitano Nemo, 1973
  (Sharif 3)
Ispaniya, 1939 (Shub 2)
Ispirazione, 1988 (Jarman 2)
Israel, 1959 (Bernstein 4)
Israel aujourd'hui, 1969 (Gélin 3)
Israel ... terre retrouvée, 1956 (Decaë 4,
  Rabier 4)
Isshinji no hyakunin-giri, 1925 (Tanaka 3)
Issy Valley. *See* Dolina Issy, 1982
Istanbul, 1957 (Flynn 3, Daniels 4, Miller 4,
  Young 4)
Istoriia grazhdenskoi voini, 1922 (Vertov 2)
Istruttoria è chiusa, dimentichi!, 1971
  (Morricone 4)
It, 1927 (Bow 3, Cooper 3, Banton 4,
  Schulberg 4)
It!, 1967 (McDowall 3)
It Ain't Hay, 1943 (Abbott and Costello 3,
  Three Stooges 3)
It Ain't No Sin. *See* Belle of the Nineties,
  1934
It All Came Out in the Wash, 1912
  (Costello 3)
It All Came True, 1940 (Bogart 3,
  Sheridan 3, Haller 4, Haskin 4, Wallis 4)
It Always Rains on Sunday, 1947
  (Hamer 2, Withers 3, Auric 4,
  Balcon 4, Rank 4, Slocombe 4)
It Came from Beneath the Sea, 1955
  (Harryhausen 4)
It Came from Outer Space, 1952 (Boyle 4)
It Came Upon the Midnight Clear, 1984
  (Rooney 3)
It Comes Up Love, 1943 (O'Connor 3)
It Conquered the World, 1956 (Corman 2,
  Van Cleef 3)
It Furthers One to Have Somewhere to Go,
  1980 (Halas and Batchelor 4)
It Grows on Trees, 1952 (Dunne 3)
It Had to Be You, 1947 (Rogers 3, Wilde 3,
  Frank 4, Maté 4)
It Had to Happen, 1936 (Raft 3, Russell 3,
  Zanuck 4)
It Happened at Lakewood Manor, 1979
  (Loy 3)
It Happened at Night. *See* Affaire d'une nuit,
  1960
It Happened at the World's Fair, 1963
  (Presley 3, Ames 4, Ruttenberg 4)
It Happened in Athens, 1962 (Mansfield 3,
  Courant 4)
It Happened in Broad Daylight. *See* Es
  geschah am hellichten Tag, 1959
It Happened in Brooklyn, 1947 (Durante 3,
  Grahame 3, Grayson 3, Sinatra 3,
  Cahn 4, Green 4, Lennart 4)
It Happened in Flatbush, 1942 (Darwell 3,
  Clarke 4, Day 4)
It Happened in Gibraltar. *See* Gibraltar, 1938
It Happened in Hollywood, 1937 (Fuller 2,
  Pangborn 3, Wray 3, Walker 4)
It Happened in Hollywood, 1972 (Craven 2)
It Happened in New York, 1935 (Miller 4)
It Happened in Pikersville, 1916 (Laurel and
  Hardy 3)
It Happened in Rome, 1957 (Rank 4)
It Happened in Spain, 1979 (D'Arrast 2)
It Happened in the Park. *See* Villa Borghese,
  1953

It Happened in the West, 1911 (Bosworth 3)
It Happened One Christmas, 1977 (Welles 2,
  Hall 4)
It Happened One Night, 1934 (Capra 2,
  Bond 3, Colbert 3, Gable 3, Cohn 4,
  Riskin 4, Walker 4)
It Happened to Jane, 1959 (Day 3,
  Lemmon 3, Duning 4)
It Happened Tomorrow, 1943 (Clair 2,
  Darnell 3, Powell 3, Metzner 4,
  Nichols 4, Schüfftan 4)
It Happens Every Spring, 1949 (Bacon 2,
  Milland 3, LeMaire 4)
It Happens Every Thursday, 1953
  (Darwell 3, Young 3, Metty 4)
It Is Hard to Please Him, But It Is Worth It,
  1917 (Cohl 4)
It Is My Music. *See* Det är min musik, 1942
It is Raining on Santiago. *See* Il pleut sur
  Santjago, 1975
It Lives Again, 1978 (Cohen 2,
  Constantine 3, Baker 4, Herrmann 4)
It Might Be You, 1947 (Cushing 3)
It Must Be Love, 1926 (LeRoy 2, Moore 3)
It Must Be Love, 1940 (Terry 4)
It Mustn't Be Forgotten, 1954
  (Bondarchuk 3)
It Only Happens to Others. *See* Ca n'arrive
  qu'aux autres, 1971
It Ought to Be a Crime, 1931 (Johnson 4)
It Pays to Advertise, 1919 (Crisp 3)
It Pays to Advertise, 1931 (Brooks 3,
  Lombard 3, Banton 4)
It Pays to Exercise, 1918 (Sennett 2)
It Pays to Wait, 1911 (Dwan 2)
It Rained All Night the Day I Left, 1979
  (Curtis 3, Thulin 3)
It Rains in My Village. *See* Bice skoro
  propast sveta, 1968
It Rains on Our Love. *See* Det regnar på vår
  kärlek, 1946
It Seemed Like a Good Idea at the Time,
  1975 (De Carlo 3)
It Should Happen to You, 1954 (Cukor 2,
  Holliday 3, Lemmon 3, Cohn 4, Kanin 4,
  Lang 4, Wald 4)
It Shouldn't Happen to a Dog, 1946
  (Basevi 4)
It Snows in the Everglades. *See* Thunder
  County, 1974
It Started in Naples, 1960 (De Sica 2,
  Gable 3, Loren 3, Cecchi D'Amico 4,
  Head 4, Surtees 4)
It Started in Paradise, 1952 (Kendall 3,
  Cardiff 4, Rank 4)
It Started in Paris, 1935 (Huston 2)
It Started in the Alps. *See* Arupusu no
  wakadaisho, 1966
It Started with a Kiss, 1959 (Ford 3,
  Reynolds 3, Lederer 4, Rose 4)
It Started with Adam. *See* It Started with
  Eve, 1941
It Started with Eve, 1941 (Durbin 3,
  Laughton 3, Kräly 4, Krasna 4, Maté 4,
  Pasternak 4, Salter 4)
It Takes a Thief. *See* Challenge, 1960
It Was een April, 1935 (Sirk 2)
It was in May. *See* Var i Maj, 1914
It Was Night in Rome. *See* Era notte a Roma,
  1960
Italia non è un paesa povero, 1960
  (Taviani 2)
Italia piccola, 1957 (Rota 4)
Italia 61, 1961 (Lenica 4)

Italia vive, 1983 (Giannini 3)

Italian, 1915 (Ince 4, Sullivan 4)

Italian Barber, 1910 (Griffith 2, Sennett 2, Pickford 3, Bitzer 4)

Italian Blood, 1911 (Griffith 2, Bitzer 4)

Italian in Warsaw. *See* Giuseppe w Warszawie, 1964

Italian Job, 1969 (Baker 3, Brazzi 3, Caine 3, Coward 4, Jones 4, Slocombe 4)

Italian Secret Service, 1968 (Comencini 2)

Italian Straw Hat. *See* **Chapeau de paille d'Italie, 1927**

Italian-American, 1974 (Scorsese 2)

Italiane e l'amore, 1961 (Zavattini 4)

Italiani brava gente, 1964 (De Santis 2, Falk 3, Kennedy 3)

Italiani sono matti, 1958 (Rota 4)

Italiano brava gente. *See* Italiani brava gente, 1964

Italiano in America, 1967 (De Sica 2, Sordi 3)

Italy 61. *See* Italia 61, 1961

Itaro jishi, 1955 (Hasegawa 3)

Itawari Asataro, 1973 (Hasegawa 3)

Itazura, 1959 (Yamamura 3, Takemitsu 4)

Itch in Time, 1943 (Blanc 4, Clampett 4)

Itihaas, 1984 (Azmi 3)

Itinéraire d'un enfant gâté, 1987 (Lelouch 2, Belmondo 3, Gélin 3, Lai 4)

Itohan monogatari, 1957 (Kyo 3)

Itoshigo to taete yukamu, 1952 (Yamada 3)

It's a Bear, 1924 (Roach 4)

It's a Bear. *See* Just a Bear, 1931

It's a Bet, 1935 (Siodmak 4)

It's a Big Country, 1951 (Brown 2, Sturges 2, Vidor 2, Wellman 2, Barrymore 3, Calhern 3, Cooper 3, Johnson 3, Kelly 3, Leigh 3, March 3, Powell 3, Alton 4, Lennart 4, Raksin 4, Schary 4)

It's a Boy, 1920 (Sennett 2)

It's a Boy, 1923 (Roach 4)

It's a Boy, 1933 (Horton 3, Balcon 4, Rank 4, Vetchinsky 4)

It's a Cinch, 1932 (Arbuckle 3)

It's a Date, 1940 (Durbin 3, Francis 3, Pidgeon 3, Krasna 4, Pasternak 4)

It's a Dog's Life. *See* Vita di cani, 1950

It's a Dog's Life, 1955 (Hayes 4)

It's a Funny, Funny World, 1978 (Golan and Globus 4)

It's a Gift, 1923 (Roach 4)

It's a Gift, 1934 (McLeod 2, Fields 3, Dreier 4, Schulberg 4, Zukor 4)

It's a Good Day, 1969 (Fields 4)

It's a Grand Life, 1953 (Dors 3)

It's a Grand Old Nag, 1947 (Clampett 4)

It's a Great Feeling, 1949 (Cooper 3, Crawford 3, Day 3, Flynn 3, Greenstreet 3, Kaye 3, Neal 3, Reagan 3, Robinson 3, Wyman 3, Cahn 4, Diamond 4, Prinz 4)

It's a Great Life, 1929 (Wood 2, Gibbons 4)

It's a Great Life. *See* Toller hecht auf krummer tour, 1962

It's a Hap-hap-happy Day, 1941 (Fleischer 4)

It's a Hard Life, 1919 (Roach 4)

It's a Mad, Mad, Mad, Mad World, 1963 (Keaton 2, Kramer 2, Lewis 2, Brown 3, Durante 3, Falk 3, Horton 3, Rooney 3, Terry-Thomas 3, Three Stooges 3, Tracy 3, Dunn 4, Edouart 4, Laszlo 4, O'Brien 4, Smith 4)

It's a Pleasure, 1945 (Henie 3)

It's a Small World, 1935 (Tracy 3, La Shelle 4, Miller 4)

It's a Small World, 1950 (Struss 4)

It's a 2′ 6″ above the Ground World, 1972 (Cleese 3, Box 4, Godfrey 4)

It's a Wild Life, 1918 (Daniels 3, Lloyd 3, Roach 4)

It's a Wise Child, 1931 (Davies 3, Booth 4)

It's a Wonderful Life, 1946 (Capra 2, Barrymore 3, Bond 3, Bondi 3, Grahame 3, Reed 3, Stewart 3, Biroc 4, Goodrich 4, Hornbeck 4, Swerling 4, Tiomkin 4, Walker 4)

It's a Wonderful World, 1939 (Van Dyke 2, Colbert 3, Stewart 3, Adrian 4, Hecht 4, Mankiewicz 4)

It's Alive, 1974 (Cohen 2, Baker 4, Herrmann 4)

It's Alive III: Island of the Alive, 1987 (Black 3, Baker 4, Herrmann 4)

It's All in the Stars, 1946 (Terry 4)

It's All True, 1942 (Welles 2)

It's All Yours, 1938 (Carroll 3, Pangborn 3, Cohn 4)

It's Always Fair Weather, 1955 (Donen 2, Charisse 3, Kelly 3, Comden and Green 4, Freed 4, Kidd 4, Previn 4, Rose 4)

It's Always Now, 1965 (Allen 4) 4)

It's an Ill Wind, 1939 (Blanc 4, Stalling 4)

It's Because of Good Weather. *See* Youki no seidayo, 1932

It's Big Country, 1951 (Kaper 4)

It's Easy to Remember, 1935 (Fleischer 4)

It's Forever Springtime. *See* E primavera, 1950

It's Good to Be Alive, 1974 (Legrand 4)

It's Great to Be Alive, 1933 (Friedhofer 4)

It's Great to Be Crazy, 1918 (Laurel and Hardy 3)

It's Great to Be Young, 1956 (Mills 3, Addison 4)

It's Hard to Be Good, 1948 (Rank 4)

It's Him, Yes! Yes!. *See* Era lui, sì! sì!, 1951

It's Hot in Hell. *See* Singe en hiver, 1962

It's Hummer Time, 1950 (Blanc 4, McKimson 4, Stalling 4)

It's in the Air, 1938 (Dearden 2, Formby 3, Dean 4)

It's in the Bag. *See* Affaire est dans le sac, 1932

It's in the Bag, 1936 (Crazy Gang 3)

It's in the Bag, 1945 (Ameche 3, Bendix 3, Carradine 3, Benchley 4, Metty 4, Reville 4, Ryskind 4)

It's Love Again, 1936 (Saville 2, Matthews 3, Terry-Thomas 3, Young 3, Balcon 4, Junge 4, Rank 4)

It's Love I'm After, 1937 (Davis 3, De Havilland 3, Howard 3, Orry-Kelly 4, Robinson 4, Wallis 4)

It's Magic. *See* Romance on the High Seas, 1948

It's My Model. *See* Det är min modell, 1946

It's My Turn, 1980 (Clayburgh 3, Douglas 3, Allen 4)

It's Never Too Late. *See* Det är aldrig för sent, 1956

It's Nice to Have a Mouse around the House, 1965 (Blanc 4, Freleng 4)

It's No Laughing Matter, 1914 (Weber 2, Bosworth 3, Marion 4)

It's Not Cricket, 1949 (Dors 3, Rank 4)

It's Not the Size That Counts. *See* Percy's Progress, 1974

It's Nothing, Only a Game. *See* No es nada mama, solo un juego, 1973

It's Only Money, 1962 (Lewis 2, Tashlin 2, Head 4)

It's Pink But Is It Mink?, 1975 (McKimson 4)

It's That Man Again, 1943 (Rank 4)

It's the Cat's, 1926 (Fleischer 4)

It's the Natural Thing to Do, 1939 (Fleischer 4)

It's the Old Army Game, 1926 (Brooks 3, Fields 3)

It's Tough to Be Famous, 1932 (Beavers 3, Polito 4)

It's Up to You, 1941 (Kazan 2)

Itsuwareru seiso, 1950 (Shindo 2, Yoshimura 2, Kyo 3, Shindo 3)

Itto d'Afrique, 1934 (Clouzot 2)

Ittouryu shinan, 1936 (Miyagawa 4)

Iumoreski, 1924 (Vertov 2)

Ivan, 1932 (Dovzhenko 2)

Ivan Franko, 1956 (Bondarchuk 3)

Ivan Grozny, 1944 (Eisenstein 2, Pudovkin 2, Cherkassov 3, Moskvin 4, Prokofiev 4, Tisse 4)

Ivan Grozny, Part II: Boyarskii Zagovor, 1958 (Eisenstein 2, Cherkassov 3, Moskvin 4, Prokofiev 4, Tisse 4)

Ivan, il figlio del diavolo bianco, 1953 (Age and Scarpelli 4)

Ivan the Terrible, Part I. *See* **Ivan Grozny, 1944**

Ivan the Terrible, Part II: The Boyars' Plot. *See* **Ivan Grozny II: Boyarskii Zagovor, 1958**

Ivanhoe, 1913 (Brenon 2)

Ivanhoe, 1952 (Fontaine 3, Sanders 3, Taylor, E. 3, Taylor, R. 3, Berman 4, Canutt 4, Junge 4, Rozsa 4, Young 4)

Ivanhoe, 1982 (Mason 3)

Ivanovo detstvo, 1962 (Tarkovsky 2)

Ivan's Childhood. *See* Ivanovo detstvo, 1962

I've Always Loved You, 1946 (Borzage 2, Chase 4, Gaudio 4)

I've Got Rings on My Fingers, 1926 (Fleischer 4)

I've Got Your Number, 1934 (Beavers 3, Blondell 3, Orry-Kelly 4)

Ivo. *See* Fluchtversuch, 1976

Ivonne, 1915 (Bertini 3)

Ivory Ape, 1980 (Palance 3)

Ivory Hunter. *See* Where No Vultures Fly, 1951

Ivory Snuff Box, 1915 (Tourneur 2, Carré 4)

Ivy, 1947 (Wood 2, Fontaine 3, Marshall 3, Bennett 4, Menzies 4, Metty 4, Orry-Kelly 4)

Ivy and John, 1965 (Warhol 2)

Iwashigumo, 1958 (Tsukasa 3)

Iz Lebiazhego soobshchaiut, 1960 (Shukshin 3)

Izakaya Chouji, 1983 (Muraki 4)

Izin, 1975 (Güney 2)

Izol no odoriko, 1967 (Takemitsu 4)

Izu no odoriko, 1933 (Tanaka 3)

Izzy Able the Detective, 1921 (Bray 4)

Izzy and His Rival. *See* Billy's Rival, 1914

Izzy and Moe, 1985 (Cooper 3)

J

J. Th. Arnfred, 1974 (Roos 2)
J-3, 1946 (Aurenche 4)
J.W. Coop, 1972 (Page 3, Robertson 3)
J. Edgar Hoover. *See* Private Files of J. Edgar Hoover, 1977
Ja se fabricam automovels em Portugal, 1939 (Oliveira 2)
Jaal, 1952 (Burman 4)
Jaan Pehchan, 1950 (Kapoor 2)
Jaaneman, 1976 (Anand 3)
Jab Pyar Kisise Hota Hai, 1961 (Anand 3)
Jabberwocky, 1971 (Švankmajer 4)
Jabberwocky, 1977 (Gilliam 2)
Jabberwocky. *See* Jan Svankmajer: Alchemist of the Surreal, 1990
Jacare, 1942 (Rozsa 4)
Jacare—Killer of the Amazon. *See* Jacare, 1942
J'accuse, 1919 (Gance 2, Burel 4, Gaumont 4)
Jáchyme hod to do stoje, 1973 (Kučera 4)
Jack Ahoy!, 1934 (Launder and Gilliat 2, Balcon 4, Junge 4, Rank 4)
Jack and the Beanstalk, 1902 (Porter 2)
Jack and the Beanstalk, 1922 (Disney 4)
Jack and the Beanstalk, 1931 (Fleischer 4)
Jack and the Beanstalk, 1933 (Iwerks 4)
Jack and the Beanstalk, 1952 (Abbott and Costello 3)
Jack and the Beanstalk, 1955 (Reiniger 4)
Jack and the Beanstalk, 1967 (Cahn 4, Mohr 4)
Jack Armstrong, 1947 (Katzman 4)
Jack et Jim, 1903 (Méliès 2)
Jack Fat and Slim Jim at Coney Island, 1910 (Bunny 3)
Jack Frost, 1923 (Roach 4)
Jack Frost, 1934 (Iwerks 4)
Jack Jaggs and Dum Dum. *See* Tom Tight et Dum Dum, 1903
Jack Knife Man, 1920 (Vidor 2)
Jack London, 1943 (Beavers 3, Hayward 3, Garmes 4)
Jack London's Klondike Fever. *See* Klondike Fever, 1980
Jack Mortimer, 1962 (Herlth 4)
Jack of All Trades, 1936 (Stevenson 2, Balcon 4, Vetchinsky 4)
Jack of Diamonds, 1911 (Dwan 2)
Jack of Diamonds, 1967 (Baker 3, Cotten 3)
Jack of Hearts, 1919 (Eason 4)
Jack of Hearts. *See* Hjärter Knekt, 1950
Jack Slade, 1953 (Malone 3, Van Cleef 3)
Jack Spurlock, Prodigal, 1918 (Edeson 4)
Jack the Ripper, 1959 (Sangster 4)
Jack the Ripper, 1976 (Kinski 3)
Jackal of Nahueltoro. *See* Chacal de Nahueltoro, 1968

Jackals, 1967 (Price 3, Burnett 4)
Jackaroo of Coolabong, 1920 (Glennon 4)
Jackass Mail, 1942 (McLeod 2, Beery 3, Sullivan 4)
Jackie, 1921 (Ford 2)
Jackie Cooper's Christmas Party, 1931 (Davies 3, Dressler 3, Gable 3, Shearer 3)
Jackie Robinson Story, 1950 (Beavers 3, Laszlo 4)
Jacknife, 1988 (De Niro 3)
Jackoman and Tetsu. *See* Jaokman to Tetsu, 1949
Jackpot, 1950 (Stewart 3, Wood 3, La Shelle 4, LeMaire 4)
Jackpot, 1975 (Alekan 4)
Jack's Pals, 1915 (Mix 3)
Jack's Shack, 1934 (Terry 4)
Jack's the Boy, 1932 (Launder and Gilliat 2, Balcon 4, Rank 4, Vetchinsky 4)
Jack's Word, 1911 (Dwan 2)
Jackson County Jail, 1976 (Corman 2, Needham 4)
Jacktown, 1962 (Rosenblum 4)
Jack-Wabbit and the Beanstalk, 1943 (Blanc 4, Freleng 4, Stalling 4)
Jacob the Liar. *See* Jakob der Lügner, 1975
Jacob Timerman: Prisoner Without a Name, Cell Without a Number, 1985 (Scheider 3)
Jacob von Günten, 1971 (Schygulla 3)
Jacobo Timerman, 1983 (Scheider 3, Ullmann 3)
Jacob's Ladder. *See* Jacobs stege, 1942
Jacob's Ladder, 1990 (Jarre 4)
Jacobs stege, 1942 (Molander 2, Fischer 4)
Jaconde, 1957 (Colpi 4)
Jacqueline, 1956 (Cusack 3, Rank 4, Unsworth 4)
Jacqueline Kennedy's Asian Journey, 1962 (Massey 3)
Jacques Copeau, 1963 (Grimault 4)
Jacques Cousteau—The First 75 Years, 1985 (Ferrer 3)
Jade Elephants. *See* Man from Downing Street, 1922
Jag älskar, du älskar, 1968 (Andersson 3)
Jag drapte, 1943 (Zetterling 2, Björnstrand 3)
Jag rödnar, 1981 (Andersson 3)
Jagd auf Menschen, 1926 (Albers 3)
Jagd nach dem Glück, 1929–30 (Reiniger 4)
Jagd nach dem Gluck, 1930 (Renoir 2, Wagner 4)
Jagd nach dem Tode, 1920 (Wiene 2, Dagover 3, Warm 4)
Jagd nach der Braut, 1927 (Warm 4)
Jagdszenden aus Niederbayern, 1969 (Winkler 3)

Jagdszenen aus Niederbayarn, 1969 (Schygulla 3)
Jäger von Fall, 1926 (Dieterle 2)
Jagged Edge, 1985 (Bridges 3, Close 3, Barry 4)
Jagirdar, 1937 (Mehboob 2, Biswas 4)
Jago hua savera, 1958 (Lassally 4)
Jagte Raho, 1956 (Kapoor 2)
Jagten paa Gentlemanrøveren, 1910 (Blom 2)
Jaguar, 1967 (Rouch 2)
Jaguar, 1979 (Brocka 2)
Jaguar Lives, 1979 (Huston 2, Lee 3, Pleasence 3)
Jaguar's Claws, 1917 (Neilan 2, Hayakawa 3, Novarro 3)
Jaguas. *See* Yagua, 1941
Jahrmarkt des Lebens, 1927 (Fröhlich 3)
J'ai bien l'honneur, 1984 (Constantine 3)
J'ai épousé une ombre, 1983 (Baye 3, Sarde 4)
J'ai perdu mon lorgnon, 1906 (Pathé 4)
J'ai quelque chose à vous dire, 1930 (Fernandel 3)
J'ai recontré le Père Noel, 1984 (Lai 4)
J'ai tout donnée, 1971 (Braunberger 4)
J'ai tué!, 1924 (Hayakawa 3)
J'ai tué Raspoutine, 1967 (Chaplin 3, Barsacq 4)
J'ai un hanneton dans mon pantalon, 1906 (Guy 2)
J'ai un idée, 1934 (Raimu 3)
Jail Bait, 1937 (Keaton 2)
Jail Bait. *See* Wildwechsel, 1972
Jail Bird, 1921 (Roach 4)
Jail Bird, 1990 (Henry 4)
Jail Birds, 1932 (Iwerks 4)
Jail Birds, 1934 (Terry 4)
Jail Break, 1946 (Terry 4)
Jail Yaatra, 1947 (Kapoor 2)
Jailbirds, 1914 (Eason 4)
Jailbreak, 1936 (Orry-Kelly 4)
Jailed, 1916 (Roach 4)
Jailed and Bailed, 1923 (Roach 4)
Jailhouse Rock, 1957 (Presley 3, Berman 4)
J'aime toutes les femmes, 1935 (Darrieux 3)
Jajauma narashi, 1966 (Muraki 4)
Jaje, 1959 (Mimica 4)
Jak być kochana, 1962 (Cybulski 3)
Jak daleko stąd, jak blisko, 1971 (Konwicki 4)
Jak na to, 1963 (Brdečka 4)
Jak se člověk naučil létat, 1958 (Brdečka 4)
Jak se moudrý Aristoteles stal jěstě moudřejším. *See* Pomsta, 1968
Jak stařeček měnil až vyměnil, 1953 (Trnka 4)
Jak zařídit byt, 1960 (Brdečka 4)

Jake Speed, 1986 (Hurt 3)

Jako yashiki, 1955 (Hasegawa 3)

Jakob der Lügner, 1975 (Brodský 3, Mueller-Stahl 3)

Jako-man to Tetsu, 1948 (Shindo 3)

Jal, 1952 (Anand 3)

Jali Note, 1960 (Anand 3)

Jalisco canta en Sevilla, 1948 (De Fuentes 2)

Jalisco nunca pierde, 1937 (Armendáriz 3, Figueroa 4)

Jalna, 1935 (Cromwell 2, Cronjager 4, Fort 4, MacGowan 4, Plunkett 4, Polglase 4, Veiller 4)

Jalousie, 1975 (Baye 3, Legrand 4)

Jalousie du barbouillé, 1928 (Cavalcanti 2)

Jalsaghar, 1958 (Chandragupta 4, Datta 4, Mitra 4)

Jalti Nishani, 1957 (Biswas 4)

Jam Session, 1944 (Donen 2, Miller 3, Cahn 4)

Jamaica Inn, 1939 (Hamer 2, Hitchcock 2, Launder and Gilliat 2, Laughton 3, Newton 3, O'Hara 3, Harrison 4, Pommer 4, Reville 4, Stradling 4)

Jamaica Run, 1953 (Milland 3, Head 4)

Jamais plus toujours, 1975 (Delerue 4)

Jambon d'Ardenne, 1977 (Girardot 3)

Jambul, 1952 (Enei 4)

James Brothers. See True Story of Jesse James, 1957

James Dean Story, 1957 (Altman 2)

James Dean—The First American Teenager, 1975 (Baker 3, Caron 3, Hopper 3, Puttnam 4)

James Wong Howe, 1974 (Lancaster 3)

Jamestown Baloos, 1957 (Breer 4)

Jamestown Exposition, 1907 (Bitzer 4)

Jamie, 1944 (Cahn 4)

Jammin' the Blues, 1944 (Burks 4, Cole 4)

Jamuna, 1949 (Anand 3)

Jan Hus, 1954 (Trnka 4)

Jan Knukke's Wedding. See Zhenitba Jana Knukke, 1934

Jan Konstantin, 1961 (Schorm 2)

Jan Roháč z dubé, 1947 (Stallich 4)

Jan Svankmajer: Alchemist of the Surreal, 1990 (Švankmajer 4)

Jan Žižka, 1955 (Trnka 4)

Jana Aranya, 1975 (Datta 4)

Jane, 1986 (Brakhage 2)

Jane and the Stranger, 1910 (Lawrence 3)

Jane Austen in Manhattan, 1980 (Ivory 2, Baxter 3, Jhabvala 4)

Jane B. par Agnès V., 1988 (Varda 2)

Jane Doe, 1983 (Saint 3)

Jane Eyre, 1944 (Stevenson 2, Welles 2, Fontaine 3, Marsh 3, Moorehead 3, O'Brien 3, Taylor 3, Barnes 4, Basevi 4, Herrmann 4, MacGowan 4)

Jane Eyre, 1971 (Hawkins 3, Scott 3, York 3, Vetchinsky 4, Williams 4)

Janet of the Chorus, 1915 (Talmadge 3)

Jangadero, 1961 (Wexler 4)

Janice Meredith, 1924 (Davies 3, Fields 3, Barnes 4)

Janie, 1944 (Curtiz 2, McDaniel 3, Benchley 4)

Janie Gets Married, 1946 (Malone 3, McDaniel 3, Benchley 4)

Janine, 1961 (Pialat 2)

Janitor, 1913 (Sennett 2)

Janitor, 1916 (Beery 3)

Janitor. See Eyewitness, 1980

Janitor's Joyful Job, 1915 (Laurel and Hardy 3)

Janitor's Vacation, 1916 (Beery 3)

Janitor's Wife's Temptation, 1915 (Sennett 2)

Janitzio, 1934 (Fernández 2)

Jánošík, 1935 (Frič 2)

January Man, 1989 (Sarandon 3, Steiger 3, Hamlisch 4)

Janus-Faced. See Januskopf, 1920

Januskopf, 1920 (Murnau 2, Lugosi 3, Veidt 3, Freund 4, Hoffmann 4)

Januskopf, 1972 (Mueller-Stahl 3)

Jaokman to Tetsu, 1949 (Mifune 3)

Japanerin, 1918 (Dupont 2, Veidt 3)

Japanese Fantasy. See Japon de fantaisie, 1909

Japanese Magic. See Japon de fantaisie, 1909

Japanese Nightingale, 1918 (Furthman 4, Miller 4)

Japanese Summer: Double Suicide. See Muri-shinju: Nippon no natsu, 1967

Japanese Swords: The Work of Kouhei Miyairi. See Nihontou: Miyairi Kouhei no waza, 1976

Japanese Youth. See Nihon no seishun, 1968

Japon de fantaisie, 1909 (Cohl 4)

Jaquar, 1967 (Braunberger 4)

Jardín de las delicias, 1970 (Saura 2, Chaplin 3)

Jardin des supplices, 1976 (Carrière 4)

Jardin qui bascule, 1974 (Moreau 3, Seyrig 3)

Jardinier. See Arroseur arrosé, 1895

Jardinier, 1973 (Fresnay 3)

Jardinier d'Argenteuil, 1966 (Gabin 3)

Jardins de Paris, 1948 (Resnais 2)

Jardins de Paris, 1961 (Fradetal 4)

Jardins du diable. See Coplan sauve sa peau, 1967

Jarnac's Treacherous Blow. See Coup de Jarnac, 1909

Järnbäraren, 1911 (Jaenzon 4, Magnusson 4)

Jarrett, 1973 (Ford 3, Quayle 3)

Jason and the Argonauts, 1963 (Harryhausen 4, Herrmann 4)

Jasper series, 1942–46 (Pal 4)

Jassy, 1947 (Lockwood 3, Rank 4, Unsworth 4)

Jatagan Mala, 1950 (Makavejev 2)

Jaune de soleil, 1971 (Duras 2)

Java, 1927 (Christian-Jaque 2)

Java Head, 1923 (Glennon 4, Young 4)

Java Head, 1934 (Dickinson 2, Richardson 3, Wong 3, Dean 4)

J'avais sept filles, 1955 (Chevalier 3)

Jawaharlal Nehru, 1985 (Benegal 2)

Jawani, 1942 (Biswas 4)

Jaws, 1975 (Spielberg 2, Dreyfuss 3, Scheider 3, Shaw 3, Fields 4, Williams 4)

Jaws: The Revenge, 1987 (Caine 3, Williams 4)

Jaws of Hell. See Balaclava, 1930

Jaws II, 1978 (Scheider 3, Williams 4)

Jayhawkers, 1959 (Frank 4, Head 4)

Jayne Mansfield Story, 1981 (Schwarzenegger 3)

Jaywalker, 1956 (Bosustow 4)

Jazz Age, 1929 (McCrea 3, Walthall 3, Plunkett 4)

Jazz Boat, 1960 (Roeg 2)

Jazz Fool, 1929 (Disney 4, Iwerks 4)

Jazz Mad, 1931 (Terry 4)

Jazz Mamas, 1929 (Sennett 2)

Jazz River, 1934 (Toland 4)

Jazz Singer, 1927 (Jolson 3, Loy 3, Berlin 4, Carré 4, Mohr 4, Warner 4, Zanuck 4)

Jazz Singer, 1953 (Curtiz 2, Prinz 4, Steiner 4)

Jazz Singer, 1980 (Olivier 3, Horner 4, Rosenman 4)

Jazz Waiter. See Caught in a Cabaret, 1914

Jazzed Honeymoon, 1919 (Daniels 3, Lloyd 3, Roach 4)

Jazzmania, 1923 (Goulding 2, Gibbons 4)

Je bridge au plafond, 1909 (Linder 3)

Je chante, 1938 (Presle 3, Matras 4)

Je hais les acteurs, 1986 (Blier 3, Hecht 4)

Je l'ai été trois fois, 1952 (Guitry 2, Blier 3)

Je m'appellerai Guillaume Apollinaire. See Guillaume Apollinaire, 1955

Je n'aime que toi, 1949 (D'Eaubonne 4)

Je reviendrai à Kandara, 1956 (Gélin 3, Kosma 4)

Je sais rien, mais je dirai tout, 1973 (Blier 3)

Je serai seule après minuit, 1968 (Clouzot 2)

Je suis avec toi, 1943 (Blier 3, Fresnay 3)

Je suis de la revue. See Botta e risposta, 1949

Je suis Pierre Rivière, 1975 (Huppert 3, Vierny 4)

Je suis un as, 1930 (Brasseur 3)

Je suis un sentimental, 1955 (Constantine 3)

Je t'aime, 1973 (Moreau 3)

Je t'aime, je t'aime, 1968 (Resnais 2)

Je t'aime, moi non plus, 1975 (Depardieu 3)

Je t'aime, tu danses, 1975 (Seyrig 3)

Je t'attendrai. See Déserteur, 1939

Je te confie ma femme, 1933 (Arletty 3)

Je te tiens, tu me tiens par la barbichette, 1978 (Presle 3)

Je tire chemin, 1968 (Barrault 3)

Je, tu, elles, 1971 (Braunberger 4)

Je tu il elle, 1974 (Akerman 2)

Je vais craquer, 1979 (Baye 3)

Je veux rentrer à la maison, 1989 (Resnais 2, Depardieu 3, Presle 3)

Je voudrais un enfant, 1909 (Linder 3)

Je vous aime, 1980 (Deneuve 3, Depardieu 3)

Je vous ferai aimer la vie, 1979 (Legrand 4)

Je vous salue, Mafia, 1965 (Constantine 3, Presle 3, Coutard 4)

Je vous salue, Paris, 1968 (Braunberger 4)

Je vous y prrrends!, 1897 (Guy 2)

Jealous Husband, 1911 (Griffith 2, Sennett 2, Bitzer 4)

Jealous Husbands, 1923 (Tourneur 2)

Jealous Lover, 1933 (Terry 4)

Jealous Rage, 1911 (Dwan 2)

Jealous Waiter, 1913 (Sennett 2)

Jealously, 1963 (Dinov 4)

Jealousy. See Revnost, 1914

Jealousy. See Eifersucht, 1925

Jealousy, 1929 (March 3, Fort 4)

Jealousy, 1934 (Ball 3)

Jealousy, 1945 (Eisler 4, Trumbo 4)

Jealousy. See Shitto, 1949

Jealousy. See Emergency Wedding, 1950

Jealousy, 1984 (Dickinson 3)

Jealousy and the Man, 1909 (Griffith 2, Bitzer 4)

Jealousy—Italian Style. See Dramma della gelosia—tutti i particolari in cronaca, 1970

Jean Cocteau, 1949 (Roos 2)

Jean Cocteau fait du cinéma, 1925 (Cocteau 2)

Jean de Florette, 1986 (Depardieu 3, Montand 3)

Jean de la Lune, 1931 (Simon 3, Achard 4, Meerson 4, Périnal 4, Trauner 4)

Jean de la lune, 1948 (Astruc 2, Darrieux 3, Achard 4)

Jean de la lune, 1977 (Guillemot 4)

Jean Effel, 1948 (Resnais 2)

Jean Intervenes, 1912 (Reid 3)

Jean la poudre, 1912 (Tourneur 2)

Jean o' the Heather, 1916 (Olcott 2)

Jean Renoir, le patron, 1966 (Rivette 2)

Jean Taris champion de natation. See Taris, 1931

Jean-Jacques Rousseau, 1957 (Leenhardt 2)

Jean-Louis Barrault—Man of the Theatre, 1984 (Moreau 3)

Jeanne, 1934 (Fradetal 4, Lourié 4, Stradling 4)

Jeanne Dielman, 23 Quai du Commerce, 1080 Bruxelles, 1975 (Akerman 2, Storck 2, Seyrig 3)

Jeanne Eagels, 1957 (Moorehead 3, Novak 3, Duning 4, Levien 4)

Jeannie, 1941 (Redgrave 3, Withers 3)

Jean-Paul Belmondo, 1965 (Lelouch 2)

J'écris dans l'espace, 1989 (Alekan 4, Carrière 4)

Jedenácté přikázání, 1935 (Frič 2, Heller 4)

Jeder für sich und Gott gegen alle, 1974 (Herzog 2)

Jedermanns Frau, 1924 (Korda 4)

Jedermanns Weib. See Jedermanns Frau, 1924

Jedna z milonu, 1935 (Stallich 4)

Jeena yahan, 1981 (Azmi 3)

Jeep, 1938 (Fleischer 4)

Jeepers Creepers, 1939 (Rogers 3, Blanc 4, Clampett 4, Stalling 4)

Jeet, 1949 (Anand 3, Biswas 4)

Jeevan Sathi, 1939 (Biswas 4)

Jeewan Jyoti, 1953 (Burman 4)

Jefe màximo, 1940 (De Fuentes 2, Armendáriz 3, Figueroa 4)

Jeff, 1969 (Delon 3)

Jeffries—Corbett Fight, 1903 (Bitzer 4)

Jeffries, Jr., 1924 (McCarey 2, Roach 4)

Jego Ostatni Czyn, 1916 (Negri 3)

Jeji lekař, 1933 (Baarová 3, Stallich 4)

Jejich svatební noc, 1922 (Heller 4)

Jelbeszéd, 1974 (Brejchová 3)

Jenatsch, 1987 (Donaggio 4)

Jengibre contra dinamita, 1939 (Cantinflas 3)

Jeniec Europy, 1989 (Carrière 4)

Jennie, 1940 (Day 4)

Jennie. See Portrait of Jennie, 1948

Jennie Gerhardt, 1933 (Astor 3, Darwell 3, Sidney 3, Schulberg 4, Shamroy 4, Zukor 4)

Jennie, Wife/Child, 1968 (Zsigmond 4)

Jennifer, 1953 (Lupino 3, Howe 4)

Jennifer, 1964 (De Palma 2)

Jennifer: a Woman's Story, 1979 (Green 4)

Jennifer on My Mind, 1971 (De Niro 3)

Jenny, 1936 (Carné 2, Barrault 3, Rosay 3, Vanel 3, D'Eaubonne 4, Kosma 4, Prévert 4)

Jenny, 1984 (Ullmann 3)

Jenny Is a Good Thing, 1969 (Lancaster 3)

Jenny Lind. See Lady's Morals, 1930

Jenny Lind, 1931 (Rosay 3)

Jenny's Pearls, 1913 (Sennett 2)

Jens Langkniv, 1940 (Henning-Jensen 2)

Jeopardy, 1953 (Sturges 2, Stanwyck 3, Rose 4, Schnee 4, Tiomkin 4)

Jeremiah Johnson, 1972 (Pollack 2, Redford 3, Anhalt 4)

Jericho, 1937 (Robeson 3)

Jéricho, 1945 (Brasseur 3, Renoir 4, Spaak 4)

Jerk, 1979 (Martin 3, Van Runkle 4)

Jerk, Too, 1984 (Biroc 4)

Jerky Turkey, 1945 (Avery 4)

Jernbanens Datter, 1911 (Psilander 3)

Jérôme Bosch, 1963 (Guillemot 4)

Jerry series, 1949–50 (Hanna and Barbera 4)

Jerry, 1924 (Gallone 2)

Jerry and the 5.15 Train, 1917 (Bray 4)

Jerry Jerry Quite Contrary, 1966 (Jones 4)

Jerusalem. See World Window, 1977

Jerusalem File, 1972 (Pleasence 3, Coutard 4)

Jesien, 1955 (Borowczyk 2)

Jess, 1912 (Cruze 2)

Jesse, 1988 (Remick 3)

Jesse and James, 1931 (Terry 4)

Jesse James, 1939 (King 2, Carradine 3, Darwell 3, Fonda 3, Power 3, Scott 3, Barnes 4, Canutt 4, Johnson 4, Zanuck 4)

Jesse James at Bay, 1941 (Rogers 3)

Jesse James vs. the Daltons, 1954 (Katzman 4)

Jessica, 1962 (Negulesco 2, Chevalier 3, Dalio 3, Dickinson 3, Moorehead 3)

Jester's Tale. See Bláznova kronika, 1964

Jesus Christ Superstar, 1973 (Jewison 2, Previn 4, Slocombe 4)

Jesus of Nazareth, 1976 (Zeffirelli 2, Bancroft 3, Cardinale 3, Cecchi d'Amico 4)

Jesusita en Chihuahua, 1942 (Infante 3)

Jet Cage, 1962 (Blanc 4, Freleng 4)

Jet Carrier, 1954 (La Shelle 4)

Jet over the Atlantic, 1959 (Raft 3, Haskin 4)

Jet Pilot, 1957 (Von Sternberg 2, Leigh 3, Wayne 3, D'Agostino 4, Furthman 4, Hoch 4, Hughes 4, Kaper 4)

Jet Storm, 1959 (Zetterling 2, Attenborough 3, Baker 3)

J'étais une aventurière, 1938 (Feuillère 3, Barsacq 4)

Jetée, 1964 (Marker 2)

Jetsons: The Movie, 1990 (Blanc 4, Hanna and Barbera 4)

Jettchen Geberts Geschichte, 1918 (Veidt 3)

Jeu avec le feu, 1974 (Noiret 3, Trintignant 3, Robbe-Grillet 4)

Jeu de coudes. See Elbowing, 1980

Jeu de la puce, 1969 (Delerue 4)

Jeu de la vérité, 1961 (Trintignant 3, Matras 4)

Jeu de massacre, 1967 (Cassel 3)

Jeu de solitaire, 1976 (Valli 3)

Jeu du solitaire, 1976 (Carrière 4)

Jeu 1, 1962 (Braunberger 4)

Jeudi on chantera comme dimanche, 1966 (Storck 2, Delerue 4)

Jeune Fille assassinée, 1974 (Vadim 2)

Jeune Fille et l'étoile, 1960 (Braunberger 4)

Jeune Fille la plus méritante de France, 1922 (Musidora 3)

Jeune Fille romanesque, 1909 (Linder 3)

Jeune Fille un seul amour. See Katya, 1960

Jeune Folle, 1952 (Trauner 4)

Jeune Homme et la mort, 1953 (Anger 2)

Jeunes Filles à marier, 1935 (Berry 3)

Jeunes filles de Paris, 1936 (Simon 3)

Jeunes Filles d'hier et d'aujourd'hui, 1916 (Musidora 3)

Jeunes filles en détresse, 1938 (Presle 3, Andrejew 4)

Jeunes Filles en détresse, 1939 (Pabst 2)

Jeunes Gens a marier, 1912 (Cohl 4)

Jeunes mariés, 1953 (D'Eaubonne 4, Spaak 4)

Jeunesse, 1934 (Stradling 4)

Jeunesse d'abord, 1935 (Brasseur 3, Prévert 4)

Jeunesse de France, 1968 (Braunberger 4)

Jeunesses musicales, 1956 (Jutra 2)

Jeux d'amour, 1960 (Saulnier 4)

Jeux dangereux, 1958 (Wakhévitch 4)

Jeux de cartes, 1916 (Cohl 4)

Jeux de la comtesse, 1980 (Cuny 3)

Jeux de l'amour, 1959 (Chabrol 2, Cassel 3, Delerue 4, Evein 4)

Jeux de l'été et de la mer, 1936 (Storck 2)

Jeux d'enfants, 1946 (Fradetal 4)

Jeux des anges, 1964 (Borowczyk 2)

Jeux interdits, 1951 (Clément 2, Aurenche 4, Bost 4)

Jeux sont faits, 1947 (Presle 3, Auric 4, Bost 4, Colpi 4, Matras 4)

Jew Suss, 1934 (Veidt 3, Balcon 4, Junge 4)

Jewel, 1933 (Hawkins 3)

Jewel of the Nile, 1985 (Douglas 3, Turner 3)

Jewel Robbery, 1932 (Dieterle 2, Francis 3, Powell 3)

Jewel Thief, 1967 (Anand 3, Burman 4)

Jeweller's Shop, 1990 (Lancaster 3, Legrand 4)

Jewels in Our Hearts. See Tokyo no koibito, 1952

Jewels of a Sacrifice, 1913 (Dwan 2)

Jewish Gauchos. See Gauchos judíos, 1975

Jewish Prudence, 1927 (Roach 4)

Jew's Christmas, 1913 (Weber 2)

Jezebel, 1938 (Huston 2, Wyler 2, Crisp 3, Davis 3, Fonda 3, Blanke 4, Friedhofer 4, Haller 4, Orry-Kelly 4, Steiner 4, Wallis 4)

Jezebel's Kiss, 1990 (McDowell 3)

Jézus Krisztus Horoszkója, 1989 (Jancsó 2)

JFK, 1991 (Costner 3, Ford 3, Lemmon 3, Matthau 3, Sheen 3, Spacek 3, Sutherland 3, Williams 4)

Jhansi ri-rani, 1952 (Haller 4)

Jidosha doroba, 1964 (Takemitsu 4)

Jigoku kaido, 1929 (Hasegawa 3)

Jigoku no mon, 1952 (Hasegawa 3)

Jigoku no mushi, 1938 (Shimura 3, Miyagawa 4)

Jigoku no soko made tsukiauze, 1959 (Yamamura 3)

Jigokubana, 1957 (Kyo 3, Yamamura 3)

Jigokumon, 1953 (Kinugasa 2, Hasegawa 3, Kyo 3)

Jigsaw, 1949 (Dietrich 3, Fonda 3, Garfield 3, Meredith 3)

Jigsaw, 1968 (Jones 4)

Jigsaw, 1972 (O'Brien 3)

Jigsaw. See Homme en colère, 1979

Jigsaw. See House on Carroll Street, 1988

Jigsaw Man, 1984 (Caine 3, Olivier 3, Francis 4)

Jihi shincho, 1927 (Mizoguchi 2)

Jihishincho, 1954 (Kagawa 3)

Jikizamurai, 1930 (Hasegawa 3)

Jilt, 1909 (Griffith 2, Bitzer 4)

Jim, 1914 (Mix 3)

Jim Bludso, 1917 (Browning 2)

Jim Bougne, boxeur, 1923 (Chevalier 3)

Jim Cameron's Wife, 1914 (Hart 3)

Jim Crow, 1912 (Vanel 3)

Jim Jam Janitor, 1928 (Sennett 2, Hornbeck 4)

Jim Jeffries—Jim Sharkey Fight, 1899 (Bitzer 4)

Jim la houlette, 1935 (Fernandel 3)

Jim the Conqueror, 1927 (Rosson 4)

Jim the Penman, 1921 (Barrymore 3, Stradling 4)

Jim Thorpe—All American, 1951 (Lancaster 3, Haller 4, Steiner 4)

Jimmy and Sally, 1933 (Trevor 3)

Jimmy B. and André, 1980 (Green 4)

Jimmy Boy, 1935 (Baxter 2)

Jimmy Hayes and Muriel, 1914 (Mix 3)

Jimmy the Gent, 1934 (Curtiz 2, Cagney 3, Darwell 3, Davis 3, Orry-Kelly 4)

Jimmy the Kid, 1983 (Gordon 3)

Jimpu Group. See Jimpuren, 1933

Jimpuren, 1933 (Mizoguchi 2)

Jinanbou garasu, 1955 (Miyagawa 4)

Jinchoge, 1966 (Kyo 3, Tsukasa 3)

Jindra, Countess Ostrovin. See Jindra, hraběnka Ostrovínová, 1933

Jinete fantasma, 1967 (Fernández 2, Figueroa 4)

Jingle Bells, 1927 (Lantz 4)

Jingle Bells, 1931 (Terry 4)

Jinks Joins the Temperance Club, 1911 (Sennett 2)

Jinkyo, 1924 (Mizoguchi 2)

Jinpinin, 1928 (Hasegawa 3)

Jinsei gekijo, 1952 (Hayasaka 4)

Jinsei gekijo seishun-hen, 1958 (Mifune 3)

Jinsei ni onimotsu, 1935 (Tanaka 3)

Jinsei o Mitsumete, 1923 (Kinugasa 2)

Jinsei tohbo-gaeri, 1955 (Yamada 3)

Jinx, 1919 (Normand 3)

Jinxed, 1982 (Siegel 2, Midler 3, Zsigmond 4)

Jinya no Shotaro, 1934 (Yamada 3)

Jirocho Fuji, 1959 (Hasegawa 3, Kyo 3)

Jirocho goshi, 1952 (Shindo 3)

Jirokichi goshi, 1952 (Hasegawa 3)

Jisei wa utsuru, 1930 (Hasegawa 3)

Jitney Elopement, 1915 (Bacon 2, Purviance 3)

Jitterbugs, 1943 (Laurel and Hardy 3, Basevi 4)

Jivaro, 1954 (Head 4)

Jive Junction, 1943 (Ulmer 2)

Jiyu gakko, 1951 (Yoshimura 2, Kyo 3, Yamamura 3)

Jízdní hlídka, 1936 (Heller 4)

Jmenuji se Fifinka, 1953 (Stallich 4)

Jo, 1971 (Blier 3, Decaë 4)

Jo Jo Dancer, Your Life is Calling, 1986 (Pryor 3)

Joachim, Put It in the Machine. See Jáchyme hod to do stoje, 1973

Joan at the Stake. See Giovanna d'Arco al rogo, 1954

Joan of Arc, 1948 (Fleming 2, Bergman 3, Bond 3, Ferrer 3, Day 4, Friedhofer 4, Hoch 4, Jeakins 4, Vorkapich 4, Wanger 4)

Joan of Paris, 1942 (Stevenson 2, Dalio 3, Henreid 3, Ladd 3, Morgan 3, Bennett 4, Metty 4)

Joan of Plattsburg, 1918 (Normand 3)

Joan of the Ozarks, 1942 (Brown 3)

Joan the Woman, 1915 (Crisp 3)

Joan the Woman, 1917 (De Mille 2, Bosworth 3, Novarro 3, Reid 3, Buckland 4, MacPherson 4)

Joanna, 1925 (Del Rio 3)

Joanna, 1968 (Sutherland 3, Lassally 4)

Joanna Francesca, 1973 (Moreau 3)

Joaquin Murieta, 1964 (Kennedy 3)

Joaquin Murieta, 1969 (Goldsmith 4)

Job in a Million, 1937 (Grierson 2)

Jobard series, 1911 (Cohl 4)

Jocelyn, 1951 (Braunberger 4)

Jocko musicien, 1903 (Guy 2)

Jocks, 1987 (Lee 3)

Joconde, 1957 (Delerue 4)

Jocular Winds, 1913 (Dwan 2)

Jodai no chokoku, 1950 (Hayasaka 4)

Joe, 1970 (Sarandon 3)

Joe and Ethel Turp Call on the President, 1939 (Brennan 3)

Joe Butterfly, 1957 (Meredith 3, Murphy 3)

Joe Chairkin Going On, 1983 (Shepard 4)

Joe Dakota, 1957 (Van Cleef 3, Salter 4)

Joe Debbs, 1917 (Lang 2)

Joe Glow the Firefly, 1941 (Blanc 4, Jones 4, Stalling 4)

Joe il Rosso, 1936 (Fusco 4)

Joe Kidd, 1972 (Sturges 2, Duvall 3, Eastwood 3, Bumstead 4, Schifrin 4)

Joe Palooka, 1973 (Three Stooges 3)

Joe Smith, American, 1942 (Gardner 3, Young 3, Schary 4)

Joe Valachi: I segreti di Cosa Nostra. See Valachi Papers, 1972

Joe Versus the Volcano, 1990 (Hanks 3, Delerue 4)

Joen no chimata, 1976 (Mizoguchi 2)

Joen no hatoba, 1951 (Kyo 3)

Joe's Bed-Stuy Barbershop: We Cut Heads, 1982 (Lee 2)

Joe's Lunch Wagon, 1934 (Terry 4)

Joey Boy, 1965 (Launder and Gilliat 2)

Jofroi, 1934 (Pagnol 2)

Jofusei, 1973 (Hasegawa 3)

Jogakusei-ki, 1941 (Takamine 3, Yamada 3)

Jogan, 1950 (Kumar 3)

Jogashima no ame, 1950 (Hasegawa 3)

Johan, 1920 (Stiller 2, Magnusson 4)

Johan Ulfstjerna, 1923 (Magnusson 4)

Johan Ulfstjerna, 1936 (Fischer 4, Jaenzon 4)

Johann Hopkins der Dritte, 1921 (Lugosi 3)

Johann Mouse, 1952 (Hanna and Barbera 4)

Johann Sebastian Bach: Fantasia G-Moll, 1965 (Švankmajer 4)

Johann Strauss, K und I. Hofballmusikdirektor. See Kaiserwalzer, 1932

Johann the Coffin Maker, 1927 (Florey 2)

Johanna d'Arc of Mongolia, 1988 (Ottinger 2, Marais 3, Seyrig 3)

Johanna Enlists, 1918 (Beery 3, Pickford 3, Marion 4, Rosher 4)

Johannas Traum, 1975 (Schroeter 2)

Johannes fils de Johannes, 1918 (Musidora 3)

Johannes Goth, 1920 (Krauss 3, Mayer 4)

Johannes Jørgensen i Assisi, 1950 (Roos 2)

Johannes Jørgensen i Svendborg, 1954 (Roos 2)

Johannes Larsen, 1957 (Roos 2)

Johannes V. Jensen, 1947 (Roos 2)

Johannestraum, 1919 (Hoffmann 4)

Johannisnacht, 1933 (Dagover 3)

John and Julie, 1955 (Sellers 3)

John and Mary, 1969 (Yates 2, Farrow 3, Hoffman 3, Jones 4)

John Barleycorn, 1914 (Bosworth 3)

John Colter's Escape, 1912 (Bosworth 3)

John Come Lately, 1943 (Cagney 3)

John Ericsson, 1937 (Sjöström 2)

John F. Kennedy: Years of Lightning, Day of Drums, 1966 (Peck 3, Schell 3)

John Gilpin, 1989 (Halas and Batchelor 4)

John Gilpin's Ride, 1908 (Hepworth 2)

John Goldfarb, Please Come Home, 1965 (MacLaine 3, Ustinov 3, Head 4, Shamroy 4, Smith 4, Williams 4)

John Halifax, Gentleman, 1915 (Pearson 2, Bennett 4)

John Halifax, Gentleman, 1938 (McDowall 4)

John Henry and the Inky Poo, 1946 (Pal 4)

John Huston and the Dubliners, 1987 (North 4)

John Huston: The Man, the Movies, the Maverick, 1988 (Mitchum 3)

John Loves Mary, 1949 (Neal 3, Reagan 3, Burks 4, Krasna 4, Wald 4)

John Meade's Woman, 1937 (D'Agostino 4, Head 4, Mankiewicz 4, Reynolds 4, Schulberg 4)

John Needham's Double, 1916 (Weber 2)

John Oakhurst, Gambler, 1911 (Bosworth 3)

John Paul Jones, 1959 (Coburn 3, Cushing 3, Davis 3, Farrow 3, Adam 4, Steiner 4)

John Petticoats, 1919 (Hart 3, August 4, Sullivan 4)

John Rance—Gentleman, 1914 (Talmadge 3)

John Smith, 1922 (Astor 3)

John Smith Wakes Up, 1940 (Greenwood 3)

John Tobin's Sweetheart, 1913 (Bunny 3)

John Wesley, 1953 (Rank 4)

Johnny Allegro, 1949 (Raft 3, Biroc 4, Duning 4)

Johnny Angel, 1945 (Trevor 3, Carmichael 4)

Johnny Angelo, 1945 (Raft 3)

Johnny Apollo, 1940 (Hathaway 2, Lamour 3, Power 3, Brown 4, Day 4, Dunne 4, Miller 4, Zanuck 4)

Johnny Banco, 1966 (Allégret 2, D'Eaubonne 4)

Johnny Belinda, 1948 (Negulesco 2, Ayres 3, Moorehead 3, Wyman 3, McCord 4, Steiner 4, Wald 4, Warner 4)

Johnny Belinda, 1967 (Farrow 3)

Johnny Bull, 1986 (Robards 3)

Johnny Come Lately, 1943 (McDaniel 3)

Johnny Comes Flying Home, 1946 (Basevi 4)

Johnny Concho, 1956 (Sinatra 3)

Johnny Cool, 1963 (Cahn 4)

Johnny Dark, 1954 (Curtis 3, Boyle 4, Salter 4)

Johnny Doesn't Live Here Anymore, 1944 (Mitchum 3, Simon 3)

Johnny Doughboy, 1942 (Alton 4, Cahn 4)

Johnny Eager, 1941 (LeRoy 2, Taylor 3, Turner 3, Kaper 4, Mayer 4, Rosson 4)

Johnny Frenchman, 1945 (Rosay 3, Balcon 4, Clarke 4, Rank 4)

Johnny Get Your Gun, 1919 (Cruze 2, Crisp 3)

Johnny Get Your Hair Cut, 1927 (Costello 3, Eason 4)

Johnny Got His Gun, 1971 (Robards 3, Sutherland 3, Trumbo 4, Van Runkle 4)

**Johnny Guitar, 1954 (Ray 2, Bond 3,
  Borgnine 3, Carradine 3, Crawford 3,
  Hayden 3, McCambridge 3,
  Maddow 4, Stradling 4, Young 4)**
Johnny Handsome, 1989 (Hill 2, Rourke 3)
Johnny haute-couture, 1934 (Brasseur 3)
Johnny Holiday, 1950 (Bendix 3,
  Carmichael 4, Mohr 4, Waxman 4)
Johnny in the Clouds. *See* Way to the Stars,
  1945
Johnny le Fligueur, 1973 (Van Cleef 3)
Johnny Mera Naam, 1970 (Anand 3)
Johnny Nobody, 1961 (Bendix 3, Cusack 3)
Johnny O'Clock, 1947 (Rossen 2, Cobb 3,
  Powell 3, Cohn 4, Duning 4, Guffey 4)
Johnny One-Eye, 1950 (Florey 2, Polglase 4)
Johnny Reno, 1966 (Andrews 3, Russell 3)
Johnny rettet Nebrador, 1953 (Albers 3)
Johnny Smith and Poker-Huntas, 1938
  (Avery 4)
Johnny Stool Pigeon, 1949 (Curtis 3,
  Duryea 3, Winters 3, Orry-Kelly 4)
Johnny Tiger, 1966 (Taylor 3, Green 4,
  Mercer 4)
Johnny Tremain, 1957 (Stevenson 2,
  Disney 4, Ellenshaw 4, Iwerks 4)
Johnny Trouble, 1957 (Barrymore 3)
Johnny, We Hardly Knew Ye, 1977
  (Meredith 3)
Johnstown Flood, 1926 (Gable 3, Gaynor 3,
  Lawrence 3)
Johnstown Flood, 1946 (Terry 4)
Joi Baba Felunath, 1978 (Chatterjee 3,
  Datta 4)
Joi Kinuyo sensei, 1936 (Tanaka 3)
Joi no Kiroku, 1941 (Tanaka 3)
Joie de revivre, 1947 (Storck 2)
Join the Circus, 1923 (Roach 4)
Join the Marines, 1937 (Brown 4)
Joi-uchi, 1967 (Mifune 3, Takemitsu 4)
Joiuchi: Hairyozuma shimatsu-ki, 1967
  (Tsukasa 3)
Joka, 1952 (Yamamura 3)
Joke of Destiny. *See* Scherzo del destinoin
  aqquato dietro l'angelo come un brigante
  di strada, 1983
Joke on the Joker, 1911 (Sennett 2)
Jokehnen, 1986 (Mueller-Stahl 3)
Jokei, 1960 (Yoshimura 2, Kyo 3, Miyagawa 4)
Jokei kazoku, 1963 (Kyo 3, Miyagawa 4,
  Yoda 4)
Joker. *See* Farceur, 1961
Joker, 1987 (Mueller-Stahl 3)
Joker Is Wild, 1957 (Vidor 2, Sinatra 3,
  Cahn 4, Head 4, Westmore Family 4)
Jokers, 1966 (Reed 3)
Jolanda la figlia del corsaro nero, 1952 (Delli
  Colli 4, De Laurentiis 4)
Jolanta—den gäckande suggan, 1945
  (Jaenzon 4)
Jolanta—the Elusive Sow. *See* Jolanta—den
  gäckande suggan, 1945
**Joli Mai, 1963 (Marker 2, Karina 3,
  Montand 3, Signoret 3, Legrand 4)**
Jolly Bad Fellow, 1964 (Barry 4)
Jolly—Clown da circo, 1923 (Camerini 2)
Jolly Green, 1970 (Coutard 4)
Jolly Jilter, 1927 (Sennett 2)
Jolly Little Elves, 1934 (Lantz 4)
Jolly Musicians, 1937 (Ptushko 4)
Jolly Whirl. *See* Singeries humaines,
  1910
Jolson Sings Again, 1949 (Jolson 3,
  Buchman 4, Cohn 4, Duning 4)

Jolson Story, 1946 (Lewis 2, Jolson 3,
  Berlin 4, Cohn 4, Cole 4, Walker 4)
Jolt for General Germ, 1931 (Fleischer 4)
Jomai, 1961 (Iwashita 3)
Jonah Man, 1904 (Hepworth 2)
**Jonah qui aura 25 ans en l'année 2000,
  1976 (Tanner 2)**
Jonah Who Will Be 25 in the Year 2000. *See*
  **Jonah qui aura 25 ans en l'année 2000,
  1976**
Jonan no Yoemon, 1931 (Hasegawa 3)
Jonathan, 1969 (Müller 4)
Jonathan, 1973 (Müller 4)
Jonathan Livingston Seagull, 1973 (Leven 4)
Jones and His New Neighbors, 1909
  (Griffith 2, Lawrence 3, Bitzer 4)
Jones and the Lady Book Agent, 1909
  (Griffith 2, Lawrence 3, Bitzer 4)
Jones Family in Hollywood, 1939 (Keaton 2)
Jones Family in Quick Millions, 1939
  (Keaton 2)
Jones Have Amateur Theatricals, 1909
  (Griffith 2, Lawrence 3, Bitzer 4)
Jonetsu, 1932 (Takamine 3)
Jonetsu no rumuba, 1950 (Yamamura 3)
Jonque, 1964 (Guillemot 4)
Joobachi, 1952 (Mori 3)
Joobachi, 1978 (Tsukasa 3)
Jordan is a Hard Road, 1915 (Dwan 2)
Jordan's Dance, 1977 (Jarman 2)
Jorjamado no cinema, 1979 (Rocha 2)
José Torres, 1960 (Takemitsu 4)
José Torres, Part II, 1965 (Takemitsu 4)
Josef Kajetán Tyl, 1925 (Heller 4)
Josef und seine Brüder, 1922 (Krauss 3)
Josei no kakugo, 1940 (Tanaka 3)
Josei no shori, 1946 (Mizoguchi 2, Shindo 2,
  Tanaka 3)
Josei tai dansei, 1950 (Yamamura 3)
Josei wa tsuyoshi, 1924 (Mizoguchi 2)
Joseph Andrews, 1977 (Richardson 2,
  Gielgud 3, Addison 4, Watkin 4)
Joseph Balsamo, 1971 (Douy 4)
Joseph in the Land of Egypt, 1914 (Cruze 2)
Josephine and Men, 1955 (Boulting 2,
  Buchanan 3, Finch 3, Addison 4)
Josephine Baker Story, 1992 (Delerue 4)
Josette, 1936 (Christian-Jaque 2,
  Fernandel 3)
Josette, 1938 (Dwan 2, Ameche 3, Simon 3,
  Young 3, Zanuck 4)
Joshila, 1973 (Anand 3)
Josh's Suicide, 1911 (Sennett 2)
Joshu to tomoni, 1956 (Hara 3, Kagawa 3,
  Tanaka 3)
Joshua Then and Now, 1985 (Arkin 3,
  Sarde 4)
Josser in the Army, 1932 (Launder and
  Gilliat 2)
Jotai, 1964 (Takemitsu 4)
Jotai, 1969 (Okada 3)
Jouens le jeu, 1952 (Brasseur 3)
Jouet, 1976 (Evein 4)
Jouet de la fatalité. *See* Adhémar, 1951
Jouets animés, 1911 (Cohl 4)
Joueur, 1948 (Rosay 3)
Joueur, 1958 (Autant-Lara 2, Blier 3,
  Philipe 3, Aurenche 4, Bost 4, Douy 4)
Joueur d'échecs, 1938 (Modot 3, Rosay 3,
  Veidt 3)
Jougasaki no ame, 1950 (Miyagawa 4)
Jougasaki's Rain. *See* Jougasaki no ame, 1950
Jouiuchi, 1967 (Muraki 4)
Joujoux savants, 1911 (Cohl 4)

Jouons le jeu . . . L'Avarice, 1952
  (Chevalier 3)
Jour à Paris, 1965 (Trintignant 3)
Jour de fête, 1949 (Tati 2)
Jour de fête, 1974 (Baye 3)
Jour de tournage, 1969 (Montand 3)
Jour du frotteur, 1932 (Cavalcanti 2)
Jour du terme, 1904 (Guy 2)
Jour et l'heure, 1962 (Piccoli 3, Signoret 3,
  Decaë 4, Evein 4)
Jour peut-être à San Pedro ou ailleurs, 1977
  (Cardinale 3)
Jour pina a demandé, 1983 (Akerman 2)
Jour "S . . .", 1984 (Lefebvre 2)
**Jour se lève, 1939 (Arletty 3, Berry 3,
  Blier 3, Gabin 3, Reggiani 3,
  Courant 4, Hakim 4, Jaubert 4,
  Prévert 4, Trauner 4)**
Journal animé, 1908 (Cohl 4)
Journal de la résistance, 1945 (Coward 4)
Journal d'un combat, 1964 (Delon 3)
**Journal d'un curé de campagne, 1950
  (Burel 4)**
Journal d'un fou, 1963 (Delerue 4)
Journal d'un scélérat, 1950 (Rohmer 2,
  Gégauff 4)
Journal d'un suicide, 1972 (Seyrig 3)
Journal d'une femme de chambre, 1964
  (Buñuel 2, Moreau 3, Piccoli 3,
  Carrière 4, Wakhévitch 4)
Journal d'une femme en blanc, 1965
  (Aurenche 4, Douy 4)
Journal masculin, 1948 (Braunberger 4)
Journal of a Crime, 1934 (Darwell 3,
  Menjou 3, Pidgeon 3, Blanke 4, Haller 4,
  Orry-Kelly 4)
Journal of Resistance, 1944 (Balcon 4)
Journal tombe à cinq heures, 1942 (Blier 3,
  Fresnay 3, Honegger 4)
Journalist. *See* Zhurnalist, 1967
Journalist's Tale, 1985 (Godfrey 4)
Journée bien remplie, 1972 (Trintignant 3)
Journée de Flambeau, 1916 (Cohl 4)
Journée naturelle, 1947 (Resnais 2)
Journey, 1959 (Litvak 2, Aimée 3,
  Brynner 3, Kerr 3, Robards 3, Auric 4,
  Fisher 4)
Journey, 1972 (Bujold 3)
Journey. *See* Viaggio, 1974
Journey, 1987 (Watkins 2)
Journey Back to Oz, 1973 (Minnelli 3,
  Rooney 3, Cahn 4)
Journey Beneath the Desert. *See* Atlantide,
  1960
Journey Beneath the Desert. *See* Antinea,
  1961
Journey for Margaret, 1942 (Van Dyke 2,
  O'Brien 3, Young 3, Schary 4,
  Waxman 4)
Journey from the Shadows, 1938 (Weiss 2)
Journey into Autumn. *See* Kvinnodröm, 1955
Journey into Fear, 1942 (Welles 2, Cotten 3,
  Del Rio 3, Moorehead 3, Sloane 3,
  Struss 4)
Journey into Fear, 1974 (Pleasence 3,
  Price 3, Winters 3, North 4)
Journey into Light, 1951 (Darwell 3,
  Hayden 3)
Journey into Medicine, 1946 (Van Dyke 2,
  Kaufman 4)
Journey into Prehistory. *See* Cesta do
  pravěku, 1955
Journey into Primeval Times. *See* Cesta do
  pravěku, 1955

Journey into the Beyond, 1977 (Carradine 3)

Journey into the Night. *See* Gang in die Nacht, 1921

Journey of Love. *See* Viaggio d'amore, 1991

Journey Out. *See* Resan bort, 1945

Journey to Avebury, 1977 (Jarman 2)

Journey to Italy. *See* **Viaggio in Italia, 1953**

Journey to Jerusalem, 1940 (Lumet 2)

Journey to Marseilles, 1944 (Warner 4)

Journey to Shiloh, 1967 (Caan 3, Ford 3)

Journey to Spirit Island, 1988 (Zsigmond 4)

Journey to the Center of the Earth, 1959 (Mason 3, Brackett 4, Cahn 4, Herrmann 4, Reisch 4, Wheeler 4)

Journey to the Center of the Earth. *See* Viaje al centro de la tierra, 1977

Journey to the Center of the Earth, 1986 (Golan and Globus 4, Watkin 4)

Journey to the Far Side of the Sun. *See* Doppelganger, 1969

Journey to the Pacific, 1968 (Fields 4)

Journey Together, 1945 (Boulting 2, Attenborough 3, Harrison 3, Love 3, Robinson 3, Rattigan 4)

Journey's End, 1930 (Pearson 2, Whale 2, Balcon 4, Sherriff 4)

Journeys from Berlin/1971, 1980 (Rainer 2)

Jours tranquilles à Clichy, 1990 (Chabrol 2, Audran 3, Rabier 4)

Jovanka e l'altri. *See* Five Branded Women, 1959

Jovanka e le altre. *See* Five Branded Women, 1959

Joven. *See* Young Ones, 1960

Joven rebelde, 1961 (Zavattini 4)

Jovenes, 1960 (Alcoriza 4)

Jovita. *See* Jowita, 1967

Jowita, 1967 (Cybulski 3, Olbrychski 3, Konwicki 4)

Joy and the Dragon, 1916 (King 2)

Joy Girl, 1918 (Dressler 3)

Joy Girl, 1927 (Dwan 2)

Joy House. *See* Félins, 1964

Joy in the Morning, 1964 (Homolka 3, Kennedy 3, Herrmann 4)

Joy of Living, 1938 (Garnett 2, Ball 3, Dunne 3, Pangborn 3, Walker 4)

Joy of Love. *See* Blaho lásky, 1965

Joy Rider, 1921 (Roach 4)

Joy Scouts, 1939 (Roach 4)

Joyeaux Microbes, 1909 (Cohl 4)

Joyeuse Prison, 1956 (Simon 3)

Joyeuses Pâques, 1984 (Belmondo 3)

Joyeux Pélerins, 1950 (Schüfftan 4)

Joyeux Tromblons, 1968 (Storck 2)

Joyless Street. *See* Freudlose Gasse, 1925

Joyless Streets. *See* Freudlose Gasse, 1925

Joys of a Jealous Wife, 1913 (Costello 3)

Joyu, 1947 (Shindo 2, Shindo 3, Yamada 3, Hayasaka 4)

Joyu Sumako no koi, 1947 (Mizoguchi 2, Tanaka 3, Yamamura 3, Yoda 4)

Jrdina jedné noci, 1935 (Stallich 4)

Jsem děvče s čertem v těle, 1933 (Heller 4, Stallich 4)

Jsouc na rece mlynář jeden, 1971 (Brdečka 4)

Juan Charrasqueado, 1947 (Armendáriz 3)

Juan sin miedo, 1938 (Fernández 2)

Juana Gallo, 1959 (Félix 3, Figueroa 4)

Juarez, 1939 (Dieterle 2, Huston 2, Calhern 3, Crisp 3, Davis 3, Garfield 3, Johnson 3, Muni 3, Rains 3, Blanke 4,

Friedhofer 4, Gaudio 4, Grot 4, Korngold 4, Orry-Kelly 4, Wallis 4, Westmore Family 4)

Jubal, 1956 (Daves 2, Borgnine 3, Bronson 3, Ford 3, Steiger 3, Cohn 4, Raksin 4, Wald 4)

Jubiaba, 1986 (Pereira Dos Santos 2)

Jubilee, 1978 (Jarman 2)

Jubilee Trail, 1954 (Young 4)

Jubilee Window, 1935 (Pearson 2, Havelock-Allan 4)

Jubilej gospodina Ikla, 1955 (Mimica 4)

Jubilo, 1920 (Rogers 3)

Jubilo. *See* Too Busy to Work, 1932

Jubilo, Jr., 1924 (Roach 4)

Jud Süss, 1940 (Staudte 2, Krauss 3, Hunte 4)

Judás, 1918 (Curtiz 2)

Judas Money. *See* Judaspengar, 1915

Judas von Tirol, 1932 (Rasp 3)

Judaspengar, 1915 (Jaenzon 4)

Judex, 1916 (Feuillade 2, Musidora 3, Gaumont 4)

Judex, 1963 (Franju 2, Fradetal 4, Jarre 4)

Judge, 1916 (Sennett 2)

Judge. *See* Domaren, 1960

Judge Alton B. Parker, 1904 (Bitzer 4)

Judge and His Hangman. *See* Richter und sein Henker, 1975

Judge and Jake Wyler, 1972 (Davis 3)

Judge and the Assassin. *See* Juge et l'assassin, 1976

Judge for a Day, 1935 (Fleischer 4)

Judge Hardy and Son, 1939 (Rooney 3, Wilson 4)

Judge Hardy's Children, 1938 (Rooney 3)

Judge Priest, 1934 (Ford 2, McDaniel 3, Rogers 3, Walthall 3, Nichols 4, Trotti 4)

Judge Rummy in Bear Facts, 1920 (La Cava 2)

Judgement at Nuremberg, 1961 (Kramer 2, Clift 3, Dietrich 3, Garland 3, Schell 3, Widmark 3)

Judgement Day, 1986 (Friedkin 2)

Judgement in Berlin, 1988 (Sheen 3)

Judgment, 1909 (Anderson 3)

Judgment at Nuremberg, 1961 (Lancaster 3, Tracy 3, Laszlo 4)

Judgment Deferred, 1951 (Baxter 2, Grierson 2, Crazy Gang 3)

Judgment House, 1917 (Blackton 2)

Judith, 1965 (Roeg 2, Finch 3, Hawkins 3, Loren 3, Hayes 4)

Judith et Holopherne, 1909 (Feuillade 2, Gaumont 4)

Judith of Bethulia, 1914 (Griffith 2, Barrymore 3, Carey 3, Gish 3, Marsh 3, Sweet 3, Walthall 3, Bitzer 4)

Judith Therpauve, 1978 (Signoret 3)

Judith Trachtenberg, 1920 (Galeen 4)

Judo Saga. *See* Sugata sanshiro, 1965

Judo School Expulsion Letter. *See* Koudoukan hamonjou, 1968

Judo senshu no koi, 1934 (Yoda 4)

Jueces de la Biblia, 1966 (Rey 3)

Juego peligroso, 1966 (Alcoriza 4)

Jugador de ajedrez, 1980 (Figueroa 4)

Jugando con la muerte, 1982 (Donaggio 4)

Juge et l'assassin, 1976 (Tavernier 2, Huppert 3, Noiret 3, Aurenche 4, Sarde 4)

Juge Fayard dit le sheriff, 1976 (Sarde 4)

Jugement de Dieu, 1949 (Kosma 4)

Jugement de minuit, 1932 (Fernandel 3,

Jeanson 4)

Jugement dernier, 1945 (Jeanson 4)

Jugend, 1922 (Rasp 3)

Jugend, 1938 (Von Harbou 4, Warm 4)

Jugend und Tollheit, 1912 (Gad 2, Nielsen 3)

Jugendrausch, 1927 (Fröhlich 3, Hoffmann 4)

Juggernaut, 1936 (Karloff 3)

Juggernaut, 1974 (Cusack 3, Harris 3, Hopkins 3, Sharif 3, Fisher 4)

Juggler, 1953 (Dmytryk 2, Kramer 2, Douglas 3, Hunt 4)

Juggler of Our Lady, 1957 (Karloff 3)

Juggling with Fate, 1913 (Mix 3)

Jugnu, 1973 (Burman 4)

Juguetes, 1978 (Bemberg 2)

Juif errant, 1926 (Artaud 3)

Juif polonais, 1931 (Baur 3, D'Eaubonne 4)

Jujin Kuki-Otoko, 1955 (Tsuburaya 4)

Jujin Yukiotoko. *See* Half Human, 1957

Jujiro, 1928 (Kinugasa 2)

Juke Box Rhythm, 1958 (Katzman 4)

Juke Girl, 1942 (Reagan 3, Sheridan 3, Deutsch 4, Glennon 4, Wald 4, Wallis 4)

Jukyu no hanayome, 1955 (Yamamura 3)

Jukyu-sai no haru, 1933 (Takamine 3)

Jules and Jim. *See* **Jules et Jim, 1962**

Jules et Jim, 1962 (Truffaut 2, Moreau 3, Werner 3, Coutard 4, Delerue 4)

Jules of the Strong Heart, 1918 (Crisp 3)

Jules Verne's Rocket to the Moon, 1967 (Terry-Thomas 3)

Julia, 1977 (Zinnemann 2, Fonda 3, Redgrave 3, Robards 3, Schell 3, Streep 3, Delerue 4, Dillon 4, Murch 4, Sargent 4, Slocombe 4)

Julia and Julia. *See* Giulia e Giulia, 1987

Julia Misbehaves, 1948 (Garson 3, Pidgeon 3, Taylor 3, Deutsch 4, Irene 4, Ruttenberg 4)

Julianwale, 1953 (Biswas 4)

Julie, 1956 (Day 3, Jourdan 3, Marsh 3)

Julie de Carneilhan, 1950 (Brasseur 3, Feuillère 3)

Julie la Rousse, 1959 (Gélin 3)

Julie Pot de Colle, 1977 (Broca 2, Carrière 4, Delerue 4)

Julie the Redhead. *See* Julie la Rousse, 1959

Juliet dans Paris, 1967 (Miller 2)

Juliet of the Spirits. *See* Giulietta degli spiriti, 1965

Julietta, 1953 (Marais 3, Moreau 3, Alekan 4, Braunberger 4, D'Eaubonne 4)

Juliette et Juliette, 1973 (Girardot 3)

Juliette ou la clé des songes, 1951 (Carné 2, Philipe 3, Alekan 4, Kosma 4, Trauner 4)

Julius Caesar, 1908 (Costello 3)

Julius Caesar, 1950 (Heston 3)

Julius Caesar, 1953 (Mankiewicz 2, Brando 3, Calhern 3, Garson 3, Gielgud 3, Kerr 3, Mason 3, O'Brien 3, Gibbons 4, Houseman 4, Rozsa 4, Ruttenberg 4)

Julius Caesar, 1970 (Gielgud 3, Heston 3, Lee 3, Robards 3)

July Days, 1923 (Roach 4)

July 14th. *See* Quatorze Juillet, 1933

Jumbo, 1962 (Berkeley 2, Walters 2, Day 3, Durante 3, Ames 4, Daniels 4, Edens 4, Gillespie 4, Pasternak 4)

Jumeaux de Brighton, 1936 (Bresson 2, Raimu 3, Simon 3)

Jument verte, 1959 (Aurenche 4, Bost 4, Douy 4)

Jump Into Hell, 1955 (Dalio 3)
Jump Your Job, 1922 (Roach 4)
Jumpin' Jack Flash, 1986 (Goldberg 3)
Jumpin' Jupiter, 1955 (Blanc 4, Jones 4, Stalling 4)
Jumping Beans, 1922 (Fleischer 4)
Jumping Beans, 1930 (Terry 4)
Jumping for Joy, 1955 (Rank 4)
Jumping Jacks, 1952 (Lewis 2, Martin 3, Bumstead 4, Head 4, Wallis 4)
Junak Markos, 1953 (Dinov 4)
June Bride, 1935 (Terry 4)
June Bride, 1948 (Davis 3, Montgomery 3, Reynolds 3, Blanke 4, Grot 4, Head 4, McCord 4)
June Madness, 1920 (Roach 4)
June Moon, 1931 (Mankiewicz 2)
June Night. See Juninatt, 1965
Junge Baron Neuhaus, 1934 (Herlth 4, Röhrig 4)
Junge Graf, 1935 (Ondra 3)
Junge Medardus, 1923 (Curtiz 2)
Jungens, 1950 (Staudte 2)
Junges Mädchen—ein junger Mann. See Knock Out, 1935
Jungfrukällen, 1960 (Von Sydow 3, Nykvist 4)
Jungle. See World Window, 1977
Jungle Book, 1942 (Johnson 3, Cooper 4, Garmes 4, Hornbeck 4, Korda, A. 4, Korda, V. 4, Périnal 4, Rozsa 4, Wheeler 4)
Jungle Book, 1967 (Sanders 3, Disney 4)
Jungle Cat, 1959 (Iwerks 4)
Jungle Fever, 1991 (Quinn 3)
Jungle Fighters. See Long and the Short and the Tall, 1961
Jungle Girl, 1941 (Canutt 4)
Jungle Jim, 1948 (Weissmuller 3, Katzman 4)
Jungle Jim in the Forbidden Land, 1952 (Weissmuller 3, Katzman 4)
Jungle Jingles, 1929 (Lantz 4)
Jungle Jitters, 1934 (Iwerks 4)
Jungle Jitters, 1938 (Freleng 4)
Jungle Jumble, 1932 (Lantz 4)
Jungle Man, 1941 (Crabbe 3)
Jungle Maneaters, 1954 (Katzman 4)
Jungle Manhunt, 1951 (Weissmuller 3, Katzman 4)
Jungle Moon-Men, 1955 (Weissmuller 3, Katzman 4)
Jungle Patrol, 1944 (Finch 3)
Jungle Princess, 1936 (Lamour 3, Milland 3, Head 4)
Jungle Raiders, 1985 (Van Cleef 3)
Jungle Rhythm, 1929 (Disney 4, Iwerks 4)
Jungle Siren, 1942 (Crabbe 3)
Jungle Trail of the Son of the Tarzan. See Son of Tarzan, 1921
Jungle Warfare, 1943 (Halas and Batchelor 4)
Jungle Woman, 1944 (Salter 4)
Jungle Woman. See Nabongo, 1944
Juninatt, 1965 (Andersson 3, Fischer 4)
Juninatten, 1940 (Bergman 3, Björnstrand 3)
Junior Bonner, 1972 (Peckinpah 2, Johnson 3, Lupino 3, McQueen 3, Preston 3, Ballard 4)
Junior Jive Bomber, 1944 (Prinz 4)
Junior Miss, 1945 (Clarke 4)
Junior Officer, 1912 (Bosworth 3)
Junkman, 1918 (Roach 4)

Juno and the Paycock, 1929 (Fitzgerald 3, Reville 4)
Junoon, 1979 (Azmi 3, Nihalani 4)
Junpaku no yoru, 1951 (Mori 3)
Jupiter. See Douze heures de bonheur, 1952
Jupiter's Darling, 1955 (Keel 3, Sanders 3, Williams 3, Gibbons 4, Pan 4, Plunkett 4, Rose 4, Rosher 4)
Jupiter's Thigh. See On a volé la cuisse de Jupiter, 1980
Jupiter's Thunderbolts. See Tonnerre de Jupiter, 1903
Jupon rouge, 1987 (Valli 3)
Jurmana, 1979 (Bachchan 3)
Jurokuya seishin, 1931 (Hasegawa 3)
Jury of Fate, 1917 (Browning 2)
Jury of One. See Testament, 1974
Jury's Evidence, 1936 (Lockwood 3, Dalrymple 4)
Jury's Secret, 1938 (Darwell 3, Wray 3, Krasner 4)
Jus' Passin' Through, 1923 (Rogers 3, Roach 4)
Jusan nichi no kinyobi, 1959 (Oshima 2)
Jusqu'à la nuit, 1984 (Branco 4, De Almeida 4)
Jusqu'au bout du monde, 1962 (Delerue 4)
Jusqu'au bout du monde, 1990 (Müller 4)
Jusqu'au coeur, 1968 (Lefebvre 2)
Jusqu'au dernier, 1956 (Moreau 3, Audiard 4, D'Eaubonne 4)
Jusques au feu exclusivement, 1971 (Fradetal 4)
Just a Bear, 1931 (Sennett 2)
Just a Clown, 1934 (Terry 4)
Just a Few Little Things, 1916 (Beery 3)
Just a Gigolo, 1931 (Milland 3)
Just a Gigolo, 1932 (Fleischer 4)
Just a Gigolo. See Schöner Gigolo—armer Gigolo, 1978
Just a Good Guy, 1924 (Roach 4)
Just a Little Bull, 1940 (Terry 4)
Just a Minute, 1924 (Roach 4)
Just a Song at Twilight, 1922 (Barthelmess 3)
Just a Wolf at Heart, 1962 (Hanna and Barbera 4)
Just Across the Street, 1952 (Sheridan 3)
Just an Echo, 1934 (Crosby 3)
Just Another Blonde, 1926 (Brooks 3, Edeson 4)
Just Another Murder, 1935 (Sennett 2)
Just Around the Corner, 1921 (Marion 4)
Just Around the Corner, 1938 (Pangborn 3, Robinson 3, Temple 3, Leven 4, Zanuck 4)
Just Ask for Diamond, 1988 (York 3)
Just Ask Jupiter, 1938 (Terry 4)
Just Before Nightfall. See Juste avant la nuit, 1971
Just Brown's Luck, 1913 (Sennett 2, Normand 3)
Just Call Me Jim, 1920 (Rogers 3)
Just Dropped In, 1919 (Daniels 3, Lloyd 3, Roach 4)
Just Ducky, 1950 (Hanna and Barbera 4)
Just for a Song, 1930 (Balcon 4)
Just For Fun, 1963 (Roeg 2)
Just for You, 1952 (Barrymore 3, Crosby 3, Wood 3, Wyman 3, Barnes 4, Friedhofer 4, Head 4, Raksin 4)
Just for You, 1956 (Carreras 4)
Just Gold, 1913 (Griffith 2, Barrymore 3, Gish 3, Bitzer 4)

Just Imagine, 1930 (Bosworth 3, O'Sullivan 3, Friedhofer 4)
Just Kids, 1913 (Sennett 2, Gish 3)
Just Like at Home. See Olyan, mint otthon, 1978
Just Like at Home, 1979 (Karina 3)
Just Like a Woman, 1912 (Griffith 2, Pickford 3, Bitzer 4)
Just Like a Woman, 1966 (Godfrey 4)
Just Like a Woman, 1992 (Box 4)
Just Like Friends. See För vänskaps skull, 1965
Just Me. See Ma Pomme, 1950
Just Mickey, 1930 (Disney 4)
Just My Luck, 1957 (Rutherford 3, Wisdom 3, Rank 4)
Just Neighbors, 1919 (Daniels 3, Lloyd 3, Roach 4)
Just Nuts, 1914 (Lloyd 3, Roach 4)
Just Off Broadway, 1924 (Gilbert 3)
Just Off Broadway, 1942 (Day 4, Raksin 4)
Just One More Chance, 1932 (Fleischer 4)
Just Pals, 1920 (Ford 2)
Just Plane Beep, 1965 (Blanc 4)
Just Rambling Along, 1919 (Laurel and Hardy 3, Roach 4)
Just Show People, 1913 (Talmadge 3)
Just Smith, 1933 (Balcon 4, Junge 4, Rank 4)
Just Spooks, 1925 (Lantz 4)
Just Suppose, 1926 (Barthelmess 3)
Just Tell Me What You Want, 1980 (Lumet 2, Loy 3, Allen 4, Morris 4)
Just This Once, 1952 (Leigh 3, Basevi 4)
Just Tony, 1922 (Mix 3)
Just William, 1939 (McDowall 3)
Juste avant la nuit, 1971 (Chabrol 2, Audran 3, Rabier 4)
Justice Cain. See Cain's Cutthroats, 1970
Justice d'abord, 1919 (Protazanov 2, Mozhukin 3)
Justice est faite, 1950 (Fresnay 3, Spaak 4)
Justice for Sale. See Night Court, 1932
Justice for Selwyn. See Prípad pro Selwyn, 1968
Justice in the Far North, 1910 (Lawrence 3)
Justice Is Done. See Justice est faite, 1950
Justice of Society. See Samhallets dom, 1912
Justice of the Range, 1935 (Bond 3)
Justice of the Sage, 1911 (Dwan 2)
Justices, 1978 (Cayatte 2, Andersson 3)
Justicière, 1925 (Périnal 4)
Justin de Marseille, 1935 (Tourneur 2, Ibert 4, Meerson 4)
Justine, 1969 (Cukor 2, Aimée 3, Bogarde 3, Dalio 3, Karina 3, Noiret 3, Berman 4, Goldsmith 4, Shamroy 4, Sharaff 4, Smith 4)
Justine and Juliet. See Marquis de Sade: Justine, 1968
Jutai, 1948 (Mori 3)
Jutro Meksyk, 1965 (Cybulski 3, Ścibor-Rylski 4)
Juve contre Fantômas, 1913 (Gaumont 4)
Juvenile Court, 1938 (Hayworth 3, Cohn 4)
Juvenile Court, 1973 (Wiseman 2)
Juvenile Love Affair, 1912 (Costello 3)
Juventude, 1950 (Pereira Dos Santos 2)
Juwelen der Fürstin Ljuba. See Wer das Scheiden hat erfunden, 1928
Juxbaron, 1927 (Dietrich 3)
Jwalamukhi, 1980 (Azmi 3)
Jwar Bhata, 1944 (Kumar 3, Biswas 4)
Jyan Arima no shugeki, 1959 (Yamamura 3)
Jyoti, 1969 (Burman 4)

K

K, 1974 (Fresnay 3)
K13 513. *See* Abenteuer eines
    Zehnmarkscheines, 1926
K-SH-E, 1932 (Shub 2)
K und K Feldermarschall. *See* Falsche
    Feldmarschall, 1930
Ka sovetskuyu rodinu, 1937 (Cherkassov 3)
Kaala, 1981 (Bachchan 3)
Kaala Patthar, 1979 (Bachchan 3)
Kaasan nagaiki shite ne, 1962 (Tanaka 3)
Kabale und Liebe. *See* Luise Millerin, 1922
Kabarett, 1954 (Henreid 3)
Kabhi Kabhie, 1976 (Bachchan 3)
Kabinett des Dr. Caligari, 1920 (Wiene 2,
    Dagover 3, Krauss 3, Veidt 3, Hunte 4,
    Mayer 4, Pommer 4, Röhrig 4, Warm 4)
Kabinett des Dr. Larifari, 1930 (Heller 4,
    Waxman 4)
Kabuliwala, 1961 (Roy 2, Shankar 4)
Kadamberi, 1975 (Azmi 3)
Kadetten, 1941 (Röhrig 4)
Kaerlighed paa Rulleskøjter, 1943 (Roos 2)
Kaerlighedens Triumf, 1914 (Psilander 3)
Kaettekita otoko, 1944 (Tanaka 3)
Kaettekita yopparai, 1968 (Toda 4)
Kaffeehaus, 1970 (Schygulla 3)
Kafka, 1991 (Guinness 3, Irons 3)
Kagaj Ke Phool Sujata, 1959 (Burman 4)
Kaga-sodo, 1953 (Yamada 3)
Kagayake nihon no josei, 1932 (Tanaka 3)
Kagayaku Showa, 1929 (Tanaka 3)
Kage no kuruma, 1970 (Iwashita 3)
Kage no Tsume, 1972 (Iwashita 3)
Kage o matoite, 1949 (Kagawa 3)
Kageboshi, 1950 (Yamada 3, Yamamura 3)
Kagemusha, 1980 (Kurosawa 2,
    Miyagawa 4, Muraki 4)
Kagero, 1969 (Shindo 2)
Kagero-gasa, 1959 (Hasegawa 3, Kagawa 3)
Kagi, 1959 (Kyo 3, Miyagawa 4)
Kagoya Dainagon, 1931 (Hasegawa 3)
Kagoya hangan, 1935 (Hasegawa 3)
Kaguyahimi, 1935 (Tsuburaya 4)
Kahin Aur Chal, 1968 (Anand 3)
Kahreden kursun, 1965 (Güney 2)
Kaidan, 1964 (Kobayashi 2, Shimura 3,
    Takemitsu 4, Toda 4)
Kaigun bakugekitai, 1940 (Hayasaka 4,
    Tsuburaya 4)
Kaigun tokubetsu nenshouhei, 1972
    (Muraki 4)
Kaiju daisenso, 1966 (Tsuburaya 4)
Kaiju soshingeki, 1968 (Tsuburaya 4)
Kaiketsu, 1941 (Yamada 3)
Kaikoku danji, 1926 (Mizoguchi 2)
Kaikoku-ki, 1928 (Hasegawa 3, Tanaka 3)
Kaikyou, 1982 (Muraki 4)

Kaintuck, 1912 (Reid 3)
Kaise Kahoon, 1964 (Burman 4)
Kaisen no zenya, 1943 (Tanaka 3)
Kaiser, The Beast of Berlin, 1918 (Chaney 3)
Kaiserwalzer, 1932 (Fröhlich 3)
Kaitchka, 1915 (Mozhukin 3)
Kaitei gunkan, 1964 (Tsuburaya 4)
Kaito Sayamaro, 1928 (Hasegawa 3,
    Tsuburaya 4)
Kaizoki-sen, 1950 (Mifune 3)
Kakedashi jidai, 1947 (Hayasaka 4)
Kako, 1961 (Yamamura 3)
Kakoe, ono, more?, 1965 (Shukshin 3)
Kakureta ninkimono, 1959 (Yoda 4)
Kakushi toride no san-akunin, 1958
    (Mifune 3, Shimura 3, Muraki 4)
Kakute kamikaze wa fuku, 1944
    (Miyagawa 4)
Kakute yume ari, 1954 (Yamamura 3)
Kal, Aaj Aur Kal, 1972 (Kapoor 2)
Kala Baazi, 1977 (Anand 3)
Kala Bazar, 1960 (Anand 3, Burman 4)
Kala Pani, 1958 (Anand 3, Burman 4)
Kaleidoscope, 1935 (Lye 4)
Kaleidoscope, 1966 (Beatty 3, York 3)
Kaleidoskop: Valeska Gert, 1979
    (Ballhaus 4)
Kalemites Visit Gibralter, 1912 (Olcott 2)
Kalina krasnaya, 1974 (Shukshin 3)
Kaliya Mardan, 1918 (Phalke 2)
Kali-Yug, Goddess of Vengeance. *See*
    Mistero del tempio indiano, 1963
Kali-Yug, la dea della vendetta. *See* Mistero
    del tempio indiano, 1963
Kalkmalerier, 1954 (Roos 2)
Kalle Karlsson fran Jularbo, 1952 (Thulin 3)
Kallelsen, 1974 (Andersson 3)
Kalyug, 1981 (Nihalani 4)
Kam čert nemuže, 1970 (Brodský 3)
Kama Sutra Rides Again, 1971 (Godfrey 4)
Kamal, 1949 (Burman 4)
Kameradschaft, 1931 (Metzner 4,
    Wagner 4)
Kamfende Herzen, 1920 (Warm 4)
Kamienne niebo, 1959 (Lomnicki 3)
Kamilla og tyven II, 1989 (Lassally 4)
Kaminari oyaji, 1937 (Takamine 3)
Kaminingyo haru no sayaki, 1926
    (Mizoguchi 2)
Kamiyui Shinza, 1932 (Hasegawa 3)
Kamla, 1984 (Azmi 3)
Kammarjunkaren, 1913 (Stiller 2, Jaenzon 4)
Kammeny tsvetok, 1946 (Ptushko 4)
Kammermusik, 1924 (Porten 3)
Kamo to negi, 1966 (Mori 3)
Kamouraska, 1973 (Jutra 2, Bujold 3)
Kampen om hans hjärta, 1916 (Stiller 2)

Kampf des Donald Westhof, 1927
    (Homolka 3, Courant 4)
Kampf um Karthago. *See* Salammbo, 1924
Kampf um Rom, 1968 (Siodmak 2, Welles 2,
    Andersson 3, Harvey 3)
Kampf um Rom II, 1969 (Harvey 3)
Kampf uns ich, 1922 (Tschechowa 3)
Kämpfende Herzen, 1920 (Lang 2, Von
    Harbou 4)
Kampfgegen Berlin, 1925 (Junge 4)
Kamyaab, 1984 (Azmi 3)
Kan su gibi akacak, 1969 (Güney 2)
Kan Gövdeyi götürdü, 1965 (Güney 2)
Kan kaerlighed kureres?, 1923 (Madsen and
    Schenstrøm 3)
Kanał, 1957 (Wajda 2, Stawiński 4)
Kanashiki hakuchi, 1924 (Mizoguchi 2)
Kanashimi wa onna dakeni, 1958 (Shindo 2,
    Kyo 3, Tanaka 3)
Kanawa, 1972 (Shindo 2)
Kanchanjanga, 1962 (Ray 2, Datta 4,
    Mitra 4)
Kancho mada shinazu, 1942 (Yoshimura 2)
Kandidat, 1980 (Kluge 2)
Kane, 1926 (Mizoguchi 2)
Kangaroo, 1952 (Milestone 2, O'Hara 3,
    Rafferty 3, Clarke 4, Newman 4)
Kangaroo Kid, 1950 (Harlan 4)
Kangaroo Steak, 1930 (Terry 4)
Kangaroom Courting, 1954 (Bosustow 4,
    Burness 4)
Kangeki jidai, 1928 (Tanaka 3)
Kanhaiya, 1959 (Kapoor 2)
Kani-ko sen, 1953 (Mori 3, Yamamura 3)
Kanimin son damlasina kadar, 1970
    (Güney 2)
Kanketsu Sasaki Kojiro, 1951 (Mifune 3)
Kanli buğday, 1965 (Güney 2)
Känn dej som Hemma, 1948 (Thulin 3)
Kanojo, 1926 (Tanaka 3)
Kanojo no hatsugen, 1946 (Tanaka 3)
Kanojo to kare, 1963 (Okada 3, Takemitsu 4)
Kanonen-Serenade, 1958 (Staudte 2)
Kanpai, 1958 (Kagawa 3)
Kanraku no onna, 1924 (Mizoguchi 2)
Kansan, 1943 (Harlan 4)
Kansas, 1988 (Dillon 3, Donaggio 4)
Kansas City Bomber, 1972 (Foster 3,
    Welch 3)
Kansas City Confidential, 1952 (Van
    Cleef 3)
Kansas City Kitty, 1944 (Donen 2, Guffey 4)
Kansas City Princess, 1934 (Blondell 3,
    Barnes 4, Orry-Kelly 4)
Kansas Cyclone, 1941 (Canutt 4)
Kansas Pacific, 1953 (Hayden 3, Wanger 4)
Kansas Raiders, 1950 (Curtis 3, Murphy 3)

Kansas Terrors, 1939 (Canutt 4)
Kanshaku rojin nikki, 1962 (Yamamura 3)
Kantaro tsukiyo-uta, 1952 (Hasegawa 3, Kagawa 3)
Kantor Idéal, 1932 (Ondra 3, Heller 4)
Kanzashi, 1941 (Tanaka 3)
Kao, 1960 (Kyo 3)
Kao no nai otoko, 1955 (Okada 3)
Kaos, 1984 (Taviani 2, Guerra 4)
Kaoyaku, 1957 (Takemitsu 4)
Kaplan von San Lorenzo, 1952 (Herlth 4)
Kapò, 1960 (Pontecorvo 2, Cristaldi 4, Gherardi 4, Solinas 4)
Kaptain Discovers the North Pole, 1960 (La Cava 2)
Käpt'n Bay-Bay. See Käpt'n, bye-bye, 1952
Käpt'n, bye-bye, 1952 (Käutner 2, Albers 3)
Kapurush-o-Mahapurush, 1965 (Chatterjee 3, Chandragupta 4, Datta 4)
Kära leken, 1959 (Andersson 3)
Kara sahin, 1964 (Güney 2)
Kära släkten, 1933 (Molander 2)
Karabotan, 1926 (Tanaka 3)
Karakter, 1914 (Psilander 3)
Karami-ai, 1962 (Yamamura 3, Takemitsu 4, Toda 4)
Karatachi no hana, 1954 (Yamada 3, Yamamura 3)
Karate Killers, 1967 (Lom 3, Terry-Thomas 3)
Karate Sanshiro, 1951 (Kagawa 3)
Kare to denen, 1929 (Tanaka 3)
Kare to jinsei, 1929 (Tanaka 3)
Kareinaru Ichizoku, 1974 (Kagawa 3, Kyo 3)
Karel Havlíčiek Borovský, 1925 (Ondra 3)
Karel Hynek Mácha, 1937 (Heller 4)
Kariera, 1955 (Konwicki 4)
Kariéra Pavla Camrdy, 1931 (Baarová 3, Stallich 4)
Karin, Daughter of Ingmar. See Karin Ingmarsdotter, 1920
Karin Ingmarsdotter, 1920 (Sjöström 2, Magnusson 4)
Karin Mansdotter, 1954 (Sjöberg 2, Nykvist 4)
Karl för sin hatt, 1940 (Björnstrand 3)
Karl May, 1974 (Käutner 2, Syberberg 2, Dagover 3)
Karl Peters, 1940 (Albers 3)
Kärlek, 1952 (Molander 2)
Kärlek och journalistik, 1916 (Stiller 2, Jaenzon 4, Magnusson 4)
Kärlek och kassabrist, 1932 (Molander 2, Jaenzon 4)
Kärlek och störtlopp, 1946 (Dahlbeck 3)
Kärlek starkare än hat, 1914 (Sjöström 2, Jaenzon 4)
Karlekan, 1980 (Josephson 3)
Kärleken segrar, 1949 (Molander 2, Thulin 3)
Kärlekens decimaler, 1960 (Dahlbeck 3)
Karm, 1977 (Azmi 3)
Karma, 1932 (Dickinson 2)
Karma, 1961 (Cotten 3)
Karneval, 1961 (Andersson 3)
Karneval und Liebe, 1934 (Heller 4)
Karnival Kid, 1929 (Disney 4, Iwerks 4)
Karol Lear, 1971 (Enei 4)
Károly Bakák, 1918 (Korda 4)
Karsky and Company. See Torguvi dom Karski, 1917
Kartiki Purnima Festival, 1914 (Phalke 2)
Karumen Junjo su, 1951 (Takamine 3)

Karumen Kokyo ni kaeru, 1951 (Takamine 3)
Karusellen, 1923 (Jaenzon 4, Magnusson 4)
Karussell des Lebens, 1919 (Negri 3)
Kasauti, 1974 (Bachchan 3)
Kaseki, 1975 (Takemitsu 4)
Kaseki no mori, 1973 (Shinoda 2, Iwashita 3, Takemitsu 4)
Kashima Paradise, 1973 (Marker 2)
Kashimanada no onna, 1959 (Yamamura 3)
Kasimpasali, 1965 (Güney 2)
Kasimpasali recep, 1965 (Güney 2)
Kăšlání a kýchani, 1950 (Brdečka 4)
Kasme Vaade, 1978 (Bachchan 3)
Kastrullresan, 1950 (Dahlbeck 3)
Kašpárek kouzelníkem, 1927 (Stallich 4)
Kataku, 1979 (Takemitsu 4)
Katana o nuite, 1937 (Shimura 3)
Katchem Kate, 1911 (Sennett 2)
Kate Bliss and the Ticker Tape Kid, 1978 (Meredith 3)
Kate Plus Ten, 1938 (Withers 3)
Katei no jijo, 1962 (Yamamura 3)
Katerina Izmailova, 1967 (Enei 4, Shostakovich 4)
Katharina, die Letzte, 1935 (Pasternak 4)
Katherine die Grosse, 1920 (Kortner 3, Freund 4)
Katherine, 1975 (Spacek 3)
Katherine Reed Story, 1965 (Altman 2)
Kathleen, 1941 (Marshall 3, Temple 3, Edens 4, Waxman 4)
Kathleen Mavourneen, 1906 (Porter 2)
Kathleen Mavourneen, 1913 (Brenon 2)
Kathleen Mavourneen, 1919 (Bara 3)
Kathy O', 1957 (Duryea 3)
Katia, 1938 (Tourneur 2, Darrieux 3)
Katia, 1960 (Schneider 3, Spaak 4)
Katie Did It, 1950 (Metty 4)
Katie: Portrait of a Centerfold, 1978 (Malone 3)
Katina. See Iceland, 1942
Katinka, 1988 (Von Sydow 3, Nykvist 4)
Katja, 1960 (D'Eaubonne 4)
Katka bumazhnyi ranet, 1926 (Enei 4, Moskvin 4)
Katka's Reinette Apple. See Katka bumazhnyi ranet, 1926
Kato and the Green Hornet, 1974 (Lee 3)
Kato hayabusa sento tai, 1944 (Tsuburaya 4)
Katok i skripka, 1960 (Tarkovsky 2)
Katrina, 1943 (Jaenzon 4)
Katrina Dead, 1967 (Warho 2)
Kats Is Kats, 1917 (Bray 4)
Kats Is Kats, 1920 (La Cava 2)
Kattorna, 1965 (Dahlbeck 3)
Katug nogenkai, 1948 (Hara 3)
Katya, 1960 (Siodmak 2, Kosma 4)
Katzelmacher, 1969 (Fassbinder 2, Schygulla 3)
Katzensteg, 1915 (Leni 2)
Kaufmann von Venedig, 1923 (Krauss 3, Porten 3, Maté 4, Warm 4)
Kauft Mariett-Aktien, 1922 (Banky 3)
Kavárna na hlavní třidě, 1954 (Brdečka 4)
Kaviarprinzessin, 1929 (Heller 4)
Kavkazskiye mineralniye vody, 1924 (Kuleshov 2)
Kawaita hana, 1963 (Takemitsu 4, Toda 4)
Kawaita hana, 1963 (Shinoda 2)
Kawaita mizuumi, 1960 (Shinoda 2, Iwashita 3, Takemitsu 4)
Kawanakajima gassen, 1941 (Hasegawa 3, Shindo 3, Yamada 3)

Kawano hotoride, 1962 (Yamamura 3)
Kaya. See Paja ubit ču te!, 1967
Kaya, I'll Kill You. See Paja ubit ču te!, 1967
Kazablan, 1973 (Golan and Globus 4)
Kazaks—Minorité nationale—Sinkiang, 1977 (Ivens 2)
Kazan, 1921 (Selig 4)
Kazan-myaku, 1950 (Mori 3)
Každý den odvahu, 1964 (Brejchová 3, Brodský 3)
Kaze futatabi, 1952 (Yamamura 3)
Kaze no naka no mendori, 1948 (Ryu 3, Tanaka 3)
Kaze no shisen, 1963 (Iwashita 3)
Kaze tachinu, 1954 (Yamamura 3)
Kazoku, 1942 (Tanaka 3)
Kazoku no jijo, 1962 (Yoshimura 2)
Kdo hledá zlaté dno, 1975 (Menzel 2)
Kdyby tisic karinetu, 1964 (Brejchová 3)
Kdybych byl tátou, 1939 (Stallich 4)
Když má svátek Dominika, 1967 (Stallich 4)
Kean, 1910 (Blom 2)
Kean, 1924 (Volkov 2, Mozhukin 3)
Kean, 1940 (Brazzi 3)
Kean, 1956 (Gassman 3, Cecchi D'Amico 4, Cristaldi 4, Di Venanzo 4)
Kean ou Désordre et Génie. See Kean, 1924
Kedlubnový kavalír v ráji, 1928 (Heller 4)
Keene, 1969 (Cotten 3)
Keep, 1983 (Box 4)
Keep 'Em Flying, 1941 (Abbott and Costello 3)
Keep 'em Growing, 1943 (Terry 4)
Keep 'em Rolling, 1934 (Huston 3, Plunkett 4, Steiner 4)
Keep 'em Slugging, 1943 (Three Stooges 3, Salter 4)
Keep Fit, 1937 (Formby 3)
Keep in Style, 1934 (Fleischer 4)
Keep It Up Downstairs, 1976 (Dors 3)
Keep Laughing, 1932 (Arbuckle 3)
Keep On Rockin', 1971 (Leacock 2)
Keep Smiling, 1925 (Bruckman 4, Garmes 4)
Keep Smiling, 1938 (Fields 3, Cronjager 4)
Keep Your Mouth Shut, 1944 (Dunning 4, McLaren 4)
Keep Your Powder Dry, 1945 (Moorehead 3, Turner 3, Irene 4)
Keep Your Seats Please, 1936 (Formby 3, Sim 3)
Keeper, 1983 (Lee 3)
Keeper of the Bees, 1925 (Bow 3)
Keeper of the Bees, 1935 (Bosworth 3)
Keeper of the Bees, 1947 (Sturges 2, Darwell 3)
Keeper of the Flame, 1942 (Cukor 2, Saville 2, Hepburn 3, Tracy 3, Adrian 4, Daniels 4, Kaper 4, Mayer 4, Stewart 4, Wheeler 4)
Keeper of the Lions, 1937 (Lantz 4)
Keepers. See Tête contre les murs, 1958
Keepers of Youth, 1931 (Launder and Gilliat 2)
Keeping Company, 1940 (Freund 4, Mankiewicz 4)
Keeping Fit, 1942 (Crawford 3)
Keeping in Shape, 1942 (Benchley 4)
Keeps Rainin' All the Time, 1934 (Fleischer 4)
Kegyelet, 1967 (Szabó 2)
Keian hi-cho, 1952 (Yamamura 3)
Keimendes Leben, 1918 (Jannings 3)

Kidnapped, 1948 (McDowall 3)

Kidnapped, 1960 (Stevenson 2, Finch 3, O'Toole 3, Dillon 4, Disney 4)

Kidnapped, 1971 (Caine 3, Hawkins 3, Howard 3, Pleasence 3, Vetchinsky 4)

Kidnapper, 1903 (Bitzer 4)

Kidnapper. See Secuestrador, 1958

Kidnappers, 1953 (Rank 4)

Kidnappers, 1964 (Meredith 3)

Kidnapping of Banker Fuxe. See Únos bankéře Fuxe, 1923

Kidnapping of the President, 1980 (Gardner 3, Johnson 3)

Kids Are Alright, 1978 (Martin 3)

Kids in the Shoe, 1935 (Fleischer 4)

Kid's Last Fight. See Life of Jimmy Dolan, 1933

Kiedy ty śpisz, 1950 (Wajda 2)

Kierunek Nowa Huta, 1951 (Munk 2)

Kiganjo no boken, 1966 (Mifune 3)

Kigeki: Keiba hissho-ho, 1967 (Shindo 3)

Kiiroi karasu, 1957 (Tanaka 3)

Kikansha C-57, 1940 (Hayasaka 4)

Kiken no eiyu, 1957 (Mifune 3, Tsukasa 3)

Kiki, 1926 (Brown 2, Colman 3, Talmadge 3, Kräly 4, Menzies 4, Schenck 4)

Kiki, 1931 (Grable 3, Ondra 3, Pickford 3, Heller 4, Newman 4, Struss 4)

Kikikomi, 1960 (Yamamura 3)

Kiko and the Honey Bears, 1936 (Terry 4)

Kiko Foils a Fox, 1936 (Terry 4)

Kiko's Cleaning Day, 1937 (Terry 4)

Kikuchi senbonyari, 1943 (Yoda 4)

Kikuchi's Thousand Spears. See Kikuchi senbonyari, 1943

Kikugoro goshi, 1932 (Hasegawa 3)

Kikyo, 1950 (Yamamura 3)

Kikyo, 1964 (Mori 3)

Kilenc hónap, 1976 (Nowicki 3)

Kilenky starého kriminálníka, 1927 (Heller 4)

Kiljoys, 1921 (Roach 4)

Kill!, 1971 (Seberg 3)

Kill a Dragon, 1967 (Palance 3)

Kill Me Tomorrow, 1957 (Fisher 2)

Kill or Be Killed, 1942 (Lye 4)

Kill or Be Killed, 1949 (Hunt 4)

Kill or Cure, 1923 (Laurel and Hardy 3, Roach 4)

Kill or Cure, 1962 (Terry-Thomas 3)

Kill Patrice, un shérif pas comme les autres, 1969 (Braunberger 4)

Kill the Killer. See Koroshiya o barase, 1969

Kill the Nerve, 1922 (Roach 4)

Kill the Other Sheik. See Oggi, domani, dopodomani, 1965

Kill the Umpire, 1950 (Bacon 2, Tashlin 2, Bendix 3)

Killdozer, 1974 (Burtt 4, Whitlock 4)

Killer. See Que la bête meure, 1969

Killer Ape, 1953 (Weissmuller 3, Katzman 4)

Killer aus Florida, 1983 (Ganz 3)

Killer Bees, 1974 (Swanson 3)

Killer by Night, 1971 (McCambridge 3, Wagner 3, Jones 4)

Killer Cop. See Polizia ha le mani legate, 1974

Killer Diller, 1948 (McQueen 3)

Killer Elite, 1975 (Peckinpah 2, Caan 3, Duvall 3)

Killer Fish, 1978 (Black 3)

Killer Force, 1975 (Lee 3, Palance 3)

Killer From Yuma. See Viva la muerte ... tua!, 1972

Killer in the Family, 1983 (Mitchum 3)

Killer Inside Me, 1975 (Carradine 3, Fraker 4)

Killer Is Loose, 1956 (Boetticher 2, Cotten 3, Ballard 4)

Killer McCoy, 1947 (Donen 2, Rooney 3, Ruttenberg 4)

Killer Meteor, 1977 (Chan 3)

Killer Nun. See Suor omicidi, 1978

Killer of Killers. See Mechanic, 1972

Killer on a Horse. See Welcome to Hard Times, 1967

Killer Shark, 1950 (Boetticher 2)

Killer That Stalked New York, 1950 (Malone 3, Biroc 4, Salter 4)

Killer Walks, 1952 (Harvey 3)

Killers, 1946 (Brooks 2, Huston 2, Siodmak 2, Gardner 3, Lancaster 3, O'Brien 3, Rozsa 4, Veiller 4)

Killers, 1964 (Cassavetes 2, Siegel 2, Dickinson 3, Marvin 3, Reagan 3, Mancini 4, Williams 4)

Killers. See Verano sangrieto, 1977

Killers Carnival. See Spie contro il mondo, 1966

Killers from Space, 1953 (Clothier 4)

Killer's Kiss, 1955 (Kubrick 2)

Killers of Kilimanjaro, 1959 (Pleasence 3, Taylor 3, Alwyn 4)

Killers on Parade. See Yuhi ni akai ore no kao, 1961

Killing, 1956 (Kubrick 2, Hayden 3, Ballard 4)

Killing Affair, 1986 (Barry 4)

Killing Cars, 1986 (Gélin 3)

Killing Dad, 1989 (Elliott 3)

Killing 'em Softly. See Man in 5A, 1983

Killing Fields, 1984 (Menges 4, Puttnam 4)

Killing Hearts, 1914 (Sennett 2)

Killing Horace, 1914 (Arbuckle 3)

Killing in Monte Carlo. See Crimen, 1960

Killing Machine, 1983 (Van Cleef 3)

Killing of a Chinese Bookie, 1976 (Cassavetes 2)

Killing of an Egg, 1977 (Driessen 4)

Killing of Sister George, 1968 (Aldrich 2, York 3, Biroc 4)

Kilroy on Deck. See French Leave, 1948

Kilroy Was Here, 1947 (Cooper 3)

Kim, 1950 (Saville 2, Flynn 3, Lukas 3, Previn 4)

Kim, 1984 (O'Toole 3)

Kimatsuri, 1984 (Takemitsu 4)

Kimi shinitamoukoto nakare, 1954 (Tsukasa 3, Hayasaka 4)

Kimi to yuku amerika-kogo, 1950 (Kagawa 3)

Kin no tamago, 1952 (Kagawa 3)

Kinare Kinare, 1963 (Anand 3)

Kincaid Gambler, 1980 (Johnson 3)

Kind Hearts and Coronets, 1949 (Hamer 2, Greenwood 3, Guinness 3, Balcon 4, Slocombe 4)

Kind Lady, 1935 (Rathbone 3, Folsey 4)

Kind Lady, 1951 (Sturges 2, Barrymore 3, Lansbury 3, Bennett 4, Plunkett 4, Raksin 4, Ruttenberg 4)

Kind of Loving, 1962 (Schlesinger 2, Bates 3)

Kind ruft, 1914 (Gad 2, Nielsen 3, Freund 4)

Kindai musha shugyo, 1928 (Tanaka 3)

Kinder der Finsternis, 1921 (Leni 2)

Kinder der Finsternis, 1922 (Freund 4)

Kinder des Generals, 1912 (Gad 2, Nielsen 3, Kräly 4)

Kinder, Mütter, und ein General, 1955 (Kinski 3, Schell 3, Pommer 4)

Kinderarzt, 1910 (Porten 3, Messter 4)

Kindergarten Cop, 1990 (Baker 3, Schwarzenegger 3)

Kindering, 1987 (Brakhage 2)

Kinderseelen klagen euch an, 1927 (Rasp 3)

Kindled Courage, 1923 (Miller 4)

Kindling, 1915 (Buckland 4)

Kindling, 1988 (De Mille 2)

Kindly Scram, 1943 (Fleischer 4)

Kindred, 1987 (Steiger 3)

Kindred of the Dust, 1923 (Walsh 2, Menzies 4)

Kinegraphy, 1955 (Takemitsu 4)

Kinema no tenchi, 1986 (Ryu 3)

Kinetic Art Show—Stockholm, 1961 (Breer 4)

King, 1930 (Langdon 3, Roach 4)

King, 1970 (Jones 3)

King: A Filmed Record ... Montgomery to Memphis, 1970 (Lumet 2, Heston 3, Lancaster 3, Quinn 3, Woodward 3)

King and Country, 1964 (Losey 2, Bogarde 3)

King and Four Queens, 1956 (Walsh 2, Gable 3, Ballard 4, North 4)

King and I, 1956 (Brynner 3, Kerr 3, Brackett 4, Newman 4, Shamroy 4, Sharaff 4, Wheeler 4)

King and the Bird. See Roi et l'oiseau, 1980

King and the Chorus Girl, 1937 (LeRoy 2, Blondell 3, Horton 3, Wyman 3, Gaudio 4, Krasna 4, Orry-Kelly 4)

King Arthur Was a Gentleman, 1942 (Rank 4)

King Cowboy, 1928 (Mix 3)

King Creole, 1958 (Curtiz 2, Matthau 3, Presley 3, Harlan 4, Head 4, Wallis 4)

King David, 1985 (Beresford 2, Gere 3, Adam 4)

King for a Day, 1940 (Fleischer 4)

King Gun. See Gatling Gun, 1973

King in New York, 1957 (Chaplin 2, Colpi 4, Périnal 4)

King Kelly of the USA, 1934 (Pangborn 3)

King Kelly of the U.S.A. See Hey! Hey! U.S.A., 1938

King Klunk, 1933 (Lantz 4)

King Kong, 1933 (Schoedsack 2, Johnson 3, Wray 3, Clothier 4, Cooper 4, Dunn 4, O'Brien 4, Plunkett 4, Polglase 4, Selznick 4, Steiner 4)

King Kong, 1976 (Bridges 3, Lange 3, Baker 4, Barry 4, De Laurentiis 4, Dunn 4)

King Kong Escapes. See Kingu Kongu no gyakushu, 1967

King Kong tai Gojira, 1962 (Tsuburaya 4)

King Kong vs. Godzilla. See King Kong tai Gojira, 1962

King Lavra. See Král Lávra, 1950

King Lear, 1909 (Costello 3)

King Lear, 1970 (Cusack 3, Wakhévitch 4)

King Lear. See **Korol Lir, 1971**

King Lear, 1983 (Hurt 3, Olivier 3)

King Lear, 1987 (Godard 2, Meredith 3, Golan and Globus 4)

King Log, 1932 (Grierson 2)

King Looney XIV, 1935 (Terry 4)

King Midas, Junior, 1929 (Fleischer 4)
King Midas, Junior, 1940 (Hubley 4)
King of Alcatraz, 1938 (Florey 2, Carey 3, Preston 3, Quinn 3, Head 4)
King of Boda. *See* Bodakunden, 1956
King of Burlesque, 1936 (Faye 3, Wyman 3, MacGowan 4, Zanuck 4)
King of Chinatown, 1939 (Quinn 3, Wong 3, Head 4)
King of Comedy, 1982 (Lewis 2, Scorsese 2, De Niro 3, Leven 4)
King of Gamblers, 1937 (Brooks 3, Crabbe 3, Trevor 3, Dreier 4, Head 4)
King of Hearts, 1936 (Withers 3)
King of Hearts. *See* Roi de coeur, 1966
King of Jazz, 1930 (Brennan 3, Crosby 3, Laemmle 4, MacArthur 4, Mohr 4)
King of Kings, 1927 (De Mille 2, Johnson 3, Carré 4, Grot 4, MacPherson 4, Westmore Family 4)
King of Kings, 1961 (Ray 2, Welles 2, Ryan 3, Krasner 4, Planer 4, Rozsa 4, Wakhévitch 4)
King of Marvin Gardens, 1972 (Rafelson 2, Burstyn 3, Dern 3, Nicholson 3, Kovacs 4)
King of Paris, 1934 (Richardson 3)
King of Soho. *See* Street of Sin, 1928
King of the Arena, 1933 (McCord 4)
King of the Cannibal Islands, 1908 (Bitzer 4)
King of the Circus. *See* Zirkuskönig, 1924
King of the Congo, 1952 (Crabbe 3, Katzman 4)
King of the Coral Sea, 1954 (Rafferty 3)
King of the Cowboys, 1943 (Rogers 3, Canutt 4)
King of the Damned, 1936 (Veidt 3, Launder and Gilliat 2, Balcon 4, Bennett 4, Rank 4)
King of the Gamblers, 1937 (Florey 2)
King of the Gypsies, 1978 (Hayden 3, Sarandon 3, Winters 3, De Laurentiis 4, Nykvist 4)
King of the Jungle, 1933 (Crabbe 3, Haller 4)
King of the Khyber Rifles. *See* Black Watch, 1929
King of the Khyber Rifles, 1953 (King 2, Herrmann 4, LeMaire 4, Shamroy 4, Wheeler 4)
King of the Mardi Gras, 1935 (Fleischer 4)
King of the Monsters. *See* Gojira, 1954
King of the Mountain, 1981 (Hopper 3)
King of the Newsboys, 1938 (Ayres 3)
King of the Pecos, 1936 (Wayne 3, Canutt 4)
King of the Ritz, 1933 (Balcon 4)
King of the Roaring Twenties, 1961 (Dors 3, Rooney 3, Swerling 4, Waxman 4)
King of the Texas Rangers, 1941 (Canutt 4)
King of the Turf, 1939 (Costello 3, Menjou 3)
King of the Underworld, 1939 (Bogart 3, Francis 3, Orry-Kelly 4)
King of the Wild, 1931 (Karloff 3, Eason 4)
King of the Wind, 1989 (Harris 3, Jackson 3, Quayle 3)
King of Wild Horses, 1924 (Roach 4)
King on Main Street, 1925 (Love 3, Menjou 3, Howe 4)
King, Queen, Knave, 1972 (Skolimowski 2, Lollobrigida 3)
King Ralph, 1991 (Hurt 3, O'Toole 3)
King Rat, 1965 (Elliott 3, Mills 3, Segal 3, Barry 4, Guffey 4)
King Richard and the Crusaders, 1954

(Harrison 3, Harvey 3, Sanders 3, Blanke 4, Steiner 4)
King Richard the Lion-Hearted, 1923 (Beery 3)
King Size Canary, 1947 (Avery 4)
King Solomon, 1918 (Laurel and Hardy 3)
King Solomon of Broadway, 1935 (D'Agostino 4, Mandell 4)
King Solomon's Mines, 1937 (Stevenson 2, Robeson 3, Balcon 4, Bennett 4, Junge 4)
King Solomon's Mines, 1950 (Granger 3, Kerr 3, Mayer 4, Plunkett 4, Surtees 4)
King Solomon's Mines, 1985 (Lom 3, Golan and Globus 4, Goldsmith 4)
King Steps Out, 1936 (Von Sternberg 2, Ballard 4, Buchman 4, Cohn 4)
King Street War; Intimita proibite di una giovane sposa, 1970 (Brazzi 3)
King Tut's Tomb, 1950 (Terry 4)
King Ubu. *See* Ubu Roi, 1976
King Zilch, 1933 (Terry 4)
Kingu Kongu no gyakushu, 1967 (Tsuburaya 4)
Kingdom of the Fairies. *See* Royaume des Fées, 1903
Kingfisher, 1982 (Harrison 3)
Kings and Queens, 1956 (Heller 4)
King's Breakfast, 1936 (Reiniger 4)
King's Cup, 1932 (Wilcox 2)
King's Dancer. *See* Tänzerin von Sanssouci, 1933
King's Daughter, 1934 (Terry 4)
King's Game, 1916 (White 3)
Kings Go Forth, 1958 (Daves 2, Curtis 3, Sinatra 3, Wood 3, Bernstein 4, Cahn 4)
King's Jester. *See* Re si diverte, 1941
King's Messenger, 1908 (Bitzer 4)
Kings of the Forest, 1912 (Selig 4)
Kings of the Road. *See* **Im Lauf der Zeit, 1976**
Kings of the Sun, 1963 (Brynner 3, Bernstein 4, Reynolds 4)
King's Pirate, 1967 (Whitlock 4)
King's Rhapsody, 1955 (Wilcox 2, Flynn 3, Neagle 3)
Kings Row, 1941 (Wood 2, Coburn 3, Rains 3, Reagan 3, Sheridan 3, Burks 4, Friedhofer 4, Howe 4, Korngold 4, Menzies 4, Orry-Kelly 4, Robinson 4, Wallis 4, Westmore Family 4)
King's Story, 1965 (Welles 2)
King's Thief, 1955 (Niven 3, Sanders 3, Plunkett 4, Rozsa 4)
King's Vacation, 1933 (Arliss 3, Powell 3, Grot 4, Orry-Kelly 4)
King's Whore. *See* Favorita del Re, 1990
Kinjite, 1989 (Bronson 3, Golan and Globus 4)
Kinkan-shoku, 1975 (Kyo 3)
Kinno inakazamurai, 1932 (Yamada 3)
Kinno inaka-zamurai, 1937 (Yamada 3)
Kinno jidai, 1973 (Hasegawa 3)
Kino v derevne, 1930 (Ptushko 4)
Kino za XX liet, 1940 (Shub 2)
Kino-Eye. *See* Kino-glaz, 1924
Kino-glaz, 1924 (Vertov 2)
Kinokawa, 1966 (Iwashita 3, Tsukasa 3, Takemitsu 4)
Kino-Nedelia, 1958 (Vertov 2)
Kino-Pravda, 1922 (Vertov 2)
Kinsei Meishobu monogatari: Ogongai no hosha, 1954 (Yamada 3)
Kinuyo monogatari, 1930 (Tanaka 3)
Kinuyo no hatsukoi, 1940 (Tanaka 3)

Kinuyo Story. *See* Kinuyo monogatari, 1930
Kipps, 1941 (Launder and Gilliat 2, Reed 2, Redgrave 3, Beaton 4, Vetchinsky 4)
Kirare no Senta, 1949 (Yamamura 3)
Kirare Yosa, 1928 (Hasegawa 3)
Kirare Yosaburou, 1960 (Miyagawa 4)
Kiri no minato, 1976 (Mizoguchi 2)
Kiri no minato no akai hana, 1962 (Kagawa 3)
Kiri no oto, 1956 (Yoda 4)
Kiri no yobanashi, 1946 (Hasegawa 3)
Kirinji, 1926 (Kinugasa 2)
Kirmes, 1960 (Staudte 2)
Kirpichiki, 1925 (Golovnya 4)
Kis lord, 1918 (Korda 4)
Kishin yuri keiji, 1924 (Kinugasa 2)
Kismat, 1943 (Biswas 4)
Kismet, 1917 (Brenon 2)
Kismet, 1920 (Gaudio 4)
Kismet, 1930 (Dieterle 2, Fröhlich 3, Johnson 3, Young 3, Estabrook 4, Seitz 4)
Kismet, 1944 (Dieterle 2, Colman 3, De Carlo 3, Dietrich 3, Cole 4, Gibbons 4, Irene 4, Rosher 4, Stothart 4)
Kismet, 1955 (Minnelli 2, Keel 3, Ames 4, Cole 4, Freed 4, Gibbons 4, Lederer 4, Previn 4, Ruttenberg 4)
Kisoji no tabigasa, 1937 (Shimura 3)
Kisoshinju, 1927 (Tanaka 3)
Kiss, 1900 (Hepworth 2)
Kiss, 1913 (Reid 3)
Kiss, 1916 (Menjou 3)
Kiss, 1921 (Glennon 4)
Kiss, 1928 (Mayer 4)
Kiss, 1929 (Feyder 2, Ayres 3, Garbo 3, Daniels 4, Day 4, Gibbons 4, Kräly 4, Lewin 4)
Kiss, 1963 (Warhol 2)
Kiss, 1969 (Popescu-Gopo 4)
Kiss and Kill. *See* Blood of Fu Manchu, 1968
Kiss and Make Up, 1934 (Grant 3, Horton 3, Sheridan 3, Banton 4, Dreier 4, Schulberg 4, Shamroy 4)
Kiss and Tell, 1945 (Temple 3, Benchley 4, Polglase 4)
Kiss Before Dying, 1956 (Astor 3, Wagner 3, Woodward 3, Ballard 4)
Kiss Before Dying, 1991 (Dillon 3, Von Sydow 3)
Kiss Before the Mirror, 1933 (Whale 2, Lukas 3, Pidgeon 3, Freund 4)
Kiss for Cinderella, 1922 (Brenon 2)
Kiss for Cinderella, 1926 (Hunt 4)
Kiss for Corliss, 1949 (Aldrich 2, Niven 3, Temple 3)
Kiss in a Taxi, 1927 (Daniels 3)
Kiss in the Dark, 1925 (Menjou 3, Polglase 4)
Kiss in the Dark, 1949 (Daves 2, Crawford 3, Niven 3, Wyman 3, Burks 4, Steiner 4)
Kiss Me Again, 1925 (Lubitsch 2, Bow 3, Kräly 4)
Kiss Me Again, 1931 (Horton 3, Pidgeon 3, Garmes 4)
Kiss Me and Die. *See* Lady in Red, 1979
Kiss Me Cat, 1953 (Blanc 4, Jones 4, Stalling 4)
Kiss Me Deadly, 1955 (Aldrich 2, Saville 2, Laszlo 4)
Kiss Me Goodbye, 1982 (Mulligan 2, Bridges 3, Caan 3, Field 3, Trevor 3)

Kiss Me Kate, 1953 (Fosse 2, Grayson 3, Keel 3, Miller 3, Pan 4, Plunkett 4, Previn 4, Rosher 4)

Kiss Me, Stupid, 1964 (Wilder 2, Martin 3, Novak 3, Blanc 4, Diamond 4, La Shelle 4, Mandell 4, Previn 4, Trauner 4)

Kiss My Hand. See Bacciamo le mani, 1973

Kiss of Death, See Dodskyssen, 1917

Kiss of Death, 1947 (Hathaway 2, Malden 3, Mature 3, Widmark 3, Hecht 4, Lederer 4, LeMaire 4, Wheeler 4, Zanuck 4)

Kiss of Evil. See Kiss of the Vampire, 1963

Kiss of Fire. See Naples au baiser de feu, 1937

Kiss of Fire, 1954 (Palance 3, Boyle 4, Salter 4)

Kiss of Hate, 1916 (Barrymore 3)

Kiss of the Spider Woman, 1985 (Babenco 2, Hurt 3)

Kiss of the Vampire, 1963 (Bernard 4, Carreras 4)

Kiss on the Cruise. See Kyssen på kryssen, 1950

Kiss the Blood off My Hands, 1948 (Fontaine 3, Lancaster 3, Newton 3, Maddow 4, Metty 4, Rozsa 4)

Kiss the Boys Goodbye, 1941 (Ameche 3, Head 4, Young 4)

Kiss the Bride Goodbye, 1944 (Simmons 3)

Kiss the Girls and Make Them Die. See Se tutte le donne del mondo, 1966

Kiss the Other Sheik. See Oggi, domani, e dopodomani, 1965

Kiss Them for Me, 1957 (Donen 2, Grant 3, Mansfield 3, Epstein 4, Krasner 4, LeMaire 4, Wald 4, Wheeler 4)

Kiss Tomorrow Goodbye, 1950 (Bond 3, Cagney 3)

Kissenga, Man of Africa. See Men of Two Worlds, 1946

Kisses, 1922 (Mathis 4)

Kisses and Kurses, 1930 (Lantz 4)

Kisses for Breakfast, 1941 (Wilde 3, Deutsch 4, Edeson 4)

Kisses for My President, 1964 (MacMurray 3, Wallach 3, Kaper 4, Surtees 4)

Kissin' Cousins, 1964 (Presley 3, Katzman 4)

Kissing Bandit, 1948 (Donen 2, Charisse 3, Grayson 3, Miller 3, Sinatra 3, Alton 4, Brown 4, Lennart 4, Pasternak 4, Plunkett 4, Surtees 4)

Kissing Cup's Race, 1930 (Carroll 3)

Kisuka, 1965 (Tsuburaya 4)

Kit & Co., 1974 (Mueller-Stahl 3)

Kit Carson, 1940 (Andrews 3, Bond 3)

Kit Carson over the Great Divide, 1925 (Walthall 3)

Kit Carson's Wooing, 1911 (Mix 3)

Kit for Kat, 1948 (Blanc 4, Freleng 4, Stalling 4)

Kita no misaki, 1976 (Tanaka 3)

Kita no san-nin, 1946 (Takamine 3, Hayasaka 4)

Kitchen, 1966 (Warhol 2)

Kitchen Lady, 1918 (Sennett 2)

Kitchen Think, 1974 (Halas and Batchelor 4)

Kitchen Toto, 1987 (Golan and Globus 4)

Kitsch, 1919 (Pick 2)

Kitten Sitter, 1949 (Terry 4)

Kitten with a Whip, 1964 (Biroc 4)

Kitty, 1929 (Saville 2)

Kitty, 1945 (Leisen 2, Goddard 3, Milland 3, Dreier 4, Young 4)

Kitty and the Cowboys, 1911 (Bunny 3)

Kitty Foiled, 1947 (Hanna and Barbera 4)

Kitty Foyle, 1940 (Rogers 3, Polglase 4, Stewart 4, Trumbo 4)

Kitty from Kansas City, 1931 (Fleischer 4)

Kitty from Killarney, 1927 (Sennett 2)

Kitty Kornered, 1946 (Blanc 4, Clampett 4, Stalling 4)

Kitty Royle, 1940 (Wood 2)

Kitty und die grosse Welt, 1956 (Schneider 3)

Kitty und die Weltkonferenz, 1939 (Käutner 2)

Kiyen ryoko, 1959 (Takemitsu 4)

Kizilirmak-Karakoyun, 1967 (Güney 2)

Kizoku no kaidan, 1959 (Yoshimura 2, Mori 3)

Kizudarake no otoko, 1950 (Hasegawa 3)

Kizudarake no sanga, 1964 (Shindo 2, Yamamura 3)

Klabzuba's Eleven. See Klapzubova jedenáctka, 1938

Klänningen, 1964 (Björnstrand 3)

Klansman, 1974 (Fuller 2, Burton 3, Marvin 3)

Klapzubova jedenáctka, 1938 (Stallich 4)

Klart till drabbning, 1937 (Fischer 4, Jaenzon 4)

Klassenfeind, 1983 (Müller 4)

Klassenverhältnisse, 1985 (Straub and Huillet)

Kleider machen Leute, 1940 (Käutner 2, Herlth 4)

Klein Dorrit, 1934 (Ondra 3, Rasp 3, Heller 4)

Kleine aus der Kongektion, 1925 (Junge 4)

Kleine Fernsehspiel, 1975 (Lenica 4)

Kleine Film einer grossen Stadt—Stadt Düsseldorf am Rhein, 1935 (Ruttman 2)

Kleine Freundin braucht jeder Mann, 1927 (Albers 3)

Kleine Godard, 1978 (Ballhaus 4)

Kleine Grenzverkehr, 1943 (Röhrig 4)

Kleine Hofkonzert, 1945 (Wagner 4)

Kleine Mutter, 1935 (Pasternak 4)

Kleine Napoleon. See So sind die Männer, 1922

Kleine Residenz, 1942 (Dagover 3)

Kleine Schornsteinfeger, 1935 (Reiniger 4)

Kleine Seitensprung, 1931 (Herlth 4, Röhrig 4)

Kleine Stadt will schlafen gehen, 1954 (Fröhlich 3)

Kleine und die grosse Liebe, 1938 (Fröhlich 3)

Kleine vom Variété, 1926 (Courant 4)

Kleinstadtsunder, 1927 (Nielsen 3)

Klepsydra, 1972 (Nowicki 3)

Kleptomaniac, 1905 (Porter 2)

Kleptomanin, 1918 (Gad 2)

Kliatva molodikh, 1944 (Vertov 2)

Klondike, 1932 (Walthall 3)

Klondike Annie, 1936 (Walsh 2, McLaglen 3, West 3, Dreier 4, Young 4)

Klondike Fever, 1980 (Dickinson 3)

Klondike Fury, 1942 (Howard 2)

Klosterfriede, 1917 (Gad 2)

Klosterjäger, 1920 (Planer 4)

Klostret I Sendomir, 1920 (Sjöström 2, Magnusson 4)

Klovnen, 1917 (Psilander 3)

Klown aus Liebe. See Zirkuskönig, 1925

Klub nravstvennosti, 1915 (Mozhukin 3)

Klute, 1971 (Pakula 2, Fonda 3, Scheider 3, Sutherland 3, Jenkins 4, Willis 4)

Kluven värld, 1948 (Sucksdorff 2)

Klyuchi shchastya, 1941 (Volkov 2)

Knabe in Blau, 1919 (Murnau 2, Hoffmann 4)

Knack—and How to Get It, 1965 (Lester 2, Barry 4, Watkin 4)

Knave of Hearts. See Monsieur Ripois, 1954

Knickerbocker Buckaroo, 1919 (Wellman 2, Fairbanks 3, Zukor 4)

Knickerbocker Holiday, 1944 (Coburn 3, Eddy 3, Huston 3, Winters 3, Brown 4, Cahn 4, Plunkett 4)

Knife in the Head. See Messer im Kopf, 1978

Knife in the Water. See **Noz w wodzie, 1962**

Kniga v derevne, 1929 (Ptushko 4)

Knight Duty, 1933 (Langdon 3)

Knight Errant, 1911 (Bosworth 3)

Knight in London, 1928 (Freund 4)

Knight of the Gold Star, 1950 (Bondarchuk 3)

Knight of the Road, 1911 (Griffith 2, Bitzer 4)

Knight of the Sword. See Santo de la espada, 1969

Knight of the Trails, 1915 (Hart 3)

Knight without Armour, 1937 (Feyder 2, Dietrich 3, Donat 3, Biro 4, Cardiff 4, Hornbeck 4, Korda 4, Marion 4, Meerson 4, Rozsa 4, Stradling 4)

Knight-Mare Hare, 1955 (Blanc 4, Jones 4, Maltese 4)

Knightriders, 1981 (Romero 2, Savini 4)

Knights and Emeralds, 1986 (Puttnam 4)

Knights and Ladies, 1910 (White 3)

Knights for a Day, 1936 (Lantz 4)

Knights Must Fall, 1949 (Blanc 4, Freleng 4, Stalling 4)

Knights of the Range, 1940 (Harlan 4, Head 4)

Knights of the Round Table, 1953 (Baker 3, Gardner 3, Taylor 3, Berman 4, Jennings 4, Junge 4, Rozsa 4, Young 4)

Knightwatch, 1988 (Alonzo 4)

Knighty Knight Bugs, 1958 (Blanc 4, Freleng 4, Foster 4, Maltese 4)

Knock, 1950 (Renoir 4)

Knock, Knock, 1940 (Lantz 4)

Knock on Any Door, 1949 (Ray 2, Bogart 3, Cohn 4, Guffey 4, Taradash 4)

Knock on the Window, the Door Is in a Jamb, 1917 (Bray 4)

Knock on Wood, 1954 (Zetterling 2, Kaye 3, Bumstead 4, Frank 4, Head 4, Kidd 4, Young 4)

Knock ou Le Triomphe de la médecine, 1950 (Jouvet 3)

Knock Out, 1935 (Heller 4)

Knocknagow, 1918 (Cusack 3)

Knockout, 1914 (Sennett 2, Arbuckle 3)

Knockout, 1923 (Roach 4)

Knockout, 1932 (Roach 4)

Knockout, 1935 (Ondra 3)

Knockout, 1941 (Kennedy 3, Quinn 3, McCord 4)

Knockout Kisses, 1933 (Sennett 2)

Knockout Reilly, 1927 (Cronjager 4)

Knocturne, 1972 (Wieland 2)

Know Your Ally: Britain, 1944 (Capra 2, Hornbeck 4)

Know Your Enemy: Germany, 1945 (Capra 2)

Know Your Enemy: Japan, 1943 (Capra 2, Andrews 3, Huston 3)

Know Your Men, 1921 (White 3, Ruttenberg 4)

Knowing Men, 1930 (Rosher 4)

Knox und die lustigen Vagabunden, 1935 (Madsen and Schenstrøm 3)

Knud, 1966 (Roos 2)

Knud Rasmussens mindeekspedition til Kap Seddon, 1982 (Roos 2)

Knute Rockne—All American, 1940 (Bacon 2, Crisp 3, Reagan 3, Buckner 4, Gaudio 4, Haskin 4, Wallis 4)

Knutzy Knights, 1954 (Three Stooges 3)

Kobanzame, 1949 (Kinugasa 2)

Koban-zame: Aizo-hen, 1949 (Hasegawa 3, Yamada 3)

Koban-zame: Dogo-hen, 1948 (Hasegawa 3)

København, Kalundborg og—?, 1934 (Holger-Madsen 2)

Kobo no seishun, 1942 (Takamine 3)

Kobo Shinsen-gumi: Zen-shi, Ko-shi, 1930 (Yamada 3)

Kocaoğlan, 1964 (Güney 2)

Kod fotografa, 1959 (Mimica 4)

Kodachi o tsukau onna, 1944 (Miyagawa 4, Yoda 4)

Kodachi o tsukau onna, 1961 (Kyo 3, Yoda 4)

Köder, 1975 (Baker 3)

Kodo nipon, 1940 (Tsuburaya 4)

Kodomo no me, 1956 (Takamine 3)

Koenigsmark, 1935 (Artaud 3, Fresnay 3, Ibert 4)

Koenigsmark, 1952 (Christian-Jaque 2)

Koffer des Herrn O.F., 1931 (Lamarr 3, Lorre 3, Rathaus 4)

Kofuku he no shotai, 1947 (Takamine 3)

Kofuku no isu, 1948 (Mori 3)

Kofuku sezu, 1959 (Tsuburaya 4)

Koga Mansion. See Koga yashiki, 1949

Koga yashiki, 1949 (Hasegawa 3, Yamada 3)

Kogda derevya byli bolshimi, 1962 (Shukshin 3)

Koge, 1964 (Tanaka 3)

Kogen no eki yo sayounara, 1951 (Kagawa 3)

Koharu kyogen, 1942 (Hayasaka 4)

Koharu's Performance. See Koharu kyogen, 1942

Kohayagawa-ke no aki, 1961 (Hara 3, Ryu 3, Tsukasa 3)

Kohinoor, 1960 (Kumar 3)

Kohlberg, 1915 (Wegener 3)

Kohlhiesels Töchter, 1920 (Lubitsch 2, Jannings 3, Porten 3, Kräly 4)

Kohlhiesels Töchter, 1930 (Porten 3)

Koho jsem včera líbal, 1935 (Stallich 4)

Koi moyo, 1930 (Yamada 3)

Koi no ikuji, 1926 (Tanaka 3)

Koi no katamichi kippu, 1960 (Shinoda 2)

Koi no Oranda-zaka, 1951 (Kyo 3)

Koi no Tokyo, 1932 (Tanaka 3)

Koi no torinawa, 1925 (Tanaka 3)

Koi okami-bi, 1948 (Yamada 3)

Koi ya koinasuna koi, 1962 (Yoda 4)

Koibumi, 1953 (Kagawa 3, Mori 3, Tanaka 3)

Koiguruma, 1930 (Yamada 3)

Koikaze gojusan-tsugi, 1952 (Yoda 4)

Koina no Ginpei, 1933 (Hasegawa 3)

Koisuru tsuma, 1947 (Hayasaka 4)

Kojak and the Marcus-Nelson Murders. See Marcus-Nelson Murders, 1973

Kojak: The Belarush File, 1985 (Von Sydow 3)

Kojin Kojitsu, 1961 (Iwashita 3)

Kojiro. See Sasaki Kojiro, 1967

Kojiro Sasaki. See Kanketsu Sasaki Kojiro, 1951

Kokila, 1937 (Biswas 4)

Kokkyo no uta, 1927 (Tanaka 3)

Ko-ko series, 1924–29 (Fleischer 4)

Koko, 1977 (Almendros 4)

Koko ni izuni ari, 1955 (Okada 3)

Kokokara hajimaru, 1965 (Tsukasa 3)

Kokoro, 1973 (Shindo 2)

Kokoro no sanmyaku, 1966 (Yoshimura 2)

Kokoru, 1955 (Mori 3)

Kokotsu no hito, 1973 (Takamine 3)

Koku Hebihime dochu, 1950 (Yamada 3)

Kokushi muso, 1932 (Yamada 3)

Kolejarskie słowo, 1953 (Munk 2)

Kolibel 'naya, 1937 (Vertov 2)

Kolik slov staci lásce, 1961 (Brejchová 3)

Kolingens galoscher, 1912 (Jaenzon 4, Magnusson 4)

Koloraturen, 1932 (Fischinger 2, Ford 2)

Komandirovka, 1962 (Shukshin 3)

Komedia smerti, 1915 (Mozhukin 3)

Komediantka, 1920 (Heller 4)

Komediantka, 1986 (Tyszkiewicz 3)

Komedianty, 1961 (Ścibor-Rylski 4)

Komedie om Geld, 1936 (Ophüls 2)

Komm' zu mir zum Rendezvous. See Amour chante, 1930

Kommando Leopard, 1985 (Kinski 3, Morricone 4)

Kommunisti, 1976 (Lomnicki 3)

Komödianten, 1912 (Gad 2, Nielsen 3)

Komödianten, 1924 (Rasp 3)

Komödianten, 1941 (Pabst 2, Porten 3)

Komödianten des Lebens, 1924 (Courant 4, Kräly 4)

Komödie der Leidenschaften, 1921 (Leni 2)

Komödie des Herzens, 1924 (Dagover 3, Herlth 4, Röhrig 4)

Komoriuta Bushu-dako, 1935 (Miyagawa 4)

Komori-zoshi, 1927 (Tsuburaya 4)

Komori zoshi, 1973 (Hasegawa 3)

Kompozitor Glinka, 1952 (Tisse 4)

Komputery, 1967 (Zanussi 2)

Komsomol. See Pesn o geroyazh, 1932

Komsomol—Leader of Electrification. See K-SH-E, 1932

Komsomol—The Guide to Electrification. See K-SH-E, 1932

Komsomolsk, 1938 (Gerasimov 2)

Kona Coast, 1968 (Blondell 3, Rafferty 3, La Shelle 4)

Koncert, 1961 (Szabó 2)

Koncert na ekrane, 1939 (Cherkassov 3)

Koncert za mašinsku pušku, 1958 (Vukotić 4)

Kondura, 1977 (Nihalani 4)

Koneč starych casu, 1989 (Menzel 2)

Konga roja, 1943 (Armendáriz 3)

Kongen af Pelikanien, 1927 (Madsen and Schenstrøm 3)

Kongen bød, 1938 (Henning-Jensen 2)

Kongo, 1932 (Huston 3, Rosson 4)

Kongres kombatantów, 1949 (Munk 2)

Kongress tanzt, 1931 (Dagover 3, Veidt 3, Herlth 4, Hoffmann 4, Pommer 4, Röhrig 4)

Koniec nocy, 1957 (Cybulski 3)

König, 1913 (Warm 4)

König für eine Nacht, 1950 (Walbrook 3)

König Pausole. See Abenteur des Königs Pausole, 1933

König und die kleinen Mädchen, 1925 (Albers 3)

König von Paris, 1930 (Courant 4)

Königin einer Nacht, 1930 (Burel 4)

Königin Luise, 1927 (Bergner 3, Schüfftan 4)

Königin vom Moulin-Rouge, 1925 (Wiene 2)

Königliche Hoheit, 1953 (Dagover 3)

Königskinder, 1950 (Käutner 2, Warm 4)

Königskinder, 1962 (Mueller-Stahl 3)

Königsliebchen, 1924 (Warm 4)

Konigsmark, 1936 (Tourneur 2)

Konigstochter von Travankore, 1917 (Hoffmann 4)

Königswalzer, 1935 (Herlth 4, Röhrig 4)

Königswalzer, 1955 (Warm 4)

Konjiki-yasha, 1933 (Hasegawa 3, Tanaka 3, Yamada 3)

Konketsuji Rika, 1973 (Yoshimura 2)

Konki, 1961 (Yoshimura 2, Kyo 3, Miyagawa 4)

Konkurs, 1963 (Ondříček 4)

Konna watashi ja nakattani, 1952 (Yamamura 3)

Kono futari ni sachi are, 1957 (Mifune 3)

Kono hiroi sora no dokokani, 1954 (Takamine 3)

Kono sora no aru kagiri, 1964 (Tanaka 3)

Kono ten no niji, 1958 (Tanaka 3)

Konohi uruwashi, 1962 (Iwashita 3)

Konoko no nanatsu no oi waini, 1982 (Iwashita 3)

Konrad Albert Pocci, der Fussballgraf vom Ammerland—Das vorläufig letzte Kapitel einer Chronik der Familie Pocci, 1967 (Syberberg 2)

Konrad Albert Pocci, the Football Count from the Ammerland— Provisionally the Last Chapter of a Chronicle of the Pocci Family. See Konrad Albert Pocci, der Fussballgraf vom Ammerland—Das vorläufig letzte Kapitel einer Chronik der Familie Pocci, 1967

Konservanbraut, 1915 (Wiene 2)

Kontract, 1981 (Zanussi 2, Caron 3, Lomnicki 3)

Kontrybucja, 1967 (Lomnicki 3)

Konyaku samba-garasu, 1956 (Tsukasa 3)

Konyaku yubiwa. See Engeiji ringu, 1950

Konyets Sankt-Peterburga, 1927 (Baranovskaya 3, Golovnya 4, Stothart 4)

Konzert, 1931 (Tschechowa 3)

Konzert, 1944 (Fröhlich 3)

Kooky Loopy, 1961 (Hanna and Barbera 4)

Ko-on, 1927 (Mizoguchi 2)

Kopf hoch, Charly, 1926 (Dietrich 3)

Kopfüber ins Gluck, 1930 (Douy 4)

Korczak, 1990 (Wajda 2, Müller 4)

Korea, 1959 (Ford 2)

Körkarlen, 1921 (Sjöström 2, Jaenzon 4, Magnusson 4)

Korkuszlar, 1965 (Güney 2)

Korol Lir, 1971 (Kozintsev 2, Shostakovich 4)

Koroshiya o barase, 1969 (Miyagawa 4)

Kort är sommaren, 1962 (Andersson 3, Ullmann 3, Fischer 4)

L.A. Story, 1991 (Martin 3)
L.B.J., 1968 (Alvarez 2)
. . . la main à couper, 1974 (Blier 3)
Laawaris, 1981 (Bachchan 3)
Laban Peterqvist Training for the Olympic
    Games. *See* Laban Petterqvist tränär för
    Olympiska spelen, 1912
Laban Petterqvist tränär för Olympiska
    spelen, 1912 (Jaenzon 4)
Labbra di lurido blu, 1976 (Morricone 4)
Labios sem beijos, 1930 (Mauro 2)
Labirynt, 1962 (Lenica 4)
Labor Goes to School, 1951 (Cloquet 4)
Laboratoire de l'angoisse, 1971
    (Braunberger 4)
Laborinto, 1966 (Storaro 4)
Laboureur, 1901 (Gaumont 4)
Laburnum Grove, 1936 (Reed 2)
Labyrint srdce, 1961 (Brejchová 3)
Labyrinth. *See* Labirynt, 1962
Labyrinth, 1986 (Lucas 2, Lassally 4)
Labyrinth of the Heart. *See* Labyrint srdce,
    1961
Labyrinthe, 1977 (Dickinson 3)
Labyrinths. *See* Labyrinthe, 1977
Lac-aux-Dames, 1934 (Allégret 2, Simon 3,
    Auric 4, Meerson 4)
Lace, 1984 (Quayle 3)
Lacemaker. *See* Dentellière, 1977
Lache Bajazzo, 1943 (Wagner 4)
Lachende Ehemann, 1926 (Albers 3)
Lachende Erben, 1933 (Ophüls 2)
Lachende Grauen, 1920 (Krauss 3, Herlth 4)
Lachende Grille, 1926 (Andrejew 4)
Lachte man gerne, 1920 (Rasp 3)
Lackey and the Lady, 1919 (Howard 3)
Lacombe Lucien, 1973 (Malle 2, Cristaldi 4,
    Delli Colli 4)
Lacrimae rerum, 1917 (Bertini 3)
Lacy and the Mississippi Queen, 1978
    (Lourié 4)
Lad—A Dog, 1961 (Glennon 4)
Lad an 'a Lamp, 1932 (Roach 4)
Lad from Old Ireland, 1910 (Olcott 2)
Lad in His Lamp, 1948 (Blanc 4,
    McKimson 4, Stalling 4)
Ladali, 1949 (Biswas 4)
Ladder, 1964 (Dunning 4)
Ladder Jinx, 1978 (Horton 3)
Laddie, 1935 (Stevens 2, Crisp 3, Berman 4,
    Biroc 4, Polglase 4, Steiner 4)
Laddie, 1940 (Cushing 3, Polglase 4)
Laddroga Maldita. *See* Opio, 1949
Ladenprinz, 1928 (Andrejew 4)
Ladies at Play, 1926 (Folsey 4, Wilson 4)
Ladies Club, 1986 (Schifrin 4)
Ladies Courageous, 1944 (Edwards 2,
    Young 3, Mohr 4, Raine 4, Tiomkin 4,
    Wanger 4)
Ladies Doctor. *See* Ginecologo della mutua,
    1977
Ladies First, 1918 (Sennett 2)
Ladies in Love, 1936 (Ameche 3, Gaynor 3,
    Lukas 3, Power 3, Simon 3, Young 3,
    Mohr 4)
Ladies in Retirement, 1941 (Vidor 2,
    Lanchester 3, Lupino 3, Barnes 4, Fort 4,
    Plunkett 4)
Ladies Love Brutes, 1930 (Astor 3, March 3,
    Mankiewicz 4, Young 4)
Ladies Love Danger, 1935 (Raphaelson 4)
Ladies' Man, 1922 (Stromberg 4)
Ladies' Man, 1931 (Francis 3, Lombard 3,
    Powell 3, Banton 4, Mankiewicz 4,
    Zukor 4)
Ladies' Man, 1946 (Cahn 4, Dreier 4)
Ladies' Man, 1961 (Lewis 2, Raft 3, Head 4)
Ladies Must Eat, 1929 (Sennett 2,
    Hornbeck 4)
Ladies Must Live, 1921 (Gilbert 3)
Ladies Must Live, 1940 (Cahn 4, McCord 4)
Ladies Must Love, 1933 (Dupont 2,
    Gaudio 4)
Ladies Must Play, 1930 (Walker 4)
Ladies of Leisure, 1926 (Lewin 4)
Ladies of Leisure, 1930 (Capra 2,
    Stanwyck 3, Cohn 4, Swerling 4,
    Walker 4)
Ladies of the Big House, 1932 (Beavers 3,
    Darwell 3, Sidney 3, Zukor 4)
Ladies of the Chorus, 1948 (Monroe 3)
Ladies of the Jury, 1932 (Steiner 4)
Ladies of the Mob, 1928 (Wellman 2,
    Bow 3)
Ladies of the Night. *See* Onna dake no yuro,
    1947
Ladies of Washington, 1944 (Quinn 3,
    Basevi 4, Clarke 4)
Ladies Past, 1930 (Stevens 2)
Ladies Should Listen, 1934 (Grant 3,
    Horton 3, Sheridan 3, Dreier 4, Head 4)
Ladies They Talk About, 1933 (Stanwyck 3,
    Orry-Kelly 4, Seitz 4)
Ladies to Board, 1924 (Mix 3)
**Ladri di biciclette, 1948 (Amidei 4, Cecchi
    D'Amico 4, Zavattini 4)**
Ladro di Bagdad, 1960 (Delli Colli 4)
Ladro lui, ladra lei, 1958 (Sordi 3)
Ladron de amor, 1930 (Furthman 4)
Ladrone, 1979 (Morricone 4)
Lady, 1925 (Borzage 2, Talmadge 3,
    Gaudio 4, Marion 4, Menzies 4,
    Schenck 4)
Lady, 1964 (Thulin 3)
Lady and Gent, 1932 (Wayne 3)
Lady and the Bandit, 1951 (Brown 4,
    Duning 4)
Lady and the Lynchings, 1977
    (Carradine 3)
Lady and the Mob, 1939 (Lupino 3)
Lady and the Monster, 1944 (Von
    Stroheim 2, Alton 4)
Lady and the Mouse, 1913 (Griffith 2,
    Barrymore 3, Gish 3, Bitzer 4, Loos 4)
Lady and the Tramp, 1955 (Disney 4,
    Iwerks 4)
Lady Audley's Secret, 1915 (Bara 3)
Lady Barber, 1924 (Sennett 2)
Lady Be Careful, 1936 (Ayres 3, Crabbe 3,
    Dreier 4, Glazer 4, Head 4)
Lady Be Gay. *See* Laugh It Off, 1939
Lady Be Good, 1928 (Folsey 4)
Lady Be Good, 1941 (Berkeley 2,
    McLeod 2, Barrymore 3, Powell 3,
    Young 3, Adrian 4, Edens 4, Folsey 4,
    Freed 4, Mayer 4)
Lady Bodyguard, 1943 (Dreier 4, Head 4)
Lady By Choice, 1934 (Lombard 3, Cohn 4,
    Swerling 4)
Lady Caroline Lamb, 1972 (Mills 3,
    Olivier 3, Richardson 3, Cristaldi 4,
    Dillon 4, Morris 4)
Lady Chatterley's Lover. *See* Amant de
    Lady Chatterley, 1955
Lady Chatterley's Lover, 1981 (Russell 4)
Lady Consents, 1936 (Marshall 3, Hunt 4,
    Polglase 4, Veiller 4)
Lady Craved Excitement, 1950 (Carreras 4)
Lady Doctor, 1910 (White 3)
Lady Escapes, 1937 (Pangborn 3, Sanders 3)
**Lady Eve, 1941 (Sturges 2, Coburn 3,
    Fonda 3, Stanwyck 3, Head 4)**
Lady Fights Back, 1937 (Krasner 4)
Lady for a Day, 1933 (Capra 2, Bosworth 3,
    Cohn 4, Riskin 4, Walker 4)
Lady for a Night, 1941 (Blondell 3,
    Wayne 3, Plunkett 4)
Lady Frankenstein. *See* Figlia di
    Frankenstein, 1971
Lady from Boston. *See* Pardon My French,
    1950
Lady from Cheyenne, 1941 (Preston 3,
    Young 3, Krasner 4)
Lady from Chunking, 1942 (Wong 3)
Lady from Frisco. *See* Rebellion, 1936
Lady from Hell, 1926 (Sweet 3)
Lady from Louisiana, 1941 (Costello 3,
    Dandridge 3, Wayne 3)
Lady from Nowhere, 1936 (Astor 3)
Lady from Paris. *See* Schöne Abenteuer,
    1924

Lady from Shanghai, 1948 (Welles 2, Hayworth 3, Sloane 3, Cohn 4)

Lady from the Sea, 1929 (Milland 3)

Lady Gambles, 1949 (Curtis 3, Preston 3, Stanwyck 3, Metty 4, Orry-Kelly 4)

Lady Gangster, 1941 (Florey 2)

Lady Godiva, 1920 (Dreier 4)

Lady Godiva, 1955 (Eastwood 3, McLaglen 3, O'Hara 3, Boyle 4, Salter 4)

Lady Godiva Rides Again, 1951 (Launder and Gilliat 2, Dors 3, Howard 3, Kendall 3, Sim 3, Alwyn 4, Korda 4, Rank 4)

Lady Hamilton, 1921 (Krauss 3, Veidt 3, Dreier 4, Hoffmann 4)

Lady Hamilton, 1941 (Leigh 3, Olivier 3, Guffey 4, Hornbeck 4, Korda, V. 4, Maté 4, Reisch 4, Rozsa 4, Sherriff 4, Wheeler 4)

Lady Hamilton—zwischen Smach und liebe, 1969 (Mills 3)

Lady Has Plans, 1942 (Goddard 3, Milland 3, Head 4, Lang 4)

Lady Helen's Escapade, 1909 (Griffith 2, Lawrence 3, Bitzer 4)

Lady Ice, 1973 (Duvall 3, Sutherland 3)

Lady in a Cage, 1964 (Caan 3, De Havilland 3, Garmes 4, Head 4, Westmore Family 4)

Lady in a Jam, 1942 (La Cava 2, Bellamy 3, Dunne 3, Mohr 4)

Lady in Black, 1913 (Loos 4)

Lady in Black. See Damen i svart, 1958

Lady in Cement, 1968 (Sinatra 3, Welch 3, Biroc 4)

Lady in Danger, 1934 (Balcon 4, Junge 4, Rank 4)

Lady in Distress, 1910 (White 3)

Lady in Distress. See Window in London, 1939

Lady in Ermine, 1927 (Bushman 3, Glazer 4)

Lady in Grey, 1922 (Lukas 3)

Lady in Love, 1930 (Adrian 4)

Lady in Question, 1940 (Vidor 2, Ford 3, Hayworth 3, Cohn 4)

Lady in Red, 1935 (Freleng 4)

Lady in Red, 1979 (Sayles 2)

Lady in the Car with Glasses and a Gun, 1970 (Audran 3, Harris 3, Perry 4, Renoir 4)

Lady in the Dark, 1944 (Leisen 2, Milland 3, Rogers 3, Dreier 4, Goodrich 4, Head 4)

Lady in the Fog, 1952 (Carreras 4)

Lady in the Iron Mask, 1952 (Laszlo 4, Tiomkin 4, Wanger 4)

Lady in the Lake, 1946 (Montgomery 3, Ames 4, Chandler 4, Gibbons 4, Irene 4, Mayer 4)

Lady in the Morgue, 1938 (Cortez 4)

Lady Is a Square, 1959 (Wilcox 2, Neagle 3)

Lady Is Willing, 1934 (Howard 3, Walker 4)

Lady Is Willing, 1942 (Leisen 2, Dietrich 3, MacMurray 3, Irene 4)

Lady Jane, 1986 (Slocombe 4)

Lady Jane's Flight, 1908 (Lawrence 3)

Lady Killer, 1933 (Cagney 3, Blanke 4, Gaudio 4)

Lady Killer of Rome. See Assassino, 1961

Lady Killers, 1916 (Roach 4)

Lady L, 1965 (Dalio 3, Loren 3, Newman 3, Niven 3, Noiret 3, Piccoli 3, Ustinov 3, Alekan 4, D'Eaubonne 4, Orry-Kelly 4, Ponti 4)

Lady Leone, 1912 (Lawrence 3)

Lady Liberty. See Mortadella, 1971

Lady Liberty, 1972 (Sarandon 3)

Lady Lies, 1929 (Colbert 3, Huston 3, Fort 4)

Lady Luck, 1946 (Young 3, D'Agostino 4)

Lady Macbeth of Mtsensk. See Sibirska Ledi Magbet, 1972

Lady Marions Sommarflirt, 1913 (Sjöström 2, Jaenzon 4, Magnusson 4)

Lady Marion's Summer Flirt. See Lady Marions Sommarflirt, 1913

Lady Marion's Summer Flirtation. See Lady Marions Sommarflirt, 1913

Lady Musashin. See Musashino Fujin, 1951

Lady Musashino. See Musashino Fujin, 1951

Lady o' the Pines, 1921 (Astor 3)

Lady of Burlesque, 1943 (Wellman 2, Stanwyck 3, Cahn 4, Head 4, Stromberg 4)

Lady of Chance, 1928 (Goulding 2, Shearer 3, Adrian 4, Booth 4, Daniels 4, Gibbons 4, Mayer 4)

Lady of Monza. See monaca di Monza, 1969

Lady of Mystery. See Close Call for Boston Blackie, 1946

Lady of Quality, 1923 (Mandell 4)

Lady of Scandal, 1930 (Rathbone 3, Adrian 4, Booth 4, Gibbons 4, Kräly 4, Miller 4)

Lady of Secrets, 1936 (Akins 4, Schulberg 4)

Lady of the Boulevards. See Nana, 1934

Lady of the Dugouts, 1919 (Van Dyke 2)

Lady of the Harem, 1926 (Walsh 2, Johnson 4)

Lady of the Lake, 1931 (Balcon 4)

Lady of the Night, 1925 (Crawford 3, Shearer 3, Gibbons 4)

Lady of the Night. See Midnight Mary, 1933

Lady of the Pavements, 1929 (Griffith 2, Pangborn 3, Berlin 4, Bitzer 4, Menzies 4, Schenck 4, Struss 4)

Lady of the Sea, 1980 (Johnson 3)

Lady of the Tropics. See His Brother's Wife, 1936

Lady of the Tropics, 1939 (Lamarr 3, Taylor 3, Folsey 4, Hecht 4, Waxman 4)

Lady on a Train, 1945 (Bellamy 3, Durbin 3, Duryea 3, Horton 3, Rozsa 4)

Lady or the Tiger?, 1942 (Zinnemann 2)

Lady Oscar, 1978 (Demy 2, Varda 2, Evein 4, Legrand 4)

Lady Paname, 1950 (Jouvet 3, Annenkov 4, D'Eaubonne 4, Jeanson 4)

Lady Pays Off, 1951 (Sirk 2, Darnell 3, Boyle 4, Daniels 4)

Lady Peggy's Escape, 1913 (Olcott 2)

Lady! Please!, 1932 (Sennett 2, Grable 3)

Lady Possessed, 1952 (Mason 3, Struss 4)

Lady Raffles, 1928 (Walker 4)

Lady Robin Hood, 1925 (Karloff 3, Berman 4)

Lady Rose's Daughter, 1920 (Miller 4)

Lady Says No!, 1951 (Niven 3, Howe 4, Orry-Kelly 4)

Lady Scarface, 1941 (Musuraca 4)

Lady Sen. See Sen-hime, 1954

Lady Sings the Blues, 1972 (Pryor 3, Alonzo 4, Legrand 4)

Lady Surrenders, 1930 (Stahl 2, Pangborn 3, Rathbone 3, Laemmle 4)

Lady Surrenders. See Love Story, 1944

Lady Takes a Chance, 1943 (Arthur 3, Wayne 3, Swerling 4)

Lady Takes a Flyer, 1958 (Turner 3)

Lady Takes a Sailor, 1949 (Curtiz 2, Arden 3, Wyman 3, McCord 4, Steiner 4)

Lady to Love, 1930 (Sjöström 2, Banky 3, Robinson 3, Gibbons 4, Howard 4, Kräly 4)

Lady Tubbs, 1935 (Brennan 3)

Lady Vanishes, 1938 (Hitchcock 2, Launder and Gilliat 2, Lockwood 3, Lukas 3, Redgrave 3, Withers 3, Reville 4, Vetchinsky 4)

Lady Vanishes, 1979 (Gould 3, Lom 3, Axelrod 4, Slocombe 4)

Lady Violette, 1922 (Lukas 3)

Lady Wants Mink, 1953 (Arden 3)

Lady Who Dared, 1931 (Gaudio 4)

Lady Windermeres Fächer, 1935 (Dagover 3)

Lady Windermere's Fan, 1925 (Lubitsch 2, Colman 3)

Lady Windermere's Fan. See Lady Windermeres Fächer, 1935

Lady Windermere's Fan. See Fan, 1949

Lady with a Lamp, 1951 (Wilcox 2, Neagle 3)

Lady with a Past, 1932 (Mohr 4, Steiner 4)

Lady with a Ribbon. See Ribon o musubu fujin, 1939

Lady with Red Hair, 1940 (Hopkins 3, Rains 3, Wilde 3, Edeson 4)

Lady with the Dog. See Dama s sobachkoi, 1960

Lady Without Camelias. See Signora senza camelie, 1952

Lady Without Passport, 1950 (Lewis 2, Lamarr 3)

Ladybug, Ladybug, 1963 (Perry 4)

Ladyfingers, 1921 (Coffee 4)

Ladyfingers, 1980 (Palance 3)

Ladyhawke, 1985 (Pfeiffer 3, Storaro 4)

Ladykillers, 1955 (Mackendrick 2, Guiness 3, Lom 3, Sellers 3, Balcon 4, Heller 4)

Lady's from Kentucky, 1939 (Beavers 3, Raft 3, Head 4)

Lady's Morals, 1930 (Beery 3, Adrian 4, Barnes 4, Booth 4, Freed 4, Gibbons 4, Kräly 4, Mayer 4, Stothart 4)

Lady's Profession, 1933 (McLeod 2, Banton 4)

Lady's Tailor, 1919 (Sennett 2)

Lafayette. See Hello Lafayette, 1926

Lafayette, 1961 (Welles 2, Renoir 4)

Lafayette Escadrille, 1957 (Wellman 2, Dalio 3, Eastwood 3, Clothier 4, Rosenman 4)

Lagourdette gentleman cambrioleur, 1916 (Musidora 3)

Lagrime e sorrisi, 1912 (Bertini 3)

Laguna Heat, 1987 (Robards 3)

Laguna negra, 1952 (Rey 3)

Lahu ke do rang, 1979 (Azmi 3)

Laila—Liebe unter der Mitternachtssonne, 1958 (Nykvist 4)

Lair of Love. See Bestiare d'amour, 1964

Lair of the White Worm, 1988 (Russell 2)

Laisen no zenya, 1943 (Yoshimura 2)

Laisse aller, c'est une valse, 1970 (Blier 2, Blier 3, D'Eaubonne 4)

Laissez tirer les tireurs, 1964 (Constantine 3, Delerue 4)

Lajawab, 1950 (Biswas 4)

Lajwanti, 1958 (Burman 4)

Lake of Illusion. See Maboroshi no mizuumi, 1982

Lake Placid Serenade, 1944 (Alton 4)
Lakharani, 1945 (Dutt 2)
Lakshkar, 1989 (Anand 3)
Lal Kunwar, 1952 (Burman 4)
Lalka, 1968 (Tyszkiewicz 3)
Lalquerida, 1949 (Armendáriz 3)
Lamb, 1915 (Fairbanks 3)
Lamb, 1918 (Lloyd 3, Roach 4)
Lamb. See Lamm, 1964
Lamb, the Woman, the Wolf, 1914 (Dwan 2, Chaney 3)
Lambertville Story, 1949 (Kaufman 4)
Lambeth Walk, 1939 (Havelock-Allan 4)
Lament for a Bandit. See Llanto por un bandido, 1964
Lamiel, 1967 (Karina 3, De Beauregard 4)
Lamjata, 1974 (Dinov 4)
Lamm, 1964 (Staudte 2)
Lamp Post Favorites, 1948 (Fleischer 4)
Lamp Still Burns, 1943 (Granger 3, Howard 3, Krasker 4, Vetchinsky 4)
Lamp Still Burns, 1948 (Rank 4)
Lampada alla finestra, 1940 (Magnani 3)
Lampe qui file, 1909 (Cohl 4)
Lancashire Luck, 1937 (Havelock-Allan 4)
Lancelot and Guinevere, 1963 (Wilde 3)
Lancelot du Lac, 1974 (Sarde 4)
Lancelot of the Lake. See Lancelot du Lac, 1974
Lancement d'un navire à La Ciotat, 1895 (Lumière 2)
Lancer Spy, 1937 (Del Rio 3, Lorre 3, Sanders 3, Dunne 4, Zanuck 4)
Land, 1942 (Flaherty 2, Crosby 4, Van Dongen 4)
Land and Freedom, 1941 (Eisenstein 2)
Land Baron of San Tee, 1911 (Dwan 2)
Land Beyond the Law, 1927 (Brown 4, Polito 4)
Land Beyond the Law, 1937 (Eason 4)
Land o'Lizards. See Silent Shelby, 1922
Land of Dead Things, 1913 (Ince 4)
Land of Death, 1911 (Dwan 2)
Land of Enchantment: Southwest U.S.A. See Southwest, 1945
Land of Fury. See Seekers, 1954
Land of Jazz, 1920 (Furthman 4)
Land of Liberty, 1939 (Macpherson 4)
Land of Long Shadows, 1917 (Van Dyke 2)
Land of Mirages. See Délibábok országa, 1983
Land of Promise, 1946 (Rotha 2, Mills 3, Alwyn 4)
Land of Promise, 1983 (Wajda 2, Olbrychski 3)
Land of the Dead. See Trésor des Îles Chiennes, 1990
Land of the Incas, 1937 (Hoch 4)
Land of the Lawless, 1927 (Fejös 2, Shamroy 4)
Land of the Midnight Fun, 1939 (Avery 4)
Land of the Minotaur. See Devil's Men, 1976
Land of the Pharaohs, 1955 (Hawks 2, Hawkins 3, Faulkner 4, Garmes 4, Harlan 4, Saulnier 4, Tiomkin 4, Trauner 4)
Land of the Soviets. See Strana Sovietov, 1937
Land of Water, 1940 (Pearson 2)
Land of White Alice, 1959 (Van Dyke 2)
Land Ohne Frauen, 1929 (Veidt 3)
Land Raiders, 1970 (Rey 3)
Land Salesman, 1913 (Sennett 2)

Land Sharks Vs. Sea Dogs, 1912 (Bosworth 3)
Land Thieves, 1911 (Dwan 2)
Land Unknown, 1957 (Salter 4, Westmore Family 4)
Land We Love. See Hero's Island, 1961
Land Without Music, 1936 (Durante 3)
Landfall, 1949 (Harvey 3)
Landing of the Pilgrims, 1940 (Terry 4)
Landlady, 1938 (Boulting 2)
Landligger-idyl vandgang, 1922 (Madsen and Schenstrøm 3)
Landloper, 1918 (Gaudio 4)
Landlord, 1970 (Ashby 2, Jewison 2, Grant 3, Boyle 4, Willis 4)
Landlord's Troubled, 1913 (Sennett 2)
Landlubber, 1922 (Roach 4)
Landru, 1963 (Charbrol 2, Melville 2, Audran 3, Darrieux 3, Morgan 3, De Beauregard 4, Ponti 4, Rabier 4, Saulnier 4)
Landscape, 1974 (Lenica 4)
Landscape After the Battle. See Krajobraz po bitwie, 1970
Landscape in the Mist. See Topio stin omichli, 1988
Landschaft im Nebel. See Topio stin omichli, 1988
Landshövdingens döttrar, 1916 (Jaenzon 4)
Landstrasse und Grosstadt, 1921 (Veidt 3, Krotner 3, Hoffmann 4)
Lane That Had No Turning, 1922 (Fleming 2)
Lang ist der Weg, 1948 (Pommer 4)
Lång-Lasse i Delsbo, 1949 (Nykvist 4)
Längste Sekunda, 1980 (Mueller-Stahl 3)
Language All My Own, 1935 (Fleischer 4)
Langue docienne, 1976 (Leenhardt 2)
Lanka Dahan, 1914 (Phalke 2)
Lantern. See Lucerna, 1925
Lanterne magique, 1903 (Méliès 2)
Lanton Mills, 1969 (Malick 2)
Lanz und Elend eines Königs. See Ludwig II, 1954
Lapin 360, 1972 (Baxter 3)
Lapland, 1957 (Iwerks 4)
Lärarinna på vift, 1941 (Fischer 4)
Larceny, 1942 (Deutsch 4)
Larceny, 1948 (Duryea 3, Winters 3, Orry-Kelly 4)
Larceny, Inc., 1942 (Bacon 2, Crawford 3, Quinn 3, Robinson 3, Wyman 3, Gaudio 4, Wald 4, Wallis 4)
Larceny Lane. See Blonde Crazy, 1931
Large Family. See Bolshaya semya, 1955
Largest Boat Ever Launched Sidewalks, 1913 (Sennett 2)
Lariat Kid, 1929 (Brennan 3, Eason 4)
Larisa, 1980 (Klimov 2)
Larks on a String. See Skřivánci na niti, 1969
Larry's Recent Behaviour, 1963 (Wieland 2)
Lars Hård, 1948 (Dahlbeck 3)
Las Vegas 500 millones, 1968 (Cobb 3, Palance 3)
Las Vegas Hillbillies, 1966 (Mansfield 3)
Las Vegas Nights, 1941 (Sinatra 3, Head 4, Prinz 4, Young 4)
Las Vegas Story, 1952 (Stevenson 2, Mature 3, Price 3, Russell 3, Carmichael 4)
Laser Mission, 1989 (Borgnine 3)
Laserblast, 1977 (McDowall 3)

Lash, 1930 (Astor 3, Barthelmess 3, Haller 4)
Lash, 1934 (Mills 3)
Lásky jedné plavovlásky, 1965 (Forman 2, Ondříček 4)
Lásky Kačenky Strnadové, 1926 (Heller 4)
Lass. See Trny a květi, 1921
Lass from the Stormy Croft. See Tösen från stormyrtorpet, 1918
Lasse-Maja, 1941 (Zetterling 2)
Lassie Come Home, 1943 (Crisp 3, Lanchester 3, McDowall 3, Taylor 3, Gibbons 4, Mayer 4, Schary 4)
Lassiter, 1984 (Hoskins 3)
Last Act, 1916 (August 4)
Last Adventure. See Aventuriers, 1966
Last Alarm, 1900 (Bitzer 4)
Last Alarm, 1926 (Costello 3)
Last American Hero, 1973 (Bridges 3)
Last American Virgin, 1982 (Golan and Globus 4)
Last Angels. See Ultimi angeli, 1977
Last Angry Man, 1959 (Muni 3, Duning 4, Howe 4)
Last Aristocrats, 1989 (Xie 2)
Last Blitzkrieg, 1959 (Johnson 3, Katzman 4)
Last Bohemian. See Poslední bohém, 1931
Last Bridge. See Letzte Brücke, 1954
Last Butterfly, 1990 (Kachyňa 2)
Last Call. See Last Performance, 1928
Last Call from Passenger Faber, 1991 (Schlöndorff 2)
Last Card. See Keno Bates, Liar, 1915
Last Castle. See Echoes of a Summer, 1975
Last Challenge, 1967 (Dickinson 3, Ford 3)
Last Chance, 1921 (Selig 4)
Last Chance, 1929 (Rooney 3)
Last Chance Motel. See Ultima chance, 1973
Last Chase, 1981 (Meredith 3)
Last Circus Show, 1975 (Cobb 3)
Last Command, 1928 (Hathaway 2, von Sternberg 2, Jannings 3, Powell 3, Biro 4, Clothier 4, Dreier 4, Glennon 4, Mankiewicz 4, Schulberg 4, Zukor 4)
Last Command, 1955 (Borgnine 3, Hayden 3, Steiner 4)
Last Company. See Letzte Kompagnie, 1930
Last Convertible, 1979 (Houseman 4)
Last Couple Out. See Sista paret ut, 1956
Last Coupon, 1932 (Launder and Gilliat 2)
Last Curtain, 1937 (Havelock-Allan 4)
Last Dance, 1991 (Zanussi 2)
Last Dawn. See Carve Her Name with Pride, 1958
Last Day, 1975 (Widmark 3)
Last Day of Summer, 1958 (Konwicki 4)
Last Days of Chez Nous, 1991 (Ganz 3)
Last Days of Dolwyn, 1948 (Burton 3, Evans 3, Heller 4, Korda 4)
Last Days of Man on Earth. See Final Program, 1973
Last Days of Patton, 1986 (Scott 3)
Last Days of Pompeii, 1935 (Schoedsack 2, Calhern 3, Rathbone 3, Cooper 4, Dunn 4, Hunt 4, O'Brien 4, Polglase 4)
Last Days of Pompeii. See Derniers Jours de Pompéi, 1948
Last Days of Pompeii. See Ultimos dias de Pompeya, 1960
Last Days of Pompeii, 1984 (Borgnine 3, Olivier 3, Quayle 3, Quinn 3)
Last Days of Sodom and Gomorrah. See Sodoma e Gomorra, 1962

Last Deal, 1909 (Griffith 2, Bitzer 4)
Last Desire. *See* Dernière jeunesse, 1939
Last Detail, 1973 (Ashby 2, Nicholson 3, Towne 4)
Last Drink of Whiskey, 1914 (Browning 2, Loos 4)
Last Drop of Water, 1911 (Griffith 2, Sennett 2, Sweet 3, Bitzer 4)
Last Embrace. *See* Hoyo, 1953
Last Embrace, 1979 (Scheider 3, Schnieder 3, Rozsa 4)
Last Emperor, 1987 (Bertolucci 2, O'Toole 3, Storaro 4)
Last Express, 1938 (Cortez 4)
Last Five Minutes. *See* Ultimi cinque minuti, 1955
Last Flight, 1931 (Dieterle 2, Barthelmess 3, Saunders 4)
Last Flight of Noah's Ark, 1980 (Bujold 3, Gould 3, Jarre 4)
Last Four Days. *See* Mussolini: ultimo atto, 1974
Last Frontier, 1926 (Johnson 3)
Last Frontier, 1932 (Canutt 4)
Last Frontier, 1955 (Mann 2, Bancroft 3, Mature 3, Preston 3, Wald 4)
Last Frontier, 1986 (Robards 3)
Last Gangster, 1937 (Beavers 3, Carradine 3, Robinson 3, Stewart 3, Adrian 4, Daniels 4, Vorkapich 4)
Last Gangster. *See* Roger Touhy, Gangster, 1944
Last Generation, 1971 (McCambridge 3)
Last Gentleman, 1934 (Arliss 3, Day 4, Newman 4, Zanuck 4)
Last Great Vaudeville Show, 1985 (O'Connor 3)
Last Grenade, 1970 (Attenborough 3, Baker 3)
Last Gunfight. *See* Ankoku-gai no taiketsu, 1960
Last Hard Men, 1976 (Heston 3, Coburn 3)
Last Holiday, 1950 (Guinness 3)
Last Hour, 1930 (Launder and Gilliat 2, Bennett 4)
Last Hours Before Morning, 1975 (Sylbert 4)
Last House on the Left, 1973 (Craven 2)
Last Hungry Cat, 1961 (Blanc 4, Freleng 4)
Last Hunt, 1956 (Brooks 2, Granger 3, Taylor 3, Harlan 4, Schary 4)
Last Hurrah, 1958 (Ford 2, Carradine 3, Crisp 3, Darwell 3, Rathbone 3, Tracy 3, Nugent 4)
Last Hurrah, 1977 (Meredith 3)
Last Hustle in Brooklyn, 1977 (Lee 2)
Last Illusion. *See* Ruf, 1949
Last Indian, 1938 (Terry 4)
Last Judgement. *See* Giudizio universale, 1961
Last Judgment. *See* Giudizio universale, 1961
Last Kiss. *See* Poslední polibek, 1922
Last Lap, 1928 (Musuraca 4)
Last Laugh. *See* **Letzte Mann, 1924**
Last Lion, 1973 (Hawkins 3)
Last Load, 1948 (Baxter 2)
Last Man on Earth. *See* Ultimo uomo della terra, 1964
Last Man to Hang?, 1956 (Fisher 2, Schlesinger 2)
Last Married Couple in America, 1980 (Segal 3, Wood 3, Head 4)
Last Match, 1990 (Borgnine 3)

Last Metro. *See* Dernier Metro, 1980
Last Mile, 1932 (Edeson 4, Miller 4)
Last Mile, 1959 (Rooney 3, Miller 4)
Last Mohican, 1963 (Arkin 3)
Last Moment, 1923 (Calhern 3)
Last Moment, 1928 (Shamroy 4)
Last Moment, 1954 (Cusack 3)
Last Moments. *See* Venditore di Palloncini, 1974
Last Mouse of Hamlin, 1955 (Terry 4)
Last Movie, 1971 (Fuller 2, Hopper 3, Kovacs 4)
Last Movie. *See* Splendor, 1989
Last Night. *See* Revolutions-hochzeit, 1927
Last Notch, 1911 (Dwan 2)
Last of England, 1987 (Jarman 2)
Last of Mrs. Cheyney, 1929 (Rathbone 3, Shearer 3, Adrian 4, Daniels 4, Gibbons 4, Kräly 4)
Last of Mrs. Cheyney, 1937 (Arzner 2, Crawford 3, Montgomery 3, Powell 3, Folsey 4, Gibbons 4, Mayer 4, Raphaelson 4)
Last of Philip Banter, 1986 (Curtis 3)
Last of Sheila, 1973 (Coburn 3, Mason 3, Perkins 3, Welch 3, Adam 4)
Last of the Buccaneers, 1950 (Henreid 3, Katzman 4)
Last of the Cavalry. *See* Army Girl, 1938
Last of the Clintons, 1935 (Carey 3)
Last of the Comanches, 1952 (Crawford 3, Canutt 4, Duning 4)
Last of the Cowboys. *See* Great Smokey Roadblock, 1978
Last of the Duanes, 1924 (Mix 3)
Last of the Duanes, 1930 (Loy 3)
Last of the Duanes, 1941 (Arden 3, Clarke 4, Day 4)
Last of the Line, 1914 (Hayakawa 3, Ince 4, Sullivan 4)
Last of the Mobile Hot-Shots. *See* Blood Kin, 1969
Last of the Mohicans, 1920 (Brown 2, Tourneur 2, Beery 3, Karloff 3)
Last of the Mohicans, 1932 (Bosworth 3, Carey 3, Canutt 4, Eason 4)
Last of the Mohicans, 1936 (Scott 3, Balderston 4, Dunne 4)
Last of the Mohicans, 1992 (Day Lewis 3)
Last of the Night Riders, 1980 (Johnson 3)
Last of the Outlaws. *See* Last Outlaw, 1936
Last of the Pagans, 1935 (Friedhofer 4, Gillespie 4, Kaper 4)
Last of the Pony Riders, 1953 (Autry 3)
Last of the Powerseekers, 1971 (Turner 3)
Last of the Red Hot Lovers, 1972 (Arkin 3)
Last of the Redmen, 1947 (Crabbe 3, Katzman 4)
Last of the Redskins. *See* Last of the Redmen, 1947
Last of the Renegades. *See* Winnetou: II Teil, 1964
Last of the Secret Agents, 1966 (Head 4)
Last Outlaw, 1919 (Ford 2, Carey 3)
Last Outlaw, 1927 (Cooper 3)
Last Outlaw, 1936 (Carey 3, Walthall 3)
Last Outpost, 1935 (Grant 3, Rains 3, Brackett 4, Dreier 4, Head 4)
Last Outpost, 1951 (Reagan 3, Head 4)
Last Page, 1952 (Dors 3, Carreras 4)
Last Pair Out. *See* Sista paret ut, 1956
Last Parade, 1931 (Karloff 3, Robinson 4, Swerling 4)

Last Party of Chauvinists. *See* Siago no jouitou, 1945
Last Performance, 1929 (Fejös 2, Veidt 3, Laemmle 4, Mohr 4)
Last Picture Show, 1971 (Bogdanovich 2, Rafelson 2, Bridges 3, Burstyn 3, Johnson 3, Kovacs 4, Surtees 4)
Last Place on Earth, 1985 (Von Sydow 3)
Last Posse, 1953 (Crawford 3, Brown 4)
Last Remake of Beau Geste, 1977 (Howard 3, Jones 3, Ustinov 3, Terry-Thomas 3, Fisher 4)
Last Ride of the Dalton Gang, 1979 (Palance 3)
Last Rites, 1988 (Watkin 4)
Last Romantic Lover, 1979 (Rey 3)
Last Round-Up, 1911 (Anderson 3)
Last Round-Up, 1934 (Hathaway 2, Scott 3)
Last Round-Up, 1943 (Terry 4)
Last Roundup, 1947 (Autry 3)
Last Run, 1971 (Huston 2, Scott 3, Goldsmith 4, Nykvist 4)
Last Safari, 1967 (Hathaway 2, Granger 3)
Last Seance, 1986 (Moreau 3)
Last Shot, 1913 (Anderson 3)
Last Shot. *See* Poslední výstřel, 1950
Last Shot. *See* Ostatni strzał, 1958
Last Song. *See* Dernière chanson, 1986
Last Squadron, 1932 (McCrea 3)
Last Stage to Santa Cruz. *See* Letzte Ritt nach Santa Cruz, 1964
Last Stagecoach West, 1957 (Van Cleef 3)
Last Stand, 1938 (Lewis 2)
Last Starfighter, 1984 (Preston 3)
Last Straw, 1934 (Terry 4)
Last Summer, 1969 (Perry 4)
Last Summer. *See* Sista leken, 1984
Last Summer at Tangiers. *See* Dernier été a Tangier, 1987
Last Sunset, 1961 (Aldrich 2, Cotten 3, Douglas 3, Hudson 3, Malone 3, Laszlo 4, Trumbo 4)
Last Supper. *See* Última cena, 1976
Last Survivors, 1975 (Sheen 3)
Last Tango in Paris, 1972 (Bertolucci 2, Varda 2, Brando 3, Léaud 3, Storaro 4)
Last Target, 1972 (Redgrave 3)
Last Temptation of Christ, 1988 (Schrader 2, Scorsese 2, Stanton 3, Ballhaus 4)
Last Ten Days. *See* letzte Akt, 1955
Last Time I Saw Archie, 1961 (Mitchum 3)
Last Time I Saw Paris, 1954 (Brooks 2, Johnson 3, Pidgeon 3, Reed 3, Taylor 3, Epstein 4, Rose 4, Ruttenberg 4)
Last Trail, 1921 (Beery 3, Furthman 4)
Last Trail, 1927 (Mix 3)
Last Trail, 1933 (Trevor 3, Miller 4)
Last Train from Bombay, 1952 (Katzman 4)
Last Train from Gun Hill, 1959 (Sturges 2, Douglas 3, Quinn 3, Head 4, Lang 4, Tiomkin 4, Trumbo 4, Wallis 4)
Last Train from Madrid, 1937 (Ayres 3, Ladd 3, Lamour 3, Quinn 3, Head 4)
Last Trick. *See* Poslední trik pana Schwarzwalldea a pana Edgara, 1964
Last Trick. *See* Jan Svankmajer: Alchemist of the Surreal, 1990
Last Tycoon, 1976 (Kazan 2, Andrews 3, Carradine 3, Curtis 3, De Niro 3, Huston 3, Milland 3, Mitchum 3, Moreau 3, Nicholson 3, Pleasence 3, Jarre 4, Pinter 4, Spiegel 4)

Last Unicorn, 1982 (Arkin 3, Bridges 3, Farrow 3, Lansbury 3, Lee 3)

Last Valley, 1970 (Caine 3, Sharif 3, Barry 4)

Last Voyage, 1960 (Malone 3, O'Brien 3, Sanders 3, Mohr 4)

Last Voyage, 1988 (Grant 3, Malden 3)

Last Wagon, 1956 (Daves 2, Widmark 3, LeMaire 4)

Last Waltz, 1978 (Scorsese 2, Kovacs 4, Leven 4, Zsigmond 4)

Last War. See Sekai dai senso, 1961

Last Warning, 1929 (Leni 2, Laemmle 4, Mohr 4)

Last Warrior. See Flap, 1970

Last Wave, 1977 (Weir 2)

Last Will and Testament of Tom Smith, 1943 (Barrymore 3, Brennan 3)

Last Witness. See Letzte Zeuge, 1960

Last Woman. See Ultima donna, 1976

Last Woman on Earth, 1958 (Corman 2, Towne 4)

Last Word, 1979 (Black 3, Harris 3)

Last Year at Marienbad. See **Année dernière à Marienbad, 1961**

Laster den Menschheit, 1927 (Nielsen 3, Krauss 2)

Lata Lena och blåögda Per, 1947 (Nykvist 4)

Late Afternoon. See Późne popołudnie, 1964

Late Autumn. See Akibiyori, 1960

Late Christopher Bean. See Christopher Bean, 1933

Late Extra, 1935 (Mason 3, Sim 3)

Late George Apley, 1947 (Mankiewicz 2, Colman 3, Marsh 3, Basevi 4, Dunne 4, La Shelle 4, Newman 4)

Late Great Planet Earth, 1979 (Welles 2)

Late Hours, 1921 (Roach 4)

Late Lamented, 1917 (Sennett 2)

Late Lamented, 1922 (Roach 4)

Late Liz, 1971 (Baxter 3)

Late Lodgers, 1921 (Roach 4)

Late Mathias Pascal. See **Feu Mathias Pascal, 1925**

Late Matthew Pascal. See **Feu Mathias Pascal, 1925**

Late Show, 1977 (Altman 2, Benton 2)

Late Spring. See **Banshun, 1949**

Latent Spark, 1911 (Bunny 3)

Latest from Paris, 1928 (Wood 2, Shearer 3, Daniels 4, Gibbons 4, Gillespie 4)

Latest in Life Saving, 1913 (Sennett 2)

Latin Lovers, 1953 (Bondi 3)

Latin Lovers, 1953 (Turner 3, Lennart 4, Pasternak 4, Rose 4, Ruttenberg 4)

Latin Quarter, 1945 (Greenwood 3)

Latino, 1985 (Wexler 4)

Latitude Zero. See Ido Zero daisakusen, 1969

Läufer von Marathon, 1933 (Metzner 4, Schüfftan 4, Von Harbou 4)

Laugh and Get Rich, 1931 (La Cava 2)

Laugh and the World Laughs. See Habit of Happiness, 1916

Laugh, Clown, Laugh, 1928 (Brenon 2, Chaney 3, Young 3, Day 4, Gibbons 4, Howe 4)

Laugh It Off, 1939 (Baxter 2, Cortez 4)

Laugh Pagliacci. See Pagliacci, 1943

Laugh That Off, 1924 (Roach 4)

Laughing, 1980 (Lanchester 3)

Laughing Anne, 1953 (Wilcox 2, Lockwood 3)

Laughing at Death, 1929 (Miller 4, Plunkett 4)

Laughing at Death. See Laughing at Trouble, 1936

Laughing at Life, 1933 (McLaglen 3, Walthall 3)

Laughing at Trouble, 1936 (Carradine 3, Darwell 3)

Laughing Bill Hyde, 1918 (Rogers 3)

Laughing Boy, 1934 (Van Dyke 2, Novarro 3, Gillespie 4, Stothart 4)

Laughing Gas, 1907 (Porter 2)

Laughing Gas, 1914 (Sennett 2)

Laughing Gas, 1931 (Iwerks 4)

Laughing Gravy, 1931 (Laurel and Hardy 3)

Laughing Irish Eyes, 1936 (Lewis 2, Krasner 4)

Laughing Ladies, 1925 (Roach 4)

Laughing Lady, 1929 (Folsey 4)

Laughing Policeman, 1973 (Dern 3, Matthau 3)

Laughing Saskia. See Nevtő Szaszkia, 1916

Laughing Sinners, 1931 (Crawford 3, Gable 3, Adrian 4, Meredyth 4, Rosher 4)

Laughter, 1930 (D'Arrast 2, March 3, Folsey 4, Mankiewicz 4, Stewart 4)

Laughter in Paradise, 1951 (Sim 3)

Laughter in Paradise, 1964 (Hepburn 3)

Laughter in the Dark, 1969 (Karina 3)

Laundress, 1914 (Beery 3)

Laundry, 1923 (Fleischer 4)

Laundry Liz, 1916 (Loos 4)

Laura, 1944 (Preminger 2, Andrews 3, Price 3, Tierney 3, Webb 3, Hoffenstein 4, Lardner 4, La Shelle 4, Raksin 4, Wheeler 4, Zanuck 4)

Laura Lansing Slept Here, 1988 (Hepburn 3)

Laurel and Hardy Murder Case, 1930 (Laurel and Hardy 3, Roach 4)

Laurel Wreath of Fame, 1912 (Bushman 3)

Laurels. See Couronnes, 1909

Lausbubengeschichten, 1964 (Käutner 2)

Lauter Liebe, 1940 (Von Harbou 4)

Lauter Lügen, 1950 (Staudte 2)

Lava. See Lawa, 1989

Lavatori della pietra, 1955 (Taviani 2)

Lavatory moderne, 1900 (Guy 2)

Lavender Hill Mob, 1951 (Crichton 2, Guinness 3, Hepburn 3, Shaw 3, Auric 4, Balcon 4, Clarke 4, Slocombe 4)

Laveuses, 1895 (Lumière 2)

Lavorano per voi, 1951 (Fusco 4)

Law and Disorder, 1940 (Sim 3)

Law and Disorder, 1958 (Crichton 2, Redgrave 3, Clarke 4)

Law and Disorder, 1974 (Passer 2, Black 3, Borgnine 3)

Law and Jake Wade, 1958 (Sturges 2, Taylor 3, Widmark 3, Plunkett 4, Surtees 4)

Law and Lawless, 1933 (Canutt 4)

Law and Order, 1921 (Roach 4)

Law and Order, 1932 (Brennan 3, Carey 3, Huston 3)

Law and Order, 1940 (Salter 4)

Law and Order, 1942 (Crabbe 3)

Law and Order, 1950 (Malone 3, Terry 4)

Law and Order, 1953 (Reagan 3)

Law and Order, 1969 (Wiseman 2)

Law and Order on Bar L Ranch, 1911 (Dwan 2)

Law and the Lady, 1924 (Costello 3)

Law and the Lady, 1951 (Garson 3, Folsey 4, Plunkett 4)

Law and the Outlaw, 1913 (Mix 3)

Law and the Woman, 1921 (Struss 4)

Law Beyond the Range, 1935 (Brennan 3)

Law Enforcers. See Polizia ringrazia, 1972

Law in Her Hands, 1936 (Orry-Kelly 4)

Law Is the Law. See Loi ... c'est la loi, 1958

Law of Compensation, 1917 (Talmadge 3)

Law of Desire. See Ley del Deseo, 1986

Law of God, 1911 (Dwan 2)

Law of Men, 1919 (Barnes 4)

Law of Nature, 1918 (Johnson 3)

Law of the Desert. See Principe del deserto, 1990

Law of the Land, 1917 (Tourneur 2, Carré 4)

Law of the Lawless, 1923 (Fleming 2)

Law of the Lawless, 1964 (Bendix 3, De Carlo 3)

Law of the Mountains, 1909 (Olcott 2)

Law of the Pampas, 1939 (Harlan 4, Head 4)

Law of the Range, 1928 (Crawford 3)

Law of the Sierras. See Salomy Jane, 1923

Law of the Snow Country, 1926 (Johnson 3)

Law of the Tropics, 1941 (Bosworth 3)

Law of the Underworld, 1938 (Musuraca 4)

Law of the West, 1912 (Ince 4)

Law of the Wild, 1934 (Canutt 4, Eason 4)

Law of the Wilds, 1915 (Eason 4)

Law vs. Billy the Kid, 1954 (Katzman 4)

Law West of Tombstone, 1938 (Bond 3, Carey 3, Hunt 4, Polglase 4)

Lawa, 1989 (Lomnicki 3, Konwicki 4)

Lawbreakers, 1960 (Burnett 4)

Lawful Cheaters, 1925 (Bow 3)

Lawful Holdup, 1911 (Dwan 2)

Lawful Larceny, 1923 (Dwan 2, Costello 3, Rosson 4)

Lawful Larceny, 1930 (Daniels 3, Hunt 4, Murfin 4, Plunkett 4)

Lawgiver. See Moses, 1975

Lawless, 1950 (Losey 2, Hunt 4)

Lawless Breed, 1952 (Walsh 2, Hudson 3, Van Cleef 3)

Lawless Eighties, 1957 (Crabbe 3)

Lawless Frontier, 1934 (Wayne 3, Canutt 4)

Lawless Land, 1987 (Corman 2)

Lawless Legion, 1929 (Brown 4)

Lawless Nineties, 1936 (Wayne 3, Canutt 4)

Lawless Range, 1935 (Wayne 3, Canutt 4)

Lawless Rider, 1954 (Canutt 4)

Lawless Street, 1955 (Lewis 2, Lansbury 3, Scott 3, Brown 4)

Lawman, 1971 (Cobb 3, Duvall 3, Lancaster 3, Ryan 3)

Lawrence of Arabia, 1962 (Lean 2, Roeg 2, Cusack 3, Ferrer 3, Guinness 3, Hawkins 3, Kennedy 3, O'Toole 3, Quayle 3, Quinn 3, Rains 3, Sharif 3, Box 4, Jarre 4, Spiegel 4, Wilson 4, Young 4)

Law's Decree, 1914 (Lawrence 3)

Lawyer Man, 1932 (Dieterle 2, Blondell 3, Powell 3, Grot 4, Orry-Kelly 4)

Lawyers, 1987 (Darrieux 3)

Lawyer's Secret, 1931 (Arthur 3, Wray 3)

Laxdale Hall, 1952 (Grierson 2)

Lazy Bones, 1925 (Borzage 2, Marion 4)

Lazy Bones. See Hallelujah, I'm a Bum, 1933

Lazy Days, 1929 (Roach 4)

Lazy Lightning, 1926 (Wyler 2, Wray 3)

Lazy Little Beaver, 1947 (Terry 4)

Lazy River, 1934 (Young 3)

Lazy River, 1968 (Dunning 4)

Lazy Wagon, 1956 (Wheeler 4)

Lazybones, 1934 (Fleischer 4)

Lazybones, 1935 (Powell and Pressburger 2)

Lea Lyon. *See* Lyon Lea, 1915

Leadbelly, 1976 (Boyle 4, Sangster 4)

Leaden Bread. *See* Olověný chléb, 1954

Leaden Times. *See* Bleierne Zeit, 1981

Leader, 1964 (Conner 2, Kumar 3)

Leading Lady, 1911 (Bunny 3, Reid 3)

Leading Lizzie Astray, 1914 (Sennett 2, Arbuckle 3)

Leading Man, 1911 (Sennett 2)

League of Gentlemen, 1959 (Dearden 2, Attenborough 3, Hawkins 3, Reed 3, Rank 4)

League of Nations, 1924 (Fleischer 4)

Leah the Forsaken, 1912 (Brenon 2)

Leak in the Foreign Office, 1914 (Cruze 2)

Léanyportre, 1971 (Szabó 2)

Leap Frog Railway, 1905 (Bitzer 4)

Leap in the Dark. *See* Salto nel vuoto, 1980

Leap into the Void. *See* Salto nel vuoto, 1979

Leap Year, 1921 (Arbuckle 3)

Leap Year Cowboy, 1911 (Dwan 2)

Leap Year Proposals, 1912 (Bunny 3)

Leapfrog as Seen by the Frog, 1900 (Hepworth 2)

Leaping Love, 1929 (Roach 4)

Learn Polikeness, 1938 (Fleischer 4)

Learning Modules for Rural Children, 1974 (Benegal 2)

Learning to Love, 1925 (Emerson 4, Loos 4, Schenck 4)

Learning Tree, 1969 (Guffey 4, Whitlock 4)

Lease of Life, 1954 (Donat 3, Elliott 3, Balcon 4, Slocombe 4)

Leather and Nylon. *See* Soleil des voyous, 1967

Leather Burners, 1943 (Mitchum 3, Harlan 4)

Leather Necker, 1935 (Langdon 3)

Leather Pushers, 1922 (Shearer 3)

Leather Saint, 1956 (Bumstead 4, Head 4)

Leather Stocking, 1909 (Bitzer 4)

Leather Stockings, 1909 (Griffith 2)

Leathernecking, 1930 (Dunne 3, Hunt 4, Murfin 4, Plunkett 4)

Leathernecks Have Landed, 1936 (Ayres 3, Bond 3, Miller 4)

Leatherpushers, 1940 (Three Stooges 3, Cortez 4, Salter 4)

Leave All Fair, 1985 (Gielgud 3)

Leave 'em Laughing, 1928 (Stevens 2, Laurel and Hardy 3, Bruckman 4)

Leave 'em Laughing, 1981 (Cooper 3, Rooney 3)

Leave Her to Heaven, 1945 (Stahl 2, Price 3, Tierney 3, Wilde 3, Newman 4, Shamroy 4, Swerling 4, Wheeler 4)

Leave it to Blanche, 1934 (Harrison 3)

Leave It to Blondie, 1945 (Planer 4)

Leave It to Dad, 1933 (Langdon 3)

Leave It to John, 1936 (Iwerks 4)

Leave It to Lester, 1930 (Green 4)

Leave It to Me, 1920 (Furthman 4)

Leave It to Me, 1922 (Roach 4)

Leave It to Smiley, 1914 (Browning 2)

Leave Well Enough Alone, 1939 (Fleischer 4)

Leavenworth Case, 1936 (Lewis 2)

Leb' wohl Christina, 1945 (Fröhlich 3)

Lebbra bianca, 1951 (Loren 3)

Leben—ein Traum, 1917 (Wiene 2)

Leben unserer Präsidenten, 1951 (Eisler 4)

Leben Wilhelm Piecks. *See* Leben unserer Präsidenten, 1951

Lebende Buddhas, 1924 (Ruttman 2, Wegener 3)

Lebende Tote, 1919 (Wiene 2, Porten 3)

Lebenshunger, 1922 (Wagner 4)

Lebenskünstler, 1925 (Holger-Madsen 2, Junge 4)

Leçon de bicyclette, 1895 (Lumière 2)

Lecon de boxe comique, 1907 (Gaumont 4)

Leçon de danse, 1897 (Guy 2)

Leçon de danse, 1900 (Guy 2)

Leçon de musique, 1971 (Braunberger 4)

Leçons de boxe, 1897 (Guy 2)

Leçons de la guerre, 1915 (Musidora 3)

Lecteur distrait, 1907 (Gaumont 4)

Lecture on Man, 1961 (Williams 4)

Lecture quotidienne, 1900 (Guy 2)

Leda. *See* A double tour, 1959

Lederstrumpf, 1918 (Lugosi 3)

Left Hand of God, 1955 (Dmytryk 2, Bogart 3, Cobb 3, Moorehead 3, Tierney 3, LeMaire 4, Planer 4, Wheeler 4, Young 4)

Left Hander, 1964 (Ivanov-Vano 4)

Left, Right, and Centre, 1959 (Launder and Gilliat 2, Sim 3)

Left-Handed Gun, 1958 (Penn 2, Newman 3)

Left-Handed Man, 1913 (Carey 3, Gish 3)

Left-Handed Woman. *See* Linkshändige Frau, 1977

Legacy. *See* Vse ostaetsia lyudyam, 1963

Legacy, 1979 (Vinton 4)

Legacy of Blood, 1973 (Carradine 3)

Legacy of the 500,000. *See* Goju man-nin no isan, 1963

Legacy of the Hollywood Blacklist, 1987 (Lancaster 3)

Legal Advice, 1916 (Mix 3)

Legal Eagles, 1986 (Redford 3, Stamp 3, Bernstein 4, Edlund 4, Kovacs 4)

Legal Light, 1915 (Mix 3)

Legend, 1985 (Scott 2, Cruise 3, Goldsmith 4)

Legend Beautiful, 1915 (Eason 4)

Legend in Leotards. *See* Return of Captain Invincible, 1983

Legend of a Cruel Giant, 1968 (Ivanov-Vano 4)

Legend of a Duel to the Death. *See* Shito no densetsu, 1963

Legend of Earl Durand, 1975 (Sheen 3)

Legend of Frenchie King. *See* Pétroleuses, 1971

Legend of Frenchy King. *See* Pétroleuses, 1971

Legend of Hell House, 1973 (McDowall 3)

Legend of Hollywood, 1924 (Struss 4)

Legend of Jimmy Blue Eyes, 1964 (Alonzo 4)

Legend of Lobo, 1962 (Disney 4)

Legend of Lylah Clare, 1968 (Aldrich 2, Borgnine 3, Finch 3, Novak 3, Biroc 4)

Legend of Provence, 1914 (Cruze 2)

Legend of Rockabye Point, 1955 (Maltese 4)

Legend of Sleepy Hollow, 1972 (Carradine 3)

Legend of the Boy and the Eagle, 1967 (Fields 4)

Legend of the Holy Drinker. *See* Leggenda del santo bevitore, 1988

Legend of the Lone Ranger, 1981 (Robards 3, Barry 4, Fraker 4, Kovacs 4)

Legend of the Lost, 1957 (Hathaway 2, Brazzi 3, Loren 3, Wayne 3, Cardiff 4, Hecht 4)

Legend of the Lost Arrow, 1912 (Bosworth 3)

Legend of the Seven Golden Vampires. *See* Golden Vampire, 1974

Legend of the Werewolf, 1974 (Cushing 3, Francis 4)

Legend of Tianyun Mountain, 1981 (Xie 2)

Legend of Walks Far Woman, 1982 (Welch 3)

Legend of William Tell. *See* Wilhelm Tell, 1934

Legend That Became a Terror. *See* Monster, 1979

Legenda del rudio malese. *See* Jungle Raiders, 1985

Légende de la fileuse, 1907 (Feuillade 2)

Légende de l'arc-en-ciel, 1909 (Gance 2)

Légende de Polichinelle, 1907 (Linder 3, Pathé 4)

Légende de Rip van Winkle, 1905 (Méliès 2)

Légende de Sainte Ursule, 1948 (Cocteau 2)

Légende des phares, 1909 (Feuillade 2, Gaumont 4)

Legge, 1959 (Brasseur 3, Mastroianni 3, Mercouri 3, Montand 3)

Legge. *See* Loi, 1959

Legge dei gangsters, 1969 (Kinski 3)

Legge violenta della squadra anticrimine. *See* Cross Shot, 1976

Leggenda de Genofeffa, 1951 (Brazzi 3)

Leggenda del santo bevitore, 1988 (Olmi 2, Quayle 3)

Leggenda di Enea, 1962 (Fusco 4)

Leggenda di Faust, 1949 (Annenkov 4, Herlth 4)

Leghorn Blows at Midnight, 1950 (Blanc 4, McKimson 4, Stalling 4)

Leghorn Swoggled, 1951 (Blanc 4, McKimson 4)

Legion Condor, 1950 (Staudte 2)

Legion of Death, 1918 (Browning 2)

Legion of Terror, 1936 (Bond 3)

Legion of the Condemned, 1928 (Wellman 2, Cooper 3, Wray 3, Saunders 4, Zukor 4)

Légion sauté sur Kolwezi, 1979 (Coutard 4, De Beauregard 4)

Legionnaires in Paris, 1927 (Plunkett 4)

Légions d'honneur, 1938 (Vanel 3, D'Eaubonne 4, Matras 4, Renoir 4)

Legion's Last Patrol. *See* Marcia o crepa, 1963

Légitime défense, 1958 (Blier 3)

Legkaya zhizn, 1964 (Maretskaya 3)

Lehrer im Wandel, 1963 (Kluge 2)

Lei da Terra—Alentejo 76, 1976 (De Almeida 4)

Leibeigenen, 1927 (Homolka 3)

Leibgardist, 1925 (Wiene 2, Metzner 4)

Leichte Isabell, 1927 (Fröhlich 3)

Leichtsinnige Jugend, 1931 (Baranovskaya 3)

Leidenschaft, 1940 (Rasp 3, Tschechowa 3)

Leidenschaftliche Bluemchen. *See* Passion Flower Hotel, 1978

Leidensweg der Inge Krafft, 1921 (Von Harbou 4)

Leidensweg der Inge Kraft, 1921 (Veidt 3)

Leise flehen meine Lieder, 1933 (Planer 4, Reisch 4)

Lek pa regnbagen, 1958 (Zetterling 2, Fischer 4)

Lekce, 1972 (Brejchová 3)

Lekcja anatomii. See Anatomie stunde, 1977

Lekkamraterna, 1914 (Stiller 2)

Lektion, 1911 (Psilander 3)

Lektion i kärlek, 1954 (Andersson 3, Björnstrand 3, Dahlbeck 3)

Lektro, 1927 (Moskvin 4)

Lelicek in the Service of Sherlock Holmes. See Lelíček ve službách Sherlocka Holmes, 1932

Lelíček ve službách Sherlocka Holmes, 1932 (Heller 4, Stallich 4)

Lelichek in Sherlock Holmes's Service. See Lelíček ve službách Sherlocka Holmes, 1932

Lemmy pour les dames, 1962 (Constantine 3, Kosma 4)

Lemon, 1969 (Frampton 2)

Lemon Drop Kid, 1934 (Neilan 2, Walthall 3)

Lemon Drop Kid, 1951 (Tashlin 2, Darwell 3, Hope 3, Head 4, Young 4)

Lemon Popsicle. See Eskimo Limon, 1977

Lemon Popsicle V. See Roman Zair, 1983

Lemon Popsicle IV. See Sapiches, 1982

Lemon Popsicle 6. See Eskimo Ohgen, 1985

Lemon Sisters, 1989 (Gould 3, Keaton 3)

Lemonade Joe. See Limonádnový Joe, 1964

Lena and the Geese, 1912 (Griffith 2, Pickford 3, Bitzer 4)

Lena Warnstetten, 1925 (Dieterle 2)

Lend Me Your Name, 1918 (Gaudio 4)

Length of a Star. See Lengte van een Ster, 1964

Lenin i 1918 godu, 1939 (Cherkassov 3)

Lenin in 1918. See Lenin i 1918 godu, 1939

Lenny, 1974 (Fosse 2, Hoffman 3)

Lenoarduv denik, 1988 (Švankmajer 4)

Leo the Last, 1969 (Winkler 4)

Leo the Last, 1970 (Boorman 2, Mastroianni 3)

Léon Morin, prêtre, 1961 (Belmondo 3)

Léon Morin, prêtre, 1963 (Melville 2)

Léon Morin—prêtre, 1963 (De Beauregard 4)

Léon Morin, prêtre, 1963 (Decaë 4)

Leon Morin, Priest See Léon Morin, prêtre, 1961

Leonard, Part 6, 1987 (Fonda 3, Bernstein 4, Edlund 4)

Leonardo da Vinci, 1952 (Kaufman 4)

Leonardo da Vinci, 1972 (Castellani 2)

Leonardo da Vinci, 1985 (Halas and Batchelor 4)

Leonardo's Diary. See Leonarduv deník, 1972

Leonardo's Diary. See Leonarduv denik, 1988

Leonardo's Dream, 1989 (Trumbull 4)

Leonarduv deník, 1972 (Švankmajer 4)

Léonce, 1913 (Gaumont 4)

Leone di Amalfi, 1950 (Gassman 3)

Leone have sept cabecas, 1970 (Léaud 3)

Léonor, 1974 (Piccoli 3)

Leonor, 1975 (Carrière 4, Morricone 4)

Leontines Ehemänner, 1928 (Wiene 2)

Leopard, 1917 (Lugosi 3)

Leopard. See Gattopardo, 1962

Leopard in the Snow, 1977 (More 3)

Leopard Man, 1943 (Tourneur 2, D'agostino 4, Lewton 4)

Leopard Woman, 1920 (Johnson 3)

Leopardi di Churchill, 1970 (Kinski 3)

Leopard's Foundling, 1914 (Mix 3)

Leopards of Kora, 1986 (Widmark 3)

Leopold le bien-aimé, 1933 (Simon 3)

Léopold le bienaimé, 1933 (Douy 4)

Leoš Janáček, 1974 (Jireš 2)

Lepke, 1974 (Curtis 3, Golan 4)

Leprosy See Trąd, 1971

Lermontov, 1941 (Prokofiev 3)

Less, 1973 (Frampton 2)

Less Than Dust, 1916 (Pickford 3, Emerson 4)

Less Than Kin, 1918 (Crisp 3, Reid 3, Buckland 4)

Less Than the Dust, 1916 (Von Stroheim 2)

Lesser Evil, 1911 (Bitzer 4)

Lesser Evil, 1912 (Griffith 2, Marsh 3, Sweet 3)

Lesson, 1910 (Griffith 2, Bitzer 4)

Lesson. See Lekce, 1972

Lesson for Life, 1916 (Eason 4)

Lesson in Love. See lektion i kärlek, 1954

Lesson in Mechanics, 1914 (Loos 4)

Lesson Number One, 1929 (Benchley 4)

Lessons for Wives See French Dressing, 1927

Lessons in Love, 1921 (Schenck 4)

Lest We Forget, 1909 (Lawrence 3)

Lest We Forget, 1934 (Baxter 2)

Lest We Forget, 1937 (Hathaway 2, Cooper 3, Taylor 3)

Lester Persky Story, 1964 (Warhol 2)

Let 'em Have It, 1935 (Wood 2)

Let 'er Buck, 1925 (Miller 4)

Let 'er Go, 1920 (Sennett 2)

Let 'er Go Gallagher, 1928 (Adrian 4)

Let 'er Go Gallagher, 19284)

Let Freedom Ring, 1939 (Barrymore 3, Eddy 3, Mclaglen 3, Hecht 4)

Let George Do It, 1940 (Dearden 2, Formby 3, Balcon 4)

Let It Be Me, 1936 (Freleng 4)

Let It Bleed, 1980 (Halas 4)

Let It Rain, 1927 (Karloff 3)

Let It Ride, 1989 (Dreyfuss 3, Allen 4)

Let Joy Reign Supreme. See Que la fête commence, 1975

Let Me Call You Sweetheart, 1932 (Fleischer 4)

Let My People Go, 1960 (Anderson 2)

Let My People Go, 1961 (Lassally 4)

Let My People Live, 1939 (Ulmer 2)

Let My People Sing, 1942 (Ustinov 3)

Let No Man Put Asunder, 1913 (Bushman 3)

Let No Man Put Asunder, 1924 (Costello 3, Webb 3)

Let No Man Write My Epitaph, 1959 (Winters 3, Seberg 3, Duning 4, Guffey 4)

Let Not Man Put Asunder, 1924 (Blackton 2)

Let the People Sing, 1942 (Baxter 2, Sim 3)

Let Them Live!, 1937 (Raksin 4)

Let There Be Light, 1946 (Huston 2)

Let Us Be Gay, 1930 (Dressler 3, Shearer 3, Adrian 4, Gibbons 4, Marion 4, Mayer 4, Shearer 4)

Let Us Be Gay. See Soyons gai, 1931

Let Us Live, 1939 (Bellamy 3, Fonda 3, O'Sullivan 3, Ballard 4, Rathaus 4, Veiller 4)

Let Women Alone, 1925 (Beery 3, Walker 4)

Lethal Obsession See Joker, 1987

Lethal Weapon, 1987 (Gibson 3)

Lethal Weapon III, 1991 (Gibson 3)

Lethal Weapon II, 1989 (Gibson 3)

Léto, 1949 (Stallich 4)

Let's All Sing Like the Birdies Sing, 1934 (Fleischer 4)

Let's Be Famous, 1939 (Balcon 4)

Let's Be Ritzy, 1934 (Ayres 3)

Let's Build, 1923 (Roach 4)

Let's Celebrake, 1938 (Fleischer 4)

Let's Dance, 1950 (McLeod 2, Astaire 3, Hutton 3, Barnes 4, Dreier 4, Head 4, Pan 4)

Let's Do It Again, 1953 (Milland 3, Wyman 3)

Let's Do It Again, 1975 (Poitier 3)

Let's Do Things, 1931 (Roach 4)

Let's Eat, 1932 (Lantz 4)

Let's Face It, 1943 (Arden 3, De Carlo 3, Hope 3, Hutton 3, Cahn 4, Head 4)

Let's Get a Divorce, 1918 (Emerson 4, Loos 4)

Let's Get Harry, 1987 (Duvall 3, Johnson 3)

Let's Get Married, 1926 (La Cava 2, Cronjager 4)

Let's Get Married, 1937 (Bellamy 3, Lupino 3)

Let's Get Married, 1960 (Adam 4, Rank 4)

Let's Get Movin', 1936 (Fleischer 4)

Let's Get Tough!, 1942 (Katzman 4)

Let's Go, 1918 (Daniels 3, Lloyd 3, Roach 4)

Let's Go, 1923 (Howard 2)

Let's Go Crazy, 1951 (Sellers 3)

Let's Go Hunting in the Woods. See Do lesíčka na čekanou, 1966

Let's Go Latin, 1947 (Fleischer 4)

Let's Go Native, 1930 (Francis 3, MacDonald 3, Banton 4)

Let's Go Places, 1929 (Grable 3)

Let's Go to the Movies, 1948 (Foreman 4)

Let's Hope It's a Girl. See Speriamo che sia femmina, 1986

Let's Live a Little, 1948 (Lamarr 3, Laszlo 4, Westmore Family 4)

Let's Live Tonight, 1935 (Walker 4)

Let's Make a Million, 1937 (Horton 3, Head 4, Struss 4)

Let's Make It Legal, 1951 (Colbert 3, Monroe 3, Wagner 3, Ballard 4, Diamond 4, LeMaire 4)

Let's Make Love, 1960 (Cukor 2, Crosby 3, Kelly 3, Monroe 3, Montand 3, Cahn 4, Cole 4, Jeakins 4, Krasna 4, Wald 4)

Let's Make Music, 1941 (Mercer 4, Polglase 4)

Let's Make Up. See Lilacs in the Spring, 1955

Let's Sing a College Song, 1947 (Fleischer 4)

Let's Sing a Love Song, 1948 (Fleischer 4)

Let's Sing a Western Song, 1947 (Fleischer 4)

Let's Sing Again, 1936 (Carré 4)

Let's Spend the Night Together, 1982 (Ashby 2)

Let's Talk It Over, 1934 (Darwell 3, Schary 4)

Let's Try Again, 1934 (Steiner 4)

Let's You and Him Fight, 1934 (Fleischer 4)

Letste Kompagnie, 1930 (Veidt 3)

Letter, 1929 (Marshall 3, Folsey 4, Fort 4)

Letter, 1940 (Wyler 2, Davis 3, Marshall 3, Friedhofer 4, Gaudio 4, Koch 4, Orry-Kelly 4, Steiner 4, Wallis 4)

Letter, 1982 (Remick 3)

Letter for Evie, 1946 (Dassin 2, Freund 4)

**Letter from an Unknown Woman, 1948
(Ophüls 2, Fontaine 3, Jourdan 3,
Banton 4, Houseman 4, Koch 4,
Planer 4)**
Letter From Bataan, 1942 (Hayward 3)
Letter from Home, 1941 (Reed 2, Johnson 3)
Letter from Siberia, 1982 (Vierny 4)
Letter M. See Slóvce M, 1964
Letter of Introduction, 1938 (Stahl 2,
Arden 3, Menjou 3, Sheridan 3)
Letter to Three Wives, 1949 (Mankiewicz 2,
Darnell 3, Douglas 3, Marsh 3, Ritter 3,
LeMaire 4, Miller 4, Newman 4,
Wheeler 4, Zanuck 4)
Lettere di condamnati a morte della
resistenza italiana, 1953 (Zavattini 4)
Lettere di una novizia, 1960 (Belmondo 3,
Ponti 4)
Letters, 1973 (Lupino 3, Stanwyck 3)
Letters from a Friend, 1943 (Ladd 3)
Letters from Marusia. See Actas de Marusia,
1985
Letters from Three Lovers, 1973 (Sheen 3)
Letters Home, 1986 (Seyrig 3)
Letters Home from Vietnam. See Dear
America, 1987
Letti selvaggi, 1979 (Vitti 3, Guerra 4)
Letting in the Sunshine, 1933 (Asquith 2)
Letto. See Secrets d'alcove, 1954
Lettre, 1930 (Fort 4)
Lettre de Paris, 1945 (Leenhardt 2)
Lettre de Sibérie, 1957 (Delerue 4)
Lettre pour vous, 1955 (Braunberger 4)
Lettres, 1914 (Feuillade 2)
Lettres d'amour, 1942 (Autant-Lara 2,
Aurenche 4)
Lettres de mon moulin, 1954 (Pagnol 2)
Lettres de Stalingrad, 1969 (Cavalcanti 2)
Letty Lynton, 1932 (Brown 2, Crawford 3,
Montgomery 3, Stromberg 4)
Letyat zhuravli, 1957 (Batalov 3)
Letzen vier von St. Paul, 1936 (Rosay 3)
Letzte Akt, 1955 (Werner 3)
Letzte Brücke, 1954 (Käutner 2, Schell 3)
Letzte Einquartierung. See Küssen ist keine
Sünd, 1926
Letzte Fort, 1928 (Wagner 4)
Letzte Illusion, 1932 (Dagover 3)
Letzte Kompagnie, 1930 (Andrejew 4)
Letzte Liebe, 1979 (Vogler 3, Winkler 3)
**Letzte Mann, 1924 (Murnau 2,
Jannings 3, Freund 4, Herlth 4,
Mayer 4, Pommer 4, Röhrig 4)**
Letzte Mann, 1955 (Albers 3, Schneider 3,
Herlth 4)
Letzte Nacht, 1949 (Schell 3)
Letzte Ritt nach Santa Cruz, 1964 (Kinski 3)
Letzte Schrei, 1977 (Seyrig 3)
Letzte Sommer, 1954 (Herlth 4)
Letzte Stunde. See Hotel Potemkin, 1924
Letzte Tag, 1913 (Warm 4)
Letzte Walzer, 1927 (Rasp 3)
Letzte Worte, 1968 (Herzog 2)
Letzte Zeuge, 1919 (Dreier 4)
Letzte Zeuge, 1960 (Staudte 2)
Letzte Zivlist, 1984 (Von Sydow 3)
Letzten Menschen, 1919 (Freund 4)
Letzten werden die Ersten sein, 1957
(Schell 3, Herlth 4)
Leuchter des Kaisers, 1936 (Rasp 3)
Leuchtfeuer, 1954 (Staudte 2)
Leuchtturm des Chaos, 1983 (Hayden 3)
Leur dernière nuit, 1953 (Gabin 3,
Barsacq 4)

Leutnant auf Befehl, 1916 (Lubitsch 2)
Lev a krotitel, 1953 (Stallich 4)
Lev farlight, 1944 (Björnstrand 3)
Lev Tolstoj, 1984 (Gerasimov 2)
Leva pa ''Hoppet'', 1951 (Thulin 3)
Levande mumien, 1916 (Magnusson 4)
Levende virkelighed, 1989 (Roos 2)
Levi, oggi, domani, 1965 (Rotunno 4)
Leviathan, 1960 (Jourdan 3)
Leviathan, 1989 (Goldsmith 4)
Lévy et Cie, 1930 (Christian-Jaque 2,
Douy 4)
Ley del Deseo, 1986 (Maura 3)
Leyenda, 1980 (Villagra 3)
Li Shizhen, The Great Pharmacologist, 1956
(Zhao 3)
Li Ting Lang, 1920 (Hayakawa 3)
Liaisons dangereuses, 1959 (Vadim 2,
Moreau 3, Philipe 3, Trintignant 3)
Lianbron, 1965 (Zetterling 2, Andersson 3,
Nykvist 4)
Lianna, 1981 (Sayles 2)
Liar, 1911 (Dwan 2)
Liars. See Menteurs, 1961
Liar's Moon, 1982 (Crawford 3, De Carlo 3,
Dillon 3)
Libaas, 1984 (Azmi 3)
Libel, 1959 (Asquith 2, Bogarde 3, De
Havilland 3, De Grunwald 4, Krasker 4)
Libeled Lady, 1936 (Harlow 3, Loy 3,
McDaniel 3, Powell 3, Tracy 3, Mayer 4)
Libera, amore mio, 1973 (Cardinale 3,
Morricone 4)
Liberated China, 1950 (Gerasimov 2)
Liberation. See Osvobozhenie, 1972
Libération de Paris, 1944 (Bost 4)
Liberation of L.B. Jones, 1970 (Wyler 2,
Cobb 3, Bernstein 4, Surtees 4)
Liberté, 1937 (Honegger 4)
Liberté en croupe, 1970 (Coutard 4,
Sarde 4)
Liberté enchaînée, 1929 (Modot 3)
Liberté ou la mort, 1989 (Ustinov 3)
Liberté surveillef. See V. Proudech, 1957
Libertine. See Matriarca, 1969
Liberty, 1929 (McCarey 2, Laurel and
Hardy 3, Harlow 3)
Liberty, 1980 (Johnson 3)
Liberty Bond short, 1918 (Gish 3)
Liberty Crown, 1967 (Conner 2)
Libido, 1967 (Giannini 3)
Libre de ne pas l'être, 1969 (Braunberger 4)
License to Kill. See Nick Carter va tout
casser, 1964
Licensed to Kill, 1965 (Cahn 4)
Licht des Lebens, 1918 (Albers 3)
Licht und der Mensch, 1955 (Auric 4)
Lichtkonzert No. 2, 1935 (Fischinger 2,
Ford 2)
Lickety Splat, 1961 (Blanc 4, Jones 4)
Lidé z maringotek, 1966 (Brodský 3,
Stallich 4)
Lidé za kamerou, 1961 (Brejchová 3,
Brdečka 4)
Lido, 1991 (Henry 4)
Lidoire, 1933 (Fernandel 3)
Lie, 1914 (Dwan 2, Chaney 3)
Lie. See No Man of Her Own, 1950
Lie Huozhong yongsheng, 1965 (Zhao 3)
Lie of Nina Petrovna. See Mensonge de Nina
Petrowna, 1937
Liebe, 1926 (Bergner 3, Warm 4)
Liebe, 1956 (Schell 3)
Liebe auf Befehl, 1931 (Tschechowa 3)

Liebe der Brüder Rott, 1929 (Tschechowa 3,
Andrejew 4, Planer 4)
Liebe der Jeanne Ney, 1927 (Rasp 3,
Hunte 4, Wagner 4, Warm 4)
Liebe der Mitzu. See Atarashiki tsuchi, 1937
Liebe des Dalai Lama. See Verbotene Land,
1924
Liebe des van Royk, 1918 (Pick 2)
Liebe geht seltsame Wege, 1937
(Tschechowa 3)
Liebe im Kunstall, 1928 (Porten 3)
Liebe im Rausch. See Colonialskandal, 1927
Liebe im Ring, 1930 (Tschechowa 3)
Liebe in Deutschland, 1983 (Wajda 2,
Schygulla 3, Olbrychski 3, Legrand 4)
Liebe in Gleitflug, 1938 (Gründgens 3)
Liebe ist kalter als der Tod, 1969 (Schygulla 3)
Liebe Lust und Lied, 1926 (Rasp 3)
Liebe macht blind, 1925 (Dagover 3,
Jannings 3, Veidt 3, Pommer 4)
Liebe, Tod, und Teufel, 1934 (Wagner 4)
Liebe und Diebe, 1928 (Porten 3)
Liebe und Heimat. See Deutsche Herzen am
Deutschen Rhein, 1925
Liebe und Telephon. See Fräulein vom Amt,
1925
Liebe und Trompetenklang. See Abenteuer
eines jungen Herrn in Polen, 1934
Liebelei, 1933 (Ophüls 2, Gründgens 3,
Tschechowa 3, Planer 4)
Liebende Buddhas, 1924 (Nielsen 3)
Liebensnest, 1922 (Wegener 3)
Lieber Karl, 1984 (Olbrychski 3)
Liebes A.B.C., 1916 (Nielsen 3)
Liebes Pielgerfahrt, 1919 (Protazanov 2)
Liebesbrief der Königin, 1916 (Wiene 2,
Messter 4)
Liebesbriefe. See Liebesnächte, 1929
Liebesbriefe der Baronin von S, 1924
(Galeen 4)
Liebesexpress, 1931 (Wiene 2)
Liebesfeuer, 1925 (Courant 4)
Liebesgeschichte, 1943 (Röhrig 4)
Liebesgeschichte, 1954 (Pommer 4)
Liebesgeschichten. See Mädels von heute,
1925
Liebesglück einer Blinden, 1909 (Porten 3,
Messter 4)
Liebeshandel, 1926 (Junge 4, Wagner 4)
Liebeshölle, 1927 (Tschechowa 3)
Liebeskarussell, 1965 (Deneuve 3)
Liebeskommando, 1931 (Fröhlich 3,
Andrejew 4)
Liebes-Korridor, 1920 (Gad 2)
Liebesleute, 1935 (Fröhlich 3)
Liebeslied, 1931 (Fröhlich 3)
Liebesnächte, 1929 (Dietrich 3)
Liebespiele im Schnee, 1967 (Siodmak 4)
Liebesreigen, 1927 (Dieterle 2)
Liebesroman im Hause Hapsburg, 1936
(Wegener 3)
Liebesspiel, 1931 (Fischinger 2, Ford 2)
Liebesspiele im Schnee, 1967 (Stallich 4)
Liebestaumel, 1920 (Veidt 3)
Liebestraum, 1991 (Novak 3)
Liebesträume, 1935 (Tschechowa 3)
Liebeswalzer, 1930 (Pommer 4)
Liebeszentrale. See Dollarprinzessin und
ihre 6 Freier, 1927
Liebfrauenmilch, 1929 (Porten 3)
Liebling der Frauen, 1911 (Freund 4)
Liebling der Frauen, 1921 (Hoffmann 4)
Liebling der Götter, 1930 (Jannings 3,
Tschechowa 3)

Liebling der Matrosen, 1937 (Sirk 2)

Lieblingsfrau des Maharadscha, 1920 (Kortner 3)

Liebschaften des Hektor Dalmore, 1921 (Veidt 3, Dreier 4)

Lied der Mutter, 1918 (Hoffmann 4)

Lied der Ströme, 1954 (Robeson 3, Shostakovich 4)

Lied, ein Kuss, ein Mädel, 1932 (Fröhlich 3)

Lied einer Nacht. See Chanson d'une nuit, 1932

Lied für Dich, 1933 (Kaper 4)

Lied ist aus, 1930 (Reisch 4)

Lied vom Leben, 1930 (Eisler 4)

Lied von der Glocke, 1907 (Freund 4)

Lien de Parenté, 1986 (Marais 3)

Liens du sang, 1978 (Chabrol 2, Audran 3, Pleasence 3, Sutherland 3, Rabier 4)

Lies My Father Told Me, 1975 (Kadár 2)

Lieu du crime, 1986 (Darrieux 3, Deneuve 3, Sarde 4)

Lieut. Danny, U.S.A., 1916 (Ince 4)

Lieutenant Kizhe. See Poruchik Kizhe, 1934

Lt. Robin Crusoe, U.S.N., 1966 (Disney 4, Ellenshaw 4)

Lieutenant Schuster's Wife, 1972 (Grant 3)

Lieutenant Smith, 1943 (Vorkapich 4)

Lieutenant souriant. See Smiling Lieutenant, 1931

Lieutenant Wore Skirts, 1955 (Tashlin 2, LeMaire 4, Wheeler 4)

Lieutenant's Last Fight, 1912 (Ince 4)

Life and Adventures of Nicholas Nickleby. See Nicholas Nickleby, 1947

Life and Death of 9413—A Hollywood Extra. See Life and Death of a Hollywood Extra, 1927

Life and Death of a Hollywood Extra, 1927 (Vorkapich 4)

Life and Death of Chico Mendes, 1992 (Menges 4)

Life and Death of Colonel Blimp, 1943 (Powell and Pressburger 2, Kerr 3, Walbrook 3, Cardiff 4, Junge 4, Périnal 4, Rank 4, Unsworth 4)

Life at Stake. See Key Man, 1954

Life at Stake. See Hra o život, 1956

Life at the Top, 1965 (Harvey 3, Simmons 3, Morris 3)

Life Begins, 1932 (Young 3)

Life Begins Again, 1942 (Alwyn 4)

Life Begins Anew. See Vita recominicia, 1945

Life Begins at 8:30, 1942 (Lupino 3, Wilde 3, Cronjager 4, Day 4, Johnson 4, Leven 4, Newman 4,)

Life Begins at Forty, 1935 (Darwell 3, Rogers 3, Trotti 4)

Life Begins at 17, 1958 (Katzman 4)

Life Begins for Andy Hardy, 1941 (Garland 3, Rooney 3)

Life Begins Now. See Nu börjar livet, 1948

Life Begins with Love, 1937 (Ballard 4)

Life Behind a Mask. See Vsyou zhizn pod maskoi, 1915

Life Continues. See Život jde dál, 1935

Life for a Kiss, 1911 (Dwan 2)

Life for Ruth, 1962 (Alwyn 4, Heller 4, Rank 4, Vetchinsky 4)

Life for the Czar. See Zhizn na Tzarya, 1911

Life Goes On, 1938 (Beavers 3)

Life Hesitates at Forty, 1935 (Roach 4)

Life in Death. See Zhizn na smerti, 1914

Life in Hollywood Number Four, 1927 (Mix 3)

Life in Sometown, U.S.A., 1938 (Keaton 2)

Life in the Balance, 1913 (Sennett 2)

Life in the Balance, 1954 (Bancroft 3, Marvin 3, Horner 4)

Life in the Citadel. See Zhizn v tsitadel, 1947

Life in the Country. See Livet på landet, 1924

Life in the Raw, 1933 (Trevor 3)

Life in Your Hands, 1975 (Lancaster 3)

Life Insurance Training Film, 1975 (Halas and Batchelor 4)

Life Is a Bed of Roses. See Vie est un roman, 1984

Life is a Circus, 1958 (Crazy Gang 3)

Life Is Cheap . . . But Toilet Paper Is Expensive, 1989 (Bernstein 4)

Life Is Nothing Without Music, 1947 (Matthews 3)

Life is Rising from the Ruins, 1945 (Kadár 2)

Life Is Short But Art Is Eternal. See Zhizn mig iskusstvo vetchno, 1916

Life Line, 1919 (Tourneur 2, Beery 3, Carré 4)

Life, Love, Death. See Vie, l'amour, la mort, 1968

Life of a Country Doctor. See Fundoshi isha, 1960

Life of a Cowboy, 1906 (Porter 2)

Life of a Film Director: Record of Kenji Mizoguchi. See Aru eiga kantoku no shogai: Mizoguchi Kenji no kiroku, 1975

Life of a Horse Dealer. See Bakuro ichidai, 1951

Life of a London Shopgirl, 1914 (Goulding 2)

Life of a Woman, 1953 (Shindo 2)

Life of an Actor. See Geidou ichidai otoko, 1941

Life of an American Cowboy, 1905 (Anderson 3)

Life of an American Fireman, 1903 (Porter 2)

Life of an American Policeman, 1905 (Porter 2)

Life of Beethoven. See Beethoven, 1927

Life of Buffalo Bill, 1910 (White 3)

Life of Chikuzan. See Chikuzan hitori-tabi, 1977

Life of Emile Zola, 1937 (De Toth 2, Dieterle 2, Calhern 3, Crisp 3, Muni 3, Blanke 4, Friedhofer 4, Gaudio 4, Grot 4, Raine 4, Steiner 4, Wallis 4, Warner 4, Westmore Family 4)

Life of General Villa, 1912 (Walsh 2)

Life of Her Own, 1950 (Cukor 2, Calhern 3, Milland 3, Turner 3, Folsey 4, Kaper 4, Lennart 4, Mayer 4, Pan 4, Rose 4)

Life of Jimmy Dolan, 1933 (Rooney 3, Temple 3, Wayne 3, Young 3, Edeson 4, Orry-Kelly 4)

Life of Juanita Castro, 1965 (Warhol 2)

Life of Lord Roberts VC, 1914 (Pearson 2)

Life of Moses, 1909 (Blackton 2)

Life of Oharu. See **Saikaku ichidai onna, 1952**

Life of Reilly, 1923 (La Cava 2)

Life of Riley, 1949 (Bendix 3, Bondi 4, Daniels 4)

Life of Simon Bolivar, 1943 (Armendáriz 3)

Life of the Molds, 1957 (Van Dyke 2)

Life of the Party, 1920 (Arbuckle 3, Brown 4)

Life of the Party, 1930 (Zanuck 4)

Life of the Party, 1937 (Dumont 3, Miller 3, Pangborn 3, Hunt 4)

Life of Vergie Winters, 1934 (Crisp 3, Berman 4, Murfin 4, Plunkett 4, Steiner 4)

Life of Wu Xun, 1950 (Zhao 3)

Life on the Mississippi, 1980 (Lassally 4)

Life on Wheels. See Lidé z maringotek, 1966

Life Saver, 1911 (Lawrence 3)

Life Savers, 1916 (Laurel and Hardy 3)

Life Size, 1973 (Lenica 4)

Life Size. See Grandeur nature, 1974

Life Size, 1976 (Piccoli 3)

Life Timer, 1913 (Mix 3)

Life Was at Stake. See Hra o život, 1956

Life with Father, 1947 (Curtiz 2, Dunne 3, Powell 3, Taylor 3, Buckner 4, Steiner 4, Stewart 4, Warner 4)

Life with Feathers, 1945 (Blanc 4, Freleng 4, Stalling 4)

Life with Fido, 1942 (Terry 4)

Life with Henry, 1941 (Niblo 2, Cooper 3, Head 4)

Life with Loopy, 1960 (Hanna and Barbera 4)

Life with the Lyons, 1954 (Daniels 3, Carreras 4)

Life with Tom, 1952 (Hanna and Barbera 4)

Lifeboat, 1944 (Hitchcock 2, Bendix 3, Basevi 4, Friedhofer 4, MacGowan 4, Swerling 4, Zanuck 4)

Lifeforce, 1985 (Golan and Globus 4, Mancini 4)

Lifelines, 1960 (Emshwiller 2)

Life's Harmony, 1916 (Borzage 2)

Life's Whirlpool, 1917 (Barrymore, E. 3, Barrymore, L. 3)

Lifespan, 1974 (Kinski 3)

Lifetime. See Toure une vie, 1974

Lifted Veil, 1917 (Barrymore 3)

Lifting the Lid, 1905 (Bitzer 4)

Liga de las muchachas, 1949 (Alcoriza 4)

Ligabue, 1978 (Zavattini 4)

Lighea, 1983 (Cecchi D'Amico 4)

Light, 1919 (Bara 3)

Light Across the Street. See Lumière d'en face, 1955

Light Ahead. See Tlatscne, 1939

Light and Shadow. See Hikaritokage, 1946

Light at Heart. See Life Begins at 8:30, 1942

Light at the Edge of the World. See Luz del fin del mundo, 1971

Light Fantastic, 1960 (Russell 2)

Light in Nature, 1960 (Hoch 4)

Light in the Dark, 1922 (Brown 2, Chaney 3, Carré 4)

Light in the Forest, 1958 (Disney 4, Ellenshaw 4)

Light in the Piazza, 1961 (Brazzi 3, De Havilland 3, Epstein 4, Freed 4, Green 4, Heller 4)

Light in the Window, 1927 (Walthall 3)

Light Machine Gun Platoon, 1941 (Hunt 4)

Light of a Distant Star, 1965 (Batalov 3)

Light of Day, 1987 (Schrader 2, Fox 3, Rowlands 3)

Light of Heart. See Life Begins at 8:30, 1942

Light of the World, 1989 (Halas and Batchelor 4)

Light of Victory, 1919 (Young 4)

Light of Western Stars, 1925 (Howard 2)

Light of Western Stars, 1930 (Lang 4)

Light of Western Stars, 1940 (Ladd 3, Harlan 4, Head 4)

Light Showers, 1922 (Roach 4)

Light, Strong and Beautiful, 1971 (Bernstein 4)

Light That Came, 1909 (Griffith 2, Pickford 3, Bitzer 4)

Light That Failed, 1923 (Clarke 4, Coffee 4)

Light That Failed, 1939 (Wellman 2, Colman 3, Huston 3, Lupino 3, Canutt 4, Dreier 4, Head 4, Young 4)

Light Touch, 1951 (Brooks 2, Granger 3, Sanders 3, Berman 4, Rose 4, Rozsa 4, Surtees 4)

Light Touch. See Touch and Go, 1955

Light Woman, 1928 (Balcon 4)

Light Years, 1987 (Close 3)

Light Years Away. See Années lumières, 1981

Lighter Burden, 1913 (Pearson 2)

Lighter Than Hare, 1960 (Blanc 4, Freleng 4)

Lighter That Failed, 1927 (Laurel and Hardy 3, Roach 4)

Lighthouse, 1906 (Bitzer 4)

Lighthouse. See Yorokobi mo Kanashimi mo ikutoshitsuki, 1957

Lighthouse by the Sea, 1924 (Garmes 4, Zanuck 4)

Lighthouse Keeper, 1911 (Pickford 3, Gaudio 4)

Lighthouse Keeper's Daughter. See Manina, la fille sans voiles, 1952

Lighthouse Love, 1932 (Sennett 2)

Lighthouse Mouse, 1955 (Blanc 4, McKimson 4)

Lighting Bryce, 1919 (Canutt 4, Glennon 4)

Lightnin', 1925 (Ford 2, August 4, Marion 4)

Lightnin', 1930 (King 2, McCrea 3, Rogers 3, Behrman 4, Levien 4)

Lightnin' Wins, 1926 (Cooper 3)

Lightning, 1927 (Stevens 2)

Lightning. See Inazuma, 1952

Lightning Bill, 1926 (Arthur 3)

Lightning Carson Rides Again, 1938 (Katzman 4)

Lightning Conductor, 1958 (Havelock-Allan 4)

Lightning Conductor, 1962 (Dinov 4)

Lightning Lariats, 1927 (Musuraca 4, Plunkett 4)

Lightning Over Water, 1981 (Wenders 2)

Lightning Raider, 1918 (Karloff 3, White 3)

Lightning Raiders, 1945 (Crabbe 3)

Lightning Rider, 1924 (Carey 3, Polito 4, Stromberg 4)

Lightning Strikes Twice, 1934 (Cronjager 4, Plunkett 4)

Lightning Strikes Twice, 1951 (Vidor 2, McCambridge 3, Blanke 4, Coffee 4, Steiner 4)

Lightning—The White Stallion, 1986 (Rooney 3, Golan and Globus 4)

Lightning Warrior, 1931 (Canutt 4)

Lights and Shadows, 1914 (Chaney 3)

Light's Diamond Jubilee, 1954 (Hecht 4)

Lights Fantastic, 1942 (Blanc 4, Freleng 4, Stalling 4)

Lights of a Great City, 1906 (Selig 4)

Lights of New York, 1927 (Warner 4)

Lights of Old Broadway, 1925 (Davis 3, Carré 4, Wilson 4)

Lights of Old Santa Fe, 1944 (Rogers 3)

Lights Out, 1942 (Terry 4)

Lights Out. See Bright Victory, 1951

Lights Out in Europe, 1939 (March 3)

Lightship, 1985 (Skolimowski 2, Brandauer 3, Duvall 3)

Ligne de démarcation, 1966 (Chabrol 2, Audran 3, Gélin 3, Seberg 3, De Beauregard 4, Gégauff 4, Rabier 4)

Ligne d'ombre, 1971 (Fradetal 4)

Ligne sans incident, 1950 (Cloquet 4)

Lignes horizontales, 1962 (McLaren 4)

Lignes verticales, 1960 (McLaren 4)

Like a Crow on a June Bug, 1974 (McCambridge 3)

Like Father, Like Son, 1987 (Moore 3)

Like Most Wives, 1914 (Weber 2, Bosworth 3, Marion 4)

Like Normal People, 1979 (Addison 4)

Likely Story, 1947 (Hunt 4, Salt 4)

Li'l Abner, 1940 (Keaton 2)

Li'l Abner, 1959 (Lewis 2, Frank 4, Mercer 4)

Lila, 1964 (Lassally 4)

Lilac Domino, 1937 (Garmes 4)

Lilac Time, 1928 (Cooper 3, Moore 3, Wilson 4)

Lilacs in the Spring, 1955 (Wilcox 2, Flynn 3, Neagle 3)

Lili, 1918 (Lugosi 3)

Lili, 1953 (Walters 2, Caron 3, Kaper 4)

Lili Lamont, 1983 (Presle 3)

Lili Marleen, 1980 (Fassbinder 2, Giannini 3, Schygulla 3)

Lilian Russell, 1940 (Day 4, Kaper 4)

Lilies of the Field, 1924 (Wong 3)

Lilies of the Field, 1930 (Korda 2, Grot 4, Korda 4)

Lilies of the Field, 1963 (Poitier 3, Goldsmith 4, Haller 4)

Liliom, 1919 (Curtiz 2)

Liliom, 1930 (Borzage 2, Behrman 4, Levien 4)

Liliom, 1934 (Lang 2, Artaud 3, Boyer 3, Maté 4, Pommer 4, Waxman 4)

Lilith, 1964 (Rossen 2, Beatty 3, Hackman 3, Seberg 3, Schüfftan 4, Sylbert 4)

Lilla Märta kommer tilbaka, 1948 (Björnstrand 3)

Lille Cirkus, 1984 (Roos 2)

Lille Lise Letpåtå, 1924 (Madsen and Schenstrøm 3)

Lille Marlene, 1950 (Baker 3)

Lillian Gish, 1984 (Moreau 3)

Lillian Russell, 1940 (Ameche 3, Faye 3, Fonda 3, Banton 4, Newman 4, Shamroy 4, Zanuck 4)

Lillies of the Field, 1930 (Garmes 4)

Lilliputian Minuet. See Menuet lilliputien, 1905

Lilliput-put, 1980 (Bozzetto 4)

Lillis Ehe, 1919 (Dreier 4)

Lilly Turner, 1933 (Brennan 3, Orry-Kelly 4)

Lily and the Rose, 1915 (Gish 3)

Lily in Love, 1985 (Smith 3)

Lily of the Dust, 1924 (Negri 3)

Lily of the Tenements, 1910 (Griffith 2, Bitzer 4)

Lily Turner, 1933 (Wellman 2)

Lily's Lovers, 1911 (Sennett 2)

Lime Street, 1985 (Wagner 3)

Limehouse Blues, 1934 (Sheridan 3, Wong 3)

Limehouse Blues, 1935 (Raft 3, Zukor 4)

Limelight, 1936 (Wilcox 2, Buchanan 3, Neagle 3)

Limelight, 1952 (Chaplin 2, Aldrich 2,

Keaton 2, Bloom 3, Chaplin 3, Purviance 3, Lourié 4, Struss 4)

Limited Mail, 1925 (Zanuck 4)

Limonádový Joe, 1964 (Brdečka 4)

Limousine Love, 1928 (Roach 4)

Limping Man, 1953 (Roberts 3)

Lin zexu, 1959 (Zhao 3)

Lina Braake, 1976 (Rasp 3)

Linarès, le jeune toréro, 1966 (Braunberger 4)

Linceul n'a pas de poches, 1974 (Gélin 3)

Lincoln Cycle, 1917 (Stahl 2)

Lincoln Highwayman, 1919 (Furthman 4)

Lincoln's Gettysburg Address, 1973 (Heston 3)

Linda, 1928 (Laszlo 4)

Lindbergh Kidnapping Case, 1976 (Cotten 3, Hopkins 3, Pidgeon 3)

Line, 1969 (Rainer 2)

Line Cruising South, 1933 (Grierson 2)

Line of Black Clouds. See Kuroun kaidou, 1948

Line of Demarcation. See Ligne de démarcation, 1966

Linea del fiume, 1976 (Hurt 3)

Linear Accelerator, 1952 (Halas and Batchelor 4)

Linear Programming, 1964 (Halas and Batchelor 4)

Liner Cruising South, 1933 (Wright 2)

Lines of White on the Sullen Sea, 1909 (Griffith 2, Bitzer 4)

Lines to Tschierva Hut, 1937 (Cavalcanti 2, Grierson 2)

Lines-Vertical. See Lignes verticales, 1960

Lines-Horizontal. See Lignes horizontales, 1962

Line-Up, 1958 (Siegel 2, Wallach 3, Mohr 4)

Linge turbulent, 1909 (Cohl 4)

Lingner Werke, 1936 (Alexeieff and Parker 4)

Linguini Incident, 1991 (Winters 3)

Link, 1986, (Stamp 3, Goldsmith 4, Morricone 4)

Linkshändige Frau, 1977 (Depardieu 3, Ganz 3, Vogler 3, Winkler 3, Müller 4)

Linus. See Linus eller Tegelhusets hemlighet, 1979

Linus eller Tegelhusets hemlighet, 1979 (Andersson 3)

Liolà, 1964 (Blasetti 2, Aimée 3, Brasseur 3, Amidei 4, Delli Colli 4)

Lion, 1962 (Holden 3, Howard 3, Arnold 4, Cardiff 4)

Lion and the Girl, 1916 (Sennett 2)

Lion and the Horse, 1952 (Steiner 4)

Lion and the House, 1932 (Sennett 2)

Lion and the Mouse, 1928 (Bacon 2, Barrymore 3)

Lion and the Mouse, 1943 (Terry 4)

Lion and the Souse, 1924 (Sennett 2)

Lion des Mogols, 1924 (Epstein 2, Mozhukin 3)

Lion Has Seven Heads. See Leone have sept cabecas, 1970

Lion Has Wings, 1939 (Powell and Pressburger 2, Oberon 3, Richardson 3, Dalrymple 4, Hornbeck 4, Korda, A. 4, Korda, V. 4, Stradling 4)

Lion Hunt, 1938 (Terry 4)

Lion Hunt, 1949 (Terry 4)

Lion Hunters, 1962 (Mirisch 4)

Lion Hunters. See Chasse au lion à l'arc, 1965

Little Märta Returns. *See* Lilla Märta kommer tilbaka, 1948

Little Mary Sunshine, 1916 (King 2, Eason 4)

Little Meena's Romance, 1916 (Fleming 2)

Little Meena's Romance, 1945 (Fleming 2)

Little Men, 1934 (McDaniel 3)

Little Men, 1940 (McLeod 2, Francis 3)

Little Mermaid. *See* Malá mořská víla, 1976

Little Minister, 1934 (Crisp 3, Hepburn 3, Berman 4, Murfin 4, Plunkett 4, Polglase 4, Steiner 4)

Little Miss Big, 1946 (Salter 4)

Little Miss Broadway, 1938 (Darwell 3, Durante 3, Temple 3, Miller 4, Zanuck 4)

Little Miss Broadway, 1947 (Katzman 4)

Little Miss Jazz, 1920 (Roach 4)

Little Miss Marker, 1934 (Menjou 3, Temple 3, Head 4, Schulberg 4)

Little Miss Marker, 1980 (Andrews 3, Curtis 3, Grant 3, Matthau 3, Mancini 4)

Little Miss Muffett. *See* Mother Goose Presents Humpty Dumpty, 1946

Little Miss Nobody, 1936 (Carey 3, Darwell 3, Glennon 4)

Little Miss Smiles, 1922 (Ford 2)

Little Miss Thoroughbred, 1938 (Sheridan 3)

Little Mo, 1978 (Baxter 3)

Little Moon of Alban, 1965 (Bogarde 3)

Little Mother, 1929 (Roach 4)

Little Mr. Jim, 1945 (Zinnemann 2, Irene 4)

Little Murders, 1971 (Arkin 3, Gould 3, Sutherland 3, Willis 4)

Little Murmurs, 1966 (Kuri 4)

Little Napoleon. *See* So sind die Männer, 1922

Little Nellie Kelly, 1940 (Garland 3, Edens 4, Freed 4, Mayer 4)

Little Nell's Tobacco, 1910 (Ince 4)

Little Nemo, 1909 (McCay 4)

Little Night Music, 1978 (Taylor 3)

Little Nikita, 1988 (Poitier 3, Hamlisch 4, Kovacs 4)

Little Nobody, 1935 (Fleischer 4)

Little Nuns. *See* Monachine, 1963

Little Old New York, 1923 (Olcott 2, Davies 3)

Little Old New York, 1940 (King 2, Bond 3, Faye 3, MacMurray 3, Balderston 4, Day 4, Newman 4, Shamroy 4, Zanuck 4)

Little Old World. *See* Piccolo mondo antico, 1941

Little Orphan, 1948 (Hanna and Barbera 4)

Little Orphan Airedale, 1947 (Blanc 4, Jones 4, Stalling 4)

Little Orphan Annie, 1919 (Moore 3)

Little Orphan Annie, 1932 (Steiner 4)

Little Orphan Annie, 1938 (Head 4)

Little Orphan Willie, 1931 (Iwerks 4)

Little Pal, 1915 (Pickford 3)

Little Pal. *See* Healer, 1935

Little Papa, 1935 (Roach 4)

Little People, 1926 (Cavalcanti 2, Dickinson 2, Pearson 2)

Little Phantasy, 1946 (McLaren 4)

Little Prince, 1974 (Donen 2, Fosse 2, Wilder 3, Barry 4, Challis 4, Russell 4)

Little Prince, 1979 (Vinton 4)

Little Princess, 1917 (Hawks 2, Neilan 2, Pickford 3, Marion 4, Rosher 4)

Little Princess, 1939 (Temple 3, Day 4, Miller 4, Zanuck 4)

Little Problems, 1951 (Terry 4)

Little Prospector, 1910 (Anderson 3)

Little Quacker, 1950 (Hanna and Barbera 4)

Little Rebel, 1911 (Lawrence 3)

Little Rebel, 1913 (Olcott 2)

Little Red Hen, 1934 (Iwerks 4)

Little Red Hen, 1955 (Terry 4)

Little Red Riding Hood, 1911 (Pickford 3)

Little Red Riding Hood, 1922 (Disney 4)

Little Red Riding Hood, 1925 (Lantz 4)

Little Red Riding Rabbit, 1944 (Blanc 4, Freleng 4, Maltese 4, Stalling 4)

Little Red Rodent Hood, 1952 (Blanc 4, Freleng 4, Stalling 4)

Little Red Walking Hood, 1937 (Avery 4, Stalling 4)

Little Robinson Corkscrew, 1924 (Sennett 2)

Little Robinson Crusoe, 1924 (Johnson 3)

Little Romance, 1979 (Hill 2, Crawford 3, Olivier 3, Bumstead 4, Delerue 4, Reynolds 4)

Little Runaway, 1952 (Hanna and Barbera 4)

Little Runaway. *See* Chiisana tobosha, 1967

Little Rural Riding Hood, 1949 (Avery 4)

Little Savage, 1929 (Miller 4, Plunkett 4)

Little Savage, 1959 (Haskin 4)

Little School Mouse, 1952 (Hanna and Barbera 4)

Little Sex, 1982 (Delerue 4)

Little Shepherd of Bargain Row, 1916 (Van Dyke 2)

Little Shepherd of Kingdom Come, 1928 (Barthelmess 3, Garmes 4, Meredyth 4)

Little Shepherd of Kingdom Come, 1960 (Crosby 4)

Little Sheriff, 1912 (Anderson 3)

Little Shoes, 1917 (Walthall 3)

Little Shop of Horrors, 1960 (Corman 2, Nicholson 3)

Little Shop of Horrors, 1986 (Martin 3)

Little Sinner, 1935 (Roach 4)

Little Sister, 1911 (Olcott 2)

Little Sister, 1914 (Mix 3)

Little Soap and Water, 1935 (Fleischer 4)

Little Soldier of '64, 1911 (Olcott 2)

Little Spies, 1986 (Rooney 3)

Little Spreewald Maiden, 1910 (Olcott 2)

Little Story. *See* Mala kronika, 1962

Little Stranger, 1936 (Fleischer 4)

Little Substitute, 1913 (Bushman 3)

Little Sunset, 1914 (Bosworth 3)

Little Swee' Pea, 1936 (Fleischer 4)

Little Sweetheart, 1988 (Hurt 3, Schifrin 4)

Little Teacher, 1909 (Griffith 2, Pickford 3, Bitzer 4)

Little Teacher, 1915 (Sennett 2, Arbuckle 3, Normand 3)

Little Tease, 1913 (Griffith 2, Walthall 3, Bitzer 4)

Little Terror, 1917 (Ingram 2)

Little Theatre of Jean Renoir. *See* Petit Théâtre de Jean Renoir, 1970

Little Tiger From Canton, 1971 (Chan 3)

Little Tinker. *See* Dráteníček, 1920

Little Tinker, 1947 (Avery 4)

Little Tokyo, U.S.A., 1942 (Day 4)

Little Tough Guys in Society, 1938 (Horton 3)

Little Train Robbery, 1905 (Porter 2)

Little Treasure, 1985 (Lancaster 3)

Little Troll Prince, 1987 (Price 3)

Little Turncoat, 1913 (Ince 4)

Little White Savage, 1919 (Young 4)

Little Widow, 1919 (Sennett 2)

Little Wild Girl, 1928 (Karloff 3)

Little Wildcat, 1922 (Laurel and Hardy 3)

Little Window. *See* Okénko, 1933

Little Women, 1933 (Cukor 2, Bennett 3, Hepburn 3, Lukas 3, Cooper 4, MacGowan 4, Murfin 4, Plunkett 4, Polglase 4, Selznick 4, Steiner 4)

Little Women, 1949 (LeRoy 2, Allyson 3, Astor 3, Brazzi 3, Leigh 3, O'Brien 3, Taylor 3, Deutsch 4, Gibbons 4, Jenkins 4, Mayer 4, Plunkett 4)

Little Women, 1978 (Young 3)

Little World of Don Camillo. *See* Petit Monde de Don Camillo, 1951

Little-Big-Cosmos. *See* Mikromakrokosmos, 1960

Littlest Horse Thieves. *See* Escape from the Dark, 1975

Littlest Outlaw, 1954 (Armendáriz 3, Disney 4)

Littlest Rebel, 1935 (Robinson 3, Temple 3, Seitz 4)

Liv Ullman's Norway. *See* Look at Liv, 1977

Live a Little, Love a Little, 1968 (Presley 3, Ames 4)

Live Again, Die Again, 1974 (Pidgeon 3)

Live and Learn, 1920 (Roach 4)

Live and Let Die, 1973 (Baker 4)

Live and Let Live. *See* Spy for a Day, 1940

Live Dangerously. *See* Lev farlight, 1944

Live for Life. *See* Vivre pour vivre, 1967

Live Ghost, 1934 (Laurel and Hardy 3, Roach 4)

Live, Love, and Believe, 1911 (Bushman 3)

Live, Love, and Learn, 1937 (Montgomery 3, Rooney 3, Russell 3, Benchley 4, Brackett 4)

Live Now, Pay Later, 1962 (Fisher 4)

Live to Love. *See* Devil's Hand, 1961

Live Today for Tomorrow. *See* Act of Murder, 1948

Live Wire, 1914 (Pearson 2)

Live Wire, 1937 (Brenon 2)

Live Wires, 1923 (Roach 4)

Lives of a Bengal Lancer, 1935 (Hathaway 2, Cooper 3, Johnson 3, Balderston 4, Banton 4, Dreier 4, Edouart 4, Head 4, Lang 4, Young 4, Zukor 4)

Lives of Bad Names. *See* Akumyo ichidai, 1967

Lives of Jenny Dolan, 1975 (Ames 4, Hunter 4)

Lives of Performers, 1972 (Rainer 2)

Livet på landet, 1924 (Jaenzon 4)

Livets Baal, 1912 (Psilander 3)

Livets konflikter, 1913 (Stiller 2, Jaenzon 4)

Livets konflikter, 1913 (Sjöström 2)

Livid Flame, 1914 (Mix 3)

Living. *See* **Ikiru, 1952**

Living Between Two Worlds, 1963 (Zsigmond 4)

Living Blackboard. *See* Cauche-mar du Fantoche, 1908

Living City, 1955 (Wexler 4)

Living Corpse. *See* Givoi troup, 1912

Living Corpse. *See* Zhivoi trup, 1928

Living Corpse. *See* Zhivoi trup, 1968

Living Dangerously, 1936 (Brenon 2)

Living Daylights, 1987 (Barry 4)

Living Dead. *See* Unheimliche Geschichten, 1932

Living Dead, 1972 (Sanders 3)

Living Dead at the Manchester Morgue. *See* Fin de semana para los muertos, 1974

Living Dead Man. *See* **Feu Mathias Pascal, 1925**
Living Death, 1915 (Browning 2)
Living Desert, 1953 (Iwerks 4)
Living Free, 1971 (Foreman 4)
Living Idol, 1957 (Lewin 4)
Living in a Big Way, 1947 (Donen 2, La Cava 2, Kelly 3, Winters 3, Berman 4, Irene 4, Ravetch 4, Rosson 4)
Living It Up, 1954 (Lewis 2, Leigh 3, Martin 3, Head 4)
Living Mummy. *See* Levande mumien, 1916
Living on Love, 1937 (Pangborn 3, Musuraca 4, Polglase 4)
Living on Velvet, 1935 (Borzage 2, Francis 3, Epstein 4, Orry-Kelly 4, Wald 4)
Living Playing Cards. *See* Cartes vivants, 1905
Living Portrait. *See* Ikiteiru gazo, 1948
Living Stream. *See* Horn i norr, 1950
Liykken draeber, 1914 (Holger-Madsen 2)
Liza. *See* Cagna, 1972
Liza and Her Double. *See* I Liza kai i alli, 1961
Lizard with a Woman's Skin. *See* Una lucertola con la pelle di donna, 1971
Lizards. *See* Basilischi, 1963
Lizzie, 1957 (Blondell 3)
Lizzie and the Iceman, 1910 (White 3)
Lizzies of the Field, 1924 (Sennett 2)
Ljusnande framtid, 1940 (Molander 2, Jaenzon 4)
Llano Kid, 1939 (Harlan 4, Head 4, Young 4)
Llanto de la tortuga, 1974 (Figueroa 4)
Llanto por un bandido, 1964 (Saura 2)
Llevame en tus brazos, 1953 (Figueroa 4)
Lloyds of London, 1936 (King 2, Carroll 3, Power 3, Sanders 3, Glennon 4, MacGowan 4, Zanuck 4)
LMNO, 1978 (Breer 4)
Lo otra, 1946 (Del Rio 3)
Lo que el viento se llevó, 1980 (Alvarez 2)
Lo que importa es vivir, 1989 (Alcoriza 4)
Lo vedi come . . . lo vedi come sei?!, 1939 (Fellini 2)
Loaded Door, 1922 (Johnson 3, Polito 4)
Loaded Pistols, 1949 (Autry 3)
Loaf. *See* Sousto, 1960
Loaf of Bread. *See* Sousto, 1960
Loafer, 1912 (Anderson 3)
Loafer's Mother, 1912 (Anderson 3)
Loan Shark, 1952 (Raft 3, Biroc 4)
Loan Shark King, 1914 (Talmadge 3)
Lobster Man from Mars, 1989 (Curtis 3)
Local Boy Makes Good, 1931 (Brown 3, Polito 4)
Local Color, 1913 (Mix 3)
Local Color, 1916 (Mix 3)
Local Hero, 1983 (Forsyth 2, Lancaster 3, Menges 4, Puttnam 4)
Local Romance. *See* Zižkovská romance, 1957
Locandiera, 1943 (Cervi 3)
Locataire, 1976 (Adjani 3, Douglas 3, Winters 3, Nykvist 4, Sarde 4)
Locataire diabolique, 1910 (Méliès 2)
Locataires d'à côté, 1909 (Cohl 4)
Locations. *See* Schauplätze, 1967
Lock, Stock, and Barrel, 1971 (Meredith 3)
Lock Up, 1989 (Stallone 3, Sutherland 3)
Lock Up Your Daughters, 1969 (York 3)
Lock Your Doors. *See* Ape Man, 1943

Locked Door, 1929 (Goddard 3, Stanwyck 3, Menzies 4, Sullivan 4)
Locked Heart, 1918 (King 2)
Locked House, 1914 (Bunny 3)
Locked Out, 1910 (White 3)
Locket, 1911 (Dwan 2)
Locket, 1913 (Bunny 3)
Locket, 1946 (Mitchum 3, D'Agostino 4, Musuraca 4)
Lockfågeln, 1971 (Björnstrand 3)
Lockspitzel Asew, 1935 (Rasp 3, Tschechowa 3)
Lockvogel. *See* Miroir aux alouettes, 1934
Loco Boy Makes Good, 1942 (Three Stooges 3, Bruckman 4)
Loco Luck, 1927 (Wray 3)
Locomotives, 1935 (Jennings 2)
Locura de amor, 1948 (Rey 3)
Locus, 1961 (Kuri 4)
Locusts, 1974 (Johnson 3)
Lodge Night, 1923 (Roach 4)
Lodger, 1926 (Hitchcock 2, Novello 3, Balcon 4)
Lodger, 1932 (Hawkins 3, Novello 3)
Lodger, 1944 (Oberon 3, Sanders 3, Ballard 4, Basevi 4, Friedhofer 4)
Lodger: A Story of the London Fog. *See* Lodger, 1926
Lodging for the Night, 1912 (Griffith 2, Pickford 3, Bitzer 4)
Loffe blir polis, 1950 (Nykvist 4)
Log kya kahenge, 1983 (Azmi 3)
Log of the Black Pearl, 1974 (Bellamy 3)
Log Rollers, 1953 (Terry 4)
Loga de la casa, 1950 (Armendáriz 3)
Logan's Run, 1976 (Ustinov 3, Goldsmith 4, Laszlo 4)
Logik des Gefühls, 1982 (Ganz 3, Vogler 3)
Lohengrin, 1907 (Porten 3, Messter 4)
Lohengrin, 1936 (De Sica 2)
Loi, 1958 (Lollobrigida 3)
Loi. *See* Legge, 1959
Loi . . . c'est la loi, 1958 (Fernandel 3, Age and Scarpelli 4, Cristaldi 4, Di Venanzo 4, Rota 4)
Loi des hommes, 1962 (Arletty 3, Dalio 3, Presle 3)
Loi des rues, 1956 (Manès 3, Trintignant 3)
Loi du 21 juin 1907, 1942 (Arletty 3)
Loi du nord, 1942 (Feyder 2, Morgan 3, Vanel 3, D'Eaubonne 4)
Loi du pardon, 1906 (Pathé 4)
Loi du printemps, 1942 (Matras 4)
Loin de Manhattan, 1980 (Branco 4)
Loin du Viêt-nam, 1967 (Guerra 2, Varda 2, Cloquet 4)
Löjen och tårar, 1913 (Sjöström 2, Jaenzon 4, Magnusson 4)
Löjtnantshjärtan, 1941 (Jaenzon 4)
Lola. *See* **Lola Montès, 1955**
Lola, 1961 (Demy 2, Aimée 3, Coutard 4, De Beauregard 4, Evein 4, Legrand 4, Ponti 4)
Lola. *See* Twinky, 1969
Lola, 1981 (Fassbinder 2, Mueller-Stahl 3)
Lola la trailera, 1983 (Fernández 2)
Lola Montès, 1955 (Ophuls 2, Ustinov 3, Walbrook 3, Werner 3, Annenkov 4, Auric 4, D'Eaubonne 4, Matras 4)
Lola Montez, 1919 (Albers 3)
Lola, the Rat, 1914 (Costello 3)
Lola Triana, 1936 (Clothier 4)
Lolas de Lola, 1976 (Léaud 3)
Lolita, 1962 (Kubrick 2, Mason 3, Sellers 3, Winters 3, Morris 4)

Lolly Madonna XXX. *See* Lolly-Madonna War, 1973
Lolly-Madonna War, 1973 (Bridges 3, Ryan 3, Steiger 3)
Lomelin, 1965 (Braunberger 4)
Lon of the Lone Mountain, 1915 (Chaney 3)
London, 1927 (Wilcox 2)
London after Midnight, 1927 (Browning 2, Chaney 3, Walthall 3, Gibbons 4, Gillespie 4, Mayer 4, Young 4)
London Belongs to Me, 1948 (Launder and Gilliat 2, Attenborough 3, Sim 3, Rank 4)
London Black-Out Murders, 1942 (Siodmak 4)
London Bobby, 1920 (Roach 4)
London Calling. *See* Hello London, 1958
London Can Take It, 1940 (Jennings 2, Watt 2, Dalrymple 4)
London Entertains, 1951 (Sellers 3)
London Melody, 1937 (Wilcox 2, Neagle 3)
London Moods, 1961 (Russell 2)
London Nobody Knows, 1967 (Mason 3)
London Scrapbook, 1942 (Love 3)
London Town, 1946 (Kendall 3, Orry-Kelly 4, Rank 4)
London University, 1961 (Lassally 4)
Londoners, 1939 (Grierson 2, Wright 2)
Londra chiama Polo Nord, 1957 (Rota 4)
Lone Chance, 1924 (Gilbert 3)
Lone Cowboy, 1915 (Walsh 2)
Lone Cowboy, 1934 (Cooper 3)
Lone Hand, 1922 (Eason 4, Miller 4)
Lone Hand, 1953 (McCrea 3)
Lone Hand Saunders, 1926 (Eason 4)
Lone Ranger, 1938 (Canutt 4)
Lone Ranger Rides Again, 1939 (Canutt 4)
Lone Rider, 1930 (McCord 4)
Lone Star, 1927 (Wyler 2)
Lone Star, 1952 (Barrymore 3, Bondi 3, Crawford 3, Gable 3, Gardner 3, Chase 4, Estabrook 4, Rosson 4)
Lone Star Ranger, 1923 (Mix 3)
Lone Star Ranger, 1930 (Miller 4)
Lone Star Ranger, 1942 (Day 4)
Lone Star Trail, 1943 (Mitchum 3, Salter 4)
Lone Stranger and Porky, 1939 (Blanc 4, Clampett 4, Stalling 4)
Lone Wolf, 1917 (Brenon 2, Hunt 4)
Lone Wolf in Paris, 1938 (Ballard 4)
Lone Wolf Returns, 1935 (Douglas 3)
Lone Wolf Spy Hunt, 1939 (Hayworth 3, Lupino 3)
Lone Wolf Strikes, 1940 (Trumbo 4)
Lone Wolf's Daughter. *See* Lone Wolf Spy Hunt, 1939
Lone World Sail, 1989 (Halas and Batchelor 4)
Lonedale Operator, 1911 (Griffith 2, Sweet 3, Bitzer 4)
Loneliness of Neglect, 1911 (Dwan 2)
Loneliness of the Long-Distance Runner, 1962 (Richardson 2, Redgrave 3, Addison 4, Lassally 4)
Lonely Are the Brave, 1962 (Douglas 3, Matthau 3, Rowlands 3, Goldsmith 4, Trumbo 4, Westmore Family 4)
Lonely Boat, 195? (Leacock 2)
Lonely Guy, 1984 (Martin 3, Goldsmith 4, Reynolds 4, Whitlock 4)
Lonely Lane. *See* Horoki, 1962
Lonely Man, 1957 (Palance 3, Perkins 3, Van Cleef 3, Head 4)
Lonely Man. *See* Samac, 1958

Lonely Man. *See* Five Bloody Graves, 1970
Lonely Night, 1951 (Leacock 2)
Lonely Passion of Judith Hearne, 1987 (Clayton 2, Hoskins 3, Smith 3, Delerue 4)
Lonely Princess, 1913 (Costello 3)
Lonely Profession, 1969 (Cotten 3)
Lonely Range, 1911 (Dwan 2)
Lonely Road, 1923 (Schulberg 4)
Lonely Road, 1936 (Dean 4, Stallich 4)
Lonely Shore, 1964 (Russell 2)
Lonely Trail, 1936 (Wayne 3, Canutt 4)
Lonely Villa, 1909 (Griffith 2, Sennett 2, Pickford 3, Bitzer 4)
Lonely Wife. *See* **Charulata, 1964**
Lonely Wives, 1931 (Horton 3)
Lonely Woman. *See* **Viaggio in Italia, 1953**
Lonely Woman. *See* Roses rouges et piments verts, 1975
Lonelyhearts, 1958 (Clift 3, Loy 3, Ryan 3, Alton 4, Schary 4)
Loner. *See* Ruckus, 1980
Loners, 1972 (Grahame 3, Katzman 4)
Lonesome, 1928 (Laemmle 4)
Lonesome Cowboys, 1968 (Warhol 2)
Lonesome Dove, 1989 (Duvall 3)
Lonesome Junction, 1908 (Bitzer 4)
Lonesome Ladies, 1927 (Coffee 4, Polito 4)
Lonesome Lenny, 1946 (Avery 4)
Lonesome Luke series, 1916–17 (Daniels 3, Lloyd 3, Roach 4)
Lonesome Mouse, 1944 (Hanna and Barbera 4)
Lonesome Robert, 1912 (Bushman 3)
Lonesome Trail, 1914 (Mix 3)
Lonesome Trail, 1930 (Canutt 4)
Long Absence. *See* Aussi Longue Absence, 1961
Long Ago Tomorrow. *See* Raging Moon, 1971
Long and the Short and the Tall, 1961 (Harris 3, Harvey 3, Mankowitz 4)
Long Arm, 1956 (Hawkins 3, Balcon 4, Rank 4)
Long Arm of Mannister, 1919 (Walthall 3)
Long Blue Road. *See* Grande strada azzurra, 1957
Long Chance, 1922 (Walthall 3, Daniels 4)
Long Dark Hall, 1951 (Harrison 3, Johnson 4)
Long Day's Journey into Night, 1962 (Lumet 2, Hepburn 3, Richardson 3, Robards 3, Kaufman 4, Previn 4, Rosenblum 4, Sylbert 4)
Long Day's Journey Into Night, 1987 (Lemmon 3)
Long des trottoirs, 1956 (Rosay 3, D'Eaubonne 4, Kosma 4)
Long Distance Wireless Photography. *See* Photographie electrique à distance, 1908
Long Duel, 1967 (Brynner 3, Howard 3, Vetchinsky 4)
Long Good Friday, 1980 (Constantine 3, Hoskins 3)
Long Goodbye, 1973 (Altman 2, Rudolph 2, Gould 3, Hayden 3, Schwarzenegger 3, Brackett 4, Chandler 4, Mercer 4, Williams 4, Zsigmond 4)
Long Gray Line, 1955 (Ford 2, Bond 3, Crisp 3, O'Hara 3, Power 3, Cohn 4, Duning 4, Wald 4)
Long Haul, 1957 (Dors 3, Mature 3)

Long Hot Summer, 1958 (Ritt 2, Welles 2, Lansbury 3, Newman 3, Remick 3, Woodward 3, Cahn 4, Faulkner 4, La Shelle 4, LeMaire 4, North 4, Ravetch 4, Wald 4, Wheeler 4)
Long Hot Summer, 1985 (Gardner 3, Robards 3)
Long John Silver, 1955 (Newton 3, Haskin 4)
Long Knife, 1958 (Rank 4)
Long Lane's Turning, 1919 (Walthall 3)
Long Live the Deceased. *See* At žije nebožtik, 1935
Long Live the King, 1923 (Sullivan 4)
Long Live the King, 1926 (McCarey 2, Laurel and Hardy 3, Roach 4)
Long Live the Lady. *See* Lunga Vita alla Signora, 1987
Long, Long Trailer, 1954 (Ball 3, Berman 4, Deutsch 4, Goodrich 4, Rose 4, Surtees 4)
Long Lost Father, 1934 (Schoedsack 2, Barrymore 3, MacGowan 4, Musuraca 4, Plunkett 4, Polglase 4, Steiner 4)
Long Memory, 1952 (Hamer 2, Mills 3, Alwyn 4, Rank 4, Vetchinsky 4)
Long Night, 1947 (Litvak 2, Fonda 3, Price 3, D'Agostino 4, Hakim 4, Lourié 4, Polito 4, Tiomkin 4)
Long Pants, 1927 (Capra 2, Garnett 2, Langdon 3, Roach 4)
Long Portage, 1913 (Ince 4)
Long Ride Home. *See* Time for Killing, 1967
Long Riders, 1980 (Hill 2)
Long Road, 1911 (Griffith 2, Sweet 3, Bitzer 4)
Long Ships, 1964 (Homolka 3, Poitier 3, Widmark 3, Adam 4, Cardiff 4, Challis 4)
Long Shot, 1980 (Frears 2, York 3)
Long Trail, 1910 (Mix 3)
Long Trail, 1929 (Brennan 3)
Long Voyage Home, 1940 (Ford 2, Bond 3, Fitzgerald 3, Wayne 3, Basevi 4, Cooper 4, Nichols 4, Toland 4, Wanger 4)
Long Wait, 1954 (Saville 2, Coburn 3, Quinn 3, Leven 4, Planer 4)
Long Walk Home, 1990 (Goldberg 3, Spacek 3)
Longest Day, 1962 (Arletty 3, Barrault 3, Burton 3, Connery 3, Fonda 3, McDowall 3, Mineo 3, Mitchum 3, More 3, O'Brien 3, Rosay 3, Ryan 3, Steiger 3, Wagner 3, Wayne 3, Barsacq 4, Jarre 4, Korda 4, Zanuck 4)
Longest Hundred Miles, 1967 (Waxman 4)
Longest Night, 1936 (Young 3)
Longest Yard, 1974 (Reynolds 3, Biroc 4, Needham 4)
Long-Haired Hare, 1949 (Blanc 4, Jones 4, Maltese 4, Stalling 4)
Longshot, 1985 (Müller 4)
Longue Marche, 1966 (Astruc 2, Trintignant 3)
Longue Nuit, 1965 (Braunberger 4)
Look at Life, 1915 (Lucas 2)
Look at Liv, 1979 (Bergman 2, Andersson 3, Finch 3, Hackman 3, Ullmann 3, Von Sydow 3)
Look Away, 1987 (Burstyn 3)
Look Back in Anger, 1959 (Richardson 2, Bloom 3, Burton 3, Evans 3, Pleasence 3, Addison 4, Morris 4)
Look Before You Love, 1948 (Lockwood 3)
Look for the Silver Lining, 1949 (Prinz 4)

Look Out!. *See* Drahoušek Klementýna, 1959
Look Out Below, 1918 (Daniels 3, Lloyd 3, Roach 4)
Look Pleasant Please, 1918 (Daniels 3, Lloyd 3, Roach 4)
Look Up and Laugh, 1935 (Fields 3, Leigh 3, More 3, Dean 4)
Look What's Happened to Rosemary's Baby, 1976 (Crawford 3, Gordon 3, Milland 3)
Look Who's Laughing, 1941 (Dwan 2, Ball 3, Polglase 4)
Look Who's Talking, 1989 (Segal 3, Travolta 3)
Look Who's Talking Too, 1990 (Pryor 3, Travolta 3)
Look Your Best, 1923 (Moore 3, Gibbons 4)
Looker, 1981 (Coburn 3, Finney 3)
Lookin' to Get Out, 1982 (Ashby 2, Voight 3, Wexler 4)
Looking at the Bright Side, 1932 (Dean 4)
Looking for His Murderer. *See* Mann, der seinen Mörder sucht, 1931
Looking for Love, 1964 (Cahn 4, Krasner 4, Pasternak 4)
Looking for Mr. Goodbar, 1977 (Brooks 2, Gere 3, Keaton 3, Weld 3, Fraker 4)
Looking for Mushrooms, 1958 (Conner 2)
Looking for Sally, 1925 (McCarey 2, Roach 4)
Looking for Trouble, 1914 (Beery 3)
Looking for Trouble, 1920 (Roach 4)
Looking for Trouble, 1934 (Wellman 2, Tracy 3, Day 4, Newman 4, Zanuck 4)
Looking Forward, 1933 (Brown 2, Barrymore 3, Adrian 4, Meredyth 4)
Looking Glass War, 1969 (Hopkins 3, Richardson 3, Box 4)
Looking Good. *See* Corky, 1972
Looking on the Bright Side, 1932 (Fields 3)
Looks and Smiles, 1981 (Loach 2, Menges 4)
Looney Looney Looney Bugs Bunny Movie, 1981 (Freleng 4)
Loop, 1986 (Brakhage 2)
Loophole, 1954 (Malone 3)
Loophole, 1980 (Finney 3, Sheen 3, York 3, Schifrin 4)
Looping, 1981 (Winters 3, Ballhaus 4)
Looping the Loop, 1928 (Krauss 3, Manès 3, Herlth 4, Hoffmann 4, Röhrig 4)
Loops, 1939 (McLaren 4)
Loopy's Hare-Do, 1961 (Hanna and Barbera 4)
Loose Ankles, 1930 (Young 3)
Loose Cannons, 1989 (Hackman 3)
Loose Change, 1921 (Roach 4)
Loose Ends, 1930 (Cardiff 4)
Loose Loot, 1953 (Three Stooges 3)
Loose Tightwad, 1923 (Roach 4)
Loot, 1970 (Attenborough 3, Remick 3)
Loot Maar, 1980 (Anand 3)
Looters. *See* Estouffade à la Carabei, 1967
Lord am Alexander-Platz, 1967 (Mueller-Stahl 3)
Lord Babs, 1932 (Launder and Gilliat 2, Balcon 4)
Lord Byron, 1922 (Veidt 3)
Lord Byron of Broadway, 1930 (Brown 4, Freed 4, Gibbons 4, Shearer 4, Tiomkin 4)
Lord Camber's Ladies, 1932 (Hitchcock 2)
Lord Chumley, 1914 (Gish 3, Loos 4)

Lord Feathertop, 1908 (Porter 2)

Lord for a Night. *See* Aru yo no tonosama, 1946

Lord Jeff, 1938 (Wood 2, Coburn 3, Rooney 3, Gibbons 4, Seitz 4)

Lord Jim, 1925 (Fleming 2)

Lord Jim, 1965 (Brooks 2, Itami 2, Hawkins 3, Lukas 3, Mason 3, O'Toole 3, Wallach 3, Kaper 4, Mathieson 4, Young 4)

Lord Love a Duck, 1966 (Gordon 3, McDowall 3, Weld 3, Axelrod 4)

Lord of the Flies, 1990 (Allen 4, Sarde 4)

Lord of the Rings, 1978 (Hurt 3, Bakshi 4, Rosenman 4)

Lord Richard in the Pantry, 1930 (Launder and Gilliat 2)

Lords of Flatbush, 1974 (Stallone 3)

Lords of Little Egypt, 1961 (Zetterling 2)

Lorelei, 1931 (Terry 4)

Lorenzaccio, 1977 (Jarre 4)

Lorenzo il Magnifico, 1911 (Bertini 3)

Lorgnon accusateur, 1905 (Guy 2)

Lorie, 1984 (Azmi 3)

Lorna Doone, 1922 (Tourneur 2, Ince 4)

Lorna Doone, 1935 (Lockwood 3, Dean 4)

Lorna Doone, 1951 (Duning 4)

Lorraine of the Lions, 1925 (Miller 4)

Los Angeles Harbour, 1913 (Sennett 2)

Lose No Time, 1921 (Roach 4)

Loser Takes All, 1956 (Brazzi 3, Greene 4, Périnal 4)

Loser Takes All, 1990 (Greene 4)

Losin' It, 1983 (Cruise 3)

Losing Fight, 1914 (Mix 3)

Losing Game. *See* Pay Off, 1930

Loss of Innocence. *See* Greengage Summer, 1961

Lost, 1955 (Green 4, Rank 4)

Lost a Cook, 1917 (Sennett 2)

Lost—A Wife, 1925 (Menjou 3)

Lost and Found, 1979 (Jackson 3, Segal 3, Frank 4, Slocombe 4)

Lost and Found on a South Sea Island, 1923 (Walsh 2, Wilson 4)

Lost and Foundling, 1944 (Blanc 4, Jones 4)

Lost and Foundry, 1937 (Fleischer 4)

Lost and Won, 1916 (De Mille 2)

Lost Angel, 1943 (Gardner 3, O'Brien 3 Irene 4, Lennart 4, Schary 4, Surtees 4)

Lost Angels, 1990 (Sutherland 3, Sarde 4)

Lost Art of Minding One's Business, 1913 (Griffith 2)

Lost Boundaries, 1949 (De Rochemont 4)

Lost Bridegroom, 1916 (Barrymore 3)

Lost Canyon, 1942 (Harlan 4)

Lost Child, 1904 (Bitzer 4)

Lost Child. *See* Munna, 1954

Lost Chord, 1933 (Hawkins 3)

Lost Combination, 1913 (Cruze 2)

Lost Command, 1966 (Cardinale 3, Delon 3, Morgan 3, Quinn 3, Segal 3, Surtees 4, Waxman 4)

Lost Continent, 1968 (Carreras 4)

Lost Dog, 1924 (Roach 4)

Lost Empire, 1929 (Cooper 4)

Lost Empires, 1986 (Olivier 3)

Lost Face. *See* Ztracená tvář, 1965

Lost Honor of Katharina Blum. *See* **Verlorene Ehre der Katharina Blum, 1975**

Lost Horizon, 1937 (Capra 2, Colman 3, Horton 3, Jaffe 3, Cohn 4, Riskin 4, Tiomkin 4, Walker 4, Westmore Family 4)

Lost Horizon, 1972 (Finch 3, Gielgud 3, Boyer 3, Ullmann 3, Ames 4, Hunter 4, Pan 4, Surtees 4)

Lost Hours, 1952 (Korda 4)

Lost House, 1915 (Gish 3, Reid 3, Loos 4)

Lost Illusion. *See* Fallen Idol, 1948

Lost Illusions, 1911 (Porter 2)

Lost in a Harem, 1944 (Abbott and Costello 3)

Lost in Alaska, 1952 (Abbott and Costello 3, Boyle 4)

Lost in America, 1985 (Jones 4)

Lost in the Alps, 1907 (Porter 2)

Lost in the Arctic, 1911 (Mix 3)

Lost in the Garden of the World, 1975 (Hoffman 3)

Lost in the Jungle, 1911 (Mix 3, Selig 4)

Lost in the Stars, 1974 (North 4)

Lost in the Stratosphere, 1934 (McDaniel 3)

Lost in Transit, 1917 (Crisp 3)

Lost Jools. *See* Stolen Jools, 1931

Lost Jungle, 1934 (Rooney 3, Canutt 4)

Lost Kingdom. *See* Antinea, 1961

Lost Lady, 1934 (Johnson 3, Stanwyck 3, Orry-Kelly 4)

Lost Man, 1969 (Poitier 3, Head 4, Jones 4)

Lost Moment, 1947 (Hayward 3, Moorehead 3, Banton 4, Mohr 4, Wanger 4)

Lost Necklace, 1910 (White 3)

Lost on the Western Front. *See* Romance of Flanders, 1937

Lost One. *See* Verlorene, 1964

Lost Patrol, 1934 (Ford 2, Karloff 3, McLaglen 3, Cooper 4, Fort 4, Nichols 4, Polglase 4, Steiner 4)

Lost People, 1949 (Zetterling 2, Attenborough 3, Lom 3, Box 4, Rank 4)

Lost Planet, 1953 (Katzman 4)

Lost Sentry. *See* Ztracená varta, 1956

Lost Sermon, 1914 (Eason 4)

Lost Shadow. *See* Verlorene Schatten, 1921

Lost Son, 1974 (Reiniger 4)

Lost Soul. *See* Anima persa, 1976

Lost Squadron, 1932 (Von Stroheim 2, Astor 3, Cronjager 4, Mankiewicz 4, Selznick 4, Steiner 4)

Lost Trail. *See* Ztracená stopa, 1956

Lost Treasure, 1914 (Eason 4)

Lost Tribe, 1949 (Weissmuller 3, Katzman 4)

Lost Volcano, 1950 (Mirisch 4)

Lost Weekend, 1945 (Wilder 2, Milland 3, Wyman 3, Brackett 4, Dreier 4, Edouart 4, Head 4, Rozsa 4, Seitz 4)

Lost World, 1925 (Beery 3, Love 3, Edeson 4, O'Brien 4, Westmore Family 4)

Lost World, 1960 (Rains 3, Bennett 4, Hoch 4, O'Brien 4)

Lost World of Sinbad. *See* Daitozuku, 1964

Lost Years, 1911 (Bushman 3)

Lost Youth. *See* Gioventù perduta, 1947

Lotna, 1959 (Polanski 2)

Lotta dell'uomo per la sua sopravvivenza, 1967 (Rossellini 2)

Lotte, 1928 (Porten 3)

Lotte Lenya Sings Kurt Weill, 1962 (Russell 2)

Lotte nell'ombra, 1939 (Amidei 4)

Lottekens Feldzug, 1915 (Wiene 2)

Lottery Bride, 1930 (Brown 3, MacDonald 3, Menzies 4, Schenck 4)

Lottery Lover, 1935 (Wilder 2, Ayres 3, Glennon 4)

Lottery Man, 1919 (Cruze 2, Reid 3)

Lotus Eater, 1921 (Neilan 2, Barrymore 3, Moore 3)

Loud Soup, 1929 (Roach 4)

Loud Visual Noises, 1987 (Brakhage 2)

Loudest Whisper. *See* These Three, 1936

Loudest Whisper. *See* Children's Hour, 1961

Louis Capet, 1954 (Leenhardt 2)

Louis Lecoin, 1966 (Delerue 4)

Louis Lumière. *See* Lumière et l'invention du cinématographe, 1953

Louis Lumière, 1964 (Rohmer 2)

Louisa, 1950 (Coburn 3, Reagan 3, Boyle 4)

Louise, 1939 (Gance 2, Courant 4, Wakhévitch 4)

Louise de Lavallière, 1921 (Freund 4)

Louisiana Hayride, 1944 (Hunter 4)

Louisiana Purchase, 1941 (Hope 3, Dreier 4, Ryskind 4, Berlin 4)

Louisiana Story, 1948 (Flaherty 2, Leacock 2, Rosenblum 4, Thomson 4, Van Dongen 4)

Loulou, 1980 (Pialat 2, Depardieu 3, Huppert 3)

Loup des Malveneur, 1943 (L'Herbier 2)

Loup et l'agneau, 1953 (Kosma 4)

Loupežníci na Chlumu, 1927 (Heller 4)

Loups chassent la nuit, 1951 (Kosma 4)

Loups entre eux, 1936 (Berry 3, Spaak 4)

Lourdes, 1958 (Russell 2)

Lourdes, 1965 (Braunberger 4)

Lourdes et ses miracles, 1954 (Demy 2)

Louve solitaire, 1967 (Lai 4)

Louves, 1957 (Moreau 3, Presle 3, Kosma 4)

Louvre Come Back to Me, 1962 (Blanc 4, Jones 4)

Louvre Museum. *See* Musée du Louvre, 1979

Lovable Cheat, 1949 (Leven 4)

Love, 1919 (Arbuckle 3)

Love, 1927 (Tourneur 2, Barrymore 3, Garbo 3, Adrian 4, Daniels 4, Gilbert 4, Gibbons 4, Marion 4, Mayer 4)

Love, 1931 (Dieterle 2)

Love. *See* Kärlek, 1952

Love. *See* Liebe, 1956

Love, 1959 (Anand 3)

Love, 1961 (Kuri 4)

Love. *See* Karlekan, 1980

Love, 1982 (Zetterling 2, Ullmann 3)

Love à la Carte. *See* Adua e le compagne, 1960

Love Affair, 1932 (Bogart 3, Cohn 4)

Love Affair, 1939 (Daves 2, Dmytryk 2, McCarey 2, Boyer 3, Dunne 3, Berman 4, Maté 4, Polglase 4, Stewart 4)

Love Affair: The Eleanor and Lou Gehrig Story, 1978 (Neal 3)

Love Affair in Toyland. *See* Drame chez les fantoches, 1908

Love Affair of a Dictator. *See* Dictator, 1935

Love Affair of the Dictator. *See* Dictator, 1935

Love Aflame, 1980 (Johnson 3)

Love Among the Millionaires, 1930 (Bow 3, Mankiewicz 4)

Love Among the Roses, 1910 (Griffith 2, Pickford 3)

Love Among the Ruins, 1975 (Cukor 2, Hepburn 3, Olivier 3, Barry 4, Dillon 4, Slocombe 4)

Love Among Thieves, 1987 (Hepburn 3, Wagner 3)

Love and Anarchy. *See* **Film d'amore e d'anarchia, 1973**

Love and Bullets, 1914 (Sennett 2)

Love and Bullets, 1979 (Bronson 3, Steiger 3, Schifrin 4)

Love and Courage, 1913 (Sennett 2, Arbuckle 3)

Love and Curses, 1938 (Maltese 4)

Love and Death, 1975 (Allen 2, Keaton 3, Cloquet 4, Rosenblum 4)

Love and Death of Ogin. *See* Oginsawa, 1979

Love and Deficit. *See* Kärlek och kassabrist, 1932

Love and Doughnuts, 1922 (Sennett 2)

Love and Downhill Skiing. *See* Kärlek och störtlopp, 1946

Love and Duty, 1916 (Laurel and Hardy 3)

Love and Dynamite, 1914 (Sennett 2)

Love and Faith of Ogin. *See* Ogin Sama, 1982

Love and Fascination. *See* Bojo no hito, 1961

Love and Gasoline, 1914 (Sennett 2)

Love and Hisses, 1937 (Simon 3, MacGowan 4)

Love and Journalism. *See* Kärlek och journalistik, 1916

Love and Kisses, 1925 (Sennett 2)

Love and Larceny. *See* Mattatore, 1960

Love and Learn, 1928 (Mankiewicz 4)

Love and Learn, 1946 (Diamond 4, Steiner 4)

Love and Lemons, 1911 (Dwan 2)

Love and Lobsters. *See* He Did and He Didn't, 1916

Love and Lunch. *See* Mabel's Busy Day, 1914

Love and Marriage, 1970 (Godfrey 4)

Love and Money, 1982 (Kinski 3)

Love and Morocco. *See* Baroud, 1931

Love and Other Crimes. *See* Alex and the Gypsy, 1976

Love and Pain, 1913 (Sennett 2)

Love and Pain and the Whole Damn Thing, 1972 (Pakula 2, Smith 3, Sargent 4, Unsworth 4)

Love and Rubbish, 1913 (Sennett 2)

Love and Salt Water, 1914 (Sennett 2)

Love and Separation in Sri Lanka. *See* Suri Lanka no ai to wakare, 1976

Love and Soda, 1914 (Beery 3)

Love and the Devil, 1929 (Korda 2, Garmes 4, Korda 4)

Love and the Frenchwoman. *See* Française et l'amour, 1960

Love and the Journalist. *See* Kärlek och journalistik, 1916

Love and the Law, 1913 (Anderson 3, Reid 3)

Love and the Zeppelin. *See* Vzucholod a láska, 1946

Love and Trouble, 1915 (Beery 3)

Love As Disorder. *See* An Affair of the Skin, 1963

Love at First Bite, 1950 (Three Stooges 3)

Love at First Flight, 1928 (Hornbeck 4)

Love at First Sight, 1928 (Sennett 2)

Love at Large, 1989 (Rudolph 2)

Love at Sea, 1936 (Havelock-Allan 4)

Love at the Top. *See* Mouton enragé, 1974

Love at Twenty. *See* Amour a vingt ans, 1962

Love Ban. *See* It's a 2′6″ Above the Ground World, 1972

Love Before Breakfast, 1936 (Lombard 3, Banton 4, D'Agostino 4, Waxman 4)

Love Begins at Twenty, 1936 (Barnes 4, Trumbo 4)

Love Birds, 1934 (Rooney 3, Mandell 4)

Love Brand, 1923 (Laemmle 4)

Love Bug, 1925 (Roach 4)

Love Bug, 1969 (Stevenson 2, Ellenshaw 4)

Love Bugs, 1917 (Laurel and Hardy 3)

Love Burglar, 1919 (Cruze 2, Beery 3, Reid 3)

Love by the Light of the Moon, 1901 (Porter 2)

Love Cage. *See* Félins, 1964

Love Cage. *See* Félins, 1964

Love Circle. *See* Metti, una sera a cena, 1969

Love Comes Along, 1930 (Daniels 3, Hunt 4, Plunkett 4)

Love Comes to Magoo, 1958 (Bosustow 4)

Love Comet, 1916 (Sennett 2)

Love Contract, 1932 (Wilcox 2)

Love Crazy, 1941 (Loy 3, Powell 3, Berman 4, Gibbons 4, Lederer 4)

Love Defender, 1919 (Polito 4)

Love Detectives, 1934 (Grable 3)

Love Doctor, 1930 (Cronjager 4, Mankiewicz 4)

Love 'em and Feed 'em, 1927 (Laurel and Hardy 3, Bruckman 4, Roach 4)

Love 'em and Leave 'em, 1926 (Brooks 3, Banton 4)

Love 'em and Weep, 1927 (Laurel and Hardy 3, Roach 4)

Love Expert, 1920 (Emerson 4, Loos 4)

Love Express. *See* Renai tokkyu, 1954

Love Film. *See* Szerelmesfilm, 1970

Love Finds a Way, 1908 (Griffith 2, Bitzer 4)

Love Finds a Way. *See* Alias French Gertie, 1930

Love Finds Andy Hardy, 1938 (Garland 3, Rooney 3, Turner 3, Edens 4)

Love Flower, 1920 (Griffith 2, Barthelmess 3, Bitzer 4)

Love from a Stranger, 1937 (Rathbone 3, Marion 4)

Love from a Stranger, 1947 (Sidney 3, Gaudio 4, Salter 4)

Love Gambler, 1922 (Gilbert 3, August 4, Furthman 4)

Love Game. *See* Den kära leken, 1959

Love God?, 1969 (O'Brien 3)

Love Habit, 1931 (Lancaster 3)

Love Happy, 1949 (Tashlin 2, Marx Brothers 3, Monroe 3)

Love Has Many Faces, 1965 (Robertson 3, Turner 3, Head 4, Raksin 4, Ruttenberg 4)

Love Heeds Not the Showers, 1911 (Pickford 3)

Love, Honor, and Behave, 1920 (Sennett 2)

Love, Honor, and Behave, 1938 (Barnes 4, Buckner 4, Wallis 4)

Love, Honor, and Goodbye, 1945 (Alton 4)

Love, Honor, and Oh Baby!, 1933 (Krasna 4)

Love, Honor, and Oh Baby!, 1940 (Cortez 4, Salter 4)

Love Hour, 1925 (Meredyth 4)

Love in a Bungalow, 1937 (Beavers 3, Krasner 4)

Love in a Cottage, 1940 (Terry 4)

Love in a Goldfish Bowl, 1961 (Head 4)

Love in a Hammock, 1901 (Porter 2)

Love in a Police Station, 1927 (Sennett 2)

Love in a Teacup. *See* Himawari-musume, 1953

Love in an Apartment Hotel, 1912 (Griffith 2, Barrymore 3, Carey 3, Marsh 3, Sweet 3, Walthall 3, Bitzer 4)

Love in Armor, 1915 (Sennett 2, Arbuckle 3)

Love in Bloom, 1935 (Glazer 4)

Love in Germany. *See* Amour en Allemagne, 1983

Love in Germany. *See* Liebe in Deutschland, 1985

Love in Goa, 1983 (Abbas 4)

Love in Las Vegas. *See* Viva Las Vegas, 1963

Love in Morocco. *See* Baroud, 1931

Love in Rome. *See* Amore a Roma, 1960

Love in Stunt Flying. *See* Liebe in Gleitflug, 1938

Love in the Afternoon, 1957 (Wilder 2, Chevalier 3, Cooper 3, Hepburn 3, Diamond 4, Mercer 4, Trauner 4, Waxman 4)

Love in the City. *See* Amore in città, 1953

Love in the Desert, 1929 (Plunkett 4)

Love in the Hills, 1911 (Griffith 2, Sweet 3, Bitzer 4)

Love in the Rough, 1930 (Montgomery 3, Gibbons 4)

Love in the Suburbs, 1900 (Bitzer 4)

Love in the Tropics. *See* Tropisk Kaerlighed, 1911

Love in the West. *See* Hell-to-Pay Austin, 1916

Love in Waiting, 1938 (Rank 4)

Love Insurance, 1919 (Crisp 3)

Love Is a Ball, 1963 (Boyer 3, Ford 3, D'Eaubonne 4, Legrand 4)

Love Is a Funny Thing. *See* Homme qui me plaît, 1969

Love Is a Headache, 1938 (Rooney 3, Adrian 4, Seitz 4)

Love Is a Many-Splendored Thing, 1955 (King 2, Holden 3, Jones 3, LeMaire 4, Newman 4, Reynolds 4, Shamroy 4, Wheeler 4)

Love Is a Racket, 1932 (Wellman 2, Raft 3)

Love Is Better Than Ever, 1952 (Taylor 3, Rose 4, Rosson 4)

Love Is Blind, 1909 (Porter 2)

Love Is Blind, 1913 (Dwan 2)

Love Is Blind. *See* Liebe macht Blind, 1925

Love Is Colder Than Death. *See* Liebe ist kalter als der Tod, 1969

Love Is Everything, 1920 (Haller 4)

Love Is in the Air, 1937 (Reagan 3)

Love Is My Profession. *See* Cas de malheur, 1958

Love Is News, 1937 (Garnett 2, Ameche 3, Darwell 3, Power 3, Sanders 3, Young 3)

Love, Laughs, and Lather, 1917 (Daniels 3, Lloyd 3, Roach 4)

Love Laughs at Andy Hardy, 1946 (Rooney 3, Irene 4)

Love Laughs at Locksmiths, 1908 (Lawrence 3)

Love Leads the Way, 1984 (Neal 3, Saint 3)

Love Lesson, 1921 (Roach 4)

Love Letters. *See* Liebesnächte, 1929

Love Letters, 1945 (Dieterle 2, Cotten 3, Jones 3, Dreier 4, Garmes 4, Head 4, Wallis 4, Young 4)

Love Letters, 1984 (Corman 2, Curtis 3)

Love Letters of a Star, 1936 (Krasner 4)

Lovers of Teruel. *See* Amants de Teruel, 1962

Lovers of Toledo. *See* Amants de Tolede, 1953

Lovers of Verona. *See* Amants de Vérone, 1948

Lovers on a Tightrope. *See* Corde raide, 1960

Lovers' Post Office, 1914 (Sennett 2, Arbuckle 3, Normand 3)

Lover's Return. *See* Revenant, 1946

Lovers Three, 1910 (White 3)

Love's A-Poppin', 1953 (Bruckman 4)

Love's Blindness, 1926 (Basevi 4, Gibbons 4)

Love's Command. *See* Liebeskommando, 1931

Love's Crucible. *See* Vem dömer, 1922

Love's Detour, 1924 (Roach 4)

Love's Devotee. *See* Elskovsleg, 1913

Love's False Faces, 1919 (Sennett 2)

Love's Family Tree. *See* Aijo no keifu, 1961

Love's Greatest Mistake, 1927 (Powell 3)

Love's Intrigue, 1924 (Sennett 2)

Love's Labor Won, 1947 (Terry 4)

Love's Languid Lure, 1927 (Sennett 2)

Love's Last Laugh, 1926 (Sennett 2)

Love's Miracle, 1912 (Cruze 2)

Loves of a Blonde. *See* Lásky jedné plavovlásky, 1965

Loves of a Dictator. *See* Dictator, 1935

Loves of a Pharaoh. *See* Weib des Pharao, 1922

Loves of an Actress, 1928 (Lukas 3, Negri 3, Vajda 4)

Loves of an Old Criminal. *See* Kilenky starého kriminálníka, 1927

Loves of Ariane. *See* Ariane, 1931

Loves of Carmen, 1927 (Walsh 2, Del Rio 3, McLaglen 3)

Loves of Carmen, 1948 (Vidor 2, Ford 3, Hayworth 3)

Loves of Colette. *See* Vie en rose, 1948

Loves of Edgar Allan Poe, 1942 (Darnell 3, Darwell 3, Day 4, Hoffenstein 4)

Loves of Hercules. *See* Amori di Ercole, 1960

Loves of Isadora. *See* Isadora, 1968

Loves of Joanna Godden, 1947 (Hamer 2, Rafferty 3, Withers 3, Balcon 4, Slocombe 4)

Loves of Kacenky Strnadova. *See* Lásky Kačenky Strnadové, 1926

Loves of Madame Du Barry. *See* I Give My Heart, 1936

Loves of Omar Khayyam. *See* Omar Khayyam, 1957

Loves of Ondine, 1967 (Warhol 2)

Loves of Pharoah. *See* Weib des Pharao, 1922

Loves of Robert Burns, 1930 (Wilcox 2)

Loves of Three Queens. *See* Eterna femmina, 1954

Loves of Zero, 1927 (Florey 2, Menzies 4)

Love's Old Dream, 1914 (Bunny 3)

Love's Option, 1928 (Dickinson 2, Pearson 2)

Love's Outcast, 1921 (Sennett 2)

Love's Quarantine, 1913 (Bunny 3)

Love's Redemption, 1921 (Talmadge 3, Hunt 4, Schenck 4)

Love's Renunciation, 1910 (White 3)

Love's Reward, 1924 (Roach 4)

Love's Sacrifice, 1914 (Ince 4)

Love's Savage Fury, 1979 (Addison 4)

Love's Stratagem, 1909 (Lawrence 3)

Love's Sweet Piffle, 1924 (Sennett 2)

Love's Western Flight, 1914 (Reid 3)

Love's Young Scream, 1919 (Roach 4)

Lovesick, 1937 (Lantz 4)

Lovesick, 1983 (Huston 2, Guinness 3, Moore 3, Sarde 4)

Lovesick Maidens of Cuddleton, 1912 (Bunny 3, Talmadge 3)

Lovey Dovey, 1923 (Roach 4)

Lovey Mary, 1926 (Gibbons 4, Gillespie 4)

Lovin' Molly, 1974 (Lumet 2, Perkins 3, Sarandon 3)

Lovin' the Ladies, 1930 (Cronjager 4)

Loving, 1957 (Brakhage 2)

Loving, 1970 (Hayden 3, Saint 3, Scheider 3, Segal 3, Willis 4)

Loving Couples. *See* Alskande par, 1964

Loving Couples, 1980 (Coburn 3, MacLaine 3, Sarandon 3)

Loving in the Rain. *See* Amour de pluie, 1974

Loving Lies, 1924 (Van Dyke 2)

Loving Memory, 1970 (Menges 4)

Loving You, 1957 (Presley 3, Head 4, Lang 4, Wallis 4)

Low Finance, 1980 (Halas and Batchelor 4)

Lowat el Hub, 1960 (Sharif 3)

Lower Depth. *See* Donzoko, 1957

Lower Depths. *See* Bas-fonds, 1936

Lower Depths. *See* Donzoko, 1957

Lower the Boom, 1949 (Fleischer 4)

Lower the River, 1968 (Terry-Thomas 3)

Low-Rank Soldiers. *See* Zouhei monogatari, 1963

Loyal 47 Ronin. *See* Chushingura, 1932

Loyal 47 Ronin. *See* Genroku chushingura, 1941

Loyal 47 Ronin. *See* Chushingura, 1962

Loyalties, 1933 (Dickinson 2, Rathbone 3, Dean 4)

Loyalty of Sylvia, 1912 (Costello 3)

L-Shaped Room, 1962 (Attenborough 3, Caron 3, Barry 4, Mathieson 4, Slocombe 4)

Luanda ya no es de San Pablo, 1976 (Alvarez 2)

Luce nelle tenebre, 1941 (Valli 3)

Lucerna, 1925 (Heller 4, Ondra 3)

Lucertola con la pelle di donna, 1971 (Baker 3, Morricone 4)

Lucette, 1924 (Feuillade 2)

Luch smerti, 1925 (Golovnya 4)

Luci del varietà, 1950 (Fellini 2, Flaiano 4, Masina 3, Pinelli 4)

Lucia, 1968 (Solas 2, Herrera 4)

Lucia di Lammermoor, 1946 (Lollobrigida 3)

Luciano Serra, pilota, 1938 (Rossellini 2)

Lucien chez les barbares, 1981 (Moreau 3)

Lucien Leuwen, 1973 (Autant-Lara 2)

Lucifer Rising, 1974 (Anger 2)

Lucifer Rising, 1980 (Anger 2)

Lucille, 1912 (Cruze 2)

Lucille Love, the Girl of Mystery, 1914 (Ford 2)

Lucio Flavio, 1978 (Babenco 2)

Luck, 1930 (Rooney 3)

Luck o' the Foolish, 1924 (Capra 2)

Luck of Ginger Coffey, 1964 (Shaw 3, Horner 4)

Luck of the Foolish, 1924 (Sennett 2)

Luck of the Foolish, 1980 (Langdon 3)

Luck of the Game. *See* Gridiron Flash, 1935

Luck of the Irish, 1920 (Dwan 2)

Luck of the Irish, 1948 (Baxter 3, Cobb 3, Power 3, Dunne 4, La Shelle 4, LeMaire 4)

Luck That Jealousy Brought, 1917 (Mix 3)

Luckiest Girl in the World, 1936 (Pangborn 3, Ryskind 4)

Lucky Beginners, 1935 (Roach 4)

Lucky Boy, 1929 (Jolson 3)

Lucky Card, 1911 (Anderson 3)

Lucky Cisco Kid, 1940 (Andrews 3)

Lucky Dan, 1922 (Howard 2)

Lucky Day. *See* Den stchastia, 1964

Lucky Days, 1935 (Havelock-Allan 4)

Lucky Deal, 1915 (Mix 3)

Lucky Devils, 1933 (Cooper 4, Hunt 4, Plunkett 4, Robinson 4, Steiner 4)

Lucky Devils, 1941 (Salter 4)

Lucky Dog, 1917 (Laurel and Hardy 3)

Lucky Duck, 1940 (Terry 4)

Lucky Ducky, 1948 (Avery 4)

Lucky Five. *See* Cinque poveri in automobile, 1952

Lucky Horseshoe, 1911 (Sennett 2)

Lucky Horseshoe, 1925 (Mix 3)

Lucky in Love, 1929 (Stradling 4)

Lucky Jim, 1909 (Griffith 2, Bitzer 4)

Lucky Jim, 1957 (Boulting 2, Terry-Thomas 3, Addison 4)

Lucky Jo, 1964 (Constantine 3, Delerue 4)

Lucky Joe, 1964 (Brasseur 3)

Lucky Jordan, 1942 (De Carlo 3, Deutsch 4, Dreier 4, Head 4, Ladd 3, Seitz 4)

Lucky Lady, 1926 (Walsh 2, Barrymore 3, Sherwood 4)

Lucky Lady, 1975 (Donen 2, Hackman 3, Minnelli 3, Reynolds 3, Unsworth 4)

Lucky Larkin, 1930 (Brown 4, McCord 4)

Lucky Leap, 1915 (Sennett 2)

Lucky Legs, 1942 (Edwards 2)

Lucky Luciano. *See* A proposito Lucky Luciano, 1973

Lucky Mascot, (Lom 3, Terry-Thomas 3, Adam 4)

Lucky Me, 1954 (Dalio 3, Day 3, Dickinson 3, Blanke 4)

Lucky Nick Cain, 1951 (Raft 3, Heller 4)

Lucky Night, 1939 (Loy 3, Taylor 3)

Lucky Number, 1921 (Roach 4)

Lucky Number, 1933 (Asquith 2, Balcon 4, Rank 4, Vetchinsky 4)

Lucky Number, 1961 (Biswas 4)

Lucky Partners, 1940 (Milestone 2, Colman 3, Rogers 3, Irene 4, Polglase 4, Tiomkin 4)

Lucky Pigs, 1970 (Le Grice 2)

Lucky Ravi, 1987 (Vogler 3)

Lucky Star, 1929 (Borzage 2, Gaynor 3, Levien 4)

Lucky Star, 1982 (Steiger 3)

Lucky Stars, 1925 (Capra 2, Sennett 2, Langdon 3)

Lucky Stiff, 1949 (Trevor 3, Laszlo 4, Lamour 3)

Lucky Stiff, 1988 (Perkins 3)

Lucky Street, 1980 (Halas and Batchelor 4)

Lucky Strike, 1915 (Laurel and Hardy 3)

Lucky Texan, 1934 (Wayne 3, Canutt 4)

Lucky to Be a Woman. *See* Fortuna di essere donna, 1955

Lucky Toothache, 1910 (Sennett 2, Pickford 3)

Lucky Transfer, 1915 (Browning 2)

Lucrèce, 1943 (Feuillère 3, Matras 4)

Lucrèce Borgia, 1935 (Gance 2, Artaud 3, Feuillère 3, Modot 3, Kaufman 4)

Lucrèce Borgia, 1952 (Armendáriz 3, Matras 4)

Lucretia Borgia. See Lucrèce Borgia, 1952

Lucretia Lombard, 1923 (Shearer 3)

Lucrezia Borgia, 1922 (Veidt 3, Freund 4)

Lucrezia Borgia. See Lucrèce Borgia, 1952

Lucy Gallant, 1955 (Ritter 3, Trevor 3, Heston 3, Wyman 3, Bumstead 4, Head 4)

Ludlow's Aeroplane, 1905 (Bitzer 4)

Ludo srce, 1959 (Mimica 4)

Ludwig, 1973 (Visconti 2, Howard 3, Mangano 3, Schneider 3, Cecchi D'Amico 4)

Ludwig: Twilight of the Gods. See Ludwig, 1973

Ludwig der Zweite, König von Bayern, 1930 (Dieterle 2)

Ludwig—Requiem for a Virgin King. See Ludwig—Requiem für einen jungfräulichen König, 1972

Ludwig—Requiem für einen jungfräulichen König, 1972 (Syberberg 2)

Ludwig II, 1954 (Kätner 2, Kinski 3, Heckroth 4, Slocombe 4)

Ludwig's Cook. See Theodor Hierneis oder: Wie man ehem. Hofkoch wird, 1972

Luffar-Petter, 1922 (Garbo 3)

Lüge, 1950 (Fröhlich 3)

Lui: Sny mimoletnye, 1941 (Volkov 2)

Lui per lei, 1971 (Ferreri 2, Morricone 4)

Luise, Königin von Preussen, 1931 (Gründgens 3, Porten 3)

Luise Millerin, 1922 (Dagover 3, Kortner 3, Krauss 3, Herlth 4, Pommer 4, Röhrig 4)

Luk královny Dorotky, povikovy, 1970 (Brejchová 3)

Luke series, 1916–17 (Daniels 3, Lloyd 3, Roach 4)

Lukrezia Borgia, 1922 (Dieterle 2, Wegener 3)

Lullaby. See Sin of Madelon Claudet, 1931

Lullaby. See Kolibel 'naya, 1937

Lullaby Bushu's Kite. See Komoriuta Bushu-dako, 1935

Lullaby of Broadway, 1951 (Day 3)

Lullaby of Hamagure. See Hamagure no komoriuta, 1973

Lulli ou le violon brisé, 1908 (Méliès 2)

Lulu, 1918 (Curtiz 2, Jannings 3)

Lulu. See Büchse der Pandora, 1928

Lulu, 1953 (Mastroianni 3)

Lulu, 1967 (Leacock 2)

Lulu, 1980 (Borowczyk 2)

Lulu Belle, 1948 (Lamour 3, Laszlo 4, MacArthur 4)

Lulu the Fool. See Classe operaia va in paradiso, 1971

Lulu's Doctor, 1912 (Costello 3)

Lumber Camp, 1937 (Lantz 4)

Lumber Chumps, 1933 (Lantz 4)

Lumber Jack Rabbit, 1954 (Blanc 4, Jones 4, Maltese 4, Stalling 4)

Lumber Jerks, 1955 (Blanc 4, Freleng 4)

Lumber Yard Gang, 1916 (Ford 2)

Lumberjack, 1944 (Harlan 4)

Lumière, 1967 (Braunberger 4)

Lumière, 1976 (Ganz 3, Moreau 3)

Lumière d'en face, 1955 (Bardot 3)

Lumière d'été, 1943 (Grémillon 2, Barrault 3, Brasseur 3, Barsacq 4, Douy 4, Prévert 4, Trauner 4)

Lumière du lac, 1988 (Barrault 3, Guillemot 4)

Lumière et l'invention du cinématographe, 1953 (Cloquet 4, Kosma 4)

Lumières de Paris, 1938 (Andrejew 4, Courant 4, Jaubert 4, Renoir 4)

Lummox, 1930 (Brenon 2, Menzies 4, Schenck 4, Struss 4)

Lumpaci Vagabundus, 1922 (Albers 3)

Lumpenkavaliere, 1932 (Madsen and Schenstrøm 3)

Lumuha Pati Mga Anghel, 1970 (Brocka 2)

Luna. See Luna, 1979

Luna, 1979 (Bertolucci 2, Clayburgh 3, Valli 3, Morricone 4, Storaro 4)

Luna de miel, 1959 (Theodorakis 4)

Luna sleva, 1928 (Cherkassov 3)

Lunch, 1897 (Guy 2)

Lunch Hound, 1927 (Lantz 4)

Luncheon at Twelve, 1933 (Roach 4)

Lune à un mètre, 1898 (Méliès 2)

Lune dans le caniveau, 1982 (Depardieu 3, Kinski 3)

Lune dans son tablier, 1909 (Cohl 4)

Lune di miel, 1985 (Baye 3)

Lunegarde, 1946 (Achard 4)

Lunes, Martes, Myerkoles . . . , 1976 (Brocka 2)

Lunettes féeriques, 1909 (Cohl 4)

Lung siuye, 1982 (Chan 3)

Lung Ta—les cavaliers du vent, 1990 (Sarde 4)

Lunga calza verde, 1960 (Zavattini 4)

Lunga manica, 1947 (Delli Colli 4)

Lunga notte del '43, 1960 (Pasolini 2, Cervi 3)

Lunga strada azzura, 1958 (Montand 3)

Lunga Vita alla Signora, 1987 (Olmi 2)

Lunghing fudai, 1987 (Chan 3)

Lunghing fudai tsuktsap, 1990 (Chan 3)

Lunkhead, 1929 (Sennett 2)

Lupa, 1953 (De Laurentiis 4)

Lupe, 1965 (Warhol 2)

Lupič nešika. See Chytte ho!, 1924

Lupinek Case. See Případ Lupínek, 1960

Lupo, 1970 (Golan and Globus 4)

Lupo della Sila, 1949 (Gassman 3, Mangano 3, De Laurentiis 4)

Lupo e l'agnello, 1980 (Audiard 4)

Lure, 1914 (Guy 2)

Lure. See Köder, 1975

Lure of Ambition, 1919 (Bara 3)

Lure of Broadway. See Bright Lights, 1916

Lure of Hollywood, 1931 (Arbuckle 3)

Lure of the Circus, 1919 (Johnson 3)

Lure of the Gown, 1909 (Griffith 2, Lawrence 3, Bitzer 4)

Lure of the Sila. See Lupo della Sila, 1949

Lure of the Wilderness, 1952 (Negulesco 2, Brennan 3, Cronjager 4, Jeakins 4, LeMaire 4, Waxman 4)

Lure of the Windigo, 1914 (Mix 3)

Lured, 1947 (Sirk 2, Ball 3, Coburn 3, Karloff 3, Sanders 3, Daniels 4, Stromberg 4)

Luring Lips, 1921 (Miller 4)

Lust for a Vampire, 1970 (Carreras 4, Sangster 4)

Lust for Evil. See Plein soleil, 1960

Lust for Gold, 1949 (Ford 3, Lupino 3, Duning 4)

Lust for Life, 1956 (Minnelli 2, Douglas 3, Quinn 3, Sloane 3, Ames 4, Gibbons 4, Harlan 4, Houseman 4, Plunkett 4, Rozsa 4, Young 4)

Lust in the Sun. See Dans la poussière du soleil, 1971

Lustgården, 1961 (Andersson 3, Björnstrand 3, Fischer 4)

Lustige Ehemann, 1919 (Lubitsch 2)

Lustige Witwer, 1929 (Reisch 4)

Lustigen Weiber, 1934 (Hoffmann 4)

Lustigen Weiber von Wien, 1931 (Andrejew 4, Reisch 4)

Lusty Men, 1952 (Ray 2, Hayward 3, Kennedy 3, Mitchum 3, D'Agostino 4, Garmes 4, Krasna 4, Wald 4)

Luther, 1927 (Herlth 4, Röhrig 4)

Luther, 1973 (Addison 4, Green 4, Anhalt 4, Young 4)

Lutte contre le gaspillage, 1951 (Decaë 4)

Lutteurs américains, 1903 (Guy 2)

Luv, 1967 (Falk 3, Ford 3, Lemmon 3, Laszlo 4, May 4)

Luxury, 1916 (Roach 4)

Luxury Girls. See Fanciulle di lusso, 1952

Luxury Liner, 1948 (Mayer 4, Pasternak 4, Rose 4)

Luxusweibchen, 1925 (Albers 3)

Luz del fin del mundo, 1971 (Brynner 3, Douglas 3, Rey 3, Decaë 4)

Lyana, 1955 (Barnet 2)

Lyautey, bâtisseur d'empire, 1947 (Ibert 4)

Lycée sur la colline, 1952 (Fradetal 4)

Lyckodrömmen, 1963 (Andersson 3, Björnstrand 3)

Lyckonälen, 1915 (Stiller 2)

Lyckoriddare, 1921 (Garbo 3)

Lyda Ssanin, 1922 (Albers 3)

Lydia, 1918 (Dreyer 2)

Lydia, 1941 (De Toth 2, Duvivier 2, Cotten 3, Oberon 3, Garmes 4, Hecht 4, Hoffenstein 4, Hornbeck 4, Korda, A. 4, Korda, V. 4, Plunkett 4, Rozsa 4)

Lydia Bailey, 1952 (Negulesco 2, Dunne 4, Friedhofer 4, LeMaire 4)

Lydia Gilmore, 1916 (Porter 2)

Lyin' Lion, 1949 (Terry 4)

Lyin' Mouse, 1937 (Freleng 4, Stalling 4)

Lyin' Tamer, 1925 (Lantz 4)

Lying in Wait Around the Corner Like a Street Bandit. See Scherzo del destinoin aqquato dietro l'angolo come un brigante di Strada, 1983

Lying Lips, 1921 (Ince 4)

Lying Lips, 1939 (Micheaux 2)

Lykkehjulet, 1926 (Madsen and Schenstrøm 3)

Lykken, 1916 (Psilander 3)

Lyman H. Howe's High Class Moving Pictures, 1983 (McCambridge 3)

Lynet, 1934 (Holger-Madsen 2)

Lynmouth, 1913 (Pearson 2)

Lyon, le regard intérieur, 1988 (Tavernier 2)

Lyon Lea, 1915 (Korda 2, Korda 4)

Lyon, place Bellecour, 1895 (Lumière 2)

Lyon, place des Cordeliers, 1895 (Lumière 2)

Lyons in Paris, 1956 (Daniels 3, Carreras 4)

Lyric of a Port. See Minato no jojoushi, 1932

Lyrosophie, 1948 (Epstein 2)

Lys de la Vie, 1920 (Clair 2)

Lyset i natten, 1953 (Roos 2)

Lyubliu tebya, 1934 (Gerasimov 2, Cherkassov 3)

Lyubov i nenavist, 1935 (Maretskaya 3)

Lyubov silna na strastyou potseluya, 1916 (Mozhukin 3)

Lyulya Bek, 1914 (Bauer 2)

M, 1931 (Gründgens 3, Lorre 3, Von Harbou 4, Wagner 4)
M, 1951 (Aldrich 2, Losey 2, Cohn 4, Hubley 4, Laszlo 4, Raine 4, Salt 4)
M, Mörder unter uns. *See* **M, 1931**
MBKS, 1973 (Le Grice 2)
M-G-M Story, 1951 (Barrymore 3)
MGM Studio Tour, 1925 (Daniels 4)
Ma and Pa, 1922 (Sennett 2)
Ma and Pa Kettle at Home, 1954 (Boyle 4)
Ma and Pa Kettle at the Fair, 1951 (Eason 4)
Ma and Pa Kettle on Vacation, 1952 (Boyle 4)
Ma come fanno a farli cosi belli?, 1980 (Bozzetto 4)
Ma Cousine de Varsovie, 1932 (Clouzot 2, Gallone 2, Courant 4)
Ma famille et ma toit. *See* Ciel est pardessus le toit, 1956
Ma femme est une panthère, 1960 (Matras 4)
Ma femme, mon gosse, et moi. *See* Amour est en jeu, 1957
Ma Jeannette et mes copains, 1954 (Kosma 4)
Ma l'amore mio non muore, 1938 (Valli 3)
Ma mère l'eau. *See* Mammy Water, 1955
Ma no kisetsu: Haru no mizuumi, 1956 (Yamamura 3)
Ma no ogon, 1950 (Mori 3)
Ma No Toki, 1985 (Iwashita 3)
Ma non è una cosa seria!, 1936 (De Sica 2)
Ma nuit chez Maud, 1969 (Trintignant 3, Almendros 4, Braunberger 4)
Ma pomme, 1950 (Chevalier 3, Alekan 4, D'Eaubonne 4)
Ma tante d'Honfleur, 1931 (Fradetal 4)
Maa, 1952 (Roy 2)
Maan, 1954 (Biswas 4)
Mabel series, 1912–22 (Sennett 2, Normand 3)
Mabel series, 1913–16 (Arbuckle 3)
Maboroshi fujin, 1949 (Yamamura 3)
Maboroshi no mizuumi, 1982 (Muraki 4)
Maboroshi-jo, 1940 (Shimura 3)
Mabuta no haha, 1931 (Yamada 3)
Mabuta no haha, 1937 (Hasegawa 3)
Macabre. *See* Macabro, 1980
Macabro, 1980 (Delli Colli 4)
Macadam, 1946 (Rosay 3, Signoret 3, D'Eaubonne 4)
Macahans, 1976 (Saint 3)
Macao, 1952 (Von Sternberg 2, Bendix 3, Grahame 3, Mitchum 3, Russell 3, D'Agostino 4)
Macao l'enfer, 1939 (Von Stroheim 2)
Macao, l'enfer du jeu, 1939 (Delannoy 2, Hayakawa 3, Auric 4, Douy 4)

Macaro, 1959 (Figueroa 4)
Macaroni. *See* Maccheroni, 1985 (Lemmon 3)
Macaroni Blues. *See* Elanprostekt nr. 4, 1986
MacArthur, 1977 (Peck 3, Goldsmith 4, Whitlock 4)
MacArthur's Children. *See* Setouchi shounen yakyu-dan, 1984
Macbeth, 1908 (Lawrence 3, Ince 4)
Macbeth, 1916 (Fleming 2, Von Stroheim 2, Emerson 4, Loos 4)
Macbeth, 1948 (Welles 2, McDowall 3, Ibert 4)
Macbeth, 1960 (Mathieson 4, Young 4)
Macbeth. *See* Makbet, 1969
Macbeth, 1971 (Schroeter 2)
Macbeth, 1972 (Polanski 2)
Maccheroni, 1985 (Mastroianni 3)
Macchia rosa, 1969 (Giannini 3)
Macchie solari, 1974 (Morricone 4)
Macchina ammazzacattivi, 1948 (Rossellini 2, Amidei 4)
MacDonald's Farm, 1951 (Fleischer 4)
Macédoine, 1970 (Brasseur 3)
Macedonian Part of Hell. *See* Makedonskiot del od pekolot, 1971
Mach' mir die Wely zum Paradies, 1930 (Reisch 4)
Macheath, 1987 (Hurt 3)
Machete, 1958 (Van Cleef 3, Struss 4)
Machi no bofu, 1934 (Tanaka 3)
Machi no hitobito, 1926 (Tanaka 3)
Machiboke no onna, 1946 (Shindo 2)
Machibuse, 1970 (Mifune 3)
''Machiko'' yori: Hana hiraku, 1948 (Takamine 3)
Machinations, 1984 (Vogler 3)
Machine Age. *See* Kalyug, 1981
Machine à parler d'amour, 1961 (Braunberger 4, Fradetal 4)
Machine à refaire la vie, 1924 (Duvivier 2)
Machine Gun Kelly, 1958 (Corman 2, Bronson 3, Crosby 4)
Machine Gun McCain. *See* Intoccabili, 1968
Machine of Eden, 1970 (Brakhage 2)
Macho, 1984 (York 3)
Macho Callahan, 1970 (Cobb 3, Seberg 3, Fisher 4)
Macho Dancer, 1988 (Brocka 2)
Machorka-Muff, 1963 (Straub and Huillet 2)
Macht der Finsternis, 1923 (Wiene 2, Andrejew 4)
Macht der Gefühle, 1983 (Kluge 2)
Macht der Versuchung, 1922 (Dagover 3)
Macht des Goldes, 1912 (Gad 2)
Maciste, 1915 (Pastrone 2)
Maciste all'inferno, 1926 (Amidei 4)

Maciste alpino, 1916 (Pastrone 2)
Maciste contre il vampiro, 1961 (De Laurentiis 4)
Maciste contro lo Sceicco, 1925 (Camerini 2)
Maciste nella gabbia dei Leoni, 1926 (Amidei 4)
Mack, 1973 (Pryor 3)
Mack At It Again, 1914 (Sennett 2, Normand 3)
Mack the Knife, 1989 (Harris 3, Golan and Globus 4)
Mackendrick, 1986 (Coburn 3)
MacKenna's Gold, 1969 (Cobb 3, Massey 3, Meredith 3, Peck 3, Quayle 3, Robinson 3, Sharif 3, Wallach 3, Foreman 4, Jones 4, Tiomkin 4)
MacKintosh and T.J., 1975 (Rogers 3)
MacKintosh Man, 1973 (Hill 2, Huston 2, Mason 3, Newman 3, Sanda 3, Jarre 4, Morris 4)
Maclovia, 1948 (Fernández 2, Armendáriz 3, Félix 3, Figueroa 4)
Macomber Affair, 1947 (Bennett 3, Peck 3, Preston 3, Francis 4, Metzner 4, Robinson 4, Rozsa 4, Struss 4)
Maçons, 1905 (Guy 2)
Mad, 1963 (Terry-Thomas 3)
Mad about Men, 1954 (Rutherford 3, Box 4, Rank 4)
Mad about Music, 1938 (Durbin 3, Marshall 3, Pangborn 3, Pasternak 4)
Mad Adventures of Rabbi Jacob. *See* Adventures de Rabbi Jacob, 1973
Mad As a Mars Hare, 1963 (Blanc 4)
Mad Atlantic. *See* Doto ichi man kairi, 1966
Mad Bridegroom. *See* Vzteklý ženich, 1919
Mad Checkmate. *See* Scacco tutto matto, 1968
Mad Doctor, 1941 (Rathbone 3, Head 4, Young 4)
Mad Doctor of Market Street, 1942 (Lewis 2, Johnson 3, Salter 4)
Mad Dog. *See* Mad Dog Morgan, 1976
Mad Dog and Glory, 1991 (Scorsese 2, De Niro 3)
Mad Dog Coll, 1961 (Hackman 3, Rosenblum 4, Sylbert 4)
Mad Dog Coll, 1991 (Golan and Globus 4)
Mad Dog Morgan, 1976 (Hopper 3)
Mad Emperor. *See* Tragédie impériale, 1938
Mad Game, 1933 (Tracy 3, Trevor 3, Miller 4)
Mad Genius, 1931 (Curtiz 2, Barrymore 3, Karloff 3, Grot 4)
Mad Ghoul, 1943 (Krasner 4, Kräly 4, Salter 4)

Mad Hatter, 1935 (Havelock-Allan 4)

Mad Hatter. *See* Breakfast in Hollywood, 1945

Mad Holiday, 1936 (Ruttenberg 4)

Mad Hour, 1928 (Haller 4, Robinson 4)

Mad House, 1934 (Terry 4)

Mad King, 1932 (Terry 4)

Mad Little Island. *See* Rockets Galore, 1958

Mad Love. *See* Mania, 1918

Mad Love, 1935 (Lorre 3, Balderston 4, Freund 4, Gibbons 4, Tiomkin 4, Toland 4)

Mad Magician, 1954 (Price 3, Glennon 4)

Mad Maid of the Forest, 1915 (Rosher 4)

Mad Man's Money. *See* Bad Men's Money, 1929

Mad Marriage, 1925 (Costello 3)

Mad Masquerade. *See* Washington Masquerade, 1932

Mad Max, 1979 (Miller 2, Gibson 3)

Mad Max: Beyond the Thunderdome, 1985 (Miller 2, Gibson 3, Jarre 4)

Mad Max II, 1982 (Gibson 3)

Mad Max III. *See* Mad Max: Beyond the Thunderdome, 1985

Mad Miss Manton, 1938 (Fonda 3, McDaniel 3, Stanwyck 3, Berman 4, Epstein 4)

Mad Monster Party, 1967 (Karloff 3)

Mad Parade, 1931 (Banton 4)

Mad Queen. *See* Locura de amor, 1948

Mad Racer, 1926 (Arthur 3)

Mad Room, 1968 (Winters 3)

Mad Wednesday, 1947 (Sturges 2, Lloyd 3, Pangborn 3, Hughes 4)

Madagascar, 1954 (Delerue 4)

Madam Kitty. *See* Salon Kitty, 1977

Madam, Permit Me to Love Your Daughter. *See* Permettete che ami vostre figlia?, 1974

Madam Satan, 1930 (Adrian 4, Gibbons 4, Macpherson 4, Mayer 4, Prinz 4, Shearer 4, Stothart 4)

Madam wünscht keine Kinder, 1926 (Freund 4)

Madama Butterfly, 1955 (Gallone 2)

Madame. *See* Madame Sans-Gêne, 1961

Madame Bovary, 1934 (Becker 2, Renoir 2, Lourié 4, Milhaud 4, Wakhévitch 4)

Madame Bovary, 1937 (Negri 3)

Madame Bovary, 1949 (Minnelli 2, Jones 3, Jourdan 3, Mason 3, Berman 4, Gibbons 4, Plunkett 4, Rozsa 4, Smith 4)

Madame Bovary, 1991 (Huppert 3, Rabier 4)

Madame Butterfly, 1915 (Olcott 2, Pickford 3, Zukor 4)

Madame Butterfly, 1933 (Grant 3, Sidney 3, Zukor 4)

Madame Butterfly, 1955 (Renoir 4)

Madame Claude, 1976 (Dalio 3, Kinski 3)

Madame Claude 2, 1981 (Lai 4)

Madame Curie, 1943 (LeRoy 2, Garson 3, Johnson 3, O'Brien 3, Pidgeon 3, Walker 3, Gibbons 4, Irene 4, Mayer 4, Sharaff 4, Stothart 4)

Madame De. . . , 1953 (De Sica 2, Boyer 3, Darrieux 3, Achard 4, Annenkov 4, D'Eaubonne 4, Matras 4)

Madame de Thèbes, 1915 (Stiller 2, Jaenzon 4, Magnusson 4)

Madame Double X, 1914 (Beery 3)

Madame Du Barry, 1934 (Dieterle 2, Del Rio 3, Blanke 4, Hunte 4, Kräly 4, Orry-Kelly 4, Polito 4)

Madame Du Barry, 1954 (Christian-Jaque 2, Jeanson 4, Matras 4)

Madame DuBarry, 1919 (Bara 3, Jannings 3, Negri 3)

Madame et le mort, 1942 (Bost 4)

Madame Guillotine, 1931 (Carroll 3)

Madame Julie. *See* Woman Between, 1931

Madame Kitty. *See* Salon Kitty, 1976

Madame Milena's Husbands. *See* Manželé paní Mileny, 1921

Madame Mystery, 1926 (Bara 3, Laurel and Hardy 3, Roach 4)

Madame Nicotine, 1908 (Gaudio 4)

Madame Peacock, 1920 (Nazimova 3)

Madame Pimpernel. *See* Paris Underground, 1945

Madame Pompadour, 1927 (Dupont 2, Wilcox 2, Marion 4)

Madame Q, 1929 (McCarey 2, Roach 4)

Madame Racketeer, 1932 (Raft 3)

Madame Récamier, 1928 (Rosay 4)

Madame Rex, 1911 (Griffith 2, Bitzer 4)

Madame Rosa. *See* Vie devant soi, 1977

Madame Sans Jane, 1925 (Roach 4)

Madame Sans Gène, 1909 (Blom 2)

Madame Sans-Gêne, 1925 (Brasseur 3, Swanson 3, Zukor 4)

Madame Sans-Gêne, 1941 (Arletty 3, Cuny 3, Aurenche 4)

Madame Sans-Gêne, 1961 (Loren 3, D'Eaubonne 4, Jeanson 4, Solinas 4)

Madame Satan, 1930 (De Mille 2, Day 4, Rosson 4)

Madame Sin, 1972 (Davis 3, Elliott 3, Wagner 4)

Madame Sourdis, 1984 (Baye 3)

Madame Souzatska, 1988 (Schlesinger 2, MacLaine 3, Jhabvala 4)

Madame Spy, 1934 (Wray 3, Freund 4)

Madame Spy, 1942 (Salter 4)

Madame Wants No Children. *See* Madame wünscht keine Kinder, 1926

Madame wünscht keine Kinder, 1926 (Dietrich 3, Balàzs 4)

Madame wünscht keine Kinder, 1933 (Wilder 2, Kaper 4)

Madame X, 1929 (Barrymore 3, Gibbons 4)

Madame X, 1937 (Wood 2, Gibbons 4, Seitz 4)

Madame X, 1966 (Meredith 3, Turner 3, Hunter 4, Metty 4, Westmore Family 4)

Madame X, 1981 (Weld 3, Anhalt 4)

Madame Yuki. *See* Yuki-fujin ezu, 1950

Madamigella di Maupin, 1965 (Gherardi 4)

Madamoiselle de la Ferté, 1948 (Cloquet 4)

Madamu to nyobo, 1931 (Tanaka 3)

Madcap Magoo, 1955 (Bosustow 4, Burness 4)

Mädchen Argentinien. *See* Fräulein aus Argentinien, 1928

Mädchen aus der Ackerstrasse, 1920 (Courant 4)

Mädchen aus Flandern, 1956 (Käutner 2, Schell 3)

Mädchen hinter gittern, 1949 (Wagner 4)

Mädchen in Uniform, 1958 (Schneider 3)

Mädchen Irene, 1936 (Dagover 3)

Mädchen Johanna, 1935 (Gründgens 3, Herlth 4, Röhrig 4)

Mädchen mit dem guten Ruf, 1938 (Tschechowa 3, Wagner 4)

Mädchen ohne Heimat, 1926 (Homolka 3)

Mädchen ohne Vaterland, 1912 (Nielsen 3)

Mädchen Schicksal, 1928 (Manès 3)

Mädchen und die Männer, 1919 (Krauss 3)

Madchen vom Moorhof, 1935 (Sirk 2)

Mädchen von Fanö, 1940 (Wegener 3, Hoffmann 4)

Mädchenjahre einer Königin, 1954 (Schneider 3)

Mädchenjahre einer Königin, 1936 (Warm 4)

Mädchenräuber, 1936 (Madsen and Schenstrøm 3)

Maddalena, 1953 (Cervi 3, Vanel 3, Bost 4, Renoir 4)

Maddalena, 1960 (Lassally 4)

Maddalena, 1970 (Kawalerowicz 2, Morricone 4)

Maddalena Ferat, 1921 (Bertini 3)

Maddalena zero in condotta, 1941 (De Sica 2)

Made a Coward, 1913 (Mix 3)

Made for Each Other, 1939 (Cromwell 2, Beavers 3, Bond 3, Coburn 3, Lombard 3, Stewart 3, Banton 4, Friedhofer 4, Menzies 4, Selznick 4, Shamroy 4, Swerling 4, Wheeler 4)

Made for Love, 1926 (Fort 4, Miller 4)

Made in Britain, 1982 (Menges 4)

Made in Heaven, 1921 (Gibbons 4)

Made in Heaven, 1952 (Rank 4, Unsworth 4)

Made in Heaven, 1987 (Rudolph 2)

Made in Italy, 1965 (Scola 2, Fabrizi 3, Magnani 3, Sordi 3)

Made in Paris, 1966 (Dalio 3, Jourdan 3, Ames 4, Jones 4, Krasner 4, Pasternak 4, Rose 4)

Made in Sweden, 1968 (Von Sydow 3, Fischer 4)

Made in the Kitchen, 1921 (Sennett 2)

Made in U.S.A., 1966 (Godard 2, Karina 3, Léaud 3, Coutard 4, De Beauregard 4, Guillemot 4)

Made Manifest, 1980 (Brakhage 2)

Made on Broadway, 1933 (Montgomery 3, Adrian 4)

Mädel aus dem Volke, 1927 (Reisch 4)

Mädel aus U.S.A., 1930 (Ondra 3, Heller 4)

Mädel mit der Peitsche, 1929 (Heller 4)

Mädel vom Ballett, 1918 (Lubitsch 2, Kräly 4)

Mädel vom Ballett, 1936 (Ondra 3)

Mädel vom Piccadilly, 1921 (Courant 4)

Mädel von der Reeperbahn, 1930 (Tschechowa 3)

Mädel von Nebenan, 1917 (Hoffmann 4)

Madeleine, 1921 (Albers 3)

Madeleine, 1950 (Lean 2, Alwyn 4, Green 4, Rank 4)

Madeleine und der Legionär, 1958 (Staudte 2)

Madeline, 1952 (Bosustow 4, Raksin 4)

Mädels von heute, 1925 (Tschechowa 3, Warm 4)

Mademoiselle, 1966 (Richardson 2, Moreau 3, Saulnier 4)

Mademoiselle Ange, 1959 (Belmondo 3, Schneider 3, Braunberger 4, D'Eaubonne 4)

Mademoiselle de la seiglière, 1921 (Burel 4)

Mademoiselle Docteur, 1937 (Von Stroheim 2, Barrault 3, Fresnay 3, Jouvet 3, Modot 3, Achard 4, Alekan 4, Annenkov 4, Heller 4, Honegger 4, Schüfftan 4)

Mademoiselle Fifi, 1944 (Wise 2, Simon 3, D'Agostino 4, Lewton 4)

Mademoiselle France. *See* Reunion, 1942

Mademoiselle from Armentieres, 1926 (Saville 2)

Mlle. Irene the Great, 1931 (Johnson 4)

Mademoiselle Josette, ma femme. *See* Fräulein Josette, meine Frau, 1926

Mademoiselle Josette ma femme, 1933 (D'Eaubonne 4)

Mademoiselle ma mère, 1937 (Brasseur 3, Darrieux 3, Burel 4)

Mademoiselle Modiste, 1926 (Barnes 4)

Mademoiselle Mozart, 1936 (Darrieux 3, Morgan 3)

Mademoiselle 100 millions, 1913 (Tourneur 2)

Mademoiselle Porte-bonheur. *See* Lucky Me, 1954

Mademoiselle X, 1945 (Achard 4, Matras 4, Wakhévitch 4)

Madge of the Mountains, 1911 (Bunny 3)

Madh Bhare Nain, 1955 (Burman 4)

Madhouse, 1974 (Cushing 3, Price 3)

Madhubala, 1950 (Anand 3)

Madhumati, 1955 (Ghatak 2)

Madhumati, 1958 (Roy 2, Kumar 3)

Madigan, 1968 (Polonsky 2, Siegel 2, Fonda 3, Widmark 3, Head 4, Metty 4, Westmore Family 4)

Madigan: Park Avenue Beat, 1973 (Widmark 3)

Madigan: The Lisbon Beat, 1973 (Widmark 3)

Madigan: The Naples Beat, 1973 (Widmark 3)

Madigan's Millions. *See* Dollaro per 7 vigliacchi, 1967

Madison Avenue, 1962 (Andrews 3, Clarke 4)

Madison Square Garden, 1932 (Brown 4)

Madla from the Brick-Kiln. *See* Madla z cihelny, 1933

Madla z cihelny, 1933 (Baarová 3, Stallich 4)

Madly, 1969 (Delon 3, Lai 4)

Madman, 1911 (Bushman 3)

Madman's Defence. *See* Dåres försvarstal, 1976

Madmen of Europe. *See* Englishman's Home, 1939

Madmen of Mandoras, 1962 (Cortez 4)

Madness of the Heart, 1949 (Lockwood 3, Bennett 4, Rank 4)

Madness of Youth, 1923 (Gilbert 3, August 4)

Mado, 1927 (Tanaka 3)

Mado, 1976 (Sautet 2, Baye 3, Schneider 3, Piccoli 3, Sarde 4)

Mado kara tobidase, 1950 (Kagawa 3)

Madone des sleepings, 1955 (Von Stroheim 2, Burel 4)

Madonna and Child, 1980 (Davies 2)

Madonna Grazia, 1917 (Gallone 2)

Madonna in The Gaucho, 1927 (Pickford 3)

Madonna of Avenue A, 1929 (Curtiz 2, Costello 3, Haskin 4, Zanuck 4)

Madonna of the Seven Moons, 1944 (Granger 3, Rank 4)

Madonna of the Storm, 1913 (Gish 3)

Madonna of the Streets, 1924 (Beery 3, Nazimova 3)

Madonna of the Streets, 1930 (Polito 4)

Madonna's Secret, 1946 (Alton 4)

Madre, 1913 (Bertini 3)

Madre folle, 1922 (Gallone 2)

Madrid, 1987 (Vogler 3)

Madriguera, 1969 (Saura 2, Chaplin 3)

Madron, 1970 (Caron 3)

Madwoman of Chaillot, 1969 (Boyer 3, Brynner 3, Evans 3, Henreid 3, Hepburn 3, Homolka 3, Kaye 3, Masina 3, Pleasence 3, Anhalt 4, Guffey 4, Renoir 4)

Mae West, 1982 (McDowall 3)

Maelstrom, 1910 (Lawrence 3)

Maelstrom, 1913 (Ince 4)

Maestrina, 1913 (Bertini 3)

Maestro, 1958 (Fabrizi 3)

Maestro, 1979 (Cassel 3)

Maestro, 1989 (McDowell 3, Halas and Batchelor 4)

Maestro d'amore, 1977 (Brazzi 3)

Maestro di Don Giovanni, 1953 (Flynn 3, Lollobrigida 3, Cardiff 4)

Maestro di Vigevano, 1963 (Bloom 3, Sordi 3, Rota 4)

Maestro e Margherita, 1972 (Cuny 3, Morricone 4)

Maffia, 1972 (Torre Nilsson 2)

Mafia. *See* In nome della legge, 1949

Mafia. *See* Giorno della civetta, 1968

Mafia. *See* maffia, 1972

Mafia Princess, 1986 (Curtis 3)

Mafia War. *See* Bacciamo le mani, 1973

Mafioso, 1962 (Ferreri 2, Lattuada 2, Sordi 3, Age and Scarpelli 4, De Laurentiis 4, Rota 4)

Mafu Cage, 1979 (Grant 3)

Magd, 1911 (Porten 3, Messter 4)

Magdalene, 1908 (Holger-Madsen 2)

Magellan, 1980 (Frampton 2)

Maggie, 1954 (Mackendrick 2, Addison 4)

Maggie, 1986 (Gardner 3)

Maggie's First False Step, 1917 (Sennett 2, Beery 3)

Maggot, 1973 (Dunning 4)

Mágia, 1917 (Korda 2, Korda 4)

Magic. *See* Mágia, 1917

Magic, 1978 (Attenborough 3, Hopkins 3, Meredith 3, Goldman 4, Goldsmith 4, Levine 4)

Magic Balloon, 1989 (Cardiff 4)

Magic Book, 1989 (Halas and Batchelor 4)

Magic Bow, 1946 (Granger 3, Rank 4)

Magic Box, 1951 (Boulting 2, Attenborough 3, Donat 3, Love 3, Olivier 3, Rutherford 3, Schell 3, Ustinov 3, Withers 3, Alwyn 4, Cardiff 4, Mathieson 4)

Magic Canvas, 1948 (Halas and Batchelor 4)

Magic Carpet, 1925 (Lantz 4)

Magic Carpet, 1951 (Ball 3, Katzman 4)

Magic Cartoons. *See* Génération spontanée, 1909

Magic Catalogue, 1956 (Vukotić 4)

Magic Christian, 1970 (Polanski 2, Attenborough 3, Brynner 3, Cleese 3, Harvey 3, Lee 3, Sellers 3, Welch 3, Unsworth 4)

Magic Donkey. *See* Peau d'âne, 1970

Magic Eggs. *See* Omelette fantastique, 1909

Magic Fan. *See* Eventail animé, 1909

Magic Fire, 1956 (Dieterle 2, Dupont 2, Cushing 3, De Carlo 3, Rasp 3, Haller 4, Herlth 4, Korngold 4)

Magic Fish, 1934 (Terry 4)

Magic Flame, 1927 (Florey 2, King 2, Banky 3, Colman 3, Barnes 4, Goldwyn 4, Mathis 4, Meredyth 4)

Magic Fluke, 1948 (Bosustow 4, Hubley 4)

Magic Flute. *See* Trollflöjten, 1974

Magic Fountain. *See* Fuente magica, 1961

Magic Fountain Pen, 1909 (Blackton 2)

Magic Garden, 1927 (Plunkett 4)

Magic Garden of Stanley Sweetheart, 1970 (Goldsmith 4)

Magic Hoop. *See* Cerceau magique, 1908

Magic Horse, 1953 (Reiniger 4)

Magic Lamp, 1924 (Lantz 4)

Magic Lantern. *See* Lanterne magique, 1903

Magic Mountain, 1982 (Steiger 3)

Magic Night. *See* Goodnight Vienna, 1932

Magic of Lassie, 1978 (Faye 3, Rooney 3, Stewart 3)

Magic on Broadway, 1937 (Fleischer 4)

Magic Pencil, 1940 (Terry 4)

Magic Shell, 1941 (Terry 4)

Magic Shoes, 1935 (Finch 3)

Magic Slipper, 1947 (Terry 4)

Magic Sounds. *See* Carobni zvuci, 1957

Magic Statue. *See* Mazou, 1938

Magic Strength, 1944 (Fleischer 4)

Magic Sword, 1962 (Rathbone 3)

Magic Town, 1947 (Wellman 2, Stewart 3, Wyman 3, Biroc 4, Hornbeck 4, Riskin 4)

Magic Voyage of Sinbad, 1962 (Coppola 2, Corman 2)

Magic Wand, 1912 (Bushman 3)

Magical Maestro, 1951 (Avery 4)

Magician, 1926 (Ingram 2, Mayer 4, Seitz 4)

Magician. *See* Magicien, 1927

Magician. *See* Ansiktet, 1958

Magician, 1980 (Halas and Batchelor 4)

Magician in Spite of Himself, 1951 (Loren 3)

Magician of Lublin. *See* Magier, 1979

Magicians of the Silver Screen. *See* Báječni muži s klikou, 1979

Magicien, 1898 (Méliès 2)

Magicien, 1927 (Wegener 3)

Magiciennes, 1960 (D'Eaubonne 4, Matras 4)

Magiciens, 1975 (Chabrol 2, Gégauff 4, Rabier 4)

Magiciens de Wanzerbé, 1949 (Rouch 2)

Magie du diamant, 1958 (Kosma 4)

Magie noire, 1904 (Guy 2)

Magier, 1979 (Arkin 3, Winters 3, Golan and Globus 4, Jarre 4)

Magique Image, 1950 (Musidora 3)

Magirama, 1956 (Gance 2)

Magistrato, 1959 (Cardinale 3)

Magliari, 1959 (Rosi 2, Sordi 3, Cecchi D'Amico 4, Cristaldi 4, Di Venanzo 4)

Mágnás Miska, 1916 (Korda 2, Korda 4)

Magnat, 1987 (Nowicki 3)

Magnate, 1973 (Cassel 3)

Magnet, 1914 (Meredyth 4)

Magnet, 1950 (Alwyn 4, Balcon 4, Clarke 4)

Magnet Laboratory, 1959 (Leacock 2)

Magnetic Monster, 1953 (Siodmak 4)

Magnificent Ambersons, 1942 (Welles 2, Wise 2, Baxter 3, Costello 3, Cotten 3, Moorehead 3, Cortez 4, D'Agostino 4, Herrmann 4)

Magnificent Bodyguard, 1978 (Chan 3)

Magnificent Brute, 1936 (McLaglen 3)

Magnificent Cuckold. *See* Magnifico cornuto, 1964

Magnificent Doll, 1946 (Borzage 2, Meredith 3, Niven 3, Rogers 3, Banton 4, Salter 4)

Magnificent Dope, 1942 (Ameche 3, Fonda 3, Horton 3, Day 4, Raksin 4)

Magnificent Flirt, 1928 (D'Arrast 2, Young 3, Mankiewicz 4, Polglase 4)

Magnificent Fraud, 1939 (Florey 2, Head 4)

Magnificent Lie, 1931 (Bellamy 3, Boyer 3, Rosay 3, Raphaelson 4)

Magnificent Life, 1931 (Lang 4)

Magnificent Matador, 1955 (Boetticher 2, O'Hara 3, Quinn 3, Ballard 4)

Magnificent Obsession, 1935 (Stahl 2, Dunne 3, Taylor 3, Waxman 4)

Magnificent Obsession, 1954 (Sirk 2, Hudson 3, Moorehead 3, Wyman 3, Hunter 4, Metty 4)

Magnificent Outcast. See Almost a Gentleman, 1939

Magnificent Rogue, 1946 (Alton 4)

Magnificent Roughnecks, 1956 (Rooney 3)

Magnificent Seven, 1960 (Sturges 2, Bronson 3, Brynner 3, Coburn 3, McQueen 3, Wallach 3, Bernstein 4, Lang 4, Mirisch 4)

Magnificent Seven Deadly Sins, 1971 (Godfrey 4)

Magnificent Seven Ride!, 1972 (Van Cleef 3, Bernstein 4)

Magnificent Showman. See Circus World, 1964

Magnificent Sinner. See Katia, 1960

Magnificent Tramp. See Archimède, le clochard, 1959

Magnificent Yankee, 1950 (Sturges 2, Calhern 3, Plunkett 4, Raksin 4, Ruttenberg 4)

Magnifico avventuriero, 1963 (Blier 3)

Magnifico cornuto, 1964 (Blier 3, Cardinale 3, Volonté 3)

Magnifique, 1974 (Belmondo 3)

Magnum Force, 1973 (Cimino 2, Eastwood 3, Schifrin 4)

Mago de Joséfa, 1964 (Douy 4)

Magoichi Saga. See Shirikurae Magoichi, 1969

Magokoro, 1953 (Tanaka 3)

Magoo series, 1953–58 (Bosustow 4, Burness 4)

Magot de Joséfa, 1964 (Autant-Lara 2, Brasseur 3, Magnani 3, Aurenche 4, Bost 4)

Magpie Madness, 1947 (Terry 4)

Magus, 1968 (Caine 3, Karina 3, Quinn 3, Green 4)

Magyarenfürstin, 1923 (Wagner 4)

Maha Geet, 1937 (Biswas 4)

Mahaan, 1983 (Bachchan 3)

Mahal, 1969 (Anand 3)

Mahanagar, 1963 (Chandragupta 4, Datta 4, Mitra 4)

Maharabata, 1989 (Carrière 4)

Maharadscha wider Willen, 1950 (Tschechowa 3)

Maharadžovo potěšení. See Harémy kouzla zbavené, 1922

Maharajah's Pleasures. See Harémy kouzla zbavené, 1922

Maharlika, 1970 (Crawford 3)

Mahatma Kabir Munna, 1954 (Biswas 4)

Mahiru no ankoku, 1956 (Yamamura 3)

Mahiru no enbukyoku, 1949 (Yoshimura 2, Tanaka 3)

Mahiru no wana, 1960 (Iwashita 3)

Mahler, 1974 (Russell 2, Puttnam 4, Russell 4)

Mahlia la métisse, 1942 (Matras 4)

Mahogany, 1975 (Perkins 3, Watkin 4)

Maid and the Man, 1911 (Dwan 2)

Maid at the Helm, 1911 (Bosworth 3)

Maid for Murder. See She'll Have to Go, 1961

Maid in China, 1938 (Terry 4)

Maid in Hollywood, 1934 (Roach 4)

Maid Mad, 1916 (Sennett 2)

Maid of Niagara, 1910 (White 3)

Maid of Salem, 1937 (Bondi 3, Colbert 3, MacMurray 3, Banton 4, Estabrook 4, Young 4)

Maid of the Mist, 1915 (Chaney 3)

Maid of the Mountains, 1909 (Anderson 3)

Maid of War, 1914 (Beery 3)

Maid or Man, 1911 (Pickford 3, Gaudio 4, Ince 4)

Maid to Order, 1916 (Laurel and Hardy 3)

Maid to Order, 1987 (Delerue 4)

Maiden and Men, 1911 (Dwan 2)

Maiden Lane, 1936 (Trevor 3)

Maidens from Wilko. See Panny z Wilka, 1978

Maiden's Trust, 1917 (Sennett 2)

Maids, 1974 (Jackson 3, York 3, Slocombe 4)

Maids à la Mode, 1933 (Roach 4)

Maids and Muslin, 1920 (Laurel and Hardy 3)

Maid's Night Out, 1911 (Normand 3)

Maid's Night Out, 1938 (Fontaine 3)

Maidstone, 1968 (Leacock 2)

Maigret, 1988 (Harris 3)

Maigret a Pigalle, 1967 (Cervi 3, Amidei 4)

Maigret dirige l'enquête, 1955 (Kosma 4)

Maigret et l'affaire Saint-Fiacre, 1958 (Delannoy 2, Gabin 3, Audiard 4)

Maigret tend un piége, 1957 (Gabin 3, Girardot 3, Audiard 4)

Maigret voit rouge, 1963 (Gabin 3)

Maihime, 1951 (Yamamura 3)

Maihime, 1989 (Shinoda 2, Miyagawa 4)

Maiko sanjushi, 1955 (Yoda 4)

Mail and Female, 1937 (Roach 4)

Mail Call, 1944 (Vorkapich 4)

Mail Early, 1939 (Mclaren 4)

Mail Early for Christmas, 1959 (McLaren 4)

Mail Order Bride, 1912 (Bushman 3)

Mail Order Bride, 1963 (Oates 3)

Mail Train. See Inspector Hornleigh Goes to It, 1941

Maillot noir, 1917 (Musidora 3)

Main, 1969 (Vierny 4)

Main à couper, 1973 (Spaak 4)

Main Attraction, 1962 (Zetterling 2, Unsworth 4)

Main chaude, 1959 (Jarre 4)

Main du diable, 1942 (Tourneur 2, Fresnay 3, Andrejew 4)

Main du professeur Hamilton ou Le Roi des dollars, 1903 (Guy 2)

Main Event, 1927 (Howard 2, Adrian 4)

Main Event, 1979 (Streisand 3)

Main mystérieuse, 1916 (Cohl 4)

Main Nashe Me Hoon, 1959 (Kapoor 2)

Main Street After Dark, 1944 (Duryea 3)

Main Street of Paris, 1939 (Cardiff 4)

Main Street to Broadway, 1953 (Garnett 2, Barrymore, E. 3, Barrymore, L. 3, Calhern 3, Harrison 3, Moorehead 3, Wilde 3, Howe 4, Raphaelson 4, Sherwood 4)

Maine-Océan, 1984 (Branco 4, De Almeida 4)

Mains d'Orlac. See Hands of Orlac, 1960

Mains negatives, 1978 (Duras 2)

Mains nettes, 1958 (Jutra 2)

Mains sales, 1951 (Brasseur 3, Gélin 3)

Mainspring, 1917 (King 2)

Mais n'te promène donc pas toute nue, 1936 (Arletty 3)

Mais où et donc ornicar?, 1978 (Chaplin 3)

Mais où sont les nègres d'antan, 1962 (Delerue 4)

Maisen, 1936 (Shimura 3)

Maisie, 1939 (Young 3, Gibbons 4)

Maisie Gets Her Man, 1942 (Stradling 4)

Maisie Goes to Reno, 1944 (Gardner 3, Irene 4)

Maisie Was a Lady, 1941 (Ayres 3, O'Sullivan 3)

Maison, 1970 (Simon 3)

Maison assassinée, 1987 (Sarde 4)

Maison aux images, 1955 (Grémillon 2)

Maison Bonnadieu, 1951 (Blier 3, Darrieux 3)

Maison dans la dune, 1934 (Matras 4, Spaak 4)

Maison de campagne, 1969 (Darrieux 3)

Maison de danses, 1931 (Tourneur 2, Vanel 3)

Maison de jade, 1988 (Sarde 4)

Maison d'en face, 1936 (Christian-Jaque 2)

Maison des bois, 1971 (Pialat 2)

Maison des Bories, 1969 (Cloquet 4)

Maison des lions, 1912 (Feuillade 2)

Maison des sept jeunes filles, 1941 (Douy 4, Spaak 4)

Maison du Fantoche, 1916 (Cohl 4)

Maison du Maltais, 1938 (Dalio 3, Jouvet 3, Courant 4, Ibert 4, Wakhévitch 4)

Maison du mystère, 1916 (Volkov 2)

Maison du mystère, 1922 (Mozhukin 3, Vanel 3)

Maison du passeur, 1965 (Prévert 4)

Maison du silence. See Voce del silenzio, 1952

Maison du souvenir. See Casa Ricordi, 1954

Maison jaune de Rio, 1930 (Vanel 3)

Maison sous la mer, 1946 (Aimée 3)

Maison sous les arbres, 1971 (Dunaway 3, Buchman 4, Perry 4)

Maisons de la misère, 1937 (Storck 2, Jaubert 4)

Maître après Dieu, 1950 (Brasseur 3)

Maître Bolbec et son mari, 1934 (D'Eaubonne 4)

Maître de forges, 1933 (Gance 2, Stradling 4)

Maître de Montpellier, 1960 (Leenhardt 2)

Maître du temps, 1970 (Guerra 2)

Maitre Galip, 1962 (Pialat 2)

Maître nageur, 1979 (Trintignant 3)

Maîtres fous, 1955 (Rouch 2, Braunberger 4)

Maitres-Nageurs, 1950 (Berry 3)

Maîtresse, 1975 (Depardieu 3, Almendros 4)

Maj på Malö, 1947 (Nykvist 3)

Maja desnuda. See Naked Maja, 1958

Maja zwischen zwei Ehen, 1938 (Dagover 3)

Majboor, 1974 (Bachchan 3)

Majesty of the Law, 1915 (Bosworth 3)

Major and the Minor, 1942 (Wilder 2, Milland 3, Rogers 3, Benchley 4, Brackett 4, Dreier 4, Head 4, Laszlo 4)

Major Barbara, 1941 (Lean 2, Harrison 3, Kerr 3, Newton 3, Beaton 4, Korda 4, Mayer 4, Walton 4)

Major Bowes' Amateur Theatre of the Air, 1935 (Sinatra 3)

Major Dundee, 1964 (Peckinpah 2,
    Coburn 3, Harris 3, Heston 3, Johnson 3,
    Oates 3)
Major from Ireland, 1912 (Olcott 2)
Major que no tuvo infancia, 1956
    (Armendáriz 3)
Majorca, 1913 (Gaumont 4)
Majordôme, 1964 (Delannoy 2, Jeanson 4)
Majority of One, 1961 (LeRoy 2,
    Guinness 3, Russell 3, Orry-Kelly 4,
    Steiner 4, Stradling 4)
Májové hvězdy, 1959 (Brejchová 3)
Makan no. 44, 1955 (Anand 3, Burman 4)
Makbet, 1969 (Wajda 2)
Make a Wish, 1937 (Rathbone 3)
Make Believe Ballroom, 1949 (Mercer 4)
Make Fruitful the Land, 1945 (Unsworth 4)
Make Haste to Live, 1954 (Bernstein 4)
Make It Real, 1948 (Ford 3)
Make It Snappy, 1921 (Roach 4)
Make Me an Offer, 1954 (Finch 3,
    Addison 4, Mankowitz 4)
Make Me a Star, 1932 (Blondell 3,
    Chevalier 3, Cooper 3, March 3,
    Sidney 3)
Make Mine Mink, 1960 (Terry-Thomas 3,
    Dillon 4, Rank 4)
Make Mine Music, 1946 (Eddy 3, Disney 4,
    Iwerks 4)
Make Up. See Kesho, 1985
Make Way for a Lady, 1936 (Marshall 3)
Make Way for Lila. See Laila—Liebe unter
    der Mitternachtssonne, 1958
Make Way for Tomorrow, 1937 (McCarey 2,
    Beavers 3, Bondi 3, Dreier 4, Head 4,
    Young 4)
Make Your Own Bed, 1944 (Wyman 3,
    Burks 4)
Makedonskiot del od pekolot, 1971
    (Mimica 4)
Maker of Men, 1930 (Wayne 3)
Makin' It, 1970 (Hitchcock 2)
Making a Living, 1914 (Sennett 2)
Making a Man of Him, 1911 (Bosworth 3)
Making a Splash, 1984 (Greenaway 2)
Making Friends, 1936 (Fleischer 4)
Making Good, 1912 (Reid 3)
Making Good, 1932 (Lantz 4)
Making It Move, 1977 (Halas and
    Batchelor 4)
Making Love, 1982 (Reynolds 4,
    Rosenman 4)
Making Michael Jackson's Thriller, 1983
    (Landis 2)
Making Mr. Right, 1987 (Seidelman 2)
Making Music Together, 1973 (Halas and
    Batchelor 4)
Making of a Legend: Gone with the Wind,
    1988 (McQueen 3)
Making of a ''Local Hero'', 1983
    (Lancaster 3)
Making of a Man, 1911 (Griffith 2, Sweet 3,
    Bitzer 4)
Making of an Automobile Tire, 1913
    (Sennett 2)
Making of Broncho Billy, 1913
    (Anderson 3)
Making of Superman: The Movie, 1980
    (Hackman 3)
Making Photoplays in Egypt, 1912 (Olcott 2)
Making Stars, 1935 (Fleischer 4)
Making the Grade, 1947 (Matthews 3)
Makioka Sisters. See Sasame-yuki, 1950
Mal. See Rage, 1966

Mal d'aimer, 1986 (Josephson 3)
Mal de mer, 1912 (Linder 3)
Mal des autres, 1959 (Delerue 4)
Mal du siècle, 1953 (Lelouch 2)
Mala hembre, 1950 (Alcoriza 4)
Mala kronika, 1962 (Mimica 4)
Malá mořská víla, 1976 (Kučera 4)
''Mala'' ordina, 1972 (Cusack 3)
Mala the Magnificent. See Eskimo, 1933
Malachi's Cove. See Seaweed Children,
    1973
Malade hydrophobe, 1900 (Méliès 2)
Malade imaginaire. See Malato imaginario,
    1979
Maladie d'amour, 1987 (Kinski 3, Piccoli 3)
Malady of Love. See Mal d'aimer, 1986
Malady of Love. See Maladie d'amour, 1987
Malaga, 1954 (O'Hara 3, Challis 4, Korda 4)
Malaga. See Moment of Danger, 1960
Malahierra, 1940 (Armendáriz 3)
Malaire, 1950 (Vanel 3)
Malakhov Kurgan, 1944 (Heifitz 2)
Malamondo. See Malamondo, 1964
Malamondo, 1964 (Morricone 4)
Malaria, 1941 (Hayakawa 3)
Mälarpirater, 1923 (Molander 2,
    Magnusson 4)
Mälarpirater, 1959 (Björnstrand 3)
Malatesta, 1970 (Constantine 3)
Malato imaginario, 1979 (Blier 3)
Malaya, 1949 (Barrymore 3, Greenstreet 3,
    Stewart 3, Tracy 3, Folsey 4, Head 4,
    Irene 4, Kaper 4)
Malcolm X, 1972 (Jones 3)
Maldone, 1927 (Grémillon 2, Honegger 4,
    Matras 4, Périnal 4)
Maldoror, 1950 (Anger 2)
Male and Female, 1919 (Daniels 3,
    Swanson 3, Buckland 4, Howe 4,
    Macpherson 4, Zukor 4)
Male Animal, 1942 (De Havilland 3,
    Fonda 3, McDaniel 3, Edeson 4,
    Epstein 4, Wallis 4)
Male Companion. See Monsieur de
    compagnie, 1964
Mâle du siècle, 1975 (Forman 2)
Male Game. See Muzne Hry, 1988
Male Hunt. See Chasse à l'homme, 1964
Male Man, 1931 (Fleischer 4)
Male oscuro, 1990 (Giannini 3)
Male oscuro, 1990 (Cecchi D'Amico 4,
    Morricone 4)
Maledetto imbroglio, 1959 (Cardinale 3)
Maléfice, 1912 (Feuillade 2)
Malencontre, 1920 (Dulac 2)
Maleta, 1960 (Ruiz 2)
Malevil, 1981 (Trintignant 3, Douy 4)
Malfray, 1948 (Resnais 2)
Malheur n'arrive jamais seul, 1903
    (Méliès 2)
Malheur qui passe, 1916 (Feuillade 2)
Malheurs de la guerre, 1962 (Storck 2)
Malheurs de Sophie, 1945 (Trauner 4)
Malia, 1918 (Bertini 3)
Malia, 1945 (Castellani 2, Brazzi 3, Cervi 3)
Malibran, 1944 (Cocteau 2, Guitry 2)
Malibu, 1983 (Coburn 3, Novak 3, Saint 3)
Malibu Beach, 1939 (Freleng 4)
Malibu Beach Party, 1940 (Blanc 4,
    Stalling 4)
Malice in Slumberland, 1929 (Fleischer 4)
Malice in the Palace, 1949 (Three Stooges 3)
Malice in Wonderland, 1985 (Taylor 3)
Malina, 1991 (Schroeter 2, Huppert 3)

Malizia, 1973 (Storaro 4)
Malkat Hakita, 1986 (Golan and Globus 4)
Mallarmé, 1964 (Rohmer 2)
Malle au mariage, 1912 (Linder 3)
Malmaison, 1963 (Fresnay 3)
Malombra, 1916 (Gallone 2)
Malombra, 1942 (Castellani 2, De
    Laurentiis 4)
Malone, 1987 (Reynolds 3, Robertson 3)
Malou, 1983 (Ballhaus 4)
Malpertuis, 1972 (Welles 2, Cassel 3,
    Delerue 4, Fisher 4)
Malquerida, 1949 (Fernández 2, Del Rio 3,
    Figueroa 4)
Malrif, aigle royal, 1960 (Jarre 4)
Malta Story, 1953 (Guinness 3, Hawkins 3,
    Alwyn 4, Krasker 4, Rank 4)
Maltese Bippy, 1969 (Daniels 4, Frank 4)
Maltese Falcon, 1931 (Daniels 3)
**Maltese Falcon, 1941 (Huston 2, Astor 3,
    Bogart 3, Bond 3, Greenstreet 3,
    Huston 3, Lorre 3, Blanke 4,
    Deutsch 4, Edeson 4, Orry-Kelly 4,
    Wallis 4)**
Malu tianshi, 1937 (Zhao 3)
Malvados, 1965 (Fernández 2)
Małżeństwo z rozsądki, 1967 (Olbrychski 3)
Mam, Behave, 1926 (Roach 4)
Mama Behave, 1926 (McCarey 2)
Mamá cumple cien años, 1979 (Saura 2,
    Chaplin 3)
Mama Loves Papa, 1933 (McLeod 2,
    Stevens 2, Johnson 4)
Mama no shinkon-ryoko, 1954 (Yamada 3,
    Yamamura 3)
Mama Steps Out, 1937 (Emerson 4, Loos 4)
Mama Turns 100, 1988 (Chaplin 3)
Mama Turns a Hundred. See Mamá cumple
    cien años, 1979
Mamaia, 1966 (Braunberger 4)
Maman Colibri, 1929 (Christian-Jaque 2,
    Duvivier 2)
Maman et la putain, 1973 (Léaud 3)
Maman Popee, 1919 (Gallone 2)
Mama's Affair, 1921 (Emerson 4, Loos 4,
    Schenck 4)
Mama's Dirty Girls, 1974 (Grahame 3)
Mama's Little Pirate, 1935 (Roach 4)
Mama's New Hat, 1939 (Freleng 4)
Mamba, 1930 (Johnson 3)
Mambo, 1954 (Rossen 2, Gassman 3,
    Mangano 3, Winters 3, Andrejew 4, De
    Laurentiis 4, Ponti 4, Rosson 4, Rota 4)
Mambo Kings, 1991 (Ballhaus 4)
Mame, 1974 (Ball 3, Preston 3, Boyle 4, Van
    Runkle 4)
Mamie Rose. See Mørke Punkt, 1911
Mamma mia, che impressione, 1951
    (Sordi 3, Zavattini 4)
Mamma Roma, 1962 (Pasolini 2, Magnani 3,
    Delli Colli 4)
Mamma's Affair, 1921 (Fleming 2)
Mamma's Boy, 1920 (Roach 4)
Mamma's Boys, 1916 (Laurel and
    Hardy 4)
Mammame, 1986 (Ruiz 2, De Almeida 4)
Mammo Kenkoku no Reimei, 1932
    (Mizoguchi 2)
Mammy, 1930 (Curtiz 2, Bosworth 3,
    Jolson 3, Berlin 4)
Mammy Water, 1955 (Braunberger 4)
Mammy Water, 1965 (Rouch 2)
Mammy's Rose, 1916 (Borzage 2)
Mamouret. See Briseur de chaînes, 1941

Mampou hattenshi: Umi no gouzoku, 1942 (Miyagawa 4)

Mamsell Josabeth, 1963 (Fischer 4)

Mamsell Nitouche, 1931 (Ondra 3, Heller 4)

Mam'selle Striptease. See Effeuillant la Marguerite, 1956

Mam'zell Pigalle. See Cette Sacrée gamine, 1955

Mam'zelle Bonaparte, 1941 (Tourneur 2, Feuillère 3)

Mam'zelle Chiffon, 1919 (Musidora 3)

Mam'zelle Cricri. See Deutschmeister, 1955

Mam'zelle Nitouche, 1931 (Allégret 2, Raimu 3, Simon 3, Braunberger 4)

Mam'zelle Nitouche, 1953 (Allégret 2, Fernandel 3, Achard 3, Aurenche 4, D'Eaubonne 4, Wakhévitch 4)

Mam'zelle Souris, 1958 (Delerue 4)

Mam'zelle Spahi, 1934 (Douy 4)

Mam'zelle Striptease. See Effeuillant la Marguerite, 1956

Man, 1910 (Griffith 2, Bitzer 4)

Man, 1921 (Carré 4)

Man, 1972 (Ayres 3, Jones 3, Meredith 3, Goldsmith 4)

Man: A Modern Drama. See Chelovek, drama nachidnya, 1912

Man, A Woman, and a Bank. See Very Big Withdrawal, 1979

Man About the House, 1946 (Korda 4, Périnal 4)

Man About the House. See Vendetta nel sole, 1947

Man About Town, 1923 (Laurel and Hardy 3, Roach 4)

Man About Town, 1932 (Howe 4)

Man About Town, 1939 (Grable 3, Lamour 3, Dreier 4, Head 4, Prinz 4, Ryskind 4, Young 4)

Man About Town. See Silence est d'or, 1947

Man Afraid, 1957 (Mancini 4, Metty 4)

Man Against Man. See Mr. "Silent" Haskins, 1915

Man Against Man. See Otoko tai otoko, 1960

Man Alive, 1945 (Menjou 3)

Man Alone, 1923 (Bosworth 3)

Man Alone, 1955 (Bond 3, Milland 3, Van Cleef 3, Young 4)

Man among Men. See Dansei No. 1, 1955

Man and a Woman. See Homme et une femme, 1966

Man and Boy, 1971 (Jones 4)

Man and His Dog Out for Air, 1958 (Breer 4)

Man and His Mate. See One Million B.C., 1939

Man and His Soul, 1916 (Bushman 3)

Man and His Tools, 1962 (Hubley 4)

Man and His World, 1967 (Vanderbeek 2, Vukotić 4)

Man and Maid, 1925 (Gibbons 4)

Man and the Girl, 1909 (Olcott 2)

Man and the Moment, 1929 (Grot 4, Polito 4)

Man and the Snake, 1972 (Fisher 4)

Man and the Woman, 1908 (Griffith 2, Bitzer 4)

Man and the Woman, 1917 (Guy 2)

Man and Wife, 1923 (Costello 3, Shearer 3)

Man at Large, 1941 (Day 4, Miller 4)

Man Bait, 1926 (Crisp 3, Rosson 4)

Man Bait. See Last Page, 1952

Man Behind the Door, 1914 (Menjou 3)

Man Behind the Gun, 1952 (Scott 3, Buckner 4, Glennon 4)

Man Behind the Mask, 1936 (Powell and Pressburger 2, Carey 3)

Man Beneath, 1919 (Hayakawa 3)

Man Betrayed, 1941 (Bond 3, Wayne 3)

Man Between, 1953 (Reed 2, Bloom 3, Mason 3, Addison 4, Andrejew 4, Korda 4)

Man braucht kein Geld, 1931 (Lamarr 3)

Man By the Roadside. See Mensch am Wege, 1923

Man Called Adam, 1966 (Levine 4)

Man Called Back, 1932 (Florey 2)

Man Called Dagger, 1967 (Kovacs 4)

Man Called Flintstone, 1966 (Hanna and Barbera 4)

Man Called Gannon, 1969 (Bumstead 4, Chase 4)

Man Called Horse, 1970 (Harris 3, Rosenman 4)

Man Called John. See . . . e venne un uomo, 1965

Man Called Peter, 1955 (Newman 4)

Man Called Sarge, 1989 (Golan and Globus 4)

Man Called Sledge, 1970 (Garner 3)

Man Called Sullivan. See Great John L., 1944

Man Could Get Killed, 1966 (Garner 3, Mercouri 3, Clarke 4)

Man Crazy, 1953 (Crosby 4)

Man for All Seasons, 1966 (Welles 2, Zinnemann 2, Hurt 3, Redgrave 3, Shaw 3, York 3, Box 4, Delerue 4)

Man for All Seasons, 1988 (Heston 3)

Man for All That, 1915 (Walsh 2)

Man for A'That, 1914 (Bushman 3)

Man for Burning. See Uomo da bruciare, 1960

Man Friday, 1975 (O'Toole 3)

Man from Bitteridge, 1955 (Metty 4)

Man from Blankley's. See Fourteenth Man, 1920

Man from Blankley's, 1930 (Barrymore 3, Young 3)

Man from Button Willow, 1965 (Keel 3)

Man from Cairo, 1953 (Raft 3)

Man from Cheyenne, 1942 (Rogers 3)

Man from Cocody. See Gentleman de Cocody, 1965

Man from Colorado, 1948 (Ford 3, Holden 3, Chase 4, Duning 4, Maddow 4)

Man from C.O.T.T.O.N. See Gone Are the Days!, 1962

Man from Dakota, 1940 (Beery 3, Del Rio 3)

Man from Del Rio, 1956 (Quinn 3, Cortez 4, Horner 4)

Man from Down Under, 1943 (Laughton 3, Reed 3, Irene 4)

Man from Downing Street, 1922 (Karloff 3)

Man from Far Away. See Uomo che viene de lontano, 1968

Man from Frisco, 1943 (Florey 2, Duryea 3)

Man from Funeral Range, 1918 (Reid 3)

Man from Galveston, 1963 (Coburn 3, Glennon 4)

Man from Hell, 1934 (Canutt 4)

Man from Hell's River, 1922 (Beery 3)

Man from Home, 1914 (Buckland 4)

Man from Home, 1914 (De Mille 2)

Man from Home, 1922 (Hitchcock 2, Miller 4)

Man from Independence, 1974 (Bernstein 4)

Man from Kangaroo, 1920 (Glennon 4, Meredyth 4)

Man from Laramie, 1955 (Mann 2, Crisp 3, Kennedy 3, Stewart 3, Cohn 4, Duning 4, Lang 4)

Man from Mexico, 1914 (Barrymore 3, Zukor 4)

Man from Monterey, 1933 (Wayne 3, McCord 4)

Man from Montreal, 1939 (Krasner 4)

Man from Morocco, 1944 (Walbrook 3)

Man from Music Mountain, 1938 (Autry 3)

Man from Music Mountain, 1943 (Rogers 3)

Man from Nowhere, 1915 (Hart 3, August 4)

Man from Oklahoma, 1945 (Rogers 3)

Man from Painted Post, 1917 (Fleming 2, Fairbanks 3)

Man from Planet X, 1951 (Ulmer 2)

Man from Red Gulch, 1925 (Carey 3, Stromberg 4)

Man from Snowy River, 1982 (Douglas 3)

Man from Texas, 1915 (Mix 3)

Man from Texas, 1924 (Carey 3)

Man from the Alamo, 1953 (Boetticher 2, Ford 3, Metty 4)

Man from the Diners' Club, 1963 (Tashlin 2, Kaye 3, Sloane 3, Stanton 3, Mohr 4)

Man from the East, 1911 (Dwan 2)

Man from the East, 1914 (Mix 3)

Man from the Folies Bergere. See Folies Bergere, 1935

Man from the Meteor, 1989 (Romero 2)

Man from the Other Side. See Chelovek s drugoi storoni, 1972

Man from the Pru, 1990 (York 3)

Man from the Restaurant. See Chelovek iz restorana, 1929

Man from Toronto, 1933 (Matthews 3, Balcon 4)

Man from Tumbleweeds, 1940 (Lewis 2)

Man from Utah, 1934 (Wayne 3, Canutt 4)

Man from Wyoming, 1930 (Cooper 3)

Man from Yesterday, 1932 (Zinnemann 2, Boyer 3, Colbert 3, Banton 4, Struss 4, Zukor 4)

Man from Yesterday, 1949 (Harvey 3)

Man Haters, 1922 (Roach 4)

Man Higher Up, 1913 (Bunny 3)

Man Hunt, 1911 (Dwan 2)

Man Hunt, 1935 (Ruttenberg 4)

Man Hunt, 1941 (Bennett 3, Carradine 3, McDowall 3, Pidgeon 3, Sanders 3, Banton 4, Day 4, MacGowan 4, Miller 4, Newman 4, Nichols 4)

Man I Killed, 1932 (Lubitsch 2, Barrymore 3, Dreier 4, Raphaelson 4, Vajda 4)

Man I Like. See Homme qui me plait, 1969

Man I Love, 1929 (Wellman 2, Banton 4, Mankiewicz 4, Selznick 4)

Man I Love, 1946 (Walsh 2, Lupino 3, Friedhofer 4, Steiner 4)

Man I Married, 1940 (Bennett 3, Day 4, Zanuck 4)

Man in a Cocked Hat. See Carlton-Browne of the F.O., 1958

Man in Black, 1950 (Carreras 4)

Man in Demand, 1955 (Lee 3)

Man in 5A, 1983 (Segal 3)

Man in Grey, 1943 (Granger 3, Lockwood 3, Mason 3, Rank 4)

Man in Half Moon Street, 1944 (Dreier 4, Fort 4, Head 4, Rozsa 4)

Man in Hiding. See Mantrap, 1953

Man in Him, 1916 (Anderson 3)

Man in Love. *See* Homme amoreux, 1987

Man in Milan, 1990 (Scorsese 2)

Man in Polar Regions, 1967 (Clarke 2)

Man in Possession, 1931 (Montgomery 3, Mayer 4)

Man in Possession. *See* Personal Property, 1937

Man in Silence, 1959 (Halas and Batchelor 4)

Man in the Attic, 1953 (Palance 3, Lemaire 4, Wheeler 4)

Man in the Box, 1908 (Bitzer 4)

Man in the Cabin, 1913 (Anderson 3)

Man in the Couch, 1914 (Browning 2)

Man in the Dark, 1953 (O'Brien 3, Crosby 4)

Man in the Glass Booth, 1975 (Schell 3, Anhalt 4)

Man in the Gray Flannel Suit, 1956 (Cobb 3, Jones 3, March 3, Peck 3, Clarke 4, Herrmann 4, Johnson 4, LeMaire 4, Smith 4, Wheeler 4, Zanuck 4)

Man in the Iron Mask, 1939 (Whale 2, Bennett 3, Cushing 3)

Man in the Iron Mask, 1977 (Jourdan 3, Richardson 3, Young 4)

Man in the Middle, 1964 (Howard 3, Mitchum 3, Barry 4)

Man in the Mirror, 1936 (Horton 3, Sim 3, Courant 4)

Man in the Moon. *See* Clair de lune espagnol, 1909

Man in the Moon, 1960 (Dearden 2, More 3, Rank 4)

Man in the Moon, 1991 (Francis 4)

Man in the Moonlight, 1919 (Moore 3)

Man in the Net, 1959 (Curtiz 2, Ladd 3, Mirisch 4, Salter 4, Seitz 4)

Man in the Raincoat. *See* Homme à l'imperméable, 1957

Man in the Road, 1957 (Cusack 3)

Man in the Saddle, 1926 (Karloff 3, Wray 3)

Man in the Saddle, 1951 (Scott 3, Brown 4, Duning 4)

Man in the Santa Claus Suit, 1980 (Astaire 3)

Man in the Shadow, 1957 (Salter 4)

Man in the Sky, 1956 (Hawkins 3, Pleasence 3, Slocombe 4)

Man in the Storm. *See* Arashi no naka no otoko, 1957

Man in the Trunk, 1942 (Day 4)

Man in the Vault, 1956 (Clothier 4)

Man in the White Suit, 1951 (Mackendrick 2, Greenwood 3, Guinness 3, Balcon 4, Slocombe 4)

Man in the Wilderness, 1971 (Huston 2, Harris 3, Fisher 4)

Man Inside, 1958 (Roeg 2, Palance 3, Pleasence 3)

Man Inside, 1990 (Baye 3)

Man Is Dead. *See* Homme est mort, 1973

Man Is Ten Feet Tall. *See* Edge of the City, 1957

Man Is to Man . . . , 1962 (Brynner 3)

Man Life Passed By, 1923 (Bosworth 3)

Man Made Monster, 1940 (Fulton 4, Salter 4)

Man Man's Ward, 1914 (Lawrence 3)

Man Must Live, 1925 (Rosson 4)

Man Next Door, 1913 (Sennett 2)

Man Next Door, 1965 (Kuri 4)

Man of Action, 1933 (Brennan 3)

Man of Affairs. *See* His Lordship, 1936

Man of a Thousand Faces, 1957 (Cagney 3, Malone 3, Westmore Family 4)

Man of Africa, 1953 (Grierson 2)

Man of Aran, 1934 (Flaherty 2, Balcon 4, Rank 4)

Man of Bronze. *See* Jim Thorpe—All American, 1951

Man of Conquest, 1939 (Fontaine 3, August 4, Canutt 4, Eason 4, Head 4, Young 4)

Man of Destiny, 1981 (Seyrig 3)

Man of Evil. *See* Fanny By Gaslight, 1944

Man of Honor, 1919 (Gaudio 4)

Man of Iron. *See* Iron Road, 1925

Man of Iron, 1935 (Astor 3)

Man of Iron. *See* Człowiek z żelaza, 1981

Man of La Mancha, 1972 (Loren 3, O'Toole 3)

Man of Marble. *See* Człowiek z marmuru, 1977

Man of Mayfair, 1931 (Buchanan 3)

Man of Music. *See* Kompozitor Glinka, 1952

Man of Nerve, 1925 (Arthur 3)

Man of Passion, 1989 (Quinn 3)

Man of Peace, 1928 (Bosworth 3)

Man of Stone, 1921 (Goulding 2)

Man of the Earth, 1915 (Lukas 3)

Man of the Forest, 1926 (Hathaway 2, Schulberg 4)

Man of the Forest, 1933 (Hathaway 2, Carey 3, Crabbe 3, Scott 3)

Man of the Hour, 1914 (Tourneur 2, Carré 4)

Man of the Hour. *See* Homme du jour, 1936

Man of the Hour. *See* Colonel Effingham's Raid, 1945

Man of the Moment. *See* Toki no ujigami, 1932

Man of the Moment, 1935 (Lockwood 3)

Man of the Moment, 1955 (Wisdom 3, Rank 4)

Man of the People, 1937 (Clarke 4)

Man of the West, 1958 (Mann 2, Cobb 3, Cooper 3, Haller 4, Mirisch 4)

Man of the World, 1931 (Lombard 3, Powell 3, Mankiewicz 4)

Man of the Year. *See* Homo eroticus, 1971

Man of Two Worlds, 1934 (Plunkett 4, Steiner 4)

Man of Wrath. *See* Wedding Group, 1936

Man on a Bus, 1955 (Lewis 2, Crawford 3)

Man on a Flying Trapeze, 1935 (Brennan 3)

Man on a String, 1960 (Borgnine 3, De Rochemont 4, Duning 4)

Man on a Swing, 1973 (Robertson 3, Schifrin 4)

Man on a Tightrope, 1953 (Kazan 2, Grahame 3, March 3, Menjou 3, LeMaire 4, Sherwood 4, Waxman 4)

Man on America's Conscience. *See* Tennessee Johnson, 1942

Man on Fire, 1957 (Crosby 3, Raksin 4, Ruttenberg 4)

Man on the Beach, 1955 (Losey 2, Carreras 4, Sangster 4)

Man on the Box, 1914 (De Mille 2, Buckland 4)

Man on the Case, 1914 (Dwan 2)

Man on the Eiffel Tower, 1949 (Laughton 3, Meredith 3, Cortez 4)

Man on the Flying Trapeze, 1934 (Fleischer 4)

Man on the Flying Trapeze, 1935 (Fields 3, Bruckman 4, Head 4)

Man on the Flying Trapeze, 1954 (Bosustow 4)

Man on the Prowl, 1957 (Musuraca 4)

Man on the Run, 1949 (Harvey 3, More 3)

Man on the Run. *See* Kidnappers, 1964

Man on the Track. *See* Człowiek na torze, 1956

Man Pasand, 1980 (Anand 3)

Man Pays, 1924 (Roach 4)

Man Power, 1927 (Cronjager 4, Schulberg 4)

Man, Pride, and Vengeance. *See* Uomo, L'orgoglio, la vendetta, 1967

Man spielt nicht mit der Liebe, 1926 (Krauss 3)

Man spielt nicht mit der Liebe, 1949 (Dagover 3)

Man steigt nach, 1927 (Metzner 4)

Man Taking Off His Gloves. *See* Tebukuro o nugasu otoko, 1946

Man There Was. *See* Terje Vigen, 1917

Man They Could Not Arrest, 1931 (Balcon 4)

Man They Could Not Hang, 1939 (Karloff 3, Brown 4)

Man Thou Gavest Me. *See* Eternal Struggle, 1923

Man to Kill. *See* Homme à abattre, 1967

Man to Man, 1922 (Carey 3)

Man to Man, 1930 (Dwan 2)

Man to Men. *See* D'homme à hommes, 1948

Man to Remember, 1938 (Kanin 4, Polglase 4, Trumbo 4)

Man to Respect. *See* Uomo da rispettare, 1972

Man Trap, 1917 (Young 4)

Man Trouble, 1930 (Zinnemann 2, August 4)

Man Under Cover, 1922 (Browning 2, Miller 4)

Man Under Suspicion, 1984 (Schell 3)

Man Under Water. *See* Clověk pod vodou, 1961

Man Upstairs, 1958 (Attenborough 3)

Man vs. Man. *See* Otoko tai otoko, 1960

Man Wanted, 1932 (Dieterle 2, Francis 3, Toland 4)

Man Who Broke the Bank at Monte Carlo, 1935 (Bennett 3, Carradine 3, Colman 3, Johnson 4, Zanuck 4)

Man Who Came Back, 1924 (Goulding 2)

Man Who Came Back, 1930 (Walsh 2, Gaynor 3, Edeson 4, Friedhofer 4)

Man Who Came Back. *See* Swamp Water, 1941

Man Who Came to Dinner, 1941 (Davis 3, Durante 3, Sheridan 3, Epstein 4, Gaudio 4, Orry-Kelly 4, Wald 4, Wallis 4)

Man Who Came to the Port. *See* Minato e kita otoko, 1952

Man Who Changed His Mind. *See* Man Who Lived Again, 1936

Man Who Cheated Himself, 1950 (Cobb 3, Harlan 4, Polglase 4)

Man Who Cheated Life. *See* Student von Prag, 1926

Man Who Committed Murder. *See* Mann, der den Mord beging, 1931

Man Who Could Cheat Death, 1959 (Fisher 2, Lee 3, Carreras 4, Sangster 4)

Man Who Could Work Miracles, 1936 (Richardson 3, Sanders 3, Hornbeck 4, Korda, A. 4, Korda, V. 4, Krasker 4, Rosson 4)

Man Who Couldn't Beat God, 1915
(Costello 3)
Man Who Dared, 1920 (Furthman 4)
Man Who Dared, 1933 (Miller 4, Nichols 4,
Trotti 4)
Man Who Dared, 1946 (Sturges 2)
Man Who Dared God, 1917 (Weber 2)
Man Who Envied Women, 1985 (Rainer 2,
Chandler 4)
Man Who Fell to Earth, 1976 (Roeg 2,
Henry 4)
Man Who Fights Alone, 1924 (Horton 3)
Man Who Finally Died, 1962 (Zetterling 2,
Baker 3, Cushing 3)
Man Who Found Himself, 1937 (Fontaine 3,
Hunt 4)
Man Who Had His Hair Cut Short. See Man
die zijn haar kort liet knippen, 1966
Man Who Haunted Himself, 1970
(Dearden 2)
Man Who Knew Too Much, 1934
(Hitchcock 2, Fresnay 3, Lorre 3,
Balcon 4, Bennett 4, Courant 4, Junge 4)
Man Who Knew Too Much, 1955
(Hitchcock 2, Day 3, Gélin 3, Stewart 3,
Bennett 4, Bumstead 4, Burks 4,
Hayes 4, Head 4, Herrmann 4,
Whitlock 4)
Man Who Laughed Last, 1929 (Hayakawa 3)
Man Who Laughs, 1928 (Leni 2, Veidt 3)
Man Who Left His Will on Film. See Tokyo
senso sengo hiwa, 1970
Man Who Lies. See Homme qui ment, 1968
Man Who Lived Again, 1936 (Launder and
Gilliat 2, Stevenson 2, Karloff 3,
Balcon 4, Balderston 4, Rank 4,
Vetchinsky 4)
Man Who Lived Twice, 1936 (Bellamy 3,
Bond 3)
Man Who Lost Himself, 1941 (Francis 3,
Salter 4)
Man Who Lost His Shadow. See Homme qui
a perdu son ombre, 1991
Man Who Loved Cat Dancing, 1973
(Cobb 3, Reynolds 3, Perry 4,
Williams 4)
Man Who Loved Redheads, 1955 (Elliott 3,
Korda 4, Périnal 4, Rattigan 4)
Man Who Loved Women. See Homme qui
aimait les femmes, 1977
Man Who Loved Women, 1983 (Edwards 2,
Andrews 3, Reynolds 3, Mancini 4,
Wexler 4)
Man Who Made the Army, 1917 (Pearson 2)
Man Who Murdered. See Mann, der den
Mord beging, 1930
Man Who Never Was, 1956 (Cusack 3,
Grahame 3, Sellers 3, Webb 3, Korda 4,
Mathieson 4, Morris 4)
Man Who Paid, 1922 (Shearer 3)
Man Who Played God, 1922 (Arliss 3,
Astor 3)
Man Who Played God, 1932 (Arliss 3,
Davis 3, Milland 3)
Man Who Reclaimed His Head, 1934
(Bennett 3, Rains 3, D'Agostino 4)
Man Who Saw Tomorrow, 1981 (Welles 2)
**Man Who Shot Liberty Valance, 1962
(Ford 2, Carradine 3, Marvin 3,
O'Brien 3, Stewart 3, Van Cleef 3,
Wayne 3, Clothier 4, Head 4,
Newman 4, Westmore Family 4)**
Man Who Stayed at Home, 1915
(Hepworth 2)

Man Who Talked Too Much, 1940
(Barthelmess 3)
Man Who Turned to Stone, 1957
(Katzman 4)
Man Who Understood Women, 1959
(Caron 3, Dalio 3, Fonda 3, Johnson 4,
Krasner 4, Wheeler 4)
Man Who Wagged His Tail. See Angel paso
sobre Brooklyn, 1957
Man Who Waited, 1922 (Pierce 4)
Man Who Watched Trains Go By. See Paris
Express, 1953
Man Who Went Out, 1913 (August 4)
Man Who Won, 1919 (Costello 3)
Man Who Won, 1923 (Wellman 2, August 4)
Man Who Would Be King, 1975 (Huston 2,
Caine 3, Connery 3, Head 4, Jarre 4,
Morris 4, Trauner 4, Whitlock 4)
Man Who Would Not Die, 1975 (Malone 3)
Man Who Wouldn't Die, 1942 (Day 4,
Raksin 4)
Man Who Wouldn't Talk, 1940 (Marsh 3,
Day 4, Miller 4)
Man Who Wouldn't Talk, 1958 (Wilcox 2,
Neagle 3, Quayle 3)
Man with a Cloak, 1951 (Calhern 3, Caron 3,
Cotten 3, Stanwyck 3, Folsey 4,
Plunkett 4, Raksin 4)
Man with a Dog, 1958 (Carreras 4)
Man with a Gun. See Chelovek s ruzhyom,
1938
Man with a Gun, 1958 (Rank 4)
Man with a Million. See Million Pound Note,
1953
Man with a Movie Camera. See **Chelovek s
kinoapparatom, 1929**
Man with an Umbrella. See Det regnar på vår
kärlek, 1946
Man with Bogart's Face, 1978 (De Carlo 3,
Lom 3, Raft 3, Duning 4)
Man with Nine Lives, 1940 (Karloff 3,
Brown 4)
Man with One Red Shoe, 1985 (Hanks 3)
Man with the Balloons. See Oggi, domani,
dopodomani, 1965
Man with the Deadly Lens. See Wrong is
Right, 1982
Man with the Electric Voice. See Fifteen
Wives, 1935
Man with the Golden Arm, 1955
(Preminger 2, Novak 3, Sinatra 3, Bass 4,
Bernstein 4)
Man with the Golden Gun, 1974 (Lee 3,
Barry 4)
Man with the Golden Touch. See Az
aranyember, 1918
Man with the Green Carnation. See Trials of
Oscar Wilde, 1960
Man with the Gun, 1955 (Dickinson 3,
Mitchum 3, Garmes 4, North 4)
Man with the Rubber Head. See Homme à la
tête de caoutchouc, 1902
Man with the Scar. See Scar Hanan, 1925
Man with the Synthetic Brain. See Blood of
Ghastly Horror, 1972
Man with the X-Ray Eyes, 1963 (Milland 3,
Crosby 4)
Man with Thirty Sons. See Magnificent
Yankee, 1950
Man with Three Wives, 1909 (Sweet 3)
Man with Two Brains, 1983 (Martin 3,
Turner 3)
Man with Two Faces, 1934 (Astor 3,
Calhern 3, Robinson 3, Gaudio 4)

Man with Two Hearts. See Ketszívü férfi,
1916
Man with Wheels in His Head. See Malade
hydrophobe, 1900
Man within, 1914 (Reid 3)
Man within, 1916 (Mix 3)
Man within, 1947 (Attenborough 3,
Greenwood 3, Redgrave 3, Box 4,
Greene 4, Rank 4, Unsworth 4)
Man without a Country, 1973 (Robertson 3)
Man without a Face, 1935 (Cusack 3)
Man without a Heart. See Muž bez srdce,
1923
Man without a Map. See Moetikuta chizu,
1968
Man without a Name. See Mann ohne
Namen, 1920
Man without a Name. See Mensch ohne
Namen, 1932
Man without a Soul. See Man Without
Desire, 1923
Man without a Star, 1955 (Vidor 2,
Douglas 3, Trevor 3, Van Cleef 3,
Chase 4, Metty 4, Salter 4)
Man without Desire, 1923 (Novello 3)
Man without Mercy. See Gone with the
West, 1975
Man, Woman, and Child, 1983 (Delerue 4)
Man, Woman, and Dog, 1964 (Kuri 4)
Man, Woman, and Sin, 1927 (Gilbert 3,
Gibbons 4)
Man, Woman, and Wife, 1929 (Mandell 4)
Managed Money, 1934 (Temple 3)
Manbeast! Myth or Monster, 1978 (Bottin 4)
Manche et la belle, 1957 (D'Eaubonne 4,
Matras 4)
**Manchurian Candidate, 1962
(Frankenheimer 2, Harvey 3,
Lansbury 3, Leigh 3, Sinatra 3,
Axelrod 4, Koch 4, Sylbert 4)**
Mandacaru vermelho, 1961 (Pereira Dos
Santos 2)
Mandalay, 1934 (Curtiz 2, Francis 3,
Temple 3, Gaudio 4, Grot 4)
Mandarin, bandit gentilhomme, 1962
(Douy 4)
Mandarin Mix-Up, 1924 (Laurel and
Hardy 3)
Mandarin Mystery, 1936 (Pangborn 3)
Mandarine, 1972 (Girardot 3, Noiret 3)
Mandarino per Teo, 1960 (Di Venanzo 4)
Mandate of Heaven, 1979 (Carradine 3)
Manden, der ville varer Skyldig, 1990
(Karina 3)
Manden uden Smil, 1916 (Holger-Madsen 2)
Mandi, 1983 (Azmi 3, Patil 3)
Mandingo, 1975 (Mason 3, De Laurentiis 4,
Jarre 4, Leven 4)
Mandragola, 1965 (Delli Colli 4, Donati 4)
Mandragora. See Galgamannen, 1945
Mandragore. See Alraune, 1952
Mandrake. See Alraune, 1927
Mandy, 1952 (Mackendrick 2, Hawkins 3,
Alwyn 4, Slocombe 4)
Maneater, 1973 (Sangster 4)
Man-Eater of Kumaon, 1948 (Haskin 4,
Salter 4)
Man-Eating Sharks, 1932 (Sennett 2)
Manèges, 1950 (Allégret 2, Blier 3,
Signoret 3, Trauner 4)
Manet ou le novateur malgré lui, 1980
(Leenhardt 2)
Mangeclous, 1988 (Blier 3, Sarde 4)
Mangetsu sanju-koku-sen, 1952 (Yamada 3)

Mangiala, 1969 (Morricone 4)

Manhã na Roça. *See* Segredo das Asas, 1944

Manhandled, 1924 (Dwan 2, Swanson 3, Rosson 4, Zukor 4)

Manhandled, 1949 (Duryea 3, Hayden 3, Lamour 3, Head 4, Laszlo 4)

Manhattan, 1924 (Rosson 4)

Manhattan, 1979 (Allen 2, Keaton 3, Streep 3, Willis 4)

Manhattan Angel, 1949 (Katzman 4)

Manhattan Cocktail, 1928 (Arzner 2, Lukas 3, Vajda 4)

Manhattan Cowboy, 1928 (Vajda 4)

Manhattan Heartbeat, 1940 (Day 4, Miller 4)

Manhattan Knights, 1928 (Johnson 3)

Manhattan Lovesong, 1934 (Pangborn 3)

Manhattan Madness, 1916 (Dwan 2, Fleming 2, Fairbanks 3, Menjou 3, Emerson 4, Loos 4)

Manhattan Madness. *See* Woman Wanted, 1935

Manhattan Madness. *See* Adventure in Manhattan, 1936

Manhattan Madness, 1945 (Fleming 2)

Manhattan Melodrama, 1934 (Mankiewicz 2, Van Dyke 2, Gable 3, Loy 3, Powell 3, Rooney 3, Howe 4, Selznick 4, Mayer 4, Vorkapich 4)

Manhattan Memories, 1947 (Fleischer 4)

Manhattan Merry-Go-Round, 1937 (Autry 3)

Manhattan Monkey Business, 1935 (Roach 4)

Manhattan Moon, 1935 (D'Agostino 4)

Manhattan Parade, 1932 (Bacon 2)

Manhattan Project, 1986 (Sarde 4)

Manhunt. *See* From Hell to Texas, 1958

Manhunt, 1986 (Borgnine 3)

Manhunt in Milan. *See* "Mala" ordina, 1972

Manhunt of Mystery Island, 1945 (Canutt 4)

Mania, 1918 (Negri 3)

Mania. *See* Flesh and the Fiends, 1960

Maniac, 1911 (Lawrence 3)

Maniac, 1962 (Carreras 4, Sangster 4)

Maniac, 1978 (Reed 3)

Maniac, 1980 (Savini 4)

Maniac Cook, 1908 (Griffith 2, Bitzer 4)

Maniac Cop, 1988 (Cohen 2)

Maniac's Desire, 1910 (White 3)

Maniacs on Wheels. *See* Once a Jolly Swagman, 1948

Manicure Girl, 1925 (Daniels 3, Hunt 4)

Manicure Lady, 1911 (Sennett 2)

Manicurist, 1916 (Sennett 2)

Manifesto, 1988 (Golan and Globus 4, Morricone 4)

Manifesto, 1989 (Makavejev 2)

Mani sporche, 1978 (Mastroianni 3, Morricone 4)

Mani sulla citta, 1963 (Steiger 3, Di Venanzo 4)

Manila Calling, 1942 (Wilde 3, Day 4, Raksin 4)

Manitou, 1977 (Curtis 3, Meredith 3, Schifrin 4)

Manja Walewska, 1936 (Tschechowa 3)

Manjudhar, 1947 (Biswas 4)

Mankinda, 1957 (Vanderbeek 2)

Manly Man, 1911 (Pickford 3, Gaudio 4, Ince 4)

Man-Made Famine, 1986 (Jackson 3)

Manmohan, 1936 (Mehboob 2)

Mann auf Abwegen, 1939 (Albers 3)

Mann auf den Schienen. *See* Człowiek na torze, 1956

Mann aus dem Jenseits, 1925 (Albers 3, Tschechowa 3, Wegener 3)

Mann, dem man den Namen stahl, 1945 (Staudte 2)

Mann, der den Mord beging, 1931 (Veidt 3, Courant 4, Warm 4)

Mann, der seinen Mörder sucht, 1931 (Siodmak 2, Wilder 2, Herlth 4, Röhrig 4, Siodmak 4)

Mann, der Sherlock Holmes war, 1937 (Albers 3, Wagner 4)

Mann der Tat, 1919 (Jannings 3)

Mann der zweimal Leben wolte, 1950 (Tschechowa 3)

Mann im Feuer, 1926 (Tschechowa 3)

Mann im Spiegel, 1916 (Freund 4, Messter 4)

Mann im Storm, 1958 (Albers 3)

Mann mit den sieben Masken, 1918 (Messter 4)

Mann mit der Pranke, 1935 (Wegener 3, Von Harbou 4)

Mann mit Grundsaltzen?, 1943 (Herlth 4)

Mann mit Herz, 1932 (Fröhlich 3)

Mann nennt es Amore, 1961 (Fusco 4)

Mann ohne Namen, 1920 (Krauss 3)

Mann seiner Frau, 1925 (Planer 4)

Mann Spiegel, 1916 (Wiene 2)

Mann um Mitternacht, 1924 (Holger-Madsen 2, Junge 4)

Mann will nach Deutschland, 1934 (Wegener 3, Wagner 4)

Mandacaru vermelho, 1961 (Pereira Dos Santos 2)

Mandalay, 1934 (Curtiz 2, Francis 3, Temple 3, Gaudio 4, Grot 4)

Människor i stad, 1947 (Sucksdorff 2)

Människor mötas och ljuv musik uppstår i hjärtat. *See* Mennesker modes och sod musik opstår i hjertet, 1967

Mannekängen, 1913 (Stiller 2, Jaenzon 4)

Mannequin, 1926 (Cruze 2, Costello 3, Pidgeon 3, Brown 4)

Mannequin, 1933 (Bennett 4)

Mannequin, 1938 (Borzage 2, Mankiewicz 2, Crawford 3, Tracy 3, Adrian 4, Folsey 4, Mayer 4)

Mannequin assassiné, 1947 (Gélin 3)

Mannequins, 1933 (D'Eaubonne 4)

Mannequins de Paris, 1956 (Audiard 4)

Männer sind zum Lieben da, 1960 (Warm 4)

Manner um Lucie. *See* Rive Gauche, 1931

Männer vom blauen kreuz. *See* Błękitny Krzyż, 1955

Mannesmann, 1937 (Ruttman 2)

Mano che nutre la morte, 1973 (Kinski 3)

Mano dello straniero, 1953 (Howard 3, Valli 3, Greene 4, Rota 4)

Mano en la trampa, 1961 (Torre Nilsson 2)

Mano nascosta di Dio, 1971 (Kinski 3)

Mano spietat della legge, 1973 (Cusack 3, Kinski 3)

Manoeuvre, 1980 (Wiseman 2)

Manolesco, roi des voleurs. *See* Manolescu, 1929

Manolescu, 1929 (Mozhukin 3, Herlth 4, Hoffmann 4, Röhrig 4)

Manolescus Memoiren, 1920 (Dreier 4)

Manolete, 1944 (Gance 2)

Manolis, 1962 (Theodorakis 4)

Manon, 1948 (Clouzot 2, Reggiani 3, Douy 4)

Manon de Montmartre, 1914 (Feuillade 2)

Manon des sources, 1952 (Pagnol 2)

Manon des sources, 1986 (Montand 3)

Manon Lescaut, 1926 (Leni 2)

Manon Lescaut, 1926 (Dietrich 3, Johnson 3, Pommer 4)

Manon Lescaut, 1940 (De Sica 2, Gallone 2, Valli 3)

Manon 70, 1968 (Deneuve 3)

Manpower, 1941 (Walsh 2, Arden 3, Bond 3, Dietrich 3, Raft 3, Robinson 3, Deutsch 4, Haller 4, Haskin 4, Wald 4, Wallis 4)

Man-Proof, 1938 (Loy 3, Pidgeon 3, Russell 3, Freund 4, Waxman 4, Young 4)

Manque de mémoire, 1929 (Maté 4)

Mans, 1971 (McQueen 3, Legrand 4)

Man's Angle, 1942 (Benchley 4)

Man's Best Friend, 1941 (Lantz 4)

Man's Calling, 1911 (Dwan 2)

Man's Castle, 1933 (Borzage 2, Tracy 3, Young 3, August 4, Cohn 4, Swerling 4)

Man's Country, 1919 (Chaney 3)

Man's Duty, 1912 (Reid 3)

Man's Duty, 1913 (Dwan 2)

Man's Enemy, 1914 (Gish 3)

Man's Favorite Sport?, 1964 (Hawks 2, Hudson 3, Harlan 4, Head 4, Mancini 4, Mercer 4)

Man's Game, 1934 (Bond 3)

Man's Genesis, 1912 (Griffith 2, Marsh 3, Bitzer 4)

Man's Great Adversary. *See* Elskovs Magt, 1912

Man's Life. *See* Hito no issho, 1928

Man's Lust for Gold, 1912 (Griffith 2, Sweet 3, Bitzer 4)

Man's Man, 1929 (Cruze 2, Daves 2, Garbo 3, Gilbert 3, Day 4, Gibbons 4)

Man's Mate, 1924 (Gilbert 3, Johnson 3)

Man's Past, 1927 (Veidt 3)

Man's Worldly Appearance. *See* Hito no yo no sugata, 1929

Mansarda, 1963 (Lomnicki 3)

Mantan Messes Up, 1946 (Horne 3)

Mantango, 1963 (Tsuburaya 4)

Mantango—Fungus of Terror. *See* Mantango, 1963

Manthan, 1976 (Patil 3, Nihalani 4)

Mantle of Charity, 1918 (Furthman 4)

Mantonnet, 1936 (Prévert 4)

Mantra-Mughdha, 1949 (Roy 2)

Mantrap, 1926 (Fleming 2, Hathaway 2, Bow 3, Head 4, Howe 4, Schulberg 4)

Mantrap, 1943 (Siodmak 4)

Mantrap, 1953 (Henreid 3, Kendall 3, Carreras 4)

Mantrap, 1961 (O'Brien 3, Head 4)

Manual of Arms, 1966 (Frampton 2)

Manuel Rodriquez, 1972 (Guzmán 2)

Manuela, 1957 (Armendáriz 3, Howard 3, Pleasence 3, Alwyn 4, Heller 4)

Manuela, 1965 (Solas 2, Herrera 4)

Manuela's Loves. *See* Jupon rouge, 1987

Manuscript Found in Saragossa. *See* Rękopis znaleziony w Saragossie, 1964

Manxman, 1928 (Hitchcock 2, Launder and Gilliat 2, Ondra 3)

Many a Pickle, 1938 (Cavalcanti 2)

Many a Pickle, 1976 (McLaren 2)

Many a Slip, 1931 (Ayres 3, Bennett 3)

Many Happy Returns, 1922 (Roach 4)

Many Happy Returns, 1934 (McLeod 2, Milland 3, Pangborn 3, Head 4)

Many Happy Returns, 1986 (Segal 3)

Many Rivers to Cross, 1955 (McLaglen 3, Taylor 3, Plunkett 4, Seitz 4)
Many Scrappy Returns, 1926 (Roach 4)
Many Tanks, 1942 (Fleischer 4)
Many Voices, 1956 (Heston 3)
Manya, die Türkin, 1915 (Kortner 3)
Manželé paní Mileny, 1921 (Heller 4)
Manzil, 1936 (Roy 2)
Manzil, 1960 (Anand 3, Burman 4)
Manzil, 1979 (Bachchan 3)
Mao le veut, 1965 (Lassally 4)
Mapuches, 1971 (Ruiz 2)
Maputo, 1976 (Alvarez 2)
Maquillage. See Da hält die Welt den Aten an, 1927
Maquillage, 1932 (Feuillère 3)
Mar, 1974 (Leduc 2)
Mar y tú, 1951 (Fernández 2, Figueroa 4)
Mara Maru, 1952 (Flynn 3, Burks 4, Steiner 4)
Maracaibo, 1958 (Wilde 3, Head 4)
Maranhão 66, 1965 (Rocha 2)
Marathon, 1919 (Daniels 3, Lloyd 3, Roach 4)
Marathon. See Maraton, 1967
Marathon Man, 1976 (Schlesinger 2, Hoffman 3, Olivier 3, Scheider 3, Goldman 4, Hall 4, Smith 4)
Marathon Runner. See Läufer von Marathon, 1933
Maraton, 1967 (Brejchová 3)
Marâtre, 1906 (Guy 2)
Marat/Sade, 1967 (Jackson 3, Watkin 4)
Marauders, 1911 (Dwan 2)
Marauders, 1955 (Duryea 3)
Marble Heart, 1913 (Cruze 2)
Marble Heart, 1916 (Brenon 2)
Marcel Achard, ou cinquante ans de vie parisienne, 1942 (Achard 4)
Marcel, ta mère t'appelle, 1962 (Grimault 4)
Marcelino, 1956 (Rey 3)
Marcelino, pan y vino, 1954 (Rey 3)
Marcella, 1920 (Gallone 2)
Marcella, 1940 (Gallone 2)
Marcellini Millions, 1917 (Crisp 3)
March Hare, 1921 (Daniels 3)
March Hare, 1956 (Cusack 3)
March of Dimes, 1942 (Gable 3)
March of Time series, 1935–51 (De Rochemont 4)
March of Time series, 1940–51 (Lye 4)
March on Marines, 1940 (Eason 4)
March or Die, 1977 (Deneuve 3, Hackman 3, Von Sydow 3, Alcott 4, Jarre 4)
March to Aldermaston, 1958 (Anderson 2, Burton 4)
Marcha del pueblo combatiente, 1980 (Alvarez 2)
Marchand d'amour, 1935 (Rosay 3, Jeanson 4)
Marchand de ballons, 1902 (Guy 2)
Marchand de coco, 1897 (Guy 2)
Marchand de notes, 1942 (Aurenche 4, Grimault 4)
Marchand de plaisir, 1923 (Autant-Lara 2)
Marchande de sable, 1931 (Christian-Jaque 2)
Marchands d'illusions, 1954 (Manès 3)
Marchands de rien, 1958 (Audiard 4)
Marché, 1895 (Lumière 2)
Marché à la volaille, 1897 (Guy 2)
Marché à la volaille, 1901 (Gaumont 4)
Marche de la faim, 1935 (Kosma 4)

Marche des machines, 1927 (Zinnemann 2, Kaufman 4)
Marche des rois, 1913 (Feuillade 2)
Marche française, 1956 (Delerue 4)
Marche nuptiale, 1928 (Christian-Jaque 2)
Marche ou crève, 1959 (Blier 3, Delerue 4)
Marchesa d'Arminiani, 1920 (Negri 3)
Marchese del Grillo, 1982 (Monicelli 2, Sordi 3)
Marcheurs de Sainte Rolende, 1968 (Storck 2)
Marcheurs de Sainte Rolende, 1975 (Storck 2)
Marching Along. See Stars and Stripes Forever, 1952
Marcia nuziale, 1966 (Ferreri 2)
Marcia o crepa, 1963 (Granger 3)
Marcia su Roma, 1962 (Gassman 3, Age and Scarpelli 4)
Marcia trionfale, 1976 (Bellocchio 2)
Marco Polo, 1983 (Cristaldi 4)
Marco the Magnificent. See Fabuleuse Aventure de Marco Polo, 1965
Marcus Welby, M.D., 1969 (Young 3)
Marcus-Nelson Murders, 1973 (Ferrer 3)
Mardi Gras, 1958 (Goulding 2, LeMaire 4, Waldo 4)
Mare, 1962 (Fusco 4)
Maré de mi corazón, 1979 (Hermosillo 2)
Mare di Napoli, 1919 (Gallone 2)
Mare matto, 1963 (Castellani 2, Belmondo 3, Lollobrigida 3, Cristaldi 4, Rota 4)
Mare Nostrum, 1926 (Ingram 2, Carré 4, Seitz 4, Mayer 4)
Mare Nostrum, 1950 (Félix 3, Rey 3)
Maresi, 1948 (Schell 3)
Maréchalferrant, 1895 (Lumière 2)
Margaret Head: Portrait of a Friend, 1977 (Rouch 2)
Marge, 1976 (Borowczyk 2, Hakim 4)
Margherita fra i tre, 1942 (De Laurentiis 4)
Margie, 1940 (Cortez 4, Salter 4)
Margie, 1946 (King 2, McDaniel 3, Basevi 4, Clarke 4, Newman 4)
Margin for Error, 1943 (Preminger 2, Bennett 3, Cronjager 4, Day 4)
Marginal, 1983 (Belmondo 3, Audiard 4)
Margo, 1970 (Golan and Globus 4)
Marguerite: 3—Eine Frau für Drei, 1939 (Käutner 2)
Marguerite de la nuit, 1956 (Autant-Lara 2, Montand 3, Morgan 3, Douy 4, Jeanson 4, Saulnier 4)
Mari a mal aux dents, 1912 (Cohl 4)
Mari à prix fixe, 1963 (Karina 3)
Mari en laisse. See If a Man Answers, 1962
Mari rêvé, 1936 (Arletty 3, Brasseur 3)
María, 1971 (Figueroa 4)
Maria and Napoleon. See Marysia i Napoleon, 1966
Maria Antonieta Rivas Mercado, 1982 (Schygulla 3)
Maria Callas Porträt, 1968 (Schroeter 2)
Maria Callas singt 1957 Rezitativ und Arie der Elvira aus Ernani 1844 von Giuseppe Verdi, 1968 (Schroeter 2)
María Candelaria, 1943 (Fernández 2, Armendáriz 3, Del Rio 3, Figueroa 4)
Maria Chapdelaine, 1934 (Duvivier 2, Gabin 3, Périnal 4)
Maria Chapdelaine, 1950 (Morgan 3)
Maria Dabrowska, 1966 (Zanussi 2)
María de la O, 1948 (Figueroa 4)

Mariá Elena, 1935 (Fernández 2, Armendáriz 3, Clothier 4, Figueroa 4)
Maria Eugenia, 1942 (Félix 3)
Maria Ilona, 1939 (Herlth 4)
Maria Magdalena, 1919 (Dreier 4)
Maria, matricula de Bilbao, 1961 (Vanel 3)
Maria no Oyuki, 1935 (Mizoguchi 2, Yamada 3)
Maria Rosa, 1916 (De Mille 2, Reid 3, Buckland 4, Macpherson 4)
Maria Stuart, 1927 (Kortner 3)
Maria Tudor, 1920 (Dreier 4)
Mariage, 1975 (Lai 4)
Mariage à la mode, 1974 (Chaplin 3, Sarde 4)
Mariage à l'américaine, 1909 (Linder 3)
Mariage à responsabilité limité, 1933 (Burel 4, Jeanson 4, Spiegel 4)
Mariage au puzzle, 1909 (Linder 3)
Mariage au téléphone, 1912 (Linder 3)
Mariage blanc, 1985 (Olbrychski 3)
Mariage d'amour, 1907 (Linder 3)
Mariage de Chiffon, 1942 (Autant-Lara 2, Blier 3, Aurenche 4)
Mariage de Figaro, 1959 (Alekan 4)
Mariage de Mademoiselle Beulemans, 1927 (Duvivier 2)
Mariage de Max. See Max se marie, 1909
Mariage de Miss Nelly, 1913 (Feuillade 2)
Mariage de raison, 1900 (Pathé 4)
Mariage de raison, 1916 (Feuillade 2)
Mariage de Victorine, 1907 (Méliès 2)
Mariage des dieux, 1969 (Braunberger 4)
Mariage forcé, 1909 (Linder 3)
Mariage imprévu, 1913 (Linder 3)
Mariage par suggestion, 1916 (Cohl 4)
Mariana, 1967 (Figueroa 4)
Marianne, 1929 (Davies 3, Adrian 4, Brown 4, Freed 4, Gibbons 4)
Marianne and Juliane. See Bleieren Zeit, 1982
Marianne de ma jeunesse, 1955 (Ophuls 2, Duvivier 3, Burel 4, D'Eaubonne 4, Ibert 4, Schüfftan 4, Wakhévitch 4)
Maria-Pilar. See Au coeur de la Casbah, 1951
Maria's Lovers, 1984 (Mikhalkov-Konchalovsky 2, Kinski 3, Mitchum 3, Savini 4)
Maricruz, 1957 (Figueroa 4)
Marido de ida y vuelta, 1955 (Rey 3)
Marie, 1985 (Spacek 3, De Laurentiis 4, Lai 4, Menges 4)
Marie Antoinette, 1938 (Duvivier 2, Van Dyke 2, Barrymore 3, Fitzgerald 3, Power 3, Shearer 3, Adrian 4, Daniels 4, Gibbons 4, Jennings 4, Mayer 4, Stewart 4, Stothart 4, Stromberg 4, Vajda 4, Vorkapich 4)
Marie Chantal Against Dr. Kha. See Marie-Chantal contre le Docteur Kha, 1965
Marie Chapdelaine, 1950 (Rosay 3)
Marie des angoisses, 1935 (Rosay 3, D'Eaubonne 4)
Marie du port, 1949 (Carné 2, Gabin 3, Alekan 4, Kosma 4, Trauner 4)
Marie Galante, 1934 (King 2, Tracy 3, Hoffenstein 4, Seitz 4)
Marie, Marie, 1984 (Darrieux 3)
Marie poupée, 1976 (Sarde 4)
Marie qui se fait attendre, 1910 (Chevalier 3)
Marie Rambert Remembers, 1960 (Russell 2)
Marie the Doll. See Marie poupée, 1976

Marie Walewska. *See* Conquest, 1937

Marie Ward, 1985 (Bernstein 4)

Marie-Antoinette, 1956 (Delannoy 2, Morgan 3, Piccoli 3)

Marie-Antoinette—Das Leben einer Königin, 1922 (Dieterle 2)

Marie-Chantal contre le Docteur Kha, 1965 (Charbrol 2, Audran 3, Reggiani 3, De Beauregard 4, Rabier 4)

Marie-Christine, 1970 (Jutra 2, Bujold 3)

Mariée est trop belle, 1956 (Bardot 3, Jourdan 3, Presle 3, D'Eaubonne 4)

Mariée était en noir, 1967 (Truffaut 2, Moreau 3, Coutard 4, Herrmann 4)

Mariée recalcitrante, 1911 (Chevalier 3)

Marie-Martine, 1943 (Berry 3, Blier 3)

Marie-Octobre, 1959 (Duvivier 2, Blier 3, Darrieux 3, Reggiani 3, Jeanson 4, Wakhévitch 4)

Mariés de l'an II, 1971 (Belmondo 3, Brasseur 3, Legrand 4, Rappeneau 4, Renoir 4, Trauner 4)

Mariés de la Tour Eiffel, 1973 (Milhaud 4)

Mariés d'un jour, 1916 (Feuillade 2, Musidora 3)

Marie's Millions. *See* Tillie's Punctured Romance, 1928

Marie-Soleil, 1964 (Bardot 3, Piccoli 3)

Marilyn, 1963 (Hudson 3)

Marilyn Monroe: Beyond the Legend, 1987 (Winters 3)

Marilyn Times Five, 1969 (Conner 2)

Marilyn's Window, 1988 (Brakhage 2)

Marinai, donne e guai, 1958 (Delli Colli 4)

Marine Law, 1913 (Dwan 2)

Marine marchande. *See* Navigation marchande, 1954

Marine Raiders, 1944 (Edwards 2, Ryan 3, Musuraca 4)

Marines, 1957 (Braunberger 4)

Marines et Cristeaux, 1928 (Gance 2)

Marines Fly High, 1940 (Ball 3)

Marines Have Landed. *See* Leathernecks Have Landed, 1936

Marines, Let's Go!, 1961 (Ballard 4, Smith 4)

Marinica, 1954 (Popescu-Gopo 4)

Marinica's Bodkin, 1955 (Popescu-Gopo 4)

Mario Banana, 1964 (Warhol 2)

Mario Prassinos, 1968 (Braunberger 4)

Mario Puzo's The Fortunate Pilgrim, 1988 (Ponti 4)

Marion, 1921 (Bertini 3)

Marionette, 1938 (Mastroianni 3)

Marionetten der Leidenschaft, 1919 (Pick 2)

Marionettiste, 1963 (Decaë 4)

Marisa la civetta, 1957 (Pasolini 2, Ponti 4)

Mariti in città, 1957 (Comencini 2, Cecchi D'Amico 4)

Marito, 1958 (Sordi 3)

Marito e moglie, 1952 (Rota 4)

Marito per Anna Zaccheo, 1953 (Zavattini 4)

Marito povero, 1946 (De Sica 2, Zavattini 4)

Marius, 1931 (Pagnol 2, Fresnay 3, Raimu 3, Junge 4, Korda, A. 4)

Mariutch, 1930 (Fleischer 4)

Mariute, 1918 (Bertini 3)

Marizza, genannt die Schmuggler-Madonna, 1922 (Murnau 2, Freund 4)

Marjorie Morningstar, 1958 (Kelly 3, Sloane 3, Trevor 3, Wood 3, Steiner 4, Stradling 4)

Mark, 1955 (Surtees 4)

Mark, 1961 (Schell 3, Steiger 3, Buchman 4, Green 4, Slocombe 4)

Mark il poliziotta, 1975 (Cobb 3)

Mark of Cain, 1916 (Chaney 3, Miller 4)

Mark of Cain, 1948 (Rank 4, Vetchinsky 4)

Mark of the Devil, 1970 (Lom 3)

Mark of the Gorilla, 1950 (Weissmuller 3, Katzman 4)

Mark of the Gun, 1965 (Kovacs 4)

Mark of the Hawk, 1958 (Poitier 3)

Mark of the Renegade, 1951 (Charisse 3, Boyle 4)

Mark of the Vampire, 1935 (Browning 2, Barrymore 3, Lugosi 3, Adrian 4, Gibbons 4, Howe 4)

Mark of Zorro, 1920 (Niblo 2, Fairbanks 3, Gaudio 4)

Mark of Zorro, 1940 (Mamoulian 2, Darnell 3, Power 3, Rathbone 3, Banton 4, Day 4, Fort 4, Friedhofer 4, Meredyth 4, Miller 4, Newman 4)

Mark of Zorro, 1974 (De Carlo 3)

Mark Twain. *See* Adventures of Mark Twain, 1985

Marked Deck. *See* Mr. ''Silent'' Haskins, 1915

Marked Man, 1917 (Ford 2, Carey 3)

Marked Men, 1919 (Ford 2, Carey 3)

Marked Timetable, 1910 (Griffith 2, Bitzer 4)

Marked Trail, 1910 (Anderson 3)

Marked Woman, 1937 (Bacon 2, Rossen 2, Bogart 3, Davis 3, Barnes 4, Burks 4, Miller 4, Orry-Kelly 4, Raksin 4, Wallis 4)

Market of Bad Names. *See* Akumyo ichiba, 1963

Market of Souls, 1919 (Sullivan 4)

Market of Vain Desire, 1916 (Sullivan 4)

Marko the Hero. *See* Junak Markos, 1953

Markurells i Wadköping, 1930 (Sjöström 2, Jaenzon 4)

Markurells i Wadköping, 1968 (Dahlbeck 3)

Markurells of Wadköping. *See* Markurells i Wadköping, 1968

Marlene, 1984 (Schell 3)

Marlowe, 1961 (Lee 3)

Marlowe, 1969 (Garner 3, Chandler 4, Daniels 4)

Marmalade Revolution. *See* Marmeladupproret, 1980

Marmara hasan, 1968 (Güney 2)

Marmeladupproret, 1980 (Andersson 3, Josephson 3)

Marnie, 1964 (Hitchcock 2, Connery 3, Dern 3, Allen 4, Boyle 4, Burks 4, Head 4, Herrmann 4, Whitlock 4)

Maroc 7, 1966 (Charisse 3, Elliott 3)

Marooned, 1969 (Sturges 2, Grant 3, Hackman 3, Peck 3, Wheeler 4)

Marquée des anciens plaisirs, 1941 (Volkov 2)

Marqueray's Duel, 1925 (Love 3)

Marquet, 1962 (Delerue 4)

Marquis de Sade: Justine, 1968 (Kinski 3, McCambridge 3, Palance 3)

Marquis d'Eon, der Spion der Pompadour, 1928 (Wagner 4)

Marquis d'Or, 1920 (Dreier 4)

Marquis of O. *See* Marquise von O, 1975

Marquis Preferred, 1929 (Menjou 3, Mankiewicz 4, Vajda 4)

Marquise von O., 1920 (Albers 3)

Marquise von O, 1975 (Ganz 3, Almendros 4)

Marquise von Pompadour, 1922 (Krauss 3)

Marquitta, 1927 (Renoir 2)

Marraine de Charley, 1959 (Cassel 3)

Marrakech, capitale du Sud, 1948 (Decaë 4)

Marriage. *See* Svadba, 1944

Marriage. *See* Kekkon, 1947

Marriage, 1959 (Anand 3)

Marriage: Year One, 1971 (Field 3, Moorehead 3)

Marriage Agency. *See* Äktenskapsbrydån, 1913

Marriage Broker. *See* Americaner Schadchen, 1939

Marriage Came Tumbling Down. *See* Ce sacre grand-père, 1967

Marriage Chance, 1922 (Walthall 3)

Marriage Cheat, 1924 (Menjou 3, Sullivan 4)

Marriage Circle, 1924 (Lubitsch 2, Menjou 3, Blanke 4)

Marriage Circus, 1925 (Sennett 2)

Marriage Clause, 1926 (Weber 2, Bushman 3, Mohr 4)

Marriage for Convenience, 1919 (Olcott 2)

Marriage Game. *See* Äktenskapsleken, 1935

Marriage Humor, 1933 (Langdon 3)

Marriage in the Revolution. *See* Revolutionsbryllup, 1914

Marriage in Transit, 1925 (Lombard 3)

Marriage Is a Private Affair, 1944 (Turner 3, Berman 4, Coffee 4, Irenc 4, Kaper 4)

Marriage Italian Style. *See* Matrimonio all'italiana, 1964

Marriage License, 1926 (Borzage 2, Pidgeon 3)

Marriage Maker, 1923 (Astor 3)

Marriage of a Young Stockbroker, 1970 (Kovacs 4)

Marriage of Convenience. *See* Børnevennerne, 1914

Marriage of Maria Braun. *See* **Ehe der Maria Braun, 1978**

Marriage of Molly O, 1916 (Marsh 3)

Marriage of Nanynky Kulickova. *See* Vdavky Nanynky Kulichovy, 1925

Marriage of William Ashe, 1916 (Hepworth 2)

Marriage on the Rocks, 1965 (Kerr 3, Martin 3, Sinatra 3, Daniels 4, Plunkett 4)

Marriage Playground, 1929 (March 3)

Marriage Playground, 1991 (Francis 3)

Marriage Ring, 1918 (Niblo 2, Barnes 4)

Marriage Rows, 1931 (Arbuckle 3)

Marriage Time. *See* Konki, 1961

Marriage Wows, 1930 (Fleischer 4)

Marriage Wrestler. *See* Äktenskapabrottaren, 1964

Marriageable Daughters. *See* Giftasvuxnar döttrar, 1933

Marriage-Go-Round, 1960 (Hayward 3, Mason 3, LeMaire 4)

Married and in Love, 1940 (Polglase 4)

Married Bachelor, 1941 (Folsey 4, Schary 4)

Married Before Breakfast, 1937 (Young 3)

Married But Single. *See* This Thing Called Love, 1941

Married by the Stork. *See* Storch hat uns getraut, 1933

Married Daughter. *See* Dcery Eviny, 1928

Married Flirts, 1924 (Shearer 3)

Married for Millions, 1906 (Bitzer 4)

Married in Haste. *See* Consolation Marriage, 1931

Married Life, 1920 (Sennett 2)

Married Too Young, 1961 (Haller 4)

Married to the Mob, 1988 (Demme 2, Pfeiffer 3)

Married Virgin, 1920 (Valentino 3)

Married Woman. *See* Femme mariée, 1964

Marry Me, 1925 (Cruze 2, Horton 3, Brown 4)

Marry Me, 1932 (Asquith 2, Balcon 4)

Marry Me, 1949 (Fisher 2, Rank 4)

Marry Me Again, 1953 (Tashlin 2)

Marry the Boss's Daughter, 1941 (Clarke 4)

Marry the Girl, 1937 (Brown 4, Raksin 4, Wallis 4)

Marrying Kind, 1952 (Cukor 2, Bronson 3, Gordon 3, Holiday 3, Cohn 4, Friedhofer 4, Horner 4, Kanin 4, Walker 4)

Mars, 1922 (Folsey 4)

Mars, 1930 (Lantz 4)

Marschall Vorwärts, 1932 (Wegener 3)

Marseille Contract, 1974 (Caine 3, Mason 3, Slocombe 4)

Marseille, premier port de France, 1945 (Decaë 4)

Marseillaise, 1912 (Cohl 4)

Marseillaise, 1938 (Becker 2, Renoir 2, Jouvet 3, Modot 3, Barsacq 4, Kosma 4, Reiniger 4, Renoir 4, Wakhévitch 4)

Marshal of Reno, 1944 (Edwards 2)

Marshall of Gunsmoke, 1944 (Salter 4)

Marshal's Capture, 1913 (Mix 3)

Marshmallow Moon. *See* Aaron Slick from Punkin Crick, 1951

Marter der Liebe, 1927 (Gallone 2, Tschechowa 3)

Martha, 1923 (Disney 4)

Martha, 1973 (Fassbinder 2, Ballhaus 4)

Martha und Ich, 1990 (Weiss 2, Piccoli 3)

Martha's Rebellion, 1912 (Bunny 3)

Martha's Vindication, 1916 (Talmadge 3)

Marthe Richard, 1937 (Von Stroheim 2, Dalio 3, Feuillère 3, Honegger 4)

Martian Through Georgia, 1962 (Blanc 4, Jones 4)

Martiens, 1973 (Vanel 3)

Martin, 1977 (Romero 2, Savini 4)

Martin Andersen Nexos sidste rejse, 1954 (Roos 2)

Martin Eden, 1914 (Bosworth 3)

Martin Fierro, 1968 (Torre Nilsson 2)

Martin Luther, 1953 (De Rochemont 4)

Martin Missil Quarterly Reports, 1957 (Brakhage 2)

Martin of the Mounted, 1926 (Wyler 2)

Martin Roumagnac, 1946 (Dietrich 3, Gabin 3, Gélin 3, Wakhévitch 4)

Martin Soldat, 1966 (Braunberger 4)

Martin the Cobbler, 1976 (Vinton 4)

Martin's Day, 1985 (Black 3, Coburn 3, Harris 3)

Marty, 1955 (Borgnine 3, Chayefsky 4, La Shelle 4)

Martyr of the Garden of the Pear Trees, 1949 (Xie 2)

Martyre, 1924 (Vanel 3)

Martyre de l'obèse, 1932 (L'Herbier 2, Spaak 4)

Martyred Presidents, 1901 (Porter 2)

Martyrium, 1920 (Negri 3, Wagner 4)

Martyrs of Love. *See* Mučedníci lásky, 1967

Maruche, 1932 (Fernandel 3)

Marvellous Wreath. *See* Guirlande merveilleuse, 1903

Marvin and Tige, 1983 (Rosenblum 4)

Marx for Beginners, 1978 (Godfrey 4)

Mary, 1931 (Tschechowa 3)

Mary Ann, 1918 (Korda 2, Korda 4)

Mary Burns, Fugitive, 1935 (Howard 2, Douglas 3, Sidney 3, Wanger 4)

Mary find the Gold, 1921 (Pearson 2)

Mary Jane's Pa, 1935 (Haller 4)

Mary Lou, 1928 (Andrejew 4)

Mary Magdalene. *See* spade e la croce, 1958

Mary, Mary, 1963 (Reynolds 3, Stradling 4)

Mary, Mary, Bloody Mary, 1975 (Carradine 3)

Mary of Scotland, 1936 (Ford 2, Carradine 3, Crisp 3, Hepburn 3, March 3, August 4, Berman 4, Nichols 4, Plunkett 4, Polglase 4)

Mary of the Mines, 1912 (Ince 4)

Mary of the Movies, 1923 (Ingram 2, Cohn 4)

Mary Poppins, 1964 (Stevenson 2, Andrews 3, Darwell 3, Lanchester 3, Disney 4, Ellenshaw 4)

Mary, Queen of Scots, 1971 (Howard 3, Jackson 3, Redgrave 3, Barry 4, Challis 3, Wallis 4)

Mary, Queen of Tots, 1925 (Roach 4)

Mary Regan, 1919 (Weber 2, Mayer 4)

Mary Stevens M.D., 1933 (Bacon 2, Francis 3, Orry-Kelly 4)

Marya Sklodowska-Curie. Ein Mädchen, das die Welt verändert, 1972 (Staudte 2)

Maryland, 1940 (King 2, Brennan 3, McDaniel 3, Barnes 4, Day 4, Newman 4, Zanuck 4)

Mary's Birthday, 1951 (Reiniger 4)

Mary's Little Lamb, 1935 (Iwerks 4)

Mary's Romance, 1910 (White 3)

Marysia i Napoleon, 1966 (Tyszkiewicz 3)

Marzia nuziale, 1915 (Gallone 2)

Más allá de las montañas, 1967 (Papas 3, Rey 3, Schell 3, Matras 4)

Más allá del amor, 1944 (Figueroa 4)

Ma's Apron Strings, 1913 (Bunny 3)

Ma's Girls, 1915 (Mix 3)

Masamod, 1920 (Lukas 3)

Mascara, 1987 (Golan and Globus 4)

Máscaras, 1976 (De Almeida 4)

Maschera di Cesare Borgia, 1941 (Stallich 4)

Mascot, 1914 (Browning 2)

Mascot of Troop 'C', 1911 (Guy 2)

Mascottchen, 1929 (Albers 3)

Masculine Feminine. *See* Masculin-Féminin, 1966

Masculin-Féminin, 1966 (Bardot 3, Léaud 3, Guillemot 4, Lai 4)

M*A*S*H, 1970 (Altman 2, Duvall 3, Gould 3, Sutherland 3, Lardner 4, Smith 4)

Mashal, 1950 (Burman 4)

Masher, 1910 (Sennett 2, Pickford 3, White 3)

Mask, 1918 (Gilbert 3)

Mask, 1921 (Selig 4)

Mask, 1961 (Vorkapich 4)

Mask, 1985 (Bogdanovich 2, Cher 3, Kovacs 4)

Mask of Comedy. *See* Gay Deceiver, 1926

Mask of Dijon, 1945 (Von Stroheim 2)

Mask of Dimitrios, 1944 (Negulesco 2, Greenstreet 3, Lorre 3, Blanke 4, Deutsch 4, Edeson 4)

Mask of Dust, 1954 (Carreras 4)

Mask of Fu Manchu, 1932 (Vidor 2, Karloff 3, Loy 3, Adrian 4, Gaudio 4)

Mask of Lopez, 1924 (Brown 4)

Mask of Love, 1916 (Chaney 3)

Mask of Riches. *See* Mask, 1918

Mask of Sheba, 1969 (Pidgeon 3, Schifrin 4)

Mask of the Avenger, 1951 (Quinn 3, Stromberg 4)

Mask-a-Raid, 1931 (Fleischer 4)

Maske, 1919 (Dupont 2)

Masked Bride, 1925 (Florey 2, Von Sternberg 2, Bushman 3, Rathbone 3, Carré 4, Gibbons 4, Mayer 4)

Masked Bride, 1978 (Chaplin 3)

Masked Mamas, 1926 (Sennett 2)

Masked Menace, 1927 (Arthur 3)

Masked Raider, 1919 (Karloff 3)

Masked Rider, 1916 (Gaudio 4)

Masked Woman, 1926 (Mathis 4)

Masked Wrestler, 1914 (Bushman 3)

Masken, 1920 (Röhrig, 4, Warm 4)

Masken, 1929 (Homolka 3, Warm 4)

Maskenfest der Liebe, 1918 (Messter 4)

Maskerade, 1934 (Tschechowa 3, Walbrook 3, Planer 4, Reisch 4)

Maskierte Liebe, 1912 (Porten 3)

Maskovaná milenka, 1940 (Baarová 3)

Masks of Death, 1984 (Mills 3)

Masks of the Devil, 1928 (Sjöström 2, Gilbert 3, Adrian 4, Gibbons 4, Marion 4)

Masoom, 1983 (Azmi 3)

Masque de fer, 1962 (Marais 3)

Masque d'horreur, 1912 (Gance 2)

Masque of the Red Death, 1964 (Corman 2, Roeg 2, Price 3)

Masque of the Red Death, 1989 (Lom 3)

Masquerada, 1949 (Armendáriz 3)

Masquerade. *See* Masquerader, 1914

Masquerade, 1924 (Fleischer 4)

Masquerade, 1929 (Clarke 4, Pierce 4)

Masquerade, 1931 (Robinson 4)

Masquerade, 1941 (Gerasimov 2)

Masquerade, 1964 (Dearden 2, Hawkins 3, Piccoli 3, Robertson 3, Goldman 4, Heller 4)

Masquerade, 1988 (Barry 4, Watkin 4)

Masquerade in Mexico, 1945 (Leisen 2, Lamour 3, Dreier 4, Head 4, Young 4)

Masquerade in Vienna. *See* Maskerade, 1934

Masquerade of Vienna. *See* Maskerade, 1934

Masquerader, 1914 (Sennett 2, Arbuckle 3)

Masquerader, 1922 (Buckland 4)

Masquerader, 1933 (Colman 3, Day 4, Estabrook 4, Goldwyn 4, Newman 4, Toland 4)

Masqueraders, 1906 (Bitzer 4)

Masques, 1952 (Alexeieff and Parker 4)

Masques, 1986 (Charbrol 2, Noiret 3, Rabier 4)

Mass Appeal, 1985 (Lemmon 3)

Mass for the Dakota Sioux, 1964 (Baillie 2)

Mass Mouse Meeting, 1943 (Fleischer 4)

Massacre, 1912 (Griffith 2, Barrymore 3, Sweet 3, Bitzer 4)

Massacre, 1934 (Barthelmess 3, Barnes 4, Orry-Kelly 4)

Massacre de la famille royale de Serbie, 1903 (Pathé 4)

Massacre en dentelles, 1951 (Audiard 4)

Massacre Hill. *See* Eureka Stockade, 1949

Massacre in Rome. *See* Rappresaglia, 1973

Massacre of Sante Fe Trail, 1912 (Ince 4)

Massada, 1981 (Quayle 3)
Massaggiatrici, 1962 (Noiret 3)
Massarati and the Brain, 1982 (Lee 3)
Massnahmen gegen Fanatiker, 1969
  (Herzog 2)
Master. See Röda tornet, 1914
Master, 1985 (Van Cleef 3)
Master and the Man, 1911 (Pickford 3,
  Gaudio 4)
Master Gunfighter, 1975 (Reynolds 4,
  Schifrin 4)
Master Hand, 1917 (Edeson 4)
Master Mind, 1914 (De Mille 2, Darwell 3)
Master of Ballantrae, 1953 (Flynn 3,
  Adam 4, Alwyn 4, Cardiff 4)
Master of Bankdam, 1947 (Fisher 2, Rank 4)
Master of Dragonard Hall. See Dragonard,
  1987
Master of Lassie. See Hills of Home, 1948
Master of Love. See Maestro d'amore, 1977
Master of Men, 1933 (Wray 3, August 4)
Master of the Islands. See Hawaiians, 1970
Master of the Vineyard, 1911 (Dwan 2)
Master of the World, 1961 (Bronson 3,
  Price 3)
Master of Woman. See Eternal Struggle,
  1923
Master Race, 1944 (Metty 4)
Master Samuel. See Mästerman, 1920
Master Touch. See uomo da rispettare, 1972
Master V. See Pimpernel Smith, 1941
Master Will Shakespeare, 1936 (Howard 3)
Mästerjuven, 1915 (Jaenzon 4)
Mästerman, 1920 (Sjöström 2, Jaenzon 4,
  Magnusson 4)
Mastermind, 1920 (Barrymore 3)
Mastermind, 1930 (Rooney 3)
Masterpiece of Murder, 1986 (Ameche 3,
  Hope 3)
Masters of the Universe, 1987 (Edlund 4,
  Golan and Globus 4)
Master's Wife, 1980 (Johnson 3)
Masterson of Kansas, 1954 (Katzman 4)
Mästertjuven, 1915 (Stiller 2)
Mastery of the Sea, 1941 (Cavalcanti 2,
  Hamer 2)
Mat, 1926 (Baranovskaya 3, Golovnya 4)
Mat, 1955 (Maretskaya 3)
Mat 1905, 1956 (Batalov 3)
Mata au hi made, 1950 (Okada 3)
Mata Hari. See Spionin, 1921
Mata Hari, 1927 (Kortner 3, Junge 4)
Mata Hari, 1932 (Barrymore 3, Garbo 3,
  Novarro 3, Daniels 4, Glazer 4,
  Mayer 4)
Mata Hari, 1984 (Golan and Globus 4)
Mata Hari—Agent H-21, 1964 (Léaud 3,
  Moreau 3, Trintignant 3, Delerue 4)
Mata Hari, the Red Dancer. See Mata Hari,
  1927
Matador, 1986 (Almodóvar 2, Maura 3)
Matador Magoo, 1957 (Bosustow 4,
  Burness 4)
Match. See Partita, 1988
Match Breaker, 1921 (Mandell 4)
Match Criqui-Ledoux, 1922 (Chevalier 3)
Match de boxe entre patineurs à roulettes,
  1912 (Linder 3)
Match de catch, 1961 (Braunberger 4)
Match des Goldes, 1912 (Nielsen 3)
Match King, 1932 (Grot 4, Orry-Kelly 4)
Match Play, 1930 (Sennett 2)
Matches, 1913 (Dwan 2)
Matching Dreams, 1916 (Eason 4)

Matchless, 1966 (Lattuada 2, Pleasence 3,
  Morricone 4)
Matchmaker, 1911 (Bunny 3, Lawrence 3)
Matchmaker, 1958 (MacLaine 3, Perkins 3,
  Deutsch 4, Hayes 4, Head 4, Lang 4,
  Westmore Family 4)
Matchmaking Mamas, 1929 (Sennett 2,
  Lombard 3, Hornbeck 4)
Mate a la vida, 1953 (Armendáriz 3)
Mate of the Alden Bessie, 1912
  (Bosworth 3)
Mate of the Sally Ann, 1917 (King 2)
Matelas alcoolique, 1906 (Guy 2)
Matelot 512, 1984 (Allio 2, Piccoli 3,
  Sanda 3)
Maten al león, 1975 (Figueroa 4)
Mater Dolorosa, 1910 (Feuillade 2)
Mater Dolorosa, 1917 (Gance 2, Artaud 3,
  Modot 3, Burel 4, Gaumont 4)
Mater Dolorosa, 1922 (Walbrook 3)
Mater Dolorosa, 1933 (Gance 2, Artaud 3)
Matériaux nouveaux, demeures nouvelles,
  1956 (Colpi 4)
Maternelle, 1933 (Fradetal 4)
Maternité, 1935 (Rosay 3, Ibert 4, Matras 4)
Maternity Hospital, 1971 (Vukotić 4)
Mates and Models, 1919 (Laurel and
  Hardy 3)
Matewan, 1987 (Sayles 2, Jones 3, Wexler 4)
Mathias Sandorf, 1921 (Modot 3)
Mathias Sandorf, 1962 (Blier 3, Jourdan 3,
  Spaak 4)
Matières nouvelles, 1964 (Storck 2)
Matilda, 1978 (Gould 3, Mitchum 3,
  Leven 4)
Matilda's Legacy, 1915 (Laurel and
  Hardy 3)
Matinee, 1976 (Hermosillo 2)
Matinee Idol, 1928 (Capra 2, Love 3,
  Cohn 4)
Matinee Idol, 1933 (Bennett 4)
Matinee Idol, 1989 (Halas and Batchelor 4)
Matinee Ladies, 1927 (Blanke 4,
  Buchman 4, Haskin 4)
Matinee Scandal. See One Rainy Afternoon,
  1936
Mating Call, 1928 (Cruze 2, Mankiewicz 4)
Mating Game, 1959 (Reynolds 3, Rose 4)
Mating of Millie, 1948 (Ford 3, Walker 4)
Mating Season, 1951 (Leisen 2, Hopkins 3,
  Ritter 3, Tierney 3, Brackett 4, Lang 4,
  Reisch 4)
Matins, 1988 (Brakhage 2)
Matisse, or The Talent for Happiness, 1960
  (Ophuls 2)
Matj, 1990 (Panfilov 2)
Matka Joanna od Aniołów, 1961
  (Kawalerowicz 2, Konwicki 4)
Matous the Shoemaker. See O ševci
  Matoušovi, 1948
Matrero, 1939 (Alton 4)
Matriarca, 1969 (Trintignant 3)
Matrices, 1964 (Halas and Batchelor 4)
Matricule 33, 1933 (Feuillère 3)
Matrimaniac, 1916 (Fleming 2, Fairbanks 3,
  Emerson 4, Loos 4)
Matrimaniac, 1945 (Fleming 2)
Matrimonial Boomerang, 1915 (Mix 3)
Matrimonial Maneuvers, 1913 (Costello 3)
Matrimonio, 1953 (De Sica 2, Sordi 3)
Matrimonio all'italiana, 1964 (Castellani 2,
  Loren 3, Mastroianni 3, Guerra 4,
  Levine 4, Ponti 4)
Matrimony, 1915 (Ince 4, Sullivan 4)

Matri-Phony, 1942 (Three Stooges 3)
Matrix and Joseph's Coat, 1973 (Le Grice 2)
Matrosowcy, 1951 (Ścibor-Rylski 4)
Matsudaira Choshichiro, 1930 (Hasegawa 3)
Matsuri-uta Mitokichi goroshi, 1932
  (Hasegawa 3)
Mattatore, 1960 (Gassman 3, Age and
  Scarpelli 4)
Mattei Affair. See Caso Mattei, 1972
Matteita otoko, 1942 (Hasegawa 3,
  Takamine 3, Yamada 3)
Matter of Dignity. See To teleftaio psemma,
  1957
Matter of Humanities. See Marcus Welby,
  M.D., 1969
Matter of Innocence. See Pretty Polly, 1967
Matter of Life and Death, 1946
  (Attenborough 3, Massey 3, Niven 3,
  Cardiff 4, Ellenshaw 4, Heckroth 4,
  Junge 4, Rank 4, Unsworth 4)
Matter of Morals. See Sista stegen, 1960
Matter of Principle, 1984 (Arkin 3)
Matter of Resistance. See Vie de château,
  1966
Matter of Sex. See What Sex Am I?, 1985
Matter of Time, 1976 (Minnelli 2,
  Bergman 3, Boyer 3, Minnelli 3, Rey 3,
  Unsworth 4)
Matter of Who, 1961 (Terry-Thomas 3)
Matthew Hopkins—Witchfinder General.
  See Witchfinder General, 1968
Matthias Kneissel, 1970 (Fassbinder 2,
  Schygulla 3)
Matto Grosso, 1932 (Crosby 4)
Matura, 1965 (Konwicki 4)
Maturareise, 1943 (Schell 3)
Maudite Galette, 1972 (Arcand 2)
Maudite soit la guerre, 1910 (Feuillade 2)
Maudits, 1947 (Dalio 3, Alekan 4, Jeanon 4)
Maulkorb, 1937 (Herlth 4)
Maulkorb, 1958 (Staudte 2)
Mauprat, 1926 (Buñuel 2, Epstein 2)
Maurice, 1987 (Ivory 2, Elliott 3)
Mauvais coeur puni, 1904 (Guy 2)
Mauvais Coups, 1960 (Signoret 3)
Mauvais Fils, 1980 (Sautet 2)
Mauvais Garçon, 1922 (Chevalier 3)
Mauvais Garçon, 1936 (Darrieux 3)
Mauvais Sang, 1986 (Piccoli 3, Reggiani 3)
Mauvaise conduite, 1984 (Almendros 4)
Mauvaise graine, 1933 (Wilder 2,
  Darrieux 3)
Mauvaise Soupe, 1897 (Guy 2)
Mauvaise soupe, 1899 (Gaumont 4)
Mauvaise Vie, 1907 (Linder 3)
Mauvaises Fréquentations, 1967 (Léaud 3)
Mauvaises Rencontres, 1955 (Astruc 2,
  Aimée 3, Piccoli 3, Douy 4, Saulnier 4)
Maverick Queen, 1956 (Stanwyck 3,
  Young 4)
Max series, 1909–17 (Linder 3)
Max and Moritz, 1978 (Halas and
  Batchelor 4)
Max Beckmann, 1961 (Fusco 4)
Max Dugan Returns, 1982 (Robards 3,
  Sutherland 3)
Max et le quinquina, 1911 (Pathé 4)
Max et les ferrailleurs, 1971 (Sautet 2,
  Piccoli 3, Schneider 3, Sarde 4)
Max mon amour, 1986 (Oshima 2, Baker 4,
  Carrière 4, Coutard 4)
Max, My Love. See Max mon amour, 1986
Maxie, 1985 (Close 3, Gordon 3,
  Delerue 4)

Maxime, 1958 (Arletty 3, Boyer 3, Morgan 3, Jeanson 4, Matras 4)

Maximum Overdrive, 1986 (De Laurentiis 4)

Maxplatte, Maxplatten, 1965 (Trnka 4)

Maxwell's Demon, 1968 (Frampton 2)

May and December, 1910 (Pickford 3)

May Blossom, 1915 (Dwan 2, Crisp 3)

May Fools. See Milou en mai, 1990

May Stars. See Májové hvězdy, 1959

May We Borrow Your Husband, 1985 (Greene 4)

Maya, 1936 (Roy 2)

Maya, 1949 (Dalio 3, Auric 4, Barsacq 4)

Maya, 1961 (Anand 3)

Maya Darpan, 1972 (Chandragupta 4)

Maybe Darwin Was Right, 1942 (Eason 4)

Maybe I'll Come Home in the Spring, 1971 (Cooper 3, Field 3)

Maybe It's Love, 1930 (Wellman 2, Bennett 3, Brown 3)

Maybe It's Love, 1934 (Brown 4, Edeson 4, Orry-Kelly 4, Wald 4)

Mayblossom, 1910 (White 3)

Mayday at 40,000 Feet, 1976 (Crawford 3, Milland 3)

Mayerling, 1936 (Litvak 2, Boyer 3, Darrieux 3, Manès 3, Achard 4, Andrejew 4, Annenkov 4, Honegger 4, Jaubert 4)

Mayerling, 1957 (Litvak 2)

Mayerling, 1968 (Deneuve 3, Gardner 3, Mason 3, Sharif 3, Alekan 4, Lai 4, Wakhévitch 4)

Mayerling to Sarajevo. See De Mayerling à Sarajevo, 1940

Mayflower, 1935 (Terry 4)

Mayflower: The Pilgrim's Adventure, 1979 (Hopkins 3)

Mayo de las tres banderas, 1980 (Alvarez 2)

Mayol, 1900 (Guy 2)

Mayor of Forty-Fourth St, 1942 (Barthelmess 3)

Mayor of Hell, 1933 (Cagney 3, Orry-Kelly 4)

Maytime, 1923 (Bow 3, Schulberg 4, Struss 4)

Maytime, 1937 (Barrymore 3, Eddy 3, MacDonald 3, Adrian 4, Mayer 4, Stothart 4, Stromberg 4, Vorkapich 4)

Maytime in Mayfair, 1949 (Wilcox 2, Neagle 3)

Mazazo macizo, 1981 (Alvarez 2)

Maze, 1953 (Menzies 4, Mirisch 4)

Mazel tov ou le mariage, 1968 (Cloquet 4)

Mazes and Monsters, 1982 (Hanks 3)

Mazo, 1952 (Yamada 3)

Mazou, 1938 (Miyagawa 4)

Mazurka, 1935 (Negri 3, Warm 4)

Mazurka di papà, 1938 (De Sica 2)

Mazzabubu ... quante come stanno quaggiu?, 1971 (Giannini 3)

McCabe and Mrs. Miller, 1971 (Altman 2, Beatty 3, Christie 3, Zsigmond 4)

McCloud, 1970 (Bumstead 4)

McConnell Story, 1955 (Allyson 3, Ladd 3, Blanke 4, Seitz 4, Steiner 4)

McDougal's Rest Farm, 1947 (Terry 4)

McFadden's Flats, 1927 (Edeson 4)

McFadden's Flats, 1935 (Darwell 3, Robinson 4)

McGuerins from Brooklyn, 1942 (Bendix 3, Roach 4)

McGuire Go Home. See High Bright Sun, 1964

McHale's Navy, 1964 (Borgnine 3)

McKee Rankin's "Forty-nine", 1911 (Bosworth 3)

McLintock!, 1963 (De Carlo 3, O'Hara 3, Wayne 3, Clothier 4, Needham 4)

McMasters, 1970 (Carradine 3, Palance 3)

McNaughton's Daughter, 1976 (Bellamy 3)

McQ, 1974 (Sturges 2, Wayne 3, Bernstein 4)

McVeagh of the South Seas, 1914 (Barrymore 3, Carey 3)

Me an' Bill, 1914 (Mix 3)

Me and Marlborough, 1935 (Saville 2, Balcon 4, Junge 4, Rank 4)

Me and My Gal, 1932 (Walsh 2, Bennett 3, Tracy 3, Walthall 3, Mayer 4, Miller 4)

Me and My Pal, 1933 (Laurel and Hardy 3)

Me and the Colonel, 1958 (Kaye 3, Rosay 3, Behrman 4, Cloquet 4, Guffey 4, Head 4, Wakhévitch 4)

Me faire ça à moi!, 1961 (Constantine 3, Legrand 4)

Me, Gangster, 1928 (Walsh 2, Brown 3, Lombard 3, Edeson 4)

Me gustan valentones, 1958 (Alcoriza 4)

Me, Natalie, 1969 (Lancaster 3, Pacino 3, Jenkins 4, Mancini 4, Smith 4)

Meadow. See Prato, 1979

Meal Ticket, 1914 (Loos 4)

Meals on Wheels, 1984 (Chan 3)

Mean Frank and Crazy Tony. See Johnny le Fligueur, 1973

Mean Johnny Barrows, 1976 (Gould 3, McDowall 3)

Mean Machine. See Longest Yard, 1974

Mean Season, 1984 (Schifrin 4)

Mean Streets, 1973 (Scorsese 2, De Niro 3)

Meanest Gal in Town, 1934 (Carradine 3, Hunt 4, Plunkett 4, Steiner 4)

Meanest Man in the World, 1923 (Sweet 3)

Meanest Man in the World, 1943 (Day 4)

Measure of a Man, 1915 (Chaney 3)

Measure of Man, 1969 (Halas and Batchelor 4)

Meat, 1975 (Wiseman 2)

Meat and Romance, 1940 (Ladd 3)

Meatcleaver Massacre, 1977 (Lee 3)

Meatless Flyday, 1944 (Blanc 4, Freleng 4, Stalling 4)

Mecánica nacional, 1971 (Alcoriza 4)

Mécaniciens de l'armée de l'air, 1959 (Lelouch 2)

Mechanic, 1972 (Bronson 3, Winkler 4)

Mechanical Bird, 1952 (Terry 4)

Mechanical Cow, 1927 (Disney 4)

Mechanical Cow, 1937 (Terry 4)

Mechanical Flea, 1964 (Ivanov-Vano 4)

Mechanical Handy Man, 1937 (Lantz 4)

Mechanical Man, 1932 (Lantz 4)

Mechanics of the Brain. See Mekhanikha golovnovo mozga, 1926

Med fuld musik, 1933 (Madsen and Schenstrøm 3)

Med livet som insats, 1940 (Sjöberg 2)

Med tuld Musik, 1933 (Holger-Madsen 2)

Médaille de sauvetage. See Max sauveteur, 1914

Medal for Benny, 1945 (Lamour 3, Dreier 4, Head 4, Young 4)

Medal for the General, 1944 (Alwyn 4)

Medan porten var stängd, 1946 (Björnstrand 3)

Medan staden sover, 1950 (Andersson 3)

Meddlers, 1911 (Dwan 2)

Meddling Women, 1924 (Barrymore, L. 3)

Medea, 1969 (Pasolini 2, Mangano 3, Donati 4)

Médécin de service, 1933 (Brasseur 3)

Médécin des lumières, 1988 (Allio 2)

Medellín '78, 1978 (Díaz 2)

Media, 1920 (Negri 3, Wegener 3)

Media luz los tres, 1957 (Alcoriza 4)

Media tono. See Donde van nuestros hijos, 1958

Medianoche, 1949 (Figueroa 4)

Mediante de Saint-Sulpice, 1923 (Modot 3)

Medic. See Toubib, 1979

Medical Story, 1975 (Ferrer 3)

Medicine Ball Caravan, 1970 (Braunberger 4)

Medicine Ball Caravan, 1979 (Scorsese 2)

Medicine Bottle, 1909 (Griffith 2, Lawrence 3, Bitzer 4)

Medicine Man, 1934 (Rooney 3)

Medico della Mutua, 1968 (Sordi 3, Amidei 4)

Medico e lo stregone, 1957 (Rota 4)

Medico e lo stregone, 1957 (De Sica 2, Monicelli 2, Mastroianni 3, Gherardi 4, Age and Scarpelli 4)

Meditation on Violence, 1948 (Deren 2)

Mediterranean Holiday, 1964 (Kelly 3)

Méditerréenne, 1969 (Braunberger 4)

Medium, 1921 (Dagover 3, Krauss 3)

Medium, 1951 (Wakhévitch 4)

Medium Cool, 1969 (Fields 4, Wexler 4)

Medusa Touch, 1978 (Burton 3, Remick 3)

Medvezhya svadba, 1926 (Tisse 4)

Meenakshi, 1942 (Roy 2)

Meer, 1927 (Tschechowa 3)

Meer ruft, 1933 (Metzner 4)

Meet Boston Blackie, 1940 (Florey 2, Planer 4)

Meet Danny Wilson, 1951 (Sinatra 3, Winters 3)

Meet Dr. Christian, 1940 (Lardner 4)

Meet John Doe, 1941 (Capra 2, Brennan 3, Cooper 3, Stanwyck 3, Barnes 4, Mandell 4, Riskin 4, Tiomkin 4, Vorkapich 4)

Meet John Doughboy, 1941 (Blanc 4, Clampett 4, Stalling 4)

Meet Marlon Brando, 1965 (Maysles 2)

Meet Me After the Show, 1951 (Grable 3, Cole 4, LeMaire 4)

Meet Me at Dawn, 1947 (Litvak 2, Rutherford 3)

Meet Me at the Fair, 1952 (Sirk 2)

Meet Me in Las Vegas, 1956 (Charisse 3, Henreid 3, Horne 3, Lorre 3, Moorehead 3, Reynolds 3, Sinatra 3, Cahn 4, Lennart 4, Pan 4, Pasternak 4, Rose 4)

Meet Me in St. Louis, 1944 (Minnelli 2, Walters 2, Astor 3, Garland 3, O'Brien 3, Edens 4, Folsey 4, Freed 4, Gibbons 4, Irene 4, Mayer 4, Sharaff 4, Smith 4)

Meet Me on Broadway, 1946 (Guffey 4)

Meet Me Tonight, 1952 (Coward 4, Dillon 4, Havelock-Allan 4, Rank 4)

Meet Mr. Joad, 1942 (Balcon 4)

Meet Mr. Lucifer, 1953 (Kendall 3)

Meet Mother Magoo, 1956 (Bosustow 4, Burness 4)

Meet My Girl, 1926 (Sennett 2)

Meet Nero Wolfe, 1936 (Hayworth 3, Schulberg 4)

Meet Sexton Blake, 1944 (Simmons 3)

Meet Simon Cherry, 1950 (Carreras 4)

Meet the Baron, 1933 (Durante 3, Three Stooges 3, Krasna 4, Mankiewicz 4, Selznick 4)

Meet the Champ, 1941 (Salter 4)

Meet the Chump, 1941 (Three Stooges 3)

Meet the Fleet, 1940 (Eason 4)

Meet the Mayor, 1932 (Pangborn 3)

Meet the Missus, 1924 (Roach 4)

Meet the Missus, 1937 (Polglase 4)

Meet the Missus, 1940 (Ladd 3)

Meet the Navy, 1946 (Unsworth 4)

Meet the Nelsons. *See* Here Come the Nelsons, 1952

Meet the People, 1944 (Allyson 3, Ball 3, Powell 3, Irene 4, Surtees 4)

Meet the Pioneers, 1948 (Anderson 2)

Meet the Prince, 1926 (Murfin 4, Struss 4)

Meet the Raisins: The Story of the California Raisins, 1988 (Vinton 4)

Meet the Stars No. 4, 1941 (Abbott and Costello 3)

Meet the Stewarts, 1942 (Holden 3)

Meet the Wildcat, 1940 (Bellamy 3, Cortez 4, Salter 4)

Meet Whiplash Willie. *See* Fortune Cookie, 1966

Meeting Again. *See* Sakai, 1953

Meeting Hearts. *See* Hjärtansom mötas, 1914

Meeting in Bucharest. *See* Setkání v Bukurešti, 1954

Meeting in Leipzig. *See* Setkání v Lipsku, 1959

Meeting in the Night. *See* Möte i natten, 1946

Meeting of the Ghost of Après Guerre. *See* Sengo-ha obake taikai, 1951

Meeting of the Ways, 1912 (Costello 3)

Meeting on the Elbe. *See* Vsetrecha na Elba, 1949

Meeting Ships. *See* Skepp som motas, 1916

Meeting Venus, 1991 (Szabó 2, Puttnam 4)

Meetings with Remarkable Men, 1979 (Stamp 3, Wakhévitch 4)

Méfaits d'un tête de veau, 1899 (Gaumont 4)

Méfiez-vous des blondes, 1950 (Audiard 4)

Méfiez-vous, mesdames!, 1963 (Darrieux 3, Morgan 3)

Még kér a nép, 1972 (Jancsó 2)

Megaforce, 1982 (Needham 4)

Megano, 1955 (Gutiérrez Alea 2)

Megapolis I, 1963 (Müller 4)

Megfelelo ember kenyes feladatra, 1985 (Tyszkiewicz 3)

Megh, 1961 (Shankar 4)

Meglin Kiddie Revue, 1929 (Garland 3)

Megumi ni kenka, 1935 (Hasegawa 3)

Meguriai, 1968 (Takemitsu 4)

Mehmaan, 1953 (Biswas 4)

Meido no kaoyaku, 1957 (Miyagawa 4)

Meigetsu somato, 1951 (Hasegawa 3)

Meijin Choji-bori, 1943 (Hasegawa 3, Yamada 3)

Meilleur de la ville, 1984 (Branco 4)

Meilleure Bobonne, 1930 (Fernandel 3)

Meilleure Part, 1955 (Allégret 2, Philipe 3, Alekan 4)

Mein Freund—der Chauffeur, 1925 (Albers 3)

Mein Freund, der Dieb, 1951 (Tschechowa 3)

Mein Herz ist eine jazzband, 1928 (Andrejew 4)

Mein in Fright, 1938 (Roach 4)

Mein Kampf, My Crimes, 1941 (Lom 3, Ustinov 3)

Mein Leben fur das deine. *See* Odette, 1928

Mein Leben für Irland, 1940 (Wegener 3)

Mein Leopold, 1931 (Fröhlich 3)

Mein Mann—der Nachtredakteur, 1919 (Gad 2)

Mein Schulefreund, 1960 (Siodmak 2)

Mein Sohn, der Herr Minister, 1937 (Rosay 3, Röhrig 4)

Mein Vater der Schauspieler, 1956 (Siodmak 2)

Mein Wille ist Gesetz, 1919 (Pick 2)

Meine Cousine aus Warschau. *See* Ma Cousine de Varsovie, 1932

Meine Frau, die Filmschauspielerin, 1919 (Kräly 4)

Meine Frau, die Hochstaplerin, 1931 (Schüfftan 4)

Meine Herren Söhne, 1945 (Wagner 4)

Meine 16 Söhne, 1955 (Dagover 3)

Meine Tante, Deine Tante, 1927 (Porten 3)

Meineid, 1929 (Andrejew 4)

Meiran, 1929 (Tsuburaya 4)

Meisouchiza, 1983 (Iwashita 3)

Meissner Porzellan, 1907 (Porten 3, Messter 4)

Meister des Welt, 1926 (Tschechowa 3)

Meito Bijomaru, 1945 (Mizoguchi 2)

Mejor alcalde, el Rey, 1973 (Rey 3)

Mejor es reir, 1930 (D'arrast 2)

Mekhanikha golovnovo mozga, 1926 (Golovnya 4)

Mela, 1948 (Kumar 3)

Melancholia, 1989 (York 3)

Melba, 1953 (Milestone 2, Andrejew 4, Spiegel 4, Stewart 4)

Melba, 1988 (Greenwood 3)

Melbourne—Olympic City, 1955 (Finch 3)

Melissokomos Patheni—O Alles Mythos, 1986 (Mastroianni 3)

Mellah de Marrakech, 1948 (Decaë 4)

Mellem muntre musikanter, 1922 (Madsen and Schenstrøm 3)

Mélo, 1986 (Resnais 2)

Melodie der Liebe, 1932 (Kaper 4)

Melodie des Herzens, 1929 (Dagover 3, Pommer 4)

Mélodie en sous-sol, 1962 (Delon 3, Gabin 3, Audiard 4)

Melodie eterne, 1940 (Cervi 3)

Mélodie pour toi, 1941 (Wakhévitch 4)

Melody, 1971 (Parker 2)

Melody and Romance, 1937 (Lockwood 3, Sim 3)

Melody Club, 1949 (Terry-Thomas 3)

Melody Cruise, 1933 (Grable 3, Cooper 4, Glennon 4, Plunkett 4, Polglase 4, Steiner 4)

Melody for Three, 1941 (Wray 3, Alton 4)

Melody for Two, 1937 (O'Connor 3)

Melody in Gray. *See* Hanare-goze Orin, 1977

Melody in Spring, 1934 (McLeod 2)

Melody Lane, 1929 (Mandell 4)

Melody Lingers On, 1935 (Dunne 4, Newman 4)

Melody of Life. *See* Symphony of Six Million, 1932

Melody of Love, 1912 (Bushman 3)

Melody of Love, 1928 (Pidgeon 3)

Melody of the Heart. *See* Melodie des Herzens, 1929

Melody of Youth. *See* They Shall Have Music, 1939

Melody Ranch, 1940 (Autry 3, Durante 3, Miller 3, Wayne 3, August 4)

Melody Time, 1948 (Rogers 3, Disney 4, Hoch 4, Iwerks 4)

Melody Trail, 1935 (Autry 3)

Mélomane, 1903 (Méliès 2)

Melomaniac. *See* Mélomane, 1903

Melting Plot, 1915 (Olcott 2)

Melusine, 1944 (Tschechowa 3, Herlth 4)

Melvin and Howard, 1980 (Demme 2, Grahame 3, Robards 3, Legrand 4)

Melvin's Revenge, 1984 (Lewis 2)

Melzer, 1983 (Volger 3)

Member of the Government. *See* Chlen pravitelstva, 1939

Member of the Wedding, 1952 (Kramer 2, Zinnemann 2, Anhalt 4, Cohn 4, Mohr 4, North 4)

Memed My Hawk, 1984 (Lom 3, Ustinov 3, Francis 4)

Memo for Joe, 1944 (Cooper 3)

Mémoire courte, 1978 (Baye 3)

Mémoire des apparences, 1987 (Ruiz 2)

Mémoire du rock, 1962 (Braunberger 4)

Mémoires d'un flic, 1955 (Simon 3)

Mémoire Tatouée, 1988 (Christie 3)

Memoirs of a Survivor, 1981 (Christie 3, Lassally 4)

Memoirs of an Invisible Man, 1992 (Fraker 4, Goldman 4)

Memoirs of Manolescu. *See* Abend-Nacht-Morgen, 1920

Memorias de un reencuentro, 1986 (Alvarez 2)

Memorias del subdessarrolo, 1968 (Gutiérrez Alea 2)

Memories. *See* Zwischengleis, 1978

Memories and Men's Souls, 1914 (Talmadge 3)

Memories from the Boston Club. *See* Minnen fran Bostonklubben, 1909

Memories of Europe, 1941 (Hoch 4)

Memories of Famous Hollywood Comedians, 1952 (Brown 3)

Memories of Me, 1988 (Connery 3, Delerue 4)

Memories of Monet, 1984 (Bloom 3)

Memories of Underdevelopment. *See* **Memorias del subdessarrolo, 1968**

Memory, 1991 (Hurt 3)

Memory Expert. *See* Man on a Flying Trapeze, 1935

Memory Lane, 1926 (Stahl 2, Booth 4, Gibbons 4, Glazer 4)

Memory of Eva Ryker, 1980 (Bellamy 3, McDowall 3)

Memory of Justice, 1976 (Ophuls 2, Puttnam 4)

Memory of Our Day, 1963 (Nemec 2)

Memory of the Heart, 1958 (Gerasimov 2)

Memory Song Book, 1952 (Fleischer 4)

Memphis Belle, 1944 (Wyler 2, Clothier 4)

Memphis Belle, 1990 (Puttnam 4, Watkin 4)

Men, 1924 (Negri 3)

Men, 1950 (Kramer 2, Zinnemann 2, Brando 3, Sloane 3, Wright 3, Foreman 4, Tiomkin 4)

Men and Beasts, 1962 (Gerasimov 2)

Men and Wolves. *See* Uomini e lupi, 1956

Men and Women, 1914 (Barrymore 3, Sweet 3)

Men Are Children Twice. *See* Valley of Song, 1952

Men Are Like That, 1930 (Wayne 3, Mankiewicz 4)

Men Are Like This. *See* So sind die Männer, 1922

Men Are Not Gods, 1936 (Harrison 3, Hopkins 3, Hornbeck 4, Korda, A. 4, Korda, V. 4, Krasker 4, Reisch 4, Rosher 4)

Men Are Such Fools, 1938 (Berkeley 2, Bogart 3, Raine 4)

Men Behind Bars. *See* Duffy of San Quentin, 1954

Men Call It Love, 1931 (Menjou 3, Rosson 4)

Men Don't Leave, 1990 (Lange 3)

Men in Black, 1934 (Three Stooges 3)

Men in Danger, 1939 (Cavalcanti 2)

Men in Her Life, 1931 (Riskin 4)

Men in Her Life, 1941 (Veidt 3, Young 3, Lemaire 4, Miller 4, Raksin 4, Stradling 4, Wilson 4)

Men in War, 1957 (Mann 2, Ryan 3, Bernstein 4, Haller 4, Maddow 4)

Men in White, 1934 (Gable 3, Loy 3, Walthall 3, Adrian 4, Folsey 4, Gibbons 4, Young 4)

Men Must Fight, 1933 (Young 3, Adrian 4, Folsey 4, Sullivan 4)

Men o' War, 1929 (Roach 4, Laurel and Hardy 3)

Men of America, 1932 (Hunt 4)

Men of Boys Town, 1941 (Cobb 3, Rooney 3, Tracy 3, Rosson 4, Stothart 4)

Men of Chance, 1932 (Astor 3, Berman 4, Musuraca 4, Steiner 4)

Men of Destiny. *See* Men of Texas, 1942

Men of Respect, 1990 (Steiger 3)

Men of Science, 1944 (Unsworth 4)

Men of Sherwood Forest, 1954 (Carreras 4)

Men of Steel, 1926 (McLaglen 3)

Men of Texas, 1942 (Brooks 2, Bellamy 3, Cooper 3, Crawford 3, Darwell 3, Krasner 4)

Men of the Blue Cross. *See* Błękitny krzyż, 1955

Men of the Desert, 1917 (Van Dyke 2)

Men of the Dragon, 1974 (Bernstein 4)

Men of the Fighting Lady, 1954 (Calhern 3, Johnson 3, Pidgeon 3, Folsey 4, Rozsa 4)

Men of the Lightship, 1940 (Cavalcanti 2, Hitchcock 2)

Men of the Night, 1935 (Bond 3)

Men of the North, 1930 (Gibbons 4, Mayer 4, Roach 4)

Men of the Sea. *See* Midshipman Easy, 1935

Men of the Sky, 1931 (Seitz 4)

Men of the Sky, 1942 (Eason 4)

Men of the Timberland, 1941 (Salter 4)

Men of the Year, 1934 (Ball 3)

Men of Tomorrow, 1932 (Crichton 2, Oberon 3, Donat 3, Korda, A. 4, Korda, V. 4)

Men of Two Worlds, 1946 (Rank 4)

Men of Yesterday, 1936 (Baxter 2)

Men on Call, 1930 (Clarke 4, Friedhofer 4)

Men on Her Mind. *See* Girl from Tenth Avenue, 1935

Men Who Tread on the Tiger's Tail. *See* Toro-no-o o fumu otokotachi, 1945

Men with Steel Faces. *See* Phantom Empire, 1935

Men with Wings, 1938 (Wellman 2, Macmurray 3, Milland 3, O'Connor 3, Head 4)

Men without Honour, 1939 (Stallich 4)

Men without Law, 1930 (McCord 4)

Men without Names, 1935 (MacMurray 3, Head 4)

Men without Souls, 1940 (Ford 3)

Men without Wings. *See* Muži bez křídel, 1945

Men without Women, 1930 (Ford 2, Wayne 3, August 4, Nichols 4)

Menace, 1913 (Dwan 2)

Menace, 1932 (Davis 3)

Menace, 1934 (Milland 3, Banton 4)

Menace, 1977 (Montand 3)

Menace de mort, 1949 (Dalio 3)

Menace to Carlotta, 1914 (Dwan 2, Chaney 3)

Menaces, 1939 (Von Stroheim 2, Braunberger 4, Heller 4)

Menage. *See* Tenue de soirée, 1986

Menagerie, 1929 (Rooney 3)

Mended Lute, 1909 (Griffith 2, Lawrence 3, Bitzer 4)

Mender of the Nets, 1912 (Griffith 2, Normand 3, Pickford 3, Bitzer 4)

Mendiante de Sainte-Sulpice, 1924 (Vanel 3)

Mendiants, 1986 (Sanda 3, Branco 4, De Almeida 4)

Mendigos, 1963 (Guerra 2)

Ménestrel de la reine Anne, 1913 (Feuillade 2)

Menino de engenho, 1965 (Rocha 2)

Mennesker modes og sod musik opstår i hjertet, 1967 (Andersson 3, Dahlbeck 3)

Men's Club, 1986 (Scheider 3)

Mensch am Wege, 1923 (Dieterle 2, Dietrich 3, Rasp 3)

Mensch gegen Mensch, 1924 (Junge 4)

Mensch ohne Namen, 1932 (Krauss 3, Herlth 4, Hoffmann 4, Röhrig 4)

Menschen am Meer, 1925 (Rasp 3)

Menschen am Sonntag, 1929 (Siodmak 2, Ulmer 2, Wilder 2, Zinnemann 2, Schüfftan 4, Siodmak 4)

Menschen hinter Gittern, 1930 (Fejös 2)

Menschen im Feuer, 1928 (Tschechowa 3)

Menschen im Hotel, 1960 (Morgan 3)

Menschen im Käfig, 1930 (Dupont 2, Kortner 3, Veidt 3)

Menschen im Rausch, 1920 (Veidt 3)

Menschen im Sturm, 1941 (Tschechowa 3)

Menschen und Masken, 1913 (Warm 4)

Menschenfeind, 1923 (Krauss 3)

Menschenopfer, 1922 (Albers 3)

Menschheit anwalt, 1920 (Röhrig 4)

Mensonge de Nina Petrowna, 1937 (Annenkov 4, Courant 4, Jeanson 4)

Mental Poise, 1938 (Benchley 4)

Mental Suicide, 1913 (Dwan 2)

Menteurs, 1961 (Chabrol 2, Modot 3)

Menuet lilliputien, 1905 (Méliès 2)

Menuisier, 1962 (Braunberger 4)

Menuisiers, 1895 (Lumière 2)

Meoto daiko, 1941 (Yoda 4)

Meoto zenzai, 1955 (Tsukasa 3)

Mephisto, 1931 (Gabin 3)

Mephisto, 1981 (Szabó 2, Brandauer 3)

Mephisto Waltz, 1970 (Goldsmith 4, Maddow 4)

Mépris, 1963 (Godard 2, Bardot 3, Palance 3, Piccoli 3, Coutard 4, De Beauregard 4, Delerue 4, Guillemot 4, Levine 4, Ponti 4)

Mer Caribe, 1955 (Decaë 4)

Mer et les jours, 1958 (Colpi 4, Delerue 4)

Meraviglie di Aladino, 1961 (O'Connor 3, Fabrizi 3, Delli Colli 4)

Meravigliose avventure di Guerrin Meschino, 1952 (Rota 4)

Mercante di Venezia, 1911 (Pathé 4)

Mercante di Venezia, 1912 (Bertini 3)

Mercante di Venezia, 1952 (Simon 3, Fusco 4)

Mercenaries, 1968 (More 3, Cardiff 4)

Mercenario, 1968 (Palance 3, Morricone 4, Solinas 4)

Mercenarios, 1983 (Fernández 2)

Mercenary. *See* Mercenario, 1968

Merchant of Venice, 1908 (Costello 3)

Merchant of Venice. *See* Mercante di Venezia, 1911

Merchant of Venice, 1914 (Weber 2)

Merchant of Venice. *See* Mercante de Venezia, 1952

Merchants of the Four Seasons. *See* Händler der vier Jahreszeiten, 1971

Merci la vie, 1991 (Depardieu 3, Girardot 3, Trintignant 3)

Mercy or Murder?, 1986 (Young 3)

Mère du moine, 1909 (Feuillade 2)

Mère et l'infant, 1959 (Demy 2)

Merely a Maid, 1920 (Roach 4)

Merely a Married Man, 1915 (Sennett 2)

Merely a Millionaire, 1912 (Bosworth 3)

Merely Mary Anne, 1931 (King 2, Gaynor 3, Furthman 4, Seitz 4)

Meri Soorat, 1963 (Burman 4)

Meridian—Kiss of the Beast, 1990 (Donaggio 4)

Meridian Zero. *See* Południk zero, 1970

Meridiano Novo, 1976 (Alvarez 2)

Merle, 1958 (McLaren 4)

Merlin and the Knights of King Arthur, 1980 (Boorman 2)

Merlin and the Sword, 1983 (McDowell 3)

Merlin the Magic Mouse, 1967 (Blanc 4)

Merlusse, 1935 (Pagnol 2)

Mermaid. *See* Sirène, 1904

Mermaids, 1990 (Cher 3, Hoskins 3)

Mermoz, 1943 (Honegger 4)

Merrill's Marauders, 1962 (Fuller 2, Clothier 4)

Merrily We Go to Hell, 1932 (Arzner 2, Grant 3, March 3, Sidney 3, Zukor 4)

Merrily We Live, 1938 (McLeod 2, Irene 4, Roach 4)

Merrily We Sing, 1944 (Fleischer 4)

Merrily Yours, 1933 (Temple 3)

Merry Andrew, 1958 (Kaye 3, Diamond 4, Kidd 4, Lennart 4, Mercer 4, Plunkett 4, Surtees 4)

Merry Chase. *See* Resa di Titi, 1945

Merry Chase, 1950 (Terry 4)

Merry Christmas Mr. Lawrence, 1983 (Oshima 2, Toda 4)

Merry Circus. *See* Veselý cirkus, 1950

Merry Dog, 1933 (Lantz 4)

Merry Dwarfs, 1929 (Stalling 4)

Merry Dwarfs, 1930 (Disney 4)

Merry Frinks, 1934 (Beavers 3, Edeson 4, Orry-Kelly 4)

Merry Mannequins, 1937 (Iwerks 4)

Merry Mavericks, 1951 (Three Stooges 3)

Merry Men, 1930 (Rooney 3)

Merry Microbes. *See* Joyeaux Microbes, 1909

Merry Mix-Up, 1956 (Three Stooges 3)

Merry Monahans, 1944 (O'Connor 3, Salter 4)

Merry Monarch. *See* Abenteur des Königs Pausole, 1933

Merry Old Soul, 1933 (Lantz 4)

Merry Old Soul, 1935 (Freleng 4)

Merry Widow, 1925 (Von Stroheim 2, Gable 3, Gilbert 3, Daniels 4, Day 4, Gibbons 4, Glazer 4, Mayer 4, Thalberg 4)

Merry Widow, 1934 (Lubitsch 2, Chevalier 3, Horton 3, MacDonald 3, Adrian 4, Gibbons 4, Loos 4, Mayer 4, Raphaelson 4, Stothart 4, Thalberg 4, Vajda 4)

Merry Widow, 1952 (Dalio 3, Turner 3, Cole 4, Levien 4, Pasternak 4, Rose 4, Surtees 4)

Merry Widow Waltz Craze, 1908 (Porter 2)

Merry Widower, 1926 (Laurel and Hardy 3, Roach 4)

Merry Wives of Gotham. *See* Lights of Old Broadway, 1925

Merry Wives of Reno, 1934 (Beavers 3, Haller 4, Orry-Kelly 4)

Merry Wives of Windsor, 1910 (Selig 4)

Merry-Go-Round, 1923 (Von Stroheim 2, Daniels 4, Day 4, Thalberg 4)

Merry-Go-Round, 1979 (Rivette 2)

Merton of the Movies, 1924 (Cruze 2, Brown 4)

Merton of the Movies, 1947 (Grahame 3, Alton 4, Irene 4, Mayer 4, Rose 4)

Merveilleuse Angélique, 1964 (Trintignant 3)

Merveilleuse Journée, 1981 (Evein 4)

Merveilleuse Vie de Jeanne d'Arc, 1928 (Modot 3)

Merveilleuse Visite, 1974 (Carné 2, Evein 4)

Merveilleux éventail vivant, 1904 (Méliès 2)

Merveilleux Parfum d'oseille, 1969 (Rosay 3)

Me's Outing. *See* Herrenpartie, 1964

Mes petites amoureuses, 1974 (Almendros 4)

Mes tantes et moi, 1936 (Morgan 3)

Mes voisins me font danser, 1909 (Linder 3)

Mesa of Lost Women, 1952 (Struss 4)

Mesalina, 1951 (Félix 3)

Mésaventure d'un charbonnier, 1897 (Guy 2)

Mésaventure d'un charbonnier, 1899 (Gaumont 4)

Mesék az írógépről, 1916 (Korda 2, Korda 4)

Meshes of the Afternoon, 1943 (Deren 2)

Meshi, 1951 (Hara 3, Yamamura 3, Hayasaka 4)

Meskal le contrabandier, 1909 (Gaumont 4)

Mesmerian Experiment. *See* Bacquet de Mesmer, 1905

Mesmerized, 1986 (Foster 3, Delerue 4)

Message, 1909 (Griffith 2, Bitzer 4)

Message, 1976 (Papas 3, Quinn 3)

Message from Geneva, 1936 (Cavalcanti 2)

Message from the Moon, 1911 (Sennett 2)

Message in the Bottle, 1911 (Pickford 3, Gaudio 4, Ince 4)

Message of Headquarters, 1913 (Cruze 2)

Message of the Arrow, 1910 (White 3)

Message of the Mouse, 1917 (Blackton 2)

Message of the Violin, 1910 (Griffith 2, Bitzer 4)

Message to Buckshot John, 1915 (Bosworth 3)

Message to Garcia, 1936 (Beery 3, Carradine 3, Hayworth 3, Stanwyck 3, Maté 4, Zanuck 4)

Message to Gracias, 1964 (Blanc 4, McKimson 4)

Message to My Daughter, 1973 (Sheen 3)

Messager, 1937 (Blier 3, Gabin 3, Achard 4, Auric 4, Lourié 4)

Messager de la lumière, 1938 (Grimault 4)

Messe de minuit, 1906 (Guy 2)

Messe e finita, 1985 (Morricone 4)

Messenger, 1918 (Laurel and Hardy 3)

Messenger Boy's Mistake, 1903 (Porter 2, Anderson 3)

Messenger of Death, 1988 (Bronson 3, Golan and Globus 4)

Messenger of the Mountains, 1963 (Watt 2)

Messenger to Kearney, 1912 (Bosworth 3)

Messer im Kopf, 1978 (Ganz 3, Winkler 3)

Messidor, 1978 (Tanner 2)

Messieurs les ronds-de-cuir, 1959 (Brasseur 3)

Messieurs Ludovic, 1946 (Berry 3, Blier 3, Kosma 4)

Messire Wołodyjowski, 1968 (Nowicki 3)

Mesuinu, 1951 (Kyo 3, Shimura 3)

Metall des Himmels, 1934 (Ruttman 2)

Metamorfeus. *See* Pomsta, 1968

Métamorphose des cloportes, 1965 (Brasseur 3, Audiard 4, Saulnier 4)

Metamorphoses comiques, 1912 (Cohl 4)

Métamorphoses du paysage industriel, 1964 (Rohmer 2)

Metamorphoses du Roi de Pique, 1904 (Pathé 4)

Metamorphosis. *See* Fantasmagorie, 1908

Metamorphosis, 1975 (Nemec 2)

Metaphors on Vision, 1990 (Brakhage 2)

Metello, 1969 (Cecchi D'Amico 4, Morricone 4)

Meteor, 1979 (Connery 3, Fonda 3, Howard 3, Malden 3, Wood 3)

Meteoro vima tou Pelargou. *See* To meteoro vima to Pelargou, 1991

Métier de fous, 1948 (Burel 4)

Metro, 1934 (Franju 2)

Métro, 1950 (Leenhardt 2)

Metro By Night. *See* Moskva Stroit metro, 1934

Metro lungo cinque, 1961 (Olmi 2)

Metropolis, 1927 (Lang 2, Fröhlich 3, Rasp 3, Freund 4, Hunte 4, Pommer 4, Schüfftan 4, Von Harbou 4)

Metropolitan, 1935 (Brennan 3, Darwell 3, Day 4, Maté 4, Meredyth 4, Newman 4, Zanuck 4)

Metropolitan Symphony. *See* Tokai kokyogaku, 1929

Metti, una sera a cena, 1969 (Girardot 3, Trintignant 3, Argento 4)

Metti, une sera a cena, 1969 (Morricone 4)

Meurtes, 1950 (Moreau 3)

Meurtre en 45 tours, 1960 (Darrieux 3)

Meurtre est un meurtre, 1972 (Chabrol 2, Audran 3)

Meurtres, 1950 (Jeanson 4)

Meurtrier, 1963 (Aurenche 4, Bost 4, Douy 4)

Meus Amigos, 1974 (De Almeida 4)

Meus oito anos, 1956 (Mauro 2)

Mexicali Rose, 1929 (Stanwyck 3, Westmore Family 4)

Mexicali Rose, 1939 (Autry 3)

Mexicali Shmoes, 1959 (Blanc 4, Freleng 4)

Mexican, 1911 (Dwan 2)

Mexican, 1914 (Mix 3)

Mexican Affair. *See* Flor de mayo, 1957

Mexican Baseball, 1947 (Terry 4)

Mexican Boarders, 1962 (Blanc 4, Freleng 4)

Mexican Cat Dance, 1963 (Blanc 4, Freleng 4)

Mexican Hayride, 1948 (Abbott and Costello 3)

Mexican Joyride, 1947 (Blanc 4, Stalling 4)

Mexican Mousepiece, 1966 (Blanc 4, McKimson 4)

Mexican Spitfire, 1939 (Polglase 4)

Mexican Spitfire Out West, 1940 (Polglase 4)

Mexican Spitfire Sees a Ghost, 1942 (Metty 4)

Mexican Sweethearts, 1909 (Griffith 2, Pickford 3, Bitzer 4)

Mexican Symphony, 1941 (Eisenstein 2)

Mexican Tragedy, 1912 (Ince 4)

Mexicanerin, 1919 (Veidt 3)

Mexicanos al grito de guerra, 1943 (Infante 3)

Mexican's Faith, 1910 (Anderson 3)

Mexican's Gratitude, 1909 (Anderson 3)

Mexico, 1930 (Lantz 4)

Mexico . . . Estamos Contigo, 1985 (Cantinflas 3)

Mexico in Flames, 1982 (Bondarchuk 3)

México mágico, 1980 (Figueroa 4)

Mexico Marches, 1941 (Eisenstein 2)

México norte, 1977 (Fernández 2)

Mexico Soon. *See* Jutro Meksyk, 1965

México 2000, 1981 (Figueroa 4)

Meyer als Soldat, 1914 (Lubitsch 2)

Meyer auf der Alm, 1913 (Lubitsch 2)

Mezi nebem a zemi, 1958 (Brodský 3)

Mezzanotte va la ronda del piacere, 1975 (Cardinale 3, Gassman 3, Giannini 3, Vitti 3)

Mezzogiorno di fuoco par Lin-Hao. *See* Mio nome è Shanghai Joe, 1973

Mi abuelo, mi perro y yo, 1983 (Fernández 2)

Mi candidato, 1938 (Armendáriz 3, Figueroa 4)

Mi General, 1986 (Rey 3)

Mi Hermano Fidel, 1977 (Alvarez 2)

Mi hijo, el Che, 1985 (Birri 2)

Mi manda piccone, 1985 (Giannini 3)

Mi negra o su negra. *See* Bestia negra, 1939

Mi permette babbo!, 1956 (Fabrizi 3, Sordi 3)

Mi viuda alegre, 1941 (Figueroa 4)

Mia signora, 1964 (Comencini 2, Mangano 3, Sordi 3)

Mia valle, 1955 (Olmi 2)

Miadzy Wroclawiem a Zielona Gora, 1972 (Kieślowski 2)

Miai-kekkon, 1958 (Kagawa 3)

Miami Exposé, 1956 (Cobb 3, Katzman 4)

Miami Story, 1954 (Katzman 4)

Miarka, Daughter of the Bear. *See* Miarka, fille l'ours, 1920

Miarka, fille l'ours, 1920 (Novello 3)

Miarka, la fille à l'ourse, 1923 (Vanel 3)

Miarka, la fille à l'ourse, 1937 (Dalio 3, Honegger 4)
Mice Follies, 1953 (Hanna and Barbera 4)
Mice Follies, 1960 (Blanc 4, McKimson 4)
Mice in Council, 1934 (Terry 4)
Mice Will Play, 1938 (Avery 4)
Michael, 1924 (Christensen 2, Dreyer 2, Freund 4, Maté 4, Pommer 4, Von Harbou 4)
Michael and Mary, 1931 (Saville 2, Marshall 3, Balcon 4, Biro 4, Vetchinsky 4)
Michael Carmichael, 1972 (Cushing 3, Carreras 4, Sangster 4)
Michael Jackson's Thriller, 1984 (Price 3)
Michael Kohlhaas—Der Rebell, 1969 (Karina 3)
Michael McShane, 1912 (Bunny 3)
Michael O'Halloran, 1937 (Brown 4)
Michael Shayne, Private Detective, 1940 (Day 4)
Michael Strogoff. See Michel Strogoff, 1926
Michael Strogoff. See Soldier and the Lady, 1936
Michael Strogoff or The Courier to the Czar, 1914 (Guy 2)
Michael the Brave, 1969 (Welles 2)
Michel Strogoff, 1926 (Mozhukin 3, Burel 4)
Michel Strogoff, 1935 (Delannoy 2, Vanel 3)
Michel Strogoff, 1956 (Barsacq 4)
Michelangelo and me, 1989 (Sharif 3)
Michele Strogoff, 1956 (Gallone 2)
Michelino la B, 1956 (Olmi 2)
Michel's Mixed Up Bird, 1978 (Legrand 4)
Michigan Kid, 1928 (Fulton 4)
Michigan Kid, 1946 (Miller 4, Salter 4)
Michki protiv Youdenitsa, 1925 (Kozintsev 2)
Michurin, 1948 (Dovzhenko 2, Bondarchuk 3, Shostakovich 4)
Mickey series, 1927–34 (Rooney 3)
Mickey, 1918 (Sennett 2, Normand 3)
Mickey, 1948 (McDaniel 3)
Mickey and His Goat, 1917 (O'Brien 4)
Mickey Mouse, 1928 (Disney 4)
Mickey One, 1965 (Penn 2, Beatty 3, Cloquet 4, Jenkins 4)
Mickey Rooney, Then and Now, 1953 (Rooney 3)
Mickey's Choo Choo, 1929 (Disney 4)
Mickey's Choo-Choo, 1929 (Iwerks 4)
Mickey's Follies, 1929 (Iwerks 4)
Mickey's Naughty Nightmares, 1917 (O'Brien 4)
Mickey's Pal, 1912 (Guy 2)
Micki and Maude, 1985 (Edwards 2, Moore 3, Legrand 4)
Micro-Phonies, 1945 (Three Stooges 3)
Mid Channel, 1920 (Edeson 4)
Midareboshi Aragami-yama, 1950 (Yamada 3)
Midaregumo, 1967 (Mori 3, Tsukasa 3, Takemitsu 4)
Midareru, 1964 (Takamine 3)
Midas Run, 1969 (Astaire 3, McDowall 3, Richardson 3, Bernstein 4)
Midas Valley, 1985 (Simmons 3)
Middies Shortening Sail, 1901 (Bitzer 4)
Middle Age Crazy, 1980 (Dern 3)
Middle of the Night, 1959 (Grant 3, March 3, Novak 3, Chayefsky 4)
Middle of the World. See Milieu du monde, 1974
Middle Watch, 1930 (Launder and Gilliat 2)

Middle Watch, 1939 (Buchanan 3)
Middleman. See Jana Aranya, 1975
Middlin' Stranger, 1927 (Karloff 3)
Midget's Revenge, 1912 (Talmadge 3)
Midlanders, 1920 (Love 3)
Midnight, 1931 (Bennett 4)
Midnight, 1934 (Bogart 3)
Midnight, 1939 (Leisen 2, Wilder 2, Ameche 3, Astor 3, Barrymore 3, Colbert 3, Brackett 4, Head 4, Irene 4, Lang 4)
Midnight, 1989 (Curtis 3)
Midnight Adventure, 1909 (Griffith 2, Pickford 3, Bitzer 4)
Midnight Alibi, 1934 (Barthelmess 3, Orry-Kelly 4)
Midnight Angel, 1941 (Siodmak 4)
Midnight at Madame Tussaud's, 1937 (Pearson 2)
Midnight Club, 1933 (Raft 3, Banton 4)
Midnight Court, 1937 (Raksin 4)
Midnight Cowboy, 1969 (Schlesinger 2, Hoffman 3, Voight 3, Barry 4, Salt 4, Smith 4)
Midnight Crossing, 1987 (Dunaway 3)
Midnight Cupid, 1910 (Griffith 2, Bitzer 4)
Midnight Daddies, 1929 (Sennett 2, Hornbeck 4)
Midnight Elopement, 1912 (Sennett 2, Normand 3)
Midnight Event. See Půlnoční příhoda, 1960
Midnight Express, 1924 (Johnson 3)
Midnight Express, 1978 (Parker 2, Stone 2, Hurt 3, Puttnam 4)
Midnight Follies, 1929 (Rooney 3)
Midnight Frolics, 1938 (Iwerks 4)
Midnight Girl, 1925 (Lugosi 3, Fort 4)
Midnight Intruder, 1938 (Krasner 4)
Midnight Kiss, 1926 (Gaynor 3)
Midnight Lace, 1960 (Day 3, Harrison 3, Loy 3, Marshall 3, McDowall 3, Hunter 4, Irene 4, Metty 4)
Midnight Life, 1928 (Bushman 3)
Midnight Lovers, 1926 (Wilson 4)
Midnight Madness, 1928 (Adrian 4)
Midnight Madness, 1980 (Fox 3)
Midnight Madonna, 1937 (Head 4)
Midnight Man, 1917 (Meredyth 4)
Midnight Man, 1974 (Lancaster 3)
Midnight Mary, 1933 (Wellman 2, Young 3, Adrian 4, Loos 4)
Midnight Menace, 1936 (Kortner 3)
Midnight Molly, 1925 (Berman 4)
Midnight Mystery, 1930 (Plunkett 4, Walker 4)
Midnight Parasites, 1972 (Kuri 4)
Midnight Patrol, 1918 (Ince 4)
Midnight Patrol, 1933 (Laurel and Hardy 3, Roach 4)
Midnight Ride of Paul Revere, 1907 (Porter 2)
Midnight Rider, 1990 (Travolta 3)
Midnight Romance, 1919 (Weber 2, Mayer 4)
Midnight Run, 1988 (De Niro 3)
Midnight Snack, 1941 (Hanna and Barbera 4)
Midnight Story, 1957 (Curtis 3, Metty 4, Salter 4)
Midnight Supper, 1909 (Porter 2)
Midnight Taxi, 1928 (Loy 3, Zanuck 4)
Midori naki shima, 1948 (Yamamura 3)
Midori no daichi, 1941 (Shindo 3, Hayasaka 4)

Midorino furusato, 1946 (Hara 3)
Midshipmaid, 1932 (Matthews 3, Mills 3)
Midshipmaid Gob. See Midshipmaid, 1932
Midshipman, 1925 (Novarro 3, Wilson 4)
Midshipman, 1932 (Balcon 4, Junge 4)
Midshipman Easy, 1935 (Lockwood 3, Dean 4)
Midshipman Jack, 1933 (D'Agostino 4, Plunkett 4, Polglase 4, Steiner 4)
Midsummer Day's Work, 1939 (Cavalcanti 2)
Midsummer Mush, 1933 (Roach 4)
Midsummer Music, 1960 (Lassally 4)
Midsummer Nightmare, 1957 (Halas and Batchelor 4)
Midsummer Night's Dream, 1909 (Costello 3)
Midsummer Night's Dream. See Sommernachtstraum, 1924
Midsummer Night's Dream, 1935 (Dieterle 2, Brown 3, Cagney 3, De Havilland 3, Powell 3, Rooney 3, Blanke 4, Grot 4, Haskin 4, Korngold 4, Mohr 4, Wallis 4, Westmore Family 4)
Midsummer Night's Dream. See Sen noci svatojánské, 1959
Midsummer Night's Dream, 1961 (Burton 3)
Midsummer Night's Sex Comedy, 1982 (Allen 2, Farrow 3, Ferrer 3, Willis 4)
Midt i byens hjerte, 1938 (Madsen and Schenstrøm 3)
Midvinterblot, 1946 (Björnstrand 3)
Midway, 1976 (Coburn 3, Fonda 3, Ford 3, Heston 3, Mifune 3, Mitchum 3, Robertson 3, Wagner 3, Mirisch 4, Williams 4)
Midwinter Blood. See Midvinterblot, 1946
Midwinter Trip to Los Angeles, 1911 (Dwan 2)
Miei primi 40 anni, 1987 (Gould 3)
Miel se fue de la luna, 1951 (Alcoriza 4)
Mientras México duerme, 1938 (Figueroa 4)
Miércoles de ceniza, 1958 (Félix 3)
Miester von Nürnberg, 1927 (Fröhlich 3)
Might Mail, 1935 (Bennett 4)
Mighty, 1929 (Cromwell 2, Hunt 4, Mankiewicz 4, Zukor 4)
Mighty Barnum, 1934 (Beery 3, Menjou 3, Day 4, Meredyth 4, Newman 4, Zanuck 4)
Mighty Barnum: A Screen Play, 1944 (Day 4)
Mighty Hunters, 1940 (Blanc 4, Jones 4, Stalling 4)
Mighty Joe Young, 1949 (Schoedsack 2, Johnson 3, Basevi 4, Cooper 4, Dunn 4, Harryhausen 4, Hunt 4, O'Brien 4)
Mighty Lak a Goat, 1942 (Gardner 3)
Mighty Lak a Rose, 1923 (Polito 4)
Mighty Like a Moose, 1926 (McCarey 2, Roach 4)
Mighty McGurk, 1947 (Beery 3, Irene 4)
Mighty Mouse series, 1945–47 (Terry 4)
Mighty Navy, 1941 (Fleischer 4)
Mighty Penny, 1942 (Balcon 4)
Mighty Treve, 1937 (Raksin 4)
Mignon, 1900 (Guy 2)
Mignon or The Child of Fate, 1912 (Guy 2)
Migrants, 1974 (Spacek 3)
Migrations. See Guerre la plus glorieuse, 1989
Mikado, 1907 (Gaumont 4)
Mikado, 1939 (Dickinson 2, Dillon 4)
Mikado, 1967 (Fisher 4, Havelock-Allan 4)

Mike, 1926 (Neilan 2)
Mike Fright, 1934 (Roach 4)
Mike's Murder, 1984 (Allen 4, Barry 4)
Mikey and Nicky, 1976 (Falk 3, Ballard 4, May 4)
Mikis Theodorakis: A Profile of Greatness, 1974 (Bates 3)
Mikkel, 1948 (Roos 2)
Mikosch rückt ein, 1928 (Metzner 4)
Mikromakrokosmos, 1960 (Brdečka 4)
Mil, 1962 (Rouch 2)
Mil amores, 1954 (Infante 3)
Mil huit cent quatorze, 1910 (Feuillade 2)
Milagro Beanfield War, 1988 (Redford 3, Allen 4)
Milan, 1946 (Kumar 3, Biswas 4)
Milan noir, 1989 (Huppert 3)
Milana the Millionairess. See Milano miliardaria, 1951
Milano '83, 1984 (Olmi 2)
Milano miliardaria, 1951 (Loren 3, Delli Colli 4)
Milano nera, 1963 (Fusco 4)
Milano odia: la polizia no puo sparare, 1974 (Morricone 4)
Milano Zero, 1983 (Bozzetto 4)
Milap, 1955 (Anand 3)
Milczenie, 1963 (Cybulski 3)
Mildred Pierce, 1945 (Curtiz 2, Arden 3, Crawford 3, McQueen 3, Friedhofer 4, Grot 4, Haller 4, Steiner 4, Wald 4)
Mile de Jules Ladoumègue, 1932 (Kaufman 4)
Mile-a-Minute Romeo, 1923 (Mix 3)
Milenky starého kriminálníka, 1927 (Ondra 3)
Miles from Home, 1988 (Gere 3, Copland 4)
Miles To Go, 1986 (Clayburgh 3)
Milestones of the Movies, 1966 (Clarke 4)
Mili, 1975 (Bachchan 3, Burman 4)
Milieu du monde, 1974 (Tanner 2)
Militaire et nourrice, 1904 (Guy 2)
Militant School Ma'am, 1914 (Mix 3)
Militant Suffragette, 1912 (Cruze 2)
Militare e mezzo, 1960 (Fabrizi 3)
Militarismo y tortura, 1969 (Ruiz 2)
Militarists. See Gunbatsu, 1970
Military Academy, 1940 (Brown 4)
Military Judas, 1913 (Ince 4)
Military Life, Pleasant Life. See Život vojenský, život veselý, 1934
Military Policemen. See Off Limits, 1952
Milk and Money, 1936 (Avery 4, Stalling 4)
Milk for Baby, 1938 (Terry 4)
Milk We Drink, 1913 (Sennett 2)
Milkfed Boy, 1914 (Crisp 3)
Milkman, 1932 (Iwerks 4)
Milkman, 1950 (Durante 3, O'Connor 3, Boyle 4)
Milky Waif, 1946 (Hanna and Barbera 4)
Milky Waif, 1950 (Hanna and Barbera 4)
Milky Way, 1922 (Van Dyke 2)
Milky Way, 1936 (McCarey 2, Lloyd 3, Menjou 3, Head 4, Zukor 4)
Milky Way. See Voie lactée, 1969
Mill Buyers, 1912 (Lawrence 3)
Mill of Life, 1914 (Costello 3, Talmadge 3)
Mill on the Floss, 1937 (Mason 3)
Mill on the Po. See Mulino del Po, 1949
Mille et deuxième nuit, 1933 (Volkov 2, Modot 3, Mozhukin, Maté 4)
Mille et une nuits, 1922 (Modot 3)

Mille et une nuits. See Meraviglie di Aladino, 1961
Mille et une nuits, 1990 (Gassman 3)
Mille et un millions. See Toute la ville accuse, 1955
Mille lire al mese, 1938 (Valli 3)
Mille milliards de dollars, 1981 (Moreau 3)
Mille villages, 1960 (Rabier 4)
Miller's Beautiful Daughter. See Bella mugnaia, 1955
Miller's Beautiful Wife. See Bella mugnaia, 1955
Miller's Crossing, 1990 (Finney 3)
Miller's Daughter, 1934 (Freleng 4)
Miller's Wife. See Bella mugnaia, 1955
Milliard dans un billard, 1965 (Spaak 4)
Millie, 1931 (Blondell 3, Brown 4, Haller 4)
Millième Fenêtre, 1960 (Fresnay 3, Trintignant 3)
Milliner. See Masamod, 1920
Millinery Bomb, 1913 (Bunny 3)
Million, 1931 (Clair 2, Meerson 4, Périnal 4)
Million a Minute, 1916 (Bushman 3)
Million Bid, 1927 (Curtiz 2, Blanke 4, Mohr 4)
Million Dollar Baby, 1941 (Reagan 3, Orry-Kelly 4, Robinson 4, Rosher 4, Wald 4, Wallis 4)
Million Dollar Bride, 1914 (Browning 2, Loos 4)
Million Dollar Cat, 1944 (Hanna and Barbera 4)
Million Dollar Face, 1981 (Curtis 3, Grant 3)
Million Dollar Kid, 1944 (Katzman 4)
Million Dollar Legs, 1932 (Dmytryk 2, Mankiewicz 2, Fields 3, Mankiewicz 4)
Million Dollar Legs, 1939 (Dmytryk 2, Crabbe 3, Grable 3, Holden 3, O'Connor 3, Head 4)
Million Dollar Mermaid, 1952 (Berkeley 2, Mature 3, Pidgeon 3, Williams 3, Deutsch 4, Folsey 4, Plunkett 4, Rose 4, Smith 4)
Million Dollar Mystery, 1914 (Cruze 2)
Million Dollar Mystery, 1987 (Cardiff 4)
Million Dollar Racket, 1937 (Katzman 4)
Million Dollar Ransom, 1934 (Darwell 3)
Million Dollar Robbery, 1914 (Guy 2)
Million Dollar Trio. See Trio: Rubenstein, Heifetz, and Piatigorsky, 1952
Million Eyes of Sumuru. See Sumuru, 1967
Million Pound Note. See Az egymillió fontos bankó, 1916
Million Pound Note, 1953 (Peck 3, Alwyn 4, Box 4, Rank 4, Unsworth 4)
Million to One, 1938 (Fontaine 3)
Millionaire, 1917 (Laurel and Hardy 3)
Millionaire, 1931 (Arliss 3, Cagney 3)
Millionaire, 1978 (Bellamy 3)
Millionaire and the Girl, 1910 (Anderson 3)
Millionaire and the Ranch Girl. See Millionaire and the Girl, 1910
Millionaire and the Squatter, 1911 (Anderson 3)
Millionaire Cowboy, 1910 (Mix 3)
Millionaire Droopy, 1956 (Avery 4)
Millionaire for Christy, 1951 (Crosby 3, MacMurray 3, Leven 4, Mandell 4, Stradling 4, Young 4)
Millionaire Merry-Go-Round. See Kicking the Moon Around, 1938
Millionaire Paupers, 1915 (Chaney 3)
Millionaire Pirate, 1919 (Young 4)

Millionaire Playboy. See Park Avenue Logger, 1937
Millionaire Playboy, 1940 (Polglase 4)
Millionaire Vagrant, 1917 (Gilbert 3)
Millionaires, 1926 (Haskin 4)
Millionaire's Double, 1917 (Barrymore 3)
Millionaires in Prison, 1940 (Three Stooges 3, Polglase 4)
Millionairess, 1960 (Asquith 2, De Sica 2, Loren 3, Sellers 3, Sim 3, Fisher 4, Mankowitz 4)
Millionär für 3 Tage, 1963 (Herlth 4)
Millionärin, 1918 (Wiene 2)
Millionenkompagnie, 1925 (Tschechowa 3)
Millionen-Mine, 1914 (Warm 4)
Millionenraub im Rivieraexpress, 1927 (Warm 4)
Million-Hare, 1963 (Blanc 4, McKimson 4)
Millionnaires d'un jour, 1949 (Brasseur 3)
Millions, 1937 (Wilcox 2)
Millions in the Air, 1935 (Prinz 4)
Millions Like Us, 1943 (Launder and Gilliat 2, Rank 4)
Millón de Madigan. See Dollaro per 7 vigliacchi, 1967
Millones de Chafian, 1938 (Armendáriz 3)
Millones de Chafian, 1938 (Figueroa 4)
Mills of the Gods, 1909 (Griffith 2, Bitzer 4)
Mills of the Gods, 1934 (Wray 3, Fort 4)
Milosierdzie platne z gory, 1975 (Zanussi 2)
Milou en mai, 1990 (Malle 2, Piccoli 3, Carrière 4)
Mimi metallurgico ferito nell'onore, 1972 (Wertmüller 2, Giannini 3)
Mimi the Metalworker. See Mimi metallurgico ferito nell'onore, 1972
Mimizuku seppo, 1958 (Tsukasa 3)
Min Ajl Imraa, 1958 (Sharif 3)
Min and Bill, 1930 (Beery 3, Dressler 3, Gibbons 4, Marion 4, Mayer 4, Shearer 4)
Min bedstefar er en stok, 1967 (Henning-Jensen 2)
Min kära är en ros, 1963 (Björnstrand 3, Fischer 4)
Min syster och jag, 1950 (Björnstrand 3)
Minami kara kaetta hito, 1942 (Takamine 3)
Minami ni kaze, 1942 (Yoshimura 2, Ryu 3)
Minami no bara, 1950 (Yoda 4)
Minami no kaze to nami, 1961 (Muraki 4)
Minamikaze, 1939 (Tanaka 3)
Minamoto Yoritsune, 1955 (Yamada 3)
Minato e kita otoko, 1952 (Mifune 3)
Minato no jojoushi, 1932 (Yoda 4)
Mind Benders, 1963 (Dearden 2, Bogarde 3, Auric 4, Mathieson 4)
Mind Cure, 1910 (White 3)
Mind of Mr. Reeder, 1939 (Junge 4)
Mind of Mr. Soames, 1970 (Stamp 3)
Mind Reader, 1933 (Orry-Kelly 4, Polito 4)
Mind Your Own Business, 1937 (McLeod 2, Head 4, Schary 4)
Minding the Baby, 1931 (Fleischer 4)
Mindwalk, 1990 (Ullmann 3)
Mine Own Executioner, 1947 (Meredith 3, Francis 4, Korda 4)
Mine Pilot. See Minlotsen, 1915
Mine with the Iron Door, 1924 (Wood 2)
Mine with the Iron Door, 1936 (Walthall 3, Carré 4)
Miner, 1922 (Laurel and Hardy 3)
Miner Affair, 1945 (Bruckman 4)
Mineral Waters of the Caucasus. See Kavkazskiye mineralniye vody, 1924

Miner's Bequest, 1913 (Anderson 3)
Miner's Daughter, 1949 (Bosustow 4)
Miners' Picnic, 1960 (Russell 2)
Miner's Romance, 1914 (Chaney 3)
Miner's Wife, 1911 (Dwan 2)
Minerva traduce el mar, 1962 (Solas 2)
Minesweeper, 1943 (Mitchum 3)
Ming Green, 1966 (Markopoulos 2)
Mini Quark, 1988 (Bozzetto 4)
Minin i Pozharsky, 1939 (Pudovkin 2,
  Golovnya 4)
Ministro y Yo, 1976 (Cantinflas 3)
Ministry of Fear, 1943 (Duryea 3, Greene 4)
Ministry of Fear, 1944 (Lang 2, Milland 3,
  Dreier 4, Head 4, Miller 4, Young 4)
Miniver Story, 1950 (Finch 3, Garson 3,
  Pidgeon 3, Junge 4, Mathieson 4,
  Mayer 4, Plunkett 4, Rozsa 4,
  Ruttenberg 4)
Minlotsen, 1915 (Stiller 2)
Minne, 1916 (Musidora 3)
Minnelli on Minnelli: Liza Remembers
  Vincente, 1987 (Minnelli 3)
Minnen fran Bostonklubben, 1909
  (Magnusson 4)
Minnie, 1922 (Neilan 2, Marion 4, Struss 4)
Minnie and Moskowitz, 1971 (Cassavetes 2,
  Rowlands 3)
Minnie the Moocher, 1932 (Fleischer 4)
Minor Love and the Real Thing. See Kleine
  und die grosse Liebe, 1938
Minshu no teki, 1946 (Hayasaka 4)
Minstrel Man, 1944 (Lewis 2)
Minstrel Mania, 1949 (Fleischer 4)
Minstrel's Song. See Slóvce M, 1964
Minuit, Place Pigalle, 1935 (Raimu 3)
Minute de vérité, 1952 (Gabin 3, Gélin 3,
  Morgan 3, Jeanson 4)
Minute to Pray, a Second to Die. See Minuto
  per pregare, un instante per morire, 1968
Minuto per pregare, un instante per morire,
  1968 (Kennedy 3, Ryan 3)
Mio, 1970 (Hani 2)
Mio caro assassino, 1972 (Morricone 4)
Mio caro Dr. Gräsler, 1990 (Von Sydow 3,
  Morricone 4, Rotunno 4)
Mio Dio, come sono caduta in basso!, 1974
  (Comencini 2, Delli Colli 4)
Mio figlio Nerone, 1956 (Bardot 3, Sordi 3,
  Swanson 3, Cristaldi 4)
Mio figlio professore, 1946 (Fabrizi 3,
  Cecchi D'Amico 4, Rota 4)
Mio figlio professore, 1976 (Cecchi
  D'Amico 4)
Mio in the Land of Faraway. See Mio, moy
  Mio, 1987
Mio, moy mio, 1987 (York 3)
Mio nome e nessuno, 1974 (Fonda 3,
  Morricone 4)
Mio nome è Shanghai Joe, 1973 (Kinski 3)
Mio Padre Monsignore, 1971 (Giannini 3)
Mioche, 1936 (Morgan 3, Spaak 4)
Miquette. See Miquette et sa mère, 1949
Miquette et sa mère, 1933 (Simon 3,
  Fradetal 4)
Miquette et sa mère, 1940 (Gélin 3)
Miquette et sa mère, 1949 (Clouzot 2,
  Jouvet 3, Wakhévitch 4)
Mir hat es immer Spass gemacht. See Wie
  dommt ein so reizendes Mädchen zu
  diesem Gewerbe?, 1970
Mira, 1971 (Delerue 4)
Mira, 1977 (Shankar 4)
Mira ka Chitra, 1960 (Biswas 4)

Miracle. See Miraklet, 1913
Miracle. See Miracolo, 1948
Miracle, 1954 (Breer 4)
Miracle, 1959 (Baker 3, Gassman 3,
  Bernstein 4, Blanke 4, Haller 4)
Miracle, 1988 (Quayle 3)
Miracle. See Keitsik, 1989
Miracle Baby, 1923 (Carey 3)
Miracle Can Happen. See On Our Merry
  Way, 1948
Miracle des loups, 1924 (Modot 3)
Miracle des loups, 1961 (Barrault 3)
Miracle des roses, 1908 (Cohl 4)
Miracle in a Manger, 1986 (O'Connor 3)
Miracle in Harlem, 1937 (Micheaux 2)
Miracle in Milan. See Miracolo a Milano,
  1950
Miracle in Soho, 1957 (Powell and
  Pressburger 2, Cusack 3, Challis 4,
  Dillon 4, Rank 4)
Miracle in the Rain, 1956 (Dalio 3,
  Johnson 3, Wyman 3, Hecht 4, Maté 4,
  Metty 4, Waxman 4)
Miracle Makers, 1923 (Van Dyke 2)
Miracle Man, 1919 (Chaney 3, Zukor 4)
Miracle Man, 1932 (McLeod 2, Bosworth 3,
  Karloff 3, Sidney 3, Laszlo 4, Young 4,
  Zukor 4)
Miracle of Fatima. See Miracle of Our Lady
  of Fatima, 1952
Miracle of Hockory, 1944 (Garson 3)
Miracle of Main Street, 1938 (Salter 4)
**Miracle of Morgan's Creek, 1944
  (Sturges 2, Hutton 3, Dreier 4, Head 4,
  Seitz 4)**
Miracle of Our Lady of Fatima, 1952
  (Burks 4, Steiner 4)
Miracle of the Bells, 1948 (Cobb 3,
  MacMurray 3, Sinatra 3, Valli 3, Cahn 4,
  Hecht 4, Lasky 4)
Miracle of the White Stallions, 1963
  (Taylor 3, Disney 4)
Miracle of the Wolves. See Miracle des
  loups, 1924
Miracle on Ice, 1981 (Malden 3)
Miracle on Main Street, 1939 (Darwell 3,
  Salter 4)
Miracle on 34th Street, 1947 (O'Hara 3,
  Ritter 3, Wood 3, Clarke 4, Day 4,
  LeMaire 4, Newman 4, Zanuck 4)
Miracle on Thirty-Fourth Street, 1974
  (McDowall 3)
Miracle Rider, 1935 (Lewis 2, Mix 3,
  Eason 4)
Miracle sous l'inquisition, 1904
  (Méliès 2)
Miracle Under the Inquisition. See Miracle
  sous l'inquisition, 1904
Miracle Woman, 1931 (Capra 2,
  Stanwyck 3, Cohn 4, Swerling 4,
  Walker 4)
Miracle Worker, 1962 (Penn 2, Bancroft 3,
  Jenkins 4)
Miracles, 1984 (Alcott 4)
Miracles de Brahmane, 1900 (Méliès 2)
Miracles for Sale, 1939 (Browning 2,
  Young 3)
Miracles n'ont lieu qu'une fois, 1951
  (Allégret 2, Marais 3, Valli 3,
  Trauner 4)
Miracles of Brahmin. See Miracles de
  Brahmane, 1900
Miracolo, 1948 (Rossellini 2)
Miracolo a loreto, 1949 (Zavattini 4)

**Miracolo a Milano, 1950 (Aldo 4, Cecchi
  D'Amico 4, Di Venanzo 4, Korda 4,
  Zavattini 4)**
Miraculé, 1987 (Moreau 3)
Miraculous Doctor. See Za opunu smrti,
  1923
Mirada de los otros, 1979 (Solanas and
  Getino 2)
Mirage, 1924 (Sullivan 4)
Mirage, 1965 (Dmytryk 2, Matthau 3,
  Peck 3, Jones 4, Whitlock 4)
Mirage in the North. See Severnoe siianie,
  1926
Mirages. See Si tu m'aimes, 1937
Mirages de Paris, 1932 (Andrejew 4,
  Douy 4, Jaubert 4, Rathaus 4)
Miraklet, 1913 (Sjöström 2, Jaenzon 4,
  Magnusson 4)
Miramar praia das rosas, 1939 (Oliveira 2)
Miranda, 1948 (Rutherford 3, Withers 3,
  Box 4, Rank 4)
Mirch Masala, 1986 (Patil 3)
Mireille, 1900 (Guy 2)
Mireille, 1906 (Feuillade 2)
Mirele Efros, 1912 (Mozhukin 3)
Miren, 1963 (Takemitsu 4)
Miroir, 1947 (Gabin 3, Gélin 3,
  Wakhévitch 4)
Miroir à deux faces, 1958 (Morgan 3)
Miroir aux alouettes, 1934 (Brasseur 3,
  Feuillère 3, Rasp 3)
Mirror, 1911 (Pickford 3, Gaudio 4)
Mirror. See Egy tukor, 1971
Mirror. See Zerkalo, 1975
Mirror Crack'd, 1980 (Chaplin 3, Curtis 3,
  Hudson 3, Lansbury 3, Novak 3,
  Taylor 3, Challis 4)
Mirror from India, 1971 (Anderson 2)
Mirror Has Two Faces. See Miroir à deux
  faces, 1958
Mirror, Mirror, 1990 (Black 3)
Mirrored Reason, 1980 (Vanderbeek 2)
Mirth and Melody. See Let's Go Places,
  1929
Misadventures of a Claim Agent, 1911
  (Dwan 2)
Misadventures of a Mighty Monarch, 1914
  (Bunny 3)
Misadventures of Buster Keaton, 1955
  (Keaton 2)
Misadventures of Merlin Jones, 1963
  (Stevenson 2, Disney 4)
Misanthrope, 1966 (Braunberger 4)
Misappropriated Turkey, 1912 (Griffith 2,
  Bitzer 4)
Misbehaving Husbands, 1940 (Langdon 3)
Misbehaving Ladies, 1930 (Seitz 4)
Miłość dwudziestolatków. See Amour à
  vingt ans, 1962
Misc. Happenings, 1961 (Vanderbeek 2)
Mischances of a Photographer, 1908
  (Méliès 2)
Mischief Maker, 1916 (Bosworth 3)
Mischievous Hedgehog, 1952 (Popescu-
  Gopo 4)
Misen ono okoku, 1937 (Takamine 3)
Miser, 1913 (August 4)
Miser. See Avaro, 1990
Miser Murphy's Wedding Present, 1914
  (Talmadge 3)
Miserabili, 1947 (Monicelli 2, Cervi 3,
  Mastroianni 3, Ponti 4)
Misérables, 1909 (Pathé 4)
Misérables, 1912 (Pathé 4)

Misérables, 1934 (Baur 3, Vanel 3, Douy 4, Honegger 4, Jaubert 4)
Miserables, 1935 (Carradine 3, Laughton 3, March 3, Newman 4, Toland 4, Zanuck 4)
Miserables. *See* Miserabili, 1948
Miserables, 1950 (Hayakawa 3)
Miserables, 1952 (Milestone 2, Lanchester 3, Newton 3, Sidney 3, Jeakins 4, La Shelle 4, LeMaire 4, Newman 4, North 4)
Misérables, 1957 (Blier 3, Gabin 3, Reggiani 3, Audiard 4)
Misérables, 1978 (Cusack 3, Gielgud 3, Johnson 3, Perkins 3)
Miseraretaru tamashii, 1953 (Yamada 3)
Misère au Borinage, 1934 (Storck 2, Van Dongen 4)
Misères de l'aiguille, 1913 (Musidora 3)
Miseria e nobiltà, 1940 (Fusco 4)
Miseria e nobiltà, 1954 (Loren 3)
Misericordia, 1919 (Pick 2)
Miserie del Signor Travet, 1946 (Cervi 3, Sordi 3, Pinelli 3, De Laurentiis 4, Rota 4)
Miser's Daughter, 1910 (Lawrence 3)
Miser's Heart, 1911 (Griffith 2, Bitzer 4)
Miser's Policy, 1914 (Eason 4)
Misery, 1990 (Bacall 3, Caan 3, Goldman 4)
Misfits, 1961 (Huston 2, Clift 3, Gable 3, Monroe 3, Ritter 3, Wallach 3, Metty 4, North 4)
Misfortune, 1973 (Loach 2)
Misfortune Never Comes Alone. *See* Malheur n'arrive jamais seul, 1903
Misguided Tour, 1980 (Halas and Batchelor 4)
Mishima: A Life in Four Chapters, 1985 (Coppola 2, Lucas 2, Schrader 2, Scheider 3)
Mishka Against Yudenich. *See* Mishki protiv Youdenitsa, 1925
Mishka, Serega, i ia, 1962 (Shukshin 3)
Mishki protiv Youdenitsa, 1925 (Enei 4)
Misión blanca, 1945 (Rey 3)
Misión Lisboa, 1965 (Rey 3)
Miska the Magnate. *See* Mágnás Miska, 1916
Misleading Lady, 1921 (Polito 4)
Misleading Lady, 1932 (Colbert 3, Folsey 4)
Misleading Widow, 1919 (Marion 4, Zukor 4)
Misplaced Foot, 1914 (Sennett 2, Arbuckle 3, Normand 3)
Misplaced Jealousy, 1911 (Sennett 2)
Miss and Mrs. Sweden, 1968 (Fischer 4)
Miss Annie Rooney, 1942 (Temple 3)
Miss April. *See* Fröken April, 1958
Miss Arabella Snaith, 1912 (Cruze 2)
Miss Arizona, 1988 (Mastroianni 3, Schygulla 3)
Miss Aubrey's Love Affair, 1912 (Bosworth 3)
Miss Bluebeard, 1925 (Daniels 3, Hunt 4)
Miss Bracegirdle Does Her Duty, 1936 (Lanchester 3, Korda 4)
Miss Brewster's Millions, 1926 (Daniels 3)
Miss Else. *See* Fräulein Else, 1929
Miss Europe. *See* Prix de beauté, 1930
Miss Fix-It. *See* Keep Smiling, 1938
Miss Gaby, 1977 (Jarman 2)
Miss George Washington, 1916 (Zukor 4)
Miss Glory, 1936 (Avery 4)
Miss Golem. *See* Slečna Golem, 1972

Miss Grant Takes Richmond, 1949 (Bacon 2, Tashlin 2, Ball 3, Holden 3)
Miss Helyett, 1926 (Delannoy 2)
Miss Hobbs, 1920 (Crisp 3, Reisch 4)
Miss India, 1957 (Burman 4)
Miss Italy, 1950 (Lollobrigida 3)
Miss Josabeth. *See* Mamsell Josabeth, 1963
Miss Julie. *See* Fräulein Julie, 1922
Miss Julie. *See* **Fröken Julie, 1951**
Miss Lina Esbrard Danseuse Cosmopolite et Serpentine, 1902 (Guy 2)
Miss London Ltd., 1943 (Rank 3)
Miss Lulu Bett, 1920 (Zukor 4)
Miss Mary, 1987 (Bemberg 2, Christie 3)
Miss Mend, 1926 (Barnet 2)
Miss Muerte, 1966 (Carrière 4)
Miss Nobody, 1926 (Pidgeon 3)
Miss Ogin. *See* Ogin sama, 1978
Miss Oyu. *See* Oyu-sama, 1951
Miss Pacific Fleet, 1935 (Blondell 3, Orry-Kelly 4)
Miss Petticoats, 1916 (Edeson 4)
Miss Pinkerton, 1932 (Bacon 2, Blondell 3)
Miss Polly, 1941 (Roach 4)
Miss Right, 1988 (Black 3)
Miss Robin Crusoe, 1954 (Dupont 2, Bernstein 4)
Miss Robin Hood, 1952 (Rutherford 3)
Miss Robinson Crusoe, 1912 (Cruze 2)
Miss Robinson Crusoe, 1953 (Miller 4)
Miss Sadie Thompson, 1953 (Bronson 3, Ferrer 3, Hayworth 3, Cohn 4, Duning 4, Wald 4)
Miss Sherlock Holmes, 1908 (Porter 2)
Miss Susie Slagle's, 1946 (Gish 3, Lake 3, Dreier 4, Head 4, Houseman 4, Lang 4)
Miss Tatlock's Millions, 1948 (Fitzgerald 3, Milland 3, Brackett 4, Dreier 4, Head 4, Lang 4, Young 4)
Miss Tulip Stays the Night, 1955 (Dors 3)
Miss Tutti Frutti, 1921 (Curtiz 2)
Miss Uyo. *See* Oyu-sama, 1951
Miss Wildcat. *See* Yamaneko rei jou, 1948
Miss with Five Zeros, 1927 (Balàzs 4)
Missed Fortune, 1952 (Three Stooges 3)
Misses Stooge, 1935 (Roach 4)
Missile, 1988 (Wiseman 2)
Missile X. *See* Teheran Incident, 1979
Missiles from Hell. *See* Battle of the V.1, 1958
Missing, 1918 (Blackton 2)
Missing, 1982 (Costa-Gavras 2, Lemmon 3, Spacek 3, Vangelis 4, Whitlock 4)
Missing Admiralty Plans. *See* Stjaalne Ansigt, 1914
Missing Are Deadly, 1975 (Ferrer 3)
Missing, Believed Married, 1937 (Rutherford 3, Havelock-Allan 4)
Missing Bride, 1914 (Sennett 2)
Missing Evidence, 1939 (Krasner 4)
Missing Guest, 1938 (Krasner 4)
Missing in Action, 1984 (Golan and Globus 4)
Missing Juror, 1944 (Boetticher 2)
Missing Link, 1927 (Zanuck 4)
Missing Link, 1989 (Baker 4)
Missing Links, 1916 (Talmadge 3)
Missing Mouse, 1950 (Hanna and Barbera 4)
Missing Ten Days. *See* Ten Days in Paris, 1939
Missing Will, 1911 (Bunny 3)
Mission, 1986 (De Niro 3, Irons 3, Menges 4, Morricone 4, Puttnam 4)

Mission à Tanger, 1949 (Audiard 4)
Mission Impossible versus the Mob, 1968 (Schifrin 4)
Mission over Korea, 1953 (O'Sullivan 3)
Mission sous la mer, 1946 (Renoir 4)
Mission to Moscow, 1943 (Curtiz 2, Siegel 2, Charisse 3, Homolka 3, Huston 3, Buckner 4, Glennon 4, Haskin 4, Koch 4, Orry-Kelly 4, Prinz 4, Steiner 4, Warner 4)
Mission to No Man's Land, 1959 (Brynner 3)
Missionaire, 1955 (Renoir 4)
Missionaires in Darkest Africa, 1912 (Olcott 2)
Missionary, 1982 (Elliott 3, Howard 3, Smith 3)
Mississippi, 1935 (Bennett 3, Crosby 3, Fields 3, Sheridan 3, Dreier 4, Head 4, Lang 4, Schary 4, Zukor 4)
Mississippi Blues, 1983 (Tavernier 2)
Mississippi Burning, 1988 (Parker 2, Hackman 3)
Mississippi Gambler, 1929 (Bennett 3, Brown 4)
Mississippi Gambler, 1942 (Three Stooges 3)
Mississippi Gambler, 1953 (Power 3, Maté 4, Miller 4)
Mississippi Hare, 1949 (Blanc 4, Jones 4)
Mississippi Mermaid. *See* Sirène du Mississippi, 1969
Mississippi Swing, 1941 (Terry 4)
Missouri Breaks, 1976 (Penn 2, Brando 3, Nicholson 3, Stanton 3, Allen 4, Williams 4)
Missouri Traveler, 1957 (Marvin 3, Hoch 4, Mercer 4)
Mist. *See* Sis, 1989
Mist in the Valley, 1922 (Hepworth 2)
Mistake, 1910 (Lawrence 3)
Mistake, 1913 (Griffith 2, Sweet 3, Walthall 3, Bitzer 4, Loos 4)
Mistake in Rustlers, 1916 (Mix 3)
Mistaken Accusation, 1913 (Bushman 3)
Mistaken Bandit, 1910 (Anderson 3)
Mistaken Masher, 1913 (Sennett 2, Normand 3)
Mistakes Will Happen, 1916 (Mix 3)
Mr. Ace, 1946 (Raft 3, Sidney 3, Struss 4)
Mr. Albert. *See* Monsieur Albert, 1932
Mr. and Mrs. Bridge, 1990 (Ivory 2, Newman 3, Woodward 3, Jhabvala 4)
Mr. and Mrs. 55, 1955 (Dutt 2)
Mr. and Mrs. Is the Name, 1934 (Freleng 4)
Mr. and Mrs. North, 1941 (Stradling 4)
Mr. and Mrs. Smith, 1941 (Hitchcock 2, Lombard 3, Montgomery 3, D'Agostino 4, Krasna 4, Polglase 4, Stradling 4)
Mr. and Mrs. Stockholm. *See* Herr och fru Stockholm, 1921
Mr. Arkadin, 1955 (Welles 2)
Mr. Ashton Was Indiscreet. *See* Senator Was Indiscreet, 1947
Mr. Barnes of New York, 1914 (Costello 3, Novarro 3)
Mr. Belvedere Goes to College, 1949 (Temple 3, Webb 3, LeMaire 4, Newman 4)
Mr. Belvedere Rings the Bell, 1951 (Webb 3, Lang 4, La Shelle 4, LeMaire 4)
Mister Big, 1943 (O'Connor 3)

Mr. Blandings Builds His Dream House, 1948 (Beavers 3, Douglas 3, Grant 3, Loy 3, McDaniel 3, Frank 4, Howe 4, Schary 4)

Mr. Bolter's Infatuation, 1912 (Bunny 3)

Mr. Bolter's Niece, 1913 (Bunny 3)

Mr. Borland Thinks Again, 1940 (Rotha 2)

Mr. Bragg, A Fugitive, 1911 (Sennett 2)

Mr. Broadway, 1933 (Ulmer 2)

Mister Buddwing, 1966 (Garner 3, Lansbury 3, Simmons 3, Rose 4)

Mr. Bug Goes to Town, 1942 (Carmichael 4)

Mr. Bunny in Disguise, 1914 (Bunny 3)

Mr. Bunnyhug Buys a Hat for His Bride, 1914 (Bunny 3)

Mr. Butler Buttles, 1912 (Talmadge 3)

Mr. Butt-In, 1906 (Bitzer 4)

Mr. Canton and Lady Rose, See Keitsik, 1989

Mr. Casanova, 1954 (Head 4)

Mr. Celebrity, 1941 (Bushman 3)

Mr. Chedworth Steps Out, 1939 (Finch 3)

Mr. Chesher's Traction Engines, 1962 (Russell 2)

Mr. Chump, 1938 (Edeson 4)

Mister Cinderella, 1936 (Krasner 4, Roach 4)

Mr. Corbett's Ghost, 1987 (Meredith 3)

Mr. Cory, 1957 (Curtis 3, Metty 4)

Mr. Deeds Goes to Town, 1936 (Capra 2, Arthur 3, Cooper 3, Pangborn 3, Cohn 4, Deutsch 4, Riskin 4, Tiomkin 4, Walker 4)

Mr. Denning Drives North, 1951 (Lom 3, Mills 3, Korda 4)

Mr. Destiny, 1990 (Caine 3)

Mr. Dippy Dipped, 1913 (Beery 3)

Mr. District Attorney, 1941 (Lorre 3, Brown 4)

Mr. District Attorney, 1947 (Glennon 4)

Mr. District Attorney in the Carter Case, 1941 (Alton 4)

Mr. Dodd Takes the Air, 1937 (Wyman 3, Deutsch 4, Edeson 4)

Mr. Dolan of New York, 1980 (Johnson 3)

Mr. Doodle Kicks Off, 1938 (Metty 4)

Mr. Dynamite, 1941 (Three Stooges 3, Salter 4)

Mr. 880, 1950 (Goulding 2, Lancaster 3, La Shelle 4, LeMaire 4, Riskin 4, Zanuck 4)

Mr. Emmanuel, 1944 (Simmons 3, Heller 4, Rank 4)

Mr. Fix-It, 1912 (Sennett 2, Normand 3)

Mr. Fix-It, 1918 (Dwan 2, Fairbanks 3, Edeson 4)

Mister Flow, 1936 (Siodmak 2, Feuillère 3, Jouvet 3, Jeanson 4)

Mr. Forbush and the Penguins, 1971 (Hurt 3, Addison 4)

Mister 420. See Shri 420, 1955

Mr. 420. See Shri 420, 1955

Mister 44, 1916 (Gaudio 4)

Mister Freedom, 1969 (Montand 3, Noiret 3, Pleasence 3, Seyrig 3, Signoret 3)

Mister Frost, 1990 (Bates 3, Cassel 3, Gélin 3)

Mr. Gallagher and Mr. Shean, 1931 (Fleischer 4)

Mr. Grouch at the Seashore, 1911 (Sennett 2)

Mr. Halpern and Mr Johnson, 1983 (Olivier)

Mr. Hayashi, 1961 (Baillie 2)

Mr. Head. See Monsieur Tête, 1959

Mr. Henpeck's Dilemma, 1913 (Pearson 2)

Mr. Hobbs Takes a Vacation, 1962 (O'Hara 3, Stewart 3, Johnson 4, Mancini 4, Mercer 4, Smith 4, Wald 4)

Mister Hobo. See Guv'nor, 1934

Mr. Hoover and I, 1989 (De Antonio 2)

Mr. Horn, 1979 (Black 3, Widmark 3, Goldman 4)

Mr. Hulot's Holiday. See **Vacances de Monsieur Hulot, 1953**

Mr. Hurry-Up, 1906 (Bitzer 4)

Mr. Hyppo, 1923 (Roach 4)

Mr. Ikla's Jubilee. See Jubilej gospodina Ikla, 1955

Mr. Imperium, 1951 (Reynolds 3, Turner 3, Folsey 4, Kaper 4, Plunkett 4)

Mister Jefferson Green, 1913 (Barrymore 3)

Mister Jericho, 1969 (Lom 3)

Mr. Johnson. See Mister Johnson, 1990

Mister Johnson, 1990 (Delerue 4)

Mr. Jones at the Ball, 1908 (Griffith 2, Lawrence 3, Bitzer 4, Macpherson 4)

Mr. Jones at the Ball, 1935 (Sennett 2)

Mr. Jones Has a Card Party, 1909 (Griffith 2, Sennett 2, Lawrence 3)

Mr. Klein, 1977 (Losey 2, Delon 3, Moreau 3, Fisher 4, Solinas 4, Trauner 4)

Mr. Know-How in Hot Water, 1961 (Dunning 4)

Mr. Lemon of Orange, 1931 (Cantor 3, August 4)

Mr. Logan, U.S.A., 1918 (Mix 3)

Mr. Lord Says No!. See Happy Family, 1952

Mr. Love, 1985 (Puttnam 4)

Mr. Lucky, 1943 (Grant 3, Barnes 4, Menzies 4)

Mr. Magoo, 1949 (Hubley 4)

Mr. Majestyk, 1974 (Bronson 3, Mirisch 4)

Mr. Marzipan's Marriage. See Zenida gospodina Marcipana, 1963

Mr. Mom, 1983 (Hughes 2)

Mr. Moses, 1965 (Baker 3, Mitchum 3, Barry 4, Morris 4)

Mr. Moto, 1937 (Lorre 3)

Mr. Moto in Danger Island, 1939 (Bond 3)

Mr. Moto Takes a Chance, 1938 (Lorre 3, Miller 4)

Mr. Moto Takes a Vacation, 1939 (Lorre 3, Clarke 4)

Mr. Moto's Gamble, 1938 (Bond 3, Lorre 3)

Mr. Moto's Last Warning, 1939 (Carradine 3, Lorre 3, Sanders 3, Miller 4, Raksin 4)

Mr. Muggs Rides Again, 1945 (Katzman 4)

Mr. Muggs Steps Out, 1943 (Katzman 4)

Mr. Music, 1950 (Coburn 3, Crosby 3, Marx Brothers 3, Barnes 4, Dreier 4, Head 4)

Mr. Natwarlal, 1979 (Bachchan 3)

Mr. Niceman's Umbrella, 1912 (Bunny 3)

Mr. Nobody. See In the Sage Brush Country, 1914

Mr. North, 1988 (Bacall 3, Huston 3, Mitchum 3, Stanton 3)

Mr. O.F.'s 13 Cases. See Koffer des Herrn O.F., 1931

Mr. Orchid. See Père tranquille, 1946

Mr. Patman, 1980 (Coburn 3)

Mr. Peabody and the Mermaid, 1948 (Powell 3, Johnson 4, Leven 4, Mercer 4, Metty 4, Westmore Family 4)

Mr. Peck Goes Calling, 1911 (Sennett 2)

Mr. Peek-a-Boo. See Garou-Garou, le passe-muraille, 1950

Mr. Perrin and Mr. Traill, 1948 (Rank 4)

Mr. Potts Goes to Moscow. See Top Secret, 1952

Mr. Prokouk in Temptation. See Pan Prokouk v pokušeni, 1947

Mr. Prokouk in the Office. See Pan Prokouk úřaduje, 1947

Mr. Prokouk Is Filming. See Pan Prokouk filmuje, 1948

Mr. Prokouk Leaves for Volunteer Work. See Brigady, 1947

Mr. Prokouk, the Animal Lover. See Pan Prokouk, přítel zvířátek, 1955

Mr. Prokouk, the Inventor. See Pan Prokouk vynálezcem, 1948

Mr. Proudfoot Shows a Light, 1941 (Launder and Gilliat 2)

Mr. Quilp, 1975 (Bernstein 4, Challis 4)

Mr. Ricco, 1975 (Martin 3, Westmore Family 4)

Mister Roberts, 1955 (Ford 2, LeRoy 2, Bond 3, Cagney 3, Fonda 3, Lemmon 3, Powell 3, Hoch 4, Nugent 4, Waxman 4)

Mr. Robinson Crusoe, 1932 (Fairbanks 3, Newman 4)

Mr. Sardonicus, 1961 (Homolka 3, Guffey 4)

Mr. Satan, 1938 (Fisher 2)

Mr. Scarface. See Padroni della città, 1977

Mister Scoutmaster, 1953 (Webb 3, La Shelle 4, LeMaire 4)

Mr. Sebastian, 1967 (Gielgud 3)

Mr. "Silent" Haskins, 1915 (Hart 3)

Mr. Skeffington, 1944 (Davis 3, Rains 3, Epstein 4, Orry-Kelly 4, Waxman 4)

Mr. Skitch, 1933 (Cruze 2, Rogers 3, Levien 4, Seitz 4)

Mr. Sleepy's Good Luck, 1914 (Phalke 2)

Mr. Smith Carries On, 1937 (Havelock-Allan 4)

Mr. Smith Goes to Washington, 1939 (Capra 2, Arthur 3, Bondi 3, Carey 3, Costello 3, Rains 3, Stewart 3, Buchman 4, Cohn 4, Tiomkin 4, Vorkapich 4, Walker 4)

Mr. Smith Wakes Up, 1929 (Lanchester 3)

Mr. Soft Touch, 1949 (Bondi 3, Ford 3, Walker 4)

Mr. Strauss Takes a Waltz, 1942 (Pal 4)

Mr. Sweeney's Masterpiece, 1910 (White 3)

Mr. Sycamore, 1975 (Simmons 3, Jarre 4)

Mister Tao, 1988 (Bozzetto 4)

Mr. Tomkins Inside Himself, 1962 (Brakhage 2)

Mr. Topaze, 1961 (Lom 3, Sellers 3)

Mr. Universe, 1950 (Tiomkin 4)

Mister V. See Pimpernel Smith, 1941

Mr. What's His Name, 1935 (Launder and Gilliat 2)

Mister Will Shakespeare, 1936 (Shearer 3)

Mr. Winkle Goes to War, 1944 (Mitchum 3, Robinson 3, Salt 4, Walker 4)

Mr. Wise Guy, 1942 (Katzman 4)

Mr. Wong at Headquarters. See Fatal Hour, 1940

Mr. Wong in Chinatown, 1939 (Karloff 3)

Mister Wu, 1918 (Pick 2)

Mr. Wu, 1927 (Chaney 3, Wong 3, Day 4, Gibbons 4, Mayer 4)

Mr. Wu. See Wu Li Chang, 1930

Mister Zehn Prozent—Miezen und Moneten, 1967 (Kinski 3)

Misteri della jungla nera, 1953 (Fusco 4)

Misteri di Roma, 1963 (Zavattini 4)

Misterio en la isla de los monstruos, 1980 (Cushing 3, Stamp 3)

Mistero del tempio indiano, 1963 (Camerini 2, Kinski 3)

Mistero di Oberwald, 1979 (Vitti 3, Guerra 4)
Mistons, 1957 (Truffaut 2)
Mistress. *See* Älaskarinnan, 1962
Mistress. *See* Maîtresse, 1975
Mrs, 1991 (Hawn 3)
Mrs. Andersson's Charlie. *See*
   Anderssonskans Kalle, 1950
Mrs. Barnacle Bill, 1934 (Roach 4)
Mrs. Death. *See* Senora Muerte, 1967
Mrs. Delafield Wants to Marry, 1986
   (Hepburn 3, Lassally 4)
Mrs. Dulska's Morals. *See* Morálka pani
   Dulské, 1958
Mrs. 'Enery 'Awkins, 1911 (Talmadge 3)
Mrs. Erricker's Reputation, 1920
   (Hepworth 2)
Mistress for the Summer. *See* Fille pour
   l'été, 1959
Mrs. Gibbons' Boys, 1962 (Dors 3)
Mrs. Jones' Burglar, 1909 (Griffith 2,
   Lawrence 3, Bitzer 4)
Mrs. Jones Entertains, 1908 (Griffith 2,
   Lawrence 3, Bitzer 4, Macpherson 4)
Mrs. Jones Has a Card Party, 1908 (Bitzer 4)
Mrs. Jones' Lover, or I Want My Hat, 1909
   (Griffith 2, Lawrence 3, Bitzer 4)
Mrs. Jones' Rest Farm, 1949 (Terry 4)
Mrs. Loring's Secret. *See* Imperfect Lady,
   1946
Mrs. Manley's Baby, 1914 (Beery 3)
Mrs. Mike, 1949 (Powell 3, Biroc 4,
   Bodeen 4, Steiner 4)
**Mrs. Miniver, 1942 (Wyler 2, Garson 3,
Pidgeon 3, Wright 3, Gibbons 4,
Gillespie 4, Mayer 4, Ruttenberg 4,
Sherriff 4, Stothart 4)**
Mrs. Murphy's Cooks, 1915 (Mix 3)
Mistress Nell, 1915 (Pickford 3)
Mistress of a Foreigner. *See* Tojin okichi,
   1930
Mistress of Paradise, 1978 (Bujold 3,
   Addison 4)
Mistress of Shenstone, 1921 (King 2)
Mrs. O'Leary's Cow, 1938 (Terry 4)
Mrs. O'Malley and Mr. Malone, 1950
   (Deutsch 4)
Mrs. Parkington, 1944 (Garnett 2, Duryea 3,
   Garson 3, Moorehead 3, Pidgeon 3,
   Irene 4, Kaper 4, Mayer 4, Ruttenberg 4)
Mrs. Peabody. *See* Number Thirteen, 1922
Mrs. Pollifax—Spy, 1971 (Russell 3,
   Biroc 4, Previn 4)
Mrs. R.—Death Among Friends. *See* Death
   Among Friends, 1975
Mrs. Skeffington, 1944 (Haller 4)
Mrs. Smithers' Boarding School, 1907
   (Bitzer 4)
Mrs. Soffel, 1985 (Armstrong 2, Gibson 3,
   Keaton 3)
Mrs. Temple's Telegram, 1920 (Cruze 2)
Mrs. Uschyck, 1973 (Jarre 4)
Mrs. Wallace Reid. *See* Linda, 1928
Mrs. Wiggs of the Cabbage Patch, 1934
   (Fields 3, Sheridan 3, Lang 4, Prinz 4,
   Zukor 4)
Mrs. Wiggs of the Cabbage Patch, 1942
   (Dreier 4, Head 4, Young 4)
Mistři zimních sportu, 1954 (Kučera 4)
Mistrigri, 1931 (Achard 4, Stradling 4)
Misty, 1961 (Garmes 4)
Misunderstood. *See* Incompreso, 1967
Misunderstood, 1984 (Hackman 3)
Misunderstood Boy, 1913 (Griffith 2,
   Barrymore 3, Gish 3, Bitzer 4)

Mit den Augen einer Frau, 1942 (Fröhlich 3,
   Tschechowa 3, Von Harbou 4)
Mit Django kam der Tod. *See* Uomo,
   L'orgoglio, la vendetta, 1967
Mit meinen Augen, 1945 (Tschechowa 3)
Mit mir will keiner spielen, 1976 (Herzog 2)
Mitad del mundo, 1963 (Figueroa 4)
Mitasareta seikatsu, 1961 (Takemitsu 4)
Mitico Gianluca, 1988 (Scola 2)
Mitico Gianluca, 1988 (Mastroianni 3)
Mitlaufer, 1984 (Mueller-Stahl 3)
Mito Komon umi o wataru, 1961
   (Hasegawa 3)
Mitsu no shinju, 1949 (Kyo 3)
Mitsuyu-sen, 1954 (Mifune 3, Hayasaka 4)
Mitt folk är icke ditt, 1944 (Björnstrand 3)
Mitt hem är Copacabana, 1965
   (Sucksdorff 2)
Mitt Me Tonight, 1941 (Bruckman 4)
Mitternacht, 1918 (Dupont 2)
Mittsu no ai, 1954 (Yamada 3)
Mivtza Kahir, 1966 (Golan and Globus 4,
   Murphy 3, Sanders 3)
Mix Me a Person, 1962 (Saville 2, Baxter 3,
   Dalrymple 4)
Mixed Babies, 1908 (Bitzer 4)
Mixed Flats, 1915 (Laurel and Hardy 3)
Mixed Magic, 1936 (Keaton 2)
Mixed Master, 1956 (Blanc 4, McKimson 4)
Mixed Nuts, 1924 (Laurel and Hardy 3)
Mixed Nuts, 1934 (Roach 4)
Mixed Values, 1915 (Loos 4)
Mixup, 1929 (Rooney 3)
Mix-Up for Maisie, 1914 (Lloyd 3, Roach 4)
Mixup in Hearts, 1917 (Laurel and Hardy 3)
Mix-Up in Movies, 1916 (Mix 3)
Mix-up in Raincoats, 1911 (Sennett 2)
Mix-up in the Galley. *See* Tripot clandestin,
   1905
Miya Bibi Raji, 1960 (Burman 4)
Miyamoto Musashi, 1940 (Miyagawa 4)
Miyamoto Musashi, 1944 (Mizoguchi 2,
   Tanaka 3)
Miyamoto Musashi, 1954 (Mifune 3)
Miyamoto Musashi: Ichijo-ji no ketto, 1941
   (Shimura 3)
Mladé dny, 1956 (Stallich 4)
Mladý muž a bílá verlyba, 1978
   (Brejchová 3)
M'liss, 1918 (Neilan 2, Pickford 3,
   Marion 4)
M'Liss, 1936 (Steiner 4)
M'Lord of the White Road, 1923
   (McLaglen 3)
Mniejsze Wiebo, 1981 (Tyszkiewicz 3)
Mo' Better Blues, 1990 (Lee 2)
Moa Moa, 1984 (Bozzetto 4)
Moan and Groans, 1935 (Terry 4)
Mob, 1951 (Borgnine 3, Bronson 3,
   Crawford 3, Duning 4, Walker 4)
Mob Town, 1941 (Salter 4)
Mobilier fidèle, 1910 (Cohl 4)
Mobilizing Mass. State Troops, 1905
   (Bitzer 4)
Moblierte Zimmer, 1929 (Albers 3)
Mobster. *See* I, Mobster 1958
Moby Dick. *See* Sea Beast, 1926
Moby Dick, 1930 (Bacon 2, Barrymore 3,
   Bennett 3, Johnson 3)
Moby Dick, 1956 (Huston 2, Welles 2,
   Lee 3, Peck 3, Francis 4, Morris 4,
   Warner 4)
Moby Duck, 1965 (Blanc 4, McKimson 4)
Moc osudu, 1968 (Brdečka 4)

Mockery, 1927 (Christensen 2, Chaney 3,
   Gibbons 4, Mayer 4)
Mod att leva, 1983 (Theodorakis 4)
Mod Lyset, 1918 (Madsen and
   Schenstrøm 3, Nielsen 3)
Mode rêvée, 1939 (L'Herbier 2, Auric 4)
Model. *See* Mannekägen, 1913
Model, 1981 (Wiseman 2)
Model and the Marriage Broker, 1951
   (Cukor 2, Ritter 3, Brackett 4, Krasner 4,
   LeMaire 4, Reisch 4, Wheeler 4)
Model and the Young Lord. *See* Moderu to
   wakatono, 1947
Model Courtship, 1903 (Bitzer 4)
Model Diary, 1922 (Terry 4)
Model Muddle, 1989 (Golan and Globus 4)
Model Murder Case. *See* Girl in the
   Headlines, 1963
Model Shop, 1969 (Demy 2, Aimée 3)
Model Wife, 1941 (Blondell 3, Powell 3,
   Salter 4)
Modeling, 1923 (Fleischer 4)
Models, Inc., 1952 (Cortez 4)
Model's Ma, 1907 (Bitzer 4)
Moderato cantabile, 1960 (Duras 2,
   Belmondo 3, Moreau 3)
Moderca zostawia ślad, 1967 (Cybulski 3)
Modern DuBarry. *See* DuBarry von Heute,
   1926
Modern Enoch Arden, 1916 (Sennett 2)
Modern Guide to Health, 1946 (Halas and
   Batchelor 4)
Modern Hero, 1934 (Pabst 2, Barthelmess 3,
   Beavers 3, Orry-Kelly 4)
Modern Hero. *See* Knute Rockne—All-
   American, 1940
Modern Husbands, 1919 (Walthall 3)
Modern Love, 1990 (Reynolds 3)
Modern Magdalen, 1915 (Barrymore 3)
Modern Marriage, 1923 (Bushman 3)
Modern Marriages, 1919 (Balàzs 3)
Modern Miracle. *See* Story of Alexander
   Graham Bell, 1939
Modern Mothers, 1928 (Walker 4)
Modern Musketeer, 1917 (Dwan 2,
   Fleming 2, Fairbanks 3, Zukor 4)
Modern Prodigal, 1910 (Griffith 2, Bitzer 4)
Modern Red Riding Hood, 1935 (Terry 4)
Modern Rip, 1911 (Bosworth 3)
Modern Rip Van Winkle. *See* Modern Rip,
   1911
Modern Rip Van Winkle, 1914 (Eason 4)
Modern Snare, 1913 (Reid 3)
**Modern Times, 1935 (Chaplin 2,
Goddard 3, Newman 4, Raksin 4)**
Moderna suffragetten, 1913 (Stiller 2)
Moderne Ecole, 1909 (Cohl 4)
Moderne Ehen, 1924 (Dieterle 2, Kortner 3)
Moderner Don Juan; Orient-Express, 1927
   (Dagover 3)
Moderní Magdalena, 1921 (Heller 4)
Moderno Barba azul, 1946 (Keaton 2)
Moderns, 1988 (Rudolph 2, Bujold 3,
   Chaplin 3)
Moderu to wakatono, 1947 (Yoda 4)
Modest Hero, 1913 (Gish 3)
Modesty Blaise, 1966 (Losey 2, Bogarde 3,
   Stamp 3, Vitti 3, Fisher 4)
Modification, 1969 (Lai 4)
Modigliani of Montparnasse. *See*
   Montparnasse 19, 1957
Modiste, 1917 (Laurel and Hardy 3)
Modré s nebe, 1983 (Brejchová 3)
Moeru aki, 1978 (Takemitsu 4)

Moeru Shanhai, 1954 (Mori 3, Yamamura 3)

Moetikuta chizu, 1968 (Takemitsu 4)

Mogambo, 1953 (Ford 2, Gable 3,
Gardner 3, Kelly 3, Junge 4, Rose 4,
Surtees 4, Young 4)

Mogli pericolose, 1958 (Comencini 2)

Moglia bionda, 1964 (Di Venanzo 4)

Moglia del prete, 1970 (Loren 3,
Mastroianni 3, Ponti 4)

Mogliamante, 1977 (Mastroianni 3)

Moglie americana, 1965 (Flaiano 4)

Moglie di mio padre, 1976 (Baker 3)

Moglie e buoi . . ., 1956 (Cervi 3)

Moglie per una notte, 1952 (Cervi 3,
Lollobrigida 3)

Moglie più bella, 1970 (Morricone 4)

Moglie virgine, 1976 (Baker 3)

Mogotona musume, 1956 (Tsukasa 3)

Mohammad, Messenger of God. See
Message, 1976

Mohammedan Conspiracy, 1914 (Cruze 2)

Mohan, 1947 (Dutt 2, Anand 3)

Mohawk, 1955 (Struss 4)

Mohawk's Way, 1910 (Griffith 2, Bitzer 4)

Mohini Bhasmasur, 1914 (Phalke 2)

Moi et l'impératrice, 1933 (Boyer 3,
Brasseur 3)

Moi, Fleur Bleue, 1978 (Foster 3)

Moi laskovyi i nezhnyi zver, 1978
(Yankovsky 3)

Moi, Pierre Rivière, ayant égorgé ma mère,
ma soeur et mon frère, 1976 (Allio 2)

Moi syn, 1928 (Cherkassov 3)

Moi, un noir, 1958 (Rouch 2, Braunberger 4)

Moi y'en a vouloir des sous, 1973 (Blier 3)

Moine, 1972 (Buñuel 2, Carrière 4, Douy 4,
Vierny 4)

Mois d'avril sont meurtriers, 1987
(Sarde 4)

Mois le plus beau, 1968 (Gélin 3)

Moisson sera belle, 1954 (Fradetal 4)

Moissons d'aujourd'hui, 1949 (Cloquet 4)

Moissons de l'espoir, 1969 (Braunberger 4)

Mokey, 1942 (Reed 3, Rosher 4)

Moko raishu: Tekikoku Kofuku, 1937
(Hasegawa 3)

Mole People, 1956 (Salter 4, Westmore
Family 4)

Molière, 1909 (Gance 2)

Molière, 1955 (Hamer 2, Belmondo 3)

Mollenard, 1938 (Siodmak 2, Baur 3,
Dalio 3, Manès 3, Alekan 4, Milhaud 4,
Schüfftan 4, Spaak 4, Trauner 4)

Molly and Me, 1929 (Brown 3)

Molly and Me, 1945 (Fields 3, McDowall 3,
Clarke 4)

Molly Bawn, 1916 (Hepworth 2)

Molly Maguires, 1970 (Ritt 2, Connery 3,
Harris 3, Howe 4, Jeakins 4, Mancini 4,
Westmore Family 4)

Molly O', 1921 (Sennett 2, Normand 3,
Goodrich 4, Hornbeck 4)

Mollycoddle, 1920 (Fleming 2, Beery 3,
Fairbanks 3)

Moloch, 1978 (Nowicki 3)

Molodaya gvardiya, 1947 (Bondarchuk 3,
Shostakovich 4)

Molti sogni per le strade, 1948 (Magnani 3,
De Laurentiis 4, Rota 4)

Môme vert-de-gris, 1953 (Constantine 3,
Modot 3)

Moment by Moment, 1978 (Travolta 3,
Horner 4)

Moment in Love, 1957 (Clarke 2)

Moment of Danger, 1960 (Dandridge 3,
Howard 3, Stewart 4)

Moment of Darkness, 1915 (Hepworth 2)

Moment of Indiscretion, 1958 (Roeg 2)

Moment of Peace, 1965 (Konwicki 4)

Moment of Terror. See Hikinige, 1966

Moment of Truth. See Minute de vérité, 1952

Moment of Truth. See Never Let Go, 1960

Moment of Truth. See Momento della verità,
1964

Moment to Moment, 1966 (LeRoy 2,
Seberg 3, Mancini 4, Mercer 4,
Stradling 4)

Momento della verità, 1964 (Di Venanzo 4)

Momento più bello, 1957 (Mastroianni 3,
Amidei 4, Rota 4)

Momentos de la vida de Martí. See Rosa
blanca, 1953

Momentos del Cardín, 1977 (Díaz 2)

Momma Don't Allow, 1956 (Reisz 2,
Richardson 2, Lassally 4)

Mommie Dearest, 1981 (Dunaway 3,
Mancini 4, Sharaff 4)

Mommy Loves Puppy, 1940 (Fleischer 4)

Momo, 1986 (Mueller-Stahl 3)

Mon ami Pierre, 1951 (Kosma 4)

Mon ami Victor, 1932 (Brasseur 3, Périnal 4)

Mon Amie Pierrette, 1967 (Lefebvre 2)

Mon Amour est près de toi, 1942
(Andrejew 4)

Mon amour, mon amour, 1967 (Piccoli 3,
Trintignant 3, Lai 4)

Mon beau-frère a tué ma soeur, 1986
(Piccoli 3, Sarde 4)

Mon cas, 1986 (Branco 4)

Mon Chapeau, 1933 (Dalio 3)

Mon chien, 1955 (Franju 2)

Mon Chien rapporte. See Chien qui rapporte,
1909

Mon Coeur et ses millions, 1931 (Berry 3)

Mon Coeur t'appelle, 1934 (Darrieux 3)

Mon curé chez les pauvres, 1956 (Burel 4)

Mon Faust, 1969 (Fresnay 3)

Mon gosse de père, 1930 (Menjou 3)

Mon gosse de Père, 1952 (Burel 4)

Mon Journal. See Journal animé, 1908

Mon Oeil, 1966 (Lefebvre 2)

Mon Oncle, 1917 (Feuillade 2, Musidora 3)

Mon Oncle, 1953 (Grimault 4)

Mon Oncle, 1958 (Tati 2)

Mon Oncle Antoine, 1971 (Jutra 2)

Mon Oncle Benjamin, 1969 (Blier 3)

Mon Oncle d'Amerique, 1980 (Resnais 2,
Depardieu 3, Saulnier 4, Vierny 4)

Mon Paris, 1928 (Dulac 2)

Mon Père avait raison, 1936 (Guitry 2)

Mon Père et mon papa, 1938 (Berry 3)

Mon premier amour, 1978 (Aimée 3, Baye 3,
Legrand 4)

Mon royaume pour un cheval, 1978 (Jarre 4)

Mona, l'étoile sans nom, 1966 (Colpi 4,
Delerue 4)

Mona Lisa, 1922 (Porten 3)

Mona Lisa, 1968 (Schroeter 2)

**Mona Lisa, 1986 (Jordan 2, Caine 3,
Hoskins 3)**

Monaca di Monza, 1947 (Brazzi 3)

Monaca di Monza, 1962 (Cervi 3, Delli
Colli 4, Fusco 4)

Monaca di Monza, 1969 (Donati 4,
Morricone 4)

Monaca di Monza, 1987 (Donaggio 4)

Monachine, 1963 (Morricone 4)

Monaco di Monza, 1962 (Gallone 2)

Monarki og demokrati, 1977 (Roos 2)

Monasterio de los buitres, 1972 (Figueroa 4)

Monastero, 1990 (Lee 3)

Monastery. See Monastero, 1990

Monastery of Sendomir. See Klostret I
Sendomir, 1920

Monday Morning in a Coney Island Police
Court, 1908 (Griffith 2, Bitzer 4)

Monday or Tuesday. See Ponedeljak ili
utorak, 1966

Monday's Child. See Chica del lunes,
1966

Monde de Paul Delvaux, 1944 (Storck 2)

Monde des marais, 1963 (Braunberger 4,
Delerue 4)

Monde desert, 1985 (Olbrychski 3)

Monde en raccourci. See Faim du monde,
1958

Monde nouveau. See Mondo nouveau 1966

Monde perdu, 1954 (Milhaud 4)

Monde tremblera, 1939 (Barsacq 4)

Monde troublant, 1953 (Decaë 4)

Mondo balordo, 1967 (Karloff 3)

Mondo dei miracoli, 1959 (De Sica 2)

Mondo di notte, 1959 (Delli Colli 4)

Mondo di notte. See Ecco, 1963

Mondo le condanna, 1952 (Reggiani 3,
Valli 3, Cecchi D'Amico 4, Flaiano 4)

Mondo Mod, 1967 (Kovacs 4, Zsigmond 4)

Mondo nuovo, 1966 (De Sica 2, Brasseur 3,
Douy 4, Zavattini 4)

Mondo nuovo, 1982 (Scola 2)

Mondo Trasho, 1969 (Waters 2)

Mondo vuole cosi, 1945 (De Sica 2,
Zavattini 4)

Moneda sangrienta, 1974 (Van Cleef 3)

Monelle. See Amoureux sont seuls au
monde, 1948

Money, 1914 (Mohr 4)

Money. See Kane, 1926

Money, 1991 (Cardinale 3, Douglas 3,
Morricone 4)

Money—a Tragicomedy. See Pengar—en
tragikomisk saga, 1946

Money and the Woman, 1940 (Howard 2)

Money Corral, 1919 (Hart 3, August 4)

Money Dance. See Zenin no odori, 1964

Money for Jam. See It Ain't Hay, 1943

Money for Speed, 1933 (Lupino 3)

Money from Home, 1954 (Lewis 2,
Martin 3, Head 4, Wallis 4)

Money Kings, 1912 (Costello 3)

Money Lender, 1914 (Eason 4)

Money Mad, 1908 (Griffith 2, Lawrence 3,
Bitzer 4)

Money Mad, 1918 (Marsh 3)

Money! Money! Money!, 1923
(Schulberg 4)

Money, Money, Money. See Cave se rebiffe,
1961

Money Money Money. See Aventure c'est
l'aventure, 1972

Money Movers, 1978 (Beresford 2)

Money on Your Life, 1938 (Kaye 3)

Money Pit, 1986 (Spielberg 2, Hanks 3,
Willis 4)

Money Talks, 1926 (Daniels 4, Gibbons 4)

Money to Burn, 1920 (Roach 4)

Money Trap, 1966 (Cotten 3, Ford 3,
Hayworth 3)

Monga, 1977 (Kuri 4)

Mongoli, 1961 (Palance 3)

Mongoloid, 1978 (Conner 2)

Mongols. See Mongoli, 1961

Mongo's Back in Town, 1971 (Field 3, Sheen 3)

Mongrel and Master, 1914 (Bushman 3)

Monica Vitti, 1990 (Vitti 3)

Monika Vogelsang, 1919 (Porten 3, Kräly 4)

Monique à Vichy, 1969 (Braunberger 4)

Monismania 1995. See Monismanien 1995, 1975

Monismanien 1995, 1975 (Andersson 3, Josephson 3, Thulin 3)

Monitors, 1969 (Arkin 3, Zsigmond 4)

Monja alférez, 1944 (Félix 3)

Monjas coronadas, 1978 (Leduc 2)

Monje blanco, 1945 (Félix 3)

Monje loco, 1940 (Figueroa 4)

Monk, 1969 (Leigh 3)

Monk. See Moine, 1972

Monkey Business, 1926 (Roach 4)

Monkey Business, 1931 (McLeod 2, Marx Brothers 3, Mankiewicz 4)

Monkey Business, 1952 (Hawks 2, Coburn 3, Grant 3, Monroe 3, Rogers 3, Diamond 4, Hecht 4, Krasner 4, Lederer 4, LeMaire 4, Wheeler 4)

Monkey Business in America, 1931 (Sennett 2)

Monkey Businessmen, 1946 (Three Stooges 3)

Monkey into Man, 1938 (Alwyn 4)

Monkey in Winter. See Singe en hiver, 1962

Monkey Meat, 1930 (Terry 4)

Monkey on My Back, 1957 (De Toth 2, Veiller 4)

Monkey Shines, 1988 (Romero 2)

Monkey Talks, 1927 (Walsh 2, Pierce 4)

Monkey Wretches, 1935 (Lantz 4)

Monkeys, Go Home!, 1967 (Chevalier 3, Disney 4, Ellenshaw 4)

Monkey's Paw, 1933 (Selznick 4, Steiner 4)

Monkey's Uncle, 1964 (Stevenson 2, Disney 4)

Monna Vanna, 1922 (Wegener 3)

Monnaie de 1.000F, 1908 (Cohl 4)

Monnaie de lapin, 1897 (Guy 2)

Monnaie de lapin, 1899 (Gaumont 4)

Monnaie de singe, 1965 (Legrand 4, Wakhévitch 4)

Mono ichidai, 1938 (Shindo 3)

Monochrome Painter Yves Kline. See Monokurohmu no gaka: Yves Kline, 1966

Monocle noir, 1961 (Blier 3)

Monocle rit Jaune, 1964 (Dalio 3)

Monocle vert, 1929 (Modot 3)

Monokurohmu no gaka: Yves Kline, 1966 (Takemitsu 4)

Monolutteur, 1904 (Guy 2)

Monpti, 1957 (Schneider 3)

Monseigneur, 1949 (Blier 3)

Monsieur, 1964 (Gabin 3, Noiret 3)

Monsieur Albert, 1932 (Baranovskaya 3, Feuillère 3, Maté 4)

Monsieur Albert, 1976 (Noiret 3, Cloquet 4)

Monsieur Albert Prophète, 1963 (Rouch 2)

Monsieur Alibi. See Copie conforme, 1946

Monsieur Badin, 1946 (Braunberger 4)

Monsieur Badin, 1977 (Guillemot 4)

Monsieur Beaucaire, 1905 (Blackton 2)

Monsieur Beaucaire, 1924 (Olcott 2, Daniels 3, Valentino 3, Braunberger 4, Westmore Family 4, Zukor 4)

Monsieur Beaucaire, 1946 (Crosby 3, Hope 3, Dreier 4, Frank 4, Head 4)

Monsieur Bébé. See Bedtime Story, 1933

Monsieur Bibi. See Faut ce qu'il faut, 1940

Monsieur Brotonneau, 1939 (Pagnol 2, Raimu 3, Courant 4)

Monsieur Clown chez les Lilliputiens, 1909 (Cohl 4)

Monsieur Cordon, 1933 (Aurenche 4)

Monsieur de compagnie, 1964 (Cassel 3, Dalio 3, Deneuve 3, Girardot 3, Coutard 4, Delerue 4)

Monsieur de Crac, 1910 (Cohl 4)

Monsieur de minuit, 1931 (Maté 4, Meerson 4)

Monsieur de Voltaire, 1963 (Leenhardt 2)

Monsieur Don't-Care, 1924 (Laurel and Hardy 3)

Monsieur et la souris, 1942 (Auric 4)

Monsieur et Madame Curie, 1953 (Franju 2, Fradetal 4)

Monsieur et Madame veulent une bonne, 1907 (Pathé 4)

Monsieur Fabre, 1951 (Fresnay 3, Renoir 4)

Monsieur Gregoire s'évadé, 1946 (Berry 3, Blier 3)

Monsieur Hector, 1940 (Fernandel 3)

Monsieur Ingres, 1967 (Leenhardt 2)

Monsieur La Bruyère, 1956 (Colpi 4)

M'sieur la caille, 1955 (Moreau 3, Kosma 4)

Monsieur la Souris, 1941 (Raimu 3)

Monsieur le Duc, 1932 (Autant-Lara 2)

Monsieur Le Maréchal, 1931 (Heller 4)

Monsieur Le Souris, 1942 (Achard 4)

Monsieur Lecocq, 1914 (Tourneur 2)

Monsieur Papa, 1977 (Baye 3)

Monsieur Personne, 1936 (Christian-Jaque 2, Berry 3)

Monsieur Pinson, policier, 1915 (Feyder 2)

Monsieur qui suit les femmes, 1906 (Pathé 4)

Monsieur Ripois, 1954 (Greenwood 3, Philipe 3, Francis 4, Morris 4)

M. Scrupule, gangster, 1953 (Dalio 3)

Monsieur Stop, 1910 (Cohl 4)

Monsieur Taxi, 1952 (Simon 3)

Monsieur Tête, 1959 (Colpi 4, Lenica 4)

Monsieur Verdoux, 1947 (Chaplin 2, Florey 2, Purviance 3, Courant 4)

Monsieur Vincent, 1947 (Fresnay 3, Renoir 4)

Monsignor, 1982 (Bujold 3, Rey 3, Williams 4)

Monsignor Quixote, 1985 (Guinness 3, Greene 4)

Monsoon, 1953 (Haller 4, Jenkins 4)

Monster. See Monstre, 1903

Monster, 1925 (Chaney 3, Mayer 4, Mohr 4, Sullivan 4)

Monster. See Monster, 1979 (Carradine 3)

Monster and the Girl, 1914 (Guy 2)

Monster and the Girl, 1941 (Lukas 3, Head 4)

Monster Club, 1980 (Carradine 3, Pleasence 3, Price 3)

Monster, Die!, 1965 (Karloff 3)

Monster from Galaxy 27, 1958 (Corman 2)

Monster from the Ocean Floor, 1954 (Corman 2, Crosby 4)

Monster in the Closet, 1987 (Carradine 3)

Monster Island. See Misterio en la isla de los monstruos, 1980

Monster Maker, 1989 (Stanton 3)

Monster Meets the Gorilla. See Bela Lugosi Meets a Brooklyn Gorilla, 1952

Monster of Highgate Pond, 1961 (Halas and Batchelor 4, Cavalcanti 2)

Monster of Terror. See Die, Monster, Die!, 1965

Monster of the Island, 1953 (Karloff 3)

Monster on the Campus, 1958 (Metty 4)

Monster Squad, 1987 (Edlund 4)

Monster Zero. See Kaiju daisenso, 1966

Monsters. See Nuovi mostri, 1977

Monsters from the Arcane Galaxy. See Monstrum z galaxie Arkana, 1981

Monsters in the Night. See Navy Versus the Night Monsters, 1965

Monstre, 1903 (Méliès 2)

Monstrum z galaxie Arkana, 1981 (Švankmajer 4, Vukotić 4)

Monstruo de la sombra, 1954 (Figueroa 4)

Montage, 1990 (Chatterjee 3)

Montagna di luce, 1949 (Risi 2)

Montagne aux météores, 1958 (Braunberger 4)

Montagne infidèle, 1923 (Epstein 2)

Montagne vivante, 1964 (Delerue 4)

Montana, 1930 (Daniels 4)

Montana, 1950 (Walsh 2, Flynn 3, Chase 4, Freund 4, Warner 4)

Montana Belle, 1952 (Dwan 2, Russell 3)

Montana Mix-Up, 1913 (Anderson 3)

Montana Moon, 1930 (Crawford 3, Adrian 4, Brown 4, Freed 4, Gibbons 4, Stothart 4)

Monte Carlo, 1926 (Daniels 4, Gibbons 4, Wilson 4)

Monte Carlo, 1928 (Bertini 3)

Monte Carlo, 1930 (Lubitsch 2, Buchanan 3, MacDonald 3, Banton 4, Dreier 4, Vajda 4, Zukor 4)

Monte Carlo. See Monte Carlo Story, 1956

Monte Carlo, 1986 (McDowell 3)

Monte Carlo Baby, 1951 (Hepburn 3)

Monte Carlo Madness. See Bomben auf Monte Carlo, 1931

Monte Carlo Nights, 1934 (Canutt 4)

Monte Carlo or Bust!. See Quei temerari sulle loro pazze, scatenate, scalcinate carriole, 1969

Monte Carlo or Bust!, 1969 (Moore 3, Terry-Thomas 3)

Monte Carlo Story, 1956 (Dietrich 3, Rotunno 4)

Monte Cassino, 1946 (Germi 2)

Monte Cristo, 1922 (Florey 2, Gilbert 3)

Monte Cristo, 1928 (Dagover 3, Modot 3)

Monte Walsh, 1970 (Marvin 3, Moreau 3, Palance 3, Barry 4, Fraker 4)

Montecarlo, 1956 (Risi 2)

Monte-charge, 1962 (Delerue 4)

Montenegro, 1981 (Josephson 3)

Montenegro—Or Pigs and Pearls. See Montenegro, 1981

Montenruba no yo wa hukete, 1952 (Kagawa 3)

Monterey Pop, 1967 (Leacock 2)

Month in the Country, 1985 (York 3)

Monthly Film Bulletin, 1955 (Adam 4)

Montiel's Widow. See Viuda de Montiel, 1979

Montmartre. See Flamme, 1923

Montmartre, 1950 (Cardiff 4)

Montmartre Nocturne, 1951 (Cardiff 4)

Montmartre-sur-Seine, 1941 (Cayatte 2, Barrault 3)

Montparnasse 19, 1957 (Aimée 3, Philipe 3, Annenkov 4, D'Eaubonne 4, Jeanson 4, Matras 4)

Montpi, 1957 (Käutner 2)

Montre, 1933 (Christian-Jaque 2)

Montréal, jour d'été, 1966 (Arcand 2)
Montrealistes, 1964 (Arcand 2)
Montreur d'ombre. *See* Schatten, 1923
Montreur d'ombres, 1959 (Delerue 4)
Monty Python and the Holy Grail, 1975
    (Gilliam 2, Cleese 3)
Monty Python Live at the Hollywood Bowl,
    1982 (Gilliam 2, Cleese 3)
Monty Python's Life of Brian, 1979
    (Gilliam 2, Cleese 3)
Monty Python's The Meaning of Life, 1983
    (Gilliam 2, Cleese 3)
Monument of Totsuseki. *See* Totsuseki iseki,
    1966
Monzaburo no Hide, 1931 (Hasegawa 3)
Moo Cow Boogie, 1943 (Dandridge 3)
Moochin' Through Georgia, 1939 (Keaton 2,
    Bruckman 4)
Moods of the Sea, 1942 (Vorkapich 4)
Moon, 1989 (McDowell 3)
Moon and Sixpence, 1942 (Marshall 3,
    Sanders 3, Lewin 4, Seitz 4, Tiomkin 4)
Moon for Your Love. *See* Lune dans son
    tablier, 1909
Moon in the Gutter. *See* Lune dans le
    caniveau, 1982
Moon Is Blue, 1953 (Preminger 2, Holden 3,
    Niven 3, Laszlo 4)
Moon Is Down, 1943 (Cobb 3, Basevi 4,
    Johnson 4, Miller 4, Newman 4)
Moon is to the Left. *See* Luna sleva, 1928
Moon over Burma, 1940 (Lamour 3,
    Preston 3, Head 4, Young 4)
Moon over Harlem, 1939 (Ulmer 2)
Moon over Las Vegas, 1944 (Bruckman 4)
Moon over Miami, 1941 (Ameche 3,
    Grable 3, Banton 4, Brown 4, Cole 4,
    Day 4, Newman 4, Pan 4, Shamroy 4)
Moon over Parador, 1988 (Mazursky 2,
    Dreyfuss 3, Rey 3, Jarre 4)
Moon Pilot, 1962 (O'Brien 3, Buckner 4,
    Disney 4)
Moon Riders, 1920 (Eason 4)
Moon Rock, 1970 (Dunning 4)
Moon Zero Two, 1969 (Carreras 4)
Moonbird, 1959 (Hubley 4)
Moonchild, 1974 (Carradine 3)
Mooncussers, 1962 (Homolka 3)
Moonfleet, 1955 (Lang 2, Granger 3,
    Greenwood 3, Sanders 3, Houseman 4,
    Plunkett 4, Rozsa 4)
Moonflower of Heaven. *See* Ten no yugao,
    1948
Moonlight and Cactus, 1932 (Arbuckle 3)
Moonlight and Cactus, 1944 (Three
    Stooges 3)
Moonlight and Melody. *See* Moonlight and
    Pretzels, 1933
Moonlight and Noses, 1925 (Laurel and
    Hardy 3, Roach 4)
Moonlight and Pretzels, 1933 (Freund 4)
Moonlight Follies, 1921 (Glennon 4)
Moonlight in Havana, 1942 (Mann 2)
Moonlight in Hawaii, 1941 (Cortez 4)
Moonlight Masquerade, 1942 (Pangborn 3,
    Alton 4)
Moonlight Murder, 1936 (Clarke 4,
    Stothart 4)
Moonlight Sonata, 1937 (Stallich 4)
Moonlighter, 1953 (Bond 3, MacMurray 3,
    Stanwyck 3, Glennon 4)
Moonlighting, 1982 (Skolimowski 2,
    Irons 3)
Moonraker, 1979 (Adam 4, Barry 4)

Moonrise, 1948 (Borzage 2, Barrymore 3)
Moon's Our Home, 1936 (Bondi 3)
Moon's Our Home, 1936 (Brennan 3,
    Fonda 3, Sullavan 3, Wanger 4)
Moon's Ray, 1914 (Bushman 3)
Moonshine, 1918 (Keaton 2, Arbuckle 3)
Moonshine County Express, 1977
    (Corman 2)
Moonshine Maid and the Man, 1914
    (Ingram 2)
Moonshine Molly, 1914 (Reid 3)
Moonshine Trail, 1919 (Blackton 2)
Moonshine Valley, 1922 (Brenon 2)
Moonshine War, 1970 (Widmark 3)
Moonshiner, 1913 (Chaney 3)
Moonshiners, 1904 (Bitzer 4)
Moonshiners, 1916 (Sennett 2, Arbuckle 3)
Moonshiner's Heart, 1912 (Anderson 3)
Moon-Spinners, 1964 (Greenwood 3,
    Negri 3, Papas 3, Wallach 3, Disney 4)
Moonstone of Fez, 1914 (Costello 3)
Moonstruck, 1988 (Jewison 2, Cher 3,
    Watkin 4)
Moonstruck, 1989 (Halas and Batchelor 4)
Moon-Struck Matador. *See* Clair de lune
    espagnol, 1909
Moontide, 1942 (Lang 2, Gabin 3, Lupino 3,
    Rains 3, Basevi 4, Clarke 4, Day 4,
    Newman 4, Reynolds 4)
Moose Hunt in Canada, 1905 (Bitzer 4)
Moose on the Loose, 1952 (Terry 4)
Mopey Dope, 1944 (Langdon 3)
Mopping Up, 1943 (Terry 4)
Mor Curé chez les pauvres, 1956 (Arletty 3)
Mor defter, 1964 (Güney 2)
Mor och dotter, 1912 (Stiller 2, Jaenzon 4,
    Magnusson 4)
Moral Code, 1917 (Barthelmess 3)
Moral der Gasse, 1925 (Krauss 3)
Moral der Ruth Halbfass, 1971 (Von
    Trotta 2)
Moral Fabric, 1916 (Ince 4, Sullivan 4)
Moral und Liebe, 1933 (Homolka 3)
Moralist. *See* Moralista, 1959
Moralista, 1959 (De Sica 2, Sordi 3)
Morálka pani Dulské, 1958 (Brejchová 3)
Morals for Women, 1931 (Love 3)
Moran of the Lady Letty, 1922 (Valentino 3,
    Glennon 4)
Moran of the Marines, 1928 (Harlow 3,
    Cronjager 4)
Moran of the Mounted, 1926 (Brown 4)
Moravia, 1955 (Taviani 2)
Morbidone, 1965 (Aimée 3, Di Venanzo 4)
Mord Em'ly, 1922 (Pearson 2)
Mörder Dmitri Karamasoff, 1931 (Kortner 3,
    Rasp 3, Rathaus 4)
Mörder sind unter uns, 1946 (Staudte 2,
    Hunte 4)
Morderca zostawia, ślad, 1967 (Ścibor-
    Rylski 4)
Mordi e fuggi, 1972 (Mastroianni 3, Reed 3)
Mords pas, on t'aime, 1975 (Allégret 2,
    Presle 3)
Mordsache Holm, 1950 (Staudte 2)
More, 1969 (Almendros 4, Gégauff 4)
More American Graffiti, 1979 (Lucas 2)
More Dead Than Alive, 1968 (Price 3)
More Milk, Evette, 1965 (Warhol 2)
More Pep, 1936 (Fleischer 4)
More Than a Miracle. *See* C'era una volta,
    1967
More Than a Secretary, 1936 (Arthur 3)
More than Meets the Eye, 1979 (Frampton 2)

More the Merrier, 1943 (Stevens 2, Arthur 3,
    Coburn 3, McCrea 3, Cohn 4)
More to Be Pitied Than Scorned, 1924
    (Cohn 4)
More Trouble, 1918 (Gilbert 3, Furthman 4)
Morfalous, 1983 (Belmondo 3, Audiard 4)
Morgan, a Suitable Case for Treatment, 1966
    (Frears 2, Redgrave 3)
Morgan il pirata, 1961 (Delli Colli 4)
Morgan le Pirate, 1909 (Gaumont 4)
Morgan le pirate, 1910 (Gaumont 4)
Morgan the Pirate. *See* Morgan il pirata,
    1961
Morgane la Sirène, 1927 (Burel 4)
Morgen werde ich verhaftet, 1939 (Herlth 4)
Morgenrot, 1933 (Herlth 4, Hoffmann 4,
    Röhrig 4)
Morgensterne, 1977 (Lassally 4)
Mori no Ishimatsu, 1949 (Shindo 2,
    Yoshimura 2)
Mori Ranmaru, 1955 (Yamamura 3)
Mori to mizuumi no matsuri, 1958
    (Kagawa 3)
Morianerna, 1965 (Dahlbeck 3)
Morianna. *See* Morianerna, 1965
Moriarty. *See* Sherlock Holmes, 1922
Morir por la patria es vivir, 1976 (Alvarez 2)
Morishaige yo doko e iku, 1956 (Kagawa 3)
Morituri, 1948 (Kinski 3, Pommer 4,
    Warm 4)
Morituri, 1965 (Brando 3, Brynner 3,
    Howard 3, Fraker 4, Goldsmith 4, Hall 4,
    Smith 4, Taradash 4)
Moriturus, 1920 (Veidt 3)
Mørke Punkt, 1911 (Psilander 3)
Mormon, 1911 (Dwan 2)
Mormon Main, 1917 (Rosher 4)
Mormonens Offer, 1911 (Psilander 3)
Morning. *See* Subah, 1983
Morning After, 1921 (Roach 4)
Morning After, 1986 (Lumet 2, Bridges 3,
    Fonda 3, Allen 4)
Morning Conflicts. *See* Asa no hamon, 1952
Morning Departure, 1950 (Attenborough 3,
    Mills 3, More 3, Alwyn 4, Rank 4,
    Vetchinsky 4)
Morning Glory, 1933 (Hepburn 3, Menjou 3,
    Berman 4, Cooper 4, Glennon 4,
    Plunkett 4, Polglase 4, Steiner 4)
Morning Judge, 1926 (Fleischer 4)
Morning, Noon and Night, 1933
    (Fleischer 4)
Morning, Noon, and Night Club, 1937
    (Fleischer 4)
Morning Papers, 1914 (Sennett 2)
Morning Star/Evening Star, 1986 (Sidney 3,
    Wright 3)
Morning Sun Shines. *See* Asahi wa
    kagayaku, 1929
Moro Affair. *See* Caso Moro, 1986
Moro Naba, 1957 (Rouch 2)
Morocco, 1930 (Hathaway 2, Von
    Sternberg 2, Cooper 3, Dietrich 3,
    Menjou 3, Ballard 4, Banton 4, Dreier 4,
    Furthman 4, Garmes 4, Zukor 4)
Morpheus Mike, 1917 (O'Brien 4)
Morphia the Death Drug, 1914 (Hepworth 2)
Mors aux dents, 1979 (Tavernier 2,
    Piccoli 3)
Morse Code Melody, 1963 (Godfrey 4)
Morsel. *See* Sousto, 1960
Mort, 1909 (Feuillade 2, Gaumont 4)
Mort de Belle, 1960 (Delerue 4)
Mort de Lucrèce, 1913 (Feuillade 2)

Mort de Mario Ricci, 1984 (Volonté 3)
Mort de Mozart, 1909 (Feuillade 2, Carré 4)
Mort de Robert Macaire et Bertrand, 1905 (Guy 2)
Mort de Vénus, 1930 (Storck 2)
Mort du cygne, 1937 (Burel 4)
Mort du Duc d'Enghien, 1912 (Gance 2)
Mort du soleil, 1921 (Dulac 2)
Mort d'un pourri, 1977 (Audran 3, Delon 3, Kinski 3, Audiard 4, Decaë 4, Sarde 4)
Mort d'un toréador, 1907 (Linder 3)
Mort en ce jardin, 1956 (Piccoli 3, Signoret 3, Vanel 3, Alcoriza 4)
Mort en direct, 1979 (Tavernier 2, Noiret 3, Schneider 3, Von Sydow 3)
Mort en fraude, 1956 (Audiard 4)
Mort en fuite, 1936 (Berry 3, Simon 3)
Mort en sautoir, 1980 (Darrieux 3)
Mort ne reçoit plus, 1944 (Berry 3, Wakhévitch 4)
Mort ne tue jamais personne, 1971 (Braunberger 4)
Mort, où est ta victoire?, 1964 (Noiret 3, Jarre 4)
Mort qui tue, 1913 (Gaumont 4)
Mort vivant, 1912 (Feuillade 2)
Mortadella, 1971 (Monicelli 2, Loren 3, Cecchi D'Amico 4, Lardner 4, Ponti 4)
Mortal Storm, 1940 (Borzage 2, Saville 2, Bond 3, Stewart 3, Sullavan 3, Young 3, Adrian 4, Daniels 4, Kaper 4)
Morte a Venezia, 1971 (Visconti 2, Bogarde 3, Mangano 3)
Morte civile, 1912 (Bertini 3)
Morte di un amico, 1960 (Pasolini 2)
Morte di un operatore, 1978 (Sarde 4)
Morte d'Isotta, 1968 (Schroeter 2)
Morte en fraude, 1956 (Gélin 3)
Morte in Vaticano, 1982 (Stamp 3, Donaggio 4)
Morte, la fatto, l'uovo, 1967 (Trintignant 3, Lollobrigida 3)
Morte non ha sesso, 1969 (Mills 3, Fusco 4)
Morte sorride all'assassino, 1973 (Kinski 3)
Mortelle randonnée, 1983 (Miller 2, Adjani 3, Audiard 4)
Morte-Saison des amours, 1961 (Gélin 3, Delerue 4, Saulnier 4, Vierny 4)
Morts en vitrine, 1957 (Colpi 4, Delerue 4)
Mosaic, 1965 (McLaren 4)
Mosaic Law, 1913 (Ince 4)
Mosaïque. See Mosaic, 1965
Mosca addio, 1987 (Olbrychski 3, Ullmann 3, Morricone 4)
Moscow Builds the Subway. See Moskva stroit metro, 1934
Moscow Does Not Believe in Tears. See Moskva slezam ne verit, 1980
Moscow Goodbye. See Mosca Addio, 1987
Moscow Nights. See Nuits moscovites, 1934
Moscow Nights, 1935 (Baur 3, Olivier 3, Quayle 3, Hornbeck 4, Korda, A. 4, Korda, V. 4)
Moscow on the Hudson, 1984 (Mazursky 2, Williams 3)
Moscow Strikes Back, 1942 (Vorkapich 4)
Mose, 1972 (Lancaster 3)
Moses. See Mose, 1972
Moses, 1975 (Papas 3, Quayle 3)
Moses and Aaron. See Moses und Aron, 1975
Moses—The Lawgiver, 1975 (Thulin 3)
Moses und Aron, 1975 (Straub and Huillet)
Moshimo kanojo ga, 1928 (Tanaka 3)

Moskau-Shanghai, 1936 (Negri 3, Wegener 3)
Moskva slezam ne verit, 1980 (Batalov 3)
Moskva stroit metro, 1934 (Shub 2)
Mosquito, 1922 (Fleischer 4)
Mosquito Coast, 1986 (Schrader 2, Weir 2, Ford 3, Jarre 4)
Moss Rose, 1947 (Barrymore 3, Mature 3, Price 3, Day 4, Furthman 4, LeMaire 4, Newman 4)
Most Beautiful. See Ichiban utsukushiku, 1944
Most Dangerous Game, 1932 (Crabbe 3, Johnson 3, McCrea 3, Wray 3, Cooper 4, Dunn 4, Steiner 4)
Most Dangerous Man Alive, 1961 (Dwan 2)
Most Dangerous Man in the World, 1969 (Peck 3, Goldsmith 4)
Most Dangerous Sin. See Crime et châtiment, 1956
Most Immoral Lady, 1929 (Pidgeon 3, Seitz 4)
Most Important Thing: Love. See Important c'est d'aimer, 1974
Most Important Thing Is Love. See Important c'est d'aimer, 1974
Most Precious Thing in Life, 1934 (Arthur 3, Bond 3, Darwell 3, Schary 4)
Most Wanted Man. See Ennemi public No 1, 1953
Most Wanted Man in the World. See Ennemi public no. 1, 1953
Most Wonderful Moment. See Momento più bello, 1957
Mostri, 1963 (Gassman 3, Age and Scarpelli 4)
Mostro, 1977 (Morricone 4)
Mostro dell'isola. See Monster of the Island, 1953
Mosura, 1961 (Kagawa 3, Shimura 3, Tsuburaya 4)
Mot de Cambronne, 1937 (Guitry 2)
Mot nya tider, 1939 (Sjöström 2, Björnstrand 3)
Möte i natten, 1946 (Dahlbeck 3)
Möte med Livet, 1952 (Thulin 3)
Möten i skymningen, 1957 (Dahlbeck 3, Fischer 4)
Moth, 1917 (Menjou 3, Talmadge 3)
Moth and the Flame, 1914 (Olcott 2)
Moth and the Spider, 1935 (Terry 4)
Mother, 1913 (Loos 4)
Mother, 1914 (Tourneur 2, Carré 4)
Mother. See **Mat, 1926**
Mother. See Okasan, 1952
Mother. See Mat, 1955
Mother. See Mat 1905, 1956
Mother. See Haha, 1963
Mother and Child. See Haha yo ko yo, 1933
Mother and Daughter. See Mor och dotter, 1912
Mother and Daughter. See Sredi dobrykh lyudei, 1962
Mother and Daughter. See Anya és leánya, 1981
Mother and Daughter—The Loving War, 1980 (Weld 3)
Mother and Son, 1967 (Nemec 2)
Mother and the Law, 1919 (Marsh 3)
Mother and the Whore. See Maman et la putain, 1973
Mother Carey's Chickens, 1938 (Brennan 3, Keeler 3, Berman 4, Hunt 4)
Mother Dear, 1982 (Brocka 2)

Mother Didn't Tell Me, 1950 (La Shelle 4, LeMaire 4)
Mother, Do Not Shame Your Name. See Haha yo kimi no na o kegasu nakare, 1928
Mother Goose Land, 1925 (Fleischer 4)
Mother Goose Land, 1933 (Fleischer 4)
Mother Goose Nightmare, 1945 (Terry 4)
Mother Goose on the Loose, 1942 (Lantz 4)
Mother Goose Presents Humpty Dumpty, 1946 (Harryhausen 4)
Mother Goose's Birthday Party, 1950 (Terry 4)
Mother Hulda, 1915 (Ince 4)
Mother India. See **Bharat Mata, 1957**
Mother Instinct, 1917 (Gilbert 3)
Mother Is a Freshman, 1949 (Bacon 2, Johnson 3, Young 3, Newman 4, Reynolds 4, Wheeler 4)
Mother Joan of the Angels. See **Matka Joanna od Aniołów, 1961**
Mother, Jugs & Speed, 1976 (Yates 2)
Mother Lode, 1983 (Heston 3)
Mother Love, 1910 (Lawrence 3)
Mothra Love. See Mutterliebe, 1929
Mother Machree, 1928 (Ford 2, McLaglen 3, Wayne 3)
Mother, Mother, 1989 (Mancini 4)
Mother, Mother, Mother, Pin a Rose on Me, 1929 (Fleischer 4)
Mother o' Mine, 1921 (Niblo 2, Sullivan 4)
Mother of Men, 1914 (Olcott 2)
Mother of Men, 1938 (Pearson 2)
Mother of Mine. See Gribiche, 1925
Mother of the Ranch, 1911 (Dwan 2, Anderson 3)
Mother Pin a Rose on Me, 1926 (Fleischer 4)
Mother—Sir!. See Navy Wife, 1956
Mother Was a Rooster, 1962 (Blanc 4, McKimson 4)
Mother Wore Tights, 1947 (Baxter 3, Grable 3, Day 4, LeMaire 4, Newman 4, Orry-Kelly 4, Trotti 4, Zanuck 4)
Mothering Heart, 1913 (Griffith 2, Gish 3, Bitzer 4)
Mother-in-Law Is Coming. See Svärmor kommer, 1930
Mother-in-Law's Day, 1945 (Hunt 4)
Mothers and Fathers, 1967 (Halas and Batchelor 4)
Mother's Atonement, 1915 (Chaney 3)
Mother's Boy, 1913 (Sennett 2, Arbuckle 3)
Mother's Boy. See Percy, 1925
Mother's Boy, 1929 (Stradling 4)
Mother's Child, 1916 (Laurel and Hardy 3)
Mother's Country Is Far. See Haruka narishi haha no kuni, 1950
Mothers Cry, 1930 (Karloff 3, Coffee 4)
Mother's Holiday, 1932 (Arbuckle 3)
Mother's Influence, 1914 (Reid 3)
Mothers-in-Law, 1923 (Schulberg 4, Struss 4)
Mother's Joy, 1923 (Laurel and Hardy 3, Roach 4)
Mother's Love, 1910 (Walsh 2)
Mother's Map. See Haha no chizu, 1942
Mother's Ordeal, 1917 (Van Dyke 2)
Mother's Tears, 1953 (Lee 3)
Mother's White Snow. See Haha shirayuki, 1956
Mothlight, 1962 (Brakhage 2)
Mothlla. See Mosura, 1961
Mothra. See Mosura, 1961
Motion and Emotion, 1990 (Müller 4)

Motion Painting No. 1, 1947 (Fischinger 2, Ford 2)

Motion Picture Giving and Taking Book, 1990 (Brakhage 2)

Motion Pictures, 1956 (Breer 4)

Motiv pro vraždu, 1974 (Brejchová 3)

Motor Boat Mamas, 1928 (Sennett 2, Hornbeck 4)

Motor Buccaneers, 1913 (Bushman 3)

Motor Friend, 1910 (White 3)

Motor Mat, 1915 (Messmer 4)

Motorcar Apaches. See Lyckonälen, 1915

Motorcyclette. See Girl on a Motorcycle, 1968

Motoring Mamas, 1929 (Sennett 2, Hornbeck 4)

Motorkavalierer, 1950 (Andersson 3)

Mots ont un sens, 1970 (Marker 2)

Mouche, 1903 (Guy 2)

Mouchette, 1967 (Bresson 2, Cloquet 4)

Mouchy, 1950 (Brdečka 4)

Mouettes, 1916 (Burel 4)

Mouid maa el Maghoul, 1958 (Sharif 3)

Moulai Hafid et Alphonse XIII, 1912 (Cohl 4)

Moule, 1936 (Delannoy 2)

Moulin Rouge, 1928 (Dupont 2, Tschechowa 3, Junge 4)

Moulin Rouge, 1934 (Ball 3, Day 4, Johnson 4, Newman 4, Rosher 4, Zanuck 4)

Moulin rouge, 1953 (Huston 2, Clayton 2, Cushing 3, Ferrer 3, Lee, 3, Anric 4, Dehn 4, Francis 4, Morris 4, Veiller 4)

Moulin Rouge, 1990 (Ophuls 2)

Mount Vernon, 1949 (Van Dyke 2)

Mountain, 1956 (Dmytryk 2, Tracy 3, Trevor 3, Wagner 3, Edouart 4, Fulton 4, Head 4, Planer 4, Westmore Family 4)

Mountain and River of Love. See Ai no sanga, 1950

Mountain Eagle, 1926 (Balcon 4)

Mountain Fighters, 1943 (Eason 4)

Mountain Justice, 1915 (Chaney 3, Furthman 4)

Mountain Justice, 1930 (Brown 4, McCord 4)

Mountain Justice, 1937 (Curtiz 2, Haller 4, Raine 4)

Mountain Language, 1988 (Pinter 4)

Mountain Law, 1911 (Anderson 3)

Mountain Mary, 1915 (Eason 4)

Mountain Men, 1980 (Heston 3)

Mountain Music, 1937 (Florey 2, Dreier 4, Glazer 4, Head 4, Lederer 4, Prinz 4, Struss 4, Young 4)

Mountain Music, 1976 (Vinton 4)

Mountain Pass. See Passe-Montagne, 1978

Mountain Pass of Love and Hate. See Aizo toge, 1934

Mountain Rat, 1914 (Crisp 3)

Mountain Rhythm, 1939 (Autry 3, Eason 4)

Mountain Road, 1960 (Stewart 3)

Mountain Romance, 1938 (Terry 4)

Mountain Woman, 1921 (White 3, Ruttenberg 4)

Mountaineer, 1914 (Reid 3)

Mountaineer's Honor, 1909 (Griffith 2, Pickford 3, Bitzer 4)

Mountains and Rivers with Scars. See kizudarake no sanga, 1964

Mountains at Dusk. See Gory o zmierzchu, 1970

Mountains of Mourne, 1930 (Wilcox 2)

Mountains of the Moon, 1958 (Van Dyke 2)

Mountains of the Moon, 1989 (Rafelson 2, Sharif 3)

Mounties Are Coming. See Vigilantes Are Coming, 1936

Mourir à Madrid, 1962 (Grimault 4, Jarre 4)

Mourir à Madrid. See To Die in Madrid, 1967

Mourir d'aimer, 1970 (Girardot 3)

Mourning Becomes Electra, 1947 (Douglas 3, Massey 3, Redgrave 3, Russell 3, Barnes 4, D'Agostino 4, Nichols 4)

Mouse, a Mystery and Me, 1987 (O'Connor 3)

Mouse and Garden, 1950 (Terry 4)

Mouse and Garden, 1960 (Blanc 4, Freleng 4)

Mouse and His Child, 1978 (Ustinov 3)

Mouse and the Lion, 1913 (Grot 4)

Mouse Cleaning, 1948 (Hanna and Barbera 4)

Mouse Comes to Dinner, 1945 (Hanna and Barbera 4)

Mouse Divided, 1953 (Blanc 4, Freleng 4, Stalling 4)

Mouse for Sale, 1953 (Hanna and Barbera 4)

Mouse Heaven, 1989 (Anger 2)

Mouse in Manhattan, 1945 (Hanna and Barbera 4)

Mouse in the House, 1947 (Hanna and Barbera 4)

Mouse Mazurka, 1949 (Blanc 4, Freleng 4, Stalling 4)

Mouse Meets Bird, 1953 (Terry 4)

Mouse Menace, 1946 (Blanc 4)

Mouse Menace, 1953 (Terry 4)

Mouse of Tomorrow, 1940 (Terry 4)

Mouse on 57th Street, 1961 (Blanc 4, Jones 4)

Mouse on the Moon, 1963 (Lester 2, Rutherford 3, Terry-Thomas 3)

Mouse That Jack Built, 1959 (Blanc 4, McKimson 4)

Mouse That Roared, 1959 (Seberg 3, Sellers 3, Foreman 4)

Mouse Trouble, 1944 (Hanna and Barbera 4)

Mouse Warming, 1952 (Blanc 4, Jones 4, Stalling 4)

Mouse Wreckers, 1949 (Blanc 4, Jones 4, Stalling 4)

Mouse-merized Cat, 1946 (Blanc 4, McKimson 4, Stalling 4)

Mouse-placed Kitten, 1959 (Blanc 4, McKimson 4)

Mouse-taken Identity, 1957 (Blanc 4, McKimson 4, Stalling 4)

Mousey, 1974 (Douglas 3, Love 3, Seberg 3)

Moussaillon, 1943 (Aurenche 4)

Moustachu, 1987 (Trintignant 3, Trauner 4)

Moutarde me monte au nez, 1974 (Decaë 4)

Mouth Agape. See Gueule ouverte, 1974

Mouthpiece, 1932 (Goddard 3, Zanuck 4)

Mouton à cinq pattes, 1953 (Fernandel 3)

Mouton enragé, 1908 (Cohl 4)

Mouton enragé, 1974 (Cassel 3, Schneider 3, Trintignant 3)

Moutonnet, 1936 (Simon 3)

Moutonnet à Paris. See Moutonnet, 1936

Moutons de Praxos. See A l'aube du troisième jour, 1963

Mouvement image par image, 1973 (McLaren 4)

Mouvement perpétuel, 1949 (Jutra 2)

Move, 1970 (Gould 3, Berman 4, Daniels 4, Hamlisch 4, Smith 4)

Move On, 1917 (Roach 4)

Move Over, Darling, 1963 (Day 3, Garner 3, Ritter 3, Smith 4)

Movers and Shakers, 1985 (Martin 3, Matthau 3)

Movie, 1922 (Roach 4)

Movie, 1958 (Conner 2)

Movie Crazy, 1932 (Lloyd 3, Bruckman 4)

Movie Daze, 1934 (Roach 4)

Movie Dummy, 1918 (Roach 4)

Movie Experience: A Matter of Choice, 1968 (Heston 3)

Movie Fans, 1920 (Sennett 2)

Movie Life of George, 1989 (Caine 3)

Movie Mad, 1931 (Iwerks 4)

Movie Madness, 1952 (Terry 4)

Movie Maniacs, 1936 (Three Stooges 3)

Movie Movie, 1978 (Donen 2, Scott 3, Wallach 3, Kidd 4)

Movie Murderer, 1970 (Kennedy 3, Oates 3, Bumstead 4)

Movie Nights, 1929 (Roach 4)

Movie Star, 1916 (Sennett 2)

Movie Stunt Pilot, 1954 (La Shelle 4)

Movies, 1925 (Arbuckle 3)

Movies, 1928 (Rooney 3)

Movies Murderer, 1980 (Kennedy 3)

Movie-Town, 1931 (Sennett 2)

Moving, 1988 (Pryor 3)

Moving Perspectives, 1967 (Sen 2)

Moving Picture Cowboy, 1914 (Mix 3)

Moving Picture Cowboy, 1914 (Mix 3)

Moving Spirit, 1951 (Halas and Batchelor 4)

Moving Target. See Harper, 1966

Moving Violation, 1976 (Corman 2)

Moviola: The Scarlett O'Hara War, 1980 (Curtis 3)

Moviola: This Year's Blonde, 1980 (Bernstein 4)

Moyuru daichi, 1940 (Hasegawa 3)

Moyuru ozora, 1940 (Hayasaka 4, Tsuburaya 4)

Mozart. See Whom the Gods Love, 1936

Mozart, 1955 (Werner 3)

Možnosti dialogu, 1982 (Švankmajer 4)

Mozu, 1940 (Yamada 3)

Mozu, 1961 (Yamada 3, Takemitsu 4)

Mrtví žijí, 1922 (Heller 4)

Ms. Don Juan. See Don Juan 1973 ou si Don Juan était une femme, 1973

Mstitel, 1959 (Stallich 4)

Mučedníci lásky, 1967 (Ondříček 4)

Much Ado About Mousing, 1964 (Jones 4)

Much Ado about Nothing, 1940 (Terry 4)

Much Ado about Nutting, 1953 (Blanc 4, Jones 4, Stalling 4)

Much Too Shy, 1942 (Formby 3)

Muchacha, 1960 (Figueroa 4)

Muchly Engaged, 1910 (White 3)

Mucho Locos, 1966 (Blanc 4, McKimson 4)

Mucho Mouse, 1956 (Hanna and Barbera 4)

Mucke, 1954 (Reisch 4)

Mud and Sand, 1922 (Laurel and Hardy 3)

Muddle in Horse Thieves, 1913 (Mix 3)

Muddy Romance, 1913 (Sennet 2)

Muddy Water. See Nigorie, 1953

Müde Tod, 1921 (Dagover 3, Herlth 4, Pommer 4, Röhrig 4, Von Harbou 4, Wagner 4, Warm 4)

Mudlark, 1950 (Negulesco 2, Dunne 3, Guinness 3, Alwyn 4, Johnson 4, Périnal 4)

Muerta viaje demasiado. *See* Humour noir, 1965

Muerte al invasor, 1961 (Alvarez 2, Gutiérrez Alea 2)

Muerte de Pio Baroja, 1957 (Bardem 2)

Muerte de un ciclista, 1955 (Bardem 2, De Beauregard 4)

Muerte de un presidente, 1970 (Rey 3)

Muertres, 1950 (Fernandel 3)

Muet Mélomane, 1899 (Pathé 4)

Mug Town, 1943 (Salter 4)

Muggsy Becomes a Hero, 1910 (Pickford 3)

Muggsy's First Sweetheart, 1910 (Griffith 2, Pickford 3, Bitzer 4)

Mughal-e-Azam, 1960 (Kumar 3)

Mugsy's Girls, 1984 (Gordon 3)

Muha, 1966 (Mimica 4)

Mühle im Schwarzwäldertal, 1952 (Rasp 3)

Mühle von Sanssouci, 1926 (Deiterle 2, Tschechowa 3, Andrejew 4)

Muhomachi no yarodomo, 1959 (Yamamura 3)

Muhomatsu no issho, 1958 (Mifune 3, Takamine 3)

Muhoumatsu no issho, 1943 (Miyagawa 4)

Muhoumono Ginpei, 1938 (Miyagawa 4)

Muj přítel Fabián, 1953 (Weiss 2)

Mujer cualquiera, 1949 (Félix 3)

Mujer de todos, 1945 (Félix 3)

Mujer en condominio, 1956 (Figueroa 4)

Mujer que yo perdí, 1949 (Infante 3)

Mujer sin alma, 1943 (De Fuentes 2, Félix 3)

Mujer sin cabeza, 1944 (Figueroa 4)

Mujer X, 1954 (Figueroa 4)

Mujeres al Borde de un Ataque de Nervios, 1987 (Maura 3)

Mujeres mandan, 1936 (De Fuentes 2, Fernández 2, Figueroa 4)

Mujers de mi general, 1950 (Infante 3)

Mukti, 1937 (Roy 2)

Mulata, 1953 (Armendáriz 3)

Mule Train, 1950 (Autry 3)

Mules and Mortgages, 1919 (Laurel and Hardy 3)

Mule's Disposition, 1926 (Lantz 4)

Mulhall's Great Catch, 1926 (Brown 4)

Mulino del Po, 1948 (Fellini 2)

Mulino del Po, 1949 (Pinelli 4, Ponti 4)

Multi-Handicapped, 1986 (Wiseman 2)

Multiple Maniacs, 1970 (Waters 2)

Mumiens Halsbaand, 1916 (Psilander 3)

Mummy, 1932 (Johnson 3, Karloff 3, Balderston 4, Freund 4, Fulton 4, Laemmle 4, Pierce 4)

Mummy, 1959 (Fischer 2, Cushing 3, Lee 3, Carreras 4, Sangster 4)

Mummy's Boys, 1936 (Polglase 4)

Mummy's Curse, 1944 (Pierce 4)

Mummy's Dummies, 1948 (Three Stooges 3)

Mummy's Ghost, 1944 (Carradine 3, Salter 4, Pierce 4)

Mummy's Hand, 1940 (Salter 4)

Mummy's Shroud, 1967 (Cushing 3, Carreras 4)

Mummy's Tomb, 1942 (Pierce 4, Salter 4)

Mum's the Word, 1926 (McCarey 2, Roach 4)

Mumsie, 1927 (Wilcox 2, Marshall 3)

Mumsy, Nanny, Sonny, and Girly, 1969 (Francis 4)

Mumyo-yumyo, 1939 (Shimura 3)

München-Berlin Wanderung, 1927 (Fischinger 2)

Münchener Bilderbogen, 1924 (Fischinger 2)

Münchhausen, 1943 (Albers 3)

Munchies, 1987 (Corman 2)

Mundo de la Mujer, 1972 (Bemberg 2)

Munekata shimai, 1950 (Tanaka 3, Ryu 3, Takamine 3, Yamamura 3)

Munekata Sisters. *See* Munekata shimai, 1950

Municipal Bandwagon, 1931 (Astaire 3)

Munimji, 1955 (Anand 3, Burman 4)

Munition Conspiracy. *See* Krigens Fjende, 1915

Munkbrogreven, 1934 (Bergman 3)

Munna, 1954 (Abbas 4)

Munster, 1966 (Terry-Thomas 3)

Munster, Go Home!, 1966 (De Carlo 3, Westmore Family 4, Whitlock 4)

Muppet Movie, 1979 (Welles 2, Coburn 3, Gould 3, Hope 3, Martin 3, Pryor 3)

Muppets Take Manhattan, 1984 (Landis 2, Gould 3)

Muqaddar ka Sikandar, 1978 (Bachchan 3)

Mur. *See* Démolition d'un mur, 1895

Mur, 1970 (Guerra 2)

Mur à Jérusalem. *See* Wall in Jerusalem, 1972

Mur de l'Atlantique, 1970 (Terry-Thomas 3, De Beauregard 4)

Mur Murs, 1980 (Varda 2)

Mura di Malapaga. *See* Au-delà des grilles, 1949

Mura hachibu, 1953 (Yamamura 3)

Mura na hanayome, 1928 (Tanaka 3)

Mura no bokujo, 1924 (Tanaka 3)

Mura no kajiya, 1929 (Tanaka 3)

Mural Murals. *See* Mur Murs, 1980

Murasaki zukin, 1958 (Yamamura 3)

Muratti greift ein, 1934 (Fischinger 2, Ford 2)

Muratti Privat, 1935 (Fischinger 2, Ford 2)

Murder, 1930 (Hitchcock 2, Marshall 3, Reville 4)

Murder, 1942 (Sanders 3)

Murder: By Reason of Insanity, 1985 (Wallach 3)

Murder à la Carte. *See* Voici le temps des assassins, 1955

Murder à la Mod, 1967 (De Palma 2)

Murder Ahoy, 1964 (Rutherford 3)

Murder Among Friends, 1941 (Clarke 4)

Murder at Monte Carlo, 1935 (Flynn 3)

Murder at the Gallop, 1963 (Rutherford 3)

Murder at the Vanities, 1934 (Leisen 2, McLaglen 3, Sheridan 3, Prinz 4, Wilson 4, Zukor 4)

Murder at the World Series, 1977 (Leigh 3)

Murder Attempt. *See* Pokus o vraždu, 1973

Murder By an Aristocrat, 1936 (Orry-Kelly 4)

Murder By Contract, 1958 (Ballard 4)

Murder By Death, 1976 (Falk 3, Guinness 3, Lanchester 3, Sellers 3, Smith 3, Booth 4, Stark 4)

Murder By Decree, 1979 (Bujold 3, Gielgud 3, Mason 3, Quayle 3, Sutherland 3)

Murder By Phone, 1981 (Barry 4)

Murder By Phone. *See* Bells, 1982

Murder By Proxy, 1955 (Carreras 4)

Murder By Rope, 1936 (Pearson 2, Havelock-Allan 4)

Murder By Television, 1935 (Lugosi 3)

Murder By the Clock, 1931 (Struss 4)

Murder Czech Style. *See* Vražda po našem, 1966

Murder for Sale. *See* Temporary Widow, 1930

Murder Goes to College, 1937 (Dmytryk 2, Crabbe 3, Head 4)

Murder, He Says, 1945 (MacMurray 3, Dreier 4, Head 4)

Murder in Aspic, 1979 (Demme 2)

Murder in Bergen. *See* Let George Do It, 1940

Murder in Greenwich Village, 1937 (Wray 3)

Murder in Music City, 1979 (Sangster 4)

Murder in Peyton Place, 1977 (Malone 3)

Murder in Soho, 1939 (Withers 3)

Murder in the Air, 1940 (Reagan 3, McCord 4)

Murder in the Big House. *See* Jailbreak, 1936

Murder in the Big House, 1942 (Johnson 3, Eason 4, McCord 4)

Murder in the Blue Room, 1944 (Diamond 4)

Murder in the Clouds, 1934 (Orry-Kelly 4, Schary 4)

Murder in the Family, 1938 (McDowall 3)

Murder in the Fleet, 1935 (Bond 3, Taylor 3, Krasner 4)

Murder in the Museum, 1934 (Walthall 3)

Murder in the Music Hall, 1946 (Alton 4)

Murder in Thornton Square. *See* Gaslight, 1944

Murder in Trinidad, 1934 (Johnson 3)

Murder Inc. *See* Enforcer, 1951

Murder, Inc., 1960 (Rosenblum 4, Sylbert 4)

Murder Is Easy, 1982 (De Havilland 3)

Murder Is My Beat, 1955 (Ulmer 2)

Murder Man, 1935 (Stewart 3, Tracy 3)

Murder Men, 1962 (Coburn 3, Dandridge 3)

Murder Most Foul, 1964 (Rutherford 3)

Murder, My Sweet, 1944 (Powell 3, Trevor 3, Chandler 4, D'Agostino 4, Paxton 4)

Murder of Dr. Harrigan, 1936 (Astor 3)

Murder of Karamazov. *See* Morder Dimitri Karamazov, 1930

Murder of Mary Phagan, 1988 (Lemmon 3)

Murder of Otsuya. *See* Otsuya goroshi, 1951

Murder of Quality, 1991 (Jackson 3)

Murder on a Bridle Path, 1936 (Musuraca 4)

Murder on a Honeymoon, 1935 (Benchley 4, MacGowan 4, Musuraca 4, Plunkett 4)

Murder on Diamond Row. *See* Squeaker, 1937

Murder on Flight 502, 1975 (Bellamy 3, Pidgeon 3)

Murder on Monday. *See* Home at Seven, 1952

Murder on the Blackboard, 1934 (MacGowan 4, Musuraca 4, Steiner 4)

Murder on the Bridge. *See* Richter und sein Henker, 1975

Murder on the Orient Express, 1974 (Lumet 2, Bacall 3, Bergman 3, Cassel 3, Connery 3, Finney 3, Gielgud 3, Perkins 3, Redgrave 3, Roberts 3, Widmark 3, Dehn 4, Unsworth 4)

Murder on the Roof, 1930 (Walker 4)

Murder on the Waterfront, 1943 (Eason 4)

Murder or Mercy, 1974 (Douglas 3)

Murder over New York, 1940 (Day 4, Miller 4)

Murder Party. *See* Night of the Party, 1934

Murder Psalm, 1980 (Brakhage 2)

Murder She Said, 1961 (Kennedy 3, Rutherford 3)

Murder Story, 1989 (Lee 3)

Murder That Wouldn't Die, 1980 (Ferrer 3)

Murder Will Out, 1930 (Seitz 4)

Murder Will Out, 1939 (Hawkins 3)

Murder with Mirrors, 1985 (Davis 3, Mills 3)

Murder with Pictures, 1936 (Ayres 3, Head 4)

Murder without Tears, 1953 (Miller 4)

Murderer. *See* Aru koroshiya, 1967

Murderer and the Girl. *See* Zbrodniarz i panna, 1963

Murderer Dimitri Karamazov. *See* Mörder Dmitri Karamasoff, 1931

Murderer Leaves a Clue. *See* Moderca zostawia ślad, 1967

Murderer Leaves Traces. *See* Morderca zostawia ślad, 1967

Murderer Lives at Number 21. *See* Assassin habite au 21, 1942

Murderer Made in Italy. *See* Segreto del vestito rosso, 1963

Murderers Are Among Us. *See* **Mörder sind unter uns, 1946**

Murderers' Row, 1966 (Martin 3, Malden 3, Schifrin 4)

Murders in the Rue Morgue, 1932 (Florey 2, Huston 2, Johnson 3, Lugosi 3, Freund 4, Laemmle 4)

Murders in the Rue Morgue, 1971 (Lom 3, Robards 3)

Murders in the Rue Morgue, 1986, (Scott 3)

Murders in the Zoo, 1933 (Darwell 3, Scott 3, Haller 4)

Murdoch's Gang, 1973 (Leigh 3)

Muriel. *See* Muriel, ou le temps d'un retour, 1963

Muriel, ou le temps d'un retour, 1963 (Resnais 2, Seyrig 3, Braunberger 4, Delerue 4, Saulnier 4, Vierny 4)

Muri-shinju: Nippon no natsu, 1967 (Toda 4)

Murmur of the Heart. *See* Soufle au coeur, 1971

Muro, 1947 (Torre Nilsson 2)

Murphy's I.O.U., 1913 (Sennett 2)

Murphy's Law, 1986 (Bronson 3, Golan 4)

Murphy's Romance, 1985 (Ritt 2, Field 3, Garner 3, Fraker 4, Ravetch 4)

Murphy's War, 1971 (Yates 2, Noiret 3, O'Toole 3, Barry 4, Slocombe 4)

Murri Affair. *See* Fatti di gente perbene, 1974

Musafir, 1955 (Ghatak 2)

Musasabi no Sankichi, 1927 (Tanaka 3)

Musashi and Kojiro. *See* Ketto ganryu-jima, 1956

Musashi Miyamoto. *See* Miyamoto Musashi, 1944

Musashibo Benkei, 1942 (Takamine 3, Yamada 3)

Musashino Fujin, 1951 (Mizoguchi 2, Mori 3, Shindo 3, Tanaka 3, Yamamura 3, Hayasaka 4, Yoda 4)

Muscle Beach Party, 1964 (Lorre 3)

Muscle Beach Tom, 1956 (Hanna and Barbera 4)

Muscle Tussle, 1953 (Blanc 4, McKimson 4, Stalling 4)

Muscle Up a Little Closer, 1956 (Three Stooges 3)

Muscle-Bound Music, 1926 (Sennett 2)

Musée, 1964 (Borowczyk 2)

Musée des grotesques, 1911 (Cohl 4)

Musée du Louvre, 1979 (Takemitsu 4)

Musée Grevin, 1958 (Cocteau 2, Demy 2, Fradetal 4)

Musée vivant, 1965 (Storck 2)

Musen fusen, 1924 (Mizoguchi 2)

Museo dei sogni, 1948 (Comencini 2)

Museo dell'amore, 1935 (Lattuada 2)

Museum Mystery, 1937 (Havelock-Allan 4)

Mush and Milk, 1933 (Roach 4)

Mushukunin Mikoshin no Joukichi, 1972 (Miyagawa 4)

Music Academy, 1989 (Halas and Batchelor 4)

Music Box, 1932 (Laurel and Hardy 3, Mayer 4, Roach 4)

Music Box, 1989 (Costa-Gavras 2, Lange 3, Mueller-Stahl 3, Sarde 4, Winkler 4)

Music for Madame, 1937 (Fontaine 3, August 4, Lasky 4, Polglase 4)

Music for Millions, 1944 (Allyson 3, Durante 3, Gardner 3, O'Brien 3, Irene 4, Pasternak 4, Surtees 4)

Music Goes 'round, 1936 (Buchman 4, Swerling 4, Walker 4)

Music Hall, 1934 (Baxter 2, Orry-Kelly 4)

Music Hall, 1985 (Olbrychski 3)

Music Hath Charms, 1936 (Lantz 4)

Music Hath Its Charms, 1915 (Browning 2)

Music in Darkness. *See* Musik i mörker, 1948

Music in Manhattan, 1944 (Darwell 3, Metty 4)

Music in My Heart, 1939 (Hayworth 3)

Music in the Air, 1930 (Waxman 4)

Music in the Air, 1934 (Wilder 2, Bosworth 3, Swanson 3, Pommer 4)

Music in Your Hair, 1934 (Roach 4)

Music Is Magic, 1935 (Daniels 3, Faye 3, McDaniel 3)

Music Lesson, 1932 (Iwerks 4)

Music Lovers, 1970 (Russell 2, Jackson 3, Previn 4, Russell 4, Slocombe 4)

Music Made Simple, 1938 (Benchley 4)

Music Man, 1938 (Halas and Batchelor 4)

Music Man, 1962 (Preston 3, Burks 4, Jeakins 4)

Music Master, 1908 (Bitzer 4)

Music Master, 1927 (Dwan 2)

Music Mice-Tro, 1967 (Blanc 4)

Music Room. *See* Jalsaghar, 1958

Musica, 1966 (Seyrig 3, Vierny 4)

Musical, 1966 (Duras 2)

Musical Madness, 1951 (Terry 4)

Musical Memories, 1935 (Fleischer 4)

Musical Mews, 1919 (Messmer 4)

Musical Mountaineers, 1939 (Fleischer 4)

Musical Poster No. 1, 1940 (Lye 4)

Musiciens de ciel, 1939 (Morgan 3, Simon 3, Alekan 4, Andrejew 4, Honegger 4, Schüfftan 4)

Musiciens de la mine, 1950 (Cloquet 4)

Musicomanie, 1910 (Cohl 4)

Musidora en Espagne. *See* Aventura de Musidora en España, 1922

Musik bei Nacht, 1953 (Herlth 4)

Musik im Blut, 1934 (Warm 4)

Musik i mörker, 1948 (Zetterling 2, Björnstrand 3)

Musik in Salzburg, 1944 (Dagover 3)

Musketeers, 1930 (Rooney 3)

Musketeers of Pig Alley, 1912 (Griffith 2, Barrymore 3, Carey 3, Gish 3, Bitzer 4)

Musodoro, 1954 (Rota 4)

Muss 'em Up, 1936 (Vidor 2, Bond 3, August 4, Berman 4, Hunt 4, Polglase 4)

Mussolini: Last Days. *See* Mussolini: ultimo atto, 1974

Mussolini: The Decline and Fall of II Duce, 1985 (Grant 3)

Mussolini: The Untold Story, 1985 (Scott 3)

Mussolini: ultimo atto, 1974 (Fonda 3, Steiger 3, Morricone 4)

Mussolini and I. *See* Io e il duce, 1985

Mussorgsky, 1950 (Cherkassov 3)

Mustang Country, 1977 (McCrea 3)

Mustang Pete's Love Affair, 1911 (Anderson 3)

Musty Musketeers, 1954 (Three Stooges 3)

Musume no boken, 1958 (Kyo 3)

Musume no naka no musume, 1958 (Yamamura 3)

Musume tabigeinen, 1941 (Yoda 4)

Musume to watashi, 1962 (Hara 3, Yamamura 3)

Musume tsuma haha, 1960 (Hara 3, Mori 3, Takamine 3)

Mut zur Sünde, 1918 (Albers 3)

Muta di Portici, 1954 (Mastroianni 3)

Mutations, 1974 (Pleasence 3, Cardiff 4)

Mute Witness, 1913 (Dwan 2)

Muteki, 1952 (Mifune 3, Shimura 3)

Mutineers, 1949 (Katzman 4)

Mutinés de l'Elseneur, 1936 (Honegger 4, Matras 4)

Mutiny, 1952 (Dmytryk 2, Lansbury 3, Laszlo 4, Tiomkin 4)

Mutiny Ain't Nice, 1938 (Fleischer 4)

Mutiny at Fort Sharp. *See* Escuadró de la muerte, 1966

Mutiny in the Arctic, 1941 (Salter 4)

Mutiny on the Bounty, 1935 (Crisp 3, Gable 3, Laughton 3, Booth 4, Clarke 4, Edeson 4, Furthman 4, Gibbons 4, Gillespie 4, Jennings 4, Kaper 4, Lewin 4, Mayer 4, Stohart 4, Thalberg 4, Westmore Family 4, Wilson 4)

Mutiny on the Bounty, 1962 (Milestone 2, Brando 3, Howard 3, Harris 3, Rafferty 3, Gillespie 4, Hall 4, Kaper 4, Lederer 4, Surtees 4)

Mutiny on the Bunny, 1950 (Blanc 4, Freleng 4, Stalling 4)

Mutiny on the Buses, 1972 (Carreras 4)

Mutiny on the Elsinore, 1938 (Lukas 3)

Mutoscope Shorts, 1897 (Bitzer 4)

Mutt in a Rut, 1959 (Blanc 4, McKimson 4)

Mutter Courage und ihre Kinder, 1955 (Douy 4)

Mütter Küsters fahrt zum Himmel, 1977 (Ballhaus 4)

Mütter Küsters Goes to Heaven. *See* Mütter Küsters fahrt zum Himmel, 1977

Mutter und Kind, 1924 (Dieterle 2, Porten 3)

Mutter und Kind, 1933 (Porten 3)

Mütter, verzaget nicht!, 1911 (Messter 4)

Mutterliebe, 1929 (Porten 3)

Mutterlied, 1937 (Von Harbou 4)

Mutts to You, 1938 (Three Stooges 3)

Muž bez srdce, 1923 (Ondra 3, Heller 4)

Muž orlem a slepici, 1978 (Brejchová 3)

Muž z Muž neznáma, 1939 (Frič 2)

Muzhskoi Razgovor, 1969 (Shukshin 3)

Muži bez křídel, 1945 (Stallich 4)

Muzne Hry, 1988 (Švankmajer 4)

Muzzle. *See* Kanonen-Serenade, 1958

Muzzle Tough, 1954 (Blanc 4, Freleng 4, Stalling 4)

My African Adventure. *See* Going Bananas, 1988

My American Uncle. *See* Mon oncle d'Amerique, 1980

My American Wife, 1923 (Wood 2, Swanson 3)

My Artistical Temperature, 1937 (Fleischer 4)

My Asylum. *See* Chiedo asilo, 1979

My Aunt's Millions. *See* Fasters miljoner, 1934

My Baby, 1912 (Griffith 2, Barrymore 3, Gish 3, Pickford 3, Walthall 3, Bitzer 4)

My Baby Just Cares for Me, 1931 (Fleischer 4)

My Beautiful Laundrette, 1985 (Frears 2, Day Lewis 3)

My Beloved, My Dead Fellow!. *See* Dorogoi moi chelovek, 1958

My Best Friend's Girl. *See* Femme de mon pote, 1982

My Best Gal, 1944 (Brooks 2, Mann 2, Pangborn 3)

My Best Girl, 1927 (Bosworth 3, Pickford 3, Rosher 4)

My Bill, 1938 (Francis 3, Orry-Kelly 4)

My Blood Runs Cold, 1965 (Duning 4)

My Blue Heaven, 1950 (Beavers 3, Grable 3, LeMaire 4, Newman 4, Trotti 4)

My Blue Heaven, 1990 (Martin 3)

My Body, My Child, 1982 (Redgrave 3)

My Bodyguard, 1980 (Dillon 3, Gordon 3, Houseman 4)

My Bonnie, 1925 (Fleischer 4)

My Boy Johnny, 1944 (Terry 4)

My Boys Are Good Boys, 1978 (Lupino 3)

My Brilliant Career, 1979 (Armstrong 2)

My Brother Down There. *See* Running Target, 1956

My Brother Talks to Horses, 1946 (Zinnemann 2, Irene 4, Plunkett 4, Rosson 4)

My Brother's Keeper, 1948 (Lee 3, Rank 4)

My Buddy, 1944 (Edwards 2)

My Bunny Lies over the Sea, 1948 (Blanc 4, Jones 4, Stalling 4)

My City. *See* Orasul meu, 1967

My Cousin, 1919 (Zukor 4)

My Cousin Rachel, 1952 (Burton 3, De Havilland 3, Jeakins 4, Johnson 4, La Shelle 4, LeMaire 4, Waxman 4, Wheeler 4)

My Darling Clementine, 1946 (Ford 2, Bond 3, Brennan 3, Darnell 3, Darwell 3, Fonda 3, Marsh 3, Mature 3, Basevi 4, Newman 4, Wheeler 4, Zanuck 4)

My Darling Clementine. *See* Drahoušek Klementýna, 1959

My Darling Daughters' Anniversary, 1973 (Massey 3, Young 3)

My Daughter and I. *See* Musume to watashi, 1962

My Daughter Joy, 1950 (Robinson 3, Korda 4, Périnal 4)

My Dear Miss Aldrich, 1937 (O'Sullivan 3, Pidgeon 3, Mankiewicz 4)

My Dear Secretary, 1948 (Douglas 3, Biroc 4)

My Dinner with Andre, 1981 (Malle 2)

My Dog Stupid, 1991 (Falk 3)

My Dream Is Yours, 1949 (Curtiz 2, Arden 3, Day 3, Menjou 3, Pangborn 3, Haller 4, Prinz 4)

My, dvoe muzhchin, 1963 (Shukshin 3)

My Enemy the Sea. *See* Taiheiyo hitoribotchi, 1963

My Face Red in the Sunset. *See* Yuhi ni akai ore no kao, 1961

My Fair Lady, 1964 (Cukor 2, Harrison 3, Hepburn 3, Beaton 4, Pan 4, Previn 4, Stradling 4, Warner 4)

My Father, My Son, 1988 (Malden 3)

My Father's House, 1947 (Crosby 4)

My Father's House, 1975 (Preston 3, Robertson 3)

My Fault, New Version. *See* Shin ono ga tsumi, 1926

My Favorite Blonde, 1942 (Carroll 3, Crosby 3, Hope 3, Dreier 4, Frank 4, Head 4)

My Favorite Brunette, 1947 (Crosby 3, Hope 3, Ladd 3, Lamour 3, Lorre 3, Dreir 4, Head 4)

My Favorite Duck, 1942 (Jones 4, Stalling 4)

My Favorite Spy, 1942 (Garnett 2, Lloyd 3, Wyman 3)

My Favorite Spy, 1951 (McLeod 2, Hope 3, Lamarr 3, Head 4, Mercer 4, Young 4)

My Favorite Wife, 1940 (McCarey 2, Dunne 3, Grant 3, Scott 3, Kanin 4, Maté 4, Polglase 4)

My Favorite Year, 1982 (O'Toole 3)

My Favourite Duck, 1942 (Blanc 4, Maltese 4)

My Feelin's Is Hurt, 1940 (Fleischer 4)

My First 40 Years. *See* Miei primi 40 anni, 1987

My Foolish Heart, 1949 (Andrews 3, Hayward 3, Day 4, Epstein 4, Garmes 4, Goldwyn 4, Head 4, Mandell 4, Young 4)

My Foolish Heart, 1990 (Babenco 2)

My Forbidden Past, 1951 (Stevenson 2, Douglas 3, Gardner 3, Mitchum 3)

My Four Years in Germany, 1918 (Cohn 4, Warner 4)

My Friend Fabian. *See* Muj přítel Fabián, 1953

My Friend Flicka, 1943 (McDowall 3, Day 4, Newman 4)

My Friend from India, 1927 (Pangborn 3, Adrian 4)

My Friend Irma, 1949 (Lewis 2, Martin 3, Bumstead 4, Dreier 4, Head 4, Wallis 4)

My Friend Irma Goes West, 1950 (Lewis 2, Martin 3, Bumstead 4, Dreier 4, Garmes 4, Head 4, Wallis 4)

My Friend Nicholas, 1961 (Brynner 3)

My Friend the Devil, 1922 (Ruttenberg 4)

My Friend the Gypsy. *See* Muj přítel Fabián, 1953

My Friend the King, 1931 (Powell and Pressburger 2)

My Friend the Monkey, 1939 (Fleischer 4)

My Friends. *See* Amici miei, 1975

My Gal Loves Music, 1944 (Mohr 4)

My Gal Sal, 1930 (Fleischer 4)

My Gal Sal, 1942 (Hayworth 3, Mature 3, Day 4, Miller 4, Newman 4, Pan 4)

My Geisha, 1962 (Maclaine 3, Montand 3, Robinson 3, Cardiff 4, Head 4, Krasna 4, Waxman 4, Westmore Family 4)

My General. *See* Mi General, 1986

My Girl Tisa, 1948 (Haller 4, Steiner 4)

My Goodness, 1920 (Sennett 2)

My Green Fedora, 1935 (Freleng 4)

My Gun is Quick, 1957 (Leven 4)

My Heart Belongs to Daddy, 1942 (Siodmak 2, Dreier 4, Head 4)

My Heart Goes Crazy. *See* London Town, 1946

My Heart Is Calling, 1934 (Launder and Gilliat 2)

My Hero, 1912 (Griffith 2, Barrymore 3, Carey 3, Bitzer 4)

My Hero. *See* Southern Yankee, 1948

My Hobo. *See* Burari burabura monogatari, 1962

My Home Is Copacabana. *See* Mitt hem är Copacabana, 1965

My Husband's Other Wife, 1919 (Blackton 2)

My Hustler, 1966 (Warhol 2)

My Irish Molly, 1939 (O'Hara 3)

My Kidnapper, My Love, 1980 (Rooney 3)

My Kingdom for a Cook, 1943 (Coburn 3, Planer 4)

My Lady Incog, 1916 (Olcott 2)

My Lady of Whims, 1926 (Bow 3)

My Lady's Garden, 1934 (Terry 4)

My Lady's Garter, 1920 (Tourneur 2, Carré 4)

My Lady's Lips, 1925 (Bow 3, Powell 3, Schulberg 4)

My Lady's Past, 1929 (Brown 3)

My Learned Friend, 1943 (Dearden 2, Hamer 2, Hay 3, Balcon 4)

My Left Foot, 1989 (Day Lewis 3, Bernstein 4)

My Life for Zarah Leander, 1986 (Sirk 2)

My Life to Live. *See* **Vivre sa vie, 1962**

My Life with Caroline, 1941 (Milestone 2, Colman 3, Miller 4)

My Life's Bright Day. *See* Waga shogai no kagayakeruhi, 1948

My Lips Betray, 1933 (Behrman 4, Friedhofer 4, Garmes 4, Kräly 4)

My Little Baby, 1916 (Bertini 3)

My Little Buckeroo, 1937 (Freleng 4)

My Little Chickadee, 1940 (Fields 3, West 3)

My Little Duckaroo, 1954 (Blanc 4, Jones 4, Maltese 4)

My Little Girl, 1986 (Jones 3, Page 3)

My Little Sister, 1919 (Ruttenberg 4)

My Love Burns. *See* Waga koi wa moenu, 1949

My Love Came Back, 1940 (De Havilland 3, Wyman 3, Buckner 4, Orry-Kelly 4, Reisch 4, Rosher 4, Wallis 4)

My Love Has Been Burning. *See* Waga koi wa moenu, 1949

My Love Is Beyond the Mountain. *See* Waga ai wa yama no kanata ni, 1948

My Love Is Like a Rose. *See* Min kära är en ros, 1963

My Lucky Star, 1933 (Crazy Gang 3)

My Lucky Star, 1938 (Henie 3, Brown 4)

My Lucky Stars, 1985 (Chan 3)

My Madonna, 1915 (Guy 2)

My Man, 1928 (Zanuck 4)

My Man and I, 1952 (Wellman 2, Trevor 3, Winters 3, Basevi 4)

My Man Godfrey, 1936 (La Cava 2, Lombard 3, Pangborn 3, Powell 3, Wyman 3, Banton 4, Ryskind 4)

My Man Godfrey, 1957 (Allyson 3, Niven 3, Daniels 4, Hunter 4)

My Man Jasper, 1945 (Pal 4)

My Marriage, 1936 (Trevor 3)

My Mother, My Daughter, 1981 (Winters 3)

My Mother the General. See Imi Hageneralit, 1979

My Mountain Song 27. See Songs, 1964–69

My Name Is Bertolt Brecht—Exile in U.S.A., 1988 (Lardner 4)

My Name Is Julia Ross, 1945 (Lewis 2, Guffey 4)

My Name Is Mistress. See Waga koi wa moenu, 1949

My Name Is Nobody, 1973 (Leone 2)

My Name Is Nobody. See Mio nome e nessuno, 1974

My Name Is Puck. See Puck heter jag, 1951

My Neighbor's Wife, 1925 (Walker 4)

My New Gown. See Boogie Woogie Dream, 1942

My New Partner II. See Ripoux contre Ripoux, 1990

My Night at Maud's. See Ma nuit chez Maud, 1969

My Official Wife, 1914 (Valentino 3)

My Official Wife, 1926 (Blanke 4, Carré 4)

My Old China, 1931 (Balcon 4)

My Old Dutch, 1911 (Costello 3)

My Old Dutch, 1934 (Balcon 4, Rank 4)

My Old Kentucky Home, 1926 (Fleischer 4)

My Old Kentucky Home, 1946 (Terry 4)

My Old Man, 1979 (Oates 3)

My Old Man's Place, 1971 (Kennedy 3)

My Other ''Husband'', 1983 (Sarde 4)

My Outlaw Brother, 1951 (Preston 3, Rooney 3)

My Own Pal, 1926 (Mix 3)

My Own True Love, 1948 (Douglas 3, Bumstead 4, Dreier 4, Head 4, Lang 4, Lewton 4)

My Pal Gus, 1952 (Widmark 3, LeMaire 4, Wheeler 4)

My Pal Paul, 1930 (Lantz 4)

My Pal, the King, 1932 (Rooney 3, Mix 3)

My Pal Trigger, 1946 (Rogers 3)

My Pal, Wolf, 1944 (Paxton 4)

My Partner Mr. Davis See Mysterious Mr. Davis, 1936

My Past, 1931 (Blondell 3, Daniels 3)

My People Are Not Yours. See Mitt folk är icke ditt, 1944

My Pony Boy, 1926 (Fleischer 4)

My Pop, My Pop, 1940 (Fleischer 4)

My Reputation, 1946 (Arden 3, Stanwyck 3, Blanke 4, Grot 4, Head 4, Howe 4, Steiner 4)

My Science Project, 1985 (Hopper 3, Baker 4)

My Seven Little Sins. See J'avais sept filles, 1955

My Sin, 1930 (March 3, Folsey 4, Green 4)

My Sister and I, 1948 (Dors 3)

My Sister and I. See Min syster och jag, 1950

My Sister Eileen, 1942 (Russell 3, Three Stooges 3, Cohn 4, Walker 4)

My Sister Eileen, 1955 (Edwards 2, Fosse 2, Leigh 3, Lemmon 3, Duning 4, Wald 4)

My Sister, My Love. See Syskonbädd 1782, 1965

My Sisters Keeper, 1986 (Barry 4)

My Six Convicts, 1952 (Kramer 2, Bronson 3, Anhalt 4, Tiomkin 4)

My Six Loves, 1963 (Reynolds 3, Robertson 3, Cahn 4, Fulton 4, Head 4)

My Son, 1925 (Bosworth 3, Nazimova 3)

My Son. See Moi syn, 1928

My Son. See Shodo satsujin: Musuko yo, 1979

My Son A-Chen, 1948 (Lee 3)

My Son Alone. See American Empire, 1942

My Son Is Guilty, 1939 (Carey 3, Ford 3, Brown 4)

My Son John, 1952 (McCarey 2, Walker 3, Head 4, Stradling 4)

My Son, My Son, 1940 (Vidor 2, Carroll 3, Coffee 4, Stradling 4)

My Son, the Hero, 1943 (Ulmer 2)

My Son, the Hero. See Arrivano i Titani, 1962

My Son, the Vampire. See Old Mother Riley Meets the Vampire, 1952

My Song for You, 1934 (Junge 4)

My Stars, 1926 (Arbuckle 3)

My Stupid Brother. See Niisan no baka, 1932

My Sweet Little Village. See Vesnicko ma strediskova, 1985

My Tail's My Ticket, 1959 (Vukotić 4)

My Teenage Daughter, 1956 (Wilcox 2, Neagle 3)

My Tender Loving Beast. See Moi laskovyi i nezhnyi zver, 1978

My Tomato, 1943 (Blenchley 4)

My Town, 1986 (Ford 3)

My True Story, 1951 (Rooney 3)

My Twelve Fathers. See Tucet mých tatínku, 1959

My Two Husbands. See Too Many Husbands, 1940

My Valet, 1915 (Sennett 2, Normand 3)

My Way. See Waga michi, 1974

My Weakness, 1933 (Ayres 3, Langdon 3, Miller 4)

My Widow and I. See Sbaglio di essere vivo, 1945

My Wife's Best Friend, 1952 (Baxter 3, LeMaire 4, Lennart 4)

My Wife's Enemy. See Nemico di mia moglie, 1959

My Wife's Family, 1941 (Greenwood 3)

My Wife's Gone to the Country, 1931 (Fleischer 4)

My Wife's Husband. See Cuisine au beurre, 1963

My Wife's Lodger, 1952 (Dors 3)

My Wife's Relations, 1922 (Keaton 2)

My Wild Irish Rose, 1947 (Burks 4, Edeson 4, Prinz 4, Steiner 4)

My Wonderful Yellow Car. See Fukeyo harukaze, 1953

Myohoin Kanpachi, 1939 (Shimura 3)

Myoreki meikenshi, 1934 (Hasegawa 3)

Myra Breckenridge, 1970 (Huston 2, Carradine 3, Welch 3, West 3, Head 4, Smith 4, Van Runkle 4)

Myriad Homes. See Countless Families, 1953

Myrt and Marge, 1933 (Three Stooges 3)

Mystère, 1949 (Rosay 3)

Mystère Barton, 1948 (Burel 4, Spaak 4)

Mystère de la chambre jaune, 1930 (L'Herbier 2, Burel 4, Meerson 4)

Mystère de la chambre jaune, 1948 (Modot 3, Reggiani 3, Douy 4)

Mystère de la Tour Eiffel, 1927 (Duvivier 2)

Mystère de l'Atelier Quinze, 1957 (Marker 2, Resnais 2, Cloquet 4, Delerue 4)

Mystères de l'ombre, 1915 (Gaumont 4)

Mystères de Paris, 1922 (Fresnay 3, Modot 3)

Mystères de Paris, 1935 (Auric 4)

Mystères de Paris, 1943 (Barsacq 4, Burel 4)

Mysteries, 1968 (Markopoulos 2)

Mystère du Palace Hôtel, 1953 (D'Eaubonne 4)

Mystère du Quai Conti, 1950 (Delerue 4)

Mystère Imberger, 1934 (Modot 3)

Mystère Koumiko, 1964 (Takemitsu 4)

Mystère Picasso, 1956 (Auric 4, Colpi 4, Renoir 4)

Mystère Saint-Val, 1945 (Fernandel 3)

Mysteries, 1978 (Müller 4)

Mysteries of India. See Indische Grabmal, 1921

Mysteries of New York. See Reggie Mixes In, 1916

Mysteries of the Novgorod Fair. See Taina niegorodskoi yamarki, 1915

Mysterious. See Chikyu boeigun, 1957

Mysterious Avenger, 1936 (Rogers 3)

Mysterious Box. See Boîte à malice, 1903

Mysterious Cafe, 1901 (Porter 2)

Mysterious Castle in the Carpathians. See Tajemstvi hradu v Karpatech, 1982

Mysterious Cowboy, 1952 (Terry 4)

Mysterious Crossing, 1936 (Krasner 4)

Mysterious Desperado, 1949 (Musuraca 4)

Mysterious Dr. Fu Manchu, 1929 (Arthur 3, Johnson 3, Zukor 4)

Mysterious House of Dr. C., 1976 (Terry-Thomas 3)

Mysterious Island, 1926 (Tourneur 2)

Mysterious Island, 1929 (Barrymore 3, Basevi 3, Gibbons 4, Mayer 4)

Mysterious Island, 1952 (Katzman 4)

Mysterious Island, 1961 (Greenwood 3, Lom 3, Harryhausen 4, Herrmann 4)

Mysterious Island. See Ile mystérieuse, 1973

Mysterious Island of Captain Nemo. See Isola misteriosa e il capitano Nemo, 1973

Mysterious Jug, 1937 (Lantz 4)

Mysterious Lady, 1928 (Niblo 2, Garbo 3, Booth 4, Daniels 4, Gibbons 4, Mayer 4, Meredyth 4)

Mysterious Lodger, 1914 (Costello 3)

Mysterious Lover of Mrs. White. See Hakufujin no yoren, 1956

Mysterious Mr. Davis, 1936 (Autant-Lara 2, Sim 3, Prévert 4)

Mysterious Mr. Moto, 1938 (Lorre 3)

Mysterious Mr. Wong, 1935 (Lugosi 3)

Mysterious Mose, 1938 (Fleischer 4)

Mysterious Mrs. M, 1917 (Weber 2)

Mysterious Mystery, 1914 (Lawrence 3)

Mysterious Mystery, 1924 (Roach 4)

Mysterious Pilot, 1937 (Canutt 4)

Mysterious Portrait. See Portrait mystérieux, 1899

Mysterious Rider, 1927 (Schulberg 4)

Mysterious Rider, 1938 (Harlan 4, Head 4)

Mysterious Rider, 1943 (Crabbe 3)

Mysterious Rose, 1914 (Ford 2)

Mysterious Shot, 1914 (Crisp 3)

Mysterious Stranger, 1947 (Terry 4)

Mysterious Stranger, 1981 (Lassally 4)

Mysterium, 1978 (Clarke 2)

Mystery at Fire Island, 1982 (Lassally 4)

Mystery at Monte Carlo. See Revenge at Monte Carlo, 1933

Mystery Castle in the Carpathians. See Tajemny hrad v Karpatech, 1981

Mystery House, 1938 (Sheridan 3)

Mystery in Mexico, 1948 (Wise 2)
Mystery in the Moonlight, 1947 (Terry 4)
Mystery Lake, 1953 (Crosby 4)
Mystery Man, 1923 (Roach 4)
Mystery Man, 1944 (Harlan 4)
Mystery Mountain, 1934 (Autry 3, Canutt 4,
    Eason 4)
Mystery of Blood. *See* Tajemství krve, 1953
Mystery of Brayton Court, 1914 (Costello 3)
Mystery of Edwin Drood, 1935 (Rains 3,
    Balderston 4, D'Agostino 4, Fulton 4)
Mystery of Leaping Fish, 1916 (Love 3)
Mystery of Marie Roget, 1942 (Salter 4)
Mystery of Mr. Wong, 1939 (Karloff 3)
Mystery of Mr. X, 1934 (Montgomery 3,
    Adrian 4)
Mystery of Monster Island. *See* Misterio en
    la isla de los monstruos, 1980
Mystery of Oberwald. *See* Mistero di
    Oberwald, 1981
Mystery of Picasso. *See* Mystère Picasso,
    1956
Mystery of Pine Tree Camp, 1913
    (Olcott 2)
Mystery of Room 643, 1914 (Bushman 3)

Mystery of the Black Jungle. *See* e Misteri
    della jungla nera, 1953
Mystery of the Blue Room. *See* Záhada
    modrého pokoje, 1933
Mystery of the Hindu Image, 1913 (Walsh 2)
Mystery of the Jewel Casket, 1905 (Bitzer 4)
Mystery of the Leaping Fish, 1916
    (Browning 2, Fleming 2, Fairbanks 3,
    Brown 4, Emerson 4)
Mystery of the Marie Celeste. *See* Phantom
    Ship, 1935
Mystery of the Night. *See* Stíny, 1921
Mystery of the Poisoned Pool, 1914
    (Rosher 4)
Mystery of the Sleeper Trunk, 1909
    (Olcott 2)
Mystery of the Wax Museum, 1933
    (Curtiz 2, Wray 3, Blanke 4, Grot 4,
    Orry-Kelly 4, Wallis, 4)
Mystery of the Yellow Aster Mine, 1913
    (Reid 3)
Mystery of the Yellow Room, 1957 (Von
    Sternberg 2)
Mystery of Wentworth Castle. *See* Doomed
    to Die, 1940

Mystery of Wickham Hall, 1914
    (Meredyth 4)
Mystery Ranch, 1932 (Johnson 3, August 4,
    Friedhofer 4)
Mystery Road, 1921 (Hitchcock 2)
Mystery Sea Raider, 1940 (Dmytryk 2,
    Dreier 4, Head 4)
Mystery Squadron, 1933 (Canutt 4)
Mystery Street, 1950 (Brooks 2, Sturges 2,
    Lanchester 3, Alton 4, Mayer 4)
Mystery Submarine, 1950 (Sirk 2, Boyle 4)
Mystery Train, 1989 (Jarmusch 2,
    Müller 4)
Mystery Woman, 1915 (Meredyth 4)
Mystery Woman, 1935 (Nichols 4)
Mystic, 1925 (Browning 2, Gibbons 4,
    Young 4)
Mystic Pink, 1976 (McKimson 4)
Mystic Swing, 1900 (Porter 2)
Mystical Flame. *See* Flamme merveilleuse,
    1903
Mystical Lovemaking. *See* Drame chez les
    fantoches, 1908
Mystical Maid of Jamasha Pass, 1911
    (Dwan 2)

N

N.E.L. Offshore News, 1975 (Arnold 4)
N.I. ni-c'est fini, 1908 (Cohl 4)
N.P., 1972 (Thulin 3)
N.P. il segreto, 1971 (Papas 3)
N.U., 1948 (Fusco 4)
N.Y. City Fire Dept., 1903 (Bitzer 4)
N. or N.W. *See* N or NW, 1938
N or NW, 1938 (Cavalcanti 2, Lye 4)
Na kometě, 1970 (Zeman 4)
Na livadi, 1957 (Mimica 4)
N'a pris les dés. *See* Eden et après, 1971
Na samotě u lesa, 1977 (Menzel 2)
Na sluneční straně, 1933 (Stallich 4)
Na tý louce zelený, 1936 (Heller 4)
Na viershina slavy, 1916 (Mozhukin 3)
Naaz, 1954 (Biswas 4)
Nabongo, 1944 (Crabbe 3)
Nacer en Leningrado, 1977 (Solas 2)
Nach dem Gesetz, 1919 (Nielsen 3)
Nach dem Sturm, 1950 (Schell 3)
Nach Meinem letzten Umzug, 1970
　(Syberberg 2)
Nach zwanzig Jahren, 1918 (Jannings 3)
Nacht, 1985 (Syberberg 2)
Nacht auf Goldenhall, 1920 (Veidt 3)
Nacht der Einbrecher, 1921 (Planer 4)
Nacht der Entscheidung, 1931
　(Tschechowa 3, Veidt 3)
Nacht der Entscheidung, 1938 (Negri 3)
Nacht der grossen Liebe, 1933 (Fröhlich 3,
　Wagner 4)
Nacht der Konigin Isabeau, 1920 (Wiene 2,
　Kortner 3)
Nacht der Medici, 1922 (Krauss 3)
Nacht der Verwandlung, 1935 (Fröhlich 3)
Nacht des Grauens, 1912 (Porten 3,
　Messter 4)
Nacht des Grauens, 1916 (Krauss 3)
Nacht des Schreckens, 1929 (Kortner 3)
Nacht gehört uns, 1929 (Albers 3, Reisch 4)
Nacht in Venedig, 1934 (Gallone 2,
　Wiene 2)
Nacht mit dem Kaiser, 1936 (Warm 4)
Nachtbesuch in der Northernbank, 1921
　(Wagner 4)
Nachtdienst. *See* Milosierdzie platne z gory,
　1975
Nächte am Bosporus. *See* Mann, der den
　Mord beging, 1930
Nächte des Grauens, 1916 (Pick 2,
　Jannings 3)
Nächte von Port Said, 1931 (Homolka 3,
　Junge 4)
Nachtfalter, 1911 (Gad 2, Nielsen 3,
　Freund 4)
Nachtgestalten, 1921 (Veidt 3, Wegener 3,
　Dreier 4, Hoffmann 4)

Nachtkolonne, 1931 (Homolka 3,
　Tschechowa 3)
Nachts auf den Strassen, 1951 (Käutner 2,
　Albers 3)
Nachts auf den Strassen, 1952 (Pommer 4)
Nachts wann der Teufel kam, 1957
　(Siodmak 2)
Nachtsonne. *See* Sole anche di notte, 1990
Nacido para la música, 1959 (Rey 3)
Nackt unter Wölfen, 1963 (Mueller-Stahl 3)
Nackte und der Satan, 1959 (Warm 4)
Nad Nemanom rassvet, 1953 (Moskvin 4)
Nad propastí, 1921 (Heller 4)
Nada, 1974 (Chabrol 2, Rabier 4)
Nada Gang. *See* Nada, 1974
Nadan, 1951 (Anand 3)
Nadare, 1952 (Shindo 2)
Nadezhda, 1954 (Gerasimov 2)
Nadezhda, 1973 (Donskoi 2)
Nadie dijo nada, 1970 (Villagra 3)
Nadie escuchaba, 1988 (Almendros 4)
Nadine, 1987 (Benton 2, Bridges 3,
　Almendros 4)
Nadiya Ke Par, 1948 (Kumar 3)
Nadja à Paris, 1964 (Rohmer 2)
Nagana, 1933 (Douglas 3, Johnson 3)
Nagana, 1954 (Auric 4)
Nagare no fu: Doran, Yoake, 1974
　(Iwashita 3, Tsukasa 3)
Nagareru, 1956 (Takamine 3, Tanaka 3,
　Yamada 3)
Nagasaki no uta wa wasureji, 1952 (Kyo 3)
Nagasaki no yuro, 1955 (Hasegawa 3)
Nagaya no shinshi roku, 1947 (Ryu 3)
Nagebushi Yasuke: Edo no maki, 1931
　(Hasegawa 3)
Nagebushi Yasuke: Michinoku no maki,
　1931 (Hasegawa 3)
Nagrody i odznaczenia, 1974 (Lomnicki 3)
Nagrodzone uczucie, 1957 (Lenica 4)
Nagurareta kochiyama, 1934 (Kinugasa 2)
Nagymama, 1916 (Korda 2, Korda 4)
Nahr el Hub, 1960 (Sharif 3)
Nai Roshani, 1941 (Biswas 4)
Naikai no wa, 1971 (Iwashita 3)
Nain, 1912 (Gaumont 4)
Nairobi Affair, 1980 (Heston 3)
Naïs, 1945 (Pagnol 2, Fernandel 3)
Naissance des cigognes, 1925 (Grémillon 2)
Naissance du cinéma, 1946 (Leenhardt 2)
Naissance du jour, 1981 (Sanda 3)
Naissance du plutonium, 1960 (Delerue 4)
Najma, 1943 (Mehboob 2)
Nakayoshi-ondo: Nippon ichi dayo, 1962
　(Hasegawa 3, Kyo 3)
Naked Alibi, 1954 (Grahame 3, Hayden 3,
　Hunter 4, Metty 4, Salter 4)

Naked and the Dead, 1958 (Walsh 2,
　Massey 3, Robertson 3, Herrmann 4, La
　Shelle 4)
Naked Angels, 1969 (Corman 2)
Naked Ape, 1973 (Alonzo 4)
Naked Autumn. *See* Mauvais Coups, 1960
Naked Cage, 1986 (Golan and Globus 4)
Naked City, 1948 (Brooks 2, Dassin 2,
　Fitzgerald 3, Daniels 4, Rozsa 4)
Naked Dawn, 1955 (Ulmer 2, Kennedy 3)
Naked Edge, 1961 (Cooper 3, Cushing 3,
　Kerr 3, Alwyn 4, Dillon 4, Mathieson 4)
Naked Eye, 1957 (Massey 3, Bernstein 4)
Naked Face, 1984 (Gould 3, Steiger 3, Golan
　and Globus 4)
Naked Face of Night. *See* Yoru no sugao,
　1958
Naked Gun, 1988 (Houseman 4)
Naked Heart. *See* Maria Chapdelaine, 1934
Naked Heart. *See* Maria Chapdelaine, 1950
Naked Jungle, 1954 (Lewis 2, Heston 3,
　Fulton 4, Haskin 4, Head 4, Laszlo 4,
　Maddow 4, Pal 4)
Naked Kiss, 1963 (Fuller 2, Cortez 4,
　Lourié 4)
Naked Lovers. *See* Naked Zoo, 1971
Naked Lunch, 1992 (Scheider 3)
Naked Maja, 1958 (Cervi 3, Gardner 3,
　Jennings 4, Rotunno 4)
Naked Night. *See* **Gycklarnas afton, 1953**
Naked Nineteen Year-Old. *See* Hadaka no
　jukyu-sai, 1970
Naked Paradise, 1957 (Corman 2, Crosby 4)
Naked Passion. *See* Pasión desnuda, 1953
Naked Prey, 1966 (Wilde 3)
Naked Runner, 1967 (Sinatra 3, Heller 4)
Naked Spur, 1953 (Mann 2, Leigh 3, Ryan 3,
　Stewart 3, Kaper 4)
Naked Street, 1955 (Bancroft 3, Quinn 3,
　Van Cleef 3, Crosby 4)
Naked Sun. *See* Hadaka no taiyo, 1958
Naked Tango, 1990 (Rey 3, Schifrin 4)
Naked Terror, 1961 (Price 3)
Naked Truth, 1958 (Terry-Thomas 3,
　Sellers 3, Rank 4)
Naked Zoo, 1971 (Hayworth 3)
Nakia, 1974 (Kennedy 3)
Nalla Thangal, 1935 (Roy 2)
Namak Halaal, 1982 (Bachchan 3, Patil 3)
Namak Haram, 1973 (Bachchan 3)
Name, Age, Occupation, 1942 (Clothier 4,
　Crosby 4)
Name of the Game Is Kill!, 1968
　(Zsigmond 4)
Name of the Rose. *See* Rosa dei nomi, 1986
　(Connery 3, Cristaldi 4, Delli Colli 4)
Name the Day, 1921 (Roach 4)

Name the Man, 1924 (Sjöström 2, Bosworth 3)

Namida no hanamichi, 1956 (Yamada 3)

Namida o shishi no tategami ni, 1962 (Shinoda 2, Yamamura 3, Takemitsu 4)

Namida-Gawa, 1967 (Yoda 4)

Naming of the Rawhide Queen, 1913 (Anderson 3)

Namkeen, 1982 (Azmi 3)

Namonaku mazushiku utsukushiku, 1961 (Takamine 3)

Nampu no oka, 1937 (Takamine 3)

Namus ve silah, 1971 (Güney 2)

Nan of Music Mountain, 1917 (Cruze 2, De Mille 2, Reid 3)

Nan o' the Backwoods, 1915 (Olcott 2)

Nan Paterson's Trial, 1905 (Bitzer 4)

Nana, 1926 (Autant-Lara 2, Renoir 2, Krauss 3, Braunberger 4)

Nana, 1934 (Ball 3, Banton 4, Day 4, Goldwyn 4, Newman 4, Toland 4)

Nana, 1954 (Christian-Jaque 2, Boyer 3, Jeanson 4, Matras 4)

Nana, 1982 (Golan and Globus 4, Morricone 4)

Nanami: Inferno of First Love. See Hatsukoi jigokuhen, 1968

Nanatsu no kao no Ginji, 1955 (Hasegawa 3, Kagawa 3)

Nanatsu no kao no onna, 1969 (Iwashita 3)

Nanatsu no umi: Teiso-hen, 1932 (Takamine 3)

Nancy Comes Home, 1918 (Gilbert 3)

Nancy Drew—Reporter, 1939 (Edeson 4)

Nancy from Nowhere, 1922 (Daniels 3, Folsey 4)

Nancy Goes to Rio, 1950 (Calhern 3, Miranda 3, Pasternak 4, Rose 4, Smith 4)

Nancy Steele Is Missing, 1937 (Carradine 3, Darwell 3, Lorre 3, McLaglen 3, Cronjager 4, Johnson 4)

Nangoku satsuma-uta, 1937 (Yamada 3)

Naniwa ereji, 1936 (Mizoguchi 2, Shimura 3, Shindo 3, Tanaka 3, Yamada 3, Yoda 4)

Naniwa hina, 1930 (Hasegawa 3)

Naniwa ni koi no monogatari, 1959 (Tanaka 3)

Naniwa onna, 1940 (Yoda 4)

Nankai no daiketto, 1966 (Tsuburaya 4)

Nankai no hanatabe, 1942 (Hayasaka 4, Tsuburaya 4)

Nankai no joka, 1950 (Yamamura 3)

Nankyoku monogatari, 1983 (Okada 3)

Nanny, 1965 (Davis 3, Carreras 4, Sangster 4)

Nanny Dear. See Tata Mia, 1986

Nanook of the North, 1922 (Flaherty 2)

Nanou, 1986 (Day Lewis 3)

Nan's Diplomacy, 1911 (Lawrence 3)

Nanshin josei, 1939 (Shindo 2)

Nanu, sie kennen Korff noch nicht?, 1938 (Rasp 3)

Nao Do Egarah, 1957 (Burman 4)

Nao ou a vã gloria de mandar, 1990 (Branco 4)

Naomi and Rufus Kiss, 1964 (Warhol 2)

Napatia, The Greek Singer, 1912 (Bushman 3)

Naples au baiser de feu, 1928 (Manès 3, Modot 3)

Naples au baiser de feu, 1937 (Dalio 3, Simon 3, Achard 4)

Naples Is a Battlefield, 1944 (Clayton 2)

Napló gyermekeimnek, 1982 (Nowicki 3)

Napló szerelmeimnek, 1987 (Nowicki 3)

Napoleon, 1927 (Gance 2, Volkov 2, Artaud 3, Manès 3, Burel 4, Honegger 4, Lourié 4)

Napoléon, 1954 (Guitry 2, Von Stroheim 2, Welles 2, Brasseur 3, Cervi 3, Darrieux 3, Gabin 3, Gélin 3, Marais 3, Montand 3, Morgan 3, Presle 3, Reggiani 3, Schell 3, Cloquet 4, Lourié 4)

Napoleon à Sainte-Hélène, 1929 (Wagner 4)

Napoleon and Josephine: A Love Story, 1987 (Perkins 3)

Napoleon and Samantha, 1972 (Douglas 3, Foster 3)

Napoleon auf St. Helena, 1929 (Krauss 3)

Napoléon Bonaparte, 1934 (Gance 2)

Napoleon Bunny-Part, 1956 (Blanc 4, Freleng 4)

Napoleon Crossing the Alps, 1903 (Gaudio 4)

Napoléon II, l'aiglon, 1961 (Cassel 3)

Napoleon und die kleine Wäscherin, 1920 (Dreier 4)

Napoléon vu par Abel Gance. See **Napoleon, 1927**

Napoleon-Gaz, 1925 (Enei 4)

Napoleon's Barber, 1928 (Ford 2)

Napoleons kleiner Brüder. See So sind die Männer, 1922

Napoleon's Little Brother. See So sind die Männer, 1922

Napoleon's Lucky Stone, 1913 (Cruze 2)

Napoletani a Milano, 1953 (Age and Scarpelli 4)

Napoli che non muore, 1939 (De Sica 2)

Napoli d'altri tempi, 1938 (De Sica 2)

Napoli e le terre d'oltremare, 1940 (Blasetti 2)

Napoli milionaria, 1950 (De Laurentiis 4, Gherardi 4, Rota 4)

Naprawde wczoraj, 1963 (Tyszkiewicz 3)

När kärleken dödar, 1913 (Stiller 2, Sjöström 2, Jeanzon 4, Magnusson 4)

Nar Kärleken kom till Byn, 1950 (Thulin 3)

När konstnärer älska, 1914 (Stiller 2, Jaenzon 4)

När larmklockan ljuder, 1913 (Stiller 2, Jaenzon 4)

När svärmor regerar, 1912 (Stiller 2)

Nar syrenerna blommar, 1952 (Nykvist 4)

Nära livet, 1958 (Andersson 3, Dahlbeck 3, Josephson 3, Thuslin 3, Von Sydow 3)

Narayamabushi-ko, 1958 (Tanaka 3)

Narazumono, 1956 (Mifune 3)

Narcissus, 1973 (McLaren 4)

Narcissus/Echo, 1971 (Braunberger 4)

Narcose, 1929 (Balàzs 4)

Narcosis. See Narcose, 1929

Narkose, 1929 (Schüfftan 4)

Narr seiner Liebe, 1929 (Tschechowa 3, Andrejew 4, Planer 4)

Narren im Schnee, 1938 (Ondra 3)

Narrow Corner, 1933 (Bellamy 3, Gaudio 4, Orry-Kelly 4)

Narrow Escape, 1913 (Loos 4)

Narrow Margin, 1990 (Hackman 3)

Narrow Path, 1918 (Miller 4)

Narrow Road, 1912 (Griffith 2, Pickford 3, Bitzer 4)

Narrow Trail, 1918 (Hart 3, August 4, Ince 4)

Narrow Valley, 1921 (Hepworth 2)

Naruto hicho, 1957 (Hasegawa 3)

Naše bláznivá rodina, 1968 (Stallich 4)

Naše Karkulka. See Drahoušek Klementýna, 1959

Nashörner, 1963 (Lenica 4)

Nashville, 1975 (Altman 2, Rudolph 2, Black 3, Chaplin 3, Christie 3, Gould 3)

Nasilje na Trgu, 1961 (Andersson 3, Crawford 3)

Nasty Habits, 1976 (Evans 3, Jackson 3, Mercouri 3, Page 3, Wallach 3, Slocombe 4)

Nasty Quacks, 1945 (Blanc 4, Stalling 4)

Nasty Rabbit, 1965 (Kovacs 4, Zsigmond 4)

Nasu no imoto, 1972 (Toda 4)

Naszdal, 1918 (Lugosi 3)

Nat Pinkerton, 1921 (Lugosi 3)

Nata di marzo, 1958 (Scola 2, Age and Scarpelli 4, Ponti 4)

Natale al campo 119, 1947 (De Sica 2, Fabrizi 3)

Natale che quasi non fu. See Christmas That Almost Wasn't, 1966

Natale in Casa di Appuntamento, 1976 (Borgnine 3)

Natalka Poltavka, 1938 (Ulmer 2)

Natasha Rostova, 1915 (Mozhukin 3)

Nate and Hayes, 1983 (Hughes 2)

Natercia, 1959 (Vierny 4)

Nathalie, 1957 (Piccoli 3)

Nathalie, 1975 (Müller 4)

Nathalie Granger, 1972 (Duras 2, Depardieu 3, Moreau 3, Cloquet 4)

Nathan der Weise, 1922 (Krauss 3)

National Barn Dance, 1944 (Benchley 4, Dreier 4, Head 4)

National Health, 1973 (Hoskins 3)

National Lampoon's Animal House, 1978 (Landis 2, Belushi 3, Sutherland 3, Bernstein 4)

National Lampoon's Class Reunion, 1982 (Hughes 2)

National Lampoon's European Vacation, 1985 (Hughes 2)

National Lampoon's Movie Madness, 1982 (Widmark 3)

National Lampoon's Vacation, 1983 (Hughes 2)

National Velvet, 1944 (Brown 2, Crisp 3, Lansbury 3, Rooney 3, Taylor 3, Berman 4, Irene 4, Mayer 4, Stothart 4)

Native Country. See Strana rodnaya, 1942

Native Drums. See Tam Tam Mayumba, 1955

Native Earth, 1946 (Finch 3)

Native Land, 1942 (Robeson 3, Maddow 4)

Native Son, 1986 (Baker 3, Dillon 3, Page 3, Van Runkle 4)

Nativity, 1978 (Schrifin 4)

Natsu no imoto, 1972 (Takemitsu 4)

Natsumaturi sando-gasa, 1951 (Yamada 3)

Natt i hamn, 1943 (Fischer 4, Björnstrand 3)

Natt på Glimmingehus, 1954 (Andersson 3)

Nattbarn, 1956 (Andersson 3, Nykvist 4)

Natten Ijus, 1957 (Björnstrand 3)

Nattens väv, 1955 (Sjöström 3)

Nattlek, 1966 (Zetterling 2, Thulin 3)

Nattmarschen i Sankt Eriks Gränd, 1909 (Magnusson 4)

Nattvardsgästerna, 1963 (Björnstrand 3, Thulin 3, Von Sydow 3)

Natura e chimica, 1959 (Olmi 2)

Natural, 1984 (Levinson 2, Close 3, Duvall 3, Redford 3, Towne 4)

Natural Born Salesman. *See* Earthworm Tractors, 1936

Natural Enemies, 1979 (Ferrer 3)

Natural Wonders of the West, 1938 (Hoch 4)

Naturalisée, 1962 (Delerue 4)

Nature in the Wrong, 1933 (Roach 4)

Nature morte, 1966 (Guillemot 4)

Nature morte, 1970 (Lenica 4)

Nature of the Beast, 1919 (Hepworth 2)

Nature retrouvée, 1968 (Gélin 3)

Nature's Workshop, 1933 (Lantz 4)

Nau Do Gyarah, 1957 (Anand 3)

Naufrageurs, 1959 (Vanel 3, Cloquet 4)

Naufragio, 1977 (Hermosillo 2)

Naughty Baby, 1928 (Fort 4, Haller 4)

Naughty Blue Knickers. *See* Follies d'elodie, 1981

Naughty Boy, 1962 (Burman 4)

Naughty But Mice, 1939 (Jones 4)

Naughty But Nice, 1927 (Moore 3, Young 3, Folsey 4, Wilson 4)

Naughty But Nice, 1939 (Powell 3, Reagan 3, Sheridan 3, Mercer 4, Wald 4)

Naughty Duck, 1950 (Popescu-Gopo 4)

Naughty Flirt, 1931 (Loy 3)

Naughty Marietta, 1935 (Van Dyke 2, Eddy 3, Lanchester 3, MacDonald 3, Adrian 4, Daniels 4, Gibbons 4, Goodrich 4, Mayer 4, Shearer 4, Stothart 4, Stromberg 4, Tiomkin 4)

Naughty! Naughty!, 1918 (Barnes 4, Sullivan 4)

Naughty Neighbors, 1939 (Blanc 4, Clampett 4, Stalling 4)

Naughty Nineties, 1945 (Abbott and Costello 3, Johnson 3)

Nauka blizej zycia, (Munk 2)

Naukri, 1954 (Roy 2)

Naulahka, 1918 (Grot 4, Menzies 4, Miller 4)

Nausicaa, 1970 (Varda 2)

Navajo, 1952 (Miller 4)

Navajo Joe. *See* Dollaro a testa, 1966

Naval Bomber Fleet. *See* Kaigun bakugekitai, 1940

Nave bianca, 1941 (Rossellini 2)

Navigation marchande, 1954 (Decaë 4)

Navigator, 1924 (Keaton 2, Crisp 3, Johnson 3, Bruckman 4, Mayer 4, Schenck 4)

Navire des hommes perdus. *See* Schiff der verlorene Menschen, 1929

Navire Night, 1978 (Duras 2, Sanda 3)

Navrat mrtvého. *See* Manželé paní Mileny, 1921

Návrat ztaceného syna, 1966 (Brejchová 3)

Navy, 1930 (Lantz 4)

Navy Blue and Gold, 1937 (Wood 2, Barrymore 3, Stewart 3, Young 3, Gibbons 4, Seitz 4)

Navy Blue Days, 1925 (Laurel and Hardy 3)

Navy Blues, 1929 (Brown 2, Gibbons 4)

Navy Blues, 1941 (Bacon 2, Sheridan 3, Gaudio 4, Howe 4, Mercer 4, Polito 4, Wald 4, Wallis 4)

Navy Comes Through, 1942 (Cooper 3, Dunn 4, Musuraca 4)

Navy Gravy, 1925 (Laurel and Hardy 3)

Navy Seals, 1990 (Alonzo 4)

Navy Secrets, 1939 (Wray 3)

Navy Spy, 1937 (Lewis 2)

Navy Steps Out. *See* Girl, a Guy, and a Gob, 1941

Navy Versus the Night Monsters, 1965 (Cortez 4)

Navy Wife. *See* Beauty's Daughter, 1935

Navy Wife, 1956 (Bennett 3, Salter 4, Wanger 4)

Navy's Special Boy Sailors. *See* Kaigun tokubetsu nenshouhei, 1972

Naxalites, 1980 (Patil 3, Abbas 4)

Naya Daur, 1957 (Kumar 3)

Naya Sansaar, 1943 (Abbas 4)

Naya Zamana, 1971 (Burman 4)

Nayak, 1966 (Chandragupta 4, Datta 4, Mitra 4)

Nayamashiki koro, 1926 (Tanaka 3)

Nayya, 1947 (Biswas 4)

Nazarín, 1958 (Buñuel 2, Figueroa 4)

Naze kanojo wa sonatta ka, 1956 (Kagawa 3)

Nazi Agent, 1942 (Dassin 2, Veidt 3, Schary 4, Stradling 4)

Nazi Hunter: The Beate Karsfield Story, 1986 (Page 3)

Nazi Hunter: The Search for Klaus Barbie. *See* Nazi Hunter: The Beate Karsfield Story, 1986

Nazis Strike. *See* **Why We Fight series, 1943–45**

Nazraana, 1961 (Kapoor 2)

Nazrana, 1987 (Patil 3)

Nazty Nuisance, 1942 (Roach 4)

Ne bougeons plus, 1903 (Guy 2)

Ne compromettez pas vos loisirs, 1949 (Decaë 4)

Né de père inconnu, 1950 (Renoir 4)

Ne jouez pas avec les Martiens, 1967 (Broca 2)

Ne le criez pas sur les toits, 1942 (Fernandel 3, Burel 4)

Ne nous fâchons pas, 1966 (Audiard 4)

Ne pleure pas, 1977 (Vanel 3)

Né pour la musique. *See* Nacido para la música, 1959

Ne réveillez pas un flic qui dort, 1988 (Delon 3, Reggiani 3, Coutard 4)

Ne tuez pas Dolly!, 1937 (Delannoy 2)

Nea, 1976 (Presle 3, Evein 4)

Neanderthal Man, 1953 (Dupont 2, Cortez 4)

Neapolitan Carousel. *See* Carosella napolitano, 1953

Neapolitan Mouse, 1953 (Hanna and Barbera 4)

Near Death, 1989 (Wiseman 2)

Near Dublin, 1924 (Laurel and Hardy 3, Roach 4)

Near to Earth, 1913 (Griffith 2, Barrymore 3, Bitzer 4)

Nearer My God to Thee, 1917 (Hepworth 2)

Nearly a Burglar's Bride, 1914 (Loos 4)

Nearly a King, 1916 (Barrymore 3, Menjou 3)

Nearly a Lady, 1915 (Bosworth 3, Marion 4)

Nearly Married, 1917 (Barthelmess 3, Edeson 4)

Near-Tragedy, 1911 (Sennett 2)

'Neath Brooklyn Bridge, 1942 (Katzman 4)

'Neath Canadian Skies, 1946 (Eason 4)

'Neath the Arizona Skies, 1934 (Wayne 3, Canutt 4)

Nebraskan, 1953 (Van Cleef 3)

Necesito dinero, 1951 (Infante 3)

Necessary Evil, 1925 (Folsey 4)

Necessary Parties, 1987 (Arkin 3)

Nechci nic slyšet, 1978 (Brejchová 3)

Neck and Neck, 1931 (Brennan 3)

Neck and Neck, 1942 (Terry 4)

Neck 'n Neck, 1927 (Disney 4)

Necklace, 1909 (Griffith 2, Lawrence 3, Pickford 3, Bitzer 4)

Necklace of Ramses, 1914 (Ingram 2)

Necromancy, 1973 (Welles 2, Hoch 4)

Ned Kelly, 1970 (Richardson 2, Fisher 4)

Ned McCobb's Daughter, 1929 (Lombard 3)

Neděle ve všedni, 1962 (Brejchová 3)

Nederland in 7 Lessen, 1964 (Hepburn 3)

Neecha Nagar, 1945 (Shankar 4)

Neel Kamal, 1947 (Kapoor 2)

Ne'er-Do-Well, 1916 (Selig 4)

Ne'er-Do-Well, 1923 (Haller 4)

Nefertite—Regina del Nilo, 1961 (Price 3)

Negatives, 1968 (Jackson 3)

Neglected Wives, 1920 (Haller 4)

Negoto dorobo, 1964 (Iwashita 3)

Negra consentida, 1948 (Alcoriza 4)

Nègre blanc, 1912 (Gance 2)

Nègre blanc, 1925 (Meerson 4)

Negro Soldier, 1944 (Capra 2)

Neige était sale, 1953 (Gélin 3)

Neiges, 1954 (Cloquet 4)

Neighbor Trouble, 1932 (Sennett 2)

Neighborhood House, 1935 (Roach 4)

Neighbors, 1907 (Bitzer 4)

Neighbors, 1911 (Sennett 2)

Neighbors, 1921 (Keaton 2)

Neighbors, 1952 (McLaren 4)

Neighbors. *See* Sąsiedzi, 1969

Neighbors, 1981 (Belushi 3)

Neighbor's Wife and Mine. *See* Madamu to nyobo, 1931

Neighbors' Wives, 1933 (Eason 4)

Neigungsehe. *See* Familie Buchholz, 1944

Neither by Day nor Night, 1973 (Robinson 3)

Neither in Nor Out. *See* Se ki, se be, 1919

Nejlepší ženská mého života, 1968 (Frič 2)

Neko to Shozo to futari no onna, 1956 (Kagawa 3, Yamada 3)

Nekri Politeia, 1951 (Papas 3)

Nel blu dipinto di blu, 1959 (De Sica 2, Di Venanzo 4, Zavattini 4)

Nel Centro del Mirino, 1983 (Bozzetto 4)

Nel gorgo della vita. *See* Lacrimae rerum, 1917

Nel nome del padre, 1971 (Cristaldi 4)

Nel segno di Roma, 1959 (Cervi 3)

Nela, 1980 (Theodorakis 4)

Nelken in Aspik, 1976 (Mueller-Stahl 3)

Nell Dale's Men Folks, 1916 (Borzage 2)

Nell Gwyn, 1935 (Wilcox 2, Neagle 3, Young 4)

Nell Gwynne, 1927 (Wilcox 2)

Nell of the Pampas, 1911 (Dwan 2)

Nell stretta morsa del ragno, 1971 (Kinski 3)

Nella città l'inferno, 1958 (Magnani 3, Masina 3, Sordi 3, Cecchi D'Amico 4)

Nella fornace, 1915 (Bertini 3)

Nell'anno del signore, 1969 (Cardinale 3, Magnani 3)

Nellie the Beautiful Cloak Model, 1924 (Bosworth 3)

Nell's Eugenic Wedding, 1914 (Loos 4)

Nell's Yells, 1939 (Iwerks 4)

Nelly la gigolette, 1914 (Bertini 3)

Nelly Raintseva, 1916 (Bauer 2)

Nelly's Folly, 1961 (Blanc 4, Jones 4)

Nellys Forlovense, 1913 (Psilander 3)

Nelly's Version, 1983 (York 3)

Nelson Affair. *See* Bequest to the Nation, 1973

Nelson Touch. *See* Corvette K-225, 1943

N'embrassez pas votre bonne, 1909 (Linder 3)

N'embrassez pas votre bonne, 1914 (Linder 3)

Nemesis, 1921 (Gallone 2)

Nemico di mia moglie, 1959 (De Sica 2, Mastroianni 3, Di Venanzo 4)

Nemrod et Compagnie, 1911 (Modot 3)

Nemureru bijo, 1968 (Yoshimura 2)

Nemuri Kyoshiro burai hikae: Majin jigoku, 1958 (Yamada 3)

Nemuri Kyoshiro no manji-giri, 1969 (Yoda 4)

Nene, 1924 (Modot 3)

Neni Sirotek Jako Sirotek, 1986 (Brodský 3)

Není stále zamračeno, 1950 (Kučera 4)

Neobychainye priklucheniya Mistera Vesta v stranye bolshevikov, 1924 (Kuleshov 2)

Neokonchennaya povest, 1955 (Bondarchuk 3)

Neon Ceiling, 1971 (Grant 3)

Neon Empire, 1989 (Anhalt 4)

Nephew of Paris, 1934 (Garmes 4)

Neppu, 1943 (Hara 3)

Neptune Disaster. *See* Neptune Factor, 1973

Neptune Factor, 1973 (Borgnine 3, Pidgeon 3, Schifrin 4)

Neptune Nonsense, 1936 (Messmer 4)

Neptune's Daughter, 1912 (Bushman 3)

Neptune's Daughter, 1914 (Brenon 2)

Neptune's Daughter, 1949 (Williams 3, Blanc 4, Hanna and Barbera 4, Irene 4, Mayer 4, Rosher 4)

Nero, 1944 (Sim 3)

Nero and the Burning of Rome, 1908 (Porter 2)

Nero Veneziamo, 1978 (Donaggio 4)

Nero Wolfe, 1977 (Baxter 3)

Nerone, 1930 (Blasetti 2)

Nerone e Messalina, 1953 (Cervi 3, Delli Colli 4)

Nero's Mistress. *See* Mio figlio Nerone, 1956

Nero's Weekend. *See* Mio figlio Nerone, 1956

Nertsery Rhymes, 1933 (Three Stooges 3)

Nerve and Gasoline, 1916 (Laurel and Hardy 3)

Nervo and Knox, 1926 (Crazy Gang 3)

Nervous Shakedown, 1947 (Bruckman 4)

Nervous Wreck, 1926 (Bosworth 3)

Nerze Nachts am Strassenrand, 1973 (Staudte 2)

Nessa no byakuran, 1951 (Yamamura 3, Hayasaka 4)

Nessa no chikai, 1940 (Hasegawa 3, Shindo 3)

Nessuno o tutti—Matti da slegare, 1974 (Bellocchio 2)

Nessuno torna indietro, 1943 (Blasetti 2, De Sica 2, Germi 2, Cervi 3)

Nest, 1927 (Stradling 4)

Nest, 1943 (Anger 2)

Nest. *See* Gniazdo, 1974

Nesting. *See* Phobia, 1979

Nesting, 1981 (Grahame 3)

Net, 1952 (Lom 3, Rank 4)

Net. *See* Madriguera, 1969

Netchaiev est de retour, 1990 (Montand 3)

Netherlands America, 1943 (Van Dongen 4)

Netsuaisha, 1961 (Yamamura 3)

Nettezza urbana. *See* N.U., 1948

Nettoyage par le vide, 1908 (Feuillade 2)

Network, 1976 (Lumet 2, Dunaway 3, Duvall 3, Finch 3, Holden 3, Chayefsky 4, Roizman 4)

Netz, 1975 (Kinski 3)

Neue Dalila, 1918 (Gad 2)

Neues vom Hexer, 1965 (Kinski 3)

Neuf à trois, ou la journée d'une vedette, 1957 (Decaë 4)

Neuf étages tout acier, 1960 (Delerue 4, Kosma 4)

Neunzing Nächte and ein Tag. *See* Sette contro la morte, 1964

Neurasia, 1968 (Schroeter 2)

Neutral Port, 1939 (Rank 4)

Neutron Bomb Incident. *See* Teheran Incident, 1979

Neuvaine, 1914 (Feuillade 2)

Nevada, 1927 (Cooper 3, Powell 3)

Nevada, 1934 (Crabbe 3)

Nevada, 1944 (Mitchum 3)

Nevada City, 1941 (Rogers 3)

Nevada Kid. *See* Conde Dracula, 1970

Nevada Smith, 1966 (Hathaway 2, Kennedy 3, Malden 3, McQueen 3, Ballard 4, Hayes 4, Head 4, Levine 4, Newman 4)

Nevada Smith, 1975 (Hayes 4)

Nevadan, 1950 (Malone 3, Scott 3, Brown 4)

Never a Dull Moment, 1943 (Pangborn 3, Salter 4)

Never a Dull Moment, 1950 (Dunne 3, MacMurray 3, Wood 3, Banton 4, Walker 4)

Never a Dull Moment, 1968 (Robinson 3, Ellenshaw 4)

Never Again!, 1910 (Sennett 2, Pickford 3)

Never Again, 1915 (Mix 3)

Never Again, 1916 (Laurel and Hardy 3)

Never Fear, 1950 (Lupino 3, Polglase 4)

Never Forget, 1991 (Mancini 4)

Never Give a Sucker an Even Break, 1941 (Dumont 3, Fields 3, Pangborn 3)

Never Give an Inch. *See* Sometimes a Great Notion, 1971

Never Kick a Woman, 1936 (Fleischer 4)

Never Let Go, 1960 (Sellers 3, Barry 4, Challis 4)

Never Let Me Go, 1953 (Brown 2, Daves 2, Gable 3, More 3, Tierney 3, Junge 4, Krasker 4, Rank 4)

Never Look Back, 1952 (Carreras 4)

Never Love a Stranger, 1957 (McQueen 3, Garmes 4)

Never on Sunday. *See* Pote tin kryiaki, 1960

Never Say Die, 1939 (Hope 3, Dreier 4, Head 4)

Never Say Goodbye, 1946 (Flynn 3, McDaniel 3, Diamond 4, Edeson 4, Grot 4)

Never Say Goodbye, 1956 (Sirk 2, Eastwood 3, Hudson 3, Sanders 3, Boyle 4)

Never Say Never Again, 1983 (Brandauer 3, Connery 3, Von Sydow 3, Legrand 4, Slocombe 4)

Never Should Have Told You, 1937 (Fleischer 4)

Never Sock a Baby, 1939 (Fleischer 4)

Never So Few, 1959 (Sturges 2, Bronson 3, Henreid 3, Lollobrigida 3, McQueen 3, Sinatra 3, Daniels 4, Friedhofer 4, Rose 4)

Never Steal Anything Small, 1958 (Cagney 3, Lederer 4)

Never Strike a Woman, Even with a Flower. *See* Zenu ani květinou neuhodiš, 1966

Never Strike a Woman with a Flower. *See* Spadla s měsíce, 1966

Never Take Candy from a Stranger. *See* Never Take Sweets from a Stranger, 1960

Never Take No for an Answer, 1952 (Havelock-Allan 4, Heller 4)

Never Take No for an Answer, 1959 (Rota 4)

Never Take Sweets from a Stranger, 1960 (Carreras 4, Francis 4)

Never the Twain Shall Meet, 1925 (Tourneur 2, Karloff 3)

Never the Twain Shall Meet, 1931 (Van Dyke 2, Howard 3)

Never Too Late, 1965 (O'Sullivan 3)

Never Too Old, 1919 (Sennett 2)

Never Too Old, 1926 (Laurel and Hardy 3, Roach 4)

Never Touched Me, 1919 (Daniels 3, Lloyd 3, Roach 4)

Never Trouble Trouble, 1931 (Oberon 3)

Never Wave at a WAC, 1953 (McLeod 2, Beavers 3, Russell 3, Bernstein 4, Daniels 4)

Never Weaken, 1921 (Lloyd 3, Roach 4)

Nevetö Szaszkia, 1916 (Korda 2)

Neveu de Beethoven, 1985 (Baye 3)

Neveu de Rameau, 1968 (Fresnay 3)

Neviditelní nepřátelé, 1950 (Brdečka 4)

Neviňátka, 1929 (Stallich 4)

Nevtelen vàr, 1920 (Lukas 3)

Nevtö Szaszkia, 1916 (Korda 4)

New Adventures of Don Juan. *See* Adventures of Don Juan, 1949

New Adventures of Get-Rich-Quick Wallingford, 1931 (Wood 2, Durante 3, MacArthur 4)

New Adventures of J. Rufus Wallingford, 1915 (Laurel and Hardy 3)

New Age of Fools. *See* Shin baka jidai, 1946

New Americans, 1945 (Vorkapich 4)

New Aunt, 1929 (Sennett 2, Hornbeck 4)

New Baby, 1911 (Sennett 2)

New Baby, 1913 (Sennett 2)

New Babylon. *See* **Novyi Vavilon, 1929**

New Bad Names. *See* Shin akumyo, 1961

New Bankroll, 1929 (Sennett 2)

New Britain, 1940 (Alwyn 4, Greene 4)

New Brooms, 1925 (Love 3)

New Butler, 1915 (Laurel and Hardy 3)

New Car, 1931 (Iwerks 4)

New Centurions, 1972 (Scott 3, Jones 4, Leven 4, Winkler 4)

New Champion, 1925 (Eason 4)

New Church Organ, 1912 (Bushman 3)

New Commandment, 1925 (Sweet 3, Haller 4)

New Conductor, 1913 (Sennett 2)

New Cowboy, 1911 (Ince 4)

New Cowpuncher, 1911 (Dwan 2)

New Deal Money, 1934 (Temple 3)

New Deal Show, 1937 (Fleischer 4)

New Delhi Times, 1985 (Mitra 4)

New Dress, 1911 (Griffith 2, Bitzer 4)

New Earth. *See* **Nieuwe Gronden, 1934**

New Earth. *See* Atarashiki tsuchi, 1937

New England Idyll, 1914 (Ince 4)

New England Visions Past and Future, 1976
(Emshwiller 2)

New Exploits of Elaine, 1915 (White 3)

New Faces, 1954 (Ballard 4, Horner 4)

New Faces of 1937, 1937 (Miller 3,
Epstein 4, Hunt 4, Polglase 4)

New Faith, 1911 (Bosworth 3)

New Fist of Fury, 1976 (Chan 3)

New Frontier, 1935 (Wayne 3)

New Frontier, 1939 (Jones 3, Wayne 3)

New Frontiers, 1940 (Ivens 2)

New Generation, 1932 (Grierson 2)

New Gentlemen. See Nouveaux Messieurs,
1928

New Gulliver. See Novy Gulliver, 1935

New Half-Back, 1929 (Sennett 2)

New Horizons. See **Vyborgskaya Storona,
1939**

New Horizons in Steel, 1977 (Benegal 2)

New House. See Novyi dom, 1947

New Interns, 1964 (Segal 3, Ballard 4)

New Janitor, 1914 (Sennett 2)

New Janko the Musician. See Nowy Janko
muzykant, 1960

New Kids, 1985 (Schifrin 4)

New Kind of Love, 1963 (Chevalier 3,
Newman 3, Ritter 3, Woodward 3,
Head 4)

New Klondike, 1926 (Milestone 2)

New Land. See Nybyggarna, 1972

New Leaf, 1971 (Matthau 3, May 4)

New Life, 1988 (Reynolds 4)

New Lot, 1936 (Dickinson 2)

New Lot, 1942 (Reed 2, Ustinov 3)

New Magdalene, 1910 (White 3)

New Magic, 1984 (Trumbull 4)

New Manager, 1911 (Bushman 3)

New Mexico, 1951 (Aldrich 2, Ayres 3)

New Minister, 1910 (Lawrence 3)

New Moon, 1919 (Talmadge 3)

New Moon, 1930 (Menjou 3, Adrian 4,
Booth 4, Mayer 4, Stothart 4)

New Moon, 1940 (Eddy 3, MacDonald 3,
Adrian 4, Daniels 4, Stothart 4)

New Morals for Old, 1932 (Loy 3,
Young 3)

New Movietone Follies of 1930. See Fox
Movietone Follies of 1930, 1930

New Neighbor, 1912 (Sennett 2, Normand 3)

New Operator, 1932 (Grierson 2)

New Order at Sjögårda. See Nyordning på
Sjögårda, 1944

New Orleans Uncensored, 1955 (Katzman 4)

New Rates, 1934 (Cavalcanti 2)

New School Teacher, 1924 (La Cava 2)

New Schoolmarm of Green River, 1913
(Anderson 3)

New Shawl, 1910 (Lawrence 3)

New Sheriff, 1913 (Anderson 3)

New Stenographer, 1911 (Bunny 3,
Costello 3)

New Superintendent, 1911 (Bosworth 3)

New Tale of Heike. See Shin Heike
monogatari, 1955

New Tale of the Taira Clan. See Shin Heike
monogatari, 1955

New Tales of the Taira Clan. See Shin Heike
monogatari, 1955

New Teacher, 1915 (Beery 3)

New Teacher, 1941 (Cushing 3)

New Toys, 1925 (Barthelmess 3, Webb 3)

New Trick, 1909 (Griffith 2, Bitzer 4)

New Typist, 1910 (White 3)

New Vision:, 1984 (Halas and Batchelor 4)

New Warriors Will Arise. See Vstanou noví
bojovníci, 1950

New Way. See Shindo: Akemi no make,
Ryota no maki, 1936

New Wine, 1941 (Estabrook 4, Korda 4)

New Wives' Conference. See Niizuma kaigi,
1949

New World. See Naya Sansaar, 1943

New World. See Nuite de Varennes, 1983

New Worlds for Old, 1936 (Rotha 2,
Alwyn 4)

New Year's Eve. See Sylvester: Tragödie
einer Nacht, 1923

New Years' Eve, 1929 (Astor 3)

New Year's Evil, 1981 (Golan and Globus 4)

New York, 1916 (Miller 4)

New York, 1927 (Powell 3, Hunt 4)

New York, 1950? (Leacock 2)

New York ballade, 1955 (Braunberger 4)

New York City—The Most, 1968
(Wallach 3)

New York Confidential, 1955 (Bancroft 3,
Crawford 3)

New York expresz kabel, 1921 (Lukas 3)

New York Eye and Ear Control, 1964
(Snow 2)

New York Girl, 1914 (Sennett 2)

New York Hat, 1912 (Griffith 2,
Barrymore 3, Gish 3, Marsh 3,
Pickford 3, Bitzer 4, Loos 4)

New York Lightboard, 1961 (McLaren 4)

New York, New York, 1977 (Scorsese 2, De
Niro 3, Minnelli 3, Kovacs 4, Leven 4,
Van Runkle 4, Winkler 4)

New York, New York Bis, 1984
(Akerman 2)

New York Nights, 1929 (Milestone 2,
Harlow 3, Jolson 3, Talmadge 3,
Furthman 4, Menzies 4, Schenck 4)

New York Stories, 1989 (Allen 2, Coppola 2,
Scorsese 2, Farrow 3, Giannini 3,
Nolte 3, Almendros 4, Nykvist 4,
Storaro 4, Tavoularis 4)

New York Town, 1941 (Vidor 2,
MacMurray 3, Preston 3, Dreier 4,
Head 4, Swerling 4)

New York University, 1952 (Van Dyke 2)

Newcomer, 1938 (Terry 4)

Newer Way, 1915 (Eason 4)

Newer Woman, 1914 (Crisp 3)

Newest Profession. See Never Wave at a
WAC, 1953

Newly Rich, 1922 (Roach 4)

Newly Rich, 1931 (Mankiewicz 2,
Lang 4)

Newlyweds, 1910 (Griffith 2, Sennett 2,
Pickford 3, Bitzer 4)

Newman Laugh-O-Grams, 1920 (Disney 4)

Newport, 1972 (Le Grice 2)

News at Eleven, 1986 (Sheen 3)

News for the Navy, 1976 (McLaren 4)

News from Home, 1977 (Akerman 2)

News No. 3, 1962 (Baillie 2)

News Review No. 2, 1945 (Van Dongen 4)

Newsboys' Home, 1938 (Cooper 3,
Krasner 4)

Newspaper Train, 1941 (Lye 4)

Newsreel of Dreams No. 1, 1968
(Vanderbeek 2)

Newsreel of Dreams No.2, 1969
(Vanderbeek 2)

Newsreel-Lightning. See Khronika-molniya,
1924

Nex de cuir, 1951 (Auric 4)

Next Aisle Over, 1918 (Daniels 3, Lloyd 3,
Roach 4)

Next Corner, 1924 (Wood 2, Chaney 3)

Next Door Neighbors. See Locataires d'à
côté, 1909

Next in Command, 1914 (Rosher 4)

Next Man, 1976 (Connery 3)

Next of Kin, 1942 (Dickinson 2, Hawkins 3,
Balcon 4, Walton 4)

Next Stop, Greenwich Village, 1976
(Mazursky 2, Winters 3)

Next Summer. See Été prochain, 1986

Next Time I Marry, 1938 (Ball 3, Kanin 4,
Metty 4)

Next Time We Love, 1936 (Sturges 2,
McDaniel 3, Milland 3, Stewart 3,
Sullavan 3, Waxman 4)

Next to No Time!, 1958 (Love 3, More 3,
Auric 4, Francis 4)

Next Voice You Hear, 1950 (Wellman 2,
Mayer 4, Raksin 4, Schary 4, Schnee 4)

Next Week-End, 1934 (Roach 4)

Nez, 1963 (Alexeieff and Parker 4)

Nez de cuir, 1952 (Allégret 2, Marais 3,
Wakhévitch 4)

Nezabyvayemyi 1919-god, 1952
(Shostakovich 4)

Nezlobte dědečka, 1934 (Heller 4)

Nezumi-kozo Jirokichi, 1932 (Hasegawa 3)

Nezumi-kozo Jirokichi: Kaiketsu-hen, 1932
(Hasegawa 3, Takamine 3)

Nezumi-kozo shinobikomi-hikae, 1956
(Hasegawa 3, Kagawa 3)

Nezumi-kozo shinobikomi-hikae: Ne-no-
koku sanjo, 1957 (Hasegawa 3)

Ni nado kruvi, 1917 (Mozhukin 3)

Ni pobres ni ricos, 1952 (Figueroa 4)

Ni sangre ni arena, 1941 (Armendáriz 3,
Cantinflas 3, Figueroa 4)

Niagara, 1953 (Hathaway 2, Cotten 3,
Monroe 3, Brackett 4, Jeakins 4,
LeMaire 4, Reisch 4, Wheeler 4)

Niagara Falls, 1932 (Arbuckle 3)

Niagara Falls, 1941 (Roach 4)

Niaye, 1964 (Sembene 2)

**Nibelungen, 1924 (Lang 2, Ruttman 2,
Hoffmann 4, Hunte 4, Pommer 4,
Reiniger 4, Schüfftan 4, Von
Harbou 4)**

Nibelungen, 1966 (Lom 3)

Nibelungen Saga. See **Nibelungen, 1924**

Nibelungen II, 1967 (Lom 3)

Nicaragua, 1969 (Schroeter 2)

Nice and Friendly, 1922 (Chaplin 2)

Nice à propos de Jean Vigo, 1984
(Oliveira 2)

Nice Couple, Chouchou and Yuni. See
Chouchou Yuji no meoto zenzai,
1965

Nice Doggy, 1952 (Terry 4)

Nice Girl?, 1941 (Brennan 3, Durbin 3,
Benchley 4, Pasternak 4)

Nice Little Bank That Should Be Robbed,
1958 (Rooney 3, LeMaire 4)

Nice People, 1922 (Daniels 3, Reid 3)

Nice Time, 1957 (Goretta 2, Tanner 2)

Nicherin to Moko daishurai, 1958
(Hasegawa 3)

Nicholas and Alexandra, 1971 (Schaffner 2,
Hawkins 3, Olivier 3, Redgrave 3, Box 4,
Korda 4, Spiegel 4, Young 4)

Nicholas Nickleby, 1947 (Cavalcanti 2,
Balcon 4, Perinal 4, Rank 4)

Nichols on Vacation, 1910 (Lawrence 3)

Nicht lange täuschte mich das Glück, 1917
(Negri 3)

Nicht versöhnt oder Es hilft nur Gewalt, wo
Gewalt herrscht, 1965 (Straub and
Huillet)

Nick Carter, 1909 (Gaumont 4, Pathé 4)

Nick Carter, 1911 (Gaumont 4)

Nick Carter casse tout. See Nick Carter va
tout casser, 1964

Nick Carter et le trefle rouge, 1965
(Constantine 3)

Nick Carter, Master Detective, 1939
(Tourneur 2, Pidgeon 3)

Nick Carter va tout casser, 1964
(Constantine 3)

Nick, Gentleman Detective. See After the
Thin Man, 1936

Nick of Time Baby, 1917 (Sennett 2,
Swanson 3)

Nick the Sting, 1976 (Cobb 3)

Nickel Hopper, 1926 (Karloff 3, Laurel and
Hardy 3, Normand 3, Roach 4)

Nickel Nurser, 1932 (Roach 4)

Nickel Queen, 1970 (Withers 3)

Nickel Ride, 1975 (Mulligan 2)

Nickelodeon, 1976 (Bogdanovich 2,
Reynolds 3, Kovacs 4, Needham 4,
Winkler 4)

Nick's Coffee Pot, 1939 (Terry 4)

Nick's Film. See Lightning Over Water,
1981

Nicky and Gino. See Dominick and Eugene,
1988

Nicky et Kitty, 1959 (Coutard 4)

Nicole, 1972 (Caron 3)

Nid d'espions. See Mademoiselle Docteur,
1936

Nido de viudas, 1977 (Lollobrigida 3,
Neal 3, Lai 4)

Nie er, 1959 (Zhao 3)

Nie weider Liebe. See Calais-Douvre, 1931

Nie wieder Liebe, 1931 (Litvak 2, Herlth 4,
Planer 4, Röhrig 4)

Niedzielny poranek, 1955 (Munk 2)

Niemand weiss es, 1920 (Pick 2)

Niemansland, 1931 (Eisler 4)

Niente rose per OSS 177, 1968 (Delli
Colli 4)

Niet!. See Habrichka el hashemersh, 1972

**Nieuwe Gronden, 1934 (Ivens 2, Eisler 4,
Van Dongen 4)**

Nieuwe polders, 1931 (Van Dongen 4)

Niewdzieczno is ic, 1979 (Tyszkiewicz 3)

Niewinni czarodzieje, 1960 (Skolimowski 2,
Wajda 2, Cybulski 3, Lomnicki 3)

Niewolnica Zmyslow, 1914 (Negri 3)

Niger—jeune république, 1961 (Jutra 2)

Nigeyuku Kodenji, 1930 (Yamada 3)

Niggard, 1914 (Reid 3)

Night, 1930 (Disney 4)

Night. See Notte, 1960

Night. See Yoru, 1976

Night Affair. See Désordre et la nuit, 1958

Night after Night, 1932 (Calhern 3, Raft 3,
West 3, Banton 4, Haller 4, Plunkett 4,
Zukor 4)

Night Ambush. See Ill Met by Moonlight,
1957

Night and Day. See Jack's the Boy, 1932

Night and Day, 1946 (Curtiz 2, Arden 3,
Grant 3, Malone 3, Wyman 3, Burks 4,
Prinz 4, Steiner 4, Warner 4)

Night and Fog. See **Nuit et brouillard,
1955**

Night and the City, 1950 (Dassin 2,
Kendall 3, Lom 3, Tierney 3, Widmark 3,
Withers 3, Lassally 4, Waxman 4)

Night and the City, 1991 (Winkler 4)

Night Angel, 1931 (Goulding 2, March 3)

Night Angel, 1990 (Black 3)

Night at Earl Carroll's, 1940 (Dreier 4,
Head 4, Reynolds 4)

Night at Glimminge Castle. See Natt på
Glimmingehus, 1954

Night at Karlstein. See Noc na Karlštejně, 1973

Night at the Biltmore Bowl, 1935 (Grable 3)

Night at the Crossroads. See Nuit du
carrefour, 1932

Night at the Movies, 1937 (Benchley 4)

**Night at the Opera, 1935 (Wood 2,
Dumont 3, Marx Brothers 3, Brown 4,
Carré 4, Freed 4, Gibbons 4, Kaper 4,
Mayer 4, Ryskind 4, Shearer 4,
Stothart 4, Thalberg 4)**

Night Beat, 1947 (Francis 3, Korda 4)

Night Before Christmas, 1912 (Costello 3)

Night Before Christmas, 1941 (Hanna and
Barbera 4)

Night Before the Divorce, 1942 (Siodmak 2)

Night Before the War Begins. See Laisen no
zenya, 1943

Night Boat to Dublin, 1945 (Lom 3,
Newton 3, Heller 4)

Night Bride, 1927 (Pangborn 3)

Night Butterfly. See Yoru no cho, 1957

Night Caller. See Peur sur la ville, 1975

Night Call Nurses, 1972 (Corman 2)

Night Club, 1928 (Florey 2, Folsey 4)

Night Club Lady, 1932 (Menjou 3, Riskin 4)

Night Club Scandal, 1937 (Barrymore 3,
Dreier 4, Head 4)

Night Court, 1932 (Van Dyke 2, Huston 3,
Raft 3)

Night Creature, 1977 (Pleasence 3)

Night Creatures. See Captain Clegg, 1962

Night Crossing, 1982 (Hurt 3, Goldsmith 4)

Night Digger. See Road Builder, 1971

Night Drum. See Yoru no tsuzumi, 1958

Night Duty. See Milosierdzie platne z gory,
1975

Night Editor, 1946 (Guffey 4)

Night Fighters. See Terrible Beauty, 1960

Night Flight, 1933 (Brown 2, Barrymore,
J. 3, Barrymore, L. 3, Gable 3, Loy 3,
Montgomery 3, Mayer 4, Selznick 4,
Stothart 4)

Night Flight. See Vol de nuit, 1978

Night Flight from Moscow. See Serpent,
1973

Night Flyer, 1928 (Daves 2)

Night Freight, 1955 (Sanders 3)

Night Gallery, 1969 (Crawford 3, Jaffe 3,
McDowall 3)

Night Games. See Nattlek, 1966

Night Games, 1974 (Schifrin 4)

Night Games, 1979 (Vadim 2)

Night Games, 1989 (Scheider 3, Donaggio 4)

Night Has a Thousand Eyes, 1948
(Robinson 3, Dreier 4, Head 4, Seitz 4,
Young 4)

Night Has Eyes, 1941 (Mason 3)

Night Hawk, 1924 (Carey 3, Stromberg 4)

Night Hawks, 1914 (Bushman 3)

Night Heaven Fell. See Bijoutiers du clair de
lune, 1957

Night Holds Terror, 1955 (Cassavetes 2)

Night Horsemen, 1921 (Mix 3)

Night in a Dormitory, 1929 (Rogers 3)

Night in Bangkok. See Bankokku no yuro,
1966

Night in Cairo. See Barbarian, 1933

Night in Casablanca, 1946 (Marx Brothers 3)

Night in Havana. See Big Boodle, 1957

Night in Hong Kong. See Honkon no yoru,
1961

Night in June. See Juninatten, 1940

Night in Karlstein. See Noc na Karlštejně,
1973

Night in London. See Nacht in London, 1928

Night in Marseilles, 1931 (Launder and
Gilliat)

Night in Montmartre, 1931 (Balcon 4,
Rank 4)

Night in New Orleans, 1942 (Johnson 3,
Dreier 4)

Night in Paradise, 1946 (Oberon 3, Banton 4,
Mohr 4, Wanger 4)

Night in the Harbor. See Natt i hamn, 1943

Night in the Show, 1915 (Chaplin 2,
Purviance 3)

Night in Town, 1910 (White 3)

Night into Morning, 1951 (Milland 3,
Basevi 4, Folsey 4)

Night Invader, 1942 (Fisher 2, Heller 4)

Night Is Ending. See Paris after Dark, 1943

Night Is My Future. See Musik i mörker,
1948

Night Is My Kingdom. See Nuit est mon
royaume, 1951

Night Is Young, 1935 (Horton 3, Novarro 3,
Russell 3, Howe 4, Stothart 4)

Night Journey. See Resa i natten, 1955

Night Key, 1937 (Bond 3, Karloff 3)

Night Kill, 1980 (Mitchum 3)

Night Life in New York, 1925 (Dwan 2)

Night Life in the Army, 1942 (Terry 4)

Night Life of the Bugs, 1936 (Lantz 4)

Night Life of the Gods, 1935 (Fulton 4,
Laemmle 4)

Night Light. See Natten ljus, 1957

Night Magic, 1985 (Audran 3)

**Night Mail, 1936 (Cavalcanti 2,
Grierson 2, Watt 2, Wright 2)**

Night Monster, 1942 (Lugosi 3, Salter 4)

'Night, Mother, 1986 (Bancroft 3, Spacek 3)

Night Moves, 1975 (Penn 2, Hackman 3,
Allen 4, Jenkins 4)

Night Must Fall, 1937 (Montgomery 3,
Russell 3, Mayer 4, Stromberg 4)

Night Must Fall, 1964 (Reisz 2, Finney 3,
Fisher 4, Francis 4)

Night My Number Came Up, 1955 (Elliott 3,
Redgrave 3, Arnold 4, Balcon 4,
Sherriff 4)

Night 'n' Gales, 1937 (Roach 4)

Night Nurse, 1931 (Wellman 2, Blondell 3,
Gable 3, Stanwyck 3)

Night of January 16th, 1941 (Daves 2,
Preston 3, Dreier 4, Head 4)

Night of June 13, 1933 (Zukor 4)

Night of Love, 1927 (Banky 3, Colman 3,
Barnes 4, Coffee 4, Goldwyn 4)

Night of Love. See Tradita, 1954

Night of Mystery, 1928 (Menjou 3,
Mankiewicz 4, Vajda 4)

Night of Mystery, 1937 (Head 4)

Night of Nights, 1939 (Milestone 2, Dreier 4,
Head 4, Stewart 4, Young 4)

Night of San Lorenzo. See Notte di San
Lorenzo, 1981

Night of Shame. See Marchandes d'illusions,
1954

Night of Terror, 1908 (Bitzer 4)
Night of Terror, 1933 (Lugosi 3)
Night of Terror, 1972 (Moorehead 3)
Night of the Askari. *See* Flüsternde Tod, 1975
Night of the Assassins. *See* Appuntamente col disonore, 1970
Night of the Beast. *See* House of the Black Death, 1965
Night of the Big Heat, 1967 (Cushing 3, Lee 3)
Night of the Blood Beast, 1958 (Corman 2)
Night of the Blood Monster. *See* Processo de las brujas, 1970
Night of the Bride. *See* Noc nevěsty, 1967
Night of the Cobra Woman, 1972 (Corman 2)
Night of the Demon, 1957 (Tourneur 2, Andrews 3, Adam 4, Bennett 4, Cohn 4)
Night of the Eagle, 1961 (Alwyn 4)
Night of the Flowers. *See* Notte dei fiori, 1972
Night of the Following Day, 1968 (Brando 3)
Night of the Fox, 1990 (Mills 3)
Night of the Full Dark Moon. *See* Silent Night, Bloody Night, 1973
Night of the Generals, 1966 (Pleasence 3, Jarre 4)
Night of the Generals, 1967 (Litvak 2, Noiret 3, O'Toole 3, Sharif 3, Decaë 4, Dehn 4, Spiegel 4, Trauner 4)
Night of the Hunter, 1955 (Gish 3, Laughton 3, Mitchum 3, Winters 3, Cortez 4)
Night of the Iguana, 1964 (Fernández 2, Huston 2, Burton 3, Gardner 3, Kerr 3, Figueroa 4, Jeakins 4, Stark 4, Veiller 4)
Night of the Lepus, 1972 (Leigh 3)
Night of the Living Dead, 1990 (Romero 2, Golan and Globus 4, Savini 4)
Night of the Living Duck, 1988 (Blanc 4)
Night of the Party, 1906 (Bitzer 4)
Night of the Party, 1934 (Powell and Pressburger 2, Junge 4)
Night of the Quarter Moon, 1959 (Moorehead 3, Cahn 4)
Night of the Shooting Stars, 1983 (Taviani 2)
Night of Thrills, 1914 (Chaney 3)
Night on Bald Mountain. *See* **Nuit sur le Mont Chauve, 1933**
Night on the Road, 1914 (Anderson 3)
Night Out, 1912 (Bosworth 3)
Night Out, 1915 (Dressler 3)
Night Owl, 1926 (Brown 4)
Night Owls, 1930 (Laurel and Hardy 3, Roach 4)
Night Parade, 1929 (Plunkett 4)
Night Passage, 1957 (Duryea 3, Murphy 3, Stewart 3, Chase 4, Daniels 4, Tiomkin 4)
Night Patrol, 1926 (Lang 4)
Night People, 1954 (Crawford 3, Peck 3, Clarke 4, Johnson 4, LeMaire 4)
Night Plane from Chungking, 1943 (Preston 3, Head 4)
Night Porter, 1973 (Bogarde 3)
Night Raiders, 1939 (Wayne 3)
Night Ride, 1929 (Robinson 3)
Night Ride, 1937 (Havelock-Allan 4)
Night Rider, 1932 (Carey 3)
Night Riders, 1939 (Canutt 4)
Night River. *See* Yoru no kawa, 1956
Night Runner, 1957 (Boyle 4)

Night Shift, 1942 (Kaye 3, Kanin 4)
Night Slaves, 1970 (Grant 3)
Night Song, 1947 (Cromwell 2, Andrews 3, Barrymore 3, Oberon 3, Ballard 4, Bodeen 4, Carmichael 4, D'Agostino 4, Orry-Kelly 4)
Night Spot, 1938 (Musuraca 4)
Night Strangler, 1973 (Carradine 3)
Night Stripes, 1944 (Kanin 4)
Night Sun. *See* Sole anche di notte, 1990
Night That Heaven Fell. *See* Bijoutiers du clair de lune, 1958
Night the World Exploded, 1957 (Katzman 4)
Night They Raided Minsky's, 1968 (Friedkin 2, Elliott 3, Gould 3, Robards 3, Wisdom 3, Rosenblum 4)
Night Tide, 1961 (Corman 2, Hopper 3, Raksin 4)
Night Time in Nevada, 1948 (Rogers 3)
Night to Remember, 1943 (Young 3, Walker 4)
Night to Remember, 1958 (More 3, Alwyn 4, Rank 4, Unsworth 4, Vetchinsky 4)
Night to Remember. *See* Kazoku no jijo, 1962
Night Train. *See* Night Train to Munich, 1940
Night Train. *See* Pociąg, 1959
Night Train to Galveston, 1952 (Autry 3)
Night Train to Mundo Fine, 1966 (Carradine 3)
Night Train to Munich, 1940 (Launder and Gilliat 2, Harrison 3, Henreid 3, Lockwood 3, Vetchinsky 4)
Night Unto Night, 1949 (Siegel 2, Crawford 3, Reagan 3, Waxman 4)
Night Visitor, 1971 (Howard 3, Ullmann 3, Von Sydow 3, Mancini 4)
Night Visitor, 1989 (Gould 3)
Night Waitress, 1936 (Quinn 3, Metty 4)
Night Walker, 1965 (Stanwyck 3, Taylor 3)
Night Watch, 1928 (Lukas 3, Biro 4, Korda 4, Struss 4)
Night Watch, 1941 (Alwyn 4)
Night Watch, 1973 (Harvey 3, Taylor 3)
Night Watchman, 1938 (Jones 4)
Night Watchman's Mistake, 1929 (Sennett 2, Hornbeck 4)
Night with a Million, 1914 (Bushman 3)
Night without Sleep, 1952 (Darnell 3, Marsh 3, Ballard 4, LeMaire 4, Newman 4)
Night without Stars, 1951 (Alwyn 4, Green 4, Rank 4)
Night Women. *See* Femme spectacle, 1964
Night Work, 1939 (O'Connor 3, Head 4)
Night World, 1932 (Berkeley 2, Ayres 3, Beavers 3, Karloff 3, Raft 3)
Nightbreaker, 1989 (Sheen 3)
Nightbreed, 1989 (Cronenberg 2)
Nightcats, 1956 (Brakhage 2)
Nightcomers, 1971 (Brando 3)
Nightfall, 1956 (Tourneur 2, Bancroft 3, Duning 4, Guffey 4)
Nighthawks, 1981 (Stallone 3, Smith 4)
Nightingale, 1914 (Barrymore 3)
Nightingale, 1982 (Challis 4)
Nightingale Sang in Berkeley Square, 1980 (Grahame 3, Niven 3)
Nightmare Series, 1978 (Brakhage 2)
Nightmare, 1942 (Barnes 4)
Nightmare, 1956 (Robinson 3, Biroc 4)

Nightmare, 1963 (Carreras 4, Francis 4, Sangster 4)
Nightmare Alley, 1947 (Goulding 2, Blondell 3, Power 3, Furthman 4, Garmes 4, LeMaire 4, Wheeler 4)
Nightmare Castle. *See* Amanti d'oltretombo, 1965
Nightmare in Badham County, 1976 (Bellamy 3)
Nightmare in the Sun, 1963 (Duvall 3, Cortez 4)
Nightmare on Elm Street, 1984 (Craven 2)
Nightmare on Elm Street 3: Dream Warriors, 1986 (Craven 2)
Nightmusic, 1986 (Brakhage 2)
Night's End. *See* Nishant, 1975
Nights in a Harem. *See* Son of Sinbad, 1955
Nights of Cabiria. *See* Notti di Cabiria, 1956
Nights of Love. *See* Liebesnächte, 1929
Nightshift, 1982 (Costner 3)
Nightwing, 1979 (Mancini 4)
Nigorie, 1953 (Yamamura 3)
Niguruma no uta, 1959 (Yoda 4)
Nihiliste, 1906 (Pathé 4)
Nihombashi, 1929 (Mizoguchi 2)
Nihon dashutsu, 1964 (Takemitsu 4)
Nihon ichi no gomasuri otoko, 1965 (Shindo 3)
Nihon ichi no yakuza otoko, 1970 (Tsukasa 3)
Nihon josei no uta, 1934 (Takamine 3)
Nihon no haha, 1942 (Tanaka 3)
Nihon no seishun, 1968 (Takemitsu 4)
Nihon tanjo, 1959 (Tanaka 3)
Nihonkai daikaisen, 1969 (Ryu 3, Tsukasa 3, Tsuburaya 4)
Nihon-maru, 1976 (Shinoda 2)
Nihon-maru Ship. *See* Nihon-maru, 1976
Nihontou: Miyairi Kouhei no waza, 1976 (Takemitsu 4)
Niisan no baka, 1932 (Tanaka 3)
Niizuma kagami, 1940 (Yamada 3)
Niizuma kaigi, 1949 (Miyagawa 4)
Niji ikutabi, 1956 (Kyo 3)
Niji o idaku shojo, 1948 (Takamine 3, Hayasaka 4)
Niji tatsu oka, 1938 (Takamine 3)
Nijinsky, 1980 (Bates 3, Irons 3, Slocombe 4)
Nijuissa no chichi, 1964 (Takemitsu 4)
Nijushi no hitomi, 1954 (Takamine 3)
Nikita, 1990 (Moreau 3)
Nikki, Wild Dog of the North, 1961 (Disney 4)
Niklashausen Journey. *See* Niklashauser Fart, 1970
Niklashauser Fart, 1970 (Schygulla 3)
Nikolai Stavrogin, 1915 (Protazanov 2, Mozhukin 3)
Nikoniko taikai: Uata no hanakago, 1946 (Tanaka 3)
Nikudan, 1980 (Ryu 3)
Nikutai no gakko, 1965 (Yamamura 3)
Nikyho velebné dobrodružtvi, 1919 (Ondra 3)
Nili, 1950 (Anand 3)
Nille, 1968 (Henning-Jensen 2)
Nilo di pietra, 1956 (Delli Colli 4)
Nils Holgerssons Underbara Resa, 1962 (Von Sydow 3)
Nina, 1956 (Aimée 3)
Nina, 1958 (D'Eaubonne 4)
Nina B. Affair. *See* Affaire Nina B., 1962
Nina de Vanghel, 1952 (Schüfftan 4)

No Place to Go, 1939 (Edeson 4)
No Place to Hide, 1959 (Menges 4)
No Place to Hide, 1974 (Stallone 3)
No Place to Hide, 1979 (Sangster 4)
No Place to Hide, 1983 (Sheen 3)
No Publicity, 1927 (Horton 3)
No Questions Asked, 1951 (Rose 4)
No Regrets for My Youth. *See* Waga seishun
    ni kuinashi, 1946
No Regrets for Our Youth. *See* Waga
    seishun ni kui nashi, 1946
No Resting Place, 1951 (Rotha 2, Alwyn 4)
No Return. *See* Vozrata net, 1974
No Road Back, 1956 (Connery 3)
No Room for the Groom, 1952 (Sirk 2,
    Curtis 3)
No Sad Songs for Me, 1950 (Sullavan 3,
    Wood 3, Duning 4, Koch 4, Maté 4,
    Walker 4)
No Sleep for Percy, 1955 (Terry 4)
No Sleep on the Deep, 1934 (Langdon 3)
No Sleep till Dawn. *See* Bombers B-52, 1957
No Small Affair, 1984 (Zsigmond 4)
No Stop-Over, 1921 (Roach 4)
No Sun in Venice. *See* Sait-on jamais?, 1957
No te engañes corazón, 1936 (Cantinflas 3)
No Time for Comedy, 1940 (Beavers 3,
    Russell 3, Stewart 3, Epstein 4, Haller 4,
    Orry-Kelly 4, Wallis 4)
No Time For Flowers, 1952 (Siegel 2)
No Time for Love, 1943 (Leisen 2,
    Colbert 3, Dreier 4, Head 4, Irene 4,
    Lang 4, Young 4)
No Time for Pity. *See* Time without Pity,
    1957
No Time for Sergeants, 1958 (LeRoy 2,
    Rosson 4)
No Time for Tears. *See* Otoko arite, 1955
No Time for Tears, 1957 (Neagle 3,
    Quayle 3)
No Time to Die, 1958 (Mature 3, Box 4)
No Time to Marry, 1938 (Astor 3)
No Trees in the Street, 1959 (Lom 3)
No Way Out, 1950 (Mankiewicz 2,
    Darnell 3, Poitier 3, Widmark 3,
    Krasner 4, LeMaire 4, Newman 4,
    Wheeler 4, Zanuck 4)
No Way Out, 1987 (Costner 3, Hackman 3,
    Alcott 4, Jarre 4)
No Way to Treat a Lady, 1968 (Remick 3,
    Segal 3, Steiger 3, Goldman 4, Jenkins 4)
No Woman Knows, 1921 (Browning 2)
Noah's Ark, 1928 (Curtiz 2, Costello 3,
    Johnson 3, Loy 3, Grot 4, Mohr 4,
    Zanuck 4)
Noah's Ark. *See* Arche de Noë, 1946
Noah's Ark, 1977 (Halas and Batchelor 4)
Noah's Lark, 1929 (Fleischer 4)
Noah's Outing, 1932 (Terry 4)
Nob Hill, 1945 (Hathaway 2, Bennett 3,
    Raft 3, Cronjager 4, Raine 4)
Nobi, 1959 (Ichikawa 2)
Nobody Home, 1919 (Garmes 4)
Nobody Listened. *See* Nadie escuchaba,
    1988
Nobody Lives Forever, 1946 (Negulesco 2,
    Brennan 3, Garfield 3, Burnett 4,
    Deutsch 4, Edeson 4)
Nobody Runs Away, 1956 (Cotten 3)
Nobody Runs Forever, 1968 (Box 4,
    Delerue 4)
Nobody Said Nothing. *See* Nadie dijo nada,
    1970
Nobody Shall Be Laughing, 1965 (Menzel 2)

Nobody's Baby, 1937 (Roach 4)
Nobody's Bridge, 1923 (Miller 4)
Nobody's Child, 1986 (Grant 3)
Nobody's Darling, 1943 (Mann 2, Calhern 3)
Nobody's Fault. *See* Little Dorrit, 1987
Nobody's Fool, 1921 (Glennon 4)
Nobody's Fool, 1936 (Horton 3)
Nobody's Kid, 1921 (Marsh 3)
Nobody's Widow, 1927 (Crisp 3, Miller 4)
Nobody's Women. *See* Femmes de
    personne, 1984
Noc na Karlštejně, 1973 (Brejchová 3,
    Kučera 4)
Noc nevěsty, 1967 (Brejchová 3)
Noc Poslubna, 1959 (Andersson 3)
Noce au lac Saint-Fargeau, 1905 (Guy 2,
    Gaumont 4)
Noces d'argent, 1915 (Feuillade 2,
    Musidora 3)
Noces de papier, 1989 (Bujold 3)
Noces de sable, 1948 (Cocteau 2)
Noces du sable, 1948 (Auric 4)
Noces rouges, 1973 (Chabrol 2, Audran 3,
    Piccoli 3, Rabier 4)
Noces sanglantes, 1915 (Feuillade 2)
Noces siciliennes, 1912 (Feuillade 2)
Noces vénetiennes. *See* Prima notte, 1958
Noche avanza, 1951 (Armendáriz 3)
Noche de los mayas, 1939 (Figueroa 4)
Noche de Reyes, 1947 (Rey 3)
Noche de sabado, 1950 (Félix 3)
Noche de tormenta, 1951 (Aimée 3)
Noche oscura, 1989 (Saura 2)
Noctiluca, 1974 (Frampton 2)
Nocturna, 1979 (Carradine 3, De Carlo 3)
Nocturne, 1919 (Feuillade 2, Gaumont 4)
Nocturne, 1946 (Raft 3, Boyle 4, Harrison 4)
Nocturne, 1954 (Alexeieff and Parker 4)
Nocturno, 1958 (Mimica 4)
Nocturno de amor, 1948 (Alcoriza 4)
Nocturno der Liebe, 1918 (Veidt 3)
Noël de Francesca, 1912 (Feuillade 2)
Noël du poilu, 1915 (Feuillade 2)
Nogent, Eldorado du dimanche, 1929
    (Carné 2)
Nogi Taisho to Kuma-san, 1926
    (Mizoguchi 2)
Nogitsune Sanji, 1930 (Hasegawa 3,
    Tsuburaya 4)
No-Good Guy, 1916 (Sullivan 4)
No-Gun Man, 1924 (Arzner 2)
Noi donne siamo fatte cosi, 1971 (Risi 2,
    Scola 2, Vitti 3, Age and Scarpelli 4)
Noi due sole, 1953 (Rota 4)
Noi gangsters, 1959 (Cervi 3)
Noi siamo le colonne, 1956 (De Sica 2)
Noi vivi, 1988 (Valli 3)
Noi vivi—addio Kira, 1942 (Brazzi 3)
Noia, 1963 (Davis 3, Guerra 4, Levine 4,
    Ponti 4)
Noire de . . , 1966 (Sembene 2)
Noire et Caline, 1977 (Alekan 4)
Noise from the Deep, 1913 (Sennett 2,
    Arbuckle 3, Normand 3)
Noise of Bombs, 1914 (Sennett 2)
Noisy Noises, 1929 (Roach 4)
Noisy Six, 1913 (Mix 3)
Noix de coco, 1938 (Simon 3, Achard 4)
Nomads of the North, 1920 (Chaney 3)
Nome della legge. *See* Mafia, 1949
Nome delle popolo italiano, 1971
    (Gassman 3)
Nommé La Rocca, 1961 (Belmondo 3,
    Cloquet 4)

Non c'è amore piu grande, 1955 (Cervi 3)
Non ci resta che piangere, 1984 (Rotunno 4)
Non coupable, 1947 (Simon 3)
Non e mai troppe tardi, 1953 (Mastroianni 3)
Non me lo dire!, 1940 (Fellini 2)
Non, ou la vaine gloire de commande. *See*
    Nao ou a vã gloria de mandar, 1990
Non si servizia un paperino, 1972 (Papas 3)
Non sono superstizioso, ma . . . !, 1943 (De
    Sica 2)
Non stuzzicate la zanzara, 1967
    (Wertmüller 2, Giannini 3, Masina 3)
Non ti conasco più amore, 1980 (Vitti 3)
Non ti conosco più, 1936 (De Sica 2)
Non toccate la donna bianca. *See* Touche pas
    la femme blanche, 1974
Non uccidere. *See* Tu ne tueras point,
    1961
None But the Brave. *See* Storm over the
    Nile, 1955
None But the Brave, 1965 (Sinatra 3,
    Daniels 4, Tsuburaya 4, Williams 4)
None But the Lonely Heart, 1944
    (Barrymore 3, Duryea 3, Fitzgerald 3,
    Grant 3, Barnes 4, D'Agostino 4,
    Eisler 4)
None Shall Escape, 1944 (De Toth 2,
    Garmes 4)
None So Blind, 1923 (Costello 3)
Nonki saiban, 1955 (Kagawa 3)
Nonna Sabella, 1957 (Delli Colli 4)
Nonsense Newsreel, 1954 (Terry 4)
Non-Skid Kid, 1922 (Roach 4)
Non-Stop Kid, 1918 (Daniels 3, Lloyd 3,
    Roach 4)
Non-Stop New York, 1937 (Stevenson 2,
    Rank 4, Siodmak 4)
Noon Whistle, 1923 (Laurel and Hardy 3,
    Roach 4)
Noon Wine, 1966 (Peckinpah 2)
Noose, 1928 (Barthelmess 3)
Noose, 1948 (Heller 4)
Noose Hangs High, 1948 (Abbott and
    Costello 3, Taradash 4)
Nor Moon By Night, 1958 (Rank 4)
Nor the Moon by Night, 1958 (Bernard 4)
Nora, 1923 (Kortner 3, Tschechowa 3,
    Pommer 4)
Nora Helmer, 1973 (Fassbinder 2)
Nora inu, 1949 (Mifune 3, Shimura 3,
    Hayasaka 4)
Nora Prentiss, 1947 (Sheridan 3, Grot 4,
    Howe 4, Waxman 4)
Nordlandrose, 1914 (Porten 3, Messter 4)
Noren, 1958 (Yamada 3)
Norliss Tapes, 1973 (Dickinson 3)
Norman Conquests in the Bayeux Tapestry,
    1967 (Evans 3)
Normandie-Niemen, 1959 (Spaak 4)
Norman Jacobson, 1967 (Emshwiller 2)
Norman Normal, 1968 (Blanc 4)
Norma Rae, 1979 (Ritt 2, Field 3, Alonzo 4,
    Ravetch 4)
Noroît, 1976 (Chaplin 3)
Norseman, 1978 (Wilde 3)
North and South, 1985 (Kelly 3, Mitchum 3,
    Simmons 3, Taylor 3)
**North by Northwest, 1959 (Hitchcock 2,
    Grant 3, Mason 3, Saint 3, Bass 4,
    Boyle 4, Burks 4, Gillespie 4,
    Herrmann 4)**
North Dallas Forty, 1978 (Nolte 3)
North of 50-50, 1924 (Roach 4)
North of 57, 1924 (Sennett 2)

North of Hudson Bay, 1923 (Ford 2, Mix 3, Furthman 4)

North of Nevada, 1924 (Brown 4)

North of the Border, 1946 (Eason 4)

North of the Great Divide, 1950 (Johnson 3, Rogers 3)

North of the Rio Grande, 1922 (Daniels 3)

North of the Rio Grande, 1937 (Cobb 3, Harlan 4, Head 4)

North of the Yukon. *See* North of Hudson Bay, 1923

North or North West. *See* N or NW, 1938

North Sea, 1938 (Cavalcanti 2, Watt 2)

North Sea Hijack. *See* Ffolkes, 1980

North Star, 1925 (Gable 3, Walker 4)

North Star, 1943 (Milestone 2, Von Stroheim 2, Andrews 3, Baxter 3, Brennan 3, Huston 3, Copland 4, Goldwyn 4, Howe 4, Mandell 4, Menzies 4)

North to Alaska, 1960 (Hathaway 2, Granger 3, Wayne 3, Shamroy 4, Smith 4)

North to the Klondike, 1942 (Crawford 3, Salter 4)

North West Mounted Police, 1940 (De Mille 2, Carroll 3, Cooper 3, Goddard 3, Preston 3, Ryan 3, Dreier 4, Head 4, Macpherson 4, Sullivan 4, Young 4)

North Woods, 1931 (Lantz 4)

Northern Frontier, 1935 (Brennan 3)

Northern Harbour. *See* Severní přístav, 1954

Northern Pursuit, 1943 (Siegel 2, Walsh 2, Flynn 3, Deutsch 4)

Northern Star. *See* Etoile du nord, 1982

Northwest Frontier, 1959 (Bacall 3, Lom 3, More 3, Nugent 4, Rank 4, Unsworth 4, Vetchinsky 4)

Northwest Hounded Police, 1946 (Avery 4)

Northwest Mounted, 1929 (Rooney 4)

Northwest Outpost, 1947 (Dwan 2, Eddy 3, Lanchester 3, Canutt 4)

Northwest Passage, 1940 (Vidor 2, Brennan 3, Tracy 3, Young 3, Jennings 4, Mayer 4, Stothart 4, Stromberg 4)

Northwest Rangers, 1942 (Carradine 3, Schary 4)

Northwest Stampede, 1948 (Eason 4)

Northwest U.S.A. *See* Pacific Northwest, 1944

Norvège, 1951 (Colpi 4)

Norway's Liv Ullman. *See* Look at Liv, 1977

Norwegian Wood, 1967 (Müller 4)

Norwood, 1970 (Wallis 4)

Nos Amours, 1983 (Pialat 2)

Nos bons étudiants, 1904 (Guy 2, Gaumont 4)

Nos Veremos en el cielo, 1950 (Armendáriz 3)

Nose. *See* Nez, 1963

Nosed Out, 1934 (Roach 4)

Nose's Story, 1911 (Gaudio 4)

Nosferatu: A Symphony of Horror. *See* **Nosferatu: Eine Symphonie des Grauens, 1922**

Nosferatu a Venezia: Il ritorno di Nosferatu, 1988 (Kinski 3, Vangelis 4)

Nosferatu: Eine Symphonie des Grauens, 1922 (Murnau 2, Galeen 4, Wagner 4)

Nosferatu—Phantom der Nacht, 1979 (Adjani 3, Ganz 3, Kinski 3)

Nosferatu the Vampire. *See* **Nosferatu: Eine Symphonie des Grauens, 1922**

Nosferatu the Vampire. *See* Zwolfte Stunde—Eine Nacht des Grauens, 1930

Nosferatu the Vampire. *See* Nosferatu—Phantom der Nacht, 1979

Nosotros los pobres, 1947 (Infante 3)

Nostalghia, 1983 (Tarkovsky 2, Josephson 3)

Nostalgia, 1971 (Frampton 2)

Nostalgia. *See* Nostalghia, 1983 (Guerra 4)

Nostalgie, 1937 (Baur 3, Manès 3, Annenkov 4, Wakhévitch 4)

Nostalgiya, 1983 (Yankovsky 3)

Nostoradamusu no daiyogen, 1974 (Tsukasa 3)

Nostra guerra, 1945 (Lattuada 2)

Nostradamus's Great Prophecy. *See* Nosutoradamusu no daiyogen, 1974

Nostri figli. *See* Vinti, 1952

Nostri mariti, 1966 (Sordi 3, Age and Scarpelli 4)

Nostri sogni, 1943 (De Sica 2, Zavattini 4)

Nostro agente a Casablanca, 1966 (Fusco 4)

Nostros dos, 1954 (Fernández 2)

Nosutoradamusu no daiyogen, 1974 (Yamamura 3, Muraki 4)

Not a Drum Was Heard, 1924 (Wellman 2, August 4)

Not a Ladies' Man, 1942 (Wray 3)

Not as a Stranger, 1955 (Kramer 2, Crawford 3, De Havilland 3, Grahame 3, Marvin 3, Mitchum 3, Sinatra 3, Anhalt 4, Planer 4)

Not By Coincidence. *See* Keine zufällige Geschichte, 1984

Not Exactly Gentlemen, 1931 (Wray 3, Nichols 4)

Not for Children. *See* Barnförbjudet, 1979

Not Guilty, 1908 (Méliès 2)

Not Guilty. *See* Non coupable, 1947

Not in Nottingham, 1963 (Hanna and Barbera 4)

Not Like Other Girls, 1912 (Lawrence 3)

Not My Kid, 1985 (Segal 3)

Not My Sister, 1916 (Sullivan 4)

Not Now, 1936 (Fleischer 4)

Not of This Earth, 1957 (Corman 2)

Not on My Account, 1943 (Metty 4)

Not on Your Life. *See* **Verdugo, 1963**

Not One Shall Die, 1957 (Guffey 4)

Not Quite Decent, 1929 (Clarke 4)

Not So Dumb, 1930 (Vidor 2, Davies 3, Pangborn 3, Adrian 4, Gibbons 4, Stewart 4)

Not So Long Ago, 1925 (Olcott 2, Howe 4)

Not So Quiet, 1930 (Lantz 4)

Not the First Time, 1976 (Frampton 2)

Not to Be Trusted, 1926 (Rooney 3)

Not Wanted, 1949 (Lupino 3)

Not Wanted on Voyage. *See* Treachery on the High Seas, 1938

Not with My Wife You Don't, 1966 (Scott 3, Bass 4, Frank 4, Head 4, Lang 4, Mercer 4, Williams 4)

Not without My Daughter, 1991 (Field 3, Goldsmith 4)

Notary. *See* Peleskei notárius, 1917

Notater om Korlighedon, 1989 (Nowicki 3)

Notch pered Rozdestvom, 1913 (Mozhukin 3)

Note in the Shoe, 1909 (Griffith 2)

Notebook on Cities and Clothes. *See* Aufzeichnungen zu Kleidern und Städten, 1989

Notes for Jerome, 1981 (Mekas 2)

Notes on a Green Revolution, 1972 (Benegal 2)

Notes on the Circus, 1966 (Mekas 2)

Notes on the Popular Arts, 1978 (Bass 4)

Notes to You, 1941 (Blanc 4, Freleng 4, Stalling 4)

Nothing But Nerves, 1941 (Benchley 4)

Nothing But Pleasure, 1940 (Keaton 2, Bruckman 4)

Nothing But the Best, 1963 (Roeg 2, Bates 3, Elliott 3, Raphael 4)

Nothing But the Night, 1972 (Cushing 3, Dors 3, Lee 3)

Nothing But the Tooth, 1948 (Blanc 4, Stalling 4)

Nothing But the Truth, 1929 (Cronjager 4)

Nothing But the Truth, 1941 (Goddard 3, Hope 3, Dreier 4, Head 4, Lang 4)

Nothing But the Truth. *See* F for Fake, 1975

Nothing But Trouble, 1918 (Daniels 3, Lloyd 3, Roach 4)

Nothing But Trouble, 1945 (Laurel and Hardy 3, Irene 4)

Nothing Else Matters, 1920 (Pearson 2)

Nothing in Common, 1986 (Hanks 3, Saint 3, Alonzo 4)

Nothing Lasts Forever, 1980 (Jaffe 3)

Nothing Personal, 1980 (Sutherland 3)

Nothing Sacred, 1937 (Wellman 2, Lombard 3, March 3, McDaniel 3, Banton 4, Hecht 4, Plunkett 4, Selznick 4, Wheeler 4)

Nothing to Wear, 1928 (Walker 4)

Nothing Underneath. *See* Sotto il vestito niente, 1985

Nothing Ventured, 1948 (Baxter 2)

Notorious, 1946 (Hitchcock 2, Bergman 3, Calhern 3, Grant 3, Rains 3, D'Agostino 4, Head 4, Hecht 4)

Notorious Affair, 1930 (Bacon 2, Francis 3, Rathbone 3, Grot 4, Haller 4)

Notorious But Nice, 1933 (Beavers 3)

Notorious Elinor Lee, 1940 (Micheaux 2)

Notorious Fanny Hill, 1965 (Kovacs 4)

Notorious Gentleman *See* Rake's Progress, 1945

Notorious Lady, 1927 (Gaudio 4, Murfin 4)

Notorious Landlady, 1962 (Edwards 2, Astaire 3, Lemmon 3, Novak 3, Duning 4)

Notorious Lone Wolf, 1946 (Guffey 4)

Notorious Sophie Lang, 1934 (Sheridan 3, Head 4, Veiller 4)

Notre Dame, cathédrale de Paris, 1957 (Franju 2, Delerue 4, Fradetal 4)

Notre histoire, 1984 (Baye 3, Delon 3, Evein 4)

Notre mariage, 1984 (Branco 4, De Almeida 4)

Notre pauvre coeur, 1916 (Feuillade 2)

Notre regrettable epoux, 1988 (Valli 3, Rabier 4)

Notre-Dame de Paris, 1931 (Epstein 2)

Notre-Dame de Paris, 1956 (Cuny 3, Lollobrigida 3, Quinn 3, Aurenche 4, Auric 4, Prévert 4)

Notte, 1960 (Antonioni 2, Mastroianni 3, Moreau 3, Vitti 3, Di Venanzo 4, Flaiano 4, Guerra 4)

Notte bianche, 1957 (Rota 4)

Notte brava, 1959 (Pasolini 2)

Notte dei fiori, 1972 (Sanda 3)

Notte delle beffe, 1940 (Sordi 3, Amidei 4)

Notte del nozze. *See* Tradita, 1954

Notte di San Lorenzo, 1982 (Taviani 2,
Guerra 4)

Notte di tempesta, 1945 (Castellani 2,
Gherardi 4)

Notte porta consiglio. *See* Roma città libera,
1946

Notti bianche, 1957 (Visconti 2, Marais 3,
Mastroianni 3, Schell 3, Cecchi
D'Amico 4, Rotunno 4)

Notti bianchi, 1957 (Cristaldi 4)

Notti di Cabiria, 1956 (Pasolini 2, Masina 3,
De Laurentiis 4, Flaiano 4, Gherardi 4,
Pinelli 4, Ponti 4, Rota 4)

Notturno, 1988 (Olbrychski 3)

Nous deux, 1979 (Deneuve 3, Lai 4)

Nous deux, Madame la vie, 1936 (Barrault 3,
Wakhévitch 4)

Nous irons à Deauville, 1962 (Constantine 3)

Nous irons à Monte Carlo, 1951 (Dalio 3,
Hepburn 3)

Nous irons à Paris, 1949 (Raft 3)

Nous irons tous au paradis, 1977 (Gélin 3)

Nous les gosses, 1941 (Modot 3, Douy 4)

Nous les jeunes. *See* Altitude 3.200, 1938

Nous Mêmes, 1962 (Alexeieff and Parker 4)

Nous ne ferons jamais de cinéma, 1932
(Cavalcanti 4)

Nous ne sommes plus des enfants, 1934
(Stradling 4)

Nous ne vieillirons pas ensemble, 1972
(Pialat 2)

Nous n'irons plus au bois, 1951 (Sautet 2)

Nous n'irons plus au bois, 1963 (Carrière 4)

Nous quatre, Cardinal, 1973 (Douy 4)

Nous sommes tous des assassins, 1952
(Spaak 4)

Nouveau Journal d'une femme en blanc,
1966 (Aurenche 4, Douy 4)

Nouveau Testament, 1936 (Guitry 2)

Nouveaux Messieurs, 1928 (Meerson 4,
Périnal 4, Spaak 4)

Nouveaux Riches, 1938 (Raimu 3, Simon 3,
Lourié 4)

Nouvelle brigades du tigre, 1987
(Constantine 3)

Nouvelle mission de Judex, 1917
(Feuillade 2, Gaumont 4)

Nouvelle Vague, 1990 (Delon 3)

Nouvelles Luttes extravagantes, 1900
(Méliès 2)

Nova sinfonia, 1982 (Alvarez 2)

Nove ospiti per un delitto, 1976 (Kennedy 3)

Novecento. *See* **1900, 1976**

Novel Affair. *See* Passionate Stranger, 1956

Novel with a Contrabass. *See* Román s
basou, 1949

Novel: Yoshida School. *See* Shousetsu
Yoshida gakkou, 1983

Novelletta, 1937 (Comencini 2)

November, 1921 (Fleischer 4)

November Days: Voices and Choices, 1990
(Ophuls 2)

Novembre à Paris, 1956 (Braunberger 4,
Delerue 4)

Novice, 1911 (Bosworth 3)

Novices, 1970 (Bardot 3, Girardot 3,
Gégauff 4)

Novio a la vista, 1953 (Bardem 2)

Novosti dnia, 1944 (Vertov 2)

Novy Gulliver, 1935 (Ptushko 4)

Novyi dom, 1947 (Cherkassov 3)

**Novyi Vavilon, 1929 (Gerasimov 2,
Kozintsev 2, Enei 4, Moskvin 4,
Shostakovich 4)**

Now, 1965 (Alvarez 2)

Now, 1970 (Brocka 2)

Now about These Women. *See* För att inte
tala om alla dessa kvinnor, 1964

Now and Forever, 1934 (Hathaway 2,
Cooper 3, Lombard 3, Temple 3,
Banton 4, Dreier 4, Zukor 4)

Now Barabbas. *See* Now Barabbas Was a
Robber . . ., 1949

Now Barabbas Was a Robber . . ., 1949
(Burton 3, More 3, De Grunwald 4,
Heller 4, Wakhévitch 4)

Now Hare This, 1958 (Blanc 4,
McKimson 4)

Now Hear This, 1963 (Blanc 4, Jones 4)

Now I'll Tell, 1934 (Faye 3, Tracy 3,
Friedhofer 4)

Now I'll Tell One, 1926 (Laurel and
Hardy 3, Roach 4)

Now I'll Tell You, 1934 (Temple 3)

Now Is the Time, 1949 (McLaren 4)

Now Let's Talk About Men. *See* Questa
volta parliamo di uomini, 1965

Now or Never, 1921 (Lloyd 3, Roach 4)

**Now, Voyager, 1942 (Davis 3, Henreid 3,
Pangborn 3, Rains 3, Friedhofer 4,
Orry-Kelly 4)**

Now We're in the Air, 1927 (Beery 3,
Brooks 3)

Now You're Talking, 1940 (Mills 3,
Balcon 4)

Nowhere to Go, 1958 (Love 3, Smith 3)

Nowhere to Hide, 1977 (Van Cleef 3,
Anhalt 4)

Nowy Janko muzykant, 1960 (Lenica 4)

Noyade interdite, 1987 (Noiret 3, Sarde 4)

**Noz w wodzie, 1962 (Polanski 2,
Skolimowski 2)**

Nozomi naki ni arazu, 1949 (Hayasaka 4)

Nseeb, 1981 (Bachchan 3)

N'te promène donc pas toute nue, 1906
(Feuillade 2)

Nth Commandment, 1923 (Borzage 2,
Moore 3, Marion 4)

Nu börjar livet, 1948 (Molander 2,
Zetterling 2)

Nu gar jag till Maxim, 1910 (Magnusson 4)

Nuage entre les dents, 1974 (Noiret 3)

Nude Bomb, 1980 (Gassman 3, Schifrin 4)

Nude in His Pocket. *See* Amour de poche,
1957

Nude Restaurant, 1967 (Warhol 2)

Nudo di donna, 1981 (Age and Scarpelli 4,
Cassel 4)

Nuestra Natacha, 1936 (Rey 3)

Nuestras vidas, 1950 (Figueroa 4)

Nuestros, 1970 (Hermosillo 2)

Nueva cenicienta, 1964 (Rey 3)

Nuevitas, 1968 (Gómez 2)

Nugget Jim's Pardner, 1916 (Borzage 2)

Nugget Nell, 1919 (Garmes 4)

Nuisance, 1921 (Laurel and Hardy 3)

Nuisance, 1933 (Toland 4)

Nuit à l'hôtel, 1931 (Dalio 3, Achard 4)

Nuit agitée, 1897 (Guy 2)

Nuit agitée, 1908 (Feuillade 2)

Nuit agitée, 1912 (Linder 3)

Nuit américaine, 1973 (Truffaut 2, Baye 3,
Léaud 3, Delerue 4, Greene 4)

Nuit au paradis, 1931 (Heller 4)

Nuit bengali, 1988 (Chatterjee 3, Hurt 3,
Carrière 4, Trauner 4)

Nuit blanche, 1948 (Brasseur 3)

Nuit bulgare, 1969 (Vanel 3)

Nuit de carrefour, 1932 (Becker 2, Renoir 4)

Nuit de Carrefour, 1984 (Vogler 3)

Nuit de décembre, 1939 (Blier 3,
D'Eaubonne 4, Jaubert 4)

Nuit de folies, 1934 (Fernandel 3)

Nuit de la revanche, 1924 (Duvivier 2,
Vanel 3)

Nuit de Sybille, 1946 (Gélin 3)

Nuit de Varennes, 1981 (Scola 2, Barrault 3,
Mastroianni 3, Piccoli 3, Schygulla 3,
Trintignant 3, Amidei 4)

Nuit de Varennes, 1983 (Gélin 3)

Nuit d'or, 1976 (Blier 3, Kinski 3, Vanel 3)

Nuit del'ocean, 1988 (Moreau 3)

Nuit des adieux, 1965 (Cherkassov 3)

Nuit des Bulgares, 1969 (Vierny 4)

Nuit des Généraux. *See* Night of the
Generals, 1967

Nuit du 11 Septembre, 1919 (Mozhukin 3)

Nuit est mon royaume, 1951 (Gabin 3,
Spaak 4)

**Nuit et brouillard, 1955 (Cloquet 4,
Colpi 4, Delerue 4, Eisler 4)**

Nuit fantastique, 1942 (L'Herbier 2, Blier 3,
Presle 3, Jeanson 4)

Nuit merveilleuse, 1940 (Fernandel 3,
Vanel 3, Matras 4)

Nuit noire, Calcutta, 1964 (Duras 2)

**Nuit sur le Mont Chauve, 1933 (Alexeieff
and Parker 4)**

Nuit terrible, 1896 (Méliès 2)

Nuit tous les chats sont gris, 1977
(Depardieu 3)

Nuits de décembre, 1939 (Reggiani 3)

Nuits de feu, 1937 (L'Herbier 2,
Annenkov 4, Lourié 4)

Nuits de Paris. *See* Mirages de Paris, 1931

Nuits de Paris, 1951 (D'Eaubonne 4)

Nuits de prince, 1930 (Manès 3)

Nuits de princes, 1928 (Burel 4)

Nuits moscovites, 1934 (Baur 3, Amidei 4,
Andrejew 4, Annenkov 4, Jaubert 4,
Planer 4)

Nukiashi sashiashi, 1934 (Yoshimura 2,
Takamine 3)

Number, 1979 (Boulting 2)

No. 111. *See* 111-es, 1919

Number One, 1969 (Dern 3, Heston 3)

Number One with a Bullet, 1986 (Golan and
Globus 4)

Number, Please, 1920 (Lloyd 3, Roach 4)

Number Please, 1931 (Bennett 4)

Number Seventeen, 1932 (Hitchcock 2,
Reville 4)

Number Thirteen, 1922 (Hitchcock 2)

Numbered Men, 1930 (Leroy 2, Polito 4)

Numbered Woman, 1938 (Bond 3, Brown 4)

Numéro deux, 1975 (Godard 2, De
Beauregard 4)

Nun. *See* Suzanne Simonin, la religieuse de
Denis Diderot, 1966

Nunca pasa nada, 1963 (Bardem 2, Cassel 3,
Delerue 4)

Nun's Night. *See* Noc nevěsty, 1967

Nun's Story, 1959 (Zinnemann 2, Evans 3,
Finch 3, Hepburn 3, Blanke 4, Planer 4,
Trauner 4, Warner 4, Waxman 4)

Nunzio, 1978 (Schifrin 4)

Nuovi angeli, 1961 (Delli Colli 4)

Nuovi mostri, 1977 (Monicelli 2,
Gassman 3, Sordi 3, Age and Scarpelli 4,
Delli Colli 4)

. . . nur ein Komödiant, 1935 (Henreid 3,
Wegener 3)

Nur um tausend Dollars, 1918 (Dupont 2)
Nuregame Botan, 1961 (Kyo 3)
Nurekami kenka tabi, 1960 (Yamada 3)
Nuremberg Trials, 1946 (Lorentz 2)
Nurse. *See* Infermiera, 1975
Nurse Edith Cavell, 1939 (Wilcox 2,
  Neagle 3, Sanders 3, August 4,
  Young 4)
Nurse from Brooklyn, 1938 (Krasner 4)
Nurse Maid, 1932 (Iwerks 4)
Nurse Mates, 1940 (Fleischer 4)
Nurse to You, 1935 (Roach 4)
Nursery Crimes, 1943 (Fleischer 4)
Nursing a Viper, 1909 (Griffith 2, Sennett 2,
  Bitzer 4)
Nusumareta koi, 1951 (Mori 3)

Nut, 1921 (Chaplin 2, Fairbanks 3)
Nut-Cracker, 1926 (Horton 3)
Nutcracker Fantasy, 1979 (Lee 3,
  McDowall 3)
Nutcracker Prince, 1990 (O'Toole 3)
Nuts, 1987 (Ritt 2, Dreyfuss 3, Malden 3,
  Streisand 3, Wallach 3, Sargent 4)
Nuts and Jolts, 1929 (Lantz 4)
Nuts and Volts, 1964 (Blanc 4, Freleng 4)
Nuts in May, 1917 (Laurel and Hardy 3)
Nutty But Nice, 1940 (Three Stooges 3,
  Bruckman 4)
Nutty Naughty Chateau. *See* Château en
  Suede, 1963
Nutty Network, 1939 (Terry 4)
Nutty News, 1942 (Blanc 4, Stalling 4)

Nutty Notes, 1929 (Lantz 4)
Nutty Professor, 1963 (Lewis 2,
  Head 4)
Nuuk 250 år, 1979 (Roos 2)
Nyan-nyan-myan-hoi, 1940 (Hayasaka 4)
Nybyggarna, 1972 (Von Sydow 3,
  Ullmann 3)
Nyckeln och ringen, 1947 (Dahlbeck 3)
Nyní hraje dechovka, 1953 (Stallich 4)
Nyobo gakko, 1961 (Mori 3)
Nyonin Mandara, 1933 (Yamada 3)
Nyonin Mandara, Part II, 1934 (Yamada 3)
Nyordning på Sjögårda, 1944
  (Björnstrand 3)
Nyubo yo, eien nare, 1955 (Mori 3,
  Tanaka 3)

O Anthropos me to garyfallo, 1980
(Theodorakis 4)
O Bôca de Ouro, 1962 (Pereira Dos
Santos 2)
O.C. and Stiggs, 1985 (Altman 2, Hopper 3)
OCIL 1958, 1958 (Delerue 4)
O canto de saudade, 1952 (Mauro 2)
O Cerco, 1970 (De Almeida 4)
O Circo, 1965 (Diegues 2)
O descobrimento do Brasil, 1937 (Mauro 2)
O despertar da redentora, 1942 (Mauro 2)
O Dreamland, 1953 (Anderson 2)
O grande momento, 1958 (Pereira Dos
Santos 2)
O.H.M.S., 1937 (Walsh 2, Mills 3, Balcon 4,
Rank 4)
O. Henry's Full House, 1952 (Hawks 2,
King 2, Negulesco 2, Baxter 3,
Laughton 3, Monroe 3, Widmark 3,
Ballard 4, Johnson 4, Krasner 4,
LeMaire 4, Newman 4, Trotti 4)
O.K. Connery, 1967 (Morricone 4)
O.K. Nero. See O.K. Nerone, 1951
O.K. Nerone, 1951 (Cervi 3)
O liudiakh i atomakh, 1983 (Batalov 3)
O Lucky Man!, 1973 (Anderson 2, Frears 2,
McDowell 3, Richardson 3, Roberts 3,
Ondříček 4)
O Lugar do morto, 1982 (Branco 4)
O lyubvi, 1971 (Yankovsky 3)
O Melissokomos, 1986 (Mastroianni 3,
Reggiani 3, Guerra 4)
O Mimi san, 1914 (Hayakawa 3, Ince 4)
O Musca cu bani, 1954 (Popescu-Gopo 4)
O Outono, 1985 (Branco 4)
O Passado e o Presente, 1972 (De
Almeida 4)
O Patio, 1958 (Rocha 2)
O Rio de Machado de Assis, 1964 (Pereira
Dos Santos 2)
O.S.S., 1946 (Ladd 3, Dreier 4)
OSS 117 n'est pas mort, 1956
(D'Eaubonne 4)
O Saisons, o châteaux, 1957 (Varda 2,
Braunberger 4)
O Samba, 1988 (Scola 2, Mastroianni 3)
O scai, 1951 (Pereira Dos Santos 2)
O Segredo das Asas, 1944 (Mauro 2)
O ševci Matoušovi, 1948 (Stallich 4)
O skleníčku vic, 1953 (Brdečka 4, Trnka 4)
**O Slavnosti a hostech, 1968 (Nemec 2,
Schorm 2, Ponti 4)**
O Sole mio, 1945 (Delli Colli 4)
O světle, 1953 (Brdečka 4)
OTC, 1969 (Vukotić 4)
O zlaté rybce, 1951 (Trnka 4)
Oasis, 1955 (Allégret 2, Morgan 3)

Oatari otoko ichidai, 1956 (Yamada 3)
Oath, 1913 (Anderson 3)
Oath, 1921 (Walsh 2, Menzies 4)
Oath and the Man, 1910 (Griffith 2, Bitzer 4)
Oath of a Viking, 1914 (Rosher 4)
Oath of His Office, 1912 (Anderson 4)
Oath of Vengeance, 1944 (Crabbe 3)
Oath of Youth. See Kliatva molodikh, 1944
Obaasan, 1944 (Takamine 3)
Oban: Kanketsu-hen, 1958 (Yamamura 3)
Obchod na korze, 1965 (Kadár 2)
Obedient Flame, 1939 (McLaren 4)
Obelisk Ampersand Encounter, 1965
(Frampton 2)
Oberdan, 1916 (Bertini 3)
Oberst Redl, 1985 (Brandauer 3)
Oberwachtmeister Schwenek, 1935
(Fröhlich 3)
Oberwald Mystery. See Mistero di
Oberwald, 1979
Obey the Law, 1933 (Bond 3)
Objec na střapaté hurce, 1962 (Stallich 4)
Object Alimony, 1929 (Walker 4)
Object Matrimony. See Help Wanted—
Male, 1920
Object of Beauty, 1991 (Watkin 4)
Objectief gezien, 1968 (Müller 4)
Objectif 500 millions, 1966 (De
Beauregard 4)
Objection, 1986 (Olbrychski 3)
Objections Overruled, 1911 (Dwan 2)
Objective, Burma!, 1945 (Flynn 3, Howe 4,
Wald 4, Warner 4, Waxman 4)
Objective Seen. See Objectief gezien, 1968
Obliging Young Lady, 1941 (Arden 3,
O'Brien 3, Pangborn 3, Musuraca 4)
Oblomok imperii, 1929 (Enei 4)
Oblong Box, 1969 (Lee 3, Price 3)
Obo Kissa, 1929 (Hasegawa 3)
Obocchan, 1926 (Tanaka 3)
Oboro kago, 1951 (Tanaka 3, Yamada 3,
Yoda 4)
Oborona Tsaritsina, 1942 (Vasiliev 2)
Oborono Sevastopolya, 1911 (Mozhukin 3)
Obrácení Ferdyše Pištory, 1931 (Stallich 4)
Obratnaya svyaz, 1977 (Yankovsky 3)
Obryv, 1913 (Mozhukin 3)
Obscure Evil. See Male oscuro, 1990
Obsession, 1934 (Vanel 3, Jaubert 4)
Obsession, 1949 (Baker 3, Newton 3,
Adam 4, Rota 4)
Obsession, 1954 (Delannoy 2, Morgan 3)
Obsession, 1976 (De Palma 2, Schrader 2,
Bujold 3, Robertson 3, Herrmann 4,
Zsigmond 4)
Obsession. See Junoon, 1979
Obuknovennoe utro, 1978 (Yankovsky 3)

Obůsku, z pytle ven!, 1956 (Brdečka 4)
Ocalenie, 1959 (Ścibor-Rylski 4)
Occhi freddi della paura, 1971 (Morricone 4)
Occhi, la bocca, 1983 (Piccoli 3)
Occhiali d'oro, 1987 (Noiret 3, Morricone 4)
Occhio alla penna, 1981 (Morricone 4)
Occhio del ragno, 1971 (Johnson 3,
Kinski 3)
Occhio nel labarinto, 1970 (Valli 3)
Occhio selvaggio, 1967 (Guerra 4)
Occident, 1938 (Berry 3, Vanel 3)
Occupe-toi d'Amélie, 1949 (Darrieux 3,
Aurenche 4, Bost 4, Douy 4)
Ocean Breakers. See Brannigar, 1935
Ocean Hop, 1927 (Disney 4)
Ocean Swells, 1934 (Stevens 2)
Ocean Waif, 1916 (Guy 2)
Oceano, 1971 (Morricone 4)
Ocean's Eleven, 1960 (Milestone 2,
Dickinson 3, MacLaine 3, Martin 3,
Raft 3, Sinatra 3, Bass 4, Cahn 4,
Daniels 4, Lederer 4)
Och en, 1978 (Josephson 3, Thulin 3,
Nykvist 4)
Ochazuke no aji, 1952 (Ryu 3)
Ochiba nikki, 1953 (Yamamura 3)
Ochimusha, 1925 (Tanaka 3)
Ochiyo toshigoro, 1937 (Miyagawa 4)
Ochiyo-gasa, 1935 (Miyagawa 4)
Ochiyo's Umbrella. See Ochiyo-gasa, 1935
Ocho años de Revolucion, 1966 (Alvarez 2)
Ochsenkrieg, 1920 (Planer 4)
Oci ciornie, 1987 (Mangano 3,
Mastroianni 3, Cecchi D'Amico 4,
Lai 4)
Oci pro plac, 1984 (Brodský 3)
Octagon, 1980 (Van Cleef 3)
Octa-Man, 1970 (Baker 4)
October. See **Oktiabr, 1928**
October. See Oktiabr, 1967
October, 1982 (Bondarchuk 3)
October Days. See Oktiabr' dni, 1958
October Man, 1947 (Greenwood 3, Mills 3,
Alwyn 4, Rank 4, Vetchinsky 4)
October Revolution, 1967 (Gielgud 3)
Octopussy, 1983 (Jourdan 3, Barry 4)
Octubre de todos, 1977 (Alvarez 2)
Odalisque, 1914 (Reid 3, Sweet 3,
Walthall 3)
Odd Couple, 1968 (Lemmon 3, Matthau 3,
Cahn 4, Westmore Family 4)
Odd Job Man, 1911 (Dwan 2)
**Odd Man Out, 1947 (Reed 2, Cusack 3,
Mason 3, Newton 3, Alwyn 4,
Krasker 4, Mathieson 4, Rank 4,
Sherriff 4)**
Odd Obsession. See Kagi, 1959

Odds Against Tomorrow, 1959 (Wise 2, Grahame 3, Ryan 3, Winters 3, Allen 4)

Oden jigoku, 1960 (Kyo 3)

Odessa File, 1974 (Schell 3, Voight 3, Morris 4)

Odessa in fiamme, 1942 (Gallone 2)

Odette, 1916 (Bertini 3)

Odette, 1928 (Bertini 3, Kortner 3)

Odette, 1950 (Wilcox 2, Howard 3, Neagle 3, Ustinov 3, Dehn 4)

Odeur des fauves, 1970 (De Sica 2, Lai 4)

Odinnadtsatii, 1928 (Vertov 2)

Odissea, 1968 (Papas 3)

Odna, 1931 (Enei 4, Moskvin 4, Shostakovich 4)

Odongo, 1956 (Alwyn 4)

Odor of the Day, 1948 (Blanc 4, Stalling 4)

Odor-able Kitty, 1945 (Blanc 4, Jones 4, Stalling 4)

Odoriko, 1957 (Kyo 3)

Odplata, 1920 (Heller 4)

Oduro Meikun, 1936 (Hasegawa 3)

Odwiedziny prezydenta, 1961 (Tyszkiewicz 3)

Odyssée du Capitaine Steve. See Walk into Paradise, 1955

Odyssée du Monsanto, 1981 (Cassel 3)

Odysseus, 1986 (Kučera 4)

Odysseus' Heimkehr, 1918 (Messter 4)

Odyssey of the North, 1914 (Bosworth 3)

Ocdipo re, 1967 (Donati 4)

Oedipus Rex. See Edipo Re, 1967

Oedipus the King, 1968 (Welles 2, Cusack 3, Sutherland 3, Lassally 4)

Oedo gonin otoko, 1951 (Yamada 3)

Oedo hara no yowa, 1938 (Shindo 3)

Oedo no kyoji, 1960 (Kagawa 3)

Oedo no oni, 1947 (Hasegawa 3, Takamine 3)

Oedo no saigon, 1928 (Tsuburaya 4)

Oeil du maître, 1957 (Resnais 2, Braunberger 4)

Oeil du malin, 1962 (Chabrol 2, Audran 3, De Beauregard 3, Ponti 4)

Oeil pour oeil, 1956 (Bost 4, Matras 4)

Oeil Torve. See Oko wykol, 1960

Oeil-du-Lynx, détective, 1936 (Kaufman 4)

Oen-dancho no koi, 1933 (Tanaka 3)

Oensan, 1955 (Tsukasa 3)

O'er Hill and Dale, 1932 (Grierson 2, Wright 2)

Oeufs brouillés, 1975 (Cassel 3, Karina 3, Carrière 4)

Oeufs de l'autruche, 1957 (Fresnay 3)

Oeuvre au noir, 1988 (Karina 3, Volonté 3)

Oeuvre immortelle, 1924 (Duvivier 2)

Oeuvre scientifique de Pasteur, 1946 (Fradetal 4)

Oeyama Shuten-doji, 1960 (Hasegawa 3)

Of A Thousand Delights. See Vaghe stelle dell'orsa, 1965

Of Cash and Hash, 1955 (Three Stooges 3)

Of Feline Bondage, 1965 (Jones 4)

Of Flesh and Blood. See Grands Chemins, 1962

Of Fox and Hounds, 1940 (Avery 4, Blanc 4, Stalling 4)

Of Human Bondage, 1934 (Cromwell 2, Davis 3, Howard 3, Berman 4, Plunkett 4, Polglase 4, Steiner 4)

Of Human Bondage, 1946 (Goulding 2, Henreid 3, Blanke 4, Friedhofer 4, Korngold 4)

Of Human Bondage, 1964 (Hathaway 2, Harvey 3, Novak 3, Box 4, Morris 4)

Of Human Hearts, 1938 (Brown 2, Bondi 3, Carradine 3, Coburn 3, Huston 3, Stewart 3, Stothart 4, Vorkapich 4)

Of Human Rights, 1950 (Van Dongen 4)

Of Life and Love. See Questa è la vita, 1954

Of Love and Desire, 1963 (Oberon 3)

Of Men and Demons, 1969 (Hubley 4, Jones 4)

Of Men and Mice, 1950 (Paxton 4)

Of Men and Music, 1950 (Aldrich 2, Crosby 4, Mohr 4)

Of Mice and Men, 1939 (Milestone 2, Meredith 3, Copland 4, Roach 4)

Of Mice and Men, 1981 (Ayres 3)

Of Pure Blood, 1986 (Remick 3)

Of Rice and Hen, 1953 (Blanc 4, McKimson 4, Stalling 4)

Of Stars and Men, 1961 (Hubley 4)

Of Thee I Sting, 1946 (Blanc 4, Freleng 4)

Off Beat, 1986 (Allen 4)

Off His Trolley, 1924 (Garnett 2, Sennett 2)

Off Limits, 1953 (Crosby 3, Hope 3, Rooney 3, Head 4)

Off the Dole, 1935 (Formby 3)

Off the Highway, 1925 (Stromberg 4)

Off the Record, 1939 (Blondell 3, Deutsch 4, Rosher 4)

Off the Trolley, 1919 (Daniels 3, Lloyd 3, Roach 4)

Off to China, 1936 (Terry 4)

Off to the Opera, 1952 (Terry 4)

Offbeat, 1960 (Zetterling 2)

Offence, 1972 (Lumet 2, Connery 3, Howard 3, Fisher 4)

Office Blues, 1930 (Rogers 3)

Office Boy, 1932 (Iwerks 4)

Office Boy's Revenge, 1903 (Porter 2)

Office Girl. See Sunshine Susie, 1931

Office Wife, 1930 (Bacon 2, Blondell 3, Bosworth 3, Zanuck 4)

Officer and a Gentleman, 1982 (Gere 3)

Officer Cupid, 1921 (Sennett 2)

Officer John Donovan, 1913 (Talmadge 3)

Officer O'Brien, 1930 (Garnett 2, Miller 4)

Officer Pooch, 1941 (Hanna and Barbera 4)

Officer 666, 1932 (Niblo 2)

Officer Thirteen, 1932 (Rooney 3)

Officer's Mess, 1931 (Lanchester 3)

Officer's Swordknot. See Tiszti kardbojt, 1915

Official Officers, 1925 (Roach 4)

Offizierstragödie. See Rosenmontag, 1924

Offret, 1986 (Tarkovsky 2, Josephson 3, Colpi 4, Nykvist 4)

Off-Shore Pirate, 1921 (Young 4)

Offspring. See From a Whisper to a Scream, 1986

Oficio más antiguo, 1968 (Alcoriza 4)

Often an Orphan, 1949 (Blanc 4, Jones 4)

Oggetti smarriti, 1979 (Ganz 3)

Oggi a me ... domani a te!, 1968 (Argento 4)

Oggi, domani, dopodomani, 1965 (Ferreri 2, Mastoianni 3, Di Venanzo 4)

O-gin Sama, 1960 (Tanaka 3)

Ogin Sama, 1978 (Yoda 4)

Ogin Sama, 1982 (Okada 3, Shimura 3)

Oginsawa, 1979 (Mifune 3)

Ognuno per se, 1968 (Kinski 3)

Ogro, 1979 (Cristaldi 4, Morricone 4)

Oh, 1965 (Vanderbeek 2)

Oh Amelia!, See Occupe-toi d'Amélie, 1949

Oh! Calcutta!, 1971 (Shepard 4)

Oh Dad, Poor Dad, Mamma's Hung You in the Closet and I'm Feelin' So Sad, 1967 (Mackendrick 2, Russell 3, Stark 4, Unsworth 4)

Oh Daddy!, 1922 (Sennett 2)

Oh, Daddy!, 1935 (Balcon 4, Rank 4)

Oh, Doctor, 1914 (Beery 3)

Oh Doctor!, 1917 (Keaton 2, Arbuckle 3)

Oh, Doctor!, 1925 (Astor 3)

Oh, Doctor!, 1937 (Arden 3, Horton 3, Krasner 4)

Oh, For a Man, 1930 (Lugosi 3, MacDonald 3, Clarke 4)

Oh! For a Man. See Will Success Spoil Rock Hunter, 1957

Oh Gentle Spring, 1942 (Terry 4)

Oh, God!, 1977 (Bellamy 3, Pleasence 3)

Oh! Heavenly Dog, 1980 (Sharif 3)

Oh! How I Hate to Get Up in the Morning, 1932 (Fleischer 4)

Oh, Johnny, How You Can Love!, 1940 (Krasner 4)

Oh, Kay!, 1928 (LeRoy 2, Moore 3, Wilson 4)

Oh Lady, Lady, 1920 (Daniels 3)

Oh les femmes. See Max et les femmes, 1912

Oh Life—A Woe Story—The A Test News, 1962 (Brakhage 2)

Oh, Mabel!, 1929 (Fleischer 4)

Oh, Mabel Behave, 1922 (Sennett 2, Normand 3)

Oh, Men! Oh, Women!, 1957 (Rogers 3, Niven 3, Pangborn 3, Clarke 4, Friedhofer 4, LeMaire 4, Johnson 4)

Oh, Mr. Porter!, 1937 (Launder and Gilliat 2, Hay 3, Rank 4, Vetchinsky 4)

Oh Money, Money, 1951 (Coburn 3)

Oh My Aunt, 1914 (Hepworth 2)

Oh, Promise Me, 1921 (Roach 4)

Oh! Que Mambo!, 1958 (Sordi 3)

Oh, Rosalinda!, 1955 (Quayle 3, Redgrave 3, Walbrook 3, Challis 4, Heckroth 4)

Oh! Such a Night, 1910 (White 3)

Oh Susanna, 1933 (Terry 4)

Oh! Susanna, 1936 (Autry 3)

Oh, Teacher, 1927 (Disney 4)

Oh, Those Eyes, 1911 (Sennett 2, Normand 3)

Oh, Uncle!, 1926 (Sennett 2)

Oh, What a Knight, 1928 (Disney 4)

Oh What a Knight, 1982 (Driessen 4)

Oh! What a Lovely War, 1969 (Attenborough 3, Bogarde 3, Cassel 3, Gielgud 3, Hawkins 3, Mills 3, More 3, Olivier 3, Redgrave, M. 3, Redgrave, V. 3, Richardson 3, Smith 3, York 3)

Oh! What a Nurse!, 1926 (Zanuck 4)

Oh, Yeah!, 1929 (Miller 4)

Oh, You Are Like a Rose. See Ack, du är some en ros, 1967

Oh You Beautiful Doll, 1926 (Fleischer 4)

Oh, You Beautiful Doll, 1949 (Stahl 2, LeMaire 4, Newman 4, Steiner 4)

Oh! You Mummy!, 1910 (White 3)

Oh! You Pearl, 1910 (White 3)

Oh! You Puppy!, 1910 (White 3)

Oh! You Scotch Lassie!, 1910 (White 3)

Oh, You Tony!, 1924 (Mix 3)

Oh, You Women!, 1919 (Emerson 4, Loos 4)

Ohan, 1985 (Ichikawa 2)

Ohanahan, 1966 (Iwashita 3)

O'Hara—Squatter and Philosopher, 1912 (Talmadge 3)

O'Hara's Wife, 1983 (Foster 3)

Ohayo, 1959 (Ozu 2, Ryu 3)
Oh-Edo gonon otoko, 1951 (Yoda 4)
Ohitsu oharetsu Somekawa Shohachi, 1931 (Yamada 3)
Ohm Krüger, 1941 (Gründgens 3, Jannings 3, Wagner 4)
Ohne Zeugen, 1919 (Kortner 3)
Ohnivé léto, 1939 (Baarová 3)
Ohtone no yogiri, 1950 (Kagawa 3)
Ohtoro-jo no hanayome, 1957 (Shimura 3, Shindo 3)
Oil and Water, 1913 (Griffith 2, Barrymore 3, Gish 3, Sweet 3, Walthall 3, Bitzer 4)
Oil Can Mystery, 1933 (Terry 4)
Oil for Aladdin's Lamp, 1942 (Ivens 2)
Oil for the Lamps of China, 1935 (Florey 2, LeRoy 2, Crisp 3, Gaudio 4)
Oil Hell of Killing Women. See Onna goroshi abura jigoku, 1949
Oil on Troubled Waters, 1913 (Dwan 2)
Oil Raider, 1934 (Crabbe 3)
Oil's Well, 1929 (Lantz 4)
Oil's Well That Ends Well, 1958 (Three Stooges 3)
Oily American, 1954 (Blanc 4, McKimson 4, Stalling 4)
Oily Hare, 1952 (Blanc 4, McKimson 4, Stalling 4)
Oily Scoundrel, 1916 (Sennett 2)
Oily to Bed, Oily to Rise, 1939 (Three Stooges 3)
Oise mairi, 1939 (Yoda 4)
Oiseau de paradis, 1962 (Jarre 4)
Oiseau rare, 1935 (Brasseur 3, Prévert 4)
Oiseau rare, 1973 (Presle 3)
Oiseau s'en vole, 1960 (Alekan 4)
Oiseaux d'Afrique, 1961 (Braunberger 4)
Oiseaux vont mourir au Pérou, 1967 (Darrieux 3)
Oiseaux vont mourir au Perou, 1968 (Brasseur 3, Seberg 3, Matras 4)
Oito Universitários, 1967 (Diegues 2)
Ojciec królowej, 1980 (Stawiński 4)
Ojo de la cerradura, 1964 (Torre Nilsson 2)
Ojo Kichiza, 1926 (Kinugasa 2)
Ojo Kissa, 1973 (Hasegawa 3)
Ojo Okichi, 1935 (Yamada 3)
Ojojoj eller sången om den eldröda hummern, 1965 (Fischer 4)
Ojos vendados, 1978 (Saura 2)
Ojosan, 1930 (Tanaka 3)
Ojo-san, 1937 (Takamine 3)
Ojosan kanpai, 1949 (Shindo 2, Hara 3)
Ok ketten, 1977 (Nowicki 3)
Oka wa hanazakari, 1952 (Yamamura 3)
Okaasan, 1952 (Okada 3)
O'Kalems' Visit to Killarney, 1912 (Olcott 2)
Okända, 1913 (Stiller 2)
Okarina, 1919 (Veidt 3)
Okasan, 1952 (Kagawa 3, Tanaka 3)
Okay America, 1932 (Ayres 3, Calhern 3, O'Sullivan 3, Miller 4)
Okay, America, 1932 (Miller 4)
O-Kay for Sound, 1937 (Launder and Gilliat 2, Crazy Gang 3, Vetchinsky 4)
Okayo no kakugo, 1939 (Tanaka 3)
Okénko, 1933 (Baarová 3, Stallich 4)
Okiku to Harima, 1954 (Hasegawa 3)
Okinu to banto, 1940 (Tanaka 3)
Oklahoma, 1955 (Zinnemann 2)

Oklahoma!, 1955 (Grahame 3, Steiger 3, Crosby 4, Deutsch 4, Levien, Orry-Kelly 4, Surtees 4)
Oklahoma, 1980 (McCrea 3)
Oklahoma Badlands, 1948 (Canutt 4)
Oklahoma Crude, 1973 (Kramer 2, Dunaway 3, Mills 3, Palance 3, Scott 3, Mancini 4, Surtees 4)
Oklahoma Kid, 1939 (Bacon 2, Bogart 3, Bond 3, Cagney 3, Crisp 3, Buckner 4, Deutsch 4, Friedhofer 4, Howe 4, Orry-Kelly 4, Steiner 4)
Oklahoma Outlaws, 1943 (Eason 4)
Oklahoma Renegades, 1939 (Canutt 4)
Oklahoma Woman, 1956 (Corman 2)
Oklahoman, 1957 (McCrea 3, Mirisch 4)
Oklahomas, 1957 (Salter 4)
Oko wykol, 1960 (Skolimowski 2)
Okomé, 1951 (Rabier 4)
Oktiabr, 1928 (Tisse 4)
Oktiabr, 1967 (Shostakovich 4)
Oktiabr' dni, 1958 (Vasiliev 2)
Okuman-choja, 1954 (Okada 3, Yamada 3)
Okuni and Gohei. See Okuni to Gohei, 1952
Okuni to Gohei, 1952 (Naruse 2, Yamamura 3)
Okusama ni goyojin, 1950 (Mori 3, Tanaka 3)
Okusama wa daigaku-sei, 1956 (Kagawa 3)
Ol' Gray Hoss, 1928 (Roach 4)
Ol' Swimmin' 'ole, 1928 (Disney 4)
Ola and Julia. See Ola och Julia, 1967
Ola och Julia, 1967 (Fischer 4)
Olaf—an Atom, 1913 (Griffith 2, Carey 3, Bitzer 4)
Olaf Laughs Last, 1942 (Bruckman 4)
Olavi, 1920 (Lukas 3)
Old Acquaintance, 1943 (Davis 3, Hopkins 3, Blanke 4, Coffee 4, Orry-Kelly 4, Polito 4, Waxman 4)
Old Actor, 1912 (Griffith 2, Marsh 3, Pickford 3, Bitzer 4)
Old Age Handicap, 1928 (Browning 2)
Old Age—The Wasted Years, 1966 (Leacock 2)
Old and New. See Staroie i novoie, 1929
Old Barn, 1929 (Sennett 2, Hornbeck 4)
Old Barn Dance, 1938 (Autry 3, Rogers 3)
Old Battersea House, 1961 (Russell 2)
Old Bill and Son, 1940 (Crichton 2, Mills 3, Dalrymple 4, Korda, A. 4, Korda, V. 4, Périnal 4)
Old Black Joe, 1926 (Fleischer 4)
Old Blackout Joe, 1940 (Hubley 4)
Old Bones of the River, 1938 (Launder and Gilliat 2, Hay 3)
Old Bookkeeper, 1911 (Griffith 2, Bitzer 4)
Old Box, 1975 (Driessen 4)
Old Boyfriends, 1979 (Schrader 2, Belushi 3, Fraker 4, Henry 4, Houseman 4)
Old Bull, 1932 (Roach 4)
Old Chisholm Trail, 1942 (Salter 4)
Old Clothes, 1925 (Crawford 3)
Old Cobbler, 1914 (Chaney 3)
Old Confectioner's Mistake, 1911 (Griffith 2, Bitzer 4)
Old Corral, 1936 (Autry 3, Rogers 3)
Old Czech Legends. See **Staré pověsti cěské, 1953**
Old Dark House, 1932 (Whale 2, Douglas 3, Karloff 3, Laughton 3, Massey 3, Edeson 4, Fulton 4, Laemmle 4, Pierce 4, Sherriff 4)
Old Dark House, 1966 (Carreras 4)
Old Dog Tray, 1935 (Terry 4)

Old Doll, 1911 (Bunny 3)
Old Dracula. See Vampira, 1973
Old Dudino. See Granitsa, 1935
Old English, 1930 (Arliss 3)
Old Enough, 1984 (Ballhaus 4)
Oldest Profession. See Plus Vieux Métier du monde, 1967
Old Explorers, 1990 (Ferrer 3)
Old Fashioned Girl, 1915 (Crisp 3)
Old Fire Horse, 1939 (Terry 4)
Old Fire Horse and the New Fire Chief, 1914 (Bunny 3)
Old Folks at Home, 1929 (Fleischer 4)
Old Glory, 1939 (Blanc 4, Jones 4, Stalling 4)
Old Greatheart. See Way Back Home, 1931
Old Grey Hare, 1944 (Blanc 4, Clampett 4, Stalling 4)
Old Grey Manor, 1935 (Hope 3)
Old Gringo, 1989 (Fonda 3, Peck 3)
Old Guard, 1941 (Gerasimov 2)
Old Gun. See Vieux Fusil, 1975
Old Heads and Young Hearts, 1910 (Lawrence 3)
Old Heidelberg, 1915 (Von Stroheim 2, Reid 3)
Old Homes of the River, 1938 (Vetchinsky 4)
Old Homestead, 1922 (Cruze 2, Brown 4, Zukor 4)
Old Homestead, 1935 (Rogers 3)
Old Hutch, 1936 (Beery 3)
Old Ironsides, 1926 (Arzner 2, Beery 3, Karloff 3, Schulberg 4)
Old Isaacs, the Pawnbroker, 1908 (Bitzer 4)
Old Lady 31, 1920 (Mathis 4)
Old Louisianna, 1937 (Hayworth 3)
Old Loves and New, 1926 (Tourneur 2, Pidgeon 3)
Old Maid, 1914 (Sweet 3)
Old Maid, 1939 (Goulding 2, Crisp 3, Davis 3, Hopkins 3, Akins 4, Blanke 4, Friedhofer 4, Gaudio 4, Orry-Kelly 4, Robinson 4, Steiner 4, Wallis 4)
Old Maid. See Vieille Fille, 1972
Old Maid's Baby, 1914 (Bunny 3)
Old Mammy's Secret Code, 1913 (Ince 4)
Old Man and Dog, 1970 (Armstrong 2)
Old Man and the Sea, 1958 (Sturges 2, Tracy 3, Crosby 4, Howe 4, Tiomkin 4)
Old Man and the Sea, 1990 (Quinn 3)
Old Man Bezouska. See Pantáta Bezoušek, 1927
Old Man Minick, 1932 (Beavers 3)
Old Man of the Mountain, 1933 (Fleischer 4)
Old Man Rhythm, 1935 (Ball 3, Grable 3, Mercer 4, Musuraca 4, Pan 4)
Old Man Who Cried Wolf, 1970 (Jaffe 3, Robinson 3)
Old Mill at Midnight, 1914 (Meredyth 4)
Old Mother Hubbard, 1935 (Iwerks 4)
Old Mother Hubbard. See Mother Goose Presents Humpty Dumpty, 1946
Old Mother Riley in Business, 1940 (Baxter 2)
Old Mother Riley in Society, 1940 (Baxter 2)
Old Mother Riley Meets the Vampire, 1952 (Lugosi 3)
Old Oaken Bucket, 1941 (Terry 4)
Old Reliable, 1914 (Talmadge 3)
Old Rockin' Chair Tom, 1947 (Hanna and Barbera 4)

On the Fire, 1918 (Daniels 3, Lloyd 3, Roach 4)

On the Firing Line, 1912 (Ince 4)

On the Front Page, 1926 (Laurel and Hardy 3, Roach 4)

On the Green Meadow. See Na tý louce zelený, 1936

On the Harmfulness of Tobacco, 1959 (Newman 3)

On the Jump, 1918 (Walsh 2, Daniels 3, Lloyd 3, Roach 4)

On the Level, 1930 (McLaglen 3, Nichols 4)

On the Little Big Horn, 1910 (Mix 3, Selig 4)

On the Loose, 1932 (Roach 4)

On the Loose, 1951 (Douglas 3, Lederer 4)

On the Moonlight Trail, 1912 (Anderson 3)

On the Move. See Utkösben, 1979

On the Night of the Fire, 1939 (Richardson 3, Rozsa 4)

On the Night Stage, 1914 (Hart 3, August 4, Ince 4, Sullivan 4)

On the Old Spanish Trail, 1947 (Rogers 3)

On the Pole, 1960 (Leacock 2)

On the Quiet, 1918 (Barrymore 3)

On the Reef, 1909 (Griffith 2, Walthall 3, Bitzer 4)

On the Riviera, 1951 (Dalio 3, Kaye 3, Tierney 3, Cole 4, LeMaire 4, Newman 4, Shamroy 4)

On the Roads of Fate. See På livets ödesväger, 1913

On the Sunny Side. See På solsidan, 1936

On the Sunny Side, 1942 (Darwell 3, McDowall 3)

On the Sunnyside. See Na sluneční straně, 1933

On the Threshold, 1925 (Walthall 3)

On the Threshold of Space, 1956 (LeMaire 4)

On the Town, 1949 (Donen 2, Kelly 3, Miller 3, Sinatra 3, Comden 4, Edens 4, Freed 4, Gibbons 4, Mayer 4, Rose 4, Rosson 4, Smith 4)

On the Waterfront, 1954 (Kazan 2, Brando 3, Cobb 3, Malden 3, Saint 3, Steiger 3, Cohn 4, Day 4, Kaufman 4, Spiegel 4)

On the Western Frontier, 1909 (Porter 2)

On the Wrong Trek, 1935 (Roach 4)

On Their Own, 1939 (Miller 3)

On Their Way, 1921 (Roach 4)

On Their Wedding Eve, 1913 (Costello 3)

On Thin Ice, 1924 (Haskin 4, Zanuck 4)

On Time, 1924 (Fort 4)

On Top of Old Smoky, 1953 (Autry 3)

On to Reno, 1927 (Cruze 2)

On Trial, 1928 (Pangborn 3, Haskin 4)

On Trial. See Affaire Mauritzius, 1953

On Wings of Eagles, 1986 (Lancaster 3)

On with the Dance, 1920 (Miller 4)

On with the New, 1938 (Fleischer 4)

On with the Show, 1929 (Brown 3, Gaudio 4)

On Your Back, 1930 (August 4)

On Your Toes, 1939 (O'Connor 3, Howe 4, Orry-Kelly 4, Wald 4)

On ze Boulevard, 1927 (Daniels 4, Gibbons 4)

Ona zashchischaet Rodinu, 1943 (Maretskaya 3)

Onai goju-ryo, 1931 (Yamada 3)

Onassis: The Richest Man in the World, 1988 (Quinn 3)

Onatsu Seijuro, 1936 (Hasegawa 3, Tanaka 3)

Onatsu torimono-cho: Torima, 1960 (Yamada 3)

Onatsu torimono-cho: Tsukiyo ni kieta onna, 1959 (Yamada 3)

Once . . . , 1990 (Price 3, Quayle 3)

Once a Crook, 1941 (Cusack 3)

Once a Gentleman, 1930 (Cruze 2, Bushman 3, Horton 3)

Once a Hero, 1931 (Arbuckle 3)

Once a Hero. See It Happened in Hollywood, 1937

Once a Jolly Swagman, 1948 (Bogarde 3, Cusack 3, Dalrymple 4, Rank 4)

Once a Lady, 1931 (Novello 3, Akins 4, Banton 4, Hoffenstein 4, Lang 4, Zukor 4)

Once a Rainy Day. See Akogare, 1966

Once a Sinner, 1931 (McCrea 3)

Once a Thief, 1935 (Pearson 2, Havelock-Allan 4)

Once a Thief, 1950 (Clothier 4, Leven 4)

Once a Thief, 1965 (Delon 3, Palance 3, Burks 4, Schifrin 4)

Once Around, 1991 (Dreyfuss 3, Rowlands 3)

Once de Pekin, 1933 (Brasseur 3)

Once Every Ten Minutes, 1914 (Lloyd 3, Roach 4)

Once in a Blue Moon, 1935 (Garmes 4, Hecht 4, MacArthur 4)

Once in a Lifetime, 1932 (Ladd 3, Laemmle 4)

Once Is Not Enough, 1975 (Douglas 3, Mercouri 3, Alonzo 4, Epstein 4, Green 4, Mancini 4)

Once More, My Darling, 1949 (Orry-Kelly 4, Montgomery 3, Harrison 4)

Once More with Feeling, 1960 (Donen 2, Brynner 3, Kendall 3, Périnal 4, Trauner 4)

Once Over, 1923 (Roach 4)

Once por cero, 1970 (Alvarez 2)

Once to Every Woman, 1920 (Valentino 3)

Once to Every Woman, 1934 (Bellamy 3, Darwell 3, Wray 3)

Once Upon a Crime, 1992 (De Laurentiis 4, Rotunno 4)

Once Upon a Dead Man, 1971 (Hudson 3)

Once Upon a Dream, 1948 (Withers 3, Rank 4)

Once Upon a Honeymoon, 1942 (McCarey 2, Grant 3, Rogers 3, Barnes 4)

Once Upon a Scoundrel, 1973 (Figueroa 4, North 4)

Once Upon a Spy, 1980 (Lee 3, Sangster 4)

Once Upon a Texas Train, 1988 (Widmark 3)

Once Upon a Thursday. See Affairs of Martha, 1943

Once Upon a Time, 1910 (Lawrence 3)

Once Upon a Time, 1944 (Grant 3, Planer 4)

Once Upon a Time, 1957 (Ivanov-Vano 4)

Once Upon a Time. See C'era una volta, 1966

Once Upon a Time in America, 1984 (Leone 2, De Niro 3, Weld 3, Delli Colli 4, Morricone 4)

Once Upon a Time in the West. See **C'era una volta il West, 1968**

Once Upon a Time . . . Is Now, 1977 (Hitchcock 2, Grant, C. 3, Grant, L. 3, Fisher 4)

Once Upon a Time There Was a King. See Byl jednou jeden král, 1954

Once Upon a Tractor, 1965 (Torre Nilsson 2)

Onda, 1955 (Olmi 2)

Ondata di calore, 1970 (Seberg 3)

Ondomane, 1961 (Delerue 4)

One Against Many, 1956 (Dieterle 2)

One Against Seven. See Counter-Attack, 1945

One Against the World, 1939 (Zinnemann 2)

One A.M., 1916 (Chaplin 2)

One Among Many. See Een blandt mange, 1961

One and One. See och En, 1978

One and Only Genuine Original Family Band, 1968 (Brennan 3, Hawn 3)

One and Yet, 1957 (Vanderbeek 2)

One Arabian Night. See Sumurun, 1920

One at a Time, 1924 (Roach 4)

One Body Too Many, 1944 (Lugosi 3)

One Born Every Minute. See Flim-Flam Man, 1967

One Busy Hour, 1909 (Griffith 2, Bitzer 4)

One But a Lion. See En, men ett lejon, 1940

One Cab's Family, 1951 (Avery 4)

One Can Say It without Getting Angry. See On peut le dire sans se fâcher!, 1978

One Clear Call, 1922 (Stahl 2, Walthall 3, Mayer 4, Meredyth 4)

One Crowded Night, 1940 (Hunt 4, Polglase 4)

One Cylinder Love, 1923 (Sennett 2)

One Day, I . . . See Aruhi watashi wa, 1959

One Day in the Life of Ivan Denisovich, 1971 (Nykvist 4)

One Deadly Summer. See Été meurtrier, 1983

One Desire, 1955 (Baxter 3, Hudson 3, Wood 3, Hunter 4)

One Exciting Adventure, 1934 (Wilder 2)

One Exciting Night, 1922 (Griffith 2)

One Exciting Night, 1944 (Heller 4)

One Exciting Week, 1946 (Three Stooges 3, Alton 4)

One Eyed Jacks, 1961 (Brando 3, Johnson 3, Malden 3, Edouart 4, Friedhofer 4, Fulton 4, Lang 4, Westmore Family 4)

One Fiancé at a Time. See Fästman i taget, 1952

One Fine Day. See Un certo giorno, 1968

One Flew Over the Cuckoo's Nest, 1975 (Forman 2, Douglas 3, Nicholson 3, Fraker 4, Wexler 4)

One Foot in Heaven, 1941 (Bondi 3, Bosworth 3, March 3, Friedhofer 4, Robinson 4, Rosher 4, Steiner 4, Wallis 4)

One Foot in Hell, 1960 (Ladd 3)

One for the Books, 1939 (Hutton 3)

One Frightened Night, 1935 (Lewis 2)

One Froggy Evening, 1955 (Blanc 4, Jones 4, Maltese 4)

One from the Heart, 1982 (Coppola 2, Kinski 3, Stanton 3, Storaro 4, Tavoularis 4)

One Glass Too Much. See O skleničků víc, 1953

One Glorious Day, 1922 (Cruze 2, Rogers 3, Brown 4)

One Good Joke Deserves Another, 1913 (Bunny 3)

One Good Turn, 1931 (Laurel and Hardy 3, Roach 4)

One Good Turn, 1954 (Wisdom 3, Addison 4, Dillon 4, Rank 4)

One Grain of Barley. *See* Hitotsubu no mugi, 1958

One Great Vision, 1953 (Lassally 4)

One Gun Gary in Nick of Time, 1939 (Terry 4)

One Ham's Family, 1943 (Avery 4)

One Heavenly Night, 1930 (Barnes 4, Brown 4, Goldwyn 4, Howard 4, Toland 4)

One Horse Farmers, 1934 (Roach 4)

One Hour Before Dawn, 1920 (King 2)

One Hour Late, 1935 (Milland 3)

One Hour Married, 1926 (Normand 3)

One Hour of Love, 1926 (Florey 2)

One Hour to Doomsday. *See* City Beneath the Sea, 1970

One Hour with You, 1932 (Cukor 2, Lubitsch 2, Chevalier 3, MacDonald 3, Dreier 4, Raphaelson 4, Zukor 4)

One Hundred a Day, 1973 (Armstrong 2)

One Hundred and One Dalmatians, 1960 (Disney 4, Iwerks 4)

One Hundred Dollar Bill, 1911 (Bunny 3)

One Hundred Killings of Flowery Yoshiwara. *See* Hana no Yoshiwara hyakunin-giri, 1960

One Hundred Per Cent Pure. *See* Girl from Missouri, 1934

One Hundred Percent American, 1918 (Pickford 3)

One Hundred Years of the Telephone, 1977 (Bass 4)

One Hysterical Night, 1929 (Brennan 3)

One in a Million, 1934 (Brown 4)

One in a Million. *See* Jedna z milonu, 1935

One in a Million, 1937 (Ameche 3, Henie 3, Menjou 3, Cronjager 4, Zanuck 4)

One in a Million, 1987 (Ameche 3)

One Is a Lonely Number, 1972 (Douglas 3, Leigh 3, Legrand 4)

One Is Business, The Other Crime, 1912 (Griffith 2, Sweet 3, Bitzer 4)

One is Guilty, 1934 (Bellamy 3)

One Little Indian, 1973 (Foster 3, Garner 3, Goldsmith 4)

One Mad Kiss, 1930 (Nichols 4)

One Magic Christmas, 1985 (Stanton 3)

One Man and His Bank, 1965 (Barry 4)

One Man Band, 1965 (Godfrey 4)

One Man Game, 1927 (Wray 3)

One Man Jury, 1978 (Palance 3)

One Man Navy, 1941 (Terry 4)

One Man's Journey, 1933 (Barrymore 3, McCrea 3, Berman 4, D'Agostino 4, Plunkett 4, Polglase 4, Steiner 4)

One Man's Story, 1948 (Alwyn 4)

One Man's War, 1990 (Hopkins 3)

One Man's Way, 1963 (Laszlo 4)

One Meat Brawl, 1947 (Blanc 4, McKimson 4)

One Mile from Heaven, 1937 (Dwan 2, Robinson 3, Trevor 3)

One Million A.D., 1973 (Carradine 3)

One Million B.C., 1940 (Mature 3, Canutt 4, Roach 4)

One Million Years B.C., 1966 (Welch 3, Carreras 4, Harryhausen 4, Roach 4)

One Minute to Play, 1926 (Wood 2, Clarke 4, Plunkett 4)

One Minute to Zero, 1952 (Garnett 2, Mitchum 3, Hunt 4, Young 4)

One More American, 1918 (Crisp 3, Rosher 4)

One More Chance, 1931 (Sennett 2, Crosby 3, Hornbeck 4)

One More Chance, 1983 (Golan and Globus 4)

One More River, 1934 (Whale 2, Laemmle 4, Sherriff 4)

One More Spring, 1935 (King 2, Darwell 3, Gaynor 3, Seitz 4)

One More Time, 1970 (Lewis 2, Cushing 3, Lee 3)

One More Tomorrow, 1946 (Sheridan 3, Wyman 3, Blanke 4, Epstein 4, Glennon 4, Grot 4, Steiner 4)

One More Train to Rob, 1970 (Needham 4)

One Mouse in a Million, 1939 (Terry 4)

One Mysterious Night, 1944 (Boetticher 2, Malone 3)

One Night. *See* En Natt, 1931

One Night and Then—, 1909 (Bitzer 4)

One Night at Dinner. *See* Metti, una sera a cena, 1969

One Night at Susie's, 1930 (Haller 4)

One Night in Lisbon, 1941 (Carroll 3, MacMurray 3, Dreier 4, Glennon 4, Head 4)

One Night in the Tropics, 1940 (Abbott and Costello 3)

One Night of Love, 1934 (Cohn 4, Newman 4, Walker 4)

One Night Stand, 1915 (Sennett 2)

One Night Stand, 1918 (Roach 4)

One Night with You, 1948 (Lee 3, Rank 4)

One Note Tony, 1947 (Terry 4)

One of Nature's Noblemen, 1911 (Bosworth 3)

One of Our Aircraft Is Missing, 1942 (Lean 2, Powell and Pressburger 2, Stevenson 2, Ustinov 3, Withers 3, Green 4, Krasker 4)

One of Our Dinosaurs Is Missing, 1976 (Stevenson 2, Ustinov 3)

One of Our Own, 1975 (Homolka 3)

One of the Best, 1927 (Lanchester 3, Balcon 4)

One of the Blood. *See* His Majesty, the American, 1919

One of the Boys, 1982 (Rooney 3)

One of the Discard, 1914 (Ince 4, Sullivan 4)

One of the Family, 1923 (Roach 4)

One of the Many, *See* Av de många, 1915.

One of the Smiths, 1931 (Roach 4)

One of Them is Named Brett, 1965 (Baker 3)

One on Reno, 1911 (Lawrence 3)

One Parisian "Knight". *See* Open All Night, 1924

One Plus One, 1968 (Guillemot 4)

One Plus One. *See* En och en, 1978

One P.M., 1971 (Leacock 2)

One Precious Year, 1933 (Rathbone 3)

One Punch O'Day, 1926 (Brown 4)

One Quarter Inch, 1917 (Roach 4)

One Quiet Night, 1931 (Arbuckle 3)

One Rainy Afternoon, 1936 (Sturges 2, Lupino 3, Day 4, Lasky 4, Newman 4)

One Romantic Night, 1930 (Dressler 3, Gish 3, Menzies 4, Schenck 4, Struss 4)

One Round O'Brien, 1911 (Sennett 2)

One Run Elmer, 1935 (Keaton 2)

One Russian Summer. *See* Giorno del furore, 1973

One Second in Montreal, 1967 (Snow 2)

One She Loved, 1912 (Griffith 2, Barrymore 3, Gish 3, Pickford 3, Walthall 3, Bitzer 4)

One Shoe Makes It Murder, 1982 (Mitchum 3)

One Single Night. *See* Enda natt, 1938

One Sings the Other Doesn't. *See* Une chante l'autre pas, 1977

One Spooky Night, 1924 (Sennett 2)

One Step to Hell, 1968 (Brazzi 3, Sanders 3)

One Stolen Night, 1922 (Laurel and Hardy 3)

One Summer Love, 1976 (Sarandon 3)

One Sunday Afternoon, 1933 (Cooper 3, Darwell 3, Wray 3, Dreier 4, Zukor 4)

One Sunday Afternoon, 1948 (Walsh 2, Malone 3, Grot 4, Wald 4)

One Sunday Morning, 1926 (Arbuckle 3)

One Swallow Doesn't Make a Summer. *See* Fluga gör ingen sommar, 1947

One Terrible Day, 1922 (Roach 4)

One That Got Away, 1957 (Rank 4)

One Third of a Nation, 1939 (Lumet 2, Sidney 3)

One Thousand Dollars a Touchdown, 1939 (Brown 3, Hayward 3, Dreier 4, Head 4)

One Thousand Nights on a Bed of Stones, 1959 (Abbas 4)

One Too Many, 1916 (Laurel and Hardy 3)

One Touch of Nature, 1908 (Griffith 2, Lawrence 3)

One Touch of Venus, 1948 (Tashlin 2, Arden 3, Gardner 3, Walker 3, Planer 4, Orry-Kelly 4)

One Track Minds, 1933 (Roach 4)

One, Two, Three, 1911 (Dwan 2)

One, Two, Three, 1961 (Wilder 2, Cagney 3, Diamond 4, Mandell 4, Mirisch 4, Previn 4, Trauner 4)

One Two Three, 1975 (Popescu-Gopo 4)

One Two Three, 1978 (Clarke 2)

One Way. *See* Senso unico, 1973

One Way or Another. *See* De cierta manera, 1977

One Way Out, 1955 (Rank 4)

One Way Passage, 1932 (Garnett 2, Francis 3, Powell 3, Grot 4, Orry-Kelly 4)

One Way Pendulum, 1964 (Yates 2)

One Way Street, 1925 (Edeson 4)

One Way Street, 1950 (Duryea 3, Hudson 3, Mason 3, Orry-Kelly 4)

One Way Ticket, 1936 (Schulberg 4)

One Way Ticket to Love. *See* koi no katamichi kippu, 1960

One Week, 1920 (Keaton 2)

One Wild Oat, 1964 (Hepburn 3)

One Wild Ride, 1925 (Roach 4)

One Wild Week, 1921 (Daniels 3)

One Woman Idea, 1929 (Rosay 3)

One Woman's Story. *See* Passionate Friends, 1949

One Wonderful Night, 1914 (Bushman 3)

One Yard to Go, 1931 (Sennett 2)

One Year Later, 1933 (Brennan 3)

One-Mama Man, 1927 (Roach 4)

One-Man Band. *See* Homme orchestre, 1900

One-Man Trail, 1921 (Howard 2)

One-Piece Bathing Suit. *See* Million Dollar Mermaid, 1952

One-Two-Three, 1914 (Beery 3)

Onesta che uccide, 1914 (Bertini 3)

Ongaku dai-shingun, 1943 (Hasegawa 3)

Oni azami, 1926 (Kinugasa 2)
Oni azami, 1950 (Hasegawa 3)
Oni no sumu yakata, 1969 (Takamine 3)
Oni srazhalis za rodinu, 1975
  (Bondarchuk 3, Shukshin 3)
Oni znali Mayakovsky, 1955 (Cherkassov 3)
Onibaba, 1964 (Shindo 2)
Oni-kenji, 1963 (Yamamura 3)
Onimasa, 1982 (Iwashita 3)
Onion Pacific, 1940 (Fleischer 4)
Onionhead, 1958 (Matthau 3, Rosson 4)
Oniromane, 1969 (Braunberger 4)
Onkel Bräsig, 1936 (Rasp 3)
Onkel og Nevø. See Fader og Søn, 1911
Only a Dancing Girl. See Bara en danserska,
  1927
Only a Farmer's Daughter, 1915 (Sennett 2)
Only a Janitor, 1919 (Beery 3)
Only a Messenger Boy, 1915 (Sennett 2)
Only a Mother. See Bara en mor, 1949
Only a Shop Girl, 1922 (Beery 3, Cohn 4)
Only a Woman. See Ich bin auch nur eine
  Frau, 1962
Only Angels Have Wings, 1939 (Hawks 2,
  Arthur 3, Barthelmess 3, Grant 3,
  Hayworth 3, Cohn 4, Furthman 4,
  Tiomkin 4, Walker 4)
Only Count the Happy Moments. See Räkna
  de lyckliga stunderna blott, 1944
Only Game in Town, 1970 (Stevens 2,
  Beatty 3, Taylor 3, Decaë 4, Jarre 4)
Only Girl, 1933 (Boyer 3, Pommer 4,
  Waxman 4)
Only One Night. See Enda natt, 1939
Only Saps Work, 1930 (Dmytryk 2,
  Mankiewicz 2)
Only Son, 1914 (De Mille 2, Darwell 3)
Only Son, 1922 (Roach 4)
Only Son. See Hotori musuko, 1936
Only the Brave, 1930 (Cooper 3, Head 4)
Only the French Can. See French Cancan,
  1955
Only the Lonely, 1991 (McDowall 3,
  O'Hara 3, Quinn 3)
Only the Valiant, 1951 (Bond 3, Peck 3,
  Waxman 4)
Only Thing, 1925 (Day 4, Gibbons 4)
Only Two Can Play, 1961 (Launder and
  Gilliat 2, Zetterling 2, Attenborough 3,
  Sellers 3, Mathieson 4)
Only Way, 1919 (Young 3)
Only Way, 1926 (Wilcox 2)
Only Way. See Ek Hi Rasta, 1939
Only When I Larf, 1968 (Dearden 2,
  Attenborough 3)
Only Woman, 1924 (Olcott 2, Talmadge 3,
  Gaudio 4, Schenck 4, Sullivan 4)
Only Yesterday, 1933 (Stahl 2, Darwell 3,
  Pangborn 3, Sullavan 3, Laemmle 4)
Only You, 1981 (Jarmusch 2)
Onna bakari no yoru, 1961 (Kagawa 3)
Onna dake no machi, 1957 (Yamada 3)
Onna dake no yuro, 1947 (Hara 3)
Onna de arukoto, 1958 (Hara 3, Kagawa 3,
  Mori 3)
Onna ga kaidan o noburu toku, 1960 (Mori 3,
  Takamine 3)
Onna goroshi abura jigoku, 1949
  (Miyagawa 4)
Onna hitori daichi o yuku, 1953 (Yamada 3)
Onna Kanja hibun: Ako-roshi, 1953
  (Yamada 3)
Onna koso ie o momore (Yoshimura 2)
Onna kumicho, 1970 (Yamada 3)

Onna no hada, 1957 (Kyo 3)
Onna no inochi, 1952 (Yamamura 3)
Onna no issho, 1953 (Shindo 3)
Onna no issho, 1962 (Kyo 3)
Onna no issho, 1967 (Iwashita 3)
Onna no koyomi, 1954 (Kagawa 3,
  Tanaka 3)
Onna no kunsho, 1961 (Yoshimura 2, Kyo 3,
  Mori 3)
Onna no mizukakami, 1951 (Takamine 3)
Onna no naka ni iru tanin, 1966 (Naruse 2)
Onna no rekishi, 1963 (Naruse 2,
  Takamine 3)
Onna no saka, 1960 (Yoshimura 2)
Onna no sono, 1954 (Takamine 3)
Onna no tatakai, 1949 (Yamamura 3)
Onna no tsuyokunaru kufu no kazukazu,
  1963 (Tsukasa 3)
Onna no uramado, 1960 (Iwashita 3)
Onna no za, 1962 (Naruse 2, Ryu 3,
  Takamine 3, Tsukasa 3)
Onna to iu shiro: Mari no maki, 1952
  (Takamine 3)
Onna to iu shiro: Yuko no maki, 1952
  (Takamine 3)
Onna to kaizoku, 1959 (Hasegawa 3, Kyo 3,
  Miyagawa 4)
Onna to umareta karanya, 1934
  (Takamine 3)
Onna wa doko he iku, 1930 (Tanaka 3)
Onna wa ikuman aritotemo, 1966 (Muraki 4)
Onna wa itsuno you nimo, 1931
  (Takamine 3)
Onna wa yoru kesho-suru, 1961 (Mori 3)
Onna-gokoro, 1959 (Mori 3)
Onna-gokoro dare ga shiru, 1951 (Kagawa 3,
  Mifune 3)
Onnagokoru, 1959 (Hara 3)
Onnagoroshi aburajigoku, 1957 (Kagawa 3)
Onna-yo ayamaru nakare, 1923 (Kinugasa 2)
Ono no sumu yakata, 1969 (Miyagawa 4)
Onorata società, 1961 (De Sica 2)
Onore vole Angelina, 1947 (Zeffirelli 2,
  Magnani 3, Cecchi D'Amico 4)
Onorevole Angelina, 1947 (Magnani 3,
  Cecchi D'Amico 4)
Onorevoli, 1963 (Cervi 3)
Onshuh junreiuta, 1936 (Miyagawa 4)
Onu Allah affetsin, 1970 (Güney 2)
Onyxkopf, 1917 (Dupont 2)
Ooh . . . You Are Awful, 1972 (Launder and
  Gilliat 2)
Ooka seidan: Yogiden: Hakuro no kamen,
  Jigokudani no taiketsu, 1954 (Yamada 3)
Ookami, 1955 (Shindo 2)
Ooku maruhi monogatari, 1967 (Yamada 3)
Oompahs, 1952 (Bosustow 4)
Oopsie Poopsie, 1980 (Loren 3,
  Mastroianni 3)
Oosaka natsu-no-jin, 1937 (Hasegawa 3)
Oosho ichidai, 1955 (Kagawa 3)
Oozora no chikai, 1952 (Kagawa 3)
Open All Night, 1924 (Menjou 3,
  Glennon 4)
Open All Night, 1934 (Pearson 2)
Open Another Bottle, 1921 (Roach 4)
Open City. See **Roma, città aperta, 1945**
Open Gate, 1909 (Griffith 2, Bitzer 4)
Open House, 1953 (Terry 4)
Open Letter. See Anichti epistoli, 1968
Open Places, 1917 (Van Dyke 2)
Open Range, 1927 (Canutt 4, Rosson 4)
Open Road. See Uppbrott, 1948
Open Season, 1974 (Holden 3)

Open Space: Death on Delivery, 1990
  (Jackson 3)
Open Switch. See Whispering Smith, 1926
Open Window, 1951 (Auric 4)
Open Windows, 1960 (Freund 4)
Opened By Mistake, 1934 (Roach 4)
Opened by Mistake, 1940 (Dreier 4, Head 4)
Opened Shutters, 1921 (Barnes 4)
Opening Day, 1938 (Benchley 4)
Opening in Moscow, 1959 (Clarke 2)
Opening Night, 1977 (Bogdanovich 2,
  Cassavetes 2, Blondell 3, Falk 3,
  Rowlands 3)
Opening Speech, 1960 (McLaren 4)
Opera, 1973 (Bozzetto 4)
Opera, 1987 (Argento 4)
Opera Cordis, 1968 (Vukotić 4)
Opéra de quatre sous. See
  Dreigroschenoper, 1931
Opéra de quatres pesos, 1970
  (Braunberger 4)
Opera do Malandro, 1986 (Guerra 2)
Opera Night, 1935 (Terry 4)
Operación abril del Caribe, 1982 (Alvarez 2)
Operacion Istanbul. See Estambul 65, 1965
Operación Relampage, 1959 (Rey 3)
Opéra-Mouffe, 1958 (Varda 2, Delerue 4)
Opéra-Musette, 1942 (Auric 4, Renoir 4)
Operation Amsterdam, 1959 (Finch 3,
  Rank 4, Vetchinsky 4)
Opération Béton, 1954 (Godard 2)
Operation Bottleneck, 1960 (Crosby 4)
Operation C.I.A., 1965 (Reynolds 3)
Operation Crossbow, 1965 (Henreid 3,
  Howard 3, Loren 3, Mills 3, Quayle 3,
  Ponti 4)
Operation Daybreak, 1975 (Decaë 4)
Operation Disaster. See Morning Departure,
  1950
Operation Eichmann, 1961 (Biroc 4)
Opération Gas-oil, 1955 (Broca 2)
Operation Head Start, 1965 (Lancaster 3)
Operation Heartbeat. See U.M.C., 1969
Operation Kid Brother. See O.K. Connery,
  1967
Operation Leontine. See Faut pas prendre les
  enfants du bon Dieu pour les canards
  sauvages, 1968
Operation M. See Hell's Bloody Devils,
  1970
Operation Mad Ball, 1957 (Edwards 2,
  Lemmon 3, Rooney 3, Boyle 4,
  Duning 4)
Opération Magali, 1952 (Kosma 4)
Operation of the K-13 Gunsight, 1944
  (Hubley 4)
Operation Ogre. See Ogro, 1979
Operation Pacific, 1951 (Bond 3, Neal 3,
  Wayne 3, Glennon 4, Steiner 4)
Operation Petticoat, 1959 (Edwards 2,
  Curtis 3, Grant 3, Harlan 4)
Operation: Rabbit, 1952 (Blanc 4, Jones 4,
  Maltese 4, Stalling 4)
Operation St. Peter's, 1968 (Robinson 3)
Operation Secret, 1952 (Malden 3, Wilde 3,
  Blanke 4, McCord 4)
Operation Snafu. See On the Fiddle, 1961
Operation Snafu. See Rosolino paternò,
  soldato . . . , 1969
Operation Snatch, 1962 (Sanders 3, Terry-
  Thomas 3)
Operation Undercover. See Report to the
  Commissioner, 1975
Operation Universe, 1959 (Carreras 4)

Operation X. *See* My Daughter Joy, 1950

Operator 13, 1934 (Cooper 3, Davies 3, McDaniel 3, Walthall 3, Adrian 4, Folsey 4, Gillespie 4)

Operazione Paradiso. *See* Se tutte le donne del mondo . . . , 1966

Opeřené stíny, 1930 (Stallich 4)

Opère sans Douleur, 1931 (Simon 3)

Opernball, 1939 (Herlth 4)

Opernring. *See* Im Sonneschein, 1936

Opfer der Gesellschaft, 1918 (Wiene 2, Veidt 3)

Ophélia, 1962 (Chabrol 2, Valli 3, Gégauff 4, Rabier 4)

Opiate '67. *See* Mostri, 1963

Opinion Makers, 1964 (Emshwiller 2)

Opinione pubblica, 1953 (Gélin 3, Spaak 4)

Opio, 1949 (Figueroa 4)

Opium, 1918 (Krauss 3)

Opium Den. *See* Opiumhalan, 1911

Opium et le bâton, 1969 (Trintignant 3)

Opium War. *See* Lin zexu, 1959

Opium Warlords, 1974 (Menges 4)

Opiumhalan, 1911 (Jaenzon 4)

Opname, 1979 (Müller 4)

Oppåt med gröna hissen, 1952 (Björnstrand 3)

Oppio per oppio, 1972 (Bozzetto 4)

Opportunity and the Man, 1911 (Lawrence 3)

Opposite Sex, 1956 (Allyson 3, Blondell 3, Miller 3, Moorehead 3, Sheridan 3, Cahn 4, Pasternak 4, Rose 4)

Opry House, 1929 (Disney 4, Iwerks 4)

Opstandelse, 1914 (Psilander 3)

Opta empfangt, 1936 (Alexeieff and Parker 4)

Optical Poem, 1937 (Fischinger 2, Ford 2)

Optimist, 1938 (Porten 3)

Optimist, 1973 (Sellers 3)

Optimist of Nine Elms. *See* Optimist, 1973

Opus I, 1921 (Ruttman 2)

Opus 1, 1947 (Roos 2)

Opus V, 1924 (Ruttman 2)

Opus II, III, IV, 1921 (Ruttman 2)

Or, 1936 (Dalio 3)

Or dans la montagne. *See* Farinet, oder das falsche Geld, 1939

Or dans la rue, 1934 (Darrieux 3, Andrejew 4)

Or de Duc, 1965 (Girardot 3)

Or des mers, 1932 (Epstein 2, Matras 4)

Or des mers, 1948 (Epstein 2)

Or du Cristobal, 1939 (Becker 2, Vanel 3, Lourié 4)

Or du duc, 1965 (Brasseur 3, Darrieux 3)

Or et le plomb, 1965 (Legrand 4)

Oracle, 1952 (Grierson 2)

Oracle de Delphes, 1903 (Méliès 2)

Oracle of Delphi. *See* Oracle de Delphes, 1903

Orage, 1938 (Barrault 3, Boyer 3, Morgan 3, Achard 4, Auric 4, Spaak 4)

Orange Blossoms for Violet, 1951 (Freleng 4)

Oranges and Lemons, 1923 (Laurel and Hardy 3, Roach 4)

Oranges de Jaffa, 1938 (Alexeieff and Parker 4, Auric 4)

Oraon, 1955 (Ghatak 2)

Orasul meu, 1967 (Popescu-Gopo 4)

Orazi e Curiazi, 1962 (Fabrizi 3, Ladd 3)

Orca, 1977 (Harris 3, De Laurentiis 4, Morricone 4)

Orchestra Rehearsal. *See* Prova d'orchestra, 1979

Orchestra Wives, 1942 (Ballard 4, Day 4, Newman 4)

Orchestre et diamants, 1961 (Rabier 4)

Orchestre rouge, 1989 (Olbrychski 3)

Orchid for the Tiger. *See* Tigre se parfume à la dynamite, 1965

Orchids and Ermine, 1927 (LeRoy 2, Moore 3, Rooney 3, Folsey 4, Wilson 4)

Orchids to You, 1935 (Dumont 3, Estabrook 4, Friedhofer 4)

Ordeal at Dry Red. *See* Terror at Black Falls, 1959

Ordeal by Innocence, 1984 (Sutherland 3)

Ordeal of Rosetta, 1918 (Goulding 2)

Order in the Court, 1920 (Roach 4)

Order of Death, 1983 (Sidney 3, Morricone 4)

Order to Kill. *See* Clan de los immorales, 1973

Orderly, 1918 (Laurel and Hardy 3)

Orderly. *See* Ordonnance, 1933

Orders Are Orders, 1954 (Grierson 2, Pleasence 3, Sellers 3)

Orders from Tokyo. *See* Port Arthur, 1936

Orders Is Orders, 1933 (Milland 3, Balcon 4, Junge 4)

Orders to Kill, 1958 (Asquith 2, Gish 3, Dehn 4, Havelock-Allan 4)

Ordet, 1943 (Molander 2, Sjöström 2)

Ordinary Matter, 1972 (Frampton 2)

Ordinary People, 1980 (Redford 3, Sutherland 3, Hamlisch 4, Sargent 4)

Ordini sono ordini, 1972 (Vitti 3, Guerra 4)

Ordonnance, 1907 (Gaumont 4)

Ordonnance, 1933 (Fernandel 3)

Ordonnance malgré lui, 1932 (Fernandel 3)

Ordre et la sécurité du monde, 1978 (Cotten 3, Hopper 3, Pleasence 3)

Ore, 1989 (Giannini 3)

Ore dell'amore, 1963 (Morricone 4)

Ore ga jigoku no tejina-shi da, 1961 (Yamamura 3)

Ore nove lezione di chimica, 1941 (Valli 3, Stallich 4)

Ore nude, 1964 (Guerra 4)

Ore Riders, 1927 (Wyler 2)

Ore was Tokichiro, 1955 (Hasegawa 3)

Oregon Trail, 1936 (Wayne 3, Canutt 4)

Oregon Trail, 1959 (Carradine 3, MacMurray 3, Canutt 4)

Orekara ikuzo, 1960 (Yamamura 3)

Orfano del ghetto, 1954 (Fusco 4)

Orfeo, 1985 (Goretta 2)

Org, 1979 (Birri 2)

Organ Grinder's Swing, 1937 (Fleischer 4)

Organic Fragment, 1942 (Fischinger 2, Ford 2)

Organization, 1971 (Poitier 3, Biroc 4, Mirisch 4)

Organizer. *See* Compagni, 1963

Orgasmo, 1969 (Baker 3)

Orgueilleux, 1953 (Morgan 3, Philipe 3, Aurenche 4, Bost 4)

Oribe's Crime. *See* Crimen de Oribe, 1950

Orient Express, 1934 (Friedhofer 4, Greene 4)

Orient Express, 1954 (Rossellini 2)

Orient qui vient, 1934 (Leenhardt 2)

Oriental Dream. *See* Kismet, 1944

Oriental Love, 1917 (Sennett 2)

Origin of Princess Moon. *See* Tsukihime keizu, 1958

Origin of Sex. *See* Sei no kigen, 1967

Original Intent, 1990 (Sheen 3)

Original Sin, 1989 (Heston 3)

Orizuru osen, 1934 (Mizoguchi 2, Yamada 3)

Orizuru-gasa, 1951 (Hasegawa 3, Yamada 3)

Orizushichi nana-henge, 1941 (Hasegawa 3)

Orlacs Hände, 1924 (Wiene 2, Kortner 3, Veidt 3)

Orlando furioso, 1972 (Storaro 4)

Orme, 1974 (Kinski 3, Storaro 4)

Ormen, 1966 (Andersson 3)

Ormens ägg. *See* Serpent's Egg, 1977

Ornament des verliebten Herzens, 1919 (Reiniger 4)

Ornament of the Loving Heart. *See* Ornament des verliebten Herzens, 1919

Oro di Napoli, 1955 (Loren 3, Mangano 3, De Laurentiis 4, Ponti 4, Zavattini 4)

Oro di Roma, 1961 (Fusco 4, Zavattini 4)

Orökseg, 1980 (Huppert 3, Nowicki 3)

Oroku kanzashi, 1935 (Yamada 3)

Orologio a cucù, 1938 (Castellani 2, De Sica 2)

Oros, 1960 (Guerra 2)

O'Rourke of the Royal Mounted. *See* Saskatchewan, 1954

Orphan, 1958 (Lee 3)

Orphan Ah-Sam. *See* Orphan, 1958

Orphan Duck, 1939 (Terry 4)

Orphan Egg, 1953 (Terry 4)

Orphan Joyce, 1916 (Van Dyke 2)

Orphan of the Ring. *See* Kid from Kokomo, 1939

Orphan of the Sage, 1928 (Musuraca 4)

Orphan of the War, 1913 (Ince 4)

Orphan Train, 1979 (Close 3)

Orphans, 1987 (Pakula 2, Finney 3, Jenkins 4)

Orphan's Mine, 1913 (Dwan 2)

Orphans of the Storm, 1921 (Griffith 2, Gish 3)

Orphan's Song, 1955 (Lee 3)

Orphan's Tragedy, 1955 (Lee 3)

Orphée, 1950 (Cocteau 2, Melville 2, Marais 3, Auric 4, D'Eaubonne 4)

Orphelin de Paris, 1923 (Feuillade 2)

Orphelin du cirque, 1926 (Vanel 3)

Orpheline, 1921 (Clair 2, Feuillade 2, Florey 2)

Orpheus. *See* **Orphée, 1950**

Orpheus in the Underworld. *See* Urfeus i underjorden, 1910

Orrori del castello di Norimberga, 1972 (Cotten 3)

Orzowei, 1975 (Allégret 2, Baker 3)

Osaka Elegy. *See* **Naniwa ereji, 1936**

Osaka monogatari, 1957 (Yoshimura 2, Kagawa 3, Yoda 4)

Osaka natsu no jin, 1937 (Yamada 3)

Osaka no onna, 1958 (Kyo 3)

Osaka Story. *See* Osaka monogatari, 1957

Osaka Woman. *See* Naniwa onna, 1940

Osaka-jo monogatari, 1961 (Kagawa 3, Mifune 3, Shimura 3, Yamada 3, Tsuburaya 4)

Osaya koisugata, 1934 (Tanaka 3)

Ösbemutató, 1974 (Szabó 2)

Oscar, 1966 (Borgnine 3, Brennan 3, Cotten 3, Crawford 3, Hope 3, Oberon 3, Sinatra 3, Cahn 4, Delerue 4, Head 4, Levine 4, Ruttenberg 4, Wakhévitch 4, Westmore Family 4)

Oscar, 1991 (Mature 3, Stallone 3, Ponti 4)

Oscar, champion de tennis, 1973 (Tati 2)
Oscar per il Signor Rossi, 1960 (Bozzetto 4)
Oscar Wilde, 1960 (Richardson 3, Périnal 4)
Ose Hangoro, 1928 (Hasegawa 3)
Ose no hangoro, 1928 (Tsuburaya 4)
O'Shaughnessy's Boy, 1935 (Beery 3,
    Cooper 3, Howe 4)
Oshidori no aida, 1956 (Yamada 3)
Osho ichidai, 1955 (Tanaka 3)
Oslerizing Papa, 1905 (Bitzer 4)
Oslo, 1963 (Roos 2)
Osmnáctiletá, 1939 (Stallich 4)
Osmosis, 1948 (Kaufman 4)
Osmy dzień tygodnia, 1957 (Cybulski 3,
    Lomnicki 3)
Osokoshi, 1985 (Ryu 3)
Ospedale del delitto, 1948 (Comencini 2)
Osram, 1957 (Alexeieff and Parker 4)
Oss tjuvar emellan eller En burk ananas,
    1945 (Dahlbeck 3)
Osseg Oder die Warheit uber Hansel und
    Gretel, 1987 (Léaud 3)
Ossessione, 1942 (De Santis 2, Visconti 2)
Ossis Tagebuch, 1917 (Lubitsch 2)
Ossuary. See Kostnice, 1970
Ossuary. See Jan Svankmajer: Alchemist of
    the Surreal, 1990
Ostatni dzień lata, 1958 (Konwicki 4)
Ostatni strzał, 1958 (Ścibor-Rylski 4)
Ostende, reine des plages, 1930 (Storck 2,
    Jaubert 4)
Osterman Weekend, 1983 (Peckinpah 2,
    Hopper 3, Hurt 3, Lancaster 3,
    Schifrin 4)
Ostia, 1969 (Pasolini 2)
Ostia, 1986 (Jarman 2)
'Ostler Joe, 1908 (Bitzer 4)
**Ostře sledované vlaky, 1966 (Menzel 2,
    Brodský 3, Ponti 4)**
Ostrich Feathers, 1937 (Lantz 4)
Ostrich Has Two Eggs. See Oeufs de
    l'autruche, 1957
Ostrov sokrovishch, 1937 (Cherkassov 3)
Osudy dobrého vojáka Svejkova, 1955
    (Trnka 4)
Osvetnic, 1958 (Vukotić 4)
Osvobozhenie, 1972 (Olbrychski 3,
    Shukshin 3)
Oswald the Lucky Rabbit, 1927 (Disney 4)
Oswego, 1943 (Van Dyke 2)
Osynliga muren, 1944 (Molander 2)
Otages, 1939 (Milhaud 4)
Otello, 1986 (Zeffirelli 2, Golan and
    Globus 4)
Otets i syn, 1917 (Mozhukin 3)
Otets Sergii, 1918 (Volkov 2, Mozhukin 3)
Othello, 1922 (Jannings 3, Krauss 3)
Othello, 1952 (Welles 2, Aldo 4, Trauner 4)
Othello, 1955 (Bondarchuk 3, Cotten 3,
    Fontaine 3)
Othello, 1966 (Olivier 3, Smith 3, Havelock-
    Allan 4, Unsworth 4)
Othello—The Black Commando, 1982
    (Curtis 3)
Other, 1972 (Mulligan 2, Goldsmith 4,
    Surtees 4)
Other, 1980 (Brakhage 2)
Other Fellow, 1912 (Bosworth 3)
Other Girl, 1914 (Bushman 3)
Other Girl, 1915 (Anderson 3)
Other Girl, 1917 (Laurel and Hardy 3)
Other Half, 1912 (Cruze 2)
Other Half, 1919 (Vidor 2)
Other Half, 1947 (Stanwyck 3)

Other Half of the Sky: A China Memoir,
    1990 (MacLaine 3)
Other Love. See Vot vspynulo utro, 1915
Other Love, 1947 (De Toth 2, Niven 3,
    Head 4, Rozsa 4)
Other Man, 1914 (Bushman 3)
Other Man, 1916 (Sennett 2, Arbuckle 3)
Other Men's Wives, 1919 (Sullivan 4)
Other Men's Women. See Steel Highway,
    1931
Other People's Business, 1914 (Sennett 2)
Other People's Money. See Argent des
    autres, 1978
Other People's Money, 1990 (Peck 3,
    Sargent 4, Wexler 4)
Other People's Sins, 1931 (Dickinson 2)
Other Side of Midnight, 1977 (Sarandon 3,
    Legrand 4, Taradash 4)
Other Side of Paradise. See Foxtrot, 1975
Other Side of the Wind, 1972
    (Bogdanovich 2, Welles 2)
Other Tomorrow, 1930 (Bacon 2, Garmes 4)
Other Wise Man, 1911 (Dwan 2)
Other Woman, 1913 (Talmadge 3)
Other Woman, 1921 (Gaudio 4)
Other Woman. See Tsuma to shite haha to
    shite, 1961
Otherwise Unexplained Fires, 1976
    (Frampton 2)
Othon, 1969 (Straub and Huillet)
Otkrytaya kniga, 1979 (Yankovsky 3)
Otley, 1968 (Schneider 3, Dillon 4,
    Foreman 4)
Otoko arite, 1955 (Mifune 3, Shimura 3)
Otoko no hanamichi, 1941 (Hasegawa 3)
Otoko no tsugunai, 1936 (Tanaka 3)
Otoko o sabaku onna, 1948 (Yamamura 3,
    Miyagawa 4)
Otoko tai otoko, 1960 (Mifune 3, Shimura 3,
    Muraki 4)
Otoko wa tsuraiyo, 1985 (Ryu 3)
Otoko wa tsuraiyo: Torajiro Haru no yume,
    1979 (Kagawa 3)
Otoko wa tsuraiyo: Torajiro junjo-shishu,
    1976 (Kyo 3)
Otoko wa tsuraiyo: Torajiro yume-makura,
    1972 (Tanaka 3)
Otoko-girai, 1964 (Mori 3)
Otokowa tsuraiyo Torajiro kokoro no tabiji,
    1988 (Ryu 3)
Otokowa tsuraiyo: Torajiro koiuta, 1971
    (Shimura 3)
Otomar Korbelář, 1960 (Stallich 4)
Otomi to Yosaburo, 1950 (Hasegawa 3,
    Yamada 3)
Otone no yogiri, 1950 (Yamamura 3)
Otoshiana, 1962 (Takemitsu 4)
Ototo, 1960 (Mori 3, Tanaka 3, Miyagawa 4)
Otra isla, 1968 (Gómez 2)
Otrantský zámek, 1977 (Švankmajer 4)
Otrávené světlo, 1921 (Ondra 3, Heller 4)
Otre l'amore, 1940 (Valli 3)
Otro Cristobal, 1963 (Alekan 4)
Otsukisama niwa waruikedo, 1954
    (Yamamura 3)
Otsuru junreika, 1937 (Yoda 4)
Otsuru's Pilgrim Song. See Otsuru junreika,
    1937
Otsuya goroshi, 1951 (Yamada 3, Yoda 4)
Otto e mezzo. See 8½, **1963**
Otto no teiso: Haru kitareba, Aki futatabi,
    1937 (Takamine 3)
Ou est au Coton, 1970 (Arcand 2)
Oublie-moi Mandoline, 1975 (Delerue 4)

Oublier Palerme. See Dimenticare, Palermo,
    1990
Oubliette, 1912 (Gaumont 4)
Oubliette, 1914 (Chaney 3)
Ouch, 1967 (Godfrey 4)
Oued, la ville aux milles coupoles, 1947
    (Fradetal 4)
Ouigours—Minorité nationale—Sinkiang,
    1977 (Ivens 2)
Ouija Board, 1920 (Fleischer 4)
Our Active Earth, 1972 (Heston 3)
Our Betters, 1933 (Cukor 2, Murfin 4,
    Rosher 4, Selznick 4, Steiner 4)
Our Better Selves, 1919 (Miller 4)
Our Blushing Brides, 1930 (Beavers 3,
    Crawford 3, Montgomery 3, Adrian 4,
    Gibbons 4, Meredyth 4, Stromberg 4,
    Tiomkin 4)
Our Children, 1913 (Sennett 2)
Our Cissy, 1973 (Parker 2)
Our Congressman, 1924 (Rogers 3, Roach 4)
Our Country, 1944 (Alwyn 4)
Our Country Cousin, 1914 (Sennett 2,
    Arbuckle 3)
Our Crazy Family. See Naše bláznivá rodina,
    1968
Our Daily Bread, 1921 (Garbo 3)
Our Daily Bread, 1930 (Murnau 2)
Our Daily Bread, 1934 (Mankiewicz 2,
    Vidor 2, Newman 4)
Our Daily Bread. See Unser täglich Brot,
    1949
Our Dancing Daughters, 1928 (Crawford 3,
    Barnes 4, Day 4, Gibbons 4, Mayer 4,
    Stromberg 4)
Our Dare Devil Chief, 1915 (Sennett 2)
Our Father, 1985 (Rey 3)
Our Fighting Navy, 1937 (Wilcox 2)
Our Gang, 1922 (Roach 4)
Our Gang, 1929 (Cooper 3)
Our Gang Follies of 1936, 1935 (Roach 4)
Our Gang Follies of 1938, 1937 (Roach 4)
Our Girl Friday, 1953 (More 3)
Our Hearts Were Growing Up, 1946
    (Dreier 4, Frank 4, Head 4, Young 4)
Our Hearts Were Young and Gay, 1944
    (Bondi 3)
Our Hearts Were Young and Gay, 1944
    (Dreier 4, Head 4)
Our Hitler. See **Hitler. Ein Film aus
    Deutschland, 1977**
Our Hospitality, 1923 (Keaton 2,
    Bruckman 4, Schenck 4)
Our Husbands. See Nostri mariti, 1966
Our Large Birds, 1914 (Sennett 2)
Our Last Spring. See Eroica, 1960
Our Leading Citizen, 1922 (Young 4)
Our Leading Citizen, 1939 (Hayward 3,
    Head 4)
Our Little Girl, 1935 (McCrea 3, Temple 3,
    Seitz 4)
Our Little Nell, 1917 (Van Dyke 2)
Our Little Nell, 1924 (Roach 4)
Our Little Red Riding Hood. See Drahoušek
    Klementýnn, 1959
Our Man Flint, 1966 (Cobb 3, Coburn 3,
    Goldsmith 4, Reynolds 4, Smith 4)
Our Man from Las Vegas. See They Came to
    Rob Las Vegas, 1968
Our Man in Havana, 1959 (Reed 2,
    Guinness 3, O'Hara 3, Richardson 3,
    Box 4, Coward 4, Greene 4, Morris 4)
Our Man in Marrakesh, 1966 (Kinski 3,
    Lom 3, Terry-Thomas 3)

Our Marriage. *See* Watakushi-tachi no kekkon, 1962

Our Miss Brooks, 1956 (Arden 3, La Shelle 4)

Our Mr. Sun, 1956 (Capra 2)

Our Mrs. McChesney, 1918 (Barrymore 3)

Our Modern Maidens, 1929 (Crawford 3, Adrian 4, Gibbons 4, Mayer 4)

Our Mother's House, 1967 (Clayton 2, Bogarde 3, Delerue 4)

Our Neighbors, the Carters, 1939 (Barnes 4, Dreier 4, Head 4, Young 4)

Our Parents-in-Law, 1910 (White 3)

Our Relations, 1936 (Laurel and Hardy 3, Maté 4, Roach 4)

Our Russian Front, 1941 (Ivens 2, Milestone 2, Huston 3, Eisler 4)

Our Story. *See* Notre histoire, 1984

Our Teacher. *See* Wareraga kyokan, 1939

Our Time, 1974 (Legrand 4)

Our Town, 1940 (Wood 2, Bondi 3, Holden 3, Copland 4, Glennon 4, Horner 4, Menzies 4)

Our Very Own, 1950 (Wood 3, Day 4, Garmes 4, Goldwyn 4, Young 4)

Our Vines Have Tender Grapes, 1945 (Moorehead 3, O'Brien 3, Robinson 3, Irene 4, Kaper 4, Surtees 4, Trumbo 4)

Our Wife, 1931 (Laurel and Hardy 3)

Our Wife, 1941 (Stahl 2, Coburn 3, Douglas 3, Cohn 4, Planer 4)

Our Younger Brother. *See* Bokura no otouto, 1933

Ouragan sur la montagne, 1922 (Duvivier 2)

Ours, 1919 (Modot 3)

Ours, 1988 (Sarde 4)

Ours et la poupée, 1970 (Bardot 3, Cassel 3)

Ousititi de Toto, 1912 (Cohl 4)

Out, 1957 (Dickinson 2)

Out Again—In Again, 1914 (Browning 2)

Out Again, in Again, 1947 (Terry 4)

Out All Night, 1933 (Temple 3, Laemmle 4)

Out and In, 1913 (Sennett 2)

Out and Out Rout, 1966 (Blanc 4)

Out California Way, 1946 (Rogers 3)

Out from the Shadow, 1911 (Crisp 3, Sweet 3)

Out of a Clear Sky, 1918 (Neilan 2)

Out of Africa, 1985 (Pollack 2, Brandauer 3, Redford 3, Streep 3, Barry 4, Watkin 4)

Out of College. *See* Gakuso o idete, 1925

Out of Darkness, 1955 (Welles 2)

Out of It, 1969 (Voight 3)

Out of Luck, 1919 (Valentino 3)

Out of Luck, 1923 (Miller 4)

Out of Petticoat Lane, 1914 (Mix 3)

Out of Rosenheim. *See* Bagdad Cafe, 1987

Out of Season, 1949 (Anderson 2)

Out of Season, 1975 (Redgrave 3, Robertson 3)

Out of the Blue, 1931 (Matthews 3)

Out of the Blue, 1980 (Hopper 3)

Out of the Box, 1942 (Cardiff 4)

Out of the Clouds, 1954 (Dearden 2)

Out of the Dark, 1988 (Black 3)

Out of the Darkness. *See* Teenage Caveman, 1958

Out of the Darkness, 1985 (Sheen 3)

Out of the Depths, 1912 (Bushman 3)

Out of the Fog, 1919 (Nazimova 3, Mathis 4)

Out of the Fog, 1941 (Litvak 2, Rossen 2, Garfield 3, Lupino 3, Blanke 4, Howe 4, Wald 4, Wallis 4)

Out of the Frying Pan into the Fire. *See* Z bláta do louže, 1934

Out of the Inkwell, 1938 (Fleischer 4)

Out of the Inkwell, 1972 (Fleischer 4)

Out of the Night, 1912 (Bushman 3)

Out of the Night. *See* Strange Illusion, 1945

Out of the Past, 1947 (Tourneur 2, Douglas 3, Mitchum 3, D'Agostino 4, Musuraca 4)

Out of the Ruins, 1928 (Barthelmess 3, Haller 4, Robinson 4)

Out of This World, 1945 (Crosby 3, Lake 3, Dreier 4, Head 4, Mercer 4, Young 4)

Out of Work, 1909 (Olcott 2)

Out on a Limb, 1987 (MacLaine 3)

Out on Bail, 1922 (Roach 4)

Out One—Out Two. *See* Spectre, 1973

Out 1: noli me tangere, 1971 (Rivette 2)

Out 1: ombre, 1974 (Rivette 2)

Out West, 1918 (Keaton 2, Arbuckle 3)

Out West, 1920 (Arbuckle 3)

Out West, 1947 (Three Stooges 3, Bruckman 4)

Out West with the Hardys, 1939 (Rooney 3)

Out with the Tide, 1928 (Shamroy 4)

Outback. *See* Wake in Fright, 1971

Outcast. *See* Avenging Conscience, 1914

Outcast, 1922 (Powell 3)

Outcast, 1928 (Seitz 4)

Outcast, 1937 (Florey 2, Head 4, Maté 4, Schary 4)

Outcast. *See* Hakai, 1962

Outcast Among Outcasts, 1912 (Griffith 2, Bitzer 4)

Outcast Among Outcasts, 1912 (Sweet 3)

Outcast Lady, 1934 (Marshall 3, Adrian 4, Akins 4, Rosher 4)

Outcast of the Islands, 1951 (Reed 2, Howard 3, Richardson 3, Francis 4, Korda, A. 4, Korda, V. 4)

Outcasts. *See* Štvaní lidé, 1933

Outcasts of Poker Flat, 1919 (Ford 2, Carey 3)

Outcasts of Poker Flat, 1952 (Baxter 3, Hopkins 3, Friedhofer 4, Jeakins 4, La Shelle 4, LeMaire 4, Reynolds 4)

Outcast's Return. *See* Tugthusfange No. 97, 1914

Outcry. *See* Grido, 1957

Outdoor Pajamas, 1924 (McCarey 2, Roach 4)

Outer and Inner Space, 1965 (Warhol 2)

Outer Limit of Solitude. *See* Hautes solitudes, 1974

Outer Space Jitters, 1956 (Three Stooges 3)

Outfit, 1973 (Black 3, Duvall 3, Ryan 3)

Outfoxed, 1949 (Avery 4)

Outland, 1981 (Connery 3)

Outlanders, 1978 (Wyman 3)

Outlaw, 1908 (Bitzer 4)

Outlaw, 1943 (Hawks 2, Huston 3, Russell 3, Furthman 4, Hughes 4, Toland 4, Young 4)

Outlaw and His Wife. *See* Berg-Ejvind och hans hustru, 1918

Outlaw and the Child, 1911 (Anderson 3)

Outlaw and the Lady, 1949 (Armendáriz 3)

Outlaw Colony, 1911 (Dwan 2)

Outlaw Dog, 1927 (Walker 4)

Outlaw Josey Wales, 1976 (Eastwood 3)

Outlaw Joukichi of Mikoshin. *See* Mushukunin Mikoshin no Joukichi, 1972

Outlaw of Gor, 1989 (Palance 3)

Outlaw of the Plains, 1946 (Crabbe 3)

Outlaw Reforms, 1914 (Meredyth 4)

Outlaw Reward, 1911 (Mix 3)

Outlaw Rule, 1934 (Canutt 4)

Outlaw Samaritan, 1911 (Anderson 3)

Outlaw Territory, 1953 (Garmes 4)

Outlawed, 1929 (Mix 3, Plunkett 4)

Outlaw's Awakening, 1915 (Anderson 3)

Outlaw's Bride, 1915 (Mix 3)

Outlaw's Deputy, 1911 (Anderson 3)

Outlaws IS Coming!, 1965 (Three Stooges 3)

Outlaws of Red River, 1927 (Mix 3)

Outlaws of the Desert, 1941 (Harlan 4)

Outlaws of the Orient, 1937 (Schoedsack 2)

Outlaw's Revenge, 1912 (Walsh 2)

Outlaw's Sacrifice, 1910 (Anderson 3)

Outlaw's Trail, 1911 (Dwan 2)

Outline Breaker, 1927 (Canutt 4)

Out-of-Towners, 1969 (Lemmon 3, Jones 4)

Outpost, 1942 (Terry 4)

Outpost in Malaya. *See* Planter's Wife, 1952

Outpost in Morocco, 1948 (Florey 2, Raft 3)

Outrage, 1915 (Hepworth 2)

Outrage, 1950 (Lupino 3, Horner 4)

Outrage, 1964 (Ritt 2, Bloom 3, Harvey 3, Newman 3, Robinson 3, Howe 4, North 4)

Outrage!, 1986 (Meredith 3, Preston 3)

Outrageous Fortune, 1987 (Midler 3)

Outriders, 1950 (McCrea 3, Novarro 3, Ames 4, Plunkett 4, Previn 4, Ravetch 4)

Outside Chance, 1978 (Corman 2)

Outside Man. *See* Homme est morte, 1973

Outside the Gates, 1915 (Chaney 3)

Outside the Law, 1921 (Browning 2, Chaney 3)

Outside the Law, 1930 (Browning 2, Robinson 3, Fort 4)

Outside the Three-Mile Limit, 1940 (Carey 3)

Outside These Walls, 1939 (Costello 3)

Outsider, 1926 (Pidgeon 3)

Outsider, 1931 (Reville 4)

Outsider, 1940 (McDowall 3, Sanders 3)

Outsider. *See* Guinea Pig, 1948

Outsider, 1961 (Curtis 3, La Shelle 4, Rosenman 4)

Outsider, 1967 (O'Brien 3)

Outsider, 1979 (Hayden 3)

Outsiders, 1983 (Coppola 2, Cruise 3, Dillon 3, Tavoularis 4)

Outward Bound, 1930 (Howard 3, Grot 4, Mohr 4)

Outwitting Dad, 1914 (Laurel and Hardy 3)

Ouvert pour cause d'inventaire, 1946 (Resnais 2)

Oveja negra, 1949 (Infante 3)

Over 21, 1945 (Buchman 4, Cohn 4)

Over Here, 1924 (Sennett 2)

Over My Dead Body. *See* Once Upon a Crime, 1992

Over Silent Paths, 1910 (Griffith 2, Bitzer 4)

Over the Andes, 1944 (Hoch 4)

Over the Bouncing Blue with Will Rogers, 1928 (Rogers 3)

Over the Brooklyn Bridge, 1984 (Gould 3, Winters 3, Donaggio 4, Golan and Globus 4)

Over the Counter, 1932 (Grable 3)

Over the Edge, 1979 (Dillon 3)

Over the Fence, 1917 (Daniels 3, Lloyd 3, Roach 4)

Over the Garden Wall, 1910 (Normand 3)

Over the Garden Wall, 1919 (Love 3)

Over the Goal, 1937 (McDaniel 3)

Over the Hill, 1922 (Ruttenberg 4)

Over the Hill, 1931 (King 2, Marsh 3, Furthman 4, Seitz 4)

Over the Hills to the Poorhouse, 1908 (Bitzer 4)

Over the Ledge, 1914 (Reid 3)

Over the Moon, 1937 (Howard 2, Harrison 3, Oberon 3, Biro 4, Hornbeck 4, Korda, A. 4, Korda, V. 4, Stradling 4)

Over the River. See One More River, 1934

Over the Top, 1986 (Stallone 3, Golan and Globus 4)

Over the Wall, 1938 (Bond 3)

Over Twenty-One, 1945 (Vidor 2, Coburn 3, Dunne 3, Buchman 4, Conn 4)

Overboard, 1978 (Dickinson 3, Robertson 3)

Overboard, 1987 (Hawn 3, McDowall 3, Alonzo 4)

Overcoat. See Cappotto, 1952

Overcoat. See Shinel, 1983

Overexposed, 1990 (Black 3)

Overland Red, 1920 (Carey 3)

Overland Riders, 1946 (Crabbe 3)

Overland Stage, 1927 (Brown 4)

Overland Stage Raiders, 1938 (Brooks 3, Wayne 3, Canutt 4)

Overland Telegraph, 1951 (Hunt 4)

Overland Trail, 1927 (Polito 4)

Overlanders, 1946 (Watt 2, Rafferty 3, Balcon 4, Rank 4)

Overnight. See That Night in London, 1933

Overtaxed. See Tartassati, 1959

Over-The-Hill Gang, 1969 (Brennan 3, Friedhofer 4)

Over-The-Hill Gang Rides Again, 1970 (Astaire 3, Brennan 3, Raksin 4)

Over There-Abouts, 1925 (Sennett 2)

Overture, 1958 (Dickinson 2)

Oviri. See Wolf at the Door, 1986

Ovoce stromů rajských jíme, 1969 (Kučera 4)

Ovod, 1955 (Enei 4, Moskvin 4, Shostakovich 4)

Owd Bob, 1938 (Stevenson 2, Launder and Gilliat 2, Lockwood 3, Vetchinsky 4)

Owen, 1975 (Black 3)

Owen Marshall, Counsellor at Law, 1981 (Sarandon 3, Bernstein 4)

Owl and the Pussycat, 1934 (Terry 4)

Owl and the Pussycat, 1939 (Terry 4)

Owl and the Pussycat, 1952 (Halas and Batchelor 4)

Owl and the Pussycat, 1970 (Segal 3, Streisand 3, Adam 4, Booth 4, Henry 4, Stark 4, Stradling 4)

Own Your Home, 1921 (Roach 4)

Ox, 1991 (Ullmann 3, Von Sydow 3, Nykvist 4)

Oxalá, 1979 (Branco 4)

Ox-Bow Incident, 1942 (Wellman 2, Andrews 3, Darwell 3, Fonda 3, Quinn 3, Basevi 4, Day 4, Miller 4, Trotti 4)

Oxford and Cambridge Boat Race, 1898 (Hepworth 2)

Oxo Parade, 1948 (Halas and Batchelor 4)

Oyashiki-zame, 1959 (Hasegawa 3)

Oyster Dredger, 1915 (Chaney 3)

Oyster Princess. See Austerprinzessin, 1919

Oysters, 1965 (Emshwiller 2)

Oyuki the Madonna. See Maria no Oyuki, 1935

Oyu-sama, 1951 (Mizoguchi 2, Shindo 3, Tanaka 3, Hayasaka 4, Miyagawa 4, Yoda 4)

Ozark Romance, 1918 (Daniels 3, Lloyd 3, Roach 4)

Ozzie of the Circus, 1929 (Lantz 4)

Ozzie of the Mounted, 1928 (Disney 4)

Ozzie Ostrich Comes to Town, 1937 (Terry 4)

P ... respecteuse, 1952 (Astruc 2, Auric 4, Bost 4, Schüfftan 4)
PBL 2, 1968 (Breer 4)
PBL 3, 1968 (Breer 4)
P.C. Josser, 1931 (Balcon 4)
P.J., 1968 (Whitlock 4)
POW—The Escape, 1986 (Golan and Globus 4)
PT 109, 1963 (Robertson 3, Surtees 4, Warner 4)
P.T. Raiders. See Ship That Died of Shame, 1955
PX, 1981 (Brocka 2)
På livets ödesvägar, 1913 (Sjöström 2, Stiller 2, Jaenzon 4)
Pa Says, 1913 (Barrymore 3, Loos 4)
På solsidan, 1936 (Molander 2, Bergman 3)
Paa Besøg hos Kong Tingeling, 1947 (Roos 2)
Paa Livets Skyggeside, 1912 (Holger-Madsen 2)
Paamenento bruu: Manatsu no koi, 1976 (Okada 3)
Paapi, 1953 (Kapoor 2)
Pablo Casals Breaks His Journey, 1958 (Dickinson 2)
Pablo y Carolina, 1955 (Infante 3)
Pace That Kills, 1928 (Laszlo 4)
Pace That Thrills, 1925 (LeRoy 2, Astor 3, McCord 4)
Pacemaker series, 1925 (Garmes 4)
Pacemakers, 1925 (Gable 3)
Pacha, 1967 (Gabin 3, Audiard 4, D'Eaubonne 4)
Pacific Blackout, 1942 (Preston 3, Dreier 4, Siodmak 4)
Pacific Destiny, 1956 (Elliott 3, Bernard 4)
Pacific Heights, 1990 (Schlesinger 2)
Pacific Liner, 1939 (Fitzgerald 3, McLaglen 3, Musuraca 4)
Pacific Northwest, 1944 (Van Dyke 2, Huston 3, Maddow 4)
Pacifist. See Pacifista, 1971
Pacifista, 1971 (Olbrychski 3, Vitti 3)
Pack of Lies, 1987 (Bates 3, Burstyn 3)
Pack Train, 1953 (Autry 3)
Pack Up Your Troubles, 1926 (Fleischer 4)
Pack Up Your Troubles, 1932 (Goddard 3, Laurel and Hardy 3, Roach 4)
Pack Up Your Troubles, 1939 (Day 4)
Package, 1989 (Hackman 3)
Package for Jasper, 1944 (Pal 4)
Packaging Story, 1964 (Bass 4)
Paco, 1975 (Ferrer 3)
Pact with the Devil. See Pacto diabolico, 1968
Pacto diabolico, 1968 (Carradine 3)

Pad (and How to Use It), 1966 (Hunter 4)
Pad Italje, 1985 (Olbrychski 3)
Paddy, 1969 (Corman 2)
Paddy O'Day, 1935 (Darwell 3, Hayworth 3, Miller 4)
Paddy O'Hara, 1917 (Ince 4)
Paddy, the Next Best Thing, 1933 (Gaynor 3, Seitz 4)
Paddy-the-Next-Best-Thing, 1923 (Wilcox 2, Marsh 3)
Padeniye Berlina, 1949 (Shostakovich 4)
Padenye dinastii romanovykh, 1927 (Shub 2)
Padlocked, 1926 (Dwan 2, Howe 4)
Padre, 1911 (Bosworth 3)
Padre, 1912 (Pastrone 2)
Padre de más de cuatro, 1938 (Figueroa 4)
Padre di famiglia, 1967 (Caron 3)
Padre padrone, 1977 (Taviani 2)
Padrecito, 1964 (Cantinflas 3)
Padri e figli, 1957 (De Sica 2, Monicelli 2, Age and Scarpelli 4, Gherardi 4)
Padroni della città, 1977 (Palance 3)
Paean. See Sanka, 1972
Paese dei campanelli, 1953 (Brazzi 3, Loren 3)
Paese senza pace, 1943 (Delli Colli 4)
Pagaille, 1991 (Age and Scarpelli 4)
Pagan, 1929 (Van Dyke 2, Crisp 3, Novarro 3, Freed 4, Gibbons 4, La Shelle 4)
Pagan Love Song, 1950 (Keel 3, Williams 3, Alton 4, Brown 4, Deutsch 4, Freed 4, Rose 4, Rosher 4)
Paganini, 1910 (Gance 2)
Paganini, 1923 (Veidt 3)
Paganini, 1989 (Blier 3, Kinski 3)
Paganini Horror, 1988 (Pleasence 3)
Page d'amour, 1977 (Aimée 3, Chaplin 3, Dalio 3)
Page de gloire, 1915 (Musidora 3)
Page Miss Glory, 1935 (Daves 2, LeRoy 2, Astor 3, Davies 3, Powell 3, Folsey 4, Orry-Kelly 4)
Page Mystery, 1917 (Edeson 4)
Pages from the Story, 1957 (Bondarchuk 3)
Pagliacci, 1936 (Eisler 4)
Pagliacci, 1943 (Valli 3)
Pagliacci, 1948 (Lollobrigida 3)
Pagliacci, 1970 (Wakhévitch 4)
Pagode, 1915 (Pick 2, Krauss 3)
Pagode, 1923 (Dieterle 2, Tschechowa 3)
Pahela Admi, 1950 (Roy 2)
Pahli Nazar, 1945 (Biswas 4)
Paid, 1930 (Wood 2, Crawford 3, Gibbons 4, MacArthur 4, Mayer, C. 4, Mayer, L. 4, Rosher 4)
Paid in Advance, 1919 (Chaney 3)

Paid in Error, 1938 (Withers 3)
Paid in Full, 1911 (Dwan 2)
Paid in Full, 1950 (Dieterle 2, Arden 3, Dreier 4, Head 4, Schnee 4, Young 4, Wallis 4)
Paid to Dance, 1937 (Hayworth 3)
Paid to Kill. See Five Days, 1954
Paid to Love, 1927 (Hawks 2, Powell 3, Glazer 4, Miller 4)
Paid with Interest. See Avenging Conscience, 1914
Paigham, 1959 (Kumar 3)
Pain de Barbarie, 1949 (Leenhardt 2)
Pain et le vin, 1964 (Cloquet 4)
Pain in the Pullman, 1936 (Three Stooges 3)
Painappuru butai, 1959 (Yamada 3)
Painless Dentistry. See Charlatan, 1901
Paint and Powder, 1921 (Roach 4)
Paint and Powder, 1925 (Polito 4, Stromberg 4)
Paint Pot Symphony, 1949 (Terry 4)
Paint Your Wagon, 1969 (Eastwood 3, Marvin 3, Seberg 3, Chayefsky 4, Fraker 4, Previn 4)
Painted Angel, 1929 (Seitz 4)
Painted Boats, 1945 (Balcon 4)
Painted Desert, 1931 (Gable 3, La Shelle 4)
Painted Faces, 1929 (Brown 3)
Painted Lady, 1912 (Griffith 2, Sweet 3, Bitzer 4)
Painted Lady, 1914 (Sweet 3)
Painted Lady's Child, 1914 (Eason 4)
Painted Lips. See Boquitas pintadas, 1974
Painted Madonna, 1917 (Ruttenberg 4)
Painted People, 1924 (Moore 3)
Painted Ponies, 1927 (Eason 4)
Painted Post, 1928 (Mix 3)
Painted Soul, 1915 (Ince 4, Sullivan 4)
Painted Stallion, 1937 (Canutt 4)
Painted Veil, 1934 (Van Dyke 2, Bondi 3, Brennan 3, Garbo 3, Marshall 3, Adrian 4, Daniels 4, Gibbons 4, Mayer 4, Stothart 4, Stromberg 4)
Painted Woman, 1932 (Tracy 3, Friedhofer 4)
Painter's Idyll, 1911 (Bosworth 3)
Painters Painting, 1972 (De Antonio 2, Emshwiller 4)
Painter's Revenge, 1908 (Porter 2)
Paintings by Ed Emshwiller, 1929 (Emshwiller 2)
Pair of Briefs, 1961 (Box 4, Rank 4)
Pair of Cupids, 1918 (Bushman 3)
Pair of Tights, 1928 (McCarey 2, Roach 4)
Paisà, 1946 (Fellini 2, Rossellini 2, Masina 3, Amidei 4)
Paisa hi paisa, 1956 (Biswas 4, Mehboob 2)

Paisan. *See* **Paisà, 1946**
Paix sur le Rhin, 1938 (Rosay 3)
Paja ubit ču te!, 1967 (Mimica 4)
Pajama Game, 1957 (Donen 2, Fosse 2,
  Day 3, Stradling 4)
Pajama Girl, 1903 (Bitzer 4)
Pajama Party, 1931 (Roach 4)
Pajama Party, 1964 (Keaton 2, Lamour 3,
  Lanchester 3, Crosby 4)
Pájaro del faro, 1971 (Alvarez 2)
Pájaros tirándole a la escopeta, 1984 (Díaz 2)
Pakbo, 1970 (Müller 4)
Pal, Canine Detective, 1949 (Hunt 4)
Pal, Fugitive Dog, 1950 (Hunt 4)
Pal Joey, 1957 (Hayworth 3, Novak 3,
  Sinatra 3, Cahn 4, Cohn 4, Duning 4,
  Pan 4)
Palace, 1985 (Legrand 4)
Palace of Nudes. *See* Crime au concert
  Mayol, 1954
Palace of Pleasure, 1926 (Glazer 4)
Palace of the Arabian Nights. *See* Palais des
  mille et une nuits, 1905
Palais des mille et une nuits, 1905 (Méliès 2)
Palais-Royale, 1951 (Braunberger 4)
Palanquin des larmes, 1988 (Aurenche 4,
  Jarre 4)
Pale Flower. *See* Kawaita hana, 1963
Pale Rider, 1985 (Eastwood 3)
Paleface, 1922 (Keaton 2)
Pale-Face, 1933 (Iwerks 4)
Paleface, 1948 (McLeod 2, Tashlin 2,
  Hope 3, Russell 3, Dreier 4, Young 4)
Palestine, 1912 (Olcott 2)
Palestinian, 1977 (Redgrave 3)
Palimpest, 1919 (Heller 4)
Palindrome, 1969 (Frampton 2)
Palio, 1932 (Blasetti 2)
Palissades, 1962 (Delerue 4)
Pallard the Punter, 1919 (Pearson 2)
Palm Beach Girl, 1926 (Daniels 3, Banton 4,
  Garmes 4)
Palm Beach Story, 1942 (Sturges 2,
  Astor 3, Colbert 3, McCrea 3,
  Pangborn 3, Dreier 4, Head 4, Irene 4,
  Young 4)
Palm Court Orchestra, 1989 (Halas and
  Batchelor 4)
Palm Springs, 1936 (Niven 3, Reynolds 4,
  Wanger 4)
Palm Springs Affair. *See* Palm Springs, 1936
Palmares des chansons, 1968 (Fernandel 3)
Palmes, 1951 (Rabier 4)
Palmier à l'huile, 1963 (Rouch 2)
Palmy Days, 1931 (Berkeley 2, Cantor 3,
  Grable 3, Raft 3, Day 4, Goldwyn 4,
  Newman 4, Ryskind 4, Toland 4)
Paloma, 1930 (Fleischer 4)
Paloma herida, 1963 (Fernández 2)
Palomas, 1964 (Rey 3)
Palombella Rossa, 1989 (Morricone 4)
Palomita blanca, 1973 (Ruiz 2)
Palooka, 1934 (Durante 3, D'Agostino 4,
  Edeson 4)
Palookah from Paducah, 1935 (Keaton 2)
Pals, 1911 (Dwan 2)
Pals, 1927 (Rooney 3)
Pals, 1987 (Ameche 3, Scott 3, Sidney 3)
Pal's Emergency, 1948 (Hunt 4)
Pals First, 1918 (Gaudio 4)
Pals First, 1926 (Del Rio 3)
Pal's Gallant Journey, 1950 (Hunt 4)
Pals in Blue, 1915 (Mix 3, Selig 4)
Pal's Oath, 1911 (Anderson 3)

Pals of the Golden West, 1951 (Rogers 3)
Pals of the Prairie, 1929 (Miller 4)
Pals of the Range, 1910 (Anderson 3)
Pals of the Saddle, 1938 (Wayne 3, Canutt 4)
Pals of the West, 1934 (Canutt 4)
Pals and Gals, 1954 (Three Stooges 3,
  Bruckman 4)
Pals and Pugs, 1920 (Laurel and Hardy 3)
Paltoquet, 1986 (Moreau 3, Piccoli 3)
Pamiętniki chłopów, 1952 (Munk 2)
Pampa gringa, 1962 (Birri 2)
Pamyati Sergo Ordzhonikidze, 1937
  (Vertov 2)
Pan, 1920 (Fejös 2)
Pan. *See* Kort är sommaren, 1962
Pan Dodek, 1971 (Lomnicki 3)
Pan Handlers, 1935 (Roach 4)
Pan Khaiye Saiya Hamara, 1984
  (Bachchan 3)
Pán na roztrhání, 1934 (Stallich 4)
Pan Passes, 1982 (Emshwiller 2)
Pan Prokouk series, 1947–72 (Zeman 4)
Pan Wołodyjowski, 1969 (Lomnicki 3,
  Olbrychski 3)
Pana a netvor, 1978 (Brejchová 3)
Panama Flo, 1932 (Fort 4, Miller 4)
Panama Hattie, 1942 (McLeod 2, Horne 3,
  Edens 4, Folsey 4, Freed 4)
Panama Lady, 1939 (Ball 3, Fort 4, Hunt 4,
  Polglase 4)
Panama Sugar and the Dog Thief, 1990
  (Reed 3)
Paname n'est pas Paris, 1927 (Vanel 3)
Pan-Americana, 1945 (Arden 3, Benchley 4)
Pan-American Exposition Electric Tower,
  1901 (Bitzer 4)
Pancho Barnes, 1988 (Hayes 4)
Pancho Villa, 1949 (Armendáriz 3)
Pancho Villa y la valentina, 1958
  (Armendáriz 3)
Pancho's Hideaway, 1964 (Blanc 4,
  Freleng 4)
Pandemonium, 1982 (O'Connor 3)
Pandilla del soborno, 1957 (Armendáriz 3)
Pandora, 1934 (Terry 4)
Pandora and the Flying Dutchman, 1951
  (Gardner 3, Mason 3, Cardiff 4, Lewin 4)
Pandora's Box, 1912 (Bunny 3)
Pandora's Box. *See* **Büchse der Pandora,**
  1928
Pandora's Box, 1943 (Terry 4)
Pandora's Box, 1985 (Andrews 3)
Pane, amore e . . . , 1955 (De Sica 2, Loren 3,
  Rotunno 4)
Pane, amore e Andulasia, 1958 (De Sica 2)
Pane, amore e fantasia, 1953 (De Sica 2,
  Lollobrigida 3)
Pane, amore e gelosia, 1954 (De Sica 2,
  Lollobrigida 3)
Pane e cioccolata, 1973 (Karina 3)
Paneless Window Washer, 1937
  (Fleischer 4)
Panels for the Walls of the World, 1967
  (Vanderbeek 2)
Panenství, 1937 (Baarová 3)
Panhandle, 1947 (Edwards 2)
Pani Helén, 1973 (Brejchová 3)
Panic. *See* Panik, 1939
Panic. *See* Panique, 1946
Panic at Lakewood Manor. *See* It Happened
  at Lakewood Manor, 1979
Panic Button, 1964 (Chevalier 3,
  Mansfield 3)
Panic in Needle Park, 1971 (Pacino 3)

Panic in the City, 1967 (Hopper 3)
Panic in the Streets, 1950 (Kazan 2,
  Palance 3, Widmark 3, Anhalt 4,
  LeMaire 4, Newman 4, Wheeler 4)
Panic in Year Zero, 1962 (Milland 3)
Panic Is On, 1931 (Roach 4)
Panic on the Air, 1936 (Ayres 3)
Panico en el Transiberiano, 1972
  (Cushing 3)
Panier à crabes, 1960 (Douy 4)
Panier de chat, 1963 (Cloquet 4)
Panik, 1939 (Björnstrand 3)
Panik in Chicago, 1931 (Wiene 2,
  Tschechowa 3)
Panique, 1946 (Duvivier 2, Simon 3, Ibert 4,
  Spaak 4)
Panny z Wilka, 1979 (Wajda 2,
  Olbrychski 3)
Panorama from Top of a Moving Train. *See*
  Panorama pris d'un train en marche,
  1898
Panorama of the Esplanade by Night, 1901
  (Porter 2)
Panorama pris d'un train en marche, 1898
  (Méliès 2)
Pantalaskas, 1959 (Bost 4)
Pantalon coupé, 1905 (Guy 2)
Pantaloons. *See* Don Juan, 1955
Pantano d'avio, 1956 (Olmi 2)
Pantáta Bezoušek, 1926 (Ondra 3, Heller 4)
Panthea, 1917 (Dwan 2, Von Stroheim 2,
  Talmadge 3, Rosson 4, Schenck 4)
Panther, 1914 (Ince 4)
Panther Squadron. *See* Men of the Fighting
  Lady, 1954
Pantoffelheld, 1922 (Courant 4)
Pantomimes, 1956 (Cocteau 2, Cloquet 4)
Pantry Panic, 1941 (Lantz 4)
Pants and Pansies, 1911 (Sennett 2)
Panurge, 1932 (Darrieux 3)
Panzergewölbe, 1914 (Leni 2)
Paola and Francesca, 1911 (Talmadge 3)
Paolo il caldo, 1973 (Giannini 3, Delli
  Colli 4)
Paolo, le petit pecheur, 1964 (Braunberger 4)
Papa, Be Good!, 1925 (Roach 4)
Papa diventa Mamma, 1952 (Fabrizi 3)
Papa Lebonnard. *See* Père Lebonnard, 1939
Papa les petits bateaux, 1971 (Dalio 3)
Papa sans le savoir, 1932 (Brasseur 3,
  Rosay 3)
Papacito lindo, 1939 (De Fuentes 2,
  Figueroa 4)
Papageno, 1935 (Reiniger 4)
Paparazzi, 1964 (Godard 2, Bardot 3,
  Piccolo 3)
Papa's Day of Rest, 1952 (Terry 4)
Papas de Francine, 1909 (Modot 3)
Papa's Delicate Condition, 1963 (Cahn 4,
  Head 4)
Papa's Little Helpers, 1952 (Terry 4)
Paper Bullets, 1941 (Ladd 3)
Paper Chase, 1973 (Houseman 4, Jenkins 4,
  Williams 4, Willis 4)
Paper Chase, 1978 (Houseman 4)
Paper Doll's Whisper of Spring. *See*
  Kaminingyo haru no sayaki, 1926
Paper Hangers, 1937 (Terry 4)
Paper Hearts, 1991 (Sheen 3)
Paper Lion, 1968 (Scheider 3)
Paper Moon, 1973 (Bogdanovich 2, Fields 4,
  Kovacs 4, Sargent 4)
Paper Nocturne. *See* Papírové nokturno,
  1949

Paper Tiger, 1974 (Mifune 3, Niven 3, Cahn 4, Levine 4)
Paperhanger's Helper, 1915 (Laurel and Hardy 3)
Papierene Brucke, 1987 (Golan and Globus 4)
Papillon, 1973 (Schaffner 2, Hoffman 3, McQueen 3, Goldsmith 4, Trumbo 4)
Papillon sur l'épaule, 1978 (Carrière 4, Guerra 4)
Papírové nokturno, 1949 (Brdečka 4)
Pappa Bom, 1949 (Björnstrand 3)
Pappa sökes, 1947 (Björnstrand 3)
Pappa, varför är du arg? Du gjorde likadant själv när du var ung, 1969 (Björnstrand 3)
Pappagalli, 1956 (Fabrizi 3, Sordi 3)
Pappagallo della zia Berta, 1912 (Bertini 3)
Pappas pojke, 1937 (Fischer 4, Jaenzon 4)
Pappi, 1934 (Warm 4)
Pappy's Puppy, 1955 (Blanc 4, Freleng 4, Stalling 4)
Paprika, 1932 (Maté 4, Pasternak 4,)
Paqueboat Tenacity, 1933 (Duvivier 2, Douy 4, Matras 4)
Paques rouges, 1914 (Feuillade 2)
Paquet embarrassant, 1907 (Feuillade 2)
Par Avion, 1958 (Breer 4)
Par habitude, 1914 (Chevalier 3)
Par habitude, 1923 (Chevalier 3)
Par habitude, 1932 (Fernandel 3)
Par le sang des autres, 1974 (Blier 3, Lai 4)
Par ordre du Tsar, 1953 (Simon 3)
Par original, 1912 (Linder 3)
Par un beau matin d'été, 1964 (Belmondo 3, Chaplin 3, Audiard 4, Wakhévitch 4)
Para gnedych, 1915 (Mozhukin 3)
Para vestir, 1955 (Torre Nilsson 2)
Paracelsus, 1943 (Pabst 2, Krauss 3, Rasp 3)
Parachute, 1969 (Anderson 2)
Parachute Battalion, 1941 (Carey 3, O'Brien 3, Preston 3, Hunt 4)
Parachute Jumper, 1933 (Brennan 3, Davis 3, Orry-Kelly 4)
Parachutistes, 1964 (Braunberger 4)
Parade, 1973 (Tati 2, Fischer 4)
Parade, 1984 (Page 3)
Parade des chapeaux, 1937 (Alexeieff and Parker 4)
Parade en sept nuits, 1941 (Barrault 3, Berry 3, Jourdan 3, Presle 3, Raimu 3, Achard 4)
Parade of the Bands, 1956 (Carreras 4)
Parade of the West, 1930 (Brown 4, McCord 4)
Parade of the Wooden Soldiers, 1933 (Fleischer 4)
Paradies im Schnee, 1923 (Courant 4, Kräly 4)
Paradigme. See Pouvoir du mal, 1985
Paradine Case, 1947 (Hitchcock 2, Barrymore 3, Coburn 3, Jourdan 3, Laughton 3, Peck 3, Valli 3, Banton 4, Garmes 4, Reville 4, Selznick 4, Waxman 4)
Paradis de Satan, 1938 (Delannoy 2, Douy 4, Lourié 4)
Paradis des pilotes perdus, 1948 (Gélin 3, D'Eaubonne 4, Kosma 4)
Paradis des riches, 1977 (Dalio 3)
Paradis perdu, 1940 (Presle 3)
Paradise. See Paradiset, 1955
Paradise Alley, 1978 (Kovacs 4)
Paradise Alley, 1991 (Stallone 3)

Paradise Bride's School. See Gokuraku hanayome-juku, 1936
Paradise Canyon, 1935 (Wayne 3, Canutt 4)
Paradise en sept nuits, 1941 (Matras 4)
Paradise for Buster, 1952 (Keaton 2)
Paradise for Three, 1938 (Astor 3, Young 3)
Paradise for Two, 1927 (La Cava 2, Cronjager 4)
Paradise for Two, 1937 (Withers 3, Hornbeck 4, Korda, A. 4, Korda, V. 4)
Paradise Garden, 1917 (Gaudio 4)
Paradise, Hawaiian Style, 1966 (Presley 3, Head 4, Wallis 4)
Paradise Island, 1930 (Glennon 4)
Paradise Lagoon. See Admirable Crichton, 1957
Paradise Lost, 1911 (Sennett 2)
Paradise Not Yet Lost, or Oona's Fifth Year, 1980 (Mekas 2)
Paradise perdu, 1939 (Matras 4)
Paradise Valley. See Pueblo Terror, 1931
Paradiset, 1955 (Dahlbeck 3)
Paradiso terrestre, 1956 (Coutard 4)
Paraiso, 1969 (Alcoriza 4)
Parakh, 1960 (Roy 2)
Parallax View, 1974 (Pakula 2, Beatty 3, Jenkins 4, Willis 4)
Paralytic, 1912 (Guy 2)
Paramount on Parade, 1930 (Arzner 2, Goulding 2, Lubitsch 2, Arthur 3, Bow 3, Chevalier 3, Cooper 3, Francis 3, March 3, Powell 3, Wray 3, Banton 4, Zukor 4)
Paranoia, 1969 (Baker 3)
Paranoiac, 1963 (Reed 3, Carreras 4, Francis 4, Sangster 4)
Paraplíčko, 1957 (Trnka 4)
Parapluie fantastique. See Tonnerre de Jupiter, 1903
Parapluies de Cherbourg, 1964 (Demy 2, Deneuve 3, Evein 4, Legrand 4, Rabier 4)
Pararazzi, 1964 (Piccoli 3)
Parash Pathar, 1957 (Chandragupta 4, Datta 4, Mitra 4, Shankar 4)
Parasite, 1925 (Schulberg 4)
Parasites. See Drag, 1929
Paratroop Command, 1958 (Corman 2)
Paratrooper. See Red Beret, 1953
Parc-Atlantique, 1966 (Arcand 2)
Pardeshi, 1957 (Biswas 4)
Pardessus de demi-saison, 1917 (Feyder 2)
Pardners, 1956 (Lewis 2, Martin 3, Moorehead 3, Van Cleef 3, Cahn 4, Head 4)
Pardon Me, 1922 (Roach 4)
Pardon My Backfire, 1953 (Three Stooges 3)
Pardon My Berth Marks, 1940 (Keaton 2, Bruckman 4)
Pardon My Clutch, 1948 (Three Stooges 3, Bruckman 4)
Pardon My French, 1921 (Olcott 2)
Pardon My French, 1950 (Henreid 3, Oberon 3, Kosma 4)
Pardon My Nerve, 1922 (Eason 4)
Pardon My Past, 1946 (Aldrich 2, MacMurray 3, Metty 4, Tiomkin 4)
Pardon My Pups, 1934 (Temple 3)
Pardon My Rhythm, 1944 (Salter 4)
Pardon My Sarong, 1942 (Abbott and Costello 3, Krasner 4)
Pardon My Scotch, 1935 (Three Stooges 3)
Pardon My Stripes, 1942 (Alton 4)
Pardon Our Nerve, 1939 (Clarke 4)

Pardon Us, 1931 (Karloff 3, Laurel and Hardy 3, Roach 4)
Paré pour accoster, 1950 (Decaë 4)
Paree, Paree, 1934 (Hope 3)
Parent Trap, 1961 (O'Hara 3, Ballard 4, Disney 4, Iwerks 4)
Parental Claim. See Lien de Parenté, 1986
Parenthood, 1989 (Martin 3, Robards 3)
Parents ne sont pas simples cette année, 1984 (Decaë 4)
Parents terribles, 1948 (Cocteau 2, Marais 3, Auric 4)
Parfum de la dame en noir, 1931 (L'Herbier 2, Meerson 4, Périnal 4)
Parfum de la dame en noir, 1949 (Modot 3, Piccoli 3, Reggiani 3, Douy 4)
Parfums, 1924 (Grémillon 2)
Pari e figli, 1957 (Mastroianni 3)
Paria, 1968 (Marais 3)
Parigi è sempre Parigi, 1951 (Rosi 2, Fabrizi 3, Mastroianni 3, Montand 3, Alekan 4, Amidei 4, Flaiano 4, Kosma 4)
Parigina a Roma, 1954 (Schüfftan 4)
Parigina a Roma, 1954 (Scola 2, Sordi 3)
Parinay, 1975 (Azmi 3)
Parineeta, 1953 (Roy 2)
Paris, 1926 (Crawford 3, Gibbons 4, Mayer 4)
Paris, 1929 (Buchanan 3, Polito 4)
Paris, 1936 (Baur 3, Ibert 4)
Paris, 1951 (Cardiff 4)
Paris à l'automne, 1958 (Resnais 2)
Paris after Dark, 1943 (Dalio 3, Sanders 3, Basevi 4, Friedhofer 4)
Paris at Midnight, 1926 (Barrymore 3, Marion 4)
Paris au jour d'hiver, 1965 (Braunberger 4)
Paris au mois d'août, 1965 (Evein 4, Jeanson 4, Renoir 4)
Paris au temps des cerises: La Commune, 1967 (Delerue 4)
Paris Blues, 1961 (Ritt 2, Newman 3, Poitier 3, Reggiani 3, Woodward 3, Matras 4, Trauner 4)
Paris Bound, 1929 (March 3)
Paris brûle-t-il?, 1966 (Welles 2, Belmondo 3, Boyer 3, Brynner 3, Caron 3, Cassel 3, Delon 3, Douglas 3, Ford 3, Gélin 3, McDowall 3, Montand 3, Perkins 3, Piccoli 3, Signoret 3, Trintignant 3, Aurenche 4, Bost 4, Jarre 4)
Paris By Night, 1988 (Delerue 4)
Paris Calling, 1941 (Bergner 3, Cobb 3, Rathbone 3, Scott 3, Glazer 4, Krasner 4)
Paris canaille, 1955 (Gélin 3)
Paris chante toujours, 1950 (Montand 3)
Paris Commune. See Zori Parizha, 1936
Paris coquin. See Paris canaille, 1955
Paris des mannequins, 1962 (Braunberger 4)
Paris des photographes, 1962 (Braunberger 4)
Paris d'hier et d'aujourd'hui, 1956 (Braunberger 4)
Paris Does Strange Things. See Élena et les hommes, 1956
Paris et le désert français, 1957 (Leenhardt 2)
Paris Exposition, 1900. See Exposition de 1900, 1900
Paris Express, 1953 (Aimée 3, Lom 3, Rains 3, Heller 4)
Paris Frills. See Falbalas, 1945
Paris Holiday, 1958 (Sturges 2, Hope 3, Cahn 4, Wakhévitch 4)

Paris Honeymoon, 1939 (Crosby 3, Horton 3, Head 4, Struss 4)

Paris in Spring, 1935 (Lupino 3, Glazer 4, Hoffenstein 4)

Paris in the Month of August. *See* Paris au mois d'août, 1965

Paris in the Spring, 1935 (Milestone 2, Dreier 4)

Paris Interlude, 1934 (Young 3, Krasner 4)

Paris la belle, 1959 (Arletty 3, Colpi 4, Prévert 4)

Paris la nuit ou Exploits d'apaches à Montamartre, 1904 (Guy 2, Gaumont 4)

Paris mange son pain, 1958 (Grimault 4, Prévert 4)

Paris, mes amours, 1935 (Fradetal 4)

Paris Model, 1953 (Goddard 3)

Paris 1900, 1947 (Resnais 2, Braunberger 4)

Paris—New York, 1939 (Von Stroheim 2, Berry 3, Simon 3, Andrejew 4)

Paris nous appartient, 1960 (Chabrol 2, Demy 2, Godard 2)

Paris on Parade, 1938 (Cardiff 4)

Paris on the Seine, 1947 (Unsworth 4)

Paris på to måder, 1949 (Roos 2)

Paris Plane, 1933 (Bennett 4)

Paris qui dort, 1923 (Clair 2)

Paris Restaurants, 1971 (Lassally 4)

Paris s'en va, 1981 (Rivette 2)

Paris, Texas, 1984 (Wenders 2, Kinski 3, Stanton 3, Müller 4, Shepard 4)

Paris tous les deux, 1957 (Fernandel 3)

Paris Trout, 1991 (Hopper 3)

Paris Underground, 1945 (Fields 3, Garmes 4)

Paris . . . un jeudi, 1954 (Kosma 4)

Paris vu par . . ., 1965 (Chabrol 2, Audran 3, Almendros 4, Rabier 4)

Paris vu par . . . 20 ans après, 1984 (Akerman 2, Léaud 3)

Paris Waltz. *See* Valse de Paris, 1949

Paris When It Sizzles, 1963 (Curtis 3, Dietrich 3, Hepburn 3, Holden 3, Axelrod 4, Coward 4, D'Eaubonne 4, Lang 4)

Paris-Beguin, 1931 (Fernandel 3, Gabin 3)

Paris-Deauville, 1935 (Delannoy 2)

Pariserinnen, 1921 (Herlth 4, Röhrig 4, Wagner 4)

Parisette, 1921 (Clair 2, Feuillade 2)

Parisian. *See* Mon gosse de père, 1930

Parisian Love, 1925 (Bow 3, Schulberg 4)

Parisian Nights, 1924 (Florey 2, Karloff 3, Haller 4)

Parisian Romance, 1916 (Menjou 3)

Parisienne, 1957 (Bardot 3, Boyer 3)

Parisiennes, 1961 (Deneuve 3, Alekan 4)

Parisiskor, 1928 (Molander 2, Jaenzon 4)

Paris-Mediterranée, 1931 (Douy 4)

Paris-Palace-Hôtel, 1956 (Boyer 3, D'Eaubonne 4, Spaak 4)

Parivar, 1956 (Roy 2)

Parivartan, 1949 (Kapoor 2)

Park Avenue Logger, 1937 (Bond 3)

Park Row, 1952 (Fuller 2)

Park Sands. *See* Jericho, 1937

Park Your Car, 1920 (Roach 4)

Parkettsessel 47, 1926 (Warm 4)

Parking, 1985 (Demy 2, Marais 3, Legrand 4)

Parking Space, 1933 (Lantz 4)

Parkstrasse 13, 1939 (Tschechowa 3)

Parlementaire, 1916 (Mozhukin 3)

Parliamo tanto di me, 1968 (Zavattini 4)

Parlor, Bedroom and Bath, 1931 (Keaton 2)

Pärlorna, 1922 (Molander 2)

Parnell, 1937 (Stahl 2, Crisp 3, Gable 3, Loy 3, Adrian 4, Behrman 4, Freund 4, Mayer 4)

Parole, 1936 (Quinn 3)

Parole de flic, 1985 (Delon 3)

Parole est du fleuve, 1961 (Delerue 4)

Parole Fixer, 1940 (Florey 2, Beavers 3, Quinn 3, Barnes 4, Head 4)

Parole Girl, 1933 (Bellamy 3, Krasna 4)

Paroles et musique, 1984 (Deneuve 3, Legrand 4)

Paroxismus, 1969 (Kinski 3)

Parque de Madrid, 1958 (Rey 3)

Parrish, 1961 (Daves 2, Colbert 3, Malden 3, Steiner 4, Stradling 4)

Parsifal, 1983 (Syberberg 2)

Parson of Panamint, 1941 (Harlan 4, Head 4)

Parson Who Fled West, 1915 (Mix 3)

Parson's Widow. *See* Prästänkan, 1920

Part de l'ombre, 1945 (Barrault 3, Feuillère 3, Auric 4, Spaak 4)

Part du feu, 1977 (Cardinale 3, Piccoli 3)

Part Time Pal, 1946 (Hanna and Barbera 4)

Part Time Wife, 1930 (McCarey 2)

Parted Curtains, 1921 (Walthall 3, Glennon 4)

Particles in Space, 1957 (Lye, 4)

Partie de campagne, 1946 (Becker 2, Visconti 2, Braunberger 4, Kosma 4, Renoir 4)

Partie de plaisir, 1975 (Chabrol 2, Gégauff 4, Rabier 4)

Partie de tric-trac, 1895 (Lumière 2)

Partie d'ecarté, 1895 (Lumière 2)

Parting Trails, 1911 (Dwan 2)

Partings. *See* Rozstanie, 1961

Partir, 1931 (Tourneur 2, Douy 4)

Partir, revenir, 1985 (Girardot 3, Piccoli 3, Trintignant 3, Legrand 4)

Partire, 1938 (De Sica 2)

Partisans in the Ukrainian Steppes. *See* Partizani v stepyakh Ukrainy, 1942

Partita, 1988 (Donaggio 4)

Partizani, 1974 (Theodorakis 4)

Partizani v stepyakh Ukrainy, 1942 (Prokofiev 4)

Partner, 1968 (Bertolucci 2, Morricone 4)

Partners, 1982 (Hurt 3, Delerue 4, Sylbert 4)

Partners Again, 1926 (King 2, Edeson 4, Goldwyn 4, Marion 4)

Partners in Crime, 1928 (Beery 3, Powell 3)

Partners in Crime, 1937 (Quinn 3, Dreier 4, Head 4)

Partners in Crime, 1942 (Launder and Gilliat 2)

Partners in Crime, 1973 (Grant 3)

Partners of the Plains, 1938 (Harlan 4, Head 4)

Partners Please, 1932 (Bennett 4)

Partners Three, 1919 (Niblo 2, Barnes 4)

Parto psicoprofiláctico, 1969 (Leduc 2)

Party. *See* Pete's Haunted House, 1926

Party, 1964 (Altman 2)

Party, 1968 (Edwards 2, Sellers 3, Ballard 4, Mancini 4)

Party, 1970 (Schepisi 2)

Party, 1984 (Nihalani 4)

Party at Kitty and Studs, 1970 (Stallone 3)

Party Crashers, 1958 (Farmer 3, Head 4)

Party Fever, 1938 (Roach 4)

Party Girl, 1958 (Ray 2, Charisse 3, Cobb 3, Taylor 3, Cahn 4, Pasternak 4, Rose 4)

Party Husbands, 1931 (Beavers 3)

Party Is Over. *See* Fin de fiesta, 1959

Party Wire, 1935 (Arthur 3)

Party's Over, 1963 (Hawkins 3, Reed 3, Barry 4)

Parvarish, 1958 (Kapoor 2)

Parvarish, 1977 (Azmi 3, Bachchan 3)

Parwana, 1972 (Bachchan 3)

Pa's Birthday, 1962 (Breer 4)

Pas de caviar pour tante Olga, 1965 (Brasseur 3, Cloquet 4)

Pas de deux, 1967 (McLaren 4)

Pas de la mule, 1930 (Epstein 2)

Pas de panique, 1965 (Brasseur 3, Manès 3)

Pas de pitié pour les caves, 1955 (Kosma 4)

Pas de problèmes, 1975 (Sarde 4)

Pas de souris dans le bizness, 1954 (Kosma 4)

Pas de Trois, 1975 (Frampton 2)

Pas de week-end pour notre amour, 1950 (Berry 3, D'Eaubonne 4)

Pas folle la guêpe, 1972 (Delannoy 2, Legrand 4, Matras 4)

Pas på Pigerne, 1930 (Madsen and Schenstrøm 3)

Pas perdus, 1964 (Morgan 3, Trintignant 3)

Pas question le samedi, 1964 (Annenkov 4)

Pas si méchant que ça, 1974 (Depardieu 3)

Pas suspendu de la cicogne. *See* To meteoro vima to Pelargou, 1991

Pas un mot à ma femme, 1931 (Fernandel 3)

Pasażerka, 1963 (Munk 2, Stawiński 4)

Pascal, 1964 (Rohmer 2)

Paseo sobre una guerra antigua, 1949 (Bardem 2, García Berlanga 2)

Pasha's Wives. *See* Esclave blanche, 1939

Pasht, 1965 (Brakhage 2)

Pasi spre lune, 1963 (Popescu-Gopo 4)

Pasion de hombre. *See* Man of Passion, 1989

Pasión desnuda, 1953 (Félix 3)

Pasión segun Berenice, 1976 (Hermosillo 2)

Paso, 1949 (Hayden 3)

Pasodoble, 1988 (Rey 3)

Pasqualino settebellezze, 1975 (Wertmüller 2, Giannini 3, Rey 3, Delli Colli 4)

Pasqualino Seven Beauties. *See* Pasqualino settebellezze, 1975

Pass the Dumpling, 1927 (Sennett 2)

Pass the Gravy, 1928 (McCarey 2)

Passage, 1979 (Lee 3, Mason 3, McDowell 3, Neal 3, Quinn 3)

Passage, 1986 (Delon 3)

Passage Home, 1955 (Cusack 3, Finch 3, Rank 4, Vetchinsky 4)

Passage Interdit, 1935 (Modot 3)

Passage of Love, 1965 (Cusack 3, Addison 4)

Passage to Algiers, 1945 (Rathbone 3)

Passage to India, 1984 (Lean 2, Guinness 3, Box 4, Jarre 4)

Passage to Marseilles, 1944 (Curtiz 2, Bogart 3, Dalio 3, Greenstreet 3, Lorre 3, Morgan 3, Rains 3, Howe 4, Robinson 4, Steiner 4, Wallis 4)

Passagem ou a Meio Caminho, 1980 (De Almeida 4)

Passager, 1928 (Vanel 3)

Passager clandestin, 1957 (Arletty 3, Reggiani 3)

Passager de la pluie, 1969 (Bronson 3, Lai 4)

Passagère. *See* Pasażerka, 1963

Passagers, 1976 (Trintignant 3)

Passagers de la Grande Ourse. *See* Gô chez les oiseaux, 1939

Passagier—Welcome to Germany, 1988 (Curtis 3)

Passagierin. *See* Pasażerka, 1963

Passant, 1943 (Alexeieff and Parker 4)

Passant par la Lorraine, 1950 (Franju 2, Fradetal 4, Kosma 4)

Passante. *See* Passante du Sans-Souci, 1981

Passante du Sans-Souci, 1981 (Piccoli 3, Schell 3, Schneider 3, Delerue 4)

Passaporto per l'Oriente, 1951 (Lollobrigida 3)

Passatore, 1947 (Fellini 2, Brazzi 3, Sordi 3, De Laurentiis 4, Pinelli 4)

Passé à vendre, 1936 (Brasseur 3)

Passé de Monique, 1917 (Feuillade 2)

Passe du diable, 1957 (Coutard 4, De Beauregard 4)

Passe ton bac d'abord, 1979 (Pialat 2)

Passeggiata, 1953 (Zavattini 4)

Passe-Montagne, 1978 (Sarde 4)

Passe-Muraille. *See* Garou-Garou, le passe-muraille, 1950

Passenger. *See* Pasażerka, 1963

Passenger. *See* **Professione: Reporter, 1975**

Passers-By, 1920 (Blackton 2)

Passes, 1982 (Emshwiller 2)

Passeurs d'hommes, 1937 (Honegger 4)

Passing of a Soul, 1915 (Hepworth 2)

Passing of Izzy, 1914 (Sennett 2)

Passing of Pete, 1916 (Mix 3)

Passing of the Beast, 1914 (Reid 3)

Passing of the Third Floor Back, 1918 (Brenon 2, Hunt 4)

Passing of the Third Floor Back, 1935 (Veidt 3, Balcon 4, Courant 4, Reville 4)

Passing of Two-Gun Hicks, 1914 (Hart 3, August 4, Sullivan 4)

Passing Shadow, 1912 (Bushman 3)

Passing Stranger, 1954 (Lassally 4)

Passing Through. *See* Good Bad Man, 1916

Passion, 1902 (Pathé 4)

Passion, 1904 (Gaumont 4)

Passion. *See* Madame DuBarry, 1919

Passion, 1954 (Dwan 2, De Carlo 3, Wilde 3, Alton 4, Polglase 4)

Passion. *See* Vášeň, 1961

Passion, 1969 (Bergman 2, Andersson 3, Josephson 3, Ullmann 3, Von Sydow 3, Nykvist 4)

Passion, 1982 (Godard 2, Huppert 3, Piccoli 3, Schygulla 3, Coutard 4)

Passion and Paradise, 1989 (Steiger 3)

Passion Béatrice, 1987 (Tavernier 2)

Passion de Jeanne d'Arc, 1928 (Dreyer 2, Artaud 3, Simon 3, Maté 4, Warm 4)

Passion Flower, 1921 (Brenon 2, Talmadge 3, Hunt 4, Schenck 4)

Passion Flower, 1930 (Francis 3, Milland 3, Adrian 4, Gibbons 4, Rosson 4)

Passion Flower Hotel, 1978 (Kinski 3, Lai 4)

Passion for Life. *See* Ecole buissonnière, 1948

Passion Fruit, 1921 (Wilson 4)

Passion Island. *See* Isla de la pasion, 1941

Passion of Anna. *See* Passion, 1969

Passion of a Woman Teacher. *See* Kyoren no onna shisho, 1926

Passion of Joan of Arc. *See* **Passion de Jeanne d'Arc, 1928**

Passion of Love. *See* Passione d'amore, 1981

Passion, travail et amour. *See* Passion, 1982

Passionate Adventure, 1924 (Hitchcock 2, Balcon 4)

Passionate Century. *See* Who Goes There!, 1952

Passionate Friends, 1949 (Howard 3, Rains 3, Green 4, Rank 4)

Passionate Plumber, 1932 (Keaton 2, Durante 4)

Passionate Quest, 1926 (Blackton 2, Musuraca 4)

Passionate Sentry. *See* Who Goes There, 1952

Passionate Stranger, 1956 (Richardson 3, Box 4, Heller 4)

Passionate Summer, 1957 (Rank 4)

Passionate Thief. *See* Risate di gioia, 1960

Passione d'amore, 1981 (Scola 2, Blier 3, Trintignant 3)

Passione secondo San Matteo, 1949 (Cervi 3)

Passionels Tagebuch, 1916 (Jannings 3)

Passions, 1984 (Woodward 3)

Passions—He Had Three, 1913 (Sennett 2, Arbuckle 3)

Passions of the Sea. *See* Lost and Found on a South Sea Island, 1923

Passion's Playground, 1920 (Valentino 3)

Passover Plot, 1976 (Pleasence 3, Golan and Globus 4, North 4)

Passport of Suez, 1939 (De Toth 2)

Passport to China. *See* Visa to Canton, 1961

Passport to Destiny, 1944 (Lanchester 3)

Passport to Fame. *See* Whole Town's Talking, 1935

Passport to Hell, 1932 (Crisp 3, Lukas 3, Friedhofer 4, Seitz 4)

Passport to Pimlico, 1949 (Rutherford 3, Auric 4, Balcon 4, Clarke 4)

Passport to Shame, 1959 (Roeg 2, Caine 3, Constantine 3, Dors 3, Lom 3)

Password Is Courage, 1962 (Bogarde 3)

Password: Korn, 1967 (Nowicki 3)

Past and Present. *See* O Passado e o Presente, 1972

Past of Mary Holmes, 1933 (Arthur 3, Plunkett 4, Polglase 4, Rosher 4, Vorkapich 4)

Past Perfumance, 1955 (Blanc 4, Jones 4)

Paste and Paper, 1922 (Roach 4)

Pasteur, 1922 (Epstein 2)

Pasteur, 1935 (Guitry 2)

Pasteur. *See* Oeuvre scientifique de Pasteur, 1946

Pastor Angelicus, 1942 (Flaiano 4)

Pastor Hall, 1940 (Boulting 2)

Pastoral Symphony. *See* Denen Kokyogaku, 1938

Pastry Panic, 1951 (Terry 4)

Pastry Pirates. *See* Porky's Baseball Broadcast, 1940

Pat and Mike, 1952 (Cukor 2, Bronson 3, Gordon 3, Hepburn 3, Tracy 3, Daniels 4, Kanin 4, Orry-Kelly 4, Raksin 4)

Pat and Patachon im Paradies. *See* Insel wird entdeckt, 1937

Pat Garrett and Billy the Kid, 1973 (Fernández 2, Peckinpah 2, Coburn 3, Robards 3, Stanton 3)

Patakin, 1982 (Gómez 2)

Patate, 1964 (Darrieux 3, Marais 3, Douy 4)

Patates, 1969 (Autant-Lara 2, Aurenche 4, Douy 4)

Patch of Blue, 1965 (Poitier 3, Winters 3, Berman 4, Burks 4, Goldsmith 4, Green 4)

Páté kolo u vozu, 1958 (Stallich 4)

Patent Leather Kid, 1927 (Barthelmess 3, Edeson 4)

Pater, 1910 (Feuillade 2, Gaumont 4)

Páter Vojtěch, 1929 (Heller 4)

Paternity, 1981 (Reynolds 3)

Pate's Dragon, 1977 (Winters 3)

Path of Glory, 1949 (Bondarchuk 3)

Path of Hope. *See* Cammino della speranza, 1950

Pather Panchali, 1955 (Chandragupta 4, Datta 4, Mitra 4, Shankar 4)

Pathfinder, 1952 (Katzman 4)

Paths into the Night. *See* Wagen in der Nacht, 1979

Paths of Glory, 1957 (Kubrick 2, Douglas 3, Menjou 3)

Pathway of Years, 1913 (Bushman 3)

Pathways of Life, 1916 (Gish 3)

Patience, 1920 (Leni 2)

Patience, 1920 (Veidt 3, Hoffmann 4)

Patient in Room 18, 1938 (Sheridan 3)

Patient Porky, 1940 (Blanc 4, Clampett 4, Stalling 4)

Patient Vanishes. *See* This Man Is Dangerous, 1941

Pâtissier et ramoneur, 1904 (Guy 2)

Patita, 1953 (Anand 3)

Patria, 1917 (Beery 3)

Patricia, 1916 (Valentino 3)

Patricia et Jean-Baptiste, 1966 (Lefebvre 2)

Patricia Neal Story, 1981 (Jackson 3)

Patricia of the Plains, 1910 (Anderson 3)

Patrick the Great, 1945 (Arden 3, O'Connor 3, Salter 4)

Patrie, 1945 (Annenkov 4, Bost 4, Spaak 4)

Patrimonio nacional, 1980 (García Berlanga 2)

Patriot, 1916 (Hart 3)

Patriot, 1928 (Lubitsch 2, Jannings 3, Clothier 4, Dreier 4, Glennon 4, Kräly 4, Zukor 4)

Patriot and the Spy, 1915 (Cruze 2)

Patriote, 1938 (Tourneur 2, Ibert 4, Jeanson 4)

Patrioten, 1937 (Baarová 3, Röhrig 4)

Patriotic Pooches, 1943 (Terry 4)

Patriotism, 1964 (Wieland 2)

Patriots. *See* Company Business, 1991

Patron est mort, 1938 (Storck 2)

Patrouille Blanche, 1941 (Hayakawa 3)

Patrouille des sables, 1954 (Dalio 3)

Patrullero 777, 1978 (Cantinflas 3)

Pat's Day Off, 1912 (Sennett 2)

Patsy, 1928 (Vidor 2, Davies 3, Dressler 3, Gibbons 4, Seitz 4)

Patsy, 1964 (Lewis 2, Carradine 3, Lorre 3, Raft 3, Sloane 3, Head 4, Raksin 4)

Pattaglia sperduta, 1954 (Cristaldi 4)

Pattern of Morality. *See* Owen Marshall, Counsellor at Law, 1971

Patterns, 1956 (Kaufman 4)

Patterns of Power. *See* Patterns, 1956

Patters, 1956 (Sloane 3)

Pattes blanches, 1949 (Grémillon 2, Barsacq 4)

Pattes de mouches, 1936 (Grémillon 2, Brasseur 3)

Patto col diavolo, 1949 (Amidei 4, Cecchi D'Amico 4)

Patton, 1970 (Coppola 2, Malden 3, Scott 3, Goldsmith 4)

Patton—Lust for Glory. *See* Patton, 1970
Patton: Lust for Glory. *See* Patton, 1970
Pattuglia di passo San Giacomo, 1954 (Olmi 2)
Patty Hearst, 1988 (Schrader 2)
Paul and Michelle, 1973 (Renoir 4)
Paul Chevrolet and the Ultimate Hallucination. *See* Paul Chevrolet en de ultieme hallucinatie, 1985
Paul Chevrolet en de ultieme hallucinatie, 1985 (Constantine 3)
Paul Claudel, 1951 (Barrault 3, Honegger 4)
Paul Delvaux ou les femmes défendues, 1968 (Storck 2)
Paul Gauguin, 1949 (Milhaud 4)
Paul Revere's Ride, 1910 (Walsh 2)
Paul Swan, 1965 (Warhol 2)
Paul Temple Returns, 1952 (Lee 3)
Paul Valéry, 1959 (Leenhardt 2)
Paula. *See* Framed, 1947
Paula, 1952 (Young 3, Duning 4, Maté 4)
Paula—''je reviens'', 1968 (Schroeter 2)
Paulina 1880, 1972 (Schell 3)
Pauline, 1914 (Warm 4)
Pauline à la plage, 1982 (Rohmer 2, Almendros 4)
Pauline at the Beach. *See* Pauline à la plage, 1982
Paura. *See* Angst, 1954
Paura e amore, 1988 (Von Trotta 2)
Paura in città, 1976 (Cusack 3)
Pauvre pompier, 1906 (Guy 2)
Pavé, 1905 (Guy 2)
Pavé de Paris, 1961 (Kosma 4)
Pavel Camrda's Career. *See* Kariera Pavla Čamrdy, 1931
Pavillon brûle, 1941 (Blier 3, Marais 3, Douy 4)
Pavlínka, 1974 (Kachyňa 2)
Pawn of Fate, 1916 (Tourneur 2, Carré 4)
Pawn Shop. *See* Stampen, 1955
Pawn Ticket 210, 1922 (Furthman 4)
Pawnbroker, 1965 (Lumet 2, Steiger 3, Jones 4, Kaufman 4, Rosenblum 4, Sylbert 4)
Pawnbroker's Heart, 1917 (Sennett 2)
Pawns of Destiny, 1914 (Lawrence 3)
Pawnshop, 1916 (Chaplin 2, Purviance 3)
Paws of the Bear, 1917 (Ince 4)
Pax, 1968 (Figueroa 4)
Pax Aeterna, 1916 (Holger-Madsen 2)
Pay as You Enter, 1928 (Bacon 2, Loy 3)
Pay as You Exit, 1935 (Roach 4)
Pay Car, 1909 (Olcott 2)
Pay Day, 1922 (Chaplin 2, Purviance 3, Fleischer 4)
Pay Dirt, 1916 (King 2, Eason 4)
Pay Me, 1916 (Chaney 3)
Pay Off, 1930 (Hunt 4, Murfin 4)
Pay or Die, 1960 (Borgnine 3, Ballard 4, Raksin 4)
Pay the Cashier, 1922 (Roach 4)
Pay the Devil, 1957 (Welles 2)
Pay Your Dues, 1919 (Daniels 3, Lloyd 3, Roach 4)
Paying Bay, 1964 (Halas and Batchelor 4)
Paying Guest, 1957 (Anand 3, Burman 4)
Paying the Penalty. *See* **Underworld, 1927**
Paying the Piper, 1921 (Miller 4)
Paying the Piper, 1949 (Blanc 4, McKimson 4)
Paymaster, 1906 (Bitzer 4)
Payment, 1916 (Sullivan 4)

Payment Deferred, 1932 (Laughton 3, Milland 3, O'Sullivan 3, Vajda 4)
Payment on Demand, 1951 (Davis 3, Head 4, Plunkett 4, Young 4)
Payoff, 1935 (Florey 2, Orry-Kelly 4)
Pay-Off, 1991 (Stanton 3)
Pays bleu, 1976 (Guillemot 4)
Pays de la terre sans arbre, 1979 (Perrault 2)
Pays d'Octobre. *See* Mississippi Blues, 1983
Pays d'où je viens, 1956 (Carné 2, Achard 4)
Pays sans bon sens, 1970 (Perrault 2)
Pays sans étoiles, 1946 (Brasseur 3, Philipe 3)
Paysage dans le brouillard. *See* Topio stin omichli, 1988
Pazza di gioia, 1940 (De Sica 2, Fusco 4)
Pazzi della domenica, 1955 (Taviani 2)
Peace. *See* Hoa-binh, 1969
Peace Game. *See* Gladiatorerna, 1969
Peace of Britain, 1936 (Rotha 2)
Peaceable Kingdom, 1971 (Brakhage 2)
Peaceful Oscar, 1927 (Arbuckle 3)
Peacemaker, 1914 (Costello 3, Talmadge 3)
Peace-Time Football, 1946 (Terry 4)
Peach Basket Hat, 1909 (Griffith 2, Lawrence 3, Pickford 3, Bitzer 4)
Peaches, 1964 (Ustinov 3, Lassally 4)
Peaches and Plumbers, 1927 (Sennett 2)
Peachy Cobbler, 1950 (Avery 4)
Peacock Alley, 1921 (Goulding 2)
Peacock Alley, 1930 (Wilson 4)
Peaks of Zelengore, 1976 (Bondarchuk 3)
Peanut Vendor, 1933 (Fleischer 4)
Peanuts and Bullets, 1915 (Sennett 2)
Pearl series, 1910–16 (White 3)
Pearl. *See* Perla, 1945
Pearl Divers, 1980 (Halas and Batchelor 4)
Pearl of Death, 1944 (Rathbone 3, Miller 4, Salter 4)
Pearl of the South Pacific, 1955 (Dwan 2, Alton 4, Jennings 4, Polglase 4)
Pearl of Tlayucan. *See* Tlayucan, 1961
Pearls Brings Tears, 1937 (Withers 3)
Pearls of the Crown. *See* Perles de la couronne, 1937
Pearls of the Deep. *See* Perličky na dně, 1965
Peasant Island, 1940 (Cardiff 4)
Peasant's Fate. *See* Krestyanskaya dolia, 1912
Peat and Repeat, 1931 (Arbuckle 3)
Peau d'âne, 1904 (Pathé 4)
Peau d'âne, 1971 (Deneuve 3, Marais 3, Presle 3, Seyrig 3, Cloquet 4, Legrand 4)
Peau de banane, 1963 (Belmondo 3, Cuny 3, Moreau 3, Rabier 4, Wakhévitch 4)
Peau de l'ours, 1957 (Cassel 3)
Peau de Torpédo, 1969 (Delannoy 2, Audran 3, Kinski 3)
Peau d'espion, 1967 (Blier 3, Jourdan 3, O'Brien 3)
Peau douce, 1964 (Truffaut 2, Léaud 3, Coutard 4, Delerue 4)
Peaux de vaches, 1988 (Coutard 4)
Pecado, 1951 (Figueroa 4)
Pecado de una madre, 1960 (Del Rio 3)
Pečat, 1955 (Makavejev 2)
Peccato, 1963 (Volonté 3)
Peccato che sia una canaglia, 1954 (De Sica 3, Loren 3, Mastroianni 3, Cecchi D'Amico 4, Flaiano 4)
Peccato degli anni verdi, o L'assegno, 1961 (Valli 3)
Peccato di castita, 1956 (Alexeieff and Parker 4, Amidei 4, Ponti 4)

Peccato di Rogelia Sanchez, 1938 (Fusco 4)
Peccato mortale, 1972 (Lollobrigida 3)
Peccato veniale, 1973 (Delli Colli 4)
Peccatrice, 1940 (De Sica 2, Cervi 3)
Pêche à la baleine, 1934 (Kosma 4)
Pêche au hareng, 1930 (Storck 2)
Pêche aux poissons rouges, 1895 (Lumière 2)
Péchés de jeunesse, 1941 (Tourneur 2, Baur 3, Spaak 4)
Pêcheur dans le torrent, 1897 (Guy 2)
Pêcheur d'Islande, 1924 (Vanel 3)
Pêcheur d'Islande, 1958 (Vanel 3, Coutard 4, De Beauregard 4)
Pêcheurs du Niger, 1962 (Rouch 2)
Pechkolavochki, 1973 (Shukshin 3)
Pechmarie, 1950 (Staudte 2)
Peck 'o' Trouble, 1953 (Blanc 4, McKimson 4, Stalling 4)
Peck Up Your Troubles, 1945 (Blanc 4, Freleng 4, Stalling 4)
Peck's Bad Boy, 1920 (Wood 2)
Peck's Bad Boy, 1934 (Cooper 3)
Peck's Bad Boy with the Circus, 1939 (Beavers 3, Young 4)
Peck's Bad Girl, 1918 (Normand 3)
Pecora nera, 1969 (Gassman 3)
Pecos Pest, 1953 (Hanna and Barbera 4)
Peculiar Patients' Pranks, 1914 (Lloyd 3, Roach 4)
Pedagogical Institution (College to You), 1942 (Fleischer 4)
Pedales sobra Cuba, 1965 (Alvarez 2)
Peddlar and the Lady. *See* Campo dei Fiori, 1943
Peddler, 1913 (Sennett 2, Arbuckle 3)
Pedestrian. *See* Fussgänger, 1974
Pédiluve, 1901 (Gaumont 4)
Pedreira de São Diogo, 1962 (Pereira Dos Santos 2)
Pedro Páramo, 1966 (Figueroa 4)
Pedro Peramo, 1977 (Morricone 4)
Pedro's Dilemma, 1912 (Sennett 2, Normand 3)
Peeks at Hollywood, 1945 (Flynn 3)
Peep Show, 1958 (Russell 2)
Peeper, 1975 (Caine 3, Wood 3, Needham 4, Winkler 4)
Peeping Penguins, 1937 (Fleischer 4)
Peeping Pete, 1913 (Sennett 2, Arbuckle 3)
Peeping Tom, 1960 (Powell and Pressburger 2, Heller 4)
Peer Gynt, 1915 (Zukor 4)
Peer Gynt, 1919 (Veidt 3)
Peer Gynt, 1934 (Albers 3, Tschechowa 3, Hoffmann 4, Warm 4)
Peer Gynt, 1945 (Heston 3)
Peer Gynt, 1965 (Bushman 3, Heston 3)
Peg Leg Pete, 1932 (Terry 4)
Peg Leg Pete the Pirate, 1935 (Terry 4)
Peg o' My Heart, 1922 (Vidor 2, Barnes 4)
Peg o' My Heart, 1933 (Davies 3, Adrian 4, Barnes 4, Booth 4, Brown 4, Freed 4, Marion 4, Stothart 4)
Peg o' the Ring, 1916 (Ford 2)
Peg of Old Drury, 1935 (Wilcox 2, Hawkins 3, Neagle 3, Young 4)
Peg Woffington, 1912 (Pearson 2)
Pegeen, 1919 (Love 3)
Peggy, 1916 (Ince 4, Sullivan 4)
Peggy, 1950 (Coburn 3, Hudson 3, Metty 4)
Peggy on a Spree. *See* Peggy på vift, 1946
Peggy på vift, 1946 (Björnstrand 3)
Peggy, Peg and Polly, 1949 (Fleischer 4)

Peggy Sue Got Married, 1986 (Coppola 2, Carradine 3, O'Sullivan 3, Turner 3, Barry 4, Tavoularis 4, Van Runkle 4)
Peggy, The Will o' th' Wisp, 1917 (Browning 2)
Peggy's Blue Skylight, 1964 (Wieland 2)
Pègre de Paris, 1906 (Guy 2)
Pehavy Max a Strasilda, 1988 (Constantine 3)
Peine du talion, 1916 (Feuillade 2, Musidora 3)
Peintre et ivrogne, 1905 (Guy 2)
Peintre neo-impressioniste, 1910 (Cohl 4)
Peintres françaises d'aujourd'hui—Edouard Pignon, 1963 (Milhaud 4)
Peking Express, 1951 (Cotten 3, Furthman 4, Head 4, Lang 4, Tiomkin 4, Wallis 4)
Peking Express, 1957 (Dieterle 2)
Peking Remembered, 1966 (Henreid 3)
Pèlerin de la beauce, 1950 (Fresnay 3)
Peleskei notárius, 1917 (Korda 4)
Pelican's Bill, 1926 (Lantz 4)
Pelileo Earthquake, 1938 (Leacock 2)
Pelle, 1981 (Cardinale 3, Lancaster 3, Mastroianni 3, Schifrin 4)
Pelle Erovraren, 1987 (Von Sydow 3)
Pelle the Conqueror. See Pelle Erovraren, 1987
Pellegrini d'amore, 1953 (Loren 3)
Pelliccia di visone, 1956 (Vitti 3, Age and Scarpelli 4, Amidei 4)
Pena de muerte, 1973 (Rey 3)
Penal Colony. See Colonia penal, 1971
Penalty, 1920 (Chaney 3)
Penalty, 1941 (Barrymore 3, Rosson 4, Schary 4)
Penderecki, Lutoslawa, 1977 (Zanussi 2)
Pendler, 1986 (Ganz 3)
Pendu, 1906 (Linder 3, Pathé 4)
Pendulum, 1969 (Seberg 3)
Penelope, 1966 (Falk 3, Wood 3, Ames 4, Head 4, Pasternak 4, Stradling 4, Williams 4)
Penelope, folle de son corps, 1974 (Fradetal 4)
Pengar—en tragikomisk saga, 1946 (Dahlbeck 3)
Penguin. See Pingwin, 1965
Penguin Parade, 1938 (Avery 4)
Penguin Pool Murder, 1932 (MacGowan 4, Steiner 4)
Péniche tragique, 1924 (Pick 2)
Penitent, 1912 (Bushman 3)
Penitent, 1988 (North 4)
Penitentiary, 1938 (Ballard 4, Miller 4)
Penn and Teller Get Killed, 1989 (Penn 2)
Penn of Pennsylvania, 1942 (Kerr 3, Alwyn 4)
Penne nere, 1952 (Mastroianni 3)
Pennies from Heaven, 1936 (McLeod 2, Crosby 3, Swerling 4)
Pennies from Heaven, 1981 (Martin 3, Adam 4, Hamlisch 4, Willis 4)
Pennington's Choice, 1915 (Bushman 3, Loos 4)
Penny and the Pownall Case, 1938 (Rank 4)
Penny and the Pownall Case, 1948 (Dors 3, Lee 3)
Penny Gold, 1973 (Cardiff 4)
Penny Journey, 1938 (Jennings 2)
Penny of Top Hill Trail, 1920 (Love 3)
Penny Paradise, 1938 (Dearden 2, Reed 2, Dean 4)
Penny Points to Paradise, 1951 (Sellers 3)

Penny Princess, 1952 (Bogarde 3, Rank 4, Unsworth 4)
Penny Serenade, 1941 (Stevens 2, Bondi 3, Dunne 3, Grant 3, Ryskind 4, Walker 4)
Penny-in-the-Slot, 1921 (Roach 4)
Peñon de las ánimas, 1942 (Félix 3)
Penrod, 1922 (Neilan 2)
Penrod and Sam, 1931 (Young 4)
Pensez à ceux qui sont en-dessous!, 1949 (Decaë 4)
Pension Groonen, 1924 (Wiene 2)
Pension Mimosas, 1935 (Feyder 2, Arletty 3, Rosay 3, Meerson 4, Spaak 4)
Pension sonnenschein, 1990 (Lomnicki 3)
Pensioners, 1911 (Dwan 2)
Pensionnaire, 1953 (Spaak 4)
Pentecost Outing. See Pfingstausflug, 1978
Penthouse, 1933 (Van Dyke 2, Loy 3, Adrian 4, Goodrich 4, Rosson 4, Stromberg 4)
Penthouse Mouse, 1963 (Jones 4)
Pentito, 1985 (Von Sydow 3, Morricone 4)
Peony Lantern. See Botab dourou, 1968
People Against O'Hara, 1951 (Sturges 2, Bronson 3, Tracy 3, Alton 4, Basevi 4, Rose 4)
People Are Bunny, 1959 (Blanc 4, McKimson 4)
People Behind the Camera. See Lidé ze kamerou, 1961
People in the Sun, 1935 (Weiss 2)
People in the Town. See Machi no hitobito, 1926
People Like Maria, 1958 (Watt 2)
People Meet. See Mennesker modes och sod musik opstår i hjertet, 1967
People Next Door, 1970 (Wallach 3, Willis 4)
People of France. See Vie est à nous, 1936
People of Småland. See Smålänningar, 1935
People of the Cumberland, 1937 (Kazan 2, Maddow 4, North 4)
People of the Simlången Valley. See Folket i Simlångsdalen, 1947
People on Sunday. See Menschen am Sonntag, 1929
People on Wheels. See Lidé z maringotek, 1966
People Soup, 1969 (Arkin 3)
People vs. Dr. Kildare, 1941 (Ayres 3, Barrymore 3)
People vs. John Doe, 1916 (Weber 2)
People vs. Nancy Preston, 1925 (Polito 4, Stromberg 4)
People Will Talk, 1935 (Head 4)
People Will Talk, 1951 (Mankiewicz 2, Grant 3, Krasner 4, LeMaire 4, Newman 4, Wheeler 4, Zanuck 4)
People's Enemy, 1935 (Coburn 3, Douglas 3, Ruttenberg 4)
People's Land, 1943 (Unsworth 4)
Peoples of Indonesia, 1943 (Van Dongen 4)
Pepe, 1960 (Cantinflas 3, Chevalier 3, Coburn 3, Crosby 3, Curtis 3, Durante 3, Garland 3, Garson 3, Leigh 3, Lemmon 3, Martin 3, Novak 3, Reed 3, Reynolds 3, Robinson 3, Sinatra 3, Green 4, Head 4, Levien 4)
Pepe El Toro, 1952 (Infante 3)
Pépé le Moko, 1937 (Duvivier 2, Dalio 3, Gabin 3, Modot 3, Hakim 4, Jeanson 4)
Pepina Rejholcová, 1932 (Stallich 4)
Pepita Jiménez, 1945 (Fernández 2)

Pepper, 1936 (Trotti 4)
Peppermint frappé, 1967 (Saura 2, Chaplin 3)
Peppino e Violetta, 1951 (Rota 4)
Peppy Polly, 1919 (Barthelmess 3)
Pequeno proscrito, 1955 (Armendáriz 3)
Pequeno salvaje, 1959 (Armendáriz 3)
Pequino proscrito. See Littlest Outlaw, 1954
Per amore, 1976 (Morricone 4)
Per amore . . . per magia, 1966 (Brazzi 3)
Per il blasone, 1914 (Bertini 3)
Per la sua gioia, 1913 (Bertini 3)
Per le antiche scale, 1976 (Mastroianni 3, Morricone 4, Pinelli 4)
Per qualche dollari in più, 1966 (Eastwood 3, Kinski 3, Van Cleef 3, Volonté 3, Morricone 4)
Per una bara piena di dollari. See Conde Dracula, 1970
Per un dollaro di gloria. See Escuadró de la muerte, 1966
Per un dollaro di gloria. See Escuadró de la muerte, 1966
Per un pugno di dollari, 1964 (Eastwood 3, Volonté 3, Morricone 4)
Pérák a SS, 1946 (Brdečka 4, Trnka 4)
Perceval, 1964 (Rohmer 2)
Perceval le Gaullois, 1978 (Rohmer 2, Almendros 4)
Perché pagare per essere felici!, 1970 (Ferreri 2)
Percy, 1925 (Ince 4)
Percy, 1971 (Elliott 3, Box 4)
Percy's Progress, 1974 (Elliott 3, Price 3, Box 4)
Perdido per cem, 1972 (Branco 4)
Père, 1971 (Fresnay 3)
Père de mademoiselle, 1953 (L'Herbier 2, Arletty 3)
Père et l'enfant, 1959 (Montand 3)
Père Goriot, 1944 (Spaak 4)
Père Lampion, 1934 (Christian-Jaque 2, Kaufman 4)
Père Lebonnard, 1939 (Brasseur 3, Ibert 4)
Père Noel a les yeux bleus, 1964 (Almendros 4)
Père Noel et fils, 1983 (Girardot 3)
Père prématuré, 1933 (Delannoy 2)
Père serge, 1941 (Volkov 2)
Père Serge, 1945 (Annenkov 4, Ibert 4)
Père tranquille, 1946 (Renoir 4)
Perfect, 1985 (Curtis 3, Travolta 3, Willis 4)
Perfect Alibi. See Birds of Prey, 1930
Perfect Clown, 1924 (Laurel and Hardy 3)
Perfect Couple, 1979 (Altman 2)
Perfect Crime, 1921 (Dwan 2, Lombard 3, Buckland 4)
Perfect Crime, 1928 (Glennon 4, Howe 4)
Perfect Day, 1929 (Laurel and Hardy 3, Roach 4)
Perfect Flapper, 1924 (Moore 3)
Perfect Friday, 1970 (Baker 3)
Perfect Furlough, 1958 (Edwards 2, Curtis 3, Dalio 3, Leigh 3)
Perfect Gentleman, 1927 (Bruckman 4)
Perfect Gentleman, 1935 (Clarke 4, Kaper 4)
Perfect Gentlemen, 1978 (Bacall 3, Gordon 3)
Perfect Kiss, 1985 (Alekan 4)
Perfect Lady, 1915 (Purviance 3)
Perfect Lady, 1924 (Roach 4)
Perfect Love, 1919 (Goulding 2)
Perfect Marriage, 1946 (Niven 3, Young 3, Head 4, Metty 4, Wallis 4)
Perfect Mother, 1970 (Brocka 2)
Perfect Murder, 1988 (Lassally 4)

Perfect Snob, 1941 (Quinn 3, Wilde 3, Clarke 4)

Perfect Specimen, 1937 (Curtiz 2, Blondell 3, Flynn 3, Horton 3, Brown 4, Haskin 4, Raine 4, Rosher 4, Wallis 4)

Perfect Strangers, 1945 (Donat 3, Kerr 3, Dalrymple 4, Korda, A. 4, Korda, V. 4, Périnal 4)

Perfect Strangers, 1950 (Ritter 3, Rogers 3, Hecht 4, Wald 4)

Perfect Thirty-Six, 1918 (Normand 3)

Perfect Understanding, 1933 (Dickinson 2, Olivier 3, Swanson 3, Courant 4)

Perfect Weekend. See St. Louis Kid, 1934

Perfect Woman, 1920 (Emerson 4, Loos 4)

Perfect Woman, 1949 (Rank 4)

Perfectionist. See Grand Patron, 1951

Perfekt gentleman, 1927 (Albers 3)

Perfidy of Mary, 1913 (Griffith 2, Barrymore 3, Bitzer 4)

Performance, 1970 (Roeg 2)

Peril. See Péril en demeure, 1984

Péril en demeure, 1984 (Piccoli 3)

Peril in the Night. See Eyewitness, 1956

Perilous Journey, 1953 (Young 4)

Perilous Voyage, 1976 (Grant 3)

Perils from the Planet Mongo. See Flash Gordon, 1936

Perils of Pauline, 1910 (White 3)

Perils of Pauline, 1914 (Miller 4)

Perils of Pauline, 1946 (Dreier 4)

Perils of Pauline, 1947 (Hutton 3, Head 4)

Perils of Pauline, 1967 (Horton 3, Terry-Thomas 3)

Perils of Pearl Pureheart, 1949 (Terry 4)

Perils of Petersboro, 1926 (Sennett 2)

Perils of the Darkest Jungle. See Tiger Woman, 1944

Perils of the Park, 1916 (Sennett 2)

Perils of the Wind, 1925 (Karloff 3)

Perinbaba, 1985 (Masina 3)

Period of Adjustment, 1962 (Hill 2, Fonda 3)

Périscope, 1915 (Gance 2, Gaumont 4)

Perjurer, 1957 (Ulmer 2)

Perla, 1945 (Armendáriz 3, Figueroa 4)

Perla del cinema, 1916 (Bertini 3)

Perle, 1932 (Feuillère 3)

Perlenkette, 1951 (Tschechowa 3)

Perles de la couronne, 1937 (Arletty 3, Barrault 3, Dalio 3, Raimu 3)

Perličky na dně, 1965 (Kučera 4)

Permanent Record, 1988 (Mancini 4)

Permanent Vacation, 1980 (Jarmusch 2)

Permanent Wave, 1929 (Lantz 4)

Permeke, 1985 (Storck 2)

Permette? Rocco Papaleo, 1971 (Mastroianni 3)

Permettete che ami vostre figlia?, 1974 (Fabrizi 3)

Permian Strata, 1969 (Conner 2)

Permission to Kill, 1975 (Bogarde 3, Gardner 3, Young 4)

Perníková chaloupka, 1927 (Stallich 4)

Perníková chaloupka, 1951 (Trnka 4)

Perón: actualización politica y doctrinaria para la toma del poder, 1971 (Solanas and Getino 2)

Perón: La revolución justicialista, 1971 (Solanas and Getino 2)

Perpetual Motion, 1920 (Fleischer 4)

Perpetual Motion, 1975 (Dinov 4)

Perpetuum & Mobile, Ltd., 1961 (Mimica 4)

Perplexed Bridegroom, 1913 (Costello 3)

Perri, 1957 (Iwerks 4)

Perroquet vert, 1928 (D'Eaubonne 4)

Perros de Dios, 1973 (Figueroa 4)

Perry Mason: The Case of the Lost Love, 1987 (Simmons 3)

Persecution, 1974 (Howard 3, Turner 3)

Persiane chiuse, 1951 (Fellini 2, Masina 3, Solinas 4)

Persistent Lover, 1912 (Bunny 3)

Person, 1904 (Bitzer 4)

Person to Bunny, 1960 (Blanc 4, Freleng 4)

Persona, 1966 (Bergman 2, Andersson 3, Björnstrand 3, Ullmann 3, Nykvist 4)

Personal Affair, 1932 (Vasiliev 2)

Personal Affair, 1953 (Tierney 3, Alwyn 4, Rank 4)

Personal Best, 1982 (Towne 4)

Personal Choice, 1989 (Sheen 3)

Personal Column. See Pièges, 1939

Personal Column. See Lured, 1947

Personal Introductions, 1914 (Bunny 3)

Personal Maid, 1931 (Freund 4)

Personal Maid's Secret, 1935 (Haskin 4)

Personal Matter. See Personal Affair, 1932

Personal Property, 1937 (Van Dyke 2, Harlow 3, Taylor 3, Daniels 4, Vajda 4, Waxman 4)

Personal Secretary, 1938 (Cortez 4)

Personality Kid, 1934 (Orry-Kelly 4)

Persons in Hiding, 1939 (Dreier 4, Head 4)

Persons Unknown. See Soliti ignoti, 1958

Perspective, 1949 (Cloquet 4)

Peru—Istituto de Verano, 1956 (Olmi 2)

Pervaya lyubov, 1933 (Cherkassov 3)

Perversion. See Cosi dolce . . . cosi perversa, 1970

Pervye eshelon, 1956 (Shostakovich 4)

Pesca a Mazzara del Vallo, 1949 (Di Venanzo 4)

Pescatorella, 1947 (Risi 2)

Pesn o geroyazh, 1932 (Eisler 4)

Pest, 1917 (Laurel and Hardy 3)

Pest, 1919 (Normand 3)

Pest, 1922 (Laurel and Hardy 3)

Pest from the West, 1939 (Keaton 2, Bruckman 4)

Pest in the House, 1947 (Blanc 4, Jones 4, Stalling 4)

Pest Man Wins, 1951 (Three Stooges 3)

Pest of Friends, 1927 (Sennett 2)

Pest Pilot, 1941 (Fleischer 4)

Pest That Came to Dinner, 1948 (Blanc 4, Stalling 4)

Pest von Florenz, 1919 (Hoffmann 4, Pommer 4, Röhrig 4, Warm 4)

Pestalozzidorf, 1953 (Dahlbeck 3)

Pestalozzos Berg, 1988 (Volonté 3)

Pests for Guests, 1955 (Blanc 4, Freleng 4)

Pet, 1921 (McCay 4)

Pet Peeve, 1954 (Hanna and Barbera 4)

Pet Problems, 1954 (Terry 4)

Pet Pyar nur Paap, 1984 (Patil 3)

Pět z milionù, 1959 (Brodský 3)

Petal on the Current, 1919 (Browning 2, Young 4)

Pete Hothead, 1952 (Bosustow 4, Burness 4)

Pete Kelly's Blues, 1955 (Leigh 3, Mansfield 3, Marvin 3, O'Brien 3, Cahn 4, Rosson 4)

Pete 'n' Tillie, 1972 (Ritt 2, Matthau 3, Page 3, Alonzo 4, Epstein 4, Head 4, Williams 4)

Pete Roleum and His Cousins, 1939 (Losey 2, Eisler 4, Van Dongen 4)

Peter der Grosse, 1922 (Jannings 3, Kortner 3, Courant 4, Dreier 4)

Peter Ibbetson, 1935 (Hathaway 2, Cooper 3, Lupino 3, Dreier 4, Edouart 4, Head 4, Lang 4, Young 4)

Peter Pan, 1924 (Brenon 2, Wong 3, Head 4, Howe 4, Zukor 4)

Peter Pan, 1953 (Cahn 4, Disney 4)

Peter Pan, 1976 (Farrow 3, Kidd 4)

Peter Pan Handled, 1925 (Lantz 4)

Peter, Paul, und Nanette, 1934 (Warm 4)

Peter Schlemihl, 1915 (Wegener 3)

Peter Schlemihl, 1919 (Galeen 4)

Peter the Great. See Peter der Grosse, 1922

Peter the Great. See Piotr Pervyi, 1937

Peter the Great, 1986 (Howard 3, Olivier 3, Redgrave 3, Sharif 3, Anhalt 4)

Peter the Pirate. See Pietro der Korsar, 1925

Peter the Tramp. See Luffar-Petter, 1922

Petering Out, 1927 (Lantz 4)

Petersburg Slums. See Petersburgskiya trushchobi, 1915

Petersburgskiya trushchobi, 1915 (Mozhukin 3)

Peterville Diamond, 1942 (Fisher 2)

Pete's Dragon, 1977 (Rooney 3)

Pete's Haunted House, 1926 (Lantz 4)

Petey and Johnny, 1961 (Leacock 2)

Petit à petit, 1970 (Rouch 2, Braunberger 4)

Petit Babouin, 1932 (Grémillon 2)

Petit Bougnat, 1970 (Adjani 3)

Petit Bournat, 1969 (De Beauregard 4)

Petit Café, 1919 (Linder 3)

Petit Café, 1930 (Chevalier 3, Rosay 3)

Petit Café, 1962 (Braunberger 4)

Petit Chantecler, 1910 (Cohl 4)

Petit Chaperon rouge, 1929 (Cavalcanti 2, Renoir 2, Jaubert 4)

Petit Chasseur, 1961 (Fradetal 4)

Petit Chose, 1938 (Arletty 3)

Petit Claus et le grand Claus, 1964 (Prévert 4)

Petit Criminel, 1990 (Sarde 4)

Petit Discours de la méthode, 1963 (Jutra 2)

Petit frère et petite soeur, 1895 (Lumière 2)

Petit Garcon de l'ascenseur, 1961 (Dalio 3, Delerue 4, Saulnier 4)

Petit Hamlet. See Hamles, 1960

Petit Hotel à louer, 1923 (Modot 3)

Petit Jacques, 1922 (Fresnay 3)

Petit Jacques, 1934 (Burel 4, D'Eaubonne 4)

Petit Jeune Homme, 1909 (Linder 3)

Petit Jour, 1963 (Godard 2, Karina 3, Coutard 4)

Petit Marcel, 1975 (Huppert 3)

Petit Matin, 1971 (Lai 4)

Petit Monde de Don Camillo, 1952 (Cervi 3, Fernandel 3)

Petit Monde des étangs, 1952 (Colpi 4)

Petit Poucet, 1900 (Pathé 4)

Petit Poucet, 1905 (Pathé 4)

Petit Poucet, 1964 (Borowczyk 2)

Petit Poucet, 1973 (Lai 4, Lenica 4)

Petit riens, 1941 (Berry 3)

Petit Roi, 1933 (Duvivier 2, Jaubert 4)

Petit Soldat, 1947 (Grimault 4, Kosma 4, Prévert 4)

Petit Soldat, 1963 (Godard 2, Karina 3, Coutard 4, De Beauregard 4, Guillemot 4)

Petit Soldat qui devient Dieu, 1908 (Cohl 4)

Petit Théâtre de Jean Renoir, 1970 (Moreau 3, Kosma 4)

Petit Trou pas cher, 1934 (Berry 3)

Petita Jimenez, 1976 (Baker 3)
Petite, 1978 (Malle 2)
Petite Andalouse, 1914 (Feuillade 2)
Petite Chocolatière, 1932 (Raimu 3,
   Simon 3, Braunberger 4, Périnal 4)
Petite danseuse, 1913 (Feuillade 2)
Petite de Montparnasse, 1932 (Waxman 4)
Petite Diligence, 1951 (Cloquet 4)
Petite Femme dans le train, 1932
   (Feuillère 3)
Petite Fille en velours bleu, 1978
   (Cardinale 3, Piccoli 3, Delerue 4)
Petite Lilie, 1929 (Milhaud 4)
Petite Lise, 1930 (Grémillon 2, Douy 4,
   Spaak 4)
Petite magicienne, 1900 (Guy 2)
Petite peste, 1938 (Presle 3)
Petite Refugiée, 1915 (Musidora 3)
Petite Republique, 1946 (Carroll 3)
Petite Rosse, 1909 (Linder 3)
Petite Sauvage, 1935 (Lourié 4)
Petite Vertu, 1967 (Brasseur 3, Audiard 4,
   Delerue 4, Rabier 4)
Petites Alliées, 1936 (Burel 4)
Petites Annonces, 1947 (Braunberger 4)
Petites apprentes, 1911 (Feuillade 2)
Petites du Quai aux Fleurs, 1943 (Blier 3,
   Gélin 3, Jourdan 3, Philipe 3, Achard 4,
   Alekan 4, Aurenche 4, Ibert 4)
Petites Filles modèles, 1952 (Rohmer 2)
Petites marionnettes, 1918 (Feuillade 2)
Petits Chats, 1959 (Deneuve 3)
Petits Coupeurs de bois vert, 1904
   (Gaumont 4, Guy 2)
Petits Matins, 1961 (Arletty 3, Blier 3,
   Brasseur 3, Gélin 3)
Petits Riens, 1941 (Fernandel 3, Raimu 3,
   Auric 4)
Petits Vagabonds, 1905 (Pathé 4)
Petra. See World Window, 1977
Petrified Forest, 1936 (Daves 2, Bogart 3,
   Davis 3, Howard 3, Blanke 4, Orry-
   Kelly 4, Polito 4)
Petrified Forest. See Kaseki no mori, 1973
Pétrole de la Gironde, 1949 (Cloquet 4)
Pétrole, pétrole, 1981 (Blier 3)
Pétroleuses, 1971 (Bardot 3, Cardinale 3,
   Presle 3, Lai 4)
Petronella, 1927 (Dieterle 2, Homolka 3)
Pétrus, 1946 (Brasseur 3, Dalio 3,
   Fernandel 3, Simon 3, Achard 4, Douy 4,
   Kosma 4)
Pett and Pott, 1934 (Cavalcanti 2,
   Grierson 2, Jennings 2, Wright 2)
Petticoat Fever, 1936 (Loy 3,
   Montgomery 3, Haller 4)
Petticoat Politics, 1941 (Ladd 3)
Pettigrew's Girl, 1919 (Zukor 4)
Petting Preferred, 1934 (Langdon 3)
Petty Girl, 1950 (Mercer 4)
Petulia, 1968 (Lester 2, Roeg 2, Christie 3,
   Cotten 3, Scott 3, Barry 4, Tavoularis 4)
Peu de soleil dans l'eau froide, 1971
   (Depardieu 3, Carrière 4, Legrand 4)
Peuple est invincible, 1969 (Ivens 2)
Peuple ne peut rien sans ses fusils, 1969
   (Ivens 2)
Peuple peut tout, 1969 (Ivens 2)
Peur. See Vertige d'un soir, 1936
Peur de l'eau. See Max a peur de l'eau,
   1913
Peur des coups, 1932 (Autant-Lara 2)
Peur sur la ville, 1975 (Belmondo 3,
   Morricone 4)

Peyton Place, 1957 (Kennedy 3, Turner 3,
   Hayes 4, Smith 4, Wald 4, Waxman 4,
   Wheeler 4)
Peyton Place—The Next Generation, 1985
   (Malone 3)
Pfarrer von Kirchfeld, 1926 (Dieterle 2)
Pfarrers Töchterlein, 1912 (Porten 3,
   Messter 4)
Pfarrhauskomödie, 1972 (Schell 3)
Pfeifen. See Dýmky, 1966
Pfingstausflug, 1978 (Bergner 3)
Pflicht zu schweigen, 1927 (Fröhlich 3,
   Planer 4)
Phaedra, 1962 (Dassin 2, Mercouri 3,
   Perkins 3, Douy 4, Theodorakis 4)
Phagun, 1973 (Burman 4)
Phantasmes, 1918 (L'Herbier 2)
Phantasmes, 1919 (Gaumont 4)
Phantasy, 1947 (McLaren 4)
Phantom, 1916 (Gilbert 3)
Phantom, 1922 (Murnau 2, Dagover 3,
   Pommer 4, Von Harbou 4, Warm 4)
Phantom, 1943 (Eason 4)
Phantom Baron. See Baron fantôme, 1943
Phantom Buster, 1927 (Karloff 3)
Phantom Carriage. See Körkalen, 1921
Phantom Carriage. See Charette fantôme,
   1939
Phantom Chariot. See Körkalen, 1921
Phantom City, 1928 (Brown 4, McCord 4)
Phantom Creeps, 1939 (Cobb 3, Lugosi 3)
Phantom Empire, 1935 (Autry 3, Canutt 4,
   Eason 4)
Phantom Express, 1932 (Bosworth 3)
Phantom Fiend. See Lodger, 1932
Phantom from Space, 1953 (Clothier 4)
Phantom in the House, 1929 (Walthall 3)
Phantom India. See Inde fantôme, 1969
Phantom Killer, 1942 (Brown 4)
Phantom Lady, 1944 (Siodmak 2,
   Harrison 4, Salter 4)
Phantom Light, 1935 (Powell and
   Pressburger 2, Vetchinsky 4)
Phantom Lovers. See Fantasmi a Roma,
   1961
Phantom of Crestwood, 1932 (Cooper 4,
   Plunkett 4, Steiner 4)
Phantom of Death, 1988 (Pleasence 3,
   Donaggio 4)
Phantom of Hollywood, 1974 (Crawford 3)
Phantom of Liberty. See Fantôme de la
   liberté, 1974
Phantom of Paris, 1931 (Gilbert 3, Meredyth 4)
Phantom of the Golden Gate. See Golden
   Gate Murders, 1979
Phantom of the North, 1929 (Karloff 3)
**Phantom of the Opera, 1925 (Chaney 3,
   Carré 4, Laemmle 4, Miller 4)**
Phantom of the Opera, 1943 (Eddy 3,
   Rains 3, Hoffenstein 4, Mohr 4)
Phantom of the Opera, 1962 (Fisher 2,
   Lom 3, Carreras 4)
Phantom of the Opera, 1983 (Schell 3)
Phantom of the Opera, 1990 (Lancaster 3,
   Golan and Globus 4)
Phantom of the Paradise, 1974 (De Palma 2)
Phantom of the Range, 1928 (Berman 4,
   Plunkett 4)
Phantom of the Rue Morgue, 1954
   (Malden 3, Blanke 4)
Phantom Outlaw, 1927 (Wyler 2)
Phantom Planet, 1962 (Bushman 3)
Phantom President, 1932 (Colbert 3,
   Durante 3, Banton 4, Laszlo 4)

Phantom Raiders, 1940 (Tourneur 2,
   Pidgeon 3)
Phantom Riders, 1918 (Ford 2, Carey 3)
Phantom Ship, 1935 (Lugosi 3)
Phantom Stockman, 1953 (Rafferty 3)
Phantom Strikes. See Gaunt Stranger, 1938
Phantom Thief, 1910 (White 3)
Phantom Toll Booth, 1971 (Jones 4)
Pharaoh. See Faraon, 1965
Phare, 1967 (Braunberger 4)
Pharmacist, 1933 (Sennett 2, Fields 3)
Phase IV, 1973 (Bass 4)
Phèdre, 1968 (Barsacq 4)
Phenomena, 1984 (Pleasence 3, Argento 4)
Phénomènes électriques, 1937 (Grimault 4)
Phenomenon No. 1, 1964 (Vanderbeek 2)
Phffft!, 1954 (Holliday 3, Lemmon 3,
   Novak 3, Axelrod 4, Cohn 4, Lang 4,
   Wald 4)
Philadelphia Experiment, 1984 (Carpenter 2)
**Philadelphia Story, 1940 (Cukor 2,
   Mankiewicz 2, Grant 3, Hepburn 3,
   Stewart 3, Adrian 4, Gibbons 4,
   Mayer 4, Ruttenberg 4, Salt 4,
   Shearer 4, Stewart 4, Waxman 4)**
Philemon, 1976 (Lourié 4)
Philibert, 1963 (Freleng 4)
Philippe Soupault et le surréalisme, 1982
   (Tavernier 2)
Philips-Radio, 1931 (Van Dongen 4)
Philosophical Story. See Filosofská historie,
   1937
Philosophy of the Boudoir. See Eugenie—
   The Story of Her Journey into
   Perversion, 1970
Phir Subah Hogi, 1958 (Kapoor 2)
Phobia, 1980 (Huston 2, Carradine 3,
   Sangster 4)
Phoenix, 1910 (Reid 3)
Phoenix. See Fujicho, 1947
Phone Call from a Stranger, 1952
   (Negulesco 2, Davis 3, Winters 3,
   Johnson 4, Krasner 4, Waxman 4)
Phoney News Flashes, 1955 (Terry 4)
Phoney Photos, 1918 (Laurel and Hardy 3)
Phonographe, 1969 (Borowczyk 2)
Phony American. See Toller hecht auf
   krummer tour, 1962
Phony Express, 1932 (Iwerks 4)
Phony Express, 1943 (Three Stooges 3)
Photo souvenir, 1978 (Carrière 4)
Photogénie de l'impondérable, 1948
   (Epstein 2)
Photogénie mécanique, 1924 (Grémillon 2)
Photographe, 1895 (Lumière 2)
Photographer, 1948 (Van Dyke 2,
   Maddow 4)
Photographie electrique à distance, 1908
   (Méliès 2)
Photographies Vivantes, 1954
   (Borowczyk 2)
Photo-souvenir, 1960 (Braunberger 4)
Phroso, 1923 (Vanel 3)
Phynx, 1970 (Berkeley 2, Blondell 3,
   Keeler 3, McQueen 3, O'Sullivan 3,
   Weissmuller 3)
Physical Culture Girls, 1903 (Bitzer 4)
Physical Culture Romance, 1914
   (Browning 2)
Physical Evidence, 1988 (Reynolds 3,
   Alonzo 4, Mancini 4)
Pia De' Tolomei, 1911 (Bertini 3)
Piacevoli notti, 1966 (Gassman 3,
   Lollobrigida 3, Vitti 3)

Piano Encores, 1954 (La Shelle 4)
Piano for Mrs. Cimino, 1982 (Davis 3)
Piano Lesson. *See* Pianolektionen, 1966
Piano Mooner, 1942 (Langdon 3)
Piano Tuner Has Arrived. *See* E'arrivato
l'accordatore, 1951
Pianolektionen, 1966 (Fischer 4)
Pianos mécanicos, 1965 (Delerue 4)
Pianos mécaniques, 1965 (Mason 3,
Mercouri 3)
Pianstvo i yevo pozledstvia, 1913
(Mozhukin 3)
Piątka z ulicy Barskiej, 1954 (Lomnicki 3)
Piatto piange, 1974 (Blier 3)
Piazza Pulita, 1972 (Papas 3)
Pibe cabeza, 1975 (Torre Nilsson 2)
Picador, 1932 (Dulac 2, Périnal 4)
Picador Porky, 1937 (Avery 4, Blanc 4,
Stalling 4)
Picari, 1987 (Monicelli 2, Blier 3,
Gassman 3, Giannini 3, Cecchi
D'Amico 4)
Picaros. *See* Picari, 1987
Picasso, 1955 (Amidei 4)
Picasso, romancero du picador, 1960
(Delerue 4)
Picasso Summer, 1972 (Brynner 3, Finney 3,
Legrand 4, Zsigmond 4)
Piccadilly, 1929 (Dupont 2, Laughton 3,
Wong 3, Junge 4)
Piccadilly Incident, 1946 (Wilcox 2,
Neagle 3)
Piccadilly Jim, 1936 (Montgomery 3,
Benchley 4, Hoffenstein 4, Ruttenberg 4)
Piccadilly null Uhr swölf, 1963 (Kinski 3)
Piccadilly Third Stop, 1960 (Zetterling 2)
Picciola, 1911 (Normand 3)
Piccioni di Piazza San Marco, 1980
(Belmondo 3)
Piccola posta, 1955 (Delli Colli 4)
Piccolo, 1960 (Vukotić 4)
Piccolo diavolo, 1988 (Matthau 3, Müller 4)
Piccolo Fonte, 1918 (Bertini 3)
Piccolo mondo antico, 1941 (Lattuada 2,
Risi 2, Valli 3, Ponti 4)
Piccolo posta, 1955 (Sordi 3)
Pick. *See* Gassenhauer, 1931
Pick a Star, 1937 (Laurel and Hardy 3,
Roach 4)
Pick and Shovel, 1923 (Laurel and Hardy 3,
Roach 4)
Pick Me Up, ur Flickorna Jackson, 1910
(Magnusson 4)
Pickaninny, 1921 (Roach 4)
Picket Guard, 1913 (Dwan 2, Reid 3)
Picking Peaches, 1924 (Capra 2, Sennett 2)
Picking Peaches, 1980 (Langdon 3)
Pickled Pink, 1965 (Freleng 4)
Pick-me-up est un sportsman, 1917 (Cohl 4)
Pick-Necking, 1933 (Terry 4)
Pickpocket, 1913 (Bunny 3)
Pickpocket, 1959 (Bresson 2, Burel 4)
Pick-Up, 1933 (Beavers 3, Raft 3, Sidney 3)
Pickup Alley. *See* Interpol, 1957
Pick-Up Artist, 1987 (Hopper 3, Delerue 4,
Towne 4, Willis 4)
Pickup on 101, 1972 (Sheen 3)
Pickup on South Street, 1953 (Fuller 2,
Ritter 3, Widmark 3, LeMaire 4,
Wheeler 4)
Pickwick Papers, 1913 (Bunny 3)
Picnic, 1955 (Holden 3, Novak 3, Robertson 3,
Russell 3, Cohn 4, Duning 4, Howe 4,
Taradash 4, Wald 4, Wexler 4)

Picnic at Hanging Rock, 1975 (Weir 2,
Roberts 3)
Picnic at Ray's, 1975 (Jarman 2)
Picnic on the Grass. *See* Déjeuner sur
l'herbe, 1959
Picnic with Papa, 1952 (Terry 4)
Picnic with Weisman. *See* Picnick mit
Weismann, 1968
Picnick mit Weismann, 1968 (Švankmajer 4)
Picnics Are Fun and Dino's Serenade, 1959
(Bosustow 4)
Picpus, 1942 (Andrejew 4)
Pictura. *See* Grant Wood, 1950
Pictura, 1953 (Price 3)
Pictura: an Adventure in Art, 1951 (Haller 4)
Picture Mommy Dead, 1966 (Ameche 3)
Picture of Dorian Gray, 1913 (Reid 3)
Picture of Dorian Gray, 1945 (Lansbury 3,
Reed 3, Sanders 3, Berman 4, Gibbons 4,
Irene 4, Lewin 4, Mayer 4, Stothart 4,
Stradling 4)
Picture of Madame Yuki. *See* Yuki Fujin
ezu, 1950
Picture of the Time. *See* Bild der Zeit,
1921
Picture Snatcher, 1933 (Bacon 2, Bellamy 3,
Cagney 3, Orry-Kelly 4, Polito 4)
Pictureland, 1911 (Gaudio 4)
Pictures at an Exhibition. *See* Tableaux
d'une exposition, 1972
Picturesque South Africa, 1936 (Hoch 4)
Picturesque West, 1899 (Bitzer 4)
Pidgin Island, 1917 (Gaudio 4)
Pie Covered Wagon, 1932 (Temple 3)
Pie in the Sky, 1934 (Kazan 2)
Piece of Cake, 1938 (Rank 4)
Piece of Pleasure. *See* Partie de plaisir,
1975
Piece of the Action, 1977 (Jones 3, Poitier 3)
Pieces of Dreams, 1970 (Legrand 4)
Pied Piper, 1924 (Lantz 4)
Pied Piper, 1942 (Preminger 2, Baxter 3,
Dalio 3, McDowall 3, Cronjager 4,
Johnson 4, Newman 4, Zanuck 4)
Pied Piper, 1972 (Dors 3, Hurt 3, Kaye 3,
Pleasence 3, Puttnam 4)
Pied Piper, 1989 (O'Toole 3)
Pied Piper Malone, 1924 (Haller 4)
Pied Piper of Guadalupe, 1961 (Blanc 4,
Freleng 4)
Pied Piper of Hamelin. *See* Rattenfänger von
Hameln, 1918
Pied Piper of Hamelin, 1961 (Johnson 3,
Rains 3, Reiniger 4)
Pied Piper Porky, 1939 (Blanc 4, Clampett 4,
Stalling 4)
Pied qui etreint, 1916 (Feyder 2, Musidora 3)
Piedestal brise, 1941 (Volkov 2)
Piednadze albo zycie, 1961 (Skolimowski 2)
Piedra libre, 1976 (Torre Nilsson 2)
Piedra sobre piedra, 1970 (Alvarez 2)
Pieds Nickelés, 1964 (Broca 2, Presle 3)
Pie-Eyed, 1925 (Laurel and Hardy 3)
Piège, 1958 (Vanel 3, Cloquet 4)
Piège à pucelles, 1972 (Chabrol 2)
Pièges, 1939 (Siodmak 2, Von Stroheim 2,
Chevalier 3, Fradetal 4, Wakhévitch 4)
Piel de verano, 1961 (Torre Nilsson 2)
Pier 13. *See* Me and My Gal, 1932
Pier 13, 1940 (Day 4, Miller 4)
Piernas de seda, 1935 (Hayworth 3)
Piero Gherardi, 1967 (Cardinale 3)
Pierre Boulez, 1965 (Braunberger 4)
Pierre dans la bouche, 1982 (Alekan 4)

Pierre et Jean, 1943 (Cayatte 2, Andrejew 4)
Pierre et Paul, 1968 (Allio 2)
Pierre of the North, 1913 (Bosworth 3)
Pierre of the Plains, 1942 (Rosher 4)
Pierre philosophe, 1912 (Gance 2)
Pierre Vallières, 1972 (Wieland 2)
Pierres oubliées, 1952 (Grimault 4)
Pierrette No. 1, 1924 (Fischinger 2)
Pierrot assassin, 1903 (Guy 2)
Pierrot des bois, 1956 (Jutra 2)
Pierrot la tendresse, 1960 (Simon 3)
Pierrot le fou, 1965 (Godard 2, Fuller 2,
Belmondo 3, Karina 3, Léaud 3,
Coutard 4, De Beauregard 4)
Pierrot Pierrette, 1924 (Feuillade 2)
Pierwszy dzień wolności, 1964 (Lomnicki 3,
Tyszkiewicz 3)
Pies and Guys, 1958 (Three Stooges 3)
Pieta per chi cade, 1953 (Pinelli 4)
Pietro, der Korsar, 1925 (Pommer 4,
Wagner 4)
Pietro Micca, 1938 (Amidei 4)
Piety. *See* Kegyelet, 1967
Piga blad pigor, 1924 (Magnusson 4)
Pigalle-Saint-Germain-des-Prés, 1950
(Cassel 3, Moreau 3)
Pigen og skoene, 1959 (Karina 3)
Pigeon, 1969 (Malone 3)
Pigeon That Took Rome, 1962 (Heston 3,
Head 4)
Pigpen. *See* Porcile, 1969
Pig's Curly Tail, 1926 (Lantz 4)
Pigs in a Polka, 1943 (Blanc 4, Freleng 4,
Stalling 4)
Pigs Is Pigs, 1914 (Bunny 3)
Pigs Is Pigs, 1937 (Freleng 4, Stalling 4)
Pigskin Capers, 1930 (Terry 4)
Pigskin Champions, 1937 (Clarke 4)
Pigskin Parade, 1936 (Garland 3, Grable 3,
Ladd 3, Miller 4, Zanuck 4)
Pigsty. *See* Porcile, 1969
Pigulki dla Aurelii, 1958 (Ścibor-Rylski 4)
Piker's Peak, 1957 (Blanc 4, Freleng 4,
Stalling 4)
Pikoo, 1981 (Ray 2)
Pikovaya drama, 1916 (Mozhukin 3)
Pilate and Others. *See* Pilatus und andere—
ein Film für Karfreitag, 1975
Pilatus und andere—ein Film für Karfreitag,
1975 (Wajda 2, Olbrychski 3)
Pile Driver. *See* Fatal Mallet, 1914
Pile ou face, 1980 (Noiret 3, Audiard 4)
Piles of Perils, 1916 (Sennett 2)
Pilgrim, 1923 (Chaplin 2, Purviance 3)
Pilgrim of Love. *See* Pellegrini d'amore,
1953
Pilgrim Porky, 1940 (Blanc 4, Clampett 4,
Stalling 4)
Pilgrimage, 1933 (Ford 2, Nichols 4)
Pilgrimage, 1972 (Delli Colli 4)
Pilgrimage Song of Grace and Grudge. *See*
Onshuh junreiuta, 1936
Pilgrimage to Ise. *See* Oise mairi, 1939
Pilgrimage to Kevlar. *See* Vallfarten till
Kevlar, 1921
Pilgrimage to the Virgin Mary. *See* Procesí k
pannence, 1961
Pilgrims of the Nights, 1921 (Gaudio 4)
Pill, 1962 (Popescu-Gopo 4)
Pill of Death. *See* Peau de Torpédo,
1969
Pill Peddlars, 1953 (Terry 4)
Pill Pounder, 1923 (La Cava 2)
Pillar of Flame, 1915 (Talmadge 3)

Pillars of Society, 1916 (Walsh 2, Walthall 3)

Pillars of the Sky, 1956 (Bond 3, Malone 3, Marvin 3)

Pillola, 1982 (Bozzetto 4)

Pillole di Ercole, 1960 (De Sica 2)

Pillow Talk, 1959 (Dalio 3, Day 3, Hudson 3, Ritter 3, Hunter 4)

Pillow to Post, 1945 (Dandridge 3, Greenstreet 3, Lupino 3)

Pills for Aurelia. See Pigulki dla Aurelii, 1958

Pilobolus and Joan, 1974 (Emshwiller 2)

Pilot, 1980 (Andrews 3, Robertson 3, Lassally 4)

Pilot No. 5, 1943 (Gardner 3, Johnson 3, Kelly 3, Schary 4)

Pilota ritorna, 1942 (Rossellini 2)

Pilote de la morte. See Flight Lieutenant, 1942

Pimpernel Smith, 1941 (Howard 3, Dalrymple 4, De Grunwald 4, Green 4)

Pin Feathers, 1933 (Lantz 4)

Pince à ongles, 1968 (Carrière 4)

Pinch Hitter, 1917 (Ince 4, Sullivan 4)

Pinch Singer, 1935 (Roach 4)

Pinched, 1917 (Daniels 3, Lloyd 3)

Pinched Bliss, 1917 (Roach 4)

Pinched in the Finish, 1917 (Sennett 2)

Pincushion Man. See Balloonland, 1935

Pine à ongles, 1968 (Forman 2)

Pine's Revenge, 1915 (Chaney 3)

Pingwin, 1965 (Cybulski 3, Stawiński 4)

Pinhamy, 1979 (Peries 2)

Pini di Roma, 1941 (Stallich 4)

Pink and Blue Blues, 1952 (Bosustow 4, Burness 4)

Pink Blue Plums. See Pink and Blue Blues, 1952

Pink Blueprint, 1965 (Freleng 4)

Pink Cadillac, 1989 (Eastwood 3)

Pink Davinci, 1975 (McKimson 4)

Pink Elephants, 1937 (Terry 4)

Pink Flamingoes, 1972 (Waters 2)

Pink Floyd: The Wall, 1982 (Parker 2, Hoskins 3)

Pink Gods, 1922 (Daniels 3, Menjou 3, Levien 4)

Pink Jungle, 1968 (Garner 3, Head 4, Metty 4)

Pink Pajamas, 1929 (Sennett 2, Hornbeck 4)

Pink Pajamas, 1964 (Freleng 4)

Pink Panther, 1964 (Edwards 2, Cardinale 3, Niven 3, Sellers 3, Wagner 3, Mancini 4, Mercer 4, Mirisch 4, Pan 4)

Pink Panther Strikes Again, 1976 (Edwards 2, Cardinale 3, Lom 3, Sellers 3, Sharif 3, Mancini 4)

Pink Phink, 1964 (Freleng 4)

Pink Pranks, 1971 (Freleng 4)

Pink Pro, 1976 (McKimson 4)

Pink Slip. See Ružové konbiné, 1932

Pink String and Sealing Wax, 1945 (Hamer 2, Withers 3, Balcon 4)

Pink Tights, 1920 (Eason 4)

Pink-Finger, 1964 (Freleng 4)

Pinky, 1949 (Kazan 2, Barrymore 3, Dunne 4, LeMaire 4, Newman 4, Nichols 4, Wheeler 4, Zanuck 4)

Pinnacle Rider, 1926 (Wyler 2)

Pinning It On, 1921 (Roach 4)

Pinocchio, 1940 (Blanc 4, Disney 4, Hubley 4)

Pinocchio, 1972 (De Sica 2, Cecchi D'Amico 4)

Pinocchio and the Emperor of the Night, 1987 (Jones 3)

Pinocchiova dobrodružstvi, 1971 (Stallich 4)

Pins Are Lucky, 1914 (Laurel and Hardy 3)

Pinthurst, 1905 (Bitzer 4)

Pinto, 1920 (Normand 3)

Pinto Ben, 1915 (Hart 3, August 4, Sullivan 4)

Pin-Up Girl, 1944 (Brown 3, Dalio 3, Grable 3, Basevi 4, Pan 4)

Pioneer Builders. See Conqueror, 1932

Pioneers in Ingolstadt. See Pionere in Ingolstadt, 1970

Pioneers of the West, 1939 (Canutt 4)

Pionere in Ingolstadt, 1970 (Schygulla 3)

Piotr Pervyi, 1937 (Cherkasov 3)

Piovra, 1918 (Bertini 3)

Piovuto dal cielo, 1953 (Zavattini 4)

Pipe Dream, 1905 (Bitzer 4)

Pipe Dreams, 1916 (Laurel and Hardy 3)

Pipe the Whiskers, 1918 (Daniels 3, Lloyd 3, Roach 4)

Piper of Strakonice. See Strakonický dudák, 1955

Piper's Price, 1916 (Chaney 3)

Piper's Tune, 1960 (Box 4)

Pipes of Pan, 1914 (Chaney 3)

Pipes of Pan, 1922 (Hepworth 2)

Pip-eye, Pup-eye, Poop-eye and Peep-eye, 1942 (Fleischer 4)

Piping Hot, 1959 (Halas and Batchelor 4)

Pippa Passes, 1909 (Griffith 2, Sennett 2, Bitzer 4)

Pir v Girmunka, 1941 (Golovnya 4)

Pirañas, 1967 (García Berlanga 2)

Piranha, 1978 (Corman 2, Dante 2, Sayles 2, Bottin 4, Donaggio 4)

Pirata sono io!, 1940 (Fellini 2)

Pirate, 1948 (Minnelli 2, Garland 3, Kelly 3, Alton 4, Edens 4, Freed 4, Gibbons 4, Goodrich 4, Mayer 4, Porter 4, Smith 4, Stradling 4)

Pirate, 1978 (Lee 3, Wallach 3)

Pirate Gold, 1912 (Griffith 2, Sweet 3, Bitzer 4)

Pirate Gold, 1920 (Grot 4)

Pirate Party on Catalina Isle, 1936 (Davies 3, Flynn 3, Grant 3)

Pirate Ship, 1933 (Terry 4)

Pirates, 1913 (Bunny 3)

Pirates. See Kaizoki-sen, 1950

Pirates, 1986 (Polanski 2, Matthau 3, Reynolds, 4, Sarde 4)

Pirate's Daughter, 1912 (Bosworth 3)

Pirates du rail, 1938 (Christian-Jaque 2, Von Stroheim 2, Dalio 3, Vanel 3)

Pirates du Rhône, 1933 (Aurenche 4)

Pirate's Gold, 1908 (Griffith 2, Bitzer 4)

Pirates of Blood River, 1962 (Lee 3, Reed 3, Carreras 4, Sangster 4)

Pirates of Capri. See Pirati de Capri, 1949

Pirates of Monterey, 1947 (Mohr 4)

Pirates of Penzance, 1983 (Lansbury 3, Slocombe 4)

Pirates of the High Seas, 1950 (Crabbe 3, Katzman 4)

Pirates of the Prairie, 1942 (Musuraca 4)

Pirates of the Sky, 1927 (Shamroy 4)

Pirates of Tortuga, 1961 (Katzman 4, Smith 4)

Pirates of Tripoli, 1955 (Henreid 3, Katzman 4)

Pirates on Horseback, 1941 (Harlan 4, Head 4)

Pirates on Lake Mälar. See Mälarpirater, 1923

Pirates on the Malaren. See Mälarpirater, 1959

Pirati della malesia, 1964 (Fusco 4)

Pirati di Capri, 1948 (Ulmer 2, Rota 4)

Pirogov, 1947 (Kozintsev 2, Cherkassov 3, Enei 4, Moskvin 4, Shostakovich 4)

Piros bugyelláris, 1917 (Korda 4)

Piroska és a farkas, 1988 (Nowicki 3)

Piscine, 1969 (Delon 3, Schneider 3, Carrière 4, Legrand 4, Levine 4)

Píseň nemilovaného, 1980 (Brejchová 3)

Píseň o sletu I, II, 1949 (Weiss 2)

Píseň života, 1925 (Heller 4)

Pisito, 1958 (Ferreri 2)

Pissarro, 1975 (Leenhardt 2)

Pissenlets par la racine, 1963 (Audiard 4)

Piste du nord. See Loi du nord, 1940

Piste du sud, 1938 (Barrault 3, Matras 4, Renoir 4)

Pistol. See Pistolen, 1973

Pistol for Ringo. See Pistola per Ringo, 1965

Pistol Harvest, 1951 (Hunt 4)

Pistol Packin' Nitwits, 1945 (Langdon 3)

Pistola per Ringo, 1965 (Morricone 4)

Pistolen, 1973 (Björnstrand 3)

Pistolero of Red River. See Last Challenge, 1967

Pistoleros de Casa Grande, 1965 (Chase 4)

Pistols for Breakfast, 1919 (Daniels 3, Lloyd 3, Roach 4)

Pit, 1914 (Tourneur 2, Carré 4)

Pit. See Ana, 1957

Pit and the Pendulum, 1913 (Guy 2)

Pit and the Pendulum, 1961 (Corman 2, Price 3, Crosby 4)

Pit and the Pendulum, 1991 (Reed 3)

Pit of Loneliness. See Olivia, 1950

Pit Stop, 1969 (Corman 2, Burstyn 3)

Pit, the Pendulum, and Hope. See Kyvadlo, jáma, a naděje, 1983

Pitchin' in the Kitchen, 1943 (Bruckman 4)

Pitfall, 1913 (Ince 4)

Pitfall, 1948 (De Toth 2)

Pitfall. See Otoshiana, 1962

Pitfalls, 1948 (Powell 3)

Pitfalls of a Big City, 1923 (Sennett 2)

Pithache Panje, 1914 (Phalke 2)

Pittori in città, 1955 (Taviani 2)

Pittsburgh, 1942 (Dietrich 3, Scott 3, Three Stooges 3, Wayne 3, Salter 4)

Pittsburgh Documents, 1971 (Brakhage 2)

Più bella serata della mia vita, 1972 (Scola 2, Brasseur 3, Simon 3, Sordi 3, Vanel 3, Amidei 4)

Piu comico spettacolo del mondo, 1953 (Struss 4)

Piu forte ragazzi!, 1972 (Cusack 3)

Pivoine, 1929 (Simon 3)

Pixilated, 1937 (Allyson 3)

Pixote, 1981 (Babenco 2)

Pizza Triangle. See Dramma della gelosia—tutti i particolari in cronaca, 1970

Pizza Tweety Pie, 1958 (Blanc 4, Freleng 4)

Pizzicato Pussycat, 1955 (Blanc 4, Freleng 4)

Place Beyond the Winds, 1916 (Chaney 3)

Place de la Concorde, 1938 (Blier 3)

Place for Gold, 1960 (Wright 2, Bernard 4, Dehn 4)

Place for Lovers. *See* Amanti, 1968

Place in a Crowd, 1989 (Menzel 2)

Place in the Sun, 1951 (Stevens 2, Clift 3, Taylor 3, Winters 3, Dreier 4, Head 4, Hornbeck 4, Waxman 4, Wilson 4)

Place of One's Own, 1945 (Lockwood 3, Mason 3, Rank 4)

Place of Skulls, 1989 (Coburn 3)

Place to Go, 1963 (Dearden 2)

Place to Live, 1941 (Maddow 4)

Placer de matar, 1988 (De Almeida 4)

Places in the Heart, 1984 (Field 3, Almendros 4)

Plácido, 1961 (García Berlanga 2)

Placier est tenance, 1910 (Cohl 4)

Plague Dogs, 1982 (Hurt 3)

Plague of the Zombies, 1966 (Bernard 4, Carreras 4)

Plain and Fancy Girls, 1925 (McCarey 2, Roach 4)

Plain Clothes, 1925 (Capra 2, Sennett 2, Langdon 3)

Plain Girl's Love, 1912 (Bosworth 3)

Plain Jane, 1916 (Ince 4, Sullivan 4)

Plain Man's Guide to Advertising, 1962 (Godfrey 4)

Plain Sailing. *See* True As a Turtle, 1956

Plain Song, 1910 (Griffith 2, Pickford 3, Bitzer 4)

Plainsman, 1936 (De Mille 2, Arthur 3, Cooper 3, Quinn 3, Dreier 4, Macpherson 4, Prinz 4, Young 4)

Plainsman, 1966 (Westmore Family 4, Williams 4)

Plainsman and the Lady, 1947 (Johnson 3)

Plaisir, 1952 (Brasseur 3, Darrieux 3, Gabin 3, Gélin 3, Simon, M. 3, Simon, S. 3, Ustinov 3, Annenkov 4, D'Eaubonne 4, Matras 4)

Plaisir d'amour, 1968 (Braunberger 4)

Plaisir de plaire, 1960 (Delerue 4)

Plaisirs de Paris, 1932 (Wakhévitch 4)

Plaisirs de Paris, 1952 (D'Eaubonne 4)

Plaisirs défendus, 1933 (Cavalcanti 2)

Plameny života, 1920 (Heller 4)

Plan Nine from Outer Space, 1959 (Lugosi 3)

Plane Crazy, 1929 (Disney 4, Iwerks 4)

Plane Daffy, 1944 (Blanc 4, Foster 4, Stalling 4)

Plane Dippy, 1936 (Avery 4)

Plane Goofy, 1940 (Terry 4)

Plane Nuts, 1933 (Three Stooges 3)

Planes, Trains and Automobiles, 1987 (Hughes 2, Martin 3)

Planet degli uomini spenti, 1960 (Rains 3)

Planet of Blood. *See* Queen of Blood, 1966

Planet of the Apes, 1968 (Schaffner 2, Heston 3, McDowall 3, Goldsmith 4, Shamroy 4, Smith 4, Wilson 4)

Planned Crops, 1943 (Lye 4)

Planter's Wife, 1908 (Griffith 2, Lawrence 3, Bitzer 4)

Planter's Wife, 1952 (Colbert 3, Hawkins 3, Rank 4, Unsworth 4)

Planton du colonel, 1897 (Guy 2)

Planton du colonel, 1907 (Gaumont 4)

Plastered in Paris, 1928 (Clarke 4)

Plastic Age, 1925 (Bow 3, Gable 3, Walthall 3, Schulberg 4)

Plastic Dome of Norma Jean, 1970 (Legrand 4)

Plastic Nightmare. *See* Shattered, 1991

Plastic Surgery in Wartime, 1941 (Cardiff 4)

Plastiques, 1963 (Storck 2)

Plateau, 1905 (Guy 2)

Platinum Blonde, 1931 (Capra 2, Harlow 3, Young 3, Cohn 4, Riskin 4, Swerling 4, Walker 4)

Platinum High School, 1960 (Duryea 3, Rooney 3, Metty 4)

Platonische Ehe, 1919 (Leni 2)

Platoon, 1986 (Stone 2, Delerue 4)

Plato's Cave Inn, 1980 (Vanderbeek 2)

Play, 1962 (Vukotić 4)

Play Ball, 1932 (Terry 4)

Play Ball, 1933 (Iwerks 4)

Play Ball, 1937 (Terry 4)

Play Dead, 1986 (De Carlo 3)

Play Dirty, 1968 (De Toth 2, Caine 3, Legrand 4)

Play Girl, 1932 (Young 3, Toland 4)

Play Girl, 1940 (Francis 3, Musuraca 4)

Play It Again, Sam, 1972 (Keaton 3, Roizman 4)

Play It As It Lays, 1972 (Perkins 3, Weld 3)

Play It Safe, 1927 (Estabrook 4)

Play Misty for Me, 1971 (Siegel 2, Eastwood 3)

Play Safe, 1936 (Fleischer 4)

Play Square, 1921 (Howard 2)

Playboy. *See* Kicking the Moon Around, 1938

Playboy, 1966 (Burton 3)

Playboy Adventure, 1936 (Havelock-Allan 4)

Playboy of Paris, 1930 (Chevalier 3, Zukor 4)

Playboy of the Western World, 1962 (Unsworth 4)

Players, 1912 (Lawrence 3)

Players, 1979 (Schell 3, Goldsmith 4, Sylbert 4)

Players, 1983 (Halas and Batchelor 4)

Playful Pest, 1943 (Fleischer 4)

Playful Polar Bears, 1938 (Fleischer 4)

Playful Pup, 1937 (Lantz 4)

Playful Puss, 1953 (Terry 4)

Playful Robot, 1956 (Vukotić 4)

Playgirl, 1954 (Winters 3)

Playgirl after Dark. *See* Too Hot to Handle, 1960

Playgirl and the War Minister. *See* Amorous Prawn, 1962

Playgirls and the Bellboy, 1962 (Coppola 2)

Playgrounds of the Mammals, 1932 (Sennett 2)

Playhouse, 1921 (Keaton 2)

Playing Around, 1930 (LeRoy 2, Grot 4, Polito 4)

Playing at Love. *See* Jeux d'amour, 1960

Playing for Time, 1980 (Redgrave 3)

Playing on the Rainbow. *See* Lek på regnbågen, 1957

Playing the Game, 1918 (Ince 4)

Playing the Ponies, 1937 (Three Stooges 3)

Playing Truant. *See* Skola skolen, 1949

Playing with Death. *See* Jugando con la muerte, 1982

Playing with Fire. *See* Jeu avec le feu, 1974

Playing with Souls, 1925 (Astor 3, Ince 4, Mohr 4, Sullivan 4)

Playing with the Devil. *See* Hrátky s čertem, 1956

Playmates. *See* Lekkamraterna, 1914

Playmates, 1918 (Laurel and Hardy 3)

Playmates, 1941 (Barrymore 3)

Playmates, 1972 (Biroc 4)

Play's the Thing, 1914 (Ince 4)

Plaything, 1929 (Milland 3)

Playthings of Destiny, 1921 (Mayer 4)

Playtime. *See* Recreation, 1960

Playtime, 1967 (Tati 2)

Playtime in Hollywood, 1956 (Lancaster 3)

Plaza Suite, 1970 (Grant 3, Matthau 3, Jarre 4)

Pleasant Journey, 1923 (Roach 4)

Pleasantville, 1976 (Lassally 4)

Please, 1933 (Crosby 3)

Please Believe Me, 1950 (Kerr 3, Walker 3, Irene 4, Lewton 4, Salter 4)

Please Don't Eat the Daisies, 1960 (Walters 2, Day 3, Niven 3, Lennart 4, Pasternak 4)

Please Go 'way and Let Me Sleep, 1931 (Fleischer 4)

Please Keep Me in Your Dreams, 1937 (Fleischer 4)

Please, Mr. Balzac. *See* Effeuillant la Marguerite, 1956

Please Murder Me, 1956 (Lansbury 3)

Please, Not Now!. *See* Bride sur le cou, 1961

Please Turn Over, 1960 (Dillon 4)

Pleased to Meet Cha, 1935 (Fleischer 4)

Pleased to Mitt You, 1940 (Bruckman 4)

Pleasure Buyers, 1925 (Walker 4)

Pleasure Garden, 1926 (Balcon 4)

Pleasure Garden, 1952 (Anderson 2, Lassally 4)

Pleasure Garden. *See* Lustgården, 1961

Pleasure Girls, 1965 (Kinski 3)

Pleasure Island, 1953 (Head 4)

Pleasure Mad, 1923 (Shearer 3, Mayer 4)

Pleasure of His Company, 1961 (Astaire 3, Reynolds 3, Burks 4, Cahn 4, Edouart 4, Fulton 4, Head 4, Newman 4, Pan 4)

Pleasure of Killing. *See* Placer de matar, 1988

Pleasure Palace, 1980 (Ferrer 3, Sharif 3)

Pleasure Party. *See* Partie de plaisir, 1975

Pleasure Seekers, 1964 (Negulesco 2, Tierney 3, Cahn 4, Smith 4)

Plein aux as, 1933 (Fradetal 4)

Plein aux as, 1939 (Modot 3)

Plein cirage, 1961 (Delerue 4)

Plein de super, 1976 (Baye 3)

Plein Fer, 1990 (Reggiani 3)

Plein Midi, 1957 (Leenhardt 2)

Plein Soleil, 1959 (Delon 3, Schneider 3, Decaë 4, Gégauff 4, Hakim 4, Rota 4)

Plein sud, 1980 (Moreau 3)

Pleine bagarre, 1961 (Constantine 3)

Pleins feux sur l'assassin, 1961 (Brasseur 3, Trintignant 3, Fradetal 4, Jarre 4)

Pleins feux sur Stanislas, 1965 (Delerue 4)

Plenty, 1985 (Schepisi 2, Gielgud 3, Streep 3)

Plenty Below Zero, 1943 (Fleischer 4)

Plenty of Money and You, 1937 (Freleng 4, Stalling 4)

Plongée tragique, 1928 (Vanel 3)

Plop Goes the Weasel, 1953 (Blanc 4, McKimson 4, Stalling 4)

Plot, 1914 (Costello 3)

Plot. *See* Attentat, 1972

Plot Against the Governor, 1913 (Cruze 2)

Plot Thickens, 1936 (Musuraca 4)

Plötzliche Reichtum der armen Leute von Kombach, 1970 (Fassbinder 2, Schlöndorff 2, Von Trotta 2)

Plouffe, 1985 (Audran 3)

Plough and the Stars, 1936 (Ford 2, Fitzgerald 3, Stanwyck 3, Nichols 4, Plunkett 4, Polglase 4)

Plow Boy, 1929 (Disney 4, Iwerks 4)

Plow Girl, 1916 (Rosher 4)

Plow That Broke the Plains, 1936 (Thomson 4)

Plow That Broke the Plains, 1989 (Lorentz 2)

Pluck of the Irish. See Great Guy, 1936

Plucked. See Morte, la fatto, l'uovo, 1967

Plum Tree, 1914 (Bushman 3)

Plumber, 1914 (Sennett 2)

Plumber, 1925 (Sennett 2)

Plumber, 1933 (Lantz 4)

Plumber, 1978 (Weir 2)

Plumber and the Lady, 1933 (Sennett 2)

Plumber's Daughter, 1927 (Sennett 2)

Plumber's Helpers, 1953 (Terry 4)

Plumbier amoureux, 1931 (Autant-Lara 2)

Plumbing Is a Pipe, 1938 (Fleischer 4)

Plunder, 1922 (White 3)

Plunder of the Sun, 1953 (Ford 3, Friedhofer 4)

Plunder Road, 1957 (Haller 4)

Plunderers, 1960 (Rosenman 4)

Plus Beaux Jours, 1957 (Decaë 4)

Plus Belles Escroqueries du monde, 1964 (Chabrol 2, Cassel 3, Deneuve 3, Coutard 4, Cristaldi 4, Delli Colli 4, Gégauff 4, Guillemot 4, Rabier 4)

Plus Grande Musée, 1985 (Huppert 3, Moreau 3)

Plus qu'on ne peut donner, 1963 (Braunberger 4)

Plus Vieux Métier du Monde, 1967 (Dalio 3, Karina 3, Moreau 3, Welch 3, Aurenche 4, Douy 4, Evein 4, Flaiano 4, Guillemot 4, Legrand 4)

Plutocrat, 1931 (Rogers 3)

Plymouth Adventure, 1952 (Brown 2, Johnson 3, Tierney 3, Tracy 3, Daniels 4, Gillespie 4, Plunkett 4, Rozsa 4, Schary 4)

Po' di cielo, 1956 (Fabrizi 3)

Po di storia del caffe, 1954 (Fusco 4)

Po: forza 50.000, 1961 (Olmi 2)

Po tu storonu Araksa, 1946 (Shub 2)

Pobeda, 1938 (Golovnya 4)

Pobediteli nochi, 1927 (Moskvin 4)

Pobočník jeho výsosti, 1933 (Heller 4)

Pobre diablo, 1940 (Armendáriz 3)

Pobres van al cielo, 1951 (Figueroa 4)

Pocharde, 1941 (Volkov 2)

Pocharde, 1952 (Brasseur 3)

Pociąg, 1959 (Cybulski 3)

Pocitani ovecek, 1982 (Brodský 3)

Pocket Money, 1972 (Malick 2, Marvin 3, Newman 3, Kovacs 4, North 4)

Pocket Policeman. See Agent de poche, 1909

Pocketful of Miracles, 1961 (Capra 2, Davis 3, Falk 3, Ford 3, Horton 3, Cahn 4, Head 4, Plunkett 4)

Pocketmaar, 1956 (Anand 3)

Pod jednou střechou, 1938 (Stallich 4)

Pod Jezevči, 1978 (Brejchová 3)

Pod kamennym nebom, 1974 (Yankovsky 3)

Poczmistrs, 1967 (Stawiński 4)

Poder local, poder popular, 1970 (Gómez 2)

Poder popular, 1979 (Guzmán 2)

Podkova pro štěstí, 1946 (Zeman 4)

Podor del deseo, 1976 (Bardem 2)

Podrugi, 1935 (Cherkassov 3, Shostakovich 4)

Podstawy w kopalni miedzi, 1972 (Kieślowski 2)

Podvig vo idach, 1928 (Vasiliev 2)

Poem Field No.1, 1967 (Vanderbeek 2)

Poem Field No.2, 1966 (Vanderbeek 2)

Poem Field No.5, 1967 (Vanderbeek 2)

Poem Field No.7, 1967 (Vanderbeek 2)

Poemat symfoniczny "Bajka" Stanisława Moniuszki, 1952 (Munk 2)

Poésie d'aujourd'hui—Un nouvel état d'intelligence, 1948 (Epstein 2)

Poet and Peasant, 1989 (Lantz 4)

Poet and the Czar. See Poet i tsar, 1927

Poet i tsar, 1927 (Cherkassov 3)

Poet Iv Montan, 1957 (Montand 3)

Poet of the Peaks, 1915 (Eason 4)

Poète et sa folle amante, 1916 (Feuillade 2, Musidora 3)

Poetic Justice, 1972 (Frampton 2)

Poet's London, 1959 (Russell 2)

Poet's Pub, 1949 (Rank 4)

Pogoń za Adamem, 1970 (Stawiński 4)

Pogo Special Birthday Special, 1971 (Jones 4)

Pohádka o Honzíkovi a Mařence, 1980 (Zeman 4)

Pohádky tisíce a jedné noci, 1974 (Zeman 4)

Poie pour l'ombre, 1960 (Gélin 3)

Poignard malais, 1930 (Douy 4)

Poil de carotte, 1925 (Duvivier 2, Feyder 2)

Poil de carotte, 1932 (Duvivier 2, Baur 3, Jaubert 4)

Poil de carotte, 1973 (Noiret 3)

Poilus de la Neuvieme, 1910 (Modot 3)

Point Blank, 1967 (Boorman 2, Dickinson 3, Marvin 3, Winkler 4)

Point de fuite, 1983 (Ruiz 2, Branco 4, De Almeida 4)

Point de mire, 1977 (Girardot 3, Decaë 4, Delerue 4)

Point du jour, 1949 (Modot 3, Piccoli 3)

Point Loma, Old Town, 1911 (Dwan 2)

Point of Order, 1963 (De Antonio 2)

Point of Terror, 1971 (Fields 4)

Pointe courte, 1955 (Resnais 2, Varda 2, Noiret 3, Delerue 4)

Pointed Heels, 1929 (Powell 3, Wray 3)

Pointin', 1979 (Cusack 3)

Pointing Finger, 1919 (Browning 2)

Pointing Finger, 1933 (Pearson 2)

Points of Reference, 1959 (Leacock 2)

Poison, 1906 (Linder 3)

Poison, 1911 (Gaumont 4)

Poison, 1951 (Guitry 2)

Poison Candy. See Little Sweetheart, 1988

Poison Gas. See Giftgas, 1929

Poison Ivy. See Môme vert-de-gris, 1953

Poison Pen, 1939 (McDowall 3, Newton 3)

Poisoned Flume, 1911 (Dwan 2)

Poisoned Light. See Otrávené světlo, 1921

Poisoned Paradise: The Forbidden Story of Monte Carlo, 1924 (Bow 3, Schulberg 4, Struss 4, Young 4)

Poisonous Arrow. See Giftpilen, 1915

Poisonous Love. See Fader og Søn, 1911

Poisson, 1951 (Simon 3)

Poisson Chinois. See Bataille silencieuse, 1937

Poisson d'avril, 1954 (Audiard 2)

Pojken i trädet, 1961 (Sucksdorff 2, Fischer 4, Jones 4)

Poker, 1920 (Fleischer 4)

Poker, 1987 (Sarde 4)

Poker Alice, 1987 (Taylor 3)

Poker at Eight, 1935 (Roach 4)

Poker Faces, 1926 (Horton 3)

Poker Windows, 1931 (Sennett 2)

Pokerspiel, 1966 (Kluge 2)

Pokhozdeniya Oktyabrini, 1924 (Kozintsev 2)

Poklad Ptačího ostrova, 1952 (Zeman 4)

Pokoj no. 13, 1915 (Negri 3)

Pokolenie, 1954 (Wajda 2, Cybulski 3, Lomnicki 3)

Pokolenie pobeditelie, 1936 (Maretskaya 3)

Pokus o vraždu, 1973 (Brejchová 3)

Polar Pals, 1939 (Blanc 4, Clampett 4, Stalling 4)

Polar Pests, 1958 (Avery 4)

Polenblut, 1934 (Ondra 3, Heller 4)

Polenta, 1980 (Ganz 3)

Polety vo sne i nayavu, 1982 (Yankovsky 3)

Polibek ze stadionu, 1948 (Frič 2)

Policarpo, ufficiale di scrittura, 1959 (Sordi 3, Age and Scarpelli 4)

Police, 1915 (Purviance 3)

Police, 1985 (Pialat 2, Depardieu 3)

Police Can't Move. See Polizia ha le mani legate, 1974

Police Car Seventeen, 1933 (Bond 3)

Police Court, 1932 (Walthall 3)

Police Fang: Razor Hanzo's Torture in Hell. See Goyoukiba: Kamisori Hanzo jigokuzeme, 1973

Police Film. See Polizeifilm, 1970

Police mondaine, 1937 (Barrault 3, Vanel 3, D'Eaubonne 4)

Police Nr. 1111, 1915 (Kortner 3)

Police Python 357, 1976 (Montand 3, Delerue 4)

Police Story, 1973 (Goldsmith 4)

Police Story. See Gingchat gusi, 1985

Police Story Part II. See Gingchat gusi tsuktsap, 1988

Police Story: The Freeway Killings, 1987 (Dickinson 3)

Policeman Hataoka. See Hataoka junsa, 1940

Policewoman. See Street Corner, 1953

Poliche, 1929 (Tschechowa 3)

Poliche, 1934 (Gance 2, Meerson 4, Stradling 4)

Polijuschka, 1958 (Gallone 2)

Polin, 1900 (Guy 2)

Polio and Communicable Diseases Hospital Trailer, 1949 (Grant 3)

Polis Paulus påskasmäll, 1924 (Molander 2, Madsen and Schenstrøm 3)

Polish Blood. See Polská krev, 1934

Polishing Up, 1914 (Bunny 3)

Polite Invasion, 1960 (Zetterling 2)

Politic Flapper. See Patsy, 1928

Political Party, 1934 (Mills 3)

Political Pull, 1924 (Roach 4)

Political Theatre. See Soushi gekijou, 1946

Politician's Dream, 1911 (Bunny 3)

Politician's Love Story, 1909 (Griffith 2, Sennett 2, Bitzer 4)

Politics, 1931 (Dressler 3)

Politics and the Press, 1914 (Talmadge 3)

Politics Film, 1972 (Falk 3)

Polizeiakte 909, 1933 (Wiene 2)

Polizeibericht meldet, 1933 (Tschechowa 3)

Polizeifilm, 1970 (Wenders 2)

Polizia è al servizio del cittadino, 1973 (Gélin 3)

Polizia ha le mani legate, 1974 (Kennedy 3)

Polizia incrimina, la legge assolve, 1973 (Rey 3)

Polizia ringrazia, 1972 (Cusack 3)
Polizia sta a guardare, 1973 (Cobb 3)
Polka-Dot Puss, 1948 (Hanna and Barbera 4)
Polkovnik v otstavke, 1976 (Yankovsky 3)
Polly Ann, 1917 (Love 3)
Polly Fulton. See B.F.'s Daughter, 1948
Polly of the Circus, 1917 (Marsh 3)
Polly of the Circus, 1932 (Davies 3, Gable 3, Milland 3, Adrian 4, Barnes 4, Wilson 4)
Polly of the Follies, 1922 (Emerson 4, Hunt 4, Loos 4, Schenck 4)
Polly of the Storm Country, 1920 (Rosson 4)
Polly Wants a Doctor, 1943 (Fleischer 4)
Polly with a Past, 1920 (Webb 3, Mathis 4)
Pollyanna, 1920 (Pickford 3, Marion 4, Rosher 4)
Pollyanna, 1960 (Crisp 3, Malden 3, Menjou 3, Moorehead 3, Wyman 3, Disney 4, Ellenshaw 4, Harlan 4, Iwerks 4, Plunkett 4)
Polo Games, Brooklyn, 1900 (Bitzer 4)
Polo Joe, 1936 (Brown 3, Wyman 3, Orry-Kelly 4)
Polo Substitute, 1912 (Bosworth 3)
Polowanie na muchy, 1969 (Wajda 2, Olbrychski 3)
Polská Krev. See Polenblut, 1934
Polska Kronika filmowa nr 52 A-B, 1959 (Munk 2)
Poltergeist, 1982 (Spielberg 2, Edlund 4, Goldsmith 4)
Poltergeist II, 1986 (Edlund 4, Goldsmith 4)
Południk zero, 1970 (Ścibor-Rylski 4)
Polvere di stelle, 1973 (Sordi 3, Vitti 3)
Polvo rojo, 1981 (Villagra 3)
Polyester, 1981 (Waters 2)
Polygamous Polonius, 1958 (Godfrey 4)
Polygamous Polonius Revisited, 1985 (Godfrey 4)
Polyushko-pole, 1956 (Maretskaya 3)
Pomme d'amour, 1932 (Périnal 4)
Pommier, 1902 (Guy 2)
Pomodoro, 1961 (Olmi 2)
Pompeii. See Warrior Queen, 1987
Pömperly's Kampf mit dem Schneeschuh, 1922 (Holger-Madsen 2)
Pompier et la servante, 1897 (Pathé 4)
Pompiers, 1895 (Lumière 2)
Pompon malencontreux 1, 1903 (Guy 2)
Pompon rouge, 1951 (Braunberger 4)
Pomsta, 1968 (Brdečka 4)
Ponedeljak ili utorak, 1966 (Mimica 4)
Ponjola, 1923 (Crisp 3)
Pont de Tancarville, 1959 (Delerue 4)
Pont d' Iéna, 1900 (Lumière 2)
Pontcarral, Colonel d'Empire, 1942 (Delannoy 2, Annenkov 4, Matras 4)
Ponti e porte de Roma, 1949 (Di Venanzo 4)
Pontius Pilate, 1964 (Rathbone 3)
Ponto di Vetro, 1940 (Brazzi 3)
Pontormo and Punks at Santa Croce, 1982 (Jarman 2)
Pony Express, 1909 (Porter 2)
Pony Express, 1925 (Cruze 2, Beery 3, Brown 4)
Pony Express, 1952 (Heston 3, Head 4)
Pony Express Days, 1940 (Eason 4)
Pony Express Rider, 1910 (Anderson 3)
Pony Express Rider, 1916 (Mix 3)
Pony Soldier, 1952 (Power 3, Newman 4, North 4, Wheeler 4)
Ponzio Pilato, 1962 (Marais 3)
Pooch, 1932 (Roach 4)
Pooja, 1940 (Biswas 4)

Pookie. See Sterile Cuckoo, 1969
Pool of London, 1950 (Dearden 2, Addison 4, Balcon 4)
Pool Sharks, 1915 (Fields 3)
Pooly-tix in Washington, 1933 (Temple 3)
Poopdeck Pappy, 1940 (Fleischer 4)
Poopsie, 1974 (Loren 3, Mastroianni 3, Ponti 4)
Poor Boob, 1919 (Crisp 3)
Poor But Beautiful. See Poveri ma belli, 1956
Poor Cinderella, 1934 (Fleischer 4)
Poor Cow, 1967 (Loach 2, McDowell 3, Stamp 3, Menges 4)
Poor Devil, 1973 (Lee 3)
Poor Fish, 1924 (McCarey 2, Roach 4)
Poor Fish, 1931 (Sennett 2)
Poor Girl. See Chudá holka, 1929
Poor Jake's Demise, 1913 (Chaney 3)
Poor Little Chap He Was Only Dreaming, 1917 (Cohl 4)
Poor Little Peppina, 1916 (Olcott 2, Pickford 3)
Poor Little Rich Girl, 1917 (Tourneur 2, Pickford 3, Carré 4, Marion 4)
Poor Little Rich Girl, 1936 (Darwell 3, Faye 3, Temple 3, Seitz 4)
Poor Little Rich Girl, 1965 (Warhol 2)
Poor Men's Wives, 1923 (Schulberg 4, Struss 4)
Poor Millionaire, 1941 (Nykvist 4)
Poor Millionaires. See Poveri milionari, 1958
Poor Nut, 1927 (Arthur 3)
Poor Old Fido, 1903 (Bitzer 4)
Poor Papa, 1928 (Disney 4)
Poor Relation, 1913 (Cruze 2)
Poor Relation, 1921 (Rogers 3)
Poor Relations, 1919 (Vidor 2)
Poor Rich, 1931 (Horton 3)
Poor Rich, 1934 (Bond 3)
Poor Rich Man, 1918 (Bushman 3)
Pop, 1970 (Kuri 4)
Pop Always Pays, 1940 (Polglase 4)
Pop and Mom in Wild Oysters, 1941 (Fleischer 4)
Pop Buell, Hoosier Farmer in Laos, 1965 (Van Dyke 2)
Pop Gear, 1965 (Unsworth 4)
Pop Goes the Easel, 1935 (Three Stooges 3)
Pop Goes the Easel, 1962 (Russell 2)
Pop Goes Your Heart, 1934 (Freleng 4)
Pop 'im Pop, 1950 (Blanc 4, McKimson 4, Stalling 4)
Popas in tabara de vara, 1958 (Mészáros 2)
Popcorn, 1931 (Terry 4)
Popcorn Story, 1949 (Bosustow 4)
Pope Joan, 1972 (De Havilland 3, Howard 3, Schell 3, Ullmann 3, Jarre 4)
Pope John Paul II, 1984 (Finney 3)
Pope Must Die, 1991 (Lom 3)
Pope of Greenwich Village, 1984 (Page 3, Rourke 3)
Popeye series, 1935–41 (Fleischer 4)
Popeye, 1980 (Altman 2, Williams 3, Rotunno 4)
Popi, 1969 (Arkin 3)
Popielusko, 1988 (Delerue 4)
Popiół i diament, 1958 (Wajda 2, Cybulski 3)
Popióły, 1965 (Wajda 2, Nowicki 3, Olbrychski 3, Tyszkiewicz 3, Ścibor-Rylski 4)

Poplach v oblacich, 1978 (Brejchová 3, Brodský 3)
Popo divorzieremo, 1940 (Amidei 4)
Popoli Morituri. See Sterbende Völker, 1922
Poppy, 1917 (Talmadge 3, Banton 4)
Poppy. See Gubijinso, 1935
Poppy, 1936 (Fields 3, Dreier 4, Head 4, Young 4)
Poppy. See Gubijinso, 1941
Poppy Girl's Husband, 1919 (Hart 3, August 4, Sullivan 4)
Poppy Is Also a Flower, 1966 (Brynner 3, Dickinson 3, Hawkins 3, Hayworth 3, Howard 3, Mastroianni 3, Quayle 3, Sharif 3, Wallach 3, Alekan 4, Auric 4)
Poprigunya, 1955 (Bondarchuk 3)
Pop's Pal, 1933 (Langdon 3)
Popsy Pop, 1971 (Baker 3, Cardinale 3)
Popular Melodies, 1933 (Fleischer 4)
Popular Power. See Poder popular, 1979
Popular Sin, 1926 (Banton 4, Garmes 4)
Por ellas aunque mal paguen, 1952 (Infante 3)
Por la puerta falsa, 1950 (De Fuentes 2)
Por mis pistolas, 1968 (Cantinflas 3)
Por primera vez elecciones libres, 1984 (Alvarez 2)
Por querer a una mujer, 1951 (Armendáriz 3)
Porcelaines tendres, 1909 (Cohl 4)
Porcile, 1969 (Ferreri 2, Léaud 3, Delli Colli 4, Donati 4)
Porco mondo, 1978 (Kennedy 3, Valli 3)
Porgy and Bess, 1959 (Preminger 2, Dandridge 3, Poitier 3, Goldwyn 4, Mandell 4, Pan 4, Previn 4, Shamroy 4, Sharaff 4)
Pork Chop Hill, 1959 (Milestone 2, Peck 3, Rosenman 4)
Pork Chop Phooey, 1963 (Hanna and Barbera 4)
Porkala, 1956 (Donner 2)
Porky and Daffy, 1938 (Blanc 4, Clampett 4, Stalling 4)
Porky and Gabby, 1937 (Blanc 4, Iwerks 4, Stalling 4)
Porky and Teabiscuit, 1939 (Blanc 4, Stalling 4)
Porky at the Crocadero, 1938 (Blanc 4, Stalling 4)
Porky Chops, 1949 (Blanc 4, Stalling 4)
Porky in Egypt, 1938 (Blanc 4, Clampett 4, Stalling 4)
Porky in Wackyland, 1938 (Blanc 4, Clampett 4, Stalling 4)
Porky of the Northwoods, 1936 (Stalling 4)
Porky Pig in Hollywood, 1986 (Blanc 4, Freleng 4, Jones 4)
Porky Pig's Feat, 1943 (Blanc 4, Stalling 4)
Porky's Ant, 1941 (Blanc 4, Jones 4, Stalling 4)
Porky's Badtime Story, 1937 (Blanc 4, Stalling 4)
Porky's Baseball Broadcast, 1940 (Blanc 4, Freleng 4, Stalling 4)
Porky's Bear Facts, 1941 (Blanc 4, Stalling 4)
Porky's Bedtime Story, 1937 (Clampett 4)
Porky's Building, 1937 (Blanc 4, Stalling 4)
Porky's Cafe, 1942 (Blanc 4, Jones 4, Stalling 4)
Porky's Double Trouble, 1937 (Blanc 4, Stalling 4)
Porky's Duck Hunt, 1937 (Avery 4, Blanc 4, Stalling 4)

Porky's Five and Ten, 1938 (Blanc 4, Clampett 4, Stalling 4)

Porky's Garden, 1937 (Avery 4, Blanc 4, Stalling 4)

Porky's Hare Hunt, 1938 (Blanc 4, Stalling 4)

Porky's Hero Agency, 1937 (Blanc 4, Clampett 4, Stalling 4)

Porky's Hired Hand, 1940 (Blanc 4, Stalling 4)

Porky's Hotel, 1939 (Blanc 4, Clampett 4, Stalling 4)

Porky's Last Stand, 1940 (Blanc 4, Clampett 4, Foster 4, Stalling 4)

Porky's Midnight Matinee, 1941 (Blanc 4, Jones 4, Stalling 4)

Porky's Movie Mystery, 1939 (Blanc 4, Clampett 4, Stalling 4)

Porky's Moving Day, 1936 (Stalling 4)

Porky's Naughty Nephew, 1938 (Blanc 4, Clampett 4, Foster 4, Stalling 4)

Porky's Party, 1938 (Blanc 4, Clampett 4, Stalling 4)

Porky's Pastry Pirates, 1942 (Blanc 4)

Porky's Phoney Express, 1938 (Blanc 4, Stalling 4)

Porky's Picnic, 1939 (Blanc 4, Clampett 4, Stalling 4)

Porky's Pooch, 1941 (Blanc 4, Clampett 4, Stalling 4)

Porky's Poor Fish, 1940 (Blanc 4, Clampett 4, Stalling 4)

Porky's Poppa, 1938 (Blanc 4, Clampett 4, Stalling 4)

Porky's Poultry Plant, 1936 (Stalling 4)

Porky's Preview, 1941 (Avery 4, Blanc 4, Stalling 4)

Porky's Prize Pony, 1941 (Blanc 4, Jones 4, Stalling 4)

Porky's Railroad, 1937 (Blanc 4, Stalling 4)

Porky's Road Race, 1937 (Blanc 4, Stalling 4)

Porky's Romance, 1937 (Blanc 4, Stalling 4)

Porky's Snooze Reel, 1941 (Blanc 4, Clampett 4, Stalling 4)

Porky's Spring Planting, 1938 (Blanc 4, Stalling 4)

Porky's Super Service, 1937 (Blanc 4, Iwerks 4, Stalling 4)

Porky's Tire Trouble, 1939 (Blanc 4, Clampett 4, Stalling 4)

Porno. See Porco mondo, 1978

Port Afrique, 1956 (Lee 3, Arnold 4, Maté 4)

Port Arthur, 1936 (Darrieux 3, Vanel 3, Walbrook 3, Heller 4)

Port Chicago, 1966 (Baillie 2)

Port de la tentation. See Temptation Harbour, 1946

Port du désir, 1954 (Gabin 3, Alekan 4, Kosma 4)

Porte aperte, 1990 (Volonté 3)

Porte de Lilas, 1957 (Clair 2, Brasseur 3, Barsacq 4)

Port of Bad Names. See Akumyo hatoba, 1963

Port of Call. See Hamnstad, 1948

Port of Escape, 1956 (Withers 3)

Port of Missing Girls, 1928 (Estabrook 4)

Port of Missing Girls, 1938 (Carey 3, Brown 4)

Port of Missing Mice, 1945 (Terry 4)

Port of New York, 1949 (Brynner 3)

Port of Seven Seas, 1938 (Sturges 2, Whale 3, Beery 3, O'Sullivan 3, Vorkapich 4, Waxman 4)

Port of Shadows. See **Quai des brumes, 1938**

Port without a Sea. See Umi no nai minato, 1931

Porta del cielo, 1946 (De Sica 2, Zavattini 4)

Porte d'Orient, 1950 (Dalio 3)

Porte du large, 1936 (Spaak 4)

Portes claquent, 1960 (Deneuve 3)

Portes claquent, 1960 (Legrand 4)

Portes de la maison, 1954 (Storck 2)

Portes de la nuit, 1946 (Brasseur 3, Montand 3, Reggiani 3, Kosma 4, Prévert 4, Trauner 4)

Porteuse de pain, 1906 (Feuillade 2)

Porteuse de pain, 1934 (Fernandel 3, Lourié 4, Stradling 4)

Porteuse de pain, 1963 (Noiret 3, Decaë 4)

Portia on Trial. See Trial of Portia Merriman, 1937

Portnoy's Complaint, 1972 (Black 3, Carradine 3, Clayburgh 3, Grant 3, Boyle 4, Legrand 4)

Portrait de la France, 1957 (Delerue 4)

Portrait de Mireille, 1909 (Gance 2)

Portrait de Raymond Depardon, 1983 (Rouch 2)

Portrait de son père, 1953 (Bardot 3)

Portrait d'Henri Goetz, 1947 (Resnais 2)

Portrait d'un assassin, 1949 (Von Stroheim 2, Arletty 3, Berry 3, Brasseur 3, Dalio 3, Spaak 4)

Portrait from Life, 1948 (Zetterling 2, Lom 3, Box 4, Rank 4)

Portrait in Black, 1960 (Quinn 3, Turner 3, Wong 3, Hunter 4, Metty 4)

Portrait mystérieux, 1899 (Méliès 2)

Portrait of a 60% Perfect Man, 1980 (Matthau 3)

Portrait of a Dead Girl. See Who Killed Miss U.S.A.?, 1970

Portrait of a Girl. See Léányportre, 1971

Portrait of a Goon, 1959 (Russell 2)

Portrait of a Hit Man, 1983 (Palance 3)

Portrait of a Mobster, 1961 (Steiner 4)

Portrait of a Showgirl, 1982 (Curtis 3)

Portrait of a Sinner. See Rough and the Smooth, 1959

Portrait of a Soviet Composer, 1961 (Russell 2)

Portrait of a Stripper, 1979 (Alonzo 4)

Portrait of a Woman, 1946 (Rosay 3)

Portrait of a Woman, Nude. See Nudo di donna, 1981

Portrait of Alison, 1955 (Green 4)

Portrait of an Album, 1985 (Jones 4)

Portrait of an Escort, 1980 (Charisse 3)

Portrait of Chieko. See Chieko-sho, 1967

Portrait of Dorian Gray. See Dorian Grays Portraet, 1910

Portrait of Dorian Gray. See Portret Doriana Greya, 1941

Portrait of Fidel Castro, 1990 (Lollobrigida 3)

Portrait of Geza Anda, 1964 (Leacock 2)

Portrait of Innocence. See Nous le Gosses, 1941

Portrait of Jason, 1967 (Clarke 2)

Portrait of Jennie, 1948 (Barrymore 3, Cotten 3, Gish 3, Jones 3, August 4, Herrmann 4, Selznick 4, Tiomkin 4)

Portrait of Maria. See **Maria Candelaria, 1943**

Portrait of Paul Burkhard, 1964 (Leacock 2)

Portrait of the Artist as a Young Man, 1977 (Gielgud 3)

Portrait of Van Cliburn, 1966 (Leacock 2)

Portrait spirite, 1903 (Méliès 2)

Porträt einer Bewährung, 1964 (Kluge 2)

Portret Doriana Greya, 1941 (Volkov 2)

Ports of Call, 1924 (Fort 4)

Ports of Industrial Scandinavia: Sweden's East Coast, 1949 (Fischer 4)

Ports of the Night. See Portes de la nuit, 1946

Poruchik Kizhe, 1934 (Prokofiev 4)

Poseidon Adventure, 1972 (Borgnine 3, Hackman 3, McDowall 3, Winters 3, Williams 4)

Position Firing, 1944 (Hubley 4)

Position Wanted, 1924 (Roach 4)

Positive Negative Electronic Faces, 1973 (Emshwiller 2)

Poslední bohém, 1931 (Stallich 4)

Poslední muž, 1934 (Frič 2)

Poslední polibek, 1922 (Heller 4)

Poslední trik pana Schwarzwalldea a pana Edgara, 1964 (Švankmajer 4)

Poslední výstřel, 1950 (Weiss 2)

Poslijednji podvig diverzanta Oblaka, 1978 (Mimica 4)

Poślizg, 1972 (Lomnicki 3)

Posse, 1975 (Dern 3, Douglas 3, Jarre 4, Wheeler 4)

Posse Cat, 1952 (Hanna and Barbera 4)

Posse from Hell, 1961 (Murphy 3, Van Cleef 3)

Possédés, 1955 (Cloquet 4)

Possédés, 1987 (Wajda 2, Huppert 3, Sharif 3, Carrière 4)

Possessed, 1931 (Brown 2, Crawford 3, Gable 3, Coffee 4, Mayer 4)

Possessed, 1947 (Crawford 3, Massey 3, Burks 4, Grot 4, Wald 4, Waxman 4)

Possessed, 1977 (Ford 3)

Possessed. See Possédés, 1987

Possession, 1929 (Bertini 3)

Possession, 1981 (Adjani 3)

Possession de l'enfant, 1909 (Feuillade 2, Gaumont 4)

Possession of Joel Delaney, 1972 (MacLaine 3)

Possessors. See Grandes Familles, 1958

Post Haste, 1934 (Grierson 2, Jennings 2, Launder and Gilliat 2)

Post No Bills, 1923 (Roach 4)

Post War Inventions, 1945 (Terry 4)

Postage Due, 1924 (Laurel and Hardy 3, Roach 4)

Postal Inspector, 1936 (Lugosi 3, McDaniel 3)

Postcards from the Edge, 1990 (Nichols 2, Dreyfuss 3, Hackman 3, MacLaine 3, Streep 3, Ballhaus 4)

Postman Always Rings Twice, 1946 (Garnett 2, Garfield 3, Turner 3, Gibbons 4, Irene 4, Mayer 4, Wilson 4)

Postman Always Rings Twice, 1981 (Rafelson 2, Huston 3, Lange 3, Nicholson 3, Jeakins 4, Jenkins 4, Nykvist 4)

Postman Didn't Ring, 1942 (Day 4, Raksin 4)

Postmark for Danger. See Portrait of Alison, 1955

Postmaster's Daughter. See Nostalgie, 1937

Posto ideale per uccidere, 1971 (Papas 3)

Postřižny, 1980 (Menzel 2)

Pot au Feu, 1965 (Altman 2)

Pot Luck, 1936 (Balcon 4, Rank 4)

Pot o'Gold, 1941 (Goddard 3, Stewart 3, Mohr 4)

Potage indigeste, 1903 (Guy 2)

Potash and Perlmutter, 1923 (Goldwyn 4, Marion 4)

Pot-Bouille, 1957 (Duvivier 2, Aimée 3, Darrieux 3, Philipe 3, Barsacq 4, Hakim 4, Jeanson 4)

Pote tin kryiaki, 1960 (Mercouri 3)

Potem nastąpi cisza, 1966 (Lomnicki 3)

Potem nastąpi cisza, 1966 (Olbrychski 3)

Potemkine, 1905 (Pathé 4)

Potent Lotion, 1989 (Halas and Batchelor 4)

Potiphar's Wife, 1931 (Lanchester 3, Olivier 3)

Potomok Chingis-khan, 1928 (Barnet 2, Golovnya 4)

Potop, 1915 (Mozhukin 3)

Potop, 1974 (Lomnicki 3)

Potop, 1974 (Olbrychski 3)

Potters, 1927 (Fields 3)

Pottsville Palooka, 1931 (Sennett 2)

Pouce!, 1972 (Cloquet 4)

Poudre d'escampette, 1971 (Piccoli 3, Legrand 4)

Poughkeepsie Regatta, 1906 (Bitzer 4)

Poule aux oeufs d'or, 1905 (Pathé 4)

Poule fantaisiste, 1903 (Guy 2)

Poule merveilleuse, 1902 (Pathé 4)

Poule mouillée qui se sèche, 1912 (Cohl 4)

Poule sur un mur, 1936 (Berry 3)

Poulet, 1963 (Cloquet 4)

Poulet au vinaigre, 1985 (Chabrol 2, Audran 3)

Poulette grise, 1947 (McLaren 4)

Poulot n'est pas sage, 1912 (Cohl 4)

Poultry Pirates, 1938 (Freleng 4)

Pound for a Pound, 1915 (Beery 3)

Poupée, 1962 (Cybulski 3, Coutard 4, Kosma 4)

Pouponnière, 1933 (Rosay 3)

Pour Bonnie, 1982 (Léaud 3)

Pour Don Carlos, 1921 (Musidora 3)

Pour être aimée, 1933 (Tourneur 2)

Pour la peau d'un flic, 1970 (Delon 3)

Pour la suite du monde, 1963 (Perrault 2)

Pour l'amour du ciel. See E più facile che un cammello ... , 1950

Pour le maillot jaune, 1939 (Burel 4)

Pour le meilleur et pour le pire, 1975 (Jutra 2)

Pour le mérite, 1938 (Röhrig 4)

Pour le mérite, 1950 (Staudte 2)

Pour le mistral, 1966 (Ivens 2)

Pour l'Espagne, 1963 (Jarre 4)

Pour mon coeur et ses millions, 1931 (Björnstrand 3)

Pour secourer la salade, 1902 (Guy 2)

Pour une nuit d'amour, 1919 (Protazanov 2)

Pour un maillot jaune, 1965 (Lelouch 2)

Pour un oui ou pour un non, 1989 (Trintignant 3)

Pour un sou d'amour, 1931 (Grémillon 2, D'Eaubonne 4)

Pour vos beaux yeux, 1986 (Storck 2)

Pourquoi le violon pleurait-il?, 1941 (Volkov 3)

Pourquoi Paris?, 1962 (Darrieux 3)

Pourquoi Paris?, 1962 (Blier 3, Girardot 3)

Pourquoi viens-tu si tard?, 1959 (Morgan 3, Audiard 4, Matras 4)

Poursuite. See Roi sans divertissement, 1963

Poursuite du vent, 1943 (Leenhardt 2)

Poursuite mouvementée, 1909 (Linder 3)

Pourvue que ce soit une fille, 1986 (Morricone 4)

Pousse des plantes, 1913 (Burel 4)

Poussière d'Empire, 1983 (Sanda 3)

Poussières, 1954 (Franju 2)

Pouvoir du mal, 1985 (Zanussi 2, Gassman 3)

Povere bimbe, 1923 (Pastrone 2)

Poveri ma belli, 1956 (Delli Colli 4)

Poveri milionari, 1958 (Delli Colli 4)

Poverty and Nobility. See Miseria e nobiltà, 1954

Povest plamennykh, 1961 (Bondarchuk 3)

Povídky z první republiky, 1965 (Brodský 3)

Povodeň, 1958 (Frič 2)

Povorot, 1978 (Yankovsky 3)

Powaqqatsi, 1988 (Golan and Globus 4)

Powder and Smoke, 1924 (Roach 4)

Powder Flash of Death, 1913 (Reid 3)

Powder River, 1953 (Cronjager 4, LeMaire 4)

Powder Town, 1942 (McLaglen 3, O'Brien 3)

Powderkeg, 1971 (Smith 4)

Powdersmoke Range, 1935 (Carey 3)

Power, 1928 (Garnett 2, Bennett 3, Lombard 3)

Power. See Jew Suss, 1934

Power, 1968 (De Carlo 3, Haskin 4, Pal 4, Rozsa 4)

Power, 1980 (Bellamy 3, Black 3, Jenkins 4)

Power. See Shakti, 1982

Power, 1986 (Lumet 2, Christie 3, Gere 3, Hackman 3)

Power Among Men, 1958 (Dickinson 2, Harvey 3, Thomson 4)

Power and Glory. See Power and the Glory, 1933

Power and the Glory, 1933 (Sturges 2, Moore 3, Tracy 3, Howe 4, Lasky 4)

Power and the Glory, 1941 (Finch 3)

Power and the Glory, 1961 (Cusack 3, Olivier 3, Scott 3, Greene 4)

Power and the Land, 1940 (Ivens 2, Crosby 4, Van Dongen 4)

Power and the Prize, 1956 (Astor 3, Coburn 3, Papas 3, Folsey 4, Kaper 4, Rose 4)

Power Dive, 1941 (Alton 4, Head 4)

Power Flash of Death, 1913 (Dwan 2)

Power for Defense, 1942 (Crosby 4)

Power of Conscience, 1913 (Bushman 3)

Power of Destiny. See Moc osudu, 1968

Power of Evil. See Pouvoir du mal, 1985

Power of Good, 1911 (Anderson 3)

Power of Love, 1911 (Dwan 2)

Power of the Camera, 1913 (Loos 4)

Power of the First. See Vlast' pervogo, 1917

Power of the Press, 1913 (Barrymore 3)

Power of the Press, 1928 (Capra 2, Cohn 4, Levien 4)

Power of the Press, 1943 (Fuller 2)

Power of Thought, 1949 (Terry 4)

Power on the Land, 1943 (Unsworth 4)

Power Play, 1978 (O'Toole 3, Pleasence 3)

Power Signal Lineman, 1953 (Lassally 4)

Power to Fly, 1953 (Halas and Batchelor 4)

Power to the People, 1972 (Benegal 2)

Power Within, 1979 (Addison 4)

Powerful Eye, 1924 (Arthur 3)

Powers Girl, 1943 (McLeod 2, Adrian 4, Cortez 4)

Powers of Darkness. See Vlast tmy, 1915

Powers of Ten, 1968 (Bernstein 4)

Powers That Prey, 1918 (King 2, Seitz 4)

Pozdniaia vstrecha, 1978 (Batalov 3)

Późne popołudnie, 1964 (Ścibor-Rylski 4)

Pozor!. See Drahoušek Klementýna, 1959

Pozzo dei miracoli, 1941 (Amidei 4)

Practical Jokers, 1938 (Roach 4)

Practically Yours, 1944 (Leisen 2, Colbert 3, De Carlo 3, MacMurray 3, Benchley 4, Dreier 4, Krasna 4, Lang 4, Young 4)

Practice Makes Perfect. See Cavaleur, 1978

Prade's Comet. See Savage Pampas, 1967

Pradlenka Jeho Jasnosti, 1930 (Heller 4)

Praesten i Vejlby, 1931 (Holger-Madsen 2)

Praestens Datter, 1916 (Holger-Madsen 2)

Prague, 1985 (Menzel 2)

Prague, 1991 (Ganz 3)

Prague Nights. See Pražské noci, 1968

Prairie Badmen, 1946 (Crabbe 3)

Prairie Chickens, 1942 (Roach 4)

Prairie King, 1927 (Eason 4)

Prairie Law, 1940 (Hunt 4)

Prairie Moon, 1938 (Autry 3)

Prairie Pioneers, 1941 (Brown, 4, Canutt 4)

Prairie Pirate, 1925 (Carey 3)

Prairie Rustlers, 1945 (Crabbe 3)

Prairie Schooners, 1939 (Canutt 4)

Prairie Thunder, 1937 (Canutt 4, Eason 4)

Prairie Trails, 1920 (Mix 3)

Prairie Wife, 1925 (Karloff 3)

Prak a drank, 1960 (Brdečka 4)

Pramen lásky, 1928 (Stallich 4)

Prämien auf den Tod, 1950 (Krauss 3)

Prancer, 1989 (Jarre 4)

Prangasiz mahkumlar, 1964 (Güney 2)

Pranke, 1931 (Rasp 3)

Präsident, 1928 (Mozhukin 3)

Präsident Barrada, 1920 (Courant 4)

Prästänkan, 1920 (Magnusson 4)

Prästen, 1914 (Sjöström 2, Jaenzon 4, Magnusson 4)

Prästen i Uddarbo, 1957 (Von Sydow 3)

Prater, 1925 (Porten 3)

Pratermizzi, 1926 (Ondra 3)

Pratermizzi, 1927 (Reisch 4)

Pratidwandi, 1970 (Datta 4)

Pratima, 1936 (Biswas 4)

Prato, 1979 (Taviani 2, Morricone 4)

Pravda, 1968 (Godard 2)

Právo na hřích, 1932 (Stallich 4)

Praxis der Liebe, 1984 (Vogler 3)

Pray for the Wildcats, 1974 (Dickinson 3)

Prayer for the Dying, 1987 (Bates 3, Hoskins 3, Rourke 3)

Prayers and Elegies of Francis Jammes, 1963 (Alwyn 4)

Pražské noci, 1968 (Brdečka 4)

Přchozí z temnot, 1921 (Ondra 3)

Précieuses ridicules, 1900 (Gaumont 4)

Precinct 45: Los Angeles Police. See New Centurions, 1972

Precio de un beso, 1930 (Nichols 4)

Precious Green Mountains, 1958 (Zhao 3)

Precious Parcel, 1916 (Laurel and Hardy 3)

Precipice. See Obryv, 1913

Precursores de la pintura argentina, 1957 (Torre Nilsson 2)

Před maturitou, 1932 (Heller 4)

Preda, 1974 (Presle 3)

Predator, 1987 (Schwarzenegger 3)

Předtucha, 1947 (Stallich 4)

Preface to a Life, 1950 (Kaufman 4)

Preface to Life, 1949 (Rathaus 4)

Prefetto di ferro, 1977 (Cardinale 3, Morricone 4)

Prega il morte e ammazza il vivo, 1970 (Kinski 3)

Prehistoric Perils, 1952 (Terry 4)

Prehistoric Porky, 1940 (Blanc 4, Clampett 4, Stalling 4)

Prehistoric Poultry, 1917 (O'Brien 4)

Prehistoric Women. *See* Slave Girls, 1968

Pre-hysterical Hare, 1958 (Blanc 4, McKimson 4)

Preis fürs Überleben, 1980 (Lassally 4)

Preiss für Überleben, 1979 (Piccoli 3)

Prélude à la gloire, 1949 (Renoir 4)

Prélude à l'apres-midi d'une faune, 1938 (Rossellini 2)

Prélude à l'Asie, 1960 (Braunberger 4)

Prélude pour orchestre, voix, et caméra, 1959 (Delerue 4)

Prelude to Fame, 1950 (Lee 3, Rank 4)

Prelude to War. *See* **Why We Fight series, 1943–45**

Preludio d'amore, 1946 (Gassman 3)

Preludio 11, 1964 (Mueller-Stahl 3)

Prem Bandhan; Sher Ka Panja, 1936 (Biswas 4)

Prem Murti. *See* Pratima, 1936

Prem Nagar, 1974 (Burman 4)

Prem Patra, 1962 (Roy 2)

Prem Pujari, 1970 (Anand 3, Burman 4)

Prem Rog, 1982 (Kapoor 2)

Prem Shastra, 1974 (Anand 3)

Premature Burial, 1962 (Coppola 2, Corman 2, Milland 3, Crosby 4)

Préméditation, 1912 (Feuillade 2)

Premier Bal, 1941 (Christian-Jaque 2, Blier 3, Spaak 4)

Premier Jour de Vacances de Poulot, 1912 (Cohl 4)

Premier May. *See* Festa di maggio, 1957

Premier Pas, 1950 (Decaë 4)

Premier prix du conservatoire, 1942 (Decaë 4)

Premier rendezvous, 1941 (Darrieux 3, Gélin 3, Jourdan 3)

Premiere, 1936 (Planer 4)

Premiere. *See* Ösbemutató, 1974

Première Cigare d'un collégien, 1906 (Linder 3)

Première Cigarette, 1904 (Guy 2)

Première croisière, 1955 (Delerue 4)

Première Fois, 1976 (Trauner 4)

Première Gamelle, 1902 (Guy 2)

Première Nuit, 1958 (Colpi 4, Delerue 4)

Première sortie, 1905 (Pathé 4)

Première Sortie d'un collégien, 1905 (Linder 3)

Premières Armes de Rocambole, 1922 (Fresnay 3)

Premiers pas de Bébé, 1985 (Lumière 2)

Premijera, 1957 (Mimica 4)

Premiya, 1974 (Yankovsky 3)

Premonition, 1970 (Rudolph 2)

Prenez des gants, 1960 (Delerue 4)

Prenez Garde à la Peinture, 1935 (Simon 3)

Prénom Carmen, 1983 (Coutard 4)

Préparez vos mouchoirs, 1978 (Depardieu 3, Delerue 4)

Prepotenti, 1958 (Fabrizi 3)

Prepotenti più di prima, 1959 (Fabrizi 3)

Pre-Production, 1973 (Le Grice 2)

Presagio, 1973 (Alcoriza 4, Figueroa 4)

Prescott Kid, 1936 (Brennan 3)

Prescription for Percy, 1954 (Terry 4)

Prescription for Romance, 1937 (Krasner 4)

Prescription: Murder, 1968 (Falk 3)

Presence, 1972 (Brakhage 2)

Présence d'Albert Camus, 1962 (Jarre 4)

Present with a Future, 1943 (Davis 3, Haller 4)

Present Arms. *See* Leathernecking, 1930

Présentation ou Charlotte et son steack, 1951 (Godard 2, Karina 3)

Presentiment. *See* Předtucha, 1947

Presenting Lily Mars, 1943 (Walters 2, Garland 3, Edens 4, Pasternak 4)

Presents, 1982 (Snow 2)

Preservation Man, 1962 (Russell 2)

President. *See* Präsident, 1928

Président, 1960 (Blier 3, Gabin 3, Audiard 4, Jarre 4)

Président Haudecoeur, 1939 (Baur 3)

President McKinley's Inauguration, 1897 (Bitzer 4)

President T. R. Roosevelt, July 4th, 1903 (Bitzer 4)

President Vanishes, 1934 (Wellman 2, Russell 3, Vorkapich 4, Wanger 4, Wilson 4)

Presidente del Borgorosso Football Club, 1970 (Amidei 4)

President's Analyst, 1967 (Coburn 3, Fraker 4, Schifrin 4)

President's Lady, 1953 (Hayward 3, Heston 3, LeMaire 4, Newman 4, Wheeler 4)

President's Mistress, 1978 (Schifrin 4)

President's Plane Is Missing, 1971 (Kennedy 3, Massey 3, McCambridge 3)

President's Women, 1977 (Rosenblum 4)

Presidio, 1988 (Connery 3, Mancini 4)

Press for Time, 1966 (Wisdom 3)

Pressing His Suit, 1914 (Roach 4)

Pressure of Guilt. *See* Shiro to kuro, 1963

Pressure Point, 1962 (Kramer 2, Falk 3, Poitier 3, Hall 4, Haller 4)

Prestige, 1932 (Garnett 2, Douglas 3, Menjou 3)

Prest-O Change-O, 1939 (Blanc 4, Jones 4, Stalling 4)

Preston Sturges: The Rise and Fall of an American Dreamer, 1990 (Hutton 3, McCrea 3)

Presumé dangereux, 1990 (Mitchum 3)

Presumed Innocent, 1990 (Pakula 2, Pollack 2, Ford 3, Jenkins 4, Williams 4, Willis 4)

Prete, fai un miracolo, 1974 (Cecchi D'Amico 4)

Prête-moi ta femme, 1936 (Brasseur 3)

Pretender, 1947 (Alton 4)

Prêtres interdits, 1973 (De Beauregard 4)

Pretty Baby, 1950 (Furthman 4)

Pretty Baby, 1978 (Malle 2, Sarandon 3, Nykvist 4)

Pretty Boy Floyd, 1959 (Falk 3, Rosenblum 4)

Pretty Girl, 1950 (Lanchester 3, Duning 4)

Pretty Hattie's Baby, 1990 (Passer 2)

Pretty in Pink, 1986 (Hughes 2, Stanton 3)

Pretty Ladies, 1925 (Crawford 3, Loy 3, Shearer 3)

Pretty Maids All in a Row, 1971 (Vadim 2, Dickinson 3, Hudson 3, McDowall 3, Schifrin 4)

Pretty Mrs. Smith, 1915 (Bosworth 3)

Pretty Poison, 1968 (Perkins 3, Weld 3, Smith 4)

Pretty Polly, 1967 (Howard 3, Green 4, Legrand 4)

Pretty Sister of Jose, 1915 (Dwan 2)

Pretty Smooth, 1919 (Young 4)

Pretty Woman, 1990 (Bellamy 3, Gere 3)

Prettykill, 1987 (York 3)

Pretzels, 1930 (Terry 4)

Preussische Liebesgeschichte, 1950 (Baarová 3)

Prevailing Craze, 1914 (Beery 3)

Preview Murder Mystery, 1936 (Florey 2, Dreier 4, Struss 4)

Přežil isem svou smrt, 1960 (Kučera 4)

Prezzo del potere, 1969 (Johnson 3)

Příběh jednoho dne, 1926 (Heller 4)

Price He Paid, 1912 (Bosworth 3)

Price of a Good Time, 1917 (Weber 2)

Price of a Party, 1924 (Astor 3, Seitz 4)

Price of a Song, 1935 (Powell and Pressburger 2)

Price of Beauty. *See* Farlige Alder, 1911

Price of Coal, 1977 (Loach 2)

Price of Death. *See* Venditore di morte, 1972

Price of Fear, 1956 (Oberon 3)

Price of Happiness, 1916 (Menjou 3)

Price of Possession, 1921 (Folsey 4)

Price of Power. *See* Prezzo del potere, 1969

Price of Pride, 1917 (Edeson 4)

Price of Redemption, 1920 (Polito 4)

Price of Silence, 1916 (Chaney 3)

Price of Survival. *See* Preis fürs Überleben, 1980

Price of the Necklace, 1914 (Ingram 2)

Price of Wisdom, 1935 (Havelock-Allan 4)

Prices Unlimited, 1944 (Mohr 4)

Příchozí z temnot, 1921 (Heller 4)

Prick Up Your Ears, 1987 (Frears 2, Jarman 2, Redgrave 3)

Pride. *See* Aan, 1952

Pride and Prejudice, 1940 (Garson 3, Olivier 3, O'Sullivan 3, Adrian 4, Freund 4, Gibbons 4, Mayer 4, Murfin 4, Stothart 4, Stromberg 4)

Pride and the Man, 1916 (Borzage 2)

Pride and the Passion, 1957 (Kramer 2, Grant 3, Loren 3, Sinatra 3, Anhalt 4, Bass 4, Planer 4)

Pride of Bluegrass, 1939 (McCord 4)

Pride of Jesse Hallam, 1981 (Wallach 3)

Pride of Lonesome, 1913 (Reid 3)

Pride of New York, 1918 (Walsh 2)

Pride of Palomar, 1922 (Borzage 2)

Pride of Pawnee, 1929 (Musuraca 4, Plunkett 4)

Pride of Pickeville, 1927 (Sennett 2)

Pride of Race. *See* Last of the Line, 1914

Pride of St. Louis, 1952 (LeMaire 4, Mankiewicz 4)

Pride of the Bowery, 1941 (Katzman 4)

Pride of the Clan, 1917 (Tourneur 2, Pickford 3, Carré 4)

Pride of the Marines, 1936 (Bond 3)

Pride of the Marines, 1945 (Garfield 3, Burks 4, Wald 4, Waxman 4)

Pride of the Plains, 1943 (Canutt 4)

Pride of the Range, 1910 (Mix 3)

Pride of the South, 1913 (Ince 4)

Pride of the West, 1938 (Harlan 4, Head 4)

Pride of the Yankees, 1942 (Wood 2, Brennan 3, Cooper 3, Duryea 3, Wright 3, Goldwyn 4, Mandell 4, Mankiewicz 4, Maté 4, Menzies 4, Swerling 4)

Pride of the Yard, 1954 (Terry 4)

Prière, 1900 (Guy 2)
Priest. *See* Prästen, 1914
Priest of Love, 1981 (Gardner 3, Gielgud 3)
Priest of Wilderness, 1910 (Olcott 2)
Priest's Wife. *See* Moglia del prete, 1970
Prigionera della torre dell cuoco, 1952
　(Brazzi 3)
Prigionieri del male, 1956 (Blier 3)
Prigioniero della montagna, 1955
　(Pasolini 2)
Prigioniero di Santa Cruz, 1941 (Amidei 4)
Prima Angélica, 1974 (Saura 2)
Prima comunione, 1950 (Fabrizi 3,
　Zavattini 4)
Prima de Cantinflas, 1940 (Cantinflas 3)
Prima della revolzione, 1964 (Morricone 4)
Prima donna che passa, 1940 (Valli 3)
Prima notte, 1958 (De Sica 2, Cardinale 3,
　Di Venanzo 4)
Prima notte di quiete, 1972 (Delon 3,
　Giannini 3, Valli 3)
Primal Call, 1911 (Griffith 2, Crisp 3,
　Bitzer 4)
Primal Lure, 1916 (Hart 3)
Primanerehe. *See* Boykott, 1930
Primanerliebe, 1927 (Albers 3, Kortner 3)
Primary, 1960 (Leacock 2, Maysles 2)
Primate, 1974 (Wiseman 2)
Primavera del papa, 1949 (Di Venanzo 4)
Prime Cut, 1972 (Hackman 3, Marvin 3,
　Spacek 3, Schifrin 4)
Prime Minister, 1941 (Dickinson 2,
　Gielgud 3)
Prime of Life. *See* Toshigoro, 1968
Prime of Miss Jean Brodie, 1969 (Johnson 3,
　Smith 3, Allen 4)
Prime of Ochiyo's Life. *See* Ochiyo
　toshigoro, 1937
Prime Time, 1959 (Black 3)
Prime Time, 1977 (Oates 3)
Primer delegado, 1975 (Alvarez 2)
**Primera carga al machete, 1969 (Gómez 2,
　Herrera 4)**
Primera fundacion de Buenos Aires, 1959
　(Birri 2)
Primeros Juegos Deportivos Militares, 1964
　(Alvarez 2)
Primerose, 1933 (Meerson 4)
Primitifs du XIII, 1960 (Arletty 3, Prévert 4)
Primitive Love. *See* Amore primitivo, 1964
Primitive Lover, 1922 (Marion 4, Schenck 4)
Primitive Peoples: Australian Aborigines,
　1949 (Finch 3)
Primitive Strain, 1916 (Van Dyke 2)
Primo amore, 1941 (Gallone 2)
Primo amore, 1958 (Camerini 2, Age and
　Scarpelli 4, Delli Colli 4)
Primo amore, 1978 (Delli Colli 4)
Primo Basilio, 1935 (Figueroa 4)
Primrose Path, 1925 (Bow 3)
Primrose Path, 1930 (Laszlo 4)
Primrose Path, 1940 (La Cava 2,
　McCrea 3, Rogers 3, August 4,
　Polglase 4)
Primrose Ring, 1917 (Rosher 4)
Primula bianca, 1946 (Ponti 4)
Prince and Betty, 1919 (Karloff 3)
Prince and the Pauper, 1915 (Porter 2)
Prince and the Pauper, 1937 (Flynn 3,
　Rains 3, Friedhofer 4, Korngold 4,
　Polito 4, Wallis 4)
Prince and the Pauper, 1977 (Borgnine 3,
　Harrison 3, Heston 3, Reed 3, Scott 3,
　Welch 3, Jarre 4)

Prince and the Showgirl, 1957 (Monroe 3,
　Olivier 3, Cardiff 4, Dillon 4, Rattigan 4,
　Warner 4)
Prince azur, 1908 (Cohl 4)
Prince Babby, 1929 (Horton 3)
Prince belge de l'Europe: Charles-Joseph de
　Ligne, 1962 (Delerue 4)
Prince Chap, 1916 (Neilan 2)
Prince charmant, 1942 (Signoret 3)
Prince Charming, 1934 (Balcon 4)
Prince Cuckoo. *See* Prinz Kukuck, 1919
Prince de galles et fallières, 1912 (Cohl 4)
Prince de Ligne. *See* Prince belge de
　l'Europe: Charles-Joseph de Ligne, 1962
Prince for Cynthia, 1953 (Box 4)
Prince Jack, 1985 (Andrews 3, Bernstein 4)
Prince of Adventurers. *See* Casanova, 1927
Prince of Arcadia, 1933 (Lupino 3)
Prince of Avenue A, 1920 (Ford 2)
Prince of Bohemia, 1914 (Eason 4)
Prince of Central Park, 1977 (Gordon 3)
Prince of Darkness, 1987 (Carpenter 2,
　Pleasence 3)
Prince of Diamonds, 1930 (Brown 4)
Prince of Foxes, 1949 (King 2, Welles 2,
　Power 3, Sloane 3, Newman 4,
　Shamroy 4)
Prince of Headwaiters, 1927 (Murfin 4)
Prince of Pirates, 1953 (Katzman 4)
Prince of Players, 1954 (Burton 3, Marsh 3,
　Massey 3, Clarke 4, Dunne 4,
　Herrmann 4, LeMaire 4)
Prince of Rogues. *See* Schinderhannes,
　1927
Prince of Tempters, 1926 (Haller 4)
Prince of the City, 1981 (Lumet 2, Allen 4)
Prince of Tides, 1991 (Nolte 3, Streisand 3)
Prince Party, 1914 (Bushman 3)
Prince Philip, 1953 (Hawkins 3)
Prince Pistachio, 1921 (Roach 4)
Prince Ruperts Drops, 1969 (Frampton 2)
Prince There Was, 1921 (Young 4)
Prince Valiant, 1954 (Hathaway 2, Crisp 3,
　Hayden 3, Leigh 3, Mason 3,
　McLaglen 3, Wagner 3, Ballard 4,
　LeMaire 4, Nichols 4, Waxman 4)
Prince Violent, 1961 (Blanc 4, Freleng 4)
Prince Who Was a Thief, 1951 (Curtis 3,
　Sloane 3, Maté 4, Salter 4)
Princesa de los Ursinos, 1947 (Rey 3)
Princess and the Pirate, 1944 (Brennan 3,
　Crosby 3, Hope 3, McLaglen 3,
　Goldwyn 4, Mandell 4)
Princess and the Plumber, 1930 (Korda 2,
　O'Sullivan 3, Friedhofer 4, Korda 4)
Princess Bride, 1987 (Falk 3, Goldman 4)
Princess Charming, 1934 (Metzner 4,
　Rank 4)
Princess Comes Across, 1936 (Howard 2,
　Lombard 3, MacMurray 3, Banton 4,
　Dreier 4)
Princess Daisy, 1983 (Cardinale 3)
Princess from Hoboken, 1927 (Karloff 3,
　Levien 4)
Princess from the Moon. *See* Taketori
　Monogatari, 1987
Princess Impudence, 1919 (Brenon 2)
Princess in the Vase, 1908 (Bitzer 4)
Princess Nicotine, 1909 (Blackton 2)
Princess of New York, 1921 (Hitchcock 2,
　Crisp 3)
Princess of the Dark, 1917 (Gilbert 3, Ince 4)
Princess of the Nile, 1954 (Van Cleef 3)
Princess Olala. *See* Prinzessin Olala, 1928

Princess O'Rourke, 1943 (Coburn 3, De
　Havilland 3, Wyman 3, Haller 4,
　Krasna 4, Orry-Kelly 4, Wallis 4)
Princess Snake's Travels. *See* Hebihime
　douchuh, 1949
Princess Tam-Tam, 1935 (Douy 4)
Princess Yang Kwei-Fei. *See* Yokihi, 1955
Princesse de Clèves, 1960 (Cocteau 2,
　Delannoy 2, Marais 3, Alekan 4, Auric 4)
Princesse Mandane, 1928 (Dulac 2)
Princesse muette, 1964 (Braunberger 4)
Princesse Tam-Tam, 1935 (Meerson 4)
Princezna se zlatou hvězdou, 1959 (Frič 2)
Principe de la iglesia. *See* Cardenal, 1951
Principe del deserto, 1990 (Sharif 3,
　Morricone 4)
Principe ribelle, 1950 (Ferreri 2)
Principessa delle Canarie, 1954
　(Mastroianni 3)
Principessa Giorgio, 1919 (Bertini 3)
Principessa straniera, 1914 (Bertini 3)
Principessa Tarahanova, 1938 (Sordi 3)
Principles of Cinematography, 1973 (Le
　Grice 2)
Prins Gustaf, 1944 (Zetterling 2)
Printemps, 1909 (Feuillade 2)
Printemps de la mer, 1958 (Braunberger 4)
Printemps, l'automne et l'amour, 1953
　(Fernandel 3)
Prinz der Legende. *See* Tragodie im Haus
　Habsburg, 1924
Prinz Kukuck, 1919 (Leni 2, Veidt 3,
　Hoffmann 4)
Prinz Sami, 1918 (Lubitsch 2)
Prinz und Bettelknabe. *See* Seine Majestat
　das Bettelkind, 1920
Prinz und die Kokotte. *See* Prinz und die
　Tanzerin, 1926
Prinz und die Tanzerin, 1926 (Albers 3)
Prinz von Arkadien, 1932 (Planer 4,
　Reisch 4)
Prinzessin Olala, 1928 (Albers 3, Dietrich 3)
Prinzessin Suwarin, 1923 (Dagover 3, Von
　Harbou 4)
Prinzessin Turandot, 1934 (Herlth 4,
　Röhrig 4, Von Harbou 4, Wagner 4)
Prinzessin von Neutralien, 1917 (Wiene 2,
　Freund 4)
Prinzessin von Urbino, 1919 (Albers 3)
Priorities on Parade, 1942 (Miller 3,
　Dreier 4, Young 4)
Případ Lupínek, 1960 (Stallich 4)
Prípad pro Selwyn, 1968 (Weiss 2)
Priscilla series, 1911 (Sennett 2)
Priscillas fahrt ins Glück, 1928 (Warm 4)
Prishell soldat s fronta, 1973 (Shukshin 3)
Prisión de suenos, 1950 (Figueroa 4)
Prisionero trece, 1933 (De Fuentes 2)
Prisioneros desparecidos, 1978
　(Villagra 3)
Prison, 1965 (Warhol 2)
Prison à l'américaine, 1971 (Braunberger 4)
Prison Break, 1938 (Bond 3)
Prison Breaker, 1936 (Mason 3)
Prison Bride. *See* Rougoku no hanayome,
　1939
Prison Farm, 1938 (Dmytryk 2, Holden 3,
　Dreier 4, Head 4)
Prison Nurse, 1938 (Cruze 2)
Prison Panic, 1930 (Lantz 4)
Prison sans barreaux, 1938 (Jeanson 4,
　Matras 4, Renoir 4, Wakhévitch 4)
Prison Ship. *See* Star Slammer, 1988
Prison sur le gouffre, 1912 (Feuillade 2)

Professeur. *See* Prima notte di quiete, 1972

Profession de géomètre expert, 1949 (Cloquet 4)

Professional Gun. *See* Mercenario, 1969

Professional Jealousy, 1907 (Bitzer 4)

Professional Soldier, 1935 (Garnett 2, McLaglen 3, Maté 4, Zanuck 4)

Professional Sweetheart, 1933 (Pangborn 3, Rogers 3, Cooper 4, Cronjager 4, Plunkett 4, Polglase 4, Steiner 4)

Professionals, 1960 (Alwyn 4)

Professionals, 1966 (Brooks 2, Bellamy 3, Cardinale 3, Lancaster 3, Palance 3, Ryan 3, Fraker 4, Hall 4, Jarre 4)

Professione Figlio, 1980 (Morricone 4)

Professione: Reporter, 1975 (Antonioni 2, Nicholson 3, Ponti 4)

Professionnel, 1981 (Belmondo 3, Audiard 4, Morricone 4)

Professor Bean's Removal, 1913 (Sennett 2, Normand 3)

Professor Beware, 1938 (Daves 2, Bond 3, Lloyd 3, Bruckman 4, Head 4, Westmore Family 4)

Prof. Guido Tersilli, primario della clinica Villa Celeste convenzionato con le mutue, 1969 (Amidei 4)

Professor My Son. *See* Mio figlio professore, 1946

Professor of the Drama, 1903 (Bitzer 4)

Professor Offkeyski, 1940 (Terry 4)

Professor Petersens plejebørn, 1924 (Madsen and Schenstrøm 3)

Prof. Small and Mr. Tall, 1943 (Fleischer 4, Hubley 4)

Professor Tom, 1948 (Hanna and Barbera 4)

Professor's Daughter, 1913 (Sennett 2, Normand 3)

Professor's Ward, 1911 (Lawrence 3)

Professor's Wooing, 1912 (Bosworth 3)

Profeta, 1967 (Gassman 3)

Profile of a Miracle, 1960 (Brynner 3)

Profile of Britain, 1940 (Lye 4)

Profit By Their Example, 1964 (Loach 2)

Profit from Loss, 1915 (Eason 4)

Profiteers, 1919 (Miller 4)

Profligate, 1911 (Bosworth 3)

Profondo rosso, 1976 (Argento 4)

Profumo di donna, 1974 (Gassman 3)

Progress for Freedom, 1962 (Ferrer 3)

Progresso in agricoltura, 1957 (Olmi 2)

Prohibition Wife, 1919 (Talmadge 3)

Proibito, 1954 (Monicelli 2, Rosi 2, Cecchi D'Amico 4, Gherardi 4, Rota 4)

Proibito rubare, 1948 (Cecchi D'Amico 4, Gherardi 4, Rota 4)

Proie du vent, 1926 (Clair 2, Vanel 3, Meerson 4)

Proie pour l'ombre, 1960 (Astruc 2, Girardot 3, Saulnier 4)

Proini Peripolos, 1987 (Chandler 4)

Project A. *See* Gaiwak, 1983

Project A: Part II. *See* Gaiwatsuktsap, 1987

Project Apollo, 1968 (Emshwiller 2)

Project Eagle. *See* Lunghing fudai tsuktsap, 1990

Project M7. *See* Net, 1952

Project X, 1967 (Hanna and Barbera 4)

Prokliatiye millioni, 1917 (Mozhukin 3)

Prokuror, 1917 (Mozhukin 3)

Proljetni zvuci, 1960 (Mimica 4)

Prolonged Time. *See* Prodloužený čas, 1984

Prom Night, 1980 (Curtis 3)

Promesse à l'inconnue, 1942 (Brasseur 3, Vanel 3)

Promesse de l'aube, 1971 (Mercouri 3, Delerue 4, Trauner 4)

Promessi sposi, 1941 (Cervi 3)

Promessi sposi, 1989 (Rey 3, Morricone 4)

Prometej s otoka Viševice, 1964 (Mimica 4)

Prométhé, 1908 (Feuillade 2)

Prométhée ... banquier, 1921 (Delluc 2, L'Herbier 2)

Prometheus, 1959 (Dinov 4)

Prometheus from Visevica Island. *See* Prometej s otoka Viševice, 1964

Prometheus XX, 1970 (Dinov 4)

Promise, 1911 (Dwan 2)

Promise, 1917 (Gaudio 4)

Promise at Dawn. *See* Promesse de l'aube, 1971

Promise Her Anything, 1966 (Beatty 3, Caron 3, Love 3, Sutherland 3, Slocombe 4)

Promised Land. *See* **Tierra prometida, 1972**

Promised Land. *See* Ziemia obiecana, 1974

Promises in the Dark, 1979 (Rosenman 4)

Promises! Promises!, 1963 (Mansfield 3, Biroc 4)

Promises to Keep, 1985 (Mitchum 3)

Promoter. *See* Card, 1952

Proof of the Man. *See* Ningen no shomei, 1977

Property Man, 1914 (Sennett 2)

Prophecy, 1972 (Rosenman 4)

Prophecy, 1979 (Frankenheimer 2, Rosenman 4)

Prophecy. *See* Yogen, 1982

Proprietà non è più un furto, 1973 (Morricone 4)

Propos de Jivago, 1962 (Alexeieff and Parker 4)

Propos de Nice, 1930 (Kaufman 4)

Propre à rien, 1956 (Decaë 4, Rabier 4)

Proscrit, 1912 (Gaumont 4)

Proscrit, L'oubliette, 1912 (Feuillade 2)

Proshchanie, 1981 (Klimov 2)

Proshu slova, 1976 (Shukshin 3)

Prospector, 1912 (Anderson 3)

Prospector, 1917 (Laurel and Hardy 3)

Prospector's Legacy, 1912 (Anderson 3)

Prospector's Vengeance, 1920 (Eason 4)

Prosperity, 1932 (Wood 2, Dressler 3)

Prosperity Race, 1962 (Zetterling 2)

Prospero's Books, 1991 (Gielgud 3, Josephson 3, Vierny 4)

Prosperous Times, 1980 (Andersson 3)

Prosseneti, 1975 (Cuny 3)

Prostaya istoriya, 1960 (Shukshin 3)

Prostituta al servizio del pubblico e in regol con le leggi dello stato, 1971 (Giannini 3)

Prostitution, 1919 (Krauss 3, Veidt 3)

Prostitution II, 1919 (Veidt 3)

Prostiye lyudi, 1956 (Enei 4, Moskvin 4, Shostakovich 4)

Prostye serdtsa, 1928 (Maretskaya 3)

Protagonisti, 1967 (Flaiano 4)

Protea I, 1913 (Gaumont 4)

Protecting San Francisco from Fire, 1913 (Sennett 2)

Protection, 1929 (Brown 3)

Protection for People, 1962 (Folsey 4)

Protector, 1985 (Chan 3)

Protégé. *See* Protegido, 1956

Protegido, 1956 (Torre Nilsson 2)

Protek the Weakerist, 1937 (Fleischer 4)

Protest at 48 Years Old. *See* Yonjuhachi-sai no teiko, 1956

Proti všem, 1957 (Trnka 4)

Protocol, 1984 (Fraker 4, Henry 4)

Protsess Eserov, 1922 (Vertov 2)

Protsess Mironova, 1919 (Vertov 2)

Proud and the Beautiful. *See* Orgueilleux, 1953

Proud and the Profane, 1956 (Holden 3, Kerr 3, Ritter 3, Head 4, Young 4)

Proud City, 1945 (Alwyn 4)

Proud Flesh, 1925 (Vidor 2, Crawford 3)

Proud Men, 1987 (Heston 3)

Proud Ones, 1956 (Brennan 3, Ryan 3, Ballard 4, LeMaire 4)

Proud Rebel, 1958 (Curtiz 2, Carradine 3, De Havilland 3, Ladd 3, McCord 4)

Proud Valley, 1940 (Robeson 3, Balcon 4)

Proudem stržena. *See* Proudy, 1922

Proudy, 1922 (Heller 4)

Prova de Fogo, 1980 (Diegues 2)

Prova d'orchestra, 1979 (Rota 4, Rotunno 4)

Provaz z oběšence, 1927 (Stallich 4)

Provesso e morte di Socrate, 1940 (Brazzi 3)

Providence, 1977 (Resnais 2, Bogarde 3, Burstyn 3, Gielgud 3, Rozsa 4, Saulnier 4)

Providence and Mrs. Urmy, 1915 (Bushman 3)

Provincial, 1990 (Lai 4)

Provinciale, 1953 (Lollobrigida 3, Aldo 4)

Provinciale, 1980 (Goretta 2, Baye 3, Ganz 3, Winkler 3)

Provocation, 1970 (Marais 3, Schell 3)

Prowler, 1951 (Aldrich 2, Losey 2, Leven 4, Miller 4, Spiegel 4, Trumbo 4)

Prowler, 1981 (Savini 4)

Prowlers of the Plains. *See* Knight of the Trails, 1915

Prowling around France with Will Rogers, 1927 (Rogers 3)

Proxy Lover: a Fable of the Future, 1929 (Fleischer 4)

Prozess der Kitty Kellermann. *See* Hokuspokus, 1930

Prozess Hauers, 1918 (Kräly 4)

Prudence and the Pill, 1968 (Evans 3, Kerr 3, Niven 3, Williams 4)

Prudence of Broadway, 1919 (Borzage 2)

Prude's Fall, 1924 (Hitchcock 2, Saville 2, Balcon 4)

Prunella, 1918 (Tourneur 2, Carré 4)

Prussian Cur, 1918 (Walsh 2)

Prussian Spy, 1909 (Griffith 2, Bitzer 4)

Przedświąteczny wieczór, 1966 (Cybulski 3, Stawiński 4)

Przekładaniec, 1968 (Wajda 2)

Przemysl, 1966 (Zanussi 2)

Przgody Pana Michala, 1982 (Lomnicki 3, Olbrychski 3)

Przy Jaciel, 1960 (Skolimowski 2)

Przypadek, 1982 (Lomnicki 3)

Przypieszenie, 1984 (Tyszkiewicz 3)

Pseudo Sultan, 1912 (Bunny 3)

Psi a lidé, 1971 (Kučera 4)

Psilander, 1914 (Psilander 3)

Psohlavci, 1954 (Stallich 4)

Psyche 59, 1964 (Neal 3)

Psyche 63, 1964 (Lassally 4)

Psyche, Lysis. *See* Du sang de la volupté et de la mort, 1947

Psychiatry in Russia, 1955 (Maysles 2)

Psycho, 1960 (Hitchcock 2, Leigh 3, Perkins 3, Bass 4, Herrmann 4)
Psycho II, 1983 (Perkins 3, Goldsmith 4, Whitlock 4)
Psycho III, 1986 (Perkins 3, Bumstead 4)
Psycho IV, 1990 (Perkins 3)
Psycho A Go-Go!. *See* Blood of Ghastly Horror, 1972
Psycho A-Go-Go!, 1965 (Zsigmond 4)
Psycho Circus. *See* Circus of Fear, 1967
Psycho Killers. *See* Flesh and the Fiends, 1960
Psychomania. *See* Living Dead, 1972
Psychopath, 1965 (Francis 4)
Psych-Out, 1968 (Dern 3, Nicholson 3, Kovacs 4)
Psychout for Murder. *See* Salvare la faccia, 1969
P'tang Yang Kipperbang, 1982 (Puttnam 4)
P'tite Lili, 1927 (Cavalcanti 2, Braunberger 4)
Puberty Blues, 1982 (Beresford 2)
Public Be Hanged. *See* World Gone Mad, 1933
Public Cowboy Number One, 1937 (Autry 3)
Public Deb No. 1, 1940 (Bellamy 3, Pangborn 3, Newman 4, Zanuck 4)
Public Defender, 1931 (Karloff 3, Cronjager 4, Steiner 4)
Public Domain, 1973 (Frampton 2)
Public Enemy, 1931 (Wellman 2, Blondell 3, Cagney 3, Harlow 3, Warner 4, Zanuck 4)
Public Enemy's Wife, 1936 (Haller 4)
Public Eye. *See* Follow Me, 1972
Public Ghost No. 1, 1935 (Roach 4)
Public Hero No. 1, 1935 (Arthur 3, Barrymore 3, Toland 4)
Public Jitterbug Number One, 1939 (Hutton 3)
Public Menace, 1935 (Arthur 3)
Public Opinion, 1916 (Sweet 3)
Public Pigeon No. 1, 1957 (McLeod 2)
Public Prosecutor. *See* Prokuror, 1917
Public Prosecutor. *See* Justice d'abord, 1919
Public Wedding, 1937 (Wyman 3)
Publicity Madness, 1927 (Loos 4)
Publicity Pays, 1924 (McCarey 2, Roach 4)
Pubs and Beaches, 1966 (Williams 4)
Puccini, 1953 (Gallone 2, Renoir 4)
Puce à l'oreille, 1967 (Kaper 4, Trauner 4)
Puce et le Privé, 1980 (Vanel 3)
Puce Moment, 1949 (Anger 2)
Puce Women, 1948 (Anger 2)
Pucérons, 1955 (Rabier 4)
Puck heter jag, 1951 (Andersson 3)
Puddle Pranks, 1931 (Iwerks 4)
Pudd'nhead Wilson, 1916 (Rosher 4)
Pudd'nhead Wilson, 1983 (Lassally 4)
Puddy the Pup and the Gypsies, 1936 (Terry 4)
Puddy's Coronation, 1937 (Terry 4)
Pudgy series, 1937–38 (Fleischer 4, Terry 4)
Puebla hoy, 1978 (Leduc 2)
Pueblerina, 1948 (Fernández 2, Figueroa 4)
Pueblito, 1961 (Fernández 2)
Pueblo, canto y esperanza, 1954 (Infante 3, Figueroa 4)
Pueblo Legend, 1912 (Griffith 2, Pickford 3, Bitzer 4)
Pueblo Terror, 1931 (Canutt 4)
Puente, 1977 (Bardem 2)
Puerta, 1968 (Alcoriza 4, Figueroa 4)
Puerta cerrada, 1939 (Alton 4)

Puerta falsa, 1950 (Armendáriz 3)
Puerta . . . joven, 1949 (Cantinflas 3)
Puerto nuevo, 1936 (Alton 4)
Pugni in tasca, 1965 (Bellocchio 2, Morricone 4)
Puissance du travail, 1925 (Simon 3)
Puits aux trois vérités, 1961 (Morgan 3, Jarre 4, Jeanson 4)
Puits fantastique, 1903 (Méliès 2)
Puits mitoyen, 1913 (Tourneur 2)
Pukar, 1983 (Bachchan 3)
Pulcherie et ses meubles, 1916 (Cohl 4)
Pull My Daisy, 1958 (Seyrig 3)
Pullman Bride, 1917 (Sennett 2, Swanson 3)
Pulnoční příhoda, 1960 (Trnka 4)
Pulp, 1972 (Caine 3, Rooney 3)
Pulsating Giant, 1971 (Benegal 2)
Pulse of Life, 1917 (Ingram 2)
Pumping Iron, 1977 (Schwarzenegger 3)
Pumpkin Eater, 1964 (Clayton 2, Bancroft 3, Finch 3, Mason 3, Smith 3, Delerue 4, Morris 4, Pinter 4)
Pumpkin Race. *See* Course aux potirons, 1907
Punch and Jody, 1974 (Ford 3)
Punch and Judy. *See* Rakvičkárna, 1966
Punch and Judy. *See* Jan Svankmajer: Alchemist of the Surreal, 1990
Punch Drunk, 1934 (Three Stooges 3)
Punch in the Nose, 1925 (Roach 4)
Punch the Clock, 1922 (Roach 4)
Punch the Magician. *See* Kašpárek kouzelníkem, 1927
Punch Trunk, 1953 (Blanc 4, Jones 4, Stalling 4)
Puncher's New Love, 1911 (Anderson 3)
Punchline, 1988 (Mazursky 2, Field 3, Hanks 3)
Punchy Cowpunchers, 1950 (Three Stooges 3)
Punchy De Leon, 1949 (Bosustow 4, Hubley 4)
Punctured Prince, 1923 (Bruckman 4)
Punishment, 1912 (Griffith 2, Sweet 3, Bitzer 4)
Punishment Island. *See* Shokei no shima, 1966
Punishment Park, 1971 (Watkins 2)
Punition, 1964 (Rouch 2, Braunberger 4)
Punition, 1973 (Dalio 3)
Puño del amo, 1958 (Figueroa 4)
Punt'a a čtyřlístek, 1954 (Weiss 2)
Punta and the Four-Leaf Clover. *See* Punt'a a čtyřlístek, 1954
Punter's Mishap, 1900 (Hepworth 2)
Puntila, 1970 (Syberberg 2)
Puny Soul of Peter Rand, 1915 (Mix 3)
Pup on a Picnic, 1953 (Hanna and Barbera 4)
Pupa del gangster, 1975 (Mastroianni 3)
Pupils of the Seventh Grade, 1938 (Protazanov 2)
Puppe, 1919 (Lubitsch 2, Kräly 4)
Puppe vom Lunapark, 1925 (Rasp 3)
Puppenheim, 1923 (Tschechowa 3)
Puppenmacher von Kiang-Ning, 1923 (Wiene 2, Krauss 3, Mayer 4)
Puppenspiel mit toten Augen, 1980 (Valli 3)
Puppet Show, 1936 (Lantz 4)
Puppetoon Movie, 1986 (Harryhausen 4)
Puppets, 1916 (Browning 2)
Puppet's Nightmare. *See* Cauche-mar du Fantoche, 1908
Puppies. *See* Štěňata, 1957
Puppy Express, 1927 (Lantz 4)

Puppy Love, 1919 (Howe 4)
Puppy Love, 1932 (Iwerks 4)
Puppy Lovetime, 1926 (Sennett 2)
Puppy Tale, 1953 (Hanna and Barbera 4)
Pups Is Pups, 1930 (Roach 4)
Pur Sang, 1931 (Autant-Lara 2)
Purchase Price, 1932 (Wellman 2, Stanwyck 3)
Pure as a Rose. *See* Come una rosa al naso, 1976)
Pure Beauté, 1954 (Alexeieff and Parker 4)
Pure Hell of St. Trinian's, 1960 (Launder and Gilliat 2, Arnold 4)
Purgation, 1910 (Griffith 2, Bitzer 4)
Puritain, 1937 (Barrault 3, Fresnay 3, Courant 4)
Puritaine, 1986 (Piccoli 3, Sarde 4)
Puritan Passions, 1923 (Astor 3)
Purity and After, 1978 (Brakhage 2)
Purlie Victorious. *See* Gone Are the Days! 1962
Purple Dawn, 1921 (Love 3)
Purple Death from Outer Space. *See* Flash Gordon Conquers the Universe, 1940
Purple Heart, 1944 (Milestone 2, Andrews 3, Baxter 3, Basevi 4, Miller 4, Newman 4, Zanuck 4)
Purple Heart Diary, 1951 (Katzman 4)
Purple Hills, 1961 (Crosby 4)
Purple Mask, 1955 (Curtis 3, Lansbury 3)
Purple Night, 1972 (Caron 3)
Purple Noon. *See* Plein Soleil, 1959
Purple People Eater, 1988 (Winters 3)
Purple Rain, 1954 (Rank 4, Unsworth 4)
Purple Rain, 1955 (Peck 3)
Purple Rose of Cairo, 1985 (Allen 2, Farrow 3, Johnson 3, Willis 4)
Purple Taxi. *See* Taxi mauve, 1977
Purple V, 1943 (Siodmak 4)
Pursued, 1947 (Walsh 2, Mitchum 3, Wright 3, Howe 4, Steiner 4)
Pursuit, 1935 (Clarke 4)
Pursuit, 1972 (Sheen 3, Goldsmith 4)
Pursuit of D.B. Cooper, 1981 (Duvall 3, Ames 4)
Pursuit of Happiness, 1934 (Bennett 3, Head 4, Struss 4, Zukor 4)
Pursuit of Happiness, 1971 (Mulligan 2, Jenkins 4)
Pursuit of the Graf Spee. *See* Battle of the River Plate, 1956
Pursuit of the Phantom, 1914 (Bosworth 3)
Pursuit to Algiers, 1945 (Salter 4)
Push-Button Kitty, 1952 (Hanna and Barbera 4)
Pusher-in-the-Face, 1928 (Florey 2, Folsey 4)
Pushover, 1954 (MacMurray 3, Malone 3, Novak 3, Wald 4)
Puss Gets the Boot, 1940 (Hanna and Barbera 4)
Puss in Boots, 1922 (Disney 4)
Puss in Boots, 1934 (Iwerks 4)
Puss in Boots, 1988 (Golan and Globus 4)
Puss 'n' Booty, 1943 (Blanc 4, Stalling 4)
Puss 'n' Toots, 1942 (Hanna and Barbera 4)
Pussycat, Pussycat, I Love You, 1970 (Delli Colli 4, Schifrin 4)
Put oko svijeta, 1964 (Vukotić 4)
Put on the Spot, 1936 (Katzman 4)
Put on Your Old Gray Bonnet, 1926 (Fleischer 4)
Put Yourself in His Place, 1912 (Cruze 2)
Putter, 1932 (Brown 3)

Puttin' on the Act, 1940 (Fleischer 4)
Puttin' on the Dog, 1944 (Hanna and
  Barbera 4)
Puttin' on the Ritz, 1930 (Bennett 3,
  Berlin 4, Menzies 4, Schenck 4)
Putting it over, 1919 (Crisp 3)
Putting Pants on Philip, 1927 (Laurel and
  Hardy 3, Stevens 2, Bruckman 4,
  Roach 4)
Putty Tat Trouble, 1951 (Blanc 4, Freleng 4,
  Stalling 4)
Puzzle, 1923 (Fleischer 4)
Puzzle of a Downfall Child, 1970
  (Dunaway 3, Scheider 3)
Puzzle of Horrors. *See* Double Face, 1969

Puzzle of the Red Orchid. *See* Rätsel der
  roten Orchidee, 1961
Pyar, 1950 (Kapoor 2, Burman 4)
Pyar Ki Kahani, 1972 (Bachchan 3)
Pyar Mohabbat, 1966 (Anand 3)
Pyasaa, 1957 (Burman 4)
Pyat dney—pyat nochey, 1960
  (Shostakovich 4)
Pygmalion, 1935 (Gründgens 3)
Pygmalion, 1938 (Asquith 2,
  Lean 2, Howard 3, Quayle 3,
  Dalrymple 4, Honegger 4, Mayer 4,
  Stradling 4)
Pygmalion, 1983 (O'Toole 3)
Pygmy Hunt, 1938 (Freleng 4)

Pygmy Island, 1951 (Weissmuller 3,
  Katzman 4)
Pyramide des Sonnengottes, 1965
  (Siodmak 2)
Pyramide humaine, 1961 (Rouch 2,
  Braunberger 4)
Pyramides bleues, 1988 (Sharif 3, Lai 4)
Pyrénées, terre de legends, 1948 (Renoir 4)
Pyrrhic Victory. *See* Manželé paní Mileny,
  1921
Pyrrhovo vítězství. *See* Manželé paní
  Mileny, 1921
Pythoness, 1989 (Halas and Batchelor 4)
Pytlákova schovanka, 1949 (Frič 2)
Pyx, 1973 (Black 3)

Q & A, 1990 (Lumet 2, Nolte 3)
Q Planes, 1939 (Olivier 3, Richardson 3,
    Dalrymple 4, Hornbeck 4, Korda, A. 4,
    Korda, V. 4, Mathieson 4, Stradling 4)
Qautre Petits Tailleurs, 1910 (Cohl 4)
Qayamat, 1983 (Patil 3)
Qingming Festival, 1936 (Zhao 3)
Qiu Jin, 1983 (Xie 2)
Quack, 1914 (Reid 3)
Quack, 1975 (Schell 3)
Quack Doctor, 1920 (Sennett 2)
Quack Quack, 1931 (Terry 4)
Quack Shot, 1954 (Blanc 4, McKimson 4,
    Stalling 4)
Quacker Tracker, 1967 (Blanc 4)
Quackodile Tears, 1962 (Blanc 4)
Quackser Fortune Has a Cousin in the
    Bronx, 1970 (Wilder 3)
Quadrate, 1934 (Fischinger 2, Ford 2)
Quadrille, 1938 (Guitry 2)
Quadrille, 1950 (Godard 2, Rivette 2)
Quadrille d'amour, 1934 (Brasseur 3)
Quadrille réaliste, 1902 (Guy 2)
Quaeta specie d'amore, 1972 (Seberg 3)
Quagmire, 1913 (Seitz 4)
Quai des blondes, 1953 (Audiard 4)
Quai des brumes, 1938 (Brasseur 3,
    Gabin 3, Morgan 3, Simon 3, Alekan 4,
    Jaubert 4, Prévert 4, Schüfftan 4,
    Trauner 4)
Quai des illusions, 1956 (Kosma 4)
Quai des Orfèvres, 1947 (Clouzot 2, Blier 3,
    Jouvet 3, Douy 4)
Quai Notre Dame, 1961 (Aimée 3)
Quail Shooting, 1905 (Bitzer 4)
Quakeress, 1913 (Ince 4)
Qualcosa di biondo, 1985 (Loren 3,
    Noiret 3)
Qualen der Nacht, 1926 (Dieterle 2, Rasp 3)
Quality Street, 1927 (Davies 3, Gibbons 4,
    Kräly 4, Lewin 4)
Quality Street, 1937 (Stevens 2, Fontaine 3,
    Hepburn 3, Berman 4, Plunkett 4)
Qualsiasi prezzo, 1968 (Kinski 3, Pidgeon 3,
    Rowlands 3)
Quand la femme s'en mêle, 1957 (Allégret 2,
    Blier 3, Delon 3, Feuillère 3,
    D'Eaubonne 4, Spaak 4)
Quand la vie était belle. See Bébé de
    l'escadron, 1935
Quand le rideau se lève, 1957 (Lelouch 2)
Quand les feuilles tombent, 1911
    (Feuillade 2)
Quand même, 1916 (Fresnay 3)
Quand midi sonne par la France, 1960
    (Kosma 4)
Quand minuit sonna, 1914 (Feyder 2)

Quand minuit sonnera, 1936 (Dalio 3,
    Kaufman 4)
Quand on est belle, 1931 (Rosay 3)
Quand passent les faisans, 1965 (Blier 3,
    Audiard 4, Legrand 4)
Quand sonnera midi, 1957 (Burel 4)
Quand tu liras cette lettre, 1953 (Melville 2,
    Alekan 4)
Quand tu nous tiens, amour, 1932
    (Fernandel 3)
Quando l'amore è sensualità, 1972
    (Morricone 4)
Quando le donne avevano la coda, 1970
    (Morricone 4)
Quando le donne persero la coda, 1972
    (Morricone 4)
Quando tramonta il sole, 1955 (Di
    Venanzo 4)
Quantez, 1957 (MacMurray 3, Malone 3)
Quarante gradi all'ombra del'lenzuolo.
    See Quarante gradi sotto il lenzuolo,
    1975
Quarante gradi sotto il lenzuolo, 1975
    (Guerra 4)
Quarantièmes Rugissants, 1982 (Christie 3)
Quarantine, 1923 (Warm 4)
Quarantined, 1970 (Jaffe 3, Duning 4)
Quare Fellow, 1962 (Havelock-Allan 4)
Quark, 1980 (Bozzetto 4)
Quark, 1987 (Bozzetto 4)
Quark, 1988 (Bozzetto 4)
Quark Economica, 1986 (Bozzetto 4)
Quarrel, 1910 (White 3)
Quarrelsome Anglers, 1898 (Hepworth 2)
Quarry Mystery, 1914 (Hepworth 2)
Quarta pagina, 1942 (Fellini 2, Cervi 3,
    Zavattini 4)
Quarta parete, 1971 (Blier 3)
Quarter Time, 1990 (Bridges 3)
Quarterback, 1926 (Cronjager 4)
Quarterback, 1940 (Head 4)
Quartermaine's Terms, 1987 (Gielgud 3)
Quartet, 1948 (Zetterling 2, Bogarde 3,
    Rosay 3, Rank 4, Sherriff 4)
Quartet, 1981 (Ivory 2, Adjani 3, Bates 3,
    Smith 3, Jhabvala 4)
Quartet That Split Up. See Kvartetten som
    sprängdes, 1950
Quartet That Was Split Up. See Kvartetten
    som sprängdes, 1950
Quartetto pazzo, 1944 (Cervi 3, Magnani 3)
Quartier Chinois, 1947 (Hayakawa 3)
Quartier Latin, 1939 (Blier 3)
Quartière, 1987 (Morricone 4)
Quartieri alti, 1944 (Castellani 2)
Quarto d'Italia, 1961 (Zavattini 4)
Quatermass and the Pit, 1967 (Carreras 4)

Quatermass Experiment, 1955 (Bernard 4,
    Carreras 4)
Quatermass II, 1957 (Bernard 4, Carreras 4)
Quatermass Xperiment. See Quatermass
    Experiment, 1955
Quaternion, 1976 (Frampton 2)
Quatorze juillet, 1932 (Clair 2, Modot 3,
    Jaubert 4, Meerson 4, Périnal 4,
    Trauner 4)
Quatorze juillet, 1954 (Gance 2)
Quatorze juillet, 1961 (Braunberger 4)
Quatre Cents Coups, 1959 (Broca 2,
    Demy 2, Truffaut 2, Léaud 3,
    Moreau 3, Decaë 4, Evein 4)
Quatre Charlots mousequetaires, 1973
    (Douy 4)
Quatre Mouches de velours gris, 1972
    (Lenica 4)
Quatre Temps, 1956 (Alexeieff and
    Parker 4)
Quatres Jambes, 1932 (Dalio 3)
Quatres Vagabonds, 1931 (Pick 2)
Quatres Vérités, 1962 (Brazzi 3, Caron 3,
    Karina 3, Vitti 3, Barsacq 4, Cecchi
    D'Amico 4)
Quatrième Pouvoir, 1985 (Noiret 3)
Quatro piccole donne, 1990 (Sharif 3)
Quattro del getto tonante, 1955 (Fusco 4)
Quattro dell'ave Maria, 1968 (Wallach 3)
Quattro giornate de Napoli, 1962 (Volonté 3)
Quattro monaci, 1962 (Fabrizi 3)
Quattro mosche di velluto grigio, 1971
    (Argento 4, Morricone 4)
Quattro moschettieri, 1963 (Fabrizi 3)
Quattro passi fra le nuvole, 1942 (Cervi 3,
    Zavattini 4)
Quattro verità. See Quatres Vérités, 1963
Que Dios me perdone, 1947 (Félix 3)
Que fait-on ce dimanche, 1977 (De
    Almeida 4)
Que Farei Eu Com Esta Espada, 1975 (De
    Almeida 4)
Que hacer, 1970 (Ruiz 2)
Qué he hecho yo para merecer esto, 1984
    (Maura 3)
Que la bete meure, 1969 (Chabrol 2, Pialat 2,
    Gégauff 4, Rabier 4)
Que la fête commence, 1975 (Tavernier 2,
    Dalio 3, Noiret 3, Aurenche 4)
Que les gros salaires lèvent le doigt!!!, 1982
    (Piccoli 3)
Que peut-il avoir, 1912 (Linder 3)
¿Qué te ha dado esa mujer?, 1951 (Infante 3)
Que viene mi marido, 1940 (Figueroa 4)
Que Viva Mexico!, 1931 (Tisse 4)
Quebec: Duplessis et après . . . , 1972
    (Arcand 2)

Queen Bee, 1955 (Crawford 3, Wray 3, Duning 4, Lang 4, Wald 4)

Queen Christina, 1933 (Mamoulian 2, Garbo 3, Gilbert 3, Adrian 4, Behrman 4, Daniels 4, Gibbons 4, Mayer 4, Stothart 4, Wagner 4)

Queen Cotton, 1941 (Alwyn 4, Cardiff 4)

Queen Dorothy's Bow. See Luk královny Dorotky, povikovy, 1970

Queen Elizabeth, 1912 (Zukor 4)

Queen for a Day, 1911 (Bunny 3)

Queen for a Day, 1951 (Friedhofer 4, Miller 4)

Queen High, 1930 (Rogers 3, Green 4)

Queen in Australia, 1955 (Finch 3)

Queen Is Crowned, 1953 (Rank 4)

Queen is Dead, 1986 (Jarman 2)

Queen Kelly, 1928 (Von Stroheim 2, Swanson 3, Plunkett 4)

Queen Louise. See Königin Luise, 1927

Queen of Apollo, 1970 (Leacock 2)

Queen of Blood, 1966 (Corman 2, Hopper 3, Rathbone 3)

Queen of Broadway, 1942 (Crabbe 3)

Queen of Destiny. See Sixty Glorious Years, 1938

Queen of Diamonds, 1972 (Cardinale 3)

Queen of Hearts, 1934 (Iwerks 4)

Queen of Hearts, 1936 (Fields 3, Dean 4)

Queen of Hearts, See Mother Goose Presents Humpty Dumpty, 1946

Queen of Modern Times. See Gendai no joo, 1924

Queen of Outer Space, 1958 (Hecht 4)

Queen of Sheba. See Regina di Saba, 1952

Queen of Spades. See Pikovaya dama, 1916

Queen of Spades. See Dame de Pique, 1937

Queen of Spades, 1948 (Clayton 2, Dickinson 2, Evans 3, Walbrook 3, Adam 4, Auric 4, De Grunwald 4, Heller 4)

Queen of Spies. See Joan of the Ozarks, 1942

Queen of the Band, 1915 (Browning 2)

Queen of the Circus. See Kyohubadan no joo, 1925

Queen of the Mob, 1940 (Bellamy 3, Ryan 3, Dreier 4, Head 4)

Queen of the Moulin Rouge, 1922 (Carré 4)

Queen of the Nightclubs, 1929 (Raft 3)

Queen of the Nile. See Nefertite—Regina del Nilo, 1961

Queen of the Quarry, 1909 (Olcott 2)

Queen of the Road, 1971 (Golan and Globus 4)

Queen Steps Out, 1951 (Terry-Thomas 3)

Queen Victoria. See Sixty Glorious Years, 1938

Queen X, 1917 (Polito 4)

Queenie, 1921 (Menjou 3)

Queenie, 1987 (Douglas 3, Topol 3)

Queenie of Hollywood, 1931 (Arbuckle 3)

Queens. See Fate, 1966

Queen's Affair, 1934 (Wilcox 2, Neagle 3, Raphaelson 4, Young 4)

Queen's Diamonds. See Three Musketeers, 1973

Queen's Guards, 1961 (Powell and Pressburger 2, Massey 3)

Queen's Husband. See Royal Bed, 1930

Queen's Jewels. See Three Musketeers, 1974

Queen's Necklace. See Affaire du collir de la reine, 1946

Queen's Royal Tour, 1954 (Rank 4)

Queen's Secret. See Taina korolevy, 1918

Queens Up, 1920 (Roach 4)

Queer Quarantine, 1914 (Beery 3)

Quei temerari sulle loro pazze, scatenate, scalcinate carriole, 1969 (Curtis 3, Hawkins 3)

Queimada!, 1969 (Brando 3, Gherardi 4, Morricone 4, Solinas 4)

Quel bandito sono io!, 1949 (Ponti 4)

Quelle drôle de blanchisserie, 1912 (Cohl 4)

Quelle drôle de gosse!, 1935 (Darrieux 3, Stradling 4)

Quelle drôle de gosse. See Sweet Devil, 1956

Quelle joie de vivre. See Che gioia vivere, 1961

Quelle strane occasioni, 1976 (Comencini 2, Sordi 3)

Quelque part, quelqu'un, 1972 (Delerue 4)

Quelques jours avec moi, 1988 (Sautet 2, Darrieux 3, Sarde 4)

Quelques pas dans la vie, 1953 (Simon 3)

Quelqu'un a tué, 1933 (Wakhévitch 4)

Quelqu'un derriére la porte, 1971 (Bronson 3, Perkins 3)

Quemando tradiciones, 1971 (Alvarez 2)

Quentin Durward. See Adventures of Quentin Durward, 1955 (Kendall 3, Taylor 3, Berman 4, Challis 4, Junge 4, Kaper 4)

Quentin Quail, 1945 (Blanc 4, Jones 4, Stalling 4)

Quequ'un a tue, 1933 (Modot 3)

Querelle, 1982 (Fassbinder 2, Moreau 3)

Querelle enfantine, 1985 (Lumière 2)

Queridísimos Verdugos, 1971 (De Almeida 4)

Quest, 1983 (Bass 4)

Quest for Fire. See Guerre du feu, 1981

Quest for Love, 1971 (Elliott 3)

Quest of Life, 1916 (Goulding 2)

Questa è la vita, 1954 (Fabrizi 3)

Questa specie d'amore, 1972 (Rey 3, Morricone 4)

Questa volta parliamo di uomini, 1965 (Wertmüller 2)

Qu'est-ce qui fait courir David?, 1982 (Aimée 3, Legrand 4)

Questi fantasmi, 1967 (Gassman 3, Loren 3, Mastroianni 3, Delli Colli 4, Ponti 4)

Questi ragazzi, 1937 (De Sica 2)

Question, 1967 (Halas and Batchelor 4)

Question, 1970 (Ghatak 2)

Question, 1977 (Tavernier 2)

Question d'assurance, 1959 (Delerue 4)

Question in Togoland, 1957 (Dickinson 2)

Question of Courage, 1914 (Crisp 3)

Question of Guilt, 1980 (Weld 3)

Question of Honor, 1915 (Eason 4)

Question of Honor. See Questione d'onore, 1965

Question of Leadership, 1981 (Loach 2)

Question of Love, 1978 (Rowlands 3)

Question of Loyalty, 1957 (Hopper 3)

Question of Rape. See Viol, 1967

Question ordinaire, 1969 (Miller 2)

Questione d'onore, 1965 (Blier 3)

Questions of Leadership, 1983 (Loach 2)

Questor Tapes, 1974 (Whitlock 4)

Quête de Marie, 1952 (Braunberger 4)

Qui?, 1970 (Schneider 3, Gégauff 4)

Qui a tué Max?, 1913 (Linder 3)

Qui comincia l'avventura, 1975 (Cardinale 3, Cristaldi 4)

Qui commande aux fusils, 1969 (Ivens 2)

Qui êtes-vous, Polly Magoo, 1966 (Noiret 3, Seyrig 3, Evein 4)

Quick, 1932 (Albers 3, Berry 3, Brasseur 3, Pommer 4)

Quick, 1932 (Siodmak 2, Albers 3, Berry 3, Brasseur 3, Pommer 4)

Quick, Before It Melts, 1965 (Ames 4, Harlan 4)

Quick Billy, 1970 (Baillie 2)

Quick Change, 1991 (Robards 3)

Quick Gun, 1964 (Murphy 3)

Quick—könig der Clowns. See Quick, 1932

Quick, Let's Get Married. See Confession, 1964

Quick Millions, 1931 (Raft 3, Tracy 3, August 4)

Quick Millions, 1939 (Day 4)

Quick Money, 1938 (Musuraca 4)

Quicksand, 1950 (Lorre 3, Rooney 3, Leven 4)

Quicksands, 1914 (Gish 3)

Quicksands, 1923 (Hawks 2, Rosson 4)

Quién me quiere a mi?, 1936 (Buñuel 2)

Quien sabe?, 1967 (Kinski 3, Volonté 3, Morricone 4, Solinas 4)

Quiet Affair. See Stilla flirt, 1934

Quiet American, 1958 (Mankiewicz 2, Murphy 3, Redgrave 3, Greene 4, Hornbeck 4, Krasker 4)

Quiet Days in Clichy. See Jours tranquilles à Clichy, 1990

Quiet Duel. See Shizukanaru ketto, 1949

Quiet Fourth, 1935 (Grable 3)

Quiet Gun, 1957 (Van Cleef 3)

Quiet Little Wedding, 1913 (Sennett 2, Arbuckle 3)

Quiet Man, 1952 (Ford 2, Bond 3, Fitzgerald 3, McLaglen 3, O'Hara 3, Wayne 3, Cooper 4, Hoch 4, Nugent 4, Young 4)

Quiet Place in the Country. See Tranquillo posto di campagna, 1968

Quiet Place to Kill. See Paranoia, 1969

Quiet Please, 1933 (Stevens 2)

Quiet Please, 1942 (Sanders 3)

Quiet Please!, 1945 (Hanna and Barbera 4)

Quiet, Please, Murder, 1942 (Day 4)

Quiet! Pleeze, 1941 (Fleischer 4)

Quiet Revolution, 1975 (Benegal 2)

Quiet Squad, 1967 (McKimson 4)

Quiet Street, 1922 (Roach 4)

Quiet Takeover, 1963 (Emshwiller 2)

Quiet Wedding, 1941 (Asquith 2, Lockwood 3, Rutherford 3, Dillon 4, Rattigan 4)

Quiet Week in a House. See Tichý týden v domě, 1969

Quijote sin mancha, 1969 (Cantinflas 3)

Qu'il est joli garçon, l'assassin de papa, 1976 (Gélin 3)

Quille, 1961 (Guillemot 4)

Quiller Memorandum, 1966 (Guinness 3, Sanders 3, Segal 3, Von Sydow 3, Barry 4, Pinter 4)

Quilombo, 1984 (Diegues 2)

Quincannon, Frontier Scout, 1956 (Biroc 4, Cahn 4)

Quincy Adams Sawyer, 1922 (Chaney 3, Sweet 3)

Quintero. See Legge dei gangsters, 1969

Quintet, 1979 (Altman 2, Andersson 3, Gassman 3, Newman 3, Rey 3)

Quinzième août, 1986 (Trintignant 3)

Quirinale, 1947 (Delli Colli 4)

Quits, 1915 (Chaney 3, Furthman 4)
Quitter, 1916 (Barrymore 3)
Quitter, 1929 (Walker 4)
Quixote, 1964 (Baillie 2)
Quiz Whiz, 1958 (Three Stooges 3)

Quo Vadis, 1901 (Pathé 4)
Quo Vadis, 1923 (Jannings 3, Courant 4)
Quo Vadis, 1951 (Huston 2, LeRoy 2,
    Kerr 3, Loren 3, Pidgeon 3, Taylor, E. 3,
    Taylor, R. 3, Ustinov 3, Behrman 4,

Ellenshaw 4, Gibbons 4, Gillespie 4,
    Levien 4, Rozsa 4, Surtees 4)
Quo Vadis, 1985 (Von Sydow 3)
Quo Vadis Homo Sapiens, 1983 (Popescu-
    Gopo 4)

R

R.A.F., 1935 (Rank 4)
R.F.D. 10,000 B.C., 1917 (O'Brien 4)
RPM, 1970 (Kamer 2, Quinn 3)
R, 1980 (Frampton 2)
R N 37, 1937 (Leenhardt 2)
R-1, 1924 (Fischinger 2)
Raag Yaman Kalyan, 1972 (Benegal 2)
Raaste Ka Patthar, 1972 (Bachchan 3)
Raaste pyare ke, 1982 (Azmi 3)
Raawan, 1984 (Patil 3)
Rabbia, 1963 (Pasolini 2)
Rabbit Every Monday, 1951 (Blanc 4,
    Freleng 4, Stalling 4)
Rabbit Fire, 1951 (Blanc 4, Jones 4,
    Maltese 4, Stalling 4)
Rabbit Hood, 1949 (Blanc 4, Jones 4,
    Maltese 4, Stalling 4)
Rabbit of Seville, 1950 (Blanc 4, Jones 4,
    Maltese 4, Stalling 4)
Rabbit Punch, 1948 (Blanc 4, Jones 4,
    Stalling 4)
Rabbit Rampage, 1955 (Blanc 4, Jones 4,
    Maltese 4)
Rabbit Romeo, 1957 (Blanc 4, McKimson 4)
Rabbit, Run, 1970 (Caan 3)
Rabbit Seasoning, 1952 (Blanc 4, Jones 4,
    Maltese 4, Stalling 4)
Rabbit Stew and Rabbits Too, 1969 (Blanc 4,
    McKimson 4)
Rabbit Test, 1978 (McDowall 3, Ballard 4)
Rabbit Transit, 1947 (Blanc 4, Freleng 4,
    Stalling 4)
Rabbit Trap, 1959 (Borgnine 3)
Rabbit's Feat, 1960 (Blanc 4, Jones 4)
Rabbit's Kin, 1952 (Blanc 4, McKimson 4,
    Stalling 4)
Rabbit's Moon, 1971 (Anger 2)
Rabbitson Crusoe, 1956 (Blanc 4, Freleng 4)
Rabindranath Tagore, 1961 (Ray 2,
    Chandragupta 4, Datta 4)
Rabotchaia slobodka, 1912 (Mozhukin 3)
Racambole. See Rocambole, 1946
Racconti d'estate, 1958 (Mastroianni 3,
    Morgan 3, Sordi 3, Amidei 4, Flaiano 4)
Racconti di Canterbury, 1972 (Welles 2,
    Delli Colli 4, Donati 4, Morricone 4)
Racconti romani, 1955 (De Sica 2, Rosi 2,
    Age and Scarpelli 4, Amidei 4)
Racconti romani di Pietro l'Aretino, 1972
    (Cervi 3)
Raccourci. See Tempo di uccidere, 1989
Race, 1914 (Sennett 2)
Race, 1933 (Rooney 3)
Race des ''Seigneurs'', 1974 (Delon 3,
    Moreau 3, Sarde 4)
Race for a Bride, 1914 (Browning 2)
Race for a Gold Mine, 1915 (Mix 3)

Race for Life. See Mask of Dust, 1954
Race for Life. See Si tous les gars du monde,
    1955
Race for the Yankee Zephyr, 1982
    (Pleasence 3)
Race Gang. See Green Cockatoo, 1937
Race Gang. See Four Dark Hours, 1939
Race Riot, 1929 (Lantz 4)
Race Street, 1948 (Bendix 3, Raft 3, Hunt 4)
Race with the Devil, 1975 (Oates 3,
    Rosenman 4)
Racers, 1955 (Cobb 3, Douglas 3, Bass 4,
    North 4, Wheeler 4)
Racetrack, 1932 (Cruze 2)
Racetrack, 1985 (Wiseman 2)
Rache der Toten, 1917 (Krauss 3)
Rache des Blutes, 1914 (Wegener 3)
Rache des Gefallenen, 1917 (Albers 3)
Rache einer Frau, 1921 (Wiene 2)
Rache ist mein, 1912 (Messter 4)
Rachel and the Stranger, 1948 (Holden 3,
    Mitchum 3, Young 3, D'Agostino 4,
    Head 4, Salt 4)
Rachel, Rachel, 1968 (Newman 3,
    Woodward 3, Allen 4)
Rachel's Man, 1975 (Rooney 3)
Rachel's Sin, 1911 (Hepworth 2)
Rächer, 1960 (Kinski 3)
Racing Fool, 1927 (Brown 4)
Racing Lady, 1937 (Carey 3, McDaniel 3)
Racing Luck. See Red Hot Tires, 1935
Racing Luck, 1948 (Katzman 4)
Racing Romance, 1926 (Brown 4)
Racing Romeo, 1927 (Wood 2, Clarke 4)
Racing Strain, 1918 (Marsh 3)
Racing the Chutes at Dreamland, 1904
    (Bitzer 4)
Rack, 1916 (Carré 4)
Rack, 1956 (Marvin 3, Newman 3,
    O'Brien 3, Pidgeon 3, Deutsch 4)
Racket, 1928 (Milestone 2, Gaudio 4)
Racket, 1951 (Cromwell 2, Mitchum 3,
    Ryan 3, Burnett 4)
Racket Buster, 1949 (Terry 4)
Racket Busters, 1938 (Rossen 2, Bogart 3,
    Deutsch 4, Edeson 4, Friedhofer 4)
Racket Cheers, 1930 (Sennett 2)
Racket Man, 1943 (Robinson 4)
Racketeer, 1929 (Lombard 3)
Racketeer Rabbit, 1946 (Blanc 4, Freleng 4,
    Maltese 4, Stalling 4)
Racketeers in Exile, 1937 (Ballard 4)
Rackety Rax, 1932 (Bond 3, McLaglen 3)
Rad, 1985 (Needham 4)
Rade, 1927 (Braunberger 4)
Radeau avec baigneurs, 1895 (Lumière 2)
Radha Krishna, 1954 (Burman 4)

Radical Lawyer, 1973 (Menges 4)
Radio City Revels, 1938 (Miller 3, Hunt 4,
    Pan 4, Veiller 4)
Radio Days, 1986 (Allen 2, Farrow 3,
    Keaton 3)
Radio Dynamics, 1942 (Fischinger 2,
    Ford 2)
Radio Follies. See Radio Parade of 1935,
    1934
Radio Girl, 1932 (Terry 4)
Radio Kisses, 1930 (Sennett 2)
Radio Lover, 1936 (Dalrymple 4)
Radio Mad, 1924 (Roach 4)
Radio Mania, 1923 (Folsey 4)
Radio On, 1979 (Menges 4)
Radio Parade of 1935, 1934 (Hay 3)
Radio Ranch. See Phantom Empire,
    1935
Radio Rhythm, 1931 (Lantz 4)
Radio Riot, 1930 (Fleischer 4)
Radioens Barndom, 1949 (Dreyer 2)
Radish and Carrot. See Daikon to ninjin,
    1965
Rafael Alberti, un retrato del poeta por
    Fernando Birri, 1983 (Birri 2)
Rafferty and the Gold Dust Twins, 1975
    (Arkin 3, Stanton 3)
Raffles, 1914 (Sennett 2)
Raffles, 1930 (D'Arrast 2, Colman 3,
    Francis 3, Barnes 4, Goldwyn 4,
    Howard 4, Menzies 4, Toland 4)
Raffles, 1940 (Wood 2, De Havilland 3,
    Niven 3, Banton 4, Basevi 4, Goldwyn 4,
    Howard 4, Toland 4, Young 4)
Raffles sur la ville, 1957 (Legrand 4)
Raffles, the Amateur Cracksman, 1905
    (Blackton 2)
Raffles, the Amateur Cracksman, 1917
    (Barrymore 3)
Raffles, the American Cracksman, 1905
    (Anderson 3)
Rafle de chiens, 1904 (Guy 2)
Rafles sur la ville, 1954 (Manès 3, Piccoli 3,
    Vanel 3)
Rafter Romance, 1933 (Rogers 3,
    Benchley 4, MacGowan 4, Plunkett 4,
    Polglase 4, Steiner 4)
Raga and the Emotions, 1971 (Benegal 2)
Ragamuffin, 1916 (Sweet 3)
Ragazza con la pistola, 1968 (Monicelli 2,
    Baker 3, Vitti 3)
Ragazza con la valigia, 1960 (Cardinale 3,
    Volonté 3)
Ragazza del bersagliere, 1967 (Blasetti 2)
Ragazza del palio, 1957 (Dors 3, Gassman 3,
    Rotunno 4)
Ragazza della Salina, 1957 (Mastroianni 3)

Ragazza di Bube, 1963 (Cardinale 3, Gherardi 4)

Ragazza di Piazza S. Pietro, 1958 (De Sica 2)

Ragazza e il generale, 1967 (Steiger 3, Morricone 4)

Ragazza in Pigiamo Giallo, 1978 (Milland 3)

Ragazza in prestito, 1965 (Brazzi 3, Girardot 3)

Ragazza in vetrina, 1961 (Pasolini 2, Flaiano 4)

Ragazze de marito, 1952 (Age and Scarpelli 4)

Ragazze de San Frediano, 1954 (Di Venanzo 4)

Ragazze delle nuvole, 1957 (Cervi 3)

Ragazze di Piazza di Spagna, 1952 (Mastroianni 3, Amidei 4)

Ragazze d'oggi, 1955 (Rosay 3, Ponti 4)

Ragazze e il generale, 1967 (Ponti 4)

Ragazze in bianco, 1949 (Antonioni 2)

Ragazzi della via Paal, 1935 (Monicelli 2)

Ragazzi di Bube, 1963 (Cristaldi 4, Di Venanzo 4)

Ragazzo del bersagliere, 1966 (Brazzi 3)

Ragazzo di borgata, 1976 (Rota 4)

Ragazzo di Calabria, 1987 (Volonté 3)

Rage, 1966 (Ford 3)

Rage, 1972 (Scott 3, Sheen 3, Schifrin 4)

Rage, 1991 (Golan and Globus 4)

Rage at Dawn, 1955 (Scott 3)

Rage de dents, 1900 (Guy 2)

Rage in Harlem, 1991 (Bernstein 4)

Rage in Heaven, 1941 (Van Dyke 2, Bergman 3, Homolka 3, Montgomery 3, Sanders 3, Kaper 4)

Rage Net, 1988 (Brakhage 2)

Rage of Paris, 1938 (Darrieux 3, Salter 4)

Rage of the Buccaneer. See Gordon, il Pirato Nero, 1961

Rage to Kill, 1989 (Reed 3)

Rågens rike, 1951 (Nykvist 4)

Ragged Angels. See They Shall Have Music, 1939

Ragged Flag. See Ranru no hata, 1974

Ragged Heiress, 1922 (Furthman 4)

Raggedy Ann and Andy, 1941 (Fleischer 4)

Raggedy Ann and Andy, 1977 (Williams 4)

Raggedy Man, 1981 (Spacek 3, Goldsmith 4, Shepard 4)

Raggedy Rawney, 1987 (Hoskins 3)

Raggedy Rose, 1926 (Laurel and Hardy 3, Normand 3)

Raggedy Rug, 1963 (Hanna and Barbera 4)

Raging Bull, 1980 (Schrader 2, Scorsese 2, De Niro 3, Winkler 4)

Raging Moon, 1971 (McDowell 3)

Raging Tide, 1951 (Winters 3, Metty 4)

Raging Waters. See Green Promise, 1949

Ragione per vivere e una per morire, 1972 (Coburn 3)

Rags, 1915 (Pickford 3)

Ragtime, 1981 (Forman 2, Cagney 3, Love 3, O'Connor 3, De Laurentiis 4, Ondříček 4)

Ragtime Bear, 1949 (Bosustow 4, Hubley 4)

Ragtime Romeo, 1931 (Iwerks 4)

Ragtime Snap Shots, 1914 (Lloyd 3, Roach 4)

Rahi, 1953 (Anand 3, Abbas 4, Biswas 4)

Raid, 1954 (Bancroft 3, Marvin 3, Ballard 4)

Raid on Entebbe, 1976 (Bronson 3, Finch 3, Sidney 3)

Raid on France, 1942 (Balcon 4)

Raid on Rommel, 1971 (Hathaway 2, Burton 3)

Raid Paris-Monte Carlo en deux heures, 1905 (Méliès 2)

Raider. See Western Approaches, 1944

Raider of the Golden Gulch, 1932 (Canutt 4)

Raiders, 1916 (Mix 3)

Raiders of Old California, 1957 (Van Cleef 3)

Raiders of San Joaquin, 1943 (Salter 4)

Raiders of the Desert, 1941 (Salter 4)

Raiders of the Lost Ark, 1981 (Kasdan 2, Lucas 2, Spielberg 2, Elliott 3, Ford 3, Burtt 4, Edlund 4, Slocombe 4, Williams 4)

Raiders of the Seven Seas, 1953 (Reed 3)

Raiding the Raiders, 1945 (Terry 4)

Raigeki tai shutsudo, 1944 (Tsuburaya 4)

Rail Rider, 1916 (Tourneur 2, Carré 4)

Railroad Man. See Ferroviere, 1956

Railroaded, 1947 (Mann 2)

Railroadin', 1929 (Roach 4)

Rail-rodder, 1965 (Keaton 2)

Rails into Laramie, 1954 (Duryea 3, Van Cleef 3)

Rain. See Sadie Thompson, 1928

Rain. See Regen, 1929

Rain, 1932 (Milestone 2, Bondi 3, Crawford 3, Huston 3, Day 4, Newman 4)

Rain, 1940 (Eisler 4)

Rain for a Dusty Summer, 1971 (Borgnine 3)

Rain Makers, 1951 (Terry 4)

Rain Man, 1988 (Levinson 2, Cruise 3, Hoffman 3)

Rain of Paris, 1980 (Dinov 4)

Rain or Shine, 1930 (Capra 2, Cohn 4, Swerling 4, Walker 4)

Rain People, 1969 (Coppola 2, Caan 3, Duvall 3, Murch 4)

Rainbow, 1989 (Russell 2, Jackson 3)

Rainbow Dance, 1936 (Cavalcanti 2, Lye 4)

Rainbow Island, 1917 (Daniels 3, Lloyd 3, Roach 4)

Rainbow Island, 1944 (De Carlo 3, Lamour 3, Dreier 4, Head 4, Struss 4)

Rainbow Jacket, 1954 (Dearden 2, Alwyn 4, Clarke 4, Heller 4)

Rainbow on the River, 1936 (Beavers 3)

Rainbow over Texas, 1946 (Rogers 3)

Rainbow Professional. See Cobra Mission, 1986

Rainbow Round My Shoulder, 1952 (Edwards 3)

Rainbow Thief, 1990 (Lee 3, O'Toole 3, Sharif 3)

Rainbow Trail, 1925 (Mix 3)

Rainbow Valley, 1935 (Wayne 3)

Rainmaker, 1956 (Hepburn 3, Lancaster 3, Head 4, Lang 4, North 4, Wallis 4)

Rainmakers, 1935 (McCord 4, Plunkett 4)

Rains Came, 1939 (Brown 2, Darwell 3, Loy 3, Power 3, Brown 4, Dunne 4, Glennon 4, Miller 4, Newman 4, Zanuck 4)

Rain's Hat, 1978 (Zetterling 2)

Rains of Ranchipur, 1955 (Negulesco 2, Burton 3, MacMurray 3, Turner 3, Friedhofer 4, Krasner 4, LeMaire 4, Rose 4)

Raintree County, 1957 (Dmytryk 2, Clift 3, Marvin 3, Moorehead 3, Saint 3, Taylor 3, Green 4, Plunkett 4, Surtees 4)

Rainy Day. See Deštivý den, 1963

Rainy Day Women, 1984 (Cusack 3)

Rainy Days, 1928 (Roach 4)

Rainy Days, 1929 (Roach 4)

Rainy Knight, 1925 (Sennett 2)

Rainy Night Duel. See Kuroobi sangokushi, 1956

Raise Ravens. See **Cria cuervos, 1976**

Raise the Rent, 1920 (Roach 4)

Raise the Titanic!, 1980 (Guinness 3, Robards 3, Barry 4)

Raisin in the Sun, 1961 (Poitier 3)

Raising a Riot, 1955 (More 3, Challis 4, Dalrymple 4, Korda 4)

Raising the Wind, 1961 (Dillon 4)

Raisins Sold Out!, 1990 (Vinton 4)

Raison avant la passion, 1968 (Wieland 2)

Raison d'état, 1978 (Cayatte 2, Vitti 3)

Ráj a peklo bohemy. See Plameny života, 1920

Raja Harishchandra, 1913 (Phalke 2)

Raja Harishchandra, 1914 (Phalke 2)

Rajah, 1919 (Daniels 3, Lloyd 3, Roach 4)

Rajgi, 1937 (Burman 4)

Raju aur Gangaram, 1964 (Biswas 4)

Rakei kazoku, 1954 (Yamamura 3)

Rake's Progress, 1945 (Launder and Gilliat 2, Harrison 3, Alwyn 4, Mathieson 4, Rank 4)

Raketbussen. See Rocket Bus, 1929

Räkna de lyckliga stunderna blott, 1944 (Dahlbeck 3)

Rakoczy-Marsch, 1933 (Fröhlich 3)

Rakudai wa shita keredo, 1930 (Ryu 3, Tanaka 3)

Rakugaki kokuban, 1959 (Shindo 2)

Rakvičkárna, 1966 (Švankmajer 4)

Rallare, 1947 (Sjöström 2)

Rally, 1980 (Lee 3)

Rally Round the Flag, 1909 (Olcott 2)

Rally 'round the Flag, Boys!, 1958 (McCarey 2, Newman 3, Weld 3, Woodward 3, LeMaire 4, Shamroy 4, Wheeler 4)

Ram Aur Shyam, 1967 (Kumar 3)

Ram Balram, 1980 (Bachchan 3)

Ramasagul, 1985 (Popescu-Gopo 4)

Rambles Through Hopland, 1913 (Pearson 2)

Ramblin' Kid, 1923 (Miller 4)

Rambling Rose, 1990 (Duvall 3)

Rambo: First Blood II, 1985 (Stallone 3, Cardiff 4, Goldsmith 4)

Rambo III, 1988 (Stallone 3, Goldsmith 4)

Ramiet and Julio, 1915 (Bray 4)

Ramkinkar, 1975 (Ghatak 2)

Ramona, 1910 (Walthall 3, Bitzer 4)

Ramona, 1916 (Crisp 3)

Ramona, 1928 (Del Rio 3, D'Agostino 4)

Ramona, 1936 (King 2, Ameche 3, Carradine 3, Darwell 3, Young 3, Newman 4, Trotti 4)

Ramoneur malgré lui, 1912 (Cohl 4)

Rampage, 1963 (Hathaway 2, Hawkins 3, Mitchum 3, Bernstein 4)

Rampage, 1987 (Friedkin 2, Morricone 4)

Rampage at Apache Wells. See Ölprinz, 1965

Ramparts We Watch, 1940 (De Rochemont 4)

Ramper, der Tiermensch, 1927 (Wegener 3)

Ramrod, 1947 (De Toth 2, Crisp 3, Lake 3, McCrea 3, Deutsch 4, Harlan 4, Head 4)

Ramsbottom Rides Again, 1956 (Baxter 2)

Ramuntcho, 1938 (Jouvet 3, Rosay 3, Douy 4, Lourié 4)
Ramuntcho, 1958 (Broca 2, Coutard 4, De Beauregard 4)
Ramuru eteruneru, 1935 (Takamine 3)
Ramuz, passage d'un poète, 1959 (Tanner 2)
Ran, 1985 (Kurosawa 2, Muraki 4, Takemitsu 4)
Ranch Chicken, 1911 (Dwan 2)
Ranch Detective, 1911 (Dwan 2)
Ranch Feud, 1913 (Anderson 3)
Ranch Girl series, 1910–13 (Anderson 3)
Ranch Girl, 1911 (Dwan 2)
Ranch Life in the Great Southwest, 1910 (Mix 3)
Ranch Life on the Range, 1911 (Dwan 2)
Ranch Romance, 1914 (Chaney 3)
Ranch Tenor, 1911 (Dwan 2)
Ranchero's Revenge, 1913 (Griffith 2, Carey 3, Bitzer 4)
Rancher's Failing, 1913 (Bosworth 3)
Rancher's Revenge, 1913 (Barrymore 3)
Ranchman series, 1909–13 (Anderson 3)
Ranchman's Marathon, 1911 (Dwan 2)
Ranchman's Nerve, 1911 (Dwan 2)
Rancho alegre, 1940 (Fernández 2)
Rancho Deluxe, 1974 (Bridges 3, Stanton 3, Fraker 4)
Rancho Grande, 1940 (Autry 3)
Rancho Notorious, 1952 (Lang 2, Dietrich 3, Kennedy 3, Friedhofer 4, Mohr 4, Taradash 4, Westmore Family 4)
Rancid Ransom, 1962 (Hanna and Barbera 4)
Rande des Schreckens, 1960 (Rasp 3)
Randolph Family. See Dear Octopus, 1943
Random Harvest, 1942 (LeRoy 2, Colman 3, Garson 3, Mayer 4, Ruttenberg 4, Stothart 4)
Randy Rides Alone, 1934 (Wayne 3, Canutt 4)
Randy Strikes Oil. See Fighting Texans, 1933
Range Boss, 1917 (Van Dyke 2)
Range Defenders, 1937 (Canutt 4)
Range Feud, 1930 (Wayne 3)
Range Girl and the Cowboy, 1915 (Mix 3)
Range Law, 1913 (Mix 3)
Range Pals, 1911 (Bosworth 3)
Range Rider, 1910 (Mix 3)
Range War, 1939 (Harlan 4, Head 4, Young 4)
Ranger and the Lady, 1940 (Johnson 3, Rogers 3, Canutt 4)
Ranger of Lonesome Gulf, 1913 (Seitz 4)
Ranger of the Big Pines, 1925 (Van Dyke 2)
Ranger's Bride, 1910 (Anderson 3)
Rangers of Fortune, 1940 (Wood 2, MacMurray 3, Dreier 4, Head 4)
Rangers of Yellowstone, 1963 (Fonda 3)
Ranger's Romance, 1914 (Mix 3)
Rango, 1931 (Schoedsack 2)
Rangun, 1927 (Tsuburaya 4)
Rangun, 1973 (Hasegawa 3)
Rank and File, 1971 (Loach 2)
Ranny v lesie, 1964 (Olbrychski 3)
Ranru no hata, 1974 (Yoshimura 2, Shimura 3, Toda 4)
Ransom, 1928 (Walker 4)
Ransom!, 1956 (Ford 3, Reed 3, Rose 4)
Ransom. See Tengoku to jigoku, 1963
Ransom, 1974 (Connery 3, Goldsmith 4, Nykvist 4)

Ransom for a Dead Man, 1971 (Falk 3, Grant 3)
Ranson's Folly, 1926 (Olcott 2, Barthelmess 3)
Rapaces diurnes et nocturnes, 1913 (Burel 4)
Rapa-Nui, 1928 (Andrejew 4)
Rape and Marriage: The Rideout Case, 1980 (Rourke 3)
Rape of Czechoslovakia, 1939 (Weiss 2)
Rape of Malaya. See Town Like Alice, 1956
Raphael et Cacolet, 1938 (Fernandel 3)
Raphaël le Tatoué, 1938 (Christian-Jaque 2)
Rapid Fire Romance, 1926 (Brown 4)
Rápido de las 9.15, 1941 (Figueroa 4)
Rapids, 1922 (Astor 3)
Rappa to musume, 1933 (Takamine 3)
Rappel immédiat, 1939 (Von Stroheim 2)
Rappin', 1985 (Golan and Globus 4)
Rapporto segreto, 1967 (Storaro 4)
Rappresaglia, 1973 (Burton 3, Mastroianni 3, Morricone 4, Ponti 4)
Rapt, 1934 (Honegger 4)
Rapto, 1953 (Fernández 2, Félix 3)
Rapture, 1965 (Douglas 3, Delerue 4, Flaiano 4)
Rapunzel, 1897 (Messter 4)
Rapunzel. See Story of Hansel and Gretel, 1951
Rare Breed, 1966 (Johnson 3, O'Hara 3, Stewart 3, Clothier 4, Needham 4, Whitlock 4, Williams 4)
Rascal. See Narazumono, 1956
Rascal, 1969 (Lanchester 3, Pidgeon 3)
Rascal of Wolfish Ways, 1915 (Sennett 2)
Rascals, 1938 (Cronjager 4)
Rascel Fifi, 1957 (Cristaldi 4, Di Venanzo 4)
Rascel Marine, 1959 (Cristaldi 4, Di Venanzo 4)
Rashomon, 1950 (Kurosawa 2, Kyo 3, Mifune 3, Mori 3, Shimura 3, Hayasaka 4, Miyagawa 4)
Raske Detektiver. See Bleka Greven, 1937
Raske Riviera rejsende, 1924 (Madsen and Schenstrøm 3)
Raskenstam, 1983 (Andersson 3)
Raskenstam—The Casanova of Sweden. See Raskenstam, 1983
Raskolnikow, 1923 (Wiene 2, Andrejew 4)
Rasp, 1931 (Powell and Pressburger 2)
Raspberry Ripple, 1988 (Dunaway 3)
Raspberry Romance, 1925 (Sennett 2)
Rasplata, 1970 (Yankovsky 3)
Raspoutine, 1954 (Brasseur 3)
Rasputin, 1931 (Veidt 3, Courant 4)
Rasputin. See Tragédie impériale, 1938
Rasputin and the Empress, 1932 (Barrymore, E. 3, Barrymore, J. 3, Barrymore, L. 3, Adrian 4, Daniels 4, MacArthur 4, Mayer 4, Stothart 4)
Rasputin the Mad Monk. See Rasputin and the Empress, 1932
Rasputin the Mad Monk, 1966 (Lee 3, Carreras 4)
Rasputin und die Frauen. See Rasputins Liebesabenteuer, 1928
Rasputins Liebesabenteuer, 1928 (Albers 3)
Rasskazi o Lenine, 1957 (Moskvin 4)
Rasslin' Round, 1934 (Iwerks 4)
Rastus and the Game-Cock, 1913 (Sennett 2)
Rastus' Rabid Rabbit Hunt, 1915 (Bray 4)
Rat, 1925 (Marsh 3, Novello 3, Balcon 4)
Rat, 1937 (Wilcox 2, Walbrook 3, Young 4)
Rat, 1960 (Zavattini 4)
Rat der Götter, 1950 (Eisler 4)

Rat Destruction, 1942 (Alwyn 4)
Rat Fink, 1965 (Zsigmond 4)
Rat Life and Diet in North America, 1968 (Wieland 2)
Rat Race, 1960 (Mulligan 2, Curtis 3, Reynolds 3, Bernstein 4, Burks 4, Head 4, Kanin 4, Westmore Family 4)
Rat Race. See Je vais craquer, 1979
Ratai, 1962 (Shindo 3, Yamada 3, Takemitsu 4)
Ratataplan, 1979 (Cristaldi 4)
Ratboy, 1986 (Baker 4)
Râtelier de la belle-mère, 1909 (Linder 3)
Rationing, 1944 (Beery 3)
Raton Pass, 1951 (Neal 3, Steiner 4)
Rats. See Ratten, 1955
Rat's Knuckles, 1924 (Roach 4)
Rats of Tobruk, 1944 (Finch 3, Rafferty 3)
Rätsel der roten Orchidee, 1961 (Kinski 3, Lee 3, Rasp 3)
Rätsel der Sphinx, 1921 (Dreier 4)
Rätsel um Beate, 1938 (Dagover 3)
Rätsel von Bangalor, 1917 (Leni 2, Veidt 3)
Ratten, 1921 (Jannings 3, Freund 4)
Ratten, 1955 (Siodmak 2, Schell 3)
Rätten att Älska, 1956 (Von Sydow 3)
Rattenfänger von Hameln, 1918 (Wegener 3, Reiniger 4)
Rattle of a Simple Man, 1964 (Box 4)
Rattled Rooster, 1948 (Blanc 4, Stalling 4)
Rattler's Hiss, 1920 (Eason 4)
Rattlesnakes and Gunpowder, 1911 (Dwan 2)
Rattornas Vinter, 1988 (Falk 3)
Raub der Mona Lisa, 1931 (Gründgens 3, Andrejew 4, Reisch 4)
Raub des Sabinerinned, 1954 (Warm 4)
Räuberbraut, 1916 (Wiene 2)
Rausch, 1919 (Nielsen 3, Freund 4, Kräly 4)
Rauschgift. See Weisse Dämon, 1932
Rauschgold, 1920 (Albers 3)
Ravagers, 1979 (Borgnine 3, Harris 3)
Raven, 1915 (Van Dyke 2, Walthall 3)
Raven, 1935 (Karloff 3, Lugosi 3, D'Agostino 4, Pierce 4, Schary 4)
Raven. See Corbeau, 1943
Raven, 1963 (Corman 2, Karloff 3, Lorre 3, Nicholson 3, Price 3, Crosby 4)
Ravin sans fond, 1917 (Gaumont 4)
Ravishing Idiot. See Ravissante idiote, 1964
Ravissante, 1960 (Noiret 3)
Ravissante Idiote, 1964 (Bardot 3, Perkins 3, Legrand 4)
Raw Deal, 1948 (Mann 2, Trevor 3)
Raw Deal, 1986 (Schwarzenegger 3)
Raw Edge, 1956 (De Carlo 3, Salter 4)
Raw Meat. See Death Line, 1972
Raw! Raw! Rooster, 1956 (Blanc 4, McKimson 4, Stalling 4)
Raw Wind in Eden, 1958 (Williams 3, Salter 4)
Rawhide, 1951 (Hathaway 2, Hayward 3, Power 3, Krasner 4, LeMaire 4, Nichols 4, Wheeler 4)
Rawhide Trail, 1958 (Struss 4)
Rawhide Years, 1956 (Curtis 3, Kennedy 3, Maté 4, Salter 4)
Ray Blas, 1947 (Auric 4)
Rayando el sol, 1945 (Armendáriz 3)
Razbitaya vaza, 1941 (Volkov 2)
Razgrom nemetzkikhy voisk pod Moskvoi. See Moscow Strikes Back, 1942
Razón de la culpa, 1942 (Infante 3)

Razor's Edge, 1946 (Goulding 2, Baxter 3, Kortner 3, Lanchester 3, Marshall 3, Power 3, Tierney 3, Webb 3, Day 4, LeMaire 4, Miller 4, Newman 4, Trotti 4, Zanuck 4)

Razor's Edge, 1984 (Elliott 3, Russell 4)

Razumov. *See* Sous les yeux d'occident, 1936

Razzberries, 1931 (Terry 4)

Razzia. *See* Razzia sur la chnouff, 1955

Razzia sur la chnouff, 1955 (Dalio 3, Félix 3, Gabin 3)

Razzle Dazzle, 1903 (Porter 2)

Re di Poggioreale, 1961 (Borgnine 3, Gherardi 4)

Re Lear, 1911 (Bertini 3, Pathé 4)

Re: Lucky Luciano. *See* A proposito Lucky Luciano, 1973

Re si diverte, 1941 (Brazzi 3, Simon 3)

Reach for the Sky, 1956 (More 3, Addison 4, Rank 4)

Reach for Tomorrow, 1958 (Fonda 3)

Reach, Mother's Song. *See* Todoke haha no uta, 1959

Reaching for the Moon, 1917 (Fleming 2, Fairbanks 3, Edeson 4, Emerson 4, Loos 4)

Reaching for the Moon, 1931 (Goulding 2, Crosby 3, Daniels 3, Fairbanks 3, Horton 3, Berlin 4, Fleischer 4, Menzies 4, Newman 4)

Reaching for the Sun, 1941 (Wellman 2, McCrea 3, Head 4, Young 4)

Readin' and Writin', 1931 (Roach 4)

Readin' 'ritin' and 'rithmetic, 1951 (Fleischer 4)

Ready for Love, 1934 (Bondi 3, Lupino 3, Shamroy 4)

Ready for the People, 1964 (Sloane 3)

Ready Money, 1914 (De Mille 2)

Ready, Set, Zoom!, 1955 (Blanc 4, Jones 4)

Ready, Willing, and Able, 1937 (Keeler 3, Wyman 3, Mercer 4, Polito 4, Wald 4)

Ready, Woolen and Able, 1960 (Blanc 4)

Real Adventure, 1922 (Vidor 2, Barnes 4)

Real Bloke, 1935 (Baxter 2)

Real Estate Fraud, 1911 (Dwan 2)

Real Genius, 1985 (Zsigmond 4)

Real Glory, 1939 (Hathaway 2, Cooper 3, Crawford 3, Niven 3, Basevi 4, Goldwyn 4, Mandell 4, Maté 4, Newman 4, Riskin 4, Swerling 4)

Real McCoy, 1929 (Roach 4)

Real McCoy, 1950 (Abbott and Costello 3)

Real Men, 1987 (Alonzo 4)

Real Thing, 1985 (Sheen 3)

Real Thing in Cowboys, 1914 (Mix 3)

Realization of a Negro's Ambition, 1916 (Johnson 3)

Really Scent, 1959 (Blanc 4, Jones 4)

Reap the Wild Wind, 1942 (De Mille 2, Beavers 3, Costello 3, Goddard 3, Hayward 3, Massey 3, McDaniel 3, Milland 3, Preston 3, Wayne 3, Bennett 4, Dreier 4, Edouart 4, Young 4)

Rear Column, 1979 (Pinter 4)

Rear Gunner, 1944 (Meredith 3)

Rear Window, 1954 (Hitchcock 2, Kelly 3, Ritter 3, Stewart 3, Burks 4, Fulton 4, Hayes 4, Head 4, Waxman 4)

Rearranged, 1979 (Kelly 3)

Rearview Mirror, 1984 (Remick 3)

Reason and Emotion. *See* Rozum a cit, 1962

Reason over Passion. *See* Raison avant la passion, 1968

Reasons of State. *See* Recurso del método, 1977

Rebecca, 1940 (Hitchcock 2, Fontaine 3, Olivier 3, Sanders 3, Barnes 4, Harrison 4, Selznick 4, Sherwood 4, Waxman 4, Westmore Family 4, Wheeler 4)

Rebecca of Sunnybrook Farm, 1917 (Neilan 2, Pickford 3, Marion 4)

Rebecca of Sunnybrook Farm, 1932 (Bellamy 3, Marsh 3, Behrman 4, Friedhofer 4, Levien 4)

Rebecca of Sunnybrook Farm, 1938 (Dwan 2, Pangborn 3, Robinson 3, Scott 3, Temple 3, Miller 4)

Rebecca's Daughter, 1990 (Forsyth 2)

Rebecca's Wedding Day, 1914 (Sennett 2, Arbuckle 3)

Rebel, 1932 (Banky 3)

Rebel. *See* Bushwackers, 1952

Rebel, 1961 (Reed 3, Sanders 3)

Rebel, 1985 (Dillon 3)

Rebel in Town, 1956 (Johnson 3)

Rebel Rabbit, 1949 (Blanc 4, McKimson 4, Stalling 4)

Rebel Rousers, 1970 (Dern 3, Stanton 3, Kovacs 4)

Rebel Set, 1959 (Struss 4)

Rebel Son, 1939 (Korda 4)

Rebel without a Cause, 1955 (Ray 2, Dean 3, Hopper 3, Mineo 3, Wood 3, Haller 4, Rosenman 4, Warner 4)

Rebel without Claws, 1961 (Blanc 4, Freleng 4)

Rebeldia, 1953 (Rey 3)

Rebelión de la sierra, 1957 (Figueroa 4)

Rebelión de los colgados, 1954 (Fernández 2, Armendáriz 3, Figueroa 4)

Rebellen. *See* One, Take Two, 1978

Rebellion, 1931 (Rooney 3)

Rebellion, 1936 (Hayworth 3)

Rebellion. *See* Hanran, 1954

Rebellion. *See* Joi-uchi, 1967

Rebellion in Cuba. *See* Chivato, 1961

Rebellion of Kitty Belle, 1914 (Gish 3)

Rebellious Blossom, 1911 (Lawrence 3)

Rebelote, 1983 (Léaud 3)

Rebels of the High Sea. *See* Shujin-sen, 1956

Rebirth of the Soil. *See* Yomigaeru daichi, 1970

Reborn. *See* Renacida, 1981

Rebound, 1931 (Loy 3, Mandell 4)

Rebound. *See* Footsteps in the Fog, 1955

Rebozo de la soledad, 1952 (Armendáriz 3, Figueroa 4)

Rebus, 1968 (Harvey 3)

Rebus, 1989 (Rotunno 4)

Rece do gory, 1967 (Skolimowski 2)

Reception of British Fleet, 1905 (Bitzer 4)

Recherche d'un appartement, 1906 (Guy 2)

Recherche du soleil, 1985 (Schroeter 2)

Recherches, 1958 (Braunberger 4)

Recht auf Liebe, 1939 (Wegener 3)

Récif de corail, 1938 (Gabin 3, Morgan 3, Spaak 4)

Récit du colonel, 1908 (Feuillade 2)

Reckless, 1935 (Fleming 2, Fleming 2, Harlow 3, Powell 3, Rooney 3, Russell 3, Adrian 4, Booth 4, Folsey 4, Gibbons 4)

Reckless, 1984 (Ballhaus 4)

Reckless Age, 1944 (Darwell 3, Pangborn 3)

Reckless Age. *See* Dragstrip Riot, 1958

Reckless Hour, 1931 (Blondell 3)

Reckless Lady, 1926 (Haller 4)

Reckless Living, 1931 (Beavers 3)

Reckless Living, 1938 (Beavers 3)

Reckless Moment, 1949 (Ophüls 2, Bennett 3, Mason 3, Cohn 4, Guffey 4, Salter 4, Wanger 4)

Reckless Romeo. *See* Cream Puff Romance, 1916

Reckless Romeo, 1917 (Keaton 2)

Reckless Rosie. *See* Naughty Baby, 1928

Reckless Wrestlers, 1916 (Lloyd 3, Roach 4)

Reckoning, 1908 (Griffith 2, Lawrence 3, Bitzer 4)

Reckoning, 1970 (Roberts 3, Arnold 4)

Recognition, 1911 (Dwan 2)

Recoil, 1917 (Grot 4, Miller 4)

Recollections of Boyhood: An Interview with Joseph Welch, 1954 (Van Dyke 2)

Récolte des betteraves, 1901 (Gaumont 4)

Reconstructed Rebel, 1912 (Bosworth 3, Mix 3)

Recontre à Paris, 1955 (Spaak 4)

Recontres sur le Rhin, 1953 (Fradetal 4)

Record Breakers, 1914 (Browning 2)

Record of a Living Being. *See* Ikimono no kiroku, 1955

Record of a Tenement Gentleman. *See* Nagaya no shinshi roku, 1947

Record of Love. *See* Aijo no keifu, 1961

Record of Manhood and Eros. *See* Kyouenroku, 1939

Record of Three Generations of Presidents. *See* Shachou sandai-ki, 1958

Records 37, 1937 (Braunberger 4)

Recours en grace, 1959 (Barsacq 4)

Recours en grâce, 1960 (Giradot 3, Jarre 4)

Recreation, 1914 (Sennett 2)

Recreation, 1960 (Seberg 3, Delerue 4)

Récréation à la Martinière, 1895 (Lumière 2)

Re-Creation of Brian Kent, 1925 (Wood 2)

Recreation I, 1956 (Breer 4)

Recreation II, 1956 (Breer 4)

Recruits in Ingolstadt. *See* Pionere in Ingolstadt, 1970

Recta final, 1964 (Fernández 2)

Recteurs et la sirène, 1948 (Epstein 2)

Recuperanti, 1969 (Olmi 2)

Recurso del método, 1977 (Cuny 3, Villagra 3)

Red, 1969 (Flaiano 4)

Red, 1976 (Krasker 4)

Red Ace, 1980 (Johnson 3)

Red and Blue, 1967 (Richardson 2, Redgrave 3)

Red and the Black. *See* Geheime Kurier, 1926

Red and the Blue, 1983 (Loach 2)

Red and the White. *See* Csillagosok, Katonák, 1967

Red Badge of Courage, 1951 (Huston 2, Murphy 3, Kaper 4, Rosson 4)

Red Ball Express, 1952 (Boetticher 2, Poitier 3, Hayes 4)

Red Baron. *See* Von Richtofen and Brown, 1971

Red Beard. *See* Akahige, 1965

Red Bells: I've Seen the Birth of the New World, 1983 (Bondarchuk 3)

Red Beret, 1953 (Baker 3, Ladd 3, Addison 4, Nugent 4)

Red Berry, 1938 (Crabbe 3)

Red Blood and Yellow, 1919 (Anderson 3)

Red Blood of Courage, 1935 (Sheridan 3)

Red Canyon, 1949 (Darwell 3)

Red Clay, 1927 (Johnson 3)

Red Courage, 1921 (Eason 4, Miller 4)
Red Crag. *See* Lie Huozhong yongsheng, 1965
Red Dance, 1928 (Walsh 2, Del Rio 3, Carré 4, Clarke 4)
Red Dancer of Moscow. *See* Red Dance, 1928
Red Danube, 1949 (Barrymore 3, Calhern 3, Lansbury 3, Leigh 3, Pidgeon 3, Rose 4, Rosher 4, Rozsa 4, Wilson 4)
Red Dawn, 1984 (Johnson 3, Stanton 3)
Red Desert. *See* **Deserto rosso, 1964**
Red Dice, 1926 (Howard 2, Macpherson 4)
Red Dragon. *See* Geheimnis der drei Dschunken, 1965
Red Dust, 1932 (Fleming 2, Hawks 2, Astor 3, Crisp 3, Gable 3, Harlow 3, Adrian 4, Mayer 4, Rosson 4, Stromberg 4)
Red Ensign, 1934 (Powell and Pressburger 2, Junge 4, Rank 4)
Red Garters, 1954 (Head 4)
Red Girl, 1908 (Griffith 2, Lawrence 3)
Red Glow over Kladno. *See* Rudá záře nad Kladnem, 1955
Red Hair, 1928 (Bow 3, Banton 4, Schulberg 4)
Red Headed Monkey, 1950 (Terry 4)
Red Heat, 1988 (Hill 2, Schwarzenegger 3)
Red, Hot, and Blue, 1949 (Hutton 3, Mature 3, Dreier 4, Head 4, Lederer 4)
Red Hot Hoofs, 1926 (Plunkett 4)
Red Hot Hottentots, 1920 (Roach 4)
Red Hot Mama, 1934 (Fleischer 4)
Red Hot Music, 1937 (Terry 4)
Red Hot Rangers, 1947 (Avery 4)
Red Hot Rhythm, 1929 (McCarey 2)
Red Hot Riding Hood, 1943 (Avery 4)
Red Hot Romance, 1913 (Sennett 2, Normand 3)
Red Hot Romance, 1922 (Fleming 2, Emerson 4, Loos 4)
Red Hot Tires, 1925 (Zanuck 4)
Red Hot Tires, 1935 (Astor 3, Grot 4, Schary 4)
Red House, 1947 (Daves 2, Robinson 3, Glennon 4, Rozsa 4)
Red Ink Tragedy, 1912 (Bunny 3)
Red Inn. *See* Auberge rouge, 1951
Red Italy, 1979 (Jarmusch 2)
Red Kimono, 1925 (Arzner 2)
Red King, White Knight, 1989 (Von Sydow 3)
Red Kitchen Murder. *See* House on Greenapple Road, 1970
Red Lantern, 1919 (Nazimova 3, Wong 3, Mathis 4)
Red Light, 1949 (Raft 3, Glennon 4, Tiomkin 4)
Red Lights, 1923 (Wilson 4)
Red Lily, 1924 (Niblo 2, Beery 3, Novarro 3, Carré 4, Meredyth 4)
Red Line 7000, 1965 (Hawks 2, Caan 3, Edouart 4, Head 4, Krasner 4)
Red Lion. *See* Akage, 1969
Red Mantle. *See* Rode kappe, 1967
Red Margaret, Moonshiner, 1913 (Dwan 2, Chaney 3)
Red Mark, 1928 (Cruze 2, Daves 2)
Red Mill, 1927 (Arbuckle 3, Davies 3, Gibbons 4, Marion 4)
Red Monarch, 1983 (Baker 3, Puttnam 4)
Red Mountain, 1951 (Dieterle 2, Kennedy 3, Ladd 3, Head 4, Lang 4, Wallis 4, Waxman 4)

Red Noses, 1932 (Roach 4)
Red Peacock. *See* Camille, 1919
Red Peacock. *See* Arme Violetta, 1920
Red Pearls, 1930 (Launder and Gilliat 2)
Red Planet Mars, 1952 (Balderston 4, Biroc 4, Horner 4, Veiller 4)
Red Pony, 1949 (Aldrich 2, Milestone 2, Calhern 3, Loy 3, Mitchum 3, Copland 4, Gaudio 4)
Red Pony, 1973 (Fonda 3, Johnson 3, O'Hara 3, Goldsmith 4)
Red Psalm. *See* **Meg ker a nep, 1972**
Red Raiders, 1927 (Brown 4)
Red Riders of Canada, 1928 (Musuraca 4)
Red Riding Hood, 1987 (Golan and Globus 4)
Red Riding Hood of the Hills, 1914 (Anderson 3)
Red Riding Hoodwinked, 1955 (Blanc 4, Freleng 4)
Red River, 1948 (Hawks 2, Brennan 3, Carey 3, Clift 3, Wayne 3, Winters 3, Chase 4, Harlan 4, Schnee 4, Tiomkin 4)
Red River Range, 1938 (Wayne 3)
Red River Valley, 1936 (Autry 3, Eason 4)
Red River Valley, 1941 (Rogers 3)
Red Roses for the Führer. *See* Rose rosse per il Fuhrer, 1968
Red Sails, 1961 (Ptushko 4)
Red Salute, 1935 (Stanwyck 3, Young 3)
Red Shoes, 1948 (Powell and Pressburger 2, Walbrook 3, Cardiff 4, Challis 4, Heckroth 4, Rank 4)
Red Skies of Montana, 1952 (Hathaway 2, Bronson 3, Widmark 3, Clarke 4, LeMaire 4, Reynolds 4, Wheeler 4)
Red Sky at Morning, 1945 (Finch 3)
Red Sky at Morning, 1971 (Bloom 3, Head 4, Wallis 4, Zsigmond 4)
Red Sonja, 1985 (Schwarzenegger 3, De Laurentiis 4, Morricone 4, Rotunno 4, Whitlock 4)
Red Stallion, 1947 (Darwell 3, Miller 4)
Red Stallion in the Rockies, 1949 (Alton 4, Canutt 4)
Red Sun. *See* Soleil rouge, 1971
Red Sundown, 1956 (Van Cleef 3, Salter 4)
Red Sword, 1929 (Musuraca 4, Plunkett 4)
Red Tent. *See* Krasnaya palatka, 1969
Red Thorns, 1976 (Nowicki 3)
Red Throwing Knives. *See* Akai shuriken, 1965
Red Tomahawk, 1967 (Crawford 3, Keel 3)
Red Viper, 1919 (Gilbert 3)
Red Wedding. *See* Noces rouges, 1973
Red White and Blue Blood, 1917 (Bushman 3)
Red Whitsun. *See* Olověný chléb, 1954
Red Widow, 1916 (Barrymore 3)
Redbird Wins, 1914 (Eason 4)
Redeemed Claim, 1913 (Anderson 3)
Redeemer, 1966 (Raksin 4)
Redeeming Sin, 1925 (Blackton 2, Nazimova 3)
Redeeming Sin, 1929 (Costello 3, Haskin 4)
Redemption, 1930 (Niblo 2, Gilbert 3, Adrian 4, Booth 4, Gibbons 4, Mayer 4)
Redemption of Broncho Billy, 1914 (Anderson 3)
Redenzione, 1915 (Gallone 2)
Redes, 1990 (Zinnemann 2)
Red-Haired Alibi, 1932 (Temple 3)

Redhead and the Cowboy, 1950 (Ford 3, O'Brien 3, Bumstead 4)
Redhead from Wyoming, 1953 (O'Hara 3, Hoch 4)
Red-Headed Woman, 1932 (Boyer 3, Harlow 3, Adrian 4, Lewin 4, Loos 4, Mayer 4, Rosson 4)
Redheads on Parade, 1935 (McLeod 2, Lasky 4)
Redivivus. *See* Příchozí z temnot, 1921
Redl Ezredes, 1985 (Szabó 2, Mueller-Stahl 3)
Redman and the Child, 1908 (Griffith 2)
Redman's View, 1909 (Griffith 2, Bitzer 4)
Redneck Country, 1979 (Winters 3)
Redonda y viene en caja cuadrada, 1979 (Díaz 2)
Redoubtable Deceased. *See* Strasnia pokoynik, 1912
Reds, 1981 (Beatty 3, Hackman 3, Keaton 3, Love 3, Nicholson 3, Allen 4, Russell 4, Storaro 4, Sylbert 4)
Redskin, 1929 (Hathaway 2, Johnson 3, Cronjager 4)
Reducing, 1931 (Dressler 3)
Reducing Creme, 1934 (Iwerks 4)
Redwood Forest Trail, 1950 (Darwell 3)
Redwood Sap, 1951 (Lantz 4)
Reel Virginian, 1924 (Sennett 2)
Reeling down the Rhine with Will Rogers, 1927 (Rogers 3)
Reencuentro, 1985 (Alvarez 2)
Reflection of Fear, 1971 (Shaw 3, Fraker 4, Kovacs 4)
Reflections in a Golden Eye, 1967 (Coppola 2, Huston 2, Brando 3, Taylor 3, Jeakins 4, Morris 4)
Reflections of Murder, 1974 (Weld 3, Leven 4)
Reflections on Black, 1955 (Brakhage 2)
Reflet de Claude Mercoeur, 1923 (Duvivier 2)
Reflexfilm, 1947 (Roos 2)
Reflux—L'Enfer au paradis, 1962 (Gégauff 4)
Reform School, 1939 (Beavers 3)
Reform School Girl, 1957 (Crosby 4)
Reformation. *See* Et Laereaar, 1914
Reformation of Sierra Smith, 1911 (Dwan 2)
Reformatory, 1938 (Bond 3)
Reformed Outlaw. *See* Scourge of the Desert, 1915
Reformed Santa Claus, 1912 (Costello 3)
Reformed Wolf, 1954 (Terry 4)
Reformer and the Redhead, 1950 (Allyson 3, Powell 3, Frank 4, Raksin 4, Rose 4)
Reformers, 1913 (Griffith 2)
Reformers, 1916 (Laurel and Hardy 3)
Refuge, 1923 (Schulberg 4)
Refuge. *See* Zuflucht, 1928
Refuge England, 1959 (Lassally 4)
Refugee, 1918 (Hepworth 2)
Refugee. *See* Three Faces West, 1940
Refugiados de la Cueva del Muertro, 1983 (Alvarez 2)
Refugiados en Madrid, 1938 (Figueroa 4)
Regain, 1937 (Pagnol 2, Fernandel 3, Honegger 4)
Regal Cavalcade. *See* Royal Cavalcade, 1935
Régard des autres. *See* Mirada de los otros, 1979
Regard sur la folie, 1953 (Colpi 4)
Regarding Henry, 1991 (Ford 3, Rotunno 4)

Regards sur la Belgique ancienne, 1936
    (Storck 2, Jaubert 4)
Regards sur l'Indochine, 1954 (Delerue 4)
Régates de San Francisco, 1960 (Autant-
    Lara 2, Aurenche 4, Bost 4, Douy 4)
Regen, 1929 (Van Dongen 4)
Regen. See Rain, 1940
Regenerates, 1917 (August 4)
Regeneration, 1915 (Walsh 2, Reid 3)
Reggie Mixes In, 1916 (Fairbanks 3, Love 3)
Reggimento Royal Cravate, 1922
    (Gallone 2)
Régime sans pain, 1985 (Ruiz 2, De
    Almeida 4)
Régiment moderne, 1906 (Guy 2)
Regimentstochter, 1933 (Heller 4)
Regina, 1982 (Gardner 3)
Regina di Navarra, 1941 (Gallone 2, Cervi 3,
    Amidei 4)
Regina di Saba, 1952 (Cervi 3, Rota 4)
Regina von Emmertiz och Gustav II Adolf,
    1910 (Jaenzon 4)
Regine, 1934 (Tschechowa 3)
Regine, 1955 (Herlth 4)
Regine, die Tragödie einer Frau, 1927
    (Homolka 3, Junge 4)
Region centrale, 1970 (Snow 2)
Registered Nurse, 1934 (Florey 2, Beavers 3,
    Bondi 3, Daniels 3, Orry-Kelly 4)
Registered Woman. See Woman of
    Experience, 1931
**Règle du jeu, 1939 (Becker 2, Dalio 3,
    Modot 3, Douy 4, Kosma 4, Renoir 4)**
Règlements de comptes, 1962 (Gélin 3)
Regnar på vår kärlek, 1946 (Björnstrand 3)
Règne de Louis XIV, 1904 (Pathé 4)
Règne du jour, 1967 (Perrault 2)
Regreso al silencio, 1967 (Villagra 3)
Regreso de Martín Corona. See Enamorado,
    1952
Regrets. See Miren, 1963
Regular Girl, 1919 (Goulding 2, Marion 4)
Regular Pal, 1920 (Roach 4)
Regular Scout, 1926 (Plunkett 4)
Réhabilitation, 1905 (Guy 2, Gaumont 4)
Rehearsal, 1974 (Dassin 2)
Rehearsal for Murder, 1982 (Preston 3)
Reifende Jugend, 1955 (Schell 3)
Reifezeugnis, 1976 (Kinski 3)
Reigen, 1920 (Nielsen 3, Veidt 3, Dreier 4,
    Hoffmann 4)
Reign of Terror, 1949 (Mann 2, Bondi 3,
    Alton 4, Menzies 4, Wanger 4)
Reign of the Vampire, 1970 (Le Grice 2)
Reijin, 1930 (Takamine 3)
Reijin, 1946 (Hara 3)
Reijin no bisho, 1931 (Takamine 3)
Reilly's Wash Day, 1919 (Sennett 2)
Reimei hachigatsu jugo-nichi, 1952
    (Kagawa 3)
Reimei izen, 1931 (Hasegawa 3)
Reina del Rio, 1940 (Armendáriz 3)
Reina Santa, 1947 (Rey 3)
Réincarnation de Serge Renaudier, 1920
    (Duvivier 2)
Reincarnation of Peter Proud, 1974
    (Goldsmith 4, Smith 4)
Reindeer People. See Sarvtid, 1943
Reine blanche, 1991 (Delerue 4)
Reine de Biarritz, 1934 (D'Eaubonne 4)
Reine des resquilleuses, 1936 (Brasseur 3)
Reine Margot, 1954 (Gance 2, Moreau 3,
    Rosay 3, Alekan 4)
Reine verte, 1964 (Carrière 4)

Re-Inforcer, 1984 (Lewis 2)
Reise in die Vergangenheit, 1943
    (Tschechowa 3)
Reise nach Wien, 1973 (Kluge 2,
    Müller 4)
Reise um die Erde in 80 Tagen, 1919
    (Veidt 3)
Reisenrad, 1961 (Schell 3)
. . . reitet für Deutschland, 1950 (Staudte 2)
Reivers, 1969 (McQueen 3, Meredith 3,
    Faulkner 4, Ravetch 4, Van Runkle 4,
    Williams 4)
Réjeanne Padovani, 1973 (Arcand 2)
Rejected Woman, 1924 (Lugosi 3, Hunt 4)
Rejedor de Milagros, 1961 (Armendáriz 3)
Rejuvenation, 1912 (Cruze 2)
Rejuvenation of Aunt Mary, 1927
    (Pangborn 3)
Reka, 1933 (Stallich 4)
Rękopis znaleziony w Saragossie, 1964
    (Cybulski 3, Tyszkiewicz 3)
Relativity, 1966 (Emshwiller 2)
Relaxe-toi, cheri, 1964 (Fernandel 3)
Relentless, 1948 (Young 3, Cronjager 4)
Relentless Outlaw, 1911 (Dwan 2)
Relic of Old Japan, 1915 (Hayakawa 3,
    Ince 4)
Religieuse. See Suzanne Simonin, la
    religieuse de Denis Diderot, 1966
Religion and Gun Practice, 1913 (Mix 3)
Relitto. See Wastrel, 1960
Reluctant Astronaut, 1967 (Whitlock 4)
Reluctant Debutante, 1958 (Minnelli 2,
    Harrison 3, Kendall 3, Lansbury 3,
    Berman 4, D'Eaubonne 4, Rose 4,
    Ruttenberg 4)
Reluctant Dragon, 1941 (Ladd 3,
    Benchley 4, Disney 4, Glennon 4,
    Hoch 4, Iwerks 4)
Reluctant Heroes, 1971 (Oates 3)
Reluctant Pup, 1953 (Terry 4)
Reluctant Saint, 1962 (Dmytryk 2, Schell 3,
    Rota 4)
Reluctant Widow, 1950 (Dillon 4, Rank 4)
Remains to Be Seen, 1953 (Allyson 3,
    Calhern 3, Dandridge 3, Johnson 3,
    Lansbury 3, Rose 4)
Remarkable Andrew, 1942 (Holden 3,
    Head 4, Trumbo 4, Young 4)
Remarkable Mr. Kipps. See Kipps, 1941
Remarkable Mr. Pennypacker, 1959
    (Coburn 3, Webb 3, Brackett 4,
    Krasner 4, LeMaire 4, Reisch 4)
Rembrandt, 1936 (Korda 2, Lanchester 3,
    Laughton 3, Hornbeck 4, Korda, A. 4,
    Korda, V. 4, Krasker 4, Périnal 4)
Rembrandt, 1942 (Röhrig 4)
Rembrandt, Etc. and Jane, 1975
    (Brakhage 2)
Remedy for Riches, 1940 (Alton 4)
Remember?, 1939 (McLeod 2, Ayres 3,
    Garson 3, Taylor 3, Folsey 4, Gibbons 4)
Remember Last Night, 1935 (Whale 2,
    Young 3, Laemmle 4, Waxman 4)
Remember Mary Magdalene, 1914 (Dwan 2,
    Chaney 3)
Remember My Name, 1978 (Altman 2,
    Rudolph 2, Chaplin 3, Perkins 3)
Remember That Face. See Mob, 1951
Remember the Day, 1941 (King 2, Colbert 3,
    Barnes 4, Day 4, Newman 4)
Remember the Night, 1940 (Leisen 2,
    Sturges 2, Bondi 3, MacMurray 3,
    Stanwyck 3, Dreier 4, Head 4)

Remember Those Poker Playing Monkeys,
    1977 (Rosenblum 4)
Remember When?, 1925 (Capra 2,
    Sennett 2, Langdon 3, Bruckman 4)
Remembrance, 1922 (Gibbons 4)
Remembrance of Love, 1982 (Douglas 3)
Reminiscences of a Journey to Lithuania,
    1972 (Mekas 2)
Re-mizeraburu, 1950 (Mori 3)
Remodeling Her Husband, 1920 (Gish 3,
    Zukor 4)
Remontons les Champs-Elysées, 1938
    (Guitry 2)
Remorques, 1941 (Cayatte 2, Grémillon 2,
    Cuny 3, Gabin 3, Morgan 3, Prévert 4,
    Spaak 4, Trauner 4)
Remote Control, 1930 (Gibbons 4)
Remote Control, 1972 (Frampton 2)
Remueménage, 1981 (Presle 3)
Renacida, 1981 (Hopper 3)
Renai tokkyu, 1954 (Muraki 4)
Renaissance, 1963 (Borowczyk 2)
Renaissance du Havre, 1951 (Fradetal 4)
Renaldo and Clara, 1977 (Stanton 3,
    Shepard 4)
Renard et le corbeau, 1971 (Braunberger 4)
Renate im Quartett, 1939 (Fröhlich 3)
Rencontre, 1914 (Feuillade 2)
Rencontre à Paris, 1956 (Matras 4)
Rencontre avec le Président Ho Chi Minh,
    1969 (Ivens 2)
Rencontre imprévue, 1908 (Linder 3)
Rencontres, 1962 (Brasseur 3, Morgan 3)
Rencontres sur le Rhin, 1952 (Colpi 4)
Rendezvous, 1923 (Neilan 2)
Rendezvous, 1935 (Howard 2, Dumont 2,
    Powell 3, Russell 3, Daniels 4,
    Mayer 4)
Rendezvous. See Darling, How Could You,
    1951
Rendez-vous, 1961 (Delannoy 2, Girardot 3,
    Noiret 3, Piccoli 3, Sanders 3,
    Aurenche 4, Bost 4)
Rendezvous, 1965 (Ghatak 2)
Rendez-vous, 1976 (Lelouch 2)
Rendezvous, 1985 (Trintignant 3, Sarde 4)
Rendez-vous à Bray, 1971 (Delvaux 2,
    Karina 3, Cloquet 4)
Rendezvous at Midnight, 1935 (Bellamy 3)
Rendezvous at Orchard Bridge, 1954 (Xie 2)
Rendez-vous aux Champs-Elysées, 1937
    (Berry 3)
Rendez-vous avec Maurice Chevalier, 1957
    (Chevalier 3)
Rendez-vous d'Anna, 1978 (Akerman 2,
    Cassel 3)
Rendez-vous d'Asnières, 1962 (Delerue 4)
Rendez-vous de Cannes, 1929 (Becker 2)
Rendezvous de juillet, 1949 (Becker 2,
    Gélin 3, Modot 3, Renoir 4)
Rendez-vous de Max, 1913 (Linder 3)
Rendez-vous de minuit, 1961 (Leenhardt 2,
    Auric 4, Evein 4)
Rendez-vous de Nöel, 1961 (Piccoli 3)
Rendezvous in Trieste. See Zwei Whisky
    und ein Sofa, 1963
Rendezvous with Annie, 1946 (Dwan 2)
Rendezvous with Dishonor. See
    Appuntamento col disonore, 1970
René la Canne, 1976 (Depardieu 3, Piccoli 3,
    Morricone 4)
Renegade, 1943 (Crabbe 3)
Renegade Ranger, 1938 (Hayworth 3)
Renegade Trail, 1939 (Harlan 4, Head 4)

Return of Mr. H. *See* Madmen of Mandoras, 1962

Return of Monte Cristo, 1946 (Siodmak 4)

Return of Ninja. *See* Zoku shinobi no mono, 1963

Return of October, 1949 (Ford 3, Duning 4, Frank 4, Maté 4)

Return of Peter Grimm, 1926 (Gaynor 3)

Return of Peter Grimm, 1935 (Barrymore 3, MacGowan 4, Plunkett 4, Polglase 4)

Return of Richard Neal, 1915 (Bushman 3)

Return of Sabata. *See* E tornato Sabata … hai chiuso, 1972

Return of Sherlock Holmes, 1929 (Crisp 3, Dean 4, Fort 4)

Return of Sophie Lang, 1936 (Milland 3, Head 4)

Return of Swamp Thing, 1989 (Jourdan 3)

Return of the Ape Man, 1944 (Carradine 3, Lugosi 3, Katzman 4)

Return of the Bad Men, 1948 (Ryan 3, Scott 3, Hunt 4)

Return of the Cisco Kid, 1939 (Bond 3, Clarke 4, Day 4, MacGowan 4, Zanuck 4)

Return of the Dragon, 1973 (Lee 3)

Return of the Edge of the World, 1978 (Powell and Pressburger 2)

Return of the Fly, 1959 (Price 3)

Return of the Golem. *See* It!, 1967

Return of the Gunfighter, 1967 (Taylor 3, Buckner 4, Salter 4)

Return of the Jedi, 1983 (Kasdan 2, Lucas 2, Ford 3, Jones 3, Burtt 4, Edlund 4, Williams 4)

Return of the Mohicans. *See* Last of the Mohicans, 1932

Return of the Musketeers, 1989 (Lester 2, Chaplin 3, Lee 3, Reed 3)

Return of the Pink Panther, 1974 (Edwards 2, Lom 3, Sellers 3, Mancini 4, Unsworth 4)

Return of the Plainsman. *See* Phantom Stockman, 1953

Return of the Prodigal. *See* Návrat ztaceného syna, 1966

Return of the Rat, 1929 (Novello 3, Balcon 4)

Return of the Scarlet Pimpernel, 1937 (Mason 3, Biro 4, Hornbeck 4, Korda 4)

Return of the Secaucus Seven, 1980 (Sayles 2)

Return of the Seven, 1966 (Cohen 2, Fernández 2, Brynner 3, Oates 3, Rey 3, Bernstein 4)

Return of the Soldier, 1982 (Bates 3, Christie 3, Jackson 3, Russell 4)

Return of the Terror, 1934 (Astor 3, Orry-Kelly 4)

Return of the Texan, 1952 (Daves 2, Brennan 3, Ballard 4, LeMaire 4, Nichols 4, Wheeler 4)

Return of the Vampire, 1944 (Lugosi 3)

Return of the Vikings, 1944 (Balcon 4)

Return of ''Widow'' Pogson's Husband, 1911 (Bunny 3)

Return of William Marr, 1912 (Bushman 3)

Return to Earth, 1976 (Bellamy 3, Robertson 3)

Return to Fantasy Island, 1978 (Cotten 3)

Return to Glennascaul, 1951 (Welles 2)

Return to Life, 1938 (Maddow 4)

Return to Macon County, 1975 (Nolte 3)

Return to Oz, 1985 (Murch 4, Vinton 4, Watkin 4)

Return to Paradise, 1953 (Cooper 3, Hoch 4, Mandell 4, Tiomkin 4)

Return to Peyton Place, 1961 (Astor 3, Ferrer 3, Weld 3, Clarke 4, Smith 4, Wald 4, Waxman 4)

Return to Salem's Lot, 1987 (Cohen 2)

Return to the Land of Demons. *See* Chiesa, 1989

Return to the River Kwai, 1988 (Schifrin 4)

Return to Witch Mountain, 1978 (Lee 3)

Return to Yesterday, 1940 (Stevenson 2, Balcon 4)

Returning Napoleon. *See* Once Upon a Crime, 1992

Reuben in the Subway, 1905 (Bitzer 4)

Reuben, Reuben, 1951 (Fleischer 4)

Reuben, Reuben, 1983 (Epstein 4)

Reunion, 1922 (Fleischer 4)

Reunion, 1932 (Newton 3)

Reunion, 1936 (McDaniel 3, Levien 4)

Reunion. *See* Reunion in France, 1942

Reunion. *See* Ami Retrouvé, 1989

Reunion at Fairborough, 1985 (Kerr 3, Mitchum 3)

Réunion des artistes, 1963 (Alekan 4)

Reunion in France, 1942 (Mankiewicz 2, Carradine 3, Crawford 3, Gardner 3, Wayne 3, Irene 4, Waxman 4)

Reunion in Rhythm, 1937 (Roach 4)

Reunion in Vienna, 1933 (Barrymore 3, Adrian 4, Folsey 4, Vajda 4)

Revak, lo schiavo di Cartagine, 1960 (Maté 4)

Revanche de Baccarat, 1946 (Brasseur 3, Burel 4)

Revanche de Roger-la-Honte, 1946 (Cayatte 2, Spaak 4)

Rêve, 1930 (Douy 4)

Rêve à la lune, 1905 (Pathé 4)

Rêve blond, 1931 (Brasseur 3)

Rêve de Noël, 1900 (Méliès 2)

Rêve de singe, 1978 (Sarde 4)

Rêve d'horloger, 1904 (Méliès 2)

Rêve du chasseur, 1904 (Guy 2)

Rêve du garçon de café. *See* Songe d'un garçon de café, 1910

Rêve du maître de ballet, 1903 (Méliès 2)

Réveil, 1925 (Vanel 3)

Réveil du jardinier, 1904 (Guy 2)

Reveille, 1924 (Pearson 2)

Reveille, das grosse Wecken, 1925 (Krauss 3)

Reveille with Beverly, 1943 (Miller 3, Pangborn 3, Sinatra 3)

Reveille-toi, chérie, 1960 (Gélin 3)

Revel Son, 1939 (Hornbeck 4)

Revelation, 1913 (Ince 4)

Revelation, 1918 (Nazimova 3)

Reveler, 1914 (Mix 3)

Revenant, 1903 (Méliès 2)

Revenant, 1913 (Feuillade 2)

Revenant, 1946 (Jouvet 3, Honegger 4, Jeanson 4)

Revenge, 1918 (Browning 2)

Revenge, 1928 (Del Rio 3)

Revenge. *See* Uomo ritorna, 1946

Revenge!, 1971 (Winters 3)

Revenge, 1979 (Wertmüller 2, Loren 3, Delli Colli 4)

Revenge, 1986 (Carradine 3)

Revenge, 1990 (Costner 3, Quinn 3)

Revenge at Monte Carlo, 1933 (Eason 4)

Revenge of Frankenstein, 1958 (Fisher 2, Fisher 2, Carreras 4, Sangster 4)

Revenge of Godzilla. *See* Gojira no gyakushu, 1955

Revenge of Hercules. *See* Vendetta di Ercole, 1960

Revenge of Milady. *See* Four Musketeers, 1974

Revenge of Suzenjinobaba. *See* Osaka monogatari, 1957

Revenge of the Colossal Beasts, 1988 (Carpenter 2)

Revenge of the Creature, 1955 (Eastwood 3)

Revenge of the Dead, 1975 (Lee 3)

Revenge of the Jedi, 1983 (Guinness 3)

Revenge of the Ninja, 1983 (Golan and Globus 4)

Revenge of the Pink Panther, 1978 (Edwards 2, Lom 3, Sellers 3, Mancini 4)

Revenge of the Zombies, 1944 (Carradine 3)

Revenger. *See* Osvetnic, 1958

Revengers, 1972 (Borgnine 3, Hayward 3, Holden 3)

Revenue Agent, 1915 (Anderson 3)

Revenue Agent, 1950 (Katzman 4)

Revenue Man and the Girl, 1911 (Bitzer 4)

Reversal of Fortune, 1990 (Close 3, Irons 3)

Rêves d'amour, 1947 (Berry 3, Trauner 4)

Rêves d'un fumeur d'Opium, 1906 (Gaumont 4)

Rêves enfantins, 1910 (Cohl 4)

Revêtement des routes, 1923 (Grémillon 2)

Revêtements routiers, 1938 (Leenhardt 2)

Revisor, 1933 (Frič 2, Stallich 4)

Revnost, 1914 (Mozhukin 3)

Revolt, 1916 (Marion 4)

Revolt in Hungary. *See* Hungarn in Flammen, 1957

Revolt of Mamie Stover, 1956 (Walsh 2, Moorehead 3, Russell 3, Friedhofer 4, LeMaire 4, Wheeler 4)

Revolt of the Slaves. *See* Rivolta degli schiavi, 1961

Révolté, 1938 (Clouzot 2)

Révolte, 1971 (Braunberger 4)

Revolte dans la prison, 1930 (Boyer 3)

Révolte des confitures. *See* Marmeladupproret, 1980

Révolte des vivants, 1939 (Von Stroheim 2)

Revolte im Erziehungshaus, 1929 (Baranovskaya 3, Homolka 3, Andrejew 4, Metzner 4)

Révoltée, 1947 (Matras 4)

Revolts in the Schoolhouse. *See* Revolte im Erziehungshaus, 1930

Revolución, 1932 (Figueroa 4)

Revolución, 1963 (Sanjinés 2)

Revoluční rok 1848, 1949 (Stallich 4)

Revolution, 1967 (Greenaway 2)

Revolution. *See* Inquilaab, 1984

Revolution, 1985 (Kinski 3, Pacino 3, Sutherland 3, Winkler 4)

Revolution d'Octobre. *See* October Revolution, 1967

Révolution française, 1989 (Delerue 4)

Revolution Marriage. *See* Revolutionsbryllup, 1914

Revolutionary, 1970 (Duvall 3, Voight 3)

Revolutionary Romance, 1911 (Guy 2)

Revolutionary Year 1948. *See* Revoluční rok 1848, 1949

Révolutionnaire, 1965 (Lefebvre 2)

Revolutionsbryllup, 1914 (Psilander 3)

Revolutions-hochzeit, 1927 (Kortner 3)

Revolver. *See* Blood in the Streets, 1976
Revolver Bill. *See* "Bad Buck" of Santa Ynez, 1915
Revólver sangriento, 1963 (Fernández 2)
Revue blanche, 1966 (Delerue 4)
Revue du Cinéma, 1966 (Burton 3)
Revue Man and the Girl, 1911 (Griffith 2)
Revue Montmartroise, 1932 (Cavalcanti 2)
Reward, 1965 (Fernández 2, Von Sydow 3, Bernstein 4, Boyle 4, Smith 4)
Reward, 1980 (Halas and Batchelor 4)
Reward for Broncho Billy, 1912 (Anderson 3)
Reward of Courage, 1913 (Dwan 2)
Reward of Patience, 1916 (Menjou 3)
Reward of Valor, 1911 (Dwan 2)
Reward Unlimited, 1944 (Selznick 4)
Rex, King of the Wild Horses, 1923 (Laurel and Hardy 3)
Rey de Africa. *See* One Step to Hell, 1968
Rey de Mexico, 1955 (Alcoriza 4)
Rey que rabío, 1944 (Rey 3)
Rey se divierte, 1944 (De Fuentes 2)
Rezzou, 1934 (Leenhardt 2)
Rhapsodia del sangre, 1958 (Baarová 3)
Rhapsody, 1954 (Vidor 2, Calhern 3, Gassman 3, Taylor 3, Green 4, Rose 4)
Rhapsody in August, 1991 (Gere 3)
Rhapsody in Blue, 1945 (Cantor 3, Coburn 3, Jolson 3, Grot 4, Haller 4, Koch 4, Lasky 4, Levien 4, Polito 4, Prinz 4, Steiner 4)
Rhapsody in Brew, 1933 (Roach 4)
Rhapsody in Rivets, 1941 (Blanc 4, Freleng 4, Stalling 4)
Rhapsody in Wood, 1947 (Pal 4)
Rhapsody of Happiness, 1947 (Zhao 3)
Rhapsody Rabbit, 1946 (Blanc 4, Freleng 4, Stalling 4)
Rheinisches Mädchen beim rheinischen Wein, 1927 (Reisch 4)
Rhinestone, 1984 (Stallone 3, Van Runkle 4)
Rhino!, 1964 (Schifrin 4)
Rhino, 1983 (Menges 4)
Rhinoceros, 1974 (Black 3, Wilder 3, Smith 4)
Rhinoceroses. *See* Nashörner, 1963
Rhode Island Red, 1968 (Rainer 2)
Rhodes. *See* Rhodes of Africa, 1936
Rhodes of Africa, 1936 (Homolka 3, Huston 3, Balcon 4)
Rhodes, the Empire Builder. *See* Rhodes of Africa, 1936
Rhubarb, 1951 (Ames 4, Head 4)
Rhumba, 1935 (Banton 4)
Rhythm, 1953 (Lye 4)
Rhythm and Weep, 1946 (Three Stooges 3)
Rhythm in the Air, 1936 (Terry-Thomas 3)
Rhythm in the Ranks, 1941 (Pal 4)
Rhythm of a City. *See* Människor i stad, 1947
Rhythm of the Rumba, 1944 (Prinz 4)
Rhythm of the Saddle, 1938 (Autry 3)
Rhythm on the Range, 1936 (Crosby 3, Farmer 3, Rogers 3, Glazer 4, Head 4, Mercer 4, Struss 4, Young 4)
Rhythm on the Range. *See* Rootin' Tootin' Rhythm, 1937
Rhythm on the Reservation, 1939 (Fleischer 4)
Rhythm on the River. *See* Freshman Love, 1935
Rhythm on the River, 1940 (Crosby 3, Rathbone 3, Head 4, Young 4)

Rhythm Parade, 1943 (De Carlo 3, Dumont 3, Foreman 4)
Rhythm Racketeer, 1937 (Terry-Thomas 3)
Rhythm Romance. *See* Some Like It Hot, 1939
Rhythmus, 1921–25 (Richter 2)
Ribon o musubu fujin, 1939 (Hayasaka 4)
Ricco, 1973 (Kennedy 3)
Rice, 1964 (Van Dyke 2)
Rice Girl. *See* Risaia, 1956
Rice Packages. *See* Sengoku dawara, 1950
Rich: A Biography of Richard Burton, 1966 (Burton 3)
Rich and Famous, 1981 (Cukor 2, Delerue 4)
Rich and Respectable. *See* Ab Morgen sind wir reich und ehrlich, 1977
Rich and Strange, 1931 (Reville 4)
Rich Are Always with Us, 1932 (Davis 3, Haller 4, Orry-Kelly 4)
Rich Full Life. *See* Cynthia, 1947
Rich Kids, 1979 (Altman 3)
Rich Man, Poor Girl, 1938 (Ayres 3, Turner 3, Young 3)
Rich Man, Poor Man, 1918 (Barthelmess 3)
Rich Man, Poor Man, 1922 (Roach 4)
Rich Man's Folly, 1931 (Cromwell 2, Laszlo 4)
Rich Man's Son. *See* Pappas pojke, 1937
Rich Men's Wives, 1922 (Schulberg 4, Struss 4)
Rich Revenge, 1910 (Griffith 2, Pickford 3, Bitzer 4)
Rich, Young, and Deadly. *See* Platinum High School, 1959
Rich, Young, and Pretty, 1951 (Dalio 3, Darrieux 3, Cahn 4, Pasternak 4)
Richard, 1972 (Carradine 3, Rooney 3)
Richard Burton, 1966 (Burton 3)
Richard Burton: My Brother, 1966 (Burton 3)
Richard Burton, Very Close Up, 1966 (Burton 3)
Richard Mortensens bevaegelige Maleri, 1944 (Roos 2)
Richard Pryor Here and Now, 1983 (Pryor 3)
Richard Pryor Is Back, 1979 (Pryor 3)
Richard Pryor, Live and Smokin', 1985 (Pryor 3)
Richard Pryor Live in Concert, 1978 (Pryor 3)
Richard Pryor Live on the Sunset Strip, 1982 (Pryor 3, Wexler 4)
Richard the Lion Hearted, 1923 (Walker 4)
Richard III, 1908 (Costello 3, Ince 4)
Richard III, 1948 (Walton 4)
Richard III, 1955 (Baker 3, Bloom 3, Gielgud 3, Olivier 3, Richardson 3, Dillon 4, Heller 4, Korda 4)
Richard III, 1985 (Ruiz 2)
Richard Wagner, 1912 (Messter 4)
Richard's Things, 1981 (Ullmann 3, Delerue 4, Raphael 4, Young 4)
Richelieu, 1914 (Dwan 2, Chaney 3)
Richest Child in the World, 1934 (Berman 4)
Richest Girl in the World, 1934 (Hopkins 3, McCrea 3, Wray 3, Krasna 4, Musuraca 4, Steiner 4)
Richest Man in the World. *See* Sins of the Children, 1930
Richter und sein Henker, 1975 (Dagover 3, Schell 3, Shaw 3, Sutherland 3, Voight 3, Morricone 4)
Richter von Zalamea, 1921 (Dagover 3, Warm 4)

Rickety Gin, 1927 (Disney 4)
Rickshaw Man. *See* Muhomatsu no issho, 1958
Riddle Gawne, 1918 (Chaney 3, Hart 3, August 4)
Riddle of Lumen, 1972 (Brakhage 2)
Riddle of the Sands, 1979 (Challis 4)
Riddle Rider, 1924 (Canutt 4)
Ride a Crooked Mile, 1938 (Farmer 3, Head 4)
Ride a Crooked Trail, 1958 (Matthau 3, Murphy 3, Chase 4)
Ride a Northbound Horse, 1969 (Johnson 3)
Ride a Wild Pony, 1976 (Addison 4, Cardiff 4)
Ride Back, 1957 (Aldrich 2, Quinn 3, Biroc 4)
Ride Beyond Vengeance, 1966 (Blondell 3, Grahame 3)
Ride Clear of Diablo, 1953 (Duryea 3, Murphy 3, Boyle 4)
Ride 'Em Cowboy, 1942 (Abbott and Costello 3)
Ride 'Em Plow Boy!, 1928 (Disney 4)
Ride for a Bride, 1913 (Sennett 2, Arbuckle 3)
Ride for Your Life, 1924 (Miller 4)
Ride Him Cowboy, 1932 (Walthall 3, Wayne 3, Krasner 4, McCord 4)
Ride in the Whirlwind, 1965 (Corman 2)
Ride, Kelly, Ride, 1941 (Miller 4)
Ride Lonesome, 1959 (Boetticher 2, Coburn 3, Van Cleef 3, Brown 4)
Ride On, Vaquero, 1941 (Raksin 4)
Ride Out for Revenge, 1957 (Grahame 3, Crosby 4)
Ride, Ranger, Ride, 1936 (Autry 3)
Ride, Tenderfoot, Ride, 1940 (Autry 3)
Ride the High Country, 1962 (McCrea 3, Oates 3, Scott 3, Ballard 4)
Ride the Pink Horse, 1947 (Montgomery 3, Boyle 4, Harrison 4, Hecht 4, Lederer 4, Metty 4)
Ride the Whirlwind, 1966 (Nicholson 3)
Ride the Wild Surf, 1964 (Biroc 4)
Ride Tonight!. *See* Rid i natt, 1942
Ride, Vaquero!, 1953 (Keel 3, Quinn 3, Taylor 3, Kaper 4, Plunkett 4, Surtees 4)
Rideau cramoisi, 1953 (Aimée 3, Cuny 3, Schüfftan 4)
Rideau rouge, 1952 (Brasseur 3, Simon 3, Kosma 4)
Rider of Death Valley, 1932 (Mix 3)
Rider of the Law, 1919 (Ford 2, Carey 3)
Rider of the Plains. *See* War Paint, 1926
Rider on the Rain. *See* Passager de la pluie, 1969
Ridere, ridere, ridere, 1955 (Vitti 3)
Riders from Tucson, 1950 (Musuraca 4)
Riders in the Sky, 1949 (Autry 3)
Riders of Destiny, 1933 (Wayne 3)
Riders of the Dark, 1927 (Van Dyke 2)
Riders of the Dawn, 1937 (Canutt 4)
Riders of the Deadline, 1943 (Mitchum 3, Harlan 4)
Riders of the Kitchen Range, 1925 (Roach 4)
Riders of the Plains, 1924 (Karloff 3)
Riders of the Purple Cows, 1924 (Sennett 2)
Riders of the Purple Sage, 1925 (Mix 3)
Riders of the Purple Sage, 1931 (Carré 4)
Riders of the Purple Sage, 1941 (Day 4)
Riders of the Range, 1949 (Hunt 4)
Riders of the Rockies, 1937 (Canutt 4)
Riders of the Storm, 1929 (Canutt 4)

Riders of the Timberline, 1941 (Harlan 4)
Riders of the Whistling Pines, 1949 (Autry 3)
Riders of the Whistling Skull, 1937 (Canutt 4)
Riders of Vengeance, 1919 (Ford 2, Carey 3)
Riders to the Stars, 1953 (Cortez 4, Siodmak 4)
Riders to the Stars, 1954 (Marshall 3)
Rid i natt, 1942 (Molander 2, Dahlbeck 3)
Ridi, pagliaccio!, 1941 (Stallich 4)
Ridicule and Tears. *See* Löjen och tårar, 1913
Ridin' a Rainbow, 1941 (Autry 3)
Ridin' Down the Canyon, 1942 (Rogers 3)
Ridin' for Love, 1926 (Wyler 2)
Ridin' Kid from Powder River, 1924 (Miller 4)
Ridin' Law, 1930 (Canutt 4)
Ridin' Mad, 1924 (Canutt 4)
Ridin' Romeo, 1921 (Mix 3)
Ridin' Rowdy, 1927 (Brennan 3)
Ridin' Wild, 1922 (Miller 4)
Ridin' Wild, 1925 (Miller 4)
Riding de Trail, 1911 (Carey 3)
Riding for a Fall. *See* Manèges, 1950
Riding for Fame, 1928 (Eason 4)
Riding High, 1943 (Lamour 3, Powell 3, Dreier 4, Head 4, Struss 4, Young 4)
Riding High, 1950 (Capra 2, Bond 3, Crosby 3, Laurel and Hardy 3, Barnes 4, Dreier 4, Head 4, Hornbeck 4, Laszlo 4)
Riding High, 1980 (Copland 4)
Riding on Air, 1937 (Brown 3)
Riding Shotgun, 1954 (De Toth 2, Bronson 3, Scott 3, Glennon 4)
Riding the Rails, 1938 (Fleischer 4)
Rien ne va plus, 1979 (Presle 3)
Rien n'est impossible à l'homme, 1910 (Cohl 4)
Rien que les heures, 1925 (Braunberger 4)
Riff Raff, 1991 (Loach 2)
Riff Raff Girls. *See* Du Rififi chez les femmes, 1959
Riff Raffy Daffy, 1948 (Blanc 4, Stalling 4)
Riffraff, 1935 (Harlow 3, Rooney 3, Tracy 3, Loos 4, Marion 4)
Rififi. *See* Du Rififi chez les hommes, 1955
Rififi à Tokyo, 1962 (Vanel 3, Delerue 4)
Rififi in Paris. *See* Du Rififi à Paname, 1966
Rififi in Tokyo. *See* Rififi à Tokyo, 1962
Right Approach, 1961 (Kanin 4)
Right Bed, 1929 (Horton 3)
Right Cross, 1950 (Sturges 2, Allyson 3, Barrymore 3, Monroe 3, Powell 3, Mayer 4, Raksin 4, Schnee 4)
Right Girl, 1910 (Lawrence 3)
Right Name But the Wrong Man, 1911 (Bosworth 3)
Right of Love, 1910 (Lawrence 3)
Right of Way, 1914 (Talmadge 3)
Right of Way, 1920 (Schenck 4)
Right of Way, 1931 (Young 3)
Right of Way, 1983 (Davis 3, Stewart 3)
Right of Youth. *See* Ungdommens Ret, 1911
Right Person, 1955 (Carreras 4)
Right Sort. *See* Ugolok, 1916
Right Stuff, 1983 (Shepard 4, Winkler 4)
Right to Die, 1987 (Welch 3)
Right to Happiness, 1915 (Eason 4)
Right to Lie, 1919 (Murfin 4)
Right to Love, 1920 (Miller 4)
Right to Love, 1930 (Lukas 3, Akins 4, Lang 4)

Right to Love. *See* Recht auf Liebe, 1939
Right to Love. *See* Rätten att Älska, 1956
Right to Love. *See* Droit d'aimer, 1972
Right to Romance, 1933 (Young 3, Buchman 4, Cooper 4, Plunkett 4, Steiner 4)
Right to the Heart, 1942 (Wilde 3, Miller 4)
Right Way, 1913 (Bushman 3)
Right Way, 1921 (Olcott 2)
Rigolboche, 1936 (Christian-Jaque 2, Berry 3)
Rigoletto, 1947 (Gallone 2)
Rika, the Mixed-Blood Girl. *See* Konketsuji Rika, 1973
Rikigun daikoshin, 1932 (Hasegawa 3)
Riki-Tiki-Tavi, 1973 (Batalov 3)
Riki-Tiki-Tavy, 1975 (Jones 4)
Riku no ooja, 1929 (Tanaka 3)
Rikugun, 1944 (Tanaka 3)
Riley and Schultz, 1912 (Sennett 2)
Riley the Cop, 1928 (Ford 2, Clarke 4)
Rime of the Ancient Mariner, 1968 (Burton 3)
Rimes, 1954 (Alexeieff and Parker 4)
Rim of the Canyon, 1949 (Autry 3)
Rimfire, 1949 (Eason 4)
Rimrock Jones, 1918 (Crisp 3, Reid 3)
Rimsky-Korsakov, 1952 (Cherkassov 3)
Rinaldo Rinaldini, 1927 (Albers 3)
Rincón cerca del cielo, 1952 (Infante 3)
Rincón de las Vírgenes, 1972 (Fernández 2)
Rinconcito madrileno, 1936 (Clothier 4)
Ring, 1910 (White 3)
Ring, 1927 (Hitchcock 2, Reville 4)
Ring, 1952 (Harlan 4)
Ring der Giuditta Foscari, 1917 (Jannings 3)
Ring of a Spanish Grandee, 1912 (Cruze 2)
Ring of Fire, 1961 (Clothier 4)
Ring of Steel, 1942 (Tracy 3, Kanin 4)
Ring Up the Curtain, 1919 (Daniels 3, Lloyd 3, Roach 4)
Ring Up the Curtain. *See* Broadway to Hollywood, 1933
Ringaleevio, 1971 (Shepard 4)
Ringards, 1978 (Lai 4)
Ringer, 1931 (Balcon 4)
Ringer, 1952 (Zetterling 2, Elliott 3, Lom 3, Arnold 4, Korda 4)
Ringo-en no shojo, 1952 (Yamamura 3)
Rings Around the World, 1966 (Ameche 3)
Rings on Her Fingers, 1942 (Mamoulian 2, Fonda 3, Tierney 3, Barnes 4, Day 4, Newman 4)
Rink, 1916 (Bacon 2, Chaplin 2, Purviance 3)
Rinty of the Desert, 1928 (Blanke 4)
Rinzo shusse-tabi, 1934 (Hasegawa 3)
Rio, 1939 (Negulesco 2, McLaglen 3, Rathbone 3, Mohr 4)
Rio Blanco, 1967 (Del Rio 3)
Rio Bravo, 1959 (Hawks 2, Bond 3, Brennan 3, Dickinson 3, Martin 3, Wayne 3, Brackett 4, Furtherman 4, Harlan 4, Tiomkin 4)
Rio Conchos, 1964 (O'Brien 3, Goldsmith 4, Smith 4)
Rio das Mortes, 1970 (Fassbinder 2, Schygulla 3)
Rio del oro, 1986 (Ganz 3)
Rio escondido, 1947 (Félix 3, Figueroa 4)
Rio Grande, 1938 (Ballard 4)
Rio Grande, 1950 (Ford 2, Johnson 3, McLaglen 3, O'Hara 3, Wayne 3, Cooper 4, Glennon 4, Young 4)

Rio Grande Patrol, 1950 (Hunt 4)
Rio Grande Romance, 1936 (Katzman 4)
Rio Hondo. *See* Comancho blanco, 1969
Rio Lobo, 1970 (Hawks 2, Wayne 3, Brackett 4, Canutt 4, Clothier 4, Goldsmith 4)
Rio Negro, 1976 (Villagra 3)
Rio Rita, 1929 (Daniels 3, Clothier 4, Steiner 4)
Rio Rita, 1942 (Abbott and Costello 3, Grayson 3, Berman 4, Folsey 4, Stothart 4)
Rio '70, 1970 (Sanders 3)
Rio y la muerte, 1954 (Buñuel 2, Alcoriza 4)
Riom le beau, 1966 (Coutard 4)
Riot, 1913 (Arbuckle 3)
Riot, 1968 (Hackman 3)
Riot in Cell Block 11, 1954 (Siegel 2, Harlan 4, Wanger 4)
Riot on Sunset Strip, 1967 (Katzman 4)
Ripe Earth, 1938 (Boulting 2)
Riporterkirály, 1917 (Korda 4)
Ripoux, 1984 (Noiret 3, Lai 4)
Ripoux contre Ripoux, 1990 (Noiret 3, Lai 4)
Ripped-Off. *See* Uomo dalle pelle dura, 1971
Rip & Stitch, Tailors, 1919 (Sennett 2)
Rip Van Winkle, 1914 (Polito 4)
Rip Van Winkle, 1934 (Terry 4)
Rip Van Winkle, 1978 (Vinton 4)
Rip's Dream. *See* Légende de Rip van Winkle, 1905
Ripstitch the Tailor, 1930 (Crosby 3)
Riptide, 1934 (Goulding 2, Brennan 3, Marshall 3, Montgomery 3, Shearer 3, Adrian 4, Booth 4, Brown 4, Freed 4, Mayer 4, Stothart 4)
Riptide. *See* Si jolie petite plage, 1948
Risaia, 1956 (Ponti 4)
Risate di gioia, 1960 (Monicelli 2, Magnani 3, Age and Scarpelli 4, Cecchi D'Amico 4, Gherardi 4)
Riscatto, 1953 (Flaiano 4, Pinelli 4)
Rise Against the Sword. *See* Abare Goemon, 1966
Rise and Fall of Emily Sprod, 1964 (Godfrey 4)
Rise and Fall of Legs Diamond, 1960 (Boetticher 2, Oates 3, Ballard 4, Rosenman 4)
Rise and Fall of the Third Reich, 1968 (Schifrin 4)
Rise and Rise of Casanova. *See* Casanova & Co., 1977
Rise and Rise of Michael Rimmer, 1970 (Cleese 3, Elliott 3, Dillon 4)
Rise and Shine, 1941 (Dwan 2, Brennan 3, Darnell 3, Cronjager 4, Day 4, Mankiewicz 4, Pan 4)
Rise of Catherine the Great. *See* Catherine the Great, 1934
Rise of Duton Lang, 1955 (Bosustow 4)
Rise of Helga. *See* Susan Lenox, Her Fall and Rise, 1931
Rise of Jenny Cushing, 1917 (Tourneur 2, Carré 4)
Rise of Michael Rimmer, 1970 (Pinter 4)
Rise of Susan, 1916 (Marion 4)
Risin' Comet, 1925 (Canutt 4)
Rising Damp, 1980 (Elliott 3)
Rising Generation, 1928 (Crazy Gang 3)
Rising of the Moon, 1957 (Ford 2, Cusack 3, Krasker 4, Nugent 4)
Rising Tide, 1933 (Rotha 2)
Risk. *See* Suspect, 1960

Risky Business, 1939 (Cortez 4)

Risky Business, 1983 (Cruise 3)

Riso amaro, 1948 (Gassman 3, Mangano 3, De Laurentiis 4)

Riso no otto, 1933 (Takamine 3)

Risque de vivre, 1979 (Braunberger 4)

Risques du métier, 1967 (Cayatte 2)

Rita Hayworth, the Love Goddess, 1983 (Schifrin 4)

Rita la zanzara, 1966 (Wertmüller 2, Giannini 3)

Rita the Mosquito. See Rita la zanzara, 1966

Rite. See Riten, 1969

Riten, 1969 (Björnstrand 3, Thulin 3, Nykvist 4)

Rito d'amore, 1990 (Donaggio 4)

Ritorno, 1940 (Brazzi 3)

Ritorno di Clint il solitario, 1972 (Kinski 3, Morricone 4)

Ritratto dell'amata, 1912 (Bertini 3)

Rittmeister Wronski, 1954 (Tschechowa 3)

Ritual. See Riten, 1969

Ritual in Transfigured Time, 1946 (Deren 2)

Ritual of Evil, 1970 (Baxter 3, Jourdan 3)

Ritz, 1976 (Lester 2, Love 3)

Ritzy, 1927 (Lang 4, Schulberg 4)

Riusciranno i nostri eroi a trovare il loro amico misteriosamente scomparso in Africa?, 1968 (Scola 2, Blier 3, Sordi 3)

Rival. See Rivale, 1974

Rival Brother's Patriotism, 1910 (White 3)

Rival Demon. See Rural Demon, 1914

Rival Romeos, 1928 (Disney 4)

Rival Romeos, 1951 (Terry 4)

Rival Stage Lines, 1914 (Mix 3)

Rival Suitors. See Fatal Mallet, 1914

Rivale, 1974 (Andersson 3)

Rivalen im Weltrekord. See Achtung! Liebe-Lebensgefahr!, 1929

Rivalité. See Rivalité de Max, 1913

Rivalité de Max, 1913 (Linder 3)

Rivalry and War, 1914 (Beery 3)

Rivals, 1912 (Sennett 2, Bosworth 3, Normand 3)

Rivals, 1928 (Rooney 3)

Rivals, 1972 (Levine 4)

Rive droit, rive gauche, 1984 (Baye 3)

Rive Gauche, 1931 (D'Arrast 2, Korda 2, Korda 4, Stradling 4)

Rivelazione, 1956 (Blier 3)

River, 1929 (Borzage 2, Fox 4)

River. See Reka, 1933

River, 1937 (Lorentz 2, Van Dyke 2, Crosby 4, Thomson 4)

River, 1951 (Renoir 2, Lourié 4, Renoir 4)

River, 1984 (Gibson 3, Spacek 3, Ondříček 4, Williams 4, Zsigmond 4)

River and Death. See Rio y la muerte, 1954

River Beat, 1954 (Green 4)

River Fuefuki. See Fuefuka-gawa, 1960

River Gang, 1945 (Salter 4)

River Inn. See Roadhouse Nights, 1930

River Ki. See Kinokawa, 1966

River Lady, 1948 (De Carlo 3, Duryea 3)

River Melodies, 1948 (Fleischer 4)

River Niger, 1976 (Jones 3)

River of Death, 1989 (Lom 3, Pleasence 3)

River of Gold, 1971 (Milland 3)

River of Mystery, 1969 (O'Brien 3)

River of No Return, 1954 (Preminger 2, Mitchum 3, Monroe 3, Cole 4, La Shelle 4, LeMaire 4, Wheeler 4)

River of Romance, 1916 (Gaudio 4)

River of Romance, 1929 (Cukor 2, Beery 3, Walthall 3)

River of Tears. See Namida-Gawa, 1967

River Patrol, 1947 (Carreras 4)

River Pirate, 1928 (Howard 2, Crisp 3, McLaglen 3, Carré 4)

River Pirates, 1905 (Bitzer 4)

River Speaks, 1956 (Lassally 4)

River Thames—Yesterday. See World Window, 1977

River Wolves, 1934 (Pearson 2, Mills 3)

River Woman, 1927 (Robinson 4)

Rivers. See Songs 1964–69

River's Edge, 1957 (Dwan 2, Milland 3, Quinn 3, Polglase 4)

River's Edge, 1987 (Hopper 3)

River's End, 1920 (Neilan 2, Carré 4)

River's End, 1930 (Curtiz 2, Carré 4)

Riverside Murder, 1935 (Sim 3)

Rivolta degli schiavi, 1961 (Cervi 3, Rey 3)

Rivoluzione sessuale, 1968 (Argento 4)

Road Agent, 1941 (Salter 4)

Road Agent, 1952 (Hunt 4)

Road Agents, 1909 (Anderson 3)

Road Agent's Love, 1912 (Anderson 3)

Road Back, 1937 (Whale 2, Sherriff 4, Tiomkin 4)

Road Builder, 1971 (Neal 3, Herrmann 4)

Road Demon, 1921 (Mix 3)

Road Demon, 1938 (Robinson 3)

Road Games, 1981 (Curtis 3)

Road Gang, 1936 (Trumbo 4)

Road Home. See Lost Angels, 1990

Road House, 1928 (Brown 3)

Road House, 1934 (Balcon 4, Junge 4, Rank 4)

Road House, 1948 (Negulesco 2, Lupino 3, Widmark 3, Wilde 3, La Shelle 4, LeMaire 4)

Road in India. See World Window, 1977

Road of the Dragon, 1932 (Cronjager 4)

Road of Truth, 1956 (Gerasimov 2)

Road Show. See Chasing Rainbows, 1930

Road Show, 1941 (Langdon 3, Menjou 3, Carmichael 4, Roach 4)

Road Through the Dark, 1918 (Edeson 4)

Road to Andalay, 1964 (Blanc 4, Freleng 4)

Road to Arcady, 1921 (Haller 4)

Road to Bali, 1952 (Hope 3, Lamour 3, Martin 3, Russell 3, Barnes 4, Head 4)

Road to Canterbury, 1952 (Korda 4)

Road to Corinth. See Route de Corinthe, 1967

Road to Denver, 1955 (Cobb 3, Van Cleef 3)

Road to Frisco. See They Drive By Night, 1940

Road to Glory, 1926 (Hawks 2, Lombard 3, August 4, Fox 4)

Road to Glory, 1936 (Hawks 2, Barrymore 3, March 3, Faulkner 4, Johnson 4, Toland 4, Zanuck 4)

Road to Happiness. See Lykken, 1916

Road to Heaven. See Himlaspelet, 1942

Road to Hollywood, 1946 (Crosby 3)

Road to Hong Kong, 1962 (Crosby 3, Hope 3, Lamour 3, Martin 3, Niven 3, Sellers 3, Sinatra 3, Cahn 4, Fisher 4, Frank 4)

Road to Hope, 1951 (Ladd 3)

Road to Mandalay, 1926 (Browning 2, Chaney 3, Walthall 3, Gibbons 4, Gillespie 4, Mankiewicz 4, Mayer 4)

Road to Morocco, 1942 (Crosby 3, De Carlo 3, Hope 3, Lamour 3, Quinn 3, Dreier 4, Head 4, Young 4)

Road to Nashville, 1966 (Zsigmond 4)

Road to Paradise, 1930 (Young 3, Seitz 4)

Road to Peace, 1949 (Crosby 3)

Road to Plaindale, 1914 (Loos 4)

Road to Reno, 1931 (Struss 4)

Road to Reno, 1938 (Scott 3)

Road to Rio, 1947 (McLeod 2, Crosby 3, Hope 3, Lamour 3, Dreier 4, Head 4, Laszlo 4)

Road to Romance, 1927 (Novarro 3, Day 4, Gibbons 4)

Road to Ruin, 1913 (Dwan 2)

Road to Salina, 1971 (Hayworth 3)

Road to Singapore, 1931 (Calhern 3, Powell 3)

Road to Singapore, 1940 (Coburn 3, Crosby 3, Hope 3, Lamour 3, Quinn 3, Dreier 4, Head 4, Prinz 4, Young 4)

Road to Success, 1913 (Dwan 2)

Road to the Barricades. See Cesta ka barikádám, 1945

Road to the Heart, 1909 (Griffith 2, Lawrence 3)

Road to the Wall, 1962 (Cagney 3)

Road to Utopia, 1945 (Crosby 3, Hope 3, Lamour 3, Benchley 4, Dreier 4, Frank 4, Head 4)

Road to Victory, 1944 (Crosby 3, Grant 3, Sinatra 3)

Road to Yesterday, 1925 (De Mille 2, Grot 4, Macpherson 4)

Road to Zanzibar, 1941 (Crosby 3, Hope 3, Johnson 3, Lamour 3, Head 4, Prinz 4, Young 4)

Road Warrior. See Mad Max II, 1982

Roadblock, 1951 (Musuraca 4)

Roadhouse Murder, 1932 (Hunt 4)

Roadhouse Nights, 1930 (Durante 3, Fort 4, Hecht 4)

Roadhouse Queen, 1933 (Sennett 2)

Roadie, 1980 (Rudolph 2)

Roads, 1980 (Halas and Batchelor 4)

Roads Across Britain, 1937 (Rotha 2, Alwyn 4)

Roads to the South. See Routes du sud, 1978

Roadside Impressario, 1917 (Crisp 3)

Roadways, 1937 (Cavalcanti 2)

Roamin' Holiday, 1937 (Roach 4)

Roamin' Vandals, 1934 (Roach 4)

Roaming Lady, 1936 (Bellamy 3, Wray 3)

Roaming Ranch. See Roaring Ranch, 1930

Roaming Romeo, 1933 (Langdon 3)

Roaming the Emerald Isle with Will Rogers, 1927 (Rogers 3)

Roar of the Dragon, 1932 (Horton 3, Selznick 4, Steiner 4)

Roar of the Iron Horse, 1951 (Katzman 4)

Roarin' Lead, 1936 (Canutt 4)

Roaring Rails, 1924 (Carey 3, Polito 4, Stromberg 4)

Roaring Ranch, 1930 (Eason 4)

Roaring Road, 1919 (Cruze 2, Reid 3)

Roaring Twenties, 1939 (Rossen 2, Walsh 2, Bogart 3, Cagney 3, Haller 4, Haskin 4, Wald 4, Wallis 4)

Roast-Beef and Movies, 1934 (Tiomkin 4)

Rob 'em Good, 1923 (Bruckman 4, Stromberg 4)

Rob Roy, the Highland Rogue, 1953 (Dillon 4, Disney 4, Ellenshaw 4, Green 4)

Robber Symphony, 1935 (Wiene 2, Rosay 3, Metzner 4)

Robbers of the Sacred Mountain. See Falcon's Gold, 1982

Robbers on the Hill. See Loupežníci na Chlumu, 1927

Robber's Roost, 1933 (O'Sullivan 3, Nichols 4)

Robbery, 1967 (Yates 2, Baker 3, Levine 4)

Robbery Under Arms, 1957 (Finch 3, Rank 4, Vetchinsky 4)

Robby the Coward, 1911 (Griffith 2)

Robe, 1953 (Burton 3, Mature 3, Simmons 3, Dunne 4, LeMaire 4, Newman 4, Shamroy 4, Wheeler 4, Zanuck 4)

Roberta, 1935 (Astaire 3, Ball 3, Dunne 3, Rogers 3, Scott 3, Berman 4, Cronjager 4, Murfin 4, Pan 4, Polglase 4, Steiner 4)

Robert De Niro: The Hero Behind the Masks, 1991 (De Niro 3)

Robert et Robert, 1978 (Lelouch 2, Morgan 3, Lai 4)

Robert Frost: A Lover's Quarrel with the World, 1963 (Clarke 2)

Robert Koch, 1939 (Jannings 3, Krauss 3)

Robert Koch, der Bekämpfer des Todes, 1939 (Wagner 4)

Robert Macaire, 1905 (Gaumont 4)

Robert Macaire et Bertrand, 1904 (Guy 2)

Robert und Bertram, 1915 (Lubitsch 2)

Robert's Lesson, 1910 (White 3)

Robie est un ange, 1941 (Alekan 4)

Robin and Marian, 1976 (Lester 2, Connery 3, Elliott 3, Harris 3, Hepburn 3, Shaw 3, Barry 4, Watkin 4)

Robin and the Seven Hoods, 1964 (Crosby 3, Falk 3, Martin 3, Robinson 3, Sinatra 3, Cahn 4, Daniels 4)

Robin Hood, 1922 (Dwan 2, Florey 2, Beery 3, Fairbanks 3, Buckland 4, Edeson 4, Grot 4, Menzies 4)

Robin Hood, 1933 (Terry 4)

Robin Hood, 1973 (Terry Thomas 3, Ustinov 3, Mercer 4)

Robin Hood and His Merrie Men. See Story of Robin Hood and His Merrie Men, 1952

Robin Hood Daffy, 1958 (Blanc 4, Jones 4)

Robin Hood in an Arrow Escape, 1936 (Terry 4)

Robin Hood, Jr, 1934 (Iwerks 4)

Robin Hood Makes Good, 1939 (Jones 4)

Robin Hood of El Dorado, 1936 (Wellman 2, Stothart 4)

Robin Hood of Texas, 1947 (Autry 3)

Robin Hood of the Pecos, 1941 (Rogers 3)

Robin Hood: Prince of Thieves, 1991 (Connery 3, Costner 3)

Robin Hoodlum, 1948 (Bosustow 4, Hubley 4)

Robin Hoodwinked, 1957 (Hanna and Barbera 4)

Robinson, 1957 (Decaë 4, Rabier 4)

Robinson Charley, 1989 (Halas and Batchelor 4)

Robinson Crusoe, 1910 (Blom 2)

Robinson Crusoe, 1917 (Daniels 4)

Robinson Crusoe, 1925 (Lantz 4)

Robinson Crusoe, 1933 (Terry 4)

Robinson Crusoe Isle, 1935 (Lantz 4)

Robinson Crusoe, Jr., 1941 (Blanc 4, Clampett 4, Stalling 4)

Robinson Crusoe on Mars, 1964 (Haskin 4, Hoch 4, Westmore Family 4)

Robinson Crusoe-Land. See Atoll K, 1950

Robinson Crusoe's Broadcast, 1938 (Terry 4)

Robinson soll nicht sterben, 1957 (Schneider 3, Heckroth 4)

Robo no ishi, 1955 (Yamada 3)

Robo no ishi, 1960 (Hara 3)

RoboCop, 1987 (Bottin 4)

Robocop II, 1990 (Rosenman 4)

Robot, 1932 (Fleischer 4)

Robot Monster, 1953 (Bernstein 4)

Robot Rabbit, 1953 (Blanc 4, Foster 4, Freleng 4, Stalling 4)

Robotnicy 71 nic o nas bez nas, 1972 (Kieślowski 2)

Robust Romeo, 1914 (Sennett 2, Arbuckle 3)

Rocambole. See Revanche de Baccarat, 1946

Rocambole, 1962 (Fusco 4)

Roccia incantata, 1950 (Zavattini 4)

Rocco and His Brothers. See **Rocco e i suoi fratelli, 1960**

Rocco e i suoi fratelli, 1960 (Visconti 2, Cardinale 3, Delon 3, Girardot 3, Cecchi D'Amico 4, Rota 4, Rotunno 4)

Rocco Papaleo. See Permette? Rocco Papaleo, 1971

Rocinante, 1986 (Hurt 3)

Rockabye, 1932 (Cukor 2, Lukas 3, McCrea 3, Pidgeon 3, Murfin 4, Rosher 4, Selznick 4, Steiner 4)

Rock-a-Bye Baby, 1958 (Lewis 2, Sturges 2, Tashlin 2, Cahn 4, Head 4)

Rock-a-Bye Bear, 1951 (Avery 4)

Rock-a-Bye Cowboy, 1933 (Stevens 2)

Rockabye Legend. See Chilly Willy in the Legend of Rockabye Point, 1955

Rock All Night, 1957 (Corman 2, Crosby 4)

Rock around the Clock, 1956 (Katzman 4)

Rock Hound Magoo, 1957 (Bosustow 4, Burness 4)

Rock 'n' Roll High School, 1979 (Dante 2, Bottin 4)

Rock of Ages, 1902 (Porter 2)

Rock of Riches, 1916 (Weber 2)

Rock, Pretty Baby, 1956 (Mineo 3, Wray 3, Mancini 4)

Rock, Rock, Rock, 1956 (Weld 3)

Rock-Cut Temples of Ellora, 1914 (Phalke 2)

Rocket Bus, 1929 (Madsen and Schenstrøm 3)

Rocket Busters, 1938 (Bacon 2)

Rocket Bye Baby, 1956 (Blanc 4, Jones 4)

Rocket Gibraltar, 1988 (Lancaster 3)

Rocket Man, 1954 (Coburn 3, Seitz 4)

Rocket Ship X-M, 1950 (Struss 4)

Rocket Squad, 1956 (Blanc 4, Jones 4)

Rocketeer, 1990 (Arkin 3)

Rockets Galore, 1958 (Rank 4)

Rockets to the Moon, 1986 (Wallach 3)

Rockin' in the Rockies, 1945 (Three Stooges 3)

Rockin' Through the Rockies, 1940 (Three Stooges 3, Bruckman 4)

Rocking Chair Rebellion, 1980 (Wright 3)

Rocking Moon, 1926 (Clarke 4, La Shelle 4)

Rocking-Horse Winner, 1950 (Mills 3, Alwyn 4, Dillon 4, Rank 4)

Rockula, 1988 (Golan and Globus 4)

Rocky, 1948 (McDowall 3)

Rocky, 1976 (Meredith 3, Stallone 3, Winkler 4)

Rocky IV, 1985 (Stallone 3, Winkler 4)

Rocky V, 1990 (Meredith 3, Stallone 3, Winkler 4)

Rocky Horror Picture Show, 1975 (Sarandon 3)

Rocky Mountain, 1950 (Flynn 3, Canutt 4, McCord 4, Steiner 4)

Rocky Mountain Grandeur, 1937 (Hoch 4)

Rocky Mountain Mystery, 1935 (Scott 3, Sheridan 3)

Rocky Rhodes, 1934 (McCord 4)

Rocky Road, 1909 (Griffith 2, Bitzer 4)

Rocky Road to Dublin, 1968 (Huston 2, Coutard 4)

Rocky Road to Ruin, 1943 (Fleischer 4)

Rocky III, 1982 (Meredith 3, Stallone 3, Winkler 4)

Rocky II, 1979 (Meredith 3, Stallone 3, Winkler 4)

Rod Laver's Wimbledon, 1969 (Heston 3)

Röda tornet, 1914 (Stiller 2, Jaenzon 4, Magnusson 4)

Rodan. See Sorano Daikaijyu Rodan, 1956

Rode kappe, 1967 (Björnstrand 3, Dahlbeck 3)

Rodelkavalier, 1918 (Lubitsch 2)

Rodent to Stardom, 1967 (Blanc 4)

Rodeo, 1929 (Sennett 2, Hornbeck 4)

Rodeo, 1951 (Mirisch 4)

Rodnoi brat, 1929 (Cherkassov 3)

Roei no uta, 1938 (Mizoguchi 2)

Rogelia, 1962 (Rey 3)

Roger Corman's Frankenstein Unbound, 1990 (Hurt 3)

Roger-la-Honte, 1946 (Cayatte 2)

Roger-la-Honte, 1966 (Papas 3)

Roger Touhy, Gangster, 1944 (McLaglen 3, Quinn 3, Basevi 4, Friedhofer 4)

Roger Wagner Chorale, 1954 (Krasner 4)

Rogopag, 1962 (Pasolini 2, Rossellini 2, Welles 2, Delli Colli 4, Donati 4, Guillemot 4, Rabier 4)

Rogue, 1918 (Laurel and Hardy 3)

Rogue Cop, 1954 (Leigh 3, Raft 3, Taylor 3, Rose 4, Seitz 4)

Rogue Male, 1975 (O'Toole 3, Sim 3)

Rogue of the Rio Grande, 1930 (Loy 3)

Rogue Regiment, 1948 (Florey 2)

Rogue Song, 1930 (Barrymore 3, Adrian 4, Booth 4, Gibbons 4, Marion 4, Mayer 4, Shearer 4, Stothart 4, Tiomkin 4)

Rogues' Gallery, 1913 (Sennett 2)

Rogue's Gallery, 1967 (Hall 4)

Rogues of Paris, 1913 (Guy 2)

Rogue's Regiment, 1948 (Powell 3, Price 3, Buckner 4, Orry-Kelly 4)

Rogue's Romance, 1919 (Valentino 3)

Roi, 1936 (Raimu 3)

Roi, 1949 (Chevalier 3)

Roi bis, 1932 (Heller 4)

Roi de Camargue, 1934 (Vanel 3, Honegger 4)

Roi de Camembert, 1931 (Maté 4)

Roi de coeur, 1966 (Bates 3, Brasseur 3, Bujold 3, Presle 3, Delerue 4)

Roi de Thulé, 1910 (Feuillade 2, Gaumont 4)

Roi de tiercé. See Gentleman d'Epsom, 1962

Roi des Champs-Elysées, 1934 (Delannoy 2, Keaton 2)

Roi des palaces, 1932 (Clouzot 2, Gallone 2, Berry 3, Simon 3)

Roi des parfums, 1910 (Gance 2)

Roi du cirage, 1931 (Douy 4)

Roi du cirque. See Zirkuskönig, 1924

Roi du maquillage, 1904 (Méliès 2)

Roi et l'oiseau, 1980 (Grimault 4, Prévert 4)

Roi Lear au village, 1911 (Gaumont 4)

Roi sans divertissement, 1963 (Vanel 3, Jarre 4)

Rois de la flotte, 1938 (Renoir 4)

Rois du sport, 1937 (Berry 3, Fernandel 3, Raimu 3, Jeanson 4)

Rok pierwszy, 1960 (Ścibor-Rylski 4)

Rok spokojnego slonca, 1984 (Zanussi 2)

Rokujo yukiyama tsumugi, 1965 (Takamine 3)

Rola, 1971 (Zanussi 2)

Role. See Bhumika, 1977

Roll on Texas Moon, 1946 (Rogers 3)

Rolle. See Rola, 1971

Rolled Stockings, 1927 (Brooks 3, Banton 4, Schulberg 4)

Rollende Kugel, 1919 (Galeen 4, Messter 4)

Rollende Rad, 1934 (Reiniger 4)

Roller Skate. See Dance Movie, 1963

Rollerball, 1975 (Jewison 2, Caan 3, Richardson 3, Box 4, Houseman 4, Previn 4, Slocombe 4)

Rollercoaster, 1977 (Fonda 3, Segal 3, Widmark 3, Schifrin 4)

Rollicking Adventures of Eliza Fraser. See Eliza Fraser, 1976

Rolling Down to Rio, 1947 (Bruckman 4)

Rolling Home, 1935 (Launder and Gilliat 2)

Rolling Man, 1972 (Moorehead 3)

Rolling Road, 1927 (Balcon 4)

Rolling Sea. See Bärande hav, 1951

Rolling Stones, 1936 (Terry 4)

Rolling Thunder, 1977 (Schrader 2)

Rollover, 1981 (Pakula 2, Fonda 3, Jenkins 4, Rotunno 4)

Roma, 1972 (Magnani 3, Mastroianni 3, Donati 4, Rota 4, Rotunno 4)

Roma a mano armato, 1976 (Kennedy 3)

Roma Bene, 1971 (Papas 3)

Roma, città aperta, 1945 (Fellini 2, Rossellini 2, Fabrizi 3, Magnani 3, Amidei 4)

Roma città libera, 1946 (De Sica 2, Cecchi D'Amico 4, Flaiano 4, Rota 4, Zavattini 4)

Roma come Chicago, 1968 (Morricone 4)

Roma ore 11, 1952 (Zavattini 4)

Roma rivuole Cesare, 1973 (Olbrychski 3)

Roman, 1910 (Bosworth 3)

Roman Behemshechim, 1985 (Topol 3)

Roman Candles, 1966 (Waters 2)

Roman Cowboy, 1917 (Mix 3)

Roman d'amour, 1904 (Pathé 4)

Roman d'amour ... et d'aventures, 1918 (Guitry 2)

Roman de la midinette, 1915 (Musidora 3)

Roman de Max, 1912 (Linder 3)

Roman de Sœur Louise, 1908 (Feuillade 2)

Roman de Werther. See Werther, 1938

Roman der Christine von Herre, 1921 (Krauss 3, Freund 4)

Roman d'un jeune homme pauvre, 1935 (Gance 2, Fresnay 3)

Roman d'un malheureux, 1907 (Pathé 4)

Roman d'un spahi, 1936 (D'Eaubonne 4)

Roman einer Opernsängerin. See Samson und Delila, 1920

Roman Gray. See Art of Crime, 1975

Roman Holiday, 1953 (Wyler 2, Hepburn 3, Peck 3, Alekan 4, Auric 4, Head 4, Planer 4, Trumbo 4)

Roman lásky a pomsty. See Probuzené svědomí, 1919

Roman Legion Hare, 1955 (Blanc 4, Foster 4, Freleng 4)

Roman Numeral Series, 1981 (Brakhage 2)

Román o ruži, 1972 (Brdečka 4)

Roman Punch, 1930 (Terry 4)

Román s basou, 1949 (Trnka 4)

Roman Scandal, 1920 (Moore 3)

Roman Scandals, 1933 (Berkeley 2, Ball 3, Cantor 3, Darwell 3, Goddard 3, Day 4, Goldwyn 4, Newman 4, Sherwood 4, Toland 4)

Roman Spring of Mrs. Stone, 1961 (Yates 2, Beatty 3, Leigh 3, De Rochemont 4)

Roman Spring of Mrs. Stone, 1962 (Love 3)

Roman Tales. See Racconti romani, 1956

Roman Zair, 1983 (Golan and Globus 4)

Romana, 1954 (Gélin 3, Lollobrigida 3, De Laurentiis 4, Flaiano 4)

Romance, 1913 (Dwan 2)

Romance. See Road to Romance, 1927

Romance, 1930 (Brown 2, Garbo 3, Adrian 4, Daniels 4, Gibbons 4, Mayer 4, Meredyth 4)

Romance, 1932 (Terry 4)

Romance and Rhythm. See Cowboy from Brooklyn, 1938

Romance and Riches. See Amazing Quest of Ernest Bliss, 1936

Romance and Rustlers, 1925 (Canutt 4)

Romance à trois, 1942 (Blier 3, Aurenche 4)

Romance de Paris, 1941 (Matras 4)

Romance for Three. See Paradise for Three, 1938

Romance in Happy Valley, 1919 (Bitzer 4)

Romance in Manhattan, 1934 (Rogers 3, Berman 4, Krasna 4, Murfin 4, Musuraca 4, Plunkett 4, Polglase 4, Steiner 4)

Romance in the Dark, 1938 (Barrymore 3)

Romance in the Jugular Vein, 1980 (Price 3)

Romance Is Sacred. See King and the Chorus Girl, 1937

Romance Land, 1923 (Mix 3)

Romance of a Horsethief, 1971 (Polonsky 2, Brynner 3, Wallach 3)

Romance of a Jewess, 1908 (Griffith 2, Lawrence 3, Bitzer 4)

Romance of an American Duchess, 1915 (Swanson 3)

Romance of an Egg, 1908 (Bitzer 4)

Romance of a Photograph, 1914 (Lawrence 3)

Romance of a War Nurse, 1908 (Porter 2)

Romance of a Will. See Kaerlighedens Triumf, 1914

Romance of Celluloid. See We Must Have Music, 1941

Romance of Digestion, 1936 (Benchley 4)

Romance of Elaine, 1915 (Barrymore 3, White 3)

Romance of Flanders, 1937 (Sim 3)

Romance of Happy Valley, 1919 (Griffith 2, Gish 3)

Romance of Old Bagdad, 1922 (McLaglen 3)

Romance of Old Erin, 1910 (Olcott 2)

Romance of Pond Cove, 1911 (Lawrence 3)

Romance of Rosy Ridge, 1947 (Johnson 3, Leigh 3, Irene 4)

Romance of Sunshine Alley, 1914 (Ince 4)

Romance of Tarzan, 1918 (Meredyth 4)

Romance of the Bar O, 1911 (Anderson 3)

Romance of the High Seas, 1948 (Pangborn 3)

Romance of the Hills, 1913 (Anderson 3)

Romance of the Hope Diamond. See Hope Diamond Mystery, 1921

Romance of the Redwoods, 1917 (De Mille 2, Pickford 3, Buckland 4, Macpherson 4)

Romance of the Redwoods, 1939 (Vidor 2)

Romance of the Rio Grande, 1911 (Mix 3)

Romance of the Rio Grande, 1929 (Edeson 4)

Romance of the Rio Grande, 1941 (Clarke 4, Day 4)

Romance of the Underworld, 1928 (Astor 3)

Romance of the West, 1912 (Anderson 3)

Romance of the Western Hills, 1910 (Griffith 2, Pickford 3, Bitzer 4)

Romance on "Bar O". See Romance of the Bar O, 1911

Romance on Bar Q Ranch. See Romance of the Bar O, 1911

Romance on the High Seas, 1948 (Day 3, Burks 4, Cahn 4, Diamond 4, Epstein 4, Grot 4)

Romance on the Orient Express, 1985 (Gielgud 3)

Romance on the Range, 1942 (Rogers 3)

Romance Ranch, 1924 (Gilbert 3)

Romance sentimentale, 1930 (Eisenstein 2, Tisse 4)

Romancing the Stone, 1984 (Zemeckis 2, Douglas 3, Turner 3)

Romanoff and Juliet, 1961 (Ustinov 3, Krasker 4, Trauner 4)

Romantic Age, 1927 (Florey 2)

Romantic Age. See Sisters under the Skin, 1934

Romantic Age, 1949 (Zetterling 2)

Romantic Comedy, 1983 (Moore 3, Hamlisch 4, Mirisch 4)

Romantic Englishwoman, 1975 (Losey 2, Caine 3, Jackson 3, Fisher 4)

Romantic Journey, 1916 (Miller 4)

Romantic Melodies, 1932 (Fleischer 4)

Romantic Rogue, 1927 (Brown 4)

Romantic Young Lady. See Jeune Fille romanesque, 1909

Romantica Avventura, 1940 (Camerini 2, Castellani 2, Cervi 3)

Romanticismo, 1951 (De Laurentiis 4)

Romany, 1923 (McLaglen 3)

Romany Tragedy, 1911 (Griffith 2, Bitzer 4)

Romanza d'amore, 1950 (Brazzi 3)

Romanze in Moll, 1943 (Käutner 2)

Romanzo a passo di danzo, 1944 (Zavattini 4)

Romanzo d'amore, 1950 (Darrieux 3, Gherardi 4)

Romanzo popolare, 1974 (Monicelli 2, Age and Scarpelli 4)

Romanzo popolare, 1991 (Age and Scarpelli 4)

Romazo d'amore, 1950 (Cecchi D'Amico 4)

Rome Adventure, 1962 (Brazzi 3, Dickinson 3, Steiner 4)

Rome Armed to the Teeth. See Roma a mano armato, 1976

Rome 11 O'Clock. See Rome ore 11, 1952

Rome Express, 1932 (Launder and Gilliat 2, Veidt 3, Balcon 4)

Rome, Open City. See **Roma, città aperta, 1945**

Rome ore 11, 1952 (Barsacq 4)

Rome Symphony. *See* World Window, 1977

Romeo and Juliet, 1916 (Bara 3, Bushman 3, Menjou 3)

Romeo and Juliet, 1924 (Sennett 2)

Romeo and Juliet, 1933 (Terry 4)

Romeo and Juliet, 1936 (Cukor 2, Barrymore 3, Howard 3, Rathbone 3, Shearer 3, Adrian 4, Booth 4, Daniels 4, Gibbons 4, Jennings 4, Mayer 4, Shearer 4, Stothart 4, Thalberg 4, Vorkapich 4)

Romeo and Juliet, 1954 (Gielgud 3, Harvey 3, Krasker 4, Rank 4)

Romeo and Juliet, 1968 (Zeffirelli 2, Olivier 3, De Laurentiis 4, Donati 4, Havelock-Allan 4, Rota 4)

Romeo and Juliet, 1990 (Previn 4)

Romeo and Juliet im Schnee, 1920 (Kräly 4)

Romeo i Julija, 1958 (Mimica 4)

Romeo, Julie a tma, 1960 (Weiss 2)

Romeo, Juliet and the Darkness. *See* Romeo, Julie a tma, 1960

Roméo pris au piége, 1905 (Guy 2)

Romeo und Julia im Schnee, 1920 (Lubitsch 2)

Romeo y Julieta, 1943 (Cantinflas 3)

Romeo-Juliet, 1990 (Hurt 3, Redgrave 3, Smith 3)

Rommel—The Desert Fox, 1951 (Mason 3)

Romola, 1924 (King 2, Colman 3, Gish 3, Powell 3)

Romona, 1910 (Griffith 2, Pickford 3)

Romy. Anatomie eines Gesichts, 1965 (Syberberg 2)

Romy. Anatomy of a Face. *See* Romy, Anatomie eines Gesichts, 1965

Ronde, 1950 (Ophüls 2, Barrault 3, Darrieux 3, Gélin 3, Philipe 3, Reggiani 3, Signoret 3, Simon 3, Walbrook 3, Annenkov 4, D'Eaubonne 4, Matras 4)

Ronde, 1964 (Vadim 2, Fonda 3, Karina 3, Decaë 4, Hakim 4)

Ronde, 1974 (Lai 4)

Ronde des heures, 1930 (D'Eaubonne 4)

Ronde des heures, 1949 (Burel 4)

Ronde enfantine, 1895 (Lumière 2)

Ronde infernale, 1928 (Boyer 3)

Rondo est sur la piste, 1948 (Braunberger 4)

Ronin fubuki, 1939 (Hasegawa 3)

Ronintabi sassho bosatsu, 1935 (Hasegawa 3)

Ronny, 1931 (Wagner 4)

Roof. *See* Tetto, 1956

Roof Needs Mowing, 1971 (Armstrong 2)

Roof of the Whale. *See* Techo de la ballena, 1982

Roof Tree, 1921 (Furthman 4, Polito 4)

Rooftops, 1989 (Wise 2, Reynolds 4)

Rooftree. *See* Tvärbalk, 1967

Rookie, 1959 (Crosby 4)

Rookie, 1990 (Eastwood 3)

Rookie of the Year, 1955 (Ford 2, Wayne 3)

Rookie Revue, 1941 (Blanc 4, Freleng 4, Stalling 4)

Rookies, 1927 (Wood 2, Gibbons 4)

Rookies. *See* Buck Privates, 1941

Rookies, 1972 (Bernstein 4)

Rookies Come Home. *See* Buck Privates Come Home, 1947

Rookies on Parade, 1941 (Brown 4, Cahn 4)

Rookie's Return, 1921 (Beery 3)

Rooks. *See* Chappaqua, 1967

Room, 1967 (Kuri 4)

Room, 1989 (Altman 2, Pleasence 3, Pinter 4)

Room and Bird, 1951 (Blanc 4, Freleng 4)

Room and Board, 1921 (Folsey 4)

Room and Bored, 1943 (Fleischer 4)

Room at the Top, 1958 (Clayton 2, Harvey 3, Signoret 3, Francis 4)

Room for One More, 1951 (Grant 3, Blanke 4, Burks 4, Steiner 4)

Room 43. *See* Passport to Shame, 1959

Room Forty-Three. *See* Passport to Shame, 1959

Room in Town. *See* Chambre en ville, 1982

Room Mates, 1933 (Stevens 2)

Room Runners, 1932 (Iwerks 4)

Room Service, 1938 (Ball 3, Marx Brothers 3, Miller 3, Berman 4, Hunt 4, Polglase 4, Ryskind 4)

Room 666, 1984 (Wenders 2)

Room to Let, 1950 (Carreras 4)

Room Upstairs. *See* Martin Roumagnac, 1946

Room with a View, 1986 (Ivory 2, Day Lewis 3, Elliott 3, Smith 3, Jhabvala 4)

Roommates. *See* Raising the Wind, 1961

Rooney, 1958 (Fitzgerald 3, Challis 4, Rank 4)

Roop Ki Rani Choron Ka Raja, 1961 (Anand 3)

Rooster, 1971 (Topol 3)

Rooster Cogburn, 1975 (Hepburn 3, Wayne 3, Ames 4, Head 4, Rosenman 4, Wallis 4)

Rooster Cogburn and the Lady. *See* Rooster Cogburn, 1975

Root of All Evil, 1947 (Rank 4)

Root of Evil, 1911 (Griffith 2, Bitzer 4)

Rootin' Tootin' Rhythm, 1937 (Autry 3, Canutt 4)

Roots in a Parched Ground, 1988 (Duvall 3)

Roots of Heaven, 1958 (Huston 2, Welles 2, Flynn 3, Howard 3, Lom 3, Lukas 3, Arnold 4, Morris 4, Zanuck 4)

Roots II, 1979 (Jones 3)

Rooty Toot Toot, 1952 (Bosustow 4, Hubley 4)

Rope, 1948 (Hitchcock 2, Stewart 3, Adrian 4)

Rope from the Hanged Man. *See* Provaz z oběšence, 1927

Rope of Sand, 1949 (Dieterle 2, Henreid 3, Jaffe 3, Lancaster 3, Lorre 3, Rains 3, Dreier 4, Head 4, Lang 4, Paxton 4, Wallis 4, Waxman 4)

Rope Trick, 1967 (Godfrey 4)

Roped, 1919 (Ford 2)

Ropin' Fool, 1922 (Rogers 3, Roach 4)

Roping a Bride, 1915 (Mix 3)

Roping a Sweetheart, 1916 (Mix 3)

Roping Her Romeo, 1917 (Sennett 2)

Roquevillard, 1922 (Duvivier 2)

Roquevillard, 1943 (Vanel 3)

Rory O'Moore, 1911 (Olcott 2)

Rosa blanca, 1953 (Fernández 2, Figueroa 4)

Rosa blanca, 1972 (Figueroa 4)

Rosa de areia, 1989 (De Almeida 4)

Rosa de los vientos, 1981 (Villagra 3)

Rosa dei nomi. *See* Name of the Rose, 1986

Rosa Diamant, 1925 (Dieterle 2)

Rosa di Tebe, 1912 (Bertini 3)

Rosa Luxemburg, 1986 (Von Trotta 2, Olbrychski 3)

Rosa per tutti, 1967 (Cardinale 3, Cristaldi 4)

Rosa rossa, 1973 (Cuny 3)

Rosa Trikot, 1919 (Kräly 4)

Rosalie, 1937 (Van Dyke 2, Eddy 3, Powell 3, Edens 4, Mayer 4, Porter 4, Stothart 4)

Rosalie, 1966 (Borowczyk 2)

Rosario, 1935 (Armendáriz 3)

Rosary, 1910 (Lawrence 3)

Rosary, 1911 (Bushman 3)

Rosary, 1922 (Beery 3, Selig 4)

Rosary, 1929 (Wilcox 2)

Rosary Murders, 1987 (Sutherland 3)

Rosauro Castro, 1950 (Armendáriz 3)

Rose, 1967 (Hunter 4)

Rose, 1979 (Bates 3, Midler 3, Stanton 3, Hall 4, Kovacs 4, Zsigmond 4)

Rose and the Ring, 1979 (Reiniger 4)

Rose Bernd, 1919 (Krauss 3, Porten 3)

Rose Bernd, 1957 (Staudte 2, Schell 3)

Rose blanche, 1913 (Feuillade 2, Gaumont 4)

Rose Bowl, 1936 (Crabbe 3, Head 4)

Rose Bowl Story, 1952 (Wood 3)

Rose de mon jardin, 1964 (Braunberger 4)

Rose der Wildnes, 1917 (Nielsen 3)

Rose des vents, 1982 (Birri 2)

Rose e spine, 1914 (Bertini 3)

Rose et Landry, 1963 (Rouch 2)

Rose et le réséda, 1947 (Barrault 3, Auric 4)

Rose et le sel, 1964 (Delerue 4)

Rose for Everyone. *See* Rosa per tutti, 1967

Rose Garden, 1989 (Ullmann 3, Wallach 3, Golan and Globus 4)

Rose Marie, 1936 (Van Dyke 2, Eddy 3, MacDonald 3, Niven 3, Stewart 3, Adrian 4, Canutt 4, Daniels 4, Goodrich 4, Mayer 4, Stothart 4, Stromberg 4)

Rose Marie, 1954 (Berkeley 2, LeRoy 2, Keel 3, Rose 4)

Rose Monday. *See* Rosenmontag, 1924

Rose o'Salem Town, 1910 (Griffith 2, Bitzer 4)

Rose o' the Sea, 1922 (Niblo 2, Meredyth 4)

Rose of Blood, 1917 (Bara 3)

Rose of Cimarron, 1952 (Leven 4, Struss 4)

Rose of Kentucky, 1911 (Griffith 2, Bitzer 4)

Rose of Kildare, 1927 (Walthall 3)

Rose of Old Mexico, 1913 (Dwan 2, Reid 3)

Rose of Paris, 1924 (Coffee 4)

Rose of the Circus, 1911 (Guy 2)

Rose of the Golden West, 1927 (Astor 3, Garmes 4, Meredyth 4)

Rose of the Rancho, 1914 (De Mille 2, Darwell 3, Buckland 4, Macpherson 4)

Rose of the Rancho, 1936 (Florey 2, Banton 4, Brackett 4, Friedhofer 4, Korngold 4)

Rose of the Winds. *See* Rosa de los vientos, 1981

Rose of the World, 1918 (Tourneur 2, Carré 4)

Rose of Thistle Island. *See* Rösen på Tistelön, 1916

Rose of Tralee, 1942 (Krasker 4)

Rose of Washington Square, 1939 (Faye 3, Jolson 3, Power 3, Day 4, Freund 4, Johnson 4, Zanuck 4)

Rose rosse per il Fuhrer, 1968 (Milland 3)

Rose scarlette, 1940 (De Sica 2)

Rose Tattoo, 1955 (Lancaster 3, Magnani 3, Head 4, Howe 4, North 4, Wallis 4)

Roseanna McCoy, 1949 (Massey 3, Friedhofer 4, Garmes 4, Goldwyn 4, Jenkins 4, Mandell 4)

Rosebud, 1975 (Preminger 2, Attenborough 3, Huppert 3, O'Toole 3)

Rosebud Beach Hotel, 1984 (Lee 3)

Rose-France, 1918 (L'Herbier 2, Gaumont 4)

Roseland, 1977 (Ivory 2, Chaplin 3, Wright 3, Jhabvala 4)

Rose-Marie, 1928 (Crawford 3, Day 4, Gibbons 4)

Rosemary's Baby, 1968 (Cassavetes 2, Polanski 2, Bellamy 3, Curtis 3, Farrow 3, Gordon 3, Edouart 4, Fraker 4, Sylbert 4)

Rosemary's Baby II. See Look What's Happened to Rosemary's Baby, 1976

Rosemunda e Alboino, 1961 (Palance 3)

Rosen aus dem Süden, 1925 (Porten 3)

Rosen aus dem Süden, 1954 (Fröhlich 3)

Rosen, die der Sturm entblättert, 1917 (Negri 3)

Rosen für Bettina, 1956 (Pabst 2)

Rosen für den Staatsanwalt, 1959 (Staudte 2)

Rosen im Herbst, 1955 (Dagover 3)

Rosen in Tirol, 1940 (Herlth 4)

Rösen på Tistelön, 1916 (Sjöström 2, Jaenzon 4, Magnusson 4)

Rosencrantz and Guildenstern are Dead, 1991 (Dreyfuss 3)

Rosengarten. See Rose Garden, 1989

Rosenkavalier, 1925 (Wiene 2)

Rosenkönig, 1984 (Branco 4)

Rosenmontag, 1924 (Warm 4)

Rosenmontag, 1930 (Herlth 4, Röhrig 4)

Rosen-resli, 1954 (Tschechowa 3)

Roses are for the Rich, 1987 (Dern 3)

Roses for the Prosecutor. See Rosen für den Staatsanwalt, 1959

Roses of Picardy, 1927 (Saville 2)

Roses of the South. See Minami no bara, 1950

Roses of Yesterday, 1913 (Selig 4)

Roses rouges et piments verts. See No encontre rosas para mi madre, 1972

Roses rouges et piments verts, 1975 (Lollobrigida 3)

Rose's Story, 1911 (Pickford 3)

Rosie, 1967 (Russell 3, Mercer 4)

Rosier de Madame Husson, 1932 (Fernandel 3, Rosay 3)

Rosier de Madame Husson, 1950 (Pagnol 2)

Rosière des Halles, 1935 (Douy 4)

Rosier miraculeux, 1904 (Méliès 2)

Rosie's Revenge, 1913 (Cruze 2)

Rosita, 1923 (Lubitsch 2, Pickford 3, Kräly 4, Menzies 4, Rosher 4)

Roslyn Romance, 1970 (Baillie 2)

Rosolino Paterno, soldato . . ., 1969 (Falk 3, Alexeieff and Parker 4, Delli Colli 4)

Rossetto, 1960 (Germi 2, Fusco 4, Zavattini 4)

Rossini, Rossini, 1990 (Cecchi D'Amico 4)

Rossiter Case, 1951 (Baker 3, Carreras 4)

Rossiya Nikolaya II i Lev Tolstoi, 1928 (Shub 2)

Rosso e nero, 1954 (Delli Colli 4)

Rötägg, 1946 (Björnstrand 3)

Rotation, 1949 (Staudte 2)

Rote Kreis, 1928 (Albers 3)

Rote Kreis, 1960 (Rasp 3)

Rote Liebe, 1982 (Constantine 3)

Rote Maus, 1925 (Warm 4)

Rote Orchideen, 1938 (Tschechowa 3)

Rote Rausch, 1962 (Kinski 3)

Rote Rosen, rote Lippen, roter Wein, 1953 (Dagover 3)

Rote Streifen, 1916 (Gad 2)

Rote Tanzerin. See Mata Hari, 1927

Rothausgasse, 1928 (Fröhlich 3, Homolka 3, Planer 4)

Rothenburger, 1918 (Pick 2)

Rothschild, 1933 (Baur 3)

Roti, 1942 (Biswas 4)

Roti Kapada Aur Makaan, 1974 (Bachchan 3)

Rotten to the Core, 1965 (Boulting 2, Vetchinsky 4, Young 4)

Roué, 1923 (Glance 2, Burel 4, Honegger 4)

Roue de la fortune, 1938 (Storck 2)

Roue tourne, 1941 (Allégret 2)

Roué's Heart, 1909 (Griffith 2, Bitzer 4)

Rouge aux lèvres, 1971 (Seyrig 3)

Rouge est mis, 1953 (Cocteau 2)

Rouge est mis, 1957 (Gabin 3, Girardot 3, Audiard 4)

Rouge et le blanc, 1971 (Autant-Lara 2)

Rouge et le noir. See Geheime Kurier, 1928

Rouge et le noir, 1954 (Autant-Lara 2, Darrieux 3, Philipe 3, Sordi 3, Aurenche 4, Bost 4, Douy 4, Saulnier 4)

Rouged Lips, 1923 (Bruckman 4)

Rough and the Smooth, 1959 (Siodmak 2, Bendix 3, Adam 4, Heller 4, Mathieson 4)

Rough Company. See Violent Men, 1954

Rough Cut, 1980 (Siegel 2, Niven 3, Reynolds 3)

Rough Diamond, 1921 (Mix 3)

Rough House, 1917 (Keaton 2, Arbuckle 3)

Rough House Rosie, 1927 (Bow 3, Rosson 4, Schulberg 4)

Rough Idea of Love, 1930 (Sennett 2)

Rough Night in Jericho, 1967 (Martin 3, Simmons 3, Metty 4, Whitlock 4)

Rough on Romeo, 1922 (Roach 4)

Rough Riders, 1927 (Astor 3, Howe 4, Schulberg 4)

Rough Riders' Roundup, 1939 (Rogers 3)

Rough Ridin', 1924 (Haller 4)

Rough Ridin' Rangers, 1935 (Canutt 4)

Rough Ridin' Red, 1928 (Musuraca 4)

Rough Romance, 1930 (Wayne 3)

Rough Seas, 1921 (Roach 4)

Rough Shod, 1922 (Eason 4)

Rough Shoot. See Shoot First, 1953

Rough, Tough, and Ready, 1945 (McLaglen 3)

Roughest Africa, 1923 (Laurel and Hardy 3, Roach 4)

Roughly Speaking, 1945 (Curtiz 2, Russell 3, Blanke 4, Steiner 4, Walker 4, Waxman 4)

Roughly Speaking, 1946 (Blanc 4, Jones 4)

Roughneck. See Conversion of Frosty Blake, 1915

Rough-Riding Romance, 1919 (Mix 3)

Roughshod, 1949 (Grahame 3, Biroc 4)

Rougoku no hanayome, 1939 (Miyagawa 4)

Roulement à billes, 1924 (Grémillon 2)

Rouletabille II: La Dernière Incarnation de Larson, 1914 (Tourneur 2)

Rouletabille I: Le Mystère de la chambre jaune, 1914 (Tourneur 2)

Roulette, 1924 (Costello 3, Selznick 4)

Round Midnight, 1986 (Tavernier 2, Noiret 3, Trauner 4, Winkler 4)

Round Up, 1920 (Keaton 2)

Rounders, 1914 (Sennett 2, Arbuckle 3)

Rounders, 1964 (Fonda 3, Ford 3, Oates 3)

Round-Up, 1920 (Arbuckle 3, Beery 3)

Roundup, 1941 (Harlan 4, Head 4)

Round-Up Time in Texas, 1937 (Autry 3)

Roustabout, 1922 (Roach 4)

Roustabout, 1964 (Presley 3, Stanwyck 3, Welch 3, Ballard 4, Head 4, Wallis 4)

Route, 1910 (Cohl 4)

Route de bagne, 1945 (Burel 4)

Route de Corinthe, 1967 (Chabrol 2, Seberg 3, Rabier 4)

Route de l'ouest, 1963 (Arcand 2)

Route de Salina. See Road to Salina, 1971

Route du bonheur, 1953 (Cassel 3)

Route d'un homme, 1967 (Barrault 3, Feuillère 3)

Route est belle, 1929 (Florey 2, Braunberger 4, Rosher 4)

Route heureuse, 1935 (Feuillère 3)

Route impériale, 1935 (L'Herbier 2)

Route Napoléon, 1953 (Delannoy 2, Fresnay 3, Burel 4)

Route sans issue, 1947 (Spaak 4)

Route sans sillage, 1963 (Delerue 4)

Routes barrées, 1956 (Colpi 4)

Routes du sud, 1978 (Montand 3, Fisher 4, Legrand 4, Traunder 4)

Rover, 1967 (Hayworth 3, Quinn 3)

Rover's Rescue, 1940 (Terry 4)

Rover's Rival, 1937 (Blanc 4, Clampett 4, Stalling 4)

Rovin' Tumbleweeds, 1939 (Autry 3, Costello 3)

Row, Row, Row, 1930 (Fleischer 4)

Rowan and Martin at the Movies, 1969 (Heston 3)

Row-Boat Romance, 1914 (Sennett 2)

Rowlandson's England, 1955 (Hamer 2, Guinness 3)

Roxanne, 1987 (Schepisi 2, Martin 3)

Roxie Hart, 1942 (Wellman 2, Menjou 3, Rogers 3, Day 4, Johnson 4, Shamroy 4)

Royal Affair. See Roi, 1949

Royal Affairs in Versailles. See Si Versailles m'était conté, 1953

Royal American, 1927 (Brown 4)

Royal Ballet, 1960 (Rank 4)

Royal Bed, 1930 (Astor 3)

Royal Blood, 1916 (Laurel and Hardy 3)

Royal Box, 1914 (Selig 4)

Royal Cat Nap, 1957 (Hanna and Barbera 4)

Royal Cavalcade, 1935 (Mills 3)

Royal Divorce, 1938 (Hawkins 3)

Royal Family of Broadway, 1930 (Cukor 2, Dmytryk 2, March 3, Banton 4, Folsey 4, Mankiewicz 4, Zukor 4)

Royal Flash, 1975 (Bates 3, Hoskins 3, McDowell 3, Reed 3, Sim 3, Unsworth 4)

Royal Flush. See Two Guys from Milwaukee, 1946

Royal Four Flush, 1925 (Roach 4)

Royal Game. See Schachnovelle, 1960

Royal Heritage, 1952 (Alwyn 4)

Royal Hunt. See Kungajakt, 1944

Royal Hunt of the Sun, 1969 (Shaw 3, Lourié 4)

Royal Johansson. See Kungliga Johansson, 1933

Royal Razz, 1924 (McCarey 2, Roach 4)

Royal Remembrances, 1929 (Hepworth 2)

Royal Rider, 1929 (Brown 4, McCord 4)

Royal River. See Distant Thames, 1951

Royal Rogue, 1917 (Sennett 2)

Royal Romance of Charles and Diana, 1982 (De Havilland 3, Granger 3, Milland 3)

Royal Scandal. *See* Hose, 1927

Royal Scandal, 1945 (Preminger 2, Baxter 3, Coburn 3, Price 3, Biro 4, Miller 4, Newman 4)

Royal Tour of New South Wales, 1956 (Finch 3)

Royal Wedding, 1947 (Neagle 3)

Royal Wedding, 1951 (Astaire 3, Green 4, Freed 4, Smith 4)

Royaume des Fées, 1903 (Méliès 2)

Royaume vous attend, 1976 (Perrault 2)

Roza, 1982 (Olbrychski 3)

Różaniec z granatow, 1969 (Olbrychski 3)

Rozdennie polzat utat ne mozet, 1914 (Mozhukin 3)

Rozeki mono, 1928 (Tsuburaya 4)

Rozmarné léto, 1968 (Menzel 2, Brodský 3)

Rozstanie, 1961 (Cybulski 3)

Roztržka, 1956 (Brejchová 3)

Rozum a cit, 1962 (Brdečka 4)

Rozwodów nie będzie, 1963 (Cybulski 3, Stawiński 4)

Ruba al prossimo tuo, 1968 (Hudson 3, Cristaldi 4, Morricone 4)

Rubber Cement, 1975 (Breer 4)

Rubber Heels, 1927 (Hunt 4)

Rubber Tires, 1927 (Love 3)

Rubberneck, 1924 (Roach 4)

Rube and the Baron, 1913 (Sennett 2, Normand 3)

Rube Brown in Town, 1907 (Bitzer 4)

Rubens, 1947 (Storck 2)

Rübezahls Hochzeit, 1916 (Wegener 3, Reiniger 4)

Rubia Servos, 1978 (Brocka 2)

Rubin and Ed, 1990 (Black 3)

Ruby Gentry, 1952 (Vidor 2, Heston 3, Jones 3, Malden 3, Harlan 4, Head 4)

Ruby Keeler, 1928 (Keeler 3)

Rückkehr, 1990 (Von Trotta 2, Delli Colli 4)

Rückkehr der Truppen von der Frühlingsparade, 1900 (Messter 4)

Ruckus, 1980 (Johnson 3)

Rudá záře nad Kladnem, 1955 (Stallich 4)

Rudd Family Goes to Town. *See* Dad and Dave Come to Town, 1938

Ruddigore, 1964 (Halas and Batchelor 4)

Rude Awakening, 1989 (Henry 4)

Rude Hostess, 1909 (Griffith 2, Bitzer 4)

Rude Journée pour la reine, 1973 (Allio 2, Depardieu 3, Signoret 3)

Rudolph Valentino, 1938 (Negri 3)

Rudolph Valentino and His 88 American Beauties, 1923 (Selznick 4)

Rudy Vallee Melodies, 1932 (Fleischer 4)

Rudyard Kipling's Jungle Book. *See* Jungle Book, 1942

Rue chinoise, 1956 (Delerue 4)

Rue de l'Estrapade, 1953 (Becker 2, Gélin 3, Jourdan 3, D'Eaubonne 4)

Rue des archives 79, 1979 (Ruiz 2)

Rue des Arcrives, 1987 (Colpi 4)

Rue des Prairies, 1959 (Gabin 3, Audiard 4)

Rue du départ, 1986 (Depardieu 3)

Rue du pied de Grue, 1979 (Tavernier 2)

Rue Fontaine, 1984 (Léaud 3)

Rue Saint-Sulpice, 1991 (Hoskins 3)

Rue sans joie, 1938 (Auric 4)

Rues de Hong Kong, 1964 (Guillemot 4)

Ruf, 1949 (Kortner 3)

Ruf aus dem Äther, 1951 (Werner 3)

Ruf des Schicksals, 1922 (Kortner 3, Wagner 4)

Ruffian, 1982 (Cardinale 3, Morricone 4)

Rug Maker's Daughter, 1915 (Bosworth 3)

Rugged Water, 1925 (Beery 3)

Ruggles of Red Gap, 1923 (Cruze 2, Horton 3, Brown 4)

Ruggles of Red Gap, 1935 (Dmytryk 2, McCarey 2, Laughton 3, Banton 4, Dreier 4, Head 4, Zukor 4)

Ruins. *See* Khandhar, 1984

Ruins of Palmyra and Baalbek. *See* World Window, 1977

Ruiscrianno i nostri eroi a trovare l'amico misteriosamente scomparso in Africa?, 1968 (Age and Scarpelli 4)

Ruisseau, 1938 (Autant-Lara 2, Rosay 3, Simon 3, Aurenche 4)

Ruka, 1965 (Trnka 4)

Ruler. *See* Herrscher, 1937

Rulers of the City. *See* Padroni della città, 1977

Rulers of the Sea, 1939 (Ladd 3, Lockwood 3, Dreier 4, Head 4, Jennings 4)

Rules of the Game. *See* **Règle du jeu, 1939**

Ruling Class, 1972 (O'Toole 3, Sim 3)

Ruling Passion, 1911 (Griffith 2, Bitzer 4)

Ruling Passion, 1916 (Brenon 2)

Ruling Passion, 1922 (Arliss 3)

Ruling Passions, 1918 (Polito 4)

Ruling Voice, 1931 (Huston 3, Young 3, Polito 4)

Rum and Wall Paper, 1915 (Sennett 2, Arbuckle 3)

Rum Runner. *See* Boulevard du rhum, 1971

Rumaensk Blod or Søstrene Corrodi, 1913 (Christensen 2)

Rumba, 1935 (Lombard 3, Raft 3, Sheridan 3, Wyman 3, Dreier 4, Prinz 4, Zukor 4)

Rumba, 1939 (McLaren 4)

Rumba, 1986 (Piccoli 3, Evein 4)

Rumble Fish, 1983 (Coppola 2, Dillon 3, Hopper 3, Rourke 3, Tavoularis 4)

Rumble on the Docks, 1956 (Katzman 4)

Rumiantsev Case. *See* Delo Rumiantseva, 1956

Rummy, 1933 (Roach 4)

Rumpelstiltskin, 1915 (August 4)

Rumpelstiltskin, 1987 (Golan and Globus 4)

Rumpus in the Harem, 1956 (Three Stooges 3)

Run a Crooked Mile, 1969 (Jourdan 3)

Run, Boy, Run, 1987 (Comencini 2)

Run for Cover, 1955 (Ray 2, Borgnine 3, Cagney 3, Bumstead 4, Head 4, Ravetch 4)

Run for the Sun, 1956 (Boulting 2, Howard 3, Widmark 3, La Shelle 4, Nichols 4)

Run for Your Money, 1949 (Guinness 3, Balcon 4, Slocombe 4)

Run for Your Wife. *See* Moglie americana, 1965

Run, Girl, Run, 1928 (Lombard 3, Hornbeck 4)

Run Home Slow, 1966 (McCambridge 3)

Run Like a Thief, 1967 (Rey 3)

Run of the Arrow, 1957 (Fuller 2, Bronson 3, Dickinson 3, Steiger 3, Biroc 4, D'Agostino 4, Young 4)

Run on Gold. *See* Midas Run, 1969

Run, Run Sweet Road Runner, 1965 (Blanc 4)

Run Silent, Run Deep, 1958 (Wise 2, Gable 3, Lancaster 3, Harlan 4, Waxman 4)

Run, Simon, Run, 1970 (Reynolds 3)

Run, Stranger, Run. *See* Happy Mother's Day—Love George, 1973

Run Wild, Run Free, 1969 (Mills 3)

Runaround, 1931 (Steiner 4)

Runaround, 1946 (Crawford 3, Banton 4)

Runaway, 1924 (Fleischer 4)

Runaway, 1926 (Bow 3, Powell 3)

Runaway!, 1973 (Johnson 3)

Runaway, 1984 (Alonzo 4, Goldsmith 4)

Runaway Barge, 1975 (Nolte 3)

Runaway Bride, 1930 (Astor 3, Crisp 3, Murfin 4)

Runaway Bus, 1954 (Rutherford 3)

Runaway Daughter. *See* Red Salute, 1935

Runaway Express, 1926 (Miller 4)

Runaway Mouse, 1954 (Terry 4)

Runaway Queen. *See* Queen's Affair, 1934

Runaway Romany, 1917 (Davies 3)

Runaway Train. *See* Runaway!, 1973

Runaway Train, 1985 (Mikhalkov-Konchalovsky 2, Voight 3, Golan and Globus 4)

Rund um eine Million, 1933 (Fröhlich 3, Stradling 4)

Rund um Europa. *See* Rote Kreis, 1928

Runner Stumbles, 1979 (Kramer 2, Kovacs 4)

Running, 1979 (Douglas 3)

Running After Luck. *See* Jagd nach dem Glück, 1923

Running after Luck. *See* Jagd nach dem Glück, 1930

Running Away, 1989 (Ponti 4)

Running Fence, 1977 (Maysles 2)

Running, Jumping, and Standing Still Film, 1960 (Lester 2, Sellers 3)

Running Man, 1963 (Frampton 2, Reed 2, Bates 3, Harvey 3, Remick 3, Rey 3, Alwyn 4, Krasker 4, Mathieson 4)

Running Man, 1987 (Schwarzenegger 3)

Running on Empty, 1988 (Lumet 2)

Running Out of Luck, 1986 (Hopper 3)

Running Target, 1956 (Hall 4)

Running Wild, 1921 (Roach 4)

Running Wild, 1927 (La Cava 2, Fields 3)

Running Wild, 1955 (Boyle 4)

Runpen to sono musume, 1931 (Tanaka 3)

Runt, 1936 (Terry 4)

Runt Page, 1932 (Temple 3)

Rupert of Cole-Slaw, 1924 (Laurel and Hardy 3, Roach 4)

Rupert of Hee-Haw. *See* Rupert of Cole-Slaw, 1924

Rupert of Hentzau, 1923 (Bosworth 3, Menjou 3)

Rupert the Runt, 1940 (Terry 4)

Rupture, 1961 (Carrière 4)

Rupture, 1970 (Chabrol 2, Audran 3, Cassel 3, Rabier 4)

Rural Conqueror, 1911 (Lawrence 3)

Rural Co-op, 1947 (Crosby 4)

Rural Demon, 1914 (Sennett 2, Arbuckle 3)

Rural Elopement, 1908 (Griffith 2, Bitzer 4)

Rural Hungary, 1939 (Hoch 4)

Rural School, 1940 (Pearson 2)

Rural Sweden, 1938 (Hoch 4)

Rural Third Degree, 1913 (Sennett 2)

Ruri no kishi, 1956 (Shindo 2)

Rusalka, 1962 (Stallich 4)
Ruscello di Ripasottile, 1941 (Rossellini 2)
Ruse, 1915 (Hart 3, August 4, Sullivan 4)
Ruse de Max, 1913 (Linder 3)
Ruses du Diable, 1965 (Piccoli 3)
Ruses, Rhymes, Roughnecks, 1914 (Lloyd 3, Roach 4)
Rush, 1991 (Towne 4)
Rush Hour, 1928 (Pangborn 3)
Rush Hour, 1941 (Asquith 2)
Rush Orders, 1921 (Roach 4)
Rush to Judgment, 1966 (De Antonio 2)
Rushin' Ballet, 1937 (Roach 4)
Rushing Roulette, 1965 (Blanc 4, McKimson 4)
Rusk. *See* Skorpan, 1957
Ruslan and Ludmila. *See* Ruslan i Ludmila, 1915
Ruslan i Ludmila, 1915 (Mozhukin 3)
Russia House, 1990 (Russell 2, Schepisi 2, Brandauer 3, Connery 3, Pfeiffer 3, Scheider 3, Goldsmith 4)
Russia of Nicholas II and Lev Tolstoy. *See* Rossiya Nikolaya II i Lev Tolstoi, 1928

Russia—the Land of Oppression, 1910 (Porter 2)
Russian Lullaby, 1931 (Fleischer 4)
Russian Rhapsody, 1944 (Blanc 4, Clampett 4, Stalling 4)
Russian Roulette, 1975 (Elliott 3, Segal 3)
Russians Are Coming, the Russians Are Coming, 1966 (Ashby 2, Jewison 2, Arkin 3, Saint 3, Biroc 4, Boyle 4)
Russians at War, 1942 (Van Dongen 4)
Russicum, 1989 (Brazzi 3, Vangelis 4)
Rustle of Silk, 1923 (Brenon 2)
Rustler Sheriff, 1911 (Dwan 2)
Rustlers, 1919 (Ford 2, Carey 3)
Rustlers, 1949 (Hunt 4)
Rustler's Hideout, 1944 (Crabbe 3)
Rustlers' Paradise, 1935 (Carey 3)
Rustler's Rhapsody, 1985 (Rey 3)
Rustler's Roundup, 1933 (Mix 3)
Rustler's Spur, 1913 (Anderson 3)
Rustler's Step-Daughter, 1913 (Anderson 3)
Rustler's Valley, 1937 (Cobb 3, Harlan 4, Head 4)
Rusty Flame. *See* Sabita honoo, 1977

Rusty Romeos, 1956 (Three Stooges 3)
Ruten, 1956 (Kagawa 3)
Ruten, 1960 (Yamada 3)
Ruten no oohi, 1960 (Kyo 3, Tanaka 3)
Ruth of the Range, 1922 (Van Dyke 2)
Ruthless, 1948 (Ulmer 2, Greenstreet 3, Glennon 4)
Ruthless Four. *See* Ognuno per se, 1968
Ruthless People, 1986 (Midler 3)
Rutschbahn, 1928 (Herlth 4, Röhrig 4)
Ruy Blas, 1909 (Costello 3)
Ruy Blas, 1947 (Cocteau 2, Darrieux 3, Marais 3, Wakhévitch 4)
Ružové konbiné, 1932 (Stallich 4)
Ryan's Daughter, 1970 (Lean 2, Howard 3, Mills 3, Mitchum 3, Havelock-Allan 4, Jarre 4, Young 4)
Rynox, 1931 (Powell and Pressburger 2)
Ryoetsu daihyojo, 1937 (Shindo 3)
Rysopis, 1964 (Skolimowski 2)
Rythmetic, 1956 (McLaren 4)
Ryuko sokitai, 1937 (Shimura 3)
Ryusei, 1949 (Yamamura 3)

S

SAS à San Salvador, 1982 (Coutard 4)
SAS—Terminate with Extreme Prejudice. *See* SAS à San Salvador, 1982
S.I., 1913 (Gad 2)
S.1., 1913 (Nielsen 3)
S.O.S., 1927 (Gallone 2)
S.O.S., 1940 (Alwyn 4)
S.O.S. Coastguard, 1937 (Lugosi 3, Canutt 4)
S.O.S. Concorde. *See* Concorde affaire, 1979
SOS: Die Insel des Tränen, 1923 (Wegener 3)
S.O.S. Eisberg, 1933 (Riefenstahl 2)
S.O.S. Foch, 1931 (Ibert 4)
S.O.S. hélicoptère, 1959 (Lelouch 2)
S.O.S. Iceberg, 1933 (Garnett 2)
SOS in the Mountains. *See* Horské volání SOS, 1929
SOS Mediterranean. *See* Alerte en Méditerranée, 1938
S.O.S. Noronha, 1956 (Demy 2, Guerra 2, Marais 3, Decaë 4)
S.O.S. Pacific, 1959 (Attenborough 3, Constantine 3, Auric 4, Green 4)
S.O.S. Sahara, 1938 (Vanel 3)
SPFX 1140, 1982 (Dreyfuss 3)
SST—Death Flight, 1977 (Meredith 3, Biroc 4)
SST—Disaster in the Sky. *See* SST—Death Flight, 1977
SST: Disaster in the Sky. *See* SST—Death Flight, 1977
S.V.D., 1927 (Enei 4, Moskvin 4)
S.W.A.L.K., 1970 (Puttnam 4)
S-a furat o bomba, 1961 (Popescu-Gopo 4)
Sa Tête, 1929 (Epstein 2)
Sa zimbeasca toti copiii, 1956 (Mészáros 2)
S. Carlino, 1950 (Di Venanzo 4)
Saadia, 1953 (Cusack 3, Simon 3, Wilde 3, Challis 4, Kaper 4, Lewin 4)
Saat Hindustani, 1971 (Bachchan 3, Abbas 4)
Sabakareru Echizen no kami, 1962 (Hasegawa 3)
Sabaku o wataru taiyo, 1960 (Yamamura 3)
Sabata. *See* Ehi, amico … c'e Sabata, hai chiuso?, 1969
Sabina, 1979 (Andersson 3)
Sabita honoo, 1977 (Takemitsu 4)
Sables, 1927 (Manès 3)
Sables, 1969 (Braunberger 4)
Sabotage, 1936 (Homolka 3, Sidney 3, Balcon 4, Bennett 4, Rathaus 4, Reville 4, Wanger 4)
Sabotage, 1952 (Andersson 3, Dahlbeck 3)
Sabotage Squad, 1942 (Planer 4)

Saboteur, 1942 (Hitchcock 2, Boyle 4, Harrison 4)
Saboteur—Code Name Morituri. *See* Morituri, 1965
Sabotier du Val de Loire, 1956 (Demy 2)
Sabre and the Arrow. *See* Last of the Comanches, 1952
Sabrina, 1954 (Wilder 2, Bogart 3, Bushman 3, Dalio 3, Hepburn 3, Holden 3, Head 4, Lang 4)
Sabrina Fair. *See* Sabrina, 1954
Sabte yar, 1972 (Güney 2)
Sac de billes, 1975 (Sarde 4)
Sac de noeuds, 1985 (Huppert 3)
Sacco and Vanzetti. *See* Sacco e Vanzetti, 1971
Sacco bello, 1979 (Morricone 4)
Sacco di Roma, 1953 (Delli Colli 4)
Sacco e Vanzetti, 1971 (Cusack 3, Volonté 3, Morricone 4)
Sacco in Plypac, 1961 (Olmi 2)
Sachche Ka Bol Bala, 1988 (Anand 3)
Sackcloth and Scarlet, 1925 (King 2, Furthman 4)
Sacré Bleu Cross, 1967 (McKimson 4)
Sacré d'Édouard VII, 1902 (Méliès 2)
Sacré Léonce, 1935 (Christian-Jaque 2)
Sacred and Profane Love, 1921 (McCord 4)
Sacred Ganges. *See* World Window, 1977
Sacred Turquoise of the Zuni, 1910 (Olcott 2)
Sacrée jeunesse, 1958 (Cassel 3)
Sacrifice, 1908 (Griffith 2, Lawrence 3, Bitzer 4)
Sacrifice. *See* **Offret, 1986**
Sacrifice of Kathleen, 1913 (Talmadge 3)
Sacrifice to Civilization, 1911 (Bosworth 3)
Sacrificial Horse. *See* Aswa medher ghora, 1981
Sacrilege, 1988 (Donaggio 4)
Saddle Buster, 1932 (McCord 4)
Saddle Girth, 1917 (Mix 3)
Saddle Hawk, 1925 (Miller 4)
Saddle Legion, 1950 (Hunt 4)
Saddle Pals, 1947 (Autry 3)
Saddle Silly, 1941 (Blanc 4, Jones 4)
Saddle the Wind, 1958 (Cassavetes 2, Crisp 3, Taylor 3, Bernstein 4, Folsey 4, Rose 4)
Saddle Tramp, 1950 (McCrea 3)
Sad Horse, 1959 (Struss 4)
Sad Idiot. *See* Kanashiki hakuchi, 1924
Sad Sack, 1957 (Lewis 2, Lorre 3, Head 4, Wallis 4)
Sadgati, 1981 (Patil 3)
Sadie and Jon, 1987 (Reynolds 3)
Sadie Goes to Heaven, 1917 (Van Dyke 2)

Sadie Hawkins Day, 1944 (Fleischer 4)
Sadie McKee, 1934 (Brown 2, Crawford 3, Adrian 4, Brown 4, Freed 4, Mayer 4)
Sadie Thompson, 1928 (Walsh 2, Barrymore 3, Swanson 3, Barnes 4, Menzies 4, Sullivan 4)
Sadist, 1963 (Zsigmond 4)
Sadist. *See* Träfracken, 1966
Sadja, 1918 (Albers 3)
Sadko, 1952 (Ptushko 4)
Sado jowa, 1934 (Yamada 3)
Sadono kuni ondeko-za, 1976 (Shinoda 2)
Sado's Ondeko—za. *See* Sadono Kuni ondeko—za, 1976
Saelfangst i Nordgrønland, 1955 (Henning-Jensen 2)
Saetta—Principe per un Giorno, 1926 (Camerini 2)
Safari, 1940 (Daves 2, Carroll 3, Dreier 4, Head 4)
Safari, 1956 (Leigh 3, Mature 3, Alwyn 4, Buckner 4, Veiller 4)
Safari diamants, 1966 (Trintignant 3)
Safari 5000. *See* Eiko eno 5000 kiro, 1969
Safari 3000. *See* Rally, 1980
Safe for Democracy, 1918 (Blackton 2)
Safe Home. *See* Pod jednou střechou, 1938
Safe in Hell, 1931 (Wellman 2, Johnson 3)
Safe in Jail, 1913 (Sennett 2)
Safe Place, 1971 (Welles 2, Nicholson 3, Weld 3)
Safecracker, 1958 (Milland 3)
Safeguarding Military Information, 1941 (Huston 3)
Safeguarding Military Information, 1944 (Rogers 3)
Safety Boots, 1965 (Dunning 4)
Safety Curtain, 1918 (Talmadge 3)
Safety First, 1941 (Cushing 3)
Safety First Ambrose, 1916 (Sennett 2)
Safety in Numbers, 1930 (Beavers 3, Lombard 3, Banton 4, Vorkapich 4)
Safety in Numbers, 1938 (Clarke 4)
Safety Last, 1923 (Lloyd 3, Roach 4, Zukor 4)
Safety Second, 1950 (Hanna and Barbera 4)
Safety Spin, 1953 (Bosustow 4, Burness 4)
Safety Worst, 1915 (Laurel and Hardy 3)
S'affranchir, 1911 (Feuillade 2, Gaumont 4)
Säg det i toner, 1929 (Jaenzon 4)
Säg det med blommer, 1952 (Björnstrand 3)
Sag' die Warhheit, 1946 (Fröhlich 3)
Saga of Anatahan. *See* Anatahan, 1953
Saga of Death Valley, 1939 (Rogers 3)
Saga of the Flying Hostesses. *See* Copacabana Palace, 1962

315

Saga of the Vagabonds. *See* Sengoku gunto-sen, 1959

Sagebrush Phrenologist, 1911 (Dwan 2)

Sagebrush Sadie, 1928 (Disney 4)

Sagebrush Tom, 1915 (Mix 3)

Sagebrush Trail, 1922 (Beery 3)

Sagebrush Trail, 1933 (Wayne 3, Canutt 4)

Sagebrush Troubadour, 1935 (Autry 3)

Sagebrusher, 1920 (Seitz 4)

Sage-femme de première classe, 1902 (Guy 2, Gaumont 4)

Sage-femme, le curé et le bon Dieu. *See* Jessica, 1962

Sagina, 1974 (Burman 4)

Sagina Mahato, 1970 (Kumar 3)

Saginaw Trail, 1953 (Autry 3)

Sagnarelle, 1907 (Linder 3)

Sagrada Família, 1972 (De Almeida 4)

Sahara, 1919 (Sullivan 4)

Sahara, 1943 (Bogart 3, Duryea 3, Brown 4, Lourié 4, Maté 4, Rozsa 4)

Sahara, 1984 (Mills 3, Golan and Globus 4, Morricone 4)

Sahara, an IV, 1960 (Delerue 4, Fradetal 4)

Sahara Hare, 1955 (Blanc 4, Freleng 4)

Sahib Bahadur, 1979 (Anand 3)

Sai cosa faceva Stalin alle donne, 1969 (Morricone 4)

Said O'Reilly to McNab, 1937 (Vetchinsky 4)

Saigo ni warau otoko, 1949 (Kyo 3)

Saigo no shinpan, 1965 (Takemitsu 4)

Saigon, 1948 (Ladd 3, Lake 3, Bumstead 4, Dreier 4, Head 4, Seitz 4)

Saikai, 1953 (Mori 3)

Saikaku ichidai onna, 1952 (Mizoguchi 2, Mifune 3, Shimura 3, Shindo 3, Tanaka 3, Yoda 4)

Saikaku's Five Women. *See* Koushoku gonin onna, 1948

Sailaab, 1956 (Dutt 2)

Sail a Crooked Ship, 1962 (Wagner 3, Biroc 4, Duning 4)

Sailboat, 1967–68 (Wieland 2)

Sailing Along, 1938 (Matthews 3, Sim 3, Junge 4)

Sailing and Village Band, 1958 (Bosustow 4)

Sailing, Sailing Over the Bounding Main, 1926 (Fleischer 4)

Sailing with a Song, 1949 (Fleischer 4)

Sailor and the Devil, 1967 (Williams 4)

Sailor Be Good, 1933 (Cruze 2)

Sailor Beware, 1951 (Lewis 2, Dean 3, Hutton 3, Martin 3, Ames 4, Head 4, Wallis 4)

Sailor Beware!, 1956 (Slocombe 4)

Sailor from Gibraltar, 1967 (Richardson 2, Welles 2, Hurt 3, Moreau 3, Redgrave 3, Courtard 4)

Sailor Jack's Reformation, 1911 (Olcott 2)

Sailor of the King, 1953 (Mathieson 4)

Sailor Papa, 1925 (Roach 4)

Sailor Takes a Wife, 1945 (Allyson 3, Walker 3, Green 4, Irene 4)

Sailor Who Fell from Grace with the Sea, 1976 (Slocombe 4)

Sailors. *See* Matrosowcy, 1951

Sailors All, 1943 (Vorkapich 4)

Sailors Beware, 1927 (Laurel and Hardy 3, Roach 4)

Sailor's Consolation, 1989 (Halas and Batchelor 4)

Sailor's Heart, 1912 (Sweet 3, Meredyth 4)

Sailor's Holiday, 1929 (Miller 4)

Sailor's Holiday, 1944 (Winters 3, Guffey 4)

Sailor's Home, 1936 (Terry 4)

Sailor's Lady, 1940 (Dwan 2, Andrews 3, Crabbe 3)

Sailor's Luck, 1933 (Walsh 2, Carré 4, Miller 4)

Sailor's Sweetheart, 1927 (Bacon 2, Loy 3)

Sailor's Three, 1940 (Balcon 4)

Sailor's Three Crowns. *See* Trois couronnes du matelo, 1982

Sailors' Wives, 1928 (Astor 3, Meredyth 4)

Saint Ilario, 1921 (Rosher 4)

Saint in London, 1939 (Sanders 3)

Saint in New York, 1938 (August 4, Polglase 4)

Saint in Palm Springs, 1941 (Sanders 3)

Saint Jack, 1979 (Bogdanovich 2, Elliott 3, Müller 4)

Saint Joan, 1957 (Preminger 2, Gielgud 3, Seberg 3, Walbrook 3, Widmark 3, Bass 4, Greene 4, Périnal 4)

Saint Meets the Tiger, 1943 (Krasker 4)

Saint prend l'affût, 1966 (Christian-Jaque 2, Marais 3)

Saint Strikes Back, 1939 (Fitzgerald 3, Sanders 3)

Saint Takes Over, 1940 (Sanders 3)

St. Benny the Dip, 1951 (Ulmer 2)

St. Elmo, 1923 (Gilbert 3, Love 3, August 4, Furthman 4)

St. Elmo Murray. *See* St. Elmo, 1923

St. Helena and Its Man of Destiny, 1936 (Hoch 4)

St. Ives, 1976 (Bronson 3, Sanders 3, Schell 3, Ballard 4, Houseman 4, Schifrin 4)

St. Louis Blues, 1939 (Walsh 2, Lamour 3, Dreier 4, Head 4)

St. Louis Blues, 1958 (Head 4)

St. Louis Exposition, 1902 (Bitzer 4)

St. Louis Kid, 1934 (Cagney 3, Orry-Kelly 4)

St. Martin's Lane, 1938 (Harrison 3, Laughton 3, Leigh 3, Pommer 4)

St. Valentine's Day Massacre, 1967 (Corman 2, Dern 3, Robards 3, Segal 3, Krasner 4, Smith 4)

St. Wenceslas. *See* Svatý Václav, 1929

Sainte Famille, 1972 (Thulin 3, Vierny 4)

Sainte Odile, 1915 (Musidora 3)

Sainte-Antoine de Padoue, 1897 (Pathé 4)

Sainted Devil, 1924 (Valentino 3, Westmore Family 4, Zukor 4)

Sainted Sisters, 1948 (Bondi 3, Fitzgerald 3, Lake 3, Bumstead 4, Dreier 4, Head 4)

Saintes Nitouches, 1962 (Blier 3)

Saint-Louis ou l'ange de la paix, 1950 (Philipe 3)

Saint's Adventure, 1917 (Walthall 3)

Saints and Sinners, 1949 (Korda 4)

Saint's Double Trouble, 1940 (Lugosi 3, Sanders 3, Hunt 4)

Saint's Girl Friday. *See* Saint's Return, 1953

Saint's Return, 1953 (Carreras 4)

Saint-Tropez Blues, 1960 (Chabrol 2, Audran 3)

Saint-Tropez, devoir de vacances, 1952 (Resnais 2, Brasseur 3, Gélin 3, Piccoli 3, Cloquet 4)

Saison in Kairo, 1933 (Herlth 4, Hoffmann 4, Reisch 4, Röhrig 4)

Saisons du plaisir, 1988 (Vanel 3)

Sais seule que j'aime, 1938 (Presle 3)

Sait-on jamais?, 1957 (Vadim 2, Saulnier 4)

Sakai, 1953 (Hayasaka 4)

Sakanaka ronin, 1930 (Yamada 3)

Sakharov, 1984 (Jackson 3, Robards 3)

Sakiko-san chotto, 1963 (Yamada 3)

Sakujitsu kieta otoko, 1941 (Hasegawa 3, Takamine 3, Yamada 3)

Sakura No Ki No Shitade, 1989 (Iwashita 3)

Sakura no mori no mankai no shita, 1975 (Shinoda 2, Iwashita 3, Takemitsu 4)

Sakura onda, 1934 (Tanaka 3)

Sakurada-mon, 1961 (Hasegawa 3)

Sakura-ondo: Kyo wa odette, 1947 (Hasegawa 3)

Sal Gordo, 1983 (Maura 3)

Sal of Singapore, 1929 (Johnson 3)

Salación, 1966 (Gómez 2, Herrera 4)

Salaire de la peur, 1953 (Clouzet 2, Montand 3, Vanti 3, Auric 4)

Salaire du péché, 1956 (Darrieux 3, Moreau 3, Alekan 4)

Salamander. *See* Salamandre, 1971

Salamander, 1981 (Cardinale 3, Lee 3, Quinn 3, Wallach 3, Goldsmith 4)

Salamandre, 1971 (Tanner 2)

Salamandre d'or, 1962 (Kosma 4)

Salammbo, 1924 (Burel 4)

Salaried Men's Loyal Ronin Story. *See* Saramiiman Chushingura, 1960

Salauds vont en enfer, 1955 (Reggiani 3)

Salavat Yulayev, 1941 (Protazanov 2)

Sale of a Heart, 1913 (Costello 3)

Sale temps pour les mouches, 1966 (Audiard 4)

Salem Came to Supper. *See* Night Visitor, 1971.

Salem's Lot, 1979 (Ayres 3, Mason 3)

Salesman, 1969 (Maysles 2)

Salesman, 1980 (Halas and Batchelor 4)

Salka Valka, 1954 (Nykvist 4)

Sallah, 1964 (Topol 3, Crosby 4, Golan and Globus 4)

Sallah Shabati. *See* Sallah, 1964

Salle à manger fantastique, 1898 (Méliès 2)

Sallie's Sure Short, 1913 (Mix 3)

Sally, 1925 (LeRoy 2, Moore 3, Mathis 4, McCord 4)

Sally, 1929 (Brown 3, Young 4, Wallis 4)

Sally and Saint Anne, 1952 (Maté 4)

Sally Bishop, 1916 (Pearson 2)

Sally in Our Alley, 1931 (Fields 3, Dean 4, Reville 4)

Sally, Irene, and Mary, 1925 (Goulding 2, Crawford 3, Gibbons 4, Mayer 4)

Sally, Irene, and Mary, 1938 (Durante 3, Faye 3)

Sally of the Sawdust, 1925 (Griffith 2, Fields 3)

Sally of the Scandals, 1928 (Love 3, Plunkett 4)

Sally Swing, 1938 (Fleischer 4)

Sally's Shoulders, 1928 (Miller 4)

Salmon Berries, 1991 (Palance 3)

Salmon Fishing, Quebec, 1905 (Bitzer 4)

Salo, o le 120 giornate di Sodoma, 1975 (Donati 4, Delli Colli 4, Morricone 4)

Salo—The 120 Days of Sodom. *See* Salo o le 120 giornate di Sodoma, 1975

Salome, 1902 (Messter 4)

Salome, 1908 (Costello 3, Lawrence 3)

Salome, 1913 (Bertini 3)

Salome, 1918 (Bara 3, Schenck 4)

Salome, 1922 (Metzner 4)

Salome, 1923 (Nazimova 3)

Salome, 1953 (Dieterle 2, Granger 3, Hayworth 3, Laughton 3, Duning 4, Hoch 4, Lang 4)

Salome, 1971 (Schroeter 2)

Salome, 1978 (Almodóvar 2)

Salome, 1980 (Brakhage 2)

Salome, 1986 (Golan and Globus 4)

Salome and Delilah, 1963 (Warhol 2)

Salome of the Tenements, 1925 (Olcott 2, Levien 4)

Salome vs. Shenandoah, 1919 (Sennett 2)

Salome, Where She Danced, 1945 (De Carlo 3, Eason 4, Mohr 4, Wanger 4)

Salome's Last Dance, 1988 (Russell 2, Jackson 3)

Salomy Jane, 1914 (Mohr 4)

Salomy Jane, 1923 (Clarke 4, Young 4)

Salomy Jane. See Wild Girl, 1932

Salon Dora Green, 1933 (Galeen 4)

Salon Kitty, 1976 (Thulin 3, Adam 4)

Salón México, 1948 (Fernández 2, Figueroa 4)

Salon nautique, 1954 (Broca 2)

Salonique, nid d'espions. See Mademoiselle Docteur, 1937

Salonwagen E 417, 1939 (Käutner 2)

Saloon Bar, 1940 (McDowall 3, Balcon 4)

Salsa, 1988 (Golan and Globus 4)

Salt in the Park, 1959 (Wieland 2)

Salt in the Wound. See Dito nell piaga, 1969

Salt of the Earth, 1954 (Wilson 4)

Salt of This Black Earth. See Sól ziemi czarnej, 1970

Salt Water Daffy, 1941 (Lantz 4)

Salt Water Tabby, 1947 (Hanna and Barbera 4)

Salt Water Taffy, 1930 (Terry 4)

Salto, 1965 (Cybulski 3, Konwicki 4)

Salto mortale, 1931 (Manès 3, Walbrook 3, Junge 4)

Salto nel vuoto, 1979 (Bellocchio 2, Aimée 3, Piccoli 3, Noiret 3)

Saltstänk och krutgubbar, 1946 (Nykvist 4)

Salty McQuire, 1937 (Terry 4)

Salty O'Rourke, 1945 (Walsh 2, Ladd 3, Dreier 4, Head 4)

Saltzburg Connection, 1971 (Anhalt 4)

Saludos Amigos, 1942 (Disney 4)

Salut la puce, 1982 (Lai 4)

Salut l'artiste, 1973 (Mastroianni 3)

Salut les Cubains, 1963 (Varda 2)

Salutary Lesson, 1910 (Griffith 2, Bitzer 4)

Salute, 1929 (Ford 2, Bond 3, Wayne 3, August 4)

Salute for Three, 1943 (De Carlo 3, Dreier 4, Head 4, Young 4)

Salute to Cuba. See Salut les Cubains, 1963

Salute to France, 1944 (Meredith 3, Kanin 4)

Salute to Romance. See Annapolis Salute, 1937

Salute to the Marines, 1943 (Beery 3)

Salute to the Theatres, 1955 (Gish 3)

Salvador, 1986 (Stone 2, Delerue 4)

Salvage, 1921 (King 2)

Salvage with a Smile, 1940 (Cavalcanti 2)

Salvare la faccia, 1969 (Brazzi 3)

Salvation. See Divine Mr. J, 1974

Salvation Army Lass, 1908 (Griffith 2, Lawrence 3, Bitzer 4)

Salvation Hunters, 1925 (Von Sternberg 2)

Salvation Nell, 1921 (D'Agostino 4, Haller 4)

Salvation Nell, 1931 (Cruze 2)

Salvatore Giuliano, 1961 (Rosi 2, Cecchi D'Amico 4, Cristaldi 4, Di Venanzo 4, Solinas 4)

Salzburg Connection, 1972 (Brandauer 3, Karina 3)

Sam Hill: Who Killed the Mysterious Mr. Foster?, 1971 (Dern 3, Jaffe 3)

Sam Lloyd's Famous Puzzles, 1917 (O'Brien 4)

Sam Marlow, Private Eye. See Man with Bogart's Face, 1979

Sam pósród miasta, 1965 (Cybulski 3)

Sam Whiskey, 1969 (Dickinson 3, Reynolds 3)

Samac, 1958 (Mimica 4)

Samaritan. See Du skal elske din Naetste, 1915

Samaritan. See Harp in Hock, 1927

Samaritan: The Mitch Snyder Story, 1986 (Sheen 3)

Same Old Story, 1982 (Driessen 4)

Same Player Shoots Again, 1967 (Wenders 2)

Same Time, Next Year, 1979 (Mulligan 2, Burstyn 3, Bumstead 4, Hamlisch 4, Mirisch 4, Surtees 4)

Sameera, 1981 (Azmi 3)

Samhallets dom, 1912 (Jaenzon 4, Magnusson 4)

Samidare zoshi, 1924 (Mizoguchi 2)

Samii yunii pioner, 1925 (Litvak 2)

Samma no aji, 1962 (Iwashita 3, Ryu 3)

Sammy and Rosie Get Laid, 1987 (Fears 2, Bloom 3)

Sammy Going South, 1963 (Mackendrick 2, Balcon 4)

Sammy in Siberia, 1919 (Daniels 3, Lloyd 3, Roach 4)

Samourai, 1967 (Melville 2, Delon 3, Decaë 4)

Sampo, 1958 (Ptushko 4)

Sam's Son, 1984 (Wallach 3)

Samson, 1914 (Lloyd 3)

Samson, 1936 (Tourneur 2, Baur 3)

Samson, 1961 (Wajda 2, Tyszkiewicz 3)

Samson and Delilah. See Samson und Delilah, 1922

Samson and Delilah, 1949 (De Mille 2, Lamarr 3, Lansbury 3, Mature 3, Sanders 3, Barnes 4, Dreier 4, Head 4, Jeakins 4, Young 4)

Samson and Delilah, 1984 (Ferrer 3, Mature 3, Schell 3, Von Sydow 3, Jarre 4)

Samson et Delila, 1902 (Pathé 4)

Samson und Dalila, 1923 (Curtiz 2)

Samson und Delila, 1920 (Korda 4)

Samson und Delila, 1922 (Lukas 3)

Samurai. See Miyamoto Musashi, 1954

Samurai, 1965 (Mifune 3, Shimura 3, Kuri 4)

Samurai. See Bianco, il giallo, il nero, 1975

Samurai Assassin. See Samurai, 1965

Samurai Banners. See Furin kaza, 1969

Samurai Daughter. See Kodachi o tsukau onna, 1961

Samurai from Nowhere. See Dojoyaburi, 1964

Samurai Nippon, 1957 (Yamada 3)

Samurai ondo, 1937 (Yoda 4)

Samurai, Part II. See Ichijoji no ketto, 1955

Samurai, Part III. See Ketto Ganryu-Jima, 1956

Samurai Pirate. See Daitozuku, 1964

Samurai Saga. See Aru kengo no shogai, 1959

Samurai Song. See Samurai ondo, 1937

Samurai Spy. See Ibun Sarutobi sasuke, 1965

Samvetsömma Adolf, 1936 (Fischer 4, Jaenzon 4)

Samvittighedsnag. See Hvem var Forbryderen?, 1912

San Antonio, 1945 (Walsh 2, Flynn 3, Buckner 4, Burnett 4, Glennon 4, Steiner 4, Waxman 4)

San Antonio Rose, 1941 (Arden 3, Three Stooges 3, Cortez 4)

San Babila ore 20: un delitto inutile, 1976 (Morricone 4)

San Demetrio London, 1943 (Hamer 2, Balcon 4)

San Diego, 1911 (Dwan 2)

San Diego, I Love You, 1944 (Keaton 2, Horton 3, Mohr 4, Salter 4)

San Domingo, 1970 (Syberberg 2)

San Fernando Valley, 1944 (Rogers 3)

San Francisco, 1906 (Bitzer 4)

San Francisco, 1936 (Van Dyke 2, Von Stroheim 2, Gable 3, MacDonald 3, Tracy 3, Adrian 4, Brown 4, Canutt 4, Edens 4, Emerson 4, Freed 4, Gibbons 4, Gillespie 4, Loos 4, Kaper 4, Mayer 4, Shearer 4, Stothart 4)

San Francisco, 1945 (Van Dyke 2)

San Francisco Celebration, 1913 (Sennett 2)

San Francisco Docks, 1941 (Fitzgerald 3, Meredith 3, Salter 4)

San Francisco International, 1970 (Johnson 3)

San Francisco Story, 1952 (De Carlo 3, McCrea 3, Friedhofer 4, Jenkins 4, Seitz 4)

San Giovanni Decollato, 1940 (Zavattini 4)

San Massenza, 1955 (Olmi 2)

San Michele aveva un gallo, 1971 (Taviani 2)

San Miniato, luglio °44, 1954 (Taviani 2, Zavattini 4)

San Quentin, 1937 (Bacon 2, Bogart 3, Sheridan 3, Raksin 4)

Sanam, 1951 (Anand 3)

Sanba, 1974 (Tanaka 3)

Sanbiki no tanuki, 1966 (Muraki 4)

Sanbyaku-rokujugo-ya, 1948 (Ichikawa 2, Takamine 3)

Sanbyaku-rokuju-go-ya, 1962 (Yamada 3)

Sancta Simplicitas, 1968 (Popescu-Gopo 4)

Sanctuary, 1961 (Richardson 2, Montand 3, Remick 3, Faulkner 4, North 4, Smith 4)

Sand, 1920 (Hart 3, August 4)

Sand, 1949 (Clarke 4)

Sand, 1971 (Ballhaus 4)

Sand Pebbles, 1966 (Wise 2, Attenborough 3, McQueen 3, Goldsmith 4, Leven 4, Reynolds 4)

Sanda tai Gailha. See Furankenshutain no kaiju—Sanda tai Gailah, 1966

Sandai kaiju chikyu saidai no kessen, 1965 (Okada 3, Shimura 3, Tsuburaya 4)

Sandakan hachi-ban-shokan: Bokyo, 1974 (Tanaka 3)

Sandakan, House No. 8. See Sandakan hachi-ban shokan: Bokyo, 1974

Sanders of the River, 1935 (Crichton 2, Robeson 3, Biro 4, Hornbeck 4, Korda, A. 4, Korda, V. 4, Périnal 4)

Sandman, 1920 (Roach 4)

Sandokan, la tigre di Monpracem, 1963 (Fusco 4)

Sandpiper, 1965 (Minnelli 2, Bronson 3, Burton 3, O'Toole 3, Saint 3, Taylor 3, Krasner 4, Sharaff 4, Trumbo 4, Wilson 4)

Sandra. *See* Vaghe stelle dell'orsa, 1965

Sands of Dee, 1912 (Griffith 2, Marsh 3, Bitzer 4)

Sands of Fate, 1914 (Crisp 3)

Sands of Iwo Jima, 1949 (Dwan 2, Wayne 3, Young 4)

Sands of the Kalahari, 1965 (Baker 3, York 3, Levine 4)

Sandwich, 1980 (Bozzetto 4)

Sandwich, 1984 (Bozzetto 4)

Sandwich Man, 1966 (Dors 3, Terry-Thomas 3, Wisdom 3)

Sandy Claws, 1955 (Blanc 4, Foster 4, Freleng 4, Stalling 4)

Sandy Gets Her Man, 1940 (Salter 4)

Sandy Is a Lady, 1940 (Krasner 4)

Sandy Steps Out, 1941 (Horton 3, Pangborn 3)

Sane Asylum, 1912 (Porter 2)

Sanford Meisner—The Theater's Best Kept Secret, 1984 (Pollack 2, Falk 3)

Sanfte Lauf, 1967 (Ganz 3)

Sang à la tête, 1955 (Gabin 3, Audiard 4)

Sang d'Allah, 1922 (Modot 3)

Sang des autres, 1973 (Vanel 3)

Sang des autres, 1983 (Chabrol 2, Audran 3, Foster 3)

Sang des bêtes, 1949 (Franju 2, Fradetal 4, Kosma 4)

Sang d'un poète, 1930 (Cocteau 2, Auric 4, D'Eaubonne 4, Périnal 4)

Sang et lumières, 1953 (Gélin 3, Audiard 4)

Sang et lumières, 1953 (García Berlanga 2, Gelin 3)

Sanga ari, 1962 (Toda 4)

Sanga Moyu, 1984 (Mifune 3)

Sangam, 1964 (Kapoor 2)

Sangaree, 1953 (Head 4)

Sången om den eldröda blomman, 1918 (Molander 2, Stiller 2, Jaenzon 4, Magnusson 4)

Sången om den eldröda blomman, 1934 (Jaenzon 4)

Sången om den eldröda blomman, 1957 (Molander 2)

Sangram, 1950 (Dutt 2)

Sangre y luces, 1953 (García Berlanga 2)

Sangue bleu, 1914 (Bertini 3)

Sanitarium, 1910 (Arbuckle 3)

Sanitarium Scandal, 1916 (Eason 4)

Sanjaku Sagohei, 1944 (Takamine 3)

Sanjh aur Savera, 1964 (Dutt 2)

Sanjog, 1972 (Bachchan 3)

Sanjuro. *See* Tsubaki Sanjuro, 1962

Sanju-san-gen-do-toshi-ya monogatari, 1945 (Hasegawa 3, Tanaka 3)

Sanka, 1972 (Shindo 2)

San-kyodai no ketto, 1960 (Hasegawa 3)

Sannin-musume kampai, 1962 (Iwashita 3)

San-nin no kaoyaku, 1960 (Hasegawa 3, Kyo 3)

Sanroku, 1962 (Yamada 3)

Sans famille, 1934 (Braunberger 4, Jaubert 4, Trauner 4)

Sans famille, 1958 (Blier 3, Brasseur 3, Cervi 3)

Sans laisser d'adresse, 1950 (Blier 3, Piccoli 3, Douy 4, Kosma 4)

Sans le joug, 1911 (Feuillade 2)

Sans lendemain, 1940 (Ophüls 2, Feuillère 3, Alekan 4, Douy 4, Lourié 4, Schüfftan 4)

Sans mobile apparent, 1971 (Audran 3, Sanda 3, Trintignant 3, Morricone 4)

Sans soleil, 1983 (Marker 2)

Sans tambour ni trompette, 1950 (Berry 3)

Sans tambour ni trompette, 1960 (Rosay 3)

Sans Toit ni loi. *See* Vagabonde, 1986

Sansar Simante, 1966 (Ghatak 2)

Sanshiro Sugata. *See* Sugata Sanshiro, 1943

Sanshiro Sugata. *See* Zoku Sugata Sanshiro, 1945

Sansho Dayu, 1954 (Mizoguchi 2, Kagawa 3, Shindo 3, Tanaka 3, Hayasaka 4, Miyagawa 4, Yoda 4)

Sansho the Bailiff. *See* **Sansho Dayu, 1954**

Sanskar, 1958 (Biswas 4)

Sånt händer inte här, 1950 (Fischer 4)

Santa Anna Winds, 1988 (Cimino 2)

Santa Catalina Islands, 1914 (Sennett 2)

Santa Catalina, Magic Isle of the Pacific, 1911 (Dwan 2)

Santa Claus: The Movie, 1985 (Meredith 3, Moore 3, Mancini 4)

Santa Elena piccolo isola, 1942 (Sordi 3)

Santa Fe, 1951 (Scott 3, Brown 4)

Santa Fe Marshall, 1940 (Harlan 4, Head 4)

Santa Fe Scouts, 1943 (Canutt 4)

Santa Fe Stampede, 1938 (Wayne 3, Canutt 4)

Santa Fe Trail, 1930 (Head 4)

Santa Fe Trail, 1940 (Curtiz 2, Bond 3, De Havilland 3, Flynn 3, Kennedy 3, Massey 3, Reagan 3, Buckner 4, Friedhofer 4, Haskin 4, Polito 4, Steiner 4, Wallis 4)

Santé à l'étable, 1957 (Braunberger 4)

Santee, 1972 (Ford 3)

Santiago, 1956 (Ladd 3, Seitz 4)

Santiago, 1970 (Brocka 2)

Santo de la espada, 1969 (Torre Nilsson 2)

Sanza shigure, 1929 (Hasegawa 3)

Saotome-ke no musumetachi, 1962 (Kagawa 3)

Sap, 1929 (Horton 3, Pangborn 3)

Sap from Syracuse, 1930 (Rogers 3, Green 4)

Saphead, 1920 (Keaton 2)

Sapho, 1934 (Douy 4, Jaubert 4)

Sapho, 1970 (D'Eaubonne 4)

Sapho 63, 1963 (Alcoriza 4)

Sapiches, 1982 (Golan and Globus 4)

Sapnon Ka Saudgar, 1968 (Kapoor 2)

Sapphire, 1959 (Dearden 2, Dillon 4, Rank 4)

Sappho, 1921 (Krauss 3, Negri 3)

Sapporo Orimpikku, 1972 (Shinoda 2)

Sapporo Winter Olympic Games. *See* Sapporo Orimpikku, 1972

Sappy Bullfighters, 1958 (Three Stooges 3)

Saps at Sea, 1940 (Langdon 3, Laurel and Hardy 3, Roach 4)

Saps in Chaps, 1942 (Blanc 4, Freleng 4, Stalling 4)

Sara lär sig folkvett, 1937 (Molander 2, Fischer 4, Jaenzon 4)

Sara Learns Manners. *See* Sara lär sig folkvett, 1937

Sara no hanano toge, 1955 (Yamamura 3)

Saraba Okite, 1971 (Iwashita 3)

Saraba rabauru, 1954 (Tsuburaya 4)

Saraband. *See* Saraband for Dead Lovers, 1948

Saraband for Dead Lovers, 1948 (Dearden 2, Granger 3, Greenwood 3, Lee 3, Quayle 3, Rosay 3, Balcon 4, Rank 4, Slocombe 4)

Saracen Blade, 1954 (Katzman 4)

Saracinesca, 1918 (Bertini 3)

Saragossa Manuscript. *See* Rękopis znaleziony w Saragossie, 1964

Sarah, 1981 (Lee 2)

Sarah and Son, 1930 (Arzner 2, March 3, Akins 4, Lang 4, Selznick 4, Zukor 4)

Sarah and the Squirrel, 1984 (Farrow 3)

Sarah et le cri de la langouste, 1985 (Seyrig 3)

Sarah Lawrence, 1940 (Van Dyke 2)

Sarah, Plain and Tall, 1991 (Close 3)

Sarah Siddons, 1938 (McDowall 3)

Sarajewo, 1955 (Kinski 3, Kortner 3)

Sarariiman Chushingura, 1960 (Tsukasa 3, Muraki 4)

Sarariiman Shimizu minato, 1962 (Tsukasa 3)

Sarati le terrible, 1938 (Baur 3, Dalio 3)

Saratoga, 1937 (Barrymore 3, Gable 3, McDaniel 3, Pidgeon 3, Gibbons 4, Loos 4)

Saratoga Trunk, 1945 (Wood 2, Bergman 3, Cooper 3, Haller 4, Robinson 4, Steiner 4, Wallis 4)

Saratoga-Koffer, 1918 (Dupont 2)

Sarga Arnyèk, 1920 (Lukas 3)

Sargam, 1950 (Kapoor 2)

Sarhad, 1960 (Anand 3)

Sarraounia, 1986 (Hondo 2)

Sarre, pleins feux, 1951 (Alekan 4, Colpi 4)

Sartana, 1968 (Kinski 3)

Sartre par lui-même, 1976 (Astruc 2)

Sarutobi. *See* Ibun Sarutobi Sasuke, 1965

Sarutobi Sasuke, 1930 (Yamada 3)

Sarvtid, 1943 (Sucksdorff 2)

Sasaki Kojiro, 1950 (Takamine 3, Tsuburaya 4)

Sasaki Kojiro, 1967 (Tsukasa 3)

Sasameyuki, 1950 (Kagawa 3, Takamine 3, Hayasaka 4)

Sasameyuki, 1959 (Kyo 3)

Sasek a kralovna, 1987 (Brodský 3)

Sasha, 1930 (Kuleshov 3)

Sąsiedzi, 1969 (Ścibor-Rylski 4)

Saskatchewan, 1954 (Walsh 2, Ladd 3, Winters 3, Salter 4, Seitz 4)

Såsom i en spegel, 1961 (Andersson 3, Björnstrand 3, Von Sydow 3, Nykvist 4)

Satan Bug, 1965 (Sturges 2, Andrews 3, Anhalt 4, Goldsmith 4, Surtees 4)

Satan McAllister's Heir, 1915 (Sullivan 4)

Satan Met a Lady, 1936 (Dieterle 2, Davis 3, Blanke 4, Orry-Kelly 4, Edeson 4)

Satan Murders, 1974 (Sarandon 3)

Satan Never Sleeps, 1962 (McCarey 2, Holden 3, Webb 3, Mathieson 4, Morris 4)

Satan Town, 1926 (Carey 3, Polito 4)

Satan Triumphant. *See* Satana likuyushchin, 1917

Satana likuyushchii, 1917 (Mozhukin 3)

Satanas, 1915 (Feuillade 2)

Satanas, 1919 (Murnau 2, Wiene 2, Kortner 3, Veidt 3, Freund 4)

Satanic Rites of Dracula, 1973 (Cushing 3, Lee 3)

Satan's Brew. *See* Satansbraten, 1976

Satan's Cheerleaders, 1977 (Carradine 3, De Carlo 3)

Satan's Sister, 1925 (Pearson 2)
Satan's Triangle, 1975 (Novak 3)
Satan's Waitin', 1954 (Blanc 4, Freleng 4, Stalling 4)
Satansbraten, 1976 (Ballhaus 4)
Satansketten, 1921 (Herlth 4, Röhrig 4)
Satdee Night, 1973 (Armstrong 2)
Satellite in the Sky, 1956 (Périnal 4)
Sati Anjana, 1934 (Mehboob 2)
Sati Mahananda, 1923 (Phalke 2)
Satin Girl, 1923 (Lawrence 3)
Satisfied Customers, 1954 (Terry 4)
Satomi ya-ken-den, 1937 (Shindo 3)
Satsueijo remansu: Renai annai, 1932 (Tanaka 3)
Satsueijo romansu, 1932 (Gosho 2)
Satsuma hikyaku, 1951 (Yamada 3)
Satsunan sodoin, 1930 (Hasegawa 3)
Satta Pe Satta, 1982 (Bachchan 3)
Saturday Afternoon, 1926 (Capra 2, Sennett 2, Langdon 3, Hornbeck 4)
Saturday Evening Puss, 1950 (Hanna and Barbera 4)
Saturday Island, 1952 (Darnell 3, Alwyn 4, Morris 4)
Saturday Men, 1962 (Menges 4)
Saturday Morning, 1922 (Roach 4)
Saturday Night, 1922 (De Mille 2, Macpherson 4, Struss 4)
Saturday Night. See Cerná sobota, 1960
Saturday Night and Sunday Morning, 1960 (Reisz 2, Richardson 2, Finney 3, Roberts 3, Francis 4)
Saturday Night Fever, 1977 (Badham 2, Travolta 3)
Saturday Night Kid, 1929 (Arthur 3, Bow 3, Harlow 3, Head 4)
Saturday, Sunday and Monday. See Sabato, Domenico e Lunedi, 1989
Saturday, Sunday, Monday, 1990 (Loren 3)
Saturday the 14th Strikes Back, 1988 (Corman 2)
Saturday's Children, 1929 (La Cava 2, Seitz 4)
Saturday's Children, 1933 (Young 3)
Saturday's Children, 1940 (Garfield 3, Rains 3, Blanke 4, Deutsch 4, Epstein 4, Howe 4, Wallis 4)
Saturday's Children, 1951 (Reed 3)
Saturday's Hero, 1951 (Bernstein 4, Garmes 4)
Saturday's Heroes, 1937 (Musuraca 4)
Saturday's Heroes, 1951 (Buchman 4)
Saturday's Lesson, 1929 (Roach 4)
Saturday's Millions, 1933 (Ladd 3)
Saturday's Shopping, 1903 (Hepworth 2)
Saturn 3, 1980 (Donen 2, Douglas 3)
Satyajit Ray, 1985 (Benegal 2)
Satyajit Ray—Film Maker, 1982 (Nihalani 4)
Satyam Shivam Sundaram, 1978 (Kapoor 2)
Satyricon, 1969 (Donati 4, Rota 4, Rotunno 4)
Sau Crore, 1990 (Anand 3)
Saucepan Journey. See Kastrullicsan, 1950
Saucy Madeline, 1918 (Sennett 2)
Saucy Sausages, 1929 (Lantz 4)
Saudagar, 1973 (Bachchan 3)
Sauerbruch—Das war mein Leben, 1954 (Herlth 4)
Saul and David, 1909 (Costello 3)
Saul and David. See Saul e David, 1964
Saul e David, 1964 (Guerra 4)
Sausalito, 1967 (Warhol 2)

Saut de l'ange, 1971 (Hayden 3)
Saut humidifié de M. Plick, 1900 (Guy 2)
Saut Perilleux, 1991 (Maura 3)
Saute ma vie, 1968 (Akerman 2)
Sautela Bhai, 1962 (Dutt 2, Biswas 4)
Sauvage, 1975 (Deneuve 3, Montand 3, Douy 4, Legrand 4, Rappeneau 4)
Sauvage et beau, 1982 (Vangelis 4)
Sauve qui peut, 1980 (Godard 2, Baye 3, Huppert 3)
Sauve-toi Lola, 1986 (Moreau 3)
Savage, 1914 (Daniels 3)
Savage, 1918 (Moore 3)
Savage, 1926 (Folsey 4, Murfin 4)
Savage, 1952 (Heston 3, Head 4, Seitz 4)
Savage. See Sauvage, 1975
Savage Bees, 1976 (Johnson 3)
Savage Brigade. See Brigade sauvage, 1939
Savage Dawn, 1985 (Black 3)
Savage Eye, 1960 (Fields 4, Maddow 4, Rosenman 4, Wexler 4)
Savage Guns. See Tierra brutal, 1962
Savage Hunt, 1981 (Theodorakis 4)
Savage Innocents, 1959 (Ray 2, Mathieson 4)
Savage Innocents, 1960 (Ray 2, O'Toole 3, Quinn 3, Wong 3, Solinas 4)
Savage Is Loose, 1974 (Scott 3)
Savage Messiah, 1972 (Jarman 2, Russell 2, Russell 4)
Savage Mutiny, 1953 (Weissmuller 3, Katzman 4)
Savage Pampas, 1967 (Taylor 3)
Savage Sam, 1963 (Disney 4)
Savage Seven, 1968 (Kovacs 4)
Savage State. See Etat sauvage, 1978
Savage Triangle. See Garçon sauvage, 1951
Savage Woman, 1918 (Edeson 4)
Savage/Love, 1981 (Clarke 2)
Savages, 1972 (Ivory 2, Lassally 4)
Savant, 1974 (Fresnay 3)
Save Our Beach. See Sunset Cove, 1978
Save the Children Fund Film, 1971 (Loach 2)
Save the Ship, 1923 (Laurel and Hardy 3, Roach 4)
Save the Tiger, 1973 (Lemmon 3, Hamlisch 4)
Save Your Money, 1921 (Roach 4)
Save Your Shillings and Smile, 1943 (Balcon 4)
Saved by a Watch, 1914 (Mix 3)
Saved by Her Horse, 1915 (Mix 3)
Saved by Love, 1908 (Porter 2)
Saved by the Belle, 1939 (Three Stooges 3)
Saved by the Pony Express, 1913 (Mix 3)
Saved by Wireless, 1915 (Sennett 2)
Saved from Himself, 1911 (Griffith 2, Normand 3, Bitzer 4)
Saved from the Torrents, 1911 (Bushman 3)
Savetier et le financier, 1909 (Feuillade 2)
Saving Grace, 1914 (Loos 4)
Saving Grace, 1943 (Balcon 4)
Saving Grace, 1986 (Giannini 3, Josephson 3, Rey 3)
Saving Mabel's Dad, 1913 (Sennett 2, Normand 3)
Saving of Bill Blewitt, 1936 (Cavalcanti 2, Grierson 2, Watt 2)
Saving Presence, 1914 (Loos 4)
Saving the Family Name, 1916 (Weber 2)
Savitri, 1961 (Biswas 4)
Savitri Stayavan, 1914 (Phalke 2)

Savoy-Hotel 217, 1936 (Albers 3, Herlth 4, Röhrig 4, Wagner 4)
Saw Mill Mystery, 1937 (Terry 4)
Sawdust and Salome, 1914 (Talmadge 3)
Sawdust and Tinsel. See Gycklarnas afton, 1953
Sawdust Paradise, 1928 (Bosworth 3, Rosson 4)
Sawdust Ring, 1917 (Love 3)
Sawdust Trail, 1924 (Miller 4)
Sawmill, 1921 (Laurel and Hardy 3)
Saxon Charm, 1948 (Hayward 3, Montgomery 3, Krasner 4)
Saxophon Susi, 1928 (Albers 3, Ondra 3, Heller 4)
Say Ah Jasper, 1944 (Pal 4)
Say Anything, 1989 (Kovacs 4)
Say Goodbye, Maggie Cole, 1972 (Hayward 3)
Say Hello to Yesterday, 1971 (Simmons 3)
Say It Again, 1926 (La Cava 2, Cronjager 4, Rosson 4)
Say It in French, 1938 (Milland 3, Head 4)
Say It with Babies, 1926 (Laurel and Hardy 3, Roach 4)
Say It With Flowers, 1934 (Baxter 2, Coburn 3)
Say It With Flowers. See Säg det med blommer, 1952
Say It with Music. See Säg det i toner, 1929
Say It with Music, 1933 (Wilcox 2)
Say It with Sables, 1928 (Capra 2, Bushman 3, Cohn 4, Walker 4)
Say It with Songs, 1929 (Bacon 2, Jolson 3, Garmes 4, Zanuck 4)
Say One for Me, 1959 (Tashlin 2, Crosby 3, Reynolds 3, Wagner 3, Cahn 4, LeMaire 4, Wheeler 4)
Say! Young Fellow, 1918 (Fairbanks 3)
Sayili kabadayilar, 1965 (Güney 2)
Sayonara, 1957 (Brando 3, Garner 3, Hopper 3, Berlin 4, Prinz 4, Waxman 4)
Saysons gais, 1930 (Rosay 3)
Saza, 1951 (Anand 3, Burman 4)
Sbaglio di essere vivo, 1945 (De Sica 2, Cervi 3)
Sbandati, 1955 (Birri 2, Di venanzo 4, Fusco 4)
Sbarco di Anzio, 1968 (Falk 3, Giannini 3, Kennedy 3, Mitchum 3, Ryan 3, De Laurentiis 4, Rotunno 4)
Sbatti il mostro in prima pagina, 1972 (Volonté 3)
Scacco tutto matto, 1968 (Robinson 3, Terry-Thomas 3)
Scalawag, 1973 (Douglas 3, Cardiff 4)
Scalp Treatment, 1952 (Lantz 4)
Scalp Trouble, 1939 (Blanc 4, Clampett 4, Stalling 4)
Scalpel, Please. See Skalpel, prosím, 1985
Scalphunters, 1968 (Pollack 2, Lancaster 3, Winters 3, Bernstein 4)
Scambio, 1990 (Giannini 3)
Scamp, 1957 (Attenborough 3, Francis 4)
Scampolo, 1958 (Schneider 3)
Scampolo '53, 1953 (Rota 4)
Scampolo, ein Kind der Strasse, 1932 (Wilder 2, Courant 4)
Scandal. See Skandalen, 1912
Scandal, 1915 (Weber 2)
Scandal. See Shubun, 1950
Scandal, 1989 (Hurt 3)
Scandal about Eva. See Skandal un Eva, 1930

Schatz, mach kasse, 1926 (Albers 3)
Schatze des Teufels, 1955 (Porten 3)
Schauplätze, 1967 (Wenders 2)
Scheherazade. *See* Shéhérazade, 1963
Schéhérezade, 1962 (Godard 2, Rey 3)
Scheidungsgrund, 1937 (Ondra 3)
Scheintote Chinese, 1928 (Reiniger 4)
Schéma d'une identification, 1946
   (Resnais 2, Philipe 3)
Schemers, 1913 (Bunny 3)
Schemers, 1916 (Laurel and Hardy 3)
Scheming Schemers, 1956 (Three Stooges 3)
Scherben, 1921 (Krauss 3, Mayer 4)
Scherzo, 1932 (Cortez 4)
Scherzo, 1939 (McLaren 4)
Scherzo del destinoin aqquato dietro l'angelo
   come un brigante di strada, 1983
   (Wertmüller 2)
Schiava del paradiso, 1967 (Brazzi 3)
Schicksal, 1924 (Veidt 3, Planer 4)
Schicksal am Lenkrad, 1953 (Eisler 4)
Schicksal aus zweiter Hand, 1949
   (Staudte 2)
Schicksal einer schönen Frau, 1932
   (Dagover 3)
Schiff der verlorene Menschen, 1929
   (Tourneur 2, Dietrich 3, Kortner 3,
   Modot 3)
Schiff in Not, 1925 (Fröhlich 3)
Schiff in Not, 1936 (Ruttman 2)
Schimbul de miine, 1959 (Mészáros 2)
Schinderhannes, 1927 (Homolka 3, Rasp 3)
Schinderhannes, 1958 (Käutner 2, Schell 3)
Schindler's List, 1990 (Scorsese 2,
   Spielberg 2)
Schirm mit dem Schwan, 1915 (Wiene 2,
   Messter 4)
Schischcksal derer von Hapsburg, 1929
   (Riefenstahl 2)
Schizoid. *See* Lucertola con la pelle di
   donna, 1971
Schizoid, 1980 (Kinski 3)
Schlagende Wetter, 1923 (Metzner 4)
Schlagerparade, 1953 (Chevalier 3)
Schlange mit dem Mädchenkopf, 1919
   (Albers 3)
Schlangenei, 1977 (Ullmann 3, De
   Laurentiis 4, Nykvist 4)
Schlangengrube und das Pendel, 1967
   (Lee 3)
Schlemihl, 1915 (Pick 2)
Schlock, 1971 (Landis 2, Baker 4)
Schloss, 1968 (Schell 3)
Schloss Hubertus: Der Fischer von
   Heiligensee, 1955 (Dagover 3)
Schloss im Süden, 1933 (Wagner 4)
Schloss Vogelöd, 1921 (Murnau 2,
   Tschechowa 3, Herlth 4, Mayer 4,
   Pommer 4, Wagner 4, Warm 4)
Schlussakkord, 1936 (Sirk 2, Dagover 3)
Schlüssakkord, 1960 (Auric 4)
Schmetterlingsschlacht, 1924 (Nielsen 3)
Schmuck des Rajah, 1918 (Gad 2)
Schneider's Anti-Noise Crusade, 1909
   (Griffith 2)
Schneider Wibbel, 1939 (Käutner 2)
Schnitz the Tailor, 1913 (Sennett 2)
Schodami w Gore, Schodami w Dol, 1988
   (Nowicki 3)
Scholar, 1918 (Laurel and Hardy 3)
Schön muss man sein, 1951 (Ondra 3)
Schöne Abenteuer, 1924 (Albers 3, Banky 3)
Schöne Abenteuer, 1932 (Arletty 3,
   Wagner 4)

Schöne Abenteuer, 1959 (Herlth 4)
Schöne Lügnerin, 1959 (Schneider 3)
Schöne Prinzessin von China, 1916
   (Reiniger 4)
Schönen Tagen von Aranjuez. *See* Adieu les
   beaux jours, 1933
Schöner Gigolo—armer Gigolo, 1978
   (Dietrich 3, Novak 3, Schell 3)
Schönheit-spflästerchen, 1937 (Dagover 3)
Schönste Geschenk, 1916 (Lubitsch 2)
School Begins, 1928 (Roach 4)
School Birds, 1937 (Terry 4)
School Days, 1932 (Fleischer 4, Iwerks 4)
School Daze, 1942 (Terry 4)
School Daze, 1988 (Lee 2)
School for Brides. *See* Two on the Tiles,
   1951
School for Husbands, 1937 (Harrison 3)
School for Sabotage. *See* They Came to
   Blow Up America, 1943
School for Scandal, 1923 (Rathbone 3)
School for Scandal, 1930 (Dickinson 2,
   Carroll 3, Harrison 3)
School for Scoundrels, 1960 (Sim 3, Terry-
   Thomas 3, Addison 4)
School for Secrets, 1946 (Attenborough 3,
   Richardson 3, Ustinov 3, Dillon 4,
   Rank 4)
School for Stars, 1935 (Havelock-Allan 4)
School for Wives, 1925 (Ruttenberg 4)
School Ma'am of Snake, 1911 (Dwan 2)
School of Love. *See* Nikutai no gakko,
   1965
School, the Basis of Life. *See* Skola, základ
   života, 1938
School Ties, 1991 (Francis 4)
Schoolgirl Diary. *See* Ore nove lezione di
   chimica, 1941
Schoolmaster of Mariposa, 1911 (Mix 3)
Schoolmistress on the Spree. *See* Lärarinna
   på vift, 1941
Schoolteacher and the Waif, 1912 (Griffith 2,
   Pickford 3, Bitzer 4)
Schornstein No. 4. *See* Voleuse, 1966
Schpountz, 1937 (Pagnol 2, Brasseur 3,
   Fernandel 3)
Schräge Vögel, 1968 (Von Trotta 2)
Schrecken. *See* Januskopf, 1920
Schreckensnacht in der Menagerie, 1921
   (Hoffmann 4)
Schritt vom Wege, 1939 (Gründgens 3)
Schubert. *See* Sinfonia d'amore, 1954
Schuberts unvollendete Symphonie. *See*
   Leise flehen meine Lieder, 1933
Schuhpalast Pinkus, 1916 (Lubitsch 2,
   Rasp 4, Kräly 4)
Schuld, 1918 (Porten 3)
Schuld der Lavinia Morland, 1920 (Leni 2)
Schuld und Sühne. *See* Raskolnikow, 1923
Schuldig, 1913 (Messter 4)
Schuldig, 1928 (Courant 4)
Schúzka se stíny, 1982 (Brejchová 3)
Schuss aus dem Fenster, 1920 (Albers 3)
Schuss am Nebelhorn, 1932 (Rasp 3)
Schüsse im ¾-Takt, 1965 (Brejchová 3)
Schuss im Morgengrauen, 1932 (Lorre 3)
Schut, 1964 (Siodmak 2)
Schützenliesl, 1926 (Reisch 4)
Schwartze Schaf, 1960 (Rasp 3)
Schwarz und Weiss wie Tage und Nächte,
   1978 (Ganz 3)
Schwarze Abt, 1963 (Kinski 3)
Schwarze Domino, 1929 (Reisch 4)
Schwarze Gesicht, 1922 (Planer 4)

Schwarze Husar, 1932 (Veidt 3, Herlth 4,
   Planer 4, Röhrig 4)
Schwarze Kobra, 1963 (Kinski 3)
Schwarze Moritz, 1915 (Lubitsch 2)
Schwarze Rosen, 1935 (Wagner 4)
Schwarze Sunde, 1989 (Straub and Huillet 2)
Schwarze Walfisch, 1934 (Jannings 3)
Schwarzer Jäger Johanna, 1934
   (Gründgens 3)
Schwarzer Jäger Johanna, 1950 (Staudte 2)
Schwarzwaldmädel, 1929 (Reisch 4)
Schwedische Nachtigall, 1941 (Herlth 4)
Schweigen im Walde, 1929 (Pasternak 4)
Schweigende Mund, 1951 (Homolka 3)
Schweikart. *See* Fräulein von Barnhelm,
   1940
Schweik's New Adventures, 1943
   (Attenborough 3)
Schweitzer, 1990 (McDowell 3)
Schwere Jungens—Leichte Mädchen, 1927
   (Fröhlich 3)
Schweres Opfer, 1911 (Porten 3, Messter 4)
Schwester Osso, 1924 (Porten 3)
Schwestern oder Die Balance des Glücks,
   1979 (Von Trotta 2)
Schwur des Peter Hergatz, 1921 (Jannings 3,
   Freund 4)
Science, 1911 (Pickford 3, Gaudio 4)
Science Friction, 1959 (Vanderbeek 2)
Scientific Card Player. *See* Scopone
   scientifico, 1972
Scientists of Tomorrow, 1968 (Ghatak 2)
Scipione detto anche l'Africano, 1971
   (Gassman 3, Mangano 3, Mastroianni 3)
Scirocco, 1987 (Donaggio 4)
Scissors, 1962 (Ghatak 2)
Sciuscià, 1946 (Amidei 4, Zavattini 4)
Scoffer, 1921 (Dwan 2)
Scolgiera del peccato, 1950 (Cervi 3)
Sconosciuto, 1979 (Schneider 3)
Sconosciuto di San Marino, 1947 (De Sica 2,
   Magnani 3, Zavattini 4)
Scoop. *See* Honor of the Press, 1932
Scoop, 1987 (Pleasence 3)
Scooper Dooper, 1947 (Bruckman 4)
Scopone scientifico, 1972 (Comencini 2,
   Cotten 3, Davis 3, Mangano 3, Sordi 3)
Scorcher, 1927 (Brown 4)
Scorchers, 1990 (Jones 3)
Scorching Sands, 1923 (Laurel and Hardy 3,
   Roach 4)
Scorned and Swindled, 1984 (Weld 3)
Scorpio, 1972 (Delon 3, Lancaster 3,
   Mirisch 4)
Scorpio Rising, 1955 (Anger 2)
Scotch, 1930 (Sennett 2)
Scotch Highball, 1930 (Terry 4)
Scotched in Scotland, 1954 (Three
   Stooges 3)
Scotland Yard, 1930 (Bennett 3, Crisp 3,
   Fort 4, Friedhofer 4)
Scotland Yard, 1941 (Balderston 4, Miller 4)
Scotland Yard Commands. *See* Lonely Road,
   1936
Scotland Yard Inspector. *See* Lady in the
   Fog, 1952
Scotland Yard Investigation, 1945 (Von
   Stroheim 2)
Scotland Yard jagt Doktor Mabuse, 1963
   (Kinski 3)
Scott of the Antarctic, 1948 (Lee 3, Mills 3,
   More 3, Balcon 4, Cardiff 4, Rank 4,
   Unsworth 4)
Scottish Mazurka, 1943 (Cardiff 4)

Scoumoune, 1972 (Belmondo 3, Cardinale 3, Depardieu 3)

Scoundrel, 1935 (Coward 4, Garmes 4, Hecht 4, MacArthur 4, Zukor 4)

Scoundrel. *See* Narazumono, 1956

Scoundrel. *See* Akuto, 1965

Scoundrel. *See* Mariés de l'an II, 1971

Scoundrel in White. *See* Docteur Popaul, 1972

Scoundrel's Toll, 1916 (Sennett 2)

Scourge of the Desert, 1915 (Hart 3)

Scoutmaster Magoo, 1958 (Bosustow 4)

Scouts to the Rescue, 1939 (Cooper 3)

Scram!, 1932 (Laurel and Hardy 3)

Scram, 1932 (Roach 4)

Scrambled Aches, 1957 (Blanc 4, Jones 4, Stalling 4)

Scrambled Brains, 1951 (Three Stooges 3)

Scrambles, 1963 (Emshwiller 2)

Scrap for Victory, 1943 (Terry 4)

Scrap Happy Daffy, 1943 (Blanc 4, Stalling 4)

Scrapper, 1917 (Ford 2)

Scrapper, 1922 (Miller 4)

Scrappily Married, 1940 (Metty 4)

Scratch as Scratch Can, 1930 (Brennan 3)

Scratch My Back, 1920 (Olcott 2)

Scream and Scream Again, 1970 (Cushing 3, Lee 3, Price 3)

Scream of Fear. *See* Taste of Fear, 1961

Scream of Stone, 1990 (Sutherland 3)

Scream, Pretty Peggy, 1973 (Davis 3)

Screamers, 1980 (Cotten 3)

Screaming Lady. *See* Screaming Woman, 1972

Screaming Mimi, 1958 (Brown 4, Guffey 4)

Screaming Skull, 1958 (Crosby 4)

Screaming Woman, 1972 (Cotten 3, De Havilland 3, Pidgeon 3, Head 4, Williams 4)

Screen Directors Playhouse. *See* Rookie of the Year, 1955

Screen—Entrance Exit, 1974 (Le Grice 2)

Screen Snapshots, 1933 (Three Stooges 3)

Screen Snapshots No. 8, 1931 (Brown 3, Love 3)

Screen Snapshots No. 11, 1934 (Cantor 3, Karloff 3)

Screen Snapshots No. 5, 1930 (Brown 3)

Screen Snapshots No. 9, 1939 (Three Stooges 3)

Screen Snapshots No. 1, 1934 (Cagney 3)

Screen Snapshots No. 107, 1942 (Barrymore 3)

Screen Snapshots No. 103, 1943 (Dietrich 3)

Screen Snapshots No. 6, 1935 (Three Stooges 3)

Screen Snapshots No. 3, 1922 (Keaton 2)

Screen Snapshots No. 206, 1952 (Baxter 3)

Screen Snapshots No. 225, 1954 (Abbott and Costello 3)

Screen Song. *See* Let Me Call You Sweetheart, 1932

Screen Test I, 1965 (Warhol 2)

Screen Test II, 1965 (Warhol 2)

Screwball Football, 1939 (Avery 4)

Screwdriver, 1941 (Lantz 4)

Screw's Adventures. *See* Sroublkova dobrodružství, 1962

Screwy Squirrel, 1944 (Avery 4)

Screwy Truant, 1945 (Avery 4)

Scribe, 1966 (Keaton 2)

Scrim, 1976 (Chaplin 3)

Scrooge, 1951 (Sim 3)

Scrooge, 1970 (Evans 3, Finney 3, Guinness 3, More 3, Morris 4)

Scrooged, 1988 (Mitchum 3, Houseman 4)

Scrub Me Mama with a Boogie Beat, 1941 (Lantz 4)

Scrubbers, 1983 (Zetterling 2)

Scrublady, 1917 (Dressler 3)

Scruffy, 1938 (McDowall 3)

Scruggs, 1965 (York 3, Coutard 4)

Scruples, 1980 (Tierney 3)

Scudda Hoo! Scudda Hay!, 1948 (Brennan 3, Monroe 3, Wood 3, LeMaire 4)

Sculptor's Landscape, 1956 (Lassally 4)

Sculptor's Nightmare, 1908 (Bitzer 4)

Sculptures au moyen-age, 1949 (Renoir 4)

Scuola del timidi, 1941 (Zavattini 4)

Scuola di Severino, 1949 (Di Venanzo 4)

Scuola elementare, 1954 (Lattuada 2, Spaak 4)

Scusa se e poco, 1982 (Vitti 3)

Scusi, facciamo l'amore, 1968 (Feuillère 3, Morricone 4)

Scusi lei è contrario o favorevole. *See* Scusi, lei è favorevole o contrario, 1966

Scusi, lei è favorevole o contrario, 1966 (Mangano 3, Sordi 3, Amidei 4)

Scwarzer Kies, 1961 (Käutner 2)

Se incontri Sartana, prega per la tua morte. *See* Sartana, 1968

Se infiel y no mires con quien, 1985 (Maura 3)

Se io fossi onesto!, 1942 (De Sica 2)

Se ki, se be, 1919 (Korda 2, Korda 4)

Se la paso la mano, 1952 (Alcoriza 4)

Se permettete parliamo di donne, 1964 (Gassman 3)

Se tutte le donne del mondo, 1966 (Terry-Thomas 3, De Laurentiis 4, Gherardi 4)

Sea, 1954 (Halas and Batchelor 4)

Sea Bat, 1930 (Karloff 3, Gibbons 4, Meredyth 4, Shearer 4)

Sea Beast, 1926 (Barrymore 3, Costello 3, Haskin 4, Meredyth 4, Westmore Family 4)

Sea Chase, 1955 (Turner 3, Wayne 3, Clothier 4)

Sea Devils, 1937 (Lupino 3, McLaglen 3, August 4, Hunt 4, Polglase 4)

Sea Devils, 1953 (Walsh 2, De Carlo 3, Hudson 3, Chase 4)

Sea Dogs, 1916 (Laurel and Hardy 3)

Sea Dog's Tale, 1926 (Sennett 2, Laurel and Hardy 3)

Sea Eagle. *See* Rösen på Tistelön, 1916

Sea Fever. *See* Rade, 1927

Sea Fort, 1940 (Cavalcanti 2, Dalrymple 4)

Sea Fury, 1958 (Baker 3, McLaglen 3, Shaw 3, Rank 4)

Sea God, 1930 (Wray 3)

Sea Going Birds, 1932 (Sennett 2)

Sea Gull, 1926 (Von Sternberg 2, Purviance 3)

Sea Gull, 1968 (Lumet 2, Elliott 3, Mason 3, Redgrave 3, Signoret 3, Fisher 4)

Sea Hawk, 1924 (Beery 3)

Sea Hawk, 1940 (Curtiz 2, Crisp 3, Flynn 3, Rains 3, Blanke 4, Friedhofer 4, Grot 4, Haskin 4, Koch 4, Korngold 4, Miller 4, Orry-Kelly 4, Polito 4, Wallis 4)

Sea Hornet, 1951 (Glennon 4)

Sea Horses, 1926 (Dwan 2, Powell 3, Howe 4)

Sea Hound, 1947 (Crabbe 3)

Sea Lion, 1921 (Bosworth 3, Love 3)

Sea Nymphs, 1914 (Sennett 2, Arbuckle 3, Normand 3)

Sea of Grass, 1947 (Kazan 2, Carey 3, Douglas 3, Hepburn 3, Tracy 3, Walker 3, Berman 4, Mayer 4, Plunkett 4, Stothart 4, Stradling 4)

Sea of Lost Ships, 1953 (Brennan 3, Raine 4)

Sea of Love, 1989 (Pacino 3)

Sea of Sand, 1958 (Attenborough 3, Green 4, Mathieson 4, Rank 4)

Sea Shall Not Have Them, 1954 (Bogarde 3, Redgrave 3, Arnold 4, Mathieson 4)

Sea Spoilers, 1936 (Wayne 3)

Sea Squaw, 1925 (Sennett 2)

Sea Squawk, 1925 (Capra 2, Langdon 3)

Sea Theme, 1949 (Hall 4)

Sea Tiger, 1927 (Astor 3, Wilson 4)

Sea Trial, 1983 (Friedkin 2)

Sea Urchin, 1913 (Chaney 3)

Sea Urchin, 1926 (Balcon 4)

Sea Wall. *See* Barrage contre le Pacifique, 1957

Sea Wall. *See* Diga sul Pacifico, 1958

Sea Wife, 1957 (Burton 3)

Sea Wolf, 1913 (Bosworth 3)

Sea Wolf, 1930 (Behrman 4)

Sea Wolf, 1941 (Curtiz 2, Rossen 2, Fitzgerald 3, Garfield 3, Lupino 3, Robinson 3, Blanke 4, Friedhofer 4, Grot 4, Haskin 4, Korngold 4, Polito 4, Wallis 4)

Sea Wolves, 1981 (Niven 3, Howard 3, Peck 3)

Seafarers, 1953 (Kubrick 2)

Seagull. *See* Kaitchka, 1915

Seagulls over Sorrento, 1954 (Kelly 3, Junge 4, Rozsa 4)

Seal. *See* Pečat, 1955

Seal of Silence, 1913 (Ince 4)

Seal Skinners, 1939 (Freleng 4)

Sealed Cargo, 1951 (Andrews 3, Rains 3)

Sealed Hearts, 1919 (Goulding 2)

Sealed Lips. *See* Förseglade löppar, 1927

Sealed Lips, 1928 (Young 4)

Sealed Lips. *See* After Tonight, 1933

Sealed Lips, 1941 (Cortez 4, Salter 4)

Sealed Room, 1909 (Griffith 2, Pickford 3, Walthall 3, Bitzer 4)

Sealed Verdict, 1948 (Crawford 3, Milland 3, Dreier 4, Friedhofer 4, Head 4)

Séance de cinématographe, 1909 (Linder 3)

Seance on a Wet Afternoon, 1964 (Attenborough 3, Barry 4)

Seapower, 1965 (Ford 3)

Search, 1948 (Zinnemann 2, Clift 3, Mayer 4)

Search. *See* Probe, 1972

Search for Beauty, 1934 (Crabbe 3, Lupino 3, Sheridan 3, Banton 4, Prinz 4, Zukor 4)

Search for Bridey Murphy, 1956 (Wright 3, Head 4)

Search for Danger, 1949 (Leven 4)

Search for Paradise, 1957 (Tiomkin 4)

Search for the Evil One, 1967 (Fields 4)

Search for the Gods, 1975 (Bellamy 3)

Search into Darkness, 1962 (Van Dyke 2)

Searchers, 1956 (Ford 2, Bond 3, Marsh 3, Wayne 3, Wood 3, Basevi 4 , Cooper 4, Hoch 4, Nugent 4, Steiner 4)

Searching Eye, 1964 (Bass 4)

Searching Wind, 1946 (Dieterle 2, Sidney 3, Young 3, Dreier 4, Garmes 4, Wallis 4, Young 4)

Seas Beneath, 1931 (Ford 2, August 4, Nichols 4)

Sea's Hold. *See* Havsbandet, 1971

Seashell and the Clergyman. *See* **Coquille et le clergyman, 1927**

Seashore Baby, 1904 (Bitzer 4)

Seashore Frolics, 1903 (Porter 2)

Seasick Sailors, 1951 (Terry 4)

Seaside Adventure, 1952 (Terry 4)

Seaside Girl, 1907 (Hepworth 2)

Season for Love. *See* Morte-Saison des amours, 1961

Season of Passion, 1961 (Baxter 3, Borgnine 3, Lansbury 3, Mills 3)

Seasons, 1963 (Ivanov-Vano 4)

Season's Greetinks, 1939 (Fleischer 4)

Seasons We Walked Together. *See* Futari de aruita ikutoshitsuki, 1962

Seated Figures, 1989 (Snow 2)

Seats of the Mighty, 1914 (Barrymore 3)

Seawards the Great Ships, 1959 (Grierson 2)

Seaweed Children, 1973 (Lassally 4)

Seawolf, 1973 (Staudte 2)

Sebastian, 1968 (Powell and Pressburger 2, Bogarde 3, Sutherland 3, York 3, Fisher 4, Goldsmith 4)

Sebastiane, 1976 (Jarman 2)

Sebastiane Wrap, 1975 (Jarman 2)

Sechs Tage Heimaturlaub, 1941 (Fröhlich 3)

Sechs Wochen unter den Apachen. *See* Achtung Harry! Augen auf!, 1926

Seclusion Near a Forest. *See* Na samotě u lesa, 1977

Second Awakening of Christa Klages. *See* Zweite Erwachen der Christa Klages, 1977

Second Best, 1972 (Bates 3)

Second Chance, 1953 (Darnell 3, Mitchum 3, Palance 3, D'Agostino 4, Maté 4)

Second Chance. *See* Si c'était à refaire, 1976

Second Chance, 1981 (Deneuve 3)

Second Chances. *See* Probation, 1932

Second Childhood, 1935 (Roach 4)

Second Choice, 1930 (Costello 3)

Second Chorus, 1940 (Astaire 3, Goddard 3, Meredith 3, Leven 4, Mercer 4, Pan 4)

Second Clue, 1914 (Eason 4)

Second Coming of Suzanne, 1974 (Dreyfuss 3)

Second Face, 1950 (Darwell 3)

Second Fiddle, 1923 (Astor 3)

Second Fiddle, 1939 (Henie 3, Power 3, Berlin 4, Glennon 4, Zanuck 4)

Second Hand Hearts, 1981 (Ashby 2, Wexler 4)

Second Hand Wife, 1932 (Bellamy 3, Clarke 4, Friedhofer 4)

Second Honeymoon, 1937 (Power 3, Trevor 3, Young 3)

Second Hundred Years, 1927 (Laurel and Hardy 3)

Second Hundred Years, 1961 (McCarey 2)

Second in Command, 1915 (Bushman 3)

Second Killing of the Dog, 1988 (Babenco 2)

Second Mate, 1950 (Baxter 2)

Second Mrs. Fenway. *See* Her Honor, The Governor, 1926

Second Mrs. Roebuck, 1914 (Reid 3, Sweet 3)

Second Serve, 1986 (Redgrave 3)

Second Sight, 1911 (Pickford 3, Gaudio 4)

Second Son Crow. *See* Jinanbou garasu, 1955

Second Thoughts, 1983 (Mancini 4)

Second Time Around, 1961 (Reynolds 3, Ritter 3, Mancini 4, Smith 4)

Second Touch. *See* Twee frouwen, 1980

Second Victory, 1986 (Von Sydow 3)

Second Victory Loan Campaign Fund, 1945 (Davis 3)

Second Wife, 1930 (Glennon 4, Plunkett 4)

Second Wife, 1936 (Bond 3, Musuraca 4)

Second Woman, 1951 (Young 3, Leven 4, Mohr 4)

Second Youth, 1924 (Hunt 4)

Seconde Vérité, 1966 (Christian-Jaque 2, Douy 4)

Seconds, 1966 (Frankenheimer 2, Hudson 3, Alonzo 4, Bass 4, Goldsmith 4, Howe 4)

Second-Story Murder, 1930 (Young 3)

Secours aux naufragés, 1903 (Guy 2)

Secret, 1974 (Noiret 3, Trintignant 3, Morricone 4)

Secret Agent, 1936 (Hitchcock 2, Carroll 3, Gielgud 3, Lorre 3, Young 3, Balcon 4, Bennett 4, Reville 4)

Secret Behind the Door, 1947 (Cortez 4)

Secret Behind the Door, 1948 (Redgrave 3, Rozsa 4)

Secret Beyond the Door, 1948 (Lang 2, Bennett 3, Banton 4, Wanger 4)

Secret Bride, 1934 (Dieterle 2, Stanwyck 3, Blanke 4, Grot 4, Orry-Kelly 4)

Secret Ceremony, 1968 (Losey 2, Farrow 3, Mitchum 3, Taylor 3, Fisher 4)

Secret Cinema, 1985 (Arden 3)

Secret Code, 1918 (Swanson 3)

Secret Command, 1944 (Planer 4)

Secret de Delhia, 1929 (Burel 4)

Secret de Mayerling, 1949 (Delannoy 2, Marais 3)

Secret de Monte-Cristo, 1948 (Brasseur 3)

Secret de Polichinelle, 1936 (Raimu 3, Rosay 3, Spaak 4)

Secret de Soeur Angèle, 1955 (D'Eaubonne 4)

Secret del Sacerdote, 1941 (Armendáriz 3)

Secret Diary of Sigmund Freud, 1984 (Baker 3, Kinski 3)

Secret du Chevalier d'eon, 1959 (Trauner 4)

Secret du Chevalier d'Eon, 1960 (Blier 3, Alekan 4)

Secret du forçat, 1913 (Feuillade 2)

Secret Flight. *See* School for Secrets, 1946

Secret Four. *See* Four Just Men, 1939

Secret Fury, 1950 (Colbert 3, Ryan 3)

Secret Game, 1917 (Hayakawa 3, Rosher 4)

Secret Garden, 1949 (Brown 2, Lanchester 3, Marshall 3, O'Brien 3, Gillespie 4, Kaper 4, Plunkett 4)

Secret Heart, 1946 (Allyson 3, Barrymore 3, Colbert 3, Pidgeon 3, Folsey 4, Irene 4, Kaper 4)

Secret Hour, 1928 (Negri 3)

Secret Interlude. *See* Storm View from Pompey's Head, 1955

Secret Invasion, 1964 (Corman 2, Granger 3, Rooney 3, Friedhofer 4)

Secret Land, 1948 (Montgomery 3, Taylor 3, Kaper 4)

Secret Life of an American Wife, 1968 (Matthau 3, Axelrod 4, Shamroy 4, Smith 4)

Secret Life of Walter Mitty, 1947 (McLeod 2, Karloff 3, Kaye 3, Garmes 4, Goldwyn 4, Jenkins 4, Raksin 4, Sharaff 4)

Secret Lives, 1937 (Heller 4)

Secret Lives of Plants, 1978 (Cloquet 4)

Secret Man, 1917 (Ford 2, Carey 3)

Secret Marriage. *See* Ett Hemligt giftermaål, 1912

Secret Meeting. *See* Marie Octobre, 1959

Secret Mission, 1942 (Granger 3, Lom 3, Mason 3, Rank 4)

Secret Motive. *See* London Black-Out Murders, 1942

Secret Night Caller, 1975 (Sidney 3)

Secret of Blood. *See* Tajemství krve, 1953

Secret of Blood Island, 1965 (Bernard 4, Carreras 4)

Secret of Convict Lake, 1951 (Barrymore 3, Cusack 3, Ford 3, Tierney 3, LeMaire 4)

Secret of Dr. Kildare, 1939 (Ayres 3, Barrymore 3)

Secret of Dorian Gray. *See* Dorian Gray, 1970

Secret of Madame Blanche, 1933 (Dunne 3, Adrian 4, Goodrich 4)

Secret of Mayerling. *See* Secret de Mayerling, 1949

Secret of My Success, 1987 (Fox 3)

Secret of Nimh, 1982 (Carradine 3)

Secret of Santa Vittoria, 1969 (Kramer 2, Giannini 3, Magnani 3, Quinn 3, Maddow 4, Rotunno 4)

Secret of Stambov, 1936 (Mason 3)

Secret of the Air, 1914 (Brenon 2)

Secret of the Black Widow. *See* Geheimnis der schwarzen Witwe, 1963

Secret of the Blue Room, 1933 (Lukas 3)

Secret of the Casbah. *See* Adventure in Algiers, 1952

Secret of the Chinese Carnation. *See* Geheimnis der chinesischen Nelke, 1964

Secret of the Ice Cave, 1989 (Golan and Globus 4)

Secret of the Incas, 1954 (Heston 3, Young 3, Head 4)

Secret of the Loch, 1934 (Bennett 4)

Secret of the Old Pit. *See* Tajemnica dzikiego szybu, 1956

Secret of the Purple Reef, 1960 (Falk 3)

Secret of the Storm Country, 1917 (Talmadge 3)

Secret of the Telegian. *See* Denso ningen, 1960

Secret of the Wastelands, 1941 (Harlan 4, Head 4)

Secret of Treasure Island, 1938 (Bosworth 3, Canutt 4)

Secret of Yolanda. *See* Ahava Ilemeth, 1982

Secret Orchard, 1915 (Sweet 3)

Secret Partner, 1960 (Dearden 2, Granger 3)

Secret People, 1951 (Dickinson 2, Reggiani 3, Rank 4)

Secret People, 1964 (Hepburn 3)

Secret Place, 1956 (Rank 4)

Secret Places, 1985 (Legrand 4)

Secret Places of the Heart, 1989 (Bujold 3)

Secret Policeman's Ball, 1979 (Cleese 3)

Secret Policeman's Other Ball, 1982 (Cleese 3)

Secret Policeman's Third Ball, 1987 (Cleese 3)

Secret Popular Character. *See* Kakureta ninkimono, 1959

Secret Scandal. *See* Scandalo segreto, 1990

Secret Scrolls. *See* Yagyu bugeicho, 1957

Secret Scrolls, Part II. *See* Soryu hiken, 1958

Secret Service, 1931 (Cronjager 4, Steiner 4)

Secret Service Man, 1912 (Reid 3)

Secret Service of the Air, 1939 (Reagan 3, McCord 4)

Secret Seven. *See* Invincibili sette, 1964

Secret Sin, 1915 (Hayakawa 3, Sweet 3)

Secret Six, 1931 (Beery 3, Bellamy 3, Gable 3, Harlow 3, Marion 4, Mayer 4, Warner 4)

Secret Society, 1991 (Keaton 3)

Secrets, 1924 (Borzage 2, Talmadge 3, Gaudio 4, Marion 4, Schenck 4, Westmore Family 4)

Secrets, 1933 (Borzage 2, Howard 3, Lawrence 3, Pickford 3, Adrian 4, Day 4, Marion 4, Newman 4)

Secrets, 1943 (Honegger 4, Matras 4)

Secrets, 1982 (Puttnam 4)

Secrets, 1984 (Challis 4)

Secrets d'alcove, 1954 (Blier 3, Amidei 4, Burel 4, Matras 4)

Secrets de la mer rouge, 1937 (Baur 3)

Secrets de la prestidigitation dévoilés, 1904 (Guy 2)

Secrets Men Can Never Share, 1988 (Wagner 3)

Secret Stranger. *See* Rough Ridin' Rangers, 1935

Secret Voice, 1936 (Pearson 2, Havelock-Allan 4)

Secret War of Harry Frigg, 1967 (Newman 3, Bumstead 4, Head 4, Henry 4, Metty 4)

Secret Ways, 1961 (Williams 4)

Secrets of a Beauty Parlor, 1917 (Sennett 2)

Secrets of a Secretary, 1931 (Colbert 3, Marshall 3, Folsey 4, Green 4, Zukor 4)

Secrets of a Soul. *See* Geheimnisse einer Seele, 1926

Secrets of a Soul. *See* Verlorene Gesicht, 1948

Secrets of an Actress, 1938 (Francis 3, Epstein 4, Gaudio 4, Orry-Kelly 4)

Secrets of Life, 1956 (Iwerks 4)

Secrets of Paris, 1922 (Stradling 4)

Secrets of the City. *See* Stadt ist voller Geheimnisse, 1955

Secrets of the East. *See* Geheimnisse des Orients, 1928

Secrets of the French Police, 1932 (Plunkett 4, Steiner 4)

Secrets of the German Ambassador. *See* Taina Germanskovo posolstva, 1914

Secrets of the Orient. *See* Shéhérazade, 1928

Secrets of the Titanic, 1987 (Sheen 3)

Secrets of Women. *See* Kvinnors väntan, 1952

Sect. *See* Setta, 1991

Secte de Marrakech. *See* Brigade mondaine, 1979

Section No. 2. *See* Scenes from Under Childhood, 1970

Section No. 3. *See* Scenes from Under Childhood, 1970

Section No. 4. *See* Scenes from Under Childhood, 1970

Section speciale, 1975 (Montand 3, Douy 4)

Secuestrador, 1958 (Torre Nilsson 2)

Sécurité et hygiène du travail dans la fabrication du sucre et de l'alcool, 1952 (Fradetal 4)

Sed Lodge, 1968 (Storaro 4)

Sedan Chair in the Mist. *See* Oboro kago, 1951

Sedicianni, 1973 (McCambridge 3)

Sedmi kontinent, 1966 (Vukotić 4)

Sedmikrásky, 1966 (Kučera 4)

Sedotta e abbandonata, 1964 (Cristaldi 4)

Seduced, 1985 (Ferrer 3)

Seduced and Abandoned. *See* Sedotta e abbandonata, 1964

Séducteurs. *See* Sunday Lovers, 1980

Seduction. *See* Yuwaku, 1948

Seduction, 1982 (Schifrin 4)

Seduction of Joe Tynan, 1979 (Douglas 3, Streep 3)

Seduction of Mimi. *See* Mimi metallurgio ferito nell'onore, 1972

Seduta spiritica, 1949 (Risi 2)

Seduttore, 1954 (Sordi 3, Cristaldi 4)

See America Thirst, 1930 (Langdon 3, Love 3, Miller 4)

See Here, Private Hargrove, 1944 (Edwards 2, Garnett 2, Reed 3, Walker 3, Benchley 4, Irene 4)

See How She Runs, 1978 (Woodward 3)

See How They Run, 1964 (Schifrin 4)

See How They Won, 1935 (Iwerks 4)

See It Now, 1952 (Berlin 4)

See My Lawyer, 1945 (Pangborn 3, Salter 4)

See No Evil. *See* Blind Terror, 1971

See No Evil, Hear No Evil, 1989 (Wilder 3)

See, Saw, Seems, 1967 (Vanderbeek 2)

See the Man Run, 1971 (Dickinson 3)

See the World, 1934 (Terry 4)

See Ya Later Gladiator, 1968 (Blanc 4)

See You in Hell, Darling. *See* American Dream, 1966

See You in Jail, 1927 (Folsey 4)

See You in the Morning, 1989 (Pakula 2, Bridges 3, Jenkins 4)

See Your Doctor, 1939 (Benchley 4)

See You Tomorrow. *See* Do widzenia do jutra, 1960

See You Tonight, 1933 (Sennett 2)

Seed, 1931 (Stahl 2, Davis 3)

Seed of Man. *See* Seme dell'uomo, 1969

Seedling. *See* Ankur, 1974

Seeds of Silver, 1913 (Bosworth 3, Selig 4)

Seein' Things, 1924 (Roach 4)

Seeing Double, 1913 (Bunny 3)

Seeing Ghosts, 1947 (Terry 4)

Seeing Nellie Home, 1924 (McCarey 2, Roach 4)

Seeing Stars, 1938 (Boulting 2)

Seeing the World, 1927 (Laurel and Hardy 3)

Seekers, 1954 (Hawkins 3, Alwyn 4, Rank 4, Unsworth 4)

Seekers, 1979 (Carradine 3)

Seelenverkäufer, 1919 (Pick 2, Dreier 4)

Seema, 1957 (Chandragupta 4)

Seemabaddha, 1971 (Ray 2, Datta 4)

Seems Like Old Times, 1980 (Hawn 3, Booth 4, Hamlisch 4, Stark 4)

Seen, 1990 (Brakhage 2)

Seeschlacht, 1917 (Krauss 3)

Seeschlacht beim Skagerak. *See* Versunkene Flotte, 1926

Segantini, il pittore della montagna, 1948 (Risi 2)

Seger i mörker, 1954 (Björnstrand 3, Fischer 4)

Segno di Venere, 1955 (De Sica 2, Sordi 3, Flaiano 4, Zavattini 4)

Segno di Zorro, 1963 (Loren 3, Brown 4)

Segodnya, 1930 (Shub 2)

Segretaria per tutti, 1932 (De Sica 2)

Segreti, segreti, 1985 (Valli 3)

Segreto del vestito rosso, 1963 (Charisse 3)

Segreto della grotta azzurra, 1922 (Gallone 2)

Segreto di Don Giovanni, 1947 (Lollobrigida 3)

Segunda Declaracion de la Habana, 1965 (Alvarez 2)

Sehnsucht, 1920 (Murnau 2, Veidt 3, Hoffmann 4)

Sehnsucht der Veronika Voss, 1982 (Fassbinder 2, Mueller-Stahl 3)

Sehnsucht des Herzens, 1950 (Warm 4)

Sehnsucht jeder Frau. *See* Lady to Love, 1930

Sehnsucht nach Afrika, 1939 (Sirk 2)

Sehnsucht, 202, 1932 (Rainer 3)

Sei mogli di Barbablu', 1950 (Loren 3)

Sei no kigen, 1967 (Shindo 2)

Seidman and Son, 1956 (Cantor 3)

Seido no Kirisuto, 1955 (Kagawa 3, Yamada 3)

Seidon, 1933 (Tanaka 3)

Seige of Syracuse. *See* Assedio di Siracusa, 1960

Seigenki, 1972 (Takemitsu 4)

Seigneurs de la forêt, 1957 (Storck 2, Welles 2)

Seigneurs des mers du sud, 1968 (Braunberger 4)

Seikatsusen ABC: Fujie nomaki, 1931 (Tanaka 3)

Seikatsusen ABC: Zenpen, 1931 (Tanaka 3)

Sein grosser Fall, 1927 (Tschechowa 3)

Sein grösster Bluff, 1927 (Dietrich 3, Galeen 4)

Sein ist das Gericht, 1921 (Metzner 4)

Sein Scheidungsgrund, 1931 (Planer 4)

Seine a rencontré Paris, 1957 (Ivens 2)

Seine Beichte, 1919 (Dreier 4)

Seine et ses marchands, 1953 (Braunberger 4)

Seine Frau, die Unbekannte, 1923 (Dagover 3, Pommer 4)

Seine Hoheit, der Eintänzer, 1927 (Reisch 4)

Seine Majestat das Bettelkind, 1920 (Korda 4)

Seine neue Nase, 1916 (Lubitsch 2)

Seine offizielle Frau. *See* Eskapade, 1936

Seine schöne Mama. *See* Flucht der Schönheit, 1915

Seine Tochter ist der Peter, 1936 (Tschechowa 3)

Seine Tochter ist der Peter, 1955 (Fröhlich 3)

Seinerzeit zu meiner Zeit, 1944 (Wegener 3)

Seins de glace, 1974 (Delon 3, Sarde 4)

Seishoku no ishizue, 1978 (Iwashita 3, Muraki 4)

Seishu Hanaoka's Wife. *See* Hanaoko Seishu no tsuma, 1967

Seishun dekameron, 1950 (Kagawa 3)

Seishun gonin otoko, 1937 (Shimura 3)

Seishun kaidan, 1955 (Yamamura 3)

Seishun kaigi, 1952 (Yamamura 3)

Seishun kokyogaku, 1929 (Tanaka 3)

Seishun no kiryu, 1942 (Kurosawa 2)

Seishun no koro, 1933 (Yoda 4)

Seishun no mon, 1975 (Muraki 4)

Seishun no mon: Jiritsu hen, 1977 (Muraki 4)

Seishun no yume ima izuko, 1932 (Tanaka 3)

Seishun no yumeji, 1976 (Mizoguchi 2)
Seishun-fu, 1930 (Tanaka 3)
Seitensprünge, 1930 (Wilder 2)
Seize the Day, 1986 (Williams 3)
Seizure, 1974 (Stone 2)
Sekai dai senso, 1961 (Yamamura 3,
   Tsuburaya 4)
Seki no Yatappe, 1930 (Hasegawa 3)
Seki no Yatappe, 1959 (Hasegawa 3)
Sekirei no kyoku, 1951 (Yamamura 3)
Sekkai no maki, 1937 (Hasegawa 3)
Sekretär der Königin, 1916 (Wiene 2,
   Messter 4)
Seksolatki, 1971 (Ścibor-Rylski 4)
Sekstet, 1963 (Thulin 3)
Sel de la terre, 1950 (Fradetal 4)
Selecting His Heiress, 1911 (Bunny 3)
Self cerca la felicità; Allegro non troppo,
   1974 (Bozzetto 4)
Self Defense, 1933 (Walthall 3)
Self Started, 1926 (Brown 4)
Self Trio, 1976 (Emshwiller 2)
Selfish Woman, 1916 (Reid 3)
Selfish Yates, 1918 (Hart 3, August 4,
   Sullivan 4)
Self-Made Hero, 1910 (Lawrence 3)
Self-Made Maids, 1950 (Three
   Stooges 3)
Selfsame Gräfin, 1961 (Rasp 3)
Selige Excellenz, 1926 (Tschechowa 3)
Seligettes, 1913 (Selig 4)
Selima, 1934 (Burman 4)
Selinunte, 1951 (Birri 2)
Seljačka buna 1573, 1975 (Mimica 4)
Sell 'em Cowboy, 1924 (Canutt 4)
Sell Out, 1976 (Reed 3, Widmark 3)
Sellout, 1952 (Malden 3, Pidgeon 3,
   Sloane 3)
Selskaya uchitelnitsa, 1947 (Maretskaya 3)
Seltsame Gräfin, 1961 (Dagover 3, Kinski 3)
Seltsame Nacht, 1926 (Holger-Madsen 2)
Seltsame Nacht der Helga Wansen, 1928
   (Holger-Madsen 2)
Seltsamen Abenteuer des Herrn Fridolin B,
   1948 (Staudte 2)
Selva de fuego, 1945 (De Fuentes 2, Del
   Rio 3)
Semaine de vacances, 1980 (Tavernier 2,
   Baye 3, Noiret 3)
Semaine en France, 1963 (Guillemot 4)
Seme dell'uomo, 1969 (Girardot 3)
Semete koyoi o, 1935 (Tanaka 3)
Seminarista, 1949 (Infante 3)
Seminole, 1953 (Boetticher 2, Hudson 3,
   Marvin 3, Quinn 3, Metty 4)
Seminole Halfbreed, 1910 (Olcott 2)
Seminole Uprising, 1955 (Katzman 4)
Seminole's Vengeance, 1911 (Olcott 2)
Semi-Tough, 1977 (Clayburgh 3, Preston 3,
   Reynolds 3, Needham 4)
Semmelweis, 1980 (Cuny 3)
Semmelweiss, 1939 (De Toth 2)
Sen no rikyu, 1989 (Mifune 3, Okada 3,
   Yoda 4)
Sen noci svatojánske, 1959 (Brdečka 4,
   Trnka 4)
Sen Yan's Devotion, 1924 (Hayakawa 3)
Senator Was Indiscreet, 1947 (Loy 3,
   Powell 3, Johnson 4, Leven 4,
   MacArthur 4)
Senator's Double, 1910 (Lawrence 3)
Senba-zuru, 1953 (Yoshimura 2, Mori 3,
   Miyagawa 4)
Senbazuru, 1969 (Kyo 3)

Send a Woman When the Devil Fails. See
   Quand la femme s'en mêle, 1957
Send Me No Flowers, 1964 (Jewison 2,
   Day 3, Hudson 3, Epstein 4)
Sendung der Lysistrata, 1961 (Kortner 3,
   Schneider 3)
Sendung des Yoghi. See Indische Grabmal,
   1921
Sénéchal le magnifique, 1957 (Fernandel 3)
Senechal the Magnificent. See Sénéchal le
   magnifique, 1957
Sengo-ha obake taikai, 1951 (Mifune 3)
Sengoki gunto-den, 1959 (Shimura 3)
Sengoku dawara, 1950 (Yoda 4)
Sengoku gunto-den, 1959 (Mifune 3,
   Tsukasa 3)
Sengoku hibun, 1955 (Yamamura 3)
Sengoku ichiban-samurai, 1938 (Shindo 3)
Sengoku-burai, 1952 (Mifune 3)
Sen-hime, 1954 (Kyo 3, Hayasaka 4)
Sen-hime goten, 1960 (Yamada 3)
Senilità, 1961 (Cardinale 3, Pinelli 4)
Senior Prom, 1959 (Three Stooges 3)
Senior Trip, 1981 (Rooney 3)
Seniors, Juniors, Colleagues. See Uwayaku
   shitayaku godouyaku, 1959
Senjin, 1935 (Miyagawa 4)
Senjo no merii kurisumasu. See Merry
   Christmas Mr. Lawrence, 1983
Senka no hate, 1950 (Yoshimura 2, Mori 3)
Senka o koete, 1950 (Takamine 3,
   Yamamura 3)
Senka the African, 1927 (Ivanov-Vano 4)
Senkyaku banrai, 1962 (Iwashita 3,
   Yamamura 3)
Sennichimae fukin, 1945 (Yoda 4)
Señor Americano, 1929 (Brown 4,
   McCord 4)
Senor Daredevil, 1926 (Brown 4, Polito 4)
Señor de la salle, 1964 (Rey 3)
Señor de Osanto, 1972 (Hermosillo 2,
   Figueroa 4)
Señor doctor, 1965 (Cantinflas 3)
Señor Droopy, 1949 (Avery 4)
Señor fotógrafo, 1952 (Cantinflas 3,
   Figueroa 4)
Señor Presidente, 1983 (Gómez 2)
Señora Ama, 1954 (Del Rio 3)
Señora de Fátima, 1951 (Rey 3)
Senora Muerte, 1967 (Carradine 3)
Senorella and the Glass Huarache, 1964
   (Blanc 4)
Señorita, 1927 (Daniels 3, Powell 3,
   Schulberg 4)
Senoritas Vivanco, 1958 (Armendáriz 3)
Senryo-hada, 1950 (Hasegawa 3)
Sens de la mort, 1921 (Clair 2, Protazanov 2)
Sensa famiglia, 1944 (Cervi 3)
Sensation Hunters, 1933 (Vidor 2)
Sensation Seekers, 1927 (Weber 2)
Sensations. See Sensations of 1945, 1944
Sensations, 1945 (Powell 3)
Sensations, 1977 (Godfrey 4)
Sensations of 1945, 1944 (Fields 3)
Sensations of 1945. See Sensations, 1945
Sense of Freedom, 1981 (Menges 4)
Sense of Loss, 1972 (Ophuls 2)
Sensi inquieti. See Climats, 1961
Sensitive Spot. See Citlivá místa, 1988
Senso, 1954 (Rosi 2, Visconti 2, Zeffirelli 2,
   Valli 3, Aldo 4, Cecchi D'Amico 4,
   Krasker 4, Rota 4, Rotunno 4)
Senso unico, 1973 (Rey 3)
Sensual Obsession. See Bad Timing, 1980

Sensualità, 1951 (De Laurentiis 4,
   Gherardi 4, Ponti 4)
Sensuikan T-57, 1959 (Tsuburaya 4)
Sensuous Assassin. See Qui?, 1970
Sentence, 1959 (Decaë 4, Evein 4,
   Saulnier 4)
Sentence of Death, 1913 (Pearson 2)
Sentimental Journey, 1946 (Bendix 3,
   O'Hara 3, Hoffenstein 4)
Sentimental Sister, 1914 (Sweet 3)
Sentimentalnyi roman, 1976 (Yankovsky 3)
Sentinel, 1977 (Carradine 3, Ferrer 3,
   Gardner 3, Kennedy 3, Meredith 3,
   Wallach 3, Smith 4)
Sentinel Asleep, 1911 (Pickford 3, Gaudio 4)
Sentinelle endormie, 1965 (Auric 4)
Sentinels of Silence, 1971 (Welles 2)
Senza buccia, 1979 (Donaggio 4)
Senza cielo, 1940 (Zavattini 4)
Senza colpa, 1915 (Gallone 2)
Senza famiglia nullatenenti, cercano affeto
   . . . , 1971 (Gassman 3, Age and
   Scarpelli 4)
Senza pietà, 1948 (Fellini 2, Masina 3,
   Gherardi 4, Pinelli 4, Ponti 4, Rota 4)
Senza sapere niente di lei, 1969
   (Comencini 2, Cecchi D'Amico 4,
   Morricone 4)
Senza veli, 1953 (Gallone 2)
Separate Beds. See Wheeler Dealers,
   1963
Separate Tables, 1958 (Hayworth 3, Kerr 3,
   Lancaster 3, Niven 3, Head 4, Horner 4,
   Lang 4, Raksin 4, Rattigan 4)
Separate Tables, 1984 (Bates 3, Christie 3)
Separate Ways, 1980 (Black 3)
Sepolta viva, 1973 (Morricone 4)
**Seppuku, 1962 (Kobayashi 2, Iwashita 3,
   Takemitsu 4, Toda 4)**
Sept ans de malheur. See Seven Years' Bad
   Luck, 1921
Sept Chateaux du diable, 1901 (Pathé 4)
Sept fois femme. See Woman Times Seven,
   1967
Sept morts sur ordonnance, 1975 (Piccoli 3,
   Vanel 3, Sarde 4)
Sept P., Cuis., S. de B., . . . a saisir, 1984
   (Varda 2)
Sept Pechés capitaux, 1910 (Gaumont 4)
Sept Péchés capitaux, 1952 (Chabrol 2,
   Morgan 3, Philipe 3, Rosay 3,
   Aurenche 4, Bost 4, Douy 4, Spaak 4,
   Trauner 4, Wakhévitch 4)
Sept Péchés capitaux, 1962 (Vadim 2,
   Cassel 3, Constantine 3, Presle 3,
   Trintignant 3, Decaë 4, Douy 4, Evein 4,
   Legrand 4, Rabier 4)
September, 1987 (Allen 2, Elliott 3,
   Farrow 3)
September Affair, 1950 (Dieterle 2,
   Cotten 3, Fontaine 3, Rosay 3, Dreier 4,
   Head 4, Lang 4, Wallis 4, Young 4)
September Gun, 1984 (Preston 3)
September in the Rain, 1937 (Freleng 4,
   Stalling 4)
September Nights. See Zářijové noci, 1957
September Storm, 1960 (Burnett 4, Haskin 4,
   Leven 4)
September 30, 1955, 1977 (Willis 4)
Sein grosser Fall, 1927 (Tschechowa 3)
Sein grösster Bluff, 1927 (Dietrich 3,
   Galeen 4)
Sein ist das Gericht, 1921 (Metzner 4)
Sequenza del fiore di carta, 1968 (Pasolini 2)

Sequestrati di Altona, 1962 (Loren 3, March 3, Schell 3, Wagner 3, Ponti 4, Rota 4, Shostakovich 4, Zavattini 4)

Séquestrée, 1908 (Cohl 4)

Sequoia, 1934 (Stothart 4, Wilson 4)

Sera'a fil Mina, 1955 (Sharif 3)

Serafino, 1968 (Germi 2, Pinelli 4)

Seraglio, 1958 (Reiniger 4)

Sérail, 1976 (Caron 3)

Seraphita's Diary, 1982 (Wiseman 2)

Sera's fil Nil, 1959 (Sharif 3)

Sera's fil Wadi, 1953 (Sharif 3)

Serenade, 1916 (Laurel and Hardy 3)

Serenade, 1921 (Walsh 2, Johnson 3, Menzies 4)

Serenade, 1927 (D'Arrast 2, Menjou 3, Vajda 4)

Serenade. See Broadway Serenade, 1939

Sérénade, 1940 (Jouvet 3)

Serenade, 1956 (Mann 2, Fontaine 3, Price 3, Blanke 4, Cahn 4)

Sérénade aux nuages, 1946 (Cayatte 2, Wakhévitch 4)

Serenade einer grossen Liebe, 1958 (Maté 4)

Serenal, 1959 (McLaren 4)

Serene Siam, 1937 (Hoch 4)

Serenity, 1953 (Markopoulos 2)

Serenyi, 1918 (Veidt 3)

Serge Panine, 1939 (Rosay 3)

Sergeant, 1968 (Steiger 3)

Sergeant Berry, 1938 (Albers 3)

Sergeant Byrne of the N.W.M.P., 1912 (Selig 4)

Sergeant Deadhead, 1965 (Keaton 2, Arden 3, Crosby 4)

Sergeant Madden, 1939 (Von Sternberg 2, Beery 3, Seitz 4)

Sergeant Murphy, 1938 (Crisp 3, Reagan 3, Eason 4, McCord 4)

Sergeant Pepper's Lonely Hearts Club Band, 1978 (Martin 3, Pleasence 3)

Sergeant Rutledge, 1960 (Ford 2, Marsh 3, Glennon 4)

Sergeant Ryker, 1963 (Marvin 3, Williams 4)

Sergeant X, 1941 (Volkov 2)

Sergeant York, 1941 (Hawks 2, Huston 2, Bond 3, Brennan 3, Cooper 3, Eason 4, Edeson 4, Friedhofer 4, Koch 4, Lasky 4, Polito 4, Steiner 4, Wallis 4)

Sergeant's Boy, 1912 (Ince 4)

Sergeants Three, 1962 (Sturges 2, Martin 3, Sinatra 3, Burnett 4, Hoch 4)

Sergent X, 1931 (Mozhukin 3)

Sergent X, 1959 (Auric 4, Renoir 4)

Sergo Ordzhonikidze, 1937 (Vertov 2)

Serial, 1980 (Lee 3, Weld 3, Schifrin 4)

Série des bouts de Zari, 1913 (Gaumont 4)

Série noire, 1955 (Von Stroheim 2, Audiard 4)

Série noire, 1979 (Blier 3)

Sérieux comme le plaisir, 1974 (Huppert 3, Carrière 4)

Serious Charge, 1959 (Périnal 4)

Serious Game. See Allvarsamma Leken, 1945

Serious Game. See Allvarsamma Leken, 1977

Serious Sixteen, 1910 (Griffith 2, Bitzer 4)

Serp i molet, 1921 (Tisse 4)

Serpe, 1919 (Bertini 3)

Serpent, 1916 (Walsh 2, Bara 3)

Serpent. See Ormen, 1966

Serpent, 1972 (Bogarde 3, Brynner 3, Fonda 3, Noiret 3, Morricone 4, Renoir 4, Saulnier 4)

Serpent and the Rainbow, 1988 (Craven 2)

Serpent of the Nile, 1953 (Katzman 4)

Serpent's Egg. See Schlangenei, 1977

Serpico, 1973 (Lumet 2, Pacino 3, Allen 4, De Laurentiis 4, Mirisch 4, Salt 4, Theodorakis 4)

Serpico: The Deadly Game, 1976 (Bernstein 4)

Servant, 1963 (Losey 2, Bogarde 3, Pinter 4, Slocombe 4)

Servante, 1969 (Gélin 3)

Servant in the House, 1921 (Gilbert 3)

Servants All, 1936 (Cusack 3)

Servants' Entrance, 1934 (Ayres 3, Gaynor 3, Friedhofer 4, Mohr 4, Raphaelson 4)

Service, 1972 (Bozzetto 4)

Service de Luxe, 1938 (Price 3)

Service de sauvetage sur la côte belge, 1930 (Storck 2)

Service for Ladies, 1927 (D'Arrast 2, Menjou 3, Glazer 4, Rosson 4, Vajda 4)

Service for Ladies, 1932 (Howard 3, Oberon 3, Biro 4, Junge 4, Korda 4, Vajda 4, Zukor 4)

Service précipité, 1903 (Guy 2)

Service with a Smile, 1937 (Fleischer 4)

Service with the Colors, 1940 (Eason 4)

Seryozha, 1960 (Bondarchuk 3)

Ses Ancêtres, 1915 (Cohl 4)

Sesso degli angeli, 1968 (Fusco 4)

Sesso di diavolo, 1970 (Brazzi 3)

Sesso in confessionale, 1974 (Morricone 4)

Sesso matto, 1973 (Giannini 3)

Sest Mušketýru, 1925 (Ondra 3)

Set Free, 1918 (Browning 2)

Sete Balas para Selma, 1967 (De Almeida 4)

Setenta veces siete, 1962 (Torre Nilsson 2)

Seth's Temptation, 1910 (Olcott 2)

Setkání v Bukurešti, 1954 (Stallich 4)

Setkání v Lipsku, 1959 (Kučera 4)

Setouchi Shonen Yakyudan, 1984 (Shinoda 2, Iwashita 3)

Setouchi shounen yakyu-dan, 1981 (Miyagawa 4)

Setřelé písmo, 1920 (Ondra 3)

Setta, 1991 (Argento 4)

Sette canne e un vestito, 1950 (Antonioni 2)

Sette chili in sette giorni, 1986 (Donaggio 4)

Sette contro la morte, 1964 (Ulmer 2)

Sette dell'orsa maggiore, 1952 (Rota 4)

Sette donne per i MacGregor, 1966 (Morricone 4)

Sette donne per una strage. See Frauen, die durch die Hölle gehen, 1966

Sette fratelli Cervi, 1967 (Reggiani 3, Volonté 3, Zavattini 4)

Sette monaci d'oro, 1966 (Fabrizi 3)

Sette peccati capitali, 1952 (Rossellini 2)

Sette piccata capitali, 1920 (Bertini 3)

Sette pistole per i MacGregor, 1966 (Morricone 4)

Sette strani cadaveri. See Morte sorride all'assassino, 1973

Sette uomini e un cervello, 1968 (Brazzi 3)

Sette volta donna. See Woman Times Seven, 1967

Setting the Style, 1914 (Bunny 3)

Setti peccati, 1942 (Zavattini 4)

Settled at the Seaside, 1915 (Sennett 2)

Settled Out of Court, 1925 (Buchanan 3)

Settlement of Love. See Aijo no kessan, 1956

Setu Bandhan, 1932 (Phalke 2)

Set-Up, 1949 (Wise 2, Ryan 3, D'Agostino 4, Krasner 4)

Seul Amour, 1943 (Presle 3, Honegger 4, Matras 4)

Seul dans la nuit, 1945 (Blier 3)

Seul ou avec d'autres, 1961 (Arcand 2)

Sève de la terre, 1955 (Alexeieff and Parker 4)

Seven Ages, 1905 (Porter 2)

Seven Ages of Man, 1906 (Ince 4)

Seven Angry Men, 1955 (Massey 3)

Seven Arts, 1958 (Popescu-Gopo 4)

Seven Beauties. See Pasqualino Settebelleze, 1975

Seven Brides for Seven Brothers, 1954 (Donen 2, Keel 3, Deutsch 4, Folsey 4, Gillespie 4, Goodrich 4, Kidd 4, Mercer 4, Plunkett 4)

Seven Brothers Meet Dracula. See Golden Vampire, 1974

Seven Capital Sins. See Sept Péchés capitaux, 1952

Seven Capital Sins. See Sept Péchés capitaux, 1962

Seven Chances, 1925 (Keaton 2, Arthur 3, Bruckman 4, Mayer 4, Schenck 4)

Seven Cities of Gold, 1955 (Quinn 3, Ballard 4, Friedhofer 4, LeMaire 4, Smith 4)

Seven Days Ashore, 1944 (Dumont 3, Metty 4)

Seven Days in May, 1964 (Frankenheimer 2, Douglas 3, Gardner 3, Lancaster 3, March 3, O'Brien 3, Goldsmith 4, Houseman 4)

Seven Days Leave, 1930 (Cooper 3, Lang 4)

Seven Days Leave, 1942 (Walters 2)

Seven Days' Leave, 1942 (Ball 3, Mature 3)

Seven Days . . . Seven Nights. See Moderato cantabile, 1960

Seven Days to Noon, 1950 (Boulting 2, Addison 4, Bernard 4, Dehn 4, Korda 4)

Seven Deadly Sins. See Sept Péchés capitaux, 1952

Seven Deadly Sins. See Sept Péchés capitaux, 1962

Seven Different Ways. See Confession, 1964

Seven Faces, 1929 (Muni 3, August 4, Friedhofer 4)

Seven Faces of Dr. Lao, 1964 (Pal 4)

Seven Footprints to Satan, 1929 (Christensen 2, Polito 4)

Seven from Heaven, 1979 (Palance 3)

Seven Guns for the MacGregors. See Sette pistole per i MacGregor, 1966

Seven Hills of Rome, 1957 (Delli Colli 4)

Seven Indians. See Saat Hindustani, 1970

Seven Keys to Baldpate, 1929 (Cronjager 4, Murfin 4, Plunkett 4)

Seven Keys to Baldpate, 1935 (Brennan 3, Plunkett 4, Polglase 4, Veiller 4)

Seven Little Foys, 1955 (Cagney 3, Hope 3, Head 4)

Seven Madmen. See Siete locos, 1973

Seven Magnificent Gladiators, 1984 (Golan and Globus 4, Morricone 4)

Seven Men from Now, 1956 (Boetticher 2, Marvin 3, Scott 3, Clothier 4)

Seven Miles from Alcatraz, 1942 (Dmytryk 2)

Seven Minutes, 1971 (Carradine 3, De Carlo 3)

Seven Minutes, 1989 (Delerue 4)

Seven Nights in Japan, 1976 (Decaë 4)

Seven Pearls, 1917 (Grot 4)

Seven Samurai. *See* **Shichinin no samurai, 1954**

Seven Seas to Calais. *See* Dominatore dei sette mari, 1960

Seven Secrets of Su-Muru. *See* Rio '70, 1970

Seven Sinners, 1925 (Milestone 2)

Seven Sinners, 1936 (Launder and Gilliat 2, Balcon 4, Metzner 4, Rank 4)

Seven Sinners, 1940 (Garnett 2, Crawford 3, Dietrich 3, Homolka 3, Wayne 3, Irene 4, Maté 4, Pasternak 4, Salter 4)

Seven Sisters, 1915 (Olcott 2)

Seven Swans, 1917 (Barthelmess 3)

Seven Sweethearts, 1942 (Borzage 2, Beavers 3, Grayson 3, Folsey 4, Pasternak 4, Reisch 4, Waxman 4)

Seven Thieves, 1960 (Hathaway 2, Robinson 3, Steiger 3, Wallach 3, Wheeler 4)

Seven Thunders, 1957 (Rank 4)

Seven Till Five, 1976 (McLaren 4)

Seven Times Seven, 1968 (Terry-Thomas 3)

Seven Waves Away. *See* Abandon Ship, 1956

Seven Ways from Sundown, 1960 (Murphy 3)

Seven Wishes of Johanna Peabody, 1978 (McQueen 3)

Seven Women, 1965 (Ford 2, Bancroft 3, Bernstein 4, La Shelle 4, Plunkett 4)

Seven Women from Hell, 1961 (Crosby 4)

Seven Women, Seven Sins, 1987 (Seyrig 3)

Seven Wonders of the World, 1955 (Garnett 2, Raksin 4)

Seven Year Itch, 1955 (Wilder 2, Homolka 3, Monroe 3, Axelrod 4, Bass 4, Cahn 4, Krasner 4, LeMaire 4, Newman 4, Wheeler 4)

Seven Years' Bad Luck, 1921 (Linder 3)

Seven-Per-Cent Solution, 1976 (Arkin 3, Duvall 3, Olivier 3, Redgrave 3, Adam 4, Addison 4, Morris 4, Reynolds 4)

Seventeen, 1917 (Zukor 4)

Seventeen, 1940 (Cooper 3, Dreier 4, Head 4)

Seventeen-Year-Olds. *See* Siebzehnjärigen, 1929

Seventh Anniversary of the Red Army. *See* Zagranichnii pokhod sudov Baltiiskogo flota kreisere 'Aurora' i uchebnogo sudna 'Komsomolts', August 8, 1925, 1925

Seventh Bandit, 1926 (Carey 3, Polito 4)

Seventh Cavalry, 1955 (Lewis 2, Scott 3, Brown 4)

Seventh Continent. *See* Sedmi kontinent, 1966

Seventh Cross, 1944 (Zinnemann 2, Moorehead 3, Tracy 3, Berman 4, Freund 4, Gibbons 4, Irene 4, Mayer 4)

Seventh Dawn, 1964 (Holden 3, York 3, Young 4)

Seventh Day, 1909 (Griffith 2, Pickford 3, Bitzer 4)

Seventh Day, 1922 (Goulding 2, King 2, Barthelmess 3)

Seventh Heaven, 1927 (Borzage 2, Gaynor 3, Glazer 4)

Seventh Heaven, 1937 (King 2, Simon 3, Stewart 3, Zanuck 4)

Seventh Heaven. *See* Sjunde himlen, 1956

Seventh Juror. *See* Septième Juré, 1962

Seventh Man, 1943 (Lewton 4)

Seventh Seal. *See* **Sjunde inseglet, 1957**

Seventh Sin, 1957 (Minnelli 2, Rosay 3, Sanders 3, Folsey 4, Rose 4, Rozsa 4)

Seventh Son, 1912 (Reid 3)

Seventh Survivor, 1941 (Fisher 2)

Seventh Veil, 1945 (Lom 3, Mason 3, Box, B. 4, Box, M. 4, Mathieson 4, Rank 4)

Seventh Victim, 1943 (Bodeen 4, D'Agostino 4, Musuraca 4)

Seventh Voyage of Sinbad, 1958 (Harryhausen 4, Herrmann 4)

Seventies People. *See* 70-Talets Människor, 1975

Seventy-Five Years of Cinema Museum, 1972 (Daves 2, Hathaway 2)

Seven-Ups, 1973 (Scheider 3)

Severed Head, 1970 (Attenborough 3, Bloom 3, Remick 3, Raphael 4)

Severní přístav, 1954 (Brdečka 4)

Severnoe siianie, 1926 (Enei 4)

Severo Torelli, 1914 (Feuillade 2, Musidora 3)

Sevillana, 1930 (Novarro 3)

Sevodiva, 1922 (Vertov 2)

Sevres Porcelain. *See* Porcelaines tendres, 1909

Sewak, 1975 (Azmi 3)

Sewer, 1912 (Guy 2)

Sex, 1920 (Niblo 2, Barnes 4, Sullivan 4)

Sex and the Married Woman, 1977 (Head 4)

Sex and the Single Girl, 1964 (Bacall 3, Curtis 3, Fonda 3, Horton 3, Wood 3, Head 4, Lang 4)

Sex Hygiene, 1941 (Ford 2, Barnes 4)

Sex Kittens Go to College, 1960 (Carradine 3, Weld 3)

Sex Life of the Polyp, 1928 (Benchley 4)

Sex, Love and Marriage. *See* Love and Marriage, 1970

Sex O'Clock U.S.A., 1976 (Braunberger 4)

Sex Power, 1970 (Vangelis 4)

Sex Quartet. *See* Fate, 1966

Sex Symbol, 1974 (Winters 3, Lai 4, Mancini 4)

Sex-Business—Made in Passing, 1969 (Syberberg 2)

Sexe faible, 1933 (Siodmak 2, Brasseur 3)

Sexmisja, 1984 (Tyszkiewicz 3)

Sextet. *See* Sekstet, 1963

Sextette, 1978 (Curtis 3, Pidgeon 3, Raft 3, West 3, Head 4)

Sexual Meditation: Faun's Room Yale. *See* Sexual Meditations, 1972

Sexual Meditation: Hotel. *See* Sexual Meditations, 1972

Sexual Meditation No. 1: Motel. *See* Sexual Meditations, 1972

Sexual Meditation: Office Suite. *See* Sexual Meditations, 1972

Sexual Meditation: Open Field. *See* Sexual Meditations, 1972

Sexual Meditation: Room with View. *See* Sexual Meditations, 1972

Sexual Meditations, 1972 (Brakhage 2)

Seytanin oğlu, 1967 (Güney 2)

Sezona mira u parizu, 1981 (Valli 3)

Sfida, 1958 (Cecchi D'Amico 4, Cristaldi 4, Di Venanzo 4)

Sfinnge, 1919 (Bertini 3)

Sfinxen, 1914 (Psilander 3)

Sfinxens Hemmelighed, 1918 (Psilander 3)

Sgt. Pepper's Lonely Hearts Club Band, 1978 (Roizman 4)

Shaan, 1980 (Bachchan 3)

Shabnam, 1949 (Kumar 3, Burman 4)

Shacho enma-cho, 1969 (Tsukasa 3)

Shacho gyojo-ki, 1966 (Tsukasa 3)

Shacho hanjo-ki, 1968 (Tsukasa 3)

Shacho ninpo-cho, 1965 (Tsukasa 3)

Shacho sandai-ki, 1958 (Tsukasa 3)

Shacho sen-ichiya, 1967 (Tsukasa 3)

Shacho shinshiroku, 1964 (Tsukasa 3)

Shacho-gaku ABC, 1970 (Tsukasa 3)

Shachou koukou-ko, 1962 (Muraki 4)

Shachou sandai-ki, 1958 (Muraki 4)

Shack Out on 101, 1955 (Marvin 3, Crosby 4)

Shackled, 1918 (Gilbert 3)

Shackles of Gold, 1922 (Brenon 2)

Shadow, 1937 (Hayworth 3, Ballard 4)

Shadow. *See* Skuggan, 1953

Shadow. *See* Cień, 1956

Shadow Army. *See* Armée des ombres, 1969

Shadow Box, 1980 (Newman 3, Sidney 3, Woodward 3, Mancini 4)

Shadow House, 1972 (Carradine 3)

Shadow in Light. *See* Stín ve světle, 1928

Shadow in the Sky, 1951 (Folsey 4, Kaper 4, Maddow 4)

Shadow in the Streets, 1975 (Andrews 3)

Shadow Line. *See* Smuga cienia, 1976

Shadow Makers. *See* Fat Man and Little Boy, 1989

Shadow of a Doubt, 1943 (Hitchcock 2, Cotten 3, Wright 3, Adrian 4, Boyle 4, Reville 4, Tiomkin 4)

Shadow of a Woman, 1946 (Deutsch 4, Glennon 4)

Shadow of Adultery. *See* Proie pour l'ombre, 1960

Shadow of Blackmail. *See* Wife Wanted, 1946

Shadow of Chinatown, 1936 (Lugosi 3)

Shadow of Darkness. *See* Yami no Kageboushi, 1938

Shadow of Doubt, 1935 (Clarke 4)

Shadow of Lightning Ridge, 1921 (Glennon 4, Meredyth 4)

Shadow of the Cat, 1961 (Theodorakis 4)

Shadow of the Eagle, 1932 (Wayne 3, Canutt 4, Eason 4)

Shadow of the Eagle, 1950 (Havelock-Allan 4)

Shadow of the Law, 1926 (Bow 3)

Shadow of the Law, 1930 (Powell 3, Lang 4)

Shadow of the Past, 1913 (Ince 4, Sullivan 4)

Shadow of the Thin Man, 1941 (Van Dyke 2, Beavers 3, Loy 3, Powell 3, Reed 3, Daniels 4, Stromberg 4)

Shadow on the Land, 1968 (Cooper 3, Hackman 3)

Shadow on the Mountain, 1931 (Grierson 2)

Shadow on the Wall, 1925 (Eason 4)

Shadow on the Wall, 1949 (Irene 4)

Shadow on the Window, 1957 (Duning 4)

Shadow Ranch, 1930 (McCord 4)

Shadow Riders, 1982 (Johnson 3)

Shadow Warrior. *See* **Kagemusha, 1980**

Shadowed, 1910 (White 3)

Shadowed, 1946 (Sturges 2)

Shadows, 1914 (Bushman 3)

Shadows, 1916 (Eason 4)

Shadows. *See* Stíny, 1921

Shadows, 1922 (Chaney 3, Schulberg 4)
Shadows, 1923 (Fleischer 4)
Shadows, 1960 (Cassavetes 2)
Shadows of Death, 1945 (Crabbe 3)
Shadows of Doubt, 1976 (Hurt 3)
Shadows of Fear. See Thérèse Raquin, 1928
Shadows of Paris, 1924 (Brenon 2, Menjou 3, Negri 3)
Shadows of the Moulin Rouge, 1913 (Guy 2)
Shadows on the Sage, 1942 (Canutt 4)
Shadows on the Snow. See Skugger över snön, 1945
Shadows Run Black, 1981 (Costner 3)
Shady Lady, 1945 (Coburn 3, Mohr 4, Siodmak 4)
Shagai, Soviet!, 1926 (Vertov 2)
Shaggy D.A., 1976 (Stevenson 2)
Shaggy Dog, 1959 (MacMurray 3, Disney 4)
Shaheed, 1948 (Kumar 3)
Shahen Shah, 1953 (Burman 4)
Shahensa, 1988 (Bachchan 3)
Shaitan el Sahara, 1954 (Sharif 3)
Shaka, 1961 (Kyo 3, Yamada 3)
Shaka Zulu, 1986 (Howard 3, Lee 3)
Shake 'em Up, 1921 (Roach 3)
Shake Hands with the Devil, 1959 (Cagney 3, Cusack 3, Harris 3, Redgrave 3, Alwyn 4)
Shake, Rattle and Rock, 1956 (Dumont 3)
Shake Your Powder Puff, 1934 (Freleng 4)
Shakedown, 1929 (Huston 2, Wyler 2)
Shakedown, 1936 (Ayres 3)
Shakedown, 1950 (Pleasence 3)
Shaker Run, 1985 (Robertson 3)
Shakespeare's Country, 1944 (Gielgud 3)
Shakespeare's Theater: The Globe Playhouse, 1950 (Colman 3)
Shakespeare Wallah, 1965 (Ivory 2, Jhabvala 4, Mitra 4)
Shakespearian Spinach, 1940 (Fleischer 4)
Shakha Proshakha, 1990 (Chatterjee 3, Depardieu 3)
Shakiest Gun in the West, 1968 (Whitlock 4)
Shakma, 1990 (McDowall 3)
Shakmatnaya goryachka, 1925 (Golovnya 4)
Shakti, 1982 (Bachchan 3, Kumar 3, Patil 3)
Shalako, 1968 (Dmytryk 2, Bardot 3, Connery 3, Hawkins 3, Mathieson 4)
Shalimar, 1978 (Harrison 3)
Shall the Children Pay?. See What Price Innocence?, 1933
Shall We Dance, 1937 (Astaire 3, Horton 3, Rogers 3, Berman 4, Pan 4, Polglase 4)
Sham Battle Shenanigans, 1942 (Terry 4)
Shama, 1981 (Azmi 3)
Shame, 1921 (Gilbert 3, Wong 3)
Shame. See Skammen, 1968
Shameful Behavior?, 1926 (Musuraca 4)
Shameful Dream. See Hazukashiiyume, 1927
Shamisen to otobai, 1961 (Shinoda 2, Mori 3)
Shampoo, 1975 (Ashby 2, Beatty 3, Christie 3, Grant 3, Hawn 3, Kovacs 4, Sylbert 4, Towne 4)
Shamrock and Roll, 1969 (Blanc 4, McKimson 4)
Shamrock and the Rose, 1927 (Costello 3)
Shamrock Handicap, 1926 (Ford 2, Gaynor 3)
Shamus, 1973 (Reynolds 3, Goldsmith 4)
Shane, 1953 (Stevens 2, Arthur 3, Johnson 3, Ladd 3, Palance 3, Head 4, Hornbeck 4, Young 4)

Shanghai, 1935 (Boyer 3, Young 3, Wanger 4)
Shanghai. See Shanghai Gesture, 1941
Shanghai Bound, 1927 (Cronjager 4)
Shanghai Drama. See Drame de Shanghaï, 1938
Shanghai Express, 1932 (Hathaway 2, Von Sternberg 2, Dietrich 3, Wong 3, Banton 4, Dreier 4, Furthman 4, Garmes 4, Zukor 4)
Shanghai Gesture, 1941 (Von Sternberg 2, Dalio 3, Huston 3, Mature 3, Tierney 3, Furthman 4, Leven 4)
Shanghai Lady, 1928 (Mohr 4)
Shanghai Madness, 1933 (Tracy 3, Wray 3, Garmes 4)
Shanghai Moon. See Shanhai no tsuki, 1941
Shanghai Orchid, 1934 (Florey 2)
Shanghai Story, 1954 (O'Brien 3, Miller 4)
Shanghaied, 1909 (Anderson 3)
Shanghaied, 1915 (Purviance 3)
Shanghaied, 1927 (Plunkett 4, Walker 4)
Shanghaied Jonah, 1917 (Sennett 2)
Shanghaied Ladies, 1924 (Sennett 2)
Shanghaied Lovers, 1924 (Capra 2)
Shanghaied Lovers, 1980 (Langdon 3)
Shanhai gaeri no Riru, 1952 (Kagawa 3)
Shanhai no tsuki, 1941 (Yamada 3)
Shanks, 1974 (Biroc 4, Leven 4, North 4)
Shannons of Broadway, 1929 (Brennan 3)
Shantata, Court Chalu Ahe, 1970 (Nihalani 4)
Shaolin Wooden Men, 1976 (Chan 3)
Shape of Things to Come, 1968 (Van Dyke 2)
Shape of Things to Come, 1979 (Palance 3)
Shaque, 1977 (Azmi 3)
Sharabi, 1964 (Anand 3)
Sharada, 1958 (Kapoor 2)
Share Cropper. See Hari Hondal Burgadar, 1980
Shark, 1920 (Ruttenberg 4)
Shark, 1970 (Kennedy 3, Reynolds 3)
Shark Monroe, 1918 (Hart 3, August 4, Sullivan 4)
Shark Reef. See She-Gods of Shark Reef, 1957
Shark River, 1953 (Cortez 4)
Sharkey's Machine, 1982 (Gassman 3, Reynolds 3, Fraker 4)
Sharkfighters, 1956 (Mature 3, Garmes 4, Mandell 4)
Sharks' Cave. See Bermuda: la fossa maledetta, 1978
Shark's Treasure, 1975 (Wilde 3)
Sharma and Beyond, 1983 (Puttnam 4)
Sharmeelee, 1971 (Burman 4)
Sharon vestida de rojo, 1968 (García Berlanga 2)
Sharp Shooters, 1928 (Scott 3, Clarke 4)
Sharpshooter, 1913 (Ince 4)
Shati el Asrar, 1957 (Sharif 3)
Shatranj Ke Khilari, 1977 (Azmi 3, Chandragupta 4, Datta 4)
Shatter. See Call Him Mr. Shatter, 1975
Shattered. See Scherben, 1921
Shattered, 1991 (Hoskins 3, Kovacs 4)
Shattered Idols, 1921 (Gaudio 4)
Shattered Spirits, 1985 (Sheen 3)
Shattered Vase. See Razbitaya vaza, 1941
Shattered Vows, 1984 (Neal 3, Winters 3)
Shaughraun, 1908 (Lawrence 3)
Shaughraun, 1912 (Olcott 2)
Shayer, 1949 (Anand 3)

Shazka o spiatchek, 1914 (Mozhukin 3)
Shchastiya bylo tak vozmotzno, 1916 (Mozhukin 3)
Shchit i mech, 1968 (Yankovsky 3)
Shchors, 1939 (Dovzhenko 2)
She, 1908 (Porter 2)
She, 1911 (Cruze 2)
She. See Kanojo, 1926
She, 1935 (Johnson 3, Scott 3, Cooper 4, Dunn 4, Hunt 4, Newman 4, Polglase 4, Steiner 4)
She, 1965 (Cushing 3, Lee 3, Bernard 4, Carreras 4)
S*H*E, 1980 (Sharif 3)
She and He. See Kanojo to kare, 1963
She and He. See Blaho lásky, 1965
She Asked for It, 1937 (Head 4, Schulberg 4, Shamroy 4)
She Conquered. See Hon segrade, 1916
She Couldn't Help It, 1921 (Daniels 3)
She Couldn't Say No, 1930 (Bacon 2, Beavers 3)
She Couldn't Say No, 1938 (Wyman 3)
She Couldn't Say No, 1939 (Withers 3)
She Couldn't Say No, 1941 (Arden 3, McCord 4)
She Couldn't Say No, 1954 (Bacon 2, Mitchum 3, Simmons 3, Orry-Kelly 4)
She Couldn't Take It, 1935 (Bennett 3, Pangborn 3, Raft 3, Cohn 4, Schulberg 4, Shamroy 4)
She Defends Her Country. See Ona zashchischaet Rodinu, 1943
She Done Him Wrong, 1933 (Beavers 3, Grant 3, West 3, Head 4, Lang 4, Zukor 4)
She Done Him Wrong. See Villain Still Pursued Her, 1940
She Fell Among Thieves, 1978 (McDowell 3)
She Fell Fainting in His Arms, 1903 (Bitzer 4)
She Gets Her Man, 1935 (Bond 3, Carradine 3, D'Agostino 4)
She Gets Her Man, 1945 (Bruckman 4)
She Goes to War, 1929 (King 2, D'Agostino 4, Estabrook 4, Gaudio 4, Saunders 4)
She Got What She Wanted, 1930 (Cruze 2)
She Had to Choose, 1934 (Crabbe 3)
She Had to Eat, 1937 (Pangborn 3)
She Had to Say Yes, 1933 (Berkeley 2, Young 3, Orry-Kelly 4)
She Is Like a Rainbow, 1969 (Müller 4)
She Knew All the Answers, 1941 (Arden 3, Bennett 3)
She Knew What She Wanted, 1936 (Withers 3)
She Landed a Big One, 1914 (Beery 3)
She Learned About Sailors, 1934 (Ayres 3, Faye 3)
She Loved a Fireman, 1938 (Sheridan 3)
She Loved a Sailor, 1916 (Sennett 2)
She Loved Him Plenty, 1918 (Sennett 2)
She Loves and Lies, 1920 (Talmadge 3)
She Loves Me Not, 1918 (Daniels 3, Lloyd 3, Roach 4)
She Loves Me Not, 1934 (Crosby 3, Hopkins 3, Glazer 4, Lang 4, Prinz 4)
She Made Her Bed, 1934 (Krasner 4, Robinson 4)
She Married an Artist, 1937 (Daves 2, Pangborn 3, Buchman 4)

She Married Her Boss, 1935 (La Cava 2, Colbert 3, Douglas 3, Buchman 4, Cohn 4, Shamroy 4)

She Needed a Doctor, 1917 (Sennett 2)

She Never Knew, 1915 (Eason 4)

She Played with Fire. *See* Fortune Is a Woman, 1957

She Reminds Me of You, 1934 (Fleischer 4)

She Stayed for Breakfast, 1940 (Schulberg 4)

She Waits, 1971 (Bondi 3)

She Walketh Alone, 1915 (Eason 4)

She Wanted a Millionaire, 1932 (Bennett 3, Tracy 3, Levien 4, Seitz 4)

She Was a Lady, 1934 (Glennon 4)

She Was an Acrobat's Daughter, 1937 (Freleng 4, Stalling 4)

She Went to the Races, 1945 (Gardner 3, Irene 4)

She Wore a Yellow Ribbon, 1949 (Ford 2, Johnson 3, McLaglen 3, Wayne 3, Basevi 4, Cooper 4, Hoch 4, Nugent 4)

She Wouldn't Say Yes, 1945 (Russell 3, Banton 4, Polglase 4, Walker 4)

She Wronged Him Right, 1934 (Fleischer 4)

Sheba, 1919 (Hepworth 2, Colman 3)

Sheba. *See* Persecution, 1974

She-Devil, 1919 (Bara 3)

She Devil, 1957 (Struss 4)

She-Devil, 1990 (Seidelman 2, Streep 3)

Sheep Ahoy, 1954 (Blanc 4, Jones 4, Maltese 4, Stalling 4)

Sheep Has Five Legs. *See* Mouton à cinq pattes, 1953

Sheep in the Deep, 1962 (Blanc 4, Jones 4)

Sheep in the Meadow, 1939 (Terry 4)

Sheep Stealers Anonymous, 1963 (Hanna and Barbera 4)

Sheepish Wolf, 1942 (Blanc 4, Freleng 4)

Sheepman, 1958 (Ford 3, MacLaine 3, Plunkett 4)

Sheepman's Daughter, 1911 (Dwan 2)

Sheepman's Escape, 1912 (Anderson 3)

Sheep's Clothing, 1914 (Bunny 3)

Sheer Madness. *See* Heller Wahn, 1982

She-Gods of Shark Reef, 1957 (Crosby 4)

Shéhérazade, 1928 (Modot 3)

Shéhérazade, 1963 (Karina 3, Matras 4, Wakhévitch 4)

Sheik, 1921 (Menjou 3, Valentino 3, Zukor 4)

Sheik Steps Out, 1937 (Novarro 3)

Sheila Levine Is Dead and Living in New York, 1975 (Scheider 3, Legrand 4)

Shelagh Delaney's Salford, 1960 (Russell 2)

Shell 43, 1916 (Gilbert 3, Sullivan 4)

She'll Have to Go, 1961 (Karina 3)

Shell Seekers, 1989 (Lansbury 3)

Shell Shocked Egg, 1948 (Blanc 4, McKimson 4, Stalling 4)

Sheltered Daughters, 1921 (Folsey 4)

Sheltering Sky, 1990 (Bertolucci 2, Storaro 4)

Shenandoah, 1965 (Stewart 3, Clothier 4, Whitlock 4)

Shenanigans, 1977 (Meredith 3, Lassally 4)

Shepherd of the Hills, 1927 (Polito 4)

Shepherd of the Hills, 1941 (Hathaway 2, Bond 3, Bondi 3, Carey 3, Wayne 3, Dreier 4, Head 4, Lang 4)

Sheriff series, 1911–13 (Anderson 3)

Sheriff and the Man, 1911 (Lawrence 3)

Sheriff and the Rustler, 1913 (Mix 3)

Sheriff Nell's Tussle, 1918 (Sennett 2)

Sheriff of Cimarron, 1945 (Canutt 4)

Sheriff of Fractured Jaw, 1958 (Walsh 2, Mansfield 3, More 3, Heller 4)

Sheriff of Sage Valley, 1942 (Crabbe 3)

Sheriff of Tombstone, 1941 (Rogers 3)

Sheriff of Toulumne, 1911 (Bosworth 3)

Sheriff of Yawapai County, 1913 (Mix 3)

Sheriff's Adopted Child, 1912 (Ince 4)

Sheriff's Baby, 1913 (Griffith 2, Barrymore 3, Carey 3, Walthall 3, Bitzer 4)

Sheriff's Blunder, 1916 (Mix 3)

Sheriff's Duty, 1916 (Mix 3)

Sheriff's Reward, 1914 (Mix 3)

Sheriff's Sisters, 1911 (Dwan 2)

Sheriff's Son, 1919 (Ince 4)

Sheriff's Streak of Yellow, 1915 (Hart 3)

Sherlock Brown, 1922 (Coffee 4)

Sherlock Holmes, 1922 (Barrymore 3, Powell 3, Hunt 4)

Sherlock Holmes, 1932 (Howard 2, Barnes 4, Friedhofer 4)

Sherlock Holmes. *See* Adventures of Sherlock Holmes, 1939

Sherlock Holmes and the Baskerville Curse, 1984 (O'Toole 3)

Sherlock Holmes and the Deadly Necklace. *See* Sherlock Holmes und das Halsband des Todes, 1962

Sherlock Holmes and the Secret Weapon, 1942 (Rathbone 3, Salter 4)

Sherlock Holmes and the Voice of Terror, 1942 (Rathbone 3)

Sherlock Holmes Faces Death, 1943 (Rathbone 3, Salter 4)

Sherlock Holmes in New York, 1976 (Huston 2)

Sherlock Holmes in Washington, 1943 (Rathbone 3)

Sherlock Holmes Jr., 1911 (Porter 2)

Sherlock Holmes I, 1908 (Holger-Madsen 2)

Sherlock Holmes III, 1908 (Holger-Madsen 2)

Sherlock Holmes und das Halsband des Todes, 1962 (Fisher 2, Lee 3, Siodmak 4)

Sherlock, Jr., 1924 (Keaton 2, Bruckman 4, Mayer 4, Schenck 4)

Sherlock Pink, 1976 (McKimson 4)

Sherlock Sleuth, 1925 (Roach 4)

Sherman Said It, 1933 (Roach 4)

Sherman Was Right, 1932 (Terry 4)

She's a Sheik, 1927 (Daniels 3, Powell 3, Hunt 4)

She's a Soldier, Too, 1944 (Bondi 3, Winters 3)

She's a Sweetheart, 1944 (Edwards 2, Darwell 3)

She's Back on Broadway, 1953 (Blanke 4, Prinz 4)

She's Dangerous, 1937 (Brennan 3, Pangborn 3, Pidgeon 3, Krasner 4, Raksin 4)

She's Gotta Have It, 1986 (Lee 2)

She's Having a Baby, 1988 (Hughes 2)

She's No Lady, 1937 (Vidor 2, Head 4, Schulberg 4)

She's Oil Mine, 1941 (Keaton 2)

She's Sighed by the Seaside, 1921 (Sennett 2)

She's the Only One. *See* Hon den enda, 1926

She's Working Her Way Through College, 1952 (Reagan 3, Cahn 4, Prinz 4)

Shestaya chast' mira, 1926 (Vertov 2)

Shestdesyat dnei, 1943 (Cherkassov 3)

She-Wolf. *See* Lupa, 1953

SH-H-H-H-H, 1955 (Avery 4)

Shi no dangai, 1951 (Hayasaka 4)

Shiawase, 1974 (Takemitsu 4)

Shibaido, 1944 (Hasegawa 3, Yamada 3)

Shichimencho no yukue, 1924 (Mizoguchi 2)

Shichi-nin no keiji: Onn o sagase, 1963 (Kagawa 3)

Shichinin no samurai, 1954 (Kurosawa 2, Mifune 3, Shimura 3, Hayasaka 4)

Shido monogatari, 1941 (Hayasaka 4)

Shield and Sword. *See* Shchit i mech, 1968

Shield for Murder, 1974 (O'Brien 3)

Shifrovanny Document, 1928 (Ptushko 4)

Shifting Sands, 1918 (Swanson 3)

Shiga Naoya, 1958 (Hani 2)

Shigure-gasa, 1928 (Hasegawa 3)

Shiinomi Gakuen, 1955 (Kagawa 3)

Shiju-hachi-nin me, 1936 (Yamada 3)

Shikamo karera wa yuku, 1931 (Mizoguchi 2)

Shikari, 1945 (Burman 4)

Shikast, 1953 (Kumar 3)

Shikibu monogatari, 1990 (Kagawa 3)

Shiki no aiyoku, 1958 (Yamada 3)

Shikko yuyo, 1950 (Hayasaka 4)

Shimai, 1931 (Takamine 3, Tanaka 3)

Shima no ratai-jiken, 1931 (Tanaka 3)

Shima-sodachi, 1963 (Iwashita 3)

Shimau-boshi, 1950 (Yoda 4)

Shimizu no Jirocho Zen-den: Kohen Ashura fukushu no maki, 1926 (Tanaka 3)

Shimmy Lugano e tarantelle e vino, 1979 (Wertmüller 2, Loren 3, Mastroianni 3)

Shin akumyo, 1961 (Yoda 4)

Shin baka jidai, 1946 (Mifune 3)

Shin Heike monogatari, 1955 (Mizoguchi 2, Shindo 3, Hayasaka 4, Miyagawa 4, Yoda 4)

Shin Heike monogatari: Shizuka to Yoshitsune, 1956 (Kagawa 3, Miyagawa 4)

Shin Heike monogatari: Yoshinaka o meguru san-nin no onna, 1956 (Kyo 3, Takamine 3)

Shin josei-kagami, 1929 (Tanaka 3)

Shin josei mondo, 1955 (Kyo 3)

Shin no shi-kotei, 1962 (Hasegawa 3, Kyo 3, Yamada 3)

Shin onna daigaku, 1960 (Tsukasa 3)

Shin ono ga tsumi, 1926 (Mizoguchi 2)

Shina no yoru, 1940 (Hasegawa 3)

Shinbone Alley, 1971 (Carradine 3)

Shindo: Akemi no maki, Ryota no maki, 1936 (Takamine 3, Tanaka 3)

Shine 'em Up, 1922 (Roach 4)

Shine On Harvest Moon, 1932 (Fleischer 4)

Shine On, Harvest Moon, 1938 (Rogers 3)

Shine On, Harvest Moon, 1944 (Sheridan 3, Edeson 4, Prinz 4, Wald 4)

Shinel, 1926 (Kozintsev 2, Enei 4, Moskvin 4)

Shinel, 1983 (Batalov 3)

Shingo jubanshobu, Part II, 1959 (Yamamura 3)

Shingun, 1930 (Tanaka 3)

Shining, 1980 (Kubrick 2, Nicholson 3, Alcott 4)

Shining Future, 1944 (Crosby 3, Durbin 3, Grant 3)

Shining Hour, 1938 (Borzage 2, Mankiewicz 2, Crawford 3, Douglas 3, McDaniel 3, Young 3, Adrian 4, Folsey 4, Murfin 4, Waxman 4)

Shining in the Red Sunset. *See* Akai yuhi ni terasarete, 1925

Shining Through, 1990 (Gielgud 3)

Shining Victory, 1941 (Crisp 3, Davis 3, Howe 4, Koch 4, Steiner 4, Wallis 4)

Shinjitsu ichiro, 1954 (Yamamura 3)

Shinju fujin, 1927 (Tanaka 3)

Shinju fujin, 1933 (Yamada 3)

Shinju ten-no-amijima, 1969 (Shinoda 2, Iwashita 3, Takemitsu 4)

Shinju yoimachigusa, 1925 (Kinugasa 2)

Shinjuku dorobo nikki, 1969 (Toda 4)

Shinkansen diabakuha, 1974 (Shimura 3)

Shinkei gyogun, 1956 (Oshima 2)

Shinkon-ryoko, 1934 (Tanaka 3)

Shinku chitai, 1952 (Okada 3)

Shinno Tsuruchiyo, 1935 (Yamada 3)

Shinpen bocchan, 1941 (Yamada 3)

Shinpen Tange Sazen: Koiguruma no maki, 1940 (Takamine 3)

Shinpen Tange Sazen: Sogan no maki, Koiguruma no maki, 1939 (Yamada 3)

Shinpen Tange Sazen: Yoto no maki, 1938 (Yamada 3)

Shinrei Jakouneko, 1940 (Miyagawa 4)

Shinrun dorobo, 1952 (Yamamura 3)

Shinryu-ro, 1938 (Takamine 3)

Shinsen-gumi, 1969 (Mifune 3, Tsukasa 3)

Shinshaku: Tojin Okichi, Funshin hen, 1938 (Tanaka 3)

Shinsho Taiheiki: Ruten Hiyoshimura, 1953 (Tanaka 3)

Shiobara tasuke, 1930 (Tsuburaya 4)

Shiosai, 1954 (Mifune 3)

Ship Ahoy, 1942 (Powell 3, Sinatra 3)

Ship Cafe, 1935 (Florey 2)

Ship Comes In, 1928 (Adrian 4, Grot 4, Levien 4)

Ship from Shanghai, 1930 (Gibbons 4)

Ship o' the Doom, 1954 (Haskin 4)

Ship of Fools, 1965 (Kramer 2, Ferrer 3, Leigh 3, Marvin 3, Segal 3, Signoret 3, Werner 3, Edouart 4, Laszlo 4, Tavoularis 4, Whitlock 4)

Ship of Lost Souls. *See* Schiff der verlorenen Menschen, 1929

Ship of Wanted Men, 1933 (Katzman 4)

Ship That Died of Shame, 1955 (Dearden 2, Attenborough 3, Alwyn 4)

Shipbuilders, 1943 (Baxter 2)

Shipmates, 1931 (Daves 2, Bosworth 3, Montgomery 3)

Shipmates Forever, 1935 (Borzage 2, Daves 2, Keeler 3, Powell 3, Orry-Kelly 4, Polito 4)

Shipmates o' Mine, 1936 (Pearson 2)

Ships. *See* Chuzhoy pidzhak, 1927

Ships Are Storming the Bastions, 1953 (Bondarchuk 3)

Ships with Wings, 1941 (Hamer 2, Balcon 4)

Shipwrecked, 1931 (Lantz 4)

Shipyard, 1933 (Rotha 2)

Shipyard Sally, 1939 (Fields 3)

Shipyard Symphony, 1943 (Terry 4)

Shirai Gonpachi, 1928 (Hasegawa 3, Tsuburaya 4)

Shiralee, 1957 (Finch 3, Addison 4)

Shirasagi, 1941 (Hayasaka 4)

Shirayuri wa nageku, 1925 (Mizoguchi 2)

Shirazu no Yataro, 1954 (Hasegawa 3)

Shiriboe Sonichi, 1969 (Miyagawa 4)

Shirikurae Magoichi, 1969 (Miyagawa 4)

Shirley Valentine, 1989 (Hamlisch 4)

Shiro to kuro, 1963 (Takemitsu 4)

Shiroi akuma, 1958 (Mori 3)

Shiroi ane, 1931 (Yoda 4)

Shiroi asa, 1964 (Takemitsu 4)

Shiroi hekiga, 1942 (Tsuburaya 4)

Shiroi yaju, 1950 (Yamamura 3)

Shishi no za, 1953 (Hasegawa 3, Tanaka 3)

Shishi-hen, 1937 (Hasegawa 3)

Shishkabugs, 1962 (Blanc 4, Freleng 4)

Shitamachi, 1957 (Mifune 3, Yamada 3)

Shito no densetsu, 1963 (Iwashita 3, Tanaka 3)

Shitoyakana kemono, 1963 (Shindo 3)

Shitto, 1949 (Shindo 2, Yoshimura 2)

Shitto, 1971 (Iwashita 3)

Shiva und die Galgenblume, 1945 (Albers 3)

Shiver and Shake, 1922 (Roach 4)

Shiver Me Timbers!, 1934 (Fleischer 4)

Shiver My Timbers, 1931 (Roach 4)

Shivering Shakespeare, 1929 (Roach 4)

Shivering Sherlocks, 1948 (Three Stooges 3)

Shivering Spooks, 1926 (Roach 4)

Shivers, 1934 (Langdon 3)

Shizen wa sabaku, 1925 (Tanaka 3)

Shizi jietou, 1937 (Zhao 3)

Shizuka gozen, 1938 (Yamada 3)

Shizukanaru ketto, 1949 (Mifune 3, Shimura 3)

Shizukanaru kyodan, 1959 (Yamamura 3)

Shkval, 1916 (Mozhukin 3)

Shli soldaty, 1958 (Bondarchuk 3)

Shlyapa, 1981 (Yankovsky 3)

Shobushi ro sono musume, 1959 (Shimura 3)

Shochiku biggu paredo, 1930 (Hasegawa 3)

Shock, 1923 (Chaney 3)

Shock, 1946 (Price 3, Leven 4)

Shock, 1972 (Carreras 4)

Shock. *See* Choc, 1982

Shock Corridor, 1963 (Fuller 2, Cortez 4, Lourié 4)

Shock Punch, 1925 (Saunders 4)

Shock to the System, 1990 (Caine 3)

Shock Treatment, 1964 (Bacall 3, McDowall 3, Smith 4)

Shock Troops. *See* Homme de trop, 1967

Shock Troops. *See* Homme qui ment, 1969

Shock Waves, 1975 (Carradine 3, Cushing 3)

Shocker, 1989 (Craven 2)

Shocking Accident, 1982 (Greene 4)

Shocking Incident, 1903 (Bitzer 4)

Shocking Miss Pilgrim, 1947 (Goulding 2, Grable 3, Basevi 4, Leven 4, Newman 4, Orry-Kelly 4, Raksin 4, Shamroy 4)

Shocking Pink, 1965 (Freleng 4)

Shockproof, 1949 (Fuller 2, Sirk 2, Wilde 3, Duning 4)

Shoddy the Tailor, 1915 (Laurel and Hardy 3)

Shodo satsujin: Musuko yo, 1979 (Takamine 3)

Shoe Shine Jasper, 1946 (Pal 4)

Shoein' Hosses, 1934 (Fleischer 4)

Shoemaker and the Hatter, 1949 (Halas and Batchelor 4)

Shoes, 1916 (Weber 2, Clarke 4)

Shoes of the Fisherman, 1968 (Gielgud 3, Olivier 3, Quinn 3, Werner 3, North 4)

Shoes That Danced, 1918 (Borzage 2)

Shoeshine. *See* **Sciuscià, 1946**

Shogun Mayeda, 1990 (Lee 3, Mifune 3)

Shogun's Samurai. *See* Yagyu ichizoku no inbo, 1978

Shohai, 1932 (Tanaka 3)

Shojo-dakara, 1950 (Takamine 3, Yamamura 3)

Shokei no shima, 1966 (Shinoda 2, Iwashita 3, Takemitsu 4, Toda 4)

Shokkaku, 1970 (Shindo 2)

Shokutaku no nai ie, 1985 (Takemitsu 4, Toda 4)

Sholay, 1975 (Bachchan 3)

Shonen, 1969 (Toda 4)

Shonen shikei-shu, 1955 (Tanaka 3)

Shonen tanteidan, 1955 (Okada 3)

Shonnenjidai, 1990 (Shinoda 2)

Shoot, 1976 (Borgnine 3, Robertson 3)

Shoot First, 1953 (Lom 3, McCrea 3, Francis 4)

Shoot on Sight, 1920 (Roach 4)

Shoot Out, 1971 (Hathaway 2, Peck 3, Wallis 4)

Shoot Straight, 1923 (Roach 4)

Shoot the Moon, 1982 (Parker 2, Finney 3, Keaton 3)

Shoot the Piano Player. *See* **Tirez sur le pianiste, 1960**

Shoot the Works, 1934 (Sheridan 3, Hecht 4)

Shoot to Kill, 1988 (Poitier 3, Sylbert 4)

Shootdown, 1988 (Lansbury 3)

Shootin' for Love, 1923 (Miller 4)

Shootin' Injuns, 1925 (Roach 4)

Shootin' Irons, 1927 (Schulberg 4)

Shootin' Mad, 1918 (Anderson 3)

Shooting, 1966 (Corman 2, Nicholson 3, Oates 3)

Shooting High, 1940 (Autry 3, Canutt 4, Day 4)

Shooting of Dan McGoo, 1945 (Avery 4)

Shooting Party, 1985 (Gielgud 3, Mason 3)

Shooting Stars, 1927 (Asquith 2)

Shooting Straight, 1930 (Cronjager 4)

Shooting Up the Movies, 1916 (Mix 3)

Shootist, 1976 (Siegel 2, Bacall 3, Carradine 3, Stewart 3, Wayne 3, Bernstein 4, De Laurentiis 4)

Shootout, 1984 (Poitier 3)

Shoot-Out at Medicine Bend, 1957 (Dickinson 3, Garner 3, Scott 3)

Shop Around the Corner, 1940 (Lubitsch 2, Stewart 3, Sullavan 3, Daniels 4, Raphaelson 4)

Shop at Sly Corner, 1946 (Dors 3, Homolka 3, Korda 4)

Shop, Look and Listen, 1940 (Freleng 4, Stalling 4)

Shop on Main Street. *See* **Obchod na korze, 1965**

Shop on the High Street. *See* **Obchod na korze, 1965**

Shop Talk, 1936 (Hope 3)

Shop-Girls of Paris. *See* Au bonheur des Dames, 1943

Shopping with Wife, 1932 (Sennett 2)

Shopworn, 1932 (Stanwyck 3, Riskin 4, Walker 4)

Shopworn Angel, 1928 (Hathaway 2, Cooper 3, Lukas 3, Estabrook 4, Lang 4)

Shopworn Angel, 1938 (Mankiewicz 2, McDaniel 3, Pidgeon 3, Stewart 3, Sullavan 3, Adrian 4, Ruttenberg 4, Salt 4, Vorkapich 4)

Shore Acres, 1920 (Ingram 2, Seitz 4)

Shore Leave, 1925 (Barthelmess 3)

Shores of Phos: A Fable, 1972 (Brakhage 2)

Shori no himade, 1945 (Takamine 3)

Shori to haiboku, 1960 (Yamamura 3)

Short and Suite, 1959 (McLaren 4)

Short and Very Short Films, 1976 (Emshwiller 2)

Short Circuit, 1986 (Badham 2)
Short Cut. *See* Tempo di uccidere, 1989
Short Cut to Hell, 1957 (Cagney 3, Greene 4, Head 4)
Short Films, 1975–76 (Brakhage 2)
Short History, 1957 (Popescu-Gopo 4)
Short Is the Summer. *See* Kort ar sommaren, 1962
Short Kilts, 1924 (Laurel and Hardy 3, Roach 4)
Short Memory. *See* Mémoire courte, 1978
Short Orders, 1923 (Laurel and Hardy 3, Roach 4)
Short Shave, 1965 (Snow 2)
Short Step, 1991 (Christie 3)
Short Tall Story, 1970 (Halas and Batchelor 4)
Short Walk to Daylight, 1972 (Whitlock 4)
Shortest Day. *See* Giorno più corto, 1963
Shoshun, 1956 (Ryu 3)
Shot. *See* Skottet, 1914
Shot and Bothered, 1966 (Blanc 4)
Shot at Dawn. *See* Schuss im Morgengrauen, 1932
Shot in the Dark, 1933 (Pearson 2, Hawkins 3)
Shot in the Dark, 1964 (Edwards 2, Lom 3, Sanders 3, Sellers 3, Challis 4, Mancini 4)
Shot in the Escape, 1943 (Bruckman 4)
Shot in the Excitement, 1914 (Sennett 2)
Shot in the Frontier, 1954 (Three Stooges 3)
Shotgun, 1955 (De Carlo 3, Hayden 3)
Shotgun Jones, 1914 (Mix 3)
Shotgun Man and the Stage Driver, 1913 (Mix 3)
Shotgun Ranchman, 1912 (Anderson 3)
Shotguns That Kick, 1914 (Sennett 2, Arbuckle 3)
Should a Doctor Tell?, 1931 (Neagle 3)
Should a Husband Forgive, 1919 (Walsh 2, Fox 4)
Should a Mother Tell, 1915 (Ingram 2)
Should a Woman Tell?, 1919 (Gilbert 3, Polito 4)
Should Crooners Marry, 1933 (Stevens 2)
Should Husbands Be Watched?, 1925 (McCarey 2, Roach 4)
Should Husbands Come First?, 1927 (Roach 4)
Should Husbands Marry, 1926 (Sennett 2)
Should Husbands Marry?, 1947 (Bruckman 4)
Should Ladies Behave?, 1933 (Barrymore 3)
Should Landlords Live?, 1924 (Roach 4)
Should Married Men Go Home?, 1928 (McCarey 2, Laurel and Hardy 3, Roach 4)
Should Men Walk Home?, 1926 (Laurel and Hardy 3, Normand 3, Roach 4)
Should Sailors Marry?, 1925 (Laurel and Hardy 3, Roach 4)
Should Sleepwalkers Marry, 1927 (Sennett 2)
Should Tall Men Marry?, 1926 (Laurel and Hardy 3, Roach 4)
Should Women Drive?, 1928 (McCarey 2, Roach 4)
Shoulder, 1964 (Warhol 2)
Shoulder Arms, 1918 (Chaplin 2, Purviance 3)
Shousetsu Yoshida gakkou, 1983 (Muraki 4)
Shout, 1978 (Skolimowski 2, Bates 3, Hurt 3, York 3)

Shout at the Devil, 1976 (Marvin 3, Jarre 4)
Shout Loud, Louder . . . I Don't Understand. *See* Spara forte, piu forte . . . non capisco, 1966
Show, 1922 (Fleischer 4)
Show, 1927 (Browning 2, Barrymore 3, Gilbert 3, Day 4, Gibbons 4, Young 4)
Show Biz Bugs, 1957 (Blanc 4, Freleng 4)
Show Boat, 1929 (Mandell 4)
Show Boat, 1936 (Whale 2, Dunne 3, Robeson 3, Laemmle 4, Prinz 4)
Show Boat, 1951 (Brown 3, Gardner 3, Grayson 3, Keel 3, Moorehead 3, Alton 4, Deutsch 4, Edens 4, Freed 4, Gibbons 4, Plunkett 4, Rosher 4, Smith 4)
Show Business, 1932 (Goddard 3, Roach 4)
Show Business, 1944 (Cantor 3, Malone 3, Duning 4)
Show Business, 1951 (Freleng 4)
Show Business at War, 1943 (Cagney 3, Hayworth 3, Loy 3)
Show Flat, 1936 (Havelock-Allan 4)
Show Folks, 1928 (Lombard 3)
Show Girl, 1928 (Grot 4, Polito 4)
Show Girl in Hollywood, 1930 (LeRoy 2, Jolson 3, Pidgeon 3, Sweet 3, Polito 4)
Show Girl's Strategum, 1911 (Lawrence 3)
Show Goes On, 1937 (Fields 3, Dean 4, Stallich 4)
Show Leader, 1966 (Baillie 2)
Show Me a Strong Town and I'll Show You a Strong Bank, 1966 (De Palma 2)
Show Me the Way to Go Home, 1932 (Fleischer 4)
Show of Force, 1990 (Duvall 3, Delerue 4)
Show of Shows, 1929 (Barrymore 3, Barthelmess 3, Bosworth 3, Buchanan 3, Costello 3, Loy 3, Young 3)
Show People, 1928 (Chaplin 2, Vidor 2, Davies 3, Gilbert 3, Hart 3, Gibbons 4)
Show Them No Mercy, 1935 (Glennon 4, Zanuck 4)
Showa no inochi, 1968 (Okada 3)
Showa zankyo-den: Karajishi jingi, 1969 (Shimura 3)
Show-Down, 1917 (Young 4)
Showdown, 1940 (Harlan 4, Head 4)
Showdown, 1950 (Brennan 3, Canutt 4)
Showdown, 1963 (Murphy 3, Salter 4)
Showdown, 1973 (Hudson 3, Martin 3, Head 4, Laszlo 4)
Showdown at Boot Hill, 1958 (Bronson 3, Carradine 3)
Showdown at Ulcer Gulch, 1958 (Crosby 3, Hope 3)
Shower. *See* Shuu, 1956
Showing Up of Larry the Lamb, 1962 (Halas and Batchelor 4)
Showman, 1962 (Maysles 2)
Show-Off, 1926 (Brooks 3, Garmes 4)
Show-Off, 1934 (Tracy 3, Howe 4, Mankiewicz 4, Mayer 4)
Show-Off, 1946 (Ames 4)
Showtime. *See* Gaiety George, 1945
Shree Krishna Janma, 1918 (Phalke 2)
Shri 420, 1955 (Nargis 3, Abbas 4)
Shriek, 1933 (Lantz 4)
Shriek in the Night, 1933 (Beavers 3, Rogers 3)
Shriek of Araby, 1923 (Sennett 2, Hornbeck 4)
Shrike, 1955 (Ferrer 3, Bass 4, Daniels 4)
Shriman Satyavadi, 1960 (Kapoor 2)

Shrimp, 1930 (Langdon 3, Roach 4)
Shrimps for a Day, 1935 (Roach 4)
Shrine of Lorna Love. *See* Death at Love House, 1976
Shriner's Daughter, 1913 (Eason 4)
Shrinking Corpse. *See* Blind Man's Bluff, 1971
Shrinking Rawhide, 1912 (Bosworth 3)
Shruti and Graces of Indian Music, 1972 (Benegal 2)
Shu to midori, 1956 (Yamamura 3, Takemitsu 4)
Shubun. *See* Sukyandaru, 1950
Shujin-sen, 1956 (Mifune 3)
Shukuzu, 1953 (Shindo 2, Yamada 3, Yamamura 3)
Shunen, 1951 (Yoda 4)
Shunju-ittoryu, 1939 (Shimura 3)
Shunkin monogatari, 1954 (Kyo 3)
Shunkin-sho: Okoto to Sasuke, 1935 (Tanaka 3)
Shunrai, 1939 (Tanaka 3)
Shunsetsu, 1950 (Yoshimura 2)
Shuppatsu, 1938 (Tanaka 3)
Shura yako: Edo no hana-osho, 1936 (Shimura 3)
Shurajo hibun, 1952 (Kinugasa 2)
Shura-jo hibun: Soryu no maki, 1952 (Hasegawa 3)
Shura-zakura, 1959 (Yamada 3)
Shurochka, 1982 (Heifitz 2)
Shusse Taikou-ki, 1938 (Miyagawa 4)
Shusse tohi, 1952 (Yamada 3)
Shut My Big Mouth, 1942 (Brown 3, Johnson 3)
Shuto Shoshitsu, 1987 (Jarre 4)
Shutsugoku yonjuhachi jikan, 1969 (Miyagawa 4)
Shuttered Room, 1967 (Reed 3)
Shuttlecock, 1990 (Bates 3)
Shuu, 1956 (Hara 3, Kagawa 3)
Shy People, 1987 (Mikhalkov-Konchalovsky 2, Clayburgh 3, Golan and Globus 4, Hamlisch 4, Menges 4)
Shylock, 1910 (Baur 3)
Shylock von Krakau, 1913 (Warm 4)
Si ça peut vous faire plaisir, 1948 (Fernandel 3)
Si ça vous chante, 1952 (Colpi 4)
Si c'était à refaire, 1976 (Aimée 3, Deneuve 3, Lai 4)
Si j'avais mille ans, 1983 (Olbrychski 3)
Si j'avais quatre dromadaires, 1966 (Marker 2)
Si je suis comme ça, c'est la faute de papa, 1978 (Deneuve 3)
Si j'étais un espion, 1967 (Blier 3)
Si jeunesse savait, 1948 (Berry 3)
Si jolie petite plage, 1949 (Allégret 2, Philipe 3, Alekan 4)
Si l'empereur savait ca!, 1930 (Feyder 2, Rosay 3, Daniels 4)
Si le roi savait ça, 1957 (Delerue 4, Wakhévitch 4)
Si le soleil ne revenait pas, 1987 (Vanel 3)
Si me han de matar mañana, 1946 (Infante 3)
Si me viera Don Porfirio, 1950 (Alcoriza 4)
Si Paris nous était conté, 1955 (Guitry 2, Darrieux 3, Morgan 3, Philipe 3, Lourié 4)
Si puo fare . . . amigo, 1971 (Palance 3)
Si salvi chi vuole, 1980 (Cardinale 3, Morricone 4)

Si, Senor, 1919 (Daniels 3, Lloyd 3, Roach 4)
Si signora, 1942 (Lattuada 2)
Si Si Senor, 1930 (Arbuckle 3)
Si te hubieses casado con migo, 1948 (Rey 3)
Si tous les gars du monde . . ., 1955 (Clouzot 2, Trintignant 3)
Si toutes les villes du monde . . ., 1951 (Kosma 4)
Si tu m'aimes, 1937 (Arletty 3, Barrault 3, Simon 3, Burel 4)
Si usted no puede, yo sí, 1950 (Buñuel 2)
Si Versailles m'était conté, 1953 (Guitry 2, Welles 2, Bardot 3, Barrault 3, Cervi 3, Colbert 3, Gélin 3, Marais 3, Philipe 3, Presle 3, Vanel 3)
Si vous ne m'aimez pas, 1916 (Feuillade 2, Musidora 3)
Si yo fuera diputado, 1951 (Cantinflas 3)
Si yo fuera millionario, 1962 (Félix 3)
Siago no joui-tou, 1945 (Miyagawa 4)
Siamo donne, 1953 (Rossellini 2, Visconti 2, Bergman 3, Magnani 3, Cecchi D'Amico 4, Zavattini 4)
Siamo tutti in libertà provvisoria, 1972 (De Sica 2, Noiret 3)
Siamo tutti inquilini, 1953 (Fabrizi 3)
Sibirska Ledi Magbet, 1972 (Wajda 2)
Sic 'em Sam!, 1918 (Fairbanks 3)
Sic 'em Towser, 1918 (Daniels 3, Lloyd 3, Roach 4)
Sicari di Hitler, 1960 (Cervi 3)
Sicario, 1961 (Germi 2, Zavattini 4)
Sicilian, 1987 (Cimino 2, Stamp 3)
Sicilian Clan. See Clan des Siciliens, 1969
Sick Abed, 1920 (Wood 2, Daniels 3, Reid 3)
Sickel and Hammer. See Serp i molet, 1921
Sidai cheutma, 1980 (Chan 3)
Siddhartha, 1972 (Nykvist 4)
Side By Side, 1975 (Terry-Thomas 3)
Side Seat Painting's Slides Sound Film, 1970 (Snow 2)
Side Show. See Two Flaming Youths, 1927
Side Show, 1928 (Walker 4)
Side Show of Life, 1924 (Brenon 2, Howe 4)
Side Street, 1928 (Musuraca 4)
Side Street, 1934 (Orry-Kelly 4)
Side Street, 1950 (Mann 2, Ruttenberg 4)
Side Streets, 1935 (Grot 4, Haskin 4)
Sideline, 1931 (Rooney 3)
Sideshow Wrestlers, 1908 (Méliès 2)
Sidetracked, 1916 (Laurel and Hardy 3)
Sidewalks of London. See St. Martin's Lane, 1938
Sidewalks of New York, 1926 (Fleischer 4)
Sidewalks of New York, 1931 (Keaton 2)
Sidney's Joujoux, 1900 (Guy 2)
Sidonie Panache, 1934 (Artaud 3, Jeanson 4)
Sieben Affären der Donna Juanita, 1973 (Mueller-Stahl 3)
Sieben Töchter der Frau Gyurkovics, 1927 (Hoffmann 4)
Siebzehnjärigen, 1929 (Baranovskaya 3)
Siècle a soif, 1958 (Colpi 4, Delerue 4)
Siege, 1978 (Sidney 3)
Siege at Red River, 1954 (Johnson 3, Cronjager 4, LeMaire 4, Wheeler 4)
Siege of Fort Bismark. See Chintao yosai bakugeki merrei, 1963
Siege of Pinchgut, 1959 (Watt 2)
Siege of Red River, 1953 (Maté 4)
Siege of Sidney Street, 1960 (Sangster 4)

Siege of Syracuse. See Assedio di Siracusa, 1960
Sieger, 1932 (Albers 3)
Siekierezada, 1986 (Olbrychski 3)
Siempre listo en las tinieblas, 1939 (Cantinflas 3)
Siempre tuya, 1950 (Fernández 2, Figueroa 4)
Siero della verità, 1949 (Risi 2)
Sierra, 1950 (Curtis 3, Murphy 3, Boyle 4, Metty 4)
Sierra de Teruel. See Espoir, 1939
Sierra Jim's Reformation, 1914 (Reid 3)
Sierra Sue, 1941 (Autry 3)
Sieshun no yume ima izuko, 1932 (Ryu 3)
Siesta, 1987 (Foster 3, Sheen 3)
Siete locos, 1973 (Torre Nilsson 2)
Siete machos, 1950 (Cantinflas 3, Alcoriza 4)
Sight and Sound, 1955 (Adam 4)
Sigillo rosso, 1950 (Cervi 3)
Sigmund, 1983 (Bozzetto 4)
Sigmund, 1988 (Bozzetto 4)
Sign Language. See Jelbeszéd, 1974
Sign of Four, 1932 (Dean 4)
Sign of Leo. See Signe du lion, 1959
Sign of the Claw, 1926 (Eason 3)
Sign of the Cross, 1932 (De Mille 2, Carradine 3, Colbert 3, Laughton 3, March 3, Buchman 4, Head 4, Prinz 4, Struss 4, Young 4, Zukor 4)
Sign of the Cross, 1944 (Nichols 4)
Sign of the Pagan, 1954 (Sirk 2, Palance 3, Metty 4, Salter 4)
Sign of the Ram, 1948 (Sturges 2, Bennett 4, Guffey 4, Salter 4)
Sign of the Snake, 1913 (Ince 4)
Sign of the Wolf, 1941 (Beavers 3)
Sign of Venus. See Segno do Venere, 1955
Sign on the Door, 1921 (Brenon 2, Talmadge 3, Hunt 4, Schenck 4)
Sign Please, 1933 (Launder and Gilliat 2, Crazy Gang 3)
Signal, 1918 (Tisse 4)
Signal Lights, 1912 (Bushman 3)
Signal rouge, 1948 (Von Stroheim 2)
Signal Tower, 1924 (Brown 2, Beery 3)
Signals Office, 1940 (Balcon 4)
Signé Arsène Lupin, 1958 (Rappeneau 4)
Signé Charlotte, 1985 (Huppert 3)
Signe du lion, 1959 (Godard 2, Audran 3, Gégauff 4)
Signed Charlotte. See Signé Charlotte, 1985
Signi del Signor Rossi, 1977 (Bozzetto 4)
Significant Other, 1991 (Willis 4)
Signo de la muerte, 1939 (Cantinflas 3)
Signor Max, 1937 (De Sica 2)
Signor Rossi al camping, 1970 (Bozzetto 4)
Signor Rossi al mare, 1961 (Bozzetto 4)
Signor Rossi a Venezia, 1972 (Bozzetto 4)
Signor Rossi compar l'automobile, 1966 (Bozzetto 4)
Signora della camelie, 1915 (Bertini 3)
Signora della camelie, 1948 (Cervi 3, Annenkov 4)
Signora della orroro, 1977 (Von Sydow 3)
Signora dell'ovest, 1942 (Brazzi 3)
Signora di tutti, 1934 (Ophüls 2)
Signora senza camelie, 1953 (Cervi 3, Cuny 3, Cecchi D'Amico 4, Fusco 4)
Signore, 1960 (Guerra 4)
Signore and signorini, buonanotte, 1976 (Gassman 3)
Signore desidera?, 1933 (De Sica 2)

Signore e signori, 1966 (Age and Scarpelli 4)
Signori e signore, buonanotte, 1976 (Comencini 2, Scola 2, Monicelli 2, Mastroianna 3, Age and Scarpelli 4)
Signori in carrozza!, 1951 (Fabrizi 3, Age and Scarpelli 4)
Signorina, 1942 (Sordi 3)
Signorina madre di famiglia, 1924 (Gallone 2)
Signorine della villa accanto, 1941 (Sordi 3)
Signorine dello 04, 1954 (Age and Scarpelli 4, Amidei 4, Delli Colli 4)
Signpost to Murder, 1965 (Woodward 3)
Signs of Life, 1989 (Kennedy 3)
Sigpress contro Scotland Yard. See Mister Zehn Prozent—Miezen und Moneten, 1967
Sikkim, 1971 (Ray 2, Datta 4)
S'il vous plaît . . . la mer?, 1978 (Presle 3)
Silaha yeminliydim, 1965 (Güney 2)
Silahlarin kanunu, 1966 (Güney 2)
Silberkoenig, 1920 (Zukor 4)
Silbermöwe, 1921 (Dieterle 2)
Silence, 1920 (Delluc 2)
Silence, 1926 (Grot 4)
Silence, 1931 (Rosher 4)
Silence. See Milczenie, 1963
Silence. See Chinmoku, 1971
Silence, 1975 (Jarre 4)
Silence . . . antenne, 1945 (Montand 3)
Silence at Bethany, 1987 (Schifrin 4)
Silence d'ailleurs, 1990 (Olbrychski 3)
Silence de la mer, 1948 (Melville 2, Decaë 4)
Silence est d'or, 1947 (Clair 2, Chevalier 3, Modot 3, Barsacq 4)
Silence of the Lambs, 1990 (Foster 3, Hopkins 3)
Silence of the North, 1981 (Burstyn 3)
Silencers, 1966 (Charisse 3, Martin 3, Bernstein 4, Guffey 4)
Silence Will Reign. See Potem nastąpi cisza, 1966
Silencioso, 1966 (Fernández 2)
Silent Barriers. See Great Barrier, 1937
Silent Battle, 1939 (Harrison 3, Havelock-Allan 4)
Silent Bell-Ringer, 1915 (Mozhukin 3)
Silent Call, 1921 (Murfin 4)
Silent Command, 1923 (Lugosi 3)
Silent Death, 1957 (Karloff 3)
Silent Duel. See Shizukanaru ketto, 1949
Silent Dust, 1948 (Auric 4)
Silent Enemy, 1957 (Harvey 3, Alwyn 4, Heller 4)
Silent Flute, 1977 (Coburn 3, Lee 3, McDowall 3, Wallach 3)
Silent Joy. See Tichá radost, 1985
Silent Lie, 1917 (Walsh 2, Fox 4)
Silent Lover, 1926 (Wilson 4)
Silent Man, 1917 (Hart 3, August 4)
Silent Message, 1910 (Anderson 3)
Silent Movie, 1976 (Brooks 2, Levinson 2, Bancroft 3, Caan 3, Minnelli 3, Reynolds 3)
Silent Night, Bloody Night, 1973 (Carradine 3)
Silent Night, Lonely Night, 1969 (Bridges 3)
Silent Partner, 1917 (Goulding 2, Neilan 2, Sweet 3)
Silent Partner, 1927 (Wyler 2)
Silent Partner, 1978 (Gould 3, York 3)
Silent Passenger, 1935 (Dickinson 2, Stallich 4)
Silent Raiders, 1954 (Bernstein 4)

Silent Running, 1971 (Cimino 2, Dern 3, Trumbull 4)
Silent Sanderson, 1925 (Carey 3, Polito 4, Stromberg 4)
Silent Sandy, 1914 (Gish 3)
Silent Shelby, 1922 (Borzage 2)
Silent Signal, 1911 (Guy 2)
Silent Sound Sense Stars Subotnick and Sender, 1962 (Brakhage 2)
Silent Stranger. See Man from Nowhere, 1915
Silent Stranger, 1924 (Brown 4)
Silent Stranger. See Step Down to Terror, 1958
Silent Tongue, 1992 (Shepard 4)
Silent Village, 1943 (Jennings 2)
Silent Voice, 1915 (Bushman 3)
Silent Voice. See Man Who Played God, 1932
Silent Voice. See Amazing Grace and Chuck, 1987
Silent Watcher, 1924 (Bosworth 3, Love 3)
Silent Wife, 1948 (Xie 2)
Silent Witness, 1932 (August 4)
Silent Witness, 1978 (More 3)
Silent Witnesses. See Rozdennie polzat utat ne mozet, 1914
Silenzio: si gira!, 1943 (Zavattini 4)
Silhouettes, 1936 (Reisch 4)
Silk Bouquet, 1926 (Wong 3)
Silk Express, 1933 (Gaudio 4, Orry-Kelly 4)
Silk Hat Kid, 1935 (Ayres 3, Schary 4)
Silk Hosiery, 1921 (Niblo 2, Barnes 4, Ince 4)
Silk Legs. See Piernas de seda, 1935
Silk Noose. See Noose, 1948
Silk Stockings, 1957 (Mamoulian 2, Astaire 3, Charisse 3, Lorre 3, Freed 4, Pan 4, Porter 4, Previn 4, Rose 4)
Silken Affair, 1956 (Niven 3)
Silken Spider, 1916 (Borzage 2)
Silks and Saddles, 1929 (Brennan 3, Mandell 4)
Silks and Saddles, 1938 (Katzman 4)
Silkwood, 1983 (Nichols 2, Cher 3, Streep 3, Delerue 4, Ondříček 4)
Silly Billies, 1936 (Hunt 4, Musuraca 4)
Silly Scandals, 1931 (Fleischer 4)
Silly Symphonies, 1930 (Disney 4)
Silsila, 1981 (Bachchan 3)
Silver Bears, 1978 (Passer 2, Audran 3, Caine 3, Jourdan 3)
Silver Bullet, 1942 (Lewis 2, Salter 4)
Silver Bullet, 1985 (De Laurentiis 4)
Silver Canyon, 1951 (Autry 3)
Silver Chalice, 1954 (Saville 2, Newman 3, Palance 3, Wood 3, Leven 4, Waxman 4)
Silver Chord, 1933 (McCrea 3)
Silver Cigarette Case, 1913 (Talmadge 3)
Silver Circle. See Ginrin, 1955
Silver City, 1951 (De Carlo 3, Fitzgerald 3, O'Brien 3, Haskin 4, Head 4)
Silver City, 1968 (Wenders 2)
Silver Cord, 1933 (Cromwell 2, Dunne 3, Berman 4, Cooper 4, Murfin 4, Plunkett 4, Rosher 4, Steiner 4)
Silver Dollar, 1932 (Daniels 3, Robinson 3)
Silver Double Suicide. See Gin-Shinju, 1956
Silver Fleet, 1943 (Richardson 3, Withers 3, Junge 4, Rank 4)
Silver Horde, 1930 (Arthur 3, McCrea 3, Sweet 3, Clothier 4)
Silver King. See Silberkoenig, 1920
Silver Lining, 1915 (Eason 4)

Silver Lining, 1931 (O'Sullivan 3)
Silver Lode, 1954 (Dwan 2, Duryea 3, Alton 4, Polglase 4)
Silver on the Sage, 1939 (Harlan 4, Head 4)
Silver Queen, 1942 (Bacon 2, Harlan 4, Young 4)
Silver River, 1948 (Walsh 2, Flynn 3, Sheridan 3, Steiner 4)
Silver Skies. See Stříbrná oblaka, 1938
Silver Spurs, 1943 (Carradine 3, Rogers 3)
Silver Streak, 1934 (Hunt 4, Plunkett 4)
Silver Streak, 1945 (Terry 4)
Silver Streak, 1976 (Clayburgh 3, Pryor 3, Wilder 3, Mancini 4)
Silver Treasure, 1926 (Fox 4)
Silver Valley, 1927 (Mix 3)
Silver Whip, 1953 (Wagner 3)
Silver Wings, 1922 (Ford 2)
Silverado, 1985 (Kasdan 2, Cleese 3, Costner 3)
Silver-Plated Gun, 1913 (Dwan 2)
Silvestre, 1980 (Branco 4, De Almeida 4)
Simba, 1955 (Bogarde 3, Rank 4, Unsworth 4)
Simon, 1956 (Lassally 4)
Simon, 1980 (Arkin 3, Comden 4)
Simon and Laura, 1955 (Finch 3, Kendall 3, Box 4, Dillon 4, Rank 4)
Simon Bolivar. See Life of Simon Bolivar, 1943
Simon Bolivar, 1969 (Blasetti 2, Schell 3)
Simón del desierto, 1965 (Buñuel 2, Figueroa 4)
Simon, Simon, 1970 (Caine 3, Sellers 3)
Simon the Jester, 1925 (Walthall 3, Marion 4)
Simone Martini, 1957 (Fusco 4)
Simp and the Sophomores, 1915 (Laurel and Hardy 3)
Simparele, 1974 (Solas 2)
Simple Charity, 1910 (Griffith 2, Pickford 3, Bitzer 4)
Simple Life, 1905 (Bitzer 4)
Simple Love, 1911 (Dwan 2)
Simple People. See Prostiye lyudi, 1956
Simple Simon, 1935 (Iwerks 4)
Simple Sis, 1927 (Loy 3)
Simple Souls, 1920 (Sweet 3)
Simple Story. See Prostaya istoriya, 1960
Simple Story. See Histoire simple, 1978
Simple Story. See Storia semplice, 1991
Simplet, 1942 (Fernandel 3, Andrejew 4)
Simpson and Godlee Story, 1956 (Lassally 4)
Sin, 1915 (Brenon 2, Bara 3)
Sin. See Grekh, 1916
Sin. See Synd, 1928
Sin. See Hřích, 1929
Sin. See Beloved, 1971
Sin of Harold Diddlebock. See Mad Wednesday, 1947
Sin of Madelon Claudet, 1931 (Young 3, MacArthur 4, Mayer 4)
Sin of Martha Queed, 1921 (Dwan 2, Gaudio 4)
Sin of Nora Morgan, 1933 (Walthall 3)
Sin of Olga Brandt, 1915 (Chaney 3)
Sin of Patricia. See Vita recominicia, 1945
Sin Ship, 1931 (Astor 3, Musuraca 4)
Sin Sister, 1929 (Clarke 4)
Sin Takes a Holiday, 1930 (Rathbone 3, Mandell 4)
Sin That Was His, 1920 (Goulding 2)
Sin Town, 1929 (Howard 2)

Sin Town, 1942 (Brooks 2, Bond 3, Bosworth 3, Crawford 3, Salter 4)
Sinai Field Mission, 1979 (Wiseman 2)
Sinatra in Israel, 1962 (Sinatra 3)
Sinbad and the Eye of the Tiger, 1977 (Harryhausen 4)
Sinbad of the Seven Seas, 1988 (Golan and Globus 4)
Sinbad the Sailor, 1935 (Iwerks 4)
Sinbad the Sailor, 1947 (O'Hara 3, Quinn 3, Barnes 4)
Since You Went Away, 1944 (Cromwell 2, Barrymore 3, Colbert 3, Cotten 3, Dandridge 3, Jones 3, McDaniel 3, Moorehead 3, Nazimova 3, Temple 3, Walker 3, Cortez 4, Garmes 4, Selznick 4, Steiner 4)
Sincerely Charlotte, 1986 (Sarde 4)
Sincerely Yours, 1955 (Blanke 4, Clothier 4)
Sincerity, 1973 (Brakhage 2)
Sincerity II, 1975 (Brakhage 2)
Sincerity III, 1978 (Brakhage 2)
Sincerity IV, 1980 (Brakhage 2)
Sincerity V, 1980 (Brakhage 2)
Sinfonia d'amore—Schubert, 1954 (Age and Scarpelli 4, Pinelli 4)
Sinful Davey, 1969 (Huston 2, Hurt 3, Huston 3, Dillon 4, Mirisch 4, Young 4)
Sing, 1938 (Carmichael 4)
Sing and Like It, 1934 (Horton 3, Cooper 4, Musuraca 4, Plunkett 4, Steiner 4)
Sing a Song, 1932 (Fleischer 4)
Sing a Song of Six Pants, 1947 (Three Stooges 3)
Sing as We Go, 1934 (Dickinson 2, Fields 3, Dean 4)
Sing, Babies, Sing, 1933 (Fleischer 4)
Sing, Baby, Sing, 1936 (Faye 3, Menjou 3, Zanuck 4)
Sing, Bing, Sing, 1933 (Sennett 2, Crosby 3)
Sing Boy Sing, 1958 (O'Brien 3)
Sing for Sweetie, 1938 (Allyson 3)
Sing for Your Supper, 1941 (Arden 3, Cahn 4, Planer 4)
Sing Me a Love Song, 1936 (Sheridan 3, Grot 4, Wald 4)
Sing Sing Prison, 1931 (Terry 4)
Sing, Sinner, Sing, 1933 (Brennan 3, Lukas 3)
Sing, Sister, Sing, 1935 (Roach 4)
Sing, Sisters, Sing!, 1933 (Fleischer 4)
Sing While You're Able, 1937 (Neilan 2)
Sing While You Work, 1948 (Fleischer 4)
Sing Your Way Home, 1945 (Mann 2)
Sing Your Worries Away, 1942 (Dumont 3)
Sing, You Sinners, 1938 (Crosby 3, MacMurray 3, O'Connor 3, Dreier 4, Head 4, Struss 4)
Singal l'antilope sacrée, 1967 (Coutard 4)
Singapore, 1947 (Gardner 3, MacMurray 3, Hornbeck 4, Miller 4)
Singapore Sue, 1932 (Grant 3)
Singapore Woman, 1941 (Negulesco 2, Deutsch 4, McCord 4)
Singaree, 1910 (Blom 2)
Singe en hiver, 1962 (Belmondo 3, Gabin 3, Audiard 4)
Singed, 1927 (Sweet 3, Clarke 4)
Singed Wings, 1922 (Daniels 3, Menjou 3)
Singende Stadt, 1930 (Gallone 2, Courant 4)
Singer and the Dancer, 1976 (Armstrong 2)
Singer Jim McKee, 1924 (Hart 3)

Singer Not the Song, 1961 (Bogarde 3, Mills 3, Alcott 4, Heller 4, Rank 4, Vetchinsky 4)

Singeries humaines, 1910 (Cohl 4)

Singin' in the Rain, 1952 (Donen 2, Charisse 3, Kelly 3, O'Connor 3, Reynolds 3, Brown 4, Comden 4, Edens 4, Freed 4, Gibbons 4, Plunkett 4, Rosson 4, Shearer 4)

Singin' the Blues, 1948 (Fleischer 4)

Singing Along, 1949 (Fleischer 4)

Singing Barbers, 1944 (Fleischer 4)

Singing Blacksmith, 1938 (Ulmer 2)

Singing Boxer, 1933 (Sennett 2)

Singing Cowboy, 1936 (Autry 3)

Singing Fool, 1928 (Bacon 2, Jolson 3, Haskin 4, Warner 4)

Singing Guns, 1950 (Bond 3, Brennan 3)

Singing Hill, 1941 (Autry 3)

Singing in the Corn, 1946 (Duning 4)

Singing Kid, 1936 (Horton 3, Jolson 3, McDaniel 3, Barnes 4, Orry-Kelly 4)

Singing Marine, 1937 (Berkeley 2, Daves 2, Darwell 3, Powell 3, Wyman 3, Mercer 4, Orry-Kelly 4)

Singing Musketeer. See Three Musketeers, 1939

Singing Nun, 1966 (Garson 3, Moorehead 3, Reynolds 3, Krasner 4)

Singing Outlaw, 1937 (Lewis 2)

Singing Plumber, 1932 (Sennett 2)

Singing Princess, 1967 (Andrews 3)

Singing River, 1921 (White 3, Furthman 4)

Singing Sap, 1930 (Lantz 4)

Singing Taxi Driver. See Taxi di notte, 1950

Singing the Blues in Red. See Fatherland, 1986

Singing Vagabond, 1935 (Autry 3)

Single Man, 1929 (Adrian 4, Gibbons 4)

Single Room Furnished, 1967 (Mansfield 3, Kovacs 4)

Single Standard, 1929 (Garbo 3, McCrea 3, Adrian 4, Gibbons 4)

Single Wives, 1924 (Walthall 3)

Single-Handed, 1914 (Anderson 3)

Single Handed, 1923 (Miller 4)

Single-Handed, 1952 (Vetchinsky 4)

Singoalla, 1949 (Matras 4)

Singular Cynic, 1914 (Lawrence 3)

Sinhalese Dance, 1950 (Peries 2)

Sinhasta or The Path to Immortality, 1968 (Benegal 2)

Sinhasta Parvani, 1914 (Phalke 2)

Sinister House. See Muss 'em Up, 1936

Sink or Swim, 1921 (Roach 4)

Sink or Swim, 1952 (Terry 4)

Sink the Bismarck!, 1960 (More 3, Challis 4)

Sinking of Japan. See Nippon chinbotsu, 1973

Sinking of the Lusitania, 1918 (McCay 4)

Sinless Sinner, 1919 (Brenon 2)

Sinner. See Sünderin, 1950

Sinners, 1920 (Folsey 4)

Sinners. See Au royaume des cieux, 1949

Sinners. See Piscine, 1968

Sinner's Holiday, 1930 (Blondell 3, Cagney 3)

Sinner's Holiday. See Christmas Eve, 1947

Sinners in Heaven, 1923 (Daniels 3)

Sinners in Love, 1928 (Plunkett 4)

Sinners in Paradise, 1938 (Whale 2)

Sinners in Silk, 1924 (Menjou 3, Glazer 4, Mayer 4, Wilson 4)

Sinners in the Sun, 1932 (Grant 3, Lombard 3, Hoffenstein 4, Young 4, Zukor 4)

Sinners of Paris. See Rafles sur la ville, 1954

Sins, 1986 (Giannini 3, Kelly 3)

Sins of Dorian Gray, 1983 (Perkins 3)

Sins of Jezebel, 1953 (Goddard 3)

Sins of Man, 1936 (Ameche 3, Friedhofer 4, MacGowan 4, Zanuck 4)

Sins of Pompeii. See Derniers Jours de Pompéi, 1948

Sins of Rachel Cade, 1961 (Dickinson 3, Finch 3, Anhalt 4, Blanke 4, Steiner 4)

Sins of Rose Bernd. See Rose Bernd, 1957

Sins of St. Anthony, 1920 (Cruze 2)

Sins of the Borgias. See Lucrèce Borgia, 1952

Sins of the Children, 1930 (Wood 2, Montgomery 3, Day 4, Gibbons 4)

Sins of the Children. See In His Steps, 1936

Sins of the Fathers, 1928 (Arthur 3, Jannings 3, Banton 4, Clothier 4)

Sins of the Parents, 1916 (Van Dyke 2)

Sins of the Parents. See Sin of Martha Queed, 1921

Sin's Pay Day, 1932 (Rooney 3)

Sintflut, 1924 (Fischinger 2)

Sioux City Sue, 1946 (Autry 3)

Sir Arne's Treasure. See **Herr Arnes Pengar, 1919**

Sir Arne's Treasure. See Herr Arnes penningar, 1954

Sir Galahad of Twilight, 1914 (Eason 4)

Sir Henry at Rawlinson End, 1980 (Howard 3)

Sir Thomas Lipton Out West, 1913 (Sennett 2)

Sired Call, 1922 (Howe 4)

Siren, 1914 (Reid 3)

Siren, 1927 (Haskin 4)

Siren of Atlantis, 1948 (Struss 4)

Siren of Bagdad, 1953 (Henreid 3, Katzman 4)

Siren of Impulse, 1912 (Griffith 2, Bitzer 4)

Siren of Seville, 1924 (Polito 4, Stromberg 4)

Sirène, 1904 (Méliès 2)

Sirène, 1907 (Feuillade 2)

Sirène, 1962 (Braunberger 4)

Sirène des tropiques, 1927 (Buñuel 2)

Sirène du Mississippi, 1969 (Truffaut 2, Belmondo 3, Deneuve 3, Guillemot 4)

Sirens of the Sea, 1919 (Young 3)

Siren's Song, 1919 (Bara 3)

Sirius Remembered, 1959 (Brakhage 2)

Sirocco, 1951 (Bogart 3, Cobb 3, Sloane 3, Guffey 4)

Sirtaki, 1966 (Storaro 4)

Sis, 1989 (Theodorakis 4)

Sis Hopkins, 1919 (Normand 3)

Sis Hopkins, 1941 (Hayward 3)

Sisimiut, 1966 (Roos 2)

Siska, 1962 (Andersson 3, Fischer 4)

Sissi, 1932 (Reiniger 4)

Sissi, 1956 (Schneider 3)

Sissi—die junge Kaiserin, 1957 (Schneider 3)

Sissi—Schichsalsjahre einer Kaiserin, 1958 (Schneider 3)

Sissignora, 1941 (Ponti 4)

Sissignore, 1968 (Guerra 4)

Sista leken, 1984 (Andersson 3)

Sista paret ut, 1956 (Sjöberg 2, Andersson, B. 3, Andersson, H. 3, Dahlbeck 3)

Sista ringen, 1955 (Nykvist 4)

Sister, 1911 (Olcott 2)

Sister, 1972 (Herrmann 4)

Sister Against Sister, 1920 (Brenon 2)

Sister Kenny, 1946 (Bondi 3, Russell 3, Banton 4, Barnes 4, Nichols 4)

Sister of Six, 1916 (Love 3)

Sister, Sister, 1982 (North 4)

Sister Stars. See Shimau-boshi, 1950

Sister to Salome, 1920 (Furthman 4)

Sisters, 1912 (Lawrence 3)

Sisters, 1914 (Crisp 3, Gish 3, Loos 4)

Sisters, 1930 (Swerling 4)

Sisters, 1938 (Litvak 2, Bondi 3, Crisp 3, Davis 3, Flynn 3, Hayward 3, Friedhofer 4, Gaudio 4, Orry-Kelly 4, Steiner 4, Wallis 4)

Sister's Love, 1911 (Griffith 2, Bitzer 4)

Sisters of Darkness. See Entre Tinieblas, 1983

Sisters of Gion. See **Gion no shimai, 1936**

Sisters of Gion. See Gion no shimai, 1956

Sisters of Nishijin. See Nishijin no shimai, 1952

Sisters of the Gion. See **Gion no shimai, 1936**

Sisters, or The Balance of Happiness. See Schwestern oder Die Balance des Glücks, 1979

Sisters under the Skin, 1934 (August 4)

Sit Tight, 1931 (Bacon 2, Bosworth 3, Brown 3)

Sitaron Se Aagey, 1958 (Burman 4)

Sitter-Downers, 1937 (Three Stooges 3)

Sittin' Pretty, 1924 (McCarey 2, Roach 4)

Sitting Pretty, 1933 (Rogers 3, Brown 4, Head 4, Krasner 4)

Sitting Pretty, 1948 (O'Hara 3, Webb 3, Young 3, LeMaire 4, Newman 4, Zanuck 4)

Sitting Target, 1972 (Reed 3)

Situation Hopeless—But Not Serious, 1965 (Guinness 3, Redford 3)

Situation of the Human World. See Hito no yo no sugata, 1929

Situm, 1984 (Patil 3)

Siukun gwaitsiu, 1979 (Chan 3)

Six Best Cellars, 1920 (Crisp 3)

Six Black Horses, 1962 (Duryea 3, Murphy 3)

Six Bridges to Cross, 1955 (Curtis 3, Mineo 3, Daniels 4, Mancini 4)

Six Characters in Search of an Author, 1976 (Houseman 4)

Six Cylinder Love, 1917 (Mix 3)

Six Cylinder Love, 1931 (Beavers 3, Horton 3, Tracy 3)

Six Day Bike Rider, 1934 (Bacon 2, Brown 3, Grot 4)

Six et demi onze, 1927 (Epstein 2, Périnal 4)

Six Feet Four, 1919 (King 2, Furthman 4)

Six Hours to Live, 1932 (Dieterle 2, Seitz 4)

Six Hundred Million People Are With You, 1958 (Ivens 2)

Six Inches Tall. See Attack of the Puppet People, 1958

Six in Paris. See Paris vu par . . ., 1965

Six Lessons from Madame La Zonga, 1941 (Three Stooges 3)

Six of a Kind, 1934 (McCarey 2, Fields 3, Dreier 4, Zukor 4)

Six petites bougies, 1962 (Delerue 4)

Six Shooter Andy, 1918 (Mix 3)

Six si petits, 1945 (Braunberger 4)

Six Thousand Enemies, 1939 (Pidgeon 3, Seitz 4)

Six Weeks, 1982 (Moore 3, Previn 4)

Six-Gun Law, 1962 (Ballard 4)

Sixième étage, 1939 (Brasseur 3)

Sixième Face du Pentagone, 1967 (Marker 2, Braunberger 4)

Sixième Jour, 1955 (Kosma 4)

Sixteen. See Sedicianni, 1973

Sixteen Candles, 1984 (Hughes 2)

Sixth and Main, 1977 (McDowall 3)

Sixth of the World. See Shestaya chast' mira, 1926

Six-Thirty Collection, 1934 (Grierson 2)

Sixty Days. See Shestdesyat dnei, 1943

Sixty Glorious Years, 1938 (Wilcox 2, Neagle 3, Walbrook 3, Young 4)

Sixtynine, 1969 (Donner 2)

Sizilianische Blutrache, 1920 (Dreier 4)

Sizzle Beach, 1986 (Costner 3)

Sjömansdansen, 1911 (Magnusson 4)

Sjörövaren, 1909 (Magnusson 4)

Sjösalavår, 1949 (Nykvist 4)

Sjunde himlen, 1956 (Björnstrand 3)

Sjunde Inseglet, 1957 (Andersson 3, Björnstrand 3, Von Sydow 3, Fischer 4)

Skaebnebaeltet, 1912 (Christensen 2)

Skaebnesvangre Logn. See Fru Potifar, 1911

Skag, 1980 (Malden 3)

Skalní ševci, 1931 (Stallich 4)

Skalpel, prosím, 1985 (Brejchová 3, Švankmajer 4)

Skammen, 1968 (Björnstrand 3, Ullmann 3, Von Sydow 3, Nykvist 4)

Skandal in Budapest, 1933 (Pasternak 4)

Skandal in der Botschaft, 1950 (Rasp 3)

Skandal in der Parkstrasse, 1932 (Metzner 4)

Skandal um Eva, 1930 (Porten 3, Wagner 4)

Skandalen, 1912 (Magnusson 4)

Skapani w ogniu, 1963 (Tyszkiewicz 3)

Skargardsnatt, 1953 (Thulin 3)

Skating Bug, 1911 (Pickford 3, Gaudio 4)

Skazka o rybake i rybke, 1937 (Ptushko 4)

Skein, 1974 (Brakhage 2)

Skeleton, 1914 (Reid 3)

Skeleton Coast, 1988 (Borgnine 3, Lom 3, Reed 3)

Skeleton Dance, 1929 (Disney 4, Iwerks 4)

Skeleton Frolic, 1937 (Iwerks 4)

Skelett des Herrn Markutius, 1920 (Wagner 4)

Skepp som motas, 1916 (Sjöström 2)

Sketches, 1975 (Brakhage 2)

Ski Bum, 1971 (Levine 4, Zsigmond 4)

Ski Fever. See Liebespiele im Schnee, 1967

Ski Party, 1965 (Hamlisch 4)

Ski Patrol, 1940 (Krasner 4)

Ski Resort, 1980 (Halas and Batchelor 4)

Ski Troop Attack, 1960 (Corman 2)

Skidding Hearts, 1917 (Sennett 2)

Skidoo, 1968 (Preminger 2, Marx Brothers 3, Meredith 3, Raft 3, Rooney 3, Shamroy 4)

Skilsmissens Børn, 1939 (Christensen 2)

Skin. See Pelle, 1981

Skin Deep, 1989 (Edwards 2, Kidd 4)

Skin Game, 1931 (Hitchcock 2, Reville 4)

Skin Game, 1971 (Garner 3)

Skin-matrix, 1984 (Emshwiller 2)

Skinners in Silk, 1925 (Sennett 2)

Skinny Gets a Goat, 1917 (Roach 4)

Skinny's False Alarm, 1917 (Roach 4)

Skinny's Finish, 1908 (Porter 2)

Skinny's Shipwrecked Sand-Witch, 1917 (Roach 4)

Skip the Maloo, 1931 (Roach 4)

Skipper. See Todd Killings, 1971

Skipper & Co., 1974 (Henning-Jensen 2)

Skipper Next to God. See Maître après Dieu, 1950

Skipper of the Osprey, 1933 (Dean 4)

Skipper Surprised His Wife, 1950 (Walker 3, Kaper 4)

Skippy, 1931 (Mankiewicz 2, McLeod 2, Cooper 3, Struss 4, Zukor 4)

Skirmish on the Home Front, 1944 (Bendix 3, Hayward 3, Hopkins 3, Hutton 3, Ladd 3, Brackett 4)

Skirts Ahoy!, 1952 (Reynolds 3, Williams 3, Lennart 4, Pasternak 4, Rose 4)

Skirt Shy, 1929 (Roach 4)

Sklaven der Sinne. See Irrende Seelen, 1920

Skok, 1969 (Olbrychski 3)

Skokie, 1981 (Kaye 3, Wallach 3)

Skola skolen, 1949 (Björnstrand 3)

Skola, základ života, 1938 (Stallich 4)

Skomakare bliv vid din läst, 1915 (Sjöström 2)

Sköna Helena, 1951 (Dahlbeck 3)

Skorpan, 1957 (Björnstrand 3)

Skorpion, panna, i lucznik, 1972 (Nowicki 3)

Skotinins. See Sud v Smolenske, 1946

Skottet, 1914 (Stiller 2, Jaenzon 4)

Skřivánci na niti, 1969 (Menzel 2)

Skuggan, 1953 (Dahlbeck 3)

Skugger över snön, 1945 (Sucksdorff 2)

Skull, 1965 (Cushing 3, Lee 3, Francis 4)

Skullduggery, 1960 (Vanderbeek 2)

Skullduggery, 1970 (Rafferty 3, Reynolds 3, Head 4, Whitlock 4)

Sky Bandits, 1986 (Watkin 4)

Sky Boy, 1929 (McCarey 2, Langdon 3, Roach 4)

Sky Bride, 1932 (Mankiewicz 2, Scott 3, Young 4)

Sky Commando, 1953 (Duryea 3, Katzman 4)

Sky Devils, 1932 (Tracy 3, Benchley 4, Gaudio 4, Hughes 4, Newman 4)

Sky Giant, 1938 (Carey 3, Fontaine 3)

Sky High, 1922 (Mix 3)

Sky Is Falling, 1947 (Terry 4)

Sky Is Red. See Cielo è rosso, 1950

Sky Larks, 1934 (Lantz 4)

Sky Murder, 1940 (Pidgeon 3)

Sky over Berlin. See Himmel über Berlin, 1987

Sky Party, 1965 (Corman 2)

Sky Patrol, 1940 (Salter 4)

Sky Pilot, 1911 (Talmadge 3)

Sky Pilot, 1921 (Vidor 2, Moore 3)

Sky Pilot, 1924 (Lantz 4)

Sky Pirate, 1914 (Sennett 2, Arbuckle 3)

Sky Plumber, 1924 (Roach 4)

Sky Princess, 1942 (Pal 4)

Sky Riders, 1976 (Coburn 3, York 3, Schifrin 4)

Sky Scraping, 1930 (Fleischer 4)

Sky Scrappers, 1928 (Disney 4)

Sky Ship, 1942 (Eason 4)

Sky Socialist, 1967 (Wieland 2)

Sky Terror. See Skyjacked, 1972

Sky, West, and Crooked, 1966 (Mills 3, Arnold 4, Dillon 4)

Skyjacked, 1972 (Heston 3, Pidgeon 3)

Skylark, 1941 (Colbert 3, Milland 3, Dreier 4, Head 4, Irene 4, Lang 4, Young 4)

Skylarking, 1923 (Sennett 2)

Skylarks, 1936 (Crazy Gang 3)

Skyldig—ikke skyldig, 1953 (Roos 2)

Skylight Sleep, 1916 (Roach 4)

Skyline, 1931 (Loy 3, O'Sullivan 3, Friedhofer 4, Nichols 4)

Skyrider, 1976 (Halas and Batchelor 4)

Skyrocket, 1926 (Neilan 2, Johnson 3, Glazer 4)

Skyscraper, 1928 (Garnett 2, Adrian 4)

Skyscraper, 1958 (Clarke 2, Van Dyke 2)

Skyscraper Caper, 1968 (Blanc 4)

Skyscraper Souls, 1932 (O'Sullivan 3, Daniels 4, Sullivan 4)

Skyscraper Symphony, 1928 (Florey 2)

Sky's No Limit, 1984 (Jarre 4)

Sky's the Limit, 1937 (Buchanan 3, Garmes 4)

Sky's the Limit, 1943 (Astaire 3, Ryan 3, Benchley 4, Mercer 4, Metty 4)

Skyward, 1981 (Davis 3)

Skywayman, 1920 (Howard 2, Furthman 4)

Sladká Josefinka, 1927 (Ondra 3, Heller 4)

Sladkaya zhenzhchina, 1976 (Yankovsky 3)

Slaedepatruljen Sirius, 1980 (Roos 2)

Slalom, 1965 (Gassman 3)

Slamdance, 1987 (Stanton 3)

Slaměnný klobouk, 1971 (Kučera 4)

Slander, 1957 (Johnson 3)

Slander the Woman, 1923 (Haskin 4)

Slanked Again, 1936 (Terry 4)

Slant, 1958 (Romero 2)

Slap. See Gifle, 1974

Slap Happy Hunters, 1941 (Terry 4)

Slap Happy Lion, 1947 (Avery 4)

Slap Happy Pappy, 1940 (Blanc 4, Clampett 4, Stalling 4)

Slap Shot, 1977 (Hill 2)

Slap Shot, 1977 (Allen 4, Bernstein 4)

Slap-Happy Mouse, 1956 (Blanc 4, McKimson 4)

Slap-Happy Sleuths, 1950 (Three Stooges 3)

Slap-Hoppy Mouse, 1956 (Stalling 4)

Slapshot, 1977 (Newman 3)

Slapstick, 1982 (Lewis 2)

Slapstick of Another Kind, 1984 (Legrand 4)

Slashed Yosaburo. See Kirare Yosaburou, 1960

Slates of the Tenpyo Period. See Tenpyo no iraka, 1979

Slattery's Hurricane, 1949 (De Toth 2, Darnell 3, Lake 3, Widmark 3, Clarke 4, Wheeler 4)

Slaughter Hotel. See Bestia uccide a sangue freddo, 1971

Slaughter on Tenth Avenue, 1957 (Duryea 3, Matthau 3)

Slaughterhouse-Five, 1972 (Hill 2, Allen 4, Bumstead 4, Ondříček 4)

Sláva, 1960 (Brdečka 4)

Slava nam, smert vragam!, 1914 (Mozhukin 3)

Slava Sovetskim Geroiniam, 1938 (Vertov 2)

Slave, 1909 (Griffith 2, Sennett 2, Lawrence 3, Pickford 3, Bitzer 4)

Slave, 1917 (Laurel and Hardy 3)

Slave Girl, 1915 (Browning 2)

Slave Girl, 1947 (Crawford 3, De Carlo 3)

Slave Girls, 1968 (Carreras 4)

Slave of Desire, 1923 (Love 3)

Slave of Fashion, 1925 (Shearer 3, Gibbons 4, Meredyth 4, Murfin 4)

Slave Ship, 1937 (Garnett 2, Beery 3, Darwell 3, Rooney 3, Sanders 3, Faulkner 4, Johnson 4, Miller 4, Newman 4, Trotti 4)

Slavers, 1977 (Howard 3, Milland 3)

Slave's Devotion, 1913 (Ince 4)

Slaves of Babylon, 1953 (Katzman 4)

Slaves of New York, 1989 (Ivory 2)

Slavey's Affinity, 1911 (Lawrence 3)

Slavka, Don't Give In!. See Slávko, nedej se!, 1938

Slavnosti sněženek, 1983 (Menzel 2)

Slay It with Flowers, 1943 (Fleischer 4)

Slečna Golem, 1972 (Brejchová 3)

Slečna od vody, 1959 (Stallich 4)

Sleep, 1963 (Warhol 2)

Sleep, My Love, 1948 (Sirk 2, Ameche 3, Colbert 3)

Sleeper, 1973 (Allen 2, Keaton 3, Rosenblum 4)

Sleeping Beauty. See Shazka o spiatchek, 1914

Sleeping Beauty, 1930 (Vasiliev 2)

Sleeping Beauty, 1954 (Reiniger 4)

Sleeping Beauty, 1958 (Disney 4, Iwerks 4)

Sleeping Beauty. See Nemureru bijo, 1968

Sleeping Beauty, 1980 (Halas and Batchelor 4)

Sleeping Beauty, 1987 (Golan and Globus 4)

Sleeping Car, 1933 (Litvak 2, Carroll 3, Novello 3, Balcon 4, Junge 4)

Sleeping Car Murder. See Compartiments tueurs, 1965

Sleeping Car to Trieste, 1949 (Rank 4)

Sleeping Dogs, 1977 (Oates 3)

Sleeping Prince. See Prince and the Showgirl, 1957

Sleeping Tiger, 1954 (Losey 2, Bogarde 3, Arnold 4, Foreman 4)

Sleeping with the Enemy, 1991 (Goldsmith 4)

Sleeping Words of the Bride. See Hanayome no negoto, 1933

Sleepless Night, 1947 (Terry 4)

Sleeps Six, 1986 (Raphael 4)

Sleepwalk, 1984 (Jarmusch 2)

Sleepy Head, 1921 (Roach 4)

Sleepy Time Down South, 1932 (Fleischer 4)

Sleepy Time Possum, 1951 (Blanc 4, McKimson 4, Stalling 4)

Sleepy-Time Tom, 1950 (Hanna and Barbera 4)

Sleigh Bells, 1907 (Olcott 2)

Sleigh Bells, 1928 (Disney 4)

Slender Thread, 1965 (Pollack 2, Bancroft 3, Poitier 3, Head 4, Jones 4)

Sleuth, 1922 (Roach 4)

Sleuth, 1925 (Laurel and Hardy 3)

Sleuth, 1972 (Mankiewicz 2, Caine 3, Olivier 3, Adam 4, Addison 4, Morris 4)

Sleuths, 1918 (Sennett 2)

Sleuths at the Floral Parade, 1913 (Sennett 2, Normand 3)

Sleuth's Last Stand, 1913 (Sennett 2)

Slick Chick, 1962 (Blanc 4, McKimson 4)

Slick Hare, 1947 (Blanc 4, Freleng 4, Stalling 4)

Slicked-Up Pup, 1950 (Hanna and Barbera 4)

Slide, Kelly, Slide, 1927 (Carey 3, Gibbons 4)

Slide, Speedy, Slide, 1931 (Sennett 2)

Slides, 1942 (Fleischer 4)

Slight Case of Larceny, 1953 (Rooney 3)

Slight Case of Murder, 1938 (Bacon 2, Robinson 3, Wallis 4)

Slight Mistake, 1911 (Bunny 3)

Slightly Daffy, 1944 (Blanc 4, Clampett 4, Maltese 4, Stalling 4)

Slightly Dangerous, 1943 (Bond 3, Brennan 3, Turner 3, Young 3, Berman 4, Irene 4, Kaper 4, Lederer 4, Rosson 4)

Slightly French, 1949 (Sirk 2, Ameche 3, Lamour 3, Duning 4)

Slightly Honorable, 1940 (Garnett 2, Arden 3, Crawford 3, Banton 4, Wanger 4)

Slightly Pregnant Man. See Evènement le plus important depuis que l'homme a marché sur la lune, 1973

Slightly Scarlet, 1930 (Mankiewicz 2, Lukas 3, Banton 4, Estabrook 4)

Slightly Scarlet, 1956 (Dwan 2, Alton 4, Polglase 4)

Slightly Static, 1935 (Rogers 3, Roach 4)

Slightly Tempted, 1940 (Salter 4)

Slightly Used, 1927 (Mohr 4)

Slim, 1937 (Daves 2, Fonda 3, Wyman 3, Steiner 4, Wallis 4)

Slim Carter, 1957 (Johnson 3)

Slim Higgins, 1915 (Mix 3)

Slim Princess, 1915 (Beery 3, Bushman 3)

Slim Princess, 1920 (Normand 3)

Slim Shoulders, 1922 (Folsey 4)

Slingshot 6⅛, 1951 (Lantz 4)

Slink Pink, 1967 (Freleng 4)

Slipper. See Tofflan-en-lycklig komedi, 1967

Slipper and the Rose, 1976 (Evans 3, Lockwood 3, More 3)

Slippery Pearls. See Stolen Jools, 1932

Slippery Silks, 1936 (Three Stooges 3)

Slippery Slickers, 1920 (Roach 4)

Slippery Slippers, 1962 (Hanna and Barbera 4)

Slipping Wives, 1927 (Laurel and Hardy 3, Roach 4)

Slippy McGee, 1923 (Moore 3, Clarke 4)

Slipstream, 1989 (Bernstein 4)

Slither, 1973 (Caan 3, Kovacs 4)

Slivers, 1977 (Emshwiller 2)

Slocum Disaster, 1904 (Bitzer 4)

Slogan, 1969 (Gélin 3)

Sloppy Bill of the Rollicking R, 1911 (Dwan 2)

Sloppy Jalopy, 1952 (Bosustow 4, Burness 4, Hubley 4, Raksin 4)

Slóvce M, 1964 (Brdečka 4)

Slovo dlya zashchity, 1976 (Yankovsky 3)

Slow But Sure, 1934 (Terry 4)

Slow Motion. See Sauve qui peut, 1979

Sluchi na stadione, 1929 (Ptushko 4)

Sluggard's Surprise, 1900 (Hepworth 2)

Slugger's Wife, 1985 (Ashby 2, Ritt 2, Booth 4, Jones 4, Stark 4)

Sluice, 1978 (Brakhage 2)

Slum, 1952 (Roos 2)

Slum Boy. See Ragazzo di borgata, 1976

Slumberland Express, 1936 (Lantz 4)

Slump Is Over. See Crise est finie, 1934

Slut, 1966 (Fischer 4)

Sluzhili dva tovarishcha, 1968 (Yankovsky 3)

Smagliature. See Faille, 1975

Smålänningar, 1935 (Fischer 4, Jaenzon 4)

Small Back Room, 1948 (Cusack 3, Hawkins 3, Challis 4, Francis 4, Heckroth 4, Korda 4)

Small Change. See Argent de poche, 1976

Small Czechoslovak Icon. See Československý ježíšek, 1918

Small Fry, 1939 (Fleischer 4)

Small Killing, 1981 (Sidney 3, Simmons 3)

Small Leaders of the ''Big Leap'', 1958 (Xie 2)

Small Man, 1935 (Baxter 2)

Small Stories of a Big Storm, 1958 (Xie 2)

Small Timers. See Ringards, 1978

Small Town Act, 1913 (Sennett 2)

Small Town Bully. See Little Teacher, 1915

Small Town Deb, 1939 (Darwell 3, Miller 4)

Small Town Girl, 1914 (Dwan 2)

Small Town Girl, 1936 (Wellman 2, Gaynor 3, Stewart 3, Taylor 3, Gibbons 4, Gillespie 4, Goodrich 4, Rosher 4, Stothart 4, Stromberg 4)

Small Town Girl, 1953 (Berkeley 2, Miller 3, Wray 3, Pasternak 4, Previn 4, Rose 4, Ruttenberg 4)

Small Town Idol, 1921 (Sennett 2, Novarro 3, Hornbeck 4)

Small Town Princess, 1927 (Sennett 2)

Small Voice, 1948 (Keel 3, Havelock-Allan 4)

Smallest Show on Earth, 1957 (Dearden 2, Launder and Gilliat 2, Rutherford 3, Sellers 3, Alwyn 4, Slocombe 4)

Smania addosso, 1962 (Gassman 3)

Smania addosso, 1963 (Cervi 3)

Smart Alecks, 1942 (Katzman 4)

Smart Blonde, 1936 (Wyman 3)

Smart Girl, 1935 (Lupino 3, Wanger 4)

Smart Girls. See Dritte, 1958

Smart Girls Don't Talk, 1948 (Burks 4, McCord 4)

Smart Money, 1931 (Cagney 3, Karloff 3, Robinson 3, Zanuck 4)

Smart Set, 1928 (Bosworth 3, Gibbons 4)

Smart Woman, 1931 (La Cava 2, Astor 3, Horton 3, Musuraca 4)

Smart Woman, 1948 (Adrian 4, Cortez 4)

Smart Work, 1931 (Arbuckle 3)

Smartest Girl in Town, 1936 (Hunt 4)

Smarty, 1934 (Blondell 3, Horton 3, Barnes 4, Orry-Kelly 4)

Smarty Cat, 1954 (Hanna and Barbera 4)

Smash and Grab, 1937 (Buchanan 3)

Smash en direct, 1962 (Auric 4)

Smashing the Crime Syndicate. See Hell's Bloody Devils, 1970

Smashing the Money Ring, 1939 (Reagan 3)

Smashing the Rackets, 1938 (Musuraca 4)

Smashing the Spy Ring, 1939 (Bellamy 3, Wray 3)

Smashing Through. See Cheyenne Cyclone, 1932

Smashing Time, 1967 (Addison 4, Ponti 4)

Smash-Up, 1947 (Hayward 3, Banton 4, Cortez 4, Wanger 4)

Smash-Up: The Story of a Woman. See Smash-Up, 1947

S'matter, Pete?, 1927 (Lantz 4)

Smerti doma, 1915 (Mozhukin 3)

Smetti di piovere. See Pacifista, 1971

Smic Smac Smoc, 1971 (Lelouch 2, Lai 4)

Smich se lepi na paty, 1987 (Brodský 3)

Smierc prowincjala, 1966 (Zanussi 2)

Smile, 1974 (Dern 3, Hall 4, Kidd 4)

Smile of a Child, 1911 (Griffith 2, Sweet 3, Bitzer 4)
Smile Please, 1924 (Capra 2, Sennett 2)
Smile Please, 1980 (Langdon 3)
Smile Wins, 1923 (Roach 4)
Smile Wins, 1927 (Roach 4)
Smiles, 1926 (Fleischer 4)
Smiles of a Summer Night. *See* **Sommarnattens leende, 1955**
Smiley, 1956 (Rafferty 3, Richardson 3, Alwyn 4, Korda 4)
Smiley Gets a Gun, 1958 (Rafferty 3)
Smilin' Guns, 1929 (Brennan 3)
Smilin' Through, 1922 (Talmadge 3, Hunt 4, Rosher 4, Schenck 4, Westmore Family 4)
Smilin' Through, 1932 (Howard 3, March 3, Shearer 3, Adrian 4, Booth 4, Garmes 4, Mayer 4, Stewart 4, Vajda 4)
Smilin' Through, 1941 (Borzage 2, Saville 2, Macdonald 3, Adrian 4, Balderston 4, Mayer 4, Stewart 4, Stothart 4)
Smiling All the Way, 1920 (Bushman 3)
Smiling Along. *See* Keep Smiling, 1938
Smiling Irish Eyes, 1929 (Moore 3, Grot 4)
Smiling Lieutenant, 1931 (Lubitsch 2, Chevalier 3, Colbert 3, Hopkins 3, Deutsch 4, Dreier 4, Folsey 4, Green 4, Raphaelson 4, Ruttenberg 4, Vajda 4, Zukor 4)
Smiling Life. *See* Hohoemu jinsei, 1930
Smith series, 1926–27 (Sennett 2)
Smith series, 1928 (Sennett 2, Hornbeck 4)
Smith, 1939 (Richardson 3)
Smith!, 1969 (Ford 3, Oates 3)
Smith, Our Friend, 1946 (Lassally 4)
Smithereens, 1982 (Seidelman 2)
Smith's Pony, 1927 (Sennett 2, Lombard 3)
Smithsonian Institution, 1965 (Bernstein 4)
Smithy, 1924 (Laurel and Hardy 3, Roach 4)
Smithy's Grandma's Party, 1913 (Beery 3)
Smitten Kitten, 1952 (Hanna and Barbera 4)
Smog, 1962 (Girardot 3)
Smoke, 1990 (Wallach 3)
Smoke in the Wind, 1971 (Brennan 3)
Smoke Menace, 1937 (Grierson 2, Wright 2)
Smoke on the 45, 1911 (Dwan 2)
Smoke Signal, 1955 (Andrews 3)
Smoked Husband, 1908 (Griffith 2, Lawrence 3, Bitzer 4)
Smoker, 1910 (Pickford 3)
Smokes and Lollies, 1975 (Armstrong 2)
Smokey, 1946 (Clarke 4)
Smokey and the Bandit, 1977 (Field 3, Reynolds 3, Needham 4)
Smokey and the Bandit II, 1980 (Field 3, Reynolds 3, Needham 4)
Smokey and the Bandit III, 1983 (Reynolds 3)
Smokey and the Bandit Ride Again. *See* Smokey and the Bandit II, 1980
Smokey Bites the Dust, 1981 (Corman 2)
Smokey Joe, 1945 (Terry 4)
Smoking Guns, 1934 (McCord 4)
Smoking Lamp. *See* Lampe qui file, 1909
Smoky, 1946 (MacMurray 3, Raksin 4)
Smoky, 1966 (Smith 4)
Smooth as Satin, 1925 (Berman 4)
Smorgasbord, 1982 (Lewis 2)
Smouldering Fires, 1924 (Brown 2)
Smouldering Spark, 1914 (Eason 4)
Smrt mouchy, 1975 (Kučera 4)
Smrt nacerno, 1976 (Brodský 3)
Smrt pana Baltisbergra, 1965 (Menzel 2)

Smuga cienia, 1976 (Wajda 2)
Smuggler and the Girl, 1911 (Dwan 2)
Smugglers. *See* Pålivets ödesväger, 1913
Smugglers. *See* Man Within, 1947
Smuggler's Cave, 1915 (Eason 4)
Smuggler's Daughter, 1912 (Anderson 3)
Smuggler's Daughter, 1914 (Laurel and Hardy 3, Meredyth 4)
Smugglers' Lass, 1915 (Rosher 4)
Smuggling Ship. *See* Mitsuyu-sen, 1954
Smultronstället, 1957 (Sjöström 2, Andersson 3, Björnstrand 3, Thulin 3, Von Sydow 3, Fischer 4)
Smurfs and the Magic Flute. *See* Flûte à six schtroumpfs, 1976
Snack Bar Budapest, 1988 (Giannini 3)
Snadný život, 1957 (Brdečka 4)
Snafu, 1946 (Benchley 4, Planer 4)
Snaiper, 1932 (Enei 4)
Snake and Crane Arts of Shaolin, 1977 (Chan 3)
Snake Eyes, 1990 (McDowell 3)
Snake in the Eagle's Shadow, 1978 (Chan 3)
Snake Pit, 1948 (Litvak 2, Bondi 3, De Havilland 3, Marsh 3, LeMaire 4, Newman 4, Wheeler 4, Zanuck 4)
Snake Princess. *See* Hebihime-sama, 1940
Snake's and Ladders, 1989 (Halas and Batchelor 4)
Snap and the Beanstalk, 1989 (Halas and Batchelor 4)
Snap Goes East, 1989 (Halas and Batchelor 4)
Snapphanar, 1942 (Björnstrand 3)
Snappy Salesman, 1930 (Lantz 4)
Snappy Snap Shots, 1953 (Terry 4)
Snappy Sneezer, 1929 (Roach 4)
Snapshots of the City, 1961 (Vanderbeek 2)
Snare of Fate, 1913 (Cruze 2)
Snare of Society, 1911 (Lawrence 3)
Snatched From a Burning Death, 1915 (Ingram 2)
Sneaking. *See* Nukiashi sashiashi, 1934
Sneak, Snoop and Snitch in Triple Trouble, 1941 (Fleischer 4)
Sneepings, 1933 (Cromwell 2)
Sneezing Breezes, 1925 (Sennett 2)
Sneezing Weasel, 1937 (Avery 4)
Sniffles and the Bookworm, 1939 (Jones 4)
Sniffles Bells the Cat, 1941 (Blanc 4, Jones 4, Stalling 4)
Sniffles Takes a Trip, 1940 (Blanc 4, Jones 4, Stalling 4)
Sniper, 1952 (Dmytryk 2, Kramer 2, Menjou 3, Anhalt 4, Guffey 4)
Snitch in Time, 1950 (Three Stooges 3)
'Sno Fun, 1951 (Terry 4)
Snob, 1921 (Wood 2)
Snob, 1924 (Gilbert 3, Shearer 3, Gibbons 4, Mayer 4)
Snobs, 1915 (De Mille 2)
Snobs!, 1961 (Kosma 4)
Snoop Sisters, 1972 (Clayburgh 3, Goddard 3)
Snooper Service, 1945 (Langdon 3)
Snoopy Loopy, 1960 (Hanna and Barbera 4)
Snorkel, 1958 (Carreras 4, Green 4, Sangster 4)
Snotchak, 1912 (Mozhukin 3)
Snow Bride, 1923 (Levien 4)
Snow Business, 1953 (Blanc 4, Stalling 4)
Snow Carnival, 1949 (Cooper 3)
Snow Country. *See* Yukiguni, 1965
Snow Creature, 1954 (Crosby 4)

Snow Cure, 1916 (Sennett 2)
Snow Excuse, 1966 (Blanc 4, McKimson 4)
Snow Goose, 1971 (Harris 3)
Snow Hawk, 1925 (Garnett 2, Laurel and Hardy 3)
Snow in the Desert, 1919 (Colman 3)
Snow Maiden, 1952 (Ivanov-Vano 4)
Snow Man, 1946 (Terry 4)
Snow Time for Comedy, 1941 (Blanc 4, Jones 4)
Snow Trail. *See* Ginrei no hate, 1947
Snow White, 1916 (Barthelmess 3)
Snow White, 1933 (Fleischer 4)
Snow White, 1987 (Golan and Globus 4)
Snow White and Rose Red, 1953 (Reiniger 4)
Snow White and the Seven Dwarfs, 1937 (Disney 4)
Snow White and The Three Stooges, 1961 (Three Stooges 3, Shamroy 4, Smith 4)
Snowball Berry Red. *See* Kalina krasnaya, 1974
Snowbeast, 1977 (Sidney 3)
Snowbird, 1916 (Cruze 2)
Snowblind, 1968 (Frampton 2)
Snowbody Loves Me, 1964 (Jones 4)
Snowbound, 1948 (Dalio 3, Lom 3, Newton 3, Rank 4)
Snowed Under, 1923 (Stromberg 4)
Snowed Under, 1936 (Orry-Kelly 4)
Snowfire, 1958 (Fields 4)
Snowman, 1908 (Bitzer 4)
Snowman, 1940 (Terry 4)
Snowman's Land, 1939 (Jones 4)
Snows of Kilimanjaro, 1952 (King 2, Dalio 3, Gardner 3, Hayward 3, Peck 3, Herrmann 4, LeMaire 4, Newman 4, Robinson 4, Shamroy 4, Wheeler 4, Zanuck 4)
Snowtime, 1938 (Iwerks 4)
Snowy Heron. *See* Shirasagi, 1941
Snubbed By a Snob, 1940 (Fleischer 4)
Sny Bezrabotnye sniatsia lis' raz, 1941 (Volkov 2)
So Big, 1924 (Beery 3, Moore 3, McCord 4)
So Big, 1932 (Wellman 2, Davis 3, Stanwyck 3, Orry-Kelly 4)
So Big, 1953 (Wise 2, Hayden 3, Wyman 3, Blanke 4, Steiner 4)
So Bright the Flame. *See* Girl in White, 1952
So Close to Life. *See* Nära livet, 1958
So Dark the Night, 1946 (Lewis 2, Friedhofer 4, Guffey 4)
So Dear to My Heart, 1948 (Bondi 3, Carey 3, Disney 4, Hoch 4)
So Does an Automobile, 1939 (Fleischer 4)
So ein Mädel, 1920 (Gad 2)
So ein Mädel vergisst man nicht, 1932 (Kortner 3)
So Ended a Great Love. *See* So endete eine Liebe, 1934
So endete eine Liebe, 1934 (Gründgens 3, Planer 4)
So Ends Our Night, 1941 (Cromwell 2, Von Stroheim 2, Ford 3, March 3, Sullavan 3, Daniels 4, Jennings 4, Lewin 4, Menzies 4, Reynolds 4)
So Evil My Love, 1948 (Milland 3, Alwyn 4, Head 4, Wallis 4, Young 4)
So Fine, 1980 (Morricone 4)
So Goes My Love, 1946 (Ameche 3, Loy 3, Salter 4)
So is This, 1983 (Snow 2)

So lang noch ein Walzer von Strauss erklingt, 1931 (Fröhlich 3)

So Little Time, 1952 (Schell 3, Morris 4)

So Long As You're Near Me. *See* Solange du da bist, 1953

So Long at the Fair, 1950 (Fisher 2, Bogarde 3, Simmons 3, Box, B. 4, Box, M. 4, Rank 4)

So Long Letty, 1920 (Moore 3)

So Long Letty, 1929 (Bacon 2)

So Long, Mr. Chumps, 1941 (Three Stooges 3, Bruckman 4)

So Much for So Little, 1949 (Freleng 4, Jones 4)

So Near, So Far, 1971 (Konwicki 4)

So Near, Yet So Far, 1912 (Griffith 2, Barrymore 3, Pickford 3, Bitzer 4)

So Nobody Knows Hadimrsku. *See* To neznáté Hadimršku, 1931

So oder so ist das Leben, 1976 (Schell 3)

So Proudly We Hail, 1943 (Colbert 3, De Carlo 3, Goddard 3, Lake 3, Dreier 4, Edouart 4, Lang 4, Rozsa 4)

So Red the Rose, 1935 (Vidor 2, Scott 3, Sullavan 3, Banton 4, Dreier 4)

So Runs the Way, 1913 (Barrymore 3, Gish 3)

So sind die Männer, 1922 (Dietrich 3)

So sind die Menschen. *See* Abschied, 1930

So Sweet . . . So Perverse. *See* Cosi dolce . . . cosi perversa, 1970

So That Men Are Free, 1962 (Van Dyke 2)

So This is Africa, 1933 (Krasna 4)

So This Is College, 1929 (Daves 2, Wood 2, McCrea 3, Montgomery 3, Gibbons 4)

So This Is Hamlet, 1923 (La Cava 2)

So This Is Harris!, 1933 (Glennon 4)

So This Is Hollywood. *See* In Hollywood with Potash and Perlmutter, 1924

So This Is London, 1930 (O'Sullivan 3, Rogers 3, Clarke 4, Levien 4)

So This Is London, 1933 (Grierson 2)

So This Is London, 1939 (Granger 3, Sanders 3)

So This Is Love, 1928 (Capra 2, Cohn 4)

So This Is Love, 1953 (Grayson 3, Blanke 4, Burks 4, Prinz 4, Steiner 4)

So This Is Marriage, 1924 (Gibbons 4, Wilson 4)

So This Is New York, 1948 (Aldrich 2, Kramer 2, Foreman 4, Tiomkin 4)

So This Is Paris, 1926 (Lubitsch 2, Loy 3, Kräly 4)

So This Is Paris, 1954 (Curtis 3, Lourié 4)

So Well Remembered, 1947 (Dmytryk 2, Howard 3, Mills 3, Eisler 4, Paxton 4, Rank 4, Young 4)

So Young, So Bad, 1950 (Henreid 3)

So You Won't Squawk, 1941 (Keaton 2)

So You Won't Talk, 1935 (Launder and Gilliat 2)

So You Won't Talk, 1940 (Brown 3)

Soak the Rich, 1936 (Hecht 4, MacArthur 4, Shamroy 4)

Soak the Sheik, 1922 (Roach 4)

Soaking the Clothes, 1914 (Roach 4)

Soap Opera. *See* Lester Persky Story, 1964

Soapdish, 1991 (Field 3, Goldberg 3)

Soapsuds Lady, 1925 (Sennett 2)

Soapy Opera, 1953 (Terry 4)

S.O.B., 1981 (Edwards 2, Andrews 3, Holden 3, Preston 3, Winters 3, Mancini 4, Van Runkle 4)

Sobaka Baskervilei, 1981 (Yankovsky 3)

Sobre el problema fronterizo entre Kampuchea y Vietnam, 1978 (Alvarez 2)

Sobre horas extras y trabajo voluntario, 1973 (Gómez 2)

Sobre las olas, 1950 (Infante 3)

Social Celebrity, 1926 (Brooks 3, Menjou 3, Garmes 4)

Social Club, 1916 (Sennett 2, Swanson 3)

Social Error, 1922 (La Cava 2)

Social Exile. *See* Declassée, 1925

Social Gangster, 1914 (Lloyd 3, Roach 4)

Social Highwayman, 1916 (Marion 4)

Social Highwayman, 1926 (Zanuck 4)

Social Leper, 1917 (Edeson 4, Marion 4)

Social Lion, 1930 (Mankiewicz 2)

Social Quicksands, 1918 (Bushman 3)

Social Register, 1934 (Neilan 2, Moore 3, Benchley 4, Loos 4)

Social Secretary, 1916 (Fleming 2, Von Stroheim 2, Talmadge 3, Emerson 4, Loos 4)

Social Secretary, 1945 (Fleming 2)

Socialisme et nihilisme, 1908 (Pathé 4)

Società Ovesticino-Dinamo, 1955 (Olmi 2)

Society, 1955 (Burman 4)

Society and Chaps, 1911 (Dwan 2)

Society Ballooning, 1906 (Bitzer 4)

Society Doctor, 1935 (Taylor 3)

Society Exile, 1919 (Menzies 4, Miller 4)

Society for Sale, 1918 (Borzage 2, Swanson 3)

Society Girl, 1932 (Tracy 3, Barnes 4)

Society Lawyer, 1939 (Pidgeon 3, Folsey 4, Goodrich 4)

Society Scandal, 1924 (Dwan 2, Swanson 3, Rosson 4)

Society Secrets, 1921 (Browning 2, McCarey 2)

Society Sensation, 1918 (Valentino 3)

Sock a Bye Baby, 1934 (Fleischer 4)

Sock a Doodle Doo, 1952 (Blanc 4, McKimson 4, Stalling 4)

Sock-a-Bye Baby, 1942 (Three Stooges 3, Bruckman 4)

Sockeroo, 1940 (Eason 4)

Soda Squirt, 1933 (Iwerks 4)

Sodom and Gomorrah. *See* Sodoma e Gomorra, 1962

Sodoma e Gomorra, 1962 (Aimée 3, Baker 3, Granger 3, Adam 4, Rozsa 4)

Sœurette, 1913 (Tourneur 2)

Soeurs Brontë, 1979 (Adjani 3, Huppert 3, Sarde 4)

Soeurs enemies, 1915 (Dulac 2)

Sofia, 1948 (Clothier 4)

Sofie, 1992 (Ullmann 3)

Sofiya Perovskaya, 1967 (Shostakovich 4)

Soft Ball Game, 1936 (Lantz 4)

Soft Beast. *See* Shitoyakana Kemono, 1963

Soft Beds and Hard Battles, 1973 (Sellers 3)

Soft Cushions, 1927 (Johnson 3, Karloff 3, Carré 4)

Soft Living, 1928 (August 4)

Soft Money, 1919 (Daniels 3, Lloyd 3, Roach 4)

Soft Shoes, 1925 (Carey 3, Polito 4, Stromberg 4)

Soft Skin. *See* Peau douce, 1964

Soft Tenderfoot, 1917 (Mix 3)

Soft-Boiled, 1923 (Mix 3)

Sogarro, 1962 (Vanel 3)

Sogeki, 1968 (Mori 3)

Soggy Bottom, U.S.A., 1981 (Johnson 3)

Sogni mostruosamente proibiti, 1982 (Valli 3)

Sogni nel cassetto, 1957 (Castellani 2)

Sogno di Butterfly, 1939 (Gallone 2)

Sogno di tutti, 1941 (Cervi 3)

Sogno di Zorro, 1951 (Gassman 3, Loren 3)

Sohn der Hagar, 1927 (Freund 4)

Sohn der weissen Berge, 1930 (Planer 4)

Sohn des Hannibal, 1926 (Planer 4)

Sohn ohne Heimat, 1955 (Krauss 3)

Söhne der Nacht, 1921 (Albers 3)

Söhne des Herrn Gaspary, 1948 (Dagover 3)

Soho Incident, 1956[?] (Adam 4)

Soif des bêtes, 1960 (Braunberger 4)

Soigne ta droite, 1987 (Godard 2)

Soigne ton gauche, 1936 (Clement 2, Tati 2)

Soikina lyubov, 1927 (Moskvin 4)

Soikin's Love. *See* Soikina lyubov, 1927

Soilers, 1923 (Laurel and Hardy 3, Roach 4)

Soilers, 1932 (Roach 4)

Soir à Tibériade, 1966 (Kosma 4)

Soir de fête, 1956 (Braunberger 4)

Soir de notre vie, 1963 (Delerue 4)

Soir de rafle, 1931 (Gallone 2, Burel 4)

Soir de Rafle, 1968 (Clouzot 2)

Soir de réveillon, 1933 (Arletty 3)

Soir . . . par hasard, 1964 (Brasseur 3)

Soir sur la plage, 1961 (Burel 4)

Soir, un train, 1968 (Delvaux 2, Aimée 3, Montand 3, Cloquet 4)

Soirée mondaine, 1917 (Chevalier 3)

Sois belle et tais-toi, 1958 (Belmondo 3, Delon 3)

Soiuzkinozhurnal No. 77, 1941 (Vertov 2)

Soiuzkinozhurnal No. 87, 1941 (Vertov 2)

Sokakta kan vardi, 1965 (Güney 2)

Sokhranivshie ogon, 1970 (Yankovsky 3)

Sol, 1974 (Brakhage 2)

Sol Madrid, 1968 (Lukas 3, Schifrin 4)

Sol no se puede tapar con un dedo, 1976 (Alvarez 2)

Sol over Danmark, 1936 (Holger-Madsen 2)

Sol y sombra, 1922 (Musidora 3)

Sól ziemi czarnej, 1970 (Olbrychski 3)

Solang' es hübsche Mädchen gibt, 1955 (Herlth 4)

Solange du da bist, 1953 (Schell 3)

Solanto un bacio, 1942 (Fusco 4)

Solar Crisis, 1990 (Heston 3, Palance 3, Edlund 4, Jarre 4)

Solar Film, 1980 (Bass 4)

Solarbabies, 1986 (Brooks 2, Edlund 4, Jarre 4)

Solaris. *See* Solyaris, 1971

Solariumagelani, 1975 (Frampton 2)

Sold, 1915 (Porter 2)

Sold at Auction, 1923 (Roach 4)

Sold for Marriage, 1916 (Gish 3)

Soldados do fogo, 1958 (Pereira Dos Santos 2)

Soldat Bom, 1948 (Björnstrand 3, Fischer 4)

Soldat der Marie, 1926 (Albers 3)

Soldatesse, 1965 (Karina 3, Delli Colli 4, Solinas 4)

Soldats d'eau douce, 1950 (Cloquet 4)

Soldier, 1982 (Kinski 3)

Soldier and the Lady, 1936 (Walbrook 3, August 4, Berman 4, Plunkett 4, Veiller 4)

Soldier Blue, 1970 (Pleasence 3)

Soldier Has Come from the Front. *See* Prishell soldat s fronta, 1973

Soldier in the Rain, 1963 (Edwards 2, McQueen 3, Weld 3, Goldman 4, Mancini 4)

Soldier Man, 1926 (Capra 2, Sennett 2, Langdon 3, Hornbeck 4)
Soldier Marched. *See* Shli soldaty, 1958
Soldier of Fortune, 1955 (Dmytryk 2, Gable 3, Hayward 3, Duning 4, Friedhofer 4, LeMaire 4, Smith 4)
Soldier of the Legion, 1980 (Johnson 3)
Soldier—Sailor, 1944 (Alwyn 4)
Soldiers and Other Cosmic Objects, 1977 (Brakhage 2)
Soldier's Duties. *See* Krigsmans erinran, 1947
Soldiers in White, 1941 (Eason 4)
Soldiers of Fortune, 1919 (Dwan 2, Beery 3, Polito 4)
Soldiers of Misfortune, 1914 (Sennett 2)
Soldiers of the King, 1933 (Horton 3, Balcon 4)
Soldier's Plaything, 1930 (Langdon 3)
Soldier's Prayer. *See* **Ningen no joken, 1959–61**
Soldier's Story, 1984 (Jewison 2)
Soldiers Three, 1951 (Garnett 2, Cusack 3, Granger 3, Newton 3, Niven 3, Pidgeon 3, Berman 4, Deutsch 4, Plunkett 4)
Soldier Who Declared Peace. *See* Tribes, 1970
Sole, 1929 (Blasetti 2)
Sole anche di notte, 1990 (Taviani 2, Vogler 3, Guerra 4, Morricone 4)
Sole anche di notte, 1990 (Kinski 3)
Sole di Montecassino, 1945 (Fusco 4)
Sole di notte. *See* Sole anche di notte, 1990
Sole sorge ancora, 1946 (De Santis 2, Pontecorvo 2)
Soledad. *See* Rebozo de Soledad, 1952
Soledad. *See* Fruits amers, 1966
Soledad de los dioses, 1985 (Alvarez 2)
Soleil, 1966 (Braunberger 4)
Soleil a toujours raison, 1941 (Brasseur 3, Presle 3, Vanel 3, Kosma 4, Prévert 4, Trauner 4, Wakhévitch 4)
Soleil dans l'oeil, 1961 (Godard 2, Karina 3, Jarre 4)
Soleil de minuit, 1943 (Berry 3, Hayakawa 3)
Soleil de pierre, 1967 (Braunberger 4)
Soleil des voyous, 1967 (Gabin 3, Lai 4)
Soleil en face, 1979 (Audran 3, Cassel 3)
Soleil éteint, 1961 (Braunberger 4)
Soleil et ombre. *See* Sol y sombra, 1922
Soleil noir, 1918 (Gance 2)
Soleil noir, 1966 (Gélin 3, Barsacq 4)
Soleil rouge, 1971 (Bronson 3, Delon 3, Mifune 3, Alekan 4, Jarre 4)
Soleils, 1960 (Rabier 4)
Soleils de l'Ile de Pâques, 1971 (Guerra 2)
Solid Gold Cadillac, 1956 (Holliday 3, Cohn 4, Lang 4, Wald 4)
Solid Ivory, 1925 (Roach 4)
Solid Serenade, 1946 (Hanna and Barbera 4)
Solid Tin Coyote, 1966 (Blanc 4)
Solidaridad Cuba y Vietnam, 1965 (Alvarez 2)
Solidarity, 1973 (Wieland 2)
Soliloques du pauvre, 1954 (Brasseur 3)
Soliloquy, 1949 (Peries 2)
Solimani il conquistatore, 1961 (Mimica 4)
Solita de Cordoue, 1946 (Cuny 3)
Solitaire, 1987 (Belmondo 3)
Solitaire Man, 1933 (Marshall 3, Adrian 4)

Solitaires, 1913 (Talmadge 3)
Soliti ignoti, 1958 (Monicelli 2, Cardinale 3, Gassman 3, Mastroianni 3, Age and Scarpelli 4, Cecchi D'Amico 4, Cristaldi 4, Di Venanzo 4, Gherardi 4)
Soliti ignoti colpiscona ancore. *See* Ab Morgen sind wir reich und ehrlich, 1977
Soliti ignoti vent'anni dopo, 1985 (Gassman 3, Mastroianni 3, Cecchi D'Amico 4, Rota 4)
Solitude du chanteur de fond, 1974 (Montand 3)
Soll man heiraten?, 1925 (Banky 3, Tschechowa 3, Warm 4)
Soll und Haben, 1924 (Tschechowa 3)
Solo, 1969 (Menges 4)
Solo for Sparrow, 1962 (Caine 3)
Solo per te, 1938 (Gallone 2)
Solomon and Sheba, 1959 (Vidor 2, Brynner 3, Lollobrigida 3, Sanders 3, Day 4, Veiller 4, Young 4)
Solomon's Heart, 1932 (Gerasimov 2)
Solstik, 1953 (Henning-Jensen 2)
Soltero. *See* Scapolo, 1955
Solution of the Mystery, 1915 (Eason 4)
Solutions françaises, 1945 (Jaubert 4)
Sølv, 1956 (Roos 2)
Solva Saal, 1958 (Burman 4)
Solving the Puzzle. *See* Champion du jeu à la mode, 1910
Solwa Sal, 1958 (Anand 3)
Solyaris, 1971 (Tarkovsky 2)
Som här inträden . . . , 1945 (Björnstrand 3)
Sombra verde, 1954 (Alcoriza 4)
Sombre dimanche, 1948 (Dalio 3)
Sombrero, 1953 (Charisse 3, De Carlo 3, Gassman 3, Pan 4, Rose 4)
Some Baby, 1914 (Lloyd 3, Roach 4)
Some Baby, 1922 (Roach 4)
Some Bull's Daughter, 1914 (Loos 4)
Some Call It Loving, 1973 (Pryor 3)
Some Came Running, 1958 (Minnelli 2, Kennedy 3, MacLaine 3, Martin 3, Sinatra 3, Bernstein 4, Cahn 4, Daniels 4, Plunkett 4)
Some Collectors, 1910 (White 3)
Some Duel, 1916 (Mix 3)
Some Girls Do, 1969 (Box 4)
Some Kind of a Nut, 1969 (Dickinson 3, Guffey 4, Kanin 4, Mirisch 4)
Some Kind of Hero, 1982 (Pryor 3)
Some Kind of Wonderful, 1987 (Hughes 2)
Some Liar, 1919 (King 2, Furthman 4)
Some Like It Hot, 1939 (Dmytryk 2, Hope 3, Dreier 4, Head 4, Hecht 4, Struss 4)
Some Like It Hot, 1959 (Wilder 2, Brown 3, Curtis 3, Lemmon 3, Monroe 3, Raft 3, Cole 4, Deutsch 4, Diamond 4, Hecht 4, Lang 4, Mirisch 4, Orry-Kelly 4)
Some Like It Not. *See* I'm Cold, 1955
Some Like It Rough, 1944 (Buchanan 3)
Some May Live, 1967 (Cotten 3, Cushing 3)
Some More of Samoa, 1941 (Three Stooges 3)
Some Nerve, 1913 (Sennett 2)
Some Nerve. *See* Gentlemen of Nerve, 1914
Some of the Best, 1949 (Barrymore 3)
Some of Us May Die. *See* Journey, 1959
Some People, 1962 (More 3)
Some Sort of Cage, 1964 (Bernstein 4)
Some Steamer Snooping, 1913 (Costello, D. 3, Costello, M. 3)

Somebody Has to Shoot the Pictures, 1990 (Scheider 3)
Somebody Killed Her Husband, 1978 (Bridges 3, North 4)
Somebody Loves Me, 1952 (Hutton 3, Barnes 4, Head 4)
Somebody Stole My Gal, 1931 (Fleischer 4)
Somebody Up There Likes Me, 1956 (Wise 2, McQueen 3, Mineo 3, Newman 3, Sloane 3, Cahn 4, Gibbons 4, Kaper 4, Ruttenberg 4, Schnee 4)
Someday, 1935 (Powell and Pressburger 2, Lockwood 3)
Someone at the Door, 1936 (Brenon 2)
Someone at the Door, 1950 (Carreras 4)
Someone Behind the Door. *See* Quelqu'un derrière la porte, 1971
Someone Else's Jacket, 1927 (Gerasimov 2)
Someone to Love, 1987 (Welles 2)
Someone to Remember, 1943 (Siodmak 2)
Someone to Watch Over Me, 1987 (Scott 2, Vangelis 4)
Something About Amelia, 1984 (Close 3)
Something Always Happens, 1928 (Johnson 3, Hunt 4, Mankiewicz 4)
Something Always Happens, 1934 (Powell and Pressburger 2)
Something Big, 1971 (Johnson 3, Martin 3, Hamlisch 4)
Something Evil, 1972 (Bellamy 3)
Something for a Lonely Man, 1968 (Oates 3)
Something for Everyone, 1970 (Lansbury 3, Lassally 4, Rosenblum 4)
Something for Joey, 1977 (Page 3)
Something for Mrs. Gibbs, 1965 (Carradine 3)
Something for the Birds, 1952 (Wise 2, Mature 3, Neal 3, Diamond 4, La Shelle 4, LeMaire 4, Wheeler 4)
Something for the Boys, 1944 (Holliday 3, Miranda 3)
Something in Common, 1986 (Burstyn 3, Wallach 3, Weld 3)
Something in Her Eye, 1915 (Laurel and Hardy 3)
Something in the Wind, 1947 (Durbin 3, O'Connor 3, Green 4, Krasner 4, Orry-Kelly 4)
Something Money Can't Buy, 1952 (Rank 4, Rota 3, Vetchinsky 4)
Something of Value, 1957 (Brooks 2, Hudson 3, Poitier 3, Berman 4, Harlan 4, Rose 4, Rozsa 4)
Something Short of Paradise, 1979 (Sarandon 3, Lassally 4)
Something Simple, 1934 (Roach 4)
Something to Do, 1919 (Crisp 3)
Something to Hide, 1971 (Finch 3, Winters 3)
Something to Live For, 1952 (Stevens 2, Fontaine 3, Marshall 3, Milland 3, Wright 3, Barnes 4, Head 4, Hornbeck 4, Young 4)
Something to Shout About, 1943 (Ameche 3, Charisse 3, Planer 4, Porter 4)
Something to Sing About, 1937 (Cagney 3)
Something to Think About, 1920 (De Mille 2, Swanson 3, Macpherson 4, Struss 4)
Something Wicked This Way Comes, 1983 (Clayton 2, Robards 3)
Something Wild, 1961 (Baker 3, Bass 4, Copland 4, Day 4, Schüfftan 4)
Something Wild, 1987 (Demme 2, Sayles 2)

Something's Wrong, 1978 (Raphael 4)
Sometimes a Great Notion, 1971 (Fonda,
   H. 3, Newman 3, Remick 3, Head 4,
   Mancini 4)
Sometimes They Come Back, 1991 (De
   Laurentiis 4)
Somewhere I'll Find You, 1942 (Gable 3,
   Johnson 3, Turner 3, Berman 4, Kaper 4,
   Reisch 4, Rosson 4)
Somewhere in Dream Land, 1936
   (Fleischer 4)
Somewhere in Egypt, 1943 (Terry 4)
Somewhere in Europe. See Valahol
   Europaban, 1947
Somewhere in France. See Foreman Went to
   France, 1942
Somewhere in Somewhere, 1925 (Roach 4)
Somewhere in Sonora, 1927 (Brown 4,
   Polito 4)
Somewhere in Sonora, 1933 (Wayne 3,
   McCord 4)
Somewhere in the City. See Backfire, 1948
Somewhere in the Night, 1946
   (Mankiewicz 2, Kortner 3, Basevi 4)
Somewhere in the Pacific, 1942 (Terry 4)
Somewhere in Time, 1980 (Wright 3,
   Barry 4)
Somewhere in Turkey, 1918 (Daniels 3,
   Lloyd 3, Roach 4)
Somewhere in Wrong, 1925 (Garnett 2,
   Laurel and Hardy 3)
Sommaren med Monika, 1953 (Andersson 3,
   Fischer 4)
Sommarkvåller på Jorden, 1987
   (Andersson 3)
Sommarlek, 1951 (Fischer 4)
Sommarnattens leende, 1955 (Andersson,
   B. 3, Andersson, H. 3, Björnstrand 3,
   Dahlbeck 3, Fischer 4)
Sommarnöje sökes, 1957 (Andersson 3,
   Björnstrand 3, Dahlbeck 3)
Sommarsaga, 1912 (Sjöström 2,
   Magnusson 4)
Sommeil d'Albertine, 1945 (Resnais 2)
Sommerfuglene, 1974 (Chaplin 3)
Sommergäste, 1975 (Ganz 3, Ballhaus 4)
Sommernachtstraum, 1924 (Albers 3,
   Krauss 3, Rasp 3, Metzner 4)
Sommersaga, 1941 (Sucksdorff 2)
Somnambul, 1929 (Kortner 3)
Son altesse l'amour, 1931 (Courant 4)
Son autre amour, 1935 (Burel 4)
Son Comes Home, 1936 (Dupont 2)
Son Copain. See Inconnue de Montréal, 1950
Son Dernier Rôle, 1946 (Dalio 3)
Son dernier verdict, 1951 (Vanel 3)
Son et Lumière, 1961 (Delerue 4)
Son Is Born, 1946 (Finch 3)
Son kizgin adam, 1970 (Güney 2)
Son nom de Venise dans Calcutta désert,
   1976 (Duras 2, Seyrig 3)
Son of a Gun, 1919 (Anderson 3)
Son of a Gunfighter, 1966 (Rey 3)
Son of Ali Baba, 1952 (Curtis 3)
Son of a Sailor, 1933 (Bacon 2, Brown 3,
   Grot 4, Orry-Kelly 4)
Son of Captain Blood. See Figlio del
   Capitano Blood, 1962
Son of David, 1919 (Colman 3)
Son of Destiny. See Madame de Thèbes,
   1915
Son of Dracula, 1943 (Siodmak 2, Salter 4,
   Siodmak 4)
Son of Dracula, 1974 (Francis 4)

Son of Fate. See Mästertjuven, 1915
Son of Flubber, 1963 (Stevenson 2,
   MacMurray 3, Disney 4, Ellenshaw 4)
Son of France, 1914 (Pearson 2)
Son of Frankenstein, 1935 (Pierce 4)
Son of Frankenstein, 1939 (Karloff 3,
   Lugosi 3, Rathbone 3)
Son of Fury, 1942 (Cromwell 2, Carradine 3,
   Farmer 3, Lanchester 3, McDowall 3,
   Power 3, Sanders 3, Tierney 3, Basevi 4,
   Day 4, Dunne 4, Newman 4, Zanuck 4)
Son of Godzilla. See Gojira no musuko, 1967
Son of His Father, 1925 (Fleming 2, Love 3)
Son of India, 1931 (Feyder 2, Novarro 3,
   Rosson 4, Vajda 4)
Son of India, 1962 (Mehboob 2)
Son of Kong, 1933 (Schoedsack 2,
   Johnson 3, O'Brien 4, Steiner 4)
Son of Lassie, 1945 (Crisp 3, Irene 4,
   Mayer 4, Stothart 4)
Son of Lifeboat, 1984 (Lewis 2)
Son of Monte Cristo, 1940 (Bennett 3,
   Sanders 3)
Son of Paleface, 1952 (De Mille 2, Tashlin 2,
   Crosby 3, Hope 3, Rogers 3, Russell 3,
   Head 4)
Son of Satan, 1924 (Micheaux 2)
Son of Sinbad, 1955 (Novak 3, Price 3,
   Young 4)
Son of Spellbound, 1984 (Lewis 2)
Son of Tarzan, 1921 (Clarke 4)
Son of the Border, 1933 (Musuraca 4,
   Steiner 4)
Son of the Gods, 1930 (Barthelmess 3,
   Haller 4)
Son of the Golden West, 1928 (Mix 3,
   Plunkett 4)
Son of the Mountains. See Syn hor, 1925
Son of the Sheik, 1921 (Young 3)
Son of the Sheik, 1926 (Banky 3,
   Valentino 3, Barnes 4, Marion 4,
   Menzies, 4, Westmore Family 4)
Son of the "Star". See Hijo del crack, 1953
Son of Zorro, 1947 (Katzman 4)
Son o' My Heart, 1930 (Borzage 2)
Son oncle de Normandie, 1938 (Berry 3,
   Auric 4)
Soñador del Kremlin, 1984 (Alvarez 2)
Sonad oskuld, 1915 (Sjöström 2)
Sonar Kella, 1974 (Chatterjee 3, Datta 4)
Sonatas, 1959 (Bardem 2, Félix 3, Rey 3)
Söndag i september, 1963 (Andersson 3)
Son-Daughter, 1932 (Brown 2, Novarro 3,
   Adrian 4, Booth 4, Stothart 4)
Sone, 1936 (Messter 4)
Sonezaki shinjuh, 1981 (Miyagawa 4)
Song, 1928 (Wong 3)
Song a Day, 1936 (Fleischer 4)
Song About Flowers, 1959 (Ioseliani 2)
Song and Dance Man, 1926 (Brenon 2,
   Love 3, Howe 4)
Song and Dance Man, 1936 (Dwan 2,
   Dumont 3, Trevor 3)
Song for Prince Charlie, 1958 (Lassally 4)
Song for Tomorrow, 1948 (Fisher 2, Lee 3)
Song from My Heart. See Waga koi waga
   uta, 1969
Song Is Born, 1947 (Hawks 2, Kaye 3,
   Friedhofer 4, Goldwyn 4, Jenkins 4,
   Mandell 4, Sharaff 4, Toland 4)
Song Lantern. See Uta-andon, 1943
Song o' My Heart, 1930 (O'Sullivan 3,
   Levien 4)
Song of Arizona, 1946 (Rogers 3)

Song of a Sad Country, 1937 (Weiss 2)
Song of Bernadette, 1943 (King 2, Cobb 3,
   Dalio 3, Darnell 3, Jones 3, Price 3,
   Basevi 4, La Shelle 4, Miller 4,
   Newman 4, Zanuck 4)
Song of Ceylon, 1934 (Cavalcanti 2,
   Grierson 2, Wright 2)
Song of Freedom, 1936 (Robeson 3)
Song of Gold. See Zpěv zlata, 1920
Song of Hate, 1915 (Ingram 2)
Song of Heroes. See Pesne o geroyazh, 1932
Song of Home. See Furusato no uta, 1925
Song of Kentucky, 1929 (Clarke 4)
Song of Life, 1922 (Stahl 2, Mayer 4,
   Meredyth 4)
Song of Life. See Píseň života, 1925
Song of Life. See Lied vom Leben, 1930
Song of Love, 1923 (Talmadge 3, Gaudio 4,
   Marion 4, Schenck 4)
Song of Love, 1929 (Arden 3, Walker 4)
Song of Love, 1947 (Brown 2, Henreid 3,
   Hepburn 3, Walker 3, Gibbons 4, Irene 4,
   Kaper 4, Mayer 4, Plunkett 4,
   Stradling 4)
Song of Mexico, 1945 (Alton 4)
Song of My Heart, 1948 (Glazer 4)
Song of Nevada, 1944 (Rogers 3)
Song of Norway, 1970 (Homolka 3,
   Robinson 3)
Song of Remembrance. See Chanson du
   souvenir (Sirk 2)
Song of Restoration. See Ishin no uta, 1938
Song of Russia, 1944 (Taylor 3, Benchley 4,
   Irene 4, Pasternak 4, Stothart 4,
   Stradling 4)
Song of Sadness. See Canto da saudade,
   1952
Song of Scheherazade, 1947 (Arden 3, De
   Carlo 3, Lourié 4, Mohr 4, Reisch 4,
   Rozsa 4)
Song of Soho, 1930 (Launder and Gilliat 2)
Song of Songs, 1933 (Mamoulian 2,
   Dietrich 3, Banton 4, Dreier 4,
   Hoffenstein 4, Zukor 4)
Song of Summer, 1968 (Russell 2)
Song of Surrender, 1949 (Leisen 2, Rains 3,
   Bumstead 4, Dreier 4, Head 4, Young 4)
Song of Texas, 1943 (Rogers 3, Canutt 4)
Song of the Birds, 1935 (Fleischer 4)
Song of the Caballero, 1930 (Brown 4,
   McCord 4)
Song of the Camp. See Roei no uta, 1938
Song of the Cart. See Niguruma no uta, 1959
Song of the Eagle, 1933 (Robinson 4)
Song of the Flame, 1930 (Garmes 4, Grot 4)
Song of the Flower Basket. See Hanakago no
   uta, 1936
Song of the Heart. See Udvari levego, 1917
Song of the Islands, 1942 (Grable 3,
   Mature 3, Day 4, Newman 4, Pan 4)
Song of the Meet, I and II. See Píseň o sletu
   I, II, 1949
Song of the Mountain Pass. See Toge no uta,
   1924
Song of the Open Road, 1944 (Fields 3)
Song of the Plough, 1933 (Baxter 2)
Song of the Prairie. See Arie prérie, 1949
Song of the Rivers. See Lied der Ströme,
   1954
Song of the Road, 1937 (Baxter 2)
Song of the Scarlet Flower. See Sängen om
   den eldröda blommon, 1918
Song of the Scarlet Flower. See Sängen om
   den eldröda blommon, 1934

Song of the Scarlet Flower. *See* Sängen om den eldröda blommon, 1957

Song of the Shirt, 1908 (Griffith 2, Lawrence 3, Bitzer 4)

Song of the Shirt, 1935 (Sennett 2)

Song of the South, 1946 (McDaniel 3, Disney 4, Iwerks 4, Toland 4)

Song of the Thin Man, 1947 (Grahame 3, Loy 3, Powell 3, Irene 4, Rosher 4)

Song of the West, 1930 (Brown 3)

Song of the West. *See* Let Freedom Ring, 1939

Song of the Wildwood Flute, 1910 (Griffith 2, Pickford 3, Bitzer 4)

Song of Victory, 1929 (Fleischer 4)

Song over Moscow. *See* Cheryomushki, 1963

Song Shop, 1929 (Day 4)

Song Shopping, 1933 (Fleischer 4)

Song to Remember, 1944 (Vidor 2, Muni 3, Oberon 3, Wilde 3, Banton 4, Buchman 4, Cahn 4, Cohn 4, Gaudio 4, Plunkett 4, Rozsa 4, Vorkapich 4)

Song 26. *See* Songs, 1969

Song without End, 1960 (Cukor 2, Vidor 2, Bogarde 3, Dalio 3, Howe 4)

Song You Gave Me, 1934 (Daniels 3)

Songe d'un garçon de café, 1910 (Cohl 4)

Songoku, 1940 (Takamine 3, Tsuburaya 4)

Songoku, 1959 (Tsuburaya 4)

Songs, 1964–69 (Brakhage 2)

Songs of Erin, 1951 (Terry 4)

Songs of Romance, 1949 (Fleischer 4)

Songs of the Rivers. *See* Lied der Ströme, 1954

Songs of the Seasons, 1948 (Fleischer 4)

Songs of Truce, 1913 (Bosworth 3, Mix 3)

Songs That Live, 1952 (Fleischer 4)

Songwriter, 1984 (Pollack 2, Rudolph 2)

Sonnenstrahl, 1933 (Fröhlich 3)

Sonnette d'alarme, 1935 (Christian-Jaque 2)

Sonnou sonjuku, 1939 (Miyagawa 4)

Sonntag des Lebens, 1930 (Goulding 2)

Sonnwendhof, 1918 (Kortner 3)

Sonny, 1922 (King 2, Barthelmess 3, Marion 4)

Sonny Boy, 1929 (Horton 3)

Sono fotogenico, 1980 (Gassman 3)

Sono hito no na wa ienai, 1951 (Yamamura 3, Hayasaka 4)

Sono hito wa honoo no yoni, 1972 (Iwashita 3)

Sono hito wa onna-kyoshi, 1970 (Iwashita 3)

Sono imoto, 1953 (Kagawa 3)

Sono Sartana, il vostro bechino, 1969 (Kinski 3)

Sono stato io!, 1937 (Valli 3)

Sono stato io, 1973 (Lattuada 2, Giannini 3)

Sono stato un'agente CIA, 1978 (Kennedy 3)

Sono un fenomeno paranormale, 1985 (Sordi 3)

Sono yo no himegoto, 1957 (Tsukasa 3)

Sono yo no onna, 1934 (Takamine 3, Tanaka 3)

Sono yo wa wasurenai, 1962 (Yoshimura 2)

Sono Zenya, 1939 (Yamada 3)

Sonoobasho no onna arite, 1962 (Tsukasa 3)

Sonora, 1933 (Walthall 3)

Sonora Kid, 1927 (Musuraca 4)

Sonotas, 1959 (Figueroa 4)

Sonoyo no bouken, 1948 (Miyagawa 4)

Sonrisa de la Virgen, 1957 (Figueroa 4)

Sons and Lovers, 1960 (Yates 2, Howard 3, Pleasence 3, Cardiff 4, Clarke 4, Francis 4, Rota 4, Wald 4)

Sons o'Guns, 1936 (Bacon 2, Blondell 3, Brown 3, Brown 4, Epstein 4, Polito 4, Wald 4)

Sons of Adventure, 1948 (Cahn 4, Canutt 4)

Sons of Ingmar. *See* Ingmarsönerna, 1919

Sons of Katie Elder, 1965 (Hathaway 2, Hopper 3, Martin 3, Wayne 3, Ballard 4, Bernstein 4, Head 4, Jennings 4, Wallis 4)

Sons of Liberty, 1939 (Curtiz 2, Rains 3)

Sons of Men, 1918 (Gilbert 3)

Sons of New Mexico, 1950 (Autry 3)

Sons of Satan. *See* Bastardi, 1968

Sons of the Desert, 1933 (Laurel and Hardy 3, Roach 4)

Sons of the Legion, 1938 (O'Connor 3, Dreier 4, Head 4)

Sons of the Musketeers. *See* At Sword's Point, 1952

Sons of the Pioneers, 1942 (Rogers 3)

Sons of the Saddle, 1930 (Brown 4, McCord 4)

Sons of the Sea. *See* Old Ironsides, 1926

Sons of the Sea. *See* Atlantic Ferry, 1941

Sons of Thunder. *See* Arrivani i titani, 1961

Son's Return, 1909 (Griffith 2, Pickford 3, Bitzer 4)

Sont morts les bâtisseurs, 1959 (Fresnay 3)

Sooky, 1931 (Mankiewicz 2, McLeod 2, Cooper 3)

Sophia Loren: Her Own Story, 1980 (Loren 3)

Sophie et le crime, 1955 (Achard 4)

Sophie Lang Goes West, 1937 (Crabbe 3, Head 4)

Sophie's Choice, 1982 (Pakula 2, Street 3, Almendros 4, Hamlisch 4, Jenkins 4)

Sophie's Place. *See* Crooks and Coronets, 1969

Sophomore, 1929 (McCarey 2, Ayres 3)

Sopralluoghi in Palestina, 1964 (Pasolini 2)

Sorano Daikaijyu Rodan, 1956 (Tsuburaya 4)

Sorcellerie culinaire, 1904 (Méliès 2)

Sorcerer, 1977 (Scheider 3, Box 4)

Sorcerer from Outer Space, 1988 (Carpenter 2)

Sorcerers, 1967 (Reeves 2, Karloff 3)

Sorcerer's Apprentice, 1955 (Powell and Pressburger 2, Francis 4, Heckroth 4)

Sorcerer's Village, 1958 (Meredith 3)

Sorceror's Apprentice, 1985 (Popescu-Gopo 4)

Sorcier, 1903 (Méliès 2)

Sorcières de Salem, 1956 (Montand 3, Piccoli 3, Signoret 3, Delerue 4, Eisler 4, Renoir 4)

Sorekara, 1986 (Ryu 3)

Sorelle, 1969 (Giannini 3)

Soria-Moria. *See* Drömda dalen, 1947

Soriso del grande tentatore, 1973 (Jackson 3, Morricone 4)

Sorority House, 1939 (Lake 3, Musuraca 4, Trumbo 4)

Sorpasso, 1962 (Gassman 3, Trintignant 3)

Sorprese dell'amore, 1959 (Comencini 2, Gassman 3)

Sorrell and Son, 1927 (Brenon 2, Howe 4, Menzies 4, Schenck 4)

Sorrell and Son, 1934 (Brenon 2, Wilcox 2)

Sorrow and the Pity. *See* **Chagrin et la pitié, 1971**

Sorrow Is Only for Women. *See* Kanashimi wa onna dakeni, 1958

Sorrowful Example, 1911 (Griffith 2, Bitzer 4)

Sorrowful Jones, 1949 (Ball 3, Hope 3, Dreier 4)

Sorrowful Shore, 1913 (Griffith 2, Bitzer 4)

Sorrows of Sarah. *See* Gorre Sarri, 1913

Sorrows of Satan, 1926 (Griffith 2, Menjou 3)

Sorrows of the Unfaithful, 1910 (Griffith 2, Pickford 3, Walthall 3, Bitzer 4)

Sorrows of Young Love. *See* Werther, 1927

Sorry, Wrong Number, 1948 (Litvak 2, Lancaster 3, Stanwyck 3, Dreier 4, Polito 4, Wallis 4, Waxman 4)

Sorte Drøm, 1911 (Gad 2, Nielsen 3, Psilander 3)

Sorte Hertug, 1907 (Holger-Madsen 2)

Sorte Kansler, 1912 (Psilander 3)

Sortie de secours, 1970 (Chabrol 2, Delon 3, Sarde 4)

Sortie des usines, 1894 or 1895 (Lumière 2)

Sortie des usines, 1895 (Lumière 2)

Sortie des usines Panhard et Levessor, 1895–97 (Gaumont 4)

Sortie d'un vapeur du port du Havre, 1901 (Gaumont 4)

Sortie du port. *See* Barque sortant du port, 1895

Sortilèges, 1944 (Piccoli 3, Prévert 4)

Sortilegio, 1966 (Storaro 4)

Sortilegio, 1970 (Ferreri 2)

Sortuz egy fekete bivalyert, 1985 (Trintignant 3)

Sorvanetch, 1914 (Mozhukin 3)

Soryu hiken. *See* Ninjitsu, 1958 (Mifune 3)

So's Your Old Man, 1926 (La Cava 2, Fields 3)

So's Your Uncle, 1943 (Bruckman 4, Krasner 4)

Soshun, 1956 (Yamamura 3)

Soshun, 1968 (Iwashita 3)

Soshu yakyoku. *See* Shina no yoru, 1940

Sosie, 1915 (Feuillade 2, Musidora 3)

Sospetto, 1975 (Girardot 3, Volonté 3, Solinas 4)

Sotelo, 1976 (Ruiz 2)

Sottaceti, 1971 (Bozzetto 4)

Sotto dieci bandiere, 1960 (Laughton 3, Volonté 3, Gherardi 4, Rota 4)

Sotto gli occhi dell'assassino, 1982 (Argento 4)

Sotto il ristorante Cinese, 1987 (Blier 3, Bozzetto 4)

Sotto il segno dello scorpione, 1969 (Taviani 2, Volonté 3)

Sotto il sole di Roma, 1948 (Sordi 3, Amidei 4)

Sotto il vestito niente, 1985 (Pleasence 3, Donaggio 4)

Sotto, Sotto, 1984 (Wertmüller 2)

Soubrette and the Simp, 1914 (Laurel and Hardy 3)

Souffle au coeur, 1971 (Gélin 3, Cristaldi 4)

Soufrière, 1977 (Herzog 2)

Soul Astray, 1914 (Eason 4)

Soul Fire, 1925 (Love 3)

Soul Herder, 1917 (Ford 2)

Soul Kiss. *See* Lady's Morals, 1930

Soul Man, 1986 (Jones 3)

Soul Mate, 1914 (Mix 3)

Soul Mates, 1925 (Basevi 4, Gibbons 4, Wilson 4)
Soul of a Monster, 1944 (Guffey 4)
Soul of a Thief, 1913 (Dwan 2)
Soul of Broadway, 1915 (Brenon 2)
Soul of Buddha, 1918 (Bara 3)
Soul of Honor, 1914 (Sweet 3, Walthall 3)
Soul of Kura-san, 1916 (Hayakawa 3)
Soul of Magdalen, 1917 (Barthelmess 3)
Soul of the Beast, 1923 (Sullivan 4)
Soul of the Sea. See Hai hun, 1957
Soulagna Rasa, 1914 (Phalke 2)
Soule, 1988 (Morricone 4)
Soulfire, 1925 (Barthelmess 3)
Soulier de satin, 1985 (Branco 4)
Soulier trop petit, 1909 (Linder 3)
Souls Adrift, 1917 (Edeson 4)
Souls at Sea, 1937 (Hathaway 2, Carey 3, Cooper 3, Raft 3, Dreier 4, Head 4, Lang 4)
Souls for Sale, 1923 (Chaplin 2, Bosworth 3)
Souls in Conflict, 1954 (Green 4)
Souls in Pawn, 1917 (King 2, Furthman 4, Seitz 4)
Souls Triumphant, 1915 (Gish 3)
Sound and the Fury, 1959 (Ritt 2, Brynner 3, Rosay 3, Woodward 3, Cahn 4, Clarke 4, Faulkner 4, North 4, Ravetch 4, Wald 4, Wheeler 4)
Sound Barrier, 1952 (Elliott 3, Richardson 3, Arnold 4, Korda, A. 4, Korda, V. 4, Rattigan 4)
Sound of Fog. See Kiri no oto, 1956
Sound of Fury, 1950 (Friedhofer 4)
Sound of Music, 1965 (Wise 2, Andrews 3, Jeakins 4, Leven 4, McCord 4, Reynolds 4)
Sound of the Mountain. See Yama no oto, 1954
Sound Sleeper, 1909 (Griffith 2, Bitzer 4)
Sound Off, 1952 (Edwards 2, Rooney 3, Duning 4)
Sounder, 1971 (Ritt 2, Alonzo 4)
Sounds From the Mountains. See Yama no oto, 1954
Soup and Fish, 1934 (Roach 4)
Soup Song, 1931 (Iwerks 4)
Soup to Nuts, 1930 (Three Stooges 3)
Soupçons, 1956 (Kosma 4)
Soupirant, 1962 (Carrière 4)
Sour Grapes, 1950 (Terry 4)
Sour Puss, 1940 (Blanc 4, Clampett 4, Stalling 4)
Source, 1900 (Guy 2)
Source, 1918 (Cruze 2, Reid 3)
Source de beauté. See Fioritures, 1916
Source of Love. See Pramen lásky, 1928
Souricière, 1950 (Blier 3)
Sourire, 1958 (Delerue 4)
Sourire aux lèvres. See Bonjour sourire, 1955
Sourire dans la tempête, 1950 (Werner 3)
Souris blanches, 1911 (Gaumont 4)
Souris chez les hommes, 1964 (Audiard 4)
Souris d'hôtel, 1928 (Meerson 4)
Sous la griffe, 1912 (Modot 3)
Sous la griffe, 1935 (Christian-Jaque 2, Spaak 4)
Sous la signe de Monte-Cristo, 1968 (Brasseur 3)
Sous la signe du taureau, 1969 (Audiard 4)
Sous la terre, 1931 (Matras 4)
Sous le ciel de Paris, 1950 (Duvivier 2)
Sous le ciel de Provence, 1956 (Fernandel 3)

Soul le Ciel d'Orient. See Shéhérazade, 1928
Sous le signe du taureau, 1969 (Gabin 3)
Sous le soleil de Satan, 1987 (Depardieu 3)
Sous les palmes de Marrakech, 1948 (Decaë 4)
Sous les ponts de Paris. See Clodoche, 1938
Sous les toits de Paris, 1930 (Clair 2, Modot 3, Meerson 4, Périnal 4, Trauner 4)
Sous les yeux d'Occident, 1936 (Barrault 3, Fresnay 3, Simon 3, Auric 4, Lourié 4)
Sous un autre soleil, 1955 (Broca 2)
Soushi gekijou, 1946 (Miyagawa 4)
Sousto, 1960 (Nemec 2)
South Advancing Women. See Nanshin josei, 1939
South American George, 1941 (Formby 3)
South o' the North Pole, 1924 (Roach 4)
South of Algiers, 1953 (Morris 4)
South of Caliente, 1951 (Rogers 3)
South of Dixie, 1944 (Beavers 3, Bruckman 4)
South of Pago-Pago, 1940 (Farmer 3, McLaglen 3)
South of St. Louis, 1949 (Malone 3, McCrea 3, Freund 4, Steiner 4)
South of Santa Fe, 1932 (Glennon 4)
South of Santa Fe, 1942 (Rogers 3)
South of Tahiti, 1941 (Crawford 3, Boyle 4)
South of the Border, 1939 (Autry 3)
South Pacific, 1958 (Brazzi 3, Jeakins 4, Newman 4, Prinz 4, Reynolds 4, Shamroy 4, Wheeler 4)
South Pole or Bust, 1934 (Terry 4)
South Riding, 1938 (Saville 2, Richardson 3, Dalrymple 4, Korda 4, Meerson 4, Stradling 4)
South Sea Adventure, 1959 (Welles 2)
South Sea Bubble, 1928 (Novello 3, Balcon 4)
South Sea Love, 1927 (Musuraca 4)
South Sea Rose, 1929 (Dwan 2, Levien 4, Rosson 4)
South Sea Sinner, 1950 (Winters 3, Orry-Kelly 4)
South Sea Woman, 1953 (Lancaster 3, McCord 4)
South Seas Adventure, 1958 (North 4)
South Seas Bouquet. See Nankai no hanatabe, 1942
South to Karanga, 1940 (Salter 4)
South West Pacific. See Rats of Tobruk, 1944
South Wind. See Minami ni kaze, 1942
South Wind and Waves. See Minami no kaze to nami, 1961
South Wind: Sequel. See Zoko minami no kaze, 1942
Southbound Duckling, 1954 (Hanna and Barbera 4)
Southern Cinderella, 1913 (Ince 4)
Southern Comfort, 1981 (Hill 2)
Southern Exposure, 1935 (Roach 4)
Southern Fried Rabbit, 1953 (Blanc 4, Freleng 4, Stalling 4)
Southern Horse-pitality, 1935 (Terry 4)
Southern Love, 1924 (Wilcox 2)
Southern Maid, 1933 (Launder and Gilliat 2, Granger 3)
Southern Maid, 1936 (Daniels 3)
Southern Pride, 1917 (King 2)
Southern Rhythm, 1932 (Terry 4)
Southern Star. See Etoile du sud, 1969
Southern Yankee, 1948 (Frank 4)

Southerner. See Prodigal, 1931
Southerner, 1945 (Aldrich 2, Renoir 2, Bondi 3, Hakim 4, Lourié 4)
Southerners, 1914 (Ingram 2)
Southside 1–1000, 1950 (Harlan 4)
Southward Ho, 1939 (Rogers 3)
Southwest, 1945 (Kaufman 4)
Southwest to Sonora. See Appaloosa, 1966
Souvenir. See Aux yeux du souvenir, 1948
Souvenir de Gibralter, 1975 (Constantine 3)
Souvenir de moi. See Vie de Jésus, 1951
Souvenir de Paris, 1955 (Guerra 2)
Souvenir d'Italie, 1957 (Sordi 3, Age and Scarpelli 4)
Souvenirs, 1938 (Pearson 2)
Souvenirs d'en France, 1975 (Moreau 3, Sarde 4)
Souvenirs perdus, 1950 (Christian-Jaque 2, Blier 3, Brasseur 3, Feuillère 3, Montand 3, Philipe 3, Jeanson 4, Kosma 4, Matras 4, Prévert 4)
Souvenirs, souvenirs, 1984 (Girardot 3, Noiret 3)
Sovetskie igrushki, 1924 (Vertov 2)
Soviet Toys. See Sovetskie igrushki, 1924
Soviet Village, 1944 (Rotha 2)
Sovversivi, 1967 (Taviani 2, Fusco 4)
Sower Reaps, 1914 (Eason 4)
Sowers, 1916 (Sweet 3, Rosher 4)
Sowing the Wind, 1916 (Hepworth 2)
Sowing the Wind, 1920 (Stahl 2, Mayer 4)
Sowizdrzal swietokrzyski, 1980 (Tyszkiewicz 3)
Soy charro de Rancho Grande, 1947 (Infante 3)
Soy puro mexicano, 1942 (Fernández 2, Armendáriz 3)
Soy un prófugo, 1946 (Cantinflas 3)
Soyez les bienvenus, 1940 (Berry 3, Gélin 3, Heller 4, Trauner 4)
Soyez ma femme. See Be My Wife, 1921
Soylent Green, 1973 (Cotten 3, Heston 3, Robinson 3, Westmore Family 4)
Soyokaze chichi to tomoni, 1940 (Takamine 3)
Soyons doncs sportifs, 1909 (Cohl 4)
Soyons gai, 1931 (Menjou 3)
Soyuz Velikogo Dela. See S.V.D., 1927
Space, 1965 (Warhol 2)
Space 1999, 1974 (Morricone 4)
Space Children, 1958 (Edouart 4, Laszlo 4)
Space Master X-7, 1958 (Three Stooges 3)
Space Passes, 1982 (Emshwiller 2)
Space Ship Sappy, 1956 (Three Stooges 3)
Spaceballs, 1987 (Brooks 2)
SpaceCamp, 1986 (Fraker 4, Williams 4)
Spacehunter: Adventures in the Forbidden Zone, 1983 (Bernstein 4)
Spaceman and King Arthur, 1979 (More 3)
Spacerek staromiejski, 1958 (Munk 2)
Spaceways, 1953 (Fisher 2, Carreras 4)
Spadaccino di Siena, 1961 (Granger 3, Delli Colli 4)
Spade e la croce, 1958 (De Carlo 3)
Spadla s měsice, 1966 (Brodský 3)
Spaedbarnet, 1953 (Roos 2)
Spaggia privata, 1986 (Blier 3)
Spaghetti, 1916 (Laurel and Hardy 3)
Spaghetti a la Mode, 1915 (Laurel and Hardy 3)
Spaghetti and Lottery, 1915 (Laurel and Hardy 3)
Spain. See Ispaniya, 1939
Spain in Flames, 1936 (Van Dongen 4)

Spalíček, 1947 (Trnka 4)
Span of Life, 1914 (Barrymore 3)
Spangles, 1926 (Bosworth 3)
Spaniard, 1925 (Walsh 2)
Spaniard and Indian, 1941 (Eisenstein 2)
Spanilá jízda, 1963 (Brdečka 4)
Spanish ABC, 1938 (Dickinson 2)
Spanish Affair, 1957 (Siegel 2)
Spanish Dancer, 1923 (Brenon 2,
    Beery 3, Menjou 3, Negri 3, Howe 4,
    Mathis 4)
Spanish Dilemma, 1912 (Sennett 2,
    Normand 3)
Spanish Earth, 1937 (Ivens 2, Renoir 2,
    Welles 2, Thomson 4, Van Dongen 4)
Spanish Fiesta, 1941 (Haller 4)
Spanish Fly, 1975 (Terry-Thomas 3)
Spanish Gardener, 1956 (Bogarde 3,
    Cusack 3, Challis 4, Rank 4)
Spanish Girl, 1909 (Anderson 3)
Spanish Gypsy, 1911 (Griffith 2, Bitzer 4,
    Macpherson 4)
Spanish Jade, 1922 (Hitchcock 2)
Spanish Love, 1922 (Powell 3)
Spanish Main, 1945 (Borzage 2, Henreid 3,
    O'Hara 3, Barnes 4, Eason 4, Eisler 4,
    Mankiewicz 4)
Spanish Onions, 1930 (Terry 4)
Spanish-American War Scenes, 1897
    (Bitzer 4)
Spanking Breezes, 1926 (Sennett 2)
Spanky, 1932 (Roach 4)
Spara forte, piu forte ... non capisco, 1966
    (Mastroianni 3, Welch 3, Cecchi
    D'Amico 4, Rota 4)
Spara per primo vivrai di più. See
    Consortium, 1968
Spare a Copper, 1940 (Dearden 2, Formby 3,
    Balcon 4)
Spare the Child, 1955 (Bosustow 4)
Spare the Rod, 1954 (Terry 4)
Spare the Rod, 1961 (Pleasence 3)
Spare Time, 1939 (Cavalcanti 2, Jennings 2)
Spark of Manhood, 1914 (Reid 3)
Sparks of Fate, 1914 (Bushman 3)
Sparky the Firefly, 1953 (Terry 4)
Sparring at N.Y. Athletic Club, 1905
    (Bitzer 4)
Sparring Partner, 1921 (Fleischer 4)
Sparrow of the Circus, 1914 (Eason 4)
Sparrows, 1926 (Pickford 3, Mohr 4,
    Rosher 4, Struss 4, Sullivan 4)
Sparsh, 1984 (Azmi 3)
Spartacus, 1960 (Kubrick 2, Curtis 3,
    Douglas 3, Laughton 3, Lom 3, Olivier 3,
    Simmons 3, Ustinov 3, Bass 4, Canutt 4,
    Ellenshaw 4, Metty 4, North 4,
    Trumbo 4)
Spartakiad. See Spartakiáda, 1956
Spartakiáda, 1956 (Stallich 4)
Sparviero del Nilo, 1949 (Gassman 3)
Spasmo, 1974 (Morricone 4)
Spasms. See Death Bite, 1982
Spassenieto, 1984 (Nowicki 3)
Spatně namalovaná slepice, 1963
    (Brdečka 4)
Spawn of the North, 1938 (Hathaway 2,
    Barrymore 3, Fonda 3, Lamour 3, Raft 3,
    Edouart 4, Furthman 4, Head 4,
    Jennings 4, Lang 4, Lewin 4, Tiomkin 4,
    Westmore Family 4)
Speak Easily, 1932 (Keaton 2, Durante 3)
Speak Easy, 1919 (Sennett 2)
Speakeasy, 1929 (Walthall 3)

Speaking from America, 1939 (Cavalcanti 2,
    Jennings 2)
Speaking of Animals Down on the Farm,
    1942 (Avery 4)
Speaking of Animals in a Pet Shop, 1942
    (Avery 4)
Speaking of Animals in the Zoo, 1942
    (Avery 4)
Speaking of Murder. See Rouge est mis,
    1957)
Speaking of Relations, 1934 (Roach 4)
Speaking of the Weather, 1937 (Stalling 4)
Spear Dance of 53 Stations. See Yari-odori
    gojusan-tsugi, 1946
Special Agent, 1935 (Davis 3, Orry-Kelly 4)
Special Day. See Giornata speciale, 1977
Special Delivery, 1927 (Arbuckle 3,
    Cantor 3, Powell 3, Schulberg 4)
Special Delivery, 1955 (Cotten 3)
Special Delivery, 1976 (Schifrin 4)
Special Effects, 1972 (Frampton 2)
Special Effects, 1985 (Cohen 2)
Special Inspector, 1939 (Hayworth 3)
Special Investigator, 1936 (Cronjager 4)
Special London Bridge Special, 1972
    (Hamlisch 4)
Special Section. See Section speciale, 1975
Species of a Mexican Man, 1980 (Johnson 3)
Speckled Band, 1931 (Massey 3, Young 4)
Spectacle Maker, 1934 (Stothart 4)
Specter of the Rose, 1946 (Hecht 4)
Specters. See Spettri, 1987
Spectre, 1973 (Léaud 3)
Spectre, 1977 (Hurt 3)
Spectre of Suspicion, 1918 (King 2)
Spectre of the Rose, 1946 (Garmes 4)
Spectre vert, 1930 (Feyder 2, Daniels 4,
    Day 4, Gibbons 4, Hecht 4)
Speed, 1931 (Sennett 2)
Speed, 1936 (Stewart 3, Gillespie 4)
Speed Crazy, 1958 (Haller 4)
Speed Demon, 1911 (Sennett 2)
Speed Demon, 1925 (Pierce 4)
Speed Fever. See Formula I, febbre della
    velocità, 1978
Speed Girl, 1921 (Daniels 3)
Speed Hound, 1927 (Cantor 3)
Speed in the Gay Nineties, 1932 (Sennett 2)
Speed Kings, 1913 (Sennett 2, Normand 3)
Speed Maniac, 1919 (Mix 3)
Speed Queen, 1913 (Sennett 2, Normand 3)
Speed Test of Tarantula, 1904 (Bitzer 4)
Speed the Plough, 1958 (Halas and
    Batchelor 4)
Speed the Swede, 1923 (Roach 4)
Speed to Spare, 1920 (Roach 4)
Speed Zone, 1989 (Van Cleef 3)
Speedway, 1929 (Gibbons 4)
Speedway, 1968 (Presley 3, Ruttenberg 4)
Speedy, 1928 (Lloyd 3, Zukor 4)
Speedy Ghost to Town, 1967 (Blanc 4)
Speedy Gonzales, 1952 (Foster 4)
Speedy Gonzales, 1955 (Blanc 4, Freleng 4,
    Stalling 4)
Speil mit dem Feuer, 1921 (Herlth 4)
Spejbl na stopě, 1955 (Trnka 4)
Spejbl on the Trail. See Spejbl na stopě, 1955
Spejblovo filmové opojení, 1931 (Stallich 4)
Spell, 1977 (Grant 3)
Spell of the Poppy, 1915 (Browning 2)
Spell on the Carpathian Key. See
    Koryatovič, 1922
Spellbinder, 1929 (Benchley 4)
Spellbinder, 1939 (Metty 4)

Spellbound, 1945 (Hitchcock 2, Bergman 3,
    Peck 3, Barnes 4, Basevi 4, Hecht 4,
    Rozsa 4, Selznick 4)
Spellbound Hound, 1950 (Bosustow 4,
    Hubley 4)
Spencer Tracy Legacy: A Tribute by
    Katharine Hepburn, 1986 (Hepburn 3)
Spencer's Mountain, 1963 (Daves 2, Crisp 3,
    Fonda 3, O'Hara 3, Steiner 4)
Spender, 1913 (Lawrence 3)
Spender, 1919 (Barrymore 3)
Spendthrift, 1922 (Terry 4)
Spendthrift, 1936 (Walsh 2, Fonda 3,
    Reynolds 4, Shamroy 4, Wanger 4)
Sperduti nel buio, 1947 (De Sica 2,
    Zavattini 4)
Speriamo che sia femmina, 1986
    (Monicelli 2, Blier 3, Deneuve 3,
    Noiret 3, Ullmann 3, Cecchi D'Amico 4)
Spessart Inn. See Wirtshaus im Spessart,
    1957
Spettri, 1987 (Pleasence 3)
Spheres. See Sphères, 1969 (McLaren 4)
Spherical Space No. 1, 1967 (Vanderbeek 2)
Sphinx. See Spynx, 1917
Sphinx, 1981 (Schaffner 2, Gielgud 3)
Spiaggia, 1953 (Ferreri 2)
Spiaggia del desiderio, 1976 (Kennedy 3)
Spiaggia privata, 1986 (Bozzetto 4)
Spice of Life. See Casse-pieds, 1948
Spices. See Mirch Masala, 1986
Spider. See Spinnen, 1920
Spider, 1931 (Friedhofer 4, Howe 4)
Spider, 1986 (Bozzetto 4)
Spider and Her Web, 1914 (Reid 3)
Spider and the Fly, 1949 (Hamer 2, Auric 4,
    Rank 4, Unsworth 4)
Spider Talks, 1932 (Terry 4)
Spider Webs, 1927 (Costello 3, Hunt 4)
Spider Woman, 1942 (Salter 4)
Spider Woman, 1944 (Rathbone 3)
Spiders. See Spinnen, 1920
Spider's Strategem. See Strategia del ragnoe,
    1969
Spider's Web. See Flashing Spurs, 1924
Spider's Web. See Spinnennets, 1988
Spie contro il mondo, 1966 (Granger 3,
    Kinski 3)
Spiel der Königin, 1923 (Pommer 4,
    Warm 4)
Spiel im Sand, 1964 (Herzog 2)
Spiel im Sommerwind, 1950 (Staudte 2)
Spiel in Farben, 1934 (Fischinger 2, Ford 2)
Spiel mit dem Feuer, 1921 (Wiene 2,
    Röhrig 4, Wagner 4)
Spiel mit dem Feuer, 1934 (Wagner 4)
Spiel mit Steinen, 1965 (Švankmajer 4)
Spiel ums Leben, 1924 (Curtiz 2)
Spiel von Liebe und Tod, 1919 (Gad 2)
Spieler, 1928 (Miller 4)
Spieler, 1938 (Baarová 3, Herlth 4)
Spieler aus Leidenschaft. See Bild der Zeit,
    1921
Spielereien einer Kaiserin, 1929 (Dagover 3)
Spielerin, 1927 (Andrejew 4)
Spies. See Spione, 1928
Spies. See Espions, 1957
Spies, 1974 (Winkler 4)
Spies A-Go-Go. See Nasty Rabbit, 1965
Spies at Work. See Spione am Werk, 1932
Spies Like Us, 1985 (Cohen 2, Costa-
    Gavras 2, Landis 2, Hope 3, Bernstein 4,
    Harryhausen 4)
Spike of Bensonhurst, 1988 (Borgnine 3)

Spring Reunion, 1957 (Andrews 3, Hutton 3, Mercer 4)

Spring Snow. *See* Shunsetsu, 1950

Spring Song, 1946 (Kendall 3)

Spring Song, 1989 (Halas 4)

Spring Sorrow of the Pipa, 1932 (Zhao 3)

Spring Symphony. *See* Fruhlingssinfonie, 1985

Spring Tonic, 1935 (Ayres 3, Trevor 3, Bruckman 4, Hecht 4)

Spring Wind on Venaya, 1959 (Bondarchuk 3)

Springende Hirsch, 1915 (Wiene 2)

Springer and SS-Men. *See* Pérák a SS, 1946

Springer and the SS-Men. *See* Pérák a SS, 1946

Springfield Rifle, 1952 (De Toth 2, Cooper 3, Steiner 4)

Springtime, 1920 (Laurel and Hardy 3)

Springtime, 1929 (Iwerks 4)

Springtime for Henry, 1934 (Lasky 4, Seitz 4)

Springtime for Thomas, 1946 (Hanna and Barbera 4)

Springtime in the Rockage, 1942 (Fleischer 4)

Springtime in the Rockies, 1937 (Autry 3)

Springtime in the Rockies, 1942 (Grable 3, Horton 3, Miranda 3, Day 4, Newman 4, Pan 4)

Springtime in the Sierras, 1947 (Rogers 3)

Springtime Serenade, 1935 (Lantz 4)

Spritsmuglerne. *See* Polis Paulus' Påskasmäll, 1925

Sprucin' Up, 1935 (Roach 4)

Sprung ins Leben, 1924 (Dietrich 3, Wagner 4)

Spurs, 1930 (Eason 4)

Spurs and Saddles, 1927 (Wray 3)

Spy, 1911 (Bosworth 3)

Spy, 1931 (Zinnemann 2)

Spy 13. *See* Operator 13, 1934

Spy Against the World. *See* Spie control il mondo, 1966

Spy for a Day, 1940 (De Grunwald 4)

Spy Has Not Yet Died. *See* Kancho mada shinazu, 1942

Spy in Black, 1939 (Veidt 3, Hornbeck 4, Korda, A. 4, Korda, V. 4, Rozsa 4)

Spy in the Pantry. *See* Ten Days in Paris, 1939

Spy in White. *See* Secret of Stambov, 1936

Spy in Your Eye. *See* Appuntamento per le spie, 1965

Spy Killer, 1969 (Sangster 4)

Spy of Napoleon, 1936 (Barthelmess 3, Courant 4)

Spy Ring, 1938 (Wyman 3)

Spy Smasher, 1942 (Canutt 4)

Spy Swatter, 1967 (Blanc 4)

Spy Train, 1980 (Halas and Batchelor 4)

Spy Who Came In from the Cold, 1966 (Ritt 2, Bloom 3, Burton 3, Cusack 3, Werner 3, Dehn 4, Morris 4)

Spy Who Loved Me, 1977 (Adam 4, Hamlisch 4, Renoir 4)

Spy with a Cold Nose, 1966 (Elliott 3, Harvey 3, Levine 4, Williams 4)

Spylarks. *See* Intelligence Men, 1965

Spynx, 1917 (Lukas 3)

Spys, 1974 (Gould 3, Sutherland 3, Fisher 4, Goldsmith 4)

Spy's Defeat, 1913 (Bushman 3)

Squabs and Squabbles, 1919 (Laurel and Hardy 3)

Squadra antimafia, 1978 (Wallach 3)

Squadron, 1964 (Robertson 3)

Squadron 992, 1940 (Cavalcanti 2, Watt 2)

Squadron Leader X, 1942 (Alwyn 4)

Squadron of Honor, 1937 (Ballard 4)

Squall. *See* Shkval, 1916

Squall, 1929 (Korda 2, Loy 3, Young 3, Korda 4, Seitz 4)

Square. *See* Tér, 1971

Square Dance, 1987 (Robards 3)

Square Deal. *See* Ruse, 1915

Square Deal, 1917 (Edeson 4, Marion 4)

Square Deal Man. *See* Ruse, 1915

Square Deal Man, 1917 (Hart 3, August 4)

Square Deal Sanderson, 1919 (Hart 3, August 4)

Square Deceiver, 1917 (Gaudio 4)

Square Jungle, 1955 (Borgnine 3, Curtis 3)

Square Mile, 1953 (Guinness 3)

Square of Violence. *See* Nasilje na Trgu, 1961

Square Peg. *See* Denial, 1925

Square Peg, 1958 (Wisdom 3, Rank 4)

Square Ring, 1953 (Dearden 2, Kendall 3, Heller 4)

Square Shooter, 1927 (Wyler 2)

Square Shooting Square, 1955 (Maltese 4)

Squarehead. *See* Mabel's Married Life, 1914

Squareheads of the Round Table, 1948 (Three Stooges 3)

Squatter's Girl, 1914 (Anderson 3)

Squaw Man, 1914 (De Mille 2, Buckland 4, Zukor 4)

Squaw Man, 1918 (De Mille 2, Buckland 4)

Squaw Man, 1931 (De Mille 2, Adrian 4, Mayer 4, Prinz 4, Rosson 4, Stothart 4)

Squaw Man's Son, 1917 (Reid 3)

Squawkin' Hawk, 1942 (Blanc 4, Jones 4)

Squaw's Love, 1911 (Griffith 2, Normand 3, Bitzer 4)

Squeak in the Deep, 1966 (Blanc 4, McKimson 4)

Squeaker, 1937 (Newton 3, Sim 3, Korda, A. 4, Korda, V. 4, Krasker 4, Périnal 4, Rozsa 4)

Squeaker. *See* Zinker, 1963

Squeaks and Squawks, 1920 (Laurel and Hardy 3)

Squealer, 1930 (Brown 4, Robinson 4)

Squeeze. *See* Controrapina, 1978

Squib Wins the Calcutta Sweep, 1922 (Pearson 2)

Squibs, 1921 (Pearson 2)

Squibs' Honeymoon, 1923 (Pearson 2)

Squibs M.P., 1923 (Pearson 2)

Squire's Son, 1914 (Ince 4)

Squirm, 1976 (Baker 4)

Squirrel Crazy, 1951 (Terry 4)

Srdce za písničku, 1933 (Stallich 4)

Sredi dobrykh lyudei, 1962 (Maretskaya 3)

Sroublkova dobrodružství, 1962 (Brdečka 4)

Staatanjo, 1963 (Yamamura 3)

Stability Versus Nobility, 1911 (Bosworth 3)

Stablemates, 1938 (Wood 2, Beery 3, Rooney 3, Seitz 4)

Stacey's Knights, 1981 (Costner 3)

Stachka, 1925 (Eisenstein 2, Tisse 4)

Stacked Cards, 1926 (Haller 4)

Staden vid vattnen, 1955 (Andersson 3)

Stadt Anatol, 1936 (Fröhlich 3)

Stadt der tausend Freuden, 1927 (Gallone 2)

Stadt in Sicht, 1923 (Pick 2, Galeen 4)

Stadt ist voller Geheimnisse, 1955 (Kortner 3)

Stadt steht Kopf, 1932 (Gründgens 3, Planer 4)

Stadt Stuttgart, 100. Cannstatter Volksfest, 1935 (Ruttman 2)

Stadt vor Versuchung, 1925 (Tschechowa 3)

Stage, 1951 (Anand 3)

Stage Door, 1937 (La Cava 2, Arden 3, Ball 3, Hepburn 3, Menjou 3, Miller 3, Pangborn 3, Rogers 3, Berman 4, Polglase 4, Ryskind 4, Veiller 4)

Stage Door Canteen, 1943 (Borzage 2, Daves 2, Bellamy 3, Darwell 3, Fields 3, Hepburn 3, Jaffe 3, Muni 3, Oberon 3, Pangborn 3, Raft 3, Weissmuller 3, Green 4, Horner 4)

Stage Door Cartoon, 1944 (Blanc 4, Freleng 4, Maltese 4, Stalling 4)

Stage Door Magoo, 1955 (Bosustow 4, Burness 4)

Stage Driver's Daughter, 1911 (Anderson 3)

Stage Fright, 1923 (Roach 4)

Stage Fright, 1938 (Metty 4)

Stage Fright, 1940 (Blanc 4, Stalling 4)

Stage Fright, 1950 (Hitchcock 2, Dietrich 3, Sim 3, Wyman 3, Reville 4)

Stage Hand, 1933 (Langdon 3)

Stage Hoax, 1952 (Lantz 4)

Stage Kisses, 1927 (Walker 4)

Stage Mother, 1933 (O'Sullivan 3, Adrian 4, Brown 4, Folsey 4, Freed 4)

Stage Note, 1910 (Lawrence 3)

Stage Robbers of San Juan, 1911 (Dwan 2)

Stage Romance, 1922 (Brenon 2)

Stage Stars Off Screen, 1925 (Buchanan 3)

Stage Struck, 1922 (Roach 4)

Stage Struck, 1925 (Dwan 2, Swanson 3, Polglase 4)

Stage Struck, 1936 (Berkeley 2, Blondell 3, Powell 3, Wyman 3, Haskin 4, Orry-Kelly 4)

Stage Struck, 1951 (Terry 4)

Stage Struck, 1958 (Lumet 2, Fonda 3, Greenwood 3, Marshall 3, North 4, Planer 4)

Stage Stunt, 1929 (Lantz 4)

Stage to Chino, 1940 (Hunt 4)

Stage to Tucson, 1949 (Brown 4)

Stagecoach, 1939 (Ford 2, Carradine 3, Trevor 3, Wayne 3, Canutt 4, Cooper 4, Glennon 4, Nichols 4, Plunkett 4, Wanger 4)

Stagecoach, 1966 (Crosby 3, Clothier 4, Goldsmith 4, Smith 4)

Stagecoach Buckaroo, 1942 (Salter 4)

Stagecoach Driver and the Girl, 1915 (Mix 3)

Stagecoach Guard, 1915 (Mix 3)

Stagecoach Kid, 1949 (Musuraca 4)

Stagecoach Outlaws, 1945 (Crabbe 3)

Stagecoach War, 1940 (Harlan 4, Head 4)

Stagione all'inferno, 1971 (Stamp 3, Jarre 4)

Stagione dei sensi, 1968 (Argento 4, Morricone 4)

Stagione del nostro amore, 1965 (Aimée 3)

Stain on the Conscience, 1968 (Vukotić 4)

Stained Glass at Fairford, 1955 (Wright 2, Donat 3)

Staircase, 1969 (Donen 2, Burton 3, Harrison 3, Moore 3, Challis 4)

Stairs, 1953 (Maddow 4)

Stairs of Sand, 1929 (Arthur 3, Beery 3)

Stairway for a Star, 1947 (Wilde 3)

Stairway to Heaven. *See* **Matter of Life and Death, 1946**

Stajio wa tenya wanya, 1957 (Kyo 3)

Stake Out on Dope Street, 1958 (Corman 2)

Stake Uncle Sam to Play Your Hand, 1918 (Normand 3)

Stake-Out. *See* Police Story, 1973

Stakeout, 1987 (Badham 2, Dreyfuss 3)

Staking His Life. *See* Conversion of Frosty Blake, 1915

Stalag 17, 1953 (Preminger 2, Wilder 2, Holden 3, Head 4, Laszlo 4, Waxman 4)

Stalingradskaya bitva, 1949 (Cherkassov 3)

Stalker, 1979 (Tarkovsky 2)

Stalking Moon, 1968 (Mulligan 2, Pakula 2, Peck 3, Saint 3, Jeakins 4, Lang 4, Sargent 4)

Stallion Road, 1947 (Walsh 2, Reagan 3, Edeson 4)

Stalowe serca, 1947 (Lomnicki 3)

Stamboul Quest, 1934 (Wood 2, Brennan 3, Loy 3, Howe 4, Mankiewicz 4, Stothart 4, Wanger 4)

Stamp Fantasia, 1961 (Kuri 4)

Stampede, 1911 (Guy 2, Pickford 3, Gaudio 4)

Stampede, 1949 (Edwards 2)

Stampeded. *See* Big Land, 1957

Stampen, 1955 (Björnstrand 3, Fischer 4)

Stan Brakhage, Ed Emshwiller, 1990 (Brakhage 2)

Stan Posiadania, 1989 (Zanussi 2)

Stand and Deliver, 1928 (Crisp 3, Adrian 4, Grot 4)

Stand By for Action, 1942 (Brennan 3, Laughton 3, Taylor 3, Balderston 4, Mankiewicz 4, Mayer 4, Rosher 4)

Stand By Me, 1986 (Dreyfuss 3)

Stand der Dinge, 1982 (Wenders 2, Alekan 4, Branco 4, Müller 4)

Stand Pat, 1922 (Roach 4)

Stand Under the Dark Clock, 1989 (Zinnemann 2)

Stand Up and Be Counted, 1972 (Cooper 3, Wheeler 4)

Stand Up and Cheer, 1934 (Pangborn 3, Temple 3)

Stand Up and Fight, 1939 (LeRoy 2, Van Dyke 2, Beery 3, Taylor 3, Murfin 4)

Standard Time, 1967 (Snow 2, Wieland 2)

Standarte, 1977 (Cushing 3, Dagover 3)

Standhafte Benjamin, 1917 (Wiene 2)

Stand-In, 1937 (Garnett 2, Blondell 3, Bogart 3, Howard 3, Clarke 4, Wanger 4)

Standing by the Treasury. *See* U pokladny stál, 1939

Standing Room Only, 1944 (De Carlo 3, Goddard 3, MacMurray 3, Dreier 4, Head 4, Lang 4)

Stanley and Iris, 1990 (De Niro 3, Fonda 3, Ravetch 4, Williams 4)

Stanley and Livingstone, 1939 (King 2, Brennan 3, Coburn 3, Tracy 3, Barnes 4, Dunne 4, MacGowan 4, Newman 4, Raksin 4, Zanuck 4)

Stanno tutti bene, 1990 (Mastroianni 3, Morgan 3, Guerra 4, Morricone 4)

Staphylokok-faren, 1960 (Roos 2)

Star, 1952 (Davis 3, Hayden 3, Wood 3, Laszlo 4, Leven 4, Orry-Kelly 4, Young 4)

Star!, 1968 (Wise 2, Andrews 3, Scheider 3, Cahn 4, Kidd 4, Laszlo 4, Leven 4, Reynolds 4)

Star Boarder, 1914 (Sennett 2)

Star Boarder, 1917 (Laurel and Hardy 3)

Star Boarder, 1920 (Sennett 2)

Star Chamber, 1983 (Douglas 3)

Star Child, 1983 (Corman 2)

Star Crash, 1979 (Barry 4)

Star Dust, 1940 (Darnell 3, Day 4, MacGowan 4, Zanuck 4)

Star 80, 1983 (Fosse 2, Baker 3, Robertson 3, Nykvist 4)

Star for a Night, 1936 (Darwell 3, McDaniel 3, Trevor 3)

Star for Two, 1990 (Bacall 3, Quinn 3)

Star Garden, 1974 (Brakhage 2)

Star in the Dust, 1956 (Eastwood 3)

Star in the Night, 1945 (Siegel 2, Burks 4)

Star Is Bored, 1956 (Blanc 4, Freleng 4)

Star Is Born, 1937 (Fleming 2, Wellman 2, Gaynor 3, March 3, Menjou 3, Pangborn 3, Turner 3, Selznick 4, Steiner 4, Wheeler 4)

Star Is Born, 1954 (Cukor 2, Bogart 3, Garland 3, Marsh 3, Mason 3, Edens 4, Sharaff 4)

Star Is Born, 1976 (Mazursky 2, Streisand 3, Surtees 4)

Star is Hatched, 1938 (Freleng 4)

Star Is Shorn, 1939 (Ballard 4)

Stark Fear, 1963 (Williams 4)

Stark Love, 1927 (Brown 4)

Stark Mad, 1929 (Bacon 2, Walthall 3)

Stark System, 1980 (Volonté 3, Morricone 4)

Star Maker, 1939 (Crosby 3, Head 4, Newman 4, Struss 4)

Star Night at the Cocoanut Grove, 1935 (Cooper 3, Crosby 3)

Star of Bethlehem, 1912 (Cruze 2)

Star of Bethlehem, 1956 (Reiniger 4)

Star of Hong Kong. *See* Honkon no hoshi, 1962

Star of India, 1913 (Guy 2)

Star of India, 1953 (Lom 3, Wilde 3, Adam 4, Rota 4)

Star of Midnight, 1935 (Powell 3, Rogers 3, Berman 4, Hunt 4, Polglase 4, Steiner 4, Veiller 4)

Star of the Circus, 1938 (Saunders 4)

Star of the Sea, 1915 (Chaney 3)

Star Packer, 1934 (Wayne 3, Canutt 4)

Star Quality, 1985 (York 3)

Star Reporter, 1931 (Powell and Pressburger 2)

Star Rock. *See* Apple, 1980

Star Said No. *See* Callaway Went Thataway, 1951

Star Slammer, 1988 (Carradine 3)

Star Spangled Rhythm, 1942 (De Mille 2, Bendix 3, Crosby 3, Goddard 3, Hayward 3, Hope 3, Hutton 3, Ladd 3, Lake 3, Lamour 3, MacMurray 3, Milland 3, Powell 3, Preston 3, Dreier 4, Frank 4, Head 4, Mercer 4)

Star Spangled Salesman, 1968 (Three Stooges 3)

Star, The Orphan, and the Butcher. *See* Evlalie quitte les champs, 1973

Star Trek IV: The Voyage Home, 1986 (Rosenman 4)

Star Trek: The Motion Picture, 1979 (Wise 2, Goldsmith 4, Trumbull 4)

Star Trek V: the Final Frontier, 1989 (Goldsmith 4)

Star Wars, 1977 (Lucas 2, Cushing 3, Ford 3, Guinness 3, Jones 3, Baker 4, Burtt 4, Edlund 4, Williams 4)

Star Without Light. *See* Etoile sans lumière, 1945

Star Witness, 1931 (Wellman 2, Huston 3)

Starci na chmelu, 1964 (Stallich 4)

Stardoom, 1970 (Brocka 2)

Stardust, 1974 (Puttnam 4)

Stardust Memories, 1980 (Allen 2, Willis 4)

Stardust on the Sage, 1942 (Autry 3)

Staré pověsti čéské, 1953 (Brdečka 4, Trnka 4)

Starets Vasili Gryaznov, 1924 (Tisse 4)

Starflight One: The Plane That Couldn't Land, 1983 (Schifrin 4)

Staright Is the Way, 1921 (Marion 4)

Stark, 1985 (Hopper 3)

Starkaste, 1929 (Sjöberg 2)

Stärker al die Liebe, 1938 (Wegener 3)

Stärker als Paragraphen, 1950 (Staudte 2)

Stärkere, 1918 (Kortner 3)

Starlift, 1951 (Cagney 3, Cooper 3, Day 3, Scott 3, Wyman 3, McCord 4, Prinz 4)

Starman, 1984 (Carpenter 2, Bridges 3, Douglas 3, Baker 4)

Staroie i novoie, 1929 (Balàzs 4, Tisse 4)

Staroye Dudino. *See* Granitsa, 1935

Starring in Western Stuff, 1916 (Mix 3)

Stars and Bars, 1917 (Sennett 2)

Stars and Bars, 1988 (Day Lewis 3, Stanton 3)

Stars and Guitars. *See* Brazil, 1944

Stars and Stripes, 1939 (McLaren 4)

Stars and Stripes Forever, 1952 (Wagner 3, Webb 3, Clarke 4, Jeakins 4, LeMaire 4, Newman 4, Trotti 4)

Stars Are Beautiful, 1974 (Brakhage 2)

Stars Are Singing, 1953 (Bumstead 4, Head 4, Young 4)

Stars in My Crown, 1950 (Tourneur 2, McCrea 3, Deutsch 4, Plunkett 4)

Stars Look Down, 1939 (Reed 2, Lockwood 3, Redgrave 3)

Stars on Horseback, 1943 (Davis 3)

Stars over Broadway, 1935 (Berkeley 2, Barnes 4, Epstein 4, Orry-Kelly 4, Wald 4)

Stars Their Courses Change, 1915 (Bushman 3)

Stars' War: The Flight of the Wild Geese, 1978 (Burton 3)

Starship Invasions. *See* Alien Encounter, 1976

Starsky and Hutch, 1975 (Schifrin 4)

Starstruck, 1982 (Armstrong 2)

Start Cheering, 1938 (Crawford 3, Durante 3, Three Stooges 3, Green 4, Walker 4)

Start in Life, 1943 (Alwyn 4)

Start the Revolution without Me, 1970 (Welles 2, Sutherland 3, Wilder 3, Addison 4)

Start the Show, 1920 (Roach 4)

Starting Over, 1979 (Pakula 2, Clayburgh 3, Reynolds 3, Hamlisch 4, Jenkins 4, Nykvist 4)

Starvation Blues, 1925 (Roach 4)

Starving for Love, 1910 (White 3)

Starý hřich, 1930 (Heller 4)

Stasera mi butto, 1967 (Giannini 3)

Stasera mi butto i due bagnani, 1968 (Giannini 3)

Stasera niente di nuovo, 1942 (Valli 3)

Stăsilo, 1957 (Mimica 4)

Stastny lev, 1959 (Brdečka 4)
State Fair, 1933 (King 2, Ayres 3, Gaynor 3, Rogers 3, Levien 4, Mohr 4)
State Fair, 1945 (Andrews 3, Levien 4, Newman 4, Shamroy 4)
State Fair, 1962 (Faye 3, Ferrer 3, Brackett 4, Newman 4, Smith 4)
State Line, 1911 (Lawrence 3)
State of Emergency, 1986 (Sheen 3)
State of Grace, 1990 (Meredith 3, Morricone 4)
State of Siege. See Etat de siège, 1972
State of the Union, 1948 (Capra 2, Hepburn 3, Johnson 3, Lansbury 3, Menjou 3, Tracy 3, Folsey 4, Hornbeck 4, Irene 4, Mayer 4, Veiller 4, Young 4)
State of Things. See Stand der Dinge, 1982
State Penitentiary, 1950 (Katzman 4)
State Secret, 1950 (Launder and Gilliat 2, Hawkins 3, Lom 3, Alwyn 4, Korda 4, Krasker 4)
State Street Sadie, 1928 (Loy 3, Zanuck 4)
Stateline Motel. See Ultima chance, 1973
States, 1967 (Frampton 2)
State's Attorney, 1932 (Barrymore 3, Selznick 4, Steiner 4)
Station Content, 1918 (Swanson 3)
Station Master, 1917 (Laurel and Hardy 3)
Station mondaine, 1951 (Braunberger 4)
Station Six Sahara, 1963 (Baker 3, Elliott 3)
Station S-T-A-R, 1932 (Wayne 3)
Station West, 1948 (Moorehead 3, Powell 3)
Stationmaster's Wife. See Bolwieser, 1978
Stato interessante, 1977 (Morricone 4)
Statue, 1905 (Guy 2)
Statue, 1970 (Cleese 3, Niven 3)
Statue animée, 1903 (Méliès 2)
Statue Parade, 1937 (Rotha 2)
Statues d'épouvante, 1953 (Cloquet 4)
Statues meurent aussi, 1953 (Marker 2, Resnais 2, Cloquet 4, Colpi 4)
Stavisky, 1974 (Resnais 2, Belmondo 3, Boyer 3, Depardieu 3, Saulnier 4, Vierny 4)
Stay As You Are. See Cosi come sei, 1978
Stay Away, Joe, 1968 (Meredith 3, Presley 3)
Stay Hungry, 1976 (Rafelson 2, Bridges 3, Field 3, Schwarzenegger 3)
Staying Alive, 1983 (Stallone 3, Travolta 3)
Staying On, 1980 (Howard 3, Johnson 3)
Staying Together, 1989 (Grant 3)
Stazione Termini, 1953 (Cervi 3, Clift 3, Jones 3, Aldo 4, Cahn 4, Morris 4, Selznick 4, Zavattini 4)
Stchastia, 1964 (Batalov 3)
Steady Company, 1915 (Chaney 3, Furthman 4)
Steagle, 1970 (Guffey 4)
Steak trop cuit, 1960 (Guillemot 4)
Steal Wool, 1957 (Blanc 4, Jones 4)
Stealers, 1920 (Shearer 3)
Stealin' Ain't Honest, 1940 (Fleischer 4)
Stealing Heaven, 1989 (Elliot 3)
Stealing Home, 1988 (Foster 3)
Steam Locomotive C-57. See Kikansha C-57, 1940
Steamboat Bill, Jr., 1928 (Keaton 2, Schenck 4)
Steamboat 'round the Bend, 1935 (Ford 2, Bosworth 3, Rogers 3, Nichols 4, Trotti 4)
Steamboat Willie, 1928 (Disney 4, Iwerks 4, Stalling 4)

Steaming, 1985 (Losey 2, Dors 3, Redgrave 3, Challis 3)
Steamlined Greta Green, 1937 (Stalling 4)
Steamroller and the Violin. See Katok i skripka, 1960
Steel, 1944 (Cardiff 4)
Steel, 1969 (Peries 2)
Steel: A Whole New Way of Life, 1971 (Benegal 2)
Steel Bayonet, 1957 (Carreras 4)
Steel Cage, 1954 (O'Sullivan 3, Alton 4)
Steel Fist, 1951 (McDowall 3)
Steel Goes to War, 1941 (Alwyn 4)
Steel Helmet, 1950 (Fuller 2)
Steel Highway, 1931 (Wellman 2, Astor 3, Blondell 3, Cagney 3)
Steel Lady, 1953 (Crosby 4)
Steel Magnolias, 1989 (Field 3, MaClaine 3, Alonzo 4, Delerue 4, Shepard 4, Stark 4)
Steel Preferred, 1926 (Bosworth 3)
Steel Rolling Mill, 1914 (Sennett 2)
Steel Town, 1952 (Sheridan 3, Hunter 4)
Steel Trap, 1952 (Aldrich 2, Cotten 3, Wright 3, Laszlo 4, Tiomkin 4)
Steel Workers, 1937 (Lantz 4)
Steeltown, 1943 (Van Dyke 2)
Steelyard Blues, 1972 (Fonda 3, Sutherland 3, Kovacs 4)
Steeple Jacks, 1951 (Terry 4)
Stein Song, 1930 (Fleischer 4)
Stein unter Steinen, 1916 (Jannings 3)
Steinbruch, 1942 (Schell 3)
Steinerne Reiter, 1923 (Hoffmann 4, Pommer 4)
Stella, 1950 (Mature 3, Sheridan 3, LeMaire 4)
Stella, 1955 (Cacoyannis 2, Mercouri 3)
Stella, 1990 (Midler 3, Van Runkle 4)
Stella Dallas, 1925 (King 2, Colman 3, Edeson 4, Goldwyn 4, Marion 4, Westmore Family 4)
Stella Dallas, 1937 (Vidor 2, Stanwyck 3, Day 4, Goldwyn 4, Maté 4, Newman 4)
Stella emigranti, 1990 (Lollobrigida 3)
Stella Maris, 1918 (Neiian 2, Pickford 3, Buckland 4, Marion 4)
Stella Parrish. See I Found Stella Parrish, 1935
Stelle emigranti, 1983 (Cardinale 3)
Stemning i April, 1947 (Henning-Jensen 2)
Sten Stensson Stéen fran Eslöv på nya äventyr, 1930 (Jaenzon 4)
Sten Stensson Stéen from Eslöv on New Adventures. See Sten Stensson Stéen fran Eslöv på nya äventyr, 1930
Štěňata, 1957 (Brejchová 3)
Stenka Rasin, 1936 (Volkov 2)
Stenographer Troubles, 1913 (Bunny 3)
Stenographer Wanted, 1912 (Bunny 3)
Step Down to Terror, 1958 (Metty 4)
Step Forward, 1922 (Sennett 2)
Step Lively, 1918 (Lloyd 3, Roach 4)
Step Lively, 1944 (Menjou 3, Sinatra 3, Cahn 4)
Step Lively Jeeves, 1937 (Pangborn 3)
Step on It, 1931 (Fleischer 4)
Step Out of Line, 1970 (Falk 3, Goldsmith 4)
Step to Darkness. See Krok do tmy, 1938
Sten Stensson Stéen fran Eslöv på nya äventyr, 1930 (Jaenzon 4)
Sten Stensson Stéen from Eslöv on New Adventures. See Sten Stensson Stéen fran Eslöv på nya äventyr, 1930

Step-Brothers, 1913 (Eason 4)
Step-Brothers. See Ibo koudai, 1957
Stepford Wives, 1974 (Goldman 4, Roizman 4, Smith 4)
Stéphane et la garde chasse, 1966 (Braunberger 4)
Stepmother, 1911 (Dwan 2)
Stepmother, 1914 (Lawrence 3)
Steppa, 1962 (Lattuada 2, Vanel 3, Donati 4, Pinelli 4)
Steppe. See Steppa, 1962
Steppe, 1977 (Bondarchuk 3)
Steppenwolf, 1974 (Sanda 3, Von Sydow 3)
Steppin' in Society, 1945 (Horton 3)
Stepping Fast, 1923 (Mix 3)
Stepping Out, 1919 (Niblo 2, Barnes 4, Sullivan 4)
Stepping Out, 1923 (Roach 4)
Stepping Out, 1929 (Roach 4)
Stepping Out, 1991 (Minnelli 3, Winters 3)
Stepping Stone, 1916 (Sullivan 4)
Stepping Toes, 1938 (Baxter 2)
Steps, 1984 (Papas 3)
Steps of Age, 1951 (Maddow 4)
Steps to the Moon. See Pasi spre lune, 1963
Stepsisters, 1910 (White 3)
Steptoe and Son Ride Again, 1973 (Dors 3)
Sterbende Modell, 1918 (Gad 2)
Sterbende Perlen, 1917 (Dupont 2)
Sterbende Völker, 1922 (Kortner 3, Wegener 3)
Stereo, 1969 (Cronenberg 2)
Sterile Cuckoo, 1969 (Pakula 2, Minnelli 3, Krasner 4, Sargent 4)
Sterimator Vesevo, 1920 (Gallone 2)
Sterling Metal. See Sporting Blood, 1940
Stern von Bethlehem, 1921 (Reiniger 4)
Stern von Damaskus, 1920 (Curtiz 2)
Stern von Valencia. See Etoile de Valencia, 1933
Sterne erlöschern nie, 1957 (Albers 3)
Stet priklyuchenni, 1929 (Ptushko 4)
Steuermann Holck, 1920 (Nielsen 3, Wegener 3)
Stevedores, 1937 (Lantz 4)
Steven Donoghue, 1926 (Balcon 4)
Stevie, 1978 (Howard 3, Jackson 3, Young 4)
Stew in the Caribbean. See Estouffade à la Carabei, 1967
Stewed, Fried and Boiled, 1929 (Benchley 4)
Stick, 1985 (Reynolds 3, Segal 3)
Stick Around, 1925 (Laurel and Hardy 3)
Stick, Start Beating!. See Obŭsku, z pytle ven!, 1956
Stick to Your Guns, 1941 (Harlan 4)
Stick to Your Story, 1926 (Brown 4)
Sticky Affair, 1916 (Laurel and Hardy 3)
Stier von Olivera, 1921 (Jannings 3, Messter 4, Metzner 4)
Stigma, 1913 (Bushman 3)
Stigmate, 1924 (Feuillade 2)
Stiletto, 1969 (Scheider 3, Levine 4)
Still Alarm, 1903 (Porter 2)
Still Alarm, 1930 (Webb 3)
Still Life, 1966 (Baillie 2)
Still Life. See Stilleben, 1969
Still of the Night, 1982 (Benton 2, Scheider 3, Streep 3, Almendros 4)
Still Watch, 1987 (Dickinson 3)
Stilla flirt, 1934 (Molander 2)
Stille nacht, 1988 (Quayle 3)

Stilleben, 1969 (Lenica 4)
Stilts. See Zancos, 1984
Stimme, 1920 (Dreier 4)
Stimme aus dem Äther, 1939 (Käutner 2)
Stimme des Anderen, 1952 (Kortner 3)
Stimulantia, 1967 (Molander 2, Andersson 3,
    Bergman 3, Björnstrand 3, Fischer 4)
Stín ve světle, 1928 (Stallich 4)
Sting, 1973 (Hill 2, Newman 3, Redford 3,
    Shaw 3, Bumstead 4, Hamlisch 4,
    Head 4, Reynolds 4, Surtees 4,
    Whitlock 4)
Sting II, 1983 (Malden 3, Reed 3, Schifrin 4)
Sting of the Lash, 1921 (King 2)
Sting of Victory, 1916 (Walthall 3)
Stingaree, 1915 (Glennon 4)
Stingaree, 1934 (Wellman 2, Dunne 3,
    Berman 4, Cooper 4, Plunkett 4,
    Steiner 4)
Stíny, 1921 (Heller 4)
Stips, 1951 (Fröhlich 3)
Stir Crazy, 1980 (Poitier 3, Pryor 3,
    Wilder 3)
Stitch in Time, 1963 (Wisdom 3)
Stjaalne Ansigt, 1914 (Psilander 3)
Sto dvadtsat tysyach v god, 1929
    (Maretskaya 3)
.Sto je radnički savjet, 1959 (Makavejev 2)
Stockade. See Cadence, 1990
Stockbroker. See För sin kärleks skull, 1913
Stock-Cars. See Tout casser, 1953
Stockholm, 1977 (Zetterling 2)
Stockholm, Pride of Sweden, 1937 (Hoch 4)
Stocks and Blondes, 1928 (Berman 4,
    Plunkett 4)
Støj, 1965 (Roos 2)
Stolen Affections. See Révoltée, 1947
Stolen Airship. See Ukradená vzducholod,
    1966
Stolen Assignment, 1955 (Fisher 2)
Stolen Birthright, 1910 (White 3)
Stolen Bride, 1913 (Gish 3, Sweet 3)
Stolen Bride, 1927 (Korda 2, Korda 4,
    Wilson 4)
Stolen by Gypsies, 1905 (Porter 2)
Stolen Face, 1952 (Fisher 2, Henreid 3,
    Carreras 4)
Stolen Frontier. See Uloupená hranice, 1947
Stolen Glory, 1912 (Sennett 2, Normand 3)
Stolen Goods, 1915 (Sweet 3)
Stolen Goods, 1924 (McCarey 2, Roach 4)
Stolen Harmony, 1935 (Raft 3, Wyman 3,
    Head 4)
Stolen Heart, See gestohlene Herz, 1934
Stolen Heaven, 1931 (Calhern 3, Folsey 4)
Stolen Heaven, 1938 (Dreier 4, Head 4)
Stolen Holiday, 1936 (Curtiz 2, Francis 3,
    Rains 3, Brown 4, Grot 4, Orry-Kelly 4,
    Robinson 4, Wallis 4)
Stolen Hours, 1963 (Hayward 3)
Stolen Jewels, 1908 (Griffith 2, Lawrence 3,
    Bitzer 4)
Stolen Jools, 1932 (Beery 3, Brown 3,
    Chevalier 3, Cooper 3, Dunne 3, Laurel
    and Hardy 3, Shearer 3)
Stolen Kiss, 1920 (Folsey 4)
Stolen Kisses. See Baisers volés, 1968
Stolen Life, 1939 (Bergner 3, Redgrave 3,
    Havelock-Allan 4)
Stolen Life, 1946 (Brennan 3, Davis 3,
    Ford 3, Friedhofer 4, Haller 4, Orry-
    Kelly 4, Polito 4, Steiner 4)
Stolen Love, 1928 (Plunkett 4)
Stolen Magic, 1915 (Sennett 2, Normand 3)

Stolen Masterpiece, 1914 (Loos 4)
Stolen Moccasins, 1913 (Mix 3)
Stolen Moments, 1920 (Valentino 3)
Stolen Paradise, 1917 (Edeson 4, Marion 4)
Stolen Purse, 1913 (Sennett 2)
Stolen Ranch, 1926 (Wyler 2)
Stolen Sweets, 1934 (Brown 4)
Stolz der 3 Kompagnie, 1931 (Walbrook 3)
Stolz der Firma, 1914 (Lubitsch 2)
Stone Age, 1922 (Roach 4)
Stone Age, 1931 (Lantz 4)
Stone Age Romeos, 1955 (Three Stooges 3)
Stone Boy, 1983 (Close 3)
Stone Boy, 1984 (Duvall 3)
Stone Flower. See Kammeny tsvetok, 1946
Stone Killer, 1973 (Bronson 3, De
    Laurentiis 4)
Stone of River Creek, 1935 (McCord 4)
Stone Pillow, 1985 (Lassally 4)
Stones Cry Out. See Let Them Live!, 1937
Stones for Ibarra, 1988 (Close 3)
Stooge, 1953 (Lewis 2, Martin 3, Head 4,
    Wallis 4)
Stooge for a Mouse, 1950 (Blanc 4,
    Freleng 4, Stalling 4)
Stooge to Conga, 1943 (Three Stooges 3)
Stool Pigeon, 1915 (Chaney 3)
Stoopnocracy, 1933 (Fleischer 4)
Stop Calling Me Baby!. See Moi, Fleur
    Bleue, 1978
Stop Kidding, 1921 (Roach 4)
Stop, Look, and Hasten!, 1954 (Blanc 4,
    Jones 4, Stalling 4)
Stop, Look, and Listen, 1926 (Laurel and
    Hardy 3, Berlin 4)
Stop, Look, and Listen, 1949 (Terry 4)
Stop! Luke! Listen!, 1917 (Daniels 3,
    Lloyd 3, Roach 4)
Stop Making Sense, 1984 (Demme 2)
Stop Me Before I Kill. See Full Treatment,
    1961
Stop Polio, 1981 (Jackson 3)
Stop That Noise, 1935 (Fleischer 4)
Stop That Tank, 1941 (Iwerks 4)
Stop the World—I Want to Get Off, 1966
    (Morris 4)
Stop Train 349. See Verspätung in
    Marienborn, 1963
Stop, You're Killing Me, 1952 (Dumont 3,
    Trevor 3, McCord 4)
Stopover Tokyo, 1957 (O'Brien 3,
    Wagner 3, Clarke 4, LeMaire 4,
    Reisch 4, Wheeler 4)
Stopping the Show, 1932 (Chevalier 3,
    Fleischer 4)
Stopping the Show. See Betty Boop's Rise to
    Fame, 1934
Stop-Press Girl, 1949 (More 3, Rank 4)
Stora äventyret, 1953 (Sucksdorff 2)
Stora famnen, 1939 (Jaenzon 4)
Stora Skrällen, 1943 (Fischer 4)
Storch hat uns getraut, 1933 (Dagover 3)
Storch streikt, 1931 (Planer 4)
Store, 1983 (Wiseman 2)
Store Fald or Malstrømmen, 1911 (Holger-
    Madsen 2)
Store Klaus og Lille Klaus, 1913
    (Christensen 2)
Store Magt, 1924 (Blom 2)
Stores and Blondes, 1928 (Miller 4)
Storia, 1986 (Comencini 2, Cardinale 3,
    Cecchi D'Amico 4)
Storia de fratelli e de cortelli, 1973 (De
    Sica 2)

Storia de Piera, 1983 (Huppert 3)
Storia de una donna, 1969 (Girardot 3)
Storia dei tredici, 1916 (Gallone 2)
Storia del pugliato degli antichi ad oggi,
    1974 (Brazzi 3)
Storia di ordinaria follia, 1981 (Sarde 4)
Storia di Piera, 1982 (Mastroianni 3,
    Schygulla 3)
Storia di una donna, 1969 (Andersson 3,
    Allen 4, Head 4, Williams 4)
Storia di un peccato, 1918 (Gallone 2)
Storia milanese, 1962 (Olmi 2)
Storia semplice, 1991 (Delli Colli 4)
Storie d'amore, 1942 (Mastroianni 3)
Storie delle invenzioni, 1959 (Bozzetto 4)
Storie di ordinaria follia, 1981 (Amidei 4,
    Delli Colli 4)
Storie di vita e malavita, 1975 (Morricone 4)
Storie scellerate, 1973 (Pasolini 2, Delli
    Colli 4)
Storie sulla sabbia, 1963 (Fusco 4)
Stories about Lenin. See Rasskazi o Lenine,
    1957
Stories of Ordinary Madness. See Storie di
    ordinaria follia, 1981
Stork Bites Man, 1947 (Cooper 3)
Stork Caliph. See Gólyakalifa, 1917
Stork Club, 1945 (Fitzgerald 3, Hutton 3,
    Benchley 4, Cahn 4, Carmichael 4,
    Head 4, Lang 4)
Stork Naked, 1955 (Blanc 4, Freleng 4)
Stork's Mistake, 1942 (Terry 4)
Storm, 1916 (Sweet 3)
Storm, 1925 (Fleischer 4)
Storm, 1930 (Huston 2, Wyler 2)
Storm, 1938 (Krasner 4)
Storm at Daybreak, 1933 (Francis 3,
    Huston 3, Adrian 4, Booth 4, Folsey 4)
Storm Boy, 1917 (Hathaway 2)
Storm Center, 1956 (Davis 3, Bass 4,
    Cohn 4, Duning 4, Guffey 4, Taradash 4)
Storm Fear, 1955 (Duryea 3, Grant 3,
    Wilde 3, La Shelle 4)
Storm in a Teacup, 1937 (Saville 2,
    Harrison 3, Leigh 3, Dalrymple 4,
    Hornbeck 4)
Storm in Tatra. See Děvčátko, neříkej ne!,
    1932
Storm of Passion. See Stürme der
    Leidenschaft, 1932
Storm of Strangers, 1970 (Maddow 4)
Storm of the Pacific. See Taiheiyo no arashi,
    1960
**Storm over Asia. See Potomok Chingis-
    Khan, 1928**
Storm over Bengal, 1938 (Canutt 4)
Storm over Lisbon, 1944 (Von Stroheim 2)
Storm over the Andes, 1935 (Schary 4)
Storm over the Nile, 1955 (Harvey 3, Lee 3,
    Korda 4, Sherriff 4)
Storm over Tjurö, 1954 (Nykvist 4)
Storm over Wyoming, 1949 (Hunt 4)
Storm View from Pompey's Head, 1955
    (Bernstein 4)
Storm Warning, 1951 (Brooks 2, Day 3,
    Reagan 3, Rogers 3, Wald 4, Westmore
    Family 4)
Storm Within. See Parents terribles, 1948
Stormfågeln, 1914 (Stiller 2, Jaenzon 4,
    Magnusson 4)
Storms of Passion. See Sturme der
    Leidenschaft, 1931
Stormswept, 1923 (Beery 3)
Stormy Era. See Showa no inochi, 1968

Stormy Knight, 1917 (Young 4)

Stormy Petrel. *See* Stormfågeln, 1914

Stormy Seas, 1932 (Iwerks 4)

Stormy, the Thoroughbred with an Inferiority Complex, 1953 (Crosby 4)

Stormy Waters. *See* Remorques, 1941

Stormy Weather, 1935 (Balcon 4, Rank 4, Vetchinsky 4)

Stormy Weather. *See* Remorques, 1941

Stormy Weather, 1943 (Horne 3, Robinson 3, Basevi 4, Garmes 4, Rose 4, Shamroy 4)

Störtebeker, 1920 (Hoffmann 4)

Story Book Review. *See* Mother Goose Presents Humpty Dumpty, 1946

Story Club, 1945 (Dreier 4)

Story from Chikamatsu. *See* **Chikamatsu monogatari, 1954**

Story in Scarlet, 1973 (Nowicki 3)

Story of Adele H. *See* Histoire d'Adèle H., 1975

Story of a Dog Who Had Fleas. *See* Historie blechatéto psa, 1958

Story of a Girl, 1949 (Zhao 3)

Story of a Love Affair. *See* Cronaca di un amore, 1950

Story of a Mosquito. *See* How a Mosquito Operates, 1912

Story of a Mother. *See* Historien om en moder, 1979

Story of a Patriot, 1957 (Herrmann 4)

Story of a Real Man, 1948 (Bondarchuk 3)

Story of a Recluse, 1987 (Granger 3)

Story of a Rose. *See* Román o ruži, 1972

Story of a Story, 1915 (Browning 2)

Story of a Twig, 1960 (Dinov 4)

Story of a Woman. *See* Storia di una donna, 1969

Story of a Woman. *See* Miei primi 40 anni, 1987

Story of Alexander Graham Bell, 1939 (Ameche 3, Coburn 3, Fonda 3, Young 3, MacGowan 4, Shamroy 4, Trotti 4, Zanuck 4)

Story of Chikamatsu. *See* **Chikamatsu monogatari, 1954**

Story of Colonel Drake, 1955 (Price 3)

Story of David, 1960 (Pleasence 3)

Story of Dr. Carver, 1938 (Zinnemann 2)

Story of Dr. Ehrlich's Magic Bullet, 1940 (Calhern 3, Crisp 3, Gordon 3, Robinson 3, Burks 4, Friedhofer 4, Howe 4, Steiner 4, Wallis 4)

Story of Dr. Wassell, 1944 (De Mille 2, Cooper 3, De Carlo 3, Bennett 4, Dreier 4, Edouart 4, Young 4)

Story of Esther Costello, 1957 (Clayton 2, Brazzi 3, Crawford 3, Love 3, Auric 4, Krasker 4)

Story of G.I. Joe, 1945 (Aldrich 2, Wellman 2, Meredith 3, Mitchum 3, Metty 4)

Story of Gilbert and Sullivan, 1953 (Launder and Gilliat 2, Finch 3, Challis 4, Heckroth 4, Korda 4)

Story of Gösta Berling. *See* **Gösta Berlings saga, 1923**

Story of Hansel and Gretel, 1951 (Harryhausen 4)

Story of Hollywood, 1988 (Reynolds 3)

Story of Irene and Vernon Castle, 1939 (Brennan 3)

Story of Jacob and Joseph, 1974 (Bates 3, Theodorakis 4)

Story of King Midas, 1953 (Harryhausen 4)

Story of Little John Bailey, 1968 (Driessen 4)

Story of Little Mook. *See* Geschichte des kleinen Muck, 1953

Story of Little Red Riding Hood, 1949 (Harryhausen 4)

Story of Louis Pasteur, 1936 (Dieterle 2, Muni 3, Blanke 4, Gaudio 4, Wallis 4, Warner 4, Westmore Family 4)

Story of Love and Revenge. *See* Probuzené svědomí, 1919

Story of Mandy. *See* Mandy, 1952

Story of Mankind, 1957 (Bushman 3, Carradine 3, Coburn 3, Colman 3, Hopper 3, Horton 3, Lamarr 3, Lorre 3, Marx Brothers 3, Moorehead 3, Pangborn 3, Price 3, Bennett 4, Musuraca 4)

Story of Michelangelo, 1949 (Flaherty 2)

Story of Montana, 1912 (Anderson 3)

Story of Monte Cristo. *See* Comte de Monte Cristo, 1961

Story of Oil, 1921 (Balcon 4)

Story of One Day. *See* Příběh jednoho dne, 1926

Story of Papworth, 1936 (Carroll 3)

Story of Piera. *See* Storia di Piera, 1982

Story of Pretty Boy Floyd, 1974 (Sheen 3)

Story of Private Pooley, 1962 (Anderson 2)

Story of Robin Hood and His Merrie Men, 1952 (Dillon 4, Disney 4, Ellenshaw 4, Green 4, Unsworth 4)

Story of Rommel. *See* Desert Fox, 1951

Story of Rosie's Rose, 1911 (Lawrence 3)

Story of Ruth, 1960 (Waxman 4)

Story of Seabiscuit, 1949 (Fitzgerald 3, Temple 3)

Story of Tank Commander Nishizumi. *See* Nishizumi sanshacho den, 1940

Story of Temple Drake, 1933 (Carradine 3, Hopkins 3, McDaniel 3, Faulkner 4, Struss 4)

Story of the Company President's Overseas Travels. *See* Shachou koukou-ko, 1962

Story of the Count of Monte Cristo. *See* Comte de Monte Cristo, 1961

Story of the Last Chrysanthemum. *See* Zangiku monogatari, 1939

Story of the Last Chrysanthemums. *See* Zangiku monogatari, 1939

Story of the Last Chrysanthemums. *See* Zangiku monogatari, 1956

Story of the Motorcar Engine, 1958 (Williams 4)

Story of the Old Gun, 1914 (Anderson 3)

Story of the Turbulent Years. *See* Povest plamennykh, 1961

Story of the Wheel, 1934 (Jennings 2)

Story of Three Loves, 1953 (Minnelli 2, Barrymore 3, Caron 3, Douglas 3, Mason 3, Moorehead 3, Ames 4, Rose 4, Rosher 4, Rosson 4, Rozsa 4)

Story of Tosca. *See* Tosca, 1940

Story of Vernon and Irene Castle, 1939 (Astaire 3, Rogers 3, Berman 4, Pan 4, Plunkett 4, Polglase 4)

Story of Vickie. *See* Mädchenjahre einer Königen, 1954

Story of Will Rogers, 1952 (Curtiz 2, Cantor 3, Wyman 3, Young 4)

Story of Women. *See* Affaire des femmes, 1989

Story on Page One, 1959 (Hayworth 3, Bernstein 4, Howe 4, Wald 4, Wheeler 4)

Story the Desert Told, 1913 (Anderson 3)

Story without a Name, 1924 (Costello 3, Rosson 4)

Stout Heart But Weak Knees, 1914 (Sennett 2)

Stowaway, 1932 (Wray 3, Shamroy 4)

Stowaway, 1936 (Faye 3, Temple 3, Young 3, Miller 4)

Stowaway, 1980 (Halas and Batchelor 4)

Stowaway Girl. *See* Manuela, 1957

Stowaway in the Sky, 1962 (Lemmon 3)

Stowaway to the Moon, 1975 (Carradine 3)

Stowaways, 1949 (Terry 4)

Strada, 1949 (Delli Colli 4)

Strada, 1954 (Fellini 2, Masina 3, Quinn 3, De Laurentiis 4, Flaiano 4, Pinelli 4, Ponti 4, Rota 4)

Strada lunga un'anno. *See* Cesta duga godinu dana, 1958

Strade di Napoli, 1947 (Risi 2)

Stradivari. *See* Stradivarius, 1935 (Fröhlich 3)

Stradivari, 1989 (Cecchi D'Amico 4, Delli Colli 4)

Stradivarius, 1935 (Feuillère 3)

Strafbare Ehe. *See* Blutschande die 173 St. G.B., 1929

Straight and Narrow, 1918 (Laurel and Hardy 3)

Straight Crook, 1921 (Roach 4)

Straight from the Heart, 1935 (Astor 3)

Straight from the Shoulder, 1921 (Laurel and Hardy 3)

Straight from the Shoulder, 1936 (Bellamy 3)

Straight on till Morning, 1972 (Carreras 4)

Straight, Place and Show, 1938 (Zanuck 4)

Straight Road, 1914 (Dwan 2)

Straight Shooter, 1940 (Katzman 4)

Straight Shootin', 1927 (Wyler 2)

Straight Shooting, 1917 (Ford 2)

Straight Time, 1978 (Hoffman 3, Stanton 3, Roizman 4, Sargent 4)

Straight to Hell, 1987 (Hooper 3)

Straightaway, 1934 (Bond 3)

Straight-Jacket, 1964 (Crawford 3)

Strained Pearl, 1916 (King 2)

Strait. *See* Kaikyou, 1982

Strait-Jacket, 1964 (Leven 4)

Straits of Love and Hate. *See* Aienkyo, 1937

Strakonický dudák, 1955 (Zeman 4)

Strana la vita, 1987 (Morricone 4)

Strana rodnaya, 1942 (Shub 2)

Strana Sovietov, 1937 (Shub 2)

Stranded, 1916 (Laurel and Hardy 3)

Stranded, 1917 (Love 3, Loos 4)

Stranded, 1927 (Loos 4)

Stranded, 1935 (Borzage 2, Daves 2, Francis 3, Grot 4, Orry-Kelly 4)

Stranded, 1987 (O'Sullivan 3)

Stranded in Arcady, 1917 (Miller 4)

Stranded in Paris, 1926 (Daniels 3, Mankiewicz 4)

Stranded in Paris. *See* Artists and Models Abroad, 1938

Strandhugg, 1950 (Sucksdorff 2)

Strange Adventure, 1932 (Shamroy 4)

Strange Affair, 1944 (Three Stooges 3, Planer 4)

Strange Affair of Uncle Harry. *See* Uncle Harry, 1945

Strange Affliction of Anton Bruckner, 1990 (Russell 2)

Strange Alibi, 1941 (Kennedy 3)

Strange Alibi. *See* Strange Triangle, 1946

Strange Bedfellows, 1965 (Hudson 3, Terry-Thomas 3, Lollobrigida 3, Frank 4)

Strange Birds, 1930 (Sennett 2)

Strange Boarder, 1920 (Rogers 3)

Strange Boarders, 1938 (Launder and Gilliat 2, Withers 3)

Strange Brew, 1983 (Von Sydow 3)

Strange Cargo, 1929 (Glazer 4, Miller 4)

Strange Cargo, 1936 (Sanders 3)

Strange Cargo, 1940 (Borzage 2, Mankiewicz 2, Crawford 3, Gable 3, Lorre 3, Lukas 3, Adrian 4, Mayer 4, Waxman 4)

Strange Case. *See* Záhadný případ, 1919

Strange Case of Captain Ramper. *See* Ramper, der Tiermensch, 1927

Strange Case of Clara Dean, 1932 (Zukor 4)

Strange Case of Dr. Jekyll and Mr. Hyde, 1968 (Homolka 3)

Strange Case of Dr. Rx, 1942 (Three Stooges 3, Salter 4)

Strange Case of Madeleine. *See* Madeleine, 1949

Strange Case of Mary Page, 1916 (Walthall 3)

Strange Case of the Cosmic Rays, 1957 (Capra 2)

Strange Case of the End of Civilisation as We Know It, 1977 (Cleese 3)

Strange Confession. *See* Imposter, 1944

Strange Conspiracy. *See* President Vanishes, 1934

Strange Death of Adolf Hitler, 1943 (Kortner 3, Salter 4)

Strange Deception. *See* Cristo proibito, 1951

Strange Door, 1951 (Karloff 3, Laughton 3, Salter 4)

Strange Evidence, 1933 (Biro 4, Korda 4)

Strange Experiment, 1937 (Sim 3)

Strange Holiday, 1945 (Rains 3)

Strange Idols, 1922 (Furthman 4)

Strange Illusion, 1945 (Ulmer 2, Page 3)

Strange Impersonation, 1946 (Mann 2)

Strange Incident. *See* **Ox-Bow Incident, 1942**

Strange Interlude, 1932 (Gable 3, O'Sullivan 3, Walthall 3, Young 3, Adrian 4, Booth 4, Garmes 4, Mayer 4, Meredyth 4, Sullivan 4, Thalberg 4)

Strange Interlude, 1988 (Ferrer 3, Jackson 3)

Strange Interval. *See* Strange Interlude, 1932

Strange Intruder, 1956 (Lupino 3)

Strange Invaders, 1982 (Addison 4)

Strange Lady in Town, 1955 (LeRoy 2, Andrews 3, Garson 3, Rosson 4, Tiomkin 4)

Strange Life!, 1988 (Morricone 4)

Strange Love Affair, 1984 (Alekan 4)

Strange Love of Martha Ivers, 1946 (Aldrich 2, Edwards 2, Milestone 2, Rossen 2, Douglas 3, Stanwyck 3, Dreier 4, Head 4, Rozsa 4, Wallis 4)

Strange Love of Molly Louvain, 1932 (Curtiz 2)

Strange Meeting, 1909 (Griffith 2, Pickford 3)

Strange New World, 1975 (Smith 4)

Strange One, 1957 (Guffey 4, Spiegel 4)

Strange Passion of a Kiss. *See* Lyubov silna na strastyou potseluya, 1916

Strange People, 1933 (Brennan 3)

Strange People. *See* Strannye lyudi, 1969

Strange Place to Meet. *See* Drole d'endroit pour une rencontre, 1988

Strange Possession of Mrs. Oliver, 1977 (Black 3)

Strange Rider, 1925 (Canutt 4)

Strange Triangle, 1946 (Basevi 4, LeMaire 4)

Strange Voyage, 1946 (Anhalt 4)

Strange Woman, 1946 (Ulmer 2, Lamarr 3, Sanders 3, Stromberg 4)

Stranger, 1910 (Olcott 2)

Stranger, 1917 (Laurel and Hardy 3)

Stranger, 1946 (Huston 2, Welles 2, Robinson 3, Young 3, D'Agostino 4, Kaper 4, Metty 4, Spiegel 4, Veiller 4)

Stranger. *See* Straniero, 1967

Stranger and the Gunfighter, 1976 (Van Cleef 3)

Stranger at Coyote, 1911 (Dwan 2)

Stranger Came Home, 1954 (Goddard 3, Carreras 4)

Stranger from Venus, 1954 (Neal 3)

Stranger in Between. *See* Hunted, 1952

Stranger in Love, 1932 (Banton 4)

Stranger in My Arms, 1959 (Käutner 2, Allyson 3, Astor 3, Coburn 3, Daniels 4, Hunter 4)

Stranger in the House, 1967 (Chaplin 3, Mason 3)

Stranger in the House, 1990 (Stamp 3, Stanton 3)

Stranger in Town, 1943 (Lennart 4, Schary 4)

Stranger Is Watching, 1982 (Schifrin 4)

Stranger on Horseback, 1955 (Tourneur 2, Carradine 3, McCrea 3)

Stranger on the Prowl, 1952 (Losey 2, Alekan 4)

Stranger on the Run, 1967 (Siegel 2, Baxter 3, Duryea 3, Fonda 3, Mineo 3)

Stranger on the Third Floor, 1940 (Lorre 3, D'Agostino 4, Musuraca 4, Polglase 4)

Stranger Rides Again, 1938 (Terry 4)

Stranger Than Fiction, 1921 (Schulberg 4)

Stranger Than Love. *See* Stärker al die Liebe, 1938

Stranger Than Paradise, 1984 (Jarmusch 2)

Stranger Walked In. *See* Love from a Stranger, 1947

Stranger Within a Woman. *See* Onna no naka ni iru tanin, 1966

Stranger Wore a Gun, 1953 (De Toth 2, Borgnine 3, Marvin 3, Scott 3, Trevor 3, Brown 4)

Strangers. *See* **Viaggio in Italia, 1953**

Strangers, 1979 (Davis 3)

Strangers All, 1935 (Vidor 2, Plunkett 4)

Stranger's Banquet, 1922 (Neilan 2, Bosworth 3)

Stranger's Hand. *See* Mano dello straniero, 1953

Strangers in Love, 1932 (Francis 3, March 3)

Strangers in 7A, 1972 (Lupino 3)

Strangers in the Night, 1944 (Mann 2)

Strangers May Kiss, 1931 (Montgomery 3, Shearer 3, Adrian 4, Daniels 4)

Strangers of the Evening, 1932 (Edeson 4)

Strangers of the Night, 1923 (Niblo 2, Mayer 4, Meredyth 4, Sullivan 4)

Strangers on a Honeymoon, 1936 (Launder and Gilliat 2)

Strangers on a Train, 1951 (Hitchcock 2, Walker 3, Burks 4, Chandler 4, Tiomkin 4)

Strangers on Honeymoon, 1936 (Balcon 4, Metzner 4)

Stranger's Return, 1933 (Vidor 2, Barrymore 3, Bondi 3, Hopkins 3, Adrian 4, Daniels 4)

Strangers: The Story of a Mother and Daughter, 1979 (Rowlands 3, Horner 4)

Strangers When We Meet, 1960 (Douglas 3, Matthau 3, Novak 3, Duning 4, Lang 4)

Strangled Eggs, 1961 (Blanc 4, McKimson 4)

Stranglehold: Delta Force II, 1990 (Golan and Globus 4)

Strangler, 1962 (Lourié 4)

Strangler of the Swamp, 1945 (Edwards 2)

Stranglers of Bombay, 1959 (Fisher 2, Bernard 4, Carreras 4)

Strangling Threads, 1922 (Hepworth 2)

Straniero, 1967 (Visconti 2, Blier 3, Karina 3, Mastroianni 3, Cecchi D'Amico 4, De Laurentiis 4, Rotunno 4)

Strannye lyudi, 1969 (Shukshin 3)

Strapless, 1989 (Ganz 3, Delerue 4)

Straschnaia miest, 1913 (Mozhukin 3)

Strasnia pokoynik, 1912 (Mozhukin 3)

Strasphere, 1983 (Zeffirelli 2)

Strass et cie, 1915 (Gaumont 4)

Strass et compagnie, 1915 (Gance 2)

Strasse des Bösen. *See* Via Mala, 1948

Strategia del ragno, 1969 (Valli 3, Storaro 4)

Strategic Air Command, 1955 (Mann 2, Allyson 3, Stewart 3, Head 4, Young 4)

Strategic Command, 1954 (Daniels 4)

Strategy, 1930 (Rooney 3)

Strategy of Broncho Billy's Sweetheart, 1914 (Anderson 3)

Stratford Adventure, 1954 (Guinness 3)

Stratos-Fear, 1933 (Iwerks 4)

Stratton Story, 1949 (Wood 2, Allyson 3, Moorehead 3, Stewart 3, Deutsch 4, Rose 4, Rosson 4)

Strauberg ist Da, 1978 (Piccoli 3)

Strauss's Great Waltz. *See* Waltzes from Vienna, 1934

Stravinsky Portrait, 1964 (Leacock 2)

Straw Dogs, 1971 (Peckinpah 2, Hoffman 3)

Straw Hat. *See* Slaměnný klobouk, 1971

Strawberry Blonde, 1941 (Walsh 2, Cagney 3, De Havilland 3, Hayworth 3, Epstein 4, Howe 4, Orry-Kelly 4, Wallis 4)

Strawberry Roan, 1933 (McCord 4)

Strawberry Roan, 1948 (Autry 3)

Strawberry Statement, 1970 (Ames 4, Winkler 4)

Straws in the Wind, 1924 (Matthews 3)

Stray Dog. *See* Norainu, 1949

Straziami ma di baci saziami, 1968 (Age and Scarpelli 4)

Stream Line. *See* linea del fiume, 1976

Streamers, 1983 (Altman 2)

Streamline Express, 1935 (Lewis 2)

Streamlined Greta Green, 1937 (Freleng 4)

Streamlined Swing, 1938 (Keaton 2)

Streams. *See* Proudy, 1922

Street Angel, 1928 (Borzage 2, Gaynor 3)

Street Angel. *See* Malu tianshi, 1937

Street Cat Named Sylvester, 1953 (Blanc 4, Foster 4, Freleng 4, Stalling 4)

Street Corner, 1948 (Miller 4)

Street Corner, 1953 (Box 4, Rank 4)

Street Corners, 1929 (Laszlo 4)

Street Girl, 1929 (Murfin 4, Plunkett 4)
Street Girls, 1974 (Corman 2, Levinson 2)
Street Hunter, 1990 (Golan and Globus 4)
Street Meat, 1959 (Vanderbeek 2)
Street of Abandoned Children, 1929
 (Negri 3)
Street of Chance, 1930 (Cromwell 2,
 Arthur 3, Francis 3, Powell 3, Coffee 4,
 Estabrook 4, Lang 4, Selznick 4)
Street of Chance, 1942 (Meredith 3,
 Trevor 3, Dreier 4, Fort 4)
Street of Forgotten Men, 1925 (Brenon 2,
 Brooks 2, Rosson 4)
Street of Illusion, 1928 (Walker 4)
Street of Memories, 1940 (Clarke 4,
 Day 4)
Street of Missing Men, 1939 (Carey 3)
Street of No Return, 1989 (Fuller 2)
Street of Shadows. See Mademoiselle
 Docteur, 1936
Street of Shadows, 1953 (Kendall 3)
Street of Shame. See Akasen chitai, 1956
Street of Sin, 1928 (Stiller 2, Jannings 3,
 Wray 3, Dreier 4, Glazer 4, Glennon 4,
 Schulberg 4)
Street of Sorrow. See Freudlose Gasse, 1925
Street of Women, 1932 (Beavers 3,
 Francis 3)
Street Scene, 1931 (Vidor 2, Bondi 3,
 Sidney 3, Barnes 4, Day 4, Goldwyn 4,
 Newman 4)
Street Scenes, 1970 (Scorsese 2)
Street Singer, 1937 (Lockwood 3)
Street Sketches. See Gaijo no suketchi, 1925
Street Smart, 1987 (Golan and Globus 4)
Street Urchin. See Uličnice, 1936
Street with No Name, 1948 (Widmark 3,
 LeMaire 4, Reynolds 4, Wheeler 4)
**Streetcar Named Desire, 1951 (Kazan 2,
 Brando 3, Leigh 3, Malden 3, Day 4,
 North 4, Stradling 4, Warner 4)**
Streetfighter. See Hard Times, 1975
Streets of Fire, 1984 (Hill 2)
Streets of Gold, 1986 (Brandauer 3)
Streets of Greenwood, 1963 (Emshwiller 2)
Streets of Illusion, 1917 (Barthelmess 3)
Streets of L.A., 1979 (Woodward 3)
Streets of Laredo, 1949 (Bendix 3, Holden 3,
 Dreier 4, Young 4)
Streets of New York, 1939 (Cooper 3)
Streets of San Francisco, 1972 (Douglas 3,
 Malden 3, Wagner 3)
Streets of Shanghai, 1927 (Wong 3)
Streets of Sorrow. See Freudlose Gasse,
 1925
Streetwalkin', 1985 (Corman 2)
Strega in amore, 1966 (Volonté 3)
Streghe, 1967 (Visconti 2, Eastwood 3,
 Girardot 3, Mangano 3, Sordi 3, Age and
 Scarpelli 4, De Laurentiis 4,
 Morricone 4, Zavattini 4)
Streit um den Knaben Jo, 1937 (Dagover 3)
Strejken, 1915 (Sjöström 2, Jaenzon 4,
 Magnusson 4)
Strength o' Ten, 1914 (Eason 4)
Strength of the Pines, 1922 (Polito 4)
Stresemann, 1956 (Aimée 3)
Stress es tres, tres, 1968 (Saura 2, Chaplin 3)
Stress is Three, Three. See Stress es tres, tres,
 1968
Stříbrná oblaka, 1938 (Stallich 4)
Strictly Business, 1910 (White 3)
Strictly Confidential. See Broadway Bill,
 1934

Strictly Dishonorable, 1931 (Stahl 2,
 Struges 2, Lukas 3, Freund 4)
Strictly Dishonorable, 1951 (Sturges 2,
 Leigh 3, Frank 4, Rose 4)
Strictly Dynamite, 1934 (Durante 3,
 Pangborn 3, Cronjager 4, Plunkett 4,
 Steiner 4)
Strictly for Pleasure. See Perfect Furlough,
 1958
Strictly in the Groove, 1943 (O'Connor 3,
 Pangborn 3, Three Stooges 3)
Strictly Modern, 1922 (Roach 4)
Strictly Personal, 1933 (Calhern 3, Head 4,
 Krasner 4, Robinson 4)
Strictly Unconventional, 1930 (Booth 4,
 Daniels 4, Gibbons 4)
Strictly Unreliable, 1932 (Roach 4)
Stride, Soviet!. See Shagai, Soviet!, 1926
Striden går vidare, 1941 (Molander 2,
 Sjöström 2)
Strife over the Boy Jo. See Streit um den
 Knaben Jo, 1937
Strife with Father, 1950 (Blanc 4,
 McKimson 4, Stalling 4)
Strike, 1909 (Porter 2)
Strike. See Strejken, 1915
Strike. See **Stachka, 1925**
Strike!. See Red Ensign, 1934
Strike at the Little Johnny Mine, 1911
 (Anderson 3)
Strike Force, 1975 (Gere 3)
Strike Me Pink, 1936 (Cantor 3, Alton 4,
 Day 4, Goldwyn 4, Newman 4, Toland 4)
Strike Up the Band, 1930 (Fleischer 4)
Strike Up the Band, 1940 (Berkeley 2,
 Garland 3, Rooney 3, Edens 4, Freed 4,
 Mayer 4, Shearer 4)
String Bean Jack, 1938 (Terry 4)
String Beans, 1918 (Ince 4, Zukor 4)
String of Pearls, 1911 (Griffith 2, Bitzer 4)
Strip, 1951 (Rooney 3, Pasternak 4, Rose 4,
 Surtees 4)
Stripes, 1981 (Oates 3, Bernstein 4)
Stripes and Stars, 1929 (Lantz 4)
Stripped to Kill, 1987 (Corman 2)
Stripper, 1963 (Trevor 3, Woodward 3,
 Goldsmith 4, Smith 4, Wald 4)
Strip-Tease, 1957 (Borowczyk 2, Lenica 4)
Strip-Tease, 1976 (Rey 3, Stamp 3)
Strogoff, 1968 (Bergner 3)
Strohfeuer, 1972 (Von Trotta 2)
Stroker Ace, 1983 (Reynolds 3, Needham 4)
**Stromboli, 1950 (Rossellini 2, Bergman 3,
 Amidei 4)**
Stromboli, terra di dio. See **Stromboli, 1950**
Strømlinjede gris, 1952 (Roos 2)
Strong Boy, 1929 (Ford 2, McLaglen 3,
 August 4)
Strong Man, 1926 (Capra 2, Garnett 2,
 Langdon 3)
Strong Medicine, 1986 (Green 4)
Strong Revenge, 1913 (Sennett 2,
 Normand 3)
Strong to the Finich, 1934 (Fleischer 4)
Stronger, 1976 (Grant 3)
Stronger Love. See Tween Two Loves, 1911
Stronger Man, 1911 (Dwan 2)
Stronger Mind, 1915 (Chaney 3)
Stronger Sex, 1931 (Lanchester 3, Balcon 4)
Stronger Than Death, 1915 (Chaney 3)
Stronger Than Death, 1920 (Guy 2,
 Nazimova 3, Carré 4)
Stronger Than Desire, 1939 (Pidgeon 3,
 Daniels 4)

Stronger Than Fear. See Edge of Doom,
 1950
Strongest, 1920 (Walsh 2, Fox 4)
Strongest. See Starkaste, 1929
Strongheart, 1914 (Barrymore 3, Sweet 3,
 Walthall 3, Gaudio 4)
Stronghold, 1952 (Lake 3, Cortex 4)
Stroszek, 1977 (Herzog 2)
Struggle, 1913 (Anderson 3)
Struggle, 1931 (Griffith 2, Emerson 4,
 Loos 4, Ruttenberg 4)
Struggle. See Borza, 1935
Struggle for His Heart. See Kampen om hans
 hjärta, 1916
Struggle in the Steeple. See Tools of
 Providence, 1915
Struggling Hearts. See Vergödö szívek, 1916
Struktura kryształu, 1969 (Olbrychski 3)
Strum in Wasserglas. See Blumenfrau von
 Lindenau, 1931
Strumfreie Junggeselle. See Moblierte
 Zimmer, 1929
Strýček z Ameriky, 1933 (Stallich 4)
Stubbs' New Servants, 1911 (Sennett 2)
Stuck on You!, 1983 (Rosenblum 4)
Stud, 1978 (Cahn 4)
Stud. Chem. Helene Willfüer, 1929
 (Tschechowa 3, Planer 4)
Studenci, 1916 (Negri 3)
Student Nurses, 1970 (Corman 2)
Student of Prague. See **Student von Prag,
 1913**
Student Prince. See Alt-Heidelberg, 1923
Student Prince, 1927 (Shearer 3, Dreier 4,
 Mayer 4)
Student Prince, 1954 (Calhern 3, Levien 4,
 Pan 4, Pasternak 4, Plunkett 4, Rose 4)
Student Prince in Old Heidelberg, 1927
 (Lubitsch 2, Novarro 3, Day 4,
 Gibbons 4, Kräly 4)
Student Teachers, 1973 (Corman 2)
Student Tour, 1934 (Durante 3, Eddy 3,
 Grable 3, Brown 4, Dunne 4, Freed 4)
**Student von Prag, 1913 (Wegener 3,
 Geleen 4)**
Student von Prag, 1926 (Krauss 3, Veidt 3,
 Galeen 4, Warm 4)
Student von Prag, 1935 (Walbrook 3,
 Warm 4)
Studies for Louisiana Story, 1967
 (Flaherty 2)
Studio Bankside, 1977 (Jarman 2)
Studio Murder Mystery, 1928 (March 3)
Studio Stoops, 1950 (Three Stooges 3)
Studs Lonigan, 1960 (Nicholson 3, Fields 4,
 Goldsmith 4, Wexler 4)
Study in Choreography for Camera, 1945
 (Deren 2)
Study in Scarlet, 1914 (Pearson 2)
Study in Scarlet, 1933 (Florey 2, Wong 3,
 Edeson 4)
Study in Terror, 1965 (Quayle 3)
Study Opus I—Man, 1976 (Popescu-
 Gopo 4)
Stuff, 1986 (Cohen 2)
Stuff Heroes Are Made Of, 1910 (Griffith 2,
 Bitzer 4)
Stuffie, 1940 (Zinnemann 2)
Stumme, 1975 (Schygulla 3)
Stunde der Versuchung, 1936 (Baarová 3,
 Fröhlich 3, Wegener 3)
Stunt Man, 1924 (Sennett 2)
Stunt Man, 1980 (O'Toole 3)
Stuntman, 1969 (Lollobrigida 3)

Stunts Unlimited, 1980 (Needham 4)

Stupid Bom. *See* Dum Bom, 1953

Stupid Cupid, 1944 (Blanc 4)

Stupor Duck, 1956 (Blanc 4, McKimson 4, Stalling 4)

Stupor Salesman, 1948 (Blanc 4, Stalling 4)

Stürme der Leidenschaft, 1931 (Siodmak 2, Jannings 3, Pommer 4)

Stürme des Lebens, 1918 (Krauss 3)

Stürme über dem Montblanc, 1930 (Riefenstahl 2)

Sturmflut, 1917 (Dupont 2)

Stürmtruppen, 1976 (Rotunno 4)

Stuttgart, die Grossstadt zwischen Wald und Reben, 1935 (Ruttman 2)

Stutzen der Gesellschaft, 1935 (Sirk 2)

Štvaní lidé, 1933 (Stallich 4)

Stydno skazat, 1930 (Maretskaya 3)

Style. *See* Andaz, 1949

Su exelencia, 1966 (Cantinflas 3)

Su última aventura, 1946 (Figueroa 4)

Subah, 1983 (Patil 3)

Subarashii akujo, 1963 (Takemitsu 4)

Subarashiki musumetachi, 1959 (Tanaka 3)

Subduing of Mrs. Nag, 1911 (Bunny 3, Normand 3)

Sube y bajo, 1958 (Cantinflas 3)

Subida al cielo, 1951 (Buñuel 2)

Subject Was Roses, 1968 (Neal 3, Sheen 3, Jenkins 4)

Submarine, 1910 (Gaudio 4)

Submarine, 1928 (Capra 2, Cohn 4, Walker 4)

Submarine Command, 1951 (Bendix 3, Holden 3, Ames 4, Head 4)

Submarine Control, 1949 (Halas and Batchelor 4)

Submarine D-1, 1937 (Bacon 2, Crawford 3, Deutsch 4, Edeson 4, Haskin 4, Steiner 4)

Submarine Patrol, 1938 (Ford 2, Bond 3, Carradine 3, Miller 4, Zanuck 4)

Submarine Pirate, 1915 (Sennett 2)

Submarine X-1, 1968 (Caan 3)

Submarine Zone. *See* Escape to Glory, 1941

Submissive. *See* Untertan, 1949

Subpoena Server, 1906 (Bitzer 4)

Substitute Minister, 1915 (Eason 4)

Substitute Model, 1912 (Bosworth 3)

Substitute Wife, 1925 (Stradling 4)

Subterraneans, 1960 (Caron 3, McDowall 3, Freed 4, Ruttenberg 4)

Suburban House. *See* Dum no předměstí, 1933

Subway, 1985 (Adjani 3, Trauner 4)

Subway Express, 1931 (Walker 4)

Subway in the Sky, 1959 (Johnson 3, Box 4)

Subway Sadie, 1926 (Edeson 4)

Succès de la prestidigitation. *See* Max escamoteur, 1912

Success, 1923 (Astor 3)

Success. *See* Successo, 1963

Success. *See* American Success Company, 1979

Success, 1991 (Keaton 3)

Success at Any Price, 1934 (Horton 3, Moore 3, Cooper 4, Plunkett 4, Steiner 4)

Success is the Best Revenge, 1984 (Skolimowski 2, Aimée 3, Hurt 3, Piccoli 3)

Successful Calamity, 1932 (Arliss 3, Astor 3, Scott 3)

Successful Failure, 1913 (Beery 3)

Successful Man. *See* Hombre de exito, 1986

Successo, 1963 (Aimée 3, Gassman 3, Trintignant 3, Morricone 4)

Such a Cook, 1914 (Sennett 2)

Such a Gorgeous Kid Like Me. *See* Belle Fille comme moi, 1972

Such a Hunter, 1914 (Bunny 3)

Such a Little Queen, 1914 (Porter 2, Crisp 3, Pickford 3)

Such a Little Queen, 1921 (Haller 4)

Such a Pretty Cloud, 1971 (Schell 3)

Such Good Friends, 1971 (Preminger 2, Meredith 3, Bass 4, May 4)

Such High Mountains, 1974 (Bondarchuk 3)

Such Is Life, 1915 (Chaney 3)

Such Is Life. *See* Takový je zivot, 1930

Such Men Are Dangerous, 1930 (Lugosi 3, Vajda 4)

Such Men Are Dangerous. *See* Racers, 1955

Sucker. *See* Life of Jimmy Dolan, 1933

Sucre, 1978 (Depardieu 3, Piccoli 3, Sarde 4)

Sud niente di nuovo, 1956 (Bertini 3)

Sud v Smolenske, 1946 (Shub 2)

Sudario a la medida. *See* Candidato per un assassino, 1969

Sudba cheloveka, 1959 (Bondarchuk 3)

Sudden Fear, 1952 (Crawford 3, Grahame 3, Palance 3, Bernstein 4, Coffee 4, Lang 4, Leven 4)

Sudden Fortune of the Poor People of Kombach. *See* Plötzliche Reichtum der armen Leute von Kombach, 1970

Sudden Impact, 1983 (Eastwood 3, Schifrin 4)

Sudden Money, 1939 (Crawford 3, Head 4)

Suddenly, 1954 (Hayden 3, Sinatra 3, Clarke 4, Raksin 4)

Suddenly. *See* Achanak, 1973

Suddenly Bad Names. *See* Akumyo niwaka, 1965

Suddenly It's Spring, 1947 (Leisen 2, Goddard 3, MacMurray 3, Dreier 4, Young 4)

Suddenly Last Summer, 1959 (Mankiewicz 2, Clift 3, Hepburn 3, McCambridge 3, Taylor 3, Arnold 4, Fisher 4, Hornbeck 4, Spiegel 4)

Suddenly, Love, 1978 (Hunter 4)

Suddenly Single, 1971 (Moorehead 3)

Suds, 1920 (Pickford 3, Rosher 4, Young 4)

Sue My Lawyer, 1938 (Langdon 3)

Sued for Libel, 1940 (Polglase 4)

Sueño del Pongo, 1970 (Alvarez 2)

Suenos de oro, 1956 (Figueroa 4)

Sueños y realidades, 1961 (Sanjinés 2)

Suez, 1938 (Dwan 2, Power 3, Young 3, Clarke 4, Dunne 4, Raksin 4, Zanuck 4)

Sufferin' Cats, 1943 (Hanna and Barbera 4)

Suffering of Susan, 1914 (Loos 4)

Suffering Shakespeare, 1924 (Roach 4)

Suffit d'une fois, 1946 (Feuillère 3, Matras 4)

Suffrageten, 1913 (Nielsen 3)

Suffragette, 1913 (Gad 2)

Suffragette. *See* Moderna suffragetten, 1913

Suffragette Minstrels, 1913 (Barrymore 3)

Sugar. *See* Sucre, 1978

Sugar and Spice, 1930 (Balcon 4)

Sugar and Spies, 1966 (Blanc 4, McKimson 4)

Sugar Daddies, 1927 (Laurel and Hardy 3)

Sugar Plum Papa, 1930 (Sennett 2)

Sugarfoot, 1951 (Massey 3, Scott 3, Cahn 4, Steiner 4)

Sugarland Express, 1974 (Spielberg 2, Hawn 3, Johnson 3, Fields 4, Williams 4, Zsigmond 4)

Sugata Sanshiro, 1943 (Shimura 3)

Sugata Sanshiro, 1955 (Yamamura 3)

Sugata Sanshiro, 1965 (Mifune 3, Okada 3)

Suhaag, 1979 (Bachchan 3)

Suhagan, 1964 (Dutt 2)

Suicidate, mi amor, 1960 (Alcoriza 4)

Suicide, 1965 (Warhol 2)

Suicide Battalion, 1944 (Huston 3)

Suicide Battalion, 1958 (Crosby 4)

Suicide Club, 1909 (Griffith 2, Bitzer 4)

Suicide Club. *See* Klub nravstvennosti, 1915

Suicide Club. *See* Trouble for Two, 1936

Suicide de Lord Stilson, 1990 (Baur 3)

Suicide Fleet, 1931 (Rogers 3, Polito 4)

Suicide Pact, 1913 (Loos 4)

Suicide Squadron. *See* Dangerous Moonlight, 1941

Suicide Troops of the Watchtower. *See* Boro no kesshitai, 1942

Suicide's Wife, 1979 (Dickinson 3)

Suikoden, 1942 (Takamine 3, Tsuburaya 4)

Suing Susan, 1912 (Bunny 3)

Suit of Armor, 1912 (Bunny 3)

Suite de la passion, 1903 (Pathé 4)

Suite de la passion, 1905 (Pathé 4)

Suite en si mineur, 1969 (Braunberger 4)

Suited to a T., 1931 (Fleischer 4)

Suitor. *See* Soupirant, 1962

Suivez cet homme!, 1953 (Blier 3)

Suivez l'oeuf, 1963 (Braunberger 4)

Suivez-moi, jeune homme, 1957 (Gélin 3)

Sujata, 1959 (Roy 2)

Sukyandaru, 1950 (Mifune 3, Shimura 3, Hayasaka 4)

Sul Ponte dei Sospiri, 1952 (Rosay 3)

Suleiman the Conqueror. *See* Solimani il conquistatore, 1961

Sullivans, 1944 (Baxter 3, Bond 3, Basevi 4, Newman 4)

Sullivan's Empire, 1967 (Schifrin 4)

Sullivan's Travels, 1941 (Sturges 2, Lake 3, McCrea 3, Pangborn 3, Dreier 4, Edouart 4, Head 4, Seitz 4)

Sultane de l'amour, 1919 (Modot 3)

Sultans, 1965 (Delannoy 2, Gélin 3, Jourdan 3, Lollobrigida 3, Noiret 3, Delli Colli 4)

Sultan's Birthday, 1944 (Terry 4)

Sultan's Cat, 1931 (Terry 4)

Sultan's Daughter, 1943 (Alton 4)

Sultan's Wife, 1917 (Sennett 2, Swanson 3)

Sultry Summer Evening. *See* Zwoele zomeravond, 1982

Summer. *See* Léto, 1949

Summer and Smoke, 1961 (Harvey 3, Page 3, Bernstein 4, Head 4, Lang 4, Wallis 4)

Summer, Autumn, 1930 (Iwerks 4)

Summer Bachelors, 1926 (Dwan 2, Ruttenberg 4)

Summer Battle of Osaka. *See* Osaka natsu no jin, 1937

Summer City, 1977 (Gibson 3)

Summer Flirtation, 1910 (White 3)

Summer Girl, 1916 (Marion 4)

Summer Girls, 1918 (Sennett 2)

Summer Guests. *See* Sommergäste, 1975

Summer Heat, 1987 (Delerue 4)

Summer Holiday, 1948 (Mamoulian 2, Huston 3, Moorehead 3, Rooney 3, Freed 4, Goodrich 4, Irene 3, Mayer 4, Plunkett 4, Smith 4)

Summer Holiday, 1962 (Walters 2, Yates 2)

Summer Idyll, 1919 (Griffith 2, Walthall 3, Bitzer 4)

Summer in the City, 1970 (Wenders 2, Müller 4)

Summer in the Fields, 1970 (Haanstra 2)

Summer Interlude. *See* Sommarlek, 1951

Summer Lightning. *See* Scudda Hoo! Scudda Hay!, 1948

Summer Love, 1958 (Wray 3, Mancini 4, Salter 4)

Summer Madness, 1955 (Brazzi 3, Hepburn 3, Korda, A. 4, Korda, V. 4)

Summer Magic, 1963 (Disney 4, Ellenshaw 4)

Summer Manoeuvres. *See* Grandes Manoeuvres, 1955

Summer Night With A Greek Profile, Almond Coloured Eyes and the Scent of Basil. *See* Note d'estate, con profilo Greco, occhi amandorla e odore di basilico, 1986

Summer of '42, 1971 (Mulligan 2, Legrand 4, Surtees 4)

Summer of Miss Forbes. *See* Verano de la Senora Forbes, 1988

Summer of Silence. *See* Sommerfuglene, 1974

Summer of the Seventeenth Doll. *See* Season of Passion, 1961

Summer on the Farm, 1943 (Alwyn 4)

Summer Place, 1959 (Daves 2, Bondi 3, Kennedy 3, Steiner 4, Stradling 4)

Summer Place Is Wanted. *See* Sommarnöje sökes, 1957

Summer Place Wanted. *See* Sommarnöje sökes, 1957

Summer School Teachers, 1975 (Corman 2)

Summer Sister. *See* Nasu no imoto, 1972

Summer Skin. *See* Piel de verano, 1961

Summer Soldiers, 1972 (Takemitsu 4)

Summer Solstice, 1981 (Fonda 3, Loy 3, Rosenblum 4)

Summer Stock, 1950 (Walters 2, Garland 3, Kelly 3, Green 4, Mayer 4, Pasternak 4, Plunkett 4, Rose 4, Smith 4)

Summer Storm, 1944 (Sirk 2, Darnell 3, Horton 3, Sanders 3, Schüfftan 4)

Summer Story, 1988 (York 3, Delerue 4)

Summer Tale. *See* Sommarsaga, 1912

Summer Tales. *See* Racconti d'estate, 1958

Summer Wishes, Winter Dreams, 1973 (Sidney 3, Woodward 3)

Summer with Monica. *See* Sommaren med Monika, 1953

Summer World, 1961 (Schaffner 2)

Summer's Lease, 1989 (Gielgud 3)

Summer's Tale. *See* Sommarsaga, 1941

Summertime, 1931 (Terry 4)

Summertime, 1935 (Iwerks 4)

Summertime. *See* Summer Madness, 1955

Summertime Killer, 1973 (Malden 3)

Summertree, 1971 (Douglas 3)

Summit, 1961 (Vanderbeek 2)

Summit, 1968 (Volonté 3)

Summit of Mount Fuji. *See* Fuji sancho, 1948

Sumo Festival. *See* Dohyou matsuri, 1944

Sumpf und Moral, 1925 (Dieterle 2)

Sumuru, 1967 (Kinski 3)

Sumurun, 1920 (Lubitsch 2, Negri 3, Wegener 3, Kräly 4, Metzner 4)

Sun Above, Death Below. *See* Sogeki, 1968

Sun Also Rises, 1957 (King 2, Dalio 3, Flynn 3, Gardner 3, Power 3, Friedhofer 4, LeMaire 4, Wheeler 4, Zanuck 4)

Sun Also Shines At Night. *See* Sole anche di notte, 1990

Sun Comes Up, 1949 (MacDonald 3, Irene 4, Previn 4)

Sun Down Limited, 1924 (Roach 4)

Sun Never Sets, 1939 (Rathbone 3)

Sun Shines Bright, 1953 (Ford 2, Darwell 3, Marsh 3, Cooper 4, Young 4)

Sun Valley Serenade, 1941 (Dandridge 3, Henie 3, Banton 4, Cronjager 4, Day 4, Pan 4)

Suna no onna, 1964 (Okada 3)

Sunbeam, 1911 (Griffith 2, Bitzer 4)

Sunbonnet Blue, 1937 (Avery 4, Stalling 4)

Sunburn, 1979 (Matthau 3)

Sunday, 1961 (De Antonio 2)

Sunday Afternoon. *See* Tarde del domingo, 1957

Sunday, Bloody Sunday, 1971 (Day Lewis 3, Finch 3, Jackson 3, Love 3)

Sunday By the Sea, 1953 (Lassally 4)

Sunday Calm, 1923 (Roach 4)

Sunday Dinner for a Soldier, 1944 (Bacon 2, Baxter 3, Darwell 3, Newman 4)

Sunday Father, 1973 (Hoffman 3)

Sunday Go to Meetin' Time, 1936 (Freleng 4)

Sunday in August. *See* Domenica d'agosto, 1950

Sunday in New York, 1964 (Fonda, J. 3, Robertson 3, Krasna 4, Orry-Kelly 4)

Sunday in September. *See* Söndag i september, 1963

Sunday in the Country, 1975 (Borgnine 3)

Sunday in the Country. *See* Dimanche à la campagne, 1984

Sunday Lovers, 1981 (Risi 2, Elliott 3, Wilder 3, Age and Scarpelli 4, Delli Colli 4)

Sunday Morning. *See* Niedzielny poranek, 1955

Sunday Punch, 1942 (Gardner 3, Schary 4)

Sunday Pursuit, 1990 (Zetterling 2)

Sunday Woman. *See* Donna della domenica, 1975

Sundays and Cybèle. *See* Cybèle, ou les dimanches de Ville d'Avray, 1962

Sündelbabel, 1925 (Junge 4)

Sünden der Vater, 1913 (Gad 2, Nielsen 3)

Sundered Ties, 1912 (Ince 4)

Sünderin, 1950 (Fröhlich 3)

Sündig und Süss, 1929 (Heller 4)

Sündige Hof, 1932 (Rasp 3)

Sundige Mutter, 1918 (Veidt 3)

Sundown, 1924 (Bosworth 3, Love 3, Marion 4)

Sundown, 1941 (Hathaway 2, Carey 3, Dandridge 3, Sanders 3, Tierney 3, Lang 4, Plunkett 4, Rozsa 4, Irene 4)

Sundown Rider, 1933 (Bond 3)

Sundown Slim, 1920 (Carey 3)

Sundown Trail, 1919 (Young 4)

Sundown Trail, 1931 (Beavers 3, McCord 4)

Sundowners, 1949 (Preston 3, Hoch 4)

Sundowners, 1960 (Zinnemann 2, Kerr 3, Mitchum 3, Rafferty 3, Ustinov 3, Fisher 4, Lennart 4, Tiomkin 4, Warner 4)

Sundowners, 1961 (Roeg 2)

Sunehere Din, 1949 (Kapoor 2)

Sunflower. *See* Girasoli, 1970

Sunflower Girl. *See* Himawari-musume, 1953

Sunghursh, 1968 (Kumar 3)

Sunk By the Census, 1940 (Metty 4)

Sunken. *See* Gesunkenen, 1925

Sunken Rocks, 1919 (Hepworth 2)

Sunken Treasure, 1936 (Terry 4)

Sunna no onna, 1963 (Takemitsu 4)

Sunny, 1930 (Haller 4)

Sunny, 1941 (Wilcox 2, Horton 3, Neagle 3, Metty 4)

Sunny Italy, 1951 (Terry 4)

Sunny Side of the Street, 1951 (Duning 4)

Sunny Side Up, 1926 (Crisp 3)

Sunny Side Up, 1929 (Brown 3, Cooper 3, Gaynor 3, Friedhofer 4)

Sunny South, 1931 (Lantz 4)

Sunny South, 1933 (Terry 4)

Sunny Spain, 1923 (Roach 4)

Sunnyside, 1919 (Chaplin 2, Purviance 3)

Sunrise, 1927 (Murnau 2, Ulmer 2, Gaynor 3, Mayer 4, Rosher 4, Struss 4)

Sunrise: A Song of Two Humans. *See* **Sunrise, 1927**

Sunrise at Campobello, 1960 (Bellamy 3, Garson 3, Harlan 4, Schary 4, Waxman 4)

Sunset, 1988 (Edwards 2, Garner 3, McDowell 3, Mancini 4)

Sunset Beach on Long Island, 1967 (Warhol 2)

Sunset Boulevard, 1950 (De Mille 2, Keaton 2, Von Stroheim 2, Wilder 2, Holden 3, Swanson 3, Brackett 4, Dreier 4, Edouart 4, Head 4, Seitz 4, Waxman 4)

Sunset Cove, 1978 (Carradine 3)

Sunset Derby, 1927 (Astor 3)

Sunset in El Dorado, 1945 (Dumont 3, Rogers 3, Canutt 4)

Sunset in the West, 1950 (Rogers 3)

Sunset in Vienna, 1938 (Wilcox 2)

Sunset in Wyoming, 1941 (Autry 3)

Sunset on the Desert, 1942 (Rogers 3)

Sunset Pass, 1929 (Hathaway 2)

Sunset Pass, 1933 (Hathaway 2, Carey 3, Scott 3)

Sunset Serenade, 1942 (Rogers 3)

Sunset, Sunrise, 1973 (Rota 4)

Sunset Trail, 1932 (Eason 4)

Sunset Trail, 1939 (Harlan 4, Head 4, Metty 4)

Sunshine, 1916 (Sennett 2)

Sunshine Alley, 1917 (Marsh 3)

Sunshine and Gold, 1917 (King 2)

Sunshine and Shadow, 1914 (Talmadge 3)

Sunshine Boys, 1975 (Matthau 3, Booth 4, Smith 4, Stark 4)

Sunshine Christmas, 1977 (Head 4)

Sunshine Dad, 1916 (Browning 2)

Sunshine Fellows Rain. *See* Driver dagg faller Regn, 1946

Sunshine in Poverty Row, 1910 (White 3)

Sunshine Molly, 1915 (Weber 2, Bosworth 3, Marion 4)

Sunshine Nan, 1918 (Barthelmess 3)

Sunshine Patriots, 1968 (Robertson 3, Sutherland 4)

Sunshine Sue, 1910 (Griffith 2, Crisp 3, Bitzer 4)

Sunshine Susie, 1931 (Saville 2, Balcon 4, Vetchinsky 4)

Sunshine Through the Dark, 1911 (Griffith 2, Bitzer 4)

Sunstone, 1979 (Emshwiller 2)
Sunsualità, 1952 (Mastroianni 3)
Sun-up, 1925 (Goulding 2)
Suo modo di fare, 1968 (Segal 3)
Suo nome faceva tremare … Interpol in
    allarme!. *See* Dio, sei proprio un
    padreterno, 1973
Suonatrice ambulante, 1912 (Bertini 3)
Suor Letizia, 1956 (Magnani 3, Di
    Venanzo 4, Zavattini 4)
Suor omicidi, 1978 (Valli 3)
Super Mouse Rides Again, 1943 (Terry 4)
Super Rabbit, 1943 (Blanc 4, Jones 4,
    Stalling 4)
Super Salesman, 1947 (Terry 4)
Super Secret Service, 1953 (Sellers 3)
Super Snooper, 1952 (Blanc 4, McKimson 4,
    Stalling 4)
Superchick, 1973 (Carradine 3)
Supercolpo da 7 miliard, 1966 (Andrews 3)
Superdome, 1978 (Johnson 3)
Supergirl, 1970 (Fassbinder 2)
Supergirl, 1984 (Dunaway 3, Farrow 3,
    O'Toole 3, Goldsmith 4)
Super-Hooper-Dyne Lizzies, 1925
    (Sennett 2)
Super-Imposition, 1968 (Vanderbeek 2)
Superloco, 1936 (Fernández 2)
Superman series, 1941–42 (Fleischer 4)
Superman, 1948 (Katzman 4)
Superman, 1978 (Benton 2, Brando 3,
    Cooper 3, Ford 3, Hackman 3, Howard 3,
    Schell 3, Stamp 3, York 3, Unsworth 4,
    Williams 4)
Superman IV: The Quest for Peace, 1987
    (Hackman 3, Golan and Globus 4,
    Williams 4)
Superman ki Wapasi, 1960 (Biswas 4)
Superman III, 1983 (Lester 2, Cooper 3,
    Hackman 3, Pryor 3)
Superman II, 1981 (Lester 2, Cooper 3,
    Hackman 3, Stamp 3, York 3,
    Unsworth 4)
Supernatural, 1933 (Lombard 3, Scott 3,
    Banton 4)
Super-Pacific, 1948 (Colpi 4)
Supersabio, 1948 (Cantinflas 3)
Super-Sleuth, 1937 (August 4, Polglase 4)
Superstar, 1990 (Hopper 3)
Superstition, 1922 (Dwan 2)
Superstizione, 1949 (Antonioni 2, Fusco 4)
Supertestimone, 1971 (Vitti 3, Guerra 4)
Supertrain, 1979 (Crawford 3, Lourié 4)
Support Your Local Gunfighter, 1971
    (Blondell 3, Garner 3)
Support Your Local Sheriff, 1968
    (Brennan 3, Dern 3, Garner 3)
Suppose They Gave a War and Nobody
    Came, 1970 (Ameche 3, Borgnine 3,
    Curtis 3, Guffey 4)
Suppressed Duck, 1965 (Blanc 4,
    McKimson 4)
Suppressed Evidence, 1915 (Anderson 3)
Sur, 1988 (Solanas and Getino 2)
Sur Faces, 1977 (Emshwiller 2)
Sur la route de Salina, 1969 (D'Eaubonne 4)
Sur le Pont d'Avignon, 1956 (Franju 2,
    Fradetal 4, Jarre 4)
Sur le Sentier de la guerre, 1909 (Modot 3)
Sur les bords de la caméra, 1932 (Storck 2)
Sur les routes de l'ete, 1936 (Storck 2)
Sur toute la gamme, 1954 (Chevalier 3)
Sur un air de Charleston, 1927
    (Braunberger 4)

Sur un arbre perché, 1971 (Chaplin 3)
Suraag, 1982 (Azmi 3)
Surboum. *See* Déchaînés, 1950
Surcouf, 1924 (Artaud 3)
Sure Fire, 1921 (Ford 2, Miller 4)
Sure Shot Morgan, 1919 (Carey 3)
Sure-Mike, 1925 (Roach 4)
Surf. *See* Brannigar, 1935
Surf. *See* Shiosai, 1954
Surf Girl, 1916 (Sennett 2)
Surface Tension, 1968 (Frampton 2)
Surfacing, 1978 (Jutra 2)
Surgeon's Heroism, 1912 (Lawrence 3)
Suri Lanka no ai to wakare, 1976'
    (Takamine 3, Muraki 4)
Surmenés, 1957 (Cassel 3, Braunberger 4,
    Delerue 4)
Suronin Chuya, 1930 (Yamada 3)
Surprise, 1923 (Fleischer 4)
Surprise, 1929 (Rooney 3)
Surprise Package, 1960 (Donen 2,
    Brynner 3, Challis 4, Coward 4)
Surprise Party, 1983 (Vadim 2)
Surprise-boogie, 1956 (Braunberger 4)
Surprises de l'affichage, 1903 (Guy 2)
Surprises de la radio, 1939 (Gélin 3)
Surrender, 1927 (Mozhukin 3)
Surrender, 1931 (Howard 2, Bellamy 3,
    Behrman 4, Grot 4, Howe 4, Levien 4)
Surrender, 1950 (Dwan 2, Brennan 3,
    Darwell 3)
Surrender, 1987 (Caine 3, Field 3, Golan and
    Globus 4)
Surrounded by Women. *See* Between Two
    Women, 1937
Surrounded House. *See* Omringgade huset,
    1922
Suruga yuhkyou-den: Yabure takka, 1964
    (Miyagawa 4)
Surveillez votre tenue, 1949 (Decaë 4)
Survival. *See* Glanz und Elend der
    Kurtisanen, 1927
Survival. *See* Guide, 1965
Survival 67, 1967 (Dassin 2)
Survival Run, 1977 (Milland 3)
Surviving, 1985 (Burstyn 3)
Survivor, 1981 (Cotten 3)
Survivors, 1983 (Matthau 3, Williams 3)
Susan and God, 1940 (Cukor 2, Crawford 3,
    Hayworth 3, March 3, Loos 4, Stothart 4,
    Stromberg 4)
Susan Lenox, Her Fall and Rise, 1931
    (Gable 3, Garbo 3, Booth 4, Daniels 4,
    Gibbons 4, Mayer 4)
Susan Slade, 1961 (Daves 2, Ballard 4,
    Steiner 4)
Susan Slept Here, 1954 (Tashlin 2, Powell 3,
    Reynolds 3, D'Agostino 4, Musuraca 4)
Susanna, 1922 (Hornbeck 4)
Susanna Pass, 1949 (Rogers 3)
Susanna tutta panna, 1957 (Delli Colli 4,
    Ponti 4)
Susannah of the Mounties, 1939
    (Lockwood 3, Scott 3, Temple 3,
    MacGowan 4, Miller 4, Zanuck 4)
Susanne im Bade, 1950 (Staudte 2)
Susie Steps Out, 1946 (Dumont 3)
Susman, 1985 (Azmi 3)
Suspect, 1945 (Siodmak 2, Laughton 3)
Suspect, 1960 (Cushing 3, Pleasence 3)
Suspect, 1987 (Yates 2, Cher 3)
Suspects, 1957 (Vanel 3)
Suspended Ordeal, 1914 (Sennett 2,
    Arbuckle 3)

Suspended Sentence, 1913 (Dwan 2)
Suspended Step of the Stork, 1991
    (Mastroianni 3, Moreau 3, Guerra 4)
Suspended Vocation. *See* Vocation
    suspendue, 1977
Suspense, 1946 (Struss 4)
Suspense au 2e Bureau, 1959
    (D'Eaubonne 4)
Suspicion, 1918 (Stahl 2)
Suspicion, 1941 (Hitchcock 2, Fontaine 3,
    Grant 3, Harrison 4, Polglase 4,
    Raphaelson 4, Reville 4, Stradling 4,
    Waxman 4)
Suspicious Henry, 1913 (Bunny 3)
Suspicious Wives, 1922 (Stahl 2)
Suspiria, 1977 (Bennett 3, Valli 3)
Suspiria, 1978 (Argento 4)
Susret u snu, 1957 (Mimica 4)
Süsse Mädel, 1926 (Warm 4)
Sussie, 1945 (Björnstrand 3)
Sussurro nel buio, 1976 (Cotten 3,
    Donaggio 4)
Susume dokuritsu-ki, 1943 (Hasegawa 3,
    Mori 3)
Sutekina konbanwa, 1965 (Iwashita 3)
Sutiejka, 1973 (Theodorakis 4)
Sutjeska, 1972 (Burton 3, Papas 3)
Sutobi kago, 1952 (Miyagawa 4)
Sutradhar, 1987 (Patil 3)
Sutter's Gold, 1936 (Cruze 2, Hawks 2,
    Carey 3, Waxman 4)
Suvarna Rekha, 1963 (Ghatak 2)
Suvorov, 1941 (Pudovkin 2, Golovnya 4)
Suwanee River, 1925 (Fleischer 4)
Suzaku Gate. *See* Suzaku-mon, 1957
Suzaku-mon, 1957 (Miyagawa 4)
Suzanna, 1922 (Sennett 2, Normand 3)
Suzanne au bain, 1930 (Storck 2)
Suzanne et les roses. *See* Jeux d'amour, 1960
Suzanne et ses brigands, 1948 (Burel 4)
Suzanne Simonin, la religieuse de Denis
    Diderot, 1966 (Karina 3, Presle 3, De
    Beauregard 4)
Suzukake no sampomichi, 1959 (Mori 3,
    Tsukasa 3)
Suzukamori, 1937 (Hasegawa 3)
Suzy, 1936 (Grant 3, Harlow 3, Coffee 4)
Sváb, 1946 (Brdečka 4)
Svadba, 1944 (Maretskaya 3)
Svadlenka, 1936 (Frič 2)
Svänger på slottet, 1959 (Björnstrand 3,
    Fischer 4)
Svärmor kommer, 1930 (Jaenzon 4)
Svart Gryning, 1987 (Andersson 3)
Svarta maskerna, 1912 (Sjöström 2, Stiller 2,
    Jaenzon 4, Magnusson 4)
Svarta palmkronor, 1968 (Andersson 3, Von
    Sydow 3, Fischer 4)
Svarta rosor, 1932 (Molander 2)
Svarta rosor, 1945 (Dahlbeck 3)
Svarte doktorn, 1911 (Holger-Madsen 2)
Svarte fugler, 1983 (Andersson 3)
Svatý Václav, 1929 (Heller 4, Stallich 4)
Svegliati e uccidi, 1966 (Volonté 3,
    Morricone 4)
Svejk at the Front. *See* Švejk na frontě, 1926
Švejk na frontě, 1926 (Heller 4)
Svengali, 1927 (Wegener 3)
Svengali, 1931 (Barrymore 3, Crisp 3,
    Grot 4)
Svengali, 1954 (Alwyn 4)
Svengali, 1983 (O'Toole 3, Barry 4)
Svengali's Cat, 1946 (Terry 4)
Svensk tiger, 1948 (Björnstrand 3)

Svět, kde se žebrá, 1938 (Stallich 4)
Svět patří nám, 1937 (Frič 2, Heller 4)
Svigersønnerne. *See* Swiegersöhne, 1926
Svítalo celou noc, 1980 (Kučera 4)
Svítání, 1933 (Stallich 4)
Svy Dager for Elisabeth, 1927 (Henie 3)
Svyloučenim veřejnosti, 1933 (Heller 4)
Swain, 1950 (Markopoulos 2)
Swallow the Leader, 1949 (Blanc 4,
    McKimson 4, Stalling 4)
Swami, 1977 (Azmi 3)
Swami Dada, 1982 (Anand 3)
Swamp, 1921 (Hayakawa 3, Love 3)
Swamp Fire, 1946 (Crabbe 3,
    Weissmuller 3)
Swamp Thing, 1982 (Craven 2, Jourdan 3)
Swamp Water, 1941 (Renoir 2, Andrews 3,
    Baxter 3, Bond 3, Brennan 3,
    Carradine 3, Huston 3, Day 4, Nichols 4)
Swamp Woman, 1956 (Corman 2)
Swan, 1925 (Menjou 3, Banton 4)
Swan. *See* One Romantic Night, 1930
Swan, 1956 (Vidor 2, Guinness 3, Jourdan 3,
    Kelly 3, Moorehead 3, Gibbons 4,
    Kaper 4, Rose 4, Ruttenberg 4, Schary 4,
    Surtees 4)
Swan Princess, 1928 (Sennett 2)
Swanee River, 1939 (Ameche 3, Jolson 3,
    Day 4, Dunne 4, Glennon 4,
    MacGowan 4, Zanuck 4)
Swann in Love, 1984 (Delon 3, Irons 3,
    Carriere 4, Nykvist 4, Saulnier 4)
Swap, 1980 (De Niro 3)
Swaralipi, 1960 (Ghatak 2)
Swarg narak, 1978 (Azmi 3)
Swarm, 1978 (Caine 3, De Havilland 3,
    Ferrer 3, Fonda 3, Grant 3, Johnson 3,
    MacMurray 3, Widmark 3, Goldsmith 4)
Swash Buckled, 1962 (Hanna and Barbera 4)
Swashbuckler, 1976 (Bujold 3, Huston 3,
    Jones 3, Shaw 3, Addison 4)
Swastika, 1973 (Puttnam 4)
Swastika Savages. *See* Hell's Bloody Devils,
    1970
Swat the Crook, 1919 (Daniels 3, Lloyd 3,
    Roach 4)
Swat the Fly, 1935 (Fleischer 4)
Sweater Girl, 1942 (Dreier 4, Young 4)
Sweden, 1960 (Van Dyke 2)
Swedenhielms, 1935 (Molander 2,
    Bergman 3)
Swedes in America, 1943 (Bergman 3)
Swedish Fly Girls. *See* Christa, 1970
Swedish Tiger. *See* Svensk tiger, 1948
Swedish Wildcats. *See* Groove Room, 1974
Sweedie Goes to College, 1915 (Beery 3,
    Swanson 3)
Sweedie series, 1914–16 (Beery 3)
Sweekar kiya maine, 1983 (Azmi 3)
Sweeney II, 1978 (Elliott 3)
Sweepings, 1933 (Barrymore 3, Cronjager 4,
    Plunkett 4, Selznick 4, Steiner 4)
Sweepstakes Winner, 1939 (Edeson 4)
Sweet Adeline, 1926 (Fleischer 4)
Sweet Adeline, 1935 (LeRoy 2, Calhern 3,
    Dunne 3, Orry-Kelly 4, Polito 4,
    Wallis 4)
Sweet Aloes. *See* Give Me Your Heart, 1936
Sweet and Hot, 1958 (Three Stooges 3)
Sweet and Lowdown, 1944 (Darnell 3,
    Ballard 4)
Sweet and Sour. *See* Dragées au poivre, 1963
Sweet and Twenty, 1909 (Griffith 2,
    Pickford 3, Bitzer 4)

Sweet Bird of Youth, 1962 (Brooks 2,
    Newman 3, Page 3, Berman 4, Krasner 4,
    Orry-Kelly 4)
Sweet Bird of Youth, 1989 (Roeg 2,
    Taylor 3)
Sweet Body of Deborah. *See* Dolce corpo di
    Deborah, 1968
Sweet By and By, 1921 (Roach 4)
Sweet Charity, 1968 (Fosse 2, MacLaine 3,
    Head 4, Surtees 4, Westmore Family 4)
Sweet Cookie, 1921 (Garmes 4)
Sweet Cookie, 1933 (Sennett 2)
Sweet Country, 1987 (Cacoyannis 2,
    Papas 3)
Sweet Daddies, 1926 (Edeson 4)
Sweet Daddy, 1924 (McCarey 2, Roach 4)
Sweet Devil, 1956 (Buchanan 3)
Sweet Dreams, 1985 (Reisz 2, Lange 3)
Sweet Genevieve, 1947 (Katzman 4)
Sweet Heart's Dance, 1988 (Sarandon 3)
Sweet Hostage, 1975 (Sheen 3)
Sweet Hours. *See* Dulces horas, 1981
Sweet Hunters, 1969 (Guerra 2, Hayden 3,
    Evein 4)
Sweet Jenny Lee, 1932 (Fleischer 4)
Sweet Kill, 1972 (Crosby 4)
Sweet Kitty Bellairs, 1930 (Pidgeon 3)
Sweet Lavender, 1915 (Hepworth 2)
Sweet Liberty, 1986 (Caine 3, Gish 3,
    Hoskins 3, Pfeiffer 3)
Sweet Light in the Dark Window. *See*
    Romeo, Julie a tma, 1960
Sweet Little Josefina. *See* Sladká Josefínka,
    1927
Sweet Memories of Yesterday, 1911
    (Pickford 3, Gaudio 4, Ince 4)
Sweet Movie, 1974 (Makavejev 2)
Sweet Music, 1935 (Gaudio 4, Wald 4)
Sweet November, 1968 (Legrand 4)
Sweet Pickle, 1925 (Sennett 2)
Sweet Revenge, 1909 (Griffith 2, Bitzer 4)
Sweet Revenge, 1913 (Beery 3)
Sweet Revenge, 1976 (Zsigmond 4)
Sweet Revenge, 1987 (Segal 3)
Sweet Ride, 1966 (Pasternak 4)
Sweet Ride. *See* Valley of the Dolls, 1967
Sweet Ride, 1968 (Smith 4)
Sweet Rosie O'Grady, 1943 (Grable 3,
    Menjou 3, Young 3, Basevi 4, Pan 4)
Sweet Secret. *See* Amai himitsu, 1971
Sweets for the Sweet, 1903 (Bitzer 4)
Sweet Sioux, 1937 (Freleng 4, Stalling 4)
Sweet Sixteen. *See* Futures vedettes, 1954
Sweet Smell of Success, 1957
    (Mackendrick 2, Curtis 3, Lancaster 3,
    Bernstein 4, Howe 4)
Sweet Sweat. *See* Amai shiru, 1964
Sweet Toronto, 1971 (Leacock 2)
Sweetheart Days, 1921 (Sennett 2)
Sweetheart of Sigma Chi, 1933 (Crabbe 3,
    Grable 3)
Sweetheart of Sigma Chi, 1946 (Cahn 4,
    Hunter 4)
Sweetheart of the Campus, 1941 (Keeler 3,
    Planer 4)
Sweethearts, 1938 (Van Dyke 2, Eddy 3,
    MacDonald 3, Adrian 4, Mayer 4,
    Stothart 4, Stromberg 4, Vorkapich 4)
Sweethearts and Wives, 1930 (Seitz 4)
Sweethearts on Parade, 1930 (Neilan 2)
Sweethearts on Parade, 1953 (Dwan 2)
Swell Guy, 1946 (Brooks 2, Gaudio 4)
Swell Hogan, 1926 (Hughes 4)
Swell-Head, 1929 (Love 3)

Swept Away by a Strange Destiny on an
    Azure August Sea. *See* Travolti da un
    insolito destino nell'azzurro mare
    d'agosto, 1974
Swiegersöhne, 1926 (Madsen and
    Schenstrøm 3)
Swift Current. *See* Gekiryu, 1952
Swim, Girl, Swim, 1927 (Hunt 4,
    Schulberg 4)
Swim or Sink, 1932 (Fleischer 4)
Swim Princess, 1928 (Capra 2, Lombard 3,
    Hornbeck 4)
Swimmer, 1968 (Pollack 2, Lancaster 3,
    Hamlisch 4, Perry 4, Wheeler 4)
Swimming Class, 1904 (Bitzer 4)
Swimming Pool. *See* Piscine, 1969
Swimming to Cambodia, 1987 (Demme 2)
Swindle. *See* Bidone, 1955
Swindlers. *See* Bidone, 1955
Swindlers. *See* Magliari, 1959
Swing, 1936 (Micheaux 2)
Swing Cleaning, 1941 (Fleischer 4)
Swing Ding Amigo, 1966 (Blanc 4,
    McKimson 4)
Swing Fever, 1943 (Gardner 3, Horne 3,
    Brown 4, Rosher 4)
Swing for Sale, 1937 (Allyson 3)
Swing Frolic, 1942 (Krasner 4)
Swing High, 1930 (Mandell 4)
Swing High, Swing Low, 1937 (Lamour 3,
    Lombard 3, MacMurray 3, Pangborn 3,
    Quinn 3, Banton 4, Dreier 4, Young 4)
Swing It, 1936 (Cronjager 4)
Swing It, Professor, 1937 (Neilan 2)
Swing Parade of 1946, 1946 (Three
    Stooges 3)
Swing School, 1938 (Fleischer 4)
Swing Shift, 1984 (Demme 2, Hawn 3)
Swing Shift Cinderella, 1945 (Avery 4)
Swing Shift Maisie, 1943 (McLeod 2,
    Irene 4, Stradling 4)
Swing, Teacher, Swing. *See* College Swing,
    1938
Swing Time, 1936 (Stevens 2, Astaire 3,
    Rogers 3, Berman 4, Pan 4, Polglase 4)
Swing with Bing, 1940 (Crosby 3)
Swing Your Baby, 1938 (Wallis 4)
Swing Your Lady, 1938 (Bogart 3,
    Reagan 3, Deutsch 4, Edeson 4,
    Friedhofer 4)
Swing Your Partners, 1918 (Lloyd 3,
    Roach 4)
Swing, You Sinner, 1938 (Fleischer 4)
Swinger, 1966 (Biroc 4, Head 4, Previn 4)
Swingin' Maiden. *See* Iron Maiden, 1963
Swingin' on a Rainbow, 1945 (Langdon 3)
Swingin' Summer, 1965 (Welch 3)
Swinging at the Castle. *See* Svänger på
    slottet, 1959
Swinging the Lambeth Walk, 1939
    (Lye 4)
Swingmen in Europe, 1977 (Rabier 4)
Swingtime Johnny, 1943 (Bruckman 4)
Swirl of Glory. *See* Sugarfoot, 1950
Swiss Army Knife with Rats and Pigeons,
    1981 (Breer 4)
Swiss Cheese, 1930 (Terry 4)
Swiss Cheeze Family Robinson, 1947
    (Terry 4)
Swiss Conspiracy, 1977 (Milland 3)
Swiss Family Robinson, 1940 (Welles 2,
    Dunn 4, Musuraca 4)
Swiss Family Robinson, 1960 (Hayakawa 3,
    Mills 3, Alwyn 4, Disney 4, Ellenshaw 4)

Swiss Miss, 1938 (Negulesco 2, Laurel and Hardy 3, Roach 4)

Swiss Miss, 1951 (Terry 4)

Swiss Ski Yodelers, 1940 (Terry 4)

Swiss Tour. *See* Four Days Leave, 1949

Switch, 1975 (Wagner 3)

Switch, 1991 (Mancini 4)

Switch Tower, 1913 (Barrymore 3)

Switched At Birth, 1991 (Hamlisch 4)

Switches and Sweeties, 1919 (Laurel and Hardy 3)

Switching Channels, 1988 (Reynolds 3, Turner 3, Hecht 4)

Swooming the Swooners, 1945 (Terry 4)

Swooner Crooner, 1944 (Blanc 4, Foster 4, Stalling 4)

Sword and Hearts, 1911 (Bitzer 4)

Sword and the Dragon, 1960 (Fields 4)

Sword and the Flute, 1959 (Ivory 2)

Sword and the Rose, 1953 (Dillon 4, Disney 4, Ellenshaw 4, Unsworth 4)

Sword for Hire. *See* Sengoku-burai, 1952

Sword in the Desert, 1949 (Andrews 3, Buckner 4)

Sword in the Stone, 1963 (Disney 4)

Sword of D'Artagnan, 1950 (Boetticher 2)

Sword of Doom. *See* Daibosatsu toge, 1966

Sword of Flying Dragon. *See* Hiryuh no ken, 1937

Sword of Gideon, 1986 (Steiger 3)

Sword of Lancelot. *See* Lancelot and Guinevere, 1963

Sword of Sherwood Forest, 1960 (Fisher 2, Cushing 3, Reed 3, Carreras 4)

Sword of the Conqueror. *See* Rosemunda e Alboino, 1961

Sword of the Valiant, 1983 (Cushing 3, Golan and Globus 4)

Sword of the Valiant: The Legend of Gawain and the Green Knight, 1983 (Connery 3, Howard 3, Young 4)

Sword of Vengeance, 1954 (Haskin 4)

Swords and Hearts, 1911 (Griffith 2)

Swords of Blood. *See* Cartouche, 1961

Swordsman, 1947 (Lewis 2, Friedhofer 4)

Swordsman of Siena. *See* Spadaccino di Siena, 1961

Sworn Enemy, 1936 (Quinn 3, Young 3)

Syanhai no tsuki, 1941 (Tsuburaya 4)

Sybil, 1976 (Field 3, Woodward 3)

Sydenham Plan, 1949 (Ferrer 3)

Sylvester and Tweety's Crazy Capers, 1986 (Freleng 4)

Sylvester: Tragödie einer Nacht, 1923 (Mayer 4)

Sylvesternacht, 1977 (Sirk 2)

Sylvia, 1965 (Baker 3, O'Brien 3, Head 4, Raksin 4, Ruttenberg 4)

Sylvia, 1984 (Rosenman 4)

Sylvia of the Secret Service, 1917 (Von Stroheim 2, Grot 4, Miller 4)

Sylvia Scarlett, 1935 (Cukor 2, Hepburn 3, Grant 3, August 4, Berman 4, Plunkett 4, Polglase 4)

Sylvie and the Ghost. *See* Sylvie et le fantôme, 1944

Sylvie and the Phantom. *See* Sylvie et le fantôme, 1944

Sylvie et le fantôme, 1944 (Tati 2, Aurenche 4)

Symmetricks, 1972 (Vanderbeek 2)

Sympathy for the Devil. *See* One Plus One, 1968

Sympathy Sal, 1915 (Loos 4)

Symphonie der Liebe. *See* Extase, 1933

Symphonie des brigands, 1936 (Schüfftan 4)

Symphonie du travail, 1943 (Alekan 4)

Symphonie eines Lebens, 1942 (Baur 3, Porten 3, Hoffman 4)

Symphonie fantastique, 1942 (Christian-Jaque 2, Barrault 3, Berry 3, Blier 3)

Symphonie New York, 1956 (Braunberger 4)

Symphonie Nr. 3 in Es-dur, Opus 55 "Eroica" von Ludwig von Beethoven, 1967 (Colpi 4)

Symphonie Nr. 9 von Franz Schubert, 1966 (Colpi 4)

Symphonie Nr. 7 von Ludwig von Beethoven, 1966 (Colpi 4)

Symphonie pastorale, 1946 (Delannoy 2, Morgan 3, Andrejew 4, Annenkov 4, Aurenche 4, Auric 4, Bost 4)

Symphonie paysanne, 1940 (Storck 2)

Symphonie pour un massacre, 1963 (Vanel 3, Barsacq 4, Renoir 4)

Symphony for a Massacre. *See* Symphonie pour un massacre, 1963

Symphony in Slang, 1951 (Avery 4)

Symphony in Two Flats, 1930 (Novello 3, Balcon 4)

Symphony of a City. *See* Människor i stad, 1947

Symphony of Love. *See* Fruhlingssinfonie, 1985

Symphony of Six Million, 1932 (La Cava 2, Dunne 3, Berman 4, Selznick 4, Steiner 4)

Symphony Orchestra, 1980 (Halas and Batchelor 4)

Syn hor, 1925 (Heller 4)

Synanon, 1965 (O'Brien 3, Stradling 4)

Synchromy, 1971 (McLaren 4)

Syncopated Sioux, 1940 (Lantz 4)

Syncopation, 1929 (Plunkett 4)

Syncopation, 1942 (Dieterle 2, Cooper 3, Menjou 3, Hunt 4)

Synd, 1928 (Molander 2, Manès 3, Jaenzon 4)

Synnöve Solbakken, 1934 (Sjöström 2)

Synnöve Solbakken, 1957 (Andersson 3, Nykvist 4)

Synthetic Sin, 1928 (Moore 3)

Synthetic Sound Experiments, 1932 (Fischinger 2, Ford 2)

Syonen hyoryuki, 1943 (Tsuburaya 4)

Syskonbädd 1782, 1965 (Andersson 3, Björnstrand 3)

System, 1964 (Reed 3)

System bouboule. *See* Deux Combinards, 1937

System ohne Schatten, 1983 (Ganz 3)

Système du Docteur Goudron et du Professeur Plume, 1912 (Tourneur 2)

Szent Péter esernyöje, 1917 (Korda 2)

Szep magyar komedia, 1970 (Tyszkiewicz 3)

Szerelmesfilm, 1970 (Szabó 2)

Szinèszno, 1920 (Lukas 3)

Szklana góra, 1960 (Tyszkiewicz 3)

Szörnyek Evadja, 1987 (Jancsó 2)

Sztandar młodych, 1958 (Lenica 4)

Sztuka młodych, 1950 (Munk 2)

Szurkerahàs hölgy, 1922 (Lukas 3)

Szyfry, 1966 (Cybulski 3)

T For Tumbleweed, 1962 (Wexler 4)

TG Psychic Rally in Heaven, 1981 (Jarman 2)

T.G.I.F., 1967 (Arkin 3)

THX 1138, 1971 (Coppola 2, Lucas 2, Duvall 3, Pleasence 3, Murch 4, Schifrin 4)

T.V.A., 1945 (Vorkapich 4)

TZ, 1979 (Breer 4)

Ta Inczacy Tastrzab, 1977 (Tyszkiewicz 3)

Ta? Ra-Ra-Boom-Der-A, 1926 (Fleischer 4)

Täällä Alkaa Seikkilu. *See* Här börjar äventyret, 1965

Tabaco, 1960 (Almendros 4)

Tabarin, 1957 (Piccoli 3)

Tabasco Road, 1957 (Stalling 4)

Tabi no hito, 1931 (Yamada 3)

Tabi no kagero, 1937 (Hasegawa 3)

Tabi yakusha, 1940 (Hayasaka 4)

Tabigaeru kokyo no uta, 1932 (Hasegawa 3)

Table aux crèves, 1951 (Fernandel 3)

Table for Five, 1983 (Voight 3, Zsigmond 4)

Table Top Dolly. *See* Breakfast, 1972

Table tournante, 1989 (Aimée 3, Grimault 4)

Tableaux d'une exposition, 1972 (Alexeieff and Parker 4)

Tableaux futuristes et incohérents, 1916 (Cohl 4)

Taboo. *See* Tabu, 1977

Taboos of the World. *See* Tabù, 1965

Tabu, 1931 (Flaherty 2, Murnau 2, Crosby 4)

Tabù, 1965 (Price 3)

Tabu, 1977 (Björnstrand 3)

Tac, tac, 1980 (Alcoriza 4)

Tacaszi vihar, 1918 (Lugosi 3)

Tacchino prepotente, 1939 (Rossellini 2)

Tacno u punoc, 1960 (Mimica 4)

Tadaima shinsatsu-chu, 1964 (Tsukasa 3)

Tadanao-kyo gyojo-ki, 1930 (Yamada 3)

Taenk på ett tal, 1969 (Andersson 3)

Tag der Freiheit: unsere Wermacht, 1935 (Riefenstahl 2)

Tag, der nie zu Ende geht, 1959 (Herlth 4)

Tagebuch des Dr. Hart, 1916 (Leni 2, Hoffmann 4)

Tagebuch einer Verliebten, 1953 (Schell 3)

Tagebuch einer Verlorenen, 1918 (Krauss 3, Veidt 3)

Tagebuch einer Verlorenen, 1929 (Brooks 3, Rasp 3, Metzner 4)

Taggart, 1964 (Duryea 3)

Tahan Na Empy, Tahan, 1977 (Brocka 2)

Tahiti Money, 1943 (Simon 3)

Tahiti Nights, 1944 (Guffey 4)

Taifu-ken no onna, 1948 (Yamamura 3)

Taiga, 1958 (Herlth 4)

Taiheiyo hitoribotchi, 1963 (Mori 3, Tanaka 3, Takemitsu 4)

Taiheiyo kiseki no sakusen: Kisuka, 1965 (Yamamura 3, Tsuburaya 4)

Taiheiyo no arashi, 1960 (Mifune 3, Shimura 3, Tsuburaya 4)

Taiheiyo no tsubasa, 1963 (Mifune 3, Tsuburaya 4)

Taiheiyo no washi, 1953 (Mifune 3, Tsuburaya 4)

Taiheiyo senso to himeyurri butai, 1962 (Yamamura 3)

Taiheyo kiseki no sakusen Kiska, 1965 (Mifune 3)

Taiko-ki, 1958 (Yamada 3)

Tail Gunner Joe, 1977 (Carradine 3, Meredith 3, Neal 3)

Tail of the Monkey, 1926 (Lantz 4)

Tail Spin, 1939 (Faye 3, Wyman 3, Brown 4, Freund 4, Zanuck 4)

Tailor from Torzhok. *See* Zakroishchik iz Torzhka, 1925

Tailor Made Man, 1922 (Irene 4)

Tailor Made Man, 1931 (Wood 2)

Tailor's Maid. *See* Padri e figli, 1957

Tailor's Story. *See* Krejčovská povíkda, 1954

Taina Germanskovo posolstva, 1914 (Mozhukin 3)

Taina korolevy, 1918 (Mozhukin 3)

Taina niegorodskoi yamarki, 1915 (Mozhukin 3)

Tainstvennie nekto, 1914 (Mozhukin 3)

Taint, 1915 (Olcott 2)

Tainted. *See* Visiteur, 1946

Tainted Money. *See* Show Them No Mercy, 1935

Tai-Pan, 1986 (Cardiff 4, De Laurentiis 4, Jarre 4)

Taiyo ni somuku mono, 1959 (Tanaka 3)

Taiyo no karyudo, 1970 (Takemitsu 4)

Taiyo wa higashi yori, 1932 (Tanaka 3)

Tajemnica dzikiego szybu, 1956 (Cybulski 3)

Tajemství hradu v Karpatech, 1982 (Brodský 3, Brdečka 4, Švankmajer 4)

Tajemství krve, 1953 (Brodský 3, Stallich 4)

Tak laska Zacina, 1975 (Brodský 3)

Takadanobaba, 1944 (Yoda 4)

Take, 1990 (Anhalt 4)

Take a Chance, 1918 (Daniels 3, Lloyd 3, Roach 4)

Take a Chance, 1933 (LeMaire 4)

Take a Giant Step, 1959 (Epstein 4)

Take a Girl Like You, 1970 (Reed 3)

Take a Hard Ride, 1975 (Andrews 3, Van Cleef 3, Goldsmith 4, Needham 4)

Take a Letter, Darling, 1942 (Leisen 2, MacMurray 3, Russell 3, Benchley 4, Dreier 4, Irene 4)

Take a Trip, 1926 (Fleischer 4)

Take Care of My Little Girl, 1951 (Negulesco 2, Epstein 4, LeMaire 4, Newman 4, Reynolds 4)

Take Cover, 1940 (Pearson 2)

Take 'em and Shake 'em, 1931 (Arbuckle 3)

Take Her, She's Mine, 1963 (Stewart 3, Ballard 4, Goldsmith 4, Johnson 4, Smith 4)

Take It or Leave It, 1944 (La Shelle 4)

Take Me Home, 1928 (Neilan 2, Brown 3, Daniels 3, Hunt 4)

Take Me Out to the Ball Game, 1910 (Anderson 3)

Take Me Out to the Ball Game, 1949 (Berkeley 2, Donen 2, Kelly 3, Sinatra 3, Williams 3, Comden 4, Deutsch 4, Edens 4, Folsey 4, Freed 4, Mayer 4, Rose 4)

Take Me to Town, 1953 (Sirk 2, Hayden 3, Sheridan 3, Hunter 4, Metty 4)

Take My Life, 1947 (Alwyn 4, Green 4, Havelock-Allan 4, Rank 4)

Take My Tip, 1937 (Launder and Gilliat 2, Metzner 4)

Take Next Car, 1922 (Roach 4)

Take One, 1990 (Burstyn 3)

Take One False Step, 1949 (Powell 3, Winters 3, Orry-Kelly 4)

Take the 5:10 to Dreamland, 1976 (Conner 2)

Take the Air, 1923 (Roach 4)

Take the Air, 1940 (Eason 4)

Take the Heir, 1930 (Horton 3)

Take the High Ground, 1953 (Brooks 2, Malden 3, Widmark 3, Alton 4, Schary 4, Tiomkin 4)

Take the Money and Run, 1969 (Allen 2, Hill 2, Hamlisch 4, Rosenblum 4)

Take the Stage. *See* Curtain Call at Cactus Creek, 1950

Take This—My Body, 1974 (Baker 3)

Take Your Medicine, 1930 (Sennett 2)

Take Your Time, 1925 (Sennett 2)

Takekurabe, 1955 (Yamada 3)

Takeshi. *See* Shonnenjidai, 1990

Taketori Monogatari, 1987 (Mifune 3)

Taki no Shiraito, 1933 (Mizoguchi 2)

Taki no Shiraito, 1952 (Kyo 3, Mori 3, Miyagawa 4, Yoda 4)

Taki no Shiraito, the Water Magician. *See* Taki no Shiraito, 1933

Taking a Chance, 1912 (Lawrence 3)

Taking a Chance, 1916 (Mix 3)

Taking a Chance, 1928 (McLeod 2)
Taking Care of Business, 1990 (Reynolds 4)
Taking His Medicine, 1911 (Sennett 2)
Taking Off, 1970 (Forman 2, Carrière 4, Henry 4)
Taking of Luke McVane, 1915 (Hart 3, August 4)
Taking of Mustang Pete, 1915 (Mix 3)
Taking of Pelham One Two Three, 1974 (Matthau 3, Shaw 3, Roizman 4)
Taking the Blame, 1935 (Fleischer 4)
Taking Ways, 1933 (Baxter 2)
Taková láska, 1959 (Weiss 2, Brdečka 4)
Takový je zivot, 1930 (Baranovskaya 3)
Takt, tone og tosser, 1925 (Madsen and Schenstrøm 3)
Tal des Lebens, 1913 (Porten 3, Messter 4)
Tal Farlow, 1980 (Lye 4)
Tala and Rhythm, 1972 (Benegal 2)
Talash, 1969 (Burman 4)
Tale of a Dead Princess, 1953 (Ivanov-Vano 4)
Tale of Archery at the Sanjusangendo. See Sanju-sangen-do toshi ya monogatari, 1944
Tale of a Shirt, 1933 (Terry 4)
Tale of a Wolf, 1958 (Hanna and Barbera 4)
Tale of Czar Sultan, 1966 (Ptushko 4)
Tale of Five Cities, 1950 (Mastroianni 3)
Tale of Five Cities. See Passaporto per l'Oriente, 1951
Tale of Genji. See Genji monogatari, 1951
Tale of John and Mary. See Pohádka o Honzíkovi a Mařence, 1980
Tale of Lost Time, 1964 (Ptushko 4)
Tale of Tales, 1980 (Norstein 4)
Tale of the Black Eye, 1913 (Sennett 2)
Tale of the Crucified Lovers. See **Chikamatsu monogatari, 1954**
Tale of the Fisherman and the Little Fish, 1937 (Ptushko 4)
Tale of the Fjords. See Drömda dalen, 1947
Tale of the Magician, 1964 (Halas and Batchelor 4)
Tale of the West or A Tail of the West, 1909 (Anderson 3)
Tale of the Wilderness, 1911 (Griffith 2, Bitzer 4)
Tale of Two Cities, 1911 (Costello 3, Talmadge 3)
Tale of Two Cities, 1917 (Dumont 3)
Tale of Two Cities, 1935 (Van Dyke 2, Colman 3, Rathbone 3, Walthall 3, Behrman 4, Gibbons 4, Mayer 4, Selznick 4, Stothart 4)
Tale of Two Cities, 1958 (Bogarde 3, Lee 3, Pleasence 3, Box 4, Clarke 4, Dillon 4, Rank 4)
Tale of Two Cities, 1980 (Cushing 3, More 3)
Tale of Two Kitties, 1942 (Blanc 4, Clampett 4, Foster 4, Stalling 4)
Tale of Two Mice, 1945 (Blanc 4, Stalling 4)
Tale of Two Worlds, 1921 (Beery 3)
Talegaon, 1914 (Phalke 2)
Talent Competition. See Konkurs, 1963
Talent for Loving, 1968 (Topol 3, Widmark 4)
Talent for Murder, 1983 (Lansbury 3, Olivier 3)
Taler De tysk. See Tausend Worte Deutsch, 1930
Tales By Capek. See Capkovy povídky, 1947

Tales from a Country by the Sea. See Kaikoku-ki, 1928
Tales from the Crypt, 1972 (Cushing 3, Richardson 3, Francis 4)
Tales from the Crypt II. See Vault of Horror, 1973
Tales from the Dark Side—The Movie, 1990 (Romero 2)
Tales from the Vienna Woods. See Geschichten aus dem Wienerwald, 1981
Tales of a Salesman, 1965 (Zsigmond 4)
Tales of Hoffman. See Hoffmanns Erzählungen, 1916
Tales of Hoffman, 1951 (Powell and Pressburger 2, Challis 4, Francis 4, Heckroth 4, Korda 4)
Tales of Hoffman. See Hoffmanovy povídky, 1962
Tales of Manhattan, 1942 (Duvivier 2, Boyer 3, Fonda 3, Hayworth 3, Lanchester 3, Laughton 3, Marsh 3, Robeson 3, Robinson 3, Rogers 3, Sanders 3, Day 4, Hecht 4, Hoffenstein 4, Leven 4, Spiegel 4, Stewart 4, Trotti 4, Walker 4)
Tales of Mystery. See Histoires extraordinaires, 1968
Tales of Ordinary Madness. See Storie di ordinaria follia, 1981
Tales of Terror, 1962 (Corman 2, Lorre 3, Price 3, Rathbone 3, Crosby 4)
Tales of the Typewriter. See Mesék az írógépröl, 1916
Tales That Witness Madness, 1973 (Hawkins 3, Novak 3, Pleasence 3, Francis 4)
Talíre nad Velkym Malikovem, 1977 (Brodský 3)
Talisman. See Amuletten, 1911
Talk about a Stranger, 1952 (Alton 4)
Talk about Work, 1971 (Menges 4)
Talk Between Men. See Muzhskoi Razgovor, 1969
Talk of the Devil, 1936 (Reed 2, Rutherford 3)
Talk of the Town, 1918 (Chaney 3)
Talk of the Town, 1942 (Stevens 2, Arthur 3, Colman 3, Grant 3, Buchman 4, Cohn 4, Irene 4)
Talk Radio, 1988 (Stone 2)
Talk to Me Like the Rain, 1959 (Sirk 2)
Talker, 1925 (Edeson 4)
Talking Feet, 1937 (Baxter 2)
Talking Heads, 1988 (Smith 3)
Talking Magpies, 1946 (Terry 4)
Talking Nicaragua, 1984 (Sarandon 3)
Talking Through My Heart, 1936 (Fleischer 4)
Tall Blond Man with One Black Shoe. See Grand Blond avec une chaussure noire, 1972
Tall Headlines, 1952 (Zetterling 2)
Tall in the Saddle, 1944 (Bond 3, Wayne 3)
Tall Lie. See For Men Only, 1951
Tall Man Riding, 1955 (Scott 3)
Tall Men, 1955 (Walsh 2, Gable 3, Marsh 3, Russell 3, Ryan 3, LeMaire 4, Nugent 4, Wheeler 4, Young 4)
Tall Story, 1960 (Fonda 3, Perkins 3, Epstein 4)
Tall Stranger, 1957 (McCrea 3, Mirisch 4, Salter 4)
Tall T, 1957 (Boetticher 2, O'Sullivan 3, Scott 3, Brown 4)
Tall Tale Teller, 1954 (Terry 4)

Tall Tales, 1940 (Van Dyke 2, Maddow 4)
Tall Target, 1951 (Mann 2, Menjou 3, Powell 3, Gibbons 4)
Tall Texan, 1953 (Cobb 3, Biroc 4)
Tall Timber, 1928 (Disney 4)
Tall Timber. See Park Avenue Logger, 1937
Tall Timber Tale, 1951 (Terry 4)
Tall Trouble. See Hell Canyon Outlaws, 1957
Tall Women. See Frauen, die durch die Hölle gehen, 1966
Talla, 1967 (Le Grice 2)
Taller de la vida, 1985 (Alvarez 2)
Tam Lin. See Devil's Widow, 1971
Tam Lin, 1971 (Cusack 3, Gardner 3, McDowall 3)
Tam na horach, 1920 (Ondra 3)
Tam Tam, 1954 (Vanel 3)
Tam Tam Mayumba, 1955 (Armendáriz 3, Mastroianni 3)
Tamahine, 1963 (Arnold 4, Unsworth 4)
Tamale Vendor, 1931 (Arbuckle 3)
Tama no sanka: Moyuru wakamono-tachi, 1962 (Iwashita 3)
Tamango, 1957 (Dandridge 3, Douy 4, Kosma 4, Wakhévitch 4)
Tamara la complaisante, 1937 (Delannoy 2, Auric 4)
Tamarind Seed, 1974 (Edwards 2, Andrews 3, Homolka 3, Quayle 3, Sharif 3, Barry 4, Pinter 4, Young 4)
Tamas, 1987 (Nihalani 4)
Tamasha, 1952 (Anand 3)
Tambíen de dolor se canta, 1950 (Infante 3)
Tambora, 1930 (Fejös 2)
Tambour. See Blechtrommel, 1978
Tambour battant, 1933 (Rosay 3)
Tamburaši u Spejbla a Hurvínka, 1953 (Stallich 4)
Tame Men and Wild Women, 1925 (Roach 4)
Tamer of Wild Horses. See Krotitelj divlijh konja, 1966
T'amerò sempre, 1933 (Camerini 2, Berry 3, Cervi 3, Valli 3, Amidei 4)
Taming a Husband, 1910 (Griffith 2, Bitzer 4)
Taming Mrs. Shrew, 1912 (Porter 2)
Taming of Dorothy. See Her Favourite Husband, 1950
Taming of Grouchy Bill, 1916 (Mix 3)
Taming of Jane, 1910 (Lawrence 3)
Taming of Texas Pete, 1913 (Mix 3)
Taming of the Shrew, 1908 (Griffith 2, Lawrence 3, Bitzer 4)
Taming of the Shrew, 1929 (Fairbanks 3, Pickford 3, Menzies 4, Struss 4)
Taming of the Shrew. See Jajauma narashi, 1966
Taming of the Shrew, 1967 (Zeffirelli 2, Burton 3, Cusack 3, Taylor 3, Cecchi d'Amico 4, Dehn 4, Donati 4, Morris 4, Rota 4, Sharaff 4)
Taming of the Snood, 1940 (Keaton 2, Bruckman 4)
Taming Target Center, 1917 (Sennett 2)
Taming the Cat, 1947 (Terry 4)
Taming the Four-Flusher. See Passing of Two-Gun Hicks, 1914
Taming the Mekong, 1965 (Van Dyke 2)
Taming Wild Animals, 1910 (Mix 3)
Tammy. See Tammy and the Bachelor, 1957

Tammy and the Bachelor, 1957 (Beavers 3, Brennan 3, Reynolds 3, Wray 3, Hunter 4)

Tammy and the Doctor, 1963 (Bondi 3, Hunter 4, Metty 4)

Tammy, Tell Me True, 1961 (Bondi 3, Hunter 4)

Tampico, 1944 (McLaglen 3, Robinson 3, Basevi 4, Clarke 4, Raksin 4)

Tampon du capiston, 1950 (Braunberger 4)

Tanganyika, 1954 (De Toth 2, Salter 4)

Tange Sazen, 1933 (Yamada 3)

Tange Sazen: Kenteki-hen, 1934 (Yamada 3)

Tangier, 1946 (Banton 4)

Tangier Assignment, 1955 (Rey 3)

Tangled Affair, 1913 (Sennett 2, Normand 3)

Tangled Fates, 1916 (Marion 4)

Tangled Hearts, 1916 (Chaney 3)

Tangled Lives, 1911 (Olcott 2)

Tangled Marriage, 1910 (White 3)

Tangled Relations, 1912 (Lawrence 3)

Tangled Tangoists, 1914 (Bunny 3)

Tangled Travels, 1944 (Fleischer 4)

Tanglewood, Music School and Music Festival. See Tanglewood Story, 1950

Tanglewood Story, 1950 (Kaufman 4)

Tango, 1936 (Pangborn 3)

Tango and Cash, 1989 (Mikhalkov-Konchalovsky 2, Palance 3, Stallone 3)

Tango del viudo, 1967 (Ruiz 2)

Tango della gelosia, 1981 (Vitti 3)

Tango für dich, 1930 (Reisch 4)

Tango notturno, 1937 (Wagner 4)

Tango notturno, 1938 (Negri 3)

Tango Tangles, 1914 (Sennett 2, Arbuckle 3)

Tangos—el exilio de Gardel, 1986 (Solanas and Getino 2)

Tangos—l'exil de Gardel. See Tangos—el exilio de Gardel, 1986

Tanin no kao, 1966 (Kyo 3, Okada 3, Takemitsu 4)

Tank, 1984 (Garner 3, Schifrin 4)

Tank Force. See No Time to Die, 1958

Tank Tactics, 1936 (Dickinson 2)

Tanks a Million, 1941 (Roach 4)

Tanks Are Coming, 1941 (Eason 4)

Tanks Are Coming, 1951 (Fuller 2)

Tanned Legs, 1929 (Neilan 2, Plunkett 4)

Tannenberg, 1950 (Staudte 2)

Tannhauser, 1913 (Cruze 2)

Tansy, 1921 (Hepworth 2)

Tant, 1970 (Douy 4)

Tant d'amour perdu, 1958 (Fresnay 3)

Tant Grun, Tant Brun, och Tant Gredelin, 1945 (Fischer 4)

Tant que je vivrai, 1945 (Feuillère 3, Matras 4)

Tant qu'il est temps: le cancer, 1960 (Braunberger 4)

Tant qu'il y aura des femmes, 1955 (Burel 4)

Tant qu'on a la santé. See Nous n'irons plus au bois, 1963

Tantalizing Fly, 1942 (Fleischer 4)

Tante Zita, 1968 (Hondo 2, Saulnier 4)

Tanuki, 1956 (Yoda 4)

Tanuki no kyujitsu, 1966 (Muraki 4)

Tanuki no taishou, 1965 (Muraki 4)

Tanya's Island, 1981 (Bottin 4)

Tanyets smerti, 1916 (Mozhukin 3)

Tanz auf dem Vulkan, 1921 (Lugosi 3)

Tanz auf dem Vulkan, 1938 (Gründgens 3)

Tanz um Liebe und Glück, 1921 (Krauss 3)

Tanzende Wien, 1927 (Andrejew 4)

Tänzer meiner Frau, 1925 (Leni 2, Korda 4)

Tänzerin. See Maihime, 1989

Tänzerin Navarro, 1922 (Nielsen 3)

Tänzerin von Sanssouci, 1933 (Dagover 3)

Tap on the Shoulder, 1965 (Loach 2)

Tap Roots, 1948 (Bond 3, Hayward 3, Karloff 3, Hoch 4, Wanger 4)

Tapis moquette, 1935 (Leenhardt 2)

Tapis volant, 1960 (Jarre 4)

Tapisserie au XXe siècle, 1955 (Kosma 4)

Tappa inte sugen, 1947 (Fischer 4)

Tappre soldaten Jönsson, 1956 (Nykvist 4)

Taps, 1981 (Cruise 3, Scott 3, Jarre 4, Roizman 4)

Tapum, la storia delle armi, 1958 (Bozzetto 4)

Taqdeer, 1943 (Mehboob 2, Nargis 3)

Tarahumara, 1965 (Alcoriza 4)

Tarakanova, 1930 (Artaud 3, D'Eaubonne 4, Wakhévitch 4)

Tarakanowa, 1938 (Magnani 3, Andrejew 4, Annenkov 4, Courant 4, Jeanson 4)

Taran, 1951 (Biswas 4)

Tarantel, 1920 (Messter 4)

Tarantelle, 1900 (Guy 2)

Tarantol dal ventre nero, 1971 (Giannini 3)

Tarantola dal ventro nero, 1971 (Morricone 4)

Tarantula, 1912 (Macpherson 4)

Tarantula, 1955 (Eastwood 3, Mancini 4, Westmore Family 4)

Taras Bulba, 1962 (Brynner 3, Curtis 3, Reynolds 4, Salt 4, Waxman 4)

Taras Shevchenko, 1951 (Bondarchuk 3)

Tarass Boulba, 1936 (Baur 3, Darrieux 3, Andrejew 4, Planer 4)

Tarde del domingo, 1957 (Saura 2)

Tare, 1911 (Gaumont 4)

Tarea, 1990 (Hermosillo 2)

Tares, 1918 (Hepworth 2)

Target, 1916 (Bosworth 3)

Target, 1952 (Hunt 4)

Target, 1985 (Penn 2, Dillon 3, Hackman 3)

Target Eagle. See Jugando con la muerte, 1982

Target Eagle, 1984 (Von Sydow 3)

Target for Killing. See Geheimnis der gelben Mönche, 1966

Target for Scandal. See Washington Story, 1952

Target for Tonight, 1941 (Hitchcock 2, Watt 2, Dalrymple 4)

Target in the Sun. See Man Who Would Not Die, 1975

Target Zero, 1955 (Bronson 3)

Targets, 1967 (Bogdanovich 2, Corman 2, Karloff 3, Fields 4, Kovacs 4)

Taris, 1931 (Vigo 2)

Taris roi de l'eau. See Taris, 1931

Tarka the Otter, 1978 (Ustinov 3)

Tarnish, 1924 (Colman 3, Carré 4, Goldwyn 4, Marion 4, Miller 4)

Tarnished Angel, 1938 (Miller 3, Musuraca 4, Polglase 4)

Tarnished Angels, 1957 (Sirk 2, Hudson 3, Malone 3, Faulkner 4)

Tarnished Lady, 1931 (Cukor 2, Banton 4, Stewart 4, Zukor 4)

Tarnished Reputation, 1920 (Guy 2)

Tarot, 1973 (Grahame 3, Rey 3)

Tarot, 1986 (Vogler 3)

Tarps Elin, 1956 (Dahlbeck 3)

Tars and Spars, 1946 (Cahn 4, Walker 4, Westmore Family 4)

Tars & Stripes, 1935 (Keaton 2)

Tartari, 1960 (Welles 2, Mature 3)

Tartarin de Tarascon, 1934 (Pagnol 2, Raimu 3, Douy 4, Milhaud 4)

Tartars. See Tartari, 1961

Tartassati, 1959 (Fabrizi 3)

Tartelette, 1968 (Grimault 4)

Tartu. See Adventures of Tartu, 1943

Tartüff, 1925 (Murnau 2, Dagover 3, Jannings 3, Krauss 3, Freund 4, Herlth 4, Mayer 4, Pommer 4, Röhrig 4)

Tartuffe. See Tartüff, 1926

Tartuffe, 1984 (Depardieu 3)

Tarzan and His Mate, 1934 (O'Sullivan 3, Weissmuller 3, Clarke 4, Gibbons 4, Gillespie 4, Mayer 4)

Tarzan and Jane Regained ... Sort Of, 1963 (Warhol 2, Hopper 3)

Tarzan and the Amazons, 1945 (Weissmuller 3)

Tarzan and the Golden Lion, 1927 (Karloff 3, Walker 4)

Tarzan and the Huntress, 1947 (Weissmuller 3)

Tarzan and the Jungle Queen. See Tarzan's Peril, 1951

Tarzan and the Leopard Woman, 1946 (Weissmuller 3, Struss 4)

Tarzan and the Mermaids, 1948 (Florey 2, Weissmuller 3, Figueroa 4, Tiomkin 4)

Tarzan and the She Devil, 1953 (Struss 4)

Tarzan and the Slave Girl, 1950 (Harlan 4, Horner 4)

Tarzan Escapes, 1936 (O'Sullivan 3, Weissmuller 3, Brown 4, Mayer 4)

Tarzan Finds a Son, 1939 (O'Sullivan 3, Weissmuller 3)

Tarzan in Manhattan, 1990 (Curtis 3)

Tarzan, the Ape Man, 1932 (Van Dyke 2, O'Sullivan 3, Weissmuller 3, Gillespie 4, Mayer 4, Rosson 4)

Tarzan, the Ape Man, 1981 (Harris 3, Storaro 4)

Tarzan the Fearless, 1933 (Crabbe 3)

Tarzan the Magnificent, 1960 (Carradine 3)

Tarzan Triumphs, 1943 (Weissmuller 3, Horner 4)

Tarzan's Desert Mystery, 1943 (Weissmuller 3, Harlan 4)

Tarzan's Greatest Adventure, 1959 (Connery 3, Quayle 3, Fisher 4)

Tarzan's Magic Fountain, 1949 (Siodmak 4, Struss 4)

Tarzan's New York Adventure, 1942 (O'Sullivan 3, Weissmuller 3, Mayer 4)

Tarzan's Peril, 1951 (Dandridge 3, Haskin 4, Struss 4)

Tarzan's Savage Fury, 1952 (Struss 4)

Tarzan's Secret Treasure, 1941 (Fitzgerald 3, O'Sullivan 3, Weissmuller 3)

Task Force, 1949 (Daves 2, Brennan 3, Cooper 3, Burks 4, Wald 4, Waxman 4)

Tassels in the Air, 1938 (Three Stooges 3)

Tassinaro, 1983 (Sordi 3)

Tassinaro a New York, 1987 (Sordi 3)

Taste for Women. See Aimez-vous des femmes, 1964

Taste of Catnip, 1966 (Blanc 4, McKimson 4)

Taste of Evil, 1971 (McDowall 3, Stanwyck 3, Sangster 4)

Taste of Fear, 1961 (Lee 3, Carreras 4, Sangster 4, Slocombe 4)

Taste of Honey, 1961 (Richardson 2, Yates 2, Addison 4, Lassally 4)

Taste the Blood of Dracula, 1970 (Lee 3, Bernard 4, Carreras 4)

Tasveer Apni Apni, 1985 (Sen 2)

Tata Mia, 1986 (Maura 3)

Tateshi Danpei, 1950 (Yamada 3)

Tateshi Danpei, 1962 (Tanaka 3)

Tateshina no shiki, 1966 (Shindo 2)

Tatiana, 1923 (Litvak 2)

Tatjana, 1923 (Tschechowa 3, Messter 4, Pommer 4)

Tatli-Bela, 1961 (Güney 2)

Tatooed Arm, 1913 (Reid 3)

Tatoué, 1968 (Gabin 3, Vierny 4)

Tatsu. See Toburoku no Tatsu, 1962

Tatsumaki bugyo, 1959 (Yamamura 3)

Tattered Web, 1971 (Crawford 3)

Tattle Television, 1940 (Hunt 4)

Tattoo. See Irezumi, 1966

Tattoo, 1981 (Dern 3, Donaggio 4, Levine 4)

Taugenichts, 1922 (Herlth 4)

Taumel. See Gehetzte Menschen, 1924

Tausend Worte Deutsch, 1930 (Madsen and Schenstrøm 3)

Tavaszni szerelem, 1921 (Banky 3)

Tavelure du pommier et du poirier, 1955 (Rabier 4)

Tavern Keeper's Daughter, 1908 (Griffith 2)

Tavern of Tragedy, 1914 (Crisp 3)

Taverna rossa, 1939 (Valli 3)

Taverne du poisson couronne, 1947 (Berry 3, Simon 3, Jeanson 4)

Tavola dei poveri, 1932 (Blasetti 2)

Tawny Pipit, 1943 (Rank 4, Vetchinsky 4)

Taxandria, 1988 (Robbe-Grillet 4)

Taxi!, 1932 (Cagney 3, Raft 3, Young 3)

Taxi, 1953 (Cassavetes 2, Page 3, Krasner 4, LeMaire 4)

Taxi Barons, 1933 (Roach 4)

Taxi Beauties, 1928 (Sennett 2, Hornbeck 4)

Taxi Dancer, 1927 (Crawford 3, Mayer 4)

Taxi di notte, 1950 (Aldo 4)

Taxi Dolls, 1929 (Sennett 2, Hornbeck 4)

Taxi Driver, 1927 (Gibbons 4)

Taxi Driver, 1954 (Anand 3, Burman 4)

Taxi Driver, 1976 (Schrader 2, Scorsese 2, De Niro 3, Foster 3, Herrmann 4, Smith 4)

Taxi for Tobruk. See Taxi pour Tobrouk, 1961

Taxi for Two, 1928 (Sennett 2, Hornbeck 4)

Taxi for Two, 1929 (Balcon 4)

Taxi mauve, 1977 (Astaire 3, Noiret 3, Ustinov 3, Delli Colli 4, Sarde 4)

Taxi, Mister, 1943 (Bendix 3, Roach 4)

Taxi, Mister. See Two Knights from Brooklyn, 1949

Taxi pour Tobrouk, 1961 (Audiard 4)

Taxi Scandal, 1928 (Sennett 2, Hornbeck 4)

Taxi Spooks, 1929 (Sennett 2, Hornbeck 4)

Taxi Talks, 1930 (Tracy 3)

Taxi! Taxi!, 1927 (Horton 3)

Taxi 13, 1928 (Neilan 2, Berman 4)

Taxi Troubles, 1931 (Sennett 2)

Taxichauffeur Bänz, 1957 (Schell 3)

Taxidi sta kythera, 1985 (Guerra 4)

Taylor Mead's Ass, 1964 (Warhol 2)

Taza, Son of Cochise, 1953 (Sirk 2, Hudson 3, Hunter 4)

Tažní ptáci, 1961 (Stallich 4)

Tchaikovsky, 1968 (Tiomkin 4)

Tchaikovsky, 1970 (Harvey 3)

Tchaikovsky, and Rachimanova. See V tylu u belych, 1925

Tchan, 1979 (Brodský 3)

Tchao Pantin, 1983 (Trauner 4)

Tchaz Boulat, 1913 (Mozhukin 3)

Tchin-Tchin, 1990 (Andrews 3, Mastroianni 3, Donaggio 4)

Te, 1963 (Szabó 2)

Te deum, 1973 (Palance 3)

Te o tsunagu ko-ra, 1964 (Takemitsu 4)

Te o tsunaqu kora, 1948 (Miyagawa 4)

Te quiero, 1978 (Figueroa 4)

Tea and Sympathy, 1956 (Minnelli 2, Kerr 3, Alton 4, Berman 4, Deutsch 4, Rose 4)

Tea for Three, 1927 (Day 4, Gibbons 4)

Tea for Two, 1950 (Arden 3, Day 3, Prinz 4)

Tea in the Garden, 1958 (Wieland 2)

Teacher and the Miracle. See Maestro, 1958

Teachers, 1984 (Grant 3, Nolte 3)

Teacher's Beau, 1935 (Roach 4)

Teacher's Pest, 1931 (Fleischer 4)

Teacher's Pests, 1932 (Lantz 4)

Teacher's Pet, 1958 (Day 3, Gable 3, Head 4)

Teaching Dad to Like Her, 1911 (Griffith 2, Bitzer 4)

Teaching of the Ittou Style. See Ittouryu shinan, 1936

Teaching the Teacher, 1921 (Roach 4)

Teahouse of the August Moon, 1956 (Brando 3, Ford 3, Kyo 3, Alton 4)

Team. See Venedig—die Insel der Glückseligen am Rande am des Untergangs, 1978

Teamwork, 1977 (Dunning 4)

Tear Me But Satiate Me with Your Kisses. See Straziami ma di baci saziami, 1968

Tear on the Page, 1915 (Loos 4)

Tear That Burned, 1914 (Gish 3, Sweet 3)

Tearin' into Trouble, 1927 (Brennan 3)

Tearin' Loose, 1925 (Arthur 3)

Tears for Simon. See Lost, 1955

Tears in the Lion's Mane. See Namida o shishi no tategami no, 1962

Tears of an Onion, 1938 (Fleischer 4)

Tease for Two, 1965 (Blanc 4, McKimson 4)

Teaser, 1925 (Barnes 4)

Tebe, Front: Kazakhstan Front, 1943 (Vertov 2)

Tebukuro o nugasu otoko, 1946 (Miyagawa 4)

Technicien du Film, 1962 (Alexeieff and Parker 4)

Technocracked, 1933 (Iwerks 4)

Techo de la ballena, 1982 (Alekan 4)

Teckman Mystery, 1954 (Korda 4, Rank 4)

Teddy at the Throttle, 1917 (Sennett 2, Beery 3, Swanson 3)

Teddy Bears, 1907 (Porter 2)

Tee for Two, 1925 (Sennett 2)

Tee for Two, 1945 (Hanna and Barbera 4)

Teen Deviyan, 1964 (Anand 3, Burman 4)

Teen Kanya, 1961 (Chatterjee 3, Chandragupta 4, Datta 4)

Teen Wolf, 1985 (Fox 3, Baker 4)

Teenage Caveman, 1958 (Crosby 4)

Teenage Doll, 1957 (Corman 2)

Teenage Rebel, 1956 (Goulding 2, Beavers 3, Rogers 3, Brackett 4, LeMaire 4, Reisch 4, Smith 4, Wheeler 4)

Teesri Kasam, 1966 (Kapoor 2)

Teeth, 1924 (Mix 3)

Teeth of Steel, 1942 (Unsworth 4)

Teheran 1943. See Teheran Incident, 1979

Teheran Incident, 1979 (Carradine 3, Delon 3)

Tehlikeli adam, 1965 (Güney 2)

Teilnehmer antwortet nicht, 1932 (Gründgens 3, Junge 4, Planer 4)

Teiva, enfant des îles, 1960 (Kosma 4)

Tejedor de milagros, 1961 (Figueroa 4)

Tejedor de Yarey, 1959 (Gómez 2)

Tekka bugyo, 1954 (Kinugasa 2, Hasegawa 3, Kagawa 3)

Tekken seisai, 1930 (Tanaka 3)

Tekki kushu, 1943 (Yoshimura 2, Tanaka 3)

Tel est pris qui croyait prendre, 1901 (Guy 2)

Telecouture sans fil, 1910 (Cohl 4)

Telefilm, 1928 (Fleischer 4)

Telefon, 1962 (Mimica 4)

Telefon, 1977 (Siegel 2, Bronson 3, Pleasence 3, Remick 3, Schifrin 4)

Telefoni bianchi, 1976 (Gassman 3)

Telefoni bianchi, 1976 (Brazzi 3)

Teleftaio Stichima, 1987 (Olbrychski 3)

Telegram from New York. See New York expresz kabel, 1921

Telegraph Trail, 1933 (Wayne 3, Canutt 4, McCord 4)

Telephone, 1956 (Fernandel 3)

Telephone. See Telefon, 1962

Telephone, 1988 (Goldberg 3, Gould 3)

Telephone Engagement, 1910 (White 3)

Telephone Girl series, 1924 (Garmes 4)

Telephone Girl, 1912 (Reid 3)

Telephone Girl, 1927 (Brenon 2)

Telephone Girl and the Lady, 1913 (Griffith 2, Barrymore 3, Marsh 3, Bitzer 4, Loos 4)

Telephone Rings in the Evening. See Denwa wa yugata ni naru, 1959

Telephone Workers, 1933 (Grierson 2)

Teletests, 1980 (Ruiz 2)

Telethon, 1978 (Leigh 3)

Television Fan. See Zavada není na vašem přijímaci, 1961

Television Spy, 1939 (Dmytryk 2, Quinn 3, Head 4)

Tell 'em Nothing, 1926 (McCarey 2, Roach 4)

Tell It to a Policeman, 1925 (Roach 4)

Tell it to a Star, 1945 (Pangborn 3)

Tell It to Sweeney, 1927 (La Cava 2, Schulberg 4)

Tell It to the Judge, 1928 (McCarey 2, Roach 4)

Tell It to the Judge, 1949 (Beavers 3, Russell 3, Walker 4)

Tell It to the Marines, 1926 (Chaney 3, Gibbons 4, Gillespie 4)

Tell Me a Riddle, 1980 (Douglas 3, Grant 3)

Tell Me Lies, 1968 (Jackson 3)

Tell Me That You Love Me, Junie Moon, 1970 (Preminger 2, Minnelli 3, Cortez 4, Kaufman 4, Wheeler 4)

Tell No Tales, 1939 (Douglas 3, Ruttenberg 4)

Tell Tale Brother, 1910 (White 3)

Tell Tale Light, 1913 (Sennett 2, Arbuckle 3)

Tell Tale Shells, 1911 (Dwan 2)

Tell Tale Wire, 1919 (Eason 4)

Tell Them Willie Boy Is Here, 1969 (Polonsky 2, Redford 3, Bumstead 4, Hall 4, Head 4, Westmore Family 4)

Tell Your Children, 1922 (Hitchcock 2, Crisp 3)

Telling the World, 1928 (Wood 2, Booth 4, Daniels 4, Gibbons 4)

Telling Whoppers, 1926 (Roach 4)

Tell-Tale Hand, 1914 (Anderson 3)

Tenero Tramonto, 1984 (Cassel 3)
Tengo fe en ti, 1979 (Alvarez 2)
Tengoku ni musubu koi, 1932 (Takamine 3)
Tengoku to jigoku, 1963 (Kagawa 3,
 Mifune 3, Shimura 3, Muraki 4)
Tengu-daoshi, 1944 (Kyo 3)
Tenichibo to iganosuke, 1933 (Kinugasa 2,
 Hasegawa 3)
Tenjodaifu, 1956 (Kagawa 3)
Tenka gomen, 1960 (Yamada 3)
Tenka no goikenban o Ikensuru otoko, 1947
 (Yoda 4)
Tenka no igagoe, 1934 (Tsuburaya 4)
Tenka o nerau bishounen, 1955
 (Miyagawa 4)
Tenka taihai, 1955 (Mifune 3, Tsukasa 3,
 Muraki 4)
Tennessee Champ, 1954 (Bronson 3,
 Winters 3, Folsey 4)
Tennessee Johnson, 1942 (Barrymore 3,
 Beavers 3, Balderston 4, Rosson 4,
 Stothart 4)
Tennessee Nights, 1989 (Steiger 3)
Tennessee's Partner, 1955 (Dwan 2,
 Dickinson 3, Reagan 3, Alton 4,
 Polglase 4)
Tennis, 1949 (Cocteau 2)
Tennis Chumps, 1949 (Hanna and
 Barbera 4)
Tennis Club, 1982 (Bozzetto 4)
Tennoji no harakiri, 1927 (Tanaka 3)
Tenpo hiken roku, 1927 (Tsuburaya 4)
Tenpo rokkasen: Jigokuno hanamichi, 1960
 (Yamada 3)
Tenpo Yasubei, 1935 (Hasegawa 3)
Tenpyo no iraka, 1979 (Takemitsu 4,
 Yoda 4)
Tenryu shibuki, 1938 (Yoda 4)
Tensai sagishi monogatari: Tanuki no
 hanamichi, 1964 (Tsukasa 3)
Tension, 1949 (Charisse 3, Previn 4,
 Stradling 4)
Tension at Table Rock, 1956 (Dickinson 3,
 Malone 3, Biroc 4, Tiomkin 4)
Tentacles. See Shokkaku, 1970
Tentacles. See Tentacoli, 1976
Tentacles of the North, 1926 (Walker 4)
Tentacoli, 1976 (Huston 2, Fonda 3,
 Winters 3)
Tentation de Barbizon, 1945 (Gélin 3)
Tentation de Saint-Antoine, 1898
 (Méliès 2)
Tentation d'Isabelle, 1985 (Sarde 4)
Tentative d'assassinat en chemin de fer,
 1904 (Guy 2)
Tentative de films abstraits, 1930 (Storck 2)
Tentazioni proibite, 1963 (Bardot 3, De
 Carlo 3, Sordi 3)
Tenth Avenue, 1948 (Surtees 4)
Tenth Avenue Angel, 1947 (Lansbury 3,
 O'Brien 3, Irene 4)
Tenth Man, 1991 (Greene 4)
Tenth Victim. See Decima vittima, 1965
Tenth Warrant, 1980 (Johnson 3)
Tenting Tonight on the Old Camp Ground,
 1943 (Salter 4)
Tent Show, 1933 (Rooney 3)
Tenue de soirée, 1986 (Depardieu 3)
Teodora, Imperatrice di Bisanzio, 1954
 (Papas 3)
Teorema, 1968 (Pasolini 2, Mangano 3,
 Stamp 3, Morricone 4)
Tepepa, 1969 (Welles 2, Morricone 4,
 Solinas 4)

Tequila Sunrise, 1988 (Gibson 3, Pfeiffer 3,
 Hall 4, Sylbert 4, Towne 4)
Tér, 1971 (Szabó 2)
Tercera palabra, 1955 (Infante 3, Alcoriza 4)
Tere Ghar Ke Samne, 1962 (Anand 3,
 Burman 4)
Tere Mere Sapne, 1971 (Anand 3, Burman 4)
Terence Davies Trilogy, 1984 (Davies 2)
Teresa, 1951 (Aldrich 2, Zinnemann 2,
 Steiger 3)
Teresa, 1987 (Risi 2)
Teresa de Jesús, 1960 (Rey 3)
Teresa la ladra, 1972 (Vitte 3, Age and
 Scarpelli 4)
Teresa the Thief. See Teresa la ladra, 1972
Teresa Venerdi, 1941 (De Sica 2, Magnani 3,
 Zavattini 4)
Teri Ankhen, 1963 (Burman 4)
Terje vigen, 1917 (Molander 2, Sjöström 2,
 Jaenzon 4, Magnusson 4)
Term of Trial, 1962 (Olivier 3, Signoret 3,
 Stamp 3, Morris 4)
Terminal Man, 1974 (Clayburgh 3,
 Segal 3)
Termination, 1966 (Baillie 2)
Terminator, 1984 (Schwarzenegger 3)
Terminator 2: Judgment Day, 1991
 (Schwarzenegger 3)
Terminus, 1961 (Schlesinger 2)
Termites of 1938, 1938 (Three Stooges 3)
Terms of Endearment, 1983 (MacLaine 3,
 Nicholson 3, Mirisch 4)
Terra bruta, 1962 (Sangster 4)
Terra di fuoco, 1938 (L'Herbier 2)
Terra incognita, 1959 (Borowczyk 2)
Terrace. See Terraza, 1962
Terra ladina, 1949 (Risi 2)
Terra madre, 1931 (Blasetti 2)
Terra promessa, 1913 (Bertini 2)
Terra straniera, 1953 (Di Venanzo 4)
**Terra trema, 1947 (Visconti 2, Zeffirelli 2,
 Aldo 4, Di Venanzo 4)**
Terrain vague, 1960 (Carné 2, Legrand 4,
 Renoir 4)
Terraza, 1962 (Torre Nilsson 2)
Terrazza, 1979 (Scola 2, Gassman 3,
 Mastroianni 3)
Terre, 1920 (Duvivier 2)
Terre d'amour, 1935 (Jaubert 4)
Terre de feu, 1938 (L'Herbier 2)
Terre de Flandre, 1938 (Storck 2)
Terre d'insectes, 1957 (Braunberger 4)
Terre d'oiseaux, 1957 (Braunberger 4)
Terre du Diable, 1922 (Modot 3)
Terre étrangère, 1987 (Piccoli 3)
Terre qui meurt, 1935 (Spaak 4)
Terres jaunes, 1989 (Deneuve 3)
Terre sous-marine, 1958 (Braunberger 4)
Terreur, 1924 (White 3)
Terreur de la Pampa, 1932 (Fernandel 3)
Terreur des Batignolles, 1931 (Clouzot 2)
Terreur en Oklahoma, 1951 (Piccoli 3,
 Douy 4)
Terrible Beauty, 1960 (Cusack 3, Harris 3,
 Mitchum 3)
Terrible Bout de papier, 1915 (Cohl 4)
Terrible Discovery, 1911 (Griffith 2,
 Bitzer 4)
Terrible Joe Moran, 1984 (Cagney 3)
Terrible Lesson, 1912 (Guy 2)
Terrible Night. See Nuit terrible, 1896
Terrible Night, 1912 (Guy 2)
Terrible Night. See Zlatcha notch, 1914
Terrible Ted, 1907 (Bitzer 4)

Terrible Teddy the Grizzly King, 1901
 (Porter 2)
Terrible Toreador, 1929 (Iwerks 4)
Terrible Toreador, 1930 (Disney 4)
Terrible Tragedy, 1916 (Laurel and Hardy 3)
Terrible Troubadour, 1933 (Lantz 4)
Terrible Turkish Executioner. See Bourreau
 turc, 1904
Terrible Vengeance. See Straschnaia miest,
 1913
Terribly Stuck Up, 1914 (Roach 4)
Terribly Talented, 1948 (Van Dyke 2,
 Kaufman 4)
Terrier Stricken, 1952 (Blanc 4, Jones 4,
 Stalling 4)
Territoire, 1981 (Alekan 4, Branco 4, De
 Almeida 4)
Territory. See Territoire, 1981
Terror, 1920 (Mix 3)
Terror, 1928 (Horton 3, Musuraca 4)
Terror, 1938 (Sim 3)
Terror, 1963 (Corman 2, Nicholson 3)
Terror, 1980 (Johnson 3)
Terror Abroad, 1933 (Banton 4)
Terror and Black Lace. See Terrór y encajes
 negros, 1986
Terror at Black Falls, 1959 (Crosby 4)
Terror by Night, 1946 (Rathbone 3, Salter 4)
Terror Faces Magoo, 1959 (Bosustow 4)
Terror from Space, 1988 (Carpenter 2)
Terror from the Year 5000, 1958 (Allen 4)
Terror House. See Night Has Eyes, 1941
Terror in a Texas Town, 1958 (Lewis 2,
 Hayden 3)
Terror in the Aisles, 1985 (Pleasence 3)
Terror in the City, 1963 (Grant 3)
Terror in the City, 1966 (Rosenblum 4)
Terror in the Crypt. See Cripta de l'incubo,
 1963
Terror in the Midnight Sun. See Invasion of
 the Animal People, 1962
Terror in the Sky, 1971 (McDowall 3)
Terror in the Wax Museum, 1973
 (Carradine 3, Crawford 3, Lanchester 3,
 Milland 3, Duning 4)
Terror Island, 1920 (Cruze 2)
Terror of Dr. Chaney. See Mansion of the
 Doomed, 1975
Terror of Manhattan, 1991 (Golan and
 Globus 4)
Terror of Sheba. See Persecution, 1974
Terror of the Tongs, 1961 (Lee 3, Bernard 4,
 Carreras 4, Sangster 4)
Terror on a Train. See Time Bomb, 1952
Terror Street. See Thirty-Six Hours, 1953
Terror Trail, 1933 (Mix 3)
Terror Train, 1980 (Curtis 3, Johnson 3,
 Alcott 4)
Terrór y encajes negros, 1986 (Alcoriza 4)
Terrore dell 'Andalusia. See Carne de horca,
 1954
Terrore sulla città, 1956 (Di Venanzo 4,
 Flaiano 4)
Terrorista, 1963 (Aimée 3, Volonté 3)
Terrorists. See Ransom, 1974
Terrors on Horseback, 1946 (Crabbe 3)
Terry Fox Story, 1983 (Duvall 3)
Terza liceo, 1954 (Amidei 4)
T'es fou, Marcel, 1974 (Montand 3)
Tesatura meccanica della linea a 220.000
 volt, 1955 (Olmi 2)
Tesha, 1928 (Saville 2)
Tesla, 1979 (Welles 2)
Tesoro del Amazonas, 1983 (Fernández 2)

Tess, 1979 (Polanski 2, Kinski 3, Cloquet 4, Sarde 4, Unsworth 4)

Tess of the D'Urbervilles, 1924 (Neilan 2, Sweet 3)

Tess of the D'Urbervilles, 1927 (Mayer 4)

Tess of the Storm Country, 1914 (Porter 2, Pickford 3)

Tess of the Storm Country, 1922 (Pickford 3, Grot 4, Rosher 4)

Tess of the Storm Country, 1932 (Gaynor 3, Behrman 4, Levien 4, Mohr 4)

Tess of the Storm Country, 1960 (Howe 4)

Test, 1909 (Griffith 2, Pickford 3, Bitzer 4)

Test, 1911 (Dwan 2, Lawrence 3)

Test, 1912 (Bosworth 3)

Test, 1914 (Reid 2)

Test. See False Bride, 1914

Test of Donald Norton, 1926 (Eason 4)

Test of Friendship, 1908 (Griffith 2, Lawrence 3, Bitzer 4)

Test of Honor, 1919 (Barrymore 3)

Test Pilot, 1938 (Fleming 2, Hawks 2, Barrymore 3, Gable 3, Loy 3, Tracy 3, Gillespie 4, Mayer 4, Vorkapich 4, Waxman 4, Young 4)

Testament, 1974 (Gabin 3, Loren 3, Ponti 4)

Testament, 1983 (Costner 3, Tavoularis 4)

Testament de Pierrot, 1904 (Guy 2)

Testament des Dr. Mabuse, 1933 (Hunte 4, Von Harbou 4, Wagner 4)

Testament d'Orphée, 1960 (Bardot 3, Brynner 3, Gélin 3, Léaud 3, Marais 3, Auric 4)

Testament du Docteur Cordelier, 1959 (Barrault 3, Modot 3, Kosma 4)

Testament d'un poete Juif assassine, 1987 (Josephson 3)

Testament of a Murdered Jewish Poet. See Testament d'un poete Juif assassine, 1987

Testament of Dr. Mabuse. See **Testament des Dr. Mabuse, 1933**

Testament of John, 1984 (Quayle 3)

Testament of Orpheus. See Testament d'Orphée, 1960

Testamenten. See Kaerlighedens Triumf, 1914

Testigos, 1968 (Villagra 3)

Testimone, 1946 (Germi 2, Zavattini 4)

Testimonies. See Vittnesbörd om henne, 1962

Testing Block, 1920 (Hart 3, August 4)

Testör, 1918 (Korda 4)

Tête, 1973 (Grimault 4)

Tête blonde, 1950 (Berry 3)

Tête contre les murs, 1958 (Aimée 3, Brasseur 3, Jarre 4, Schüfftan 4)

Tête d'horloge, 1969 (Fresnay 3)

Tête d'un homme, 1933 (Duvivier 2, Baur 3, Manès 3, Wakhévitch 4)

Têtes de femmes, femmes de tête, 1916 (Feyder 2)

Tetsu no shojo, 1928 (Tanaka 3)

Tetto, 1956 (Zavattini 4)

Teufel, 1918 (Dupont 2)

Teufel führt Regie. See Dämonische Liebe, 1950

Teufel in Seide, 1955 (Herlth 4)

Teufel und die Madonna, 1919 (Dreier 4)

Teufelsanbeter, 1918 (Lugosi 3)

Teufelskerl, 1935 (Baarová 3, Fröhlich 3)

Teufelsreporter, 1929 (Wilder 2)

Teure Heimat, 1929 (Albers 3)

Teutonic Knights. See Krzyżacy, 1960

Tevye and His Seven Daughters. See Diamonds, 1975

Tex, 1982 (Dillon 3, Johnson 3, Donaggio 4)

Texan, 1920 (Mix 3, Furthman 4)

Texan, 1930 (Cromwell 2, Hathaway 2, Cooper 3, Wray 3, Canutt 4, Zukor 4)

Texan Meets Calamity Jane, 1950 (Struss 4)

Texans, 1938 (Bennett 3, Brennan 3, Scott 3, Edouart 4, Head 4)

Texan's Honor, 1929 (Canutt 4)

Texans Never Cry, 1951 (Autry 3)

Texas, 1941 (Ford 3, Holden 3, Trevor 3)

Texas Across the River, 1966 (Delon 3, Martin 3, Cahn 4, Metty 4)

Texas Bad Man, 1932 (Mix 3)

Texas Bearcat, 1925 (Eason 4)

Texas, Brooklyn, and Heaven, 1948 (Murphy 3)

Texas Carnival, 1951 (Walters 2, Keel 3, Miller 3, Williams 3, Pan 4, Rose 4)

Texas Chainsaw Massacre Part II, 1986 (Hopper 3, Golan and Globus 4)

Texas Cyclone, 1932 (Brennan 3, Wayne 3)

Texas in 1999, 1931 (Fleischer 4)

Texas Kelly at Bay, 1913 (Ince 4)

Texas Kid, 1920 (Eason 4)

Texas Lady, 1955 (Colbert 3)

Texas Masquerade, 1943 (Harlan 4)

Texas Rangers, 1936 (Vidor 2, MacMurray 3, Cronjager 4, Dreier 4, Head 4)

Texas Rangers Ride Again, 1940 (Crawford 3, Quinn 3, Ryan 3, Head 4)

Texas Rose. See Return of Jack Slade, 1955

Texas Stampede, 1939 (Ballard 4)

Texas Steer, 1927 (Rogers 3)

Texas Terror, 1935 (Wayne 3)

Texas Tom, 1950 (Hanna and Barbera 4)

Texas Tornado, 1928 (Berman 4)

Texas Tornado, 1934 (Canutt 4)

Texas to Tokyo. See We've Never Been Licked, 1943

Texas Trail, 1925 (Carey 3)

Texas Trail, 1937 (Harlan 4, Head 4)

Texasville, 1990 (Bogdanovich 2, Bridges 3)

Texican, 1966 (Crawford 3, Murphy 3)

Text of Light, 1974 (Brakhage 2)

Thanatopsis, 1962 (Emshwiller 2)

Thank Heaven for Small Favors. See Drôle de paroissien, 1963

Thank You, 1925 (Ford 2, Marion 4)

Thank You, 1937 (Lorre 3)

Thank You, Jeeves, 1936 (Niven 3)

Thank You Madame. See Im Sonneschein, 1936

Thank You, Mr. Moto, 1937 (Miller 4)

Thank Your Lucky Stars, 1943 (Bogart 3, Cantor 3, Davis 3, De Havilland 3, Flynn 3, Garfield 3, Horton 3, Lupino 3, McDaniel 3, Sheridan 3, Edeson 4, Frank 4, Grot 4, Prinz 4)

Thanks a Million, 1935 (Powell 3, Johnson 4, Zanuck 4)

Thanks for Everything, 1938 (Menjou 3, Brown 4, Zanuck 4)

Thanks for the Memory, 1938 (Hope 3, Freier 4, Fleischer 4, Head 4, Struss 4)

Thark, 1932 (Wilcox 2)

That Awful Brother, 1911 (Lawrence 3)

That Cat. See Až přijde kocour, 1963

That Certain Age, 1938 (Cooper 3, Douglas 3, Durbin 3, Pasternak 4)

That Certain Feeling, 1937 (Wallis 4)

That Certain Feeling, 1956 (Hope 3, Saint 3, Sanders 3, Bumstead 4, Diamond 4, Frank 4, Head 4)

That Certain Summer, 1972 (Sheen 3)

That Certain Thing, 1928 (Capra 2, Cohn 4, Walker 4)

That Certain Woman, 1937 (Goulding 2, Crisp 3, Davis 3, Fonda 3, Haller 4, Orry-Kelly 4, Steiner 4)

That Championship Season, 1982 (Dern 3, Mitchum 3, Sheen 3, Golan and Globus 4)

That Chink at Golden Gulch, 1910 (Griffith 2, Bitzer 4)

That Cold Day in the Park, 1969 (Altman 2, Kovacs 4)

That Crying Baby, 1910 (White 3)

That Dangerous Age, 1950 (Loy 3, Korda 4, Périnal 4)

That Dare Devil, 1911 (Sennett 2)

That Darn Cat, 1965 (Stevenson 2, Lanchester 3, McDowall 3, Disney 4)

That Devil Bateese, 1918 (Chaney 3)

That Forsyte Woman, 1949 (Flynn 3, Garson 3, Leigh 3, Pidgeon 3, Young 3, Kaper 4, Plunkett 4, Ruttenberg 4)

That Funny Feeling, 1965 (O'Connor 3, Whitlock 4)

That Gal of Burke's, 1916 (Borzage 2)

That Gang of Mine, 1940 (Lewis 2, Katzman 4)

That Girl from College. See Sorority House, 1939

That Girl from Paris, 1936 (Ball 3, Berman 4, Hunt 4)

That Girl Montana, 1921 (Sweet 3)

That Hagen Girl, 1947 (Reagan 3, Temple 3, Freund 4, Waxman 4)

That Hamilton Woman. See Lady Hamilton, 1941

That House in the Outskirts. See Aquella Casa en las Afueras, 1980

That I May Live, 1937 (Dwan 2)

That Inferior Feeling, 1939 (Benchley 4)

That is the Port Light. See Are ga minato no tomoshibi da, 1961

That Kind of Girl. See Models, Inc., 1952

That Kind of Love. See Taková láska, 1959

That Kind of Woman, 1959 (Lumet 2, Loren 3, Sanders 3, Head 4, Kaufman 4, Ponti 4)

That Lady, 1955 (De Havilland 3, Lee 3, Rosay 3, Addison 4, Junge 4, Krasker 4, Veiller 4)

That Lady in Ermine, 1948 (Lubitsch 2, Preminger 2, Grable 3, LeMaire 4, Newman 4, Pan 4, Raphaelson 4, Shamroy 4, Wheeler 4)

That Little Band of Gold, 1915 (Sennett 2, Arbuckle 3, Normand 3)

That Little Big Fellow, 1918 (Fleischer 4)

That Lucky Touch, 1975 (Cassel 3, Cobb 3, Winters 3, York 3)

That Mad Mr. Jones. See Fuller Brush Man, 1947

That Man from Rio. See Homme de Rio, 1964

That Man in Istanbul. See Estambul 65, 1965

That Man's Here Again, 1937 (Trumbo 4)

That Midnight Kiss, 1949 (Barrymore 3, Grayson 3, Ames 4, Mayer 4, Pasternak 4, Surtees 4)

That Minstrel Man, 1914 (Sennett 2, Arbuckle 3)

That Model from Paris, 1926 (Florey 2)

That Mothers Might Live, 1938 (Zinnemann 2)

That Navy Spirit. *See* Hold 'em Navy, 1937

That Night, 1917 (Sennett 2, Beery 3)

That Night, 1928 (McCarey 2, Roach 4)

That Night Adventure. *See* Sonoyo no bouken, 1948

That Night in London, 1933 (Donat 3, Korda 4)

That Night in Rio, 1941 (Ameche 3, Faye 3, Miranda 3, Banton 4, Day 4, Meredyth 4, Newman 4, Pan 4, Shamroy 4)

That Night with You, 1945 (Keaton 2, Salter 4)

That Noise, 1961 (Godfrey 4)

That Obscure Object of Desire. *See* Cet obscur objet de désir, 1977

That Old Gang of Mine, 1931 (Fleischer 4)

That Other Girl, 1910 (White 3)

That Other Woman, 1942 (Duryea 3, Day 4)

That Party in Person, 1929 (Cantor 3)

That Ragtime Band, 1913 (Sennett 2)

That Riviera Touch, 1966 (Heller 4)

That Royle Girl, 1926 (Griffith 2, Fields 3)

That Sinking Feeling, 1979 (Forsyth 2)

That Splendid November. *See* Bellissimo novembre, 1968

That Springtime Fellow, 1915 (Sennett 2)

That Summer of White Roses, 1989 (Steiger 3)

That Touch of Mink, 1962 (Day 3, Grant 3, Duning 4, Lourié 4, Metty 4, Westmore Family 4)

That Uncertain Feeling, 1941 (Lubitsch 2, Arden 3, Douglas 3, Meredith 3, Oberon 3, Barnes 4, Irene 4, Reisch 4, Stewart 4)

That Way with Women, 1947 (Greenstreet 3, McCord 4)

That Wonderful Urge, 1948 (Power 3, Tierney 3, Clarke 4, LeMaire 4, Newman 4)

Thatch of Night, 1990 (Brakhage 2)

That'll Be the Day, 1973 (Puttnam 4)

That's a Good Girl, 1932 (Buchanan 3)

That's Dancing!, 1985 (Kelly 3, Minnelli 3, Mancini 4)

That's Entertainment, 1974 (Astaire 3, Crosby 3, Kelly 3, Minnelli 3, Rooney 3, Sinatra 3, Stewart 3, Taylor 3, Laszlo 4, Mancini 4, Metty 4)

That's Entertainment, Part II, 1976 (Astaire 3, Kelly 3, Bass 4, Folsey 4)

That's Gratitude, 1934 (Pangborn 3)

That's Him, 1918 (Lloyd 3, Roach 4)

That's Life, 1986 (Andrews 3, Lemmon 3, Mancini 4)

That's Me, 1962 (Arkin 3)

That's My Baby, 1926 (Garnett 2)

That's My Boy, 1932 (Crabbe 3, Marsh 3, August 4, Krasna 4)

That's My Boy, 1951 (Lewis 2, Marsh 3, Martin 3, Garmes 4, Head 4, Wallis 4)

That's My Line, 1931 (Arbuckle 3)

That's My Man, 1947 (Borzage 2, Ameche 3, Canutt 4, Gaudio 4, Salter 4)

That's My Meat, 1931 (Arbuckle 3)

That's My Mommy, 1955 (Hanna and Barbera 4)

That's My Pup, 1952 (Hanna and Barbera 4)

That's My Uncle, 1935 (Pearson 2)

That's My Wife, 1929 (Laurel and Hardy 3, Roach 4)

That's Right—You're Wrong, 1939 (Ball 3, Horton 3, Menjou 3, Duning 4, Metty 4, Polglase 4)

That's the Spirit, 1945 (Keaton 2, Salter 4)

That's Where the Action Is, 1965 (De Antonio 2)

That's Worth While, 1921 (Calhern 3)

Thau le pêcheur, 1957 (Coutard 4)

Thaumaturge chinois, 1904 (Méliès 2)

Thaumetopoea, 1960 (Guillemot 4)

Thé à la menthe, 1962 (Cybulski 3)

Thé chez la concierge, 1907 (Feuillade 2)

Theater in Trance, 1981 (Fassbinder 2)

Théâtre de Monsieur et Madame Kabal, 1965 (Borowczyk 2)

Théâtre National Populaire, 1956 (Philipe 3, Fradetal 4, Jarre 4)

Theatre of Blood, 1973 (Dors 3, Hawkins 3, Price 3)

Theatre of Death, 1967 (Lee 3)

Theatre of Life. *See* Jinsei gekijo, 1952

Theatre of Life. *See* Jinsei gekijo seishunhen, 1958

Theatre Royal. *See* Royal Family of Broadway, 1931

Theatre Royal, 1943 (Baxter 2, Crazy Gang 3)

Theban Plays by Sophocles, 1986 (Gielgud 3, Quayle 3)

Theft of the Mona Lisa. *See* Raub der Mona Lisa, 1931

Their Big Moment, 1934 (Plunkett 4, Steiner 4)

Their Bridal Night. *See* Jejich svatební noc, 1922

Their Cheap Vacation, 1914 (Beery 3)

Their Compact, 1917 (Bushman 3)

Their Everyday Life. *See* Ich dzień powszedni, 1963

Their Fates Sealed, 1911 (Sennett 2)

Their First Acquaintance, 1914 (Crisp 3)

Their First Divorce Case, 1911 (Sennett 2)

Their First Execution, 1913 (Sennett 2)

Their First Kidnapping Case, 1911 (Sennett 2)

Their First Mistake, 1932 (Laurel and Hardy 3, Roach 4)

Their First Misunderstanding, 1911 (Gaudio 4, Ince 4)

Their Hero Son, 1911 (Dwan 2)

Their Honeymoon, 1916 (Laurel and Hardy 3)

Their Hour, 1915 (Meredyth 4)

Their Husbands, 1913 (Sennett 2)

Their Masterpiece, 1913 (Dwan 2)

Their Own Desire, 1929 (Montgomery 3, Shearer 3, Adrian 4, Daniels 4, Day 4, Gibbons 4, Marion 4)

Their Promise, 1913 (Anderson 3)

Their Purple Moment, 1928 (Laurel and Hardy 3, Roach 4)

Their Secret Affair. *See* Top Secret Affair, 1957

Their Social Splash, 1915 (Sennett 2)

Their Ups and Downs, 1914 (Sennett 2, Arbuckle 3)

Their Vacation, 1916 (Laurel and Hardy 3)

Theirs Is the Glory, 1946 (Challis 4, Rank 4)

Thelema Abbey, 1955 (Anger 2)

Thelma and Louise, 1991 (Sarandon 3)

Thelma Jordan. *See* File on Thelma Jordan, 1949

Thelonious Monk: Straight No Chaser, 1989 (Eastwood 3)

Them!, 1954 (Kaper 4)

Them Thar Hills, 1934 (Laurel and Hardy 3, Roach 4)

Them Was the Happy Days, 1916 (Lloyd 3, Roach 4)

Them Were the Happy Days, 1917 (Messmer 4)

Thèmes et variations, 1928 (Dulac 2)

Themroc, 1973 (Piccoli 3)

Then Came Bronson, 1969 (Sheen 3)

Then I'll Come Back to You, 1916 (Marion 4)

Then kurote-gume, 1937 (Yamada 3)

Then the Light Fades, 1913 (Dwan 2)

Theodora Goes Wild, 1936 (Douglas 3, Dunne 3, Buchman 4, Cohn 4, Walker 4)

Theodore et Cie, 1933 (Raimu 3, Douy 4)

Theodor Hierneis oder: Wie man ehem. Hofkoch wird, 1972 (Syberberg 2)

Theorum. *See* Teorema, 1968

There Ain't No Justice, 1939 (Balcon 4)

There Ain't No Santa Claus, 1926 (Roach 4)

There Are Mountains and Rivers. *See* Sanga ari, 1962

There Auto Be a Law, 1953 (Blanc 4, McKimson 4, Stalling 4)

There Burned a Flame. *See* Det brinner en eld, 1943

There Goes My Girl, 1937 (Musuraca 4, Walker 4)

There Goes My Heart, 1938 (McLeod 2, Langdon 3, March 3, Irene 4, Roach 4)

There Goes the Bride, 1925 (Roach 4)

There Goes the Bride, 1932 (Matthews 3, Balcon 4)

There Goes the Bride, 1980 (Crawford 3)

There Goes the Groom, 1937 (Meredith 3, Krasner 4)

There He Goes, 1925 (Capra 2, Sennett 2, Langdon 3)

There Is Another Sun, 1951 (Harvey 3)

There Is a Season, 1953 (Van Dyke 2)

There Is No Escape, 1952 (Henreid 3)

There Must Be a Pony, 1986 (Taylor 3, Wagner 3)

There They Go-Go-Go, 1956 (Blanc 4, Jones 4, Stalling 4)

There Was a Crooked Man, 1960 (Wisdom 3, York 3)

There Was a Crooked Man, 1970 (Benton 2, Mankiewicz 2, Douglas 3, Fonda 3, Grant 3, Meredith 3, Oates 3, Westmore Family 4)

There Was a Father. *See* Chichi ariki, 1942

There Was a Lad. *See* Zhivet takoi paren, 1964

There Was a Miller on the River. *See* Jsouc na rece mlynář jeden, 1971

There Was Once a King. *See* Bly jednou jeden Král, 1955

There Were Days . . . and Moons. *See* Il y a des jours . . . et des lunes, 1990

There Will Be No Leave Today, 1959 (Tarkovsky 2)

There You Are!, 1926 (Garnett 2, Gibbons 4, Gillespie 4)

There's a Future in It, 1944 (Alwyn 4)

There's a Girl in My Soup, 1970 (Boulting 2, Dors 3, Hawn 3, Sellers 3)

There's Always a Price Tag. *See* Retour de Manivelle, 1957

There's Always a Woman, 1938 (Astor 3, Blondell 3, Douglas 3, Hayworth 3, Cohn 4, Ryskind 4)

There's Always Tomorrow, 1934 (Taylor 3)

There's Always Tomorrow, 1956 (Sirk 2, Bennett 3, Darwell 3, MacMurray 3, Stanwyck 3, Hunter 4, Metty 4)

There's a Magic in the Music, 1941 (Head 4)

There's Magic in Music, 1941 (Dreier 4)

There's Music in the Hair, 1913 (Bunny 3)

There's No Business Like Show Business, 1954 (Monroe 3, O'Connor 3, Alton 4, Berlin 4, Cole 4, LeMaire 4, Newman 4, Shamroy 4, Trotti 4, Wheeler 4)

There's No Place Like Home, 1917 (Weber 2)

There's One Born Every Minute, 1942 (Taylor 3, Salter 4)

There's Something about a Soldier, 1934 (Fleischer 4)

There's Something about a Soldier, 1943 (Beavers 3, Fleischer 4)

There's Something Wrong in Paradise, 1984 (Black 3)

There's That Woman Again, 1938 (Costello 3, Douglas 3, Cohn 4, Epstein 4, Walker 4)

Therese, 1916 (Sjöström 2, Jaenzon 4, Magnusson 4)

Thérèse. See Thérèse Desqueyroux, 1962

Thérèse, 1986 (Evein 4)

Thérèse and Isabelle, 1968 (Auric 4)

Thérèse Desqueyroux, 1962 (Franju 2, Noiret 3, Jarre 4, Matras 4)

Thérèse Martin, 1938 (Ibert 4)

Thérèse Raquin, 1919 (Kuleshov 2)

Thérèse Raquin, 1928 (Manès 3, Andrejew 4)

Thérèse Raquin, 1953 (Signoret 3, Hakim 4, Spaak 4)

Thermogenesis, 1972 (Emshwiller 2)

These Are the Damned. See Damned, 1963

These Blessed Two. See Två Saliga, 1985

These Children Are Safe, 1939 (Alwyn 4)

These Dangerous Years, 1957 (Wilcox 2, Neagle 3)

These Foolish Things. See Daddy Nostalgie, 1990

These Foolish Times. See Shin baka jidai, 1946

These Glamour Girls, 1939 (Ayres 3, Turner 3, Walker 3)

These Kids Are Grown-Ups. See Ils sont grands ces petits, 1979

These Thousand Hills, 1958 (Clarke 4, LeMaire 4, Wheeler 4)

These Three, 1936 (Wyler 2, Brennan 3, Hopkins 3, McCrea 3, Oberon 3, Day 4, Goldwyn 4, Mandell 4, Newman 4, Toland 4)

These Wilder Years, 1956 (Cagney 3, Pidgeon 3, Stanwyck 3, Ames 4, Folsey 4, Rose 4)

They All Came Out, 1939 (Tourneur 2)

They All Died Laughing. See Jolly Bad Fellow, 1964

They All Kissed the Bride, 1942 (Crawford 3, Douglas 3, Cohn 4, Irene 4, Walker 4)

They All Laughed, 1983 (Bogdanovich 2, Hepburn 3, Müller 4)

They Also Kill. See Some May Live, 1967

They Asked for It, 1939 (Cortez 4)

They Call It Sin, 1932 (Calhern 3, Young 3)

They Call Me Mister Tibbs!, 1970 (Poitier 3, Jones 4, Mirisch 4)

They Came By Night, 1940 (Launder and Gilliat 2)

They Came from Beyond Space, 1967 (Francis 4)

They Came to a City, 1944 (Dearden 2, Withers 3, Balcon 4)

They Came to Blow Up America, 1943 (Bond 3, Sanders 3, Basevi 4, Friedhofer 4)

They Came to Cordura, 1959 (Rossen 2, Cooper 3, Hayworth 3, Cahn 4, Guffey 4)

They Came to Rob Las Vegas. See Las Vegas 500 millones, 1968

They Dare Not Love, 1941 (Whale 2, Cushing 3, Lukas 3, Bennett 4, Planer 4, Vajda 4)

They Died With Their Boots On, 1941 (Walsh 2, Bosworth 3, De Havilland 3, Flynn 3, Greenstreet 3, Kennedy 3, McDaniel 3, Quinn 3, Canutt 4, Eason 4, Glennon 4, Orry-Kelly 4, Steiner 4, Wallis 4)

They Done Him Right, 1933 (Lantz 4)

They Drive By Night, 1940 (Walsh 2, Bogart 3, Lupino 3, Raft 3, Sheridan 3, Burks 4, Deutsch 4, Edeson 4, Haskin 4, Wald 4, Wallis 4)

They Flew Alone, 1942 (Wilcox 2, Neagle 3, Newton 3, Alwyn 4)

They Fought for the Country. See Oni srazhalis za rodinu, 1975

They Fought for the Motherland. See Oni srazhalis za rodinu, 1975

They Gave Him a Gun, 1937 (Van Dyke 2, Tracy 3, Rosson 4)

They Go Boom, 1929 (Laurel and Hardy 3, Roach 4)

They Got Me Covered, 1942 (Preminger 2, Hope 3, Lamour 3, Goldwyn 4, Head 4, Mandell 4, Maté 4, Mercer 4)

They Had to See Paris, 1929 (Borzage 2, Rogers 3, Levien 4)

They Knew Mayakovsky. See Oni znali Mayakovsky, 1955

They Knew Mr. Knight, 1945 (Greenwood 3, Rank 4)

They Knew What They Wanted, 1940 (Carey 3, Laughton 3, Lombard 3, Malden 3, Kanin 4, Newman 4, Polglase 4, Pommer 4, Stradling 4)

They Leap Into Life. See Sprung ins Leben, 1924

They Learned About Women, 1930 (Wood 2, Love 3, Gibbons 4)

They Live, 1988 (Carpenter 2)

They Live Again, 1938 (Zinnemann 2)

They Live By Night, 1948 (Ray 2, D'Agostino 4, Houseman 4, Schary 4, Schnee 4)

They Loved Life. See Kanał, 1957

They Made Me a Criminal, 1939 (Berkeley 2, Bond 3, Garfield 3, Rains 3, Sheridan 3, Glazer 4, Grot 4, Howe 4, Steiner 4, Wallis 4)

They Made Me a Fugitive, 1947 (Howard 3, Heller 4)

They Met in Argentina, 1941 (O'Hara 3, Hunt 4)

They Met in a Taxi, 1936 (Bond 3, Wray 3)

They Met in Bombay, 1941 (Brown 2, Gable 3, Lorre 3, Russell 3, Adrian 4, Daniels 4, Loos 4, Stothart 4, Stromberg 4)

They Met in the Dark, 1943 (Mason 3, Heller 4, Rank 4)

They Might Be Giants, 1971 (Scott 3, Woodward 3, Barry 4)

They Only Kill Their Masters, 1972 (Allyson 3, Garner 3, O'Brien 3)

They Passed This Way. See Four Faces West, 1948

They Ran for Their Lives, 1968 (Carradine 3)

They Rode West, 1954 (Reed 3, Nugent 4, Wald 4)

They Serve Abroad, 1942 (Boulting 2)

They Shall Have Music, 1939 (Brennan 3, McCrea 3, Goldwyn 4, Newman 4, Riskin 4, Toland 4)

They Shoot Horses, Don't They?, 1969 (Pollack 2, Dern 3, Fonda, J. 3, York 3, Green 4, Horner 4, Winkler 4)

They Staked Their Lives. See Med livet som insats, 1940

They Wanted to Marry, 1937 (Pangborn 3, Metty 4)

They Were Expendable, 1945 (Edwards 2, Ford 2, Bond 3, Montgomery 3, Reed 3, Wayne 3, August 4, Mayer 4, Stothart 4)

They Were Five. See Belle equipe, 1936

They Were Not Divided, 1950 (Lee 3, Rank 4)

They Were Sisters, 1945 (Mason 3, Rank 4)

They Who Dare, 1954 (Milestone 2, Bogarde 3, Elliott 3)

They Won't Believe Me, 1947 (Hayward 3, Young 3, Boyle 4, Harrison 4)

They Won't Forget, 1937 (LeRoy 2, Rossen 2, Rains 3, Turner 3, Deutsch 4, Edeson 4, Warner 4)

They Would Elope, 1909 (Griffith 2, Pickford 3, Bitzer 4)

They're a Weird Mob, 1966 (Powell and Pressburger 2, Rafferty 3)

They're Off, 1933 (Crazy Gang 3)

They've Kidnapped Anne Benedict. See Abduction of Saint Anne, 1973

Thicker Than Water, 1935 (Laurel and Hardy 3, Roach 4)

Thief, 1920 (White 3)

Thief, 1952 (Milland 3)

Thief, 1971 (Dickinson 3)

Thief. See Ladrone, 1979

Thief, 1981 (Caan 3, Weld 3)

Thief and the Cobbler, 1981 (Price 3)

Thief and the Girl, 1911 (Griffith 2, Bitzer 4)

Thief Catcher, 1914 (Sennett 2)

Thief in Paradise, 1925 (Colman 3, Goldwyn 4, Grot 4, Marion 4, Miller 4)

Thief in the Dark, 1928 (Edeson 4)

Thief of Bagdad, 1924 (Walsh 2, Fairbanks 3, Johnson 3, Wong 3, Edeson 4, Grot 4, Menzies 4)

Thief of Bagdad, 1940 (Crichton 2, Powell and Pressburger 2, Veidt 3, Biro 4, Ellenshaw 4, Hornbeck 4, Korda, A. 4, Korda, V. 4, Krasker 4, Menzies 4, Périnal 4, Rozsa 4, Unsworth 4)

Thief of Bagdad. See Ladro di Bagdad, 1960

Thief of Baghdad, 1978 (McDowall 3, Stamp 3, Ustinov 3)

Thief of Baghdad, 1940 (Mathieson 4)

Thief of Damascus, 1952 (Henreid 3, Katzman 4)

Thief of Paris. See Voleur, 1967

Thief Who Came to Dinner, 1973 (Hill 2, Clayburgh 3, Oates 3, Mancini 4)

Thief's Wife, 1911 (Dwan 2)

Thieves, 1976 (Fosse 2, McCambridge 3)

Thieves After Dark, 1983 (Fuller 2, Presle 3)
Thieves Fall Out, 1939 (Darwell 3)
Thieves Fall Out, 1941 (Quinn 3)
Thieves' Gold, 1918 (Ford 2, Carey 3)
Thieves' Highway, 1949 (Dassin 2, Cobb 3, LeMaire 4, Newman 4, Wheeler 4)
Thieves Like Us, 1974 (Altman 2)
Thigh Line Lyre Triangular, 1961 (Brakhage 2)
Thin Air. See Body Stealers, 1969
Thin Ice, 1937 (Henie 3, Power 3, Cronjager 4)
Thin Ice, 1981 (Gish 3)
Thin Ice, 1989 (Halas and Batchelor 4)
Thin Man, 1934 (Van Dyke 2, Loy 3, O'Sullivan 3, Powell 3, Gibbons 4, Goodrich 4, Howe 4, Mayer 4, Shearer 4, Stromberg 4)
Thin Man Goes Home, 1944 (Loy 3, Powell 3, Freund 4, Irene 4, Riskin 4)
Thin Red Line, 1964 (Arnold 4)
Thin Twins, 1929 (Roach 4)
Thing, 1951 (D'Agostino 4, Dunn 4, Harlan 4, Lederer 4, Tiomkin 4)
Thing, 1982 (Carpenter 2, Pleasence 3, Bottin 4, Morricone 4, Whitlock 4)
Thing from Another World. See Thing, 1951
Thing That Couldn't Die, 1958 (Metty 4)
Thing We Love, 1918 (Reid 3)
Thing with Two Heads, 1972 (Milland 3, Baker 4)
Things Are Looking Up, 1934 (Leigh 3, Balcon 4, Rank 4)
Things Change, 1988 (Ameche 3)
Things Happen at Night, 1948 (Lassally 4)
Things in Life. See Choses de la vie, 1970
Things in Their Season, 1974 (Neal 3)
Things of Life. See Choses de la vie, 1970
Things to Come, 1936 (Crichton 2, Massey 3, Richardson 3, Sanders 3, Biro 4, Hornbeck 4, Korda, A. 4, Korda, V. 4, Krasker 4, Mathieson 4, Menzies 4, Périnal 4)
Think, 1964 (Bernstein 4)
Think Fast, Mr. Moto, 1937 (Lorre 3)
Think of a Number. See Taenk på ett tal, 1969
Think Twentieth, 1967 (Hayward 3, Heston 3)
Third Alarm, 1930 (Bosworth 3)
Third Bad Name. See Daisan no Akumyo, 1963
Third Bell. See Třeti zvoněni, 1938
Third Day, 1965 (Marshall 3, McDowall 3, Surtees 4)
Third Degree, 1926 (Curtiz 2, Costello, D. 3, Blanke 4, Mohr 4)
Third Eye, 1969 (Meredith 3)
Third Finger, Left Hand, 1940 (Costello 3, Douglas 3, Loy 3, Folsey 4)
Third Generation. See Dritte Generation, 1979
Third Girl from the Left, 1973 (Curtis 3, Novak 3)
Third Key. See Long Arm, 1956
Third Lover. See Oeil du malin, 1962
Third Man, 1949 (Reed 2, Welles 2, Cotten 3, Howard 3, Valli 3, Greene 4, Korda, A. 4, Korda, V. 4, Krasker 4, Selznick 4)
Third Man on the Mountain, 1959 (Lom 3, Alwyn 4, Disney 4)
Third Part of the Night, 1971 (Nowicki 3)
Third Party Risk, 1955 (Carreras 4)

Third Secret, 1964 (Crichton 2, Attenborough 3, Hawkins 3, Slocombe 4)
Third Squad. See Třeti rota, 1931
Third String, 1932 (Pearson 2)
Third Time Lucky, 1931 (Launder and Gilliat 2, Balcon 4)
Third Time Lucky, 1948 (Adam 4, Rank 4)
Third Voice, 1960 (O'Brien 3, Haller 4)
Thirst, 1917 (Sennett 2)
Thirst. See Desert Nights, 1929
Thirst. See Törst, 1949
Thirteen. See Twelve Plus One, 1969
Thirteen Chairs. See Tretton stolar, 1945
Thirteen Down, 1915 (Bushman 3)
Thirteen Ghosts, 1960 (Biroc 4)
Thirteen Hours by Air, 1936 (Leisen 2, Bennett 3, MacMurray 3, Head 4)
Thirteen Men and a Girl. See Letste Kompagnie, 1930
Thirteen Most Beautiful Boys, 1965 (Warhol 2)
Thirteen Most Beautiful Women, 1965 (Warhol 2)
Thirteen Steps to Death. See Why Must I Die?, 1959
Thirteen Trunks of Mr. O.F. See Koffer des Herrn O.F., 1931
Thirteen West Street, 1962 (Ladd 3, Steiger 3, Duning 4)
Thirteen Women, 1932 (Dunne 3, Loy 3, Steiner 4)
Thirteenth Chair, 1929 (Browning 2, Lugosi 3, Adrian 4, Day 4, Gibbons 4)
Thirteenth Chair, 1937 (Clarke 4)
Thirteenth Guest, 1932 (Rogers 3)
Thirteenth Hour, 1927 (Barrymore 3)
Thirteenth Juror, 1927 (Bushman 3, Pidgeon 3)
Thirteenth Letter, 1950 (Preminger 2, Boyer 3, Darnell 3, Rosay 3, Koch 4, La Shelle 4, LeMaire 4, North 4, Wheeler 4)
Thirteenth Man, 1913 (Bushman 3)
Thirty Day Princess, 1934 (Sturges 2, Grant 3, Sidney 3, Schulberg 4, Shamroy 4)
Thirty Days, 1916 (Laurel and Hardy 3)
Thirty Days, 1922 (Cruze 2, Reid 3, Brown 4)
Thirty Days. See Silver Lining, 1931
Thirty Foot Bride of Candy Rock, 1957 (Abbott and Costello 3)
Thirty is a Dangerous Age, Cynthia, 1968 (Moore 3)
Thirty Seconds over Tokyo, 1944 (Edwards 2, LeRoy 2, Johnson 3, Mitchum 3, Tracy 3, Walker 3, Gibbons 4, Gillespie 4, Irene 4, Mayer 4, Rosson 4, Shearer 4, Stothart 4, Surtees 4, Trumbo 4, Wheeler 4)
Thirty Years of Fun, 1963 (Keaton 2)
Thirty-Nine Steps, 1935 (Hitchcock 2, Carroll 3, Donat 3, Balcon 4, Bennett 4, Reville 4)
Thirty-Nine Steps, 1960 (More 3, Box 4, Rank 4)
Thirty-Nine Steps, 1979 (Mills 3)
Thirty-Six Hours, 1953 (Duryea 3, Carreras 4)
This Above All, 1942 (Litvak 2, Fontaine 3, Power 3, Day 4, Miller 4, Newman 4, Sherriff 4, Zanuck 4)
This Ancient Law. See Alte Gesetz, 1923

This Angry Age. See Barrage contre le Pacifique, 1958
This Animal World, 1955 (O'Brien 4)
This Charming Couple, 1949 (Van Dyke 2)
This Could Be the Night, 1957 (Wise 2, Simmons 3, Cahn 4, Harlan 4, Lennart 4, Pasternak 4)
This Day and Age, 1933 (De Mille 2, Carradine 3, Dreier 4, Zukor 4)
This Dusty World. See Jinkyo, 1924
This Earth Is Mine, 1959 (King 2, Hudson 3, Rains 3, Cahn 4, Friedhofer 4, Metty 4, Robinson 4)
This England, 1923 (Matthews 3)
This England, 1941 (McDowall 3)
This Girl for Hire, 1983 (Ferrer 3, McDowall 3)
This Greedy Old Skin. See Gametsui yatsu, 1960
This Gun for Hire, 1942 (De Carlo 3, Ladd 3, Lake 3, Preston 3, Burnett 4, Dreier 4, Greene 4, Head 4, Seitz 4)
This Happy Breed, 1944 (Lean 2, Johnson 3, Mills 3, Newton 3, Coward 4, Green 4, Havelock-Allan 4, Rank 4)
This Happy Feeling, 1958 (Edwards 2, Astor 3, Reynolds 3, Hunter 4)
This Hero Stuff, 1919 (King 2, Furthman 4)
This House of Vanity. See Vanity's Price, 1924
This House Possessed, 1981 (Bennett 3)
This Is a Life?, 1955 (Blanc 4, Freleng 4)
This Is Cinerama, 1952 (Schoedsack 2, Cooper 4, O'Brien 4, Steiner 4)
This Is Colour, 1942 (Cardiff 4)
This Is Dynamite, 1952 (Head 4)
This Is Heaven, 1929 (Banky 3, Barnes 4, Goldwyn 4, Toland 4)
This Is it, 1982 (Snow 2)
This Is Korea!, 1951 (Ford 2)
This Island Earth, 1955 (Mancini 4, Salter 4, Westmore Family 4)
This Is Lloyd's, 1962 (Quayle 3)
This Is London, 1956 (Harrison 3)
This Is My Affair, 1937 (Carradine 3, McLaglen 3, Stanwyck 3, Taylor 3, MacGowan 4, Trotti 4)
This Is My Affair. See I Can Get It for You Wholesale, 1951
This Is My Ducky Day, 1961 (Hanna and Barbera 4)
This Is My Love, 1954 (Darnell 3, Duryea 3, Reed 3, Waxman 4)
This Is My Street, 1963 (Hurt 3)
This Is Russia, 1957 (Wilson 4)
This is Spinal Tap, 1984 (Huston 3)
This Is the Air Force, 1947 (Halas and Batchelor 4)
This Is the Army, 1943 (Curtiz 2, Costello 3, Reagan 3, Berlin 4, Glennon 4, Orry-Kelly 4, Polito 4, Prinz 4, Robinson 4, Steiner 4, Wallis 4)
This Is the Life, 1914 (Beery 3)
This is the Life, 1917 (Walsh 2)
This Is the Life, 1933 (Milland 3)
This Is the Life, 1935 (Neilan 2, Trotti 4)
This Is the Life, 1944 (O'Connor 3, Wray 3, Mohr 4)
This Is the Night, 1932 (Grant 3)
This Kind of Love. See Quaeta specie d'amore, 1972
This Land Is Full of Life. See Din tillvaros land, 1940

This Land Is Mine, 1943 (Renoir 2, Laughton 3, O'Hara 3, Sanders 3, D'Agostino 4, Lourié 4, Nichols 4)

This Land Is Mine, 1959 (Simmons 3)

This Life We Live, 1913 (Anderson 3)

This Little Piggie Went to Market, 1934 (Fleischer 4)

This Love of Ours, 1945 (Dieterle 2, Oberon 3, Rains 3, Ballard 4, Banton 4, Salter 4)

This Love Thing, 1970 (Halas and Batchelor 4)

This Mad World, 1930 (Rathbone 3, Adrian 4, Gibbons 4, Rosson 4)

This Man in Paris, 1939 (Sim 3, Havelock-Allan 4)

This Man Is Dangerous, 1941 (Mason 3)

This Man Is Dangerous, 1952 (Crawford 3)

This Man is Dangerous. See Cet homme est dangereux, 1953

This Man Is Mine, 1934 (Bellamy 3, Dunne 3, Murfin 4, Plunkett 4, Polglase 4, Steiner 4)

This Man Is News, 1938 (Dearden 2, Sim 3, Havelock-Allan 4, Head 4)

This Man Must Die. See Que la bête meure, 1969

This Man Reuter. See Dispatch from Reuters, 1940

This Man's Navy, 1945 (Edwards 2, Wellman 2, Beery 3, Chase 4, Irene 4)

This Marriage Business, 1938 (August 4)

This Modern Age, 1931 (Bosworth 3, Crawford 3, Rosher 4)

This Modern Age, Number Sixteen. See British—Are They Artistic?, 1947

This Must Not be Forgotten. See It Mustn't Be Forgotten, 1954

This Other Eden, 1959 (Box 4)

This Precious Freedom, 1942 (Surtees 4)

This Property Is Condemned, 1966 (Coppola 2, Pollack 2, Bronson 3, Redford 3, Wood 3, Edouart 4, Head 4, Houseman 4, Howe 4, Westmore Family 4)

This Reckless Age, 1932 (Mankiewicz 2)

This Rugged Land, 1962 (Bronson 3)

This Savage Land, 1969 (Scott 3, Rosenman 4)

This Side of Heaven, 1934 (Howard 2, Barrymore 3, Rosson 4)

This Special Friendship. See Amitiés particulières, 1964

This Sporting Age, 1932 (Nichols 4)

This Sporting Genius, 1927 (Mayer 4)

This Sporting Life, 1963 (Anderson 2, Reisz 2, Harris 3, Jackson 3, Roberts 3)

This Strange Passion. See El, 1953

This Thing Called Love, 1929 (Harlow 3)

This Thing Called Love, 1941 (Cobb 3, Douglas 3, Russell 3, Cohn 4, Walker 4)

This Time for Keeps, 1942 (Gardner 3)

This Time for Keeps, 1947 (Donen 2, Durante 3, Williams 3, Freund 4, Irene 4, Pasternak 4)

This Time Let's Talk About Men. See Questa volta parliamo di uomini, 1965

This Transient Life, 1971 (Okada 3)

This Was a Woman, 1947 (Adam 4, Lassally 4)

This Was Japan, 1945 (Wright 2)

This Way Out, 1915 (Laurel and Hardy 3)

This Way Please, 1937 (Florey 2, Grable 3, Dreier 4, Head 4, Prinz 4)

This Week of Grace, 1933 (Fields 3)

This Woman, 1924 (Bow 3)

This Woman Is Dangerous, 1952 (McCord 4)

This Woman Is Mine, 1941 (Brennan 3, Krasner 4, Miller 4)

This World. See Kataku, 1979

This'll Make You Whistle, 1936 (Wilcox 2, Buchanan 3, Terry-Thomas 3)

Thodisi bewafai, 1980 (Azmi 3)

Thomas Crown Affair, 1968 (Ashby 2, Hill 2, Jewison 2, Wiseman 2, Dunaway 3, McQueen 3, Boyle 4, Legrand 4, Van Runkle 4, Wexler 4)

Thomas Graals bästa barn, 1914 (Sjöström 2)

Thomas Graals bästa barn, 1918 (Molander 2, Stiller 2, Magnusson 4)

Thomas Graals bästa film, 1914 (Sjöström 2)

Thomas Graals bästa film, 1917 (Molander 2, Stiller 2, Magnusson 4)

Thomas Graal's Best Child. See Thomas Graals bästa barn, 1918

Thomas Graal's Best Film. See Thomas Graals bästa film, 1917

Thomas Graal's Best Picture. See Thomas Graals bästa film, 1917

Thomas Graal's First Child. See Thomas Graals bästa barn, 1918

Thomas Graals myndling, 1922 (Molander 2)

Thomas Graal's Ward. See Thomas Graals myndling, 1922

Thomasine and Bushrod, 1974 (Ballard 4)

Thomas l'imposteur, 1964 (Cocteau 2, Auric 4, Fradetal 4)

Thomas the Imposter. See Thomas l'imposteur, 1964

Thompson's Last Run, 1986 (Mitchum 3)

Thompson's Night Out, 1908 (Bitzer 4)

Thorn Birds, 1983 (Simmons 3)

Thorns and Flowers. See Trny a květi, 1921

Thorns and Orange Blossoms, 1922 (Schulberg 4, Struss 4)

Thoroughbred, 1916 (Sullivan 4)

Thoroughbreds. See Silks and Saddles, 1928

Thoroughbreds Don't Cry, 1937 (Garland 3, Rooney 3, Brown 4, Mayer 4)

Thoroughly Modern Millie, 1967 (Hill 2, Andrews 3, Bernstein 4, Cahn 4, Hunter 4, Metty 4, Previn 4, Westmore Family 4, Whitlock 4)

Thorvaldsen, 1949 (Dreyer 2)

Those Athletic Girls, 1918 (Sennett 2)

Those Awful Hats, 1909 (Griffith 2, Lawrence 3, Bitzer 4)

Those Beautiful Dames, 1934 (Freleng 4)

Those Bitter Sweets, 1915 (Sennett 2)

Those Boys, 1909 (Griffith 2, Bitzer 4)

Those Calloways, 1965 (Brennan 3, Disney 4, Steiner 4)

Those College Girls, 1915 (Sennett 2)

Those Country Kids, 1914 (Sennett 2, Arbuckle 3, Normand 3)

Those Daring Young Men in Their Jaunty Jalopies. See Quei temerari sulle loro pazze, scatenate, scalcinate carriole, 1969

Those Endearing Young Charms, 1945 (Young 3)

Those Fantastic Flying Fools. See Jules Verne's Rocket to the Moon, 1967

Those Gentlemen Who Have a Clean Sheet. See Herren mit der weissen Weste, 1970

Those Glory Glory Days, 1983 (Puttnam 4)

Those Good Old Days, 1913 (Sennett 2, Normand 3)

Those Happy Days, 1914 (Sennett 2, Arbuckle 3)

Those Hicksville Boys, 1911 (Sennett 2)

Those High Grey Walls, 1939 (Vidor 2)

Those Love Pangs, 1914 (Sennett 2)

Those Magnificent Men in Their Flying Machines, 1965 (Cassel 3, Sordi 3, Terry-Thomas 3, Challis 4, Zanuck 4)

Those Redheads from Seattle, 1953 (Moorehead 3, Head 4, Mercer 4)

Those Three French Girls, 1930 (Freed 4, Gibbons 4, Mayer 4)

Those Troublesome Tresses, 1913 (Bunny 3)

Those We Love, 1932 (Florey 2, Astor 3, Edeson 4)

Those Were the Days, 1934 (Launder and Gilliat 2, Hay 3, Mills 3)

Those Were the Days, 1940 (Holden 3, Ladd 3, Dreier 4, Head 4, Young 4)

Those Were the Years. See C'eravamo tanti amati, 1974

Those Who Are Late. See Spóźnieni przechodnie, 1962

Those Who Dance, 1924 (Love 3, Sweet 3)

Those Who Make Tomorrow. See Asu o tsukuru hitobito, 1946

Those Who Pay, 1918 (Ince 4, Sullivan 4)

Those Wise Guys Who Fool Around, 1956 (Lee 3)

Those Without Sin, 1917 (Neilan 2, Sweet 3)

Thot Fal'n, 1978 (Brakhage 2)

Thou Shalt Not, 1910 (Griffith 2, Walthall 3, Bitzer 4)

Thou Shalt Not Covet, 1912 (Bunny 3)

Thou Shalt Not Kill. See Tu ne tueras point, 1961

Thou Shalt Not Kill, 1982 (Grant 3)

Thou Shalt Not Steal, 1917 (Ruttenberg 4)

Thousand and One Nights, 1945 (Wilde 3, Winters 3)

Thousand and One Nights. See Fiore delle mille e una notte, 1974

Thousand Clowns, 1965 (Holliday 3, Robards 3, Rosenblum 4)

Thousand Cranes. See Senba-zuru, 1953

Thousand Cranes. See Senbazuru, 1969

Thousand Dollar Husband, 1916 (Sweet 3)

Thousand Dollars a Touchdown, 1939 (Daves 2)

Thousand to One, 1920 (Bosworth 3)

Thousands Cheer, 1938 (Allyson 3)

Thousands Cheer, 1943 (Astor 3, Ball 3, Charisse 3, Garland 3, Grayson 3, Horne 3, Kelly 3, O'Brien 3, Powell 3, Reed 3, Rooney 3, Edens 4, Folsey 4, Gibbons 4, Irene 4, Mayer 4, Pasternak 4, Stothart 4)

Thread of Destiny, 1910 (Griffith 2, Pickford 3, Bitzer 4)

Thread of Life, 1911 (Dwan 2)

Threads of Fate, 1915 (Chaney 3)

Threat, 1960 (Cronjager 4)

Threatening Sky, 1965 (Anderson 2)

Three Act Tragedy, 1987 (Ustinov 3)

Three Ages, 1923 (Keaton 2, Beery 3, Laurel and Hardy 3, Bruckman 4, Schenck 4)

Three American Beauties, 1906 (Porter 2)

Three American LPs. See Drei amerikanische LPs, 1969

Three Amigos!, (Landis 2, Martin 3, Bernstein 4)

Three Apples, 1979 (Popescu-Gopo 4)
Three Arabian Nuts, 1951 (Three Stooges 3)
Three Badgers. *See* Sanbiki no tanuki, 1966
Three Bad Men, 1926 (Ford 2)
Three Bad Men and a Girl, 1915 (Ford 2)
Three Bears, 1925 (Lantz 4)
Three Bears, 1934 (Terry 4)
Three Bears, 1935 (Iwerks 4)
Three Bears, 1939 (Terry 4)
Three Bites of the Apple, 1967 (Fabrizi 3)
Three Black Bags, 1913 (Bunny 3)
Three Blind Mice, 1938 (Darwell 3,
    McCrea 3, Niven 3, Pangborn 3,
    Young 3, Zanuck 4)
Three Blind Mice, 1945 (Dunning 4)
Three Blondes in His Life, 1959 (Haller 4)
Three Brave Men, 1957 (Borgnine 3,
    Milland 3, Clarke 4, Dunne 4, LeMaire 4,
    Salter 4)
Three Brothers, 1915 (Reid 3)
Three Brothers. *See* Tre fratelli, 1981
Three Caballeros, 1944 (Disney 4, Iwerks 4)
Three Came Home, 1938 (Clarke 4)
Three Came Home, 1950 (Negulesco 2,
    Colbert 3, Hayakawa 3, Friedhofer 4,
    Johnson 4, Krasner 4, LeMaire 4)
Three Came Home, 1986 (Colbert 3)
Three Cases of Murder, 1954 (Welles 2,
    Dalrymple 4, Korda 4, Mathieson 4,
    Périnal 4)
Three Cheers for Love, 1936 (Dmytryk 2,
    Head 4, Young 4)
Three Cheers for the Irish, 1940 (Bacon 2,
    Deutsch 4, Rosher 4, Wald 4, Wallis 4)
Three Chumps Ahead, 1934 (Roach 4)
Three Clear Sundays, 1965 (Loach 2)
Three Cockeyed Sailors. *See* Sailors Three,
    1940
Three Coins in the Fountain, 1954
    (Negulesco 2, Brazzi 3, Jourdan 3,
    Webb 3, Cahn 4, Jeakins 4, Krasner 4,
    LeMaire 4, Reynolds 4, Wheeler 4,
    Young 4)
Three Comrades, 1938 (Borzage 2,
    Mankiewicz 2, Sullavan 3, Taylor 3,
    Young 3, Gibbons 4, Mayer 4,
    Ruttenberg 4, Sherriff 4, Vorkapich 4,
    Waxman 4)
Three Crosses. *See* Krizova trojka, 1948
Three Daring Daughters, 1948
    (MacDonald 3, Ames 4, Irene 4,
    Levien 4, Pasternak 4, Stothart 4)
Three Dark Horses, 1952 (Three Stooges 3)
Three Daughters of the West, 1911 (Dwan 2)
Three Dawns to Sydney, 1948 (Alwyn 4)
Three Days of the Condor, 1975 (Pollack 2,
    Dunaway 3, Redford 3, Robertson 3,
    Von Sydow 3, De Laurentiis 4,
    Houseman 4, Roizman 4)
Three Days of Victor Chernyshev. *See* Tri
    dnia Viktora Chernysheva, 1968
Three Days to a Kill, 1991 (Golan and
    Globus 4)
Three Dumb Clucks, 1937 (Three Stooges 3,
    Bruckman 4)
Three Encounters. *See* Tri vstrechi, 1948
Three Fables of Love. *See* Quatres Vérités,
    1962
Three Faces East, 1926 (Walthall 3,
    Sullivan 4)
Three Faces East, 1930 (Von Stroheim 2)
Three Faces of Eve, 1957 (Cobb 3,
    Woodward 3, Cortez 4, Johnson 4,
    LeMaire 4, Wheeler 4)

Three Faces of Sin. *See* Puits aux trois
    vérités, 1961
Three Faces West, 1940 (Coburn 3,
    Wayne 3, Alton 4, Young 4)
Three Fat Men, 1965 (Batalov 3)
Three Films, 1965 (Brakhage 2)
Three Foolish Wives, 1924 (Sennett 2)
Three for All, 1974 (Dors 3)
Three for Bedroom C, 1952 (Dumont 3,
    Swanson 3, Laszlo 4)
Three for the Show, 1954 (Grable 3,
    Duning 4, Wald 4)
Three for the Show, 1955 (Lemmon 3,
    Carmichael 4, Cole 4)
Three Forbidden Stories. *See* Tre storie
    proibite, 1952
Three Friends, 1912 (Griffith 2,
    Barrymore 3, Sweet 3, Walthall 3,
    Bitzer 4)
Three Fugitives, 1989 (Jones 3, Nolte 3,
    Wexler 4)
Three Gamblers, 1913 (Anderson 3)
Three Generations of Danjuro. *See* Danjuro
    sandai, 1944
Three Girls About Town, 1941 (Blondell 3,
    Benchley 4, Planer 4)
Three Girls from Rome. *See* Ragazze di
    Piazza di Spagna, 1952
Three Girls Lost, 1931 (Wayne 3, Young 3)
Three Godfathers, 1936 (Mankiewicz 2,
    Brennan 3, Ruttenberg 4)
Three Godfathers, 1948 (Ford 2,
    Armendáriz 3, Bond 3, Darwell 3,
    Johnson 3, Marsh 3, Basevi 4, Cooper 4,
    Hoch 4, Nugent 4)
Three Gold Coins, 1920 (Mix 3)
Three Grandfathers, 1948 (Wayne 3)
Three Guys Named Mike, 1951 (Walters 2,
    Johnson 3, Keel 3, Wyman 3, Kaper 4)
Three Hams on Rye, 1950 (Three Stooges 3)
Three Hearts for Julia, 1943 (Douglas 3,
    Folsey 4, Irene 4, Stothart 4)
Three Heroines. *See* Tri geroini, 1938
Three Hollywood Girls, 1930 (Arbuckle 3)
Three Hours, 1927 (Bosworth 3)
Three Hours to Kill, 1954 (Andrews 3,
    Reed 3, Brown 4)
Three Hundred Spartans. *See* Lion of Sparta,
    1961
Three Husbands, 1950 (Arden 3, Darwell 3,
    Planer 4)
Three in a Closet, 1920 (Bruckman 4)
Three Installations, 1952 (Anderson 2,
    Copland 4, Lassally 4)
Three into Two Won't Go, 1969 (Bloom 3,
    Steiger 3, Lai 4, Lassally 4)
Three Is a Crowd, 1951 (Terry 4)
Three Is a Family, 1944 (McDaniel 3)
Three Jumps Ahead, 1923 (Ford 2, Mix 3)
Three Keys, 1924 (Haller 4)
Three Kids and a Queen, 1935
    (D'Agostino 4, Waxman 4)
Three Kings and a Queen, 1939 (Hutton 3)
Three Lazy Mice, 1935 (Lantz 4)
Three Little Beers, 1935 (Three Stooges 3,
    Bruckman 4)
Three Little Bops, 1956 (Blanc 4, Foster 4,
    Freleng 4)
Three Little Ghosts, 1922 (Goulding 2)
Three Little Girls in Blue, 1946 (Newman 4)
Three Little Pigskins, 1934 (Three
    Stooges 3)
Three Little Pirates, 1946 (Three Stooges 3,
    Bruckman 4)

Three Little Powders, 1914 (Beery 3)
Three Little Pups, 1953 (Avery 4)
Three Little Sew and Sews, 1939 (Three
    Stooges 3, Ballard 4)
Three Little Twerps, 1943 (Three Stooges 3)
Three Little Words, 1950 (Astaire 3,
    Reynolds 3, Mayer 4, Pan 4, Previn 4,
    Rose 4)
Three Live Ghosts, 1922 (Hitchcock 2,
    Miller 4, Zukor 4)
Three Live Ghosts, 1929 (Bennett 3,
    Montgomery 3, Menzies 4)
Three Live Ghosts, 1936 (Howe 4,
    Sullivan 4)
Three Lives, 1953 (Dmytryk 2, Heston 3)
Three Lives of Thomasina, 1963 (Disney 4,
    Iwerks 4)
Three Loan Wolves, 1946 (Three Stooges 3)
Three Loves. *See* Frau, nach der Man sich
    sehnt, 1929
Three Loves Has Nancy, 1938 (Gaynor 3,
    Montgomery 3, Adrian 4, Daniels 4,
    Krasna 4)
Three Magic Feathers. *See* Tři čarovná péra,
    1970
Three Married Men, 1936 (Dmytryk 2,
    Cronjager 4)
Three Maxims, 1937 (Wilcox 2, Neagle 3)
Three Men and a Baby, 1987 (Hamlisch 4)
Three Men and a Girl, 1919 (Neilan 2,
    Barthelmess 3)
Three Men and a Girl, 1949 (Adam 4, De
    Grunwald 4, Heller 4)
Three Men from Texas, 1940 (Harlan 4,
    Head 4, Young 4)
Three Men in a Boat, 1933 (Dean 4)
Three Men in a Boat, 1956 (Clayton 2,
    Harvey 3, Addison 4)
Three Men in a Hidden Fortress. *See*
    Kakushitoride no san akunin, 1958
Three Men in a Tub, 1938 (Roach 4)
Three Men in White, 1944 (Barrymore 3,
    Gardner 3, Johnson 3, Walters 3,
    Irene 4)
Three Men Missing. *See* Ztracenci, 1957
Three Men of the North. *See* Kita no sannin,
    1945
Three Men on a Horse, 1936 (LeRoy 2,
    Blondell 3, Orry-Kelly 4, Polito 4)
Three Men to Pay, 1922 (Love 3)
Three Mesquiteers, 1936 (Carey 3)
Three Miles Out, 1924 (Emerson 4, Loos 4)
Three Million Dollars, 1911 (Dwan 2)
Three Minus Me. *See* Tres menos eu, 1988
Three Missing Links, 1938 (Three
    Stooges 3)
Three Mountaineers, 1980 (Halas and
    Batchelor 4)
Three Mounted Men, 1918 (Ford 2,
    Carey 3)
Three Moves to Freedom. *See*
    Schachnovelle, 1960
Three Murderesses. *See* Faibles femmes,
    1959
Three Musketeers, 1921 (Niblo 2,
    Fairbanks 3, Menjou 3, Edeson 4,
    Menzies 4)
Three Musketeers, 1933 (Wayne 3, Canutt 4)
Three Musketeers, 1935 (Ball 3, Lukas 3,
    Nichols 4, Plunkett 4, Polglase 4,
    Steiner 4)
Three Musketeers, 1938 (Ivanov-Vano 4)
Three Musketeers, 1939 (Dwan 2,
    Ameche 3, Carradine 3)

Thunder in the City, 1937 (Richardson 3, Rozsa 4, Sherwood 4)

Thunder in the Dust. *See* Sundowners, 1949

Thunder in the East. *See* Battle, 1934

Thunder in the East, 1953 (Vidor 2, Boyer 3, Kerr 3, Ladd 3, Friedhofer 4, Garmes 4, Head 4, Swerling 4)

Thunder in the Night, 1935 (Glennon 4)

Thunder in the Sun, 1959 (Hayward 3, Cortez 4, LeMaire 4, Leven 4)

Thunder in the Valley, 1947 (Basevi 4, Clarke 4, LeMaire 4)

Thunder Island, 1963 (Nicholson 3)

Thunder of Drums, 1961 (Bronson 3)

Thunder of the Sea, 1936 (Anhalt 4)

Thunder on the Hill, 1951 (Sirk 2, Colbert 3, Daniels 4, Salter 4)

Thunder over Mexico, 1933 (Eisenstein 2)

Thunder over Texas, 1934 (Ulmer 2)

Thunder over the Plains, 1953 (De Toth 2, Scott 3, Glennon 4)

Thunder Pass, 1954 (Carradine 3)

Thunder Riders, 1928 (Wyler 2)

Thunder Road, 1958 (Mitchum 3)

Thunder Rock, 1942 (Boulting 2, Mason 3, Redgrave 3)

Thunder Trail, 1937 (Head 4, Struss 4)

Thunderball, 1965 (Connery 3, Adam 4, Barry 4, Douy 4)

Thunderbirds, 1952 (Bond 3, Young 4)

Thunderbolt, 1912 (Cruze 2)

Thunderbolt, 1929 (Hathaway 2, Von Sternberg 2, Wray 3, Dreier 4, Furthman 4, Mankiewicz 4)

Thunder-Bolt, 1947 (Wyler 2)

Thunderbolt and Lightfoot, 1974 (Cimino 2, Bridges 3, Eastwood 3)

Thunderhead, Son of Flicka, 1945 (McDowall 3, Clarke 4)

Thunderheart, 1991 (Shepard 4)

Thundering Dawn, 1923 (Wong 3, Coffee 4)

Thundering Fleas, 1926 (Laurel and Hardy 3, Roach 4)

Thundering Gunslingers, 1944 (Crabbe 3)

Thundering Herd, 1925 (Hathaway 2, Howard 2)

Thundering Herd, 1933 (Hathaway 2, Carey 3, Crabbe 3, Scott 3)

Thundering Hoofs, 1941 (Hunt 4)

Thundering Landlords, 1925 (Roach 4)

Thundering Romance, 1924 (Arthur 3)

Thundering Taxis, 1933 (Roach 4)

Thundering Through, 1925 (Arthur 3)

Thundering Toupees, 1929 (Roach 4)

Thundering West, 1939 (Ballard 4)

Thunderstorm, 1957 (Lee 3)

Thursday the Twelfth. *See* Pandemonium, 1982

Thursday's Child, 1943 (Granger 3)

Thursday's Child, 1983 (Rowlands 3)

Thursday's Children, 1953 (Anderson 2, Burton 3, Lassally 4)

Thursday's Game, 1974 (Burstyn 3, Wilder 3, Biroc 4)

Thus the Divine Wind Arrives. *See* Kakute kamikaze wa fuku, 1944

Thwarted Vengeance, 1911 (Anderson 3)

Thy Name Is Woman, 1924 (Niblo 2, Novarro 3, Carré 4, Mayer 4, Meredyth 4)

Ti attende una corda . . . Ringo. *See* Ritorno di Clint il solitario, 1972

Ti conosco, mascherina!, 1943 (Baarová 3)

Ti ho sempre amato, 1953 (Delli Colli 4)

Ti ho sposato per allegria, 1967 (Vittí 3, Age and Scarpelli 4)

Ti presento un'amica, 1988 (Cecchi D'Amico 4)

Ti ritroverò, 1948 (Fusco 4)

Tiara Tahiti, 1962 (Lom 3, Mason 3, Mills 3, Heller 4, Rank 4, Vetchinsky 4)

Tiburoneros, 1962 (Alcoriza 4)

Tic, 1908 (Feuillade 2)

Tichá radost, 1985 (Brejchová 3)

Tichý týden v domě, 1969 (Švankmajer 4)

. . . Tick . . . Tick . . . Tick . . ., 1969 (March 3)

Tick Tock Tuckered, 1944 (Blanc 4, Clampett 4, Stalling 4)

Ticket of Leave, 1936 (Havelock-Allan 4)

Ticket of Leave Man, 1910 (White 3)

Ticket to Paradise. *See* Biljett till paradiset, 1962

Ticket to Ride, 1988 (Brazzi 3)

Ticket to Tomahawk, 1950 (Baxter 3, Brennan 3, Monroe 3, LeMaire 4)

Tickle Me, 1965 (Presley 3)

Ticklish Affair, 1963 (Gillespie 4, Krasner 4, Pasternak 4)

Tide of Empire, 1929 (Dwan 2, Gibbons 4, Young 4)

Tide of Fortune, 1910 (Lawrence 3)

Tides of Barnegat, 1917 (Neilan 2, Sweet 3)

Tides of Passion, 1925 (Blackton 2, Marsh 3)

Tie Me Up! Tie Me Down!. *See* ¡Atame!, 1989

Tie That Binds, 1915 (Anderson 3)

Tied for Life, 1933 (Langdon 3)

Tief im Böhmerwald, 1908 (Porten 3, Messter 4)

Tiefland, 1922 (Dagover 3)

Tiempo de silencio, 1986 (Rey 3)

Tiempo es el viento, 1976 (Alvarez 2)

Tiempo libre a la roca, 1981 (Alvarez 2)

Tiens, vous êtes à Poitiers?, 1916 (Feyder 2)

Tiera sedienta, 1945 (Rey 3)

Tierarzt Dr. Vlimmen, 1945 (Wegener 3)

Tierra baja, 1950 (Armendáriz 3)

Tierra brutal, 1962 (Rey 3)

Tierra de los toros, 1924 (Musidora 3)

Tierra de pasiónes, 1944 (Armendáriz 3)

Tierra del Fuego se apaga, 1955 (Fernández 2, Figueroa 4)

Tierra prometida, 1972 (Villagra 3)

Tierra y el cielo, 1977 (Gómez 2)

Tieta d'agreste, 1981 (Loren 3)

Tifusari, 1963 (Mimica 4)

Tiger, 1930 (Hoffmann 4)

Tiger and the Flame. *See* Jhansi ri-rani, 1952

Tiger and the Pussycat. *See* Tigre, 1967

Tiger Balm, 1972 (Frampton 2)

Tiger Bay, 1933 (Wong 3)

Tiger Bay, 1959 (Mills 3, Rank 4)

Tiger—Fruhling in Wien, 1985 (Constantine 3)

Tiger Hunt in Assam, 1958 (Van Dyke 2)

Tiger in the Sky. *See* McConnell Story, 1955

Tiger in the Smoke, 1956 (Arnold 4, Rank 4)

Tiger Likes Fresh Blood. *See* Tigre aime la chair fraiche, 1964

Tiger Love, 1924 (Hawks 2, Clarke 4)

Tiger Makes Out, 1967 (Hoffman 3, Wallach 3)

Tiger Man, 1918 (Hart 3, August 4)

Tiger Morse, 1967 (Warhol 2)

Tiger Rose, 1923 (Goulding 2, Rosher 4)

Tiger Rose, 1929 (MacMurray 3, Gaudio 4)

Tiger Shark, 1932 (Hawks 2, Robinson 3, Gaudio 4, Orry-Kelly 4)

Tiger Thompson, 1924 (Carey 3, Eason 4, Stromberg 4)

Tiger Town, 1983 (Scheider 3)

Tiger Walks, 1964 (Disney 4)

Tiger Woman, 1917 (Bara 3)

Tiger Woman, 1944 (Canutt 4)

Tigerin, 1921 (Hoffmann 4)

Tiger's Club, 1920 (Ruttenberg 4)

Tiger's Cub, 1921 (White 3)

Tigers Don't Cry, 1976 (Quinn 3)

Tight Little Island. *See* Whisky Galore!, 1949

Tight Shoes, 1923 (Roach 4)

Tight Shoes, 1941 (Crawford 3, Three Stooges 3, Salter 4)

Tight Spot, 1955 (Robinson 3, Rogers 3, Duning 4, Guffey 4, Wald 4)

Tightrope, 1984 (Bujold 3, Eastwood 3)

Tigra, 1953 (Torre Nilsson 2)

Tigre, 1967 (Gassman 3, Age and Scarpelli 4)

Tigre aime la chair fraiche, 1964 (Chabrol 2, Rabier 4)

Tigre de Yautepec, 1933 (De Fuentes 2)

Tigre reale, 1916 (Pastrone 2)

Tigre se parfume à la dynamite, 1965 (Chabrol 2, Rabier 4)

Tigress, 1914 (Guy 2)

Tigress, 1927 (Walker 4)

Tigress. *See* Tigra, 1953

Tigullio minore, 1947 (Risi 2)

Tih Minh, 1918 (Feuillade 2)

Tijera de oro, 1958 (Alcoriza 4)

Tijuana Story, 1957 (Katzman 4)

'Til We Meet Again, 1940 (Goulding 2, Oberon 3, Orry-Kelly 4, Wallis 4)

Till Eulenspiegel, 1966 (Ophuls 2)

Till glädje, 1950 (Sjöström 2, Fischer 4)

Till I Come Back to You, 1918 (De Mille 2, Buckland 4, Rosher 4)

Till Österland, 1926 (Molander 2, Jaenzon 4, Magnusson 4)

Till the Clouds Roll By, 1946 (Minnelli 2, Allyson 3, Charisse 3, Garland 3, Horne 3, Johnson 3, Lansbury 3, Sinatra 3, Walker 3, Williams 3, Alton 4, Folsey 4, Freed 4, Irene 4, Mayer 4, Rose 4, Stradling 4)

Till the End of Time, 1946 (Dmytryk 2, Edwards 2, Mitchum 3, D'Agostino 4, Schary 4)

Till Tomorrow Comes. *See* Asu aru kagiri, 1962

Till We Meet Again, 1922 (Goulding 2, Marsh 3)

Till We Meet Again, 1936 (Florey 2, Marshall 3, Head 4)

'Till We Meet Again, 1940 (Gaudio 4, Haskin 4)

Till We Meet Again, 1944 (Borzage 2, Milland 3, Coffee 4, Dreier 4, Head 4)

Tilli the Toiler, 1941 (Pangborn 3)

Tillie series, 1915 (Dressler 3)

Tillie and Gus, 1933 (Fields 3, Zukor 4)

Tillie the Toiler, 1927 (Davies 3, Daniels 4)

Tillie the Toiler, 1927 (Day 4, Gibbons 4)

Tillie Wakes Up, 1917 (Marion 4)

Tillie's Punctured Romance, 1914 (Sennett 2, Arbuckle 3, Normand 3)

Tillie's Punctured Romance, 1928 (Fields 3)

Tilly the Tomboy, 1909 (Hepworth 2)

Tim, 1979 (Gibson 3)

Timber, 1942 (Salter 4)

Timber Queen, 1922 (Roach 4)

Timber Tramps, 1975 (Garnett 2, Cotten 3)

Timber Wolf, 1925 (Van Dyke 2)

Timberjack, 1954 (Hayden 3, Menjou 3, Carmichael 4, Mercer 4, Young 4)

Timbuktu. See Legend of the Lost, 1957

Timbuktu, 1959 (Tourneur 2, De Carlo 3, Mature 3, Veiller 4)

Time, 1967 (Vukotić 4)

Time after Time, 1979 (McDowell 3, Rozsa 4)

Time after Time, 1985 (Gielgud 3, Howard 3)

Time & Fortune Vietnam Newsreel, 1969 (Mekas 2)

Time and Tide, 1916 (Eason 4)

Time Bandits, 1981 (Gilliam 2, Cleese 3, Connery 3, Richardson 3)

Time Bomb, 1952 (Ford 3, Addison 4, Junge 4, Young 4)

Time Flies, 1944 (Rank 4)

Time for Action. See Tip on a Dead Jockey, 1957

Time for Dying, 1971 (Boetticher 2, Ballard 4)

Time for Killing, 1967 (Ford, G. 3, Ford, H. 3, Stanton 3, Anhalt 4, Brown 4)

Time for Love, 1927 (Powell 3)

Time for Love, 1935 (Fleischer 4)

Time for Loving, 1971 (Noiret 3, Legrand 4)

Time for Miracles, 1980 (Brazzi 3)

Time for Terror. See Flesh Feast, 1973

Time Gallops On, 1952 (Terry 4)

Time Gentlemen Please, 1952 (Grierson 2)

Time Has Stopped. Time Stood Still. See Tempo si è fermato, 1959

Time in the Sun, 1939 (Eisenstein 2)

Time Is Money, 1913 (Brenon 2)

Time Is Money, 1923 (Rasp 3)

Time Is On Our Side, 1983 (Ashby 2)

Time Limit, 1957 (Widmark 3)

Time Limit, 1990 (Malden 3)

Time Lock, 1957 (Connery 3)

Time Lost and Time Remembered. See Passage of Love, 1965

Time Machine, 1959 (Pal 4)

Time of Destiny, 1988 (Hurt 3, Bumstead 4, Morricone 4)

Time of Indifference. See Indifferenti, 1963

Time of Indifference. See Gli indifferente, 1989

Time of the Heathen, 1961 (Emshwiller 2)

Time of Their Lives, 1946 (Abbott and Costello 3)

Time of Your Life, 1948 (Bendix 3, Bond 3, Cagney 3, Crawford 3, Darwell 3, Howe 4)

Time of Youth. See Seishun no koro, 1933

Time on My Hands, 1932 (Fleischer 4)

Time Out for Love. See Grandes Personnes, 1960

Time Out for Murder, 1938 (Darwell 3, Miller 4)

Time Out for Rhythm, 1941 (Miller 3, Three Stooges 3, Cahn 4, Planer 4, Prinz 4)

Time Out for Romance, 1937 (Trevor 3)

Time Out of Mind, 1947 (Siodmak 2, Rozsa 4)

Time the Comedian, 1924 (Florey 2)

Time the Great Healer, 1914 (Hepworth 2)

Time, the Place, and the Girl, 1946 (Edeson 4, Prinz 4)

Time to Die, 1983 (Morricone 4)

Time to Kill, 1942 (Chandler 4, Clarke 4, Day 4)

Time to Live, 1985 (Minnelli 3)

Time to Live, a Time to Die. See Feu follet, 1963

Time to Love, 1927 (Schulberg 4)

Time to Love and a Time to Die, 1958 (Sirk 2, Kinski 3, Metty 4, Rozsa 4)

Time to Remember. See Miracle in a Manger, 1986

Time to Sing, 1968 (Katzman 4)

Time Travelers, 1964 (Kovacs 4, Zsigmond 4)

Time Travelers, 1976 (Lourié 4)

Time without Memory. See Seigenki, 1972

Time without Pity, 1957 (Losey 2, Cushing 3, Redgrave 3, Francis 4)

Timely Interception, 1913 (Griffith 2, Barrymore 3, Gish 3, Bitzer 4)

Times Gone By. See Altri tempi, 1952

Times Square, 1929 (Robinson 4)

Times Square Lady, 1935 (Taylor 3)

Times Square Playboy, 1936 (Orry-Kelly 4)

Timestalkers, 1987 (Kinski 3)

Timid Rabbit, 1937 (Terry 4)

Timid Tabby, 1956 (Hanna and Barbera 4)

Timid Toreador, 1940 (Blanc 4, Clampett 4, Stalling 4)

Timid Young Man, 1935 (Keaton 2, Sennett 2)

Timidité vaincue, 1909 (Linder 3)

Timothy Dobbs, That's Me, 1916 (Beery 3)

Timothy's Quest, 1922 (Olcott 2)

Timothy's Quest, 1936 (Schary 4)

Tin Can Tourist, 1937 (Terry 4)

Tin Drum. See Blechtrommel, 1978

Tin Gods, 1926 (Dwan 2, Powell 3)

Tin Hats, 1926 (Gibbons 4, Lewin 4)

Tin Man, 1935 (Roach 4)

Tin Men, 1987 (Dreyfuss 3)

Tin Pan Alley, 1940 (Faye 3, Grable 3, Banton 4, Day 4, MacGowan 4, Newman 4, Shamroy 4)

Tin Pan Alley Cats, 1943 (Blanc 4, Clampett 4, Foster 4, Stalling 4)

Tin Star, 1957 (Mann 2, Fonda 3, Perkins 3, Van Cleef 3, Bernstein 4, Head 4, Nichols 4)

Tindous, 1955 (Kosma 4)

Tingel-Tangel, 1927 (Reisch 4)

Tingler, 1960 (Price 3)

Tiniest of Stars, 1913 (Cruze 2)

Tinkering with Trouble, 1914 (Lloyd 3, Roach 4)

Tin-minh, 1919 (Gaumont 2)

Tinsel Tree, 1941 (Anger 2)

Tinted Venus, 1921 (Hepworth 2)

Tintin et le mystère de la Toison d'Or, 1961 (Vanel 3)

Tintomara, 1970 (Dahlbeck 3)

Tip, 1917 (Daniels 3, Lloyd 3, Roach 4)

Tip on a Dead Jockey, 1957 (Dalio 3, Malone 3, Taylor 3, Folsey 4, Lederer 4, Rose 4, Rozsa 4)

Tip Toes, 1927 (Wilcox 2, Rogers 3)

Tipo difícil de matar, 1965 (Fernández 2)

Tip-Off, 1931 (Rogers 3)

Tip-Off Girls, 1938 (Quinn 3, Head 4)

Tire au flanc, 1928 (Renoir 2, Simon 3, Braunberger 4)

Tire au flanc, 1933 (Simon 3)

Tire Man, Spare My Tires, 1942 (Langdon 3, Bruckman 4)

Tire Trouble, 1942 (Terry 4)

Tire Troubles, 1923 (Roach 4)

Tire-au-flanc 62, 1961 (Coutard 4)

Tired, Absent-Minded Man, 1911 (Bunny 3)

Tired and Feathered, 1965 (Blanc 4)

Tired Business Men, 1927 (Roach 4)

Tired Feet, 1933 (Langdon 3)

Tirez s'il vous plait, 1908 (Berry 3)

Tirez sur le pianiste, 1960 (Truffaut 2, Braunberger 4, Coutard 4, Delerue 4)

Tiro a segno per uccidere. See Geheimnis der gelben Mönche, 1966

Tiroir secret, 1986 (Moreau 3, Morgan 3)

Tirol in Waffen, 1914 (Porten 3, Messter 4)

Tis an Ill Wind That Blows No Good, 1909 (Griffith 2, Bitzer 4)

Tiszti kardbojt, 1915 (Korda, A. 2, Korda, V. 4)

Tit for Tat. See Bonne Farce avec ma tête, 1904

Tit for Tat, 1935 (Laurel and Hardy 3, Roach 4)

Titan, 1949 (Flaherty 2)

Titan Find, 1984 (Kinski 3)

Titanic, 1953 (Negulesco 2, Ritter 3, Stanwyck 3, Wagner 3, Webb 3, Brackett 4, Jeakins 4, LeMaire 4, Reisch 4, Wheeler 4)

Titan-Michaelangelo, 1949 (March 3)

Titans. See Arrivani i titani, 1961

Titfield Thunderbolt, 1952 (Crichton 2, Auric 4, Clarke 4, Slocombe 4)

Titicut Follies, 1967 (Wiseman 2)

Title for the Sin. See Právo na hřich, 1932

Title Match of Magic. See Ninjutsu senshuken jiai, 1956

Title Shot, 1979 (Curtis 3)

Tito's Guitar, 1929 (Fleischer 4)

Tizoc, 1956 (Félix 3, Infante 3)

Tkada-no-baba, 1927 (Tanaka 3)

Tlatsche, 1939 (Ulmer 2)

Tlayucan, 1961 (Alcoriza 4)

T-Men, 1948 (Mann 2, Alton 4)

TNT Jackson, 1974 (Corman 2)

To Be a Crook. See Fille et des fusils, 1964

To Be Called For, 1914 (Mix 3)

To Be or Not to Be, 1942 (Lubitsch 2, Lombard 3, Irene 4, Korda, A. 4, Korda, V. 4, Maté 4, Plunkett 4)

To Be or Not to Be, 1983 (Brooks 2, Bancroft 3, Ferrer 3)

To Be Seven in Belfast, 1975 (Menges 4)

To Beat the Band, 1935 (Mercer 4, Musuraca 4, Plunkett 4)

To Bed or Not to Bed. See Diavolo, 1963

To Beep or Not to Beep, 1963 (Blanc 4)

To Catch a King, 1984 (Wagner 3)

To Catch a Thief, 1954 (Hitchcock 2, Grant 3, Kelly 3, Vanel 3, Burks 4, Hayes 4, Head 4)

To Commit a Murder. See Peau d'espion, 1967

To Die in Madrid. See Mourir à Madrid, 1962

To Die in Madrid, 1967 (Gielgud 3)

To Dig a Pit. See Cavar un foso, 1966

To Dorothy, a Son, 1954 (Winters 3, Box 4)

To Duck or Not to Duck, 1943 (Blanc 4, Jones 4, Stalling 4)

To Each His Own, 1946 (Leisen 2, De Havilland 3, Brackett 4, Dreier 4, Head 4, Young 4)

To, è morta la nonna, 1969 (Monicelli 2)

To Find a Man, 1970 (Booth 4)

To Forget Palermo,. *See* Dimenticare Palermo, 1990

To Forget Venice. *See* Dimenticare Venezia, 1979

To Hare Is Human, 1956 (Blanc 4, Jones 4, Maltese 4)

To Have and Have Not, 1944 (Hawks 2, Bacall 3, Bogart 3, Brennan 3, Dalio 3, Carmichael 4, Faulkner 4, Furthman 4, Mercer 4, Waxman 4)

To Have and to Hold, 1916 (Reid 3)

To Have and to Hold, 1922 (Miller 4)

To Have and to Hold, 1951 (Carreras 4)

To Hear Your Banjo Play, 1940 (Leacock 2, Van Dyke 2)

To Heir is Human, 1944 (Langdon 3)

To Hell and Back, 1955 (Murphy 3)

To Hell with the Kaiser, 1918 (Mathis 4)

To Itch His Own, 1958 (Blanc 4, Jones 4, Stalling 4)

To iu onna, 1971 (Iwashita 3)

To John Bunny's, 1915 (Bunny 3)

To Joy. *See* Till glädje, 1950

To Kill a Clown, 1971 (Lassally 4)

To Kill a Mockingbird, 1962 (Pakula 2, Duvall 3, Peck 3, Bernstein 4, Bumstead 4, Harlan 4, Westmore Family 4)

To Kill a Stranger, 1982 (Pleasence 3)

To Kill or to Die. *See* Mio nome è Shanghai Joe, 1973

To Kill With Intrigue, 1978 (Chan 3)

To koritsi me ta mavra, 1955 (Lassally 4)

To Live. *See* **Ikiru, 1952**

To Live and Die in L.A., 1985 (Müller 4)

To Live in Peace. *See* Vivere in pace, 1946

To Love. *See* Att älska, 1964

To maend i ødemarken, 1972 (Roos 2)

To Mary—with Love, 1936 (Cromwell 2, Loy 3, Pangborn 3, Trevor 3, MacGowan 4)

To Melody a Soul Responds, 1915 (Eason 4)

To meteoro vima to Pelargou. *See* Suspended Step of the Stork, 1991

To neznáte Hadimršku, 1931 (Heller 4)

To Our Children's Children, 1969 (Halas and Batchelor 4)

To Our Loves. *See* Nos Amours, 1983

To Paris with Love, 1954 (Hamer 2, Guinness 3, Buckner 4)

To Parsifal, 1963 (Baillie 2)

To Please a Lady, 1950 (Brown 2, Gable 3, Menjou 3, Stanwyck 3, Basevi 4, Kaper 4, Mayer 4, Rose 4, Rosson 4)

To Please One Woman, 1921 (Weber 2)

To Rent—Furnished, 1915 (Eason 4)

To Russia with Elton, 1979 (Moore 3)

To Save Her Soul, 1909 (Griffith 2, Pickford 3, Bitzer 4)

To Sir with Love, 1967 (Poitier 3)

To teleftaio psemma, 1957 (Lassally 4)

To the Aid of Stonewall Jackson, 1911 (Olcott 2)

To the Devil a Daughter, 1976 (Elliott 3, Kinski 3, Lee 3, Widmark 3, Watkin 4)

To the Ends of the Earth, 1948 (Stevenson 2, Powell 3, Buchman 4, Duning 4, Guffey 4)

To the Ladies, 1923 (Cruze 2, Astor 3, Horton 3)

To the Last Man, 1923 (Fleming 2, Hathaway 2, Howe 4)

To the Last Man, 1933 (Hathaway 2, Carradine 3, Crabbe 3, Scott 3, Temple 3)

To the Moon, Alice, 1990 (Wexler 4)

To the Moon and Beyond, 1964 (Trumbull 4)

To the North-West, 1934 (Zhao 3)

To the Orient. *See* Till Österland, 1926

To the Public Danger, 1948 (Fisher 2)

To the Rescue, 1932 (Lantz 4)

To the Shores of Tripoli, 1942 (O'Hara 3, Scott 3, Cronjager 4, Newman 4, Trotti 4, Zanuck 4)

To the Victor. *See* Owd Bob, 1938

To the Victor, 1948 (Brooks 2, Daves 2, Malone 3, Burks 4, Wald 4)

To the Western World, 1981 (Huston 2)

To Woody Allen, From Europe With Love, 1981 (Delvaux 2)

To Your Health, 1956 (Halas and Batchelor 4)

To Z, 1956 (Snow 2)

Toâ, 1949 (Guitry 2)

Toast of New Orleans, 1950 (Grayson 3, Niven 3, Cahn 4, Green 4, Mayer 4, Pasternak 4, Plunkett 4, Rose 4)

Toast of New York, 1937 (Farmer 3, Grant 3, Nichols 4, Polglase 4)

Toast of New York, 1983 (Grant 3)

Toast of Song, 1952 (Fleischer 4)

Toast of the Legion. *See* Kiss Me Again, 1931

Toast to a Young Miss. *See* Ojosan kanpai, 1949

Tobacco Road, 1941 (Ford 2, Andrews 3, Bond 3, Tierney 3, Banton 4, Basevi 4, Day 4, Johnson 4, La Shelle 4, Miller 4, Newman 4, Zanuck 4)

Tobasco Road, 1957 (Blanc 4)

Tobias Buntschuh, 1921 (Holger-Madsen 2)

Tobias Wants Out, 1913 (Mix 3)

Tobie est un ange, 1941 (Allégret 2)

Tobira o hiraku onna, 1946 (Miyagawa 4, Yoda 4)

Tobisuke boken ryoko, 1949 (Hayasaka 4)

Tobisuke's Adventures. *See* Tobisuke boken ryoko, 1949

Toboggan, 1934 (Burel 4)

Tobruk, 1967 (Hudson 3, Bumstead 4, Harlan 4, Kaper 4, Whitlock 4)

Toburoku no Tatsu, 1962 (Mifune 3)

Toby and the Tall Corn, 1954 (Leacock 2, Van Dyke 2)

Toby Tyler, or Ten Weeks with a Circus, 1959 (Disney 4, Iwerks 4)

Toccata for Toy Trains, 1957 (Bernstein 4)

Tochan no po ga kikoeru, 1971 (Tsukasa 3)

Tocher, 1937 (Reiniger 4)

Tochter der Landstrasse, 1914 (Gad 2, Nielsen 3)

Tochter des Bajazzo, 1919 (Albers 3)

Tochter des Mehemed, 1919 (Jannings 3)

Tochter des Regiments, 1933 (Ondra 3)

Tochter des Samurai. *See* Atarashiki tsuchi, 1937

Tod des Empedokles, 1987 (Straub and Huillet 2)

Tod in Sevilla, 1913 (Gad 2, Nielsen 3)

Tod ritt Dienstags. *See* Giorno dell'ira, 1967

Toda máquina, 1951 (Infante 3)

Toda-ke no kyodai, 1941 (Ryu 3)

Today. *See* Sevodiva, 1922

Today, 1930 (D'Agostino 4, Howe 4, Miller 4)

Today. *See* Segodnya, 1930

Today and Tomorrow, 1945 (Alwyn 4)

Today is Forever. *See* Griffin and Phoenix: A Love Story, 1976

Today It's Me—Tomorrow You. *See* Oggi a me … domani a te!, 1968

Today We Live, 1933 (Hawks 2, Cooper 3, Crawford 3, Young 3, Faulkner 4)

Today We Live, 1937 (Rotha 2)

Todd Killings, 1971 (Grahame 3, Rosenman 4)

Todesreigen, 1921 (Tschechowa 3)

Todesritt in Riesenrad, 1912 (Planer 4)

Todessmaragd. *See* Knabe in Blau, 1919

Tödlicher Irrtum, 1970 (Mueller-Stahl 3)

Todo es posible en Granada, 1954 (Oberon 3)

Todoke haha no sakebi, 1959 (Yamada 3)

Todoke haha no uta, 1959 (Yoda 4)

Todo modo, 1976 (Mastroianni 3, Piccoli 3, Volonté 3, Morricone 4)

Toets, 1967 (Müller 4)

Tofflan-en lycklig komedi, 1967 (Björnstrand 3)

Tog Dogs, 1989 (Halas and Batchelor 4)

Toge no uta, 1924 (Mizoguchi 2)

Together, 1956 (Anderson 2, Lassally 4)

Together. *See* Amo non Amo, 1978

Together Again, 1944 (Vidor 2, Boyer 3, Coburn 3, Dunne 3, Cohn 4, Polglase 4, Walker 4)

Together in the Weather, 1946 (Pal 4)

Together We Stand, 1986 (Gould 3)

Togger, 1937 (Rasp 3)

Tohjin Okichi, 1935 (Hayakawa 3)

Toho senichiya, 1947 (Hasegawa 3, Takamine 3, Yamada 3)

Toho shoboto, 1946 (Takamine 3)

Toi de faire, Mignonne, 1963 (Constantine 3)

Toi que j'adore, 1933 (Feuillère 3)

Toilers, 1919 (Colman 3)

Toilet Section Chief. *See* Toiretto buchou, 1961

Toiretto buchou, 1961 (Muraki 4)

Tojin Okichi, 1930 (Kinugasa 2, Mizoguchi 2)

Tojin Okichi, 1954 (Yamada 3)

Tojuro no koi, 1937 (Hasegawa 3)

Tojuro no koi, 1955 (Hasegawa 3, Kyo 3, Shindo 3, Yoda 4)

Toka kan no jinsei, 1941 (Tanaka 3)

Tokai kokyogaku, 1929 (Mizoguchi 2)

Tokaku omna to iu mono wa, 1932 (Yoda 4)

Toki no ujigami, 1932 (Mizoguchi 2)

Tokio Jokio, 1943 (Blanc 4, Stalling 4)

Tokojiro of Katsukake. *See* Kutsukake Tokojiro, 1961

Tokyo 1958, 1958 (Hani 2)

Tokyo Bay on Fire. *See* Tokyo-wan enjou, 1975

Tokyo Blackout. *See* Shuto Shoshitsu, 1987

Tokyo boshoku, 1957 (Hara 3, Ryu 3, Yamada 3, Yamamura 3)

Tokyo hika, 1951 (Mori 3)

Tokyo Joe, 1949 (Bogart 3, Hayakawa 3)

Tokyo koshinkyoku, 1929 (Mizoguchi 2)

Tokyo March. *See* Tokyo koshinkyoku, 1929

Tokyo monogatari, 1953 (Imamura 2, Hara 3, Kagawa 3, Ryu 3, Yamamura 3)

Tokyo mushuku, 1950 (Yamamura 3)

Tokyo no ekubo, 1952 (Takamine 3)

Tokyo no gassho, 1931 (Takamine 3)

Tokyo no hiroin, 1950 (Mori 3)
Tokyo no koibito, 1952 (Mifune 3)
Tokyo no kyujitsu, 1958 (Hara 3, Kagawa 3, Mifune 3, Tsukasa 3)
Tokyo no onna, 1933 (Tanaka 3)
Tokyo no sora no shita niwa, 1955 (Yamada 3)
Tokyo no yado, 1935 (Ozu 2)
Tokyo Olympiad. *See* Tokyo Orimpikku, 1965
Tokyo Orimpikku, 1965 (Miyagawa 4)
Tokyo Rose, 1945 (Edwards 2)
Tokyo saiban, 1983 (Takemitsu 4)
Tokyo senso sengo hiwa, 1970 (Takemitsu 4, Toda 4)
Tokyo Story. *See* **Tokyo monogatari, 1953**
Tokyo Sweetheart. *See* Tokyo no koibito, 1952
Tokyo Trial. *See* Tokyo saiban, 1983
Tokyo Twilight. *See* Tokyo boshoku, 1957
Tokyo Woman. *See* Tokyo no onna, 1933
Tokyo-ga, 1985 (Wenders 2, Ryu 3)
Tokyo-hen, 1948 (Takamine 3)
Tokyo's Chorus. *See* Tokyo no gassho, 1931
Tokyo-wan enjou, 1975 (Muraki 4)
Tol'able David, 1921 (Goulding 2, King 2, Barthelmess 3)
Tol'able David, 1930 (Carradine 3, Walthall 3, Glazer 4)
Tol'able Romeo, 1926 (Roach 4)
Told at Twilight, 1917 (King 2)
Told in the Hills, 1919 (Howe 4)
Tolg ol disturbo, 1990 (Sanda 3)
Tolgo il disturbo, 1990 (Risi 2, Gassman 3, Gould 3)
Toll Bridge Troubles, 1929 (Fleischer 4)
Toll Gate, 1920 (Hart 3, August 4)
Toll of the Marshes, 1913 (Bushman 3)
Toll of the Sea, 1922 (Wong 3, Marion 4)
Tolle Bomberg, 1957 (Albers 3)
Tolle Heirat von Laló, 1918 (Pick 2)
Tolle Miss. *See* Miss Hobbs, 1921
Tolle Nacht, 1943 (Fröhlich 3)
Toller Einfall, 1932 (Kaper 4)
Toller hecht auf krummer tour, 1962 (Bendix 3)
Tom and Chérie, 1955 (Hanna and Barbera 4)
Tom and Jerry Mix, 1917 (Mix 3)
Tom and Jerry: The Movie, 1990 (Mancini 4)
Tom Brown of Culver, 1932 (Wyler 2, Power 3)
Tom Brown's Schooldays, 1940 (Stevenson 2, Biroc 4, Musuraca 4, Polglase 4)
Tom Brown's Schooldays, 1951 (Newton 3)
Tom, Dick, and Harry, 1941 (Meredith 3, Rogers 3, Kanin 4, Polglase 4)
Tom Horn, 1980 (McQueen 3, Alonzo 4)
Tom Jones, 1963 (Richardson 2, Evans 3, Finney 3, Greenwood 3, York 3, Addison 4, Lassally 4)
Tom Mix in Arabia, 1922 (Mix 3)
Tom Sawyer, 1917 (Zukor 4)
Tom Sawyer, 1930 (Cromwell 2, Darwell 3, Lang 4)
Tom Sawyer, 1973 (Foster 3, Oates 3, Williams 4)
Tom Sawyer, Detective, 1938 (O'Connor 3, Head 4)
Tom Thumb, 1936 (Iwerks 4)
Tom Thumb, 1958 (Matthews 3, Sellers 3, Terry-Thomas 3, Pal 4, Périnal 4)

Tom Thumb in Trouble, 1940 (Blanc 4, Jones 4, Stalling 4)
Tom Tight et Dum Dum, 1903 (Méliès 2)
Tom Toms of Mayumba. *See* Tam Tam Mayumba, 1955
Tom Turk and Daffy, 1944 (Blanc 4, Jones 4, Stalling 4)
Tomahawk, 1951 (De Carlo 3, Hudson 3, Salter 4)
Tomalio, 1933 (Arbuckle 3)
Tomate, 1960 (Almendros 4)
Tomb, 1986 (Carradine 3)
Tomb of Ligeia, 1965 (Corman 2, Price 3, Towne 4)
Tombeau sous L'Arc de Triomphe, 1927 (Wiene 2)
Tombola, paradiso nero, 1947 (Fabrizi 3)
Tomboy, 1909 (Olcott 2)
Tomboy and the Champ, 1960 (Johnson 3, Clothier 4)
Tomboy Bessie, 1911 (Sennett 2, Normand 3)
Tomboy on Bar Z, 1912 (Anderson 3)
Tomboys, 1905 (Selig 4)
Tombstone Terror, 1937 (Katzman 4)
Tombstone, the Town Too Tough to Die, 1942 (Harlan 4)
Tomei ningen, 1954 (Tsuburaya 4)
Tommy, 1931 (Protazanov 2)
Tommy, 1974 (Russell 2, Nicholson 3, Reed 3, Russell 4)
Tommy Gets His Sister Married, 1910 (White 3)
Tommy Tucker's Tooth, 1923 (Disney 4)
Tomorrow, 1971 (Faulkner 4)
Tomorrow and Tomorrow, 1932 (Lukas 3, Lang 4, Zukor 4)
Tomorrow at Eight, 1933 (Plunkett 4)
Tomorrow at Midnight. *See* For Love or Money, 1939
Tomorrow at Ten, 1963 (Shaw 3)
Tomorrow Begins Today, 1976 (Benegal 2)
Tomorrow Is Another Day, 1951 (Blanke 4, Burks 4)
Tomorrow Is Forever, 1946 (Welles 2, Colbert 3, Wood 3, Coffee 4, Steiner 4)
Tomorrow Mexico. *See* Jutro Meksyk, 1965
Tomorrow Never Comes, 1978 (Pleasence 3, Reed 3)
Tomorrow the World, 1944 (March 3, Moorehead 3, Lardner 4)
Tomorrow We Live, 1942 (Ulmer 2, Lom 3, De Grunwald 4, Heller 4)
Tomorrow's Island, 1968 (Crichton 2)
Tomorrow's Love, 1925 (Glennon 4)
Tomorrow's Youth, 1935 (Darwell 3, Pangborn 3)
Tomoshibi, 1954 (Kagawa 3)
Tom's Gang, 1927 (Musuraca 4)
Tom's Photo Finish, 1956 (Hanna and Barbera 4)
Tom's Sacrifice, 1916 (Mix 3)
Tom's Strategy, 1916 (Mix 3)
Tom-Tom Tomcat, 1953 (Blanc 4, Freleng 4, Stalling 4)
Tomuraishi tachi, 1968 (Miyagawa 4)
Ton ombre est la mienne, 1962 (Jarre 4)
Tondeur de chiens, 1897 (Guy 2)
Tong Man, 1919 (Hayakawa 3)
Tongues, 1982 (Clarke 2)
Tongues of Flame, 1925 (Love 3)
Tongues of Scandal, 1927 (Laszlo 4, Shamroy 4)
Toni, 1928 (Christian-Jaque 2, Buchanan 3)

Toni, 1935 (Becker 2, Renoir 4)
Tonic, 1928 (Lanchester 3)
Tonight at 8:30. *See* Meet Me Tonight, 1952
Tonight and Every Night, 1945 (Saville 2, Hayworth 3, Winters 3, Cahn 4, Cohn 4, Cole 4, Maté 4)
Tonight at Twelve, 1929 (Mandell 4)
Tonight for Sure, 1962 (Coppola 2)
Tonight Is Ours, 1933 (Leisen 2, Colbert 3, March 3, Struss 4, Zukor 4)
Tonight Let's All Make Love in London, 1968 (Christie 3, Marvin 3, Redgrave 3)
Tonight or Never, 1931 (LeRoy 2, Douglas 3, Karloff 3, Swanson 3, Goldwyn 4, Newman 4, Toland 4, Vajda 4)
Tonight or Never. *See* I natt eller aldrig, 1941
Tonight We Raid Calais, 1943 (Bondi 3, Cobb 3, Dalio 3, Ballard 4, Day 4, Salt 4)
Tonight We Sing, 1953 (Leisen 2, Bancroft 3, LeMaire 4, Newman 4, Shamroy 4)
Tonight's the Night. *See* Happy Ever After, 1954
Tonio Kroger, 1964 (Flaiano 4)
Tonka, 1958 (Mineo 3, Disney 4)
Tonnelier, 1897 (Guy 2)
Tonnelier, 1899 (Gaumont 4)
Tonnerre, 1948 (Epstein 2)
Tonnerre de Dieu, 1965 (Gabin 3)
Tonnerre de Jupiter, 1903 (Méliès 2)
Tontons flingueurs, 1973 (Blier 3, Audiard 4)
Tony Arzenta. *See* Big Guns, 1973
Tony Freunde, 1967 (Fassbinder 2)
Tony Rome, 1967 (Rowlands 3, Sinatra 3, Biroc 4, Smith 4)
Tony Runs Wild, 1926 (Mix 3)
Tony the Fiddler, 1913 (Bushman 3)
Too Ardent Lover, 1903 (Bitzer 4)
Too Bad She's Bad. *See* Peccato che sia una canaglia, 1954
Too Beautiful for You. *See* Trop belle pour toi, 1989
Too Busy to Work, 1932 (Beavers 3, Powell 3, Rogers 3, Clarke 4)
Too Busy to Work, 1939 (Cronjager 4)
Too Early, Too Late. *See* Trop tot, trop tard, 1983
Too Far to Go, 1978 (Close 3, Lassally 4)
Too Hop to Handle, 1956 (Blanc 4, McKimson 4)
Too Hot to Handle, 1938 (Gable 3, Loy 3, Pidgeon 3, Rosson 4, Waxman 4)
Too Hot to Handle, 1960 (Lee 3, Mansfield 3)
Too Late Blues, 1961 (Cassavetes 2, Head 4, Raksin 4)
Too Late for Divorce, 1956 (Lee 3)
Too Late for Tears, 1949 (Duryea 3, Kennedy 3, Haskin 4, Stromberg 4)
Too Late the Hero, 1970 (Aldrich 2, Caine 3, Elliott 3, Fonda 3, Robertson 3, Biroc 4)
Too Many Blondes, 1941 (Three Stooges 3, Krasner 4)
Too Many Brides, 1914 (Sennett 2)
Too Many Burglars, 1911 (Sennett 2)
Too Many Chefs, 1916 (Mix 3)
Too Many Chefs. *See* Who Is Killing the Great Chefs of Europe?, 1978
Too Many Cooks, 1920 (Howard 3)
Too Many Cooks, 1931 (Musuraca 4)

Too Many Crooks, 1930 (Olivier 3, Murfin 4)

Too Many Crooks, 1959 (Terry-Thomas 3, Rank 4)

Too Many Girls, 1910 (Porter 2)

Too Many Girls, 1940 (Ball 3, Johnson 3, Miller 3, Polglase 4)

Too Many Highballs, 1933 (Sennett 2, Bruckman 4)

Too Many Husbands, 1931 (Sennett 2)

Too Many Husbands, 1940 (Arthur 3, Douglas 3, MacMurray 3, Cohn 4, Prinz 4, Walker 4)

Too Many Kisses, 1925 (Marx Brothers 3, Powell 3, Rosson 4, Saunders 4)

Too Many Mamas, 1924 (McCarey 2, Roach 4)

Too Many Millions, 1918 (Cruze 2, Reid 3, Rosher 4)

Too Many Parents, 1936 (Dmytryk 2, Farmer 3, Head 4, Struss 4)

Too Many Suspects,. See Ellery Queen, 1975

Too Many Thieves, 1966 (Falk 3)

Too Many Too Soon, 1961 (Peries 2)

Too Many Wives, 1937 (Musuraca 4, Polglase 4)

Too Many Women. See God's Gift to Women, 1931

Too Many Women, 1932 (Roach 4)

Too Much, 1987 (Golan and Globus 4)

Too Much Burglar, 1914 (Costello 3)

Too Much Business, 1978 (Horton 3)

Too Much Harmony, 1933 (Mankiewicz 2, Crosby 3, Prinz 4)

Too Much Johnson, 1919 (Crisp 3)

Too Much Johnson, 1938 (Welles 2, Holliday 3)

Too Much Money, 1926 (Folsey 4)

Too Much Speed, 1921 (Reid 3)

Too Much Sun, 1990 (Arkin 3)

Too Much, Too Soon, 1958 (Flynn 3, Malone 3, Blanke 4, Musuraca 4, Orry-Kelly 4)

Too Scared to Scream, 1985 (O'Sullivan 3)

Too Soon To Love, 1959 (Nicholson 3)

Too Tough to Kill, 1935 (Bond 3)

Too Wise Wives, 1921 (Weber 2, Calhern 3)

Too Young for Love, 1959 (Head 4)

Too Young to Kiss, 1951 (Allyson 3, Johnson 3, Goodrich 4, Green 4, Kaper 4, Rose 4, Ruttenberg 4)

Too Young to Know, 1945 (Malone 3)

Too Young to Love, 1959 (Love 3, Box 4)

Too Young to Marry, 1931 (LeRoy 2, Young 3)

Tooi kumo, 1955 (Takamine 3)

Tools of Providence, 1915 (Hart 3)

Toote Khilone, 1978 (Azmi 3)

Tooth Will Out, 1951 (Three Stooges 3)

Toot! Toot!, 1926 (Fleischer 4)

Tootsie, 1982 (Pollack 2, Hoffman 3, Lange 3, May 4, Roizman 4, Smith 4)

Tootsie and Tamales, 1919 (Laurel and Hardy 3)

Top Crack, 1967 (Terry-Thomas 3)

Top Flat, 1935 (Roach 4)

Top Gun, 1955 (Hayden 3)

Top Gun, 1986 (Cruise 3)

Top Hat, 1934 (Astaire 3, Ball 3, Horton 3, Rogers 3, Berlin 4, Berman 4, Pan 4, Polglase 4, Steiner 4)

Top Hat and Tails: The Story of Jack Buchanan, 1943 (Buchanan 3)

Top Job, Grand Slam. See Ad ogni costo, 1967

Top Man, 1943 (Beavers 3, Gish 3, O'Connor 3, Mohr 4)

Top o' the Morning, 1949 (Crosby 3, Fitzgerald 3, Bumstead 4, Dreier 4)

Top of New York, 1922 (Levien 4)

Top of the Bill, 1931 (Bosworth 3)

Top of the Form, 1952 (Rank 4)

Top of the Hill, 1980 (Duning 4)

Top of the World, 1924 (Clarke 4)

Top of the World, 1955 (Clothier 4)

Top Secret, 1952 (Homolka 3, Lee 3)

Top Secret!, 1984 (Cushing 3, Sharif 3, Challis 4, Jarre 4)

Top Secret Affair, 1957 (Cromwell 2, Douglas 3, Hayward 3, Cortez 4, LeMaire 4)

Top Sergeant, 1942 (Salter 4)

Top Speed, 1930 (LeRoy 2, Brown 3, Grot 4)

Topaz, 1969 (Hitchcock 2, Piccoli 3, Bumstead 4, Folsey 4, Head 4, Jarre 4, Whitlock 4)

Topaze, 1933 (D'Arrast 2, Pagnol 2, Barrymore 3, Feuillère 3, Jouvet 3, Loy 3, MacGowan 4, Selznick 4, Steiner 4)

Topaze, 1936 (Pagnol 2)

Topaze, 1951 (Pagnol 2, Fernandel 3)

Topaze, 1970 (Noiret 3)

Topeka Terror, 1945 (Canutt 4)

Topio stin omichli, 1988 (Guerra 4)

Topkapi, 1964 (Dassin 2, Mercouri 3, Schell 3, Ustinov 3, Alekan 4, Douy 4)

Toplitsky and Company, 1913 (Sennett 2)

Topper, 1937 (McLeod 2, Grant 3)

Topper Returns, 1941 (Blondell 3, Roach 4)

Topper Takes a Trip, 1939 (McLeod 2, Pangborn 3, Friedhofer 4, Irene 4, Roach 4)

Tops, 1969 (Bernstein 4)

Tops Is the Limit. See Anything Goes, 1936

Tops with Pops, 1956 (Hanna and Barbera 4)

Topsy and Eva, 1927 (Johnson 3)

Topsy Turvy Villa, 1900 (Hepworth 2)

Topsy-Turvy Sweedie, 1914 (Beery 3)

Tor der Freiheit, 1919 (Albers 3)

Tora! Tora! Tora!, 1970 (Cotten 3, Robards 3, Yamamura 3, Day 4, Goldsmith 4, Muraki 4, Smith 4, Zanuck 4)

Torajiro Shinjitsu Ichiro. See Otoko wa Tsuraiyo, 1985

Tora-ko, 1935 (Shimura 3)

Tora's Pure Love. See Otoko wa tsuraiyo: Torajiro junjo-shishu, 1976

Tora's Spring Dream. See Otoko wa tsuraiyo: Torajiro Haru no yume, 1979

Tora-San Goes North, 1988 (Mifune 3)

Tora-San Goes to Vienna. See Otokowa Tsuraiyoo Toraijiro kokoro no tabiji, 1988

Tora-San's Forbidden Love. See Otoko wa Tsuraiyo, 1985

Torch, 1949 (Armendáriz 3, Goddard 3, Figueroa 4)

Torch Singer, 1933 (Colbert 3, Banton 4, Coffee 4, Struss 4)

Torch Song, 1953 (Walters 2, Crawford 3, Ames 4, Deutsch 4, Hayes 4, Rose 4, Schnee 4)

Torch Song Trilogy, 1988 (Bancroft 3)

Torchy Blane in Panama, 1938 (Gaudio 4)

Torchy Plays with Dynamite, 1939 (Wyman 3)

Torchy's Millions, 1921 (Shearer 3)

Tordenstenene, 1927 (Madsen and Schenstrøm 3)

Tordeuse orientale, 1955 (Rabier 4)

Torero, 1954 (Bardem 2)

Torero, 1957 (Del Rio 3)

Torgus. See Verlogene Moral, 1921

Torguvi dom Karski, 1917 (Mozhukin 3)

Toribe-yama shinju, 1928 (Hasegawa 3)

Toribeyama shinju: Osome Hankuro, 1936 (Hasegawa 3)

Torii Kyozaemon, 1942 (Shimura 3)

Torino nei centi'anni, 1961 (Rossellini 2)

Torment, 1924 (Tourneur 2, Love 3)

Torment. See Hets, 1944

Torment. See Scélérats, 1960

Tormented, 1960 (Laszlo 4)

Tormento, 1950 (Rosi 2)

Torn Between Two Lovers, 1979 (Remick 3)

Torn Curtain, 1966 (Hitchcock 2, Andrews 3, Newman 3, Addison 4, Head 4, Heckroth 4, Whitlock 4)

Tornado, 1917 (Ford 2)

Tornavara, 1941 (Hayakawa 3)

Toro negro, 1959 (Alcoriza 4)

Toro-no-o o fumu otokotachi, 1945 (Mori 3)

Toros, 1967 (Braunberger 4)

Torpedo Bay. See Finchè dura la tempesta, 1964

Torpedo Raider. See Brown on Resolution, 1935

Torpedo Run, 1958 (Borgnine 3, Ford 3, Folsey 4, Gillespie 4)

Torpedo Squadron, 1942 (Ford 2)

Torpido Yilmaz, 1965 (Güney 2)

Torreani, 1951 (Fröhlich 3)

Torrent, 1917 (L'Herbier 2)

Torrent, 1920 (Glennon 4)

Torrent, 1925 (Mayer 4)

Torrent. See Honryu, 1926 (Garbo 3, Daniels 4, Gibbons 4, Stromberg 4)

Torrents of Spring, 1989 (Skolimowski 2, Kinski 3)

Torrid Toreador, 1942 (Terry 4)

Torrid Zone, 1940 (Cagney 3, Sheridan 3, Deutsch 4, Haskin 4, Howe 4, Wald 4, Wallis 4)

Torro de falisco, 1940 (Armendáriz 3)

Torso. See Corpi presentano tracce di violenza carnale, 1973

Törst, 1949 (Fischer 4)

Torticola contre Frankensberg, 1952 (Brasseur 3, Gélin 3, Piccoli 3, Kosma 4)

Tortilla Flaps, 1958 (Blanc 4, McKimson 4)

Tortilla Flat, 1942 (Fleming 2, Garfield 3, Lamarr 3, Tracy 3, Freund 4, Glazer 4)

Tortoise Beats Hare, 1941 (Avery 4, Blanc 4, Stalling 4)

Tortoise Wins Again, 1946 (Terry 4)

Tortoise Wins By a Hare, 1943 (Blanc 4, Clampett 4, Foster 4, Stalling 4)

Tortue et le renard, 1970 (Braunberger 4)

Torture Garden, 1967 (Cushing 3, Meredith 3, Palance 3, Bernard 4, Francis 4)

Torture par l'espérance, 1928 (Modot 3, Spaak 4)

Tortured Dust, 1984 (Brakhage 2)

Tosca, 1918 (Bertini 3)

Tosca, 1940 (Visconti 2, Brazzi 3, Simon 3)

Tosca. See Devanti a lui tremava tutta Roma, 1946

Tosca, 1956 (Gallone 2, Rotunno 4)

Tosca, 1973 (Fabrizi 3, Gassman 3, Vitti 3)

Toscanini, Hymn of the Nations, 1945 (Kaufman 4)

Toselli. See Romanzo d'amore, 1950

Tösen från stormyrtorpet, 1918 (Sjöström 2, Magnusson 4)

Toshigoro, 1968 (Muraki 4)

Toss of the Coin, 1911 (Pickford 3, Gaudio 4)

Tot samyi Myunkhauzen, 1979 (Yankovsky 3)

Tot Watchers, 1957 (Hanna and Barbera 4)

Tota no o o fumu otokotachi, 1945 (Shimura 3)

Total Recall, 1990 (Schwarzenegger 3, Goldsmith 4)

Total War in Britain, 1945 (Rotha 2, Mills 3, Alwyn 4)

Totem, 1963 (Emshwiller 2)

Totem Mark, 1911 (Bosworth 3, Mix 3)

Toten Augen, 1917 (Negri 3)

Toten Augen von London, 1961 (Kinski 3)

Toteninsel, 1920 (Dagover 3, Herlth 4, Warm 4)

Toteninsel, 1921 (Röhrig 4)

Totenklaus. See Verlogene Moral, 1921

Totentanz, 1912 (Gad 2, Nielsen 3)

Totentanz, 1919 (Krauss 3, Warm 4)

Tötet nicht mehr!, 1919 (Pick 2)

Toto, 1925 (Florey 2)

Toto, 1933 (Tourneur 2, Douy 4)

Totò a colori, 1952 (Delli Colli 4, Age and Scarpelli 4, De Laurentiis 4)

Toto aéronaute, 1907 (Gaumont 4)

Totò cerca casa, 1950 (Monicelli 2, Age and Scarpelli 4, Ponti 4)

Totò cerca moglie, 1950 (Age and Scarpelli 4)

Totò contro i quattro, 1963 (Fabrizi 3)

Totò d'Arabia. See Totò de Arabia, 1965

Totò de Arabia, 1965 (Rey 3)

Toto devient anarchiste, 1910 (Cohl 4)

Totò e Carolina, 1955 (Monicelli 2, Flaiano 4)

Totò e i re di Roma, 1952 (Monicelli 2, Risi 2, Sordi 3, Rota 4)

Totò e le donne, 1953 (Monicelli 2, Delli Colli 4, Age and Scarpelli 4)

Totò e Marcellino, 1958 (Cardinale 3)

Totò e Peppino divisi a Berlino, 1962 (Age and Scarpelli 4)

Totò, Fabrizi e i giovani d'oggi, 1960 (Fabrizi 3)

Totò in Colour. See Totò a colori, 1952

Totò le Moko, 1949 (Age and Scarpelli 4)

Totò, Peppino, e . . . la malafemmina, 1956 (De Laurentiis 4)

Totò, Peppino, e le fanatiche, 1958 (Age and Scarpelli 4)

Totò Tarzan, 1950 (Age and Scarpelli 4)

Totò, Vittorio e la dottoressa, 1957 (De Sica 2)

Toto Wants a Home. See Totò cerca casa, 1950

Toto-Gâte-Sauce, 1905 (Pathé 4)

Toton, 1919 (Borzage 2)

Toto's Troubles, 1919 (Roach 4)

Totsugu hi, 1956 (Yoshimura 2)

Totsuseki iseki, 1966 (Shindo 2)

Toubib, 1979 (Delon 3, Renoir 4, Sarde 4)

Touch. See Toets, 1967

Touch. See Beröringen, 1971

Touch, 1990 (Zanussi 2)

Touch All the Bases, 1922 (Roach 4)

Touch and Die, 1990 (Sheen 3)

Touch and Go, 1955 (Hawkins 3, Love 3, Addison 4, Balcon 4, Slocombe 4)

Touch and Go. See Poudre d'escampette, 1971

Touch of a Child, 1918 (Hepworth 2)

Touch of a Stranger, 1988 (Winters 3)

Touch of Class, 1973 (Jackson 3, Segal 3, Cahn 4, Frank 4)

Touch of Evil, 1958 (Welles 2, Cotten 3, Dietrich 3, Heston 3, Leigh 3, McCambridge 3, Mancini 4, Metty 4)

Touch of Hell. See Serious Charge, 1959

Touch of Larceny, 1960 (Mason 3, Sanders 3, Head 4)

Touch of Love, 1915 (Eason 4)

Touch of Night. See Dotknięcie nocy, 1960

Touch of Scandal, 1984 (Dickinson 3)

Touch of the Sun, 1979 (Cushing 3)

Touch Wood, 1980 (Armstrong 2)

Touchdown, 1931 (McLeod 2)

Touchdown Army, 1938 (Head 4)

Touchdown Demons, 1940 (Terry 4)

Touché and Go, 1957 (Blanc 4, Jones 4)

Touche à tout, 1935 (Berry 3, Barsacq 4, Burel 4)

Touche pas la femme blanche, 1974 (Cuny 3, Deneuve 3, Fabrizi 3, Noiret 3, Piccoli 3, Sarde 4)

Touché, Pussy Cat, 1954 (Hanna and Barbera 4)

Touchez pas au Grisbi, 1953 (Gabin 3, Moreau 3, D'Eaubonne 4)

Touchez pas au Grisbi, 1988 (Sautet 2)

Touchez pas le femme blanche, 1974 (Mastroianni 3)

Tough As They Come, 1942 (Salter 4)

Tough Egg, 1936 (Terry 4)

Tough Enough, 1983 (Oates 3)

Tough Game. See Hårda leken, 1955

Tough Guy, 1935 (Cooper 3)

Tough Guys, 1986 (Douglas 3, Lancaster 3, Wallach 3)

Tough Guys Don't Dance, 1987 (Coppola 2, Golan and Globus 4, Towne 4)

Tough Kid's Waterloo, 1900 (Bitzer 4)

Tough Luck, 1920 (Roach 4)

Tough Winter, 1922 (Roach 4)

Tough Winter, 1930 (Roach 4)

Toughlove, 1985 (Dern 3, Remick 3)

Touha, 1958 (Brejchová 3, Kučera 4)

Touiste encore, 1963 (Cloquet 4)

Toujin Okichi, 1955 (Yoda 4)

Toukai's Suiko Story. See Toukai Suiko-den, 1945

Toukai Suiko-den, 1945 (Miyagawa 4)

Toulouse-Lautrec, 1950 (Braunberger 4)

Toulouse-Lautrec, 1985 (Halas and Batchelor 4)

Tour, 1928 (Clair 2, Périnal 4)

Tour au large, 1926 (Grémillon 2)

Tour de Babel, 1951 (Honegger 4)

Tour de chant, 1933 (Cavalcanti 2)

Tour de cochon, 1934 (Wakhévitch 4)

Tour de Nèsle, 1955 (Gance 2, Brasseur 3, Straub and Huillet)

Tour du monde d'un policier, 1906 (Pathé 4)

Tour du monde en bateau-stop, 1954 (Storck 2)

Tour Eiffel, 1900 (Lumière 2)

Tour Pour rien, 1933 (Rosay 3)

Tour Rheumatism. See Mabel's Latest Prank, 1914

Tourbiers, 1964 (Guillemot 4)

Tourbillon de Paris, 1928 (Duvivier 2, Dagover 3)

Toure une vie, 1974 (Lai 4)

Tourelle III, 1939 (Christian-Jaque 2, Blier 3)

Tourist, 1921 (Laurel and Hardy 3)

Tourist, 1925 (Arbuckle 3)

Tourist Trap, 1979 (Donaggio 4)

Touristes revenant d'une excursion, 1895 (Lumière 2)

Tourists, 1911 (Sennett 2, Normand 3)

Tourment, 1912 (Feuillade 2)

Tournament of Roses, 1954 (La Shelle 4)

Tous les chemins mènent à Rome, 1948 (Philipe 3, Presle 3, Barsacq 4, Matras 4)

Tous les deux, 1948 (Burel 4)

Tous les garçons s'appellent Patrick, 1957 (Godard 2, Braunberger 4)

Tous les vents, 1945 (Decaë 4)

Tous peuvent me tuer, 1957 (Broca 2, Aimée 3)

Tous vedettes, 1979 (Caron 3, Evein 4)

Tout ça ne vaut pas l'amour, 1931 (Tourneur 2, Gabin 3)

Tout casser, 1953 (Colpi 4, Decaë 4)

Tout casser. See Consortium, 1968

Tout chante autour de moi, 1954 (Piccoli 3)

Tout dépend des filles, 1979 (Presle 3, De Beauregard 4)

Tout est à nous, 1979 (Chaplin 3)

Tout est bien qui finit bien. See Max et son rival, 1909

Tout feu, 1981 (Montand 3)

Tout feu, tout flamme. See Ca va etre ta fête, 1961

Tout feu, tout flamme, 1982 (Adjani 3, Montand 3, Rappeneau 4)

Tout la mémoire du monde, 1956 (Cloquet 4)

Tout le monde il est beau, tout le monde il est gentil, 1972 (Blier 3)

Tout l'or du monde, 1961 (Clair 2, Noiret 3, Barsacq 4)

Tout Petit Faust, 1910 (Cohl 4)

Tout peut arriver, 1969 (Deneuve 3)

Tout pour l'amour, 1933 (Clouzot 2)

Tout pour le tout, 1958 (Guerra 2)

Tout pour rien, 1933 (Douy 4)

Tout s'arrange, 1931 (Fradetal 4)

Tout va bien, 1972 (Godard 2, Fonda, J. 3, Montand 3)

Toutankhamon et son royaume, 1967 (Decaë 4)

Toute Innocence, 1987 (Baye 3, Rabier 4)

Toute la mémoire du monde, 1956 (Resnais 2, Braunberger 4, Delerue 4, Jarre 4)

Toute la ville accuse, 1955 (Burel 4)

Toute révolution est un coup de dés, 1977 (Straub and Huillet 4)

Toutes folles de lui, 1967 (Audiard 4, Wakhévitch 4)

Toutes les femmes se ressemblent, 1990 (Gélin 3)

Tout's Remembrance, 1910 (Anderson 3)

Tovarich, 1937 (Litvak 2, Boyer 3, Colbert 3, Rathbone 3, Deutsch 4, Grot 4, Lang 4, Orry-Kelly 4, Robinson 4, Steiner 4, Wallis 4)

Tovaritch, 1935 (Delannoy 2)

Toward the Decisive Battle in the Sky,. See Kessen no ozura e, 1943

Toward the Unknown, 1956 (Garner 3, Holden 3, Rosson 4)

Towards New Times. *See* Mot nya tider, 1939

Towed in a Hole, 1932 (Laurel and Hardy 3)

Tower of Jewels, 1920 (Costello 3)

Tower of Lies, 1925 (Sjöström 2, Chaney 3, Shearer 3, Basevi 4, Gibbons 4, Mayer 4, Wilson 4)

Tower of London, 1939 (Karloff 3, Price 3, Rathbone 3, Salter 4)

Tower of London, 1962 (Coppola 2, Corman 2, Price 3)

Towering Inferno, 1974 (Astaire 3, Dunaway 3, Holden 3, Jones 3, McQueen 3, Newman 3, Wagner 3, Biroc 4, Westmore Family 4, Williams 4)

Town, 1941 (Von Sternberg 2)

Town by the Sea. *See* Staden vid vattnen, 1955

Town Called Bastard. *See* Town Called Hell, 1971

Town Called Hell, 1971 (Rey 3, Shaw 3)

Town Like Alice, 1956 (Finch 3, Rank 4, Unsworth 4, Vetchinsky 4)

Town on Trial. *See* Processo alla città, 1952

Town on Trial, 1957 (Coburn 3, Mills 3)

Town People. *See* Machi no hitobito, 1926

Town Tamer, 1965 (Andrews 3)

Town That Cried Terror. *See* Maniac, 1978

Town That Dreaded Sundown, 1977 (Johnson 3)

Town That Forgot God, 1922 (Ruttenberg 4)

Town Went Wild, 1944 (Horton 3)

Town without Pity, 1961 (Douglas 3, Tiomkin 4, Trumbo 4)

Towne Hall Follies, 1935 (Lantz 4)

Towser and the Tramp, 1907 (Gaumont 4)

Toy, 1982 (Pryor 3, Booth 4, Kovacs 4)

Toy Grabbers. *See* Up Your Teddy Bear, 1970

Toy Parade, 1932 (Iwerks 4)

Toy Shoppe, 1934 (Lantz 4)

Toy Soldiers, 1991 (Elliott 3)

Toy Town Hall, 1936 (Freleng 4, Stalling 4)

Toy Trouble, 1941 (Blanc 4, Jones 4, Stalling 4)

Toy Wife, 1938 (Douglas 3, Rainer 3, Young 3, Adrian 4, Akins 4, Cooper 4)

Toyland, 1932 (Terry 4)

Toyland Premiere, 1934 (Lantz 4)

Toymaker on the Brink and the Devil, 1910 (Porter 2)

Toyo no haha, 1934 (Takamine 3, Tanaka 3)

Toyotomi's Record of Promotion. *See* Shusse Taikou-ki, 1938

Toys in the Attic, 1963 (Hill 2, Martin 3, Page 3, Tierney 3, Biroc 4, Duning 4, Mirisch 4)

Toys of Fate, 1909 (Porter 2)

Toys of Fate, 1918 (Nazimova 3)

T.R. Baskin, 1971 (Caan 3)

Tra i gorghi, 1916 (Gallone 2)

Tra moglie e Mario, 1975 (Sordi 3)

Tracce di una vita amorosa, 1990 (Morricone 4)

Track of the Cat, 1954 (Wellman 2, Bondi 3, Mitchum 3, Wright 3, Clothier 4)

Track of Thunder, 1967 (Fields 4)

Track 29, 1988 (Roeg 2)

Trackdown: Finding the Goodbar Killer, 1983 (Segal 3)

Tracked by the Police, 1927 (Zanuck 4)

Tracked Down, 1912 (Bushman 3)

Tracking the Sleeping Death, 1938 (Zinnemann 2)

Tracks, 1922 (Johnson 3)

Tracks, 1976 (Hopper 3)

Trąd, 1971 (Ścibor-Rylski 4)

Trade Gun Bullet, 1912 (Bosworth 3)

Trade Tattoo, 1937 (Grierson 2, Lye 4)

Trade Winds, 1938 (Garnett 2, Bellamy 3, Bennett 3, March 3, Irene 4, Maté 4, Newman 4, Wanger 4)

Trader Horn, 1931 (Van Dyke 2, Carey 3, Mayer 4)

Trädgårdsmästaren, 1912 (Sjöström 2, Jaenzon 4, Magnusson 4)

Tradimento, 1951 (Monicelli 2, Gassman 3)

Trading Places, 1983 (Landis 2, Ameche 3, Bellamy 3, Curtis 3, Elliott 3, Murphy 3, Bernstein 4)

Tradita, 1954 (Bardot 3, Delli Colli 4)

Tradition de minuit, 1939 (Dalio 3, Aurenche 4)

Traffic. *See* Trafic, 1971

Traffic in Souls. *See* Cargaison blanche, 1937

Traffic Jam. *See* Ingorgo, 1979

Trafic, 1971 (Haanstra 2, Tati 2)

Trafic Jam, 1988 (Girardot 3)

Trafiquant, 1911 (Feuillade 2)

Träfracken, 1966 (Björnstrand 3)

Tragala, pervo, 1981 (Rey 3)

Tragedia di un uomo ridicolo, 1981 (Aimée 3, Morricone 4)

Tragédie de Carmen, 1983 (Carrière 4, Nykvist 4, Wakhévitch 4)

Tragédie impériale, 1938 (Baur 3, Lourié 4, Milhaud 4)

Tragedy of a Dress Suit, 1911 (Sennett 2)

Tragedy of a Ridiculous Man. *See* Tragedia di un uomo ridiculo, 1981

Tragedy of Carmen. *See* Tragédie de Carmen, 1983

Tragedy of Love. *See* Tragödie der Liebe, 1923

Tragedy of the Desert, 1912 (Olcott 2)

Tragedy of the Orient, 1914 (Hayakawa 3)

Tragedy of the Street. *See* Dirnentragödie, 1927

Tragedy of Whispering Creek, 1914 (Dwan 2, Chaney 3)

Tragic General. *See* Higegi no shogun Yamashita Yasubumi, 1953

Tragic Love, 1908 (Griffith 2, Bitzer 4)

Tragic Pursuit. *See* Caccia tragica, 1947

Tragic Ship. *See* Eld ombord, 1923

Tragico ritorno, 1952 (Mastroianni 3)

Tragikomödie, 1922 (Krauss 3)

Tragique Amour de Mona Lisa, 1910 (Gance 2)

Tragödie, 1925 (Porten 3)

Tragödie der Liebe, 1923 (Leni 2, Dietrich 3, Jannings 3)

Tragödie einer Leidenschaft, 1949 (Warm 4)

Tragödie eines Verlorenen, 1927 (Junge 4)

Tragödie eines verschollenen Fürstensohnes. *See* Versunkene Welt, 1920

Tragödie im Haus Habsburg, 1924 (Korda 4)

Tragoedia, 1975 (Brakhage 2)

Traidores de San Angel, 1966 (Torre Nilsson 2)

Trail Beyond, 1934 (Wayne 3, Canutt 4)

Trail Drive, 1934 (McCord 4)

Trail Guide, 1952 (Musuraca 4)

Trail of Hate, 1917 (Ford 2)

Trail of '98, 1929 (Brown 2, Tourneur 2, Carey 3, Del Rio 3, Glazer 4, Mayer 4, Seitz 4, Young 4)

Trail of Robin Hood, 1950 (Rogers 3)

Trail of the Books, 1911 (Griffith 2, Bitzer 4)

Trail of the Eucalyptus, 1911 (Dwan 2)

Trail of the Horse Thieves, 1928 (Musuraca 4)

Trail of the Law, 1924 (Shearer 3)

Trail of the Lonesome Pine, 1916 (De Mille 2, Buckland 4, Macpherson 4)

Trail of the Lonesome Pine, 1922 (Howe 4)

Trail of the Lonesome Pine, 1926 (Fleischer 4)

Trail of the Lonesome Pine, 1936 (Hathaway 2, Bondi 3, Fonda 3, MacMurray 3, Sidney 3, Canutt 4, Dreier 4, Friedhofer 4, Wanger 4)

Trail of the Pink Panther, 1982 (Edwards 2, Lom 3, Sellers 3, Mancini 4)

Trail of the Snake Band, 1913 (Anderson 3)

Trail of the Swordfish, 1931 (Sennett 2)

Trail of the Vigilantes, 1940 (Dwan 2, Crawford 3, Krasner 4, Salter 4)

Trail Rider, 1925 (Van Dyke 2)

Trail Street, 1947 (Ryan 3, Scott 3, Hunt 4)

Trail to San Antone, 1947 (Autry 3)

Trailblazer Magoo, 1956 (Bosustow 4, Burness 4)

Trailed to the Hills. *See* Trailed to the West, 1910

Trailed to the West, 1910 (Anderson 3)

Trailer, 1959 (Breer 2)

Trailer Life, 1937 (Terry 4)

Trailer Thrills, 1937 (Lantz 4)

Trailin', 1921 (Mix 3)

Trailin' West, 1936 (McCord 4)

Trailing the Counterfeit, 1911 (Sennett 2)

Train, 1964 (Frankenheimer 2, Lancaster 3, Moreau 3, Simon 3, Jarre 4)

Train, 1966 (Greenaway 2)

Train, 1973 (Schneider 3, Trintignant 3, Sarde 4, Saulnier 4)

Train, 1987 (Sanda 3)

Train de 8 h 47, 1934 (Fernandel 3)

Train d'enfer, 1984 (Legrand 4)

Train des suicides, 1931 (Fradetal 4)

Train en marche, 1973 (Marker 2)

Train of Events, 1949 (Crichton 2, Finch 3, Balcon 4, Clarke 4)

Train of Incidents, 1914 (Bunny 3)

Train on Jacob's Ladder, Mt. Washington, 1899 (Bitzer 4)

Train pour Venise, 1938 (D'Eaubonne 4)

Train Robbers, 1973 (Johnson 3, Wayne 3, Clothier 4)

Train sans yeux, 1925 (Cavalcanti 2, Manès 3)

Train to Alcatraz, 1948 (Darwell 3)

Train Trouble, 1940 (Halas and Batchelor 4)

Trained Nurse at Bar Z, 1911 (Dwan 2)

Training Pigeons, 1936 (Fleischer 4)

Trains de plaisir, 1930 (Storck 2)

Trains sans fumée, 1951 (Rabier 4)

Traitement de choc, 1972 (Delon 3, Girardot 3)

Traitor, 1914 (Weber 2, Bosworth 3, Marion 4)

Traitors, 1957 (Lee 3)

Traitor's Gate, 1965 (Kinski 3, Francis 4)

Traitors of San Angel. *See* Traidores de San Angel, 1966

Tramonte, 1913 (Bertini 3)

Tramp, 1915 (Bacon 2, Purviance 3)

Tramp and the Dog, 1896 (Selig 4)

Tramp and the Dog, 1906 (Selig 4)

Tramp and the Mattress-Makers. *See* Cardeuse de Matelas, 1906

Tramp, the Boys are Marching, 1926 (Fleischer 4)

Tramp, Tramp, Tramp, 1926 (Capra 2, Crawford 3, Langdon 3)

Tramping Tramps, 1930 (Lantz 4)

Tramplers. *See* Uomini dal passo pesante, 1966

Tramps, 1915 (Laurel and Hardy 3)

Tramp's Gratitude, 1911 (Dwan 2)

Tranches de vie, 1985 (Cassel 3)

Tranquillo posto di campagna, 1968 (Redgrave 3, Guerra 4, Morricone 4)

Trans, 1978 (Clarke 2)

Transatlantic, 1931 (Howard 2, Loy 3, Friedhofer 4, Howe 4)

Transatlantic Merry-Go-Round, 1934 (Newman 4)

Transatlantic Tunnel. *See* Tunnel, 1935

Transatlantisches, 1926 (Amidei 4)

Trans-Europ Express, 1966 (Trintignant 3, Robbe-Grillet 4)

Transfer, 1966 (Cronenberg 2)

Transfigurations, 1909 (Cohl 4)

Transformation, 1959 (Emshwiller 2)

Transformation of Mike, 1911 (Griffith 2, Sweet 3, Bitzer 4)

Transformations, 1897 (Guy 2)

Transformations, 1904 (Guy 2)

Transforms, 1970 (Vanderbeek 2)

Transfusion, 1910 (Lawrence 3)

Transgression, 1931 (Brenon 2, Francis 3, Steiner 4)

Transgression of Manuel, 1913 (Dwan 2)

Transient Lady, 1935 (Carradine 3)

Transmutations. *See* Underworld, 1986

Transmutations imperceptibles, 1904 (Méliès 2)

Transport from Paradise. *See* Transport z rje, 1963

Transport z rje, 1963 (Brodský 3)

Transports urbains, 1948 (Braunberger 4)

Transylvania 6-5000, 1963 (Blanc 4)

Trap, 1913 (Chaney 3)

Trap, 1922 (Chaney 3, Miller 4)

Trap, 1959 (Cobb 3, Widmark 3, Frank 4, Head 4)

Trap, 1966 (Reed 3, Krasker 4)

Trap. *See* Gabbia, 1985

Trap for Santa Claus, 1909 (Griffith 2, Bitzer 4)

Trap Happy, 1946 (Hanna and Barbera 4)

Trap Happy Porky, 1945 (Blanc 4, Jones 4, Stalling 4)

Trapeze, 1956 (Reed 2, Curtis 3, Lancaster 3, Lollobrigida 3, Arnold 4, Krasker 4, Mankowitz 4)

Trapped, 1923 (Fleischer 4)

Trapped Beneath the Sea, 1974 (Cobb 3)

Trapped by Bloodhounds, or The Lynching at Cripple Creek, 1905 (Selig 4)

Trapped by Fear. *See* Distractions, 1960

Trapped by Television, 1936 (Astor 3)

Trapp-Familie, 1956 (Herlth 4)

Trapp-Familie in Amerika, 1958 (Herlth 4)

Traqué, 1950 (Signoret 3, Schüfftan 4)

Traque, 1974 (Renoir 4)

Traquenard. *See* Haine, 1979

Trash, 1970 (Warhol 2, Spacek 3)

Trás-os-Montes, 1976 (De Almeida 4)

Trastevere, 1971 (De Sica 2)

Tratta della bianche, 1952 (Loren 3)

Tratta delle bianche, 1952 (Gassman 3, De Laurentiis 4)

Traum des Hauptmann Loy, 1961 (Brejchová 3)

Trauma, 1979 (Cotten 3)

Traumende Mund, 1932 (Bergner 3, Jaubert 4, Mayer 4)

Traumende Mund, 1953 (Schell 3)

Traumkönig, 1925 (Dieterle 2)

Traumulus, 1936 (Jannings 3)

Travail, 1969 (Chabrol 2)

Travailleurs de la mer, 1918 (Duvivier 2)

Travaux du tunnel sous l'Escaut, 1932 (Storck 2, Kaufman 4)

Traveler's Joy, 1949 (Rank 4)

Travelin' Fast; Fast and Fearless, 1924 (Arthur 3)

Travelin' On, 1922 (Hart 3, August 4)

Traveling Actors. *See* Tabi yakusha, 1940

Traveling Executioner, 1970 (Goldsmith 4)

Traveling Husbands, 1931 (Steiner 4)

Traveling Saleslady, 1935 (Blondell 3, McDaniel 3, Barnes 4, Grot 4)

Traveling Salesman, 1921 (Arbuckle 3, Brown 4)

Traveller's Joy, 1949 (Withers 3)

Travellin' On, 1914 (Carey 3)

Travelling Matte, 1971 (Frampton 2)

Travels of Princess Snake. *See* Hebihime douchuh, 1949

Travels of Teddy, 1915 (Messmer 4)

Travels with Anita. *See* Viaggio con Anita, 1978

Travels with My Aunt, 1972 (Cukor 2, Smith 3, Allen 4, Box 4, Greene 4, Slocombe 4)

Traversata nera, 1939 (Amidei 4)

Traversée de la France, 1961 (Leenhardt 2)

Traversée de Paris, 1956 (Gabin 3, Aurenche 4, Bost 4, Douy 4, Saulnier 4)

Travestie, 1988 (Sarde 4)

Travestis du diable, 1963 (Jarre 4)

Traviata, 1982 (Zeffirelli 2)

Traviata '53, 1953 (Fusco 4, Pinelli 4)

Travolti da un insolito destino nell'azzurro mare d'agosto, 1974 (Wertmüller 2, Giannini 3)

Tre aquilotta, 1942 (Rossellini 2, Sordi 3)

Tre colonne in cronaca, 1990 (Volonté 3, Morricone 4)

Tre corsari, 1952 (De Laurentiis 4, Delli Colli 4)

Tre eccetera del colonnello. *See* Trois etc . . . du colonel, 1959

Tre fili fino a Milano, 1958 (Olmi 2)

Tre fratelli, 1981 (Noiret 3, Vanel 3)

Tre ladri, 1954 (Simon 3)

Tre nel mille, 1971 (Guerra 4, Morricone 4)

Tre notti d'amore, 1964 (Fusco 4, Gherardi 4)

Tre önskningar, 1960 (Dahlbeck 3)

Tre passi a nord, 1951 (Fabrizi 3)

Tre piger i Paris, 1963 (Gélin 3)

Tre ragazze cercano marito, 1944 (Sordi 3)

Tre sergenti del Bengala, 1965 (Fusco 4)

Tre storie proibite, 1952 (Cervi 3, Aldo 4)

Tre straniere a Roma, 1958 (Cardinale 3)

Tre volti, 1965 (Harris 3, Sordi 3)

Tre volti della paura. *See* Black Sabbath, 1964

Treachery of Broncho Billy's Pal, 1914 (Anderson 3)

Treachery on the High Seas, 1938 (Daniels 3)

Treachery Within. *See* Double Crime sur la Ligne Maginot, 1938

Tread Softly Stranger, 1958 (Dors 3, Slocombe 4)

Treason, 1918 (Polito 4)

Treason. *See* Old Louisianna, 1937

Treasure. *See* Schatz, 1923

Treasure Blues, 1935 (Roach 4)

Treasure Hunt, 1952 (De Grunwald 4)

Treasure Hunt, 1980 (Halas and Batchelor 4)

Treasure Island, 1920 (Tourneur 2, Chaney 3, Carré 4, Furthman 4)

Treasure Island, 1934 (Fleming 2, Barrymore 3, Beery 3, Cooper 3, Mayer 4, Rosson 4, Stothart 4, Stromberg 4)

Treasure Island. *See* Ostrov sokrovishch, 1937

Treasure Island, 1950 (Newton 3, Disney 4, Ellenshaw 4, Haskin 4, Young 4)

Treasure Island, 1972 (Welles 2, Mankowitz 4)

Treasure Island. *See* Ile au trésor, 1985

Treasure Island, 1990 (Heston 3, Lee 3, Reed 3)

Treasure of Bird Island. *See* Poklad Ptačího ostrova, 1952

Treasure of Ice Cake Island, 1989 (Halas and Batchelor 4)

Treasure of Kalifa. *See* Steel Lady, 1953

Treasure of Lost Canyon, 1951 (Metty 4)

Treasure of Matecumbe, 1976 (Ustinov 3)

Treasure of Pancho Villa, 1955 (Winters 3)

Treasure of Ruby Hills, 1955 (Van Cleef 3)

Treasure of San Teresa, 1959 (Constantine 3, Lee 3)

Treasure of Silver Lake, 1962 (Lom 3)

Treasure of the Amazon, 1985 (Pleasence 3)

Treasure of the Four Crowns, 1983 (Morricone 4)

Treasure of the Golden Condor, 1953 (Daves 2, Bancroft 3, Wilde 3, Wray 3, Cronjager 4, Jeakins 4, LeMaire 4, Newman 4, Wheeler 4)

Treasure of the Lost Canyon, 1951 (Powell 3)

Treasure of the Sierra Madre, 1948 (Huston 2, Bogart 3, Huston 3, Sheridan 3, Blanke 4, McCord 4, Steiner 4, Warner 4)

Treasure of the Yankee Zephyr. *See* Race for the Yankee Zephyr, 1982

Treasure Trove, 1911 (Bunny 3)

Treasurer's Report, 1928 (Benchley 4)

Treasures of Satan. *See* Trésors de Satan, 1902

Treat 'em Rough, 1919 (Mix 3)

Treat 'em Rough, 1942 (Salter 4)

Treating 'em Rough, 1919 (Sennett 2)

Treatise on Japanese Rowdy Songs. *See* Nippon shunka-ko, 1967

Tree, 1966 (Greenaway 2)

Tree Cornered Tweety, 1956 (Blanc 4, Freleng 4)

Tree for Two, 1943 (Fleischer 4)

Tree for Two, 1952 (Blanc 4, Foster 4, Freleng 4, Stalling 4)

Tree Grows in Brooklyn, 1945 (Kazan 2, Blondell 3, Marsh 3, Newman 4, Shamroy 4, Wheeler 4, Zanuck 4)

Tree Grows in Brooklyn, 1974 (Robertson 3, Goldsmith 4)

Tree in a Test Tube, 1943 (Laurel and Hardy 3)

Tree of Hands, 1988 (Bacall 3)
Tree of Liberty. *See* Howards of Virginia, 1940
Trees and Jamaica Daddy, 1958 (Bosustow 4)
Tree Saps, 1931 (Fleischer 4)
Trèfle à cinq feuilles, 1972 (Noiret 3, Coutard 4)
Treize à table, 1955 (Girardot 3, Presle 3)
Treize jours en France, 1968 (Lai 4)
Trelawney of the Wells, 1916 (Hepworth 2)
Trelawny of the Wells. *See* Actress, 1928
Tren para las estrellas, 1987 (Diegues 2)
Trenchcoat, 1983 (Delli Colli 4)
Trenck, 1932 (Tschechowa 3)
Trenck, der Pandur, 1940 (Albers 3)
Treno crociato, 1942 (Brazzi 3)
Treno popolare, 1933 (Rota 4)
Trenta minuti d'amore, 1983 (Vitti 3)
Trenta secondi d'amore, 1936 (Magnani 3)
Trente secondes d'amour. *See* Trenta secondi d'amore, 1936
Trent's Last Case, 1929 (Hawks 2, Crisp 3, Rosson 4)
Trent's Last Case, 1952 (Welles 2, Wilcox 2, Lockwood 3)
Trepidazione, 1946 (Delli Colli 4)
Tres Berretines, 1933 (Alton 4)
Tres calaveras, 1964 (Figueroa 4)
Tres cantos, 1954 (García Berlanga 2)
Tres citas con el destino, 1953 (De Fuentes 2)
Tres Garcia, 1946 (Infante 3)
Tres huastecos, 1948 (Infante 3)
Tres menos eu, 1988 (Branco 4)
Tres mosqueteros, 1942 (Cantinflas 3, Figueroa 4)
Très Moutarde, 1908 (Linder 3)
Tres tristes tigres, 1968 (Villagra 3)
Tres y dos, 1985 (Díaz 2)
Trésor de Cantenac, 1950 (Guitry 2)
Trésor des hommes bleus, 1961 (Kosma 4)
Trésor des Îles Chiennes, 1990 (Branco 4)
Trésor des Pieds-Nickelés, 1949 (Braunberger 4)
Trésor d'Ostende, 1955 (Storck 2, Kosma 4)
Trésors de Satan, 1902 (Méliès 2)
Trespasser, 1929 (Swanson 3, Walthall 3, Barnes 4, Toland 4)
Trespasser. *See* Night Editor, 1946
Trespasser, 1947 (Alton 4)
Trespasses, 1987 (Johnson 3)
Třetí rota, 1931 (Stallich 4)
Třeti zvonění, 1938 (Heller 4)
Tretton stolar, 1945 (Nykvist 4)
Trêve, 1968 (Gélin 3, Guillemot 4)
Trevico-Torino ... Viaggio nel Fiat Nam, 1973 (Scola 2)
Trey of Hearts, 1914 (Meredyth 4)
Tři čarovná péra, 1970 (Brdečka 4)
Tri dnia Viktora Chernysheva, 1968 (Shukshin 3)
Tri geroini, 1938 (Vertov 2)
Tři kroky od těla, 1934 (Heller 4)
Tri pensi o Lenine, 1934 (Vertov 2)
Tři veteráni, 1983 (Švankmajer 4)
Tri vstrechi, 1948 (Ptushko 4)
Tři zlaté vlasy děda Vševěda, 1963 (Frič 2)
Triage, 1940 (Clement 2)
Trial, 1955 (Ford 3, Kennedy 3, Schary 4, Schnee 4)
Trial. *See* **Procès, 1963**
Trial, 1991 (Pinter 4)
Trial and Error. *See* Dock Brief, 1962

Trial Balloons, 1982 (Breer 4)
Trial by Combat, 1976 (Cushing 3, Mills 3, Pleasence 3)
Trial in Smolensk. *See* Sud v Smolenske, 1946
Trial Marriage, 1929 (Berman 4, Levien 4, Walker 4)
Trial Marriages, 1906 (Bitzer 4)
Trial of Billy Jack, 1974 (Bernstein 4)
Trial of Joan of Arc. *See* Procès de Jeanne d'Arc, 1962
Trial of Mary Dugan, 1929 (Shearer 3, Adrian 4, Daniels 4, Gibbons 4, Mayer 4, Shearer 4)
Trial of Mary Dugan, 1941 (McLeod 2, Young 3, Folsey 4)
Trial of Mironov. *See* Protsess Mironova, 1919
Trial of Mr. Wolf, 1941 (Blanc 4, Freleng 4, Maltese 4, Stalling 4)
Trial of '98, 1929 (Gibbons 4)
Trial of Portia Merriman, 1937 (Bosworth 3)
Trial of the Catonsville Nine, 1972 (Peck 3, Wexler 4)
Trial of the Social Revolutionaries. *See* Protsess Eserov, 1922
Trial of Vivienne Ware, 1932 (Howard 2, Bennett 3, Friedhofer 4)
Trial Run, 1984 (Grant 3)
Trials of Oscar Wilde, 1960 (Roeg 2, Finch 3, Mason 3, Adam 4)
Triangle. *See* Idée fixe, 1962
Triangulo de Cuatro, 1975 (Bemberg 2)
Tribal Law, 1912 (Reid 3)
Tribe. *See* Tribu, 1991
Tribe That Hides from Man, 1970 (Menges 4)
Tribes, 1970 (Day 4, Metty 4, Smith 4)
Tribe's Penalty, 1911 (Anderson 3)
Tribu, 1934 (Fernández 2)
Tribu, 1991 (Sarde 4)
Tribulations d'un chinois en Chine, 1965 (Belmondo 3, Delerue 4)
Tribute, 1980 (Lemmon 3, Remick 3)
Tribute to a Bad Man, 1956 (Wise 2, Cagney 3, Papas 3, Van Cleef 3, Plunkett 4)
Tribute to a Bad Man, 1956 (Rozsa 4, Surtees 4)
Třicet jedna ve stínu, 1965 (Weiss 2)
Tricheurs, 1958 (Belmondo 3, Renoir 4, Spaak 4)
Tricheurs, 1983 (Branco 4, Müller 4)
Trick for Trick, 1933 (Menzies 4)
Trick of Hearts, 1928 (Eason 4)
Trick or Tweet, 1959 (Blanc 4, Freleng 4)
Trick That Failed, 1909 (Griffith 2, Pickford 3, Bitzer 4)
Tricking the Government, 1914 (Olcott 2)
Tricks, 1926 (Cooper 3)
Tricky Business, 1942 (Terry 4)
Tricky Dicks, 1953 (Three Stooges 3)
Tricky Painter's Fate, 1908 (Méliès 2)
Triebmörder. *See* Bestia uccide a sangue freddo, 1971
Tried for His Own Murder, 1915 (Costello 3)
Trieste File, 1980 (Van Cleef 3)
Triflers, 1924 (Schulberg 4)
Trifling Woman, 1922 (Ingram 2, Novarro 3, Seitz 4, Vorkapich 4)
Trigger Finger, 1924 (Eason 4)
Trigger Happy. *See* Deadly Companions, 1961
Trigger Tricks, 1930 (Eason 4)

Trilby, 1915 (Tourneur 2)
Trilby, 1917 (Carré 4)
Trilby's Love Disaster, 1916 (Mix 3)
Trilogy, 1969 (Page 3, Perry 4, Rosenblum 4)
Trilogy of Terror, 1975 (Black 3)
Trimmed, 1922 (Polito 4)
Trimmed in Furs, 1934 (Langdon 3)
Trimmed in Gold, 1926 (Sennett 2)
Trimmed with Red. *See* Help Yourself, 1920
Trimming of Paradise Gulch, 1910 (Mix 3)
Třináctý revír, 1945 (Stallich 4)
Trinkets of Tragedy, 1914 (Bushman 3)
Trio, 1950 (Simmons 3, Rank 4, Sherriff 4, Unsworth 4)
Trio, 1975 (Brakhage 2)
Trio Film, 1968 (Rainer 2)
Trio infernal, 1974 (Piccoli 3, Schneider 3, Morricone 4)
Trionfo di Ringo, 1965 (Morricone 4)
Trio: Rubenstein, Heifetz, and Piatigorsky, 1952 (Laszlo 4)
Trip, 1967 (Bogdanovich 2, Dern 3, Hopper 3, Nicholson 3)
Trip Around the World. *See* Put oko svijeta, 1964
Trip for Tat, 1960 (Blanc 4, Freleng 4)
Trip Through a Hollywood Studio, 1935 (Cagney 3, Del Rio 3)
Trip to Bountiful, 1985 (Page 3)
Trip to Chinatown, 1926 (Wong 3)
Trip to Door, 1971 (Brakhage 2)
Trip to Paradise, 1921 (Glazer 4, Mathis 4)
Trip to Terror. *See* Blood of the Iron Maiden, 1970
Trip to the Moon. *See* **Voyage dans la lune, 1902**
Triple Cross, 1966 (Brynner 3, Howard 3, Schneider 3, Alekan 4)
Triple Crossed, 1958 (Three Stooges 3)
Triple Deception. *See* House of Secrets, 1956
Triple Echo, 1973 (Jackson 3, Reed 3)
Triple Entente, 1915 (Musidora 3)
Triple Justice, 1940 (Hunt 4)
Triple Play, 1981 (Scorsese 2)
Triple Threat, 1948 (Katzman 4)
Triple Trouble, 1918 (Chaplin 2, Purviance 3)
Triple Trouble. *See* Kentucky Kernels, 1934
Triple Trouble, 1944 (Metty 4)
Triple Trouble, 1947 (Terry 4)
Triplet Trouble, 1952 (Hanna and Barbera 4)
Trip-Off Girls, 1938 (Crabbe 3)
Tripoli, 1950 (O'Hara 3, Howe 4)
Tripoli, bel suol d'amore, 1954 (Sordi 3)
Triporteur, 1957 (Legrand 4)
Tripot clandestin, 1905 (Méliès 2)
Trishul, 1978 (Bachchan 3)
Tristan and Isolde. *See* Tristan et Iseult, 1973
Tristan et Iseult, 1973 (Cusack 3)
Tristan Tzara, dadaismens fader, 1949 (Roos 2)
Tristana, 1970 (Buñuel 2, Deneuve 3, Rey 3)
Tristano e Isotta, 1911 (Bertini 3)
Triste Fin d'un vieux savant, 1904 (Guy 2)
Tristi amori, 1943 (Gallone 2, Berry 3, Cervi 3, Amidei 4)
Triumph, 1916 (Chaney 3)
Triumph, 1924 (De Mille 2, Glennon 4, Macpherson 4)
Triumph, 1928 (Rooney 3)
Triumph des Lebens. *See* Ich lebe für dich, 1929

Triumph des Willens, 1935 (Riefenstahl 2)

Triumph eines Genies. *See* Friedrich
Schiller, 1940

Triumph of Lester Snapwell, 1963
(Keaton 2)

Triumph of the Heart. *See* Hjärtats triumf,
1929

Triumph of the Rat, 1926 (Novello 3,
Balcon 4)

Triumph of the Will. *See* **Triumph des
Willens, 1935**

Triumph of Will, 1940 (Buñuel 2)

Triumphs of a Man Called Horse, 1982
(Harris 3)

Triumph Tiger '57. *See* Hempas bar, 1977

Triúnfo de un hombre llamado caballo, 1982
(Alcott 4)

Trny a květi, 1921 (Heller 4)

Trocadero, 1944 (Fleischer 4)

Trödler von Amsterdam, 1925 (Krauss 3,
Andrejew 4)

Trog, 1970 (Crawford 3, Francis 4)

Troika. *See* Vot mchitza troika potchtovaia,
1913

Troika, 1930 (Tschechowa 3)

Troîka, sur la piste blanche, 1937 (Dalio 3,
Vanel 3)

Trois Argentines à Montmartre, 1939
(Brasseur 3)

Trois cents à l'heure, 1934 (Fradetal 4)

Trois Chambres à Manhattan, 1965 (Carné 2,
Girardot 3, Barsacq 4, Schüfftan 4)

Trois Couronnes du matelot, 1982 (Branco 4,
Vierny 4)

Trois etc ... du colonel, 1959 (Gélin 3)

Trois femmes, trois âmes, 1951 (Alekan 4)

Trois filles à Paris. *See* Tre piger i Paris,
1963

Trois font la paire, 1957 (Guitry 2, Simon 3)

Trois hommes à abattre, 1980 (Delon 3)

Trois hommes dur un cheval, 1969
(Braunberger 4)

Trois hommes en Corse, 1950 (Decaë 4)

Trois jours à vivre, 1957 (Gélin 3, Moreau 3,
Audiard 4, Kosma 4)

Trois Masques, 1929 (Christian-Jaque 2)

Trois milliards sans ascenseur, 1972
(Reggiani 3)

Trois minutes—les saisons, 1938 (Auric 4)

Trois Mousquetaires, 1932 (Baur 3,
Fradetal 4, Wakhévitch 4)

Trois Mousquetaires, 1953 (Cervi 3,
Audiard 4)

Trois Pages d'un journal. *See* Tagebuch
einer Verlorenen, 1929

Trois places pour le 26, 1988 (Montand 3,
Evein 4)

Trois Rats, 1915 (Musidora 3)

Trois télégrammes, 1950 (Kosma 4)

Trois Themes, 1980 (Alexeieff and Parker 4)

Trois Valses, 1938 (Fresnay 3,
D'Eaubonne 4, Schüfftan 4)

Trois Vies une corde, 1933 (Storck 2,
Jaubert 4)

Troisième Dalle, 1942 (Berry 3)

Troisième Larron, 1916 (Musidora 3)

Trois-Mâts, 1935 (Storck 2)

Trois-Mâts ''Mercator'', 1935 (Jaubert 4)

Trois-six-neuf, 1937 (Blier 3, Barsacq 4)

Trojan Horse, 1946 (Terry 4)

Trojan Women, 1971 (Bujold 3, Hepburn 3,
Papas 3, Redgrave 3, Theodorakis 4)

Trollenberg Terror, 1958 (Sangster 4)

Trolley Troubles, 1921 (Roach 4)

Trolley Troubles, 1927 (Disney 4)

Trollflöjten, 1974 (Nykvist 4)

Trommelfeuer der Liebe, 1927 (Reisch 4)

Trommeln Asiens, 1921 (Planer 4)

Trompe-l'oeil, 1974 (Presle 3)

Trompé mais content, 1902 (Guy 2)

Trompette anti-neurasthenique, 1915
(Cohl 4)

Tron, 1982 (Bridges 3)

Trône de France, 1937 (Alexeieff and
Parker 4)

Troop Beverly Hills, 1989 (Hamlisch 4, Van
Runkle 4)

Trooper Hook, 1957 (McCrea 3,
Stanwyck 3)

Trooper of Troop K, 1916 (Johnson 3)

Trooper O'Neill, 1922 (Howard 2)

Troopers Three, 1930 (Eason 4)

Troopship. *See* Farewell Again, 1937

Trop aimée, 1909 (Linder 3)

Trop belle pour toi, 1989 (Blier 2,
Depardieu 3, Lai 4)

Trop c'est trop, 1975 (Dalio 3, Gélin 3)

Trop crédules, 1908 (Chevalier 3)

Trop tot, trop tard, 1983 (Straub and Huillet)

Tropennächte, 1931 (Rasp 3)

Trophée du zouave, 1915 (Musidora 3)

Tropic Fury, 1939 (Johnson 3)

Tropic Holiday, 1938 (Lamour 3, Milland 3,
Head 4, Prinz 4)

Tropic Madness, 1928 (Musuraca 4,
Plunkett 4)

Tropic of Cancer, 1969 (Burstyn 3)

Tropic Zone, 1953 (Reagan 3, Head 4)

Tropical Fish, 1933 (Terry 4)

Tropicana. *See* Heat's On, 1943 (Planer 4)

Tropisk Kaerlighed, 1911 (Psilander 3)

Troppo forte, 1986 (Sordi 3)

Troppo tardi t'ho conosciuta, 1939 (De
Laurentiis 4)

Trots, 1952 (Molander 2, Andersson 3,
Dahlbeck 3)

Trotta, 1984 (Schell 3)

Trottie True, 1949 (Lee 3, Rank 4)

Trotting Through Turkey, 1920 (Roach 4)

Trou, 1959 (Cloquet 4)

Trou dans le mur, 1930 (Brasseur 3)

Trou normand, 1952 (Bardot 3)

Troubador Girl. *See* Musume tabigeinen,
1941

Troubadour's Triumph, 1912 (Weber 2)

Trouble, 1922 (Beery 3)

Trouble Along the Way, 1953 (Curtiz 2,
Coburn 3, Reed 3, Wayne 3, Steiner 4)

Trouble Back Stairs. *See* Krach im
Hinterhaus, 1935

Trouble Brewing, 1939 (Formby 3,
Withers 4)

Trouble Bruin, 1961 (Hanna and Barbera 4)

Trouble Enough, 1916 (Lloyd 3, Roach 4)

Trouble for Two, 1936 (Montgomery 3,
Russell 3, Clarke 4, Waxman 4)

Trouble Indemnity, 1950 (Bosustow 4,
Burness 4, Hubley 4)

Trouble in Mind, 1985 (Rudolph 2, Bujold 3)

Trouble in Morocco, 1937 (Schoedsack 2)

Trouble in Panama. *See* Torchy Blane in
Panama, 1938

Trouble in Paradise, 1932 (Lubitsch 2,
Francis 3, Hopkins 3, Horton 3,
Marshall 3, Banton 4, Dreier 4,
Raphaelson 4, Zukor 4)

Trouble in Store, 1953 (Rutherford 3,
Wisdom 3, Rank 4, Vetchinsky 4)

Trouble in Sundown, 1939 (Bond 3)

Trouble in Texas, 1937 (Hayworth 3,
Canutt 4)

Trouble in the Air, 1948 (Rank 4)

Trouble in the Glen, 1954 (Welles 2,
Wilcox 2, Lockwood 3, McLaglen 3,
Nugent 4, Young 4)

Trouble in the Morning. *See* Asa no hamon,
1952

Trouble in the Sky. *See* Code of Silence,
1960

Trouble Shooter, 1924 (Mix 3)

Trouble Shooter. *See* Man With the Gun,
1955

Trouble with Angels, 1966 (Lupino 3,
Russell 3, Goldsmith 4)

Trouble with Girls, 1969 (Carradine 3,
Presley 3, Price 3)

Trouble with Harry, 1955 (Hitchcock 2,
MacLaine 3, Burks 4, Hayes 4, Head 4,
Herrmann 4)

Trouble with Husbands, 1940 (Benchley 4)

Trouble with Michael Caine, 1989 (Caine 3)

Trouble with Spies, 1987 (Sutherland 3)

Trouble with Women, 1947 (Milland 3,
Dreier 4, Head 4, Young 4)

Troubled Waters, 1936 (Mason 3,
Rutherford 3, Sim 3)

Troublemaker, 1964 (Henry 4)

Troublemakers. *See* Once Upon a Crime,
1992

Troublesome Satchel, 1909 (Griffith 2,
Bitzer 4)

Troublesome Secretaries, 1911 (Normand 3)

Troublesome Stepdaughters, 1912 (Bunny 3,
Talmadge 3)

Trouper's Heart, 1911 (Dwan 2)

Trouping with Ellen, 1924 (Rathbone 3,
Hunt 4)

Trousers. *See* Hose, 1927

Trout. *See* Truite, 1982

Trout Fishing, Rangeley Lakes, 1905
(Bitzer 4)

Trouvaille de Bûchu, 1917 (Feyder 2)

Trovatore, 1910 (Bertini 3)

Trovatore, 1949 (Gallone 2)

Truands, 1956 (Constantine 3, Modot 3)

Truant Soul, 1917 (Walthall 3)

Truants, 1907 (Bitzer 4)

Trübe Wasser, 1958 (Eisler 4)

Truc du brésilien, 1932 (Cavalcanti 2,
D'Eaubonne 4)

Truce Hurts, 1948 (Hanna and Barbera 4)

Truck Busters, 1943 (Eason 4, Haskin 4)

Truck That Flew, 1943 (Pal 4)

Truckload of Trouble, 1949 (Terry 4)

Trude, die Sechzehnjährige, 1926 (Ondra 3,
Tschechowa 4)

True As a Turtle, 1956 (Rank 4)

True Chivalry, 1910 (White 3)

True Confession, 1937 (Barrymore 3,
Lombard 3, MacMurray 3, McDaniel 3,
Dreier 4, Head 4, Lewin 4)

True Confessions, 1981 (Cusack 3, De
Niro 3, Duvall 3, Meredith 3, Delerue 4,
Roizman 4, Winkler 4)

True Glory, 1945 (Reed 2, Ustinov 3,
Alwyn 4, Kanin 4)

True Grit, 1969 (Hathaway 2, Duvall 3,
Hopper 3, Wayne 3, Ballard 4,
Bernstein 4, Jeakins 4, Wallis 4)

True Grit, 1978 (Oates 3)

True Story of Camille. *See* Vera storia della
signora della camelie, 1980

True Story of Jesse James, 1957 (Ray 2,
	Carradine 3, Moorehead 3, Wagner 3)
True Story of Lilli Marlene, 1944
	(Jennings 2)
True Story of Lynn Stuart, 1958 (Guffey 4)
True Story of the Civil War, 1956
	(Massey 3)
True Story of the Lyons Mail, 1915
	(Pearson 2)
True to Life, 1943 (De Carlo 3, Powell 3,
	Carmichael 4, Dreier 4, Head 4, Lang 4,
	Mercer 4, Young 4)
True to the Army, 1941 (Miller 3, Young 4)
True to the Navy, 1930 (Bow 3, March 3,
	Mankiewicz 4)
True-Heart Susie, 1919 (Griffith 2, Gish 3,
	Bitzer 4)
Truite, 1982 (Losey 2, Cassel 3, Huppert 3,
	Moreau 3, Alekan 4, Trauner 4)
Truman at Potsdam, 1976 (Houseman 4)
Trumpet Blows, 1934 (Menjou 3, Raft 3)
Trumpet Call. See Rough Riders, 1927
Trumpet Island, 1920 (Haller 4)
Trunk Conveyor, 1952 (Anderson 2)
Trunk Crime, 1939 (Boulting 2)
Trunk Mystery, 1927 (Shamroy 4)
Trunk to Cairo. See Mivtza Kahir, 1966
Trust, 1911 (Gaumont 4)
Trust, 1915 (Chaney 3)
Trusting Wives, 1929 (Horton 3)
Trut!, 1944 (Sucksdorff 2)
Truth, 1920 (Hunt 4)
Truth. See Vérité, 1960
Truth about Angela Jones, 1950 (Rathaus 4)
Truth about Spring, 1965 (Mills 3)
Truth about Women, 1958 (Zetterling 2,
	Harvey 3, Lee 3, Beaton 4, Box 4,
	Heller 4)
Truth about Youth, 1930 (Loy 3, Young 3,
	Miller 4)
Truth Juggler, 1922 (Roach 4)
Truthful Liar, 1924 (Rogers 3, Roach 4)
Truthful Tulliver, 1917 (Hart 3, August 4)
Trutze von Trutzberg, 1921 (Planer 4)
Truxtonia. See Truxton King, 1923
Truxton King, 1923 (Gilbert 3, August 4)
Try and Get It, 1924 (Horton 3, Furthman 4)
Try and Get Me. See Sound of Fury, 1950
Try This One for Size, 1989 (Steiger 3)
Try, Try Again, 1921 (Roach 4)
Tryanniske fästmannen, 1912 (Stiller 2,
	Magnusson 4)
Trygon Factor, 1966 (Granger 3)
Trying to Fool, 1911 (Sennett 2)
Trying to Get Along, 1919 (Sennett 2)
Trying to Get Arrested, 1909 (Griffith 2)
Trying to Get Married, 1909 (Bitzer 4)
Tryout, 1916 (Laurel and Hardy 3)
Tryst, 1929 (Launder and Gilliat 2)
Trzy koniety, 1957 (Lomnicki 3)
Trzy starty, 1955 (Cybulski 3)
Tschetan, der Indianerjunge, 1973
	(Ballhaus 4)
Tsubaki Sanjuro, 1962 (Kurosawa 2,
	Mifune 3, Shimura 3, Muraki 4)
Tsubakuro-gasa, 1955 (Hasegawa 3)
Tsubasa no gaika, 1942 (Kurosawa 2)
Tsubasa wa kokoro ni tsukete, 1978
	(Kagawa 3)
Tsuchiya Chikara: Rakka no make, 1937
	(Hasegawa 3)
Tsui Hsiang Nien Tê Chi Chieh, 1984
	(Hou 2)
Tsujigahana, 1972 (Iwashita 3)

Tsuki kara kita otoko, 1951 (Hasegawa 3)
Tsuki no wataridori, 1951 (Hasegawa 3)
Tsuki wa noborinu, 1955 (Tanaka 3)
Tsukigata Hanpeita, 1925 (Kinugasa 2)
Tsukigata Hanpeita, 1929 (Hasegawa 3)
Tsukigata Hanpeita, 1933 (Yamada 3)
Tsukigata Hanpeita, 1934 (Hasegawa 3)
Tsukigata Hanpeita, 1952 (Yamada 3)
Tsukigata Hanpeita, 1956 (Kinugasa 2,
	Hasegawa 3, Kyo 3, Yamamura 3)
Tsukihime keizu, 1958 (Miyagawa 4)
Tsukimiso, 1959 (Oshima 2)
Tsukiyo garasu, 1939 (Yoda 4)
Tsukiyo no kasa, 1955 (Tanaka 3)
Tsuma no kokoro, 1956 (Naruse 2, Mifune 3,
	Takamine 3)
Tsuma to iu na no onnatachi, 1963
	(Tsukasa 3)
Tsuma to onna kisha, 1950 (Hayasaka 4)
Tsuma to shite haha to shite, 1961
	(Takamine 3)
Tsuma to shite onnato shite, 1961 (Mori 3)
Tsurigane-so, 1940 (Takamine 3)
Tsurugi no ketsuen, 1928 (Hasegawa 3)
Tsurugi o koete, 1930 (Yamada 3)
Tsuruhachi Tsurijiro, 1938 (Hasegawa 3,
	Yamada 3)
Tsuruhachi Tsurujiro, 1956 (Yamamura 3)
Tsuyu no atosaki, 1956 (Takemitsu 4)
Tsuzurikata kyodai, 1958 (Kagawa 3)
Tsuzurikata kyoshitsu, 1938 (Takamine 3)
Tu seras vedette, 1942 (Alekan 4)
Tu, solo tu, 1949 (Alcoriza 4)
Tu Ten Kámen, 1923 (Ondra 3, Heller 4)
Tu enfanteras sans douleur, 1956 (Delerue 4)
Tu es danse et vertige, 1967 (Coutard 4)
Tu m'appartiens, 1929 (Bertini 3)
Tu m'as sauvé la vie, 1950 (Guitry 2,
	Fernandel 3)
Tu ne tueras point, 1961 (Aurenche 4,
	Bost 4, Douy 4)
Tu n'epouseras jamais un avocat, 1914
	(Musidora 3)
Tua donna, 1954 (Neal 3)
Tuba, 1976 (Frampton 2)
Tubby the Tuba, 1947 (Pal 4)
Tubog Sa Ginto, 1970 (Brocka 2)
Tucet mých tatínku, 1959 (Brdečka 4)
Tucker. See Tucker: The Man and His
	Dream, 1988
Tucker: The Man and His Dream, 1988
	(Coppola 2, Lucas 2, Bridges 3,
	Storaro 4, Tavoularis 4)
Tudor Princess, 1913 (Ingram 2)
Tudor Rose, 1936 (Stevenson 2, Launder and
	Gilliat 2, Mills 3, Balcon 4,
	Vetchinsky 4)
Tuesday in November, 1945 (Hubley 4,
	Koch 4, Thomson 4)
Tueur, 1971 (Blier 3, Depardieu 3, Gabin 3,
	Renoir 4)
Tueur triste, 1984 (Feuillère 3)
Tueurs de San Francisco. See Once a Thief,
	1965
Tugboat Annie, 1933 (LeRoy 2, Beery 3,
	Dressler 3, O'Sullivan 3, Young 3,
	Mayer 4, Raine 4, Toland 4)
Tugboat Annie Sails Again, 1940 (Reagan 3,
	Wyman 3, Deutsch 4, Edeson 4)
Tugboat Granny, 1956 (Blanc 4, Freleng 4)
Tugboat Princess, 1936 (Trumbo 4)
Tugboat Romeos, 1916 (Sennett 2)
Tugthusfange No. 97, 1914 (Psilander 3)
Tulák. See Aničko, vrať se!, 1926

Tulip Time. See Seven Sweethearts, 1942
Tulipa, 1967 (Gómez 2)
Tulipe noire, 1963 (Delon 3, Decaë 4)
Tulips Shall Grow, 1942 (Pal 4)
Tull-Bom, 1951 (Björnstrand 3)
Tulsa, 1949 (Armendáriz 3, Hayward 3,
	Preston 3, Fulton 4, Hoch 4, Nugent 4,
	Wanger 4)
Tumbleweed, 1953 (Murphy 3, Van Cleef 3,
	Hunter 4, Metty 4)
Tumbleweeds, 1925 (Hart 3, August 4,
	Sullivan 4)
Tumbling River, 1927 (Mix 3)
Tumbling Tumbleweeds, 1935 (Autry 3,
	Rogers 3)
Tummy Trouble, 1989 (Turner 3)
Tumultes, 1931 (Boyer 3)
Tuna Clipper, 1949 (McDowall 3)
Tune in Tomorrow. See Aunt Julia and the
	Scriptwriter, 1990
Tune Up and Sing, 1934 (Fleischer 4)
Tunel, 1988 (Rey 3)
Tunes of Glory, 1960 (Guinness 3, Mills 3,
	York 3, Arnold 4)
Tung, 1966 (Baillie 2)
Tunisian Victory, 1944 (Boulting 2, Capra 2,
	Huston 2, Meredith 3, Alwyn 4,
	Hornbeck 4, Veiller 4)
Tunnel, 1919 (Warm 4)
Tunnel, 1933 (Gabin 3, Hoffmann 4)
Tunnel, 1935 (Arliss 3, Huston 3, Balcon 4,
	Metzner 4, Siodmak 4)
Tunnel of Love, 1958 (Day 3, Kelly 3,
	Widmark 3, Rose 4)
Tunnel sous la manche ou Le Cauchemar
	franco-anglais, 1907 (Méliès 2)
Tunnel to the Sun. See Korube no taiyo,
	1968
Tunnel 28, 1962 (Siodmak 2)
Tunnell, 1933 (Gründgens 3)
Turbina, 1940 (Baarová 3)
Turbina nr. 3, 1927 (Moskvin 4)
Turbine d'odio, 1914 (Gallone 2)
Turbine no. 3. See Turbina nr. 3, 1927
Turco napoletano, 1953 (Struss 4)
Turf Sensation. See Women First, 1924
Turkey Dinner, 1936 (Lantz 4)
Turkey Hunt, Pinehurst, 1905 (Bitzer 4)
Turkeys in a Row. See Shichimencho no
	yukue, 1924
Turkey Time, 1933 (Balcon 4, Junge 4,
	Rank 4)
Turkish Delight, 1927 (Garnett 2,
	Sullivan 4)
Turm des schweigens, 1924 (Pommer 4)
Tür mit den sieben Schlössern, 1962
	(Kinski 3)
Turmoil, 1924 (Mandell 4)
Turn Back the Clock, 1933 (Three Stooges 3,
	Adrian 4, Gillespie 4, Hecht 4, Rosson 4,
	Stothart 4, Vorkapich 4)
Turn Back the Hours, 1928 (Loy 3,
	Pidgeon 3, Robinson 4)
Turn in the Road, 1919 (Vidor 2)
Turn of the Tide, 1935 (Rank 4)
Turn Off the Moon, 1937 (Dmytryk 2,
	Pangborn 3, Dreier 4, Head 4, Prinz 4,
	Young 4)
Turn the Key Softly, 1953 (Rank 4,
	Unsworth 4)
Turn to the Right, 1922 (Ingram 2, Mathis 4,
	Seitz 4)
Turnabout, 1940 (Astor 3, Menjou 3,
	Pangborn 3, Roach 4)

Turned Out Nice Again, 1941 (Dearden 2, Hamer 2, Formby 3, Balcon 4)

Turner, 1972 (Rosenblum 4)

Turner and Hooch, 1989 (Hanks 3)

Turning a Blind Eye, 1985 (Richardson 2)

Turning Point, 1952 (Dieterle 2, Holden 3, O'Brien 3, Head 4)

Turning Point, 1977 (Bancroft 3, MacLaine 3, Reynolds 4, Surtees 4)

Turno, 1981 (Gassman 3)

Turn-Tale Wolf, 1952 (Blanc 4, McKimson 4, Stalling 4)

Turtle Diary, 1985 (Jackson 3, Pinter 4)

Tusalava, 1929 (Lye 4)

Tutankhamen. See Tu Ten Kámen, 1923

Tutta la città canta, 1943 (Fellini 2)

Tutti a casa, 1960 (Reggiani 3, Sordi 3, Alexeieff and Parker 4, De Laurentiis 4)

Tutti dentro, 1984 (Sordi 3)

Tutti innamorati, 1959 (Mastroianni 3)

Tuttles of Tahiti, 1942 (Vidor 2, Laughton 3, Musuraca 4)

Tutto a posto e niente in ordine, 1974 (Wertmüller 2, Rotunno 4)

Tütün zamani, 1959 (Güney 2)

Tutyu and Totyo. See Tutyu és Totyo, 1915

Tutyu és Totyo, 1914 (Korda 2, Korda 4)

Tuxedo Warrior, 1982 (Lassally 4)

Tüzoltó utca 25, 1973 (Szabó 2)

TV Dante, 1990 (Gielgud 3)

TV Dante—Canto 5, 1984 (Greenaway 2)

T.V. Interview, 1967 (Vanderbeek 2)

TV of Tomorrow, 1953 (Avery 4)

Två konungar, 1924 (Jaenzon 4)

Två kvinnor, 1947 (Björnstrand 3, Dahlbeck 3)

Två kvinnor, 1975 (Andersson 3)

Två människor, 1945 (Fischer 4)

Två man om en änka, 1933 (Jaenzon 4)

Två Saliga, 1985 (Andersson 3)

Två Sköna Juveler, 1954 (Thulin 3)

Två Svenska emigranters aventyr i Amerika, 1912 (Jaenzon 4, Magnusson 4)

Två trappor över gården, 1950 (Andersson 3)

Tvár, 1973 (Brdečka 4)

Tvärbalk, 1967 (Andersson 3)

Twa Corbies, 1989 (Halas and Batchelor 4)

Twarza w twarz, 1968 (Zanussi 2)

'Twas Ever Thus, 1915 (Bosworth 3, Marion 4)

Twee frouwen, 1980 (Andersson 3, Perkins 3)

Tween Two Loves, 1911 (Pickford 3)

Tweet and Lovely, 1959 (Blanc 4, Freleng 4)

Tweet and Sour, 1956 (Blanc 4, Freleng 4)

Tweet Dreams, 1959 (Blanc 4, Freleng 4)

Tweet, Tweet, Tweety, 1951 (Blanc 4, Stalling 4)

Tweetie Pie, 1947 (Blanc 4, Freleng 4)

Tweety and the Beanstalk, 1957 (Blanc 4, Freleng 4)

Tweety Zoo, 1957 (Blanc 4, Freleng 4)

Tweety's Circus, 1955 (Blanc 4, Foster 4, Freleng 4)

Tweety's S.O.S., 1951 (Blanc 4, Foster 4, Freleng 4, Stalling 4)

Twelve Angry Men, 1957 (Lumet 2, Cobb 3, Fonda 3, Kaufman 4)

Twelve Chairs, 1970 (Brooks 2)

Twelve Crowded Hours, 1939 (Ball 3, Fort 4, Musuraca 4)

Twelve Good Men, 1936 (Launder and Gilliat 2)

Twelve Hours to Kill, 1960 (Crosby 4)

Twelve Miles Out, 1927 (Crawford 3, Gilbert 3, Gibbons 4, Mayer 4)

Twelve O'Clock and All Ain't Well, 1941 (Terry 4)

Twelve O'Clock High, 1949 (King 2, Peck 3, Newman 4, Shamroy 4, Wheeler 4, Zanuck 4)

Twelve Plus One. See Una su tredici, 1969

Twelve Tasks of Asterix, 1973 (Halas and Batchelor 4)

Twelve: Ten, 1919 (Brenon 2)

Twelve to the Moon, 1960 (Bushman 3, Alton 4, Bodeen 4)

Twentieth Century, 1934 (Hawks 2, Barrymore 3, Lombard 3, August 4, Cohn 4, Hecht 4, MacArthur 4)

Twenty Four Eyes. See Nijushi no hitomi, 1954

Twenty Horses, 1932 (Johnson 4)

Twenty Legs Under the Sea, 1931 (Fleischer 4)

Twenty Million Dollar Mystery, 1915 (Cruze 2)

Twenty Million Sweethearts, 1934 (Powell 3, Rogers 3, Orry-Kelly 4, Wald 4)

Twenty Minutes at Warner Brothers Studios, 1927 (Barrymore 3)

Twenty Minutes of Love, 1914 (Sennett 2)

Twenty One, 1923 (Barthelmess 3, Folsey 4)

Twenty Plus Two, 1961 (Moorehead 3)

Twenty Shades of Pink, 1976 (Wallach 3)

Twenty Thousand Leagues Under the Sea, 1980 (Johnson 3)

Twenty Thousand Men a Year, 1939 (Scott 3)

Twenty Thousand Years in Sing Sing, 1933 (Curtiz 2, Calhern 3, Davis 3, Tracy 3, Grot 4, Haskin 4, Orry-Kelly 4)

Twenty Years of Cinema. See Kino za XX liet, 1940

Twenty-Fifth Hour. See 25e Heure, 1967

Twenty-Four-Dollar Island, 1927 (Flaherty 2)

Twenty-Four Hours, 1931 (Francis 3, Hopkins 3, Haller 4)

Twenty-Four Hours of Shanghai, 1933 (Zhao 3)

Twenty-Four Hours to Kill, 1965 (Rooney 3)

Twenty-Nine, 1967 (Godfrey 4)

Twenty-One Carat Snatch. See Popsy Pop, 1971

Twenty-One Hours at Munich, 1976 (Holden 3, Quayle 3)

Twenty-Three Paces to Baker Street, 1956 (Hathaway 2, Johnson 3, Krasner 4, LeMaire 4)

Twice a Man, 1963 (Markopoulos 2)

Twice a Woman. See Twee frouwen, 1980

Twice Blessed, 1945 (Irene 4)

Twice Branded, 1936 (Mason 3)

Twice in a Lifetime, 1985 (Burstyn 3, Hackman 3)

Twice 'round the Daffodils, 1962 (Dillon 4)

Twice Two, 1920 (Howard 3)

Twice Two, 1933 (Laurel and Hardy 3, Roach 4)

Twice Upon a Time, 1953 (Powell and Pressburger 2, Hawkins 3, Challis 4, Francis 4, Korda 4)

Twice-Told Tales, 1963 (Price 3)

Twilight, 1912 (Bushman 3)

Twilight. See Belle Aventure, 1945

Twilight. See Alkony, 1971

Twilight for the Gods, 1958 (Charisse 3, Hudson 3, Kennedy 3, Raksin 4)

Twilight in the Sierras, 1950 (Rogers 3)

Twilight in Tokyo. See Tokyo boshoku, 1957

Twilight Meeting. See Möten i skymningen, 1957

Twilight Meetings. See Möten i skymningen, 1957

Twilight of Honor, 1963 (Rains 3, Green 4)

Twilight on the Prairie, 1944 (Bruckman 4, Salter 4)

Twilight on the Rio Grande, 1947 (Autry 3, Canutt 4)

Twilight on the Trail, 1937 (Fleischer 4)

Twilight on the Trail, 1941 (Harlan 4)

Twilight Path. See Daikon to ninjin, 1965

Twilight Time, 1983 (Malden 3)

Twilight Women. See Women of Twilight, 1952

Twilight Zone—The Movie, 1983 (Dante 2, Landis 2, Miller 2, Spielberg 2, Bottin 4, Goldsmith 4)

Twilight's Last Gleaming, 1977 (Aldrich 2, Cotten 3, Douglas 3, Lancaster 3, Widmark 3, Goldsmith 4)

Twin Beds, 1929 (Polito 4)

Twin Beds, 1942 (Bennett 3, Irene 4, Mohr 4, Tiomkin 4)

Twin Brothers, 1909 (Griffith 2)

Twin Detectives, 1976 (Gish 3)

Twin Flats, 1916 (Laurel and Hardy 3)

Twin Kiddies, 1917 (King 2)

Twin Screws, 1933 (Roach 4)

Twin Sisters, 1915 (Laurel and Hardy 3)

Twin Sisters of Kyoto. See Koto, 1963

Twin Triplets, 1935 (Roach 4)

Twinkle in God's Eye, 1955 (Rooney 3)

Twinkle, Twinkle, Lucky Stars, 1985 (Chan 3)

Twinkletoes, 1926 (LeRoy 2, Moore 3)

Twinkletoes Gets the Bird, 1941 (Fleischer 4)

Twinkletoes in Hat Stuff, 1941 (Fleischer 4)

Twinkletoes—Where He Goes Nobody Knows, 1941 (Fleischer 4)

Twinky, 1969 (Bronson 3, Hawkins 3, Howard 3, Lassally 4)

Twins, 1916 (Sennett 2)

Twins, 1925 (Laurel and Hardy 3)

Twins, 1988 (Schwarzenegger 3, Delerue 4)

Twins from Suffering Creek, 1920 (Wellman 2, Furthman 4)

Twins of Evil, 1971 (Cushing 3, Carreras 4)

Twisker Pitcher, 1937 (Fleischer 4)

Twist. See Folies bourgeoises, 1976

Twist Again à Moscou, 1986 (Blier 3, Noiret 3)

Twist Again in Moscow. See Twist Again à Moscou, 1986

Twist around the Clock, 1961 (Katzman 4)

Twist, ninfette e vitelloni, 1962 (Fabrizi 3)

Twist of Fate. See Beautiful Stranger, 1954

Twisted Justice, 1990 (Black 3)

Twisted Lives. See Menteurs, 1961

Twisted Nerve, 1968 (Boulting 2, Herrmann 4)

Twisted Road. See **They Live By Night, 1948**

Twisted Trail, 1910 (Griffith 2, Pickford 3, Bitzer 4)

Twisted Trails, 1916 (Mix 3)

Twisted Triggers, 1926 (Arthur 3)

Twister, 1989 (Stanton 3)

Twixt Love and Fire, 1914 (Sennett 2, Arbuckle 3)

Two, 1965 (Ray 2)

Two Against the World, 1932 (Orry-Kelly 4, Rosher 4)

Two Against the World, 1936 (Bogart 3)

Two Alone, 1934 (Bondi 3, Steiner 4)

Two Americans, 1929 (Huston 3)

Two and Two Make Six, 1962 (Francis 4)

Two April Fools, 1954 (Bruckman 4)

Two Arabian Knights, 1927 (Milestone 2, Astor 3, Karloff 3, August 4, Gaudio 4, Hughes 4, Menzies 4)

Two Are Guilty. See Glaive et la balance, 1963

Two Bagatelles, 1952 (McLaren 4)

Two Barbers, 1944 (Terry 4)

Two Baroque Churches in Germany, 1959 (Bernstein 4)

Two Before Zero, 1962 (Rathbone 3)

Two Blondes and a Redhead, 1947 (Katzman 4)

Two Bottle Babies, 1904 (Bitzer 4)

Two Bright Boys, 1939 (Cooper 3)

Two Brothers, 1910 (Griffith 2, Pickford 3, Bitzer 4)

Two Brothers. See Brüder Schellenberg, 1926

Two Can Play, 1926 (Bow 3)

Two Colonels. See Duo colonelli, 1962

Two: Creeley/McClure, 1965 (Brakhage 2)

Two Crooks, 1917 (Sennett 2)

Two Crowded Hours, 1931 (Powell and Pressburger 2)

Two Crows from Tacos, 1956 (Blanc 4, Freleng 4)

Two Daughters. See Teen Kanya, 1961

Two Daughters of Eve, 1912 (Griffith 2, Gish 3, Bitzer 4)

Two Dinky Dramas of a Non-Serious Kind, 1914 (Beery 3)

Two Dollar Bettor, 1951 (Leven 4)

Two Down, One to Go, 1945 (Capra 2, Hornbeck 4)

Two English Girls. See Deux Anglaises et le continent, 1971

Two Evil Eyes. See Due occhi diabolici, 1990

Two Faces of Dr. Jekyll, 1960 (Lee 3, Reed 3, Carreras 4, Mankowitz 4)

Two Fathers, 1911 (Lawrence 3)

Two Fathers, 1944 (Asquith 2)

Two Fedors. See Dva Fedora, 1959

Two Fister, 1927 (Wyler 2)

Two Flags West, 1950 (Wise 2, Cotten 3, Darnell 3, Wilde 3, LeMaire 4, Newman 4, Nugent 4, Robinson 4, Shamroy 4, Wheeler 4)

Two Flaming Youths, 1927 (Fields 3, Mankiewicz 4)

Two Flats West, 1950 (Friedhofer 4)

Two Fools in a Canoe, 1898 (Hepworth 2)

Two for the Money, 1971 (Brennan 3, Dreyfuss 3, McCambridge 3)

Two for the Road, 1966 (Donen 2, Finney 3, Hepburn 3, Challis 4, Mancini 4, Raphael 4)

Two for the Seesaw, 1962 (Wise 2, MacLaine 3, Mitchum 3, Leven 4, McCord 4, Mirisch 4, Orry-Kelly 4, Previn 4, Westmore Family 4)

Two for the Zoo, 1941 (Fleischer 4)

Two for Tonight, 1935 (Bennett 3, Crosby 3, Head 4, Struss 4)

Two from One Housing Block. See Two from the Same Block, 1957

Two from the Same Block, 1957 (Bondarchuk 3)

Two Frosts. See Dva mrazíci, 1954

Two Fugitives, 1911 (Anderson 3)

Two Girls and a Sailor, 1944 (Allyson 3, Durante 3, Gardner 3, Horne 3, Johnson 3, Irene 4, Pasternak 4, Surtees 4)

Two Girls on Broadway, 1940 (Blondell 3, Turner 3, Brown 4, Folsey 4, Freed 4)

Two Girls Wanted, 1927 (Gaynor 3, Miller 4)

Two Gophers from Texas, 1948 (Blanc 4, Stalling 4)

Two Grilled Fish, 1968 (Kuri 4)

Two Gun Cupid. See Bad Man, 1941

Two Gun Hicks. See Passing of Two Gun Hicks, 1914

Two Guns, 1917 (Carey 3)

Two Guys Abroad, 1961 (Raft 3)

Two Guys from Milwaukee, 1946 (Bacall 3, Bogart 3, Pangborn 3, Diamond 4, Edeson 4)

Two Guys from Texas, 1948 (Malone 3, Cahn 4, Diamond 4, Edeson 4)

Two Headed Giant, 1939 (Terry 4)

Two Hearts in Waltz Time, 1934 (Gallone 2)

Two Hearts that Beat as Ten, 1915 (Beery 3)

Two in a Crowd, 1936 (Bennett 3, McCrea 3)

Two in a Taxi, 1941 (Florey 2)

Two in Revolt, 1936 (Steiner 4)

Two in the Bush. See Rally, 1980

Two in the Dark, 1936 (Musuraca 4)

Two in the Shadow. See Midaregumo, 1967

Two Jakes, 1990 (Nicholson 3, Wallach 3, Towne 4, Zsigmond 4)

Two Kinds of Love, 1920 (Eason 4)

Two Kinds of Women, 1932 (Hopkins 3, Head 4, Struss 4)

Two Kings. See Två konungar, 1924

Two Knights from Brooklyn, 1949 (Bendix 3)

Two Latins from Manhattan, 1941 (Cahn 4)

Two Lazy Crows, 1936 (Iwerks 4)

Two Little Bears, 1961 (Crosby 4)

Two Little Indians, 1952 (Hanna and Barbera 4)

Two Little Lambs, 1935 (Lantz 4)

Two Little Rabbits, 1952 (Popescu-Gopo 4)

Two Little Rangers, 1912 (Guy 2)

Two Little Waifs, 1910 (Griffith 2, Bitzer 4)

Two Lives of Mattia Pascal. See Due vite di Mattia Pascal, 1985

Two Living, One Dead, 1961 (Fischer 4)

Two Lovers, 1928 (Niblo 2, Banky 3, Colman 3, Lukas 3, Barnes 4, Goldwyn 4)

Two Loves, 1961 (Walters 2, Harvey 3, Hawkins 3, MacLaine 3, Kaper 4, Maddow 4, Ruttenberg 4)

Two Lunatics, 1910 (White 3)

Two Memories, 1909 (Griffith 2, Bitzer 4)

Two Men, 1910 (Lawrence 3)

Two Men and a Girl. See Honeymoon, 1947

Two Men and a Widow. See Tva man om en änka, 1933

Two Men of Sandy Bar, 1916 (Bosworth 3)

Two Men of the Desert, 1913 (Griffith 2, Carey 3, Crisp 3, Sweet 3, Walthall 3, Bitzer 4)

Two Minds for Murder. See Quelqu'un derrière la porte, 1971

Two Minutes to Play, 1937 (Katzman 4)

Two Mrs. Carrolls, 1947 (Bogart 3, Stanwyck 3, Burks 4, Grot 4, Head 4, Waxman 4)

Two Mrs. Grenvilles, 1987 (Colbert 3)

Two Mouseketeers, 1952 (Hanna and Barbera 4)

Two Mugs from Brooklyn. See Two Knights from Brooklyn, 1949

Two Mules for Sister Sara, 1970 (Boetticher 2, Siegel 2, Eastwood 3, MacLaine 3, Figueroa 4, Morricone 4, Westmore Family 4)

Two Nights with Cleopatra. See Due notti con Cleopatra, 1954

Two O'Clock Courage, 1945 (Mann 2)

Two of a Kind, 1951 (O'Brien 3, Duning 4, Guffey 4)

Two of a Kind, 1983 (Reed 3, Robertson 3, Travolta 3)

Two of Them. See Schimbul de miine, 1959

Two of Them. See Ok ketten, 1977

Two of Us. See Jack of All Trades, 1936

Two of Us. See Vieil Homme et l'enfant, 1966

Two Off the Cuff, 1968 (Godfrey 4)

Two Old Tars, 1913 (Sennett 2)

Two on a Doorstep, 1936 (Havelock-Allan 4)

Two on a Guillotine, 1965 (Steiner 4)

Two on the Tiles, 1951 (Lom 3)

Two Orphans, 1911 (Selig 4)

Two Orphans, 1915 (Brenon 2, Bara 3)

Two Orphans. See Due orfanelle, 1942

Two Outlaws, 1928 (Miller 4)

Two Overcoats, 1911 (Bunny 3)

Two Paths, 1910 (Griffith 2, Crisp 3, Bitzer 4)

Two People. See Två människor, 1945

Two People, 1971 (Wise 2, Baye 3, Decaë 4, Reynolds 4)

Two Pigeons. See Deux Pigeons, 1962

Two Plus Fours, 1930 (Crosby 3)

Two Ranchmen, 1913 (Anderson 3)

Two Reformations, 1911 (Anderson 3)

Two Rode Together, 1961 (Ford 2, Marsh 3, Stewart 3, Widmark 3, Duning 4, Nugent 4)

Two Scents Worth, 1955 (Blanc 4, Jones 4)

Two Scrambled, 1918 (Lloyd 3, Roach 4)

Two Seconds, 1932 (LeRoy 2, Robinson 3, Grot 4, Polito 4)

Two Sentences, 1915 (Eason 4)

Two Sides, 1911 (Griffith 2, Bitzer 4)

Two Sides to Every Story, 1974 (Snow 2)

Two Sisters, 1929 (Karloff 3)

Two Sisters from Boston, 1946 (Allyson 3, Durante 3, Grayson 3, Pasternak 4, Rose 4, Surtees 4)

Two Smart People, 1946 (Dassin 2, Ball 3, Freund 4, Irene 4)

Two Solitudes, 1978 (Jutra 2, Jarre 4)

Two Stage Sisters. See **Wutai Jiemie, 1964**

Two Tars, 1928 (McCarey 2, Stevens 2, Laurel and Hardy 3)

Two Texas Knights. See Two Guys from Texas, 1948

Two Thousand Women, 1944 (Launder and Gilliat 2)

Two Thousand Years Later, 1969 (Horton 3)

Two Tickets to Broadway, 1951 (Berkeley 2, Leigh 3, Miller 3, Cahn 4, Cronjager 4)

Two Tickets to London, 1943 (Fitzgerald 3, Morgan 3, Krasner 4)

Two Tickets to Paris, 1962 (Rosenblum 4)

Two Together. *See* Ninin sugata, 1942

Two Too Young, 1935 (Roach 4)

Two Topers, 1905 (Bitzer 4)

Two Tough Tenderfeet, 1918 (Sennett 2)

Two Twins, 1923 (Stromberg 4)

Two Wagons, Both Covered, 1923 (Rogers 3, Roach 4)

Two Way Street, 1931 (Launder and Gilliat 2, Bennett 4)

Two Weeks, 1920 (Emerson 4, Loos 4)

Two Weeks in Another Town, 1962 (Minnelli 2, Charisse 3, Douglas 3, Robinson 3, Trevor 3, Houseman 4, Krasner 4, Plunkett 4, Raksin 4, Schnee 4)

Two Weeks in September. *See* Coeur joie, 1967

Two Weeks to Live, 1943 (Pangborn 3)

Two Weeks with Love, 1950 (Berkeley 2, Calhern 3, Reynolds 3, Ames 4, Mayer 4, Plunkett 4)

Two Weeks with Pay, 1921 (Daniels 3)

Two Western Paths, 1913 (Anderson 3)

Two White Arms, 1932 (Niblo 2, Menjou 3)

Two Who Dared. *See* Woman Alone, 1936

Two Widows, 1913 (Sennett 2)

Two Women. *See* Två kvinnor, 1947

Two Women. *See* Ciociara, 1960

Two Women. *See* Två Kvinnor, 1975

Two Women. *See* Ok ketten, 1977

Two Women. *See* Twee frouwen, 1980

Two Women and a Man, 1909 (Griffith 2, Bitzer 4)

Two Worlds, 1930 (Dupont 2, Junge 4, Rosher 4)

Two Yanks in Trinidad, 1942 (Cahn 4)

Two Years Before the Mast, 1946 (Bendix 3, Fitzgerald 3, Ladd 3, Dreier 4, Laszlo 4, Miller 4, Young 4)

Two-Alarm Fire, 1934 (Fleischer 4)

Two-Faced Wolf, 1960 (Hanna and Barbera 4)

Two-Faced Woman, 1941 (Cukor 2, Douglas 3, Garbo 3, Gordon 3, Adrian 4, Alton 4, Behrman 4, Kaper 4, Mayer 4, Ruttenberg 4)

Two-Fisted, 1935 (Cruze 2)

Two-Fisted Justice, 1932 (Canutt 4)

Two-Fisted Law, 1932 (Brennan 3, Wayne 3)

Two-Fisted Sheriff, 1925 (Canutt 4)

Two-Gun Gussie, 1918 (Daniels 3, Lloyd 3, Roach 4)

Two-Gun Man, 1911 (Anderson 3)

Two-Headed Spy, 1958 (De Toth 2, Caine 3, Hawkins 3, Pleasence 3)

Two-Lane Blacktop, 1971 (Oates 3, Stanton 3)

Two-Minute Warning, 1976 (Cassavetes 2, Heston 3, Pidgeon 3, Rowlands 3)

Twonky, 1953 (Biroc 4)

Two's a Crowd, 1950 (Blanc 4, Jones 4, Stalling 4)

Two-Way Street, 1960 (Box 4)

Two-Way Stretch, 1960 (Sellers 3)

Ty pomnis li?, 1914 (Mozhukin 3)

Tyaag, 1977 (Burman 4)

Tycoon, 1947 (Quinn 3, Wayne 3, Chase 4, D'Agostino 4)

Type bien, 1990 (Gélin 3)

Type comme moi ne devrait jamais mourir, 1976 (Guillemot 4)

Typhoid. *See* Tifusari, 1963

Typhon sur Nagasaki, 1956 (Darrieux 3, Marais 3, Alekan 4)

Typhoon, 1914 (Hayakawa 3, Ince 4)

Typhoon, 1940 (Preston 3, Dreier 4, Head 4, Reynolds 4)

Typical Budget, 1925 (Buchanan 3)

Tyrannical Fiancée. *See* Tryanniske fästmannen, 1912

Tyrant Is Dead, 1910 (Costello 3)

Tyrant of Red Gulch, 1928 (Musuraca 4)

Tyrant of the Sea, 1950 (Katzman 4)

Tyrant of Toledo. *See* Amants de Tolède, 1953

Tyrtéc, 1912 (Feuillade 2)

Tystnaden, 1963 (Thulin 3, Nykvist 4)

Tyvepak, 1921 (Madsen and Schenstrøm 3)

U

U oluji, 1952 (Mimica 4)
U ozera, 1969 (Shukshin 3)
U pokladny stál, 1939 (Stallich 4)
U snědeného krámu, 1933 (Frič 2)
U sv. Matěje, 1928 (Stallich 4)
UFO Incident, 1975 (Jones 3)
U-47: Kapitänleutnant Prien, 1958
    (Tschechowa 3)
U.M.C., 1969 (Robinson 3, La Shelle 4)
U.S. Army in San Francisco, 1915
    (Sennett 2)
U.S. Naval Militia, 1900 (Bitzer 4)
USA en vrac, 1953 (Lelouch 2)
U.S.S. Maine, Havana Harbor, 1897
    (Bitzer 4)
Ubåt 39, 1952 (Andersson 3, Dahlbeck 3)
Uber Alles in der Welt, 1941 (Röhrig 4)
Uberfall, 1928 (Metzner 4)
Uberflussige Menschen, 1926 (Krauss 3,
    Rasp 3, Andrejew 4)
Übernachtung in Tirol, 1973 (Von Trotta 2)
Ubit Drakona, 1989 (Yankovsky 3)
U-Boat 29. *See* Spy in Black, 1939
U-Boat 39. *See* Ubåt 39, 1952
U-Boat Prisoner, 1944 (Guffey 4)
Ubu and the Great Gidouille. *See* Ubu et la
    Grande Gidouille, 1979
Ubu et la Grande Gidouille, 1979 (Lenica 4)
Ubu Roi, 1976 (Lenica 4)
Uccelacci e uccellini, 1966 (Pasolini 2,
    Delli Colli 4, Donati 4, Morricone 4)
Uccello dalle piume di cristallo, 1969
    (Argento 4, Morricone 4, Storaro 4)
Uccidere in silenzio, 1972 (Cervi 3)
Uccidete il vitello grasso ed arrostitelo, 1970
    (Morricone 4)
Uchiiri zenya, 1941 (Shimura 3)
Uchu daikaiju Dogora, 1964 (Tsuburaya 4)
Uchu daisensu, 1959 (Tsuburaya 4)
Uchveli uzh davno krisantemi v sadu, 1916
    (Mozhukin 3)
Ücünüzü de mihlarim, 1965 (Güney 2)
Udayer Pathey, 1944 (Roy 2)
Uddhar, 1949 (Anand 3)
Udeippon, 1930 (Yamada 3)
Udflytterne, 1972 (Roos 2)
Udienza, 1971 (Ferreri 2, Cardinale 3,
    Cuny 3, Gassman 3, Piccoli 3,
    Cristaldi 4)
Udvari levego, 1917 (Lukas 3)
Uemon torimono-cho: Uemon Edo-sugata,
    1940 (Shimura 3)
Uerreichbare, 1982 (Zanussi 2, Caron 3)
Uforia, 1985 (Stanton 3)
Ugetsu monogatari, 1953 (Mizoguchi 2,
    Kyo 3, Mori 3, Tanaka 3, Hayasaka 4,
    Miyagawa 4, Yoda 4)

Ugly American, 1963 (Brando 3, Okada 3)
Ugly Dachshund, 1966 (Disney 4)
Ugly Dino, 1942 (Fleischer 4)
Ugly Duckling, 1959 (Carreras 4)
Ugolok, 1916 (Mozhukin 3)
Uijin, 1933 (Hasegawa 3)
Ukamau, 1966 (Sanjinés 2)
Ukelele Sheiks, 1926 (Roach 4)
Ukigumo, 1955 (Mori 3, Takamine 3)
Ukigusa, 1959 (Ozu 2, Kyo 3, Ryu 3,
    Miyagawa 4)
Ukiyo kouji, 1939 (Yoda 4)
Ukradená vzducholod, 1966 (Zeman 4)
Ulička v Ráji, 1936 (Heller 4)
Uličnice, 1936 (Heller 4)
Ulisse, 1954 (Douglas 3, Mangano 3,
    Quinn 3, De Laurentiis 4, Hecht 4,
    Ponti 4, Rosson 4, Schüfftan 4)
Ulla, min Ulla, 1930 (Jaenzon 4)
Ulla, My Ulla. *See* Ulla, min Ulla, 1930
Uloupená hranice, 1947 (Weiss 2,
    Brodský 3)
Ulrik fortaeller en historie, 1972 (Roos 2)
Ultima carrozzella, 1943 (Fellini 2,
    Fabrizi 3, Magnani 3)
Ultima cena, 1976 (Villagra 3)
Ultima chance, 1973 (Wallach 3)
Ultima donna, 1976 (Baye 3, Depardieu 3,
    Sarde 4)
Ultima Mazurka, 1986 (Josephson 3)
Ultima nemica, 1938 (Valli 3)
Ultima Sentenza. *See* Son dernier verdict,
    1951
Ultima Thule, 1968 (Roos 2)
Ultimata donna, 1976 (Piccoli 3)
Ultimate Solution of Grace Quigley, 1983
    (Hepburn 3, Nolte 3, Addison 4, Golan
    and Globus 4)
Ultimate Warrior, 1975 (Brynner 3, Von
    Sydow 3)
Ultimatum, 1938 (Siodmak 2, Von
    Stroheim 2, Wiene 2, Fradetal 4)
Ultimatum, 1971 (Lefebvre 2)
Ultimatum. *See* Ultimatum alla città, 1975
Ultimatum alla città, 1975 (Cobb 3)
Ultimi angeli, 1977 (Kennedy 3)
Ultimi cinque minuti, 1955 (Brazzi 3,
    Darnell 3)
Ultimi filibustieri, 1943 (Amidei 4)
Ultimi giorni di Pompei. *See* Derniers Jours
    de Pompéi, 1948
Ultimi zar, 1928 (Amidei 4)
Ultimo addio, 1942 (Cervi 3)
Ultimo amante, 1955 (Ponti 4)
Ultimo amore, 1946 (De Santis 3)
Ultimo ballo, 1941 (Amidei 4)
Ultimo incontro, 1951 (Valli 3)

Ultimo Lord. *See* Femme en homme, 1931
Ultimo paradiso, 1946 (Flaiano 4)
Ultimo sogno, 1921 (Bertini 3)
Ultimo tango a Parigi. *See* **Last Tango in**
    Paris, 1972
Ultimo treno della notte, 1975 (Morricone 4)
Ultimo uomo della terra, 1964 (Price 3)
Ultimo uomo di Sara, 1972 (Morricone 4)
Ultimos de Filipinas, 1945 (Rey 3)
Ultimos dias de Pompeya, 1960 (Rey 3)
Ultraman, 1967 (Tsuburaya 4)
Ultus series, 1915–17 (Pearson 2)
Ulvejaegerne, 1926 (Madsen and
    Schenstrøm 3)
Ulysse, 1983 (Varda 2)
Ulysse ou Les Mauvaises rencontres, 1949
    (Astruc 2)
Ulysses. *See* Ulisse, 1954
Ulzana's Raid, 1972 (Aldrich 2, Lancaster 3,
    Biroc 4)
Um Adeus Português, 1985 (De Almeida 4)
Um apólogo, 1939 (Mauro 2)
Um das Lächeln einer Frau, 1919 (Wiene 2)
Um dia na rampa, 1957 (Rocha 2)
Um Haaresbreite, 1913 (Porten 3, Messter 4)
Um Liebe und Thron, 1922 (Planer 4)
Um môco de 74 anos, 1963 (Pereira Dos
    Santos 2)
Um seine Ehre. *See* Perfekt gentleman, 1927
Um Thron und Liebe. *See* Sarajewo, 1955
Uma, 1941 (Kurosawa 2, Takamine 3)
Umanità, 1946 (Cervi 3)
Umanoide, 1979 (Morricone 4)
Umarete wa mita keredo, 1932 (Ryu 3)
Umarmungen und andere Sachen, 1976
    (Léaud 3)
Umbartha. *See* Subah, 1983
Umberto D, 1952 (De Sica 2, Aldo 4,
    Zavattini 4)
Umbracle, 1970 (Lee 3)
Umbrellas of Cherbourg. *See* **Parapluies de**
    Cherbourg, 1964
Umbrellas to Men, 1912 (Bunny 3)
Umi no hanabi, 1951 (Yamada 3)
Umi no nai minato, 1931 (Yoda 4)
Umi no yaju, 1949 (Yamamura 3)
Umi no yarodomo, 1957 (Shindo 2)
Umi o wataru sairei, 1941 (Shimura 3)
Umi o yuku bushi, 1939 (Yoda 4)
Umon torimonocho: Harebare gojusan-tsugi,
    1936 (Shimura 3)
Umweg zur Ehe, 1918 (Wiene 2)
Umwege zum Glück, 1939 (Dagover 3)
Un Certo giorno, 1968 (Olmi 2)
Un, deux, trois . . . , 1974 (Grimault 4)
Un, deux, trois, quatre. *See* Black Tights,
    1960

Un, deux, trois, quatre!. *See* Mademoiselle, 1966

Una su tredici, 1969 (De Sica 2, Welles 2, Gassman 3, Terry-Thomas 3)

Unaccustomed as We Are, 1929 (Laurel and Hardy 3, Roach 4)

Unafraid, 1915 (De Mille 2, Buckland 4, Macpherson 4)

Unafraid, 1918 (King 2)

Unanoide, 1979 (Kennedy 3)

Unashamed, 1932 (Beavers 3, Young 3, Adrian 4)

Unbändiges Spanien, 1962 (Eisler 4)

Unbearable Bear, 1943 (Blanc 4, Jones 4, Stalling 4)

Unbearable Lightness of Being, 1988 (Day Lewis 3, Josephson 3, Olbrychski 3, Carrière 4, Murch 4, Nykvist 4)

Unbekannte Gast, 1931 (Metzner 4)

Unbekannte Morgen, 1923 (Krauss 3, Lukas 3, Korda 4)

Unbeliever, 1918 (Von Stroheim 2)

Unbezähmbare Leni Peickert, 1969 (Kluge 2)

Uncanny, 1977 (Cushing 3, Greenwood 3, Milland 3, Pleasence 3)

Uncensored, 1942 (Asquith 2, Rattigan 4, Vetchinsky 4)

Uncensored Cartoons, 1981 (Freleng 4, Jones 4)

Uncensored Movies, 1923 (Rogers 3, Roach 4)

Uncertain Glory, 1944 (Walsh 2, Flynn 3, Lukas 3, Buckner 4, Deutsch 4)

Uncertain Lady, 1934 (Horton 3, Freund 4)

Unchained, 1955 (Miller 4, North 4)

Unchained Goddess, 1958 (Capra 2)

Unchanging Sea, 1910 (Griffith 2, Pickford 3, Bitzer 4)

Uncharted Channels, 1920 (King 2)

Uncharted Seas, 1921 (Valentino 3, Seitz 4)

Uncharted Waters, 1933 (Grierson 2)

Unchastened Woman, 1925 (Bara 3)

Uncivil War Brides, 1946 (Bruckman 4)

Uncivil Warbirds, 1946 (Three Stooges 3)

Uncivil Warriors, 1935 (Three Stooges 3)

Uncle!, 1909 (Griffith 2, Pickford 3, Bitzer 4)

Uncle. *See* Zio indegno, 1989

Uncle Buck, 1989 (Hughes 2)

Uncle from America. *See* Strýček z Ameriky, 1933

Uncle Harry. *See* Strange Affair of Uncle Harry, 1945 (Siodmak 2, Sanders 3, Banton 4, Harrison 4, Lourié 4, Salter 4)

Uncle Jake, 1933 (Sennett 2)

Uncle Joe Shannon, 1978 (Winkler 4)

Uncle Joey, 1941 (Terry 4)

Uncle Joey Comes to Town, 1941 (Terry 4)

Uncle John's Arrival in Stockholm. *See* Fabror Johannes ankomst till Stockholm, 1912

Uncle Josh at the Moving Picture Show, 1902 (Porter 2)

Uncle Sam's Songs, 1951 (Fleischer 4)

Uncle Silas, 1947 (Simmons 3, Krasker 4, Rank 4)

Uncle Tom, 1929 (Sennett 2, Hornbeck 4)

Uncle Tom Without the Cabin, 1919 (Sennett 2)

Uncle Tom's Bungalow, 1937 (Avery 4, Stalling 4)

Uncle Tom's Cabana, 1947 (Avery 4)

Uncle Tom's Cabin, 1903 (Porter 2)

Uncle Tom's Cabin, 1910 (Costello 3, Talmadge 3)

Uncle Tom's Cabin, 1918 (Zukor 4)

Uncle Tom's Cabin, 1927 (Beavers 3, Mandell 4)

Uncle Tom's Cabin, 1957 (Massey 3)

Uncle Tom's Cabin, 1968 (Lom 3)

Uncle Tom's Cabin, 1987 (Dern 3)

Uncle Tom's Uncle, 1926 (Roach 4)

Uncle Vanya. *See* Dyadya Vanya, 1970

Uncle Was a Vampire. *See* Tempi duri per vampiri, 1959

Uncle Yanco, 1967 (Varda 2)

Uncommon Valor, 1983 (Hackman 3)

Unconquered, 1917 (Bosworth 3)

Unconquered, 1947 (De Mille 2, Bond 3, Cooper 3, Goddard 3, Johnson 3, Karloff 3, Bennett 4, Dreier 4, Edouart 4, Westmore Family 4, Young 4)

Unconscious London Strata, 1982 (Brakhage 3)

Unconventional Linda. *See* Holiday, 1938

Uncovered Wagon, 1923 (Roach 4)

Und das am Montagmorgen, 1959 (Comencini 2)

Und deine Liebe auch, 1962 (Mueller-Stahl 3)

... und führe uns nicht in Versuchung, 1957 (Herlth 4)

... und keiner schämte sich, 1960 (Fröhlich 3)

und über uns der Himmel, 1947 (Albers 3)

Und Wandern sollst du ruhelos, 1917 (Pommer 4)

Undead, 1956 (Corman 2)

Undefeated, 1969 (Hudson 3, Johnson 3, Wayne 3, Clothier 4, Needham 4)

Under a Shadow, 1915 (Chaney 3)

Under a Texas Moon, 1930 (Curtiz 2, Loy 3)

Under Age, 1941 (Dmytryk 2)

Under Burning Skies, 1912 (Griffith 2, Sweet 3, Bitzer 4)

Under California Skies, 1948 (Rogers 3)

Under Capricorn, 1949 (Hitchcock 2, Bergman 3, Cotten 3, Cardiff 4)

Under Cover of Night, 1937 (Clarke 4)

Under Crimson Skies, 1920 (Johnson 3)

Under False Colors, 1914 (Talmadge 3)

Under False Colors. *See* Under falsk flagg, 1935

Under False Pretences, 1911 (Dwan 2)

Under falsk flagg, 1935 (Molander 2)

Under Fiesta Stars, 1941 (Autry 3, Brown 4)

Under Fire, 1926 (Arthur 3)

Under Fire, 1983 (Hackman 3, Nolte 3, Trintignant 3, Goldsmith 4)

Under Handicap, 1917 (Gaudio 4)

Under Mexican Skies, 1912 (Anderson 3)

Under Milk Wood, 1971 (Burton 3, O'Toole 3, Taylor 3)

Under My Skin, 1950 (Negulesco 2, Garfield 3, Presle 3, La Shelle 4, LeMaire 4, Robinson 4)

Under Nevada Skies, 1946 (Rogers 3, Canutt 4)

Under Pressure, 1935 (Walsh 2, McLaglen 3, Chase 4, Mohr 4)

Under Royal Patronage, 1914 (Bushman 3)

Under Sheriff, 1914 (Sennett 2, Arbuckle 3)

Under Siege, 1986 (Ayres 3)

Under Södra Korset, 1952 (Nykvist 4)

Under Suspicion, 1918 (Bushman 3)

Under Suspicion. *See* Garde à Vue, 1980

Under Ten Flags. *See* Sotto dieci bandiere, 1960

Under Texas Skies, 1939 (Canutt 4)

Under the Bamboo Tree, 1905 (Bitzer 4)

Under the Banner of Samurai. *See* Furin kaza, 1969

Under the Big Top, 1938 (Brown 4)

Under the Black Eagle, 1927 (Van Dyke 2)

Under the Cherry Blossoms. *See* Sakura no mori no mankai no shita, 1975

Under the Cherry Moon, 1986 (Ballhaus 4, Sylbert 4)

Under the Clock. *See* Clock, 1945

Under the Daisies, 1913 (Talmadge 3)

Under the Gaslight, 1914 (Barrymore 3)

Under the Greenwood Tree, 1929 (Launder and Gilliat 2)

Under the Gun, 1950 (Jaffe 3, Orry-Kelly 4)

Under the Lash, 1921 (Wood 2, Swanson 3)

Under the Military Flag. *See* Gunki hatameku shitani, 1972

Under the Old Apple Tree, 1907 (Bitzer 4)

Under the Pampas Moon, 1935 (Hayworth 3)

Under the Rainbow, 1981 (Arden 3)

Under the Red Robe, 1924 (Powell 3)

Under the Red Robe, 1937 (Sjöström 2, Massey 3, Veidt 3, Biro 4, Howe 4, Périnal 4)

Under the Roofs of Paris. *See* Sous les toits de Paris, 1930

Under the Sign of Scorpio. *See* Sotto il segno dello scorpione, 1969

Under the Southern Cross. *See* Under Södra Korset, 1952

Under the Sun of Rome. *See* Sotto il sole di Roma, 1948

Under the Tonto Rim, 1928 (Hathaway 2, Schulberg 4)

Under the Tonto Rim, 1933 (Hathaway 2)

Under the Tonto Rim, 1947 (Hunt 4)

Under the Top, 1918 (Cruze 2, Crisp 3, Emerson 4, Loos 4)

Under the Volcano, 1984 (Fernández 2, Huston 2, Finney 3, Figueroa 4, North 4)

Under the Yoke, 1918 (Bara 3)

Under the Yoke of Sin. *See* Vo vlasti gretcha, 1915

Under the Yum Yum Tree, 1963 (Lemmon 3, Biroc 4, Cahn 4)

Under Two Flags, 1916 (Bara 3)

Under Two Flags, 1922 (Browning 2)

Under Two Flags, 1936 (Carradine 3, Colbert 3, Colman 3, McLaglen 3, Russell 3, Meredyth 4, Zanuck 4)

Under Two Jags, 1923 (Laurel and Hardy 3, Roach 4)

Under Western Skies, 1910 (Anderson 3)

Under Western Skies, 1926 (Miller 4)

Under Western Skies, 1945 (Bruckman 4)

Under Western Stars, 1938 (Rogers 3)

Under Your Hat, 1940 (Henreid 3, Terry-Thomas 3)

Under Your Spell, 1936 (Preminger 2)

Underbara lögnen, 1955 (Nykvist 4)

Underbare Lüge der Nina Poetrowna, 1929 (Pommer 4)

Undercover, 1943 (Baker 3, Balcon 4)

Undercover, 1987 (Golan and Globus 4)

Undercover Doctor, 1939 (Crawford 3, Head 4)

Undercover Hero. *See* Soft Beds and Hard Battles, 1973

Undercover Maisie, 1947 (Irene 4)

Under-Cover Man, 1932 (Raft 3, Fort 4, Head 4)

Undercover Man, 1942 (Harlan 4)

Undercover Man, 1949 (Lewis 2, Rossen 2, Ford 3, Duning 4, Guffey 4)

Undercurrent, 1946 (Minnelli 2, Hepburn 3, Mitchum 3, Taylor 3, Berman 4, Freund 4, Irene 4, Previn 4, Stothart 4)

Undercurrent. See Yoruno kawa, 1956

Underdog, 1932 (Lantz 4)

Underground, 1928 (Asquith 2)

Underground, 1941 (Deutsch 4, Wallis 4)

Underground. See Undercover, 1943

Underground, 1976 (De Antonio 2, Wexler 4)

Underground Guerillas. See Undercover, 1943

Underground U.S.A., 1980 (Jarmusch 2)

Underneath the Arches, 1937 (Crazy Gang 3)

Under-Pup, 1939 (Bondi 3, Mohr 4, Pasternak 4)

Undersea Kingdom, 1936 (Lewis 2, Eason 4)

Understanding Heart, 1927 (Crawford 3, Gibbons 4)

Understudy, 1912 (Bushman 3)

Understudy, 1915 (Costello 3)

Undertakers. See Tomuraishi tachi, 1968

Undertow, 1930 (Mandell 4)

Undertow, 1949 (Hudson 3, Orry-Kelly 4)

Underwater, 1955 (Sturges 2, Russell 3, D'Agostino 4)

Underwater Odyssey. See Neptune Factor, 1973

Underwater Warrior, 1958 (Biroc 4)

Undia de vida, 1950 (Fernández 2)

Undici moschettieri, 1951 (Delli Colli 4)

Undine, 1912 (Cruze 2)

Undying Flame, 1917 (Tourneur 2, Carré 4)

Undying Monster, 1942 (Ballard 4, Day 4, Raksin 4)

Une chante l'autre pas, 1977 (Varda 2)

Une et l'autre, 1967 (Noiret 3)

Unearthly, 1957 (Carradine 3)

Uneasy Three, 1925 (McCarey 2, Roach 4)

Unendliche Fahrt—aber begrenzt, 1965 (Kluge 2)

Unerreichbare Nahe, 1984 (Von Trotta 2)

Unexpected. See Anhonee, 1952

Unexpected Father, 1939 (Darwell 3)

Unexpected Fireworks. See Feu d'artifice improvisé, 1905

Unexpected Help, 1910 (Griffith 2, Bitzer 4)

Unexpected Pest, 1956 (Blanc 4, McKimson 4, Stalling 4)

Unexpected Review, 1911 (Bunny 3)

Unexpected Romance, 1915 (Anderson 3)

Unexpected Santa Claus, 1908 (Porter 2)

Unexpected Uncle, 1941 (Daves 2, Garnett 2, Coburn 3)

Unfaithful, 1931 (Cromwell 2, Lukas 3, Lang 4)

Unfaithful, 1947 (Arden 3, Ayres 3, Sheridan 3, Burks 4, Haller 4, Steiner 4, Wald 4)

Unfaithful Wife, 1903 (Bitzer 4)

Unfaithful Wife. See Femme infidèle, 1969

Unfaithfully Yours, 1948 (Sturges 2, Darnell 3, Harrison 3, LeMaire 4, Newman 4, Wheeler 4, Zanuck 4)

Unfaithfully Yours, 1984 (Levinson 2, Kinski 3, Moore 3)

Unfinished Business, 1941 (La Cava 2, Dunne 3, Montgomery 3, Waxman 4)

Unfinished Dance, 1947 (Charisse 3, O'Brien 3, Irene 4, Mayer 4, Pasternak 4, Rose 4, Stothart 4, Surtees 4)

Unfinished Fresco, 1924 (Volkov 2)

Unfinished Journey, 1943 (Gielgud 3)

Unfinished Love Song, 1919 (Kuleshov 2)

Unfinished Rainbows, 1941 (Ladd 3)

Unfinished Story. See Neokonchennaya povest, 1955

Unfinished Symphony. See Leise flehen meine Lieder, 1933

Unfinished Symphony, 1934 (Asquith 2)

Unfinished Tale. See Neokonchennaya povest, 1955

Unfit or The Strength of the Weak, 1914 (Hepworth 2)

Unfoldment, 1922 (Lawrence 3, Mohr 4)

Unforeseen Metamorphosis, 1912 (Cohl 4)

Unforgettable Year 1919. See Nezabyvayemyi 1919-god, 1952

Unforgiven, 1960 (Huston 2, Gish 3, Hepburn 3, Lancaster 3, Murphy 3, Jeakins 4, Maddow 4, Planer 4, Tiomkin 4)

Unforgiven, 1992 (Bumstead 4)

Unforseen Complication, 1910 (White 3)

Unfriendly Enemies, 1925 (Laurel and Hardy 3, Roach 4)

Unfriendly Fruit, 1916 (Lloyd 3)

Unfug der Liebe, 1928 (Wiene 2)

Ung flukt, 1959 (Ullmann 3)

Ungarische Rhapsodie, 1913 (Porten 3, Messter 4)

Ungarische Rhapsodie, 1928 (Dagover 3, Hoffmann 4, Pommer 4)

Ungarmädel. See Zigeunerblut, 1934

Ungarn in Flammen, 1957 (Schell 3)

Ungdommens Ret, 1911 (Psilander 3)

Ungekusst soll man nicht schlaten geh'n, 1936 (Stradling 4)

Ungkarlspappan, 1934 (Molander 2)

Unglassed Windows Cast a Terrible Reflection, 1953 (Brakhage 2)

Unguarded Hour, 1936 (Wood 2, Young 3, Irene 4)

Unguarded Moment, 1956 (Russell 3, Williams 3, Daniels 4)

Unguarded Women, 1924 (Astor 3, Daniels 3)

Unhappy Finish, 1921 (Sennett 2)

Unheilbar, 1916 (Jannings 3)

Unheimliche Geschichten, 1919 (Veidt 3, Hoffmann 4)

Unheimliche Geschichten, 1932 (Wegener 3)

Unheimlichen Wünsche, 1939 (Tschechowa 3)

Unholy, 1988 (Howard 3)

Unholy Four. See Stranger Came Home, 1954

Unholy Garden, 1931 (Colman 3, Wray 3, Barnes 4, Day 4, Goldwyn 4, Hecht 4, MacArthur 4, Newman 4, Toland 4)

Unholy Love. See Alraune, 1927

Unholy Night, 1929 (Barrymore 3, Karloff 3, Adrian 4, Day 4, Gibbons 4, Hecht 4)

Unholy Night. See Spectre vert, 1930

Unholy Partner, 1941 (Robinson 3)

Unholy Partners, 1941 (LeRoy 2, Dalio 3, Barnes 4, Gibbons 4)

Unholy Rollers, 1972 (Corman 2)

Unholy Three, 1925 (Browning 2, Chaney 3, McLaglen 3, Gibbons 4, Mayer 4, Young 4)

Unholy Three, 1930 (Chaney 3, Gibbons 4, Mayer 4, Shearer 4)

Unholy Wife, 1957 (Bondi 3, Dors 3, Steiger 3, Ballard 4, D'Agostino 4)

Unicorn. See Enhörningen, 1955

Unicorn Fist, 1973 (Lee 3)

Unicorn in the Garden, 1953 (Bosustow 4, Raksin 4)

Unidentified Flying Oddball. See Spaceman and King Arthur, 1979

Uniform Lovers. See Hold 'em Yale, 1935

Uniformes et grandes manoeuvres, 1950 (Fernandel 3)

Uninhibited. See Pianos mécaniques, 1965

Uninvited, 1944 (Crisp 3, Milland 3, Brackett 4, Dreier 4, Head 4, Lang 4, Young 4)

Uninvited Pests, 1946 (Terry 4)

Union Depot, 1932 (Blondell 3, Polito 4)

Union Pacific, 1939 (De Mille 2, McCrea 3, Preston 3, Quinn 3, Stanwyck 3, Dreier 4, Edouart 4, Head 4, Macpherson 4, Sullivan 4)

Union Pacific Railroad Scenes, 1901 (Bitzer 4)

Union Pacific Railroad Shots, 1899 (Bitzer 4)

Union sacrée, 1915 (Feuillade 2, Musidora 3)

Union Square, 1950 (Fitzgerald 3)

Union Station, 1950 (Holden 3, Dreier 4, Maté 4)

United Action, 1940 (Maddow 4)

United States Mail. See Appointment with Danger, 1951

United States Smith, 1927 (Robinson 4)

Univermag, 1922 (Vertov 2)

Universe, 1961 (Meredith 3)

Universe d'Utrillo, 1954 (Jarre 4)

Unkissed Man, 1929 (McCarey 2, Harlow 3)

Unknown, 1927 (Browning 2, Chaney 3, Crawford 3, Day 4, Gibbons 4, Mayer 4, Young 4)

Unknown Blonde, 1934 (Pangborn 3)

Unknown Cavalier, 1926 (Brown 4, Polito 4)

Unknown Claim, 1910 (Anderson 3)

Unknown Guest, 1943 (Tiomkin 4)

Unknown Man, 1951 (Pidgeon 3, Rose 4)

Unknown Purple, 1923 (Walthall 3)

Unknown Soldier, 1926 (Walthall 3)

Unknown Terror, 1957 (Biroc 4)

Unknown Valley, 1933 (Bond 3)

Unknown Violinist, 1912 (Bunny 3)

Unknown Woman. See Okända, 1913

Unlawful Trade, 1914 (Dwan 2, Chaney 3)

Unlucky Woman. See Boogie Woogie Dream, 1942

Unmarried, 1939 (Crabbe 3, O'Connor 3, Head 4)

Unmarried. See Glasberget, 1953

Unmarried Bachelor, 1941 (Young 3)

Unmarried Woman, 1977 (Mazursky 2, Bates 3, Clayburgh 3)

Unmentionables, 1963 (Blanc 4, Freleng 4)

Unmögliche, 1936 (Von Harbou 4)

Unmögliche Frau, 1936 (Fröhlich 3)

Unmögliche Liebe, 1932 (Nielsen 3)

Unnatural Hare, 1959 (Blanc 4)

Uno tra la folla, 1946 (Fusco 4)

Unos bankéré Fuxe, 1923 (Ondra 3, Heller 4)

Unpainted Woman, 1919 (Browning 2, Young 4)

Unpardonable Sin, 1916 (Gaudio 4)

Unpardonable Sin, 1919 (Neilan 2, Beery 3, Sweet 3)
Unplanned Elopement, 1914 (Bushman 3)
Unpopular Mechanic, 1936 (Lantz 4)
Unprotected, 1916 (Sweet 3)
Unprotected Female, 1903 (Bitzer 4)
Unpublished Story, 1942 (Launder and Gilliat 2, Dillon 4, Havelock-Allan 4, Rank 4)
Unremarkable Life, 1989 (Winters 3)
Unruly Hare, 1945 (Blanc 4, Stalling 4)
Uns et les autres, 1981 (Lelouch 2, Caan 3, Chaplin 3, Olbrychski 3, Lai 4)
Unseeing Eyes, 1923 (Barrymore 3)
Unseen, 1945 (Marshall 3, McCrea 3, Chandler 4, Dreier 4, Houseman 4, Seitz 4)
Unseen Defense, 1913 (Bosworth 3)
Unseen Enemy, 1912 (Griffith 2, Carey 3, Gish 3, Bitzer 4)
Unseen Hands, 1924 (Beery 3)
Unseen Heroes. See Battle of the V 1, 1958
Unseen Vengeance, 1914 (Eason 4)
Unser Mann in Dschungel, 1986 (Mueller-Stahl 3)
Unser täglich Brot, 1949 (Eisler 4)
Unsere Leichen Leben Noch, 1981 (Preminger 2)
Unshrinkable Jerry Mouse, 1964 (Jones 4)
Unsichtbare Front, 1932 (Pasternak 4)
Unsichtbare Gegner, 1933 (Homolka 3, Lorre 3, Schüfftan 4, Spiegel 4)
Unsinkable Molly Brown, 1964 (Walters 2, Reynolds 3, Ames 4, Edens 4, Gillespie 4)
Unsterbliche Herz, 1939 (Wegener 3, Warm 4)
Unsterbliche Lump, 1930 (Fröhlich 3, Herlth 4, Hoffmann 4, Röhrig 4)
Unsuspected, 1947 (Curtiz 2, Rains 3, Burks 4, Grot 4, Meredyth 4, Waxman 4)
Untamable Whiskers. See Roi du maquillage, 1904
Untamed, 1920 (Mix 3)
Untamed, 1929 (Crawford 3, Montgomery 3, Brown 4, Day 4, Freed 4, Gibbons 4, Mayer 4, Polglase 4)
Untamed, 1940 (Darwell 3, Milland 3, Dreier 4, Head 4, Young 4)
Untamed, 1955 (King 2, Hayward 3, Moorehead 3, Power 3, Jennings 4, Waxman 4)
Untamed. See Arakure, 1957
Untamed Breed, 1948 (Brown 4, Duning 4)
Untamed Frontier, 1952 (Cotten 3, Van Cleef 3, Winters 3, Salter 4)
Untamed Lady, 1926 (Swanson 3)
Untel Pere et Fils, 1943 (Duvivier 2, Jourdan 3, Jouvet 3, Morgan 3, Raimu 3, Achard 4, Spaak 4)
Unter Ausschluss der Öffentlichkeit, 1927 (Dieterle 2, Krauss 3)
Unter Ausschluss der Öffentlichkeit, 1937 (Baarová 3, Tschechowa 3, Wegener 3)
Unter den Brücken, 1945 (Käutner 2)
Unter falscher Flagge, 1932 (Fröhlich 3, Pasternak 4)
Unter Geiern, 1964 (Granger 3)
Unter Geschäftsaufsich. See Wehe, wenn er losgelassen, 1932
Unter heissem Himmel, 1936 (Albers 3, Herlth 4, Röhrig 4, Wagner 4)
Unter Palmen am blauen Meer, 1957 (Dagover 3)

Unter Räubern und Bestien, 1921 (Hoffmann 4)
Unternehman Michael, 1937 (Röhrig 4)
Untertan, 1949 (Staudte 2)
Until September, 1984 (Barry 4)
Until They Get Me, 1917 (Borzage 2)
Until They Sail, 1957 (Wise 2, Fontaine 3, Newman 3, Simmons 3, Cahn 4, Raksin 4, Ruttenberg 4, Schnee 4)
Untitled Film of Geoffrey Holder's Wedding, 1955 (Brakhage 2)
Untitled Film on Pittsburgh, 1959 (Brakhage 2)
Unto the Third Generation, 1913 (Lawrence 3)
Untouchables, 1987 (De Palma 2, Connery 3, Costner 3, De Niro 3, Morricone 4)
Unvanquished. See Aparajito, 1956
Unveiling, 1911 (Griffith 2, Bitzer 4)
Unwelcome Children. See Kreuzzug des Weibes, 1926
Unwelcome Guest, 1912 (Griffith 2, Pickford 3, Bitzer 4)
Unwelcome Guest, 1913 (Gish 3)
Unwelcome Mrs. Hatch, 1914 (Dwan 2)
Unwelcome Quest, 1912 (Carey 3)
Unwiderstehliche, 1937 (Ondra 3)
Unwilling Hero, 1921 (Gibbons 4)
Unwritten Code, 1944 (Edwards 2, Guffey 4)
Uogashi shunjitsu, 1952 (Yamamura 3)
Uomini . . . che mascalzoni, 1932 (De Sica 2)
Uomini, che mascalzoni!, 1953 (Age and Scarpelli 4, Rota 4)
Uomini contro, 1970 (Rosi 2, Cuny 3, Volonté 3, Guerra 4)
Uomini dal passo pesante, 1966 (Cotten 3)
Uomini e lupi, 1956 (Armendáriz 3, Mangano 3, Montand 3, Guerra 4, Zavattini 4)
Uomini e no, 1980 (Morricone 4)
Uomini e nobiluomini, 1959 (De Sica 2)
Uomini in piú, 1950 (Antonioni 2)
Uomini nella nebbia, 1955 (Fusco 4)
Uomini non guardano il cielo, 1951 (De Sica 2)
Uomini non sono ingrati, 1937 (Cervi 3)
Uomini sono nemici, 1948 (Mangano 3)
Uomo a metà, 1966 (Morricone 4)
Uomo che sorride, 1936 (De Sica 2)
Uomo che viene de lontano, 1968 (Van Cleef 3)
Uomo da bruciare, 1962 (Taviani 2, Volonté 3)
Uomo da rispettare, 1972 (Douglas 3, Delli Colli 4)
Uomo dai calzoni corti, o L'amore piu grande, 1958 (Valli 3)
Uomo dai cinque palloni, 1965 (Mastroianni 3)
Uomo dalle due ombre, 1971 (Mason 3)
Uomo dalle pelle dura, 1971 (Borgnine 3)
Uomo della croce, 1943 (Rossellini 2)
Uomo della Mancha. See Man of La Mancha, 1972
Uomo di Corleone, 1977 (Papas 3)
Uomo di paglia, 1957 (Germi 2, Cristaldi 4)
Uomo di rispettare, 1973 (Morricone 4)
Uomo, la bestia e la virtu, 1953 (Welles 2)
Uomo, l'orgoglio, la vendetta, 1967 (Kinski 3, Cecchi D'Amico 4)
Uomo ritorna, 1946 (Cervi 3, Magnani 3)
Uomo senza domenica, 1957 (De Santis 2)
Uomo venuto dal mare, 1941 (Fusco 4)

Up, 1980 (Halas and Batchelor 4)
Up a Tree, 1930 (Arbuckle 3)
Up and at 'em, 1924 (Roach 4)
Up and Going, 1922 (Mix 3)
Up for Murder, 1931 (Ayres 3, Beavers 3, Freund 4)
Up from the Beach, 1965 (Lumet 2, Crawford 3, Robertson 3, Rosay 3)
Up Goes Maisie, 1945 (Irene 4)
Up in Alf's Place, 1919 (Sennett 2)
Up in Arms, 1944 (Andrews 3, Calhern 3, Dumont 3, Kaye 3, Day 4, Goldwyn 4, Mandell 4)
Up in Central Park, 1948 (Durbin 3, Price 3, Green 4, Krasner 4)
Up in Daisy's Penthouse, 1953 (Three Stooges 3, Bruckman 4)
Up in Mabel's Room, 1926 (Garnett 2, Rosson 4)
Up in Mabel's Room, 1944 (Dwan 2)
Up in the Clouds. See Akash Kusum, 1965
Up in the World, 1956 (Wisdom 3, Rank 4)
Up Periscope!, 1959 (Garner 3, Oates 3, O'Brien 3)
Up Pops the Devil, 1931 (Lombard 3, Banton 4, Struss 4)
Up Pops the Duke, 1931 (Arbuckle 3)
Up Romance Road, 1918 (King 2)
Up San Juan Hill, 1909 (Bosworth 3, Mix 3, Selig 4)
Up She Goes. See Up Goes Maisie, 1945
Up the Creek, 1958 (Sellers 3)
Up the Down Staircase, 1967 (Mulligan 2, Pakula 2, Jenkins 4)
Up the Junction, 1965 (Loach 2, Havelock-Allan 4)
Up the MacGregors. See Sette donne per i MacGregor, 1966
Up the River, 1930 (Ford 2, Bogart 3, Brown 3, Tracy 3, August 4)
Up the River, 1938 (Darwell 3, Robinson 3)
Up the Sandbox, 1972 (Streisand 3, Horner 4, Willis 4, Winkler 4)
Up the Thames to Westminster, 1910 (Olcott 2)
Up to Date, 1989 (Dunaway 3)
Up to His Ears. See Tribulations d'un chinois en Chine, 1965
Up to His Neck, 1954 (Rank 4, Vetchinsky 4)
Up to Mars, 1930 (Fleischer 4)
Up with the Green Lift. See Oppåt med gröna hissen, 1952
Up Your Anchor. See Eskimo Ohgen, 1985
Up Your Teddy Bear, 1970 (Jones 4)
Upfront, 1951 (Metty 4)
Upheaval, 1916 (Barrymore 3)
Uphill All the Way, 1986 (Reynolds 3)
Upholding the Law, 1917 (August 4)
Upir z ferratu, 1982 (Brejchová 3)
Upkeep, 1973 (Hubley 4)
Upland Rider, 1928 (Brown 4, McCord 4)
Upon This Rock, 1970 (Bogarde 3, Evans 3)
Uppbrott, 1948 (Sucksdorff 2)
Uppehall i Myrlandet. See 4×4, 1965
Upper Crust, 1981 (Crawford 3)
Upper Hand, 1914 (Ingram 2)
Upper Hand. See Du Rififi à Paname, 1966
Upper Underworld, 1931 (Polito 4)
Uppercut, 1922 (Roach 4)
Uppercut O'Brien, 1929 (Sennett 2)
Upperworld, 1934 (Astor 3, Rogers 3, Rooney 3, Gaudio 4, Grot 4, Hecht 4)
Upright and Wrong, 1947 (Dunning 4)

Upright Sinner. *See* Brave Sünder, 1931
Uprising. *See* Aufstand, 1980
Ups and Downs, 1911 (Bunny 3)
Ups and Downs, 1914 (Beery 3)
Ups and Downs, 1915 (Laurel and Hardy 3)
Upstage, 1926 (Shearer 3, Gaudio 4,
  Gibbons 4, Gillespie 4, Mayer 4)
Upstairs, 1919 (Normand 3)
Upstairs and Downstairs, 1959 (Cardinale 3,
  Box 4, Rank 4)
Up-standing Sitter, 1948 (Blanc 4,
  McKimson 4)
Upstream, 1927 (Ford 2, Johnson 3,
  Clarke 4)
Upstream, 1931 (Grierson 2)
Upswept Hare, 1953 (Blanc 4, McKimson 4,
  Stalling 4)
Uptight, 1968 (Dassin 2, Hubley 4,
  Kaufman 4, Trauner 4)
Up-To-Date Conjurer. *See* Impressioniste fin
  de siècle, 1899
Uptown Saturday Night, 1974 (Poitier 3,
  Pryor 3)
Upturned Glass, 1947 (Mason 3, Rank 4)
Uragirareta mono, 1926 (Tanaka 3)
Urakaidan, 1965 (Tsukasa 3)
Ural, 1919 (Kuleshov 2)
Uran Khatola, 1955 (Kumar 3)
Uranium Boom, 1956 (Katzman 4)
Uranium Conspiracy, 1977 (Golan and
  Globus 4)
Uranus, 1991 (Depardieu 3, Noiret 3)
Urashima Taro no koei, 1946 (Takamine 3)

Urban Cowboy, 1980 (Travolta 3)
Urbanisme africain, 1962 (Rouch 2)
Ureshii koro, 1934 (Yamada 3)
Urfeus i underjorden, 1910 (Magnusson 4)
Urgano sul Po, 1955 (Schell 3)
Uriel Acosta, 1920 (Hoffmann 4)
Urlaub und Ehrenwort, 1937 (Röhrig 4)
Urlo, 1965 (Storaro 4)
Urodziny Matyldy, 1974 (Stawiński 4)
Urodziny młodego warszawiaka, 1980
  (Stawiński 4)
Ursule et Grelu, 1973 (Dalio 3, Girardot 3)
Uruhashiki ai, 1931 (Takamine 3)
Uruhashiki shuppatsu, 1939 (Takamine 3)
Us Paar, 1974 (Burman 4)
Us Two. *See* Nous deux, 1979
Used Cars, 1980 (Spielberg 2, Zemeckis 2)
Useful Sheep, 1912 (Sennett 2)
Userer, 1910 (Bitzer 4)
Users, 1978 (Curtis 3, Fontaine 3, Jarre 4)
Usmev diabla, 1988 (Tyszkiewicz 3)
Usne Kaha Tha, 1960 (Roy 2)
Ustedes los ricos, 1948 (Infante 3)
Usual Way, 1913 (Beery 3)
Usurer, 1910 (Griffith 2, Walthall 3)
Ut Mine Stromtid, 1920 (Dreier 4)
Uta-andon, 1943 (Yamada 3)
Utae wakodo-tachi, 1963 (Iwashita 3)
Utage, 1967 (Iwashita 3)
Utah, 1945 (Rogers 3)
Utah Blaine, 1956 (Katzman 4)
Utah Kid, 1930 (Karloff 3)
Uta-kichi andon, 1938 (Yamada 3)

Utamaro and Five Women. *See* Utamaro o
  mehuru go-nin no onna, 1946
Utamaro and His Five Women. *See* Utamaro
  o meguru gonin no onna, 1946
Utamaro o meguru gonin no onna,
  1946 (Mizoguchi 2, Tanaka 3,
  Yoda 4)
Utamaro o meguru gonin no onna, 1959
  (Hasegawa 3)
Utěky domů, 1979 (Brejchová 3)
Utinapló, 1989 (Mészáros 2)
Utközben, 1979 (Nowicki 3,
  Tyszkiewicz 3)
Utopia. *See* Atoll K, 1950
Utopia, 1978 (Sanda 3)
Utrpení mladé lásky. *See* Werther, 1927
Utsukishisa to kanashimi to, 1965
  (Yamamura 3)
Utsukushii hito, 1954 (Kagawa 3)
Utsukushiki batsu, 1949 (Yamamura 3)
Utsukushisa to kanashimi to, 1965
  (Takemitsu 4)
Utsukushisa to kanashimi to, 1965
  (Shinoda 2)
Utvandrarna, 1971 (Ullmann 3, Von
  Sydow 3)
Uwaki no susume, 1960 (Iwashita 3)
Uwasa no onna, 1954 (Mizoguchi 2,
  Shindo 3, Tanaka 3, Miyagawa 4,
  Yoda 4)
Uwayaku shitayaku godouyaku, 1959
  (Muraki 4)
Uzu, 1961 (Iwashita 3)

V blouzněni, 1928 (Stallich 4)
V boynoi slepote strastei, 1916
    (Mozhukin 3)
V for Victory, 1939 (McLaren 4)
V gorakh Ala-Tau, 1944 (Vertov 2)
V polnotch na kladbische, 1914
    (Mozhukin 3)
V prachu hvězd, 1975 (Brejchová 3)
V. Proudech, 1957 (Saulnier 4)
V roukatch bespotchadnogo roka, 1914
    (Mozhukin 3)
V tylu u belych, 1925 (Enei 4)
VI, 1944 (Jennings 2)
V.I. Warshawski, 1991 (Turner 3)
V.I.P.s, 1963 (Asquith 2, Welles 2,
    Burton 3, Jourdan 3, Rutherford 3,
    Smith 3, Taylor 3, Booth 4, De
    Grunwald 4, Fisher 4, Rattigan 4,
    Rozsa 4)
VTIK Train. See Agitpoezd VTsIK, 1921
VVVC Journal, 1931 (Ivens 2)
Va banque, 1930 (Dagover 3, Gründgens 3,
    Reisch 4)
Va voir maman, papa travaille, 1977
    (Presle 3, Delerue 4)
Vacances, 1938 (Storck 2)
Vacances au paradis, 1959 (Delerue 4)
Vacances blanches, 1951 (Decaë 4)
Vacances conjugales, 1933 (Brasseur 3)
**Vacances de Monsieur Hulot, 1953 (Tati 2,
    Grimault 4)**
Vacances du diable, 1930 (Goulding 2)
Vacances en enfer, 1961 (Fradetal 4)
Vacances explosives, 1956 (Arletty 3)
Vacances portugaises, 1962 (Deneuve 3,
    Gélin 3, Coutard 4, Delerue 4)
Vacanza, 1969 (Redgrave 3)
Vacanza, 1988 (Scola 2, Mastroianni 3)
Vacanza del diavolo, 1930 (Goulding 2)
Vacanze a Ischia, 1957 (De Sica 2)
Vacanze d'inverno, 1959 (De Sica 2,
    Morgan 3, Sordi 3)
Vacanze in Valtrebbia, 1981 (Bellocchio 2)
Vacation, 1924 (Fleischer 4)
Vacation. See Vacanza, 1969
Vacation Days, 1947 (Katzman 4)
Vacation from Love, 1938 (Adrian 4)
Vacation from Marriage. See Perfect
    Strangers, 1945
Vacation Loves, 1930 (Sennett 2)
Vache et le prisonnier, 1959 (Fernandel 3,
    Jeanson 4)
Vacuum Cleaner, 1980 (Halas and
    Batchelor 4)
Vad veta val männen?, 1933 (Jaenzon 4)
Vaeddeløberen, 1919 (Madsen and
    Schenstrøm 3)

Vagabond, 1916 (Bacon 2, Chaplin 2,
    Purviance 3)
Vagabond. See Aničko, vrať se!, 1926
Vagabond. See **Awara, 1951**
Vagabond. See Vagabonde, 1986
Vagabond Club, 1929 (Miller 4)
Vagabond King, 1930 (MacDonald 3,
    Banton 4, Dreier 4, Mankiewicz 4,
    Zukor 4)
Vagabond King, 1956 (Curtiz 2, Grayson 3,
    Price 3, Bumstead 4, Burks 4, Young 4)
Vagabond Lady, 1935 (Young 3, Roach 4)
Vagabond Loafers, 1949 (Three Stooges 3)
Vagabond Lover, 1929 (Neilan 2, Dressler 3,
    Plunkett 4)
Vagabond Queen, 1929 (Rosher 4)
Vagabond Trail, 1924 (Wellman 2,
    August 4)
Vagabond Violinist. See Broken Melody,
    1934
Vagabonde, 1918 (Musidora 3)
Vagabonde, 1931 (Fradetal 4)
Vagabonde, 1986 (Varda 3)
Vagabonds, 1912 (Olcott 2)
Vagabonds du rêve, 1949 (Rosay 3)
Vagabond's Galoshes. See Kolingens
    galoscher, 1912
Vägen till Kolckrike, 1953 (Nykvist 4)
Vaghe stelle dell'orsa, 1965 (Visconti 2,
    Cardinale 3, Cecchi D'Amico 4,
    Cristaldi 4)
Vagues, 1901 (Guy 2)
Vainqueur de la course pédestre, 1909
    (Feuillade 2)
Vaisseau sur la colline, 1960 (Delerue 4)
Val d'enfer, 1943 (Tourneur 2)
Valachi Papers, 1972 (Bronson 3, De
    Laurentiis 4)
Valahol Europaban, 1947 (Balàzs 4)
Valborgsmassoafton, 1935 (Sjöström 2,
    Bergman 3)
Valdez Horses. See Valdez il mezzosanque,
    1973
Valdez il mezzosanque, 1973 (Sturges 2,
    Bronson 3)
Valdez Is Coming, 1971 (Lancaster 3)
Valdez the Halfbreed. See Valdez il
    mezzosanque, 1973
Valencia, 1926 (Karloff 3, Gibbons 4,
    Gillespie 4, Mayer 4)
Valentin De Las Sierras, 1967 (Baillie 2)
Valentina, 1965 (Félix 3)
Valentina, 1981 (Panfilov 2, Quinn 3)
Valentina—The Virgin Wife. See Moglie
    virgine, 1976
Valentine Girl, 1917 (Barthelmess 3,
    Menjou 3)

Valentino, 1951 (Banton 4, Estabrook 4,
    Mandell 4, Stradling 4)
Valentino, 1977 (Russell 2, Caron 3,
    Russell 4, Winkler 4)
Valentino en Angleterre, 1923 (Florey 2)
Valerie, 1957 (Hayden 3, Laszlo 4)
Valet's Wife, 1908 (Lawrence 3, Bitzer 4)
Valfångare, 1939 (Fischer 4, Jaenzon 4)
Valiant, 1929 (Howard 2, Muni 3, Carré 4)
Valiant, 1962 (Mills 3, Shaw 3)
Valiant Is the Word for Carrie, 1936
    (Carey 3, McDaniel 3, Banton 4)
Valiant Tailor, 1934 (Iwerks 4)
Valientes no mueren, 1961 (Armendáriz 3)
Valigia dei sogni, 1953 (Comencini 2)
Valise, 1974 (Sarde 4)
Valise diplomatique, 1909 (Cohl 4)
Valise enchantée, 1903 (Guy 2)
Valle de las espadas, 1963 (Rey 3, Valli 3)
Vallée, 1972 (Almendros 4, Gégauff 4)
Vallée aux loups, 1966 (Fresnay 3)
Vallée fantôme, 1987 (Tanner 2,
    Trintignant 3)
Valley. See Vallée, 1972
Valley Forge, 1974 (Fonda 3)
Valley of Decision, 1915 (Bennett 3)
Valley of Decision, 1945 (Garnett 2,
    Barrymore 3, Crisp 3, Duryea 3,
    Garson 3, Peck 3, Gillespie 4, Irene 4,
    Levien 4, Mayer 4, Ruttenberg 4,
    Stothart 4)
Valley of Eagles, 1951 (Rota 4)
Valley of Esopus, 1906 (Bitzer 4)
Valley of Fire, 1951 (Autry 3)
Valley of Gwangi, 1969 (Harryhausen 4)
Valley of Head Hunters, 1953
    (Weissmuller 3)
Valley of Hell, 1927 (Stevens 2)
Valley of Night, 1919 (Barrymore 3)
Valley of Silent Men, 1922 (Borzage 2)
Valley of Song, 1952 (Roberts 3)
Valley of the Dolls, 1967 (Dreyfuss 3,
    Grant 3, Hayward 3, Daniels 4, Day 4,
    Previn 4, Smith 4, Williams 4)
Valley of the Dolls, 1981 (Simmons 3)
Valley of the Eagles, 1951 (Lee 3)
Valley of the Giants, 1919 (Cruze 2, Reid 3,
    Zukor 4)
Valley of the Giants, 1927 (McCord 4)
Valley of the Giants, 1938 (Crisp 3,
    Trevor 3, Deutsch 4, Friedhofer 4,
    Miller 4, Polito 4)
Valley of the Head Hunters, 1953
    (Katzman 4)
Valley of the Kings, 1954 (Taylor 3,
    Plunkett 4, Rozsa 4, Smith 4, Surtees 4)
Valley of the Moon, 1914 (Bosworth 3)

Valley of the Sun, 1942 (Ball 3)
Valley of Tomorrow, 1920 (Furthman 4)
Valley of Vengeance, 1944 (Crabbe 3)
Valley Town, 1940 (Van Dyke 2, Maddow 4)
Vallfarten till Kevlar, 1921 (Magnusson 4)
Valmiki, 1946 (Kapoor 2)
Valmont, 1989 (Forman 2, Carrière 4, Ondříček 4)
Valparaiso, Valparaiso, 1971 (Cuny 3)
Vals, 1985 (Carradine 3)
Valse brillante, 1936 (Ophüls 2, Planer 4)
Valse brillante, 1949 (Annenkov 4, Burel 4)
Valse de Paris, 1949 (Astruc 2, Fresnay 3, Achard 4, Matras 4)
Valse du gorille, 1959 (Vanel 3, Renoir 4)
Valse eternelle, 1936 (Brasseur 3)
Valse renversante, 1914 (Chevalier 3)
Valse royale, 1935 (Grémillon 2)
Valse Triste, 1977 (Conner 2)
Valseuses, 1973 (Depardieu 3, Huppert 3, Moreau 3)
Value for Money, 1955 (Dors 3, Pleasence 3, Rank 4, Unsworth 4, Vetchinsky 4)
Valvaire d'Amour, 1923 (Vanel 3)
Vamonos con Pancho Villa, 1935 (De Fuentes 2, Figueroa 4)
Vamos a matar, compañeros!, 1970 (Palance 3, Rey 3, Morricone 4)
Vamp, 1918 (Barnes 4, Ince 4, Sullivan 4)
Vamp till Ready, 1935 (Roach 4)
Vampir, 1969 (Lee 3)
Vampira, 1973 (Niven 3)
Vampiras, 1969 (Carradine 3)
Vampire. See Vampyren, 1912
Vampire, 1915 (Guy 2)
Vampire Ambrose, 1916 (Sennett 2)
Vampire Bat, 1933 (Douglas 3, Wray 3)
Vampire Beast Craves Blood. See Blood Beast Terror, 1968
Vampire Circus, 1972 (Carreras 4)
Vampire de Düsseldorf, 1964 (De Beauregard 4)
Vampire Happening. See Gebissen wird nur Nachts—Happening der Vampire, 1971
Vampire Hookers, 1978 (Carradine 3)
Vampire Lovers, 1970 (Cushing 3, Carreras 4)
Vampire Men of the Lost Planet. See Horror of the Blood Monsters, 1970
Vampire over London. See Old Mother Riley Meets the Vampire, 1952
Vampires, 1914 (Feuillade 2, Feyder 2, Musidora 3, Gaumont 4)
Vampires, 1915 (Feuillade 2)
Vampires. See Vampiras, 1969
Vampire's Ghost, 1945 (Brackett 4)
Vampyr ou l'étrange aventure de David Gray, 1932 (Dreyer 2, Fradetal 4, Maté 4, Warm 4)
Vampyren, 1912 (Sjöström 2, Jaenzon 4, Magnusson 4)
Vampyres, 1975 (Love 3)
Vampyres, Daughters of Darkness. See Vampyres, 1975
Van Gogh, 1948 (Resnais 2, Braunberger 4)
Vanderbeekiana, 1968 (Vanderbeek 2)
Vanderbilt Cup Auto Race, 1904 (Bitzer 4)
Vanessa: Her Love Story, 1935 (Howard 2, Crisp 3, Montgomery 3, Coffee 4, Selznick 4, Stothart 4)
Vanganza, 1957 (Rey 3)
Vangelo '70. See Amore e rabbia, 1969

Vangelo secondo Matteo, 1964 (Pasolini 2, Delli Colli 4, Donati 4)
Vanille fraise, 1989 (Cristaldi 4)
Vanina, 1922 (Nielsen 3, Wegener 3, Mayer 4, Pommer 4)
Vanina Vanini. See Vanina, 1922
Vanina Vanini, 1961 (Rossellini 2, Solinas 4)
Vanish, 1978 (Kuri 4)
Vanished, 1971 (Widmark 3, Young 3)
Vanishing Act, 1986 (Gould 3)
Vanishing American, 1955 (Van Cleef 3)
Vanishing Body. See Black Cat, 1934
Vanishing Cornwall, 1958 (Redgrave 3)
Vanishing Duck, 1957 (Hanna and Barbera 4)
Vanishing Lady. See Escamotage d'une dame chez Robert-Houdin, 1896
Vanishing Legion, 1931 (Carey 3, Canutt 4, Eason 4)
Vanishing Pioneer, 1928 (Powell 3)
Vanishing Point, 1970 (Alonzo 4)
Vanishing Prairie, 1954 (Iwerks 4)
Vanishing Race, 1911 (Dwan 2)
Vanishing Race, 1928 (Zukor 4)
Vanishing Rider, 1928 (Karloff 3)
Vanishing Shadow, 1934 (Cobb 3)
Vanishing Virginian, 1942 (Borzage 2, Beavers 3, Grayson 3)
Vanishing West, 1928 (Canutt 4)
Vanity, 1927 (Crisp 3, Johnson 3, Adrian 4, Grot 4, Miller 4, Sullivan 4)
Vanity and Its Cure, 1911 (Lawrence 3)
Vanity Fair, 1911 (Bunny 3)
Vanity Fair, 1923 (Bosworth 3)
Vanity Fair, 1932 (Loy 3)
Vanity Street, 1932 (August 4)
Vanity's Price, 1924 (Mohr 4)
Vanity's Price, 1957 (Von Sternberg 2)
Vánočni, 1946 (Zeman 4)
Vanquished. See Vinti, 1952
Vanquished, 1953 (Head 4)
Väntande vatten, 1965 (Fischer 4)
Vantour de la Sierra, 1909 (Gaumont 4)
Vaquero's Vow, 1908 (Griffith 2, Lawrence 3, Bitzer 4)
Var i Maj, 1914 (Sjöström 2)
Var sin väg, 1948 (Björnstrand 3, Dahlbeck 3)
Varan the Unbelievable. See Daikaiju Baran, 1958
Vargtimmen, 1968 (Josephson 3, Thulin 3, Ullmann 3, Von Sydow 3, Nykvist 4)
Varhaník v sv. Víta, 1929 (Frič 2)
Variable Studies, 1960 (Emshwiller 2)
Variációk egy témára, 1961 (Szabó 2)
Variaciones, 1963 (Solas 2)
Variations No. 5, 1965 (Vanderbeek 2)
Variations on a Mechanical Theme, 1959 (Russell 2)
Variations on a Theme. See Variációk egy témára, 1961
Variation sur le geste, 1962 (Storck 2)
Variété, 1925 (Jannings 3, Freund 4, Pommer 4, Schüfftan 4)
Variétés, 1935 (Albers 3, Gabin 3)
Varietes, 1971 (Bardem 2, Matras 4)
Variety. See **Variété, 1925**
Variety, 1966 (Burton 3)
Variety, 1977 (Canutt 4)
Variety Girl, 1947 (De Mille 2, Tashlin 2, Bendix 3, Cooper 3, Crosby 3, Fitzgerald 3, Goddard 3, Hayden 3, Holden 3, Hope 3, Ladd 3, Lake 3, Lamour 3, Lancaster 3, Milland 3, Preston 3, Stanwyck 3, Dreier 4, Head 4)

Variety Lights. See Luci del varietà, 1950
Variety Show, 1937 (Barnes 4)
Variola vera, 1982 (Josephson 3)
Var-matin, 1976 (Leenhardt 2)
Varmlanningarne, 1909 (Magnusson 4)
Várostérkép, 1977 (Szabó 2)
Varsity, 1928 (Estabrook 4)
Varsity Girl. See Fair Co-ed, 1927
Varsity Show, 1937 (Berkeley 2, Powell 3, Mercer 4, Polito 4, Wald 4)
Vascular Passes, 1982 (Emshwiller 2)
Vášeň, 1961 (Trnka 4)
Vases of Hymen, 1914 (Bunny 3)
Vash syn i brat, 1965 (Shukshin 3)
Vassa, 1983 (Panfilov 2)
Vasundhara, 1983 (Chatterjee 3)
Vas-y maman, 1978 (Girardot 3)
Vatan, 1938 (Biswas 4)
Vater und Sonhe, 1988 (Ganz 3)
Vater werden ist nicht schwer . . . , 1926 (Wagner 4)
Vatican Affair. See Qualsiasi prezzo, 1968
Vatican Pimpernel, 1982 (Gielgud 3)
Vatican Story. See Qualsiasi prezzo, 1968
Vaudeville, 1924 (Fleischer 4)
Vaughan Williams, 1984 (Russell 2)
Vault of Horror, 1973 (Elliott 3, Terry-Thomas 3)
Vautrin, 1943 (Simon 3)
Vautrin the Thief. See Vautrin, 1943
Vavasour Ball, 1914 (Talmadge 3)
Vavocka, 1941 (Volkov 2)
Vdavky Nanynky Kulichovy, 1925 (Ondra 3, Heller 4)
Veau, 1908 (Cohl 4)
Veau gras, 1939 (Kaufman 4)
Vecchia guardia, 1934 (Blasetti 2)
Vecchia signora, 1932 (De Sica 2)
Vecchie amicizie, 1956 (Delli Colli 4)
Večery s Jindřichem Plachtou, 1954 (Stallich 4)
Ved Faengslets Port, 1911 (Psilander 3)
Ved Vejen. See Katinka, 1988
. . . Veda silahlara veda . . . , 1966 (Güney 2)
Vedo nudo, 1969 (Vitti 3)
Vedova, 1957 (Milestone 2)
Vedova allegro, 1949 (Age and Scarpelli 4)
Vedova scaltra, 1922 (Gallone 2)
Vedovo, 1959 (Sordi 3)
Veena, 1948 (Biswas 4)
Veertig Jaren, 1938 (Heller 4)
Vegas, 1978 (Allyson 3, Curtis 3)
Vegas Strip War, 1984 (Hudson 3, Jones 3)
Vegetarian's Dream, 1912 (Cohl 4)
Veilchenfresser, 1926 (Dagover 3, Andrejew 4)
Veiled Lady, 1910 (White 3)
Veiled Woman, 1929 (Lugosi 3, Clarke 4)
Veille d'Armes, 1926 (Modot 3)
Veille d'armes, 1935 (L'Herbier 2, Spaak 4)
Veils of Baghdad, 1953 (Mature 3)
Veinard. See That Lucky Touch, 1975
Veinards, 1962 (Broca 2)
Vein of Gold, 1910 (Anderson 3)
Veine d'Anatole. See Gros Lot, 1933
Vel' d'hiv', 1960 (Audiard 4, Jarre 4)
Velbound uchem jehly, 1926 (Ondra 3)
Veleno della parole, 1914 (Bertini 3)
Velha a Fiar, 1964 (Mauro 2)
Velia, 1980 (Cecchi D'Amico 4)
Veliki strah, 1958 (Vukotić 4)
Velikii grazhdanin, 1938 (Shostakovich 4)

Veliky put', 1927 (Shub 2)
Velké dobrodružství, 1952 (Brdečka 4)
Velour, 1967 (Bujold 3)
Velvet Fingers, 1920 (Grot 4)
Velvet Paw, 1916 (Tourneur 2, Carré 4)
Velvet Touch, 1948 (Greenstreet 3, Russell 3, Trevor 3, Banton 4, Walker 4)
Velvet Underground, 1966 (Warhol 2)
Velvet Vampire, 1971 (Corman 2)
Vem dömer, 1922 (Sjöström 2, Jaenzon 4, Magnusson 4)
Vem Skot?, 1916 (Magnusson 4)
Vendanges, 1922 (Epstein 2)
Vendémiaire, 1918 (Feuillade 2, Gaumont 4)
Vendetta, 1905 (Pathé 4)
Vendetta, 1920 (Jannings 3, Negri 3)
Vendetta, 1946 (Ophüls 2)
Vendetta, 1950 (Sturges 2, Burnett 4, Hughes 4, Planer 4)
Vendetta. See Joaquin Murieta, 1964
Vendetta di Aquila Nera, 1951 (Brazzi 3)
Vendetta di Ercole, 1960 (Crawford 3)
Vendetta di una pazza, 1951 (Baarová 3)
Vendetta e un piatto che si serve freddo, 1971 (Kinski 3)
Vendetta en Camargue, 1950 (Kosma 4)
Vendetta nel sole, 1947 (Lollobrigida 3)
Vendetta of Samurai. See Ketto kagiya no tsuji, 1952
Venditore di morte, 1972 (Kinski 3)
Venditore di palloncini, 1974 (Cobb 3, Cusack 3)
Venedig—die Insel der Glückseligen am Rande am des Untergangs, 1978 (Ballhaus 4)
Venere imperiale, 1962 (Castellani 2, Lollobrigida 3, Presle 3, Aurenche 4)
Venetian Affair, 1967 (Karloff 3, Krasner 4, Schifrin 4)
Venetian Bird, 1952 (Box 4, Rank 4, Rota 4)
Venetian Lies. See Footloose, 1979
Venezia città minore, 1958 (Olmi 2)
Venezia, la luna, e tu, 1958 (Sordi 3, Delli Colli 4)
Venezia, una Mostra per il cinema, 1982 (Blasetti 2)
Veneziana, 1986 (Morricone 4)
Venezianische Nacht, 1914 (Freund 4)
Venganza de Heraclio Bernal, 1957 (Figueroa 4)
Vengeance. See Haevnet, 1911
Vengeance, 1930 (Cohn 4)
Vengeance, 1962 (Francis 4)
Vengeance. See Pomsta, 1968
Vengeance. See Noroît, 1976
Vengeance de Riri, 1908 (Cohl 4)
Vengeance d'Edgar Poe, 1912 (Gance 2)
Vengeance des esprits. See Jobard fiance par interim, 1911
Vengeance du domestique, 1912 (Linder 3)
Vengeance du sergent de ville, 1913 (Feuillade 2)
Vengeance du serpent à plumes, 1984 (Decaë 4)
Vengeance d'une femme, 1990 (Huppert 3)
Vengeance d'une orpheline russe, 1965 (Braunberger 4)
Vengeance Is Mine, 1917 (Miller 4)
Vengeance Is Mine. See **Fukushu suru wa ware ni ari, 1979**
Vengeance of Fate, 1912 (Ince 4)
Vengeance of Fu Manchu, 1967 (Lee 3)
Vengeance of Galora, 1913 (Barrymore 3)
Vengeance of She, 1968 (Carreras 4)

Vengeance of the 47 Ronin. See Chushingura, 1932
Vengeance of the West, 1916 (Chaney 3)
Vengeance that Failed, 1911 (Dwan 2)
Vengeance Trail. See Vendetta e un piatto che si serve freddo, 1971
Vengeance Valley, 1950 (Folsey 4, Plunkett 4)
Vengeance Valley, 1951 (Lancaster 3, Walker 3, Ravetch 4)
Venice. See Venedig—die Insel der Glückseligen am Rande am des Untergangs, 1978
Venice, the Moon, and You. See Venezia, la luna, e tu, 1958
Venice: Themes and Variations, 1957 (Ivory 2)
Venir du Havre, 1962 (Braunberger 4)
Venise et ses amants, 1950 (Cocteau 2)
Venise, une nuit, 1937 (Christian-Jaque 2)
Venom, 1982 (Hayden 3, Kinski 3, Reed 3)
Vent d'est, 1970 (Ferreri 2, Godard 2, Volonté 3)
Vent'anni, 1950 (Zavattini 4)
Vent se lève, 1958 (Bost 4)
Vent souffle où il veut. See **Condamné à mort s'est échappé, 1956**
Vento del sud, 1959 (Cardinale 3, Cristaldi 4, Di Venanzo 4)
Vento mi ha cantato una canzone, 1948 (Sordi 3)
Ventriloquist Cat, 1950 (Avery 4)
Ventriloquist Cat, 1955 (Avery 4)
Ventriloquist's Trunk, 1911 (Bunny 3)
Vénus, 1928 (Burel 4)
Vénus aveugle, 1941 (Gance 2, Alekan 4, Burel 4)
Vénus de l'or, 1938 (Delannoy 2)
Vénus et Adonis, 1900 (Guy 2)
Vénus impériale. See Venere imperiale, 1962
Venus in Furs. See Paroxismus, 1969
Venus in the East, 1918 (Crisp 3)
Venus Makes Trouble, 1937 (Ballard 4)
Venus Model, 1918 (Normand 3)
Venus of Venice, 1927 (Neilan 2, Barnes 4, Schenck 4)
Venus Victrix, 1916 (Dulac 2)
Venus von Montmartre, 1925 (Albers 3, Tschechowa 3)
Vera Cruz, 1954 (Aldrich 2, Borgnine 3, Bronson 3, Cooper 3, Lancaster 3, Cahn 4, Chase 4, Friedhofer 4, Laszlo 4)
Vera Holgk und ihre Töchter. See Unmögliche Liebe, 1932
Vera Panina, 1918 (Gad 2)
Vera storia della signora delle Camelie, 1981 (Huppert 3, Rey 3, Volonté 3, Morricone 4)
Verano de la Señora Forbes, 1988 (Hermosillo 2, Schygulla 3)
Verano sangrieto, 1977 (Van Cleef 3)
Verboten, 1958 (Fuller 2, Biroc 4)
Verbotene Land, 1924 (Banky 3)
Verbotene Stadt, 1920 (Wiene 2)
Verbotene Weg, 1920 (Galeen 4)
Verbotene Weg, 1923 (Pick 2)
Verdadera vocación de Magdalena, 1971 (Hermosillo 2)
Verdict, 1946 (Siegel 2, Greenstreet 3, Lorre 3, Burks 4, Haller 4)
Verdict. See Testament, 1974
Verdict, 1982 (Lumet 2, Mason 3, Newman 3)

Verdugo, 1963 (García Berlanga 2, Delli Colli 4, Flaiano 4)
Verdugo de Sevilla, 1942 (Figueroa 4)
Verdun, visions d'histoire, 1928 (Artaud 3)
Veredas, 1977 (De Almeida 4)
Vererbte Triebe, 1929 (Albers 3)
Vererbte Triebe: Der Kampf ums neue Geschlecht, 1929 (Albers 3)
Verflucht dies Amerika, 1973 (Chaplin 3)
Verfuhrte, 1914 (Wegener 3)
Verführte Heilige, 1919 (Wiene 2)
Vergangenheit rächt sich, 1917 (Gad 2)
Vergiftete Brunnen, 1921 (Gad 2)
Vergine del Roncador, 1953 (Fusco 4)
Vergine de Norimberga, 1964 (Lee 3)
Vergine di Roma, 1961 (Jourdan 3, Piccoli 3)
Vergine moderna, 1954 (De Sica 2, Flaiano 4)
Vergine per il principe, 1965 (Gassman 3)
Vergiss, wenn Du kannst, 1956 (Fröhlich 3)
Vergödö szívek, 1916 (Korda 2, Korda 4)
Vergogna schifosi, 1968 (Morricone 4)
Verhängnisvolle Andenken, 1918 (Gad 2)
Verirrte Jugend, 1929 (Baranovskaya 3)
Veritáaa, 1982 (Zavattini 4)
Veritas Vincit, 1920 (Leni 2)
Vérité, 1960 (Clouzot 2, Bardot 3, Vanel 3)
Vérité sur Bébé Donge, 1951 (Darrieux 3, Gabin 3, Burel 4)
Vérités et mensonges. See F for Fake, 1975
Verkannt, 1910 (Porten 3, Messter 4)
Verliebte Frima, 1932 (Ophüls 2, Fröhlich 3, Verliebte Hotel, 1933 (Ondra 3, Heller 4)
Verliebtes Abenteuer, 1938 (Tschechowa 3)
Verlobten des Todes. See Fidanzati della morte, 1956
Verlogene Moral, 1921 (Freund 4, Mayer 4)
Verlorene, 1964 (Lorre 3)
Verlorene Ehre der Katharina Blum, 1975 (Schlöndorff 2, Von Trotta 2, Winkler 3)
Verlorene Gesicht, 1948 (Fröhlich 3)
Verlorene Schatten, 1920 (Wegener 3, Freund 4, Reiniger 4)
Verlorene Schuh, 1923 (Tschechowa 3, Pommer 4)
Vermachtnis des Inka, 1966 (Rey 3)
Vermilion Pencil, 1922 (Hayakawa 3, Love 3)
Vermischte Nachrichten, 1987 (Kluge 2)
Verna—USO Girl, 1978 (Hurt 3, Spacek 3)
Věrni zustaneme, 1945 (Weiss 2)
Verona Trial. See Processo a Verona, 1963
Veronika Voss. See Sehnsucht der Veronika Voss, 1982
Véronique et son cancre, 1958 (Rohmer 2)
Verrat. See Kampf um Rom II, 1969
Verrat an Deutschland, 1955 (Warm 4)
Verrat ist kein Gesselschaftsspiel, 1972 (Staudte 2)
Verräter, 1936 (Baarová 3, Röhrig 4)
Verräterin, 1911 (Gad 2)
Vers de la grappe, 1955 (Rabier 4)
Vers l'abine, 1934 (Rosay 3)
Vers l'extase, 1959 (Matras 4, Spaak 4)
Versailles. See Si Versailles m'était conté, 1954
Versailles, 1969 (Alekan 4)
Versailles et ses fantômes, 1948 (Braunberger 4)
Versatile Villain, 1915 (Sennett 2)
Verschleierte Dame, 1917 (Pommer 4)
Verschlossene Tür, 1917 (Gad 2)

Verschollene Inka-Gold, 1978 (Staudte 2)
Verschwörung zu Genua. *See* Fiesco, 1921
Version latine, 1969 (Chabrol 2)
Versions/Stages, 1989 (Emshwiller 2)
Verso la vita, 1946 (Risi 2)
Verso sera, 1990 (Mastroianni 3)
Verspätung in Marienborn, 1963 (Ferrer 3)
Verspieltes Leben, 1949 (Herlth 4)
Versprich mir nichts!, 1937 (Von Harbou 4)
Versuchung, 1981 (Zanussi 2)
Versuchung in Sommerwind, 1972
    (Käutner 2)
Versunkene Flotte, 1926 (Albers 3)
Versunkene Welt, 1922 (Lukas 3, Korda 4)
Vertauschte Braut, 1915 (Krauss 3)
Vertauschte Braut, 1925 (Junge 4)
Vertauschte Braut, 1934 (Ondra 3,
    Heller 4)
Vertauschte Braut, 1934 (Walbrook 3)
Vertauschte Gesichter, 1929 (Warm 4)
Vertical Features Remake, 1978
    (Greenaway 2)
Vertige, 1926 (L'Herbier 2)
Vertige, 1934 (Arletty 3)
Vertige d'un soir, 1936 (Vanel 3)
Vertiges, 1985 (Branco 4, De Almeida 4)
Vertigine d'Amore, 1948 (Vanel 3)
Vertigo. *See* Dourman, 1912
Vértigo, 1945 (Félix 3)
Vertigo, 1958 (Hitchcock 2, Novak 3,
    Stewart 3, Bass 4, Bumstead 4,
    Burks 4, Edouart 4, Fulton 4, Head 4,
    Herrmann 4, Mathieson 4)
Vertigo, 1986 (Emshwiller 2)
Vertu de Lucette, 1912 (Feuillade 2)
Veruschka—Poesia di una donna, 1971
    (Morricone 4)
Verwegene Musikanten, 1956 (Dagover 3)
Verwehte Spuren. *See* Auf gefährlichen
    Spuren, 1924
Verwehte Spuren, 1938 (Von Harbou 4,
    Warm 4)
Very Big Withdrawal, 1979 (Sutherland 3)
Very Busy Gentlemen. *See* Pán na roztrhání,
    1934
Very Close Quarters, 1986 (Winters 3)
Very Confidential, 1927 (August 4)
Very English Murder. *See* Chisto angliiskoe
    ubiistvo, 1973
Very Eye of Night, 1959 (Deren 2)
Very Good Young Man, 1919 (Crisp 3)
Very Handy Man. *See* Liola, 1964
Very Handy Man. *See* Stagione del nostro
    amore, 1965
Very Happy Alexander. *See* Alexandre le
    bienheureux, 1968
Very Honorable Guy, 1934 (Bacon 2,
    Brown 3, Orry-Kelly 4)
Very Idea, 1929 (Plunkett 4)
Very Important Person, 1961 (Rank 4)
Very Merry Cricket, 1971 (Jones 4)
Very Missing Person, 1972 (Arden 3)
Very Private Affair. *See* Vie privée, 1962
Very Special Favor, 1965 (Boyer 3, Caron 3,
    Hudson 3)
Very Thought of You, 1944 (Daves 2,
    Bondi 3, Glennon 4, Wald 4, Waxman 4)
Very Young Lady, 1941 (Cronjager 4,
    Day 4)
Ves v pohraniči, 1948 (Weiss 2)
Veselý cirkus, 1950 (Trnka 4)
Vesire gli ignudi, 1953 (Flaiano 4)
Vesna, 1947 (Cherkassov 3)
Vesnicko ma strediskova, 1985 (Menzel 2)

Vessel of Wrath, 1938 (Lanchester 3,
    Laughton 3, Newton 3, Pommer 4)
Vestervovvov, 1927 (Madsen and
    Schenstrøm 3)
Vestire gli ignudi, 1953 (Brasseur 3,
    Spaak 4)
Vesuvius Express, 1953 (Clarke 4)
Vesyoli musikanti, 1937 (Ptushko 4)
Veszelyban a pokol, 1921 (Banky 3)
Vêtements Sigrand, 1938 (Alexeieff and
    Parker 4)
Veuve Couderc, 1971 (Delon 3, Signoret 3,
    Saulnier 4)
Veuve en or, 1969 (Audiard 4,
    D'Eaubonne 4)
Veuve joyeuse, 1934 (Achard 4)
Vezelay, 1950 (Fresnay 3)
Vézélay, 1969 (Milhaud 4)
Vězěn no Bezděze, 1932 (Stallich 4)
Vi går landsvagen, 1937 (Jaenzon 4)
Vi haenger i en tråd, 1962 (Roos 2)
Vi som går köksvägen, 1932 (Molander 2)
Vi som går scenvägen, 1938 (Björnstrand 3)
Vi tre debutera, 1953 (Björnstrand 3,
    Fischer 4)
Vi två, 1939 (Björnstrand 3)
Via Cabaret, 1913 (Reid 3)
Via Crucis, 1918 (Blom 2)
Via libre a la zafra del '64, 1964 (Alvarez 2)
Via Mala, 1945 (Hoffmann 4, Röhrig 4, Von
    Harbou 4)
Via Mala, 1985 (Morricone 4)
Via Montenapoleone, 1987 (Gélin 3)
Via Padova 46, 1954 (Sordi 3, Rota 4)
Via Pony Express, 1933 (Canutt 4)
Viaccia, 1961 (Germi 2, Belmondo 3,
    Cardinale 3)
Viadukt, 1982 (Mueller-Stahl 3)
Viager, 1972 (Depardieu 3)
Viaggio, 1974 (Burton 3, Loren 3,
    Ponti 4)
Viaggio con Anita, 1978 (Monicelli 2,
    Hawn 3, Delli Colli 4, Morricone 4,
    Pinelli 4)
Viaggio d'amore, 1991 (Guerra 4)
Viaggio de lavoro, 1968 (Mangano 3)
Viaggio di Capitan Fracassa, 1991 (Scola 2,
    Age and Scarpelli 4)
Viaggio in Italia, 1953 (Rossellini 2,
    Bergman 3, Sanders 3)
Viaggio lungo il Tirreno. *See* Chi legge?,
    1960
Viaggio nella vertigini, 1975 (Thulin 3)
Viaje al centro de la tierra, 1977 (More 3)
Viale della speranza, 1952 (Mastroianni 3)
Vibes, 1988 (Falk 3, Edlund 4)
Vice and Virtue. *See* Vice et la vertu, 1962
Vice et la vertu, 1962 (Vadim 2, Deneuve 3,
    Girardot 3, Gégauff 4)
Vice Raid, 1959 (Cortez 4)
Vice Squad, 1931 (Cromwell 2, Francis 3,
    Lukas 3, Lang 4)
Vice Squad, 1953 (Goddard 3, Robinson 3,
    Van Cleef 3, Biroc 4)
Vice Squad, 1982 (Alcott 4)
Vice Versa, 1947 (Ustinov 3, Dillon 4,
    Rank 4)
Vicenta, 1920 (Musidora 3)
Vicious Circle, 1948 (Kortner 3)
Vicious Circle. *See* Circle, 1957
Vicious Circle. *See* Chakra, 1980
Vicious Circle, 1985 (Moreau 3, Sharif 3)
Vicki, 1953 (Horner 4, Krasner 4)
Vicomte de Bragelonne, 1954 (Astruc 2)

Vicomte règle ses comptes, 1967 (O'Brien 3,
    Rey 3)
Victim. *See* Avenging Conscience, 1914
Victim, 1961 (Dearden 2, Bogarde 3,
    Heller 4, Rank 4, Vetchinsky 4)
Victim, 1972 (Bumstead 4)
Victim of Circumstances, 1911 (Sennett 2)
Victim of Jealousy, 1910 (Griffith 2,
    Pickford 3, Bitzer 4)
Victimas del pecado, 1950 (Fernández 2,
    Figueroa 4)
Victimes de l'alcoolisme, 1902 (Pathé 4)
Victims, 1982 (Schifrin 4)
Victims of Terror, 1967 (Lee 3)
Victims of the Mormon. *See* Mormonens
    Offer, 1911
Victims of Vesuvius. *See* Victims of Terror,
    1967
Victoire en chantant, 1976 (Douy 4)
Victor, 1915 (Beery 3)
Victor, 1951 (Gabin 3)
Victor Brockdorff—en portrætskitse, 1989
    (Roos 2)
Victor Hugo, 1951 (Leenhardt 2)
Victor I, 1968 (Wenders 2)
Victoria Cross, 1912 (Reid 3)
Victoria Cross, 1917 (Hayakawa 3)
Victoria the Great, 1937 (Wilcox 2,
    Henreid 3, Neagle 3, Walbrook 3,
    Young 4)
Victors, 1963 (Finney 3, Mercouri 3,
    Moreau 3, Schneider 3, Wallach 3,
    Bass 4, Challis 4, Foreman 4)
Victor/Victoria, 1982 (Edwards 2,
    Andrews 3, Garner 3, Preston 3,
    Mancini 4)
Victory, 1919 (Tourneur 2, Beery 3,
    Chaney 3, Carré 4, Furthman 4)
Victory. *See* Pobeda, 1938
Victory, 1940 (Cromwell 2, March 3,
    Balderston 4, Dreier 4, Head 4,
    Veiller 4)
Victory, 1981 (Caine 3, Stallone 3, Von
    Sydow 3)
Victory and Peace, 1918 (Brenon 2)
Victory at Entebbe, 1976 (Douglas 3,
    Dreyfuss 3, Hopkins 3, Lancaster 3,
    Taylor 3)
Victory at Yorktown, 1965 (Hawkins 3)
Victory in the Dark. *See* Seger i mörker,
    1954
Victory of the Night. *See* Pobediteli nochi,
    1927
Victory of Women. *See* Josei no shori, 1946
Victory Song. *See* Hisshoka, 1945
Victory through Air Power, 1943 (Disney 4)
Victory Wedding, 1944 (Mills 3)
Victory Wedding, 1978 (Matthews 3)
Victuailles de Gretchen se revoltent, 1916
    (Cohl 4)
Vid Vgen. *See* Katinka, 1988
Vida cambia, 1976 (Figueroa 4)
Vida en rosa, 1988 (Díaz 2)
Vida es magnifica. *See* Voleur du Tibidabo,
    1964
Vida no vale nada, 1954 (Infante 3,
    Alcoriza 4)
Vidas, 1983 (Branco 4, De Almeida 4)
Videodrome, 1983 (Cronenberg 2, Baker 4)
Videospace, 1972 (Vanderbeek 2)
Vidya, 1948 (Anand 3, Burman 4)
Vie, 1958 (Straub and Huillet 2, Schell 3,
    Renoir 4)
Vie. *See* Sauve qui peut, 1980

Vie à deux, 1958 (Guitry 2, Brasseur 3, Darrieux 3, Fernandel 3, Feuillère 3, Philipe 3)

Vie chantée, 1950 (Burel 4)

Vie commence demain, 1950 (Milhaud 4)

Vie continue. *See* Vie devant soi, 1977

Vie continue, 1982 (Cassel 3, Girardot 3, Delerue 4)

Vie dans l'herbe, 1957 (Braunberger 4)

Vie de Bohème, 1916 (Carré 4, Marion 4)

Vie de Bohême, 1943 (L'Herbier 2, Jourdan 3, Wakhévitch 4)

Vie de château, 1966 (Borowczyk 2, Belmondo 3, Brasseur 3, Dalio 3, Deneuve 3, Noiret 3, Legrand 4, Rappeneau 4, Saulnier 4)

Vie de chien, 1941 (Fernandel 3)

Vie de Christ, 1906 (Guy 2)

Vie de Jésus, 1951 (Braunberger 4)

Vie de plaisir, 1943 (Spaak 4)

Vie de Polichinelle, 1905 (Linder 3)

Vie de Raimu, 1948 (Raimu 3)

Vie del Petrolio, 1964 (Bertolucci 2)

Vie des oiseaux en Mauritanie, 1963 (Braunberger 4)

Vie des termites, 1958 (Braunberger 4)

Vie des travailleurs italiens en France, 1926 (Grémillon 2)

Vie devant soi, 1977 (Signoret 3, Almendros 4, Evein 4, Sarde 4)

Vie drole, 1914 (Gaumont 4)

Vie du Christ, 1897 (Guy 2, Gaumont 4)

Vie du Christ, 1906 (Gaumont 4)

Vie du marin, 1906 (Guy 2)

Vie du moyen age, 1955 (Rabier 4)

Vie d'un grand journal, 1934 (Epstein 2)

Vie d'un homme, 1938 (Auric 4)

Vie d'un honnête homme, 1953 (Guitry 2, Simon 3)

Vie d'un joueur, 1903 (Pathé 4)

Vie d'une femme, 1920 (Gallone 2)

Vie d'une fleuve: La Seine, 1932 (Jaubert 4, Kaufman 4)

Vie en rose, 1948 (Jeanson 4)

Vie est à nous, 1936 (Becker 2, Modot 3, Eisler 4, Renoir 4)

Vie est un long fleuve tranquille, 1988 (Gélin 3)

Vie est un roman, 1984 (Resnais 2, Chaplin 3, Gassman 3, Saulnier 4)

Vie est un songe, 1987 (Ruiz 2)

Vie et rien d'autre, 1989 (Tavernier 2, Noiret 3)

Vie, l'amour, la mort, 1968 (Girardot 3, Lai 4)

Vie miraculeuse de Thérèse Martin, 1929 (Christian-Jaque 2, Duvivier 2)

Vie ou la mort, 1912 (Feuillade 2)

Vie parisienne, 1936 (Siodmak 2, Morgan 3, Jaubert 4)

Vie privée, 1962 (Bardot 3, Mastroianni 3, Decaë 4, Evein 4, Rappeneau 4)

Vie sentimentale de Georges le Tueur, 1971 (Braunberger 4)

Vie telle qu'elle est series, 1911–13 (Feuillade 2)

Vieil Homme et l'enfant, 1966 (Simon 3, Delerue 4)

Vieille Fille, 1972 (Girardot 3, Noiret 3, Legrand 4)

Vieilles Estampes, 1904 (Guy 2)

Vieilles Femmes de l'hospice, 1917 (Feyder 2, Gaumont 4)

Vienna Burgtheater. *See* Burgtheater, 1936

Vienna Waltzes. *See* Wien tantz, 1951

Viennese Nights, 1930 (Lugosi 3, Pidgeon 3)

Viens l'chercher, 1905 (Pathé 4)

Vient de paraître, 1949 (Fresnay 3)

Viento norte, 1937 (Alton 4)

Vier gesellen, 1938 (Bergman 3)

Vier um die Frau. *See* Kamfende Herzen, 1920

Vier vom Bob, 1931 (Rasp 3)

Vierge d'Argos, 1910 (Feuillade 2)

Vierge du Rhin, 1953 (Gabin 3)

Vierge folle, 1928 (Fresnay 3)

Vièrges, 1962 (Schüfftan 4)

Viernes de la eternidad, 1981 (Schifrin 4)

Vierte kommt nicht, 1939 (Wagner 4)

Viertelstunde Grossstadtstatistik, 1933 (Fischinger 2, Ford 2)

Vietnam! Vietnam!, 1971 (Ford 2, Heston 3)

Vieux Chaland, 1932 (Epstein 2)

Vieux de la vieille, 1960 (Fresnay 3, Gabin 3, Audiard 4)

Vieux Fusil, 1975 (Noiret 3, Schneider 3)

Vieux garçon, 1931 (Tourneur 2)

Vieux Pays ou Rimbaud est mort, 1977 (Lefebvre 2)

View from Pompey's Head, 1955 (Dunne 4, LeMaire 4)

View from the Bridge. *See* Vu du pont, 1962

View to a Kill, 1985 (Barry 4)

Viewing Sherman Institute for Indians at Riverside, 1915 (Sennett 2)

Vigil, 1914 (Hayakawa 3, Ince 4)

Vigil in the Night, 1940 (Stevens 2, Cushing 3, Lombard 3, Newman 4, Plunkett 4, Polglase 4)

Vigilantes Are Coming, 1936 (Canutt 4)

Vigilante's Return, 1947 (Miller 4)

Vigile, 1960 (De Sica 2, Sordi 3)

Vigilia di natale, 1913 (Bertini 3)

Vignes du seigneur, 1932 (D'Eaubonne 4)

Vignes du seigneur, 1958 (Fernandel 3)

Vijaya, 1942 (Biswas 4)

Vijeta, 1983 (Nihalani 4)

Viking, 1929 (Crisp 3)

Viking Queen, 1967 (Carreras 4)

Vikings, 1958 (Welles 2, Borgnine 3, Curtis 3, Douglas 3, Leigh 3, Cardiff 4, Saulnier 4)

Viking's Daughter, 1908 (Lawrence 3)

Viktor and Viktoria, 1933 (Walbrook 3)

Viktoria, 1934 (Hoffmann 4)

Vilaine histoire, 1934 (Christian-Jaque 2)

Vildfagel, 1921 (Magnusson 4)

Vildfåglar, 1955 (Sjöberg 2)

Villa Borghese, 1953 (Presle 3, Amidei 4, Flaiano 4)

Villa dei mostri, 1950 (Antonioni 2, Fusco 4)

Villa des mille joies, 1928 (Modot 3)

Villa Destin, 1921 (Autant-Lara 2, L'Herbier 2)

Villa dévalisée, 1905 (Guy 2)

Villa im Tiergarten, 1926 (Albers 3)

Villa Miranda, 1970 (Brocka 2)

Villa of the Movies, 1917 (Sennett 2)

Villa Rides, 1968 (Bronson 3, Brynner 3, Lom 3, Mitchum 3, Rey 3, Jarre 4, Towne 4)

Villa Santo-Sospir, 1952 (Cocteau 2)

Villa vuelve, 1949 (Armendáriz 3)

Village. *See* Pestalozzidorf, 1953

Village Barber, 1931 (Iwerks 4)

Village Blacksmith, 1916 (Sennett 2)

Village Blacksmith, 1922 (Ford 2, Love 3)

Village Blacksmith, 1933 (Terry 4)

Village Blacksmith, 1938 (Terry 4)

Village Bride. *See* Mura na hanayome, 1928

Village Chestnut, 1918 (Sennett 2)

Village Cut-Up, 1906 (Bitzer 4)

Village dans Paris, 1939 (Clair 2)

Village dans Paris: Montmartre, 1940 (Jaubert 4)

Village de la France Australe, 1954 (Decaë 4)

Village du milieu des brumes, 1961 (Decaë 4)

Village Hero, 1911 (Sennett 2)

Village in India. *See* World Window, 1977

Village magique, 1954 (Kosma 4)

Village of the Damned, 1960 (Sanders 3)

Village of the Giants, 1965 (Edouart 4)

Village on the Frontier. *See* Ves v pohraniči, 1948

Village perdu, 1947 (Honegger 4)

Village Romance, 1912 (Lawrence 3)

Village Scandal, 1915 (Sennett 2, Arbuckle 3)

Village School of Emperor Supporters. *See* Sonnou sonjuku, 1939

Village School-teacher. *See* Selskaya uchitelnitsa, 1947

Village Smithy, 1919 (Sennett 2)

Village Smithy, 1936 (Avery 4, Stalling 4)

Village Smitty, 1931 (Iwerks 4)

Village Specialist, 1932 (Iwerks 4)

Village Squire, 1935 (Leigh 3, Havelock-Allan 4)

Village Tale, 1935 (Scott 3, Musuraca 4, Plunkett 4, Polglase 4)

Village Vampire, 1916 (Sennett 2)

Villain, 1917 (Laurel and Hardy 3)

Villain, 1971 (Burton 3, Challis 4)

Villain, 1979 (Douglas 3, Schwarzenegger 3, Needham 4)

Villain Foiled, 1911 (Sennett 2)

Villain Still Pursued Her, 1937 (Terry 4)

Villain Still Pursued Her, 1940 (Keaton 2, Pangborn 3, Ballard 4)

Villain's Curse, 1932 (Terry 4)

Villanelle des Rubans, 1932 (Epstein 2)

Ville à Chandigarh, 1966 (Tanner 2)

Ville Bidon, 1975 (Cloquet 4)

Ville de Madame Tango, 1914 (Musidora 3)

Ville de pirates, 1984 (Branco 4, De Almeida 4)

Ville de silences, 1979 (Cassel 3)

Ville della Brianza, 1955 (Taviani 2)

Vim, Vigor and Vitaliky, 1936 (Fleischer 4)

Vina Vladimira Olmera, 1956 (Brejchová 3)

Vince il sistema, 1949 (Risi 2)

Vincent, 1983 (Price 3)

Vincent and Theo, 1990 (Altman 2, Cassel 3)

Vincent, François, Paul, and the Others. *See* Vincent, François, Paul, et les autres, 1974

Vincent, François, Paul, et les autres, 1974 (Sautet 2, Audran 3, Depardieu 3, Montand 3, Piccoli 3, Reggiani 3, Sarde 4)

Vincent Lopez and His Orchestra, 1939 (Hutton 3)

Vincent the Dutchman, 1971 (Zetterling 2)

Vincent—The Life and Death of Vincent Van Gogh, 1987 (Hurt 3)

Vinden från våster, 1943 (Sucksdorff 2)

Vinden och floden, 1951 (Sucksdorff 2)

Vindicta, 1923 (Feuillade 2)

Vine Bridge. *See* Lianbron, 1965

Vine Garden. *See* Lianbron, 1965

Vingarne, 1916 (Stiller 2, Jaenzon 4, Magnusson 4)

Vingeskudt, 1913 (Christensen 2)

Vingt-cinquième Heure. See 25e Heure, 1967

Vingt-quatre heures d'amant, 1964 (Lelouch 2)

Vingt-quatre heures de la vie d'un clown, 1946 (Melville 2)

Vingt-quatre heures de la vie d'une femme, 1968 (Darrieux 3)

Vingt-quatre heures de perm', 1940 (Heller 4)

Vingt-quatre heures de perm', 1945 (Wakhévitch 4)

Vingt-quatre heures en trente minutes, 1928 (Kaufman 4)

Vintage, 1957 (Morgan 3, Raksin 4, Ruttenberg 4)

Vintage of Fate, 1912 (Bosworth 3)

Vinti, 1952 (Rosi 2, Cecchi D'Amico 4, Fusco 4)

Vinyl, 1965 (Warhol 2)

Viol, 1967 (Andersson 3)

Violanta, 1977 (Depardieu 3)

Violantha, 1927 (Dieterle 2, Porten 3)

Violence. See Boryoku, 1952

Violence at Noon. See Hakuchu no torima, 1966

Violence in the Cinema: Part I, 1971 (Miller 2)

Violent City. See Città violenta, 1970

Violent Four. See Banditi a Milano, 1968

Violent Hour. See Dial 1119, 1950

Violent Is the Word for Curly, 1938 (Three Stooges 3, Ballard 4)

Violent Journey, 1966 (Jeakins 4)

Violent Men, 1955 (Ford 3, Robinson 3, Stanwyck 3, Guffey 4, Maté 4, Steiner 4, Wald 4)

Violent Playground, 1958 (Dearden 2, Baker 3, Cushing 3, Rank 4)

Violent Saturday, 1955 (Borgnine 3, Marvin 3, Mature 3, Sidney 3, Clarke 4, Friedhofer 4, LeMaire 4, Wheeler 4)

Violent Streets. See Thief, 1981

Violent Summer. See Estate violenta, 1959

Violenza: quinto potere, 1972 (Morricone 4)

Violenza segreta, 1962 (Fusco 4, Gherardi 4)

Violets Are Blue, 1986 (Spacek 3)

Violette. See Violette Nozière, 1978

Violette and François. See Violette et François, 1977

Violette et François, 1977 (Adjani 3, Reggiani 3, Sarde 4)

Violette Nozière, 1978 (Chabrol 2, Audran 3, Huppert 3, Rabier 4)

Violettes impériales, 1952 (Barsacq 4, Matras 4)

Violin Maker, 1915 (Chaney 3)

Violin Maker of Cremona, 1909 (Griffith 2, Pickford 3, Bitzer 4)

Violin Maker of Nuremberg, 1911 (Guy 2)

Violinist of Florence. See Geiger von Florenz, 1926

Violins Came with the Americans, 1986 (Ferrer 3)

Violon de Crémone, 1968 (Delerue 4)

Violon et agent. See Violoniste, 1908

Violoniste, 1908 (Cohl 4)

Violons d'Ingres, 1940 (Jaubert 4)

Violons du bal, 1974 (Trintignant 3)

Violons parfois, 1977 (Guillemot 4)

Vip mio fratello superuomo, 1968 (Bozzetto 4)

Vipères, 1911 (Gaumont 4)

Virgen de medianoche, 1942 (Figueroa 4)

Virgen que forjó una Patria, 1942 (Novarro 3, Figueroa 4)

Virgin Island, 1958 (Cassavetes 2, Poitier 3, Francis 4, Lardner 4)

Virgin Lips, 1928 (Walker 4)

Virgin of Stamboul, 1920 (Browning 2, Beery 3)

Virgin Paradise, 1921 (White 3, Ruttenberg 4)

Virgin Queen, 1923 (Blackton 2)

Virgin Queen, 1955 (Davis 3, Marshall 3, Brackett 4, Clarke 4, LeMaire 4, Waxman 4)

Virgin Soldiers, 1970 (Foreman 4)

Virgin Spring. See Jungfrukällen, 1960

Virgin Who Embraces a Rainbow. See Niji o idaku shojo, 1948

Virgin Wife. See Moglie virgine, 1976

Virginia, 1941 (Beavers 3, Carroll 3, Hayden 3, MacMurray 3, Dreier 4, Edouart 4, Glennon 4, Head 4, Young 4)

Virginia City, 1940 (Curtiz 2, Bogart 3, Bond 3, Flynn 3, Hopkins 3, Scott 3, Buckner 4, Canutt 4, Friedhofer 4, Haskin 4, Koch 4, Polito 4, Steiner 4, Wallis 4)

Virginia Courtship, 1922 (Rosson 4)

Virginia Judge, 1935 (Krasner 4)

Virginia Romance, 1916 (Bushman 3)

Virginian, 1914 (De Mille 2, Buckland 4)

Virginian, 1923 (Lang 4, Schulberg 4)

Virginian, 1929 (Fleming 2, Hathaway 2, Cooper 3, Huston 3, Scott 3, Estabrook 4, Head 4, Hunt 4, Zukor 4)

Virginian, 1946 (McCrea 3, Dreier 4, Edouart 4, Goodrich 4, Head 4)

Virginia's Death, 1968 (Schroeter 2)

Virginie, 1962 (Braunberger 4, Matras 4)

Virginity. See Panenství, 1937

Viridiana, 1961 (Bardem 2, Buñuel 2, Rey 3)

Virtue, 1932 (Bond 3, Lombard 3, Riskin 4, Walker 4)

Virtue Is Its Own Reward, 1914 (Chaney 3)

Virtue of Rags, 1912 (Bushman 3)

Virtuous Bigamist. See Sous le ciel de Provence, 1956

Virtuous Husband, 1931 (Arthur 3)

Virtuous Liars, 1924 (Costello 3)

Virtuous Scoundrel. See Vie d'un honnête homme, 1952

Virtuous Sin, 1930 (Cukor 2, Francis 3, Huston 3)

Virtuous Sinners, 1919 (Valentino 3)

Virtuous Thief, 1919 (Niblo 2, Barnes 4, Sullivan 4)

Virtuous Vamp, 1919 (Emerson 4, Loos 4)

Virtuous Wives, 1919 (Mayer 4)

Virus Story, 1953 (Rotha 4)

Visa to Canton, 1961 (Carreras 4)

Visage mysterieux d'Océanie, 1970 (Braunberger 4)

Visages de femmes, 1939 (Brasseur 3)

Visages de France, 1936 (Honegger 4)

Visages d'enfants, 1923 (Burel 4)

Visages de Paris, 1955 (Braunberger 4)

Viscount. See Vicomte règle ses comptes, 1967

Vishwasghaat, 1976 (Azmi 3)

Visible Manifestations, 1961 (Dunning 4)

Vision. See Deedar, 1951

Vision, 1987 (Remick 3)

Vision Beautiful, 1912 (Bosworth 3)

Vision Quest, 1985 (Roizman 4)

Visioniii, 1958 (Vanderbeek 2)

Visions in Meditation #1, 1989 (Brakhage 2)

Visions in Meditation #2, 1990 (Brakhage 2)

Visions of Eight, 1973 (Forman 2, Ichikawa 2, Lelouch 2, Penn 2, Schlesinger 2, Zetterling 2, Allen 4, Lassally 4, Mancini 4)

Visit. See Besuch, 1964

Visit. See Het bezoek, 1971

Visit, 1987 (Arkin 3)

Visit from Space, 1964 (Vukotić 4)

Visit to a Chief's Son, 1974 (Lai 4)

Visit to a Small Planet, 1960 (Lewis 2, Head 4)

Visit to the Spiritualist, 1899 (Blackton 2)

Visit with Darius Milhaud, 1955 (Auric 4)

Visita, 1963 (De Santis 2, Scola 2)

Visita que no toco al timbre, 1954 (Alcoriza 4)

Visitatore, 1980 (Peckinpah 2, Winters 3)

Visite, 1955 (Rivette 2, Truffaut 2)

Visite à César Domela, 1947 (Resnais 2)

Visite à Félix Labisse, 1947 (Resnais 2)

Visite à Hans Hartung, 1947 (Resnais 2)

Visite à Lucien Coutaud, 1947 (Resnais 2)

Visite à Maurice Chevalier, 1954 (Chevalier 3)

Visite à Oscar Dominguez, 1947 (Resnais 2)

Visite au Haras, 1951 (Decaë 4)

Visite sous-marine du Maine, 1898 (Méliès 2)

Visiteur, 1946 (Fresnay 3)

Visiteurs du soir, 1942 (Arletty 3, Berry 3, Cuny 3, Signoret 3, Barsacq 4, Kosma 4, Prévert 4, Trauner 4, Wakhévitch 4)

Visiting Hours, 1982 (Grant 3)

Visitor, 1910 (White 3)

Visitor, 1978 (Ford 3)

Visitor. See Visitatore, 1980

Visitor, 1991 (Matthau 3)

Visitors, 1972 (Kazan 2)

Viskningar och rop, 1972 (Andersson 3, Josephson 3, Thulin 3, Ullmann 3, Nykvist 4)

Vispa Teresa, 1939 (Rossellini 2)

Vita agra, 1964 (Amidei 4)

Vita, a volta è molto dura, vero Provvidenza, 1972 (Morricone 4)

Vita da cani, 1950 (Monicelli 2, Fabrizi 3, Lollobrigida 3, Mastroianni 3, Amidei 4, Ponti 4, Rota 4)

Vita difficile, 1961 (Gassman 3, Mangano 3, Sordi 3)

Vita è bella, 1943 (Magnani 3)

Vita in scatola; L'uomo e il suo mondo, 1967 (Bozzetto 4)

Vita katten, 1950 (Björnstrand 3)

Vita recominicia, 1945 (Valli 3)

Vita venduta, 1977 (Morricone 4)

Vita violenta, 1965 (Solinas 4)

Vitamin C, 1950 (Brdečka 4)

Vitamin G-Man, 1943 (Fleischer 4, Hubley 4)

Vitamin Hay, 1941 (Fleischer 4)

Vittel, 1926 (Autant-Lara 2)

Vitelloni, 1953 (Fellini 2, Baarová 3, Sordi 3, Flaiano 4, Pinelli 4, Rota 4)

Vittima dell'ideale, 1916 (Bertini 3)

Vittnesbörd om henne, 1962 (Fischer 4)

Vittorio De Sica, il Regista, l'attore, l'uomo, 1974 (De Sica 2)

Viuda de Montiel, 1979 (Chaplin 3, Villagra 3)

Viva Benito Canales, 1965 (Figueroa 4)

Viva Cisco Kid, 1940 (Clarke 4)

Viva el Presidente. See Recurso del método, 1977

Viva Italia!. See Nuovi mostri, 1977

Viva Knievel!, 1977 (Kelly 3)

Viva la muerte … tua!, 1972 (Wallach 3)

Viva la vie, 1984 (Piccoli 3, Trintignant 3)

Viva Las Vegas. See Meet Me in Las Vegas, 1956

Viva Las Vegas, 1964 (Presley 3, Biroc 4)

Viva l'Italia, 1960 (Rossellini 2, Amidei 4)

Viva Maria, 1965 (Malle 2, Bardot 3, Moreau 3, Carrière 4, Decaë 4, Delerue 4, Evein 4)

Viva Max, 1969 (Ustinov 3)

Viva mi desgracia, 1943 (Infante 3)

Viva revolución, 1956 (Armendáriz 3)

Viva Villa!, 1934 (Hawks 2, Beery 3, Walthall 3, Wray 3, Clarke 4, Hecht 4, Howe 4, Mayer 4, Selznick 4, Stothart 4, Vorkapich 4)

Viva Willie, 1934 (Iwerks 4)

Viva Zapata!, 1952 (Kazan 2, Brando 3, Quinn 3, LeMaire 4, Newman 4, North 4, Wheeler 4, Zanuck 4)

Vivacious Lady, 1938 (Stevens 2, Bondi 3, Coburn 3, Pangborn 3, Rogers 3, Stewart 3, Berman 4, Irene 4, Polglase 4)

Vivarium, 1958 (Braunberger 4)

Vive eau, 1967 (Braunberger 4, Coutard 4)

Vive Henry IV, vive l'amour, 1962 (Autant-Lara 2, De Sica 2, Blier 3, Brasseur 3, Darrieux 3, Mercouri 3, Aurenche 4, Douy 4, Jeanson 4)

Vive la classe, 1931 (Fernandel 3)

Vive la France; Comment réussir quand on est con et pleurnichard, 1973 (Audiard 4)

Vive la vie, 1937 (Epstein 2)

Vive la vie, 1984 (Lelouch 2, Aimée 3)

Vive le sabotage!, 1907 (Feuillade 2, Gaumont 4)

Vive le Tour!, 1965 (Delerue 4)

Vive les femmes!, 1984 (Trauner 4)

Vivement dimanche!, 1983 (Truffaut 2, Trintignant 3, Almendros 4, Delerue 4)

Vivere a sbafo, 1949 (Alexeieff and Parker 4)

Vivere ancora, 1944 (Cervi 3)

Vivere in pace, 1946 (Fabrizi 3, Cecchi D'Amico 3, Ponti 4, Rota 4)

Vivi, o preferibilmente morti, 1969 (Flaiano 4)

Vivian, 1964 (Conner 2)

Viviana, 1916 (Eason 4)

Vivre à San Francisco, 1968 (Braunberger 4)

Vivre pour vivre, 1967 (Girardot 3, Montand 3, Lai 4)

Vivre sa vie, 1962 (Godard 2, Karina 3, Braunberger 4, Coutard 4, Guillemot 4, Legrand 4)

Vixen, 1916 (Bara 3)

Vixen. See Jotai, 1969

Vixen and the Hare, 1973 (Norstein 4)

Vladimir et Rosa, 1971 (Godard 2)

Vladimir Horowitz, the Last Romantic, 1986 (Maysles 2)

Vlast' pervogo, 1917 (Baranovskaya 3)

Vlast tmy, 1915 (Mozhukin 3)

Vlast vítá, 1945 (Stallich 4)

Vlasteli byta, 1932 (Ptushko 4)

Vlastně se nič nestalo, 1989 (Schorm 2, Brejchová 3)

Vlčí jáma, 1957 (Weiss 2, Brejchová 3, Brdečka 4)

Vlyublen po sobstvennomu zhelaniyu, 1982 (Yankovsky 3)

Vnimanie, cherpakha!, 1969 (Batalov 3)

Vo imya zhizni, 1946 (Cherkassov 3)

Vo vlasti gretcha, 1915 (Mozhukin 3)

Vocation d'André Carrel. See Puissance du travail, 1925

Vocation irrésistible, 1934 (Delannoy 2)

Vocation suspendue, 1977 (Vierny 4)

Voce, 1982 (Brazzi 3)

Voce del silenzio, 1952 (Pabst 2, Fabrizi 3, Gélin 3, Marais 3, Bost 4, Zavattini 4)

Voce della luna, 1990 (Delli Colli 4, Morricone 4, Pinelli 4)

Voce nel tuo cuore, 1949 (Gassman 3)

Voce, una chitarra, un po' di luna, 1956 (Delli Colli 4)

Voci bianche, 1964 (Aimée 3)

Vogel, 1963 (Müller 4)

Vogelhändler, 1935 (Dagover 3)

Voglia da morire, 1966 (Girardot 3)

Voglia di vivere, 1989 (Sanda 3)

Voglia matta, 1962 (Morricone 4)

Vogliamo di colonnelli, 1973 (Monicelli 2, Age and Scarpelli 4)

Voglio Tradire mio Marito, 1925 (Camerini 2)

Voglio vivere con Letizia, 1938 (Cervi 3)

Vogues of 1938, 1937 (Bennett 3, Irene 4, Wanger 4, Young 4)

Voi vivi, 1942 (Valli 3)

Voice from the Dead, 1908 (Porter 2)

Voice from the Deep, 1911 (Sennett 2)

Voice from the Minaret, 1923 (Talmadge 3, Gaudio 4, Marion 4, Schenck 4)

Voice in the Fog, 1916 (Rosher 4)

Voice in the Mirror, 1958 (Matthau 3, Daniels 4, Mancini 4)

Voice in the Night, 1934 (Bond 3)

Voice in the Night. See Freedom Radio, 1940

Voice le temps des assassins, 1956 (Duvivier 2)

Voice of Bugle Ann, 1936 (Barrymore 3, O'Sullivan 3, Haller 4, Hoffenstein 4)

Voice of Conscience, 1912 (Bushman 3)

Voice of Hollywood, 1930 (Dressler 3)

Voice of Hollywood, 1932 (Cooper 3)

Voice of Hollywood No. 13, 1932 (Wayne 3)

Voice of Hollywood Nos. 1–2, 1930 (Mix 3)

Voice of La Raza, 1972 (Quinn 3)

Voice of Scandal. See Here Comes Carter, 1936

Voice of the Blood. See Blodets röst, 1913

Voice of the Child, 1911 (Griffith 2, Bitzer 4)

Voice of the City, 1929 (Gibbons 4, Mayer 4, Shearer 4)

Voice of the Moon. See Voce della luna, 1990

Voice of the Storm, 1929 (Plunkett 4)

Voice of the Turtle, 1947 (Arden 3, Reagan 3, Polito 4, Steiner 4)

Voice of the Viola, 1914 (Reid 3)

Voice of the Violin, 1909 (Griffith 2, Bitzer 4)

Voice of the World, 1932 (Grierson 2)

Voice on the Wire, 1980 (Johnson 3)

Voices Across the Sea, 1928 (Gilbert 3, Shearer 3)

Voices of the City, 1922 (Chaney 3)

Voices of the Moon. See Voce della luna, 1990

Voici des fleurs, 1963 (Fradetal 4)

Voici le temps des assassins, 1955 (Gabin 3)

Voie lactée, 1969 (Cuny 3, Piccoli 3, Seyrig 3, Carrière 4, Matras 4)

Voilà vous, 1951 (Rabier 4)

Voiles à Val, 1959 (Guillemot 4)

Voiles bas et en travers, 1983 (Perrault 2)

Voina i mir, 1912 (Mozhukin 3)

Voina i mir, 1959 (Bondarchuk 3)

Voisin trop gourmand, 1915 (Cohl 4)

Voisin … voisin, 1911 (Linder 3)

Voisins. See Neighbors, 1952

Voisins n'aiment pas la musique, 1970 (Braunberger 4)

Voiture cellulaire, 1906 (Guy 2)

Voitures d'eau, 1969 (Perrault 2)

Voix d'enfants, 1935 (Milhaud 4)

Voix des anches, 1957 (Decaë 4)

Voix d'Orly, 1965 (Coutard 4, Delerue 4)

Voix humaine, 1948 (Cocteau 2)

Voix humaine, 1970 (Cocteau 2)

Voix sans visage, 1933 (Schüfftan 4)

Vol, 1923 (Vanel 3)

Vol de nuit, 1978 (Howard 3)

Volare. See Nel blu dipinto di blu, 1959

Volcano, 1926 (Howard 2, Beery 3, Daniels 3)

Volcano. See Vulcano, 1949 (Dieterle 2)

Volcano, 1976 (Burton 3)

Volé par les bohemiens, 1904 (Gaumont 4)

Voleur, 1933 (Simon 3)

Voleur, 1934 (Tourneur 2, Courant 4)

Voleur, 1963 (Braunberger 4)

Voleur, 1967 (Belmondo 3, Carrière 4, Decaë 4, Saulnier 4)

Voleur de bicyclette, 1905 (Pathé 4)

Voleur de crimes, 1969 (Trintignant 3)

Voleur de femmes, 1936 (Gance 2, Berry 3)

Voleur de paratonnerres, 1944 (Aurenche 4, Grimault 4)

Voleur du Tibidabo, 1964 (Karina 3)

Voleur sacrilège, 1903 (Guy 2)

Voleurs de la nuit. See Thieves After Dark, 1983

Voleuse, 1966 (Duras 2, Piccoli 3, Schneider 3)

Volga Boatman, 1926 (De Mille 2, Adrian 4, Coffee 4, Grot 4, Miller 4)

Volga en flammes, 1934 (Darrieux 3, Andrejew 4)

Volga Volga, 1934 (Volkov 2)

Volki, 1925 (Baranovskaya 3)

Volksfeind, 1937 (Warm 4)

Volles Herz und leere Tashcen, 1964 (Cervi 3, Rosay 3)

Volley ball, 1965 (Arcand 2)

Volochayevskiye dni, 1937 (Vasiliev 2, Shostakovich 4)

Volontär, 1919 (Warm 4)

Volpone, 1940 (Tourneur 2, Baur 3, Jouvet 3, Barsacq 4)

Voltaire, 1933 (Arliss 3, Gaudio 4, Orry-Kelly 4)

Voltati Eugenio, 1980 (Comencini 2, Blier 3)

Voltera, comune medievale, 1955 (Taviani 2)

Volti dell'amore, 1923 (Gallone 2)

Volume 2: Directors, 1990 (Chatterjee 3)

Voltige, 1895 (Lumière 2)

Volunteer, 1943 (Richardson 3, Junge 4, Powell and Pressburger 2)

Volunteers, 1985 (Hanks 3)

Vom Blitz zum Fernsehbild, 1937 (Milhaud 4)

Vom Freudenhaus in die Ehe,. *See* Mädchen ohne Heimat, 1926

Vom Mann. *See* Miss Hobbs, 1921

Vom Niederrhein, 1925 (Dieterle 2)

Vom Schicksal verfolgten, 1927 (Dieterle 2)

Vom Teufel gejagt, 1950 (Albers 3)

Von der Liebe reden wir später, 1953 (Fröhlich 3)

Von Himmel gefallen. *See* Special Delivery, 1955

Von Morgens bis Mitternachts, 1920 (Hoffmann 4)

Von Richtofen and Brown, 1971 (Friedhofer 4)

Von Rummelplatz, 1930 (Ondra 3, Heller 4)

Von Ryan's Express, 1965 (Howard 3, Sinatra 3, Daniels 4, Goldsmith 4, Smith 4)

Voodoo Island. *See* Silent Death, 1957

Voodoo Man, 1944 (Carradine 3, Lugosi 3, Katzman 4)

Voodoo Tiger, 1952 (Weissmuller 3, Katzman 4)

Voor Recht en Vrijheid te Kortrijk, 1939 (Storck 2)

Vor Liebe wird gewarnt, 1937 (Ondra 3)

Vor Sonnenuntergang, 1956 (Albers 3)

Vor Tids Dame, 1912 (Psilander 3)

Vordertreppe und Hintertreppe, 1914 (Gad 2, Nielsen 3, Freund 4)

Vore venners vinter, 1923 (Madsen and Schenstrøm 3)

Vorn Teufel gejagt, 1950 (Dagover 3)

Vors uns liegt das Leben, 1948 (Warm 4)

Vortex, 1927 (Novello 3, Balcon 4)

Vortex. *See* Blondy, 1975

Vortice, 1953 (Papas 3)

Voruntersuchung, 1931 (Siodmak 2, Fröhlich 3, Pommer 4)

Vot mchitza troika potchtovaia, 1913 (Mozhukin 3)

Vot vspynulo utro, 1915 (Mozhukin 3)

Vote. *See* Voto, 1950

Vote for Huggett, 1949 (Dors 3, Box 4, Rank 4)

Voto, 1950 (Loren 3, Delli Colli 4)

Vot'permis, 1905 (Pathé 4)

Votre Devoue, Blake, 1954 (Constantine 3)

Votre santé!, 1950 (Fradetal 4)

Voulez-vous danser avec moi, 1959 (Bardot 3)

Vous n'aurez pas l'Alsace et la Lorraine, 1976 (Douy 4)

Vous n'avez rien à déclarer?, 1936 (Allégret 2, Brasseur 3, Raimu 3, Aurenche 4, Braunberger 4, Fradetal 4)

Vous n'avez rien à déclarer?, 1959 (Jarre 4)

Vous n'avez rien contre la jeunesse, 1958 (Guillemot 4)

Vous pigez?, 1955 (Constantine 3, Burel 4)

Vous verrez la semaine prochaine, 1929 (Cavalcanti 2)

Voyage. *See* Viaggio, 1973

Voyage à Biarritz, 1962 (Arletty 3, Fernandel 3, Audiard 4)

Voyage à Galveston, 1970 (Moore 3)

Voyage à la Côte d'Azur, 1913 (Gaumont 4)

Voyage au Congo, 1926 (Braunberger 4)

Voyage autour d'un étoile, 1906 (Pathé 4)

Voyage autour d'une main, 1983 (Ruiz 2)

Voyage d'Abdallah, 1953 (Jarre 4)

Voyage d'agrément, 1935 (Christian-Jaque 2)

Voyage dans la lune, 1902 (Méliès 2)

Voyage de Mr. Perrichon, 1933 (Arletty 3, Wakhévitch 4)

Voyage de noces. *See* Voyage de noces en Espagne, 1912

Voyage de noces, 1932 (Brasseur 3)

Voyage de noces, 1975 (Baye 3, Trintignant 3)

Voyage de noces. *See* Jalousie 1976, 1976

Voyage de noces en Espagne, 1912 (Linder 3)

Voyage du Capitaine Fracasse. *See* Viaggio di Capitan Fracassa, 1990

Voyage du père, 1966 (Fernandel 3, Noiret 3)

Voyage en Amérique, 1951 (Fresnay 3, Alekan 4)

Voyage en Amérique, 1975 (Seyrig 3)

Voyage en Boscavie, 1958 (Guillemot 4)

Voyage en Camardie, 1971 (Braunberger 4)

Voyage en douce, 1981 (Chaplin 3, Sanda 3)

Voyage en Espagne, 1906 (Guy 2)

Voyage imaginaire, 1925 (Clair 2)

Voyage imprévu, 1934 (Spaak 4)

Voyage of Captain Fracassa. *See* Viaggio di Capitan Fracassa, 1990

Voyage of Terror; the Achille Lauro Affair, 1989 (Morricone 4)

Voyage of the Damned, 1976 (Welles 2, Dunaway 3, Elliott 3, Ferrer 3, Grant 3, McDowell 3, Rey 3, Schell 3, Von Sydow 3, Werner 3, Schifrin 4)

Voyage Round My Father, 1982 (Bates 3, Olivier 3)

Voyage sans espoir, 1943 (Christian-Jaque 2, Marais 3)

Voyage to America. *See* Voyage en Amérique, 1951

Voyage to America, 1964 (Houseman 4, Thomson 4)

Voyage to a Prehistoric Planet, 1967 (Rathbone 3)

Voyage to Italy. *See* **Viaggio in Italia, 1953**

Voyage to Next, 1974 (Hubley 4)

Voyage to the Bottom of the Sea, 1961 (Fontaine 3, Lorre 3, Pidgeon 3, Bennett 4, Hoch 4, Smith 4)

Voyager, 1911 (Bosworth 3)

Voyager, 1991 (Shepard 4)

Voyage-surprise, 1946 (Kosma 4, Prévert 4, Trauner 4)

Voyageur de la Toussaint, 1943 (Berry 3, Reggiani 3)

Voyageur sans bagages, 1943 (Fresnay 3, Matras 4)

Voyante, 1923 (Baur 3)

Voyou, 1970 (Trintignant 3, Lai 4)

Voz do carnaval, 1933 (Miranda 3)

Vozrata net, 1974 (Batalov 3)

Vozrozhdennia, 1915 (Mozhukin 3)

Vozvrascheniye Maksima. *See* **Vozvrascheniye Maksima, 1937**

Vozvrashcheniye Maksima, 1937 (Kozintsev 2, Enei 4, Moskvin 4, Shostakovich 4)

Vrai Visage de Thérèse de Lisieux, 1961 (Grimault 4)

Vražda po našem, 1966 (Weiss 2)

Vredens dag, 1943 (Dreyer 2)

Vsadniki vetra, 1930 (Cherkassov 3)

Vse ostaetsia lyudyam, 1963 (Cherkassov 3)

Vserusski starets Kalinin, 1920 (Vertov 2)

Vsetrecha na Elba, 1949 (Tisse 4)

Všichni dobří rodáci, 1968 (Kučera 4)

Vskrytie moschei Sergeia Radonezhskogo, 1919 (Vertov 2)

Vspomnim, Tovarisc, 1987·(Heifitz 2)

Vstanou noví bojovníci, 1950 (Weiss 2)

Vstrecha na Elbe, 1949 (Shostakovich 4)

Vstrechnyi, 1932 (Shostakovich 4)

Vsyou zhizn pod maskoi, 1915 (Mozhukin 3)

Vu du pont, 1962 (Lumet 2, Aurenche 4, Saulnier 4)

Vuelen los Garcia, 1946 (Infante 3)

Vulcan Entertains. *See* Hell's Fire, 1934

Vulcano, 1949 (Brazzi 3, Magnani 3)

Vulture, 1966 (Crawford 3)

Vultures. *See* Morfalous, 1983

Vultures and Doves, 1912 (Costello 3)

Vultures of the Sea, 1928 (Karloff 3)

Vyborg Side. *See* **Vyborgskaya Storona, 1939**

Vyborgskaya Storona, 1939 (Kozintsev 2, Enei 4, Moskvin 4, Shostakovich 4)

Vynález zkásy, 1958 (Brdečka 4, Zeman 4)

Vyšši princip, 1960 (Brejchová 3)

Výstřely ve ¾ taktu. *See* Schüsse im ¾-Takt, 1965

Vzorná výchova, 1953 (Stallich 4)

Vzteklý ženich, 1919 (Heller 4)

Vzucholod a láska, 1946 (Brdečka 4)

W

W. Bialy dzie in, 1980 (Nowicki 3)
W Plan, 1930 (Launder and Gilliat 2,
    Saville 2, Caroll 3, Young 4)
W Starym Dworku, 1984 (Tyszkiewicz 3)
W.C. Fields and Me, 1976 (Steiger 3,
    Head 4, Mancini 4)
W.C. Fields: Straight Up, 1986 (Moore 3)
W.R.: Misterije organizma, 1971
    (Makavejev 2)
W.R.—Mysteries of the Organism. See
    W.R.: Misterije organizma, 1971
W.S.P., 1974 (Lassally 4)
WUSA, 1970 (Harvey 3, Newman 3,
    Perkins 3, Woodward 3, Schifrin 4)
W.V.S., 1942 (Alwyn 4)
W.W. and the Dixie Dancekings, 1975
    (Reynolds 3, Needham 4)
Wabash Avenue, 1950 (Grable 3, Mature 3,
    Lederer 4, LeMaire 4)
Wabbit Twouble, 1941 (Blanc 4, Clampett 4,
    Stalling 4)
Wabbit Who Came to Supper, 1942
    (Blanc 4, Freleng 4, Stalling 4)
Wachsfigurenkabinett, 1924 (Dieterle 2,
    Wiene 2, Jannings 3, Krauss 3, Veidt 3,
    Galeen 4, Junge 4)
Wackiest Ship in the Army, 1961
    (Lemmon 3, Rafferty 3, Duning 4)
Wackiki Wabbit, 1943 (Blanc 4, Jones 4,
    Stalling 4)
Wacky Blackouts, 1942 (Blanc 4,
    Clampett 4, Stalling 4)
Wacky Wabbit, 1942 (Blanc 4, Clampett 4,
    Foster 4, Stalling 4)
Wacky Wildlife, 1940 (Avery 4, Blanc 4,
    Stalling 4)
Wacky World of Mother Goose, 1967
    (Rutherford 3)
Wacky Worm, 1941 (Blanc 4, Freleng 4,
    Jones 4, Stalling 4)
Waco, 1966 (Keel 3, Russell 3, Head 4)
Wade Brent Pays, 1914 (Mix 3)
Waffen der Jugend, 1912 (Wiene 2)
Waga ai wa yama no kanata ni, 1948
    (Hayasaka 4)
Waga haha no sho, 1936 (Tanaka 3)
Waga koi no tabiji, 1961 (Shinoda 2,
    Iwashita 3, Yamamura 3)
Waga koi waga uta, 1969 (Iwashita 3)
Waga koi wa moenu, 1949 (Mizoguchi 2,
    Shindo 2, Tanaka 3, Yoda 4)
Waga koiseshi otome, 1946 (Hara 3)
Waga michi, 1974 (Shindo 2)
Waga seishun ni kuinashi, 1946 (Hara 3,
    Shimura 3)
Waga shogai no kagayakeru hi, 1948
    (Shindo 2, Yoshimura 2, Mori 3)

Wagaya wa tanoshi, 1951 (Takamine 3,
    Yamada 3)
Wagen in der Nacht, 1979 (Zanussi 2)
Wages for Wives, 1925 (Borzage 2)
Wages of Fear. See **Salaire de la peur, 1952**
Wages of Sin, 1903 (Bitzer 4)
Wages of Tin, 1924 (Roach 4)
Wages of Virtue, 1924 (Dwan 2, Swanson 3)
Waggily Tale, 1958 (Blanc 4, Freleng 4)
Wagner, 1983 (Burton 3, Gielgud 3,
    Greenwood 3, Olivier 3, Redgrave 3,
    Richardson 3, Russell 4, Storaro 4)
Wagon Heels, 1945 (Blanc 4, Clampett 4,
    Stalling 4)
Wagon Master, 1929 (Brown 4, McCord 4)
Wagon Master, 1950 (Ford 2, Bond 3,
    Darwell 3, Johnson 3, Basevi 4,
    Cooper 4, Glennon 4, Nugent 4)
Wagon Show, 1928 (Costello 3, Brown 4)
Wagon Team, 1952 (Autry 3)
Wagon Tracks, 1919 (Hart 3, August 4,
    Ince 4, Sullivan 4)
Wagon Trail, 1935 (Carey 3)
Wagon Train, 1940 (Polglase 4)
Wagon Wheels, 1934 (Scott 3, Sheridan 3)
Wagon Wheels West, 1943 (Eason 4)
Wagons Roll at Night, 1941 (Bogart 3,
    Sidney 3, Haskin 4, Wallis 4)
Wags to Riches, 1949 (Avery 4)
Wags to Riches, 1955 (Avery 4)
Wahnsinn, 1919 (Veidt 3, Hoffmann 4)
Wahrheit über Rosemarie, 1959 (Warm 4)
Waikiki Wedding, 1937 (Crosby 3, Quinn 3,
    Head 4, Prinz 4, Struss 4, Young 4)
Wail. See Dokoku, 1952
Waise von Lowood, 1926 (Rasp 3)
Waisenhauskind, 1917 (Nielsen 3)
Wait Till the Sun Shines, Nellie, 1932
    (Fleischer 4)
Wait till the Sun Shines, Nellie, 1952
    (King 2, LeMaire 4, Newman 4,
    Shamroy 4)
Wait Until Dark, 1967 (Arkin 3, Hepburn 3,
    Jenkins 4, Lang 4, Mancini 4)
Wait Until Spring, Bandini, 1989
    (Dunaway 3)
Waiter from the Ritz, 1926 (Cruze 2)
Waiter No. 5, 1910 (Griffith 2, Pickford 3,
    Bitzer 4)
Waiters' Ball, 1916 (Sennett 2, Arbuckle 3)
Waiters' Picnic, 1913 (Sennett 2,
    Arbuckle 3)
Waiting for Baby, 1941 (Benchley 4)
Waiting for Godot, 1983 (Jarman 2)
Waiting for the Light, 1989 (MacLaine 3)
Waiting People, 1953 (Rotha 2)
Waiting Water. See Väntande vatten, 1965

Waiting Women. See Kvinnors väntan, 1952
Wakai hitotachi, 1954 (Yoshimura 2)
Wakai koibito-tachi, 1959 (Tsukasa 3)
Wakai sensei, 1941 (Hayasaka 4)
Wakaki hi no chuji, 1925 (Kinugasa 2)
Wakaki ushio, 1955 (Yamada 3)
Wakamono yo naze naku ka, 1930
    (Tanaka 3)
Wakare, 1959 (Yamada 3)
Wakaret ikiru toki mo, 1961 (Tanaka 3,
    Tsukasa 3)
Wakasama zamurai torimonocho: Nazo no
    noh-men yashiki, 1950 (Kagawa 3)
Wakasama zamurai torimonocho: Noroi no
    ningyo-shi, 1951 (Kagawa 3)
Wake in Fright, 1971 (Rafferty 3)
Wake Island, 1942 (Bendix 3, Preston 3,
    Burnett 4, Dreier 4, Head 4)
Wake Me When It's Over, 1960 (LeRoy 2,
    Cahn 4, Shamroy 4, Wheeler 4)
Wake of the Red Witch, 1948 (Wayne 3)
Wake Up and Die. See Svegliati e uccidi,
    1966
Wake Up and Dream, 1934 (Darwell 3,
    Mandell 4)
Wake Up and Dream, 1946 (Bacon 2,
    Wheeler 4)
Wake Up and Live, 1937 (Faye 3,
    Cronjager 4, MacGowan 4, Zanuck 4)
Wakefield Express, 1952 (Anderson 2,
    Lassally 4)
Wakiki hi no yorokobi, 1943 (Takamine 3)
Waking Up the Town, 1925 (Cruze 2,
    Shearer 3, Edeson 4)
Wakodo no yume, 1928 (Ozu 2, Ryu 3)
Wak-Wak, ein Märchenzauber. See
    Geschichte des Prinzen Achmed, 1922
Walden, 1968 (Mekas 2)
Waldwinter, 1956 (Kinski 3)
Wales—Green Mountain, Black Mountain,
    1942 (Alwyn 4)
Walk a Tightrope, 1963 (Duryea 3)
Walk, Don't Run, 1966 (Walters 2, Grant 3,
    Jones 4, Stradling 4)
Walk East on Beacon, 1952 (De
    Rochemont 4)
Walk in the Forest, 1975 (Friedhofer 4)
Walk in the Old City of Warsaw. See
    Spacerek staromiejski, 1958
Walk in the Shadow. See Life for Ruth, 1962
Walk in the Spring Rain, 1970 (Bergman 3,
    Quinn 3, Bernstein 4, Green 4, Lang 4)
Walk in the Sun, 1946 (Milestone 2,
    Rossen 2, Andrews 3, Harlan 4)
Walk into Hell. See Walk into Paradise, 1956
Walk into Paradise, 1956 (Rafferty 3,
    Auric 4, Guillemot 4)

Walk Like a Man, 1987 (Frank 4)

Walk on the Wild Side, 1962 (Dmytryk 2, Edwards 2, Baxter 3, Fonda 3, Harvey 3, Stanwyck 3, Bass 4, Bernstein 4, LeMaire 4, Sylbert 4)

Walk Softly, Stranger, 1950 (Stevenson 2, Cotten 3, Valli 3, Schary 4)

Walk Tall, 1960 (Crosby 4)

Walk the Proud Land, 1956 (Bancroft 3, Murphy 3, Salter 4)

Walk Through H, 1978 (Greenaway 2)

Walk with Love and Death, 1969 (Hondo 2, Huston 2, Huston 3, Delerue 4)

Walkabout, 1971 (Roeg 2, Barry 4)

Walkin' My Baby Back Home, 1953 (O'Connor 3)

Walkie Talkie, 1986 (York 3)

Walking After Midnight, 1988 (Coburn 3, Sheen 3)

Walking Along the Main Road. See Vi går landsvagen, 1937

Walking Back, 1928 (Adrian 4, Grot 4)

Walking Dead, 1936 (Curtiz 2, Karloff 3, Mohr 4, Orry-Kelly 4, Westmore Family 4)

Walking Down Broadway. See Hello, Sister, 1933

Walking Down Broadway, 1938 (Trevor 3, Miller 4)

Walking Hills, 1949 (Sturges 2, Kennedy 3, Scott 3, Brown 4)

Walking My Baby Back Home, 1953 (Bacon 2, Leigh 3)

Walking on Air, 1936 (Hunt 4)

Walking Trip of Revenge. See Adauchi hizakurige, 1936

Walking Woman Work. See New York Eye and Ear Control, 1964

Walkout, 1923 (Roach 4)

Walkover. See Walkower, 1965

Walkower, 1965 (Skolimowski 2)

Walky Talky Hawky, 1946 (Blanc 4, McKimson 4, Stalling 4)

Wall. See Muro, 1947

Wall. See Deewar, 1975

Wall, 1982 (Roberts 3, Wallach 3, Rosenman 4)

Wall Between, 1916 (Bushman 3)

Wall in Jerusalem, 1972 (Burton 3)

Wall of Death. See There Is Another Sun, 1951

Wall of Money, 1913 (Dwan 2, Reid 3)

Wall of Noise, 1963 (Ballard 4)

Wall of Tyrrany, 1988 (Golan and Globus 4)

Wall Street, 1929 (Beavers 3)

Wall Street, 1987 (Stone 2, Douglas 3, Sheen 3, Stamp 3)

Wall Street Blues, 1924 (Sennett 2)

Wall Street Cowboy, 1939 (Rogers 3)

Wall Walls. See Mur Murs, 1980

Wallenberg: A Hero's Story, 1985 (Andersson 3)

Wallflower, 1922 (Moore 3)

Wallflower, 1948 (Freund 4)

Wallflowers, 1928 (Arthur 3, Plunkett 4)

Wallop, 1921 (Ford 2, Carey 3, Johnson 3)

Walls of Jericho, 1948 (Stahl 2, Baxter 3, Darnell 3, Douglas 3, Wilde 3, LeMaire 4, Miller 4, Newman 4, Trotti 4)

Walls of Malapaga. See Au-delà des grilles, 1949

Walpurgis Night. See Valborgsmassoafton, 1935

Walter, 1982 (Menges 4)

Walter & Carlo i Amerika, 1989 (Curtis 3)

Walter and June, 1983 (Menges 4)

Walter Wanger's Vogues of 1938. See Vogues of 1938, 1937

Walternacht, 1917 (Kräly 4)

Waltz at Noon. See Mahiru no enbukyoku, 1949

Waltz Dream. See Walzertraum, 1925

Waltz Me Around, 1920 (Roach 4)

Waltz of the Toreadors, 1962 (Cusack 3, Sellers 3, Mathieson 4, Rank 4)

Waltz Time, 1933 (Junge 4)

Waltz Time, 1945 (Kendall 3)

Waltz Time in Vienna. See Walzerkrieg, 1933

Waltz War. See Walzerkrieg, 1933

Waltzes from Vienna, 1934 (Matthews 3, Junge 4, Reville 4)

Walzer um den Stephanstrum, 1935 (Tschechowa 3)

Walzer von Strauss, 1925 (Reisch 4)

Walzerkönig. See Heut Spielt der Strauss, 1928

Walzerkrieg, 1933 (Arletty 3, Walbrook 3, Herlth 4, Hoffmann 4, Röhrig 4)

Walzertraum, 1925 (Pommer 4, Schüfftan 4)

Wanda, 1983 (Vogler 3)

Wanda la peccatrice, 1952 (Rosay 3, Pinelli 4)

Wanda Nevada, 1979 (Fonda 3)

Wanderer, 1911 (Dwan 2)

Wanderer, 1913 (Griffith 2, Barrymore 3, Walthall 3, Bitzer 4)

Wanderer, 1926 (Walsh 2, Beery 3, Carey 3, Head 4, Menzies 4)

Wanderer of the Wasteland, 1924 (Zukor 4)

Wanderer of the Wasteland, 1934 (Crabbe 3)

Wanderers. See Girovaghi, 1956

Wanderer's Notebook. See Horoki, 1962

Wanderers of the Desert. See World Window, 1977

Wandering. See Bloudĕni, 1965

Wandering Daughters, 1923 (Coffee 4)

Wandering Fires, 1925 (Stradling 4)

Wandering Gypsy, 1911 (Dwan 2)

Wandering Husbands, 1924 (Sullivan 4)

Wandering Jew, 1933 (Veidt 3)

Wandering Papas, 1925 (Laurel and Hardy 3, Roach 4)

Wandering Willies, 1926 (Sennett 2)

Wanderlust. See Mary Jane's Pa, 1935

Wandernde Bild, 1920 (Von Harbou 4)

Wandernde Licht, 1916 (Wiene 2, Porten 3, Messter 4)

Wandernder Held. See Wandernde Bild, 1920

Waning Sex, 1926 (Shearer 3, Gibbons 4, Mayer 4)

Wanted, 1970 (Brocka 2)

Wanted: A Baby. See Bachelor's Baby, 1927

Wanted—A Bad Man, 1917 (Laurel and Hardy 3)

Wanted, a Child, 1909 (Griffith 2, Bitzer 4)

Wanted, A Grandmother, 1912 (Costello 3)

Wanted: Babysitter. See Baby-Sitter, 1975

Wanted—$5000, 1918 (Daniels 3, Lloyd 3, Roach 4)

Wanted Men. See Wolves, 1930

Wanters, 1923 (Stahl 2, Shearer 3, Mayer 4)

Wanton Countess. See Senso, 1954

War Against Mrs. Hadley, 1942 (Johnson 3, Freund 4, Schary 4)

War and Peace. See Voina i mir, 1912

War and Peace, 1956 (Camerini 2, Vidor 2, Fonda 3, Gassman 3, Hepburn 3, Homolka 3, Lom 3, Mills 3, Cardiff 4, De Laurentiis 4, Gherardi 4, Ponti 4, Rota 4)

War and Peace. See **Voina i mir, 1959**

War and Peace. See Krieg und frieden, 1983

War and Pieces, 1964 (Blanc 4)

War and Remembrance, 1988 (Gielgud 3, Mitchum 3)

War Arrow, 1954 (O'Hara 3, Daniels 4, Hayes 4)

War at Sea from Hawaii to Malaya. See Hawai-Marei oki kaisen, 1942

War Babies, 1932 (Temple 3)

War Between Men and Women, 1972 (Lemmon 3, Robards 3, Hamlisch 4)

War Between the Tates, 1977 (Barry 4)

War Bonnet. See Savage, 1952

War Brides, 1916 (Brenon 2, Barthelmess 3, Nazimova 3, Hunt 4)

War Comes to America. See **Why We Fight series, 1943–45**

War Correspondent, 1932 (Swerling 4)

War Dogs, 1943 (Hanna and Barbera 4)

War Drums, 1956 (Johnson 3)

War Feathers, 1926 (Roach 4)

War Game, 1961 (Zetterling 2)

War Game, 1962 (Menges 4)

War Game, 1966 (Watkins 2)

War Games. See Suppose They Gave a War and Nobody Came?, 1970

War Gods of the Deep, 1965 (Tourneur 2, Marion 4)

War Hunt, 1962 (Pollack 2, Redford 3, McCord 4)

War in the Mediterranean, 1943 (Howard 3)

War Is Over. See Guerre est finie, 1966

War Lord. See West of Shanghai, 1937

War Lord, 1965 (Schaffner 2, Heston 3, Bumstead 4, Metty 4, Salter 4, Westmore Family 4, Whitlock 4)

War Lover, 1962 (McQueen 3, Wagner 3, Koch 4, Mathieson 4)

War Mamas, 1931 (Roach 4)

War Nurse, 1930 (Montgomery 3, Gibbons 4, Rosher 4)

War of the Gargantuas. See Furankenshutain no kaiju—Sanda tai Gailah, 1966

War of the Roses, 1989 (Douglas 3, Turner 3, Bass 4)

War of the Satellites, 1958 (Corman 2, Crosby 4)

War of the Wildcats. See In Old Oklahoma, 1943

War of the Worlds, 1953 (Barnes 4, Haskin 4, Head 4, Pal 4)

War on the Plains, 1912 (Anderson 3, Bosworth 3, Ince 4)

War Paint, 1926 (Van Dyke 2)

War Relief, 1917 (Fairbanks 3)

War Requiem, 1989 (Jarman 2, Olivier 3)

War Shock. See Woman's Devotion, 1956

War Wagon, 1967 (Fernández 2, Dern 3, Douglas 3, Keel 3, Wayne 3, Clothier 4, Needham 4, Tiomkin 4, Westmore Family 4, Whitlock 4)

Ward of the King, 1913 (Cruze 2)

Wardrobe, 1958 (Dunning 4)

Ware Case, 1938 (Stevenson 2, Balcon 4)

Ware hitotsubu no mugi naredo, 1965 (Takamine 3)

Ware nakinurete, 1948 (Mori 3)

Warenhausprinzessin, 1926 (Albers 3)

Warera sarariiman, 1963 (Tsukasa 3)
Wareraga kyokan, 1939 (Takamine 3)
WarGames, 1983 (Burtt 4, Fraker 4)
Waris, 1954 (Biswas 4)
Warlock, 1959 (Dmytryk 2, Fonda 3,
    Malone 3, Quinn 3, Widmark 3,
    LeMaire 4)
Warlock, 1989 (Goldsmith 4)
Warlords of Atlantis, 1978 (Charisse 3)
Warlords of the 21st Century. See
    Battletruck, 1981
Warm Corner, 1930 (Saville 2, Balcon 4)
Warm Current. See Danryu, 1939
Warm December, 1973 (Poitier 3)
Warm Reception, 1916 (Laurel and Hardy 3)
Warmakers, 1913 (Costello 3)
Warming Up, 1928 (Arthur 3, Cronjager 4)
Warn London, 1934 (Bennett 4)
Warning, 1910 (White 3)
Warning, 1914 (Anderson 3, Crisp 3)
Warning, 1927 (Walker 4)
Warning, 1982 (Bardem 2)
Warning Hand, 1912 (Bushman 3)
Warning Shadows. See Schatten, 1923
Warning Shot, 1967 (Gish 3, Pidgeon 3,
    Sanders 3, Biroc 4, Edouart 4,
    Goldsmith 4, Head 4)
Warning to Wantons, 1949 (Rank 4)
Warnung vor einer heiligen Nutte, 1970
    (Constantine 3, Schygulla 3, Ballhaus 4)
Warpath, 1951 (O'Brien 3, Haskin 4)
Warrant, 1975 (Anand 3)
Warrens of Virginia, 1915 (De Mille 2,
    Sweet 3, Buckland 4)
Warrior and the Demon, 1988 (Carpenter 2)
Warrior of the Lost Word, 1984
    (Pleasence 3)
Warrior Queen, 1987 (Pleasence 3)
Warriors, 1930 (Rooney 3)
Warriors. See Dark Avenger, 1955
Warriors, 1979 (Hill 2)
Warriors 5. See Guerra continua, 1961
Warrior's Husband, 1933 (Levien 4, Mohr 4)
Warriors of Faith. See Jan Roháč z dubé,
    1947
Warrior's Rest. See Repos du guerrier, 1962
Warrior Who Crosses the Sea. See Umi o
    yuku bushi, 1939
Warschauer Zitadelle, 1937 (Warm 4)
Wartezimmer zum Jenseits, 1964 (Kinski 3)
Warui yatsu hodo yoku nemuru, 1960
    (Kagawa 3, Mifune 3, Mori 3, Ryu 3,
    Shimura 3, Muraki 4)
Warum lauft Herr R amok?, 1969
    (Schygulla 3)
Was bin ich ohne Dich?, 1934
    (Tschechowa 3, Von Harbou 4)
Was es der im dritten Stock?, 1938
    (Porten 3)
Was Frauen träumen, 1933 (Wilder 2,
    Fröhlich 3, Lorre 3)
Was geschah in dieser Nacht, 1941
    (Wagner 4)
Was He a Coward?, 1911 (Griffith 2,
    Sweet 3, Bitzer 4)
Was ist los mit Nanette, 1928 (Holger-
    Madsen 2)
Was Justice Served?, 1909 (Griffith 2,
    Bitzer 4)
Washed Ashore, 1922 (Roach 4)
Washee Ironee, 1934 (Roach 4)
Washington at Valley Forge, 1908 (Olcott 2)
Washington Cowboy. See Rovin'
    Tumbleweeds, 1939

Washington Masquerade, 1932
    (Barrymore 3, McDaniel 3, Adrian 4,
    Toland 4)
Washington Melodrama, 1941 (Rosson 4)
Washington Merry-Go-Round, 1932
    (Swerling 4, Wanger 4)
Washington Story, 1952 (Calhern 3,
    Johnson 3, Neal 3, Alton 4, Rose 4,
    Schary 4)
Wasp, 1915 (Eason 4)
Wasp Woman, 1959 (Corman 2)
Wasser für Canitoga, 1939 (Albers 3)
Wasted Love, 1930 (Wong 3)
Wasted Night, 1972 (Nowicki 3)
Wastrel, 1960 (Cacoyannis 2, Cecchi
    D'Amico 4)
Wasureenu bojo, 1956 (Yamamura 3)
Watakushi-tachi no kekkon, 1962
    (Shinoda 2)
Watan, 1938 (Mehboob 2)
Wataridori itsukaeru, 1955 (Takamine 3,
    Tanaka 3)
Watashi iwa kai ni naritai, 1959 (Muraki 4)
Watashi niwa otto ga aru, 1940 (Tanaka 3)
Watashi no na wa joufu. See Waga koi wa
    moenu, 1949
Watashi no niisan, 1934 (Hasegawa 3,
    Tanaka 3)
Watashi no papa-san mamaga suki, 1931
    (Takamine 3)
Watashi wa Bellet, 1964 (Oshima 2)
Watch Dog, 1923 (Roach 4)
Watch Dog, 1945 (Terry 4)
Watch Him Step, 1922 (Mohr 4)
Watch it Sailor!, 1961 (Carreras 4)
Watch on the Rhine, 1943 (Bondi 3, Davis 3,
    Lukas 3, Friedhofer 4, Mohr 4, Orry-
    Kelly 4, Steiner 4, Wallis 4, Warner 4)
Watch Out, 1924 (Sennett 2)
Watch the Birdie, 1935 (Hope 3)
Watch the Birdie, 1950 (Miller 3)
Watch the Birdie, 1954 (Godfrey 4)
Watch the Birdie, 1963 (Russell 2)
Watch Your Neighbors, 1918 (Sennett 2)
Watch Your Stern, 1960 (Dillon 4)
Watch Your Wife, 1922 (Roach 4)
Watcha Watchin', 1962 (Hanna and
    Barbera 4)
Watchdog, 1939 (Terry 4)
Watcher in the Woods, 1980 (Baker 3,
    Davis 3)
Watchtower over Tomorrow, 1945 (Hecht 4)
Water, 1975 (Greenaway 2)
Water, 1985 (Caine 3, Slocombe 4)
Water Babies, 1978 (Greenwood 3)
Water Cure, 1916 (Laurel and Hardy 3)
Water Dog, 1914 (Sennett 2, Arbuckle 3)
Water Duel, 1900 (Bitzer 4)
Water for Firefighting, 1948 (Halas and
    Batchelor 4)
Water Gipsies, 1932 (Dean 4, Reville 4)
Water Hole, 1928 (Mankiewicz 4)
Water Magician. See Taki no shiraito, 1952
Water Nymph, 1912 (Sennett 2, Normand 3)
Water Wagons, 1925 (Sennett 2)
Water War, 1911 (Dwan 2)
Water, Water Every Hare, 1952 (Blanc 4,
    Jones 4, Maltese 4, Stalling 4)
Water, Water Everywhere, 1920 (Rogers 3)
Water Wrackets, 1975 (Greenaway 2)
Watercolor, 1958 (Ioseliani 2)
Waterfront, 1928 (Garmes 4, Robinson 4)
Waterfront, 1939 (Bond 3)
Waterfront, 1944 (Carradine 3)

Waterfront, 1950 (Burton 3, Newton 3,
    Mathieson 4)
Waterfront Lady, 1935 (Lewis 2, Bond 3)
Waterfront Women. See Waterfront, 1950
Waterhole Number Three, 1967 (Blondell 3,
    Coburn 3, Dern 3, Burks 4)
Waterloo, 1928 (Vanel 3, Wagner 4)
Waterloo, 1970 (Welles 2, Bondarchuk 3,
    Hawkins 3, Steiger 3, De Laurentiis 4,
    Rota 4)
Waterloo Bridge, 1931 (Whale 2, Davis 3,
    Edeson 4, Fulton 4, Laemmle 4)
Waterloo Bridge, 1940 (LeRoy 2, Leigh 3,
    Taylor 3, Adrian 4, Behrman 4,
    Gillespie 4, Mayer 4, Ruttenberg 4,
    Stothart 4)
Waterloo Road, 1944 (Launder and Gilliat 2,
    Granger 3, Mills 3, Sim 3, Rank 4,
    Vetchinsky 4)
Waters of Time, 1950 (Wright 2, Dehn 4)
Watersark, 1964 (Wieland 2)
Watership Down, 1978 (Elliott 3, Hurt 3,
    Richardson 3)
Wattstax, 1973 (Pryor 3)
Wave. See Redes, 1990
Wave of Unrest, 1954 (Xie 2)
Wavelength, 1967 (Snow 2, Wieland 2)
Wavell's 30,000, 1942 (Dalrymple 4)
Wax Experiments, 1946 (Fischinger 2)
Wax Works, 1934 (Lantz 4)
Waxworks. See Wachsfigurenkabinett,
    1924
Way Ahead, 1944 (Reed 2, Howard 3,
    Niven 3, Ustinov 3, Alwyn 4, Green 4,
    Mathieson 4, Rank 4)
Way Back Home, 1931 (Davis 3, Berman 4,
    Hunt 4, Murfin 4, Steiner 4, Westmore
    Family 4)
Way Back When series, 1942 (Fleischer 4)
Way Down East, 1920 (Griffith 2,
    Barthelmess 3, Gish 3, Shearer 3,
    Bitzer 4)
Way Down East, 1935 (King 2, Fonda 3,
    Estabrook 4, Friedhofer 4)
Way Down South, 1939 (Young 4)
Way Down Yonder in the Corn, 1943
    (Fleischer 4)
Way for a Sailor, 1930 (Wood 2, Beery 3,
    Gilbert 3, Milland 3, Gibbons 4,
    MacArthur 4, Mayer 4)
Way in the Wilderness, 1940 (Zinnemann 2)
Way of a Gaucho, 1952 (Tourneur 2,
    Sloane 3, Tierney 3, Dunne 4, LeMaire 4,
    Newman 4, Wheeler 4)
Way of a Girl, 1925 (Gibbons 4)
Way of a Man, 1909 (Sennett 2)
Way of a Man with a Maid, 1918 (Crisp 3)
Way of a Woman, 1914 (Reid 3)
Way of a Woman, 1919 (Talmadge 3,
    Schenck 4)
Way of All Flesh, 1927 (Fleming 2,
    Jannings 3, Biro 4, Furthman 4, Zukor 4)
Way of All Flesh, 1940 (Coffee 4,
    Furthman 4, Head 4, Young 4)
Way of All Pants, 1927 (Roach 4)
Way of Drama. See Shibaido, 1944
Way of Man, 1909 (Griffith 2, Lawrence 3,
    Pickford 3, Bitzer 4)
Way of the Beast. See Kemonomichi, 1965
Way of the Dragon. See Return of the
    Dragon, 1973
Way of the Redman, 1914 (Mix 3)
Way of the Rem Redman, 1916 (Mix 3)
Way of the Strong, 1926 (Cohn 4)

Way of the Strong, 1928 (Capra 2)
Way of the West, 1911 (Dwan 2)
Way of the World, 1910 (Griffith 2, Bitzer 4)
Way of the World, 1916 (Bosworth 3)
Way Out West, 1930 (Niblo 2, Gibbons 4,
Shearer 4)
Way Out West, 1937 (Laurel and Hardy 3,
Roach 4)
Way Perilous, 1913 (Bushman 3)
Way to Love, 1933 (Chevalier 3, Horton 3,
Glazer 4, Lang 4, Zukor 4)
Way to Shadow Garden, 1954 (Brakhage 2)
Way to the Gold, 1957 (Brennan 3,
LeMaire 4)
Way to the Heights. See Cesty k výšinam,
1921
Way to the Sea, 1936 (Rotha 2)
Way to the Skies. See Droga do nieba, 1958
Way to the Stars, 1945 (Howard 3, Mills 3,
Redgrave 3, Simmons 3, De Grunwald 4,
Dillon 4, Green 4, Rank 4, Rattigan 4)
Way Up Thar, 1935 (Sennett 2, Rogers 3)
Way . . . Way Out, 1966 (Lewis 2, Clothier 4,
Schifrin 4, Smith 4)
Way We Live, 1946 (Rank 4)
Way West, 1967 (Douglas 3, Field 3,
Mitchum 3, Widmark 3, Clothier 4,
Kaper 4, Maddow 4, Needham 4,
Previn 4)
Way We Were, 1973 (Pollack 2, Redford 3,
Streisand 3, Booth 4, Hamlisch 4,
Sharaff 4, Stark 4)
Ways in the Night. See Wagen in der Nacht,
1979
Ways of Fate, 1913 (Dwan 2, Reid 3)
Ways of Love. See Amore, 1948
Wayside People. See Robo no ishi, 1960
Wayward, 1932 (Green 4, Head 4)
Wayward Bus, 1957 (Mansfield 3,
Brackett 4, Clarke 4, LeMaire 4)
Wayward Life. See Provinciale, 1952
Wayward Youth. See Verirrte Jugend, 1929
We Aim to Please, 1934 (Fleischer 4)
We All Help, 1941 (Cushing 3)
We All Loved Each Other So Much. See
C'eravamo tanto amati, 1974
We Americans, 1928 (Laemmle 4)
We Are Building. See Wy brouwen, 1929
We Are in the Navy Now. See We Joined the
Navy, 1962
We Are Not Alone, 1939 (Goulding 2,
Muni 3, Blanke 4, Gaudio 4, Haskin 4,
Steiner 4, Wallis 4)
We Are the Lambeth Boys, 1958
(Lassally 4)
We Are the Marines, 1942 (De
Rochemont 4)
We Can't Have Everything, 1918 (De
Mille 2, Buckland 4)
We Did It, 1936 (Fleischer 4)
We Dive at Dawn, 1943 (Asquith 2, Mills 3,
Rank 4)
We Faw Down, 1928 (McCarey 2, Laurel
and Hardy 3)
We from the Theatre. See Vi som går
scenvägen, 1938
We Go Fast, 1941 (Day 4)
We Go Through the Kitchen. See Vi som går
köksvägen, 1932
We har manje namn, 1976 (Zetterling 2)
We Have Come for Your Daughters. See
Medicine Ball Caravan, 1970
We Have Many Names. See We har manje
namn, 1976

We Have Our Moments, 1937 (Niven 3,
Pangborn 3, Krasner 4)
We Humans. See Young America, 1932
We Joined the Navy, 1962 (Bogarde 3,
More 3, Heller 4)
We Live Again, 1934 (Mamoulian 2,
Sturges 2, Jaffe 3, March 3, Day 4,
Goldwyn 4, Jennings 4, Newman 4,
Toland 4)
We Live in Two Worlds, 1937 (Cavalcanti 2,
Grierson 2, Jaubert 4)
We Moderns, 1925 (LeRoy 2, Moore 3,
Mathis 4, McCord 4)
We Must Have Music, 1941 (Garland 3)
We Never Sleep, 1917 (Daniels 3, Lloyd 3,
Roach 4)
We Owe It to Our Children, 1955 (Lee 3)
We Sail at Midnight, 1943 (Ford 2)
We Search and Strike, 1942 (Dalrymple 4)
We Serve, 1941 (Johnson 3)
We Slip Up. See We Faw Down, 1928
We Still Kill the Old Way. See Ciascuno il
sou, 1967
We, the Animals, Squeak, 1941 (Blanc 4,
Clampett 4, Stalling 4)
We the Living. See Noi vivi, 1988
We the Women. See Siamo donne, 1953
We Think the World of You, 1988 (Bates 3)
We Three. See Compromised, 1931
We Three Debutantes. See Vi tre debutera,
1953
We Two. See Vi två, 1939
We Want Our Mummy, 1939 (Three
Stooges 3)
We Were Dancing, 1942 (Douglas 3,
Gardner 3, Shearer 3, Kaper 4)
We Were Strangers, 1949 (Huston 2,
Armendáriz 3, Garfield 3, Jones 3,
Novarro 3, Metty 4, Spiegel 4)
We Who Are Young, 1940 (Turner 3,
Freund 4, Kaper 4, Trumbo 4)
We Who Are Young, 1952 (Lassally 4)
Weak and the Wicked, 1953 (Dors 3, Love 3,
Roberts 3)
Weak-End Party, 1922 (Laurel and Hardy 3)
Weaker Brother, 1911 (Dwan 2)
Weaker Sex, 1948 (Rank 4)
Weaker's Strength, 1914 (Anderson 3)
Weakly Reporter, 1944 (Blanc 4, Jones 4,
Stalling 4)
Wealth of the Poor, 1915 (Anderson 3)
Wealth of Waters, 1953 (Rotha 2)
Weapon, 1913 (Costello 3)
Weapon, 1957 (Marshall 3)
Wear a Very Big Hat, 1965 (Loach 2)
Wear Willies, 1929 (Lantz 4)
Wearing of the Grin, 1951 (Blanc 4, Jones 4,
Maltese 4)
Weary River, 1929 (Barthelmess 3, Haller 4)
Weasel Stop, 1956 (Blanc 4, McKimson 4)
Weasel While You Work, 1958 (Blanc 4,
McKimson 4)
Weather Forecast, 1934 (Grierson 2)
Weather Wizards, 1939 (Zinnemann 2)
Weavers. See Weber, 1927
Web, 1947 (Bendix 3, O'Brien 3, Price 3,
Salter 4)
Web, 1956 (Watkins 2)
Web. See Après le vent des sables, 1974
Web. See Netz, 1975
Web of Desire, 1917 (Marion 4)
Web of Evidence. See Beyond This Place,
1959
Web of Fear. See Constance aux enfers, 1964

Web of Passion. See A double tour, 1959
Web of the Spider. See Nell stretta morsa del
ragno, 1971
Weber, 1927 (Dieterle 2, Wegener 3,
Andrejew 4)
Webster Boy, 1962 (Cassavetes 2)
Wedding, 1905 (Bitzer 4)
Wedding. See Svadba, 1944
Wedding. See Wesele, 1972
Wedding, 1978 (Altman 2, Cromwell 2,
Chaplin 3, Farrow 3, Gassman 3, Gish 3,
Zsigmond 4)
Wedding at Ulfåsa. See Bröllopet på Ulfåsa,
1911
Wedding Bells, 1921 (Schenck 4)
Wedding Bells, 1927 (Schulberg 4)
Wedding Bells. See Royal Wedding, 1951
Wedding Bells Out of Tune, 1921
(Sennett 2)
Wedding Belts, 1942 (Fleischer 4)
Wedding Breakfast. See Catered Affair,
1956
Wedding Day. See Bröllopsdagen, 1960
Wedding Dress, 1911 (Dwan 2)
Wedding Gown, 1913 (Loos 4)
Wedding Group, 1936 (Sim 3)
Wedding in Blood. See Noces rouges, 1973
Wedding in Monaco, 1956 (Kelly 3)
Wedding in the Eccentric Club. See Hochzeit
in Ekzentrik Klub, 1917
Wedding in White, 1973 (Pleasence 3)
Wedding March, 1928 (Von Stroheim 2,
Wray 3, Day 4, Mohr 4, Zukor 4)
Wedding Night, 1935 (Vidor 2, Bellamy 3,
Brennan 3, Cooper 3, Goldwyn 4,
Newman 4, Toland 4)
Wedding Night. See Noc Poslubna, 1959
Wedding of Jack and Jill, 1930 (Garland 3)
Wedding Party, 1969 (De Palma 2,
Clayburgh 3, De Niro 3)
Wedding Present, 1936 (Bennett 3, Grant 3,
Dreier 4, Head 4, Schulberg 4,
Shamroy 4)
Wedding Rehearsal, 1932 (Korda 2,
Oberon 3, Biro 4, Korda, A. 4, Korda,
V. 4)
Wedding Rings, 1929 (Haller 4)
Wedlock, 1918 (Gilbert 3)
Wedlock Deadlock, 1947 (Bruckman 4)
Wedlock House: An Intercourse, 1959
(Brakhage 2)
Wednesday, 1974 (Lemmon 3)
Wednesday's Child, 1934 (Berman 4,
MacGowan 4, Plunkett 4, Steiner 4)
Wednesday's Luck, 1936 (Pearson 2,
Havelock-Allan 4)
Wee Geordie. See Geordie, 1955
Weeds, 1987 (Nolte 3)
Week End Husbands, 1924 (Costello 3)
Wee Lady Betty, 1917 (Borzage 2,
Love 3)
Wee MacGregor's Sweetheart, 1922
(Pearson 2)
Wee Sandy, 1962 (Reiniger 4)
Wee Wee Monsieur, 1938 (Three Stooges 3)
Wee Willie Winkie, 1937 (Ford 2,
McLaglen 3, Temple 3, Miller 4,
Newman 4, Zanuck 4)
**Week-end, 1967 (Godard 2, Léaud 3,
Coutard 4, Gégauff 4, Guillemot 4)**
Weekend à Zuydcoote, 1964 (Belmondo 3,
Decaë 4, Hakim 4, Jarre 4)
Weekend at Dunkirk. See Weekend à
Zuydcoote, 1964

Weekend at the Waldorf, 1945 (Walters 2, Johnson 3, Pidgeon 3, Rogers 3, Turner 3, Benchley 4, Green 4, Irene 4)

Weekend for Three, 1941 (Garnett 2, Horton 3, Pangborn 3, Metty 4)

Weekend in Havana, 1941 (Faye 3, Miranda 3, Day 4, Newman 4, Pan 4)

Weekend Marriage, 1932 (Young 3, Orry-Kelly 4)

Weekend Murders. See Concerto per pistola solista, 1970

Weekend of a Champion, 1972 (Polanski 2)

Week-end Pass, 1944 (Bruckman 4)

Weekend sur deux, 1990 (Baye 3, Guillemot 4)

Week-end total, 1965 (Braunberger 4)

Weekend with Father, 1951 (Sirk 2, Neal 3, Boyle 4)

Weekend with Lulu, 1961 (Carreras 4)

Weekend Wives, 1928 (Launder and Gilliat 2)

Weekends Only, 1932 (Bennett 3, Mohr 4)

Weekly Reels. See Kino-Nedelia, 1958

Week's Vacation. See Semaine de vacances, 1980

Weg der ins Verderben fuhrt. See Berlin W., 1920

Weg des Todes, 1917 (Veidt 3)

Weg zum Nachbarn, 1966 (Lenica 4)

Wege im Zwielicht, 1948 (Fröhlich 3)

Wege nach Rio, 1931 (Homolka 3)

Wege zu Kraft und Schönheit, 1925 (Pommer 4)

Wege zur gutten Ehe, 1933 (Tschechowa 3)

Wehe, wenn er losgelassen, 1932 (Heller 4)

Wehe, wenn sie losgelassen, 1926 (Porten 3, Courant 4)

Weib des Pharao, 1922 (Lubitsch 2, Jannings 3, Wegener 3, Kräly 4, Metzner 4)

Weib in Flammen, 1928 (Albers 3, Planer 4)

Weighing the Baby, 1903 (Bitzer 4)

Weight for Me, 1989 (Halas and Batchelor 4)

Weird Science, 1985 (Hughes 2)

Weird Woman, 1944 (Miller 4, Salter 4)

Weir-Falcon Saga, 1970 (Brakhage 2)

Weiss Rausch, 1931 (Riefenstahl 2)

Weisse Abenteuer, 1951 (Herlth 4)

Weisse Dämon, 1932 (Albers 3, Lorre 3, Hoffmann 4)

Weisse Hölle von Piz Palü, 1929 (Metzner 4)

Weisse Pfau, 1920 (Leni 2)

Weisse Rosen, 1914 (Gad 2, Nielsen 3, Kräly 4)

Weisse Schatten, 1951 (Käutner 2)

Weisse Stadion, 1928 (Ruttmann 2)

Weisse Teufel, 1930 (Volkov 2, Dagover 3, Mozhukin 3, Courant 4)

Weissen Rosen von Ravensberg, 1929 (Warm 4)

Weisses Hölle vom Piz Palü, 1929 (Riefenstahl 2)

Welcome Burglar, 1908 (Griffith 2, Bitzer 4)

Welcome Danger, 1929 (Lloyd 3, Bruckman 4, Zukor 4)

Welcome Home, 1925 (Cruze 2, Brown 4)

Welcome Home, 1935 (Miller 4)

Welcome Home. See Vlast vítá, 1945

Welcome Home, 1989 (Schaffner 2, Mancini 4)

Welcome Home, Johnny Bristol, 1972 (Sheen 3, Schifrin 4)

Welcome Intruder, 1913 (Griffith 2, Barrymore 3, Bitzer 4)

Welcome Little Stranger, 1941 (Terry 4)

Welcome Stranger, 1947 (Crosby 3, Fitzgerald 3, Dreier 4, Head 4)

Welcome to Arrow Beach, 1973 (Harvey 3)

Welcome to Blood City, 1977 (Palance 3)

Welcome to Britain, 1943 (Asquith 2, Hope 3, Meredith 3, Alwyn 4)

Welcome to Hard Times, 1967 (Fonda 3, Oates 3)

Welcome to L.A., 1976 (Altman 2, Rudolph 2, Chaplin 3, Spacek 3)

Welfare, 1975 (Wiseman 2)

Welfare of the Workers, 1940 (Jennings 2)

Well, 1913 (Barrymore 3)

Well, 1951 (Laszlo 4, Tiomkin 4)

We'll Meet Again, 1982 (York 3)

We'll Meet in the Gallery. See Ci troviamo in Galleria, 1953

We'll Smile Again, 1942 (Baxter 2, Crazy Gang 3)

Well Well Well. See Ojojoj eller sången om den eldröda hummern, 1965

Well Worn Daffy, 1965 (Blanc 4, McKimson 4)

Well-Digger's Daughter. See Fille du puisatier, 1940

Well-Filled Day. See Journée bien remplie, 1972

Well-Groomed Bride, 1946 (De Havilland 3, Milland 3, Dreier 4, Head 4, Seitz 4)

Wells Fargo, 1937 (McCrea 3, Dreier 4, Estabrook 4, Head 4, Young 4)

Welsh Singer, 1915 (Evans 3)

Welt ohne Maske, 1934 (Tschechowa 3)

Welt ohne Waffen, 1918 (Wegener 3)

Welt will belogen sein, 1926 (Courant 4)

Weltbrand, 1920 (Gad 2, Kortner 3)

Weltspiegel, 1918 (Pick 2)

Weltstrasse See—Welthafen Hamburg, 1938 (Ruttman 2)

Wendy and Joyce, 1985 (Wieland 2)

Wenn am Sonntagabend die Dorfmusik spielt, 1933 (Warm 4)

Wenn das Herz in Hass erglüht, 1918 (Negri 3)

Wenn der junge Wein blüht, 1943 (Porten 3)

Wenn der weisse Flieder wieder blüht, 1953 (Schneider 3)

Wenn die Maske fällt, 1912 (Gad 2, Nielsen 3)

Wenn die Musik nicht wär, 1935 (Gallone 2)

Wenn die Schwalben heimwärts ziehn, 1928 (Fröhlich 3)

Wenn die Sonne wieder scheint, 1943 (Wegener 3, Herlth 4)

Wenn du einmal dein Herz verschenkst, 1929 (Wagner 4)

Wenn ein Weib den Weg verliert. See Café Electric, 1927

Wenn Frauen lieben und hassen, 1917 (Krauss 3)

Wenn ich König wär!, 1934 (Warm 4)

Wenn Männer Schlange stehen. See Chikita, 1961

Wenn Tote sprechen, 1917 (Veidt 3)

Wenn vier dasselbe Tun, 1917 (Lubitsch 2, Jannings 3)

Went the Day Well?, 1942 (Balcon 4, Greene 4, Walton 4)

Wer das Scheiden hat erfunden, 1928 (Albers 3)

Wer nimmt die Liebe ernst?, 1931 (Courant 4)

Werdegeng. See Reigen, 1920

We're All Gamblers, 1927 (Cruze 2, Glennon 4)

We're Going to Be Rich, 1938 (Fields 3, McLaglen 3)

We're in the Army Now. See Pack Up Your Troubles, 1939

We're in the Money, 1935 (Blondell 3, Brown 4)

We're in the Navy Now, 1926 (Beery 3, Schulberg 4)

We're No Angels, 1955 (Curtiz 2, Bennett 3, Bogart 3, Rathbone 3, Ustinov 3)

We're No Angels, 1989 (Jordan 2, De Niro 3)

We're Not Dressing, 1934 (Crosby 3, Lombard 3, Milland 3, Dreier 4, Glazer 4, Lang 4)

We're Not Married, 1952 (Goulding 2, Arden 3, Calhern 3, Darwell 3, Marvin 3, Monroe 3, Rogers 3, Johnson 4, LeMaire 4)

We're Not the Jet Set, 1977 (Duvall 3)

We're on the Jury, 1937 (Musuraca 4)

We're Only Human, 1936 (Darwell 3, Hunt 4)

We're Rich Again, 1934 (Crabbe 3, Musuraca 4, Plunkett 4, Steiner 4)

Werewolf, 1956 (Katzman 4)

Werewolf of London, 1935 (D'Agostino 4, Fulton 4, Pierce 4)

Werther, 1922 (Dulac 2)

Werther, 1927 (Heller 4)

Werther, 1938 (Douy 4, Lourié 4)

Wesele, 1972 (Wajda 2, Olbrychski 3)

Wesoła II, 1952 (Ścibor-Rylski 4)

West 11, 1963 (Dors 3, Heller 4)

West and Soda, 1965 (Bozzetto 4)

West is West, 1920 (Carey 3)

West of Broadway, 1931 (Bellamy 3, Gilbert 3, Meredyth 4)

West of Hot Dog, 1924 (Laurel and Hardy 3)

West of Shanghai, 1937 (Karloff 3)

West of the Divide, 1934 (Wayne 3, Canutt 4)

West of the Pecos, 1934 (Beavers 3)

West of the Pecos, 1935 (Metty 4)

West of the Pecos, 1945 (Mitchum 3)

West of the Pesos, 1960 (Blanc 4, McKimson 4)

West of Zanzibar, 1928 (Browning 2, Chaney 3, Johnson 3, Day 4, Gibbons 4, Young 4)

West of Zanzibar, 1954 (Watt 2)

West Point, 1927 (Dwan 2, Crawford 3)

West Point of the Air, 1935 (Beery 3, O'Sullivan 3, Russell 3, Taylor 3, Young 3, Saunders 4)

West Point Story, 1950 (Cagney 3, Day 3, Cahn 4, Prinz 4)

West Point Widow, 1941 (Siodmak 2, Dreier 4, Head 4, Kräly 4)

West Side Story, 1961 (Wise 2, Wood 3, Bass 4, Dunn 4, Green 4, Leven 4, Mirisch 4, Sharaff 4)

West Virginian. See Reel Virginian, 1924

Westbound, 1959 (Boetticher 2, Scott 3, Blanke 4)

Western Approaches, 1944 (Cardiff 4, Dalrymple 4)

Western Blood, 1918 (Mix 3)

Western Chivalry, 1910 (Anderson 3)

Western Courage, 1935 (Bond 3)

Western Cyclone, 1943 (Crabbe 3)

Western Daze, 1941 (Pal 4)

402 WESTERN DOCTOR'S PERIL

Western Doctor's Peril, 1911 (Dwan 2)
Western Dreamer, 1911 (Dwan 2)
Western Girls, 1912 (Anderson 3)
Western Girl's Sacrifice, 1911 (Anderson 3)
Western Governor's Humanity, 1980
   (Johnson 3)
Western Hearts, 1911 (Mix 3)
Western Hearts, 1912 (Anderson 3)
Western History, 1971 (Brakhage 2)
Western Isles, 1941 (Alwyn 4, Cardiff 4)
Western Jamboree, 1938 (Autry 3)
Western Justice, 1907 (Anderson 3, Selig 4)
Western Justice, 1937 (Katzman 4)
Western Law That Failed, 1913
   (Anderson 3)
Western Love, 1913 (Guy 2)
Western Maid, 1910 (Anderson 3)
Western Masquerade, 1916 (Mix 3)
Western Redemption, 1911 (Anderson 3)
Western Sister's Devotion, 1913
   (Anderson 3)
Western Story. See Gal Who Took the West,
   1949
Western Trail, 1936 (Terry 4)
Western Union, 1941 (Lang 2, Carradine 3,
   Scott 3, Young 3, Banton 4, Brown 4,
   Canutt 4, Cronjager 4, Day 4)
Western Waif, 1911 (Dwan 2)
Western Way, 1915 (Anderson 3)
Western Woman's Way, 1910 (Anderson 3)
Westerner, 1940 (Wyler 2, Andrews 3,
   Brennan 3, Cooper 3, Basevi 4,
   Goldwyn 4, Mandell 4, Newman 4,
   Swerling 4, Tiomkin 4, Toland 4)
Westerners, 1919 (Seitz 4)
Westerner's Way, 1910 (Anderson 3)
Westfront 1918, 1930 (Pabst 2, Metzner 4,
   Wagner 4)
Westinghouse A.B.C., 1965 (Bernstein 4)
Westward Bound, 1930 (Canutt 4)
Westward Ho, 1935 (Wayne 3, Canutt 4)
Westward Ho!, 1940 (Dickinson 2)
Westward Ho the Wagons!, 1956 (De
   Toth 2, Disney 4, Iwerks 4)
Westward Passage, 1932 (Olivier 3,
   Selznick 4, Steiner 4)
Westward the Wagon. See Hitched, 1971
Westward the Women, 1951 (Capra 2,
   Wellman 2, Taylor 3, Plunkett 4,
   Schary 4, Schnee 4)
Westworld, 1973 (Brynner 3)
Wet Hare, 1962 (Blanc 4, McKimson 4)
Wet Knight, 1932 (Lantz 4)
Wet Parade, 1932 (Fleming 2, Durante 3,
   Huston 3, Loy 3, Young 3, Adrian 4,
   Barnes 4, Mayer 4, Stromberg 4)
Wet Weather, 1922 (Roach 4)
Wetherby, 1985 (Redgrave 3)
Wetterleuchten, 1925 (Dieterle 2)
Wetterwart, 1923 (Pommer 4)
We've Come a Long, Long Way, 1943
   (Horne 3)
We've Come a Long Way, 1952 (Halas and
   Batchelor 4)
We've Never Been Licked, 1943
   (Mitchum 3, Krasner 4, Raine 4,
   Wanger 4)
Whale for the Killing, 1981 (Widmark 3,
   Lourié 4)
Whalers. See Valfångare, 1939
Whales of August, 1987 (Anderson 2,
   Davis 3, Gish 3, Price 3)
Wham Bam Slam, 1955 (Three Stooges 3,
   Bruckman 4)

Wharf, 1968 (Le Grice 2)
Wharf Angel, 1934 (McLaglen 3,
   Hoffenstein 4, Menzies 4)
Wharf Rat, 1916 (Marsh 3, Loos 4)
Wharves and Strays, 1935 (Korda 4)
What?, 1971 (Breer 4)
What?. See Che?, 1972
What a Blonde, 1945 (Hunt 4)
What a Bozo, 1931 (Roach 4)
What a Carve Up!, 1961 (Pleasence 3)
What a Cinch, 1915 (Laurel and Hardy 3)
What a Crazy World, 1963 (Heller 4)
What a Funeral. See Funebrák, 1932
What a Life, 1932 (Iwerks 4)
What a Life, 1939 (Wilder 2, Head 4)
What a Lion!, 1938 (Hanna and Barbera 4)
What a Little Sneeze Will Do, 1941
   (Terry 4)
What a Man. See Never Give a Sucker an
   Even Break, 1941
What a Night!, 1928 (Daniels 3, Cronjager 4,
   Mankiewicz 4)
What a Night, 1935 (Terry 4)
What a Way to Go!, 1964 (Dumont 3,
   Kelly 3, MacLaine 3, Martin 3,
   Mitchum 3, Newman 3, Comden 4,
   Head 4, Shamroy 4, Smith 4, Westmore
   Family 4)
What a Whopper, 1921 (Roach 4)
What a Widow!, 1930 (Dwan 2, Swanson 3,
   Barnes 4)
What a Woman!, 1943 (Russell 3, Winters 3,
   Banton 4, Polglase 4, Walker 4)
What a Woman Can Do, 1911 (Anderson 3)
What about Bob?, 1991 (Dreyfuss 3,
   Ballhaus 4, Sargent 4)
What Are Best Friends For?, 1973 (Grant 3,
   Lourié 4)
What Came to Bar Q, 1914 (Anderson 3)
What Demoralized the Barber Shop, 1901
   (Porter 2)
What Did You Do in the War, Daddy?, 1966
   (Edwards 2, Coburn 3, Dunn 4,
   Mancini 4)
What Do Men Know?. See Vad veta val
   männen?, 1933
What Do Men Want?, 1921 (Weber 2)
What Does Dorrie Want?, 1982 (Keaton 3)
What Drink Did, 1909 (Griffith 2, Bitzer 4)
What Ever Happened to Uncle Fred, 1967
   (Godfrey 4)
What Every Iceman Knows, 1927 (Roach 4)
What Every Woman Knows, 1934 (La
   Cava 2, Crisp 3, Adrian 4, Lewin 4,
   Rosher 4, Stothart 4)
What Every Woman Learns, 1919 (Niblo 2,
   Barnes 4)
What Father Saw, 1913 (Sennett 2)
What Fools Men Are, 1922 (Carré 4)
What Happened to Jones, 1920 (Cruze 2)
What Happened to Rosa?, 1921 (Menjou 3,
   Normand 3)
What Happens at Night, 1941 (Terry 4)
What Have I Done to Deserve This?. See
   Qué he hecho yo para merecer esto, 1984
What He Forgot, 1915 (Laurel and Hardy 3)
What I Didn't Say to the Prince, 1975
   (Brdečka 4)
What Is a Computer, 1967 (Halas and
   Batchelor 4)
What Is a Workers' Council. See Sto je
   radnički savjet, 1959
What Kind of Fool Am I, 1961 (Godfrey 4)
What Life!, 1939 (Cooper 3)

What Love Forgives, 1919 (Polito 4)
What Love Will Do, 1921 (Howard 2)
What Makes Daffy Duck, 1948 (Blanc 4,
   Stalling 4)
What Makes David Run?. See Qu'est-ce qui
   fait courir David?, 1981
What Makes Lizzy Dizzy, 1942 (Langdon 3)
What Money Can Buy, 1928 (Carroll 3)
What Money Can't Buy, 1917 (Cruze 2,
   Bosworth 3)
What Next, Corporal Hargrove?, 1945
   (Edwards 2, Walker 3, Irene 4)
What! No Beer, 1933 (Keaton 2, Durante 3,
   Wilson 4)
What No Spinach?, 1936 (Fleischer 4)
What Papa Got, 1910 (White 3)
What Pearl's Pearl Did, 1910 (White 3)
What Price Beauty, 1928 (Loy 3, Adrian 4,
   Menzies 4)
What Price Fame?. See Hollywood
   Hoodlum, 1934
What Price Fleadom, 1948 (Avery 4)
What Price Glory, 1926 (Walsh 2, Del Rio 3,
   McLaglen 3)
What Price Glory, 1952 (Ford 2, Cagney 3,
   Wagner 3, LeMaire 4, Newman 4)
What Price Goofy?, 1925 (McCarey 2,
   Roach 4)
What Price Hollywood?, 1932 (Cukor 2,
   Beavers 3, Berman 4, Murfin 4,
   Rosher 4, Selznick 4, Steiner 4,
   Vorkapich 4)
What Price Innocence?, 1933 (Beavers 3,
   Grable 3)
What Price Melody. See Lord Byron of
   Broadway, 1930
What Price Porky, 1938 (Blanc 4,
   Clampett 4, Stalling 4)
What Price Taxi, 1932 (Roach 4)
What Price Vengeance, 1937 (Cohn 4)
What Sex Am I?, 1985 (Grant 3)
What Shall I Do?, 1924 (Walker 4)
What Shall We Do with Our Old?, 1910
   (Griffith 2, Crisp 3, Bitzer 4)
What the Birds Knew. See Ikimoto no kiroki,
   1955
What the Butler Saw, 1950 (Carreras 4)
What the Daisy Said, 1910 (Griffith 2,
   Pickford 3, Bitzer 4)
What the Doctor Ordered, 1911 (Sennett 2)
What the Scotch Started, 1933 (Harlow 3)
What the Swedish Butler Saw. See Groove
   Room, 1974
What Time Is It?. See Che ora e?, 1990
What to Do, 1928 (Ptushko 4)
What Who How, 1957 (Vanderbeek 2)
What Will People Say?, 1916 (Guy 2)
What Women Did for Me, 1927 (Roach 4)
What Women Dream. See Was Frauen
   träumen, 1933
What Women Will Do, 1921 (Hunt 4)
What Would You Do Chums?, 1939
   (Baxter 3)
Whatever Happened to Aunt Alice?, 1969
   (Aldrich 2, Gordon 3, Page 3, Biroc 4)
Whatever Happened to Baby Jane?, 1962
   (Aldrich 2, Crawford 3, Davis 3,
   Haller 4)
Whatever Happened to Green Valley?, 1973
   (Weir 2)
What's a Nice Girl Like You . . . ?, 1971
   (McDowall 3, O'Brien 3, Price 3)
What's a Nice Girl Like You Doing in a
   Place Like This, 1963 (Scorsese 2)

What's Brewin', Bruin?, 1948 (Blanc 4,
Jones 4, Stalling 4)

What's Buzzin', Buzzard?, 1943 (Avery 4)

What's Buzzin Cousin?, 1943 (Miller 3,
Walker 4)

What's Cookin', 1942 (O'Connor 3,
Pangborn 3)

What's Cookin', Doc?, 1944 (Blanc 4,
Clampett 4, Stalling 4)

What's Cooking?, 1947 (Halas and
Batchelor 4)

What's Good for the Goose, 1969
(Wisdom 3, Golan and Globus 4)

What's Happened to Sugar, 1945
(Flaherty 2)

What's Happened to Sugar, 1967
(Flaherty 2)

What's Happening: The Beatles in the USA,
1964 (Maysles 2)

What's His Name, 1914 (De Mille 2,
Buckland 4)

What's Important Is to Live. See Lo que
importa es vivir, 1989

What's in a Number, 1948 (Lassally 4)

What's My Lion?, 1961 (Blanc 4,
McKimson 4)

What's New Pussycat?, 1965 (Allen 2,
Burton 3, O'Toole 3, Schneider 3,
Sellers 3, Saulnier 4, Sylbert 4,
Williams 4)

What's Opera, Doc?, 1957 (Blanc 4, Jones 4,
Maltese 4)

What's Sauce for the Goose, 1916 (Laurel
and Hardy 3)

What's So Bad about Feeling Good?, 1968
(Ritter 3, Bumstead 4, Head 4)

What's the Matador?, 1942 (Three
Stooges 3)

What's the Matter with Helen?, 1971
(Moorehead 3, Reynolds 3, Winters 3,
Ballard 4, Lourié 4, Raksin 4,
Reynolds 4)

What's the World Coming To?, 1926
(Roach 4)

What's Up, Doc?, 1950 (Blanc 4,
McKimson 4, Stalling 4)

What's Up, Doc?, 1972 (Benton 2,
Bogdanovich 2, Streisand 3, Fields 4,
Henry 4, Kovacs 4)

What's Up Front, 1964 (Zsigmond 4)

What's Up, Tiger Lily?, 1966 (Allen 2)

What's Worth While?, 1921 (Weber 2)

What's Wrong with Women?, 1922
(Folsey 4)

What's Your Hurry, 1909 (Griffith 2,
Pickford 3, Bitzer 4)

What's Your Hurry?, 1920 (Wood 2, Reid 3)

Wheeeeels No. 1, 1958 (Vanderbeek 2)

Wheeeeels No. 2, 1959 (Vanderbeek 2)

Wheel of Chance, 1928 (Haller 4)

Wheel of Fortune. See Man Betrayed, 1941

Wheel of Life, 1914 (Reid 3)

Wheel of Life, 1929 (Cronjager 4)

Wheeler Dealers, 1963 (Garner 3, Remick 3,
Lang 4)

Wheels of Chance, 1928 (Barthelmess 3)

Wheels of Destiny, 1934 (McCord 4)

Wheels of Justice, 1911 (Mix 3)

Wheels of Terror, 1987 (Reed 3)

When a Feller Needs a Friend, 1932
(Cooper 3, Rosson 4)

When a Girl Loves, 1919 (Weber 2)

When a Man Loves, 1910 (Griffith 2,
Pickford 3, Bitzer 4)

When a Man Loves, 1927 (Barrymore 3,
Costello 3, Johnson 3, Carré 4, Haskin 4,
Meredyth 4)

When a Man Rides Alone, 1919 (King 2,
Furthman 4)

When a Man Sees Red, 1934 (McCord 4)

When a Man's a Prince, 1926 (Sennett 2)

When a Stranger Calls, 1979 (Roberts 3)

When a Woman Ascends the Stairs. See
Onna ga kaidan o noboru toku, 1960

When a Woman Guides, 1914 (Loos 4)

When a Woman Loses Her Way. See Café
Electric, 1927

When a Woman Sins, 1918 (Bara 3)

When a Woman Won't, 1913 (Dwan 2)

When Ambrose Dared Walrus, 1915
(Sennett 2)

When Artists Love. See När konstnärer
älska, 1914

When Bearcat Went Dry, 1919 (Chaney 3)

When Bess Got in Wrong, 1914
(Meredyth 4)

When Boys Leave Home. See Downhill,
1927

When Comedy was King, 1960 (Keaton 2)

When Cupid Slipped, 1916 (Mix 3)

When Dawn Came, 1920 (Moore 3)

When Dinosaurs Ruled the Earth, 1970
(Carreras 4)

When Do We Eat, 1918 (Niblo 2, Barnes 4,
Ince 4)

When Doctors Disagree, 1919 (Normand 3)

When Dreams Come True, 1913 (Sennett 2)

When East Comes West, 1911 (Dwan 2)

When East Comes West, 1922 (Eason 4)

When Edith Played Judge and Jury, 1912
(Bosworth 3)

When Eight Bells Toll, 1971 (Hawkins 3,
Hopkins 3)

When Empty Hearts Are Filled, 1915
(Eason 4)

When He Wants a Dog He Wants a Dog,
1917 (Cohl 4)

When Hell Broke Loose, 1958 (Bronson 3)

When Hell Was in Season, 1979 (Saint 3)

When Husbands Flirt, 1925 (Arzner 2,
Wellman 2)

When I Fall in Love. See Everybody's All-
American, 1988

When I Grow Up, 1951 (Preston 3, Laszlo 4,
Spiegel 4)

When I was a Kid, I Didn't Dare. See Si je
suis comme ça, c'est la faute de papa,
1978

When I Yoo Hoo, 1936 (Freleng 4)

When in Rome, 1952 (Brown 2, Johnson 3,
Buckner 4, Daniels 4, Schnee 4)

When Jim Returned, 1913 (Reid 3)

When Johnny Comes Marching Home, 1943
(O'Connor 3)

When Kings Were the Law, 1912 (Griffith 2,
Crisp 3, Bitzer 4)

When Knighthood Was in Flower, 1922
(Davies 3, Powell 3)

When Knights Were Bold, 1908
(Bitzer 4)

When Knights Were Bold, 1936
(Buchanan 3, Fitzgerald 3, Wray 3,
Young 4)

When Knights Were Bold, 1941 (Terry 4)

When Knights Were Cold, 1922 (Laurel and
Hardy 3)

When Ladies Meet, 1933 (Loy 3,
Montgomery 3, Adrian 4, Mayer 4)

When Ladies Meet, 1941 (Crawford 3,
Garson 3, Marshall 3, Taylor 3, Adrian 4,
Kaper 4, Loos 4)

When Lee Surrenders, 1912 (Ince 4)

When Lilacs Blossom. See Nar syrenerna
blommar, 1952

When Love and Honor Called, 1911
(Anderson 3)

When Love and Honor Called, 1915
(Anderson 3)

When Love is Blind, 1919 (Sennett 2)

When Love is Young, 1910 (White 3)

When Love is Young, 1937 (Brennan 3,
Pangborn 3)

When Love Kills. See När kärleken dödar,
1913

When Love Took Wings, 1915 (Sennett 2,
Arbuckle 3)

When Luck Changes, 1913 (Dwan 2, Reid 3)

When Magoo Flew, 1955 (Bosustow 4,
Burness 4)

When Men Desire, 1919 (Bara 3)

When Men Would Kill, 1914 (Olcott 2)

When Mercy Tempers Justice, 1912
(Cruze 2)

When Michael Calls, 1971 (Douglas 3)

When Money Comes, 1929 (McCarey 2,
Roach 4)

When Mousehood Was in Flower, 1953
(Terry 4)

When My Baby Smiles at Me, 1948
(Grable 3, LeMaire 4, Newman 4,
Trotti 4, Zanuck 4)

When My Ship Comes in, 1934 (Fleischer 4)

When Reuben Fooled the Bandits, 1914
(Sennett 2)

When Soul Meets Soul, 1913 (Bushman 3)

When Strangers Marry, 1944 (Mitchum 3,
Tiomkin 4)

When Strangers Meet, 1933 (Bond 3)

When Strangers Meet. See Einer frisst den
anderern, 1964

When Summer Comes, 1922 (Sennett 2)

When the Alarm Bell Rings. See När
larmhlockan ljuder, 1913

When the Bough Breaks, 1947 (Box 4,
Rank 4)

When the Boys Meet the Girls, 1964
(Katzman 4)

When the Cat's Away, 1929 (Disney 4,
Iwerks 4, Stalling 4)

When the Chrysanthemums Fade. See
Uchveli uzh davno krisantemi v sadu, 1916

When the Clouds Roll By, 1919 (Fleming 2,
Fairbanks 3)

When the Cook Fell Ill, 1914 (Mix 3)

When the Daltons Rode, 1940 (Crawford 3,
Francis 3, Scott 3)

When the Dead Return, 1911 (Olcott 2)

When the Desert Calls, 1922 (Carré 4)

When the Door Opened. See Escape, 1940

When the Fire Bells Rang, 1911 (Sennett 2)

When the Girls Meet the Boys. See Girl
Crazy, 1943

When the Gods Played a Badger Game, 1915
(Chaney 3)

When the Law Rides, 1928 (Musuraca 4,
Plunkett 4)

When the Legends Die, 1972 (Widmark 3)

When the Lights Go on Again, 1944
(Howard 2)

When the Mother-in-Law Reigns,. See När
svärmor regerar, 1912

When the Pie Was Opened, 1941 (Lye 4)

When the Press Speaks, 1913 (Bunny 3)
When the Red Red Robin Comes Bob Bob Bobbin' Along, 1932 (Fleischer 4)
When the Redskins Rode, 1951 (Katzman 4)
When the Road Parts, 1915 (Loos 4)
When the Studio Burned, 1913 (Cruze 2)
When the Trees Were Tall. See Kogda derevya byli bolshimi, 1962
When the Wind Blows, 1920 (Roach 4)
When the Wind Blows, 1930 (Roach 4)
When the Wind Blows. See Make Way for Tomorrow, 1937
When the Wind Blows, 1986 (Mills 3)
When Thief Meets Thief, 1937 (Walsh 2)
When Time Ran Out, 1980 (Borgnine 3, Holden 3, Meredith 3, Newman 3, Foreman 4, Schifrin 4)
When Tomorrow Comes, 1939 (Stahl 2, Boyer 3, Dunne 3, Orry-Kelly 4)
When Villains Wait, 1914 (Sennett 2)
When Wealth Torments, 1912 (Bushman 3)
When We Are Married, 1943 (Baxter 2)
When We Are Old, 1983 (Ryu 3)
When We Were in Our Teens, 1910 (Pickford 3)
When We Were Twenty-One, 1921 (King 2)
When Were You Born?, 1938 (Wong 3)
When Wifey Holds the Purse Strings, 1911 (Sennett 2)
When Willie Comes Marching Home, 1950 (Ford 2, Marsh 3, LeMaire 4, Newman 4, Wheeler 4)
When Women Kill, 1983 (Grant 3)
When Worlds Collide, 1951 (Edouart 4, Head 4, Maté 4, Pal 4, Seitz 4)
When You and I Were Young, 1917 (Guy 2)
When You Come Home, 1947 (Baxter 2)
When You Comin' Back, Red Ryder?, 1978 (Grant 3)
When You Remember Me, 1990 (Burstyn 3)
When Your Telephone Rings, 1948 (Rathaus 4)
When You're in Love, 1937 (Brooks 3, Grant 3, Cohn 4, Newman 4, Riskin 4, Walker 4)
When You're Married. See Mabel's Married Life, 1914
When Yuba Plays the Rumba on the Tuba, 1933 (Fleischer 4)
Whence and Where To. See Kudy kam, 1956
When's Your Birthday, 1936 (Clampett 4)
When's Your Birthday, 1937 (Brown 3)
Where Am I?, 1923 (Roach 4)
Where Angels Go . . . Trouble Follows, 1968 (Johnson 3, Russell 3, Taylor 3, Schifrin 4, Wheeler 4)
Where Are My Children?, 1916 (Weber 2)
Where Are the Children?, 1986 (Clayburgh 3)
Where Are the Dreams of Youth?. See Sieshun no yume ima izuko, 1932
Where Are We. See Hello Lafayette, 1926
Where Are Your Children?, 1943 (Cooper 3)
Where Broadway Meets the Mountains, 1911 (Dwan 2)
Where Charity Begins, 1910 (White 3)
Where Chimneys Are Seen. See Entotsu no mieru basho, 1953
Where Danger Lives, 1950 (Mitchum 3, O'Sullivan 3, Rains 3, Bennett 4, Musuraca 4)
Where Destiny Guides, 1913 (Dwan 2)
Where Did You Get That Girl?, 1941 (Pangborn 3, Salter 4)

Where Does It Hurt?, 1972 (Sellers 3)
Where Do We Go from Here?, 1945 (Preminger 2, MacMurray 3, Quinn 3, Raksin 4, Ryskind 4, Shamroy 4)
Where Eagles Dare, 1968 (Burton 3, Canutt 4)
Where East Is East, 1929 (Browning 2, Chaney 3, Gibbons 4, Young 4)
Where Hazel Met the Villain, 1914 (Sennett 2)
Where History Has Been Written, 1913 (Pearson 2)
Where Is My Wandering Boy This Evening, 1923 (Sennett 2)
Where Is Parsifal, 1984 (Welles 2, Curtis 3, Pleasence 3)
Where It's At, 1969 (Guffey 4, Kanin 4)
Where Lights Are Low, 1921 (Hayakawa 3)
Where Love Has Gone, 1964 (Dmytryk 2, Davis 3, Hayward 3, Cahn 4, Hayes 4, Head 4, Levine 4)
Where No Vultures Fly, 1951 (Watt 2, Balcon 4)
Where Now Are the Dreams of Youth?. See Seishun no yume ima izuko, 1932
Where Pigeons Go to Die, 1990 (Rosenman 4)
Where Sinners Meet, 1934 (Biroc 4, Musuraca 4, Plunkett 4, Steiner 4)
Where the Boys Are, 1960 (Ames 4, Pasternak 4)
Where the Breakers Roar, 1908 (Griffith 2, Lawrence 3, Bitzer 4)
Where the Daltons Rode, 1940 (Mohr 4)
Where the Devil Cannot Get. See Kam čert nemuže, 1970
Where the Forest Ends, 1915 (Chaney 3)
Where the Heart Is, 1990 (Boorman 2)
Where the Hot Wind Blows. See Loi, 1959
Where the Ladies Go, 1980 (Black 3)
Where the Lilies Bloom, 1974 (Stanton 3)
Where the Mountains Meet, 1913 (Anderson 3)
Where the Pavement Ends, 1923 (Ingram 2, Novarro 3, Seitz 4)
Where the River Bends. See Bend of the River, 1952
Where the Sidewalk Ends, 1950 (Preminger 2, Andrews 3, Malden 3, Tierney 3, Hecht 4, La Shelle 4, LeMaire 4, Wheeler 4)
Where the Spies Are, 1965 (Cusack 3, Niven 3)
Where the West Begins, 1919 (King 2, Furthman 4)
Where the Worst Begins, 1925 (Haskin 4)
Where There's a Heart, 1911 (Dwan 2)
Where There's a Will, 1936 (Fisher 2, Launder and Gilliat 2, Hay 3, Balcon 4, Rank 4, Vetchinsky 4)
Where There's Life, 1947 (Bendix 3, Hope 3, Dreier 4, Head 4, Lang 4)
Where Were You When the Lights Went Out?, 1968 (Day 3, Terry-Thomas 3)
Where's Charley, 1952 (Kidd 4)
Where's Jack, 1969 (Baker 3, Bernstein 4)
Where's Piconi?. See Mi manda piccone, 1985
Where's Poppa?, 1970 (Gordon 3, Segal 3)
Where's Sally, 1936 (Launder and Gilliat 2)
Where's That Fire, 1939 (Hay 3)
Where's the Fire?, 1921 (Roach 4)
Wherever We Are, 1987 (Zanussi 2)

Which Is Witch?, 1949 (Blanc 4, Freleng 4, Stalling 4)
Which Is Witch?, 1989 (Halas and Batchelor 4)
Which Side Are You On?, 1985 (Loach 2, Menges 4)
Which Way Did He Go?, 1913 (Bunny 3)
Which Way Is Up?, 1977 (Pryor 3, Alonzo 4)
Which Way to the Front?, 1970 (Lewis 2)
Which Woman, 1918 (Browning 2)
Whiffs, 1975 (Gould 3, Cahn 4)
While America Sleeps, 1939 (Zinnemann 2)
While I Run This Race, 1966 (Heston 3)
While Paris Sleeps, 1923 (Tourneur 2, Chaney 3, Gilbert 3)
While Paris Sleeps, 1932 (Dwan 2, McLaglen 3)
While the Cat's Away, 1911 (Pickford 3, Gaudio 4)
While the City Sleeps, 1928 (Chaney 3, Day 4, Gibbons 4)
While the City Sleeps. See Medan staden sover, 1950
While the City Sleeps, 1956 (Lang 2, Andrews 3, Lupino 3, Marsh 3, Price 3, Sanders 3, Fields 4, Laszlo 4, Robinson 4)
While the Door Was Locked. See Medan porten var stängd, 1946
While the Patient Slept, 1935 (Brown 4, Edeson 4)
While the Sun Shines, 1947 (Asquith 2, Rutherford 3, Rattigan 4)
While There's War, There's Hope. See Finche c'è guerra c'è speranza, 1974
Whip, 1917 (Tourneur 2, Carré 4)
Whip Hand, 1913 (Bushman 3)
Whip Hand, 1951 (Menzies 4, Musuraca 4)
Whip Woman, 1928 (Young 3, Haller 4)
Whiplash, 1948 (Arden 3, Waxman 4)
Whipped. See Underworld Story, 1950
Whipsaw, 1935 (Wood 2, Loy 3, Tracy 3, Howe 4, Mayer 4)
Whirl of Life, 1915 (Gordon 3)
Whirlpool, 1934 (Arthur 3, Bond 3)
Whirlpool, 1949 (Preminger 2, Ferrer 3, Tierney 3, Hecht 4, LeMaire 4, Miller 4, Newman 4, Raksin 4, Wheeler 4)
Whirlpool, 1959 (Rank 4, Unsworth 4)
Whirls and Girls, 1929 (Sennett 2)
Whirlwind, 1930 (Rooney 3)
Whirlwind, 1951 (Autry 3)
Whirlwind. See Dai-tatsumaki, 1964
Whirlwind of Youth, 1927 (Schulberg 4)
Whisky Galore!, 1949 (Greenwood 3, Balcon 4)
Whisper in the Dark. See Sussurro nel buio, 1976
Whisperers, 1967 (Evans 3, Barry 4)
Whispering, 1922 (Wilcox 2)
Whispering Chorus, 1918 (De Mille 2, Buckland 4, Macpherson 4)
Whispering City, 1947 (Lukas 3)
Whispering Death. See Flüsternde Tod, 1975
Whispering Devils, 1920 (Gaudio 4)
Whispering Enemies, 1939 (Costello 3)
Whispering Ghosts, 1942 (Carradine 3, Ballard 4, Day 4, Raksin 4)
Whispering Shadows, 1933 (Lugosi 3, Walthall 3)
Whispering Smith, 1926 (Clarke 4, La Shelle 4)

Whispering Smith, 1948 (Crisp 3, Ladd 3, Preston 3, Deutsch 4, Dreier 4, Head 4)

Whispering Smith Hits London, 1952 (Baker 3, Lom 3, Carreras 4)

Whispering Smith vs. Scotland Yard. *See* Whispering Smith Hits London, 1952

Whispering Tongues, 1934 (Pearson 2)

Whispering Whiskers, 1926 (Sennett 2)

Whispers in the Dark, 1937 (Fleischer 4)

Whistle, 1921 (Hart 3, August 4)

Whistle at Eaton Falls, 1951 (Siodmak 2, Borgnine 3, De Rochemont 4)

Whistle Blower, 1987 (Caine 3, Gielgud 3)

Whistle Down the Wind, 1961 (Attenborough 3, Bates 3, Alcott 4, Arnold 4, Rank 4)

Whistle in My Heart. *See* Anzukko, 1958

Whistle Stop, 1946 (Gardner 3, McLaglen 3, Raft 3, Metty 4, Tiomkin 4)

Whistling in Brooklyn, 1943 (Irene 4)

Whistling in the Dark, 1941 (Arden 3, Veidt 3, Kaper 4)

White Angel, 1936 (Dieterle 2, Crisp 3, Francis 3, Blanke 4, Gaudio 4, Grot 4, Orry-Kelly 4)

White Banners, 1938 (Goulding 2, Cooper 3, Rains 3, Blanke 4, Rosher 4, Steiner 4, Wallis 4)

White Black Sheep, 1926 (Olcott 2, Barthelmess 3)

White Blacksmith, 1922 (Roach 4)

White Buffalo, 1977 (Bronson 3, Carradine 3, Novak 3, Barry 4, De Laurentiis 4)

White Bus, 1967 (Anderson 2, Hopkins 3, Ondříček 4)

White Caps, 1905 (Porter 2)

White Cargo, 1942 (Saville 2, Lamarr 3, Pidgeon 3, Kaper 4, Mayer 4, Stradling 4)

White Cat. *See* Vita katten, 1950

White Christmas, 1954 (Curtiz 2, Crosby 3, Kaye 3, Alton 4, Berlin 4, Frank 4, Head 4, Krasna 4)

White Circle, 1920 (Tourneur 2, Gilbert 3, Furthman 4)

White Cliffs of Dover, 1944 (Brown 2, Dunne 3, Johnson 3, McDowall 3, Taylor 3, Folsey 4, Gillespie 4, Irene 4, Mayer 4, Stothart 4)

White Cockatoo, 1935 (Blanke 4, Gaudio 4)

White Comanche. *See* Comancho blanco, 1969

White Corridors, 1951 (Withers 3)

White Cradle Inn, 1947 (Carroll 3, Dillon 4)

White Dawn, 1974 (Oates 3, Mancini 4)

White Demon. *See* Weisse Dämon, 1932

White Devil. *See* Weisse Teufel, 1930

White Dog, 1982 (Fuller 2)

White Dove, 1920 (King 2)

White Eagle, 1922 (Van Dyke 2)

White Eagle, 1941 (Howard 3, Canutt 4)

White Eagles, 1932 (Bond 3)

White Elder Sister. *See* Shiroi ane, 1931

White Face, 1932 (Balcon 4)

White Fang, 1925 (Murfin 4)

White Fang, 1936 (Carradine 3, Darwell 3, Freidhofer 4, Miller 4, Zanuck 4)

White Feather, 1955 (Daves 2, Wagner 3, Ballard 4, Friedhofer 4, Smith 4)

White Field Duration, 1972 (Le Grice 2)

White Flannels, 1927 (Bacon 2)

White Flood, 1940 (Eisler 4, Maddow 4)

White Gold, 1927 (Garnett 2, Howard 2, Fort 4, Grot 4, Sullivan 4)

White Hands, 1922 (Bosworth 3, Sullivan 4)

White Heat, 1934 (Weber 2)

White Heat, 1949 (Walsh 2, Cagney 3, O'Brien 3, Steiner 4)

White Heather, 1919 (Tourneur 2, Gilbert 3, Carré 4)

White Hell of Piz Palü. *See* Weisse Hölle von Piz Palü, 1929

White Horses of Summer. *See* Bianchi cavalli d'Agosto, 1975

White House Years, 1977 (Barry 4)

White Hunter, Black Heart, 1990 (Eastwood 3)

White Knights, 1985 (Skolimowski 2)

White Legion, 1936 (Brown 4)

White Lies, 1934 (Wray 3)

White Lightning, 1953 (Van Cleef 3)

White Lightning, 1973 (Reynolds 3)

White Lily Laments. *See* Shirayuri wa nageku, 1925

White Line. *See* Cuori senza fontiere, 1950

White Mama, 1980 (Cooper 3, Davis 3)

White Man, 1924 (Gable 3, Schulberg 4, Struss 4)

White Man's Law, 1918 (Hayakawa 3, Rosher 4)

White Medicine Man, 1911 (Bosworth 3)

White Mice, 1926 (Powell 3)

White Mischief, 1987 (Chaplin 3, Howard 3, Hurt 3)

White Moll, 1920 (White 3)

White Moor. *See* De-as fi Harap Alb, 1965

White Morning. *See* Shiroi asa , 1964

White Moth, 1924 (Tourneur 2)

White Mouse, 1914 (Mix 3)

White Nights. *See* Fehér éjszakák, 1916

White Nights. *See* Notti bianche, 1957

White Nights, 1985 (Page 3, Watkin 4)

White Oak, 1921 (Hart 3, August 4)

White Orchid of the Heating Desert. *See* Nessa no byakuran, 1951

White Outlaw, 1929 (Laszlo 4)

White Palace, 1990 (Pollack 2, Sarandon 3, Sargent 4)

White Parade, 1934 (Darwell 3, Young 3, La Shelle 4, Lasky 4, Levien 4, Miller 4)

White Paradise. *See* Bílý Ráj, 1924

White Raven, 1917 (Barrymore 3)

White Red Man, 1911 (Porter 2)

White Rider. *See* White Thunder, 1925

White Rock, 1976 (Coburn 3, Challis 4)

White Rose, 1913 (Bushman 3)

White Rose. *See* Fehér Rosza, 1919

White Rose, 1923 (Griffith 2, Marsh 3, Novello 3, Bitzer 4)

White Rose, 1967 (Conner 2)

White Rose of the Wilds, 1911 (Griffith 2, Sennett 2, Sweet 3, Bitzer 4)

White Roses, 1911 (Bushman 3, Pickford 3)

White Savage. *See* South of Tahiti, 1941

White Savage, 1943 (Brooks 3)

White Scar, 1915 (Bosworth 3)

White Scourge. *See* Bílá nemoc, 1937

White Shadow, 1924 (Saville 2, Balcon 4)

White Shadows. *See* White Shadow, 1924

White Shadows in the South Seas, 1928 (Van Dyke 2, Mayer 4, Stromberg 4)

White Sheep, 1924 (Roach 4)

White Sheep, 1970 (Stevens 2)

White Sheik. *See* Sceicco bianco, 1952

White Shoulders, 1922 (Schulberg 4)

White Shoulders, 1931 (Astor 3)

White Sister, 1923 (King 2, Colman 3, Gish 3)

White Sister, 1933 (Fleming 2, Gable 3, Adrian 4, Booth 4, Daniels 4, Stewart 4, Stothart 4, Stromberg 4)

White Sister. *See* Bianco, rosso, e . . . , 1972

White Slave Catchers, 1914 (Browning 2, Loos 4)

White Slave Trade. *See* Tratta della bianche, 1952

White Stallion, 1984 (Borgnine 3)

White Star, 1985 (Hopper 3)

White Telephones. *See* Telefoni bianchi, 1976

White Thread of the Waterfall. *See* Taki no shiraito, 1952

White Thunder, 1925 (Canutt 4)

White Tie and Tails, 1946 (Bendix 3, Duryea 3)

White Tiger, 1923 (Browning 2, Beery 3)

White Tower, 1950 (Aldrich 2, Ford 3, Homolka 3, Rains 3, Valli 3)

White Treachery, 1911 (Dwan 2)

White Unicorn, 1947 (Greenwood 3, Lockwood 3, Rank 4)

White Voices. *See* Voci bianche, 1964

White Water Summer, 1987 (Alcott 4)

White Wilderness, 1958 (Iwerks 4)

White Wings, 1922 (Laurel and Hardy 3, Roach 4)

White Wings. *See* Yankee Clipper, 1927

White Wing's Bride, 1925 (Capra 2, Langdon 3)

White Witch Doctor, 1953 (Hathaway 2, Hayward 3, Mitchum 3, Herrmann 4, Jeakins 4, LeMaire 4, Shamroy 4, Wheeler 4)

White Woman, 1933 (Johnson 3, Laughton 3, Lombard 3, Dreier 4, Head 4, Hoffenstein 4, Raine 4, Zukor 4)

White Zombie, 1932 (Lugosi 3)

Whitechapel, 1920 (Dupont 2)

Whitsun Outing. *See* Pfingstausflug, 1978

Whity, 1970 (Fassbinder 2, Schygulla 3, Balhaus 4)

Who?, 1974 (Gould 3, Howard 3)

Who Am I This Time?, 1982 (Sarandon 3)

Who Are My Parents?, 1922 (Ruttenberg 4)

Who Believes in the Stork. *See* Kto wierzy w bociany, 1971

Who Bombed Birmingham?, 1990 (Hurt 3)

Who Dares Wins. *See* Final Option, 1982

Who Done It?, 1942 (Abbott and Costello 3, Bendix 3, Salter 4)

Who Done It?, 1949 (Three Stooges 3)

Who Done It?, 1955 (Dearden 2, Clarke 4, Heller 4, Rank 4)

Who Framed Roger Rabbit?, 1988 (Spielberg 2, Zemeckis 2, Hoskins 3, Turner, 3, Blanc 4, Jones 4, Williams 4)

Who Gets the Friends, 1988 (Clayburgh 3)

Who Goes Next?, 1938 (Hawkins 3, Dillon 4)

Who Goes There, 1952 (Korda 4, Mathieson 4)

Who Got the Reward, 1911 (Sennett 2)

Who Has Been Rocking My Dream Boat, 1941 (Anger 2)

Who Has Seen the Wind?, 1965 (Baker 3, Head 4)

Who Has Seen the Wind?, 1977 (Ferrer 3)

Who Ho Ray No. 1, 1972 (Vanderbeek 2)

Who I Kissed Yesterday. *See* Koho jsem včera líbal, 1935

Who Is Harry Kellerman and Why Is He Saying Those Terrible Things about Me?, 1971 (Hoffman 3, Horner 4, Smith 4)

Who Is Hope Schuyler?, 1942 (Miller 4, Raksin 4)

Who Is in the Box, 1910 (White 3)

Who Is Killing the Great Chefs of Europe?, 1978 (Cassel 3, Noiret 3, Segal 3, Alcott 4, Mancini 4)

Who Is the Black Dahlia?, 1975 (McCambridge 3)

Who Is the Man?, 1924 (Gielgud 3)

Who Is to Blame?, 1918 (Borzage 2)

Who Killed Cock Robin?, 1933 (Terry 4)

Who Killed Doc Robbin, 1948 (Roach 4)

Who Killed Doc Robin?, 1931 (Balcon 4)

Who Killed Gail Preston?, 1938 (Hayworth 3)

Who Killed Max?. See Qui a tué Max?, 1913

Who Killed Miss U.S.A.?, 1970 (Bumstead 4)

Who Killed Santa Claus. See Assassinat du Père Noël, 1941

Who Killed Teddy Bear?, 1965 (Mineo 3)

Who Killed Who?, 1943 (Avery 4)

Who Knows, 1916 (Eason 4)

Who Loved Him Best, 1918 (Polito 4)

Who Pays, 1915 (King 2)

Who Pays My Wife's Bill?. See Be My Wife, 1921

Who Pulled the Trigger, 1980 (Johnson 3)

Who Scent You?, 1960 (Blanc 4, Jones 4)

Who Seeks the Gold Bottom. See Kdo hledá zlaté dno, 1975

Who Slew Aunty Roo?, 1971 (Richardson 3, Winters 3, Sangster 4)

Who So Diggeth a Pit, 1914 (Reid 3)

Who Stole Bunny's Umbrella, 1912 (Bunny 3)

Who Stole the Doggies?, 1915 (Laurel and Hardy 3)

Who Stole the Shah's Jewels?, 1974 (Kinski 3)

Who Was That Lady?, 1960 (Curtis 3, Leigh 3, Martin 3, Cahn 4, Krasna 4, Previn 4, Stradling 4)

Who Was the Goat, 1910 (White 3)

Who Will Marry Me?, 1919 (Levien 4)

Who Writes to Switzerland, 1937 (Cavalcanti 2)

Whoa, Be Gone, 1958 (Blanc 4, Jones 4)

Whole Town's Talking, 1926 (Del Rio 3, Horton 3, Loos 4)

Whole Town's Talking, 1935 (Ford 2, Arthur 3, Ball 3, Robinson 3, August 4, Burnett 4, Cohn 4, Riskin 4, Swerling 4)

Whole Truth, 1923 (Laurel and Hardy 3)

Whole Truth, 1958 (Clayton 2, Granger 3, Reed 3, Sanders 3)

Whole Truth, 1964 (Loach 2)

Who'll Stop the Rain, 1978 (Nolte 3, Weld 3)

Wholly Moses!, 1980 (Moore 3, Pryor 3, Houseman 4)

Wholly Smoke, 1938 (Blanc 4, Stalling 4)

Whom God Hath Joined, 1912 (Cruze 2)

Whom the Gods Destroy, 1916 (Brenon 2)

Whom the Gods Destroy, 1919 (Borzage 2)

Whom the Gods Destroy, 1934 (Bosworth 3, Young 3, Buchman 4)

Whom the Gods Love, 1936 (Dickinson 2, Andrejew 4, Dean 4, Stallich 4)

Whom the Gods Wish to Destroy. See Nibelungen, 1966

Whoopee!, 1930 (Berkeley 2, Cantor 3, Grable 3, Brown 4, Day 4, Garmes 4, Goldwyn 4, Goodrich 4, Newman 4, Toland 4)

Whoopee Boys, 1986 (Elliott 3)

Whoops Apocalypse, 1987 (Lom 3)

Whoops! I'm a Cowboy, 1937 (Fleischer 4)

Whoops! I'm an Indian, 1937 (Three Stooges 3, Bruckman 4)

Whore, 1991 (Russell 2)

Who's Afraid of the Avant-Garde, 1968 (Leacock 2)

Who's Afraid of Virginia Woolf?, 1966 (Nichols 2, Burton 3, Segal 3, Taylor 3, North 4, Sharaff 4, Stradling 4, Sylbert 4, Warner 4, Wexler 4)

Who's Been Sleeping in My Bed?, 1963 (Martin 3, Duning 4, Head 4, Ruttenberg 4)

Who's Got the Action?, 1962 (Martin 3, Matthau 3, Turner 3, Duning 4, Head 4, Ruttenberg 4)

Who's Got the Black Box?. See Route de Corinthe, 1967

Who's Kitten Who?, 1952 (Blanc 4, Foster 4, McKimson 4, Stalling 4)

Who's Minding the Mint?, 1967 (Brennan 3, Biroc 4, Schifrin 4)

Who's Minding the Store?, 1963 (Lewis 2, Tashlin 2, Moorehead 3, Head 4)

Who's That Girl?, 1987 (Mills 3)

Who's That Knocking at My Door, 1968 (Scorsese 2)

Who's To Win, 1912 (Bunny 3)

Who's Who, 1906 (Selig 4)

Who's Who in the Jungle, 1945 (Terry 4)

Who's Who in the Zoo, 1931 (Sennett 2)

Who's Who in the Zoo, 1942 (Blanc 4, Stalling 4)

Who's Your Father?, 1918 (Mix 3)

Who's Your Friend, 1925 (Garnett 2)

Who's Your Lady Friend?, 1937 (Reed 2, Lockwood 3)

Whose Baby. See Nick of Time Baby, 1916

Whose Baby, 1917 (Sennett 2)

Whose Life Is It Anyway?, 1981 (Badham 2, Dreyfuss 3)

Whose Little Girl Are You?. See Better Late Than Never, 1982

Whose Little Wife Are You, 1918 (Sennett 2)

Whose Wife?, 1917 (Seitz 4)

Whose Zoo, 1918 (Laurel and Hardy 3)

Why?. See Detenuto in attesa di giudizio, 1970

Why?, 1972 (Garmes 4)

Why Albert Pinto Is Angry. See Albert Pinto ko gussa kyon aata hai, 1981

Why Aren't You Laughing?. See Proč se nesměješ, 1922

Why Be Good?, 1929 (Moore 3, Grot 4, Wilson 4)

Why Beaches Are Popular, 1919 (Sennett 2)

Why Bother to Knock. See Don't Bother to Knock, 1961

Why Bri?, 1961 (Lassally 4)

Why Bring That Up?, 1929 (Hunt 4)

Why Change Your Wife?, 1920 (De Mille 2, Daniels 3, Swanson 3)

Why Daddy?, 1944 (Benchley 4)

Why Do I Dream Those Dreams, 1934 (Freleng 4)

Why Do You Smile, Mona Lisa?. See Proč se usmíváš, Mona Lisa?, 1966

Why Does Mr. R Run Amok?. See Warum lauft Herr R amok?, 1969

Why Foxy Grandpa Escaped Ducking, 1903 (Bitzer 4)

Why Girls Go Back Home, 1926 (Loy 3)

Why Girls Love Sailors, 1927 (Laurel and Hardy 3, Roach 4)

Why Girls Say No, 1927 (Laurel and Hardy 3, Roach 4)

Why Go Home?, 1920 (Roach 4)

Why He Gave Up, 1911 (Sennett 2)

Why Husbands Go Mad, 1924 (McCarey 2, Roach 4)

Why Is a Plumber?, 1929 (McCarey 2, Roach 4)

Why Man Creates, 1968 (Bass 4)

Why Men Leave Home, 1924 (Stahl 2, Booth 4, Polito 4)

Why Men Work, 1924 (McCarey 2, Roach 4)

Why Mrs. Jones Got a Divorce, 1900 (Porter 2)

Why Mules Leave Home, 1934 (Terry 4)

Why Must I Die?, 1959 (Haller 4)

Why Not Stay for Breakfast, 1979 (Challis 4)

Why Pick on Me?, 1918 (Daniels 3, Lloyd 3, Roach 4)

Why Reginald Reformed, 1914 (Cruze 2)

Why Sailors Go Wrong, 1928 (Johnson 3)

Why Smith Left Home, 1919 (Crisp 3)

Why the Actor Was Late, 1908 (Méliès 2)

Why the Sheriff Is a Bachelor, 1914 (Mix 3)

Why Their News is Bad News, 1984 (Christie 3)

Why UNESCO?. See Proč UNESCO?, 1958

Why We Fight series, 1943–45:
  Battle of Britain, 1943 (Capra 2, Huston 3, Hornbeck 4, Tiomkin 4, Veiller 4)
  Battle of China, 1944 (Capra 2, Litvak 2, Hornbeck 4, Tiomkin 4, Veiller 4)
  Battle of Russia, 1944 (Capra 2, Litvak 2, Hornbeck 4, Tiomkin 4, Veiller 4)
  Nazis Strike, 1943 (Capra 2, Litvak 2, Hornbeck 4, Tiomkin 4, Veiller 4)
  Prelude to War, 1943 (Capra 2, Friedhofer 4, Hornbeck 4, Veiller 4)
  War Comes to America, 1945 (Capra 2, Litvak 2, Hornbeck 4, Tiomkin 4, Veiller 4)

Why Women Love, 1925 (Sweet 3)

Why Worry?, 1923 (Lloyd 3, Roach 4, Zukor 4)

Wiano, 1964 (Lomnicki 3)

Wichita, 1955 (Tourneur 2, Mirisch 4, Salter 4)

Wicked, 1931 (Dwan 2, McLaglen 3)

Wicked As They Come, 1954 (Marshall 3, Arnold 4)

Wicked Darling, 1919 (Browning 2, Chaney 3)

Wicked Dreams of Paula Schultz, 1968 (Lewin 4)

Wicked Lady, 1945 (Fisher 2, Lockwood 3, Mason 3, Rank 4)

Wicked Lady, 1983 (Bates 3, Dunaway 3, Elliott 3, Gielgud 3, Cardiff 4, Golan and Globus 4)

Wild Orchids, 1929 (Garbo 3, Adrian 4, Daniels 4, Gibbons 4, Kräly 4)

Wild over You, 1953 (Blanc 4, Jones 4, Stalling 4)

Wild Papa, 1925 (Roach 4)

Wild Party, 1929 (Arzner 2, Bow 3, March 3, Banton 4)

Wild Party, 1956 (Quinn 3, Horner 4)

Wild Party, 1974 (Ivory 2, Welch 3, Lassally 4)

Wild Poses, 1933 (Roach 4)

Wild Racers, 1967 (Corman 2, Almendros 4, Fields 4)

Wild Ride, 1958 (Corman 2, Nicholson 3)

Wild River, 1960 (Kazan 2, Clift 3, Dern 3, Remick 3, Reynolds 4, Wheeler 4)

Wild Rovers, 1971 (Edwards 2, Holden 3, Malden 3, Roberts 3, Goldsmith 4)

Wild Seed, 1964 (Fraker 4, Hall 4)

Wild Stallion, 1952 (Johnson 3, Mirisch 4)

Wild Strawberries. See Smultronstället, 1957

Wild Thing, 1987 (Sayles 2)

Wild Times, 1980 (Hopper 3)

Wild West, 1928 (Rooney 3)

Wild West Days. See Pony Express Days, 1940

Wild West Love, 1914 (Sennett 2)

Wild Westerners, 1962 (Katzman 4)

Wild Wife, 1954 (Blanc 4, McKimson 4, Stalling 4)

Wild, Wild Susan, 1925 (Daniels 3, Hunt 4)

Wild, Wild World, 1960 (Blanc 4, McKimson 4)

Wild, Wild World of Jayne Mansfield, 1967 (Mansfield 3)

Wild Women, 1918 (Ford 2, Carey 3)

Wild Youth, 1918 (Cruze 2)

Wildcat. See Bergkatze, 1921

Wildcat, 1942 (Crabbe 3)

Wildcat Bus, 1940 (Ladd 3, Wray 3)

Wildcat Trooper, 1936 (Bosworth 3, Canutt 4)

Wildcats, 1931 (Rooney 3)

Wildcats, 1986 (Hawn 3, Leven 4)

Wildcats of St. Trinians, 1980 (Launder and Gilliat 2)

Wildcatter, 1937 (Bond 3, McDaniel 3, Cortez 4)

Wildcatters, 1980 (Malden 3)

Wildente. See Haus der Lüge, 1925

Wildente, 1976 (Ganz 3, Seberg 3, Müller 4)

Wildentes, 1925 (Rasp 3)

Wilderness Mail, 1914 (Mix 3)

Wilderness Trail, 1919 (Mix 3, Moore 3)

Wilderness Woman, 1926 (Haller 4)

Wildfire, 1915 (Barrymore 3, Edeson 4)

Wildfire, 1925 (Hunt 4)

Wildfire, 1988 (Jarre 4, Van Runkle 4)

Wildflower, 1914 (Dwan 2)

Wildwechsel, 1972 (Schygulla 3)

Wilfredo Lam, 1978 (Solas 2)

Wilful Ambrose, 1915 (Sennett 2)

Wilful Peggy, 1910 (Griffith 2, Pickford 3, Bitzer 4)

Wilhelm Tell, 1923 (Veidt 3)

Wilhelm Tell, 1934 (Veidt 3)

Wilhelm von Kobell, 1966 (Syberberg 2)

Will, 1968 (Vanderbeek 2)

Will Get You. See Hunter, 1980

Will He Conquer Dempsey?, 1923 (Selznick 4)

Will of His Grace. See Hans nåds testamente, 1919

Will of James Waldron, 1911 (Dwan 2)

Will Penny, 1967 (Dern 3, Heston 3, Johnson 3, Pleasence 3, Ballard 4, Raskin 4, Westmore Family 4)

Will Power, 1910 (White 3)

Will Success Spoil Rock Hunter?, 1957 (Tashlin 2, Blondell 3, Mansfield 3, Marx Brothers 3, Axelrod 4, LeMaire 4, Wheeler 4)

Will There Really Be a Morning, 1983 (Grant 3)

Will Tomorrow Ever Come?. See That's My Man, 1947

Willa, 1979 (Barry 4)

Willard, 1971 (Borgnine 3, Lanchester 3, North 4)

Willful Willie, 1942 (Terry 4)

Willi Tobler and the Wreck of the Sixth Fleet. See 'Zu böser Schlacht schleich' ich heut' Nacht so bang', 1977

William McKinley at Canton, Ohio, 1896 (Bitzer 4)

William Tell, 1934 (Lantz 4)

William Tell. See Guglielmo Tell, 1949

Williamsburg, 1957 (Herrmann 4)

Willie, 1914 (Roach 4)

Willie and Phil, 1980 (Mazursky 2, Wood 3)

Willie Becomes an Artist, 1911 (Sennett 2)

Willie Goes to Sea, 1914 (Roach 4)

Willie Minds the Dog, 1913 (Sennett 2)

Willie the Kid, 1952 (Bosustow 4)

Willie Walrus and the Awful Confession, 1914 (Meredyth 4)

Willie's Camera, 1903 (Bitzer 4)

Willie's Disguise, 1910 (White 3)

Willie's Great Scheme, 1910 (White 3)

Willie's Haircut, 1914 (Roach 4)

Willoughby's Magic Hat, 1943 (Fleischer 4)

Willow, 1988 (Lucas 2)

Willow Springs, 1973 (Schroeter 2)

Willow Tree in the Ginza. See Ginza no yanagi, 1932

Willows of Ginza. See Ginza no yanagi, 1932

Willy and Phil, 1980 (Nykvist 4)

Willy Wonka and the Chocolate Factory, 1971 (Wilder 3)

Wilmar 8, 1980 (Grant 3)

Wilmington 10, USA 10,000, 1978 (Gerima 2)

Wilson, 1944 (King 2, Bushman 3, Coburn 3, Dalio 3, Price 3, Basevi 4, Newman 4, Shamroy 4, Trotti 4, Zanuck 4)

Wily Weasel, 1937 (Lantz 4)

Wimmin Hadn't Oughta Drive, 1940 (Fleischer 4)

Wimmin Is a Myskery, 1940 (Fleischer 4)

Winchester '73, 1950 (Mann 2, Curtis 3, Duryea 3, Hudson 3, Stewart 3, Winters 3, Chase 4, Daniels 4)

Winchester '73, 1967 (Blondell 3, Duryea 3)

Wind, 1928 (Sjöström 2, Gish 3, Gibbons 4, Marion 4, Mayer 4)

Wind Across the Everglades, 1958 (Ray 2, Falk 3, Sylbert 4)

Wind and the Lion, 1975 (Huston 2, Connery 3, Goldsmith 4)

Wind and the River. See Vinden och floden, 1951

Wind Cannot Read, 1958 (Bogarde 3, Pleasence 3, Box 4, Rank 4)

Wind from the East. See Vent d'est, 1970

Wind from the West. See Vinden från våster, 1943

Wind Is My Lover. See Singoalla, 1949

Wind of Change, 1961 (Pleasence 3)

Wind Rose. See Windrose, 1957

Windbag the Sailor, 1936 (Fisher 2, Launder and Gilliat 2, Hay 3, Balcon 4, Vetchinsky 4)

Windblown Hare, 1949 (Blanc 4, Foster 4, McKimson 4, Stalling 4)

Windfall, 1935 (Withers 3)

Windfall in Athens, 1953 (Cacoyannis 2)

Winding Stair, 1925 (Struss 4)

Windjammer, 1926 (Brown 4)

Windjammer, 1958 (De Rochemont 4)

Windmill in Barbados, 1933 (Cavalcanti 2, Grierson 2, Wright 2)

Windmill Revels, 1937 (More 3)

Windmills of the Gods, 1988 (Wagner 3)

Windom's Way, 1957 (Finch 3, Bernard 4, Challis 4, Rank 4)

Window, 1949 (Kennedy 3, D'Agostino 4)

Window, 1965 (Kuri 4)

Window, 1975 (Brakhage 2)

Window Dummy, 1925 (Sennett 2)

Window in London, 1939 (Lukas 3, Redgrave 3, Dalrymple 4)

Window Suite of Children's Songs. See Songs, 1964–69

Window Water Baby Moving, 1959 (Brakhage 2)

Windows, 1975 (Greenaway 2)

Windows, 1980 (Morricone 4, Willis 4)

Windprints, 1989 (Hurt 3)

Windrose, 1956 (Cavalcanti 2, Pontecorvo 2, Signoret 3, Alekan 4, Solinas 4)

Winds of Chance, 1925 (Bosworth 3, McLaglen 3)

Winds of Change, 1978 (Ustinov 3)

Winds of the Wasteland, 1936 (Wayne 3, Canutt 4)

Winds of War, 1983 (Mitchum 3, Topol 3)

Windwalker, 1981 (Howard 3)

Windy Day, 1968 (Hubley 4)

Windy Riley Goes Hollywood, 1931 (Arbuckle 3, Brooks 3)

Wine, 1913 (Sennett 2)

Wine, 1924 (Florey 2, Bow 3)

Wine of Youth, 1924 (Vidor 2, Wilson 4)

Wine Opener, 1905 (Bitzer 4)

Wine, Women, and Horses, 1937 (Sheridan 3)

Wine, Women, and Song, 1915 (Anderson 3)

Wine, Women and Song, 1933 (Brenon 2)

Wing and a Prayer, 1944 (Edwards 2, Hathaway 2, Ameche 3, Andrews 3, Friedhofer 4, Wheeler 4)

Winged Horse, 1932 (Lantz 4)

Winged Horseman, 1929 (Eason 4)

Winged Idol, 1915 (Ince 4, Sullivan 4)

Winged Victory, 1944 (Cukor 2, Ritt 2, Cobb 3, Holliday 3, Malden 3, O'Brien 3, Horner 4, Wheeler 4, Zanuck 4)

Winging 'round Europe with Will Rogers, 1927 (Rogers 3)

Wings. See Vingarne, 1916

Wings, 1927 (Wellman 2, Bow 3, Cooper 3, Walthall 3, Clothier 4, Head 4, Saunders 4, Zukor 4)

Wings and the Woman. See They Flew Alone, 1942

Wings and Wheels, 1916 (Sennett 2)

Wings for the Eagle, 1942 (Bacon 2, Sheridan 3, Haskin 4)

Wings in the Dark, 1935 (Grant 3, Loy 3, Dreier 4, Head 4, Zukor 4)

Wings of a Serf. *See* Krylya kholopa, 1926

Wings of Danger, 1952 (Kendall 3, Carreras 4)

Wings of Desire. *See* Himmel über Berlin, 1987

Wings of Eagles, 1957 (Ford 2, Bond 3, Marsh 3, O'Hara 3, Wayne 3, Plunkett 4, Schnee 4)

Wings of Fame, 1990 (O'Toole 3)

Wings of Fire, 1967 (Bellamy 3)

Wings of Steel, 1941 (Eason 4)

Wings of the Hawk, 1953 (Boetticher 2)

Wings of the Morning, 1937 (Fonda 3, Cardiff 4)

Wings of the Navy, 1939 (Bacon 2, De Havilland 3, Edeson 4, Mercer 4, Orry-Kelly 4, Wallis 4)

Wings over Empire, 1937 (Alwyn 4)

Wings over Everest, 1934 (Balcon 4)

Wings over Honolulu, 1937 (Beavers 3, Milland 3, Raksin 4)

Wings Up, 1944 (Gable 3)

Winifred Wagner und die Geschichte des Hauses Wahnfried von 1914–1975, 1975 (Syberberg 2)

Winner, 1914 (Beery 3)

Winner, 1926 (Brown 4)

Winner. *See* Coeur gros comme ça, 1961

Winners, 1930 (Rooney 3)

Winners and Sinners, 1983 (Chan 3)

Winners of the Wilderness, 1927 (Van Dyke 2, Crawford 3)

Winning of La Mesa, 1911 (Dwan 2)

Winning of the West, 1953 (Autry 3)

Winning Punch, 1910 (Lawrence 3)

Winning Punch, 1912 (Lawrence 3)

Winning Punch, 1916 (Sennett 2)

Winning Steak. *See* Stacey's Knights, 1981

Winning Team, 1952 (Day 3, Reagan 3)

Winning the Futurity, 1926 (Stromberg 4)

Winning the West, 1946 (Terry 4)

Winning Ticket, 1935 (Clarke 4)

Winning Way. *See* All-American, 1953

Winning Your Wings, 1942 (Stewart 3)

Winonah's Vengeance, 1910 (White 3)

Wins Out, 1932 (Lantz 4)

Winslow Boy, 1948 (Asquith 2, Donat 3, Alwyn 4, Andrejew 4, De Grunwald 4, Korda 4, Rattigan 4, Young 4)

Winsor McCay, 1911 (McCay 4)

Winsor McCay and His Jersey Skeeters, 1916 (McCay 4)

Winsor McCay's Drawings, 1911 (Bunny 3)

Winter Carnival, 1939 (Sheridan 3, Walker 3, Wanger 4)

Winter Dusk, 1957 (Konwicki 4)

Winter Flight, 1984 (Menges 4, Puttnam 4)

Winter Garden, 1989 (Halas and Batchelor 4)

Winter Kill, 1974 (Nolte 3, Goldsmith 4)

Winter Kills, 1979 (Huston 2, Bridges 3, Hayden 3, Malone 3, Mifune 3, Perkins 3, Taylor 3, Wallach 3, Boyle 4, Jarre 4, Zsigmond 4)

Winter Light,. *See* Nattvardsgästerna, 1963

Winter Meeting, 1948 (Davis 3, Blanke 4, Haller 4, Steiner 4)

Winter of Our Discontent, 1983 (Sutherland 3, Weld 3)

Winter on the Farm, 1942 (Alwyn 4)

Winter Solstice, 1974 (Frampton 2)

Winter Sports and Pastimes of Coronado Beach, 1911 (Dwan 2)

Winter Sports Champions. *See* Mistři zimních sportu, 1954

Winter Wonderland, 1947 (Alton 4)

Winter's Tale, 1966 (Harvey 3, Morris 4)

Winterset, 1936 (Ball 3, Carradine 3, Meredith 3, Berman 4, Polglase 4, Steiner 4, Veiller 4)

Wintertime, 1943 (Henie 3, Wilde 3, Basevi 4, Brown 4, Clarke 4, Friedhofer 4, Newman 4)

Wiping Something Off the Slate, 1900 (Hepworth 2)

Wir brauchen kein Geld. *See* Man braucht kein Geld, 1931

Wir Kinder der Hölle. *See* **Hitler: Ein Film aus Deutschland, 1977**

Wir machen Musik, 1942 (Käutner 2)

Wir sind vom k.u.k. Infanterie-Regiment, 1926 (Albers 3)

Wir um schalten auf Hollywood, 1931 (Menjou 3)

Wirtshaus im Spessart, 1957 (Herlth 4)

Wise Aristotle Gets Still Wiser. *See* Pomsta, 1968

Wise Blood, 1979 (Huston 2, Stanton 3, North 4)

Wise Flies, 1930 (Fleischer 4)

Wise Girl, 1937 (Dumont 3, Hopkins 3, Milland 3)

Wise Girls, 1929 (Booth 4, Daniels 4, Day 4, Gibbons 4)

Wise Guy, 1926 (Astor 3, Furthman 4)

Wise Guys, 1937 (Crazy Gang 3)

Wise Guys, 1986 (De Palma 2)

Wise Guys Prefer Brunettes, 1926 (Laurel and Hardy 3, Roach 4)

Wise Kid, 1922 (Browning 2)

Wise Old Elephant, 1913 (Bosworth 3)

Wise Owl, 1940 (Iwerks 4)

Wise Quackers, 1949 (Blanc 4, Freleng 4, Stalling 4)

Wise Quacking Duck, 1943 (Blanc 4, Clampett 4, Foster 4, Stalling 4)

Wise Quacks, 1939 (Blanc 4, Clampett 4, Foster 4, Stalling 4)

Wise Quacks, 1953 (Terry 4)

Wise Virgin, 1924 (Walker 4)

Wise Wife, 1926 (Garnett 2, Adrian 4)

Wiser Age. *See* Onna no za, 1962

Wiser Sex, 1932 (Zinnemann 2, Colbert 3, Douglas 3, Folsey 4, Green 4)

Wishing Ring, 1914 (Tourneur 2, Carré 4)

Wishing Ring Man, 1919 (Love 3)

Wishing Seat, 1913 (Dwan 2)

Wistful Widow. *See* Wistful Widow of Wagon Gap, 1947

Wistful Widow of Wagon Gap, 1947 (Abbott and Costello 3)

Witch. *See* Strega in amore, 1966

Witch of Salem, 1913 (Ince 4, Sullivan 4)

Witch of the Range, 1911 (Dwan 2)

Witches, 1966 (Fontaine 3, Carreras 4)

Witches. *See* Streghe, 1967

Witches, 1989 (Roeg 2, Zetterling 2, Huston 3)

Witches Brew, 1978 (Turner 3)

Witches' Cradle, 1943 (Deren 2)

Witches of Eastwick, 1987 (Miller 2, Cher 3, Nicholson 3, Pfeiffer 3, Sarandon 3, Bottin 4, Williams 4, Zsigmond 4)

Witches of Salem. *See* Sorcières de Salem, 1956

Witchfinder General, 1968 (Reeves 2, Price 3)

Witchfire, 1986 (Winters 3)

Witching Hour, 1934 (Hathaway 2, Head 4)

Witchita, 1955 (McCrea 3)

Witch's Cat, 1947 (Terry 4)

Witch's Revenge. *See* Sorcier, 1903

Witch's Tangled Hare, 1959 (Blanc 4)

With a Kodak, 1911 (Sennett 2)

With a Little Help from His Friends. *See* Making of a "Local Hero", 1983

With a Smile. *See* Avec le sourire, 1936

With a Song in My Heart, 1952 (Hayward 3, Ritter 3, Wagner 3, LeMaire 4, Newman 4, Shamroy 4, Trotti 4)

With Baited Breath. *See* Col cuore in gola, 1967

With Beauty and Sorrow. *See* Utsukishisa to kanashimi to, 1965

With General Pancho Villa in Mexico, 1914 (Rosher 4)

With Her Card, 1909 (Griffith 2, Bitzer 4)

With Her Rival's Help, 1910 (White 3)

With Hoops of Steel, 1919 (Walthall 3)

With Intent to Kill, 1984 (Malden 3)

With Lee in Virginia, 1913 (Ince 4)

With Love and Hisses, 1927 (Laurel and Hardy 3, Roach 4)

With Love From Truman, 1966 (Maysles 2)

With Neatness and Dispatch, 1918 (Bushman 3)

With Potash and Perlmutter. *See* Partners Again, 1926

With Six You Get Egg Roll, 1968 (Day 3, Stradling 4)

With the Aid of the Law, 1915 (Mix 3)

With the Blood of Others. *See* Par le sang des autres, 1974

With the Enemy's Help, 1912 (Pickford 3, Sweet 3)

With Will Rogers series, 1927 (Rogers 3)

Within Hail. *See* Bilocation, 1973

Within Man's Power, 1954 (Kaufman 4)

Within Our Gates, 1920 (Micheaux 2)

Within the Law, 1923 (Talmadge 3, Gaudio 4, Marion 4, Schenck 4)

Within the Law, 1939 (Lederer 4)

Without a Clue, 1988 (Caine 3, Mancini 4)

Without Anesthetic. *See* Bez znieczulenia, 1977

Without Apparent Motive. *See* Sans mobile apparent, 1971

Without Benefit of Clergy, 1921 (Karloff 3)

Without Each Other, 1961 (Tiomkin 4)

Without Honor, 1950 (Moorehead 3, Hakim 4, Steiner 4)

Without Honors, 1932 (Carey 3)

Without Love, 1945 (Ball 3, Grahame 3, Hepburn 3, Tracy 3, Freund 4, Irene 4, Kaper 4, Stewart 4)

Without Mercy, 1925 (Clarke 4)

Without Orders, 1936 (Bond 3, Hunt 4)

Without Pity. *See* Senza pietà, 1948

Without Regret, 1935 (Niven 3, Brackett 4)

Without Reservations, 1946 (LeRoy 2, Colbert 3, Grant 3, Wayne 3, Krasner 4, Lasky 4)

Without Warning. *See* Invisible Menace, 1938

Without Warning, 1952 (Biroc 4)

Without Warning, 1980 (Palance 3)

Witness, 1942 (Benchley 4)

Witness. *See* Temps du ghetto, 1961

Witness. *See* Temoin, 1978

Witness, 1985 (Weir 2, Ford 3, Jarre 4)

Witness for the Defense, 1919 (Menzies 4, Miller 4)

Witness for the Prosecution, 1957 (Wilder 2, Dietrich 3, Lanchester 3, Laughton 3, Power 3, Harlan 4, Head 4, Mandell 4, Trauner 4)

Witness for the Prosecution, 1982 (Kerr 3, Pleasence 3, Richardson 3)

Witness Out of Hell. *See* Gorge trave, 1965

Witness to Murder, 1954 (Sanders 3, Stanwyck 3, Alton 4)

Witness to the Will, 1914 (Ingram 2)

Witnesses. *See* Temps du ghetto, 1961

Witnesses, 1986 (Mills 3)

Wittold Lutoslawski, 1991 (Zanussi 2)

Wives and Lovers, 1963 (Johnson 3, Leigh 3, Winters 3, Anhalt 4, Ballard 4, Head 4, Wallis 4)

Wives and Other Wives, 1918 (Furthman 4)

Wives Beware. *See* Two White Arms, 1932

Wives Never Know, 1936 (Beavers 3, Menjou 3, Head 4)

Wives of Jamestown, 1913 (Olcott 2)

Wives of Men, 1918 (Stahl 2)

Wives of the Prophet, 1926 (Costello 3)

Wives Under Suspicion, 1938 (Whale 2)

Wiz, 1978 (Lumet 2, Horne 3, Pryor 3, Allen 4, Jones 4, Morris 4, Whitlock 4)

Wizard of Arts, 1941 (Fleischer 4)

Wizard of Babylon. *See* Bauer von Babylon, 1983

Wizard of Baghdad, 1960 (Katzman 4)

Wizard of Mars, 1965 (Carradine 3)

Wizard of Oz, 1910 (Selig 4)

Wizard of Oz, 1924 (Laurel and Hardy 3)

Wizard of Oz, 1939 (Fleming 2, LeRoy 2, Garland 3, Adrian 4, Edens 4, Freed 4, Gibbons 4, Gillespie 4, Mayer 4, Rosson 4, Shearer 4, Smith 4, Stothart 4)

Wizard of the Saddle, 1928 (Plunkett 4)

Wizards, 1977 (Bakshi 4)

Wizja Lokalna—1901, 1981 (Olbrychski 3)

Wo ist Coletti?, 1913 (Warm 4)

Wo ist Herr Belling?, 1944 (Jannings 3)

Wo ist mein Schatz?, 1916 (Lubitsch 2)

Woe Oh Ho No, 1972 (Emshwiller 2)

Woes of a Waitress, 1914 (Costello 3)

Woes of a Wealthy Lady, 1911 (Bunny 3)

Woes of Roller Skates, 1908 (Méliès 2)

Wold Shadow, 1972 (Brakhage 2)

Wolf at the Door, 1986 (Sutherland 3, Von Sydow 3, Carrière 4)

Wolf Dog, 1933 (Walthall 3, Canutt 4)

Wolf Echoes. *See* Wilcze echa, 1967

Wolf Fangs, 1927 (Miller 4)

Wolf Hounded, 1958 (Hanna and Barbera 4)

Wolf Hunters, 1949 (Boetticher 2)

Wolf in Cheap Clothing, 1936 (Terry 4)

Wolf in Sheepdog's Clothing, 1963 (Hanna and Barbera 4)

Wolf Larsen, 1958 (Crosby 4)

Wolf Lowry, 1917 (Hart 3, August 4)

Wolf Man, 1924 (Gilbert 3, Shearer 3)

Wolf Man, 1941 (Bellamy 3, Lugosi 3, Rains 3, Pierce 4, Salter 4, Siodmak 4)

Wolf Song, 1929 (Fleming 2, Hathaway 2, Cooper 3, Head 4)

Wolf Trap. *See* Vlčí jáma, 1957

Wolf unter Wölfen, 1965 (Mueller-Stahl 3)

Wolf with Child. *See* Kozure ohkami, 1972

Wolf! Wolf!, 1934 (Lantz 4)

Wolf! Wolf!, 1944 (Terry 4)

Wolf Woman, 1916 (Sullivan 4)

Wolfen, 1981 (Finney 3)

Wolfhound, 1916 (Terry 4)

Wolf's Clothing, 1927 (Haskin 4)

Wolf's Pardon, 1947 (Terry 4)

Wolf's Side of the Story, 1938 (Terry 4)

Wolf's Tale, 1944 (Terry 4)

Wolga-Wolga, 1928 (Andrejew 4, Planer 4)

Wolves. *See* Volki, 1925

Wolves, 1930 (Laughton 3)

Wolves. *See* Ookami, 1955

Wolves of the Air, 1927 (Costello 3)

Wolves of the Rail, 1918 (August 4)

Wolves of the Road, 1925 (Canutt 4)

Wolves of the Sea, 1938 (Bosworth 3)

Wolves of the Trail, 1918 (Hart 3)

Woman, 1915 (Purviance 3)

Woman, 1918 (Tourneur 2, Carré 4)

Woman, 1921 (Carré 4)

Woman, 1939 (Stromberg 4)

Woman Accused, 1933 (Calhern 3, Grant 3, Struss 4)

Woman Across the Way. *See* Frau gegenüber, 1978

Woman Against Woman, 1938 (Astor 3)

Woman Alone, 1917 (Edeson 4, Marion 4)

Woman Alone. *See* Sabotage, 1936

Woman and Pirates. *See* Onna to kauzoku, 1959

Woman and the Hunter, 1957 (Sheridan 3)

Woman and the Law, 1918 (Walsh 2)

Woman at Her Window. *See* Femme à sa fenêtre, 1976

Woman Basketball Player Number Five, 1957 (Xie 2)

Woman Between, 1931 (Launder and Gilliat 2, Hunt 4)

Woman Between. *See* Woman I Love, 1937

Woman Chases Man, 1937 (Crawford 3, Hopkins 3, McCrea 3, Day 4, Goldwyn 4, Mandell 4, Newman 4, Toland 4)

Woman Commands, 1932 (Negri 3, Rathbone 3, Brown 4, Krasner 4, Mandell 4, Mohr 4)

Woman Conquers, 1922 (Karloff 3, Schulberg 4)

Woman Destroyed. *See* Smash-Up, 1947

Woman Destroyed. *See* Donna spezzata, 1988

Woman Disputed, 1928 (Florey 2, King 2, Talmadge 3, Menzies 4, Schenck 4, Sullivan 4)

Woman for Joe, 1955 (Rank 4)

Woman from Headquarters, 1950 (Salter 4)

Woman from Hell, 1929 (Astor 3, Carré 4)

Woman from Mellon's, 1909 (Griffith 2, Pickford 3, Bitzer 4)

Woman from Monte Carlo, 1932 (Curtiz 2, Dagover 3, Huston 3, Haller 4)

Woman from Moscow, 1928 (Lukas 3, Negri 3)

Woman from Warren's, 1915 (Browning 2)

Woman Gives, 1920 (Talmadge 3)

Woman God Forgot, 1917 (De Mille 2, Bosworth 3, Reid 3, Buckland 4, Macpherson 4)

Woman Hater, 1948 (Feuillère 3, Granger 3, Dillon 4, Rank 4)

Woman Haters, 1913 (Sennett 2, Arbuckle 3)

Woman Haters, 1934 (Brennan 3, Three Stooges 3)

Woman He Loved, 1922 (Gaudio 4)

Woman He Loved, 1988 (De Havilland 3)

Woman He Married, 1922 (Niblo 2, Meredyth 4)

Woman He Scorned, 1930 (Negri 3)

Woman Hungry, 1931 (Polito 4)

Woman Hunt. *See* Au Royaume des cieux, 1947

Woman Hunt, 1961 (Crosby 4)

Woman Hunt, 1974 (Corman 2)

Woman Hunter, 1972 (Duning 4)

Woman I Love, 1929 (Miller 4, Plunkett 4)

Woman I Love, 1937 (Litvak 2, Hopkins 3, Muni 3, Plunkett 4, Polglase 4, Rosher 4, Veiller 4)

Woman I Love, 1971 (Dunaway 3)

Woman I Stole, 1933 (Wray 3)

Woman in a Dressing Gown, 1957 (Quayle 3)

Woman in a Leopardskin Coat. *See* Kvinna i leopard, 1958

Woman in Black, 1914 (Barrymore 3, Gaudio 4)

Woman in Bondage. *See* Impassive Footman, 1932

Woman in Brown. *See* Vicious Circle, 1948

Woman in Command. *See* Soldiers of the King, 1933

Woman in Green, 1945 (Rathbone 3, Miller 4, Salter 4)

Woman in Her Thirties. *See* Side Streets, 1935

Woman in Hiding, 1949 (Lupino 3, Orry-Kelly 4, Daniels 4)

Woman in His House, 1920 (Stahl 2)

Woman in His House. *See* Animal Kingdom, 1932

Woman in His Life, 1933 (Adrian 4)

Woman in Leopardskin. *See* Kvinna i leopard, 1958

Woman in Question, 1950 (Bogarde 3, Dillon 4)

Woman in Red, 1935 (Florey 2, Stanwyck 3, Brown 4, Orry-Kelly 4, Polito 4)

Woman in Red, 1984 (Wilder 3)

Woman in Room 13, 1932 (King 2, Bellamy 3, Loy 3, Friedhofer 4, Seitz 4)

Woman in the Case. *See* Allotment Wives, 1945

Woman in the Dark, 1934 (Bellamy 3, Douglas 3, Wray 3, Plunkett 4)

Woman in the Dunes. *See* **Suna no onna, 1963**

Woman in the Hall, 1947 (Simmons 3, Dalrymple 4, Mathieson 4, Rank 4)

Woman in the Moon. *See* Frau im Mond, 1929

Woman in the Night. *See* Tesha, 1928

Woman in the Suitcase, 1919 (Niblo 2, Barnes 4, Ince 4)

Woman in the Ultimate, 1913 (Gish 3)

Woman in the Window, 1944 (Lang 2, Bennett 3, Duryea 3, Massey 3, Robinson 3, Fields 4, Friedhofer 4, Johnson 4, Krasner 4)

Woman in Two Minds. *See* ketlekü asszony, 1917

Woman in White, 1929 (Wilcox 2, Sweet 3)

Woman in White, 1948 (Greenstreet 3, Moorehead 3, Blanke 4, Burks 4, Steiner 4)

Woman in White. *See* Kvinna i vitt, 1949

Woman Inside, 1981 (Blondell 3)

Woman Is a Woman. *See* Femme est une femme, 1961

Woman Is the Judge, 1939 (Brown 4)

Woman Like Satan. *See* Femme et le pantin, 1958

Woman Next Door. *See* Femme d'à côté, 1981

Woman Obsessed, 1959 (Hathaway 2, Hayward 3, Friedhofer 4, LeMaire 4, Smith 4, Wheeler 4)

Woman of Affairs, 1928 (Brown 2, Bosworth 3, Garbo 3, Gilbert 3, Adrian 4, Daniels 4, Gibbons 4, Mayer 4, Meredyth 4)

Woman of Arizona, 1912 (Anderson 3)

Woman of Bronze, 1923 (Vidor 2)

Woman of Distinction, 1950 (Ball 3, Milland 3, Russell 3, Walker 4)

Woman of Dolwyn. *See* Last Days of Dolwyn, 1948

Woman of Experience, 1931 (Pangborn 3, Brown 4, Mohr 4)

Woman of Mystery, 1914 (Guy 2)

Woman of No Importance. *See* Frau ohne Bedetung, 1936

Woman of Otowi Crossing, 1974 (Koch 4)

Woman of Paris, 1923 (Chaplin 2, Menjou 3, Purviance 3)

Woman of Pleasure, 1919 (Sweet 3)

Woman of Pleasure. *See* Kanraku no onna, 1924

Woman of Rome. *See* Romana, 1954

Woman of Rumor. *See* Uwasa no onna, 1954

Woman of Rumors. *See* Uwasa no onna, 1954

Woman of Sin. *See* Woman Scorned, 1911

Woman of Straw, 1964 (Dearden 2, Connery 3, Lollobrigida 3, Richardson 3, Adam 4, Heller 4, Mathieson 4)

Woman of Summer. *See* Stripper, 1963

Woman of the Circus. *See* Carola Lamberti—Eine vom Zirkus, 1954

Woman of the Jury, 1924 (Love 3)

Woman of the North Country, 1952 (Raine 4)

Woman of the River. *See* Donne del fiume, 1954

Woman of the Rumor. *See* Uwasa no onna, 1954

Woman of the Sea. *See* Sea Gull, 1926

Woman of the Sleeping Forest. *See* Sleeping Beauty, 1930

Woman of the Town, 1943 (Trevor 3, Harlan 4, Rozsa 4)

Woman of the World, 1925 (Negri 3, Glennon 4)

Woman of the Year, 1942 (Mankiewicz 2, Stevens 2, Bendix 3, Hepburn 3, Tracy 3, Adrian 4, Lardner 4, Mayer 4, Ruttenberg 4, Waxman 4)

Woman of the Year, 1976 (Ames 4)

Woman of Tomorrow. *See* Zhemtshina zavtrastchevo dnia, 1914

Woman of Wonders. *See* Donna delle meraviglie, 1985

Woman on Pier 13, 1950 (Stevenson 2, Ryan 3, Musuraca 4)

Woman on the Beach, 1947 (Renoir 2, Bennett 3, Ryan 3, D'Agostino 4, Eisler 4)

Woman on the Jury, 1924 (Bosworth 3, Walthall 3)

Woman on the Run, 1950 (Sheridan 3, Leven 4, Mohr 4)

Woman on Trial, 1927 (Stiller 2, Negri 3, Glennon 4, Schulberg 4)

Woman One Longs For. *See* Frau, nach der Man sich sehnt, 1929

Woman Opening a Door. *See* Tobira o hiraku onna, 1946

Woman Opening the Door. *See* Tobira o hiraku onna, 1946

Woman Opposite, 1968 (Polanski 2)

Woman or Two. *See* Femme ou deux, 1985

Woman Pays, 1914 (Cruze 2)

Woman Possessed, 1958 (Roeg 2)

Woman Racket, 1930 (Sweet 3, Gibbons 4)

Woman Racket. *See* Cargaison blanche, 1937

Woman Rebels, 1936 (Crisp 3, Hepburn 3, Marshall 3, Berman 4, Polglase 4, Vajda 4, Veiller 4)

Woman Scorned, 1911 (Griffith 2, Sweet 3, Bitzer 4)

Woman Tamer. *See* She Couldn't Take It, 1935

Woman the Flower. *See* Femme-Fleur, 1965

Woman There Was, 1919 (Bara 3)

Woman They Almost Lynched, 1953 (Dwan 2)

Woman Times Seven, 1967 (Arkin 3, Brazzi 3, Caine 3, Gassman 3, MacLaine 3, Noiret 3, Sellers 3, Evein 4, Levine 4, Matras 4, Zavattini 4)

Woman to Woman, 1923 (Hitchcock 2, Saville 2, Balcon 4, Reville 4)

Woman to Woman, 1929 (Saville 2, Balcon 4)

Woman Trap, 1929 (Wellman 2)

Woman Trap, 1936 (Brackett 4, Head 4)

Woman Under Oath, 1919 (Stahl 2)

Woman Under the Cross. *See* Žena pod křížem, 1937

Woman Under the Influence, 1974 (Cassavetes 2, Falk 3, Rowlands 3)

Woman Using a Small Sword. *See* Kodachi o tsukau onna, 1944

Woman Using a Small Sword. *See* Kodachi o tsukau onna, 1961

Woman, Wake Up!, 1922 (Calhern 3, Barnes 4)

Woman Wanted, 1935 (Calhern 3, McCrea 3, O'Sullivan 3, Clarke 4)

Woman, Ways of Love. *See* Amore, 1947

Woman Who Convicts Men. *See* Otoko o sabaku onna, 1948

Woman Who Did Not Care, 1913 (Cruze 2)

Woman Who Gave, 1918 (Ruttenberg 4)

Woman Who Is Waiting. *See* Machiboke no onna, 1946

Woman Who Knows What She Wants. *See* Žena, která ví, co chce, 1934

Woman Who Sinned, 1924 (Mohr 4)

Woman Who Touched Legs. *See* Ashi ni sawatta onna, 1952

Woman Who Walked Alone, 1922 (Glennon 4, Howe 4)

Woman Who Wouldn't Die. *See* Catacombs, 1965

Woman Wise, 1928 (Pidgeon 3)

Woman with a Dagger. *See* Zhenshchina s kinzhalom, 1916

Woman with Four Faces, 1923 (Brenon 2, Howe 4)

Woman with No Name, 1950 (Burton 3, Heller 4)

Woman with the Orchid. *See* Frau mit den Orchiden, 1919

Woman without a Face. *See* Kvinna utan ansikte, 1947

Woman Without a Face. *See* Mister Buddwing, 1966

Womanhandled, 1925 (La Cava 2, Cronjager 4)

Woman-Proof, 1923 (Astor 3, Haller 4)

Woman's Decision. *See* Bilans kwartalny, 1975

Woman's Decoration. *See* Onna no kunsho, 1961

Woman's Descent. *See* Onna no saka, 1960

Woman's Devotion, 1956 (Henreid 3)

Woman's Face. *See* Kvinnas ansikte, 1938

Woman's Face, 1941 (Cukor 2, Saville 2, Crawford 3, Douglas 3, Veidt 3, Adrian 4, Kaper 4, Mayer 4, Stewart 4)

Woman's Fool, 1918 (Ford 2, Carey 3)

Woman's Heart. *See* Onnagokoru, 1959

Woman's Honor, 1913 (Dwan 2)

Woman's Life. *See* Onna no rekishi, 1963

Woman's Past, 1915 (Ingram 2)

Woman's Place, 1921 (Fleming 2, Emerson 4, Hunt 4, Loos 4, Schenck 4)

Woman's Revenge, 1910 (White 3)

Woman's Secret, 1924 (Marsh 3)

Woman's Secret, 1949 (Ray 2, Douglas 3, Grahame 3, O'Hara 3, Mankiewicz 4)

Woman's Secret. *See* Fujinkai no himitsu, 1959

Woman's Side, 1922 (Schulberg 4)

Woman's Status. *See* Onna no za, 1962

Woman's Touch. *See* Woman Chases Man, 1937

Woman's Vengeance, 1947 (Boyer 3, Lourié 4, Metty 4, Orry-Kelly 4, Rozsa 4)

Woman's Way, 1908 (Griffith 2, Lawrence 3)

Woman's Way, 1916 (Marion 4)

Woman's Woman, 1922 (Goodrich 4)

Woman's World, 1954 (Negulesco 2, Allyson 3, Bacall 3, MacMurray 3, Webb 3, Wilde 3, Brackett 4, LeMaire 4)

Woman-Wise, 1937 (Dwan 2)

Womb of Power, 1979 (Nihalani 4)

Women, 1939 (Cukor 2, Crawford 3, Dumont 3, Fontaine 3, Goddard 3, McQueen 3, Russell 3, Shearer 3, Adrian 4, Loos 4, Mayer 4, Murfin 4, Ruttenberg 4)

Women, 1973 (Brakhage 2)

Women Against Women, 1938 (Marshall 3)

Women and Gold, 1925 (Daniels 4)

Women and Roses, 1914 (Reid 3)

Women and War, 1913 (Dwan 2)

Women and War. *See* Arrêtez les tambours, 1961

Women Are Like That, 1938 (Francis 3, Orry-Kelly 4)

Women Are Strong. *See* Josei wa tsuyoshi, 1924

Women Are Weak. *See* Faibles femmes, 1959

Women Everywhere, 1930 (Korda 2, Biro 4, Korda 4)

Women Family. *See* Jokei kazoku, 1963

Women First, 1924 (Eason 4)

Women in Cages, 1971 (Corman 2)

Women in Chains, 1972 (Lupino 3)

Women in Love, 1969 (Russell 2, Bates 3, Jackson 3, Reed 3, Delerue 4, Russell 4)

Women in Our Time, 1948 (Arnold 4)

Women in Prison. *See* Joshu to tomoni, 1957

Women in Revolt, 1972 (Warhol 2)
Women in the Wind, 1939 (Arden 3, Francis 3, Orry-Kelly 4)
Women in War, 1940 (Cushing 3)
Women in White,. See Journal d'une femme en blanc, 1965
Women Left Alone, 1913 (Dwan 2)
Women Love Diamonds, 1927 (Goulding 2, Barrymore 3, Gibbons 4, Gillespie 4, Young 4)
Women Love Once, 1931 (Lukas 3, Akins 4, Struss 4)
Women Make Movies. See Gold Diggers, 1984
Women Men Forget, 1920 (Stahl 2)
Women Men Marry, 1931 (Scott 3, Shamroy 4)
Women Must Dress, 1935 (Krasner 4)
Women of All Nations, 1931 (Walsh 2, Bogart 3, Lugosi 3, McLaglen 3, Carré 4)
Women of Glamour, 1937 (Douglas 3)
Women of Paris. See Parisiskor, 1928
Women of the Ginza. See Ginza no onna, 1955
Women of the Night. See Yoru no onnatachi, 1948
Women of the World. See Donna del mondo, 1963
Women of Twilight, 1952 (Harvey 3, De Grunwald 4)
Women of Valor, 1986 (Sarandon 3)
Women on the Verge of a Nervous Breakdown. See Mujeres al Borde de un Ataque de Nervios, 1987
Women: So We Are Made. See Noi donne siamo fatte cosi, 1971
Women Tend to . . . See Tokaku omna to iu mono wa, 1932
Women They Talk About, 1928 (Bacon 2)
Women Trouble. See Molti sogni per le strade, 1947
Women Unveiled. See Onnade arukoto, 1958
Women without Men. See Dirnentragödie, 1927
Women without Men, 1956 (Carreras 4)
Women without Names, 1940 (Florey 2, Beavers 3, Dreier 4, Head 4, Lang 4)
Women without Names. See Donne senza nome, 1950
Women Won't Tell, 1933 (Darwell 3)
Women's Origin. See Fukeizu, 1962
Women's Prison, 1955 (Lupino 3)
Women's Red Army Detachment, 1960 (Xie 2)
Women's Room, 1980 (Remick 3)
Women's Scroll. See Jokei, 1960
Won By a Fish, 1911 (Sennett 2, Pickford 3)
Won By a Neck, 1930 (Arbuckle 3)
Won in a Closet, 1914 (Sennett 2, Normand 3)
Won Through a Medium, 1911 (Sennett 2)
Won Ton Ton, the Dog Who Saved Hollywood, 1976 (Blondell 3, Borgnine 3, Carradine 3, Charisse 3, Crawford 3, De Carlo 3, Dern 3, Faye 3, Mature 3, Pidgeon 3, Weissmuller 3)
Wonder Bar, 1934 (Bacon 2, Berkeley 2, Darwell 3, Del Rio 3, Francis 3, Jolson 3, Powell 3, Orry-Kelly 4, Polito 4)
Wonder Boy. See Wunder unserer Tage, 1951
Wonder Gloves, 1951 (Bosustow 4)
Wonder Kid. See Wunder unserer Tage, 1951

Wonder Man, 1945 (Kaye 3, Banton 4, Fulton 4, Goldwyn 4, Mandell 4)
Wonder of Women, 1929 (Brown 2, Day 4, Gibbons 4, Meredyth 4)
Wonder of Wool, 1960 (Halas and Batchelor 4)
Wonder Ring, 1955 (Brakhage 2)
Wonder Woman, 1974 (Biroc 4)
Wonder World, 1972 (Takemitsu 4)
Wonderful Adventure, 1915 (Ingram 2)
Wonderful Adventures of Herr Munchausen. See Monsieur de Crac, 1910
Wonderful Bad Woman. See Subarashii akujo, 1963
Wonderful Chance, 1920 (Valentino 3)
Wonderful Country, 1959 (Armendáriz 3, Mitchum 3, Crosby 4, Horner 4, North 4)
Wonderful Eye, 1911 (Sennett 2)
Wonderful Lie of Nina Petrovna. See wunderbare Lüge der Nina Petrowna, 1929
Wonderful Living Fan. See Merveilleux éventail vivant, 1904
Wonderful Nights of Peter Kinema, 1913 (Pearson 2)
Wonderful Rose Tree. See Rosier miraculeux, 1904
Wonderful Statue, 1913 (Bunny 3)
Wonderful Story, 1922 (Wilcox 2)
Wonderful Thing, 1921 (Brenon 2, Talmadge 3, Carré 4, Schenck 4)
Wonderful Things, 1958 (Wilcox 2, Neagle 3)
Wonderful to Be Young. See Young Ones, 1961
Wonderful World of Jack Paar, 1959 (McLaren 4)
Wonderful World of the Brothers Grimm, 1962 (Bloom 3, Bondi 3, Harvey 3, Homolka 3, Terry-Thomas 3, Pal 4)
Wonderful Years. See Restless Years, 1958
Wonderland, 1931 (Lantz 4)
Wonders of Aladdin. See meraviglie di Aladino, 1961
Wooden Horse, 1950 (Finch 3, Dalrymple 4, Korda 4)
Wooden Indian, 1949 (Terry 4)
Wooden Leg, 1909 (Griffith 2, Bitzer 4)
Woodland, 1932 (Terry 4)
Woodman Spare That Tree, 1951 (Terry 4)
Woodpecker in the Rough, 1952 (Lantz 4)
Woods Are Full of Cuckoos, 1937 (Stalling 4)
Woodstock, 1970 (Scorsese 2)
Woody Woodpecker, 1941 (Lantz 4)
Woody Woodpecker Polka, 1951 (Lantz 4)
Wooers of Mountain Kate, 1911 (Dwan 2)
Wooing of Miles Standish, 1908 (Olcott 2)
Wooing of Winifred, 1911 (Costello 3)
Woolen Under Where, 1963 (Blanc 4, Jones 4)
Word. See Ordet, 1943
Word, 1978 (Chaplin 3)
Word of Honor, 1981 (Malden 3)
Wordless Message, 1913 (Dwan 2, Mix 3)
Words and Music, 1929 (Bond 3, Wayne 3, Clarke 4)
Words and Music, 1948 (Allyson 3, Charisse 3, Garland 3, Horne 3, Kelly 3, Leigh 3, Rooney 3, Alton 4, Edens 4, Freed 4, Mayer 4, Rose 4, Rosher 4, Smith 4, Stradling 4)
Words for Battle, 1941 (Jennings 2, Olivier 3)

Work, 1915 (Chaplin 2, Purviance 3)
Work Party, 1942 (Lye 4)
Worker and Warfront, 1945 (Alwyn 4)
Workers' Quarters. See Rabotchaia slobodka, 1912
Workers 71. See Robotnicy 71 nic o nas bez nas, 1972
Working and Playing to Health, 1953 (Van Dyke 2)
Working Class Goes to Heaven. See Classe operaia va in paradiso, 1971
Working for Hubby, 1912 (Bunny 3)
Working Girl, 1988 (Nichols 2, Ford 3, Weaver 3, Ballhaus 4)
Working Girls, 1931 (Arzner 2, Lukas 3, Akins 4)
Working Man, 1933 (Arliss 3, Davis 3, Orry-Kelly 4)
Working Trip. See Komandirovka, 1962
Works and Days, 1969 (Frampton 2)
Workshop for Peace, 1959 (Dickinson 2)
World According to Garp, 1982 (Hill 2, Close 3, Williams 3, Bumstead 4, Ondříček 4)
World Against Him, 1916 (Polito 4)
World and His Wife, 1920 (Marion 4)
World and His Wife. See State of the Union, 1948
World and Its Women, 1919 (Gibbons 4)
World and the Flesh, 1932 (Cromwell 2, Hopkins 3, Struss 4)
World Apart, 1917 (Reid 3)
World Apart, 1987 (Menges 4)
World at Her Feet, 1927 (Schulberg 4)
World Belongs to Us. See Svět patří nám, 1937
World Changes, 1933 (LeRoy 2, Astor 3, Muni 3, Rooney 3, Gaudio 4, Orry-Kelly 4, Wallis 4)
World Flier, 1931 (Sennett 2)
World for Ransom, 1954 (Aldrich 2, Duryea 3)
World for Sale, 1918 (Blackton 2)
World Gardens, 1942 (Unsworth 4)
World Gone Mad, 1933 (Calhern 3)
World Gone Wild, 1988 (Dern 3)
World in Flames, 1940 (Head 4)
World in His Arms, 1952 (Walsh 2, Peck 3, Quinn 3, Chase 4, Metty 4)
World in My Corner, 1956 (Murphy 3)
World in My Pocket, 1961 (Steiger 3)
World Is Full of Married Men, 1979 (Baker 3)
World Is Peaceful. See Tenka taihei, 1955
World Is Rich, 1947 (Rotha 2)
World Moves On, 1934 (Ford 2, Carroll 3, Friedhofer 4, Steiner 4)
World of Abbott and Costello, 1965 (Abbott and Costello 3)
World of Andrew Wyeth, 1977 (Fonda 3)
World of Apu. See **Apur Sansar, 1959**
World of Darkness. See Yugsjömordet, 1966
World of Dong Kingman. See Dong Kingman, 1955
World of Henry Orient, 1964 (Hill 2, Lansbury 3, Sellers 3, Bernstein 4, Johnson 4, Kaufman 4, Smith 4)
World of Ingmar Bergman, 1975 (Donner 2)
World of Little Ig, 1956 (Halas and Batchelor 4)
World of Plenty, 1943 (Rotha 2, Alwyn 4, Mayer 4)
World of Sam Smith, 1974 (Lassally 4)
World of Sport Fishing, 1972 (Crosby 3)

World of Suzie Wong, 1960 (Holden 3,
Box 4, Cahn 4, Duning 4, Stark 4,
Unsworth 4)
World of Wall Street, 1929 (Lukas 3)
World Premiere, 1941 (Barrymore 3,
Farmer 3, Head 4)
World, the Flesh, and the Devil, 1959
(Rozsa 4)
World War III, 1982 (Hudson 3)
World Was His Jury, 1958 (O'Brien 3,
Katzman 4)
World Window, 1977 (Cardiff 4)
World Without End, 1953 (Rotha 2,
Wright 2)
Worldly Goods, 1924 (Glennon 4)
Worldly Madonna, 1922 (Edeson 4)
World's a Stage, 1922 (Haskin 4)
Worlds Apart, 1991 (O'Toole 3)
World's Applause, 1923 (Daniels 3,
Menjou 3)
World's Best Bride. *See* Hanayome san wa
sekai-ichi, 1959
Worlds Beyond, 1986 (Black 3)
Worlds Beyond: The Black Tomb, 1987
(Wallach 3)
World's Champion, 1922 (Reid 3)
World's Greatest Athlete, 1972 (Hamlisch 4)
World's Greatest Lover, 1977 (Wilder 3)
World's Oldest Living Thing, 1914
(Sennett 2)
Worm's Eye View, 1951 (Dors 3)
Worst of Farm Disasters, 1941 (Ivens 2)
Worst of Friends, 1916 (Sennett 2)
Worst Woman in Paris?, 1933 (Menjou 3,
Mohr 4)
Worth of a Life, 1914 (Ince 4)
Wot Dot, 1970 (Halas and Batchelor 4)
Woton's Wake, 1963 (De Palma 2)
Wot's All th' Shootin, Fer, 1940 (Terry 4)
Wotta Nitemare, 1939 (Fleischer 4)
Would Be Shriner, 1911 (Sennett 2)
Would You Believe It?. *See* Tryst, 1929

Would You Forgive?, 1920 (Furthman 4)
Would-Be Heir, 1911 (Dwan 2)
Wounded in Honour. *See* Mimi metallurgico
ferito nell'onore, 1972
Wounded in the Forest. *See* Ranny v lesie,
1964
Wow, 1969 (Jutra 2)
Woyzeck, 1979 (Herzog 2, Kinski 3)
Wozzeck, 1947 (Warm 4)
Wraki, 1957 (Cybulski 3)
Wrath of God, 1972 (Hayworth 3,
Mitchum 3, Schifrin 4)
Wrath of the Gods, 1914 (Hayakawa 3,
Ince 4)
Wreath in Time, 1908 (Griffith 2, Bitzer 4)
Wreath of Orange Blossoms, 1910
(Griffith 2, Crisp 3, Bitzer 4)
Wreck of the Hesperus, 1926 (Adrian 4)
Wreck of the Hesperus, 1944 (Terry 4)
Wreck of the Mary Deare, 1959 (Cooper 3,
Harris 3, Heston 3, Redgrave 3,
Duning 4, Ruttenberg 4, Young 4)
Wrecker, 1928 (Balcon 4)
Wrecker, 1933 (Bond 3)
Wreckety Wrecks, 1933 (Roach 4)
Wrecking Crew, 1968 (Martin 3)
Wrecking Crew, 1979 (Lee 3)
Wrecks. *See* Wraki, 1957
Wrestlers, 1933 (Sennett 2)
Wrestler's Bride. *See* Wrestlers, 1933
Wrestling, N.Y. Athletic Club, 1905 (Bitzer 4)
Wrestling Sextette. *See* Nouvelles Luttes
extravagantes, 1900
Wrestling Swordfish, 1931 (Sennett 2)
Wringing Good Joke, 1900 (Porter 2)
Written Law, 1931 (Carroll 3)
**Written on the Wind, 1956 (Sirk 2,
Bacall 3, Hudson 3, Malone 3, Cahn 4,
Metty 4)**
Wrong Again, 1929 (McCarey 2, Laurel and
Hardy 3)
Wrong All Around, 1914 (Browning 2)

Wrong Arm of the Law, 1962 (Caine 3,
Sellers 3)
Wrong Box, 1966 (Caine 3, Mills 3,
Moore 3, Richardson 3, Sellers 3,
Barry 4)
Wrong is Right, 1982 (Connery 3)
Wrong Man, 1956 (Hitchcock 2, Fonda 3,
Quayle 3, Burks 4)
Wrong Move. *See* Falsche Bewegung, 1974
Wrong Movement. *See* Falsche Bewegung,
1974
Wrong Patient, 1911 (Bunny 3)
Wrong Road, 1937 (Cruze 2)
Wrong Room, 1939 (Lake 3)
Wrongdoers, 1925 (Barrymore 3)
Wspólny pokój, 1959 (Tyszkiewicz 3)
Wszystko na sprzedaż, 1968 (Wajda 2,
Olbrychski 3, Tyszkiewicz 3)
Wu Li Chang, 1930 (Gibbons 4, Marion 4)
Wüger der Welt, 1919 (Dupont 2)
Wunder unserer Tage, 1951 (Werner 3,
Korda 4, Krasker 4)
Wunderbare Lüge der Nina Petrowna, 1929
(Herlth 4, Hoffmann 4, Jaubert 4,
Röhrig 4)
Wunderbaren Sommer. *See* Gluck auf der
Alm, 1958
Wutai Jiemei, 1964 (Xie 2)
Wuthering Heights, 1939 (Wyler 2, Crisp 3,
Niven 3, Oberon 3, Olivier 3, Basevi 4,
Goldwyn 4, Hecht 4, MacArthur 4,
Mandell 4, Newman 4, Toland 4)
Wuthering Heights, 1970 (Legrand 4)
Wuya yu Maque, 1948 (Zhao 3)
Wy brouwen, 1929 (Van Dongen 4)
Wyoming, 1928 (Van Dyke 2, Selznick 4)
Wyoming, 1940 (Beery 3)
Wyoming, 1947 (Alton 4, Canutt 4)
Wyoming Kid. *See* Cheyenne, 1947
Wyoming Mail, 1950 (Metty 4)
Wyoming Outlaw, 1939 (Wayne 3, Canutt 4)
Wyoming Whirlwind, 1932 (Canutt 4)

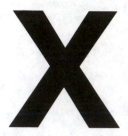

X. *See* Man with the X-Ray Eyes, 1963

X the Unknown, 1956 (Bernard 4, Carreras 4, Sangster 4)

X, Y, and Zee. *See* Zee and Company, 1971

Xala, 1974 (Sembene 2)

Xanadu, 1980 (Kelly 3)

X-Diagnosis. *See* Diagnoza X, 1933

Xeroscopy, 1980 (Halas and Batchelor 4)

X-15, 1961 (Bronson 3)

Xiao Lingzi, 1936 (Zhao 3)

Xochimilco. *See* **María Candelária, 1943**

X-Ray Glasses. *See* Lunettes féeriques, 1909

Y

Y el cielo fue tomado por asalto, 1973 (Alvarez 2)

Y el projimo?, 1973 (Chaplin 3)

. . . y la noche se hizo arcoiris, 1978 (Alvarez 2)

. . . y mañana seran mujeres!, 1954 Y tenemos sabor, 1967 (Gómez 2)

Y'a Bon les blancs, 1988 (Piccoli 3)

Ya, Frantsisk skorina, 1970 (Yankovsky 3)

Yaarana, 1981 (Bachchan 3)

Yabu no naka no kuroneko, 1968 (Shindo 2)

Yabure amigasa, 1973 (Hasegawa 3)

Yabure kabure, 1970 (Kyo 3)

Yabure-daiko, 1949 (Mori 3)

Yacht on the High Seas, 1955 (LeMaire 4)

Yagua, 1930 (Fejös 2)

Yagua, 1941 (Rathaus 4)

Yagui, 1916 (Bosworth 3)

Yagyu bugei-cho, 1957 (Kagawa 3, Mifune 3)

Yagyu ichizoku no inbo, 1978 (Yamada 3)

Yahudi, 1958 (Roy 2, Kumar 3)

Yaji Kita, 1933 (Hasegawa 3)

Yaji Kita bijn sodo, 1932 (Hasegawa 3)

Yakko Kagami-san, 1934 (Hasegawa 3)

Yakko no Koman, 1927 (Tanaka 3)

Yakuza, 1975 (Schrader 2, Mitchum 3, Towne 4)

Yakuza kiji, 1937 (Shindo 3)

Yale Laundry, 1907 (Bitzer 4)

Yalis, la vergine del Roncador. See Vergine del Roncador, 1953

Yalta Conference, 1944 (Gerasimov 2)

Yama no gaika, 1929 (Tanaka 3)

Yama no oto, 1954 (Hara 3, Yamamura 3)

Yama no sanka: Moyuru wakamono-tachi, 1962 (Shinoda 2, Yamada 3, Yamamura 3)

Yamabiko gakko, 1952 (Okada 3)

Yamada Nagamasa Oja no tsurugi, 1959 (Hasegawa 3)

Yamamoto Isoroku, 1968 (Mori 3, Tsukasa 3, Tsuburaya 4)

Yamamoto Isoruku, 1968 (Mifune 3)

Yamaneko rei jou, 1948 (Yoda 4)

Yamaneko Tomi no hanashi, 1943 (Takamine 3)

Yamashita Yasubumi. See Higegi no shogun Yamashita Yasubumi, 1953

Yamata, 1919 (Korda 2, Korda 4)

Yami no Kageboushi, 1938 (Miyagawa 4)

Yami o yokogire, 1959 (Yamamura 3)

Yamile sous le Cèdres, 1939 (Vanel 3)

Yamiuchi tosei, 1932 (Yamada 3)

Yanapanacuna, 1970 (Alvarez 2)

Yang-tse Incident, 1957 (Wilcox 2)

Yangyu. See Yagyu bugei-cho, 1957

Yank at Eton, 1942 (Rooney 3, Freund 4, Kaper 4)

Yank at Oxford, 1938 (Launder and Gilliat 2, Barrymore 3, Leigh 3, O'Sullivan 3, Taylor 3, Balcon 4, Booth 4, Mayer 4, Rosson 4, Saunders 4)

Yank Came Back, 1947 (Meredith 3)

Yank in Dutch. See Wife Takes a Flyer, 1942

Yank in Indo-China, 1952 (Katzman 4)

Yank in Korea, 1951 (Katzman 4)

Yank in London, 1945 (Wilson 2, Darwell 3, Harrison 3, Neagle 3, Heller 4)

Yank in Rome. See Americano in vacanza, 1945

Yank in the R.A.F., 1941 (King 2, Grable 3, Power 3, Banton 4, Basevi 4, Day 4, Newman 4, Shamroy 4, Zanuck 4)

Yank on the Burma Road, 1942 (Schary 4)

Yankee at King Arthur's Court. See Connecticut Yankee, 1931

Yankee Buccaneer, 1952 (Boyle 4, Metty 4)

Yankee Clipper, 1927 (Fort 4, Sullivan 4)

Yankee Dood It, 1956 (Blanc 4, Freleng 4)

Yankee Doodle Andy, 1941 (Bruckman 4)

Yankee Doodle Boy, 1926 (Fleischer 4)

Yankee Doodle Bugs, 1954 (Blanc 4, Freleng 4)

Yankee Doodle Cricket, 1974 (Jones 4)

Yankee Doodle Daffy, 1943 (Blanc 4, Freleng 4, Stalling 4)

Yankee Doodle Dandy, 1942 (Curtiz 2, Cagney 3, Huston 3, Buckner 4, Howe 4, Prinz 4, Wallis 4)

Yankee Doodle Dixie, 1913 (Bosworth 3)

Yankee Doodle Dude, 1926 (Sennett 2)

Yankee Doodle in Berlin, 1919 (Sennett 2)

Yankee Doodle Mouse, 1944 (Hanna and Barbera 4)

Yankee from the West, 1915 (Reid 3)

Yankee Girl, 1910 (White 3)

Yankee Girl, 1915 (Bosworth 3)

Yankee in King Arthur's Court. See Connecticut Yankee in King Arthur's Court, 1949

Yankee in London. See I Live in Grosvenor Square, 1945

Yankee Pasha, 1954 (Cobb 3, Salter 4)

Yankee Princess, 1919 (Love 3)

Yankee Senor, 1926 (Mix 3)

Yanks, 1979 (Schlesinger 2, Gere 3, Redgrave 3, Roberts 3, Russell 4)

Yanks Ahoy, 1942 (Roach 4)

Yanqui No, 1960 (Leacock 2)

Yaoke mae, 1953 (Yoshimura 2)

Yaps and Yokels, 1919 (Laurel and Hardy 3)

Yaqui, 1968 (Fernández 2)

Yaqui Cur, 1913 (Griffith 2, Barrymore 3, Bitzer 4)

Yarali kartal, 1965 (Güney 2)

Yari no Gonza, 1985 (Shinoda 2, Iwashita 3, Miyagawa 4, Takemitsu 4)

Yari no Gonzo, 1929 (Hasegawa 3)

Yari-odori gojusan-tsugi, 1946 (Miyagawa 4)

Yarn about Yarn, 1941 (Terry 4)

Yashagaike, 1979 (Shinoda 2)

Yashu Honno-ji, 1934 (Hasegawa 3)

Yataro-gasa, 1955 (Yamada 3)

Yato kaze no naka o hashiru, 1961 (Ryu 3)

Yatoro-gasa: Kyorai no maki, Dokuho no maki, 1932 (Yamada 3)

Yatsu no hajiki wa jigoku daze, 1958 (Yamamura 3)

Yawar mallku, 1969 (Sanjinés 2)

Ye Happy Pilgrims, 1934 (Lantz 4)

Ye Olde Melodies, 1926 (Fleischer 4)

Ye Olde Saw Mill, 1935 (Sennett 2)

Ye Olde Songs, 1932 (Terry 4)

Ye Olde Swap Shoppe, 1940 (Iwerks 4)

Ye Olde Toy Shop, 1935 (Terry 4)

Ye Olden Grafter, 1915 (Sennett 2)

Year Around, 1948 (Fleischer 4)

Year of Living Dangerously, 1982 (Weir 2, Gibson 3, Weaver 3, Jarre 4)

Year of the Comet, 1991 (Goldman 4)

Year of the Dragon, 1985 (Cimino 2, Stone 2, Rourke 3, De Laurentiis 4)

Year of the Gun, 1990 (Allen 4)

Year of the Horse, 1966 (Hubley 4)

Year of the Mouse, 1965 (Jones 4)

Year of the Quiet Sun, 1986 (Zanussi 2)

Year of the Woman, 1973 (Beatty 3)

Yearling, 1946 (Brown 2, Peck 3, Wyman 3, Gibbons 4, Irene 4, Mayer 4, Rosher 4, Stothart 4)

Yearning. See Midareru, 1964

Years Are So Long. See Make Way for Tomorrow, 1937

Years Between, 1946 (Redgrave 3, Box, J. 4, Box, M. 4)

Years of Change, 1950 (Van Dyke 2)

Years to Come, 1922 (Roach 4)

Years without Days. See Castle on the Hudson, 1940

Yeh Gulistan Hamara, 1972 (Anand 3, Burman 4)

Yeh kaisa insaaf, 1980 (Azmi 3)

Yellow Balloon, 1952 (More 3)

Yellow Cab Man, 1950 (Deutsch 4, Stradling 4)

Yellow Canary, 1943 (Wilcox 2, Neagle 3, Rutherford 3, Bodeen 4)

Yellow Canary, 1963 (Crosby 4)

You Can't Buy Luck, 1937 (Hunt 4)

You Can't Cheat an Honest Man, 1939 (Fields 3, Krasner 4)

You Can't Do That to Me. *See* Maisie Goes to Reno, 1944

You Can't Do without Love. *See* One Exciting Night, 1944

You Can't Escape, 1942 (Deutsch 4)

You Can't Escape Forever, 1941 (Gaudio 4)

You Can't Fool Your Wife, 1923 (Glennon 4, Young 4)

You Can't Fool Your Wife, 1940 (Ball 3, Hunt 4, Polglase 4)

You Can't Get Away with Murder, 1939 (Bogart 3, Buckner 4, Friedhofer 4, Polito 4)

You Can't Go Home Again, 1975 (Ray 2)

You Can't Go Home Again, 1979 (Grant 3)

You Can't Have Everything, 1937 (Ameche 3, Faye 3)

You Can't Ration Love, 1944 (Dreier 4, Head 4)

You Can't Run Away from It, 1956 (Allyson 3, Beavers 3, Lemmon 3, Powell 3, Duning 4, Mercer 4, Wald 4)

You Can't Shoe a Horsefly, 1940 (Fleischer 4)

You Can't Sleep Here. *See* I Was a Male War Bride, 1949

You Can't Take It with You, 1938 (Capra 2, Arthur 3, Barrymore 3, Miller 3, Stewart 3, Cohn 4, Irene 4, Riskin 4, Tiomkin 4, Walker 4)

You Can't Win 'em All, 1970 (Bronson 3, Curtis 3, Mathieson 4)

You Can't Win Them All, 1974 (Challis 4)

You Do, I Do, We Do, 1972 (Vanderbeek 2)

You Don't Need Pajamas at Rosie's. *See* First Time, 1968

You Gotta Be a Football Hero, 1935 (Fleischer 4)

You Gotta Stay Happy, 1948 (Fontaine 3, Stewart 3, Metty 4)

You, John Jones, 1943 (Cagney 3)

You Know What Sailors Are, 1954 (Arnold 4, Rank 4)

You Leave Me Breathless, 1938 (Fleischer 4)

You Lie So Deep, My Love, 1975 (Pidgeon 3)

You Made Me Love You, 1933 (Launder and Gilliat 2)

You Must Be Joking!, 1965 (Elliott 3, Terry-Thomas 3, Godfrey 4, Unsworth 4)

You Nazty Spy, 1940 (Three Stooges 3, Bruckman 4)

You Never Can Tell, 1920 (Daniels 3)

You Never Can Tell, 1951 (Powell 3)

You Never Know. *See* You Can Never Tell, 1951

You Never Know Women, 1926 (Wellman 2, Glazer 4, Vajda 4)

You Only Live Once, 1937 (Lang 2, Bond 3, Fonda 3, Sidney 3, Mandell 4, Newman 4, Shamroy 4, Wanger 4)

You Only Live Twice, 1967 (Connery 3, Pleasence 3, Adam 4, Barry 4, Young 4)

You Ought to Be in Pictures, 1940 (Blanc 4, Freleng 4, Stalling 4)

You Remember Ellen, 1911 (Olcott 2)

You Said a Hatful!, 1934 (Roach 4)

You Said a Mouthful, 1932 (Bacon 2, Brown 3, Rogers 3, Orry-Kelly 4)

You Shouldn't Die. *See* Kimi shinitamau koto nakare, 1954

You Sinners, 1938 (Carmichael 4)

You Took the Words Right Out of My Heart, 1938 (Fleischer 4)

You Try Somebody Else, 1932 (Fleischer 4)

You Were Meant for Me, 1948 (Bacon 2, LeMaire 4, Reynolds 4)

You Were Never Duckier, 1948 (Blanc 4, Jones 4, Stalling 4)

You Were Never Lovelier, 1942 (Daves 2, Astaire 3, Hayworth 3, Menjou 3, Cohn 4, Irene 4, Mercer 4)

You Who Are About to Enter . . . *See* I som här inträden . . . , 1945

You Will Remember, 1940 (McDowall 3)

You Will Send Me to Bed, Eh?, 1903 (Bitzer 4)

You Wouldn't Believe It, 1920 (Sennett 2)

You'd Be Surprised, 1926 (Benchley 4, Furthman 4, Schulberg 4)

You'd Be Surprised, 1930 (Launder and Gilliat 2)

Youki no seidayo, 1932 (Yoda 4)

You'll Find Out, 1940 (Karloff 3, Lorre 3, Lugosi 3, Mercer 4, Polglase 4)

You'll Never Get Rich, 1941 (Astaire 3, Hayworth 3, Alton 4, Benchley 4, Cohn 4, Porter 4)

You'll Never Walk Alone, 1952 (Keel 3)

Young America, 1932 (Borzage 2, Beavers 3, Bellamy 3, Tracy 3)

Young America, 1942 (Darwell 3)

Young America Flies, 1940 (Daves 2, Eason 4)

Young and Beautiful, 1934 (Pangborn 3, Schary 4)

Young and Eager. *See* Claudelle Inglish, 1961

Young and Innocent, 1937 (Bennett 4, Harrison 4, Junge 4, Reville 4)

Young and the Brave, 1963 (Bendix 3)

Young and the Damned. *See* **Olvidados, 1950**

Young and the Passionate. *See* **Vitelloni, 1953**

Young and Willing, 1943 (Hayward 3, Holden 3, Benchley 4, Dreier 4, Head 4, Young 4)

Young and Willing. *See* Weak and the Wicked, 1953

Young and Willing. *See* Wild and the Willing, 1962

Young April, 1926 (Crisp 3, Love 3, Adrian 4, Grot 4, Macpherson 4)

Young as You Feel, 1931 (Borzage 2, Rogers 3)

Young as You Feel, 1940 (Lake 3, Clarke 4)

Young at Heart, 1938 (Gaynor 3)

Young at Heart, 1954 (Barrymore 3, Day 3, Malone 3, Sinatra 3, Blanke 4, Coffee 4, Epstein 4, McCord 4)

Young Bess, 1953 (Granger 3, Kerr 3, Laughton 3, Simmons 3, Plunkett 4, Rosher 4, Rozsa 4)

Young Bill Hickok, 1940 (Rogers 3, Canutt 4)

Young Billy Young, 1969 (Dickinson 3, Mitchum 3)

Young Bride, 1932 (Fort 4, Miller 4, Murfin 4, Steiner 4)

Young Buffalo Bill, 1940 (Rogers 3)

Young Captives, 1959 (Head 4)

Young Cassidy, 1965 (Ford 2, Christie 3, Evans 3, Redgrave 3, Smith 3, Cardiff 4)

Young Country, 1970 (Brennan 3)

Young Days. *See* Mladé dny, 1956

Young Diana, 1922 (Davies 3)

Young Dillinger, 1965 (Cortez 4)

Young Dr. Kildare, 1938 (Ayres 3, Barrymore 3, Mayer 4, Seitz 4)

Young Doctors, 1961 (Ashby 2, March 3, Segal 3, Bernstein 4, Sylbert 4)

Young Doctors in Love, 1982 (Stanton 3, Jarre 4)

Young Donovan's Kid, 1931 (Niblo 2, Cooper 3, Karloff 3, Cronjager 4, Steiner 4)

Young Don't Cry, 1957 (Mineo 3, Haller 4)

Young Eagles, 1930 (Wellman 2, Arthur 3, Lukas 3)

Young Einstein, 1988 (Morricone 4)

Young Frankenstein, 1974 (Brooks 2, Hackman 3, Wilder 3, Jeakins 4)

Young Fugitives, 1938 (Salter 4)

Young Fury, 1965 (Bendix 3)

Young Girl at the University. *See* Daigaku no oneichan, 1959

Young Girl Dares to Pass. *See* Oneichan makari touru, 1959

Young Girls of Rochefort. *See* Demoiselles de Rochefort, 1967

Young Guard. *See* Molodaya gvardiya, 1947

Young Guns, 1959 (Fraker 4)

Young Guns, 1988 (Palance 3, Stamp 3)

Young Guns II, 1990 (Coburn 3)

Young Have No Morals. *See* Dragueurs, 1959

Young Ideas, 1943 (Dassin 2, Astor 3, Gardner 3, Marshall 3, Schary 4)

Young in Heart, 1938 (Goddard 3, Bennett 4, Menzies 4, Selznick 4, Shamroy 4, Waxman 4, Wheeler 4)

Young Invaders. *See* Darby's Rangers, 1958

Young Ironsides, 1932 (Goddard 3, Roach 4)

Young Joe, the Forgotten Kennedy, 1977 (Barry 4)

Young Lady, 1941 (Cahn 4)

Young Lady from the Riverside. *See* Slečna od vody, 1959

Young Lady in a Dream. *See* Yume no naka no ojousan, 1934

Young Land, 1957 (Hopper 3, Hoch 4, Tiomkin 4)

Young Lawyers, 1969 (Pryor 3, Schifrin 4)

Young Lions, 1958 (Dmytryk 2, Brando 3, Clift 3, Martin 3, Schell 3, Van Cleef 3, Anhalt 4, Friedhofer 4, LeMaire 4, Wheeler 4)

Young Lord. *See* Bonchi, 1960

Young Love: Lemon Popsicle VII, 1988 (Golan and Globus 4)

Young Lovers. *See* Never Fear, 1950

Young Lovers, 1954 (Havelock-Allan 4, Rank 4)

Young Lovers, 1964 (Biroc 4)

Young Man of Manhattan, 1930 (Colbert 3, Rogers 3)

Young Man of Music. *See* Young Man with a Horn, 1950

Young Man with a Horn, 1950 (Bacall 3, Day 3, Douglas 3, Cahn 4, Carmichael 4, Foreman 4, McCord 4, Wald 4)

Young Man with Ideas, 1952 (Leisen 2, Ford 3, Ruttenberg 4)

Young Man's Fancy, 1920 (Sennett 2)

Young Man's Fancy, 1939 (Stevenson 2, Balcon 4)

Young Master. *See* Sidai cheutma, 1980

Young Master Feng, 1925 (Zhao 3)

Young Mr. Jazz, 1919 (Daniels 3, Lloyd 3, Roach 4)

Young Mr. Lincoln, 1939 (Ford 2, Bond 3, Fonda 3, Day 4, Glennon 4, MacGowan 4, Miller 4, Newman 4, Trotti 4, Zanuck 4)

Young Mr. Pitt, 1942 (Reed 2, Launder and Gilliat 2, Donat 3, Lom 3, Mills 3, Beaton 4, Vetchinsky 4, Young 4)

Young Mrs. Eames, 1913 (Bosworth 3)

Young Nowheres, 1929 (Barthelmess 3, Haller 4)

Young Nurses, 1972 (Corman 2)

Young Oldfield, 1924 (McCarey 2, Roach 4)

Young Ones, 1961 (Figueroa 4, Slocombe 4)

Young Onions, 1932 (Sennett 2)

Young Painter, 1922 (Astor 3)

Young People, 1940 (Dwan 2, Marsh 3, Temple 3, Brown 4, Cronjager 4, Day 4, Newman 4)

Young People. *See* Wakai hitotachi, 1954

Young Philadelphians, 1959 (Newman 3, Stradling 4)

Young Racers, 1963 (Coppola 2, Corman 2, Crosby 4, Golan and Globus 4)

Young Rajah, 1922 (Valentino 3, Mathis 4, Zukor 4)

Young Rebel. *See* Cervantes, 1968

Young Runaways, 1968 (Dreyfuss 3, Katzman 4)

Young Savages, 1961 (Frankenheimer 2, Pollack 2, Lancaster 3, Winters 3, Anhalt 4)

Young Scarface. *See* Brighton Rock, 1947

Young Sherlock Holmes, 1985 (Levinson 2, Spielberg 2)

Young Sherlocks, 1922 (Roach 4)

Young Sinners, 1931 (Seitz 4)

Young Stranger, 1957 (Frankenheimer 2, Bass 4, Rosenman 4)

Young Teacher. *See* Wakai sensei, 1941

Young Tom Edison, 1940 (Rooney 3, Schary 4)

Young Toscanini. *See* Giovane Toscanini, 1988

Young Veteran, 1941 (Cavalcanti 2, Crichton 2, Dearden 2)

Young Warriors, 1983 (Borgnine 3)

Young Whirlwind, 1928 (Miller 4)

Young Widow, 1946 (De Toth 2, Beavers 3, Russell 3, Garmes 4, Stromberg 4)

Young Winston, 1972 (Attenborough 3, Bancroft 3, Hawkins 3, Hopkins 3, Mills 3, Shaw 3, Foreman 4)

Young Wives' Tale, 1951 (Greenwood 3)

Young Wives' Tales, 1964 (Hepburn 3)

Young Woodley, 1930 (Carroll 3)

Young World. *See* Mondo nuovo, 1966

Youngblood Hawke, 1964 (Daves 2, Astor 3, Steiner 4)

Younger Brothers, 1949 (Burks 4)

Younger Generation, 1929 (Capra 2, Cohn 4, Levien 4)

Youngest Profession, 1943 (Garson 3, Moorehead 3, Pidgeon 3, Powell 3, Taylor 3, Turner 3, Irene 4, Lederer 4, Schary 4)

Youngsters. *See* Štěňata, 1957

Your Body is Mine, 1983 (Brocka 2)

Your Cheatin' Heart, 1964 (Katzman 4)

Your Children and You, 1946 (Alwyn 4)

Your Children's Ears, 1945 (Alwyn 4)

Your Children's Eyes, 1944 (Alwyn 4)

Your Children's Sleep, 1948 (Alwyn 4)

Your Children's Teeth, 1945 (Alwyn 4)

Your Girl and Mine, 1914 (Mix 3)

Your Husband's Past, 1926 (Roach 4)

Your Key to the Future, 1956 (Kidd 4)

Your Last Act, 1941 (Zinnemann 2)

Your Lips No. 1, 1970 (Le Grice 2)

Your Lips 3, 1971 (Le Grice 2)

Your Own Back Yard, 1925 (Roach 4)

Your Own Land. *See* Din tillvaros land, 1940

Your Past Is Showing. *See* Naked Truth, 1958

Your Red Wagon. *See* **They Live By Night, 1948**

Your Son and Brother. *See* Vash syn i brat, 1965

Your Technocracy and Mine, 1933 (Benchley 4)

Your Ticket Is No Longer Valid, 1980 (Harris 3, Moreau 3)

Your Time on Earth. *See* Din stund pa jorden, 1972

Your Turn Darling. *See* Toi de faire, Mignonne, 1963

Your Uncle Dudley, 1935 (Horton 3, Schary 4)

Your Witness, 1950 (Baker 3, Montgomery 3, Adam 4, Arnold 4, Harrison 4)

You're a Big Boy Now, 1966 (Coppola 2, Black 3, Page 3)

You're a Sweetheart, 1937 (Faye 3)

You're Darn Tootin', 1928 (Laurel and Hardy 3, Roach 4)

You're Driving Me Crazy, 1931 (Fleischer 4)

You're Fired, 1919 (Cruze 2, Reid 3)

You're in the Army Now. *See* O.H.M.S., 1937

You're in the Army Now, 1941 (Durante 3)

You're in the Navy Now, 1941 (Wyman 3)

You're in the Navy Now, 1951 (Bronson 3, Cooper 3, Marvin 3, LeMaire 4, Wheeler 4)

You're My Everything, 1949 (Keaton 2, Baxter 3, LeMaire 4, Newman 4, Trotti 4)

You're Never Too Young, 1955 (Lewis 2, Martin 3, Cahn 4, Head 4)

You're Next, 1921 (Roach 4)

You're Not Built That Way, 1936 (Fleischer 4)

You're Not So Tough, 1940 (Salter 4)

You're Only Young Once, 1938 (Rooney 3)

You're Only Young Twice, 1952 (Grierson 2)

You're Pinched, 1920 (Roach 4)

You're Telling Me!, 1932 (Roach 4)

You're Telling Me, 1934 (Crabbe 3, Fields 3, Banton 4)

You're Telling Me!, 1941 (Launder and Gilliat 2, Salter 4)

You're the Doctor, 1938 (Withers 3)

You're the One, 1941 (Horton 3, Head 4, Mercer 4)

Yours for the Asking, 1936 (Costello 3, Lupino 3, Raft 3, Banton 4, Dreier 4)

Yours, Mine, and Ours, 1968 (Ball 3, Fonda 3, Johnson 3)

Youth. *See* Jugend, 1938

Youth, 1977 (Xie 2)

Youth and His Amulet. *See* Gen to Fudo-myoh, 1961

Youth and Jealousy, 1913 (Dwan 2, Reid 3)

Youth Gets a Break, 1941 (Losey 2)

Youth in Fury. *See* Kawaita mizuumi, 1960

Youth in Poland, 1957 (Maysles 2)

Youth in Revolt. *See* Altitude 3200, 1938

Youth of Maxim. *See* **Yunost Maxima 1935**

Youth on Parade, 1943 (De Carlo 3, Cahn 4)

Youth on Parole, 1938 (Dumont 3)

Youth on Trial, 1944 (Boetticher 2)

Youth Runs Wild, 1944 (Lewton 4)

Youth Speaks. *See* Pesne o geroyazh, 1932

Youth Takes a Fling, 1938 (McCrea 3, Maté 4, Pasternak 4)

Youth Will Be Served, 1940 (Darwell 3, Cronjager 4, Day 4)

Youthful Sinners. *See* Tricheurs, 1958

Youth's Gamble, 1925 (Brown 4)

Youth's Oath. *See* Kliatva molodikh, 1944

You've Got to Walk It Like You Talk It or You'll Lose That Beat, 1971 (Craven 2, Pryor 3)

Yovita. *See* Jowita, 1967

Yugato, 1953 (Kagawa 3)

Yugsjömordet, 1966 (Dahlbeck 3)

Yuhi ni akai ore no kao, 1961 (Shinoda 2)

Yuhrei ressha, 1949 (Miyagawa 4)

Yuhu ni ore no akai kao, 1961 (Iwashita 3)

Yukan naru koi, 1925 (Tanaka 3)

Yuki Fujin ezu, 1950 (Mizoguchi 2, Yamamura 3, Hayasaka 4, Yoda 4)

Yuki no honoo, 1955 (Tsukasa 3, Yamamura 3)

Yuki no wataridori, 1957 (Hasegawa 3)

Yukiguni, 1965 (Iwashita 3)

Yukiko, 1955 (Imai 2)

Yukiko to Natsuko, 1941 (Yamada 3)

Yukon Jake, 1924 (Sennett 2)

Yukovsky, 1950 (Pudovkin 2, Golovnya 4)

Yukubo, 1953 (Miyagawa 4)

Yukyo gonin otoko, 1958 (Hasegawa 3)

Yukyo no mure, 1948 (Hasegawa 3, Yamamura 3)

Yuma, 1971 (Duning 4)

Yume de aritai, 1962 (Yamamura 3)

Yume no naka no ojousan, 1934 (Yoda 4)

Yume Utsutsu, 1935 (Tanaka 3)

Yunost Maksima. *See* **Yunost Maxima, 1935**

Yunost Maxima, 1935 (Enei 4, Moskvin 4, Shostakovich 4)

Yurakucho de aimasho, 1958 (Kyo 3)

Yurei akatsuki ni shisu, 1948 (Hasegawa 3)

Yurei hanjo-ki, 1960 (Kagawa 3)

Yuri Norstein, 1980 (Norstein 4)

Yushima no shiraume, 1955 (Mori 3)

Yuwaku, 1948 (Shindo 2, Yoshimura 2, Hara 3)

Yuyake-gume, 1956 (Yamada 3)

Yves Montand chante en U.S.S.R. *See* Poet Iv Montan, 1957

Yvette, 1927 (Cavalcanti 2, Braunberger 4)

Yvonne la nuit, 1949 (Cervi 3)

Z

Z, 1969 (Costa-Gavras 2, Montand 3, Papas 3, Trintignant 3, Coutard 4, Theodorakis 4)
Z bláta do louže, 1934 (Stallich 4)
Z českých mlýnu, 1929 (Stallich 4)
Z.P.G., 1971 (Chaplin 3, Reed 3)
Za opunu smrti, 1923 (Heller 4)
Za rodnou hroudu, 1930 (Stallich 4)
Za sciana, 1971 (Zanussi 2)
Za svobudu národa, 1920 (Heller 4)
Za trnkovým keřem, 1979 (Brejchová 3)
Za trynkovým kefem, 1981 (Brejchová 3)
Za život radostný, 1951 (Kučera 4)
Žabec. See Trny a květi, 1921
Zabijaka, 1967 (Stawiński 4)
Zabil jsem Einsteina, pánové, 1969 (Brejchová 3)
Zabriskie Point, 1970 (Antonioni 2, Ford 3, Guerra 4, Ponti 4, Shepard 4, Tavoularis 4)
Zabudnite na Mozarta, 1985 (Mueller-Stahl 3)
Začarovaný klíček karpatsky. See Koryatovič, 1922
Zaczęło się w Hiszpanii, 1950 (Munk 2)
Zaduszki, 1961 (Tyszkiewicz 3, Konwicki 4)
Zagranichnii pokhod sudov Baltiiskogo flota kreisere 'Aurora' i uchebnogo sudna 'Komsomolts', August 8, 1925, 1925 (Vertov 2)
Zagreb Title, 1984 (Vukotić 4)
Záhada modrého pokoje, 1933 (Stallich 4)
Záhada Noci. See Stíny, 1921
Záhadný případ, 1919 (Heller 4)
Zahrada, 1968 (Švankmajer 4)
Zaida, die Tragödie eines Modells, 1923 (Holger-Madsen 2)
Zakroishchik iz Torzhka, 1925 (Maretskaya 3)
Zaliczenie, 1969 (Zanussi 2)
Zaloga-Crew, 1952 (Lomnicki 3)
Zalzala, 1952 (Anand 3)
Zamach, 1959 (Stawiński 4, Lomnicki 3)
Zamanat, 1977 (Azmi 3)
Zameer, 1975 (Bachchan 3)
Zámek Gripsholm, 1960 (Brejchová 3)
Zampó y yo, 1965 (Rey 3)
Zancos, 1984 (Saura 2)
Zander the Great, 1925 (Daves 2, Bosworth 3, Davies 3, Barnes 4, Marion 4)
Zandra Rhodes, 1981 (Greenaway 2)
Zandunga, 1937 (De Fuentes 2)
Zandy's Bride, 1974 (Hackman 3, Ullmann 3)
Zangiku monogatari, 1939 (Mizoguchi 2, Yoda 4)

Zangiku monogatari, 1956 (Hasegawa 3, Yoda 4)
Zánik domu Usheru, 1981 (Švankmajer 4)
Zánik samoty Berhof, 1983 (Brejchová 3)
Zanjeer, 1973 (Bachchan 3)
Zanna bianca, 1973 (Rey 3)
Zansho, 1978 (Tsukasa 3)
Zany Adventures of Robin Hood, 1984 (McDowall 3, Segal 3)
Zanzibar, 1940 (Krasner 4, Salter 4)
Zapadlí vlastenci, 1932 (Heller 4)
Zapatas Bande, 1914 (Gad 2, Nielsen 3, Freund 4)
Zapfenstreich am Rhein, 1930 (Planer 4)
Zaporosch Sa Dunayem, 1938 (Ulmer 2)
Zapotecan Village, 1941 (Eisenstein 2)
Zapped Again, 1989 (Black 3)
Zaproszenie do wnętrza, 1978 (Wajda 2)
Zarak, 1957 (Mature 3, Alwyn 4, Box 4)
Zarco, 1957 (Armendáriz 3)
Zarco—The Bandit. See Zarco, 1957
Zardoz, 1973 (Boorman 2, Connery 3, Unsworth 4)
Zářijové noci, 1957 (Brodský 3, Kučera 4)
Zärliche Haie, 1966 (Karina 3)
Zärtlichkeit der Wölfe, 1973 (Fassbinder 2)
Zasadil dědek řepu, 1945 (Trnka 4)
Zastihla me noc, 1985 (Brejchová 3)
Zatoichi: A Thousand Dollar Price on His Head. See Zatouichi senryo kubi, 1964
Zatoichi: Abare Himatsuri, 1970 (Mori 3)
Zatoichi hatashi-jo, 1968 (Shimura 3)
Zatoichi Meets Yojimbo. See Zatoichi to Yojimbo, 1970
Zatoichi to Yojimbo, 1970 (Mifune 3)
Zatoichi's Conspiracy, 1973 (Okada 3, Shimura 3)
Zatouichi abare himatsuri, 1970 (Miyagawa 4)
Zatouichi Breaking Out of Prison. See Zatouichi rouyaburi, 1967
Zatouichi Challenge Letter. See Zatouichi hatashijou, 1968
Zatouichi hatashijou, 1968 (Miyagawa 4)
Zatouichi Meets Yojimbo. See Zatouichi to Yojimbo, 1970
Zatouichi no uta ga kikoeru, 1966 (Miyagawa 4)
Zatouichi rouyaburi, 1967 (Miyagawa 4)
Zatouichi senryo kubi, 1964 (Miyagawa 4)
Zatouichi to Yojimbo, 1970 (Miyagawa 4)
Zatouichi: Wild Fire Festival. See Zatouichi abare himatsuri, 1970
Zatouichi's Song Is Heard. See Zatouichi no uta ga kikoeru, 1966
Zauberberg, 1982 (Ballhaus 4)

Zavada není na vašem přijímaci, 1961 (Brdečka 4)
Zaza, 1915 (Porter 2, Zukor 4)
Zaza, 1923 (Dwan 2, Swanson 3, Rosson 4)
Zaza, 1939 (Cukor 2, Dmytryk 2, Colbert 3, Marshall 3, Nazimova 3, Akins 4, Dreier 4, Head 4, Lang 4, Lewin 4)
Zaza, 1942 (Castellani 2, Rota 4)
Zazanie, 1978 (Renoir 4)
Zazie. See Zazie dans le métro, 1960
Zazie dans le métro, 1960 (Noiret 3, Evein 4, Rappeneau 4)
Zbabělec, 1962 (Weiss 2)
Zbrodniarz i panna, 1963 (Cybulski 3)
Zdjęcia próbne, 1976 (Olbrychski 3)
Zeb vs. Paprika, 1924 (Laurel and Hardy 3, Roach 4)
Zed and Two Noughts, 1986 (Greenaway 2, Vierny 4)
Zeder: Voices from Darkness, 1983 (Delli Colli 4)
Zee and Co. See Zee and Company, 1971
Zee and Company, 1971 (Caine 3, Taylor 3, York 3)
Zehn Minuten Mozart, 1930 (Reiniger 4)
Zehnte Pavillon der Zitadelle, 1916 (Jannings 3)
Zeigfeld Follies, 1946 (Astaire 3)
Zelená knížka, 1948 (Stallich 4)
Zelené obzory, 1962 (Brejchová 3)
Zelenyi Zmii, 1926 (Maretskaya 3)
Zelig, 1983 (Allen 2, Farrow 3, Willis 4)
Zelly and Me, 1988 (Donaggio 4)
Zelyonyi pauk, 1916 (Volkov 2)
Zemliaka, 1975 (Shukshin 3)
Zemma, 1951 (Mori 3, Yamamura 3)
Zemsta, 1958 (Tyskiewicz 3)
Žena, která ví co chce, 1934 (Heller 4, Stallich 4)
Žena pod křižem, 1937 (Lom 3)
Zenida gospodina Marcipana, 1963 (Mimica 4)
Zenigata Heiji, 1951 (Hasegawa 3)
Zenigata Heiji torimon-hikae, 1952 (Hasegawa 3)
Zenigata Heiji torimon-hikae series, 1951–61 (Hasegawa 3)
Zenin no odori, 1964 (Miyagawa 4)
Zenobia, 1939 (Langdon 3, Laurel and Hardy 3, McDaniel 3, Roach 4, Struss 4)
Zenu ani květinou neuhodiš, 1966 (Brejchová 3)
Zerbrochene Krug, 1937 (Jannings 3, Herlth 4, Von Harbou 4, Wagner 4)
Zerkalo, 1975 (Tarkovsky 2, Yankovsky 3)
Zero, 1960 (Asquith 2)

Zéro de conduite, 1933 (Vigo 2, Jaubert 4, Kaufman 4)

Zero Fighter. *See* Dai kusen, 1966

Zero Hour, 1921 (Roach 4)

Zero Hour, 1939 (Darwell 3, Fort 4)

Zero Hour, 1957 (Andrews 2, Darnell 3, Hayden 3, Leven 4)

Zero Murder Case. *See* Uncle Harry, 1945

Zero Population Growth. *See* Z.P.G., 1971

Zerstorte Heimat. *See* Dornenweg einer Fürstin, 1928

Zerwany most, 1963 (Lomnicki 3)

Zeugin aus der Hölle, 1965 (Papas 3)

Zeyno, 1970 (Güney 2)

Zezowate szczęście, 1960 (Stawiński 4)

Zhdi menya, Ana, 1969 (Yankovsky 3)

Zhemtshina zavtrastchevo dnia, 1914 (Mozhukin 3)

Zhenitba Jana Knukke, 1934 (Cherkassov 3)

Zhenshchina s kinzhalom, 1916 (Mozhukin 3)

Zhivet takoi paren, 1964 (Shukshin 3)

Zhivoi trup, 1928 (Maretskaya 3, Golovnya 4)

Zhivoi trup, 1968 (Batalov 3)

Zhizn mig iskusstvo vetchno, 1916 (Mozhukin 3)

Zhizn na smerti, 1914 (Mozhukin 3)

Zhizn na Tzarya, 1911 (Mozhukin 3)

Zhizn v tsitadel, 1947 (Enei 4)

Zhurnalist, 1967 (Girardot 3, Shukshin 3)

Ziddi, 1948 (Anand 3)

Ziddi, 1964 (Burman 4)

Ziegfeld Follies, 1946 (Minnelli 2, Walters 2, Ball 3, Charisse 3, Garland 3, Grayson 3, Horne 3, Johnson 3, Kelly 3, Powell 3, Rooney 3, Williams 3, Alton 4, Edens 4, Folsey 4, Freed 4, Gibbons 4, Levien 4, Mayer 4, Raphaelson 4, Rose 4, Rosher 4, Sharaff 4, Smith 4)

Ziegfeld Girl, 1941 (Berkeley 2, Arden 3, Cooper 3, Garland 3, Horton 3, Lamarr 3, Stewart 3, Turner 3, Adrian 4, Berman 4, Brown 4, Edens 4, Levien 4, Mayer 4, Stothart 4)

Ziemia obiecana, 1974 (Wajda 2, Olbrychski 3)

Zigano. *See* Zigano, der Brigant vom Monte Diavolo, 1925

Zigeuner der Nacht, 1932 (Metzner 4, Schüfftan 4)

Zigeuner-baron, 1935 (Walbrook 3)

Zigeunerblut, 1910 (Nielsen 3)

Zigeunerblut, 1934 (Warm 4)

Zigeunergaron, 1927 (Andrejew 4)

Zigeunerliebe, 1922 (Ondra 3)

Ziggy's Gift, 1982 (Williams 4)

Zigomar, 1907 (Gaumont 4)

Zigomar, 1911 (Gaumont 4)

Zigomar peau d'anguille, 1913 (Gaumont 4)

Zig-Zag, 1970 (Wallach 3)

Zig-zag, 1974 (Deneuve 2)

Zimba gibi delikanli, 1964 (Güney 2)

Zimowy zmierzch, 1957 (Konwicki 4)

Zinc laminé et architecture, 1958 (Delerue 4)

Zindagi Zindagi, 1972 (Burman 4)

Zinker, 1931 (Frič 2, Rasp 3, Heller 4)

Zinker, 1963 (Kinski 3, Rasp 3)

Zio indegno, 1989 (Gassman 3, Giannini 3)

Zip 'n' Snort, 1961 (Blanc 4, Jones 4)

Zipp, the Dodger, 1914 (Sennett 2, Arbuckle 3)

Zipping Along, 1953 (Blanc 4, Jones 4, Stalling 4)

Zirkus des Lebens, 1921 (Krauss 3, Warm 4)

Zirkus Saran. *See* Knox und die lustigen Vagabunden, 1935

Zirkusblut, 1916 (Krauss 3)

Zirkuskönig, 1924 (Banky 3, Linder 3)

Zis Boom Bah, 1941 (Katzman 4)

Zitelloni, 1958 (De Sica 2)

Zitra vstanu a oparim se cajem, 1977 (Brodský 3)

Život jde dál, 1935 (Heller 4, Stallich 4)

Zivot je pes, 1933 (Frič 2)

Život vojenský, život veselý, 1934 (Stallich 4)

Zizanie, 1978 (Girardot 3)

Žižkovská romance, 1957 (Brejchová 3)

Zlatcha notch, 1914 (Mozhukin 3)

Zlaté ptáče , 1932 (Stallich 4)

Zlaty gori, 1931 (Shostakovich 4)

Zlatý pavouk, 1956 (Brejchová 3)

Zločin v dívčí škole, 1965 (Menzel 2)

Zločin v šantánu, 1968 (Menzel 2, Brodský 3)

Złote koło, 1971 (Ścibor-Rylski 4)

Zły chłopiec, 1950 (Wajda 2)

Zmrzly dřevař, 1962 (Brdečka 4)

Známosti z ulice, 1929 (Heller 4)

Zo o kutta renchu, 1947 (Yoshimura 2)

Zoë, 1953 (Alekan 4)

Zoe bonne, 1966 (Chabrol 2)

Zoko minami no kaze, 1942 (Yoshimura 2)

Zoko Miyamoto Musashi, 1955 (Mifune 3)

Zoko Shimizu-minato, 1940 (Shimura 3)

Zoku aizen katsura, 1939 (Tanaka 3)

Zoku Ako-jo, 1952 (Yamada 3)

Zoku aoi sanmyaku, 1957 (Tsukasa 3)

Zoku Fukei-zu, 1942 (Hasegawa 3, Takamine 3, Yamada 3)

Zoku haikei tenno heika sama, 1964 (Iwashita 3)

Zoku Hebihime dochu, 1949 (Hasegawa 3, Kyo 3)

Zoku Hebihime-sama, 1940 (Hasegawa 3)

Zoku hesokuri shacho, 1956 (Tsukasa 3)

Zoku jirocho Fuji, 1960 (Hasegawa 3)

Zoku Kageboshi, 1950 (Yamada 3)

Zoku Minamoto Toshitsune, 1956 (Yamada 3)

Zoku namo naku mazushiku utsukushiku; Chichi to ko, 1967 (Takamine 3)

Zoku ningen kakumei, 1976 (Shimura 3, Muraki 4)

Zoku Ooka seidan: Mazo kaiketsu-hen, 1931 (Yamada 3)

Zoku otoko wa tsuraiyo, 1969 (Shimura 3)

Zoku sarariiman Chushingura, 1961 (Tsukasa 3)

Zoku sarariiman Shimizu minato, 1962 (Tsukasa 3)

Zoku Sasaki Kojiro, 1951 (Takamine 3)

Zoku shacho enma-cho, 1969 (Tsukasa 3)

Zoku shacho gyogo-ki, 1966 (Tsukasa 3)

Zoku shacho hanjo-ki, 1968 (Tsukasa 3)

Zoku shacho ninpo-cho, 1965 (Tsukasa 3)

Zoku shacho sandai-ki, 1958 (Tsukasa 3)

Zoku shacho sen-ichiya, 1967 (Tsukasa 3)

Zoku shacho shinshiroku, 1964 (Tsukasa 3)

Zoku shacho-gaku ABC, 1970 (Tsukasa 3)

Zoku shinobi no mono, 1963 (Yamamura 3)

Zoku Sugata Sanshiro, 1945 (Mori 3)

Zołnierz zwycięstwa, 1953 (Lomnicki 3)

Zolotoi eshelon, 1959 (Shukshin 3)

Zolotoi klyuchik, 1939 (Ptushko 4)

Zoltan . . . Hound of Dracula, 1977 (Ferrer 3)

Zombie, 1978 (Argento 4)

Zombies of Mora Tau, 1957 (Katzman 4)

Zombies on Broadway, 1945 (Lugosi 3, D'Agostino 4)

Zona, 1916 (Negri 3)

Zona roja, 1975 (Fernández 2)

Zone, 1928 (Périnal 4)

Zone de la mort, 1917 (Gance 2, Modot 3, Burel 4)

Zone de mort, 1917 (Gaumont 4)

Zone Moment, 1956 (Brakhage 2)

Zoo, 1933 (Lantz 4)

Zoo, 1962 (Haanstra 2)

Zoo. *See* Chiriakhana, 1967

Zoo and You, 1938 (Alwyn 4)

Zoo Babies, 1938 (Alwyn 4)

Zoo in Budapest, 1933 (Young 3, Friedhofer 4, Garmes 4, Lasky 4)

Zoo Is Company, 1961 (Hanna and Barbera 4)

Zoo zéro, 1978 (Kinski 3, Valli 3)

Zoom and Bored, 1957 (Blanc 4, Jones 4, Stalling 4)

Zoom at the Top, 1962 (Blanc 4, Jones 4)

Zoot Cat, 1944 (Hanna and Barbera 4)

Zora. *See* Silent Night, Bloody Night, 1973

Zorba the Greek, 1964 (Cacoyannis 2, Bates 3, Papas 3, Quinn 3, Lassally 4, Theodorakis 4)

Zori Parizha, 1936 (Maretskaya 3)

Zorns Lemma, 1970 (Frampton 2)

Zorro, 1975 (Baker 3, Delon 3)

Zorro de Jalisco, 1940 (Fernández 2)

Zorro Rides Again, 1937 (Canutt 4)

Zorro's Black Whip, 1944 (Canutt 4)

Zorro's Fighting Legion, 1939 (Canutt 4)

Zotz!, 1962 (Dumont 3)

Zouhei monogatari, 1963 (Miyagawa 4)

Zouzou, 1934 (Gabin 3, Douy 4, Kaufman 4, Meerson 4)

Zoya, 1944 (Shostakovich 4)

Zoya, 1954 (Batalov 3)

Zpěv zlata, 1920 (Ondra 3, Heller 4)

Ztracená stopa, 1956 (Kučera 4)

Ztracená tvář, 1965 (Brejchová 3)

Ztracená varta, 1956 (Brdečka 4)

Ztracenci, 1957 (Brdečka 4)

'Zu böser Schlacht schleich' ich heut' Nacht so bang', 1977 (Kluge 2)

Zu jedem kommt einmal die Liebe. *See* Alte Lied, 1930

Zu jung für die Liebe, 1961 (Käutner 2)

Zu neuen Ufern, 1937 (Sirk 2)

Zu spät, 1911 (Messter 4)

Zucker und Zimt, 1915 (Lubitsch 2)

Zuckerkandl!, 1968 (Hubley 4)

Zuflucht, 1928 (Porten 3)

Zügelloses Blut, 1917 (Negri 3)

Zuiderzee Dike, 1931 (Van Dongen 4)

Zula Hula, 1937 (Fleischer 4)

Zulu, 1963 (Baker 3, Burton 3, Caine 3, Hawkins 3, Barry 4)

Zulu Dawn, 1979 (Elliott 3, Hoskins 3, Lancaster 3, Mills 3, O'Toole 3, Bernstein 4)

Zulu-Land, 1911 (Selig 4)

Zulu's Heart, 1908 (Griffith 2, Lawrence 3, Bitzer 4)

Zum Goldenen Anker. *See* Marius, 1931

Zum Paradies der Damen, 1922 (Pick 2)

Zum Tee bei Dr. Borsig, 1963 (Herlth 4)

Zum Tode gehetz, 1912 (Gad 2, Nielsen 3)

Zuppa di pesce, 1992 (De Almeida 4)

Zur Chronik von Grieshuus, 1925 (Dagover 3, Herlth 4, Von Harbou 4, Röhrig 4, Wagner 4)